C000296372

Published by Collins
An imprint of HarperCollins Publishers
1 London Bridge Street,
London SE1 9GF

www.harpercollins.co.uk

First published by Geographia Ltd 1977

22nd edition 2016

Mapping generated from Collins Bartholomew digital databases

London Underground and Overground Maps by permission of Transport Trading Limited
Registered User No. 16/2986/P

Information on fixed speed camera locations provided by PocketGPSWorld.Com Ltd.

The grid on this map is the National Grid taken from the Ordnance Survey map with the permission of the Controller of Her Majesty's Stationery Office.

Printed by RR Donnelley APS Co Ltd

Paperback ISBN 978 0 00 811279 0

10 9 8 7 6 5 4 3 2

Queries concerning this product to be addressed to:
Collins RoadCheck,
Collins Geo,
HarperCollins Publishers,
Westerhill Road,
Bishopbriggs,
Glasgow,
G64 2QT

e-mail: roadcheck@harpercollins.co.uk

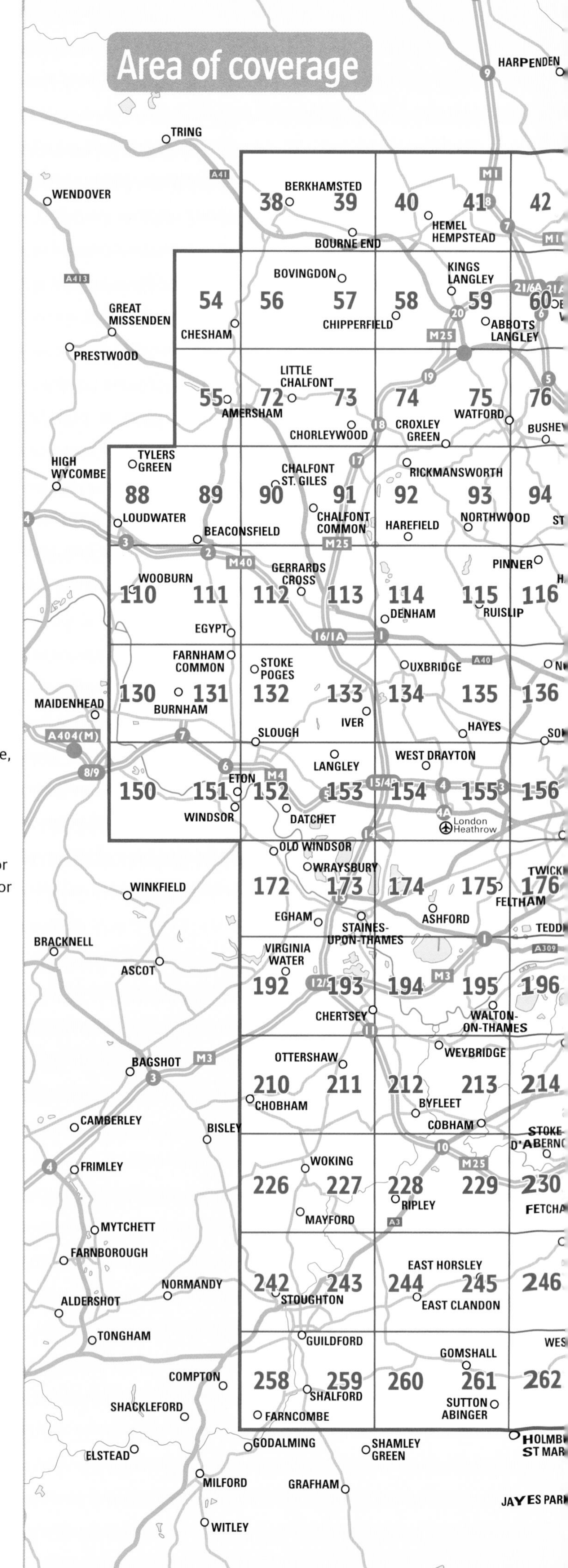

WELWYN

WHEATHAMPSTEAD 28 29 WELWYN GARDEN CITY 30 31 32 HERTFORD WARE 33 34 HUNSDON 35 SAWBRIDGEWORTH 36 SHEERING 37 OLD HARLOW LEADEN RODING

43 ST. ALBANS 44 HATFIELD 45 WELHAM GREEN ESSENDON 46 47 48 BROXBOURNE HODDESDON 49 50 LOWER NAZEING HARLOW 51 POTTER STREET 52 53 M11

61 LONDON COLNEY 62 SHENLEY A1(M) 63 BROOKMANS PARK POTTERS BAR 64 65 CUFFLEY 66 CHESHUNT 67 68 WALTHAM ABBEY 69 EPPING 70 NORTH WEALD BASSETT 71 CHIPPING ONGAR A414 M25

77 78 BOREHAMWOOD 79 BARNET 80 NEW BARNET 81 82 ENFIELD 83 84 LOUGHTON 85 THEYDON BOIS 86 ABRIDGE 87 STAPLEFORD ABBOTTS KELVEDON HATCH INGATESTONE 108 109 BRENTWOOD BILLERICAY

95 96 EDGWARE EAST BARNET 97 FINCHLEY 98 SOUTHGATE 99 WOOD GREEN 100 EDMONTON 101 102 WOODFORD 103 CHIGWELL 104 105 COLLIER ROW 106 HAROLD HILL 107 A10 M11

117 118 HENDON 119 120 121 WALTHAMSTOW 122 STOKE NEWINGTON 123 LEYTON 124 WANSTEAD 125 ILFORD 126 127 ROMFORD HORNCHURCH 128 129 UPMINSTER LAINDON BULPHAN A406 A12 A127

WEMBLEY HAMPSTEAD WILLESDEN 137 138 139 140 141 142 143 144 145 146 147 DAGENHAM RAINHAM 148 149 SOUTH OCKENDON AVELEY STANFORD-LE-HOPE STRATFORD WEST HAM

272-273 274-275 276-277 278-279 280-281 282-283 284-285 286-287 288-289 290-291 292-293 MARYLEBONE STEPNEY London City

ACTON HAMMERSMITH WESTMINSTER LAMBETH 294-295 296-297 298-299 300-301 302-303 304-305 WOOLWICH ERITH PURFLEET GRAYS CHADWELL ST. MARY

157 158 KEW 159 160 161 162 163 164 165 166 167 168 169 170 171 TILBURY 306-307 308-309 310-311 312-313 314-315 BATTERSEA BRIXTON GREENWICH A205

RICHMOND WANDSWORTH CATFORD BEXLEY DARTFORD NORTHFLEET GRAVESEND 177 178 179 180 181 182 183 184 185 186 SIDCUP 187 188 189 190 191 WIMBLEDON STREATHAM CHISLEHURST A3 A20

KINGSTON UPON THAMES MERTON MITCHAM BECKENHAM BROMLEY SWANLEY SOUTH DARENTH LONGFIELD 197 SURBITON 198 199 200 201 202 CROYDON 203 204 205 ORPINGTON 206 RAMSDEN 207 208 FARNINGHAM 209 A24 A232 M25 M2 MEOPHAM

215 216 EWELL EPSOM 217 218 SUTTON 219 PURLEY 220 ADDINGTON SANDERSTEAD 221 222 FARNBOROUGH 223 DOWNE 224 CHELSFIELD 225 M20 WEST KINGSDOWN CULVERSTONE GREEN

BANSTEAD COULSDON WARLINGHAM BIGGIN HILL KNOCKHOLT OTFORD KEMSING WROTHAM M26 231 232 ASHTEAD LEATHERHEAD 233 TADWORTH 234 235 236 237 238 TATSFIELD 239 240 241 RIVERHEAD SEVENOAKS WEST MALLING IGHTHAM A23 A25

WALTON ON THE HILL CATERHAM 247 248 249 250 251 7/8 252 GODSTONE 253 OXTED 254 WESTERHAM 255 256 257 MEREWORTH REIGATE REDHILL SHIPBOURNE

DORKING BROCKHAM SOUTH GODSTONE MARLPIT HILL EAST PECKHAM A21 263 264 NORTH HOLMWOOD 265 LEIGH 266 267 SALFORDS BLINDLEY HEATH EDENBRIDGE LINGFIELD A22

BEARE GREEN HORLEY M23 268 269 NEWCHAPEL CHARLWOOD London Gatwick A24 HOLTYE COMMON ROYAL TUNBRIDGE WELLS

Coverage at 1:20,000
3·2 inches to 1 mile / 5 cm to 1 km

Coverage at 1:10,000
6·3 inches to 1 mile / 10 cm to 1 km
See pages 270–271 for Key to central London maps

Collins
GREATER LONDON STREET ATLAS

CONTENTS

INFORMATION PAGES

M25 London orbital motorway 2–3
London Underground map 4
London Overground map 5
Transport index 6–7
Congestion Charging Zone 8
Low Emission Zone 9
West End theatres & cinemas, shopping 10
Places of interest index 11
Airport plans 12

ROUTE PLANNING MAPS

Key to route planning maps 13
Key to map symbols 13
Route planning maps 14–25

LONDON STREET MAPS

Key to London street maps 26–27
Key to map symbols 27
London street maps 28–269

CENTRAL LONDON MAPS

Key to central London maps 270–271
Key to map symbols 270–271
Central London maps 272–315

Index to street names, places of interest, place names, stations, hospitals, schools, colleges and universities 316–480
Administrative areas 482–483

M25 London orbital motorway

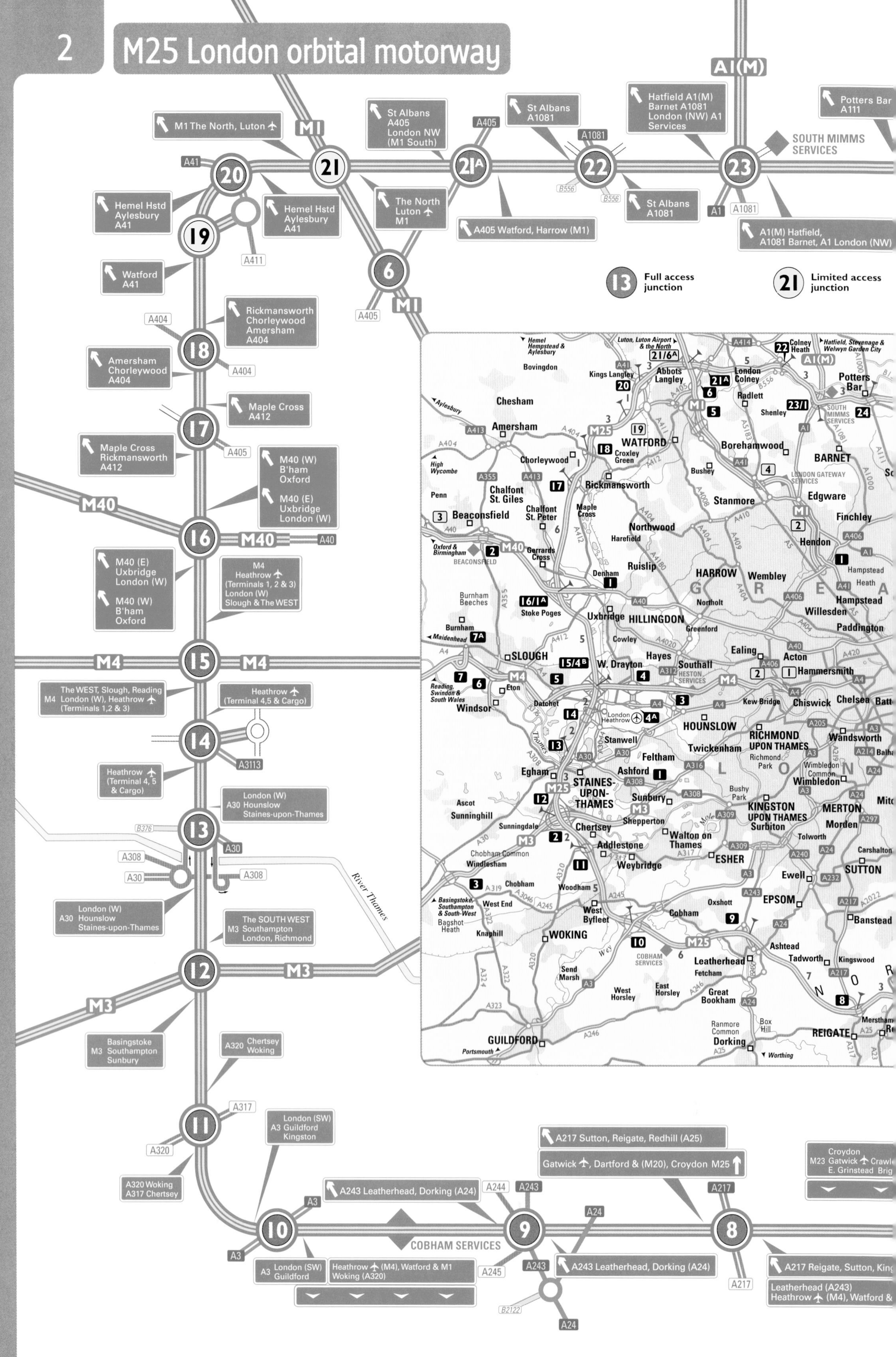
M1 The North, Luton
St Albans A405 London NW (M1 South)
St Albans A1081
Hatfield A1(M) Barnet A1081 London (NW) A1 Services
Potters Bar A111
SOUTH MIMMS SERVICES
Hemel Hstd Aylesbury A41
The North Luton M1
A405 Watford, Harrow (M1)
St Albans A1081
A1(M) Hatfield, A1081 Barnet, A1 London (NW)
Full access junction
Limited access junction
Watford A41
Rickmansworth Chorleywood Amersham A404
Amersham Chorleywood A404
Maple Cross A412
Maple Cross Rickmansworth A412
M40 (W) B'ham Oxford
M40 (E) Uxbridge London (W)
M40 (E) Uxbridge London (W)
M40 (W) B'ham Oxford
M4 Heathrow (Terminals 1, 2 & 3) London (W) Slough & The WEST
The WEST, Slough, Reading M4 London (W), Heathrow (Terminals 1,2 & 3)
Heathrow (Terminal 4,5 & Cargo)
Heathrow (Terminal 4, 5 & Cargo)
London (W) A30 Hounslow Staines-upon-Thames
London (W) A30 Hounslow Staines-upon-Thames
The SOUTH WEST M3 Southampton London, Richmond
River Thames
Basingstoke M3 Southampton Sunbury
A320 Chertsey Woking
London (SW) A3 Guildford Kingston
A320 Woking A317 Chertsey
A217 Sutton, Reigate, Redhill (A25)
Gatwick, Dartford & (M20), Croydon M25
Croydon M23 Gatwick Crawley E. Grinstead Brig
A243 Leatherhead, Dorking (A24)
COBHAM SERVICES
A3 London (SW) Guildford
Heathrow (M4), Watford & M1 Woking (A320)
A243 Leatherhead, Dorking (A24)
A217 Reigate, Sutton, King
Leatherhead (A243) Heathrow (M4), Watford &

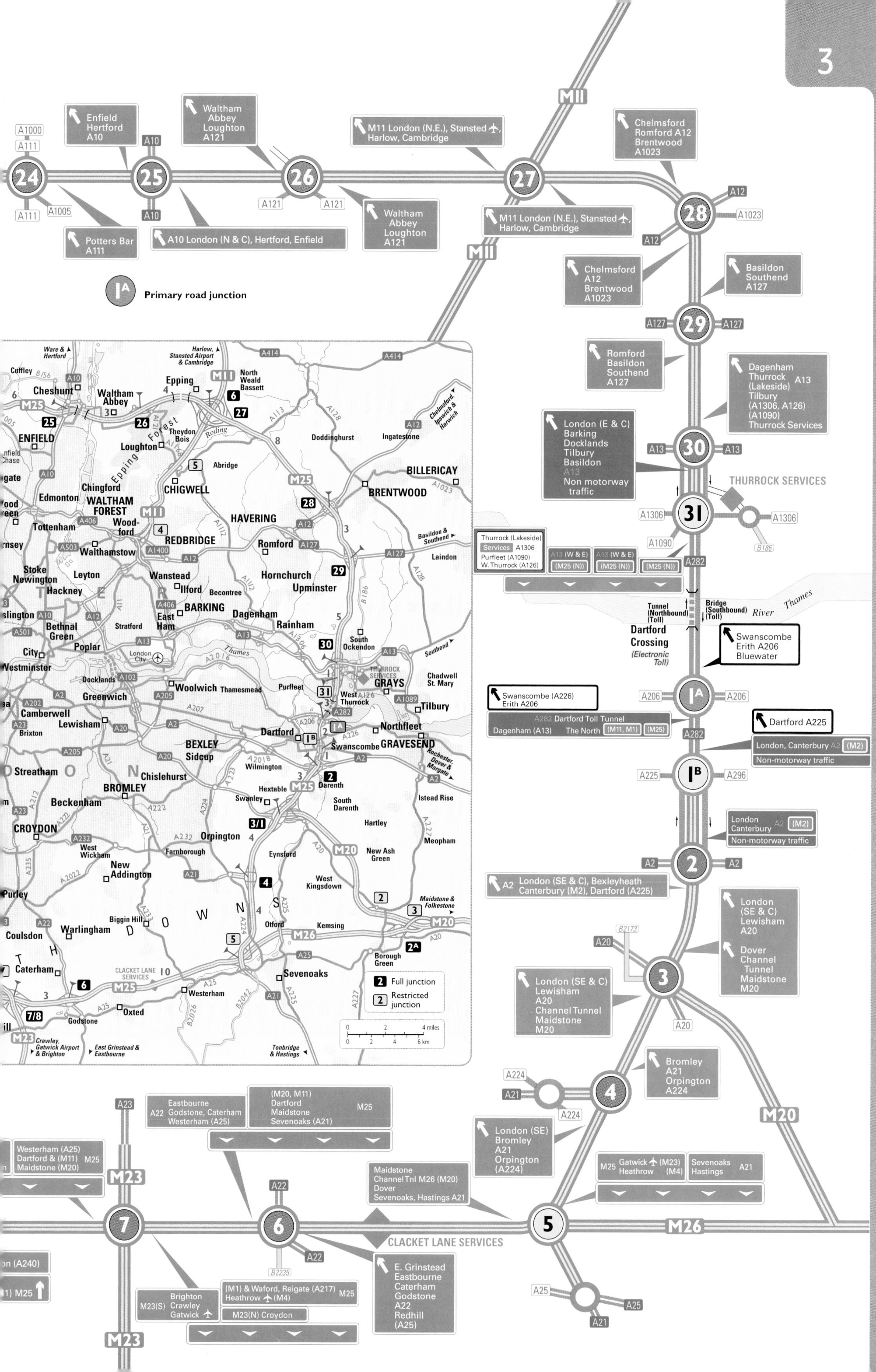

24
A1000
A111
A111
A1005
Potters Bar A111

25
Enfield Hertford A10
A10
A10
A10 London (N & C), Hertford, Enfield

26
Waltham Abbey Loughton A121
A121
A121
Waltham Abbey Loughton A121

27
M11
M11 London (N.E.), Stansted, Harlow, Cambridge
M11 London (N.E.), Stansted, Harlow, Cambridge

28
Chelmsford Romford A12 Brentwood A1023
A12
A1023
A12
Chelmsford A12 Brentwood A1023

29
Basildon Southend A127
A127
A127
Romford Basildon Southend A127

30
Dagenham Thurrock A13 (Lakeside) Tilbury (A1306, A126) (A1090) Thurrock Services
A13
A13
London (E & C) Barking Docklands Tilbury Basildon A13 Non motorway traffic

THURROCK SERVICES

31
A1306
A1306
B186
A1090
A282
Thurrock (Lakeside) Services A1306 Purfleet (A1090) W. Thurrock (A126)
A13 (W & E) (M25 (N))
A13 (W & E) (M25 (N))
(M25 (N))

Tunnel (Northbound) (Toll)
Bridge (Southbound) (Toll)
River Thames
Dartford Crossing (Electronic Toll)
Swanscombe Erith A206 Bluewater

1A
A206
A206
Swanscombe (A226) Erith A206
A282 Dartford Toll Tunnel
Dagenham (A13) The North (M11, M1) (M25)
A282
Dartford A225
London, Canterbury A2 (M2)
Non-motorway traffic

1B
A225
A296
London Canterbury A2 (M2)
Non-motorway traffic

2
A2
A2
A2 London (SE & C), Bexleyheath Canterbury (M2), Dartford (A225)

3
London (SE & C) Lewisham A20
Dover Channel Tunnel Maidstone M20
B2173
A20
A20
London (SE & C) Lewisham A20 Channel Tunnel Maidstone M20

4
A224
A21
A224
Bromley A21 Orpington A224
London (SE) Bromley A21 Orpington (A224)
M20
M25 Gatwick (M23) Heathrow (M4)
Sevenoaks Hastings A21

5
M26
A25
A25
A21
Maidstone Channel Tnl M26 (M20) Dover Sevenoaks, Hastings A21

6
A22
A22
B2235
CLACKET LANE SERVICES
E. Grinstead Eastbourne Caterham Godstone A22 Redhill (A25)
Eastbourne A22 Godstone, Caterham Westerham (A25)
(M20, M11) Dartford Maidstone Sevenoaks (A21) M25

7
M23
A23
Westerham (A25) Dartford & (M11) M25 Maidstone (M20)
...on (A240)
...1) M25
Brighton M23(S) Crawley Gatwick
(M1) & Waford, Reigate (A217) Heathrow (M4) M25
M23(N) Croydon

1A Primary road junction

2 Full junction
2 Restricted junction

0 2 4 miles
0 2 4 6 km

London Underground map

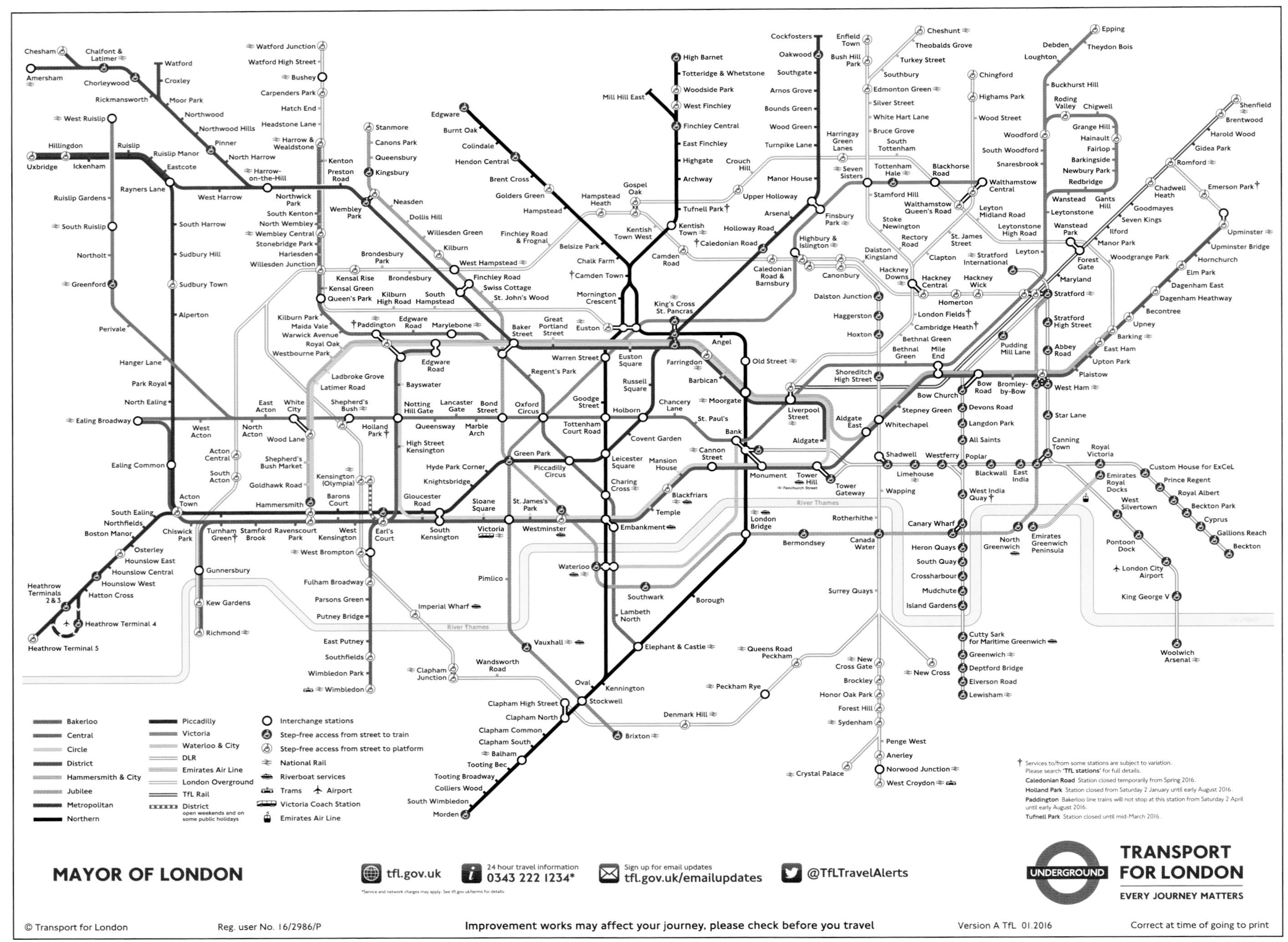

Romford — Emerson Park — Upminster
TfL Rail | District

Romford to Upminster services end at 2141/2154 Mondays to Saturdays and 1941/1954 Sundays

Cheshunt
Theobalds Grove
Turkey Street
Southbury
Enfield Town
Bush Hill Park
Edmonton Green
Silver Street
White Hart Lane
Bruce Grove
South Tottenham
Seven Sisters (Victoria)
Stamford Hill
Stoke Newington
Rectory Road
Hackney Downs

Chingford
Highams Park
Wood Street
Walthamstow Central (Victoria)
St. James Street
Clapton
London Fields†
Cambridge Heath†
Bethnal Green
Liverpool Street (Central, Circle, Hammersmith & City, Metropolitan, TfL Rail, Trains to Southend and Stansted)

Watford Junction
Watford High Street
Bushey
Carpenders Park
Hatch End
Headstone Lane
Harrow & Wealdstone
Kenton
South Kenton
North Wembley
Wembley Central
Stonebridge Park
Harlesden
Willesden Junction (Bakerloo)
Kensal Green
Queen's Park (Bakerloo)
Kilburn High Road
South Hampstead
Euston (Northern, Victoria)

Harringay Green Lanes
Crouch Hill
Upper Holloway
Gospel Oak
Blackhorse Road (Victoria)
Walthamstow Queen's Road
Leyton Midland Road
Leytonstone High Road
Wanstead Park (TfL Rail Forest Gate 300m)
Woodgrange Park
Barking (District, Hammersmith & City)

Richmond
Kew Gardens
Gunnersbury (District)
South Acton
Acton Central
Kensal Rise
Brondesbury Park
Brondesbury
West Hampstead (Jubilee 100m, 100m, Trains to Luton)
Finchley Road & Frognal
Hampstead Heath
Kentish Town West
Camden Road
Caledonian Road & Barnsbury
Highbury & Islington (Victoria)
Canonbury
Dalston Kingsland
Hackney Central
Homerton
Hackney Wick
Stratford (Central, Jubilee, DLR, TfL Rail, Trains to Southend)

Shepherd's Bush (Central 100m)
Kensington (Olympia) (District line open weekends, public holidays and some Olympia events; District)
West Brompton (District)
Imperial Wharf
Clapham Junction (Trains to Gatwick)

Dalston Junction
Haggerston
Hoxton
Shoreditch High Street
Whitechapel (District, Hammersmith & City)
Shadwell (DLR 100m)
Wapping
Rotherhithe
Canada Water (Jubilee)
Surrey Quays
New Cross
New Cross Gate
Brockley
Honor Oak Park
Forest Hill
Sydenham
Crystal Palace
Penge West
Anerley
Norwood Junction
West Croydon (Tramlink)

Battersea Park
Wandsworth Road
Clapham High Street (Northern, Clapham North 100m)
Denmark Hill
Peckham Rye
Queens Road Peckham

River Thames
River Thames

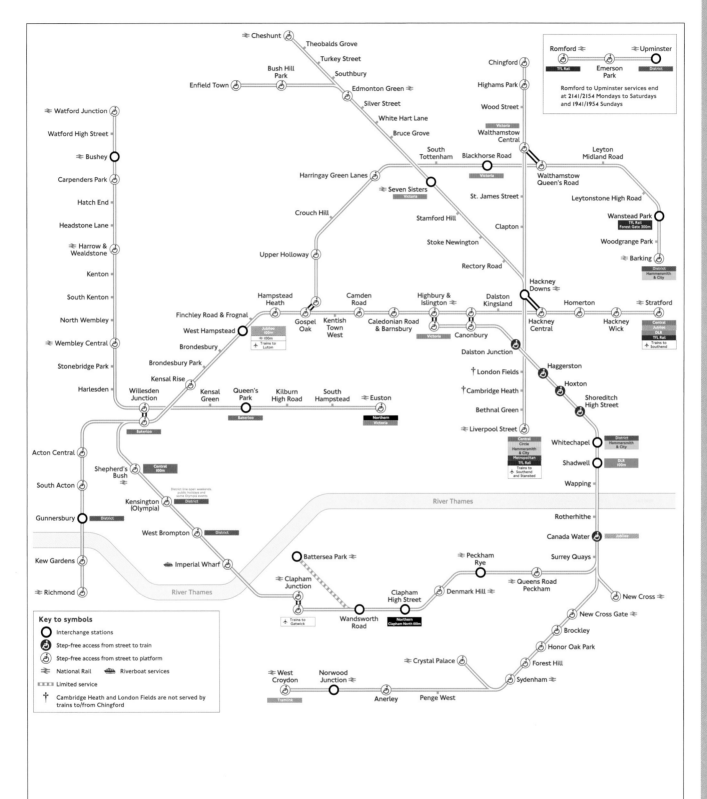

Key to symbols

- Interchange stations
- Step-free access from street to train
- Step-free access from street to platform
- National Rail
- Riverboat services
- Limited service
- † Cambridge Heath and London Fields are not served by trains to/from Chingford

Reg. user No. 16/2986/P 10.2015

MAYOR OF LONDON

Transport index

Key to symbols :-

- ⇌ Railway station
- ○ London Overground station
- ⊖ London Underground station
- DLR Docklands Light Railway station
- Tra Tramlink station
- Riv Pedestrian ferry landing stage
- ◆ Bus station

All entries are followed by the page number and grid reference on which the name will be found. So, for example, the first entry, **Abbey Road,** will be found on page **281** in square J10.

All entries are indexed to the largest scale map on which they are shown.

DLR	Abbey Road	281	J10
⇌	Abbey Wood	166	EW76
○	Acton Central	138	CR74
⇌	Acton Main Line	138	CQ72
⊖	Acton Town	158	CN75
Tra	Addington Village	221	EA107
◆	Addington Village Interchange	221	EA107
Tra	Addiscombe	202	DU102
⇌	Addlestone	212	BK105
⇌	Albany Park	186	EX89
⊖	Aldgate	288	A9
◆	Aldgate	288	A9
⊖	Aldgate East	288	B8
⇌	Alexandra Palace	99	DL54
DLR	All Saints	290	E10
⊖	Alperton	138	CL67
⇌	Amersham	55	AQ38
⊖	Amersham	55	AQ38
Tra	Ampere Way	201	DM102
⇌	Anerley	182	DV94
○	Anerley	182	DV94
⊖	Angel	276	F10
⇌	Angel Road	100	DW50
⇌	Apsley	58	BL25
⊖	Archway	121	DJ61
Tra	Arena	202	DW99
⊖	Arnos Grove	99	DJ49
⊖	Arsenal	121	DN62
⇌	Ashford	174	BL91
⇌	Ashtead	231	CK117
Tra	Avenue Road	203	DX96
⊖	Baker Street	284	F6
⇌	Balham	181	DH88
⊖	Balham	181	DH88
⊖	Bank	287	L9
DLR	Bank	287	L9
Riv	Bankside Pier	299	J1
⇌	Banstead	217	CY114
⇌	Barbican	287	H6
⊖	Barbican	287	H6
⇌	Barking	145	EQ66
○	Barking	145	EQ66
⊖	Barking	145	EQ66
⊖	Barkingside	125	ER56
⇌	Barnehurst	167	FC82
⇌	Barnes	159	CU83
⇌	Barnes Bridge	158	CS82
⊖	Barons Court	294	E10
⇌	Bat & Ball	257	FJ121
⇌	Battersea Park	309	J6
⇌	Bayford	47	DN18
⊖	Bayswater	283	L10
⇌	Beaconsfield	89	AL52
⇌	Beckenham Hill	183	EC92
⇌	Beckenham Junction	203	EA95
Tra	Beckenham Junction	203	EA95
Tra	Beckenham Road	203	DY95
DLR	Beckton	293	L7
DLR	Beckton Park	293	K10
⊖	Becontree	146	EW66
Tra	Beddington Lane	201	DJ100
Tra	Belgrave Walk	200	DD97
⇌	Bellingham	183	EB90
⇌	Belmont	218	DA110
⊖	Belsize Park	274	D3
⇌	Belvedere	166	FA76
⇌	Berkhamsted	38	AW18
⊖	Bermondsey	300	D6
⇌	Berrylands	198	CN98
⇌	Betchworth	248	CR132
○	Bethnal Green	288	E4
⊖	Bethnal Green	288	G3
⇌	Bexley	186	FA88
⇌	Bexleyheath	166	EY82
⇌	Bickley	204	EL97
⇌	Birkbeck	202	DW97
Tra	Birkbeck	202	DW97
⇌	Blackfriars, North Entrance	286	G10
	South Entrance	298	G1
Riv	Blackfriars Pier	286	G10
⇌	Blackheath	315	K10
Tra	Blackhorse Lane	202	DU101
○	Blackhorse Road	123	DX56
⊖	Blackhorse Road	123	DX56
DLR	Blackwall	302	F1
◆	Bluewater	189	FU88
⊖	Bond Street	285	H9
◆	Bondway	310	B2
⇌	Bookham	230	BZ123
⊖	Borough	299	K5
⊖	Boston Manor	157	CG77
⊖	Bounds Green	99	DK51
DLR	Bow Church	290	B3
⇌	Bowes Park	99	DL51
⊖	Bow Road	290	A2
⇌	Boxhill & Westhumble	247	CH131
⊖	Brent Cross	119	CX59
⇌	Brentford	157	CJ79
⇌	Brentwood	108	FW48
⇌	Bricket Wood	60	CA30
⇌	Brimsdown	83	DY41
⇌	Brixton	161	DN84
⊖	Brixton	161	DN84
⇌	Brockley	313	M10
○	Brockley	313	M10
⊖	Bromley-by-Bow	290	D4
⇌	Bromley North	204	EG95
◆	Bromley North	204	EG95
⇌	Bromley South	204	EG97
○	Brondesbury	272	G6
○	Brondesbury Park	272	E8
⇌	Brookmans Park	63	CX27
⇌	Broxbourne	49	EA20
○	Bruce Grove	100	DT54
◆	Brunel	132	AT74
⊖	Buckhurst Hill	102	EK47
⇌	Burnham	131	AK72
⊖	Burnt Oak	96	CQ53
○	Bushey	76	BX44
○	Bush Hill Park	82	DT44
⇌	Byfleet & New Haw	212	BK110
Riv	Cadogan Pier	308	D3
⊖	Caledonian Road	276	B4
○	Caledonian Road & Barnsbury	276	D6
○	Cambridge Heath	278	E10
○	Camden Road	275	L7
⊖	Camden Town	275	K8
○	Canada Water	301	H5
⊖	Canada Water	301	H5
⊖	Canary Wharf	302	C3
DLR	Canary Wharf	302	B2
Riv	Canary Wharf Pier	301	P2
⊖	Canning Town	291	K8
DLR	Canning Town	291	K8
◆	Canning Town	291	K8
⇌	Cannon Street	299	L1
⊖	Cannon Street	299	L1
○	Canonbury	277	J3
⊖	Canons Park	96	CL52
○	Carpenders Park	94	BX48
⇌	Carshalton	218	DF105
⇌	Carshalton Beeches	218	DF107
⇌	Castle Bar Park	137	CF71
⇌	Caterham	236	DU124
⇌	Catford	183	EA87
⇌	Catford Bridge	183	EA87
Tra	Centrale	202	DQ103
⇌	Chadwell Heath	126	EX59
⇌	Chafford Hundred	169	FV77
⇌	Chalfont & Latimer	72	AW39
⊖	Chalfont & Latimer	72	AW39
⊖	Chalk Farm	274	F6
⊖	Chancery Lane	286	E7
⇌	Charing Cross	298	A2
⊖	Charing Cross	298	A2
⇌	Charlton	304	B10
⇌	Cheam	217	CY108
Riv	Chelsea Harbour Pier	308	A7
⇌	Chelsfield	224	EV106
⇌	Chertsey	193	BF102
⊖	Chesham	54	AQ31
⇌	Cheshunt	67	DZ30
○	Cheshunt	67	DZ30
⇌	Chessington North	216	CL106
⇌	Chessington South	215	CK108
⊖	Chigwell	103	EP49
⇌	Chilworth	259	BE140
○	Chingford	102	EE45
◆	Chingford	102	EE45
⇌	Chipstead	234	DF118
⇌	Chislehurst	205	EN96
⇌	Chiswick	158	CQ80
⊖	Chiswick Park	158	CQ77
⇌	Chorleywood	73	BD42
⊖	Chorleywood	73	BD42
Tra	Church Street	201	DP103
⇌	City Thameslink	286	G9
⇌	Clandon	244	BH129
⊖	Clapham Common	161	DJ84
○	Clapham High Street	161	DK83
⇌	Clapham Junction	160	DD84
○	Clapham Junction	160	DD84
⊖	Clapham North	161	DL83
⊖	Clapham South	181	DH86
○	Clapton	122	DV61
⇌	Claygate	215	CD107
⇌	Clock House	203	DY96
⇌	Cobham & Stoke D'Abernon	230	BY117
⊖	Cockfosters	80	DG42
⊖	Colindale	118	CS55
⊖	Colliers Wood	180	DD94
Tra	Coombe Lane	220	DW106
⇌	Coulsdon South	235	DK116
⇌	Coulsdon Town	235	DL115
⊖	Covent Garden	286	A10
⇌	Crayford	187	FE86
⇌	Crews Hill	65	DM34
⇌	Cricklewood	119	CX63
⇌	Crofton Park	183	DZ85
◆	Cromwell Road	198	CL95
DLR	Crossharbour	302	D6
○	Crouch Hill	121	DM59
⊖	Croxley	75	BP44
⇌	Crystal Palace	182	DU93
○	Crystal Palace	182	DU93
⇌	Cuffley	65	DM29
DLR	Custom House for ExCeL	292	B10
DLR	Cutty Sark for Maritime Greenwich	314	E3
DLR	Cyprus	293	M10
⇌	Dagenham Dock	146	EZ68
⊖	Dagenham East	127	FC64
⊖	Dagenham Heathway	146	EZ65
○	Dalston Junction	278	A5
○	Dalston Kingsland	277	P4
⇌	Dartford	188	FL86
⇌	Datchet	152	AV81
⊖	Debden	85	EQ42
⇌	Denham	114	BG59
⇌	Denham Golf Club	113	BD59
⇌	Denmark Hill	311	L9
○	Denmark Hill	311	L9
⇌	Deptford	314	A4
DLR	Deptford Bridge	314	B6
DLR	Devons Road	290	C4
⊖	Dollis Hill	119	CU64
⇌	Dorking	247	CJ134
⇌	Dorking Deepdene	247	CJ134
⇌	Dorking West	263	CG135
⇌	Drayton Green	137	CF72
⇌	Drayton Park	276	F2
Tra	Dundonald Road	179	CZ94
⇌	Dunton Green	241	FF119
⇌	Ealing Broadway	137	CK73
⊖	Ealing Broadway	137	CK73
⊖	Ealing Common	138	CM74
⊖	Earl's Court	295	K9
⇌	Earlsfield	180	DC88
⇌	Earlswood	266	DF136
⊖	East Acton	139	CT72
⊖	Eastcote	116	BW59
⇌	East Croydon	202	DR103
Tra	East Croydon	202	DR103
⇌	East Dulwich	162	DS84
⊖	East Finchley	120	DE56
⊖	East Ham	144	EL66
DLR	East India	291	H10
⊖	East Putney	179	CY85
⇌	Ebbsfleet International	190	GA86
⇌	Eden Park	203	EA99
⊖	Edgware	96	CP51
◆	Edgware	96	CN51
⊖	Edgware Road	284	C7
⇌	Edmonton Green	100	DU47
○	Edmonton Green	100	DU47
◆	Edmonton Green	100	DU47
⇌	Effingham Junction	229	BU123
⇌	Egham	173	BA92
⇌	Elephant & Castle	299	J8
⊖	Elephant & Castle	299	J8
⇌	Elmers End	203	DX98
Tra	Elmers End	203	DX98
⊖	Elm Park	127	FH63
⇌	Elmstead Woods	184	EL93
⇌	Elstree & Borehamwood	78	CM42
⇌	Eltham	185	EM85
◆	Eltham	185	EM85
DLR	Elverson Road	314	D9
⊖	Embankment	298	B2
Riv	Embankment Pier	298	C2
○	Emerson Park	128	FL59
◆	Empress Approach Bus Terminus	307	J2
⇌	Enfield Chase	82	DQ41
⇌	Enfield Lock	83	DY37
○	Enfield Town	82	DS42
⊖	Epping	70	EU31
⇌	Epsom	216	CR113
⇌	Epsom Downs	233	CV115
⇌	Erith	167	FE78
⇌	Esher	197	CD103
⇌	Essex Road	277	J7
⇌	Euston	285	M2
○	Euston	285	M2
⊖	Euston	285	M2
◆	Euston	285	N3
⊖	Euston Square	285	M4
⇌	Ewell East	217	CV110
⇌	Ewell West	216	CS109
◆	Fairfield	198	CL96
⊖	Fairlop	103	ER53
⇌	Falconwood	165	EQ84
⇌	Farncombe	258	AT144
⇌	Farningham Road	208	FP96
⇌	Farringdon	286	F6
⊖	Farringdon	286	F6
⇌	Feltham	175	BV88
⇌	Fenchurch Street	287	P10
Riv	Festival Pier	298	C2
Tra	Fieldway	221	EB108
⊖	Finchley Central	98	DA53
⊖	Finchley Road	273	N4
○	Finchley Road & Frognal	273	N3
⇌	Finsbury Park	121	DN61
⊖	Finsbury Park	121	DN61
◆	Finsbury Park	121	DN61
⇌	Forest Gate	281	P2
⇌	Forest Hill	182	DW89
○	Forest Hill	182	DW89
⊖	Fulham Broadway	307	K4
⇌	Fulwell	177	CD91
DLR	Gallions Reach	293	P10
⊖	Gants Hill	125	EN58
⇌	Garston	76	BX35
⇌	Gatwick Airport	269	DH152
Tra	George Street	202	DQ103
⇌	Gerrards Cross	112	AY57
⇌	Gidea Park	128	FJ56
⇌	Gipsy Hill	182	DS92
⊖	Gloucester Road	295	P8
⊖	Golders Green	120	DA59
◆	Golders Green	120	DA60
⊖	Goldhawk Road	294	A5
⇌	Gomshall	261	BR139
⊖	Goodge Street	285	M6
⇌	Goodmayes	126	EU60
⇌	Gordon Hill	81	DP39
○	Gospel Oak	275	H1
⊖	Grange Hill	103	ER49
⇌	Grange Park	81	DP43
Tra	Gravel Hill	221	DY108
⇌	Gravesend	191	GG87
⇌	Grays	170	GA79
⊖	Great Portland Street	285	K5
⇌	Greenford	137	CD67
⊖	Greenford	137	CD67
⇌	Greenhithe for Bluewater	189	FU85
Riv	Greenland Pier	301	N7
⊖	Green Park	297	L3
⇌	Greenwich	314	D4
DLR	Greenwich	314	D4
Riv	Greenwich Pier	314	E2
⇌	Grove Park	184	EG90
◆	Grove Park	184	EH90
⇌	Guildford	258	AW135
◆	Guildford	258	AX135
○	Gunnersbury	158	CP78
⊖	Gunnersbury	158	CP78
⇌	Hackbridge	201	DH103
○	Hackney Central	278	E4
⇌	Hackney Downs	278	E3
○	Hackney Downs	278	E3
○	Hackney Wick	280	A5
⇌	Hadley Wood	80	DC38
○	Haggerston	278	A8
⊖	Hainault	103	ES52
⊖	Hammersmith	294	B9
◆	Hammersmith	294	B9
⊖	Hampstead	120	DC63
○	Hampstead Heath	274	D1
⇌	Hampton	196	CA95
⇌	Hampton Court	197	CE98
⇌	Hampton Wick	197	CJ95
⊖	Hanger Lane	138	CM69
⇌	Hanwell	137	CE73
○	Harlesden	138	CR68
⊖	Harlesden	138	CR68
◆	Harlow	35	ER14
⇌	Harlow Mill	36	EW10
⇌	Harlow Town	35	ER12
⇌	Harold Wood	106	FM53
⇌	Harringay	121	DN58
○	Harringay Green Lanes	121	DP58
Tra	Harrington Road	202	DW97
◆	Harrow	117	CE58
⇌	Harrow & Wealdstone	117	CE56
○	Harrow & Wealdstone	117	CE56
⊖	Harrow & Wealdstone	117	CE56
⇌	Harrow on the Hill	117	CE58
⊖	Harrow on the Hill	117	CE58
○	Hatch End	94	BZ52
⇌	Hatfield	45	CW17
⊖	Hatton Cross	155	BT84
◆	Hatton Cross	155	BT84
⇌	Haydons Road	180	DC92
⇌	Hayes	204	EF102
⇌	Hayes & Harlington	155	BT76
○	Headstone Lane	94	CB53
⇌	Heathrow Airport Terminal 4	175	BP85
⊖	Heathrow Airport Terminal 4	175	BP85
⇌	Heathrow Airport Terminal 5	154	BJ83
⊖	Heathrow Airport Terminal 5	154	BJ83
⇌	Heathrow Airport Terminals 2-3	155	BP83
⊖	Heathrow Airport Terminals 2-3	155	BP83
⇌	Hemel Hempstead	40	BG23
◆	Hemel Hempstead	40	BJ20
⇌	Hendon	119	CU58
⊖	Hendon Central	119	CW57
⇌	Herne Hill	181	DP86
DLR	Heron Quays	302	B3
⇌	Hersham	196	BY104
⇌	Hertford East	32	DS09
⇌	Hertford North	31	DP09
⇌	Highams Park	101	ED51
⊖	High Barnet	80	DA42
⇌	Highbury & Islington	276	F5
○	Highbury & Islington	276	F5
⊖	Highbury & Islington	276	F5
⊖	Highgate	121	DH58
⊖	High Street Kensington	295	L5
⊖	Hillingdon	114	BN64
Riv	Hilton Docklands Nelson Dock Pier	301	N2
⇌	Hinchley Wood	197	CF104
⇌	Hither Green	184	EE86
⊖	Holborn	286	B8
⊖	Holland Park	294	G3
⊖	Holloway Road	276	D2
○	Homerton	279	J4
⇌	Honor Oak Park	183	DX86
○	Honor Oak Park	183	DX86
⇌	Horley	269	DH149
⊖	Hornchurch	128	FK62
⇌	Hornsey	121	DM56
⇌	Horsley	245	BS125
⇌	Hounslow	176	CB85
⊖	Hounslow Central	156	CA83
⊖	Hounslow East	156	CC82
⊖	Hounslow West	156	BY82
⇌	How Wood	60	CC28
○	Hoxton	287	P1
⇌	Hurst Green	254	EF132
⊖	Hyde Park Corner	296	G4
⊖	Ickenham	115	BQ63
⇌	Ilford	125	EN62
○	Imperial Wf	307	P7
DLR	Island Gardens	302	E9
⇌	Isleworth	157	CF82
⇌	Iver	153	BF75
⇌	Kempton Park	175	BV94
⇌	Kenley	220	DQ114
⊖	Kennington	298	G10

Kensal Green 282 B2
Kensal Green 282 B2
Kensal Rise 282 B1
Kensington (Olympia) 294 E6
Kensington (Olympia) 294 E6
Kensington (Olympia) 294 E6
Kent House 203 DY95
Kentish Town 275 L3
Kentish Town 275 L3
Kentish Town West 275 H5
Kenton 117 CH58
Kenton 117 CH58
Kew Bridge 158 CM78
Kew Gardens 158 CM81
Kew Gardens 158 CM81
Kidbrooke 164 EH83
Kilburn 272 F5
Kilburn High Road 273 K9
Kilburn Park 273 J10
King George V 305 M3
King Henry's Drive 221 EB109
Kingsbury 118 CN57
King's Cross 286 A1
King's Cross St. Pancras 286 A1
Kings Langley 59 BQ30
Kingston 198 CL95
Kingswood 233 CZ121
Knightsbridge 296 E5
Knockholt 224 EY109
Ladbroke Grove 282 F8
Ladywell 183 EB85
Lakeside 169 FV76
Lambeth North 298 E5
Lancaster Gate 284 A10
Langdon Park 290 D7
Langley 153 BA75
Latimer Road 282 D10
Lea Bridge 123 DY10
Leatherhead 231 CG121
Lebanon Road 202 DS103
Lee 184 EG86
Leicester Square 285 P10
Lewisham 314 D10
Lewisham 314 E10
Lewisham 314 E10
Leyton 123 EC62
Leyton Midland Road 123 EC60
Leytonstone 124 EE60
Leytonstone High Road 124 EE61
Limehouse 289 L9
Limehouse 289 L9
Liverpool Street 287 N7
Liverpool Street 287 N7
Liverpool Street 287 N7
Lloyd Park 220 DT105
London Bridge 299 N3
London Bridge 299 N3
London Bridge City Pier 299 N2
London City Airport 304 G2
London Eye Pier 298 C4
London Fields 278 E7
London Gatwick Airport 269 DH152
London Heathrow Airport Central 155 BP83
London Heathrow Airport Terminal 4 175 BQ85
London Road (Guildford) 242 AY134
Longcross 192 AT102
Loughborough Junction 311 H10
Loughton 84 EL43
Lower Sydenham 183 DZ92
Maida Vale 283 M2
Malden Manor 198 CS101
Manor House 121 DP59
Manor Park 124 EK63
Mansion House 287 K10
Marble Arch 284 F10
Maryland 281 J4
Marylebone 284 E5
Marylebone 284 E5
Masthouse Terrace Pier 302 B10
Maze Hill 315 J2
Merstham 251 DJ128
Merton Park 200 DA95
Mile End 289 N4
Millbank Pier 298 B9
Mill Hill Broadway 96 CS51
Mill Hill East 97 CX52
Mitcham 200 DE98
Mitcham Eastfields 200 DG96
Mitcham Junction 200 DG99
Mitcham Junction 200 DG99
Monument 287 M10
Moorgate 287 L7
Moorgate 287 L7
Moor Park 93 BR48
Morden 200 DB97
Morden Road 200 DB96
Morden South 200 DA99
Mornington Crescent 275 L10
Mortlake 158 CQ83
Motspur Park 199 CV99
Mottingham 184 EL88
Mudchute 302 D9
Neasden 118 CS64
New Addington 221 EC110
New Barnet 80 DD43
New Beckenham 183 DZ94
Newbury Park 125 ER58
New Cross 313 P5
New Cross 313 P5
New Cross Gate 313 L5
New Cross Gate 313 L5
New Eltham 185 EP88
New Malden 198 CS97
New Southgate 99 DH50
Norbiton 198 CN95
Norbury 201 DM95
North Acton 138 CR70
North Dulwich 182 DR85
North Ealing 138 CM72
Northfields 157 CH76
Northfleet 190 GA86
North Greenwich 303 J4
North Greenwich 303 J4
North Harrow 116 CA57
Northolt 136 CA66
Northolt Park 116 CB63
North Sheen 158 CN84
Northumberland Park 100 DV53
North Wembley 117 CK62
North Wembley 117 CK62
Northwick Park 117 CG59
Northwood 93 BS52
Northwood Hills 93 BU54
Norwood Junction 202 DT98
Norwood Junction 202 DT98
Notting Hill Gate 295 J1
Nunhead 312 G9
Nutfield 267 DL136
Oakleigh Park 98 DD45
Oakwood 81 DJ43
Ockendon 149 FX69
Old Street 287 L3
Old Street 287 L3
Orpington 205 ET103
Orpington 205 ET103
Osterley 157 CD80
Oval 310 E3
Oxford Circus 285 L9
Oxshott 214 CC113
Oxted 254 EE129
Paddington 284 A8
Paddington 284 A8
Palmers Green 99 DM49
Parkhouse 45 CT17
Park Royal 138 CN70
Park Street 61 CD26
Parsons Green 307 H7
Peckham Rye 312 C8
Peckham Rye 312 C8
Penge East 182 DW93
Penge West 182 DV93
Penge West 182 DV93
Perivale 137 CG68
Petts Wood 205 EQ99
Phipps Bridge 200 DC97
Piccadilly Circus 297 M1
Pimlico 297 N10
Pinner 116 BY56
Plaistow 281 M10
Plumstead 165 ER77
Ponders End 83 DX43
Pontoon Dock 304 C3
Poplar 302 C1
Potters Bar 64 DA32
Preston Road 118 CL60
Prince Regent 292 C10
Prince Regent 292 D10
Pudding Mill Lane 280 C9
Purfleet 168 FN78
Purley 219 DP112
Purley Oaks 220 DQ109
Putney 159 CY84
Putney Bridge 306 G10
Putney Pier 306 E10
Queensbury 118 CM55
Queen's Park 282 F1
Queen's Park 282 F1
Queens Road Peckham 312 F6
Queens Road Peckham 312 F6
Queenstown Road (Battersea) 309 K6
Queensway 295 M1
Radlett 77 CG35
Rainham 147 FF70
Ravensbourne 183 ED94
Ravenscourt Park 159 CU77
Rayners Lane 116 BZ59
Raynes Park 199 CW96
Rectory Road 122 DT62
Redbridge 124 EK58
Redhill 250 DG133
Redhill 250 DG133
Reedham 219 DM113
Reeves Corner 201 DP103
Regent's Park 285 J5
Reigate 250 DA133
Richmond 158 CL84
Richmond 158 CL84
Richmond 158 CL84
Richmond 177 CK85
Rickmansworth 92 BK45
Rickmansworth 92 BK45
Riddlesdown 220 DR113
Roding Valley 102 EK49
Romford 127 FE58
Romford 127 FE58
Rotherhithe 301 H4
Royal Albert 292 G10
Royal Oak 283 M7
Royal Victoria 291 N10
Roydon 34 EG13
Ruislip 115 BS60
Ruislip Gardens 115 BU63
Ruislip Manor 115 BU60
Russell Square 286 A5
Rye House 49 EC15
St. Albans Abbey 43 CD22
St. Albans City 43 CE20
St. Helier 200 DA100
St. James's Park 297 N6
St. James Street 123 DY57
St. Johns 314 B8
St. John's Wood 274 A10
St. Katharine's Pier 300 A2
St. Margarets (SG12) 33 EC11
St. Margarets (TW1) 177 CH86
St. Mary Cray 206 EU98
St. Pancras International 286 A1
St. Paul's 287 J8
Salfords 266 DG142
Sanderstead 220 DR109
Sandilands 202 DT103
Seer Green & Jordans 89 AR52
Selhurst 202 DS99
Seven Kings 125 ES60
Sevenoaks 256 FG124
Sevenoaks 257 FJ125
Seven Sisters 122 DS57
Seven Sisters 122 DS57
Seven Sisters 122 DS57
Shadwell 288 F10
Shadwell 288 F10
Shalford 258 AY140
Shenfield 109 GA45
Shepherd's Bush 294 D4
Shepherd's Bush 294 D4
Shepherd's Bush 294 C4
Shepherd's Bush Market 294 A3
Shepperton 195 BQ99
Shoreditch High Street 287 P5
Shoreham 225 FG111
Shortlands 204 EE96
Sidcup 186 EU89
Silver Street 100 DT50
Slade Green 167 FG81
Sloane Square 296 G9
Slough 132 AT74
Snaresbrook 124 EG57
South Acton 158 CQ76
Southall 156 BZ75
South Bermondsey 300 G10
Southbury 82 DV42
South Croydon 220 DR106
South Ealing 157 CJ76
Southfields 179 CZ88
Southgate 99 DJ46
South Greenford 137 CE69
South Hampstead 273 P7
South Harrow 116 CC62
South Kensington 296 B8
South Kenton 117 CJ60
South Kenton 117 CJ60
South Merton 199 CZ97
South Quay 302 D5
South Ruislip 116 BW63
South Ruislip 116 BW63
South Tottenham 122 DT57
Southwark 298 G3
South Wimbledon 180 DB94
South Woodford 102 EG54
Staines 174 BG92
Staines 173 BF92
Stamford Brook 159 CT77
Stamford Hill 122 DS59
Stanmore 95 CK50
Star Lane 291 J5
Stepney Green 289 J5
Stockwell 310 B8
Stoke Newington 122 DT61
Stonebridge Park 138 CN66
Stonebridge Park 138 CN66
Stone Crossing 189 FS85
Stoneleigh 217 CU106
Stratford 280 G6
Stratford 280 G6
Stratford 280 G6
Stratford 280 G6
Stratford 280 G6
Stratford High Street 280 G7
Stratford International 280 D5
Strawberry Hill 177 CE90
Streatham 181 DL92
Streatham Common 181 DK94
Streatham Hill 181 DL89
Sudbury & Harrow Road 117 CH64
Sudbury Hill 117 CE63
Sudbury Hill Harrow 117 CE63
Sudbury Town 137 CH65
Sunbury 195 BT95
Sundridge Park 184 EH94
Sunnymeads 152 AY83
Surbiton 197 CK100
Surrey Quays 301 J8
Sutton 218 DC107
Sutton Common 200 DB103
Swanley 207 FD98
Swanscombe 190 FZ85
Swiss Cottage 274 A6
Sydenham 182 DW91
Sydenham 182 DW91
Sydenham Hill 182 DT90
Syon Lane 157 CG80
Tadworth 233 CW122
Taplow 130 AF72
Tattenham Corner 233 CV118
Teddington 177 CG93
Temple 286 D10
Thames Ditton 197 CF101
Theobalds Grove 67 DX32
Therapia Lane 201 DL101
Theydon Bois 85 ET36
Thornton Heath 202 DQ98
Thornton Heath 201 DN99
Tilbury Town 170 GE82
Tolworth 198 CP103
Tooting 180 DG93
Tooting Bec 180 DF90
Tooting Broadway 180 DE92
Tottenham Court Road 285 N8
Tottenham Hale 122 DV55
Tottenham Hale 122 DV55
Totteridge & Whetstone 98 DB47
Tower Gateway 288 B10
Tower Hill 287 P10
Tufnell Park 121 DJ63
Tulse Hill 181 DP89
Turkey Street 82 DW37
Turnham Green 158 CS77
Turnpike Lane 121 DN55
Turnpike Lane 121 DP55
Twickenham 177 CF87
Upminster 128 FQ61
Upminster 128 FQ61
Upminster 128 FQ61
Upminster Bridge 128 FN61
Upney 145 ET66
Upper Halliford 195 BS96
Upper Holloway 121 DK61
Upper Warlingham 236 DU118
Upton Park 144 EH67
Uxbridge 134 BK66
Vauxhall 310 B2
Vauxhall 310 B2
Victoria 297 K8
Victoria 297 K8
Victoria Bus Sta 297 K7
Victoria Coach Sta 297 J9
Virginia Water 192 AY99
Waddon 219 DN105
Waddon Marsh 201 DN103
Wallington 219 DH107
Waltham Cross 67 DY34
Waltham Cross 67 DY34
Walthamstow Central 123 EA56
Walthamstow Central 123 EA56
Walthamstow Central 123 EA56
Walthamstow Central 123 EA56
Walthamstow Queens Road 123 DZ57
Walton-on-Thames 213 BU105
Wandle Park 201 DN103
Wandsworth Common 180 DF88
Wandsworth Riverside Quarter Pier 160 DA84
Wandsworth Road 309 M9
Wandsworth Town 160 DB84
Wanstead 124 EH58
Wanstead Park 124 EH63
Wapping 300 G3
Ware 33 DY07
Warren Street 285 M4
Warwick Avenue 283 N5
Waterloo 298 E4
Waterloo 298 E4
Waterloo East 298 E3
Watford 75 BT41
Watford High Street 76 BW42
Watford Junction 76 BW40
Watford Junction 76 BW40
Watford North 76 BW37
Welham Green 45 CX23
Wellesley Road 202 DQ103
Welling 166 EU82
Welwyn Garden City 29 CY09
Welwyn Garden City 29 CX08
Wembley Central 118 CL64
Wembley Central 118 CL64
Wembley Central 118 CL64
Wembley Park 118 CN62
Wembley Stadium 118 CM64
West Acton 138 CN72
Westbourne Park 283 H6
West Brompton 307 K1
West Brompton 307 K1
West Brompton 307 K1
West Byfleet 212 BG112
Westcombe Park 315 P1
West Croydon 202 DQ102
West Croydon 202 DQ102
West Croydon 202 DQ102
West Croydon 202 DQ102
West Drayton 134 BL74
West Dulwich 182 DR88
West Ealing 137 CH73
Westferry 290 A10
West Finchley 98 DB51
West Ham 291 K2
West Ham 291 K2
West Ham 291 J2
West Hampstead 273 K5
West Hampstead 273 L5
West Hampstead (Thameslink) 273 K4
West Harrow 116 CC58
West India Quay 302 C1
West Kensington 294 G10
Westminster 298 B5
Westminster Pier 298 B4
West Norwood 181 DP90
West Ruislip 115 BQ61
West Ruislip 115 BQ61
West Silvertown 303 P3
West Sutton 218 DA105
West Wickham 203 EC101
Weybridge 212 BN107
Whitechapel 288 E6
Whitechapel 288 E6
White City 294 B1
White City 294 B2
White Hart Lane 100 DT52
Whitton 176 CC87
Whyteleafe 236 DT117
Whyteleafe South 236 DU119
Willesden Green 272 B4
Willesden Junction 139 CT69
Willesden Junction 139 CT69
Wimbledon 179 CZ93
Wimbledon 179 CZ93
Wimbledon 179 CZ93
Wimbledon Chase 199 CY96
Wimbledon Park 180 DA90
Winchmore Hill 99 DN46
Windsor & Eton Central 151 AR81
Windsor & Eton Riverside 151 AR80
Woking 227 AZ117
Woldingham 237 DX122
Woodford 102 EH51
Woodgrange Park 124 EK64
Wood Green 99 DM54
Wood Lane 294 B1
Woodmansterne 235 DH116
Woodside 202 DV100
Woodside Park 98 DB49
Wood Street 123 EC56
Woolwich Arsenal 305 P8
Woolwich Arsenal 305 P8
Woolwich Arsenal Pier 305 P6
Woolwich Dockyard 305 J8
Worcester Park 199 CU102
Worplesdon 226 AV124
Wraysbury 173 BA86

The London Congestion Charging Zone was introduced to reduce traffic congestion within Central London.

- The congestion charging zone operates inside the 'Inner Ring Road' linking Marylebone Road, Euston Road, Pentonville Road, Tower Bridge, Elephant and Castle, Vauxhall Bridge and Park Lane. The route around the zone is exempt from charge (see map below).

- The daily operating time is from 7am to 6pm, Monday to Friday, excluding public holidays and the period between Christmas Day and New Year's Day.

- Payment of the daily £11.50 Congestion Charge, either in advance or on the day of travel, allows the registered vehicle to enter, drive around and leave the congestion zone as many times as required on that one day.

- Payments can be made in a variety of ways but in all cases the vehicle registration number and the dates to be paid for must be given.
Charges can be paid:
  - online at www.tfl.gov.uk/roadusers/congestioncharging
  - by Congestion Charging Auto Pay by registering online
  - by phone on 0343 222 2222
  - by text message to 81099 for drivers who have pre-registered on the website or telephone.
  - by post, ten days before travel, by requesting an application form from Congestion Charging, PO Box 4780, Worthing, BN11 9PQ, or downloading the form from the website and posting to the same address.

- Further information, including vehicles eligible for exemption or a discount, can be found on the website **www.tfl.gov.uk/roadusers/congestioncharging** or by telephoning 0343 222 2222

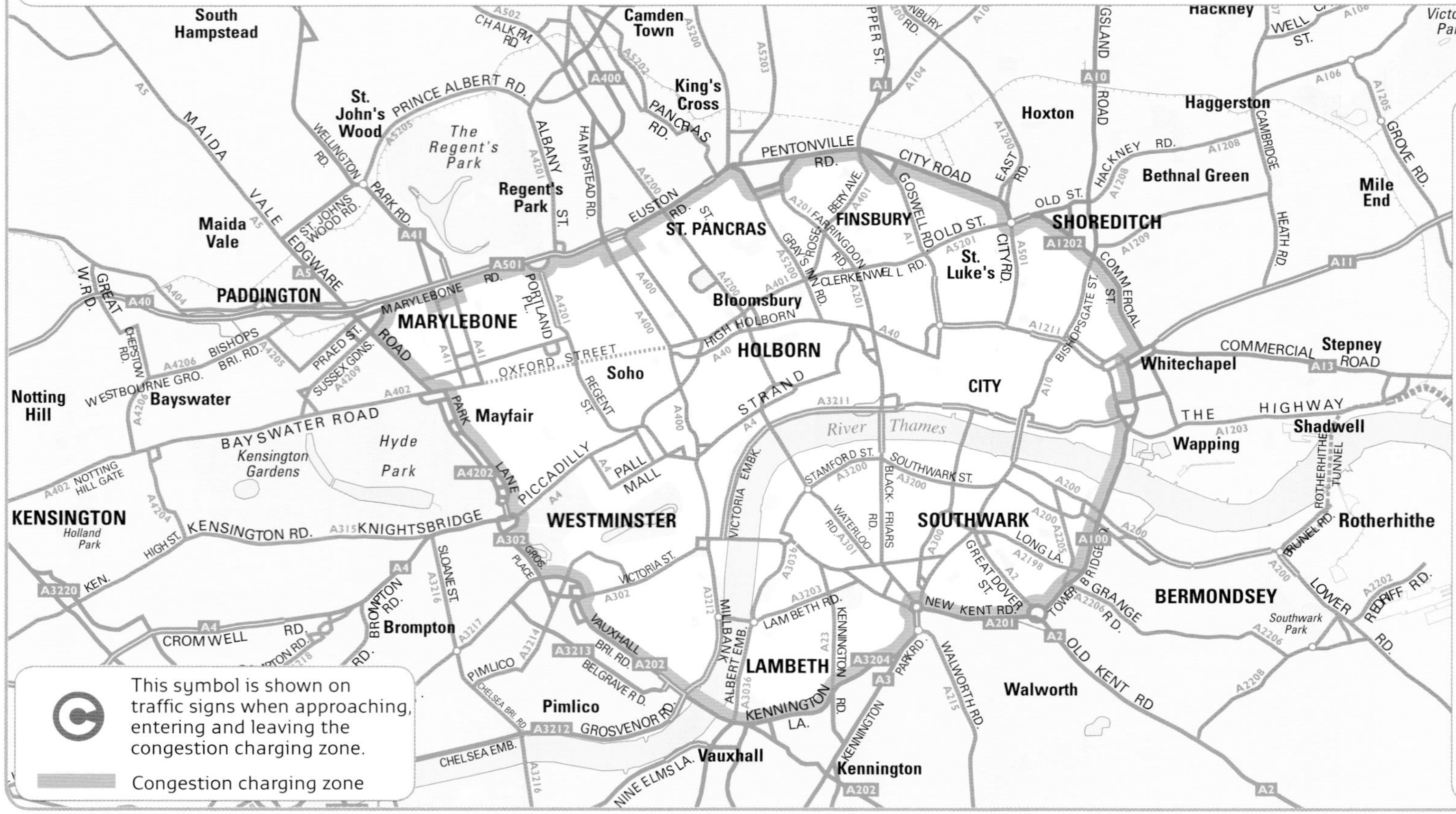

- Residents inside the congestion zone are eligible for a 90% discount upon payment of an annual £10 registration fee.

- On paying the charge the car registration number is held on a database. Cameras in and around the congestion zone record all vehicle number plates and check them against the database.
  - Drivers can pay the £11.50 charge until midnight on the day of travel.
  - Drivers who forget to pay by midnight on the day of travel can pay by midnight on the following charging day but they will then incur a £2.50 surcharge making the total charge £14. This charge can only be paid by telephone or online.

Any driver who has not paid before midnight on the following charging day will be sent a £130 Penalty Charge Notice (PCN).
Payment within 14 days will reduce this to £65. Failure to pay within 28 days will result in the penalty being increased to £195.

This symbol is shown on traffic signs when approaching, entering and leaving the congestion charging zone.

Congestion charging zone

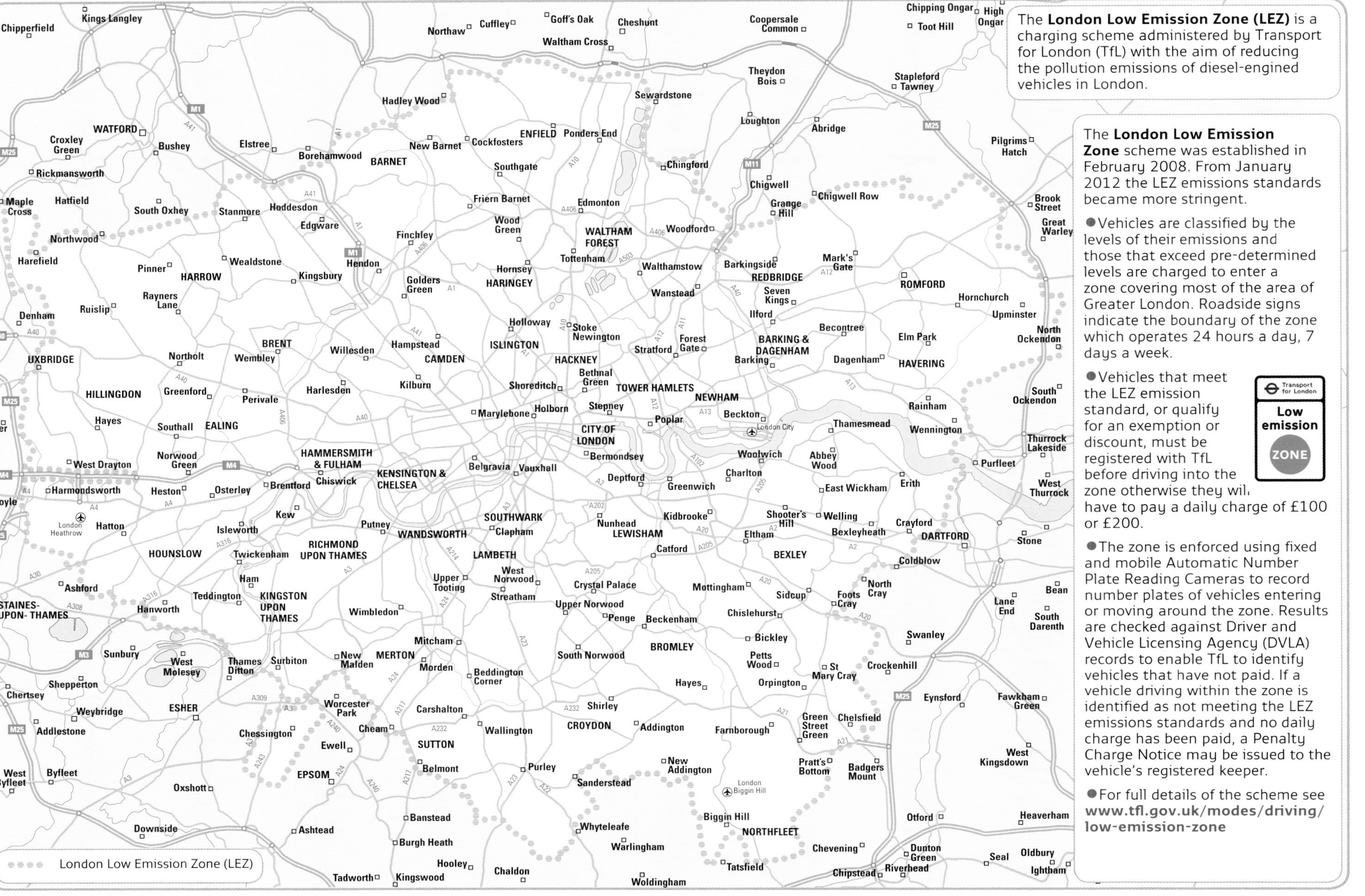

The **London Low Emission Zone (LEZ)** is a charging scheme administered by Transport for London (TfL) with the aim of reducing the pollution emissions of diesel-engined vehicles in London.

The **London Low Emission Zone** scheme was established in February 2008. From January 2012 the LEZ emissions standards became more stringent.

- Vehicles are classified by the levels of their emissions and those that exceed pre-determined levels are charged to enter a zone covering most of the area of Greater London. Roadside signs indicate the boundary of the zone which operates 24 hours a day, 7 days a week.
- Vehicles that meet the LEZ emission standard, or qualify for an exemption or discount, must be registered with TfL before driving into the zone otherwise they will have to pay a daily charge of £100 or £200.
- The zone is enforced using fixed and mobile Automatic Number Plate Reading Cameras to record number plates of vehicles entering or moving around the zone. Results are checked against Driver and Vehicle Licensing Agency (DVLA) records to enable TfL to identify vehicles that have not paid. If a vehicle driving within the zone is identified as not meeting the LEZ emissions standards and no daily charge has been paid, a Penalty Charge Notice may be issued to the vehicle's registered keeper.
- For full details of the scheme see **www.tfl.gov.uk/modes/driving/low-emission-zone**

West End theatres & cinemas

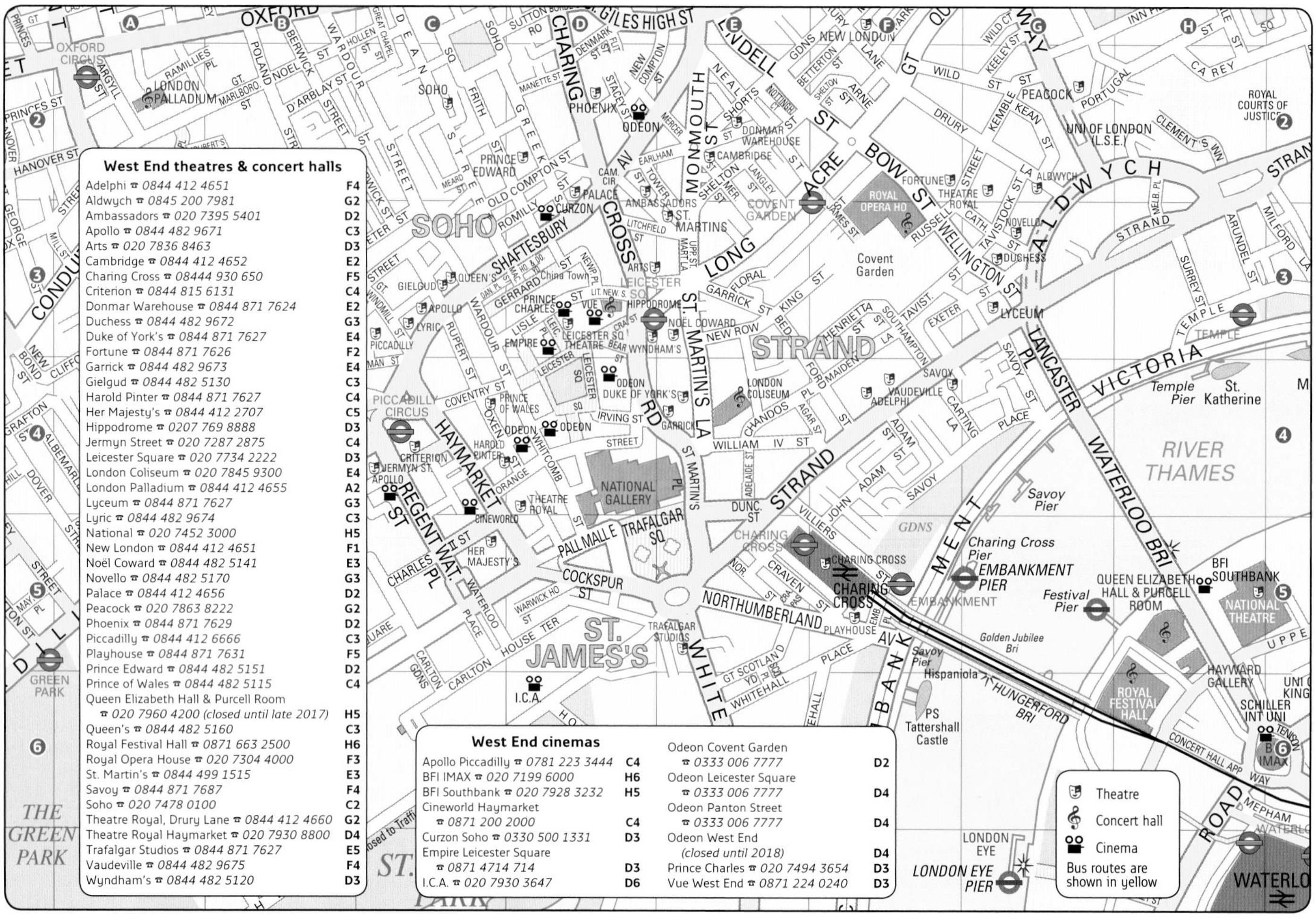

West End theatres & concert halls

Adelphi ☎ *0844 412 4651*	F4
Aldwych ☎ *0845 200 7981*	G2
Ambassadors ☎ *020 7395 5401*	D2
Apollo ☎ *0844 482 9671*	C3
Arts ☎ *020 7836 8463*	D3
Cambridge ☎ *0844 412 4652*	E2
Charing Cross ☎ *08444 930 650*	F5
Criterion ☎ *0844 815 6131*	C4
Donmar Warehouse ☎ *0844 871 7624*	E2
Duchess ☎ *0844 482 9672*	G3
Duke of York's ☎ *0844 871 7627*	E4
Fortune ☎ *0844 871 7626*	F2
Garrick ☎ *0844 482 9673*	E4
Gielgud ☎ *0844 482 5130*	C3
Harold Pinter ☎ *0844 871 7627*	C4
Her Majesty's ☎ *0844 412 2707*	C5
Hippodrome ☎ *0207 769 8888*	D3
Jermyn Street ☎ *020 7287 2875*	C4
Leicester Square ☎ *020 7734 2222*	D3
London Coliseum ☎ *020 7845 9300*	E4
London Palladium ☎ *0844 412 4655*	A2
Lyceum ☎ *0844 871 7627*	G3
Lyric ☎ *0844 482 9674*	C3
National ☎ *020 7452 3000*	H5
New London ☎ *0844 412 4651*	F1
Noël Coward ☎ *0844 482 5141*	E3
Novello ☎ *0844 482 5170*	G3
Palace ☎ *0844 412 4656*	D2
Peacock ☎ *020 7863 8222*	G2
Phoenix ☎ *0844 871 7629*	D2
Piccadilly ☎ *0844 412 6666*	C3
Playhouse ☎ *0844 871 7631*	F5
Prince Edward ☎ *0844 482 5151*	D2
Prince of Wales ☎ *0844 482 5115*	C4
Queen Elizabeth Hall & Purcell Room ☎ *020 7960 4200 (closed until late 2017)*	H5
Queen's ☎ *0844 482 5160*	C3
Royal Festival Hall ☎ *0871 663 2500*	H6
Royal Opera House ☎ *020 7304 4000*	F3
St. Martin's ☎ *0844 499 1515*	E3
Savoy ☎ *0844 871 7687*	F4
Soho ☎ *020 7478 0100*	C2
Theatre Royal, Drury Lane ☎ *0844 412 4660*	G2
Theatre Royal Haymarket ☎ *020 7930 8800*	D4
Trafalgar Studios ☎ *0844 871 7627*	E5
Vaudeville ☎ *0844 482 9675*	F4
Wyndham's ☎ *0844 482 5120*	D3

West End cinemas

Apollo Piccadilly ☎ *0781 223 3444*	C4
BFI IMAX ☎ *020 7199 6000*	H6
BFI Southbank ☎ *020 7928 3232*	H5
Cineworld Haymarket ☎ *0871 200 2000*	C4
Curzon Soho ☎ *0330 500 1331*	D3
Empire Leicester Square ☎ *0871 4714 714*	D3
I.C.A. ☎ *020 7930 3647*	D6
Odeon Covent Garden ☎ *0333 006 7777*	D2
Odeon Leicester Square ☎ *0333 006 7777*	D4
Odeon Panton Street ☎ *0333 006 7777*	D4
Odeon West End *(closed until 2018)*	D4
Prince Charles ☎ *020 7494 3654*	D3
Vue West End ☎ *0871 224 0240*	D3

Theatre
Concert hall
Cinema
Bus routes are shown in yellow

West End shopping

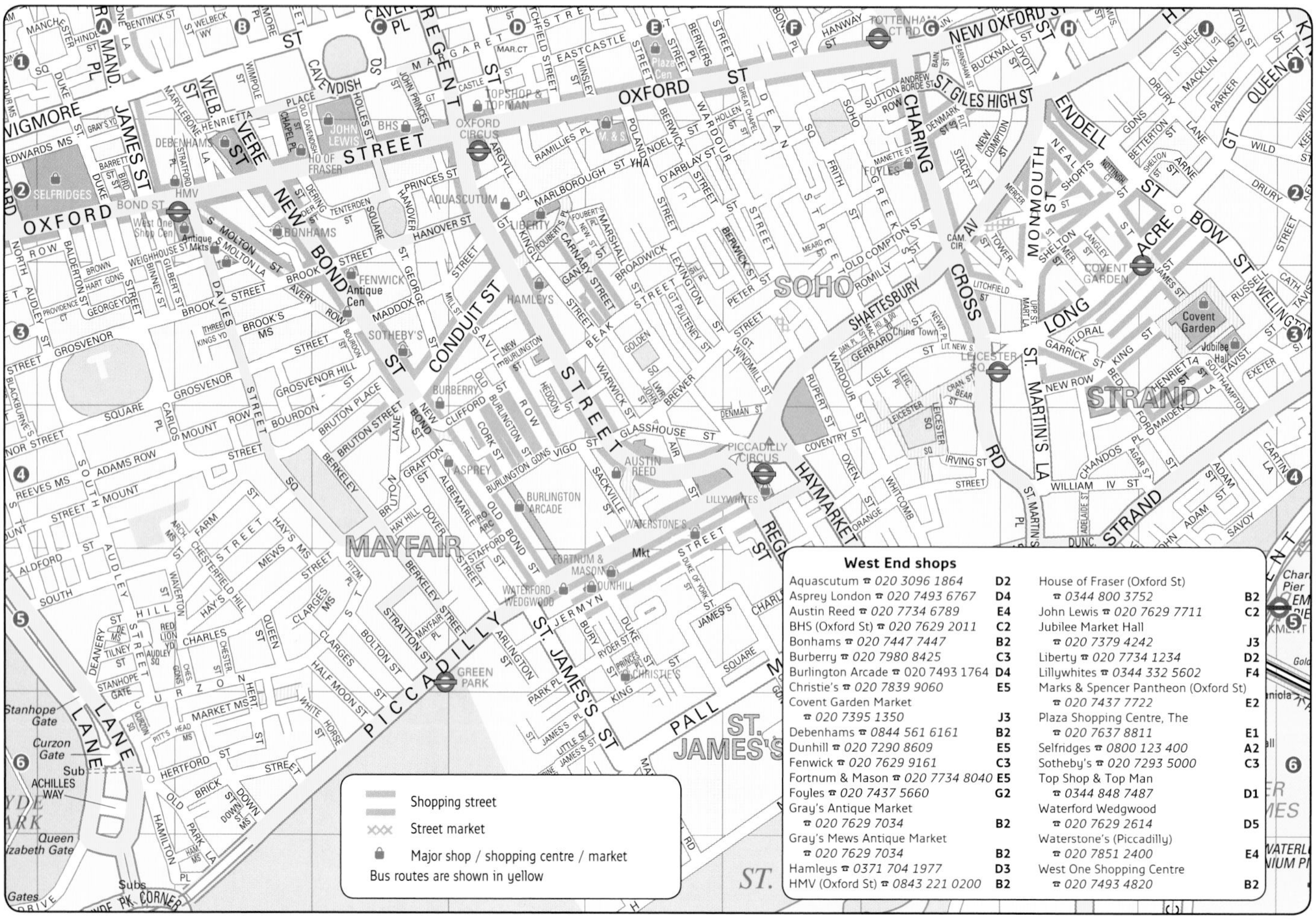

West End shops

Aquascutum ☎ *020 3096 1864*	D2
Asprey London ☎ *020 7493 6767*	D4
Austin Reed ☎ *020 7734 6789*	E4
BHS (Oxford St) ☎ *020 7629 2011*	C2
Bonhams ☎ *020 7447 7447*	B2
Burberry ☎ *020 7980 8425*	C3
Burlington Arcade ☎ *020 7493 1764*	D4
Christie's ☎ *020 7839 9060*	E5
Covent Garden Market ☎ *020 7395 1350*	J3
Debenhams ☎ *0844 561 6161*	B2
Dunhill ☎ *020 7290 8609*	E5
Fenwick ☎ *020 7629 9161*	C3
Fortnum & Mason ☎ *020 7734 8040*	E5
Foyles ☎ *020 7437 5660*	G2
Gray's Antique Market ☎ *020 7629 7034*	B2
Gray's Mews Antique Market ☎ *020 7629 7034*	B2
Hamleys ☎ *0371 704 1977*	D3
HMV (Oxford St) ☎ *0843 221 0200*	B2
House of Fraser (Oxford St) ☎ *0344 800 3752*	B2
John Lewis ☎ *020 7629 7711*	C2
Jubilee Market Hall ☎ *020 7379 4242*	J3
Liberty ☎ *020 7734 1234*	D2
Lillywhites ☎ *0344 332 5602*	F4
Marks & Spencer Pantheon (Oxford St) ☎ *020 7437 7722*	E2
Plaza Shopping Centre, The ☎ *020 7637 8811*	E1
Selfridges ☎ *0800 123 400*	A2
Sotheby's ☎ *020 7293 5000*	C3
Top Shop & Top Man ☎ *0344 848 7487*	D1
Waterford Wedgwood ☎ *020 7629 2614*	D5
Waterstone's (Piccadilly) ☎ *020 7851 2400*	E4
West One Shopping Centre ☎ *020 7493 4820*	B2

Shopping street
Street market
Major shop / shopping centre / market
Bus routes are shown in yellow

2 Willow Rd, NW3 120 DE63
Admiralty Arch, SW1 297 P2
Africa Cen, WC2 286 A10
Air Forces Mem, Egh. TW20 172 AX91
Albert Mem, SW7 296 A4
Aldenham Country Pk, Borwd. WD6 77 CG43
Alexander Fleming Laboratory Mus, W2 284 B8
Alexandra Palace, N22 99 DK54
All Hallows-on-the-Wall C of E Ch, EC2 287 M7
Altura Twr, SW11 308 A9
Amersham Mus, Amer. HP7 55 AP40
Apollo Hammersmith, W6 294 B10
Apollo Thea, W1 285 N10
Apollo Victoria Thea, SW1 297 L7
Aquatic Experience, Brent. TW8 157 CH81
ArcelorMittal Orbit, E20 280 D8
Arsenal FC, N5 276 E1
Arthur Jacob Nature Reserve, Slou. SL3 153 BC83
Avery Hill Pk, SE9 185 EQ86
Bank of England, EC2 287 L9
Bank of England Mus, EC2 287 M9
Bankside Gall, SE1 299 H1
Banqueting Ho, SW1 298 A3
Barbican Arts & Conf Cen, EC2 287 K6
Barnes Common, SW13 159 CU83
Barnet Mus, Barn. EN5 off Wood St 79 CY42
Battersea Dogs & Cats Home, SW8 309 K5
Battersea Park, SW11 308 F4
Bayhurst Wood Country Pk, Uxb. UB9 114 BM56
Beacon Wd Country Pk, Dart. DA2 189 FV91
Bekonscot Model Village, Beac. HP9 89 AK51
Bentley Priory Battle of Britain Mus, Stan. HA7 95 CF48
Bentley Priory Open Space, Stan. HA7 95 CF49
Berkhamsted Castle, Berk. HP4 38 AX18
Big Ben (Elizabeth Tower), SW1 298 B5
Bigbury Cl, N17 100 DS52
Blackheath, SE3 315 M7
Black Park Country Pk, Slou. SL3 133 AZ67
Bomber Command Mem, W1 297 J4
Borough Mkt, SE1 299 L3
Boston Manor Ho, Brent. TW8 157 CH78
Bourne Hall Mus & Lib, Epsom KT17 217 CT109
Brentford FC, Brent. TW8 157 CK79
Brentwood Mus, Brwd. CM14 108 FW49
Brewery, The, EC1 287 K6
British Dental Assoc Mus, W1 285 J7
British Lib, NW1 285 P2
British Lib Newspapers (Former), NW9 118 CS55
British Med Assoc, WC1 285 P4
British Mus, The, WC1 285 P7
Brockwell Park, SE24 181 DP86
Brompton Oratory, SW7 296 C7
Brooklands Mus, Wey. KT13 212 BN109
Bruce Castle Mus, N17 100 DS53
BruneGall, WC1 285 P6
Brunel Mus & Engine Ho, SE16 300 G4
Buckingham Palace, SW1 297 K5
Burgh Ho (Hampstead Mus), NW3 off New End Sq 120 DD63
Burpham Court Fm Pk, Guil. GU4 243 AZ128
Bushy Park, Tedd. TW11 197 CF95
Business Design Cen, N1 276 F9
Camden Arts Cen, NW3 273 N3
Camden Lock Mkt & Waterbuses, NW1 275 J7
Camley St Natural Pk, NW1 275 P10
Carlyle's Ho, SW3 308 C3
Cassiobury Park, Wat. WD18 75 BS41
Cathedral of the Holy Spirit Guildford, Guil. GU2 242 AV134
Cecilia Colman Gall, NW8 274 B10
Cecil Sharp Ho, NW1 275 H8
Cenotaph, The, SW1 298 A4
Central Criminal Ct, (Old Bailey), EC4 287 H8
Charles Dickens Mus, WC1 286 D4
Charlton Athletic FC, SE7 304 D10
Charterhouse, EC1 287 H5
Chartwell, West. TN16 255 ET131
Chelsea Antique Mkt, SW3 308 B2
Chelsea FC, SW6 307 L4
Chelsea Physic Gdn, SW3 308 E2
Chenies Manor, Rick. WD3 73 BA38
Chertsey Mus, Cher. KT16 off Windsor St 194 BG100
Chessington World of Adventures, Chess. KT9 215 CJ110
Chiltern Open Air Mus, Ch.St.G. HP8 91 AZ47
Chinatown, W1 off Gerrard St 285 P10
Chislehurst Caves, Chis. BR7 off Caveside Cl 205 EN95
Chiswick Ho, W4 158 CS79
Chobham Common National Nature Reserve, Wok. GU24 210 AS105
Churchill Mus & Cabinet War Rooms, SW1 297 P4
City of Westminster Archives Cen, SW1 297 P6
Clandon Park, Guil. GU4 244 BG132
Clapham Common, SW4 160 DG84
Claremont Landscape Gdn, Esher KT10 214 BZ108
Clarence Ho, SW1 297 M4
Cleopatra's Needle, WC2 298 C2
Climate Change (DECC), SW1 298 A3
Clink Prison Mus, SE1 299 L2
Cliveden, Maid. SL6 110 AD64
Clockmakers' Museum, The, (Guildhall Lib), EC2 287 K8
College of Arms, EC4 287 H10
Copper Box, E20 280 B5
Coram's Flds, WC1 286 B5
Coronet Thea, SE1 299 H7
County Hall, SE1 298 C4
Courtauld Inst of Art, WC2 286 C10
Covent Garden, WC2 286 B10
Crossness Pumping Sta, SE2 146 EY72
Crystal, The, E16 303 N1
Crystal Palace FC, SE25 202 DS98
Crystal Palace Nat Sports Cen, SE19 182 DU93
Crystal Palace Pk, SE19 182 DT92
Cuming Mus, SE17 off Walworth Rd 299 J9
Cutty Sark, SE10 314 E2
Danson Park, Well. DA16 166 EW84
Dartford Heath, Dart. DA1 187 FG88
Dartford Mus, Dart. DA1 188 FL87
De Havilland Aircraft Heritage Cen, St.Alb. AL2 62 CP29
Denham Aerodrome, Uxb. UB9 113 BD57
Department for Environment, Food & Rural Affairs (Defra), SW1 298 A7
Department for Transport (DfT), SW1 297 P8
Department of Energy & Climate Change (DECC), SW1 298 A3
Department of Health, SW1 298 A4
Design Mus, SE1 300 B3
Diana Princess of Wales Mem, W2 296 C4
Doctor Johnson's Ho, EC4 286 F9
Dominion Thea, W1 285 P8
Dorking & District Mus, Dor. RH4 263 CG136
Dorney Ct, Wind. SL4 150 AG77
Down Ho - Darwin Mus, Orp. BR6 223 EN112
Dulwich Coll Picture Gall, SE21 182 DS87
Ealing Common, W5 138 CL74
Eastbury Manor Ho, Bark. IG11 145 ET67
East Ham Nature Reserve & Visitor Cen, E6 293 K4
East Surrey Mus, Cat. CR3 236 DU124
East Village London, E20 280 E3
EDF Energy London Eye, SE1 298 C4
Egham Mus, Egh. TW20 173 BA92
Elmbridge Mus, Wey. KT13 212 BN105
Elstree Aerodrome, Borwd. WD6 77 CF41
Eltham Palace, SE9 184 EL87
Emirates Air Line, E16/SE10 303 L3
Epping Forest, Epp. CM16 & Loug. IG10 84 EJ39
Epping Forest District Mus, Wal.Abb. EN9 off Sun St 67 EC33
Epsom Downs Racecourse, Epsom KT18 233 CT118
Erith Lib & Mus, Erith DA8 off Walnut Tree Rd 167 FE78
Eros, W1 297 N1
Estorick Collection of Modern Italian Art, N1 277 H5
ExCeL London, E16 304 B1
Eynsford Castle, Dart. DA4 208 FL103
Fairfield Halls, Croy. CR0 202 DR104
Fan Mus, SE10 314 F4
Faraday Mus, W1 297 L1
Fenton Ho, NW3 120 DC62
Finsbury Park, N4 121 DP59
Firepower, SE18 305 P6
Florence Nightingale Mus, SE1 298 C5
Foreign & Commonwealth Office, SW1 297 P4
Fortnum & Mason, W1 297 L2
Forty Hall & Mus, Enf. EN2 82 DT38
Forum, The, NW5 275 K2
Foundling Mus, WC1 286 B4
Freemason's Hall (United Grand Lo of England), WC2 286 B8
Freightliners Fm, N7 276 D4
Freud Mus, NW3 274 A4
Fulham FC, SW6 306 C7
Fulham Palace, SW6 306 E9
Fuller's Griffin Brewery, W4 159 CT79
Garden Museum, SE1 298 C7
Gasworks Gall, SE11 310 D2
Gatwick Airport (London), Gat. RH6 268 DD153
Geffrye Mus, E2 287 P1
George Inn, SE1 299 L3
Golden Hinde, SE1 299 L2
Goldsmiths' Hall, EC2 287 J8
Gorhambury, St.Alb. AL3 42 BW19
Gravesham Mus, Grav. DA11 191 GH86
Gray's Inn, WC1 286 D6
Great Bookham Common, Lthd. KT23 230 BZ121
Greek Orthodox Cath of the Divine Wisdom (St. Sophia), W2 283 K10
Green Park, The, SW1 297 K3
Greenwich Heritage Cen, SE18 305 N6
Greenwich Pk, SE10 315 J4
Guards Mus, SW1 297 M5
Guildford Castle, Guil. GU1 258 AX136
Guildford House Gall, Guil. GU1 off High St 258 AX135
Guildford Mus, Guil. GU1 258 AX136
Guildhall, The, EC2 287 L8
Guildhall Art Gall, (Guildhall Lib), EC2 287 K8
Gunnersbury Park, W3 158 CM77
Gunnersbury Park Mus, W3 158 CN76
Hackney City Fm, E2 288 C1
Hackney Marsh, E9 123 DY62
Hackney Mus, E8 278 F5
Hainault Forest Country Pk, Chig. IG7 104 EW47
Hall Pl, Bex. DA5 187 FC86
Ham Ho, Rich. TW10 177 CJ88
Hamleys, W1 285 L10
Hampstead Heath, NW3 120 DD61
Hampton Court Palace & Pk, E.Mol. KT8 197 CE97
Harlequins RL, Twick. TW2 177 CE87
Harrods, SW1 296 E6
Harrow Arts Cen, Pnr. HA5 94 CB52
Harrow Mus, Har. HA2 116 CB55
Hatchlands Ho & Pk, Guil. GU4 244 BM131
Hatfield Ho & Pk, Hat. AL9 45 CX18
Hayward Gall, SE1 298 D2
Headley Heath, Epsom KT18 248 CP128
Heathrow Airport (London), Houns. TW6 155 BP81
Hertford Mus, Hert. SG14 32 DR09
Highgate Cem, N6 120 DG60
H.M.S. Belfast, SE1 299 P2
H.M.S. President, EC4 298 F1
H.M. Treasury, SW1 298 A4
Hogarth's Ho, W4 off Hogarth La 158 CS79
Holland Pk, W8 294 G4
Home Office, SW1 297 P7
Honeywood Heritage Cen, Cars. SM5 218 DF106
Horniman Mus, SE23 182 DV88
Horse Guards Par, SW1 297 P3
Horton Country Pk, Epsom KT19 216 CM110
Horton Park Children's Fm, Epsom KT19 216 CN110
Hounslow Heath, TW4 176 BY86
Houses of Parliament, SW1 298 B5
H.Q.S. Wellington, Master Mariners' Hall, WC2 286 E10
Hurlingham Club, SW6 159 CZ83
Hurlingham Park, SW6 307 H10
Hyde Park, W2 296 C2
ICC London, E16 304 B1
Imperial War Mus, SE1 298 F7
Institute of Contemporary Arts (I.C.A.), SW1 297 P3
IsmailCen, SW7 296 B8
Jewel Twr (Hos of Parliament), SW1 298 A6
Jewish Mus, NW1 275 J9
Jubilee Gdns, SE1 298 C3
Keats Ho, NW3 274 C1
Kempton Park Racecourse, Sun. TW16 176 BW94
Kensal Green Cem, W10 282 A3
Kensington Gdns, W2 295 P3
Kensington Palace, W8 295 M3
Kenwood Ho, NW3 120 DE60
Kew Observatory, Rich. TW9 157 CH83
Kew Palace (Royal Botanic Gdns), Rich. TW9 158 CL80
Kia Oval, The (Surrey CCC), SE11 310 D2
Kibes La, Ware SG12 33 DX06
Kingsbury Watermill, St.Alb. AL3 42 CB19
Kings Pl, N1 276 B10
Kingston Mus & Heritage Cen, Kings.T. KT1 198 CL96
Knole Ho & Pk, Sev. TN15 257 FL126
Lambeth Palace, SE1 298 C7
Lancaster Ho, SW1 297 L4
Langley Park Country Pk, Slou. SL3 133 BA70
Leatherhead Mus of Local History, Lthd. KT22 231 CH122
Lee Valley Hockey & Tennis Cen, E20 280 C1
Lee Valley Pk, E10 67 DZ31
Lee Valley VeloPark, E20 280 D2
Lee Valley White Water Cen, Waltham Cross EN9 67 EA33
Lee Vw, Enf. EN2 81 DP39
Leighton Ho Mus, W14 295 H6
Lesnes Abbey (ruins), Erith DA18 166 EX77
Leyton Orient FC, E10 123 EB62
Liberty, W1 285 L9
Lifetimes Mus (Croydon Cen Lib), Croy. CR0 202 DQ104
Liffler Rd, SE18 165 ES78
Lincoln's Inn, WC2 286 D8
Linley Sambourne Ho, W8 295 K5
Little Holland Ho, Cars. SM5 218 DE108
Little Venice (Waterbuses), W2 283 N6
Lloyd's of London, EC3 287 N9
London Aquatics Cen, E20 280 E7
London Biggin Hill Airport, West. TN16 222 EK113
London Brass Rubbing Cen (St. Martin-in-the-Fields Ch), WC2 298 A1
London Bridge Experience & The London Tombs, The, SE1 299 M2
London Canal Mus, The, N1 off New Wf Rd 276 B10
London Cen Mosque, NW8 284 D2
London City Airport, E16 304 G2
London Coliseum, WC2 298 A1
London Dungeon, The, SE1 299 M3
London Fire Brigade Mus, SE1 299 J4
London Gatwick Airport, Gat. RH6 268 DD153
London Heathrow Airport, Houns. TW6 155 BP81
London Met Archives, EC1 286 F4
London Motor Mus, Hayes UB3 155 BT76
London Mus of Water & Steam, Brent. TW8 158 CM78
London Palladium, W1 285 L9
London Peace Pagoda, SW11 308 F4
London Regatta Cen, E16 304 F1
London Stone, EC4 287 L10
London Television Cen, SE1 298 E2
London Tombs, The, SE1 299 M2
London Transport Mus, WC2 286 B10
Lord's (Marylebone CC & Mus, Middlesex CCC), NW8 284 B2
Lordsbury Fld, Wall. SM6 219 DJ110
Loseley Ho & Pk, Guil. GU3 258 AS140
Lowewood Mus, Hodd. EN11 49 EA18
Lullingstone Park Visitor Cen, Dart. DA4 225 FG107
Lullingstone Roman Vil, Dart. DA4 207 FH104
Lyric Hammersmith, W6 294 A9
Madame Tussauds, NW1 284 G5
Magna Carta Monument, Egh. TW20 172 AX89
Mall Galleries, SW1 297 P2
Mansion Ho, EC4 287 L9
Marble Arch, W1 284 F10
Marble Hill Ho, Twick. TW1 177 CJ87
Marlborough Ho, SW1 297 M3
MedicGalleries, W1 297 L1
Menier Chocolate Factory, SE1 off Southwark St 299 K3
Methodist Cen Hall, SW1 297 P5
Met Collection, The, SW6 307 J2
MI5 (Security Service) Thames Ho, SW1 298 A8
Mill Green Mus, Hat. AL9 45 CX15
Millwall FC, SE16 313 H1
Milton's Cottage, Ch.St.G. HP8 90 AV48
Ministry of Defence, SW1 298 A4
Ministry of Justice, SW1 297 M6
Monument, The, EC3 287 M10
Moor Park, Rick. WD3 92 BN48
Morden Hall Pk NT, Mord. SM4 200 DB97
Museum of Childhood at Bethnal Grn, E2 288 F2
Museum of Croydon, Croy. CR0 202 DQ104
Museum of Harlow, Harl. CM20 36 EV12
Museum of Instruments (Royal Coll of Music), SW7 296 A6
Museum of London, EC2 287 J7
Museum of London Docklands, E14 302 B1
Museum of Richmond, Rich. TW9 177 CK85
Museum of St. Albans, St.Alb. AL1 43 CE19
National Archives, The, Rich. TW9 158 CP80
National Army Mus, SW3 308 F2
National Gall, WC2 297 P1
National Maritime Mus, SE10 314 G3
National Portrait Gall, WC2 297 P1
National Thea, SE1 298 D2
Natural History Mus, SW7 296 A7
NEC Harlequins RFC, Twick. TW2 177 CE87
Nelson's Column, WC2 298 A2
New Scotland Yd, SW1 297 N6
Nonsuch Mansion, Sutt. SM3 217 CW107
O2, The, SE10 303 J3
O2 Academy Brixton, SW9 310 E10
Old Admiralty Bldg (MOD), SW1 297 P3
Old Amersham Rd, Ger.Cr. SL9 113 BB60
Old Billingsgate, EC3 299 N1
Old Curiosity Shop, WC2 286 C8
Old Operating Thea Mus & Herb Garret, SE1 299 M3
Old Town Hall Arts Cen, Hem.H. HP1 40 BK19
Olympia, W14 294 F7
Olympic Stadium, E20 280 C7
Orbis Wf, SW11 308 A10
Orleans Ho Gall, Twick. TW1 177 CH88
Osterley Park Ho, Islw. TW7 156 CC78
Painshill Park, Cob. KT11 213 BS114
Passport Office, SW1 297 K8
Percival David Foundation of Chinese Art, WC1 off Gordon Sq 285 P5
Peter Pan Statue, W2 296 A2
Petrie Mus of Egyptian Archaeology, WC1 off Malet Pl 285 N5
Photographers' Gall, W1 285 L9
Physical Energy Statue, W2 295 P3
Pitzhanger Manor Ho & Gall, W5 137 CJ74
Polesden Lacey, Ho & Gdn, Dor. RH5 246 CA130
Polish Inst & Sikorsk Mus, SW7 off Princes Gate 296 B5
Pollock's Toy Mus, W1 285 M6
Poppy Factory Mus, The, Rich. TW10 177 CK86
Portcullis Ho, SW1 off Bridge St 298 B5
Prince Henry's Room, EC4 286 E9
P.S. Tattershall Castle, SW1 298 B3
Pumphouse Ed Mus, Rotherhithe, SE16 301 M2
Quebec Ho (Wolfe's Ho), West. TN16 255 ER126
Quebec Ms, W1 284 F9
Queen Elizabeth Hall & Purcell Room, SE1 298 C2
Queen Elizabeth Olympic Pk, E20 280 C3
Queen Elizabeth IConf Cen, SW1 297 P5
Queen Elizabeth's Hunting Lo, E4 102 EF45
Queen Mary's Gdns, NW1 284 G3
Queen's Club, The (Tennis Cen), W14 306 E1
Queen's Gall, The, SW1 297 K5
Queen's Ho, The, SE10 314 G3
Queen's Ice & Bowl, W2 295 M1
Queens Park Rangers FC, W12 139 CV74
Queen's Twr, SW7 296 A6
Queen Victoria Mem, SW1 297 L4
R.A.F. Northolt, Ruis. HA4 115 BT64
Ragged Sch Mus, E3 289 M6
Rainham Hall, Rain. RM13 147 FG70
Ranelagh Gdns, SW3 308 G1
Ranmore Common, Dor. RH5 246 CB133
Red Ho, The (William Morris Ho), Bexh. DA6 166 EY84
Regent's Park, The, NW1 284 F1
Rich Mix Cen, The, E1 off Bethnal Grn Rd 288 B4
Richmond Park, Rich. TW10 178 CN88
Ripley's Believe It or Not!, W1 297 N1
Roosevelt Mem, W1 285 H10
Royal Acad of Arts, W1 297 L1
Royal Acad of Dramatic Art (R.A.D.A.), WC1 285 P6
Royal Air Force Mus, NW9 97 CU54
Royal Albert Hall, SW7 296 A5
Royal Berkshire Yeomanry Mus (Windsor TA Cen), Wind. SL4 151 AR83
Royal Botanic Gdns, Kew, Rich. TW9 158 CL80
Royal Coll of Surgeons of England, WC2 286 D8
Royal Courts of Justice, WC2 286 D9
Royal Dress Collection (Kensington Palace), W8 295 M3
Royal Festival Hall, SE1 298 D3
Royal Geographical Society, SW7 296 A5
Royal Horticultural Society Gdn Wisley, Wok. GU22 228 BL119
Royal Horticultural Society (Lawrence Hall), SW1 297 N7
Royal Horticultural Society (Lindley Hall), SW1 297 N8
Royal Hosp Chelsea & Mus, SW3 308 G1
Royal Mews, The, SW1 297 K6
Royal National Rose Society - Gdns of the Rose, The, St.Alb. AL2 60 BY26
Royal Observatory Greenwich (Flamsteed Ho), SE10 315 H4
Royal Opera Arc, SW1 297 N2
Royal Opera Ho, WC2 286 B10
Rugby Football Union Twickenham, Twick. TW1 177 CE86
SaatchGall, The, SW3 296 F9
Sadler's Wells Thea, EC1 286 G2
St. Albans Cath, St.Alb. AL3 43 CD20
St. Albans Organ Mus, St.Alb. AL1 off Camp Rd 43 CH21
St. Bartholomew-the-Great Ch, EC1 287 H7
St. Bride's Ch, EC4 286 G9
St. Clement Danes Ch, WC2 286 D9
St. James's Palace, SW1 297 M4
St. James's Park, SW1 297 N4
St. John's Gate & Mus of the Order of St. John, EC1 286 G5
St. John's Jerusalem, Dart. DA4 188 FP94
St. Katharine Docks, E1 300 B1
St. Lawrence Jewry Ch, EC2 287 K8
St. Martin-in-the-Fields Ch, WC2 298 A1
St. Mary at Hill Ch, EC3 299 N1
St. Mary-le-Bow Ch, EC2 287 K9
St. Paul's Cath, EC4 287 J9
Sandown Park Racecourse, Esher KT10 196 CB104
Saracens RFC, Wat. WD18 75 BV43
Science Mus, SW7 296 B7
Scoop at More London, SE1 off Tooley St 299 P3
Sea Life London Aquarium, SE1 298 C4
Selfridges, W1 284 G9
Serpentine, The, W2 296 C3
Serpentine Gall, W2 296 B3
Serpentine Sackler Gallery, W8 296 C2
Sevenoaks Mus, Sev. TN13 257 FJ125
Shakespeare's Globe Thea, SE1 299 J1
Shard, The, SE1 299 M3
Shell Cen, SE1 298 D3
Shere Mus, Guil. GU5 260 BN139
Sherlock Holmes Mus, NW1 284 F5
Sir John Soane's Mus, WC2 off Lincoln's Inn Flds 286 C8
Skinners' Hall, EC4 off Dowgate Hill 287 L10
Slough Mus, Slou. SL1 152 AU75
Somerset Ho, WC2 286 C10
South London Art Gall, SE5 311 P6
Southwark Cath, SE1 299 L2
Speaker's Cor, W2 284 F10
Spencer Ho, SW1 297 L3
Spitalfields City Fm, E1 288 C5
Squerryes Ct & Gdns, West. TN16 255 EQ128
Stapleford Aerodrome, Rom. RM4 86 EZ40
Stave Hill Ecological Pk, SE16 301 L4
Sternberg Cen, N3 98 DB54
Stock Exchange, EC4 287 H8
Strawberry Hill Ho, Twick. TW1 177 CF90
Surrey Docks Fm, SE16 301 N5
Sutton Ho, E9 278 G3
Sutton Pl, Guil. GU4 243 BA127
Syon Ho & Pk, Brent. TW8 157 CJ81
Tate Britain, SW1 298 A9
Tate Modern, SE1 299 H2
Telecom Twr, W1 285 L6
Temple, The, EC4 286 E10
Temple Bar, EC4 287 H9
Temple Bar Mem, EC4 286 E9
Thames Barrier Information & Learning Cen, SE18 304 E6
Theatre Royal, WC2 286 B9
Thorpe Park, Cher. KT16 193 BE98
Tilbury Fort, Til. RM18 171 GJ84
Tottenham Hotspur FC, N17 100 DT52
Tower Br Exhib, SE1 300 A3
Tower of London, EC3 300 A1
Tower Pier, EC3 299 P2
Trent Park Country Pk, Barn. EN4 80 DG40
Trinity Ho, EC3 287 P10
Upminster Tithe Barn Mus of Nostalgia, Upmin. RM14 128 FQ59
Valence Ho Mus, Dag. RM8 126 EX62
Valley Gdns, The, Egh. TW20 192 AS96
Verulamium Mus & Pk, St.Alb. AL3 42 CB20
Victoria & Albert Mus, SW7 296 B7
Victoria Embankment Gdns, WC2 298 B1
Victoria Park, E9 279 L8
Vincentia Ct, SW11 307 P9
Wallace Collection, W1 284 G8
Waltham Abbey (ruins), Wal.Abb. EN9 67 EC33
Walworth Garden Fm - Horticultural Training Cen, SE17 311 H1
Wandsworth Mus, SW18 180 DA85
Ware Mus, Ware SG12 33 DX06
Watermans Art Cen, Brent. TW8 158 CL79
Watford FC, Wat. WD18 75 BV43
Watford Mus, Wat. WD17 76 BW42
Weald Country Pk, Brwd. CM14 108 FS45
Wellington Arch, W1 297 H4
Wellington Mus, W1 296 G4
Wembley Arena, Wem. HA9 118 CN63
Wembley Stadium, Wem. HA9 118 CN63
Wentworth Golf Course, Vir.W. GU25 192 AT100
Wesley's Ho, EC1 287 L5
West Ham United FC, E13 144 EJ68
Westminster Abbey, SW1 298 A6
Westminster Abbey Mus, SW1 298 A6
Westminster Cath, SW1 297 L7
Westminster City Hall, SW1 297 M6
Whitechapel Art Gall, E1 288 B8
White Cube, N1 off Hoxton Sq 287 N3
White Cube, SW1 297 M2
William Morris Gall, E17 off Lloyd Pk 123 EA55
Wimbledon (All England Tennis & Croquet Club), SW19 179 CY91
Wimbledon Common, SW19 179 CT91
Wimbledon Windmill Mus, SW19 179 CV89
Windsor Castle, Wind. SL4 152 AS80
Windsor Great Pk, Ascot SL5, Egh. TW20 & Wind. SL4 172 AS93
Windsor Racecourse (Royal), Wind. SL4 151 AM79
Woolwich Common, SE18 165 EM80
Wrotham Pk, Barn. EN5 79 CZ36
WWT London Wetland Cen, SW13 159 CV80
Wyllyotts Cen & Potters Bar Mus, Pot.B. EN6 63 CZ32
ZSL London Zoo, NW1 274 G10

Key to map symbols

- P Short stay car park
- P Mid stay car park
- P Long stay car park
- London Underground station
- Railway station
- Docklands Light Railway station
- Monorail station
- Information centre for tourists
- Bus station
- Major hotel

London City

Tel. 020 7646 0000
www.londoncityairport.com

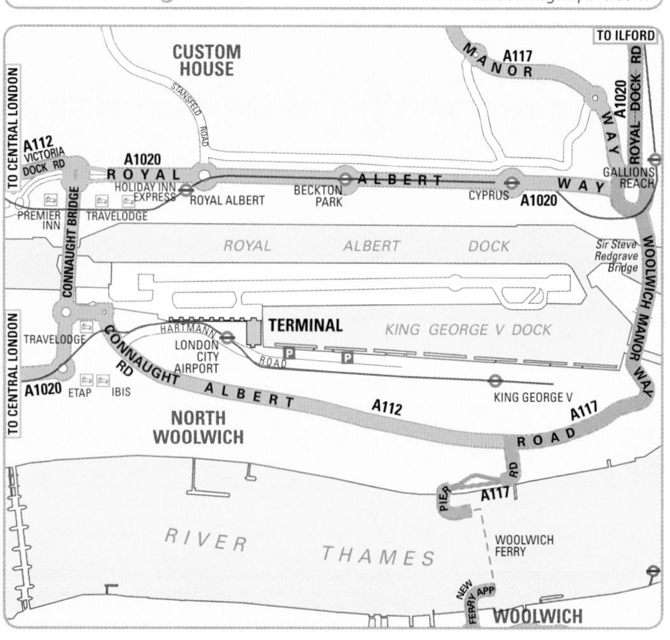

London Luton

Tel. 01582 405100
www.london-luton.co.uk

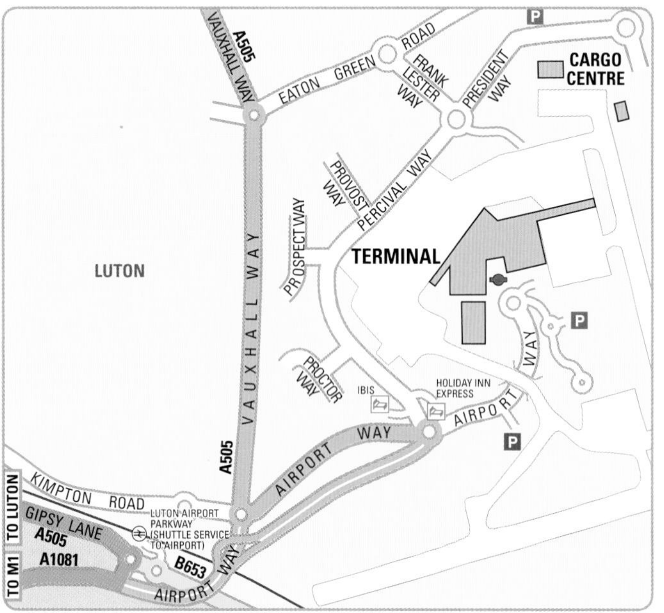

Stansted

Tel. 0844 335 1803
www.stanstedairport.com

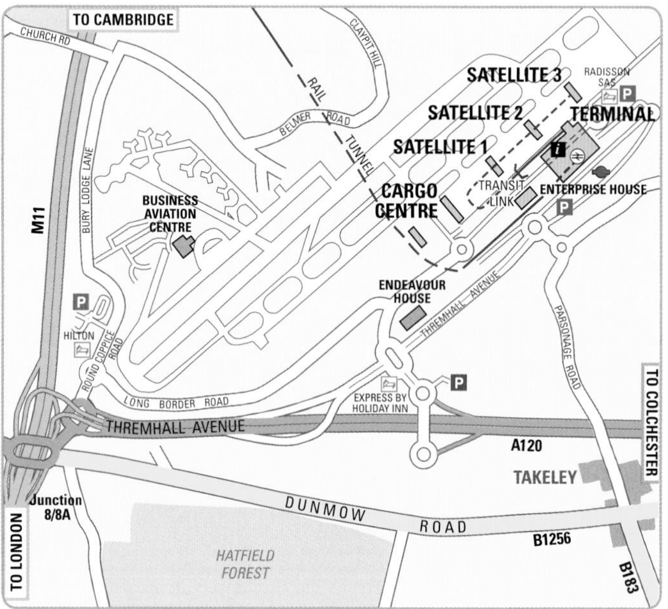

Heathrow

Tel. 0844 335 1801
www.heathrowairport.com

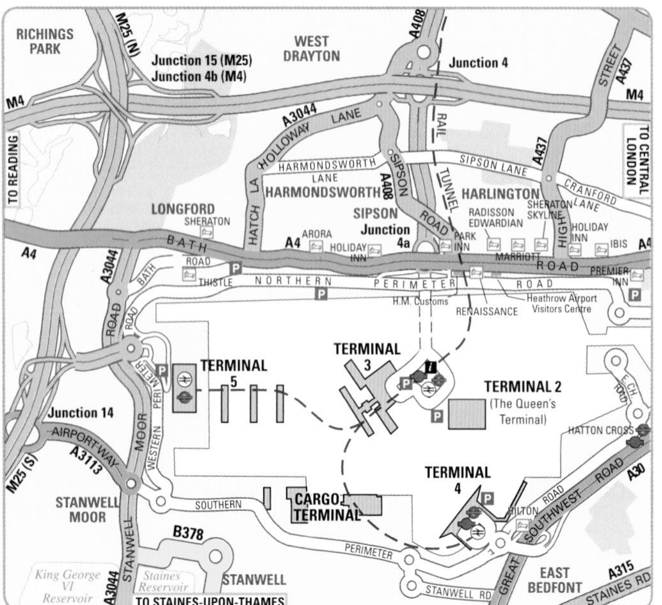

Gatwick

Tel. 0844 892 0322
www.gatwickairport.com

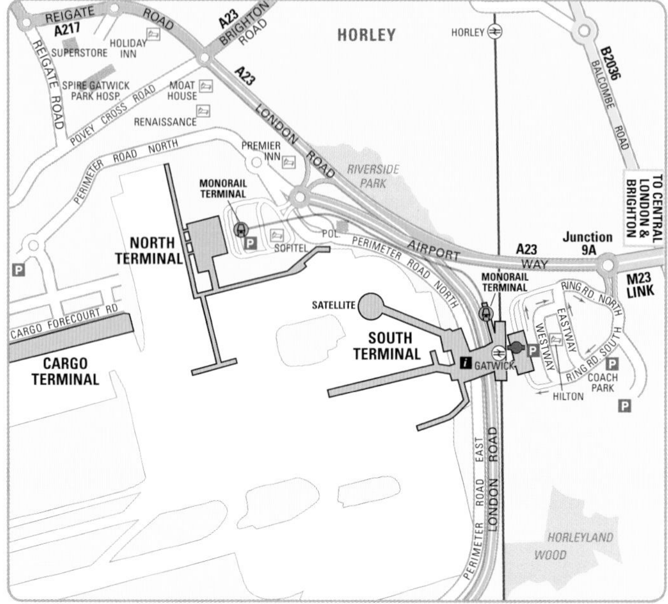

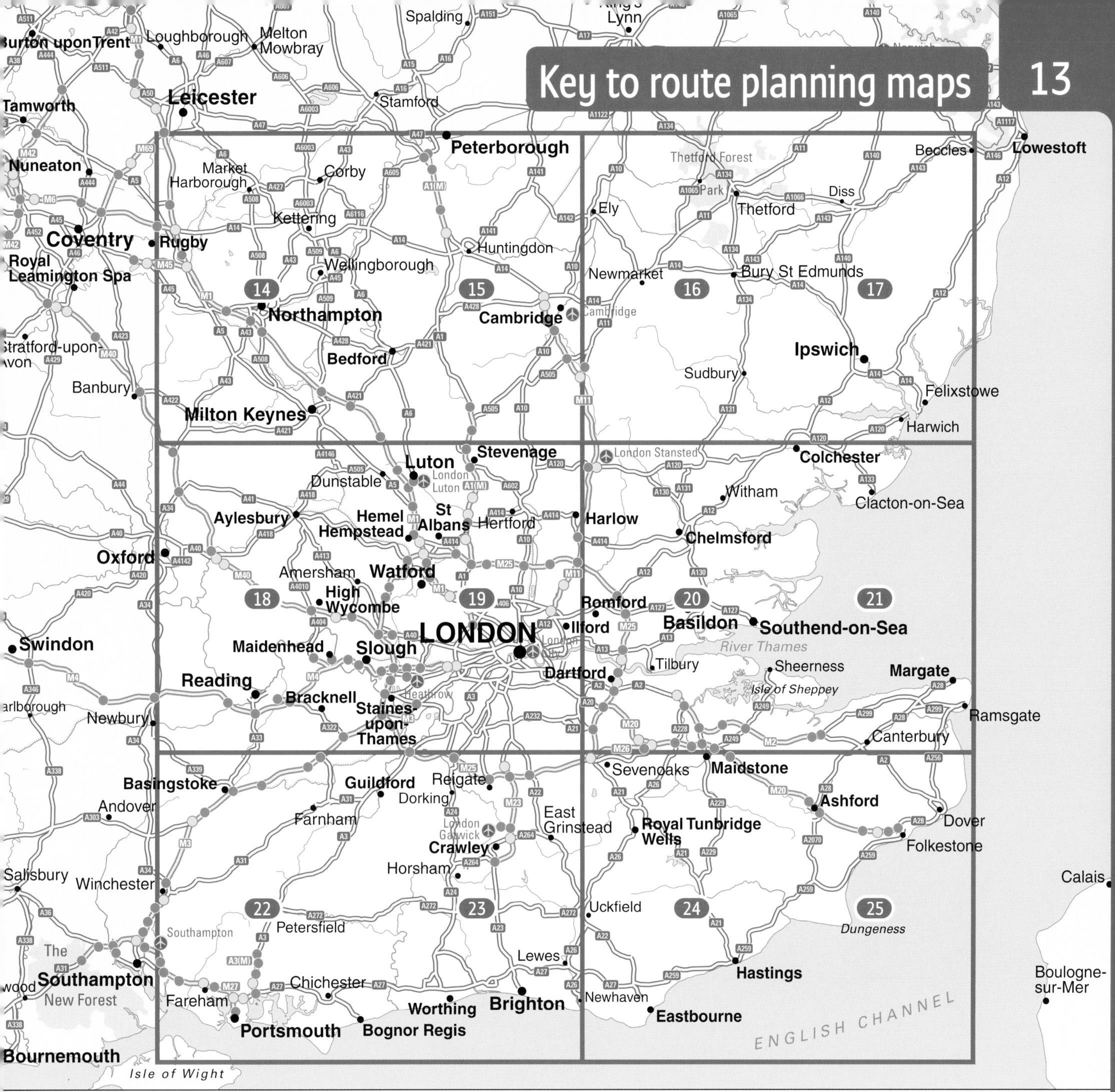

SCALE

0 2 4 6 miles
0 2 4 6 8 10 kilometres

4.2 miles to 1 inch / 2.6 km (1.6 miles) to 1 cm

Key to map symbols on pages 14-25

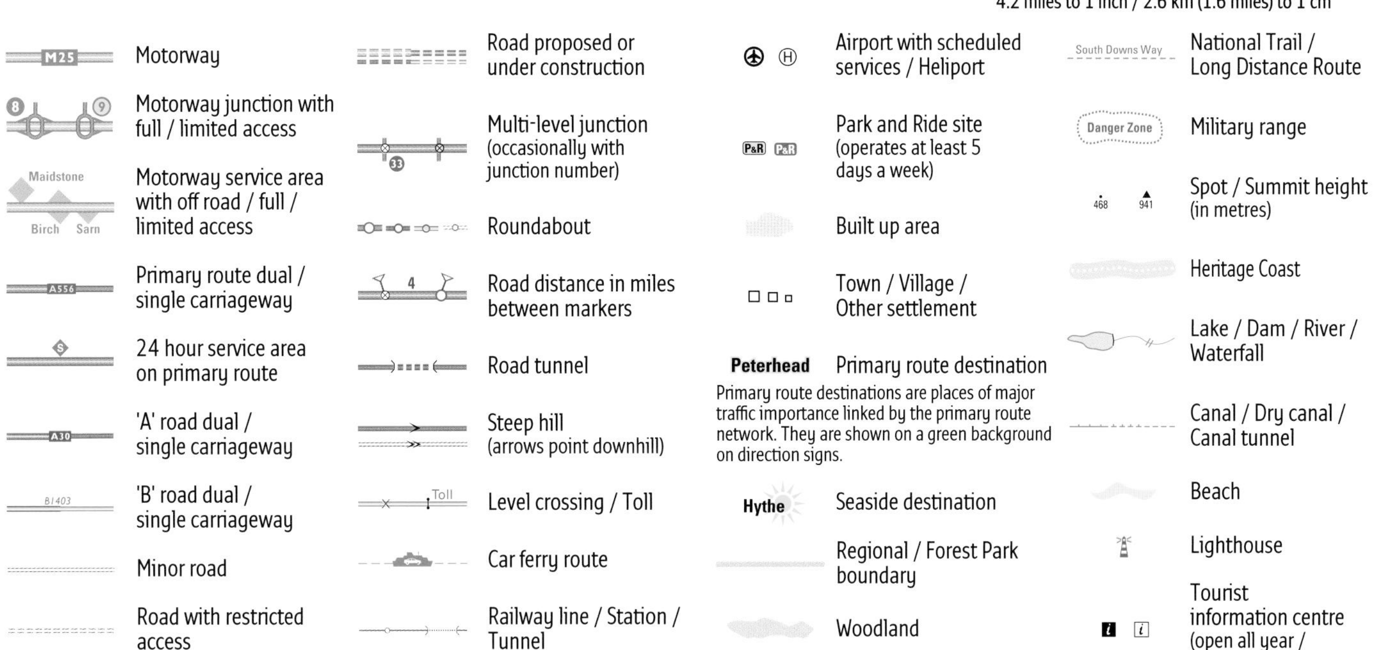
M25
Motorway
Motorway junction with full / limited access
Maidstone
Birch Sarn
Motorway service area with off road / full / limited access
A556
Primary route dual / single carriageway
24 hour service area on primary route
A30
'A' road dual / single carriageway
B1403
'B' road dual / single carriageway
Minor road
Road with restricted access
Road proposed or under construction
33
Multi-level junction (occasionally with junction number)
Roundabout
4
Road distance in miles between markers
Road tunnel
Steep hill (arrows point downhill)
Toll
Level crossing / Toll
Car ferry route
Railway line / Station / Tunnel
Airport with scheduled services / Heliport
P&R
Park and Ride site (operates at least 5 days a week)
Built up area
Town / Village / Other settlement
Peterhead
Primary route destination
Primary route destinations are places of major traffic importance linked by the primary route network. They are shown on a green background on direction signs.
Hythe
Seaside destination
Regional / Forest Park boundary
Woodland
South Downs Way
National Trail / Long Distance Route
Danger Zone
Military range
468
941
Spot / Summit height (in metres)
Heritage Coast
Lake / Dam / River / Waterfall
Canal / Dry canal / Canal tunnel
Beach
Lighthouse
Tourist information centre (open all year / open seasonally)

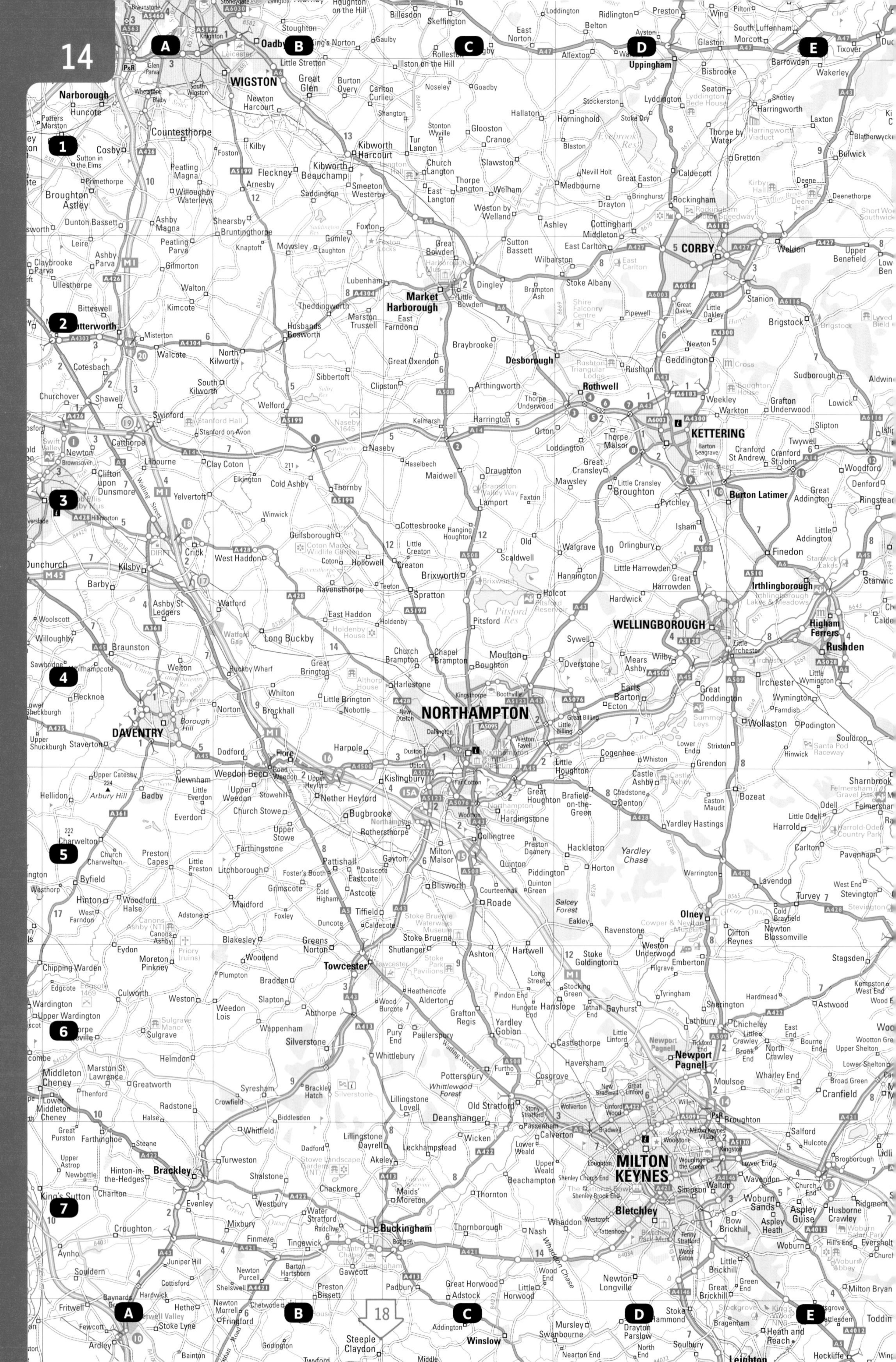
14
A
B
C
D
E
1
2
3
4
5
6
7
WIGSTON
Oadby
Narborough
Countesthorpe
Uppingham
CORBY
Kibworth Harcourt
Market Harborough
Desborough
Rothwell
KETTERING
Burton Latimer
Irthlingborough
WELLINGBOROUGH
Higham Ferrers
Rushden
DAVENTRY
NORTHAMPTON
Towcester
Brackley
Buckingham
MILTON KEYNES
Newport Pagnell
Olney
Bletchley
Winslow
Leighton
18

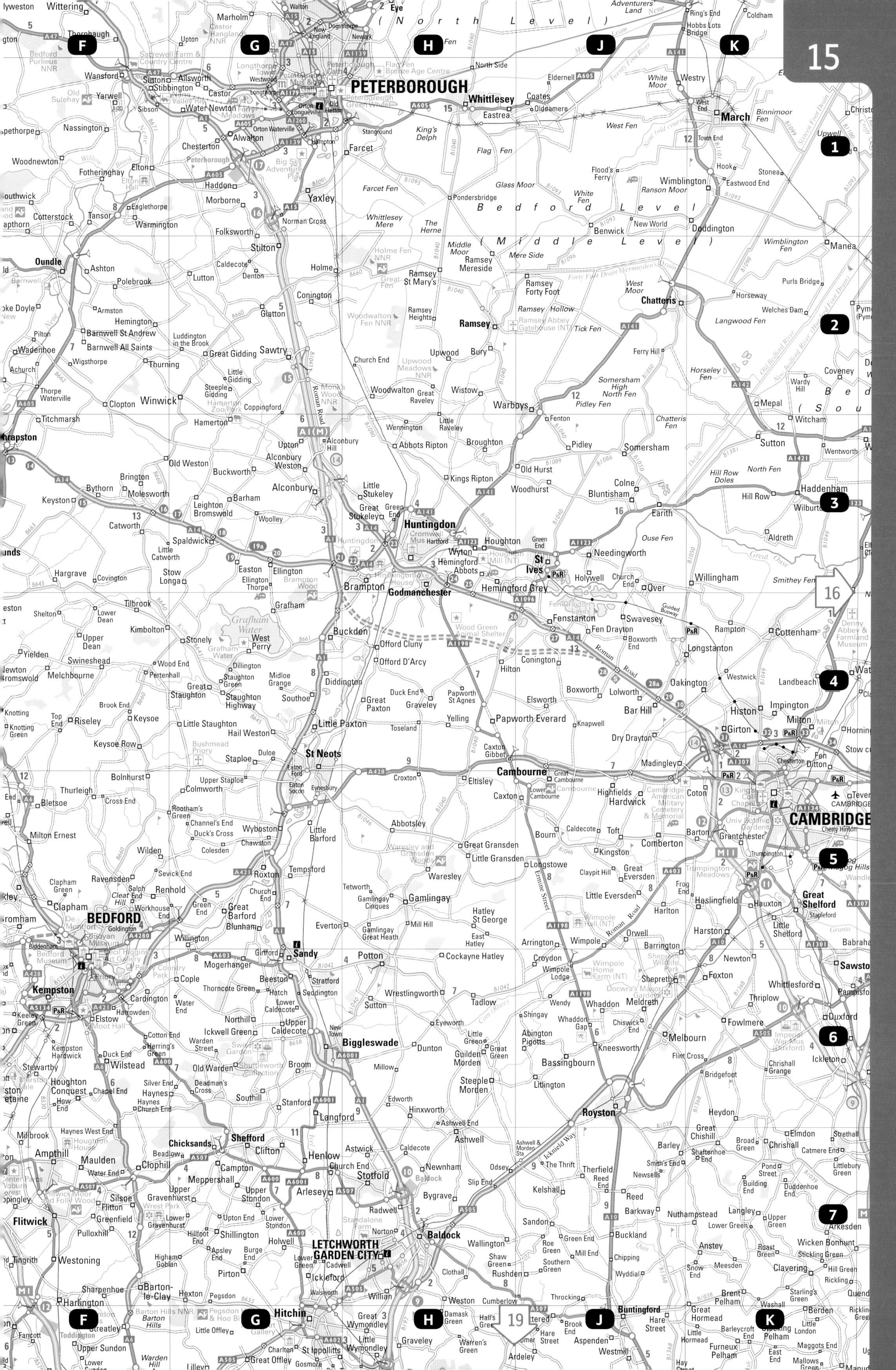
F
G
H
J
K
1
2
3
4
5
6
7
16
19
PETERBOROUGH
Eye
(North Level)
Whittlesey
March
Wansford
Stilton
Yaxley
Oundle
Ramsey
Chatteris
Bedford Level (Middle Level)
Warboys
Somersham
Huntingdon
Godmanchester
St Ives
Brampton
St Neots
Cambourne
CAMBRIDGE
BEDFORD
Kempston
Sandy
Biggleswade
Royston
Baldock
LETCHWORTH GARDEN CITY
Hitchin
Shefford
Ampthill
Flitwick
Buntingford
Alconbury
Sawtry
Kimbolton
Thrapston
Histon
Girton
Cottenham
Willingham
Haddenham
Sutton
Manea
Great Shelford
Melbourn
Stotfold
Arlesey
Potton
Gamlingay
Papworth Everard
Bar Hill
Fenstanton
Hemingford Grey
Needingworth
Doddington
Chesterton
Alwalton
Farcet
Harlington
Westoning
Henlow
Clifton
Wilstead
Cardington
Clapham
Buckden
Little Paxton
Comberton
Harston
Whittlesford
Duxford
Sawston
Ickleton
Bassingbourn
Ashwell
Barkway
Linton

A B C D E

1 2 3 4 5 6 7

Laddus Fens, Upwell, North District, Three Holes, Nordelph, Denver, Wereham, Boughton, Oxborough, Oxburgh Hall (NT), Gooderstone, Great Cressingham, Hilborough, Threxton Hill, Little Cressingham, Bodney

Euximoor Fen, Upwell Fen, South District, Fordham, Hilgay, Wretton, Stoke Ferry, Whittington, Foulden, Beckett End, Northwold, Little London

March, Binnimoor Fen, Christchurch, Lakes End, Ten Mile Bank, Southery, Methwold, Methwold Hythe, Cranwich, Ickburgh, Tottington, Danger Zone

Upwell Fen, Tipps End, Welney, Hilgay Fen, Southery Fens, Methwold Fens, Queen's Ground, Mundford, West Tofts, Lynford

Hook, Stonea, Wimblington, Eastwood End, Gold Hill, Brandon Creek, Feltwell, THETFORD, Doddington, The Apes Hall

Wimblington Fen, Manea, Mare Fen, Little Ouse, Brandon Bank, Feltwell Fens, Hockwold cum Wilton, Weeting, Weeting Castle, Grime's Graves, The Thetford Forest Pk, BRECKLAND, Weeting Heath NNR

Purls Bridge, Fodder Fen, Burnt Fen, Hockwold Fens, Brandon, Town Street, Santon Downham, Croxton

Horseway, Welches Dam, Pymore (Pymoor), Littleport, Longwood Fen, Wangford Fen, Grime Fen, Shippea Hill, Shippea Hill Sta, High Lodge Forest Centre, Brandon Park, FOREST PARK, THETFORD

Horseley Fen, Coveney, Little Downham, Little Street, West Fen, Chettisham, Queen Adelaide, Padnal Fen, Prickwillow, Lakenheath, Wangford, Wangford Warren, Thetford Warren Lodge, Thetford Warren, Priory, Ancient House Mus

Wardy Hill, Mepal, Witcham, Bedford Level (South Level), Ely, Ely Cathedral, Ely Road & Rail Distribution Centre, Middle Fen, Undley, The Delph, Lakenheath Warren, Center Parcs, Kennyhill, Elveden

Sutton, Wentworth, Witchford, Stuntney, Great Fen, Mildenhall Fen, Wilde Street, Eriswell, Barnham

Hill Row Doles, North Fen, Haddenham, Hill Row, Wilburton, Stretham, Little Thetford, Broad Hill, Isleham Fen, Barway, Soham Cotes, Thistley Green, Beck Row, Holywell Row, Berner's Heath, THETFORD FOREST PARK, Culfordheath

West Row, Mildenhall, Worlington, Barton Mills, Priory Church, Isleham, Soham Mere, Soham, Aldreth, Elford Closes, Downfields, Icklingham, West Stow Country Park, Wordwell, Troston

Willingham, Smithey Fen, Chittering, Wicken Fen NNR (NT), Upware, Wicken, Fordham, Freckenham, Tuddenham, Cavenham Heath NNR, Red Lodge, Herringswell, Cavenham, Lackford, Lackford Lakes, West Stow, Flempton, Culford, Ingham, Ampton, Timworth, Timworth Green

15

North Fen, River Bank, Adventurers' Fen, Little Fen, Fordham Abbey, Chippenham, Chippenham Fen NNR, Kennett, Fornham All Saints, Hengrave

Rampton, Cottenham, Denny Abbey & Farmland Museum, Landwade, Snailwell, Burwell, Reach, Risby, Fornham St Martin, Great Barton

Longstanton, Westwick, Landbeach, Waterbeach, Clayhithe, Swaffham Prior, Exning, Kentford, Needham Street, Higham, Westley, BURY ST EDMUNDS, Moyse's Hall Mus

Oakington, Histon, Impington, Milton, Commercial End, Lode, Anglesey Abbey (NT), National Horseracing Museum, Newmarket, Moulton, Gazeley, Burthorpe, Barrow, Great Saxham, Little Saxham, Newmarket Heath

Girton, Horningsea, Swaffham Bulbeck, Stow cum Quy, Bottisham, Cheveley, Ashley, Dalham, Denham, Dunstall Green, Horringer, Ickworth (NT), Theatre Royal (NT), Nowton Park, Nowton, Low Green, High Green, Rushbrooke

Chesterton, Fen Ditton, Teversham, Little Wilbraham, Great Wilbraham, CAMBRIDGE CITY, CAMBRIDGE, Cherry Hinton, Kings Coll Chapel, Univ Botanic Gardens, Coton, Barton, Grantchester, Trumpington, Fulbourn, Six Mile Bottom, Dullingham, Stetchworth, Ditton Green, Little Ditton, Saxon Street, Woodditton, Broad Green, Upend, Ousden, Back Street, Lidgate, Hargrave, Hargrave Green, Chevington, Tan Office Green, Stonecross Green, Hawstead, Whepstead, Chedburgh, Baxter's Green, Depden Green, Depden, Sicklesmere, Great Welnetham, Bradfield Combust, Mickley Green

Westley Waterless, Kirtling, Dullingham Ley, Burrough Green, Kirtling Green, Mill End, Lark Hall, Ashfield Green, Thorns, Wickhambrook, Rede, Brockley, Stanningfield, Hoggard's Green, Harrow Green, Windsor Green

Gog Magog Hills, Wandlebury, Trumpington Meadows, Frog End, Haslingfield, Hauxton, Great Shelford, Stapleford, Worsted Lodge, Willingham Green, Brinkley, Widgham Green, East Green, Cowlinge, Pound Green, Attleton Green, Malting End, Clopton Green, Wickham Street, Farley Green, Hawkedon, Lawshall, Audley End, Somerton, Cross Green, Hartest, Lawshall Green, Hibb's Green

Harston, Little Shelford, Weston Colville, West Wratting, Carlton, Great Bradley, Little Bradley, Hobbles Green, Stradishall, Denston, Stansfield, Assington Green, Weston Green, Carlton Green, Little Thurlow, Little Thurlow Green, Sowley Green, Boxted, Shimpling, Shimpling Street, Alpheton

Newton, Babraham, Balsham, Temple End, Great Thurlow, Chilford Hall, West Wickham, Chimney Street, Barnardiston, Hundon, Stanstead, Brook Street, Bridge Street, Kentwell Hall

Foxton, Sawston, Little Abington, Great Abington, Hildersham, Streetly End, Withersfield, Great Wratting, Mount Pleasant, Poslingford, Glemsford, Whittlesford, Thriplow, Pampisford, Little Linton, Linton, Horseheath, Little Wratting, Brockley Green, Chilton Street, Kedington, Cavendish, High Street, Melford Hall (NT)

Fowlmere, Melbourn, Duxford, Imperial War Mus (Duxford), Linton Zoo, Bartlow, Cardinal's Green, Mill Green, Haverhill, Calford Green, Clare, Pentlow, Pentlow Street, Long Melford, Foxearth, Liston

Flint Cross, Hinxton, Stump Cross, Hadstock, Shudy Camps, Nosterfield End, Sturmer, Boyton End, Clare Castle, Clare Priory, Rodbridge Corner, Newman's Green

Chrishall Grange, Bridgefoot, Ickleton, Great Chesterford, Little Chesterford, Castle Camps, Wiggens Green, Stevenston End, Ashdon, Helions Bumpstead, Baythorn End, Ashen, Stoke by Clare, Ovington, Belchamp St Paul, Church Street, Belchamp Otten, Borley Green, Borley, Gainsborough's House, Sudbury

Heydon, Great Chishill, Little Walden, Church End, Camps End, Olmstead Green, Water End, Steeple Bumpstead, Smith's Green, Birdbrook, Ridgewell, Knowl Green, Tilbury Green, Puttock End, Belchamp Walter, Ballingdon, Bulmer, Middleton

Elmdon, Strethall, Littlebury, Audley End, Saffron Walden, Red Oaks Hill, Stocking Green, Great Yeldham, Little Yeldham, Bulmer Tye, Gestingthorpe, Henny Street, Great Henny

Broad Green, Chrishall, Catmere End, Littlebury Green, Sewards End, Pleasant Valley, Wimbish, Hempstead, Chapelend Way, Stambourne, Stambourne Green, Toppesfield, Hedingham Castle, Audley End, Twinstead

Shaftenhoe End, Pond Street, Building End, Duddenhoe End, Wendens Ambo, Audley End Sta, Radwinter, Cornish Hall End, Pool Street, Robinhood End, Gainsford End, Barr Hall, Highstreet Green, Castle Hedingham, Wickham St Paul, Alphamstone

Langley, Upper Green, Lower Green, Shortgrove, Upper Green, Howlett End, Wimbish Green, Great Sampford, Sible Hedingham, Great Maplestead, Little Maplestead, Cross End, Pebmarsh

Arkesden, Anstey, Wicken Bonhunt, Roast Green, Stickling Green, Newport, Elder Street, Debden, Tindon End, Debden Cross, Debden Green, Little Sampford, Howe Street, Finchingfield, Bridge End, Brickkiln Green, Snow End, Meesden, Clavering, Hill Green, Rickling, Widdington, Prior's Hall Barn, Wethersfield, Boose's Green

Brent Pelham, Washall Green, Starling's Green, Quendon, Rickling Green, Hamperden End, Cutlers Green, Thaxted, Bardfield End Green, Little Bardfield, Great Bardfield, Bardfield, Blackmore End, Whiteash Green, Halstead, Colne Engaine, White Colne

Great Hormead, Little Hormead, Barleycroft End, Stocking Pelham, Berden, Little London, Ugley, Ugley Green, Maggots End, Manuden, Cherry Green, Henham, Chickney, Broxted, Holder's Green, Sibley's Green, Duton Hill, Lindsell, Duck End, Oxen End, Shalford, Church End, Shalford Green, Jasper's Green, High Garrett, Gosfield, Greenstead Green, Earls Colne, Colne Valley, Chappel

Furneux Pelham, East End, Mallows Green, Hay Street, Elsenham, Pledgdon

20

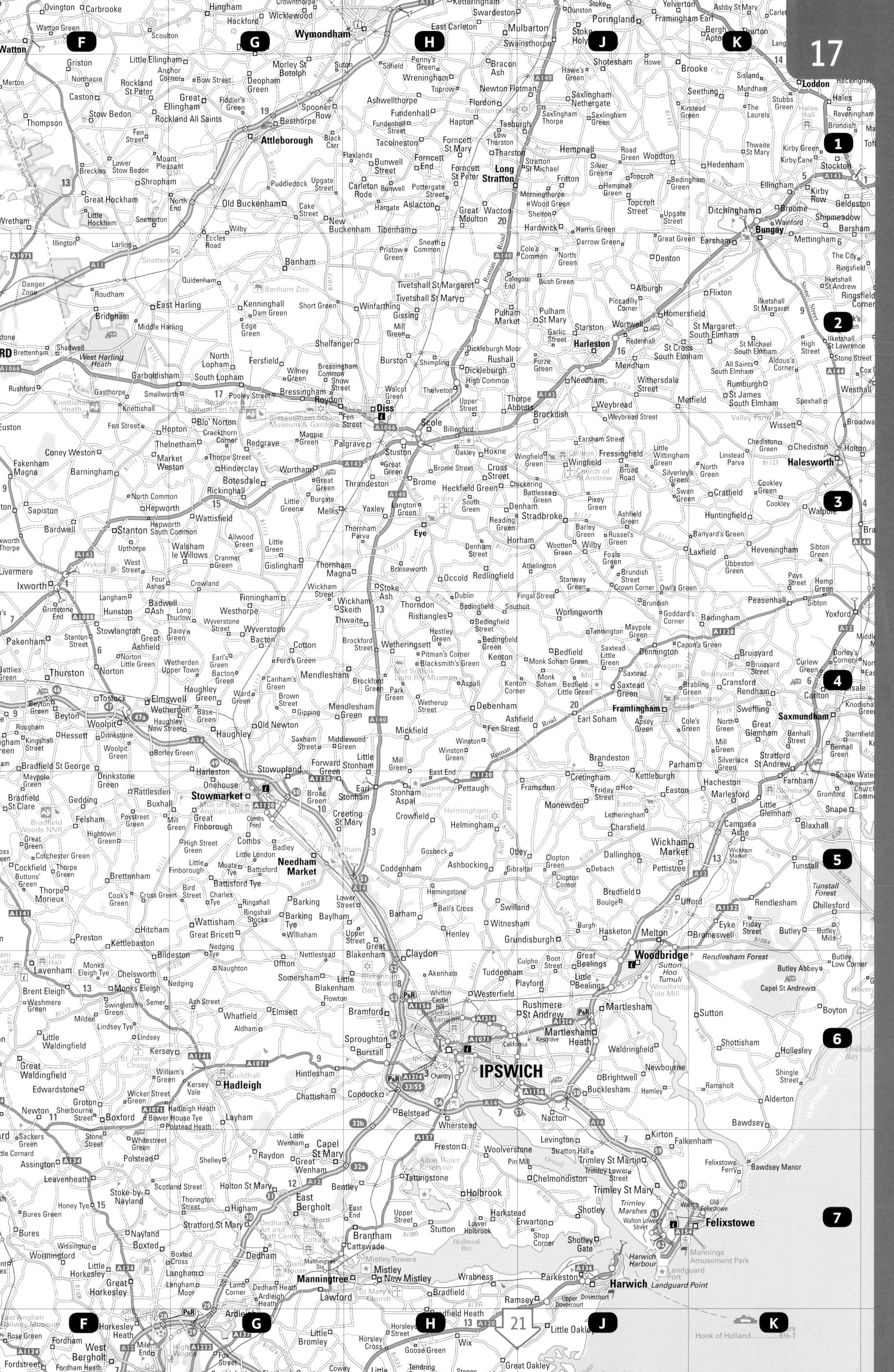
Wymondham
Attleborough
Watton
Long Stratton
Loddon
Bungay
Diss
Harleston
Halesworth
Eye
Framlingham
Saxmundham
Stowmarket
Needham Market
Debenham
Wickham Market
Woodbridge
IPSWICH
Hadleigh
Felixstowe
Harwich
Manningtree
Lavenham
Thurston
Ixworth
Botesdale
Scole
Yoxford
Rendlesham Forest
Tunstall Forest
Banham Zoo
Hook of Holland
F
G
H
J
K
1
2
3
4
5
6
7
21

14
OXFORD
AYLESBURY
HIGH WYCOMBE
READING
MAIDENHEAD
WOKINGHAM
BRACKNELL
CAMBERLEY
AMERSHAM
ABINGDON
SLOUGH
Bicester
Thame
Wallingford
Didcot
Henley-on-Thames
Marlow
Princes Risborough
Wendover
Tring
Leighton Buzzard
Chesham
Beaconsfield
Windsor
Winslow
Watlington
Wheatley
Crowthorne
Sandhurst
Yateley
Tadley
Pangbourne
Theale
Twyford
Burnham
Ascot
Bagshot
Frimley
C H I L T E R N H I L L S
The Three Hundreds of Aylesbury
22

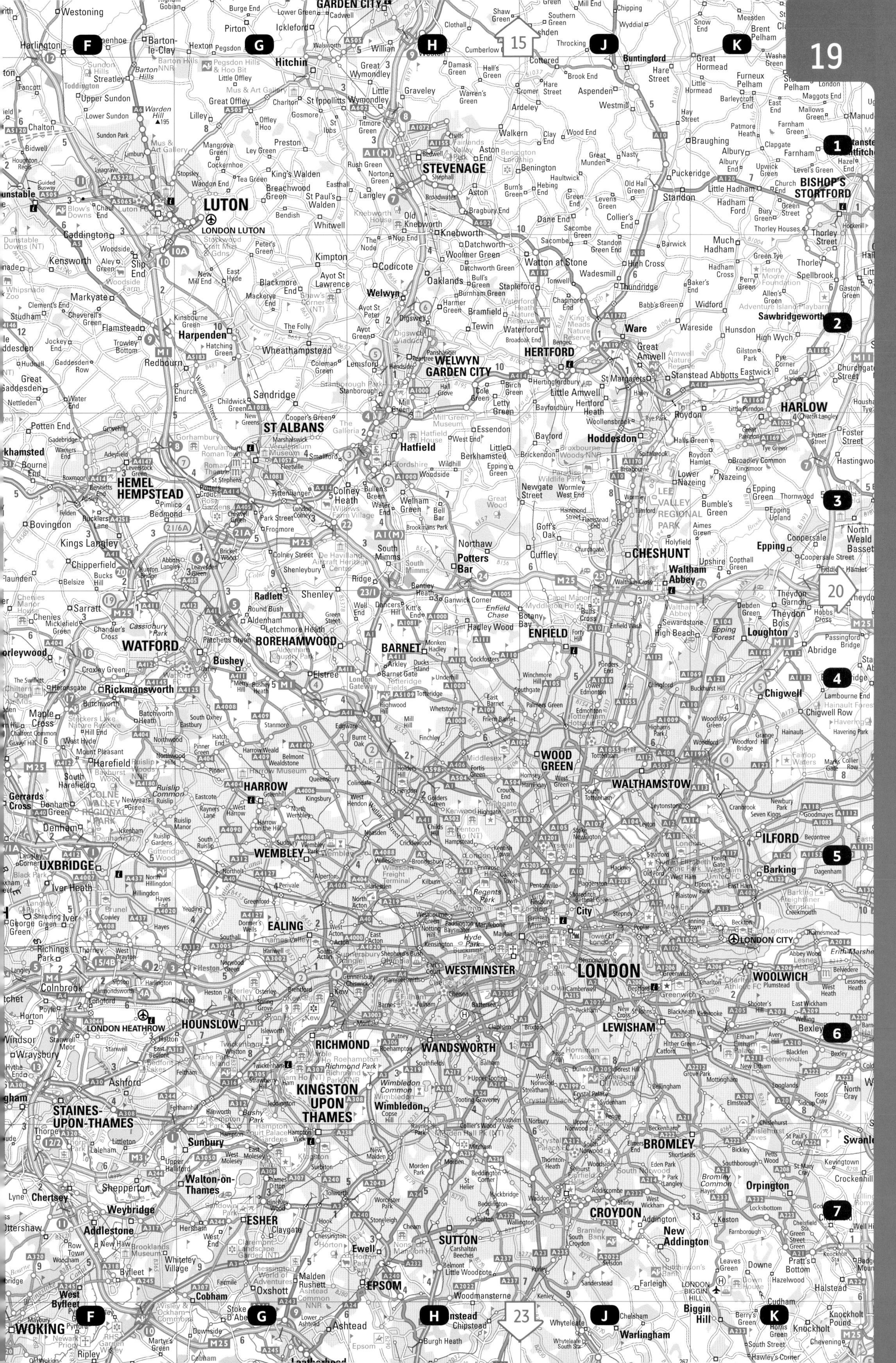
F
G
H
J
K
15
20
23
1
2
3
4
5
6
7
LUTON
LONDON LUTON
STEVENAGE
Hitchin
BISHOP'S STORTFORD
Harpenden
Welwyn
WELWYN GARDEN CITY
HERTFORD
Ware
HARLOW
ST ALBANS
Hatfield
HEMEL HEMPSTEAD
Hoddesdon
CHESHUNT
Waltham Abbey
Epping
Potters Bar
Radlett
WATFORD
BOREHAMWOOD
BARNET
ENFIELD
Loughton
Rickmansworth
Bushey
Chigwell
WOOD GREEN
WALTHAMSTOW
HARROW
UXBRIDGE
WEMBLEY
ILFORD
Barking
EALING
City
LONDON CITY
WESTMINSTER
LONDON
WOOLWICH
HOUNSLOW
LONDON HEATHROW
RICHMOND
WANDSWORTH
LEWISHAM
KINGSTON UPON THAMES
Wimbledon
STAINES-UPON-THAMES
Sunbury
Walton-on-Thames
BROMLEY
CROYDON
Orpington
Weybridge
Addlestone
ESHER
Chertsey
SUTTON
New Addington
Ewell
EPSOM
Cobham
WOKING
West Byfleet
Biggin Hill
Warlingham
Ashtead
Leatherhead
Dunstable
Tring
Westoning
Barton-le-Clay
Buntingford
Sawbridgeworth
Wheathampstead
Redbourn
Kings Langley
Borehamwood
Elstree
Hadley Wood
Edgware
Stanmore
Ruislip
Denham
Gerrards Cross
Iver Heath
Colnbrook
Ashford
Shepperton
Oxshott
Banstead
Chipstead
Knockholt
Halstead
Bexley
Swanley

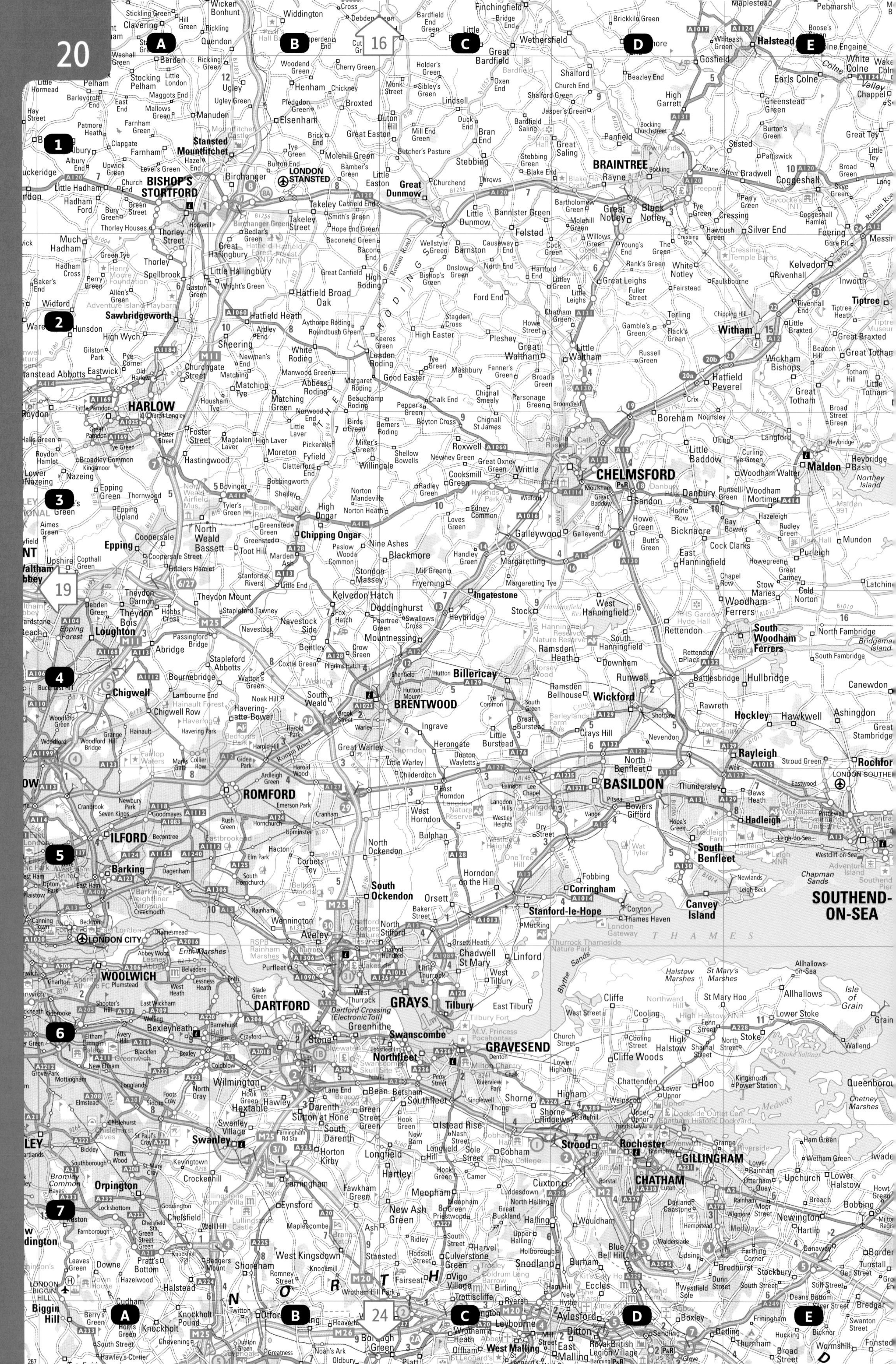
16
19
24
A
B
C
D
E
1
2
3
4
5
6
7
BISHOP'S STORTFORD
Stansted Mountfitchet
LONDON STANSTED
Great Dunmow
Halstead
BRAINTREE
Coggeshall
Kelvedon
Tiptree
Witham
Hatfield Peverel
Sawbridgeworth
HARLOW
Epping
Chipping Ongar
CHELMSFORD
Maldon
South Woodham Ferrers
Billericay
BRENTWOOD
Wickford
Rayleigh
Hockley
Rochford
BASILDON
Hadleigh
South Benfleet
Canvey Island
SOUTHEND-ON-SEA
Chigwell
Loughton
ROMFORD
ILFORD
Barking
WOOLWICH
LONDON CITY
DARTFORD
GRAYS
Tilbury
Stanford-le-Hope
Corringham
South Ockendon
Swanscombe
Northfleet
GRAVESEND
Strood
Rochester
CHATHAM
GILLINGHAM
Swanley
Orpington
Biggin Hill
Aylesford
Snodland
West Malling
THAMES

F
G
H
J
K
17
25
1
2
3
4
5
6
7
Wormingtord
Little Horkesley
Great Horkesley
Boxted Cross
Langham
Dedham
Lamb Corner
Manningtree
Mistley
Mistley Towers
New Mistley
Lawford
Wrabness
Parkeston
Harwich
Harwich Harbour
Landguard Fort
Landguard Point
Upper Dovercourt
Hook of Holland
Bradfield Heath
Horsleycross Street
Horsley Cross
Little Oakley
Great Oakley
Wix
Ardleigh
Little Bromley
Great Bromley
Goose Green
Tendring
Tendring Green
Stones Green
Stone Point
Horsey Island
The Naze
Beaumont
Thorpe Green
Hamford Water NNR
Kirby le Soken
Walton on the Naze
New Walton Pier
Thorpe-le-Soken
Kirby Cross
Frinton-on-Sea
Great Holland
Holland-on-Sea
Sandy Point
Weeley
Weeley Heath
Aingers Green
Great Bentley
Little Bentley
Raven's Green
Balls Green
Hare Green
Elmstead Market
Elmstead Heath
Crockleford Heath
Frating
Thorrington
Alresford
Row Heath
Little Clacton
Great Clacton
Clacton Common
CLACTON-ON-SEA
Clacton Pier
Jaywick
St Osyth
St Osyth Marsh
Point Clear
Seawick
Colne Point
Gunfleet Sand
Brightlingsea
Brightlingsea Reach
Hurst Green
Wivenhoe
Rowhedge
Fingringhoe
COLCHESTER
Horkesley Heath
Fordham
Fordham Heath
West Bergholt
Rose Green
Fordstreet
Eight Ash Green
Aldham
Stanway
Marks Tey
Stanway Green
Copford Green
Heckfordbridge
Easthorpe
Birch
Hardy's Green
Birch Green
Layer de la Haye
Malting Green
Abberton
Abberton Reservoir
Layer Breton
Smythe's Green
Layer Marney
Peldon
Tolleshunt Knights
Great Wigborough
Virley
Salcott
Tolleshunt D'Arcy
Tollesbury
Mersea Island
East Mersea
West Mersea
Cudmore Grove
Mersea Flats
Cobmarsh Island
Great Cob Island
Virley Channel
The Nass
Goldhanger
Bradwell Waterside
Sales Point
St Peter's Flat
East End
Osea Island
Blackwater
Ramsey Island
Bradwell-on-Sea
St Lawrence
Tillingham
Dengie Flat
Steeple
Maylandsea
Mayland
Dengie
Asheldham
Dengie Marshes
Southminster
Ray Sand
Althorne
Mangapps Railway Museum
Stoneyhills
Eves Corner
Ostend
Old Montsale
Deal Hall
Burnham-on-Crouch
Holliwell Point
Foulness Sands
Foulness Point
Crouch
Paglesham Churchend
Wallasea Island
Courtsend
Churchend
Ballards Gore
Paglesham Eastend
Potton Island
Foulness Island
Barling
Havengore Island
Little Wakering
Great Wakering
Maplin Sands
North Shoebury
Southchurch
Shoeburyness
Thorpe Bay
Shoebury Ness
Sheerness
Marine Town
Mile Town
West Minster
Halfway Houses
Minster
East End
Eastchurch
Warden
Warden Point
Leysdown-on-Sea
ISLE OF SHEPPEY
Elmley Marshes NNR
Elmley Island
Eastchurch Marshes
Isle of Harty
The Swale NNR
Shell Ness
Kingshill
The Swale
Kemsley
Sittingbourne & Kemsley Light Railway
SITTINGBOURNE
Conyer
Murston
Bapchild
Teynham
Deerton Street
Luddenham Court
Uplees
Oare
Faversham
Preston
Goodnestone
Graveney
Rodmersham
Rodmersham Green
Lynsted
Lewson Street
Ospringe
Dungate
Milstead
Doddington
Newnham
Whitehill
North Street
Eastling
Sheldwich
Wichling
Whitstable
Seasalter
Tankerton
Swalecliffe
Chestfield
South Street
Clapham Hill
Yorkletts
Highstreet
Dargate
Hernhill
Staplestreet
Boughton Street
Dunkirk
Oversland
Chartham Hatch
Harbledown
Rough Common
Blean
Tyler Hill
Pean Hill
Honey Hill
Blean Woods NNR
CANTERBURY
Canterbury Cathedral
St Augustine's Abbey
Herne Bay
Hampton
Beltinge
Herne
Herne Common
Hunters Forstal
Broomfield
Highstead
Maypole
Hoath
West End
Wildwood
Calcott
Broadoak
Westbere
Sturry
Hersden
Fordwich
Reculver
Reculver Country Park
Hillborough
Boyden Gate
Chislet
Upstreet
Roman Road
Sarre
St Nicholas at Wade
West Stourmouth
Plucks Gutter
East Stourmouth
Grove
Westmarsh
Preston
Elmstone
Wingham
Ickham
Littlebourne
Bramling
Stodmarsh
Stodmarsh NNR
Birchington
Acol
ISLE OF THANET
Monkton
Minster
Gore Street
Manston
MARGATE
Tudor House
Westgate on Sea
Westbrook
Cliftonville
Kingsgate
Foreness
Long Nose Spit
South Channel
Salmestone Grange
Quex House & Gdns
Spitfire & Hurricane Memorial
RAF Manston
Haine
Northwood
Cliffs End
Pegwell
Ramsgate
St Augustine's Cross
Pegwell Bay
Sandwich & Pegwell Bay NNR
Richborough Castle
Sandwich Flats
Stonar Cut
Royal St. Georges
Sandwich Bay
Great Stonar
Sandwich
Cop Street
Ash
Roman Amphitheatre
Marshborough
Shatterling
Staple
Woodnesborough
Toll

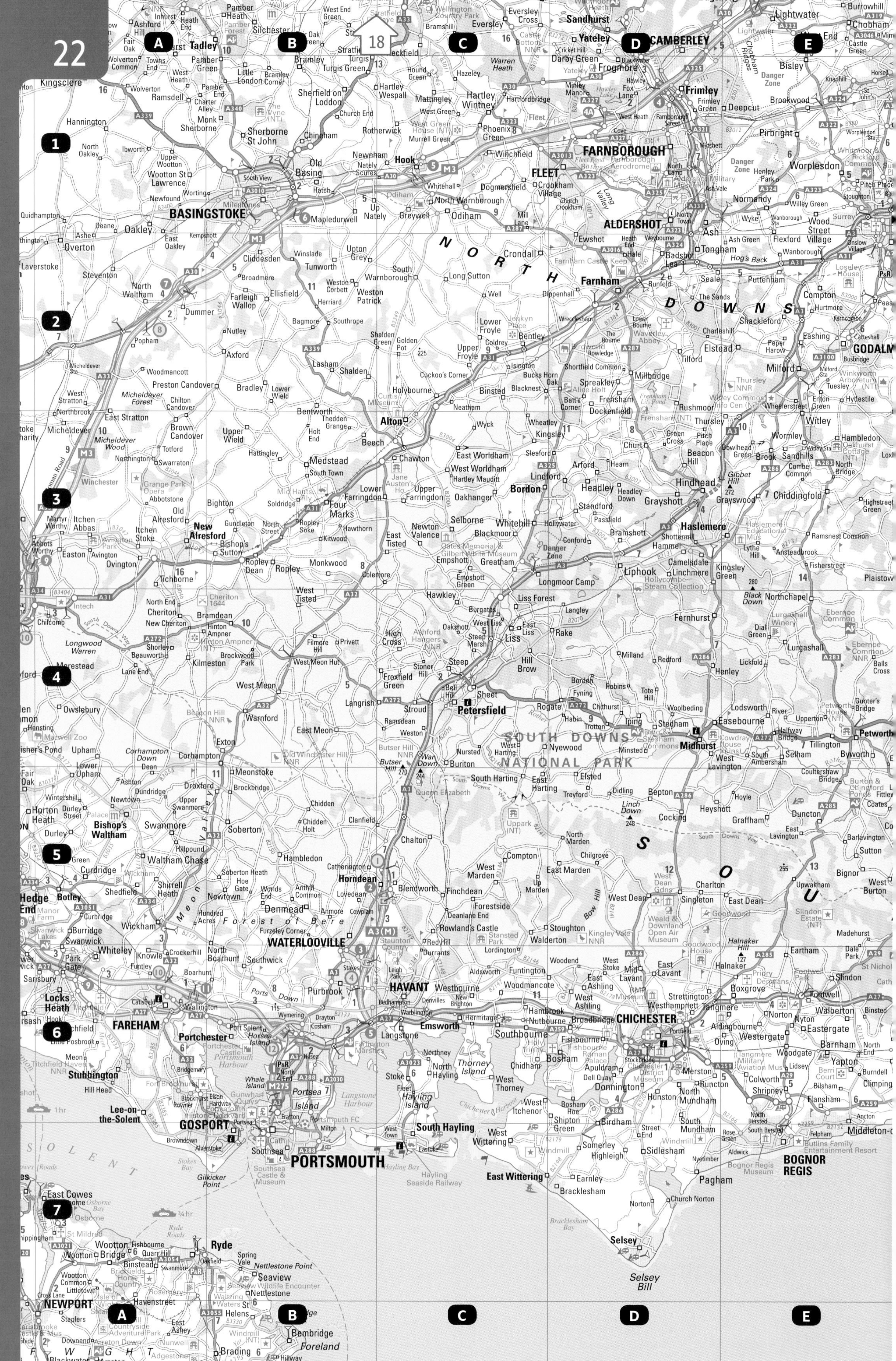
18
A
B
C
D
E
1
2
3
4
5
6
7
BASINGSTOKE
FARNBOROUGH
CAMBERLEY
ALDERSHOT
FLEET
Farnham
Alton
Petersfield
Midhurst
Haslemere
Hindhead
Bordon
Liphook
Liss
New Alresford
Bishop's Waltham
WATERLOOVILLE
HAVANT
FAREHAM
GOSPORT
PORTSMOUTH
CHICHESTER
BOGNOR REGIS
Emsworth
South Hayling
Selsey
Selsey Bill
East Wittering
Ryde
NEWPORT
East Cowes
Lee-on-the-Solent
Portchester
Tadley
Hook
Odiham
Oakley
Frimley
Yateley
Sandhurst
Petworth
GODALMING
Milford
Witley
Chiddingfold
Horndean
Denmead
Wickham
Botley
Hedge End
Locks Heath
Stubbington
NORTH DOWNS
SOUTH DOWNS NATIONAL PARK
SOLENT
Portsea Island
Hayling Island
Thorney Island
Selsey Bill
Bembridge Foreland
ISLE OF WIGHT

F
G
H
J
K
19
24
1
2
3
4
5
6
7
WOKING
Byfleet
Cobham
EPSOM
Ewell
Banstead
Woodmansterne
Biggin Hill
Warlingham
Leatherhead
Ashtead
Tadworth
Caterham
Oxted
Westerham
GUILDFORD
Dorking
REIGATE
Redhill
Godstone
Bletchingley
Edenbridge
Horley
LONDON GATWICK
Lingfield
East Grinstead
CRAWLEY
Forest Row
HORSHAM
Cranleigh
Billingshurst
Haywards Heath
HAYWARDS HEATH
Cuckfield
Burgess Hill
Uckfield
Pulborough
Storrington
Steyning
Henfield
Hurstpierpoint
Lewes
Arundel
LITTLEHAMPTON
WORTHING
Lancing
Shoreham-by-Sea
Southwick
Portslade-by-Sea
HOVE
BRIGHTON
Rottingdean
Peacehaven
Newhaven
Seaford
Dieppe

A
B
C
D
E
1
2
3
4
5
6
7
20
23
West Kingsdown
Stansted
Culverstone Green
Snodland
Burham
Eccles
Shoreham
Otford
Kemsing
Wrotham
Borough Green
Addington
Leybourne
West Malling
East Malling
Aylesford
Ditton
Boxley
Detling
Thurnham
Bearsted
MAIDSTONE
Hollingbourne
Harrietsham
Tatsfield
Westerham
Brasted
Sundridge
Chipstead
Riverhead
SEVENOAKS
Seal
Ightham
Platt
Kings Hill
Mereworth
Wateringbury
Teston
East Farleigh
Loose
Langley
Limpsfield
Oxted
Crockham Hill
Ide Hill
Sevenoaks Weald
Shipbourne
Plaxtol
West Peckham
Hadlow
Nettlestead
Yalding
Hunton
Coxheath
Linton
Chart Sutton
Sutton Valence
Ulcombe
Boughton Malherbe
Marlpit Hill
Four Elms
Bough Beech
Hildenborough
Tonbridge
East Peckham
Laddingford
Chainhurst
Headcorn
Edenbridge
Chiddingstone
Leigh
Penshurst
Five Oak Green
Capel
Paddock Wood
Marden
Staplehurst
Smarden
Dormansland
Southborough
Pembury
Matfield
Brenchley
Horsmonden
Frittenden
Cowden
Speldhurst
Langton Green
ROYAL TUNBRIDGE WELLS
Lamberhurst
Goudhurst
Biddenden
Hammerwood
Ashurst
Groombridge
Frant
Kilndown
Sissinghurst
Cranbrook
Forest Row
Hartfield
Withyham
Eridge Green
Hartley
Benenden
Tenterden
THE WEALD
CROWBOROUGH
Ashdown Forest
Mark Cross
Wadhurst
Flimwell
Hawkhurst
Rolvenden
Rotherfield
Ticehurst
Stonegate
Sandhurst
Newenden
Wittersham
Nutley
Mayfield
Hurst Green
Etchingham
Bodiam
Northiam
Beckley
Maresfield
Five Ashes
Burwash
Robertsbridge
Peasmarsh
Fletching
Buxted
Heathfield
Broad Oak
Newick
Uckfield
Rye
Framfield
Punnett's Town
Brightling
Mountfield
Udimore
Dallington
Netherfield
Sedlescombe
Brede
Horam
Rushlake Green
Whatlington
Barcombe
East Hoathly
Battle
Westfield
Icklesham
Laughton
Ringmer
Herstmonceux
Ninfield
Crowhurst
Lewes
Hailsham
Fairlight
Glynde
Pevensey Levels
St Leonards
HASTINGS
BEXHILL
Rodmell
West Firle
Selmeston
Alciston
Polegate
Westham
Pevensey
Pevensey Bay
Berwick
Wilmington
Tarring Neville
Alfriston
South Heighton
Telscombe
Piddinghoe
Newhaven
Bishopstone
Jevington
Seaford
Westdean
Friston
East Dean
EASTBOURNE
Beachy Head
Royal Sovereign
Birling Gap
Dieppe hours 4

F
G
H
J
K
1
2
3
4
5
6
7
21
Bapchild
Teynham
Rodmersham
Rodmersham Green
Lewson Street
Faversham
Preston
Goodnestone
Dargate
Highstreet
Hernhill
Staplestreet
Boughton Street
Dunkirk
Ospringe
Whitehill
North Street
Gushmere
Oversland
Sheldwich
Sheldwich Lees
Selling
Newnham
Doddington
Eastling
Throwley
Frith
Badlesmere
Old Wives Lees
Payden Street
Otterden Place
Leaveland
Shottenden
Chilham
Chilham Castle
Warren Street
Stalisfield Green
Molash
Challock
Godmersham
Lenham Heath
Charing
Charing Heath
Westwell Leacon
Westwell
Eastwell Park
Boughton Aluph
Boughton Lees
Bilting
Crundale
Sole Street
Waltham
Imperial College at Wye
Wye
Hassell Street
Kempe's Corner
Little Chart
Ram Lane
Pluckley
Pluckley Thorne
Hothfield
Kennington
Brook
Hastingleigh
Whatsole Street
Wye NNR
ASHFORD
Great Chart
Willesborough Lees
Willesborough
Hinxhill
Sevington
Mersham
Daniel's Water
Ashford Designer Outlet
Beaver Green
Kingsnorth
Cheeseman's Green
The Forstal
Smeeth
Brabourne Lees
Brabourne
West Brabourne
Bull Green
Brissenden Green
Shadoxhurst
Bromley Green
Hengherst
Redbrook Street
Sugarloaf
Orlestone
Stone Cross
Aldington
Bonnington
Stonestreet Green
Woodchurch
Brook Street
Ham Street
Ham Street Woods NNR
Ruckinge
Bilsington
The Leacon
Hamstreet
Warehorne
Kenardington
Leigh Green
Shirley Moor
Reading Street
Appledore Heath
Appledore
Appledore Sta
Snave
Shargate
Brenzett Green
Brenzett
Ivychurch
Isle of Oxney
Stone
The Stocks
Fairfield
Brookland
Iden
Playden
East Guldeford
East Guldeford Level
Rye
Rye Harbour
Camber
Camber Sands Holiday Centre
Rye Bay
Winchelsea
Winchelsea Beach
Walland Marsh
Romney Marsh
Newchurch
Burmarsh
St Mary in the Marsh
Dymchurch
St Mary's Bay
Old Romney
New Romney
Littlestone-on-Sea
Romney Sands
Greatstone-on-Sea
LYDD (LONDON ASHFORD)
Lydd
Lydd-on-Sea
Denge Marsh
Danger Zone
Denge Beach
Dungeness NNR
Dungeness
West Road
East Road
Romney, Hythe & Dymchurch Railway
Port Lympne
Port Lympne Wild Animal Park
Lympne
West Hythe
Botolph's Bridge
Hythe
Palmarsh
Saltwood
Court-at-Street
Newingreen
Sellindge
Stanford
Newington
Cheriton
Sandgate
Channel Tunnel Terminal
FOLKESTONE
Capel le Ferne
Hawkinge
Paddlesworth
Etchinghill
Postling
Newbarn
Lyminge
Monks Horton
Stowting
Woodland
Ottinge
Rhodes Minnis
Mount
Elham
Sixmile
Maxted Street
Bodsham Green
Stelling Minnis
Lyminge Forest
Stone Street
Densole
Swingfield Minnis
Acrise Place
Selstead
Wingmore
Bladbean
Breach
Denton
Wootton
Elham Valley
Derringstone
Barham
Bossingham
Upper Hardres Court
Kingston
Bishopsbourne
Lower Hardres
Bridge
Patrixbourne
Bekesbourne
Petham
Garlinge Green
Anvil Green
Chartham
Shalmsford Street
Chartham Hatch
Nackington
Thanington
Harbledown
Upper Harbledown
Rough Common
Blean
Blean Woods NNR
Honey Hill
Pean Hill
Druidstone Park & Arts Park
Broadoak
Calcott
Westbere
Hersden
Sturry
Fordwich
CANTERBURY
Canterbury Cathedral
St Martin's Church
St Augustine's Abbey
Howletts Wild Animal Park
Wickhambreaux
Ickham
Littlebourne
Bramling
Stodmarsh NNR
Grove
Westmarsh
East Stourmouth
Stourmouth
Elmstone
Wingham
Wingham Well
Wingham Wildlife Park
Hoaden
Shatterling
Staple
Goodnestone
Goodnestone Park
Adisham
Aylesham
Ratling
Nonington
Chillenden
Knowlton
Easole Street
Womenswold
Woolage Village
Woolage Green
Barfrestone
Lower Eythorne
Eythorne
Shepherdswell
Coldred
Lydden
Lydden Temple Ewell NNR
Ewell Minnis
Alkham
South Alkham
St Radigund's Abbey
West Hougham
Temple Ewell
River
Buckland
Whitfield
Ash
Cop Street
Marshborough
Barnsole
Richborough
Richborough Castle
Roman Amphitheatre
Sandwich
Woodnesborough
Worth
Ham
Eastry
Hacklinge
Finglesham
Betteshanger
Northbourne
Tilmanstone
Elvington
Great Mongeham
Sholden
Deal
Deal Castle
Walmer
Ripple
East Studdal
Sutton
Walmer Castle & Gardens
Kingsdown
Ringwould
Ashley
West Langdon
Martin Mill Sta
East Langdon
Guston
West Cliffe
St Margaret's Bay
The Pines
South Foreland
South Foreland Lighthouse (NT)
Gateway to the White Cliffs
DOVER
Dover Castle
De Bradelei Wharf
Maxton
Women's Land Army Mus
Knights Templar Church
Samphire Hoe
Dover - Folkestone Heritage Coast
East Wear Bay
Channel Tunnel Folkestone to Calais 35mins
Calais
Dunkerque
STRAITS OF
Pegwell
Sandwich & Pegwell Bay NNR
M2
M20
A2
A20
A28
A252
A251
A2070
A2042
A259
A260
A261
A2034
A256
A257
A258
A290
A2050
B2068
B2067
B2046
B2011
B2075
B2080
Roman Road

Key to London street maps

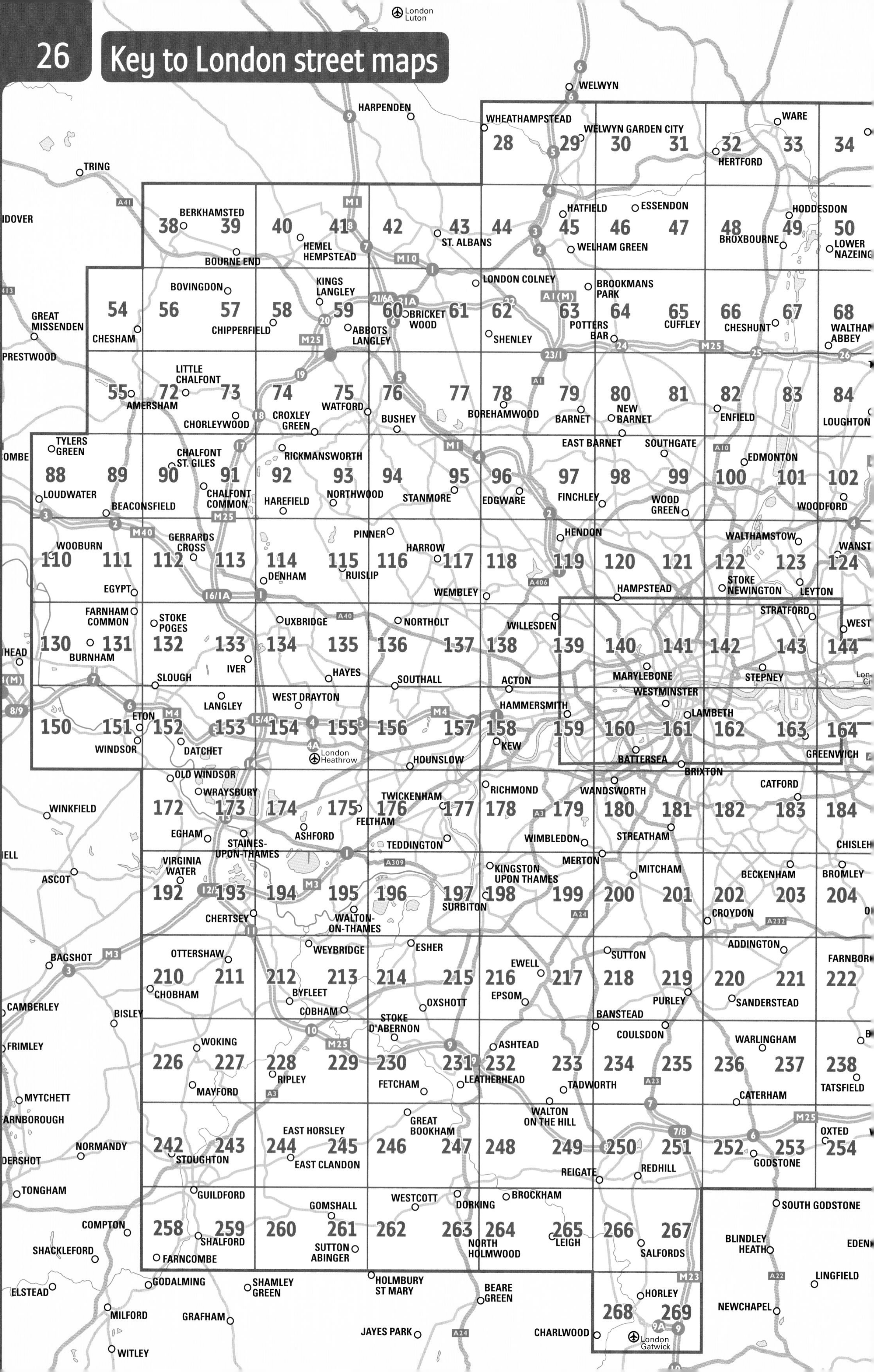

London Luton
WELWYN
HARPENDEN
WHEATHAMPSTEAD
WELWYN GARDEN CITY
WARE
28 29 30 31 32 33 34
HERTFORD
TRING
A41
IDOVER
HATFIELD
ESSENDON
HODDESDON
BERKHAMSTED
38 39 40 41 42 43 44 45 46 47 48 49 50
HEMEL HEMPSTEAD
ST. ALBANS
WELHAM GREEN
BROXBOURNE
LOWER NAZEING
BOURNE END
M1
M10
A413
BOVINGDON
KINGS LANGLEY
LONDON COLNEY
BROOKMANS PARK
A1(M)
GREAT MISSENDEN
54 56 57 58 59 60 61 62 63 64 65 66 67 68
BRICKET WOOD
CHESHAM
CHIPPERFIELD
ABBOTS LANGLEY
SHENLEY
POTTERS BAR
CUFFLEY
CHESHUNT
WALTHAM ABBEY
M25
PRESTWOOD
LITTLE CHALFONT
55 72 73 74 75 76 77 78 79 80 81 82 83 84
AMERSHAM
WATFORD
CHORLEYWOOD
CROXLEY GREEN
BUSHEY
BOREHAMWOOD
BARNET
NEW BARNET
ENFIELD
LOUGHTON
A1
TYLERS GREEN
CHALFONT ST. GILES
RICKMANSWORTH
EAST BARNET
SOUTHGATE
EDMONTON
OMBE
88 89 90 91 92 93 94 95 96 97 98 99 100 101 102
LOUDWATER
CHALFONT COMMON
HAREFIELD
NORTHWOOD
STANMORE
EDGWARE
FINCHLEY
WOOD GREEN
WOODFORD
BEACONSFIELD
A10
M40
GERRARDS CROSS
PINNER
HENDON
WALTHAMSTOW
WANST
WOOBURN
HARROW
110 111 112 113 114 115 116 117 118 119 120 121 122 123 124
DENHAM
RUISLIP
STOKE NEWINGTON
EGYPT
WEMBLEY
A406
HAMPSTEAD
LEYTON
16/1A
FARNHAM COMMON
STOKE POGES
UXBRIDGE
A40
NORTHOLT
WILLESDEN
STRATFORD
WEST
HEAD
130 131 132 133 134 135 136 137 138 139 140 141 142 143 144
BURNHAM
IVER
HAYES
MARYLEBONE
STEPNEY
SLOUGH
SOUTHALL
ACTON
WESTMINSTER
Lon Ci
WEST DRAYTON
HAMMERSMITH
LANGLEY
M4
ETON
LAMBETH
150 151 152 153 154 155 156 157 158 159 160 161 162 163 164
WINDSOR
DATCHET
London Heathrow
KEW
HOUNSLOW
BATTERSEA
GREENWICH
OLD WINDSOR
BRIXTON
WRAYSBURY
RICHMOND
WANDSWORTH
CATFORD
WINKFIELD
TWICKENHAM
172 173 174 175 176 177 178 179 180 181 182 183 184
FELTHAM
EGHAM
ASHFORD
STAINES-UPON-THAMES
A3
WIMBLEDON
STREATHAM
CHISLEH
ELL
TEDDINGTON
A309
VIRGINIA WATER
KINGSTON UPON THAMES
MERTON
MITCHAM
BECKENHAM
BROMLEY
ASCOT
M3
192 193 194 195 196 197 198 199 200 201 202 203 204
SURBITON
CROYDON
A24
A232
CHERTSEY
WALTON-ON-THAMES
OTTERSHAW
WEYBRIDGE
ESHER
ADDINGTON
BAGSHOT
SUTTON
FARNBOR
EWELL
210 211 212 213 214 215 216 217 218 219 220 221 222
CHOBHAM
BYFLEET
EPSOM
OXSHOTT
PURLEY
SANDERSTEAD
CAMBERLEY
COBHAM
BISLEY
BANSTEAD
STOKE D'ABERNON
COULSDON
WARLINGHAM
FRIMLEY
WOKING
ASHTEAD
226 227 228 229 230 231 232 233 234 235 236 237 238
LEATHERHEAD
MAYFORD
RIPLEY
FETCHAM
TADWORTH
A23
CATERHAM
TATSFIELD
MYTCHETT
A3
WALTON ON THE HILL
FARNBOROUGH
GREAT BOOKHAM
EAST HORSLEY
OXTED
NORMANDY
242 243 244 245 246 247 248 249 250 251 252 253 254
STOUGHTON
EAST CLANDON
GODSTONE
DERSHOT
REIGATE
REDHILL
TONGHAM
GUILDFORD
WESTCOTT
BROCKHAM
SOUTH GODSTONE
GOMSHALL
DORKING
COMPTON
258 259 260 261 262 263 264 265 266 267
SHALFORD
LEIGH
NORTH HOLMWOOD
BLINDLEY HEATH
EDEN
SHACKLEFORD
SUTTON ABINGER
SALFORDS
FARNCOMBE
M23
A22
LINGFIELD
GODALMING
SHAMLEY GREEN
HOLMBURY ST MARY
BEARE GREEN
HORLEY
ELSTEAD
268 269
MILFORD
GRAFHAM
NEWCHAPEL
JAYES PARK
A24
CHARLWOOD
London Gatwick
WITLEY

Key to map symbols on pages 28-269

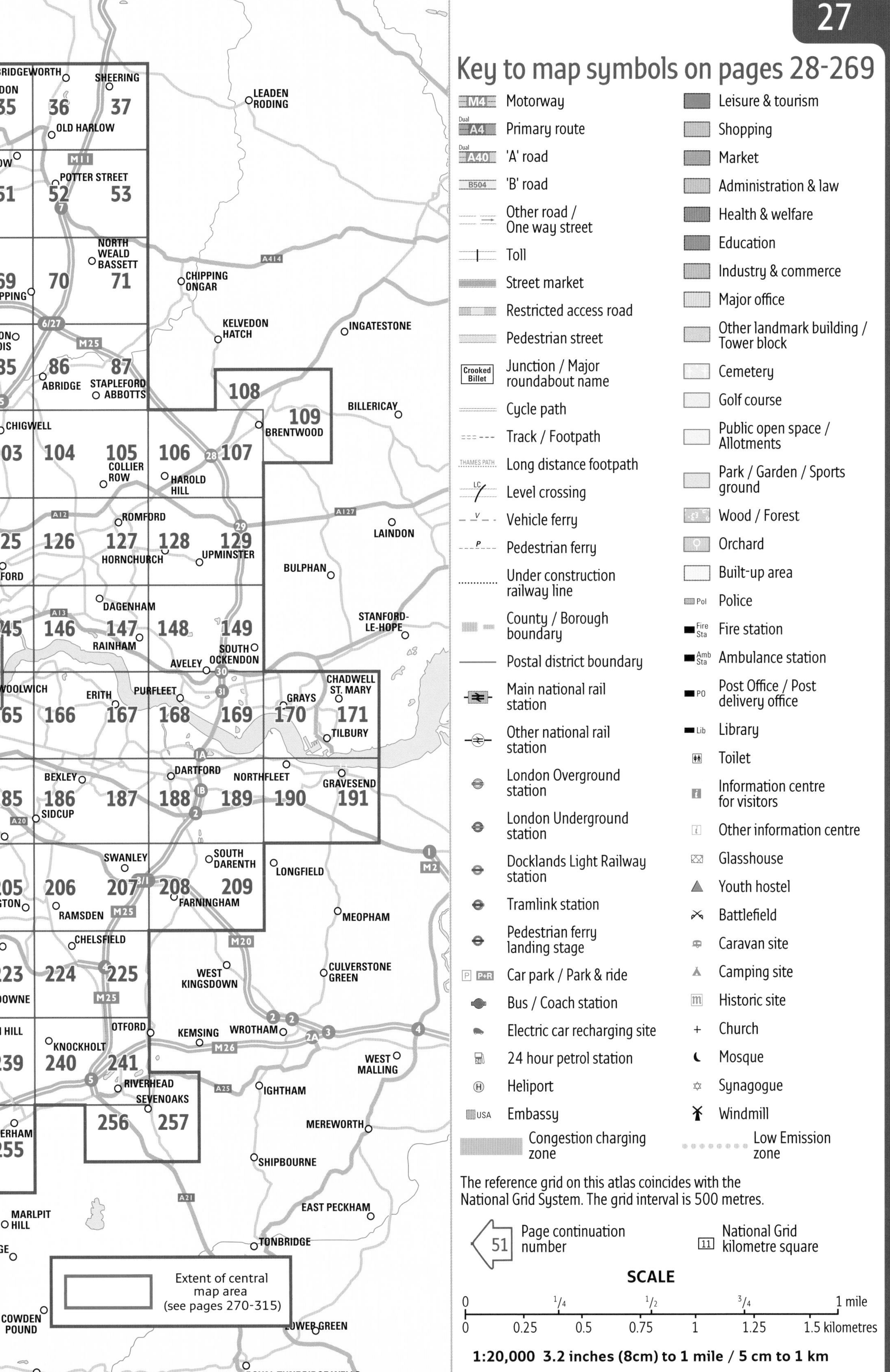

M4	Motorway
Dual A4	Primary route
Dual A40	'A' road
B504	'B' road
	Other road / One way street
	Toll
	Street market
	Restricted access road
	Pedestrian street
Crooked Billet	Junction / Major roundabout name
	Cycle path
	Track / Footpath
THAMES PATH	Long distance footpath
LC	Level crossing
V	Vehicle ferry
P	Pedestrian ferry
	Under construction railway line
	County / Borough boundary
	Postal district boundary
	Main national rail station
	Other national rail station
	London Overground station
	London Underground station
	Docklands Light Railway station
	Tramlink station
	Pedestrian ferry landing stage
P P+R	Car park / Park & ride
	Bus / Coach station
	Electric car recharging site
24	24 hour petrol station
H	Heliport
USA	Embassy
	Congestion charging zone
	Leisure & tourism
	Shopping
	Market
	Administration & law
	Health & welfare
	Education
	Industry & commerce
	Major office
	Other landmark building / Tower block
	Cemetery
	Golf course
	Public open space / Allotments
	Park / Garden / Sports ground
	Wood / Forest
	Orchard
	Built-up area
Pol	Police
Fire Sta	Fire station
Amb Sta	Ambulance station
PO	Post Office / Post delivery office
Lib	Library
	Toilet
i	Information centre for visitors
i	Other information centre
	Glasshouse
	Youth hostel
	Battlefield
	Caravan site
	Camping site
m	Historic site
+	Church
	Mosque
	Synagogue
	Windmill
	Low Emission zone

The reference grid on this atlas coincides with the National Grid System. The grid interval is 500 metres.

51 Page continuation number

11 National Grid kilometre square

SCALE

0 — 1/4 — 1/2 — 3/4 — 1 mile

0 — 0.25 — 0.5 — 0.75 — 1 — 1.25 — 1.5 kilometres

1:20,000 3.2 inches (8cm) to 1 mile / 5 cm to 1 km

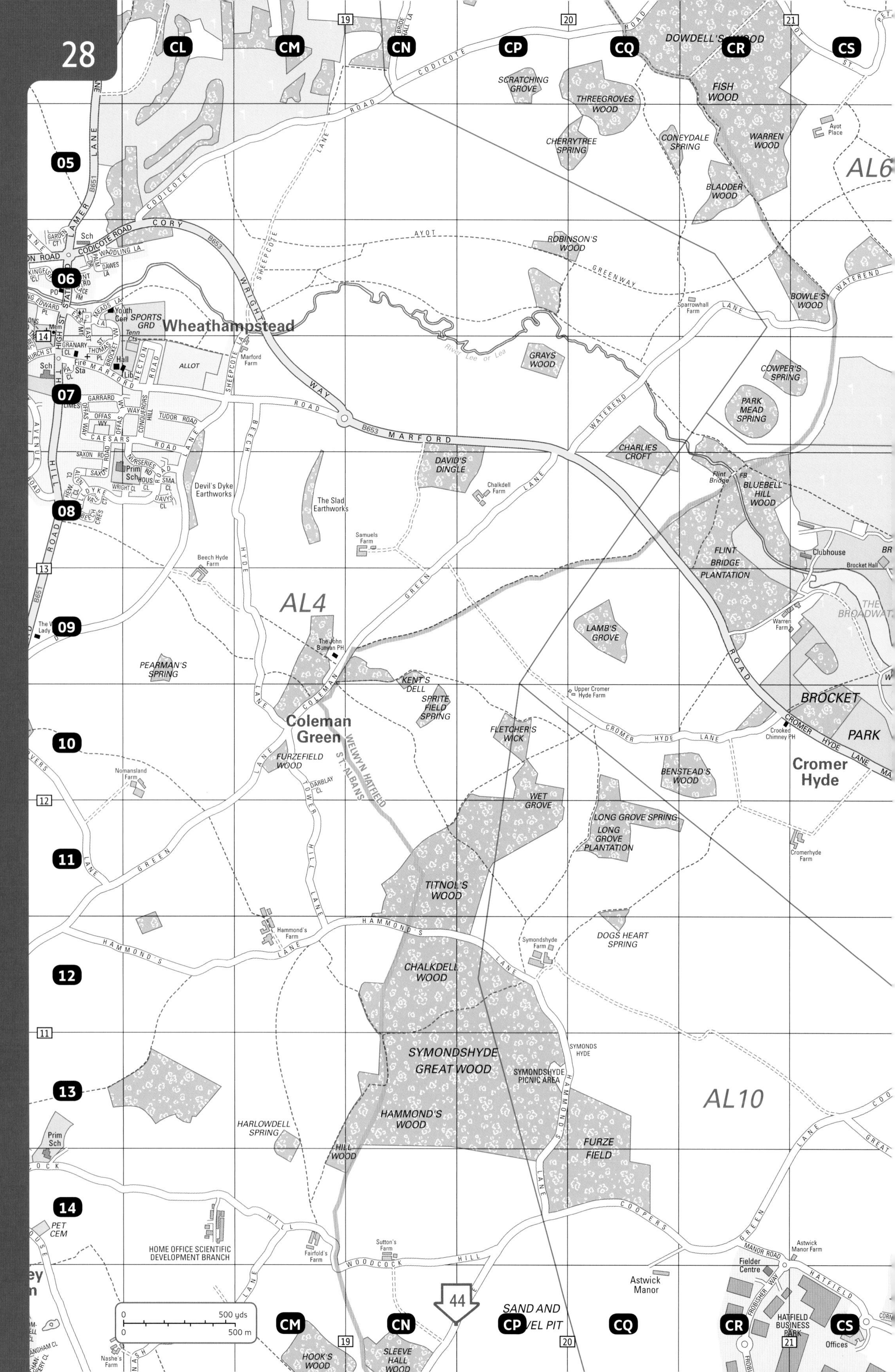
Wheathampstead
Coleman Green
Cromer Hyde
BROCKET PARK
AL4
AL6
AL10
DOWDELL'S WOOD
FISH WOOD
WARREN WOOD
BLADDER WOOD
SCRATCHING GROVE
THREEGROVES WOOD
CHERRYTREE SPRING
CONEYDALE SPRING
ROBINSON'S WOOD
BOWLE'S WOOD
GRAYS WOOD
COWPER'S SPRING
PARK MEAD SPRING
CHARLIES CROFT
DAVID'S DINGLE
BLUEBELL HILL WOOD
FLINT BRIDGE PLANTATION
LAMB'S GROVE
PEARMAN'S SPRING
KENT'S DELL
SPRITE FIELD SPRING
FLETCHER'S WICK
FURZEFIELD WOOD
BENSTEAD'S WOOD
WET GROVE
LONG GROVE SPRING
LONG GROVE PLANTATION
TITNOL'S WOOD
DOGS HEART SPRING
CHALKDELL WOOD
SYMONDSHYDE GREAT WOOD
SYMONDSHYDE PICNIC AREA
HAMMOND'S WOOD
HARLOWDELL SPRING
HILL WOOD
FURZE FIELD
HOOK'S WOOD
SLEEVE HALL WOOD
SAND AND GRAVEL PIT
HOME OFFICE SCIENTIFIC DEVELOPMENT BRANCH
Astwick Manor
HATFIELD BUSINESS PARK
Fielder Centre
Offices
The Slad Earthworks
Devil's Dyke Earthworks
The John Bunyan PH
Crooked Chimney PH
Clubhouse
Brocket Hall
Ayot Place
Sparrowhall Farm
Marford Farm
Chalkdell Farm
Samuels Farm
Beech Hyde Farm
Nomansland Farm
Hammond's Farm
Symondshyde Farm
Upper Cromer Hyde Farm
Warren Farm
Cromerhyde Farm
Sutton's Farm
Fairfold's Farm
Astwick Manor Farm
Nashe's Farm
SPORTS GRD
ALLOT
River Lee or Lea
AYOT GREENWAY
CODICOTE ROAD
MARFORD ROAD
WATEREND LANE
COLEMAN GREEN LANE
CROMER HYDE LANE
HAMMOND'S LANE
WOODCOCK HILL
COOPERS GREEN LANE
WELWYN HATFIELD
ST. ALBANS
0 500 yds
0 500 m
44
CL CM CN CP CQ CR CS
05 06 07 08 09 10 11 12 13 14

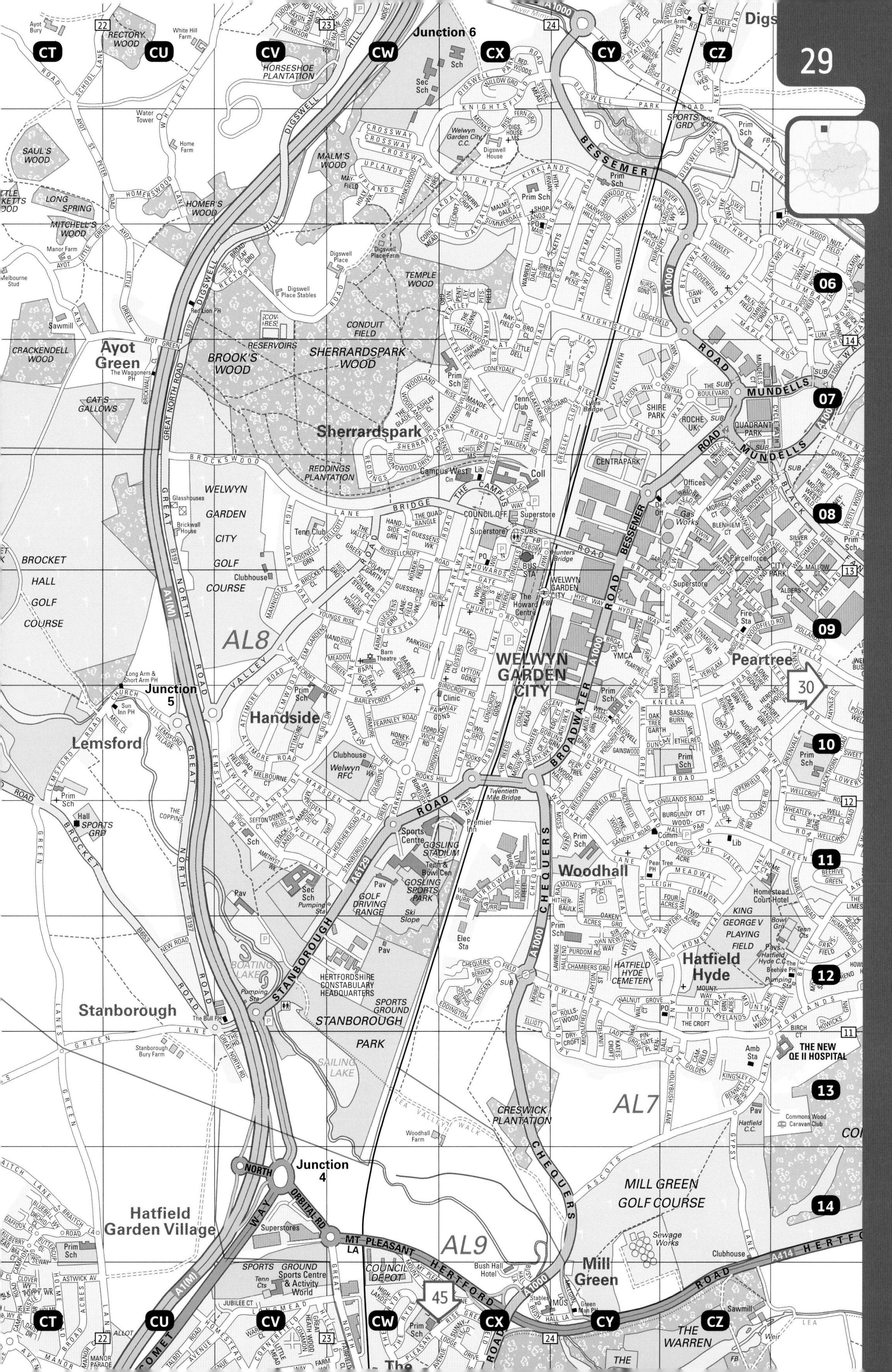

CT
CU
CV
CW
CX
CY
CZ
Junction 6
Junction 5
Junction 4
RECTORY WOOD
HORSESHOE PLANTATION
SAUL'S WOOD
LONG SPRING
MITCHELL'S WOOD
HOMER'S WOOD
MALM'S WOOD
TEMPLE WOOD
CONDUIT FIELD
BROOK'S WOOD
SHERRARDSPARK WOOD
REDDINGS PLANTATION
CRACKENDELL WOOD
Ayot Green
CAT'S GALLOWS
Sherrardspark
WELWYN GARDEN CITY GOLF COURSE
BROCKET HALL GOLF COURSE
AL8
AL7
AL9
WELWYN GARDEN CITY
Handside
Lemsford
Peartree
Woodhall
Hatfield Hyde
KING GEORGE V PLAYING FIELD
HATFIELD HYDE CEMETERY
THE NEW QE II HOSPITAL
Stanborough
STANBOROUGH PARK
SAILING LAKE
BOATING LAKE
HERTFORDSHIRE CONSTABULARY HEADQUARTERS
GOSLING STADIUM
GOSLING SPORTS PARK
GOLF DRIVING RANGE
CRESWICK PLANTATION
MILL GREEN GOLF COURSE
Mill Green
Hatfield Garden Village
THE WARREN
DIGSWELL LAKE
BESSEMER ROAD
MUNDELLS
BROADWATER ROAD
CHEQUERS
STANBOROUGH ROAD
GREAT NORTH ROAD
HERTFORD ROAD
MT PLEASANT
ORBITAL RD
NORTH WAY
A1(M)
A1000
A6129
A414
B197
B653
B195
B1000
30
45
06
07
08
09
10
11
12
13
14

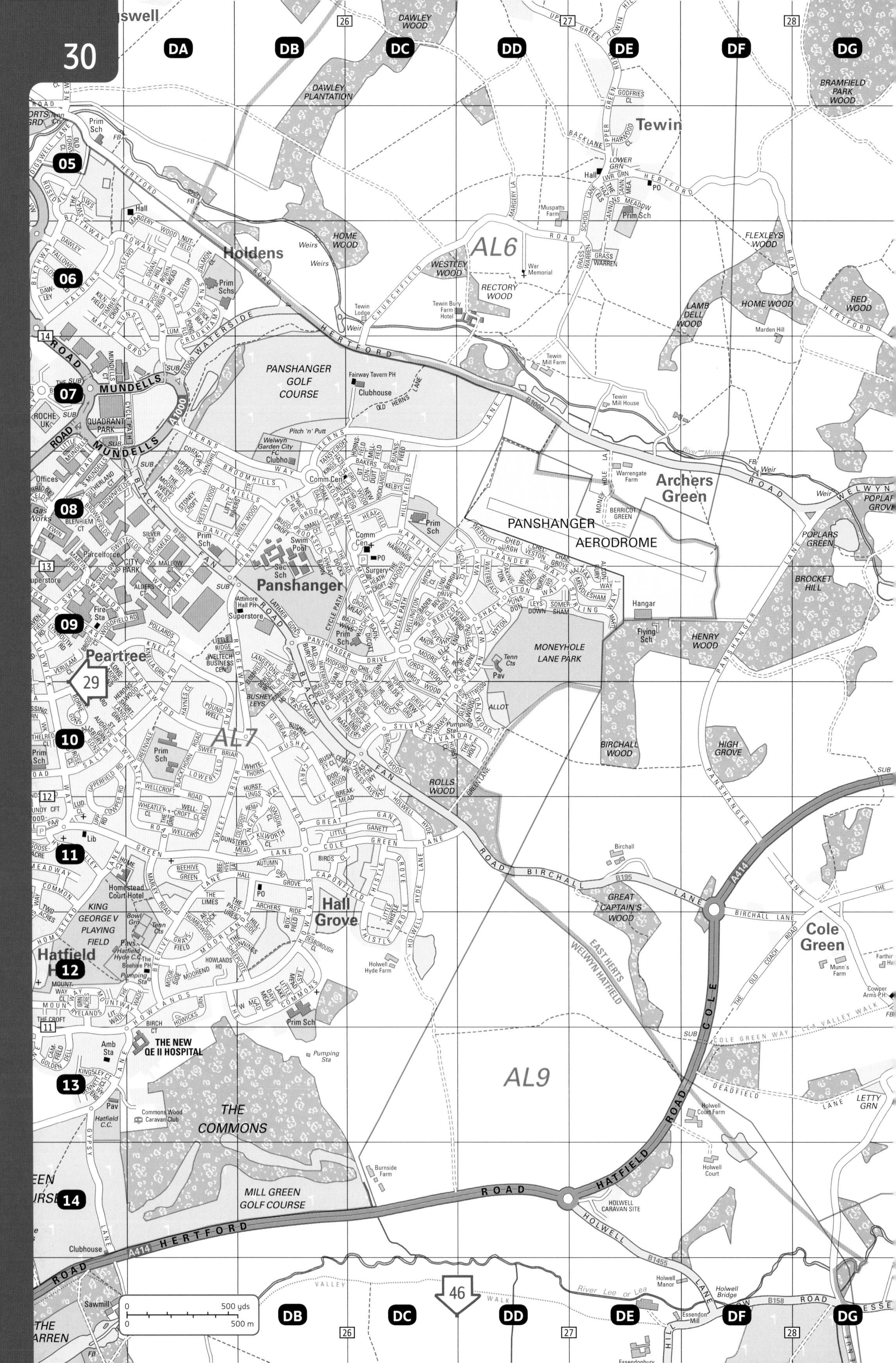
DA
DB
DC
DD
DE
DF
DG
DAWLEY WOOD
DAWLEY PLANTATION
BRAMFIELD PARK WOOD
Tewin
Holdens
HOME WOOD
AL6
WESTLEY WOOD
RECTORY WOOD
FLEXLEYS WOOD
LAMB DELL WOOD
HOME WOOD
RED WOOD
PANSHANGER GOLF COURSE
Fairway Tavern PH
Clubhouse
Welwyn Garden City FC Clubho
Archers Green
PANSHANGER AERODROME
POPLARS GREEN
BROCKET HILL
Panshanger
Peartree
29
MONEYHOLE LANE PARK
HENRY WOOD
BIRCHALL WOOD
HIGH GROVE
ROLLS WOOD
AL7
Hall Grove
GREAT CAPTAIN'S WOOD
Cole Green
KING GEORGE V PLAYING FIELD
Hatfield Hyde
THE NEW QE II HOSPITAL
AL9
THE COMMONS
MILL GREEN GOLF COURSE
HOLWELL CARAVAN SITE
Holwell Court Farm
Holwell Court
Burnside Farm
LETTY GRN
River Lee or Lea
46
Holwell Bridge
Essendon Mill
THE WARREN
05
06
07
08
09
10
11
12
13
14
26
27
28
0 500 yds
0 500 m

Bramfield
Bramfield Place Farm
PRIEST WOOD
Waterford Hall
BARLEYCROFT GROVE
DH
DJ
DK
DL
DM
DN
DP
BRAMFIELD
VICARAGE
LANE
SACOMBE
Waterford
WATERFORD PLANTATION
WATERFORD HEATH COMMUNITY NATURE PARK
WATERFORD MARSH
TIMBER ORCHARD
HIGH
NORTH ROAD
A119
TATTLE
HILL
Bacon's Farm
GREAT MOLE WOOD
THE ORCHARD
06
Goldings Hall
GOLDINGS
OAKFIELD PLANTATION
GREAT MOLEWOOD
HOOK'S BUSHES
BARNSLEYS WOOD
CHATTERSFIELD PLANTATION
HANGING GROVE
Broadoak End
ICEHOUSE WOOD
Windyridge Farm
HIGH MOLEWOOD
07
SELEBROOM WOOD
ARCHER'S SPRING
LONG WOOD
ELEVEN ACRE WOOD
Bengeo
LITTLE MOLE WOOD
Lafarge Redlands Aggregates
Comm Cen
HERTFORD CEMETERY
ALLOT
08
WELWYN ROAD
Prim Sch
EVERGREEN WOOD
BROADWATER
GARDEN WOOD
BLAKEMORE WOOD
Golden Griffin PH
B1000
Weir
SAND PIT
Sec Sch
HERTFORD NORTH
09
SG14
LADY HUGHES'S WOOD
CHESHER'S PLANTATION
HERTFORD COUNTY HOSP
32
HERTFORD
OSIER BEDS
CHELMSFORD WOOD
HERTINGFORDBURY
BYPASS
A414
Mill Farm
Epcombs
10
GREEN
CHISEL SHELF
THE COURTYARD
THE MILL
Hertingfordbury
White Horse Hotel
Hall
Prince of Wales PH
Hertford Town FC
Pav
ALLOT
Tenn Cts
Cricket Ground
THE OLD COACH ROAD
War Memorial
Hertingfordbury C.C.
Sch
TERRACE WOOD
Terrace Wood Nursery
The Bury Farm
COLE GREEN WAY
LEA VALLEY WALK
11
KIT'S
Birch Green
Birch Grove Nursery
FOXDELLS
River Lee or Lea
12
Riverside Garden Centre
SPORTS GRD
Letty Green Fruit Farm
PONTERS GROVE
Eastendgreen Farm
SOUTHFIELD WOOD
Bayfordbury Park Farm
Letty Green
Rochfords Nursery
Pipers End
East End Green
CHALK DELL
SG13
THE PINETUM
13
GROTTO WOOD
Bayfordbury
Bayfordbury Mansion
GRAVEL PIT
Roxford
Uni of Herts-Field Station & Observatory
Glasshouse
14
Woolmers Park
HATFIELD
GRAVEFIELD GROVE
Home Farm
THE PIGHTLE
SPRING WOOD
LARCH PLANTATION
HOOK'S GROVE
SAILOR'S GROVE
47
Water Hall Farm
BROADGREEN WOOD
The Home Field
LOWER ROAD
29
30
31

DQ
DR
DS
DT
DU
DV
DW
33
34
35
05
06
07
08
09
10
11
12
13
14
SG14
SG13
ST JOHNS WOOD
OAK WOOD
Pumping Sta
Elec Sta
Depot
WATERFORD HEATH COMMUNITY PASTURE PARK
EIGHT ACRE PLANTATION
COWSHED CORNER
Ware Park Farm
Ware Park
Ware Park Manor
MONASTERY
Bardon Farm
Nursery
GREAT MOLE WOOD
BENGEO MEADOWS
Kennel Corner
WARE CEM
WESTMILL ROAD
WATTON ROAD
Sec Sch
Prim Sch
Swim Pool
SPORTS GRD
Lido
RIVER LEE OR LEA
LEA VALLEY WALK
KING'S MEADS
Chadwell Spring
Clubhouse
CHADWELL SPRINGS GOLF COURSE
HERTFORD ROAD
Bengeo
LITTLE MOLE WOOD
THE WARREN
HARTHAM COMMON
LOCK HOUSE IND EST
MEAD LANE IND EST
MEAD BUSINESS CENTRE
DICKER MILL IND EST
HERTFORD EAST
Superstore
WARE ROAD
STANSTEAD ROAD
A119
A414
A10
B1502
Fitness Cen
Madford Retail Pk
Fire Sta
Royal Mail Delivery Off
FOXHOLES BUSINESS PARK
BALLSHILL GRO
Foxholes Roundabout
LONDON ROAD
Foxholes Farm
Rush Green Farm
HERTFORD
GASCOYNE WAY
Castle
County Hall
BURIAL GRD
Sec Sch
Hertford Cricket Club
BALLS PARK
THE CANAL
Jenningsbury Court
Moat
Amwell Place Farm
Dunkirks Farm
Caravan Club Site
Hertford Town FC
COUNTY HALL
Cricket Ground
SPORTS GRD
Comm Cen
GREAT STOCK WOOD
LITTLE STOCK WOOD
Hertford Heath
SPORTS GRD
Water Tower
Swallow Grove Farm
HERTFORD HEATH NATURE RESERVE
BALLS WOOD
HIGH WOOD
Bayfordbury Mansion
Research Centre
Brickendonbury
HOBBYHORSE WOOD
SAILOR'S GROVE
THE GROVE
Blackfields Farm
East Herts Equestrian Centre
EAST HERTS
BOX
ERMINE STREET (ROMAN ROAD)
31
48
500 yds
500 m

DX
DY
DZ
EA
EB
EC
ED
36
37
38
Great Cozens
Morley Hall
Moat
JACKSON'S GROVE
Swades Farm
Newhole Farm
Ford
HARCAMLOW WAY
KING GEORGE'S FLD
THE VINEYARD
PRIOR'S WOOD
SG12
DOGHOUSE WOOD
LADY GROVE
Waters Place Farm
Easneye
YOUNGS WOOD
WARE
VIADUCT
AMWELL END
HIGH ST
A1170
B1004
WIDBURY HILL
Brokengall Hill
Widburyhill Farm
WIDBURY BARNS
WIDBURY WOOD
MEAD WOOD
The Dairy Farm
14
06
07
08
09
10
11
12
13
EASNEYE WOOD
All Nations Christian Coll
SPORTS GRD
PETER'S WOOD
POST WOOD
LONDON ROAD
Hardmead Lock
LEE VALLEY REGIONAL PARK
PRESDALES RECREATION GROUND
Amwellbury Farm
AMWELL QUARRY NATURE RESERVE
LEE VALLEY CYCLE ROUTE
HOLLYCROSS ROAD
CAPPELL ROAD
Van Hage Garden Centre
Great Amwell
War Memorial
34
St. Margarets
Stanstead Lock
Stanstead Abbotts
The Maltings
Glasshouses
LEAFYOAK WOOD
MUCH WOOD
Amwell Roundabout
B181
STATION ROAD
St. Margaretsbury Rec Grd
GOLDING'S WOOD
A414
LEE VALLEY REGIONAL PARK
SPORTS GROUND
HAILEY WOOD
Haileybury Sports Complex
Hailey
The Galley Hall PH
Ryegate Farm
RYE MEADS NATURE RESERVE
RSPB RYE MEADS
Visitor Centre
Filter Beds
Sewage Works
Sludge Lagoons
EN11
A10 HODDESDON BYPASS
DELLS WOOD
Woollensbrook
CEM
Rye House Gatehouse
Showman's Caravan Site
RYE HOUSE SPEEDWAY
RYE HOUSE
49

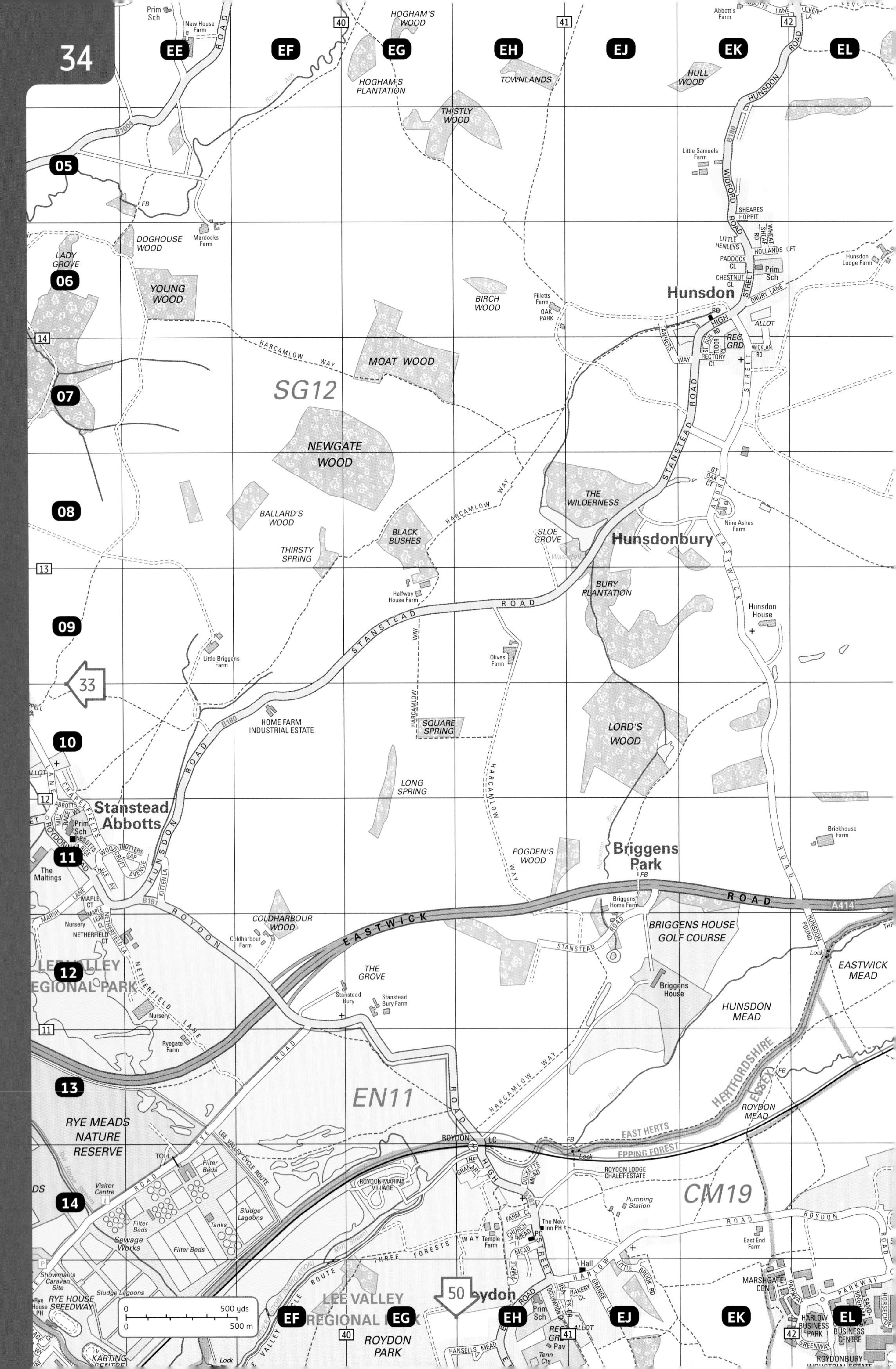
Hunsdon
Hunsdonbury
Stanstead Abbotts
Briggens Park
SG12
EN11
CM19
NEWGATE WOOD
MOAT WOOD
LORD'S WOOD
THE WILDERNESS
BRIGGENS HOUSE GOLF COURSE
RYE MEADS NATURE RESERVE
LEE VALLEY REGIONAL PARK
HUNSDON MEAD
EASTWICK MEAD
ROYDON MEAD
ROYDON PARK
HARCAMLOW WAY
STANSTEAD ROAD
EASTWICK ROAD
A414
HERTFORDSHIRE
ESSEX
33
50

CM21
CM20
GOLDEN GROVE
SAYES COPPICE
THE MANOR OF GROVES GOLF COURSE AND COUNTRY CLUB
Gilston Park
Pye Corner
Eastwick
Eastwick Lodge Roundabout
Burnt Mill Roundabout
Crown Gate Roundabout
Mark Hall
Netteswell
Little Parndon
PRINCESS ALEXANDRA HOSPITAL
HARLOW
TOWN PARK
CANONS BROOK GOLF COURSE
HARLOW STADIUM
PARNDON MEAD
HOLLINGSON MEADS
SAND AND GRAVEL PIT
EASTWICK ROAD
EDINBURGH WAY
FIFTH / ALLENDE AVENUE
HERTFORDSHIRE
36
51

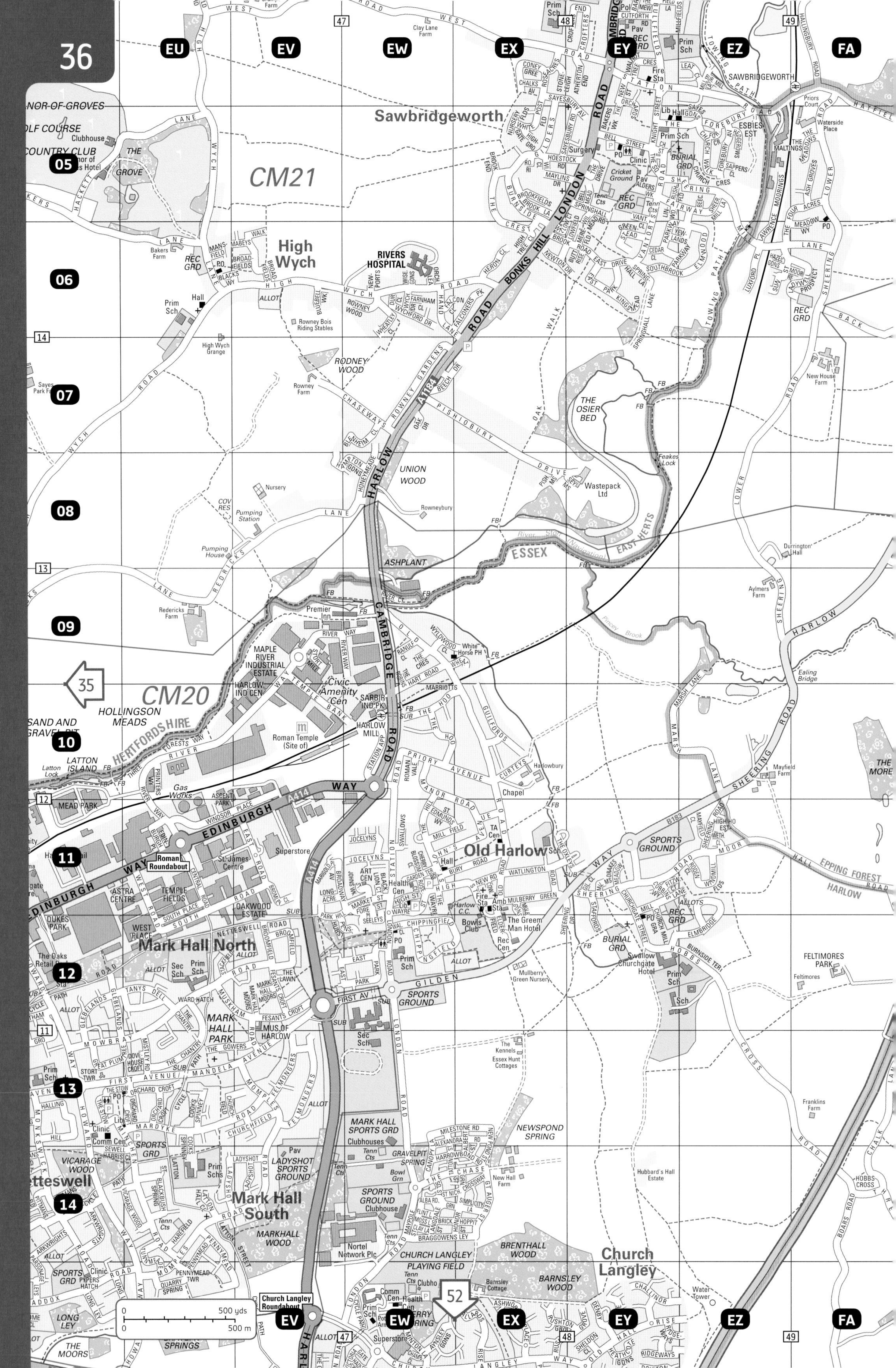
EU
EV
EW
EX
EY
EZ
FA
05
06
07
08
09
10
11
12
13
14
Sawbridgeworth
CM21
High Wych
RIVERS HOSPITAL
RODNEY WOOD
UNION WOOD
THE OSIER BED
Wastepack Ltd
ESSEX
EAST HERTS
ASHPLANT
CAMBRIDGE ROAD
LONDON ROAD
HARLOW ROAD
BONKS HILL
A1184
MAPLE RIVER INDUSTRIAL ESTATE
HARLOW IND CEN
Civic Amenity Cen
SARBIR IND PK
HARLOW MILL
Roman Temple (Site of)
CM20
HOLLINGSON MEADS
SAND AND GRAVEL PIT
HERTFORDSHIRE
LATTON ISLAND
MEAD PARK
Gas Works
EDINBURGH WAY
A414
Roman Roundabout
St James Centre
TEMPLE FIELDS
ASTRA CENTRE
DUKES PARK
WEST PLACE
OAKWOOD ESTATE
Mark Hall North
Superstore
Old Harlow
Hallowbury
Chapel
SPORTS GROUND
EPPING FOREST
HARLOW
BURIAL GRD
Swallow Churchgate Hotel
FELTIMORES PARK
Mullberry Green Nursery
The Green Man Hotel
Bowls Club
MARK HALL PARK
MUS OF HARLOW
Sec Sch
MARK HALL SPORTS GRD
NEWSPOND SPRING
LADYSHOT SPORTS GROUND
VICARAGE WOOD
Netteswell
Mark Hall South
MARKHALL WOOD
Nortel Network Plc
CHURCH LANGLEY PLAYING FIELD
BRENTHALL WOOD
BARNSLEY WOOD
Church Langley
Church Langley Roundabout
THE MOORS
Hubbard's Hall Estate
Franklins Farm
HOBBS CROSS
Durrington Hall
Aylmers Farm
Ealing Bridge
Mayfield Farm
THE MORE
New House Farm
Priors Court
Waterside Place
ESBIES EST
35
52
0 500 yds
0 500 m

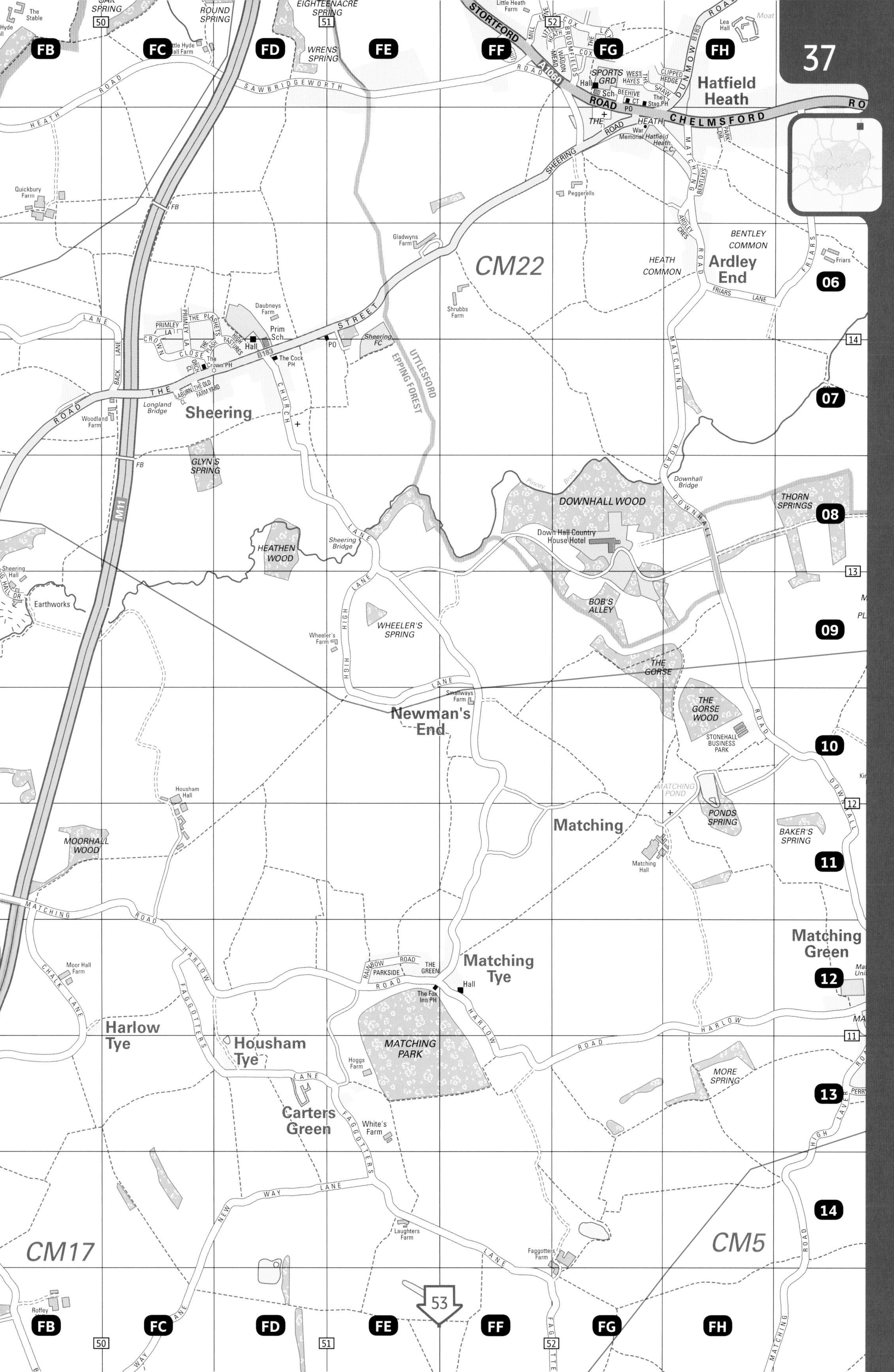
FB
FC
FD
FE
FF
FG
FH
Hatfield Heath
Ardley End
BENTLEY COMMON
HEATH COMMON
CM22
Sheering
Newman's End
Matching
Matching Tye
Matching Green
Harlow Tye
Housham Tye
Carters Green
CM17
CM5
DOWNHALL WOOD
Down Hall Country House Hotel
BOB'S ALLEY
THE GORSE
THE GORSE WOOD
STONEHALL BUSINESS PARK
PONDS SPRING
BAKER'S SPRING
THORN SPRINGS
HEATHEN WOOD
WHEELER'S SPRING
GLYN'S SPRING
MOORHALL WOOD
MATCHING PARK
MORE SPRING
WRENS SPRING
ROUND SPRING
EIGHTEENACRE SPRING
UTTLESFORD
EPPING FOREST
M11
A1060
B183
SAWBRIDGEWORTH ROAD
CHELMSFORD ROAD
SHEERING ROAD
THE STREET
CHURCH LANE
HIGH LANE
DOWNHALL ROAD
MATCHING ROAD
HARLOW ROAD
FAGGOTTERS LANE
NEW WAY LANE
CHALK LANE
FRIARS LANE
HIGH LAVER
Daubneys Farm
Shrubbs Farm
Gladwyns Farm
Quickbury Farm
Woodland Farm
Longland Bridge
Sheering Bridge
Downhall Bridge
Wheeler's Farm
Smallways Farm
Housham Hall
Matching Hall
Moor Hall Farm
Hoggs Farm
White's Farm
Laughters Farm
Faggotters Farm
Roffey
Sheering Hall
Earthworks
Peggerells
Lea Hall
Friars
The Fox Inn PH
The Cock PH
The Crown PH
53
06
07
08
09
10
11
12
13
14
50
51
52

NORTHCHURCH COMMON NT
AS
AT
AU
AV
AW
AX
AY
98
99
00
FIRTHSDEN BEECHES
NATIONAL TRUST
Pumping Station
15
16
17
18
19
20
21
22
23
24
09
08
07
06
Gorseside Farm
Northchurch Farm
Hill Farm
Dudswell
GRAND UNION CANAL
BERKHAMSTED GOLF COURSE
HP4
BERKHAMSTED
Northchurch
HIGH STREET
A4251
B4506
NEW ROAD
CEM
Sch
PO
Social Cen
Sec Sch
New Farm
BERKHAMSTED PLACE
SPORTS GRD
Clubhouse
The Mansion
Well Farm
Hospice
THE ROOKERY
Woodcock Hill
COX DELL
THE PLANTATION
Youth Club
Sports Cen
Health Cen
GOSSOMS END
BERKHAMSTED CASTLE (ruins)
Berkhamsted Town FC
Superstore
THE MOOR
CIVIC CEN
Fit Cen
Prim Sch
Prep Sch
REC GRD
ALLOT
KINGS ROAD
A416
KINGSHILL WAY
PLAYING FIELD
National Film & Television Archive
Tower
Ashlyns Farm
Ashlyns Hall
BERKHAMSTED A41 BYPASS
A41
LONDON ROAD
PANCAKE WOOD
FIRS WOOD
WILLOW WOOD
HOCKERIDGE WOOD
CHESHAM ROAD
Johns Lane Farm
William Hill Farm
Hockeridge Farm
SANDPIT GREEN
DROPPING'S WOOD
COKER'S SPRING
Haresfoot Farm
Harriotts End Farm
THE LARCHES
HEATHEN GROVE
HP5
Brickies Farm
Snowhill Farm
Old Oak Farm
Sewage Works
Ashley Green
Hall
Flamstead Farm
DACORUM
HERTFORDSHIRE
CHILTERN
BUCKINGHAMSHIRE
Whelpley Hill Farm
Kenmore Farm
GREAT WOOD
SHORT WOOD
Sale's Farm
Spencer's Farm
Hemming's Farm
SWING GATE LANE
SUB
0 500 yds
0 500 m
56

AZ
BA
BB
BC
BD
BE
BF
01
02
03
GREAT FRITHDEN COPSE
NATIONAL TRUST
LITTLE FRITHSDEN COPSE
FRITHSDEN VINES
Hollybush Farm
Alford Arms PH
NETTLEDEN ROAD
Crossways Farm
HERDIN'S WOOD
Strathgade Farm
Bingham's Park Farm
Poultry Farm
BROWN'S SPRING WOOD
HOLLYBUSH WOOD
Rumblers Farm
POTTEN END HILL
War Memorial
BERKHAMSTED GOLF COURSE
Grims Ditch
SPORTS GRD
Pav
ALLOT
Woodcroft Farm
Potten End Farm
CATSTAIL WOOD
16
Potten End
THE SQUARE
THE FRONT
Sch
Hall
RAMBLING WAY
DELL WOOD
09
Martins Pond PH
HEMPSTEAD LANE
Boxted Farm
17
Bowling Green
COV RES
BERKHAMSTED ROAD
Gutteridge Farm
Little Heath Park
Little Heath Farm
LITTLE HEATH NT
Boxted Pig Farm
FIELDS END LANE
Gadebridge
SPORTS GROUND
18
GUTTERIDGE WOOD
Little Heath Great Farm
Lower Little Heath Farm
Fields End Farm
08
WARNERS END
Warners End
Sec Sch
Prim Sch
19
BULLBEGGAR'S WOOD
HAWTHORNE LANE
CHAULDEN LANE
40
HP1
SHRUB HILL COMMON
William Crook House
Comm Cen
NORTHRIDGE PARK
20
Chaulden
Prim Schs
07
21
Berkhamsted Sewage Works
GRAND UNION CANAL
River Bulbourne
Lock
A4251
Pix Farm
PIX FARM LANE
Pouchen End Farm
Broadway Farm
LONDON ROAD
The Three Horseshoes PH
CHAULDEN LANE PLAYING FIELD
Rugby Ground
CONVENT
SUGAR LANE
Watermill Hotel
Cress Farm
White Horse PH & The Anchor PH
Bourne End Farm
22
A41
KINGS LANGLEY BYPASS
Bourne End
BOURNE END MILLS
Moorend Farm
ROAD
06
HEMEL HEMPSTEAD
Swan PH
Lower Farm
STONEY LANE
Premier Inn
BERKHAMSTED BYPASS
GREEN CROFT
Vale Farm
HAY WOOD
Sch
23
UPPER ROUGHDOWN
Prep Sch
HANGING WOOD
Clubhouse
LITTLE HAY GOLF COMPLEX
BOXMOOR GOLF COURSE
24
COLESHILL WOOD
HP3
BOX LANE
SHEETHANGER COMMON
Howe's Retreat
Felden Lodge
GORSEFIELD WOOD
57
BURY WOOD
Tower Farm
Felden Grange
Felden Manor
Longcroft Farm
COVERED RESERVOIR

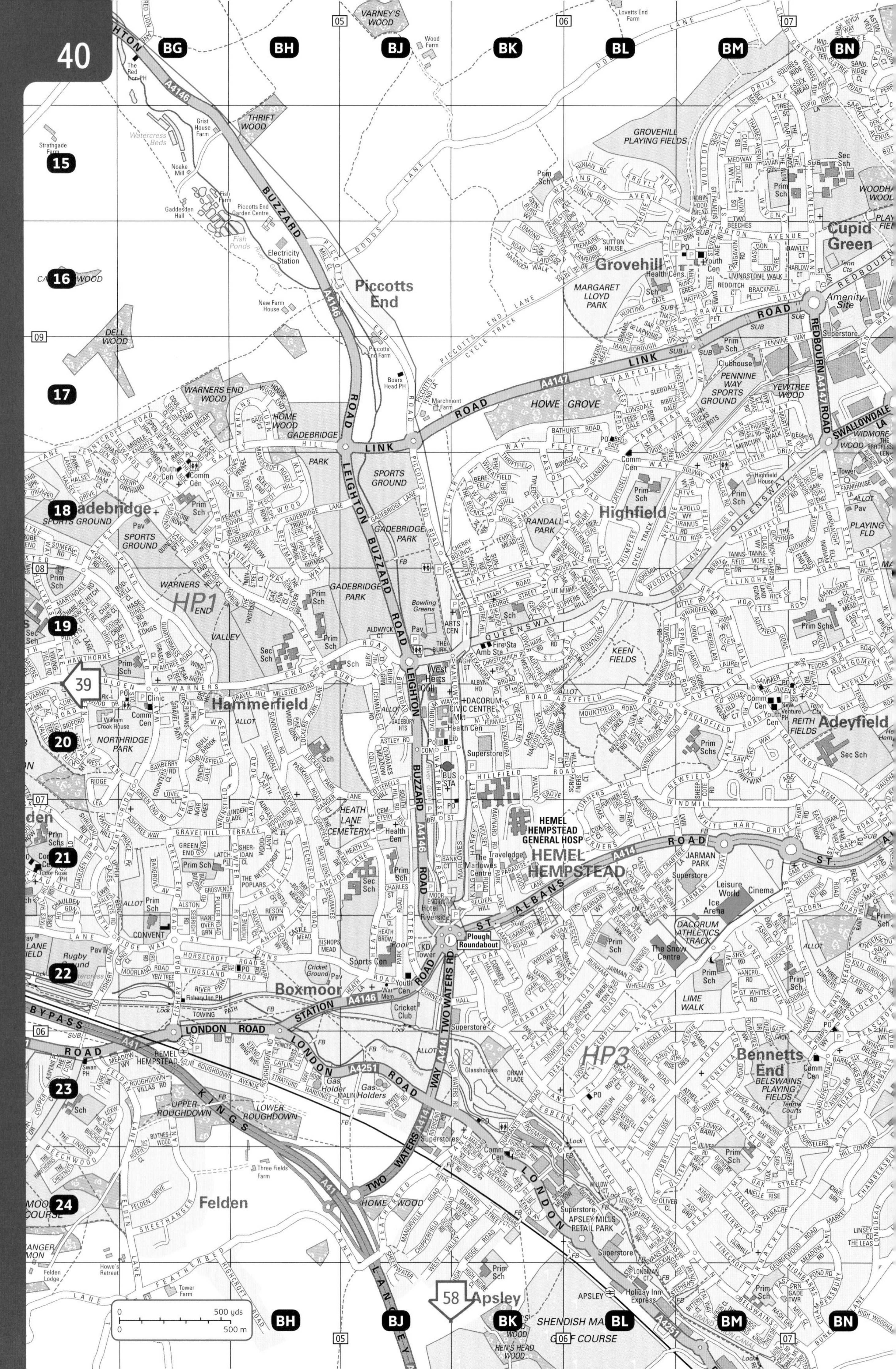

BG
BH
BJ
BK
BL
BM
BN
15
16
17
18
19
20
21
22
23
24
VARNEY'S WOOD
Wood Farm
Lovetts End Farm
The Red Lion PH
THRIFT WOOD
Grist House Farm
Watercress Beds
Strathgade Farm
Noake Mill
Fish Farm
Gaddesden Hall
Piccotts End Garden Centre
Fish Ponds
Electricity Station
Piccotts End
New Farm House
DELL WOOD
Piccotts End Farm
Boars Head PH
Marchmont Farm
GROVEHILL PLAYING FIELDS
Grovehill
MARGARET LLOYD PARK
Cupid Green
Amenity Site
Superstore
Clubhouse
PENNINE WAY SPORTS GROUND
YEWTREE WOOD
HOWE GROVE
WARNERS END WOOD
HOME WOOD
GADEBRIDGE
LINK ROAD
BUZZARD ROAD
LEIGHTON BUZZARD ROAD
A4146
A4147
REDBOURN ROAD
SWALLOWDALE LA
WIDMORE WOOD
SPORTS GROUND
Gadebridge
SPORTS GROUND
GADEBRIDGE PARK
Highfield
RANDALL PARK
PLAYING FLD
HP1
WARNERS END
VALLEY
Bowling Greens
ARTS CEN
QUEENSWAY
Fire Sta
Amb Sta
KEEN FIELDS
39
Hammerfield
West Herts Coll
DACORUM CIVIC CENTRE
Mkt
Health Cen
Superstore
BUS STA
NORTHRIDGE PARK
REITH FIELDS
Adeyfield
HEATH LANE CEMETERY
HEMEL HEMPSTEAD GENERAL HOSP
HEMEL HEMPSTEAD
Travelodge
The Marlowes Centre
ST. ALBANS ROAD
A414
JARMAN PARK
Leisure World
Cinema
Ice Arena
DACORUM ATHLETICS TRACK
The Snow Centre
CONVENT
Rugby Ground
Plough Roundabout
KD Tower
Sports Cen
Cricket Ground
Boxmoor
STATION ROAD
TWO WATERS RD
Cricket Club
LONDON ROAD
A41
HEMEL HEMPSTEAD
Fishery Inn PH
Superstore
LIME WALK
HP3
Bennetts End
BELSWAINS PLAYING FIELDS
Glasshouses
ORAM PLACE
Gas Holder
Gas Holders
UPPER ROUGHDOWN
LOWER ROUGHDOWN
KINGS LANGLEY BYPASS
A4251
Three Fields Farm
Felden
HOME WOOD
TWO WATERS WAY
Superstores
Superstore
APSLEY MILLS RETAIL PARK
Superstore
Felden Lodge
Howe's Retreat
Tower Farm
58
Apsley
SHENDISH MANOR GOLF COURSE
HEN'S HEAD WOOD
APSLEY
Holiday Inn Express
GRAND UNION CANAL
0
500 yds
0
500 m

HP2
AL3
WD5
Leverstock Green
Junctions 7 & 8
Buncefield Terminal
Oil Tanks
HEMEL HEMPSTEAD INDUSTRIAL ESTATE
MAYLANDS AVENUE
BREAKSPEAR WAY
HEMEL HEMPSTEAD ROAD
PUNCH BOWL LANE
HOGG END LANE
CHERRY TREE LANE
BUNCEFIELD LANE
WESTWICK ROW
BEDMOND ROAD
WOODWELLS FARM CEMETERY
KENTISH WOOD
WINDMILLHILL WOOD
THE VISTAS
BRUCE'S PLANTATION
BRICKKILN WOOD
GORHAMBURY
BLACKWATER WOOD
POTTERS CROUCH PLANTATION
LONGFIELD SPRING
APPSPOND WOOD
LONG DEANS
M1
A4147
A414
42
59

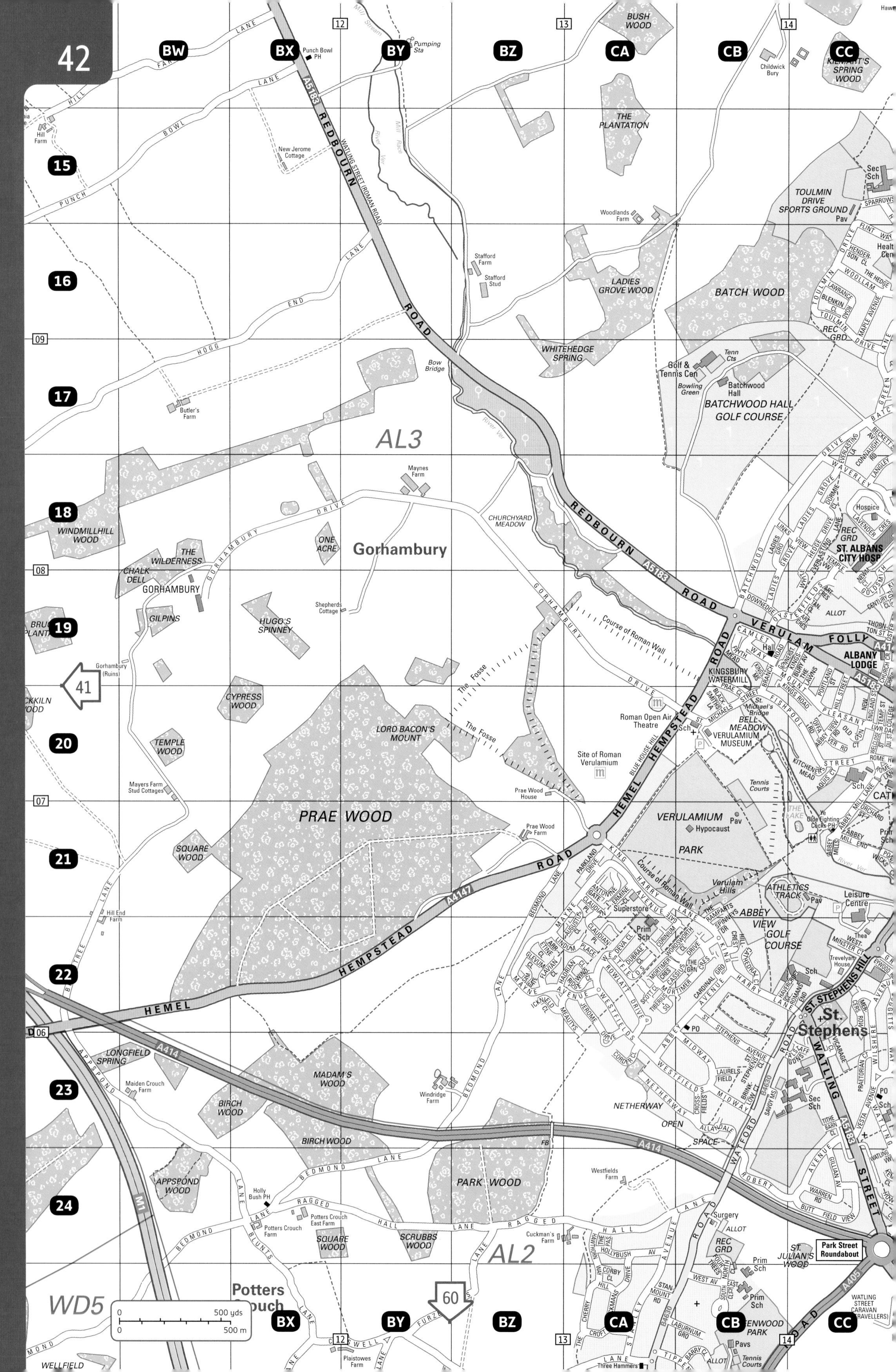
BW
BX
BY
BZ
CA
CB
CC
12
13
14
15
16
17
18
19
20
21
22
23
24
09
08
07
06
Punch Bowl PH
Pumping Sta
Mill Stream
BUSH WOOD
Childwick Bury
KIEMANT'S SPRING WOOD
FARM LANE
HILL
Hill Farm
PUNCH BOWL LANE
New Jerome Cottage
A5183 REDBOURN ROAD
WATLING STREET (ROMAN ROAD)
River Ver
Mill Race
THE PLANTATION
Woodlands Farm
TOULMIN DRIVE SPORTS GROUND
Pav
Sec Sch
Stafford Farm
Stafford Stud
LADIES GROVE WOOD
BATCH WOOD
HOGG END LANE
WHITEHEDGE SPRING
Bow Bridge
Golf & Tennis Cen
Tenn Cts
Bowling Green
Batchwood Hall
BATCHWOOD HALL GOLF COURSE
Butler's Farm
AL3
Maynes Farm
WINDMILLHILL WOOD
THE WILDERNESS
CHALK DELL
GORHAMBURY
GORHAMBURY DRIVE
ONE ACRE
Gorhambury
CHURCHYARD MEADOW
REDBOURN ROAD
ST. ALBANS CITY HOSP
Hospice
GILPINS
Shepherds Cottage
HUGO'S SPINNEY
Course of Roman Wall
VERULAM ROAD
FOLLY
ALBANY LODGE
Gorhambury (Ruins)
41
CYPRESS WOOD
The Fosse
KINGSBURY WATERMILL
Roman Open Air Theatre
LORD BACON'S MOUNT
BELL MEADOW
VERULAMIUM MUSEUM
TEMPLE WOOD
Site of Roman Verulamium
HEMEL HEMPSTEAD ROAD
Mayers Farm Stud Cottages
Prae Wood House
PRAE WOOD
Prae Wood Farm
VERULAMIUM PARK
Hypocaust
Tennis Courts
SQUARE WOOD
ATHLETICS TRACK
Leisure Centre
Hill End Farm
A4147
Superstore
Prim Sch
ABBEY VIEW GOLF COURSE
HEMEL HEMPSTEAD ROAD
St. Stephens
LONGFIELD SPRING
A414
Maiden Crouch Farm
MADAM'S WOOD
Windridge Farm
BIRCH WOOD
NETHERWAY
OPEN SPACE
BIRCH WOOD
BEDMOND LANE
PARK WOOD
Westfields Farm
APPSPOND WOOD
Holly Bush PH
Potters Crouch East Farm
Potters Crouch Farm
SQUARE WOOD
SCRUBBS WOOD
RAGGED HALL LANE
Cuckman's Farm
AL2
Surgery
REC GRD
Prim Sch
ST. JULIAN'S WOOD
Park Street Roundabout
M1
WD5
Potters Crouch
60
500 yds
500 m
Plaistowes Farm
WELLFIELD
Three Hammers
WATLING STREET CARAVAN (TRAVELLERS)
A405
A5183 WATLING STREET

43
HOME OFFICE SCIENTIFIC DEVELOPMENT BRANCH
CD
CE
CF
CG
CH
CJ
CK
15
16
17
09
08
07
06
16
17
18
19
20
21
22
23
24
44
61
New Greens
Townsend
Jersey Farm
JERSEY FARM WOODLAND PARK
Marshalswick
ST. ALBANS
Fleetville
The Camp
AL1
AL4
WOOLLAMS PLAYING FIELD
SANDRIDGEBURY LANE
BEECH BOTTOM DYKE
THE GLEN
THE WICK
SKYS WOOD
HOME WOOD
HIGHFIELD PARK
LONGACRES PLAYING FIELD
CLARENCE PARK
ST. ALBANS CEMETERY
VERULAM GOLF COURSE
St. Julians
Sopwell House Hotel
NORTH ORBITAL COMMERCIAL PARK
CHALKDELL WOOD
VERULAMIAN RFC
London Colney Rbt
Tyttenhanger
Junction 1
HARPENDEN ROAD
SANDRIDGE ROAD
ST. ALBANS ROAD
HATFIELD ROAD
LONDON ROAD
NORTH ORBITAL ROAD
A1081
A1057
A414
A5183
St. Albans City
SPORTS GROUND

CL
CM
CN
CP
CQ
CR
CS
28
HOME OFFICE SCIENTIFIC DEVELOPMENT BRANCH
SAND AND GRAVEL PIT
SAND & GRAVEL PIT
HOOK'S WOOD
SLEEVE HALL WOOD
BALL'S COVERT
OAK WOOD
ROUND WOOD
HOME COVERT
ASH GREEN
Astwick Manor
HATFIELD BUSINESS PARK
AL10
University of Hertfordshire de Havilland Campus
ST. ALBANS ROAD WEST
Wilkin's Green
Ellenbrook
Smallford
HATFIELD ROAD
BAGGYMEAD SPRING
Oaklands Coll
Junction 3
AL4
Sleapshyde
JOHNSON'S SPRING
Bullen's Green
Colney Heath
Roestock
Tyttenhanger
SAND AND GRAVEL PIT
KNIGHT'S WOOD
BLOUNT SPRING
THE WARREN
FREDERICK'S WOOD
NORTH ORBITAL ROAD
43
62
GARDEN WOOD
THE NEW PLANTATION
COPPICE
0 500 yds
0 500 m
15
16
17
18
19
20
21
22
23
24

45
Junction
CT
CU
CV
CW
CX
CY
CZ
Hatfield Garden Village
29
MILL GREEN GOLF COURSE
Sewage Works
Clubhouse
Mill Green
Bush Hall Hotel
MUS
Green Man PH
Superstores
MT PLEASANT
HERTFORD ROAD
COUNCIL DEPOT
SPORTS GROUND
Sports Centre & Activity World
Sawmill
THE WARREN
Weir
THE BROADWATER
VINEYARD
HOME PARK
The Ryde
Birchwood
COMET WAY
A1(M)
HATFIELD TUNNEL
Premier Inn
T-Mobile
Fire Sta
HATFIELD
Old Hatfield
Red Lion PH
Superstore
Swim Pool
Roe Green
OLD TUDOR PALACE
HATFIELD HOUSE
NEW POND
HATFIELD PARK
POLLARD WOOD
THE LONG RIDE
16
17
18
19
20
21
22
23
24
09
08
07
06
CONDUIT WOOD
BRICKKILN WOOD
WELLINGTON WOOD
THE ROUGHS
46
Memorial BURIAL GRD
HOWE DELL
Oxlease
SPORTS GRD
Home Farm
Reservoir
COOMBE WOOD
Park Dairy
University of Hertfordshire (College Lane Campus)
HAZEL GROVE
South Hatfield
Leisure Centre
OXLEYS WOOD
HALFWAYOAK POND
MILLWARD'S PARK
Woodside
Woodside Place Farm
Quality Hotel
SOUTHWAY
GREAT NORTH ROAD
A1000
A1001
WELWYN HATFIELD DISTRICT CEMETERY
New Barnfield
Marshmoor Nurseries
AL9
Junction 2
Welham Green
ALPHA BUSINESS PARK
WELHAM GREEN
Marshmoor Bridge
Lower Woodside
Elec Sta
TOLLGATE WOOD
BUSH WOOD
REC GRD
Hope & Anchor PH
Sibthorpe Arms PH
Skimpans Bridge
Potterells Farm
Comm Cen
Rockwater Nursery
Bell Bar Nursery
M.K.M. Nurseries
Nursery
THE FIRS PARK
THE LEGG
PELPIN'S WOOD
ROUND WOOD
Tennis Courts
BROOKMANS PARK GOLF COURSE
Clubhouse
North Mymms
63
Med Cen
POTTERELLS

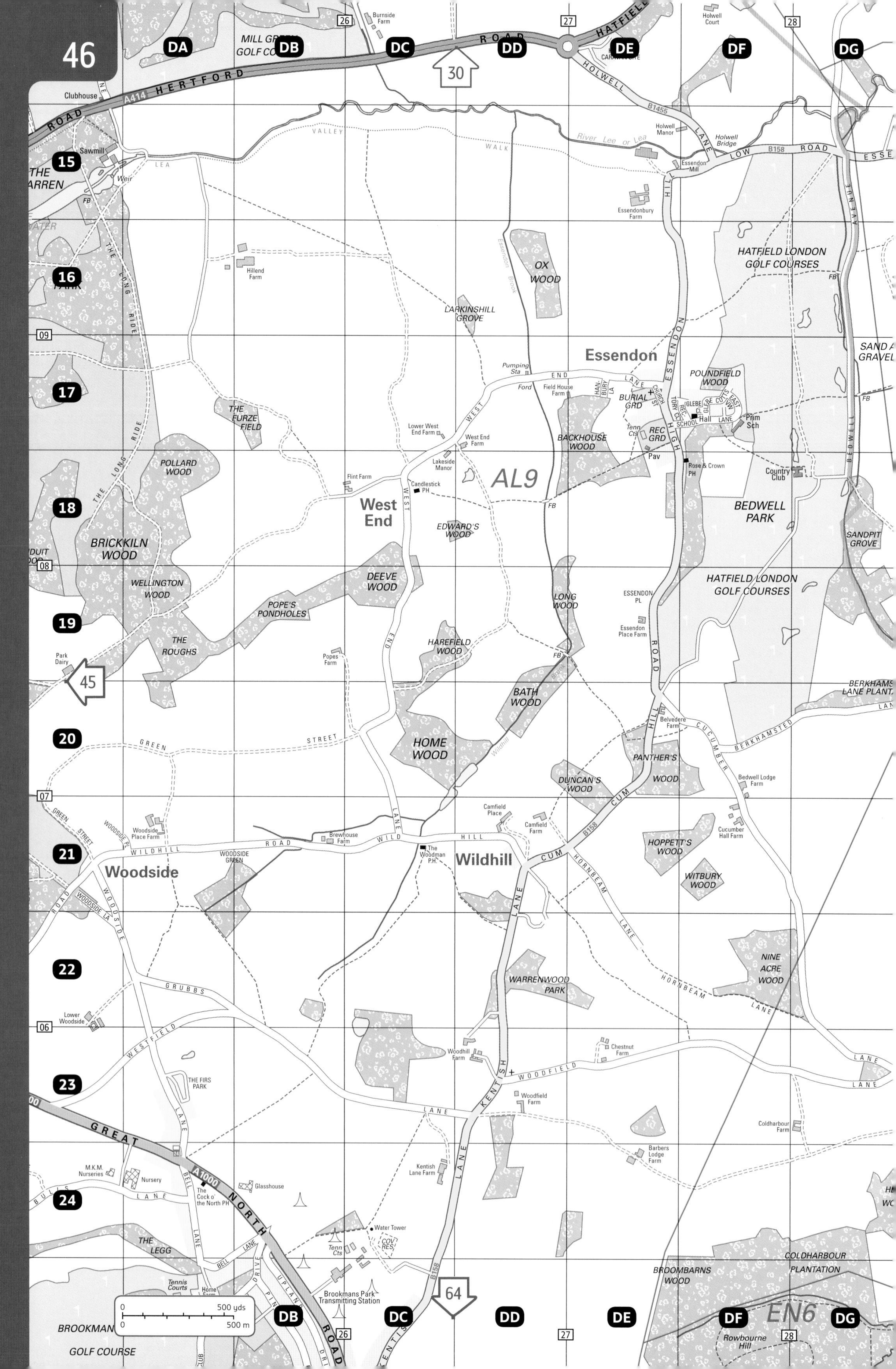

HERTFORD ROAD
A414
HATFIELD
Mill Green Golf Course
Burnside Farm
Holwell Court
30
Clubhouse
Sawmill
THE WARREN
Weir
LEA VALLEY WALK
River Lee or Lea
Holwell Manor
Holwell Bridge
HOLWELL LANE
B1455
LOW ROAD
B158
Essendon Mill
Essendonbury Farm
HIGH ROAD
THE LONG RIDE
Hillend Farm
OX WOOD
Essendon Brook
LARKINSHILL GROVE
HATFIELD LONDON GOLF COURSES
AVENUE
BEDWELL AVENUE
Essendon
ESSENDON HIGH ROAD
Pumping Sta
Ford
END LANE
Field House Farm
BURIAL GRD
POUNDFIELD WOOD
REC GRD
SCHOOL LANE
Hall
Prim Sch
THE FURZE FIELD
WEST END LANE
Lower West End Farm
West End Farm
Lakeside Manor
BACKHOUSE WOOD
Pav
Rose & Crown PH
Country Club
POLLARD WOOD
Flint Farm
Candlestick PH
AL9
FB
BEDWELL PARK
West End
EDWARD'S WOOD
SANDPIT GROVE
BRICKKILN WOOD
DEEVE WOOD
WELLINGTON WOOD
POPE'S PONDHOLES
LONG WOOD
ESSENDON PL
Essendon Place Farm
THE ROUGHS
HAREFIELD WOOD
Park Dairy
Popes Farm
45
BATH WOOD
BERKHAMSTED LANE PLANTATION
GREEN STREET
HOME WOOD
Wildhill
Belvedere Farm
CUCUMBER LANE
BERKHAMSTED LANE
PANTHER'S WOOD
DUNCAN'S WOOD
Bedwell Lodge Farm
Camfield Place
Camfield Farm
CUCUMBER HILL
Woodside Place Farm
WOODSIDE PL
WILDHILL ROAD
Brewhouse Farm
WILDHILL
The Woodman P.H.
HOPPETT'S WOOD
Cucumber Hall Farm
WOODSIDE GREEN
Woodside
HORNBEAM LANE
WITBURY WOOD
WOODSIDE LA
WOODSIDE ROAD
KENTISH LANE
GRUBBS LANE
WARRENWOOD PARK
NINE ACRE WOOD
Lower Woodside
WESTFIELD LANE
Woodhill Farm
Chestnut Farm
WOODFIELD LANE
THE FIRS PARK
Woodfield Farm
GREAT NORTH ROAD
A1000
Coldharbour Farm
Barbers Lodge Farm
M.K.M. Nurseries
Nursery
Glasshouse
Kentish Lane Farm
BULLS LANE
BELL LANE
The Cock o' the North PH
Water Tower
COV RES
THE LEGG
Tenn Cts
COLDHARBOUR PLANTATION
Tennis Courts
Home Farm
UPLANDS
BROOMBARNS WOOD
Brookmans Park Transmitting Station
64
500 yds
500 m
BROOKMANS PARK GOLF COURSE
EN6
Rowbourne Hill
DA DB DC DD DE DF DG
15 16 17 18 19 20 21 22 23 24
26 27 28
09 08 07 06

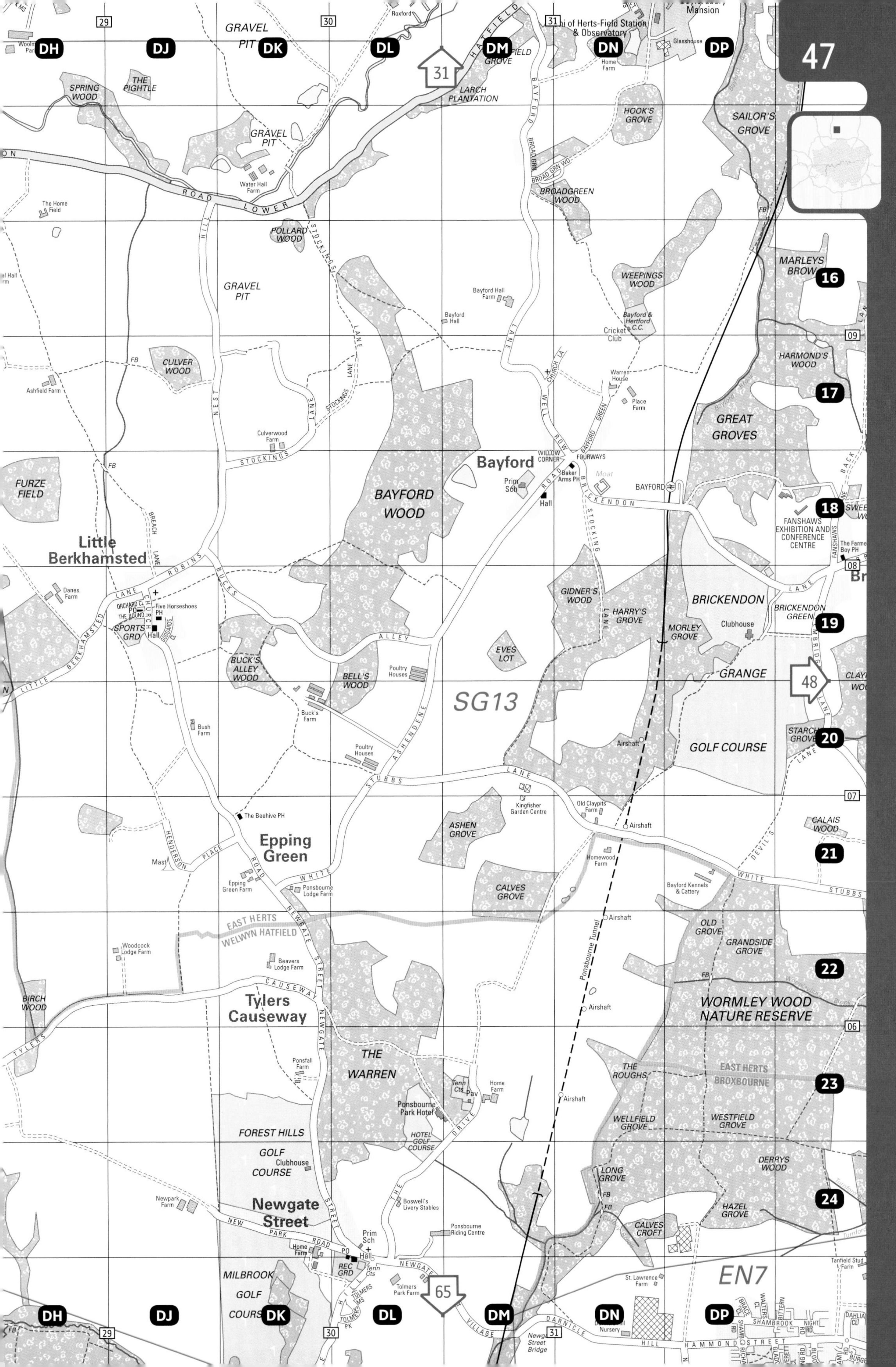
Bayford
Little Berkhamsted
Epping Green
Tylers Causeway
Newgate Street
BAYFORD WOOD
SG13
EN7
BRICKENDON
GRANGE
GOLF COURSE
WORMLEY WOOD NATURE RESERVE
FOREST HILLS GOLF COURSE
MILBROOK GOLF COURSE
THE WARREN
GREAT GROVES
SAILOR'S GROVE
MARLEYS BROW
HARMOND'S WOOD
HOOK'S GROVE
BROADGREEN WOOD
WEEPINGS WOOD
LARCH PLANTATION
SPRING WOOD
THE PIGHTLE
GRAVEL PIT
POLLARD WOOD
CULVER WOOD
FURZE FIELD
BUCK'S ALLEY WOOD
BELL'S WOOD
EVES LOT
GIDNER'S WOOD
HARRY'S GROVE
MORLEY GROVE
ASHEN GROVE
CALVES GROVE
OLD GROVE
GRANDSIDE GROVE
THE ROUGHS
WELLFIELD GROVE
WESTFIELD GROVE
DERRYS WOOD
LONG GROVE
HAZEL GROVE
CALVES CROFT
BIRCH WOOD
CALAIS WOOD
STARCH GROVE
FANSHAWS EXHIBITION AND CONFERENCE CENTRE
Ponsbourne Tunnel
Ponsbourne Park Hotel
Bayford Hall Farm
Water Hall Farm
Culverwood Farm
Ashfield Farm
Danes Farm
Bush Farm
Buck's Farm
Kingfisher Garden Centre
Old Claypits Farm
Homewood Farm
Bayford Kennels & Cattery
Epping Green Farm
Ponsbourne Lodge Farm
Woodcock Lodge Farm
Beavers Lodge Farm
Ponsfall Farm
Newpark Farm
Boswell's Livery Stables
Ponsbourne Riding Centre
Tolmers Park Farm
St. Lawrence Farm
Tanfield Stud Farm
The Beehive PH
Five Horseshoes PH
Baker Arms PH
EAST HERTS
WELWYN HATFIELD
BROXBOURNE
DH DJ DK DL DM DN DP
16 17 18 19 20 21 22 23 24
31
48
65

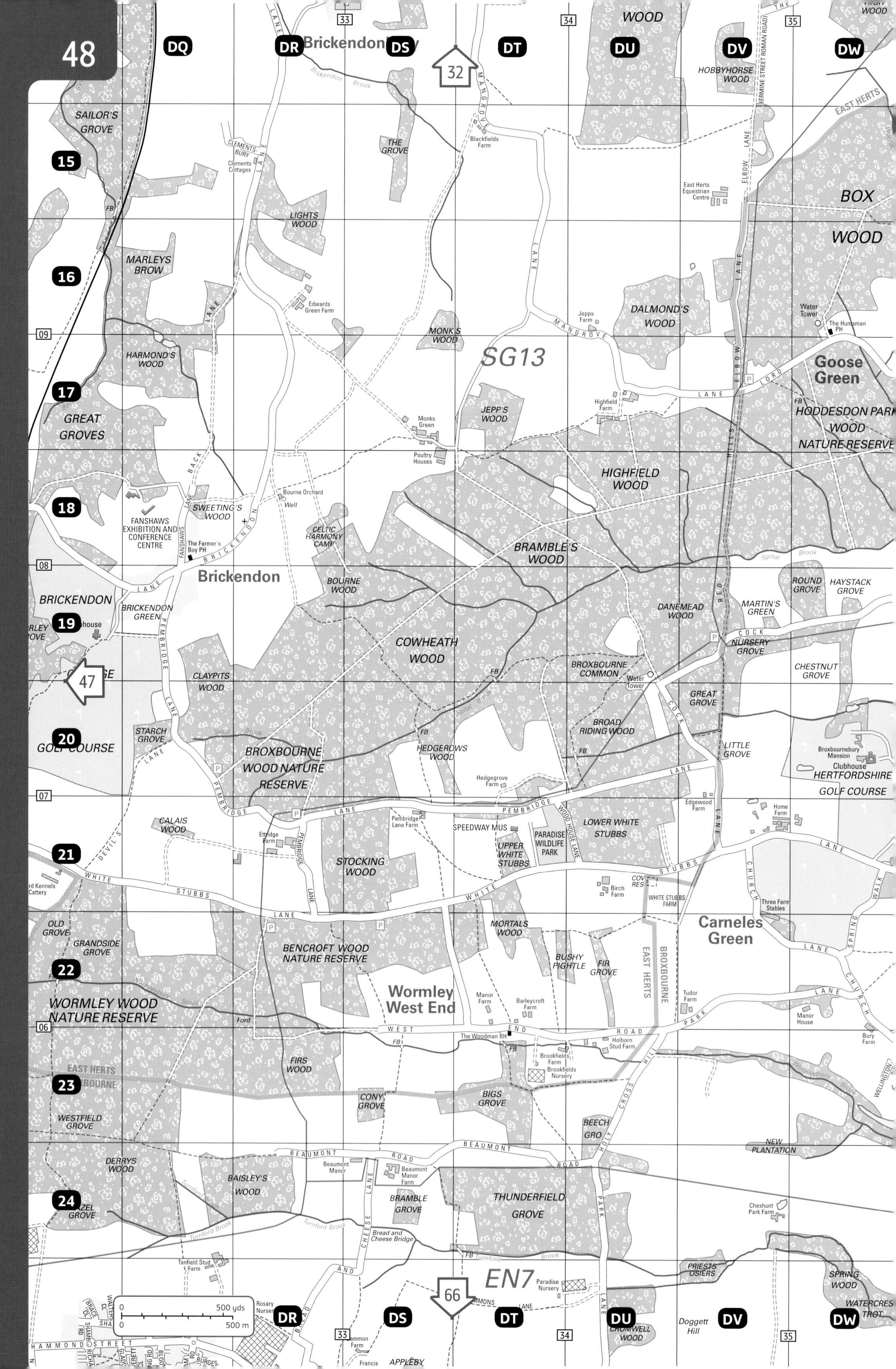
Brickendon
SG13
Brickendon
Goose Green
Carneles Green
Wormley West End
EN7
SAILOR'S GROVE
MARLEYS BROW
HARMOND'S WOOD
GREAT GROVES
LIGHTS WOOD
THE GROVE
MONKS WOOD
JEPP'S WOOD
HIGHFIELD WOOD
DALMOND'S WOOD
BOX WOOD
HOBBYHORSE WOOD
HODDESDON PARK WOOD NATURE RESERVE
BRAMBLE'S WOOD
COWHEATH WOOD
BOURNE WOOD
CELTIC HARMONY CAMP
SWEETING'S WOOD
FANSHAWS EXHIBITION AND CONFERENCE CENTRE
The Farmer's Boy PH
BRICKENDON GREEN
CLAYPITS WOOD
STARCH GROVE
BROXBOURNE WOOD NATURE RESERVE
HEDGEROWS WOOD
BROXBOURNE COMMON
BROAD RIDING WOOD
DANEMEAD WOOD
MARTIN'S GREEN
NURSERY GROVE
ROUND GROVE
HAYSTACK GROVE
CHESTNUT GROVE
GREAT GROVE
LITTLE GROVE
Broxbournebury Mansion
Clubhouse
HERTFORDSHIRE GOLF COURSE
CALAIS WOOD
STOCKING WOOD
SPEEDWAY MUS
PARADISE WILDLIFE PARK
UPPER WHITE STUBBS
LOWER WHITE STUBBS
WHITE STUBBS FARM
MORTALS WOOD
BUSHY PIGHTLE
FIR GROVE
BENCROFT WOOD NATURE RESERVE
OLD GROVE
GRANDSIDE GROVE
WORMLEY WOOD NATURE RESERVE
FIRS WOOD
CONY GROVE
BIGS GROVE
BEECH GRO
WESTFIELD GROVE
DERRYS WOOD
BAISLEY'S WOOD
BRAMBLE GROVE
THUNDERFIELD GROVE
NEW PLANTATION
PRIESTS OSIERS
SPRING WOOD
CROMWELL WOOD
Doggett Hill
EAST HERTS
BROXBOURNE
WHITE STUBBS LANE
WEST END ROAD
BEAUMONT ROAD
PEMBRIDGE LANE
MANGROVE LANE
LORD LANE
ELBOW LANE
COCK LANE
CHURCH LANE
SPRING WALK
PARK LANE
HOLY CROSS HILL
CHEESE LANE
The Woodman PH
The Huntsman PH
Bread and Cheese Bridge
Tanfield Stud Farm
Paradise Nursery
500 yds
500 m
32
47
66

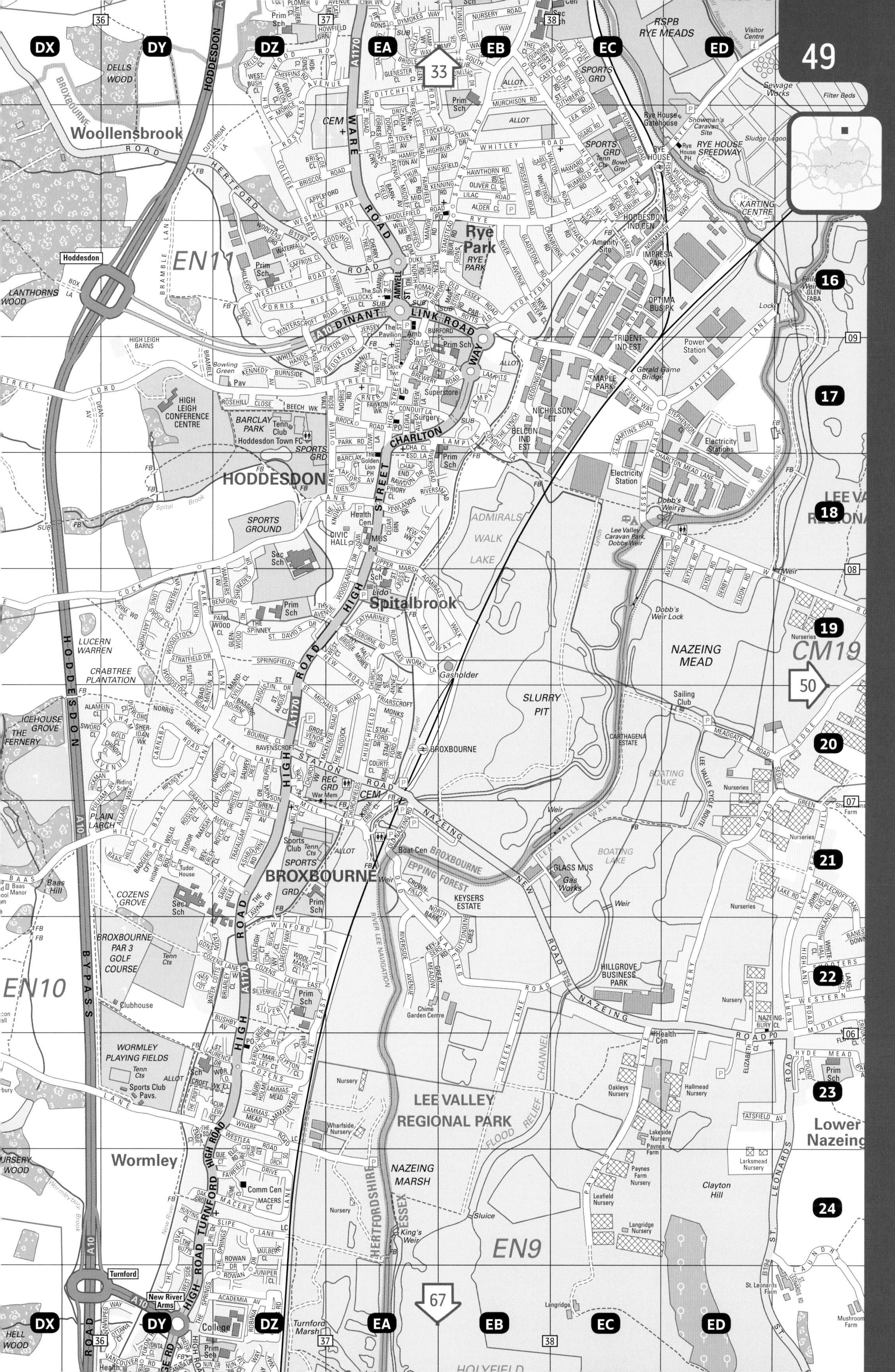
DX
DY
DZ
EA
EB
EC
ED
33
RSPB RYE MEADS
Woollensbrook
DELLS WOOD
HODDESDON BYPASS
A10
A1170
EN11
Hoddesdon
LANTHORNS WOOD
HIGH LEIGH BARNS
HIGH LEIGH CONFERENCE CENTRE
BARCLAY PARK
Hoddesdon Town FC
HODDESDON
Rye Park
RYE HOUSE SPEEDWAY
KARTING CENTRE
Sewage Works
Filter Beds
Rye House Gatehouse
IMPRESA PARK
OPTIMA BUS PK
TRIDENT IND EST
Power Station
Gerald Game Bridge
MAPLE PARK
NICHOLSON CT
BELCON IND EST
Electricity Stations
Electricity Station
Dobb's Weir
Lee Valley Caravan Park, Dobbs Weir
ADMIRALS WALK LAKE
Spitalbrook
Dobb's Weir Lock
NAZEING MEAD
CM19
50
LUCERN WARREN
CRABTREE PLANTATION
ICEHOUSE GROVE
THE FERNERY
Gasholder
SLURRY PIT
Sailing Club
CARTHAGENA ESTATE
BROXBOURNE
BOATING LAKE
LEE VALLEY CYCLE ROUTE
PLAIN LARCH
Baas Hill
COZENS GROVE
BROXBOURNE
EPPING FOREST
KEYSERS ESTATE
GLASS MUS
BROXBOURNE PAR 3 GOLF COURSE
EN10
HILLGROVE BUSINESS PARK
Chime Garden Centre
WORMLEY PLAYING FIELDS
LEE VALLEY REGIONAL PARK
FLOOD RELIEF CHANNEL
Oakleys Nursery
Hallmead Nursery
Lakeside Nursery
Paynes Farm
Larksmead Nursery
Lower Nazeing
Wormley
NAZEING MARSH
HERTFORDSHIRE
ESSEX
King's Weir
Clayton Hill
EN9
Leafield Nursery
Langridge Nursery
Turnford
New River Arms
HELL WOOD
Turnford Marsh
College
67
St. Leonards Farm
Mushroom Farm
HOLYFIELD
16
17
18
19
20
21
22
23
24
09
08
07
06
36
37
38

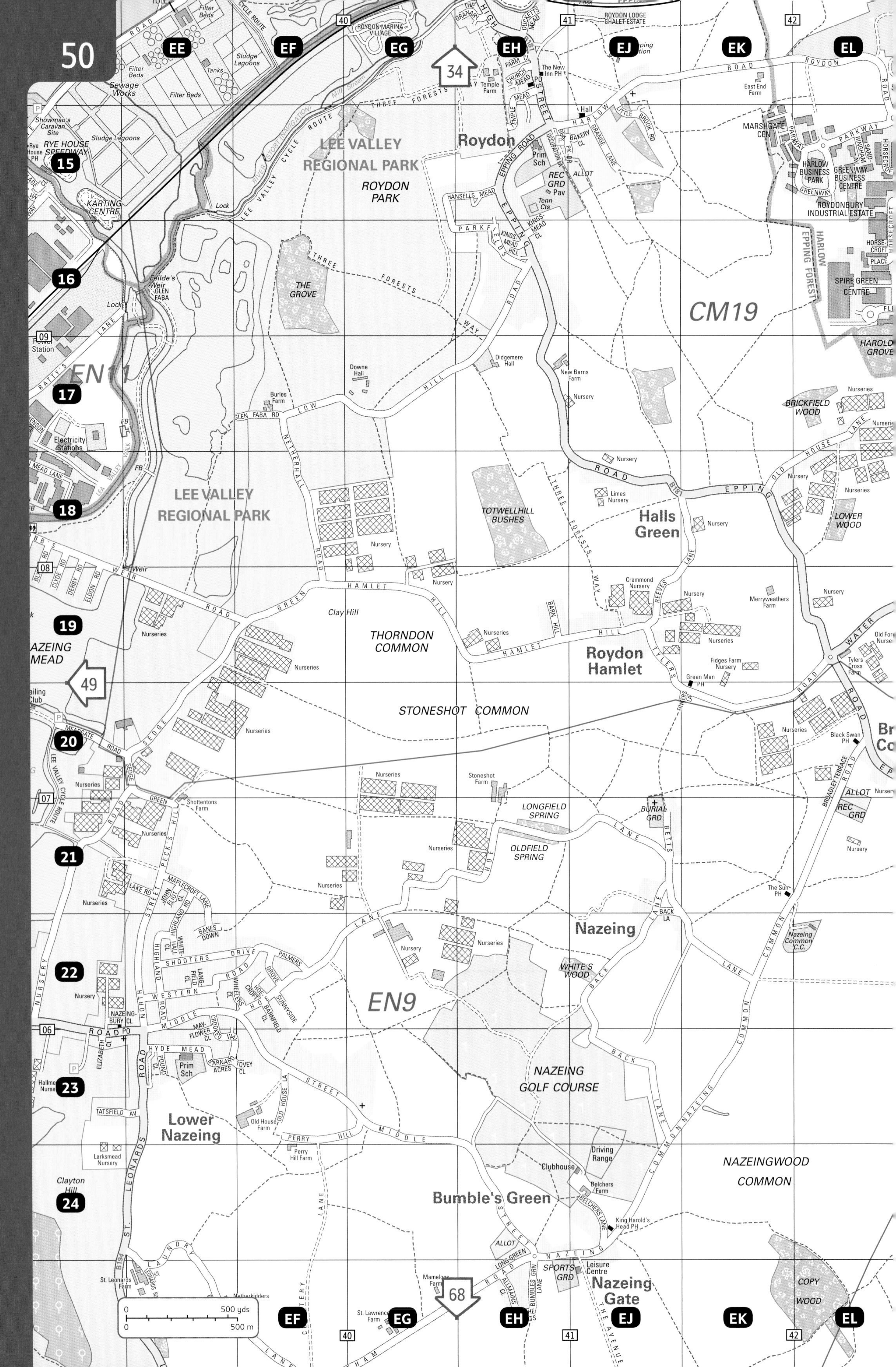

Roydon
LEE VALLEY REGIONAL PARK
ROYDON PARK
THE GROVE
CM19
EN11
EN9
RYE HOUSE SPEEDWAY
KARTING CENTRE
Sewage Works
Filter Beds
Sludge Lagoons
Showman's Caravan Site
Power Station
Electricity Stations
ROYDON MARINA VILLAGE
ROYDON LODGE CHALET ESTATE
East End Farm
MARSHGATE CEN
HARLOW BUSINESS PARK
GREENWAY BUSINESS CENTRE
ROYDONBURY INDUSTRIAL ESTATE
SPIRE GREEN CENTRE
HAROLD GROVE
BRICKFIELD WOOD
LOWER WOOD
Didgemere Hall
New Barns Farm
Downe Hall
Burles Farm
TOTWELLHILL BUSHES
Halls Green
Crammond Nursery
Merryweathers Farm
Roydon Hamlet
THORNDON COMMON
Clay Hill
STONESHOT COMMON
Stoneshot Farm
Shottentons Farm
LONGFIELD SPRING
OLDFIELD SPRING
Nazeing
WHITE'S WOOD
NAZEING GOLF COURSE
Lower Nazeing
Old House Farm
Perry Hill Farm
Larksmead Nursery
Clayton Hill
Bumble's Green
Belchers Farm
Clubhouse
Driving Range
NAZEINGWOOD COMMON
COPY WOOD
Nazeing Gate
Leisure Centre
St. Leonards Farm
St. Lawrence Farm
NAZEING MEAD
Nazeing Common C.C.
Tylers Cross Farm
Black Swan PH
Green Man PH
The Sun PH
King Harold's Head PH
34
49
68
EE EF EG EH EJ EK EL
15 16 17 18 19 20 21 22 23 24
0 500 yds
0 500 m

CANONS BROOK GOLF COURSE
HARLOW STADIUM
Little Parndon
PRINCESS ALEXANDRA HOSPITAL
Netteswell
CM20
Harlow College
HARLOW
Crown Gate Roundabout
SECOND AVENUE
A1025
THE MOORS
Pinnacles
JEAN McALPINE PARK
COLDHARBOUR PINNACLES ESTATE
HARLOW BUSINESS CENTRE
Hare Street
Whitehall Roundabout
THIRD AVENUE
NEW FRONTIERS SCIENCE PARK
NETTLESWELL PLANTATION
CM18
PLAYING FIELD
Great Parndon
PARNDON WOOD
Brays Grove
Tye Green
Passmores
UPPER WOOD
Katherines
KATHERINES WAY
A1169
SOUTHERN WAY
Latton Bush
Stewards
THE LATTON BUSH CENTRE
Sumners
MAUND'S WOOD
BURNETT'S WOOD
Kingsmoor
PARNDON WOOD CEM
PARNDON WOOD NATURE RESERVE
RISDEN'S WOOD
Jacks Hatch
Rye Hill
HOSPITAL WOOD
HARLOW
EPPING FOREST
CM16
Epping Green
EPPING LONG GRN
Epping Upland
B181
EM
EN
EP
EQ
ER
ES
ET
43
44
45
35
52
69
16
17
18
19
20
21
22
23
24
09
08
07
06

EU
EV
EW
EX
EY
EZ
FA
36
47
48
49
Mark Hall South
MARKHALL WOOD
LADYSHOT SPORTS GROUND
SPORTS GROUND
Nortel Network Plc
CHURCH LANGLEY PLAYING FIELD
BRENTHALL WOOD
BARNSLEY WOOD
Church Langley
Hubbard's Hall Estate
HOBBS CROSS
New Hall Farm
Church Langley Roundabout
Clock Tower Roundabout
Water Tower
GRAVEPIT SPRINGS
THE MOORS
CM20
A1025
AVENUE
HARLOW
PLAYING FLDS
PERRY SPRING
Superstore
Potter Street
Foster Street Farm
Wayside Farm
Hoggs Farm
Searles Farm
Greenways
BUSH FAIR PLAYING FIELDS
Brays Grove
NICHOLLS FIELD
POTTER
A1169
WAY
Windyridge
CM17
STREET
LATTON COMMON
Latton Bush
SPORTS GRD
CM18
HARLOW
EPPING FOREST
A414
HARLOW PARK
HASTINGWOOD BUS CEN
The Retreat
Hastingwood
LATTON PARK
MARK BUSHES
BYPASS
51
The Rainbow & Dove PH
Junction 7
Hastingwood Interchange
M11
St. Clare Hospice
Hastingwood Farm
Paris Hall Farm
RUNDELL'S GROVE
Harlow Garden Centre
CANES
Latton Priory Farm
Canes
Rivetts Farm
The Herb Farm
Seed Mill
A414
LANE
Delved Bridge
Cripsey Brook
Esgors Farm
CM16
Garden Centre
Rose Farm
Thornwood Sewage Treatment Works
Hayleys Manor Farm
BARN MEADOW
Golf Range
UPPER CLAPTON FC
WEALD HALL FARM COMMERCIAL CENTRE
North Weald Golf Centre Driving Range
70
0 500 yds
0 500 m
07
08
09
06
15
16
17
18
19
20
21
22
23
24

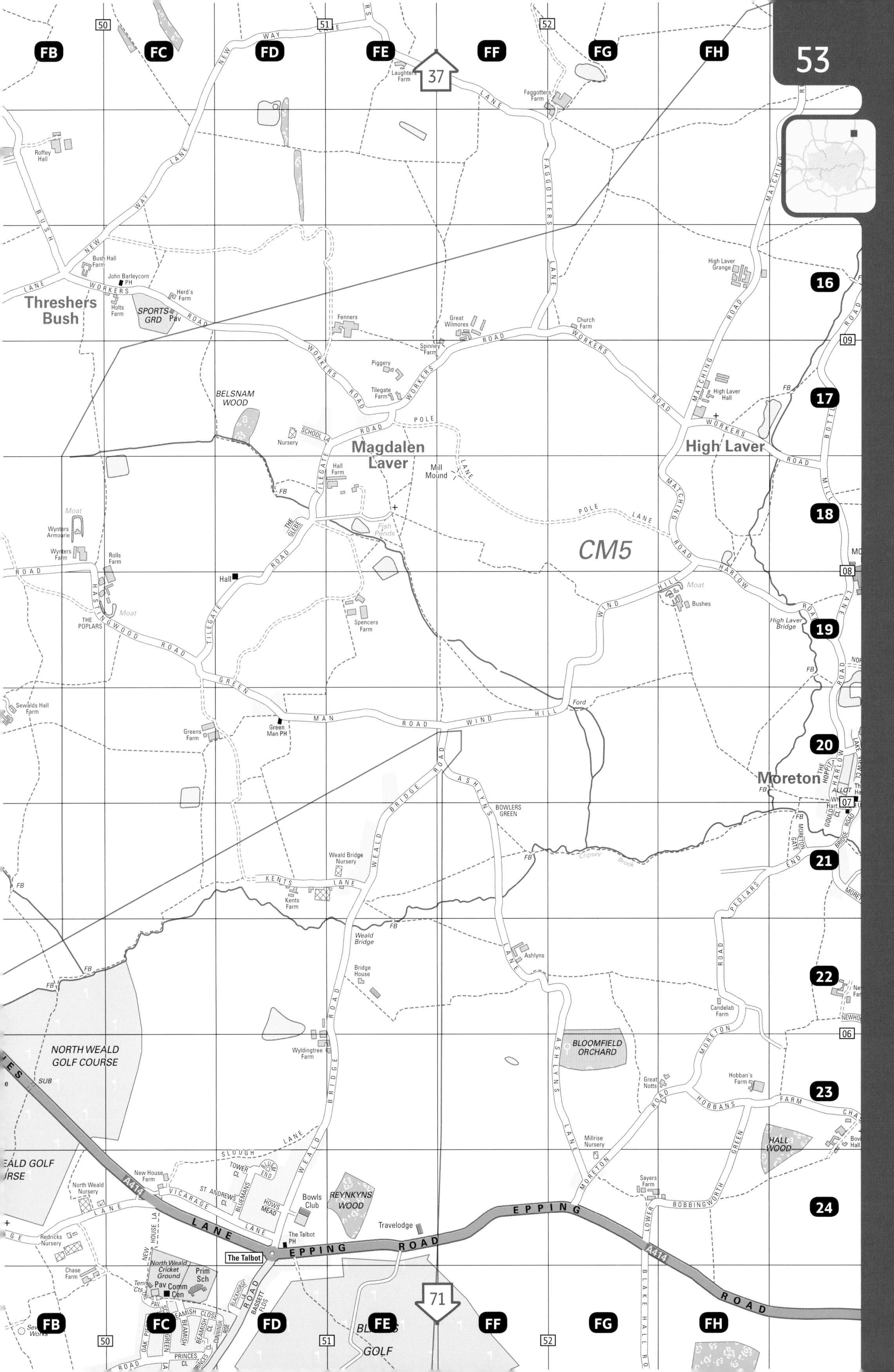
FB
FC
FD
FE
FF
FG
FH
50
51
52
37
71
Threshers Bush
Magdalen Laver
High Laver
Moreton
CM5
Roffey Hall
Bush Hall Farm
John Barleycorn PH
Herd's Farm
Holts Farm
SPORTS GRD
Pav
Fenners
Great Wilmores
Church Farm
Spinney Farm
Piggery
Tilegate Farm
BELSNAM WOOD
Nursery
Hall Farm
Mill Mound
Laughters Farm
Faggotters Farm
High Laver Grange
High Laver Hall
High Laver Bridge
Bushes
Wynters Armourie
Wynters Farm
Rolls Farm
THE POPLARS
Hall
Spencers Farm
Fish Ponds
Sewalds Hall Farm
Greens Farm
Green Man PH
Ford
BOWLERS GREEN
Weald Bridge Nursery
Kents Farm
Weald Bridge
Bridge House
Ashlyns
Cripsey Brook
Candelab Farm
BLOOMFIELD ORCHARD
Wyldingtree Farm
NORTH WEALD GOLF COURSE
Great Notts
Hobban's Farm
HALL WOOD
Millrise Nursery
Sayers Farm
New House Farm
North Weald Nursery
REYNKYNS WOOD
Bowls Club
Travelodge
The Talbot PH
The Talbot
Redricks Nursery
Chase Farm
North Weald Cricket Ground
Prim Sch
Pav
Comm Cen
NEW WAY LANE
BUSH LANE
WORKERS ROAD
FAGGOTTERS LANE
MATCHING ROAD
POLE LANE
SCHOOL LA
TILEGATE ROAD
THE GLEBE
HASTINGWOOD ROAD
GREEN MAN ROAD
WIND HILL
HARLOW ROAD
WEALD BRIDGE ROAD
ASHLYNS LANE
KENTS LANE
PEDLARS END
MORETON ROAD
HOBBANS FARM
GREEN
BOBBINGWORTH
LOWER
BLAKE HALL RD
EPPING ROAD
A414
SLOUGH LANE
VICARAGE LANE
TOWER CL
BLUEMANS END
BLUEMANS
ST. ANDREWS CL
HOWS MEAD
BEAMISH CLOSE
PRINCES CL
BASSETT FLDS
BLACKHORSE LA
16
17
18
19
20
21
22
23
24
09
08
07
06

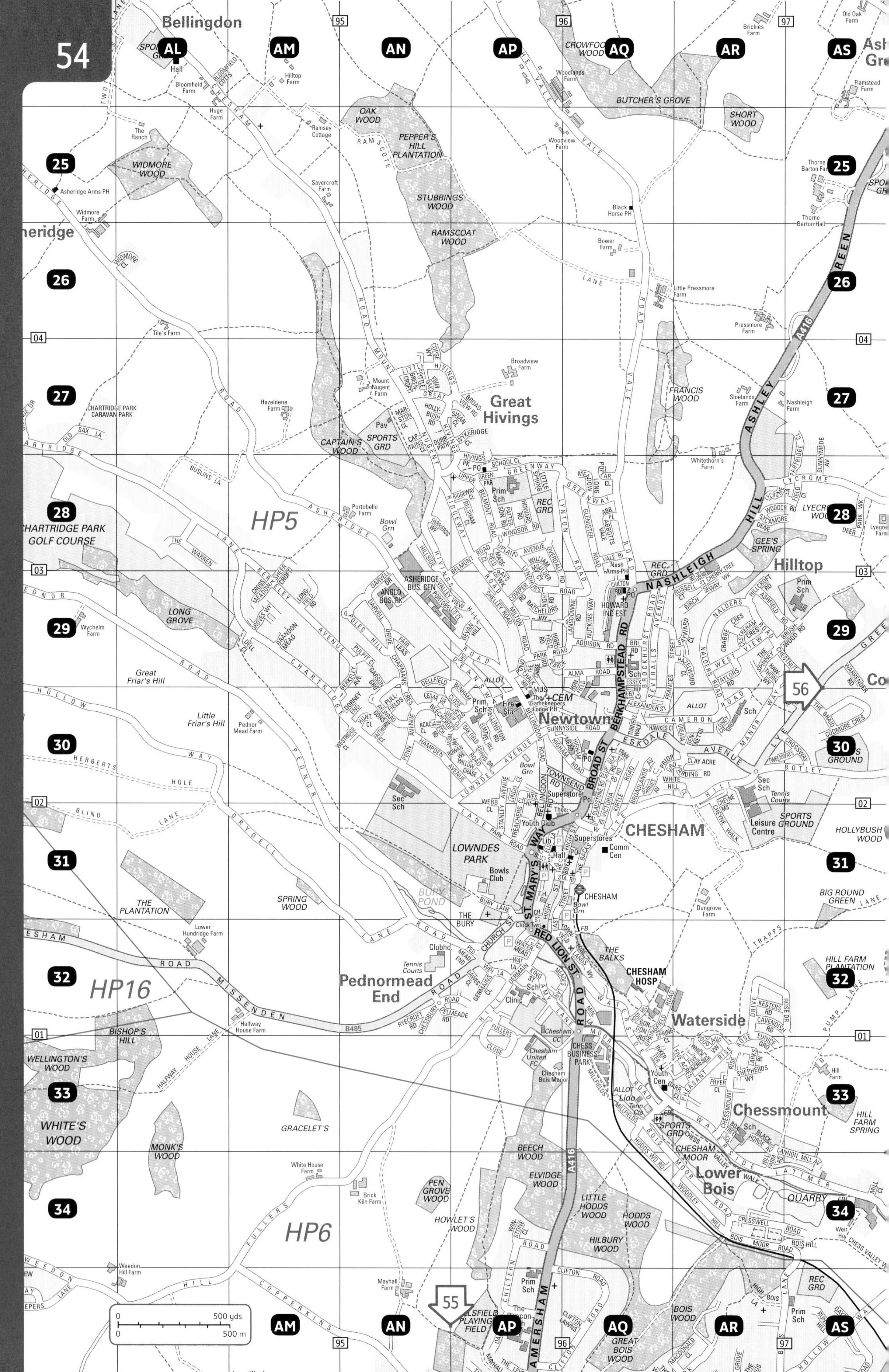
Bellingdon
AL
AM
AN
AP
AQ
AR
AS
95
96
97
CROWFOOT WOOD
BUTCHER'S GROVE
SHORT WOOD
OAK WOOD
PEPPER'S HILL PLANTATION
WIDMORE WOOD
STUBBINGS WOOD
RAMSCOAT WOOD
Great Hivings
CAPTAIN'S WOOD
FRANCIS WOOD
HP5
CHARTRIDGE PARK GOLF COURSE
LONG GROVE
Hilltop
Newtown
CHESHAM
LOWNDES PARK
Pednormead End
HP16
Waterside
Chessmount
Lower Bois
WELLINGTON'S WOOD
WHITE'S WOOD
MONK'S WOOD
GRACELET'S
HP6
BEECH WOOD
ELVIDGE WOOD
LITTLE HODDS WOOD
HODDS WOOD
HILBURY WOOD
BOIS WOOD
GREAT BOIS WOOD
THE PLANTATION
SPRING WOOD
HILLFARM SPRING
HOLLYBUSH WOOD
BIG ROUND GREEN
HILL FARM PLANTATION
56
55
A416
B485
25
26
27
28
29
30
31
32
33
34
04
03
02
01
500 yds
500 m

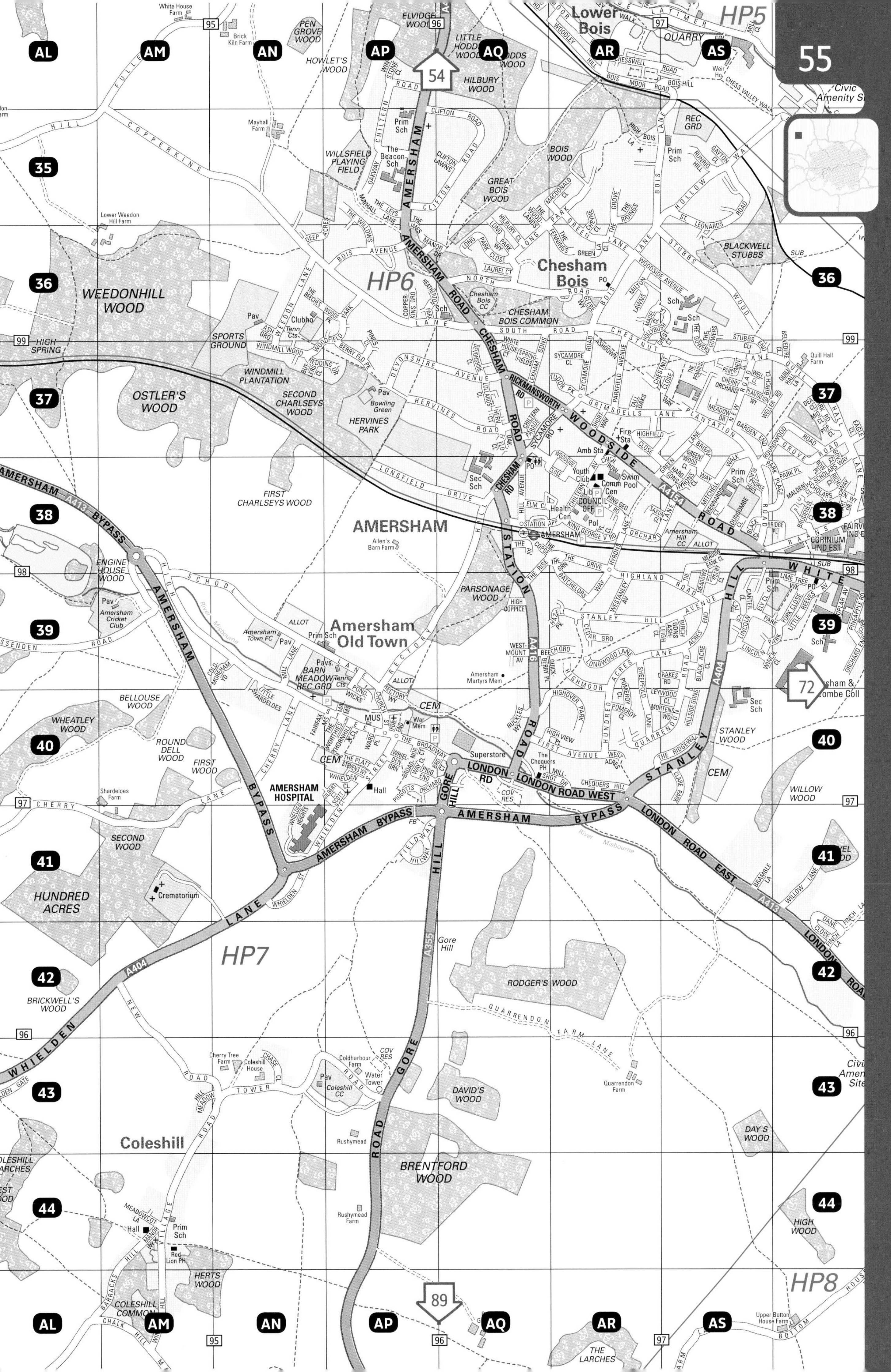
Lower Bois
HP5
QUARRY
Chesham Bois
BOIS WOOD
GREAT BOIS WOOD
HILBURY WOOD
LITTLE HODDS WOOD
HODDS WOOD
ELVIDGE WOOD
PEN GROVE WOOD
HOWLET'S WOOD
WILLSFIELD PLAYING FIELD
REC GRD
BLACKWELL STUBBS
CHESHAM BOIS COMMON
HP6
WEEDONHILL WOOD
HIGH SPRING
SPORTS GROUND
WINDMILL PLANTATION
OSTLER'S WOOD
SECOND CHARLSEYS WOOD
HERVINES PARK
FIRST CHARLSEYS WOOD
AMERSHAM
ENGINE HOUSE WOOD
PARSONAGE WOOD
Amersham Old Town
AMERSHAM HOSPITAL
BELLOUSE WOOD
WHEATLEY WOOD
ROUND DELL WOOD
FIRST WOOD
SECOND WOOD
HUNDRED ACRES
Crematorium
STANLEY WOOD
WILLOW WOOD
HP7
Gore Hill
RODGER'S WOOD
BRICKWELL'S WOOD
DAVID'S WOOD
DAY'S WOOD
Coleshill
BRENTFORD WOOD
HIGH WOOD
HERTS WOOD
COLESHILL COMMON
HP8
THE LARCHES
AMERSHAM BYPASS
LONDON ROAD WEST
LONDON ROAD EAST
STATION ROAD
WOODSIDE ROAD
RICKMANSWORTH RD
CHESHAM ROAD
AMERSHAM ROAD
GORE ROAD
WHIELDEN LANE
QUARRENDON FARM LANE
54
72
89

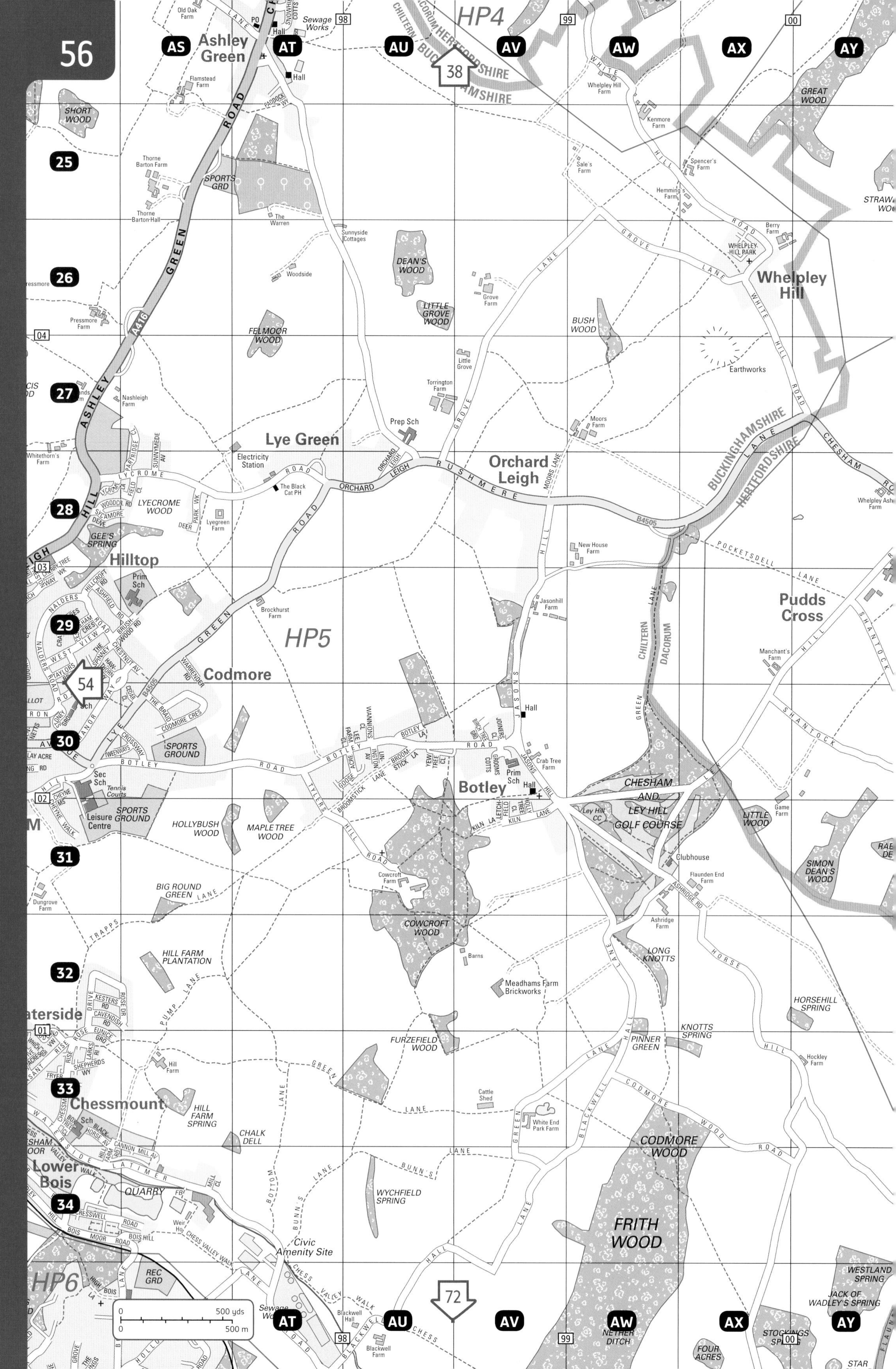

HP4
HP5
HP6
Ashley Green
Lye Green
Orchard Leigh
Whelpley Hill
Hilltop
Codmore
Botley
Pudds Cross
Chessmount
Lower Bois
SHORT WOOD
DEAN'S WOOD
LITTLE GROVE WOOD
FELMOOR WOOD
BUSH WOOD
GREAT WOOD
LYECROME WOOD
GEE'S SPRING
HOLLYBUSH WOOD
MAPLE TREE WOOD
BIG ROUND GREEN
HILL FARM PLANTATION
COWCROFT WOOD
FURZEFIELD WOOD
HILL FARM SPRING
CHALK DELL
WYCHFIELD SPRING
CODMORE WOOD
FRITH WOOD
LONG KNOTTS
KNOTTS SPRING
PINNER GREEN
HORSEHILL SPRING
LITTLE WOOD
SIMON DEAN'S WOOD
WESTLAND SPRING
JACK OF WADLEY'S SPRING
FOUR ACRES
NETHER DITCH
CHESHAM AND LEY HILL GOLF COURSE
SPORTS GRD
SPORTS GROUND
REC GRD
QUARRY
Leisure Centre
Civic Amenity Site
Electricity Station
Earthworks
Meadhams Farm Brickworks
BUCKINGHAMSHIRE
HERTFORDSHIRE
CHILTERN
DACORUM
ASHLEY GREEN ROAD
A416
B4505
B4505
38
54
72
0 500 yds
0 500 m

HP1
HP3
WD3
WD4
Bovingdon
Hogpits Bottom
Flaunden
Belsize
H.M. THE MOUNT PRISON
COLESHILL WOOD
HANGING WOOD
LITTLE HAY GOLF COMPLEX
BOXMOOR GOLF COURSE
SHEETHANGER COMMON
RAMACRE WOOD
GORSEFIELD WOOD
BURY WOOD
RAINHILL SPRING
RAINHILL DELL
KINGSHILL DELL
SHORTRIDGE WOOD
OLD DEAN
HOMEFIELD SPRING
BOVINGDON GREEN
BAKER'S WOOD
WOODMAN'S WOOD
LOWER PLANTATION
FLAUNDEN SPRING
LIMEDELL SPRING
HANGING CROFT
DEBARDINE WOOD
ROSEHALL WOOD
PLOUGH WOOD
HILLMEADS SPRING
TOP SPRING
OLDCROFT WOOD
HANGINGLANE WOOD
BRAMBLE CROFT
DAFFODIL SPRING
PENMAN'S GREEN
Disused Airfield
Bryants Nurseries
Wyevale Garden Centre
Stoney Lane Nursery
Macdonald Bobsleigh Hotel
Cottingham Farm
Woodman's Farm
Cherry Tree Farm
Rose Hall Farm
Great Sarratt Hall
R.A.F. Chenies
DACORUM
THREE RIVERS

39
58
73

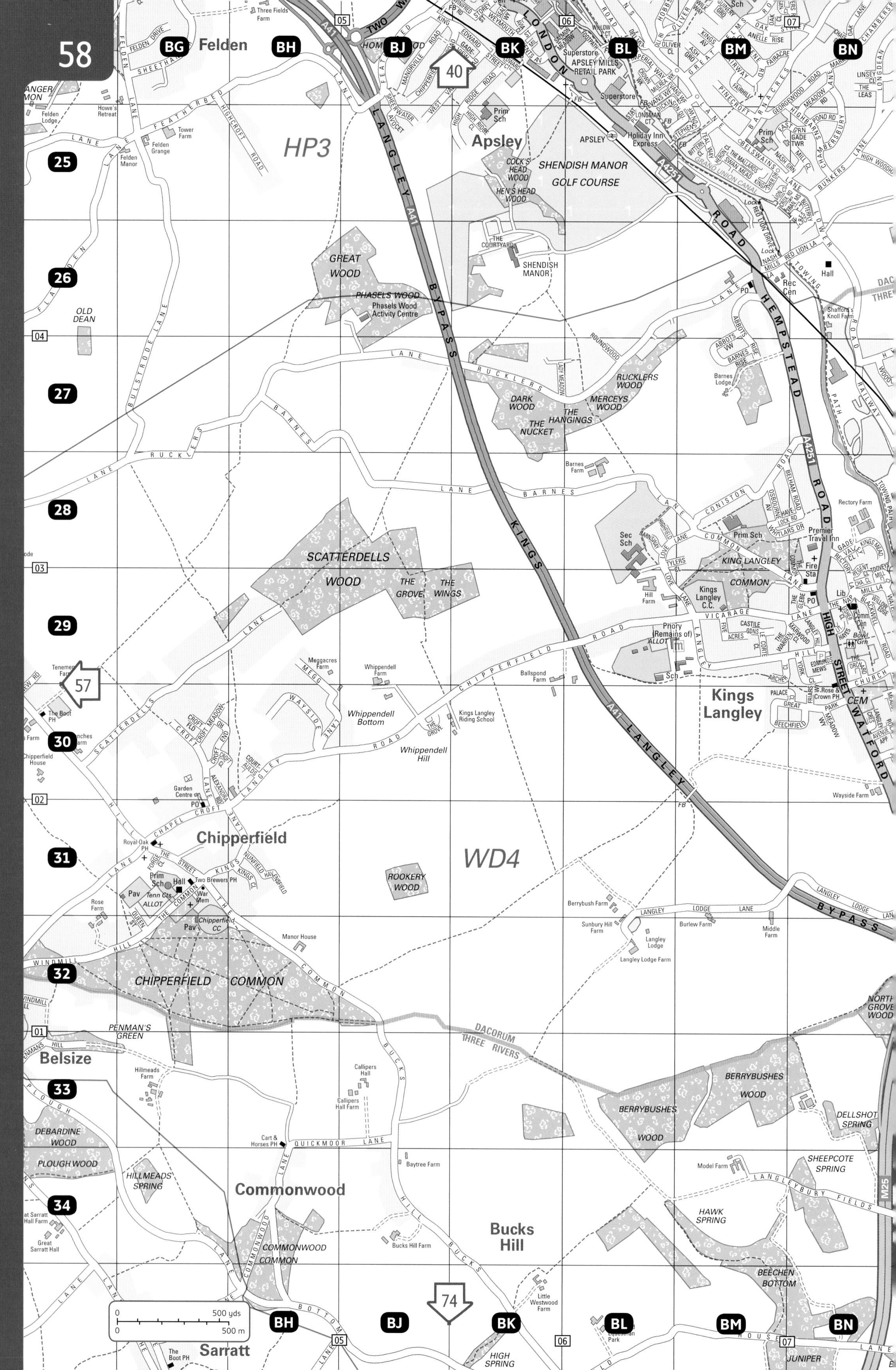
Felden
HP3
Apsley
SHENDISH MANOR
GOLF COURSE
GREAT
WOOD
PHASELS WOOD
RUCKLERS
WOOD
DARK
WOOD
THE
HANGINGS
MERCEYS
WOOD
THE
NUCKET
SCATTERDELLS
WOOD
THE
GROVE
THE
WINGS
Whippendell
Bottom
Kings
Langley
Chipperfield
WD4
ROOKERY
WOOD
CHIPPERFIELD
COMMON
Belsize
BERRYBUSHES
WOOD
DEBARDINE
WOOD
PLOUGH WOOD
Commonwood
HAWK
SPRING
Bucks
Hill
BEECHEN
BOTTOM
Sarratt
HIGH
SPRING
KINGS LANGLEY BYPASS
A41
A4251
M25
DACORUM
THREE RIVERS
40
57
74

HP3
WD5
WD25
POTTERS CROUCH PLANTATION
LONG DEANS
WELLFIELD SPRING
DEADMAN WOOD
BEDMOND WOOD
PIECORNER WOOD
HANGING WOOD
FURZEFIELD WOOD
JOB'S WOOD
Bedmond
BEDMOND PLAYING FIELDS
MOOR WOOD
LONG SPRING
HYDE LANE SPRING
NEW PLANTATION
GREAT NOTLEY
LITTLE NOTLEY
STOWES WOOD
LONG WOOD
ROUND WOOD
BLOOM WOOD
ABBOTS LANGLEY
MANOR HOUSE GROUNDS
TANNERS WOOD
LEAVESDEN COUNTRY PARK
Junction 20
Hunton Bridge
Langleybury
Leavesden Green
Woodside
Kingswood
Garston
WOODSIDE STADIUM
ALBAN WOOD
WOODSIDE PLAYING FIELDS
SOUTH WAY PLAYING FLD
Warner Bros. Studios Leavesden
NORTH WATFORD CEMETERY
STANBOROUGH PARK
KINGS LANGLEY
KINGLEY PK
KINGS PARK IND. EST.
MONACO WORKS
Wind Turbine & Renewable Energy Systems
KINGSWAY (NORTH ORBITAL ROAD)
NORTH WESTERN AVENUE
WATFORD ROAD
ST. ALBANS THREE RIVERS
M25
M1
A405
A41
41
60
75
BP
BQ
BR
BS
BT
BU
BV
26
27
28
29
30
31
32
33
34

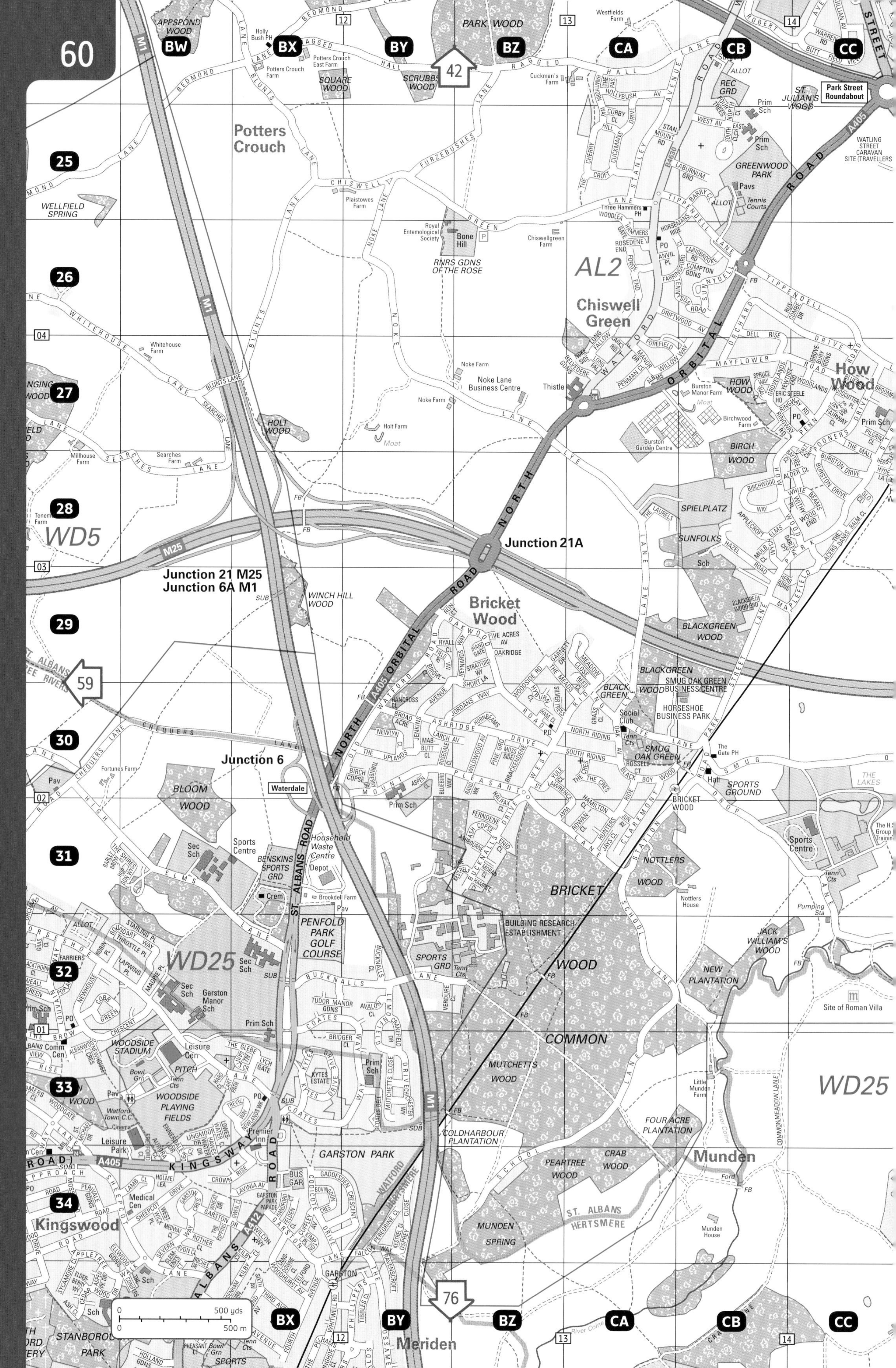
Potters Crouch
Chiswell Green
AL2
How Wood
Bricket Wood
WD5
WD25
Junction 21A
Junction 21 M25
Junction 6A M1
Junction 6
Waterdale
Park Street Roundabout
Munden
Kingswood
Meriden
BRICKET WOOD COMMON
GARSTON PARK
PENFOLD PARK GOLF COURSE
WOODSIDE PLAYING FIELDS
BUILDING RESEARCH ESTABLISHMENT
Site of Roman Villa
Royal Entemological Society
RNRS GDNS OF THE ROSE
Noke Lane Business Centre
HORSESHOE BUSINESS PARK
SMUG OAK GREEN BUSINESS CENTRE
NORTH ORBITAL ROAD
ST. ALBANS ROAD
KINGSWAY
BW BX BY BZ CA CB CC
25 26 27 28 29 30 31 32 33 34
42
59
76
500 yds
500 m

AL1
AL2
AL4
WD7
Park Street
Frogmore
Colney Street
LONDON COLNEY
KINGSLEY GREEN
RADLETT
SHENLEY PARK
PORTERS PARK GOLF COURSE
GRAVEL PIT
Harper Lane Rail Depot
ALL SAINTS PASTORAL CENTRE
BROAD COLNEY LAKES NATURE RESERVE
VERULAMIANS RFC
COLUMBANS SPORTS GRD
CHALKDELL WOOD
HOUND'S WOOD
NINE ACRES
RADLETT GOLF CENTRE
SAND PLANTATION
The Shenley Cricket Centre
Oakridge Lane Sewage Treatment Works
London Colney Rbt
NORTH ORBITAL ROAD
WATLING STREET
HARPER LANE
SHENLEY LANE
M25
A414
A5183
A1081
B5378
B556
43
62
77

LONDON COLNEY
Junction 22
AL4
AL2
WD7
WD6
Ridge Hill
Shenley
Ridge
GARDEN WOOD
THE NEW PLANTATION
FREDERICK'S WOOD
COPPICE WOOD
(SITE OF SPECIAL SCIENTIFIC INTEREST)
WALSINGHAM WOOD
COBS ASH
ROUND WOOD
REDWELL WOOD
BIG MAYFIELD WOOD
RIVERSIDE ESTATE
Colney Fields Shopping Park
BROAD COLNEY LAKES NATURE RESERVE
Gordon Hall Building
UNIVERSITY COLLEGE LONDON SPORTS GROUNDS
Arsenal FC Training Ground
DE HAVILLAND AIRCRAFT HERITAGE CENTRE
Salisbury Hall
R.S.P.C.A. Southridge Animal Centre
DELL GROVE
COMBE WOOD
COW BANKS
SHENLEY PARK
LITTLERIDGE WOOD
BIG PURSLEY WOOD
LITTLE PURSLEY WOOD
CROSS OAKS WOOD
THE GORSE
The Shenley Cricket Centre
London Colney C.C.
SAND AND GRAVEL PIT
THE WARREN
Tyttenhanger Farm
Tyttenhanger House
Coursers Farm
Redwell Wood Farm
Rectory Farm
Shenley Hill Stud Farm
Rabley Park Farm
Ravenscroft Farm
Crossoaks Farm
Pursley Farm
Tokonoma Bonsai
The Garden Nursery
The White Horse PH
NORTH ORBITAL ROAD A414
LONDON COLNEY BYPASS A1081
COURSERS ROAD
BELL LANE
ST. ALBANS ROAD
SHENLEYBURY
BLACK LION HILL
LONDON ROAD
RECTORY LANE
MIMMS LANE
PACKHORSE LANE
CROSSOAKS LANE
M25
B556
B5378
44
61
78
CL CM CN CP CQ CR CS
25 26 27 28 29 30 31 32 33 34
0 500 yds
0 500 m

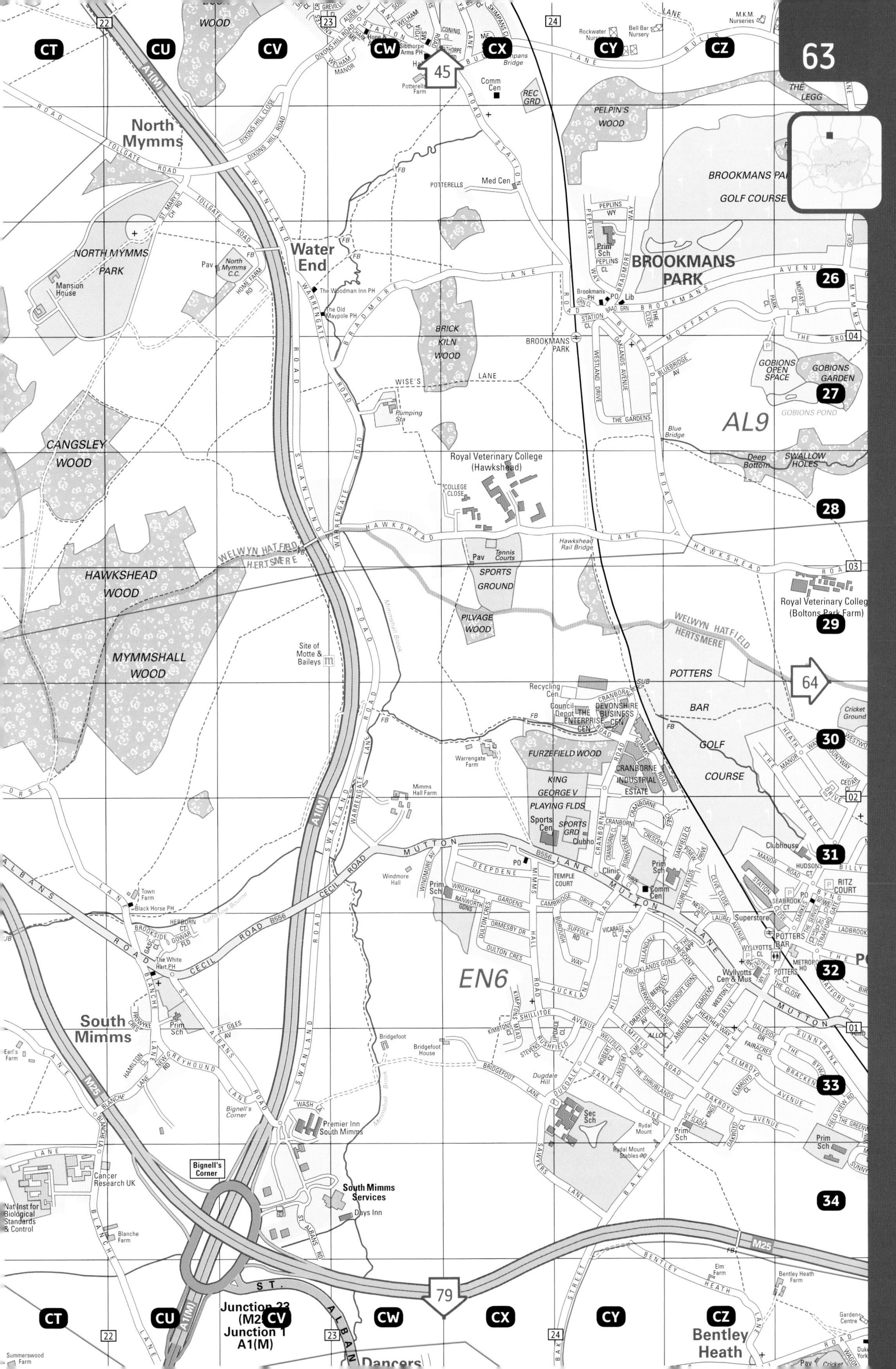
North Mymms
NORTH MYMMS PARK
Mansion House
Water End
CANGSLEY WOOD
HAWKSHEAD WOOD
MYMMSHALL WOOD
BRICK KILN WOOD
Royal Veterinary College (Hawkshead)
SPORTS GROUND
PILVAGE WOOD
PELPIN'S WOOD
BROOKMANS PARK GOLF COURSE
BROOKMANS PARK
GOBIONS OPEN SPACE
GOBIONS GARDEN
GOBIONS POND
AL9
Deep Bottom
SWALLOW HOLES
Royal Veterinary College (Boltons Park Farm)
POTTERS BAR GOLF COURSE
FURZEFIELD WOOD
KING GEORGE V PLAYING FLDS
CRANBORNE INDUSTRIAL ESTATE
EN6
South Mimms
Bignell's Corner
Cancer Research UK
Nat Inst for Biological Standards & Control
South Mimms Services
Premier Inn South Mimms
Days Inn
Junction 23 (M25) Junction 1 A1(M)
Bentley Heath
Dancers
WELWYN HATFIELD
HERTSMERE
A1(M)
M25
45
64
79
CT CU CV CW CX CY CZ
22 23 24
26 27 28 29 30 31 32 33 34

DA
DB
DC
DD
DE
DF
DG
26
27
28
46
63
80
25
26
27
28
29
30
31
32
33
34
04
03
02
01
Nursery
Glasshouse
The Cock o' the North PH
Kentish Lane Farm
Water Tower
COV RES
Tenn Cts
Brookmans Park Transmitting Station
THE LEGG
ROUND WOOD
Tennis Courts
Home Farm
Clubhouse
Sec Sch
BROOKMANS PARK
GOLF COURSE
GEORGE'S WOOD
GEORGE'S WOOD ROAD
CALDER AVENUE
THE GROVE
GOBIONS OPEN SPACE
GOBIONS GARDEN
GOBIONS POND
AL9
GOBIONS WOOD
Deep Bottom
SWALLOW HOLES
NORTH ROAD
GREAT NORTH ROAD
A1000
KENTISH
B158
SHEPHERDS WAY
B157
SPORTS GROUND
Tenn Cen
Tennis Courts
CHAPEL CL
Queenswood Sch
LEGGATTS WOOD
ROWBOURNE PLACE
WELL ROAD
WELL WOOD
THE RIDGEWAY
BROOMBARNS WOOD
COLDHARBOUR PLANTATION
Rowbourne Hill
GREAT
HAWKSHEAD ROAD
SWANLEY BAR LANE
Royal Veterinary College (Boltons Park Farm)
JUDGES HILL
B156
NORTHAW PLACE
Northaw House
The Sun PH
Prim Sch
War Mem
Two Brewers PH
Stud Farm
SPORTS GRD
Tenn Cts
Northaw
NORTHAW ROAD
THE VINEYARD
NYN POND
HOOK LANE
HOOK WOOD
EN6
COOPERS LANE
SPORTS GROUND
Pav
Tennis Courts
THE FORGE
Chequers PH
Cricket Ground
Sch
Prim Sch
Sec Sch
CHURCH ROAD
MOUNT GRACE ROAD
Clubhouse
BILLY LOWS LANE
RITZ COURT
PARKFIELD OPEN SPACE
Elec Sta
BUS GAR
Lib
Pol
THE CAUSEWAY
COTTON ROAD
OAKMERE LANE
OAKMERE PARK
Superstore
POTTERS BAR
POTTERS BAR
Wyllyotts Cen & Mus
Potters Bar Town FC Grd
Cricket Club
Bowls Club
Med Cen
Amb Sta
Fire Sta
War Mem
CEM
MUTTON LANE
HIGH STREET
HATFIELD ROAD
BARNET RD
SOUTHGATE ROAD
A111
ALLOT
Prim Sch
Youth & Comm Cen
FIVE ACRE WOOD
FIR WOOD
Oshwal Centre
Derasar
Hooke Hill
Foxhole Hill
POND WOOD
Turkey Brook
HERTSMERE
WELWYN HATFIELD
ENFIELD
POTTERS BAR COMMUNITY HOSP
Prim Sch
M25
THE RIDGEWAY
A1005
STAGG
New Cottage Farm
Prep. Sch
Junction 24
Fenny Shade Hill
Elm Farm
Bentley Heath Farm
Chase Farm
FIR WOOD
Plumridge Hill
Ind Sch
Bentley Heath
Duke of York PH
Ganwick Corner
0
500 yds
0
500 m

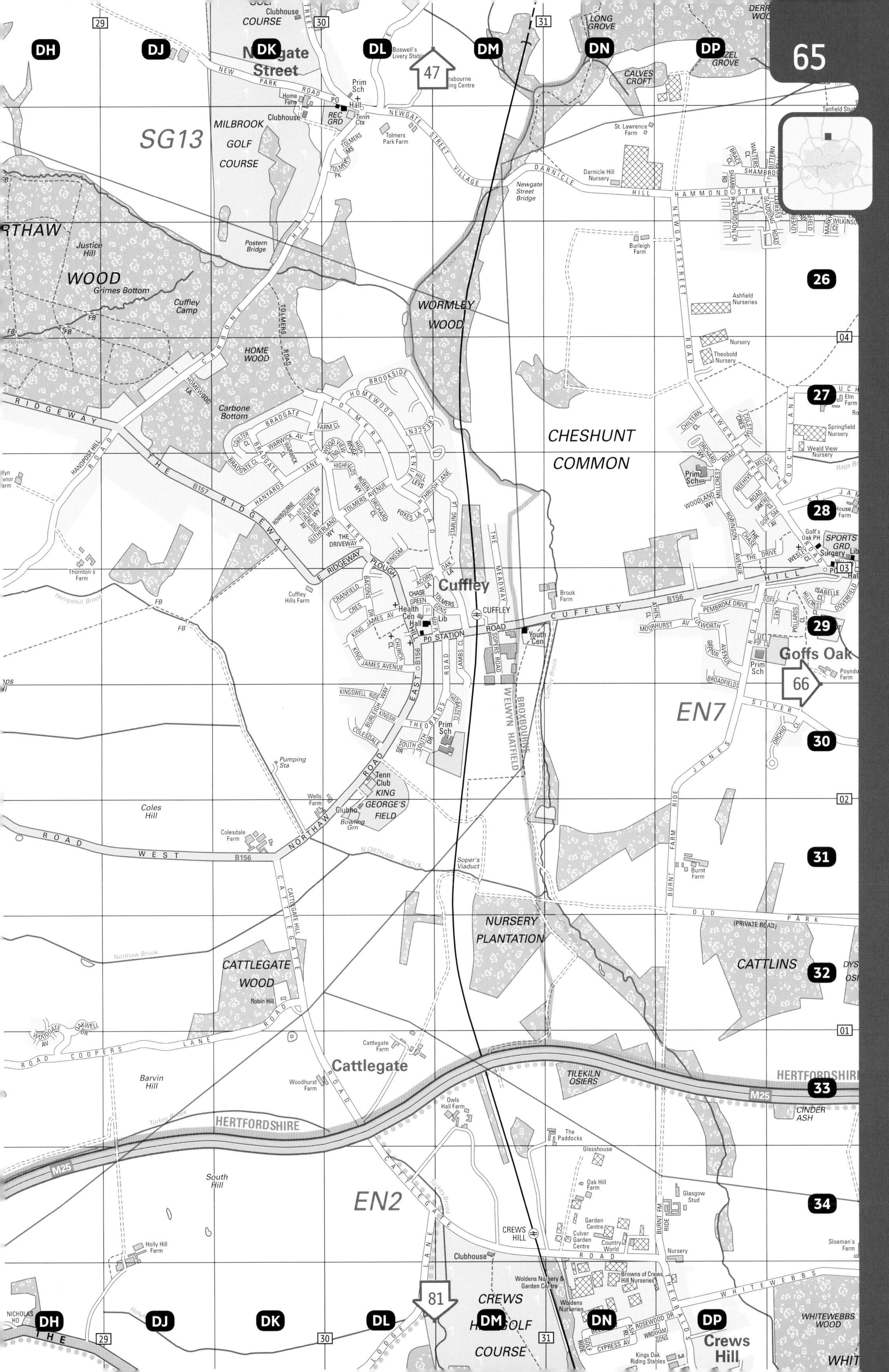
Newgate Street
SG13
MILBROOK GOLF COURSE
NORTHAW WOOD
WORMLEY WOOD
HOME WOOD
CHESHUNT COMMON
Cuffley
Goffs Oak
EN7
NURSERY PLANTATION
CATTLEGATE WOOD
CATTLINS
Cattlegate
TILEKILN OSIERS
HERTFORDSHIRE
M25
EN2
CREWS HILL GOLF COURSE
Crews Hill
WHITEWEBBS WOOD
CALVES CROFT
LONG GROVE
KING GEORGE'S FIELD
Coles Hill
Barvin Hill
South Hill
47
66
81

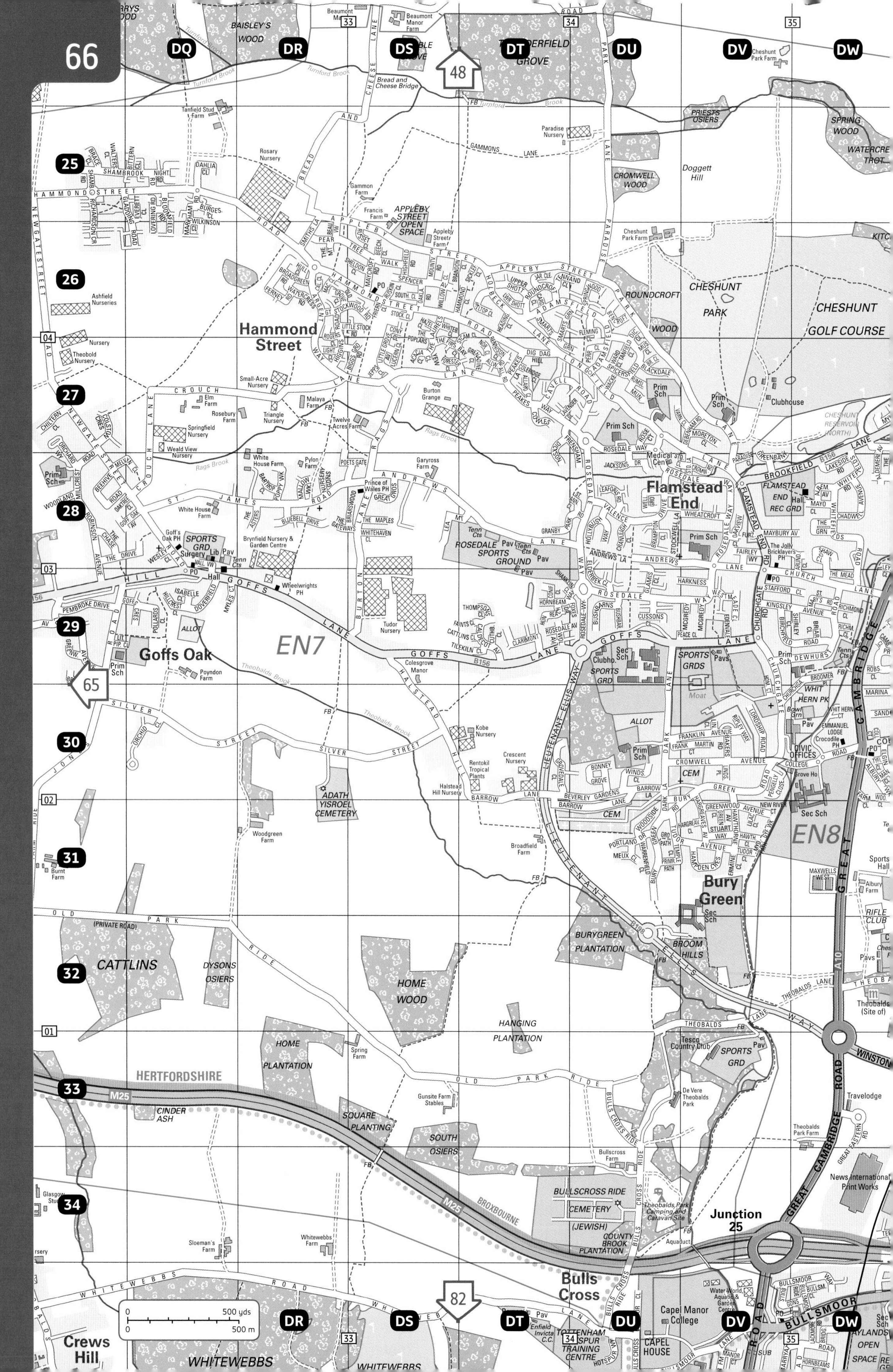
DQ
DR
DS
DT
DU
DV
DW
48
BAISLEY'S WOOD
Turnford Brook
Beaumont Manor Farm
Bread and Cheese Bridge
TEMPLERFIELD GROVE
PARK LANE
Cheshunt Park Farm
PRIESTS OSIERS
SPRING WOOD
WATERCRESS TROT
Tanfield Stud Farm
Rosary Nursery
Gammon Farm
GAMMONS LANE
Paradise Nursery
CROMWELL WOOD
Doggett Hill
25
SHAMBROOK
HAMMOND STREET
NEWGATESTREET
APPLEBY STREET OPEN SPACE
Appleby Street Farm
Cheshunt Park Farm
26
Ashfield Nurseries
CHESHUNT PARK
ROUNDCROFT
CHESHUNT GOLF COURSE
WOOD
Hammond Street
Theobold Nursery
Nursery
04
27
Small-Acre Nursery
CROUCH LANE
Elm Farm
Malaya Farm
Rosebury Farm
Triangle Nursery
Twelve Acres Farm
Burton Grange
Springfield Nursery
Weald View Nursery
Rags Brook
Prim Sch
Clubhouse
CHESHUNT RESERVOIR (NORTH)
White House Farm
Pylon Farm
Garyross Farm
Prince of Wales PH
ANDREWS LANE
Flamstead End
FLAMSTEAD END REC GRD
BROOKFIELD LANE
28
ST JAMES ROAD
White House Farm
Goff's Oak PH
SPORTS GRD
Surgery
Lib
Pav
Tenn Cts
Bryntfield Nursery & Garden Centre
ROSEDALE SPORTS GROUND
Pav
Tenn Cts
03
Wheelwrights PH
GOFFS LANE
Tudor Nursery
29
Goffs Oak
Prim Sch
EN7
ALLOT
Colesgrove Manor
Poyndon Farm
Theobalds Brook
65
SILVER STREET
30
Kobe Nursery
Rentokil Tropical Plants
Crescent Nursery
Halstead Hill Nursery
ADATH YISROEL CEMETERY
BARROW LANE
02
Woodgreen Farm
Broadfield Farm
LIEUTENANT ELLIS WAY
SPORTS GRDS
ALLOT
Prim Sch
CEM
Sec Sch
EN8
CIVIC OFFICES
31
Burnt Farm
Bury Green
Sec Sch
BROOM HILLS
BURYGREEN PLANTATION
OLD PARK
(PRIVATE ROAD)
CATTLINS
DYSONS OSIERS
32
HOME WOOD
HANGING PLANTATION
RIDE
GREAT CAMBRIDGE ROAD
THEOBALDS LANE
Theobalds (Site of)
RIFLE CLUB
Sports Hall
01
HOME PLANTATION
Spring Farm
Tesco Country Club
SPORTS GRD
Pav
33
HERTFORDSHIRE
M25
CINDER ASH
OLD PARK RIDE
Gunsite Farm Stables
De Vere Theobalds Park
Travelodge
SQUARE PLANTING
SOUTH OSIERS
BULLS CROSS RIDE
Bullscross Farm
Theobalds Park Farm
News International Print Works
34
BROXBOURNE
BULLSCROSS RIDE CEMETERY (JEWISH)
Theobalds Park Camping and Caravan Site
COUNTY BROOK PLANTATION
Junction 25
Sloeman's Farm
Whitewebbs Farm
Aquaduct
WHITEWEBBS ROAD
82
Bulls Cross
Water World Aquatic & Garden Centre
Capel Manor College
BULLSMOOR
0
500 yds
500 m
Crews Hill
WHITEWEBBS
Enfield Invicta C.C.
TOTTENHAM HOTSPUR TRAINING CENTRE
CAPEL HOUSE
33
34
35
OPEN SPACE

DX
DY
DZ
EA
EB
EC
ED
49
68
83
26
27
28
29
30
31
32
33
34
EN10
EN9
Turnford
Turnford Marsh
Holyfield Marsh
HOLYFIELD LAKE
LEE VALLEY REGIONAL PARK
Holyfield
Hayes Hill
Lee Valley Park Farm & Information Service
Grubbs Hill
HOMEFIELD WOOD
KENNEL WOOD
Clayton Hill
COLEMAN'S SHAW
NAZEING MARSH
THE NIGHTLEYS
NORTH METROPOLITAN PIT
SEVENTY ACRES LAKE
CHESHUNT LAKE
Cheshunt Lock
Turnershill Marsh
Thistly Marsh
RIVER LEE NAVIGATION
WALTHAM ABBEY WOODS
Cornmill Meadows
BOWYER'S WATER
Cheshunt Marsh
Waltham Marsh
ROYAL GUNPOWDER MILLS
Lee Valley White Water Centre
WALTHAM CROSS
Holdbrook
TOWN MEAD
WALTHAM ABBEY (Ruins)
ABBEY GARDENS
CHESHUNT
GRUNDY PARK
Freezywater
RAMMEY MARSH
Sewardstone Roundabout
M25
A10
A121
A1055
B194
HERTFORDSHIRE
ESSEX
EPPING FOREST
BROXBOURNE

EE
EF
EG
EH
EJ
EK
EL
Bumble's Green
50
NAZEINGWOOD COMMON
Hill Farm
Clubhouse
Range
Belchers Farm
King Harold's Head PH
ALLOT
SPORTS GRD
Leisure Centre
Nazeing Gate
COPY WOOD
St. Leonards Farm
Netherkidders Farm
Mushroom Farm
Mamelons Farm
St. Lawrence Farm
Harold's Park Farm
LONGFIELD SHAW
COLEMAN'S SHAW
Coach & Horses PH
Denver Lodge Farm
GALLEYHILL GREEN
THE SPRINGS
DEERPARK WOOD
Parvills Farm
Marsh Hill
Galley Hill
Kennels
Peartree Farm
Claverhambury Manor
Claverhambury Farm
Claverhambury Carp Farm
Holyfield
GALLEYHILL WOOD
BROADGATE SPRINGS
BRAYSHILL SPRING
Reevesgate Farm
LONGCROFT GROVE
Three Gates
Aimes Green
STOCKING GROVE
Cobbinsend Farm
Aimesgreen Farm
Nightingales
Maynards Farm
EN9
MAPLE SPRINGS
67
BREACH BARNS PARK
KENNEL WOOD
Breach Barns Farm
Fernhall Farm
FERNHALL WOOD
Oakwood Nursery
Fourways Nursery
Dallance Farm
Obelisk
BROOKMEADOW WOOD
Newhouse Farm
Nicholls Farm
Home Farm
Monkswood Nursery
Mushroom Farm
COBBIN POND
Obelisk Farm
COPPED HALL GREEN
Springfield Nursery
Upshire Nursery
Glyn Gates
Abbey View Nursery
Knollys Nursery
GDNS
Lea Valley Nursery
The Temple
Warlies Park House
WARLIES PARK
Burgess Farm
Paternoster Nursery
Paternoster House
Paternoster Hill Nursery
Upshire
Hall
Warlies Lodge
The Horseshoes PH
Queens Head PH
Jubilee Ct
Sports Cen
Sec Sch
Prim Schs
Prim Sch
SPORTS GROUND
OXLEYS WOOD
Copthall Green
Crown Hill Nursery
Clubho.
LARSENS REC GRD
Woodgreen Farm
POTKILN WOOD
BRAMBLY SHAW
Green Lane Bungalows
Woodredon House
Southend Farm
Upshire Hall
CLAY PIGEON RANGE
Marriott Waltham Abbey
Prim Schs
WALTHAM ABBEY
SPORTS GROUND
Swim Pool
WALTHAM ABBEY FC
CONYBURY WOOD
WOODBINE CLOSE
Woodbine Inn PH
Sudbury Farm
The Lodge
Skillet Hill Farm
84
Woodredon Farm
STABLES SHAW
Woodredon Riding School
Volunteer PH
HONEY LANE
SKILLET HILL
A121
M25
DOWDING WAY
Quinton Hill Farm
Sewardstone Roundabout
500 yds
500 m
40
41
42
25
26
27
28
29
30
31
32
33
34

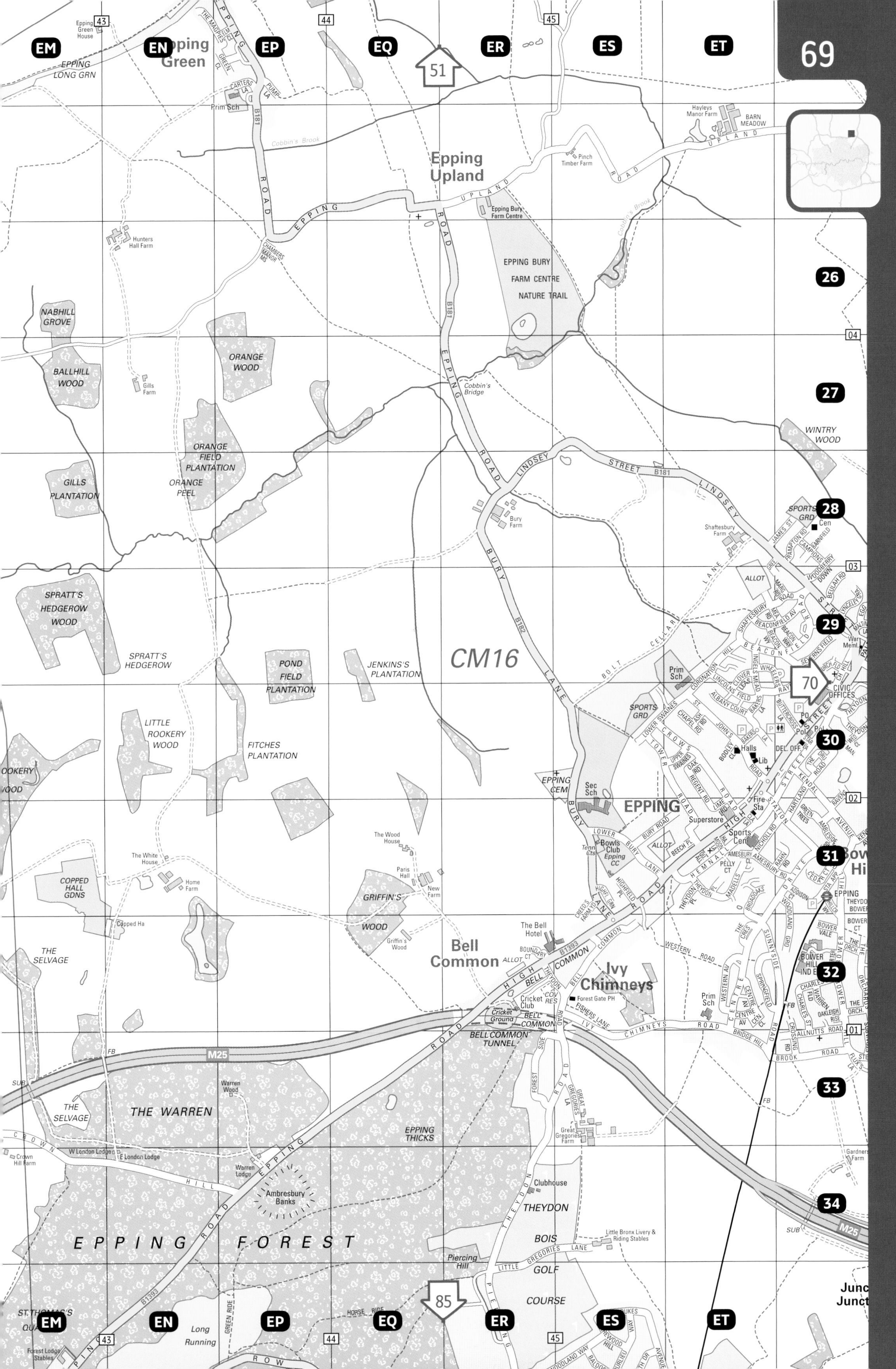
Epping Green
Epping Upland
EPPING BURY FARM CENTRE NATURE TRAIL
Epping Bury Farm Centre
Hayleys Manor Farm
BARN MEADOW
Pinch Timber Farm
Hunters Hall Farm
NABHILL GROVE
BALLHILL WOOD
ORANGE WOOD
Gills Farm
Cobbin's Bridge
ORANGE FIELD PLANTATION
ORANGE PEEL
GILLS PLANTATION
WINTRY WOOD
Bury Farm
Shaftesbury Farm
SPRATT'S HEDGEROW WOOD
SPRATT'S HEDGEROW
POND FIELD PLANTATION
JENKINS'S PLANTATION
CM16
LITTLE ROOKERY WOOD
FITCHES PLANTATION
EPPING CEM
EPPING
CIVIC OFFICES
The Wood House
The White House
Home Farm
COPPED HALL GDNS
Paris Hall
New Farm
GRIFFIN'S WOOD
Griffin's Wood
Copped Ha
THE SELVAGE
The Bell Hotel
Bell Common
Ivy Chimneys
Forest Gate PH
Cricket Club
BELL COMMON TUNNEL
M25
Warren Wood
THE WARREN
THE SELVAGE
EPPING THICKS
Great Gregories Farm
W London Lodge
E London Lodge
Crown Hill Farm
Warren Lodge
Ambresbury Banks
Clubhouse
THEYDON BOIS GOLF COURSE
Little Bronx Livery & Riding Stables
EPPING FOREST
Piercing Hill
Gardners Farm
Long Running
Forest Lodge Stables
51
70
85

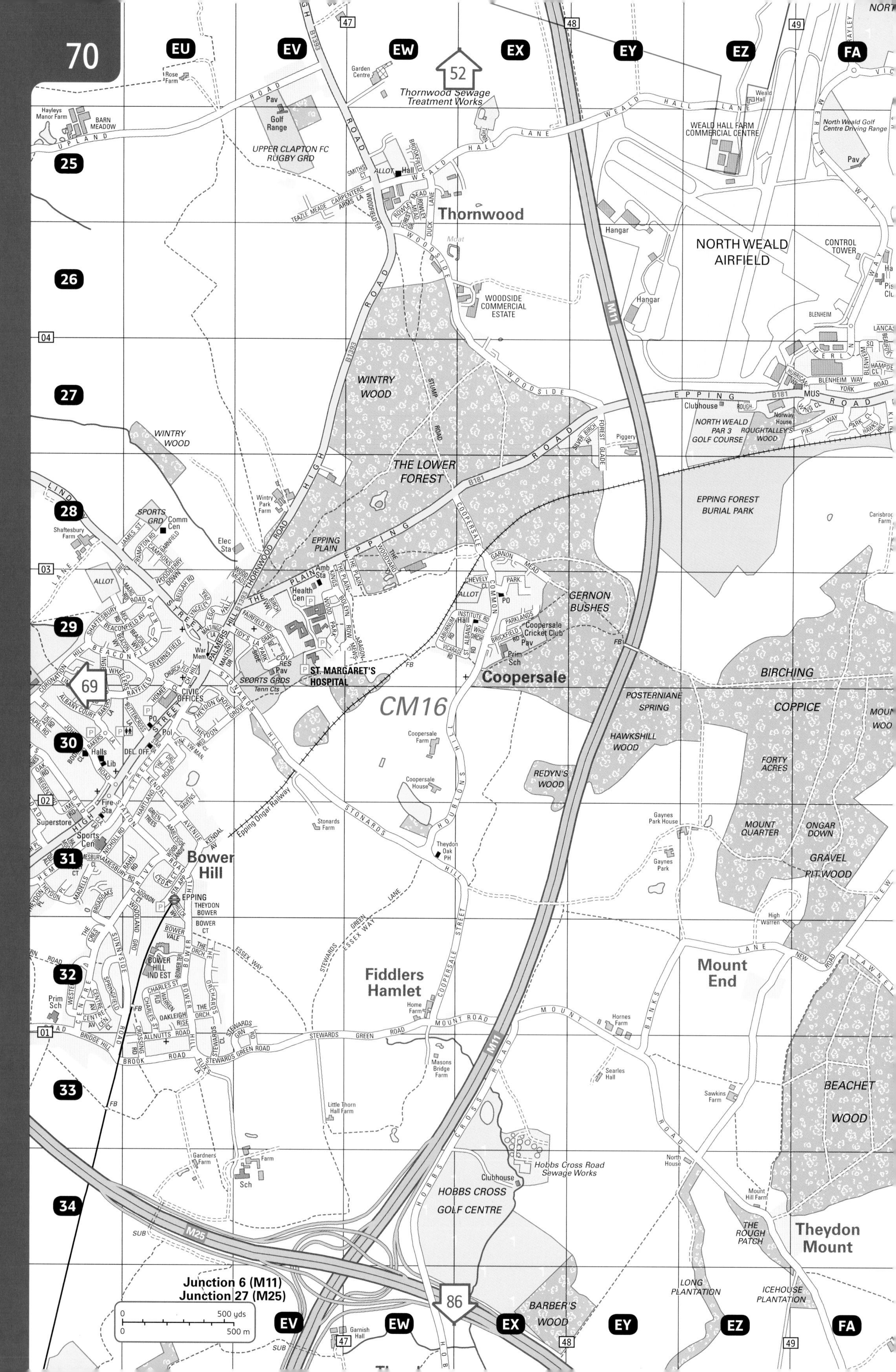
EU
EV
EW
EX
EY
EZ
FA
52
Thornwood Sewage Treatment Works
Rose Farm
Garden Centre
Hayleys Manor Farm
BARN MEADOW
UPLAND ROAD
Pav
Golf Range
UPPER CLAPTON FC RUGBY GRD
WEALD HALL LANE
WEALD HALL FARM COMMERCIAL CENTRE
North Weald Golf Centre Driving Range
Thornwood
Hangar
NORTH WEALD AIRFIELD
CONTROL TOWER
WOODSIDE COMMERCIAL ESTATE
BLENHEIM
WINTRY WOOD
THE LOWER FOREST
EPPING ROAD
Clubhouse
NORTH WEALD PAR 3 GOLF COURSE
ROUGHTALLEY'S WOOD
Piggery
EPPING FOREST BURIAL PARK
Carisbrook Farm
Wintry Park Farm
SPORTS GRD
Comm Cen
Shaftesbury Farm
Elec Sta
EPPING PLAIN
ALLOT
Health Cen
GERNON BUSHES
Coopersale Cricket Club
ST MARGARET'S HOSPITAL
SPORTS GRDS
Tenn Cts
Coopersale
BIRCHING COPPICE
POSTERNIANE SPRING
HAWKSHILL WOOD
CM16
69
CIVIC OFFICES
Coopersale Farm
Coopersale House
REDYN'S WOOD
FORTY ACRES
Superstore
Stonards Farm
Epping Ongar Railway
Gaynes Park House
Gaynes Park
MOUNT QUARTER
ONGAR DOWN
GRAVEL PIT WOOD
Bower Hill
Theydon Oak PH
EPPING
THEYDON BOWER
BOWER HILL IND EST
ESSEX WAY
High Warren
Fiddlers Hamlet
Mount End
Home Farm
MOUNT ROAD
Hornes Farm
STEWARDS GREEN ROAD
M11
Masons Bridge Farm
Searles Hall
BEACHET WOOD
Sawkins Farm
Little Thorn Hall Farm
Gardners Farm
Farm
Sch
Hobbs Cross Road Sewage Works
Clubhouse
HOBBS CROSS GOLF CENTRE
North House
Mount Hill Farm
THE ROUGH PATCH
Theydon Mount
M25
Junction 6 (M11)
Junction 27 (M25)
LONG PLANTATION
ICEHOUSE PLANTATION
86
BARBER'S WOOD
0 500 yds
0 500 m
Garnish Hall
25
26
27
28
29
30
31
32
33
34

North Weald Bassett
Toot Hill
Greensted Green
Clatterford End
BLAKES GOLF COURSE
TOOT HILL GOLF COURSE
EPPING ROAD
EPPING LANE
HIGH ROAD
BLAKE HALL ROAD
TOOT HILL ROAD
GREENSTED ROAD
SCHOOL ROAD
BERWICK LANE
TAWNEY COMMON
MUTTON ROW
OLD RECTORY ROAD
ESSEX WAY
Epping Ongar Railway
North Weald
Ongar Park Hall
Clubhouse
Water Tower
PEWLEY WOOD
MILLER'S GROVE
DOLMAN'S SPRING
GREENSTED WOOD
HIGH WOOD
ONGAR PARK WOOD
NORTHLANDS WOOD
KNIGHTSLAND WOOD
LONG SPRING
HANGING SPRING
ROUND SPRING
WELL EAVES
ICEHOUSE WOOD
TWENTYACRE WOOD
BERWICK HAM
REYNKYNS WOOD
The Talbot
Travelodge
CM5
RM4
53
87

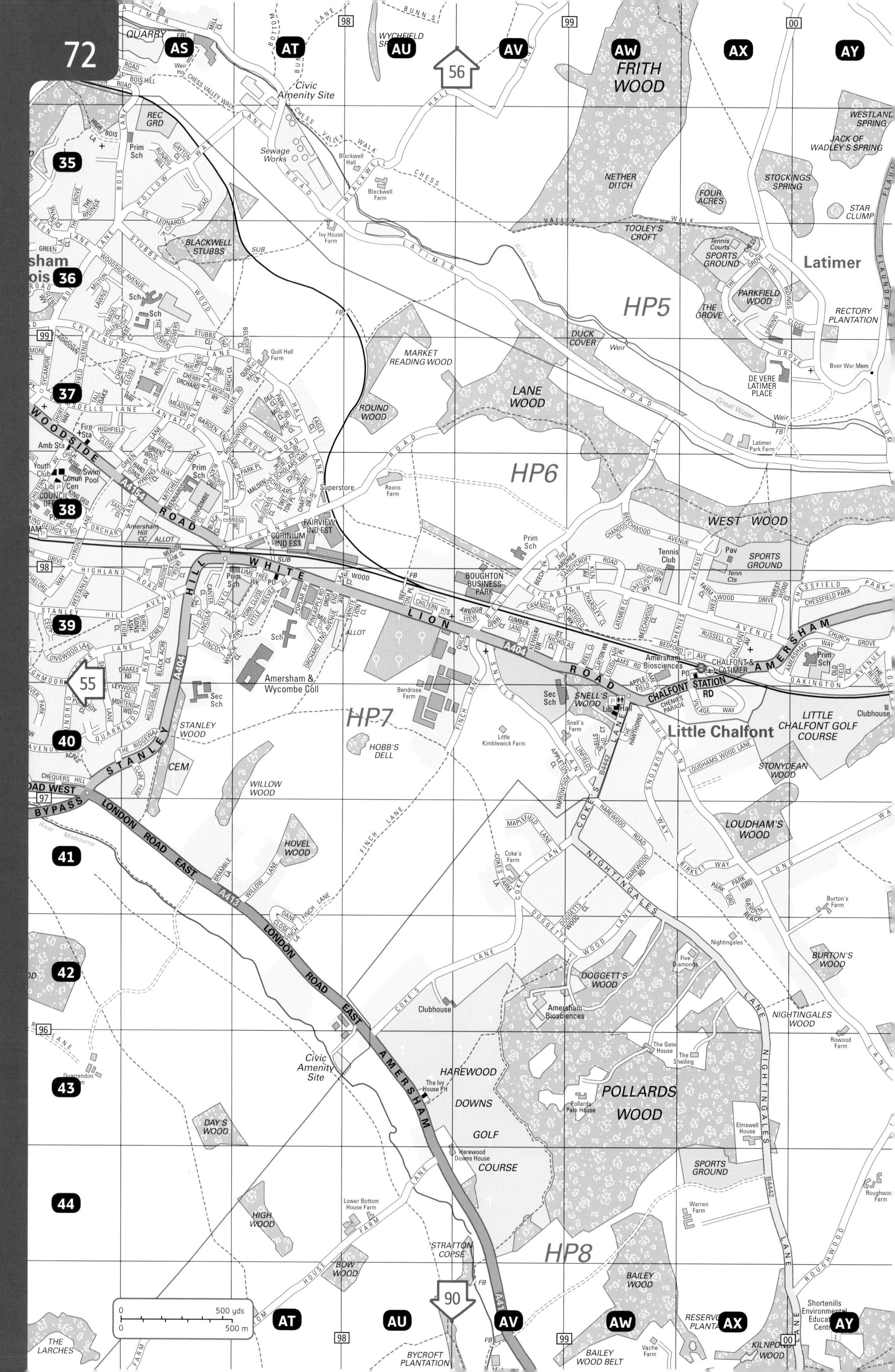
AS
AT
AU
AV
AW
AX
AY
98
99
00
56
FRITH WOOD
WESTLAND SPRING
JACK OF WADLEY'S SPRING
Civic Amenity Site
Sewage Works
Blackwell Hall
Blackwell Farm
CHESS VALLEY WALK
QUARRY
REC GRD
Prim Sch
35
36
37
38
39
40
41
42
43
44
NETHER DITCH
STOCKINGS SPRING
FOUR ACRES
STAR CLUMP
BLACKWELL STUBBS
TOOLEY'S CROFT
Ivy House Farm
Tennis Courts
SPORTS GROUND
Latimer
PARKFIELD WOOD
THE GROVE
RECTORY PLANTATION
HP5
DUCK COVER
Weir
Quill Hall Farm
MARKET READING WOOD
DE VERE LATIMER PLACE
Boer War Mem
LANE WOOD
ROUND WOOD
Great Water
Latimer Park Farm
Fire Sta
Amb Sta
Youth Club
Comm Cen
Swim Pool
COUNCIL OFF
Lib
WOODSIDE
A4154
Superstore
Raans Farm
HP6
Prim Sch
Amersham Hill CC
ALLOT
FAIRVIEW IND EST
CORINIUM IND EST
WEST WOOD
Tennis Club
Pav
SPORTS GROUND
Tenn Cts
BOUGHTON BUSINESS PARK
WHITE LION ROAD
A404
HILL
Sch
ALLOT
Amersham & Wycombe Coll
Amersham Biosciences
CHALFONT & LATIMER
CHALFONT STATION RD
Prim Sch
55
Sec Sch
STANLEY WOOD
Bendrose Farm
HP7
HOBB'S DELL
Little Kimblewick Farm
SNELL'S WOOD
Lib
Hall
Snell's Farm
Little Chalfont
LITTLE CHALFONT GOLF COURSE
Clubhouse
STONYDEAN WOOD
CEM
WILLOW WOOD
STANLEY
BYPASS
97
LONDON ROAD EAST
A413
HOVEL WOOD
LOUDHAM'S WOOD
Coke's Farm
Burton's Farm
Nightingales
BURTON'S WOOD
Five Diamonds
DOGGETT'S WOOD
Clubhouse
Amersham Biosciences
NIGHTINGALES WOOD
Rowood Farm
96
Quarrendon Farm
Civic Amenity Site
HAREWOOD DOWNS GOLF COURSE
The Ivy House PH
The Gate House
The Sheiling
POLLARDS WOOD
Pollards Park House
DAY'S WOOD
Elmswell House
Harewood Downs House
SPORTS GROUND
B4442
Roughwood Farm
HIGH WOOD
Lower Bottom House Farm
Warren Farm
STRATTON COPSE
HP8
BOW WOOD
BAILEY WOOD
90
FB
Shortenills Environmental Education Centre
RESERVOIR PLANTATION
THE LARCHES
BYCROFT PLANTATION
BAILEY WOOD BELT
Vache Farm
KILNPOND WOOD
0 500 yds
0 500 m

73
AZ
BA
BB
BC
BD
BE
BF
01
02
03
57
74
91
36
37
38
39
40
41
42
43
44
96
97
98
99
HP3
WD3
HANGING CROFT
LONG WOOD
FLAUNDEN GROVE
BALDWIN'S WOOD
OLDFIELD SPRING
WALLACE'S WOOD
Mast
R.A.F. Chenies
Martin Top Farm
Moonshine Farm
DACORUM
THREE RIVERS
BRAGMANS
CHENIES HILL
TOP SPRING
OLDCROFT WOOD
HANGINGLANE WOOD
BRAMBLE CROFT
LIMESHILL WOOD
DAFFODIL SPRING
WOOD
PLOUGH WOOD
Great Sarratt Hall Farm
Great Sarratt Hall
DAWES COMMON
SANDFIELD WOOD
Valley Farm
HOLLOWAY LANE
Moor Cottage
Watercress Beds
MOUNT WOOD
CHESS VALLEY WALK
River Chess
Mill Farm
CHENIES BOTTOM
Chenies Place
LATIMER ROAD
PLACEHOUSE COPSE
CONEY WOOD
WALK WOOD
Greathouse Farm
Prim Sch
Chenies Manor
Bedford Arms PH
BACK LANE
Mountwood Farm
NICHOLAS SPRING
TURVEYLANE WOOD
Chenies
BEDFORD CL
Chenies Garden Centre
Chenies & Latimer CC
Pav
Football Ground
WYBURN WOOD
AMERSHAM ROAD
A404
Sarrattmill Bridge
Water Works
MEAD SPRING
Weir
Weirs
FB
SCRUBBS WOOD
BLUNTS WOOD
Green End Business Cen
ALLOT
CHURCH ROAD
CHILTON'S WOOD
CHILTERN
OLD HANGING WOOD
NEW HANGING WOOD
LODGE COPSE
Lodge Farm
HALSEY'S WOOD
Great Greenstreet Farm
Little Greenstreet Farm
Stubbs Farm
GREEN STREET
BUCKINGHAMSHIRE
HERTFORDSHIRE
CHENIES ROAD
NORTH HILL
Sec Sch
Field Study Centre
Tennis Club
Chorleywood House
DELL WOOD
CEM
RICKMANSWORTH ROAD
WHITELANDS WOOD
HILLAS WOOD
CARPENTER'S WOOD
WHITELANDS AVENUE
CARPENTERS WOOD DRIVE
Newhouse Farm
Prim Sch
Arts Centre
Clubhouse Hall
CHORLEYWOOD COMMON
CHORLEYWOOD GOLF COURSE
Chorleywood Cricket Club
Prim Sch
White Horse PH
The Cedars
HOME WOOD
Black Horse PH
Chorleywood
CHORLEYWOOD
PO
Lib
CROSSLANE WOOD
BURTONS LANE
CHALFONT LANE
Fairfield Farm & Livery Stables
Roughwood Park
BLACKETTS WOOD
COMMON GATE ROAD
BERRY LANE
Berry Farm
THE SCREEN
West Herts Riding School
PHEASANTS WOOD
SOLOMON'S WOOD
Penn Farm
The Hall Farm
Hill Farm
Chorleywood Bottom
SHEPHERDS LANE
The Swillet
ALLOT
OLD SHIRE LANE
Bullsland Farm
GROVE WOOD
Heronsgate
M25
Prim Sch

Commonwood
Bucks Hill
Sarratt
WD4
WD3
Chandler's Cross
Loudwater
Croxley Green
Junction 19
Junction 18
M25
A404
BG
BH
BJ
BK
BL
BM
BN
35
36
37
38
39
40
41
42
43
44
58
73
92
05
06
07
99
98
97
96
HILLMEADS SPRING
Great Sarratt Hall
COMMONWOOD COMMON
Baytree Farm
Bucks Hill Farm
Model Farm
BEECHEN BOTTOM
JUNIPER HILL
Little Westwood Farm
Great Westwood Equestrian Park
HIGH SPRING
The Boot PH
SPORTS GROUND
Tennis Courts
Poultry Houses
Newhall Farm
Buckshill Bottom
TEMPLEPAN WOOD
TEMPLEPAN LANE
DAWS COMMON
SANDFIELD WOOD
Adams Nurseries
ALLOT
Green End Business Cen
Yew Court Farm
Potten's Farm
BIRCH SPRING
DARTPATH WOOD
WHITE SHACK LANE
Mickleford Green Farm
GREAT WOOD
SHEEPYARD SPRING
SAWPIT SPRING
New Model Farm
Coltspring Riding Stables
Coltyard Farm
Cottage Farm
Blacketts Nurseries
SCRUBBS WOOD
BLUNTS WOOD
WILLOW WOOD
HARROCKS WOOD
Sarrattmill Bridge
MEAD SPRING
Redhall Farm
WELLING GROVE
MERLIN'S WOOD
MERLIN'S SPRING
Micklefield Hall Farm
Micklefield Hall
Beechen Hill
BEECHENGROVE WOOD
MILLFIELD PLANTATION
ROUND SPRING
LONG SPRING
UPPER PLANTATION
York Ho Sch
Model Farm
WATERDELL SPRING
Highlands Water Gardens
Solesbridge Mill Water Gardens
Waterdell House
Killingdown Farm
Croxley House
LITTLE LADY'S WOOD
Loudwater House
Mont Au Source
Whitestocks Farm
PARROT'S DELL
White Horse PH
HOME WOOD
Glen Chess
Loudwater Farm
COPTHORNE WOOD
BALDWINS LANE RECREATION GROUND
ROUND SPRING
SPORTS GROUND
Coach & Horses PH
SOLOMON'S WOOD
THE SCREEN
West Herts Riding School
PHEASANTS WOOD
The Royal Masonic Sch
HOCKEY GRD
PLAYING FIELD
CRICKET GRD
Clubhouse
FORTUNE COMMON
CROXLEY HALL WOOD
LONG VALLEY WOOD
SPORTS GROUND
RICKMANSWORTH PARK
CHORLEYWOOD ROAD
WATFORD ROAD
SCOTS HILL
CHESS VALLEY WALK
River Chess
500 yds
500 m

BP
BQ
BR
BS
BT
BU
BV
08
09
10
59
Langleybury
THE ROOKERY
SPORTS GROUND
Langleybury Children's Farm
Leavesden Green
Kingswood
NORTH ORBITAL ROAD
KINGSWAY (NORTH ORBITAL ROAD)
NORTH WESTERN AVENUE
A41
A405
Hunton Bridge Interchange
Leavesden Green
THREE RIVERS
WATFORD
NORTH WATFORD CEMETERY
STANBOROUGH PARK
The Mosque
The Dome
36
37
38
39
40
41
42
43
44
HEATH WOOD
The Grove Hotel
THE GROVE GOLF COURSE
Clubhouse
WD24
Watford Tunnels
NORTH WATFORD
CALLOWLAND REC GRD
HEMPSTEAD ROAD
A411
ST. ALBANS ROAD
A412
WHIPPENDELL WOOD
WEST HERTS GOLF COURSE
Jacotts Hill
ROUGH WOOD
SPORTS GROUND
CASSIOBURY PARK
Paddling Pools
NATURE RESERVE
THE EMPIRE CENTRE
TRIDENT CENTRE
IMPERIAL PARK
Holiday Inn Express
76
WATFORD JUNCTION
British Telecom
West Herts College
THE COLOSSEUM
WATFORD
TOWN HALL
WD17
BEECHEN GROVE
Intu Watford
WATFORD HIGH STREET
RICKMANSWORTH ROAD
CASSIO ROAD
A4178
WEST WATFORD
VICARAGE RD CEMETERY
VICARAGE ROAD
VICARAGE RD STADIUM WATFORD FC
WATFORD GENERAL HOSP
WIGGENHALL ROAD
WD18
HAGDEN LANE
GRAND UNION CANAL
CROXLEY GREEN BUSINESS PARK
WATFORD BUSINESS PARK
Holywell
HOLYWELL IND EST
LONG VALLEY WOOD
COMMON MOOR
RIVERSIDE PARK
Electricity Transmission Station
KING GEORGE V PLAYING FIELDS
93
TOLPITS LANE
EASTBURY ROAD
DEACONS HILL
WATFORD METRO CEN
ORBITAL 25 BUSINESS PARK
MOOR PARK INDUSTRIAL

BW
BX
BY
BZ
CA
CB
CC
35
36
37
38
39
40
41
42
43
44
60
75
94
Garston
STANBOROUGH PARK
Meriden
MUNDEN SPRING
PEARTREE WOOD
Munden House
The Dome
A41 AVENUE
COLNE WAY (NORTH WESTERN AVENUE)
OTTERSPOOL WAY
A412
ST ALBANS ROAD
NORTH WATFORD
SPORTS GROUND
Superstore
Superstore 24hr
THE WENTA BUSINESS CEN
ODHAMS TRADING EST
WATFORD NORTH LC
SANDOWN RD IND EST
PARAMOUNT IND EST
MOWAT IND EST
TOP GOLF GAME CENTRE
Clubhouse
Elec Sta
Colne Bridge
M1
Junction 5
Berrygrove Interchange
ALDENHAM GOLF COURSE & COUNTRY CLUB
WALL HALL MANSION
Aldenham
Round Bush
WD25
WD24
WD17
WD23
WD19
HERTSMERE
WATFORD
BERRY GROVE LANE
BERRY WAY
Busheymill Bridge
Bushey Hall Farm
REC GRD
Watford R.F.C.
THE EMPIRE CENTRE
HOLLY IND PARK
TRIDENT CENTRE
PENFOLD TRADING EST
IMPERIAL PARK
WATFORD JUNCTION
Hartswood
Hilton Watford
ELTON WAY (NORTH WESTERN AVENUE)
WINFIELD MOBILE HOME PARK
Patchetts Equestrian Centre
Three Compasses PH
Delrow House
Holland Farm
Prim Sch
Comm Cen
Fitness Cen
The Purcell School
PLAYING FIELD
BUSHEY JEWISH CEMETERY
SCOTTS WOOD
BUSHEY HALL GOLF COURSE
RADLETT ROAD PLAYING FIELDS
STEPHENSON
A4008
METROPOLITAN POLICE BUSHEY SPORTS GROUND
Queens' Sch
The Lincolnsfields Centre
SPORTS GRD
Leisure Cen
Sports Cen
ICEDALE WOODS
GREATHAM RD IND EST
British Telecom
BEECHEN GROVE
Intu Watford
Charter Place
YMCA
Travelodge
Premier Inn
WATFORD HIGH STREET
Waterfields Retail Park
Waterfields
WATERFIELDS WAY
Colne Valley Retail Park
Veolia Water
Gas Works
Theatre & Arts Cen
Watford Arches Retail Park
DALTON WAY
LWR HIGH ST
WIGGENHALL ROAD
VICARAGE RD
WATFORD FC STADIUM
FISHER'S IND EST
WIGGENHALL RD GOODS YD
SPORTS GROUND
OXHEY
OXHEY PARK
A4125
DEACONS HILL
A4178
CHALK HILL
LONDON ROAD
HIGH ROAD
A411
BUSHEY
BUSHEY GOLF COURSE & COUNTRY CLUB
BURIAL GRD
DRIVING RANGE
Haydon Hill House
Watford Equestrian Centre
Watford Borough Council Nursery
ALDENHAM ROAD
Sec Sch
MOAT FIELD REC GRD
KING GEORGE REC GROUND
SPARROWS
Caravan Site
0 500 yds
0 500 m

RADLETT
Battlers Green
Letchmore Heath
ELSTREE AERODROME
HILFIELD PARK RESERVOIR
ALDENHAM COUNTRY PARK
ALDENHAM RESERVOIR
ALDENHAM PARK WOODLAND
ELSTREE
WD7
WD6
WATLING STREET
ELSTREE OPEN SPACE
THE GORSE
National Grid Elstree 400kV Substation
TYLERS WAY (NORTH WESTERN AV)
M1
61
78
95

CL
CM
CN
CP
CQ
CR
CS
62
77
96
19
20
21
99
98
97
96
35
36
37
38
39
40
41
42
43
44
WD7
WD6
BIG PURSLEY WOOD
LITTLE PURSLEY WOOD
CROSS OAKS WOOD
BIRCH WOOD
Green Street
Well End
THE MEADOWS
AYCLIFFE ROAD PITCHES
SPORTS GROUND
ABERFORD PARK
MEADOW PARK
BOREHAMWOOD
B.B.C. Elstree Studios
Elstree Film Studios
Borehamwood Shopping Park
BOREHAMWOOD IND PARK
DEVONSHIRE BUSINESS PARK
ELSTREE BUSINESS CENTRE
KENILWORTH PARK
RIPON PARK
ROWLEY LANE SPORTS GRD
ROWLEY LANE GOLF COURSE
A1 DRIVING RANGE
DRIVING RANGE
GOLF COURSE
HERTSMERE BOROUGH COUNCIL CEMETERY
ELSTREE & BOREHAMWOOD
STIRLING IND CEN
Stirling Corner
Stirling Retail Pk
Furze Hill
Deacons Hill
DEACONS HILL OPEN SPACE
SCRATCH WOOD
FROGHALL WOOD
BOYS HILL WOOD
THISTLE WOOD
ELSTREE OPEN SPACE
ELSTREE TUNNEL
BARNET LANE
A411
A1 BARNET BY PASS
ELSTREE WAY
A5135
SHENLEY ROAD
B5378
ALLUM LANE
ELSTREE HILL NORTH
ELSTREE HILL SOUTH
Catherine Bourne
London Colney C.C.
Tokonoma Bonsai
The Garden Nursery
The White Horse PH
Pursley Farm
Auriol Farm
Wood Hall Farm
Wood Hall
Kitwells Farm
Villa Scalabrini
Lyndhurst
Silver Hill
High Canons
High Canons Farm
Holmshill House
Crossoaks Farm
Bucketsland Farm
Wheatsheaf Farm
Maxwelton Nurseries
Well End Farm
Cowley Hill Farm
Organ Hall Farm
Strangeways Farm
Rowley Farm
Mops & Brooms PH
Travelodge
Holiday Inn
Woodcock Hill Farm
Airshafts
BUPA Nursing Home
Elstree Manor
Penniwells Farm
Hyver Hall
ARKLEY PARK
ELSTREE PARK
Elli Dani Farm (Stables)
South Medburn Farm
Clubhouse
Hertswood School (Upper School)
War Memorial
Superstore
Gas Works
0
500 yds
500 m

Bignell's Corner
South Mimms Services
Days Inn
Research UK
Blanche Farm
63
M25
Junction 23
(M25)
Junction 1
A1(M)
A1 BYPASS
BARNET
Dancers Hill
Laurel Lodge
Laurel House
Dancershill House
DANCERS HILL ROAD
BENTLEY HEATH LANE
Elm Farm
Bentley Heath
Norfolk Lodge
Mausoleum
Wrotham Park
Tennis Courts
Pool
WROTHAM PARK
Deadman's Bottom
BOTTOM
DYRHAM LANE
Dyrham Park Farm
TROTTERS
DYRHAM PARK GOLF COURSE
Country Club
Pool
Tennis Courts
DYRHAM PARK
Valentine's Farm
Green Dragon Inn PH
Knightsland Farm
Lower Kitt's End Farm
Wrotham Business Park
Kitt's End
Kitt's End Farm
A1081
ST. ALBANS ROAD
THE SHIRE LONDON GOLF COURSE
ALLOTMENTS
Clubhouse
OLD FOLD MANOR GOLF COURSE
MOAT
Old Fold Manor
Monken Hadley
Battle of Barnet 1471
Rectory Farm
80
GALLEY LANE
Fold Farm
EN5
Electricity Sta
High Barnet
BYNG ROAD PLAYING FIELDS
Homestead Farm
POOR CLARE MONASTERY
HERTFORDSHIRE
HERTSMERE
BARNET
SPORTS GROUND
Barnet Elizabethans R.F.C.
ALLOT
DENIS BLAND NATURE RESERVE
Prim Sch
Sec Sch
Swim Pool
HADLEY GREEN
HADLEY HIGHSTONE
GREAT NORTH ROAD
A1000
Hadley
KING GEORGE'S FIELD
BARNET
SPORTS GROUND
Woodlands Farm
ARKLEY LANE
ARKLEY OPEN SPACE
ARKLEY GOLF COURSE
ARKLEY RISE ESTATE OPEN SPACE
Rowley Green
Nursery
Three Elms Farm
WOOD STREET
A411
WHALEBONE PARK
BARNET HOSP
THE BULL THEATRE
Barnet and Southgate Coll
Sports Cen
HIGH BARNET
CHIPPING BARNET
CEMETERY
BELLS HILL ALLOT
ALLOT
Arkley Manor Farm
Clubhouse
War Memorial
Water Tower
Arkley
BARNET ROAD
WHITINGS HILL OPEN SPACE
Prim Sch
Prim Schs
Comm Cen
Valley Cen
Clubhouse
Underhill
SPORTS GROUND
BARNET PLAYING FIELDS
KING GEORGE V PLAYING FIELDS
Barnet Gate
SPORTS GROUND
Ducks Island
Whitings Hill Farm
Cottage Farm
GRANGE PLAYING FIELDS
PLAYING FIELD
Tennis Courts
LONDON LOOP / DOLLIS VALLEY GREENWALK
Dollis Brook
OLD ELIZABETHANS (BARNET) MEMORIAL PLAYING FIELDS
Brent Lodge Farm
MAYS LANE
97
Sec Sch
N20
SOUTH HERTS GOLF COURSE
OAKLANDS ROAD
CT
CU
CV
CW
CX
CY
CZ
36
37
38
39
40
41
42
43
44

DA
DB
DC
DD
DE
DF
DG
POTTERS BAR COMMUNITY HOSP
M25
64
Junction 24
THE RIDGEWAY
A1005
STAGG HILL
35
Bentley Heath
Ganwick Corner
CHASE WOOD
FIR WOOD
Fenny Shade Hill
Plumridge Hill
PLUMRIDGE WOOD
VAULT HILL WOOD
36
Wrotham Park
WROTHAM PARK
Three Oak Hill
Hornbeam Hills
HERTFORDSHIRE
Cockshot Hill
Deadman's Bottom
SPOILBANK WOOD
Slopers Pond Farm
Roundhedge Hill
37
Wrotham Business Park
WAGGON ROAD
ENFIELD
38
BARTRAMS QUASH
West Lodge Park Hotel
ASH WOOD
HADLEY WOOD
Great Broadgates Hill
FERNY HILL
COCKFOSTERS ROAD
39
Monken Hadley
Battle of Barnet
79
BEECH HILL PARK
HADLEY WOOD GOLF COURSE
FERNYHILL WOOD
ROUGH LOT
SEEDFIELD SPINNEY
40
Bournwell Hill
MONKEN HADLEY COMMON
COVERT WAY OPEN SPACE
Sewit's Hill
EN4
OAK WOOD
Priddeon's Hill
Newman's Hill
BEECH HILL LAKE
Hadley
TUDOR GOLF COURSE
KING GEORGE'S FIELD
EN5
Jewish Comm. Sec Sch
41
SPORTS GROUND
TRENT PARK CEM
VICTORIA REC GRD
COCKFOSTERS
42
NEW BARNET
BARNET
COCKFOSTERS
A110
43
Underhill SPORTS GROUND
BARNET PLAYING FIELDS
44
KING GEORGE V PLAYING FIELDS
EAST BARNET
WYATTS FARM OPEN SPACE
OAK HILL PARK
Oak Hill College
N20
98
OAKLEIGH PARK
0 500 yds
0 500 m

M25
DH
DJ
DK
DL
DM
DN
DP
29
30
31
South Hill
65
Holly Hill Farm
CREWS HILL
Oak Hill Farm
Garden Centre
Culver Garden Centre
Country World
Glasgow Stud
BURNT FM RIDE
Nursery
Sloeman's Farm
Clubhouse
CREWS HILL GOLF COURSE
Woldens Nursery & Garden Centre
Woldens Nurseries
Browns of Crews Hill Nurseries
WHITEWEBBS
BEECH AV
CYPRESS AV
ROSEWOOD DR
WROXHAM GDNS
Kings Oak Riding Stables
TINGEYS TOP LANE
Crews Hill
Wilfwoods Water Garden Centre
WILDWOOD
Glasshouses
Hill Side Nursery
NICHOLAS HO
THE RIDGEWAY
Botany Bay
EAST LODGE LANE
Pav
Botany Bay C.C.
Botany Bay Farm
Kings Oak Plain
SUB
LITTLE BEECHILL WOOD
A1005
Prim Sch
ST. JOHNS PK HOME EST
STRAYFIELD ROAD
FLASH LANE
North Enfield CC
The Fallow Buck PH
Anglo Aquarium Plant
Queenswood Farm
Kingswood
LONDON LOOP
RECTORY FARM ROAD
Rectory Farm
Turkey Brook
STRAYFIELD ROAD CEMETERY
Rendlesham Viaduct
Clay Hill
CHASE
LONDON LOOP/RECTORY FARM ROAD
EN2
HILLY FIELDS PARK
LAVENDER HILL CEMETERY
Cuckolds Hill
Park Farms
THE KING'S OAK HOSPITAL
CHASE FARM HOSPITAL
Royal Chace Hotel
FOUR HILLS EST
HADLEY ROAD
Parkside Farm
Pumping Station
Amb Sta
MOAT WOOD
Camlet Hill
RIDE WOOD
Vicarage Farm
Leeging Beech Gutter
GORDON HILL
LAVENDER HILL
Salmon's Brook
Hog Hill
WILLIAMS WOOD
ICEHOUSE WOOD
Fish Pond
Well
Monument
SHAWS WOOD
NUFFIELD HOSP
82
Comfort Hotel
Tennis Courts
Pav
SPORTS GROUND
TRENT PARK GOLF COURSE
Merryhills Brook
SLADES HILL
WINDMILL HILL
A110
World's End
ENFIELD GOLF COURSE
Clubhouse
ENFIELD CHASE
TRIANGULAR WOOD
South Lodge Farm
ENFIELD ROAD
Trent Park Equestrian Centre
Driving Range
Clubhouse
Sec Sch
Prim Sch
CHEYNE WALK
GRANGE PARK
OAKWOOD
BRAMLEY ROAD
PRIORY
Health Cen
Superstore
SPORTS GROUND
N21
OAKWOOD PARK
Pitch 'n' Putt
Ice Well
YACHTING POND
Hounsden Gutter
SPORTS GRD
99
WINCHMORE HILL
N14
GROVELANDS
Leisure Cen
36
37
38
39
40
41
42
43
44

DQ
DR
DS
DT
DU
DV
DW
66
81
100
35
36
37
38
39
40
41
42
43
44
Junction 25
BULLSCROSS RIDE
CEMETERY (JEWISH)
Theobalds Park Camping and Caravan Site
COUNTY BROOK PLANTATION
Bulls Cross
Capel Manor College
CAPEL HOUSE
TOTTENHAM HOTSPUR TRAINING CENTRE
Crews Hill
WHITEWEBBS WOOD
WHITEWEBBS PARK
WHITEWEBBS GOLF COURSE
White Webbs House
Wilfwoods Water Garden Centre
WILDWOOD
EN2
Clay Hill
Kingswood
HILLY FIELDS PARK
FORTY HALL COUNTRY PARK
Forty Hill
FORTY HALL & MUSEUM
ALLOTMENTS
BULLS CROSS FIELD
SPORTS GROUND
Bullsmoor
CEMETERY
Crematorium
ALLOTMENTS
ENFIELD CEMETERY (JEWISH)
QUEEN ELIZABETH STADIUM
EN1
ENFIELD PLAYING FIELDS
ENFIELD
BASEBALL GROUND
ENFIELD TOWN
ENFIELD CHASE
TOWN PARK
BUSH HILL PARK GOLF COURSE
BUSH HILL PARK
GRANGE PARK
N21
SOUTHBURY
MARTINBRIDGE TRADING ESTATE
HASLEMERE BUSINESS CENTRE
GREAT CAMBRIDGE IND EST
ENFIELD RETAIL PK
JUBILEE PARK
GREAT CAMBRIDGE ROAD
SOUTHBURY ROAD
HERTFORD ROAD
0
500 yds
500 m

Holdbrook
Freezywater
RAMMEY MARSH
LEE VALLEY REGIONAL PARK
GUNPOWDER PARK
Enfield Lock
Enfield Wash
EN3
EN9
Sewardstone
KING GEORGE'S RESERVOIR
Brimsdown
E4
CHINGFORD GOLF COURSE
THE HAWK WOOD
Sewardstone Roundabout
M25
MOLLISON AVENUE
MERIDIAN WAY
SEWARDSTONE ROAD
LEA VALLEY ROAD

EE
EF
EG
EH
EJ
EK
EL
68
WALTHAM ABBEY
Junction 26
HONEY LANE
M25
A121
DOWDING WAY
WOODRIDDEN
EN9
Sewardstone Roundabout
SPORTS GROUND
Swim Pool
Prim Schs
Marriott Waltham Abbey
CLAY PIGEON RANGE
CONYBURY WOOD
STABLES SHAW
BRAMBLY SHAW
POTKILN WOOD
LORD PADGETS WOOD
POPLARS SHAW
WALTHAM ABBEY CEMETERY (JEWISH)
HONEY LANE PLAIN
HONEY LANE QUARTERS
SUNSHINE PLAIN
Round Hills
BEECH HILL PARK
HIGH BEECH GOLF COURSE
AVEY LANE
PYNEST GRN
THOMPSON'S WOOD
MOTT STREET
ALDERGROVE WOOD
High Beach
LITTLE MONK WOOD
EPPING FOREST
IG10
Loughton Camp
Epping Forest Field Cen
Duke of Wellington PH
King's Oak PH
Robin Hood PH
HILL WOOD
Police Training Centre
Owl PH
FERNHILL WOOD
WEST ESSEX GOLF COURSE
Clubhouse
Sewardstonebury
E4
BANCHET FIELD
WHITEHOUSE PLAIN
ROUND THICKET
ALMHOUSE PLAIN
North Long Hills
Long Hills
Strawberry Hill
Fairmead Bottom
WOODMAN'S GLADE
BURY WOOD
Cuckoo Pits
Grimston's Oak
Magpie Hill
CHINGFORD GOLF COURSE
CHINGFORD PLAIN
QUEEN ELIZABETH'S HUNTING LODGE
A1069
A104
EPPING NEW ROAD
102
Buckhurst Hill
Warren Hill
Oaklands Sch
LOUGHTON
83
Barn Hill
35
36
37
38
39
40
41
42
43
44
99
98
97
96
500 yds
500 m

EPPING FOREST
69
86
103
EM
EN
EP
EQ
ER
ES
ET
36
37
38
39
40
41
42
43
44
THEYDON BOIS GOLF COURSE
Theydon Bois
CM16
RM4
IG7
Debden Green
Debden
OUGHTON
LOUGHTON GOLF COURSE
HILLYFIELDS OPEN SPACE
WOOLSTON MANOR GOLF & COUNTRY CLUB
Junction 5
Wake Arms
Rolls Park Roundabout
Little London
ST. THOMAS'S QUARTERS
Long Running
Jacks Hill
Oak Hill
Dulsmead Hollow
COPLEY PLAIN
SHELTER PLAIN
FURZE GROUND
GREAT MONK WOOD
BROADSTROOD PLAIN
BIRCH WOOD
RED OAK WOOD
GAUNT'S WOOD
THEYDON PLAIN
THE COPPICE
Piercing Hill
LONG SHAW
BROADFIELD SHAW
THEYDON MEAD
THEYDON BOIS CEMETERY
Theydon Hall
Ripley Grange
Debden Ho Cen
IMPRIMO PARK
PROSPECT BUSINESS PARK
LOUGHTON BUSINESS CEN
OAKWOOD HILL INDUSTRIAL ESTATE
Epping Forest Col
SPORTS GROUND
Printing Works
Little Bronx Livery & Riding Stables
GOLDINGS HILL
RECTORY LANE
CHIGWELL LANE
LONDON ROAD
GRAVEL LANE
ABRIDGE ROAD
COPPICE ROW
EPPING ROAD
THEYDON PARK ROAD
LOUGHTON LANE
M11
A121
A1168
A113
A1112
B172
B1393

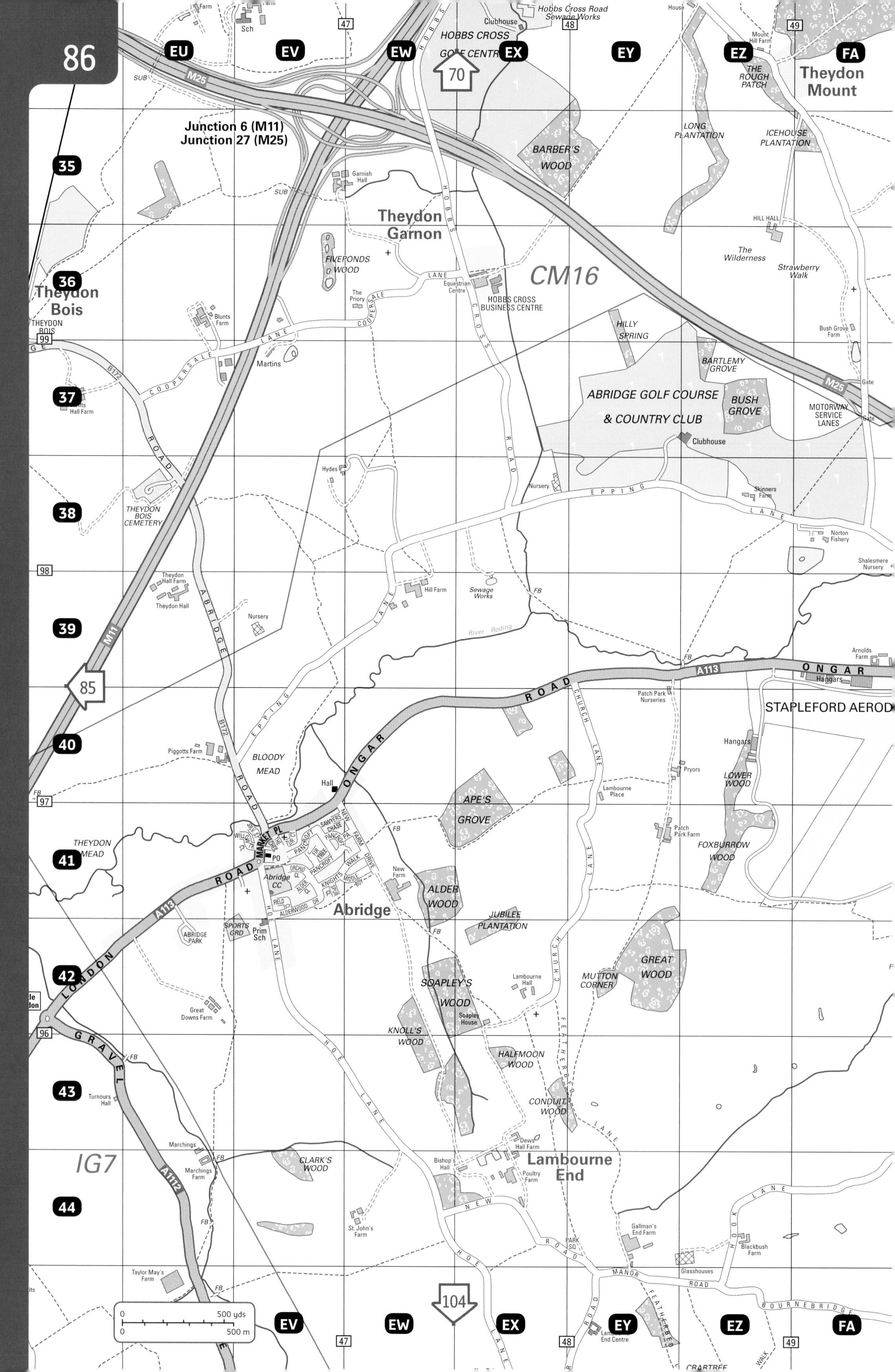

Junction 6 (M11)
Junction 27 (M25)
M25
M11
Theydon Bois
Theydon Garnon
Theydon Mount
HOBBS CROSS GOLF CENTRE
Hobbs Cross Road Sewage Works
BARBER'S WOOD
CM16
FIVEPONDS WOOD
Garnish Hall
Blunts Farm
Martins
The Priory
Equestrian Centre
HOBBS CROSS BUSINESS CENTRE
LONG PLANTATION
ICEHOUSE PLANTATION
THE ROUGH PATCH
Mount Hill Farm
HILL HALL
The Wilderness
Strawberry Walk
Bush Grove Farm
HILLY SPRING
BARTLEMY GROVE
ABRIDGE GOLF COURSE & COUNTRY CLUB
BUSH GROVE
Clubhouse
MOTORWAY SERVICE LANES
Skinners Farm
Norton Fishery
Shalesmere Nursery
Hydes
Nursery
THEYDON BOIS CEMETERY
Blunts Hall Farm
Theydon Hall Farm
Theydon Hall
Hill Farm
Sewage Works
River Roding
Arnolds Farm
ONGAR ROAD
A113
Hangars
STAPLEFORD AEROD
Patch Park Nurseries
Piggotts Farm
BLOODY MEAD
Hall
Pryors
LOWER WOOD
Lambourne Place
APE'S GROVE
THEYDON MEAD
Patch Park Farm
FOXBURROW WOOD
Abridge
Abridge CC
PO
New Farm
ALDER WOOD
JUBILEE PLANTATION
ABRIDGE PARK
SPORTS GRD
Prim Sch
GREAT WOOD
MUTTON CORNER
SOAPLEY'S WOOD
Soapley House
Lambourne Hall
KNOLL'S WOOD
Great Downs Farm
HALFMOON WOOD
CONDUIT WOOD
Turnours Hall
Marchings
Marchings Farm
IG7
CLARK'S WOOD
Dews Hall Farm
Bishop's Hall
Lambourne End
Poultry Farm
A1112
St. John's Farm
Gallman's End Farm
Blackbush Farm
Glasshouses
Taylor May's Farm
MANOR ROAD
BOURNEBRIDGE
Lambourne End Centre
CRABTREE
HOE LANE
CHURCH LANE
FEATHERBED LANE
HOOK LANE
NEW ROAD
GRAVEL
LONDON ROAD
EPPING LANE
COOPERSALE LANE
ABRIDGE ROAD
HOBBS CROSS ROAD
500 yds
500 m
EU EV EW EX EY EZ FA
35 36 37 38 39 40 41 42 43 44
47 48 49 96 97 98 99
70 85 104

Stapleford Tawney
Stapleford Abbotts
Bounce Hill
Nuper's Hatch
RM4
CM5
CM14
TWENTYACRE WOOD
BERWICK HAM
TENACRE WOOD
ICEHOUSE WOOD
BOB'S BARN WOOD
LANGFORD BOTTOM
SHALES MORE
RAILMEAD PLANTATION
SUTTONS MANOR
STONYROCKS PLANTATION
BROOM WOOD
CURTISMILL GREEN
STAPLEFORD ABBOTTS GOLF COURSE
EPPING FOREST
BRENTWOOD
LONDON ROAD
A113
M25
B175
Passingford Bridge
Mitchells Farm
Howletts Hall
Dabbs Farm
Albyns Farm
Albyns Hall
Bons Farm
Hammonds Farm
Waters Farm
Great Tawney Hall
Little Tawney Farm
Howfields
Murrells Farm
Traceys Farm
Shonk's Mill Bridge
Green Farm
Grafton Farm
40 Acre Farm
Lodge Farm
Brook Farm
Jenkins Farm
Spring Farm
Tyseahill Farm
Olives Farm
Stapleford Hall Farm
High House Farm
Woodlands Farm
Church Farm
Battles Hall
Belmont Farm
Skips Corner Farm
WATTON'S GREEN
The Rabbits PH
Prim Sch
Village Hall
Nursery
Crown Park Farm
FB
FC
FD
FE
FF
FG
FH
36
37
38
39
40
41
42
43
44
50
51
52
71
105

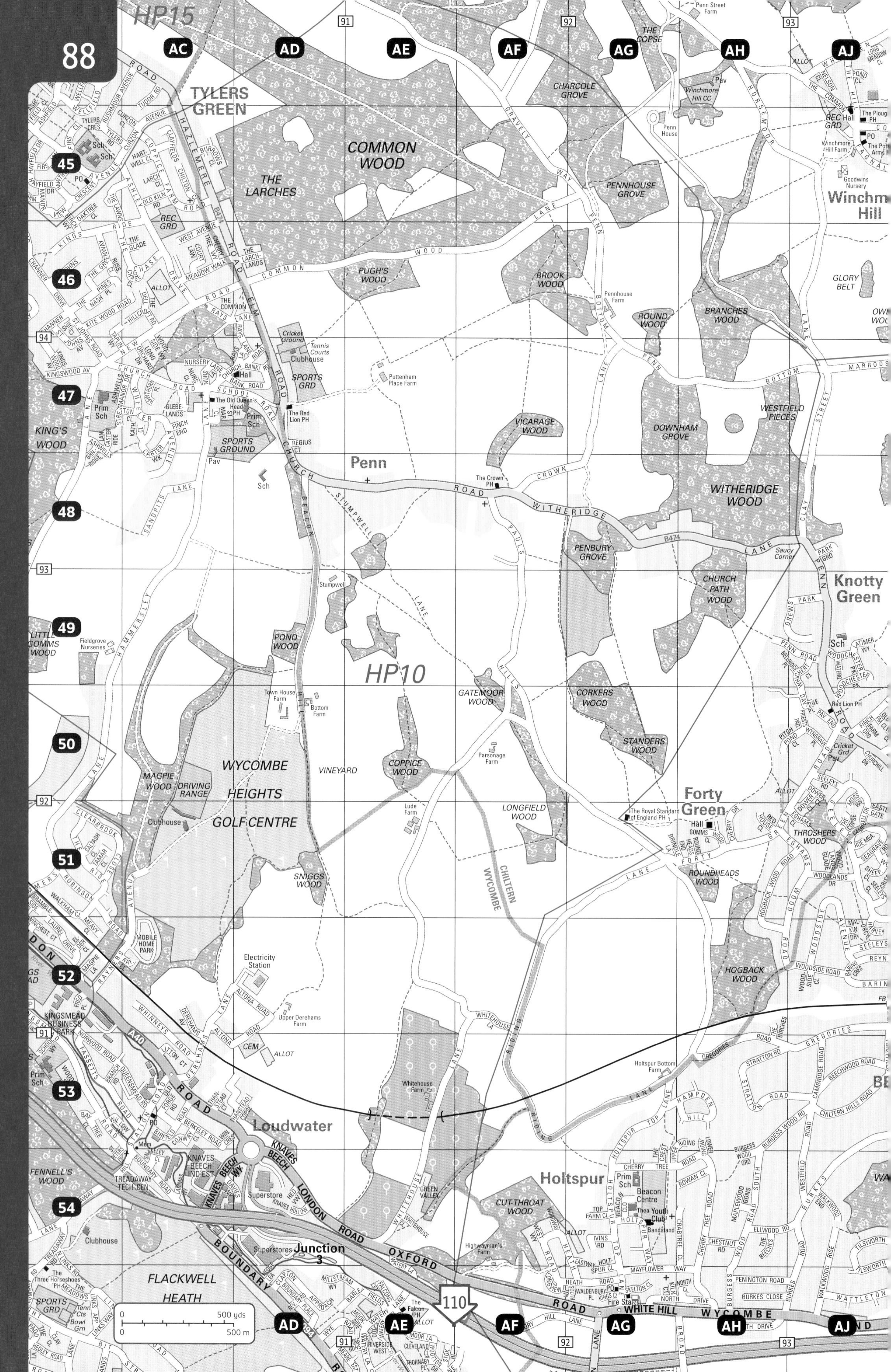
HP15
AC
AD
AE
AF
AG
AH
AJ
TYLERS GREEN
COMMON WOOD
THE LARCHES
CHARCOLE GROVE
PENNHOUSE GROVE
Winchmore Hill
PUGH'S WOOD
BROOK WOOD
ROUND WOOD
BRANCHES WOOD
GLORY BELT
SPORTS GRD
Penn
VICARAGE WOOD
DOWNHAM GROVE
WESTFIELD PIECES
WITHERIDGE WOOD
KING'S WOOD
SPORTS GROUND
PENBURY GROVE
CHURCH PATH WOOD
Knotty Green
POND WOOD
HP10
GATEMOOR WOOD
CORKERS WOOD
STANDERS WOOD
WYCOMBE HEIGHTS GOLF CENTRE
MAGPIE WOOD
DRIVING RANGE
VINEYARD
COPPICE WOOD
LONGFIELD WOOD
Forty Green
THROSHERS WOOD
SNIGGS WOOD
ROUNDHEADS WOOD
CHILTERN WYCOMBE
HOGBACK WOOD
Electricity Station
KINGSMEAD BUSINESS PARK
Loudwater
KNAVES BEECH IND EST
FENNELL'S WOOD
TREADAWAY TECH CEN
Holtspur
CUT-THROAT WOOD
Junction 3
FLACKWELL HEATH
OXFORD ROAD
LONDON ROAD
WHITE HILL
WYCOMBE
A40
B474
110
0 500 yds
0 500 m

HP7
HP8
HP9
SL9
Seer Green
BEACONSFIELD
HODGEMOOR WOODS
GREAT BEARD'S WOOD
BROWN'S WOOD
BEACONSFIELD GOLF COURSE
THE MOUNT
AMERSHAM ROAD
A355
COLESHILL COMMON
HERTS WOOD
HERTFORDSHIRE WOOD
LITTLE LUCKINGS WOOD
TALLY WOOD
GREAT LUCKINGS WOOD
ONGAR HILL DELLS
OWSLEARS WOOD
STARVEACRE WOOD
BOTTOM WOOD
BIRCHEN SPRING
PEGGS WOOD
BLUE CLOSE WOOD
CLEARE CRAFT WOOD
HILL'S WOOD
HEATHFIELD GROVE
HALES WOOD
WELPLEY'S WOOD
THE LARCHES
RAWLINGS DELL
BIG COPSE
LITTLE COPSE
SANDELS WOOD
NETHERLANDS WOOD
LEDBOROUGH WOOD
OLDFIELDS FURZE
YOUNG'S WOOD
GREEN WOOD
WALK WOOD
LITTLE WALK WOOD
WHEATSHEAF WOOD
DEAN WOOD
PITLANDS WOOD
BIRCHLAND WOOD
MODEL VILLAGE
Chiltern Woodland Burial Park
Sewage Works
Beaconsfield Cricket Club
SEER GREEN & JORDANS
LONDON END
LONDON ROAD
WYCOMBE END
OXFORD ROAD
PARK LANE
LOWER PYEBUSHES
PYEBUSHES
55
90
111
46
47
48
49
50
51
52
53
54

AS
AT
AU
AV
AW
AX
AY
HP7
HP8
HP9
45
46
47
48
49
50
51
52
53
54
72
89
112
HIGH WOOD
BOW WOOD
STRATTON COPSE
BAILEY WOOD
RESERVOIR PLANTATION
Shortenills Environmental Education Centre
KILNPOND WOOD
THE LARCHES
BYCROFT PLANTATION
BAILEY WOOD BELT
SHORTENILLS WOOD
OAK PLANTATION
DELLGARDEN PLANTATION
HALES WOOD
WELPLEY'S WOOD
PERRYFIELD PLANTATION
RUSHCROFT WOOD
MILLFIELD PLANTATION
Chalfont St. Giles
GEMOOR WOODS
MILTON'S COTTAGE
TURNER'S WOOD
RAWLINGS DELL
BIG COPSE
Butlers Cross
OAKLAND PARK GOLF COURSE
DRIVING RANGE
PLAYING FIELD
FOXDELL WOOD
Dibden Hill
LITTLE COPSE
LONG WOOD
FARM WOOD
OUTFIELD PLANTATION
GREEN WOOD
ROUND WOOD
MIDDLE WOOD
CHALFONT GROVE
Seer Green
Jordans
POND WARREN WOOD
BIRCH PLANTATION
MONTAGUE'S DELL
CRUTCHES WOOD
GROVE WOOD
OLD JORDANS & MAYFLOWER BARN
WELDERS WOOD
SPRING WOOD
DEAN WOOD
WEEDONS DELL
MOUNTHILL WOOD
THE ASH BEDS
THIRTY ACRE KNOLL
GREAT LEGS WOOD
Layter's Green
GOLDHILL COMMON
MALMS WOOD
BIRCHLAND WOOD
HIGH WOOD
BEECH WOOD
BIRCH WOOD
AUSTENWOOD COMMON
LONDON ROAD
AMERSHAM ROAD
GRAVEL HILL
A413
A40
0 500 yds
0 500 m

Chorleywood Bottom
The Swillet
Heronsgate
Mill End
Junction 17
GROVESPRING WOOD
PHILIPSHILL WOOD
NEWLAND GORSE
NEWLAND PARK
Buckinghamshire Chilterns University College
CHILTERN OPEN AIR MUSEUM
SPORTS GROUND
BOTTOM WOOD
LADYWALK WOOD
WD3
Maple Cross Roundabout
FIVE PLANTATIONS
POLLARDSHILL WOOD
Maple Cross
Chalfont Common
KILN WOOD
BEECHEN WOOD
FRANKLINS SPRING
Maple Lodge Sewage Treatment Works
PLAYING FIELDS
ROBERT'S WOOD
SL9
ROUND ROCKET PLANTATION
QUARRY & LANDFILL SITE
MIDDLE WOOD
LYNSTERS LAKE
UB9
West Hyde
BLOOM WOOD
PYNESFIELD LAKE
GRAVEL PIT
CHALFONT ST. PETER
HOGTROUGH WOOD
Horseshoe Bay
Sailing Club
GERRARDS CROSS GOLF COURSE
LITTLE HANGING WOOD
Denham Grove
NOCKHILL WOOD
JUNIPER WOOD
THREE RIVERS
SOUTH BUCKS
HERTFORDSHIRE
BUCKINGHAMSHIRE
M25
A412
A405
DENHAM WAY
NORTH ORBITAL ROAD
73
92
113

92
74
91
114
BG
BH
BJ
BK
BL
BM
BN
SOLOMON'S WOOD
Mill End
Moneyhill
RICKMANSWORTH
CROXLEY HALL WOODS
LONG VALLEY WOOD
SPORTS GROUND
HOCKEY PLAYING FIELD
CRICKET GRD
FORTUNE COMMON
RICKMANSWORTH PARK
Batchworth Roundabout
RIVERSIDE DRIVE
BATCHWORTH LAKE
THE AQUADROME
BURY LAKE
WD3
Batchworth
RICKMANSWORTH
MOOR PARK GOLF COURSE
BATCHWORTH PARK GOLF COURSE
Moor Park Farm
Clubhouse
Batchworth Heath
STOCKER'S LAKE
STOCKER'S LAKE NATURE RESERVE
Stocker's Lock
GRAND UNION CANAL
Stocker's Farm
Mill End Pumping Sta
Froghall Farm
GARRETT WOOD
HIGH WOOD
CHALK PIT
SPRINGWELL CHALK PIT
Springwell Lock
SPRINGWELL LAKE
WOODCOCK HILL CEMETERY
Andrews Ley Farm
Juniper Dell
Greenbroom Spring
Sandfield Spring
WOODCOCK HILL INDUSTRIAL ESTATE
Pipers Farm
Bush Spring
HERTFORDSHIRE
THREE RIVERS
HILLINGDON
LONDON LOOP
COCKS WOOD
Maple Lodge Sewage Treatment Works
Filter Beds
Sludge Beds
Rose & Crown PH
LONG SPRING
PARK WOOD
Cripps House Farm
BISHOP'S WOOD
POORFIELD
LOCKWELL WOOD
PEARSON'S WOOD
Waybeards Farm
White Heath Farm
Hill End
LYNSTERS LAKE
Harefield Grove
WATTS COMMON
TAYLORS MEADOW
PARK WOOD
Nature Reserve
MOUNT PLEASANT SPORTS GRD
UB9
HAREFIELD HOSPITAL
COVERED RESERVOIR
Battlers Wells Farm
FRENCH GROVE
BATTLERS WELLS WOOD
Little Bourne Farm (Equestrian Stables)
Shepherds Hill Farm
Shepherds Hill House
HAREFIELD
FURZEFIELD
DEADMAN'S GROVE
Horseshoe Bay
Sailing Club
Black Jack's Lock
ASHAIN SPRING
SCARLET SPRING
KILN POND
CLAYPITS
DELL
RAVENERS SPRING
Shooting School
HIGHBONES
Knightscote Farm
Langley Farm
Bourne Farm
Harefield United FC
Harefield CC
0 500 yds
0 500 m

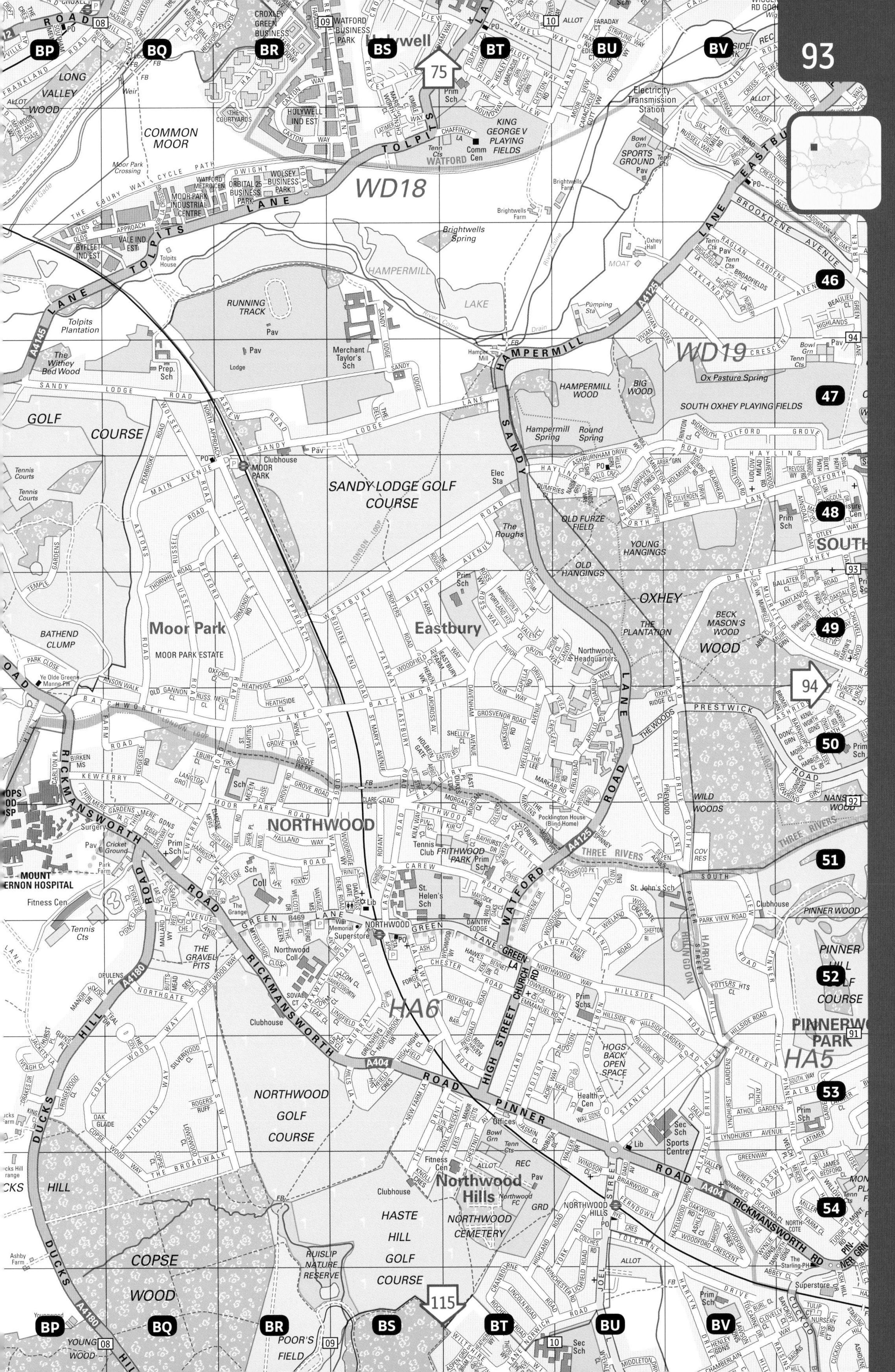
BP
BQ
BR
BS
BT
BU
BV
75
Holywell
CROXLEY GREEN BUSINESS PARK
WATFORD BUSINESS PARK
HOLYWELL IND EST
LONG VALLEY WOOD
COMMON MOOR
KING GEORGE V PLAYING FIELDS
Electricity Transmission Station
SPORTS GROUND
WD18
TOLPITS LANE
THE EBURY WAY CYCLE PATH
WATFORD METRO CEN
ORBITAL 25 BUSINESS PARK
WOLSEY BUSINESS PARK
MOOR PARK INDUSTRIAL CENTRE
VALE IND EST
BYFLEET IND EST
Tolpits House
Brightwells Spring
Brightwells Farm
HAMPERMILL LAKE
Oxhey Hall
MOAT
RUNNING TRACK
Merchant Taylor's Sch
Tolpits Plantation
The Withey Bed Wood
A4145
A4125
HAMPERMILL LANE
WD19
Ox Pasture Spring
SOUTH OXHEY PLAYING FIELDS
HAMPERMILL WOOD
BIG WOOD
Hampermill Spring
Round Spring
SANDY LODGE ROAD
GOLF COURSE
SANDY LODGE GOLF COURSE
MOOR PARK
The Roughs
OLD FURZE FIELD
YOUNG HANGINGS
OLD HANGINGS
OXHEY
THE PLANTATION
BECK MASON'S WOOD
WOOD
SOUTH
Moor Park
MOOR PARK ESTATE
Eastbury
Northwood Headquarters
BATHEND CLUMP
BATCHWORTH LANE
94
46
47
48
49
50
51
52
53
54
PRESTWICK ROAD
WILD WOODS
THREE RIVERS
NORTHWOOD
RICKMANSWORTH ROAD
MOUNT VERNON HOSPITAL
Fitness Cen
FRITHWOOD PARK
Pocklington House (Blind Home)
St. Helen's Sch
NORTHWOOD
THE GRAVEL PITS
Northwood Coll
GREEN LANE
WATFORD ROAD
PINNER WOOD
PINNER HILL GOLF COURSE
HA6
HA5
A4180
A404
PINNER ROAD
HIGH STREET
HOGS BACK OPEN SPACE
NORTHWOOD GOLF COURSE
DUCKS HILL
Northwood Hills
NORTHWOOD CEMETERY
HASTE HILL GOLF COURSE
RUISLIP NATURE RESERVE
COPSE WOOD
POOR'S FIELD
115
YOUNG WOOD
NORTHWOOD HILLS
Superstore
Sec Sch
Sports Centre

STANMORE
BUSHEY HEATH
HARROW WEALD
BELMONT
QUEENSBURY
WEALDSTONE
HA7
HA3
HA8
WD6
STANMORE COMMON
BENTLEY PRIORY OPEN SPACE
STANMORE COUNTRY PARK (NATURE RESERVE)
STANMORE GOLF COURSE
ROYAL NATIONAL ORTHOPAEDIC HOSP
SPIRE HOSPITAL
Junction 4
ELSTREE HILL OPEN SPACE
CENTENNIAL PARK
WATFORD BYPASS
ELSTREE ROAD
UXBRIDGE ROAD
LONDON ROAD
HONEYPOT LANE
BROCKLEY HILL
EDGWARE WAY
CANONS PARK
77
96
117

CL
CM
CN
CP
CQ
CR
CS
78
95
118
45
46
47
48
49
50
51
52
53
54
19
20
21
94
93
92
91
DEACONS HILL OPEN SPACE
Deacons Hill
SCRATCH WOOD
FROGHALL WOOD
BOYS HILL WOOD
THISTLE WOOD
CLUMP OF TREES WOOD
TARGET WOOD
GRAVEL PIT WOOD
MILL HILL GOLF COURSE
NUT WOOD
HEMMINGS WOOD
STONEY WOOD
STONEY WOOD LAKE
LEG OF MUTTON POND
ELSTREE OPEN SPACE
WD6
HERTSMERE
BARNET
M1
A1
A41
A410
A411
A5
A5100
A5109
A4140
BARNET LA
Stirling Corner
Stirling Retail Pk
ELSTREE PARK
ARKLEY PARK
Hyver Hall
Woodcock Hill Farm
BUPA Nursing Home
Elstree Manor
Penniwells Farm
Corus Hotel
Junction 4
London Gateway Services
Days Hotel
Bury Farm
EDGWAREBURY CEMETERY
REC GRD
SPORTS GRD
Clubhouse
EDGWAREBURY PARK
Tennis Courts
BROCKLEY HILL DRIVING RANGE
EDGWAREBURY GOLF COURSE
BROCKLEY PARK
SPORTS GROUND
Canons Corner
EDGWARE WAY (WATFORD BYPASS)
Apex Corner
NORTHWAY CIRCUS
CONVENT
STONEGROVE PARK
STONEGROVE
EDGWARE
HA8
HA7
N London Collegiate Sch
KING GEORGE V MEML GDNS
CANONS PARK
THE LAKE
THE BASIN
Broadwalk Shopping Centre
BUS STA
BUS DEPOT
Masons Arms PH
Premier Inn
CHANDOS RECREATION GROUND
PRINCE EDWARD PLAYING FIELD
HONEYPOT BUSINESS CEN
BARNET FC
EDGWARE COMMUNITY HOSPITAL
MILL YD IND EST
BURNT OAK
WATLING PARK
SPORTS GROUND
SILKSTREAM PARK
WILLIAM ELLIS SPORTS GROUND
MONTROSE PLAYING FIELDS
PUBLIC HEALTH ENGLAND COLINDALE
NHS BLOOD AND TRANSPLANT
COLINDALE
COLINDALE BUSINESS PK
CAPITOL IND PK
THE TECHNOLOGY PK
ADASTRAL ESTATE
LYNDHURST PARK
MILL HILL BROADWAY
The Flying Eagle Tavern PH
QUEENSBURY
Superstore
STA PAR
MILL HILL
MARSH
SELVAGE LANE
HALE LANE
DEANSBROOK ROAD
BURNT OAK BROADWAY
EDGWARE ROAD
HIGH STREET
STATION ROAD
HONEYPOT LANE
WHITCHURCH LANE
STONEGROVE
WATLING AVENUE
Gas Works
STANMORE MARSH
Pitch 'n' Putt
0 500 yds
0 500 m

CT
CU
CV
CW
CX
CY
CZ
22
23
24
79
Barnet Gate
Ducks Island
GRANGE PLAYING FIELDS
PLAYING FIELD
PLAYING FIELDS
OLD ELIZABETHANS (BARNET) MEMORIAL PLAYING FIELDS
Brent Lodge Farm
Dollis Brook
N20
OLD CHOLMELEIAN SPORTS GROUND
TOTTERIDGE FIELDS NATURE RESERVE
Mote End Farm
TOTTERIDGE PARK
TOTTERIDGE COMMON
A5109
TOTTERIDGE
TOTTERIDGE VILLAGE
46
47
48
49
50
51
52
53
54
93
94
92
91
HENDON PARK WOOD
HIGHWOOD HILL
Highwood Hill
HIGHWOOD PARK
Holcombe Dales
TOTTERIDGE GREEN
Consolata Missionary Coll
DARLANDS LAKE NATURE RESERVE
Folly Brook
Folly Farm
SPORTS GROUND
Clubhouses
Burtonhole Farm
SPORTS GROUND
N12
98
NW7
THE MILL FIELD
CHALET ESTATE
MARSHALL ESTATE
Mill Hill Circus
Natl Inst for Medical Research
THE RIDGEWAY
B552
Drivers Hill
Watch Tower House
Frith Manor Farm
Frith Manor Equestrian Centre
MILL HILL
ARRANDENE OPEN SPACE
Milespit Hill
Featherstone Hill
INGLIS BARRACKS
FINCHLEY GOLF COURSE
Nether Court (Clubhouse)
MILL HILL PARK
WATFORD WAY
MILL HILL CEM
BITTACY HILL PARK
Council Depot
MILL HILL EAST
Pentavia Retail Park
CHASE LODGE PLAYING FIELD
METRO GOLF RANGE
Leisure Cen
HENDON GOLF
ALLIANZ PARK STADIUM (SARACENS RFC)
Crematorium
HENDON CEMETERY
Barnet and Southgate College
Junction 2
Five Ways Corner
COPTHALL PLAYING FIELDS
COPTHALL SPORTS GROUND
COURSE
HOLDERS HILL
CHURCH END
N3
FINCHLEY CENTRAL
A1
M1
A41
A504
GREAT NORTH WAY
NW4
SUNNY HILL PARK
RAF MUSEUM
Hendon RFC
WINDSOR OPEN SPACE
Hendon Hall Hotel
HENDON
119
NW9
EAST END ROAD
REGENTS PARK

DA
DB
DC
DD
DE
DF
DG
80
97
120
45
46
47
48
49
50
51
52
53
54
EAST BARNET
OAK HILL PARK
Oak Hill College
SOUTH HERTS GOLF COURSE
N20
BROOK FARM OPEN SPACE
WYATTS FARM OPEN SPACE
KING GEORGE V PLAYING FIELDS
BARNET PLAYING FIELDS
EN4
OAKLEIGH PARK
DAME ALICE OWEN'S GRD
TOTTERIDGE LANE
VILLAGE
TOTTERIDGE GREEN
TOTTERIDGE & WHETSTONE
WHETSTONE
SWAN LANE OPEN SPACE
NORTH MIDDLESEX GOLF COURSE
BRUNSWICK PARK
MIDDLESEX UNI
BETHUNE PARK GOLF COURSE
FRIARY PARK
FRIERN BARNET
N12
WOODSIDE PARK
NORTH FINCHLEY
COPPETTS WOOD
COPPETTS CENTRE
WEST FINCHLEY
FINCHLEY MEMORIAL HOSP
GLEBELANDS OPEN SPACE
NATURE RESERVE
NORTH CIRCULAR ROAD
A406
A1000
HIGH ROAD
VICTORIA PARK
FINCHLEY
N3
FINCHLEY CENTRAL
CHURCH END
MUSWELL HILL SPORTS GROUND
COPPETTS WOOD HOSP
ST. PANCRAS & ISLINGTON CEMETERY
Crematorium
COLDFALL WOOD
N2
EAST END RD
EAST FINCHLEY
REGENTS PARK
0
500 yds
500 m

DH
DJ
DK
DL
DM
DN
DP
81
OAKWOOD
OAKWOOD PARK
YACHTING POND
WINCHMORE HILL
GROVELANDS PARK
N14
N21
N13
N11
N22
OSIDGE
SOUTHGATE
Barnet and Southgate College
PRIORY HOSPITAL
THE BOURNE
CHASE SIDE
WOODCROFT WILDSPACE
THE PAULIN GROUND
Sports Hall
CLOWES SPORTS GROUND
SOUTHGATE CEMETERY
SOUTHGATE CEMETERY
PALMERS GREEN
ARNOS PARK
NEW SOUTHGATE
BROOMFIELD PARK
HAZELWOOD SPORTS GRD
ALDERMANS HILL
CANNON HILL
GREEN LANES
HEDGE LANE
NORTH CIRCULAR ROAD
BOWES ROAD
Clockhouse Junction
BOWES PARK
TOTTENHALL SPORTS GROUND
BOUNDARY PLAYING FIELDS
FRIERN BRIDGE RETAIL PARK
ENFIELD
HARINGEY
NEW RIVER SPORTS CENTRE
ST. GEORGE'S IND EST
MUSWELL HILL GOLF COURSE
SCOUT PARK
RECREATION GROUND
WOODSIDE PARK
CEM
PLAYING FIELD
TRAIN DEPOT
WOOD GREEN
LORDSHIP LANE
NOEL PARK
REC GRD
ALEXANDRA PALACE
ALEXANDRA PALACE
ALEXANDRA PARK
SPORTS GROUND
RESERVOIR
HORNSEY WATER TREATMENT WORKS
121
THE DECORIUM
WD GRN COMMON
The Mall
BELMONT REC GRD
MUSWELL HILL
THE GROVE
HORNSEY
TURNPIKE LANE
HIGH ROAD
WESTBURY AVENUE
DOWNHILLS WAY
46
47
48
49
50
51
52
53
54
100
29
30
31
91
92
93
94

DQ
DR
DS
DT
DU
DV
DW
82
45
46
47
48
49
50
51
52
53
54
99
122
N21
N13
N9
N18
N17
N22
LOWER EDMONTON
EDMONTON
UPPER EDMONTON
TOTTENHAM
TOTTENHAM HALE
TOTTENHAM MARSHES
JUBILEE PARK
KING GEORGE'S FLD
EDMONTON CEMETERY
FIRS FARM PLAYING FIELDS
CHURCH STREET REC GRD
CHURCHFIELD REC GRD
THE PAULIN GROUND
CLOWES SPORTS GROUND
PYMMES PARK
TATEM PARK REC GRD
HOLLYWOOD GDNS
TOTTENHALL SPORTS GROUND
BOUNDARY PLAYING FIELDS
TOTTENHAM CEMETERY
BRUCE CASTLE PARK
LORDSHIP RECREATION GROUND
DOWN LANE REC GRD
EDMONTON FEDERATION CEMETERY (JEWISH)
TOTTENHAM PARK CEMETERY
MONTAGU RECREATION GROUND
WESTERN SYNAGOGUE CEMETERY
CRAIG PARK
NORTH MIDDLESEX UNIVERSITY HOSPITAL
Great Cambridge Junction
GREAT CAMBRIDGE ROAD
NORTH CIRCULAR ROAD
STERLING WAY
ANGEL ROAD
MERIDIAN WAY
HERTFORD ROAD
FORE STREET
HIGH ROAD
THE ROUNDWAY
LORDSHIP LANE
BRUCE GROVE
WATERMEAD WAY
GREEN LANES
RIDGE AVENUE
SILVER STREET
WHITE HART LANE
EDMONTON GREEN
Kenninghall
TRIUMPH TRADING EST
MOWLEM TRADING ESTATE
MILMEAD INDUSTRIAL CENTRE
TOWER GDNS
BROADWATER FARM EST
LOCKWOOD RESERVOIR
LOW MAYNARD RESERVOIR
SPORTS GRD
ALLOTMENTS
500 yds
500 m

DX
DY
DZ
EA
EB
EC
ED
36
37
38
83
102
123
46
47
48
49
50
51
52
53
54
91
92
93
94
CHINGFORD
LEE VALLEY
WILLIAM GIRLING RESERVOIR
GOLF COURSE
DEEPHAMS SEWAGE TREATMENT WORKS
Lidl UK GmbH Distribution Centre
LEE VALLEY REGIONAL PARK
THE HAWK WOOD
POLE HILL
MANSFIELD PARK
CHINGFORD
E4
RIDGEWAY PARK
FRIDAY HILL
PIMP HALL PARK
CHINGFORD MOUNT CEMETERY
CHINGFORD HATCH
LARKSWOOD PLAYING FIELDS
LARKS WOOD
JUBILEE SPORTS GRD
SOUTH CHINGFORD
CHINGFORD HALL PARK
WAR MEMORIAL REC GRD
HIGHAMS PARK
HALE END
IG8
EPPING
AINSLIE WOOD (Nat Res)
ROLLS SPORTS GRD
BANBURY RESERVOIR
MUSLIM BURIAL GROUND
FAIRWAY GOLF RANGE
BRITANNIA SPORTS GROUND
GOALS CHINGFORD
THE LONDON HOSPITAL SPORTS GRD
Crooked Billet
Cooks Ferry
Hall La
Wood Street
The Bell
E17
LLOYD PARK
HIGHAM HILL
WALTHAMSTOW
Sir George Monoux Coll
WALTHAM FOREST TRACK
CHESTNUTS SHOWGROUND
Waltham Forest Coll
THORPE COOMBE HOSP
WALTHAMSTOW FOREST
WALTHAM FOREST
UPLANDS BUSINESS PARK
HIGHAMS LODGE BUSINESS CEN
LEA VALLEY VIADUCT
NORTH CIRCULAR RD
SOUTHEND RD
NEW ROAD
HATCH LA
KINGS HEAD HILL
SEWARDSTONE ROAD
MANSFIELD HILL
OLD CHURCH ROAD
CHINGFORD MOUNT ROAD
CHINGFORD ROAD
HALL LANE
NEW ROAD
LARKSHALL ROAD
FOREST ROAD
WALTHAM WAY
MERIDIAN WAY
LEE PARK WAY
CHINGFORD GOLF COURSE

EE
EF
EG
EH
EJ
EK
EL
84
40
41
42
IG10
CHINGFORD PLAIN
QUEEN ELIZABETH'S HUNTING LODGE
A1069
RANGERS ROAD
Buckhurst Hill
THE WARREN
HATCH FOREST
CHINGFORD GREEN
WHITEHALL PLAIN
E4
WHITEHALL ROAD
FRIDAY HILL
PIMP HALL PARK
BLUEHOUSE GROVE
SPORTS GROUND
HATCH FOREST
HATCH GROVE
REED'S FOREST
HOLLY HOUSE HOSP
IG9
LORD'S BUSHES
Knighton Wood
Woodford Wells
RODING VALLEY
LUXBOROUGH LANE TREATMENT WORKS
LOUGHTON R.F.C.
SPORTS GRD
NEW ROAD
HATCH LA
WOODFORD GOLF COURSE
The Lops
WOODFORD GREEN
101
HIGHAMS PARK
THE HIGHAMS PARK
IG8
RAY PARK
ASHTON PLAYING FIELD
RUNNING TRACK
HALE END
WOODFORD R.F.C.
BROADMEAD
WOODFORD
A1009
EPPING FOREST
WALTHAMSTOW FOREST
ORCHARD EST
PLAYING FLDS
DARTNALLS PLAYING FLD
WANSTEAD Clubhouse RFC
SOUTHEND ROAD
NORTH CIRCULAR RD
Waterworks Corner
George Lane Roundabout
Charlie Brown's Roundabout
SOUTH WOODFORD
E17
E18
124
Junction
45
46
47
48
49
50
51
52
53
54
94
93
92
91
500 yds
500 m

EM
EN
EP
EQ
ER
ES
ET
85
104
125
46
47
48
49
50
51
52
53
54
43
44
45
91
92
93
94
WOOLSTON
MANOR GOLF
& COUNTRY CLUB
Rolls Park
Roundabout
ROLLS
PARK
ABRIDGE
ROAD
LANE
PUDDING LANE
River Roding
RIVERSIDE
SPORTS
GROUND
LOUGHTON
FC
Fitness
Centre
Pool
Coll
RODING LANE
CHIGWELL LANE
M11
A113
A123
A112
CHIGWELL GRANGE
Bramstones
Rodings
Pav
Fives
&
Heronians
C.C.
Old
Farm
Pettits
Hall
Burnt
House
Fulham's
Farm
Brownings
Farm
Taylor
IG7
CHIGWELL ROW
WATER WORKS
Filter
Beds
Reservoir
Settling
Tanks
Res
GRAVEL LANE
Chase Farm
Riding Stables
Miller's
Farm
CHASE LANE
CHIGWELL HALL
Chigwell
Hall
METROPOLITAN POLICE
SPORTS GRD
CEM
Sch
Prim
Sch
Rose Bridge
Oaks
Farm
Hillside
White
Ridge
COV
RES
VICARAGE LANE
GREEN LANE
LONDON LOOP
Chigwell Brook
Chigwell
Lib
Hall
CHIGWELL
New Barns
Farm
OLD
LOUGHTONIANS
HOCKEY
CLUB
Pressure
Reduction Sta
SPORTS
GROUND
Luxborough
Nursery
Chigwell
Nursery
Nursery Farm
CHIGWELL
CEMETERY
FROGHALL LANE
HIGH ROAD
HAINAULT ROAD
CHIGWELL
GOLF COURSE
Clubhouse
Sec
Sch
CONVENT OF THE
SACRED HEART
Sch
MANOR ROAD
FENCEPIECE ROAD
GRANGE
HILL
Grange Hill
LONDON
UNDERGROUND
DEPOT
LAMBOURNE ROAD
Forest
House
Sch and
Training Cen
Chig Well
(Site of)
Fairview
PLAYING
FIELD
Woodview
REC
GRD
BROCKET WAY
MANFORD WAY
Prim
Sch
Health Cen
Lib
Comm
Cen
Pol
Fire Sta
HAINAULT
P & O
Nedlloyd
ALLOT
FOREST ROAD
PLAYING
FIELD
HAINAULT
RECREATION
GROUND
Bowl
Club
ILFORD
WANDERERS
R.F.C.
FAIRLOP
OAK
PLAYING
FIELD
SPORTS
GROUND
Clubho.
Pavs
Pitches
FOREST
INDUSTRIAL
PARK
BRACKEN
INDUSTRIAL
ESTATE
Sailing
Centre
FAIRLOP
WATER
DRIVING
RANGE
IG6
FAIRLOP
WATERS
GOLF COURSE
Riding
School
PAINTERS
IG2
Aldborough
Hall Farm
ALDBOROUGH
HATCH
Menzies
Prince Regent
Hotel
Findlay House
(Guide Dogs
for the Blind)
Kennels
Pav
Cricket
Ground
Woodford Bridge
Claybury
Hall
HOSPITAL HILL
WOOD
Claybury
Woods
Hospital
Hill
EGG
CLUMP
COCKED HAT
PLANTATION
IG5
ASH
PLANTATION
RAVENSBOURNE GARDENS
COCKED HAT
PLANTATION
Clinic
Youth
Cen
Sec
Sch
CLAYHALL
TIPTREE
ESTATE
GARDEN
OF
REST
BARKINGSIDE
CEM
BARKINGSIDE
REC
GRD
BARKINGSIDE
BARNARDOS
VILLAGE
Barnardo's
SPORTS
GROUND
Sports
Cen
FAIRLOP
Fullwell
Cross
Health
Cen
Lib
Swim
Pool
Sec
Sch
HIGH ST
Old
Maypole PH
Schs
ALLOT
Sec
Sch
Prim
Sch
Forest
Farm
FOREST ROAD

Chigwell Row
IG7
HAINAULT
FOREST COUNTRY
PARK
HAINAULT
FOREST
GOLF
COURSE
Havering Park
Collier Row
Mark's Gate
RM6
IG6
RM7
ROMFORD ROAD
GRAVEL LANE
MANOR ROAD
WHALEBONE LANE NORTH
HAINAULT ROAD
FOREST ROAD
LAMBOURNE ROAD
FIVE OAKS LANE
FOX BURROW ROAD
HAINAULT LODGE NATURE RES
REDBRIDGE CYCLING CENTRE
FOREST PARK CEMETERY
GARDENS OF PEACE CEMETERY
HAINAULT BUSINESS PARK
FOREST ROAD PLAYING FIELD
HAINAULT RECREATION GROUND
SPORTS GROUND
THREE CORNERS PLAIN
SPURGATE PLAIN
TAYLOR'S PLAIN
WEDDRELL'S PLAIN
CABIN PLAIN
SANDHILLS
LOWER SANDHILLS
MILE PLANTATION
CRABTREE HILL
Dog Kennel Hill
Cabin Hill
WELLGATE COMMUNITY FARM
NORTHGATE IND PK
86
103
126
500 yds
500 m

FB
FC
FD
FE
FF
FG
FH
87
106
127
CM14
RM4
RM5
RM1
RM3
RM2
46
47
48
49
50
51
52
53
54
Nuper's Hatch
Havering-atte-Bower
HAVERING COUNTRY PARK
PYRGO PARK
FOXBURROW WOOD
BEDFORD'S PARK
Chase Cross
RISEBRIDGE GOLF COURSE
ROMFORD GOLF COURSE
RAPHAEL PARK
Gidea Park
GIDEA PARK SPORTS GRD
WEALD PARK
NOAK HILL ROAD
TYSEA HILL
BROXHILL ROAD
LOWER BEDFORDS ROAD
HAVERING ROAD
EASTERN AVENUE
MAIN ROAD
ST. FRANCIS HOSPICE
STRAIGHTS PLANTATION
PALACE PLANTATION
SANDPITS PLANTATION
WITCH HILL PLANTATION
HILLY PARK
TRENCH POND PLANTATION
SOUTH PARK PLANTATION
PHEASANT WOOD
AVENUE WOOD
BOWER WOOD
SPRING WOODS
LARCH WOOD
NURSERY WOOD
KILN WOOD
ROUND WOOD
PINE WOOD
FURRY FIELD
BIG FIELD
BEAN FIELD
EPPING FOREST
ESSEX
HAVERING
BRENTWOOD
LAWNS REC GRD
KING GEORGE'S PLAYING FIELDS
HUBBINET IND EST
Water Works
BEDFORDS LAKE
Superstore
VICTORIA

FJ
FK
FL
FM
FN
FP
FQ
45
46
47
48
49
50
51
52
53
54
105
128
PRIORS GOLF COURSE
ESSEX
BRENTWOOD
HAVERING
CURTIS PLANTATION
WABBING'S PLANTATION
SEVENACRE PLANTATION
LOCKSMITH WOOD
GOLDSMITH WOOD
Frieze Hall
The Chequers PH
Weald Bridge
Old Macdonalds Farm
Wright's Bridge
Wrightsbridge Farm
Wealdside
Rochetts Farm
St. Vincent's Hamlet
M25
RM4
Widdrington Farm
TRENCH POND PLANTATION
SPICE PITS WOOD
Spice Pits Farm
Pentowan Farm
NOAK HILL SPORTS GRD
Hill Farm
Hall
Noak Hill
THE OSIERS
BURNT WOOD
FOXBURROW
Manor Farm
FIR WOOD
DAGNAM PARK
COCK WOOD
MAYLANDS GOLF COURSE
ALDER WOOD
Havering Coll
HATTER'S WOOD
DUCK WOOD NATURE RESERVE
CENTRAL PARK
Harold Hill
LONG WOOD
SALE WOOD
Ardleigh Green Cricket Club
SHOULDER OF MUTTON WOOD
RM3
Youth Centre
Leisure Cen
Health Cen
Comm Cen
Clubhouse
Maylands
SPORTS GRD
Putwell Bridge
COLCHESTER ROAD
A12
PLAYING FIELD
Harold Park
BATES INDUSTRIAL EST
Paine's Bridge
HALL TERRACE
HAROLD HILL INDUSTRIAL ESTATE
FALCON BUS. CEN
Harold Court
Sludge Beds
Tylers Common Fishery
Roots & Shoots Garden Cen
HAROLD COURT WOODS
Gallows Corner
AVENUE INDUSTRIAL ESTATE
GIDEA PARK SPORTS GRD
HAROLD WOOD
King Harold PH
Ivy Lodge Farm
Cockabourne Bridge
Pages Farm
Riding Stables
RM14
RM2
MAIN ROAD
SOUTHEND ARTERIAL ROAD
A127
STAFFORD INDUSTRIAL ESTATE
HAROLD WOOD PARK
Harold Wood Cricket Club
PAGES WOOD
Ingrebourne Farm
Health Club
0 500 yds
0 500 m

108
109
129
CM15
CM14
CM13
WEALD
COUNTRY
PARK
BRENTWOOD
South
Weald
Brook
Street
Warley
Great
Warley
WARLEY
COUNTRY
PARK
Junction
28
BRENTWOOD BYPASS
A12
A128
A1023
B186
M25
BRENTWOOD
HAVERING
ESSEX
LONDON ROAD
BROOK STREET
HIGH STREET
SHENFIELD ROAD
INGRAVE ROAD
ONGAR ROAD
WEALD ROAD
KINGS ROAD
QUEENS ROAD
WARLEY HILL
WARLEY ROAD
EAGLE WAY
WOODMAN ROAD
HARTSWOOD ROAD
MAGPIE LANE
DARK LANE
MASCALLS LANE
NAGS HEAD LANE
GREAT WARLEY STREET
HOLE FARM LANE
BIRD LANE
WARLEY GAP
LANGTONS WOOD
FOXDOWN WOOD
HIGH WOOD
LARKINS PLAYING FIELDS
THE SPINNEY
THE PARK
BELVEDERE FIELD
LODGE FIELD
MARSH FIELD
LAKE FIELD
SOUTH WEALD LAKE
FRONT PARK
VICARAGE WOOD
LOWER VICARAGE WOOD
CLEMENT'S WOOD
LOWER BELT
BACHELOR'S WALK
TOP PLANTATION
TYLERS SHAW
JACKSONS WOOD
WORMWALK SHAW
JERMAINS WOOD
BRIDGE WOOD
TYLERS WOOD
FOXBURROW WOOD
COOMBE WOOD
WARLEY PLACE NATURE RESERVE
HOLDEN'S WOOD
ELLEN'S WOOD
RUSHY PIECE
DONKEY LANE PLANTATION
BARRACK WOOD
CEMETERY
WARLEY PLAYING FIELDS
WARLEY HILL BUSINESS PK
MARILLAC HOSPITAL
SPIRE HARTSWOOD HOSP
ESSEX NUFFIELD HOSP
BRENTWOOD LEISURE PARK
WARLEY PARK GOLF COURSE
SPORTS GROUND
SPORTS GRD
Brentwood Centre
Sawyer's Hall Farm
Langtons Farm
Calcott Hall Farm
Halfway House Farm
Tower Arms PH
Nags Head PH
Holiday Inn Brentwood
Tomlins Nursery
Mascalls
Leverton House
Leverton Hall
Boyles Court Farm
Thatchers Arms PH
Stonyhills Farm
Stonyhills House
Coombe Lodge
Foxburrows
Tooks Farm
Clap Gate Farm
Pump Farm
Warley Lea Farm
Hole Farm
Suttons Farm
Tylers Hall
Bennett's Farm
Old Vicarage
Little Warley Lodge
Clubhouse
Driving Range
FR
FS
FT
FU
FV
FW
FX
57
58
59
46
47
48
49
50
51
52
53
54
91
92
93
94

Bentley
Crow Green
Pilgrim's Hatch
CM15
WEALD COUNTRY PARK
CM14
BRENTWOOD
South Weald
Brook Street
Warley
WARLEY COUNTRY PARK
Junction 28
106
107
500 yds
500 m

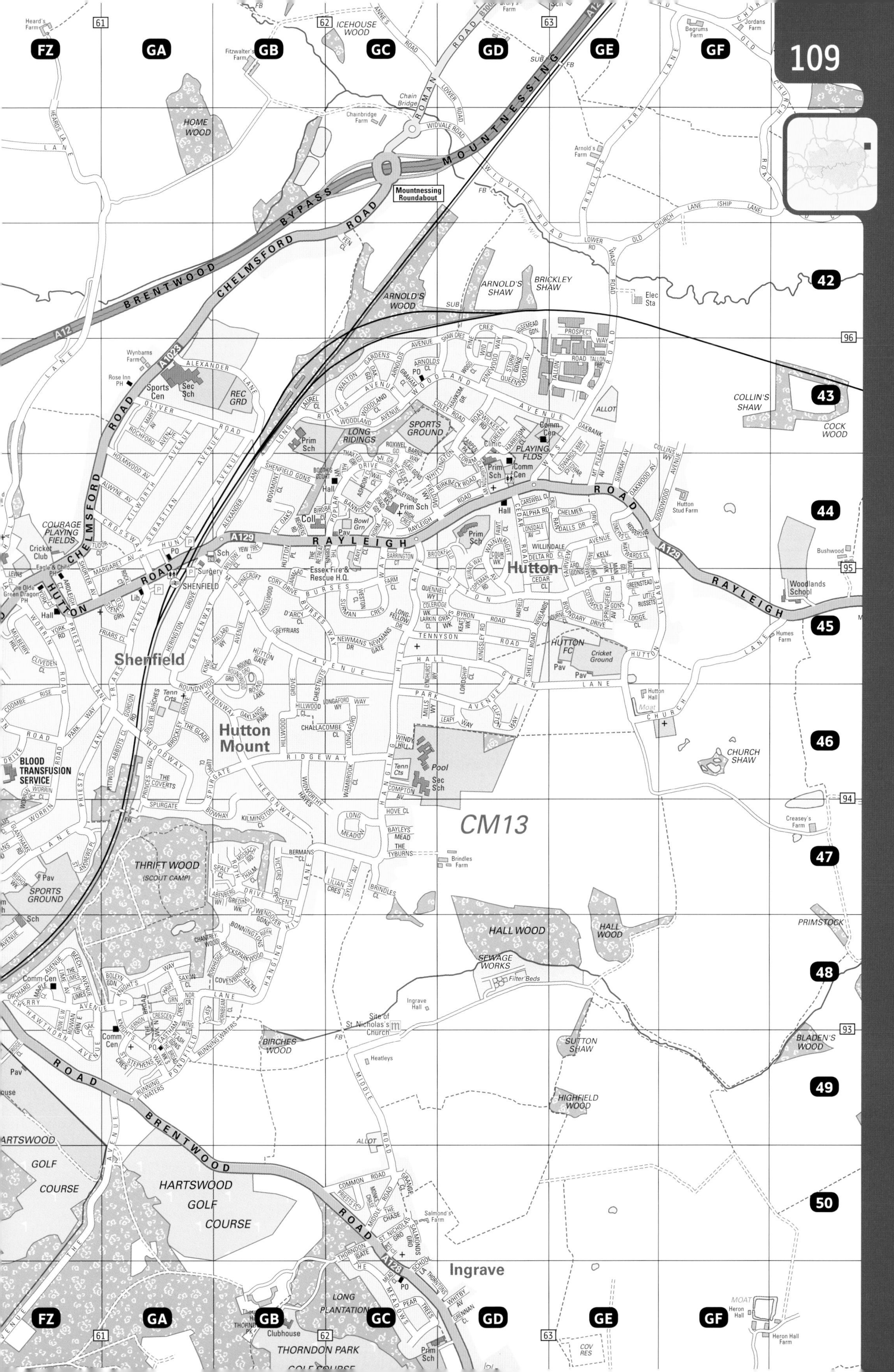
Shenfield
Hutton
Hutton Mount
Ingrave
CM13
BRENTWOOD BYPASS
MOUNTNESSING
Mountnessing Roundabout
CHELMSFORD ROAD
RAYLEIGH ROAD
HUTTON ROAD
BRENTWOOD ROAD
HOME WOOD
ICEHOUSE WOOD
ARNOLD'S WOOD
ARNOLD'S SHAW
BRICKLEY SHAW
COLLIN'S SHAW
COCK WOOD
CHURCH SHAW
THRIFT WOOD
HALL WOOD
SEWAGE WORKS
BIRCHES WOOD
SUTTON SHAW
HIGHFIELD WOOD
BLADEN'S WOOD
PRIMSTOCK
HARTSWOOD GOLF COURSE
LONG PLANTATION
THORNDON PARK
Woodlands School
Essex Fire & Rescue H.Q.
BLOOD TRANSFUSION SERVICE
COURAGE PLAYING FIELDS
SPORTS GROUND
LONG RIDINGS
Hutton FC
Cricket Ground
Heard's Farm
Fitzwalter's Farm
Chainbridge Farm
Begrums Farm
Jordans Farm
Arnold's Farm
Wynbarns Farm
Hutton Stud Farm
Bushwood
Humes Farm
Creasey's Farm
Brindles Farm
Ingrave Hall
St Nicholas's Church
Heatleys
Salmond's Farm
Heron Hall
Heron Hall Farm
Clubhouse
FZ
GA
GB
GC
GD
GE
GF
61
62
63
42
43
44
45
46
47
48
49
50
96
95
94
93

FLACKWELL HEATH GOLF COURSE
Junction 3
Holtspur
Wooburn Green
HP10
Wooburn
WOOBURN PARK
BOURNE END
SL8
WOOLMAN'S WOOD
HEDSOR PARK
BURWOOD ESTATE
SL6
SL1
LAMBOURNE GOLF COURSE
HOLLYBUSH WOOD
HEDSOR GOLF COURSE
ODDS FARM PARK
CLIVEDEN NT
Cookham
WYMERS WOOD
88
130
500 yds
500 m

AK
AL
AM
AN
AP
AQ
AR
89
HP9
SL9
SL2
Junction 2
WYCOMBE END
LONDON END
LONDON ROAD
OXFORD ROAD
A40
A355
M40
PARK LANE
Wilton Park Farm
Beaconsfield Cricket Club
SPORTS GROUND
PITLANDS WOOD
BIRCHLAND WOOD
Chiltern Woodland Burial Park
Sewage Works
LOWER PYEBUSHES
PYEBUSHES
Oak Lodge Meadows
Beaconsfield RFC
REC GRD
Royal Saracens Head
War Mem
Garden Centre
Bellhouse Hotel
Hyde Farm
Hall Barn Gardens
Beaconsfield SYCOB FC & Slough Town FC
HEDGERLEY LANE
GREEN BROOM
DUKE'S UNDERWOOD
Wapsey's Land
SAND AND GRAVEL PIT
THE GROVE
Beaconsfield Service Area
WINDSOR ROAD
CAVE WOOD
BIRCHEN SPRING COPPICE
HILL WOOD
BURTLEY WOOD
HILLMOTTS WOOD
Hillmotts Farm
HOLLYBUSH WOOD
Woodlands Farm
BOWER WOOD
Slade Farm
HILLMOTTS FURZE
HANGINGS WOOD
Downey Bottom
COMMON ROAD
BROOMHILL COPPICE
JENNINGS WOOD
SUTTON'S WOOD
Mount Pleasant Farm
HICKNAHAM PLANTATION
Jennings Farm
Dorney Bottom
112
PENNLANDS WOOD
MOLL HAYES WOOD
Hedgerley
The White Horse PH
Gas Works
Pennlands Farm
Hall
HAREHATCH LANE
KILN LANE
LITTLE WOOD
KILN WOOD
BOVENEY WOOD
HEALY'S GORSE
COLLINSWOOD ROAD
Water Tower
The Yew Tree PH
HANGING WOOD
TREETOPS CAMPSITE
Abbey Park Farm
SUMMERLINS WOOD
PARISH LANE
FOOTPATH WOOD
Hollybush Corner
BLACK GROVE
LITTLE BURNT COPPICE
Boveney Wood Farm
HEATHFIELD WOOD
PONDS WOOD
ALLOT
COV RES
STAPLEFURZE WOOD
The One Pin PH
COLLUM
The Blackwood Arms PH
SCHOOL WOOD
TWELVE ACRE WOOD
TIMBER WOOD
EGYPT WOODS
Littleworth Corner
WHITESPARK WOOD
GREAT BURNT COPPICE
NINE ACRE WOOD
Clubhouse SPORTS GRD
DORNEY WOOD
HARTLEY COURT MOAT
BEACONSFIELD ROAD
EGYPT
Prim Sch
FLEET WOOD
TOWER WOOD
BURNHAM BEECHES
INGRAM'S COPSE
BROCKHURST WOOD
LORD MAYORS DRIVE
131
Pumpkin Hill
JUNIPER GROVE
EAST BURNHAM COMMON
Farnham Common
PARSON'S WOOD
56
57
58
59
60
61
62
63
64
94
95
96

BIRCHLAND WOOD
HIGH WOOD
BEECH WOOD
BIRCH WOOD
Bellhouse Hotel
OXFORD ROAD
A40
SIBLET'S WOOD
CHANTRY WOOD
Wapsey's Wood Landfill Site
SAND AND GRAVEL PIT
FURTHER WARREN WOOD
WEST PLANTATION
SL9
BULSTRODE PARK
Bulstrode
MENAGERIE WOOD
GROVE PLANTATION
Bulstrode Camp
GERRARDS CROSS
GERRARDS CROSS COMMON
HEDGERLEY LANE
SUTTON'S WOOD
Hedgerley
LEITH GROVE
RSPB NATURE RESERVE
CHURCH WOOD
HANGING WOOD
MOUNTHILL WOOD
HEDGERLEY PARK
BLACK GROVE
DUKE'S ORCHARD
PARKSIDE CEMETERY
PICKERIDGE WOOD
TIMBER WOOD
STOKE WOOD
HAY WOOD
SL3
Fulmer
SL2
STOKE COMMON
FRAME WOOD
BROCKHURST WOOD
PENN WOOD
M40
WINDSOR ROAD
90
111
132
500 yds
500 m

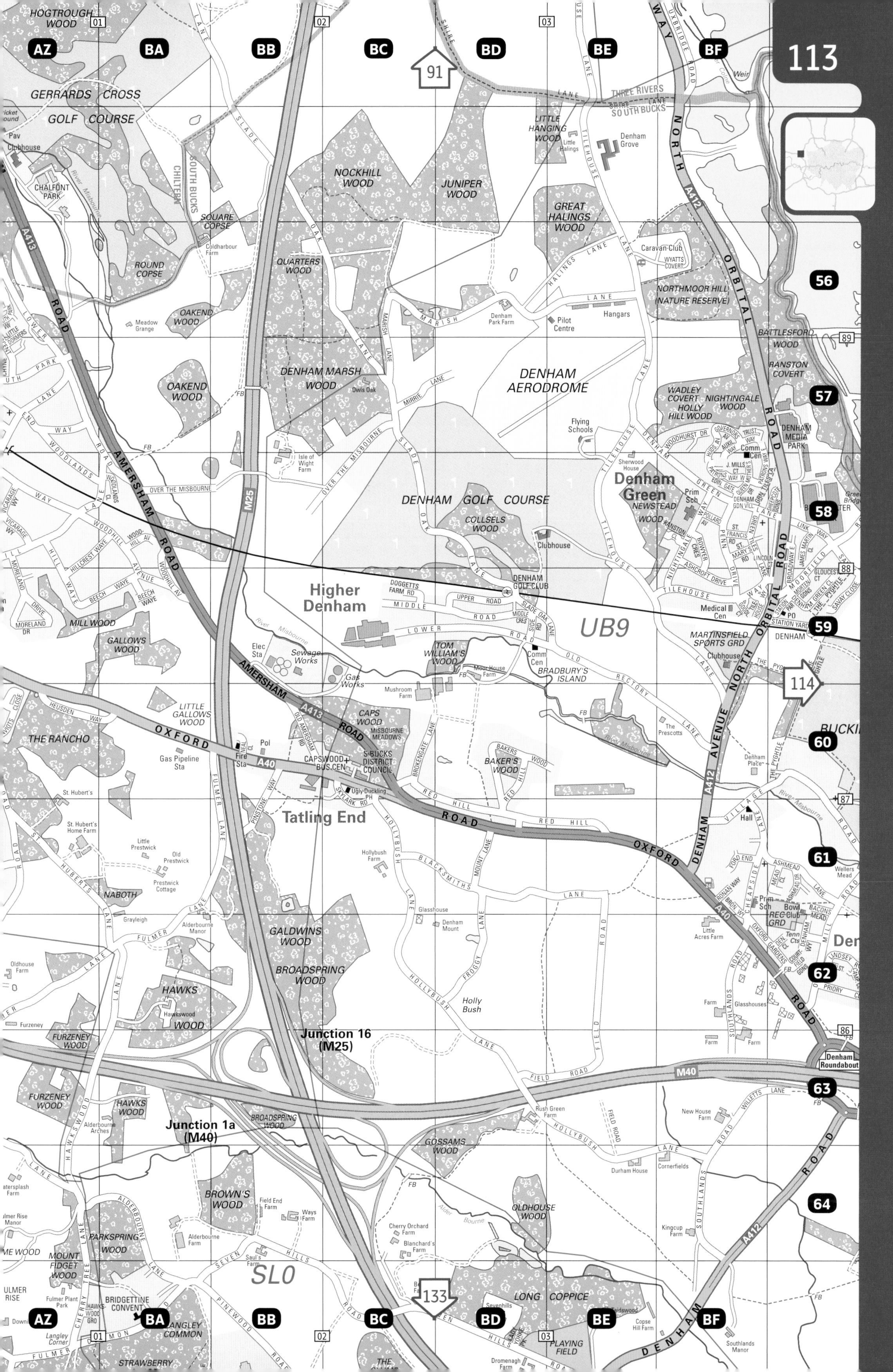
HOGTROUGH WOOD
GERRARDS CROSS GOLF COURSE
Clubhouse
CHALFONT PARK
SQUARE COPSE
Coldharbour Farm
ROUND COPSE
CHILTERN
SOUTH BUCKS
SLADE LANE
NOCKHILL WOOD
JUNIPER WOOD
LITTLE HANGING WOOD
Little Halings
Denham Grove
THREE RIVERS
SOUTH BUCKS
GREAT HALINGS WOOD
Caravan Club
WYATTS COVERT
NORTHMOOR HILL (NATURE RESERVE)
NORTH ORBITAL ROAD
A412
UXBRIDGE ROAD
Weir
QUARTERS WOOD
OAKEND WOOD
Meadow Grange
A413
AMERSHAM ROAD
MARISH LANE
HALINGS LANE
Denham Park Farm
Pilot Centre
Hangars
DENHAM MARSH WOOD
Owls Oak
MIRRIE LANE
DENHAM AERODROME
BATTLESFORD WOOD
RANSTON COVERT
WADLEY COVERT
NIGHTINGALE WOOD
HOLLY HILL WOOD
DENHAM MEDIA PARK
Flying Schools
Isle of Wight Farm
OVER THE MISBOURNE
M25
DENHAM GOLF COURSE
COLLSELS WOOD
Clubhouse
Sherwood House
Denham Green
NEWSTEAD WOOD
Prim Sch
Comm Cen
DENHAM GOLF CLUB
Higher Denham
UPPER ROAD
MIDDLE ROAD
LOWER ROAD
MILL WOOD
GALLOWS WOOD
UB9
Medical Cen
PO
STATION YARD
DENHAM
MARTINSFIELD SPORTS GRD
Clubhouse
Elec Sta
Sewage Works
Gas Works
TOM WILLIAM'S WOOD
Moor House Farm
Comm Cen
BRADBURY'S ISLAND
OLD RECTORY LANE
Mushroom Farm
The Prescotts
LITTLE GALLOWS WOOD
THE RANCHO
OXFORD ROAD
Fire Sta
Pol
Gas Pipeline Sta
A40
CAPS WOOD
MISBOURNE MEADOWS
CAPSWOOD BUS.CEN
S.BUCKS DISTRICT COUNCIL
BAKER'S WOOD
NORTH ORBITAL AVENUE
DENHAM AVENUE
Denham Place
St. Hubert's
St. Hubert's Home Farm
Ugly Duckling PH
Tatling End
RED HILL
Hall
Little Prestwick
Old Prestwick
Prestwick Cottage
Hollybush Farm
BLACKSMITHS LANE
NABOTH
Grayleigh
Alderbourne Manor
Glasshouse
Denham Mount
Prim Sch
REC GRD
Little Acres Farm
Oldhouse Farm
GALDWINS WOOD
BROADSPRING WOOD
HAWKS WOOD
Hawkswood
Furzeney
FURZENEY WOOD
Holly Bush
Junction 16 (M25)
Glasshouses
Farm
Denham Roundabout
M40
FURZENEY WOOD
HAWKS WOOD
Alderbourne Arches
Junction 1a (M40)
BROADSPRING WOOD
Rush Green Farm
New House Farm
GOSSAMS WOOD
HOLLYBUSH LANE
Durham House
Cornerfields
FIELD ROAD
WILLETTS LANE
Watersplash Farm
Fulmer Rise Manor
BROWN'S WOOD
Field End Farm
Ways Farm
Cherry Orchard Farm
Blanchard's Farm
OLDHOUSE WOOD
Kingcup Farm
SOUTHLANDS ROAD
PARKSPRING WOOD
MOUNT FIDGET WOOD
Alderbourne Farm
Saul's Farm
SEVEN HILLS ROAD
SL0
LONG COPPICE
Sevenhills
Copse Hill Farm
FULMER RISE
Fulmer Plant Park
BRIDGETTINE CONVENT
LANGLEY COMMON
Langley Corner
PINEWOOD ROAD
PLAYING FIELD
Dromenagh Farm
Southlands Manor
DENHAM ROAD
STRAWBERRY
91
114
133
AZ
BA
BB
BC
BD
BE
BF
01
02
03
56
57
58
59
60
61
62
63
64
89
88
87
86

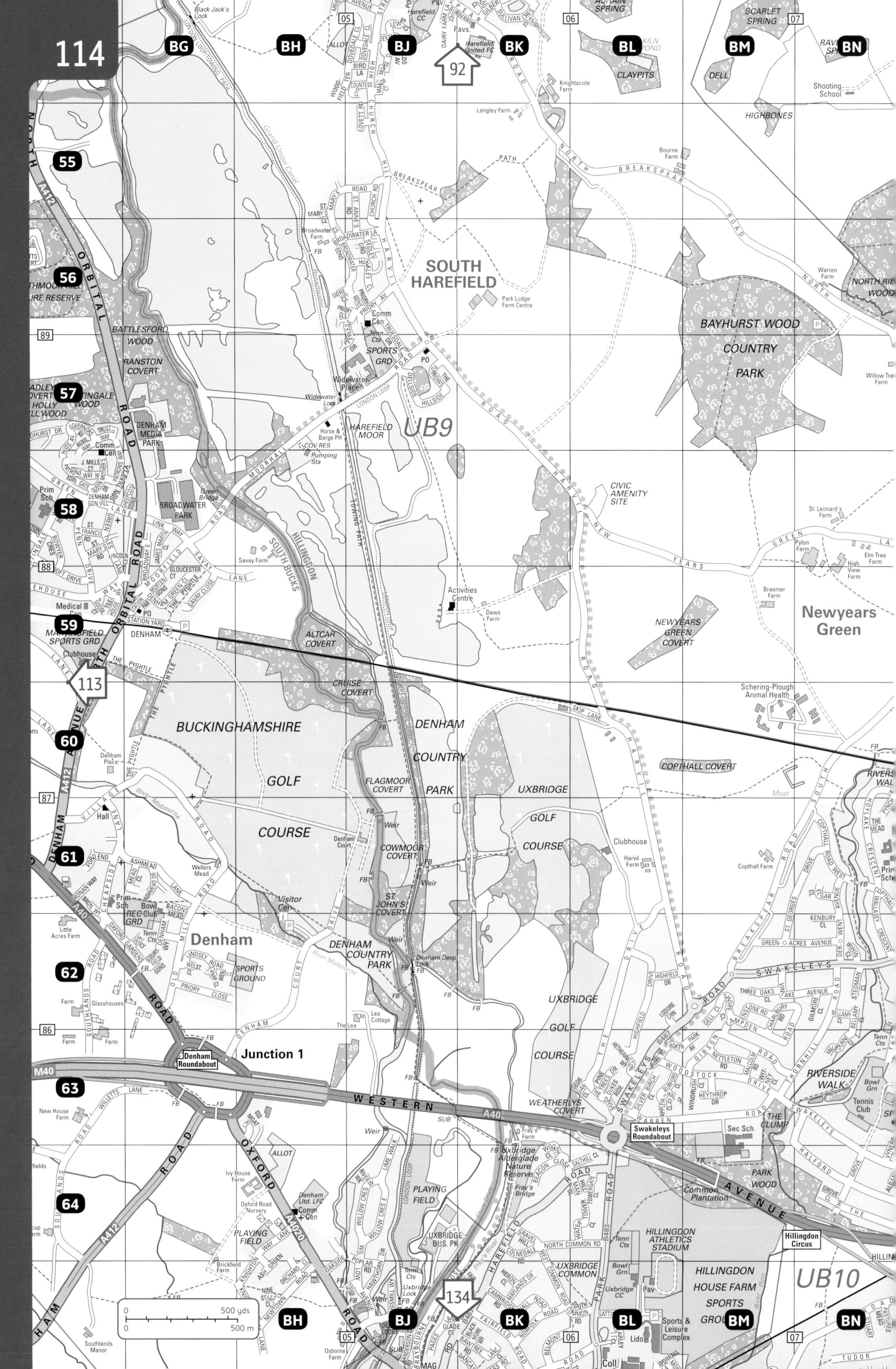
BG
BH
BJ
BK
BL
BM
BN
92
SOUTH HAREFIELD
UB9
HAREFIELD MOOR
BAYHURST WOOD COUNTRY PARK
CLAYPITS
DELL
HIGHBONES
SCARLET SPRING
Shooting School
NORTH BREAKSPEAR ROAD
BREAKSPEAR
Newyears Green
NEWYEARS GREEN COVERT
CIVIC AMENITY SITE
Activities Centre
Dews Farm
Savay Farm
SAVAY LANE
MOORHALL ROAD
HARVIL ROAD
NEW YEARS GREEN LANE
Schering-Plough Animal Health
SKIP LANE
COPTHALL COVERT
BUCKINGHAMSHIRE GOLF COURSE
DENHAM COUNTRY PARK
UXBRIDGE GOLF COURSE
FLAGMOOR COVERT
COWMOOR COVERT
ST. JOHN'S COVERT
ALTCAR COVERT
CRUISE COVERT
BROADWATER PARK
DENHAM MEDIA PARK
BATTLESFORD WOOD
RANSTON COVERT
NORTH ORBITAL ROAD
A412
Denham
DENHAM
Junction 1
Denham Roundabout
M40
WESTERN AVENUE
A40
Swakeleys Roundabout
SWAKELEYS ROAD
RIVERSIDE WALK
PARK WOOD
Common Plantation
HILLINGDON ATHLETICS STADIUM
HILLINGDON HOUSE FARM SPORTS GROUND
UB10
Hillingdon Circus
UXBRIDGE COMMON
UXBRIDGE BUS. PK
PLAYING FIELD
OXFORD ROAD
A4020
Uxbridge Alderglade Nature Reserve
WEATHERLYS COVERT
SPORTS GROUND
113
134
55
56
57
58
59
60
61
62
63
64
05
06
07
89
88
87
86
500 yds
500 m

Northwood Hills
93
COPSE WOOD
HA6
YOUNG WOOD
MAD BESS WOOD
RUISLIP NATURE RESERVE
HILL GOLF COURSE
POOR'S FIELD
RUISLIP LIDO
PARK WOOD
RUISLIP COMMON
Breakspear Crematorium
Hillingdon Borough FC
HA5
EASTCOTE VILLAGE
EASTCOTE HO GRD
Haydon Hall
Eastcote Hockey & Badminton Club
KINGS COLLEGE PLAYING FIELDS
HA4
RUISLIP
WARRENDER PARK
EASTCOTE
116
RUISLIP GOLF COURSE
DRIVING RANGE
RUISLIP MANOR
CAVENDISH REC GRD
PINE GDNS
BESSINGBY FIELD
ICKENHAM
KING GEORGE V PLAYING FIELD
MAD FIELD COVERT
NEW POND FARM FIELDS
RUISLIP GARDENS
BRAINTREE INDUSTRIAL ESTATE
ODYSSEY BUSINESS PARK
SOUTH RUISLIP
RAF NORTHOLT
Ickenham Marsh
FREEZELAND COVERT
135
HA4
SPORTS GROUND
BP
BQ
BR
BS
BT
BU
BV
08
09
10
56
57
58
59
60
61
62
63
64
89
88
87
86

BW
BX
BY
BZ
CA
CB
CC
94
115
136
55
56
57
58
59
60
61
62
63
64
MONTESOLE PLAYING FIELDS
PINNER GREEN
LITTLE COMMON
CEM
BLOOMSBURY COURT
CHISWICK COURT
Pinner Park Farm
REC GRD
CUCKOO HILL
PINNER MEMORIAL PARK
PINNER
PINNER NEW CEMETERY
Training Cen
HEADSTONE MANOR RECREATION GROUND
Harrow Mus
SPORTS GROUND
HEADSTONE
Old Lyonian Sports Club
HA5
EASTCOTE VILLAGE
PINNER VILLAGE GARDENS
The Pinner Arms
NORTH HARROW
THE CROFT PLAYING FIELD
EASTCOTE
WEST HARROW REC GRD
WEST HARROW
Streamside Reservation
ROXBOURNE PARK
RAYNERS LANE
SPORTS GRD
HA2
CAVENDISH REC GRD
PINE GDNS
BESSINGBY FIELD
RECREATION GROUND
NEWTON PARK WEST
NEWTON FM ECOLOGY PK
SOUTH HARROW
DEANE PARK
ADDISON IND EST
ALEXANDRA PARK
SOUTH RUISLIP
PLAYING FIELD
Ruislip Retail Park
Victoria Retail Park
IMPERIAL PARK
Brook Retail Park
HA4
Civic Amenity Site
ODYSSEY BUSINESS PARK
EARLSMEAD STADIUM
Harrow Borough FC
NORTHOLT RECREATION GRD
UB5
Air Traffic Radio Sta
LORD HALSBURY MEMORIAL GRD
HILLINGDON
EALING
A404
A4090
A312
B466
0 500 yds
0 500 m

CD
CE
CF
CG
CH
CJ
CK
95
117
HA7
QUEENSBURY
WEALDSTONE
WEALDSTONE CEM
HA3
KENTON
KENTON RECREATION GROUND
ST. LUKE'S HOSPICE
WOODCOCK PARK
56
57
58
59
60
61
62
63
64
HARROW & WEALDSTONE
HARROW ON THE HILL
HARROW
HA1
HARROW SCHOOL PLAYING FIELDS
NORTHWICK PARK HOSP
ST. MARK'S HOSP
University of Westminster
OLYMPIC MEDICAL INSTITUTE
NORTHWICK PARK
PRESTON
118
JOHN BILLAM SPORTS GRD
PRESTON PARK
HARROW SCHOOL GOLF COURSE
BOWDEN HOUSE
ROXETH
NORTH WEMBLEY
HA9
JOHN LYON RBT
CLEMENTINE CHURCHILL HOSPITAL
CHASEWOOD PARK
VALE FARM SPORTS GROUND
WEMBLEY COMMERCIAL CENTRE
KING EDWARD VII PARK
UB6
SUDBURY
BARHAM PARK
HA0
WEMBLEY CENTRAL
SUDBURY HILL
SUDBURY HILL HARROW
SUDBURY & HARROW ROAD
SUDBURY TOWN
SOUTH KENTON
NORTH WEMBLEY
KENTON
137
A4006
A404
A409
A312
A4005
A4088
A4090
A4089

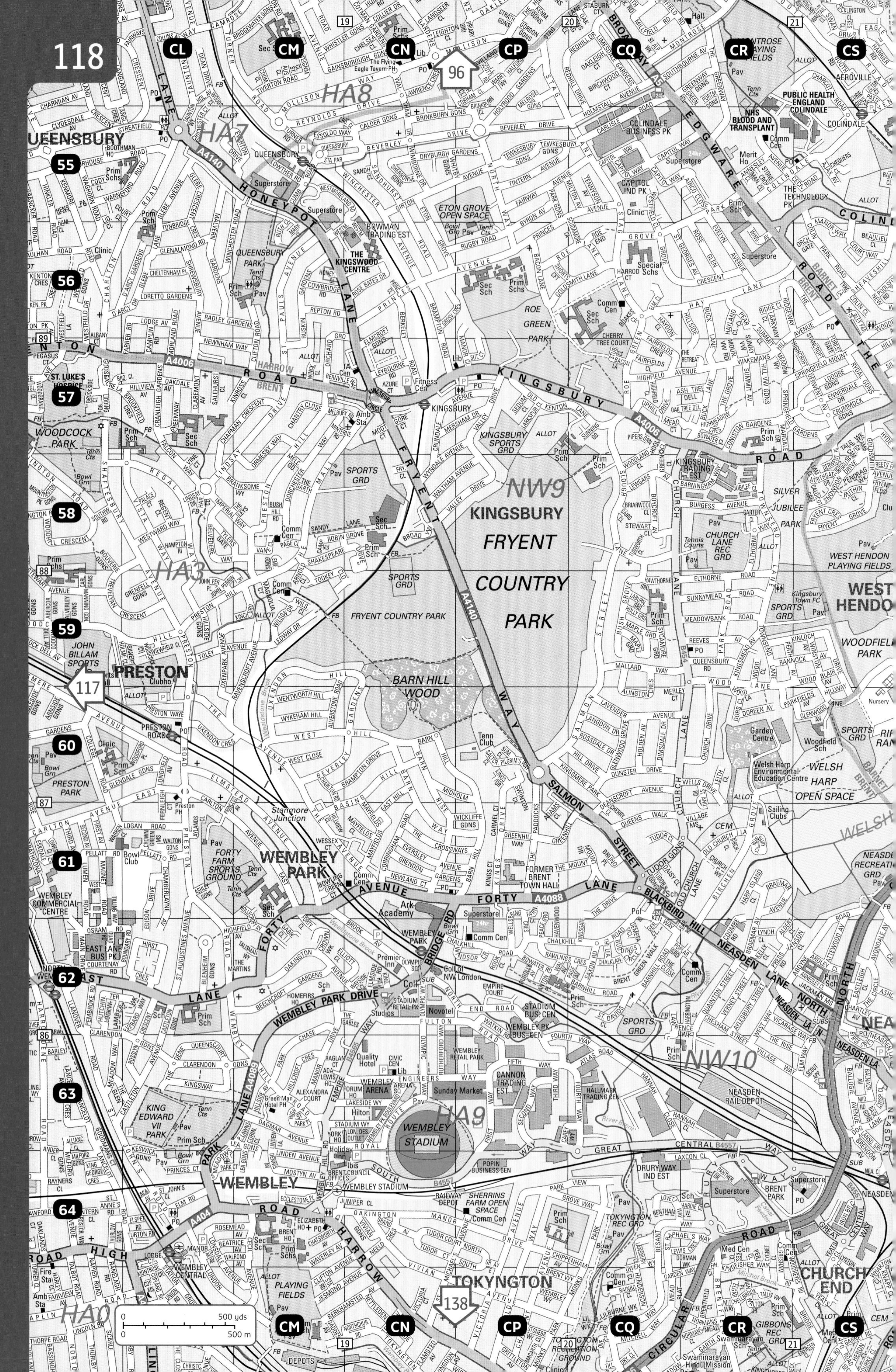
CL
CM
CN
CP
CQ
CR
CS
96
HA8
HA7
QUEENSBURY
COLINDALE BUSINESS PK
PUBLIC HEALTH ENGLAND COLINDALE
NHS BLOOD AND TRANSPLANT
CAPITOL IND PK
THE TECHNOLOGY PK
ETON GROVE OPEN SPACE
BOWMAN TRADING EST
THE KINGSWOOD CENTRE
QUEENSBURY PARK
ROE GREEN PARK
KINGSBURY
NW9
KINGSBURY FRYENT COUNTRY PARK
FRYENT COUNTRY PARK
BARN HILL WOOD
SILVER JUBILEE PARK
WEST HENDON PLAYING FIELDS
WOODFIELD PARK
WELSH HARP OPEN SPACE
Welsh Harp Environmental Education Centre
HA3
WOODCOCK PARK
ST. LUKE'S HOSPICE
JOHN BILLAM SPORTS
PRESTON
117
PRESTON PARK
WEMBLEY PARK
FORTY FARM SPORTS GROUND
WEMBLEY COMMERCIAL CENTRE
EAST LANE BUS PK
Stanmore Junction
FORMER BRENT TOWN HALL
WEMBLEY RETAIL PARK
CANNON TRADING EST
HALLMARK TRADING CEN
WEMBLEY ARENA
HA9
WEMBLEY STADIUM
STADIUM RETAIL PK
WEMBLEY PK BUS CEN
POPIN BUSINESS CEN
SHERRINS FARM OPEN SPACE
KING EDWARD VII PARK
WEMBLEY
WEMBLEY CENTRAL
TOKYNGTON
TOKYNGTON REC GRD
NW10
NEASDEN RAIL DEPOT
DRURY WAY IND EST
BRENT PARK
CHURCH END
GIBBONS REC GRD
PLAYING FIELDS
138
HA0
55
56
57
58
59
60
61
62
63
64
19
20
21
86
87
88
89
A4140
A4006
A4088
A4089
A404
A5
B4557
B4565
B455
B457
0 500 yds
0 500 m

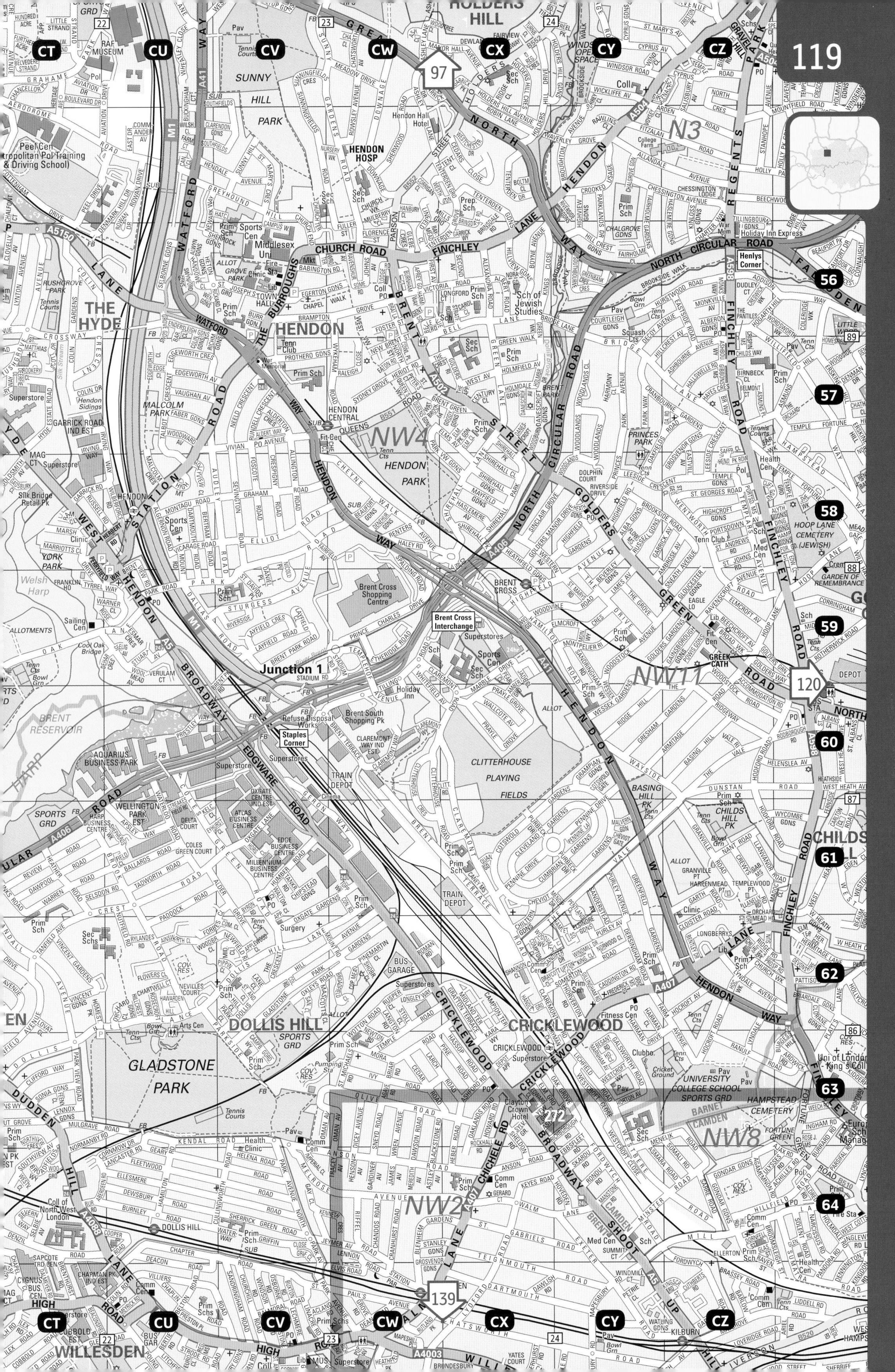
CT
CU
CV
CW
CX
CY
CZ
97
HOLDERS HILL
SUNNY HILL PARK
HENDON HOSP
N3
THE HYDE
HENDON
NW4
HENDON PARK
Henlys Corner
56
57
58
59
60
61
62
63
64
Brent Cross Shopping Centre
Brent Cross Interchange
Junction 1
Staples Corner
BRENT RESERVOIR
Welsh Harp
NW11
HOOP LANE CEMETERY (JEWISH)
GARDEN OF REMEMBRANCE
120
CLITTERHOUSE PLAYING FIELDS
CHILDS HILL
DOLLIS HILL
GLADSTONE PARK
CRICKLEWOOD
HAMPSTEAD CEMETERY
NW8
NW2
139
WILLESDEN
KILBURN
NORTH CIRCULAR ROAD
HENDON WAY
EDGWARE ROAD
FINCHLEY ROAD
WATFORD WAY

DA
DB
DC
DD
DE
DF
DG
98
26
27
28
55
56
57
58
59
60
61
62
63
64
88
89
87
86
119
140
273
274
N3
N2
N6
NW11
NW3
NORTH CIRCULAR ROAD
EAST END RD
EAST FINCHLEY CEMETERY
Crematorium
EAST FINCHLEY
FORTIS GREEN
COLDFALL WOOD
HIGHGATE WOOD
ST.LUKE'S WOODSIDE HOSPITAL
Henlys Corner
Holiday Inn Express
FALLODEN WAY
LYTTELTON ROAD
AYLMER ROAD
GREAT NORTH ROAD
ARCHWAY
LITTLE WOOD
BIG WOOD
HAMPSTEAD GARDEN SUBURB
HIGHGATE GOLF COURSE
Clubhouse
HOOP LANE CEMETERY (JEWISH)
GARDEN OF REMEMBRANCE
GOLDERS GREEN
HAMPSTEAD HEATH EXTENSION
HAMPSTEAD GOLF COURSE
Bunkers Hill
TURNERS WOOD
NORTH WOOD
Kenwood House
KENWOOD
HAMPSTEAD HEATH
SANDY HEATH
NORTH END ROAD
GOLDERS HILL PARK
CHILDS HILL
WEST HEATH
HEATHLANDS
QUEEN MARY'S HOSP
PARLIAMENT HILL
HIGHGATE PONDS
HIGHGATE MEN'S POND
KENWOOD LADIES POND
HAMPSTEAD PONDS
ATHLETICS TRACK
HAMPSTEAD
ROYAL FREE HOSP
WEST HAMPSTEAD
HAMPSTEAD CEMETERY
FINCHLEY ROAD
HAVERSTOCK HILL
ROSSLYN HILL
HENDON WAY
REGENTS PARK ROAD
MAITLAND PARK ESTATE
ST. DOMINIC'S PRIORY
LISMORE CIRCUS
BELSIZE SQUARE
FINCHLEY ROAD & FROGNAL
WEST HAMPSTEAD (THAMESLINK)
O2 Centre
European Sch of Management
Uni of London King's Coll
BARNET
CAMDEN
HARINGEY
0 500 yds
0 500 m

DH
DJ
DK
DL
DM
DN
DP
99
NOEL PARK
ALEXANDRA PALACE
ALEXANDRA PARK
N22
MUSWELL HILL
HORNSEY
SPORTS GROUND
HORNSEY WATER TREATMENT WORKS
PRIORY PARK
N8
CROUCH END PLAYING FIELDS
QUEEN'S WOOD
HARRINGAY
CROUCH END
STROUD GREEN
STATIONERS PARK
ALLOTMENTS
SPORTS GRD
FINSBURY PARK
N4
AMERICAN GDNS
HARRINGAY GREEN LANES
RAILWAY FLDS
WHITTINGTON HOSPITAL
WATERLOW PARK
HIGHGATE CEMETERY
N19
UPPER HOLLOWAY
WHITTINGTON PARK
DARTMOUTH PARK
TUFNELL PARK
HOLLOWAY
N7
H.M. PRISON HOLLOWAY
LOWER HOLLOWAY
EMIRATES STADIUM ARSENAL FC
N5
HIGHBURY
HIGHBURY FIELDS
KENTISH TOWN
NW5
PENTONVILLE PRISON
CANONBURY
NATURE RESERVE
HOLLOWAY ROAD
SEVEN SISTERS ROAD
CAMDEN ROAD
CALEDONIAN ROAD
ARCHWAY ROAD
HORNSEY ROAD
CROUCH HILL
GREEN LANES
HIGH ROAD
PARK ROAD
TOTTENHAM LANE
PRIORY ROAD
JUNCTION ROAD
BRECKNOCK ROAD
122
141
56
57
58
59
60
61
62
63
64
275
276
29
30
31

DQ
DR
DS
DT
DU
DV
DW
100
33
34
35
LORDSHIP RECREATION GROUND
N22
N17
N15
N16
N4
N5
E5
E8
BELMONT REC GRD
WEST GREEN
DOWNHILLS PARK
BRUCE GROVE
DOWN LANE REC GRD
TOTTENHAM HALE
TOTTENHAM MARSHES
LOCKWOOD RESERVOIR
MILMEAD INDUSTRIAL CENTRE
LOCKWOOD INDUSTRIAL PARK
LEE VALLEY TECHNOPARK
MONUMENT WAY
FERRY LANE
Tottenham Hale Retail Park
THE HIGH CROSS CENTRE
LOW MAYNARD RESERVOIR
Walthamstow Wetlands Nature Park
TOWN HALL
BROAD LANE
SEVEN SISTERS
Seven Sisters
CHESTNUTS PARK
ST ANN'S HOSPITAL
SOUTH TOTTENHAM
MARKFIELD REC GRD
Markfield Beam Engine
RESERVOIR NUMBER TWO
RESERVOIR NUMBER ONE
RESERVOIR NUMBER THREE
WARWICK RESERVOIR EAST
WARWICK RESERVOIR WEST
COPPERMILL PLAYING FIELD
LEE VALLEY REGIONAL
HARRINGAY GREEN LANES
Arena Shopping Park
Baseball Ground
WOODBERRY DOWN ESTATE
Skinners' Acad
FINSBURY
MANOR HOUSE
121
EAST RESERVOIR
WEST RESERVOIR
AMHURST PARK
STAMFORD HILL
SPRINGHILL SPORTS GRD
SPRINGFIELD PARK
CLAPTON COMMON
Walthamstow Marsh Nature Reserve
STAMFORD HILL ESTATE
GUINNESS TRUST EST
UPPER CLAPTON
ABNEY PARK CEMETERY
STOKE NEWINGTON
CLISSOLD PARK
SPORTS GROUND
KINGS CRES ESTATE
NORTHWOLD ESTATE
NORTH MILLFIELDS RECREATION GROUND
SOUTH MILLFIELDS
SHACKLEWELL
HACKNEY DOWNS
277
278
HIGHBURY
Uni-Met Lon.
Petchey Academy
HACKNEY DOWNS
DALSTON KINGSLAND
DALSTON JUNCTION
HACKNEY CENTRAL
KINGSLAND
HACKNEY
142
HIGHBURY & ISLINGTON
BALLS POND ROAD
DALSTON LANE
GRAHAM ROAD
500 yds
500 m
55
56
57
58
59
60
61
62
63
64
86
87
88
89

DX
DY
DZ
EA
EB
EC
ED
101
HIGHAM HILL
LLOYD PARK
WALTHAMSTOW
UPPER WALTHAMSTOW
E17
THORPE COOMBE HOSP
Blackhorse Road
The Bell
Wood Street
Whipps Cross
WHIPPS CROSS UNIVERSITY HOSPITAL
WALTHAMSTOW CEM
ST. JAMES'S PARK
LOW HALL SPORTS GROUND
LEYTON IND VILLAGE
LEYTONSTONE
E10
LEYTON
LEYTON ORIENT FC
ST. PATRICK'S RC CEMETERY
THE WATERWORKS NATURE RESERVE
LEE VALLEY PITCH & PUTT GOLF COURSE
SEYMOUR ROAD PLAYING FIELD
LAYTON JUBILEE PARK
TEMPLE MILLS DEPOT
New Spitalfields Market
HACKNEY MARSH
LEE VALLEY REGIONAL PARK
LEA BRIDGE
LOWER CLAPTON
CLAPTON PARK
HOMERTON
HACKNEY WICK
E9
E15
E20
WICK WOODLAND
Lea Interchange
BMX Track
Lee Valley VeloPark
QUEEN ELIZABETH OLYMPIC PARK
EAST VILLAGE
STRATFORD INTERNATIONAL
STRATFORD
143
124
279
280
56
57
58
59
60
61
62
63
64

SOUTH WOODFORD
EPPING FOREST
E18
SNARESBROOK
WHIPPS CROSS UNIVERSITY HOSPITAL
LEYTONSTONE
E11
WANSTEAD
WANSTEAD FLATS
WANSTEAD PARK
WANSTEAD GOLF COURSE
ALDERSBROOK
CITY OF LONDON CEMETERY
MANOR PARK
MANOR PARK CEMETERY
WEST HAM CEMETERY
FOREST GATE
E15
E7
IG4
SPIRE RODING HOSP
RODING VALLEY PARK
Junction 4
Charlie Brown's Roundabout
Redbridge Roundabout
Waterworks Corner
Whipps Cross
Snaresbrook Crown Court
Eastern Avenue
North Circular Road
Woodford New Road
Hollybush Hill
Hermon Hill
Blake Hall Road
Aldersbrook Road
Romford Road
Woodgrange Road
Leytonstone Road
High Road
Green Man Roundabout
Woodgrange Park Cemetery
Plashet Jewish Cemetery
Jewish Cemetery
102
123
144
281
EE EF EG EH EJ EK EL
55 56 57 58 59 60 61 62 63 64
0 500 yds
0 500 m

EM
EN
EP
EQ
ER
ES
ET
103
CLAYHALL
IG5
GARDEN OF REST
BARKINGSIDE CEM
BARKINGSIDE
BARNARDOS VILLAGE
FAIRLOP WATERS
GOLF COURSE
DRIVING RANGE
IG6
ALDBOROUGH HATCH
GANTS HILL
NEWBURY PARK
EASTERN AVENUE
WOODFORD AVENUE
CRANBROOK ROAD
IG2
VALENTINES PARK
MELBOURNE FIELD
SEVEN KINGS
SEVEN KINGS PARK
FORD'S SPORTS GROUND
NE LONDON TREATMENT CENTRE
126
CRANBROOK
IG1
IG3
ILFORD
SOUTH PARK
LOXFORD PARK
LOXFORD
LITTLE ILFORD PARK
BARKING PARK
E12
145
56
57
58
59
60
61
62
63
64

EU
EV
EW
EX
EY
EZ
FA
104
Mark's Gate
47
48
49
55
56
57
58
59
60
61
62
63
64
89
88
87
86
125
146
IG2
IG3
IG11
RM6
RM8
RM9
EASTERN AVENUE
A12
KING GEORGE HOSPITAL
GOODMAYES HOSPITAL
NE LONDON TREATMENT CENTRE
Redbridge College
CHADWELL HEATH
CHADWELL HEATH CEM
GOODMAYES
GOODMAYES PARK
BECONTREE
VALENCE PARK
PARSLOES PARK
MAYESBROOK PARK
KINGS PARK
WESTLANDS PLAYING FIELDS
WEST HAM UNITED FC TRAINING GROUND
CRANFIELD GOLF CENTRE
MIRRAVALE TRADING ESTATE
ELDENWALL ESTATE
CHADWELL HEATH IND PARK
NEWTON IND EST
WHALEBONE LANE NORTH
WHALEBONE LANE SOUTH
HIGH ROAD
LONGBRIDGE ROAD
GREEN LANE
WOOD LANE
HEATHWAY
PAINTERS ROAD
BILLET ROAD
World War II Gun Emplacements
Becontree Heath
500 yds
500 m

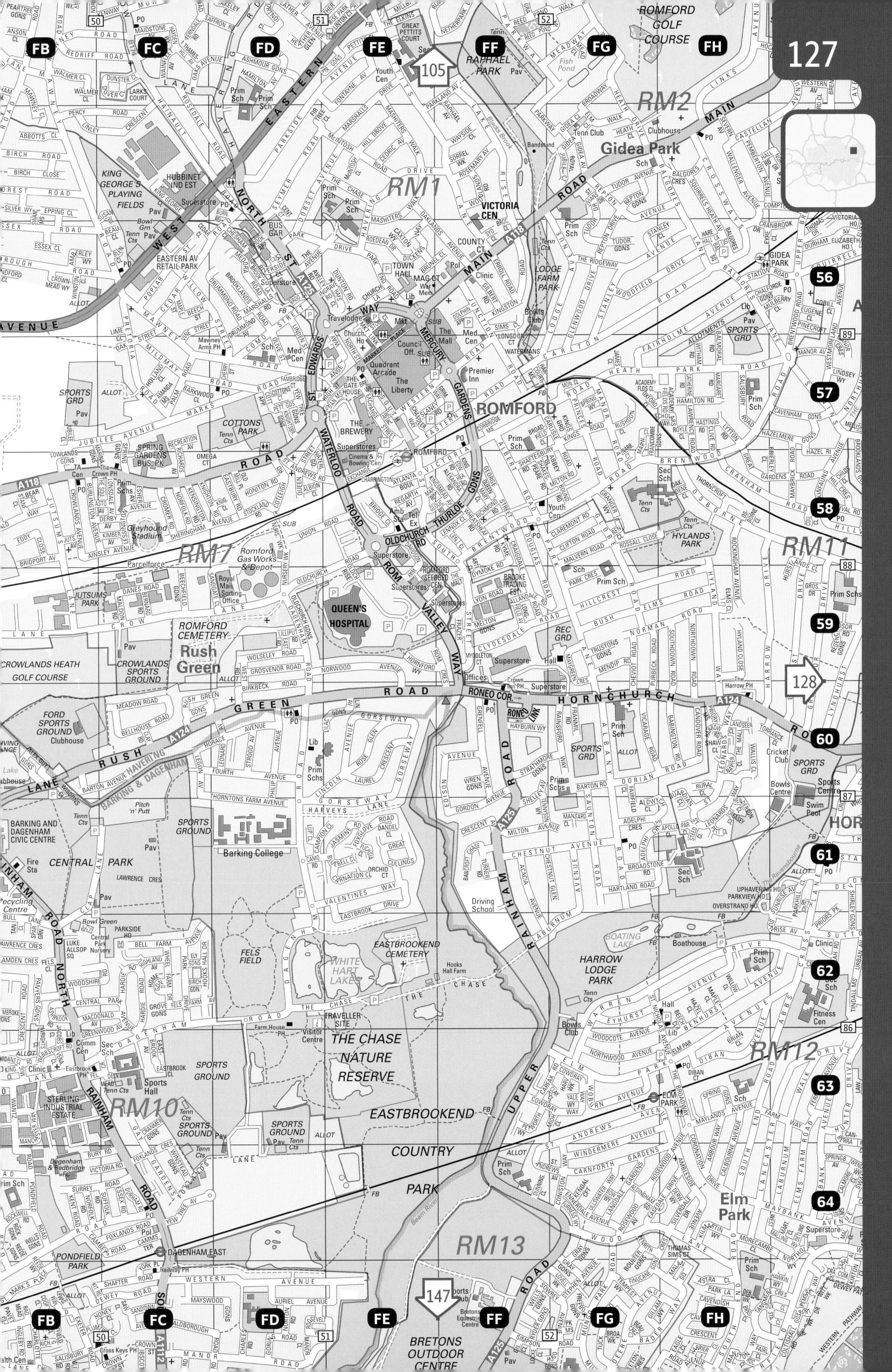
FB
FC
FD
FE
FF
FG
FH
105
ROMFORD GOLF COURSE
RAPHAEL PARK
RM2
Gidea Park
RM1
VICTORIA CEN
KING GEORGE'S PLAYING FIELDS
HUBBINET IND EST
EASTERN AV RETAIL PARK
WEST AVENUE
NORTH ST
MAIN ROAD
LODGE FARM PARK
GIDEA PARK
56
57
58
59
60
61
62
63
64
ROMFORD
COTTONS PARK
THE BREWERY
Quadrant Arcade
The Liberty
The Mall
ROMFORD
SPRING GARDENS BUS PK
Greyhound Stadium
RM7
Romford Gas Works & Depot
JUTSUMS PARK
QUEEN'S HOSPITAL
RM11
HYLANDS PARK
128
ROMFORD CEMETERY
Rush Green
CROWLANDS HEATH GOLF COURSE
CROWLANDS SPORTS GROUND
FORD SPORTS GROUND
RUSH GREEN ROAD
RONEO COR.
HORNCHURCH ROAD
BARKING AND DAGENHAM CIVIC CENTRE
CENTRAL PARK
Barking College
FELS FIELD
EASTBROOKEND CEMETERY
WHITE HART LAKES
HARROW LODGE PARK
BOATING LAKE
THE CHASE NATURE RESERVE
EASTBROOKEND COUNTRY PARK
RM10
STERLING INDUSTRIAL ESTATE
RM12
ELM PARK
Elm Park
RAINHAM ROAD NORTH
UPPER RAINHAM ROAD
RM13
PONDFIELD PARK
DAGENHAM EAST
147
BRETONS OUTDOOR CENTRE
50
51
52

128
HAROLD WOOD
106
RM3
PAGES WOOD
RM2
Ardleigh Green
Emerson Park
RM11
127
UPMINSTER GOLF COURSE
HORNCHURCH
UPMINSTER
RM12
GAYNES PARKWAY
ST. GEORGES HOSPITAL
Hacton
Elm Park
Corbets Tey
148
SOUTHEND ARTERIAL ROAD
A127
HIGH STREET
UPMINSTER ROAD
A124
ST. MARY'S LANE
Havering College of Further Educ
ST. MARY'S CONVENT
ST. ANDREW'S PARK
HORNCHURCH CEM
HORN-CHURCH STADIUM
UPMINSTER PARK
PARKLANDS OPEN SPACE
ELLIOT PLAYING FIELDS
FJ
FK
FL
FM
FN
FP
FQ
55
56
57
58
59
60
61
62
63
64
500 yds
500 m

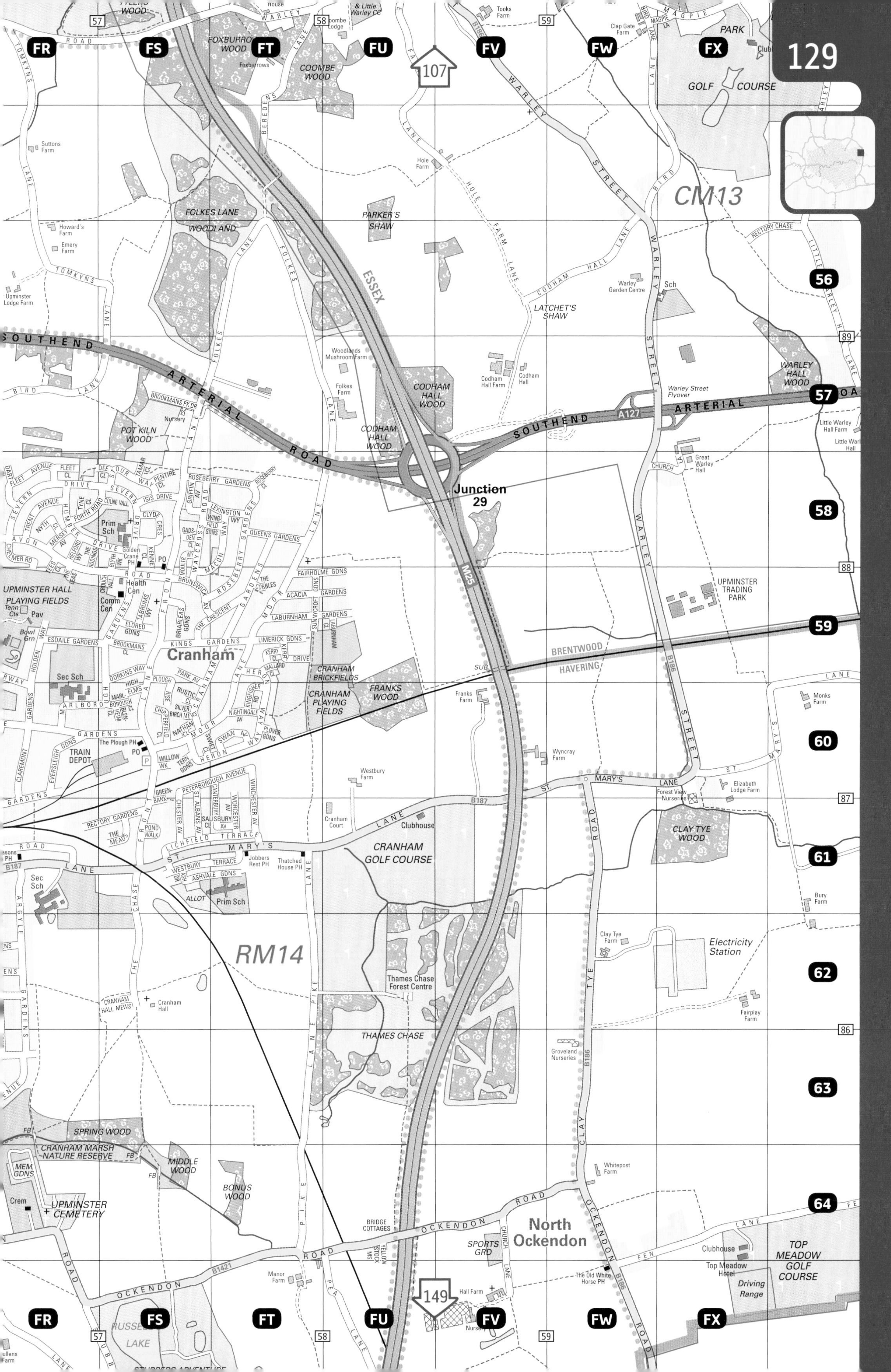

Cranham
North Ockendon
CM13
RM14
Junction 29
ESSEX
M25
A127
SOUTHEND ARTERIAL ROAD
WARLEY STREET
ST. MARY'S LANE
OCKENDON ROAD
CLAY TYE ROAD
PIKE LANE
FOLKES LANE
BRENTWOOD
HAVERING
FOXBURROWS WOOD
COOMBE WOOD
FOLKES LANE WOODLAND
PARKER'S SHAW
LATCHET'S SHAW
CODHAM HALL WOOD
POT KILN WOOD
WARLEY HALL WOOD
GOLF COURSE
UPMINSTER HALL PLAYING FIELDS
UPMINSTER TRADING PARK
CRANHAM BRICKFIELDS
CRANHAM PLAYING FIELDS
FRANKS WOOD
CLAY TYE WOOD
CRANHAM GOLF COURSE
Electricity Station
Thames Chase Forest Centre
THAMES CHASE
SPRING WOOD
CRANHAM MARSH NATURE RESERVE
MIDDLE WOOD
BONUS WOOD
UPMINSTER CEMETERY
TOP MEADOW GOLF COURSE
Driving Range
RUSSELL LAKE
FR FS FT FU FV FW FX
56 57 58 59 60 61 62 63 64
107
149

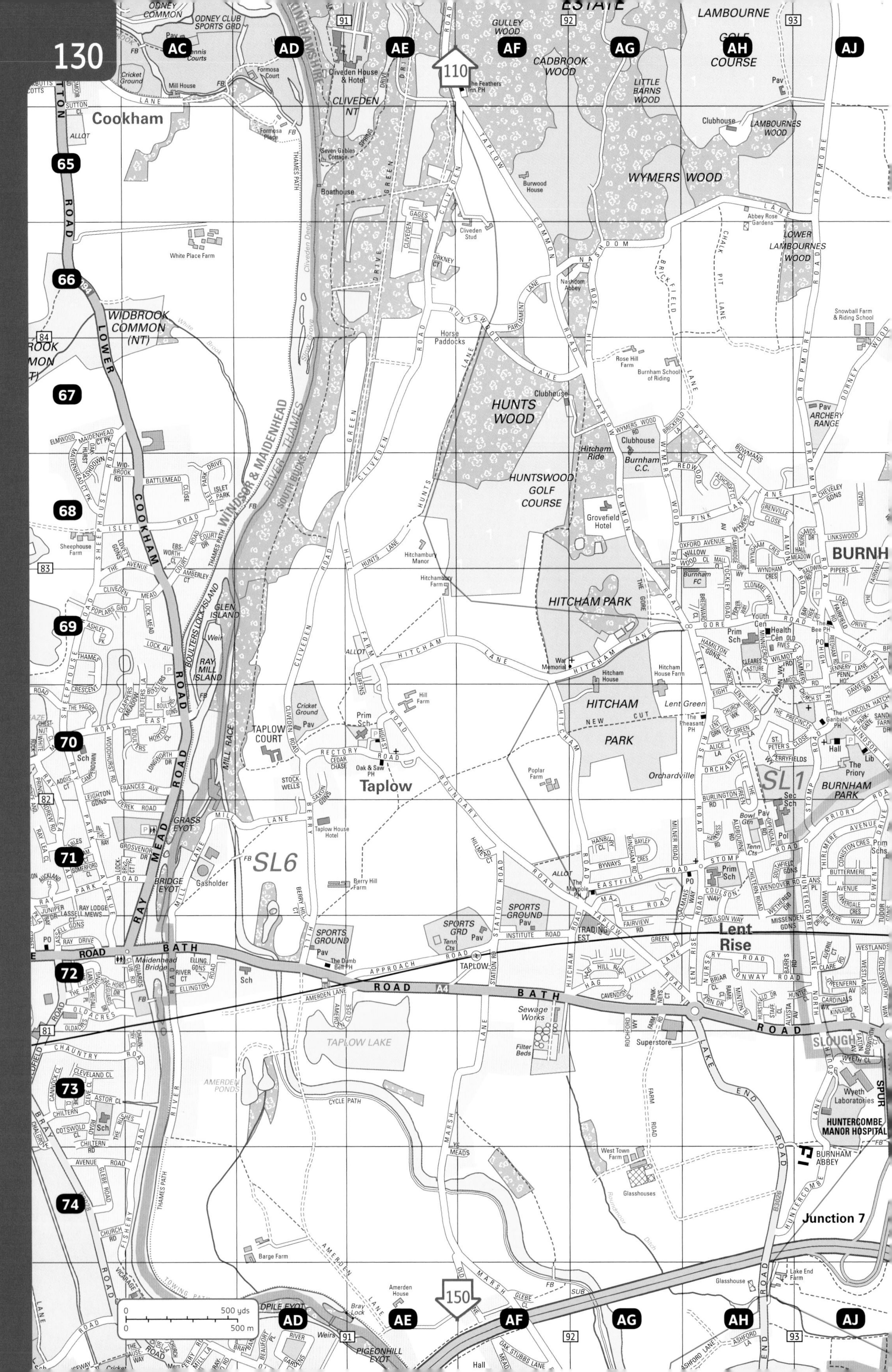
AC
AD
AE
AF
AG
AH
AJ
110
150
91
92
93
84
83
82
81
65
66
67
68
69
70
71
72
73
74
ODNEY COMMON
ODNEY CLUB SPORTS GRD
Tennis Courts
Cricket Ground
Mill House
Formosa Court
Formosa Place
Cookham
ALLOT
Cliveden House & Hotel
CLIVEDEN NT
Seven Gables Cottage
Boathouse
The Feathers Inn PH
GULLEY WOOD
CADBROOK WOOD
LAMBOURNE GOLF COURSE
LITTLE BARNS WOOD
Clubhouse
LAMBOURNES WOOD
WYMERS WOOD
Burwood House
Abbey Rose Gardens
LOWER LAMBOURNES WOOD
White Place Farm
Cliveden Stud
GAGES
ORKNEY CT
Nashdom Abbey
NASHDOM LANE
CHALK PIT LANE
BRICKFIELD LANE
DROPMORE ROAD
Snowball Farm & Riding School
WIDBROOK COMMON (NT)
White Brook
Horse Paddocks
HUNTSWOOD LANE
PARLIAMENT LANE
Rose Hill Farm
Burnham School of Riding
HUNTS WOOD
Clubhouse
ARCHERY RANGE
Pav
LOWER COOKHAM ROAD
WINDSOR & MAIDENHEAD
SOUTH BUCKS
RIVER THAMES
THAMES PATH
ELMWOOD
MAIDENHEAD CT PK
BATTLEMEAD CLOSE
ISLET PARK DRIVE
ISLET ROAD
Sheephouse Farm
SHEEPHOUSE ROAD
Hitcham Ride
Burnham C.C.
HUNTSWOOD GOLF COURSE
Grovefield Hotel
POYLE LANE
BOWMANS CL
REDWOOD
PINK LANE
CHEVELEY GDNS
BURNH
OXFORD AVENUE
Burnham FC
HITCHAM PARK
Hitchambury Manor
Hitchambury Farm
HUNTS LANE
GLEN ISLAND
BOULTERS LOCK ISLAND
Weir
RAY MILL ISLAND
MILL RACE
GORE ROAD
Prim Sch
Health Cen
Youth Cen
The Bee PH
ALLOT
HITCHAM LANE
War Memorial
Hitcham House
Hitcham House Farm
HITCHAM PARK
NEW CUT
Lent Green
The Pheasant PH
The Garibaldi PH
Hall
Lib
The Priory
Hill Farm
Cricket Ground
TAPLOW COURT
Prim Sch
RECTORY ROAD
Oak & Saw PH
Taplow
Poplar Farm
Orchardville
SL1
BURNHAM PARK
Sec Sch
Pol
Prim Schs
SL6
GRASS EYOT
BRIDGE EYOT
Gasholder
Taplow House Hotel
Berry Hill Farm
RAY MEAD ROAD
BOUNDARY ROAD
The Maypole PH
EASTFIELD ROAD
Prim Sch
PO
SPORTS GROUND
SPORTS GRD
Tenn Cts
TRADING EST
Lent Rise
BATH ROAD
Maidenhead Bridge
The Dumb Bell PH
TAPLOW
APPROACH ROAD
A4
Sch
Sewage Works
Filter Beds
Superstore
SLOUGH
TAPLOW LAKE
AMERDEN PONDS
CYCLE PATH
Wyeth Laboratories
HUNTERCOMBE MANOR HOSPITAL
BURNHAM ABBEY
West Town Farm
Glasshouses
Roundmoor Ditch
MARSH LANE
Junction 7
Barge Farm
Amerden House
Glasshouse
Lake End Farm
TOWING PATH
Bray Lock
Weirs
PIGEONHILL EYOT
500 yds
500 m
Hall
OAK STUBBS LANE

AK
AL
AM
AN
AP
AQ
AR
111
BURNHAM
BEECHES
EAST BURNHAM
COMMON
Ingram's Copse
Farnham Common
Parson's Wood
Old Orchard Wood
Dorneywood House
Pumpkin Hill
Seven Ways Plain
Juniper Grove
Hawthorn Dell
BURNHAM
BEECHES
GOLF
COURSE
Fox Den
Clubhouse
Thompkins Wood
SL2
East Burnham
Kennedy's Garden Centre
Lock's Bottom
Civic Amenity Site
East Burnham Park
Farnham Common Nursery
Farnham Park Farm
FARNHAM PARK
GOLF
COURSE
Clubhouses
FARNHAM
PARK
Farnham Royal
Burnham Beeches Hotel
Grove Wood
Cherry Orchard Nature Park
George Pitcher Memorial Rec Grd
Deepwood
SOUTH BUCKS
Cocksherd Wood
STOKE
PARK
GOLF
COURSE
Sports Centre
Tennis Courts
Stoke Park Club
132
Britwell Estate
KENNEDY PARK
Manor Park
BUCKINGHAMSHIRE
Haymill Valley
Mars Ltd
Slough Heat & Power
SLOUGH TRADING ESTATE
Perth Trading Est
Granville Playing Field
Godolphin Playing Fields
BURNHAM
Progress Business Cen
Rec Grd
Superstores
Cockfield Bridge
BATH ROAD
A4
Westgate Retail Park
Slough Retail Park
Slough Business Park
Village Green
Mercian Recreation Ground
Salt Hill Park
SLOUGH
Ice Arena
Sports Centre
Allotments
Cippenham
Sludge Beds
Holiday Inn
151
A355
BEACONSFIELD ROAD
FARNHAM ROAD
66
67
68
69
70
71
72
73
74
94
95
96

STOKE COMMON
BROCKHURST WOOD
FRAME WOOD
PENN WOOD
FULMER COMMON
STOKE POGES
FARNHAM PARK GOLF COURSE
Wexham Street
NUFFIELD HOSP
SL2
WEXHAM PARK GOLF COURSE
STOKE PARK GOLF COURSE
GRAY'S FIELD
GARDEN OF REMEMBRANCE
Stoke Green
WEXHAM PARK HOSPITAL
SL3
THE LANES GOLF COURSE
Stoke Place Hotel and Country Club
CEMETERY
Crematorium
ARTS CENTRE
George Green
SL1
SLOUGH
SALT HILL PARK
BLOOM PARK
UPTON WOOD
ROWLEY WOOD
Pinewood Hotel
UXBRIDGE ROAD
WELLINGTON ST
Queensmere Shop Centre
500 yds
500 m

BLACK PARK COUNTRY PARK
LANGLEY PARK COUNTRY PARK
IVER HEATH
IVER
Shreding Green
IVER GOLF COURSE
LONG COPPICE
PLAYING FIELD
NATURE RESERVE
Pinewood Film Studios
Heatherden Hall
Five Points
SLOUGH ROAD
DENHAM ROAD
CHURCH ROAD
UB9
SL0
BUCKINGHAMSHIRE
SLOUGH
SOUTH BUCKS
Grand Union Canal (Slough Arm)
LANGLEY BUSINESS CENTRE
Recycling Centre
CHANDLERS HILL
BROWN'S WOOD
OLDHOUSE WOOD
THE CLUMP
BROOM WARREN
DIAMOND WOOD
CHESTNUT WOOD
COLUMN LARCHES
FOXES GUTTER
ROUGHGROUND WOOD
ARBORETUM
LANGLEY PARK WOOD
RHODODENDRON GARDENS
STRAWBERRY WOOD
LANGLEY COMMON
HEATHFIELD PLANTATION
PARKSPRING WOOD
MOUNT FIDGET WOOD
BRIDGETTINE CONVENT
Sewage Works
113
134
153
AZ BA BB BC BD BE BF
01 02 03
66 67 68 69 70 71 72 73 74
84 83 82 81

BG
BH
BJ
BK
BL
BM
BN
114
133
154
65
66
67
68
69
70
71
72
73
74
UB9
UB10
UB8
UB7
SL0
UXBRIDGE
UXBRIDGE MOOR
COWLEY
YIEWSLEY
IVER
HILLINGDON
WEST DRAYTON
Hillingdon Circus
HILLINGDON ATHLETICS STADIUM
HILLINGDON HOUSE FARM SPORTS GROUNDS
UXBRIDGE COMMON
Uxbridge College (Uxbridge Campus)
HILLINGDON COURT PARK
Brunel University
BRUNEL UNIVERSITY SPORTS PARK
HILLINGDON HOSPITAL
HILLINGDON GOLF COURSE
HILLINGDON & UXBRIDGE CEMETERY
HUNTSMOOR PARK
FARLOWS LAKE
LITTLE BRITAIN LAKE
COWLEY LAKE
Electricity Sub Station
Water Treatment Works
Sewage Works
CHILTERN BUSINESS VILLAGE
SARUM COMPLEX
TRADE CITY BUSINESS PARK
COWLEY BUSINESS PARK
BRIDGE WORKS
TOMO INDUSTRIAL EST
ZODIAC BUSINESS PARK
RAINBOW INDUSTRIAL ESTATE
HORTON IND PARK
COWLEY ROAD
HIGH STREET
COWLEY HIGH ROAD
HILLINGDON ROAD
HILLINGDON HILL
FALLING LANE
PARK VIEW RD
STOCKLEY RD
ROCKINGHAM RD
ST. JOHNS ROAD
OXFORD ROAD
PARK ROAD
A4020
A4007
A408
A437
M25
Apple Tree Rbt
Colham Roundabout
Grand Union Canal (Slough Arm)
GOLF COURSE
0 500 yds
0 500 m

RAF NORTHOLT
115
HA4
ODYSSEY BUSINESS PARK
WESTERN AVENUE
A40
NORTH HILLINGDON
FREEZELAND COVERT
CUTTHROAT WOOD
GUTTERIDGE WOOD
NATURE RESERVE
MEADOWS NATURE RESERVE
Polish War Memorial
C & L GOLF & COUNTRY CLUB
WEST END ROAD
Down Barns Moated Site
UB5
WEST LONDON SHOOTING SCHOOL
THE GORSE
SPORTS GROUND
Hillingdon Abbots R.F.C.
HARE PLANTATION
HOME COVERT
POLE HILL OPEN SPACE
YEADING BROOK MEADOWS NATURE RESERVE
GROSVENOR PLAYING FIELD
Brook House F.C.
Hayes R.F.C.
GRANGE PK
YEADING
136
HAYES SHRUB
HAYES PARK
Mellow Lane Farm
Dalton's Farm
UB4
BELMORE PLAYING FIELDS
HAYES END
RECREATION GROUND
UXBRIDGE ROAD
A4020
ROSEDALE PARK
GRASSY MEADOW
MEMORIAL GDNS
Hayes Cricket Club
HAYES
BARRA HALL PARK
BELL HOUSE FLD
Uxbridge College Hayes Community Campus
Lombardy Retail Park
Ossie Garvin Roundabout
HEXAGON BUSINESS CENTRE
HAYES METRO CENTRE
WARREN PARK
THE PARKWAY
A312
HAYES BYPASS
MINET COUNTRY PARK
STOCKLEY PARK GOLF COURSE
STOCKLEY PARK
The Arena
DAWLEY ROAD
UB3
UB11
E.M.I. SPORTS GROUND
Grand Union Canal
WATERWAY BUSINESS PARK
SPEEDWAY IND. EST
HAYES TOWN
155
ARGENT BUSINESS CEN
PROVIDENT IND. EST
PASADENA TRADING EST
Stilwell Roundabout
HARLINGTON ROAD
STOCKLEY ROAD
BP BQ BR BS BT BU BV
08 09 10
66 67 68 69 70 71 72 73 74 81 82 83 84

BW
BX
HA4
BY
BZ
CA
CB
CC
116
Civic Amenity Site
NORTHOLT RECREATION GRD
Air Traffic Radio Sta
65
SPORTS GROUND
Polish War Memorial
LORD HALSBURY MEMORIAL REC GRD
HILLINGDON
EALING
NORTHOLT
ISLIP MANOR PARK
BELVUE BUSINESS CENTRE
NORTHOLT TRADING ESTATE
KELVIN INDUSTRIAL ESTATE
66
C & L GOLF & COUNTRY CLUB
SPORTS GROUND
WESTERN AVENUE
LIME TREE PARK GOLF COURSE
West London Academy
Target Roundabout
BELVUE PARK
EALING GOLF RANGE
THE METROPOLITAN CENTRE
LONDON MARATHON PLAYING FIELDS
67
Down Barns Moated Site
UB5
WEST LONDON SHOOTING SCHOOL
LIME TREE PARK
NORTHALA FIELDS
MARNHAM FIELDS
NORTHOLT GOLF COURSE
SMITHS FARM EST
68
White Hart Roundabout
RECTORY PARK
RUISLIP ROAD
THE PARKWAY (HAYES BYPASS)
69
GREENFORD
RAVENOR PARK
135
YEADING
SOUTHALL CRICKET CLUB
KING GEORGE'S FIELD
70
GREENFORD PARK REC GRD
THE BROADWAY
Willow Tree Roundabout
UB4
71
JUBILEE PARK
GREENFORD PARK CEMETERY
WARREN PARK
BROOKSIDE
WILLOWTREE MARINA
72
SPIKES BRIDGE PARK
Lombardy Retail Park
Ossie Garvin Roundabout
UXBRIDGE ROAD
73
DORMER'S WELLS
WEST MIDDLESEX GOLF COURSE
HEXAGON BUSINESS CENTRE
HAYES BRIDGE RETAIL PARK
HAYES METRO CENTRE
SOUTHALL
THE BROADWAY
HIGH STREET
UB1
SOUTHALL PARK
74
SPRINGFIELD RD BUS. CEN
BROOK INDUSTRIAL ESTATE
MINET COUNTRY PARK
HEATHROW PURPLE PARKING
BARRATT IND EST
SOUTHALL RAILWAY CENTRE
156
0 500 yds
0 500 m
BX
BY
BZ
CA
CB
CC
FEATHERSTONE IND EST
GLADE LANE CANALSIDE PARK
THE BRIDGE BUSINESS

CD
CE
CF
CG
CH
CJ
CK
117
SUDBURY
HA0
BARHAM PARK
WHITTON AVENUE WEST
WHITTON AVENUE EAST
HARROW ROAD
SUDBURY & HARROW ROAD
SUDBURY TOWN
WEMBLEY
GLAXCO WELLCOME
HORSENDEN WOOD
HOME MEAD
SPORTS GROUND
BERKELEY FIELDS
GREAT BRAMSTONES
HORSENDEN HILL GOLF COURSE
HORSENDEN HILL
SUDBURY GOLF COURSE
GRAND UNION CANAL (PADDINGTON BRANCH)
ALPERTON CEMETERY
ONE TREE HILL OPEN SPACE
UB6
Westway Shopping Pk
GREENFORD
GREENFORD GRN BUS. PK
Royal Mail Centre
PERIVALE WOOD (Nature Reserve)
OLDFIELD REC GRD
PERIVALE
PERIVALE PARK
PERIVALE NEW BUSINESS CENTRE
WADSWORTH BUSINESS CENTRE
FLEETWAY BUSINESS PARK
SHERATON BUSINESS CEN
ALPERTON
ABERCORN COMMERCIAL CENTRE
CAPITAL BUSINESS CEN
ALPERTON SPORTS GROUND
Greenford Roundabout
EALING CENTRAL SPORTS GRD
SOUTH GREENFORD
Perivale
WESTERN AVENUE
A40
ATHLETICS TRACK
PERIVALE PARK SPORTS GROUND
EALING GOLF COURSE
PITSHANGER PARK
PERIVALE PARK GOLF COURSE
138
66
67
68
69
70
71
72
73
74
BRENT VALLEY PARK
CUCKOO PARK
CLEVELAND PARK
W7
W5
W13
BRENT VALLEY GOLF COURSE
DRAYTON GREEN
WEST EALING
EALING
EALING BROADWAY
CHURCHFIELDS RECREATION GROUND
KENSINGTON & CHELSEA CEMETERY
HANWELL
HANWELL CEMETERY
WALPOLE PARK
PITZHANGER MANOR HOUSE & GALL
EALING HOSPITAL N.H.S. TRUST
University of West London
LAMMAS PARK
UXBRIDGE ROAD
BROADWAY
NEW BROADWAY
157

CL
CM
CN
CP
CQ
CR
CS
WEMBLEY
WEMBLEY STADIUM
118
TOKYNGTON
CHURCH END
HA0
HA9
65
66
67
68
69
70
71
72
73
74
ONE TREE HILL OPEN SPACE
ALPERTON
NORTHFIELDS INDUSTRIAL ESTATE
STONEBRIDGE
Princess Royal Distribution Centre
TOKYNGTON RECREATION GROUND
GIBBONS REC GRD
PREMIER PARK
TOWNSEND INDUSTRIAL ESTATE
UNITED BISCUITS-McVITIE
HARLESDEN
PARK ROYAL
PARK ROYAL CEN
CENTRAL MIDDLESEX HOSPITAL
GENESIS BUSINESS PARK
Twyford Abbey
Diageo
Hanger Lane
137
HANGER HILL PARK
WESTERN AVENUE
A40
A406
NORTH CIRCULAR ROAD
POWERGATE BUSINESS PARK
FROGMORE INDUSTRIAL ESTATE
BUSH INDUSTRIAL EST
ACTON CEMETERY
NORTH ACTON
WESTERN TRADING EST
WESTPOINT TRADING EST
WESTWOOD PARK TRADING EST
ROYALE LEISURE PARK
NORTH ACTON PLAYING FIELDS
Gypsy Corner
VICTORIA IND EST
BARCLAYS BANK SPORTS GROUND
WEST ACTON
W3
ACTON MAIN LINE
EALING BROADWAY
EALING COMMON
Ealing Common
UXBRIDGE ROAD
GUNNERSBURY AVENUE
TWYFORD AVENUE SPORTS GRD
London Wasps RFC Training Grd
ACTON
EAST ACTON
ACTON PARK
ACTON CENTRAL
HIGH STREET
W5
University of West London
158
ACTON TOWN
ACTON PARK ESTATE
0 500 yds
0 500 m
19
20
21

CT
CU
CV
CW
CX
CY
CZ
119
140
159
22
23
24
66
67
68
69
70
71
72
73
74
81
82
83
84
WILLESDEN
WILLESDEN GREEN
BRONDESBURY
BRONDESBURY PARK
NW2
NW6
NW10
W9
W10
W12
W8
KENSAL RISE
KENSAL GREEN
KENSAL TOWN
KILBURN
WEST KILBURN
MAIDA HILL
NORTH KENSINGTON
NOTTING HILL
SHEPHERD'S BUSH
KENSINGTON
OLD OAK COMMON
WORMWOOD SCRUBS
WILLESDEN NEW CEMETERY
ROUNDWOOD PARK
PADDINGTON OLD CEMETERY
QUEEN'S PARK
ST. MARY'S RC CEMETERY
KENSAL GREEN CEMETERY
GRAND UNION CANAL (Paddington Branch)
LITTLE WORMWOOD SCRUBS
LINFORD CHRISTIE STADIUM
QUEEN CHARLOTTE & CHELSEA HOSP
HAMMERSMITH HOSPITAL
H.M. PRISON WORMWOOD SCRUBS
ST. CHARLES HOSP
LOFTUS ROAD STADIUM QPR FC
HOLLAND PARK
WESTWAY
UXBRIDGE ROAD
HARROW ROAD
WILLESDEN LANE
WOOD LANE
WEST CROSS ROUTE
HOLLAND PARK AVENUE
Savoy Circus
Holland Park Rbt

140
DA
DB
DC
DD
DE
DF
DG
120
65
66
67
68
69
70
71
72
73
74
139
160
WEST HAMPSTEAD
NW6
SOUTH HAMPSTEAD
BELSIZE PARK
NW3
PRIMROSE HILL
KILBURN
NW8
ST. JOHN'S WOOD
THE REGENT'S PARK
NW1
ZSL LONDON ZOO
LORD'S CRICKET GROUND
MAIDA VALE
LISSON GROVE
W9
MAIDA HILL
WESTBOURNE GREEN
PADDINGTON
MARYLEBONE
W2
BAYSWATER
KENSINGTON GARDENS
HYDE PARK
W8
KENSINGTON
HOLLAND PARK
SW7
THE SERPENTINE
ROUND POND
KENSINGTON PALACE
QUEEN MARY'S GARDENS
PADDINGTON RECREATION GROUND
OXFORD STREET where marked is closed to through traffic (except buses & taxis) from 7a.m.-7p.m. Monday - Saturday
500 yds
500 m

DH
DJ
DK
DL
DM
DN
DP
121
HOLLOWAY
LOWER HOLLOWAY
KENTISH TOWN
CAMDEN TOWN
KING'S CROSS
BARNSBURY
ISLINGTON
N1
N7
PENTONVILLE PRISON
SOMERS TOWN
ST. PANCRAS
FINSBURY
CLERKENWELL
EC1
WC1
BLOOMSBURY
BRITISH MUSEUM
HOLBORN
WC2
W1
SOHO
STRAND
EC4
BLACKFRIARS
SOUTHWARK
SE1
THE BOROUGH
WATERLOO
ST. JAMES'S
ST. JAMES'S PARK
SW1
THE GREEN PARK
MAYFAIR
REGENT'S PARK
66
67
68
69
70
71
72
73
74
142
161
29
30
31
84
83
82
81
PENTONVILLE RD
EUSTON RD
CALEDONIAN ROAD
YORK WAY
CAMDEN ROAD
UPPER STREET
GOSWELL RD
FARRINGDON RD
GRAY'S INN RD
KINGSWAY
ALDWYCH
VICTORIA EMBANKMENT
HOLBORN VIADUCT
NEWGATE ST
OXFORD STREET
REGENT STREET
PICCADILLY
SHAFTESBURY AV
CHARING CROSS
WHITEHALL
WESTMINSTER BR
WATERLOO BR
BLACKFRIARS BR
SOUTHWARK ST
RIVER THAMES

DQ
DR
DS
DT
DU
DV
DW
122
CANONBURY
KINGSLAND
HACKNEY
DALSTON
SOUTH HACKNEY
DE BEAUVOIR TOWN
HOXTON
HAGGERSTON
BETHNAL GREEN
ST. LUKE'S
CLERKENWELL
SHOREDITCH
BROADGATE
BARBICAN
STEPNEY
WHITECHAPEL
WAPPING
SHADWELL
SOUTHWARK
BOROUGH
141
162
65
66
67
68
69
70
71
72
73
74
N1
E8
E2
EC1
EC2
EC3
EC4
E1
SE1
RIVER THAMES
TOWER OF LONDON
LONDON BRIDGE
GUY'S HOSPITAL
TATE MODERN
0 500 yds
0 500 m

HOMERTON
HACKNEY WICK
QUEEN ELIZABETH OLYMPIC PARK
E9
E20
E15
STRATFORD
VICTORIA PARK
OLD FORD
Olympic Stadium
London Aquatics Centre
Westfield Stratford City
STRATFORD INTERNATIONAL
BOW
MILE END
E3
TOWER HAMLETS CEMETERY PARK
BROMLEY
LEE VALLEY REGIONAL PARK
Three Mills Studios
LIMEHOUSE
E14
POPLAR
WEST INDIA DOCKS
ISLE
CANARY WHARF
SE16
SE10
The O2
NORTH GREENWICH
RIVER THAMES
MILE END STADIUM
BOW CREEK ECOLOGICAL PARK
CANNING TOWN
WEST HAM
STAR LANE
123
144
163
DX
DY
DZ
EA
EB
EC
ED
66
67
68
69
70
71
72
73
74

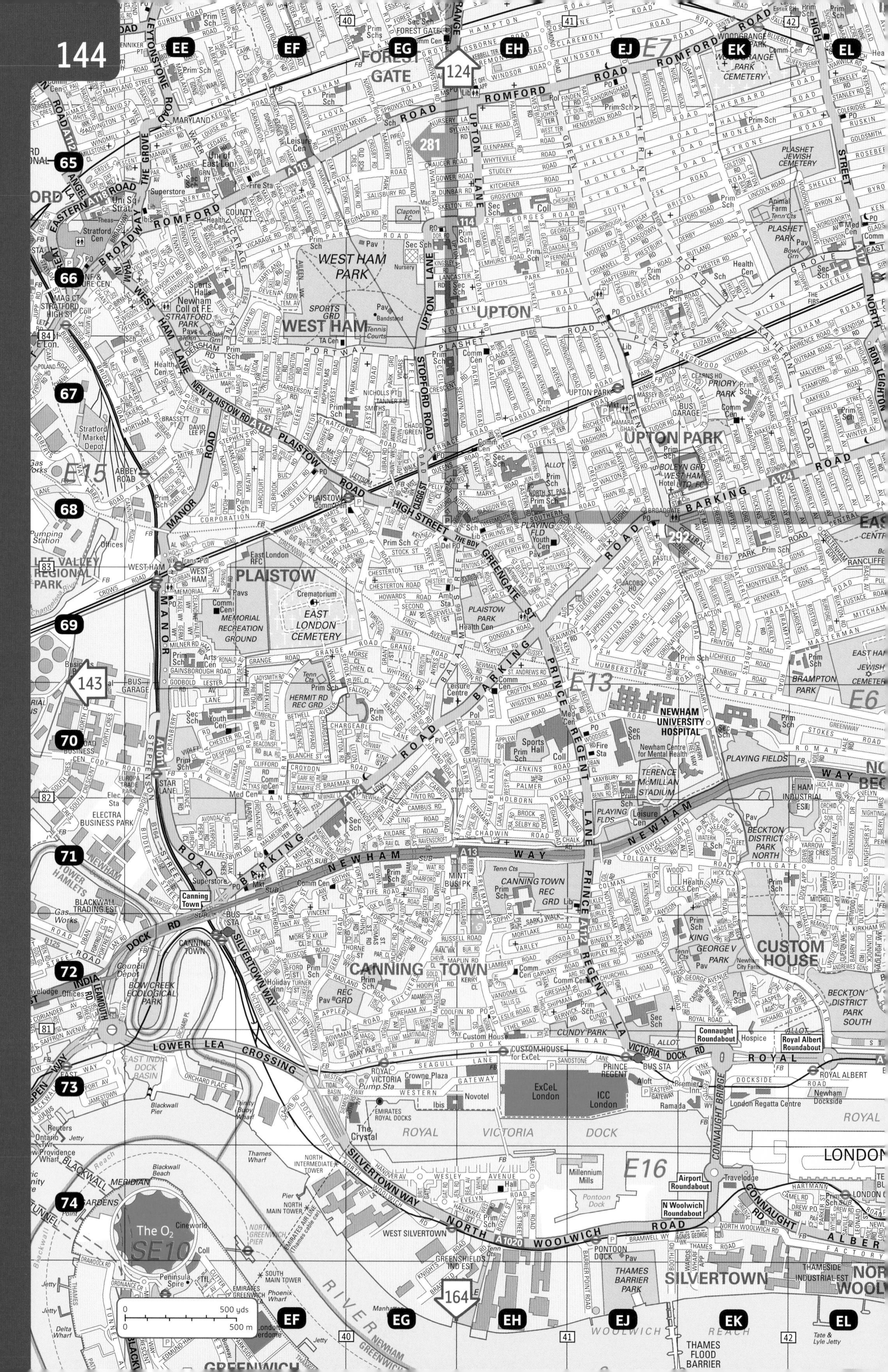
EE
EF
EG
EH
EJ
EK
EL
40
41
42
FOREST GATE
124
E7
WOODGRANGE PARK CEMETERY
ROMFORD ROAD
281
WEST HAM PARK
WEST HAM
UPTON
PLASHET JEWISH CEMETERY
PLASHET PARK
UPTON PARK
PRIORY PARK
BOLEYN GRD WEST HAM UTD FC
E15
Stratford Market Depot
PLAISTOW
EAST LONDON CEMETERY
MEMORIAL RECREATION GROUND
LEE VALLEY REGIONAL PARK
PLAISTOW PARK
HERMIT RD REC GRD
292
143
E13
E6
NEWHAM UNIVERSITY HOSPITAL
TERENCE McMILLAN STADIUM
BRAMPTON PARK
ELECTRA BUSINESS PARK
CANNING TOWN REC GRD
CANNING TOWN
Canning Town
CUSTOM HOUSE
KING GEORGE V PARK
BECKTON DISTRICT PARK NORTH
BECKTON DISTRICT PARK SOUTH
BOW CREEK ECOLOGICAL PARK
LOWER LEA CROSSING
Connaught Roundabout
Royal Albert Roundabout
ExCeL London
ICC London
ROYAL VICTORIA DOCK
E16
Airport Roundabout
N Woolwich Roundabout
LONDON
The O2
SE10
WEST SILVERTOWN
THAMES BARRIER PARK
SILVERTOWN
164
RIVER
WOOLWICH REACH
THAMES FLOOD BARRIER
GREENWICH
65
66
67
68
69
70
71
72
73
74
0 500 yds
0 500 m

EM
EN
EP
EQ
ER
ES
ET
LOXFORD
125
LITTLE ILFORD PARK
BARKING PARK
THE LAKE
Indoor Bowl Club
BARKING PARK REC GRD
LONGBRIDGE ROAD
FANSHAWE AV
NORTHERN RELIEF ROAD
SPORTS GROUND
BARKING COMMUNITY HOSPITAL
UPNEY
RIPPLE ROAD
RIPPLESIDE BURIAL GROUND
BARKING
ABBEY RETAIL PARK
BARKING ROAD REC GRD
NORTH CIRCULAR ROAD
A406
A124
A123
A13
IG11
BARKING INDUSTRIAL PARK
ALFREDS WAY IND ESTATE
WAYSIDE COMMERCIAL EST
ALFREDS WAY
BARKING BYPASS
Movers Lane
LYON BUSINESS PARK
KATELLA TRADING EST
ABBEY WHARF INDUSTRIAL ESTATE
BARKING BUSINESS CENTRE
RIVER ROAD BUSINESS PARK
IO CENTRE
TRAFALGAR BUSINESS CENTRE
BUZZARD CREEK INDUSTRIAL ESTATE
CREEKMOUTH
146
FLANDERS RD PLAYING FLDS
293
ALLOTMENTS
GOOSELEY'S PLAYING FIELDS
Refuse Transfer Station
PITCHES
Filter Beds
BECKTON SEWAGE TREATMENT WORKS
BECKTON TRIANGLE RETAIL PARK
GATEWAY RETAIL PARK
Beckton Alps
NEWHAM WAY
LONDON IND EST
BECKTON RETAIL PARK
BECKTON
Gallions Reach Shopping Park
GEMINI BUSINESS PARK
BARKING FLOOD BARRIER
Gas Works
DLR DEPOT
NEW BECKTON PARK
MARGARET NESS OR TRIPCOCK POINT
GALLIONS REACH
Cyprus Roundabout
Gallions Roundabout
ALBERT DOCK
Uni of East London
Sir Steve Redgrave Bri
ALBERT BASIN
CITY AIRPORT
KING GEORGE V DOCK
KING GEORGE V
ROYAL DOCK ROAD
WOOLWICH MANOR WAY
THAMESMEAD
SE28
GALLIONS HILL
THAMESMEAD WEST
165
305
H.M. PRISON
ROYAL VICTORIA GDNS
STANDARD INDUSTRIAL ESTATE
Woolwich Ferry Pier
66
67
68
69
70
71
72
73
74
43
44
45

EU
EV
EW
EX
EY
EZ
FA
126
145
166
65
66
67
68
69
70
71
72
73
74
PARSLOES PARK
RM9
DAGENHAM HEATHWAY
BECONTREE
Barking Sporthouse & Gym.
Boating Lake
RIPPLESIDE BURIAL GROUND
Lodge Avenue Junction
BARKING INDUSTRIAL PARK
ALFREDS WAY IND ESTATE
WAYSIDE COMMERCIAL EST
CASTLE GREEN
GORESBROOK SPORTS GROUND
BARKING R.F.C.
GORESBROOK PARK
RIPPLESIDE COMMERCIAL ESTATE
PORTLAND COMM EST
MAYBELLS COMM EST
SCRATTONS FARM ECO-PARK
Freight Depot
FORD MOTOR WORKS
DAGENHAM DOCK
BARKING BUSINESS CENTRE
RIVERSIDE INDUSTRIAL ESTATE
The Ripple Nature Reserve
IG11
POWER STATION
CREEKMOUTH
TRAFALGAR BUSINESS CENTRE
BUZZARD CREEK INDUSTRIAL ESTATE
THAMES GATEWAY PARK
Horse Shoe Corner
Power Station
Oil Storage Depot
BARKING & DAGENHAM
Gravel Works
Barking or False Point
CROSSNESS LIGHTHOUSE
THAMESMEAD NORTH
Ecology Study Area
Driving Range
Crossness Pumping Station
SE2
RIVERSIDE GOLF
THAMESVIEW GOLF COURSE
Crossness Sewage Treatment Works
Sludge Incinerator
THAMESMEAD
MANORWAY GREEN
Thamesmead Town FC
CROSSWAY PARK
PHOENIX POINT
SPORTS GROUND
SOUTHMERE PARK
ERITH MARSHES
CROSSNESS NATURE RESERVE
LAKESIDE CENTRE
SOUTHMERE
BIRCHMERE PARK
SE28
DA18
WOODLAND WAY
The Business Academy Bexley
ABBEY WOOD PARK
A13
A1153
A1240
A2016
0 500 yds
0 500 m

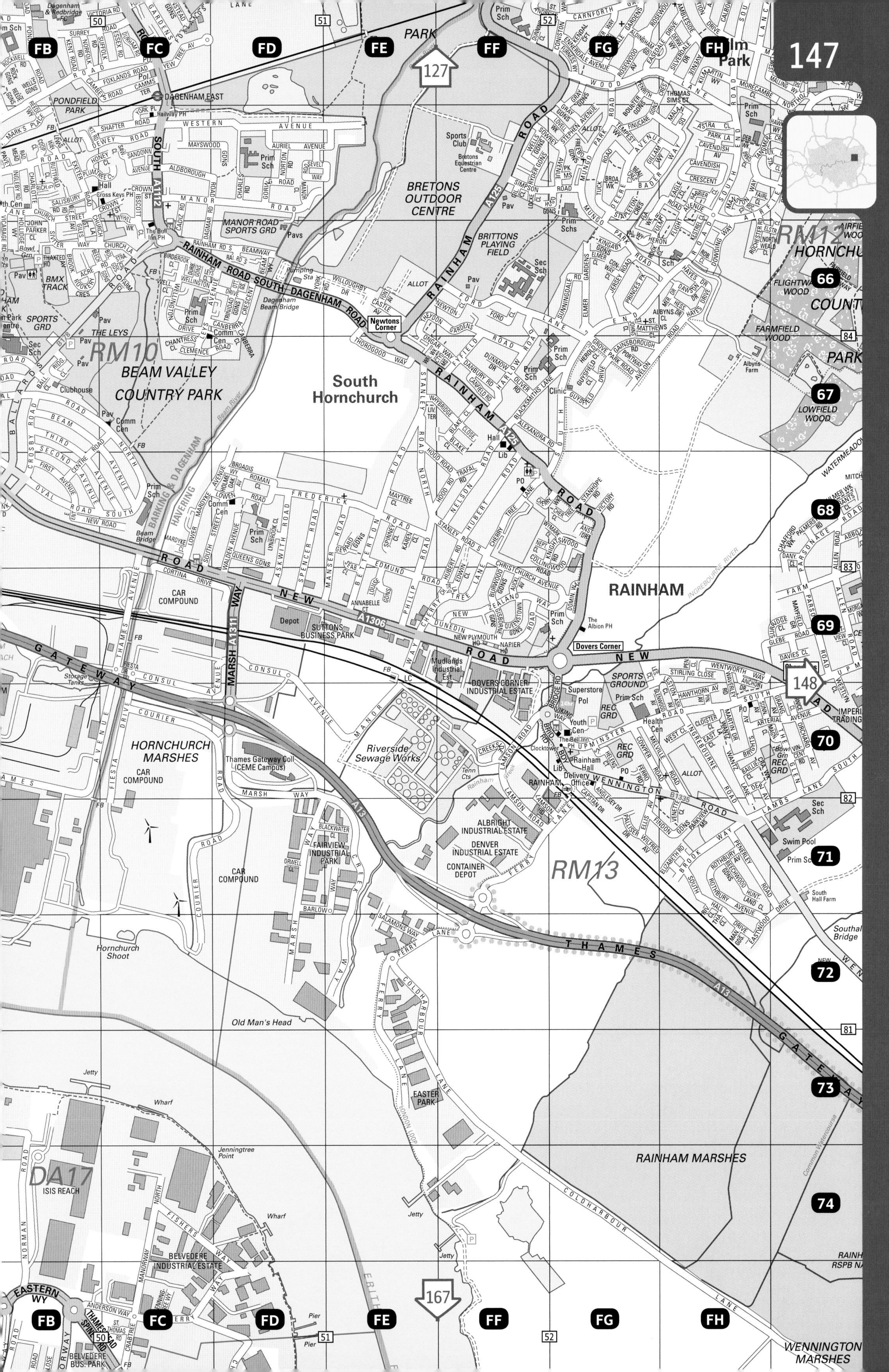
South Hornchurch
RAINHAM
RM10
RM12
RM13
DA17
BEAM VALLEY COUNTRY PARK
BRETONS OUTDOOR CENTRE
BRITTONS PLAYING FIELD
HORNCHURCH MARSHES
RAINHAM MARSHES
WENNINGTON MARSHES
Riverside Sewage Works
FAIRVIEW INDUSTRIAL PARK
ALBRIGHT INDUSTRIAL ESTATE
DENVER INDUSTRIAL ESTATE
CONTAINER DEPOT
DOVERS CORNER INDUSTRIAL ESTATE
Mudlands Industrial Est
SUTTONS BUSINESS PARK
BELVEDERE INDUSTRIAL ESTATE
EASTER PARK
Newtons Corner
Dovers Corner
DAGENHAM EAST
Thames Gateway Coll (CEME Campus)
Old Man's Head
Hornchurch Shoot
Jenningtree Point
ISIS REACH
FLIGHTWAYS WOOD
FARMFIELD WOOD
LOWFIELD WOOD
PONDFIELD PARK
MANOR ROAD SPORTS GRD
BMX TRACK
THE LEYS
RAINHAM ROAD SOUTH
DAGENHAM ROAD
RAINHAM ROAD
NEW ROAD
THAMES GATEWAY
FERRY LANE
COLDHARBOUR LANE
WENNINGTON ROAD
UPMINSTER ROAD
BRIDGE RD
MARSH WAY
FB FC FD FE FF FG FH
127
148
167
50 51 52
66 67 68 69 70 71 72 73 74
84 83 82 81

RM12
HORNCHURCH
COUNTRY
PARK
AIRFIELD WOOD
PINEWOOD
FLIGHTWAY WOOD
FARMFIELD WOOD
LOWFIELD WOOD
ABBEY WOOD
BERWICK GLADES
BERWICK WOODS
BERWICK POND
BONNETTS WOOD
Civic Amenity Site
DAMYNS HALL AERODROME
SAND AND GRAVEL PIT
SAND & GRAVEL PIT
Corbets Tey
PARKLANDS OPEN SPACE
WARWICK WOOD
WHITE POST WOOD
White Post Corner
RAINHAM CEMETERY (JEWISH)
SPRING FARM PARK
IMPERIAL TRADING EST
Chandlers Corner
RM13
Swim Pool
Sec Sch
Prim Sch
Southall Bridge
NEW COTTAGES
East Hall Farm
Wennington
Wennington Hall
Premier Travel Inn
Willow Farm
Lennards
Fire Sta
New Farm
Sandy Lane Farm
Moor Hall
KENNINGTON PARK
Bretts Farm
Sir Henry Gurnett PH
RAINHAM MARSHES RSPB NATURE RESERVE
WENNINGTON MARSHES
AVELEY MARSHES
THURROCK COM CENTRE
PURFLEET IND PARK
SPORTS GROUND
A13
A1306
NEW ROAD
LONDON ROAD
GATEWAY
SANDY LANE B1335
WARWICK LANE
128
147
168
FJ FK FL FM FN FP FQ
65 66 67 68 69 70 71 72 73 74
54 55 56
84 83 82 81
500 yds
500 m

North Ockendon
SOUTH OCKENDON
Aveley
North Stifford
RM14
RM15
RM16
UPMINSTER CEMETERY
MIDDLE WOOD
BONUS WOOD
TOP MEADOW GOLF
Top Meadow Hotel
Driving Range
RUSSELL'S LAKE
STUBBERS ADVENTURE CENTRE
COYS LAKE
SAND AND GRAVEL PIT
FREEMAN'S SHAW
THE WILDERNESS
HAVERING
THURROCK
OCKENDON ROAD
DENNISES LANE
PEA LANE
STUBBERS LANE
SUNNINGS LANE
FEN LANE
NORTH ROAD
M25
129
169
WHITEHALL WOOD
BELHUS WOODS COUNTRY PARK
LITTLE BRICKKILN WOOD
BRICKKILN WOOD
BELHUS CHASE
LONG POND
OAK WOOD
ASH PLANTATION
ROOKERY
SPORTS GROUND
THE SHRUBBERY
BELHUS PARK GOLF COURSE
BELHUS PARK
The Ockendon Academy
BONNYGATE WOOD
SOUTH OCKENDON REC GRD
Thurrock Garden Centre
LITTLE PALMER'S SHAW
GREAT PALMER'S SHAW
MARDYKE VALLEY GOLF COURSE
DILKES PARK
Culver Centre
STIFFORD ROAD
B1335
AVELEY BYPASS
HANGMAN'S WOOD
MILLARD'S GARDEN
BRANNETT'S WOOD
MARDYKE WOODS
DAVY DOWN RIVERSIDE PARK
FIELDS OF PEACE
Junction 30
LOW WELL WOOD
BRICKBARN WOOD
COMBE WOOD
ARENA ESSEX RACEWAY
KARTING CEN
LAKESIDE COACH PARK
Thurrock Services
A13
ARTERIAL ROAD
PILGRIMS LANE
STIFFORD HILL
FR FS FT FU FV FW FX
57 58 59
66 67 68 69 70 71 72 73 74
84 83 82 81

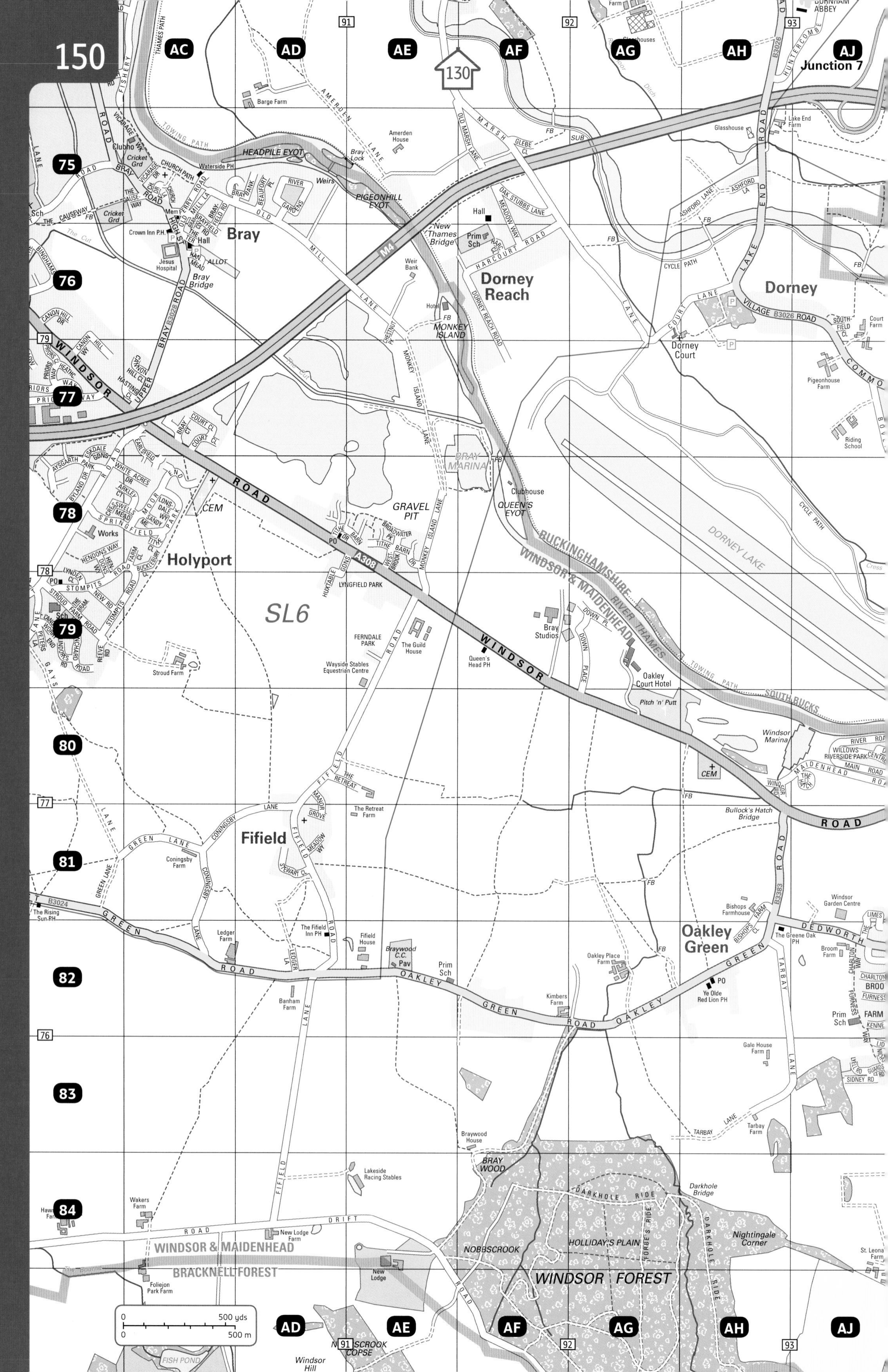
130
Junction 7
Bray
Dorney Reach
Dorney
Holyport
SL6
Fifield
Oakley Green
WINDSOR FOREST
Bray Bridge
New Thames Bridge
HEADPILE EYOT
PIGEONHILL EYOT
MONKEY ISLAND
BRAY MARINA
QUEEN'S EYOT
GRAVEL PIT
DORNEY LAKE
BUCKINGHAMSHIRE
WINDSOR & MAIDENHEAD
RIVER THAMES
SOUTH BUCKS
BRACKNELL FOREST
Barge Farm
Amerden House
Bray Lock
Weirs
Jesus Hospital
Crown Inn P.H.
Dorney Court
Pigeonhouse Farm
Riding School
Lake End Farm
Glasshouse
Bray Studios
Oakley Court Hotel
Pitch 'n' Putt
Windsor Marina
Bullock's Hatch Bridge
Queen's Head PH
The Guild House
Wayside Stables Equestrian Centre
Ferndale Park
Lyngfield Park
Stroud Farm
The Retreat Farm
Coningsby Farm
Ledger Farm
The Fifield Inn PH
Fifield House
Braywood C.C.
Banham Farm
Kimbers Farm
Oakley Place Farm
Ye Olde Red Lion PH
Bishops Farmhouse
The Greene Oak PH
Windsor Garden Centre
Broom Farm
Gale House Farm
Tarbay Farm
Braywood House
BRAY WOOD
Lakeside Racing Stables
Darkhole Bridge
DARKHOLE RIDE
HOLLIDAY'S PLAIN
NOBBSCROOK
Nightingale Corner
St. Leonards Farm
Wakers Farm
New Lodge Farm
New Lodge
Foliejon Park Farm
The Bourne
FISH POND
NOBBSCROOK COPSE
Windsor Hill
The Rising Sun PH
WINDSOR ROAD
A308
GREEN ROAD
B3024
OAKLEY GREEN
DRIFT ROAD
LAKE END ROAD
B3026
B3383
M4
0 500 yds
0 500 m
AC AD AE AF AG AH AJ
75 76 77 78 79 80 81 82 83 84
91 92 93

Cippenham
Chalvey
SL1
Junction 6
Eton Wick
DORNEY COMMON
Boveney
SL4
ROYAL WINDSOR RACECOURSE
Clewer Village
ETON
ETON COLLEGE GOLF COURSE
Dedworth
Clewer Green
Clewer New Town
WINDSOR
WASTE WATER TREATMENT WORKS
JUBILEE RIVER
RIVER THAMES
MAIDENHEAD ROAD
WINDSOR & ETON RELIEF ROAD
WINDSOR GREAT PARK
QUEEN MARY'S PLANTATION
HOG COMMON
ASH PLANTATION
WINDSOR CEMETERY
KING EDWARD VII HOSP
PRINCESS MARGARET HOSP
131
152
AK
AL
AM
AN
AP
AQ
AR
76
77
78
79
80
81
82
83
84

SLOUGH
WINDSOR
DATCHET
Upton Park
Upton
UPTON COURT PARK
DITTON PARK
THE HOME PARK
THE HOME PARK RECREATION GROUND
DATCHET GOLF COURSE
AGARS PLOUGH PLAYING FIELDS
THAMES VALLEY ATHLETICS CENTRE
WINDSOR CASTLE
HAM ISLAND
Southlea
Sunnymeads
SL1
SL4
132
151
172

IVER GOLF COURSE
BUCKINGHAMSHIRE
SLOUGH
SOUTH BUCKS
Recycling Centre
LANGLEY
LANGLEY BUSINESS CENTRE
E. Berkshire Coll
MEMORIAL GROUND
Chequer Bridge
Withy Bridge
Richings Park
RICHINGS PARK GOLF COURSE AND COUNTRY CLUB
HOME WOOD
SL0
Junction 15 (M25)
Junction 4B (M4)
M4
OAK PLANTATION
SLOUGH OLD WOOD
Sewage Works
LAKESIDE IND EST
Swimming Pool
HARVEY PARK
Royal Mail Distribution Centre
AXIS PARK
Junction 5
Marriott Hotel
Brands Hill
Quality Hotel Heathrow
COLNBROOK BYPASS
A4
Colnbrook
Incinerator
Sailing Club
REC GRD
THE QUEEN MOTHER RESERVOIR
SL3
Colnbrook Bridge
Pond
PIPPINS PARK
Arora Park Hotel
Poyle
Hilton London Heathrow Airport Terminal 5
COLNBROOK GOLF RANGE
BRITANNIA INDUSTRIAL EST
MCKAY TRADING ESTATE
POLYGON BUSINESS CEN.
TRIDENT INDUSTRIAL ESTATE
Horton
Arthur Jacob Nature Reserve
Junction 14
HILLINGDON
AIRPORT
M25
TW19
WINDSOR & MAIDENHEAD
SURREY
WRAYSBURY
133
154
173

BP
BQ
BR
BS
BT
BU
BV
135
UB11
HAYES TOWN
UB3
MINET COUNTRY PARK
Junction 4
Junction 3
Junction 4A
IMPERIAL COLLEGE SPORTS GROUND
LITTLE HARLINGTON FIELD
HARLINGTON
CRANFORD COUNTRYSIDE PARK
AVENUE PARK
CRANFORD
TW5
156
TW4
HEATHROW AIRPORT (LONDON)
TERMINAL 2
HATTON
TW14
175
HOUNSLOW HEATH GOLF COURSE
DONKEY WOOD
Waggoners Roundabout
Hatton Cross
BATH ROAD
GREAT SOUTH-WEST ROAD
THE PARKWAY
NORTH HYDE ROAD
STATION ROAD
HIGH STREET
PROLOGIS PARK HEATHROW
BOURNE FARM FIELD
PINKWELL PARK
CHERRY LANE CEMETERY
SAM PHILIP REC GRD
SPORTS GROUND
CRANE MEADOW
BRITISH AIRWAYS SPORTS GROUND
INTERNATIONAL TRADING EST
SQUIRRELS TRADING ESTATE
E.M.I. SPORTS GROUND
76
77
78
79
80
81
82
83
84

BW
BX
BY
BZ
CA
CB
CC
136
SOUTHALL
UB1
MINET COUNTRY PARK
UB3
HEATHROW PURPLE PARKING
SOUTHALL RAILWAY CENTRE
MIDDLESEX BUSINESS CENTRE
THE BRIDGE BUSINESS CENTRE
GLADE LANE CANALSIDE PARK
TENTELOW LANE SPORTS GROUND
BEAVER INDUSTRIAL PARK
INTERNATIONAL TRADING EST
BULLSBRIDGE IND EST
SOUTHALL REC GRD
ENDSLEIGH IND EST
UB2
NORWOOD GREEN
NORTH HYDE
AIRLINKS
GOLF
COURSE
SQUARE ONE
Western International Market
Junction 3
SPITFIRE ESTATE
AIR LINKS INDUSTRIAL ESTATE
Heston Services
BRITISH AIRWAYS SPORTS GROUND
PARKWAY TRADING ESTATE
OSTERLEY PARK HOUSE
Osterley Park Farm
HESTON PARK
HESTON INDUSTRIAL MALL
HESTON
OSTERLEY
Brentford FC Training Ground
155
TW5
SUTTON PLAYING FIELD
LAMPTON
LAMPTON PARK
HOUNSLOW CIVIC CENTRE
Waggoners Roundabout
Henlys Roundabout
HOUNSLOW WEST
BEAVERSFORD PARK
HOUNSLOW
HOUNSLOW CENTRAL
HOUNSLOW EAST
TW4
TW3
INWOOD PARK
HEATHROW CAUSEWAY CENTRE
HEATHROW INT TRADING ESTATE
RIFLE RANGE
GREEN LANE OPEN SPACE
DONKEY WOOD
HOUNSLOW HEATH
CENTRAL PARK EST
176
75
76
77
78
79
80
81
82
83
84
0 500 yds
0 500 m

157
HANWELL
W7
W13
W5
LITTLE EALING
BRENTFORD
TW7
TW8
TW9
TW1
OSTERLEY PARK NT
WYKE GREEN GOLF COURSE
SPRING GROVE
WOODLANDS
ISLEWORTH
SYON PARK
SYON HOUSE
BOTANIC GA
KEW
ROYAL MID-SURREY GOLF COURSE (OLD DEER PARK)
OLD DEER PARK RECREATION GROUND
RICHMOND GREEN
ST. MARGARETS
MOGDEN SEWAGE TREATMENT WORKS
BOSTON MANOR HOUSE
BOSTON MANOR PARK
WEST MIDDLESEX UNIVERSITY HOSP
EALING HOSPITAL N.H.S. TRUST
GREAT WEST ROAD
UXBRIDGE ROAD
BROADWAY
LONDON ROAD
TWICKENHAM ROAD
HIGH STREET
M4
A4
A3002
A315
A310
A316
Junction 2
Gillette Corner
St. Margarets Roundabout
Richmond Circus
Battles of Brentford 1016 & 1642
137
158
177

CL
CM
CN
CP
CQ
CR
CS
W5
W3
W4
TW8
TW9
SW14
138
157
178
75
76
77
78
79
80
81
82
83
84
EALING COMMON
ACTON PARK
SOUTH ACTON
BEDFORD PARK
GUNNERSBURY PARK
GUNNERSBURY
SOUTH EALING CEMETERY
KENSINGTON CEMETERY
CLAYPONDS HOSP
Junction 1
Chiswick Rbt
Junction 2
Gunnersbury Park
Kew Bridge
BRENTFORD
BRENTFORD AIT
CHISWICK
CHISWICK HOUSE GROUNDS
CHISWICK HOUSE
KEW
Kew Green
KEW PALACE
ROYAL BOTANIC GARDENS
OLIVER'S ISLAND
THE NATIONAL ARCHIVES
GROVE PARK
RIVER THAMES
UNIVERSITY OF WESTMINSTER SPORTS GROUND
DUKE'S MEADOW
DUKE'S MEADOWS GOLF CHISWICK BRIDGE
NORTH SHEEN
NORTH SHEEN CEMETERY
HAMMERSMITH CEMETERY
MORTLAKE
Chalkers Corner
Manor Circus
Richmond Circus
Milestone Green
EAST SHEEN
RICHMOND ATHLETIC GROUND
ROYAL HOSP
QUEEN'S COTTAGE GARDENS
PESTHOUSE COMMON
EAST SHEEN COMMON (NT)
NATIONAL TENNIS CENTRE
PALEWELL COMMON
HOUNSLOW
RICHMOND UPON THAMES
CHISWICK HIGH ROAD
GREAT WEST RD
LOWER MORTLAKE ROAD
UPPER RICHMOND ROAD
UPPER RICHMOND ROAD WEST
SOUTH CIRCULAR ROAD
NORTH CIRCULAR ROAD
KEW ROAD
MORTLAKE ROAD
CLIFFORD AVENUE
CHERTSEY ROAD
BURLINGTON LANE
ELLESMERE ROAD
HOGARTH LANE
500 yds
500 m

CT
CU
CV
CW
CX
CY
CZ
139
SHEPHERD'S BUSH
KENSINGTON
HOLLAND PARK
W14
W8
W12
W6
HAMMERSMITH
KENSINGTON (OLYMPIA)
OLYMPIA
EARLS COURT
SW5
CASTELNAU
SW13
WWT LONDON WETLAND CENTRE
SW6
FULHAM
PARSONS GREEN
BARNES
SW15
PUTNEY
WANDSWORTH
ROEHAMPTON
BARN ELMS PLAYING FIELDS
BARNES COMMON
FULHAM PALACE GARDENS
HURLINGHAM PARK
RIVER THAMES
CHARING CROSS HOSP
HAMMERSMITH CEMETERY
FULHAM CEMETERY
BISHOP'S PARK
160
179
294
306
76
77
78
79
80
81
82
83
84
22
23
24
UXBRIDGE ROAD
GOLDHAWK ROAD
KING STREET
GREAT WEST ROAD
HAMMERSMITH FLYOVER
TALGARTH ROAD
HAMMERSMITH ROAD
KENSINGTON HIGH ST
HOLLAND ROAD
LILLIE ROAD
DAWES ROAD
FULHAM PALACE ROAD
FULHAM ROAD
NEW KINGS RD
UPPER RICHMOND ROAD
LOWER RICHMOND ROAD
PUTNEY HIGH ST
PUTNEY BRIDGE
WANDSWORTH BRIDGE
ROEHAMPTON LANE
ROCKS LANE

KENSINGTON GARDENS
HYDE PARK
THE SERPENTINE
KENSINGTON
HOLLAND PARK
SOUTH KENSINGTON
EARLS COURT
WEST BROMPTON
BROMPTON
BELGRAVIA
CHELSEA
SANDS END
WALHAM GREEN
PARSONS GREEN
BATTERSEA PARK
CLAPHAM JUNCTION
WANDSWORTH
W8
SW7
SW5
SW10
SW3
SW6
SW11
SW15
SW18
DA
DB
DC
DD
DE
DF
DG
75
76
77
78
79
80
81
82
83
84
140
159
180
307
308
NATURAL HISTORY MUSEUM
SCIENCE MUSEUM
VICTORIA & ALBERT MUSEUM
ROYAL HOSPITAL CHELSEA
THE ROYAL MARSDEN
ROYAL BROMPTON HOSP
CHELSEA & WEST. HOSP
STAMFORD BRIDGE CHELSEA FC
BROMPTON CEMETERY
HURLINGHAM PARK
KENSINGTON ROAD
KNIGHTSBRIDGE
CROMWELL ROAD
BROMPTON ROAD
FULHAM ROAD
KING'S ROAD
CHELSEA EMBANKMENT
CHEYNE WALK
BATTERSEA BRIDGE
ALBERT BRIDGE
WANDSWORTH BRIDGE
LAVENDER HILL
CLAPHAM COMMON
500 yds
500 m

DH
DJ
DK
DL
DM
DN
DP
141
THE GREEN PARK
ST. JAMES'S PARK
SW1
BUCKINGHAM PALACE
ST. JAMES'S
WESTMINSTER
VICTORIA
PIMLICO
SOUTHWARK
WATERLOO
SE1
LAMBETH
SE11
VAUXHALL
KENNINGTON
RIVER THAMES
NINE ELMS
SW8
SOUTH LAMBETH
STOCKWELL
SW9
SE5
BATTERSEA
CLAPHAM
SW4
BRIXTON
SE24
HOUSES OF PARLIAMENT
ST. THOMAS' HOSP
LAMBETH PALACE
TATE BRITAIN
THE KIA OVAL (SURREY C.C.C.)
KENNINGTON PARK
MYATT'S FIELDS PARK
LAMBETH HOSPITAL
TRINITY HOSPICE
CLAPHAM COMMON
76
77
78
79
80
81
82
83
84
162
309
310
181
29
30
31

DQ
DR
DS
DT
DU
DV
DW
142
WAPPING
SOUTHWARK
SE1
LONDON BRIDGE
GUY'S HOSPITAL
TOWER BRIDGE EXHIBITION
THE BOROUGH
BERMONDSEY
NEWINGTON
SE17
WALWORTH
BURGESS PARK
SOUTHWARK PARK
161
CAMBERWELL
PECKHAM
SE5
SE15
MAUDSLEY HOSPITAL
KING'S COLLEGE HOSPITAL
RUSKIN PARK
311
312
SE24
SE22
PECKHAM RYE COMMON
PECKHAM RYE PARK
DULWICH COMMUNITY HOSP
182
75
76
77
78
79
80
81
82
83
84
0
500 yds
0
500 m

DX
DY
DZ
EA
EB
EC
ED
143
ISLE
OF
DOGS
WEST INDIA DOCKS
MILLWALL
CUBITT
TOWN
MUDCHUTE
FARM
E14
ISLAND
GARDENS
SE10
SE16
OTHERHITHE
DEPTFORD
SE8
DEPTFORD PARK
PEPYS PARK
SE14
NEW CROSS GATE
NEW CROSS
ST JOHN'S
GREENWICH
GREENWICH PARK
164
NATIONAL MARITIME MUSEUM
ROYAL OBSERVATORY GREENWICH (Flamsteed House)
QUEEN'S HOUSE
BLACKHEATH
SE3
SE4
HILLY FIELDS
LEWISHAM
SE13
BROCKLEY
BROCKLEY CEMETERY
LADYWELL CEMETERY
LADYWELL
UNIVERSITY HOSPITAL
MANOR PARK
183
EVELYN STREET
CREEK ROAD
BLACKHEATH ROAD
BLACKHEATH HILL
SHOOTERS HILL
LEWISHAM WAY
LOAMPIT VALE
LOAMPIT HILL
MANCHESTER ROAD
WESTFERRY ROAD
TRAFALGAR ROAD
ROMNEY RD
LEE HIGH RD
SOUTHWARK
TOWER HAMLETS
76
77
78
79
80
81
82
83
84
36
37
38
313
314

EE
EF
EG
EH
EJ
EK
EL
144
The O2
GREENWICH PENINSULA
NORTH GREENWICH
E16
SILVERTOWN
WEST SILVERTOWN
N Woolwich Roundabout
Airport Roundabout
PONTOON DOCK
THAMES BARRIER PARK
THAMESIDE INDUSTRIAL EST
RIVER THAMES
WOOLWICH REACH
THAMES FLOOD BARRIER
GREENWICH PENINSULA ECOLOGY PARK
BUGSBY'S WAY
NEW CHARLTON
MERIDIAN TRADING ESTATE
ANCHORAGE POINT IND EST
Stone Lake Roundabout
WOOLWICH ROAD
SE10
MARYON PARK
MARYON WILSON PARK
THE VALLEY CHARLTON ATHLETIC FC
EAST GREENWICH PLEASAUNCE
WESTCOMBE PARK
TRAFALGAR RD
MAZE HILL
CHARLTON
SE7
CHARLTON PARK
163
GREENWICH PARK
ROYAL OBSERVATORY GREENWICH
NATIONAL MARITIME MUSEUM
Sun-in-the-Sands
SHOOTERS HILL ROAD
BLACKHEATH
SE3
HORNFAIR PARK
KIDBROOKE
Kidbrooke Interchange
ROCHESTER WAY RELIEF RD
BLACKHEATH PARK
LEE
SE12
SE13
GREENWICH CEMETERY
SUTCLIFFE PARK
Lee Green
ELTHAM ROAD
184
SIDCUP RD
Yorkshire Grey
75
76
77
78
79
80
81
82
83
84
500 yds
500 m

KING GEORGE V DOCK
EM
EN
EP
EQ
ER
ES
ET
145
THAMESMEAD WEST
SE28
H.M. PRISON BELMARSH
WOOLWICH CROWN CT
WEST THAMESMEAD BUSINESS PARK
GALLIONS REACH
305
NEWHAM
GREENWICH
WOOLWICH FREE FERRY
WOOLWICH FOOT TUNNEL
ROYAL VICTORIA GDNS
STANDARD INDUSTRIAL ESTATE
BROADWATER GRN
WOOLWICH ARSENAL
WOOLWICH
PLUMSTEAD
PLUMSTEAD HIGH STREET
PLUMSTEAD COMMON
SE2
SE18
WINN'S COMMON
BARRACK FIELD
WOOLWICH COMMON
ROYAL ARTILLERY BARRACKS
WOOLWICH GARRISON
WOOLWICH CEMETERY
EAST WICKHAM
EAST WICKHAM OPEN SPACE
SHREWSBURY PARK
SHOOTERS HILL GOLF COURSE
SHOOTER'S HILL
HILLVIEW CEMETERY
ELTHAM COMMON
MEMORIAL HOSPITAL
CASTLE WOOD
JACK WOOD
OXLEAS WOOD
OXLEAS MEADOW
SHEPHERDLEAS WOOD
FALCONWOOD
DA16
DA15
SE9
ELTHAM CEMETERY
ELTHAM PARK SOUTH
ELTHAM WARREN GOLF COURSE
WELLING
166
185
76
77
78
79
80
81
82
83
84

EU
EV
EW
EX
EY
EZ
FA
146
LAKESIDE CENTRE
SOUTHMERE PARK
ERITH MARSHES
BIRCHMERE PARK
SE28
DA18
WOODLAND WAY
ABBEY WOOD PARK
THISTLEBROOK INDUSTRIAL EST
KENCOT CL BUS PARK
EASTERN IND EST
SE18
ABBEY WOOD
Lesnes Abbey (ruins)
PLUMSTEAD GARDENS
ABBEY WOOD CARAVAN CLUBS SITE
SE2
BOSTALL HEATH
HURST ESTATE
WEST HEATH
ALBERT ROAD ESTATE
BOSTALL WOODS
CLAM FIELD RECREATION GROUND
GOLDIE LEIGH HOSPITAL
165
WOOLWICH CEMETERY
PLUMSTEAD CEMETERY
EAST WICKHAM
EAST WICKHAM OPEN SPACE
DA16
STEVENS PARK
DA7
WELLING
BEXLEYHEATH
BEXLEYHEATH CEMETERY
DANSON
PARK
DA6
186
75
76
77
78
79
80
81
82
83
84
500 yds
500 m
47
48
49

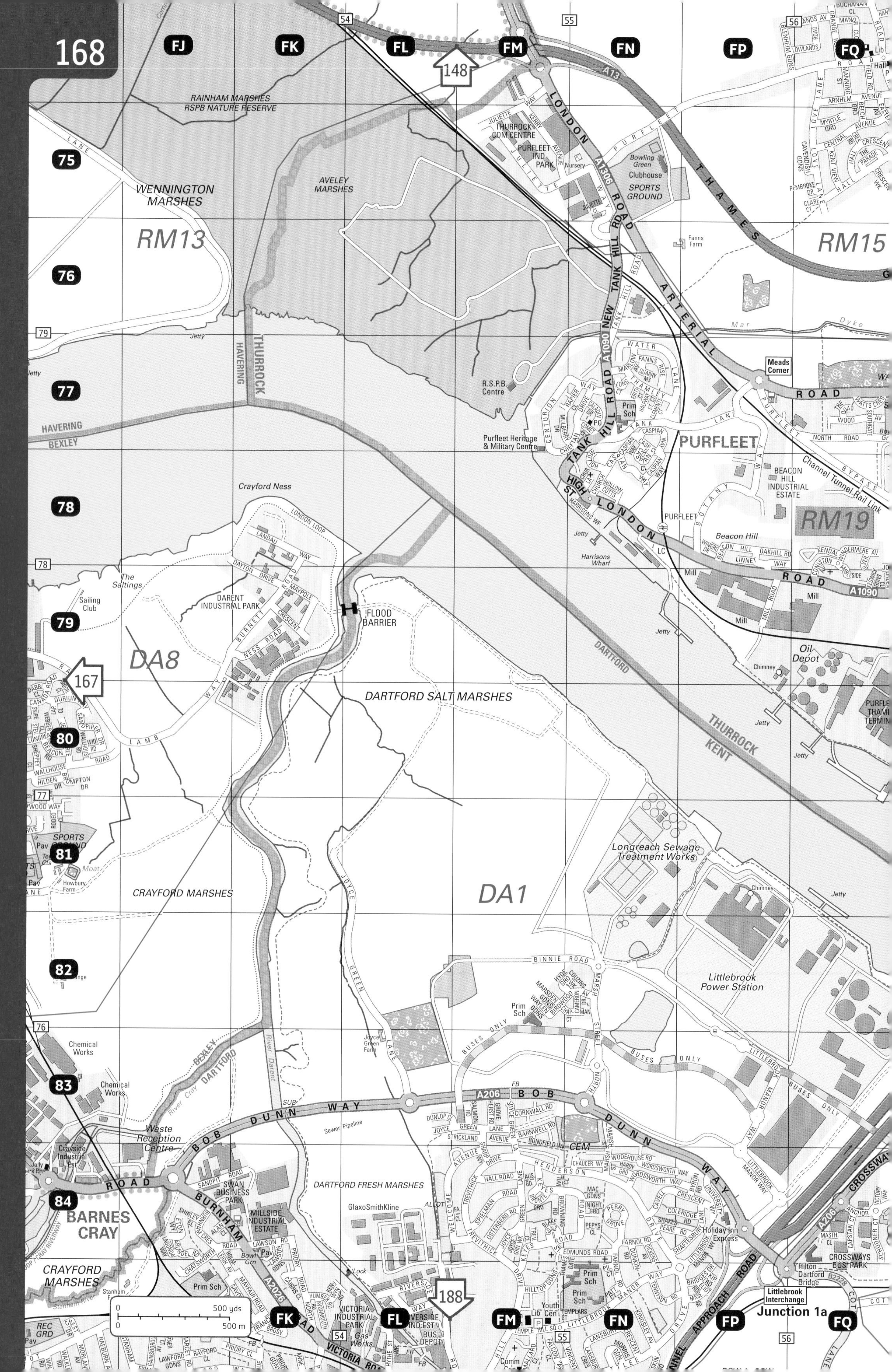
FJ
FK
FL
FM
FN
FP
FQ
148
RAINHAM MARSHES
RSPB NATURE RESERVE
WENNINGTON MARSHES
RM13
AVELEY MARSHES
RM15
THURROCK
HAVERING
BEXLEY
Crayford Ness
Purfleet Heritage & Military Centre
PURFLEET
BEACON HILL INDUSTRIAL ESTATE
RM19
Beacon Hill
Meads Corner
Harrisons Wharf
DARENT INDUSTRIAL PARK
FLOOD BARRIER
DA8
167
DARTFORD SALT MARSHES
Oil Depot
THURROCK
KENT
DARTFORD
Longreach Sewage Treatment Works
CRAYFORD MARSHES
DA1
Littlebrook Power Station
Chemical Works
Waste Reception Centre
BOB DUNN WAY
A206
BARNES CRAY
SWAN BUSINESS PARK
MILLSIDE INDUSTRIAL ESTATE
DARTFORD FRESH MARSHES
GlaxoSmithKline
Holiday Inn Express
Hilton Dartford Bridge
CROSSWAYS BUS PARK
Littlebrook Interchange
Junction 1a
188
VICTORIA INDUSTRIAL PARK
RIVERSIDE IND EST
BUS DEPOT
75
76
77
78
79
80
81
82
83
84
0 500 yds
0 500 m

Junction 30
Junction 31
West Thurrock
CHAFFORD HUNDRED
RM16
South Stifford
RM20
DA2
DA9
DA10
Stone
Greenhithe
RIVER THAMES
ST. CLEMENT'S OR FIDDLER'S REACH
STONENESS LIGHTHOUSE
WEST THURROCK MARSHES
Oil Storage Depot
Chemical Works
Electricity Sub Station
WILDLIFE SANCTUARY
Thurrock Services
ARTERIAL ROAD
A13
M25
A126
A1306
A1090
A282
A226
CANTERBURY WAY
QUEEN ELIZABETH II BRIDGE (TOLL)
DARTFORD TUNNEL
CROSSWAYS BOULEVARD
LONDON ROAD
OLIVER ROAD
THURROCK WAY
STONENESS RD
Intu Lakeside
LAKESIDE RETAIL PK
ARENA ESSEX RACEWAY
KARTING CEN
Stonehouse Corner
THURROCK TRADE PARK
ACORN TRADING ESTATE
GLADE BUSINESS CENTRE
WATERGLADE INDUSTRIAL PK
FROGMORE ESTATE
J31 PARK
LYNDALE ESTATE
MAGNET ESTATE
THAMES EUROPORT
Johnson's Wharf
Bell Wharf
SWANSCOMBE MARSHES
BRANNETT'S WOOD
BRICKBARN WOOD
COMBE WOOD
LOW WELL WOOD
HANGMAN'S WOOD
MARDYKE WOODS
WARREN GORGE
LION GORGE
GALLEY HILL TRADE PARK
149
170
189
FR FS FT FU FV FW FX
57 58 59
76 77 78 79 80 81 82 83 84

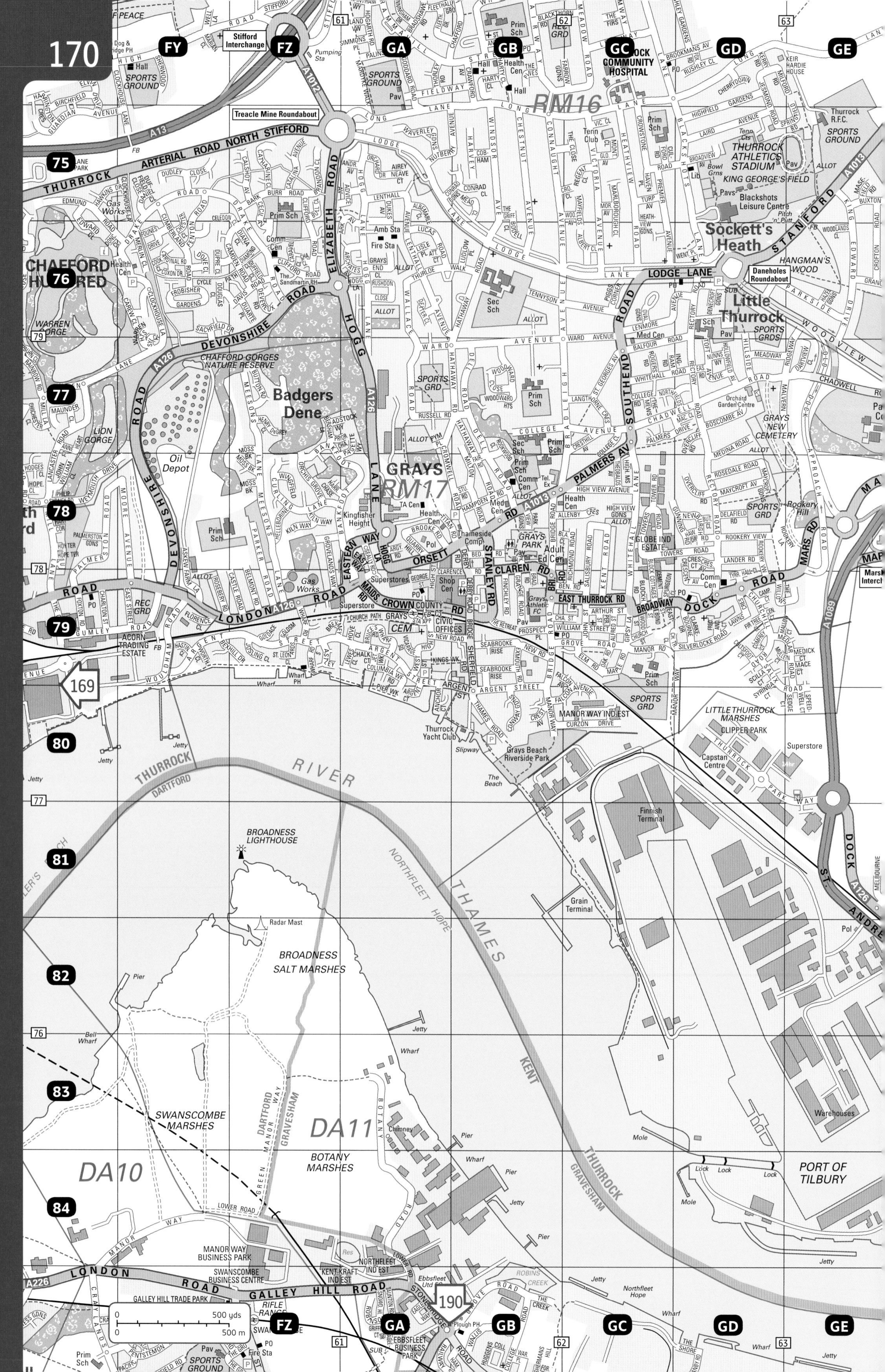

FY
FZ
GA
GB
GC
GD
GE
Stifford Interchange
Treacle Mine Roundabout
Daneholes Roundabout
RM16
RM17
DA10
DA11
GRAYS
CHAFFORD HUNDRED
Sockett's Heath
Little Thurrock
Badgers Dene
CHAFFORD GORGES NATURE RESERVE
WARREN GORGE
LION GORGE
Oil Depot
THURROCK ARTERIAL ROAD NORTH STIFFORD
ELIZABETH ROAD
HOGG LANE
DEVONSHIRE ROAD
LODGE LANE
SOUTHEND ROAD
PALMERS AV
STANFORD ROAD
DOCK ROAD
LONDON ROAD
ORSETT RD
EAST THURROCK RD
STANLEY RD
BROADWAY
ST. ANDREWS
THURROCK COMMUNITY HOSPITAL
THURROCK ATHLETICS STADIUM
KING GEORGE'S FIELD
Blackshots Leisure Centre
Thurrock R.F.C.
HANGMAN'S WOOD
GRAYS NEW CEMETERY
GLOBE IND ESTATE
ACORN TRADING ESTATE
MANOR WAY IND EST
Thameside Compl
Kingfisher Height
Thurrock Yacht Club
Grays Beach Riverside Park
LITTLE THURROCK MARSHES
CLIPPER PARK
Capstan Centre
Superstore
Finnish Terminal
Grain Terminal
Warehouses
PORT OF TILBURY
RIVER THAMES
NORTHFLEET HOPE
BROADNESS LIGHTHOUSE
Radar Mast
BROADNESS SALT MARSHES
SWANSCOMBE MARSHES
BOTANY MARSHES
MANOR WAY BUSINESS PARK
SWANSCOMBE BUSINESS CENTRE
KENT KRAFT IND EST
NORTHFLEET IND EST
GALLEY HILL TRADE PARK
GALLEY HILL ROAD
EBBSFLEET BUSINESS PARK
ROBINS CREEK
Northfleet Hope
THURROCK
DARTFORD
KENT
GRAVESHAM
169
190
500 yds
500 m

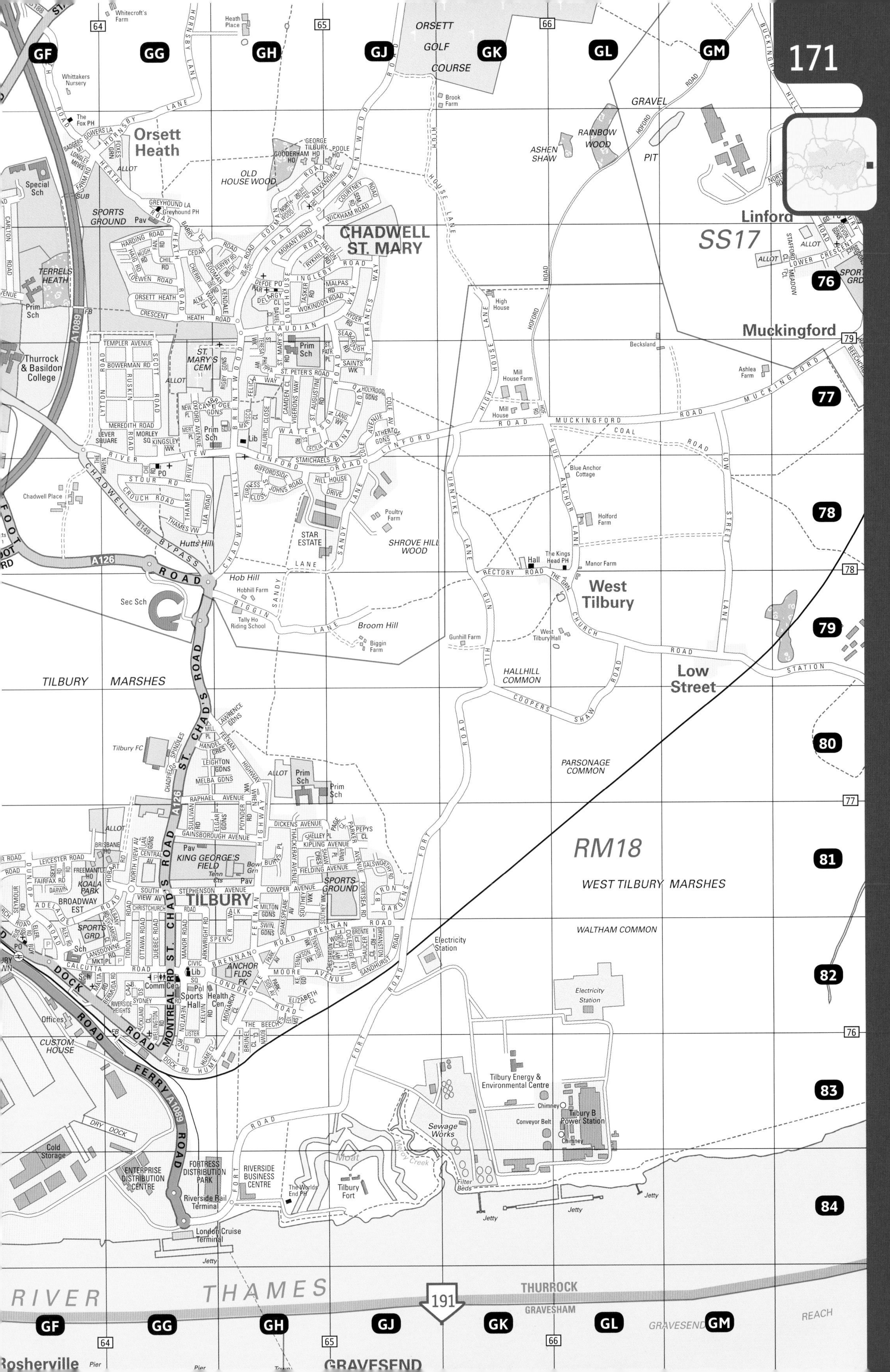
Orsett Heath
CHADWELL ST. MARY
Linford
SS17
Muckingford
West Tilbury
Low Street
TILBURY
RM18
TILBURY MARSHES
WEST TILBURY MARSHES
WALTHAM COMMON
PARSONAGE COMMON
HALLHILL COMMON
ORSETT GOLF COURSE
RAINBOW WOOD
ASHEN SHAW
GRAVEL PIT
OLD HOUSE WOOD
SHROVE HILL WOOD
Hob Hill
Broom Hill
Hutts Hill
Tilbury Fort
Tilbury Energy & Environmental Centre
Tilbury B Power Station
Sewage Works
London Cruise Terminal
RIVER THAMES
GRAVESHAM
THURROCK
GRAVESEND
REACH
Rosherville
191

AS
AT
AU
AV
AW
AX
AY
152
192
OLD WINDSOR
SL4
SL5
TW20
Sunnymeads
COLNE VALLEY REGIONAL PARK
REMENHAM PARK
Englefield Green
Egham Wick
Ripley Springs
WINDSOR GREAT PARK
RUNNYMEDE PARK
THE SAVILL GARDENS
Savill Court Hotel
Brunel University, Runnymede Campus
University of London Royal Holloway College
Royal Holloway Coll (Hall of Residence)
Battersea Dogs & Cats Home
Anglo Saxon Palace (site of)
Old Windsor Lock
FRIARY ISLAND
MAGNA CARTA ISLAND
Magna Carta Monument
John F Kennedy Memorial
Air Forces Memorial
Benedictine Nunnery (remains)
OLD WINDSOR WOOD
LIDDELL PLANTATION
DUKE OF YORK PLANTATION
WILD BOAR ENCLOSURE
GORE PLANTATION
Cookes Hill
KING GEORGE VI CORONATION GROVE
CONSERVATORY COVERT
GREENBROOM COVERT
CUMBERLAND LODGE
Royal Lodge
CHAPEL WOOD
WILDERNESS
SMITH'S LAWN
POLO GROUND
SCARLETOAK PLANTATION
OBELISK POND
ALBERT ROAD
STRAIGHT ROAD
WINDSOR ROAD
PRIEST HILL
ST. JUDE'S ROAD
EGHAM HILL
BISHOPSGATE ROAD
CRIMP HILL
A308
A328
A30
B376
B3021
500 yds
500 m

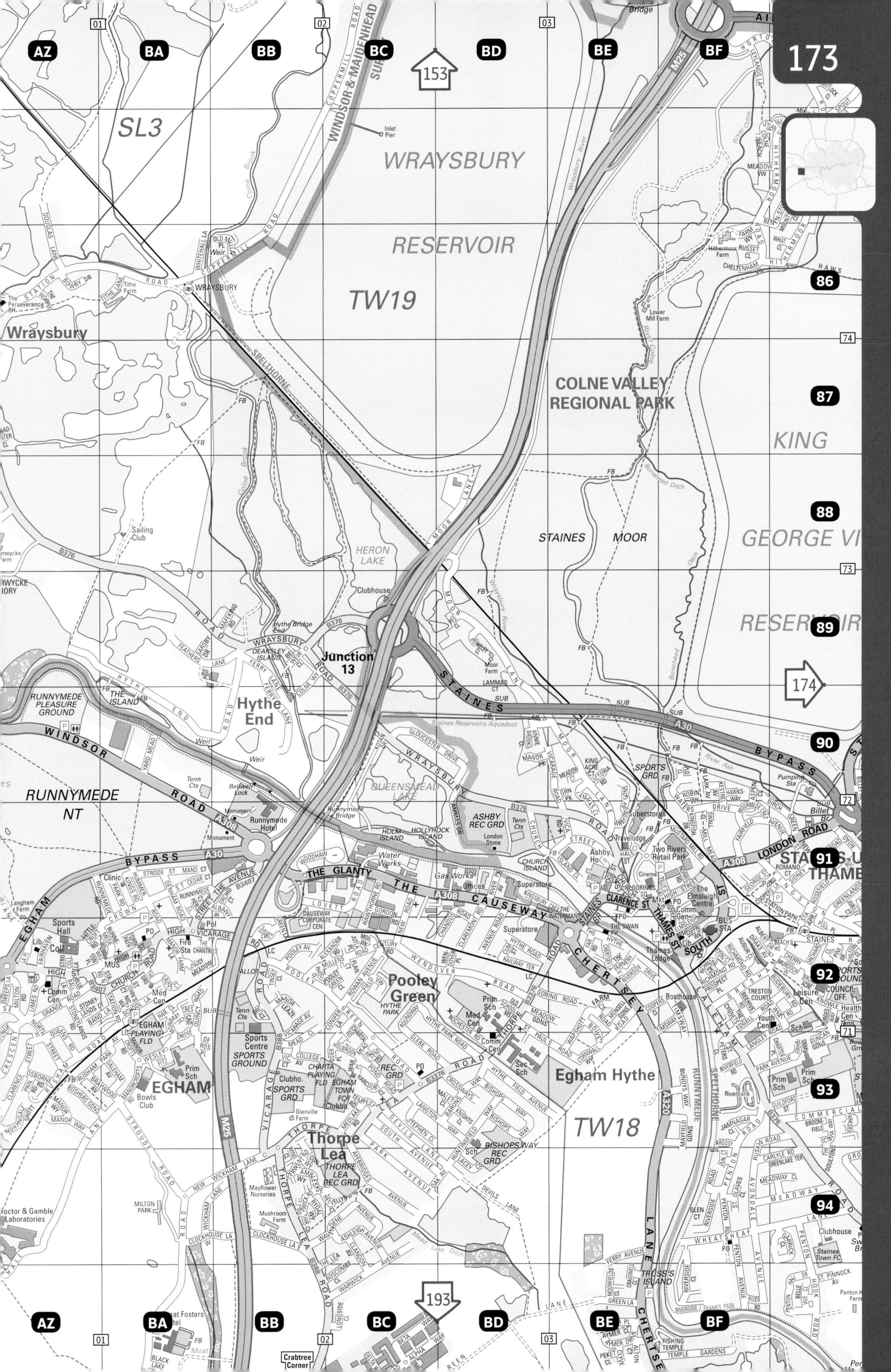
WRAYSBURY
RESERVOIR
TW19
SL3
Wraysbury
COLNE VALLEY
REGIONAL PARK
STAINES
MOOR
KING
GEORGE VI
RESERVOIR
HERON
LAKE
Junction
13
Hythe
End
RUNNYMEDE
PLEASURE
GROUND
RUNNYMEDE
NT
QUEENSMEAD
LAKE
ASHBY
REC GRD
Pooley
Green
EGHAM
Egham Hythe
TW18
Thorpe
Lea
THORPE
LEA
REC GRD
SPORTS
GROUND
BISHOPS WAY
REC
GRD
STAINES BYPASS
WINDSOR ROAD
THE CAUSEWAY
THE GLANTY
LONDON ROAD
CHERTSEY LANE
WINDSOR & MAIDENHEAD
SPELTHORNE
RUNNYMEDE
Two Rivers
Retail Park
Elmsleigh
Centre
Crabtree
Corner
153
174
193
86
87
88
89
90
91
92
93
94

STANWELL MOOR
KING GEORGE VI RESERVOIR
STAINES RESERVOIRS
TW19
STANWELL
STAINES-UPON-THAMES
ASHFORD
TW17
TW18
QUEEN MARY
ASHFORD MANOR GOLF COURSE
ASHFORD HOSPITAL
Crooked Billet Roundabout
Fordbridge Roundabout
CARGO TERMINAL
BRITISH AIRWAYS CARGO CENTRE
BLACKBURN TRADING ESTATE
H.M. Prison Bronzefield
SHORTWOOD COMMON
RECREATION GROUND
GRAVEL PIT
154
173
194
500 yds
500 m

BP
BQ
BR
BS
BT
BU
BV
08
09
10
155
HATTON
HATTON CROSS
TW6
TERMINAL 4
TW14
DUKE OF NORTHUMBERLAND'S RIVER
HOUNSLOW URBAN FARM
HATTON CEM
BEDFONT RECREATION GROUND
GREAT SOUTH WEST ROAD
STAINES ROAD
Clockhouse Roundabout
NORTH FELTHAM TRADING EST
FALCON EST
MERCURY CENTRE
MARLIN PARK
GRIFFIN CENTRE
Asylum & Immigration Tribunal
SPORTS GROUND
BEDFONT LANE REC GRD
FELTHAM ARENAS
GLEBELANDS PLAYING FIELDS
FELTHAM PARK
HARLINGTON ROAD WEST
86
87
88
89
90
91
92
93
94
EAST BEDFONT
BEDFONT LAKES COUNTRY PARK
Information Centre
H.M. Young Offenders Institution & Remand Centre
GROSVENOR PARK
LOWER FELTHAM
FELTHAM
FELTHAM BUSINESS COMPLEX
FELTHAMBROOK IND. EST
176
HIGH STREET
ASHFORD RD
CEM
TW13
ASHFORD IND EST
SNAKEY LANE
Staines R.F.C.
LAKESIDE SPORTS GROUND
FELTHAMHILL
KING GEORGE'S FIELD
TW15
TW16
BP Sunbury Business Park
Pumping Station
Filter Beds
STAINES ROAD WEST
SPORTS GROUND
KEMPTON PARK
Grandstand
Sunbury Cross
Junction 1
SUNBURY
ASHFORD COMMON WATER TREATMENT WORKS
195
M3
LONDON
RACECOURSE

BW
BX
BY
BZ
CA
CB
CC
156
175
196
TW4
TW3
TW14
TW13
TW12
TW16
HOUNSLOW HEATH
HOUNSLOW HEATH GOLF COURSE
HOUNSLOW HEATH GOLF COURSE
CENTRAL PARK EST
STAINES ROAD
WHITTON
HOUNSLOW
CRANE PARK
HANWORTH PARK
HANWORTH
KEMPTON PARK
KEMPTON PARK RESERVOIRS
FULWELL PARK
FULWELL GOLF COURSE
TWICKENHAM PARK GOLF CENTRE
TWICKENHAM CEMETERY
BOROUGH CEMETERY
HEATHFIELD REC GRD
MILL FARM BUSINESS PARK
West Thames Coll
FELTHAM BUSINESS COMPLEX
HAMPTON BUSINESS PARK
HANWORTH TRADING ESTATE
APEX RETAIL PARK
GREAT CHERTSEY ROAD
TWICKENHAM RD
UXBRIDGE ROAD
HAMPTON ROAD WEST
HOUNSLOW ROAD
HANWORTH ROAD
HARLINGTON ROAD WEST
HARLINGTON ROAD EAST
SWIFT WAY
CARLISLE PARK
HALF MOON COVERT
KINGSWAY BUSINESS PARK
HAMPTON
Open Air Pool
MURRAY PARK
PLAYING FIELD
85
86
87
88
89
90
91
92
93
94
0 500 yds
0 500 m

CD
CE
CF
CG
CH
CJ
CK
TW9
OLD DEER PARK RECREATION GROUND
MOGDEN SEWAGE TREATMENT WORKS
TW6
ST. MARGARETS
St. Margarets Roundabout
157
RICHMOND GREEN
RICHMOND
THE RUGBY FOOTBALL UNION TWICKENHAM
TWICKENHAM TRADING EST
Whitton Rd Roundabout
London Road Roundabout
MOOR MEAD GRD
CHERTSEY ROAD
THE AVENUE
RICHMOND ROAD
TW2
RICHMOND UPON THAMES COLLEGE
MARBLE HILL
MARBLE HILL HOUSE
MARBLE HILL PARK
TW1
PETERSHAM MEADOWS
GLOVER'S ISLAND
MEADOWBANK
RIVER THAMES
ORLEANS HOUSE GALLERY
YORK HOUSE
EEL PIE ISLAND
HAM HOUSE (NT)
HAM HOUSE GARDENS
TWICKENHAM
TWICKENHAM RIFLE CLUB
KING GEORGE'S FIELD
REC GRD
SPORTS GROUND
TW10
HAM
HAM COMMON
ST. MICHAEL'S CONVENT
THE CASSEL
STRAWBERRY HILL
STRAWBERRY HILL GOLF COURSE
STRAWBERRY HILL HO
St. Mary's Coll
Thames Young Mariners Base
HAM FIELDS
Teddington Lock
Teddington Weir
Teddington Studios
The Lensbury Hotel
TEDDINGTON CEM
TEDDINGTON
HAMPTON HILL
CANAL PLANTATION
NATIONAL PHYSICAL LABORATORY
BUSHY HOUSE
TW11
ROUND PLANTATION
BUSHY PARK
197
178
KT2
TROWLOCK ISLAND
STEVEN'S EYOT
HAMPTON WICK
86
87
88
89
90
91
92
93
94

RICHMOND PARK
RICHMOND
PETERSHAM
HAM COMMON
EAST SHEEN
SW14
TW10
KT2
COOMBE
RICHMOND GOLF COURSE
COOMBE HILL GOLF COURSE
COOMBE WOOD GOLF COURSE
EAST SHEEN COMMON (NT)
PESTHOUSE COMMON
EAST SHEEN CEMETERY
RICHMOND CEMETERY
PALEWELL COMMON
PALEWELL PLAYING FIELDS
TECK PLANTATION
SHEEN WOOD
The Bog
SHEEN CROSS WOOD
POLO FIELD
CONDUIT WOOD
SAW PIT PLANTATION
JUBILEE PLANTATION
DUCHESS WOOD
WHITE LODGE PLANTATIONS
The Royal Ballet Sch
KIDNEY WOOD
SIDMOUTH WOOD
QUEEN ELIZABETH'S PLANTATION
KING GEORGE V JUBILEE PLANTATION
DEER PARK
TREEBOX WOOD
SPANKER'S HILL WOOD
POND PLANTATION
LAWN PLANTATION
White Ash Lodge
Pembroke Lodge
KING HENRY VIII MOUND
PETERSHAM MEADOWS
GLOVER'S ISLAND
Tercentenary Plantation
Pond Slade
PRINCE CHARLES'S SPINNEY
GIBBET WOOD
HAM CROSS PLANTATION
ISABELLA PLANTATION
Broomfield Hill
BROOMFIELD HILL PLANTATION
Kingston Uni (Dorich House)
Kingston University (Kingston Hill)
HIGH WOOD
Deer Fold
Ham Dip
Ham Bottom
CORONATION PLANTATION
Thatchedhouse Lodge
Kings Clump
Dark Hill
Ladderstile Gate
Warren House Conference Cen
THE WATERGARDENS
KINGSTON PARK EST
Kingston Lodge Hotel
American Uni in London
Richmond Hill Hotel
Royal Star & Garter Home
Ormeley Lodge
Parkgate House
Open during daylight hours only
UPPER RICHMOND ROAD WEST
PETERSHAM ROAD
RICHMOND ROAD
KINGSTON HILL
COOMBE LANE WEST
SAWYER'S HILL
QUEEN'S RIDE
HAM GATE AVENUE
ROBIN HOOD WAY
CL CM CN CP CQ CR CS
158
177
198
85 86 87 88 89 90 91 92 93 94
0 500 yds
0 500 m

CT
CU
CV
CW
CX
CY
CZ
159
ROEHAMPTON
PUTNEY
WANDSWORTH
SW15
PUTNEY HEATH
ROEHAMPTON GOLF COURSE
Southlands College
Digby Stuart College
Roehampton University
Froebel College
QUEEN MARY'S UNI HOSP
ROEHAMPTON PLAYING FIELDS
S. Thames Coll Downshire Ho
MARYFIELD CONVENT
Roehampton Uni-Whitelands College
ST MARY'S CONVENT
Tibbet's Corner
Roehampton Lane
ROYAL HOSPITAL
UPPER RICHMOND ROAD
EAST PUTNEY
SOUTHFIELDS
SW18
WIMBLEDON PARK Stadium
Kingsfarm Plantation
RICHMOND PARK GOLF COURSE
Jerry's Hill
Crematorium
PUTNEY VALE CEMETERY
Stag Lane
WINDMILL MUSEUM
PUTNEY VALE
WIMBLEDON
LONDON SCOTTISH GOLF COURSE
WIMBLEDON PARK GOLF COURSE
WIMBLEDON PARK
ALL ENGLAND LAWN TENNIS & CROQUET CLUB
PARKSIDE HOSPITAL
SW19
COMMON
BLUEGATE GRAVEL PIT (DISUSED)
Queen's Butt (Site of)
Gravelly Hill
Farm Bog
Farm Ravine
Caesar's Camp
CANNIZARO PARK
Cannizaro House Hotel
Fishponds Wood Nature Reserve
Mill Corner
ROYAL WIMBLEDON GOLF COURSE
Shadwell Wood
LADY JANE'S WOOD
HIGH ST WIMBLEDON
WIMBLEDON HILL RD
WIMBLEDON
SPORTS GROUND
COPSE HILL
SW20
OBERON PLAYING FIELD
DUNDONALD REC GRD
COTTENHAM PARK
KINGSTON ROAD
180
199
86
87
88
89
90
91
92
93
94
22
23
24
71
72
73
74

DA
DB
DC
DD
DE
DF
DG
160
179
200
85
86
87
88
89
90
91
92
93
94
WANDSWORTH
WANDSWORTH RIVERSIDE QUARTER PIER
CLAPHAM JUNCTION
CLAPHAM COMMON
WANDSWORTH COMMON
SW11
SW18
SW17
SW19
SOUTHFIELDS
EARLSFIELD
SUMMERSTOWN
BALHAM
UPPER TOOTING
TOOTING GRAVENEY
COLLIER'S WOOD
SOUTH WIMBLEDON
WIMBLEDON PARK
FURZE
H.M. PRISON WANDSWORTH
WANDSWORTH CEMETERY
CENTRAL LONDON GOLF CENTRE
SPRINGFIELD HOSPITAL
STREATHAM CEMETERY
WIMBLEDON STADIUM
WIMBLEDON CEMETERY
LAMBETH CEMETERY
ST. GEORGE'S HOSPITAL
LONDON ROAD CEMETERY
FIGGE'S MARSH
SPENCER PARK
KING GEORGE'S PARK
GARRATT GREEN
GARRATT PARK
WANDLE MEADOW NAT. PK
MERTON INDUSTRIAL PARK
Wandsworth Town
Earlsfield
Wimbledon Park
Haydons Road
Tooting Bec
Tooting Bdy
Tooting
Wimbledon
Colliers Wood
WANDSWORTH HIGH ST
WEST HILL
ARMOURY WAY
GARRATT LANE
MERTON ROAD
DURNSFORD ROAD
TRINITY ROAD
BURNTWOOD LANE
PLOUGH LANE
HAYDONS ROAD
MERTON HIGH STREET
MERANTUN WAY
THE BROADWAY
KINGSTON ROAD
TOOTING HIGH ST
UPPER TOOTING RD
BALHAM HIGH ROAD
MITCHAM ROAD
CLAPHAM COMMON W SIDE
NIGHTINGALE LANE
BELLEVUE RD
ALEXANDRA RD
A3
A24
A214
A217
A218
A219
A238
A205
0 500 yds
0 500 m

DH
DJ
DK
DL
DM
DN
DP
161
182
201
86
87
88
89
90
91
92
93
94
BRIXTON
CLAPHAM PARK
CLAPHAM COMMON
SW4
SW2
SE24
SE21
SE27
SE19
SW16
BROCKWELL PARK
STREATHAM HILL
TOOTING BEC COMMON
STREATHAM PARK
STREATHAM
STREATHAM COMMON
STREATHAM VALE
NORWOOD GROVE RECREATION GROUND
NORBURY PARK
NORBURY
WEST NORWOOD CEMETERY
TULSE HILL
H.M. PRISON BRIXTON
BRIXTON HILL
STREATHAM HIGH ROAD
CHRISTCHURCH ROAD
POYNDERS ROAD
CAVENDISH ROAD
BEC ROAD
MITCHAM ROAD
NORWOOD ROAD
DULWICH ROAD
THURLOW PARK ROAD
KNIGHTS HILL
BEULAH HILL
CROWN LANE
STREATHAM COMMON NORTH
ACRE LANE
COLDHARBOUR LANE
BALHAM HILL
CLAPHAM COMMON SOUTH SIDE
ATKINS RD
TOOTING GRAVENEY COMMON
BIGGIN WOOD
PLAYING FIELD
THE ROOKERY

DQ
DR
DS
DT
DU
DV
DW
162
181
202
85
86
87
88
89
90
91
92
93
94
SE24
SE22
SE21
SE27
SE26
SE19
SE20
HERNE HILL
EAST DULWICH
DULWICH
TULSE HILL
WEST DULWICH
WEST NORWOOD
UPPER SYDENHAM
SYDENHAM
NORWOOD
NORWOOD NEWTOWN
UPPER NORWOOD
PENGE
PECKHAM RYE COMMON
PECKHAM RYE PARK
CAMBERWELL OLD CEMETERY
BROCKWELL PARK
DULWICH PARK
DULWICH & SYDENHAM HILL GOLF COURSE
SYDENHAM HILL WOOD (NATURE RESERVE)
DULWICH WOOD
WEST NORWOOD CEMETERY
NORWOOD PARK
CRYSTAL PALACE PARK
CRYSTAL PALACE NATIONAL SPORTS CENTRE
HERNE HILL VELODROME
SOUTH BANK UNIVERSITY SPORTS GROUND
DULWICH COMMUNITY HOSP
DULWICH PICTURE GALL
HALF MOON LANE
LORDSHIP LANE
CROXTED ROAD
DULWICH COMMON
LONDON ROAD
THURLOW PARK ROAD
DULWICH WOOD PK
WESTWOOD HILL
CRYSTAL PALACE PARK ROAD
KIRKDALE
DARTMOUTH ROAD
ANERLEY HILL
ANERLEY ROAD
CENTRAL HILL
CROWN DALE
BEULAH HILL
WESTOW HILL
CHURCH ROAD
KNIGHTS HILL
NORWOOD HIGH ST
0 500 yds
0 500 m

BROCKLEY
SE4
LADYWELL
UNIVERSITY HOSPITAL LEWISHAM
LEWISHAM PARK
SE13
HITHER GREEN
HONOR OAK PARK
SE23
CATFORD
Catford Gyratory
SE6
FOREST HILL
BELL GREEN
BELLINGHAM
LOWER SYDENHAM
SOUTHEND
NEW BECKENHAM
BECKENHAM PLACE PARK
BR3
BECKENHAM
BR2
SHORTLANDS GOLF COURSE
BROMLEY PARK
THE SLOANE HOSPITAL
FORSTER MEMORIAL PARK
MOUNTSFIELD PARK PLAYING FIELDS
BLYTHE HILL FIELDS
LADYWELL FIELDS
BROCKLEY HILL PARK
CAMBERWELL NEW CEMETERY
HONOR OAK SPORTS GRD
BROCKLEY CEMETERY
LADYWELL CEMETERY
KENT C.C.C.
CRYSTAL PALACE FC TRAINING GROUND
ROYAL BANK OF SCOTLAND SPORTS GOUND
LEWISHAM BOROUGH SPORTS GROUND
MIDLAND BANK SPORTS GROUND
WARREN AVE PLAYING FIELDS
SUMMERHOUSE HILL WOOD
ASH PLANTATION
GOLF COURSE
163
184
203
DX
DY
DZ
EA
EB
EC
ED
86
87
88
89
90
91
92
93
94

EE
EF
EG
EH
EJ
EK
EL
164
183
204
85
86
87
88
89
90
91
92
93
94
SE13
SE12
SE6
BR1
BR2
HITHER GREEN
GROVE PARK
MOTTINGHAM
ELTHAM
DOWNHAM
PLAISTOW
SUNDRIDGE
ELMSTEAD
ELMSTEAD WOOD
Widmore Green
MANOR PARK
MANOR HOUSE GARDENS
HITHER GREEN CEMETERY
Crematorium
GROVE PARK CEMETERY
NORTHBROOK PARK
SUTCLIFFE PARK
OLD COLFEIANS SPORTS GROUND
MIDDLE PARK FIELD
QUEENSCROFT REC GRD
KING JOHN PLAYING FIELDS
UNI OF GREENWICH ATHLETIC GRD
CHINBROOK MEADOWS
MOTTINGHAM SPORTS GROUND
LOWER MARVELS WOOD
MARVELS WOOD
SUNDRIDGE PARK GOLF COURSE
ROCKPIT WOOD
ELMSTEAD WOODS
LOGSHILL WOOD
SHAFTESBURY PARK REC GRD
KING'S MEADOW PLAYING FIELDS
DOWNHAM PLAYING FIELDS
DOWNHAM FIELDS
LEWISHAM BOROUGH SPORTS GROUND
MIDLAND BANK SPORTS GROUND
WARREN AVE PLAYING FIELDS
SHORTLANDS GOLF
BROMLEY PARK
THE SLOANE HOSPITAL
BROMLEY NORTH
Clifton's Roundabout
Yorkshire Grey
LEWISHAM
GREENWICH
ELTHAM ROAD
SIDCUP ROAD
WESTHORNE AVENUE
BURNT ASH HILL
BURNT ASH ROAD
BARING ROAD
BURNT ASH LANE
LONDON ROAD
BROMLEY HILL
S CIRCULAR ROAD
ST. MILDREDS ROAD
ROCHESTER WAY
A20
A205
A210
A212
A2212
A2213
A21
B226
0 500 yds
0 500 m

ELTHAM
AVERY HILL
BLACKFEN
DA15
DA16
LAMORBEY
SE9
NEW ELTHAM
LONGLANDS
SIDCUP
DA14
BR7
CHISLEHURST WEST
CHISLEHURST
SCADBURY PARK
NATURE RESERVE
ROYAL BLACKHEATH GOLF COURSE
University of Greenwich Avery Hill Campus
CHISLEHURST COMMON
CAMDEN PARK
CHISLEHURST GOLF COURSE
PARK WOOD
165
186
205
86
87
88
89
90
91
92
93
94

EU
EV
EW
EX
EY
EZ
FA
166
DA16
DANSON
PARK
THE LAKE
The Boathouse
DA6
BEXLEYHEATH
BROADWAY
The Mall Bexleyheath
BEXLEYHEATH GOLF COURSE
ROCHESTER WAY
A2
Danson Interchange
BLACKFEN ROAD
A210
BLACKFEN
HOLLY OAK WOOD PK
BEXLEY
BEXLEY PARK WOOD
PENHILL PARK
SIDCUP GOLF COURSE
DA15
Rose Bruford College
LAMORBEY PARK
RUTLAND SHAW
HURST ROAD
A222
ABBEYHILL PARK
DA5
KING GEORGE'S REC GRD
SIDCUP
185
WARING PARK
Sidcup Arts Cen
GOLDSMITH COLLEGE SPORTS GRD
THE ALDERS
NORTH CRAY
NORTH CRAY WOOD
STABLE MEADOW
DA14
FOOTS CRAY MEADOWS
GATTONS WOOD
GATTONS PLANTATION
SIDCUP HIGH STREET
SIDCUP PLACE
QUEEN MARY'S HOSP
Frognal Corner
GARDEN SHAW
FOOTS CRAY
SCADBURY PARK
NATURE RESERVE
A20
RUXLEY CORNER INDUSTRIAL ESTATE
Ruxley Corner
RUXLEY WOOD
Crittall's Corner
SIDCUP BYPASS
BR5
206
RUXLEY PARK GOLF COURSE
CRAYFIELDS BUSINESS PARK
CRAY VALLEY
Scadbury Moated Manor House Site
85
86
87
88
89
90
91
92
93
94
0 500 yds
0 500 m

FB
FC
FD
FE
FF
FG
FH
167
BARNES CRAY
CRAYFORD MARSHES
DA1
CRAYFORD
WATLING STREET
LONDON ROAD (WATLING STREET)
BOURNE ROAD
CRAYFORD ROAD
DARTFORD ROAD
CRAYFORD GREYHOUND STADIUM
HALL PLACE GARDENS
HALL PLACE
Black Prince Interchange
EAST ROCHESTER WAY
ROCHESTER WAY
OLD BEXLEY
DARTFORD HEATH
DARTFORD BYPASS
Dartford Heath
SHEPHERDS LANE
OLD BEXLEY LANE
DARTFORD GOLF COURSE
North West Kent College
Coldblow
BEXLEY LANE
DARTFORD ROAD
VICARAGE ROAD
Bracton Centre
188
JOYDEN'S WOOD
Hook Green
DA2
ROWHILL WOOD
Joydens Wood
BIRCHWOOD PARK GOLF CENTRE
Hextable
BR8
Swanley Village
DARTFORD
SEVENOAKS
KENT
86
87
88
89
90
91
92
93
94
74
73
72
71
50
51
52
207

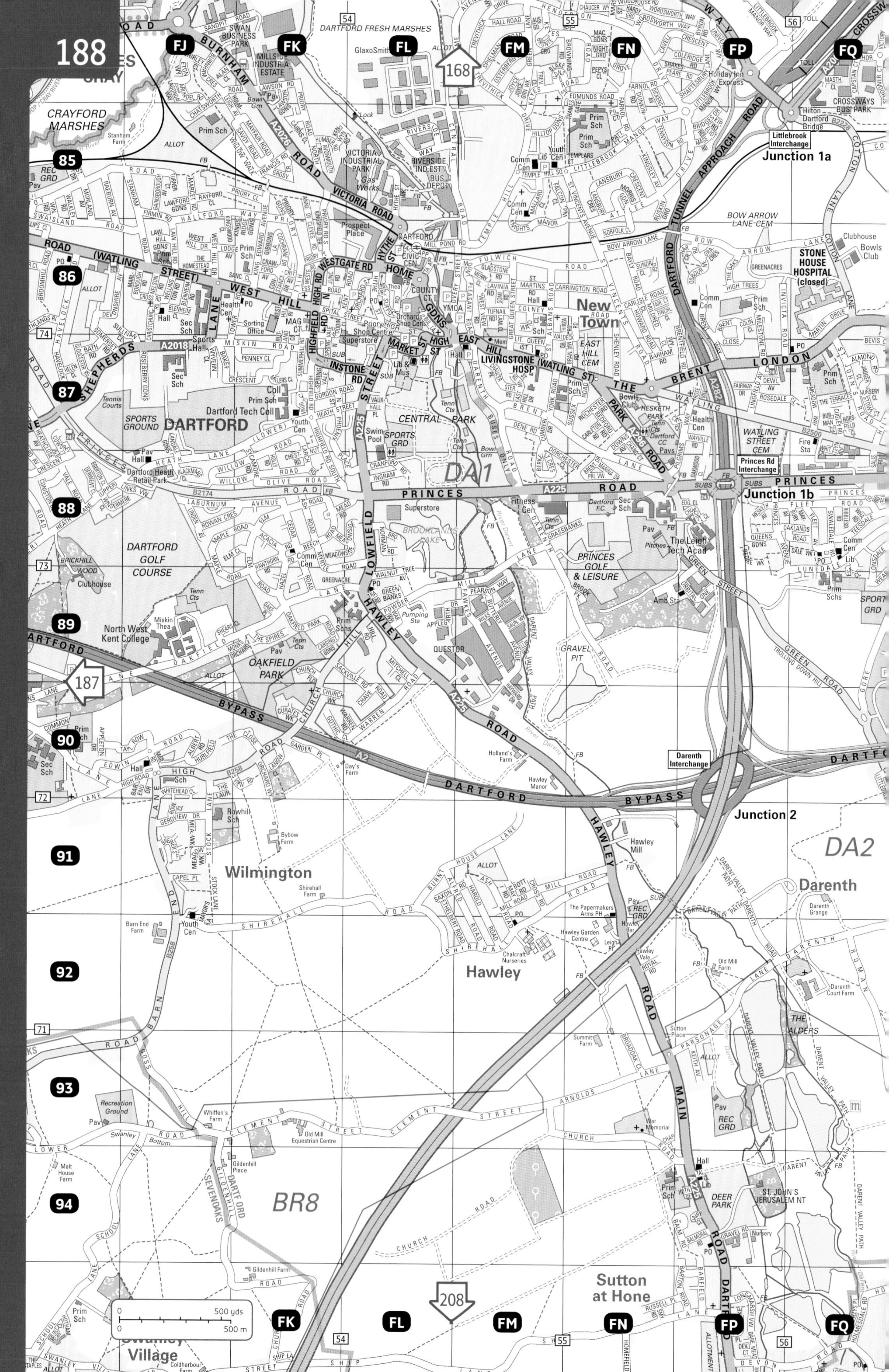
DARTFORD FRESH MARSHES
CRAYFORD MARSHES
FJ
FK
FL
FM
FN
FP
FQ
168
187
208
54
55
56
74
73
72
71
85
86
87
88
89
90
91
92
93
94
BURNHAM ROAD
VICTORIA ROAD
Victoria Industrial Park
Riverside Ind Est
Bus Depot
Millside Industrial Estate
Swan Business Park
GlaxoSmith
Holiday Inn Express
Littlebrook Interchange
Junction 1a
Crossways Bus Park
Hilton Dartford Bridge
DARTFORD TUNNEL APPROACH ROAD
BOW ARROW LANE CEM
STONE HOUSE HOSPITAL (closed)
Clubhouse
Bowls Club
New Town
EAST HILL CEM
LIVINGSTONE HOSP
CENTRAL PARK
SPORTS GRD
DA1
DARTFORD
Dartford Tech Coll
SPORTS GROUND
Dartford Heath Retail Park
WEST HILL
WATLING STREET
SHEPHERDS LANE
PRINCES ROAD
Junction 1b
Princes Rd Interchange
WATLING STREET CEM
LONDON ROAD
THE BRENT
BROOKLANDS LAKE
PRINCES GOLF & LEISURE
The Leigh Tech Acad
DARTFORD GOLF COURSE
BRICKHILL WOOD
Clubhouse
North West Kent College
OAKFIELD PARK
LOWFIELD STREET
HAWLEY ROAD
GRAVEL PIT
GREEN STREET GREEN ROAD
DARTFORD BYPASS
Darenth Interchange
Junction 2
DA2
Darenth
Wilmington
Hawley
Hawley Mill
Hawley Manor
Holland's Farm
Day's Farm
Bybow Farm
Shirehall Farm
Barn End Farm
SHIREHALL ROAD
Darenth Grange
Darenth Court Farm
THE ALDERS
DARENT VALLEY PATH
Summit Farm
Sutton Place
MAIN ROAD
Whiffen's Farm
Old Mill Equestrian Centre
CLEMENT STREET
Recreation Ground
Malt House Farm
Gildenhill Place
Gildenhill Farm
BR8
ST. JOHN'S JERUSALEM NT
DEER PARK
Sutton at Hone
War Memorial
Swanley Village
Coldharbour Farm
SHIP LANE
0 500 yds
0 500 m

FR
FS
FT
FU
FV
FW
FX
57
58
59
169
190
209
Crossways Boulevard
Newtons Court
Quadrant Court
Superstore
Johnson's Wharf
Thames Europort
Travelodge
Stone Crossing
Elizabeth Street
Stone
Greenhithe for Bluewater
London Road
A226
St. Clements Way
Greenhithe
Knockhall
Ingress Abbey
Swanscombe Heritage Park
Nat Res
Leisure Centre
DA9
DA10
DA13
DA4
Stone Rec Grd
Stone Cem
Bluewater Parkway
Bluewater Shopping Centre
The Village
Cinema
Plaza
Bus Sta
Stone Castle
Western Cross Farm
Alkerden Farm
Watling Street
A296
Darent Valley Hospital
Chalk Pit
Bean Interchange
A2
Dartford Bypass
Darenth Country Park
Knoxfield Caravan Park
Arrow Riding & Carriage Driving Centre for the Disabled
Darenth Wood
Badger's Mount
The Thrift
Bean
Bean Farm
The Royal Oak PH
Caravan Site
Cov Res
Youth Club
Prim Sch
Beacon Wood Country Park
Cherwell Farm
Ladies Wood
Lords Wood
Waller Park
Lane End
Betsham Hill
Betsham C.C.
Highcross Road
Sandbanks
Green Street Green
Manor Farm Garden Centre
Shellbank
Westwood Farm
Wheatsheaf PH
Hook Green
St. Margaret's Road
St. Margaret's Farm
South Darenth
Gill's Road
Gill's Farm
Walnut Tree Farm
Ryecroft Farm
Ryecroft Wood
Chalkcroft
Quarry
Sports Grd
Dartford
Sevenoaks
Green Street Green Road
86
87
88
89
90
91
92
93
94
71
72
73
74

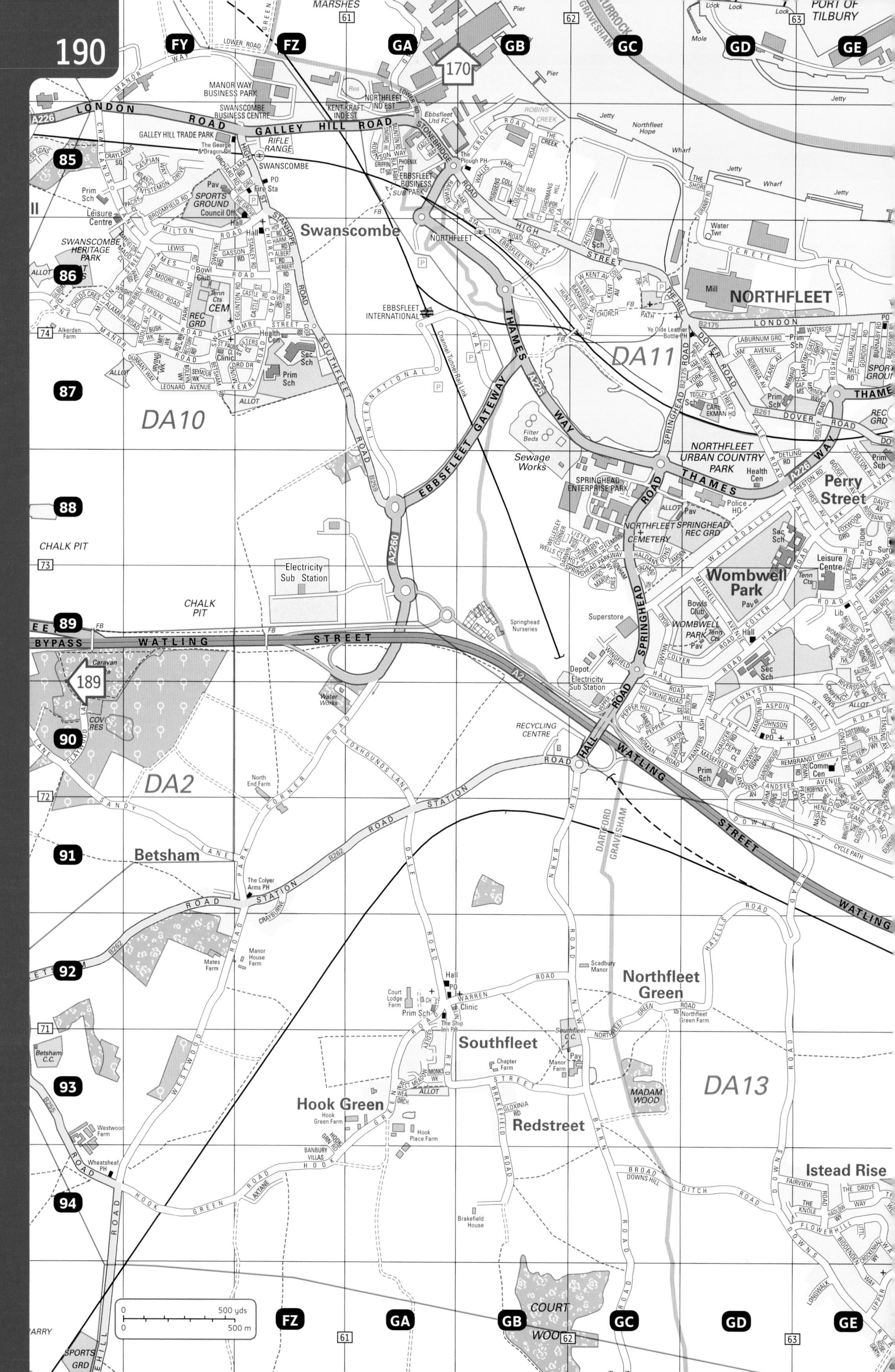
Swanscombe
NORTHFLEET
DA11
DA10
DA2
DA13
Perry Street
Wombwell Park
Betsham
Northfleet Green
Southfleet
Hook Green
Redstreet
Istead Rise
PORT OF TILBURY
EBBSFLEET INTERNATIONAL
WATLING STREET
LONDON ROAD
GALLEY HILL ROAD
EBBSFLEET GATEWAY
THAMES WAY
SPRINGHEAD ROAD
NORTHFLEET URBAN COUNTRY PARK
MADAM WOOD
COURT WOOD
170
189

RIVER THAMES
THURROCK
GRAVESHAM
GRAVESEND
Milton
Denton
Windmill Hill
Westcourt
Kings Farm
Parrock Farm
Riverview Park
Singlewell
Ifield
DA12
RM18
MID KENT GOLF COURSE
CLAYLANE WOOD
WATLING STREET
WROTHAM ROAD
ROCHESTER ROAD
171

AS
AT
AU
AV
AW
AX
AY
172
FUZZY CLUMP
ALDER COVERT
Cumberland Obelisk
OBELISK POND
SCARLETOAK PLANTATION
POLO GROUND
Flying Barn
Pav
Breakheart Hill
95
DARKHOLE CLUMP
HEATHER GARDEN
High Flyer's Hill
WINTER GARDEN
OXHED CLUMP
CANADIAN MEMORIAL AVENUE
The Punch Bowl
THE VALLEY GARDENS
96
Egham Wick
EGHAM WICK PLANTATION
Eton Bridge
Larch Bri
Totem Pole
WICK POND
VIRGINIA WATER PLANTATION
BROAD HILLS RIDE
Blays House
Viatel
LARKSFIELD
ST DAVID'S DR
ROBERTS WY
BAKEHAM LANE
SIMONS WALK
LONDON ROAD
A30
CUT HILLS
ACS Egham International Sch
Royal Holloway College
Callow Hill
WOODLEE CL
GREAT WOOD
Whitehall Farm
69
FROSTFARM PLANTATION
VIRGINIA WATER
Botany Bay Point
97
BLACKNEST ROAD
A329
Roman Ruins (Leptis Magna)
Virginia Lodge
Cascade Bridge
BELVEDERE WOOD
98
Fort Belvedere
CEDAR DRIVE
SL5
68
99
VIRGINIA BEECHES
HOLLOW LANE
THE DELL
Stroude Farm
Stroude Crossing
CHRISTCHURCH ROAD
B389
WATERFALL CL
WOODSIDE WY
Prim Sch
WAVERLEY DRIVE
STUART WY
QUENTIN WY
KING'S COPSE
WAVERLEY COPSE
GENERAL'S COPSE
DUKE'S COPSE
SPRING WOODS
LAKE RD
WOODLANDS RD
PIPERS END
GORSE HILL ROAD
HEATH RISE
MORELLA CL
PLAYING FLD
TROTSWORTH AVENUE
TROTSWORTH CT
GU25
ABBOTS DRIVE
BROCK WAY
VIRGINIA DRIVE
FRIARS RD
STATION APP
Hall
MONKS ROAD
ABBEY ROAD
LAKE ROAD
BADGERS HILL
NUNS WALK
OAKWOOD RD
KEEPERS WK
THE GLEBE
VIRGINIA WATER
PO
Lib
STATION PAR
PINEWOOD
STAYNE END
LINDALE CLOSE
CHESTNUT AV
PORTNALL DRIVE
PORTNALL ROAD
Broom Hill
WENTWORTH DRIVE
WENTWORTH POND
WELLINGTON AVENUE
Wellington Bri
The Bourne
Clubhouse
Tennis Courts
MEADOW ROAD
SHERBOURNE DR
FIRWOOD ROAD
NORTH DRIVE
WENTWORTH
The Dormy House
Wentworth
Ingliston House
Podenhale
100
67
HARPESFORD AVENUE
SUNDON CRES
HILLSIDE
WOODSHORE CL
EAST DRIVE
Comm Cen
BEECHMONT AV
BOURNE RD
Prim Sch
CABRERA AVENUE
MERESIDE PL
TRUMPS GREEN AV
THE PA
PO
LYNE ROAD
Waterloo Bridge
The Klondyke Piggeries
HEATHERSIDE DR
CROWN ROAD
Pav
KING GEORGE V PLAYING FIELD
Tenn Cts
TITHE CL
TITHE MEADOWS
TRUMPS GREEN ROAD
THE MOUNT
CROWN LA
FURNIVAL CL
HOME
THE PADDOCKS
LYNE
FAIRWAY
OAK TREE CL
UMBERSTONES
BOURNESIDE
WEST DRIVE
SOUTH DRIVE
KNOWLE GRO CL
KNOWLE GROVE
KNOWLE HILL
Fairview Farm
Trumps Farm
101
GOLF COURSE
BEECH WOOD
BEECHWOOD ROAD
Knowle Hill
CORRIE GDNS
KNOWLE GROVE
BLUEBELLE WOOD
GREAT WOOD
Longcross Bri
Burnt Hill
102
RUNNYMEDE
M3
CHOBHAM LANE
KITSMEAD
LONGCROSS
66
Little Arm
GU24
SURREY HEATH ROAD
CHERTSEY COMMON
BOG WOOD
103
Ship Hill
Long Arm
BARROWHILLS
Pav
Tenn Cts
BARROW HILLS GOLF COURSE
DICKEN'S WOOD
Hersham Farm
Grangewood
KITSMEAD LANE
BURMA ROAD
FB
SUB
CHOBHAM ROAD
Longcross
WOOD CL
TANGLEWOOD CL
HOLLY CL
ALBURY CL
B386
LONGCROSS ROAD
104
Flutters Hill
ACCOMMODATION ROAD
Oystershell Hill
CHERTSEY ROAD
Rushy Pond
Lily Pond Farm
Glasshouse
210
CHOBHAM COMMON NATIONAL NATURE RESERVE
0 500 yds
0 500 m
98
99
00

AZ
BA
BB
BC
BD
BE
BF
01
02
03
173
194
211
TW20
TW18
KT16
KT15
Great Fosters Hotel
Crabtree Corner
THORPE INDUSTRIAL EST
EGHAM BUSINESS VILLAGE
TRUSS'S ISLAND
FISHING TEMPLE
PENTON HOOK ISLAND
PENTON HOOK MARINA
PENTON PARK (Caravan Park)
Luddington House
Stroude
Oaktree Nursery
LONGSIDE LAKE
Thorpe
TASIS England
CEMEX UK
MANOR LAKE
THORPE PARK
Mountbatten Pavilion
Abbey Lake
ST. ANN'S LAKE
Britannia Arena
SPORTS GROUND
THE MOAT
WATER GARDENS
Manor Farm
Woodcock Farm
Spring Farm
Hurst Stud Farm
THORPE GREEN
Thorpe Green
Rose & Crown PH
ANCHOR COPSE
Junction 2 (M3), Junction 12 (M25)
St. Anne's Chapel (remains of)
ST. ANN'S HILL PARK
Sludge Lagoons
Lyne Sewage Works
Filter Beds
Recycling Centre
Redlands Farm
Lyne Hill Farm
Ruxbury Farm
Twynersh House PH
Chertsey Cricket Club
ABBEYFIELDS REC GRD
ELM FARM CARAVAN PARK
Almner Priory
Lynefield Farm
Hillside Farm
Nursery
The Brooks Riding Centre
THE ROUGH
Merrywood Farm
Lyne Court
Lyne Place Manor
Piggery
Lyne
LYNE COPSE
RECREATION GROUND
Pantiles Nurseries
HERSHAM COPSE
FAN GROVE
FANGROVE PARK
Lynwood Farm
Lyne Acres Farm
Great Cockcrow Railway
Cockcrow Hill
Hardwick Court Farm
GOGMORE FM PK
CHERTSEY
ALLOTMENTS
REC GRD
SANDGATES
Pannells Farm
SPORTS GROUND
Sec Sch
ADDLESTONE CEMETERY
Trys Hill Farm
Fan Court
Westbrook Farm
Squires Nursery
Fox Hills Farm
White Lodge Centre
RUNNYMEDE HOSP
ST. PETER'S HOSP
Silverlands Farm
FOXHILLS GOLF COURSE
Clubhouse
Foxhills Country Club
Foxhills
HOME WOOD
Botleys Mansion
HOMEWOOD PARK
Hillswood Business
Church Farm
Kitchenride Corner
Woodside Farm
Junction 11
M25
M3
A320
B388
B389
B386
A317
THORPE BYPASS
MILL HOUSE LANE
THORPE LEA ROAD
STAINES LANE
STAINES ROAD
CHERTSEY LANE
LYNE CROSSING
RUXBURY ROAD
ALMNERS ROAD
WATERY LANE
HARDWICK LANE
GUILDFORD ROAD
PYRCROFT ROAD
EASTWORTH RD
CHILSEY GREEN RD
TRYS HILL
HOLLOWAY HILL
ST. PETER'S WAY
STONEHILL ROAD
96
97
98
99
100
101
102
103
104

BG
BH
BJ
BK
BL
BM
BN
GRAVEL
174
QUEEN
MARY
RESERVOIR
TW18
Staines Town FC
Penton Hook Farm
SPORTS GROUND
Clubhouse
Garden Centre
Penton Hook Lock
PENTON HOOK ISLAND
PENTON HOOK
PENTON HOOK MARINA
Yacht Basin
PENTON PARK
(Caravan Park)
Mountbatten Pavilion
Abbey Lake
Pumping Sta
Intake Channel
Gas Pipeline Sta
ROUND COPSE
Glasshouse
Manor Farm
Prim Sch
Hall
Youth Club
Three Horseshoes PH
SPORTS GRD
LALEHAM
Nursery
Rowing Club
LALEHAM PARK
Laleham Abbey
LALEHAM PARK SPORTS GROUND
Camp Site
LALEHAM GOLF COURSE
LALEHAM BURWAY
RESERVOIR
Filter Beds
Water Works
Shepperton Studios
THE GREEN
Squires Bridge
Laleham Nurseries
REC GRD
Staines Road Farm
Sailing Club
KT16
M3
193
Earthworks
ABBEYFIELDS REC GRD
Abbey Bridge
Abbey Chase House
Chertsey Cricket Club
Chertsey Town
MUS
Old TH
GOGMORE FM PK
Health Club
CHERTSEY
Prim Sch
SPORTS GROUND
Weir
Chertsey Lock
ABBEYFIELDS MOBILE HOME PARK
KINGFISHER PH
RECREATION GROUND
Dumsey Eyot
Riversleigh Farm
Marina
FORDWATER TRADING EST
Fordwater Bridge
CHERTSEY MEADS
Dockett Point
PHARAOH'S ISLAND
Shepperton Lock
LOCK ISLAND
HAMHAUGH ISLAND
Hamhaugh Point
Hamm Court Farm
The Bull Dogs
Fire Sta
Woburn Park Farm
Hatch Farm
CEM
ADDLESTONE MOOR
ADDLESTONE CEMETERY
ABBEY MOOR GOLF COURSE
Clubho.
WOBURN PARK
Tennis Cen
St. George's College
The Plantation Nursery
KT15
VICTORY PARK
Bowl Grn
SPORTS GRD
Superstore
212
BOURNE BUS PK
AHM Culinary Brands
WEYBRIDGE BUSINESS PARK
Black Boy Bridge
Weybridge Lock
HOSP
WEYBRIDGE
Junction 11
Woodside Farm
0 500 yds
0 500 m

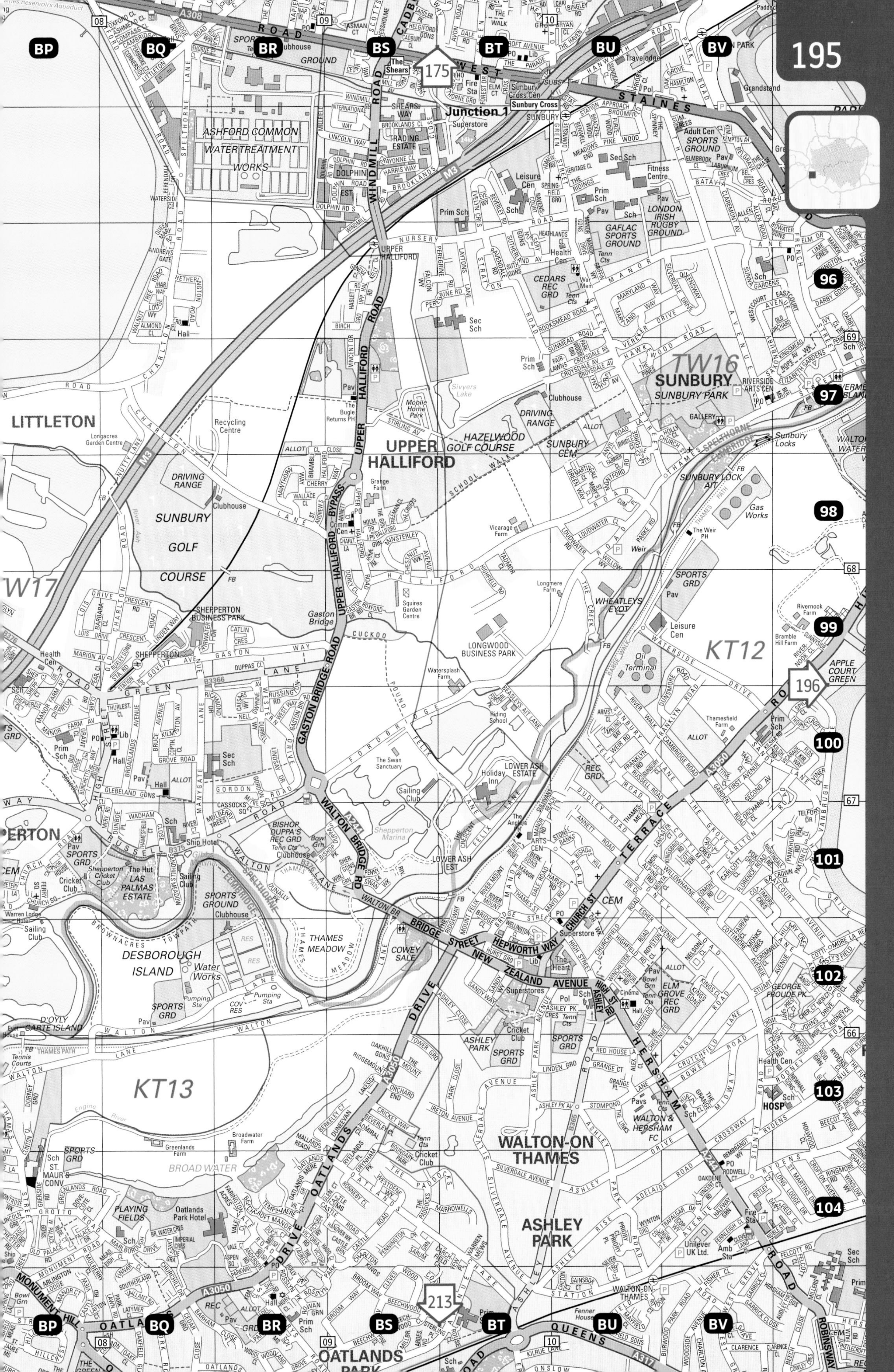
BP
BQ
BR
BS
BT
BU
BV
175
Junction 1
Sunbury Cross
ASHFORD COMMON WATER TREATMENT WORKS
LITTLETON
UPPER HALLIFORD
HAZELWOOD GOLF COURSE
TW16
SUNBURY
SUNBURY PARK
LONDON IRISH RUGBY GROUND
GAFLAC SPORTS GROUND
CEDARS REC GRD
SUNBURY GOLF COURSE
DRIVING RANGE
TW17
SHEPPERTON BUSINESS PARK
SHEPPERTON
LONGWOOD BUSINESS PARK
WHEATLEYS EYOT
KT12
APPLE COURT GREEN
196
96
97
98
99
100
101
102
103
104
LOWER ASH ESTATE
Holiday Inn
Shepperton Marina
BISHOP DUPPA'S REC GRD
LAS PALMAS ESTATE
DESBOROUGH ISLAND
D'OYLY CARTE ISLAND
THAMES MEADOW
COWEY SALE
KT13
BROAD WATER
Oatlands Park Hotel
PLAYING FIELDS
ELM GROVE REC GRD
GEORGE FROUDE PK
WALTON & HERSHAM FC
WALTON-ON THAMES
ASHLEY PARK
OATLANDS PARK
213
Sunbury Locks
Gas Works
Oil Terminal
A308
A3050
A244
M3
B375
B376
B3366
A317
08
09
10
66
67
68
69

BW
BX
BY
BZ
CA
CB
CC
KEMPTON
PARK
RACECOURSE
TW16
HALF MOON COVERT
PLAYING FIELD
176
HAMPTON
Open Air Pool
KINGSWAY BUSINESS PARK
KEMPTON GATE
HYDES FIELD
Portlane Bridge
UPPER SUNBURY ROAD
EAST
A308
STAIN HILL RESERVOIRS
UPON THAMES
RICHMOND
KENTON COURT MEADOW
CONFERENCE CENTRE
SUNBURY COURT
GRAND JUNCTION ISLE
SUNBURY COURT ISLAND
GRAND JUNCTION RESERVOIR
TW12
PLATT'S EYOT
SUNNYSIDE RESERVOIR
GARRICK'S AIT
HURST PARK
SURREY
RIVER THAMES
ELMBRIDGE
SWAN'S REST ISLAND
RIVERMEAD ISLAND
MOLESEY RESERVOIRS NATURE RESERVE
HURST ROAD
A3050
SUNBURY
SPELTHORNE
Sunbury Locks
SUNBURY LOCK AIT
WALTON ADVANCED WATER TREATMENT WORKS
Gas Works
BESSBOROUGH RESERVOIR
KNIGHTS RESERVOIR
WALTON ROAD
B369
KT12
KT8
WEST MOLESEY
HOSP
NEILSON PLAYING FIELD
SPORTS GROUND
Sailing Club
APPLE COURT GREEN
195
QUEEN ELIZABETH II RESERVOIR
SAND & GRAVEL PIT
ISLAND BARN RESERVOIR
River Mole
River Ember
KT10
Sewage Works
RYDENS
NORTH WEYLANDS INDUSTRIAL ESTATE
EMBER CENTRE
DRIVING RANGE
HERSHAM
HERSHAM VILLAGE GOLF COURSE
CORONATION RECREATION GROUND
RIVER-MOLE BUSINESS PARK
SANDOWN IND PK
Lower Green
SANDOWN GOLF COURSE
SANDOWN PARK RACECOURSE
Grandstand & Exhibition Centre
Karting Centre
Wayneflete's or Wolsey's Tower
THE WARREN
214
ESHER
95
96
97
98
99
100
101
102
103
104
69
68
67
66
12
13
14
0 500 yds
0 500 m

BUSHY PARK
TW11
HAMPTON WICK
HAMPTON COURT PARK
(HOME PARK)
HAMPTON COURT PALACE
GOLF COURSE
KT8
EAST MOLESEY
THAMES DITTON
KT7
WESTON GREEN
HINCHLEY WOOD
LONG DITTON
KT6
KT9
LITTLEWORTH COMMON
SURBITON
THE ROYAL PADDOCKS
HAMPTON COURT PALACE
THAMES DITTON ISLAND
BOYLE FM ISLAND
RAVENS AIT
TAGG'S ISLAND
ASH ISLAND
THAMES DITTON & ESHER GOLF COURSE
DITTON COMMON
Scilly Isles
Hook Junction
KINGSTON BYPASS
PORTSMOUTH ROAD
HAMPTON COURT WAY
HAMPTON COURT ROAD
KINGSTON ROAD
WARREN PLANTATION
HALF MOON PLANTATION
OVAL PLANTATION
BROOM CLUMPS
WATERHOUSE WOODLAND GARDEN
Diana Fountain
Kingston University
Cockcrow Hill
SURREY
177
215
198
CD
CE
CF
CG
CH
CJ
CK
96
97
98
99
100
101
102
103
104

CL
CM
CN
CP
CQ
CR
CS
178
197
216
COOMBE
COOMBE WOOD GOLF COURSE
KT2
KINGSTON HOSPITAL
NORBITON
KINGSTON UPON THAMES
KINGSTON CEMETERY
KT1
NEW MALDEN
SURBITON CEMETERY
BERRYLANDS
KT3
KT5
HOGSMILL PUBLIC OPEN SPACE
SURBITON
SURBITON FISHPONDS OPEN SPACE
KT6
HOGSMILL OPEN SPACE
OLD MALDEN
MAORI SPORTS GROUND
TOLWORTH HOSPITAL
TOLWORTH
KINGSTON UNIVERSITY SPORTS GRD
RIVERHILL SPORTS GRD
KING GEORGES FIELD
KT9
WANDGAS ATHLETIC GROUND
KING GEORGE'S FIELD AURIOL PARK
KINGSTON BYPASS
Hook Junction
Tolworth Junction
SURREY
95
96
97
98
99
100
101
102
103
104
0 500 yds
0 500 m

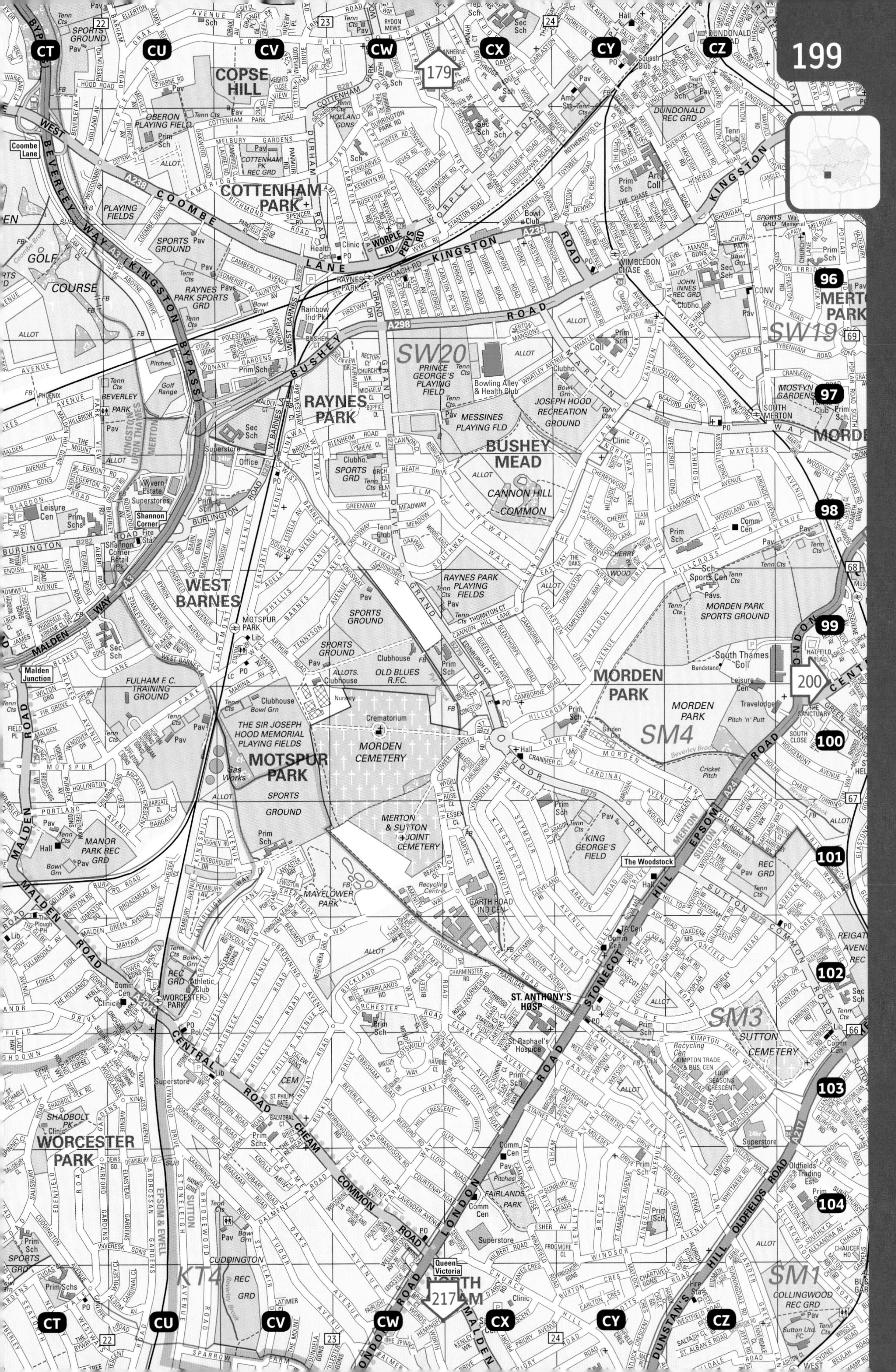
CT
CU
CV
CW
CX
CY
CZ
179
COPSE HILL
OBERON PLAYING FIELD
COTTENHAM PARK
COTTENHAM PK REC GRD
COOMBE LANE
PLAYING FIELDS
SPORTS GROUND
GOLF COURSE
RAYNES PARK SPORTS GRD
KINGSTON BY-PASS
BEVERLEY WAY
KINGSTON ROAD
WORPLE ROAD
DUNDONALD REC GRD
WIMBLEDON CHASE
Art Coll
SW20
SW19
PRINCE GEORGE'S PLAYING FIELD
Bowling Alley & Health Club
RAYNES PARK
BUSHEY ROAD
JOSEPH HOOD RECREATION GROUND
MESSINES PLAYING FLD
BUSHEY MEAD
CANNON HILL COMMON
BEVERLEY PARK
KINGSTON UPON THAMES
MERTON
MERTON PARK
MOSTYN GARDENS
SOUTH MERTON
MORDEN
96
97
98
99
100
101
102
103
104
WEST BARNES
RAYNES PARK PLAYING FIELDS
SPORTS GROUND
OLD BLUES R.F.C.
MORDEN PARK SPORTS GROUND
South Thames Coll
MORDEN PARK
SM4
200
Malden Junction
FULHAM F.C. TRAINING GROUND
THE SIR JOSEPH HOOD MEMORIAL PLAYING FIELDS
MOTSPUR PARK
Crematorium
MORDEN CEMETERY
MERTON & SUTTON JOINT CEMETERY
KING GEORGE'S FIELD
The Woodstock
MANOR PARK REC GRD
MAYFLOWER PARK
GARTH ROAD IND CEN
ST. ANTHONY'S HOSP
St. Raphael's Hospice
SM3
SUTTON CEMETERY
KIMPTON TRADE & BUS. CEN
WORCESTER PARK
CENTRAL ROAD
CHEAM COMMON ROAD
LONDON ROAD
STONECOT HILL
EPSOM ROAD
FAIRLANDS PARK
Queen Victoria
NORTH CHEAM
217
KT4
CUDDINGTON REC GRD
EPSOM & EWELL
SUTTON
SM1
COLLINGWOOD REC GRD
Sutton Utd. FC
Oldfields Trading Est
ST. DUNSTAN'S HILL
OLDFIELDS ROAD
22
23
24

DA
DB
DC
DD
DE
DF
DG
180
SOUTH WIMBLEDON
COLLIER'S WOOD
LONDON ROAD CEMETERY
MERTON HIGH
MERANTUN WAY
MERTON
MERTON PARK
SW19
KINGSTON ROAD
MORDEN ROAD
WESTERN ROAD
LOMBARD BUSINESS PARK
MERTON INDUSTRIAL PARK
NELSON TRADING EST
ABBEY REC GRD
NURSERY ROAD PLAYING FIELDS
MOSTYN GARDENS
MORDEN
MORDEN HALL PARK
MORDEN HALL ROAD
PHIPPS BRIDGE
BURIAL GROUND
MITCHAM
FIGGE'S MARSH
STREATHAM ROAD
LONDON ROAD
COMMONSIDE WEST
CRICKET GRN
MADEIRA RD
CRANMER RD
CARSHALTON ROAD
MITCHAM GOLF COURSE
MITCHAM JUNCTION
RAVENSBURY PARK
LIONGATE ENTERPRISE PARK
BROOKMEADS EST
WATERMEADS NT
POULTER PARK
SM4
MORDEN PARK SPORTS GROUND
MORDEN SOUTH
MORDEN REC GRD
CENTRAL ROAD
ST. HELIER AVENUE
BISHOPSFORD ROAD
MORETON GREEN
ST. HELIER
THOMAS WALL PARK
Rose Hill
SUTTON ARENA
ST. HELIER OPEN SPACE
SM5
Mitcham R.U.F.C.
ROSEHILL
ROSEHILL PARK EAST
GREENSHAW WOOD
ST. HELIER HOSP
QUEEN MARY'S HOSP FOR CHILDREN
ROSEHILL RECREATION GROUND
REIGATE AVENUE
REIGATE AVENUE REC GRD
SM3
SUTTON CEMETERY
BENHILTON
ROYSTON PARK
THE WRYTHE
THE WRYTHE REC GRD
DALE PARK
WILDERNESS ISLAND
LIMES GRN
SM1
SUTTON COMMON
OLDFIELDS ROAD
EPSOM ROAD
NIGHTINGALE
CARSHALTON
199
218
95
96
97
98
99
100
101
102
103
104
26
27
28
66
67
68
69
0
500 yds
500 m

DH
DJ
DK
DL
DM
DN
DP
STREATHAM VALE
181
NORBURY PARK
NORBURY
SW16
STREATHAM PARK
CEMETERY
PLAYING FIELDS
POLLARDS HILL
CR7
THORNTON HEATH
CR4
MITCHAM
PLAYING FIELD
COMMON
SPORTS GRD
CROYDON CEMETERY
MAYDAY UNIVERSITY HOSPITAL
BROAD GREEN
202
QUEENS ROAD CEMETERY
96
97
98
99
100
101
102
103
104
Thornton Heath Pond
Lombard Rbt
CR0
WADDON
WANDLE PARK
WADDON MARSH
HACKBRIDGE
SM6
BEDDINGTON
BEDDINGTON PARK
THE GRANGE GARDENS
CROYDON SUB STATION
MILL LANE TRADING ESTATE
DUPPAS HILL
WEST CROYDON
219
Fiveways
LONDON ROAD
PURLEY WAY
MITCHAM ROAD
CROYDON ROAD
A23
A236
A232
29
30
31

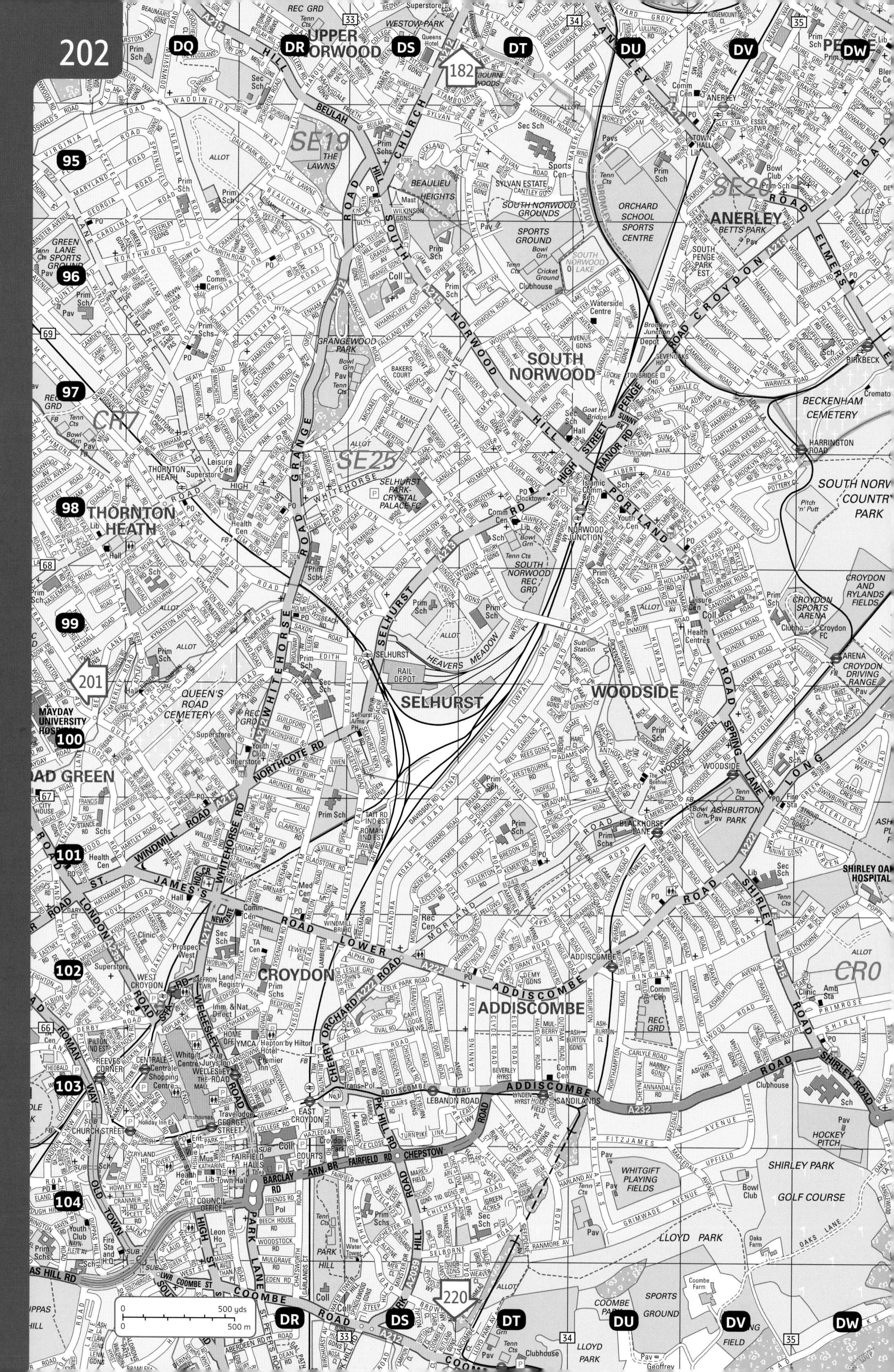
DQ
DR
DS
DT
DU
DV
DW
182
201
220
33
34
35
95
96
97
98
99
100
101
102
103
104
UPPER NORWOOD
SE19
THE LAWNS
BEAULIEU HEIGHTS
SOUTH NORWOOD GROUNDS
SPORTS GROUND
ORCHARD SCHOOL SPORTS CENTRE
ANERLEY
SE20
BETTS PARK
GREEN LANE SPORTS GROUND
GRANGEWOOD PARK
SOUTH NORWOOD
BECKENHAM CEMETERY
CR7
SE25
SELHURST PARK CRYSTAL PALACE FC
THORNTON HEATH
SOUTH NORWOOD COUNTRY PARK
SOUTH NORWOOD REC GRD
CROYDON AND RYLANDS FIELDS
CROYDON SPORTS ARENA
MAYDAY UNIVERSITY HOSPITAL
QUEEN'S ROAD CEMETERY
SELHURST
WOODSIDE
CROYDON DRIVING RANGE
ASHBURTON PARK
SHIRLEY OAKS HOSPITAL
CROYDON
ADDISCOMBE
CR0
SHIRLEY PARK GOLF COURSE
WHITGIFT PLAYING FIELDS
LLOYD PARK
SPORTS GROUND
COOMBE PARK
HOCKEY PITCH
500 yds
500 m

DX
DY
DZ
EA
EB
EC
ED
183
BECKENHAM
NEW BECKENHAM
CATOR PARK
KENT HOUSE
BECKENHAM ROAD
BECKENHAM JUNCTION
CLOCK HOUSE
AVENUE ROAD
BECKENHAM HOSPITAL
CROYDON RD REC GROUND
BR3
KELSEY PARK
ELMERS END
THE SLOANE HOSPITAL
SHORTLANDS
BR2
96
97
98
99
100
101
102
103
104
204
PARK LANGLEY
EDEN PARK
HARVINGTON PLAYING FIELD
UPPER ELMERS END
CROUCH OAK WOOD
MONKS ORCHARD
BETHLEM ROYAL HOSPITAL
HIGH BROOM WOOD
LANGLEY PARK GOLF COURSE
THE ROOKERY
WEST WICKHAM
BLAKE REC GRD
BR4
SHIRLEY
FOXES WOOD
PINEWOODS
SPRING PARK WOOD
SPRING PARK
SPARROWS DEN PLAYING FIELDS
CONEY HALL REC GRD
KENNEL WOOD
THE ADDINGTON
221
36
37
38

EE
EF
EG
EH
EJ
EK
EL
184
40
41
42
BROMLEY PARK
SHORTLANDS GOLF COURSE
THE SLOANE HOSPITAL
SHORTLANDS
BROMLEY
Bromley North
Widmore Green
WIDMORE
BR1
BR2
BR4
BROMLEY SOUTH
BROMLEY CIVIC CENTRE
Intu Bromley
QUEEN'S MEAD REC GRD
CHURCH HOUSE GDNS
MARTIN'S HILL
HAVELOCK REC GRD
WHITEHALL REC GRD
LOGSHILL WOOD
PLAYING FIELD
SOUTH HILL WOOD
CUPOLA WOOD
NORMAN PARK RECREATION GROUND
ATHLETICS TRACK
SCROGGINHALL WOOD
Bromley College of Further & Higher Education
LORDS WOOD
BROOK WOOD
MAZZARDS WOOD
WOODCOCK GROVE
BOLDS WOOD
THE GROVE SPORTS GRD
BARNET WOOD
PARKHOUSE F.C. RUGBY GROUND
COLYERS WOOD
PADMALL WOOD
HAYES COMMON
HAYES
PRIORY HOSP. HAYES GROVE
THE KNOLL
Coney Hall
WEST WICKHAM COMMON
CONEY HALL REC GRD
Old Beccehamian R.F.C.
LANGLEY PARK COURSE
Keston Mark
RAVENSBOURNE BUSINESS CEN
THE EMMAUS CENTRE
203
222
95
96
97
98
99
100
101
102
103
104
69
68
67
66
0 500 yds
0 500 m

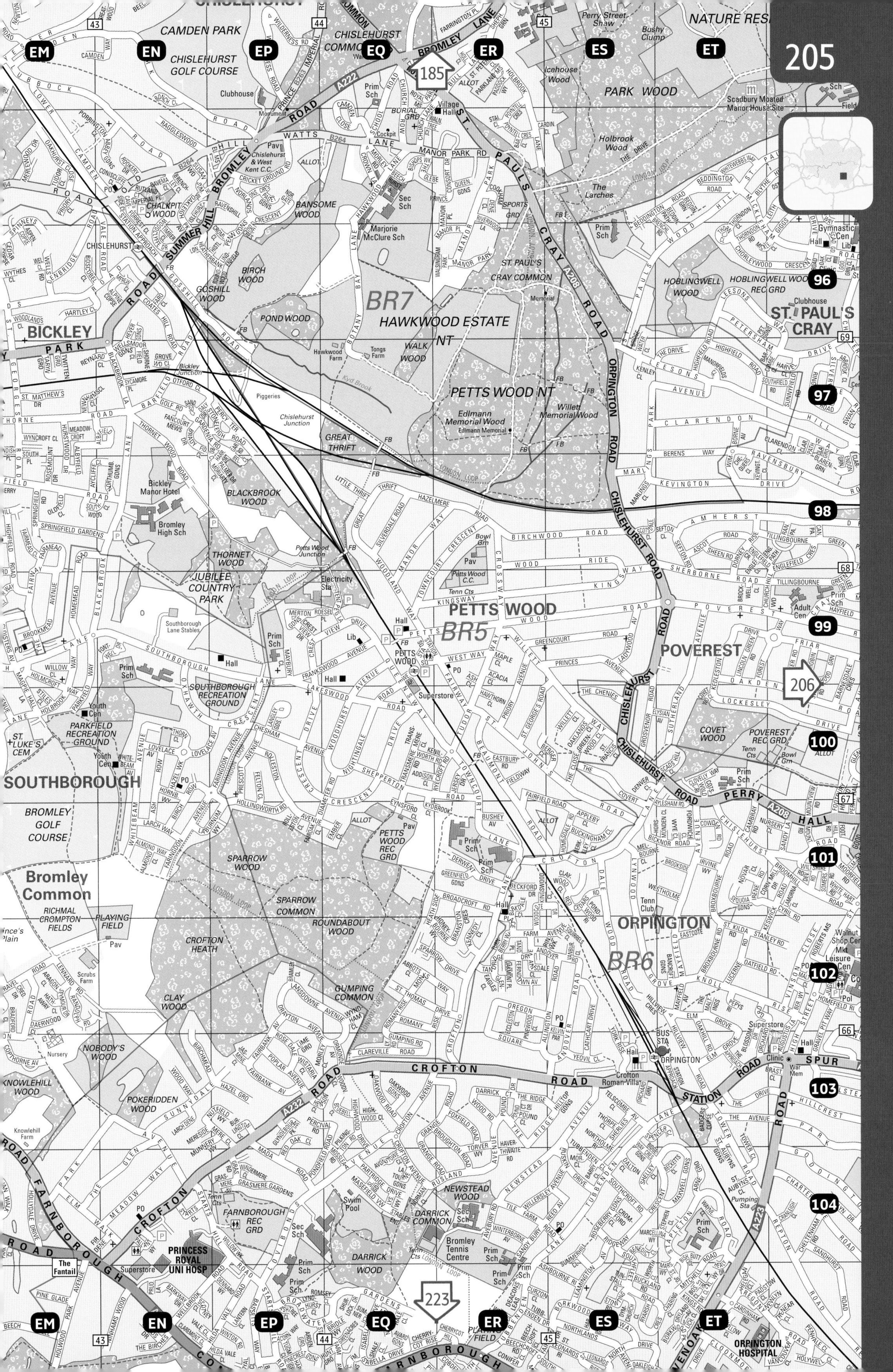
EM
EN
EP
EQ
ER
ES
ET
CAMDEN PARK
CHISLEHURST GOLF COURSE
CHISLEHURST COMMON
185
Perry Street Shaw
Bushy Clump
NATURE RESE
Icehouse Wood
PARK WOOD
Scadbury Moated Manor House Site
Holbrook Wood
The Larches
BICKLEY
Chislehurst & West Kent C.C.
BANSOME WOOD
Marjorie McClure Sch
CHALKPIT WOOD
SUMMER HILL
CHISLEHURST
BIRCH WOOD
GOSHILL WOOD
POND WOOD
BR7
HAWKWOOD ESTATE NT
WALK WOOD
ST. PAUL'S CRAY COMMON
HOBLINGWELL WOOD
HOBLINGWELL WOOD REC GRD
ST. PAUL'S CRAY
96
97
98
99
100
101
102
103
104
PETTS WOOD NT
Edlmann Memorial Wood
Willett Memorial Wood
Chislehurst Junction
Bickley Junction
GREAT THRIFT
Bickley Manor Hotel
Bromley High Sch
BLACKBROOK WOOD
THORNET WOOD
JUBILEE COUNTRY PARK
Petts Wood Junction
PETTS WOOD
BR5
Petts Wood C.C.
POVEREST
206
COVET WOOD
POVEREST REC GRD
SOUTHBOROUGH RECREATION GROUND
PARKFIELD RECREATION GROUND
ST. LUKE'S CEM
SOUTHBOROUGH
BROMLEY GOLF COURSE
Bromley Common
RICHMAL CROMPTON FIELDS
PLAYING FIELD
SPARROW WOOD
SPARROW COMMON
ROUNDABOUT WOOD
CROFTON HEATH
PETTS WOOD REC GRD
CLAY WOOD
NOBODY'S WOOD
GUMPING COMMON
ORPINGTON
BR6
KNOWLEHILL WOOD
POKERIDDEN WOOD
Crofton Roman Villa
NEWSTEAD WOOD
FARNBOROUGH REC GRD
DARRICK COMMON
DARRICK WOOD
Bromley Tennis Centre
PRINCESS ROYAL UNI HOSP
The Fantail
223
ORPINGTON HOSPITAL
CROFTON ROAD
FARNBOROUGH ROAD
CHISLEHURST ROAD
ORPINGTON ROAD
ST PAULS CRAY ROAD
PERRY HALL
STATION ROAD
SPUR ROAD

EU
EV
EW
EX
EY
EZ
FA
186
205
224
SIDCUP BYPASS
A20
DA14
BR5
BR6
BR7
Crittall's Corner
EDGINGTON
RUXLEY WOOD
Ruxley Manor Garden Centre
Scadbury Moated Manor House Site
Field Study Centre
Youth Cen
SEVENOAKS WAY
A224
CRAYFIELDS BUSINESS PARK
CRAYFIELDS IND PARK
RUXLEY PARK GOLF COURSE
CRAY VALLEY GOLF COURSE
DRIVING RANGE
Clubhouse
Ski Centre
Fitness Cen
Pilgrim Hill
Barnfield Bank
CHAPMANS LANE
Lower Hockenden Farm
The Small House
Simon's Field Shaw
HOBLINGWELL WOOD REC GRD
ST. PAUL'S CRAY
PAULS CRAY HILL PARK
HIGHLANDS WOOD
HOCKENDEN WOOD
Hogspring Cottages
Milewood
MURRAY BUSINESS CEN
Gas Works
SPRINGVALE RETAIL PARK
BROOK IND PK
ST MARY CRAY
STAR LANE
CEM
SANDWAY PK
NUGENT SHOPPING PARK
NUGENT IND PARK
BLACKSMITHS LANE
THE WARREN
Sheepcote Farm
Ringland Farm
CHILD'S WOOD
POVEREST
POVEREST REC GRD
COVET WOOD
ST MARY CRAY REC GRD
RIVERSIDE GDNS
METRO CEN
Derry Downs
GRIGG'S CROSS
KYNASTON WOOD
Blueberry Farm
Kevington Farm
Waldens Farm
Crouch Farm
CROCKENHILL ROAD
B258
Walden Manor
Heather's Holdings
Bleak House Farm
PERRY HALL ROAD
A208
HIGH ST
COURT ROAD (ORPINGTON BYPASS)
PRIORY GARDENS
BURIAL GRD
GRASSMEADE RECREATION GROUND
RAMSDEN
Eastwood Farm
GRIFF'S WOOD
HOLLINGBOURNE TWR
BEKESBOURNE TWR
Piggery
Byways Nurseries
SAGE WENTS
SPUR ROAD
A232
A223
Goddington Manor
Goddington
GODDINGTON PARK
ROUNDS SMALLAMS
Bowling Green
Cookham Hill Farm
Cookham Farm
Crownwood Farm
LILLY'S WOOD
BLACK BUSH WOOD
ORPINGTON HOSPITAL
Tennis Courts
500 yds
500 m
95
96
97
98
99
100
101
102
103
104
47
48
49
66
67
68
69

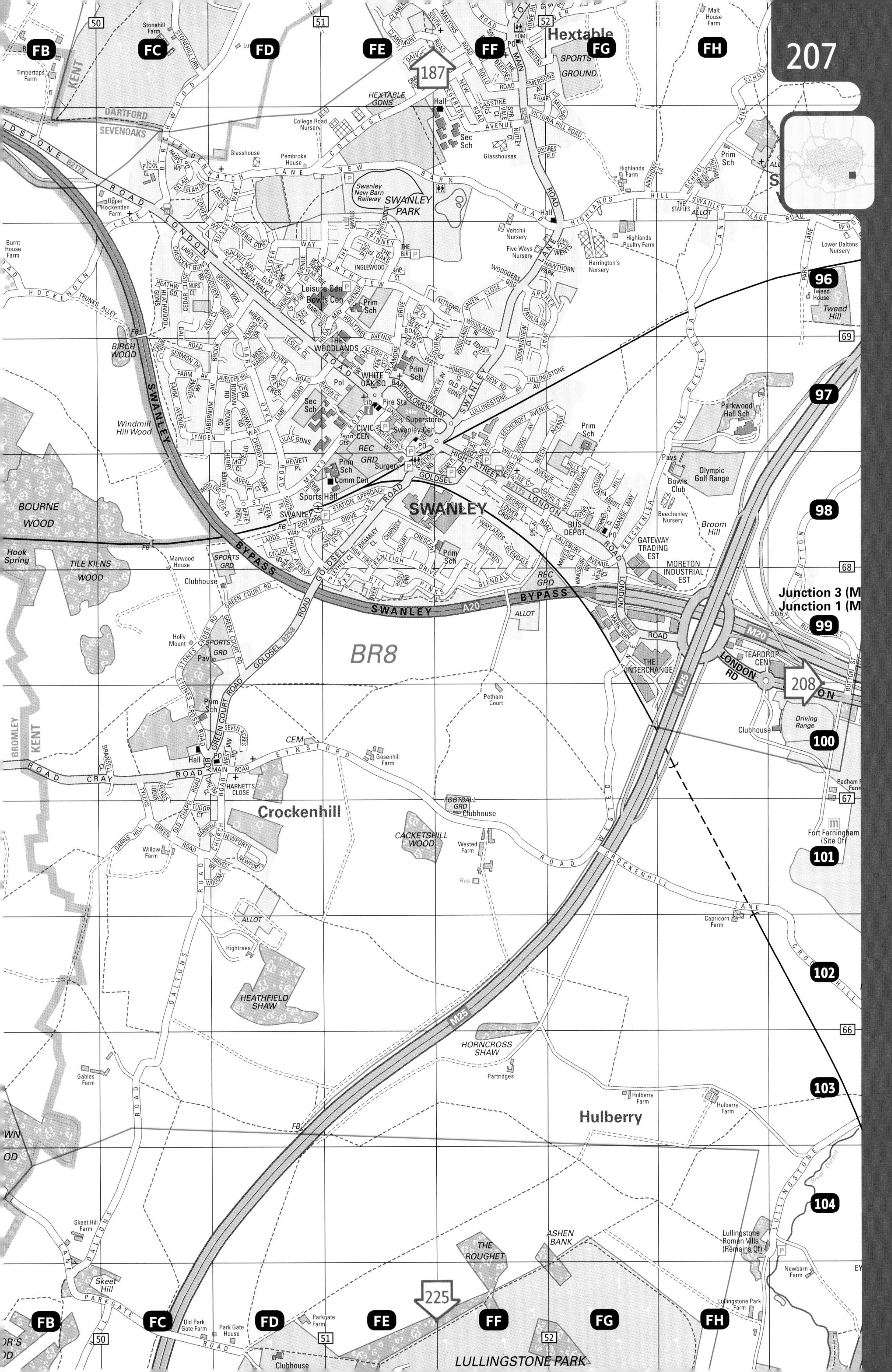
FB
FC
FD
FE
FF
FG
FH
50
51
52
187
Hextable
SPORTS GROUND
Malt House Farm
Stonehill Farm
Timbertops Farm
KENT
DARTFORD
SEVENOAKS
HEXTABLE GDNS
College Road Nursery
Glasshouse
Pembroke House
Sec Sch
Glasshouses
Highlands Farm
Prim Sch
HIGHLANDS HILL
SWANLEY VILLAGE ROAD
THE STAPLES
ALLOT
Upper Hockenden Farm
Swanley New Barn Railway
SWANLEY PARK
NEW BARN ROAD
Veitchii Nursery
Five Ways Nursery
Highlands Poultry Farm
Harrington's Nursery
Lower Daltons Nursery
Burnt House Farm
HOCKENDEN
TRUNKS ALLEY
Leisure Cen
Bowls Cen
Prim Sch
BIRCH WOOD
THE WOODLANDS
WHITE OAK SQ
Pol
Fire Sta
Lib
Superstore
Swanley Cen
CIVIC CEN
REC GRD
Sec Sch
Tweed House
Tweed Hill
96
97
98
99
100
101
102
103
104
69
68
67
66
Parkwood Hall Sch
Windmill Hill Wood
Olympic Golf Range
Bowls Club
Beechenlea Nursery
Broom Hill
SWANLEY
BOURNE WOOD
Hook Spring
TILE KILNS WOOD
Marwood House
SPORTS GRD
Clubhouse
Sports Hall
Comm Cen
Surgery
BUS DEPOT
GATEWAY TRADING EST
MORETON INDUSTRIAL EST
Junction 3 (M
Junction 1 (M
SWANLEY BY-PASS
A20
M20
M25
REC GRD
ALLOT
BR8
THE INTERCHANGE
TEARDROP CEN
LONDON RD
208
Driving Range
Clubhouse
Holly Mount
SPORTS GRD
Pav
Prim Sch
GREEN COURT ROAD
GOLDSEL ROAD
Petham Court
Pedham Farm
CEM
Gosenhill Farm
EYNSFORD ROAD
CRAY ROAD
BROMLEY
KENT
Crockenhill
HARNETTS CLOSE
FOOTBALL GRD
Clubhouse
CACKETSHILL WOOD
Westerd Farm
Fort Farningham (Site Of)
Willow Farm
Res
CROCKENHILL LANE
Capricorn Farm
ALLOT
Hightrees
HEATHFIELD SHAW
DALTONS ROAD
HORNCROSS SHAW
Partridges
Gables Farm
Hulberry Farm
Hulberry
Skeet Hill Farm
Skeet Hill
THE ROUGHET
ASHEN BANK
Lullingstone Roman Villa (Remains Of)
Newbarn Farm
Lullingstone Park Farm
225
PARKGATE ROAD
Old Park Gate Farm
Park Gate House
Parkgate Farm
Clubhouse
LULLINGSTONE PARK

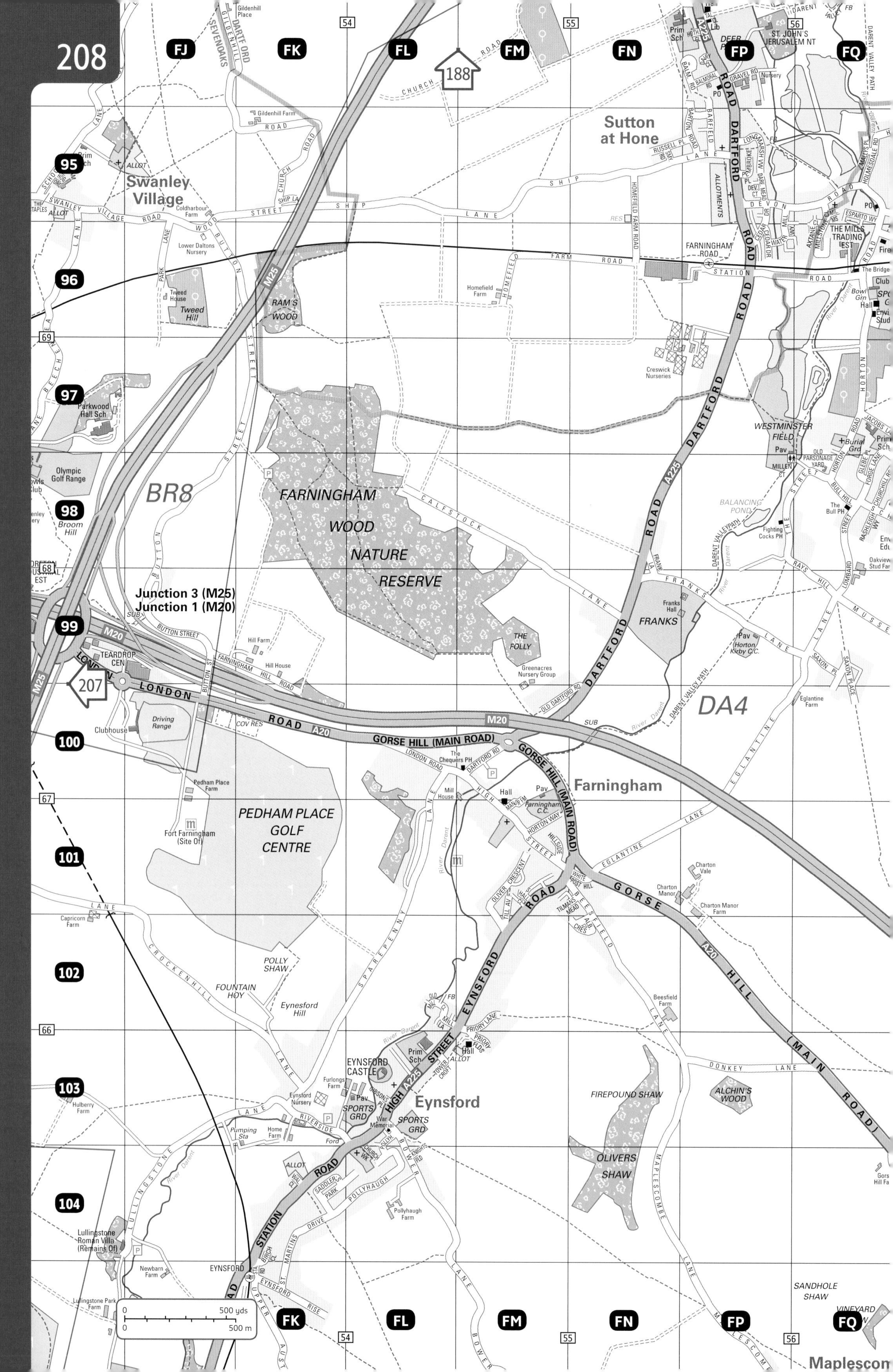

FJ
FK
FL
FM
FN
FP
FQ
54
55
56
188
207
95
96
97
98
99
100
101
102
103
104
69
68
67
66
Swanley Village
Sutton at Hone
Farningham
Eynsford
BR8
DA4
FARNINGHAM WOOD NATURE RESERVE
PEDHAM PLACE GOLF CENTRE
Junction 3 (M25)
Junction 1 (M20)
M25
M20
A20
A225
DARTFORD ROAD
LONDON ROAD
GORSE HILL (MAIN ROAD)
SHIP LANE
SWANLEY VILLAGE ROAD
BUTTON STREET
CALFSTOCK LANE
FARM ROAD
STATION ROAD
EYNSFORD ROAD
HIGH STREET
DONKEY LANE
MAPLESCOMBE LANE
SPAREPENNY LANE
CROCKENHILL LANE
LULLINGSTONE LANE
ST. JOHN'S JERUSALEM NT
Olympic Golf Range
Tweed Hill
RAM'S WOOD
THE FOLLY
FRANKS
WESTMINSTER FIELD
THE MILLS TRADING EST
Creswick Nurseries
Greenacres Nursery Group
Fort Farningham (Site Of)
POLLY SHAW
FOUNTAIN HOY
Eynesford Hill
EYNSFORD CASTLE
FIREPOUND SHAW
ALCHIN'S WOOD
OLIVERS SHAW
SANDHOLE SHAW
Lullingstone Roman Villa (Remains Of)
Lullingstone Park Farm
Newbarn Farm
Pollyhaugh Farm
Beesfield Farm
Charton Manor
Charton Manor Farm
Eglantine Farm
Capricorn Farm
Hulberry Farm
Pedham Place Farm
Driving Range
Clubhouse
TEARDROP CEN
Hill Farm
Hill House
Homefield Farm
Gildenhill Farm
Coldharbour Farm
Lower Daltons Nursery
Parkwood Hall Sch
Broom Hill
Maplescombe
0
500 yds
500 m

South Darenth
Pinden
Mile End Green
Dean Bottom
Horton Kirby
Hartley Green
Fawkham Green
DA2
DA3
TN15
HORTON WOOD
GROVE WOOD
CHURCHDOWN WOOD
FAWKHAM VALLEY GOLF COURSE
REDLIBBETS GOLF COURSE
FAWKHAM MANOR HOSPITAL
SAXTEN'S WOOD
CHOAKS WOOD
GABRIEL SPRING WOOD
BRANDS HATCH MOTOR RACING CIRCUIT
LONGFIELD
M20

Longcross
192
226
CHOBHAM COMMON
NATIONAL NATURE
RESERVE
Oystershell Hill
Rushy Pond
Staple Hill
Chickabiddy Hill
Albury Bottom
Earthworks
ROUNDPOND CLUMP
ROUND POND
FIR CLUMP
Car Breakers Yard
Round Pond Nursery
Langshot Bog
Langshot Equestrian Centre
Albury Farm
Butts Hill
Gracious Pond
Gracious Pond Farm
Old Slade
Earthworks
Lily Pond Farm
Glasshouse
Upper Childown
Childown
Fish Pond
Stonehill
Fern Hill
Stanners Hill
Stannershill Farm
DUNSTALL GREEN
Home Farm
Burrowhill
Ram Bridge
Rambridge Farm
Westways Farm
Brimshot Farm
LITTLE HEATH
GU24
Chobham Park Farm
Henage Corner
Buckstone Farm
Little Heath Farm
Little Heath Nursery
Burrow Hill Nursery
Clubhouse
Chobham R.F.C.
Sch
Youth Cen
Nursery
Larkenshaw
Larkenshaw Farm
CHOBHAM BUSINESS CENTRE
Hangars
Stanyards Farm
SOW MOOR PLANTATION
SOW MOOR
Fishpool Bridge
Copyhold
Riverside Nursery
Brooklands Farm
Kelmstone Arabian Stud
Little Goldbridge Farm
Burnside Nursery
Sunfield Farm
CHOBHAM
Millbourne Bri
Fire Sta
Prim Sch
CEM
Cricket Ground
Hall
Tenn Cts
REC
GRD
Pav
Grant's Bri
Willow Farm
Poplar Grove Farm
Rothwell Nursery
Broadford
Broadford Farm
Focklesbrook Farm
Chobham Farm
MILFORD GREEN
Sewage Works
Cox Hill
Milford House
Daydown Nursery
Mimbridge
White Lodge Farm
COXHILL GREEN
Border Farm
Mimbridge Garden Centre
Deep Pool Farm
Castle Grove PH
Castle Grn
Millbrook Animal Centre (R.S.P.C.A.)
Studley Grange Farm
Grove Herb Farm
Young Stroat Farm
Scotchers Farm
Shaws Farm
Wapshott Farm
Heather Farm
GU21
SURREY HEATH
WOKING
HORSELL COMMON
NUFFIELD HOSPITAL
Knaphill Manor Farm
Knaphill Manor
Graylands Farm
Westbury Farm
Garden Supplies
Mink Farm
Parley Brook Farm
Garden Centre
Parley Bridge
Knapwood House
Mizen's
Rec Cen
Sec Sch
HORSELL BIRCH
Mill Bourne
The Bourne
Parley Brook
M3
A319
A3046
B386
B383
CHERTSEY ROAD
LONGCROSS ROAD
STAPLE HILL
STAPLE HILL ROAD
WINDSOR ROAD
ACCOMMODATION ROAD
GRACIOUS POND ROAD
STONEHILL ROAD
STONEHILL CRES
CLEARMOUNT
HEATHER WAY
GORSE LA
KILLY HILL
BROOM LANE
RED LION ROAD
BRIMSHOT LANE
MINCING LANE
THE AVENUE
MEDHURST CL
OAKDENE
BRACKEN WAY
ELM DRIVE
DELTA
BURR HILL LANE
CHOBHAM PARK LANE
LITTLE HEATH ROAD
TURFHOUSE LA
WINDSOR CT RD
BOWLING GRN RD
OAKHURST
SANDY LA
BURROW HILL
LESLIE ROAD
THE GRANGE
MACDONALD ROAD
HIGH STREET
BAGSHOT ROAD
BROOK LANE
STATION ROAD
SANDPIT HALL ROAD
MOUNT ROAD
PHILPOT LANE
TROTTERS LANE
BROADFORD LANE
BROADFORD ROAD
GROVE ROAD
GUILDFORD ROAD
LAKESIDE DRIVE
GROSVENOR RD
CARTHOUSE LANE
CHOBHAM ROAD
LITTLEWICK ROAD
HORSELL COMMON ROAD
DEEP POOL LANE
YOUNGSTROAT LANE
STROAT LA
KETTLEWELL HILL
COMMON CLOSE
SOUTH ROAD
CHEAPSIDE
VIGGORY LANE
HEATHER CL
HORSELL BIRCH
500 yds
500 m

OTTERSHAW
ROW TOWN
WOODHAM
SHEERWATER
Pyrford
KT16
KT15
KT14
GU22
Junction 11
RUNNYMEDE HOSP
ST. PETER'S HOSP
QUEENWOOD GOLF COURSE
Foxhills Country Club
OTTERSHAW PARK
GREAT WOOD
BIRCH WOOD
HOYT WOOD
BROX COPSE
NEW ZEALAND GOLF COURSE
McLaren Technology Centre
HORSELL COMMON
WEST BYFLEET GOLF COURSE
GUILDFORD ROAD
CHOBHAM ROAD
MURRAY ROAD
SPINNEY HILL
ST. PETER'S WAY
WOODHAM LANE
SHEERWATER ROAD
CHERTSEY ROAD
WOODHAM ROAD
OLD WOKING ROAD
BASINGSTOKE CANAL
193
212
227

MOOR GOLF COURSE
Junction 11
ADDLESTONE
WEYBRIDGE ROAD
A317
ST. PETER'S WAY
CHERTSEY ROAD
HIGH STREET
BRIGHTON ROAD
STATION ROAD
CHURCH ROAD
NEW HAW ROAD
A318
KT15
ROW TOWN
NEW HAW
BYFLEET ROAD
OYSTER LANE
BROOKLANDS
BROOKLANDS MUSEUM
MERCEDES-BENZ WORLD
Brooklands College
BROOKLANDS COMMUNITY PARK
WELLINGTON WAY
BARNES WALLIS DR
SOPWITH DR
WOODHAM
WOODHAM LANE
CAMPHILL INDUSTRIAL ESTATE
HEATHERVALE REC GRD
PARVIS ROAD
A245
DARTNELL PARK
KT14
WEST BYFLEET
BYFLEET
OLD WOKING ROAD
GU22
GU23
TRADITIONS GOLF COURSE
TOP GOLF ADDLESTONE GOLF COURSE
CENTRAL VETERINARY LABORATORY
SAYES COURT PUBLIC OPEN SPACE
Weybridge Junction
Addlestone Junction
Byfleet & New Haw
River Wey
M25
194
211
228
BG
BH
BJ
BK
BL
BM
BN
105
106
107
108
109
110
111
112
113
114
0 500 yds
0 500 m

BP
BQ
BR
BS
BT
BU
BV
195
ASHLEY PARK
OATLANDS PARK
BURWOOD PARK
Oatlands Park Hotel
PLAYING FIELDS
WALTON-ON-THAMES
Unilever UK Ltd.
MONUMENT HILL
OATLANDS DRIVE
QUEENS ROAD
A3050
A317
HERSHAM
Haine's Bridge
GlaxoSmithKline
THE HEATH
KT12
KT13
KT11
WALTON COMMON
UPPER COMMON
SPORTS GROUND
Whiteley Village C.C.
WHITELEY VILLAGE
BURHILL GOLF COURSE
(OLD COURSE)
BURHILL GOLF COURSE
(NEW COURSE)
Dick Turpin's Cottage
ST. GEORGE'S HILL
FLAGSTAFF HOUSE CONFERENCE CENTRE
ST. GEORGE'S HILL GOLF COURSE
COVERED RESERVOIRS
WARREN POND
UPPER POND
Strawberry Hill
Beards Hill
CONVENT
Notre Dame Sch
Seven Hills Estate
BURWOOD PARK
Hook's Corner
Chestnut Lodge Farm
Chippings Farm
West Lodge
ACS Cobham International School
Riverside Farm
Burhill Kennels
Squire's Garden Centre
CEM
SEVEN HILLS ROAD
B365
BYFLEET ROAD
A245
ESHER ROAD
A3
PORTSMOUTH ROAD
FOXHOLM COVERT
SILVERMERE GOLF COURSE
SILVER MERE
Squash Club
Home Farm
Hilton Cobham
PAINSHILL PARK
Painshill
THE BROOM
Gothic Temple
Chinese Bridge
GROTTO
THE LAKE
Wood Hill
Visitor Centre
Cobham Br
Weir
Long Orchard Farm
Bramble Hedge Farm
Foxwarren Park
Red Hill
Oak Pollard
Gothic Tower
WHEEL ISLAND
BELL WOOD
GUILDFORD ROAD
REDHILL ROAD
B368
COBHAM COMMUNITY HOSP
Superstore
BETWEEN STREETS
HIGH ST
RIVERHILL
MILL RD
STOKE
COBHAM
ROSE LODGE WOOD
Cobham Court Farm
Cobham FC
Health Cen
Youth Cen
Lib
214
229
106
107
108
109
110
111
112
113
114
08
09
10
61
62
63
64

BW
BX
BY
BZ
CA
CB
CC
196
213
230
HERSHAM
WEST END
ESHER
KT12
KT11
HERSHAM VILLAGE GOLF COURSE
SANDOWN PARK RACECOURSE
CORONATION RECREATION GROUND
HERSHAM RIVERSIDE PARK
PRINCESS ALICE HOSPICE
MOORE PLACE GOLF COURSE
CLAREMONT PARK GOLF COURSE
WEST END COMMON
CLAREMONT LANDSCAPE GARDEN (NT)
Claremont Park
HORSESHOE CLUMP
WINTERDOWN WOOD
ESHER COMMON
FAIRMILE COMMON
OXSHOTT HEATH
LITTLE HEATH COMMON
Fairmile
COBHAM COMMUNITY HOSP
KNOWLE HILL PARK
HERSHAM BYPASS
ESHER ROAD
PORTSMOUTH ROAD
ESHER BYPASS
COPSEM LANE
WARREN LANE
BLACKHILLS
LAMMAS LANE
BURHILL ROAD
SANDY LANE
FAIRMILE LANE
BURHILL GOLF COURSE (NEW COURSE)
ACS Cobham International School
DRIVING RANGE
COBHAM R.F.C.
OXSHOTT
ARBROOK COMMON
THE FURZE
CLAY PLANTATION
ROSE LODGE WOOD
0
500 yds
500 m

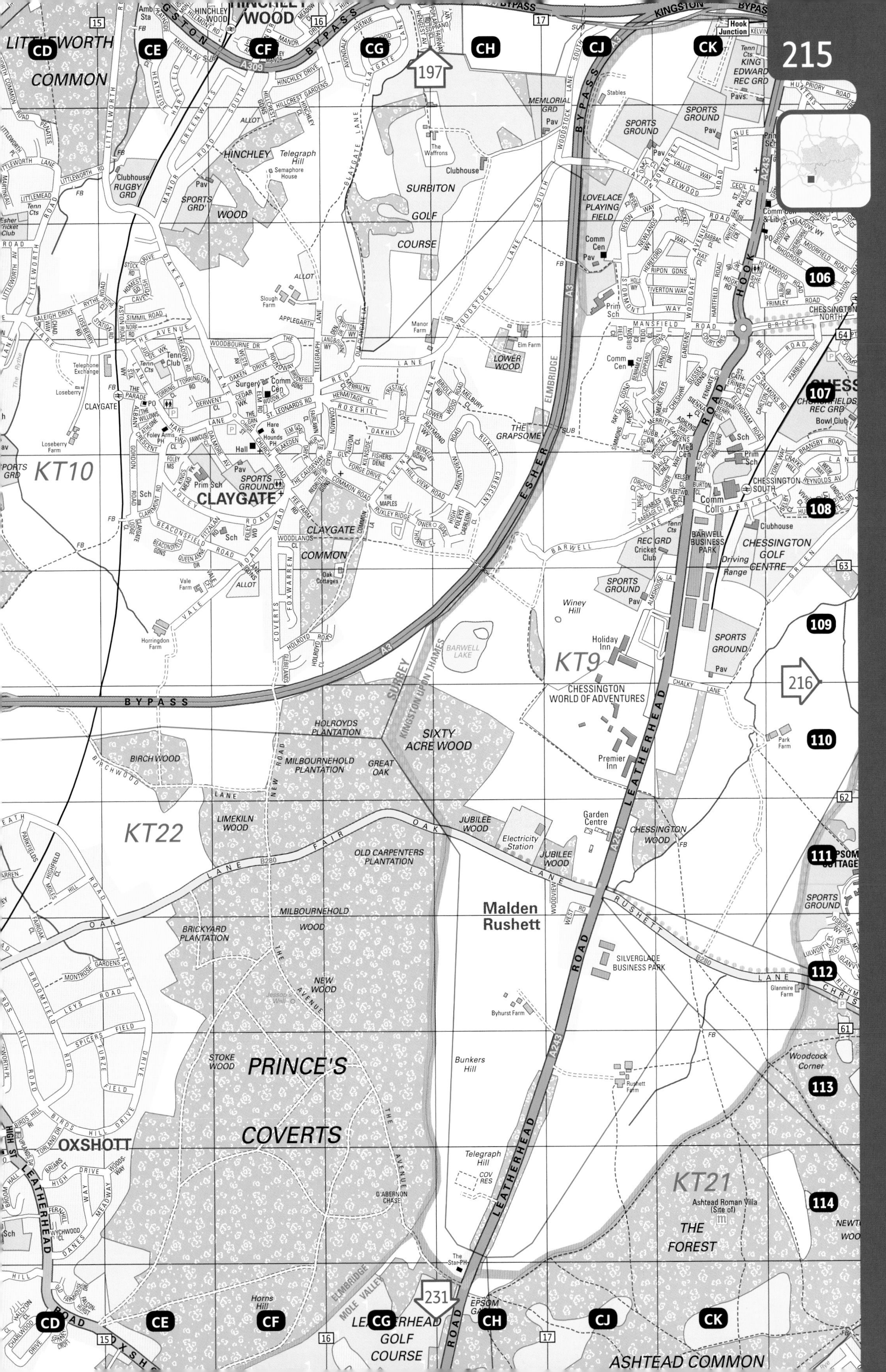
LITTLEWORTH
COMMON
HINCHLEY WOOD
KINGSTON BYPASS
Hook Junction
KING EDWARD REC GRD
SPORTS GROUND
MEMORIAL GRD
SURBITON GOLF COURSE
HINCHLEY WOOD
Telegraph Hill
Semaphore House
RUGBY GRD
SPORTS GRD
LOVELACE PLAYING FIELD
CHESSINGTON NORTH
LOWER WOOD
Elm Farm
Manor Farm
Slough Farm
CLAYGATE
KT10
THE GRAPSOME
CHESS
CHESSINGTON SOUTH
REC GRD
Bowl Club
CLAYGATE COMMON
SPORTS GROUND
CHESSINGTON GOLF CENTRE
BARWELL BUSINESS PARK
Oak Cottages
Vale Farm
Horringdon Farm
Winey Hill
BARWELL LAKE
Holiday Inn
KT9
CHESSINGTON WORLD OF ADVENTURES
SURREY
KINGSTON UPON THAMES
HOLROYDS PLANTATION
SIXTY ACRE WOOD
BIRCH WOOD
MILBOURNEHOLD PLANTATION
GREAT OAK
Premier Inn
Park Farm
KT22
LIMEKILN WOOD
JUBILEE WOOD
Electricity Station
Garden Centre
CHESSINGTON WOOD
OLD CARPENTERS PLANTATION
MILBOURNEHOLD WOOD
Malden Rushett
BRICKYARD PLANTATION
SILVERGLADE BUSINESS PARK
NEW WOOD
Byhurst Farm
Glanmire Farm
EPSOM COTTAGE
SPORTS GROUND
STOKE WOOD
PRINCE'S COVERTS
Bunkers Hill
Rushett Farm
Woodcock Corner
OXSHOTT
Telegraph Hill
D'ABERNON CHASE
KT21
Ashtead Roman Villa (Site of)
THE FOREST
Horns Hill
LEATHERHEAD GOLF COURSE
ASHTEAD COMMON
A3
A243
A309
B280
LEATHERHEAD ROAD
ESHER BYPASS
OAKLEY LANE
FAIR OAK LANE
RUSHETT LANE
CD
CE
CF
CG
CH
CJ
CK
197
216
231
15
16
17
106
107
108
109
110
111
112
113
114
61
62
63
64

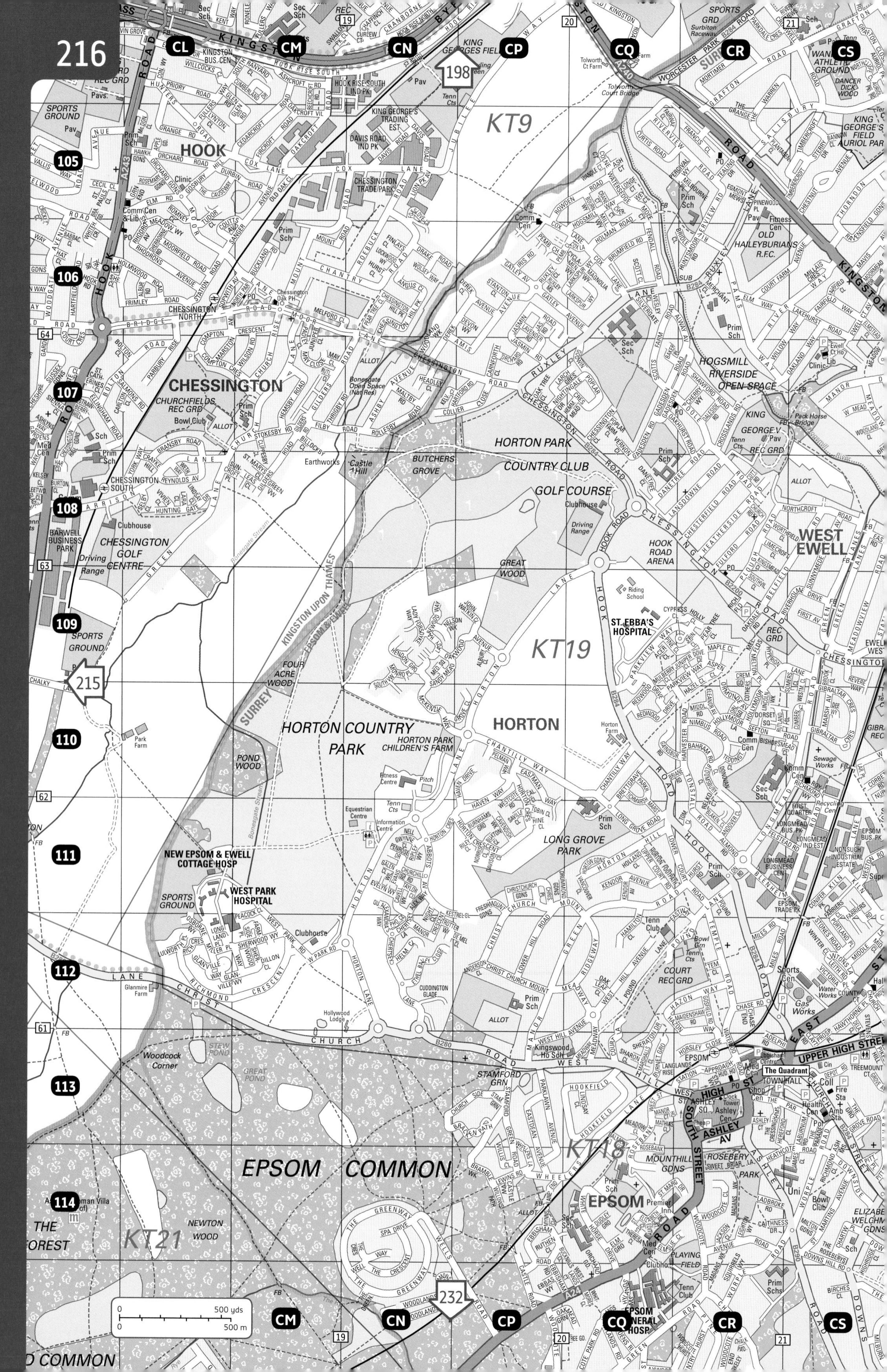
CL
CM
CN
CP
CQ
CR
CS
198
KT9
HOOK
KINGSTON BY PASS
SPORTS GROUND
CHESSINGTON
CHESSINGTON NORTH
CHESSINGTON SOUTH
CHURCHFIELDS REC GRD
CHESSINGTON GOLF CENTRE
BARWELL BUSINESS PARK
KING GEORGE'S TRADING EST
DAVIS ROAD IND PK
CHESSINGTON TRADE PARK
HOOK RISE SOUTH IND PK
KING GEORGES FIELD
Castle Hill
BUTCHERS GROVE
HORTON PARK COUNTRY CLUB GOLF COURSE
HOGSMILL RIVERSIDE OPEN SPACE
KING GEORGE V REC GRD
OLD HAILEYBURIANS R.F.C.
WEST EWELL
HOOK ROAD ARENA
GREAT WOOD
KT19
ST. EBBA'S HOSPITAL
HORTON
HORTON COUNTRY PARK
HORTON PARK CHILDREN'S FARM
FOUR ACRE WOOD
POND WOOD
LONG GROVE PARK
NEW EPSOM & EWELL COTTAGE HOSP
WEST PARK HOSPITAL
COURT REC GRD
215
EPSOM COMMON
KT18
EPSOM
KT21
NEWTON WOOD
THE FOREST
The Quadrant
TOWN HALL
EPSOM GENERAL HOSP
232
105
106
107
108
109
110
111
112
113
114
0 500 yds
0 500 m

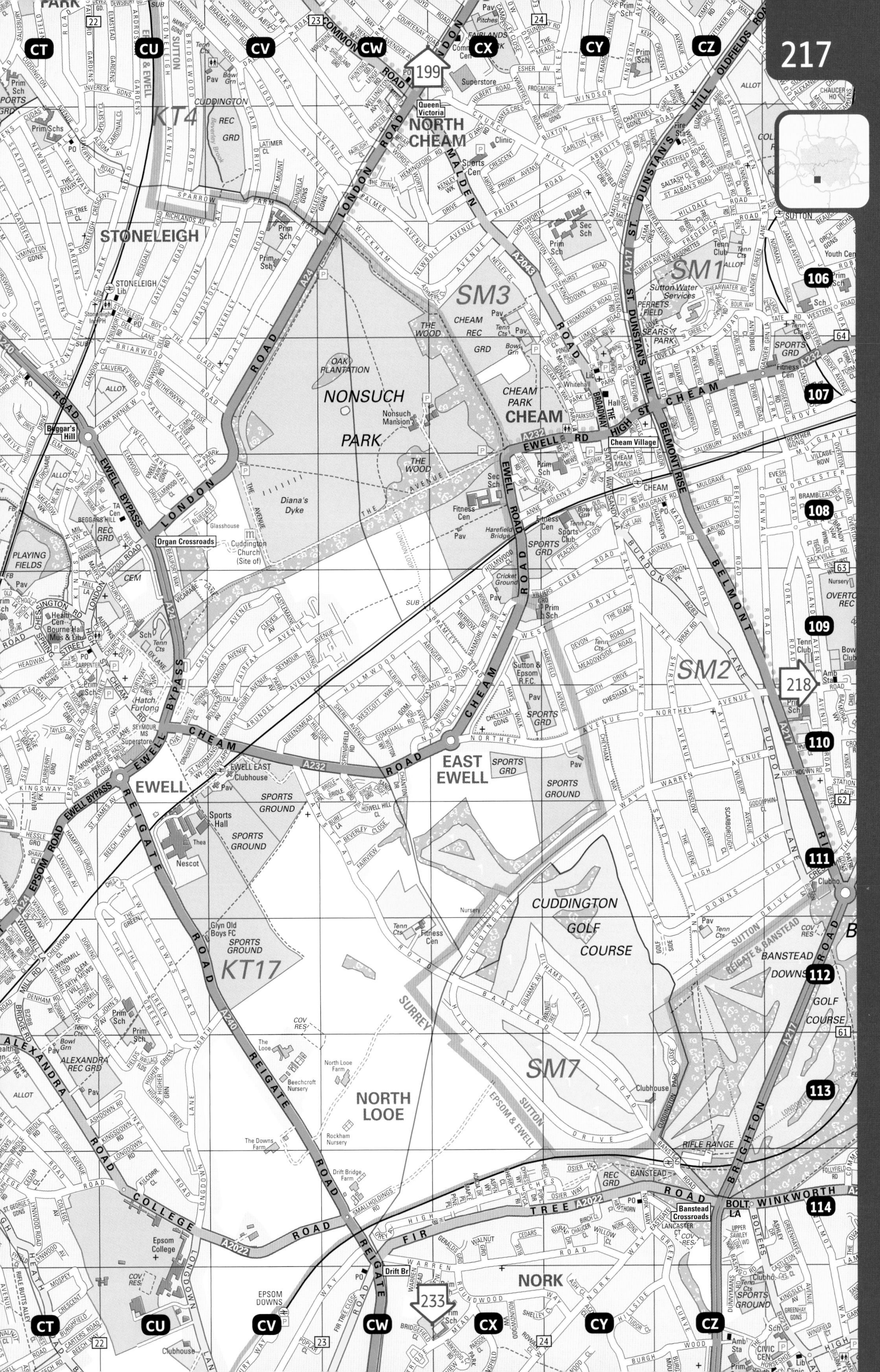

CT
CU
CV
CW
CX
CY
CZ
199
NORTH CHEAM
Queen Victoria
Superstore
CUDDINGTON REC GRD
KT4
STONELEIGH
STONELEIGH Lib
Beggar's Hill
EWELL BYPASS
LONDON ROAD
Organ Crossroads
Cuddington Church (Site of)
Glasshouse
NONSUCH PARK
OAK PLANTATION
Nonsuch Mansion
THE WOOD
Diana's Dyke
THE AVENUE
SM3
CHEAM REC GRD
CHEAM PARK
CHEAM
Cheam Village
EWELL RD
HIGH ST
BROADWAY
BELMONT RISE
ST. DUNSTAN'S HILL
SM1
Sutton Water Services
PERRETS FIELD
SEARS PARK
SUTTON
106
107
108
109
110
111
112
113
114
218
BELMONT
SM2
EWELL ROAD
CHEAM ROAD
Harefield Bridge
Cricket Ground
Sutton & Epsom R.F.C.
SPORTS GRD
EAST EWELL
EWELL
EWELL EAST
Clubhouse
SPORTS GROUND
Nescot
KT17
REIGATE ROAD
EPSOM ROAD
PLAYING FIELDS
CEM
Hatch Furlong
Bourne Hall Mus & Lib
Health Cen
CUDDINGTON GOLF COURSE
SM7
SURREY
EPSOM & EWELL
SUTTON
REIGATE & BANSTEAD
BANSTEAD DOWNS GOLF COURSE
RIFLE RANGE
Clubhouse
NORTH LOOE
The Looe
North Looe Farm
Beechcroft Nursery
Rockham Nursery
The Downs Farm
Drift Bridge Farm
Glyn Old Boys FC
ALEXANDRA REC GRD
Epsom College
COLLEGE ROAD
FIR TREE ROAD
A2022
Drift Br
EPSOM DOWNS
233
NORK
Banstead Crossroads
BANSTEAD
WINKWORTH
BRIGHTON ROAD
A217
A24
A232
A240
22
23
24

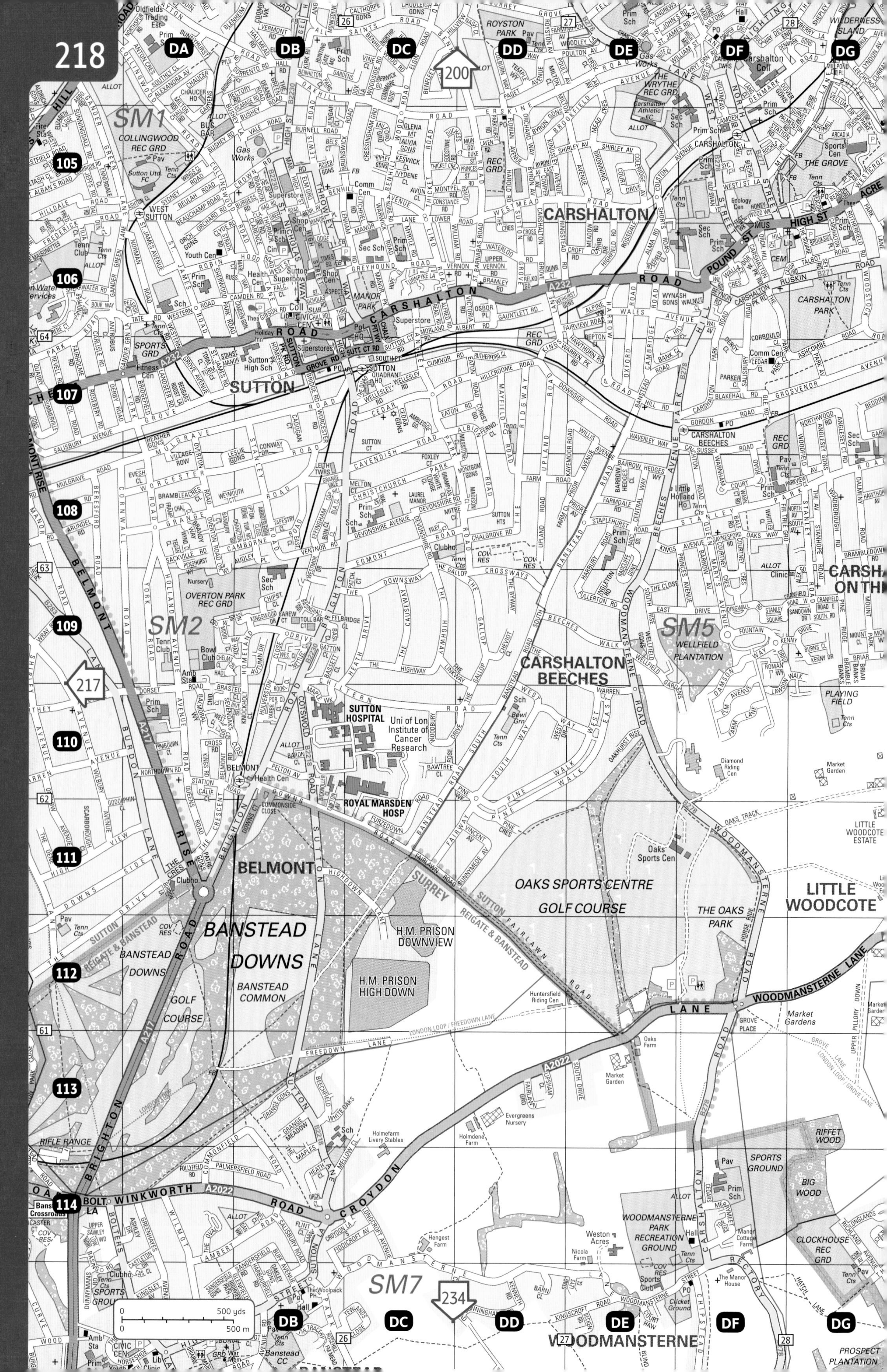
DA
DB
DC
DD
DE
DF
DG
200
SM1
COLLINGWOOD REC GRD
Sutton Utd. FC
WEST SUTTON
CARSHALTON
CARSHALTON ROAD
HIGH ST
POUND ST
THE WRYTHE REC GRD
THE GROVE
CARSHALTON PARK
SUTTON
GROVE RD
SUTTON HIGH SCH
CARSHALTON BEECHES
OVERTON PARK REC GRD
SM2
SM5
WELLFIELD PLANTATION
CARSHALTON BEECHES
SUTTON HOSPITAL
Uni of Lon Institute of Cancer Research
ROYAL MARSDEN HOSP
BELMONT
BANSTEAD DOWNS
BANSTEAD COMMON
BANSTEAD DOWNS GOLF COURSE
H.M. PRISON DOWNVIEW
H.M. PRISON HIGH DOWN
OAKS SPORTS CENTRE GOLF COURSE
THE OAKS PARK
LITTLE WOODCOTE
Oaks Sports Cen
WOODMANSTERNE LANE
WOODMANSTERNE PARK RECREATION GROUND
SPORTS GROUND
RIFFET WOOD
BIG WOOD
CLOCKHOUSE REC GRD
PROSPECT PLANTATION
SM7
WOODMANSTERNE
WINKWORTH ROAD
CROYDON ROAD
BRIGHTON ROAD
BELMONT RISE
RIFLE RANGE
217
234
105
106
107
108
109
110
111
112
113
114
500 yds
500 m

BEDDINGTON PARK
CROYDON ROAD
DUPPAS HILL RD
DUPPAS HILL
WALLINGTON
SM6
BANDON HILL CEMETERY
MELLOWS PARK
SOUTH BEDDINGTON
ROUNDSHAW PLAYING FIELD
ROUNDSHAW OPEN SPACE
PURLEY WAY PLAYING FIELDS
CR0
CR2
SOUTH CROYDON
HALING PARK
WOODCOTE
PURLEY
Purley Cross
Fiveways
PURLEY WAR MEM. HOSP
CR8
CR5
Woodcote Park
WOODCOTE PARK GOLF COURSE
FOXLEY WOOD
HIGHER DRIVE REC GRD
WOODCOTE GROVE REC GRD
RIDDLESDOWN WOOD
FOXLEY LANE
LITTLE WOODCOTE LANE
SMITHAM BOTTOM LANE
BRIGHTON ROAD
GODSTONE ROAD
DOWNS COURT ROAD
WOODCOTE ROAD
WOODCOTE GROVE ROAD
MANOR ROAD
STAFFORD ROAD
PLOUGH LANE
PURLEY WAY
SANDY LANE
KENLEY
COULSDON TOWN
HARTLEY BUSHES
201
220
235
DH
DJ
DK
DL
DM
DN
DP
106
107
108
109
110
111
112
113
114
29
30
31
61
62
63
64

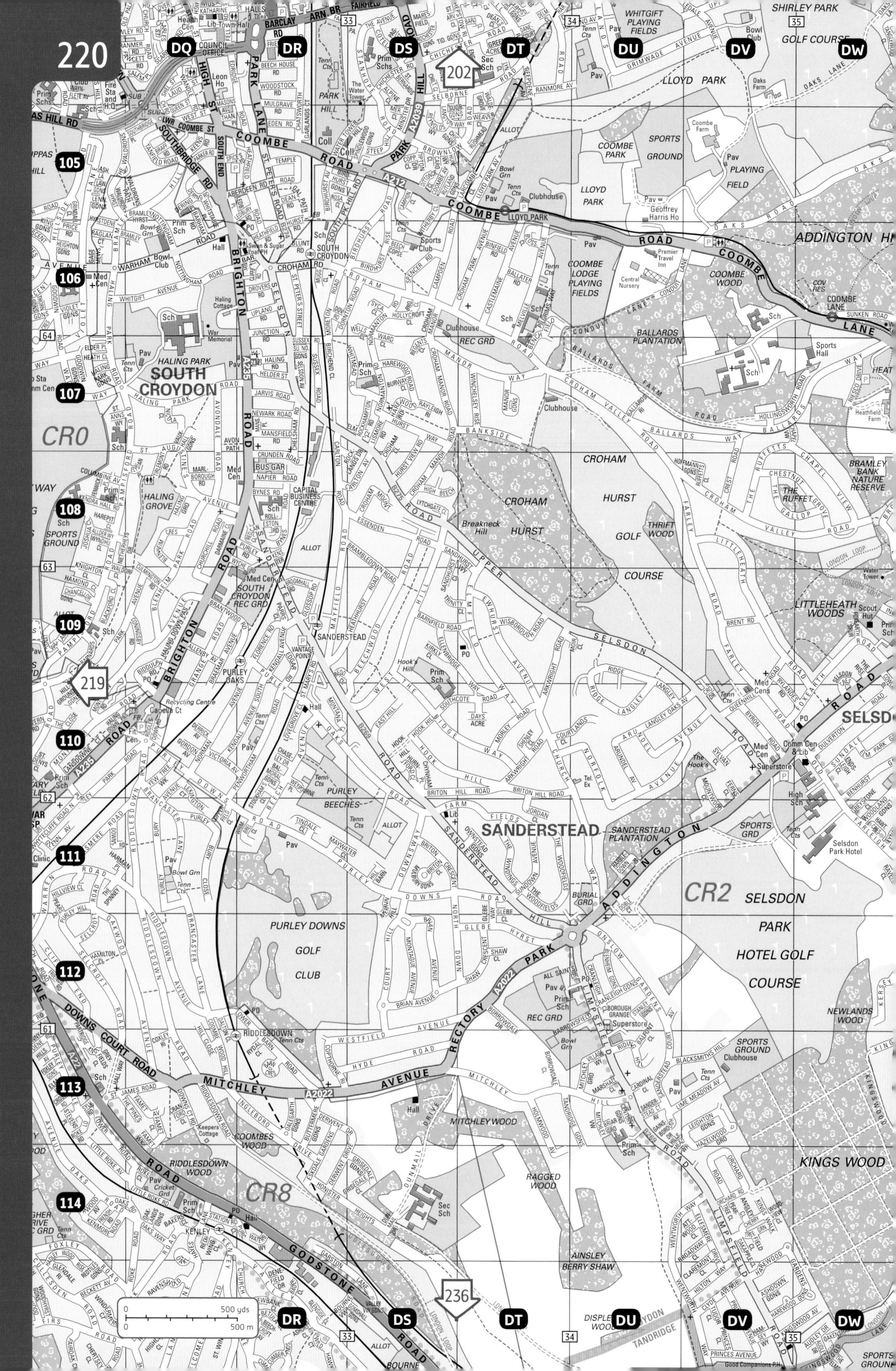
DQ
DR
DS
DT
DU
DV
DW
202
SHIRLEY PARK
GOLF COURSE
WHITGIFT
PLAYING
FIELDS
LLOYD PARK
COOMBE
PARK
SPORTS
GROUND
LLOYD
PARK
PLAYING
FIELD
COOMBE ROAD
PARK LANE
HIGH ST
SOUTH END
SOUTHBRIDGE RD
BRIGHTON ROAD
A235
A212
A2039
A2022
A22
ADDINGTON HI
COOMBE
LODGE
PLAYING
FIELDS
COOMBE
WOOD
BALLARDS
PLANTATION
COOMBE LANE
105
106
107
108
109
110
111
112
113
114
HALING PARK
SOUTH
CROYDON
CR0
CR2
CR8
HALING
GROVE
CROHAM
HURST
GOLF
COURSE
CROHAM
HURST
Breakneck
Hill
THRIFT
WOOD
LITTLEHEATH
WOODS
BRAMLEY
BANK
NATURE
RESERVE
THE
RUFFET
SELSDON ROAD
UPPER SELSDON ROAD
SANDERSTEAD ROAD
SANDERSTEAD
SANDERSTEAD
PLANTATION
ADDINGTON ROAD
PURLEY
OAKS
PURLEY
BEECHES
PURLEY DOWNS
GOLF
CLUB
SELSDON
PARK
HOTEL GOLF
COURSE
Selsdon
Park Hotel
NEWLANDS
WOOD
RECTORY PARK
MITCHLEY AVENUE
MITCHLEY WOOD
RIDDLESDOWN
RIDDLESDOWN
WOOD
COOMBES
WOOD
RAGGED
WOOD
AINSLEY
BERRY SHAW
KINGS WOOD
LIMPSFIELD ROAD
DOWNS COURT ROAD
GODSTONE ROAD
KENLEY
219
236
0
500 yds
0
500 m
33
34
35
TANDRIDGE
LONDON LOOP

ADDINGTON
ADDINGTON PALACE GOLF COURSE
THE ADDINGTON GOLF CLUB
FORESTDALE
NEW ADDINGTON
ADDINGTON VALE
ADDINGTON COURT GOLF COURSE
FARLEIGH COURT GOLF COURSE
FARLEIGH
SELSDON WOOD NT
SPRING PARK
KENT GATE WAY
SELSDON PARK ROAD
GRAVEL HILL
FIELDWAY
KING HENRY'S DRIVE
NEW ADDINGTON
ADDINGTON VILLAGE
CR0
CR6
BR4
203
222
237
DX
DY
DZ
EA
EB
EC
ED
106
107
108
109
110
111
112
113
114

EE
EF
EG
EH
EJ
EK
EL
40
41
42
204
Coney Hall
HAYES COMMON
F.C. RUGBY GROUND
COLYERS WOOD
Sec Sch
Wyevale Garden Centre
ALLOT
Keston Mark
CROYDON ROAD
A232
GLEBE WAY
CROYDON RD
WICKHAM COMMON
Hall
HARVEST BANK RD
HARVEST BANK ROAD
ROBINS GRO
HARTFIELD CRESCENT
LAWRENCE RD
KINGSWAY
QUEENSWAY
CHURCH DRIVE
CONEY HALL REC GRD
Tenn Cts
Bowl Grn
Pav
BURIAL GRD
Sch
105
THE EMMAUS CENTRE
SYLVAN WAY
HAWTHORN DRIVE
CHESTNUT AVENUE
BIRCH TREE AVENUE
CHERRY TREE WALK
LIME TREE WALK
MONARCH CL
Prim Sch
GATES GREEN ROAD
BASTON MANOR ROAD
The Lodge
Hast Hill
Baston Manor
The Oasthouse
WEST COMMON ROAD
BASTON ROAD
B265
PADMALL WOOD
OAKFIELD LANE
COMMONSIDE
J.B. Stables
Greyhound PH
LAKES ROAD
PO
The Fox PH
HEATHFIELD
KESTON AV
RAVENSBOURNE OPEN SPACE
RAVENSBOURNE BUSINESS CEN
OAKLEY ROAD
FOREST DRIVE
BEECHWOOD DR
LONDON WOOD
Prim Sch
KESTON COMMON
Forest Lodge
BR4
Rouse Farm
WELL WOOD
LAYHAMS ROAD
106
FOX LANE
HERITAGE HILL
Keston
LEAFY GROVE
FISHPONDS ROAD
War Mem
SOUTH PARK
Earthworks
64
BROMLEY
CROYDON
107
LONG SHAW
COOPER'S WOOD
Elm Farm Cottage
NASH LANE
North Pole Farm
NORTH POLE LANE
Layham's Cattery
Graylings Farm
Fortune Bank Farm
Nash Farm
Longfield Farm & Cottage
ALLOT
JACKASS LANE
Foxhill Farm
JACKASS SHAW
Hall
WESTERHAM ROAD
Cricket Ground
Caesar's Camp
The Courtyard
CASTLE HILL RUFFS
Stables
FULLER'S WOOD
JAMES'S WOOD
A233
Wilberforce Court
Holwood
BRADMANSHILL WOOD
Five Oaks Stables
War Bank
The Temple (Roman Mausoleum)
Tenn Cts
108
Mickleham Way Electricity Sta
RUSHFIELD SHAW
Metropolitan Police Dog Training Establishment
BROOMFIELDBANK SHAW
BR2
Keston Court Poultry Farm
Roman Villa
RECTORY ROAD
Scout Camp
LONDON LOOP
Milchden
CHURCH ROAD
63
NEW ADDINGTON
ROWDOWN WOOD
Glebe Farm
ORCHARD PLACE
DOWNE ROAD
BLACKNESS LANE
109
Leaves Green
Layham's Farm
Kimberley Farm
ADDINGTON VALE
221
VULCAN WAY
Gas Works
110
Prim Sch
FURZE BOTTOM
GREEN LANE
The Vale Farm
Crown Inn PH
Clubhouse
SPORTS GROUND
62
Holmshaw Farm
HOPPERSNATCH SHAW
Greyhound Training Kennels
Bradmore
ASHMORE LANE
High House Farm
Greenacres Riding School
Colinette Farm
LEAVES GREEN CRES
Milking Lane Farm
MILKING LANE
111
UVEDALE
MILNE PARK
CATOR CL
HENRY CRESCENT
COV RES
Croydon R.F.C.
Higham's Hill
Highams Hill Farm
The Kings Arms PH
Clubhouse
112
FAIRCHILDES AVENUE
Prim Sch
Sec Sch
TERMINAL
MAIN ROAD
61
SHEEPBARN LANE
JEWELS HILL
JEWELS WOOD
REC GRD
Tenn Cts
GRICE AV
KEITH PARK CR
113
BOGRAMS WOOD
North Lodge
South Lodge
SALT BOX HILL
OAKLANDS LANE
Hangars
LONDON BIGGIN HILL AIRPORT
TN16
SOW WOOD
CHURCH WAY
Hangars
CUDHAM LODGE WOODS
White Bear Inn PH
Fairchildes Farm
FAIRCHILDES LANE
BLACKMANS LANE
Blackman's Cottages
Cox's Cottage
CR6
114
TANDRIDGE
SURREY
BROMLEY
SKID HILL LANE
CROWN ASH HILL
AIRPORT INDUSTRIAL ESTATE
BIGGIN HILL BUSINESS PARK
Hangar
GREAT HILL SHAW
Skid Hill House
238
0 500 yds
0 500 m
CHRISTY ROAD
Costains Farm
MIDDLEY SHAW

EM
EN
EP
EQ
ER
ES
ET
43
44
45
205
224
239
106
107
108
109
110
111
112
113
114
64
63
62
61
FARNBOROUGH
COMMON
ROAD
CROFTON
The Fantail
Superstore
PRINCESS ROYAL UNI HOSP
REC GRD
DARRICK WOOD
NEWSTEAD WOOD
Bromley Tennis Centre
PLAYING FIELD
ORPINGTON HOSPITAL
SEVENOAKS ROAD
SEVENOAKS WAY
HIGH STREET
Green Street Green
RAMUS WOOD
COCKSETT PLANTATION
Cocksett Hill
Rose & Crown PH
Chelsfield Hall Farm
GLENTRAMMON REC GRD
ROUNDS WOOD
A21
A223
B2158
NINHAMS WOOD
LAKE WOOD
COVERED RESERVOIRS
BROOM BANK
SPORTS GRD
Sports Club
Mill Hill
CHURCH END PLANTATION
BR6
Sevenoaks Lodge
SHIRE LANE
LOWER HOOK BUSINESS PARK
North End Farm
North End Farm Cottages
LONDON LOOP
BLACKLANDS
HIGH ELMS COUNTRY PARK
Nature Centre
Woodpiece
Clubhouse
Clockhouse
THE ROOKERY
HIGH ELMS GOLF COURSE
NATURE FIELD
WHITELANDS WOOD
Denbarn Farm
Farthings
Farthing Street Farm
Orange Court
Meadow Cottage
Green Acres
Hazels
Little Crowhill
The Rookery
Gorringes Farm
CUCKOO WOOD
Cuckoo Lodge
BURNT GORSE
LITTLE MOLLOMS WOOD
GREAT MOLLOMS WOOD
Grasslands Farm
Avondale Farm
SPORTS GRD
Prim Sch
Downe
The Queens Head PH
Downe Hall
Hall
Petleys Farm
Petleys
Long Acre
Christmas Tree Farm
Hang Grove Farm
SQUARE SHAW
THOMPSON WOOD
HAZEL WOOD
Hazelwood
The Shack
Endsleigh
White Earth
Snag Farm
Southfields
Rose Cottage
The Oaks
Snag Lane Farm
FOXBERRY WOOD
HOMEFIELD SPRING
Downe Lodge
Downe Court Manor
Downe Court Farm
DOWN HOUSE - DARWIN MUSEUM
DOWNE BANK NATURE RESERVE
LORDFIELD SHAW
The Shaws (Girl Guide Camp)
Mace Farm
Mace Farm Cottages
BROOM WOOD
HIGH WOOD
KANGLES WOOD
WEST KENT GOLF COURSE
Buxton Browne Research Institute
Downe C.C.
Pav
HANG GROVE
Beechwood
The Boundary
Hostye Farm
MACE LANE
TN14
Church Hill Farm
FOXBURROW WOOD
NEW YEARS WOOD
HOOK WOOD
NEWLANDS WOOD
LADIES WOOD
SPENCERS GROVE
BIRD HOUSE WOOD
DOWNE ACTIVITY CENTRE
Clock Tower
Luxted Farm
TWENTY ACRE SHAW
LEASONS WOOD
BROMLEY CROFT
Open Air Pool
Single Street
CHURCH APPROACH
Bottom Farm
Black Horse PH
SPORTS GRD
Tenn Cts
New Year Cottage
BIRCHES CROFT
JOCKEY WOOD
LORD DARBY MS
Cacket's Cottages
Cottage Farm
AKES SHAW
NORSTED LANE
Norsted Manor Farm

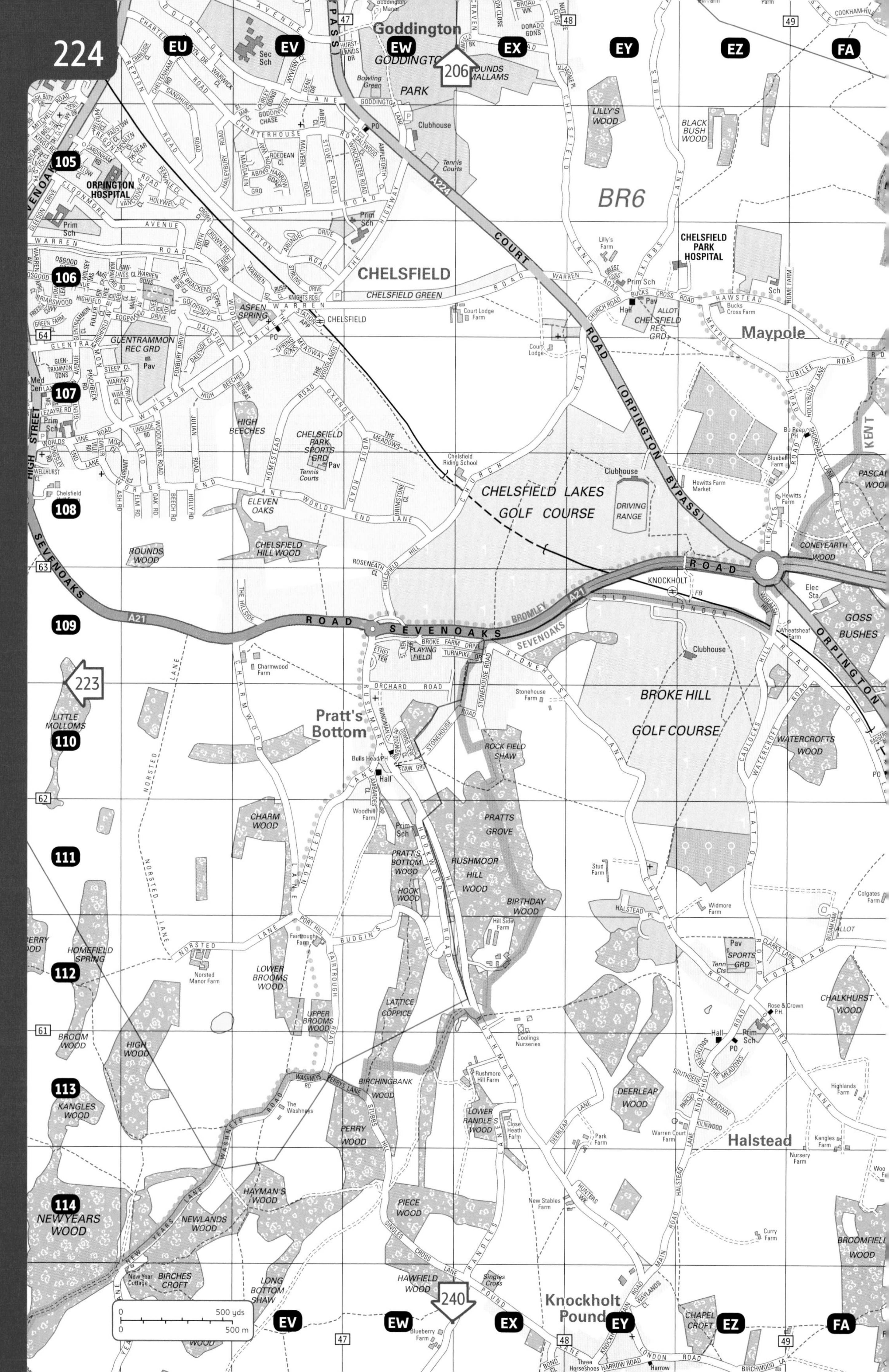

EU
EV
EW
EX
EY
EZ
FA
47
48
49
Goddington
GODDINGTON PARK
206
Sec Sch
Bowling Green
Clubhouse
Tennis Courts
A224
COURT ROAD (ORPINGTON BYPASS)
LILLY'S WOOD
BLACK BUSH WOOD
BR6
Lilly's Farm
CHELSFIELD PARK HOSPITAL
105
ORPINGTON HOSPITAL
Prim Sch
106
CHELSFIELD
CHELSFIELD GREEN
Court Lodge Farm
Court Lodge
Prim Sch
Hall
Pav
CHELSFIELD REC GRD
BUCKS CROSS ROAD
HAWSTEAD ROAD
Bucks Cross Farm
Sch
Maypole
MAYPOLE LANE
JUBILEE ROAD
ASPEN SPRING
PO
64
GLENTRAMMON REC GRD
Pav
107
HIGH STREET
HIGH BEECHES
CHELSFIELD PARK SPORTS GRD
Tennis Courts
Chelsfield Riding School
Bo Peep PH
Bluebell Farm
Hewitts Farm Market
Hewitts Farm
KENT
PASCAL WOOD
CHELSFIELD LAKES GOLF COURSE
Clubhouse
DRIVING RANGE
108
ELEVEN OAKS
WORLDS END LANE
CHELSFIELD HILL WOOD
ROUNDS WOOD
63
ROSENEATH CL
KNOCKHOLT
FB
CONEYEARTH WOOD
Elec Sta
GOSS BUSHES
109
SEVENOAKS ROAD
A21
BROMLEY
OLD LONDON
Wheatsheaf Farm
ORPINGTON
Clubhouse
223
Charmwood Farm
BROKE FARM DRIVE
PLAYING FIELD
TURNPIKE DR
ORCHARD ROAD
STONEHOUSE ROAD
Stonehouse Farm
BROKE HILL GOLF COURSE
LITTLE MOLLOMS
110
Pratt's Bottom
ROCK FIELD SHAW
WATERCROFTS WOOD
Bulls Head PH
Hall
62
CHARM WOOD
Woodhill Farm
Prim Sch
PRATTS GROVE
111
PRATT'S BOTTOM WOOD
RUSHMOOR HILL WOOD
HOOK WOOD
BIRTHDAY WOOD
Stud Farm
Widmore Farm
Colgates Farm
Hill Side Farm
Fairtrough Farm
HALSTEAD PL
Pav
SPORTS GRD
Tenn Cts
HOMEFIELD SPRING
NORSTED LANE
112
Norsted Manor Farm
LOWER BROOMS WOOD
LATTICE COPPICE
Rose & Crown P.H.
CHALKHURST WOOD
61
BROOM WOOD
UPPER BROOMS WOOD
Coolings Nurseries
Hall
Prim Sch
PO
HIGH WOOD
113
KANGLES WOOD
BIRCHINGBANK WOOD
Rushmore Hill Farm
DEERLEAP WOOD
Highlands Farm
The Washneys
PERRY WOOD
LOWER RANDLE'S WOOD
Close Heath Farm
Park Farm
Warren Court Farm
Halstead
Kangles Farm
Nursery Farm
HAYMAN'S WOOD
114
NEWYEARS WOOD
NEWLANDS WOOD
PIECE WOOD
New Stables Farm
Curry Farm
BROOMFIELD WOOD
New Year Cottage
BIRCHES CROFT
LONG BOTTOM SHAW
HAWFIELD WOOD
240
Singles Cross
Knockholt Pound
CHAPEL CROFT
500 yds
500 m
Blueberry Farm
Three Horseshoes
Harrow
HARROW ROAD
LONDON ROAD
BIRCHWOOD LA

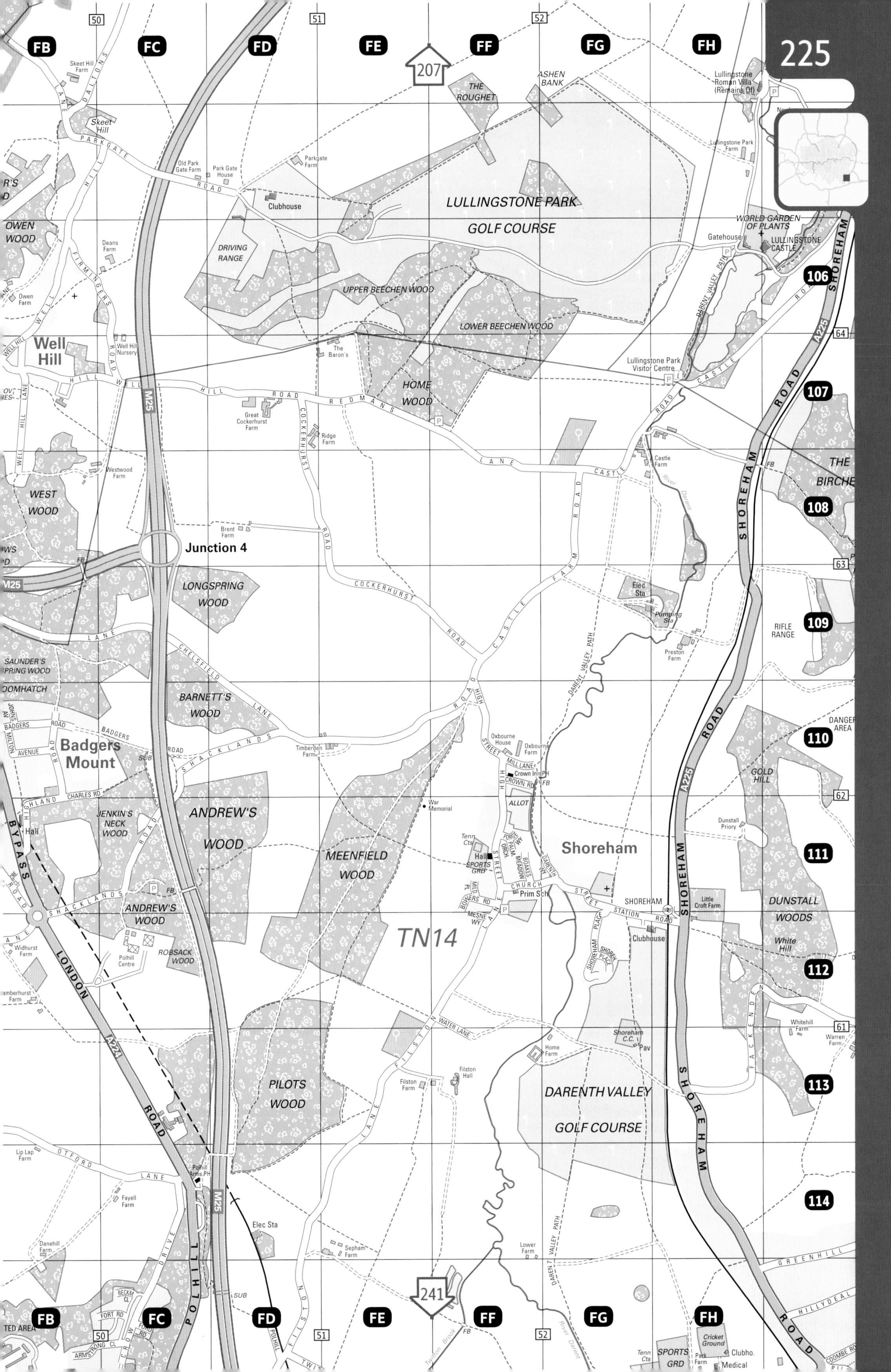

207
241
LULLINGSTONE PARK
GOLF COURSE
THE ROUGHET
ASHEN BANK
Lullingstone Roman Villa (Remains Of)
Lullingstone Park Farm
WORLD GARDEN OF PLANTS
Gatehouse
LULLINGSTONE CASTLE
Clubhouse
DRIVING RANGE
UPPER BEECHEN WOOD
LOWER BEECHEN WOOD
HOME WOOD
Lullingstone Park Visitor Centre
Skeet Hill Farm
Skeet Hill
Parkgate Farm
Old Park Gate Farm
Park Gate House
Deans Farm
OWEN WOOD
Owen Farm
Well Hill
Well Hill Nursery
The Baron's
Great Cockerhurst Farm
Ridge Farm
Westwood Farm
WEST WOOD
Brent Farm
Junction 4
LONGSPRING WOOD
Castle Farm
THE BIRCHE
Elec Sta
Pumping Sta
Preston Farm
RIFLE RANGE
SAUNDER'S SPRING WOOD
BARNETT'S WOOD
Badgers Mount
Timberden Farm
Oxbourne House
Oxbourne Farm
Crown Inn PH
ALLOT
GOLD HILL
DANGER AREA
JENKIN'S NECK WOOD
ANDREW'S WOOD
MEENFIELD WOOD
War Memorial
Shoreham
Dunstall Priory
Prim Sch
SHOREHAM
Little Croft Farm
DUNSTALL WOODS
White Hill
Clubhouse
ROBSACK WOOD
Polhill Centre
Widhurst Farm
TN14
PILOTS WOOD
Shoreham C.C.
Pav
Home Farm
Whitehill Farm
Warren Farm
Filston Hall
Filston Farm
DARENTH VALLEY
GOLF COURSE
Lip Lap Farm
Polhill Arms PH
Fayell Farm
Elec Sta
Danehill Farm
Sepham Farm
Lower Farm
Cricket Ground
SPORTS GRD
Medical
FB FC FD FE FF FG FH
50 51 52
61 62 63 64
106 107 108 109 110 111 112 113 114
M25
A225
A224
SHOREHAM ROAD
LONDON ROAD
POLHILL
DARENT VALLEY PATH
River Darent

AS
AT
AU
AV
AW
AX
AY
210
242
98
99
00
GU21
GU24
GU3
115
116
117
118
119
120
121
122
123
124
59
58
57
56
HORSELL COMMON
Horsell
Goldsworth Park
Knaphill
St. John's
Mount Hermon
Hook Heath
Mayford
LOCKFIELD DRIVE
A324
A320
A3046
B380
KETTLEWELL HILL
GOLDSWORTH PARK REC GRD
GOLDSWORTH PARK TRADING ESTATE
TRACIOUS COPSE
LITTLEWICK COMMON
HORSELL BIRCH
WATERERS PARK
LANSBURY ESTATE
WOKING CEMETERY
Crematorium
Basingstoke Canal
WOKING GOLF COURSE
WORPLESDON GOLF COURSE
SUTTON GREEN GOLF COURSE
HOE VALLEY LINEAR PARK
SMART'S HEATH
PREY HEATH
MARTLANDS IND EST
BRIDLEY COPSE
WHITMOOR POND
Fisher's Hill
Burdenshot Hill
Beech Hill
Pye Hill
WORPLESDON
HORSELL MOOR
The Living Planet Centre
The Peacocks Centre
Mizen's Railway
0
500 yds
500 m

WEST BYFLEET
Pyrford
WOKING
Maybury
GU22
HOEBRIDGE GOLF CENTRE
Old Woking
Westfield
GU23
GU4
Send
Send Marsh
PYRFORD COMMON
THE ROUGH
Pyrford Village
Newark Priory (Remains)
211
228
243

BG
BH
BJ
BK
BL
BM
BN
05
06
07
212
KT14
TRADITIONS GOLF COURSE
Heath Club
Tennis Courts
Nursery
Clubhouse
Lees Farm
Dodd's Bridge
Murray's Bridge
WOKING
GUILDFORD
MURRAYS LANE
COMMON MEADOWS
River Wey
Manor House
THE ISLAND
Park Barn Farm
BUXTON WOOD
M25
Sewage Works
Filter Beds
Church Farm
Wisley Bridge
Wisley
CHITTENDEN COTTS
SPORTS GRD
Pav
Tennis Cts
WOOLGER'S WOOD
Pond Farm
PEATMOOR WOOD
Pyrford Marina
LOCK COPSE
The Anchor PH
Pyrford Lock
Pyrford Place Farm
PYRFORD GOLF COURSE
THE WISLEY GOLF COURSE
Clubhouse
DRIVING RANGE
Wren's Nest
Pinetum
WISLEY COMMON
River Wey Navigation NT
115
116
117
118
119
120
121
122
123
124
59
58
57
56
GU22
Pyrford Green
Green Farm
Home Farm
Pyrford Place
Aberconway House
Bicentenary Glasshouse
OCKHAM VILLAGE GRN
Battleston Hill
Church Farm
Lady Place
Pyrford Village
The Prae
Wheelers Farm
Ockham Mill Farm
Nursery
ROYAL HORTICULTURAL SOCIETY GARDEN WISLEY
OCKHAM COMMON
Elm Corner
PORTSMOUTH ROAD
Abbey Stream
Newark Priory (Remains)
Walsham Lock
WALSHAM PLANTATION
Weir
Warren Farm Home Park
Irish Hole
Ockham Mill
Ockham Park
Stratford Bridge
227
Newark New Bridge
Newark Lock
Mill House
Newark Mill Bridge
WALSHAM MEADOW
Dunsborough Farm
Dunsborough Park
RIPLEY GREEN
Nutberry Fruit Farm
Conduits
Sewage Works
SPORTS GRD
Half Moon PH
The Seven Stars PH
Homewood Farm
NEWARK LANE
Old Rectory Farm
Chestnut Farm
Ockham
Hall
War Memorial
Prim Sch
Hall
Chapel Farm
Sch
Ripley
ALLOT
OCKHAM PARK
Ockham Park House
GU23
Devonia Farm
PARK WOOD
Ockham Park Farm
Sailing Club
Guileshill Farm
RIPLEY BYPASS
A3
Manor Rd
Send Marsh
Grove Heath Farm
Jovial Sailor PH
GROVE HEATH
LOVELAND'S COPSE
ROBOROW WOOD
BACHELOR'S COPSE
Ryde Farm
HUNGRY HILL
GARLICK'S ARCH COPSE
GROVE HEATH CT
BRAMBLERIDE COPSE
244
Nursery
SHEPPARDSGROVE COPSE
0 500 yds
0 500 m

PAINSHILL PARK
213
KT11
Junction 10
Wisley Interchange
OCKHAM COMMON
CHATLEY WOOD
CHATLEY HEATH
HATCHFORD WOOD
HATCHFORD PARK
THE BOGS
BREACH HILL WOOD
LODGE COPSE
BRAMBLE WOOD
Halfpenny Cross
Downside
DOWNSIDE COMMON
COBHAM PARK
Cobham Park Nursery
Cobham Stud Farm
Downside Bridge
ROSE LODGE WOOD
Cobham Court Farm
Pointers Green
BRICKFIELD COPSE
LITTLE BRICKFIELD COPSE
NORTON WOOD
Cold Norton Farm
Hazeldene Farm
Poultry Houses
Highway Farm
Bull Riding Farm
230
Martyr's Green
The Black Swan PH
Pound Farm
TANNERS COPSE
ELMBRIDGE
GUILDFORD
OLD OAK COMMON
THE NEW PRESERVE
PEAKED ROUGH
ROUNDABOUT
Hurst Hill
May's Green
CHAFFERS COPSE
HOOK WOOD
TRULLIBER COPSE
STUMPS GROVE
Barnsthorns
CLAMP ROUGH
GALLOWS GROVE
BUSHY THICKET
THICKET COPSE
Banks Way House
Newmarsh Farm
Gun Club
KT24
EFFINGHAM JUNCTION
EFFINGHAM COMMON
THE DRIFT GOLF COURSE
Clubhouse
BARNSTHORNS WOOD
Blue Ride
THE DRIFT
THE FOREST
245
Slater's Oak
Norwood Farm
Effingham C.C.
Cricket Club
Lower Farm
Hook Farm
Indian Farm
HORSLEY CAMPING & CARAVAN SITE
Broom House
SPORTS GRD
Manor Farm
EVEN WOOD
Slade Farm
Blackmoor Farm
Upton Farm
Bridge End Farm
Wilderness Farm
HUNT'S COPSE
Appstree Farm
SPORTS GROUND
ALMS HEATH
School Farm
BOLDER MERE
Hut Hill
Hut Hill Cottage
CURRIE'S CLUMP
Sandpit Hill
Cockrow Hill
Redhill Bottom
Red Hill
Oak Pollard
Gothic Tower
Tower Hill
WHEEL ISLAND
GROTTO
Chinese Bridge
THE LAKE
Gothic Temple
THE BROOM
Wood Hill
Visitor Centre
BELL WOOD
Long Orchard Farm
Bramble Hedge Farm
Foxwarren Park
Queen Anne's Cottage
Chatley Farm
Chatley Semaphore
Telegraph Hill
Poynters Farm
Pondtail Farm
Cossins House
Cossins Farm
New Barn Farm
Days Inn
M25
A3
PORTSMOUTH ROAD
POINTERS ROAD
OCKHAM LANE
HORSLEY ROAD
PLOUGH LANE
CHILBROOK ROAD
NORTON LANE
GOOSE GREEN
COBHAM PARK ROAD
DOWNSIDE ROAD
BOOKHAM ROAD
OLD LANE
OCKHAM ROAD NORTH
HATCH LANE
DRIFT ROAD
FOREST ROAD
EFFINGHAM COMMON ROAD
LOWER FARM ROAD
BANKS LANE
BETWEEN STREETS
HIGH ST
RIVERHILL
ANVIL LANE
CHURCH ST
River Mole
BP
BQ
BR
BS
BT
BU
BV
116
117
118
119
120
121
122
123
124
08
09
10
56
57
58
59

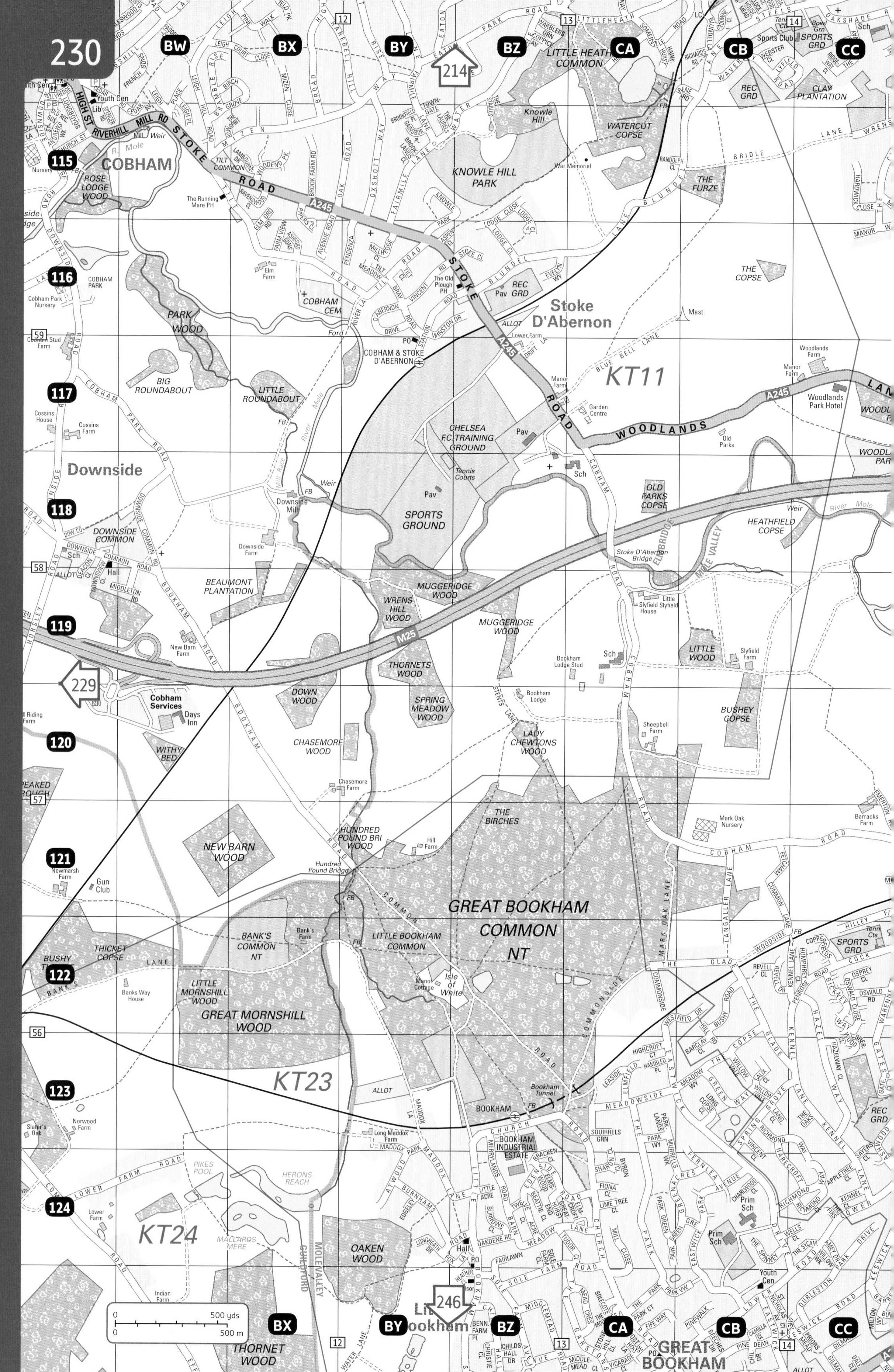
BW
BX
BY
BZ
CA
CB
CC
214
COBHAM
Stoke D'Abernon
KT11
KT23
KT24
Downside
LITTLE HEATH COMMON
KNOWLE HILL PARK
WATERCUT COPSE
THE FURZE
ROSE LODGE WOOD
PARK WOOD
BIG ROUNDABOUT
LITTLE ROUNDABOUT
COBHAM CEM
COBHAM & STOKE D'ABERNON
CHELSEA F.C. TRAINING GROUND
SPORTS GROUND
DOWNSIDE COMMON
BEAUMONT PLANTATION
MUGGERIDGE WOOD
WRENS HILL WOOD
THORNETS WOOD
SPRING MEADOW WOOD
DOWN WOOD
CHASEMORE WOOD
LADY CHEWTONS WOOD
OLD PARKS COPSE
HEATHFIELD COPSE
LITTLE WOOD
BUSHEY COPSE
Woodlands Park Hotel
WOODLANDS
M25
A245
229
Cobham Services
WITHY BED
NEW BARN WOOD
HUNDRED POUND BRI WOOD
THE BIRCHES
GREAT BOOKHAM COMMON NT
LITTLE BOOKHAM COMMON
BANK'S COMMON NT
THICKET COPSE
LITTLE MORNSHILL WOOD
GREAT MORNSHILL WOOD
BOOKHAM
BOOKHAM INDUSTRIAL ESTATE
OAKEN WOOD
THORNET WOOD
GREAT BOOKHAM
Little Bookham
246
MOLE VALLEY
0 500 yds
0 500 m

CD
CE
CF
CG
CH
CJ
CK
KT9
215
THE FOREST
Horns Hill
LEATHERHEAD GOLF COURSE
EPSOM GAP
ASHTEAD COMMON
OXSHOTT ROAD
KINGSTON ROAD
A244
A243
Pachesham Park
Clubhouse
WOODLANDS PARK
Prince's Coverts
Clouds Hill Farm
Queen Elizabeth's Foundation Coll
Tyrwhitt House
M25
Junction 9
KT21
Paddock Lodge Stables
Ashley Court
WOOD FIELD
ASHTEAD
116
117
118
119
120
121
122
123
124
59
58
57
56
15
16
17
Rowhurst Forge
Queen Elizabeth's Foundation (Dev Cen)
TEAZLE WOOD
DRIVING RANGE
PACHESHAM PARK GOLF CENTRE
Superstores
REGENT PARK
BALANCING PONDS
Leatherhead Common
Sewage Works
Brook Willow Farm
Amenity Site
Pachesham Equestrian Centre
THE MOUNTS
Earthworks
BUSHY PLATT
Lower Ashtead
SPORTS FLD
Prim Sch
Youth Cen
ASHTEAD REC GRD
Lib
Clinic
232
ASHTEAD HOSP
RANDALLS ROAD
MOLE VALLEY PREDATORS FC
KT22
Crematorium
RANDALLS PARK CEMETERY
A245
BYPASS ROAD
Junction 9
LEATHERHEAD BYPASS RD
LEATHERHEAD
A24
Barnetwood Farm
ALLOT
Cannon Grove Nursery
LEATHERHEAD
MOLE BUSINESS PARK
LEATHERHEAD TRADE PARK
STATION RD
BULL HILL
KINGSTON ROAD
SPORTS GROUND
SPORTS GRD
Knoll Rbt
HOSP
REC GRD
Bowl Club
River Mole
Tenn Club
REC GRD
FRIARS ORCHARD
Fire Sta
MILL POND
Leatherhead Bridge
Leatherhead FC
SPORTS GRD
Leatherhead & Cobham C.C. Clubhouse
Leisure Centre
Thorncroft Manor
Fetcham
Water Works
Filter Beds
Hawk's Hill
COV RES
Rifle Range
DORKING ROAD
B2450
B2122
B2033
HEADLEY ROAD
REIGATE ROAD
Beaverbrook Roundabout
SHEPHERDS CLOSE
Downside Farm
LEATHERHEAD BYPASS
A246
YOUNG STREET
Bocketts Farm Park
GUILDFORD ROAD
Givons Grove Roundabout
247
GIVONS GROVE
THE GARDEN

EPSOM COMMON
NEWTON WOOD
216
WOOD FIELD
ASHTEAD
ASHTEAD PARK
Ashtead Park
City of London Freemen's School
ASHTEAD HOSP
KT21
231
EPSOM GENERAL HOSP
Woodcote
RAC WOODCOTE PARK GOLF COURSE
Woodcote Park Country Club
THE GROVE
WORLDS END
HALFMOON CLUMP
LANGLEY BOTTOM WOOD
Langley Vale
THE WARREN
KT18
ExxonMobil House
Chase Farm Stud
ADDLESTEAD WOOD
Addlestead Farm
M25
Tyrrell's Wood
TYRRELL'S WOOD
HAMBLETON WOOD
HEADLEY COURT
HOOK WOOD
GREAT HURST WOOD
LITTLE HURST WOOD
Beaverbrook Roundabout
COVERED RESERVOIR
Highlands Farm
Clubhouse
PIGNUT WOOD
KT22
NOWER WOOD
OYSTER HILL NT
TYRRELL'S WOOD GOLF COURSE
COSTAL WOOD
248
Headley
0 500 yds
0 500 m

CT
CU
CV
CW
CX
CY
CZ
217
KT17
EPSOM DOWNS
Epsom College
COLLEGE ROAD
A2022
REIGATE ROAD
FIR TREE ROAD
Drift Bridge Hotel
Drift Br
NORK
SM7
Banstead Crossroads
BOLTERS LA
Clubho.
SPORTS GROUND
Amb Sta
CIVIC CEN
Prim Schs
Youth Cen
116
GARRATTS LANE
B2219
South Hatch Stables
BURGH HEATH ROAD
B284
B288
SOUTH LANE
B291
PARK WOOD
Comm Cen
Football Pitch
NORK PARK
SPORTS GROUND
BUCKLE'S GAP
YEW TREE BOTTOM ROAD
EPSOM GOLF COURSE
Heights Stables
Derby Stables
Nork Park Farm
Toyota(GB)
59
117
CHIPSTEAD ROAD
PARK WOOD
TATTENHAM WAY RECREATION GROUND
Tenn Cts
Pav
Grandstands
TATTENHAM CORNER ROAD
B290
RACE DAY PARKING
EPSOM DOWNS RACECOURSE
EPSOM DOWNS
The Hill
Tattenham Corner
Race Stables
TATTENHAM CRESCENT
Clinic
Lib
Prim Sch
Tattenham Corner
TATTENHAMS WAY
B2221
A240
Superstore
COVERED RESERVOIR
PAGES ACRE
118
Sch
CANONS WOOD
58
BRIGHTON ROAD
A217
Burgh Heath
Hall
BURGH HEATH
Premier Inn
Canons Farm
119
234
LANGLEY VALE
SPORTS GRD
Banstead Athletic FC
REC GRD
Youth Cen
Swim Pool
PIT WOOD
Med Cen
IND EST
EPSOM & EWELL
REIGATE & BANSTEAD
WALTON DOWNS
WALTON ROAD
120
SPORTS GROUND
Legal & General
57
KT20
Garden Farm
THE CHILDRENS TRUST
121
KINGSWOOD
WATERHOUSE LANE
TADWORTH
Prim Sch
Med Cen
TADWORTH
BONSOR DRIVE
B2032
122
Wingfield Stud Farm
Tumble Beacon PH
WORKHOUSE POND
56
Kingswood Warren
Police Training School
Sch
Tadworth CC
Clubho.
KINGSWOOD
123
SPORTS GRD
B290
MILL ROAD
War Memorial
Clubhouse
MERE POND
B2220
SPORTS GRD
BANSTEAD HEATH
124
Ebbisham Farm
SANDHILL WOOD
Walton Manor
Prim Sch
BURIAL GRD
Hall
The Clock Tower Riding Centre
Walton Manor Farm
Comm Hall
Walton on the Hill
Sch
249
CHIPSTEAD LANE
BEECHEN
SPORTS GRD
COPSE
Pav
22
23
24
SPORTS GROUND
Clubhouse
BANSTEAD
Fidelity

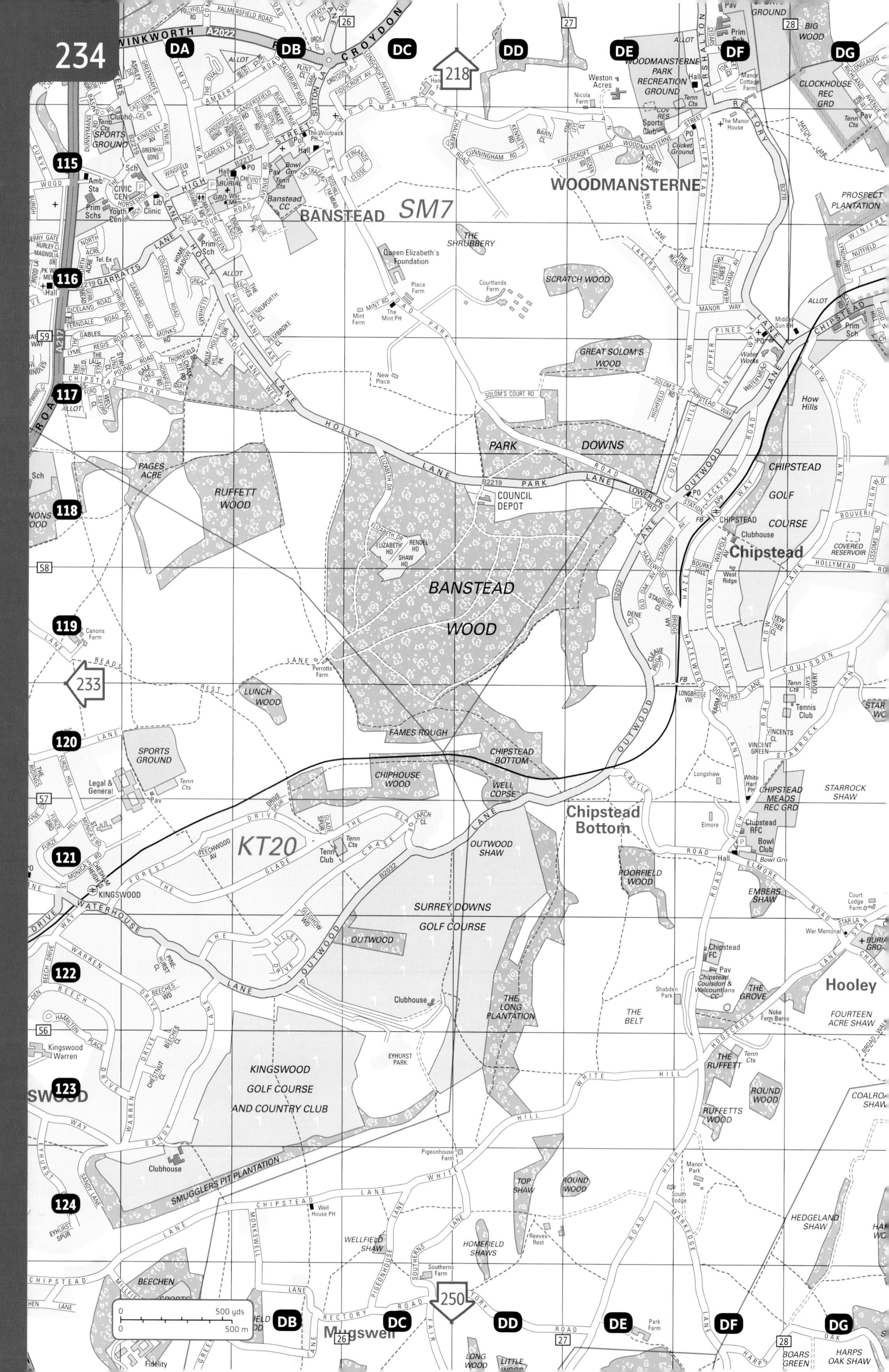
DA
DB
DC
DD
DE
DF
DG
218
WINKWORTH
A2022
CROYDON
BANSTEAD
SM7
WOODMANSTERNE
WOODMANSTERNE PARK RECREATION GROUND
Weston Acres
Nicola Farm
CLOCKHOUSE REC GRD
BIG WOOD
PROSPECT PLANTATION
THE SHRUBBERY
Queen Elizabeth's Foundation
SCRATCH WOOD
Courtlands Farm
Place Farm
Mint Farm
The Mint PH
New Place
GREAT SOLOM'S WOOD
SOLOM'S COURT RD
Banstead CC
SPORTS GROUND
CIVIC CEN
PAGES ACRE
RUFFETT WOOD
PARK
DOWNS
COUNCIL DEPOT
HOLLY LANE
B2219
LOWER PK RD
CHIPSTEAD GOLF COURSE
Chipstead
How Hills
COVERED RESERVOIR
BANSTEAD WOOD
ELIZABETH HO
RENDEL HO
SHAW HO
Canons Farm
Perrotts Farm
233
LUNCH WOOD
FAMES ROUGH
CHIPSTEAD BOTTOM
CHIPHOUSE WOOD
WELL COPSE
Chipstead Bottom
Legal & General
KT20
KINGSWOOD
OUTWOOD SHAW
SURREY DOWNS GOLF COURSE
OUTWOOD
OUTWOOD LANE
B2032
Tennis Club
STARROCK SHAW
CHIPSTEAD MEADS REC GRD
Chipstead RFC
POORFIELD WOOD
EMBERS SHAW
Court Lodge Farm
War Memorial
Chipstead FC
Chipstead, Coulsdon & Walcountians CC
Shabden Park
THE GROVE
Hooley
FOURTEEN ACRE SHAW
THE BELT
THE LONG PLANTATION
Clubhouse
EYHURST PARK
Kingswood Warren
KINGSWOOD GOLF COURSE AND COUNTRY CLUB
THE RUFFETT
ROUND WOOD
RUFFETTS WOOD
WHITE HILL
COALROAD SHAW
SMUGGLERS PIT PLANTATION
Pigeonhouse Farm
TOP SHAW
ROUND WOOD
Manor Park
South Lodge
HEDGELAND SHAW
Well House PH
WELLFIELD SHAW
HOMEFIELD SHAWS
Reeves Rest
Southerns Farm
250
BEECHEN
Mugswell
Park Farm
LONG WOOD
BOARS GREEN
HARPS OAK SHAW
Fidelity
0 500 yds
0 500 m
115
116
117
118
119
120
121
122
123
124
56
57
58
59
26
27
28

WOODCOTE PARK GOLF COURSE
COULSDON
KENLEY
CR8
HARTLEY BUSHES
COULSDON MANOR GOLF COURSE
STONYFIELD SHAW
FARTHING OR FAIRDEAN DOWNS
New Hill
Old Coulsdon
CR5
GRANGE PARK
COULSDON COMMON
HAPPY VALLEY PARK
DEVILS DEN WOOD
FIGGS WOOD
THE GULLET
BOXERS WOOD
DITCHES SHAW
PETERSHOLE SHAW
NETHERNE WOOD
SURREY NATIONAL GOLF COURSE
BROAD WOOD
PILES WOOD
CHURCH GREEN
FRYERN BROOM WOOD
Chaldon
CR3
WILLEY BROOM WOOD
FURZEFIELD WOOD
ALDERSTEAD HEATH
LORD'S WOOD
GRASSCUTS SHAW
SPARTICLES WOOD
RH1
Junction 7
BRIGHTON ROAD
A23
A237
B2032
B2030
B276
B2031
219
236
251
DH
DJ
DK
DL
DM
DN
DP
116
117
118
119
120
121
122
123
124
CROYDON
TANDRIDGE
SURREY

DQ
DR
DS
DT
DU
DV
DW
220
235
252
KENLEY
CR8
CR2
CR5
CR3
KENLEY COMMON
KENLEY AERODROME
Whyteleafe
UPPER WARLINGHAM
Caterham-on-the-Hill
CATERHAM
SURREY NATIONAL GOLF COURSE
COULSDON COMMON
MANOR PARK
WHYTELEAFE RECREATION GROUND
BETTS MEAD RECREATION GROUND
RIDDLESDOWN WOOD
RAGGED WOOD
AINSLEY BERRY SHAW
DISPLEY'S WOOD
CROYDON
TANDRIDGE
SURREY
LONDON LOOP
PLAYING FIELDS
SPORTS GROUND
THE DOBBIN
TITHEPIT SHAW
COXES WOOD
BLIZE WOOD
RYDON'S WOOD
WINDMILL SHAW
ROUND SHAW
Stony Hill
PARK SHAW
QUEEN'S PARK
RUGBY GROUND
CATERHAM DENE HOSP
THE NORTH DOWNS HOSP
GODSTONE ROAD
CATERHAM BYPASS
A22
B2031
B2030
B269
B270
Ofcom (Spectrum Management Office)
Surrey Hills Gliding Club
RAF Mem
Joysons Hill
Burntwood Hill
WESTWAY COMMON
Hamsey Green
KINGS WOOD
115
116
117
118
119
120
121
122
123
124
33
34
35
56
57
58
59
0
500 yds
500 m

FARLEIGH
Chelsham
CR6
WARLINGHAM
Woldingham Garden Village
Woldingham
GREAT PARK WOOD
HOLT WOOD
HENLEY WOOD
MILL COMMON
GREENLAWN MEMORIAL PARK
WOLDINGHAM GOLF COURSE
HALLILOO PLANTATION
COTTERSHILL SHAW
WORMS HEATH
SLINES GREEN
SLINES OAK
WASHPOND SHAW
OLDBURY SHAW
BIRCHEN SHAW
CONY CROOK
ASHEN SHAW
GREENHILL SHAW
WHISTLERS WOOD
HELL SHAW
CHALK PITS
THE BUSHES
LITTLE CHURCH WOOD
TEMPLEHILL PLANTATION
GREAT CHURCH WOOD NATURE RESERVE
MOSSYHILL SHAW
OAKEN SHAW
MOSESHILL SHAW
CREWE'S WOOD
MOUNT HOPPER
LITTLEPARK WOOD
GT FARLEIGH GRN
LITTLE FARLEIGH GREEN
LITTLE GREAT HILL
GREAT HILL SHAW
FIVE ACRE SHAW
MIDDLEY SHAW
HONEYOAK WOOD
THE GRIPES
BULL GREEN
CHELSHAM COMMON
Warlingham NATS Radio Station
High Breach
Hovings Hole
Water Tower
Masts
DX
DY
DZ
EA
EB
EC
ED
221
238
253
36
37
38
56
57
58
59
116
117
118
119
120
121
122
123
124

BIGGIN HILL
Tatsfield
Titsey
CR6
CR3
RH8
AIRPORT INDUSTRIAL ESTATE
BIGGIN HILL BUSINESS PARK
BIGGIN HILL CEM
MOLLARDS WOOD
OWLS WOOD
LONG COPPICE
ROUND WOOD
LUMBERDINE WOOD
ASHEN SHAW
PITCHERS WOOD
TITSEY PLANTATION
TITSEY PLACE AND GARDENS
PARK WOOD GOLF COURSE
SPORTS GROUND
BEAVER WATER WORLD
HONEYOAK WOOD
GREAT HILL SHAW
MIDDLEY SHAW
JERRY REDDINGS SHAW
CHERRY TREE SHAW
SHEPHERDS SHAW
LONGLANDS SHAW
WHITE BANK
CONY CROOK
COWYARD SHAW
HOME WOOD
ISLE SHAW
PARSONS SHAW
LIMEHOUSE BOTTOM
WESTMORE GREEN
CLARKS LANE SHAW
HIGH TREES
COLDHARBOUR BEECHES
HELL SHAW
BARTON SHAW
CHURCH WOOD
CLACKET WOOD
Botley Hill
MAIN ROAD
CLARKS LANE
CROYDON ROAD
BEDDLESTEAD LANE
HESIERS ROAD
LUSTED HALL LANE
TITSEY HILL
PILGRIMS LANE
222
237
254
0 500 yds
0 500 m

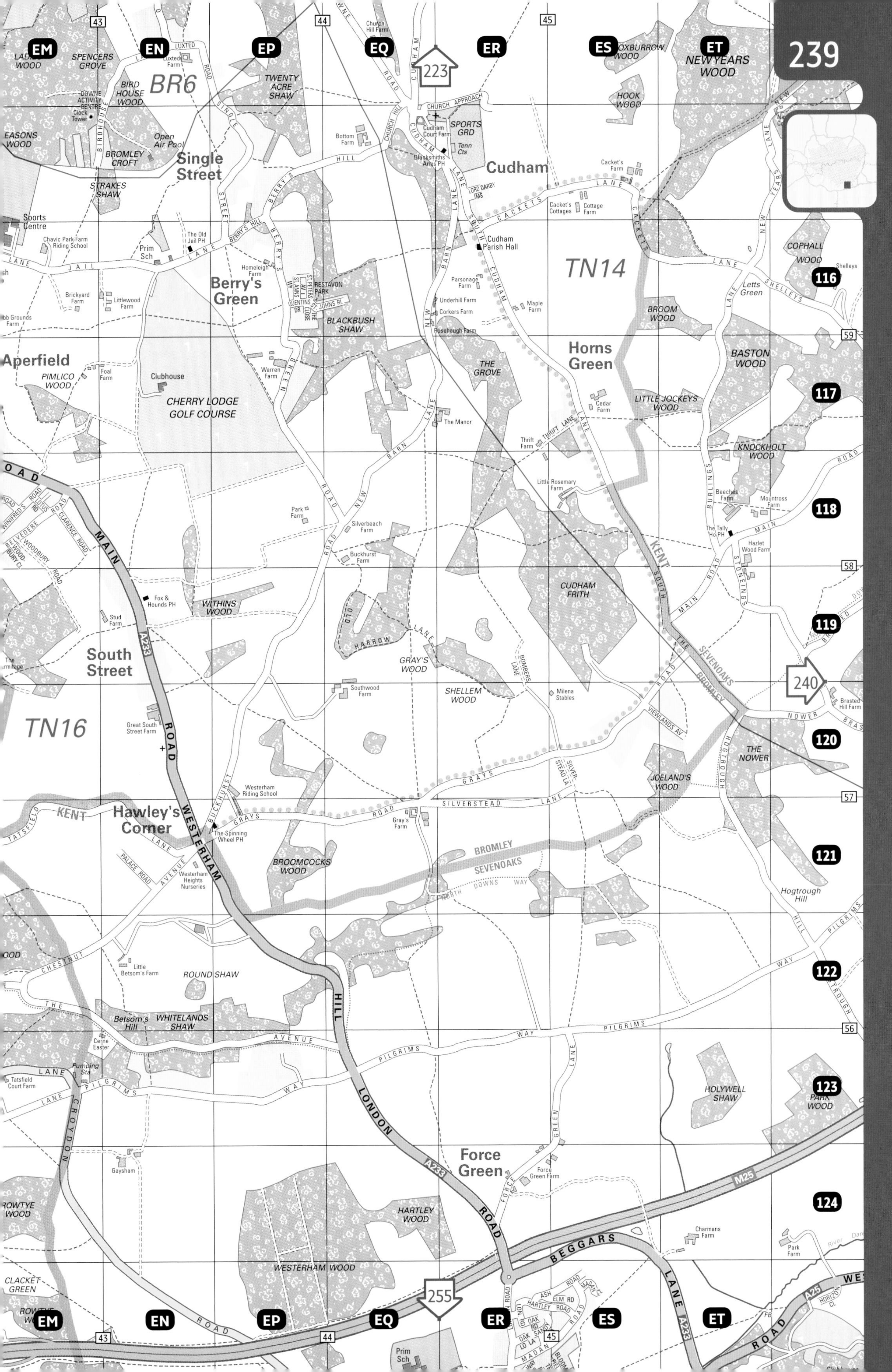
EM
EN
EP
EQ
ER
ES
ET
43
44
45
223
255
240
116
117
118
119
120
121
122
123
124
59
58
57
56
BR6
TN14
TN16
LADIES WOOD
SPENCERS GROVE
Luxted Farm
LUXTED ROAD
BIRD HOUSE WOOD
DOWNE ACTIVITY CENTRE
Clock Tower
EASONS WOOD
BIRDHOUSE
BROMLEY CROFT
Open Air Pool
TWENTY ACRE SHAW
SINGLE STREET
Single Street
STRAKES SHAW
Sports Centre
Chavic Park Farm Riding School
The Old Jail PH
Prim Sch
JAIL LANE
BERRY'S HILL
Homeleigh Farm
Berry's Green
Brickyard Farm
Littlewood Farm
Aperfield
PIMLICO WOOD
Foal Farm
Clubhouse
CHERRY LODGE GOLF COURSE
Church Hill Farm
CUDHAM ROAD
CHURCH HILL
CHURCH APPROACH
Cudham Court Farm
SPORTS GRD
Tenn Cts
Bottom Farm
Blacksmiths Arms PH
Cudham
LORD DARBY MS
CACKETS LANE
Cacket's Farm
Cacket's Cottages
Cottage Farm
Cudham Parish Hall
Parsonage Farm
Underhill Farm
Corkers Farm
Rosehaugh Farm
Maple Farm
RESTAVON PARK
ST PETERS AV
ST ANNS WY
QUENTINS DR
JOHNS RI
BLACKBUSH SHAW
Warren Farm
BERRY'S GREEN
NEW BARN LANE
THE GROVE
Horns Green
Cedar Farm
The Manor
Thrift Farm
THRIFT LANE
Little Rosemary Farm
OXBURROW WOOD
HOOK WOOD
NEWYEARS WOOD
NEW YEARS LANE
COPHALL WOOD
Shelleys
Letts Green
SHELLEYS
BROOM WOOD
BASTON WOOD
LITTLE JOCKEYS WOOD
KNOCKHOLT WOOD
BURLINGS
Beeches Farm
Mountross Farm
The Tally Ho PH
Hazlet Wood Farm
MAIN ROAD
STONEINGS
KENT
SOUTH
MAIN ROAD
LOTUS RD
WINIFRED'S ROAD
CLARENCE ROAD
BELVEDERE
WOODBURY CL
WOODBURY ROAD
Park Farm
Silverbeach Farm
Buckhurst Farm
NEW ROAD
Fox & Hounds PH
WITHINS WOOD
Stud Farm
CUDHAM FRITH
OLD HARROW LANE
GRAY'S WOOD
SHELLEM WOOD
BOMBERS LANE
Milena Stables
South Street
The Armitage
A233
Southwood Farm
Great South Street Farm
SEVENOAKS ROAD
THE SEVENOAKS
BROMLEY
VIEWLANDS AV
NOWER
THE NOWER
HOGTROUGH
JOELAND'S WOOD
Brasted Hill Farm
GRAYS ROAD
SILVERSTEAD LA
SILVERSTEAD LANE
Westerham Riding School
BUCKHURST
Hawley's Corner
TATSFIELD
KENT
Gray's Farm
The Spinning Wheel PH
WESTERHAM ROAD
PALACE ROAD
AVENUE
Westerham Heights Nurseries
BROOMCOCKS WOOD
BROMLEY
SEVENOAKS
NORTH DOWNS WAY
Hogtrough Hill
HILL
PILGRIMS WAY
CHESTNUT
Little Betsom's Farm
ROUND SHAW
Betsom's Hill
WHITELANDS SHAW
THE AVENUE
Cerne Easter
Pumping Sta
Tatsfield Court Farm
LANE
CROYDON
PILGRIMS WAY
LONDON
HOLYWELL SHAW
PARK WOOD
Gaysham
Force Green
FORCE GREEN LANE
Force Green Farm
ROWTYE WOOD
HARTLEY WOOD
M25
Charmans Farm
Park Farm
River Darent
WESTERHAM WOOD
BEGGARS LANE
CLACKET GREEN
ROAD
ASH ROAD
ELM RD
HARTLEY ROAD
OAK RD
LONDON RD
MADAN CL
MADAN
SANDY LA
Prim Sch
FB
A25
HORIZON CL

EU
EV
EW
EX
EY
EZ
FA
224
239
47
48
49
59
58
57
56
115
116
117
118
119
120
121
122
123
124
HAYMAN'S WOOD
NEWLANDS WOOD
NEW YEARS LANE
New Year Cottage
BIRCHES CROFT
LONG BOTTOM SHAW
HAWFIELD WOOD
SINGLES CROSS LANE
Singles Cross
RANDLES LANE
POUND LANE
New Stables Farm
HUNTERS WK
HILL
HALSTEAD ROAD
Curry Farm
BROOMFIELD WOOD
Knockholt Pound
MAIN ROAD
WAYLANDS CL
OLD KNOCKHOLT MAIN ROAD
CHAPEL CROFT
JOCKEY'S WOOD
Blueberry Farm
BOND CL
Three Horseshoes PH
HARROW ROAD
Harrow Inn PH
LONDON ROAD
BIRCHWOOD LA
Warren Farm
Rose Cottage Farm
Coolings Garden Centre
Clinic
IVY LA
Ivy Farm
The Grange
Comm Cen
Mast
Bowl Grn
Football Pitch
CHEVENING LANE
The Mill House
STAR HILL
LEES WOOD
DUTCHMORE WOOD
COPHALL WOOD
Shelleys
CHINE FM PL
Letts Green
SHELLEYS LANE
Homefield
BLUEBERRY LANE
COOPER'S WOOD
Court Lodge
DOWNS
Knockholt
War Mem
Prim Sch
SUNDRIDGE LANE
NORTH
BASTON WOOD
ASHFIELD WOOD
STAR HILL WOOD
ASHPLATT
KNOCKHOLT BEECHES
CHATHAM'S
LORD
RIDE
MINNY WOOD
KNOCKHOLT WOOD
Masts
SAND BANKS
COV RES
Keepers Cottage
Beeches Farm
Mountross Farm
CHEVENING PARK
The Tally Ho PH
Hazlet Wood Farm
SUMMERHOUSE WOOD
PARK WOOD
THE SPINNEY
PILGRIMS WAY
STONEINGS
Chevening
HAGBUSH WOOD
ROUGHFIELDS WOOD
NORTH DOWNS
BRASTED
Well
Chevening House
Shootfield
BURIAL GRD
Home Farm
SEVENOAKS
BROMLEY
Brasted Hill Farm
SHOOTFIELD WOOD
TN14
NOWER
THE NOWER
OVENDEN
HOME WOOD
Chevening Cross
Grove House
CLAYPIT SHAW
Oveny Green Farm
Combe Bank Farm
Ovenden Lodge
OVENDEN ROAD
M25
Junction 5
Hogtrough Hill
COMBEBANK WOOD
Combe Bank Wood
B2211
Court Lodge Farm
HOGTROUGH HILL
TN16
COMBE WOOD
COMBE BANK DRIVE
Sch
Pumping Station
STATION ROAD
ST. MARTINS MEADOW
GLEBE COTTS
THORNS MEADOW
COLES LANE
Tanners
RECTORY LANE
Pav
SPORTS GROUND
Pumping Sta
Council Yard
River Darent
Offices
Stanhope Arms PH
Mill Farm
The Old Rectory
PYM ORCHARD
PO
Bowling Green
Warren Farm
A25
MAIN ROAD
White Horse PH
Sundridge
Brasted
THE OLD YARD
Hall
MANOR RD
CHAPMANS ROAD
CHAPMANS CL
The Old Rectory
Charmans Farm
CHURCH
WILKINS WY
MILL CL
WATER
STREET
White Hart Inn PH
THE CARRIAGEWAY
WOODSIDE ROAD
NEW ROAD
Park Farm
SPORTS GRD
Tennis Courts
Bull Inn PH
ELLIOTTS LA
MULBERRY PL
Orchard Farm
Brasted Place
Prim Sch
ST MARY'S CH RD
THE WARREN
WESTERHAM HIGH
RD
WEST END
LANE
CHART
THE ROOKERIES
Brasted Place Farm
A233
0
500 yds
500 m
Long Barn
GREYSTONE PK
CHURCH
Sundridge Place
Sundridge

FB
FC
FD
FE
FF
FG
FH
225
Twitton
Otford
TN14
Dunton Green
Longford
Chipstead
Riverhead
Bessels Green
TN13
SEVENOAKS WILDLIFE RESERVE
EAST LAKE
WEST LAKE
CHIPSTEAD LAKE
GRAVEL PIT
OTFORD CEMETERY
ORCHARD HEY
BLUEBELL WOOD
HOME WOOD
RYE WOOD
ALDER SHAW
EDWARD SHAW
RAKEFIELD WOOD
COLD ARBOR WOOD
ASH PLAT WOOD
ANT WOOD
MONTREAL PARK
OBELISK WOOD
LITTLE BRITAIN'S WOOD
MIDDLINGS WOOD
RIVERHEAD PARKLAND
CHIPSTEAD COMMON
OLD GROVE
QINETIQ FORT HALSTEAD
NORTH DOWNS BUSINESS PARK
Morants Court Cross
Bat and Ball Junction
DUNTON GREEN
SEVENOAKS
POLHILL
M25
M26
A224
A225
A25
A21
SEVENOAKS BYPASS
WESTERHAM ROAD
LONDON ROAD
OTFORD ROAD
BRADBOURNE VALE ROAD
AMHERST HILL
ST. JOHN'S HILL
DARTFORD ROAD
STATION ROAD
HIGH STREET
116
117
118
119
120
121
122
123
124
256
257
50
51
52
56
57
58
59

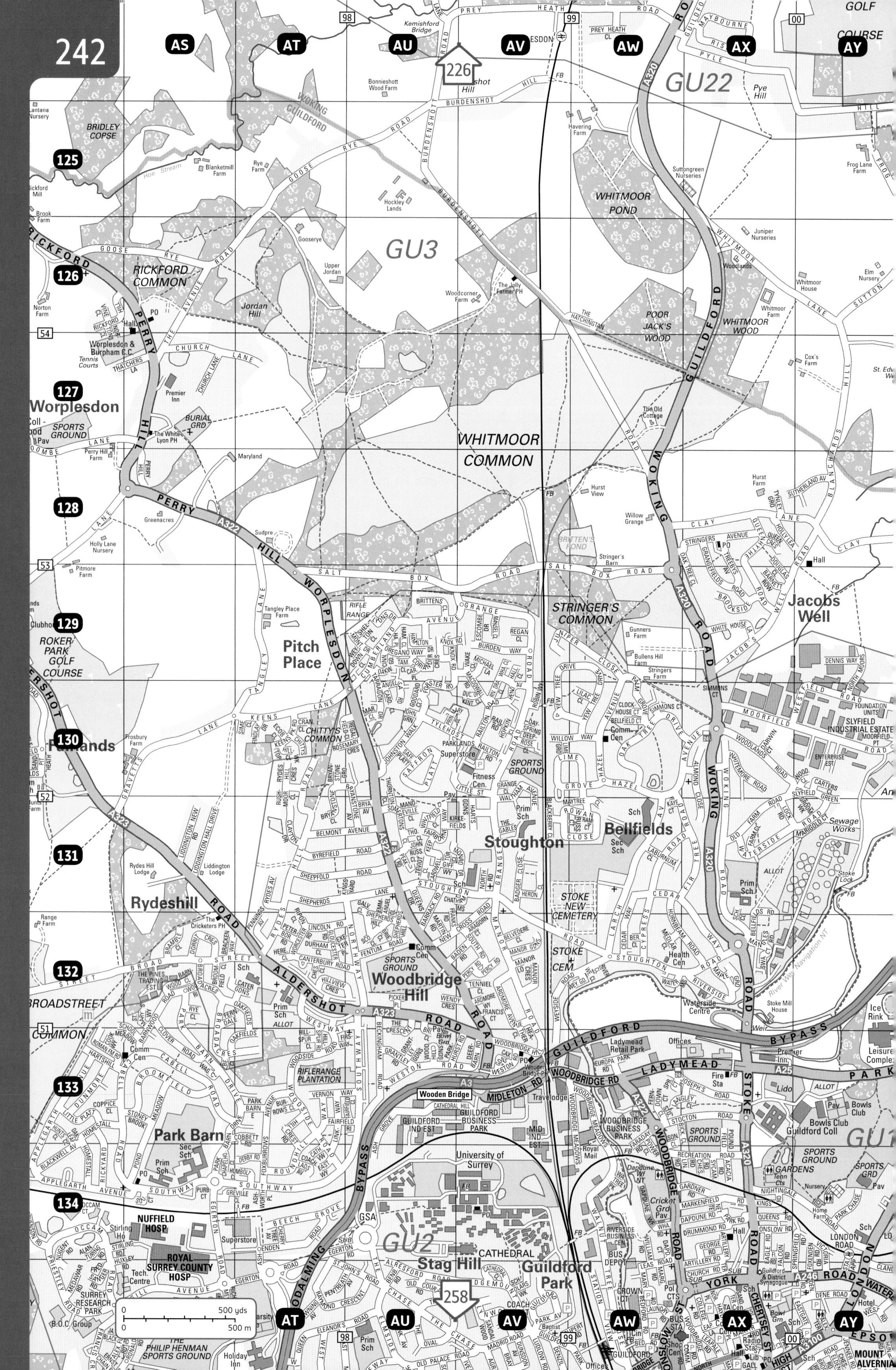
AS
AT
AU
AV
AW
AX
AY
226
GU22
GU3
GU2
GOLF COURSE
BRIDLEY COPSE
WOKING
GUILDFORD
Hoe Stream
Blanketmill Farm
Rye Farm
Bonnieshott Wood Farm
Kemishford Bridge
PREY HEATH ROAD
PREY HEATH CL
BURDENSHOT HILL
BURDENSHOT ROAD
GOOSE RYE ROAD
Hockley Lands
Havering Farm
Suttongreen Nurseries
WHITMOOR POND
Pye Hill
Frog Lane Farm
Juniper Nurseries
Woodlands
Elm Nursery
Whitmoor House
Whitmoor Farm
SUTTON LANE
RICKFORD COMMON
Gooserye
Upper Jordan
Jordan Hill
Woodcorner Farm
The Jolly Farmer PH
THE HATCHINGTAN
POOR JACK'S WOOD
WHITMOOR WOOD
Cox's Farm
Norton Farm
Brook Farm
Rickford Mill
Lantana Nursery
PERRY HILL
Worplesdon & Burpham C.C.
Tennis Courts
THATCHERS LA
CHURCH LANE
Premier Inn
BURIAL GRD
The Old Cottage
Worplesdon
SPORTS GROUND
The White Lyon PH
Perry Hill Farm
Maryland
WHITMOOR COMMON
WOKING ROAD
GUILDFORD ROAD
Hurst View
Hurst Farm
BLANCHARDS HILL
SUTHERLAND AV
Willow Grange
BRITTEN'S POND
Stringer's Barn
CLAY LANE
Greenacres
Sudpre
Holly Lane Nursery
Pitmore Farm
SALT BOX ROAD
A322
A320
A323
A3
A25
A246
Tangley Place Farm
Pitch Place
RIFLE RANGE
STRINGER'S COMMON
Gunners Farm
Bullens Hill Farm
Stringers Farm
Jacobs Well
ROKER PARK GOLF COURSE
TANGLEY LANE
KEENS LANE
CHITTY'S COMMON
Prosbury Farm
Fairlands
SLYFIELD INDUSTRIAL ESTATE
FOUNDATION UNITS
ENTERPRISE EST
Sewage Works
Superstore
Fitness Cen.
SPORTS GROUND
Stoughton
Bellfields
Sec Sch
Prim Sch
Rydes Hill Lodge
Liddington Lodge
LIDDINGTON HALL DRIVE
Rydeshill
The Cricketers PH
Range Farm
STOKE NEW CEMETERY
STOKE CEM
ALLOT
Stoke Lock
River Wey Navigation NT
Woodbridge Hill
SPORTS GROUND
THE PINES TRADING EST
BROADSTREET COMMON
BROAD STREET
ALDERSHOT ROAD
RIFLERANGE PLANTATION
Wooden Bridge
GUILDFORD BYPASS
Ladymead Retail Park
EUROPA PARK
LADYMEAD
Offices
Premier Inn
Ice Rink
Leisure Complex
Lido
Bowls Club
Bowls Club Guildford Coll
Travelodge
WOODBRIDGE MEADOWS
WOODBRIDGE BUSINESS PARK
Royal Mail
Park Barn
Sec Sch
NUFFIELD HOSP
ROYAL SURREY COUNTY HOSP
Tech. Centre
SURREY RESEARCH PARK
B.O.C. Group
THE PHILIP HENMAN SPORTS GROUND
GUILDFORD IND EST
GUILDFORD BUSINESS PARK
MID IND EST
University of Surrey
Stag Hill
CATHEDRAL
Guildford Park
Cricket Grd
RIVERSIDE BUSINESS CEN
BUS DEPOT
CROWN CT
Dapdune Wharf NT
Guildford & District Synagogue
Nursery
GARDENS
Home Farm
258
Holiday Inn
Prim Sch
Hotel
Baptist
MOUNT ALVERNIA
500 yds
500 m

Send
Send Marsh
Sutton Green
Westfield Farm
Runtley Wood Farm
Cricketshill Farm
Pav
Concorde C.C.
Triggs Lock Bridge
Triggs Lock
Sendholme
Wareham's Farm
REC GRD
Sutton Green House
Manor House
Sutton Park House
SUTTON PARK
Sutton Place
BURPHAM COURT FARM PARK
Burpham Court Farm
Bower's Lock
Bower's Mill
Bower's Cottages
RIVERSIDE PARK
Sendcourt Farm
Send Grove
Sendgrove
CEM
GU23
Woodhill House Farm
Sendhurst Grange
Old Timbers
Nutbourne Fruit Farm
Tudor Barn Farm
Stables
Sendbarns
HIGHCOTTS WOOD
Dedswell Manor Farm
WOKING
GUILDFORD
River Wey
RIVER WEY NAVIGATION
Whitehouse Farm
Nuthill Farm
Broadoak Bridge
Weir
Burpham
LONDON ROAD
A3
RIPLEY ROAD
BYPASS
FRITHYS WOOD
COTTS WOOD
GU4
Gosden Hill Farm
THE COPSE
Superstore
SUTHERLAND MEMORIAL PARK
Burpham
COPSE EDGE
SPORTS GROUND
DEPOT
MERROW IND EST
MERROW BUSINESS CEN
MERROW COMMON
Clandon Park Garden Centre
REGT. MUS
Clandon Park NT
THE WILDERNESS
CHALK PIT
THE WILD WOOD
Surrey Cricket Centre
Sec Sch
Abbotswood
Miniature Railway
Clubhouse
Bushy Hill
Merrow
Bowling Green
Merrow CC
Fitness Cen
Tennis Courts
Dance Coll
Horse & Groom PH
Clinic
GUILDFORD GOLF COURSE
Clubhouse
MERROW DOWNS
WALNUT TREE BOTTOM
SPORTS GROUND
EPSOM ROAD
A25
A246
A3100
A247
B2215
B2234
227
244
259
126
127
128
129
130
131
132
133
134
AZ
BA
BB
BC
BD
BE
BF
01
02
03
51
52
53
54

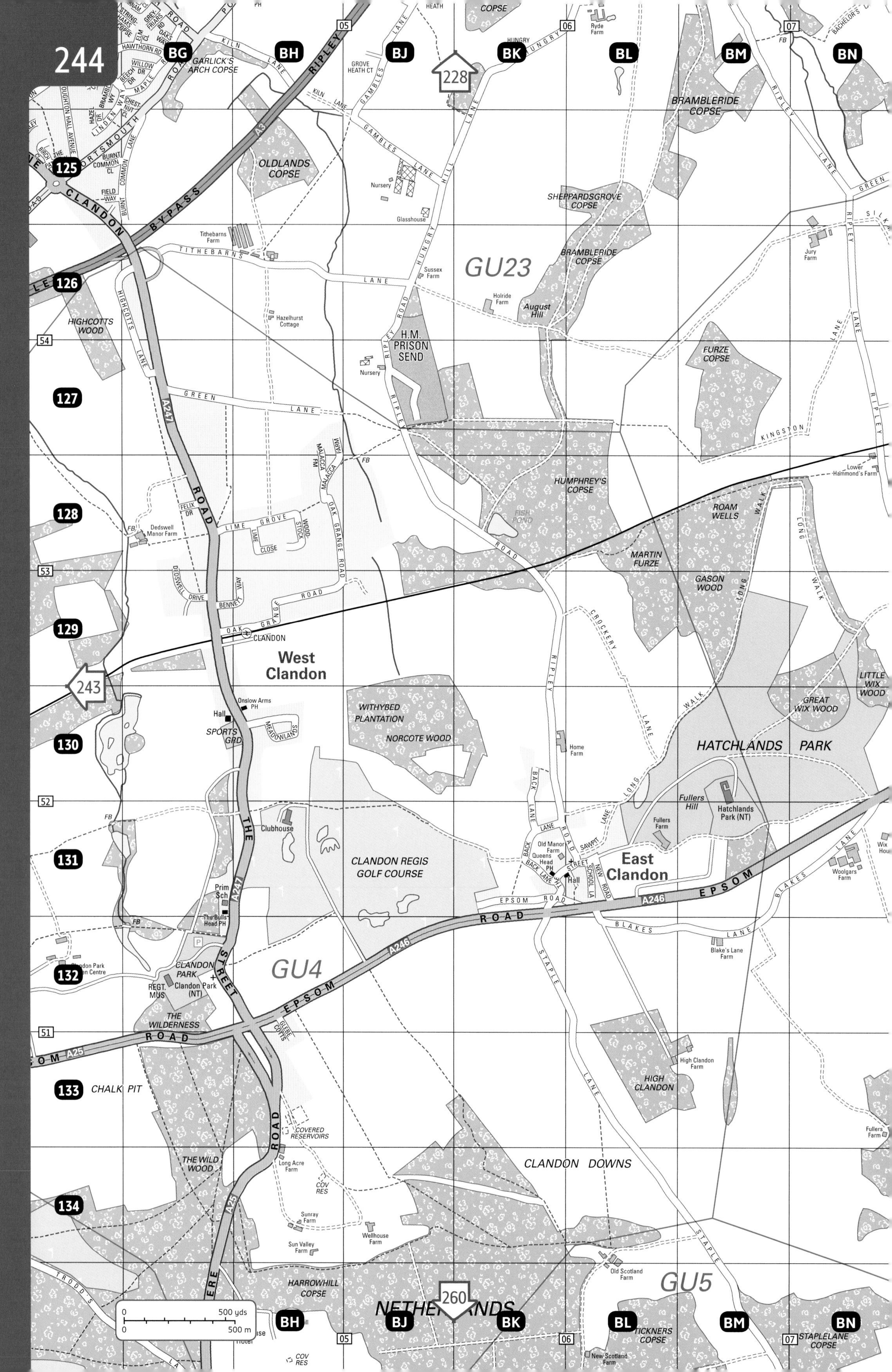

West Clandon
East Clandon
GU23
GU4
GU5
HATCHLANDS PARK
CLANDON REGIS GOLF COURSE
H.M. PRISON SEND
CLANDON DOWNS
OLDLANDS COPSE
BRAMBLERIDE COPSE
SHEPPARDSGROVE COPSE
HUMPHREY'S COPSE
MARTIN FURZE
GASON WOOD
ROAM WELLS
FURZE COPSE
GREAT WIX WOOD
LITTLE WIX WOOD
WITHYBED PLANTATION
NORCOTE WOOD
HIGHCOTTS WOOD
HIGH CLANDON
HARROWHILL COPSE
THE WILD WOOD
THE WILDERNESS
CHALK PIT
TICKNERS COPSE
STAPLELANE COPSE
CLANDON BYPASS
EPSOM ROAD
THE STREET
RIPLEY ROAD
HUNGRY HILL LANE
GREEN LANE
TITHEBARNS LANE
KINGSTON LANE
BLAKES LANE
STAPLE LANE
CROCKERY LANE
LONG WALK
228
243
260
0 500 yds
0 500 m

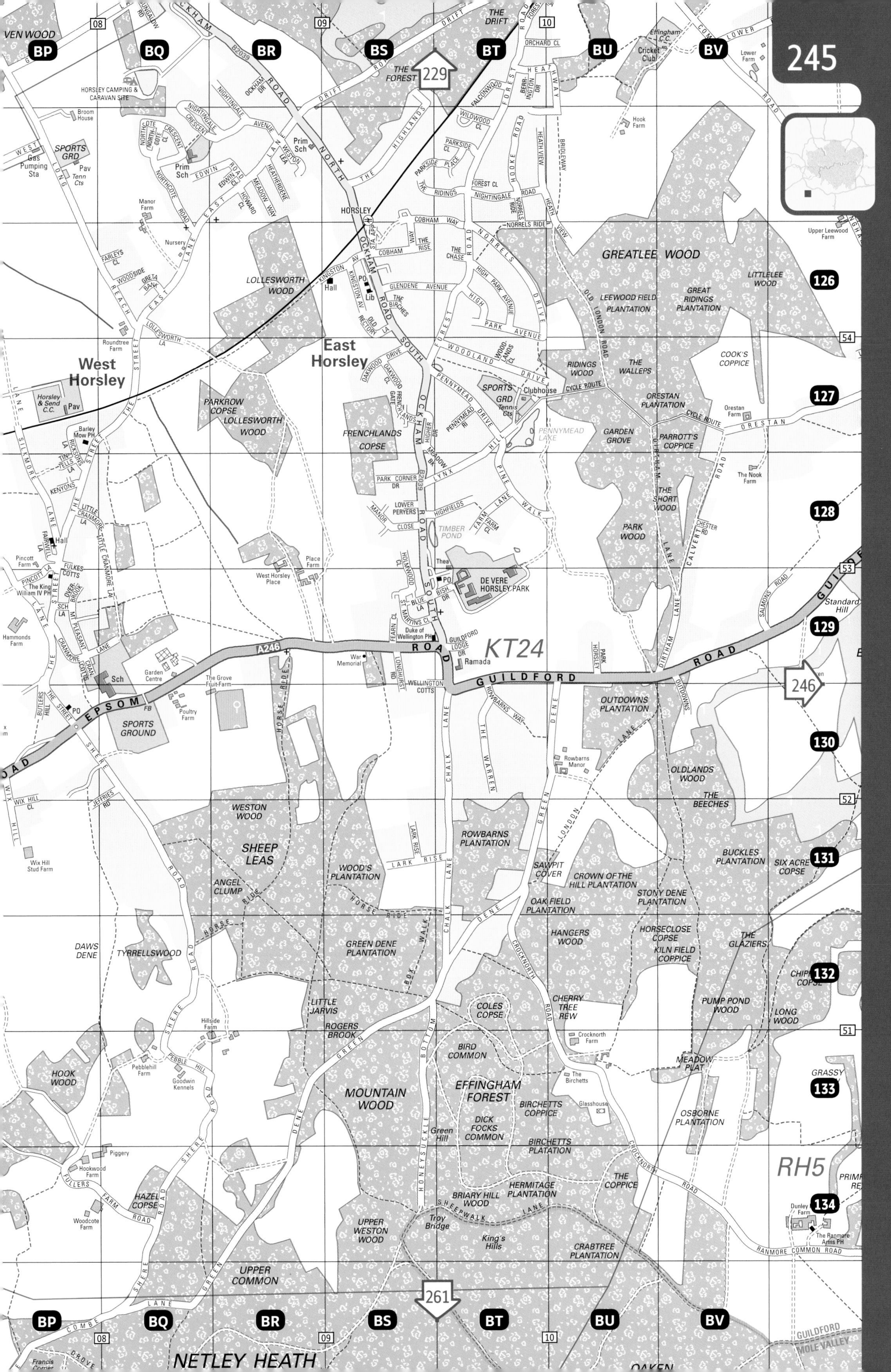
BP
BQ
BR
BS
BT
BU
BV
08
09
10
229
246
261
VEN WOOD
HORSLEY CAMPING & CARAVAN SITE
Broom House
SPORTS GRD
Gas Pumping Sta
Pav
Tenn Cts
Prim Sch
Manor Farm
Nursery
West Horsley
Horsley & Send C.C.
Roundtree Farm
Barley Mow PH
Hall
Pincott Farm
The King William IV PH
Hammonds Farm
Sch
Garden Centre
The Grove Fruit Farm
Poultry Farm
SPORTS GROUND
Wix Hill Stud Farm
WESTON WOOD
SHEEP LEAS
ANGEL CLUMP
DAWS DENE
TYRRELLSWOOD
HOOK WOOD
Hillside Farm
Pebblehill Farm
Goodwin Kennels
Piggery
Hookwood Farm
HAZEL COPSE
Woodcote Farm
UPPER COMMON
NETLEY HEATH
Francis Corner
EPSOM ROAD
A246
GUILDFORD ROAD
KT24
East Horsley
HORSLEY
LOLLESWORTH WOOD
PARKROW COPSE
FRENCHLANDS COPSE
West Horsley Place
Place Farm
War Memorial
Duke of Wellington PH
Ramada
DE VERE HORSLEY PARK
TIMBER POND
Thea
PO
Lib
SPORTS GRD
Clubhouse
PENNYMEAD LAKE
WOOD'S PLANTATION
GREEN DENE PLANTATION
LITTLE JARVIS
ROGERS BROOK
MOUNTAIN WOOD
UPPER WESTON WOOD
Troy Bridge
Green Hill
BIRD COMMON
EFFINGHAM FOREST
DICK FOCKS COMMON
COLES COPSE
BRIARY HILL WOOD
HERMITAGE PLANTATION
King's Hills
CRABTREE PLANTATION
THE COPPICE
BIRCHETTS COPPICE
BIRCHETTS PLATATION
The Birchetts
Glasshouse
Crocknorth Farm
CHERRY TREE REW
HANGERS WOOD
OAK FIELD PLANTATION
SAWPIT COVER
CROWN OF THE HILL PLANTATION
ROWBARNS PLANTATION
Rowbarns Manor
OUTDOWNS PLANTATION
OLDLANDS WOOD
THE BEECHES
BUCKLES PLANTATION
STONY DENE PLANTATION
HORSECLOSE COPSE
KILN FIELD COPPICE
THE GLAZIERS
PUMP POND WOOD
MEADOW PLAT
OSBORNE PLANTATION
SIX ACRE COPSE
LONG WOOD
GRASSY
RH5
Dunley Farm
The Ranmore Arms PH
RANMORE COMMON ROAD
GUILDFORD
MOLE VALLEY
Standard Hill
GREATLEE WOOD
LITTLELEE WOOD
LEEWOOD FIELD PLANTATION
GREAT RIDINGS PLANTATION
COOK'S COPPICE
RIDINGS WOOD
THE WALLEPS
ORESTAN PLANTATION
Orestan Farm
GARDEN GROVE
PARROTT'S COPPICE
The Nook Farm
THE SHORT WOOD
PARK WOOD
Upper Leewood Farm
Hook Farm
Effingham C.C.
Cricket Club
Lower Farm
THE DRIFT
THE FOREST
CYCLE ROUTE
126
127
128
129
130
131
132
133
134
54
53
52
51

BW
BX
BY
BZ
CA
CB
CC
230
245
262
Little Bookham
GREAT BOOKHAM
Effingham
KT23
KT24
OAKEN WOOD
THORNET WOOD
LITTLELEE WOOD
COOK'S COPPICE
EFFINGHAM GOLF COURSE
Standard Hill
STARS WOOD
White Hill
SIX ACRE COPSE
HAZEL BUCKET
CHIPPENS COPSE
PUMP POND WOOD
LONG WOOD
BURROWS WOOD
ROBINSGROVE WOOD
GRASSY SHAW
OSBORNE PLANTATION
PRIMROSE REW
STONYROCK COPSE
ROUND LIONS COPSE
HOGDEN COPSE
LONG SHAW
MOLE VALLEY
BIG HIGH GROVE
Polesden Lacey
POLESDEN LACEY NT
PRESERVE COPSE
CHERRYTREE COPSE
ROUND COPSE
YEWTREE SHAW
BELCHAM'S COPSE
CONNICUT WOOD
CROOKSFIELD WOOD
BAGDEN WOOD
RANMORE COMMON NT
KESWICK PLANTATION
RANMORE ROUNDABOUT
THE SPAINS
LILLIES COPSE
THE ROUNDABOUTS
GREAT COPSE
BURNETTS LEAP
NATIONAL TRUST
HORLEY'S COPSE
GUILDFORD ROAD
LEATHERHEAD ROAD
RANMORE COMMON ROAD
Wyvenhoe Riding Centre
Goldstone Farm
Kenilworth Riding Stables
High Barn Farm
Effingham Hill Farm
Ranmore Farm
Dog Kennel Green Farm
Dunley Hill Farm
The Ranmore Arms PH
Landbarn Farm
Y.H.A.
0 500 yds
0 500 m

CD
CE
CF
CG
CH
CJ
CK
15
16
17
231
248
263
126
127
128
129
130
131
132
133
134
54
53
52
51
KT22
KT20
RH5
RH4
LEATHERHEAD BYPASS
Givons Grove Roundabout
YOUNG STREET
GUILDFORD ROAD
GUIL. RD
A246
A24
A2003
B2209
B2038
Downside Farm
Bocketts Farm Park
Givons Grove
DORKING ROAD
Cherkley Court & Gardens
STANE STREET (ROMAN ROAD)
THE HAZELS
FETCHAM DOWNS
UPDOWN WOOD
WALNUT TREE CLUMP
Roaringhouse Farm
Denshire Hill
THE SHRUBS
NORBURY PARK
Norbury Park House
ICEHOUSE COMBE
Norbury Tunnel
LONGBURY WOOD
Norbury Park Farm
River Mole
Weir
MICKLEHAM BYPASS
BOOKHAM WOOD
SPORTS GROUND
Swanworth Farm
SWANWORTH LANE
DELL CLOSE
Hall
Mickleham
MICKLEHAM DOWNS
WHITE HILL NT
Warren Farm
CHARLEY MOUNT
Mickleham Hall
DRUIDS GROVE
Juniper Hill
JUNIPERHILL WOOD
COWSLIP LANE
Cowslip Farm
Fredley Manor
HEADLEY ROAD
Juniper Hall
Bridleways Equestrian Centre
BEECHY WOOD
Ham Bank
NICOLS FIELD
St. Faiths
FREDLEY PARK
JUNIPER TOP
CRABTREE LANE
FOXBURY SHAW
NT
Pinehurst
Bagden Hill
CHAPEL WOOD
Chapel Hill
Lodge Hill
DOWNS
THE THORNS
THE ZIG ZAG
CHAPEL LANE
Chapel Farm
CAMILLA DRIVE
Mercure Burford Bridge Hotel
BOX HILL NT
Bagden Farm
Westhumble
CLEVELAND CT
BOXHILL & WESTHUMBLE
WESTHUMBLE STREET
The Stepping Stones PH
Burford Lodge
Pav
SPORTS GROUND
THE WHITES
DORKING WOOD
ASHCOMBE WOOD
NORTH DOWNS WAY
Denbies Wine Estate
BRADLEY LANE
Salomon's Memorial
GREATLEE WOOD
PLAYING FIELDS
Pixholme Court
Denbies Farm
GREEN TERRACE
VINEYARD
Friends Provident
PIXHAM END
Pixham
Sewage Works
RANMORE COMMON ROAD
Denbies
DORKING
ASHCOMBE ROAD
DORKING DEEPDENE
DORKING CEMETERY
Boxhill
RANMORE ROAD
PILGRIMS WAY
MEADOWBANK
RH4
ALLOT
Prim Sch
DORKING WEST
CHALKPIT
DEEPDENE AV
REIGATE ROAD
Travelodge
DORKING BUSINESS PARK
Dorking FC
COUNCIL OFF
Sports Cen
Theatre
BETCHWORTH
CLAY
Pipp Brook
Water

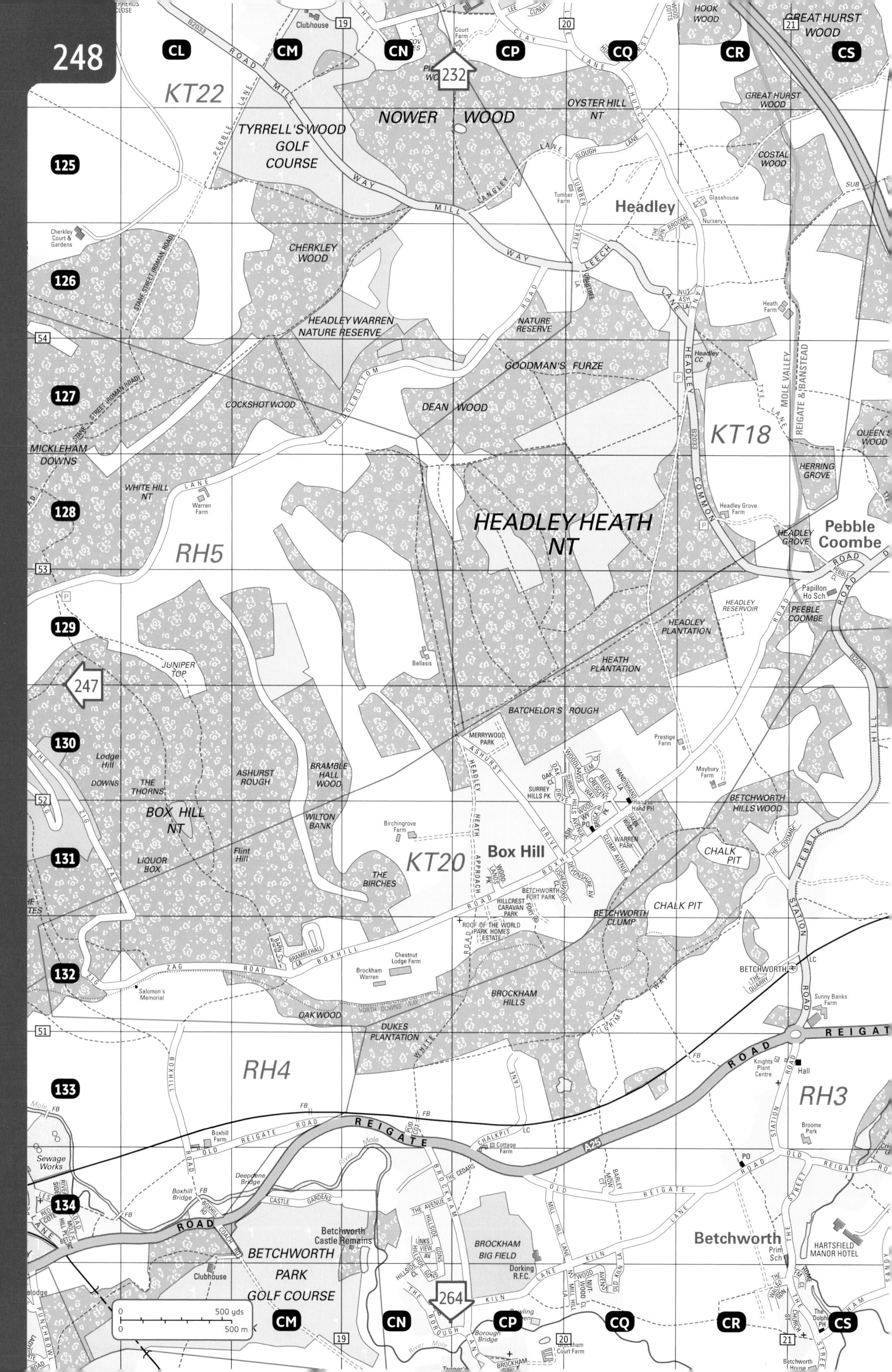
NOWER WOOD
TYRRELL'S WOOD GOLF COURSE
OYSTER HILL NT
Headley
CHERKLEY WOOD
HEADLEY WARREN NATURE RESERVE
NATURE RESERVE
GOODMAN'S FURZE
COCKSHOT WOOD
DEAN WOOD
MICKLEHAM DOWNS
WHITE HILL NT
HEADLEY HEATH NT
Pebble Coombe
HEADLEY PLANTATION
HEATH PLANTATION
BATCHELOR'S ROUGH
JUNIPER TOP
ASHURST ROUGH
BRAMBLE HALL WOOD
BOX HILL NT
Box Hill
BETCHWORTH HILLS WOOD
CHALK PIT
BETCHWORTH CLUMP
BROCKHAM HILLS
OAK WOOD
DUKES PLANTATION
Betchworth
BETCHWORTH PARK GOLF COURSE
BROCKHAM BIG FIELD
KT22
KT18
KT20
RH5
RH4
RH3
500 yds
500 m

232
247
264

Walton on the Hill
BANSTEAD HEATH
BANSTEAD
KT20
HEATH
WALTON HEATH GOLF COURSE
WALTON HEATH
CHUSSEX PLAIN
Lower Kingswood
Mogador
GAS STATION
Pfizer
LITTLE HEATH
ROUND WOOD
DEWRIDING PLANTATION
Lady Hill
Thistle Hill
Buckland Hills
Mount Hill
Conybury Hill
Juniper Hill
Colley Hill
THE HORSESHOE
THE SADDLE KNOB
QUEEN'S PARK
MARGERY WOOD NT
COVERED RESERVOIR
FOUR ACRE UPPER WOODS
THE BEECHES
NORTHLAND SHAW
BUSHY SHAW
COLLEYLAND SHAW
BUSHFIELD COPPICE
COLLEY COPSE
COLLEY WOOD
Buckland
RH2
TAP WOOD
SAND AND GRAVEL PIT
ROUND ALDERS
THE ALDERS
REIGATE HEATH GOLF COURSE
REIGATE HEATH
REIGATE
PRIORY PARK
REIGATE PARK
BRIGHTON ROAD
A217
M25
A25
BUCKLAND ROAD
WEST STREET
HIGH STREET
DORKING ROAD
NORTH DOWNS WAY
PILGRIMS WAY
MOLE VALLEY
REIGATE & BANSTEAD
CT CU CV CW CX CY CZ
22 23 24
51 52 53 54
126 127 128 129 130 131 132 133 134
233 250 265

DA
DB
DC
DD
DE
DF
DG
234
26
27
28
Clubhouse
Well House PH
Manor Park
South Lodge
TOP SHAW
HEDGELAND SHAW
WELLFIELD SHAW
OMEFIELD SHAWS
Reeves Rest
Southerns Farm
BEECHEN
SPORTS GRD
Pav
COPSE
MILLFIELD WOOD
Mugswell
RECTORY ROAD
Park Farm
125
Fidelity Investments Int.
FURZEFIELD COPSE
LONG WOOD
LITTLE WOOD
UPPER GATTON WOOD
BOARS GREEN SHAW
HARPS OAK SHAW
Boars Green Farm
GRUB WOOD
CR5
COLTS BUSHES
UPPER GATTON PARK
DELL WOOD
FURZEFIELD SHAW
126
GREEN LANE
ALLOT
GATWICK WOOD
54
Home Field Farm
Highways Livery Stables
Ashtead Hill
Lower Kingswood
Upper Gatton
127
Orchard Cottage Riding Stables
JUBILEE PLANTATIONS
PARK SHAW
Hall
Tenn Cts
Pav
Prim Sch
REC GRD
BABYLON LANE
Crossways Farm
REIGATE H
GATTON BOTTOM
Gatton
Driving Range
GOLF COU
Clubhouse
Kingswood Manor
KT20
THE CROSSWAYS
MAJORITY PLANTATION
MANSHIPS SHAW
Kingswood Hill
GATTON FIELD SHAW
CATSBRAIN EAST
M25
Whitehall Farm
128
BRIGHTON ROAD
A217
GROVE SHAW
GLEBE SHAW
TOWER WOOD
GATLANDS SHAW
53
HIGH BEECHES
High Beeches
JUBILEE PLANTATIONS
CATSBRAIN SHAW
Sch
129
COVERED RESERVOIR
Margery
Margery Hall Stud
Reigate Hill Interchange
GATTON PARK
Tennis Courts
Margery Farm
249
Junction 8
HALFMOON CLUMP
HOP GARDEN POND
ENGINE POND
REIGATE HILL
THE BURPIT
SPORTS GROUND
THE LAKE
Water Tower
TWO ACRE WOOD
BLACKHORSE WOOD
GREAT BUCK WOOD
RH2
SERPENTINE WOOD
Margery Hall
Mast
WINGATE HILL
Kingswood Hall
130
NT
GREENCLUMP HILL
TEMPLE WOOD
FOUR ACRE UPPER WOODS
Water Tower
Rock Farm
QUEEN'S PARK
Mast
REIGATE FORT
NUTWOOD NT
Stables
52
THE BEECHES
REIGATE HILL NT
PARK ROAD
A242
Coles Meads
East Surrey Coll
131
Broadleas
Yew Tree PH
Sec Sch
Sec Sch
Manor Hotel
GATTON ROAD
132
COLLEY WOOD
SPORTS GROUND
Sch
WRAY COMMON
Tennis Courts
Prim Sch
MEML PARK
51
Club
Pav
Sch
Cricket Ground
Surrey Fire & Rescue Service HQ
Comm Cen
Fire Sta
Prim Sch
ALLOT
Prim Sch
Offices
133
Superstore
Surgery
Offices
Reigate Coll
Bowls Club
TA Centre
Sports Cen
Johnston House
ALLOT
STATION RD
QUEENSWAY
Belfry Shop Cen
Comm Cen
REDHILL
LONDON ROAD
A23
Hall
TOWN HALL
Site of Reigate Castle
HIGH STREET
CHURCH STREET
A25
134
Reigate Priory C.C.
Pav
Superstore
PO
REIGATE
Tennis Courts
Sec Sch
Bowl Grn
SPORTS GROUND
Sch
REIGATE CEMETERY
Prim Sch
Clinic
REDHILL
REDSTONE MANOR
Airshaft
KINGSFIELD BUSINESS CEN
Reigate R.F.C.
PRIORY POND
PRIORY PARK
Pav
Site of Priory
Tenn Cts
BLACKBOROUGH ROAD
The Garibaldi PH
0 500 yds
0 500 m
DB
DC
266
DD
DE
REDHILL COMMON
DF
DG
26
27
28
Clinic
Sch
Gas Works
REIGATE PARK

DH
DJ
DK
DL
DM
DN
DP
235
SPARTICLES WOOD
Airshafts
ALDERSTEAD HEATH
FRYERN BROOM WOOD
DEAN LANE
ROOK LANE
B2031
Rook Hill
Hall
Prim Sch
WILLEY BROOM WOOD
Clubhouse
SIX BROTHERS FIELD
CR3
Mersham Tunnel
Junction 7
COVERED RESERVOIR
Alderstead Farm
THE SHRUBBERY
ALDERSTEAD HILL
Tollsworth Manor
Uplands Farm
RIDGEBUSHES WOOD
Earthworks
PILGRIMS' LANE
Hilltop Farm
Masts
PILGRIMS WAY
NORTH DOWNS WAY
Willey Park Farm
126
SHEPHERDS HILL
CHURCH HILL
LIME WORKS ROAD
JOLLIFFE RD
M23
Ockley Hill
Junction 8 (M23), Junction 7 (M25)
OCKLEY WOOD
BEDLAMS BANK
White Hill
127
ROCKSHAW ROAD
SPRINGBOTTOM ROAD
HERONSWOOD MERE
WITHY SHAW
Merstham
MERSTHAM
Hall
Pav
Merstham CC
Home Farm
GATTON PARK
FURZEFIELD WOOD
128
RADSTOCK ROAD
Comm Cen
PENDELL WOOD
BLACK BUSHES
Prim Sch
THE GROVE
Prim Sch
M25
129
Warwick Wold
OAKWOOD RD
BLETCHINGLEY ROAD
Health Cen
Lib
Sch
Darby House
BLACK BUSHES
252
Tennis Courts
SPORTS GROUND
ALLOT
South Merstham
SEWAGE WORKS
REIGATE & BANSTEAD
TANDRIDGE
130
QUARRYSIDE BUSINESS PARK
Pendell Farm
WATER LANE
MERCERS PARK COUNTRY PARK
RH1
Pendell House
PENDELL CT
Sch
Brewer Street Farm
131
HOLMETHORPE IND EST
THE LAGOON
Ford Bridge
NUTFIELD MARSH ROAD
Lake Farm
Holmethorpe
Cricket Ground
Inn on the Pond PH
CHILMEAD LANE
Chilmead Farm
PEYTON'S COTTAGES
COCKLEY PLANTATION
132
Nursery
Bletchingley
Glebe House
ALLOT
LITTLE COMMON
Nutfield Court
PUBLIC TIP
PARK WOOD
Nutfield
CASTLE STREET
133
Castle Hill
Capenor Nursery
Robert Denholm House
COOMBES COPPICE
STANLEY'S WOOD
NUTFIELD CEMETERY
HIGH STREET
ROAD
A25
FOX HOLE
HOLMESDALE PARK
NORTH PARK
Nutfield Priory Hotel
SPORTS GRD
Furze Hill
Castle Hill Farm
134
Nutfield Lodge
Stockers Hill
Priory Farm Plant Centre
STENERS HILL
Priory Farm
NUTFIELD PRIORY LAKE
267
HOGTROUGH LANE
REDSTONE CEMETERY
Bower Hill
Kentwyns
KENTWYNS RISE
Prim Sch
Lyttel Hall
Sandhills Farm

DQ
DR
DS
DT
DU
DV
DW
236
251
125
126
127
128
129
130
131
132
133
134
CR3
RH1
CATERHAM
Rook Hill
Fryern Farm
QUEEN'S PARK
SPORTS GRD
RUGBY GROUND
Clubhouse
THE NORTH DOWNS HOSP
CARR'S CROFT
Sports Centre
Sch
EIGHT ACRE WOOD
The Chalet Farm
The Chalet
Paddock Barn
PADDOCK WOOD
OCKLEY WOOD
White Hill
GRUBS WOOD
The Harrow PH
QUARRY HANGERS
SPRING BOTTOM
Arthur's Seat
OLDPARK SHAW
TEN ACRE SHAW
TUPWOOD SCRUBS
THE DEVILS HOLE
DIALBANK WOOD
FOSTERDOWN WOOD
QUARRY WOOD
Quarry Farm
Quarry Hall Farm
ROCKY SHAW
The Mound
Gravelly Hill
Weather Station
Fosterdown Fort
KENNEL SHAW
Kennels and Cattery
GODSTONE VINEYARD
PENDELL WOOD
BLACK BUSHES
CONDUIT SHAW
Roughets House
Godstone Interchange
Junction 6
M25
A22
Fire Sta
Orpheus Centre
KITCHEN COPSE
BLACK BUSHES
Place Farm
Pendell Farm
Water Works
ELM PLATT
SAND PIT
Brewer Street Farm
Brewer Street
Godstone
Bay Pond
BLETCHINGLEY ROAD
Knights Garden Centre Ivy Mill
Stangrave Hall Stables
HILLBROW COTTAGES
BLETCHINGLEY GOLF COURSE
Bletchingley
Nursery
Dormers Farm
SUNNYBANK VILLAS
Waterhouse Farm
A25
Clubhouse
Court Lodge Farm
The Plough Inn PH
Castle Hill
STANLEY'S WOOD
Bowling Green
Garston Park
HARLINGS SHAW
GODSTONE FARM
TILBURSTOWHILL PLANTATION
Tilburstow Hill
Castle Hill Farm
Sandhills
GRAVELHILL WOOD
Coldharbour House
Coldharbour Farm
ELEVEN ACRE SHAW
LONG SHAW
CROOKEDFIELD SHAW
Sandhills Farm
Tilburstowhill Farm
M23
0 500 yds
0 500 m

OXTED
Tandridge
RH8
NORTH DOWNS GOLF COURSE
GODSTONE GOLF COURSE
TANDRIDGE GOLF COURSE
OXTED QUARRY
CHALK PIT
CHALK PITS
THE ABBEYS
SAND PIT
MASTER PARK
GODSTONE ROAD
OXTED ROAD
WEST ROAD
GODSTONE BYPASS
EASTBOURNE ROAD
M25
A25
A22
B2236
TANDRIDGE LANE
TANDRIDGE HILL LANE
BARROW GREEN ROAD
SANDY LANE
CHALKPIT LANE
GANGERS HILL
FLOWER LANE
HOGTROUGH LANE
SOUTHLANDS LANE
BROADHAM GREEN ROAD
GIBBS BROOK LANE
SPRING LANE
JACKASS LANE
LEIGH PLACE LANE
CHURCH LANE
WHISTLERS WOOD
STUBBS COPSE
THE RUMPS
HAZEL SHAW
HORSE SHAW
HANGING WOOD
ROBINS GROVE WOOD
RYE WOOD
ARMITAGE WOOD
LODGE WOOD
HAMFIELD SHAW
FIVE ACRE SHAW
CHALKPIT WOOD
THE BOGS
THE MOUNT
THE BIRCHES
NEW BUSTONS WOOD
BUSTONS WOOD
ROUND WOOD
STONEPIT SHAW
OLDPARK WOOD
CASTLEHILL WOOD
REDDINGS WOOD
SOUTHLANDS SHAWS
SOUTHLANDS WOOD
DEAN SHAW
STOW COPPICE
HOPGARDEN WOOD
MOORE'S SHAW
FLOWER WOOD
PALMERS WOOD OILFIELD
MARDEN PARK
BEECH PLANTATION NT
OXTED DOWNS NT
SPORTS GROUND
BUSHEY CROFT REC GRD
Sewage Works
Barrow Green Court
Barrow Green Farm
Ridgeway Manor
Tandridge Priory
Tandridge Court
Tandridge Court Farm
Tandridge Hall
Barley Mow PH
Little Court Farm
Knights Garden Centre
Leigh Mill House
The Glebe House
Leigh Place
Stockett's Manor
Perrysfield Farm
Rose Farm
Southlands Lodge
Newhouse Farm
Hollybush Farm
Haycutter PH
Stonehall Farm
Mill Barn
BROADHAM GREEN
Clubhouse
Airshaft
Oxted Tunnel
237
254
DX
DY
DZ
EA
EB
EC
ED
36
37
38
126
127
128
129
130
131
132
133
134

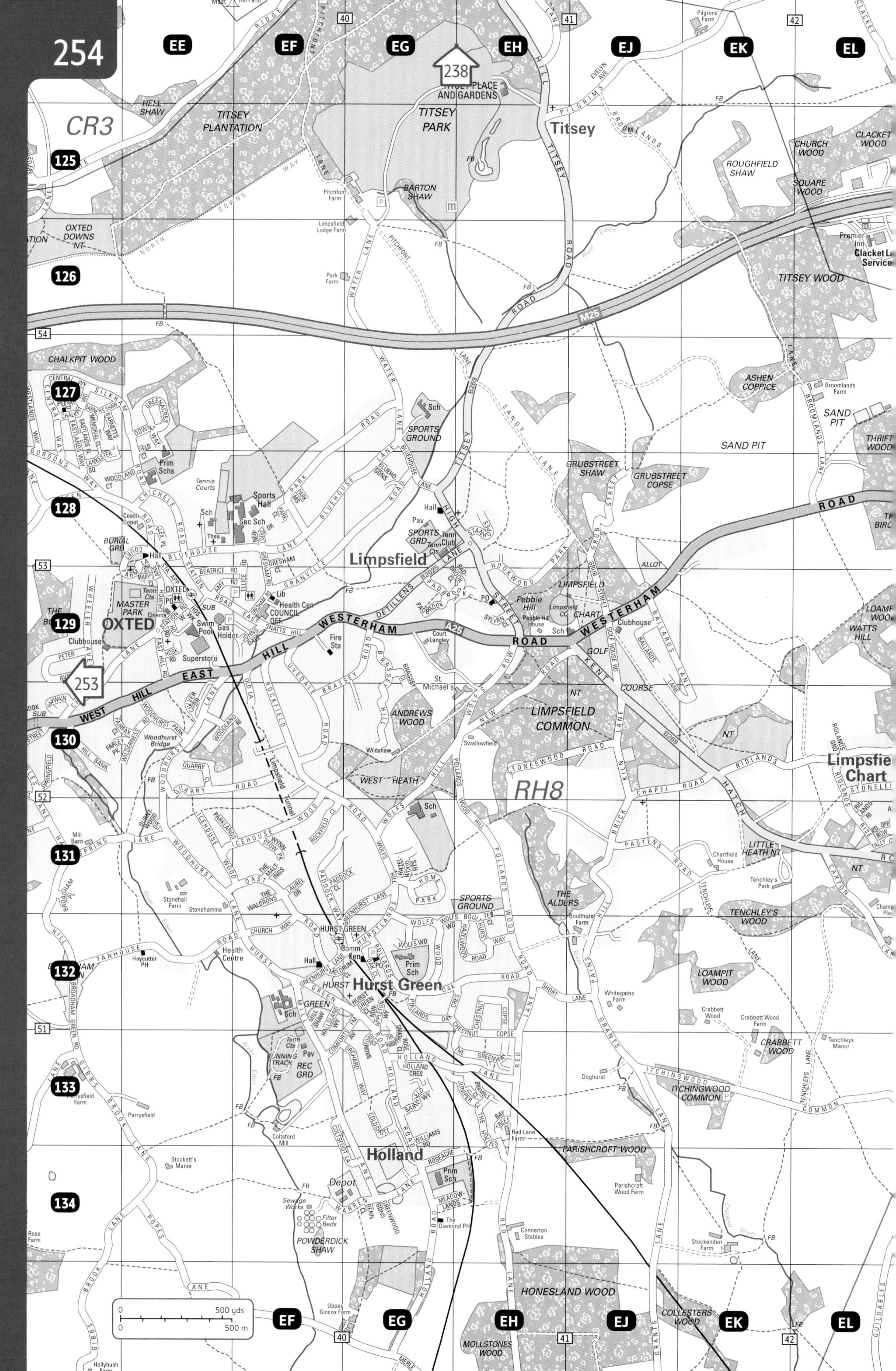

EE
EF
EG
EH
EJ
EK
EL
238
TITSEY PLACE AND GARDENS
CR3
HELL SHAW
TITSEY PLANTATION
TITSEY PARK
Titsey
CHURCH WOOD
CLACKET WOOD
ROUGHFIELD SHAW
SQUARE WOOD
BARTON SHAW
Pitchfont Farm
Limpsfield Lodge Farm
OXTED DOWNS NT
Premier Inn
Clacket L Service
TITSEY WOOD
Park Farm
M25
CHALKPIT WOOD
ASHEN COPPICE
Broomlands Farm
SAND PIT
SAND PIT
SPORTS GROUND
GRUBSTREET SHAW
GRUBSTREET COPSE
Tennis Courts
Sports Hall
Sec Sch
Prim Schs
Limpsfield
BURIAL GRD
ALLOT
LIMPSFIELD CHART
OXTED
MASTER PARK
Health Cen
COUNCIL OFF
Swim Pool
Gas Holder
Superstore
Fire Sta
Clubhouse
GOLF COURSE
WATTS HILL
253
WESTERHAM ROAD
EAST HILL
WEST HILL
ANDREWS WOOD
LIMPSFIELD COMMON
NT
Woodhurst Bridge
Limpsfield Tunnel
WEST HEATH
RH8
Limpsfie Chart
LITTLE HEATH NT
Mill Barn
Stonehall Farm
Stonehamme
SPORTS GROUND
THE ALDERS
Boulthurst Farm
TENCHLEY'S WOOD
Tenchley's Park
Haycutter PH
Health Centre
HURST GREEN
Hurst Green
Prim Sch
LOAMPIT WOOD
Whitegates Farm
Crabbett Wood
Crabbett Wood Farm
CRABBETT WOOD
Tenchleys Manor
REC GRD
RUNNING TRACK
Perrysfield Farm
Perrysfield
Doghurst
ITCHINGWOOD COMMON
Coltsford Mill
Red Lane Farm
PARISHCROFT WOOD
Stockett's Manor
Holland
Prim Sch
Depot
Parishcroft Wood Farm
Sewage Works
Filter Beds
POWDERDICK SHAW
The Diamond PH
Connerton Stables
Rose Farm
Stockenden Farm
HONESLAND WOOD
COLLESTERS WOOD
Upper Gincox Farm
MOLLSTONES WOOD
Hollybush Farm
0 500 yds
0 500 m
125
126
127
128
129
130
131
132
133
134
40
41
42
51
52
53
54

239
WESTERHAM
WESTERHAM WOOD
Westerham
Goodley Stock
Kent Hatch
Hosey Hill
TN16
SQUERRYES PARK
SQUERRYES COURT & GDNS
HOSEY COMMON
TOWER WOOD
CROCKHAMHILL COMMON
Froghole
Crockham Hill
TN8
Moorhouse
Moorhouse Bank
MOORHOUSE BANK COMMON NT
CRONKLANDS
THE HIGH CHART
THE CHART
SCEARN BANK
ROUNDMEAD SHAW
LODGES WOOD
SPRING SHAW
DUNSDALE
WOOD
KING GEORGE'S FIELD
QUEBEC HOUSE NT
CHARTWELL NT
BUDDLES WOOD
CHANDLER WOOD
DERBY WOOD
GUDGE WOOD
PERRY WOOD
PRIORY WOOD
ROW WOOD
BROWN'S OVEN WOOD
MANNING'S WOOD
WESTERHAM GOLF COURSE
LONGCROFT WOOD
HATCROFT WOOD
GUILDABLES WOOD
WET WOOD
DEVIL OF KENT
SAND PIT
ROWTYE WOOD
CLACKET GREEN
FARLEY COMMON
SURREY
KENT
TANDRIDGE
SEVENOAKS
BEGGARS LANE
WESTERHAM ROAD
HIGH STREET
HOSEY HILL
HOSEY COMMON ROAD
FRENCH STREET
MAPLETON ROAD
PUDDLEDOCK LANE
SMITHS LANE
MAIN ROAD
SPOUT LANE
POOTINGS ROAD
DAIRY LANE
DENNETTSLAND ROAD
KENT HATCH ROAD
TREVEREUX HILL
GOODLEY STOCK ROAD
CROYDON ROAD
M25
A25
A233
B2026
B2024
B269
EM
EN
EP
EQ
ER
ES
ET
43
44
45
51
52
53
54
126
127
128
129
130
131
132
133
134

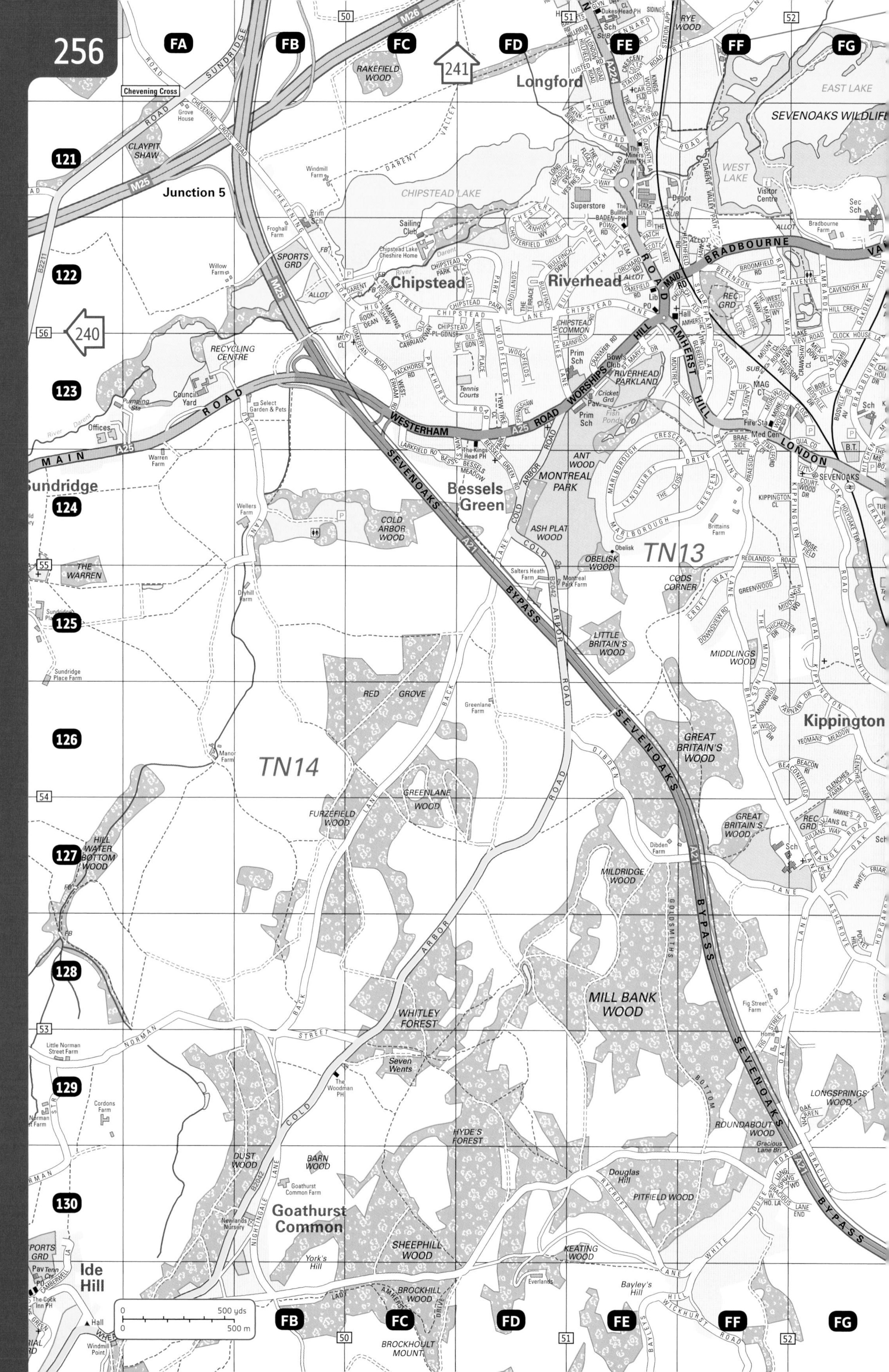
FA
FB
FC
FD
FE
FF
FG
121
122
123
124
125
126
127
128
129
130
241
240
Longford
Chevening Cross
Grove House
CLAYPIT SHAW
RAKEFIELD WOOD
RYE WOOD
EAST LAKE
SEVENOAKS WILDLIFE
WEST LAKE
Visitor Centre
Junction 5
M25
M26
A224
CHIPSTEAD LAKE
Windmill Farm
Superstore
Depot
Sailing Club
Chipstead Lake Cheshire Home
Froghall Farm
SPORTS GRD
Willow Farm
ALLOT
Chipstead
Riverhead
Bradbourne Farm
BRADBOURNE
RECYCLING CENTRE
Council Yard
Pumping Sta
Offices
Select Garden & Pets
Tennis Courts
WESTERHAM
ROAD
MAIN
A25
Warren Farm
Sundridge
Wellers Farm
COLD ARBOR WOOD
The Kings Head PH
BESSELS MEADOW
Bessels Green
ANT WOOD
MONTREAL PARK
ASH PLAT WOOD
RIVERHEAD PARKLAND
Cricket Grd
Fish Ponds
Prim Sch
Bowls Club
MAG CT
Fire Sta
Med Cen
LONDON
SEVENOAKS
THE WARREN
Salters Heath Farm
Montreal Park Farm
Obelisk
OBELISK WOOD
TN13
CODS CORNER
Dryhill Farm
SEVENOAKS BYPASS
A21
B2042
LITTLE BRITAIN'S WOOD
MIDDLINGS WOOD
Sundridge Place Farm
RED GROVE
Greenlane Farm
GREAT BRITAIN'S WOOD
Kippington
Manor Farm
TN14
GREENLANE WOOD
FURZEFIELD WOOD
GREAT BRITAIN'S WOOD
HILL WATER BOTTOM WOOD
Dibden Farm
MILDRIDGE WOOD
MILL BANK WOOD
WHITLEY FOREST
Fig Street Farm
Little Norman Street Farm
NORMAN STREET
Seven Wents
The Woodman PH
Cordons Farm
LONGSPRINGS WOOD
HYDE'S FOREST
ROUNDABOUT WOOD
Gracious Lane Bri
DUST WOOD
BARN WOOD
Goathurst Common Farm
Douglas Hill
PITFIELD WOOD
Goathurst Common
Newlands Nursery
SHEEPHILL WOOD
KEATING WOOD
York's Hill
Everlands
Bayley's Hill
Ide Hill
BROCKHILL WOOD
BROCKHOULT MOUNT
The Cock Inn PH
Hall
Windmill Point
500 yds
500 m
50
51
52
53
54
55
56

Greatness
TN14
Seal
Wildernesse
SEVENOAKS
Godden Green
TN15
KNOLE PARK GOLF COURSE
DEER PARK
Sevenoaks Common
Underriver
WILDERNESSE GOLF COURSE
FAWKE COMMON
Bat and Ball Junction
SEVENOAKS HOSP
Knole NT
SEAL ROAD
HIGH STREET
MAIDSTONE ROAD
TONBRIDGE ROAD
RIVER HILL
A25
A225
FH
FJ
FK
FL
FM
FN
FP
122
123
124
125
126
127
128
129
130

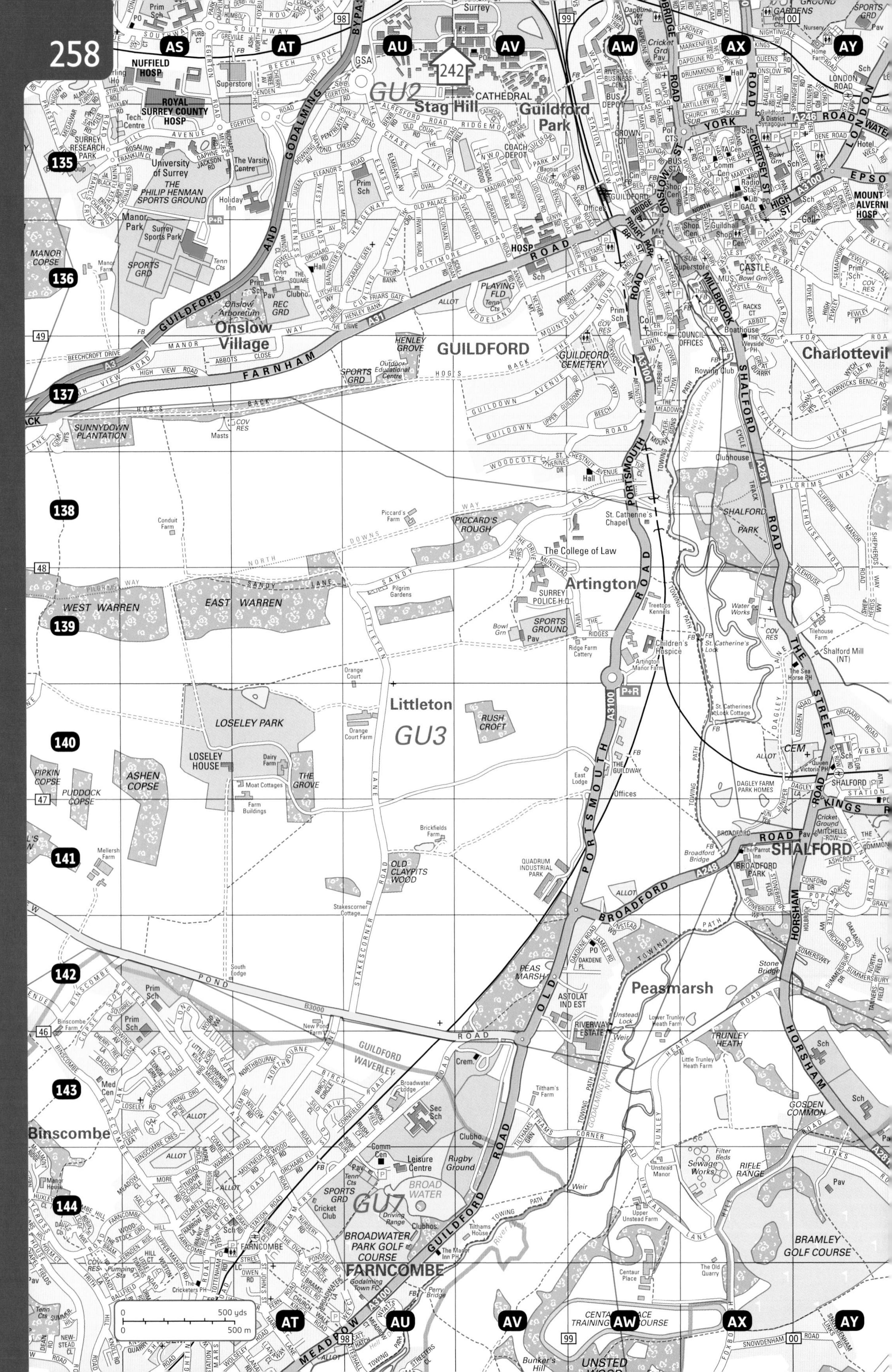
AS
AT
AU
AV
AW
AX
AY
242
NUFFIELD HOSP
ROYAL SURREY COUNTY HOSP
SURREY RESEARCH PARK
University of Surrey
THE PHILIP HENMAN SPORTS GROUND
The Varsity Centre
Holiday Inn
Manor Park
Surrey Sports Park
SPORTS GRD
MANOR COPSE
GU2
Stag Hill
CATHEDRAL
Guildford Park
Onslow Village
Onslow Arboretum
REC GRD
GUILDFORD
GUILDFORD CEMETERY
Charlotteville
HENLEY GROVE
Outdoor Educational Centre
SUNNYDOWN PLANTATION
SHALFORD PARK
PICCARD'S ROUGH
St. Catherine's Chapel
The College of Law
Artington
SURREY POLICE H.Q.
SPORTS GROUND
Children's Hospice
WEST WARREN
EAST WARREN
Pilgrim Gardens
LOSELEY PARK
LOSELEY HOUSE
Littleton
GU3
RUSH CROFT
ASHEN COPSE
PIPKIN COPSE
PUDDOCK COPSE
THE GROVE
OLD CLAYPITS WOOD
QUADRUM INDUSTRIAL PARK
SHALFORD
Peasmarsh
PEAS MARSH
ASTOLAT IND EST
RIVERWAY ESTATE
TRUNLEY HEATH
GOSDEN COMMON
RIFLE RANGE
BRAMLEY GOLF COURSE
Binscombe
GU7
BROAD WATER
BROADWATER PARK GOLF COURSE
FARNCOMBE
Leisure Centre
Rugby Ground
SPORTS GRD
Cricket Club
CENTAUR PLACE TRAINING COURSE
UNSTED WOOD
135
136
137
138
139
140
141
142
143
144
0 500 yds
0 500 m

GUILDFORD GOLF COURSE
MERROW DOWNS
WALNUT TREE BOTTOM
HAREWARREN
THE ROUGHS
SPORTS GROUND
GU1
GU4
GU5
PEWLEY DOWN
ALBURY DOWNS
CHANTRIES
FARTHING COPSE
HALFPENNY COPSE
St. Martha's Hill
LIDWELL COPSE
Chilworth Manor
MUD WOOD
Chilworth
DORKING ROAD
CHRISTMAS HILL
SHALFORD COMMON
BRADSTONE BROOK SPORTS GROUND
WONERSH COMMON
Tangley Hill
FRANCISCAN FRIARY
ROSEMARY HILL
NATIONAL TRUST
LOCKNER HOLT
Blackheath
Chinthurst Hill
Derry's Hill
DERRY'S WOOD
NORTHBROOK HILL
BARNETT HILL CONFERENCE CENTRE
ST. MARY'S DERRYWOOD
St. John's Seminary
Wonersh
Bramley
HEATHFIELDS
CUCKOO COPSE
243
260
136
137
138
139
140
141
142
143
144

244
259
NETHERLANDS
HARROWHILL COPSE
TICKNERS COPSE
STAPLELANE COPSE
CHANTRY WOOD
GU4
ALBURY DOWNS
WEST HANGER
Mother Webb's Corner
THE BOXWOOD
COMBE BOTTOM
Juniper Hill
NETLEY PLANTATION
Manor House Hotel
Newlands Corner
Visitor Centre
Old Scotland Farm
New Scotland Farm
Sun Valley Farm
Wellhouse Farm
Sunray Farm
Harrowhill
Newbarn
SHERBOURNE POND
SILENT POOL
Sherbourne Farm
Silent Pool Junction
SHERBOURNE COTTS
SAND PIT
WESTON WOOD
FARM HILL WOOD
SILVERWOOD COTTAGES
SILVER WOOD
Water Lane Farm
WATERLOO POND
POSTFORD POND
CHILWORTH RD
DORKING ROAD
GUILDFORD LA
THE STREET
A248
A25
SHERE ROAD
Weston House
Weston Farm
Albury
The Mansion
GU5
Chantry Bridge
The Old Rectory
OAK POLLARD
BELMOUNT COPSE
CUCKOO COPSE
Birget Hill
Birmingham Farm
ALBURY WARREN
ALBURY PARK
Sher
THE PLANTATION
SHERE HEATH
Shere Heath Crossing
Parklands Farm
Albury Heath
ALBURY HEATH
William IV PH
KILN ROUGH
Ford Crossing
Little Ford Farm
SPORTS GRD
Clubho.
WARNERS LANE
Brook Crossing
Brook Farm
Brook
Ponds Farm
Cotterells Farm
BLACKHEATH
BROOMFIELDS
MUSTARD COPSE
JUGS COPSE
FOXHOLES WOOD
HEATHFIELDS
EDGELEY CARAVAN PARK
JELLEY'S COPSE
ROMPIN DOWNS
Farley Green
FARLEY HEATH
KINGSFIELD
Lockhurst Hatch Farm
DILTON COPSE
FAR PLANTATION
NEW FIELD
SKEMP
MAYORHOUSE HOLT
Holmcroft Nursery
Hound House Farm
500 yds
500 m

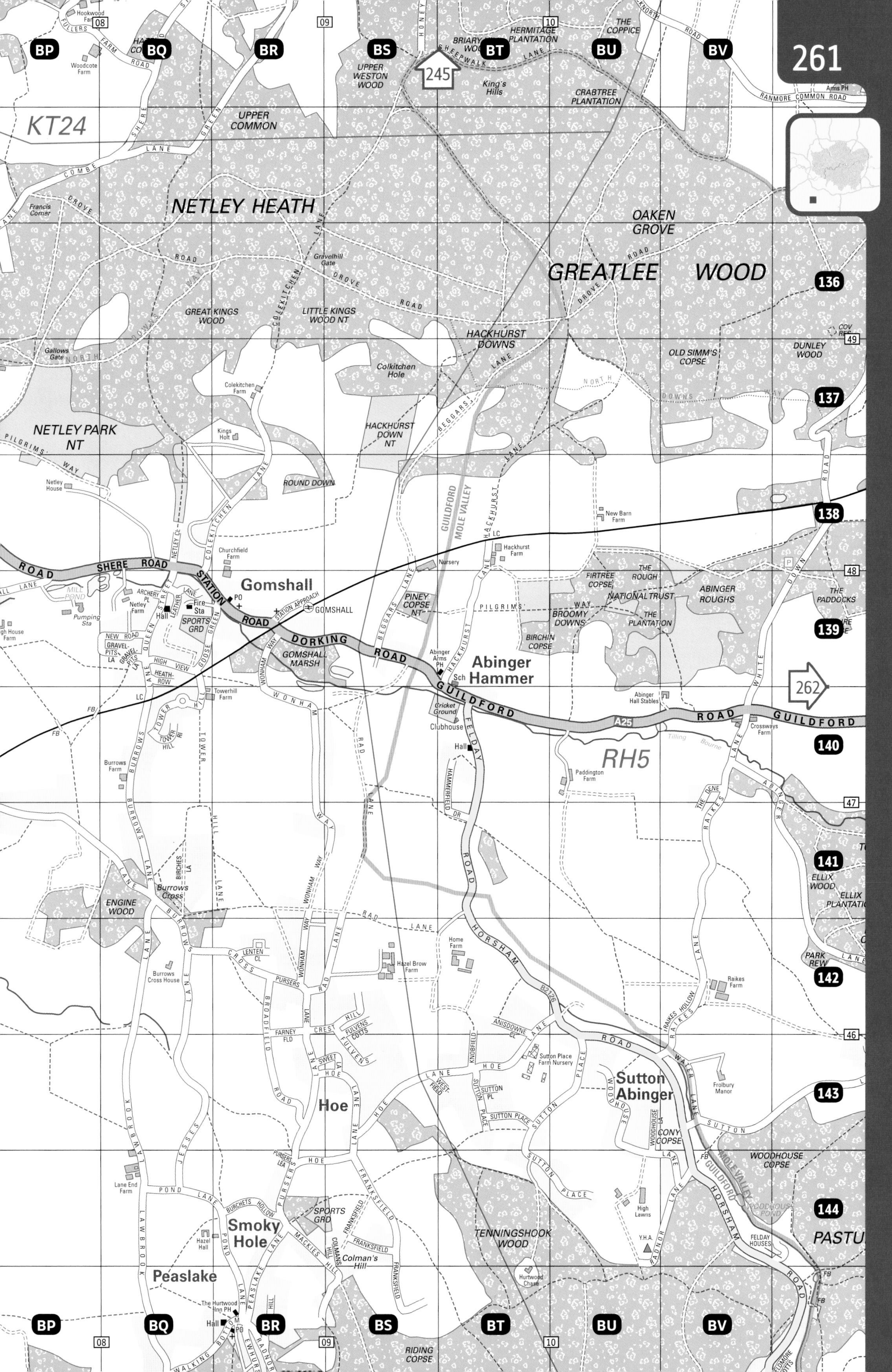

NETLEY HEATH
GREATLEE WOOD
OAKEN GROVE
UPPER COMMON
KT24
RH5
Gomshall
Abinger Hammer
Sutton Abinger
Hoe
Smoky Hole
Peaslake
NETLEY PARK NT
HACKHURST DOWNS
HACKHURST DOWN NT
LITTLE KINGS WOOD NT
GREAT KINGS WOOD
UPPER WESTON WOOD
King's Hills
CRABTREE PLANTATION
HERMITAGE PLANTATION
THE COPPICE
OLD SIMM'S COPSE
DUNLEY WOOD
ABINGER ROUGHS
THE ROUGH
NATIONAL TRUST
FIRTREE COPSE
BROOMY DOWNS
BIRCHIN COPSE
THE PLANTATION
THE PADDOCKS
PINEY COPSE NT
GOMSHALL MARSH
ROUND DOWN
Colkitchen Hole
ENGINE WOOD
Burrows Cross
TENNINGSHOOK WOOD
WOODHOUSE COPSE
CONY COPSE
ELLIX WOOD
RIDING COPSE
Colman's Hill
SHERE ROAD
STATION ROAD
DORKING ROAD
GUILDFORD ROAD
HORSHAM ROAD
A25
B2126
245
262
136
137
138
139
140
141
142
143
144
BP
BQ
BR
BS
BT
BU
BV
08
09
10
46
47
48
49

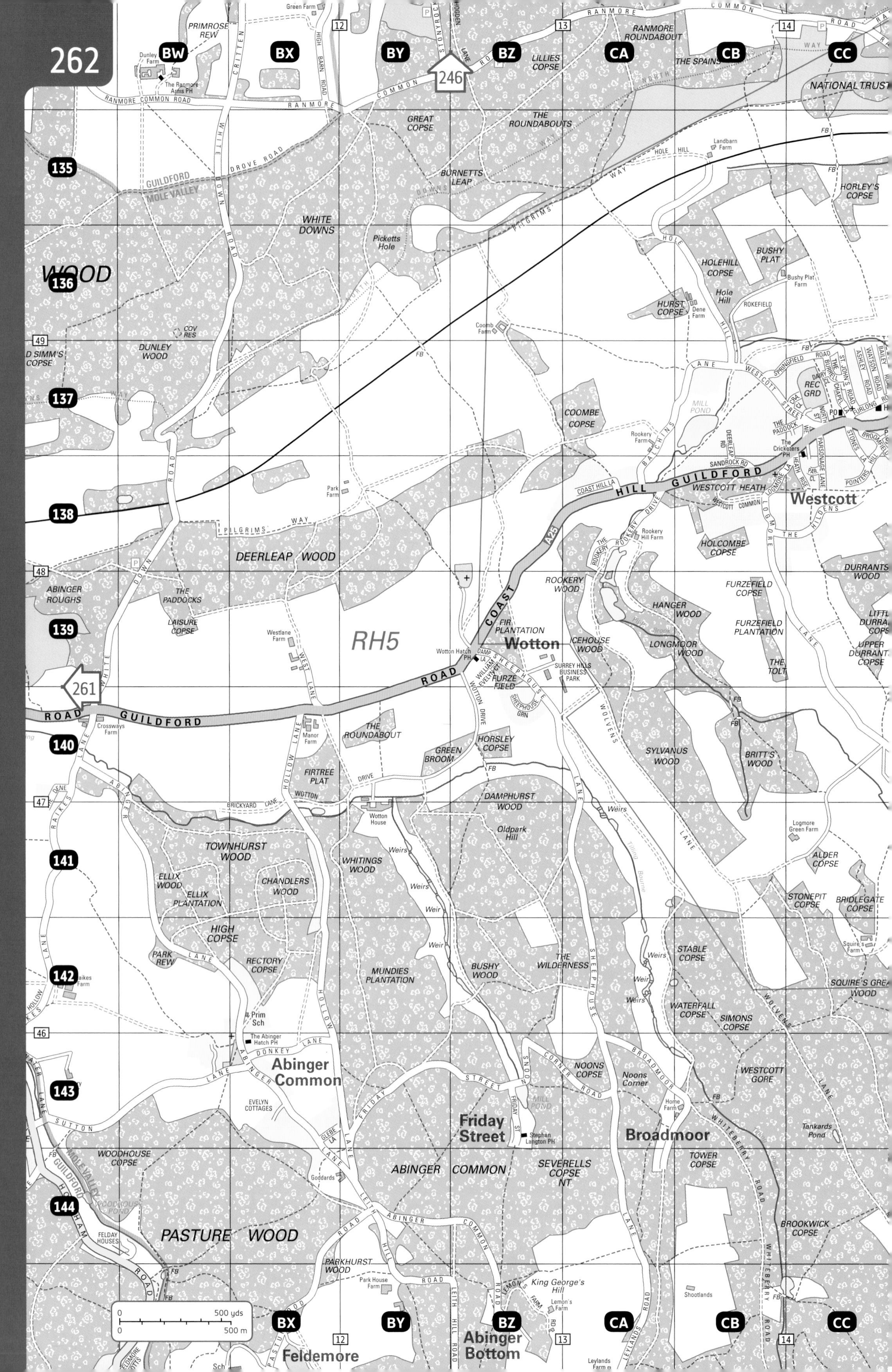

BW
BX
BY
BZ
CA
CB
CC
12
13
14
246
261
Green Farm
PRIMROSE REW
Dunley Farm
The Ranmore Arms PH
RANMORE COMMON ROAD
RANMORE COMMON
CRITTEN
HIGH BARN ROAD
STONYROCK
HOGDEN LANE
LILLIES COPSE
RANMORE ROUNDABOUT
THE SPAINS
NATIONAL TRUST
NORTH
WAY
GREAT COPSE
THE ROUNDABOUTS
Landbarn Farm
HOLE HILL
FB
135
136
137
138
139
140
141
142
143
144
47
46
48
49
GUILDFORD
MOLE VALLEY
DROVE ROAD
WHITE DOWN ROAD
BURNETTS LEAP
DOWNS
WHITE DOWNS
PILGRIMS WAY
Picketts Hole
HORLEY'S COPSE
BUSHY PLAT
Bushy Plat Farm
HOLEHILL COPSE
Hole Hill
ROKEFIELD
HURST COPSE
Dene Farm
WOOD
COV RES
DUNLEY WOOD
D SIMM'S COPSE
Coomb Farm
Westcott
SPRINGFIELD ROAD
WESTCOTT STREET
REC GRD
MILL POND
COOMBE COPSE
Rookery Farm
BALCHINS
DEERLEAP RD
THE PADDOCK
The Cricketers PH
SANDROCK RD
PARSONAGE LANE
HEATH RISE
LOGMORE LA
POINTERS
STONES LA
BROOMFIELD
COAST HILL LA
HILL GUILDFORD
WESTCOTT HEATH
WESTCOTT COMMON
HILDENS
Park Farm
PILGRIMS WAY
DEERLEAP WOOD
ABINGER ROUGHS
THE PADDOCKS
LAISURE COPSE
Rookery Hill Farm
THE ROOKERY
ROOKERY DRIVE
HOLCOMBE COPSE
DURRANTS WOOD
A25
COAST
ROOKERY WOOD
FURZEFIELD COPSE
HANGER WOOD
FURZEFIELD PLANTATION
FIR PLANTATION
Wotton
ICEHOUSE WOOD
LONGMOOR WOOD
THE TOLT
UPPER DURRANT COPSE
Westlane Farm
WEST LANE
RH5
Wotton Hatch PH
DAMP LA
WILLIAM EVELYN CT
SHEEPHOUSE
SURREY HILLS BUSINESS PARK
FURZE FIELD
SHEEPHOUSE GRN
ROAD
GUILDFORD
Crossways Farm
Manor Farm
THE ROUNDABOUT
WOTTON DRIVE
HORSLEY COPSE
GREEN BROOM
WOLVENS
SYLVANUS WOOD
BRITT'S WOOD
FIRTREE PLAT
HOLLOW LANE
DRIVE
WOTTON
BRICKYARD LANE
ABINGER
RAIKES
DENE
Wotton House
DAMPHURST WOOD
Oldpark Hill
Weirs
Weir
Tilling Bourne
LANE
Logmore Green Farm
TOWNHURST WOOD
ELLIX WOOD
ELLIX PLANTATION
CHANDLERS WOOD
WHITINGS WOOD
ALDER COPSE
STONEPIT COPSE
BRIDLEGATE COPSE
HIGH COPSE
PARK REW
RECTORY COPSE
MUNDIES PLANTATION
BUSHY WOOD
THE WILDERNESS
STABLE COPSE
Squire's Farm
SQUIRE'S GREAT WOOD
Raikes Farm
HOLLOW
Prim Sch
The Abinger Hatch PH
DONKEY LANE
Abinger Common
WATERFALL COPSE
SIMONS COPSE
NOONS COPSE
Noons Corner
BROADMOOR
CORNER ROAD
WESTCOTT GORE
Home Farm
FRIDAY STREET
EVELYN COTTAGES
SUTTON
WOODHOUSE COPSE
Friday Street
Stephan Langton PH
MILL POND
Broadmoor
WHITEBERRY ROAD
Tankards Pond
GLEBE LA
SEVERELLS COPSE NT
TOWER COPSE
Goddards
ABINGER COMMON
PASTURE WOOD
FELDAY HOUSES
WOODHOUSE POND
HORSHAM ROAD
LEITH HILL
ABINGER COMMON
BROOKWICK COPSE
PARKHURST WOOD
Park House Farm
King George's Hill
Lemon's Farm
LEMONS FARM RD
LEITH HILL ROAD
LEYLANDS ROAD
Shootlands
0
500 yds
500 m
Feldemore
Abinger Bottom
Leylands Farm
Sch

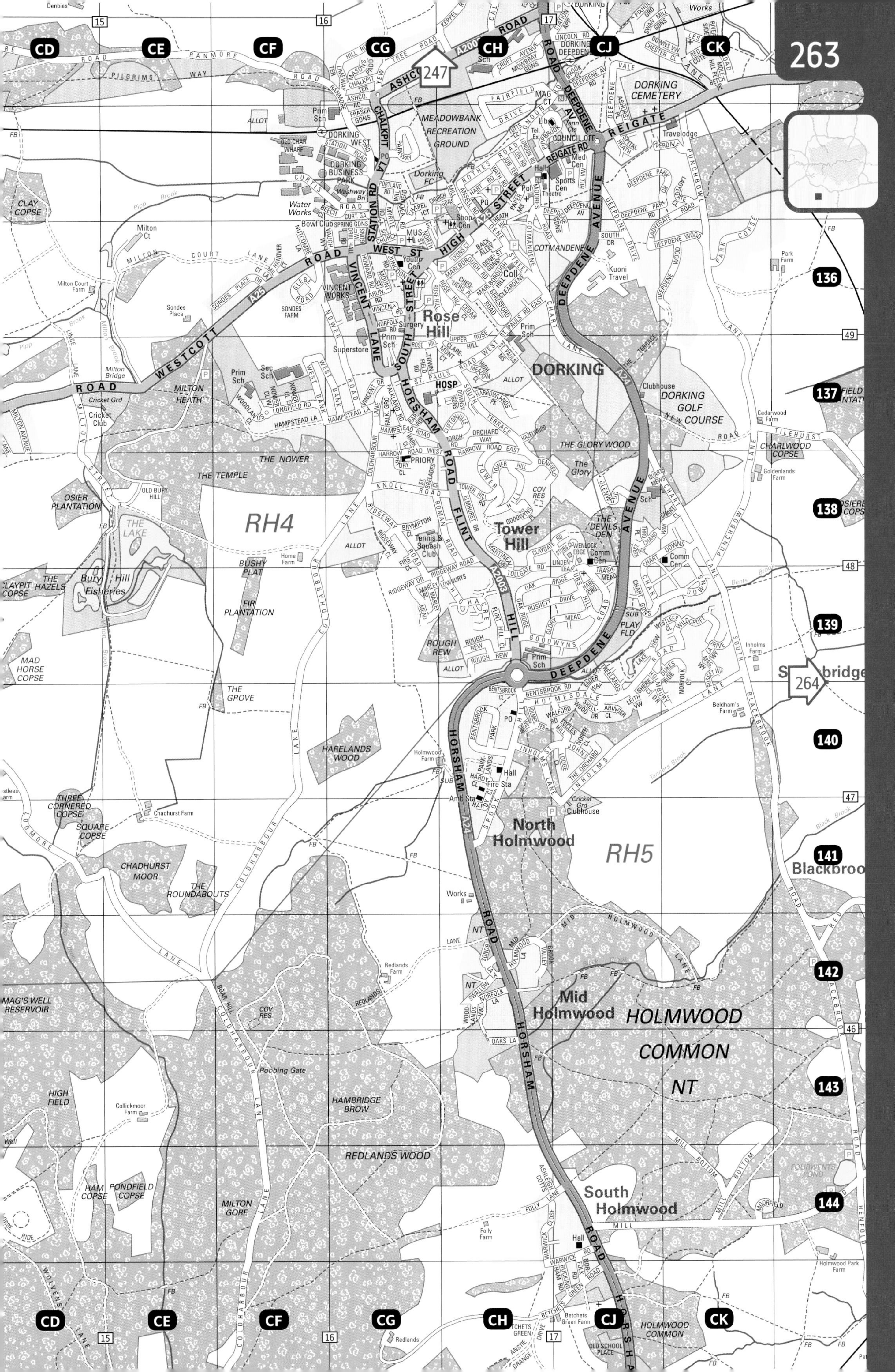
CD
CE
CF
CG
CH
CJ
CK
247
264
DORKING
Rose Hill
Tower Hill
North Holmwood
Mid Holmwood
South Holmwood
RH4
RH5
HOLMWOOD COMMON NT
DORKING CEMETERY
MEADOWBANK RECREATION GROUND
DORKING GOLF COURSE
THE GLORY WOOD
THE NOWER
THE TEMPLE
MILTON HEATH
OSIER PLANTATION
THE LAKE
Bury Hill Fisheries
THE HAZELS
CLAYPIT COPSE
CLAY COPSE
MAD HORSE COPSE
BUSHY PLAT
FIR PLANTATION
THE GROVE
HARELANDS WOOD
ROUGH REW
THREE CORNERED COPSE
SQUARE COPSE
CHADHURST MOOR
THE ROUNDABOUTS
MAG'S WELL RESERVOIR
HIGH FIELD
HAM COPSE
PONDFIELD COPSE
MILTON GORE
HAMBRIDGE BROW
REDLANDS WOOD
Robbing Gate
CHARLWOOD COPSE
WESTCOTT ROAD
RANMORE ROAD
PILGRIMS WAY
REIGATE ROAD
DEEPDENE AVENUE
HIGH STREET
WEST ST
STATION RD
VINCENT LANE
SOUTH STREET
HORSHAM ROAD
FLINT HILL
COLDHARBOUR LANE
PUNCHBOWL LANE
BLACKBROOK ROAD
MILL ROAD
Blackbroo
136
137
138
139
140
141
142
143
144
15
16
17
46
47
48
49

Betchworth
Brockham
Strood Green
Stonebridge
Blackbrook
Bunce Common
BETCHWORTH PARK GOLF COURSE
BETCHWORTH PARK
HIGHRIDGE WOOD
SCAMMELLS GROVE
RH3
RH4
RH5
248
263

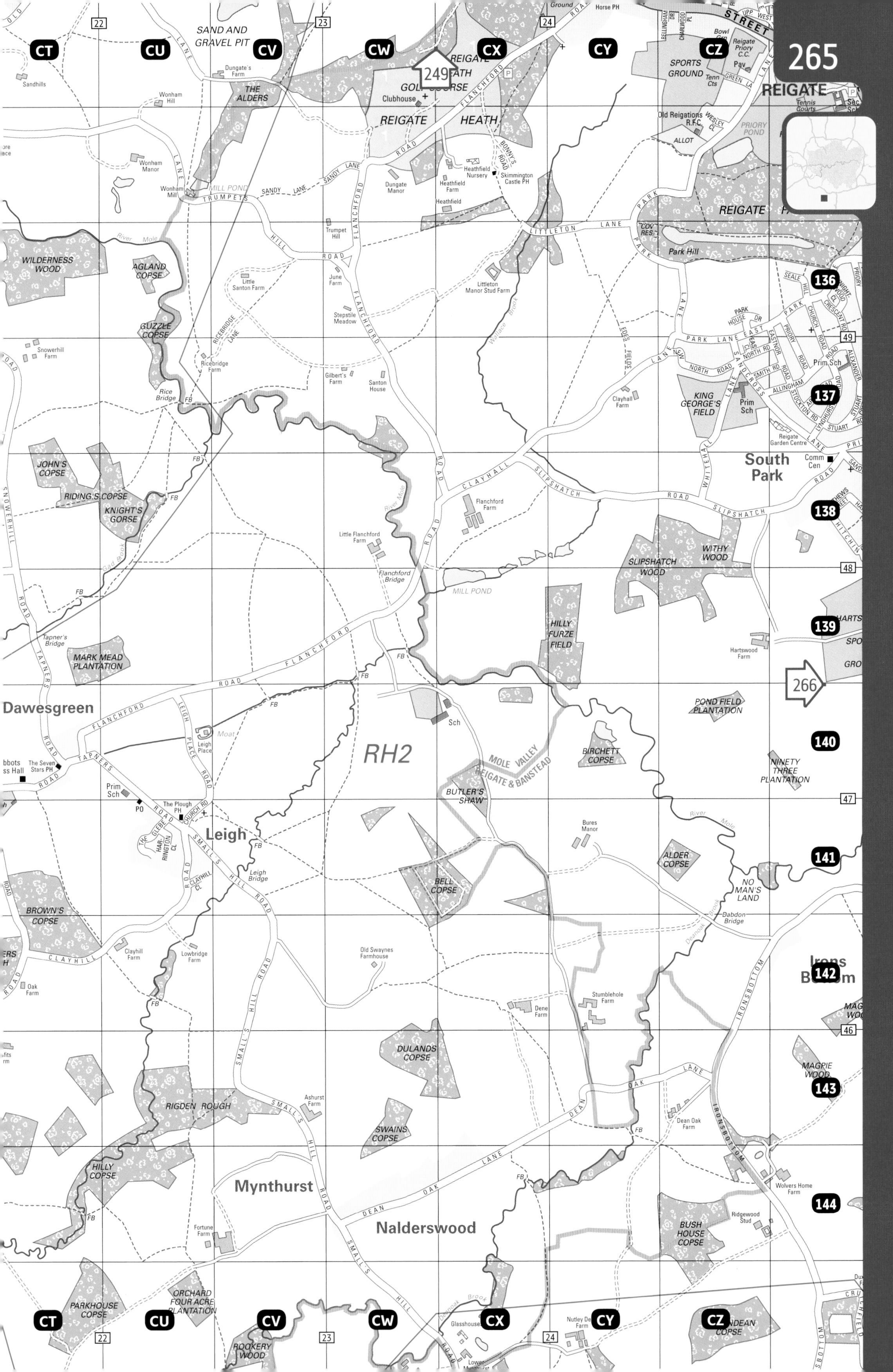
REIGATE
South Park
Dawesgreen
Leigh
Mynthurst
Nalderswood
RH2
REIGATE HEATH
REIGATE HEATH GOLF COURSE
WILDERNESS WOOD
AGLAND COPSE
GUZZLE COPSE
JOHN'S COPSE
RIDING'S COPSE
KNIGHT'S GORSE
MARK MEAD PLANTATION
BROWN'S COPSE
SLIPSHATCH WOOD
WITHY WOOD
HILLY FURZE FIELD
POND FIELD PLANTATION
BIRCHETT COPSE
NINETY THREE PLANTATION
BUTLER'S SHAW
BELL COPSE
ALDER COPSE
DULANDS COPSE
SWAINS COPSE
RIGDEN ROUGH
HILLY COPSE
BUSH HOUSE COPSE
PARKHOUSE COPSE
ORCHARD FOUR ACRE PLANTATION
ROOKERY WOOD
KING GEORGE'S FIELD
MAGPIE WOOD
SAND AND GRAVEL PIT
THE ALDERS
River Mole
MILL POND
FLANCHFORD ROAD
CLAYHALL LANE
SLIPSHATCH ROAD
LITTLETON LANE
DEAN OAK LANE
SMALL'S HILL ROAD
TAPNERS ROAD
IRONSBOTTOM
MOLE VALLEY
REIGATE & BANSTEAD
249
266
136
137
138
139
140
141
142
143
144

REIGATE
REDHILL
Earlswood
Mead Vale
Woodhatch
South Park
Doversgreen
Sidlow
Irons Bottom
Salfords
RH2
RH6
250
265
268
DA
DB
DC
DD
DE
DF
DG
135
136
137
138
139
140
141
142
143
144
49
48
47
46
26
27
28
REIGATE PARK
PRIORY PARK
PRIORY POND
REIGATE CEMETERY
SPORTS GROUND
REDHILL COMMON
EARLSWOOD COMMON
REDHILL AND REIGATE GOLF COURSE
EARLSWOOD LAKES
EARLSWOOD SEWAGE WORKS
EAST SURREY HOSPITAL
FELLAND COPSE
PETRIDGEWOOD COMMON
HOME GROVE
BENTING WOOD
HOLLOW SHAW
HARTSWOOD SPORTS GROUND
WITHY WOOD
KILN FIELD PLANTATION
TWELVE ACRE PLANTATION
NINETY THREE PLANTATION
POND FARM PLANTATION
TURNER'S SHAW
NO MAN'S LAND
MAGPIE WOOD
FONTIGARRY FARM BUSINESS PARK
SAXLEY HILL
BUSH HOUSE COPSE
COLLENDEAN COPSE
BIRCHFIELD COPSE
KING GEORGE'S FIELD
HIGH STREET
CHURCH STREET
BELL STREET
REIGATE ROAD
BLACKBOROUGH ROAD
COCKSHOT HILL
WOODHATCH ROAD
DOVERS GREEN ROAD
BRIGHTON ROAD
HORLEY ROAD
THE CUTTING
LONESOME LANE
IRONSBOTTOM
KINNERSLEY MANOR
LODGE LANE
MEATH GREEN LANE
DUXHURST LANE
BONEHURST ROAD
PEAR TREE HILL
A25
A23
A217
A2044
B2034
River Mole
Earlswood Brook
Salfords Stream
Burstow Stream
Dovers Farm
Hartswood Farm
Sidlow Farm
Sidlow Bridge
Riverside Meadow Farm
White Owl Farm
Lonesome Farm
Kinnersley Manor
Kinnersley Manor Farm
New Riverunook Farm
Lower Duxhurst Farm
Horseshoe Farm Stables
Wick Farm
Ladyland Farm
Wolvers Home Farm
Ridgewood Stud
Duxhurst Farm
Dean Oak Farm
Brookside Farm
Maple Manor
Burnt Oak Farm
New Pond Farm
Glasshouse
Premier Inn
Salfords Bridge
Cheswick Farm
Moat Farm
Little Orchard Farm
Meath Green Farm
Cambridge Hotel
Bonehurst Bridge
Dabdon Bridge
0 500 yds
0 500 m

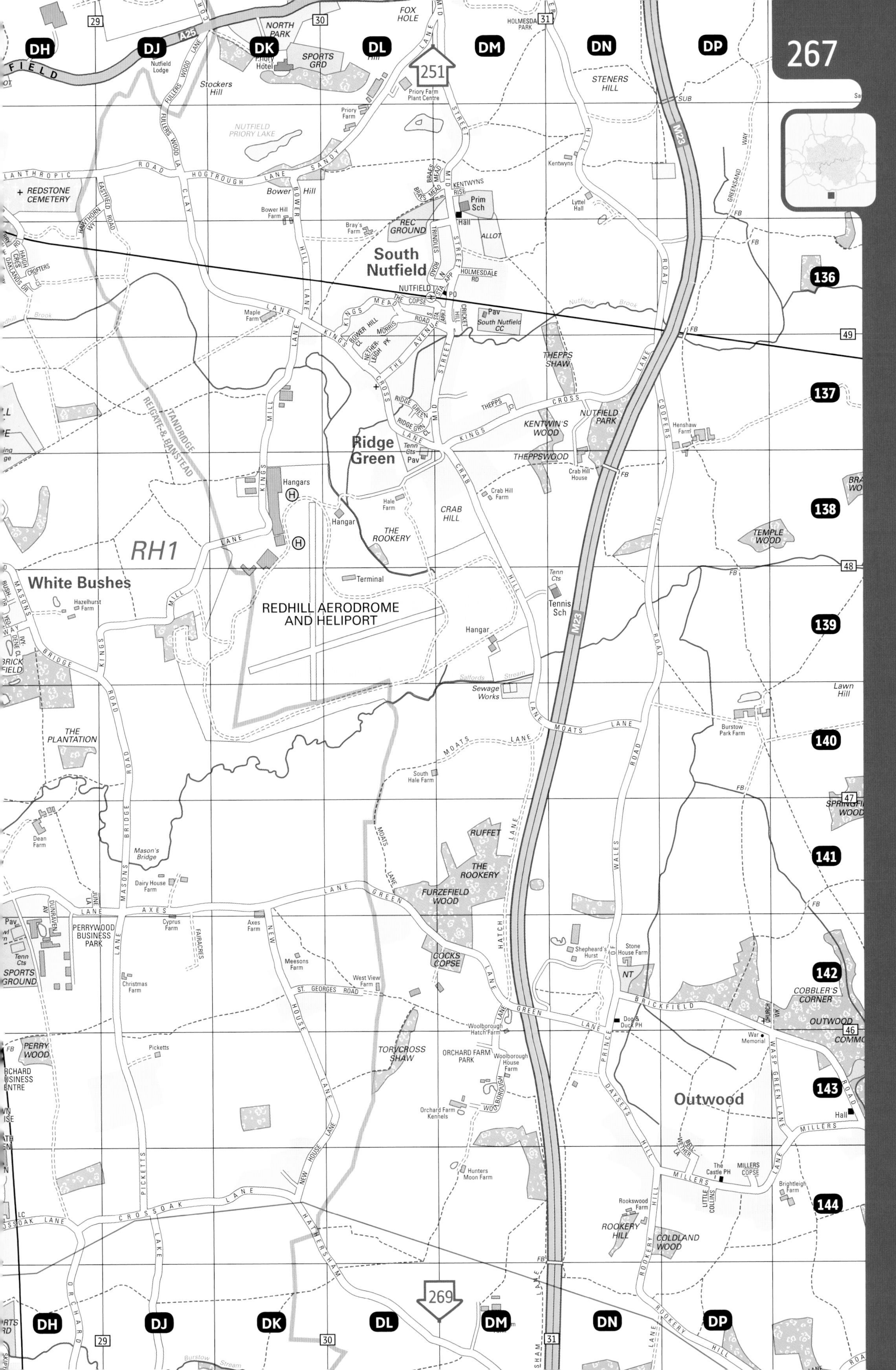
South Nutfield
Ridge Green
White Bushes
Outwood
REDHILL AERODROME AND HELIPORT
RH1
M23
A25
NORTH PARK
SPORTS GRD
Priory Hotel
Nutfield Lodge
Stockers Hill
NUTFIELD PRIORY LAKE
Priory Farm Plant Centre
Priory Farm
FOX HOLE
HOLMESDALE PARK
STENERS HILL
Kentwyns
Lyttel Hall
REDSTONE CEMETERY
Bower Hill
Bower Hill Farm
Bray's Farm
REC GROUND
Prim Sch
Hall
ALLOT
NUTFIELD
PO
Pav
South Nutfield CC
Maple Farm
THEPPS SHAW
KENTWIN'S WOOD
NUTFIELD PARK
THEPPSWOOD
Crab Hill House
Crab Hill Farm
CRAB HILL
Henshaw Farm
TEMPLE WOOD
Hangars
Hangar
Hale Farm
THE ROOKERY
Terminal
Tenn Cts
Tennis Sch
Hazelhurst Farm
THE PLANTATION
Sewage Works
Burstow Park Farm
Lawn Hill
South Hale Farm
Dean Farm
Mason's Bridge
RUFFET
THE ROOKERY
FURZEFIELD WOOD
COCKS COPSE
Dairy House Farm
Cyprus Farm
Axes Farm
PERRYWOOD BUSINESS PARK
SPORTS GROUND
Christmas Farm
Meesons Farm
West View Farm
Shepheard's Hurst
Stone House Farm
NT
Dog & Duck PH
War Memorial
COBBLER'S CORNER
OUTWOOD COMMON
PERRY WOOD
Picketts
TORYCROSS SHAW
ORCHARD FARM PARK
Woolborough Hatch Farm
Woolborough House Farm
Orchard Farm Kennels
Hunters Moon Farm
The Castle PH
MILLERS COPSE
Brightleigh Farm
Rookswood Farm
ROOKERY HILL
COLDLAND WOOD
Hall
DH DJ DK DL DM DN DP
29 30 31
136 137 138 139 140 141 142 143 144
49 48 47 46
251
269

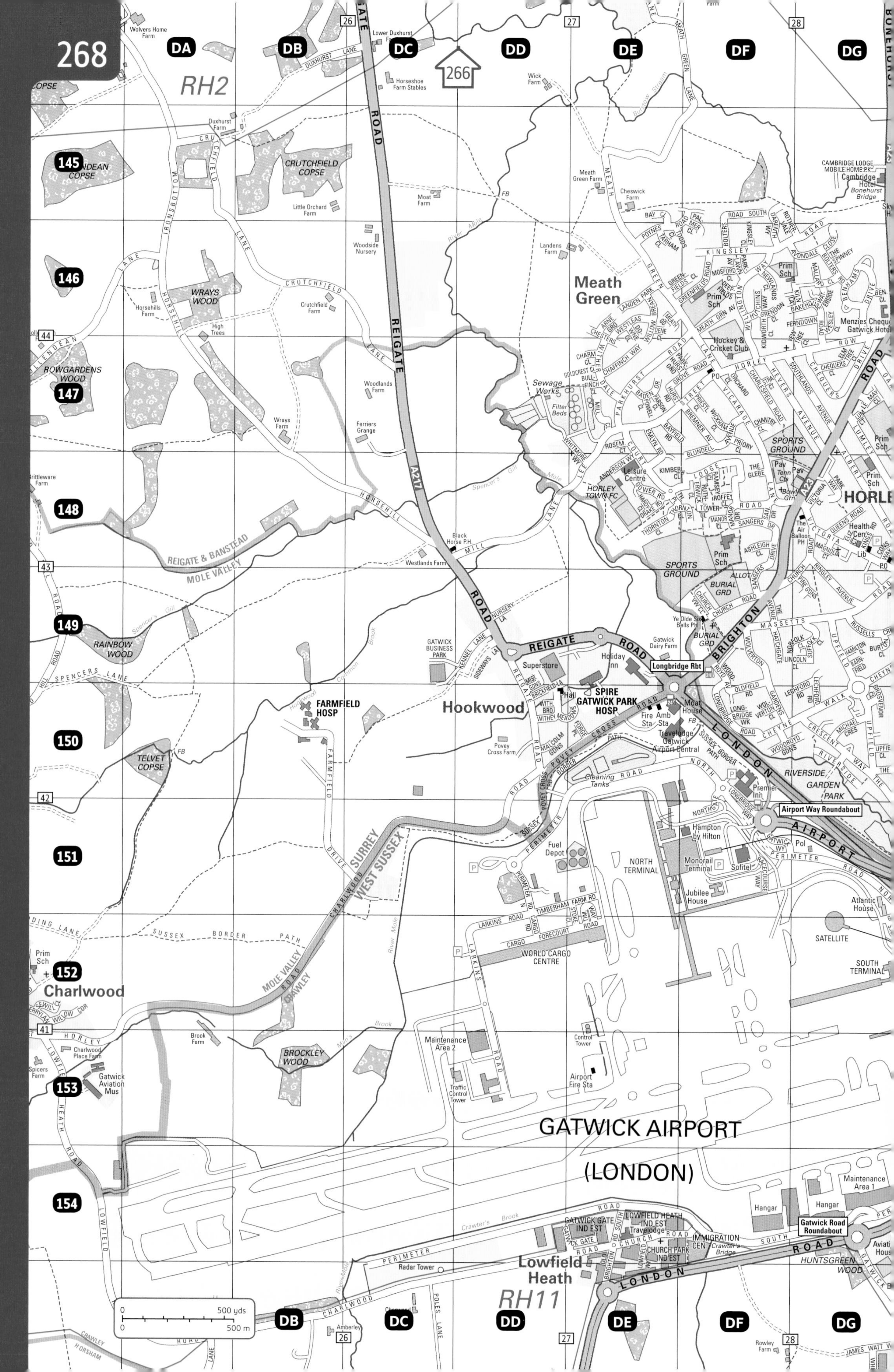
RH2
Meath Green
Hookwood
GATWICK AIRPORT
(LONDON)
Charlwood
Lowfield Heath
RH11
REIGATE ROAD
BRIGHTON ROAD
LONDON ROAD
AIRPORT WAY
Longbridge Rbt
Airport Way Roundabout
Gatwick Road Roundabout
NORTH TERMINAL
SOUTH TERMINAL
WORLD CARGO CENTRE
SPIRE GATWICK PARK HOSP
FARMFIELD HOSP
SURREY
WEST SUSSEX
REIGATE & BANSTEAD
MOLE VALLEY
CRUTCHFIELD COPSE
WRAYS WOOD
ROWGARDENS WOOD
RAINBOW WOOD
TELVET COPSE
BROCKLEY WOOD
HUNTSGREEN WOOD
SPORTS GROUND
BURIAL GRD
RIVERSIDE GARDEN PARK
Sewage Works
Holiday Inn
Superstore
Premier Inn
Hampton by Hilton
Sofitel
Travelodge Gatwick Airport Central
Moat House
Jubilee House
Fuel Depot
Maintenance Area 1
Maintenance Area 2
Control Tower
Airport Fire Sta
Radar Tower
Gatwick Aviation Mus
SATELLITE
266
0 500 yds
0 500 m

DH
DJ
DK
DL
DM
DN
DP
267
RH1
RH6
RH10
146
147
148
149
150
151
152
153
154
29
30
31
44
43
42
41
Hunters Moon Farm
The Castle PH
MILLERS COPSE
Rookswood Farm
ROOKERY HILL
COLDLAND WOOD
Hathersham Farm
THE ROOKERY
COURTOAK GREEN
LONGYARDS SHAW
Greatlake Farm
Burstow Manor
BURSTOW BUSINESS CENTRE
Hollesley Farm
Elec Sta
The Farmhouse PH
Tanyard Farm
BROOK WOOD
Sewage Works
Smallfield Grid Sub Station
ALDER BED
LOST SEVENS
LANGSHOTT WOOD
OAK BED
WEATHERHILL COMMON
GATWICK METRO CENTRE
Gas Holder Sta
Prim Sch
Swim Pool
Sec Sch
Harrowsley Green Farm
Wilgers Farm
Farney Glen Farm
Haroldslea Poultry Farm
Site of Thunderfield Castle
Lower Broadbridge Farm
Broadmead Farm
BRIDGEHAM WOOD
Smallfield
SPORTS GRD
The Plough PH
PLAYING FIE
Green Farm
Hall
THE ROUGHS
THE PLANTATION
REIGATE & BANSTEAD
TANDRIDGE
Flightpath Farm
Broadbridge Stables
COLLINS WOOD
BELLHATCH WOOD
Junction 9a
Junction 9
Airport Way Roundabout East
SUSSEX BORDER PATH
M23
Monorail Terminal
First Point
Hilton
Schlumberger House
BUS/COACH STA
GATWICK AIRPORT
BRIDGES WOOD
WEST SUSSEX
SURREY
Broadfield Farm
Fern Court Farm
Gatwick House
Mushroom Farm
Burstow
EASTLANDS SHAW
Redeham Hall
Keepers Corner
Rivington Farm
Teizers Farm
Burstow Hall
Burstow Nurseries
The Shipley Bridge Inn PH
Shipley Bridge
KILN HEATH
HORLEYLAND WOOD
Filter Beds
Sludge Lagoons
Sewage Works
UPPER PICKETT'S
ALLEN'S WOOD
Courtlands
Riding School
Burstow Park Farm
Burstow Park
New House Farm
The Parsons Pig PH
Oldlands Farm
The Greyhound PH
BLACKCORNER WOOD
Hollybush Farm
KING GEORGE'S FIELD
Pav
GATWICK INTERNATIONAL DISTRIBUTION CENTRE

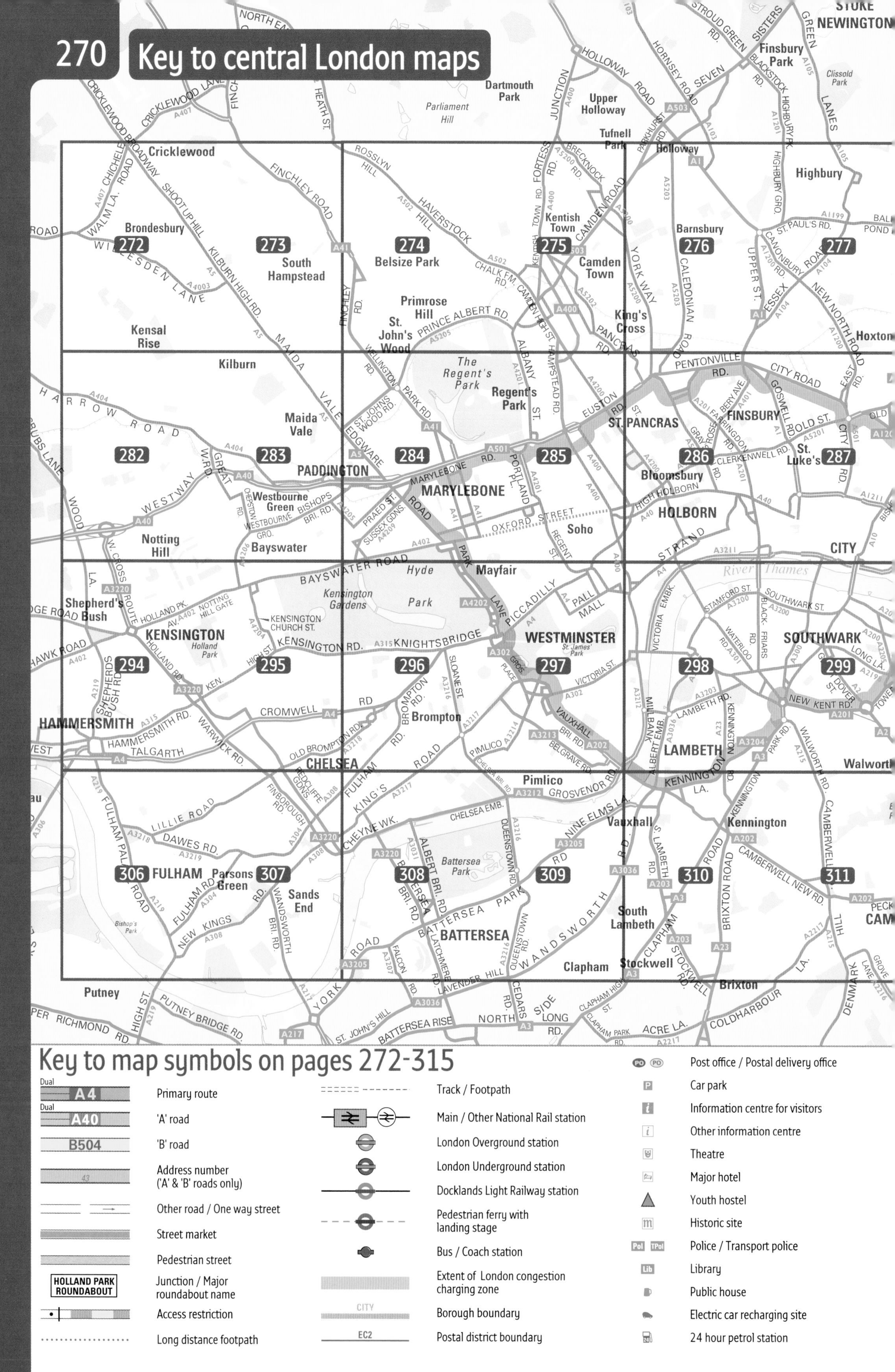
272
273
274
275
276
277
282
283
284
285
286
287
294
295
296
297
298
299
306
307
308
309
310
311
Key to map symbols on pages 272-315
Dual A4
Primary route
Dual A40
'A' road
B504
'B' road
Address number ('A' & 'B' roads only)
Other road / One way street
Street market
Pedestrian street
HOLLAND PARK ROUNDABOUT
Junction / Major roundabout name
Access restriction
Long distance footpath
Track / Footpath
Main / Other National Rail station
London Overground station
London Underground station
Docklands Light Railway station
Pedestrian ferry with landing stage
Bus / Coach station
Extent of London congestion charging zone
CITY
Borough boundary
EC2
Postal district boundary
Post office / Postal delivery office
Car park
Information centre for visitors
Other information centre
Theatre
Major hotel
Youth hostel
Historic site
Police / Transport police
Library
Public house
Electric car recharging site
24 hour petrol station

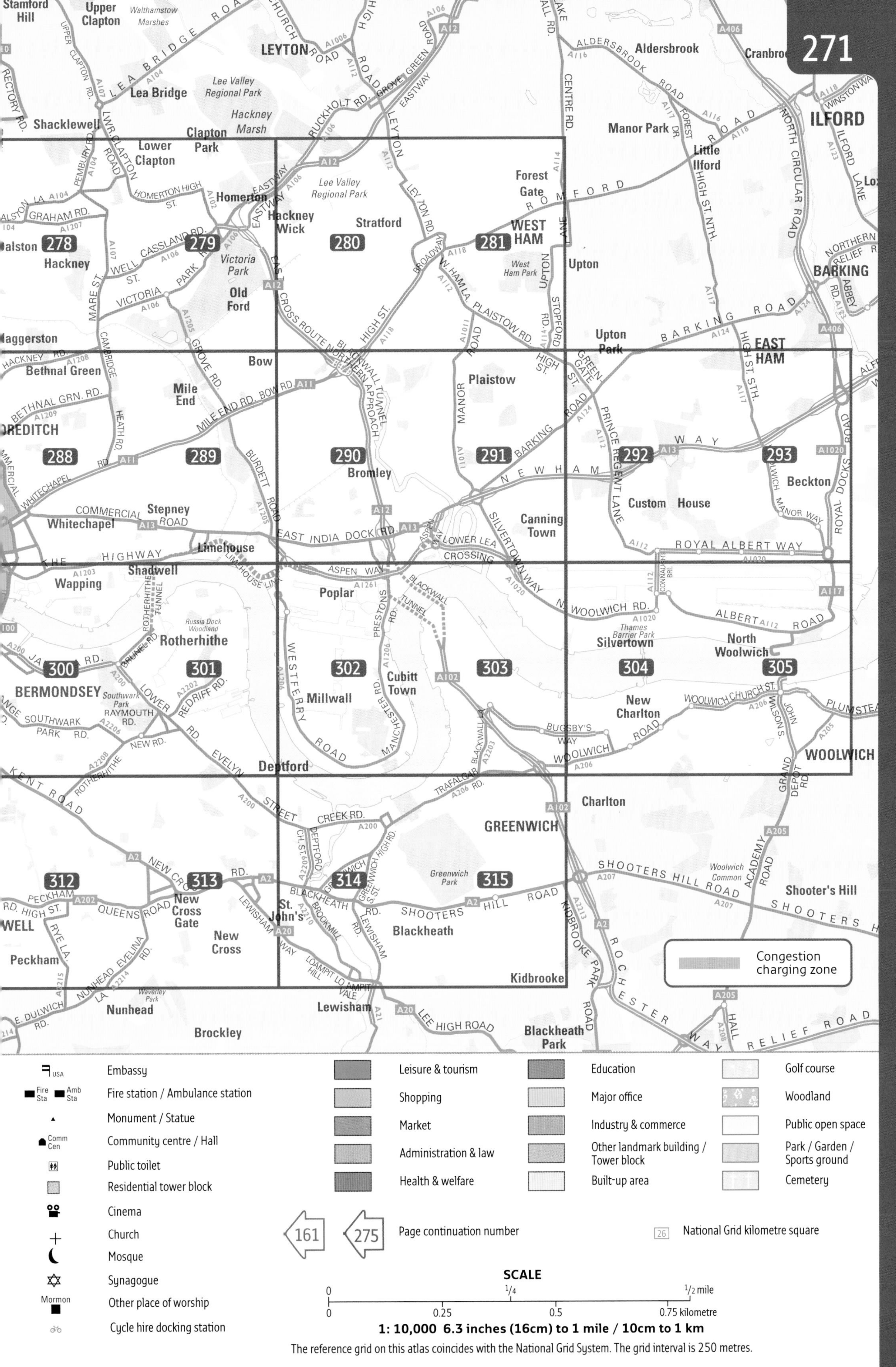
Stamford Hill
Upper Clapton
Walthamstow Marshes
LEYTON
Aldersbrook
Cranbrook
ILFORD
Lea Bridge
Lee Valley Regional Park
Hackney Marsh
Shacklewell
Lower Clapton
Clapton Park
Manor Park
Little Ilford
Forest Gate
Homerton
Hackney Wick
Lee Valley Regional Park
Stratford
WEST HAM
West Ham Park
Upton
BARKING
Dalston
Hackney
Victoria Park
Old Ford
Haggerston
Upton Park
EAST HAM
Bethnal Green
Bow
Mile End
Plaistow
SHOREDITCH
Bromley
Beckton
Custom House
Whitechapel
Stepney
Canning Town
Limehouse
Wapping
Shadwell
Poplar
Silvertown
North Woolwich
Thames Barrier Park
Russia Dock Woodland
Rotherhithe
BERMONDSEY
Southwark Park
Millwall
Cubitt Town
New Charlton
WOOLWICH
Deptford
Charlton
GREENWICH
Greenwich Park
Woolwich Common
Shooter's Hill
Peckham
New Cross Gate
New Cross
St. John's
Blackheath
Kidbrooke
Nunhead
Waverley Park
Lewisham
Brockley
Blackheath Park
278
279
280
281
288
289
290
291
292
293
300
301
302
303
304
305
312
313
314
315
Congestion charging zone
Embassy
Fire station / Ambulance station
Monument / Statue
Community centre / Hall
Public toilet
Residential tower block
Cinema
Church
Mosque
Synagogue
Other place of worship
Cycle hire docking station
Leisure & tourism
Shopping
Market
Administration & law
Health & welfare
Education
Major office
Industry & commerce
Other landmark building / Tower block
Built-up area
Golf course
Woodland
Public open space
Park / Garden / Sports ground
Cemetery
161
275
Page continuation number
26
National Grid kilometre square
SCALE
0
1/4
1/2 mile
0
0.25
0.5
0.75 kilometre
1: 10,000 6.3 inches (16cm) to 1 mile / 10cm to 1 km
The reference grid on this atlas coincides with the National Grid System. The grid interval is 250 metres.

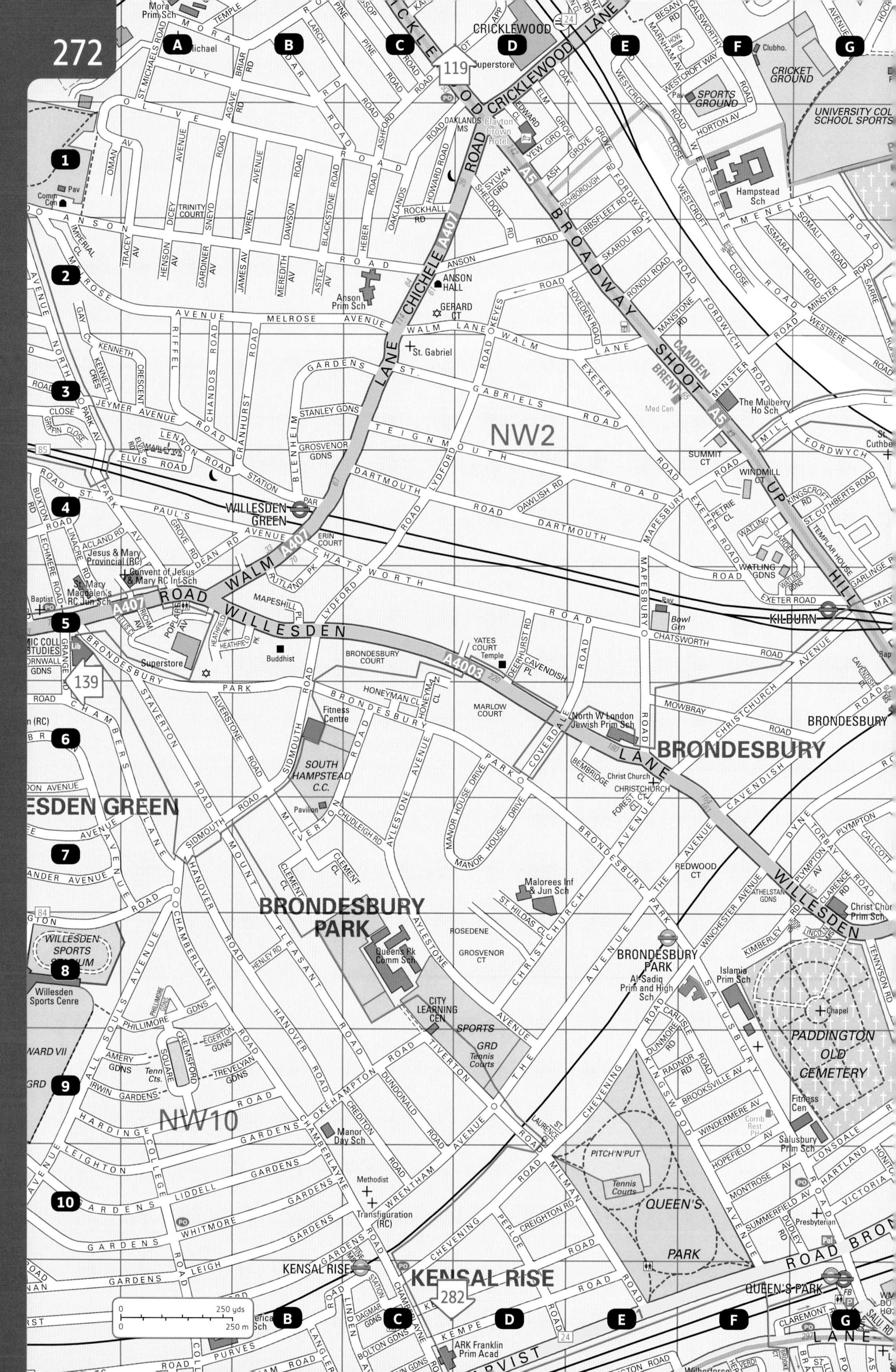

A
B
C
D
E
F
G
1
2
3
4
5
6
7
8
9
10
CRICKLEWOOD
CRICKLEWOOD LANE
CRICKLEWOOD BROADWAY
119
Superstore
CRICKET GROUND
SPORTS GROUND
UNIVERSITY COL SCHOOL SPORTS
Hampstead Sch
Clayton Crown Hotel
OAKLANDS MS
ANSON HALL
GERARD CT
Anson Prim Sch
St. Gabriel
NW2
CAMDEN
BRENT
Med Cen
The Mulberry Ho Sch
SUMMIT CT
WINDMILL CT
WATLING GDNS
KILBURN
EXETER ROAD
Bowl Grn
WILLESDEN GREEN
ERIN COURT
Jesus & Mary Provincial (RC)
Convent of Jesus & Mary RC Inf Sch
St. Mary Magdalen's RC Jun Sch
Baptist
Lib
139
Superstore
Buddhist
YATES COURT
Temple
BRONDESBURY COURT
MARLOW COURT
North W London Jewish Prim Sch
BRONDESBURY
Christ Church
CHRISTCHURCH CT
Fitness Centre
SOUTH HAMPSTEAD C.C.
Pavilion
ESDEN GREEN
WILLESDEN SPORTS STADIUM
Willesden Sports Centre
BRONDESBURY PARK
Queens Pk Comm Sch
CITY LEARNING CEN
SPORTS GRD
Tennis Courts
Malorees Inf & Jun Sch
ROSEDENE
GROSVENOR CT
REDWOOD CT
BRONDESBURY PARK
Al-Sadiq Prim and High Sch
Islamia Prim Sch
Chapel
PADDINGTON OLD CEMETERY
Christ Church Prim Sch
Fitness Cen
Salusbury Prim Sch
Corrib Rest PH
Presbyterian
NW10
Manor Day Sch
Methodist
Transfiguration (RC)
PITCH'N'PUT
Tennis Courts
QUEEN'S PARK
KENSAL RISE
282
QUEEN'S PARK
ARK Franklin Prim Acad
0 250 yds
0 250 m
CHICHELE ROAD
A407
A5
SHOOT UP HILL
WALM LANE
WILLESDEN LANE
A4003
MAPESBURY ROAD
CHATSWORTH ROAD
DARTMOUTH ROAD
TEIGNMOUTH ROAD
ANSON ROAD
MELROSE AVENUE
OLIVE ROAD
CHAMBERLAYNE ROAD
BRONDESBURY PARK
SALUSBURY ROAD
CHEVENING ROAD
HARDINGE ROAD
LEIGHTON GARDENS
LIDDELL GARDENS
WHITMORE GARDENS
CHRISTCHURCH AVENUE
AYLESTONE AVENUE
MANOR HOUSE DRIVE
SIDMOUTH ROAD
HANOVER ROAD
MOUNT PLEASANT ROAD
TIVERTON ROAD
WRENTHAM AVENUE
KEMPE ROAD
HARVIST

H
J
K
L
M
N
P
120
1
2
3
4
5
6
7
8
9
10
274
283
HAMPSTEAD
NW3
NW6
NW8
WEST HAMPSTEAD
SOUTH HAMPSTEAD
KILBURN
FINCHLEY ROAD
WEST END LANE
FORTUNE GREEN
FORTUNE GRN RD
FROGNAL
FITZJOHN'S AV
HEATH ST
HAMPSTEAD HIGH
FINCHLEY ROAD & FROGNAL
WEST HAMPSTEAD (THAMESLINK)
WEST HAMPSTEAD
FINCHLEY ROAD
SOUTH HAMPSTEAD
KILBURN HIGH ROAD
KILBURN PARK
KILBURN HIGH ROAD
BELSIZE ROAD
ABBEY ROAD
MAIDA VALE
CARLTON VALE
BRONDESBURY VILLAS
MAYGROVE PEACE PARK
KILBURN GRANGE PARK
HAMPSTEAD C.C.
CAMDEN ARTS CEN
FREUD MUSEUM
University Coll Sch
EVERYMAN
VUE Superstore
O2 Centre
Superstore
ABBEY ROAD ESTATE
MORTIMER ESTATE
WEBHEATH ESTATE
CAMDEN
WESTMINSTER
BOUNDARY ROAD
HILGROVE ROAD
ADELAIDE ROAD
COLLEGE CRES
George Eliot Inf & Jun Schs
Quintin Kynaston Sch
The American Sch in London
St. Augustine's HighSch
St. Mary's Kilburn C of E Prim Sch
EUROPEAN SCH OF MANAGEMENT
Emmanuel C of E Prim Sch
Beckford Prim Sch
Kingsgate Prim Sch
Charteris Comm Sports Cen
HOSP OF ST JOHN & ST. ELIZA

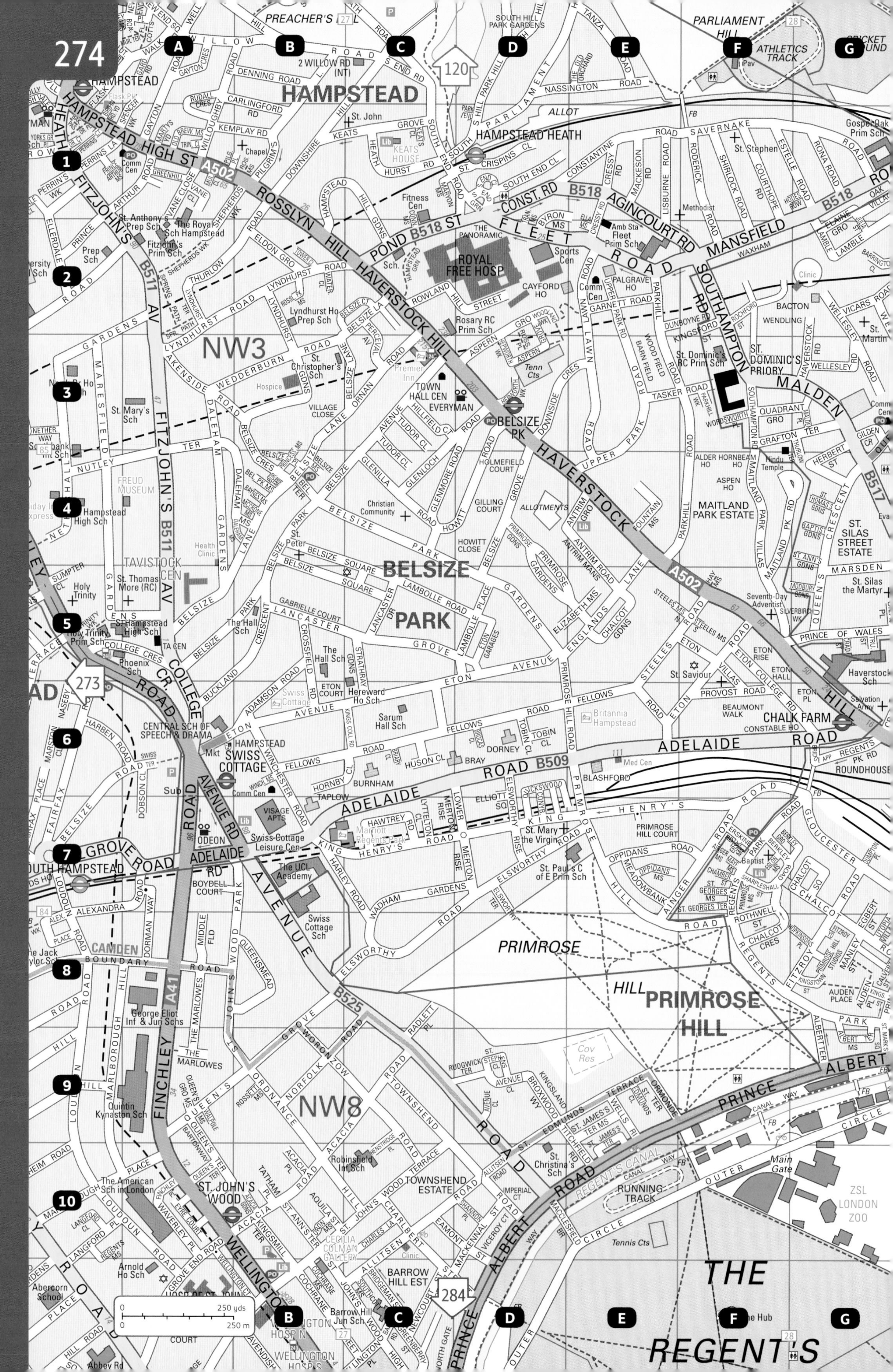
A
B
C
D
E
F
G
1
2
3
4
5
6
7
8
9
10
PREACHER'S
PARLIAMENT HILL
ATHLETICS TRACK
CRICKET GROUND
SOUTH HILL PARK GARDENS
HAMPSTEAD
HAMPSTEAD
2 WILLOW RD (NT)
DENNING ROAD
CARLINGFORD RD
KEMPLAY RD
NASSINGTON ROAD
PARLIAMENT
ALLOT
HAMPSTEAD HEATH
HAMPSTEAD HIGH ST
A502
ROSSLYN HILL
HAVERSTOCK HILL
St. John
KEATS GROVE
KEATS HOUSE
DOWNSHIRE
PILGRIM'S
SOUTH END ROAD
SOUTH END CL
ST. CRISPINS CL
CONSTANTINE
SAVERNAKE ROAD
St. Stephen
Gospel Oak Prim Sch
AGINCOURT RD
B518
MANSFIELD
FLEET ROAD
Fleet Prim Sch
Sports Cen
ROYAL FREE HOSP
POND ST
THE PANORAMIC
FITZJOHN'S AV
B511
St. Anthony's Prep Sch
The Royal Sch Hampstead
Fitzjohn's Prim Sch
Prep Sch
ELLERDALE
THURLOW
LYNDHURST ROAD
LYNDHURST GDNS
Lyndhurst Ho Prep Sch
ROWLAND HILL STREET
Rosary RC Prim Sch
CAYFORD HO
Comm Cen
GARNETT ROAD
PALGRAVE HO
PARKHILL
SOUTHAMPTON RD
St. Dominic's RC Prim Sch
ST. DOMINIC'S PRIORY
MALDEN
WELLESLEY
St. Martin
NW3
WEDDERBURN ROAD
St. Christopher's Sch
Hospice
VILLAGE CLOSE
Premier Inn
TOWN HALL CEN
EVERYMAN
BELSIZE PK
HAVERSTOCK
St. Mary's Sch
MARESFIELD
NUTLEY TER
FREUD MUSEUM
Hampstead High Sch
TAVISTOCK CEN
St. Thomas More (RC)
Holy Trinity
Health Clinic
Christian Community
HOLMEFIELD COURT
GILLING COURT
HOWITT CLOSE
ALLOTMENTS
PRIMROSE GARDENS
ANTRIM ROAD
FOUNTAIN MS
MAITLAND PARK ESTATE
ALDER HO
HORNBEAM HO
ASPEN HO
Hindu Temple
ST. SILAS STREET ESTATE
St. Silas the Martyr
Seventh-Day Adventist
BELSIZE
PARK
BELSIZE SQUARE
St. Peter
LAMBOLLE ROAD
GABRIELLE COURT
LANCASTER GROVE
The Hall Sch
ETON AVENUE
St. Saviour
ETON RISE
ETON HALL
Haverstock Sch
Salvation Army
CHALK FARM
ADELAIDE ROAD
ROUNDHOUSE
PRINCE OF WALES RD
St. Hampstead High Sch
Holy Trinity Prim Sch
Phoenix Sch
COLLEGE CRES
TA CEN
273
CENTRAL SCH OF SPEECH & DRAMA
HAMPSTEAD
SWISS COTTAGE
Mkt
Comm Cen
VISAGE APTS
Sarum Hall Sch
Hereward Ho Sch
ETON COURT
Swiss Cottage
FELLOWS ROAD
DORNEY
TOBIN CL
BRAY
BURNHAM
TAPLOW
HUSON CL
Britannia Hampstead
BLASHFORD
Med Cen
ROAD B509
ELLIOTT SQ
St. Mary the Virgin
PRIMROSE HILL COURT
OPPIDANS ROAD
MEADOWBANK
Baptist
CHALCOT SQ
GLOUCESTER
ODEON
Swiss Cottage Leisure Cen
Marriott Regents Park
KING HENRY'S ROAD
HAWTREY
The UCL Academy
St. Paul's C of E Prim Sch
GROVE ROAD
SOUTH HAMPSTEAD
BOYDELL COURT
AVENUE RD
FINCHLEY ROAD
A41
Swiss Cottage Sch
WADHAM GARDENS
ELSWORTHY ROAD
PRIMROSE
HILL
PRIMROSE HILL
ALEXANDRA
CAMDEN
BOUNDARY ROAD
George Eliot Inf & Jun Schs
THE MARLOWES
QUEENSMEAD
B525
RADLETT PL
Cov Res
NW8
Quintin Kynaston Sch
NORFOLK
ORDNANCE
TOWNSHEND ROAD
ACACIA
Robinsfield Inf Sch
TOWNSHEND ESTATE
ST. JOHN'S WOOD
The American Sch in London
Arnold Ho Sch
Abercorn School
HOSP OF ST. JOHN
WELLINGTON HOSP N
WELLINGTON HOSP S
CECILIA COLMAN GALLERY
Clinic
BARROW HILL EST
Barrow Hill Jun Sch
284
PRINCE ALBERT ROAD
St. Christina's Sch
REGENT'S CANAL
RUNNING TRACK
OUTER CIRCLE
Main Gate
ZSL LONDON ZOO
Tennis Cts
THE REGENT'S
The Hub
250 yds
250 m

TUFNELL PARK
GOSPEL OAK
NW5
N7
KENTISH TOWN
KENTISH TOWN WEST
CAMDEN TOWN
NW1
N1
KING'S CROSS
REGENT'S PARK
H.M.P. HOLLOWAY
HILLDROP ESTATE
BRECKNOCK ROAD ESTATE
AGAR GROVE ESTATE
CLARENCE WAY EST
CANTELOWES GDNS
CAMDEN SQ GDNS
ST. PANCRAS GARDENS
ST. MARTIN'S GARDENS
ST. PANCRAS HOSPITAL
MORNINGTON CRESCENT
CAMDEN ROAD
ST. PANCRAS
PANCRAS SQ
Camden Lock Mkt
Stables Mkt
Tufnell Pk Prim Sch
Holloway School
LONDON MET UNI - Halls of Residence
Camden Sch for Girls
Royal Mail Delivery Off
Carlton Prim Sch
Parcelforce
ROYAL VETERINARY COLL
Gloucester Gate
Cecil Sharp House
JEWISH MUS
REGENT'S PARK BARRACKS
DEPOT
HIGHGATE ROAD
GORDON HO RD
FORTESS ROAD
KENTISH TOWN ROAD
CAMDEN ROAD
BRECKNOCK ROAD
CAMDEN PARK RD
YORK WAY
CAMDEN HIGH ST
CAMDEN ST
ROYAL COLLEGE ST
ST. PANCRAS WAY
PANCRAS ROAD
MIDLAND ROAD
PARKWAY
DELANCEY STREET
CHALK FARM RD
MALDEN CRES
FERDINAND ST
PRINCE OF WALES ROAD
LEIGHTON RD
TORRIANO AV
AGAR GROVE
CROWNDALE RD
EVERSHOLT ST
HAMPSTEAD RD
ALBANY ST
OAKLEY SQ
A400
A5200
A503
A5202
A5205
B518
B512
121
276
285
H
J
K
L
M
N
P
1
2
3
4
5
6
7
8
9
10

HOLLOWAY
LOWER HOLLOWAY
BARNSBURY
ISLINGTON
KING'S CROSS
PENTONVILLE
N7
N1
EMIRATES STADIUM ARSENAL FC
H.M.P. HOLLOWAY
H.M.P. PENTONVILLE
CALEDONIAN PARK
HIGHBURY FIELDS
PARADISE PARK
BARNARD PARK
THORNHILL SQ
BARNSBURY SQ GDN
HOLLOWAY ROAD
CALEDONIAN ROAD
CALEDONIAN ROAD & BARNSBURY
DRAYTON PARK
HIGHBURY & ISLINGTON
ANGEL
NAGS HEAD
CENTRAL ST. MARTINS COLLEGE OF ART AND DESIGN (KING'S CROSS)
BUSINESS DESIGN CEN
KINGS PLACE
REGENT'S CANAL
COPENHAGEN STREET
CAMDEN ROAD
YORK WAY
LIVERPOOL ROAD
UPPER STREET
PENTONVILLE ROAD
TOLLINGTON ROAD
121
275
286
0 250 yds
0 250 m

N16
N5
N1
E8
HIGHBURY
CANONBURY
KINGSLAND
DE BEAUVOIR TOWN
HOXTON
DALSTON KINGSLAND
DALSTON JUNCTION
HAGGERSTON
SHOREDITCH PARK
SHOREDITCH PARK GARDEN
ROSEMARY GDNS
BUTTERFIELD GREEN
ESSEX ROAD
CANONBURY
NEW NORTH ROAD
BALLS POND ROAD
ST. PAUL'S ROAD
KINGSLAND ROAD
STOKE NEWINGTON HIGH ST
SOUTHGATE ROAD
EAGLE WHARF ROAD
REGENT'S CANAL
KINGSLAND BASIN
WENLOCK BASIN
CITY ROAD BASIN
GEFFRYE MUSEUM
122
278
287

A
B
C
D
E
F
G
1
2
3
4
5
6
7
8
9
10
N16
SHACKLEWELL
122
HACKNEY DOWNS
Stormont Ho Spec Sch
Downsview Spec Sch
Mossbourne Comm. Academy
Petchey Academy
CRICKETFIELD ROAD
A104
PEMBURY ROAD
CLAPTON RD
A102 LWR CLAPTON ROAD
LWR CLAPTON RD
DALSTON LANE
A107
AMHURST ROAD
HACKNEY DOWNS
HACKNEY CENTRAL
DALSTON KINGSLAND
Kingsland Shopping Cen
RIDLEY ROAD
DALSTON A104
KINGSLAND HIGH ST
STOKE NEWINGTON RD
A10
DALSTON JUNCTION
GRAHAM ROAD
A1207
HACKNEY
HACKNEY TOWN HALL
HACKNEY EMPIRE
MARE STREET
E8
DALSTON
LONDON FIELDS
LONDON FIELDS
LONDON FIELDS
277
QUEENSBRIDGE ROAD
B108
KINGSLAND ROAD
HAGGERSTON
REGENTS ROW
HAGGERSTON PARK
SPORTS GROUND
BUS DEPOT
Gas Works
CAMBRIDGE HEATH
CAMBRIDGE HEATH ROAD
VICTORIA PARK ROAD
WELL STREET
A106
SOUTH HACKNEY
E2
HACKNEY ROAD
A1208
288
Hackney City Farm
Haggerston Sch
Bridge Academy
Geffrye Museum
WHITMORE ESTATE
N1
BISHOPS WAY
B127
250 yds
250 m
MALMES

H
J
K
L
M
N
P
CLAPTON PARK
123
HACKNEY MARSH
LEE VALLEY REGIONAL PARK
LOWER CLAPTON
E5
Rushmore Prim Sch
Rushmore Inf Sch
St. Jude
Daubeney Prim Sch
Word of God
Kingsmead Prim Sch
KINGSMEAD EST
CLAPTON PARK EST
LANDMARK HEIGHTS
Sports Pav
SKY APARTMENTS
Marshgate Bridge
WICK WOODLAND
HOMERTON UNIVERSITY HOSPITAL
Christchurch
HOMERTON
MABLEY GREEN
HOMERTON HIGH STREET
MARSH HILL
The City Academy
St. Barnabas
BANNISTER HOUSE
NISBET HOUSE
JOHN HOWARD CEN
Berger Prim Sch
St. Luke
St. Dominic's RC Prim Sch
Immaculate Heart (RC)
St. Mary of Eton
TROWBRIDGE ESTATE
Gainsborough Comm Sch
HACKNEY WICK
E9
280
VICTORIA PK IND EST
WELL STREET COMMON
Queens Gate
Bowling Green
St. John of Jerusalem
St. John of Jerusalem C of E Prim Sch
Orchard Prim Sch
St. Mark
OLD FORD
WAVERTON HO
VICTORIA PARK
VICTORIA FOUNTAIN
Bandstand
Gunmakers Gate
Royal Gate East
St. Agnes Gate
PARKSIDE ESTATE
Lauriston Prim Sch
DEER PARK
Crown Gate
HERTFORD UNION CANAL
Three Colt Br
Skew Bridge
LAKEVIEW EST
CHISENHALE GALL
Chisenhale Prim Sch
Methodist
St. Paul
Old Ford Prim Sch
Comm Hall & Health Cen
BRODICK HO
BOW
289
St. Elizabeth's Prim Sch
PK VIEW EST
St. James
Gatehouse Sch
SEWARDSTONE RD
WENNINGTON GRN
St. Barnabas
Jehovah's Witness
Olga Prim Sch
MILE END PARK
E3
CROWN CL BUSINESS
1
2
3
4
5
6
7
8
9
10

A
B
C
D
E
F
G
1
2
3
4
5
6
7
8
9
10
E10
E9
E20
E3
SPORTS GROUND
Market
Lee Valley Hockey and Tennis Centre
RUCKHOLT ROAD
A106
A12
OLD RIVER LEA
ST THERESA'S CL
Sports Pav
B112
ROAD
LEA INTERCHANGE
NORTHWALL ROAD
BMX TRACK
Lee Valley VeloPark
WICK WOODLAND
HACKNEY CUT
TEMPLE MILLS LANE
TEMPLE MILL LA
Superstore
123
38
Sub
SPORTS GRD
DRAPERS FIELD REC GRD
LEYTON ROAD
LEYTON MAJOR RD
Downsell Prim Sch
FRITH
MILLAIS
LESLIE
DOWNSELL
STEWART
DRAPERS
CROWNFIELD
COLEGRAVE
CHANDOS
CHOBHAM
A112
Baptist
Chobham Academy
WESTDOWN
NUTFIELD RD
ETCHINGHAM RD
CRANBOURNE RD
GORDON RD
Pav
QUEEN ELIZABETH OLYMPIC PARK
WATERDEN ROAD
HONOUR LEA AVENUE
SUNRISE CL
NAPA CL
LOGAN CL
SCARLET CL
PARADE
VICTORY
CELEBRATION AV
East Village
LIBERTY BRIDGE ROAD
MEDALS WY
RIBBONS WK
MIRABELLE GARDENS
ORIENS MEWS
DE COUBERTIN ST
PENNY BROOKES STREET
DORSET CRES
A12
OLYMPIC PARK AVENUE
ANTHEMS WAY
INTERNATIONAL WAY
STRATFORD INTERNATIONAL
HITCHCOCK LANE
ROUNDHOUSE LANE
STATION LA
MONTFICHET ROAD
Premier Inn
VUE CINEMA
Westfield Stratford City
STRATFORD
WESTFIELD AVENUE
BUS STA
GREAT EASTERN
HACKNEY WICK
Gainsborough Comm Sch
BERKSHIRE ROAD
Copper Box
Energy Centre
CLARNICO LANE
WHITE POST LA
HEPSCOTT RD
VICTORIA PK IND EST
TREGO ROAD
279
Carpenters Road Lock
WATERWORKS RIVER
London Aquatics Centre
Mem
Olympic Stadium
ArcelorMittal Orbit
CITY MILL RIVER
RIVER LEE OR LEA
Old Ford Lock
LEA VALLEY WK
OMEGA WKS
ROACH ROAD
WYKE ROAD
SMEED ROAD
BEACHY ROAD
STOUR ROAD
BREAM ST
DACE ROAD
MONIER ROAD
WICK LANE
EAST CROSS ROUTE
Lock
St. Mark's
WINFORD HO
WAVERTON HO
LOCTON GRN
RUSTON ST
OLD FORD RD
Health Cen
CROWN CLOSE BUSINESS CEN
ATLEY RD
ICELAND RD
AUTUMN ST
DYE HO LA
MAVERTON RD
PARNELL RD
B142
GARRISON
ICENI COURT
TREDEGAR RD
PANCRAS WAY
Youth Cen
FAIRFIELD RD
WICK LANE
MANHATTAN BLDG
BLACKWALL TUNNEL NORTHERN APPROACH
290
GROVE HALL PARK
Baptist
PUDDING MILL LANE
City Mill Lock
View Tube
MARSHGATE LANE
BOW BACK RIVER
COOK'S ROAD
GEORGE HUDSON TWR
CENTRAL HO
SUGAR HOUSE LA
THREE MILLS WALL RIVER
HIGH STREET
A118
STRATFORD HIGH ST
Sports Cen
BUILDING CRAFTS COLL
DENNISON POINT
GIBBINS RD
CARPENTERS ROAD
Comm Cen
JAMES RILEY PT
ICONA PT
LUND PT
Carpenters Prim Sch
Holiday Inn Ex
WARTON ROAD
BRIDGEWATER RD
HALO
UNI OF E LON
POLAND HO
BURFORD WF APTS
ALBERT BIGG PT
AUBREY MOORE PT
ABBEY LANE
ABBEY RD
BISSON ROAD
LEGGATT RD
RIVERSIDE ROAD
BOW INDUSTRIAL PARK
LEE VALLEY PARK
PUMPING STA
0 250 yds
0 250 m

H
J
K
L
M
N
P
1
2
3
4
5
6
7
8
9
10
124
144
291
FOREST GATE
WEST HAM
MARYLAND
E7
E13
E15
JEWISH CEMETERY
WEST HAM CEMETERY
WEST HAM PARK
SPORTS GROUND
STRATFORD PARK
FOREST LANE PK
CLAPTON FC
AVENUE ROAD ESTATE
STRATFORD MARKET DEPOT
ABBEY ROAD
PLAISTOW
FOREST GATE
UPTON LANE
WOODGRANGE ROAD
ROMFORD ROAD
A118
A112
A11
A114
A1011
B164
B165
B161
HIGH ROAD LEYTONSTONE
LEYTONSTONE ROAD
WATER LANE
THE GROVE
BROADWAY
VICARAGE LANE
PORTWAY
PLASHET ROAD
STOPFORD ROAD
NEW PLAISTOW RD
PLAISTOW ROAD
HIGH STREET
MANOR ROAD
FOREST LANE
EARLHAM GROVE
KNOX ROAD
PARK ROAD
DENSHAM RD
WEST HAM LA
CORPORATION ROAD
GREENWAY
UNI OF EAST LONDON (Stratford Campus)
NEWHAM COLL OF FURTHER ED (Stratford Campus)
The Stratford Centre
THEATRE ROYAL
Superstore
Maryland Prim Sch
Earlham Prim Sch
Odessa Inf Sch
Forest Gate Comm Sch
Azhar Academy Girls Sch
Portway Prim Sch
Selwyn Prim Sch
Curwen Prim Sch
Ranelagh Prim Sch
Manor Prim Sch
Colegrave Prim Sch
Park Prim Sch
Sarah Bonnell Sch
John F. Kennedy Sch
West Ham Ch Prim Sch
Tennis Courts
Bandstand
Nursery
Channelsea Ho Bus C
East London R.F.C.

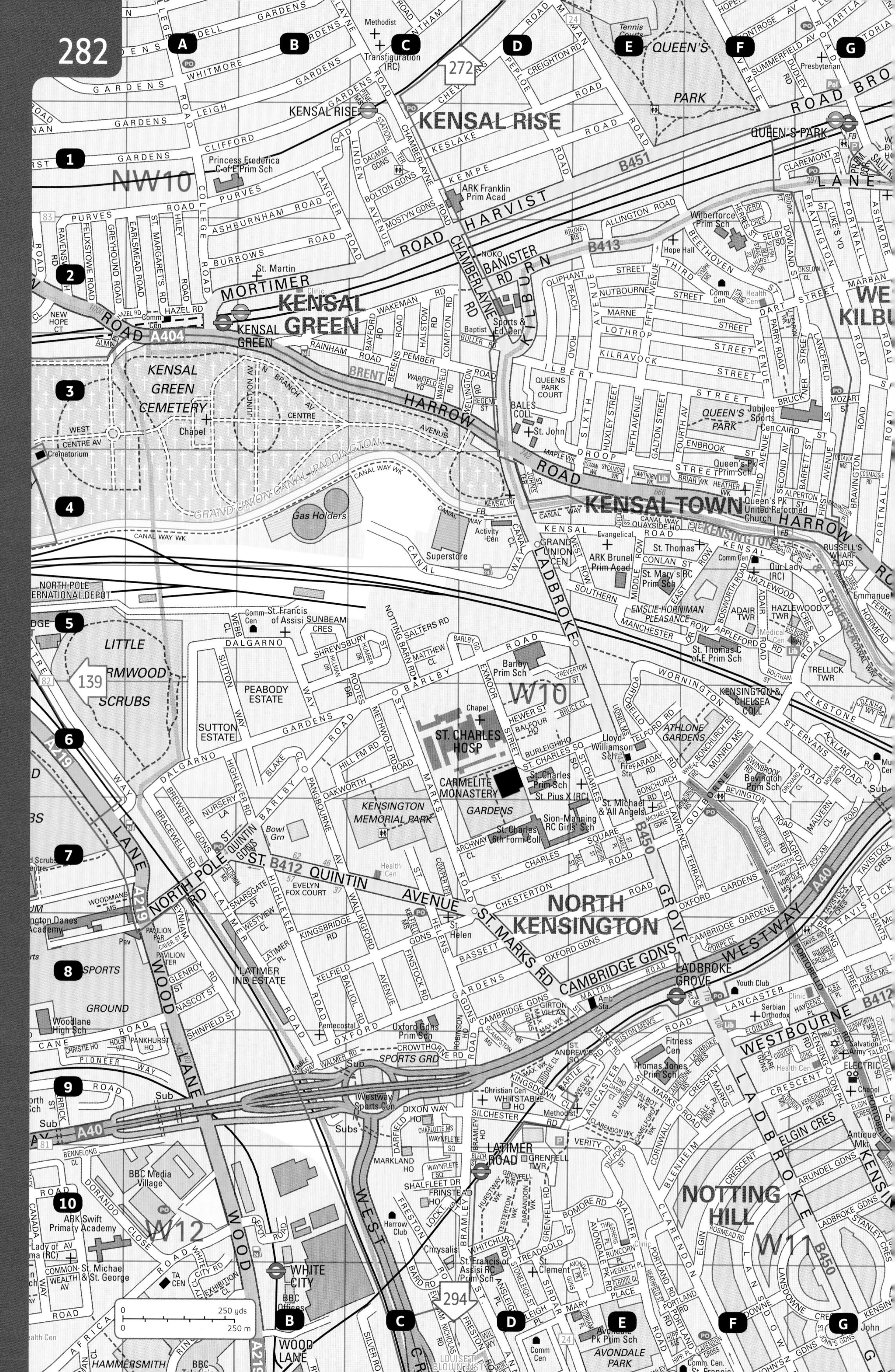
A
B
C
D
E
F
G
1
2
3
4
5
6
7
8
9
10
KENSAL RISE
KENSAL GREEN
KENSAL TOWN
NORTH KENSINGTON
NOTTING HILL
NW10
W10
W11
W12
QUEEN'S PARK
KENSAL GREEN CEMETERY
LITTLE WORMWOOD SCRUBS
SPORTS GROUND
GRAND UNION CANAL (PADDINGTON)
Gas Holders
Superstore
KENSINGTON MEMORIAL PARK
ST. CHARLES HOSP
CARMELITE MONASTERY
EMSLIE HORNIMAN PLEASANCE
ATHLONE GARDENS
SPORTS GRD
BBC Media Village
WHITE CITY
LATIMER ROAD
LADBROKE GROVE
WESTBOURNE PARK
KENSAL RISE
QUEEN'S PARK
HARROW ROAD
LADBROKE GROVE
WESTWAY
WOOD LANE
WEST CROSS
CHAMBERLAYNE RD
ST. QUINTIN AVENUE
ST. MARKS RD
CAMBRIDGE GDNS
PORTOBELLO RD
ELGIN CRES
A404
A40
A219
B412
B413
B450
B451
272
139
294
0
250 yds
0
250 m

KILBURN
KILBURN PARK
MAIDA VALE
MAIDA HILL
W9
NW8
W6
W2
ST. JOHN'S
WESTBOURNE GREEN
PADDINGTON
BAYSWATER
ROYAL OAK
WARWICK AVENUE
Little Venice
PADDINGTON RECREATION GROUND
ATHLETICS TRACK
CRICKET GROUND
CARLTON VALE
MAIDA VALE
SHIRLAND ROAD
HARROW ROAD
WESTWAY
ELGIN AVENUE
SUTHERLAND AVENUE
CLIFTON GDNS
BLOMFIELD ROAD
ABBEY ROAD
HAMILTON TERRACE
GROVE END ROAD
EDGWARE ROAD
WESTBOURNE PARK ROAD
WESTBOURNE GROVE
BISHOPS BRIDGE RD
EASTBOURNE TER
CRAVEN ROAD
QUEENSWAY
PORCHESTER RD
CHEPSTOW ROAD
PEMBRIDGE VILLAS
LEDBURY ROAD
GT WESTERN RD
KILBURN PARK ROAD
BAYSWATER ROAD
Paddington Sports Club
BBC Studios
Bowling Greens
Abbey Rd Studios
St. George's Catholic School, Maida Vale
Westminster Academy
Paddington Academy
City of Westminster Coll (Maida Vale Cen)
Whiteleys Shop Cen
St. Mary's Hosp
273
284
295
H
J
K
L
M
N
P
1
2
3
4
5
6
7
8
9
10

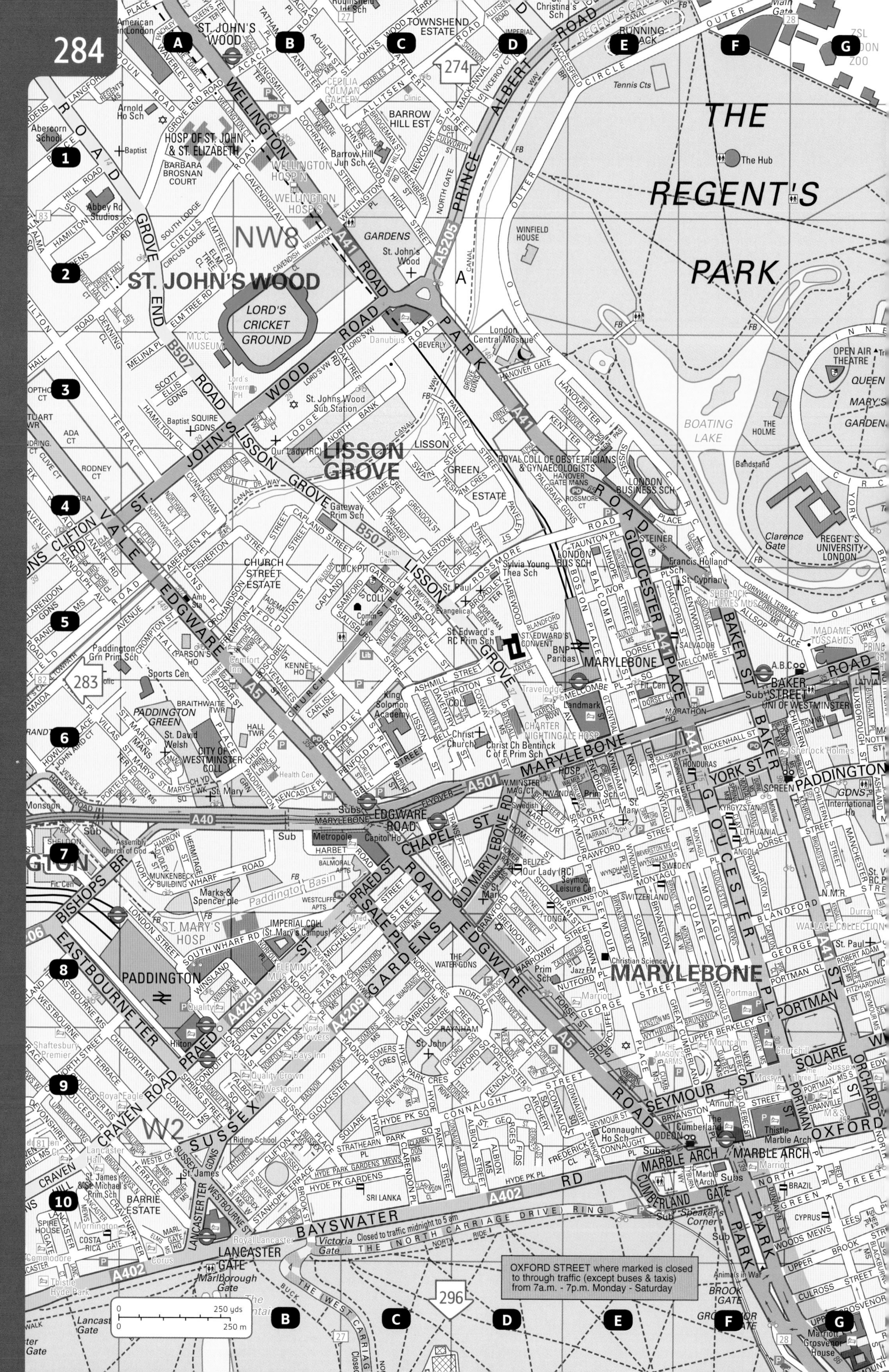
ST. JOHN'S WOOD
NW8
LORD'S CRICKET GROUND
THE REGENT'S PARK
LISSON GROVE
MARYLEBONE
PADDINGTON
W2
OXFORD STREET where marked is closed to through traffic (except buses & taxis) from 7a.m. - 7p.m. Monday - Saturday
Closed to traffic midnight to 5 am
283
274
296

REGENT'S PARK
NW1
SOMERS TOWN
EUSTON
WC1
BLOOMSBURY
THE BRITISH MUSEUM
W1
SOHO
MAYFAIR
BRITISH LIBRARY
ST. PANCRAS INT.
UNIVERSITY OF LONDON
OXFORD CIRCUS
PICCADILLY CIRCUS
TOTTENHAM COURT RD
LEICESTER SQ
BOND ST
GOODGE ST
WARREN ST
EUSTON SQUARE
GT. PORTLAND ST
REGENT'S PARK
MORNINGTON CRESCENT
EUSTON ROAD
OXFORD ST
HAMPSTEAD ROAD
TOTTENHAM COURT RD
GOWER ST
CHARING CROSS RD
NATIONAL GALLERY
275
286
297
H
J
K
L
M
N
P
1
2
3
4
5
6
7
8
9
10

A
B
C
D
E
F
G
1
2
3
4
5
6
7
8
9
10
NW1
SOMERS TOWN
KING'S CROSS
ST. PANCRAS
PENTONVILLE
FINSBURY
WC1
BLOOMSBURY
HOLBORN
WC2
STRAND
ANGEL
FARRINGDON
CHANCERY LANE
COVENT GARDEN
TEMPLE
RUSSELL SQ
LEICESTER SQ
CITY THAMESLINK
BLACKFRIARS PIER
PENTONVILLE ROAD
EUSTON RD
GRAY'S INN RD
KING'S CROSS RD
FARRINGDON RD
CLERKENWELL RD
THEOBALD'S ROAD
HIGH HOLBORN
HOLBORN
NEW OXFORD ST
KINGSWAY
ALDWYCH
STRAND
VICTORIA EMBANKMENT
CHARTERHOUSE
FLEET STREET
CHANCERY LANE
SOUTHAMPTON ROW
CHARING CROSS RD
MIDLAND ROAD
PANCRAS ROAD
CALEDONIAN RD
ROSEBERY AV
SKINNER ST
CITY ROAD
BRITISH LIBRARY
THE BRITISH MUSEUM
CORAM'S FIELDS
RUSSELL SQUARE GARDENS
GRAY'S INN GARDENS
LINCOLN'S INN FIELDS
ROYAL COURTS OF JUSTICE
HOSP FOR CHILDREN
EASTMAN DENTAL HOSP
MOUNT PLEASANT MAIL CENTRE
ROYAL OPERA HO
SOMERSET HOUSE
NATIONAL GALLERY
UNIVERSITY OF LONDON
LONDON SCH OF ECO & POL SCI
KING'S COLL
BOURNE ESTATE
THE TEMPLE
H.Q.S. WELLINGTON MASTER MARINERS'
H.M.S. PRESIDENT
Temple Pier
Savoy Pier
THAMES
276
285
298
0 250 yds
0 250 m

H
J
K
L
M
N
P
1
2
3
4
5
6
7
8
9
10
277
288
299
N1
EC1
EC2
EC3
EC4
E1
HOXTON
ST. LUKE'S
BARBICAN
BROADGATE
SHOREDITCH PARK
CITY ROAD BASIN
WENLOCK BASIN
REGENT'S CANAL
NEW NORTH RD
SHEPHERDESS WALK
OLD STREET
CITY ROAD
GREAT EASTERN STREET
KINGSLAND
SHOREDITCH HIGH STREET
BISHOPSGATE
CURTAIN RD
GOSWELL RD
ALDERSGATE ST
BUNHILL FIELDS
BUNHILL ROW
CHISWELL ST
FINSBURY SQ
MOORGATE
LIVERPOOL STREET
LONDON WALL
HOUNDSDITCH
COMMERCIAL
MINORIES
CHEAPSIDE
CANNON
QUEEN VICTORIA
MANSION HOUSE
BANK
MONUMENT
FENCHURCH ST
TOWER HILL
TOWER OF LONDON
ST. PAUL'S CATHEDRAL
ST. BARTHOLOMEW'S HOSPITAL
MOORFIELDS EYE HOSP
BLACKFRIARS
MILLENNIUM BRIDGE
SOUTHWARK
Swan Lane Pier
Southwark Bridge Steps
Bank of England
Tower 42

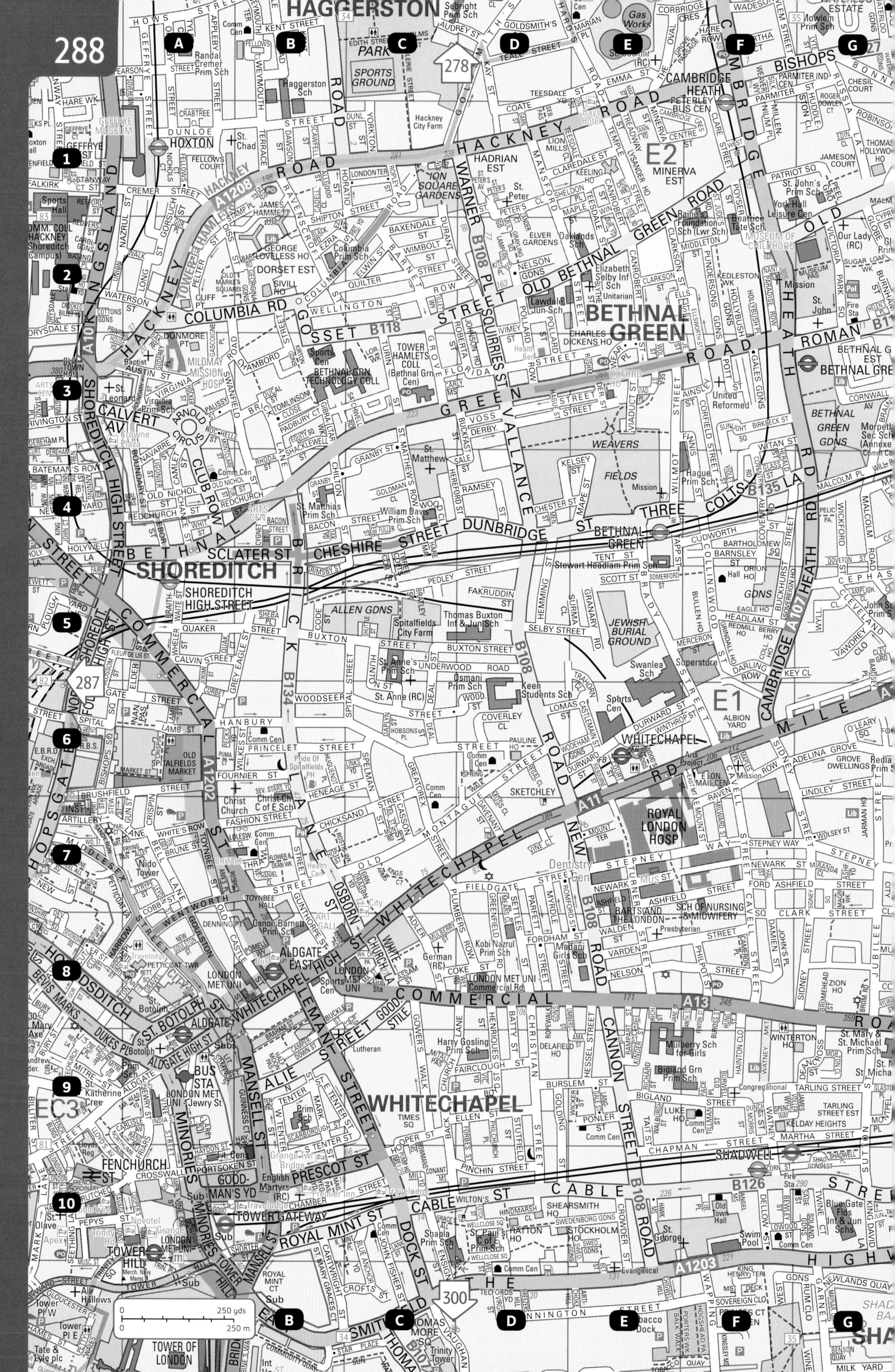
HAGGERSTON
HOXTON
SHOREDITCH
BETHNAL GREEN
WHITECHAPEL
E2
E1
EC3
HACKNEY ROAD
KINGSLAND
SHOREDITCH HIGH STREET
COMMERCIAL ST
COMMERCIAL Rd
WHITECHAPEL RD
WHITECHAPEL HIGH ST
MILE END RD
CAMBRIDGE HEATH RD
OLD BETHNAL GREEN ROAD
BETHNAL GREEN ROAD
COLUMBIA RD
VALLANCE RD
BRICK LANE
CHESHIRE STREET
DUNBRIDGE ST
THREE COLTS LA
NEW ROAD
CANNON STREET ROAD
CABLE ST
ROYAL MINT ST
LEMAN STREET
MANSELL ST
MINORIES
HOUNDSDITCH
BISHOPSGATE
ROMAN ROAD
WEAVERS FIELDS
ALLEN GDNS
JEWISH BURIAL GROUND
ROYAL LONDON HOSP
OLD SPITALFIELDS MARKET
Spitalfields City Farm
Hackney City Farm
ARNOLD CIRCUS
BETHNAL GREEN GDNS
MUSEUM OF CHILDHOOD
GEFFRYE MUSEUM
FENCHURCH ST
TOWER HILL
TOWER GATEWAY
ALDGATE
ALDGATE EAST
SHADWELL
TOWER OF LONDON
0
250 yds
0
250 m
A
B
C
D
E
F
G
1
2
3
4
5
6
7
8
9
10
278
287
300

H
J
K
L
M
N
P
279
BOW
ROMAN ROAD
B119
SEWARDSTONE RD
B127
B118
FORD
MACE ST
GROVE ROAD
MILE END PARK
REGENT'S CANAL
MEATH GARDENS
SPORTS GRD
ALLOT
MILE END
E3
MALMESBURY ROAD
COBORN ROAD
TREDEGAR ROAD
BOW ROAD
A11
MILE END ROAD
MILE END HOSPITAL
JEWISH BURIAL GROUND
QUEEN MARY UNI OF LONDON
Guardian Angels RC Prim Sch
GREEN BRIDGE
MILE END
BURDETT ROAD
A1205
TOWER HAMLETS CEMETERY PARK
UNI OF CUMBRIA (TOWER HAMLETS)
STEPNEY GREEN
OCEAN ESTATE
GLOBE ROAD
B120
BANCROFT ROAD
HARFORD ST
SHANDY PARK
Ben Jonson Prim Sch
Mile End Park Leisure Cen
MILE END STADIUM
RAGGED SCHOOL MUSEUM
SPORTS GROUND
Gas Works
290
1
2
3
4
5
6
7
8
9
10
STEPNEY
STEPNEY GREEN PARK
B121
B140
BEN JONSON ROAD
ST. PAULS WAY
LONDON INDEP HOSP
STEPNEY GREEN
Stepney Grn Sch
St. Dunstan & All Saints
WHITE HORSE ROAD
Sir John Cass's Foundation & Redcoat Sch
TOWER HAMLETS COLL
E14
LOCKSLEY ESTATE
MILE END PARK
LIMEHOUSE CUT
COMMERCIAL ROAD
A13
LIMEHOUSE
LIMEHOUSE BASIN
B126
CABLE STREET
ROTHERHITHE TUNNEL
ROPEMAKERS FIELD
A1203
NARROW STREET
KING EDWARD VII MEMORIAL PK
Ratcliffe Cross Stairs
Stone Stairs
Victoria Wharf
Blyth's Wharf
Free Trade Wharf
Duke Shore Wharf
Limehouse Hole Stairs
Lavender Wharf
301
THAMES
WESTFERRY
W. INDIA DOCK RD
EAST INDIA DOCK
LINK
WESTFERRY RD

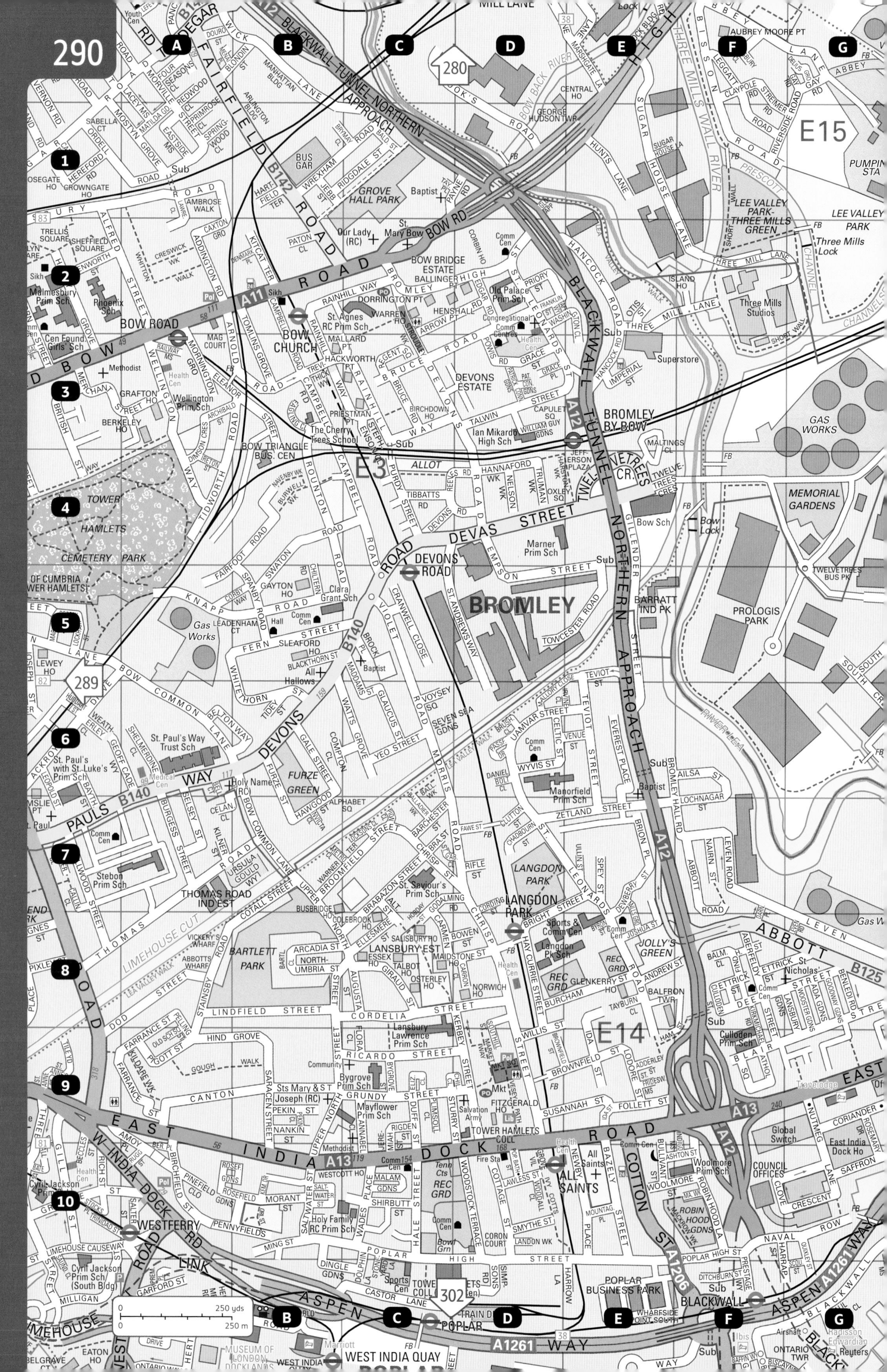
A
B
C
D
E
F
G
1
2
3
4
5
6
7
8
9
10
280
289
302
E15
E3
E14
BOW ROAD
BOW CHURCH
DEVONS ROAD
BROMLEY
BROMLEY BY BOW
LANGDON PARK
ALL SAINTS
WESTFERRY
BLACKWALL
POPLAR
WEST INDIA QUAY
BLACKWALL TUNNEL NORTHERN APPROACH
FAIRFIELD ROAD
TREDEGAR RD
BOW RD
A11
B142
A12
A13
A1261
A1206
B140
B125
DEVAS STREET
DEVONS ROAD
ST PAULS WAY
EAST INDIA DOCK ROAD
ASPEN WAY
LIMEHOUSE CUT
TOWER HAMLETS CEMETERY PARK
GROVE HALL PARK
BARTLETT PARK
FURZE GREEN
LANGDON PARK
JOLLY'S GREEN
MEMORIAL GARDENS
PROLOGIS PARK
GAS WORKS
LEE VALLEY PARK
THREE MILLS GREEN
Three Mills Lock
Three Mills Studios
Superstore
BOW BRIDGE ESTATE
DEVONS ESTATE
LANSBURY EST
BOW TRIANGLE BUS. CEN
THOMAS ROAD IND EST
BARRATT IND PK
TWELVETREES BUS PK
POPLAR BUSINESS PARK
RIVER LEA
THREE MILLS WALL RIVER
BOW BACK RIVER
PRESCOTT CHANNEL
CHANNELSEA
Bow Lock
Bow Sch
Marner Prim Sch
Old Palace Prim Sch
St Agnes RC Prim Sch
Malmesbury Prim Sch
Phoenix Sch
Wellington Prim Sch
Clara Grant Sch
The Cherry Trees School
St. Paul's Way Trust Sch
Stebon Prim Sch
St. Saviour's Prim Sch
Manorfield Prim Sch
Lansbury Lawrence Prim Sch
Bygrove Prim Sch
Mayflower Prim Sch
Holy Family RC Prim Sch
Woolmore Prim Sch
Culloden Prim Sch
Cyril Jackson Prim Sch
Global Switch
East India Dock Ho
COUNCIL OFFICES
MUSEUM OF LONDON DOCKLANDS
250 yds
250 m

PLAISTOW
E13
CANNING TOWN
E16
MEMORIAL RECREATION GROUND
EAST LONDON CEMETERY
HERMIT ROAD RECREATION GROUND
RECREATION GROUND
BOW CREEK ECOLOGICAL PARK
EAST INDIA DOCK BASIN
WEST HAM
PLAISTOW
STAR LANE
CANNING TOWN
ROYAL VICTORIA
ABBEY ROAD
EMIRATES ROYAL DOCKS
BARKING ROAD
NEWHAM WAY
MANOR ROAD
LOWER LEA CROSSING
281
292
303

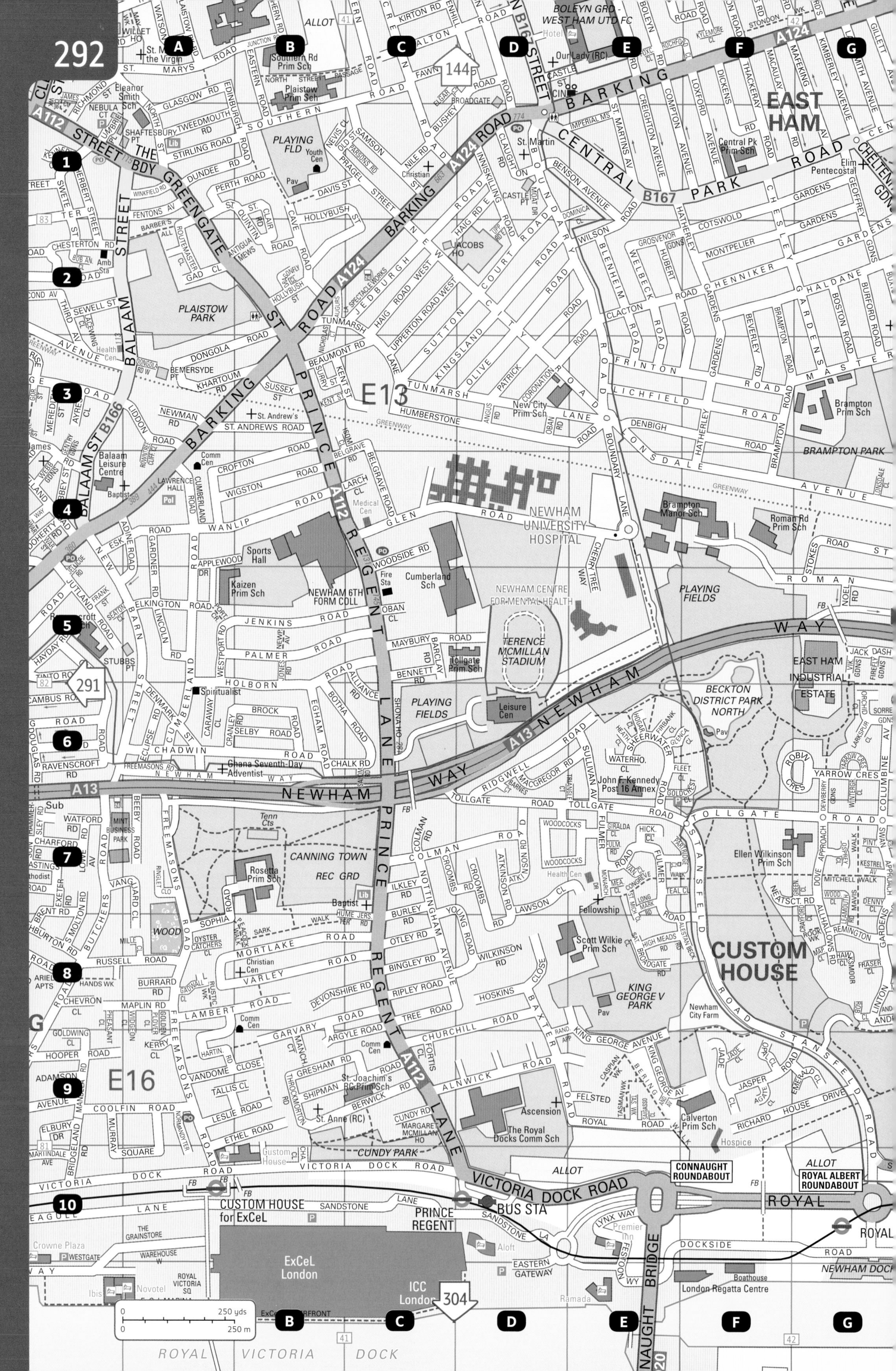
A
B
C
D
E
F
G
1
2
3
4
5
6
7
8
9
10
BOLEYN GRD - WEST HAM UTD FC
144
EAST HAM
BARKING ROAD
CENTRAL PARK ROAD
A124
A112
B167
B166
PLAYING FLD
PLAISTOW PARK
E13
NEWHAM UNIVERSITY HOSPITAL
NEWHAM CENTRE FOR MENTAL HEALTH
TERENCE MCMILLAN STADIUM
PLAYING FIELDS
BECKTON DISTRICT PARK NORTH
EAST HAM INDUSTRIAL ESTATE
BRAMPTON PARK
A13
NEWHAM WAY
PRINCE REGENT LANE
BALAAM STREET
GREENGATE ST
291
CANNING TOWN REC GRD
CUSTOM HOUSE
KING GEORGE V PARK
E16
CUNDY PARK
VICTORIA DOCK ROAD
CONNAUGHT ROUNDABOUT
ROYAL ALBERT ROUNDABOUT
CUSTOM HOUSE for ExCeL
PRINCE REGENT
BUS STA
ExCeL London
ICC London
304
London Regatta Centre
NEWHAM DOCK
ROYAL VICTORIA DOCK
CONNAUGHT BRIDGE
250 yds
250 m

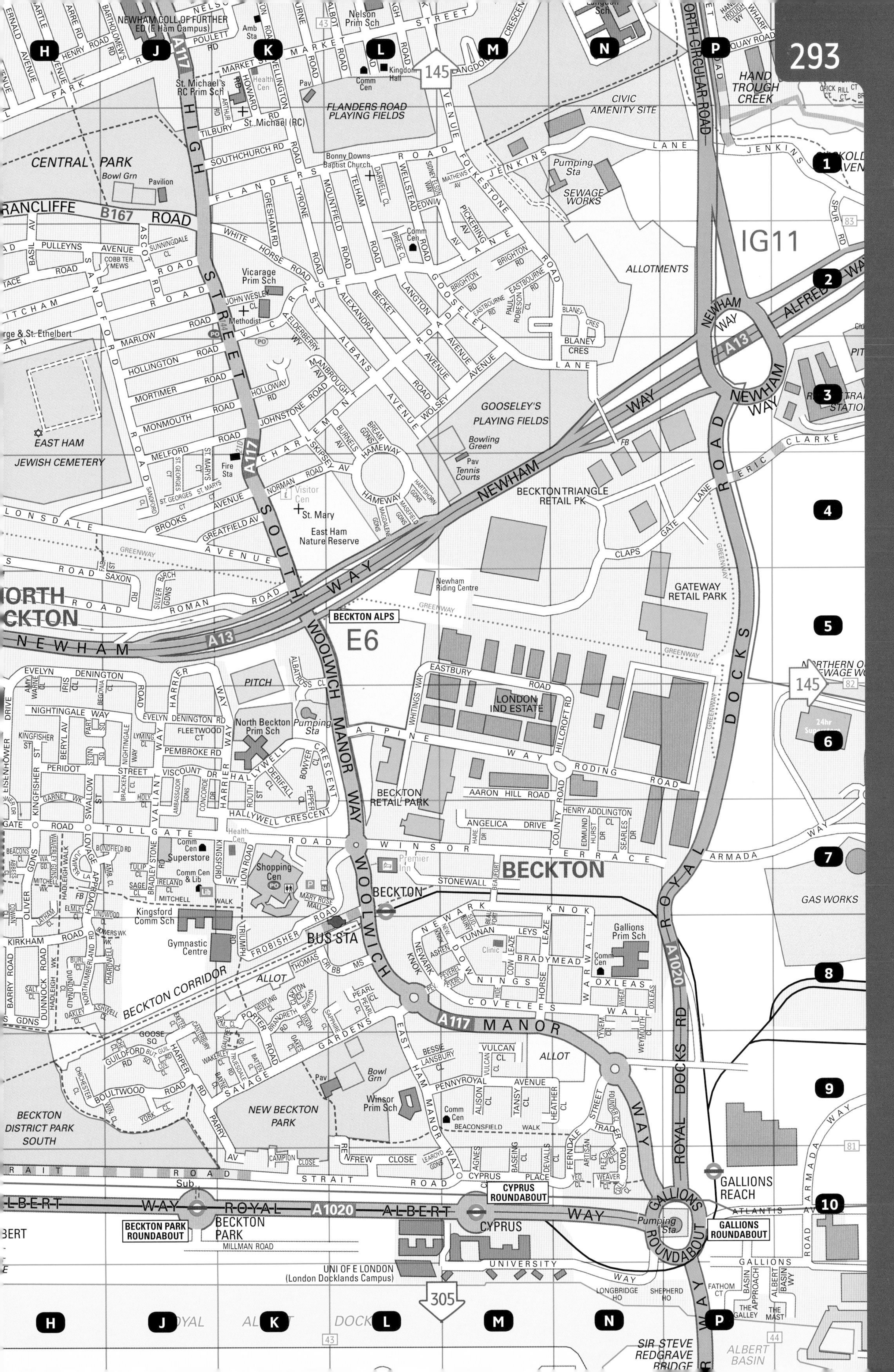

BECKTON
NORTH BECKTON
E6
IG11
CENTRAL PARK
EAST HAM JEWISH CEMETERY
FLANDERS ROAD PLAYING FIELDS
GOOSELEY'S PLAYING FIELDS
BECKTON TRIANGLE RETAIL PK
GATEWAY RETAIL PARK
LONDON IND ESTATE
BECKTON RETAIL PARK
East Ham Nature Reserve
BECKTON ALPS
NEW BECKTON PARK
BECKTON DISTRICT PARK SOUTH
CIVIC AMENITY SITE
SEWAGE WORKS
ALLOTMENTS
GAS WORKS
HAND TROUGH CREEK
BECKTON PARK ROUNDABOUT
CYPRUS ROUNDABOUT
GALLIONS ROUNDABOUT
GALLIONS REACH
UNI OF E LONDON (London Docklands Campus)
SIR STEVE REDGRAVE BRIDGE
ALBERT BASIN
NEWHAM WAY
ROYAL DOCKS ROAD
ROYAL ALBERT WAY
NORTH CIRCULAR ROAD
WOOLWICH MANOR WAY
HIGH STREET SOUTH
145
305

BBC Media Village
WOOD LANE
WHITE CITY
BBC Offices
BBC Television Centre (Closed)
HAMMERSMITH PARK
W12
AFRICA
RING ROAD
ARIEL WAY
SHEPHERD'S BUSH
Westfield
VUE CINEMA
WEST CROSS ROUTE
A3220
NOTTING HILL
W11
AVONDALE PARK
Avondale Pk Prim Sch
HOLLAND PARK
LADBROKE GROVE
LANSDOWNE
HOLLAND PARK ROUNDABOUT
SHEPHERD'S BUSH MARKET
UXBRIDGE ROAD
A4020
SHEPHERDS BUSH COMMON
SHEPHERDS BUSH GREEN
West 12 Shopping Cen
GOLDHAWK ROAD
A402
A219
HOLLAND ROAD
ADDISON GARDENS
W14
ADDISON ROAD
KENSINGTON (OLYMPIA)
OLYMPIA
BLYTHE HOUSE
BROOK GREEN
St. Paul's Girls Sch
W6
SPORTS GROUND
The Godolphin & Latymer Sch
GLENTHORNE ROAD
BEADON RD
HAMMERSMITH
HAMMERSMITH BROADWAY
KING STREET
A315
LYRIC
HAMMERSMITH FLYOVER
TALGARTH ROAD
A4
BARONS COURT
WEST KENSINGTON
NORTH END ROAD
HAMMERSMITH CEMETERY
FULHAM PALACE ROAD
QUEEN CAROLINE ESTATE
RIVERSIDE STUDIOS
IMPERIAL COLL
HAMMERSMITH BRIDGE RD
159
282
306
0 250 yds
0 250 m
A B C D E F G
1 2 3 4 5 6 7 8 9 10

H
J
K
L
M
N
P
1
2
3
4
5
6
7
8
9
10
283
296
307
W2
W8
SW7
SW5
KENSINGTON GARDENS
KENSINGTON
SOUTH KENSINGTON
EARLS COURT
ROUND POND
NOTTING HILL GATE
QUEENSWAY
HIGH ST. KENSINGTON
EARL'S COURT
GLOUCESTER ROAD
BAYSWATER ROAD
KENSINGTON ROAD
KENSINGTON GORE
CROMWELL ROAD
WEST CROMWELL RD
BROMPTON ROAD
KENSINGTON HIGH ST
KENSINGTON CHURCH ST
PALACE GARDENS TER
QUEEN'S GATE
GLOUCESTER RD
EARLS COURT RD
PEMBROKE RD
WARWICK GARDENS
HOLLAND WALK
CAMPDEN HILL
KENSINGTON PALACE
Albert Memorial
Speke Monument
Physical Energy Statue
Peter Pan
Lancaster Gate
Black Lion Gate
Orme Square Gate
Diana Mem Playground
Queen's Gate
Palace Gate
KENSINGTON TOWN HALL
Holland Park Sch
CRICKET GROUND
LEIGHTON HO MUS
ROYAL COLL OF ART
ROYAL COLL OF MUSIC
Imp. Coll & Sci. Mus Libs
IMPERIAL COLLEGE
NATURAL HISTORY MUSEUM
CROMWELL HOSP
LONDON ELECTRONICS COLL
LILLE BRIDGE DEPOT
Empress State Building
A402
A4
A3220
A3218
B325
B415

HYDE PARK
KENSINGTON GARDENS
W2
SW7
SW3
BROMPTON
BAYSWATER RD
KENSINGTON RD
KENSINGTON GORE
KNIGHTSBRIDGE
BROMPTON ROAD
CROMWELL RD
THURLOE PL
FULHAM ROAD
SLOANE STREET
PONT STREET
KING'S ROAD
LOWER SLOANE ST
PARK LANE
MARBLE ARCH
LANCASTER GATE
THE LONG WATER
THE SERPENTINE
SERPENTINE ROAD
ROTTEN ROW
SOUTH CARRIAGE DRIVE
NORTH CARRIAGE DRIVE
WEST CARRIAGE DRIVE
Speakers' Corner
Bird Sanctuary
Peter Pan
Speke Monument
Physical Energy Statue
Queens Temple
Serpentine Sackler Gallery
Serpentine Gallery
Lido
Pier
Diana Princess of Wales Memorial
Holocaust Memorial
Albert Memorial
ROYAL ALBERT HALL
ROYAL COLL OF ART
IMPERIAL COLL
ROYAL COLL OF MUSIC
SCIENCE MUSEUM
NATURAL HISTORY MUSEUM
VICTORIA & ALBERT MUSEUM
Brompton Oratory
SOUTH KENSINGTON
HARRODS
KNIGHTSBRIDGE
SLOANE SQ
THE ROYAL MARSDEN
ROYAL BROMPTON HOSP
Saatchi Gallery
Chelsea Old Town Hall
0 250 yds
0 250 m

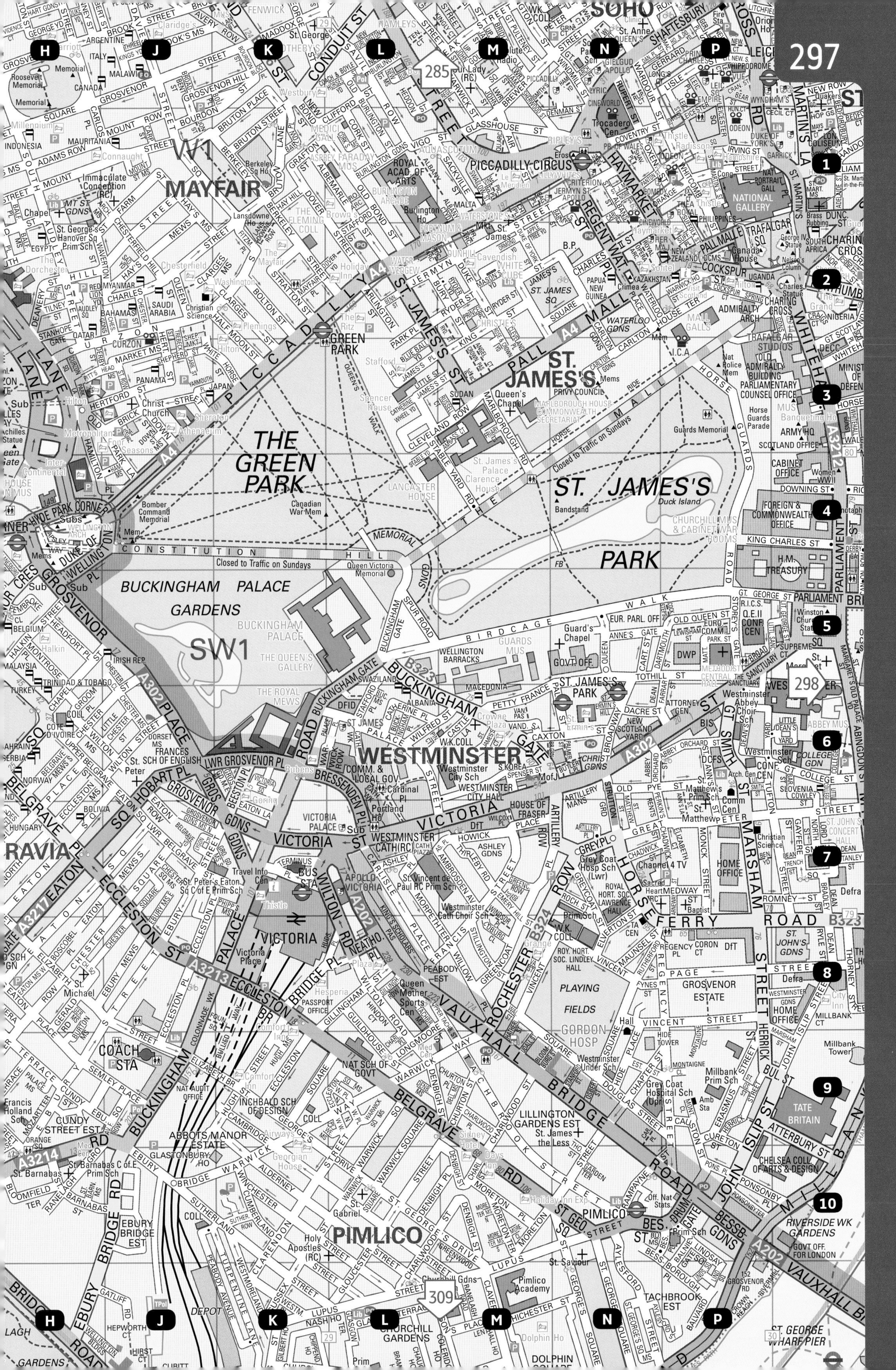
SOHO
MAYFAIR
W1
PICCADILLY CIRCUS
PICCADILLY
GREEN PARK
THE GREEN PARK
ST. JAMES'S
ST. JAMES'S PARK
BUCKINGHAM PALACE GARDENS
BUCKINGHAM PALACE
SW1
WESTMINSTER
VICTORIA
PIMLICO
RAVIA
NATIONAL GALLERY
TRAFALGAR SQ
H.M. TREASURY
FOREIGN & COMMONWEALTH OFFICE
HOME OFFICE
TATE BRITAIN
PLAYING FIELDS
PALL MALL
THE MALL
HORSE GUARDS
CONSTITUTION HILL
BIRDCAGE WALK
VICTORIA ST
VAUXHALL BRIDGE ROAD
BELGRAVE RD
BUCKINGHAM PALACE ROAD
GROSVENOR PLACE
HORSEFERRY ROAD
MILLBANK
HYDE PARK CORNER
COACH STA
285
298
309
H
J
K
L
M
N
P
1
2
3
4
5
6
7
8
9
10

298
A
B
C
D
E
F
G
1
2
3
4
5
6
7
8
9
10
286
297
310
STRAND
WC2
RIVER THAMES
KING'S REACH
VICTORIA EMBANKMENT
WATERLOO BRI
WESTMINSTER BRI
LAMBETH BRI
BLACKFRIARS BRI
NATIONAL GALLERY
TRAFALGAR SQ
CHARING CROSS
EMBANKMENT
TEMPLE
WATERLOO
WESTMINSTER
LAMBETH NORTH
VAUXHALL
KENNINGTON
HOUSES OF PARLIAMENT
WESTMINSTER ABBEY
ROYAL FESTIVAL HALL
NATIONAL THEATRE
ST. THOMAS' HOSP
LAMBETH
SE11
SW1
TATE BRITAIN
MILLBANK
GERALDINE MARY HARMSWORTH PARK
IMPERIAL WAR MUS
KENNINGTON ROAD
LAMBETH ROAD
ST. GEORGE'S ROAD
BLACKFRIARS ROAD
WATERLOO ROAD
STAMFORD STREET
THE CUT
WHITEHALL
PARLIAMENT ST
MARSHAM STREET
ALBERT EMBANKMENT
KENNINGTON LANE
0 250 yds
0 250 m

H
J
K
L
M
N
P
287
EC4
SOUTHWARK
BLACKFRIARS
MILLENNIUM BRIDGE
Southwark Bridge Steps
CANNON ST
Swan Lane Pier
MONUMENT
TOWER HILL
BANKSIDE PIER
SHAKESPEARE'S GLOBE THEATRE
SAM WANAMAKER PLAYHOUSE
TATE MODERN
Financial Times
Old Billingsgate
H. M. Revenue & Customs
TOWER OF LONDON
EC3
TOWER PIER
LONDON BRIDGE CITY PIER
LONDON BRIDGE HOSP.
SOUTHWARK CATHEDRAL
H.M.S. BELFAST
TOWER BRIDGE
THE SCOOP
MORE LONDON RIVERSIDE
CITY HALL (Greater London Authority)
POTTERS FIELDS PARK
Blue Fin Building
PEABODY TRUST
Borough Mkt
The Shard
LONDON BRIDGE
SE1
SOUTHWARK
UNION STREET
SOUTHWARK STREET
BOROUGH HIGH STREET
TOOLEY STREET
ST. THOMAS STREET
GUY'S HOSP.
BERMONDSEY STREET
CRUCIFIX LA
DRUID STREET
LONG LANE
LEATHERMARKET GARDENS
THE BOROUGH
BOROUGH ROAD
SOUTHWARK BRIDGE ROAD
MARSHALSEA RD
GREAT DOVER STREET
TABARD GARDENS
TABARD GARDENS ESTATE
ABBEY STREET
ELIM ESTATE
LONDON SOUTH BANK UNI
NEWINGTON CAUSEWAY
NEWINGTON GDNS
ROCKINGHAM ESTATE
KING'S COLLEGE (Hall Of Residence)
GRANGE ROAD
300
ELEPHANT & CASTLE
NEW KENT ROAD
BRICKLAYER'S ARMS ROUNDABOUT
OLD KENT RD
NEWINGTON
TOWER BRIDGE ROAD
Bricklayer's Arms Distribution Centre
Royal Mail
WALWORTH ROAD
WALWORTH
SE17
EAST STREET
SURREY SQUARE PARK
KINGLAKE EST
Superstores
DUNTON ROAD
AYLESBURY EST
FARADAY GARDENS
BURGESS PARK
Walworth Academy
311
1
2
3
4
5
6
7
8
9
10

A
B
C
D
E
F
G
1
2
3
4
5
6
7
8
9
10
288
299
312
TOWER OF LONDON
TOWER HILL
TOWER GATEWAY
TOWER PIER
EC3
E1
SE1
SE16
WAPPING
BERMONDSEY
SOUTHWARK
TOWER HAMLETS
SOUTHWARK
TOWER BRIDGE
TOWER BRIDGE RD
TOWER BRIDGE APP
H.M.S. BELFAST
CITY HALL (Greater London)
THE SCOOP
POTTERS' FIELDS PARK
TOWER BRIDGE EXHIBITION
BUTLERS WHARF
DESIGN MUSEUM
UPPER POOL
THE POOL
LOWER POOL
ST. KATHARINE'S PIER
ST. KATHARINE DOCKS
EAST SMITHFIELD
ROYAL MINT ST
CABLE ST
THE HIGHWAY
A1203
B126
PRESCOT ST
DOCK ST
THOMAS MORE ST
VAUGHAN WAY
PENNINGTON STREET
Tobacco Dock
WAPPING HIGH ST
WAPPING LANE
WAPPING WALL
KENNET STREET
Wapping Old Stairs
Wapping New Stairs
Wapping Dock Stairs
Alderman Stairs
George's Stairs
Mill Stairs
East Lane Stairs
Cherry Garden Pier
King's Stairs
Princes Stairs
KING'S STAIRS GARDENS
BERMONDSEY WALL EAST
BERMONDSEY WALL WEST
JAMAICA ROAD
A200
DRUID STREET
SHAD THAMES
TANNER ST
ABBEY ST
SPA ROAD
GRANGE RD
A2206
SOUTHWARK PARK ROAD
SOUTHWARK PARK
RAYMOUTH RD
ROTHERHITHE NEW ROAD
LYNTON ROAD
ROLLS ROAD
B204
B202
B203
DUNTON ROAD
CATLIN STREET
OLD KENT ROAD
A2
PATERSON PARK
BERMONDSEY SPA GDNS
DICKENS ESTATE
NECKINGER EST
LONGFIELD ESTATE
MANOR ESTATE
KIRBY ESTATE
RENNIE ESTATE
MAWBEY ESTATE
ADMIRAL HYSON TRADING EST
SIX BRIDGES TRADING EST
Superstores
Walworth Academy
Harris Academy Bermondsey
City of London Academy
250 yds
250 m

LIMEHOUSE
289
RIVER THAMES
ROTHERHITHE
CANADA WATER
SURREY QUAYS
GREENLAND DOCK
SOUTH DOCK
DEPTFORD
E14
SE8
302
313
SALTER ROAD
REDRIFF ROAD
LOWER ROAD
EVELYN STREET
PLOUGH WAY
GROVE STREET
ROTHERHITHE NEW ROAD
ROTHERHITHE STREET
WESTFERRY ROAD
WESTFERRY CIRCUS
NARROW STREET
LIMEHOUSE HOLE STAIRS
LIMEHOUSE REACH
ROTHERHITHE TUNNEL
MELLISH SPORTS GROUND
ECOLOGICAL PARK
Stave Hill
RUSSIA DOCK WOODLAND
SURREY WATER
CANADA WATER
Surrey Quays Shopping Centre
ODEON SURREY QUAYS
MAST LEISURE PK
Associated Newspapers Print Works
Surrey Docks Farm
REDRIFF ESTATE
ALBION ESTATE
AYLTON ESTATE
KING EDWARD VII MEMORIAL PK
HILTON DOCKLANDS NELSON DOCK PIER
CANARY WHARF PIER
GREENLAND PIER
West India Dock Pier
Surrey Docks Water Sports Cen
PEPYS PARK
DEPTFORD PARK
SAYES COURT PARK
CANNON WHARF BUSINESS CENTRE
THE DEN MILLWALL FC
TOWER HAMLETS
SOUTHWARK
LEWISHAM
A200
A2202
A1203
B205
B206
B207
H J K L M N P
1 2 3 4 5 6 7 8 9 10

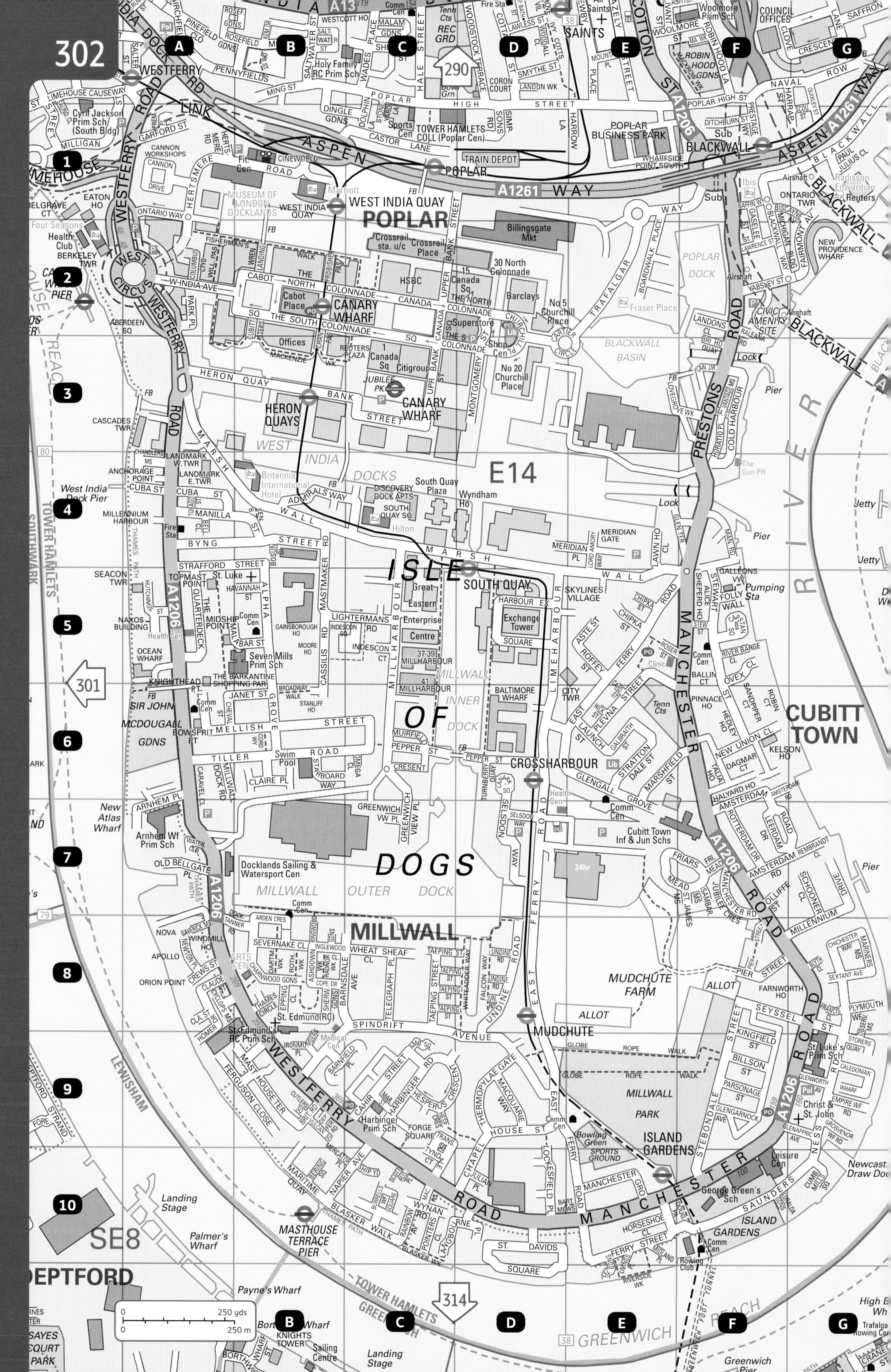

290
301
314
A
B
C
D
E
F
G
1
2
3
4
5
6
7
8
9
10
POPLAR
E14
ISLE
OF
DOGS
MILLWALL
CUBITT TOWN
SE8
DEPTFORD
WESTFERRY
LIMEHOUSE CAUSEWAY
Cyril Jackson Prim Sch (South Bldg)
MILLIGAN
CANNON WORKSHOPS
CINEWORLD
ASPEN
WAY
A1261
POPLAR
WEST INDIA QUAY
MUSEUM OF LONDON DOCKLANDS
Marriott
Billingsgate Mkt
Crossrail sta. u/c
Crossrail Place
30 North Colonnade
HSBC
15 Canada Sq
Barclays
No 5 Churchill Place
Fraser Place
CABOT
NORTH
COLONNADE
CANADA
Cabot Place
CANARY WHARF
Superstore
Shop Cen
No 20 Churchill Place
1 Canada Sq
Citigroup
REUTERS PLAZA
Offices
HERON QUAY
BANK
STREET
JUBILEE PK
HERON QUAYS
CANARY WHARF
BLACKWALL BASIN
POPLAR DOCK
CARTIER CIRCLE
TRAFALGAR WAY
WEST INDIA DOCKS
Britannia International Hotel
DISCOVERY DOCK APTS
South Quay Plaza
Wyndham Ho
SOUTH QUAY SQ
Hilton
MARSH WALL
SOUTH QUAY
MERIDIAN GATE
SKYLINES VILLAGE
HARBOUR EX
Exchange Tower
SQUARE
Great Eastern Enterprise Centre
37-39 MILLHARBOUR
41 MILLHARBOUR
MILLWALL INNER DOCK
BALTIMORE WHARF
CITY TWR
CROSSHARBOUR
MANCHESTER
PRESTONS ROAD
A1206
LIMEHARBOUR
Seven Mills Prim Sch
THE BARKANTINE SHOPPING PAR
SIR JOHN MCDOUGALL GDNS
Swim Pool
GREENWICH VIEW PL
Docklands Sailing & Watersport Cen
MILLWALL OUTER DOCK
Arnhem Wf Prim Sch
New Atlas Wharf
West India Dock Pier
Cubitt Town Inf & Jun Schs
24hr
MUDCHUTE FARM
ALLOT
MUDCHUTE
MILLWALL PARK
ISLAND GARDENS
St. Edmund's RC Prim Sch
Harbinger Prim Sch
FORGE SQUARE
MASTHOUSE TERRACE PIER
George Green's Sch
Leisure Cen
St. Luke's Prim Sch
Christ & St. John
ISLAND GARDENS
Rowing Club
GREENWICH FOOT TUNNEL
GREENWICH
Greenwich Pier
Landing Stage
Palmer's Wharf
Payne's Wharf
TOWER HAMLETS
GREENWICH
LEWISHAM
SOUTHWARK
RIVER
REACH
Jetty
Pier
Lock
250 yds
250 m
KNIGHTS TOWER
Sailing Centre
Newcastle Draw Dock
Tower Hamlets Coll (Poplar Cen)
TRAIN DEPOT
POPLAR BUSINESS PARK
BLACKWALL
COUNCIL OFFICES
Woolmore Prim Sch
ROBIN HOOD GDNS
Holy Family RC Prim Sch
SAINTS
Radisson Edwardian
Reuters
NEW PROVIDENCE WHARF
CIVIC AMENITY SITE
The Gun PH
KELSON HO
Pumping Sta

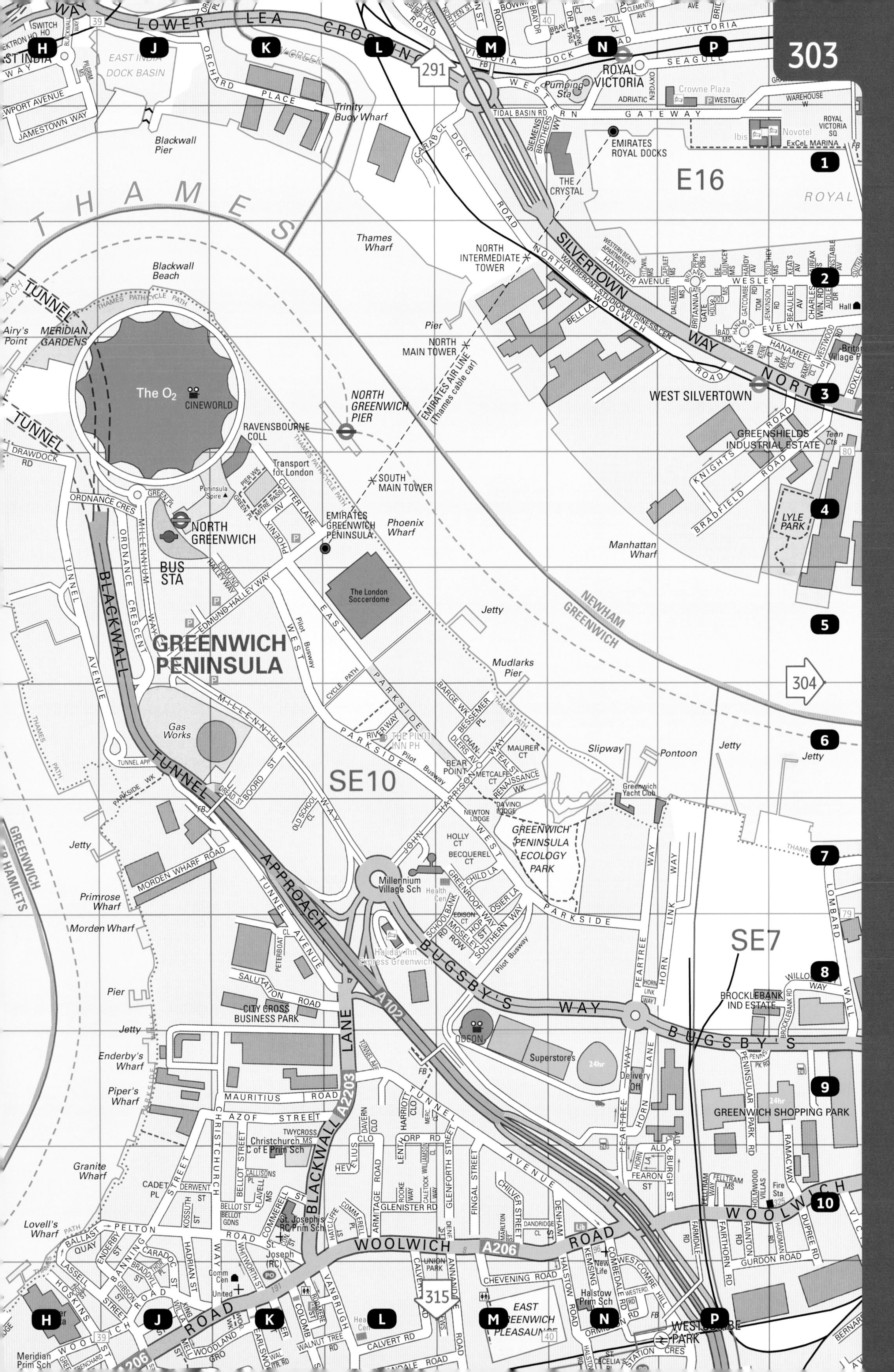
THAMES
E16
SE10
SE7
GREENWICH PENINSULA
The O_2
CINEWORLD
NORTH GREENWICH
BUS STA
ROYAL VICTORIA
WEST SILVERTOWN
EMIRATES AIR LINE (Thames cable car)
EMIRATES ROYAL DOCKS
EMIRATES GREENWICH PENINSULA
NORTH GREENWICH PIER
THE CRYSTAL
The London Soccerdome
GREENWICH PENINSULA ECOLOGY PARK
GREENWICH SHOPPING PARK
BROCKLEBANK IND ESTATE
GREENSHIELDS INDUSTRIAL ESTATE
LYLE PARK
SILVERTOWN WAY
BLACKWALL TUNNEL APPROACH
BUGSBY'S WAY
WOOLWICH ROAD
LOWER LEA CROSSING
EAST INDIA DOCK BASIN
Blackwall Pier
Thames Wharf
Phoenix Wharf
Manhattan Wharf
Mudlarks Pier
Greenwich Yacht Club
ODEON
Superstores
CITY CROSS BUSINESS PARK
EAST GREENWICH PLEASAUNCE
WESTCOMBE PARK
291
304
315

VICTORIA DOCK ROAD
CONNAUGHT ROUNDABOUT
ROYAL ALBERT ROUNDABOUT
CUSTOM HOUSE for ExCeL
ExCeL London
ICC London
ExCeL WATERFRONT
ExCeL MARINA
ROYAL VICTORIA DOCK
E16
CONNAUGHT BRIDGE
A1020
JET CENTRE
London Regatta Centre
AIRPORT ROUNDABOUT
MILLENNIUM MILLS
PONTOON DOCK
WESLEY AVENUE
EVELYN ROAD
Britannia Village Prim Sch
N WOOLWICH ROUNDABOUT
CONNAUGHT ROAD
HARTMANN ROAD
NORTH WOOLWICH ROAD
FACTORY ROAD
THAMES ROAD
GREENSHIELDS INDUSTRIAL ESTATE
LYLE PARK
THAMES BARRIER PARK
SILVERTOWN
THAMESIDE INDUSTRIAL
WOOLWICH REACH
RIVER
Tate & Lyle Jetty
THAMES FLOOD BARRIER
303
292
Barrier Gardens Pier
BARRIER CONTROL BUILDING
MELLISH IND ESTATE
HARRINGTON WAY
BOWATER ROAD
THAMES PATH
ANCHORAGE PT INDUSTRIAL EST
RIVERSIDE
MERIDIAN TRADING ESTATE
ROPERY BUSINESS PARK
NEW CHARLTON
STONE LAKE RETAIL PARK
SE7
STONE LAKE ROUNDABOUT
WOOLWICH ROAD
A206
GREENWICH SHOPPING PARK
BROCKLEBANK IND ESTATE
BUGSBY'S WAY
ROYAL GREENWICH UNI TECH COLL
Windrush Prim Sch
St. Catherine (RC)
MARYON PARK
MARYON WILSON PARK
ANIMAL PARK
THE VALLEY -CHARLTON ATHLETIC FC
CHARLTON
164
WESTCOMBE PARK
250 yds
250 m

BECKTON PARK ROUNDABOUT
BECKTON PARK
CYPRUS ROUNDABOUT
CYPRUS
GALLIONS ROUNDABOUT
GALLIONS REACH
A1020
293
UNI OF E LONDON
(London Docklands Campus)
UNIVERSITY WAY
MILLMAN ROAD
ROYAL ALBERT DOCK
SIR STEVE REDGRAVE BRIDGE
ALBERT BASIN
Airport
KING GEORGE V DOCK
KING GEORGE V
HARTMANN ROAD
NEWLAND STREET
NORTH WOOLWICH
STANDARD INDUSTRIAL ESTATE
ALBERT ROAD
A112
A117
WOOLWICH MANOR WAY
ROYAL VICTORIA GDNS
THE SIDINGS APARTMENTS
Waldair Wharf
North Woolwich Pier
Woolwich Ferry Pier
PIER ROAD
THAMES
NEWHAM
GREENWICH
WOOLWICH FOOT TUNNEL
WOOLWICH FREE FERRY
165
WOOLWICH ARSENAL PIER
WOOLWICH
GREENWICH HERITAGE CEN
FIREPOWER
THAMES PATH
South Pontoon
NEW FERRY APP
WOOLWICH HIGH ST
CHURCH STREET
A206
WOOLWICH DOCKYARD IND EST
WOOLWICH DOCKYARD
St. Mary Magdalene
SE18
BERESFORD ST
PLUMSTEAD RD
WOOLWICH ARSENAL
Crossrail sta. u/c
ROYAL CARRIAGE MEWS
GREENWICH COMMUNITY COLL (Burrage Cen)
JOHN WILSON ST
A205
B210
WELLINGTON STREET
TOWN HALL
WOOLWICH CENTRE
ARTILLERY PLACE
HILLREACH
HEATH
ROYAL ARTILLERY BARRACKS
REPOSITORY ROAD
BARRACK FIELD
DEPOT ROAD
GRAND DEPOT RD
Mulgrave Pond
Mulgrave Sch
Woodhill Prim Sch
Cardwell Prim Sch
St. Peter's RC Prim Sch
Foxfield Prim Sch
Nightingale Prim Sch
St. Margaret's C of E Prim Sch
The Royal Garrison Church of St. George
DAWSON CL
RAGLAN RD
FREDERICK PLACE
BURRAGE PLACE
H J K L M N P
1 2 3 4 5 6 7 8 9 10

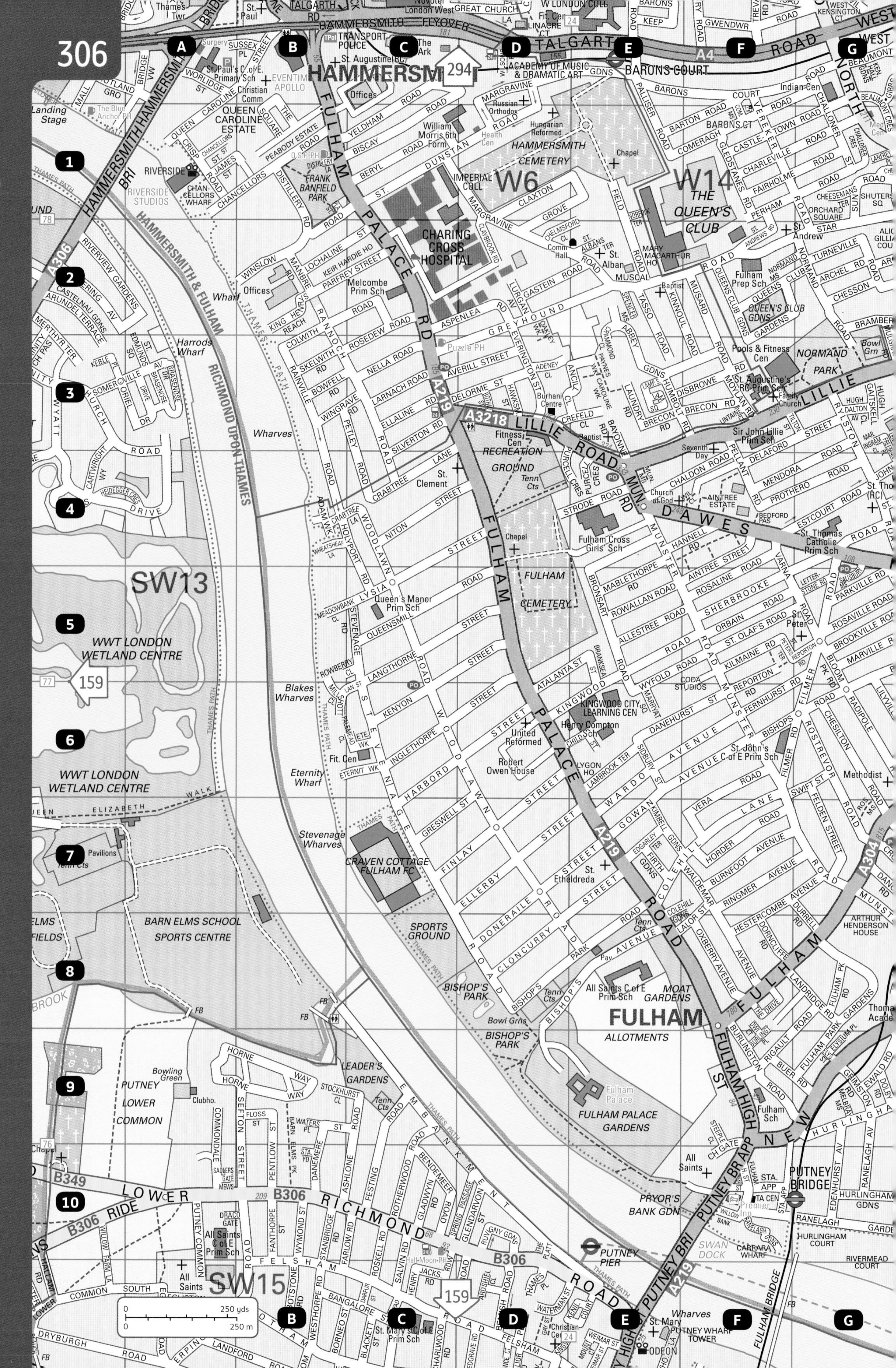
HAMMERSMITH
FULHAM
W6
W14
SW13
SW15
THE QUEEN'S CLUB
CHARING CROSS HOSPITAL
HAMMERSMITH CEMETERY
FULHAM CEMETERY
RECREATION GROUND
WWT LONDON WETLAND CENTRE
BARN ELMS SCHOOL SPORTS CENTRE
PUTNEY LOWER COMMON
CRAVEN COTTAGE FULHAM FC
SPORTS GROUND
BISHOP'S PARK
FULHAM PALACE GARDENS
MOAT GARDENS
ALLOTMENTS
LEADER'S GARDENS
PRYOR'S BANK GDN
PUTNEY BRIDGE
PUTNEY PIER
BARONS COURT
HAMMERSMITH FLYOVER
HAMMERSMITH BRIDGE
PUTNEY BRIDGE
FULHAM BRIDGE
RICHMOND UPON THAMES
HAMMERSMITH & FULHAM
FULHAM PALACE RD
LILLIE ROAD
DAWES ROAD
TALGARTH ROAD
LOWER RICHMOND ROAD
FULHAM ROAD
NEW KINGS ROAD
FULHAM HIGH ST
PUTNEY HIGH ST
A4
A219
A3218
A306
A304
B306
B349
294
159
Landing Stage
Riverside Studios
Harrods Wharf
Wharves
Blakes Wharves
Eternity Wharf
Stevenage Wharves
Swan Dock
Carrara Wharf
Fulham Palace
Fulham Cross Girls' Sch
Kingwood City Learning Cen
Henry Compton Sch
Queen's Manor Prim Sch
All Saints C of E Prim Sch
Fulham Prep Sch
Academy of Music & Dramatic Art
THAMES PATH
250 yds
250 m
A B C D E F G
1 2 3 4 5 6 7 8 9 10

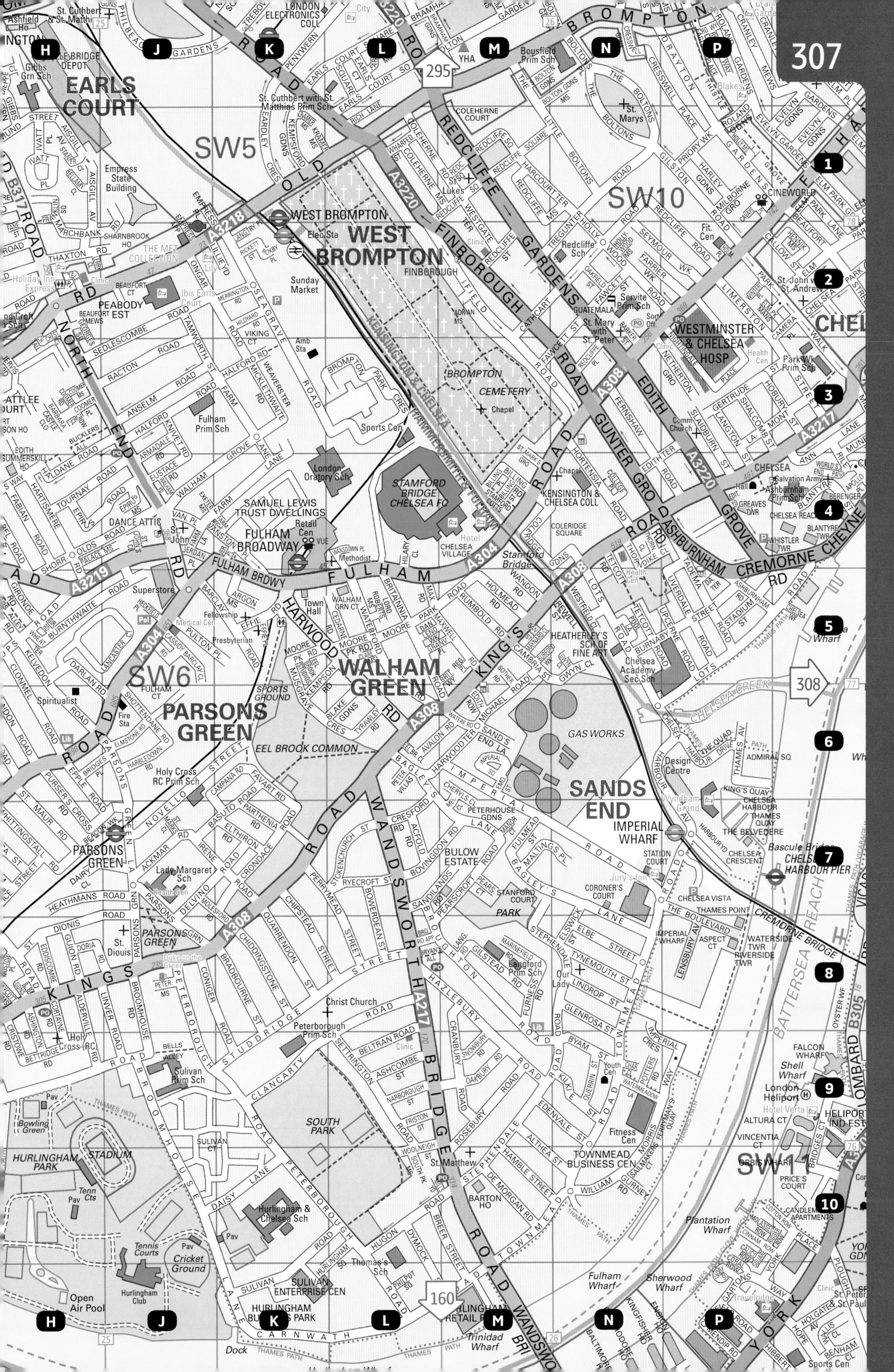

EARLS COURT
SW5
SW10
SW6
WEST BROMPTON
BROMPTON CEMETERY
STAMFORD BRIDGE CHELSEA FC
FULHAM BROADWAY
WALHAM GREEN
PARSONS GREEN
SANDS END
EEL BROOK COMMON
SOUTH PARK
HURLINGHAM PARK
GAS WORKS
WESTMINSTER & CHELSEA HOSP
KENSINGTON & CHELSEA COLL
OLD BROMPTON ROAD
REDCLIFFE GARDENS
FINBOROUGH ROAD
FULHAM ROAD
KING'S ROAD
WANDSWORTH BRIDGE ROAD
NORTH END ROAD
CREMORNE ROAD
LOTS ROAD
IMPERIAL ROAD
HARWOOD ROAD
NEW KING'S ROAD
EDITH GROVE
GUNTER GRO
FULHAM BRDWY
WEST BROMPTON
PARSONS GREEN
IMPERIAL WHARF
CHELSEA HARBOUR
CHELSEA HARBOUR PIER
BATTERSEA REACH
CREMORNE BRIDGE
London Heliport
Hurlingham Club
Open Air Pool
Cricket Ground
Fulham Wharf
Sherwood Wharf
Plantation Wharf
Trinidad Wharf
Lombard B305
CINEWORLD
295
308
160
H
J
K
L
M
N
P
1
2
3
4
5
6
7
8
9
10

CHELSEA
SW3
SW10
SW11
SW6
BATTERSEA PARK
BATTERSEA
FULHAM ROAD
KING'S ROAD
CHEYNE WALK
CHELSEA EMBANKMENT
CREMORNE RD
BATTERSEA BRI
ALBERT BRI
ALBERT BRIDGE ROAD
BATTERSEA BRIDGE ROAD
BATTERSEA PARK ROAD
PRINCE OF WALES DR
LATCHMERE ROAD
WESTBRIDGE ROAD
LOMBARD ROAD
FALCON ROAD
ROYAL HOSPITAL ROAD
OAKLEY STREET
BEAUFORT ST
THE ROYAL MARSDEN
ROYAL BROMPTON HOSP
WESTMINSTER & CHELSEA HOSP
CHELSEA PHYSIC GARDEN
NATIONAL ARMY MUSEUM
BURTON'S COURT
ROYAL HOSP CHELSEA
CADOGAN PIER
CHELSEA HARBOUR PIER
Bascule Bridge
London Heliport
CHILDREN'S ZOO
Peace Pagoda
REC GRDS
ROYAL COLL OF ART
ROYAL ACAD OF DANCE
KENSINGTON & CHELSEA
WANDSWORTH
THAMES PATH
BATTERSEA REACH
Chelsea Wharf
St. Mary's Wharves
Plantation Wharf
YORK GDNS
WINSTANLEY EST
Theatre503
Superstores
CINEWORLD
Chelsea Old Town Hall
Chelsea Old Ch
Crosby Hall
Carlyle's Ho (NT)
296
307
160
A B C D E F G
1 2 3 4 5 6 7 8 9 10
0 250 yds
0 250 m

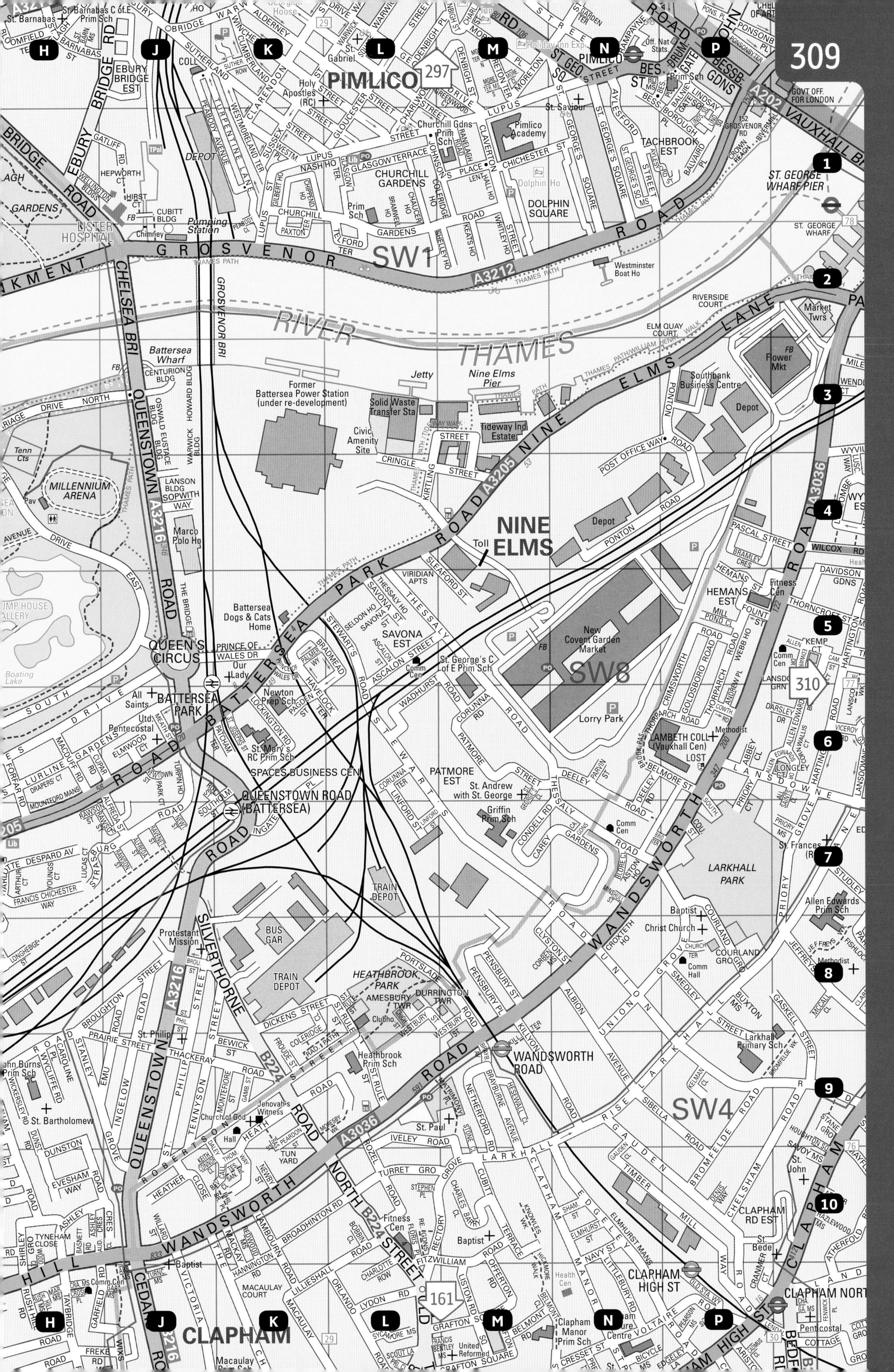
PIMLICO
297
Holy Apostles (RC)
Churchill Gdns Prim Sch
Pimlico Academy
St. Saviour
TACHBROOK EST
CHURCHILL GARDENS
DOLPHIN SQUARE
Dolphin Ho
Pimlico
GOVT OFF. FOR LONDON
VAUXHALL BRIDGE
A202
ST. GEORGE WHARF PIER
ST. GEORGE WHARF
EBURY BRIDGE EST
EBURY BRIDGE ROAD
LISTER HOSPITAL
Pumping Station
GROSVENOR ROAD
A3212
SW1
Westminster Boat Ho
THAMES PATH
RIVER THAMES
CHELSEA BRI
GROSVENOR BRI
Battersea Wharf
Former Battersea Power Station (under re-development)
Jetty
Nine Elms Pier
Solid Waste Transfer Sta
Civic Amenity Site
Tideway Ind Estate
RIVERSIDE COURT
ELM QUAY COURT
Market Twrs
Flower Mkt
Southbank Business Centre
Depot
NINE ELMS LANE
A3205
PONTON ROAD
POST OFFICE WAY
CRINGLE STREET
KIRTLING STREET
NINE ELMS
Toll
MILLENNIUM ARENA
QUEENSTOWN ROAD
A3216
Marco Polo Ho
SOPWITH WAY
PRINCE OF WALES DR
QUEEN'S CIRCUS
Battersea Dogs & Cats Home
BATTERSEA PARK ROAD
BATTERSEA PARK
All Saints
Utd Pentecostal
Newton Prep Sch
St. Mary's RC Prim Sch
SAVONA EST
St. George's C of E Prim Sch
New Covent Garden Market
SW8
Lorry Park
NINE ELMS
HEMANS EST
Fitness Cen
WILCOX RD
A3036
WANDSWORTH ROAD
LAMBETH COLL (Vauxhall Cen)
Methodist
LARKHALL PARK
PATMORE EST
St. Andrew with St. George
Griffin Prim Sch
SPACES BUSINESS CEN
QUEENSTOWN ROAD (BATTERSEA)
TRAIN DEPOT
BUS GAR
Protestant Mission
SILVERTHORNE ROAD
HEATHBROOK PARK
AMESBURY TWR
DURRINGTON TWR
Heathbrook Prim Sch
St. Philip
Jehovah's Witness
Church of God
WANDSWORTH ROAD
St. Paul
Baptist
Christ Church
COURLAND GRO
Allen Edwards Prim Sch
St. Frances
Larkhall Primary Sch
SW4
310
St. John
CLAPHAM RD EST
St. Bede
CLAPHAM HIGH ST
CLAPHAM NORTH
Pentecostal
Fitness Cen
161
Clapham Manor Prim Sch
United Reformed
GRAFTON SQUARE
CLAPHAM
Macaulay Prim Sch
St. Bartholomew
John Burns Prim Sch
Comm Cen
Health Cen
B224
NORTH STREET
LARKHALL RISE
CEDARS RD
H J K L M N P
1 2 3 4 5 6 7 8 9 10

A
B
C
D
E
F
G
1
2
3
4
5
6
7
8
9
10
298
309
161
VAUXHALL
SW1
SE11
SW8
SW9
SW4
KENNINGTON
SOUTH LAMBETH
STOCKWELL
ST. GEORGE WHARF PIER
RIVERSIDE WK GARDENS
VAUXHALL BRI
BRIDGEFOOT
WANDSWORTH RD
BUS STATION
PARRY ST
LANE
SIS/MI6
ALBERT EMBANKMENT
KENNINGTON LANE
HARLEYFORD ROAD
KENNINGTON OVAL
THE KIA OVAL (SURREY C.C.C.)
GAS WORKS
GASWORKS GALLERY
SPRING GDNS
VAUXHALL PARK
KENNINGTON PARK
SPORTS GRD
KENNINGTON ROAD
KENNINGTON PARK ROAD
CAMBERWELL
OVAL
SOUTH LAMBETH ROAD
CLAPHAM ROAD
BRIXTON ROAD
STOCKWELL ROAD
LANSDOWNE WAY
FENTIMAN ROAD
WYVIL ROAD
LARKHALL PARK
SLADE GDNS
MAX ROACH PARK
LAMBETH HOSPITAL
CLAPHAM NORTH
STOCKWELL PARK ESTATE
LOUGHBOROUGH ESTATE
ANGELL TOWN ESTATE
COWLEY ESTATE
CALDWELL GARDENS ESTATE
STUDLEY ESTATE
MURSELL ESTATE
STOCKWELL GARDENS EST
CLAPHAM RD EST
WYCK GARDENS
BUS GAR
Flower Mkt
Depot
O2 ACADEMY BRIXTON
250 yds
250 m
A202
A3036
A3204
A203
A3
A23

WALWORTH
SE17
SURREY GDNS
SURREY SQUARE PARK
FARADAY GARDENS
AYLESBURY EST
ELIZABETH EST
BURGESS PARK
Kart Track
ALBANY ROAD
B214
SE15
BURGESS BUSINESS PARK
ELMINGTON ESTATE
DOWLAS ESTATE
WYNDHAM ESTATE
CAMBERWELL
CAMBERWELL ROAD
A215
A202
MEDLAR ST
GREEK CATHEDRAL
CAMBERWELL GREEN
CAMBERWELL CHURCH ST
PECKHAM ROAD
BRUNSWICK PARK
SCEAUX GDNS
CAMBERWELL COLL OF ARTS
S LONDON GALL
TOWN HALL
LUCAS GDNS
MYATT'S FIELDS PARK
DENMARK HILL
SE5
CRAWFORD ESTATE
VALMAR TRADING ESTATE
MAUDSLEY HOSPITAL
KING'S COLLEGE HOSPITAL
CHAMPION PK
WILLIAM BOOTH COLL
CHAMPION PARK EST
RUSKIN PARK
LOUGHBOROUGH JUNCTION
A2217
A2216
DOG KENNEL HILL EST
CHAMPION HILL ESTATE
COLDHARBOUR LANE
DOG KENNEL HILL
GROVE PARK
ALLOT
299
312
162
H
J
K
L
M
N
P
1
2
3
4
5
6
7
8
9
10

A
B
C
D
E
F
G
1
2
3
4
5
6
7
8
9
10
300
311
162
SE5
SE1
SE15
SE5
PECKHAM
ROLLS ROAD
CATLIN STREET
ROTHERHITHE NEW ROAD
VERNEY ROAD
OLD KENT ROAD
TRAFALGAR AV
B215
SUMNER RD
WILLOWBROOK RD
PECKHAM HILL STREET
PECKHAM PARK ROAD
B216
PECKHAM HIGH STREET
QUEENS ROAD
A202
A2
A2215
A2214
HANOVER PK
RYE LANE
PECKHAM RYE
NUNHEAD LANE
EVELINA ROAD
CHOUMERT ROAD
CHADWICK ROAD
LYNDHURST GROVE
COMMERCIAL WAY
FENHAM ROAD
ASYLUM ROAD
CLIFTON CRES
CULMORE ROAD
GOLDSMITH ROAD
MEETING HOUSE LANE
BRAYARDS ROAD
KIMBERLEY AVENUE
ILDERTON ROAD
STUBBS DRIVE
ABERCORN WAY
PATERSON PARK
Superstores
Walworth Academy
Methodist
Fire Sta
St. Philip & St. Mark
MAWBEY ESTATE
Phoenix Prim Sch
SIX BRIDGES TRADING EST
Comm Cen
Cobourg Prim Sch
SPORTS GRD
Football Pitch
Pav
GESS PARK
SURREY LINEAR CANAL PARK
Christ Apostolic
24hr Superstore
Cantium Retail Park
Mountain of Fire
KENT PARK IND EST
Southwark Reuse & Recycling Centre
Gas Works
Christ Church
NICE BUS. PK
TUSTIN ESTATE
Pilgrims' Way Prim Sch
Tuke Sch
Gloucester Prim Sch
Haymerle Sch
Church of Christ
LINDLEY ESTATE
LEYTON SQ
FRIARY ESTATE
St. Francis RC Prim Sch
FRANCISCAN FRIARY
Our Lady of Sorrows (RC)
Baptist
LEDBURY EST
Camelot Prim Sch
CAROLINE GARDENS
Superstore
SPORTS GRD
BRIMMINGTON PARK
St. John with St. Andrew
St. Luke
BELLS GARDEN EST
Apostolic
Peckham Pk Sch
OLIVER-GOLDSMITH ESTATE
Oliver Goldsmith Prim Sch
CAMBERWELL COLL OF ARTS
S LONDON GALL
Assemblies of God
St. James the Gt RC Prim Sch
Pulse Fitness Cen
Lib
PO
Pol
QUEENS ROAD PECKHAM
Methodist
John Donne Prim Sch
COSSALL PARK
St. Thomas the Apostle Coll
PELICAN ESTATE
Harris Academy Peckham
Highshore Sch
Aylesham Centre
BUS STA
CLIFTON ESTATE
WITCOMBE PT
PREMIER
PECKHAM RYE
St. James (RC)
SPORTS GROUND
WARWICK GDNS
All Saints
BUS GAR
St. Mary Magdalene Prim Sch
Church of God
SOUTHWARK ADULT ED (Thomas Calton Cen)
Bellenden Prim Sch
Evangelical
Gospel Hall
Salvation Army
Faith Chapel
Revival Church
St. Saviour
Dog Kennel Hill Prim Sch
DOG KENNEL HILL EST
Child Care Cen
Child Health Cen
Health Cen
Comm Cen
Rye Oak Sch
St. Anthony
St. John's & St. Clement's Prim Sch
BRAYARDS RD EST
0
250 yds
250 m

H
J
K
L
M
N
P
DEPTFORD
SE8
SE14
SE4
NEW CROSS GATE
NEW CROSS
DEPTFORD PARK
THE DEN MILLWALL FC
GEMINI PROJECT
Power Station
Chimney
ORION BUS. CEN
Recycling Cen
SURREY CANAL ROAD
BRIDGE MEADOWS
BRIDGE HOUSE MEADOWS
DEPTFORD TRADING EST
FOLKESTONE GARDENS
PARKSIDE BUSINESS ESTATE
SAYES COURT PARK
Sir Francis Drake Prim Sch
GRINSTEAD ROAD
EVELYN STREET
DEPTFORD HIGH STREET
EDWARD STREET
SANFORD STREET
PAGNELL ST
AMERSHAM VALE
FORDHAM PARK
Deptford Grn Sch
Childeric Prim Sch
NEW CROSS ROAD
LEWISHAM WAY
AMERSHAM RD
FLORENCE RD
Superstore
NEW CROSS GATE
HATCHAM MS BUSINESS CEN
St James Hatcham C of E Prim Sch
UNI OF LONDON GOLDSMITHS COLL
St. James
BUS GARAGE
Haberdashers Aske's Hatcham Coll
NEW CROSS GATE CUTTING NATURE RESERVE
ALLOT
TELEGRAPH HILL PARK
Bandstand
Edmund Waller Prim Sch
Hatcham Temple Grove Free Sch
ECKINGTON GDNS
Myatt Gdn Prim Sch
FRIENDLY GARDENS
Lucas Vale Prim Sch
DRAKEFELL ROAD
B2142 ROAD
Haberdashers Aske's Hatcham Coll
CROSSWAYS SIXTH FORM
BROCKLEY
John Stainer Prim Sch
NUNHEAD CEMETERY
HABERDASHERS ASKE'S PLAYING FIELD
NUNHEAD
Hollydale Prim Sch
LAUSANNE ROAD
GELLATLY RD
KENDER A202 STREET
POMEROY B2227 STREET
301
314
163
1
2
3
4
5
6
7
8
9
10

A
B
C
D
E
F
G
1
2
3
4
5
6
7
8
9
10
DEPTFORD
Palmer's Wharf
MASTHOUSE TERRACE PIER
Payne's Wharf
Borthwick Wharf
KNIGHTS TOWER
Sailing Centre
Landing Stage
TOWER HAMLETS
GREENWICH
E14
GREENWICH REACH
ISLAND GARDENS
MANCHESTER ROAD
302
SE8
GREENWICH PIER
Greenwich Pier
Wood Wharf
CUTTY SARK
Old Royal Navy Coll.
TRINITY COLL OF MUSIC
UNI OF GREENWICH (MaritimeGreenwich Campus)
ROMNEY ROAD
A206
QUEEN'S HOUSE
NATIONAL MARITIME MU
CREEK ROAD
A200
McMILLAN STUDENT VILLAGE
St. Nicholas with St. Lukes
Laban
BROOKMARSH IND EST
DEPTFORD CHURCH STREET
DEPTFORD HIGH STREET
DEPTFORD
Tidemill Academy Prim Sch
Leisure Centre
FAIRCHARM TRADING EST
GREENWICH
GREENWICH HIGH ROAD
James Wolfe Prim Sch
GREENWICH CEN BUS. PK
ROYAL HILL
Circus Gate
King George Street Gate
SE10
GREENWICH SOUTH STREET
LEWISHAM SOUTHWARK COLL (Deptford Campus)
A2209
313
DEPTFORD BRIDGE
BLACKHEATH ROAD
EGERTON DRIVE
B208
CROOMS HILL
Our Lady (RC)
St. Ursula's Convent Sch
B209
BLACKHEATH HILL
A2
SHOOTERS HILL
FLORENCE ROAD
B218
BROOKMILL ROAD
A2210
Lucas Vale Prim Sch
FRIENDLY GARDENS
St. Stephen's C of E Prim Sch
Water Works
LEWISHAM ROAD
SE13
BLACKHEATH BUS. EST
Morden Mt Prim Sch
ST. JOHN'S
ST. JOHNS
Ashmead Jun Sch
LEWISHAM WAY
ELVERSON ROAD
A2211
LEWISHAM SOUTHWARK COLL (Lewisham Way Campus)
SE14
LOAMPIT HILL
A20
LOAMPIT VALE
THURSTON RD
LEWISHAM
GRANVILLE PK ADULT LEARNING CEN
BUS STA
LOAMPIT VALE
163
Lewisham Br Prim Sch
LEWISHAM
LEWISHAM HIGH ST
Lewisham Centre
BELMONT HILL
0 250 yds
0 250 m
HILLY FIELDS

H
J
K
L
M
N
P
1
2
3
4
5
6
7
8
9
10
Lovell's Wharf
Power Sta
Meridian Prim Sch
TRAFALGAR ROAD
A206
WOOLWICH ROAD
Arches Leisure Cen
MAZE HILL
EAST GREENWICH PLEASAUNCE
WESTCOMBE PARK
SE7
SE3
GREENWICH PARK
ONE TREE HILL
ROYAL OBSERVATORY GREENWICH (FLAMSTEED HOUSE)
Peter Harrison Planetarium
THE GARDENS
THE WILDERNESS (DEER PARK)
Bandstand
Blackheath Gate
Vanbrugh Park Gate
Maze Hill Gate
Maze Hill House Gate
Creed Place Gate
Park Row Gate
RANGER'S HOUSE
John Roan Sec Sch
Blackheath High Sch
Invicta Inf Sch
Kingdom Hall
The Pointer Sch
Bardon Lodge
VANBRUGH PARK
SHOOTERS HILL ROAD
A2
B210
CHARLTON WAY
BLACKHEATH
PRINCE OF WALES ROAD
STRATHEDEN ROAD
Blackheath Nursery & Prep Sch
Morden College
All Saints Cof E Prim Sch
John Ball Sch
Blackheath High Sch (Jun Dept)
Clarendon Hotel
BLACKHEATH HALLS
Our Lady (RC)
St. Michael & All Angels
Brooklands JMI Sch
SPORTS GROUNDS
St. Matthew Academy
BLACKHEATH HOSP
LEE TERRACE
B220
LEE ROAD
B212
164
303
A102
A2213
KIDBROOKE PARK ROAD
Wingfield Prim Sch
KIDB

Notes on how to use the index

The index starting on page 318 combines entries for street names, place names, places of interest, stations, hospitals, schools, colleges and universities.

Place names are shown in capital letters,
e.g. **ACTON**, W3 .... **138** CN74
These include towns, villages and other localities within the area covered by this atlas.

Places of interest are shown with a star symbol,
e.g. ★ **British Mus, The** WC1 ... **285** P7
These include parks, museums, galleries, other important buildings and tourist attractions.

Other features are shown by symbols as listed :-

- Railway station
- London Overground station
- London Underground station
- DLR Docklands Light Railway station
- Tra Tramlink station
- Riv Pedestrian ferry landing stage
- Bus station
- H Hospital
- Sch School
- Coll College
- Uni University
- Jct Road junction
- ● Selected industrial estate / commercial building
- Selected major shop / shopping centre / market

All other entries are for street names.

When there is more than one feature with exactly the same name then that name is shown only once in the index.
It is then followed by a list of entries for each postal district that contains a feature with that same name. London postal district references are given first in alpha-numeric order and are followed by either the post town or locality in alphabetical order. For example, there are three streets called **Ardley Close** in this atlas and the index entry shows that one of these is in London postal district NW10, one is in London postal district SE6 and one is in Ruislip HA4.
e.g. **Ardley Cl**, NW10 ....**118** CS62
SE6..............................**183** DY90
Ruislip HA4 ....**115** BQ59

In cases where there are two or more streets of the same name in the same postal area, extra information is given in brackets to aid location.
Some postal areas are abbreviated and a full list of locality and post town abbreviations used in this atlas is given on the following page.

All entries are followed by the page number and grid reference on which the name will be found. So, in the example above, **Ardley Close,** NW10 will be found on page **118** in square CS62.

All entries are indexed to the largest scale map on which they are shown.

The index also contains some features which are not actually named on the maps because there is not enough space. In these cases the adjoining or nearest named thoroughfare to such a street is shown in *italic.* The reference indicates where the unnamed street is located *off* the named thoroughfare.
e.g. **Baird Cl**, E10 *off Marconi Rd*. **123** EA60

A strict letter-by-letter alphabetical order is followed in this index. Entries beginning with numerals appear at the beginning of the index.

Names beginning with a definite article (i.e. **The**) are indexed from their second word onwards with the definite article being placed at the end of the name.
e.g. **Avenue, The**, E4................. **101** ED51

Standard terms such as **Avenue, Close, Rise** and **Road** are abbreviated in the index but are ordered alphabetically as if given in full. So, for example, **Abbots Ri** comes before **Abbots Rd.** A list of these abbreviations is given below.

General abbreviations

A&E	Accident & Emergency
Acad	Academy
All	Alley
App	Approach
Apts	Apartments
Arc	Arcade
Assoc	Association
Av	Avenue
Ave	Avenue
BUPA	British United Provident Association
Bdy	Broadway
Bk	Bank
Bldg	Building
Bldgs	Buildings
Boul	Boulevard
Bowl	Bowling
Br	Bridge
C of E	Church of England
Cath	Cathedral, Catholic
CCC	County Cricket Club
Cem	Cemetery
Cen	Central, Centre
Cft	Croft
Cfts	Crofts
Ch	Church
Chyd	Churchyard
Circ	Circus
Cl	Close
Co	County
Coll	College
Comb	Combined
Comm	Community
Comp	Comprehensive
Conf	Conference
Cont	Continuing
Conv	Convent
Cor	Corner
Cors	Corners
Cotts	Cottages
Cres	Crescent
Ct	Court
Ctyd	Courtyard
Del	Delivery
Dep	Depot
Dept	Department
Dev	Development
Dr	Drive
Dws	Dwellings
E	East
Ed	Education, Educational
Embk	Embankment
Est	Estate
Ex	Exchange
Exhib	Exhibition
Ext	Extension
FC	Football Club
Fit Cen	Fitness Centre
Fld	Field
Flds	Fields
Fm	Farm
GM	Grant Maintained
Gall	Gallery
Gar	Garage
Gdn	Garden
Gdns	Gardens
Gen	General
Gra	Grange
Gram	Grammar
Grd	Ground
Grds	Grounds
Grn	Green
Grns	Greens
Gro	Grove
Gros	Groves
Gt	Great
HQ	Headquarters
Ho	House
Hos	Houses
Hosp	Hospital
HPRU	Human Psycho-pharmacology Research Unit
Hts	Heights
Ind	Industrial
Indep	Independent
Inf	Infant(s)
Inst	Institute
Int	International
JM	Junior Mixed
JMI	Junior Mixed & Infant(s)
Jun	Junior
Junct	Junction
La	Lane
Las	Lanes
Lib	Library
Lit	Literary
Lo	Lodge
Lwr	Lower
Mans	Mansions
Med	Medical
Med	Medicine
Mem	Memorial
Met	Metropolitan
Mid	Middle
Mkt	Market
Ms	Mews
Mt	Mount
Mus	Museum
N	North
NHS	National Health Service
Nat	National
Nurs	Nursery
Off	Office
PO	Post Office
PRU	Pupil Referral Unit
Par	Parade
Pas	Passage
Pk	Park
Pl	Place
Pol	Police
Poly	Polytechnic
Prec	Precinct
Prep	Preparatory
Prim	Primary
Prom	Promenade
Pt	Point
Quad	Quadrant
RC	Roman Catholic
Rbt	Roundabout
Rd	Road
Rds	Roads
Rehab	Rehabilitation
Ri	Rise
S	South
Sch	School
Schs	Schools
Sec	Secondary
Sen	Senior
Shop	Shopping
Spec	Special
Sq	Square
St	Street
St.	Saint
Sta	Station
Sts	Streets
Sub	Subway
TA	Territorial Army
Tech	Technical, Technology
Tenn	Tennis
Ter	Terrace
Thea	Theatre
Trd	Trading
Twr	Tower
Twrs	Towers
Uni	University
Upr	Upper
VA	Voluntary Aided
VC	Voluntary Controlled
Vet	Veterinary
Vil	Villas
Vil	Villa
Vw	View
W	West
Wd	Wood
Wds	Woods
Wf	Wharf
Wk	Walk
Wks	Works
Yd	Yard

Locality & post town abbreviations

Note: In the following list of abbreviations post towns are in **bold** type.

Abb.L.	**Abbots Langley**
Abin.Com.	Abinger Common
Abin.Ham.	Abinger Hammer
Add.	**Addlestone**
Alb.Hth	Albury Heath
Ald.	Aldenham
Amer.	**Amersham**
Amer.O.T.	Amersham Old Town
Art.	Artington
Ash.Grn	Ashley Green
Ashf.	**Ashford**
Ashtd.	**Ashtead**
Ayot St.P.	Ayot Saint Peter
B.End	Bourne End
B.Stort.	Bishop's Stortford
Bad.Dene	Badgers Dene
Bad.Mt	Badgers Mount
Bans.	**Banstead**
Bark.	**Barking**
Barn.	**Barnet**
Barne.	Barnehurst
Beac.	**Beaconsfield**
Beck.	**Beckenham**
Bedd.	Beddington
Bedd.Cor.	Beddington Corner
Bell.	Bellingdon
Belv.	**Belvedere**
Berk.	**Berkhamsted**
Berry's Grn	Berry's Green
Bet.	**Betchworth**
Bex.	**Bexley**
Bexh.	**Bexleyheath**
Bigg.H.	Biggin Hill
Birch Grn	Birch Green
Bkhm	Bookham
Bletch.	Bletchingley
Borwd.	**Borehamwood**
Bov.	Bovingdon
Box H.	Box Hill
Bramfld	Bramfield
Brent.	**Brentford**
Brick.Wd	Bricket Wood
Broad.Com.	Broadley Common
Brock.	Brockham
Brom.	Bromley
Brook.Pk	Brookmans Park
Brox.	**Broxbourne**
Brwd.	**Brentwood**
Buck.H.	**Buckhurst Hill**
Burgh Hth	Burgh Heath
Burn.	Burnham
Bushey Hth	Bushey Heath
Carp.Pk	Carpenders Park
Cars.	**Carshalton**
Cat.	**Caterham**
Ch.End	Church End
Ch.Lang.	Church Langley
Ch.St.G.	**Chalfont Saint Giles**
Chad.Hth	Chadwell Heath
Chad.Spr.	Chadwell Springs
Chad.St.M.	Chadwell Saint Mary
Chaff.Hun.	Chafford Hundred
Chal.St.P.	Chalfont Saint Peter
Chan.Cr.	Chandlers Cross
Chap.End	Chapmore End
Charl.	Charlwood
Chel.	Chelsham
Chels.	Chelsfield
Cher.	**Chertsey**
Chesh.	**Chesham**
Chesh.B.	Chesham Bois
Chess.	**Chessington**
Chev.	Chevening
Chig.	**Chigwell**
Chilw.	Chilworth
Chipper.	Chipperfield
Chis.	**Chislehurst**
Chob.Com.	Chobham Common
Chorl.	Chorleywood
Chsht	Cheshunt
Cipp.	Cippenham
Clay.	Claygate
Cob.	**Cobham**
Cockfos.	Cockfosters
Cole Grn	Cole Green
Colesh.	Coleshill
Coll.Row	Collier Row
Coln.Hth	Colney Heath
Coln.St	Colney Street
Colnbr.	Colnbrook
Cooper.	Coopersale
Couls.	**Coulsdon**
Cran.	Cranford
Craw.	Crawley
Cray.	Crayford
Crock.	Crockenhill
Crock.H.	Crockham Hill
Crox.Grn	Croxley Green
Croy.	**Croydon**
Dag.	**Dagenham**
Dance.H.	Dancers Hill
Dart.	**Dartford**
Denh.	Denham
Dor.	**Dorking**
Dorney R.	Dorney Reach
Down.	Downside
Dunt.Grn	Dunton Green
E.Barn.	East Barnet
E.Bed.	East Bedfont
E.Burn.	East Burnham
E.Clan.	East Clandon
E.Ewell	East Ewell
E.Hors.	East Horsley
E.Mol.	**East Molesey**
E.Til.	East Tilbury
Earls.	Earlswood
Eastcote Vill.	Eastcote Village
Eden.	Edenbridge
Edg.	**Edgware**
Eff.	Effingham
Eff.Junct.	Effingham Junction
Egh.	**Egham**
Elm Pk	Elm Park
Elm.Wds	Elmstead Woods
Els.	Elstree
Enf.	**Enfield**
Eng.Grn	Englefield Green
Epp.	**Epping**
Epp.Grn	Epping Green
Epp.Upl.	Epping Upland
Epsom Com.	Epsom Common
Essen.	Essendon
Ewell E.	Ewell East
Ewell W.	Ewell West
Eyns.	Eynsford
Far.Grn	Farley Green
Farn.Com.	Farnham Common
Farn.Royal	Farnham Royal
Farnboro.	Farnborough
Farnc.	Farncombe
Fawk.	Fawkham
Fawk.Grn	Fawkham Green
Felt.	**Feltham**
Fetch.	Fetcham
Flack.Hth	Flackwell Heath
Flam.	Flamstead
Flaun.	Flaunden
Fnghm	Farningham
Forty Grn	Forty Green
Frog.	Frogmore
Gat.	Gatwick
Gdmg.	Godalming
Gdse.	**Godstone**
Geo.Grn	George Green
Ger.Cr.	**Gerrards Cross**
Gidea Pk	Gidea Park
Gilston Pk	Gilston Park
Godden Grn	Godden Green
Goms.	Gomshall
Grav.	**Gravesend**
Green.	**Greenhithe**
Grn St Grn	Green Street Green
Grnf.	**Greenford**
Gt Amwell	Great Amwell
Gt Warley	Great Warley
Guil.	**Guildford**
H.Wyc.	High Wycombe
Hackbr.	Hackbridge
Had.Wd	Hadley Wood
Halst.	Halstead
Han.	Hanworth
Har.	**Harrow**
Har.Hill	Harrow on the Hill
Har.Wld	Harrow Weald
Hare.	Harefield
Harl.	**Harlow**
Harling.	Harlington
Harm.	Harmondsworth
Harold Wd	Harold Wood
Hast.	Hastingwood
Hat.	**Hatfield**
Hat.Hth	Hatfield Heath
Hav.at.Bow.	Havering-atte-Bower
Haz.	Hazlemere
Hedg.	Hedgerley
Hem.H.	**Hemel Hempstead**
Herons.	Heronsgate
Hert.	**Hertford**
Hert.Hth	Hertford Heath
Hext.	Hextable
High Barn.	High Barnet
Hinch.Wd	Hinchley Wood
Hkwd	Hookwood
Hlgdn	Hillingdon
Hmptn H.	Hampton Hill
Hmptn W.	Hampton Wick
Hmptn.	**Hampton**
Hodd.	**Hoddesdon**
Holm.	Holmwood
Holm.St.M.	Holmbury Saint Mary
Holt.	Holtspur
Holy.	Holyport
Horl.	**Horley**
Horn.	**Hornchurch**
Hort.Kir.	Horton Kirby
Houns.	**Hounslow**
Houns.W.	Hounslow West
Hunt.Br.	Hunton Bridge
Hutt.	Hutton
Hyde Hth	Hyde Heath
Ickhm	Ickenham
Ilf.	**Ilford**
Islw.	**Isleworth**
Ken.	**Kenley**
Kes.	**Keston**
Kgfld	Kingfield
Kgswd	Kingswood
Kings L.	**Kings Langley**
Kings.T.	**Kingston upon Thames**
Knap.	Knaphill
Knock.	Knockholt
Knock.P.	Knockholt Pound
Knot.Grn	Knotty Green
Lamb.End	Lambourne End
Let.Hth	Letchmore Heath
Letty Grn	Letty Green
Lmpfld	Limpsfield
Lmpfld Cht	Limpsfield Chart
Lmsfd	Lemsford
Lon.Col.	London Colney
Lon.Gat.Air.	London Gatwick Airport
Lon.Hthrw Air.	London Heathrow Airport
Lon.Hthrw Air.N	London Heathrow Airport N
Long Dit.	Long Ditton
Long.	**Longfield**
Longcr.	Longcross
Loud.	Loudwater
Loug.	**Loughton**
Lt.Berk.	Little Berkhamsted
Lt.Chal.	Little Chalfont
Lt.Hth	Little Heath
Lt.Warley	Little Warley
Lthd.	**Leatherhead**
Lvsdn	Leavesden
Lwfld Hth	Lowfield Heath
Lwr Kgswd	Lower Kingswood
Lwr Naze.	Lower Nazeing
Magd.Lav.	Magdalen Laver
Maid.	Maidenhead
Map.Cr.	Maple Cross
Mark Hall N.	Mark Hall North
Match.Grn	Matching Green
Match.Tye	Matching Tye
Mdgrn	Middlegreen
Merst.	Merstham
Mick.	Mickleham
Mid Holm.	Mid Holmwood
Mimbr.	Mimbridge
Mitch.	**Mitcham**
Mitch.Com.	Mitcham Common
Mord.	**Morden**
Mots.Pk	Motspur Park
Mtnsg	Mountnessing
N.Har.	North Harrow
N.Holm.	North Holmwood
N.Mal.	**New Malden**
N.Mymms	North Mymms
N.Ock.	North Ockendon
N.Stfd	North Stifford
N.Wld Bas.	North Weald Bassett
N.Wld Bas.N.	North Weald Bassett North
Nave.	Navestock
Nave.S.	Navestock Side
Naze.	Nazeing
Naze.Gate	Nazeing Gate
New Adgtn	New Addington
New Barn.	New Barnet
Newgate St	Newgate Street
Northumb.Hth	Northumberland Heath
Nthch	Northchurch
Nthflt	Northfleet
Nthlt.	**Northolt**
Nthwd.	**Northwood**
Nutfld	Nutfield
Oakl.	Oaklands
Oakley Grn	Oakley Green
Ock.	Ockham
Old Harl.	Old Harlow
Old Wind.	Old Windsor
Old Wok.	Old Woking
Ong.	Ongar
Ons.Vill.	Onslow Village
Orch.L.	Orchard Leigh
Orp.	**Orpington**
Ott.	Ottershaw
Oxt.	**Oxted**
Pans.	Panshanger
Park St	Park Street
Peasl.	Peaslake
Peasm.	Peasmarsh
Petts Wd	Petts Wood
Picc.End	Piccotts End
Pilg.Hat.	Pilgrim's Hatch
Pnr.	**Pinner**
Pond.End	Ponders End
Port.Wd	Porters Wood
Pot.B.	**Potters Bar**
Pott.Cr.	Potters Crouch
Pott.End	Potten End
Pott.St	Potter Street
Pr.Bot.	Pratt's Bottom
Pur.	**Purley**
Purf.	**Purfleet**
Putt.	Puttenham
Rad.	**Radlett**
Rain.	**Rainham**
Ran.Com.	Ranmore Common
Rayners La	Rayners Lane
Red.	**Redhill**
Redbn	Redbourn
Reig.	**Reigate**
Rich.	**Richmond**
Rick.	**Rickmansworth**
Rod.Val.	Roding Valley
Roe Grn	Roe Green
Rom.	**Romford**
Rosh.	Rosherville
Ruis.	**Ruislip**
Runny.	Runnymede
Rush Grn	Rush Green
Rvrhd	Riverhead
Rydes.	Rydeshill
S.Croy.	**South Croydon**
S.Darenth	South Darenth
S.Har.	South Harrow
S.Holm.	South Holmwood
S.Merst.	South Merstham
S.Mimms	South Mimms
S.Nutfld	South Nutfield
S.Ock.	**South Ockendon**
S.Oxhey	South Oxhey
S.Park	South Park
S.Ruis.	South Ruislip
S.Stfd	South Stifford
S.Wld	South Weald
S.le H.	Stanford-le-Hope
Salf.	Salfords
Sand.	Sandridge
Saw.	**Sawbridgeworth**
Scad.Pk	Scadbury Park
Seer Grn	Seer Green
Send M.	Send Marsh
Sev.	**Sevenoaks**
Shalf.	Shalford
Sham.Grn	Shamley Green
Sheer.	Sheerwater
Shenf.	Shenfield
Shep.	**Shepperton**
Shipley Br	Shipley Bridge
Shore.	Shoreham
Short.	Shortlands
Sid.	**Sidcup**
Slade Grn	Slade Green
Slou.	**Slough**
St.Alb.	**Saint Albans**
St.Geo.H.	Saint George's Hill
St.John's	Saint John's
St.M.Cray	Saint Mary Cray
St.P.Cray	Saint Paul's Cray
Stai.	**Staines-upon-Thames**
Stan.	**Stanmore**
Stanboro.	Stanborough
Stanfd.Riv.	Stanford Rivers
Stans.Abb.	Stanstead Abbotts
Stanw.	Stanwell
Stanw.M.	Stanwell Moor
Stap.Abb.	Stapleford Abbotts
Stap.Taw.	Stapleford Tawney
Sthflt	Southfleet
Sthl Grn	Southall Green
Sthl.	**Southall**
Stoke D'Ab.	Stoke D'Abernon
Stoke P.	Stoke Poges
Strood Grn	Strood Green
Sun.	Sunbury-on-Thames
Sund.	Sundridge
Surb.	**Surbiton**
Sutt.	**Sutton**
Sutt.Grn	Sutton Green
Sutt.H.	Sutton at Hone
Swan.	**Swanley**
Swans.	**Swanscombe**
T.Ditt.	**Thames Ditton**
Tad.	**Tadworth**
Tand.	Tandridge
Tap.	Taplow
Tats.	Tatsfield
Tedd.	**Teddington**
Th.Hth.	**Thornton Heath**
They.B.	Theydon Bois
They.Gar.	Theydon Garnon
They.Mt	Theydon Mount
Thnwd	Thornwood
Thres.B.	Threshers Bush
Til.	**Tilbury**
Tkgtn	Tokyngton
Turnf.	Turnford
Twick.	**Twickenham**
Tyr.Wd	Tyrrell's Wood
Tytten.	Tyttenhanger
Undrvr	Underriver
Upmin.	**Upminster**
Uxb.	**Uxbridge**
Vir.W.	**Virginia Water**
W.Byf.	**West Byfleet**
W.Clan.	West Clandon
W.Ewell	West Ewell
W.Hors.	West Horsley
W.Hyde	West Hyde
W.Mol.	**West Molesey**
W.Thur.	West Thurrock
W.Til.	West Tilbury
W.Wick.	**West Wickham**
Wal.Abb.	**Waltham Abbey**
Wal.Cr.	**Waltham Cross**
Wall.	**Wallington**
Walt.	**Walton-on-Thames**
Walt.Hill	Walton on the Hill
Warl.	**Warlingham**
Wat.	**Watford**
Wat.Oak.	Water Oakley
Waterf.	Waterford
Wdf.Grn.	**Woodford Green**
Wdhm	Woodham
Wealds.	Wealdstone
Well.	**Welling**
Welw.	Welwyn
Welw.G.C.	**Welwyn Garden City**
Wem.	**Wembley**
Wenn.	Wennington
West Dr.	**West Drayton**
West.	**Westerham**
Westc.	Westcott
Westh.	Westhumble
Wey.	**Weybridge**
Wheat.	Wheathampstead
Whel.Hill	Whelpley Hill
Whiteley Vill.	Whiteley Village
Whyt.	Whyteleafe
Wilm.	Wilmington
Winch.Hill	Winchmore Hill
Wind.	**Windsor**
Wink.	Winkfield
Wok.	**Woking**
Wold.	Woldingham
Won.	Wonersh
Woob.Grn	Wooburn Green
Woob.Moor	Wooburn Moor
Wor.Pk.	**Worcester Park**
Worp.	Worplesdon
Wrays.	Wraysbury
Wyc.End	Wycombe End
Yiew.	Yiewsley

● 1 Canada Sq, E14 302 C3
Uni 200 Pentonville Rd, Hall of Res, N1 286 C1
★ 2 Willow Rd, NW3 120 DE63
● 30 St. Mary Axe, EC3 off St. Mary Axe 287 P8
5 Pancras Sq (Camden Council & Pancras Sq Leisure), N1 276 A10
8 Walworth Rd - Strata, SE1 299 J8
● 99 Bishopsgate, EC2 off Bishopsgate 287 N8

A

Aaron Hill Rd, E6 293 M6
Abady Ho, SW1 off Page St 297 P8
Abberley Ms, SW4 off Cedars Rd 161 DH83
Abberton Wk, Rain. RM13 off Ongar Way 147 FE66
Abbess Cl, E6 293 H7
SW2 181 DP88
Abbess Ter, Loug. IG10 85 EP41
Abbeville Ms, SW4 161 DK84
Abbeville Rd, N8 off Barrington Rd 121 DK56
SW4 181 DJ86
Abbey Av, St.Alb. AL3 42 CA23
Wembley HA0 138 CL68
Abbey Chyd, Wal.Abb. EN9 67 EC33
Abbey Cl, E5 122 DU63
SW8 309 P6
Hayes UB3 135 BV74
Northolt UB5 off Invicta Gro 136 BZ69
Pinner HA5 115 BV55
Romford RM1 127 FG58
Slough SL1 131 AL73
Woking GU22 227 BE116
Sch Abbey C of E Prim Sch, The, St.Alb. AL1 off Grove Rd 43 CD21
Abbey Ct, Wal.Abb. EN9 67 EB34
Abbey Cres, Belv. DA17 166 FA77
Abbeydale Cl, Harl. CM17 52 EW16
Abbeydale Rd, Wem. HA0 138 CN67
Abbey Dr, SW17 off Church La 180 DG92
Abbots Langley WD5 59 BU32
Dartford DA2 187 FE89
Staines-upon-Thames TW18 194 BJ98
Abbeyfield Cl, Mitch. CR4 200 DE96
Abbeyfield Est, SE16 off Abbeyfield Rd 300 G8
Abbeyfield Rd, SE16 300 G8
Abbeyfields Cl, NW10 138 CN68
Abbeyfields Mobile Home Pk, Cher. KT16 194 BK101
Abbey Gdns, NW8 283 N1
SE16 300 D8
SW1 off Great Coll St 298 A6
W6 306 E2
Ashford TW15 175 BP92
Chertsey KT16 194 BG100
Chislehurst BR7 205 EN95
Waltham Abbey EN9 67 EC33
Abbey Grn, Cher. KT16 194 BG100
Abbey Gro, SE2 166 EV77
Abbeyhill Rd, Sid. DA15 186 EW89
● Abbey Ind Est, Mitch. CR4 200 DF99
Wembley HA0 138 CM67
Abbey La, E15 280 F10
Beckenham BR3 183 EA94
Sch Abbey Manor Coll, John Evelyn Ed Cen, SE4 off Dressington Av 183 EA86
● Abbey Mead Ind Pk, Wal.Abb. EN9 67 EC34
Abbey Meadows, Cher. KT16 194 BJ101
Abbey Ms, E17 off Leamington Av 123 EA57
Isleworth TW7 157 CH81
Abbey Mill End, St.Alb. AL3 42 CC21
Abbey Mill La, St.Alb. AL3 42 CC21
Abbey Mills, St.Alb. AL3 42 CC21
Abbey Orchard St, SW1 297 P6
Abbey Par, SW19 off Merton High St 180 DC94
W5 off Hanger La 138 CM69
Abbey Pk, Beck. BR3 183 EA94
Abbey Pk La, Burn. SL1 111 AL61
Abbey Pl, Dart. DA1 off Priory Rd N 188 FK85
Sch Abbey Prim Sch, Mord. SM4 off Glastonbury Rd 200 DB101
Abbey Retail Pk, Bark. IG11 145 EP67
DLR Abbey Road 281 J10
Abbey Rd, E15 281 H10
NW6 273 L7
NW8 273 N9
NW10 138 CP68
SE2 166 EX77
SW19 180 DC94
Barking IG11 145 EP66
Belvedere DA17 166 EX77
Bexleyheath DA7 166 EY84
Chertsey KT16 194 BH101
Croydon CR0 201 DP104
Enfield EN1 82 DS43
Gravesend DA12 191 GL88
Greenhithe DA9 189 FW85
Ilford IG2 125 ER57
Shepperton TW17 194 BN102
South Croydon CR2 221 DX110
Virginia Water GU25 192 AX99
Waltham Cross EN8 67 DY34
Woking GU21 226 AW117
Abbey Rd Est, NW8 273 L9
Abbey St, E13 291 P4
SE1 299 P6
Abbey Ter, SE2 166 EW77
● Abbey Trd Est, SE26 183 DZ92
Abbey Vw, NW7 97 CT48
Radlett WD7 77 CF35
Waltham Abbey EN9 67 EB33
Watford WD25 76 BX36
Abbey Vw Rd, St.Alb. AL3 42 CC20
Jct Abbey Vw Rbt, Wal.Abb. EN9 67 EB33
Abbey Wk, W.Mol. KT8 196 CB97
Abbey Way, SE2 166 EX76
● Abbey Wf Ind Est, Bark. IG11 145 ER68
ABBEY WOOD, SE2 166 EV76
⇌ Abbey Wood 166 EW76
Abbey Wd La, Rain. RM13 148 FK68
Abbey Wd Rd, SE2 166 EV77
Abbot Cl, Byfleet KT14 212 BK110
Staines-upon-Thames TW18 174 BK94
Abbot Ct, SW8 off Hartington Rd 310 A5
Abbot Rd, Guil. GU1 258 AX136
Abbots Av, Epsom KT19 216 CN111
St. Albans AL1 43 CE23
Abbots Av W, St.Alb. AL1 43 CD23
Abbotsbury Cl, E15 280 F10
W14 294 F5
Abbotsbury Gdns, Pnr. HA5 116 BW58
Abbotsbury Ms, SE15 162 DW83
Sch Abbotsbury Prim Sch, Mord. SM4 off Abbotsbury Rd 200 DB99
Abbotsbury Rd, W14 294 F4
Bromley BR2 204 EF103
Morden SM4 200 DB99
● Abbots Business Pk, Kings L. WD4 58 BN28
Abbots Cl, Guil. GU2 258 AS137
Orpington BR5 205 EQ102
Rainham RM13 148 FJ68
Ruislip HA4 116 BX62
Shenfield CM15 109 GA46
Abbots Dr, Har. HA2 116 CA61
Virginia Water GU25 192 AW98
Abbots Fld, Grav. DA12 off Ruffets Wd 191 GJ93
Sch Abbotsfield Sch, Hlgdn UB10 off Clifton Gdns 135 BP68
Abbotsford Av, N15 122 DQ56
Abbotsford Cl, Wok. GU22 off Onslow Cres 227 BA117
Abbotsford Gdns, Wdf.Grn. IG8 102 EG52
Abbotsford Lo, Nthwd. HA6 93 BS50
Abbotsford Rd, Ilf. IG3 126 EU61
Abbots Gdns, N2 120 DD56
W8 295 L7
Abbots Grn, Croy. CR0 221 DX107
Abbotshade Rd, SE16 301 K2
Abbotshall Av, N14 99 DJ48
Abbotshall Rd, SE6 183 ED88
Sch Abbot's Hill Sch, Hem.H. HP3 off Bunkers La 59 BP25
Abbots La, SE1 299 P3
Kenley CR8 236 DQ116
ABBOTS LANGLEY, WD5 59 BR31
Sch Abbots Langley Sch, Abb.L. WD5 off Parsonage Cl 59 BT30
Abbotsleigh Cl, Sutt. SM2 218 DB108
Abbotsleigh Rd, SW16 181 DJ91
Abbots Manor Est, SW1 297 J9
Abbotsmede Cl, Twick. TW1 177 CF89
Abbots Pk, SW2 181 DN88
St. Albans AL1 43 CF22
Abbots Pl, Borwd. WD6 78 CP37
Abbot's Pl, NW6 273 L8
Abbots Ri, Kings L. WD4 58 BM26
Redhill RH1 250 DG132
Abbots Rd, Abb.L. WD5 59 BS30
Edgware HA8 96 CQ52
Abbot's Rd, E6 144 EK67
Abbots Ter, N8 121 DL58
Abbotstone Rd, SW15 159 CW83
Abbot St, E8 278 A4
Abbots Vw, Kings L. WD4 58 BM27
Abbots Wk, W8 295 L7
Windsor SL4 151 AL82
Abbots Way, Beck. BR3 203 DY99
Chertsey KT16 193 BF101
Guildford GU1 243 BD133
Abbotsweld, Harl. CM18 51 ER18
Sch Abbotsweld Prim Sch, Harl. CM18 off Partridge Rd 51 ER17
Abbotswell Rd, SE4 183 DZ85
ABBOTSWOOD, Guil. GU1 243 AZ132
Abbotswood, Guil. GU1 243 AZ131
Abbotswood Cl, Belv. DA17 off Coptefield Dr 166 EY76
Guildford GU1 243 AZ131
Abbotswood Dr, Wey. KT13 213 BR110
Abbotswood Gdns, Ilf. IG5 125 EM55
Abbotswood Rd, SE22 162 DS84
SW16 181 DK90
Abbotswood Way, Hayes UB3 135 BV74
Abbots Yd, Guil. GU1 off Walnut Tree Cl 258 AW135
Abbott Av, SW20 199 CX96
Abbott Cl, Hmptn. TW12 176 BY93
Northolt UB5 136 BZ65
Abbott Rd, E14 290 E7
Abbotts Cl, N1 277 J5
SE28 146 EW73
Romford RM7 127 FB55
Swanley BR8 207 FG98
Uxbridge UB8 134 BK71
Abbotts Cres, E4 101 ED49
Enfield EN2 81 DP40
Abbotts Dr, Wal.Abb. EN9 68 EG33
Wembley HA0 117 CH61
Abbotts Pk Rd, E10 123 EC59
Abbotts Pl, Chesh. HP5 54 AQ28
Abbotts Ri, Stans.Abb. SG12 33 ED11
Abbotts Rd, Barn. EN5 80 DB42
Mitcham CR4 201 DJ98
Southall UB1 136 BY74
Sutton SM3 199 CZ104
Abbott's Tilt, Hersham KT12 196 BY104
Abbotts Vale, Chesh. HP5 54 AQ28
Abbotts Wk, Bexh. DA7 166 EX80
Caterham CR3 off Gaist Av 236 DV122
Abbotts Way, Slou. SL1 131 AK74
Stanstead Abbotts SG12 33 ED11
Abbotts Wf, E14 290 A8
Abbs Cross Gdns, Horn. RM12 128 FJ60
Abbs Cross La, Horn. RM12 128 FJ63
Sch Abbs Cross Sch, Horn. RM12 off Abbs Cross La 128 FJ62
Abchurch La, EC4 287 M10
Abchurch Yd, EC4 287 L10
Abdale Rd, W12 139 CV74
Abel Cl, Hem.H. HP2 40 BM20
Sch Abel Smith Sch, Hert. SG13 off Churchfields 32 DR09
Abenberg Way, Hutt. CM13 109 GB47
● Abenglen Ind Est, Hayes UB3 155 BR75
Aberavon Rd, E3 289 M3
Abercairn Rd, SW16 181 DJ94
Aberconway Rd, Mord. SM4 200 DB97
Abercorn Cl, NW7 97 CY52
NW8 283 N1
South Croydon CR2 221 DX112
● Abercorn Commercial Cen, Wem. HA0 137 CK67
Abercorn Cres, Har. HA2 116 CB60
Abercorn Dell, Bushey WD23 94 CC47
Abercorn Gdns, Har. HA3 117 CK59
Romford RM6 126 EV58
Abercorn Gro, Ruis. HA4 115 BR56
Abercorn Ms, Rich. TW10 off Kings Rd 158 CM84
Abercorn Pl, NW8 283 N2
Abercorn Rd, NW7 97 CY52
Stanmore HA7 95 CJ52
Sch Abercorn Sch, NW8 283 P1
Abercorn Wk, NW8 283 N2
Abercorn Way, SE1 300 C10
Woking GU21 226 AU118
Abercrombie Dr, Enf. EN1 off Linwood Cres 82 DU39
Abercrombie St, SW11 308 D8
Abercrombie Way, Harl. CM18 51 EQ16
Aberdale Ct, SE16 off Garter Way 301 J5
Aberdale Gdns, Pot.B. EN6 63 CZ33
Aberdare Cl, W.Wick. BR4 203 EC103
Aberdare Gdns, NW6 273 M7
NW7 97 CX52
Aberdare Rd, Enf. EN3 82 DW42
Aberdeen Av, Slou. SL1 131 AN73
Aberdeen La, N5 277 H2
Aberdeen Par, N18 off Angel Rd 100 DV50
Aberdeen Pk, N5 277 H2
Aberdeen Pk Ms, N5 277 K1
Aberdeen Pl, NW8 284 A5
Aberdeen Rd, N5 277 J1
N18 100 DV50
NW10 119 CT64
Croydon CR0 220 DQ105
Harrow HA3 95 CF54
Aberdeen Sq, E14 301 P2
Aberdeen Ter, SE3 314 G8
Aberdour Rd, Ilf. IG3 126 EV62
Sch Aberdour Sch, Burgh Hth KT20 off Brighton Rd 233 CZ118
Aberdour St, SE1 299 N8
Aberfeldy St, E14 290 F8
Aberford Gdns, SE18 164 EL81
Aberford Rd, Borwd. WD6 78 CN40
Aberfoyle Rd, SW16 181 DK93
Abergeldie Rd, SE12 184 EH86
Abernethy Rd, SE13 164 EE84
Abersham Rd, E8 278 B2
Abery St, SE18 165 ES77
Abigail Ms, Rom. RM3 off King Alfred Rd 106 FM54
Ability Twrs, EC1 287 J2
Abingdon Cl, NW1 275 N5
SE1 300 B10
SW19 180 DC93
Uxbridge UB10 134 BM67
Woking GU21 226 AV118
Wor.Pk. KT4 199 CV104
Abingdon Pl, Pot.B. EN6 64 DB32
Abingdon Rd, N3 98 DC54
SW16 201 DL96
W8 295 J6
Abingdon St, SW1 298 A6
Abingdon Vil, W8 295 J7
Abingdon Way, Orp. BR6 224 EV105
Abinger Av, Sutt. SM2 217 CW109
Abinger Cl, Bark. IG11 126 EU63
Bromley BR1 204 EL97
New Addington CR0 221 EC107
North Holmwood RH5 263 CJ140
Wallington SM6 219 DL106
ABINGER COMMON, Dor. RH5 262 BX143
Abinger Common Rd, Dor. RH5 262 BY144
Sch Abinger Common Sch, Abin.Com. RH5 off Abinger La 262 BX142
Abinger Dr, Red. RH1 266 DE136
Abinger Gdns, Islw. TW7 157 CE83
Abinger Gro, SE8 313 N3
ABINGER HAMMER, Dor. RH5 261 BT139
Sch Abinger Hammer Village Sch, Abin.Ham. RH5 off Hackhurst La 261 BT139
Sch Abinger Keep, Horl. RH6 off Langshott La 269 DJ147
Abinger La, Dor. RH5 261 BV140
Abinger Ms, W9 283 J4
Abinger Rd, W4 158 CS76
Abinger Way, Guil. GU4 243 BB129
Ablett St, SE16 312 G1
Abney Gdns, N16 off Stoke Newington High St 122 DT61
Aboyne Dr, SW20 199 CU96
Aboyne Est, SW17 180 DD90
Sch Aboyne Lo Sch, St.Alb. AL3 off Etna Rd 43 CD19
Aboyne Rd, NW10 118 CS62
SW17 180 DD90
Abraham Cl, Wat. WD19 93 BV49
Abraham Ct, Upmin. RM14 128 FN61
ABRIDGE, Rom. RM4 86 EV41
Abridge Cl, Wal.Cr. EN8 83 DX35
Abridge Gdns, Rom. RM5 104 FA51
Abridge Pk, Abridge RM4 86 EU42
Abridge Rd, Abridge RM4 86 EU39
Chigwell IG7 85 ER44
Theydon Bois CM16 85 ES36
Abridge Way, Bark. IG11 146 EV68
Abyssinia Cl, SW11 off Cairns Rd 160 DE84
Abyssinia Rd, SW11 off Auckland Rd 160 DE84
Acacia Av, N17 100 DR52
Brentford TW8 157 CH80
Hayes UB3 135 BT72
Hornchurch RM12 127 FF61
Mitcham CR4 off Acacia Rd 201 DH96
Ruislip HA4 115 BU60
Shepperton TW17 194 BN99
Wembley HA9 118 CL64
West Drayton UB7 134 BM73
Woking GU22 226 AX120
Wraysbury TW19 152 AY84
● Acacia Business Cen, E11 off Howard Rd 124 EE62
Acacia Cl, SE8 301 L9
SE20 off Selby Rd 202 DU96
Chesham HP5 54 AN30
Cheshunt EN7 66 DS27
Petts Wood BR5 205 ER99
Stanmore HA7 95 CE51
Woodham KT15 211 BF110
Acacia Ct, Wal.Abb. EN9 off Farthingale La 68 EG34
Acacia Dr, Bans. SM7 217 CX114
Sutton SM3 199 CZ102
Upminster RM14 128 FN63
Woodham KT15 211 BF110
Acacia Gdns, NW8 274 B10
Upminster RM14 129 FT59
West Wickham BR4 203 EC103
Acacia Gro, SE21 182 DR89
Berkhamsted HP4 38 AV20
New Malden KT3 198 CR97
Acacia Ms, Harm. UB7 154 BK79
Acacia Pl, NW8 274 B10
Acacia Rd, E11 124 EE61
E17 123 DY58
N22 99 DN53
NW8 274 B10
SW16 201 DL95
W3 138 CQ73
Beckenham BR3 203 DZ97
Dartford DA1 188 FK88
Enfield EN2 82 DR39
Greenhithe DA9 189 FS86
Guildford GU1 242 AX134
Hampton TW12 176 CA93
Mitcham CR4 201 DH96
Staines-upon-Thames TW18 174 BH92
Acacias, The, Barn. EN4 80 DD43
Acacia St, Hat. AL10 45 CU21
Acacia Wk, Swan. BR8 207 FD96
Acacia Way, Sid. DA15 185 ET88
Academia Ave, Brox. EN10 67 DZ25
Academia Way, N17 100 DS51
Academy Ct, Borwd. WD6 78 CN42
Dagenham RM8 126 EU63
Academy Flds Cl, Rom. RM2 127 FG57
Academy Flds Rd, Rom. RM2 127 FH57
Academy Gdns, W8 295 J4
Croydon CR0 202 DT102
Northolt UB5 136 BX68
Academy Pl, SE18 165 EM81
Islw. TW7 157 CE81
Academy Rd, SE18 165 EM81
Academy Way, Dag. RM9 126 EV63
Acanthus Dr, SE1 300 C10
Acanthus Rd, SW11 308 G10
Accommodation La, Harm. UB7 154 BJ79
Accommodation Rd, NW11 119 CZ59
Longcross KT16 192 AX104
A.C. Ct, T.Ditt. KT7 off Harvest La 197 CG100
Acer Av, Hayes UB4 136 BY71
Rainham RM13 148 FK69
Acer Cl, Epsom 216 CQ109
Acer Ct, Enf. EN3 83 DY41
Acer Rd, Bigg.H. TN16 238 EK116
E8 278 B6
Acers, Park St AL2 60 CC28
Aces Ct, Houns. TW3 156 CC82
Acfold Rd, SW6 307 L7
Achilles Cl, SE1 300 D10
Hemel Hempstead HP2 40 BM18
Achilles Pl, Wok. GU21 226 AW117
Achilles Rd, NW6 273 H2
Achilles St, SE14 313 N5
Achilles Way, W1 296 G3
Acklam Rd, W10 282 G7
Acklington Dr, NW9 96 CS53
Ackmar Rd, SW6 307 J7
Ackroyd Dr, E3 289 P6
Ackroyd Rd, SE23 183 DX87
Sch Acland Burghley Sch, NW5 off Burghley Rd 121 DJ63
Acland Cl, SE18 off Clothworkers Rd 165 ER80
Acland Cres, SE5 162 DR83
Acland Rd, NW2 139 CV65
Acle Cl, Ilf. IG6 103 EP52
Acme Rd, Wat. WD24 75 BU38
Acock Gro, Nthlt. UB5 116 CB63
Acol Cres, Ruis. HA4 115 BV64
Acol Rd, NW6 273 K7
Aconbury Rd, Dag. RM9 146 EV67
Acorn Cl, E4 101 EA50
Banstead SM7 233 CY115
Chislehurst BR7 185 EQ92
Enfield EN2 81 DP39
Hampton TW12 176 CB93
Horley RH6 269 DJ147
Romford RM1 off Pettits La 105 FE54
Slough SL3 off Tamar Way 153 BB78
Stanmore HA7 95 CH52
Acorn Ct, Ilf. IG2 125 ES58
Acorn Gdns, SE19 202 DT95
W3 138 CR71
Acorn Gro, Hayes UB3 155 BT80
Kingswood KT20 233 CY124
Ruislip HA4 115 BT63
Woking GU22 off Old Sch Pl 226 AY121
● Acorn Ind Pk, Dart. DA1 187 FF85
Acorn La, Cuffley EN6 65 DL29
Acorn Ms, Harl. CM18 51 ET17
Acorn Par, SE15 312 E5
Acorn Pl, Wat. WD24 75 BU37
Acorn Rd, Dart. DA1 187 FF85
Hemel Hempstead HP3 40 BN21
Acorns, The, Chig. IG7 103 ES49
Smallfield RH6 269 DP148
Sch Acorns Inf Sch, The, Betchworth Site, Bet. RH3 off The Street 248 CR134
Leigh Site, Leigh RH2 off Tapners Rd 265 CU140
Acorn St, Hunsdon SG12 34 EK08
Acorns Way, Esher KT10 214 CC106
Acorn Trading Est, Grays RM20 170 FY79
Acorn Wk, SE16 301 M2
Acorn Way, SE23 183 DX90
Beckenham BR3 203 EC99
Orpington BR6 223 EP105
Acre Dr, SE22 162 DU84
Acrefield Rd, Chal.St.P. SL9 112 AX55
Acre La, SW2 161 DL84
Carshalton SM5 218 DG105
Wallington SM6 218 DG105
Acre Pas, Wind. SL4 151 AR81
Acre Path, Nthlt. UB5 off Arnold Rd 136 BY65
Acre Rd, SW19 180 DD93
Dagenham RM10 147 FB66
Kingston upon Thames KT2 198 CL95
Acres End, Amer. HP7 55 AS39
Acres Gdns, Tad. KT20 233 CX119
Acre Vw, Horn. RM11 128 FL56
Acre Way, Nthwd. HA6 93 BT53
Acrewood, Hem.H. HP2 40 BL20
Acrewood Way, St.Alb. AL4 44 CM20
Acris St, SW18 180 DC85
Sch ACS Cobham Int Sch, Cob. KT11 off Portsmouth Rd 214 BW110
Sch ACS Egham International School, Egh. TW20 off London Rd 192 AW96
Sch ACS Hillingdon Int Sch, Hlgdn UB10 off Vine La 134 BM67
ACTON, W3 138 CN74
Coll Acton & W London Coll, W3 off Gunnersbury La 138 CP74
⊖ Acton Central 138 CR74
Acton Cl, N9 100 DU47
Cheshunt EN8 67 DY31
Sch Acton High Sch, W3 off Gunnersbury La 158 CN75
Acton Hill Ms, W3 off Uxbridge Rd 138 CP74
Acton Ho, W3 138 CQ72
Acton La, NW10 138 CS68
W3 158 CQ75
W4 158 CR76
⇌ Acton Main Line 138 CQ72
Acton Ms, E8 278 A8
● Acton Pk Est, W3 158 CR75
Actons La, High Wych CM21 35 EQ05
Acton St, WC1 286 C3
⊖ Acton Town 158 CN75
Acuba Rd, SW18 180 DB89
Acworth Cl, N9 100 DW45
Ada Cl, N11 98 DF48
Ada Ct, W9 283 P3
Ada Gdns, E14 290 G8
E15 281 L9
Adair Cl, SE25 202 DV97
Adair Gdns, Cat. CR3 236 DQ121
Adair Rd, W10 282 F5
Adair Twr, W10 282 F5
Ada Lewis Ho, Wem. HA9 118 CM63
Adam & Eve Ct, W1 285 M8
Adam & Eve Ms, W8 295 K6
Adam Cl, SE6 183 DZ91
Slough SL1 131 AN74
Adam Ct, SW7 295 P8
Adam Meere Ho, E1 off Tarling St 288 G9
Adam Rd, E4 101 DZ51
Adams Cl, N3 98 DA52
NW9 118 CP61
Surbiton KT5 198 CM100
Adams Ct, EC2 287 M8
Adamsfield, Wal.Cr. EN7 66 DU27
Adams Gdns Est, SE16 300 G4
Adams Ho, N16 off Stamford Hill 122 DT60
Harlow CM20 off Post Office Rd 35 ER14
Adams Ms, N22 99 DM52
SW17 180 DF89
Adamson Rd, E16 291 P9
NW3 274 B6
Adamson Way, Beck. BR3 203 EC99
Adams Pl, N7 276 D3
Adamsrill Cl, Enf. EN1 82 DR44
Sch Adamsrill Prim Sch, SE26 off Adamsrill Rd 183 DY90
Adamsrill Rd, SE26 183 DY91
Adams Rd, N17 100 DR54
Beckenham BR3 203 DY99
Adams Row, W1 297 H1
Adams Sq, Bexh. DA6 off Regency Way 166 EY83
Adam St, WC2 298 B1
Adams Wk, Kings.T. KT1 198 CL96
Adams Way, Croy. CR0 202 DT100
Adam Wk, SW6 306 B4
Ada Pl, E2 278 D9
Adare Wk, SW16 181 DM90
Ada Rd, SE5 311 N5
Wembley HA0 117 CJ62
Adastral Est, NW9 96 CS53
Ada St, E8 278 E9
Adcock Wk, Orp. BR6 off Borkwood Pk 223 ET105
Adderley Gdns, SE9 185 EN91
Adderley Gro, SW11 off Culmstock Rd 180 DG85
Adderley Rd, Har. HA3 95 CF53
Adderley St, E14 290 E9
Sch Addey & Stanhope Sch, SE14 314 A6
ADDINGTON, Croy. CR0 221 DZ106
Addington Border, Croy. CR0 221 DY110
Addington Cl, Wind. SL4 151 AN83
Addington Ct, SW14 158 CR83
Addington Dr, N12 98 DC51
Addington Gro, SE26 183 DY91
Sch Addington High Sch, New Adgtn CR0 off Fairchildes Av 222 EE112
Addington Rd, E3 290 A2
E16 291 K5
N4 121
DN59
Croydon CR0 201 DN102
South Croydon CR2 220 DU111
West Wickham BR4 204 EE103
Addington Sq, SE5 311 K4
Addington St, SE1 298 D5
Tram Addington Village 221 EA107
Addington Village Interchange 221 EA107
Addington Village Rd, Croy. CR0 221 EA106
Addis Cl, Enf. EN3 83 DX39
ADDISCOMBE, Croy. CR0 202 DT102
Tram Addiscombe 202 DU102
Addiscombe Av, Croy. CR0 202 DU101
Addiscombe Cl, Har. HA3 117 CJ57
Addiscombe Ct Rd, Croy. CR0 202 DS102
Addiscombe Gro, Croy. CR0 202 DR103
Addiscombe Rd, Croy. CR0 202 DS103
Watford WD18 75 BV42
Addison Av, N14 81 DH44
W11 294 E2
Hounslow TW3 156 CC81
Addison Br Pl, W14 294 G8
Addison Cl, Cat. CR3 236 DR122
Northwood HA6 93 BU53
Petts Wood BR5 205 EQ100
Addison Ct, Epp. CM16 70 EU31
Addison Cres, W14 294 F6
Addison Dr, SE12 184 EH85
Addison Gdns, W14 294 C6
Grays RM17 off Palmers Dr 170 GC77
Surbiton KT5 198 CM98
Addison Gro, W4 158 CS76
● Addison Ind Est, Ruis. HA4 116 BY63

Addison Pl, W11 294 E3
Southall UB1
off Atherton Pl 136 CA73
Sch **Addison Prim Sch**, W14 294 C6
Addison Rd, E11 124 EG58
E17 123 EB57
SE25 202 DU98
W14 294 G6
Bromley BR2 204 EJ99
Caterham CR3 236 DR121
Chesham HP5 54 AQ29
Enfield EN3 82 DW39
Guildford GU1 258 AY135
Ilford IG6 103 EQ53
Teddington TW11 177 CH93
Woking GU21
off Chertsey Rd 227 AZ117
Addison's Cl, Croy. CR0 203 DZ103
Addison Way, NW11 119 CZ56
Hayes UB3 135 BU72
Northwood HA6 93 BT53
Addle Hill, EC4 287 H10
ADDLESTONE, KT15 212 BJ106
⇌ **Addlestone** 212 BK105
ADDLESTONE MOOR,
Add. KT15 194 BG103
Addlestone Moor, Add. KT15 194 BJ103
Addlestone Pk, Add. KT15 212 BH106
Addlestone Rd, Add. KT15 212 BL105
Addy Ho, SE16 301 H9
Adecroft Way, W.Mol. KT8 196 CC97
Adela Av, N.Mal. KT3 199 CV99
Adelaide Av, SE4 163 DZ84
Adelaide Cl, SW9
off Broughton Dr 161 DN84
Enfield EN1 82 DS38
Slough SL1
off Amerden Way 151 AN75
Stanmore HA7 95 CG49
Adelaide Cotts, W7 157 CF75
Adelaide Ct, E9 279 L3
Waltham Cross EN8
off Queens Way 67 DZ34
Adelaide Gdns, Rom. RM6 126 EY57
Adelaide Gro, W12 139 CU74
Adelaide Pl, Wey. KT13 213 BR105
Adelaide Rd, E10 123 EB62
NW3 274 B7
SW18 *off Putney Br Rd* 180 DA85
W13 137 CG74
Ashford TW15 174 BK92
Chislehurst BR7 185 EP92
Hounslow TW5 156 BY81
Ilford IG1 125 EP61
Richmond TW9 158 CM84
Southall UB2 156 BY77
Surbiton KT6 198 CL99
Teddington TW11 177 CF93
Tilbury RM18 171 GF81
Walton-on-Thames KT12 195 BU104
Adelaide Sq, Wind. SL4 151 AR82
Adelaide St, WC2 298 A1
St. Albans AL3 43 CD19
Adelaide Ter, Brent. TW8 157 CK78
Adelaide Wf, E2
off Queensbridge Rd 278 B9
Adela St, W10 282 E4
Adelina Gro, E1 288 G6
Adelina Ms, SW12 181 DK88
Adeline Pl, WC1 285 P7
Adeliza Cl, Bark. IG11
off North St 145 EQ66
Adelphi Ct, SE16
off Garter Way 301 J5
Adelphi Cres, Hayes UB4 135 BT69
Hornchurch RM12 127 FG61
Adelphi Gdns, Slou. SL1 152 AS75
Adelphi Rd, Epsom KT17 216 CR113
Adelphi Ter, WC2 298 B1
Adelphi Way, Hayes UB4 135 BT69
Adeney Cl, W6 306 D3
Aden Gro, N16 277 L1
Adenmore Rd, SE6 183 EA87
Aden Rd, Enf. EN3 83 DY42
Ilford IG1 125 EP59
Aden Ter, N16 122 DR63
ADEYFIELD, Hem.H. HP2 40 BN20
Adeyfield Gdns, Hem.H. HP2 40 BM19
Adeyfield Rd, Hem.H. HP2 40 BM20
Sch **Adeyfield Sch**, Hem.H. HP2
off Longlands 40 BN20
Adhara Rd, Nthwd. HA6
off Vega Cres 93 BU50
Adhern Ct, St.Alb. AL1 43 CJ22
Adie Rd, W6 294 A7
Adine Rd, E13 292 A4
Adisham Ho, E5
off Pembury Rd 278 E2
● **Adler Ind Est**, Hayes UB3 155 BR75
Adlers La, Westh. RH5 247 CG131
Adler St, E1 288 C8
Adley St, E5 279 M1
Adlington Cl, N18 100 DR50
Admaston Rd, SE18 165 EQ80
Admiral Cl, Orp. BR5 206 EX98
Weybridge KT13 195 BS103
Admiral Ct, NW4
off Barton Cl 119 CU57
Admiral Ho, Tedd. TW11
off Twickenham Rd 177 CG91
● **Admiral Hyson Trd Est**, SE16 300 E9
Admiral Pl, N8 121 DP56
SE16 301 M2
Admirals Cl, E18 124 EH56
Colney Heath AL4 44 CR23
Admirals Ct, Guil. GU1 243 BB133
Admiral Seymour Rd, SE9 165 EM84
Admirals Gate, SE10 314 D6
Admiral Sq, SW10 307 P6
Admiral's Rd,
Lthd. KT22, KT23 247 CD126
Admiral Stirling Ct, Wey. KT13
off Weybridge Rd 212 BM105
Admiral St, SE8 314 B7
Hertford SG13 32 DU09
Admirals Wk, NW3 120 DC62
Coulsdon CR5 235 DM120
Green. DA9 189 FV85
Hoddesdon EN11 49 EA19
St. Albans AL1 43 CG23
Admiral's Wk, Dor. RH5 246 CB130
Admirals Way, E14 302 B4
Gravesend DA12 191 GK86
★ **Admiralty Arch**, SW1 297 P2
Admiralty Cl, SE8 314 A6
West Drayton UB7 154 BL75
Admiralty Way, Tedd. TW11 177 CF93
Admiral Wk, W9 283 K6
Admiral Way, Berk. HP4 38 AT17
Adnams Wk, Rain. RM13
off Lovell Wk 147 FF65
Adolf St, SE6 183 EB91
Adolphus Rd, N4 121 DP61
Adolphus St, SE8 313 P4
Adomar Rd, Dag. RM8 126 EX62
Adpar St, W2 284 A5
Adrian Av, NW2
off North Circular Rd 119 CV60
Adrian Cl, Barn. EN5 79 CX44
Harefield UB9 92 BK53
Hemel Hempstead HP1 40 BH21
Adrian Ms, SW10 307 M2
Adrian Rd, Abb.L. WD5 59 BS31
Adrians Wk, Slou. SL2 132 AT74
Adriatic, E16 291 N10
Adriatic Bldg, E14 289 L10
Adrienne Av, Sthl. UB1 136 BZ70
● **Adrienne Business Cen**,
Sthl. UB1 *off Adrienne Ave* 136 BZ69
Adstock Ms, Chal.St.P. SL9
off Church La 90 AX53
Adstock Way, Bad.Dene RM17 170 FZ77
Coll **ADT Coll**, SW15
off West Hill 179 CZ85
Coll **Adult Coll of Barking**
& Dagenham, The, Dag. RM9
off Fanshawe Cres 126 EZ64
Coll **Adult Ed Coll Bexley**, Brampton Rd
Adult Ed Cen, Bexh. DA7
off Brampton Rd 166 EX83
Crayford Manor Ho Adult Ed Cen,
Dart. DA1 *off Mayplace Rd E* 167 FE83
Southlake Cen, SE2
off Seacourt Rd 166 EX75
Advance Rd, SE27 182 DQ91
Advent Ct, Wdf.Grn. IG8
off Wood La 102 EF50
Adventurers Ct, E14
off Newport Av 303 H1
Advent Way, N18 101 DX50
Advice Av, Grays RM16 170 GA75
Adys Rd, SE15 312 B10
Aegean Apts, E16
off Western Gateway 303 P1
Sch **Aerodrome Prim Sch**, Croy. CR0
off Goodwin Rd 219 DP106
Aerodrome Rd, NW4 97 CT54
NW9 97 CT54
Aerodrome Way, Houns. TW5 156 BW79
Watford WD25 59 BT34
Aeroville, NW9 96 CS54
Affleck St, N1 286 D1
Afghan Rd, SW11 308 C9
★ **Africa Cen**, WC2 286 A10
Afton Dr, S.Ock. RM15 149 FV72
Agamemnon Rd, NW6 273 H2
Agar Cl, Surb. KT6 198 CM103
Agar Gro, NW1 275 M7
Agar Gro Est, NW1 275 M7
Agar Pl, NW1 275 M7
Agars Pl, Datchet SL3 152 AU79
Agar St, WC2 298 A1
Agate Cl, E16 292 F9
NW10 138 CN69
Agate Rd, W6 294 A6
Agates La, Ashtd. KT21 231 CK118
Agatha Cl, E1 300 F2
Agaton Rd, SE9 185 EQ89
Agave Rd, NW2 272 A1
Agdon St, EC1 286 G4
Ager Ave, Dag. RM8 126 EX60
Agincourt Rd, NW3 274 E1
Agister Rd, Chig. IG7 104 EU50
Agnes Av, Ilf. IG1 125 EP63
Agnes Cl, E6 293 M10
Agnesfield Cl, N12 98 DE51
Agnes Gdns, Dag. RM8 126 EX63
Agnes George Wk, E16 304 E3
Agnes Rd, W3 139 CT74
Agnes Scott Ct, Wey. KT13
off Palace Dr 195 BP104
Agnes St, E14 289 P8
Agnew Rd, SE23 183 DX87
Agraria Rd, Guil. GU2 258 AV135
Agricola Ct, E3 279 P9
Agricola Pl, Enf. EN1 82 DT43
Aidan Cl, Dag. RM8 126 EY63
Aileen Wk, E15 281 M6
Ailsa Av, Twick. TW1 177 CG85
Ailsa Rd, Twick. TW1 177 CH85
Ailsa St, E14 290 F6
AIMES GREEN, Wal.Abb. EN9 68 EF28
Ainger Ms, NW3 274 F7
Ainger Rd, NW3 274 E7
Ainsdale Cl, Orp. BR6 205 ER102
Ainsdale Cres, Pnr. HA5 116 CA55
Ainsdale Dr, SE1 312 C1
Ainsdale Rd, W5 137 CK70
Watford WD19 94 BW48
Ainsdale Way, Wok. GU21 226 AU118
Ainsley Av, Rom. RM7 127 FB58
Ainsley Cl, N9 100 DS46
Ainsley St, E2 288 F3
Ainslie Wk, SW12 181 DH87
Ainslie Wd Cres, E4 101 EB50
Ainslie Wd Gdns, E4 101 EB49
Sch **Ainslie Wd Prim Sch**, E4
off Ainslie Wd Rd 101 EB50
Ainslie Wd Rd, E4 101 EA50
Ainsty Est, SE16 301 J5
Ainsworth Cl, NW2 119 CU62
SE15 311 P8
Ainsworth Rd, E9 278 G7
Croydon CR0 201 DP103
Ainsworth Way, NW8 273 N8
Aintree Av, E6 144 EL67
Aintree Cl, Colnbr. SL3 153 BE81
Gravesend DA12 191 GH90
Uxbridge UB8 135 BP72
Aintree Cres, Ilf. IG6 103 EQ54
Aintree Est, SW6 306 F4
Aintree Gro, Upmin. RM14 128 FM62
Aintree Rd, Perivale UB6 137 CH68
Aintree St, SW6 306 F5
Airco Cl, NW9 118 CR55
Aird Ct, Hmptn. TW12
off Oldfield Rd 196 BZ95
Aird Ho, SE1
off Rockingham St 299 J7
Airdrie Cl, N1 276 C7
Hayes UB4
off Glencoe Rd 136 BY71
Airedale, Hem.H. HP2
off Wharfedale 40 BL17
Airedale Av, W4 159 CT77
Airedale Av S, W4
off Netheravon Rd S 159 CT78
Airedale Cl, Dart. DA2 188 FQ88
Airedale Rd, SW12 180 DF87
W5 157 CJ76
Aire Dr, S.Ock. RM15 149 FV70
Airey Neave Ct, Grays RM17 170 GA75
Airfield Way, Horn. RM12 147 FH65
★ **Air Forces Mem**, Egh. TW20 172 AX91
Airlie Gdns, W8 295 J3
Ilford IG1 125 EP60
● **Air Links Ind Est**,
Houns. TW5 156 BW78
Air Pk Way, Felt. TW13 175 BV89
● **Airport Gate Business Cen**,
West Dr. UB7 154 BM80
● **Airport Ind Est**, Bigg.H. TN16 222 EK114
Jct **Airport Rbt**, E16 304 E2
Airport Way, Gat. RH6 268 DG151
Staines-upon-Thames TW19 153 BF84
Jct **Airport Way Rbt**, Horl. RH6 268 DF151
Jct **Airport Way Rbt E**,
Horl. RH6 269 DH151
Air Sea Ms, Twick. TW2 177 CD89
Air St, W1 297 M1
Airthrie Rd, Ilf. IG3 126 EV61
Aisgill Av, W14 307 H1
Aisher Rd, SE28 146 EW73
Aisher Way, Rvrhd TN13 256 FE121
Aislibie Rd, SE12 164 EE84
Aissele Pl, Esher KT10 214 CB105
Aiten Pl, W6
off Standish Rd 159 CU77
Aitken Cl, E8 278 C8
Mitcham CR4 200 DF101
Aitken Rd, SE6 183 EB89
Barnet EN5 79 CW43
Aitman Dr, Brent. TW8
off Chiswick High Rd 158 CN78
Ait's Vw, W.Mol. KT8
off Victoria Av 196 CB97
Ajax Av, NW9 118 CS55
Slough SL1 131 AP73
Ajax Rd, NW6 273 H2
● **Ajax Wks**, Bark. IG11 145 EP66
Akabusi Cl, Croy. CR0 202 DU100
Akehurst La, Sev. TN13 257 FJ125
Akehurst St, SW15 179 CU86
Akeman Cl, St.Alb. AL3
off Meautys 42 BZ22
Akenside Rd, NW3 274 A3
Akerman Rd, SW9 310 G7
Surbiton KT6 197 CJ100
Akers Ct,
Wal.Cr. EN8 *off High St* 67 DX32
Akers Way, Chorl. WD3 73 BD44
Sch **Akiva Prim Sch**, N3
off East End Rd 98 DA54
Alabama St, SE18 165 ER80
Alacross Rd, W5 157 CJ75
Alamaro Lo, SE10
off Renaissance Wk 303 M6
Alamein Cl, Brox. EN10 49 DX20
Alamein Gdns, Dart. DA2 189 FR87
Alamein Rd, Swans. DA10 189 FX86
Alana Hts, E4
off Kings Head Hill 101 EB45
Alanbrooke, Grav. DA12 191 GJ87
Alan Cl, Dart. DA1 168 FJ84
Alandale Dr, Pnr. HA5 93 BV54
Aland Ct, SE16 301 M7
Alander Ms, E17 123 EC56
Alan Dr, Barn. EN5 79 CY44
Alan Gdns, Rom. RM7 126 FA59
Alan Hilton Ct, Ott. KT16
off Cheshire Cl 211 BD107
Alan Hocken Way, E15 291 J1
Alan Rd, SW19 179 CY92
Alanthus Cl, SE12 184 EF86
Alan Way, Geo.Grn SL3 132 AY72
Alaska, E16
off Seagull La 291 N10
Alaska Bldg, SE13
off Deals Gateway 314 C7
Alaska St, SE1 298 E3
Alba Cl, Hayes UB4
off Ramulis Dr 136 BX70
Albacore Cres, SE13 183 EB86
Albacore Way, Hayes UB3 135 BT73
Alba Gdns, NW11 119 CY58
Albain Cres, Ashf. TW15 174 BL89
Alba Ms, SW18 180 DA89
Alban Av, St.Alb. AL3 43 CD18
Sch **Alban City Sch**, St.Alb. AL1 43 CE19
Alban Cres, Borwd. WD6 78 CP39
Farningham DA4 208 FN102
Alban Highwalk, EC2
off London Wall 287 K7
Alban Pk, St.Alb. AL4 44 CM20
Albans Vw, Wat. WD25 59 BV33
Alban Way Cycle Route,
Hat. AL10 44 CQ20
St. Albans AL1, AL4 43 CK20
Albanwood, Wat. WD25 59 BV33
Sch **Alban Wd Prim Sch**, Wat. WD25
off The Brow 59 BV32
Albany, W1 297 L1
Albany, The, Wdf.Grn. IG8 102 EF49
Albany Cl, N15 121 DP56
SW14 158 CP84
Bexley DA5 186 EW87
Bushey WD23 77 CD44
Esher KT10 214 CA109
Reigate RH2 250 DA132
Uxbridge UB10 114 BN64
Albany Ct, E4
off Chelwood Cl 83 EB44
E10 123 EA59
Epping CM16 69 ET30
Harrow HA3 117 CK56
Albany Ctyd, W1 297 M1
Albany Cres, Clay. KT10 215 CE107
Edgware HA8 96 CN52
Albany Gate, Chesh. HP5
off Bellingdon Rd 54 AP30
Albany Hts, Grays RM17
off Hogg La 170 GA78
H **Albany Lodge Comm**
Treatment Cen, St.Alb. AL3 42 CC19
Albany Mans, SW11 308 D5
Albany Ms, N1 276 E6
SE5 311 K3
Bromley BR1 184 EG93
Kingston upon Thames KT2 177 CK93
St. Albans AL2 60 CA27
Sutton SM1 *off Camden Rd* 218 DB106
Ware SG12 *off Albany Quay* 33 DY06
⇌ **Albany Park** 186 EX89
Albany Pk, Colnbr. SL3 153 BD81
Albany Pk Av, Enf. EN3 82 DW39
Albany Pk Rd, Kings.T. KT2 177 CK93
Leatherhead KT22 231 CG119
Albany Pas, Rich. TW10 178 CM85
Albany Pl, Brent. TW8
off Albany Rd 158 CL79
Egham TW20 173 BA91
Albany Quay, Ware SG12 33 DY06
Albany Rd, E10 123 EA59
E12 124 EK63
E17 123 DY58
N4 121 DM58
N18 100 DV50
SE5 311 L3
SE17 311 L3
SW19 180 DB92
W13 137 CH73
Belvedere DA17 166 EZ79
Bexley DA5 186 EW87
Brentford TW8 157 CK79
Chislehurst BR7 185 EP92
Enfield EN3 83 DX37
Hersham KT12 214 BX105
Hornchurch RM12 127 FG60
New Malden KT3 198 CR98
Old Windsor SL4 172 AU85
Pilgrim's Hatch CM15 108 FV44
Richmond TW10 *off Albert Rd* 178 CL85
Romford RM6 126 EZ58
Tilbury RM18 171 GG81
Windsor SL4 151 AQ82
Albanys, The, Reig. RH2 250 DA131
Sch **Albany Sch, The**, Horn.
RM12 *off Broadstone Rd* 127 FH61
Albany St, NW1 275 J10
Albany Vw, Buck.H. IG9 102 EG46
Albany Way, Stai. TW18 174 BK93
Alba Pl, W11 282 G8
Alba Rd, Harl. CM17 36 EW14
Albatross Cl, E6 293 K5
Albatross Ct, Hert. SG13
off Tee Side 32 DV08
Albatross Gdns, S.Croy. CR2 221 DX111
Albatross St, SE18 165 ES80
Albatross Way, SE16 301 J5
Hatfield AL10 44 CR18
Albemarle, SW19 179 CX89
Albemarle App, Ilf. IG2 125 EP58
Albemarle Av, Chsht EN8 66 DW28
Potters Bar EN6 64 DB33
Twickenham TW2 176 BZ88
Albemarle Cl, Grays RM17 170 GA75
Albemarle Gdns, Ilf. IG2 125 EP58
New Malden KT3 198 CR98
Albemarle Pk, Stan. HA7
off Marsh La 95 CJ50
Sch **Albemarle Prim Sch**, SW19
off Princes Way 179 CY89
Albemarle Rd, Beck. BR3 203 EB95
East Barnet EN4 98 DE45
Albemarle St, W1 297 K1
Albemarle Way, EC1 286 G5
Albeny Gate, St.Alb. AL1 43 CD21
Albermarle Pk, Beck. BR3
off Albemarle Rd 203 EB95
Alberon Gdns, NW11 119 CZ56
Alberta Av, Sutt. SM1 217 CY105
Alberta Dr, Smallfield RH6 269 DN148
Alberta Est, SE17 299 H10
Alberta Rd, Enf. EN1 82 DT44
Erith DA8 167 FC81
Alberta St, SE17 298 G10
Albert Av, E4 101 EA49
SW8 310 C5
Chertsey KT16 194 BG97
Albert Barnes Ho, SE1 299 J7
Albert Basin, E16 305 P1
Albert Basin Way, E16 305 P1
Albert Bigg Pt, E15 280 F9
Albert Br, SW3 308 D3
SW11 308 D3
Albert Br Rd, SW11 308 D4
Albert Carr Gdns, SW16 181 DL92
Albert Cl, E9 278 F9
N22 99 DK53
Grays RM16 170 GC76
Slough SL1 *off Hencroft St S* 152 AT76
Albert Ct, SW7 296 A5
Waltham Cross EN8
off Queens Way 67 DZ34
Albert Cres, E4 101 EA49
Albert Dr, SW19 179 CY89
Staines-upon-Thames TW18 173 BF92
Woking GU21 211 BD114
Albert Embk, SE1 310 B1
Albert Gdns, E1 289 J9
Harlow CM17 52 EX16
Albert Gate, SW1 296 F4
Albert Gro, SW20 199 CX95
Albert Hall Mans, SW7 296 A5
Albert Ho, SE28
off Erebus Dr 165 EQ76
Albertine Cl, Epsom KT17 233 CV116
Albertine St, Harl. CM17 36 EX13
Albert Mans, SW11 308 E6
★ **Albert Mem**, SW7 296 A4
Albert Ms, E14
off Narrow St 289 L10
N4 121 DM60
SE4 *off Arabin Rd* 163 DY84
W8 295 N6
Redhill RH1 *off Reed Dr* 266 DG137
Albert Murray Cl, Grav. DA12
off Armoury Dr 191 GJ87
Albert Pl, N3 98 DA53
N17 *off High Rd* 122 DT55
W8 295 M5
Eton Wick SL4 *off Common Rd* 151 AN78
Albert Rd, E10 123 EC61
E16 305 H3
E17 123 EA57
E18 124 EH55
N4 121 DM60
N15 122 DS58
N22 99 DJ53
NW4 119 CX56
NW6 283 H1
NW7 97 CT50
SE9 184 EL90
SE20 183 DX94
SE25 202 DU98
W5 137 CH70
Addlestone KT15 194 BK104
Ashford TW15 174 BM92
Ashtead KT21 232 CM118
Belvedere DA17 166 EZ78
Bexley DA5 186 FA86
Bromley BR2 204 EK99
Buckhurst Hill IG9 102 EK47
Chelsfield BR6 224 EU106
Chesham HP5 54 AQ31
Dagenham RM8 126 EZ60
Albert Rd, Dartford DA2 188 FJ90
East Barnet EN4 80 DC42
Englefield Green TW20 172 AX93
Epsom KT17 217 CT113
Hampton Hill TW12 176 CC92
Harrow HA2 116 CC55
Hayes UB3 155 BS76
Horley RH6 268 DG147
Hounslow TW3 156 CA84
Ilford IG1 125 EP62
Kingston upon Thames KT1 198 CM96
Mitcham CR4 200 DF97
New Malden KT3 199 CT98
Richmond TW10 178 CL85
Romford RM1 127 FF57
St. Mary Cray BR5 206 EV100
South Merstham RH1 251 DJ129
Southall UB2 156 BX76
Sutton SM1 218 DD106
Swanscombe DA10 190 FZ86
Teddington TW11 177 CF93
Twickenham TW1 177 CF88
Warlingham CR6 237 DZ117
West Drayton UB7 134 BL74
Windsor SL4 152 AS84
Albert Rd Est, Belv. DA17 166 EZ78
Albert Rd N, Reig. RH2 249 CZ133
Watford WD17 75 BV41
Albert Rd S, Wat. WD17 75 BV41
Albert Sleet Ct, N9
off Colthurst Dr 100 DV48
Albert Sq, E15 281 K3
SW8 310 C5
Albert St, N12 98 DC50
NW1 275 K9
St. Albans AL1 43 CD21
Slough SL1 152 AT76
Warley CM14 108 FW50
Windsor SL4 151 AP81
Albert Ter, NW1 274 G8
NW10 138 CR67
W6 *off Beavor La* 159 CU78
Buckhurst Hill IG9 102 EK47
Albert Ter Ms, NW1 274 G9
Albert Wk, E16
off Pier Rd 305 M4
Albert Way, SE15 312 E4
Albion Av, N10 98 DG53
SW8 309 N8
Albion Cl, W2 284 D10
Hertford SG13 32 DS08
Romford RM7 127 FD58
Slough SL2 132 AU74
Albion Cres, Ch.St.G. HP8 90 AV48
Albion Dr, E8 278 A7
Albion Est, SE16 301 J5
Albion Gro, N16 122 DS63
Albion Hill, Hem.H. HP2
off Wolsey Rd 40 BK21
Loughton IG10 84 EJ43
Albion Ho, E16
off Church St 305 N3
Woking GU21 227 AZ117
Albion Ms, N1 276 E8
NW6 272 G6
W2 284 D9
W6 *off Galena Rd* 159 CV77
Albion Par, N16
off Albion Rd 122 DR63
Gravesend DA12 191 GK86
Albion Pk, Loug. IG10 84 EK43
Albion Pl, EC1 286 G6
W6 159 CV77
Windsor SL4 151 AN82
Sch **Albion Prim Sch**, SE16 301 H5
Albion Riverside Bldg, SW11 308 D4
Albion Rd, E17 123 EC55
N16 277 M2
N17 100 DT54
Bexleyheath DA6 166 EZ84
Chalfont St. Giles HP8 90 AV47
Gravesend DA12 191 GJ87
Hayes UB3 135 BS72
Hounslow TW3 156 CA84
Kingston upon Thames KT2 198 CQ95
Reigate RH2 266 DC135
St. Albans AL1 43 CF20
Sutton SM2 218 DD107
Twickenham TW2 177 CE88
Albion Sq, E8 278 A7
Albion St, SE16 301 H5
W2 284 D9
Croydon CR0 201 DP102
Albion Ter, E8 278 A7
Gravesend DA12 191 GJ86
Albion Vil Rd, SE26 182 DW90
Albion Wk, N1 286 B1
Albion Way, EC1 287 J7
SE13 163 EC84
Wembley HA9
off North End Rd 118 CP62
Albion Yd, N1 286 B1
E1 288 F6
Albon Ho, SW18
off Neville Gill Cl 180 DB86
● **Albright Ind Est**, Rain. RM13 147 FF71
Albrighton Rd, SE22 162 DS83
Albuhera Cl, Enf. EN2 81 DN39
ALBURY, Guil. GU5 260 BJ139
Albury Av, Bexh. DA7 166 EY82
Isleworth TW7 157 CF80
Sutton SM2 217 CW109
Albury Cl, Epsom KT19 216 CP109
Hampton TW12 176 CA93
Longcross KT16 192 AU104
Albury Ct, Sutt. SM1
off Ripley Gdns 218 DC105
Albury Dr, Pnr. HA5 94 BX52
Albury Gro Rd, Chsht EN8 67 DX30
ALBURY HEATH, Guil. GU5 260 BL141
Albury Heath, Albury GU5 260 BL141
Albury Keep, Horl. RH6
off Langshott La 269 DH147
Albury Ms, E12 124 EJ60
Albury Pk, Albury GU5 260 BL140
Albury Ride, Chsht EN8 67 DX31
Albury Rd, Chess. KT9 216 CL106
Guildford GU1 259 AZ135
Hersham KT12 213 BS107
South Merstham RH1 251 DJ129
Albury St, SE8 314 A3
Albury Wk, Chsht EN8 66 DW30
Albyfield, Brom. BR1 205 EM97
Albyn Ho, Hem.H. HP2 40 BK19

Albyn Rd, SE8 314 A7
Albyns Cl, Rain. RM13 147 FG66
Albyns La, Rom. RM4 87 FC40
Alcester Cres, E5 122 DV61
Alcester Rd, Wall. SM6 219 DH105
Alcock Cl, Wall. SM6 219 DK108
Alcock Rd, Houns. TW5 156 BX80
Alcocks Cl, Kgswd KT20 233 CY120
Alcocks La, Kgswd KT20 233 CY120
Alconbury, Welw.G.C. AL7 30 DE08
Alconbury Cl, Borwd. WD6 78 CM39
Alconbury Rd, E5 122 DU61
Alcorn Cl, Sutt. SM3 200 DA103
Alcott Cl, W7
off Westcott Cres 137 CF71
Alcuin Ct, Stan. HA7 95 CJ52
Sch Aldborough E-Act Free Sch, Ilf. IG3 125 ES59
ALDBOROUGH HATCH, Ilf. IG2 125 ES55
Aldborough Rd, Dag. RM10 147 FC65
Upminster RM14 128 FM61
Aldborough Rd N, Ilf. IG2 125 ET57
Aldborough Rd S, Ilf. IG3 125 ES60
Aldborough Spur, Slou. SL1 132 AS72
Aldbourne Rd, W12 139 CT74
Burnham SL1 130 AH71
Aldbridge St, SE17 299 P10
Aldburgh Ms, W1 285 H8
Aldbury Av, Wem. HA9 138 CP66
Aldbury Cl, St.Alb. AL4
off Larkswood Ri 43 CJ15
Watford WD25 76 BX36
Aldbury Gro, Welw.G.C. AL7 30 DB09
Aldbury Ms, N9 100 DR45
Aldbury Rd, Mill End WD3 91 BF45
Aldebert Ter, SW8 310 B5
Aldeburgh Cl, E5
off Southwold Rd 122 DV61
Aldeburgh Pl, SE10 303 P9
Woodford Green IG8 102 EG49
Aldeburgh St, SE10 303 N10
Aldemere Av, Chsht EN8 66 DW28
Alden Av, E15 291 L3
ALDENHAM, Wat. WD25 76 CB38
Aldenham Av, Rad. WD7 77 CG36
Aldenham Cl, Slou. SL3 152 AX76
★ Aldenham Country Pk, Borwd. WD6 77 CG43
Aldenham Dr, Uxb. UB8 135 BP70
Aldenham Gro, Rad. WD7 61 CH34
Aldenham Rd, Bushey WD23 76 BZ42
Elstree WD6 77 CH42
Letchmore Heath WD25 77 CE39
Radlett WD7 77 CG35
Watford WD19 76 BX44
Sch Aldenham Sch, Els. WD6
off Aldenham Rd 77 CF40
Aldenham St, NW1 285 M1
Aldenholme, Wey. KT13 213 BS107
Aldensley Rd, W6 159 CV76
Alden Vw, Wind. SL4 151 AK81
Alder Av, Upmin. RM14 128 FM63
Alderbourne La, Fulmer SL3 112 AX63
Iver SL0 113 BA64
Sch Alderbrook Prim Sch, SW12
off Oldridge Rd 181 DH87
Alderbrook Rd, SW12 181 DH86
Alderbury Rd, SW13 159 CU79
Slough SL3 153 AZ75
Alderbury Rd W, Slou. SL3 153 AZ75
Alder Cl, SE15 312 B3
Englefield Green TW20 172 AY92
Erith DA18 166 EZ75
Hoddesdon EN11 49 EB15
Park Street AL2 60 CB28
Slough SL1 131 AM74
Aldercombe La, Cat. CR3 252 DS127
Alder Ct, N11
off Cline Rd 99 DJ51
Aldercroft, Couls. CR5 235 DM116
Alder Dr, S.Ock. RM15
off Laburnum Gro 149 FW70
Alder Gro, NW2 119 CV61
Aldergrove Gdns, Houns. TW3
off Bath Rd 156 BY82
Aldergrove Wk, Horn. RM12
off Pembrey Way 148 FJ65
Alder Ho, NW3 274 F4
Alderley Ct, Berk. HP4 38 AV20
Alderman Av, Bark. IG11 146 EU69
Aldermanbury, EC2 287 K8
Aldermanbury Sq, EC2 287 K7
Alderman Cl, Dart. DA1 187 FE87
North Mymms AL9 45 CW24
Alderman Judge Mall, Kings.T. KT1 off Eden St 198 CL96
Aldermans Hill, N13 99 DL49
Alderman's Wk, EC2 287 N7
Aldermary Rd, Brom. BR1 204 EG95
Alder Ms, N19 off Bredgar Rd 121 DJ61
Aldermoor Rd, SE6 183 DZ90
Alderney Av, Houns. TW5 156 CB80
Alderney Gdns, Nthlt. UB5 136 BZ66
Alderney Ho, N1 off Arran Wk 277 K5
Alderney Ms, SE1 299 L6
Alderney Rd, E1 289 J4
Erith DA8 167 FG80
Alderney St, SW1 297 K10
Alder Rd, SW14 158 CR83
Denham UB9 134 BJ65
Iver SL0 133 BC68
Sidcup DA14 185 ET90
Alders, The, N21 81 DN44
SW16 181 DJ91
Feltham TW13 176 BY91
Hounslow TW5 156 BZ79
West Byfleet KT14 212 BJ112
West Wickham BR4 203 EB102
Alders Av, Wdf.Grn. IG8 102 EE51
ALDERSBROOK, E12 124 EH61
Aldersbrook Av, Enf. EN1 82 DS40
Aldersbrook Dr, Kings.T. KT2 178 CM93
Aldersbrook La, E12 125 EM62
Sch Aldersbrook Prim Sch, E12
off Ingatestone Rd 124 EJ60
Aldersbrook Rd, E11 124 EH61
E12 124 EK62
Alders Cl, E11 124 EH61
W5 157 CK76
Edgware HA8 96 CQ50
● Alders Ct, Welw.G.C. AL7 30 DA09
Aldersey Gdns, Bark. IG11 145 ER65
Aldersey Rd, Guil. GU1 243 AZ134
Aldersford Cl, SE4 183 DX85
Aldersgate St, EC1 287 J8
Alders Gro, E.Mol. KT8 197 CD99
Aldersgrove, Wal.Abb. EN9
off Roundhills 68 EE34
Aldersgrove Av, SE9 184 EJ90
Aldershot Rd, NW6 273 H8
Guildford GU2, GU3 242 AT132
Alderside Wk, Eng.Grn TW20 172 AY92
Aldersmead Av, Croy. CR0 203 DX100
Aldersmead Rd, Beck. BR3 183 DY94
Alderson Pl, Sthl. UB2 136 CC74
Alderson St, W10 282 F4
Alders Rd, Edg. HA8 96 CQ50
Reigate RH2 250 DB132
Alderstead La, Merst. RH1 251 DK126
Alders Wk, Saw. CM21 36 EY05
Alderton Cl, NW10 118 CR62
Loughton IG10 85 EN42
Pilgrim's Hatch CM15 108 FV43
Alderton Cres, NW4 119 CV57
Alderton Hall La, Loug. IG10 85 EN42
Alderton Hill, Loug. IG10 84 EL43
Sch Alderton Inf Sch, Loug. IG10
off Alderton Hall La 85 EN43
Sch Alderton Jun Sch, Loug. IG10
off Alderton Hall La 85 EN43
Alderton Ms, Loug. IG10
off Alderton Hall La 85 EN42
Alderton Ri, Loug. IG10 85 EN42
Alderton Rd, SE24 162 DQ83
Croydon CR0 202 DT101
Alderton Way, NW4 119 CV57
Loughton IG10 85 EM43
Alderville Rd, SW6 307 H8
Alder Wk, Ilf. IG1 125 EQ64
Watford WD25
off Aspen Pk Dr 75 BV35
Alder Way, Swan. BR8 207 FD96
Alderwick Dr, Houns. TW3 157 CD83
Alderwood Cl, Abridge RM4 86 EV41
Caterham CR3 252 DS125
Alderwood Dr, Abridge RM4 86 EV41
Alderwood Ms, Barn. EN4 80 DC38
Sch Alderwood Prim Sch, SE9
off Rainham Cl 185 ES86
Alderwood Rd, SE9 185 ER86
Aldford St, W1 296 G2
⊖ Aldgate 288 A9
● Aldgate 288 A9
Aldgate, EC3 288 A9
Aldgate Av, E1 288 A8
⊖ Aldgate East 288 B8
Aldgate High St, EC3 288 A9
Aldham Dr, S.Ock. RM15 149 FW71
Aldin Av N, Slou. SL1 152 AU75
Aldin Av S, Slou. SL1 152 AU75
Aldine Ct, W12 294 B4
Aldine Pl, W12 294 B3
Aldine St, W12 294 B4
Aldingham Ct, Horn. RM12
off Easedale Dr 127 FG64
Aldingham Gdns, Horn. RM12 127 FG64
Aldington Cl, Dag. RM8 126 EW59
Aldington Rd, SE18 304 F7
Aldis Ms, SW17 180 DE92
Enfield EN3 83 EA37
Aldis St, SW17 180 DE92
Aldock, Welw.G.C. AL7 30 DA12
Aldred Rd, NW6 273 J2
Aldren Rd, SW17 180 DC90
Aldrich Cres, New Adgtn CR0 221 EC109
Aldriche Way, E4 101 EC51
Aldrich Gdns, Sutt. SM3 199 CZ104
Aldrich Ter, SW18
off Lidiard Rd 180 DC89
Aldridge Av, Edg. HA8 96 CP48
Enfield EN3 83 EA38
Ruislip HA4 116 BX61
Stanmore HA7 96 CL53
Aldridge Ri, N.Mal. KT3 198 CS101
Aldridge Rd, Slou. SL2 131 AN70
Aldridge Rd Vil, W11 283 H7
Aldridge Wk, N14 99 DL45
Aldrien Ct, N9
off Galahad Rd 100 DU48
Aldrington Rd, SW16 181 DJ92
Aldsworth Cl, W9 283 L5
Aldwick, St.Alb. AL1 43 CH22
Aldwick Cl, SE9 185 ER90
Aldwick Rd, Croy. CR0 201 DM104
Aldworth Gro, SE13 183 EC86
Aldworth Rd, E15 281 J7
Aldwych, WC2 286 C10
Aldwych Av, Ilf. IG6 125 EQ56
Aldwych Cl, Horn. RM12 127 FG61
Aldwych Underpass, WC2
off Kingsway 286 C9
Aldwyck Ct, Hem.H. HP1 40 BJ19
Aldykes, Hat. AL10 45 CT18
Alers Rd, Bexh. DA6 186 EX85
Alesia Cl, N22 99 DL52
Alestan Beck Rd, E16 292 F8
Alexa Ct, W8 295 L8
Sutton SM2 off Mulgrave Rd 218 DA107
Alexander Av, NW10 139 CV66
Alexander Cl, Barn. EN4 80 DD42
Bromley BR2 204 EG102
Sidcup DA15 185 ES85
Southall UB2 136 CC74
Twickenham TW2 177 CF89
Alexander Ct, Chsht EN8 67 DX30
Alexander Cres, Cat. CR3 236 DQ121
Alexander Evans Ms, SE23 183 DX88
Sch Alexander First Sch, Oakley Grn SL4 off Kenneally Row 150 AJ82
★ Alexander Fleming Laboratory Mus, W2 284 B8
Alexander Godley Cl, Ashtd. KT21 232 CM119
Alexander Ho, Kings.T. KT2
off Kingsgate Rd 198 CL95
Alexander La, Brwd. CM13, CM15 109 GB44
Sch Alexander McLeod Prim Sch, SE2 off Fuchsia St 166 EV78
Alexander Ms, SW16 181 DJ92
W2 283 L8
Harlow CM17 52 EX17
Alexander Pl, SW7 296 C8
Oxted RH8 254 EE128
Alexander Rd, N19 121 DL62
Bexleyheath DA7 166 EX82
Chislehurst BR7 185 EP92
Coulsdon CR5 235 DH115
Egham TW20 173 BB92
Greenhithe DA9 189 FW85
Hertford SG14 31 DN09
London Colney AL2 61 CJ25
Reigate RH2 266 DA137
Alexander Sq, SW3 296 C8
Alexander St, W2 283 K8
Chesham HP5 54 AQ30
Alexanders Wk, Cat. CR3 252 DT126
Alexandra Av, N22 99 DK53
SW11 308 G6
W4 158 CR80
Harrow HA2 116 BZ60
Southall UB1 136 BZ73
Sutton SM1 200 DA104
Warlingham CR6 237 DZ117
Alexandra Cl, SE8 313 N2
Ashford TW15 175 BR94
Grays RM16 171 GH75
Harrow HA2 116 CA62
Staines-upon-Thames TW18 174 BK93
Swanley BR8 207 FE96
Walton-on-Thames KT12 195 BU103
Alexandra Cotts, SE14 313 P7
Alexandra Ct, N14 81 DJ43
N16 277 P1
W9 283 P4
Ashford TW15 175 BR93
Waltham Cross EN8
off Alexandra Way 67 DZ34
Wembley HA9 118 CM63
Alexandra Cres, Brom. BR1 184 EF93
Alexandra Dr, SE19 182 DS92
Surbiton KT5 198 CN101
Alexandra Gdns, N10 121 DH56
W4 158 CS80
Carshalton SM5 218 DG109
Hounslow TW3 156 CB82
Alexandra Gro, N4 121 DP60
N12 98 DB50
Sch Alexandra Inf Sch, Beck. BR3
off Kent Ho Rd 183 DX94
Kingston upon Thames KT2
off Alexandra Rd 178 CN94
Sch Alexandra Jun Sch, SE26
off Cator Rd 183 DX93
Alexandra Ms, N2 120 DF55
SW19 off Alexandra Rd 179 CZ93
Watford WD17 75 BU40
Sch Alexandra Nurs & Inf & Jun Schs, Houns. TW3
off Denbigh Rd 156 CB82
★ Alexandra Palace, N22 99 DK54
⇌ Alexandra Palace 99 DL54
Alexandra Palace Way, N22 121 DJ55
Alexandra Pk Rd, N10 99 DH54
N22 99 DK54
Sch Alexandra Pk Sch, N11
off Bidwell Gdns 99 DJ53
Alexandra Pl, NW8 273 P8
SE25 202 DR99
Croydon CR0
off Alexandra Rd 202 DS102
Guildford GU1 259 AZ136
Sch Alexandra Prim Sch, N22
off Western Rd 99 DM54
Alexandra Rd, E6 293 L2
E10 123 EC62
E17 123 DZ58
E18 124 EH55
N8 121 DN55
N9 100 DV45
N10 99 DH51
N15 122 DR57
NW4 119 CX56
NW8 273 P8
SE26 183 DX93
SW14 158 CR83
SW19 179 CZ93
W4 158 CR75
Addlestone KT15 212 BK105
Ashford TW15 175 BR94
Biggin Hill TN16 238 EH119
Borehamwood WD6 78 CR38
Brentford TW8 157 CK79
Brentwood CM14 108 FW48
Chadwell Heath RM6 126 EX58
Chipperfield WD4 58 BG30
Croydon CR0 202 DS102
Enfield EN3 83 DX42
Englefield Green TW20 172 AW93
Epsom KT17 217 CT113
Erith DA8 167 FF79
Gravesend DA12 191 GL87
Harlow CM17 36 EW13
Hemel Hempstead HP2 40 BK20
Hounslow TW3 156 CB82
Kings Langley WD4 58 BN29
Kingston upon Thames KT2 178 CN94
Mitcham CR4 180 DE94
Rainham RM13 147 FF67
Richmond TW9 158 CM82
Romford RM1 127 FF58
St. Albans AL1 43 CE20
Sarratt WD3 74 BG36
Slough SL1 151 AR76
Thames Ditton KT7 197 CF99
Tilbury RM18 171 GF82
Twickenham TW1 177 CJ86
Uxbridge UB8 134 BK68
Warlingham CR6 237 DY117
Watford WD17 75 BU40
Windsor SL4 151 AR82
Sch Alexandra Sch, S.Har. HA2
off Alexandra Av 116 CA61
Alexandra Sq, Mord. SM4 200 DA99
Alexandra St, E16 291 N6
SE14 313 M4
Alexandra Ter, Guil. GU1 258 AY135
Alexandra Wk, SE19
off Alexandra Dr 182 DS92
South Darenth DA4
off Gorringe Av 209 FS96
Alexandra Way, Epsom KT19 216 CN111
Waltham Cross EN8 67 DZ34
Alexandria Rd, W13 137 CG73
Alex Ct, Hem.H. HP2
off Alexandra Rd 40 BK19
Alex Guy Gdns, Rom. RM8 127 FB60
Alexis St, SE16 300 C8
Alfan La, Dart. DA2 187 FD92
Alfearn Rd, E5 122 DW63
Alford Cl, Guil. GU4 243 AZ131
Alford Grn, New Adgtn CR0 221 ED107
Alford Ho, N6 121 DJ58
Alford Pl, N1 287 K1
Alford Rd, Erith DA8 167 FD78
Alfoxton Av, N15 121 DP56
Alfreda St, SW11 309 J6
Alfred Cl, W4 158 CR77
Alfred Ct, Whyt. CR3
off Godstone Rd 236 DU119
Alfred Gdns, Sthl. UB1 136 BY73
Alfred Ms, W1 285 N6
Alfred Pl, WC1 285 N6
Northfleet DA11 191 GF88
Alfred Prior Ho, E12 125 EN63
Alfred Rd, E15 281 L2
SE25 202 DU99
W2 283 K6
W3 138 CQ74
Aveley RM15 148 FQ74
Belvedere DA17 166 EZ78
Brentwood CM14 108 FX47
Buckhurst Hill IG9 102 EK47
Feltham TW13 176 BW89
Gravesend DA11 191 GH89
Hawley DA2 188 FL91
Kingston upon Thames KT1 198 CL97
Sutton SM1 218 DC106
Sch Alfred Salter Prim Sch, SE16 301 K5
Alfred's Gdns, Bark. IG11 145 ES68
Alfred St, E3 289 P1
Grays RM17 170 GC79
Alfreds Way, Bark. IG11 145 EQ69
● Alfreds Way Ind Est, Bark. IG11 146 EU67
Alfreton Cl, SW19 179 CX90
Alfriston, Surb. KT5 198 CM99
Alfriston Av, Croy. CR0 201 DL101
Harrow HA2 116 CA58
Alfriston Cl, Dart. DA1 187 FE86
Surbiton KT5 198 CM100
Alfriston Rd, SW11 180 DF85
Sch Alfriston Sch, Knot.Grn HP9
off Penn Rd 88 AJ49
Algar Cl, Islw. TW7
off Algar Rd 157 CG83
Stanmore HA7 95 CF50
Algar Rd, Islw. TW7 157 CG83
Algarve Rd, SW18 180 DB88
Algernon Rd, NW4 119 CU58
NW6 273 J9
SE13 314 C10
Algers Cl, Loug. IG10 84 EK43
Algers Mead, Loug. IG10 84 EK43
Algers Rd, Loug. IG10 84 EK43
Algiers Rd, SE13 163 EA84
Alibon Gdns, Dag. RM10 126 FA64
Alibon Rd, Dag. RM9, RM10 126 EZ64
Alice Cl, New Barn. EN5 80 DC42
Alice Ct, SW15 159 CZ84
Alice Gilliatt Ct, W14 306 G2
Alice La, E3 279 N9
Burnham SL1 130 AH70
Alice Ms, Tedd. TW11
off Luther Rd 177 CF92
Alice Ruston Pl, Wok. GU22 226 AW119
Alice Shepherd Ho, E14
off Stewart St 302 F5
Alice St, SE1 299 N7
Alice Thompson Cl, SE12 184 EJ89
Alice Wk, W5 137 CJ71
Alice Walker Cl, SE24
off Shakespeare Rd 161 DP84
Alice Way, Houns. TW3 156 CB84
Alicia Av, Har. HA3 117 CH56
Alicia Cl, Har. HA3 117 CJ56
Alicia Gdns, Har. HA3 117 CH56
Alie St, E1 288 B9
Alington Cres, NW9 118 CQ60
Alington Gro, Wall. SM6 219 DJ109
Alison Cl, E6 293 M9
Croydon CR0
off Shirley Oaks Rd 203 DX102
Eastcote HA5 115 BV58
Woking GU21 226 AY115
Aliwal Rd, SW11 160 DE84
Alkerden La, Green. DA9 189 FW86
Swanscombe DA10 189 FW86
Alkerden Rd, W4 158 CS78
Alkham Rd, N16 122 DT61
Allan Barclay Cl, N15 122 DT58
Allan Cl, N.Mal. KT3 198 CR99
Allandale, Hem.H. HP2 40 BK18
St. Albans AL3 42 CB23
Allandale Av, N3 119 CY55
Allandale Cres, Pot.B. EN6 63 CY32
Allandale Pl, Orp. BR6 206 EX104
Allandale Rd, Enf. EN3 83 DX36
Hornchurch RM11 127 FF59
Allan Way, W3 138 CQ71
Allard, NW9 off Boulevard Dr 97 CT54
Allard Cl, Chsht EN7 66 DT27
Orpington BR5 206 EW101
Allard Cres, Bushey Hth WD23 94 CC46
Allard Gdns, SW4 181 DK85
Allard Way, Brox. EN10 49 DY21
Allardyce St, SW4 161 DM84
Allbrook Cl, Tedd. TW11 177 CE92
Allcot Cl, Felt. TW14 175 BT88
Allcroft Rd, NW5 275 H3
Allder Way, S.Croy. CR2 219 DP108
Alldicks Rd, Hem.H. HP3 40 BM22
Allenby Av, S.Croy. CR2 220 DQ109
Allenby Cl, Grnf. UB6 136 CA69
Allenby Cres, Grays RM17 170 GB78
Allenby Dr, Horn. RM11 128 FL60
Sch Allenby Prim Sch, Sthl. UB1
off Allenby Rd 136 CA72
Allenby Rd, SE23 183 DY90
SE28 165 EQ76
Biggin Hill TN16 238 EL117
Southall UB1 136 CA72
Allen Cl, Mitch. CR4 201 DH95
Shenley WD7 off Russet Dr 62 CL32
Sunbury-on-Thames TW16 195 BV95
Allen Ct, Dor. RH4
off High St 263 CH136
Greenford UB6 117 CF64
Hatfield AL10 off Drakes Way 45 CV20
Allendale Av, Sthl. UB1 136 CA72
Allendale Cl, SE5 311 L8
SE26 183 DX92
Dartford DA2 off Princes Rd 189 FR88
Allendale Rd, Grnf. UB6 137 CH65
Allende Av, Harl. CM20 35 ER13
Allen Edwards Dr, SW8 310 A6
Sch Allen Edwards Prim Sch, SW4 310 A7
Allenford Ho, SW15
off Tunworth Cres 179 CT86
Allen Ho Pk, Wok. GU22 226 AW120
Allen Pl, Twick. TW1
off Church St 177 CG88
Allen Rd, E3 279 N10
N16 122 DS63
Beckenham BR3 203 DX96
Bookham KT23 246 CB126
Croydon CR0 201 DM101
Rainham RM13 148 FJ69
Sunbury-on-Thames TW16 195 BV95
Allensbury Pl, NW1 275 P7
Allens Mead, Grav. DA12 191 GM88
Allens Rd, Enf. EN3 82 DW43
Allen St, W8 295 K6
Allenswood, SW19
off Albert Dr 179 CY88
Allenswood Rd, SE9 164 EL83
Allen Way, Datchet SL3 152 AW81
Allerds Rd, Farn.Royal SL2 131 AM67
Allerford Ct, Har. HA2 116 CB57
Allerford Ms, Har. HA2
off Allerford Ct 116 CB57
Allerford Rd, SE6 183 EB91
Allerton Cl, Borwd. WD6 78 CM38
Allerton Ct, NW4
off Holders Hill Rd 97 CX54
Allerton Rd, N16 122 DQ61
Borehamwood WD6 78 CL38
Allerton Wk, N7
off Durham Rd 121 DM61
Allestree Rd, SW6 306 E5
Alleyn Cres, SE21 182 DR89
Alleyndale Rd, Dag. RM8 126 EW61
Alleyn Pk, SE21 182 DR89
Southall UB2 156 BZ77
Alleyn Rd, SE21 182 DR90
Sch Alleyn's Sch, SE22
off Townley Rd 182 DS85
Allfarthing La, SW18 180 DB86
Sch Allfarthing Prim Sch, SW18
off St. Ann's Cres 180 DC86
Allgood Cl, Mord. SM4 199 CX100
Allgood St, E2 288 B1
Allhallows La, EC4 299 L1
★ All Hallows-on-the-Wall C of E Ch, EC2 287 M7
Allhallows Rd, E6 292 G7
All Hallows Rd, N17 100 DS53
Allhusen Gdns, Fulmer SL3
off Alderbourne La 112 AY63
Alliance Cl, Houns. TW4
off Vimy Cl 176 BZ85
Wembley HA0 117 CK63
● Alliance Ct, W3
off Alliance Rd 138 CP71
Alliance Rd, E13 292 C5
SE18 166 EU79
W3 138 CP70
Allied Ct, N1 277 P7
Allied Way, W3
off Larden Rd 158 CS75
Allingham Cl, W7 137 CF73
Allingham Ct, Gdmg. GU7
off Summers Rd 258 AT144
Allingham Ms, N1 277 J10
Allingham Rd, Reig. RH2 266 DA137
Allingham St, N1 277 J10
Allington Av, N17 100 DS51
Allington Cl, SW19
off High St Wimbledon 179 CX92
Gravesend DA12
off Farley Rd 191 GM88
Greenford UB6 136 CC66
Allington Ct, Enf. EN3 83 DX43
Slough SL2 132 AT73
Allington Rd, NW4 119 CV57
W10 282 E2
Harrow HA2 116 CC57
Orpington BR6 205 ER103
Allis Ms, Harl. CM17
off Tatton St 36 EW14
Allison Cl, SE10 314 F7
Waltham Abbey EN9 68 EG33
Allison Gro, SE21 182 DS88
Allison Rd, N8 121 DN57
W3 138 CQ72
Allitsen Rd, NW8 284 C1
Allmains Cl, Naze.Gate EN9 68 EH25
Coll All Nations Christian Coll, Easneye SG12 33 EC08
Allnutts Rd, Epp. CM16 70 EU33
Allnutt Way, SW4 181 DK85
Alloa Rd, SE8 301 K10
Ilford IG3 126 EU61
Allonby Dr, Ruis. HA4 115 BP59
Allonby Gdns, Wem. HA9 117 CJ60
Allonby Ho, E14 289 L7
Allotment La, Sev. TN13 257 FJ122
Allotment Way, NW2
off Midland Ter 119 CX62
Alloway Cl, Wok. GU21
off Inglewood 226 AV118
Alloway Rd, E3 289 M2
Allport Ms, E1 289 H5
DLR All Saints 290 E10
Sch All Saints Benhilton C of E Prim Sch, Sutt. SM1
off All Saints Rd 200 DB104
Sch All Saints Carshalton C of E Prim Sch, Cars. SM5
off Rotherfield Rd 218 DG106
Sch All Saints Cath Sch & Tech Coll, Dag. RM8
off Terling Rd 126 FA60
All Saints Cl, N9 100 DT47
SW8 310 A6
Chigwell IG7 104 EU48
Swanscombe DA10
off High St 190 FZ85
Sch All Saints C of E Jun Sch, SE19 off Upper Beulah Hill 202 DS95
Sch All Saints C of E Prim Sch, SE3 315 J8
SW6 306 E8
SW15 306 A10
SW19 off East Rd 180 DC94
Sch All Saints' C of E Prim Sch, N20
off Oakleigh Rd N 98 DD47
NW2 off Cricklewood La 119 CZ62
All Saints Cres, Wat. WD25 60 BX33
All Saints Dr, SE3 315 K8
South Croydon CR2 220 DT112
Sch All Saints Inf Sch, SE19
off Upper Beulah Hill 202 DS95
All Saints La, Crox.Grn WD3 74 BN44
All Saints Ms, Har. HA3 95 CE51
All Saints Pas, SW18
off Wandsworth High St 180 DA85
All Saints Rd, SW19 180 DC94
W3 158 CQ76
W11 282 G7
Northfleet DA11 191 GF88
Sutton SM1 200 DB104
All Saints St, N1 276 C10
Allsop Pl, NW1 284 F5
All Souls Av, NW10 139 CV68
Sch All Souls C of E Prim Sch, W1 285 L7

All Souls Pl, W1 285 K7
Allum Cl, Els. WD6 78 CL42
Allum Gro, Tad. KT20 233 CV121
Allum La, Els. WD6 78 CM42
Allum Way, N20 98 DC46
Allwood Cl, SE26 183 DX91
Allwood Rd, Chsht EN7 66 DT27
Allyn Cl, Stai. TW18
off Penton Rd 173 BF93
Alma Av, E4 101 EC52
Hornchurch RM12 128 FL63
Alma Barn Ms, Orp. BR5 206 EX103
Almack Rd, E5 278 G1
Alma Cl, Knap. GU21 226 AS118
Alma Ct, Har. HA2
off Hornbuckle Cl 117 CD61
Alma Cres, Sutt. SM1 217 CY106
Alma Cut, St.Alb. AL1 43 CE21
Alma Gro, SE1 300 B9
Almanza Pl, Bark. IG11 146 EV68
Alma Pl, NW10
off Harrow Rd 139 CV69
SE19 182 DT94
Thornton Heath CR7 201 DN99
Watord WD25 76 BY36
Sch Alma Prim Sch, SE16 300 D8
Enfield EN3 *off Alma Rd* 83 DX43
Alma Rd, N10 98 DG52
SW18 180 DC85
Carshalton SM5 218 DE106
Chesham HP5 54 AQ29
Enfield EN3 83 DY43
Esher KT10 197 CE102
Eton Wick SL4 151 AM77
Northchurch HP4 38 AS17
Orpington BR5 206 EX103
Reigate RH2 250 DB133
St. Albans AL1 43 CE21
Sidcup DA14 186 EU90
Southall UB1 136 BY73
Swanscombe DA10 190 FZ85
Windsor SL4 151 AQ82
Alma Row, Har. HA3 95 CD53
Alma Sq, NW8 283 P2
Alma St, E15 280 G4
NW5 275 K4
Alma Ter, SW18 180 DD87
W8 *off Allen St* 295 K7
Almeida St, N1 276 G7
Almeric Rd, SW11 160 DF84
Almer Rd, SW20 179 CU94
Almington St, N4 121 DL60
Almners Rd, Lyne KT16 193 BC100
Almond Av, W5 158 CL76
Carshalton SM5 200 DF103
Uxbridge UB10 115 BP62
West Drayton UB7 154 BN76
Woking GU22 226 AX121
Almond Cl, SE15 312 D9
Bromley BR2 205 EN101
Englefield Green TW20 172 AV93
Feltham TW13
off Highfield Rd 175 BU88
Grays RM16 171 GG76
Guildford GU1 242 AX130
Hayes UB3 135 BS73
Ruislip HA4 115 BT62
Shepperton TW17 195 BQ96
Windsor SL4 151 AP82
Almond Dr, Swan. BR8 207 FD96
Almond Gro, Brent. TW8 157 CH80
Almond Rd, N17 100 DU52
SE16 300 F8
Burnham SL1 130 AH68
Dartford DA2 188 FQ87
Epsom KT19 216 CR111
Almonds, The, St.Alb. AL1 43 CH24
Almonds Av, Buck.H. IG9 102 EG47
Almond Wk, Hat. AL10
off Southdown Rd 45 CU21
Almond Way, Borwd. WD6 78 CP42
Bromley BR2 205 EN101
Harrow HA2 94 CB54
Mitcham CR4 201 DK99
Almons Way, Slou. SL2 132 AV71
Almorah Rd, N1 277 L7
Hounslow TW5 156 BX81
Alms Heath, Ock. GU23 229 BP121
Almshouse La, Chess. KT9 215 CJ109
Enfield EN1 82 DV37
Almshouses, The, Dor. RH4
off Cotmandene 263 CH135
Alnwick Gro, Mord. SM4
off Bordesley Rd 200 DB98
Alnwick Rd, E16 292 C9
SE12 184 EH87
ALPERTON, Wem. HA0 138 CM67
⊖ **Alperton** 138 CL67
Sch Alperton Comm Sch,
Lwr Sch, Wem. HA0
off Ealing Rd 138 CL67
Upr Sch & 6th Form Cen, Wem.
HA0 *off Stanley Av* 138 CL66
Alperton La, Perivale UB6 137 CK69
Wembley HA0 137 CK69
Alperton St, W10 282 F4
Alphabet Gdns, Cars. SM5 200 DD100
Alphabet Sq, E3 290 B6
● **Alpha Business Pk**,
N.Mymms AL9 45 CW23
Alpha Cl, NW1 284 D4
Alpha Ct, Whyt. CR3 236 DU118
Alpha Est, Hayes UB3 155 BS75
Alpha Gro, E14 302 B5
Alpha Pl, NW6 273 K10
SW3 308 D2
Sch Alpha Prep Sch, Har. HA1
off Hindes Rd 117 CE57
Alpha Rd, E4 101 EB48
N18 100 DU51
SE14 313 P6
Chobham GU24 210 AT110
Croydon CR0 202 DS102
Enfield EN3 83 DY42
Hutton CM13 109 GD44
Surbiton KT5 198 CM100
Teddington TW11 177 CD92
Uxbridge UB10 135 BP70
Woking GU22 227 BB116
Alpha St, SE15 312 C9
Alpha St N, Slou. SL1 152 AU75
Alpha St S, Slou. SL1 152 AT76
Alpha Way, Egh. TW20 193 BC95
Alphea Cl, SW19 180 DE94
Alpine Av, Surb. KT5 198 CQ103
Alpine Cl, Croy. CR0 202 DS104
Epsom KT19 *off Cox La* 216 CQ106
Alpine Copse, Brom. BR1 205 EN96
Alpine Gro, E9 279 H7
Alpine Rd, E10 123 EB61
SE16 301 H9
Redhill RH1 250 DG131
Walton-on-Thames KT12 195 BU101
Alpine Vw, Cars. SM5 218 DE106
Alpine Wk, Stan. HA7 95 CE47
Alpine Way, E6 293 L6
Alresford Rd, Guil. GU2 258 AU135
Alric Av, NW10 138 CR66
New Malden KT3 198 CS97
Alroy Rd, N4 121 DN59
Alsace Rd, SE17 299 N10
Sch Al-Sadiq Boys & Girls Prim & High School, NW6 273 F8
Alscot Rd, SE1 300 B8
Alscot Way, SE1 300 A8
Alsford Wf, Berk. HP4 38 AX19
Alsike Rd, SE2 166 EX76
Erith DA18 166 EY76
Alsom Av, Wor.Pk. KT4 217 CU105
Alsop Cl, Lon.Col. AL2 62 CL27
Alston Cl, Long Dit. KT6 197 CH101
Alston Rd, N18 100 DV50
SW17 180 DD91
Barnet EN5 79 CY41
Hemel Hempstead HP1 40 BG21
● **Alston Wks**, Barn. EN5 79 CY41
Altair Cl, N17 100 DT51
Altair Way, Nthwd. HA6 93 BT49
Altash Way, SE9 185 EM89
Altenburg Av, W13 157 CH76
Altenburg Gdns, SW11 160 DF84
Alterton Cl, Wok. GU21 226 AU117
Alt Gro, SW19
off St. George's Rd 179 CZ94
Altham Gdns, Wat. WD19 94 BX49
Altham Gro, Harl. CM20 35 ET12
Altham Rd, Pnr. HA5 94 BY52
Althea St, SW6 307 M9
Althorne Gdns, E18 124 EF56
Althorne Rd, Red. RH1 266 DG136
Althorne Way, Dag. RM10 126 FA61
Althorp Cl, Barn. EN5 97 CU45
Althorpe Gro, SW11 308 B6
Althorpe Ms, SW11 308 B7
Althorpe Rd, Har. HA1 116 CC57
Althorp Rd, SW17 180 DF88
St. Albans AL1 43 CE19
Altitude Apts, Croy. CR0 202 DR104
Altmore Av, E6 145 EM66
Sch Altmore Inf Sch, E6
off Altmore Av 145 EM67
Alto Ct, E15
off Plaistow Gro 281 L9
Altona Rd, Loud. HP10 88 AC52
Alton Av, Stan. HA7 95 CF52
Altona Way, Slou. SL1 131 AP72
Alton Cl, Bex. DA5 186 EY88
Isleworth TW7 157 CF82
Alton Ct, Stai. TW18 193 BE95
Alton Gdns, Beck. BR3 183 EA94
Twickenham TW2 177 CD87
Alton Ho, E3
off Bromley High St 290 D2
Alton Rd, N17 122 DR55
SW15 179 CU88
Croydon CR0 201 DN104
Richmond TW9 158 CL84
Sch Alton Sch, The, SW15
off Danebury Av 178 CS86
Alton St, E14 290 C7
★ **Altura Twr**, SW11 308 A9
Altwood Cl, Slou. SL1 131 AL71
Altyre Cl, Beck. BR3 203 DZ99
Altyre Rd, Croy. CR0 202 DR103
Altyre Way, Beck. BR3 203 DZ99
Aluric Cl, Grays RM16 171 GH77
Alvanley Gdns, NW6 273 L2
Alva Way, Wat. WD19 94 BX47
Alverstoke Rd, Rom. RM3 106 FL52
Alverstone Av, SW19 180 DA89
East Barnet EN4 98 DE45
Alverstone Gdns, SE9 185 EQ88
Alverstone Rd, E12 125 EN63
NW2 272 A6
New Malden KT3 199 CT98
Wembley HA9 118 CM60
Alverston Gdns, SE25 202 DS99
Alverton, St.Alb. AL3
off Green La 42 CC17
Alverton St, SE8 313 N1
Alveston Av, Har. HA3 117 CH55
Alveston Sq, E18 102 EG54
Alvey Est, SE17 299 N9
Alvey St, SE17 299 N10
Alvia Gdns, Sutt. SM1 218 DC105
Alvington Cres, E8 278 A2
Alvista Av, Tap. SL6 130 AH72
Alway Av, Epsom KT19 216 CQ106
Alwen Gro, S.Ock. RM15 149 FV71
Alwin Pl, Wat. WD18 75 BS42
Alwold Cres, SE12 184 EH86
Alwyn Av, W4 158 CR78
Alwyn Cl, Els. WD6 78 CM44
New Addington CR0 221 EB108
Alwyne Av, Shenf. CM15 109 GA44
Alwyne Ct, Wok. GU21 226 AY116
Alwyne La, N1 277 H6
Alwyne Pl, N1 277 J5
Alwyne Rd, N1 277 H6
SW19 179 CZ93
W7 137 CE73
Alwyne Sq, N1 277 J4
Alwyne Vil, N1 277 H6
Alwyn Gdns, NW4 119 CU56
W3 138 CP72
Alwyns Cl, Cher. KT16
off Alwyns La 194 BG100
Alwyns La, Cher. KT16 193 BF100
Alyngton, Nthch HP4 38 AS16
Alyth Gdns, NW11 120 DA58
Alzette Ho, E2 289 J2
Amalgamated Dr, Brent. TW8 157 CG79
Amanda Cl, Chig. IG7 103 ER51
Amanda Ct, Slou. SL3 152 AX76
Amanda Ms, Rom. RM7 127 FC57
Amazon Apts, N8
off New River Av 121 DM56
Amazon St, E1 288 E9
Ambassador Cl, Houns. TW3 156 BY82
Ambassador Gdns, E6 293 J7
Ambassador's Ct, SW1 297 M3
Ambassador Sq, E14 302 C9
Amber Av, E17 101 DY53
Amber Cl, New Barn. EN5 80 DB44
Amber Ct, SW17 180 DG91
Staines-upon-Thames TW18
off Laleham Rd 173 BF92
Ambercroft Way, Couls. CR5 235 DP119
Amberden Av, N3 120 DA55
Ambergate St, SE17 299 H10
Amber Gro, NW2 119 CX60
Amber La, Ilf. IG6 103 EP52
Amberley Cl, Orp. BR6 223 ET106
Pinner HA5 116 BZ55
Send GU23 243 BF125
Amberley Ct, Maid. SL6 130 AC69
Sidcup DA14 186 EW92
Amberley Dr, Wdhm KT15 211 BF110
Amberley Gdns, Enf. EN1 100 DS45
Epsom KT19 217 CT105
Amberley Gro, SE26 182 DV91
Croydon CR0 202 DT101
Amberley Pl, Wind. SL4
off Peascod St 151 AR81
Amberley Rd, E10 123 EA59
N13 99 DM47
SE2 166 EX79
W9 283 K6
Buckhurst Hill IG9 102 EJ46
Enfield EN1 100 DT45
Slough SL2 131 AL71
Amberley Way, Houns. TW4 176 BW85
Morden SM4 199 CZ101
Romford RM7 127 FB56
Uxbridge UB10 134 BL69
Amber Ms, N22
off Brampton Pk Rd 121 DN55
Amberry Ct, Harl. CM20 35 ER14
Amberside Cl, Islw. TW7 177 CD86
Amberside Ct, Hem.H. HP3
off Hardings Cl 40 BH23
Amber St, E15 281 H5
Amber Wf, E2 278 A9
Amberwood Cl, Wall. SM6 219 DL106
Amberwood Ri, N.Mal. KT3 198 CS100
Ambient Ho, Enf. EN3
off Tysoe Av 83 DZ36
Amblecote, Cob. KT11 214 BY111
Amblecote Cl, SE12 184 EH90
Amblecote Meadows, SE12 184 EH90
Amblecote Rd, SE12 184 EH90
Sch Ambler Prim Sch, N4
off Blackstock Rd 121 DP61
Ambler Rd, N4 121 DP62
Ambleside, SW19
off Albert Dr 179 CY88
Bromley BR1 183 ED93
Epping CM16 70 EU31
Purfleet RM19 168 FQ78
Ambleside Av, SW16 181 DK91
Beckenham BR3 203 DY99
Hornchurch RM12 127 FH64
Walton-on-Thames KT12 196 BW102
Ambleside Cl, E9 279 H2
E10 123 EB59
N17 *off Drapers Rd* 122 DT55
Redhill RH1 267 DH139
Ambleside Cres, Enf. EN3 83 DX41
Ambleside Dr, Felt. TW14 175 BT88
Ambleside Gdns, SW16 181 DK92
Ilford IG4 124 EL56
South Croydon CR2 221 DX109
Sutton SM2 218 DC107
Wembley HA9 117 CK60
Ambleside Pt, SE15 312 G4
Ambleside Rd, NW10 139 CT66
Bexleyheath DA7 166 FA82
Ambleside Wk, Uxb. UB8
off High St 134 BK67
Ambleside Way, Egh. TW20 173 BB94
Ambrey Way, Wall. SM6 219 DK109
Ambrooke Rd, Belv. DA17 166 FA76
Ambrosden Av, SW1 297 M7
Ambrose Av, NW11 119 CY59
Ambrose Cl, E6 293 J7
Crayford DA1 167 FF84
Orpington BR6
off Stapleton Rd 205 ET104
Ambrose Ms, SW11 308 E9
Ambrose St, SE16 300 E8
Ambrose Wk, E3 290 A1
● **AMC Business Cen**, NW10 138 CP69
Amelia, NW9
off Boulevard Dr 97 CT54
Amelia Cl, W3 138 CP74
Amelia St, SE17 299 H10
Amelle Gdns, Rom. RM3 106 FP51
Amen Cor, EC4 287 H9
SW17 180 DF93
Amen Ct, EC4 287 H8
Amenity Way, Mord. SM4 199 CW101
Amerden Cl, Tap. SL6 130 AD72
Amerden La, Tap. SL6 130 AD74
Amerden Way, Slou. SL1 151 AN75
Sch American Sch in London, The, NW8 274 A10
America Sq, EC3 288 A10
America St, SE1 299 J3
Ameriand Rd, SW18 179 CZ86
AMERSHAM, HP6 & HP7 55 AP38
⇌ **Amersham** 55 AQ38
⊖ **Amersham** 55 AQ38
Coll Amersham & Wycombe Coll,
Amersham Campus,
Amer. HP7 *off Stanley Hill* 72 AT39
Amersham Av, N18 100 DR51
Amersham Bypass, Amer. HP7 55 AN41
Amersham Cl, Rom. RM3 106 FM51
Amersham Dr, Rom. RM3 106 FL51
Amersham Gro, SE14 313 N4
H Amersham Hosp, Amer. HP7 55 AN41
★ **Amersham Mus**, Amer. HP7 55 AP40
AMERSHAM OLD TOWN,
Amer. HP7 55 AP39
Amersham Pl, Amer. HP7 72 AW39
Amersham Rd, SE14 313 N5
Beaconsfield HP9 89 AM53
Chalfont St. Giles HP8 72 AU43
Chalfont St. Peter SL9 90 AX49
Chesham HP5 55 AP35
Chesham Bois HP6 55 AP36
Coleshill HP7 89 AP46
Croydon CR0 202 DQ100
Gerrards Cross SL9 113 BB59
Little Chalfont HP6 72 AX39
Rickmansworth WD3 73 BB39
Romford RM3 106 FM51
Sch Amersham Sch, The,
Amer. HP7 *off Stanley Hill* 55 AS40
Amersham Vale, SE14 313 P4
Amersham Wk, Rom. RM3 106 FM51
Amersham Way, Amer. HP6 72 AX39
Amery Gdns, NW10 139 CV67
Romford RM2 128 FK55
Amery Rd, Har. HA1 117 CG61
Amesbury, Wal.Abb. EN9 68 EG32
Amesbury Av, SW2 181 DL89
Amesbury Cl, Epp. CM16 69 ET31
Wor.Park KT4 199 CW102
Amesbury Dr, E4 83 EB44
Amesbury Rd, Brom. BR1 204 EK97
Dagenham RM9 146 EX66
Epping CM16 69 ET31
Feltham TW13 176 BX89
Slough SL1 151 AM75
Amesbury Twr, SW8 309 L8
Ames Rd, Swans. DA10 190 FY86
Amethyst Cl, N11 99 DK52
Amethyst Ct, Enf. EN3
off Enstone Rd 83 DY41
Amethyst Rd, E15 281 H1
Amethyst Wk, Welw.G.C. AL8 29 CV11
Amey Dr, Bkhm KT23 230 CC124
Amherst Av, W13 137 CJ72
Amherst Cl, Orp. BR5 206 EU98
Amherst Dr, Orp. BR5 205 ET98
Amherst Hill, Sev. TN13 256 FE122
Amherst Pl, Sev. TN13 256 FF122
Amherst Rd, W13 137 CJ72
Sevenoaks TN13 257 FH122
Sch Amherst Sch, Rvrhd TN13
off Witches La 256 FE123
Amhurst Gdns, Islw. TW7 157 CF81
Amhurst Par, N16
off Amhurst Pk 122 DT59
Amhurst Pk, N16 122 DR59
Amhurst Pas, E8 278 C1
Amhurst Rd, E8 278 E3
N16 122 DT63
Amhurst Ter, E8 278 C1
Amhurst Wk, SE28
off Roman Sq 146 EU74
Amias Dr, Edg. HA8 96 CL49
Amicia Gdns, Stoke P. SL2 132 AT67
Amidas Gdns, Dag. RM8 126 EV63
Amiel St, E1 289 H4
Amies St, SW11 308 E10
Amina Way, SE16 300 C7
Amis Av, Epsom KT19 216 CP107
New Haw KT15 212 BG111
Amis Rd, Wok. GU21 226 AS119
Amity Gro, SW20 199 CW95
Amity Rd, E15 281 L8
Ammanford Grn, NW9
off Ruthin Cl 118 CS58
Amner Rd, SW11 180 DG86
Amor Rd, W6 294 A7
Amott Rd, SE15 162 DU83
Amoy Pl, E14 290 A9
Ampere Ho, W3 *off Warple Way* 158 CS75
Ampere Way, Croy. CR0 201 DL101
Tr Ampere Way 201 DM102
Ampleforth Cl, Orp. BR6 224 EW105
Ampleforth Rd, SE2 166 EV75
Amport Pl, NW7 97 CY51
Ampthill Sq Est, NW1 285 M1
Ampton Pl, WC1 286 C3
Ampton St, WC1 286 C3
Amroth Cl, SE23 182 DV88
Amroth Grn, NW9
off Fryent Gro 118 CS58
Amstel Way, Wok. GU21 226 AT118
Amsterdam Rd, E14 302 F7
Amundsen Ct, E14
off Napier Av 302 B10
Amwell Cl, Enf. EN2 82 DR43
Watford WD25 *off Phillipers* 76 BY35
Amwell Common,
Welw.G.C. AL7 30 DB10
Amwell Ct, Hodd. EN11 49 EA16
Waltham Abbey EN9 68 EF33
Amwell Ct Est, N4 122 DQ60
Amwell End, Ware SG12 33 DX06
Amwell Hill, Gt Amwell SG12 33 DZ08
Amwell La, Ware SG12 33 EA09
Amwell Pl, Hert.Hth SG13 32 DW11
Jct Amwell Rbt, Ware SG12 33 DZ11
Amwell St, EC1 286 E2
Hoddesdon EN11 49 EA17
Sch Amwell Vw Sch, Stans. Abb.
SG12 *off Station Rd* 33 EB11
Amyand Cotts, Twick. TW1
off Amyand Pk Rd 177 CH86
Amyand La, Twick. TW1
off Marble Hill Gdns 177 CH87
Amyand Pk Gdns, Twick. TW1
off Amyand Pk Rd 177 CH87
Amyand Pk Rd, Twick. TW1 177 CG87
Amy Cl, Wall. SM6 219 DL108
Sch Amy Johnson Prim Sch,
Wall. SM6 *off Mollison Dr* 219 DL108
Amy La, Chesh. HP5 54 AP32
Amy Rd, Oxt. RH8 254 EE129
Amyruth Rd, SE4 183 EA85
Amy Warne Cl, E6 293 H6
Anatola Rd, N19
off Dartmouth Pk Hill 121 DH61
Ancaster Cres, N.Mal. KT3 199 CU100
Ancaster Ms, Beck. BR3 203 DX97
Ancaster Rd, Beck. BR3 203 DX97
Ancaster St, SE18 165 ES80
Anchorage Cl, SW19 180 DA92
Anchorage Pt, E14 301 P4
● **Anchorage Pt Ind Est**, SE7 304 C7
Anchor & Hope La, SE7 304 B7
● **Anchor Bay Ind Est**,
Erith DA8 167 FG79
Anchor Boul, Dart. DA2 168 FQ84
Anchor Cl, Bark. IG11 146 EV69
Cheshunt EN8 67 DX28
Anchor Ct, Grays RM17 170 GA80
Anchor Dr, Rain. RM13 147 FH69
Anchor Ho, SW18
off Smugglers Way 160 DB84
Anchor La, Hem.H. HP1 40 BH21
Anchor Ms, N1 277 P5
SW11 *off Westbridge Rd* 308 B7
SW12 181 DH86
🔒 **Anchor Retail Pk**, E1 289 H5
Anchor St, SE16 300 E8
Anchor Ter, E1 289 H5
Anchor Wf, E3 *off Watts Gro* 290 C6
Anchor Yd, EC1 287 K4
Ancill Cl, W6 306 D3
Ancona Rd, NW10 139 CU68
SE18 165 ER78
Andace Pk Gdns, Brom. BR1 204 EJ95
Andalus Rd, SW9 161 DL83
Ander Cl, Wem. HA0 117 CK63
Andermans, Wind. SL4 151 AK81
Anderson Cl, N21 81 DM43
W3 138 CR72
Epsom KT19 216 CP112
Guildford GU2 *off Tylehost* 242 AV130
Harefield UB9 92 BG53
Sutton SM3 200 DA102
Anderson Ct, Red. RH1 266 DG137
Anderson Dr, Ashf. TW15 175 BQ91
Anderson Ho, Bark. IG11
off The Coverdales 145 ER68
Anderson Pl, Houns. TW3 156 CB84
Anderson Rd, E9 279 J4
Shenley WD7 62 CN33
Weybridge KT13 195 BR104
Woodford Green IG8 124 EK55
Andersons Sq, N1 276 G9
Anderson St, SW3 296 E10
Anderson Way, Belv. DA17 167 FB75
Horley RH6 268 DE148
Anderton Cl, SE5 162 DR83
Andmark Ct, Sthl. UB1
off Herbert Rd 136 BZ74
Andover Av, E16 292 E9
Andover Cl, Epsom KT19 216 CR111
Feltham TW14 175 BT88
Greenford UB6 136 CB70
Uxbridge UB8 134 BH68
Andover Est, N7 121 DM61
Andover Pl, NW6 273 L10
Andover Rd, N7 121 DM61
Orpington BR6 205 ER102
Twickenham TW2 177 CD88
Andrea Av, Grays RM16 170 GA75
Andre St, E8 278 D2
Andrew Borde St, WC2 285 P8
Andrew Cl, Dart. DA1 187 FD85
Ilford IG6 103 ER51
Shenley WD7 62 CM33
Andrewes Gdns, E6 292 G8
Andrewes Ho, EC2
off The Barbican 287 K7
Andrew Hill La, Hedg. SL2 111 AQ61
Andrew Pl, SW8 309 P6
Andrew Reed Ho, SW18
off Linstead Way 179 CY87
Andrews Cl, E6 292 G8
Buckhurst Hill IG9 102 EJ47
Epsom KT17 217 CT114
Harrow HA1 117 CD59
Hemel Hempstead HP2
off Church St 40 BK18
Orpington BR5 206 EX97
Worcester Park KT4 199 CX103
Andrews Crosse, WC2 286 E9
Andrewsfield, Welw.G.C. AL7 30 DC09
Andrews Gate, Shep. TW17 195 BQ96
Andrews La, Chsht EN7 66 DU28
Sch Andrews La Prim Sch,
Chsht EN7 *off Andrews La* 66 DV28
Andrews Pl, SE9 185 EP86
Dartford DA2 187 FE89
Andrew's Rd, E8 278 E9
Andrew St, E14 290 E8
Andrews Wk, SE17 311 H3
Andromeda Ct,
Rom. RM3 *off Myrtle Rd* 106 FJ51
Andwell Cl, SE2 166 EV75
Anelle Ri, Hem.H. HP3 40 BM24
Anemone Ct, Enf. EN3
off Enstone Rd 83 DY41
ANERLEY, SE20 202 DV95
⇌ **Anerley** 182 DV94
⊖ **Anerley** 182 DV94
Anerley Gro, SE19 182 DT94
Anerley Hill, SE19 182 DT93
Anerley Pk, SE20 182 DU94
Anerley Pk Rd, SE20 182 DV94
Anerley Rd, SE19 182 DU94
SE20 182 DU94
Anerley Sta Rd, SE20 202 DV95
Anerley St, SW11 308 F8
Anerley Vale, SE19 182 DT94
Anfield Cl, SW12
off Belthorn Cres 181 DJ87
Angas Ct, Wey. KT13 213 BQ106
⊖ **Angel** 276 F10
Angela Carter Cl, SW9
off Wiltshire Rd 310 F10
Angel All, E1 288 B8
● **Angel Building**, EC1 286 F1
🔒 **Angel Cen**, N1 276 F10
Angel Cl, N18 100 DT49
Hampton Hill TW12
off Windmill Rd 176 CC93
Angel Cor Par, N18
off Fore St 100 DU49
Angel Ct, EC2 287 M8
SW1 297 M3
SW17 180 DF91
Croydon CR0 202 DS103
Jct Angel Edmonton, N18
off Angel Rd 100 DU50
Angelfield, Houns. TW3 156 CB84
Angel Gate, EC1 287 H2
Guildford GU1 *off High St* 258 AX136
Angel Hill, Sutt. SM1 200 DB104
Angel Hill Dr, Sutt. SM1 200 DB104
Angelica Cl, West Dr. UB7
off Lovibonds Av 134 BM72
Angelica Dr, E6 293 M7
Angelica Gdns, Croy. CR0 203 DX102
Angelica Rd, Guil. GU2 242 AU130
Angelis Apts, N1
off Graham St 287 H1
Angel La, E15 281 H4
EC4 *off Upper Thames St* 299 L1
Hayes UB3 135 BR71
Angell Pk Gdns, SW9 310 F10
Angell Rd, SW9 310 F10
Angell Town Est, SW9 310 E8
Angel Ms, E1 288 F10
N1 286 F1
SW15 179 CU87
Angelo Ms, SW16 201 DM97
Angel Pl, N18 100 DU50
SE1 299 L4
Reigate RH2
off Cockshot Hill 266 DB137
⇌ **Angel Road** 100 DW50
Angel Rd, N18 100 DV50
Harrow HA1 117 CE58
Thames Ditton KT7 197 CG101
● **Angel Rd Wks**, N18 100 DW50
Angel Southside, EC1 286 F1
Angel Sq, EC1 286 F1
Angel St, EC1 287 J8
Angel Wk, W6 294 A9
Angel Way, Rom. RM1 127 FE57
Angel Wf, N1
off Eagle Wf Rd 277 K10

Angerstein La, SE3 315 M6
Angle Cl, Uxb. UB10 134 BN67
Anglefield Rd, Berk. HP4 38 AU19
Angle Grn, Dag. RM8 126 EW60
Angle Pl, Berk. HP4 38 AU19
Angle Rd, Grays RM20 169 FX79
Anglers Cl, Rich. TW10
off Locksmeade Rd 177 CJ91
Angler's La, NW5 275 K5
Anglers Reach, Surb. KT6 197 CK99
Anglesea Av, SE18 305 N9
Anglesea Ms, SE18 305 N9
Anglesea Pl, Grav. DA11
off Clive Rd 191 GH86
Anglesea Rd, SE18 305 N9
Kingston upon Thames KT1 197 CK98
Orpington BR5 206 EW100
Anglesea Ter, W6
off Wellesley Av 159 CV76
Anglesey Cl, Ashf. TW15 174 BN90
Anglesey Ct Rd, Cars. SM5 218 DG107
Anglesey Dr, Rain. RM13 147 FG70
Anglesey Gdns, Cars. SM5 218 DG107
Anglesey Rd, Enf. EN3 82 DV42
Watford WD19 94 BW50
Anglesmede Cres, Pnr. HA5 116 CA55
Anglesmede Way, Pnr. HA5 116 BZ55
Angles Rd, SW16 181 DL91
Anglia Cl, N17
off Park La 100 DV52
Anglia Ct, Dag. RM8
off Spring Cl 126 EX60
Anglia Ho, E14 289 M9
Anglian Cl, Wat. WD24 76 BW40
Anglian Rd, E11 123 ED62
Anglia Wk, E6 145 EM67
● Anglo Business Pk,
Chesh. HP5 54 AN29
Anglo Rd, E3 279 P10
Angrave Ct, E8 278 B8
Angrave Pas, E8 278 B8
Angus Cl, Chess. KT9 216 CN106
Angus Dr, Ruis. HA4 116 BW63
Angus Gdns, NW9 96 CR53
Angus Rd, E13 292 D3
Angus St, SE14 313 M4
Anhalt Rd, SW11 308 D4
Anisdowne Cl, Abin.Ham. RH5 261 BT142
Ankerdine Cres, SE18 165 EP81
Ankerwycke Priory,
Wrays. TW19 172 AY89
Anlaby Rd, Tedd. TW11 177 CE92
Anley Rd, W14 294 C5
Anmersh Gro, Stan. HA7 95 CK53
Annabel Cl, E14 290 C9
Annabelle Ct, Rain. RM13 147 FE69
Annabels Ms, W5 137 CK70
Anna Cl, E8 278 B8
Annalee Gdns, S.Ock. RM15 149 FV71
Annalee Rd, S.Ock. RM15 149 FV71
Annandale Gro, Uxb. UB10 115 BQ62
Annandale Rd, SE10 315 L1
W4 158 CS77
Croydon CR0 202 DU103
Guildford GU2 258 AV136
Sidcup DA15 185 ES87
Anna Neagle Cl, E7
off Dames Rd 124 EG63
Annan Way, Rom. RM1 105 FD53
Anne Boleyn Ct, SE9
off Avery Hill Rd 185 ER86
Anne Boleyn's Wk,
Kings.T. KT2 178 CL92
Sutton SM3 217 CX108
Anne Case Ms, N.Mal. KT3
off Sycamore Gro 198 CR97
Anne Compton Ms, SE12 184 EF87
Anne Goodman Ho, E1
off Jubilee St 288 G8
Anne Heart Cl,
Chaff.Hun. RM16 169 FX77
Anne Ms, Bark. IG11 145 EQ66
Anne of Cleeves Ct, SE9
off Avery Hill Rd 185 ER86
Anne of Cleves Rd, Dart. DA1 188 FK85
Anners Cl, Egh. TW20 193 BC97
Annesley Av, NW9 118 CR55
Annesley Cl, NW10 118 CS62
Annesley Dr, Croy. CR0 203 DZ104
Annesley Rd, SE3 164 EH81
Annesley Wk, N19
off Highgate Hill 121 DJ61
Annesmere Gdns, SE3
off Highbrook Rd 164 EK83
Anne St, E13 291 N4
Anne's Wk, Cat. CR3 236 DS120
Annett Cl, Shep. TW17 195 BS98
Annette Cl, Har. HA3 95 CE54
Annette Cres, N1 277 K7
Annette Rd, N7 121 DM63
Annett Rd, Walt. KT12 195 BU101
Anne Way, Ilf. IG6 103 EQ51
West Molesey KT8 196 CB98
Annie Besant Cl, E3 279 P9
Annie Brooks Cl, Stai. TW18 173 BD90
Annie Taylor Ho, E12
off Walton Rd 125 EN63
Annifer Way, S.Ock. RM15 149 FV71
Anningsley Pk, Ott. KT16 211 BD110
Anning St, EC2 287 P4
Annington Rd, N2 120 DF55
Annis Rd, E9 279 L5
Ann La, SW10 308 A4
Ann Moss Way, SE16 300 G6
Ann's Cl, SW1 296 F5
Ann's Pl, E1 288 A7
Ann St, SE18 165 ER77
Annsworthy Av, Th.Hth. CR7
off Grange Pk Rd 202 DR97
Annsworthy Cres, SE25
off Grange Rd 202 DR96
Sch Annunciation RC Inf Sch,
The, Edg. HA8
off Thirleby Rd 96 CR53
Sch Annunciation RC Jun Sch,
The, Edg. HA8 off The Meads 96 CR51
Ansculf Rd, Slou. SL2 131 AN69
Ansdell Rd, SE15 312 G8
Ansdell St, W8 295 M6
Ansdell Ter, W8 295 M6
Ansell Gro, Cars. SM5 200 DG102
Ansell Rd, SW17 180 DE90
Dorking RH4 263 CH135
Anselm Cl, Croy. CR0 202 DT104
Anselm Rd, SW6 307 J3
Pinner HA5 94 BZ52
Ansford Rd, Brom. BR1 183 EC92
Ansleigh Pl, W11 294 D1
Ansley Cl, S.Croy. CR2 220 DV114
Anslow Gdns, Iver SL0 133 BD68
Anslow Pl, Slou. SL1 130 AJ71
Anson Cl, Bov. HP3 57 AZ27
Romford RM7 105 FB54
St. Albans AL1 43 CH22
Anson Ho, E1 289 L5
Anson Pl, SE28 165 ER75
Sch Anson Prim Sch, NW2 272 C2
Anson Rd, N7 275 M1
NW2 272 C2
Anson Ter, Nthlt. UB5 136 CB65
Anson Wk, Nthwd. HA6 93 BQ49
Anstead Dr, Rain. RM13 147 FG68
Anstey Rd, SE15 312 C10
Anstey Wk, N15 121 DP56
Anstice Cl, W4 158 CS80
Anston Ct, Guil. GU2
off Southway 242 AS134
Anstridge Path, SE9 185 ER86
Anstridge Rd, SE9 185 ER86
Antelope Av, Grays RM16
off Hogg La 170 GA76
Antelope Rd, SE18 305 J6
Antelope Wk, Surb. KT6
off Maple Rd 197 CK99
Anthems Way, E20 280 D4
Anthony Cl, NW7 96 CS49
Dunton Green TN13 256 FE121
Watford WD19 94 BW46
Anthony La, Swan. BR8 207 FG95
Anthony Rd, SE25 202 DU100
Borehamwood WD6 78 CM40
Greenford UB6 137 CE68
Welling DA16 166 EU81
Sch Anthony Roper Prim Sch,
The, Eyns. DA4 off High St 208 FL103
Anthonys, Wok. GU21 211 BB112
Anthony St, E1 288 F8
Anthony Way, N18 101 DX51
Slough SL1 131 AK73
Anthony W Ho, Brock. RH3
off Wheelers La 264 CP136
Anthorne Cl, Pot.B. EN6 64 DB31
Anthus Ms, Nthwd. HA6 93 BS52
Antigua Cl, SE19 182 DR92
Antigua Ms, E13 292 B2
Antigua Wk, SE19 182 DR92
Antill Rd, E3 289 L2
N15 122 DU56
Antill Ter, E1 289 J8
Antlands La, Shipley Br RH6 269 DK153
Antlands La E, Horl. RH6 269 DL153
Antlands La W, Horl. RH6 269 DL153
Antlers Hill, E4 83 EB43
Antoinette Ct, Abb.L. WD5 59 BT29
Anton Cres, Sutt. SM1 200 DA104
Antoneys Cl, Pnr. HA5 94 BX54
Antonine Gate, St.Alb. AL3 42 CA21
Antonine Hts, SE1 299 N5
Anton Pl, Wem. HA9 118 CP62
Anton Rd, S.Ock. RM15 149 FV70
Anton St, E8 278 D2
Antony Ho, E5
off Pembury Pl 278 E3
Antrim Gro, NW3 274 E4
Antrim Mans, NW3 274 D4
Antrim Rd, NW3 274 E4
Antrobus Cl, Sutt. SM1 217 CZ106
Antrobus Rd, W4 158 CQ77
Anvil Cl, SW16 181 DJ94
Bovingdon HP3
off Yew Tree Dr 57 BB28
Anvil Ct, Langley SL3
off Blacksmith Row 153 BA77
Anvil La, Cob. KT11 213 BU114
Anvil Pl, St.Alb. AL2 60 CA26
Anvil Rd, Sun. TW16 195 BU97
Anvil Ter, Dart. DA2
off Pinewood Pl 187 FE89
Anworth Cl, Wdf.Grn. IG8 102 EH51
Anyards Rd, Cob. KT11 213 BV113
Anzio Gdns, Cat. CR3 236 DQ121
Apeldoorn Dr, Wall. SM6 219 DL109
Aperdele Rd, Lthd. KT22 231 CG118
APERFIELD, West. TN16 239 EM117
Aperfield Rd, Bigg.H. TN16 238 EL117
Erith DA8 167 FF79
Apers Av, Wok. GU22 227 AZ121
Apex Cl, Beck. BR3 203 EB95
Jct Apex Cor, NW7 96 CR49
● Apex Ind Est, NW10
off Hythe Rd 139 CT70
🛍 Apex Retail Pk, Felt. TW13 176 BZ90
● Apex Twr, N.Mal. KT3 198 CS97
Apley Rd, Reig. RH2 266 DA137
Aplin Way, Islw. TW7 157 CE81
Apollo, E14 302 A8
Apollo Av, Brom. BR1
off Rodway Rd 204 EH95
Northwood HA6 93 BU50
Apollo Cl, Horn. RM12 127 FH61
★ Apollo Hammersmith, W6 294 B10
Apollo Pl, E11 124 EE62
SW10 308 A4
St. John's GU21
off Church Rd 226 AU119
★ Apollo Thea, W1 285 N10
★ Apollo Victoria Thea, SW1 297 L7
Apollo Way, SE28
off Broadwater Rd 165 ER76
Hemel Hempstead HP2 40 BM18
Apostle Way, Th.Hth. CR7 201 DP96
Apothecary St, EC4 286 G9
Appach Rd, SW2 181 DN85
Apperlie Dr, Horl. RH6 269 DJ150
Apple Blossom Ct, SW8
off Pascal St 309 P4
Appleby Cl, E4 101 EC51
N15 122 DR57
Petts Wood BR5 205 ES101
Twickenham TW2 177 CD89
Uxbridge UB8 135 BQ72
Appleby Ct, W3
off Newport Rd 158 CQ75
Appleby Dr, Crox.Grn WD3 75 BP42
Romford RM3 106 FJ50
Appleby Gdns, Felt. TW14 175 BT88
Appleby Grn, Rom. RM3
off Appleby Dr 106 FJ50
Appleby Rd, E8 278 D6
E16 291 M9
Appleby St, E2 278 A10
Cheshunt EN7 66 DT26
Apple Cotts, Bov. HP3 57 BA27
Applecroft, Nthch HP4 38 AS17
Park Street AL2 60 CB28
Applecroft Rd, Welw.G.C. AL8 29 CV09
Sch Applecroft Sch, Welw.G.C. AL8
off Applecroft Rd 29 CV10
Appledore Av, Bexh. DA7 167 FC81
Ruislip HA4 115 BV62
Appledore Cl, SW17 180 DF89
Bromley BR2 204 EF99
Edgware HA8 96 CN53
Romford RM3 106 FJ53
Appledore Cres, Sid. DA14 185 ES90
Appledore Way, NW7
off Tavistock Av 97 CX52
Appledown Ri, Couls. CR5 235 DJ115
Applefield, Amer. HP7 72 AW39
Appleford Cl, Hodd. EN11 49 DZ15
Appleford Rd, W10 282 F5
Apple Garth, Brent. TW8 157 CK77
Applegarth, Clay. KT10 215 CF106
New Addington CR0 221 EB108
Applegarth Dr, Dart. DA1 188 FL89
Ilford IG2 125 ET56
Applegarth Ho, Erith DA8 167 FF82
Sch Applegarth Nurs & Inf & Jun Schs,
New Adgtn CR0 off Bygrove 221 EB107
Applegarth Rd, SE28 146 EV74
W14 294 C7
Applegate, Brwd. CM14 108 FT43
Apple Gro, Chess. KT9 216 CL105
Enfield EN1 82 DS41
Harrow HA2 116 CA60
Twickenham TW1 177 CG86
Apple Mkt, Kings.T. KT1
off Eden St 197 CK96
Apple Orchard, Swan. BR8 207 FD98
Apple Orchard, The,
Hem.H. HP2 off Highfield La 40 BM18
Apple Rd, E11 124 EE62
Appleshaw Cl, Grav. DA11 191 GG92
Appleton Cl, Amer. HP7 72 AV40
Bexleyheath DA7 167 FB82
Harlow CM19 51 EQ16
Appleton Dr, Dart. DA2 187 FH90
Appleton Gdns, N.Mal. KT3 199 CU100
Appleton Rd, SE9 164 EL83
Loughton IG10 85 EP41
Appleton Sq, Mitch. CR4
off Silbury Av 200 DE95
Appleton Way, Horn. RM12 128 FK60
Apple Tree Av, Uxb. UB8 134 BM71
West Drayton UB7 134 BM71
Appletree Cl, SE20
off Jasmine Gro 202 DV95
Leatherhead KT22 230 CC124
Appletree Ct, Guil. GU4 243 BD131
Appletree Gdns, Barn. EN4 80 DE42
Appletree La, Slou. SL3 152 AW76
Jct Apple Tree Rbt,
West Dr. UB7 134 BM73
Appletree Wk, Chesh. HP5
off Cresswell Rd 54 AR34
Watford WD25 59 BV34
Apple Tree Yd, SW1 297 M2
Applewood Cl, N20 98 DE46
NW2 119 CV62
Ickenham UB10 114 BL63
Applewood Dr, E13 292 A4
Appold St, EC2 287 N6
Erith DA8 167 FF79
Apprentice Gdns, Nthlt. UB5 136 BZ69
Apprentice Way, E5
off Clarence Rd 122 DV63
Approach, The, NW4 119 CX57
W3 138 CR72
Enfield EN1 82 DV40
Orpington BR6 205 ET103
Potters Bar EN6 63 CZ32
Upminster RM14 128 FP62
Approach Cl, N16 277 N2
Approach Rd, E2 288 G1
SW20 199 CW96
Ashford TW15 175 BQ93
Barnet EN4 80 DD42
Edgware HA8 96 CP51
Purley CR8 219 DP112
St. Albans AL1 43 CE21
Taplow SL6 130 AE72
West Molesey KT8 196 CA99
Apps Meadow Cl, W.Mol. KT8 196 BZ98
Appspond La, Pott.Cr. AL2 41 BV23
Aprey Gdns, NW4 119 CW56
April Cl, W7 137 CE73
Ashtead KT21 232 CM117
Feltham TW13 175 BU90
Orpington BR6 223 ET106
April Glen, SE23 183 DX90
April St, E8 278 B1
Aprilwood Cl, Wdhm KT15 211 BF111
Apsledene, Grav. DA12
off Miskin Way 191 GK93
Apsley, Hem.H. HP3 58 BK25
⇌ Apsley 58 BL25
Apsley Cl, Har. HA2 116 CC57
Apsley Gra, Hem.H. HP3
off London Rd 58 BL25
🛍 Apsley Mills Retail Pk,
Hem.H. HP3 40 BL24
Apsley Rd, SE25 202 DV98
New Malden KT3 198 CQ97
Apsley Way, NW2 119 CU61
W1 297 H4
● Aquarius Business Pk, NW2 119 CT60
Aquarius Way, Nthwd. HA6 93 BU50
★ Aquatic Experience,
Brent. TW8 157 CH81
Aquila Cl, Lthd. KT22 232 CL121
Aquila St, NW8 274 B10
Aquinas St, SE1 298 F2
Aquis Ct, St.Alb. AL3 42 CC20
Arabella Dr, SW15 158 CS84
Arabia Cl, E4 101 ED45
Arabin Rd, SE4 163 DY84
Arado, NW9 off Boulevard Dr 97 CT54
Araglen Av, S.Ock. RM15 149 FV71
Aragon Av, Epsom KT17 217 CV109
Thames Ditton KT7 197 CF99
Aragon Cl, Brom. BR2 205 EM102
Enfield EN2 81 DM38
Hemel Hempstead HP2 41 BQ15
Loughton IG10 84 EL44
New Addington CR0 222 EE110
Romford RM5 105 FB51
Sunbury-on-Thames TW16 175 BT94
Aragon Ct, SE11
off Hotspur St 298 E10
Aragon Dr, Ilf. IG6 103 EQ52
Ruislip HA4 116 BX60
Aragon Ms, Epp. CM16 70 EW29
Aragon Pl, Mord. SM4 199 CX101
Sch Aragon Prim Sch,
Mord. SM4 off Aragon Rd 199 CY101
Aragon Rd, Kings.T. KT2 178 CL92
Morden SM4 199 CX100
Aragon Twr, SE8 301 N9
Aragon Wk, Byfleet KT14 212 BM113
Aragorn Ct, Guil. GU2 242 AV132
Aran Ct, Wey. KT13
off Mallards Reach 195 BR103
Arandora Cres, Rom. RM6 126 EV59
Aran Dr, Stan. HA7 95 CJ49
Aran Hts, Ch.St.G. HP8 90 AV49
Aran Ms, N7
off Barnsbury Gro 276 E6
Arbery Rd, E3 289 L2
Arbor Cl, Beck. BR3 203 EB96
Arbor Ct, N16 122 DR61
Arboretum Pl, Bark. IG11
off Ripple Rd 145 EQ66
Arborfield Cl, SW2 181 DM88
Slough SL1 152 AS76
Arbor Ho, Orp. BR6
off Station Rd 205 ET103
Arbor Rd, E4 101 ED48
Arbour, The, Hert. SG13 32 DR11
Arbour Cl, Fetch. KT22 231 CF123
Warley CM14 108 FW50
Arbour Rd, Enf. EN3 83 DX42
Arbour Sq, E1 289 J9
Sch Arbour Vale Sch, Slou. SL2
off Farnham Rd 131 AP69
Arbour Vw, Amer. HP7 72 AV39
Arbour Way, Horn. RM12 127 FH64
Arbroath Grn, Wat. WD19 93 BU48
Arbroath Rd, SE9 164 EL83
Arbrook Chase, Esher KT10 214 CC107
Arbrook Cl, Orp. BR5 206 EU97
Arbrook La, Esher KT10 214 CC107
Arbury Ter, SE26 182 DU90
Arbuthnot La, Bex. DA5 186 EY86
Arbuthnot Rd, SE14 313 J8
Arbutus Cl, Red. RH1 266 DC136
Arbutus Rd, Red. RH1 266 DC136
Arbutus St, E8 278 A8
Arcade, The, EC2 287 N7
Croydon CR0 off High St 202 DQ104
Hatfield AL10 off Wellfield Rd 45 CV17
Romford RM3 106 FK50
Arcade Pl, Rom. RM1 127 FE57
Arcadia Av, N3 98 DA53
Arcadia Caravans, Stai. TW18 194 BH95
🛍 Arcadia Cen, The, W5 137 CK73
Arcadia Cl, Cars. SM5 218 DG105
Arcadian Av, Bex. DA5 186 EY86
Arcadian Cl, Bex. DA5 186 EY86
Arcadian Gdns, N22 99 DM52
Arcadian Pl, SW18 179 CY87
Arcadian Rd, Bex. DA5 186 EY86
Arcadia St, E14 290 B8
Arcany Rd, S.Ock. RM15 149 FV70
Arc Ct, N11
off Friern Barnet Rd 99 DH49
★ ArcelorMittal Orbit, E20 280 D8
Archangel St, SE16 301 K5
Archates Av, Grays RM16 170 GA76
Sch Archbishop Lanfranc Sch, The,
Croy. CR0 off Mitcham Rd 201 DL100
Archbishops Pl, SW2 181 DM86
Sch Archbishop Sumner C of E
Prim Sch, SE11 298 F9
Sch Archbishop Tenison's C of E
High Sch, Croy. CR0
off Selborne Rd 202 DT104
Sch Archbishop Tenison's Sch,
SE11 310 D3
Archdale Pl, N.Mal. KT3 198 CP97
Archdale Rd, SE22 182 DT85
Sch Archdeacon Cambridge's
C of E Prim Sch, Twick. TW2
off The Green 177 CE89
Archel Rd, W14 306 G2
Coll Archer Acad, The, N2
off Beaumont Cl 120 DE56
Archer Cl, Barn. EN5 79 CZ44
Kings L. WD4 58 BM29
Kingston upon Thames KT2 178 CL94
Archer Ho, N1
off Phillipp St 277 P9
SW11 308 A8
Archer Ms, Hmptn H. TW12
off Windmill Rd 176 CC93
SW9 310 A10
Archer Rd, SE25 202 DV98
Orpington BR5 206 EU99
Archers, Harl. CM19 51 EP20
Archers Cl, Hert. SG14 32 DQ08
Archers Ct, S.Ock. RM15 149 FV71
Archers Dr, Enf. EN3 82 DW40
Archers Fld, St.Alb. AL1 43 CF18
ARCHERS GREEN, Welw. AL6 30 DE08
Archer Sq, SE14 313 L3
Archers Ride, Welw.G.C. AL7 30 DB11
Archer St, W1 285 N10
Archer Ter, West Dr. UB7
off Yew Av 134 BL73
Archer Way, Swan. BR8 207 FF96
Archery Cl, W2 284 D9
Harrow HA3 117 CF55
Archery La, Brom. BR2 204 EK100
Archery Pl, Goms. GU5 261 BQ139
Archery Rd, SE9 185 EM85
Archery Steps, W2
off St. Georges Flds 284 D10
Arches, SW9 161 DP83
off Ridgeway Rd
Arches, The, SW6 306 G8
SW8 off New Covent Gdn Mkt 309 P4
WC2 298 B2
Harrow HA2 116 CB61
Windsor SL4 151 AQ81
Archfield, Welw.G.C. AL7 29 CY06
● Archgate Business Cen, N12
off High Rd 98 DC50
Archibald Cl, Enf. EN3 83 DX36
Archibald Ms, W1 297 H1
Archibald Rd, N7 275 N1
Romford RM3 106 FN53
Archibald St, E3 290 A3
Archie Cl, West Dr. UB7 154 BN75
Archie St, SE1 299 P5
Coll Architectural Assoc Sch of
Architecture, WC1 285 P7
Arch Rd, Hersham KT12 196 BX104
Arch St, SE1 299 J7
⊖ Archway 121 DJ61
Archway, Rom. RM3 105 FH51
● Archway Business Cen, N19
off Wedmore St 121 DK62
Uni Archway Campus, The, N19
off Highgate Hill 121 DJ61
Archway Cl, N19
off Archway Rd 121 DJ61
SW19 180 DB91
W10 282 C7
Wallington SM6 201 DK104
Archway Mall, N19 121 DJ61
Archway Ms, SW15
off Putney Br Rd 159 CY84
Dorking RH4 off Chapel Ct 263 CG135
Archway Pl, Dor. RH4
off Chapel Ct 263 CG135
Archway Rd, N6 120 DG58
N19 121 DJ60
Archway St, SW13 158 CS83
Arcola St, E8 278 A2
Arcon Dr, Nthlt. UB5 136 BY70
Arctic St, NW5 275 J3
Arcus Rd, Brom. BR1 184 EE93
Ardbeg Rd, SE24 182 DR86
Arden Cl, SE28 146 EX72
Bovingdon HP3 57 BA28
Bushey Heath WD23 95 CF45
Harrow HA1 117 CD62
Reigate RH2 266 DB138
Twick. TW2 176 BZ87
Arden Ct Gdns, N2 120 DD58
Arden Cres, E14 302 B8
Dagenham RM9 146 EW66
Arden Est, N1 287 N1
Arden Gro, Orp. BR6 223 EP105
Arden Ho, SW9 310 B9
Arden Ms, E17 123 EB57
Arden Mhor, Pnr. HA5 115 BV56
Arden Rd, N3 119 CY55
W13 137 CJ73
Ardens Way, St.Alb. AL4 43 CK18
Ardent Cl, SE25 202 DS97
Ardesley Wd, Wey. KT13 213 BS105
Ardfern Av, SW16 201 DN97
Ardfillan Rd, SE6 183 ED88
Ardgowan Rd, SE6 184 EE87
Ardilaun Rd, N5 122 DQ63
Ardingly Cl, Croy. CR0 203 DX104
Ardleigh Cl, Horn. RM11 128 FK55
Ardleigh Ct, Shenf. CM15 109 FZ45
Ardleigh Gdns, Hutt. CM13
off Fairview Av 109 GE44
Sutton SM3 200 DA101
ARDLEIGH GREEN,
Horn. RM11 128 FJ56
Sch Ardleigh Grn Inf Sch, Horn.
RM11 off Ardleigh Grn Rd 128 FK55
Sch Ardleigh Grn Jun Sch, Horn.
RM11 off Ardleigh Grn Rd 128 FK55
Ardleigh Grn Rd, Horn. RM11 128 FK57
Ardleigh Ms, Ilf. IG1
off Bengal Rd 125 EP62
Ardleigh Rd, E17 101 DZ53
N1 277 M5
Ardleigh Ter, E17 101 DZ53
Ardley Cl, NW10 118 CS62
SE6 183 DY90
Ruislip HA4 115 BQ59
Ardley Cres, Hat.Hth CM22 37 FH05
ARDLEY END, B.Stort. CM22 37 FH06
Ardlui Rd, SE27 182 DQ89
Ardmay Gdns, Surb. KT6 198 CL99
Ardmere Rd, SE13 183 ED86
Ardmore Av, Guil. GU2 242 AV132
Ardmore La, Buck.H. IG9 102 EH45
Ardmore Pl, Buck.H. IG9 102 EH45
Ardmore Rd, S.Ock. RM15 149 FV70
Ardmore Way, Guil. GU2 242 AV132
Ardoch Rd, SE6 183 ED89
Ardra Rd, N9 101 DX48
Ardrossan Cl, Slou. SL2 131 AQ70
Ardrossan Gdns, Wor.Pk. KT4 199 CU104
Ardross Av, Nthwd. HA6 93 BS50
Ardshiel Cl, SW15
off Bemish Rd 159 CX83
Ardshiel Dr, Red. RH1 266 DE136
Ardwell Av, Ilf. IG6 125 EQ57
Ardwell Rd, SW2 181 DL89
Ardwick Rd, NW2 120 DA63
Tra Arena 202 DW99
● Arena, The, Enf. EN3 83 DZ38
🛍 Arena Shop Pk, N4 121 DP58
Arena Sq, Wem. HA9 118 CN63
Arewater Grn, Loug. IG10 85 EM39
Argali Ho, Erith DA18
off Kale Rd 166 EY76
Argall Av, E10 123 DX59
Argall Way, E10 123 DX60
Argenta Way, NW10 138 CP66
● Argent Business Cen,
Hayes UB3 155 BU75
Argent Cl, Egh. TW20 173 BC93
Argent Ct, Barn. EN5 80 DC42
Grays RM17 170 GA80
Argento Twr, SW18 180 DB86
Argent St, Grays RM17 170 FY79
Argent Way, Chsht EN7 66 DR26
Argles Cl, Green. DA9
off Cowley Av 189 FU85
Argon Ms, SW6 307 K5
Argon Rd, N18 100 DW50
Argosy Gdns, Stai. TW18 173 BF93
Argosy La, Stanw. TW19 174 BK87
Argus Cl, Rom. RM7 105 FB53
Argus Way, Nthlt. UB5 136 BY69
Argyle Av, Houns. TW3 176 CA86
Argyle Cl, W13 137 CG70
Argyle Ct, Wat. WD18 75 BT42
Argyle Gdns, Upmin. RM14 129 FR61
Argyle Pas, N17 100 DT53
Argyle Pl, W6 159 CV77
Sch Argyle Prim Sch, WC1 286 A2
Argyle Rd, E1 289 J4
E15 281 J1
E16 292 B9
N12 98 DA50
N17 100 DU53
N18 100 DU49
W13 137 CG71
Barnet EN5 79 CW42
Greenford UB6 137 CF69
Harrow HA2 116 CB58
Hounslow TW3 176 CB85
Ilford IG1 125 EN61
Sevenoaks TN13 257 FH125
Teddington TW11 177 CE92
Argyle Sq, WC1 286 B2
Argyle St, WC1 286 A2
Argyle Wk, WC1 286 B3
Argyle Way, SE16 312 D1
Argyll Av, Slou. SL1 131 AN73
Southall UB1 136 CB74

Argyll Cl, SW9 310 C10
Argyll Gdns, Edg. HA8 96 CP54
Argyll Rd, SE18 165 EQ76
W8 295 J5
Grays RM17 170 GA78
Hemel Hempstead HP2 40 BL15
Argyll St, W1 285 L9
Aria Ho, WC2 286 B8
Arica Ho, SE16 300 F6
Arica Rd, SE4 163 DY84
Ariel Apts, E16
off Fords Pk Rd 291 P8
Ariel Cl, Grav. DA12 191 GM91
Ariel Rd, NW6 273 J5
Ariel Way, W12 294 B2
Hounslow TW4 155 BV83
Arisdale Av, S.Ock. RM15 149 FV71
Aristotle Rd, SW4 161 DK83
Arizona Bldg, SE13
off Deals Gateway 314 C7
Sch Ark Acad, Wem. HA9
off Forty Av 118 CN61
Sch ARK Academy Putney, SW15 off Pullman Gdns 179 CW86
Ark Av, Grays RM16 170 GA76
Sch ARK Brunel Prim Acad, W10 282 E4
Arkell Gro, SE19 181 DP94
Sch ARK Franklin Prim Acad, NW6 282 C1
Arkindale Rd, SE6 183 EC90
Arklay Cl, Uxb. UB8 134 BM70
ARKLEY, Barn. EN5 79 CU43
Arkley Ct, Hem.H. HP2
off Arkley Rd 41 BP15
Arkley Cres, E17 123 DZ57
Arkley Dr, Barn. EN5 79 CU42
Arkley La, Barn. EN5 79 CU41
Arkley Pk, Barn. EN5 78 CR44
Arkley Rd, E17 123 DZ57
Hemel Hempstead HP2 41 BP15
Arkley Vw, Barn. EN5 79 CV42
Arklow Ct, Chorl. WD3
off Station App 73 BD42
Arklow Ho, SE17 311 L2
Arklow Ms, Surb. KT6
off Vale Rd S 198 CL103
Arklow Rd, SE14 313 N3
Sch ARK Swift Prim Acad, W12 off Australia Rd 139 CV73
Arkwright Rd, NW3 273 N3
Colnbrook SL3 153 BE82
South Croydon CR2 220 DT110
Tilbury RM18 171 GG82
Arkwrights, Harl. CM20 35 ET14
Arlesey Cl, SW15 179 CY85
Arlesford Rd, SW9 310 B10
Arlingford Rd, SW2 181 DN85
Arlingham Ms, Wal.Abb. EN9
off Sun St 67 EC33
Arlington, N12 98 DA48
Arlington Av, N1 277 K9
Arlington Bldg, E3 280 B10
Arlington Cl, SE13 183 ED85
Sidcup DA15 185 ES87
Sutton SM1 200 DA103
Twickenham TW1 177 CJ86
Arlington Ct, W3
off Mill Hill Rd 138 CP74
Hayes UB3 off Shepiston La 155 BR78
Reigate RH2 off Oakfield Dr 250 DB132
Arlington Cres, Wal.Cr. EN8 67 DY34
Arlington Dr, Cars. SM5 200 DF103
Ruislip HA4 115 BR58
Arlington Gdns, W4 158 CQ78
Ilford IG1 125 EN60
Romford RM3 106 FL53
Arlington Grn, NW7 97 CX52
Arlington Ho, SE8
off Evelyn St 313 P2
SW1 off Arlington St 297 L2
West Drayton UB7
off Porters Way 154 BM75
Arlington Lo, SW2 161 DM84
Weybridge KT13 213 BP105
Arlington Ms, Twick. TW1
off Arlington Rd 177 CJ86
Arlington Pl, SE10 314 E5
Arlington Rd, N14 99 DH47
NW1 275 K9
W13 137 CH72
Ashford TW15 174 BM92
Richmond TW10 177 CK89
Surbiton KT6 197 CK100
Teddington TW11 177 CF91
Twickenham TW1 177 CJ86
Woodford Green IG8 102 EG53
Arlington Sq, N1 277 K9
Arlington St, SW1 297 L2
Arlington Way, EC1 286 F2
Arliss Way, Nthlt. UB5 136 BW67
Arlow Rd, N21 99 DN46
Armada Ct, SE8 314 A3
Grays RM16 off Hogg La 170 GA76
Armadale Cl, N17 122 DV56
Armadale Rd, SW6 307 J4
Feltham TW14 175 BU85
Woking GU21 226 AU117
Armada Way, E6 145 EQ73
Armagh Rd, E3 279 P9
Armand Cl, Wat. WD17 75 BT38
Armfield Cl, W.Mol. KT8 196 BZ99
Armfield Cres, Mitch. CR4 200 DF96
Armfield Rd, Enf. EN2 82 DR39
Arminger Rd, W12 139 CV74
Armistice Gdns, SE25 202 DU97
Armitage Cl, Loud. WD3 74 BK42
Armitage Rd, NW11 119 CZ60
SE10 303 L10
Armor Rd, Purf. RM19 169 FR77
Armour Cl, N7 276 C5
Armoury Dr, Grav. DA12 191 GJ87
Armoury Rd, SE8 314 D9
Armoury Way, SW18 180 DA85
Armstead Wk, Dag. RM10 146 FA66
Armstrong Av, Wdf.Grn. IG8 102 EE51
Armstrong Cl, E6 293 K8
Borehamwood WD6 78 CQ41
Bromley BR1 204 EL97
Dagenham RM8 126 EX59
Halstead TN14 241 FB115
London Colney AL2 62 CL27
Pinner HA5 115 BU58
Walton-on-Thames KT12 195 BU100
Armstrong Cres, Cockfos. EN4 80 DD41
Armstrong Gdns, Shenley WD7 62 CL32
Armstrong Ho, Uxb. UB8
off High St 134 BJ66
Armstrong Pl, Hem.H. HP1
off High St 40 BK19
Armstrong Rd, NW10 138 CS66
SE18 165 EQ76
SW7 296 A7
W3 139 CT74
Englefield Green TW20 172 AW93
Feltham TW13 176 BY92
Armstrong Way, Sthl. UB2 156 CB75
Armytage Rd, Houns. TW5 156 BX80
Arnal Cres, SW18 179 CY87
Arncliffe Cl, N11 98 DG51
Arncroft Ct, Bark. IG11
off Renwick Rd 146 EV69
Arndale Wk, SW18
off Garratt La 180 DB85
Arndale Way, Egh. TW20
off Church Rd 173 BA92
Arne Gro, Horl. RH6 268 DE146
Orpington BR6 205 ET104
Arne Ho, SE11 298 C10
Arne St, WC2 286 B9
Arnett Cl, Rick. WD3 74 BG44
Sch Arnett Hills JMI Sch, Rick. WD3 off Berry La 74 BG44
Arnett Sq, E4 101 DZ51
Arnett Way, Rick. WD3 74 BG44
Arne Wk, SE3 164 EF84
Arneways Av, Rom. RM6 126 EX55
Arneway St, SW1 297 P7
Arnewood Cl, SW15 179 CU88
Oxshott KT22 214 CB113
Arney's La, Mitch. CR4 200 DG100
Arngask Rd, SE6 183 ED87
Arnhem Av, Aveley RM15 148 FQ74
Arnhem Dr, New Adgtn CR0 221 ED111
Arnhem Pl, E14 302 A7
Arnhem Way, SE22
off East Dulwich Gro 182 DS85
Arnhem Wf, E14
off Arnhem Pl 302 A7
Sch Arnhem Wf Prim Sch, E14 302 A7
Arnison Rd, E.Mol. KT8 197 CD98
Arnold Av E, Enf. EN3 83 EA38
Arnold Av W, Enf. EN3 83 DZ38
Arnold Bennett Way, N8
off Burghley Rd 121 DN55
Arnold Circ, E2 288 A3
Arnold Cl, Har. HA3 118 CM59
Arnold Cres, Islw. TW7 177 CD85
Arnold Dr, Chess. KT9 215 CK107
Arnold Est, SE1 300 B5
Arnold Gdns, N13 99 DP50
Sch Arnold Ho Sch, NW8 284 A1
Arnold Pl, Til. RM18 171 GJ81
Arnold Rd, E3 290 A2
N15 122 DT55
SW17 180 DF94
Dagenham RM9, RM10 146 EZ66
Gravesend DA12 191 GJ89
Northolt UB5 136 BX65
Staines-upon-Thames TW18 174 BJ94
Waltham Abbey EN9 83 EC36
Woking GU21 227 BB116
Arnolds Av, Hutt. CM13 109 GC43
Arnolds Cl, Hutt. CM13 109 GC43
Arnolds Fm La, Mtnsg CM13 109 GE41
Arnolds La, Sutt.H. DA4 188 FM93
⊖ Arnos Grove 99 DJ49
Arnos Gro, N14 99 DK49
Arnos Rd, N11 99 DJ50
Arnott Cl, SE28
off Applegarth Rd 146 EW73
W4 158 CR77
Arnould Av, SE5 162 DR84
Arnsberg Way, Bexh. DA7 166 FA84
Arnside Gdns, Wem. HA9 117 CK60
Arnside Rd, Bexh. DA7 166 FA81
Arnside St, SE17 311 K2
Arnulf St, SE6 183 EB91
Arnulls Rd, SW16 181 DN93
Arodene Rd, SW2 181 DM86
Arosa Rd, Twick. TW1 177 CK86
Arpley Sq, SE20
off High St 182 DW94
Arragon Gdns, SW16 181 DL94
West Wickham BR4 203 EB104
Arragon Rd, E6 144 EK67
SW18 180 DB88
Twickenham TW1 177 CG87
Arran Cl, Erith DA8 167 FD79
Hemel Hempstead HP3 41 BQ22
Wallington SM6 219 DH105
Arran Dr, E12 124 EK60
Arran Grn, Wat. WD19
off Prestwick Rd 94 BX49
Arran Ms, W5 138 CM74
Arranmore Ct, Bushey WD23 76 BY42
Arran Rd, SE6 183 EB89
Arran Wk, N1 277 J6
Arran Way, Esher KT10 196 CB103
Arras Av, Mord. SM4 200 DC99
Arretine Cl, St.Alb. AL3 42 BZ22
Arreton Mead, Horsell GU21 210 AY114
Arrol Ho, SE1 299 K7
Arrol Rd, Beck. BR3 202 DW97
Arrow Rd, E3 290 C2
Arrowscout Wk, Nthlt. UB5
off Wayfarer Rd 136 BY69
Arrowsmith Cl, Chig. IG7 103 ET50
Arrowsmith Ho, SE11 298 C10
Arrowsmith Path, Chig. IG7 103 ET50
Arrowsmith Rd, Chig. IG7 103 ES50
Loughton IG10 84 EL41
⊖ Arsenal 121 DN62
★ Arsenal FC, N5 276 E1
Arsenal Rd, SE9 165 EM82
Arsenal Way, SE18 165 EQ76
Arta Ho, E1 289 H9
Uni Art & Design,
Back Hill Site, EC1 286 F5
Byam Shaw Sch of Art, N19
off Elthorne Rd 121 DK61
King's Cross N1 276 A9
Artemis Cl, Grav. DA12 191 GL87
Arterberry Rd, SW20 179 CW94
Arterial Av, Rain. RM13 147 FH70
Arterial Rd N Stifford, Grays RM17 170 FY75
Arterial Rd Purfleet, Purf. RM19 168 FN76
Arterial Rd W Thurrock, Grays RM16, RM20 169 FU76
Artesian Cl, NW10 138 CR66
Hornchurch RM11 127 FF58
Artesian Gro, Barn. EN5 80 DC41
Artesian Rd, W2 283 J9
Artesian Wk, E11 124 EE62
Arthingworth St, E15 281 J8
Arthur Ct, SW11 309 H7
W2 283 L8
Arthurdon Rd, SE4 183 EA85
Arthur Gro, SE18 165 EQ77
Arthur Henderson Ho, SW6 306 G8
Arthur Horsley Wk, E7 281 M2
★ Arthur Jacob Nature Reserve, Slou. SL3 153 BC83
Arthur Newton Ho, SW11
off Lavender Rd 308 B10
Arthur Rd, E6 145 EM68
N7 121 DM63
N9 100 DT47
SW19 180 DA90
Biggin Hill TN16 238 EJ115
Kingston upon Thames KT2 178 CN94
New Malden KT3 199 CV99
Romford RM6 126 EW59
St. Albans AL1 43 CH20
Slough SL1 151 AR75
Windsor SL4 151 AP81
Arthur's Br Rd, Wok. GU21 226 AW117
Arthur St, EC4 299 M1
Bushey WD23 76 BX42
Erith DA8 167 FF80
Gravesend DA11 191 GG87
Grays RM17 170 GC79
Arthur St W, Grav. DA11 191 GG87
Arthur Toft Ho, Grays RM17
off New Rd 170 GB79
Arthur Vil, Epsom KT17 217 CT112
Arthur Walls Ho, E12
off Grantham Rd 125 EN62
Artichoke Dell, Chorl. WD3 73 BE43
Artichoke Hill, E1 300 E1
Artichoke Pl, SE5 311 L6
Artillery Cl, Ilf. IG2
off Horns Rd 125 EQ58
Artillery La, E1 287 P7
W12 139 CU72
Artillery Mans, SW1 297 N6
Artillery Pas, E1 287 P7
Artillery Pl, SE18 305 K9
SW1 297 N7
Harrow HA3 off Chicheley Rd 94 CC52
Artillery Rd, Guil. GU1 258 AX135
Artillery Row, SW1 297 N7
Gravesend DA12 191 GJ87
Artillery Ter, Guil. GU1 242 AX134
ARTINGTON, Guil. GU3 258 AW139
Artington Cl, Orp. BR6 223 EQ105
Artington Wk, Guil. GU2 258 AW137
Artisan Cl, E6 293 N10
Artisan Cres, St.Alb. AL3 42 CC19
Artizan St, E1 287 P8
Sch Arts Ed Sch London, The, W4 off Bath Rd 158 CS77
Arundel Av, Epsom KT17 217 CV110
Morden SM4 199 CZ98
South Croydon CR2 220 DU110
Arundel Cl, E15 281 K1
SW11 180 DE85
Bexley DA5 186 EZ86
Cheshunt EN8 66 DW28
Croydon CR0 201 DP104
Hampton Hill TW12 176 CB92
Hemel Hempstead HP2 41 BP19
Arundel Ct, N12 98 DE51
Harrow HA2 116 CA63
Slough SL3 152 AX77
Arundel Dr, Borwd. WD6 78 CQ43
Harrow HA2 116 BZ63
Orpington BR6 224 EV106
Woodford Green IG8 102 EG52
Arundel Gdns, N21 99 DN46
W11 282 G10
Edgware HA8 96 CR52
Ilford IG3 126 EU61
Arundel Gt Ct, WC2 286 D10
Arundel Gro, N16 277 N2
St. Albans AL3 43 CD15
Arundel Pl, N1 276 E5
Arundel Rd, Abb.L. WD5 59 BU32
Cockfosters EN4 80 DE41
Croydon CR0 202 DR100
Dartford DA1 168 FJ84
Dorking RH4 263 CG136
Hounslow TW4 156 BW83
Kingston upon Thames KT1 198 CP96
Romford RM3 106 FM53
Sutton SM2 217 CZ108
Uxbridge UB8 134 BH68
Arundel Sq, N7 276 E5
Arundel St, WC2 286 D10
Arundel Ter, SW13 159 CV79
Arvon Rd, N5 276 F2
Asbaston Ter, Ilf. IG1
off Buttsbury Rd 125 EQ64
Ascalon Ho, SW8
off Ascalon St 309 L5
Ascalon St, SW8 309 L5
Ascension Rd, Rom. RM5 105 FC51
Ascent, NW9 off Boulevard Dr 97 CT54
● Ascent Pk, Harl. CM20 36 EU10
Ascham Dr, E4
off Rushcroft Rd 101 EB52
Ascham End, E17 101 DY53
Ascham St, NW5 275 L2
Aschurch Rd, Croy. CR0 202 DT101
Ascot Cl, Els. WD6 78 CN43
Ilford IG6 103 ES51
Northolt UB5 116 CA64
Ascot Gdns, Enf. EN3 82 DW37
Hornchurch RM12 128 FL63
Southall UB1 136 BZ71
Ascot Ms, Wall. SM6 219 DJ109
Ascot Rd, E6 293 J2
N15 122 DR57
N18 100 DU49
SW17 180 DG93
Feltham TW14 174 BN88
Gravesend DA12 191 GH90
Orpington BR5 205 ET98
Watford WD18 75 BS43
Ascots La, Welw.G.C. AL7 29 CY14
Ascott Av, W5 158 CL75
Ascot Ter, Gt Amwell SG12
off Yearling Cl 33 DZ08
Ashanti Ms, E8 278 F3
Ashbeam Cl, Gt Warley CM13 107 FW51
Ashbourne, St.Alb. AL2 60 BZ31
Ashbourne Av, E18 124 EH56
N20 98 DF47
NW11 119 CZ57
Bexleyheath DA7 166 EY80
Harrow HA2 117 CD61
Ashbourne Cl, N12 98 DB49
W5 138 CN71
Coulsdon CR5 235 DJ118
Ashbourne Ct, E5
off Daubeney Rd 123 DY63
Ashbourne Gdns, Hert. SG13 32 DS11
Ashbourne Gro, NW7 96 CR50
SE22 182 DT85
W4 158 CS78
Ashbourne Ho, Slou. SL1 152 AS75
Coll Ashbourne Indep 6th Form Coll, W8 295 L4
Ashbourne Par, W5
off Ashbourne Rd 138 CM70
Ashbourne Ri, Orp. BR6 223 ER105
Ashbourne Rd, W5 138 CM71
Broxbourne EN10 49 DZ21
Mitcham CR4 180 DG93
Romford RM3 106 FJ49
Ashbourne Sq, Nthwd. HA6 93 BS51
Ashbourne Ter, SW19 180 DA94
Ashbourne Way, NW11 119 CZ57
Ashbridge Rd, E11 124 EE59
Ashbridge St, NW8 284 C5
Ashbrook Rd, N19 121 DK60
Dagenham RM10 127 FB62
Old Windsor SL4 172 AV87
Ashburn Gdns, SW7 295 N8
Ashburnham Av, Har. HA1 117 CF58
Ashburnham Cl, N2 120 DD55
Sevenoaks TN13
off Fiennes Way 257 FJ127
Watford WD19 93 BU48
Ashburnham Dr, Wat. WD19 93 BU48
Ashburnham Gdns, Har. HA1 117 CF58
Upminster RM14 128 FP60
Ashburnham Gro, SE10 314 D5
Ashburnham Pk, Esher KT10 214 CC105
Ashburnham Pl, SE10 314 D5
Sch Ashburnham Prim Sch, SW10 308 A4
Ashburnham Retreat, SE10 314 D5
Ashburnham Rd, NW10 282 A2
SW10 307 P5
Belvedere DA17 167 FC77
Richmond TW10 177 CH90
Ashburnham Twr, SW10
off Blantyre St 308 A4
Ashburn Pl, SW7 295 N8
Ashburton Av, Croy. CR0 202 DV102
Ilford IG3 125 ES63
Ashburton Cl, Croy. CR0 202 DU102
Ashburton Ct, Pnr. HA5 116 BX55
Ashburton Gdns, Croy. CR0 202 DU103
Sch Ashburton Jun & Inf Sch, Croy. CR0 off Long La 202 DV100
Ashburton Rd, E16 291 P8
Croydon CR0 202 DU102
Ruislip HA4 115 BU61
Ashburton Ter, E13 281 N10
Ashburton Triangle, N5
off Drayton Pk 121 DN63
Ashbury Cl, Hat. AL10 44 CS18
Ashbury Cres, Guil. GU4 243 BC132
Ashbury Dr, Uxb. UB10 115 BP61
Ashbury Gdns, Rom. RM6 126 EX57
Ashbury Pl, SW19 180 DC93
Ashbury Rd, SW11 308 G10
Ashby Av, Chess. KT9 216 CN107
Ashby Cl, Hornchurch RM11
off Holme Rd 128 FN60
West Wickham BR4 203 ED104
Ashby Gdns, St.Alb. AL1 43 CD24
Ashby Gro, N1 277 K6
Ashby Ho, N1 277 K6
Ashby Ms, SE4 313 N9
SW2 off Prague Pl 181 DL85
Ashby Rd, N15 122 DU57
SE4 313 P9
Watford WD24 75 BU38
Ashby St, EC1 287 H3
Ashby Wk, Croy. CR0 202 DQ100
Ashby Way, Sipson UB7 154 BN80
Ashchurch Gro, W12 159 CU75
Ashchurch Pk Vil, W12 159 CU76
Ashchurch Ter, W12 159 CU76
Ash Cl, SE20 202 DW96
Abbots Langley WD5 59 BR32
Banstead SM7 233 CY115
Brookmans Park AL9 64 DA25
Carshalton SM5 200 DF103
Edgware HA8 96 CQ49
Harefield UB9 92 BK53
New Malden KT3 198 CR96
Petts Wood BR5 205 ER99
Pilgrim's Hatch CM15 108 FT43
Pyrford GU22 228 BG115
Romford RM5 105 FB52
Sidcup DA14 186 EV90
Slough SL3 153 BB76
South Merstham RH1 251 DJ130
Stanmore HA7 95 CG51
Swanley BR8 207 FC96
Tadworth KT20 248 CQ131
Watford WD25 75 BV35
Woking GU22 226 AY120
Ashcombe, Welw.G.C. AL8 29 CY05
Ashcombe Av, Surb. KT6 197 CK101
Ashcombe Cl, Ashf. TW15 174 BK90
Ashcombe Gdns, Edg. HA8 96 CN49
Ashcombe Ho, Enf. EN3 83 DX41
Ashcombe Pk, NW2 118 CS62
Ashcombe Rd, SW19 180 DA92
Carshalton SM5 218 DG107
Dorking RH4 247 CG134
Merstham RH1 251 DJ127
Sch Ashcombe Sch, The, Dor. RH4 off Ashcombe Rd 247 CH134
Ashcombe Sq, N.Mal. KT3 198 CQ97
Ashcombe St, SW6 307 L9
Ashcombe Ter, Tad. KT20 233 CV120
Ash Copse, Brick.Wd AL2 60 BZ31
Ash Ct, N11 off Cline Rd 99 DJ51
Epsom KT19 216 CQ105
Ashcroft, Pnr. HA5 94 CA51
Shalford GU4 258 AY141
Ashcroft Av, Sid. DA15 186 EU86
Ashcroft Ct, N20 98 DD47
Broxbourne EN10
off Winford Dr 49 DZ22
Burnham SL1 130 AH68
Ashcroft Cres, Sid. DA15 186 EU86
Ashcroft Dr, Denh. UB9 113 BF58
Ashcroft Pk, Cob. KT11 214 BY112
Ashcroft Pl, Lthd. KT22 231 CJ121
Ashcroft Ri, Couls. CR5 235 DL116
Ashcroft Rd, E3 289 L3
Chessington KT9 198 CM104
Ashcroft Sq, W6 294 A9
Ashdale, Bkhm KT23 246 CC126
Ashdale Cl, Stai. TW19 174 BL89
Twickenham TW2 176 CC87
Ashdale Gro, Stan. HA7 95 CF51
Ashdale Rd, SE12 184 EH88
Ashdales, St.Alb. AL1 43 CD24
Ashdale Way, Twick. TW2
off Ashdale Cl 176 CC87
Ashdene, SE15 312 E6
Pinner HA5 116 BW55
Ashdene Cl, Ashf. TW15 175 BQ94
Ashdon Cl, Hutt. CM13
off Poplar Dr 109 GC44
South Ockendon RM15
off Afton Dr 149 FV72
Woodford Green IG8 102 EH51
Ashdon Rd, NW10 138 CS67
Bushey WD23 76 BX41
Ashdown Cl, Beck. BR3 203 EB96
Bexley DA5 187 FC87
Reigate RH2 266 DB138
Woking GU22
off Guildford Rd 226 AY118
Ashdown Ct, E17 101 EC54
Ashdown Cres, NW5 274 G3
Cheshunt EN8 67 DY28
Ashdown Dr, Borwd. WD6 78 CM40
Ashdown Gdns, S.Croy. CR2 236 DV115
Ashdown Pl, T.Ditt. KT7 197 CG100
Ashdown Rd, Enf. EN3 82 DW41
Epsom KT17 217 CT113
Kingston upon Thames KT1 198 CL96
Reigate RH2 266 DB138
Uxbridge UB10 134 BN68
Ashdown Wk, E14 302 B8
Romford RM7 105 FB54
Ashdown Way, SW17 180 DG89
Amersham HP6 55 AR37
Ash Dr, Hat. AL10 45 CU21
Redhill RH1 267 DH136
Ashen, E6 293 L8
Jct Ashen Cross, Slou. SL3 133 BB71
Ashenden, SE17 299 J8
Ashendene Rd, Bayford SG13 47 DL20
Ashenden Rd, E5 279 K2
Guildford GU2 258 AT135
Ashenden Wk, Farn.Com. SL2 111 AR63
Ashen Dr, Dart. DA1 187 FG86
Ashen Gro, SW19 180 DA90
Ashentree Ct, EC4 286 F9
Ashen Vale, S.Croy. CR2 221 DX109
● Asheridge Business Cen, Chesh. HP5 54 AN29
Asheridge Rd, Chesh. HP5 54 AM28
Asher Loftus Way, N11 98 DF51
Asher Way, E1 300 D2
Ashfield Av, Bushey WD23 76 CB44
Feltham TW13 175 BV88
Ashfield Cl, Ashtd. KT21 232 CL119
Beckenham BR3 183 EA94
Richmond TW10 178 CL88
Sch Ashfield Jun Sch, Bushey WD23 off School La 94 CB45
Ashfield La, Chis. BR7 185 EQ93
Ashfield Par, N14 99 DK46
Ashfield Rd, N4 122 DQ58
N14 99 DJ48
W3 139 CT74
Chesham HP5 54 AR29
Ashfields, Loug. IG10 85 EM40
Reigate RH2 250 DB132
Watford WD25 75 BT35
Ashfield St, E1 288 E7
Ashfield Yd, E1 288 G7
ASHFORD, TW15 174 BM92
⇌ Ashford 174 BL91
Ashford Av, N8 121 DL56
Ashford TW15 175 BP93
Brentwood CM14 108 FV48
Hayes UB4 136 BX72
Ashford Cl, E17 123 DZ58
Ashford TW15 174 BL91
Sch Ashford C of E Prim Sch, Ashf. TW15 off School Rd 175 BP93
Ashford Cres, Ashf. TW15 174 BL90
Enfield EN3 82 DW40
Ashford Gdns, Cob. KT11 230 BX116
Ashford Grn, Wat. WD19 94 BX50
H Ashford Hosp, Ashf. TW15 174 BL89
● Ashford Ind Est, Ashf. TW15 175 BQ91
Ashford La, Dorney SL4 150 AH75
Maidenhead SL6 150 AG75
Ashford Ms, N17 100 DU53
Sch Ashford Pk Prim Sch, Ashf. TW15 off Station Cres 174 BK91
Ashford Rd, E6 145 EN65
E18 102 EH54
NW2 272 C1
Ashford TW15 175 BQ94
Feltham TW13 175 BT90
Iver SL0 133 BC66
Staines-upon-Thames TW18 194 BK95
Ashford St, N1 287 N2
Ash Grn, Denh. UB9 134 BH65
Ash Gro, E8 278 F9
N10 121 DH56
N13 100 DQ48
NW2 272 D1
SE20 202 DW96
W5 158 CL75
Amersham HP6 55 AN36
Enfield EN1 100 DS45
Feltham TW14 175 BS88
Guildford GU2 242 AU134
Harefield UB9 92 BK53
Hayes UB3 135 BR73
Hemel Hempstead HP3 40 BM24
Hounslow TW5 156 BX81
Southall UB1 136 CA71
Staines-upon-Thames TW18 174 BJ93
Stoke Poges SL2 132 AT66
Wembley HA0 117 CG63
West Drayton UB7 134 BM73
West Wickham BR4 203 EC103
Ashgrove Rd, Ashf. TW15 175 BQ92
Bromley BR1 183 ED93
Ilford IG3 125 ET60
Sevenoaks TN13 256 FG127
Ash Gros, Saw. CM21 36 FA05
Sch Ashgrove Sch, Brom. BR1
off Widmore Rd 204 EH96
Ash Hill Cl, Bushey WD23 94 CB46
Ash Hill Dr, Pnr. HA5 116 BW55
Ash Ho, SE1
off Longfield Est 300 B9
● Ash Ind Est, Harl. CM19 51 EM16
Ashingdon Cl, E4 101 EC48
Ashington Ho, E1
off Barnsley St 288 F4

Ashington Rd, SW6 307 H8
Ash Island, E.Mol. KT8 197 CD97
Ashlake Rd, SW16 181 DL91
Ashland Pl, W1 284 G6
Ash La, Horn. RM11
off Wiltshire Av 128 FM56
Romford RM1 105 FG51
Windsor SL4 151 AK82
Ashlar Pl, SE18 305 N9
Ashlea Rd, Chal.St.P. SL9 90 AX54
Ashleigh Av, Egh. TW20 173 BC94
Ashleigh Cl, Amer. HP7 55 AS39
Horley RH6 268 DF148
Ashleigh Cotts, Dor. RH5 263 CH144
Ashleigh Ct, Wal.Abb. EN9
off Lamplighters Cl 68 EG34
Wat. WD17 off Loates La 76 BW41
Ashleigh Gdns, Sutt. SM1 200 DB103
Upminster RM14 129 FR62
Ashleigh Ms, SE15 312 B10
Ashleigh Pt, SE23
off Dacres Rd 183 DX90
Ashleigh Rd, SE20 202 DV97
SW14 158 CS83
Ashley Av, Epsom KT18 216 CR113
Ilford IG6 103 EP54
Morden SM4 200 DA99
Ashley Cen, Epsom KT18 216 CR113
Ashley Cl, NW4 97 CW54
Bookham KT23 246 BZ125
Hemel Hempstead HP3 40 BM22
Pinner HA5 93 BV54
Sevenoaks TN13 257 FH124
Walton-on-Thames KT12 195 BT102
Welwyn Garden City AL8 29 CW07
Sch Ashley C of E Prim Sch,
Walt. KT12 off Ashley Rd 195 BU102
Ashley Ct, Epsom KT18 216 CR113
Hatfield AL10 45 CU17
Woking GU21 226 AT118
Ashley Cres, N22 99 DN54
SW11 309 H10
Ashley Dr, Bans. SM7 218 DA114
Borehamwood WD6 78 CQ43
Isleworth TW7 157 CE79
Penn HP10 88 AC45
Twickenham TW2 176 CB87
Walton-on-Thames KT12 195 BU104
Ashley Gdns, N13 100 DQ49
SW1 297 M7
Orpington BR6 223 ES106
Richmond TW10 177 CK90
Shalford GU4 259 AZ141
Wembley HA9 118 CL61
ASHLEY GREEN, Chesh. HP5 38 AS24
Ashley Grn Rd, Chesh. HP5 54 AR27
Ashley Gro, Loug. IG10
off Staples Rd 84 EL41
Ashley La, NW4 97 CW54
NW7 97 CW54
Croydon CR0 219 DP105
ASHLEY PARK, Walt. KT12 195 BT104
Ashley Pk Av, Walt. KT12 195 BT103
Ashley Pk Cres, Walt. KT12 195 BT102
Ashley Pk Rd, Walt. KT12 195 BU103
Ashley Pl, SW1 297 L7
Ashley Ri, Walt. KT12 213 BU105
Ashley Rd, E4 101 EA50
E7 144 EJ66
N17 122 DU55
N19 121 DL60
SW19 180 DB93
Enfield EN3 82 DW40
Epsom KT18 216 CR114
Hampton TW12 196 CA95
Hertford SG14 31 DN10
Richmond TW9
off Jocelyn Rd 158 CL83
St. Albans AL1 43 CJ20
Sevenoaks TN13 257 FH123
Thames Ditton KT7 197 CF100
Thornton Heath CR7 201 DM98
Uxbridge UB8 134 BH68
Walton-on-Thames KT12 195 BU102
Westcott RH4 262 CC137
Woking GU21 226 AT118
Ashleys, Rick. WD3 91 BF45
Ashley Sq, Epsom KT18 216 CR113
Ashley Wk, NW7 97 CW52
Ashling Rd, Croy. CR0 202 DU102
Ashlin Rd, E15 281 H1
Ashlone Rd, SW15 306 B10
Ashlyn Cl, Bushey WD23 76 BY42
Ashlyn Gro, Horn. RM11 128 FK55
Ashlyns Ct, Berk. HP4 38 AV20
Ashlyns La, Ong. CM5 53 FG23
Ashlyns Pk, Cob. KT11 214 BY113
Ashlyns Rd, Berk. HP4 38 AV20
Epping CM16 69 ET30
Sch Ashlyns Sch, Berk. HP4
off Chesham Rd 38 AW21
Ashlyns Way, Chess. KT9 215 CK107
Ashmead, N14 81 DJ43
Ashmead Cl, Ashf. TW15 175 BQ94
Ashmead Dr, Denh. UB9 114 BG61
Ashmead Gate, Brom. BR1 204 EJ95
Ashmead Ho, E9
off Kingsmead Way 279 M2
Ashmead La, Denh. UB9 114 BG61
Ashmead Ms, SE8
off Ashmead Rd 314 A8
Ashmead Pl, Amer. HP7 72 AW39
Sch Ashmead Prim Sch, SE8 314 A8
Ashmead Rd, SE8 314 A8
Feltham TW14 175 BU88
Ashmeads Ct, Shenley WD7 61 CK33
Ashmere Av, Beck. BR3 203 ED96
Ashmere Cl, Sutt. SM3 217 CW106
Ashmere Gro, SW2 161 DL84
Ash Ms, Epsom KT18 216 CS113
Ashmill St, NW1 284 C6
Ashmole Pl, SW8 310 D3
Sch Ashmole Prim Sch, SW8 310 D3
Sch Ashmole Sch, N14
off Cecil Rd 99 DJ46
Ashmole St, SW8 310 D3
Ashmore Cl, SE15 312 B5
Ashmore Ct, Houns. TW5
off Wheatlands 156 CA79
Ashmore Gdns, Hem.H. HP3 41 BP21
Northfleet DA11 190 GD91
Ashmore Gro, Well. DA16 165 ER83
Ashmore La, Kes. BR2 222 EH111
Ashmore Rd, W9 283 H4
Ashmount Cres, Slou. SL1 151 AN75
Sch Ashmount Hill Prim Sch, N8 121 DL59
Ashmount Rd, N15 122 DT57
N19 121 DJ59
Ashmount Ter, W5 157 CK77
Ashmour Gdns, Rom. RM1 105 FD54
Ashneal Gdns, Har. HA1 117 CD62
Ashness Gdns, Grnf. UB6 137 CH65
Ashness Rd, SW11 180 DF85
Ash Platt, The,
Seal TN14, TN15 257 FL121
Ash Platt Rd, Seal TN15 257 FL121
Ash Ride, Enf. EN2 81 DN35
Ashridge Cl, Bov. HP3 57 AZ28
Harrow HA3 117 CJ58
Ashridge Cres, SE18 165 EQ80
Ashridge Dr, Brick.Wd AL2 60 BY30
Watford WD19 94 BW50
Ashridge Gdns, N13 99 DK50
Pinner HA5 116 BY56
Ashridge Ri, Berk. HP4 38 AT18
Ashridge Rd, Chesh. HP5 56 AW31
Ashridge Way, Mord. SM4 199 CZ97
Sunbury-on-Thames TW16 175 BU93
Ash Rd, E15 281 K2
Croydon CR0 203 EA103
Dartford DA1 188 FK88
Gravesend DA12 191 GJ91
Hawley DA2 188 FM91
Orpington BR6 223 ET108
Shepperton TW17 194 BN98
Sutton SM3 199 CY101
Westerham TN16 255 ER125
Woking GU22 226 AX120
Ash Row, Brom. BR2 205 EN101
ASHTEAD, KT21 232 CL118
⇌ Ashtead 231 CK117
Ashtead Common,
Ashtd. KT21 231 CJ115
Ashtead Gap, Lthd. KT22 231 CH116
H Ashtead Hosp, Ashtd. KT21 232 CL119
ASHTEAD PARK, Ashtd. KT21 232 CN118
Ashtead Rd, E5 122 DU59
Ashtead Wds Rd, Ashtd. KT21 231 CJ117
Ashton Cl, Hersham KT12 213 BV107
Sutton SM1 218 DA105
Ashton Ct, E4
off Connington Cres 102 EE48
Romford RM6 126 EY58
Ashton Gdns, Houns. TW4 156 BZ84
Romford RM6 126 EY58
Sch Ashton Ho Sch, Islw. TW7
off Eversley Cres 157 CD81
Ashton Rd, E15 280 G3
Enfield EN3 83 DY36
Romford RM3 106 FK52
Woking GU21 226 AT117
Ashton St, E14 290 F10
Ashtree Av, Mitch. CR4 200 DD96
Ash Tree Cl, Croy. CR0 203 DY100
Surbiton KT6 198 CL102
Ashtree Cl, Orp. BR6 223 EP105
Ashtree Ct, St.Alb. AL1
off Granville Rd 43 CF20
Waltham Abbey EN9
off Farthingale La 68 EG34
Ash Tree Dell, NW9 118 CQ57
Ash Tree Fld, Harl. CM20 35 EN13
Ash Tree Rd, Wat. WD24 75 BV36
Ash Tree Way, Croy. CR0 203 DY99
Ashtree Way, Hem.H. HP1 40 BG21
Ashurst Cl, SE20 202 DV95
Dartford DA1 167 FF83
Kenley CR8 236 DR115
Leatherhead KT22 231 CG121
Northwood HA6 93 BS52
Ashurst Dr, Box H. KT20 248 CP130
Ilford IG2, IG6 125 EP58
Shepperton TW17 194 BL99
Ashurst Pl, Dor. RH4 247 CJ134
Ashurst Rd, N12 98 DE50
Barnet EN4 80 DF43
Tadworth KT20 233 CV121
Ashurst Wk, Croy. CR0 202 DV103
Ash Vale, Map.Cr. WD3 91 BD50
Ashvale Dr, Upmin. RM14 129 FS61
Ashvale Gdns, Rom. RM5 105 FD50
Upminster RM14 129 FS61
Ashvale Rd, SW17 180 DF92
Ashview Cl, Ashf. TW15 174 BL93
Ashview Gdns, Ashf. TW15 174 BL92
Ashville Rd, E11 123 ED61
Ash Wk, SW2 181 DM88
South Ockendon RM15 149 FX69
Wembley HA0 117 CJ63
Ashwater Rd, SE12 184 EG88
Ashway Cen, The,
Kings.T. KT2 off Elm Cres 198 CL95
Ashwell Cl, E6 293 H8
Ashwell Pl, Wat. WD24 75 BU37
Ashwells Manor Dr,
Penn HP10 88 AC47
Ashwells Rd, Pilg.Hat. CM15 108 FS41
Ashwell St, St.Alb. AL3 43 CD19
Ashwells Way, Ch.St.G. HP8 90 AW47
Ashwick Cl, Cat. CR3 252 DU125
Ashwindham Ct, Wok. GU21
off Raglan Rd 226 AT118
Ashwin St, E8 278 A4
Ashwood, Warl. CR6 236 DW120
Ashwood Av, Rain. RM13 147 FH70
Uxbridge UB8 134 BN72
Ashwood Dr, Chesh. HP5 54 AP30
Ashwood Gdns, Hayes UB3
off Cranford Dr 155 BT77
New Addington CR0 221 EB107
Ashwood Ms, St.Alb. AL1
off Prospect Rd 43 CD22
Ashwood Pk, Fetch. KT22 230 CC124
Woking GU22 227 BA118
Ashwood Pl, Bean DA2
off Bean La 189 FV90
Ashwood Rd, E4 101 ED48
Englefield Green TW20 172 AV93
Potters Bar EN6 64 DB33
Woking GU22 227 AZ118
Ashworth Cl, SE5 311 L8
Ashworth Pl, Guil. GU2 242 AT134
Harlow CM17 52 EX15
Ashworth Rd, W9 283 M2
Asker Ho, N7
off Tufnell Pk Rd 121 DL63
Askern Cl, Bexh. DA6 166 EX84
Aske St, N1 287 N3
Askew Cres, W12 159 CT75
Askew Fm La, Grays RM17 170 FY78
Askew Rd, W12 139 CT74
Northwood HA6 93 BR47
Askham Ct, W12 139 CU74
Askham Rd, W12 139 CU74
Askill Dr, SW15 179 CY85
Askwith Rd, Rain. RM13 147 FD69
Asland Rd, E15 281 J9
Aslett St, SW18 180 DB87
Asmara Rd, NW2 272 F2
Asmar Cl, Couls. CR5 235 DL115
Asmuns Hill, NW11 120 DA57
Asmuns Pl, NW11 119 CZ57
Asolando Dr, SE17 299 K9
Aspasia Cl, St.Alb. AL1 43 CF21
Aspdin Rd, Nthflt DA11 190 GD90
Aspect Ct, SW6 307 P8
Aspects, Sutt. SM1 218 DB106
Aspects Ct, Slou. SL1
off Windsor Rd 152 AS75
Aspen Cl, N19 off Hargrave Pk 121 DJ61
W5 158 CM75
Bricket Wood AL2 60 BY30
Epsom KT19 216 CR109
Guildford GU4 243 BD131
Orpington BR6 224 EU106
Slough SL2 off Birch Gro 131 AP71
Staines-upon-Thames TW18 173 BF90
Stoke D'Abernon KT11 230 BY116
Swanley BR8 207 FD95
West Drayton UB7 134 BM74
Aspen Copse, Brom. BR1 205 EM96
Aspen Ct, Brwd. CM13 109 GA48
Hayes UB3 155 BS77
Virginia Water GU25 192 AY98
Aspen Dr, Wem. HA0 117 CG63
Aspen Gdns, W6 159 CV78
Ashford TW15 175 BQ92
Mitcham CR4 200 DG99
Aspen Grn, Erith DA18 166 EZ76
Aspen Gro, Pnr. HA5 115 BT55
Upminster RM14 128 FN63
Aspen Ho, NW3 274 F4
Warlingham CR6
off East Parkside 237 EB115
Aspen La, Nthlt. UB5 136 BY69
Aspenlea Rd, W6 306 C2
Aspen Pk Dr, Wat. WD25 75 BV35
Aspens Pl, Hem.H. HP1 39 BF23
Aspen Sq, Wey. KT13 195 BR104
Aspen Vale, Whyt. CR3
off Whyteleafe Hill 236 DT118
Aspen Way, E14 302 B1
Banstead SM7 217 CX114
Enfield EN3 83 DX35
Feltham TW13 175 BV90
South Ockendon RM15 149 FX69
Welwyn Garden City AL7 30 DC10
Aspern Gro, NW3 274 D3
Aspfield Row, Hem.H. HP1 40 BH18
Aspinall Rd, SE4 313 K10
Aspinden Rd, SE16 300 F8
Aspley Rd, SW18 180 DB85
Asplins Rd, N17 100 DU53
Asprey Ct, Cat. CR3 236 DT123
Asprey Gro, Cat. CR3 236 DU124
Asprey Ms, Beck. BR3 203 DZ99
Asprey Pl, Brom. BR1
off Chislehurst Rd 204 EL96
Asquith Cl, Dag. RM8 126 EW60
Assam St, E1 288 C8
Assata Ms, N1 277 H4
Assembly Pas, E1 289 H6
Assembly Wk, Cars. SM5 200 DE101
Assher Rd, Hersham KT12 196 BY104
Assheton Rd, Beac. HP9 89 AK51
Astall Cl, Har. HA3 95 CE53
Astbury Business Pk, SE15
off Station Pas 312 G6
Astbury Ho, SE11 298 E7
Astbury Rd, SE15 312 G6
Astede Pl, Ashtd. KT21 232 CM118
Astell St, SW3 296 D10
Aster Ct, E5 122 DW61
Asters, The, Chsht EN7 66 DR28
Aste St, E14 302 E5
Asteys Row, N1 277 H7
Asthall Gdns, Ilf. IG6 125 EQ56
Astleham Rd, Shep. TW17 194 BL97
Astle St, SW11 308 G8
Astley, Grays RM17 170 FZ79
Astley Av, NW2 272 B2
Sch Astley Cooper Sch, The,
Hem.H. HP2 off St. Agnells La 40 BN15
Astley Ho, SE1
off Rowcross St 300 B10
Astley Rd, Hem.H. HP1 40 BJ20
● Astolat Ind Est, Peasm. GU3 258 AV142
Aston Av, Har. HA3 117 CJ59
Aston Cl, Ashtd. KT21 231 CJ118
Bushey WD23 76 CC44
Sidcup DA14 186 EU90
Watford WD24 76 BW40
Aston Ct, N4 off Queens Dr 122 DQ61
Aston Gra, Hert. SG14 32 DR07
Aston Grn, Houns. TW4 156 BW82
Aston Ho, SW8 309 N7
Sch Aston Ho Sch, Jun Sch, W5
off Aston Rd 137 CK72
Sen Sch, W5
off Montpelier Rd 137 CK71
Aston Mead, Wind. SL4 151 AL80
Aston Ms, Rom. RM6 126 EW59
Aston Pl, SW16
off Averil Gro 181 DP93
Aston Rd, SW20 199 CW96
W5 137 CK72
Claygate KT10 215 CE106
Astons Rd, Nthwd. HA6 93 BQ48
Aston St, E14 289 L8
Aston Ter, SW12
off Cathles Rd 181 DH86
Astonville St, SW18 180 DA88
Aston Way, Epsom KT18 233 CT115
Potters Bar EN6 64 DD32
Astor Av, Rom. RM7 127 FC58
Astor Cl, Add. KT15 212 BK105
Kingston upon Thames KT2 178 CP93
Astoria, NW9
off Boulevard Dr 97 CT54
Astoria Ct, Pur. CR8
off High St 219 DN111
Astoria Wk, SW9 161 DN83
● Astra Business Cen,
Red. RH1 266 DG144
● Astra Cen, Harl. CM20 35 ET11
Astra Cl, Horn. RM12 147 FH65
Astra Dr, Grav. DA12 191 GL92
Astrop Ms, W6 294 A6
Astrop Ter, W6 294 A6
Astwick Av, Hat. AL10 45 CT15
Astwood Ms, SW7 295 N8
Asylum Arch Rd, Red. RH1 266 DF137
Asylum Rd, SE15 312 F4
Atalanta Cl, Pur. CR8 219 DN110
Atalanta St, SW6 306 D6
Atbara Ct, Tedd. TW11 177 CH93
Atbara Rd, Tedd. TW11 177 CH93
Atcham Rd, Houns. TW3 156 CC84
Atcost Rd, Bark. IG11 146 EU71
Atheldene Rd, SW18 180 DB88
Sch Athelney Prim Sch, SE6
off Athelney St 183 EA90
Athelney St, SE6 183 EA90
Athelstan Cl, Rom. RM3 106 FM53
Athelstane Gro, E3 289 N1
Athelstane Ms, N4
off Stroud Grn Rd 121 DN60
Athelstan Gdns, NW6 272 F7
Athelstan Ho, E9
off Kingsmead Way 279 N2
Sch Athelstan Ho Sch,
Hmptn. TW12 off Percy Rd 196 CA95
Athelstan Rd, Hem.H. HP3 40 BM23
Kingston upon Thames KT1 198 CM98
Romford RM3 106 FM53
Athelstan Wk N, Welw.G.C. AL7 29 CY10
Athelstan Wk S, Welw.G.C. AL7 29 CX10
Athelstan Way, Orp. BR5 206 EU95
Athelstone Rd, Har. HA3 95 CD54
Athena Cl, Har. HA2
off Byron Hill Rd 117 CE61
Kingston upon Thames KT1 198 CM97
Athena Ct, SE1 off Long La 299 N5
Athenaeum Ct, N5 277 K1
Athenaeum Pl, N10 121 DH55
Athenaeum Rd, N20 98 DC46
Athena Pl, Nthwd. HA6
off The Drive 93 BT53
Athenia Cl, Goffs Oak EN7 65 DN29
Athenlay Rd, SE15 183 DX85
Athens Gdns, W9 283 J5
Atherden Rd, E5 122 DW63
Atherfield Rd, Reig. RH2 266 DC137
Atherfold Rd, SW9 310 A10
Atherley Way, Houns. TW4 176 BZ87
Atherstone Ct, W2 283 M6
Atherstone Ms, SW7 295 P8
Atherton Cl, Shalf. GU4 258 AY140
Stanwell TW19 174 BK86
Atherton Ct, Eton SL4
off Meadow La 151 AR80
Atherton Dr, SW19 179 CX91
Atherton Gdns, Grays RM16 171 GJ77
Atherton Hts, Wem. HA0 137 CJ65
Atherton Ms, E7 281 M4
Atherton Pl, Har. HA2 117 CD55
Southall UB1 136 CA73
Atherton Rd, E7 281 M3
SW13 159 CU80
Ilford IG5 102 EL54
Atherton St, SW11 308 D8
Athlone, Clay. KT10 215 CE107
Athlone Cl, E5 278 F2
Radlett WD7 77 CG36
Athlone Ct, E17 123 EC55
Athlone Rd, SW2 181 DM87
Athlone Sq, Wind. SL4
off Ward Royal 151 AQ81
Athlone St, NW5 275 H4
Athlon Rd, Wem. HA0 137 CK68
Athol Cl, Pnr. HA5 93 BV53
Athole Gdns, Enf. EN1 82 DS43
Athol Gdns, Pnr. HA5 93 BV53
Atholl Ho, W9 283 N3
Atholl Rd, Ilf. IG3 126 EU59
Athol Rd, Erith DA8 167 FC78
Athol Sq, E14 290 F9
Athol Way, Uxb. UB10 134 BN69
Atkin Cl, Ruis HA4 115 BU58
Atkins Cl, Bigg.H. TN16 222 EJ112
Wok. GU21
off Greythorne Rd 226 AU118
Atkins Dr, W.Wick. BR4 203 ED103
Atkinson Cl, Bushey WD23 95 CE45
Orp. BR6 off Martindale Av 224 EU106
Atkinson Ho, SW11
off Austin Rd 308 G7
Atkinson Rd, E16 292 D7
Atkins Rd, E10 123 EB58
SW12 181 DK87
Atlanta Boul, Rom. RM1 127 FE58
Atlanta Bldg, SE13
off Deals Gateway 314 C7
Atlantic, E16
off Seagull La 291 N10
Atlantic Cl, Swans. DA10 190 FY85
Atlantic Rd, SW9 161 DN84
Atlantis Av, E16 293 P10
Atlantis Cl, Bark. IG11 146 EV69
● Atlas Business Cen, NW2 119 CV61
Atlas Cres, Edg. HA8 96 CP47
Atlas Gdns, SE7 304 C8
Atlas Ms, E8 278 B4
N7 276 D5
Atlas Rd, E13 291 P1
N11 99 DH51
NW10 138 CS69
Dartford DA1 off Cornwall Rd 168 FM83
Wembley HA9 118 CQ63
● Atlas Trade Pk, Erith DA8 167 FD78
Atley Rd, E3 280 A9
● Atlip Cen, Wem. HA0
off Atlip Rd 138 CL67
Atlip Rd, Wem. HA0 138 CL67
Atney Rd, SW15 159 CY84
Atria Rd, Nthwd. HA6 93 BU50
● Atrium, The, Uxb. UB8
off Harefield Rd 134 BJ66
Attenborough Cl, Wat. WD19 94 BY48
Atterbury Cl, West. TN16 255 ER126
Atterbury Rd, N4 121 DN58
Atterbury St, SW1 297 P9
Attewood Av, NW10 118 CS62
Attewood Rd, Nthlt. UB5 136 BY65
Attfield Cl, N20 98 DD47
Attimore Cl, Welw.G.C. AL8 29 CV10
Attimore Rd, Welw.G.C. AL8 29 CV10
Attle Cl, Uxb. UB10 134 BN68
Attlee Cl, Hayes UB4 135 BV69
Thornton Heath CR7 202 DQ100
Attlee Ct, Grays RM17 170 GA76
Attlee Dr, Dart. DA1 188 FN85
Attlee Rd, SE28 146 EV73
Hayes UB4 135 BU69
Attlee Ter, E17 123 EB56
Attneave St, WC1 286 E3
Attock Ms, E17 123 EB57
Attwood Cl, S.Croy. CR2 220 DV114
Atwater Cl, SW2 181 DN88
Atwell Cl, E10
off Belmont Pk Rd 123 EB58
Atwell Pl, T.Ditt. KT7 197 CF102
Atwell Rd, SE15 312 D9
Atwood, Bkhm KT23 230 BY124
Atwood Av, Rich. TW9 158 CN82
Sch Atwood Prim Sch,
S.Croy. CR2 off Limpsfield Rd 220 DU113
Atwood Rd, W6 159 CV77
Atwoods All, Rich. TW9 158 CN81
Auber Cl, Hodd. EN11 33 DZ14
Aubert Ct, N5 121 DP63
Aubert Pk, N5 121 DP63
Aubert Rd, N5 121 DP63
Aubrey Av, Lon.Col. AL2 61 CJ26
Aubrey Beardsley Ho, SW1
off Vauxhall Br Rd 297 M9
Aubrey Moore Pt, E15 280 F10
Aubrey Pl, NW8 283 N1
Aubrey Rd, E17 123 EA55
N8 121 DL57
W8 295 H2
Aubreys Rd, Hem.H. HP1 39 BE21
Aubrey Wk, W8 295 H3
Aubrietia Cl, Rom. RM3 106 FL53
Auburn Cl, SE14 313 L5
Aubyn Hill, SE27 182 DQ91
Aubyn Sq, SW15 159 CU84
Auckland Av, Rain. RM13 147 FF69
Auckland Cl, SE19 202 DT95
Enfield EN1 82 DV37
Tilbury RM18 171 GG82
Auckland Gdns, SE19 202 DS95
Auckland Hill, SE27 182 DQ91
Auckland Ri, SE19 202 DS95
Auckland Rd, E10 123 EB62
SE19 202 DT95
SW11 160 DE84
Caterham CR3 236 DS122
Ilford IG1 125 EP60
Kingston upon Thames KT1 198 CM98
Potters Bar EN6 63 CY32
Auckland St, SE11 310 C1
Auden Dr, Borwd. WD6 78 CN43
Auden Pl, NW1 274 G8
Sutton SM3
off Wordsworth Dr 217 CW105
Audleigh Pl, Chig. IG7 103 EN51
Audley Cl, N10 99 DH52
SW11 309 H10
Addlestone KT15 212 BH106
Borehamwood WD6 78 CN41
Audley Ct, E18 124 EF56
Pinner HA5
off Rickmansworth Rd 94 BW54
Audley Dr, E16 304 A2
Warlingham CR6 236 DW115
Audley Firs, Hersham KT12 214 BW105
Audley Gdns, Ilf. IG3 125 ET61
Loughton IG10 85 EQ40
Waltham Abbey EN9 67 EC34
Audley Pl, Sutt. SM2 218 DB108
Sch Audley Prim Sch, Cat. CR3
off Whyteleafe Rd 236 DT121
Audley Rd, NW4 119 CV58
W5 138 CM71
Enfield EN2 81 DP40
Richmond TW10 178 CM85
Audley Sq, W1 297 H2
Audley Wk, Orp. BR5 206 EW100
Audrey Cl, Beck. BR3 203 EB100
Audrey Gdns, Wem. HA0 117 CH61
Audrey Rd, Ilf. IG1 125 EP62
Audrey St, E2 278 C10
Audric Cl, Kings.T. KT2 198 CN95
Audwick Cl, Chsht EN8 67 DX28
Augur Cl, Stai. TW18 173 BF92
Augurs La, E13 292 B2
Augusta Cl, W.Mol. KT8
off Freeman Dr 196 BZ97
Augusta Rd, Twick. TW2 176 CC89
Augusta St, E14 290 C8
August End, Geo.Grn SL3 132 AY72
Augustine Cl, Colnbr. SL3 153 BE83
Augustine Ct, Wal.Abb. EN9
off Beaulieu Dr 67 EB33
Whyteleafe CR3
off Godstone Rd 236 DU119
Augustine Rd, W14 294 C7
Gravesend DA12 191 GJ87
Harrow HA3 94 CB53
Orpington BR5 206 EX97
August La, Albury GU5 260 BK144
Augustus Cl, W12
off Goldhawk Rd 159 CV75
Brentford TW8 157 CJ80
St. Albans AL3 42 CA22
Stanmore HA7 95 CK48
Augustus Ct, SE1 299 N8
Augustus Ho, NW1
off Augustus St 285 L2
Augustus La, Orp. BR6 206 EU103
Augustus Rd, SW19 179 CY88
Augustus St, NW1 285 K1
Aulay Lawrence Ct, N9
off Menon Dr 100 DV48
Aultone Way, Cars. SM5 200 DF104
Sutton SM1 200 DB103
Aultone Yd, Cars. SM5 200 DF104
Aulton Pl, SE11 310 F1
Aurelia Gdns, Croy. CR0 201 DM99
Aurelia Rd, Croy. CR0 201 DL100
Auriel Av, Dag. RM10 147 FD65
Auriga Ms, N1 277 M2
Auriol Cl, Wor.Pk. KT4
off Auriol Pk Rd 198 CS104
Auriol Dr, Grnf. UB6 137 CD66
Uxbridge UB10 134 BN65
Sch Auriol Jun Sch, Ewell KT19
off Vale Rd 217 CT105
Auriol Pk Rd, Wor.Pk. KT4 198 CS104
Auriol Rd, W14 294 E9
Aurora Cl, Wat. WD25 60 BW34
Aurora Ct, Edg. HA8
off Fortune Ave 96 CP53
Grav. DA12 off Canal Rd 191 GJ86
Aurum Cl, Horl. RH6 269 DH149
Austell Gdns, NW7 96 CS48
Austen Apts, SE20
off Croydon Rd 202 DV96
Austen Cl, SE28 146 EV74
Greenhithe DA9 189 FW85
Loughton IG10 85 ER41
Tilbury RM18
off Coleridge Rd 171 GJ82
Austen Gdns, Dart. DA1 168 FM84
Austen Ho, NW6 283 J2
Austen Rd, Erith DA8 167 FB80
Guildford GU1 259 AZ135
Harrow HA2 116 CB61
Austenway, Chal.St.P. SL9 112 AX55
Austen Way, Slou. SL3 153 AZ79

Austenwood Cl, Chal.St.P. SL9 90 AW54
Austenwood La, Chal.St.P. SL9 90 AX54
Austin Av, Brom. BR2 204 EL99
Austin Cl, SE23 183 DZ87
Coulsdon CR5 235 DP118
Twickenham TW1 177 CJ85
Austin Ct, E6 *off Kings Rd* 144 EJ67
Austin Friars, EC2 287 M8
Austin Friars Pas, EC2 287 M8
Austin Friars Sq, EC2 287 M8
Austin Rd, SW11 41 G7
Hayes UB3 155 BT75
Northfleet DA11 191 GF88
Orpington BR5 206 EU100
Austin's La, Uxb. UB10 115 BQ62
Austins Mead, Bov. HP3 57 BB28
Austins Pl, Hem.H. HP2
off St. Mary's Rd 40 BK19
Austin St, E2 288 A3
Austin Waye, Uxb. UB8 134 BJ67
Austral Cl, Sid. DA15 185 ET90
Austral Dr, Horn. RM11 128 FK59
Australia Rd, W12 139 CV73
Slough SL1 132 AV74
Austral St, SE11 298 G8
Austyn Gdns, Surb. KT5 198 CP102
Austyns Pl, Ewell KT17 217 CU109
Autumn Cl, SW19 180 DC93
Enfield EN1 82 DU39
Slough SL1 131 AM74
Autumn Dr, Sutt. SM2 218 DB109
Autumn Glades, Hem.H. HP3 41 BQ22
Autumn Gro, Brom. BR1 184 EH93
Welwyn Garden City AL7 30 DB11
Autumn St, E3 280 B9
Auxiliaries Way, Uxb. UB9 113 BF57
Avalon Cl, SW20 199 CY96
W13 137 CG71
Enfield EN2 81 DN40
Orpington BR6 206 EX104
Watford WD25 60 BY32
Avalon Ct, Bushey WD23 76 CA40
Avalon Rd, SW6 307 L6
W13 137 CG70
Orpington BR6 206 EW103
Avante Ct, Kings.T. KT1 197 CK97
Sch Avanti Ct Prim Sch, Barkingside IG6
off Carlton Dr 125 ER55
Avard Gdns, Orp. BR6 223 EQ105
Avarn Rd, SW17 180 DF93
Avebury, Slou. SL1 131 AN74
Avebury Ct, N1
off Avebury St 277 L9
Hemel Hempstead HP2 40 BN17
Avebury Pk, Surb. KT6 197 CK101
Avebury Rd, E11 123 ED60
off Southwest Rd
SW19 199 CZ95
Orpington BR6 205 ER104
Avebury St, N1 277 L9
AVELEY, S.Ock. RM15 149 FR73
Aveley Bypass, S.Ock. RM15 148 FQ73
Aveley Cl, Aveley RM15 149 FR74
Erith DA8 167 FF79
Sch Aveley Prim Sch, Aveley RM15 *off Stifford Rd* 149 FS74
Aveley Rd, Rom. RM1 127 FD56
Upminster RM14 148 FP65
Aveline St, SE11 310 E1
Aveling Cl, Pur. CR8 219 DM113
Aveling Pk Rd, E17 101 EA54
Avelon Rd, Rain. RM13 147 FG67
Romford RM5 105 FD51
Avenell Rd, N5 121 DP62
Avening Rd, SW18
off Brathway Rd 180 DA87
Avening Ter, SW18 180 DA86
Avenons Rd, E13 291 N5
Avenue, The, E4 101 ED51
E11 (Leytonstone) 124 EF61
E11 (Wanstead) 124 EH58
N3 98 DA54
N8 121 DN55
N10 99 DJ54
N11 99 DH49
N17 100 DS54
NW6 272 E7
NW10 *off Hillside* 138 CR67
SE10 314 G4
SW4 180 DG85
SW11 180 DE87
SW18 180 DE87
W4 158 CS76
W13 137 CH73
Amersham HP7 55 AQ38
Barnet EN5 79 CY41
Beckenham BR3 203 EB95
Bexley DA5 186 EX87
Brentwood CM13 107 FW51
Brockham RH3 248 CN134
Bromley BR1 204 EK97
Bushey WD23 76 BZ42
Carshalton SM5 218 DG108
Cheam SM3 217 CW108
Chobham GU24 210 AT109
Claygate KT10 215 CE107
Coulsdon CR5 235 DK115
Cowley UB8 134 BK70
Cranford TW5 155 BU81
Croydon CR0 202 DS104
Datchet SL3 152 AV81
Egham TW20 173 BB91
Epsom KT17 217 CV108
Farnham Common SL2 111 AP64
Gravesend DA11 191 GG88
Greenhithe DA9 169 FV84
Hampton TW12 176 BZ93
Harrow HA3 95 CF53
Hatch End HA5 94 CA52
Hemel Hempstead HP1 39 BE19
Hertford SG14 31 DP07
Hoddesdon EN11 49 DZ19
Horley RH6 268 DF149
Hornchurch RM12 128 FJ61
Hounslow TW3 176 CB85
Ickenham UB10 114 BN63
Isleworth TW7 157 CD79
Keston BR2 204 EK104
Leatherhead KT22 215 CF112
Loughton IG10 84 EK44
Nazeing EN9 68 EJ25
New Haw KT15 212 BG110
Northwood HA6 93 BQ51
Old Windsor SL4 172 AV85
Orpington BR6 205 ET103
Pinner HA5 116 BZ58
Potters Bar EN6 63 CZ30
Radlett WD7 61 CG33
Avenue, The, Richmond TW9 158 CM82
Romford RM1 127 FD56
St. Paul's Cray BR5 186 EV94
South Nutfield RH1 267 DL137
Staines-upon-Thames TW18 194 BH95
Sunbury-on-Thames TW16 195 BV95
Surbiton KT5 198 CM100
Sutton SM2 217 CZ109
Tadworth KT20 233 CV122
Twickenham TW1 177 CJ85
Watford WD17 75 BU40
Wembley HA9 118 CM61
West Drayton UB7 154 BL76
West Wickham BR4 203 EC101
Westerham TN16 239 EM122
Whyteleafe CR3 236 DU119
Worcester Park KT4 199 CT103
Worplesdon GU3 242 AS121
Wraysbury TW19 152 AX83
Avenue App, Kings L. WD4 58 BN30
Avenue Cl, N14 81 DJ44
NW8 274 D9
Hounslow TW5 155 BU81
Romford RM3 106 FM52
Tadworth KT20 233 CV122
West Drayton UB7 154 BK76
Avenue Ct, Tad. KT20
off The Avenue 233 CV123
Avenue Cres, W3 158 CP75
Hounslow TW5 155 BV80
Avenue Dr, Slou. SL3 133 AZ71
Avenue Elmers, Surb. KT6 198 CL99
Avenue Gdns, SE25 202 DU97
SW14 158 CS83
W3 158 CP75
Horley RH6 269 DJ149
Hounslow TW5 155 BU80
Teddington TW11 177 CF94
Avenue Gate, Loug. IG10 84 EJ44
● **Avenue Ind Est**, E4 101 DZ51
Romford RM3 106 FK54
Ave Maria La, EC4 287 H9
Avenue Ms, N10 121 DH55
Avenue Pk Rd, SE27 181 DP89
Sch Avenue Prim Sch, E12
off Meanley Rd 124 EL64
Cheam SM2
off Avenue Rd 218 DA110
Avenue Ri, Bushey WD23 76 CA43
Avenue Road 203 DX96
Avenue Rd, E7 124 EH64
N6 121 DJ59
N12 98 DC49
N14 99 DH45
N15 122 DR57
NW3 274 A6
NW8 274 B7
NW10 139 CT68
SE20 202 DW95
SE25 202 DU96
SW16 201 DK96
SW20 199 CV96
W3 158 CP75
Banstead SM7 234 DB115
Beckenham BR3 202 DW95
Belvedere DA17 167 FC77
Bexleyheath DA7 166 EY83
Brentford TW8 157 CJ78
Caterham CR3 236 DR122
Chadwell Heath RM6 126 EV59
Cobham KT11 230 BX116
Epsom KT18 216 CR114
Erith DA8 167 FC80
Feltham TW13 175 BT90
Hampton TW12 196 CB95
Harold Wood RM3 106 FM52
Hoddesdon EN11 49 ED19
Isleworth TW7 157 CF81
Kingston upon Thames KT1 198 CL97
New Malden KT3 198 CS98
Pinner HA5 116 BY55
St. Albans AL1 43 CE19
Sevenoaks TN13 257 FJ123
Southall UB1 156 BZ75
Staines-upon-Thames TW18 173 BD92
Sutton SM2 218 DA110
Tatsfield TN16 238 EL120
Teddington TW11 177 CG94
Theydon Bois CM16 85 ER36
Wallington SM6 219 DJ108
Warley CM14 108 FW49
Woodford Green IG8 102 EJ51
Avenue Rd Est, E11
off High Rd Leytonstone 123 ED63
Avenue S, Surb. KT5 198 CM101
Avenue Ter, N.Mal. KT3
off Kingston Rd 198 CQ97
Watford WD19 76 BY44
Averil Ct, Tap. SL6 130 AJ72
Averil Gro, SW16 181 DP93
Averill St, W6 306 C3
Avern Gdns, W.Mol. KT8 196 CB98
Avern Rd, W.Mol. KT8 196 CB99
Avery Fm Row, SW1 297 J9
Avery Gdns, Ilf. IG2 125 EM57
AVERY HILL, SE9 185 EQ86
★ **Avery Hill Pk**, SE9 185 EQ86
Avery Hill Rd, SE9 185 ER86
Avery Row, W1 285 J10
Avey La, High Beach IG10 84 EH39
Waltham Abbey EN9 83 ED36
Avia Cl, Hem.H. HP3 40 BK24
Avian Ave, Frog. AL2 61 CE28
Aviary Cl, E16 291 M7
Aviary Rd, Wok. GU22 228 BG116
Aviation Dr, NW9 97 CT54
● **Aviator Pk**, Add. KT15 194 BK104
Aviemore Cl, Beck. BR3 203 DZ99
Aviemore Way, Beck. BR3 203 DY99
Sch Avigdor Hirsch Torah Temimah Prim Sch, NW2
off Parkside 119 CV63
Avignon Rd, SE4 313 K10
Avington Cl, Guil. GU1
off London Rd 242 AY134
Avington Ct, SE1
off Old Kent Rd 299 P9
Avington Gro, SE20 182 DW94
Avion Cres, NW9 97 CU53
Avior Dr, Nthwd. HA6 93 BT49
Avis Gro, Croy. CR0 221 DY110
Avis Sq, E1 289 K8
Avoca Rd, SW17 180 DG91
Avocet, Hem.H. HP3 40 BJ24
Avocet Cl, SE1 300 C10
St. Albans AL3 42 CC17
Avocet Ms, SE28 165 ER76
Avon Cl, Add. KT15 212 BG107
Gravesend DA12 191 GK89
Hayes UB4 136 BW70
Slough SL1 131 AL73
Sutton SM1 218 DC105
Watford WD25 60 BW34
Worcester Park KT4 199 CU103
Avon Ct, Buck.H. IG9
off Chequers 102 EH46
Greenford UB6 *off Braund Av* 136 CB70
Avondale Av, N12 98 DB50
NW2 118 CS62
Barnet EN4 98 DF46
Esher KT10 197 CG104
Staines-upon-Thames TW18 173 BF94
Worcester Park KT4 199 CT102
Avondale Cl, Hersham KT12
off Pleasant Pl 214 BW106
Horley RH6 268 DF146
Loughton IG10 103 EM45
Avondale Ct, E11 124 EE60
E16 291 K6
E18 102 EH53
Avondale Cres, Enf. EN3 83 DY41
Ilford IG4 124 EK57
Avondale Dr, Hayes UB3 135 BU74
Loughton IG10 103 EM45
Avondale Gdns, Houns. TW4 176 BZ85
Avondale Ho, SE1
off Avondale Sq 312 C1
Avondale Pk Gdns, W11 294 E1
Sch Avondale Pk Prim Sch, W11 294 E1
Avondale Pk Rd, W11 282 E10
Avondale Ri, SE15 312 A10
Avondale Rd, E16 291 K6
E17 123 EA59
N3 98 DC53
N13 99 DN47
N15 121 DP57
SE9 184 EL89
SW14 158 CR83
SW19 180 DB92
Ashford TW15 174 BK90
Bromley BR1 184 EE93
Harrow HA3 117 CF55
South Croydon CR2 220 DQ107
Welling DA16 166 EW82
Avondale Sq, SE1 312 C1
Avon Grn, S.Ock. RM15 149 FV72
Sch Avon Ho Sch, Wdf.Grn. IG8
off High Rd Woodford Grn 102 EG49
Avonley Rd, SE14 313 H5
Avonmead, Wok. GU21
off Silversmiths Way 226 AW118
Avon Ms, Pnr. HA5 94 BZ53
Avonmore Av, Guil. GU1 243 AZ133
Avonmore Gdns, W14
off Avonmore Rd 294 G9
Avonmore Pl, W14 294 F8
Sch Avonmore Prim Sch, W14 294 F8
Avonmore Rd, W14 294 G8
Avonmor Ms, Ripley GU23 228 BH122
Avonmouth Rd, Dart. DA1 188 FK85
Avonmouth St, SE1 299 J6
Avon Path, S.Croy. CR2 220 DQ107
Avon Pl, SE1 299 K5
Avon Rd, E17 123 ED55
SE4 314 A10
Greenford UB6 136 CA70
Sunbury-on-Thames TW16 175 BT94
Upminster RM14 129 FR58
Avon Sq, Hem.H. HP2 40 BM15
Avonstowe Cl, Orp. BR6 205 EQ104
Avontar Rd, S.Ock. RM15 149 FV70
Avon Way, E18 124 EG55
Avonwick Rd, Houns. TW3 156 CB82
Avril Way, E4 101 EC50
Avro, NW9
off Boulevard Dr 97 CT54
Avro Way, Wall. SM6 219 DL108
Weybridge KT13 212 BL110
Awlfield Av, N17 100 DR53
Awliscombe Rd, Well. DA16 165 ET82
Axes La, Red. RH1 267 DJ141
Axe St, Bark. IG11 145 EQ67
Axholme Av, Edg. HA8 96 CN53
Axiom Apts, Rom. RM1
off Mercury Gdns 127 FF56
● **Axis Cen**, Lthd. KT22 231 CF119
Axis Ct, SE10 315 J2
SE16 *off East La* 300 D4
● **Axis Pk**, Langley SL3 153 BB78
Axminster Cres, Well. DA16 166 EW81
Axminster Rd, N7 121 DL62
Axon Pl, Ilf. IG1 125 EQ61
Axtaine Rd, Orp. BR5 206 EX101
Axtane, Sthflt DA13 190 FZ94
Axtane Cl, Sutt.H. DA4 208 FQ96
Axwood, Epsom KT18 232 CQ115
Aybrook St, W1 284 G7
Aycliffe Cl, Brom. BR1 205 EM98
Aycliffe Dr, Hem.H. HP2 40 BL16
Sch Aycliffe Dr Prim Sch, Hem.H. HP2 *off Aycliffe Dr* 40 BL16
Aycliffe Rd, W12 139 CT74
Borehamwood WD6 78 CL39
Ayebridges Av, Egh. TW20 173 BC94
Aylands Cl, Wem. HA9 118 CL61
Aylands Rd, Enf. EN3 82 DW36
Sch Aylands Sch, Enf. EN3
off Keswick Dr 82 DW36
Aylesbury Cl, E7 281 M4
Aylesbury Ct, Sutt. SM1
off Benhill Wd Rd 200 DC104
Aylesbury Cres, Slou. SL1 131 AR72
Aylesbury End, Beac. HP9 89 AL54
Aylesbury Est, SE17 311 M1
Aylesbury Rd, SE17 311 M1
Bromley BR2 204 EG97
Aylesbury St, EC1 286 G5
NW10 118 CR62
Aylesford Av, Beck. BR3 203 DY99
Aylesford St, SW1 297 N10
🔒 **Aylesham Cen**, SE15 312 C7
Aylesham Cl, NW7 97 CU52
Aylesham Rd, Orp. BR6 205 ET101
Ayles Rd, Hayes UB4 135 BV69
Aylestone Av, NW6 272 C8
Aylesworth Av, Slou. SL2
off Doddsfield Rd 131 AN69
Aylesworth Spur, Old Wind. SL4 172 AV87
Aylets Fld, Harl. CM18 51 ES19
Aylett Rd, SE25 202 DV98
Isleworth TW7 157 CE82
Upminster RM14 128 FQ61
Ayley Cft, Enf. EN1 82 DU43
Ayliffe Cl, Kings.T. KT1
off Cambridge Gdns 198 CN96
Aylmer Cl, Stan. HA7 95 CG49
Aylmer Dr, Stan. HA7 95 CG49
Aylmer Par, N2 120 DF57
Aylmer Rd, E11 124 EF60
N2 120 DE57
W12 158 CS75
Dagenham RM8 126 EY62
Ayloffe Rd, Dag. RM9 146 EZ65
Sch Ayloff Prim Sch, Elm Pk RM12
off South End Rd 127 FH63
Ayloffs Cl, Horn. RM11 128 FL57
Ayloffs Wk, Horn. RM11 128 FK57
Aylsham Dr, Uxb. UB10 115 BR62
Aylsham La, Rom. RM3 106 FJ49
Aylsham Rd, Hodd. EN11 49 EC15
Aylton Est, SE16 301 H5
Sch Aylward Acad, N18
off Windmill Rd 100 DR49
Aylward Gdns, Chesh. HP5 54 AN30
Sch Aylward Prim Sch, Stan. HA7
off Pangbourne Dr 95 CK50
Aylward Rd, SE23 183 DX89
SW20 199 CZ96
Aylwards Ri, Stan. HA7 95 CG49
Aylward St, E1 288 G8
Aylwyn Est, SE1 299 P6
Aymer Cl, Stai. TW18 193 BE95
Aymer Dr, Stai. TW18 193 BE95
Aynhoe Rd, W14 294 D8
Aynho St, Wat. WD18 75 BV43
Aynscombe Angle, Orp. BR6 206 EV101
Aynscombe La, SW14 158 CQ83
Aynscombe Path, SW14
off Thames Bk 158 CQ82
Aynsley Gdns, Harl. CM17 52 EW15
AYOT GREEN, Welw. AL6 29 CU07
Ayot Grn, Welw. AL6 29 CU06
Ayot Greenway, St.Alb. AL4 28 CN06
Ayot Little Grn, Ayot St.P. AL6 29 CT06
Ayot Path, Borwd. WD6 78 CN37
Ayot St. Peter Rd, Welw. AL6 29 CT05
Ayr Ct, W3 138 CN71
Ayres Cl, E13 291 P3
Ayres St, SE1 299 K4
Ayr Grn, Rom. RM1 105 FE52
Ayron Rd, S.Ock. RM15 149 FV70
Ayrsome Rd, N16 122 DS62
Ayrton Gould Ho, E2 289 K2
Ayrton Rd, SW7 296 A6
Ayr Way, Rom. RM1 105 FE52
Aysgarth Ct, Sutt. SM1
off Sutton Common Rd 200 DB104
Aysgarth Rd, SE21 182 DS86
Aytoun Pl, SW9 310 D9
Aytoun Rd, SW9 310 D9
Azalea Cl, W7 137 CF74
Ilford IG1 125 EP64
London Colney AL2 61 CH27
Azalea Ct, Pur. CR8
off Whytecliffe Rd S 219 DP111
Wok. GU22 226 AX119
Woodford Green IG8
off The Bridle Path 102 EE52
Azalea Dr, Swan. BR8 207 FD98
Azalea Ho, Felt. TW13
off Bedfont La 175 BV88
Azalea Wk, Pnr. HA5 115 BV57
Azalea Way, Geo.Grn SL3
off Blinco La 132 AY72
Azania Ms, NW5 275 J4
Azenby Rd, SE15 312 A8
Sch Azhar Acad Girl's Sch, E7 281 N4
Azile Everitt Ho, SE18
off Blendon Ter 165 EQ78
Azof St, SE10 303 K9
Azura Ct, E15
off Warton Rd 280 F8
Azure Ct, NW9 118 CN57
Azure Pl, Houns. TW3
off Holly Rd 156 CB84

B

Baalbec Rd, N5 277 H3
Baas Hill, Brox. EN10 49 DX21
Baas Hill Cl, Brox. EN10 49 DY21
Baas La, Brox. EN10 49 DY21
Babbacombe Cl, Chess. KT9 215 CK106
Babbacombe Gdns, Ilf. IG4 124 EL56
Babbacombe Rd, Brom. BR1 204 EG95
Baber Br Caravan Site, Felt. TW14 176 BW85
Baber Dr, Felt. TW14 176 BW86
Babington Ct, WC1
off Ormond Cl 286 B6
Sch Babington Ho Sch, Chis. BR7 *off Grange Dr* 185 EM93
Babington Ri, Wem. HA9 138 CN65
Babington Rd, NW4 119 CV56
SW16 181 DK92
Dagenham RM8 126 EW64
Hornchurch RM12 127 FH60
Babmaes St, SW1 297 N1
Babylon La, Lwr Kgswd KT20 250 DA127
Bacchus Wk, N1 287 N1
Bachelors Acre, Wind. SL4 151 AR81
Bachelor's La, Wok. GU23 228 BN124
Baches St, N1 287 M3
Back, The, Pott.End HP4 39 BB16
Back All, Dor. RH4 263 CH136
Back Ch La, E1 288 C10
Back Grn, Hersham KT12 214 BW107
Back Hill, EC1 286 E5
Backhouse Pl, SE17 299 P9
Back La, N8 121 DL57
NW3 *off Heath St* 120 DC63
Bexley DA5 186 FA87
Brentford TW8 157 CK79
Buckhurst Hill IG9 102 EK47
Chalfont St. Giles HP8 90 AU48
Chenies WD3 73 BB38
East Clandon GU4 244 BK130
Edgware HA8 96 CQ53
Godden Green TN15 257 FN124
Hertford SG13 48 DQ18
Ide Hill TN14 256 FC126
Letchmore Heath WD25 77 CE39
Nazeing EN9 50 EJ23
North Stifford RM16 149 FW74
Purfleet RM19 169 FS76
Richmond TW10 177 CJ90
Romford RM6 *off Station Rd* 126 EX59
Sheering CM22 36 FA06
Tewin AL6 30 DE05
Backley Gdns, SE25 202 DU100
Back of High St, Chobham GU24 *off High St* 210 AS111
Back Path, Red. RH1 252 DQ133
Back Rd, Sid. DA14 186 EU91
Backs, The, Chesh. HP5 54 AQ31
Back St, Harl. CM17
off Broadway Av 36 EW11
Bacon Gro, SE1 300 A7
Bacon La, NW9 118 CP56
Edgware HA8 96 CN53
Bacon Link, Rom. RM5 105 FB51
Sch Bacon's Coll, SE16 301 L4
Bacons Dr, Cuffley EN6 65 DL29
Bacons La, N6 120 DG60
Bacons Mead, Denh. UB9 114 BG61
Bacon St, E1 288 B4
E2 288 B4
Bacon Ter, Dag. RM8
off Fitzstephen Rd 126 EV64
Bacton, NW5 274 F2
Bacton St, E2 289 H2
Badburgham Ct, Wal.Abb. EN9 68 EF33
Baddeley Cl, Enf. EN3 83 EA37
Baddow Cl, Dag. RM10 146 FA67
Woodford Green IG8 102 EK51
Baddow Wk, N1 277 J8
Baden Cl, Stai. TW18 174 BG94
Baden Dr, E4 83 EB42
Horley RH6 268 DE147
Baden Pl, SE1 299 L4
Baden Powell Cl, Dag. RM9 146 EY67
Surbiton KT6 198 CM103
Sch Baden-Powell Prim Sch, E5
off Ferron Rd 122 DV62
Baden Powell Rd, Sev. TN13 256 FE121
Baden Rd, N8 121 DK56
Guildford GU2 242 AU132
Ilford IG1 125 EP64
Bader Cl, Ken. CR8 236 DR115
Welwyn Garden City AL7 30 DC09
Bader Gdns, Slou. SL1 151 AN75
Bader Wk, Nthflt DA11 190 GE90
Bader Way, SW15 179 CU86
Rainham RM13 147 FG65
Badger Cl, Felt. TW13 175 BV90
Guildford GU2 242 AV131
Hounslow TW4 156 BW83
Ilford IG2 125 EQ59
Badgers Cl, Ashf. TW15 174 BM92
Borehamwood WD6
off Kingsley Av 78 CM40
Enfield EN2 81 DP41
Harrow HA1 117 CD58
Hayes UB3 135 BS73
Hertford SG13 32 DV09
Woking GU21 226 AW118
Badgers Copse, Orp. BR6 205 ET103
Worcester Park KT4 199 CT103
Badgers Cft, N20 97 CY46
SE9 185 EN90
Broxbourne EN10 49 DY21
Hemel Hempstead HP2 41 BR21
Badgers Dell, Chorl. WD3 73 BB42
BADGERS DENE, Grays RM17 170 FZ77
Badgers Hill, Vir.W. GU25 192 AW99
Badgers Hole, Croy. CR0 221 DX105
Badgers La, Warl. CR6 236 DW120
BADGERS MOUNT, Sev. TN14 225 FB110
Badgers Mt, Orsett RM16 171 GF75
Badgers Ri, Bad.Mt TN14 224 FA110
Badgers Rd, Bad.Mt TN14 225 FB110
Badgers Wk, Chorl. WD3 73 BF42
New Malden KT3 198 CS96
Purley CR8 219 DK111
Whyteleafe CR3 236 DT119
Badgers Wd, Chaldon CR3 252 DQ125
Farnham Common SL2 111 AQ64
Badger Way, Hat. AL10 45 CV20
Badingham Dr, Fetch. KT22 231 CE123
Badlis Rd, E17 101 EA54
Badlow Cl, Erith DA8 167 FE80
Badma Cl, N9
off Hudson Way 100 DW48
Badminton Cl, Borwd. WD6 78 CN40
Harrow HA1 117 CE56
Northolt UB5 136 CA65
Badminton Ms, E16 303 P2
Badminton Pl, Brox. EN10 49 DY20
Badminton Rd, SW12 180 DG86
Badric Ct, SW11 308 B9
Badsworth Rd, SE5 311 J5
Baffin Way, E14 302 F1
Bafton Gate, Brom. BR2 204 EH102
Bagden Hill, Westh. RH5 247 CD130
Bagley Cl, West Dr. UB7 154 BL75
Bagley's La, SW6 307 M7
Bagleys Spring, Rom. RM6 126 EY56
Bagot Cl, Ashtd. KT21 232 CM116
Bagshot Ct, SE18
off Prince Imperial Rd 165 EN81
Bagshot Rd, Enf. EN1 100 DT45
Englefield Green TW20 172 AW94
Bagshot St, SE17 311 P1
Bahram Rd, Epsom KT19 216 CR110
Baildon St, SE8 313 P5
Bailey Cl, E4 101 EC49
N11 99 DK52
SE28 145 ES74
Purfleet RM19 *off Gabion Av* 169 FR77
Windsor SL4 151 AN82
Bailey Cres, Chess. KT9 215 CK108
Bailey Ho, SE18
off Berber Par 164 EL81
Bailey Ms, SW2 181 DN85
W4 *off Herbert Gdns* 158 CP79
Bailey Pl, N16 *off Gillett St* 277 P3
SE26 183 DX93
Bailey Rd, Westc. RH4 262 CC137
Baillie Cl, Rain. RM13 147 FH70
Baillie Rd, Guil. GU1 259 AZ135
Baillies Wk, W5
off Liverpool Rd 157 CK75
Bainbridge Cl, Ham TW10
off Latchmere Cl 178 CL92
Bainbridge Rd, Dag. RM9 126 EZ63
Bainbridge St, WC1 285 P8
Baines Cl, S.Croy. CR2
off Brighton Rd 220 DR106
Baines Wk, Chesh. HP5
off High St 54 AP31
Bainton Mead, Wok. GU21 226 AU117
Baird Av, Sthl. UB1 136 CB73
Baird Cl, E10
off Marconi Rd 123 EA60
NW9 118 CQ58
Bushey WD23 *off Ashfield Av* 76 CB44
Slough SL1 151 AP75

A
B

B

Baird Gdns, SE19 182 DS91
Baird Rd, Enf. EN1 82 DV42
Baird St, EC1 287 K4
Bairny Wd App, Wdf.Grn. IG8
off Broadway Cl 102 EH51
Bairstow Cl, Borwd. WD6 78 CL39
Baizdon Rd, SE3 315 J9
Bakeham La,
Eng.Grn TW20 172 AW94
Bakehouse Ms,
Hmptn. TW12 176 CA94
Bakehouse Rd, Horl. RH6 268 DF146
Baker Boy La, Croy. CR0 221 DZ112
Baker Cres, Dart. DA1 188 FJ87
Baker Hill Cl, Nthflt DA11 191 GF91
Baker La, Mitch. CR4 200 DG96
Baker Pas, NW10
off Baker Rd 138 CS67
Baker Pl, Epsom KT19 216 CQ107
Baker Rd, NW10 138 CS67
SE18 164 EL80
Bakers Av, E17 123 EB58
Bakers Cl, Ken. CR8 220 DQ114
St. Albans AL1 43 CG21
Bakers Ct, SE25 202 DS97
Bakerscroft, Chsht EN8 67 DX28
Bakers End, SW20 199 CY96
Bakers Fld, N7 121 DK63
Bakers Gdns, Cars. SM5 200 DE103
Bakers Gro,
Welw.G.C. AL7 30 DC08
Bakers Hall Ct, EC3
off Great Tower St 299 P1
Bakers Hill, E5 122 DW60
New Barnet EN5 80 DB40
Bakers La, N6 120 DF58
Epping CM16 69 ET30
High Wych CM21 35 ET05
Bakers Mead, Gdse. RH9 252 DW130
Bakers Ms, Orp. BR6 223 ET107
Baker's Ms, W1 284 G8
Bakers Orchard,
Woob.Grn HP10 110 AE58
Bakers Pas, NW3 273 P1
Baker's Rents, E2 288 A3
Bakers Rd, Chsht EN7 66 DV30
Uxbridge UB8 134 BK66
Bakers Row, E15 281 J10
Baker's Row, EC1 286 E5
⊖ Baker Street 284 F6
Baker St, NW1 284 F5
W1 284 F6
Enfield EN1 82 DR41
Hertford SG13 32 DS09
Potters Bar EN6 79 CY35
Weybridge KT13 212 BN105
Bakers Wk, Saw. CM21 36 EY05
Bakers Wd, Denh. UB9 113 BD60
Baker's Yd, EC1 286 E5
Uxbridge UB8
off Bakers Rd 134 BK66
Bakery Cl, SW9 310 D6
Roydon CM19 50 EJ15
Bakery Path, Edg. HA8
off Station Rd 96 CP51
Bakery Pl, SW11
off Altenburg Gdns 160 DF84
Bakewell Way, N.Mal. KT3 198 CS96
Balaams La, N14 99 DK47
Balaam St, E13 291 P4
Balaclava Rd, SE1 300 B9
Surbiton KT6 197 CJ101
Bala Grn, NW9
off Snowdon Dr 118 CS58
Balcary Gdns, Berk. HP4 38 AS20
Balcaskie Rd, SE9 185 EM85
Balchen Rd, SE3 164 EK82
Balchier Rd, SE22 182 DV86
Balchins La, Westc. RH4 262 CA138
Balcombe Cl, Bexh. DA6 166 EX84
Balcombe Gdns, Horl. RH6 269 DJ149
Balcombe Rd, Horl. RH6 269 DH147
Balcombe St, NW1 284 E5
Balcon Ct, W5
off Boileau Rd 138 CM72
Balcon Way, Borwd. WD6 78 CQ39
Balcorne St, E9 279 H7
Balder Ri, SE12 184 EH89
Balderton St, W1 285 H9
Baldocks Rd, They.B. CM16 85 ES35
Baldock St, E3 290 C1
Ware SG12 33 DX06
Baldock Way, Borwd. WD6 78 CM39
Baldry Gdns, SW16 181 DL93
Baldwin Cres, SE5 311 J6
Guildford GU4 243 BC132
Baldwin Gdns, Houns. TW3
off Chamberlain Gdns 156 CC81
Baldwin Rd, SW11 180 DG86
Beaconsfield HP9 89 AP54
Burnham SL1 130 AJ69
Watford WD17 75 BU38
Baldwins, Welw.G.C. AL7 30 DB09
Baldwin's Gdns, EC1 286 E6
Baldwins Hill, Loug. IG10 85 EM40
Baldwins La,
Crox.Grn WD3 74 BN42
Baldwins Shore, Eton SL4 151 AR79
Baldwin St, EC1 287 L3
Baldwin Ter, N1 277 J10
Baldwyn Gdns, W3 138 CQ73
Baldwyns Pk, Bex. DA5 187 FD89
Baldwyns Rd, Bex. DA5 187 FD89
Balearic Apts, E16
off Western Gateway 303 P1
Bale Rd, E1 289 L6
Coll Bales Coll, W10 282 D3
Balfern Gro, W4 158 CS78
Balfern St, SW11 308 D7
Balfe St, N1 286 B1
Balfont Cl, S.Croy. CR2 220 DU113
Balfour Av, W7 137 CF74
Woking GU22 226 AY122
● Balfour Business Cen,
Sthl. UB2 156 BX76
Balfour Gro, N20 98 DF48
Balfour Ho, Ilf. IG1
off High Rd 125 ER61
W10 282 D6
Balfour Ms, N9 100 DU48
W1 297 H2
Bovingdon HP3 57 AZ27
Balfour Pl, SW15 159 CV84
W1 297 H1
Balfour Rd, N5 277 J1
SE25 202 DU98
SW19 180 DB94
W3 138 CQ71
W13 157 CG75
Bromley BR2 204 EK99
Carshalton SM5 218 DF108
Grays RM17 170 GC77
Harrow HA1 117 CD57
Hounslow TW3 156 CB83
Ilford IG1 125 EP61
Southall UB2 156 BX76
Weybridge KT13 212 BN105
Balfour St, SE17 299 L8
Hertford SG14 32 DQ08
Balfron Twr, E14 290 E8
Balgonie Rd, E4 101 ED46
Balgores Cres, Rom. RM2 127 FH55
Balgores La, Rom. RM2 127 FH55
Balgores Sq, Rom. RM2 127 FH56
Balgowan Cl, N.Mal. KT3 198 CS99
Sch Balgowan Prim Sch,
Beck. BR3 off Balgowan Rd 203 DY96
Balgowan Rd, Beck. BR3 203 DY97
Balgowan St, SE18 165 ET77
BALHAM, SW12 180 DF88
≠ Balham 181 DH88
⊖ Balham 181 DH88
Balham Continental Mkt,
SW12 off Shipka Rd 181 DH88
Balham Gro, SW12 180 DG87
Balham High Rd, SW12 180 DG88
SW17 180 DG89
Balham Hill, SW12 181 DH87
Balham New Rd, SW12 181 DH87
Balham Pk Rd, SW12 180 DF88
Balham Rd, N9 100 DU47
Balham Sta Rd, SW12 181 DH88
Balkan Wk, E1 300 E1
Balladier Wk, E14 290 C7
Ballamore Rd, Brom. BR1 184 EG90
Ballance Rd, E9 279 K4
Ballands N, The, Fetch. KT22 231 CE122
Ballands S, The, Fetch. KT22 231 CE123
Ballantine St, SW18 160 DC84
Ballantyne Cl, SE9 184 EL91
Ballantyne Dr, Kgswd KT20 233 CZ121
Ballard Cl, Kings.T. KT2 178 CR94
Ballard Grn, Wind. SL4 151 AL80
Ballards Cl, Dag. RM10 147 FB67
Ballards Fm Rd, Croy. CR0 220 DU107
South Croydon CR2 220 DU107
Ballards Grn, Tad. KT20 233 CY119
Ballards La, N3 98 DA53
N12 98 DA53
Oxted RH8 254 EJ129
Ballards Ms, Edg. HA8 96 CN51
Ballards Ri, S.Croy. CR2 220 DU107
Ballards Rd, NW2 119 CU61
Dagenham RM10 147 FB67
Ballards Way, Croy. CR0 220 DV107
South Croydon CR2 220 DU107
Ballast Quay, SE10 303 H10
Ballater Cl, Wat. WD19 94 BW49
Ballater Rd, SW2 161 DL84
South Croydon CR2 220 DT106
Ball Ct, EC3
off Castle Ct 287 M9
Ballenger Ct, Wat. WD18 75 BV41
Ballina St, SE23 183 DX87
Ballin Ct, E14
off Stewart St 302 F5
Ballingdon Rd, SW11 180 DG86
Ballinger Ct, Berk. HP4 38 AV20
Ballinger Pt, E3 290 C2
Ballinger Way, Nthlt. UB5 136 BY70
Balliol Av, E4 101 ED49
Balliol Rd, N17 100 DS53
W10 282 B8
Welling DA16 166 EV82
Balloch Rd, SE6 183 ED88
Ballogie Av, NW10 118 CS63
Ballota Ct, Edg. HA8
off Fortune Ave 96 CP53
Ballow Cl, SE5 311 N5
Balls Pk, Hert. SG13 32 DT11
Balls Pond Pl, N1 277 M4
Balls Pond Rd, N1 277 M4
Balmain Cl, W5 137 CK74
Balmer Rd, E3 289 N1
Balmes Rd, N1 277 M8
Balmoral Apts, W2 off Praed St 284 C7
Balmoral Av, N11 98 DG50
Beckenham BR3 203 DY98
Balmoral Cl, SW15 179 CX86
Park Street AL2 60 CC28
Slough SL1 131 AL72
Balmoral Ct, Wor.Pk. KT4 199 CV103
Balmoral Cres, W.Mol. KT8 196 CA97
Balmoral Dr, Borwd. WD6 78 CR43
Hayes UB4 135 BT71
Southall UB1 136 BZ70
Woking GU22 227 BC116
Balmoral Gdns, W13 157 CG76
Bexley DA5 186 EZ87
Ilford IG3 125 ET60
South Croydon CR2 220 DR110
Windsor SL4 151 AR83
Balmoral Gro, N7 276 C5
Balmoral Ms, W12 159 CT76
Balmoral Rd, E7 124 EJ63
E10 123 EB61
NW2 139 CV65
Abbots Langley WD5 59 BU32
Enfield EN3 83 DX36
Harrow HA2 116 CA63
Hornchurch RM12 128 FK62
Kingston upon Thames KT1 198 CM98
Pilgrim's Hatch CM15 108 FV44
Romford RM2 127 FH56
Sutton at Hone DA4 188 FP94
Watford WD24 76 BW38
Worcester Park KT4 199 CV104
Balmoral Way, Sutt. SM2 218 DA110
Balmore Cl, E14 290 F8
Balmore Cres, Barn. EN4 80 DG43
Balmore St, N19 121 DH61
Balmuir Gdns, SW15 159 CW84
Balnacraig Av, NW10 118 CS63
Balniel Gate, SW1 297 P10
Balquhain Cl, Ashtd. KT21 231 CK117
Balsams Cl, Hert. SG13 32 DR11
Baltic Apts, E16
off Western Gateway 303 P1
Baltic Cl, SW19 180 DD94
Baltic Ct, SE16 301 K4
Baltic Pl, N1 277 P9
Baltic Quay, SE16 301 M8
Baltic St E, EC1 287 J5
Baltic St W, EC1 287 J5
Baltic Wf, Grav. DA11 191 GG86
Baltimore Ho, SW18 160 DC84
Baltimore Pl, Well. DA16 165 ET82
Baltimore Wharf, E14 302 D6
Balvaird Pl, SW1 309 P1
Balvernie Gro, SW18 179 CZ87
Bamber Ho, Bark. IG11
off St. Margarets 145 EQ67
Bamber Rd, SE15 312 A6
Bamboo Ct, E5 122 DW61
Bamborough Gdns, W12 294 B5
Bamford Av, Wem. HA0 138 CM67
Bamford Rd, Bark. IG11 145 EQ65
Bromley BR1 183 EC92
Bamford Way, Rom. RM5 105 FB50
Bampfylde Cl, Wall. SM6 201 DJ104
Bampton Dr, NW7 97 CU52
Bampton Rd, SE23 183 DX90
Romford RM3 106 FL52
Bampton Way, Wok. GU21 226 AU118
Banavie Gdns, Beck. BR3 203 EC95
Banbury Av, Slou. SL1 131 AM71
Banbury Cl, Enf. EN2
off Holtwhites Hill 81 DP39
Banbury Ct, WC2 286 A10
Sutton SM2 218 DA108
● Banbury Enterprise Cen,
Croy. CR0 off Factory La 201 DP103
Banbury Rd, E9 279 J7
E17 101 DX52
Banbury St, SW11 308 D8
Watford WD18 75 BU43
Banbury Vil, Grav. DA13 190 FZ94
Banbury Wk, Nthlt. UB5
off Brabazon Rd 136 CA68
Banchory Rd, SE3 164 EH80
Bancroft Av, N2 120 DE57
Buckhurst Hill IG9 102 EG47
Bancroft Chase, Horn. RM12 127 FF61
Bancroft Cl, Ashf. TW15
off Feltham Hill Rd 174 BN92
Bancroft Ct, SW8 310 A6
Northolt UB5 136 BW67
Reigate RH2 250 DB134
Bancroft Gdns, Har. HA3 94 CC53
Orpington BR6 205 ET102
Bancroft Rd, E1 289 H3
Harrow HA3 94 CC54
Reigate RH2 250 DA134
Sch Bancroft's Sch, Wdf.Grn.
IG8 off High Rd Woodford Grn 102 EG48
Banders Ri, Guil. GU1 243 BC133
Band La, Egh. TW20 173 AZ92
Bandon Cl, Uxb. UB10 134 BM67
Sch Bandon Hill Prim Sch
(Meadow Field), Wall. SM6
off Sandy La S 219 DK107
Sch Bandon Hill Prim Sch
(Wood Field), Cars. SM5 218 DF108
Bandon Ri, Wall. SM6 219 DK106
Banes Down, Lwr Naze. EN9 50 EE22
Banfield Ct, Lon.Col. AL2 61 CH26
Banfield Rd, SE15 162 DV83
Sch Bangabandhu Prim Sch, E2 289 H3
Bangalore St, SW15 159 CW83
Bangor Cl, Nthlt. UB5 116 CB64
Bangors Cl, Iver SL0 133 BE72
Bangors Rd N, Iver SL0 133 BD67
Bangors Rd S, Iver SL0 133 BE71
Banim St, W6 159 CV76
Banister Ms, NW6 273 L6
Banister Rd, W10 282 D2
⊖ Bank 287 L9
DLR Bank 287 L9
Bank, The, N6
off Cholmeley Pk 121 DH60
Bank Av, Mitch. CR4 200 DD96
Bank Ct, Dart. DA1
off High St 188 FL86
Hemel Hempstead HP1 40 BJ21
Bank End, SE1 299 K2
Bankfoot, Bad.Dene RM17 170 FZ77
Bankfoot Rd, Brom. BR1 184 EE91
Bankhurst Rd, SE6 183 DZ87
Bank La, SW15 178 CS85
Kingston upon Thames KT2 178 CL94
Bank Ms, Sutt. SM1
off Sutton Ct Rd 218 DC107
Bank Mill, Berk. HP4 38 AY19
Bank Mill La, Berk. HP4 38 AY20
★ Bank of England, EC2 287 L9
★ Bank of England Mus, EC2 287 M9
Bank Pl, Brwd. CM14
off High St 108 FW47
Bank Rd, Penn HP10 88 AC47
Banks Ho, SE1 299 J7
Banksian Wk, Islw. TW7 157 CE81
Banksia Rd, N18 100 DW50
Bankside, SE1 299 J1
Dunton Green TN13 256 FE121
Enfield EN2 81 DP39
Epsom KT17 233 CW116
Northfleet DA11 190 GC86
South Croydon CR2 220 DT107
Southall UB1 136 BX74
Woking GU21
off Wyndham Rd 226 AV118
Bankside Av, SE13 163 EB83
Northolt UB5
off Townson Av 135 BU68
Bankside Cl, N4 122 DQ58
Bexley DA5 187 FD91
Biggin Hill TN16 238 EJ118
Carshalton SM5 218 DE107
Harefield UB9 92 BG51
Isleworth TW7 157 CF84
Bankside Dr, T.Ditt. KT7 197 CH102
★ Bankside Gall, SE1 299 H1
Bankside Lofts, SE1 299 H2
Pier Bankside Pier 299 J1
Bankside Rd, Ilf. IG1 125 EQ64
Bankside Way, SE19
off Lunham Rd 182 DS93
Banks La, Bexh. DA6 166 EZ84
Epp. CM16 70 EY32
Bank's La, Eff. KT24 229 BV122
Banks Rd, Borwd. WD6 78 CQ40
Banks Spur, Slou. SL1
off Cooper Way 151 AP75
Bank St, E14 302 B3
Gravesend DA12 191 GH86
Sevenoaks TN13 257 FH125
Banks Way, E12 125 EN63
Guildford GU4 243 AZ131
Banks Yd, Houns. TW5 156 BZ79
Bankton Rd, SW2 161 DN84
Bankwell Rd, SE13 164 EE84
Bann Cl, S.Ock. RM15 149 FV73
Banner Cl, Purf. RM19
off Brimfield Rd 169 FR77
Bannerman Ho, SW8 310 C3
Banner St, EC1 287 K5
Banning St, SE10 315 J1
Bannister Cl, SW2 181 DN88
Greenford UB6 117 CD64
Slough SL3 152 AY75
Bannister Dr, Hutt. CM13 109 GC44
Bannister Gdns, Orp. BR5
off Main Rd 206 EW97
Bannister Ho, E9 279 J3
Harrow HA3
off Headstone Dr 117 CE55
Bannister's Rd, Guil. GU2 258 AT136
Sch Bannockburn Prim Sch, SE2 166 EU77
Sch Bannockburn Prim Sch -
Plumstead, SE18
off Plumstead High St 165 ET77
Bannockburn Rd, SE18 165 ES77
Bannow Cl, Epsom KT19 216 CS105
★ Banqueting Ho, SW1 298 A3
BANSTEAD, SM7 234 DB115
≠ Banstead 217 CY114
Sch Banstead Comm Jun Sch,
Bans. SM7 off The Horseshoe 233 CZ115
Banstead Ct, W12
off Hilary Rd 139 CT73
Jct Banstead Crossroads,
Bans. SM7 217 CZ114
Banstead Gdns, N9 100 DS48
Sch Banstead Inf Sch,
Bans. SM7 off The Horseshoe 233 CZ115
Banstead Rd, Bans. SM7 217 CX112
Carshalton SM5 218 DE107
Caterham CR3 236 DR121
Epsom KT17 217 CV110
Purley CR8 219 DN111
Banstead Rd S, Sutt. SM2 218 DD110
Banstead St, SE15 312 G10
Banstead Way, Wall. SM6 219 DL106
Banstock Rd, Edg. HA8 96 CP51
Banting Dr, N21 81 DM43
Banton Cl, Enf. EN1
off Central Av 82 DV40
Bantry Rd, Slou. SL1 151 AM75
Bantry St, SE5 311 M5
Banwell Rd, Bex. DA5
off Woodside La 186 EX86
Banyard Rd, SE16 300 F7
Banyards, Horn. RM11 128 FL56
Bapchild Pl, Orp. BR5
off Okemore Gdns 206 EW98
Baptist Gdns, NW5 274 G4
Barandon Wk, W11 282 D10
Barataria Pk, Ripley GU23 227 BF121
Barbara Brosnan Ct, NW8 284 A1
Barbara Castle Cl, SW6 307 H3
Barbara Cl, Shep. TW17 195 BP99
Barbara Hucklesby Cl, N22
off The Sandlings 99 DP54
Sch Barbara Speake Stage Sch,
W3 off East Acton La 138 CS73
Barbauld Rd, N16 122 DS62
Barbel Cl, Wal.Cr. EN8 67 EA34
Barber Cl, N21 99 DN45
Barberry Cl, Rom. RM3 106 FJ52
Barberry Rd, Hem.H. HP1 40 BG20
Barber's All, E13 292 A2
BARBICAN, EC2 287 J7
≠ Barbican 287 H6
⊖ Barbican 287 H6
★ Barbican Arts & Conf Cen,
EC2 287 K6
Barbican Rd, Grnf. UB6 136 CB72
Barb Ms, W6 294 B7
Barbon Cl, WC1 286 B6
Barbot Cl, N9 100 DU48
Barchard St, SW18 180 DB85
Barchester Cl, W7 137 CF74
Uxbridge UB8 134 BJ70
Barchester Rd, Har. HA3 95 CD54
Slough SL3 153 AZ75
Barchester St, E14 290 C7
Barclay Cl, SW6 307 J5
Fetcham KT22 230 CB123
Hertford Heath SG13 32 DV11
Watford WD18 75 BU44
Barclay Ct, Hodd. EN11 49 EA18
Slough SL1 151 AQ75
Barclay Oval, Wdf. Grn. IG8 102 EG49
Barclay Path, E17 123 EC57
Sch Barclay Prim Sch, E10
off Canterbury Rd 123 ED58
Barclay Rd, E11 124 EE60
E13 292 C5
E17 123 EC57
N18 100 DR51
SW6 307 J5
Croydon CR0 202 DR104
Barclay Way, W.Thur. RM20 169 FT78
Barcombe Av, SW2 181 DL89
Barcombe Cl, Orp. BR5 205 ET97
Barden Cl, Hare. UB9 92 BJ52
Barden St, SE18 165 ES80
Bardeswell Cl, Brwd. CM14 108 FW47
Bardfield Av, Rom. RM6 126 EX55
Bardney Rd, Mord. SM4 200 DB98
Bardolph Av, Croy. CR0 221 DZ109
Bardolph Rd, N7 121 DL63
Richmond TW9
off St. Georges Rd 158 CM83
Bardon Wk, Wok. GU21
off Bampton Way 226 AV117
Bard Rd, W10 294 C1
Bards Cor, Hem.H. HP1
off Laureate Way 40 BH19
Bardsey Pl, E1 288 G5
Bardsey Wk, N1 277 K5
Bardsley Cl, Croy. CR0 202 DT104
Bardsley La, SE10 314 E3
Bardwell Ct, St.Alb. AL1 43 CD21
Bardwell Rd, St.Alb. AL1 43 CD21
Barfett St, W10 282 G4
Barfield, Sutt.H. DA4 208 FP95
Barfield Av, N20 98 DE47
Barfield Rd, E11 124 EF60
Bromley BR1 205 EN97
Barfields, Bletch. RH1 251 DP133
Loughton IG10 85 EN42
Barfields Gdns, Loug. IG10
off Barfields 85 EN42
Barfields Path, Loug. IG10 85 EN42
Barfleur La, SE8 301 N9
Barfolds, N.Mymms AL9
off Dixons Hill Rd 45 CW23
Barford Cl, NW4 97 CU53
Barford St, N1 276 F9
Barforth Rd, SE15 162 DV83
Barfreston Way, SE20 202 DV95
Bargate Cl, SE18 165 ET78
New Malden KT3 199 CU101
Bargate Ct, Guil. GU2
off Chapelhouse Cl 242 AS134
Barge Ct, Green. DA9 169 FW84
Barge Ho Rd, E16 305 N3
Barge Ho St, SE1 298 F2
Barge La, E3 279 M9
Bargery Rd, SE6 183 EB88
Barge Wk, SE10 303 M6
E.Mol. KT8 197 CD97
Kingston upon Thames
KT1, KT2 197 CK95
Walton-on-Thames KT12 196 BX97
Bargrove Av, Hem.H. HP1 40 BG21
Bargrove Cl, SE20 182 DU94
Bargrove Cres, SE6
off Elm La 183 DZ89
Barham Av, Els. WD6 78 CM41
Barham Cl, Brom. BR2 204 EL102
Chislehurst BR7 185 EP92
Gravesend DA12 191 GM88
Romford RM7 105 FB54
Wembley HA0 137 CH65
Weybridge KT13 213 BQ105
Sch Barham Prim Sch, Wem.
HA0 off Danethorpe Rd 137 CJ65
Barham Rd, SW20 179 CU94
Chislehurst BR7 185 EP92
Dartford DA1 188 FN87
South Croydon CR2 220 DQ105
Baring Cl, SE12 184 EG89
Baring Cres, Beac. HP9 88 AJ52
Sch Baring Prim Sch, SE12
off Linchmere Rd 184 EG87
Baring Rd, SE12 184 EG87
Beaconsfield HP9 88 AJ52
Cockfosters EN4 80 DD41
Croydon CR0 202 DU102
Baring St, N1 277 L9
Baritone Ct, E15
off Church St 281 L9
Barkantine Shop Par, The,
E14 302 A5
Bark Burr Rd, Grays RM16 170 FZ75
Barker Cl, Cher. KT16 193 BE101
New Malden KT3
off England Way 198 CP98
Northwood HA6 93 BT52
Richmond TW9 158 CP82
Barker Dr, NW1 275 M7
Barker Ms, SW4 161 DH84
Barker Rd, Cher. KT16 193 BE101
Barker St, SW10 307 N2
Barker Wk, SW16 181 DK90
Barkham Rd, N17 100 DR52
Barkham Ter, SE1 298 F6
Bark Hart Rd, Orp. BR6 206 EV102
BARKING, IG11 145 EP67
≠ Barking 145 EQ66
⊖ Barking 145 EQ66
⊖ Barking 145 EQ66
Sch Barking Abbey Sch,
Lwr Sch, Bark. IG11
off Longbridge Rd 125 ES64
Upr Sch, Bark. IG11
off Sandringham Rd 145 ET65
Barking & Dagenham Civic Cen,
Dag. RM10 127 FB61
● Barking Business Cen,
Bark. IG11 146 EU69
Coll Barking Coll, Rush Grn RM7
off Dagenham Rd 127 FD61
H Barking Comm Hosp,
Bark. IG11 145 ET66
● Barking Ind Pk, Bark. IG11 145 ET67
Barking Rd, E6 292 D1
E13 292 A3
E16 291 L7
BARKINGSIDE, Ilf. IG6 125 EP55
⊖ Barkingside 125 ER56
Bark Pl, W2 283 L10
Barkston Gdns, SW5 295 L10
Barkston Path, Borwd. WD6 78 CN37
Barkway Ct, N4
off Queens Dr 122 DQ61
Barkway Dr, Orp. BR6 223 EN105
Barkwood Cl, Rom. RM7 127 FC57
Barkworth Rd, SE16 312 F1
Barlborough St, SE14 313 H4
Barlby Gdns, W10 282 C5
Sch Barlby Prim Sch, W10 282 D5
Barlby Rd, W10 282 C6
Barlee Cres, Uxb. UB8 134 BJ71
Barle Gdns, S.Ock. RM15 149 FV72
Barley Brow, Wat. WD25 59 BV31
Barley Cl, Bushey WD23 76 CB43
Wembley HA0 117 CK63
Barleycorn Way, E14 289 N10
Hornchurch RM11 128 FM58
Barley Cft, Harl. CM18 51 ER19
Hemel Hempstead HP2 41 BQ20
Hertford SG14 32 DR07
Barleycroft Grn, Welw.G.C. AL8 29 CW09
Barleycroft Rd, Welw.G.C. AL8 29 CW10
Barley Flds, Woob.Grn HP10 110 AE55
Barleyfields Cl, Rom. RM6 126 EV59
Barley Ho, NW7
off Morphou Rd 97 CY50
Barley La, Ilf. IG3 126 EU60
Romford RM6 126 EV58
Sch Barley La Prim Sch,
Chad.Hth RM6 off Huxley Dr 126 EV59
Barley Mow Caravan Pk,
St.Alb. AL4 44 CM22
Barley Mow Ct, Bet. RH3 248 CQ134
Barley Mow La, St.Alb. AL4 44 CL23
Barley Mow Pas, EC1 287 H7
W4 158 CR78
Barley Mow Rd, Eng.Grn TW20 172 AW92
Barley Mow Way, Shep. TW17 194 BN98
Barley Ponds Cl, Ware SG12 33 DZ06
Barley Ponds Rd, Ware SG12 33 DZ06
● Barley Shotts Business Pk,
W10 off Acklam Rd 282 G6
Barlow Cl, Hat. AL10 44 CR16
Wallington SM6 219 DL108
Barlow Dr, SE18 164 EL81
Barlow Ho, SE16
off Rennie Est 300 F9
Barlow Pl, W1 297 K1
Barlow Rd, NW6 273 H4
W3 138 CP74
Hampton TW12 176 CA94
Barlow St, SE17 299 M8
Barlow Way, Rain. RM13 147 FD71
Barmeston Rd, SE6 183 EB89
Barmor Cl, Har. HA2 94 CB54

Barmouth Av, Perivale UB6 137 CF68
Barmouth Rd, SW18 180 DC86
Croydon CR0 203 DX103
Barnabas Ct, N21
off Cheyne Wk 81 DN43
Barnabas Rd, E9 279 K3
Barnaby Cl, Har. HA2 116 CC61
Barnaby Pl, SW7 296 A9
Barnaby Way, Chig. IG7 103 EP48
Barnacre Cl, Uxb. UB8 134 BK72
Barnacres Rd, Hem.H. HP3 58 BM25
Barnard Acres, Lwr Naze. EN9 50 EE23
Barnard Cl, SE18 305 M8
Chislehurst BR7 205 ER95
Sunbury-on-Thames TW16
off Oak Gro 175 BV94
Wallington SM6 219 DK108
Barnard Ct, Wok. GU21 226 AS118
Barnard Gdns, Hayes UB4 135 BV70
New Malden KT3 199 CU98
Barnard Grn, Welw.G.C. AL7 29 CZ10
Barnard Gro, E15 281 L7
Barnard Hill, N10 98 DG54
Barnard Ms, SW11 160 DE84
Barnardo Dr, Ilf. IG6 125 EQ56
Barnardo Gdns, E1 289 J10
Barnardo St, E1 289 J9
Barnardos Village, Ilf. IG6 125 EQ55
Barnard Rd, SW11 160 DE84
Enfield EN1 82 DV40
Mitcham CR4 200 DG97
Warlingham CR6 237 EB119
Barnard's Inn, EC1 off Holborn 286 F8
Barnards Pl, S.Croy. CR2 219 DP109
Barnard Way, Hem.H. HP3 40 BL21
Barnato Cl, W.Byf. KT14 212 BL112
Barnby Cl, Ashtd. KT21 231 CJ117
Barnby Sq, E15 281 J8
Barnby St, E15 281 J8
NW1 285 M1
Barn Cl, Ashf. TW15 175 BP92
Banstead SM7 234 DD115
Epsom KT18
off Woodcote Side 232 CP115
Farnham Common SL2 111 AP63
Hemel Hempstead HP3 40 BM23
Northolt UB5 136 BW68
Radlett WD7 77 CG35
Tadworth KT20 248 CM132
Welwyn Garden City AL8 29 CW09
Barn Cres, Pur. CR8 220 DR113
Stanmore HA7 95 CJ51
Barncroft Cl, Loug. IG10 85 EN43
Uxbridge UB8 135 BP71
Barncroft Grn, Loug. IG10 85 EN43
Sch Barn Cft Prim Sch, E17
off Brunel Rd 123 DY58
Sch Barncroft Prim Sch,
Hem.H. HP2 off Washington Av 40 BK15
Barncroft Rd, Berk. HP4 38 AT20
Loughton IG10 85 EN43
Barncroft Way, St.Alb. AL1 43 CG21
Barndicott, Welw.G.C. AL7 30 DC09
Barneby Cl, Twick. TW2
off Rowntree Rd 177 CE88
BARNEHURST, Bexh. DA7 167 FD83
⇌ Barnehurst 167 FC82
Barnehurst Av, Bexh. DA7 167 FC81
Erith DA8 167 FC81
Barnehurst Cl, Erith DA8 167 FC81
Sch Barnehurst Inf Sch,
Northumb.Hth DA8
off Barnehurst Cl 167 FC81
Sch Barnehurst Jun Sch,
Northumb.Hth DA8
off Barnehurst Cl 167 FC81
Barnehurst Rd, Bexh. DA7 167 FC82
Barn Elms Cl, Wor.Pk. KT4 198 CS104
Barn Elms Pk, SW15 306 B9
Sch Barn End Cen, Wilm. DA2
off High Rd 188 FJ90
Barn End Dr, Dart. DA2 188 FJ90
Barn End La, Dart. DA2 188 FJ92
BARNES, SW13 159 CU82
⇌ Barnes 159 CU83
Barnes Av, SW13 159 CU80
Chesham HP5 54 AQ30
Southall UB2 156 BZ77
⇌ Barnes Bridge 158 CS82
Barnes Br, SW13 158 CS82
W4 158 CS82
Barnesbury Ho, SW4 181 DK85
Barnes Cl, E12 124 EK63
★ Barnes Common, SW13 159 CU83
Barnes Ct, E16 292 D6
Barnet EN5 80 DB42
Woodford Green IG8 102 EK50
BARNES CRAY, Dart. DA1 167 FH84
Barnes Cray Cotts, Dart. DA1
off Maiden La 187 FG85
Barnes Cray Rd, Dart. DA1 167 FG84
Barnesdale Cres, Orp. BR5 206 EU100
Barnes End, N.Mal. KT3 199 CU99
Barnes High St, SW13 159 CT82
H Barnes Hosp, SW14 158 CS83
Barnes Ho, Bark. IG11
off St. Marys 145 ER67
Barnes La, Kings L. WD4 58 BH27
Barnes Pikle, W5 137 CK73
Sch Barnes Prim Sch, SW13
off Cross St 159 CT83
Barnes Ri, Kings L. WD4 58 BM27
Barnes Rd, N18 100 DW49
Godalming GU7 258 AS143
Ilford IG1 125 EQ64
Barnes St, E14 289 L9
Barnes Ter, SE8 313 P1
Barnes Wallis Cl, Eff. KT24 246 BX127
Barnes Wallis Dr, Wey. KT13 212 BL111
Barnes Way, Iver SL0 133 BF73
Wal.Abb. EN9 68 EG32
BARNET, EN4 & EN5 79 CZ41
Coll Barnet & Southgate Coll,
Grahame Pk campus, NW9
off Grahame Pk Way 97 CT53
Southgate campus, N14
off High St 99 DK47
Wood St campus, Barn. EN5 79 CZ42
Barnet Bypass, Barn. EN5 78 CS41
Borehamwood WD6 78 CS41
Barnet Dr, Brom. BR2 204 EL103
BARNET GATE, Barn. EN5 79 CT44
Barnet Gate La, Barn. EN5 79 CT44
Barnet Gro, E2 288 C2
Barnet Hill, Barn. EN5 80 DA42
H Barnet Hosp, Barn. EN5 79 CX42
Barnet La, N20 97 CZ46
Barnet EN5 79 CZ44
Elstree WD6 77 CK44
★ Barnet Mus, Barn. EN5
off Wood St 79 CY42
Barnet Rd, Barn. EN5 79 CV43
London Colney AL2 62 CL27
Potters Bar EN6 80 DA35
Barnett Cl, Erith DA8 167 FF82
Leatherhead KT22 231 CH119
Wonersh GU5 259 BC143
Barnett La, Won. GU5 259 BB144
● Barnet Trd Est,
High Barn. EN5 79 CZ41
Barnett Row,
Jacobs Well GU4 242 AX129
Barnetts Ct, Har. HA2
off Leathsail Rd 116 CB62
Barnetts Shaw, Oxt. RH8 253 ED127
Barnett St, E1 288 E8
Barnetts Way, Oxt. RH8 253 ED127
Sch Barnett Wd Inf Sch,
Ashtd. KT21 off Barnett Wd La 231 CK117
Barnett Wd La, Ashtd. KT21 231 CJ119
Leatherhead KT22 231 CH120
Barnet Way, NW7 96 CR45
Barnet Wd Rd, Brom. BR2 204 EJ103
Barney Cl, SE7 304 C10
Barn Fld, NW3 274 E3
Barnfield, Bans. SM7 218 DB114
Epping CM16 70 EU28
Gravesend DA11 191 GG89
Hemel Hempstead HP3 40 BM23
Horley RH6 268 DG149
Iver SL0 133 BE72
New Malden KT3 198 CS100
Slough SL1 131 AK74
Barnfield Av, Croy. CR0 202 DW103
Kingston upon Thames KT2 177 CK91
Mitcham CR4 201 DH98
Barnfield Cl, N4
off Crouch Hill 121 DL59
SW17 180 DC90
Coulsdon CR5 236 DQ119
Greenhithe DA9 189 FT86
Hoddesdon EN11 49 EA15
Lower Nazeing EN9 50 EF22
Swanley BR8 207 FC101
Barnfield Gdns, SE18
off Barnfield Rd 165 EP79
Kingston upon Thames KT2 178 CL91
Barnfield Pl, E14 302 B9
Sch Barnfield Prim Sch,
Edg. HA8 off Silkstream Rd 96 CQ53
Barnfield Rd, SE18 165 EP79
W5 137 CJ70
Belvedere DA17 166 EZ79
Edgware HA8 96 CQ53
Orpington BR5 206 EX97
St. Albans AL4 43 CJ17
Sevenoaks TN13 256 FD123
South Croydon CR2 220 DS109
Tatsfield TN16 238 EK120
Welwyn Garden City AL7 29 CY11
Barnfield Way, Oxt. RH8 254 EG133
Barnfield Wd Cl, Beck. BR3 203 ED100
Barnfield Wd Rd, Beck. BR3 203 ED100
Barnham Dr, SE28 145 ET74
Barnham Rd, Grnf. UB6 136 CC69
Barnham St, SE1 299 P4
Barnhill, Pnr. HA5 116 BW57
Barn Hill, Roydon CM19 50 EH19
Wembley HA9 118 CP61
Barnhill Av, Brom. BR2 204 EF99
Sch Barnhill Comm High Sch,
Hayes UB4 off Yeading La 136 BW69
Barnhill La, Hayes UB4 135 BV69
Barnhill Rd, Hayes UB4 135 BV70
Wembley HA9 118 CQ62
Barnhurst Path, Wat. WD19 94 BW50
Barningham Way, NW9 118 CR58
Barn Lea, Mill End WD3 92 BG46
Barnlea Cl, Felt. TW13 176 BY89
Barnmead, Chobham GU24 210 AT110
Barn Mead, Harl. CM18 51 ER17
Theydon Bois CM16 85 ES36
Toot Hill CM5 71 FE29
Barnmead Gdns, Dag. RM9 126 EZ64
Barn Meadow, Epp.Upl. CM16
off Upland Rd 69 ET25
Barn Meadow La, Bkhm KT23 230 BZ124
Barnmead Rd, Beck. BR3 203 DY95
Dagenham RM9 126 EZ64
Barnock Cl, Dart. DA1 187 FE87
Barn Ri, Wem. HA9 118 CN60
BARNSBURY, N1 276 D6
Barnsbury Cl, N.Mal. KT3 198 CQ98
Barnsbury Cres, Surb. KT5 198 CQ102
Barnsbury Est, N1 276 D9
Barnsbury Gro, N7 276 D5
Barnsbury La, Surb. KT5 198 CP103
Barnsbury Pk, N1 276 E6
Sch Barnsbury Prim Sch,
Wok. GU22 off Hawthorn Rd 226 AX121
Barnsbury Rd, N1 276 E10
Barnsbury Sq, N1 276 E7
Barnsbury St, N1 276 E7
Barnsbury Ter, N1 276 D7
Barns Ct, Harl. CM19 51 EN20
Waltham Abbey EN9 68 EG32
Barnscroft, SW20 199 CV97
Barnsdale Av, E14 302 B8
Barnsdale Cl, Borwd. WD6 78 CM39
Barnsdale Rd, W9 283 H4
Barnsfield Pl, Uxb. UB8 134 BJ66
Barnside Ct, Welw.G.C. AL8 29 CW09
Barnsley Rd, Rom. RM3 106 FM52
Barnsley St, E1 288 F4
Barnstaple La, SE13
off Lewisham High St 163 EC84
Barnstaple Path, Rom. RM3 106 FJ50
Barnstaple Rd, Rom. RM3 106 FJ50
Ruislip HA4 116 BW62
Barnston Wk, N1 277 J8
Barnston Way, Hutt. CM13 109 GC43
Barn St, N16 122 DS61
Barnsway, Kings L. WD4 58 BL28
Barnway, Eng.Grn TW20 172 AW92
Barn Way, Wem. HA9 118 CN60
Barnwell Rd, SW2 181 DN85
Dartford DA1 168 FM83
Barnwood Cl, N20 97 CZ46
W9 283 L5
Guildford GU2 242 AS132
Ruislip HA4 115 BR61
Barnwood Rd, Guil. GU2 242 AS133
Barnyard, The, Walt.Hill KT20 233 CU124
Baron Cl, N11 98 DG50
Sutton SM2 218 DB110
Baroness Rd, E2 288 B2
Baronet Gro, N17 100 DU53
Baronet Rd, N17 100 DU53
Baron Gdns, Ilf. IG6 125 EQ55
Baron Gro, Mitch. CR4 200 DE98
Baron Ho, SW19
off Chapter Way 200 DD95
Baron Rd, Dag. RM8 126 EX60
Barons, The, Twick. TW1 177 CH86
⊖ Barons Court 294 E10
Barons Ct, Wall. SM6
off Whelan Way 201 DK104
Barons Ct Rd, W14 294 E10
Baronsfield Rd, Twick. TW1 177 CH86
Barons Gate, Barn. EN4 80 DE44
Barons Hurst, Epsom KT18 232 CQ116
Barons Keep, W14 294 E10
Barons Mead, Har. HA1 117 CE56
Baronsmead Rd, SW13 159 CU81
Baronsmede, W5 158 CM75
Baronsmere Rd, N2 120 DE56
Barons Pl, SE1 298 F5
Baron St, N1 276 E10
Barons Wk, Croy. CR0 203 DY100
Barons Way, Egh. TW20 173 BD93
Reigate RH2 266 DA138
Baronswood, Eng.Grn TW20 172 AX92
Baron Wk, E16 291 L6
Mitcham CR4 200 DE98
Baroque Ct, Houns. TW3
off Prince Regent Rd 156 CC83
Barque Ms, SE8 314 A2
Barrack La, Wind. SL4 151 AR82
Barrack Path, Wok. GU21 226 AT118
Barrack Rd, Guil. GU2 242 AU132
Hounslow TW4 156 BX84
Barrack Row, Grav. DA11 191 GH86
Barracks, The, Add. KT15 194 BH104
Barracks Hill, Colesh. HP7 89 AM45
Barracks La, Barn. EN5
off High St 79 CY41
Barra Cl, Hem.H. HP3 41 BP23
Barra Hall Circ, Hayes UB3 135 BS72
Barra Hall Rd, Hayes UB3 135 BS73
Barrards Way, Seer Grn HP9 89 AQ51
Barrass Cl, Enf. EN3 83 EA37
Barratt Av, N22 99 DM54
● Barratt Ind Est,
Southall UB1 156 CA75
● Barratt Ind Pk, E3 290 E5
Barratt Way, Har. HA3
off Tudor Rd 117 CD55
Barrenger Rd, N10 98 DF53
Barrens Brae, Wok. GU22 227 BA118
Barrens Cl, Wok. GU22 227 BA118
Barrens Pk, Wok. GU22 227 BA118
Barrett Cl, Rom. RM3 105 FH52
Barrett Rd, E17 123 EC56
Fetcham KT22 230 CC124
Barretts Grn Rd, NW10 138 CQ68
Barretts Gro, N16 277 P2
Barretts Rd, Dunt.Grn TN13 241 FD120
Barrett St, W1 285 H9
Barrhill Rd, SW2 181 DL89
Barricane, Wok. GU21 226 AV119
Barrie Cl, Couls. CR5 235 DJ115
Barriedale, SE14 313 M8
Barrie Est, W2 284 A10
Barrier App, SE7 304 E7
Barrier Pt Rd, E16 304 C3
Barrier Pt Twr, E16
off Barrier Pt Rd 304 C4
Barringer Sq, SW17 180 DG91
Barrington Cl, NW5 274 G2
Ilford IG5 103 EM53
Loughton IG10 85 EQ42
Barrington Ct, W3
off Cheltenham Pl 158 CP75
Dorking RH4
off Barrington Rd 263 CG137
Hutton CM13 109 GC44
N10 off Colney Hatch La 98 DG54
Barrington Dr, Fetch. KT22 247 CD125
Harefield UB9 92 BG52
Barrington Grn, Loug. IG10 85 EQ42
Barrington Lo, Wey. KT13 213 BQ106
Barrington Ms, Welw.G.C. AL7 30 DB10
Barrington Pk Gdns,
Ch.St.G. HP8 90 AX46
Sch Barrington Prim Sch, Bexh. DA7
off Barrington Rd 166 EX82
Barrington Rd, E12 145 EN65
N8 121 DK57
SW9 161 DP83
Bexleyheath DA7 166 EX82
Dorking RH4 263 CG137
Loughton IG10 85 EQ41
Purley CR8 219 DJ112
Sutton SM3 200 DA102
Barrington Vil Cl, SE18 165 EN81
Barrow Av, Cars. SM5 218 DF108
Barrow Cl, N21 99 DP48
Barrowdene Cl, Pnr. HA5
off Paines La 94 BY54
Barrowell Grn, N21 99 DP47
Barrowfield Cl, N9 100 DV48
Barrow Gdns, Red. RH1 251 DH132
Barrowgate Rd, W4 158 CQ78
Barrow Grn Rd, Oxt. RH8 253 EC128
Barrow Hedges Cl, Cars. SM5 218 DE108
Sch Barrow Hedges Prim Sch,
Cars. SM5 off Harbury Rd 218 DE108
Barrow Hedges Way,
Cars. SM5 218 DE108
Barrow Hill, Wor.Pk. KT4 198 CS103
Barrow Hill Cl, Wor.Pk. KT4 198 CS103
Barrow Hill Est, NW8 284 C1
Sch Barrow Hill Jun Sch, NW8 284 C1
Barrow Hill Rd, NW8 284 C1
Barrow La, Chsht EN7 66 DT30
Barrow Pt Av, Pnr. HA5 94 BY54
Barrow Pt La, Pnr. HA5 94 BY54
Barrow Rd, SW16 181 DK93
Croydon CR0 219 DN106
Barrowsfield, S.Croy. CR2 220 DT112
Barrows Rd, Harl. CM19 51 EM15
Barrow Wk, Brent. TW8 157 CJ79
Barr Rd, Grav. DA12 191 GM89
Potters Bar EN6 64 DC33
Barrsbrook Fm Rd,
Cher. KT16 193 BE102
Barrsbrook Hall, Cher. KT16 193 BE102
Barrs Rd, NW10 138 CR66
Barr's Rd, Tap. SL6 130 AH72
Barry Av, N15 122 DT58
Bexleyheath DA7 166 EY80
Windsor SL4 151 AQ80
Barry Cl, Grays RM16 171 GG75
Orpington BR6 205 ES104
St. Albans AL2 60 CB25
Barry Ho, SE16
off Rennie Est 300 F10
Barry Rd, E6 293 H8
NW10 138 CQ66
SE22 182 DU86
Bars, The, Guil. GU1 258 AX135
Barset Rd, SE15 312 G10
Barson Cl, SE20 182 DW94
Barston Rd, SE27 182 DQ89
Barstow Cres, SW2 181 DM88
Bartel Cl, Hem.H. HP3 41 BR22
Bartelotts Rd, Slou. SL2 131 AK70
Barter St, WC1 286 B7
Barters Wk, Pnr. HA5
off High St 116 BY55
Barth Ms, SE18 165 ES77
Bartholomew Cl, EC1 287 J7
SW18 160 DC84
Bartholomew Ct, E14
off Newport Av 303 H1
Dorking RH4 off South St 263 CG137
Bartholomew Dr,
Harold Wd RM3 106 FK54
Bartholomew Ho, W10
off Appleford Rd 282 F5
Bartholomew La, EC2 287 M9
Bartholomew Pl, EC1 287 J7
Bartholomew Rd, NW5 275 M5
Bartholomew Sq, E1 288 F4
EC1 287 K4
Bartholomew St, SE1 299 L7
Bartholomew Vil, NW5 275 L5
Bartholomew Way,
Swan. BR8 207 FE97
Barth Rd, SE18 165 ES77
Bartle Av, E6 144 EL68
Bartle Rd, W11 282 D9
Bartlett Cl, E14 290 B8
Bartlett Ct, EC4 286 F8
Bartlett Ms, E14
off East Ferry Rd 302 D10
Bartlett Rd, Grav. DA11 191 GG88
Westerham TN16 255 EQ126
Bartletts, Chal.St.P. SL9 90 AY52
Bartletts Mead, Hert. SG14 32 DR06
Bartletts Pas, EC4 286 F8
Bartlett St, S.Croy. CR2 220 DR106
Bartlow Gdns, Rom. RM5 105 FD53
Barton, The, Cob. KT11 214 BX112
Barton Av, Rom. RM7 127 FB60
Barton Cl, E6 293 K8
E9 279 H2
NW4 119 CU57
SE15 312 F10
Addlestone KT15 212 BG107
Bexleyheath DA6 186 EY85
Chigwell IG7 103 EQ47
Shepperton TW17 195 BP100
Barton Ct, Whyt. CR3 236 DU119
Barton Grn, N.Mal. KT3 198 CR96
Barton Ho, E3
off Bow Rd 290 C2
N1 277 H6
SW6 307 M10
Barton Meadows, Ilf. IG6 125 EQ56
Barton Pl, Guil. GU4
off London Rd 243 BB131
Barton Rd, W14 306 E1
Bramley GU5 259 BA144
Hornchurch RM12 127 FG60
Sidcup DA14 186 EY93
Slough SL3 153 AZ75
Sutton at Hone DA4 208 FP95
Bartons, The, Els. WD6 77 CK44
Barton St, SW1 298 A6
Bartonway, NW8 274 A9
Barton Way, Borwd. WD6 78 CN40
Croxley Green WD3 75 BP43
Bartram Cl, Uxb. UB8 135 BP70
Bartram Rd, SE4 183 DY85
Bartrams La, Barn. EN4 80 DC38
Bartrop Cl, Goffs Oak EN7 66 DR28
Barts Cl, Beck. BR3 203 EA99
Barville Cl, SE4
off St. Norbert Rd 163 DY84
● Barwell Business Pk,
Chess. KT9 215 CK108
Barwell Cres, Bigg.H. TN16 222 EJ113
Barwell La, Chess. KT9 215 CJ108
Barwick Dr, Uxb. UB8 135 BP71
Barwick Ho, W3 158 CQ75
Barwick Rd, E7 124 EH63
Barwood Av, W.Wick. BR4 203 EB102
Bascombe Gro, Dart. DA1 187 FE87
Bascombe St, SW2 181 DN86
Basden Gro, Felt. TW13 176 CA89
Basedale Rd, Dag. RM9 146 EV66
Baseing Cl, E6 293 M10
Basevi Way, SE8 314 C2
Basford Way, Wind. SL4 151 AK83
Bashley Rd, NW10 138 CR70
Basil Av, E6 293 H2
Basildene Rd, Houns. TW4 156 BX82
Basildon Av, Ilf. IG5 103 EN53
Basildon Cl, Sutt. SM2 218 DB109
Watford WD18 75 BQ44
Basildon Rd, SE2 166 EU78
Basildon Sq, Hem.H. HP2 40 BM16
Basil Gdns, SE27 182 DQ92
Croydon CR0 off Primrose La 203 DX102
Basil Ms, Harl. CM17
off Square St 36 EW14
Basilon Rd, Bexh. DA7 166 EY82
Basil St, SW3 296 E6
Basin App, E14 289 M9
E16 305 P1
Basing Cl, T.Ditt. KT7 197 CF101
Basing Ct, SE15 312 B7
Basingdon Way, SE5 162 DR84
Basing Dr, Bex. DA5 186 EZ86
Basingfield Rd, T.Ditt. KT7 197 CF101
Basinghall Av, EC2 287 L7
Basinghall Gdns, Sutt. SM2 218 DB109
Basinghall St, EC2 287 L8
Basing Hill, NW11 119 CZ60
Wembley HA9 118 CM61
Basing Ho, Bark. IG11
off St. Margarets 145 ER67
Basing Ho Yd, E2 287 P2
Basing Pl, E2 287 P2
Basing Rd, Bans. SM7 217 CZ114
Mill End WD3 91 BF46
Basing St, W11 282 G8
Basing Way, N3 120 DA55
Thames Ditton KT7 197 CF101
Basire St, N1 277 J8
Baskerville Gdns, NW10 118 CS63
Baskerville Rd, SW18 180 DE87
Basket Gdns, SE9 184 EL85
Baslow Cl, Har. HA3 95 CD53
Baslow Wk, E5 123 DX63
Basnett Rd, SW11 309 H10
Basque Ct, SE16 301 J4
Bassano St, SE22 182 DT85
Bassant Rd, SE18 165 ET79
Bass Ct, E15
off Plaistow Gro 281 L9
Bassein Pk Rd, W12 159 CT75
Basset Cl, New Haw KT15 212 BH110
Bassett Cl, Sutt. SM2 218 DB109
Bassett Dr, Reig. RH2 250 DA133
Bassett Flds, N.Wld Bas. CM16 71 FD25
Bassett Gdns, Islw. TW7 156 CC80
North Weald Bassett CM16 71 FB26
Bassett Ho, SW19
off Durnsford Rd 180 DB92
Bassett Rd, W10 282 D8
Uxbridge UB8 off Oxford Rd 134 BJ66
Woking GU22 227 BC116
Bassetts, Tats. TN16 238 EJ121
Bassetts Cl, Orp. BR6 223 EP105
Bassett St, NW5 274 G3
Bassetts Way, Orp. BR6 223 EP105
Bassett Way, Grnf. UB6 136 CB72
Slough SL2
off Pemberton Rd 131 AL70
Bassil Rd, Hem.H. HP2 40 BK21
Bassingbourne Cl, Brox. EN10 49 DZ20
Bassingburn Wk, Welw.G.C. AL7 29 CZ10
Bassingham Rd, SW18 180 DC87
Wembley HA0 137 CK65
Bassishaw Highwalk, EC2
off Aldermanbury Sq 287 K7
Basswood Cl, SE15
off Candle Gro 162 DV83
Bastable Av, Bark. IG11 145 ES68
Bastion Highwalk, EC2 287 J7
● Bastion Ho, EC2
off London Wall 287 J7
Bastion Rd, SE2 166 EU78
Baston Manor Rd, Brom. BR2 204 EH104
Baston Rd, Brom. BR2 204 EH102
Sch Baston Sch, Hayes BR2
off Baston Rd 204 EH103
Bastwick St, EC1 287 J4
Basuto Rd, SW6 307 J7
⇌ Bat & Ball 257 FJ121
Jct Bat & Ball Junct,
Sev. TN14 257 FH121
Bat & Ball Rd, Sev. TN14 257 FJ121
Batavia Cl, Sun. TW16 196 BW95
Batavia Ms, SE14 313 M5
Batavia Rd, SE14 313 M5
Sunbury-on-Thames TW16 195 BV95
Batchelor St, N1 276 E10
Batchelors Way, Amer. HP7 55 AR39
Chesham HP5 54 AP29
Batchwood Dr, St.Alb. AL3 42 CC17
Batchwood Gdns, St.Alb. AL3 43 CD17
Batchwood Grn, Orp. BR5 206 EU97
Batchwood Hall, St.Alb. AL3 42 CB17
Sch Batchwood Sch, St.Alb. AL3
off Townsend Dr 43 CD17
Batchwood Vw, St.Alb. AL3 42 CC18
BATCHWORTH, Rick. WD3 92 BM47
BATCHWORTH HEATH, Rick. WD3 92 BN49
Batchworth Heath Hill,
Rick. WD3 92 BN49
Batchworth Hill, Rick. WD3 92 BM48
Batchworth La, Nthwd. HA6 93 BS50
Jct Batchworth Rbt, Rick. WD3 92 BK46
Bateman Cl, Bark. IG11
off Glenny Rd 145 EQ65
Bateman Ct, Croy. CR0
off Harry Cl 202 DQ100
Bateman Ho, SE17 310 G3
Bateman Rd, E4 101 EA51
Croxley Green WD3 74 BN44
Bateman's Bldgs, W1 285 N9
Batemans Ms, Warley CM14
off Vaughan Williams Way 108 FV49
Bateman's Row, EC2 287 P4
Bateman St, W1 285 N9
● Bates Business Cen, Harold Wd.
RM3 off Church Rd 106 FN52
Bates Cl, Geo.Grn SL3 132 AY72
Bates Cres, SW16 181 DJ94
Croydon CR0 219 DN106
● Bates Ind Est,
Harold Wd RM3 106 FP52
Bateson St, SE18 165 ES77
Bateson Way, Wok. GU21 211 BC114
Bates Rd, Rom. RM3 106 FN52
Bate St, E14 289 P10
Bates Wk, Add. KT15 212 BJ108
● B.A.T. Export Ho,
Wok. GU21 226 AY117
Batford Cl, Welw.G.C. AL7 30 DB10
Bath Cl, SE15 312 F5
Bath Ct, EC1 286 E5
EC1 (St. Luke's Est)
off St. Luke's Est 287 L3
Bathgate Rd, SW19 179 CX90
Bath Ho, SE1
off Bath Ter 299 K6
Bath Ho Rd, Croy. CR0 201 DL102
Bath Pas, Kings.T. KT1
off St. James Rd 197 CK96
Bath Pl, EC2 287 N3
Barnet EN5 79 CZ41
Bath Rd, E7 144 EK65
N9 100 DV47
W4 158 CS77
Colnbrook SL3 153 BB79
Dartford DA1 187 FH87
Harlington UB3 155 BQ81
Hounslow TW3, TW4,
TW5, TW6 156 BX82
Romford RM6 126 EY58
Slough SL1 131 AP74
Taplow SL6 130 AF72
West Drayton UB7 154 BK81
Baths Rd, Brom. BR2 204 EK98
Bath St, EC1 287 K3
Gravesend DA11 191 GH86
Bath Ter, SE1 299 J7
Bathurst Av, SW19
off Brisbane Av 200 DB95
Bathurst Cl, Iver SL0 153 BF75
Bathurst Gdns, NW10 139 CV68
Bathurst Ms, W2 284 A10
Bathurst Rd, Hem.H. HP2 40 BK17
Ilford IG1 125 EP60
Bathurst St, W2 284 A10
Bathurst Wk, Iver SL0 153 BE75

B

Bathway, SE18 305 M8
Batley Cl, Mitch. CR4 200 DF101
Batley Pl, N16 122 DT62
Batley Rd, N16
off Stoke Newington High St 122 DT62
Enfield EN2 82 DQ39
Batman Cl, W12 139 CV74
Baton Cl, Purf. RM19 169 FR77
Batoum Gdns, W6 294 B6
Batsford Ho, SW19
off Durnsford Rd 180 DB91
Batson Ho, E1
off Fairclough St 288 D9
Batson St, W12 159 CU75
Batsworth Rd, Mitch. CR4 200 DD97
Batten Av, Wok. GU21 226 AS119
Battenburg Wk, SE19
off Brabourne Cl 182 DS92
Batten Cl, E6 293 K9
Batten St, SW11 308 D10
Batterdale, Hat. AL9 45 CW17
Battersby Rd, SE6 183 ED89
BATTERSEA, SW11 308 F6
Battersea Br, SW3 308 B4
SW11 308 B4
Battersea Br Rd, SW11 308 C5
● Battersea Business Cen, SW11
off Lavender Hill 160 DG83
Battersea Ch Rd, SW11 308 B6
★ Battersea Dogs & Cats Home, SW8 309 K5
Battersea High St, SW11 308 B7
★ Battersea Park, SW11 308 F4
⇌ Battersea Park 309 J6
Battersea Pk Rd, SW8 309 J6
SW11 308 C9
Sch Battersea Pk Sch, SW11 308 F7
Battersea Ri, SW11 180 DE85
Battersea Sq, SW11
off Battersea High St 308 B7
Battery Rd, SE28 165 ES75
Battis, The, Rom. RM1
off South St 127 FE57
Battishill Gdns, N1
off Waterloo Ter 276 G7
Battishill St, N1 276 G7
Battlebridge Ct, N1 276 B10
Battle Br La, SE1
off Tooley St 299 N3
Battlebridge La, Merst. RH1 251 DH130
Battle Cl, SW19 180 DC93
Battledean Rd, N5 276 G2
Battlefield Rd, St.Alb. AL1 43 CF18
Battlemead Cl, Maid. SL6 130 AC68
Battle Rd, Belv. DA17 167 FC77
Erith DA8 167 FC77
BATTLERS GREEN, Rad. WD7 77 CE37
Battlers Grn Dr, Rad. WD7 77 CE37
Batts Hill, Red. RH1 250 DE132
Reigate RH2 250 DD132
Batty St, E1 288 D8
Batwa Ho, SE16 312 F1
Baudwin Rd, SE6 184 EE89
Baugh Rd, Sid. DA14 186 EW92
Baulk, The, SW18 180 DA87
Bavant Rd, SW16 201 DL96
Bavaria Rd, N19 121 DL61
Bavdene Ms, NW4
off The Burroughs 119 CV56
Bavent Rd, SE5 311 K9
Bawdale Rd, SE22 182 DT85
Bawdsey Av, Ilf. IG2 125 ET56
Bawtree Cl, Sutt. SM2 218 DC110
Bawtree Rd, SE14 313 L4
Uxbridge UB8 134 BK65
Bawtry Rd, N20 98 DF48
Baxendale, N20 98 DC47
Baxendale St, E2 288 C2
Baxter Av, Red. RH1 250 DE134
Baxter Cl, Brom. BR1
off Stoneleigh Rd 205 EP97
Slough SL1 152 AS76
Southall UB2 156 CB75
Uxbridge UB10 135 BP69
Baxter Gdns, Noak Hill RM3
off North End 106 FJ47
Baxter Ho, E3
off Bromley High St 290 C2
Baxter Rd, E16 292 D8
N1 277 M5
N18 100 DV49
NW10 138 CS70
Ilford IG1 125 EP64
Watford WD24 75 BU36
Baxter Wk, SW16 181 DK89
Bayards, Warl. CR6 236 DW118
Bay Cl, Horl. RH6 268 DE145
Bay Ct, W5 158 CL76
Baycroft Cl, Pnr. HA5 116 BW55
Baydon Ct, Brom. BR2 204 EF97
Bayes Cl, SE26 182 DW92
Bayeux, Tad. KT20 233 CX122
Bayfield Rd, SE9 164 EK84
Horley RH6 268 DE147
BAYFORD, Hert. SG13 47 DM18
⇌ Bayford 47 DN18
BAYFORDBURY, Hert. SG13 31 DM13
Bayford Cl, Hem.H. HP2 41 BQ15
Hertford SG13 32 DQ11
Bayford Grn, Bayford SG13 47 DN18
Bayford La, Bayford SG13 31 DM14
Bayford Ms, E8 278 F7
Sch Bayford Prim Sch, Bayford SG13 off Ashendene Rd 47 DM18
Bayford Rd, NW10 282 C3
Bayford St, E8 278 F7
Baygrove Ms, Hmptn W. KT1 197 CJ95
Bayham Pl, NW1 275 L10
Bayham Rd, W4 158 CR76
W13 137 CH73
Morden SM4 200 DB98
Sevenoaks TN13 257 FJ123
Bayham St, NW1 275 L9
Bayhorne La, Horl. RH6 269 DJ150
Bayhurst Dr, Nthwd. HA6 93 BT51
★ Bayhurst Wood Country Pk, Uxb. UB9 114 BM56
Bayleaf Cl, Hmptn H. TW12 177 CD92
Bayley Cres, Burn. SL1 130 AG71
Bayleys Mead, Hutt. CM13 109 GC47
Bayley St, WC1 285 N7
Bayley Wk, SE2
off Woolwich Rd 166 EY78
Baylie Ct, Hem.H. HP2
off Baylie La 40 BL18
Baylie La, Hem.H. HP2 40 BL18
Sch Baylis Ct Sch, Slou. SL1
off Gloucester Av 131 AR71
Baylis Ms, Twick. TW1 177 CG87
Baylis Par, Slou. SL1
off Oatlands Dr 132 AS72
Baylis Pl, Brom. BR1 204 EL97
Baylis Rd, SE1 298 E5
Slough SL1 131 AR73
Bayliss Av, SE28 146 EX73
Bayliss Cl, N21 81 DL43
Southall UB1 136 CB72
Bayliss Ct, Guil. GU1
off Mary Rd 258 AW135
Bayly Rd, Dart. DA1 188 FN86
Bay Manor La, Grays RM20 169 FT79
Baymans Wd, Shenf. CM15 108 FY47
Bayne Cl, E6 293 K9
Bayne Hill Cl, Seer Grn HP9 89 AR52
Baynes Cl, Enf. EN1 82 DU40
Baynes Ms, NW3 274 B4
Baynes St, NW1 275 M7
Baynham Cl, Bex. DA5 186 EZ86
Baynton Rd, Wok. GU22 227 BB120
Bayonne Rd, W6 306 E3
Bays Fm Ct, West Dr. UB7 154 BJ80
Bayshill Ri, Nthlt. UB5 136 CB65
Bayston Rd, N16 122 DT62
BAYSWATER, W2 283 M9
⊖ Bayswater 283 L10
Bayswater Cl, N13 99 DP49
Bayswater Rd, W2 284 B10
Baythorne St, E3 289 P6
Bay Tree Av, Lthd. KT22 231 CG120
Baytree Cen, Brwd. CM14
off High St 108 FW47
Bay Tree Cl, Brom. BR1 204 EJ95
Ilford IG6
off Hazel La 103 EP52
Baytree Cl, Chsht EN7 66 DT27
Park St AL2 60 CB27
Sidcup DA15 185 ET88
Bay Tree Ct, Burn. SL1 130 AJ69
Baytree Ho, E4
off Dells Cl 101 EB45
Baytree Ms, SE17 299 L8
Baytree Rd, SW2 161 DM84
Bay Trees, Oxt. RH8 254 EH133
Baytree Wk, Wat. WD17 75 BT38
Baywood Sq, Chig. IG7 104 EV49
Bazalgette Cl, N.Mal. KT3 198 CR99
Bazalgette Ct, W6
off Great W Rd 159 CU78
Bazalgette Gdns, N.Mal. KT3 198 CR99
Bazely St, E14 290 E10
Bazile Rd, N21 81 DN44
Beacham Cl, SE7 164 EK78
Beachborough Rd, Brom. BR1 183 EC91
Beachcroft Av, Sthl. UB1 136 BZ74
Beachcroft Rd, E11 124 EE62
Beachcroft Way, N19 121 DK60
Beach Gro, Felt. TW13 176 CA89
Beach's Ho, Stai. TW18 174 BG92
Beachy Rd, E3 280 A7
Beacon Cl, Bans. SM7 233 CX116
Beaconsfield HP9 88 AG54
Chalfont St. Peter SL9 90 AY52
Uxbridge UB8 114 BK64
Beacon Dr, Bean DA2 189 FV90
Beaconfield Av, Epp. CM16 69 ET29
Beaconfield Rd, Epp. CM16 69 ET29
Beaconfields, Sev. TN13 256 FF126
Beaconfield Way, Epp. CM16 69 ET29
Beacon Gate, SE14 313 J9
Beacon Gro, Cars. SM5 218 DG105
Beacon Hill, N7 276 A2
Penn HP10 88 AD48
Purfleet RM19 168 FP78
Woking GU21 226 AW118
● Beacon Hill Ind Est, Purf. RM19 168 FP78
Sch Beacon Hill Sch, S.Ock. RM15
off Erriff Dr 149 FU71
Post 16 Provision, S.Ock. RM15
off Fortin Cl 149 FU73
Beacon Ri, Sev. TN13 256 FG126
Beacon Rd, SE13 183 ED86
Erith DA8 167 FH80
London Heathrow Airport TW6 174 BN86
Ware SG12 33 EA05
Jct Beacon Rd Rbt, Lon.Hthrw Air. TW6 175 BP86
Beacons, The, Hat. AL10
off Beaconsfield Cl 45 CW17
Loughton IG10 85 EN38
Sch Beacon Sch, The, Bans. SM7
off Picquets Way 233 CY117
Chesham Bois HP6
off Amersham Rd 55 AP35
Beacons Cl, E6 293 H7
BEACONSFIELD, HP9 88 AJ53
⇌ Beaconsfield 89 AL52
Beaconsfield Cl, N11 98 DG49
SE3 315 N2
W4 158 CQ78
Hatfield AL10 45 CW17
Beaconsfield Common La, Slou. SL2 111 AQ57
Beaconsfield Gdns, Clay. KT10 215 CE108
Sch Beaconsfield High Sch, Beac. HP9 off Wattleton Rd 89 AL54
Beaconsfield Par, SE9
off Beaconsfield Rd 184 EL91
Beaconsfield Pl, Epsom KT17 216 CS112
Sch Beaconsfield Prim Sch, Sthl. UB1 off Beaconsfield Rd 156 BY75
Beaconsfield Rd, E10 123 EC61
E16 291 L5
E17 123 DZ58
N9 100 DU49
N11 98 DG48
N15 122 DS56
NW10 139 CT65
SE3 315 M3
SE9 184 EL89
SE17 311 M1
W4 158 CR76
W5 157 CJ75
Bexley DA5 187 FE88
Bromley BR1 204 EK97
Claygate KT10 215 CE108
Croydon CR0 202 DR100
Enfield EN3 83 DX37
Epsom KT18 232 CR119
Hatfield AL10 45 CW17
Hayes UB4 136 BW74
New Malden KT3 198 CR96
Beaconsfield Rd, St. Albans AL1 43 CE20
Slough SL2 131 AQ68
Southall UB1 136 BX74
Surbiton KT5 198 CM101
Twickenham TW1 177 CH86
Woking GU22 227 AZ120
Sch Beaconsfield Sch, The, Beac. HP9
off Wattleton Rd 89 AL54
Beaconsfield St, N1 276 A9
Beaconsfield Ter Rd, W14 294 E7
Beaconsfield Wk, E6 293 M9
SW6 307 H7
Beacontree Av, E17 101 ED53
Beacontree Rd, E11 124 EF59
Beacon Way, Bans. SM7 233 CX116
Rickmansworth WD3 92 BG45
★ Beacon Wd Country Pk, Dart. DA2 189 FV91
Beadles La, Oxt. RH8 253 ED130
Beadlow Cl, Cars. SM5
off Olveston Wk 200 DD100
Beadman Pl, SE27
off Norwood High St 181 DP91
Beadman St, SE27 181 DP91
Beadnell Rd, SE23 183 DX88
Beadon Rd, W6 294 A9
Bromley BR2 204 EG98
Beads Hall La, Pilg.Hat. CM15 108 FV42
Beaford Gro, SW20 199 CY97
Beagle Cl, Felt. TW13 175 BV91
Radlett WD7 77 CF37
Beagles Cl, Orp. BR5 206 EX103
Beak St, W1 285 M10
Beal Cl, Well. DA16 166 EU81
Beale Cl, N13 99 DP50
Beale Pl, E3 279 N10
Beale Rd, E3 279 N9
Beales La, Wey. KT13 194 BN104
Beales Rd, Bkhm KT23 246 CB127
Sch Beal High Sch, Ilf. IG4
off Woodford Br Rd 124 EL56
Bealings End, Beac. HP9 89 AK50
Beal Rd, Ilf. IG1 125 EN61
Beam Av, Dag. RM10 147 FB67
Beames Rd, NW10 138 CR67
Beaminster Gdns, Ilf. IG6 103 EP54
Beaminster Ho, SW8
off Dorset Rd 310 C4
Beamish Cl, N.Wld Bas. CM16 71 FC25
Beamish Dr, Bushey Hth WD23 94 CC46
Beamish Ho, SE16
off Rennie Est 300 G9
Beamish Rd, N9 100 DU46
Orpington BR5 206 EW101
Sch Beam Prim Sch, Dag. RM10
off Oval Rd N 147 FC68
Beamway, Dag. RM10 147 FD66
BEAN, Dart. DA2 189 FV90
Beanacre Cl, E9 279 P4
Beane Cft, Grav. DA12 191 GM88
Beane River Vw, Hert. SG14 32 DQ09
Beane Rd, Hert. SG14 31 DP09
Jct Bean Interchange, Dart. DA2 189 FU89
Bean La, Bean DA2 189 FV89
Sch Bean Prim Sch, Bean DA2
off School La 189 FW91
Bean Rd, Bexh. DA6 166 EX84
Greenhithe DA9 189 FV85
Beanshaw, SE9 185 EN91
Beansland Gro, Rom. RM6 104 EY54
Bear All, EC4 286 G8
Bear Cl, Rom. RM7 127 FB58
Beardell St, SE19 182 DT93
Beardow Gro, N14 81 DJ44
Beard Rd, Kings.T. KT2 178 CM92
Beardsfield, E13 281 N9
Beard's Hill, Hmptn. TW12 196 CA95
Beard's Hill Cl, Hmptn. TW12
off Beard's Hill 196 CA95
Beardsley Ter, Dag. RM8
off Fitzstephen Rd 126 EV64
Beardsley Way, W3 158 CR75
Beards Rd, Ashf. TW15 175 BS93
Bearfield Rd, Kings.T. KT2 178 CL94
Bear Gdns, SE1 299 J2
Bearing Cl, Chig. IG7 104 EU49
Bearing Way, Chig. IG7 104 EU49
Bear La, SE1 299 H2
Bear Pt, SE10 303 M6
Bear Rd, Felt. TW13 176 BX92
Bears Den, Kgswd KT20 233 CZ122
Bears Rails Pk, Old Wind. SL4 172 AT87
Bearstead Ri, SE4 183 DZ85
Bearsted Ter, Beck. BR3 203 EA95
Bear St, WC2 285 P10
Bearswood End, Beac. HP9 89 AL51
Bearwood Cl, Add. KT15
off Ongar Pl 212 BG107
Potters Bar EN6 64 DD31
Beasleys Ait La, Sun. TW16 195 BT100
Beasleys Yd, Uxb. UB8
off Warwick Pl 134 BJ66
Beaton Cl, SE15 312 B6
Greenhithe DA9 169 FV84
Beatrice Av, SW16 201 DM97
Wembley HA9 118 CL64
Beatrice Cl, E13 291 N4
Pinner HA5 115 BU56
Beatrice Ct, Buck.H. IG9 102 EK47
Beatrice Gdns, Nthflt DA11 190 GE89
Beatrice Pl, W8 295 L7
Beatrice Rd, E17 123 EA57
N4 121 DN59
N9 100 DW45
SE1 300 D9
Oxted RH8 254 EE129
Richmond TW10
off Albert Rd 178 CM85
Southall UB1 136 BZ74
Sch Beatrice Tate Sch, E2 288 F2
Beatrice Wilson Flats, Sev. TN13 off Rockdale Rd 257 FH125
Sch Beatrix Potter Prim Sch, SW18 off Magdalen Rd 180 DC88
Beatson Wk, SE16 301 L2
Beattie Cl, Bkhm KT23 230 BZ124
Feltham TW14 175 BT88
Beattock Ri, N10 121 DH56
Beatty Av, Guil. GU1 243 BA133
Beatty Rd, N16 122 DS63
Stanmore HA7 95 CJ51
Waltham Cross EN8 67 DZ34
Beatty St, NW1 275 L10
Beattyville Gdns, Ilf. IG6 125 EN55
Beauchamp Cl, W4
off Beaumont Rd 158 CQ76
Beauchamp Ct, Stan. HA7
off Hardwick Cl 95 CJ50
Beauchamp Gdns, Mill End WD3 92 BG46
Beauchamp Pl, SW3 296 D6
Beauchamp Rd, E7 144 EH66
SE19 202 DR95
SW11 160 DE84
East Molesey KT8 196 CB99
Sutton SM1 218 DA106
Twickenham TW1 177 CG87
West Molesey KT8 196 CB99
Beauchamps, Welw.G.C. AL7 30 DB10
Beauchamp St, EC1 286 E7
Beauchamp Ter, SW15
off Dryburgh Rd 159 CV83
Beauclare Cl, Lthd. KT22
off Delderfield 231 CK121
Sch Beauclerc Inf Sch, Sun. TW16 off French St 196 BW97
Beauclerc Rd, W6 159 CV76
Beauclerk Cl, Felt. TW13 175 BV88
Beaudesert Ms, West Dr. UB7 154 BL75
Beaufort, E6 293 M8
Beaufort Av, Har. HA3 117 CG56
Beaufort Cl, E4
off Higham Sta Av 101 EB51
SW15 179 CV87
W5 138 CM71
Chafford Hundred RM16
off Clifford Rd 170 FZ76
North Weald Bassett CM16 70 FA27
Reigate RH2 249 CZ133
Romford RM7 127 FC56
Woking GU22 227 BC116
Sch Beaufort Comm Prim Sch, Wok. GU21 off Kirkland Av 226 AT116
Beaufort Ct, SW6 307 J2
Richmond TW10 177 CJ91
Beaufort Dr, NW11 120 DA56
Beaufort Gdns, E1 289 K6
NW4 119 CW58
SW3 296 D6
SW16 181 DM94
Hounslow TW5 156 BY81
Ilford IG1 125 EN60
Beaufort Ms, SW6 307 H2
Beaufort Pk, NW11 120 DA56
Beaufort Pl, Bray SL6 150 AD75
Beaufort Rd, W5 138 CM71
Kingston upon Thames KT1 198 CL98
Reigate RH2 249 CZ133
Richmond TW10 177 CJ91
Ruislip HA4 off Lysander Rd 115 BR61
Twickenham TW1 177 CJ87
Woking GU22 227 BC116
Beauforts, Eng.Grn TW20 172 AW92
Beaufort St, SW3 308 B3
Beaufort Way, Epsom KT17 217 CU108
Beaufoy Rd, N17 100 DS52
Beaufoy Wk, SE11 298 D9
Beaulieu Av, E16 304 A2
SE26 182 DV91
Beaulieu Cl, NW9 118 CS56
SE5 311 M10
Datchet SL3 152 AV81
Hounslow TW4 176 BZ85
Mitcham CR4 200 DG95
Twickenham TW1 177 CK87
Watford WD19 94 BW46
Beaulieu Dr, Pnr. HA5 116 BX58
Waltham Abbey EN9 67 EB32
Beaulieu Gdns, N21 100 DQ45
Beaulieu Pl, W4 158 CQ76
Beauly Way, Rom. RM1 105 FE53
Beaumanor Gdns, SE9 185 EN91
Beaumaris Dr, Wdf.Grn. IG8 102 EK52
Beaumaris Gdns, SE19 182 DQ94
Beaumaris Grn, NW9
off Goldsmith Av 118 CS58
Beaumaris Twr, W3 158 CP75
Beaumayes Cl, Hem.H. HP1 40 BH21
Beaumont Av, W14 294 G10
Harrow HA2 116 CB58
Richmond TW9 158 CM83
St. Albans AL1 43 CH18
Wembley HA0 117 CJ64
Beaumont Cl, N2 120 DE56
Kingston upon Thames KT2 178 CN94
Romford RM2 106 FJ54
Beaumont Cres, W14 294 G10
Rainham RM13 147 FG65
Beaumont Dr, Ashf. TW15 175 BR92
Northfleet DA11 190 GE87
Worcester Park KT4 199 CV102
Beaumont Gdns, NW3 120 DA62
Hutton CM13 off Bannister Dr 109 GC44
Beaumont Gate, Rad. WD7 77 CG35
Beaumont Gro, E1 289 J5
Beaumont Ms, W1 285 H6
Pinner HA5 116 BY55
Beaumont Pk Dr, Roydon CM19 50 EH15
Beaumont Pl, W1 285 M4
Barnet EN5 79 CZ39
Isleworth TW7 177 CF85
Watford WD18 75 BU43
Sch Beaumont Prim Sch, E10
off Burchell Rd 123 EB60
Purley CR8 off Old Lo La 219 DN114
Beaumont Ri, N19 121 DK60
Beaumont Rd, E10 123 EB59
E13 292 B3
SE19 182 DQ93
SW19 179 CY87
W4 158 CQ76
Broxbourne EN10 48 DR24
Petts Wood BR5 205 ER100
Purley CR8 219 DN113
Slough SL2 131 AR70
Windsor SL4 151 AQ82
Beaumonts, Red. RH1 266 DF143
Sch Beaumont Sch, St.Alb. AL4
off Oakwood Dr 43 CJ19
Beaumont Sq, E1 289 J6
Beaumont St, W1 285 H6
Beaumont Vw, Chsht EN7 66 DR26
Beaumont Wk, NW3 274 F6
● Beaumont Wks, St.Alb. AL1
off Hedley Rd 43 CH20
Beauvais Ter, Nthlt. UB5 136 BX69
Beauval Rd, SE22 182 DT86
Beaverbank Rd, SE9 185 ER88
Jct Beaverbrook Rbt, Lthd. KT22 231 CK123
Beaver Cl, SE20
off Lullington Rd 182 DU94
Hampton TW12 196 CB95
Morden SM4 199 CW101
Beaver Gro, Nthlt. UB5
off Jetstar Way 136 BY69
● Beaver Ind Pk, Sthl. UB2 156 BW76
Beaver Rd, Ilf. IG6 104 EW50
Beavers Cl, Guil. GU3 242 AS133
Sch Beavers Comm Prim Sch, Houns. TW4 off Arundel Rd 156 BW83
Beavers Cres, Houns. TW4 156 BW84
Beavers La, Houns. TW4 156 BW83
Beaverwood Rd, Chis. BR7 185 ES93
Sch Beaverwood Sch for Girls, Chis. BR7 off Beaverwood Rd 185 ES93
Beavor Gro, W6 off Beavor La 159 CU78
Beavor La, W6 159 CU77
Beazley Cl, Ware SG12 33 DY05
Bebbington Rd, SE18 165 ES77
Beblets Cl, Orp. BR6 223 ET106
Beccles Dr, Bark. IG11 145 ES65
Beccles St, E14 289 P10
Bec Cl, Ruis. HA4 116 BX62
Beck Cl, SE13 314 C7
Beck Ct, Beck. BR3 203 DX97
BECKENHAM, BR3 203 EA95
● Beckenham Business Cen, Beck. BR3 183 DY93
Beckenham Gdns, N9 100 DS48
Beckenham Gro, Brom. BR2 203 ED96
⇌ Beckenham Hill 183 EC92
Beckenham Hill Rd, SE6 183 EB92
Beckenham BR3 183 EB92
H Beckenham Hosp, Beck. BR3 203 DZ96
⇌ Beckenham Junction 203 EA95
Tram Beckenham Junction 203 EA95
Beckenham La, Brom. BR2 204 EE96
Beckenham Pl Pk, Beck. BR3 183 EB94
Tram Beckenham Road 203 DY95
Beckenham Rd, Beck. BR3 203 DX95
West Wickham BR4 203 EB101
Beckenshaw Gdns, Bans. SM7 234 DE115
Beckers, The, N16 122 DU63
Becket Av, E6 293 L2
Becket Cl, SE25 202 DU100
Great Warley CM13 107 FW51
Becket Fold, Har. HA1
off Courtfield Cres 117 CF57
Becket Ho, Brwd. CM14 108 FW47
Becket Rd, N18 100 DW49
Beckets Sq, Berk. HP4
off Bridle Way 38 AU17
Becket St, SE1 299 L6
Beckett Av, Ken. CR8 235 DP115
Beckett Chase, Slou. SL3
off Olivia Dr 153 AZ78
Beckett Cl, NW10 138 CR65
SW16 181 DK89
Belvedere DA17
off Tunstock Way 166 EY76
Beckett Ho, SW9 310 B9
Beckett Rd, Couls. CR5 235 DK122
Becketts, Hert. SG14 31 DN10
Beckett's Av, St.Alb. AL3 42 CC17
Becketts Cl, Bex. DA5 187 FC88
Feltham TW14 175 BV86
Orpington BR6 205 ET104
Becketts Pl, Hmptn W. KT1 197 CK95
Beckett Wk, Beck. BR3 183 DY93
Beckford Cl, W14 295 H9
Beckford Dr, Orp. BR5 205 ER101
Beckford Pl, SE17 311 K1
Sch Beckford Prim Sch, NW6 273 H3
Beckford Rd, Croy. CR0 202 DT100
Beckham Ho, SE11
off Marylee Way 298 D9
Beckingham Rd, Guil. GU2 242 AU132
Beckings Way, Flack.Hth HP10 110 AC56
Beck La, Beck. BR3 203 DX97
Becklow Gdns, W12 159 CU75
Becklow Ms, W12
off Becklow Rd 159 CT75
Becklow Rd, W12 159 CU75
Beckman Cl, Halst. TN14 241 FC115
Sch Beckmead Sch, Beck. BR3
off Monks Orchard Rd 203 EA102
Beck River Pk, Beck. BR3 203 DZ95
Beck Rd, E8 278 E8
Becks Rd, Sid. DA14 186 EU90
BECKTON, E6 293 M7
DLR Beckton 293 L7
Jct Beckton Alps, E6 293 L5
DLR Beckton Park 293 K10
Jct Beckton Pk Rbt, E16 293 J10
Beckton Retail Pk, E6 293 L6
Beckton Rd, E16 291 M6
Beckton Triangle Retail Pk, E6 293 M4
Beck Way, Beck. BR3 203 DZ97
Beckway Rd, SW16 201 DK96
Beckway St, SE17 299 M9
Beckwell Rd, Slou. SL1 151 AQ75
Beckwith Rd, SE24 182 DR86
Beclands Rd, SW17 180 DG93
Becmead Av, SW16 181 DK91
Harrow HA3 117 CH57
Becondale Rd, SE19 182 DS92
BECONTREE, Dag. RM8 126 EY62
⊖ Becontree 146 EW66
Becontree Av, Dag. RM8 126 EV63
BECONTREE HEATH, Dag. RM8 126 FA60
Sch Becontree Prim Sch, Dag. RM8 off Stevens Rd 126 EV62
Bequerel Ct, SE10 303 M7
Bective Pl, SW15
off Bective Rd 159 CZ84
Bective Rd, E7 124 EG63
SW15 159 CZ84
Becton Pl, Erith DA8 167 FB80
Bedale Rd, Enf. EN2 82 DQ38
Romford RM3 106 FN50
Bedale St, SE1 299 L3
Bedale Wk, Dart. DA2 188 FP88
BEDDINGTON, Croy. CR0 201 DK103
BEDDINGTON CORNER, Mitch. CR4 200 DG101
Beddington Cross, Croy. CR0 201 DK102
Beddington Fm Rd, Croy. CR0 201 DL102
Beddington Gdns, Cars. SM5 218 DG107
Wallington SM6 219 DH107
Beddington Grn, Orp. BR5 205 ET95
Beddington Gro, Wall. SM6 219 DK106
Sch Beddington Inf Sch, Wall. SM6 off Croydon Rd 219 DJ105
Tram Beddington Lane 201 DJ100
Beddington La, Croy. CR0 201 DJ99
● Beddington La Ind Est, Croy. CR0 201 DJ100
Sch Beddington Pk Prim Sch, Bedd. CR0 off Mallinson Rd 201 DK104
Beddington Path, Orp. BR5 205 ET95
Beddington Rd, Ilf. IG3 125 ET59
Orpington BR5 205 ES96

● Beddington Trd Pk, Croy. CR0 201 DL102
Beddlestead La, Warl. CR6 238 EF117
Bede Cl, Pnr. HA5 94 BX53
Bedelsford Sch, Kings.T. KT1 off Grange Rd 198 CL97
Bedens Rd, Sid. DA14 186 EY93
Bede Rd, Rom. RM6 126 EW58
Bede Sq, E3 289 P5
Bedevere Rd, N9 100 DU48
Bedfont Cl, Felt. TW14 175 BQ86
Mitcham CR4 200 DG96
Bedfont Ct, Stai. TW19 154 BH84
Bedfont Ct Est, Stai. TW19 154 BG83
Bedfont Grn Cl, Felt. TW14 175 BQ88
Bedfont Inf & Nurs & Jun Schs, E.Bed. TW14 off Hatton Rd 175 BS86
Bedfont La, Felt. TW13, TW14 175 BT87
Bedfont Rd, Felt. TW13, TW14 175 BS89
Stanwell TW19 174 BL86
Bedford Av, WC1 285 P7
Amersham HP6 72 AW39
Barnet EN5 79 CZ43
Hayes UB4 135 BV72
Slough SL1 131 AM72
Bedfordbury, WC2 286 A10
Bedford Cl, N10 98 DG52
W4 158 CS79
Chenies WD3 73 BB38
Woking GU21 226 AW115
Bedford Cor, W4 158 CS77
Bedford Ct, WC2 298 A1
Bedford Cres, Enf. EN3 83 DY35
Bedford Dr, Farn.Com. SL2 111 AP64
Bedford Gdns, W8 295 J3
Hornchurch RM12 128 FJ61
Bedford Hill, SW12 181 DH88
SW16 181 DH88
Bedford Ho, SW4 161 DL84
Guildford GU1 off Bedford Rd 258 AW135
Bedford Ms, N2 120 DE55
SE6 183 EB89
BEDFORD PARK, W4 158 CR76
Bedford Pk, Croy. CR0 202 DQ102
Bedford Pk Cor, W4 off Bath Rd 158 CS77
Bedford Pk Rd, St.Alb. AL1 43 CE20
Bedford Pas, SW6 306 F4
Bedford Pl, WC1 286 A6
Croydon CR0 202 DR102
Bedford Rd, E6 145 EN67
E17 101 EA54
E18 102 EG54
N2 120 DE55
N8 121 DK58
N9 100 DV45
N15 122 DS56
N22 99 DL53
NW7 96 CS47
SW4 161 DL83
W4 158 CR76
W13 137 CH73
Dartford DA1 188 FN87
Grays RM17 170 GB78
Guildford GU1 258 AW135
Harrow HA1 116 CC58
Ilford IG1 125 EP62
Northfleet DA11 191 GF89
Northwood HA6 93 BQ48
Orpington BR6 206 EV103
Ruislip HA4 115 BT63
St. Albans AL1 43 CE21
Sidcup DA15 185 ES90
Twickenham TW2 177 CD90
Worcester Park KT4 199 CW103
Bedford Row, WC1 286 D6
Bedford Sq, WC1 285 P7
Bedford St, WC2 286 A10
Berkhamsted HP4 38 AX19
Watford WD24 75 BV39
Bedford Ter, SW2 off Lyham Rd 181 DL85
Bedford Way, WC1 285 P5
Bedgebury Ct, E17 off Hawker Pl 101 EC54
Bedgebury Gdns, SW19 179 CY89
Bedgebury Rd, SE9 164 EK84
Bedivere Rd, Brom. BR1 184 EG90
Bedlam Ms, SE11 298 E8
Bedlam Way, Houns. TW3 156 BZ84
Bedlow Way, Croy. CR0 219 DM105
BEDMOND, Abb.L. WD5 59 BS27
Bedmond Hill, Pimlico HP3 59 BS25
Bedmond La, Abb.L. WD5 59 BV25
St. Albans AL2, AL3 58 BX24
Bedmond Rd, Abb.L. WD5 59 BT29
Hemel Hempstead HP3 41 BS23
Bedmond Village Prim & Nurs Sch, Bedmond WD5 off Meadow Way 59 BT28
Bedonwell Inf Sch, Belv. DA17 off Bedonwell Rd 166 EY79
Bedonwell Jun Sch, Belv. DA17 off Bedonwell Rd 166 EY79
Bedonwell Rd, SE2 166 EY79
Belvedere DA17 166 FA79
Bexleyheath DA7 166 FA79
Bedser Cl, SE11 310 D2
Thornton Heath CR7 202 DQ97
Woking GU21 227 BA116
Bedser Dr, Grnf. UB6 117 CD64
Bedster Gdns, W.Mol. KT8 196 CB96
Bedwardine Rd, SE19 182 DS94
Bedwell Av, Essen. AL9 46 DG18
Bedwell Cl, Croy. CR0 202 DR99
Welw.G.C. AL7 29 CY10
Bedwell Gdns, Hayes UB3 155 BS78
Bedwell Pk, Essen. AL9 46 DF18
Bedwell Rd, N17 100 DS53
Belvedere DA17 166 FA78
Beeby Rd, E16 292 A7
Beech Av, N20 98 DE46
W3 138 CS74
Brentford TW8 157 CH80
Brentwood CM13 109 FZ48
Buckhurst Hill IG9 102 EH47
Effingham KT24 246 BX129
Enfield EN2 81 DN35
Radlett WD7 61 CG33
Ruislip HA4 115 BV60
Sidcup DA15 186 EU87
South Croydon CR2 220 DR111
Swanley BR8 207 FF98
Tatsfield TN16 238 EK119
Upminster RM14 128 FP62
Beech Bottom, St.Alb. AL3 43 CD17
Beech Cl, N9 82 DU44
SE8 313 P3
SW15 179 CU87
SW19 179 CW93
Ashford TW15 175 BR92
Byfleet KT14 212 BL112
Carshalton SM5 200 DF103
Cobham KT11 214 CA112
Dorking RH4 263 CF135
Effingham KT24 246 BX128
Hatfield AL10 45 CU19
Hersham KT12 214 BW105
Hornchurch RM12 127 FH62
Loughton IG10 85 EP41
Stanwell TW19 off St. Mary's Cres 174 BK87
Sunbury-on-Thames TW16 off Harfield Rd 196 BX96
Ware SG12 33 DX08
West Drayton UB7 154 BN76
Beech Cl Ct, Cob. KT11 214 BZ111
Beech Copse, Brom. BR1 205 EM96
South Croydon CR2 220 DS106
Beech Ct, SE9 184 EL86
Ilford IG1 125 EN62
Beech Cres, Box H. KT20 248 CQ130
Beechcroft, Ashtd. KT21 232 CM119
Chislehurst BR7 185 EN94
Beechcroft Av, NW11 119 CZ59
Bexleyheath DA7 167 FD81
Croxley Green WD3 75 BQ44
Harrow HA2 116 CA59
Kenley CR8 236 DR115
New Malden KT3 198 CQ95
Beechcroft Cl, Houns. TW5 156 BY80
Orpington BR6 223 ER105
Beechcroft Gdns, Wem. HA9 118 CM62
Beechcroft Lo, Sutt. SM2 off Devonshire Rd 218 DC108
Beechcroft Manor, Wey. KT13 195 BR104
Beechcroft Rd, E18 102 EH54
SW14 158 CQ83
SW17 180 DE89
Bushey WD23 76 BY43
Chesham HP5 54 AN30
Chessington KT9 216 CM105
Orpington BR6 223 ER105
Beechdale, N21 99 DM47
Beechdale Rd, SW2 181 DM86
Beech Dell, Kes. BR2 223 EM105
Beechdene, Tad. KT20 233 CV122
Beech Dr, N2 120 DF55
Berkhamsted HP4 38 AW20
Borehamwood WD6 78 CM40
Kingswood KT20 233 CZ122
Reigate RH2 250 DD134
Ripley GU23 228 BG124
Sawbridgeworth CM21 36 EW07
Beechen Cliff Way, Islw. TW7 off Henley Cl 157 CF81
Beechen Gro, Pnr. HA5 116 BZ55
Watford WD17 76 BW42
Beechen La, Lwr Kgswd KT20 249 CZ125
Beechenlea La, Swan. BR8 207 FH97
Beechen Wd, Map.Cr. WD3 91 BD49
Beeches, The, Amer. HP6 55 AN36
Banstead SM7 234 DB116
Beaconsfield HP9 88 AH54
Bramley GU5 259 AZ144
Brentwood CM14 108 FV48
Chorleywood WD3 73 BF43
Fetcham KT22 231 CE124
Hounslow TW3 156 CB81
Park Street AL2 61 CE27
Swanley BR8 187 FF94
Tilbury RM18 171 GH82
Beeches Av, Cars. SM5 218 DE108
Beeches Cl, SE20 202 DW95
Kingswood KT20 234 DA123
Beeches Dr, Bookham KT23 246 CB125
Farnham Common SL2 111 AP64
Beeches Pk, Beac. HP9 89 AK53
Beeches Rd, SW17 180 DE90
Farnham Common SL2 111 AP64
Sutton SM3 199 CY102
Beeches Wk, Cars. SM5 218 DD109
Beeches Way, B.End SL8 110 AD61
Beeches Wd, Kgswd KT20 234 DA122
Beech Fm Rd, Warl. CR6 237 EC120
Beechfield, Bans. SM7 218 DB113
Hoddesdon EN11 33 EA13
Kings Langley WD4 58 BM30
Sawbridgeworth CM21 36 EZ05
Beechfield Cl, Borwd. WD6 78 CL40
Beechfield Cotts, Brom. BR1 off Widmore Rd 204 EJ96
Beechfield Gdns, Rom. RM7 127 FC59
Beechfield Rd, N4 122 DQ58
SE6 183 DZ88
Bromley BR1 204 EJ96
Erith DA8 167 FE80
Hemel Hempstead HP1 40 BH21
Ware SG12 33 DZ05
Welwyn Garden City AL7 29 CY11
Beechfield Sch, Wat. WD24 off Gammons La 75 BU37
Beechfield Wk, Wal.Abb. EN9 83 ED35
Beech Gdns, EC2 off White Lyon Ct 287 J6
W5 158 CL75
Dagenham RM10 147 FB66
Woking GU21 226 AY115
Beech Gro, Add. KT15 212 BH105
Amersham HP7 55 AQ39
Aveley RM15 148 FQ74
Bookham KT23 246 CA127
Caterham CR3 252 DS126
Croydon CR0 221 DY110
Epsom KT18 233 CV117
Guildford GU2 242 AT134
Ilford IG6 103 ES51
Mayford GU22 226 AX123
Mitcham CR4 201 DK98
New Malden KT3 198 CR97
Beech Hall, Ott. KT16 211 BC108
Beech Hall Cres, E4 101 ED52
Beech Hall Rd, E4 101 EC52
Beech Hill, Barn. EN4 80 DD38
Woking GU22 226 AX123
Beech Hill Av, Barn. EN4 80 DC39
Beech Hill Ct, Berk. HP4 38 AX18
Beech Hill Gdns, Wal.Abb. EN9 84 EH37
Beechhill Rd, SE9 185 EN85
Beech Holt, Lthd. KT22 231 CJ122
Beech Ho, NW3 off Maitland Pk Vil 274 F4
Croydon CR0 221 EB107
Beech Ho Rd, Croy. CR0 202 DR104
Beech Hurst Cl, Chis. BR7 205 EQ95
Beech Hyde La, Wheat. AL4 28 CM07
Beech La, Buck.H. IG9 102 EH47
Guildford GU2 258 AW137
Jordans HP9 90 AS52
Beech Lawn, Guil. GU1 259 AZ135
Beech Lawns, N12 98 DD50
Beech Lo, Stai. TW18 off Farm Cl 173 BE92
Beechmeads, Cob. KT11 214 BX113
Beechmont Av, Vir.W. GU25 192 AX99
Beechmont Cl, Brom. BR1 184 EE92
Beechmont Rd, Sev. TN13 257 FH129
Beechmore Gdns, Sutt. SM3 199 CX103
Beechmore Rd, SW11 308 F7
Beechmount Av, W7 137 CD71
Beecholme, Bans. SM7 217 CY114
Beecholme Av, Mitch. CR4 201 DH95
Beecholme Est, E5 122 DV62
Beecholme Prim Sch, Mitch. CR4 off Edgehill Rd 201 DH95
Beecholm Ms, Chsht EN8 67 DX28
Beech Pk, Amer. HP6 72 AV39
Beechpark Way, Wat. WD17 75 BS37
Beech Pl, Epp. CM16 69 ET31
St. Albans AL3 43 CD17
Beech Rd, N11 99 DL51
SW16 201 DL96
Biggin Hill TN16 238 EH118
Dartford DA1 188 FK88
Epsom KT17 233 CT115
Feltham TW14 175 BS87
Merstham RH1 251 DJ126
Orpington BR6 224 EU108
Reigate RH2 250 DA131
St. Albans AL3 43 CE17
Sevenoaks TN13 off Victoria Rd 257 FH125
Slough SL3 152 AY75
Watford WD24 75 BU37
Weybridge KT13 off St. Marys Rd 213 BR105
Beechrow, Ham TW10 178 CL91
Beech St, EC2 287 J6
Romford RM7 127 FC56
Beechtree Av, Eng.Grn TW20 172 AV93
Beech Tree Cl, N1 276 E6
Fetcham KT23 247 CD125
Stanmore HA7 95 CJ50
Beech Tree Glade, E4 102 EF46
Beechtree La, St.Alb. AL3 41 BV22
Beech Tree La, Stai. TW18 off Staines Rd 194 BH96
Beech Tree Pl, Sutt. SM1 off St. Nicholas Way 218 DB106
Beech Vale, Wok. GU22 off Hill Vw Rd 227 AZ118
Beechvale Cl, N12 98 DE50
Beech Wk, NW7 96 CS51
Dartford DA1 167 FG84
Epsom KT17 217 CU111
Hoddesdon EN11 49 DZ17
Beech Way, NW10 138 CR66
Epsom KT17 233 CT115
South Croydon CR2 221 DX113
Twickenham TW2 176 CA90
Beechway, Bex. DA5 186 EX86
Guildford GU1 243 BB133
Beech Waye, Ger.Cr. SL9 113 AZ59
Beechwood Av, N3 119 CZ55
Amersham HP6 72 AW38
Chorleywood WD3 73 BB42
Coulsdon CR5 235 DH115
Greenford UB6 136 CB69
Harrow HA2 116 CB62
Hayes UB3 135 BR73
Kingswood KT20 234 DA121
Orpington BR6 223 ES106
Potters Bar EN6 64 DB33
Richmond TW9 158 CN81
Ruislip HA4 115 BT61
St. Albans AL1 43 CH18
Staines-upon-Thames TW18 174 BH93
Sunbury-on-Thames TW16 175 BU93
Thornton Heath CR7 201 DP98
Uxbridge UB8 134 BN72
Weybridge KT13 213 BS105
Beechwood Circle, Har. HA2 off Beechwood Gdns 116 CB62
Beechwood Cl, NW7 96 CR50
Amersham HP6 72 AW39
Cheshunt EN7 66 DS26
Hertford SG13 32 DT09
Knaphill GU21 226 AS117
Long Ditton KT6 197 CJ101
Weybridge KT13 213 BS105
Beechwood Ct, Cars. SM5 218 DF105
Sunbury-on-Thames TW16 175 BU93
Beechwood Cres, Bexh. DA7 166 EX83
Beechwood Dr, Cob. KT11 214 CA111
Keston BR2 222 EK105
Woodford Green IG8 102 EF50
Beechwood Gdns, NW10 off St. Annes Gdns 138 CM69
Caterham CR3 236 DU122
Harrow HA2 116 CB62
Ilford IG5 125 EM57
Rainham RM13 147 FH71
Slough SL1 152 AS75
Beechwood Gro, W3 138 CS73
Long Ditton KT6 197 CJ101
Beechwood La, Warl. CR6 237 DX119
Beechwood Manor, Wey. KT13 213 BS105
Beechwood Ms, N9 100 DU47
Beechwood Pk, E18 124 EG55
Chorleywood WD3 73 BF42
Hemel Hempstead HP3 39 BF24
Leatherhead KT22 231 CJ123
Beechwood Ri, Chis. BR7 185 EP91
Watford WD24 75 BV36
Beechwood Rd, E8 278 A4
N8 121 DK56
Beaconsfield HP9 88 AJ53
Caterham CR3 236 DU122
Knaphill GU21 226 AS117
Slough SL2 131 AR71
South Croydon CR2 220 DS109
Virginia Water GU25 192 AU101
Beechwood Sch, SW16 off Leigham Ct Rd 181 DL90
Slough SL2 off Long Readings La 131 AP69
Beechwoods Ct, SE19 off Crystal Palace Par 182 DT92
Beechwood Vil, Red. RH1 266 DG144
Beechworth Cl, NW3 120 DA61
Beecot La, Walt. KT12 196 BW103
Beecroft La, SE4 off Beecroft Rd 183 DY85
Beecroft Ms, SE4 off Beecroft Rd 183 DY85
Beecroft Rd, SE4 183 DY85
Beehive Cl, E8 278 A6
Elstree WD6 77 CK44
Uxbridge UB10 off Honey Hill 134 BM66
Beehive Ct, Rom. RM3 off Arundel Rd 106 FM52
Beehive Grn, Welw.G.C. AL7 30 DA11
Beehive La, Ilf. IG1, IG4 125 EM58
Welwyn Garden City AL7 30 DA12
Beehive Pas, EC3 287 N9
Beehive Pl, SW9 161 DN83
Beehive Rd, Goffs Oak EN7 65 DP28
Staines-upon-Thames TW18 173 BF92
Beehive Way, Reig. RH2 266 DB138
Beeken Dene, Orp. BR6 off Isabella Dr 223 EQ105
Beel Cl, Amer. HP7 72 AW39
Beeleigh Rd, Mord. SM4 200 DB98
Beesfield La, Fnghm DA4 208 FN101
Beeston Cl, E8 278 C2
Watford WD19 94 BX49
Beeston Dr, Chsht EN8 67 DX27
Beeston Pl, SW1 297 K7
Beeston Rd, Barn. EN4 80 DD44
Beeston Way, Felt. TW14 176 BW86
Beethoven Rd, Els. WD6 77 CJ44
Beethoven St, W10 282 F2
Beeton Cl, Pnr. HA5 94 CA52
Beeton Way, SE27 182 DR91
Begbie Rd, SE3 164 EJ81
Beggars Bush La, Wat. WD18 75 BR43
Beggars Hill, Epsom KT17 217 CT108
Beggar's Hill, Epsom KT17 217 CT107
Beggars Hollow, Enf. EN2 82 DR37
Beggars La, Abin.Ham. RH5 261 BT137
Westerham TN16 255 ER125
Beggars Roost La, Sutt. SM1 218 DA107
Begonia Cl, E6 293 H6
Begonia Pl, Hmptn. TW12 off Gresham Rd 176 CA93
Begonia Wk, W12 off Du Cane Rd 139 CT72
Beira St, SW12 181 DH87
Beis Chinuch Lebonos Girls Sch, N4 off Woodberry Gro 122 DQ59
Beis Malka Girls' Sch, N16 off Alkham Rd 122 DT60
Beis Rochel D'Satmar Girls' Sch, N16 off Amhurst Pk 122 DS59
Beis Yaakov Prim Sch, NW9 off Edgware Rd 118 CR55
Beken Ct, Wat. WD25 off First Av 76 BW35
Bekesbourne St, E14 289 L9
Bekesbourne Twr, Orp. BR5 206 EX102
★ Bekonscot Model Village, Beac. HP9 89 AK51
Belcher Rd, Hodd. EN11 off Amwell St 49 EA16
Belchers La, Naze.Gate EN9 50 EJ24
● Belcon Ind Est, Hodd. EN11 49 EB17
Belcroft Cl, Brom. BR1 184 EF94
Beldam Haw, Halst. TN14 224 FA112
Beldham Gdns, W.Mol. KT8 196 CB97
Belfairs Dr, Rom. RM6 126 EW59
Belfairs Grn, Wat. WD19 94 BX50
Belfast Av, Slou. SL1 131 AQ72
Belfast Rd, N16 122 DT61
SE25 202 DV98
Belfield Gdns, Harl. CM17 52 EW16
Belfield Rd, Epsom KT19 216 CR109
Belfont Wk, N7 276 B1
Belford Gro, SE18 305 L9
Belford Rd, Borwd. WD6 78 CM38
Belfort Rd, SE15 313 H8
Belfour Ter, N3 off Squires La 98 DB54
Belfry Av, Hare. UB9 92 BG53
Belfry Cl, SE16 300 F10
Bromley BR1 205 EP98
Belfry La, Rick. WD3 92 BJ46
Belfry Shop Cen, Red. RH1 250 DF133
Belgrade Rd, N16 277 P1
Hampton TW12 196 CB95
Belgrave Av, Rom. RM2 128 FJ55
Watford WD18 75 BT43
Belgrave Cl, N14 off Prince George Av 81 DJ43
NW7 96 CR50
W3 off Avenue Rd 158 CP75
Hersham KT12 213 BV105
Orpington BR5 206 EW98
St. Albans AL4 43 CJ16
Belgrave Ct, E14 301 P1
Belgrave Cres, Sun. TW16 195 BV95
Belgrave Dr, Kings L. WD4 59 BQ28
Belgrave Gdns, N14 81 DK43
NW8 273 M9
Stanmore HA7 off Copley Rd 95 CJ50
Belgrave Hts, E11 124 EG60
Belgrave Manor, Wok. GU22 226 AY119
Belgrave Ms, Uxb. UB8 134 BK70
Belgrave Ms N, SW1 296 G5
Belgrave Ms S, SW1 297 H6
Belgrave Ms W, SW1 296 G6
Belgrave Pl, SW1 297 H6
Belgrave Rd, E10 123 EC60
E11 124 EG61
E13 292 B4
E17 123 EA57
SE25 202 DT98
SW1 297 L9
SW13 159 CT80
Hounslow TW4 156 BZ83
Ilford IG1 125 EM60
Mitcham CR4 200 DD97
Slough SL1 132 AS73
Sunbury-on-Thames TW16 195 BV95
Belgrave Sq, SW1 296 G6
Belgrave St, E1 289 K9
Belgrave Ter, Wdf.Grn. IG8 102 EG48
Belgrave Walk 200 DD97
Belgrave Wk, Mitch. CR4 200 DD97
Belgrave Yd, SW1 297 J7
BELGRAVIA, SW1 296 G7
Belgravia Cl, Barn. EN5 79 CZ41
Belgravia Gdns, Brom. BR1 184 EE93
Belgravia Ho, SW4 181 DK86
Belgravia Ms, Kings.T. KT1 197 CK98
Belgrove St, WC1 286 A2
Belham Rd, Kings L. WD4 58 BM28
Belham Wk, SE5 off Mary Datchelor Cl 311 M6
Belhaven Ct, Borwd. WD6 78 CM39
Belhus Chase, Aveley RM15 149 FR71
Belhus Pk, Aveley RM15 149 FS73
Belinda Rd, SW9 161 DP83
Belitha Vil, N1 276 D6
Bell, The, E17 123 EA55
Bellamy Cl, E14 302 A4
W14 307 H1
Edgware HA8 96 CQ48
Uxbridge UB10 114 BN62
Watford WD17 75 BU39
Bellamy Dr, Stan. HA7 95 CH53
Bellamy Ho, SW17 off Garratt La 180 DD91
Hounslow TW5 156 CA79
Bellamy Rd, E4 101 EB51
Cheshunt EN8 67 DY29
Enfield EN2 82 DR40
Bellamy St, SW12 181 DH87
Bel La, Felt. TW13 off Butts Cotts 176 BZ90
Bellarmine Cl, SE28 165 ET75
Bellasis Av, SW2 181 DL89
Bell Av, Rom. RM3 105 FH53
West Drayton UB7 154 BM77
Bell Br Rd, Cher. KT16 193 BF102
Bellchambers Cl, Lon.Col. AL2 61 CJ26
Bell Cl, Beac. HP9 89 AM53
Bedmond WD5 59 BT27
Greenhithe DA9 189 FT85
Pinner HA5 94 BW54
Ruislip HA4 115 BT62
Slough SL2 132 AV71
Bellclose Rd, West Dr. UB7 154 BL75
BELL COMMON, Epp. CM16 69 ER32
Bell Common, Epp. CM16 69 ES32
Bell Common Tunnel, Epp. CM16 69 ER33
Bell Ct, Surb. KT5 off Barnsbury La 198 CP103
Bell Cres, Couls. CR5 off Maple Way 235 DH121
Bell Dr, SW18 179 CY87
Bellefield, SL1 151 AM75
Bellefield Rd, Orp. BR5 206 EV99
Bellefields Rd, SW9 161 DM83
Bellegrove Cl, Well. DA16 165 ET82
Bellegrove Par, Well. DA16 off Bellegrove Rd 165 ET83
Bellegrove Rd, Well. DA16 165 ER82
Bellenden Prim Sch, SE15 312 C10
Bellenden Rd, SE15 312 B8
Bellerbys Coll, SE8 314 B3
Bellestaines Pleasaunce, E4 101 EA47
Belleville Prim Sch, SW11 off Webbs Rd 180 DF85
SW11 160 DG84
Belleville Rd, SW11 180 DF85
Belle Vue, Grnf. UB6 137 CD67
Belle Vue Cl, Stai. TW18 194 BG95
Belle Vue Est, NW4 off Bell La 119 CW56
Belle Vue La, Bushey Hth WD23 95 CD46
Bellevue Ms, N11 98 DG50
Bellevue Par, SW17 off Bellevue Rd 180 DE88
Belle Vue Pk, Th.Hth. CR7 202 DQ97
Bellevue Pl, E1 288 G5
Slough SL1 152 AT76
Belle Vue Rd, E17 101 ED54
NW4 119 CW56
Downe BR6 off Standard Rd 223 EN110
Ware SG12 33 DZ06
Bellevue Rd, N11 98 DG49
SW13 159 CU82
SW17 180 DE88
W13 137 CH70
Bexleyheath DA6 186 EZ85
Hornchurch RM11 128 FM60
Kingston upon Thames KT1 198 CL97
Romford RM5 105 FC51
Bellevue Ter, Hare. UB9 92 BG52
Bellew St, SW17 180 DC90
Bell Fm Av, Dag. RM10 127 FC62
Bell Fm Jun Sch, Hersham KT12 off Hersham Rd 214 BW105
Bellfield, Croy. CR0 221 DY109
Bellfield Cl, SE3 315 P4
Bellfield Ct, Guil. GU1 242 AW130
BELLFIELDS, Guil. GU1 242 AW131
Bellfields Rd, Guil. GU1 242 AX132
Bellflower Cl, E6 292 G6
Bellflower Path, Rom. RM3 106 FJ52
Bell Gdns, E17 off Markhouse Rd 123 DZ57
Orpington BR5 206 EW99
Bellgate, Hem.H. HP2 40 BL17
Bellgate Ms, NW5 off York Ri 121 DH62
Bellgate Prim Sch, Hem.H. HP2 off Fletcher Way 40 BL18
BELL GREEN, SE6 183 DZ90
Bell Grn, SE26 183 DZ90
Bovingdon HP3 57 BB27
Bell Grn La, SE26 183 DY92
Bellhaven, E15 281 H4
Bell Hill, Croy. CR0 off Surrey St 202 DQ103
Bellhouse La, Pilg.Hat. CM14 108 FS43
Bellhouse Rd, Rom. RM7 127 FC60
Bellina Ms, NW5 275 K1
● Bell Ind Est, W4 off Cunnington St 158 CQ77
Bellingdon Rd, Chesh. HP5 54 AP31
BELLINGHAM, SE6 183 EB90
⇌ Bellingham 183 EB90
Bellingham Ct, Bark. IG11 off Renwick Rd 146 EV69
Bellingham Dr, Reig. RH2 249 CZ134
Bellingham Grn, SE6 183 EA90
Bellingham Rd, SE6 183 EB90
● Bellingham Trd Est, SE6 off Franthorne Way 183 EB90
Bell Inn Yd, EC3 287 M9
Bell La, E1 288 A7
E16 303 N2
NW4 119 CX56
Amersham HP6, HP7 72 AV39
Bedmond WD5 59 BT27
Berkhamsted HP4 38 AS18
Brookmans Park AL9 64 DA25
Broxbourne EN10 49 DY21
Enfield EN3 83 DX38
Eton Wick SL4 151 AM77
Feltham TW14 175 BQ87
Fetcham KT22 231 CD123

Bell La, Hertford SG14 32 DR09
Hoddesdon EN11 49 EA17
London Colney AL2 62 CL29
Twickenham TW1
off The Embankment 177 CG88
Wembley HA9
off Magnet Rd 117 CK61
Bell La Cl, Fetch. KT22 231 CD123
Sch Bell La Comb Sch, Lt.Chal. HP6
off Bell La 72 AV38
Sch Bell La Prim Sch, NW4
off Bell La 119 CX56
Bellmaker Ct, E3 290 A6
Bellman Av, Grav. DA12 191 GL88
Bellmarsh Rd, Add. KT15 212 BH105
Bell Mead, Saw. CM21 36 EY05
Bell Meadow, SE19
off Dulwich Wd Av 182 DS91
Godstone RH9 252 DV132
Bellmount Wd Av, Wat. WD17 75 BS39
Bello Cl, SE24 181 DP87
Bellot Gdns, SE10 303 K10
Bellot St, SE10 303 K10
Bell Par, Wind. SL4
off St. Andrews Av 151 AM82
Bellridge Pl, Knot.Grn HP9 88 AH49
Bellring Cl, Belv. DA17 166 FA79
Bell Rd, E.Mol. KT8 197 CD99
Enfield EN1 82 DR39
Hounslow TW3 156 CB84
Bells All, SW6 307 J9
Bells Gdn Est, SE15 312 C5
Bells Hill, Barn. EN5 79 CX43
Bell's Hill, Stoke P. SL2 132 AU67
Bells Hill Grn, Stoke P. SL2 132 AU66
Bells La, Horton SL3 153 BB83
Bell St, NW1 284 C6
SE18 164 EL81
Reigate RH2 250 DA134
Sawbridgeworth CM21 36 EY05
Bellswood La, Iver SL0 133 BB71
Belltrees Gro, SW16 181 DM92
Bell Vw, St.Alb. AL4 43 CK20
Windsor SL4 151 AM83
Bell Vw Cl, Wind. SL4 151 AM82
Bell Water Gate, SE18 305 M6
Bell Weir Cl, Stai. TW19 173 BB89
Bellwether La, Outwood RH1 267 DP143
Bell Wf La, EC4 299 K1
Bellwood Rd, SE15 163 DX84
Bell Yd, WC2 286 E8
Bell Yd Ms, SE1 299 P5
Belmarsh Rd, SE28
off Western Way 165 ES75
BELMONT, Har. HA3 95 CG54
BELMONT, Sutt. SM2 218 DB111
⇌ Belmont 218 DA110
Sch Belmont, Mill Hill Prep Sch,
NW7 off The Ridgeway 97 CU48
Belmont, Slou. SL2 131 AN71
Weybridge KT13
off Egerton Rd 213 BQ107
Belmont Av, N9 100 DU46
N13 99 DL50
N17 122 DQ55
Barnet EN4 80 DF43
Guildford GU2 242 AT131
New Malden KT3 199 CU99
Southall UB2 156 BY76
Upminster RM14 128 FM61
Welling DA16 165 ES83
Wembley HA0 138 CM67
Belmont Circle, Har. HA3 95 CH53
Belmont Cl, E4 101 ED50
N20 98 DB46
SW4 161 DJ83
Cockfosters EN4 80 DF42
Uxbridge UB8 134 BK65
Woodford Green IG8 102 EH49
Belmont Cotts, Colnbr. SL3
off High St 153 BC80
Belmont Ct, NW11 119 CZ57
Belmont Gro, SE13 314 G10
W4 off Belmont Ter 158 CR77
Belmont Hall Ct, SE13
off Belmont Gro 163 ED83
Belmont Hill, SE13 163 ED83
St. Albans AL1 43 CD21
Sch Belmont Inf Sch, N22
off Rusper Rd 122 DQ55
Sch Belmont Jun Sch, N22
off Rusper Rd 122 DQ55
Belmont La, Chis. BR7 185 EQ92
Stanmore HA7 95 CJ52
Belmont Ms, SW19
off Chapman Sq 179 CX89
Belmont Pk, SE13 163 ED84
Belmont Pk Cl, SE13 163 ED84
Belmont Pk Rd, E10 123 EB58
Sch Belmont Pk Sch, E10
off Leyton Grn Rd 123 EC58
Sch Belmont Prim Sch, W4
off Belmont Rd 158 CR77
Erith DA8 off Belmont Rd 166 FA80
Belmont Ri, Sutt. SM2 217 CZ107
Belmont Rd, N15 122 DQ56
N17 122 DQ56
SE25 202 DV99
SW4 161 DJ83
W4
off Chiswick High Rd 158 CR77
Beckenham BR3 203 DZ96
Bushey WD23 76 BY43
Chesham HP5 54 AP29
Chislehurst BR7 185 EP92
Erith DA8 166 FA80
Grays RM17 170 FZ78
Harrow HA3 117 CF55
Hemel Hempstead HP3 40 BL24
Hornchurch RM12 128 FK62
Ilford IG1 125 EQ62
Leatherhead KT22 231 CG122
Reigate RH2 266 DC135
Sutton SM2 218 DA110
Twickenham TW2 177 CD89
Uxbridge UB8 134 BK66
Wallington SM6 219 DH106
Sch Belmont Sch, Har.Wld HA3
off Hibbert Rd 95 CF54
Belmont St, NW1 275 H6
Belmont Ter, W4 158 CR77
Belmor, Els. WD6 78 CN43
Belmore Av, Hayes UB4 135 BU72
Woking GU22 227 BD116
Belmore La, N7 275 P3
Sch Belmore Prim Sch,
Hayes UB4 off Owen Rd 135 BV69
Belmore St, SW8 309 N6
Beloe Cl, SW15 159 CU83
Belper Ct, E5
off Pedro St 123 DX63
Belsham Cl, Chesh. HP5 54 AP28
Belsham St, E9 278 G4
BELSIZE, Rick. WD3 57 BF33
Belsize Av, N13 99 DM51
NW3 274 B4
W13 157 CH76
Belsize Cl, Hem.H. HP3 40 BN21
St. Albans AL4 43 CJ15
Belsize Ct, NW3 274 B2
Sutt. SM1 218 DB105
Belsize Cres, NW3 274 B3
Belsize Gro, NW3 274 D4
Belsize La, NW3 274 A5
Belsize Ms, NW3 274 B4
BELSIZE PARK, NW3 274 C5
⊖ Belsize Park 274 D3
Belsize Pk, NW3 274 A5
Belsize Pk Gdns, NW3 274 B4
Belsize Pk Ms, NW3 274 B4
Belsize Pl, NW3 274 B4
Belsize Rd, NW6 273 P7
Harrow HA3 95 CD52
Hemel Hempstead HP3 40 BN21
Belsize Sq, NW3 274 B4
Belsize Ter, NW3 274 B4
Belson Rd, SE18 305 J8
Belswains Grn, Hem.H. HP3
off Belswains La 40 BL23
Belswains La, Hem.H. HP3 58 BM25
Sch Belswains Prim Sch,
Hem.H. HP3 off Barnfield 40 BM24
Beltana Dr, Grav. DA12 191 GL91
Beltane Dr, SW19 179 CX90
Belthorn Cres, SW12 181 DJ87
Beltinge Rd, Rom. RM3 128 FM55
Beltona Gdns, Chsht EN8 67 DX27
Belton Rd, E7 144 EH66
E11 124 EE63
N17 122 DS55
NW2 139 CU65
Berkhamsted HP4 38 AU18
Sidcup DA14 186 EU91
Belton Way, E3 290 A6
Beltran Rd, SW6 307 L9
Beltwood Rd, Belv. DA17 167 FC77
BELVEDERE, DA17 167 FB77
⇌ Belvedere 166 FA76
Belvedere, The, SW10 307 P7
Belvedere Av, SW19 179 CY92
Ilford IG5 103 EP54
Belvedere Bldgs, SE1 299 H5
● Belvedere Business Pk,
Belv. DA17 167 FB75
Belvedere Cl, Amer. HP6 72 AT36
Esher KT10 214 CB106
Gravesend DA12 191 GJ88
Guildford GU2 242 AV132
Teddington TW11 177 CE92
Weybridge KT13 212 BN106
Belvedere Ct, N1 277 N8
N2 120 DD57
Belvedere Dr, SW19 179 CY92
Belvedere Gdns, St.Alb. AL2 60 CA27
West Molesey KT8 196 BZ99
Belvedere Gro, SW19 179 CY92
Belvedere Ho, Felt. TW13 175 BU88
Belvedere Ind Est,
Belv. DA17 167 FC76
Sch Belvedere Inf Sch, Belv. DA17
off Mitchell Cl 167 FB76
Sch Belvedere Jun Sch, Belv. DA17
off Mitchell Cl 167 FB76
Belvedere Ms, SE3 315 P5
SE15 162 DW83
Belvedere Pl, SE1 299 H5
SW2 161 DM84
Belvedere Rd, E10 123 DY60
SE1 298 D4
SE2 146 EX74
SE19 182 DT94
W7 157 CF76
Bexleyheath DA7 166 EZ83
Biggin Hill TN16 239 EM118
Brentwood CM14 108 FT48
Belvederes, The, Reig. RH2 266 DB137
Belvedere Sq, SW19 179 CY92
Belvedere Strand, NW9 97 CT54
Belvedere Way, Har. HA3 118 CL58
Belvoir Cl, SE9 184 EL90
Belvoir Ho, SW1
off Vauxhall Br Rd 297 M8
Belvoir Rd, SE22 182 DU87
● Belvue Business Cen,
Nthlt. UB5 136 CB66
Belvue Cl, Nthlt. UB5 136 CA66
Belvue Rd, Nthlt. UB5 136 CA66
Sch Belvue Sch, Nthlt. UB5
off Rowdell Rd 136 CA67
Bembridge Cl, NW6 272 E6
Bembridge Ct, Slou. SL1
off Park St 152 AT75
Bembridge Gdns, Ruis. HA4 115 BR61
Bembridge Pl, Wat. WD25 59 BU33
Bemersyde Pt, E13 292 A3
Bemerton Est, N1 276 B7
Bemerton St, N1 276 C8
Bemish Rd, SW15 159 CX83
Bempton Dr, Ruis. HA4 115 BV61
Bemsted Rd, E17 123 DZ55
Benares Rd, SE18 165 ET77
Benbow Cl, St.Alb. AL1 43 CH22
Benbow Rd, W6 159 CV76
Benbow St, SE8 314 B2
Benbow Waye, Uxb. UB8 134 BJ71
Benbrick Rd, Guil. GU2 258 AU135
Benbury Cl, Brom. BR1 183 EC92
Bence, The, Egh. TW20 193 BB97
Bench Fld, S.Croy. CR2 220 DT107
Benchleys Rd, Hem.H. HP1 39 BF21
Bench Manor Cres,
Chal.St.P. SL9 90 AW54
Bencombe Rd, Pur. CR8 219 DN114
Bencroft, Chsht EN7 66 DU26
Bencroft Rd, SW16 181 DJ94
Hemel Hempstead HP2 40 BL20
Bencurtis Pk, W.Wick. BR4 203 ED104
Bendall Ms, NW1 284 D6
Bendemeer Rd, SW15 306 C10
Bendish Pt, SE28 165 EQ75
Bendish Rd, E6 144 EL66
Bendmore Av, SE2 166 EU78
Bendon Valley, SW18 180 DB87
Bendysh Rd,
Bushey WD23 76 BY41
Benedict Cl, Belv. DA17
off Tunstock Way 166 EY76
Orpington BR6 205 ES104
Benedict Dr, Felt. TW14 175 BR87
Benedictine Gate, Wal.Cr. EN8 67 DY27
Sch Benedict Prim Sch, Mitch. CR4
off Church Rd 200 DD97
Benedict Rd, SW9 310 D10
Mitcham CR4 200 DD97
Benedicts Wf, Bark. IG11
off Town Quay 145 EP67
Benedict Way, N2 120 DC55
Benenden Grn, Brom. BR2 204 EG99
Benen-Stock Rd, Stai. TW19 173 BF85
Benets Rd, Horn. RM11 128 FN60
Benett Gdns, SW16 201 DL96
Benfleet Cl, Cob. KT11 214 BY112
Sutton SM1 200 DC104
Benfleet Way, N11 98 DG47
Benford Rd, Hodd. EN11 49 DZ19
Bengal Ct, EC3
off Birchin La 287 M9
Bengal Rd, Ilf. IG1 125 EP63
Bengarth Dr, Har. HA3 95 CD54
Bengarth Rd, Nthlt. UB5 136 BX67
BENGEO, Hert. SG14 32 DQ07
Bengeo Gdns, Rom. RM6 126 EW58
Bengeo Meadows, Hert. SG14 32 DR06
Bengeo Ms, Hert. SG14 32 DQ06
Sch Bengeo Prim Sch, Hert. SG14
off The Avenue 32 DQ06
Bengeo St, Hert. SG14 32 DQ08
Bengeworth Rd, SE5 311 J10
Harrow HA1 117 CG61
Ben Hale Cl, Stan. HA7 95 CH49
Benham Cl, SW11 160 DD83
Chesham HP5 54 AP29
Chessington KT9 215 CJ107
Coulsdon CR5 235 DP118
Benham Gdns, Houns. TW4 176 BZ85
Benham Rd, W7 137 CE71
Benhams Cl, Horl. RH6 268 DG146
Benhams Dr, Horl. RH6 268 DG146
Benhams Pl, NW3
off Holly Wk 120 DC63
Benhill Av, Sutt. SM1 218 DB105
Benhill Rd, SE5 311 M5
Sutton SM1 200 DC104
Benhill Wd Rd, Sutt. SM1 200 DC104
BENHILTON, Sutt. SM1 200 DB103
Benhilton Gdns, Sutt. SM1 200 DB104
Benhurst Av, Horn. RM12 127 FH62
Benhurst Cl, S.Croy. CR2 221 DX110
Benhurst Ct, SW16 181 DN92
Benhurst Gdns, S.Croy. CR2 220 DW110
Benhurst La, SW16 181 DN92
Sch Benhurst Prim Sch,
Elm Pk RM12 off Benhurst Av 127 FH62
Beningfield Dr, Lon.Col. AL2 61 CH27
Benington Ct, N4
off Brownswood Rd 122 DQ61
Benin St, SE13 183 ED87
Benison Ct, Slou. SL1
off Hencroft St S 152 AT76
Benjafield Cl, N18 100 DV49
Benjamin Cl, E8 278 D9
Hornchurch RM11 127 FG58
Benjamin La, Wexham SL3 132 AV70
Benjamin Ms, SW12 181 DJ87
Benjamin St, EC1 286 G6
Ben Jonson Ho, EC2
off The Barbican 287 K6
Sch Ben Jonson Prim Sch, E1 289 M5
Ben Jonson Rd, E1 289 K7
Benledi Rd, E14 290 G8
Benlow Wks, Hayes UB3
off Silverdale Rd 155 BU75
Benn Cl, Oxt. RH8 254 EG134
Bennelong Cl, W12 139 CV73
Bennerley Rd, SW11 180 DE85
Bennet Ms, N19
off Wedmore St 121 DK62
Bennets Ctyd, SW19
off Watermill Way 200 DC95
Bennetsfield Rd, Uxb. UB11 135 BP74
Bennet's Hill, EC4 287 H10
Bennet St, SW1 297 L2
Bennett Cl, Cob. KT11 213 BU113
Hampton Wick KT1 197 CJ95
Hounslow TW4 176 BY85
Northwood HA6 93 BT52
Welling DA16 166 EU82
Welwyn Garden City AL7 29 CZ13
Bennett Gro, SE13 314 D7
Bennett Ho, SW1
off Page St 297 P8
Bennett Pk, SE3 315 L10
Bennett Rd, E13 292 C5
N16 277 N1
SW9 310 F9
Romford RM6 126 EY58
Bennetts, Chesh. HP5 54 AR30
Bennetts Av, Croy. CR0 203 DY103
Greenford UB6 137 CE67
Bennetts Castle La, Dag. RM8 126 EW63
Bennetts Cl, N17 100 DT51
Colney Heath AL4 44 CR23
Mitcham CR4 201 DH95
Slough SL1 131 AN74
Bennetts Copse, Chis. BR7 184 EL93
BENNETTS END, Hem.H. HP3 40 BM21
Bennetts End Cl, Hem.H. HP3 40 BM21
Bennetts End Rd, Hem.H. HP3 40 BM21
Bennetts Fm Pl, Bkhm KT23 246 BZ125
Bennetts Fld, Bushey WD23 76 BY43
Bennetts Gate, Hem.H. HP3
off Kimps Way 40 BN23
Bennett St, W4 158 CS79
Bennetts Way, Croy. CR0 203 DY103
Bennetts Yd, SW1 297 P7
Uxbridge UB8
off High St 134 BJ66
Bennett Way, Lane End DA2 189 FR91
West Clandon GU4 244 BG129
Benning Cl, Wind. SL4 151 AK83
Benning Dr, Dag. RM8 126 EY60
Benningfield Gdns, Berk. HP4 38 AY17
Benningholme Rd, Edg. HA8 96 CS51
Bennington Dr, Borwd. WD6 78 CM39
Bennington Rd, N17 100 DS53
Woodford Green IG8 102 EE52
Bennions Cl, Horn. RM12
off Franklin Rd 148 FK65
Bennison Dr, Harold Wd RM3 106 FK54
Benn St, E9 279 M4
Benn's Wk, Rich. TW9
off Rosedale Rd 158 CL84
Benrek Cl, Ilf. IG6 103 EQ53
Bensbury Cl, SW15 179 CV87
Bensham Cl, Th.Hth. CR7 202 DQ98
Bensham Gro, Th.Hth. CR7 202 DQ96
Bensham La, Croy. CR0 201 DP101
Thornton Heath CR7 201 DP98
Bensham Manor Rd,
Th.Hth. CR7 202 DQ98
Sch Bensham Manor Sch, Th.Hth.
CR7 off Ecclesbourne Rd 202 DQ99
Bensington Ct, Felt. TW14 175 BR86
Benskin Rd, Wat. WD18 75 BU43
Benskins La,
Noak Hill RM4 106 FK46
Bensley Cl, N11 98 DF50
Ben Smith Way, SE16 300 D6
Benson Av, E6 292 D1
Benson Cl, Houns. TW3 156 CA84
Slough SL2 132 AU74
Uxbridge UB8 134 BL71
Benson Ct, SW8
off Hartington Rd 310 A6
Enfield EN3
off Harston Dr 83 EA38
Sch Benson Prim Sch, Croy. CR0
off West Way 203 DY104
Benson Quay, E1 300 G1
Benson Rd, SE23 182 DW88
Croydon CR0 201 DN104
Grays RM17 170 GB79
Bentall Cen, The,
Kings.T. KT1 197 CK96
Bentfield Gdns, SE9
off Aldersgrove Av 184 EJ90
Benthall Gdns, Ken. CR8 236 DQ117
Sch Benthal Prim Sch, N16
off Benthal Rd 122 DU62
Benthal Rd, N16 122 DU61
Bentham Av, Wok. GU21 227 BC115
Bentham Ct, N1 277 J7
Bentham Ho, SE1
off Falmouth Rd 299 L6
Bentham Rd, E9 279 J5
SE28 146 EV73
Bentham Wk, NW10 118 CQ64
Ben Tillet Cl, Bark. IG11 146 EU66
Ben Tillett Cl, E16 305 J3
Bentinck Cl, NW8
off Prince Albert Rd 284 D1
Gerrards Cross SL9 112 AX57
Bentinck Ms, W1 285 H8
Bentinck Rd, West Dr. UB7 134 BK74
Bentinck St, W1 285 H8
Bentine La, Wat. WD18 75 BV41
Bentley Ct, SE13
off Whitburn Rd 163 EC84
Bentley Dr, NW2 119 CZ62
Harlow CM17 52 EW16
Ilford IG2 125 EQ58
Weybridge KT13 212 BN109
BENTLEY HEATH, Barn. EN5 79 CZ35
Bentley Heath La, Barn. EN5 63 CY34
Bentley Ms, Enf. EN1 82 DR44
Bentley Pk, Burn. SL1 131 AK68
★ Bentley Priory Battle of Britain Mus,
Stan. HA7 95 CF48
★ Bentley Priory Open Space,
Stan. HA7 95 CF49
Bentley Rd, N1 277 P5
Hertford SG14 31 DL08
Slough SL1 131 AN74
Bentleys, Hat.Hth CM22 37 FH05
Bentley St, Grav. DA12 191 GJ86
Bentley Way, Stan. HA7 95 CG50
Woodford Green IG8 102 EG48
Sch Bentley Wd High Sch for Girls,
Stan. HA7 off Bridges Rd 95 CF50
Benton Rd, Ilf. IG1 125 ER60
Watford WD19 94 BX50
Bentons La, SE27 182 DQ91
Bentons Ri, SE27 182 DR92
Bentry Cl, Dag. RM8 126 EY61
Bentry Rd, Dag. RM8 126 EY61
Bentsbrook Cl, N.Holm. RH5 263 CH140
Bentsbrook Pk, N.Holm. RH5 263 CH140
Bentsbrook Rd, N.Holm. RH5 263 CH140
Bentsley Cl, St.Alb. AL4 43 CJ16
Sch Bentworth Prim Sch, W12
off Bentworth Rd 139 CV72
Bentworth Rd, W12 139 CV72
Benville Ho, SW8 310 D5
Benwell Ct, Sun. TW16 195 BU95
Benwell Rd, N7 276 E1
Benwick Cl, SE16 300 F8
Benworth St, E3 289 P2
Sch Benyon Prim Sch,
S.Ock. RM15 off Tyssen Pl 149 FW68
Benyon Rd, N1 277 M8
Benyon Wf, E8 277 P8
Beomonds Row, Cher. KT16
off Heriot Rd 194 BG101
Sch Beormund Sch, SE1 299 M5
Berberis Cl, Guil. GU1 242 AW132
Berberis Ho, Felt. TW13
off Highfield Rd 175 BU89
Berberis Wk, West Dr. UB7 154 BL77
Berber Par, SE18 164 EL81
Berber Pl, E14 290 A10
Berber Rd, SW11 180 DF85
Berberry Cl, Edg. HA8
off Larkspur Gro 96 CQ49
Berceau Wk, Wat. WD17 75 BS39
Bercta Rd, SE9 185 EQ89
Berdan Ct, Enf. EN3
off George Lovell Dr 83 EA37
Bere Cl, Green. DA9 189 FW85
Berecroft, Harl. CM18 51 ER20
Beredens La,
Gt Warley CM13 129 FT55
Berefeld, Hem.H. HP2 40 BK18
Berengers Ct, Rom. RM6 126 EZ59
Berengers Pl, Dag. RM9 146 EV65
Berenger Twr, SW10 308 A4
Berenger Wk, SW10
off Blantyre St 308 A4
Berens Rd, NW10 282 C3
Orpington BR5 206 EX99
Berens Way, Chis. BR7 205 ET98
Beresford Av, N20 98 DF47
W7 137 CD71
Slough SL2 132 AW74
Surbiton KT5 198 CP102
Twickenham TW1 177 CJ86
Wembley HA0 138 CM67
Beresford Dr, Brom. BR1 204 EL97
Woodford Green IG8 102 EJ49
Beresford Gdns, Enf. EN1 82 DS42
Hounslow TW4 176 BZ85
Romford RM6 126 EY57
Beresford Rd, E4 102 EE46
E17 101 EB53
N2 120 DE55
N5 277 L3
N8 121 DN57
Dorking RH4 263 CH136
Harrow HA1 117 CD57
Kingston upon Thames KT2 198 CM95
Mill End WD3 91 BF46
New Malden KT3 198 CQ98
Northfleet DA11 190 GE87
St. Albans AL1 43 CH21
Southall UB1 136 BX74
Sutton SM2 217 CZ108
Beresford Sq, SE18 305 N8
Beresford St, SE18 305 N7
Beresford Ter, N5 277 K3
Berestede Rd, W6 159 CT78
Bere St, E1 289 K10
Bergenia Ho, Felt. TW13
off Bedfont La 175 BV88
Bergen Sq, SE16 301 M6
Berger Cl, Petts Wd BR5 205 ER100
Sch Berger Prim Sch, E9 279 J4
Berger Rd, E9 279 J4
Berghem Ms, W14 294 D7
Berghers Hill, Woob.Grn HP10 110 AF59
Bergholt Av, Ilf. IG4 124 EL57
Bergholt Cres, N16 122 DS59
Bergholt Ms, NW1 275 M7
Berglen Ct, E14 289 L9
Bericot Way, Welw.G.C. AL7 30 DC09
Bering Sq, E14 302 B10
Bering Wk, E16 292 E9
Berisford Ms, SW18 180 DB86
Berkeley Av, Bexh. DA7 166 EX81
Chesham HP5 54 AN30
Greenford UB6 137 CE65
Hounslow TW4 155 BU82
Ilford IG5 103 EN54
Romford RM5 105 FC52
Berkeley Cl, Abb.L. WD5 59 BT32
Chesham HP5 off Berkeley Av 54 AN30
Elstree WD6 78 CN43
Hornchurch RM11 128 FP61
Kingston upon Thames KT2 178 CL94
Petts Wood BR5 205 ES101
Potters Bar EN6 63 CY32
Ruislip HA4 115 BU62
Staines-upon-Thames TW19 173 BD89
Ware SG12 32 DW05
Berkeley Ct, N14 81 DJ44
Croxley Green WD3
off Mayfare 75 BR43
Guildford GU1
off London Rd 242 AY134
Wallington SM6 201 DJ104
Weybridge KT13 195 BR103
Berkeley Cres, Barn. EN4 80 DD43
Dartford DA1 188 FM88
Berkeley Dr, Horn. RM11 128 FN60
West Molesey KT8 196 BZ97
Berkeley Gdns, N21 100 DR45
W8 295 K3
Claygate KT10 215 CG107
Walton-on-Thames KT12 195 BT101
West Byfleet KT14 211 BF114
Berkeley Ho, E3 289 P3
Berkeley Ms, W1 284 F8
Berkeley Pl, SW19 179 CX93
Epsom KT18 232 CR115
Sch Berkeley Prim Sch,
Heston TW5 off Cranford La 156 BX80
Berkeley Rd, E12 124 EL64
N8 121 DK57
N15 122 DR58
NW9 118 CN56
SW13 159 CU81
Loudwater HP10 88 AC53
Uxbridge UB10 135 BQ66
Berkeleys, The, Fetch. KT22 231 CE124
Berkeley Sq, W1 297 K1
Berkeley St, W1 297 K1
Berkeley Twr, E14 301 P2
Berkeley Wk, N7
off Durham Rd 121 DM61
Berkeley Waye, Houns. TW5 156 BX80
Berkerley Ms, Sun. TW16 196 BW97
Berkhampstead Rd, Belv. DA17 166 FA78
Chesham HP5 54 AQ30
BERKHAMSTED, HP4 38 AW17
⇌ Berkhamsted 38 AW18
Berkhamsted Av, Wem. HA9 138 CM65
Berkhamsted Bypass,
Berk. HP4 38 AV21
Hemel Hempstead HP1 39 BB23
★ Berkhamsted Castle,
Berk. HP4 38 AX18
Sch Berkhamsted Collegiate Sch,
Castle Campus, Berk. HP4
off Castle St 38 AW19
Kings Campus, Berk. HP4
off Kings Rd 38 AV19
Prep Sch, Berk. HP4 off Kings Rd 38 AV19
Berkhamsted Hill, Berk. HP4 38 AY17
Berkhamsted La, Essen. AL9 46 DF20
Berkhamsted Pl, Berk. HP4 38 AW17
Berkhamsted Rd, Hem.H. HP1 39 BD17
Berkley Av, Wal.Cr. EN8 67 DX34
Berkley Cl, St.Alb. AL4 43 CJ16
Berkley Ct, Berk. HP4
off Mill St 38 AW19
Berkley Cres, Grav. DA12
off Milton Rd 191 GJ86
Berkley Gro, NW1 274 F7
Berkley Rd, NW1 274 F7
Beaconsfield HP9 89 AK49
Gravesend DA12 191 GH86
Berks Hill, Chorl. WD3 73 BC43
Berkshire Av, Slou. SL1 131 AP72
Berkshire Cl, Cat. CR3 236 DR122
Berkshire Gdns, N13 99 DN51
N18 100 DV50
Berkshire Rd, E9 279 P4
Berkshire Sq, Mitch. CR4
off Berkshire Way 201 DL98
Berkshire Way, Horn. RM11 128 FN57
Mitcham CR4 201 DL98
Bermans Cl, Hutt. CM13 109 GB47
Bermans Way, NW10 118 CS63
Bermer Rd, Wat. WD24 76 BW39
BERMONDSEY, SE1 300 A7
⊖ Bermondsey 300 D6
Bermondsey Sq, SE1 299 P6
Bermondsey St, SE1 299 N3
● Bermondsey Trd Est, SE16
off Rotherhithe New Rd 300 G10
Bermondsey Wall E, SE16 300 D5
Bermondsey Wall W, SE16 300 C4

Bermuda Rd, Til. RM18 171 GG82
Bermuda Way, E1 289 K6
Bernal Cl, SE28
off Haldane Rd 146 EX73
Bernard Ashley Dr, SE7 164 EH78
Bernard Av, W13 157 CH76
Bernard Cassidy St, E16 291 M6
Bernard Gdns, SW19 179 CZ92
Bernard Gro, Wal.Abb. EN9
off Beaulieu Dr 67 EB33
Bernard Rd, N15 122 DT57
Romford RM7 127 FC59
Wallington SM6 219 DH105
Bernards Cl, Ilf. IG6 103 EQ51
Bernard Shaw Ho, NW10
off Knatchbull Rd 138 CR67
Sch Bernards Heath Inf Sch,
St.Alb. AL1 off Sandridge Rd 43 CF18
Sch Bernards Heath Jun Sch,
St.Alb. AL3 off Watson Av 43 CE17
Bernard St, WC1 286 A5
Gravesend DA12 191 GH86
St. Albans AL3 43 CD19
Bernays Cl, Stan. HA7 95 CJ51
Bernays Gro, SW9 161 DM84
Bernel Dr, Croy. CR0 203 DZ104
Berne Rd, Th.Hth. CR7 202 DQ99
Berners Cl, Slou. SL1 131 AL73
Berners Dr, W13 137 CG72
Broxbourne EN10
off Berners Way 49 DZ23
St. Albans AL1 43 CD23
Bernersmede, SE3 315 N10
Berners Ms, W1 285 M7
Berners Pl, W1 285 M8
Berners Rd, N1 276 F10
N22 99 DN53
Berners St, W1 285 M7
Berners Way, Brox. EN10 49 DZ23
Berney Rd, Croy. CR0 202 DR101
Bernhardt Cres, NW8 284 C4
Bernhart Cl, Edg. HA8 96 CQ52
Bernice Cl, Rain. RM13 148 FJ70
Bernville Way, Har. HA3 118 CM57
Bernwell Rd, E4 102 EE48
Berricot Grn, Tewin AL6 30 DE08
Berridge Grn, Edg. HA8 96 CN52
Berridge Ms, NW6 273 J2
Berridge Rd, SE19 182 DS92
Berries, The, Sand. AL4 43 CG16
Berriman Rd, N7 121 DM62
Berrington Dr, E.Hors. KT24 229 BT124
Berrington Ms, Slou. SL1 131 AN74
Berriton Rd, Har. HA2 116 BZ60
Berry Av, Wat. WD24 75 BU36
Berrybank Cl, E4
off Greenbank Cl 101 EC47
Berry Cl, N21 99 DP46
Dagenham RM10 126 FA64
Hornchurch RM12
off Airfield Way 128 FJ64
Rickmansworth WD3 92 BH45
Berry Ct, Houns. TW4
off Raglan Cl 176 BZ85
Berrydale Rd, Hayes UB4 136 BY70
Berryfield, Slou. SL2 132 AW72
Berryfield Cl, E17 123 EB56
Bromley BR1 204 EL95
Berry Fld Pk, Amer. HP6 55 AP37
Berryfield Rd, SE17 299 H10
Jct Berrygrove Interchange,
Wat. WD25 76 CA38
Berry Gro La, Wat. WD25 76 CA39
Sch Berrygrove Prim Sch,
Wat. WD25 off Fourth Av 76 BX35
Berryhill, SE9 165 EP84
Berry Hill, Stan. HA7 95 CK49
Taplow SL6 130 AD71
Berry Hill Ct, Tap. SL6 130 AD71
Berryhill Gdns, SE9 165 EP84
BERRYLANDS, Surb. KT5 198 CM99
≠ Berrylands 198 CN98
Berrylands, SW20 199 CW97
Orpington BR6 206 EW104
Surbiton KT5 198 CN99
Berrylands Rd, Surb. KT5 198 CM100
Berry La, SE21 182 DR91
Hersham KT12
off Burwood Rd 214 BX106
Rickmansworth WD3 92 BH46
Berryman Cl, Dag. RM8
off Bennetts Castle La 126 EW62
Berrymans La, SE26 183 DX91
Berrymead, Hem.H. HP2 40 BM19
Berry Meade, Ashtd. KT21 232 CM117
Berry Meade Cl, Ashtd. KT21
off Berry Meade 232 CM117
Berrymead Gdns, W3 138 CQ74
Sch Berrymede Inf Sch, W3
off Park Rd N 158 CP75
Sch Berrymede Jun Sch, W3
off Osborne Rd 158 CP75
Berrymede Rd, W4 158 CR76
Berry Pl, EC1 287 H3
Berryscroft Ct, Stai. TW18 174 BJ94
Berryscroft Rd, Stai. TW18 174 BJ94
Berry's Grn Rd,
Berry's Grn TN16 239 EP116
Berry's Hill, Berry's Grn TN16 239 EP115
Berrys La, Byfleet KT14 212 BK111
BERRY'S GREEN, West. TN16 239 EP116
Berry St, EC1 287 H4
Berry Wk, Ashtd. KT21 232 CM119
Berry Way, W5 158 CL76
Rickmansworth WD3 92 BH45
Bersham La, Bad.Dene RM17 170 FZ77
Bertal Rd, SW17 180 DD91
Bertelli Pl, Felt. TW13 175 BV88
Berther Rd, Horn. RM11 128 FK59
Berthold Ms, Wal.Abb. EN9 67 EB33
Berthon St, SE8 314 B4
Bertie Rd, NW10 139 CU65
SE26 183 DX93
Bertram Cotts, SW19 180 DA94
Bertram Rd, NW4 119 CU58
Enfield EN1 82 DU42
Kingston upon Thames KT2 178 CN94
Bertram St, N19 121 DH61
Bertram Way, Enf. EN1 82 DT42
Bertrand St, SE13 314 C10
Bertrand Way, SE28 146 EV73
Bert Rd, Th.Hth. CR7 202 DQ99
Berwick Av, Hayes UB4 136 BX72
Slough SL1 131 AP73
Berwick Cl, Beac. HP9 89 AP54
Stanmore HA7 95 CF51
Twickenham TW2 176 CA87
Waltham Cross EN8 67 EA34
Berwick Cres, Sid. DA15 185 ES86
Berwick Gdns, Sutt. SM1 200 DC104
Berwick La, Stanfd.Riv. CM5 87 FF36
Berwick Pl, Welw.G.C. AL7 29 CX12
Berwick Pond Cl, Rain. RM13 148 FK68
Berwick Pond Rd, Rain. RM13 148 FL68
Upminster RM14 148 FM66
Berwick Rd, E16 292 C9
N22 99 DP53
Borehamwood WD6 78 CM38
Rainham RM13 148 FK68
Welling DA16 166 EV81
Berwick St, W1 285 N9
Berwick Way, Orp. BR6 206 EU102
Sevenoaks TN14 257 FH121
Berwyn Av, Houns. TW3 156 CB81
Berwyn Rd, SE24 181 DP88
Richmond TW10 158 CP84
Beryl Av, E6 293 H6
Beryl Ho, SE18
off Spinel Cl 165 ET78
Beryl Rd, W6 306 C1
Berystede, Kings.T. KT2 178 CP94
Besant Ct, N1 277 M3
Besant Pl, SE22
off Hayes Gro 162 DT84
Besant Rd, NW2 119 CY63
Besant Wk, N7
off Newington Barrow Way 121 DM61
Besant Way, NW10 118 CQ64
Besley St, SW16 181 DJ93
Bessant Dr, Rich. TW9 158 CP81
Bessborough Gdns, SW1 297 P10
Bessborough Pl, SW1 297 N10
Bessborough Rd, SW15 179 CU88
Harrow HA1 117 CD60
Bessborough St, SW1 297 N10
BESSELS GREEN, Sev. TN13 256 FC124
Bessels Grn Rd, Sev. TN13 256 FD123
Bessels Meadow, Sev. TN13 256 FD124
Bessels Way, Sev. TN13 256 FC124
Bessemer Cl, Slou. SL3 153 AZ78
Sch Bessemer Gra Prim Sch,
SE5 off Dylways 162 DR84
Bessemer Pl, SE10 303 M6
Bessemer Rd, SE5 311 K9
Welwyn Garden City AL7, AL8 29 CY05
Bessie Lansbury Cl, E6 293 L9
Bessingby Rd, Ruis. HA4 115 BU61
Bessingham Wk, SE4
off Aldersford Cl 183 DX85
Besson St, SE14 313 J6
Bessy St, E2 289 H2
Bestobell Rd, Slou. SL1 131 AQ72
Bestwood St, SE8 301 K9
Beswick Ms, NW6 273 M3
Betam Rd, Hayes UB3 155 BR75
Beta Pl, SW4
off Santley St 161 DM84
Beta Rd, Chobham GU24 210 AT110
Woking GU22 227 BB116
Beta Way, Egh. TW20 193 BC95
BETCHWORTH, RH3 248 CR134
≠ Betchworth 248 CR132
Betchworth Fort Pk, Tad. KT20 248 CP131
Betchworth Pl, Dor. RH4 247 CK134
Betchworth Rd, Ilf. IG3 125 ES61
Betchworth Way,
New Adgtn CR0 221 EC109
Betenson Av, Sev. TN13 256 FF122
Betham Rd, Grnf. UB6 137 CD69
Bethany Cl, Horn. RM12 128 FJ61
Bethany Pl, Wok. GU21 226 AX118
Bethany Waye, Felt. TW14 175 BS87
Bethecar Rd, Har. HA1 117 CE57
Bethell Av, E16 291 L4
Ilford IG1 125 EN59
Bethel Rd, Sev. TN13 257 FJ123
Welling DA16 166 EW83
Bethersden Cl, Beck. BR3 183 DZ94
Sch Beth Jacob Gram Sch for
Girls, NW4 off Stratford Rd 119 CX56
H Bethlem Royal Hosp,
Beck. BR3 203 EA101
BETHNAL GREEN, E2 288 E2
⊖ Bethnal Green 288 E4
⊖ Bethnal Green 288 G3
Bethnal Grn Est, E2 288 G3
Bethnal Grn Rd, E1 288 A4
E2 288 A4
Sch Bethnal Grn Tech Coll, E2 288 B3
Sch Beths Gram Sch, Bex. DA5
off Hartford Rd 187 FB86
Bethune Av, N11 98 DF49
Bethune Rd, N16 122 DR59
NW10 138 CR70
Bethwin Rd, SE5 311 H4
Betjeman Cl, Chsht EN7
off Rosedale Way 66 DU28
Coulsdon CR5 235 DM117
Pinner HA5 116 CA56
Betjeman Ct, West Dr. UB7 134 BK74
Betjeman Gdns, Chorl. WD3 73 BD42
Betjeman Way, Hem.H. HP1 40 BH18
Betley Ct, Walt. KT12 195 BV104
Betony Cl, Croy. CR0
off Primrose La 203 DX102
Betony Rd, Rom. RM3 106 FJ51
Betoyne Av, E4 102 EE49
BETSHAM, Grav. DA13 190 FY91
Betsham Rd, Erith DA8 167 FF80
Southfleet DA13 189 FX92
Swanscombe DA10 190 FY87
Betstyle Rd, N11 99 DH49
Betterton Dr, Sid. DA14 186 EY89
Betterton Rd, Rain. RM13 147 FE69
Betterton St, WC2 286 A9
Bettles Cl, Uxb. UB8 134 BJ68
Bettoney Vere, Bray SL6 150 AC75
Bettons Pk, E15 281 K9
Bettridge Rd, SW6 307 H9
Betts Cl, Beck. BR3 203 DY96
Betts La, Naze. EN9 50 EJ21
Betts Ms, E17 123 DZ58
Betts St, E1 300 E1
Betts Way, SE20 202 DV95
Long Ditton KT6 197 CH102
Sch Betty Layward Prim Sch,
N16 off Clissold Rd 122 DR62
Betula Cl, Ken. CR8 236 DR115
Betula Wk, Rain. RM13 148 FK69
Between Sts, Cob. KT11 213 BU114
Beulah Av, Th.Hth. CR7
off Beulah Rd 202 DQ96
Beulah Cl, Edg. HA8 96 CP48
Beulah Cres, Th.Hth. CR7 202 DQ96
Beulah Gro, Croy. CR0 202 DQ100
Beulah Hill, SE19 181 DP93
Sch Beulah Inf & Nurs Sch,
Th.Hth. CR7 off Furze Rd 202 DQ97
Sch Beulah Jun Sch,
Th.Hth. CR7 off Beulah Rd 202 DQ97
Beulah Path, E17
off Addison Rd 123 EB57
Beulah Rd, E17 123 EB57
SW19 179 CZ94
Epping CM16 70 EU29
Hornchurch RM12 128 FJ62
Sutton SM1 218 DA105
Thornton Heath CR7 202 DQ97
Beulah Wk, Wold. CR3 237 DY120
Beult Rd, Dart. DA1 167 FG83
Bevan Av, Bark. IG11 146 EU66
Bevan Cl, Hem.H. HP3 40 BK22
Bevan Ct, Croy. CR0 219 DN106
Bevan Hill, Chesh. HP5 54 AP29
Bevan Ho, Grays RM16
off Laird Av 170 GD75
Bevan Pk, Epsom KT17 217 CT111
Bevan Pl, Swan. BR8 207 FF98
Bevan Rd, SE2 166 EV78
Barnet EN4 80 DF42
Bevans Cl, Green. DA9 189 FW86
Bevan St, N1 277 K9
Bevan Way, Horn. RM12 128 FM63
Bev Callender Cl, SW8 309 J10
Bevenden St, N1 287 M2
Bevercote Wk, Belv. DA17
off Osborne Rd 166 EZ79
Beveridge Rd, NW10 138 CS66
Beverley Av, SW20 199 CT95
Hounslow TW4 156 BZ84
Sidcup DA15 185 ET87
Beverley Cl, N21 100 DQ46
SW11 off Maysoule Rd 160 DD84
SW13 159 CT82
Addlestone KT15 212 BK106
Broxbourne EN10 49 DY21
Chessington KT9 215 CJ105
Enfield EN1 82 DS42
Epsom KT17 217 CW111
Hornchurch RM11 128 FM59
Weybridge KT13 195 BS103
Beverley Cotts, SW15
off Kingston Vale 178 CS90
Beverley Ct, N14 99 DJ45
N20 off Farnham Cl 98 DC45
SE4 313 P10
Beverley Cres, Wdf.Grn. IG8 102 EH53
Beverley Dr, Edg. HA8 118 CP55
Beverley Gdns, NW11 119 CY59
SW13 159 CT83
Cheshunt EN7 66 DT30
Hornchurch RM11 128 FM59
St. Albans AL4 43 CK16
Stanmore HA7 95 CG53
Welwyn Garden City AL7 30 DC09
Wembley HA9 118 CM60
Worcester Park KT4
off Green La 199 CU102
Beverley Hts, Reig. RH2 250 DB132
Beverley Hyrst, Croy. CR0 202 DT103
Beverley La, SW15 179 CT90
Kingston upon Thames KT2 178 CS94
Beverley Ms, E4
off Beverley Rd 101 ED51
Beverley Path, SW13 159 CT82
Beverley Rd, E4 101 ED51
E6 292 F2
SE20 off Wadhurst Cl 202 DV96
SW13 159 CT83
W4 159 CT78
Bexleyheath DA7 167 FC82
Bromley BR2 204 EL103
Dagenham RM9 126 EY63
Kingston upon Thames KT1 197 CJ95
Mitcham CR4 201 DK98
New Malden KT3 199 CU98
Ruislip HA4 115 BU61
Southall UB2 156 BY77
Sunbury-on-Thames TW16 195 BT95
Whyteleafe CR3 236 DS116
Worcester Park KT4 199 CW103
● Beverley Trd Est, Mord. SM4
off Garth Rd 199 CX101
Beverley Way, SW20 199 CT95
New Malden KT3 199 CT95
Beverly, NW8 284 C3
Beversbrook Rd, N19 121 DK62
Beverstone Rd, SW2 181 DM85
Thornton Heath CR7 201 DN98
Beverston Ms, W1 284 E7
Bevil Ct, Hodd. EN11
off Molesworth 33 EA14
Bevill Allen Cl, SW17 180 DF92
Bevill Cl, SE25 202 DU97
Bevin Cl, SE16 301 L2
Bevin Ct, WC1 286 D2
Bevington Path, SE1
off Tanner St 300 A5
Sch Bevington Prim Sch, W10 282 F6
Bevington Rd, W10 282 F6
Beckenham BR3 203 EB96
Bevington St, SE16 300 D5
Bevin Rd, Hayes UB4 135 BU69
Bevin Sq, SW17 180 DF90
Bevin Way, WC1 286 E2
Bevis Cl, Dart. DA2 188 FQ87
Bevis Marks, EC3 287 P8
Bewcastle Gdns, Enf. EN2 81 DL42
Bew Ct, SE22
off Lordship La 182 DU87
Bewdley St, N1 276 E6
Bewick Ms, SE15 312 E5
Bewick St, SW8 309 K9
Bewley Cl, Chsht EN8 67 DX31
Bewley St, E1 288 F10
SW19 180 DC93
Bewlys Rd, SE27 181 DP92
Bexhill Cl, Felt. TW13 176 BY89
Bexhill Dr, Grays RM17 170 FY79
Bexhill Rd, N11 99 DK50
SE4 183 DZ87
SW14 158 CQ83
Bexhill Wk, E15 281 K9
BEXLEY, DA5 186 FA86
≠ Bexley 186 FA88
Coll Bexley Cen for Music & Dance,
Sid. DA15 off Station Rd 186 EU90
Bexley Cl, Dart. DA1 187 FE85
Coll Bexley Coll, Holly Hill Campus,
Belv. DA17
off Holly Hill Rd 167 FB78
Bexley Gdns, N9 100 DR48
Chadwell Heath RM6 126 EV57
Sch Bexley Gram Sch,
Well. DA16 off Danson La 166 EV84
BEXLEYHEATH, DA6 & DA7 186 EZ85
≠ Bexleyheath 166 EY82
Sch Bexleyheath Sch,
Bexh. DA6 off Graham Rd 166 FA83
Bexley High St, Bex. DA5 186 FA87
Bexley La, Dart. DA1 187 FE85
Sidcup DA14 186 EW90
Bexley Rd, SE9 185 EP85
Erith DA8 167 FC80
Bexley St, Wind. SL4 151 AQ81
Beyers Gdns, Hodd. EN11 33 EA14
Beyers Prospect, Hodd. EN11 33 EA13
Beyers Ride, Hodd. EN11 33 EA13
Beynon Rd, Cars. SM5 218 DF106
Bézier Apts, EC1 287 M4
Bianca Ct, NW7
off Marchant Cl 96 CS51
Bianca Rd, SE15 312 C3
Bibsworth Rd, N3 97 CZ54
Bibury Cl, SE15 311 P3
Bicester Rd, Rich. TW9 158 CN83
Bickenhall St, W1 284 F6
Bickersteth Rd, SW17 180 DF93
Bickerton Rd, N19 121 DJ61
BICKLEY, Brom. BR1 205 EM97
≠ Bickley 204 EL97
Bickley Cres, Brom. BR1 204 EL98
Bickley Pk Rd, Brom. BR1 204 EL97
Sch Bickley Pk Sch,
Nurs & Pre-Prep, Brom. BR1
off Page Heath La 204 EK97
Sch Bickley Prim Sch,
Brom. BR1 off Nightingale La 204 EJ96
Bickley Rd, E10 123 EB59
Bromley BR1 204 EK96
Bickley St, SW17 180 DE92
Bicknell Cl, Guil. GU1 242 AW133
Bicknell Rd, SE5 162 DQ83
Bickney Way, Fetch. KT22 230 CC122
Bicknoller Cl, Sutt. SM2 218 DB110
Bicknoller Rd, Enf. EN1 82 DT39
Bicknor Rd, Orp. BR6 205 ES101
Bicycle Ms, SW4 161 DK83
Bidborough Cl, Brom. BR2 204 EF99
Bidborough St, WC1 286 A3
Biddenden Way, SE9 185 EN91
Istead Rise DA13 190 GE94
Biddenham Turn, Wat. WD25 76 BW35
Bidder St, E16 291 J6
Biddestone Rd, N7 276 C1
Biddles Cl, Slou. SL1 131 AL74
Biddulph Rd, W9 283 L3
South Croydon CR2 220 DQ109
Bideford Av, Perivale UB6 137 CH68
Bideford Cl, Edg. HA8 96 CN53
Feltham TW13 176 BZ90
Romford RM3 106 FJ53
Bideford Gdns, Enf. EN1 100 DS45
Bideford Rd, Brom. BR1 184 EF90
Enfield EN3 83 DZ38
Ruislip HA4 115 BV62
Welling DA16 166 EV80
Bideford Spur, Slou. SL2 131 AP69
Bidhams Cres, Tad. KT20 233 CW121
Bidwell Gdns, N11 99 DJ52
Bidwell St, SE15 312 F7
★ Big Ben
(Elizabeth Tower), SW1 298 B5
★ Bigbury Cl, N17 100 DS52
Big Common La, Bletch. RH1 251 DP133
Biggerstaff Rd, E15 280 E8
Biggerstaff St, N4 121 DN61
Biggin Av, Mitch. CR4 200 DF95
BIGGIN HILL, West. TN16 238 EH116
Biggin Hill, SE19 181 DP94
● Biggin Hill Business Pk,
West. TN16 238 EK115
Biggin Hill Cl, Kings.T. KT2 177 CJ92
Sch Biggin Hill Prim Sch,
Bigg.H. TN16
off Old Tye Av 238 EL116
Biggin La, Grays RM16 171 GH79
Biggin Way, SE19 181 DP94
Bigginwood Rd, SW16 181 DP94
Biggs Gro Rd, Chsht EN7 66 DR27
Biggs Row, SW15
off Felsham Rd 159 CX83
Biggs Sq, E9
off Felstead St 279 P5
Big Hill, E5 122 DV60
Sch Bigland Grn Prim Sch, E1 288 E9
Bigland St, E1 288 E9
Bignell Rd, SE18 165 EP78
Jct Bignell's Cor,
S.Mimms EN6 63 CU34
Bignold Rd, E7 281 P1
Bigwood Rd, NW11 120 DB57
Biko Cl, Uxb. UB8
off Sefton Way 134 BJ72
Billet Cl, Rom. RM6 126 EX55
Billet La, Berk. HP4 38 AU18
Hornchurch RM11 128 FK60
Iver SL0 133 BB69
Slough SL3 133 BB73
Billet Rd, E17 101 DX54
Romford RM6 126 EV55
Staines-upon-Thames TW18 174 BG90
Billets Hart Cl, W7 157 CE75
● Billet Wks, E17 101 DZ53
Bill Faust Ho, E1
off Tarling St 288 G9
Bill Hamling Cl, SE9 185 EM89
Billingford Cl, SE4 163 DX84
Billing Pl, SW10 307 M4
Billing Rd, SW10 307 M4
Billings Cl, Dag. RM9
off Ellerton Rd 146 EW66
🔒 Billingsgate Mkt, E14 302 D2
Billing St, SW10 307 M4
Billington Ms, W3
off High St 138 CP74
Billington Rd, SE14 313 J5
Billinton Hill, Croy. CR0 202 DR103
Billiter Sq, EC3 287 P10
Billiter St, EC3 287 P9
Bill Nicholson Way, N17
off High Rd 100 DT52
Billockby Cl, Chess. KT9 216 CM107
Billson St, E14 302 F9
Billy Lows La, Pot.B. EN6 64 DA31
Bilsby Gro, SE9 184 EK91
Bilton Cl, Poyle SL3 153 BE82
Bilton Rd, Erith DA8 167 FG80
Perivale UB6 137 CH67
Bilton Twrs, W1
off Great Cumberland Pl 284 F9
Bilton Way, Enf. EN3 83 DY39
Hayes UB3 155 BV75
Bina Gdns, SW5 295 N9
Bincote Rd, Enf. EN2 81 DM41
Binden Rd, W12 159 CT76
Bindon Grn, Mord. SM4 200 DB98
Binfield Rd, SW4 310 B7
Byfleet KT14 212 BL112
South Croydon CR2 220 DT106
Bingfield St, N1 276 B8
Bingham Cl, Hem.H. HP1 39 BF18
South Ockendon RM15 149 FV72
Bingham Ct, N1 277 H6
Bingham Dr, Stai. TW18 174 BK94
Woking GU21 226 AT118
Bingham Pl, W1 284 G6
Bingham Pt, SE18 305 P9
Bingham Rd, Burn. SL1 130 AG71
Croydon CR0 202 DU102
Bingham St, N1 277 L4
Bingley Rd, E16 292 C8
Greenford UB6 136 CC71
Hoddesdon EN11 49 EC17
Sunbury-on-Thames TW16 175 BU94
Binley Ho, SW15
off Highcliffe Dr 179 CU86
Binne Ho, SE1
off Bath Ter 299 J7
Binney St, W1 285 H10
Binnie Rd, Dart. DA1 168 FM82
Binns Rd, W4 158 CS78
Binns Ter, W4
off Binns Rd 158 CS78
Binscombe Cres, Gdmg. GU7 258 AS144
Binsey Wk, SE2 146 EW74
Binstead Cl, Hayes UB4 136 BY71
Binyon Cres, Stan. HA7 95 CF50
Birbetts Rd, SE9 185 EM89
Birchall La, Cole Grn SG14 30 DF12
Birchall Wd, Welw.G.C. AL7 30 DC10
Bircham Path, SE4
off Aldersford Cl 183 DX85
Birchanger Rd, SE25 202 DU99
Birch Av, N13 100 DQ48
Caterham CR3 236 DR124
Leatherhead KT22 231 CF120
West Drayton UB7 134 BM72
Birch Circle, Gdmg. GU7 258 AT143
Birch Cl, E16 291 K6
N19 121 DJ61
SE15 312 D9
Amersham HP6 55 AS37
Banstead SM7 217 CY114
Brentford TW8 157 CH80
Buckhurst Hill IG9 102 EK48
Eynsford DA4 208 FK104
Hounslow TW3 157 CD83
Iver SL0 133 BD68
New Haw KT15 212 BK109
Romford RM7 127 FB55
Send GU23 243 BF125
Sevenoaks TN13 257 FH123
South Ockendon RM15 149 FX69
Teddington TW11 177 CG92
Woking GU21 226 AW119
Birch Copse, Brick.Wd AL2 60 BY30
Birch Ct, Nthwd. HA6
off Rickmansworth Rd 93 BQ51
Rom. RM6 126 EW58
Welwyn Garden City AL7 30 DA12
Birch Cres, Horn. RM11 128 FL56
South Ockendon RM15 149 FX69
Uxbridge UB10 134 BM67
Birchcroft Cl, Chaldon CR3 252 DQ125
Birchdale, Ger.Cr. SL9 112 AX60
Birchdale Cl, W.Byf. KT14 212 BJ111
Birchdale Gdns, Rom. RM6 126 EX59
Birchdale Rd, E7 124 EJ64
Birchdene Dr, SE28 166 EU75
Birchdown Ho, E3 290 C3
Birch Dr, Hat. AL10 45 CU19
Maple Cross WD3 91 BD50
Birchen Cl, NW9 118 CR61
Birchend Cl, S.Croy. CR2 220 DR107
Birchen Gro, NW9 118 CR61
Bircherley Ct, Hert. SG14
off Priory St 32 DR09
🔒 Bircherley Grn Shop Cen,
Hert. SG14 off Green St 32 DR09
Bircherley St, Hert. SG14 32 DR09
Birches, The, E12
off Station Rd 124 EL63
N21 81 DM44
SE7 164 EH79
Beaconsfield HP9 88 AH53
Brentwood CM13 108 FY48
Bushey WD23 76 CC43
East Horsley KT24 245 BS126
Hemel Hempstead HP3 39 BF23
North Weald Bassett CM16 71 FB26
Orpington BR6 223 EN105
Swanley BR8 207 FE96
Waltham Abbey EN9
off Honey La 68 EF34
Woking GU22
off Heathside Rd 227 AZ118
Birches Cl, Epsom KT18 232 CS115
Mitcham CR4 200 DF97
Pinner HA5 116 BY57
Birches La, Goms. GU5 261 BQ141
Birchfield, N.Stfd RM16 149 FX74
Birchfield Cl, Add. KT15 212 BH105
Coulsdon CR5 235 DM116
Birchfield Gro, Epsom KT17 217 CW110
Birchfield Rd, Chsht EN8 66 DV29
Birchfield St, E14 290 A10
Birch Gdns, Amer. HP7 55 AS39
Dagenham RM10 127 FC62
Birchgate Ms, Tad. KT20
off Bidhams Cres 233 CW121
BIRCH GREEN, Hert. SG14 31 DJ11
Birch Grn, NW9
off Clayton Fld 96 CS52
Hemel Hempstead HP1 39 BF19
Hertford SG14 31 DJ12
Staines-upon-Thames TW18 174 BG91
Birch Gro, E11 124 EE62
SE12 184 EF87
W3 138 CN74
Cobham KT11 214 BW114
Kingswood KT20 233 CY124
Potters Bar EN6 64 DA32
Shepperton TW17 195 BS96
Slough SL2 131 AP71
Welling DA16 166 EU84
Windsor SL4 151 AK81
Woking GU22 227 BD115
Birchgrove Ho, Rich. TW9 158 CP80
Birch Hill, Croy. CR0 221 DX106

Birchington Cl, Bexh. DA7 167 FB81
Orpington BR5 off Hart Dyke Rd 206 EW102
Birchington Ho, E5 278 E2
Birchington Rd, N8 121 DK58
NW6 273 K8
Surbiton KT5 198 CM101
Windsor SL4 151 AN82
Birchin La, EC3 287 M9
Birchlands Av, SW12 180 DF87
Birch La, Flaun. HP3 57 BB33
Purley CR8 219 DL111
Birch Leys, Hem.H. HP2 off Hunters Oak 41 BQ15
Birchmead, Orp. BR6 205 EN103
Watford WD17 75 BT38
Birchmead Av, Pnr. HA5 116 BW56
Birchmead Cl, St.Alb. AL3 43 CD17
● Birchmere Business Pk, SE28 166 EU75
Birchmere Row, SE3 315 M9
Birchmore Wk, N5 122 DQ62
Birch Pk, Har. HA3 94 CC52
Birch Pl, Green. DA9 189 FS86
Birch Rd, Felt. TW13 176 BX92
Godalming GU7 258 AT143
Romford RM7 127 FB55
Birch Row, Brom. BR2 205 EN101
Birch Tree Av, W.Wick. BR4 222 EF106
Birch Tree Gro, Ley Hill HP5 56 AV30
Birch Tree Wk, Wat. WD17 75 BT37
Birch Tree Way, Croy. CR0 202 DV103
Birch Vale, Cob. KT11 214 CA112
Birch Vw, Epp. CM16 70 EV29
Birch Wk, Borwd. WD6 78 CN39
Erith DA8 167 FC79
Ilford IG3 off Craigen Gdns 125 ES63
Mitcham CR4 201 DH95
West Byfleet KT14 212 BG112
Birch Way, Chesh. HP5 54 AR29
Hatfield AL10 off Crawford Rd 45 CV16
London Colney AL2 61 CK27
Redhill RH1 267 DH136
Warlingham CR6 237 DY118
Birchway, Hayes UB3 135 BU74
BIRCHWOOD, Hat. AL10 45 CU16
Birchwood, Shenley WD7 62 CN34
Waltham Abbey EN9 off Roundhills 68 EE34
Birchwood Av, N10 120 DG55
Beckenham BR3 203 DZ98
Hatfield AL10 45 CU16
Sidcup DA14 186 EV89
Wallington SM6 200 DG104
Sch Birchwood Av Prim Sch, Hat. AL10 off Birchwood Av 45 CV16
Birchwood Cl, Gt Warley CM13 107 FW51
Hatfield AL10 45 CU16
Horley RH6 269 DH147
Morden SM4 200 DB98
Birchwood Ct, N13 99 DP50
Edgware HA8 96 CQ54
Birchwood Dr, NW3 120 DB62
Dartford DA2 187 FE91
West Byfleet KT14 212 BG112
Birchwood Gro, Hmptn. TW12 176 CA93
Birchwood La, Chaldon CR3 251 DP125
Esher KT10 215 CD110
Knockholt Pound TN14 240 EZ115
Leatherhead KT22 215 CD110
Birchwood Pk Av, Swan. BR8 207 FE97
Birchwood Rd, SW17 181 DH92
Dartford DA2 187 FE92
Petts Wood BR5 205 ER98
Swanley BR8 207 FC95
West Byfleet KT14 212 BG112
Birchwood Ter, Swan. BR8 off Birchwood Rd 207 FC95
Birchwood Way, Park St AL2 60 CB28
Birdbrook Cl, Dag. RM10 147 FC66
Hutton CM13 109 GB44
Birdbrook Rd, SE3 164 EJ83
Birdcage Wk, SW1 297 M5
Harlow CM20 35 EQ14
Coll Bird Coll, Sid. DA14 off Birkbeck Rd 186 EU90
Birdcroft Rd, Welw.G.C. AL8 29 CW09
Birdham Cl, Brom. BR1 204 EL99
Birdhouse La, Downe BR6 239 EN115
Birdhurst Av, S.Croy. CR2 220 DR105
Birdhurst Gdns, S.Croy. CR2 220 DR105
Birdhurst Ri, S.Croy. CR2 220 DS106
Birdhurst Rd, SW18 160 DC84
SW19 180 DE93
South Croydon CR2 220 DS106
Birdie Way, Hert. SG13 32 DV08
Bird in Bush Rd, SE15 312 D4
Bird-in-Hand La, Brom. BR1 204 EK96
Bird-in-Hand Ms, SE23 off Dartmouth Rd 182 DW89
Bird-in-Hand Pas, SE23 off Dartmouth Rd 182 DW89
Bird in Hand Yd, NW3 273 P1
Bird La, Gt Warley CM13 129 FX55
Harefield UB9 92 BJ54
Upminster RM14 129 FR57
Birds Cl, Welw.G.C. AL7 30 DB11
Birds Fm Av, Rom. RM5 105 FB53
Birdsfield La, E3 279 N8
Birds Hill Dr, Oxshott KT22 215 CD113
Birds Hill Ri, Oxshott KT22 215 CD113
Birds Hill Rd, Oxshott KT22 215 CD112
Bird St, W1 285 H9
Birdswood Dr, Wok. GU21 226 AS119
Bird Wk, Twick. TW2 176 BZ88
Birdwood Av, Dart. DA1 168 FM82
SE13 183 ED86
Birdwood Cl, S.Croy. CR2 221 DX111
Teddington TW11 177 CE91
Birfield Rd, Loud. HP10 88 AC53
⇌ Birkbeck 202 DW97
Tram Birkbeck 202 DW97
Birkbeck Av, W3 138 CQ73
Greenford UB6 136 CC67
Uni Birkbeck Coll, Main Bldg, WC1 285 P5
Clore Management Cen, WC1 285 P5
Gordon Ho & Ingold Laboratories, WC1 285 N4
Gordon Sq, WC1 285 P4
Russell Sq, WC1 285 P6
Birkbeck Gdns, Wdf.Grn. IG8 102 EF47
Birkbeck Gro, W3 158 CR75
Birkbeck Hill, SE21 181 DP89
Birkbeck Ms, E8 278 A3
W3 138 CR74
Birkbeck Pl, SE21 182 DQ88
Sch Birkbeck Prim Sch, Sid. DA14 off Alma Rd 186 EV90
Birkbeck Rd, E8 278 A3
N8 121 DL56
N12 98 DC50
N17 100 DT53
NW7 97 CT50
SW19 180 DB92
W3 138 CR74
W5 157 CJ77
Beckenham BR3 202 DW96
Enfield EN2 82 DR39
Hutton CM13 109 GD44
Ilford IG2 125 ER57
Romford RM7 127 FD60
Sidcup DA14 186 EU90
Birkbeck St, E2 288 F3
Birkbeck Way, Grnf. UB6 136 CC67
Birkdale Av, Pnr. HA5 116 CA55
Romford RM3 106 FM52
Birkdale Cl, SE16 312 E1
SE28 146 EX72
Orpington BR6 205 ER101
Birkdale Gdns, Croy. CR0 221 DX105
Watford WD19 94 BX48
Birkdale Rd, SE2 166 EU77
W5 138 CL70
Birkenhead Av, Kings.T. KT2 198 CM96
Birkenhead St, WC1 286 B2
Birken Ms, Nthwd. HA6 93 BP50
Birkett Way, Ch.St.G. HP8 72 AX41
Birkhall Rd, SE6 183 ED88
Birkheads Rd, Reig. RH2 250 DA133
Birklands La, St.Alb. AL1 61 CH25
Birkwood Cl, SW12 181 DK87
Birley Rd, N20 98 DC47
Slough SL1 131 AR72
Birley St, SW11 308 G9
Birling Rd, Erith DA8 167 FD80
Birnam Cl, Send M. GU23 228 BG124
Birnam Rd, N4 121 DM61
Birnbeck Cl, NW11 119 CZ57
Birnbeck Ct, NW11 off Finchley Rd 119 CZ57
Birrell Ho, SW9 310 C9
Birse Cres, NW10 118 CS63
Birstall Grn, Wat. WD19 94 BX49
Birstall Rd, N15 122 DS57
Birtchnell Cl, Berk. HP4 38 AU18
Birtley Path, Borwd. WD6 78 CL39
Biscayne Av, E14 302 F1
Biscay Rd, W6 306 C1
Biscoe Cl, Houns. TW5 156 CA79
Biscoe Way, SE13 163 ED83
Bisenden Rd, Croy. CR0 202 DS103
Bisham Cl, Cars. SM5 200 DF102
Bisham Gdns, N6 120 DG60
Bishop Butt Cl, Orp. BR6 205 ET104
Bishop Cen, Tap. SL6 130 AF72
Sch Bishop Challoner Cath Collegiate Sch, E1 289 H9
Sch Bishop Challoner Sch, Short. BR2 off Bromley Rd 203 ED96
Sch Bishop David Brown Sch, The, Sheer. GU21 off Albert Dr 211 BD113
Sch Bishop Douglass Sch, N2 off Hamilton Rd 120 DC55
Bishop Duppa's Pk, Shep. TW17 195 BR101
Bishop Fox Way, W.Mol. KT8 196 BZ98
Sch Bishop Gilpin C of E Prim Sch, SW19 off Lake Rd 179 CZ92
Sch Bishop John Robinson Prim Sch, SE28 off Hoveton Rd 146 EW73
Sch Bishop Justus C of E Sch, Brom. BR2 off Magpie Hall La 204 EL101
Bishop Ken Rd, Har. HA3 95 CF54
Bishop Kings Rd, W14 294 F8
Sch Bishop Perrin C of E Prim Sch, Whitton TW2 off Hospital Br Rd 176 CB88
Bishop Ramsey Cl, Ruis. HA4 115 BT59
Sch Bishop Ramsey C of E Sch, Ruis. HA4 off Hume Way 115 BU59
Sch Bishop Ridley C of E Prim Sch, Well. DA16 off Northumberland Av 165 ES84
Bishop Rd, N14 99 DH45
Bishops Av, Brom. BR1 204 EJ96
Elstree WD6 78 CM43
Northwood HA6 93 BS49
Romford RM6 126 EW58
Bishop's Av, E13 144 EH67
SW6 306 D8
Bishops Av, The, N2 120 DD59
Bishops Br, W2 283 P8
Bishops Br Rd, W2 283 M9
Bishops Cl, E17 123 EB56
SE9 185 EQ89
W4 158 CQ78
Barnet EN5 79 CX44
Enf. EN1 off Central Av 82 DV40
Hatfield AL10 45 CT18
Richmond TW10 177 CK90
St. Albans AL4 43 CG16
Uxb. UB10 134 BN68
Bishop's Cl, N19 121 DJ62
Couls. CR5 235 DN118
Sutt. SM1 200 DA104
Bishops Ct, Abb.L. WD5 59 BT31
Cheshunt EN8 off Churchgate 66 DV30
Greenhithe DA9 189 FS85
Bishop's Ct, EC4 286 G8
WC2 286 E8
Bishops Dr, Felt. TW14 175 BR86
Northolt UB5 136 BY67
Bishops Fm Cl, Oakley Grn SL4 150 AH82
Bishopsfield, Harl. CM18 51 ES18
Sch Bishopsford Comm Sch, Mord. SM4 off Lilleshall Rd 200 DD100
Bishopsford Rd, Mord. SM4 200 DC101
Bishops Garth, St.Alb. AL4 off Bishops Cl 43 CG16
Bishopsgate, EC2 287 N9
Bishopsgate Arc, EC2 287 P7
Bishopsgate Chyd, EC2 287 N7
Coll Bishopsgate Inst, EC2 287 P7
Bishopsgate Rd, Eng.Grn TW20 172 AT90
Sch Bishopsgate Sch, Egh. TW20 off Bishopsgate Rd 172 AU90
Bishops Grn, Brom. BR1 off Upper Pk Rd 204 EJ95
Bishops Gro, N2 120 DD58
Hampton TW12 176 BZ91
Bishop's Hall, Kings.T. KT1 197 CK96
Bishops Hall Rd, Pilg.Hat. CM15 108 FV44
Sch Bishopshalt Sch, Hlgdn UB8 off Royal La 134 BM69
Sch Bishop's Hatfield Girls' Sch, Hat. AL10 off Woods Av 45 CU18
Bishops Hill, Walt. KT12 195 BU101
Bishops Ho, SW8 off South Lambeth Rd 310 B5
Bishopsmead, SE5 off Camberwell Rd 311 K5
Bishops Mead, Hem.H. HP1 40 BH22
Bishopsmead Cl, E.Hors. KT24 off Ockham Rd S 245 BS128
Epsom KT19 216 CR110
Bishopsmead Dr, E.Hors. KT24 245 BT129
Bishopsmead Par, E.Hors. KT24 off Ockham Rd S 245 BS129
Bishops Orchard, Farn.Royal SL2 131 AP69
Bishop's Pk, SW6 306 C8
Bishops Pk Rd, SW16 201 DL95
Bishop's Pk Rd, SW6 306 D8
Bishops Pl, Sutt. SM1 off Lind Rd 218 DC106
● Bishop Sq, Hat. AL10 44 CS17
Bishops Ri, Hat. AL10 45 CT22
Bishops Rd, N6 120 DG58
SW6 306 G5
W7 157 CE75
Croydon CR0 201 DP101
Hayes UB3 135 BQ71
Slough SL1 152 AU75
Bishop's Rd, SW11 308 D4
Bishops Sq, E1 287 P6
Bishops Ter, SE11 298 F8
Bishopsthorpe Rd, SE26 183 DX91
Sch Bishop Stopford's Sch, Enf. EN1 off Brick La 82 DV40
Bishop St, N1 277 J8
Bishops Wk, Chis. BR7 205 EQ95
Croydon CR0 221 DX106
Woob.Grn HP10 110 AE58
Bishop's Wk, Pnr. HA5 off High St 116 BY55
Bishops Way, E2 278 F10
Egham TW20 173 BD93
Bishops Wd, Wok. GU21 226 AT117
H Bishops Wood Hosp, Nthwd. HA6 93 BP51
Bishopswood Rd, N6 120 DF59
Sch Bishop Thomas Grant Catholic Sch, SW16 off Belltrees Gro 181 DM92
Bishop Wk, Shenf. CM15 109 FZ47
Sch Bishop Wand C of E Sch, The, Sun. TW16 off Laytons La 195 BT96
Bishop Wilfred Wd Cl, SE15 312 D8
Sch Bishop Winnington-Ingram C of E Prim Sch, Ruis. HA4 off Southcote Ri 115 BR59
Biskra, Wat. WD17 75 BU39
Bisley Cl, Wal.Cr. EN8 67 DX33
Worcester Park KT4 199 CW102
Bisley Ho, SW19 179 CX89
Bispham Rd, NW10 138 CM69
Bisson Rd, E15 280 F10
Bisterne Av, E17 123 ED55
● Bittacy Busines Cen, NW7 97 CY52
Bittacy Cl, NW7 97 CX51
Bittacy Ct, NW7 off Bittacy Hill 97 CY52
Bittacy Hill, NW7 97 CX51
Bittacy Pk Av, NW7 97 CX51
Bittacy Ri, NW7 97 CW51
Bittacy Rd, NW7 97 CX51
Bittams La, Cher. KT16 211 BE105
Bittern Cl, Chsht EN7 66 DQ25
Hayes UB4 136 BX71
Hemel Hempstead HP3 58 BM25
Bitterne Dr, Wok. GU21 226 AT117
Bittern Ho, West Dr. UB7 off Wraysbury Dr 134 BK73
Bittern Pl, N22 99 DM54
Bittern St, SE1 299 J5
Bittoms, The, Kings.T. KT1 197 CK97
Bixley Cl, Sthl. UB2 156 BZ77
Black Acre Cl, Amer. HP7 55 AS39
Blackacre Rd, They.B. CM16 85 ES37
Blackall St, EC2 287 N4
Blackberry Cl, Guil. GU1 242 AV131
Shepperton TW17 off Cherry Way 195 BS98
Blackberry Fm Cl, Houns. TW5 156 BY80
Blackberry Fld, Orp. BR5 206 EU95
Blackbird Hill, NW9 118 CQ61
Blackbirds La, Ald. WD25 77 CD35
Blackbird Yd, E2 288 B2
Blackborne Rd, Dag. RM10 146 FA65
Blackborough Cl, Reig. RH2 250 DC134
Blackborough Rd, Reig. RH2 266 DC135
Black Boy La, N15 122 DQ57
Black Boy Wd, Brick.Wd AL2 60 CA30
Blackbridge Rd, Wok. GU22 226 AX119
BLACKBROOK, Dor. RH5 264 CL141
Blackbrook La, Brom. BR1, BR2 205 EN97
Blackbrook Rd, Dor. RH5 263 CK140
Black Bull Yd, EC1 off Hatton Wall 286 E6
Blackburn, The, Bkhm KT23 off Little Bookham St 230 BZ124
Blackburne's Ms, W1 284 G10
Blackburn Rd, NW6 273 L5
● Blackburn Trd Est, Stanw. TW19 174 BM86
Blackburn Way, Houns. TW4 176 BY85
Blackbury Cl, Pot.B. EN6 64 DC31
Blackbush Av, Rom. RM6 126 EX57
Blackbush Cl, Sutt. SM2 218 DB108
Blackbush Spring, Harl. CM20 36 EU14
Black Cut, St.Alb. AL1 43 CE21
Blackdale, Chsht EN7 66 DU27
Blackdown Av, Wok. GU22 227 BE115
Blackdown Cl, N2 98 DC54
Woking GU22 227 BC116
Blackdown Ter, SE18 off Prince Imperial Rd 165 EM80
Black Eagle Cl, West. TN16 255 EQ127
Black Eagle Dr, Nthflt DA11 190 GA85
Black Eagle Sq, West. TN16 off High St 255 EQ127
Blackett Cl, Stai. TW18 193 BE96
Blackett St, SW15 159 CX83
Blacketts Wd Dr, Chorl. WD3 73 BB43
Black Fan Cl, Enf. EN2 82 DQ39
Black Fan Rd, Welw.G.C. AL7 30 DB09
BLACKFEN, Sid. DA15 185 ET87
Blackfen Par, Sid. DA15 off Blackfen Rd 186 EU86
Blackfen Rd, Sid. DA15 185 ES85
Sch Blackfen Sch for Girls, Sid. DA15 off Blackfen Rd 186 EV86
Blackford Cl, S.Croy. CR2 219 DP109
Blackford Rd, Wat. WD19 94 BX50
Blackford's Path, SW15 off Roehampton High St 179 CU87
⇌ Blackfriars, North Entrance 286 G10
South Entrance 298 G1
Blackfriars Br, EC4 286 G10
SE1 286 G10
Blackfriars Ct, EC4 286 G10
Black Friars La, EC4 286 G10
Blackfriars Pas, EC4 286 G10
Pier Blackfriars Pier 286 G10
Blackfriars Rd, SE1 298 G5
Black Gates, Pnr. HA5 off Moss La 116 BZ55
Black Grn Wd Cl, Park St AL2 60 CB29
Blackhall La, Sev. TN15 257 FK123
BLACKHEATH, SE3 315 K7
Guil. GU4 259 BE142
★ Blackheath, SE3 315 M7
⇌ Blackheath 315 K10
Blackheath Av, SE10 315 H5
● Blackheath Business Est, SE10 314 E7
Coll Blackheath Conservatoire of Music & The Arts, SE3 315 L10
Blackheath Gro, SE3 315 L9
Wonersh GU5 259 BB143
Sch Blackheath High Sch, Jun Dept, SE3 315 M9
Sen Dept, SE3 315 N4
Blackheath Hill, SE10 314 D7
H Blackheath Hosp, The, SE3 164 EE83
Blackheath La, Albury GU5 260 BH140
Guildford GU4, GU5 259 BD143
Sch Blackheath Nurs & Prep Sch, SE3 315 N6
BLACKHEATH PARK, SE3 164 EF84
Blackheath Pk, SE3 315 M10
Blackheath Ri, SE13 314 E9
Blackheath Rd, SE10 314 C6
Blackheath Vale, SE3 315 K8
Blackheath Village, SE3 315 L9
Blackhills, Esher KT10 214 CA109
Blackhorse Av, Chesh. HP5 54 AR33
Blackhorse Cl, Amer. HP6 55 AS38
Black Horse Cl, Wind. SL4 151 AK82
Black Horse Ct, SE1 299 M6
Blackhorse Cres, Amer. HP6 55 AS38
Tram Blackhorse Lane 202 DU101
Blackhorse La, E17 123 DX55
Croydon CR0 202 DU101
North Weald Bassett CM16 71 FD25
Reigate RH2 250 DB129
South Mimms EN6 62 CS30
● Blackhorse Ms, E17 off Blackhorse La 123 DX55
Black Horse Pl, Uxb. UB8 off Waterloo Rd 134 BJ67
⇌ Blackhorse Road 123 DX56
⊖ Blackhorse Road 123 DX56
Jct Blackhorse Rd, E17 123 DX56
Blackhorse Rd, E17 123 DX56
SE8 313 M2
Sidcup DA14 186 EU91
Woking GU22 226 AS122
Blackhouse Fm, Egh. TW20 off Coldharbour La 193 BC97
Black Lake Cl, Egh. TW20 193 BA95
Blacklands Dr, Hayes UB4 135 BQ70
Blacklands Meadow, Nutfld RH1 251 DL133
Blacklands Rd, SE6 183 EC91
Blacklands Ter, SW3 296 E9
Blackley Cl, Wat. WD17 75 BT37
Black Lion Ct, Harl. CM17 36 EW11
Black Lion Hill, Shenley WD7 62 CL32
Black Lion La, W6 159 CU77
Black Lion Ms, W6 off Black Lion La 159 CU77
Blackmans Cl, Dart. DA1 188 FJ88
Blackmans La, Warl. CR6 222 EE114
Blackmead, Rvrhd TN13 256 FE121
Blackmoor La, Wat. WD18 75 BR43
Blackmore Av, Sthl. UB1 137 CD74
Blackmore Cl, Grays RM17 170 GB78
Blackmore Ct, Wal.Abb. EN9 68 EG33
Blackmore Cres, Wok. GU21 227 BB115
Blackmore Dr, NW10 138 CP66
Blackmore Rd, Buck.H. IG9 102 EL45
Blackmores, Harl. CM19 51 EP15
Blackmores Gro, Tedd. TW11 177 CG93
Blackmore Way, Uxb. UB8 134 BK65
Blackness La, Kes. BR2 222 EK109
Woking GU22 226 AY119
★ Black Park Country Pk, Slou. SL3 133 AZ67
Black Pk Rd, Slou. SL3 133 AZ68
Black Path, E10 123 DX59
Blackpond La, Slou. SL2 131 AP66
Blackpool Gdns, Hayes UB4 135 BS70
Blackpool Rd, SE15 312 E9
Black Prince Cl, Byfleet KT14 212 BM114
Jct Black Prince Interchange, Bex. DA5 187 FB86
Black Prince Rd, SE1 298 C9
SE11 298 D9
Black Rod Cl, Hayes UB3 155 BT76
Blackshaw Rd, SW17 180 DC91
Blackshots La, Grays RM16 170 GD75
Blacksmith Cl, Ashtd. KT21 232 CM119
Blacksmith La, Chilw. GU4 259 BC139
Blacksmith Rd, Horl. RH6 269 DJ146
Blacksmith Row, Slou. SL3 153 BA77
Blacksmiths Cl, Gt Amwell SG12 33 EA08
Romford RM6 126 EW58
Blacksmiths Hill, S.Croy. CR2 220 DU113
Blacksmiths La, Cher. KT16 194 BG101
Denham UB9 113 BC61
Orpington BR5 206 EW99
Rainham RM13 147 FF67
St. Albans AL3 42 CB20
Staines-upon-Thames TW18 194 BH97
Blacksmiths Way, High Wych CM21 36 EU06
Blacks Rd, W6 294 A9
Blackstock Ms, N4 off Blackstock Rd 121 DP61
Blackstock Rd, N4 121 DP61
N5 121 DP61
Blackstone Cl, Red. RH1 266 DE135
Blackstone Est, E8 278 D7
Blackstone Hill, Red. RH1 266 DE135
Blackstone Ho, SW1 off Churchill Gdns 309 L1
Blackstone Rd, NW2 272 B2
Black Swan Cl, Ware SG12 off Baldock St 33 DX06
Black Swan Yd, SE1 299 N4
Black's Yd, Sev. TN13 off Bank St 257 FJ125
Blackthorn Av, West Dr. UB7 154 BN77
Blackthorn Cl, Reig. RH2 266 DC136
St. Albans AL4 43 CJ17
Watford WD25 59 BV32
Blackthorn Ct, Houns. TW5 156 BY80
Blackthorn Dell, Slou. SL3 152 AW76
Blackthorne Av, N7 276 E5
Croy. CR0 202 DW101
Blackthorne Cl, Hat. AL10 45 CT21
Blackthorne Cres, Colnbr. SL3 153 BE83
Blackthorne Dr, E4 101 ED49
Blackthorne Rd, Bigg.H. TN16 238 EK116
Bookham KT23 246 CC126
Colnbrook SL3 153 BE83
Blackthorn Gro, Bexh. DA7 166 EX83
Blackthorn Rd, Ilf. IG1 125 ER64
Reigate RH2 266 DC136
Welwyn Garden City AL7 30 DA10
Blackthorn St, E3 290 B5
Blackthorn Way, Warley CM14 108 FX50
Blacktree Ms, SW9 161 DN83
DLR Blackwall 302 F1
Blackwall La, SE10 303 K10
Blackwall Pier, E14 303 J1
● Blackwall Trd Est, E14 291 H7
Blackwall Tunnel, E14 302 G1
Blackwall Tunnel App, SE10 303 J5
Blackwall Tunnel Northern App, E3 280 B10
E14 290 E2
Blackwall Way, E14 302 F1
Blackwater Cl, E7 281 M1
Rainham RM13 147 FD71
Blackwater La, Hem.H. HP3 41 BS23
Blackwater Rd, Sutt. SM1 off High St 218 DB105
Blackwater St, SE22 182 DT85
Blackwell Cl, E5 123 DX63
N21 81 DL43
Harrow HA3 95 CD52
Blackwell Dr, Wat. WD19 76 BW44
Blackwell Gdns, Edg. HA8 96 CN48
Blackwell Hall La, Chesh. HP5 56 AW33
Blackwell Rd, Kings L. WD4 58 BN29
Blackwood Av, N18 off Harbet Rd 101 DX50
Blackwood Cl, W.Byf. KT14 212 BJ112
Blackwood Ct, Brox. EN10 off Groom Rd 67 DZ26
Blackwood St, SE17 299 L10
Blade Ct, Rom. RM7 off Oldchurch Rd 127 FE58
Blade Ms, SW15 159 CZ84
Bladen Cl, Wey. KT13 213 BR107
Blades Cl, Lthd. KT22 231 CK120
Blades Ct, SW15 159 CZ84
Bladindon Dr, Bex. DA5 186 EW87
Bladon Cl, Guil. GU1 243 BA133
Bladon Gdns, Har. HA2 116 CB58
Blagdens Cl, N14 99 DJ47
Blagdens La, N14 99 DK47
Blagdon Rd, SE13 183 EB86
New Malden KT3 199 CT98
Blagdon Wk, Tedd. TW11 177 CJ93
Blagrove Cres, Ruis HA4 115 BV58
Blagrove Rd, W10 282 F7
Blair Av, NW9 118 CS59
Esher KT10 196 CC103
Blair Cl, N1 277 K4
Hayes UB3 155 BU77
Sidcup DA15 185 ES85
Blairderry Rd, SW2 181 DL89
Blair Dr, Sev. TN13 257 FH123
Blairhead Dr, Wat. WD19 93 BV48
Blair Ho, SW9 310 C8
Sch Blair Peach Prim Sch, Sthl. UB1 off Beaconsfield Rd 136 BX74
Blair Rd, Slou. SL1 132 AS74
Blair St, E14 290 F9
Blake Apts, N8 off New River Av 121 DM55
Blake Av, Bark. IG11 145 ES67
Blakeborough Dr, Harold Wd RM3 106 FL54
Blake Cl, W10 282 B6
Carshalton SM5 200 DE101
Hayes UB4 135 BR68
Rainham RM13 147 FF67
St. Albans AL1 43 CG23
Welling DA16 165 ES81
Blakeden Dr, Clay. KT10 215 CF107
Blakefield Gdns, Couls. CR5 235 DM118
Blake Gdns, SW6 307 L6
Dartford DA1 168 FM84
Blake Hall Cres, E11 124 EG60
Blake Hall Rd, E11 124 EG59
Ongar CM5 71 FG25
Blakehall Rd, Cars. SM5 218 DF107
Blake Ho, Beck. BR3 183 EA93
Blakemere Rd, Welw.G.C. AL8 29 CX07
Blake Ms, Rich. TW9 off High Pk Rd 158 CN81
Blakemore Gdns, SW13 off Lonsdale Rd 159 CV79
Blakemore Rd, SW16 181 DL90
Thornton Heath CR7 201 DM99
Blakemore Way, Belv. DA17 166 EY76
Blakeney Av, Beck. BR3 203 DZ95
Blakeney Cl, E8 278 C2
N20 98 DC46
NW1 275 N7
Epsom KT19 216 CR111
Blakeney Rd, Beck. BR3 183 DZ94
Blakenham Rd, SW17 180 DF91
Blaker Ct, SE7 off Fairlawn 164 EJ80
Blake Rd, E16 291 L5
N11 99 DJ52
Croydon CR0 202 DS103
Mitcham CR4 200 DE97
Blaker Rd, E15 280 E9
Blakes Av, N.Mal. KT3 199 CT99
Blakes Ct, Saw. CM21 off Church St 36 EY05
Blake's Grn, W.Wick. BR4 203 EC102
Blakes La, E.Clan. GU4 244 BL132
New Malden KT3 199 CT99
West Horsley KT24 244 BM131
Blakesley Av, W5 137 CJ72
Blakesley Ho, E12 off Grantham Rd 125 EN62

B

Blakesley Wk, SW20
off Kingston Rd 199 CZ96
Blakes Rd, SE15 311 P4
Blakes Ter, N.Mal. KT3 199 CU99
Blake St, SE8 314 A2
Blakesware Gdns, N9 100 DR45
Blakes Way, Til. RM18
off Coleridge Rd 171 GJ82
Blake Twr, EC2 287 J6
Blakewood Cl, Felt. TW13 176 BW91
Blanchard Cl, SE9 184 EL90
Blanchard Dr, Wat. WD18
off Cassio Pl 75 BS42
Blanchard Gro, Enf. EN3 83 EB38
Blanchard Ms, Harold Wd RM3 106 FM52
Blanchards Hill, Guil. GU4 242 AY128
Blanchard Way, E8 278 D5
Blanch Cl, SE15 312 G5
Blanchedowne, SE5 162 DR84
Blanche La, S.Mimms EN6 63 CT34
Blanche Nevile Sch, N10
off Burlington Rd 120 DG55
Blanche St, E16 291 L5
Blanchland Rd, Mord. SM4 200 DB99
Blanchmans Rd, Warl. CR6 237 DY118
Blandfield Rd, SW12 180 DG86
Blandford Av, Beck. BR3 203 DY96
Twickenham TW2 176 CB88
Blandford Cl, N2 120 DC56
Croydon CR0 201 DL104
Romford RM7 127 FB56
Slough SL3 152 AX76
Woking GU22 227 BB117
Blandford Ct, Slou. SL3
off Blandford Rd S 152 AX76
Blandford Cres, E4 101 EC45
Blandford Rd, W4 158 CS76
W5 157 CK75
Beckenham BR3 202 DW96
St. Albans AL1 43 CG20
Southall UB2 156 CA77
Teddington TW11 177 CD92
Blandford Rd N, Slou. SL3 152 AX76
Blandford Rd S, Slou. SL3 152 AX76
Blandford Sq, NW1 284 D5
Blandford St, W1 284 F8
Blandford Waye, Hayes UB4 136 BW72
Bland St, SE9 164 EK84
Blaney Cres, E6 293 N3
Blanford Ms, Reig. RH2 250 DD134
Blanford Rd, Reig. RH2 266 DC135
Blanmerle Rd, SE9 185 EP88
Blann Cl, SE9 184 EK86
Blantyre St, SW10 308 A4
Blantyre Twr, SW10 308 A4
Blantyre Wk, SW10
off Blantyre St 308 A4
Blashford, NW3 274 E6
Blashford St, SE13 183 ED87
Blasker Wk, E14 302 B10
Blattner Cl, Els. WD6 78 CL42
Blawith Rd, Har. HA1 117 CE56
Blaxland Ter, Chsht EN8
off Davison Dr 67 DX28
Blaydon Cl, N17 100 DV52
Ruislip HA4 115 BS59
Blaydon Wk, N17 100 DV52
Blays Cl, Eng.Grn TW20 172 AW93
Blays La, Eng.Grn TW20 172 AV94
Bleak Hill La, SE18 165 ET79
Bleak Ho La, W4
off Chiswick High Rd 158 CR78
Blean Gro, SE20 182 DW94
Bleasdale Av, Perivale UB6 137 CG68
Blechynden St, W10 282 D10
Bleddyn Cl, Sid. DA15 186 EW86
Bledlow Cl, NW8 284 B5
SE28 146 EW73
Bledlow Ri, Grnf. UB6 136 CC68
Bleeding Heart Yd, EC1 286 F7
Blegborough Gdns, Berk. HP4 38 AS19
Blegborough Rd, SW16 181 DJ93
Blemundsbury, WC1
off Dombey St 286 C6
Blencarn Cl, Wok. GU21 226 AT116
Blendon Dr, Bex. DA5 186 EX86
Blendon Path, Brom. BR1
off Hope Pk 184 EF94
Blendon Rd, Bex. DA5 186 EX86
Blendon Ter, SE18 165 EQ78
Blendworth Pt, SW15
off Wanborough Dr 179 CV88
Blenheim Av, Ilf. IG2 125 EN58
Blenheim Cen, The,
Houns. TW3 156 CB82
Blenheim Cen, SE20 182 DW94
Blenheim Cl, N21 100 DQ46
SE12 184 EH88
SW20 199 CW97
Dartford DA1 188 FJ86
Greenford UB6
off Leaver Gdns 137 CD68
Romford RM7 127 FC56
Sawbridgeworth CM21 36 EW07
Slough SL3 133 AZ74
Upminster RM14 129 FS60
Wallington SM6 219 DJ108
Watford WD19 94 BX45
West Byfleet KT14
off Madeira Rd 211 BF113
Blenheim Ct, N19 121 DL61
Bromley BR2 off Durham Av 204 EF98
Sidcup DA14 185 ER90
Sutton SM2 off Wellesley Rd 218 DC107
Waltham Cross EN8
off Eleanor Cross Rd 67 DZ34
Woodford Green IG8
off Navestock Cres 102 EJ53
Blenheim Cres, W11 282 E10
Ruislip HA4 115 BR61
South Croydon CR2 220 DQ108
Blenheim Dr, Well. DA16 165 ET81
Blenheim Gdns, NW2 272 B4
SW2 181 DM86
Aveley RM15 148 FP74
Kingston upon Thames KT2 178 CP94
South Croydon CR2 220 DU112
Wallington SM6 219 DJ107
Wembley HA9 118 CL62
Woking GU22 226 AV119
Blenheim Gro, SE15 312 B9
Blenheim High Sch, Epsom KT19
off Longmead Rd 216 CR110
Blenheim Ms, Shenley WD7 62 CL33
Blenheim Pk Rd, S.Croy. CR2 220 DQ109
Blenheim Pas, NW8 273 N10
Blenheim Pl, Tedd. TW11 177 CF92
Blenheim Prim Sch, Orp. BR6
off Blenheim Rd 206 EW103
Blenheim Ri, N15 122 DT56
Blenheim Rd, E6 292 E2
E15 124 EE63
E17 123 DX55
NW8 273 N10
SE20 off Maple Rd 182 DW94
SW20 199 CW97
W4 158 CS76
Abbots Langley WD5 59 BU33
Barnet EN5 79 CX41
Bromley BR1 204 EL98
Dartford DA1 188 FJ86
Epsom KT19 216 CR111
Harrow HA2 116 CB58
Northolt UB5 136 CB65
Orpington BR6 206 EW103
Pilgrim's Hatch CM15 108 FU44
St. Albans AL1 43 CF19
Sidcup DA15 186 EW88
Slough SL3 152 AX77
Sutton SM1 200 DA104
Blenheim Sq,
N.Wld Bas. CM16 70 FA27
Blenheim St, W1 285 J9
Blenheim Ter, NW8 273 N10
Blenheim Way, Islw. TW7 157 CG81
North Weald Bassett CM16 70 FA27
Blenhiem Ct, Welw.G.C. AL7 29 CZ08
Blenkarne Rd, SW11 180 DF86
Blenkin Cl, St.Alb. AL3 42 CC16
Bleriot Rd, Houns. TW5 156 BW80
Blessbury Rd, Edg. HA8 96 CQ53
Blessed Dominic RC Prim Sch,
NW9 off Lanacre Av 97 CT54
Blessed Sacrament RC
Prim Sch, N1 276 C9
Blessington Cl, SE13 163 ED83
Blessington Rd, SE13 163 ED83
Blessing Way, Bark. IG11 146 EW68
BLETCHINGLEY, Red. RH1 252 DQ132
Bletchingley Adult Ed Cen,
Bletch. RH1 off Stychens La 252 DQ133
Bletchingley Cl, Merst. RH1 251 DJ129
Thornton Heath CR7 201 DP98
Bletchingley Rd, Gdse. RH9 252 DU131
Merstham RH1 251 DJ129
Nutfield RH1 251 DN133
Bletchley Ct, N1 287 L1
Bletchley St, N1 287 K1
Bletchmore Cl, Harling. UB3 155 BR78
Bletsoe Wk, N1 277 K10
Blewbury Ho, SE2 166 EX75
off Yarnton Way
Bligh Rd, Grav. DA11 191 GG86
Bligh's Ct, Sev. TN13
off Bligh's Wk 257 FH125
Bligh's Rd, Sev. TN13
off High St 257 FJ125
Bligh's Wk, Sev. TN13 257 FH125
Blincoe Cl, SW19 179 CX89
Blinco La, Geo.Grn SL3 132 AY72
Blind La, Bans. SM7 234 DE115
Betchworth RH3 264 CQ137
High Beach IG10 84 EE40
Waltham Abbey EN9 68 EJ33
Blindman's La, Chsht EN8 67 DX30
Bliss Cres, SE13 314 D8
Blissett St, SE10 314 E6
Bliss Ho, Enf. EN1 82 DT38
Bliss Ms, W10 282 F2
Blisworth Cl, Hayes UB4 136 BY70
Blithbury Rd, Dag. RM9 146 EV65
Blithdale Rd, SE2 166 EU77
Blithfield St, W8 295 L7
Blockhouse Rd, Grays RM17 170 GC79
Blockley Rd, Wem. HA0 117 CH61
Bloemfontein Av, W12 139 CV74
Bloemfontein Rd, W12 139 CV73
Bloemfontein Way, W12
off Bloemfontein Rd 139 CV74
Blomfield Ct, SW11 308 B7
Blomfield Ms, W2 283 N7
Blomfield Rd, W9 283 N6
Blomfield St, EC2 287 M7
Blomfield Vil, W2 283 M7
Blomville Rd, Dag. RM8 126 EY62
Blondell Cl, Harm. UB7 154 BK79
Blondel St, SW11 308 G8
Blondin Av, W5 157 CJ77
Blondin St, E3 280 A10
Bloomburg St, SW1 297 M9
Bloomfield Cl, Knap. GU21 226 AS118
Bloomfield Ct, E10
off Brisbane Rd 123 EB62
Bloomfield Cres, Ilf. IG2 125 EP58
Bloomfield Pl, W1 285 K10
Bloomfield Rd, N6 120 DG58
SE18 165 EP78
Bromley BR2 204 EK99
Cheshunt EN7 66 DQ25
Kingston upon Thames KT1 198 CL98
Bloomfield Ter, SW1 297 H10
Westerham TN16 255 ES125
Bloom Gro, SE27 181 DP90
Bloomhall Rd, SE19 182 DR92
Bloom Pk Rd, SW6 306 G5
BLOOMSBURY, WC1 285 P7
Bloomsbury Cl, NW7 97 CU52
W5 138 CM73
Epsom KT19 216 CR110
Bloomsbury Ct, WC1 286 B7
Guildford GU1 off St. Lukes Sq 259 AZ135
Pinner HA5 116 BZ55
Bloomsbury Ho, SW4 181 DK86
Bloomsbury Ms, Wdf.Grn. IG8
off Waltham Rd 102 EL51
Bloomsbury Pl, SW18 180 DC85
WC1 286 B6
Bloomsbury Sq, WC1 286 B7
Bloomsbury St, WC1 285 P7
Bloomsbury Way, WC1 286 A8
Blore Cl, SW8 309 N7
Blore Ct, W1 285 N9
Blossom Ave, Har. HA2 116 CB61
Blossom Cl, W5 158 CL75
Dagenham RM9 146 EZ67
South Croydon CR2 220 DT106
Blossom Dr, Orp. BR6 205 ET103
Blossom Ho Sch, SW20
off The Drive 179 CW94
Blossom La, Enf. EN2 82 DQ39
Blossom St, E1 287 P6
Blossom Way, Uxb. UB10 134 BM66
West Drayton UB7 154 BN77
Blossom Waye, Houns. TW5 156 BY80
Blount St, E14 289 M8
Bloxam Gdns, SE9 184 EL85
Bloxhall Rd, E10 123 DZ60
Bloxham Cres, Hmptn. TW12 176 BZ94
Bloxworth Cl, Wall. SM6 201 DJ104
Blucher Rd, SE5 311 K5
Blucher St, Chesh. HP5 54 AP31
Blue Anchor All, Rich. TW9
off Kew Rd 158 CL84
Blue Anchor La, SE16 300 D8
West Tilbury RM18 171 GL77
Blue Anchor Yd, E1 288 C10
Blue Ball La, Egh. TW20 173 AZ92
Blue Ball Yd, SW1 297 L3
Blue Barn La, Wey. KT13 212 BN111
Bluebell Av, E12 124 EK64
Bluebell Cl, E9 278 G8
SE26 182 DT91
Hemel Hempstead HP1
off Sundew Rd 39 BE21
Hertford SG13 32 DU09
Northolt UB5 136 BZ65
Orpington BR6 205 EQ103
Park Street AL2 60 CC27
Rush Green RM7 127 FE61
Wallington SM6 201 DH102
Bluebell Ct, Wok. GU22 226 AX119
Bluebell Dr, Bedmond WD5 59 BT27
Cheshunt EN7 66 DR28
Bluebell La, East Horsley KT24 245 BS129
Stoke D'Abernon KT11 230 CA117
Bluebell Wk, High Wych. CM21 36 EV06
Bluebell Way, Hat. AL10 28 CT14
Ilford IG1 145 EP65
Blueberry Cl, St.Alb. AL3 43 CD16
Watford WD19 94 BW45
Woodford Green IG8 102 EG51
Blueberry Gdns, Couls. CR5 235 DM116
Blueberry La, Knock. TN14 240 EW116
Bluebird La, Dag. RM10 146 FA66
Bluebird Way, SE28 165 ER75
Bricket Wood AL2 60 BY30
Bluebridge Av, Brook.Pk AL9 63 CY27
Bluebridge Rd, Brook.Pk AL9 63 CY26
Blue Cedars, Bans. SM7 217 CX114
Blue Cedars Pl, Cob. KT11 214 BX112
Bluecoat Ct, Hert. SG14
off Railway St 32 DR09
Bluecoats Av, Hert. SG14 32 DR09
Bluecoat Yd, Ware SG12 33 DX06
Bluefield Ct, Hmptn. TW12 176 CA92
Blue Gate Flds Inf & Jun Schs,
E1 288 G10
Bluegates, Ewell KT17 217 CU108
Bluehouse Gdns, Oxt. RH8 254 EG128
Blue Ho Hill, St.Alb. AL3 42 CA20
Bluehouse La, Oxt. RH8 254 EG127
Bluehouse Rd, E4 102 EE48
Blue Leaves Av, Couls. CR5 235 DK121
Bluelion Pl, SE1 299 N6
Bluemans, N.Wld Bas. CM16 53 FD24
Bluemans End,
N.Wld Bas. CM16 53 FD24
Blueprint Apts, SW12
off Balham Gro 181 DH87
Blue Sch, The, Islw. TW7
off North St 157 CG83
Bluett Rd, Lon.Col. AL2 61 CK27
Bluewater 189 FU88
Bluewater Ho, SW18
off Smugglers Way 160 DB84
Bluewater Parkway,
Bluewater DA9 189 FS87
Bluewater Shop Cen,
Green. DA9 189 FT87
Blumfield Ct, Slou. SL1 131 AK70
Blumfield Cres, Slou. SL1 131 AK70
Blundel La, Stoke D'Ab. KT11 214 CB114
Blundell Av, Horl. RH6 268 DF148
Blundell Cl, E8 278 C2
St. Albans AL3 43 CD16
Blundell Rd, Edg. HA8 96 CR53
Blundell St, N7 276 B6
Blunden Cl, Dag. RM8 126 EW60
Blunden Dr, Slou. SL3 153 BB77
Blunesfield, Pot.B. EN6 64 DD31
Blunt Rd, S.Croy. CR2 220 DR106
Blunts Av, Sipson UB7 154 BN80
Blunts La, St.Alb. AL2 60 BW27
Blunts Rd, SE9 185 EN85
Blurton Rd, E5 279 H1
Blyth Cl, E14 302 G8
Borehamwood WD6 78 CM39
Twickenham TW1
off Grimwood Rd 177 CF86
Blythe Cl, SE6 183 DZ87
Iver SL0 133 BF72
Blythe Hill, SE6 183 DZ87
Orpington BR5 205 ET95
Blythe Hill La, SE6 183 DZ87
Blythe Hill Pl, SE23
off Brockley Pk 183 DY87
Blythe Ms, W14 294 C6
Blythe Rd, W14 294 E8
Hoddesdon EN11 49 ED19
Blythe St, E2 288 E2
Blytheswood, Hem.H. HP3 40 BG23
Blytheswood Pl, SW16
off Curtis Fld Rd 181 DM91
Blythe Vale, SE6 183 DZ88
Blyth Rd, E17 123 DZ59
SE28 146 EW73
Bromley BR1 204 EF95
Hayes UB3 155 BS75
Blyth's Wf, E14 301 M1
Blythswood Rd, Ilf. IG3 126 EU60
Blyth Wk, Upmin. RM14 129 FS58
Blythway, Welw.G.C. AL7 29 CZ06
Blyth Wd Pk, Brom. BR1
off Blyth Rd 204 EF95
Blythwood Rd, N4 121 DL59
Pinner HA5 94 BX53
Blyton Cl, Beac. HP9 89 AK51
BMI Hendon Hosp, NW4 119 CW55
Bnois Jerusalem Sch, N16
off Amhurst Pk 122 DS59
Boades Ms, NW3 274 A1
Boadicea Cl, Slou. SL1 131 AK74
Boadicea St, N1 276 C9
Boakes Cl, NW9 118 CQ56
Boakes Meadow, Shore. TN14 225 FF111
Boar Cl, Chig. IG7 104 EU50
Boardman Av, E4 83 EB43
Boardman Cl, Barn. EN5 79 CY43
Board School Rd, Wok. GU21 227 AZ116
Boardwalk Pl, E14 302 E2
Boar Hill, Dor. RH5 263 CF142
Boarlands Cl, Slou. SL1 131 AM73
Boarlands Path, Slou. SL1
off Brook Path 131 AM73
Boar's Head Yd, Brent. TW8
off Brent Way 157 CK80
Boars Rd, Harl. CM17 36 FA14
Boatemah Wk, SW9
off Peckford Pl 310 E9
Boathouse Wk, SE15 312 B4
Richmond TW9 158 CL81
Boat Lifter Way, SE16 301 M8
Bob Anker Cl, E13 291 P2
Bobbin Cl, SW4 309 L10
Bobby Moore Way, N10 98 DF52
Bark. IG11 off Broadway 145 EQ67
Bob Dunn Way, Dart. DA1 168 FJ84
Bob Marley Way, SE24
off Mayall Rd 161 DN84
Bobs La, Rom. RM1 105 FG52
Bocketts La, Lthd. KT22 231 CF124
Bockhampton Rd,
Kings.T. KT2 178 CM94
Bocking St, E8 278 E8
Boddicott Cl, SW19 179 CY89
Boddington Gdns, W3 158 CN75
Bodell Cl, Grays RM16 170 GB76
Bodiam Cl, Enf. EN1 82 DR40
Bodiam Rd, SW16 181 DK94
Bodiam Way, NW10 138 CM69
Bodicea Ms, Houns. TW4 176 BZ87
Bodle Av, Swans. DA10 190 FY87
Bodley Cl, Epp. CM16 69 ET30
New Malden KT3 198 CS99
Bodley Manor Way, SW2
off Hambridge Way 181 DN87
Bodley Rd, N.Mal. KT3 198 CR100
Bodmin Av, Slou. SL2 131 AN71
Bodmin Cl, Har. HA2 116 BZ62
Orpington BR5 206 EW102
Bodmin Gro, Mord. SM4 200 DB99
Bodmin St, SW18 180 DA88
Bodnant Gdns, SW20 199 CU97
Bodney Rd, E8 278 E3
Bodwell Cl, Hem.H. HP1 39 BF19
Boeing Way, Sthl. UB2 155 BV76
Boevey Path, Belv. DA17 166 EZ79
Bogey La, Orp. BR6 223 EN108
Bognor Gdns, Wat. WD19 94 BW50
Bognor Rd, Well. DA16 166 EX81
Bohemia, Hem.H. HP2 40 BL19
Bohemia Pl, E8 278 F4
Bohn Rd, E1 289 L6
Bohun Gro, Barn. EN4 80 DE44
Boileau Par, W5
off Boileau Rd 138 CM72
Boileau Rd, SW13 159 CU80
W5 138 CM72
Bois Av, Amer. HP6 55 AP36
Bois Hall Rd, Add. KT15 212 BK105
Bois Hill, Chesh. HP5 54 AS34
Bois La, Amer. HP6 55 AR35
Bois Moor Rd, Chesh. HP5 54 AQ33
Boissy Cl, St.Alb. AL4 44 CL21
Bolberry Rd, Coll.Row RM5 105 FD50
Bolden St, SE8 314 C8
Bolderwood Way, W.Wick. BR4 203 EB103
Boldmere Rd, Pnr. HA5 116 BW59
Boleyn Av, Enf. EN1 82 DV39
Epsom KT17 217 CV110
Boleyn Cl, E17 123 EA56
Chafford Hundred RM16
off Clifford Rd 170 FZ76
Hemel Hempstead HP2
off Parr Cres 41 BQ15
Loughton IG10
off Roding Gdns 84 EL44
Staines-upon-Thames TW18
off Chertsey La 173 BE92
Boleyn Ct, Brox. EN10 49 DY21
Buckhurst Hill IG9 102 EG46
Boleyn Dr, Ruis. HA4 116 BX61
St. Albans AL1 43 CD22
West Molesey KT8 196 BZ97
Boleyn Gdns, Brwd. CM13 109 GA48
Dagenham RM10 147 FC66
West Wickham BR4 203 EB103
Boleyn Gro, W.Wick. BR4 203 EC103
Boleyn Rd, E6 144 EK68
E7 281 P7
N16 277 P3
Boleyn Row, Epp. CM16 70 EV29
Boleyn Wk, Lthd. KT22 231 CF120
Boleyn Way, Barn. EN5 80 DC41
Ilford IG6 103 EQ51
Swanscombe DA10 190 FY87
Bolina Rd, SE16 301 H10
Bolingbroke Acad, SW11 180 DE85
Bolingbroke Cl, Cockfos. EN4 80 DF41
Bolingbroke Gro, SW11 160 DE84
Bolingbroke Rd, W14 294 D6
Bolingbroke Wk, SW11 308 B5
Bolingbroke Way, Hayes UB3 135 BR74
Bolingbrook, St.Alb. AL4 43 CG16
Bolliger Ct, NW10
off Park Royal Rd 138 CQ70
Bollo Br Rd, W3 158 CP76
Bollo La, W3 158 CP75
W4 158 CQ77
Bolney Gate, SW7 296 C5
Bolney St, SW8 310 C5
Bolney Way, Felt. TW13 176 BY90
Bolsover Gro, Merst. RH1 251 DL129
Bolsover St, W1 285 K5
Bolstead Rd, Mitch. CR4 201 DH95
Bolster Gro, N22 99 DK52
Bolt Cellar La, Epp. CM16 69 ES29
Bolt Ct, EC4 286 F9
Bolters La, Bans. SM7 217 CZ114
Bolters Rd, Horl. RH6 268 DG146
Bolters Rd S, Horl. RH6 268 DF146
Boltmore Cl, NW4 119 CX55
Bolton Av, Wind. SL4 151 AQ83
Bolton Cl, SE20
off Selby Rd 202 DU96
Chessington KT9 215 CK107
Bolton Cres, SE5 310 F3
Windsor SL4 151 AQ83
Bolton Dr, Mord. SM4 200 DC101
Bolton Gdns, NW10 282 C1
SW5 295 L10
Bromley BR1 184 EF93
Teddington TW11 177 CG93
Bolton Gdns Ms, SW10 295 N10
Bolton Rd, E15 281 M5
N18 100 DT50
NW8 273 M9
NW10 138 CS67
W4 158 CQ80
Chessington KT9 215 CK107
Harrow HA1 116 CC56
Windsor SL4 151 AQ83
Boltons, The, SW10 295 N10
Wembley HA0 117 CF63
Woodford Green IG8 102 EG49
Boltons Cl, Wok. GU22 228 BG116
Boltons La, Harling. UB3 155 BQ80
Woking GU22 228 BG116
Boltons Pl, SW5 295 N10
Bolton St, W1 297 K2
Bolton Wk, N7
off Durham Rd 121 DM61
Bombay St, SE16 300 E8
Bomber Command Mem, W1 297 J4
Bombers La, West. TN16 239 ER119
Bomer Cl, Sipson UB7 154 BN80
Bomore Rd, W11 282 D10
Bonar Pl, Chis. BR7 184 EL94
Bonar Rd, SE15 312 C5
Bonaventure Ct, Grav. DA12 191 GM91
Bonchester Cl, Chis. BR7 185 EN94
Bonchurch Cl, Sutt. SM2 218 DB108
Bonchurch Rd, W10 282 E6
W13 137 CH74
Bond Cl, Iver SL0 133 BB66
Knockholt Pound TN14 240 EX115
West Drayton UB7 134 BM72
Bond Ct, EC4 287 L9
Bondfield Av, Hayes UB4 135 BU69
Bondfield Rd, E6 293 H7
Bondfield Wk, Dart. DA1 168 FM84
Bond Gdns, Wall. SM6 219 DJ105
Bonding Yd Wk, SE16 301 M5
Bond Prim Sch, Mitch. CR4
off Bond Rd 200 DF96
Bond Rd, Mitch. CR4 200 DE96
Surbiton KT6 198 CM103
Warlingham CR6 237 DX118
Bonds La, Mid Holm. RH5 263 CH142
Bond Street 285 H9
Bond St, E15 281 J2
W4 158 CS77
W5 137 CK73
Englefield Green TW20 172 AV92
Grays RM17 170 GC79
Bondway 310 B2
Bondway, SW8 310 B3
Bonehurst Rd, Horl. RH6 266 DG144
Salfords RH1 266 DG142
Bone Mill La, Gdse. RH9
off Eastbourne Rd 253 DY134
Boneta Rd, SE18 305 J7
Bonfield Rd, SE13 163 EC84
Bonham Cl, Belv. DA17 166 EZ78
Bonham Gdns, Dag. RM8 126 EX61
Bonham Rd, SW2 181 DM85
Dagenham RM8 126 EX61
Bonham Way, Nthflt. DA11 190 GC88
Bonheur Rd, W4 158 CR75
Bonhill St, EC2 287 M5
Boniface Gdns, Har. HA3 94 CB52
Boniface Rd, Uxb. UB10 115 BP62
Boniface Wk, Har. HA3 94 CB52
Bonington Ho, Enf. EN1
off Ayley Cft 82 DU43
Bonington Rd, Horn. RM12 128 FK64
Bonita Ms, SE4 313 J10
Bonks Hill, Saw. CM21 36 EX06
Bon Marche Ter Ms, SE27
off Gipsy Rd 182 DS91
Bonner Ct, Chsht EN8
off Coopers Wk 67 DX28
Bonner Hill Rd, Kings.T. KT1 198 CM97
Bonner Prim Sch, E2 289 H1
Bonner Rd, E2 278 G10
Bonners Cl, Wok. GU22 226 AY122
Bonnersfield Cl, Har. HA1 117 CF58
Bonnersfield La, Har. HA1 117 CG58
Bonner St, E2 289 H1
Bonner Wk, Grays RM16
off Clifford Rd 170 FZ76
Bonnett Ms, Horn. RM11 128 FL60
Bonneville Gdns, SW4 181 DJ86
Bonneville Prim Sch, SW4
off Bonneville Gdns 181 DJ86
Bonney Gro, Chsht EN7 66 DU30
Bonneygrove Prim Sch, Chsht EN7
off Dark La 66 DU30
Bonney Way, Swan. BR8 207 FE96
Bonnington Ho, N1
off Killick St 286 C1
Bonningtons, Brwd. CM13 109 GB48
Bonnington Sq, SW8 310 C2
Bonnington Twr, Brom. BR2 204 EL100
Bonnygate Prim Sch, S.Ock. RM15
off Arisdale Av 149 FV71
Bonny's Rd, Reig. RH2 265 CX135
Bonny St, NW1 275 L7
Bonser Rd, Twick. TW1 177 CF89
Bonsey Cl, Wok. GU22 226 AY121
Bonsey La, Wok. GU22 226 AY121
Bonseys La, Chobham GU24 211 AZ110
Bonsor Dr, Kgswd KT20 233 CY122
Bonsor St, SE5 311 N5
Bonus Pastor Cath Coll,
Lwr Sch, Brom. BR1
off Churchdown 184 EE91
Upr Sch, Brom. BR1
off Winlaton Rd 184 EE91
Bonville Gdns, NW4
off Handowe Cl 119 CU56
Bonville Rd, Brom. BR1 184 EF92
Bookbinders' Cotts, N20
off Manor Dr 98 DF48
Booker Cl, E14 289 P7
Booker Rd, N18 100 DU50
Bookham 230 BZ123
Bookham Ct, Lthd. KT23
off Church Rd 230 BZ123
Mitcham CR4 200 DD97
Bookham Gro, Bkhm KT23 246 CB126
Bookham Ind Est,
Bkhm KT23 230 BZ123
Bookham Rd, Down. KT11 230 BW119
Book Ms, WC2 285 P9
Boone Ct, N9 100 DW48
Boones Rd, SE13 164 EE84
Boone St, SE13 164 EE84
Boord St, SE10 303 K6
Boot All, St.Alb. AL1
off Market Pl 43 CD20
Boothby Rd, N19 121 DK61
Booth Cl, E9 278 F9
SE28 146 EV73
Booth Dr, Stai. TW18 174 BK93
Booth Ho, Brent. TW8
off London Rd 157 CJ80
Booth La, EC4 287 J10
Boothman Ho, Har. HA3 117 CK55

B

Booth Rd, E16 304 D3
NW9 96 CS54
Croydon CR0
off Waddon New Rd 201 DP103
Booths Cl, N.Mymms AL9 45 CX24
Booth's Ct, Hutt. CM13 109 GB44
Booth's Pl, W1 285 M7
Boot St, N1 287 N3
Bordars Rd, W7 137 CE71
Bordars Wk, W7 137 CE71
Borden Av, Enf. EN1 82 DR44
Border Cres, SE26 182 DV92
Border Gdns, Croy. CR0 221 EB105
Bordergate, Mitch. CR4 200 DE95
Border Rd, SE26 182 DV92
Borderside, Slou. SL2 132 AU72
Borders La, Loug. IG10 85 EN42
Bordesley Rd, Mord. SM4 200 DB98
Bordon Wk, SW15 179 CU87
Boreas Wk, N1 287 H1
Boreham Av, E16 291 N9
Boreham Cl, E11
off Hainault Rd 123 EC60
Boreham Holt, Els. WD6 78 CM42
Boreham Rd, N22 100 DQ54
BOREHAMWOOD, WD6 78 CP41
● Borehamwood Ind Pk, Borwd. WD6 78 CR40
Borehamwood Shop Pk, Borwd. WD6 78 CN41
Borgard Rd, SE18 305 J8
Borham Ms, Hodd. EN11 33 EA13
Borkwood Pk, Orp. BR6 223 ET105
Borkwood Way, Orp. BR6 223 ES105
Borland Cl, Green. DA9
off Steele Av 189 FU85
Borland Rd, SE15 162 DW84
Teddington TW11 177 CH93
Bornedene, Pot.B. EN6 63 CY31
Borneo St, SW15 159 CW83
⊖ Borough 299 K5
BOROUGH, THE, SE1 299 J5
Borough, The, Brock. RH3 264 CN135
Borough Gra, S.Croy. CR2 220 DU112
Borough High St, SE1 299 J5
Borough Hill, Croy. CR0 201 DP104
★ Borough Mkt, SE1 299 L3
Borough Rd, SE1 298 G6
Isleworth TW7 157 CE81
Kingston upon Thames KT2 198 CN95
Mitcham CR4 200 DE96
Tatsfield TN16 238 EK121
Borough Sq, SE1 299 J5
Borough Way, Pot.B. EN6 63 CY32
Borrell Cl, Brox. EN10 49 DZ20
Borrett Cl, SE17 311 J1
Borrodaile Rd, SW18 180 DB86
Borromeo Way, Brwd. CM14 108 FV46
Borrowdale Av, Har. HA3 95 CG54
Borrowdale Cl, N2 98 DC54
Egham TW20 off Derwent Rd 173 BB94
Ilford IG4 124 EL56
South Croydon CR2 220 DT113
Borrowdale Ct, Enf. EN2 82 DQ39
Hemel Hempstead HP2 40 BL17
Borrowdale Dr, S.Croy. CR2 220 DT112
Borthwick Ms, E15 281 J1
Borthwick Rd, E15 281 J1
NW9 off West Hendon Bdy 119 CT58
Borthwick St, SE8 314 A1
Borwick Av, E17 123 DZ55
Bosanquet Cl, Uxb. UB8 134 BK70
Bosanquet Rd, Hodd. EN11 49 EC15
Bosbury Rd, SE6 183 EC90
Boscastle Rd, NW5 121 DH62
Boscobel Cl, Brom. BR1 205 EM96
Boscobel Pl, SW1 297 H8
Boscobel St, NW8 284 B5
Bosco Cl, Orp. BR6 223 ET105
Boscombe Av, E10 123 ED59
Grays RM17 170 GD77
Hornchurch RM11 128 FK60
Boscombe Circ, NW9
off Warmwell Av 96 CR54
Boscombe Cl, E5 279 L2
Egham TW20 193 BC95
Boscombe Gdns, SW16 181 DL93
Boscombe Rd, SW17 180 DG93
SW19 200 DB95
W12 139 CU74
Worcester Park KT4 199 CW102
Bose Cl, N3 97 CY53
Bosgrove, E4 101 EC46
Boshers Gdns, Egh. TW20 173 AZ93
Boss Ho, SE1 300 A4
Boss St, SE1 300 A4
Bostall Heath, SE2 166 EW78
Bostall Hill, SE2 166 EU78
Bostall La, SE2 166 EV78
Bostall Manorway, SE2 166 EV77
Bostall Pk Av, Bexh. DA7 166 EY80
Bostall Rd, Orp. BR5 186 EV94
Bostal Row, Bexh. DA7
off Harlington Rd 166 EZ83
Bostock Ho, Houns. TW5 156 CA79
Boston Gdns, W4 158 CS79
W7 157 CG77
Brentford TW8 157 CG77
Boston Gro, Ruis. HA4 115 BQ58
Slough SL1 131 AQ72
⊖ Boston Manor 157 CG77
★ Boston Manor Ho, Brent. TW8 157 CH78
Boston Manor Rd, Brent. TW8 157 CH77
Boston Pk Rd, Brent. TW8 157 CJ78
Boston Pl, NW1 284 E5
Boston Rd, E6 292 G2
E17 123 EA58
W7 137 CE74
Croydon CR0 201 DM100
Edgware HA8 96 CQ52
Bostonthorpe Rd, W7 157 CE75
Boston Vale, W7 157 CG77
Bosun Cl, E14 302 B4
Bosville Av, Sev. TN13 256 FG123
Bosville Dr, Sev. TN13 256 FG123
Bosville Rd, Sev. TN13 256 FG123
Boswell Cl, Orp. BR5
off Killewarren Way 206 EW100
Shenley WD7 62 CL32
Boswell Ct, WC1 286 B6
Boswell Path, Hayes UB3
off Croyde Av 155 BT77
Boswell Rd, Th.Hth. CR7 202 DQ98
Boswell Row, Cat. CR3
off Croydon Rd 236 DU122
Boswell St, WC1 286 B6
Bosworth Cl, E17 101 DZ53
Bosworth Ct, Slou. SL1 130 AJ73
Bosworth Cres, Rom. RM3 106 FJ51
Bosworth Ho, Erith DA8
off Saltford Cl 167 FE78
Bosworth Rd, N11 99 DK51
W10 282 F5
Barnet EN5 80 DA41
Dagenham RM10 126 FA63
BOTANY BAY, Enf. EN2 81 DK36
Botany Bay La, Chis. BR7 205 EQ97
Botany Cl, Barn. EN4 80 DE42
Botany Rd, Nthflt DA11 170 GA83
Botany Way, Purf. RM19 168 FP78
Boteley Cl, E4 101 ED47
Botery's Cross, Red. RH1 251 DP133
Botham Cl, Edg. HA8 96 CQ52
Botham Dr, Slou. SL1 152 AS76
Botha Rd, E13 292 B6
Bothwell Cl, E16 291 M7
Bothwell Rd, New Adgtn CR0 221 EC110
Bothwell St, W6 306 D3
BOTLEY, Chesh. HP5 56 AV30
Botley La, Chesh. HP5 56 AU30
Botley Rd, Chesh. HP5 56 AT30
Hemel Hempstead HP2 40 BN15
Botolph All, EC3 287 N10
Botolph La, EC3 299 M1
Botsford Rd, SW20 199 CY96
Bottom Ho Fm La, Ch.St.G. HP8 90 AT45
Bottom La, Chesh. HP5 56 AT34
Kings Langley WD4 74 BH35
Seer Green HP9 89 AP51
Bottrells Cl, Ch.St.G. HP8 90 AT47
Bottrells La, Ch.St.G. HP8 90 AT47
Coleshill HP7 89 AP46
Bott Rd, Hawley DA2 188 FM91
Botts Ms, W2 283 K9
Botts Pas, W2 283 K9
Botwell Common Rd, Hayes UB3 135 BR73
Botwell Cres, Hayes UB3 135 BS72
Sch Botwell Ho RC Prim Sch, Hayes UB3
off Botwell La 155 BT75
Botwell La, Hayes UB3 135 BS74
Boucher Cl, Tedd. TW11 177 CF92
Boucher Dr, Nthflt DA11 191 GF90
Bouchier Wk, Rain. RM13
off Deere Av 147 FG65
Boughton Av, Brom. BR2 204 EF101
● Boughton Business Pk, Amer. HP6 72 AV39
Boughton Hall Av, Send GU23 227 BF124
Boughton Rd, SE28 165 ES76
Boughton Way, Amer. HP6 72 AW38
Boulcott St, E1 289 K9
Boulevard, The, SW6 307 P7
SW17 off Balham High Rd 180 DG89
SW18 off Smugglers Way 160 DB84
Greenhithe DA9
off Ingress Pk Av 169 FW84
Watford WD18 75 BR43
Welwyn Garden City AL7 29 CZ07
Wembley HA9
off Engineers Way 118 CN63
Woodford Green IG8 103 EN51
Boulevard Dr, NW9 97 CT54
Boulmer Rd, Uxb. UB8 134 BJ69
Boulogne Rd, Croy. CR0 202 DQ100
Boulter Cl, Brom. BR1 205 EP97
Boulter Gdns, Rain. RM13 147 FG65
Boulters Cl, Maid. SL6 130 AC70
Slough SL1 off Amerden Way 151 AN75
Boulters Ct, Maid. SL6 130 AC70
Boulters Gdns, Maid. SL6 130 AC70
Boulters La, Maid. SL6 130 AC70
Boulters Lock Island, Maid. SL6 130 AC69
Boulthurst Way, Oxt. RH8 254 EH132
Boulton Ho, Brent. TW8
off Green Dragon La 158 CL78
Boulton Rd, Dag. RM8 126 EY62
Boultwood Rd, E6 293 H9
Bounce, The, Hem.H. HP2 40 BK18
BOUNCE HILL, Rom. RM4 87 FH39
Bounces La, N9 100 DV47
Bounces Rd, N9 100 DV46
Boundaries Rd, SW12 180 DF89
Feltham TW13 176 BW88
Boundary, The, Lt.Berk. SG13 47 DJ19
Boundary Av, E17 123 DZ59
● Boundary Business Cen, Wok. GU21 227 BA115
● Boundary Business Ct, Mitch. CR4 200 DD97
Boundary Cl, SE20
off Haysleigh Gdns 202 DU96
Barnet EN5 79 CZ39
Ilford IG3 off Loxford La 125 ES63
Kingston upon Thames KT1 198 CP97
Southall UB2 156 CA78
Boundary Ct, Epp. CM16 69 ER32
N18 100 DT51
Welwyn Garden City AL7
off Boundary La 29 CZ13
Boundary Dr, Hert. SG14 32 DR07
Hutton CM13 109 GE45
Boundary La, E13 292 E3
SE17 311 K3
Welwyn Garden City AL7 29 CY12
Boundary Pk, Wey. KT13 195 BS103
Boundary Pas, E2 288 A4
Boundary Pl, Woob.Grn HP10 110 AD55
Boundary Rd, E13 292 D1
E17 123 DZ59
N9 82 DW44
N22 121 DP55
NW8 273 M9
SW19 180 DD93
Ashford TW15 174 BJ92
Barking IG11 145 EQ68
Carshalton SM5 219 DH107
Chalfont St. Peter SL9 90 AX52
High Wycombe HP10 88 AC54
Pinner HA5 116 BX58
Romford RM1 127 FG58
St. Albans AL1 43 CE18
Sidcup DA15 185 ES85
Taplow SL6 130 AE70
Upminster RM14 128 FN62
Wallington SM6 219 DH107
Wembley HA9 118 CL62
Woking GU21 227 BA116
Boundary Row, SE1 298 G4
Boundary St, E2 288 A3
Erith DA8 167 FF80
Boundary Way, Croy. CR0 221 EA106
Hemel Hempstead HP2 41 BQ18
Watford WD25 59 BV32
Woking GU21 227 BA115
Boundary Yd, Wok. GU21
off Boundary Rd 227 BA116
Boundfield Rd, SE6 184 EE90
⊖ Bounds Green 99 DK51
● Bounds Grn Ind Est, N11 99 DH51
Sch Bounds Grn Inf Sch, N11
off Bounds Grn Rd 99 DK52
Sch Bounds Grn Jun Sch, N11
off Bounds Grn Rd 99 DL52
Bounds Grn Rd, N11 99 DJ51
N22 99 DJ51
Bourbon La, W12 294 C3
Bourchier Cl, Sev. TN13 257 FH126
Bourchier St, W1 285 N10
Bourdon Pl, W1 285 K10
Bourdon Rd, SE20 202 DW96
Bourdon St, W1 285 K10
Bourke Cl, NW10 138 CS65
SW4 181 DL86
Bourke Hill, Chipstead CR5 234 DF118
Bourlet Cl, W1 285 L7
Bourn Av, N15 122 DR56
Barnet EN4 80 DD43
Uxbridge UB8 134 BN70
Bournbrook Rd, SE3 164 EK83
Bourne, The, N14 99 DK46
Bovingdon HP3 57 BA27
Ware SG12 33 DX05
Bourne Av, N14 99 DL47
Chertsey KT16 194 BG97
Hayes UB3 155 BQ76
Ruislip HA4 116 BW64
Windsor SL4 151 AQ84
Bournebridge Cl, Hutt. CM13 109 GE45
Bournebridge La, Stap.Abb. RM4 104 EZ45
● Bourne Business Pk, Add. KT15 212 BK105
Bourne Cl, Brox. EN10 49 DZ20
Chilworth GU4 259 BB140
Isleworth TW7 157 CE83
Thames Ditton KT7 197 CF103
Ware SG12 33 DX05
West Byfleet KT14 212 BH113
Bourne Ct, Ruis. HA4 115 BV64
Bourne Dr, Mitch. CR4 200 DD96
BOURNE END, Hem.H. HP1 39 BC22
Bourne End, Horn. RM11 128 FN59
Bourne End La, Hem.H. HP1 39 BC22
● Bourne End Mills, Hem.H. HP1 39 BB22
Bourne End Rd, Maid. SL6 110 AD62
Northwood HA6 93 BS49
Bourne Est, EC1 286 E6
Bournefield Rd, Whyt. CR3
off Godstone Rd 236 DT118
Bourne Gdns, E4 101 EB49
Bourne Gro, Ashtd. KT21 231 CK119
Bournehall Av, Bushey WD23 76 CA43
Bournehall La, Bushey WD23 76 CA44
★ Bourne Hall Mus & Lib, Epsom KT17 217 CT109
Sch Bournehall Prim Sch, Bushey WD23
off Bournehall Av 76 CB43
Bournehall Rd, Bushey WD23 76 CA44
Bourne Hill, N13 99 DL46
Bourne Hill Cl, N13
off Bourne Hill 99 DM47
● Bourne Ind Pk, Dart. DA1 187 FE85
Bourne La, Cat. CR3 236 DR121
Bourne Mead, Bex. DA5 187 FD85
Bournemead, Bushey WD23 76 CB44
Bournemead Av, Nthlt. UB5 135 BU68
Bournemead Cl, Nthlt. UB5 135 BU68
Bourne Meadow, Egh. TW20 193 BB98
Bournemead Way, Nthlt. UB5 135 BV68
Bourne Ms, Gdse. RH9 252 DW130
Bournemouth Cl, SE15 312 D9
Bournemouth Rd, SE15 312 D9
SW19 200 DA95
Bourne Pk Cl, Ken. CR8 236 DS115
Bourne Pl, W4 158 CR78
Chertsey KT16 194 BH102
Sch Bourne Prim Sch, Ruis. HA4
off Cedar Av 136 BW65
Bourne Rd, E7 124 EF62
N8 121 DL58
Berkhamsted HP4 38 AT18
Bexley DA5 187 FB86
Bromley BR2 204 EK98
Bushey WD23 76 CA43
Dartford DA1 187 FC86
Godalming GU7 258 AT143
Gravesend DA12 191 GM89
Slough SL1 151 AQ75
South Merstham RH1 251 DJ130
Virginia Water GU25 192 AX99
Bourneside, Vir.W. GU25 192 AU101
Bourneside Cres, N14 99 DK46
Bourneside Gdns, SE6 183 EC92
Bourneside Rd, Add. KT15 212 BK105
Bourne St, SW1 296 G9
Croydon CR0
off Waddon New Rd 201 DP103
Bourne Ter, W2 283 L6
Bourne Vale, Brom. BR2 204 EG101
Bournevale Rd, SW16 181 DL91
Bourne Vw, Grnf. UB6 137 CF65
Kenley CR8 236 DR115
Bourne Way, Add. KT15 212 BJ106
Bromley BR2 204 EF103
Epsom KT19 216 CQ105
Sutton SM1 217 CZ106
Swanley BR8 207 FC97
Woking GU22 226 AX122
Bournewood Rd, SE18 166 EU80
Orpington BR5 206 EV101
Bournville Rd, SE6 183 EA87
Bournwell Cl, Barn. EN4 80 DF41
Bourton Cl, Hayes UB3 135 BU74
Sch Bousfield Prim Sch, SW5 295 N10
Bousfield Rd, SE14 313 J8
Bousley Ri, Ott. KT16 211 BD108
Sch Boutcher C of E Prim Sch, SE1 300 A8
Boutflower Rd, SW11 160 DE84
Boutique Hall, SE13
off Lewisham Cen 163 EC84
Bouton Pl, N1
off Waterloo Ter 276 G7
Bouverie Gdns, Har. HA3 117 CK58
Purley CR8 219 DL114
Bouverie Ms, N16 122 DS61
Bouverie Pl, W2 284 B8
Bouverie Rd, N16 122 DS61
Chipstead CR5 234 DG118
Harrow HA1 116 CC59
Bouverie St, EC4 286 F9
Bouverie Way, Slou. SL3 152 AY78
Bouvier Rd, Enf. EN3 82 DW38
BOVENEY, Wind. SL4 151 AK79
Boveney Cl, Slou. SL1
off Amerden Way 151 AN75
Boveney New Rd, Eton Wick SL4 151 AL77
Boveney Rd, SE23 183 DX87
Dorney SL4 150 AJ77
Boveney Wd La, Burn. SL1 110 AJ62
Bovey Way, S.Ock. RM15 149 FV71
Bovill Rd, SE23 183 DX87
BOVINGDON, Hem.H. HP3 57 BA28
Bovingdon Av, Wem. HA9 138 CN65
Bovingdon Cl, N19
off Brookside Rd 121 DJ61
Bovingdon Cres, Wat. WD25 60 BX34
Bovingdon La, NW9 96 CS53
Sch Bovingdon Prim Sch, Bov. HP3
off High St 57 BB27
Bovingdon Rd, SW6 307 L7
Bovingdon Sq, Mitch. CR4
off Leicester Av 201 DL98
BOW, E3 289 M1
Bow Arrow La, Dart. DA1, DA2 188 FN86
Bowater Cl, NW9 118 CR57
SW2 181 DL86
Bowater Gdns, Sun. TW16 195 BV96
Bowater Pl, SE3 164 EH80
Bowater Ridge, St.Geo.H. KT13 213 BR110
Bowater Rd, SE18 304 F7
Wembley HA9 118 CP62
Bow Br Est, E3 290 C2
DLR Bow Church 290 B3
Bow Chyd, EC4 287 K9
Bow Common La, E3 289 N5
Bowden Cl, Felt. TW14 175 BS88
Bowden Dr, Horn. RM11 128 FL60
H Bowden Ho, Har.Hill HA1 117 CE61
Bowden St, SE11 310 F1
Bowditch, SE8 301 N10
Bowdon Rd, E17 123 EA59
Bowen Dr, SE21 182 DS90
Bowen Rd, Har. HA1 116 CC59
Bowen St, E14 290 D8
Bowens Wd, Croy. CR0 221 DZ109
Bowen Way, Couls. CR5 235 DK122
Bower Av, SE10 315 K5
Bower Cl, Nthlt. UB5 136 BW68
Romford RM5 105 FD52
Bower Ct, Epp. CM16 70 EU32
Woking GU22
off Princess Rd 227 BB116
Bowerdean St, SW6 307 L7
Bower Fm Rd, Hav.at.Bow. RM4 105 FC48
BOWER HILL, Epp. CM16 70 EU31
Bower Hill, Epp. CM16 70 EU32
Bower Hill Cl, S.Nutfld RH1 267 DL137
● Bower Hill Ind Est, Epp. CM16 70 EU32
Bower Hill La, S.Nutfld RH1 267 DK135
Bower La, Eyns. DA4 208 FL103
Bowerman Av, SE14 313 M3
Bowerman Rd, Grays RM16 171 GG77
Sch Bower Pk Sch, Rom. RM1
off Havering Rd 105 FE51
Bower Rd, Swan. BR8 187 FG94
Bowers Av, Nthflt DA11 191 GF91
Bowers Cl, Guil. GU4
off Cotts Wd Dr 243 BA129
Bowers Fm Dr, Guil. GU4 243 BA130
Bowers La, Guil. GU4 243 BA129
Bowers Rd, Shore. TN14 225 FF111
Bower St, E1 289 J9
Bowers Wk, E6 293 H8
Bower Ter, Epp. CM16 70 EU32
Bower Vale, Epp. CM16 70 EU32
Bower Way, Slou. SL1 131 AM73
Bowery Ct, Dag. RM10
off St. Mark's Pl 147 FB65
Bowes Cl, Sid. DA15 186 EV86
Bowes-Lyon Cl, Wind. SL4
off Ward Royal 151 AQ81
Bowes-Lyon Ms, St.Alb. AL3 43 CD20
BOWES PARK, N22 99 DL51
≠ Bowes Park 99 DL51
Sch Bowes Prim Sch, N11
off Bowes Rd 99 DK50
Bowes Rd, N11 99 DH50
N13 99 DL50
W3 138 CS73
Dagenham RM8 126 EW63
Staines-upon-Thames TW18 173 BE92
Walton-on-Thames KT12 195 BV103
Bowfell Rd, W6 306 B3
Bowford Av, Bexh. DA7 166 EY81
Bowgate, St.Alb. AL1 43 CE19
Bowhay, Hutt. CM13 109 GA47
Bowhill Cl, SW9 310 F4
Bowie Cl, SW4 181 DK87
Bowland Rd, SW4 161 DK84
Woodford Green IG8 102 EJ51
Bowland Yd, SW1 296 F5
Bow La, EC4 287 K9
N12 98 DC53
Morden SM4 199 CY100
Bowl Ct, EC2 287 P5
Bowlers Grn, Magd.Lav. CM5 53 FF21
Bowlers Orchard, Ch.St.G. HP8 90 AU48
Bowles Grn, Enf. EN1 82 DV36
Bowley Cl, SE19 182 DT93
Bowley La, SE19 182 DT92
Bowling Cl, Uxb. UB10
off Birch Cres 134 BM67
Bowling Ct, Wat. WD18 75 BU42
Bowling Grn Cl, SW15 179 CV87
Bowling Grn Ct, Wem. HA9 118 CM61
Bowling Grn La, EC1 286 F4
Bowling Grn Pl, SE1 299 L4
Bowling Grn Rd, Chobham GU24 210 AS109
Bowling Grn Row, SE18 305 J7
Bowling Grn St, SE11 310 E2
Bowling Grn Wk, N1 287 N2
Bowling Rd, Ware SG12 33 DY06
Bowls, The, Chig. IG7 103 ES49
Bowls Cl, Stan. HA7 95 CH50
Bowman Av, E16 291 M10
Bowman Ms, SW18 179 CZ88
Bowmans Cl, W13 137 CH74
Burnham SL1 130 AH67
Potters Bar EN6 64 DD32
Bowmans Ct, Hem.H. HP2 40 BK18
Bowmans Grn, Wat. WD25 76 BX36
Sch Bowmansgreen Prim Sch, Lon.Col. AL2 off Telford Rd 61 CJ27
Bowmans Lea, SE23 182 DW87
Bowmans Meadow, Wall. SM6 201 DH104
Bowmans Ms, E1 288 C10
Bowman's Ms, N7
off Seven Sisters Rd 121 DL62
Bowmans Pl, N7
off Holloway Rd 121 DL62
Bowmans Rd, Dart. DA1 187 FF87
● Bowman Trd Est, NW9 118 CN56
Bowmead, SE9 185 EM89
Bowmont Cl, Hutt. CM13 109 GB44
Bowmore Wk, NW1 275 P6
Bown Cl, Til. RM18 171 GH82
Bowness Cl, E8 278 A5
Bowness Cres, SW15 178 CS92
Bowness Dr, Houns. TW4 156 BY84
Bowness Rd, SE6 183 EB87
Bexleyheath DA7 167 FB82
Bowness Way, Horn. RM12 127 FG64
Bowood Rd, SW11 160 DG84
Enfield EN3 83 DX40
Bowring Grn, Wat. WD19 94 BW50
⊖ Bow Road 290 A2
Bow Rd, E3 289 P3
Bowrons Av, Wem. HA0 137 CK66
Bowry Dr, Wrays. TW19 173 AZ86
Sch Bow Sch, E3 290 B1
E3 290 E4
Bowsher Ct, Ware SG12 33 DY06
Bowsley Ct, Felt. TW13
off Highfield Rd 175 BU89
Bowsprit, The, Cob. KT11 230 BW115
Bowsprit Pt, E14 302 A6
Bow St, E15 281 J3
WC2 286 B9
Bowstridge La, Ch.St.G. HP8 90 AW51
● Bow Triangle Business Cen, E3 290 B3
Bowyer Cl, E6 293 K6
Bowyer Ct, E4
off The Ridgeway 101 EC46
Bowyer Cres, Denh. UB9 113 BF58
Bowyer Dr, Slou. SL1 131 AL74
Bowyer Pl, SE5 311 K4
Bowyers, Hem.H. HP2 40 BK18
Bowyers Cl, Ashtd. KT21 232 CM118
Bowyers Ct, Twick. TW1 157 CH84
Bowyer St, SE5 311 J4
Boxall Rd, SE21 182 DS86
Box Elder Cl, Edg. HA8 96 CQ50
Boxfield, Welw.G.C. AL7 30 DB12
Boxford Cl, S.Croy. CR2 221 DX112
Boxgrove Av, Guil. GU1 243 BA132
Boxgrove La, Guil. GU1 243 BA133
Sch Boxgrove Prim Sch, SE2
off Boxgrove Rd 166 EW76
Guildford GU1
off Boxgrove La 243 BB133
Boxgrove Rd, SE2 166 EW76
Guildford GU1 243 BA133
BOX HILL, Tad. KT20 248 CP131
Boxhill, Hem.H. HP2 40 BK18
≠ Boxhill & Westhumble 247 CH131
Boxhill Rd, Box H. KT20 248 CP131
Dorking RH4 248 CL133
Sch Box Hill Sch, Mick. RH5
off Old London Rd 247 CH127
Boxhill Way, Strood Grn RH3 264 CP138
Box La, Bark. IG11 146 EV68
Hemel Hempstead HP3 39 BE24
Hoddesdon EN11 49 DX16
Boxley Rd, Mord. SM4 200 DC98
Boxley St, E16 304 A3
BOXMOOR, Hem.H. HP1 40 BH22
Sch Boxmoor Ho Sch, Hem.H. HP3
off Box La 39 BF23
Sch Boxmoor Prim Sch, Hem.H. HP1
off Cowper Rd 40 BG21
Boxmoor Rd, Har. HA3 117 CH56
Romford RM5 105 FC50
Boxoll Rd, Dag. RM9 126 EZ63
Box Ridge Av, Pur. CR8 219 DM112
Boxted Cl, Buck.H. IG9 102 EL46
Boxted Rd, Hem.H. HP1 39 BF18
Box Tree Cl, Chesh. HP5 54 AR33
Boxtree La, Har. HA3 94 CC53
Boxtree Rd, Har. HA3 95 CD52
Boxtree Wk, Orp. BR5 206 EX102
Box Tree Wk, Red. RH1 266 DC136
Box Wk, Lthd. KT24 245 BS132
Boxwell Rd, Berk. HP4 38 AV19
Boxwood Cl, West Dr. UB7
off Hawthorne Cres 154 BM75
Boxwood Way, Warl. CR6 237 DX117
Boxworth Cl, N12 98 DD50
Boxworth Gro, N1 276 D8
Boyard Rd, SE18 305 N10
Boyce Cl, Borwd. WD6 78 CL39
Boyce St, SE1 298 D3
Boyce Way, E13 291 N4
Boycroft Av, NW9 118 CQ58
Boyd Av, Sthl. UB1 136 BZ74
Boyd Cl, Kings.T. KT2 178 CN94
Boydell Ct, NW8 274 A7
Boyd Rd, SW19 180 DD93
Boyd St, E1 288 C9
Boyd Way, SE3 164 EJ84
Boyes Cres, Lon.Col. AL2 61 CH26
Boyfield St, SE1 299 H5
Boyland Rd, Brom. BR1 184 EF92
Boyle Av, Stan. HA7 95 CG51
Boyle Cl, Uxb. UB10 134 BM68
Boyle Fm Island, T.Ditt. KT7 197 CG100
Boyle Fm Rd, T.Ditt. KT7 197 CG100
Boyle St, W1 285 L10
Boyne Av, NW4 119 CX56
Boyne Rd, SE13 314 F10
Dagenham RM10 126 FA62
Boyne Ter Ms, W11 294 G2
Boyseland Ct, Edg. HA8 96 CQ47
Boyson Rd, SE17 311 L2
Boyton Cl, E1 289 H4
N8 121 DL55
Boyton Rd, N8 121 DL55
Brabant Ct, EC3 287 N10
Brabant Rd, N22 99 DM54
Brabazon Av, Wall. SM6 219 DL108
Brabazon Rd, Houns. TW5 156 BW80
Northolt UB5 136 CA68
Brabazon St, E14 290 C8
Brabiner Gdns, Croy. CR0 221 ED110
Brabourne Cl, SE19 182 DS92
Brabourne Cres, Bexh. DA7 166 EZ79
Brabourne Hts, NW7 96 CS48
Brabourne Ri, Beck. BR3 203 EC99

Brabourn Gro, SE15 312 G9
Brace Cl, Chsht EN7 65 DP25
Bracer Ho, N1 off Nuttall St 277 P10
Bracewell Av, Grnf. UB6 117 CF64
Bracewell Rd, W10 282 A7
Bracewood Gdns, Croy. CR0 202 DT104
Bracey Ms, N4 off Bracey St 121 DL61
Bracey St, N4 121 DL61
Bracken, The, E4
off Hortus Rd 101 EC47
Bracken Av, SW12 180 DG86
Croydon CR0 203 EB104
Brackenbridge Dr, Ruis. HA4 116 BX62
Brackenbury Gdns, W6 159 CV76
Sch Brackenbury Prim Sch, W6
off Dalling Rd 159 CV76
Brackenbury Rd, N2 120 DC55
W6 159 CV76
Bracken Cl, E6 293 J7
Bookham KT23 230 BZ124
Borehamwood WD6 78 CP39
Farnham Common SL2 111 AR63
Sunbury-on-Thames TW16 175 BT93
Twickenham TW2 176 CA87
Woking GU22 227 AZ118
Bracken Ct, Hat. AL10 29 CT14
Brackendale, N21 99 DM47
Potters Bar EN6 64 DA33
Brackendale Cl,
Epping Green TW20 172 AY92
Hounslow TW3 156 CB81
Brackendale Gdns,
Upmin. RM14 128 FQ63
Brackendene, Brick.Wd AL2 60 BZ30
Dartford DA2 187 FE91
Brackendene Cl, Wok. GU21 227 BA115
Bracken Dr, Chig. IG7 103 EP51
Bracken End, Islw. TW7 177 CD85
Brackenfield Cl, E5 122 DV62
Brackenforde, Slou. SL3 152 AW75
Bracken Gdns, SW13 159 CU82
Brackenhill, Berk. HP4 38 AY18
Cobham KT11 214 CA111
Ruis. HA4 116 BY63
Bracken Hill Cl, Brom. BR1 204 EF95
Bracken Hill La, Brom. BR1 204 EF95
● Bracken Ind Est, Ilf. IG6 103 ET53
Bracken Ms, E4 off Hortus Rd 101 EC46
Romford RM7 126 FA58
Bracken Path, Epsom KT18 216 CP113
Brackens, The, Enf. EN1 100 DS45
Hemel Hempstead HP2
off Heather Way 40 BK19
Orpington BR6 224 EU106
Brackens Dr, Warley CM14 108 FW50
Brackenside, Horl. RH6
off Stockfield 269 DH147
Bracken Way, Chobham GU24 210 AT110
Guildford GU3 242 AS132
Brackenwood, Sun. TW16 195 BU95
Brackley, Wey. KT13 213 BR106
Brackley Av, SE15 162 DV83
Brackley Cl, Wall. SM6 219 DL108
Brackley Rd, W4 158 CS78
Beckenham BR3 183 DZ94
Brackley Sq, Wdf.Grn. IG8 102 EK52
Brackley St, EC1 287 J6
Brackley Ter, W4 158 CS78
Bracklyn Cl, N1 277 L10
Bracklyn Ct, N1 277 L10
Bracklyn St, N1 277 L10
Bracknell Cl, N22 99 DN53
Bracknell Gdns, NW3 273 L1
Bracknell Gate, NW3 273 L2
Bracknell Pl, Hem.H. HP2 40 BM16
Bracknell Way, NW3 273 L1
Bracondale, Esher KT10 214 CC107
Bracondale Rd, SE2 166 EU77
H Bracton Cen, The, Dart. DA2 187 FF89
Bracton La, Dart. DA2 187 FF89
Bradbery, Map.Cr. WD3 91 BD50
Bradbourne Pk Rd, Sev. TN13 256 FG123
Bradbourne Rd, Bex. DA5 186 FA87
Grays RM17 170 GB79
Sevenoaks TN13 257 FH122
Bradbourne St, SW6 307 K8
Bradbourne Vale Rd,
Sev. TN13 256 FF122
Bradbury Cl, Borwd. WD6 78 CP39
Southall UB2 156 BZ77
Bradbury Ct, SW20
off Clifton Pk Av 199 CW96
Bradbury Gdns, Fulmer SL3 112 AX63
Bradbury Ms, N16 277 P3
Bradbury St, N16 277 P3
Bradd Cl, S.Ock. RM15 149 FW69
Braddock Cl, Coll.Row RM5 105 FC51
Isleworth TW7 157 CF83
Braddon Rd, Rich. TW9 158 CM83
Braddyll St, SE10 315 J1
Bradenham Av, Well. DA16 166 EU84
Bradenham Cl, SE17 311 L2
Bradenham Rd, Har. HA3 117 CH56
Hayes UB4 135 BS69
Bradenhurst Cl, Cat. CR3 252 DT126
Braden St, W9 283 L5
Bradfield Cl, Guil. GU4 243 BA131
Woking GU22 226 AY118
Bradfield Dr, Bark. IG11 126 EU64
Bradfield Ho, SW8
off Wandsworth Rd 309 N8
Bradfield Rd, E16 303 P4
Ruislip HA4 116 BY64
Bradford Cl, N17 100 DT51
SE26 off Coombe Rd 182 DV91
Bromley BR2 205 EM102
Bradford Dr, Epsom KT19 217 CT107
Bradford Rd, W3
off Warple Way 158 CS75
Heronsgate WD3 91 BC45
Ilford IG1 125 ER60
Slough SL1 131 AN72
Bradfords Cl, Buck.H. IG9 102 EK49
Bradgate, Cuffley EN6 65 DK27
Bradgate Cl, Cuffley EN6 65 DK28
Bradgate Rd, SE6 183 EA86
Brading Cres, E11 124 EH61
Brading Rd, SW2 181 DM87
Croydon CR0 201 DM100
Brading Ter, W12 159 CV76
Bradiston Rd, W9 283 H2
Bradleigh Av, Grays RM17 170 GC77
Bradley Cl, N1 276 F10
N7 276 B5
Belmont SM2 off Station Rd 218 DA110
Bradley Gdns, W13 137 CH72
Bradley Ho, E3
off Bromley High St 290 D1
SE16 off Nelldale Rd 300 F8
Bradley La, Dor. RH5 247 CG132
Bradley Lynch Ct, E2
off Morpeth St 289 J2
Bradley Ms, SW17 180 DF88
Bradley Rd, N22 99 DM54
SE19 182 DQ93
Enfield EN3 83 DY38
Slough SL1 131 AR73
Waltham Abbey EN9 83 EC36
Bradley Stone Rd, E6 293 J7
Bradman Row, Edg. HA8
off Pavilion Way 96 CQ52
Bradmead, SW8 309 K5
Bradmore Ct, Enf. EN3
off Enstone Rd 83 DY41
Bradmore Grn, Brook.Pk AL9 63 CY26
Coulsdon CR5
off Coulsdon Rd 235 DM118
Bradmore La, Brook.Pk AL9 63 CW27
Bradmore Pk Rd, W6 159 CV76
Bradmore Way, Brook.Pk AL9 63 CY26
Coulsdon CR5 235 DL117
Bradshaw Cl, SW19 180 DA93
Windsor SL4 151 AL81
Bradshaw Dr, NW7 97 CX52
Bradshawe Waye, Uxb. UB8 134 BL71
Bradshaw Rd, Wat. WD24 76 BW39
Bradshaws, Hat. AL10 45 CT22
Bradshaws Cl, SE25 202 DU97
Bradstock Rd, E9 279 K5
Epsom KT17 217 CU106
Bradstone Brook, Shalf. GU4 259 BA141
Bradstowe Ho, Har. HA1
off Junction Rd 117 CE58
Brad St, SE1 298 F3
Bradwell Av, Dag. RM10 126 FA61
Bradwell Cl, E18 124 EF56
Hornchurch RM12 147 FH65
Bradwell Ct, Whyt. CR3
off Godstone Rd 236 DU119
Bradwell Grn, Hutt. CM13 109 GC44
Bradwell Ms, N18
off Lyndhurst Rd 100 DU49
Bradwell Rd, Buck.H. IG9 102 EL46
Bradwell St, E1 289 K3
Brady Av, Loug. IG10 85 EQ40
Brady Ct, Dag. RM8 126 EX60
Brady Dr, Brom. BR1 205 EN97
Bradymead, E6 293 M8
Sch Brady Prim Sch, Rain. RM13
off Wennington Rd 148 FJ71
Brady St, E1 288 E5
Braemar Av, N22 99 DL53
NW10 118 CR62
SW19 180 DA89
Bexleyheath DA7 167 FC84
South Croydon CR2 220 DQ109
Thornton Heath CR7 201 DN97
Wembley HA0 137 CK66
Braemar Cl, SE16 300 E10
Braemar Gdns, NW9 96 CR53
Hornchurch RM11 128 FN58
Sidcup DA15 185 ER90
Slough SL1 151 AN75
West Wickham BR4 203 EC102
Braemar Rd, E13 291 M5
N15 122 DS57
Brentford TW8 157 CK79
Worcester Park KT4 199 CV104
Braemer Ho, W9 283 N3
Braeside, Beck. BR3 183 EA92
New Haw KT15 212 BH111
Braeside Av, SW19 199 CY95
Sevenoaks TN13 256 FF124
Braeside Cl, Pnr. HA5 94 CA52
Sevenoaks TN13 256 FF123
Braeside Cres, Bexh. DA7 167 FC84
Braeside Rd, SW16 181 DJ94
Sch Braeside Sch,
Jun Sch, Buck.H. IG9
off Palmerston Rd 102 EJ47
Sen Sch, Buck.H. IG9
off High Rd 102 EH46
Braes Mead, S.Nutfld RH1 267 DL135
Braes St, N1 277 H6
Braesyde Cl, Belv. DA17 166 EZ77
Brafferton Rd, Croy. CR0 220 DQ105
Braganza St, SE17 298 G10
Bragg Cl, Dag. RM8
off Porters Av 146 EV65
Braggowens Ley, Harl. CM17 36 EW14
Bragmans La, Flaun. HP3 57 BB34
Sarratt WD3 57 BE33
Braham St, E1 288 B9
Braid, The, Chesh. HP5 54 AS30
Braid Av, W3 138 CS72
Braid Cl, Felt. TW13 176 BZ89
Braid Ct, W4
off Lawford Rd 158 CQ80
Braidwood Pas, EC1
off Cloth St 287 J6
Braidwood Rd, SE6 183 ED88
Braidwood St, SE1 299 N3
Brailsford Cl, Mitch. CR4 180 DE94
Brailsford Rd, SW2 181 DN85
Brain Cl, Hat. AL10 45 CV18
Sch Braintcroft Prim Sch, NW2
off Warren Rd 119 CT61
Brainton Av, Felt. TW14 175 BV87
Braintree Av, Ilf. IG4 124 EL56
● Braintree Ind Est, Ruis. HA4 115 BV63
Braintree Rd, Dag. RM10 126 FA62
Ruislip HA4 115 BV63
Braintree St, E2 288 G4
Braithwaite Av, Rom. RM7 126 FA59
Braithwaite Gdns, Stan. HA7 95 CJ53
Braithwaite Ho, EC1 287 K4
Braithwaite Rd, Enf. EN3 83 DZ41
Braithwaite St, E1 288 A5
Braithwaite Twr, W2 284 A6
Brakefield Rd, Sthflt DA13 190 GB93
Brakey Hill, Bletch. RH1 252 DS134
Brakynbery, Nthch HP4 38 AS16
Bramah Rd, SW9 310 F7
Bramalea Cl, N6 120 DG58
Bramall Cl, E15 281 L2
Bramall Ct, N7 276 C4
Bramber Ct, Brent. TW8
off Sterling Pl 158 CL77
Slough SL1 131 AN74
Bramber Ho, Kings.T. KT2
off Kingsgate Rd 198 CL95
Bramber Rd, N12 98 DE50
W14 306 G2
Bramber Way, Warl. CR6 237 DZ116
Brambleacres Cl, Sutt. SM2 218 DA108
Bramble Av, Bean DA2 189 FW90
Bramble Banks, Cars. SM5 218 DG109
Bramblebury Rd, SE18 165 EQ78
Bramble Cl, N15 122 DU56
Beckenham BR3 203 EC99
Chalfont St. Peter SL9
off Garners Rd 90 AY51
Chigwell IG7 103 EQ46
Croydon CR0 221 EA105
Guildford GU3 242 AS132
Oxted RH8 254 EH133
Redhill RH1 266 DG136
SE19 202 DR95
Shepperton TW17
off Halliford Cl 195 BR97
Stanmore HA7 95 CK52
Uxbridge UB8 134 BM71
Watford WD25 59 BU34
Bramble Cft, Erith DA8 167 FC77
Brambledene Cl, Wok. GU21 226 AW118
Brambledown, Stai. TW18 194 BG95
Brambledown Cl,
W.Wick. BR4 204 EE99
Brambledown Rd, Cars. SM5 218 DG108
South Croydon CR2 220 DS108
Wallington SM6 219 DH108
Bramblefield Cl, Long. DA3 209 FX97
Bramble Gdns, W12 139 CT73
Bramblehall La, Tad. KT20 248 CM132
Bramble La, Amer. HP7 55 AS41
Hampton TW12 176 BZ93
Hoddesdon EN11 49 DY17
Sevenoaks TN13 257 FH128
Upminster RM14 148 FQ67
Bramble Mead, Ch.St.G. HP8 90 AU48
Bramble Ri, Cob. KT11 230 BW115
Harlow CM20 35 EQ14
Bramble Rd, Hat. AL10 44 CR18
Brambles, The, Chsht EN8 67 DX31
Chigwell IG7
off Clayside 103 EQ51
St. Albans AL1 43 CD22
West Drayton UB7 154 BL77
Brambles Cl, Cat. CR3 236 DS122
Isleworth TW7 157 CG80
Brambles Fm Dr, Uxb. UB10 134 BN69
Sch Brambletye Jun Sch, Red. RH1
off Brambletye Pk Rd 266 DG136
Brambletye Pk Rd, Red. RH1 266 DG135
Bramble Wk, Epsom KT18 216 CP114
Bramble Way, Ripley GU23 227 BF124
Bramblewood, Merst. RH1 251 DH129
Bramblewood Cl, Cars. SM5 200 DE102
Brambling Cl, Bushey WD23 76 BY42
Green. DA9 189 FU86
Brambling Ri, Hem.H. HP2 40 BL17
Bramblings, The, E4 101 ED49
Bramcote Av, Mitch. CR4 200 DF98
Bramcote Ct, Mitch. CR4
off Bramcote Av 200 DF98
Bramcote Gro, SE16 300 G10
Bramcote Rd, SW15 159 CV84
Bramdean Cres, SE12 184 EG88
Bramdean Gdns, SE12 184 EG88
Bramerton Rd, Beck. BR3 203 DZ97
Bramerton St, SW3 308 C2
Bramfield, Wat. WD25
off Garston La 60 BY34
Bramfield Ct, N4
off Queens Dr 122 DQ61
Bramfield La, Waterf. SG14 31 DL05
Bramfield Rd, SW11 180 DE86
Hertford SG14 31 DL06
Bramford Ct, N14 99 DK47
Bramford Rd, SW18 160 DC84
Bramham Gdns, SW5 295 L10
Chessington KT9 215 CK105
Bramhope La, SE7 164 EH79
Bramlands Cl, SW11 160 DE83
Bramleas, Wat. WD18 75 BT42
Bramley Av, Couls. CR5 235 DJ115
● Bramley Business Cen,
Bramley GU5
off Station Rd 259 AZ144
Bramley Cl, E17 101 DY54
N14 81 DH43
NW7 96 CS48
Chertsey KT16 194 BH102
Eastcote HA5 115 BT55
Hayes UB3 135 BU73
Istead Rise DA13 191 GF94
Orpington BR6 205 EP102
Redhill RH1
off Abinger Dr 266 DE136
South Croydon CR2 219 DP106
Staines-upon-Thames TW18 174 BJ93
Swanley BR8 207 FE98
Twickenham TW2 176 CC86
Woodford Green IG8
off Orsett Ter 102 EJ52
Bramley Ct, Wat. WD25
off Orchard Av 59 BV31
Welling DA16 166 EV81
Bramley Cres, SW8 309 P4
Ilford IG2 125 EN58
Bramley Gdns, Wat. WD19 94 BW50
Bramley Gro, Ashtd. KT21 232 CL119
Bramley Hill, S.Croy. CR2 219 DP106
Bramley Ho, SW15
off Tunworth Cres 179 CT86
W10 282 D9
Bramley Ho Ct, Enf. EN2 82 DR37
Bramley Hyrst, S.Croy. CR2 220 DQ105
Bramley Par, N14 81 DJ42
Bramley Pl, Dart. DA1 167 FG84
Bramley Rd, N14 81 DH43
W5 157 CJ76
W10 282 D10
Cheam SM2 217 CX109
Sutton SM1 218 DD106
Sch Bramley Sch, Walt.Hill KT20
off Chequers La 249 CU125
Bramley Shaw, Wal.Abb. EN9 68 EF33
Bramley Wk, Horl. RH6 269 DJ148
Bramley Way, Ashtd. KT21 232 CM117
Hounslow TW4 176 BZ85
St. Albans AL4 43 CJ21
West Wickham BR4 203 EB103
Brammas Cl, Slou. SL1 151 AQ76
Brampton Cl, E5 122 DV61
Cheshunt EN7 66 DU28
Brampton Gdns, N15 122 DQ57
Hersham KT12 214 BW106
Brampton Gro, NW4 119 CV56
Harrow HA3 117 CG56
Wembley HA9 118 CN60
Brampton La, NW4 119 CW56
Sch Brampton Manor Sch, E6 292 E4
Brampton Pk Rd, N22 121 DN55
Sch Brampton Prim Sch, E6 292 G3
Bexleyheath DA7
off Brampton Rd 166 EX82
Brampton Rd, E6 292 F4
N15 122 DQ57
NW9 118 CN56
SE2 166 EW79
Bexleyheath DA7 166 EX80
Croydon CR0 202 DT101
Hillingdon UB10 135 BP68
St. Albans AL1 43 CG19
Watford WD19 93 BU48
Brampton Ter, Borwd. WD6 78 CN38
Bramshaw Gdns, Wat. WD19 94 BX50
Bramshaw Ri, N.Mal. KT3 198 CS100
Bramshaw Rd, E9 279 K5
Bramshill Cl, Chig. IG7
off Tine Rd 103 ES50
Bramshill Gdns, NW5 121 DH62
Bramshill Rd, NW10 139 CT68
Bramshot Av, SE7 315 P1
Bramshot Way, Wat. WD19 93 BU47
Bramston Cl, Ilf. IG6 103 ET51
Bramston Rd, NW10 139 CU68
SW17 180 DC90
Bramwell Cl, Sun. TW16 196 BX96
Bramwell Ho, SE1
off Harper Rd 299 K7
SW1 309 L1
Bramwell Ms, N1 276 D8
Bramwell Way, E16 304 D3
Brancaster Dr, NW7 97 CT52
Brancaster Gro, Ashtd. KT22 232 CL121
Brancaster La, Pur. CR8 220 DQ112
Brancaster Pl, Loug. IG10 85 EM41
Brancaster Rd, E12 125 EM63
SW16 181 DL90
Ilford IG2 125 ER58
Brancepeth Gdns, Buck.H. IG9 102 EG47
Branch Cl, Hat. AL10 45 CW16
Branch Hill, NW3 120 DC62
Branch Pl, N1 277 M8
Branch Rd, E14 289 L10
Ilford IG6 104 EV50
Park Street AL2 61 CD27
St. Albans AL3 42 CB19
Branch St, SE15 311 P5
Brancker Rd, Har. HA3 117 CK55
Brancroft Way, Enf. EN3 83 DY39
Brand Cl, N4 121 DP60
Brandesbury Sq, Wdf.Grn. IG8 103 EN51
Sch Brandlehow Prim Sch, SW15
off Brandlehow Rd 159 CZ84
Brandlehow Rd, SW15 159 CZ84
Brandon Cl, Chaff.Hun. RM16 170 FZ75
Cheshunt EN7 66 DS26
Brandon Est, SE17 311 H3
Brandon Gros Av, S.Ock. RM15 149 FW69
Brandon Mead, Chesh. HP5 54 AM29
Brandon Ms, EC2
off The Barbican 287 L7
Brandon Rd, E17 123 EC55
N7 276 A6
Dartford DA1 188 FN87
Southall UB2 156 BZ78
Sutton SM1 218 DB105
Brandon St, SE17 299 J9
Gravesend DA11 191 GH87
Brandram Ms, SE13 164 EE83
Brandram Rd, SE13 164 EE83
Brandreth Ct, Har. HA1
off Sheepcote Rd 117 CF58
Brandreth Rd, E6 293 K8
SW17 181 DH89
Brandries, The, Wall. SM6 201 DK104
BRANDS HILL, Slou. SL3 153 BB79
Brandsland, Reig. RH2 266 DB138
Brands Rd, Slou. SL3 153 BB79
Brand St, SE10 314 E5
Brandville Gdns, Ilf. IG6 125 EP56
Brandville Rd, West Dr. UB7 154 BL75
Brandy Way, Sutt. SM2 218 DA108
Sch Branfil Inf Sch, Upmin. RM14
off Cedar Av 128 FN63
Sch Branfil Jun Sch, Upmin. RM14
off Cedar Av 128 FN63
Branfill Rd, Upmin. RM14 128 FP61
Brangbourne Rd, Brom. BR1 183 EC92
Brangton Rd, SE11 310 D1
Brangwyn Cres, SW19 200 DD95
Branksea St, SW6 306 E5
Branksome Av, N18 100 DT51
Branksome Cl, Hem.H. HP2 40 BN19
Teddington TW11 177 CD91
Walton-on-Thames KT12 196 BX103
Branksome Rd, SW2 181 DL85
SW19 200 DA95
Branksome Way, Har. HA3 118 CL58
New Malden KT3 198 CQ95
Bransby Rd, Chess. KT9 216 CL107
Branscombe Gdns, N21 99 DN45
Branscombe St, SE13 314 D10
Bransdale Cl, NW6 273 K8
Bransell Cl, Swan. BR8 207 FC100
Bransgrove Rd, Edg. HA8 96 CM53
Branston Cl, Wat. WD19 94 BW45
Branston Cres, Petts Wd BR5 205 ER102
Branstone Rd, Rich. TW9 158 CM81
Branton Rd, Green. DA9 189 FT86
Brants Wk, W7 137 CE70
Brantwood Av, Erith DA8 167 FC80
Isleworth TW7 157 CG84
Brantwood Cl, E17 123 EB55
West Byfleet KT14
off Brantwood Gdns 212 BG113
Brantwood Ct, W.Byf. KT14
off Brantwood Dr 211 BF113
Brantwood Dr, W.Byf. KT14 211 BF113
Brantwood Gdns, Enf. EN2 81 DL42
Ilford IG4 124 EL56
West Byfleet KT14 211 BF113
Brantwood Rd, N17 100 DT51
SE24 182 DQ85
Bexleyheath DA7 167 FB82
South Croydon CR2 220 DQ109
Brantwood Way, Orp. BR5 206 EW97
Brasenose Dr, SW13 306 A3
Brasher Cl, Grnf. UB6 117 CD64
Brassett Pt, E15 281 K9
Brassey Cl, Felt. TW14 175 BU88
Oxted RH8 254 EG129
Brassey Hill, Oxt. RH8 254 EG130
Brassey Rd, NW6 273 H4
Oxted RH8 254 EF130
Brassey Sq, SW11 308 G10
Brassie Av, W3 138 CS72
Brass Tally All, SE16 301 K5
BRASTED, West. TN16 240 EW124
Brasted Cl, SE26 182 DW91
Bexleyheath DA6 186 EX85
Orpington BR6 205 ET103
Sutton SM2 218 DA110
Brasted Hill, Knock. TN14 240 EU120
Brasted Hill Rd, Brasted TN16 240 EV121
Brasted La, Knock. TN14 240 EU119
Brasted Rd, Erith DA8 167 FE80
Westerham TN16 255 ES126
Brathway Rd, SW18 180 DA87
Bratley St, E1 288 C5
Brattle Wd, Sev. TN13 257 FH129
Braund Av, Grnf. UB6 136 CB70
Braundton Av, Sid. DA15 185 ET88
Braunston Dr, Hayes UB4 136 BY70
Bravington Cl, Shep. TW17 194 BM99
Bravington Pl, W9 282 G4
Bravington Rd, W9 282 G4
Bravingtons Wk, N1 286 B1
Brawlings La, Chal.St.P. SL9 91 BA49
Brawne Ho, SE17 311 H3
Braxfield Rd, SE4 163 DY84
Braxted Pk, SW16 181 DM93
BRAY, Maid. SL6 150 AC76
Bray, NW3 274 D6
Brayards Rd, SE15 312 E9
Brayards Rd Est, SE15
off Firbank Rd 312 F8
Braybank, Bray SL6 150 AC75
Braybourne Cl, Uxb. UB8 134 BJ65
Braybourne Dr, Islw. TW7 157 CF80
Braybrooke Gdns, SE19
off Fox Hill 182 DS94
Braybrook St, W12 139 CT71
Brayburne Av, SW4 309 M9
Bray Cl, Borwd. WD6 78 CQ39
Bray SL6 150 AC76
Bray Ct, Maid. SL6 150 AC77
Braycourt Av, Walt. KT12 195 BV101
Bray Cres, SE16 301 J4
Braydon Rd, N16 122 DT60
Bray Dr, E16 291 M10
Brayfield Rd, Bray SL6 150 AC75
Brayfield Ter, N1 276 E7
Brayford Sq, E1 289 H8
Bray Gdns, Wok. GU22 227 BE116
Bray Pas, E16 291 N10
Bray Pl, SW3 296 E9
Bray Rd, NW7 97 CX51
Guildford GU2 258 AV135
Stoke D'Abernon KT11 230 BY116
BRAYS GROVE, Harl. CM18 52 EU17
Sch Brays Gro Comm Coll, Harl. CM18
off Tracyes Rd 52 EV17
Brays Mead, Harl. CM18 51 ET17
Bray Springs, Wal.Abb. EN9
off Roundhills 68 EE34
Brayton Gdns, Enf. EN2 81 DK42
Braywood Av, Egh. TW20 173 AZ93
Sch Braywood C of E First Sch,
Oakley Grn SL4
off Oakley Grn Rd 150 AE82
Braywood Rd, SE9 165 ER84
Brazier Cres, Nthlt. UB5 136 BZ70
Braziers Fld, Hert. SG13 32 DT09
Brazil Cl, Bedd. CR0 201 DL101
Breach Barns La, Wal.Abb. EN9 68 EF30
Breach Barns Pk, Wal.Abb. EN9 68 EH29
Breach La, Dag. RM9 146 FA69
Little Berkhamsted SG13 47 DJ18
Breach Rd, Grays RM20 169 FT79
Bread & Cheese La, Chsht EN7 66 DR25
Bread St, EC4 287 K9
Breakfield, Couls. CR5 235 DL116
Breakmead, Welw.G.C. AL7 30 DB10
Breakneck Hill, Green. DA9 189 FV85
Breakspear Av, St.Alb. AL1 43 CF21
Breakspear Ct, Abb.L. WD5 59 BT30
Breakspear Ct, Wat. WD24 75 BV38
Breakspeare Rd, Abb.L. WD5 59 BS31
Sch Breakspeare Sch, Abb.L. WD5
off Gallows Hill La 59 BS31
Sch Breakspear Inf & Jun Schs,
Ickhm UB10 off Bushey Rd 114 BN61
Breakspear Path, Hare. UB9 114 BJ55
Breakspear Pl, Abb.L. WD5
off Hanover Gdns 59 BT30
Breakspear Rd, Ruis. HA4 115 BP59
Breakspear Rd N, Hare. UB9 114 BN57
Breakspear Rd S,
Ickhm UB9, UB10 114 BM62
Breakspears Dr, Orp. BR5 206 EU95
Breakspears Ms, SE4 314 A9
Breakspears Rd, SE4 314 A10
Breakspear Way, Hem.H. HP2 41 BQ20
Breaks Rd, Hat. AL10 45 CV18
Bream Cl, N17 122 DV56
Bream Gdns, E6 293 L3
Breamore Cl, SW15 179 CU88
Breamore Rd, Ilf. IG3 125 ET61
Bream's Bldgs, EC4 286 E8
Bream St, E3 280 B7
Breamwater Gdns, Rich. TW10 177 CH90
Brearley Cl, Edg. HA8 96 CQ52
Uxbridge UB8 134 BL65
Sch Breaside Prep Sch, Brom. BR1
off Orchard Rd 204 EK95
Breasley Cl, SW15 159 CV84
Brechin Pl, SW7 295 P9
Brecken Cl, St.Alb. AL4 43 CG16
Sch Brecknock Prim Sch, NW1 275 P4
Brecknock Rd, N7 275 N2
N19 121 DJ63
Brecknock Rd Est, N19 275 M1
Breckonmead, Brom. BR1
off Wanstead Rd 204 EJ96
Brecon Cl, Mitch. CR4 201 DL97
Worcester Park KT4 199 CW103
Brecon Grn, NW9
off Goldsmith Av 118 CS58
Brecon Ms, N7 275 N3
Brecon Rd, W6 306 F3
Enfield EN3 82 DW42
Brede Cl, E6 293 L2
Bredgar, SE13 183 EC85
Bredgar Rd, N19 121 DJ61
Bredhurst Cl, SE20 182 DW93
Bredinghurst, SE22 182 DU87
Sch Bredinghurst Sch, SE15
off Stuart Rd 163 DX84
Bredon Rd, Croy. CR0 202 DT101
Bredune, Ken. CR8 236 DR115
Bredward Cl, Burn. SL1 130 AH69
Breech La, Walt.Hill KT20 233 CU124
Breer St, SW6 307 L10
Breezers Hill, E1 300 D1
Breeze Ter, Chsht EN8
off Collet Cl 67 DX28

B

Bremher Rd, Har. HA2 116 CC61
Bremer Ms, E17 123 EB56
Bremer Rd, Stai. TW18 174 BG90
Bremner Av, Horl. RH6 268 DF147
Bremner Cl, Swan. BR8 207 FG98
Bremner Rd, SW7 295 P5
Brenchley Av, Grav. DA11 191 GH92
Brenchley Cl, Brom. BR2 204 EF100
Chislehurst BR7 205 EN95
Brenchley Gdns, SE23 182 DW86
Brenchley Rd, Orp. BR5 205 ET95
Bren Ct, Enf. EN3
off Colgate Pl 83 EA37
Brendans Cl, Horn. RM11 128 FL60
Brenda Rd, SW17 180 DF89
Brenda Ter, Swans. DA10
off Manor Rd 190 FY87
Brende Gdns, W.Mol. KT8 196 CB98
Brendon Av, NW10 118 CS63
Brendon Cl, Erith DA8 167 FE81
Esher KT10 214 CC107
Harlington UB3 155 BQ80
Brendon Ct, Rad. WD7 61 CH34
Brendon Dr, Esher KT10 214 CC107
Brendon Gdns, Har. HA2 116 CB63
Ilford IG2 125 ES57
Brendon Gro, N2 98 DC54
Brendon Rd, SE9 185 ER89
Dagenham RM8 126 EZ60
Brendon St, W1 284 D8
Brendon Way, Enf. EN1 100 DS45
Brenley Cl, Mitch. CR4 200 DG97
Brenley Gdns, SE9 164 EK84
Brennan Rd, Til. RM18 171 GH82
Brent, The, Dart. DA1, DA2 188 FN87
Coll Brent Adult Coll, NW10
off Morland Gdns 138 CR67
Brent Cl, Bex. DA5 186 EY88
Dartford DA2 188 FP86
Brentcot Cl, W13 137 CH70
Brent Cres, NW10 138 CM68
⊖ Brent Cross 119 CX59
Brent Cross Gdns, NW4
off Cooper Rd 119 CX58
Jct Brent Cross Interchange, The, NW2 119 CX59
Brent Cross Shop Cen, NW4 119 CW59
Brentfield, NW10 138 CP66
Brentfield Cl, NW10 138 CR65
Brentfield Gdns, NW2
off Hendon Way 119 CX59
Brentfield Ho, NW10
off Stonebridge Pk 138 CR66
Sch Brentfield Prim Sch, NW10
off Meadow Garth 138 CR65
Brentfield Rd, NW10 138 CR65
Dartford DA1 188 FN86
BRENTFORD, TW8 157 CK79
⇌ Brentford 157 CJ79
● Brentford Business Cen, Brent. TW8 157 CH80
Brentford Cl, Hayes UB4 136 BX70
★ Brentford FC, Brent. TW8 157 CK79
Sch Brentford Sch for Girls, Brent. TW8
off Boston Manor Rd 157 CK79
Brent Grn, NW4 119 CW57
Brent Grn Wk, Wem. HA9 118 CQ62
Brenthall Twrs, Harl. CM17 52 EW17
Brentham Way, W5 137 CK70
Brenthouse Rd, E9 278 G6
Brenthurst Rd, NW10 119 CT64
Sch Brent Knoll Sch, SE23
off Mayow Rd 183 DX90
Brentlands Dr, Dart. DA1 188 FN88
Brent La, Dart. DA1 188 FM87
Brent Lea, Brent. TW8 157 CJ80
Brentmead Cl, W7 137 CE73
Brentmead Gdns, NW10 138 CM68
Brentmead Pl, NW11
off North Circular Rd 119 CX58
● Brent New Enterprise Cen, NW10
off Cobbold Rd 139 CT65
Brenton St, E14 289 M8
Brent Pk, NW10 118 CR64
Brent Pk Rd, NW4 119 CV59
NW9 119 CU60
Brent Pl, Barn. EN5 80 DA43
Sch Brent Prim Sch, The, Dart. DA2
off London Rd 188 FQ87
Brent Rd, E16 291 P8
SE18 165 EP80
Brentford TW8 157 CJ79
South Croydon CR2 220 DV109
Southall UB2 156 BW76
Brent Side, Brent. TW8 157 CJ79
Brentside Cl, W13 137 CG70
● Brentside Executive Cen, Brent. TW8 157 CH79
Sch Brentside High Sch, W7
off Greenford Av 137 CE70
Sch Brentside Prim Sch, W7
off Kennedy Rd 137 CE70
Brent S Shop Pk, NW2 119 CW60
Brent St, NW4 119 CW56
Brent Ter, NW2 119 CW61
Brentvale Av, Sthl. UB1 137 CD74
Wembley HA0 138 CM67
Brent Vw Rd, NW9 119 CU59
Brent Waters Business Pk., Brent. TW8
off The Ham 157 CJ80
Brent Way, N3 98 DA51
Brentford TW8 157 CK80
Dartford DA2 188 FP86
Wembley HA9 138 CP65
Brentwick Gdns, Brent. TW8 158 CL77
BRENTWOOD, CM13 - CM15 108 FU47
⇌ Brentwood 108 FW48
Brentwood Bypass, Brwd. CM14, CM15 107 FR49
Brentwood Cl, SE9 185 EQ88
H Brentwood Comm Hosp & Minor Injuries Unit, Brwd. CM15 108 FY46
Sch Brentwood Co High Sch, Brwd. CM14
off Seven Arches Rd 108 FX48
Brentwood Ct, Add. KT15 212 BH105
Brentwood Ho, SE18
off Shooters Hill Rd 164 EK80
★ Brentwood Mus, Brwd. CM14 108 FW49
Brentwood Pl, Brwd. CM15 108 FX46
Sch Brentwood Prep Sch, Brwd. CM15
off Middleton Hall La 108 FY46
Brentwood Rd, Brwd. CM13 109 GA49
Grays RM16 171 GH77
Romford RM1, RM2 127 FF58
Sch Brentwood Sch, Brwd. CM15
off Ingrave Rd 108 FX47
Sch Brentwood Ursuline Conv High Sch, Brwd. CM14 off Queens Rd 108 FX47
Brereton Ct, Hem.H. HP3 40 BL22
Brereton Rd, N17 100 DT52
Bressay Dr, NW7 97 CU52
Bressenden Pl, SW1 297 K6
Bressey Av, Enf. EN1 82 DU39
Bressey Gro, E18 102 EF54
Brettlands Rd, Cher. KT16 193 BE103
Breton Ho, EC2
off The Barbican 287 K6
Brett Cl, N16 122 DS61
Northolt UB5
off Broomcroft Av 136 BX69
Brett Ct, N9 100 DW47
Cheshunt EN8
off Coopers Wk 67 DX28
Brettell St, SE17 311 M1
Brettenham Av, E17 101 EA53
Sch Brettenham Prim Sch, N18
off Brettenham Rd 100 DU49
Brettenham Rd, E17 101 EA54
N18 100 DU49
Brett Gdns, Dag. RM9 146 EY66
Brettgrave, Epsom KT19 216 CQ110
Brett Ho Cl, SW15
off Putney Heath La 179 CX86
Brett Pas, E8 278 F3
Brett Pl, Wat. WD24 75 BU37
Brett Rd, E8 278 F3
Barnet EN5 79 CW43
Brevet Cl, Purf. RM19 169 FR77
Brewer's Fld, Dart. DA2 188 FJ91
Brewer's Grn, SW1 297 N6
Brewers Hall Gdns, EC2 287 K7
Brewers La, Rich. TW9 177 CK85
Brewer St, W1 285 M10
Bletchingley RH1 252 DQ131
★ Brewery, The, EC1 287 K6
Brewery, The, Rom. RM1 127 FE57
Brewery Cl, Wem. HA0 117 CG64
Brewery La, Byfleet KT14 212 BL113
Hoddesdon EN11 49 EA17
Sevenoaks TN13 off High St 257 FJ125
Brewery Rd, N7 276 A6
SE18 165 ER78
Bromley BR2 204 EL102
Hoddesdon EN11 49 EA17
Woking GU21 226 AX117
Brewery Sq, EC1 286 G4
SE1 300 A3
Brewery Wk, Rom. RM1 127 FE57
Brewhouse La, E1 300 F3
SW15 159 CY83
Hertford SG14 32 DQ09
Brewhouse Rd, SE18 305 K8
Brew Ho Rd, Strood Grn RH3
off Tanners Meadow 264 CP138
Brewhouse Wk, SE16 301 L3
Brewhouse Yd, EC1 287 H4
Gravesend DA12
off Queen St 191 GH86
Brewood Rd, Dag. RM8 146 EV65
Brewster Gdns, W10 282 A6
Brewster Ho, E14 289 N10
Brewster Pl, Kings.T. KT1 198 CG96
Brewster Rd, E10 123 EB60
Brian Av, S.Croy. CR2 220 DS112
Brian Cl, Horn. RM12 127 FH63
Briane Rd, Epsom KT19 216 CQ110
Brian Rd, Rom. RM6 126 EW57
Briant Est, SE1 298 E7
Briant Ho, SE1 298 D7
Briants Cl, Pnr. HA5 94 BZ54
Briant St, SE14 313 J6
Briar Av, SW16 181 DM94
Briarbank Rd, W13 137 CG72
Briar Banks, Cars. SM5 218 DG109
Briarcliff, Hem.H. HP1 39 BE19
Briar Cl, N2 120 DB55
N13 100 DQ48
Buckhurst Hill IG9 102 EK47
Cheshunt EN8 66 DW29
Hampton TW12 176 BZ92
Isleworth TW7 177 CF85
Potten End HP4 39 BA16
Taplow SL6 130 AH72
Warlingham CR6 237 EA116
West Byfleet KT14 212 BH111
Briar Ct, Sutt. SM3 217 CW105
Briar Cres, Nthlt. UB5 136 CB65
Briardale Gdns, NW3 120 DA62
Briarfield Av, N3 98 DB54
Briarfield Cl, Bexh. DA7 166 FA82
Briar Gdns, Brom. BR2 204 EF102
Briar Gro, S.Croy. CR2 220 DU113
Briar Hill, Pur. CR8 219 DL111
Briaris Cl, N17 100 DV52
Briar La, Cars. SM5 218 DG110
Croydon CR0 221 EB105
Briarleas Gdns, Upmin. RM14 129 FS59
Briarley Cl, Brox. EN10 49 DZ22
Briar Pas, SW16 201 DL97
Briar Pl, SW16 201 DM97
Briar Rd, NW2 119 CW63
SW16 201 DL97
Bexley DA5 187 FD90
Harrow HA3 117 CJ57
Romford RM3 106 FJ52
St. Albans AL4 43 CJ17
Send GU23 227 BB123
Shepperton TW17 194 BM99
Twickenham TW2 177 CE88
Watford WD25 59 BU34
Briars, The, Bushey Hth WD23 95 CE45
Cheshunt EN8 67 DY31
Harlow CM18 51 ES18
Hertford SG13 32 DU09
Sarratt WD3 74 BH36
Slough SL3 153 AZ78
Briars Cl, Hat. AL10 45 CU18
Briars Ct, Oxshott KT22 215 CD114
Briars La, Hat. AL10 45 CU18
Briars Wk, Rom. RM3 106 FL54
Briarswood, Goffs Oak EN7 66 DS28
Briars Wd, Hat. AL10 45 CT18
Horley RH6 269 DJ147
Briarswood Way, Orp. BR6 223 ET106
Briar Wk, SW15 159 CV84
W10 282 E4
Edgware HA8 96 CQ52
West Byfleet KT14 212 BG112
Briarway, Berk. HP4 38 AW20
Briar Way, Guil. GU4 243 BB130
Slough SL2 131 AQ71
West Drayton UB7 154 BN75
Briarwood, Bans. SM7 234 DA115
Briarwood Cl, NW9 118 CQ58
Feltham TW13 175 BS90
Briar Wd Cl, Brom. BR2
off Gravel Rd 204 EL104
Briarwood Ct, Wor.Pk. KT4
off The Avenue 199 CU102
Briarwood Dr, Nthwd. HA6 93 BU54
Briarwood Rd, SW4 181 DK85
Epsom KT17 217 CU107
Briary Cl, NW3 274 C6
Briary Ct, E16 291 M9
Sidcup DA14 186 EV92
Briary Gdns, Brom. BR1 184 EH92
Briary Gro, Edg. HA8 96 CP54
Briary La, N9 100 DT48
Brick Ct, EC4 286 E9
Grays RM17
off Columbia Wf Rd 170 GA79
Brickcroft, Brox. EN10 67 DY26
Brickcroft Hoppit, Harl. CM17 36 EW14
Brickenden Ct, Wal.Abb. EN9 68 EF33
BRICKENDON, Hert. SG13 48 DQ19
BRICKENDONBURY, Hert. SG13 32 DR14
Brickendon Grn, Brickendon SG13 48 DQ19
Brickendon La, Hert. SG13 48 DQ18
Bricket Rd, St.Alb. AL1 43 CD20
Brickett Cl, Ruis. HA4 115 BQ57
BRICKET WOOD, St.Alb. AL2 60 BZ29
⇌ Bricket Wood 60 CA30
Brick Fm Cl, Rich. TW9 158 CP81
Brickfield, Hat. AL10 45 CU21
Brickfield Av, Hem.H. HP3 41 BP21
Brickfield Cl, E9 278 F5
Brentford TW8 157 CJ80
Brickfield Cotts, SE18 165 ET79
Brickfield Fm Gdns, Orp. BR6 223 EQ105
Brickfield La, Barn. EN5 79 CT44
Burnham SL1 130 AG67
Harlington UB3 155 BR79
Hookwood RH6 268 DD150
Brickfield Ms, Wat. WD19 76 BY44
Brickfield Rd, SW19 180 DB91
Coopersale CM16 70 EX29
Outwood RH1 267 DN142
Thornton Heath CR7 201 DP95
Brickfields, Har. HA2 117 CD61
Brickfields, The, Ware SG12 32 DV05
● Brickfields Ind Est, Hem.H. HP2 41 BP16
Brickfields La, Cooper. CM16
off Brickfield Rd 70 EX29
Brickfields Way, West Dr. UB7 154 BM76
Brick Kiln Cl, Wat. WD19 76 BY44
Brick Kiln La, Oxt. RH8 254 EJ131
Brick Knoll Pk, St.Alb. AL1 43 CJ21
Brickland Ct, N9
off The Broadway 100 DU47
Brick La, E1 288 B4
E2 288 B3
Enfield EN1, EN3 82 DV40
Nthlt. UB5 136 BZ69
Stanmore HA7 95 CK52
● Bricklayer's Arms Distribution Cen, SE1 299 P9
Jct Bricklayer's Arms Rbt, SE1 299 L8
Brickmakers La, Hem.H. HP3 41 BP21
Brick St, W1 297 J3
Brickwall Cl, Ayot St.P. AL6 29 CU07
Brickwall La, Ruis. HA4 115 BS60
Brickwood Cl, SE26 182 DV90
Brickwood Rd, Croy. CR0 202 DS103
Brickyard La, Wotton RH5 262 BW141
Brideale Cl, SE15 312 B3
Bride Ct, EC4 286 G9
Bride La, EC4 286 G9
Bridel Ms, N1 276 G9
Brides Pl, N1 277 N7
Bride St, N7 276 D5
Bridewain St, SE1 300 A6
Bridewell Pl, E1 300 F3
EC4 286 G9
Bridford Ms, W1 285 K6
Bridge, The, SW8 309 J5
Harrow HA3 117 CE55
Kings Langley WD4 59 BP29
Sch Bridge Acad, E2 278 B9
Bridge App, NW1 274 G6
Bridge Av, W6 159 CW78
W7 137 CD71
Upminster RM14 128 FN61
Bridge Barn La, Wok. GU21 226 AW117
● Bridge Business Cen, Sthl. UB2 156 CA75
Bridge Cl, W10 282 D9
Brentwood CM13 109 FZ49
Byfleet KT14 212 BM112
Dartford DA2 169 FR83
Enfield EN1 82 DV40
Romford RM7 127 FE58
Slough SL1 131 AM73
Staines-upon-Thames TW18 173 BE91
Teddington TW11 177 CF91
Walton-on-Thames KT12 195 BT101
Woking GU21 226 AW117
Bridge Cotts, Upmin. RM14 129 FU64
Bridge Ct, E14
off Newport Av 291 H10
Grays RM17 off Bridge Rd 170 GB79
Har. HA2 116 CC61
Welwyn Garden City AL7 29 CZ09
Woking GU21 226 AX117
Bridge Dr, N13 99 DM49
Bridge End, E17 101 EC53
Bridge End Cl, Kings.T. KT2
off Clifton Rd 198 CN95
Bridgefield Cl, Bans. SM7 233 CW115
Bridgefield Rd, Sutt. SM1 218 DA107
Bridgefields, Welw.G.C. AL7 29 CZ08
Bridgefoot, SE1 310 A1
Ware SG12 off High St 33 DX06
Bridgefoot La, Pot.B. EN6 63 CX33
Bridge Gdns, N16 277 L1
Ashford TW15 175 BQ94
East Molesey KT8 197 CD98
Bridge Gate, N21 100 DQ45
● Bridgegate Cen, Welw.G.C. AL7
off Martinfield 29 CZ08
Bridgeham Cl, Wey. KT13
off Mayfield Rd 212 BN106
Bridgeham Way, Smallfield RH6 269 DP148
Bridge Hill, Epp. CM16 69 ET33
Bridgehill Cl, Guil. GU2 242 AU133
Wembley HA0 137 CK67
Bridge Ho, NW3
off Adelaide Rd 274 G6
SW8 off St. George Wf 310 A1
Bridge Ho Quay, E14 302 F3
● Bridge Ind Est, Horl. RH6 269 DH148
Bridgeland Rd, E16 291 P10
Bridgelands Cl, Beck. BR3 183 DZ94
Bridge La, NW11 119 CY57
SW11 308 D7
Virginia Water GU25 192 AY99
Bridgeman Dr, Wind. SL4 151 AN82
Bridgeman Rd, N1 276 C7
Teddington TW11 177 CG93
Bridgeman St, NW8 284 C1
Bridge Meadows, SE14 313 J2
Bridge Ms, Wok. GU21
off Bridge Barn La 226 AX117
Bridgend Rd, SW18 160 DC84
Enfield EN1 82 DW35
Bridgenhall Rd, Enf. EN1 82 DT39
Bridgen Rd, Bex. DA5 186 EY86
Bridge Pk, SW18 180 DA85
Guildford GU4 243 BC131
Bridge Pl, SW1 297 K8
Amersham HP6 55 AS38
Croydon CR0 202 DR101
Watford WD17
off Lower High St 76 BX43
Bridgepoint Pl, N6
off Hornsey La 121 DJ60
Bridgeport Pl, E1 300 D2
Bridger Cl, Wat. WD25 60 BX33
Bridge Rd, E6 145 EM66
E15 281 H7
E17 123 DZ59
N9 off Fore St 100 DU48
N22 99 DL53
NW10 138 CS65
Beckenham BR3 183 DZ94
Bexleyheath DA7 166 EY82
Chertsey KT16 194 BH101
Chessington KT9 216 CL106
East Molesey KT8 197 CE98
Epsom KT17 217 CT112
Erith DA8 167 FF81
Grays RM17 170 GB78
Hounslow TW3 157 CD83
Hunton Bridge WD4 59 BQ33
Isleworth TW7 157 CD83
Orpington BR5 206 EV100
Rainham RM13 147 FF70
Southall UB2 156 BZ75
Sutton SM2 218 DB107
Twickenham TW1 177 CH86
Uxbridge UB8 134 BJ68
Wallington SM6 219 DJ106
Welwyn Garden City AL7, AL8 29 CW08
Wembley HA9 118 CN62
Weybridge KT13 212 BM105
Bridge Rd E, Welw.G.C. AL7 29 CY08
Bridge Row, Croy. CR0
off Cross Rd 202 DR102
Sch Bridge Sch, The,
Prim Dept, N7 275 P4
Sec Dept, N7 275 P1
Bridges Cl, Horl. RH6 269 DK148
Bridges Ct, SW11 308 A10
Bridges Dr, Dart. DA1 188 FP85
Bridges La, Croy. CR0 219 DL105
Bridges Pl, SW6 307 H6
Bridges Rd, SW19 180 DB93
Stanmore HA7 95 CF50
Bridges Rd Ms, SW19
off Bridges Rd 180 DB93
Bridge St, SW1 298 A5
W4 158 CR77
Berkhamsted HP4 38 AX19
Colnbrook SL3 153 BD80
Guildford GU1 258 AW135
Hemel Hempstead HP1 40 BJ21
Leatherhead KT22 231 CG122
Pinner HA5 116 BX55
Richmond TW9 177 CK85
Staines-upon-Thames TW18 173 BE91
Walton-on-Thames KT12 195 BT102
Bridge Ter, E15 281 H7
SE13 off Mercator Rd 163 ED84
Bridgetown Cl, SE19
off Georgetown Cl 182 DS92
Bridge Vw, W6 294 A10
Greenhithe DA9 169 FV84
Bridgeview Ct, Ilf. IG6 103 ER51
● Bridge Wks, Uxb. UB8 134 BJ70
Bridgewater Cl, Chis. BR7 205 ES97
Bridgewater Ct, Slou. SL3 153 BA78
Bridgewater Gdns, Edg. HA8 96 CM54
Bridgewater Hill, Nthch HP4 38 AT16
Bridgewater Rd, E15
off Warton Rd 280 E9
Berkhamsted HP4 38 AU17
Wembley HA0 137 CJ66
Weybridge KT13 213 BR107
Sch Bridgewater Sch, Berk. HP4
off Bridle Way 38 AU17
Bridgewater Sq, EC2 287 J6
Bridgewater St, EC2 287 J6
Bridgewater Ter, Wind. SL4 151 AR81
Bridgewater Way, Bushey WD23 76 CB44
Windsor SL4
off Bridgewater Ter 151 AR81
Bridge Way, N11
off Pymmes Grn Rd 99 DJ48
NW11 119 CZ57
Chipstead CR5 234 DE119
Cobham KT11 213 BT113
Twickenham TW2 176 CC87
Uxbridge UB10 115 BP64
Bridgeway, Bark. IG11 145 ET66
Wembley HA0 138 CL66
Bridgeway St, NW1 285 M1
Bridge Wf, Cher. KT16 194 BJ101
Bridge Wf Rd, Islw. TW7
off Church St 157 CH83
Bridgewood Cl, SE20 182 DV94
Bridgewood Rd, SW16 181 DK94
Worcester Park KT4 217 CU105
Bridge Yd, SE1 299 M2
Bridgford St, SW18 180 DC90
Bridgman Rd, W4 158 CQ76
Bridgwater Cl, Rom. RM3 106 FK50
Bridgwater Rd, Rom. RM3 106 FJ50
Ruislip HA4 115 BU63
Bridgwater Wk, Rom. RM3 106 FK50
Bridle Cl, Enf. EN3 83 DZ37
Epsom KT19 216 CR106
Hoddesdon EN11 33 EA13
Kingston upon Thames KT1 197 CK98
St. Albans AL3 43 CE18
Sunbury-on-Thames TW16
off Forge La 195 BU97
Bridle End, Epsom KT17 217 CT114
Bridle La, W1 285 M10
Cobham KT11 230 CB115
Leatherhead KT22 230 CB115
Loudwater WD3 74 BK41
Twickenham TW1 177 CH86
Bridle Ms, Barn. EN5
off High St 79 CZ42
Bridle Path, Bedd. CR0 201 DM104
Watford WD17 75 BV40
Bridle Path, The, Epsom KT17 217 CV110
Woodford Green IG8 102 EE52
Bridlepath Way, Felt. TW14 175 BS88
Bridle Rd, Clay. KT10 215 CH107
Croydon CR0 203 EA104
Epsom KT17 217 CT113
Pinner HA5 116 BW58
Bridle Rd, The, Pur. CR8 219 DL110
Bridle Way, Berk. HP4 38 AU17
Croydon CR0 221 EA106
Great Amwell SG12 33 EA09
Hoddesdon EN11 33 EA14
Orpington BR6 223 EQ105
Bridle Way, The, Croy. CR0 221 DY110
Bridleway, The, Wall. SM6 219 DJ105
Bridleway Cl, Epsom KT17 217 CW110
Bridle Way N, Hodd. EN11 33 EA13
Bridle Way S, Hodd. EN11 33 EA14
Bridlington Cl, Bigg.H. TN16 238 EH119
Bridlington Rd, N9 100 DV45
Watford WD19 94 BX48
Bridlington Spur, Slou. SL1 151 AP76
Bridport Av, Rom. RM7 127 FB58
Bridport Pl, N1 277 M10
Bridport Rd, N18 100 DS50
Greenford UB6 136 CB67
Thornton Heath CR7 201 DN97
Bridport Ter, SW8 309 N7
Bridport Way, Slou. SL2 131 AP70
Bridstow Pl, W2 283 K8
Brief St, SE5 310 G8
Brier Lea, Lwr Kgswd KT20 249 CZ126
Brierley, New Adgtn CR0 221 EB107
Brierley Av, N9 100 DW46
Brierley Cl, SE25 202 DU98
Hornchurch RM11 128 FJ58
Brierley Rd, E11 123 ED63
SW12 181 DJ89
Brierly Cl, Guil. GU2 242 AU132
Brierly Gdns, E2 289 H1
Brier Rd, Tad. KT20 233 CV119
Briery Ct, Chorl. WD3 74 BG42
Hemel Hempstead HP2 40 BN19
Briery Fld, Chorl. WD3 74 BG42
Briery Way, Amer. HP6 55 AS37
Hemel Hempstead HP2 40 BN18
Brigade Cl, Har. HA2 117 CD61
Brigade Pl, Cat. CR3 236 DQ122
Brigade St, SE3 315 L9
Brigadier Av, Enf. EN2 82 DQ39
Brigadier Hill, Enf. EN2 82 DQ38
Briggeford Cl, E5 122 DU61
BRIGGENS PARK, Ware SG12 34 EJ11
Briggs Cl, Mitch. CR4 201 DH95
Bright Cl, Belv. DA17 166 EX77
Brightfield Rd, SE12 184 EF85
Bright Hill, Guil. GU1 258 AX136
Brightlands, Nthflt DA11 190 GE91
Brightlands Rd, Reig. RH2 250 DC132
Brightling Rd, SE4 183 DZ86
Brightlingsea Pl, E14 289 N10
Brightman Rd, SW18 180 DD88
Brighton Av, E17 123 DZ57
Brighton Cl, Add. KT15 212 BJ106
Uxbridge UB10 135 BP66
Brighton Dr, Nthlt. UB5 136 CA65
Brighton Gro, SE14 313 L6
Brighton Rd, E6 293 M2
N2 98 DC54
N16 122 DS63
Addlestone KT15 212 BJ105
Banstead SM7 217 CZ114
Coulsdon CR5 235 DJ119
Horley RH6 268 DF149
Purley CR8 220 DQ110
Redhill RH1 266 DF135
South Croydon CR2 220 DQ106
Surbiton KT6 197 CJ100
Sutton SM2 218 DB109
Tadworth KT20 233 CY119
Watford WD24 75 BU38
Brighton Spur, Slou. SL2 131 AP70
Brighton Ter, SW9 161 DM84
Redhill RH1 off Hooley La 266 DF135
Brights Av, Rain. RM13 147 FH70
Brightside, The, Enf. EN3 83 DX39
Brightside Av, Stai. TW18 174 BJ94
Brightside Rd, SE13 183 ED86
Bright St, E14 290 D8
Brightview Cl, Brick.Wd AL2 60 BY29
Brightwell Cl, Croy. CR0
off Sumner Rd 201 DN102
Brightwell Cres, SW17 180 DF92
Brightwell Rd, Wat. WD18 75 BU43
Brightwen Gro, Stan. HA7 95 CG47
Sch Brigidine Sch Windsor, Wind. SL4
off King's Rd 151 AR83
Brig Ms, SE8 314 A3
Brigstock Rd, Belv. DA17 167 FB77
Coulsdon CR5 235 DH115
Thornton Heath CR7 201 DN99
Brill Pl, NW1 285 P1
Brimfield Rd, Purf. RM19 169 FR77
Brim Hill, N2 120 DC56
Brimpsfield Cl, SE2 166 EV76
BRIMSDOWN, Enf. EN3 83 DY41
⇌ Brimsdown 83 DY41
Brimsdown Av, Enf. EN3 83 DY40
● Brimsdown Ind Est, Enf. EN3 83 DY39
Sch Brimsdown Inf & Jun Schs, Enf. EN3 off Green St 83 DX41
Brimshot La, Chobham GU24 210 AS109
Brimstone Cl, Orp. BR6 224 EW108
Brimstone Ho, E15
off Victoria St 281 J6
Brimstone La, Dor. RH5 264 CM143
Brimstone Wk, Berk. HP4 38 AT17
Sch Brindishe Prim Sch, SE12
off Wantage Rd 184 EF85
Brindle Gate, Sid. DA15 185 ES88
Brindle La, Forty Grn HP9 88 AG51
Brindles, Horn. RM11 128 FL56
Brindles, The, Bans. SM7 233 CZ117
Brindles Cl, Hutt. CM13 109 GC47
Brindley Cl, Bexh. DA7 167 FB83
Wembley HA0 137 CJ67
Brindley Ho, SW2
off New Pk Rd 181 DL87
Brindley St, SE14 313 N7

Brindley Way, Brom. BR1 184 EG92
Hemel Hempstead HP3
off London Rd 58 BM25
Southall UB1 136 CB73
Brindwood Rd, E4 101 DZ48
Brinkburn Cl, SE2 166 EU77
Edgware HA8 96 CP54
Brinkburn Gdns, Edg. HA8 118 CN55
Brinkley, Kings.T. KT1
off Burritt Rd 198 CN96
Brinkley Rd, Wor.Pk. KT4 199 CV103
Brinklow Ct, St.Alb. AL3 42 CB23
Brinklow Cres, SE18 165 EP80
Brinklow Ho, W2 283 K6
Brinkworth Rd, Ilf. IG5 124 EL55
Brinkworth Way, E9 279 P4
Brinley Cl, Chsht EN8 66 DW31
Brinsdale Rd, NW4 119 CX56
Brinsley Ho, E1
off Tarling St 288 G9
Brinsley Rd, Har. HA3 95 CD54
Brinsmead, Frog. AL2 61 CD27
Brinsmead Rd, Rom. RM3 106 FN54
Brinsworth Cl, Twick. TW2 177 CD89
Brinton Wk, SE1 298 G3
Brion Pl, E14 290 E7
Brisbane Av, SW19 200 DB95
Brisbane Ho, Til. RM18 171 GF81
Brisbane Rd, E10 123 EB61
W13 157 CG75
Ilford IG1 125 EP59
Brisbane St, SE5 311 L5
Briscoe Cl, E11 124 EF61
Hoddesdon EN11 49 DZ15
Briscoe Ms, Twick. TW2 177 CD89
Briscoe Rd, SW19 180 DD93
Hoddesdon EN11 49 DZ15
Rainham RM13 148 FJ68
Briset Rd, SE9 164 EK83
Briset St, EC1 286 G6
Briset Way, N7 121 DM61
Brisson Cl, Esher KT10 214 BZ107
Bristol Cl, Houns. TW4
off Harvey Rd 176 CA87
Stanwell TW19 174 BL86
Wallington SM6 219 DL108
Bristol Gdns, SW15
off Portsmouth Rd 179 CW87
W9 283 M5
Bristol Ho, SE11
off Lambeth Wk 298 E7
Bristol Ms, W9 283 M5
Bristol Pk Rd, E17 123 DY56
Bristol Rd, E7 144 EJ65
Gravesend DA12 191 GK90
Greenford UB6 136 CB67
Morden SM4 200 DC99
Bristol Way, Slou. SL1 132 AS74
Briston Gro, N8 121 DL58
Briston Ms, NW7 97 CU52
Bristowe Cl, SW2 181 DN86
Bristow Rd, SE19 182 DS92
Bexleyheath DA7 166 EY81
Croydon CR0 219 DL105
Hounslow TW3 156 CC83
Britannia Bldg, N1
off Ebenezer St 287 L2
● **Britannia Business Pk**,
Wal.Cr. EN8 67 DZ34
Britannia Cl, SW4
off Bowland Rd 161 DK84
Erith DA8 167 FF79
Northolt UB5 136 BX69
Britannia Ct, Kings.T. KT2
off Skerne Wk 197 CK95
Britannia Dr, Grav. DA12 191 GM92
Britannia Gate, E16 303 P2
● **Britannia Ind Est**,
Colnbr. SL3 153 BD82
Britannia La, Twick. TW2 176 CC87
Britannia Rd, E14 302 B9
N12 98 DC48
SW6 307 L5
Chesham HP5 54 AQ29
Ilford IG1 125 EP62
Surbiton KT5 198 CM101
Waltham Cross EN8 67 DZ34
Warley CM14 108 FW50
Britannia Row, N1 277 H8
Britannia St, WC1 286 C2
Sch **Britannia Village Prim Sch**, E16 304 A3
Britannia Wk, N1 287 L2
Britannia Way, NW10 138 CP70
SW6 307 M5
Stanwell TW19 174 BK87
★ **British Dental Assoc Mus**, W1 285 J7
British Gro, W4 159 CT78
British Gro N, W4
off Middlesex Ct 159 CT78
British Gro Pas, W4 159 CT78
British Gro S, W4
off British Gro Pas 159 CT78
British Legion Rd, E4 102 EF47
★ **British Lib**, NW1 285 P2
★ **British Lib Newspapers** (Former), NW9 118 CS55
★ **British Med Assoc**, WC1 285 P4
★ **British Mus, The**, WC1 285 P7
Coll **British Sch of Osteopathy**, SE1 299 K5
British St, E3 289 P3
Coll **British Transport Pol Training Sch**, Walt.Hill KT20
off Sandlands Gro 233 CU123
Briton Cl, S.Croy. CR2 220 DS111
Briton Cres, S.Croy. CR2 220 DS111
Briton Hill Rd, S.Croy. CR2 220 DS110
Coll **BRIT Sch for Performing Arts & Tech, The**, Croy. CR0
off The Crescent 202 DR100
Brittain Rd, Dag. RM8 126 EY62
Hersham KT12 214 BX106
Brittains La, Sev. TN13 256 FF123
Brittany Ho, Enf. EN2
off Chantry Cl 82 DQ38
Brittany Pt, SE11 298 E9
Britten Cl, NW11 120 DB60
Elstree WD6 off Rodgers Cl 77 CK44
Brittenden Cl, Orp. BR6 223 ES107
Brittenden Par, Grn St Grn BR6
off Glentrammon Rd 223 ET107
Britten Dr, Sthl. UB1 136 CA72
Brittens Cl, Guil. GU2 242 AU129
Britten St, SW3 308 C1
Brittidge Rd, NW10
off Paulet Way 138 CS66
Britton Av, St.Alb. AL3 43 CD20
Britton Cl, SE6
off Brownhill Rd 183 ED87
Sch **Brittons Sch**, Rain. RM13
off Ford La 147 FF66
Britton St, EC1 286 G5
Britwell Dr, Berk. HP4 38 AY17
Britwell Est, Slou. SL2 131 AM70
Britwell Gdns, Burn. SL1 131 AK69
Britwell Rd, Burn. SL1 131 AK69
Brixham Cres, Ruis. HA4 115 BU60
Brixham Gdns, Ilf. IG3 125 ES64
Brixham Rd, Well. DA16 166 EX81
Brixham St, E16 305 K3
BRIXTON, SW2 161 DL84
⇌ **Brixton** 161 DN84
⊖ **Brixton** 161 DN84
Brixton Hill, SW2 181 DL87
Brixton Hill Pl, SW2 181 DL87
Brixton Oval, SW2 161 DN84
Brixton Rd, SW9 310 E5
Watford WD24 75 BV39
Brixton Sta Rd, SW9 161 DN84
🛍 **Brixton Village Mkt**, SW9
off Coldharbour La 161 DN84
Brixton Water La, SW2 181 DM85
Broad Acre, Brick.Wd AL2 60 BY30
Broadacre, Stai. TW18 174 BG92
Broadacre Cl, Uxb. UB10 115 BP62
Broad Acres, Gdmg. GU7 258 AS143
Hatfield AL10 45 CT15
Broadacres, Guil. GU3 242 AS132
Broadbent Cl, N6 121 DH60
Broadbent St, W1 285 J10
Broadberry Ct, N18 100 DV50
Broadbridge Cl, SE3 315 N4
Broadbridge La,
Smallfield RH6 269 DN148
Broad Cl, Hersham KT12 196 BX104
Broad Common Est, N16
off Osbaldeston Rd 122 DU60
Broadcoombe, S.Croy. CR2 220 DW108
Broad Ct, WC2 286 B9
Welwyn Garden City AL7 29 CY09
Broadcroft, Hem.H. HP2 40 BK18
Broadcroft Av, Stan. HA7 95 CK54
Broadcroft Rd, Petts Wd BR5 205 ER101
Broad Ditch Rd, Sthflt DA13 190 GC94
Broadeaves Cl, S.Croy. CR2 220 DS106
Broadfield, Harlow CM20 35 ES14
● **Broadfield Cl**, Croy. CR0
off Progress Way 201 DM103
Broadfield Cl, NW2 119 CW62
Romford RM1 127 FF57
Tadworth KT20 233 CW120
Broadfield Ct,
Bushey Hth WD23 95 CE47
Sch **Broadfield Inf Sch**,
Hem.H. HP2
off Broadfield Rd 40 BM20
Sch **Broadfield Jun Sch**,
Hem.H. HP2
off Windmill Rd 40 BM20
Broadfield La, NW1 276 A6
Broadfield Pl, Welw.G.C. AL8 29 CV10
Broadfield Rd, SE6 184 EE87
Hemel Hempstead HP2 40 BM20
Peaslake GU5 261 BR142
Broadfields, E.Mol. KT8 197 CD100
Goffs Oak EN7 65 DP29
Harrow HA2 94 CB54
High Wych CM21 36 EV06
Broadfields Av, N21 99 DN45
Edgware HA8 96 CP49
Sch **Broadfields Co Prim Sch**,
Harl. CM20
off Freshwaters 35 ES14
Broadfields Hts, Edg. HA8 96 CP49
Broadfields La, Wat. WD19 93 BV46
Sch **Broadfields Prim Sch**, Edg. HA8
off Broadfields Av 96 CN47
Broadfield Sq, Enf. EN1 82 DV40
Broadfields Way, NW10 119 CT64
Broadfield Way, Ald. WD25 76 CB36
Buck.H. IG9 102 EJ48
Broadford, Shalf. GU4 258 AX141
Broadford La, Chobham GU24 210 AT112
● **Broadford Pk**, Shalf. GU4 258 AX141
Sch **Broadford Prim Sch**,
Harold Hill RM3
off Faringdon Av 106 FK51
Broadford Rd, Peasm. GU3 258 AW142
BROADGATE, EC2 287 M6
Broadgate, E13 144 EJ68
Waltham Abbey EN9 68 EF33
Broadgate Circle, EC2 287 N6
Broadgate Rd, E16 292 E8
Broadgates Av, Barn. EN4 80 DB39
Broadgates Rd, SW18
off Ellerton Rd 180 DD88
BROAD GREEN, Croy. CR0 201 DN100
Broad Grn, Bayford SG13 47 DM15
Broad Grn Av, Croy. CR0 201 DP101
Broadgreen Rd, Chsht EN7 66 DR26
Broad Grn Wd, Bayford SG13 47 DM15
Broadham Grn Rd, Oxt. RH8 253 ED132
Broadham Pl, Oxt. RH8 253 ED131
Broadhead Strand, NW9 97 CT53
Broadheath Dr, Chis. BR7 185 EM92
Broad Highway, Cob. KT11 214 BX114
Broadhinton Rd, SW4 309 K10
Broadhurst, Ashtd. KT21 232 CL116
Broadhurst Av, Edg. HA8 96 CP49
Ilford IG3 125 ET63
Broadhurst Cl, NW6 273 N5
Richmond TW10
off Lower Gro Rd 178 CM85
Broadhurst Gdns, NW6 273 L5
Chigwell IG7 103 EQ49
Reigate RH2 266 DB137
Ruislip HA4 116 BW61
Broadhurst Wk, Rain. RM13 147 FG65
Broadis Way, Rain. RM13 147 FD68
Broadlake Cl, Lon.Col. AL2 61 CK27
Broadlands, Bad.Dene RM17
off Bankfoot 170 FZ78
Hanworth TW13 176 BZ90
Horley RH6 269 DJ147
Broadlands Av, SW16 181 DL89
Chesham HP5 54 AQ31
Enfield EN3 82 DV41
Shepperton TW17 195 BQ100
Broadlands Cl, N6 120 DG59
SW16 181 DL89
Enfield EN3 82 DV41
Waltham Cross EN8 67 DX34
Broadlands Dr, Warl. CR6 236 DW119
Broadlands Rd, N6 120 DF59
Bromley BR1 184 EH91
Broadlands Way, N.Mal. KT3 199 CT100
Broad La, EC2 287 N6
N8 off Tottenham La 121 DM57
N15 122 DT56
Beaconsfield HP9 110 AH55
Dartford DA2 187 FG91
Hampton TW12 176 CA93
Wooburn Green HP10 110 AG58
Broad Lawn, SE9 185 EN89
Broadlawns Ct, Har. HA3 95 CF53
Broadleaf Gro, Welw.G.C. AL8 29 CV06
BROADLEY COMMON,
Wal.Abb. EN9 50 EL20
Broadley Gdns, Shenley WD7
off Queens Way 62 CL32
Broadley Rd, Harl. CM19 51 EM19
Broadley St, NW8 284 B6
Broadley Ter, NW1 284 D5
Waltham Abbey EN9 50 EL21
Broadmark Rd, Slou. SL2 132 AV73
Broadmayne, SE17 299 K10
Broadmead, SE6 183 EA90
Ashtead KT21 232 CM117
Horley RH6 269 DJ147
Broadmead Av, Wor.Pk. KT4 199 CU101
Broadmead Cl, Hmptn. TW12 176 CA93
Pinner HA5 94 BY52
Sch **Broadmead Junior, Inf & Nurs Sch**,
Croy. CR0
off Sydenham Rd 202 DR101
Broadmead Rd, Hayes UB4 136 BY70
Northolt UB5 136 BY70
Woking GU22, GU23 227 BB122
Woodford Green IG8 102 EG51
Broadmeads, Send GU23
off Broadmead Rd 227 BB122
Ware SG12 33 DX06
Sch **Broadmere Comm Prim Sch**,
Sheer. GU21
off Devonshire Av 211 BD113
BROADMOOR, Dor. RH5 262 CA143
Broadmoor, Dor. RH5 262 CA143
Broad Oak, Slou. SL2 131 AQ70
Sunbury-on-Thames TW16 175 BT93
Woodford Green IG8 102 EH50
Broadoak Av, Enf. EN3 83 DX35
Broad Oak Cl, E4 101 EA50
Orpington BR5 206 EU96
Broadoak Cl, Sutt.H. DA4 188 FN93
Broadoak Ct, SW9
off Gresham Rd 161 DN83
Broad Oak Ct, Slou. SL2 131 AQ70
BROADOAK END, Hert. SG14 31 DM07
Broad Oak La, Hert. SG14 31 DM07
Broad Oak Manor, Hert. SG14 31 DM07
Broadoak Rd, Erith DA8 167 FD80
Broadoaks, Epp. CM16 69 ET31
Broadoaks Cres,
W.Byf. KT14 212 BH114
Broadoaks Way, Brom. BR2 204 EF99
Broad Platts, Slou. SL3 152 AX76
Broad Ride, Egh. TW20 192 AU96
Broad Rd,
Swanscombe DA10 190 FY86
Watford WD24 75 BU36
Broad Sanctuary, SW1 297 P5
Broadstone Pl, W1 284 G7
Broadstone Rd, Horn. RM12 127 FG61
Broad St, Chesh. HP5 54 AQ30
Dagenham RM10 146 FA66
Hemel Hempstead HP2 40 BK19
Rydeshill GU3 242 AS132
Teddington TW11 177 CF93
Broad St Av, EC2 287 N7
Broad St Pl, EC2 287 M7
Broadstrood, Loug. IG10 85 EN38
Broad Vw, NW9 118 CN58
Broadview Av, Grays RM16 170 GD75
Broadview Ho, Enf. EN3
off Tysoe Av 83 DZ36
Broadview Rd, SW16 181 DJ94
Chesham HP5 54 AP27
Broadwalk, E18 124 EF55
Harrow HA2 116 CA57
Broad Wk, N21 99 DM47
NW1 285 J3
SE3 164 EJ83
W1 296 G2
Caterham CR3 236 DT122
Coulsdon CR5 234 DG123
Croydon CR0 221 DY110
Epsom KT18 233 CX119
Harlow CM20 35 ER14
Hounslow TW5 156 BX81
Orpington BR6 206 EX104
Richmond TW9 158 CM80
Sevenoaks TN15 257 FL128
Broad Wk, The, W8 295 M1
East Molesey KT8 197 CF97
Broadwalk, The, Nthwd. HA6 93 BQ54
Broadwalk Ct, W8 295 K2
Broad Wk La, NW11 119 CZ59
Broad Wk N, The, Brwd. CM13 109 GA49
🛍 **Broadwalk Shop Cen**,
Edg. HA8 96 CN51
Broad Wk S, The,
Brwd. CM13 109 GA49
Broadwall, SE1 298 F2
Broadwater, Berk. HP4 38 AW18
Potters Bar EN6 64 DB30
Broadwater Cl,
Hersham KT12 213 BU106
Woking GU21 211 BD112
Wraysbury TW19 173 AZ87
Broadwater Cres,
Welw.G.C. AL7 29 CX10
Broad Water Cres, Wey. KT13 195 BQ104
Broadwater Fm Est, N17 100 DR54
Sch **Broadwater Fm Prim Sch**, N17
off Moira Cl 100 DR54
Broadwater Gdns, Hare. UB9 114 BH56
Orpington BR6 223 EP105
Broadwater La, Hare. UB9 114 BH56
● **Broadwater Pk**, Denh. UB9 114 BG58
Broadwater Pk, Maid. SL6 150 AE78
Broadwater Pl, Wey. KT13
off Oatlands Dr 195 BS103
Sch **Broadwater Prim Sch**, SW17
off Broadwater Rd 180 DE91
Broadwater Ri, Guil. GU1 243 BA134
Broadwater Rd, N17 100 DS53
SE28 165 ER76
SW17 180 DE91
Welwyn Garden City AL7 29 CY10
Broadwater Rd N,
Hersham KT12 213 BT106
Broadwater Rd S,
Hersham KT12 213 BT106
Sch **Broadwater Sch**, Farnc. GU7
off Summers Rd 258 AU143
Broadway, E15 281 H7
SW1 297 N6
W7 137 CG74
W13 137 CG74
Barking IG11 145 EQ67
Bexleyheath DA6, DA7 166 EY84
Grays RM17 170 GC79
Nthwd. HA6
off Joel St 93 BU54
Potters Bar EN6
off Darkes La 63 CZ32
Rainham RM13 147 FG70
Romford RM2 127 FG55
Staines-upon-Thames TW18
off Kingston Rd 174 BH93
Swanley BR8 207 FC100
Tilbury RM18 171 GF82
Broadway, The, E4 101 EC51
E13 292 A1
N8 121 DL58
N9 100 DU47
N14 off Winchmore Hill Rd 99 DK46
N22 99 DN54
NW7 96 CS50
SW13 off The Terrace 158 CS82
SW19 179 CZ93
W5 137 CK73
W7 off Cherington Rd 137 CE74
Amersham HP7 55 AP40
Beaconsfield HP9
off Penn Rd 89 AK52
Cheam SM3 217 CY107
Chesham HP5 54 AP31
Croydon CR0
off Croydon Rd 219 DL105
Dagenham RM8 126 EZ61
Farnham Common SL2 131 AQ65
Greenford UB6 136 CC70
Hatfield AL9 45 CW17
Hornchurch RM12 127 FH63
Laleham TW18 194 BJ97
Loughton IG10 85 EQ42
New Haw KT15 212 BG110
Pinner HA5 94 BZ52
Southall UB1 136 BX73
Stanmore HA7 95 CJ50
Sutton SM1 off Manor La 218 DC106
Thames Ditton KT7
off Hampton Ct Way 197 CE102
Watford WD17 76 BW41
Wealdstone HA3 95 CE54
Wembley HA9 off East La 118 CL62
Woking GU21 227 AZ117
Woodford Green IG8 102 EH51
Wycombe End HP9 89 AL54
Broadway Av, Croy. CR0 202 DR99
Harlow CM17 36 EV11
Twickenham TW1 177 CH86
Broadway Cl, Amer. HP7 55 AP40
South Croydon CR2 220 DV114
Woodford Green IG8 102 EH51
Broadway Ct, SW19 179 CZ93
Amersham HP7 55 AP40
Broadway E, Denh. UB9 114 BG59
Broadway Est, Til. RM18 171 GF81
Broadway Gdns, Mitch. CR4 200 DE98
🛍 **Broadway Mkt**, SW17 180 DF91
Broadway Mkt, E8 278 D9
Broadway Mkt Ms, E8 278 D9
Broadway Ms, E5 122 DT59
N13 off Elmdale Rd 99 DM50
N21 99 DP46
Broadway Par, N8 121 DL58
Hayes UB3
off Coldharbour La 135 BU74
Hornchurch RM12
off The Broadway 127 FH63
Broadway Pl, SW19
off Hartfield Rd 179 CZ93
🛍 **Broadway Shop Cen**, W6 294 B9
Broadway Wk, E14 302 B6
Broadwick St, W1 285 M10
Broadwood, Grav. DA11 191 GH92
Broadwood Av, Ruis. HA4 115 BS58
Broadwood Rd, Couls. CR5 235 DK121
Broadwood Ter, W8
off Pembroke Rd 295 H8
Broad Yd, EC1 286 G5
Brocas Cl, NW3 274 D6
Brocas St, Eton SL4 151 AR80
Brocas Ter, Eton SL4 151 AQ80
Brockbridge Ho, SW15
off Tangley Gro 179 CT86
Brockdene Dr, Kes. BR2 222 EK105
Brockdish Av, Bark. IG11 125 ET64
Brockenhurst, W.Mol. KT8 196 BZ100
Brockenhurst Av, Wor.Pk. KT4 198 CS102
Brockenhurst Cl, Wok. GU21 211 AZ114
Brockenhurst Gdns, NW7 96 CS50
Ilford IG1 125 EQ64
Brockenhurst Ms, N18 100 DU49
Brockenhurst Rd, Croy. CR0 202 DV101
Brockenhurst Way, SW16 201 DK96
Brocket Cl, Chig. IG7
off Brocket Way 103 ET50
Brocket Pk, Lmsfd AL8 28 CS10
Brocket Rd, Grays RM16 171 GG76
Hoddesdon EN11 49 EA17
Welwyn Garden City AL8 29 CT11
Brockett Cl, Welw.G.C. AL8 29 CV09
Brocket Way, Chig. IG7 103 ES50
Brock Grn, S.Ock. RM15
off Cam Grn 149 FV72
BROCKHAM, Bet. RH3 264 CP136
Brockham Cl, SW19 179 CZ92
Brockham Cres,
New Adgtn CR0 221 ED108
Brockham Dr, SW2
off Fairview Pl 181 DM87
Ilford IG2 125 EP58
Brockham Grn, Brock. RH3 264 CP135
Brockham Hill Pk, Box H. KT20 248 CQ131
Brockhamhurst Rd, Bet. RH3 264 CN141
Brockham Keep, Horl. RH6
off Langshott La 269 DJ147
Brockham La, Brock. RH3 248 CN134
Sch **Brockham Sch**, Brock. RH3
off Wheelers La 264 CP136
Brockham St, SE1 299 K6
Brockhill, Wok. GU21 226 AU117
Brockhurst Cl, Stan. HA7 95 CF51
Brockhurst Rd, Chesh. HP5 54 AQ29
Brockill Cres, SE4 163 DY84
Brocklebank Cl, Whyt. CR3 236 DU118
Brocklebank Ho, E16
off Glenister St 305 M3
● **Brocklebank Ind Est**, SE7 303 P8
Brocklebank Rd, SE7 304 A9
SW18 180 DC87
Brocklehurst St, SE14 313 K4
Brocklesbury Cl, Wat. WD24 76 BW41
Brocklesby Rd, SE25 202 DV98
Brockles Mead, Harl. CM19 51 EQ19
BROCKLEY, SE4 183 DY85
⇌ **Brockley** 313 M10
⊖ **Brockley** 313 M10
Brockley Av, Stan. HA7 96 CL48
Brockley Cl, Stan. HA7 96 CL49
Brockley Combe, Wey. KT13 213 BR105
Brockley Cres, Rom. RM5 105 FC52
Brockley Cross, SE4 313 N10
Brockley Footpath, SE15 162 DW84
Brockley Gdns, SE4 313 N8
Brockley Gro, SE4 183 DZ85
Hutton CM13 109 GA46
Brockley Hall Rd, SE4 183 DY86
Brockley Hill, Stan. HA7 95 CJ46
Brockley Ms, SE4 183 DY85
Brockley Pk, SE23 183 DY87
Stanmore HA7 96 CL48
Sch **Brockley Prim Sch**, SE4
off Brockley Rd 183 DZ85
Brockley Ri, SE23 183 DY86
Brockley Rd, SE4 313 M10
Brockleyside, Stan. HA7 95 CK49
Brockley Vw, SE23 183 DY87
Brockley Way, SE4 183 DX85
Brockman Ri, Brom. BR1 183 ED91
Brock Pl, E3 290 C5
Brock Rd, E13 292 B6
Brocks Dr, Sutt. SM3 199 CY104
Brockshot Cl, Brent. TW8 157 CK79
Brocksparkwood, Brwd. CM13 109 GB48
Brock St, NW1 285 L4
SE15 312 G10
Brockswood La,
Welw.G.C. AL8 29 CU08
Brockton Cl, Rom. RM1 127 FF56
Brock Way, Vir.W. GU25 192 AW99
Brockway Cl, E11 124 EE60
Guildford GU1 243 BB132
Brockweir, E2 288 G1
Brockwell Av, Beck. BR3 203 EB99
Brockwell Cl, Orp. BR5 205 ET99
★ **Brockwell Park**, SE24 181 DP86
Brockwell Pk Gdns, SE24 181 DN87
Brockwell Pk Row, SW2 181 DN86
Broderick Gro, Bkhm KT23
off Lower Shott 246 CA126
Brodewater Rd, Borwd. WD6 78 CP40
Brodia Rd, N16 122 DS62
Brodick Ho, E3 279 N10
Brodie Ho, SE1
off Coopers Rd 300 B10
Brodie Rd, E4 101 EC46
Enfield EN2 82 DQ38
Guildford GU1 258 AY135
Brodie St, SE1 300 B10
Brodlove La, E1 289 J10
Brodrick Gro, SE2 166 EV77
Brodrick Rd, SW17 180 DE89
Brograve Gdns, Beck. BR3 203 EB96
Broke Ct, Guil. GU4
off Speedwell Cl 243 BC131
Broke Fm Dr, Orp. BR6 224 EW109
Broken Furlong, Eton SL4 151 AP78
Brokengate La, Denh. UB9 113 BC60
Broken Wf, EC4 287 J10
Brokes Cres, Reig. RH2 250 DA132
Brokesley St, E3 289 N3
Brokes Rd, Reig. RH2 250 DA132
Broke Wk, E8 278 B8
Bromar Rd, SE5 311 P10
Bromborough Grn, Wat. WD19 94 BW50
Bromefield, Stan. HA7 95 CJ53
Bromefield Ct, Wal.Abb. EN9 68 EG33
Bromehead Rd, E1 288 G8
Bromehead St, E1 288 G8
Bromell's Rd, SW4 161 DJ84
Brome Rd, SE9 165 EM83
Bromet Cl, Wat. WD17 75 BT38
Sch **Bromet Prim Sch**, Wat. WD19
off Oxhey Rd 94 BX45
Bromfelde Rd, SW4 309 P10
Bromfelde Wk, SW4 309 P9
Bromfield St, N1 276 F10
Bromford Cl, Oxt. RH8 254 EG133
Bromhall Rd, Dag. RM8, RM9 146 EV65
Bromhedge, SE9 185 EM90
Bromholm Rd, SE2 166 EV76
Bromleigh Cl, Chsht EN8 67 DY28
Bromleigh Ct, SE23 182 DV89
BROMLEY, BR1 & BR2 204 EF96
E3 290 D5
Bromley, Grays RM17 170 FZ79
Coll **Bromley Adult Ed Coll**,
Kentwood Cen, SE20
off Kingsdale Rd 183 DX94
Poverest Cen, Orp. BR5
off Poverest Rd 206 EU99
Widmore Cen, Brom. BR1
off Nightingale La 204 EJ97
Bromley Av, Brom. BR1 184 EE94
⊖ **Bromley-by-Bow** 290 D4
Bromley Cl, Harl. CM20 36 EV11
Coll **Bromley Coll of Further & Higher Ed**,
Beckenham Learning Cen, Beck. BR3
off Beckenham Rd 203 DZ95
Bromley Campus BR2
off Rookery La 204 EK100
Orpington Campus BR6
off The Walnuts 206 EU102
BROMLEY COMMON,
Brom. BR2 205 EM101
Bromley Common, Brom. BR2 204 EJ98
Bromley Cres, Brom. BR2 204 EF97
Ruislip HA4 115 BT63
Bromley Gdns, Brom. BR2 204 EF97
Bromley Gro, Brom. BR2 203 ED96
Bromley Hall Rd, E14 290 E6
Sch **Bromley High Sch GDST**, Brom. BR1
off Blackbrook La 205 EN98
Bromley High St, E3 290 C2
Bromley Hill, Brom. BR1 184 EE92
● **Bromley Ind Cen**,
Brom. BR1 204 EJ97
Bromley La, Chis. BR7 185 EQ94
⇌ **Bromley North** 204 EG95
Bromley North 204 EG95
BROMLEY PARK, Brom. BR1 204 EE95
Bromley Pk, Brom. BR1
off London Rd 204 EF95
Bromley Pl, W1 285 L6

B

Bromley Rd, E10 123 EB58
E17 101 EA54
N17 100 DT53
N18 100 DR48
SE6 183 EB88
Beckenham BR3 203 EB95
Chislehurst BR7 205 EP95
Downham BR1 183 EC91
Shortlands BR2 203 EC96
Sch **Bromley Rd Inf Sch**, Beck. BR3
off Bromley Rd 203 EB95
● **Bromley Rd Retail Pk**, SE6
off Bromley Rd 183 EB89
⇌ **Bromley South** 204 EG97
Bromley St, E1 289 K7
BROMPTON, SW3 296 C7
Brompton Arc, SW3 296 E5
Brompton Cl, SE20
off Selby Rd 202 DU96
Hounslow TW4 176 BZ85
Brompton Dr, Erith DA8 167 FH80
Brompton Gro, N2 120 DE56
★ **Brompton Oratory**, SW7 296 C7
Brompton Pk Cres, SW6 307 L3
Brompton Pl, SW3 296 D6
Brompton Rd, SW1 296 D6
SW3 296 C8
SW7 296 D6
Brompton Sq, SW3 296 C6
Bromwich Av, N6 120 DG61
Bromyard Av, W3 138 CS74
Bromyard Ho, SE15 312 E4
W3 138 CS74
Bromycroft Rd, Slou. SL2 131 AN69
BRONDESBURY, NW2 272 E6
⊃ **Brondesbury** 272 G6
Brondesbury Ct, NW2 272 C5
Brondesbury Ms, NW6 273 J7
BRONDESBURY PARK, NW6 272 B7
⊃ **Brondesbury Park** 272 E8
Brondesbury Pk, NW2 139 CV65
NW6 272 E7
Brondesbury Rd, NW6 272 G10
Brondesbury Vil, NW6 273 H10
Bronsart Rd, SW6 306 E5
Bronsdon Way, Denh. UB9 113 BF61
Bronson Rd, SW20 199 CX96
Bronte Cl, E7
off Bective Rd 124 EG63
Erith DA8 167 FB80
Ilford IG2 125 EN57
Slough SL1 152 AS75
Tilbury RM18 171 GJ82
Bronte Ct, Borwd. WD6
off Chaucer Gro 78 CN42
Bronte Gro, Dart. DA1 168 FM84
Bronte Ho, NW6 283 K2
Sch **Bronte Sch**, Grav. DA11
off Pelham Rd 191 GG87
Bronte Vw, Grav. DA12 191 GJ88
Bronti Cl, SE17 311 K1
Bronze Age Way, Belv. DA17 167 FC76
Erith DA8 167 FC76
Bronze St, SE8 314 B4
BROOK, Guil. GU5 260 BL142
Brook Av, Dag. RM10 147 FB66
Edgware HA8 96 CP51
Wembley HA9 118 CN62
Brookbank, Enf. EN1 82 DV37
Wooburn Green HP10 110 AC60
Brookbank Av, W7 137 CD71
Brookbank Rd, SE13 163 EA83
● **Brook Business Cen**, Uxb. UB8
off St. Johns Road 134 BH68
Brook Cl, NW7 97 CY52
SW17 180 DG89
SW20 199 CV97
W3 138 CN74
Borehamwood WD6 78 CP41
Dorking RH4 247 CJ134
Epsom KT19 216 CS109
Romford RM2 105 FF53
Ruislip HA4 115 BS59
Stanwell TW19 174 BM87
Sch **Brook Comm Prim Sch**,
E8 278 D3
Brook Ct, Bark. IG11
off Spring Pl 145 EQ68
Buckhurst Hill IG9 102 EH46
Brook Cres, E4 101 EA49
N9 100 DV49
Slough SL1 131 AL72
Brookdale, N11 99 DJ49
Brookdale Av, Upmin. RM14 128 FN62
Brookdale Cl, Upmin. RM14 128 FP62
Brookdale Rd, E17 123 EA55
SE6 183 EB86
Bexley DA5 186 EY86
Brookdene Av, Wat. WD19 93 BV45
Brookdene Dr, Nthwd. HA6 93 BT52
Brookdene Rd, SE18 165 ET77
Brook Dr, SE11 298 F7
Harrow HA1 116 CC56
Radlett WD7 61 CF33
Ruislip HA4 115 BS58
Brooke Av, Har. HA2 116 CC62
Brooke Cl, Bushey WD23 94 CC45
Brooke Ct, W10 282 F1
Brookehowse Rd, SE6 183 EB90
Brook End, Saw. CM21 36 EX05
Brookend Rd, Sid. DA15 185 ES88
Brooke Rd, E5 122 DU62
E17 123 EC56
N16 122 DT62
Grays RM17 170 GA78
Brooker Rd, Wal.Abb. EN9 67 EC34
Brookers Cl, Ashtd. KT21 231 CJ117
Brooke's Ct, EC1 286 E6
Brookes Mkt, EC1 286 F6
Brooke St, EC1 286 E7
● **Brooke Trading Est**,
Rom. RM1 127 FF59
Brooke Way, Bushey WD23 94 CC45
Brook Fm Rd, Cob. KT11 230 BX115
Brookfield, N6 120 DG62
Godalming GU7 258 AU143
Thornwood CM16 70 EW25
Woking GU21 226 AV116
Coll **Brookfield Adult Learning Cen**,
Uxb. UB8 *off Park Rd* 134 BL65
Brookfield Av, E17 123 EC56
NW7 97 CV51
W5 137 CK70
Sutton SM1 218 DD105
● **Brookfield Cen**, Chsht EN8 67 DX27
Brookfield Cl, NW7 97 CV51
Ashtead KT21 232 CL120
Hutton CM13 109 GC44
Ottershaw KT16 211 BD107
Redhill RH1 266 DG140
Brookfield Ct, Grnf. UB6 136 CC69
Harrow HA3 117 CK57
Brookfield Cres, NW7 97 CV51
Harrow HA3 118 CL57
Brookfield Dr, Horl. RH6 269 DH146
Brookfield Gdns, Chsht EN8 67 DX27
Claygate KT10 215 CF107
Sch **Brookfield Ho Sch**, Wdf.Grn. IG8
off Alders Av 102 EE51
Brookfield La E, Chsht EN8 67 DX27
Brookfield La W, Chsht EN8 66 DV28
Brookfield Pk, NW5 121 DH62
Brookfield Path, Wdf.Grn. IG8 102 EE51
Brookfield Pl, Cob. KT11 230 BY115
Sch **Brookfield Prim Sch**, N19
off Chester Rd 121 DH61
Sutton SM3 *off Ridge Rd* 199 CY102
● **Brookfield Retail Pk**,
Chsht EN8 67 DX26
Brookfield Rd, E9 279 M5
N9 100 DU48
W4 158 CR75
Wooburn Green HP10 110 AD60
Brookfields, Enf. EN3 83 DX42
Sawbridgeworth CM21 36 EX05
Brookfields Av, Mitch. CR4 200 DE99
Brook Gdns, E4 101 EB49
SW13 159 CT83
Kingston upon Thames KT2 198 CQ95
Brook Gate, W1 296 F1
Brook Grn, W6 294 D8
Chobham GU24
off Brookleys 210 AT110
Brook Hill, Far.Grn GU5 260 BK143
Oxted RH8 253 EC130
Brookhill Cl, SE18 165 EP78
East Barnet EN4 80 DE43
Brookhill Rd, SE18 165 EP78
Barnet EN4 80 DE43
Brookhouse Dr,
Woob.Grn HP10 110 AC60
Brookhouse Gdns, E4 102 EE49
Brookhurst Rd, Add. KT15 212 BH107
● **Brook Ind Est**, Hayes UB4 136 BX74
Brooking Cl, Dag. RM8 126 EW62
Brooking Rd, E7 281 P2
Brookland Cl, NW11 120 DA56
Brookland Garth, NW11 120 DB56
Brookland Hill, NW11 120 DA56
Sch **Brookland Inf & Jun Schs**, NW11
off Hill Top 120 DB56
Sch **Brookland Inf Sch**, Chsht EN8
off Elm Dr 67 DY28
Sch **Brookland Jun Sch**, Chsht EN8
off Elm Dr 67 DY28
Brookland Ri, NW11 120 DA56
BROOKLANDS, Wey. KT13 212 BM109
Brooklands, Dart. DA1 188 FL88
Brooklands App, Rom. RM1 127 FD56
Brooklands Av, SW19 180 DB89
Sidcup DA15 185 ER89
Brooklands Cl, Cob. KT11 230 BY115
Romford RM7
off Marshalls Rd 127 FD56
Sunbury-on-Thames TW16 195 BS95
Coll **Brooklands Coll**, Ashford Campus,
Ashf. TW15 *off Church Rd* 174 BM91
Weybridge Campus, Wey. KT13
off Heath Rd 212 BM107
Brooklands Ct, New Haw KT15 212 BK110
St. Albans AL1 43 CE20
Weybridge KT13 213 BP108
Brooklands Dr, Perivale UB6 137 CJ67
Weybridge KT13 212 BM110
Brooklands Gdns, Horn. RM11 128 FJ57
Potters Bar EN6 63 CY32
● **Brooklands Ind Pk**,
Wey. KT13 212 BL110
Brooklands La, Rom. RM7 127 FD56
Weybridge KT13 212 BM107
★ **Brooklands Mus**, Wey. KT13 212 BN109
Brooklands Pk, SE3 315 N10
Brooklands Pas, SW8 309 N6
Brooklands Pl, Hmptn. TW12 176 CB92
Sch **Brooklands Prim Sch**, SE3 315 P10
Brooklands Rd, Rom. RM7 127 FD56
Thames Ditton KT7 197 CF102
Weybridge KT13 213 BP107
Sch **Brooklands Sch**, Reig. RH2
off Wray Pk Rd 250 DB132
Brooklands Way, Red. RH1 250 DE132
Brook La, SE3 164 EH82
Albury GU5 260 BL142
Berkhamsted HP4 38 AV18
Bexley DA5 186 EX86
Bromley BR1 184 EG93
Sawbridgeworth CM21 36 EX05
Send GU23 227 BE122
● **Brook La Business Cen**, Brent. TW8
off Brook La N 157 CK78
Brooklane Fld, Harl. CM18 52 EV18
Brook La N, Brent. TW8 157 CK78
Brooklea Cl, NW9 96 CS53
Brookleys, Chobham GU24 210 AT110
Brooklyn Av, SE25 202 DV98
Loughton IG10 84 EL42
Brooklyn Cl, Cars. SM5 200 DE103
Woking GU22 226 AY119
Brooklyn Ct, Wok. GU22
off Brooklyn Rd 226 AY119
Brooklyn Gro, SE25 202 DV98
Brooklyn Pas, W12 294 A5
Brooklyn Rd, SE25 202 DV98
Bromley BR2 204 EK99
Woking GU22 226 AY118
Brooklyn Way, West Dr. UB7 154 BK76
Brookmans Av, Brook.Pk AL9 63 CY26
Brookmans Cl, Upmin. RM14 129 FS59
BROOKMANS PARK, Hat. AL9 63 CY26
⇌ **Brookmans Park** 63 CX27
Brookmans Pk Dr, Upmin. RM14 129 FS57
Sch **Brookmans Pk Prim Sch**,
Brook.Pk AL9
off Bradmore Way 63 CY26
● **Brookmarsh Ind Est**, SE10 314 C4
Brook Mead, Epsom KT19 216 CS107
Brookmead Av, Brom. BR1 205 EM99
Brookmead Cl, Orp. BR5 206 EV101
● **Brookmead Ind Est**,
Croy. CR0 201 DJ100
Brook Meadow, N12 98 DB49
Brook Meadow Cl,
Wdf.Grn. IG8 102 EE51
Brookmeadow Way, Wal.Abb. EN9
off Breach Barn Mobile
Home Pk 68 EH30
Brookmead Rd, Croy. CR0 201 DJ100
Brookmeads Est, Mitch. CR4 200 DE99
Brookmead Way, Orp. BR5 206 EV100
Brook Ms, N13 99 DN50
Chig. IG7 103 EP48
Brook Ms N, W2 283 P10
Brookmill Cl, Wat. WD19
off Brookside Rd 93 BV45
Brookmill Rd, SE8 314 B6
Brook Par, Chig. IG7
off High Rd 103 EP48
Brook Pk, Dart. DA1 188 FN89
Brook Pk Cl, N21 81 DP44
Brook Path, Loug. IG10 84 EL42
Slough SL1 131 AM73
Brook Pl, Barn. EN5 80 DA43
● **Brook Retail Pk**, Ruis. HA4 116 BX64
Brook Ri, Chig. IG7 103 EN48
Brook Rd, N8 121 DL56
N22 121 DM55
NW2 119 CU61
Borehamwood WD6 78 CN40
Brentwood CM14 108 FT48
Buckhurst Hill IG9 102 EG47
Chilworth GU4 259 BC140
Epping CM16 70 EU33
Ilford IG2 125 ES58
Loughton IG10 84 EL43
Merstham RH1 251 DJ129
Northfleet DA11 190 GE88
Redhill RH1 266 DF135
Romford RM2 105 FF53
Sawbridgeworth CM21 36 EX06
Surbiton KT6 198 CL103
Swanley BR8 207 FD97
Thornton Heath CR7 202 DQ98
Twickenham TW1 177 CG86
Waltham Cross EN8 67 DZ34
Brook Rd S, Brent. TW8 157 CK79
Brooks Av, E6 293 J4
Brooksbank St, E9 279 J5
Brooksby Ms, N1 276 F6
Brooksby St, N1 276 F7
Brooksby's Wk, E9 279 J2
Brooks Cl, SE9 185 EN89
Weybridge KT13 212 BN110
Brooks Ct, Hert. SG14 31 DM08
Brookscroft, Croy. CR0 221 DY110
Brookscroft Rd, E17 101 EB53
Brooksfield, Welw.G.C. AL7 30 DB08
Brookshill, Har. HA3 95 CD50
Brookshill Av, Har. HA3 95 CD50
Brookshill Dr, Har. HA3 95 CD50
Brookshill Gate, Har.Wld HA3 95 CD50
Sch **Brookside**, Ilf. IG3
off Barley La 126 EU58
Brookside, N21 81 DM44
Carshalton SM5 218 DG106
Chertsey KT16 193 BE101
Colnbrook SL3 153 BC80
East Barnet EN4 80 DE44
Harlow CM19 51 EM17
Hatfield AL10 44 CR18
Hertford SG13 32 DS09
Hoddesdon EN11 49 DZ17
Hornchurch RM11 128 FL57
Ilford IG6 103 EQ51
Jacobs Well GU4 242 AX129
Orpington BR6 205 ET101
South Mimms EN6 63 CU32
Uxbridge UB10 134 BM66
Waltham Abbey EN9
off Broomstick Hall Rd 68 EE32
Wat. WD24
off North Western Ave 76 BX36
Brookside Av, Ashf. TW15 174 BJ92
Wraysbury TW19 152 AY83
Brookside Cl, Barn. EN5 79 CY44
Feltham TW13 175 BU90
Kenton HA3 117 CK57
South Harrow HA2 116 BY63
Brookside Cres, Cuffley EN6 65 DL27
Worcester Park KT4
off Green La 199 CU102
Brookside Gdns, Enf. EN1 82 DV37
Sch **Brookside Inf & Jun Schs**, Harold
Hill RM3 *off Dagnam Pk Dr* 106 FL50
Sch **Brookside Prim Sch**, Hayes UB4
off Perth Av 136 BW69
Brookside Rd, N9 100 DV49
N19 121 DJ61
NW11 119 CY58
Hayes UB4 136 BW73
Istead Rise DA13 191 GF94
Watford WD19 93 BV45
Brookside S, E.Barn. EN4 98 DG45
Brookside Wk, N3 97 CY54
N12 98 DA51
NW4 119 CY56
NW11 119 CY56
Brookside Way, Croy. CR0 203 DX100
Brooks La, W4 158 CN79
Brook's Ms, W1 285 J10
Brook Sq, SE18
off Barlow Dr 164 EL81
Brooks Rd, E13 281 N9
W4 158 CN78
BROOK STREET, Brwd. CM14 108 FS49
Brook St, N17
off High Rd 100 DT54
W1 285 H10
W2 284 B10
Belvedere DA17 167 FB78
Brentwood CM14 108 FS50
Erith DA8 167 FB79
Kingston upon Thames KT1 198 CL96
Windsor SL4 151 AR82
Brooksville Av, NW6 272 F9
Brooks Way, Orp. BR5 206 EW96
Brook Vale, Erith DA8 167 FB81
Brook Valley, Mid Holm. RH5 263 CH142
Brookview Rd, SW16 181 DJ92
Brookville Rd, SW6 306 G5
Brook Wk, N2 98 DD53
Edgware HA8 96 CR51
Brookway, SE3 164 EG83
Brook Way, Chig. IG7 103 EN48
Leatherhead KT22 231 CG118
Rainham RM13 147 FH71
Brookwood, Horl. RH6
off Stockfield 269 DH147
Brookwood Av, SW13 159 CT83
Brookwood Cl, Brom. BR2 204 EF98
Brookwood Rd, SW18 179 CZ88
Hounslow TW3 156 CB81
Broom Av, Orp. BR5 206 EV96
Broom Cl, Brom. BR2 204 EL100
Cheshunt EN7 66 DU27
Esher KT10 214 CB106
Hatfield AL10 45 CT21
Teddington TW11 177 CK94
Broomcroft Av, Nthlt. UB5 136 BW69
Broomcroft Cl, Wok. GU22 227 BD116
Broomcroft Dr, Wok. GU22 227 BD115
Broome Cl, Headley KT18 248 CQ126
Broome Ho, E5 278 E2
Broome Pl, Aveley RM15 149 FR74
Broome Rd, Hmptn. TW12 176 BZ94
Broomer Pl, Chsht EN8 66 DW29
Broome Way, SE5 311 L5
Broom Fm Est, Wind. SL4 150 AJ82
Broomfield, E17 123 DZ59
Guildford GU2 242 AS133
Harlow CM20 36 EV12
Park Street AL2 60 CC27
Staines-upon-Thames TW18 174 BG93
Sunbury-on-Thames TW16 195 BU95
Broomfield Av, N13 99 DM50
Broxbourne EN10 67 DY26
Loughton IG10 85 EM44
Broomfield Cl, Guil. GU3 242 AS132
Romford RM5 105 FD52
Broomfield Ct, Wey. KT13 213 BP107
Broomfield Gate, Slou. SL2 131 AP70
Sch **Broomfield Ho Sch**, Kew TW9
off Broomfield Rd 158 CM81
Broomfield La, N13 99 DM49
Broomfield Pk, Westc. RH4 262 CC137
Broomfield Pl, W13 137 CH74
Broomfield Ride,
Oxshott KT22 215 CD112
Broomfield Ri, Abb.L. WD5 59 BR32
Broomfield Rd, N13 99 DL50
W13 137 CH74
Beckenham BR3 203 DY97
Bexleyheath DA6 186 FA85
New Haw KT15 212 BH111
Richmond TW9 158 CM81
Romford RM6 126 EX59
Sevenoaks TN13 256 FF122
Surbiton KT5 198 CM102
Swanscombe DA10 190 FY86
Teddington TW11
off Melbourne Rd 177 CJ93
Broomfields, Esher KT10 214 CC106
Sch **Broomfield Sch**, N14
off Wilmer Way 99 DK50
Broomfield St, E14 290 B7
Broom Gdns, Croy. CR0 203 EA104
Broom Gro, Wat. WD17 75 BU38
Broomgrove Gdns, Edg. HA8 96 CN53
Broomgrove Rd, SW9 310 D9
Broom Hall, Oxshott KT22 215 CD114
Broomhall End, Wok. GU21
off Broomhall La 226 AY116
Broomhall La, Wok. GU21 226 AY116
Broomhall Rd, S.Croy. CR2 220 DR109
Woking GU21 226 AY116
Broom Hill, Hem.H. HP1 39 BE21
Stoke Poges SL2 132 AU66
Broomhill Ct, Wdf.Grn. IG8
off Broomhill Rd 102 EG51
Broomhill Ri, Bexh. DA6 186 FA85
Broomhill Rd, SW18 180 DA85
Dartford DA1 187 FH86
Ilford IG3 126 EU61
Orpington BR6 206 EU101
Woodford Green IG8 102 EG51
Broomhills, Sthflt DA13
off Betsham Rd 190 FY91
Welwyn Garden City AL7 30 DA08
Broomhill Wk, Wdf.Grn. IG8 102 EF52
Broom Ho, Slou. SL3 153 AZ77
Broomhouse La, SW6 307 J9
Broomhouse Rd, SW6 307 J8
Broomlands La, Oxt. RH8 254 EJ125
Broom La, Chobham GU24 210 AS109
Broomleys, St.Alb. AL4 43 CK17
Broomloan La, Sutt. SM1 200 DA103
Broom Lock, Tedd. TW11 177 CJ93
Broom Mead, Bexh. DA6 186 FA85
Broom Pk, Tedd. TW11 177 CK94
Broom Rd, Croy. CR0 203 EA104
Teddington TW11 177 CJ93
Brooms Cl, Welw.G.C. AL8 29 CX06
● **Broomsleigh Business Pk**, SE26
off Worsley Br Rd 183 DZ92
Broomsleigh St, NW6 273 H3
Broomstick Hall Rd,
Wal.Abb. EN9 68 EE33
Broomstick La, Chesh. HP5 56 AU30
Broom Water, Tedd. TW11 177 CJ93
Broom Water W, Tedd. TW11 177 CJ92
Broom Way, Wey. KT13 213 BS105
Broomwood Cl, Bex. DA5 187 FD89
Croydon CR0 203 DX99
Broomwood Gdns,
Pilg.Hat. CM15 108 FU44
Sch **Broomwood Hall Sch**, SW12
off Nightingale La 180 DG87
Broomwood Rd, SW11 180 DF86
Orpington BR5 206 EV96
Broseley Gdns, Rom. RM3 106 FL49
Broseley Gro, SE26 183 DY92
Broseley Rd, Rom. RM3 106 FL49
Brosse Way, Brom. BR2 204 EL101
Broster Gdns, SE25 202 DT97
Brougham Rd, E8 278 C8
W3 138 CQ72
Brougham St, SW11 308 F8
Brough Cl, SW8 310 B5
Kingston upon Thames KT2 177 CK92
Broughinge Rd, Borwd. WD6 78 CP40
Broughton Av, N3 119 CY55
Richmond TW10 177 CH90
Broughton Dr, SW9 161 DN84
Broughton Gdns, N6 121 DJ58
Broughton Rd, SW6 307 L7
W13 137 CH73
Orpington BR6 205 ER103
Otford TN14 241 FG116
Thornton Heath CR7 201 DN100
Broughton Rd App, SW6 307 L8
Broughton St, SW8 309 J8
Broughton Way, Rick. WD3 92 BG45
Brouncker Rd, W3 158 CQ75
Brow, The, Ch.St.G. HP8 90 AX48
Redhill RH1 *off Spencer Way* 266 DG139
Watford WD25 59 BV33
Brow Cl, Orp. BR5
off Brow Cres 206 EX101
Brow Cres, Orp. BR5 206 EW102
Browells La, Felt. TW13 175 BV89
Brownacres Towpath,
Wey. KT13 195 BP102
Brown Cl, Wall. SM6 219 DK108
Browne Cl, Brwd. CM14 108 FV46
Romford RM5 105 FB50
Woking GU22 227 BB120
Brownell Pl, W7 157 CF75
Brownfields, Welw.G.C. AL7 29 CZ08
Brownfields Ct, Welw.G.C. AL7
off Brownfields 30 DA08
Brownfield St, E14 290 D9
Browngraves Rd, Harling. UB3 155 BQ80
Brown Hart Gdns, W1 285 H10
Brownhill Rd, SE6 183 EB87
Browning Av, W7 137 CF72
Sutton SM1 218 DE105
Worcester Park KT4 199 CV102
Browning Cl, E17 123 EC56
W9 283 P5
Collier Row RM5 104 EZ52
Hampton TW12 176 BZ91
Welling DA16 165 ES81
Browning Ct, Borwd. WD6
off Chaucer Gro 78 CN42
Browning Ms, W1 285 J7
Browning Rd, E11 124 EF59
E12 145 EM65
Dartford DA1 168 FM84
Enfield EN2 82 DR38
Fetcham KT22 247 CD125
Browning St, SE17 299 K10
Browning Wk, Til. RM18
off Coleridge Rd 171 GJ82
Browning Way, Houns. TW5 156 BX81
Brownlea Gdns, Ilf. IG3 126 EU61
Brownlow Cl, Barn. EN4 80 DD43
Brownlow Ms, WC1 286 D5
Brownlow Rd, E7
off Woodford Rd 124 EG63
E8 278 B8
N3 98 DB52
N11 99 DL51
NW10 138 CS66
W13 137 CG74
Berkhamsted HP4 38 AW18
Borehamwood WD6 78 CN42
Croydon CR0 220 DS105
Redhill RH1 250 DE134
Brownlow St, WC1 286 D7
Brownrigg Rd, Ashf. TW15 174 BN91
Brown Rd, Grav. DA12 191 GL88
Brown's Bldgs, EC3 287 P9
Brownsea Wk, NW7 97 CX51
Browns La, NW5 275 J3
Effingham KT24 246 BX127
Brownspring Dr, SE9 185 EP91
Browns Rd, E17 123 EA55
Surbiton KT5 198 CM101
Sch **Brown's Sch**, Orp. BR6
off Hawstead La 224 EZ106
Browns Spring, Pott.End HP4 39 BC16
Brown St, W1 284 E8
Brownswell Rd, N2 98 DD54
Brownswood Rd, N4 121 DP62
Beaconsfield HP9 89 AK51
Broxash Rd, SW11 180 DG86
BROXBOURNE, EN10 49 DZ21
⇌ **Broxbourne** 49 EA20
Broxbourne Av, E18 124 EH56
Broxbournebury Ms, Brox. EN10
off White Stubbs La 48 DW21
● **Broxbourne Business Cen**, Chsht EN8
off Fairways 67 DX26
Sch **Broxbourne C of E Prim Sch**, Brox.
EN10
off Mill La 49 DZ21
Broxbourne Common,
Brox. EN10 48 DU19
Broxbourne Rd, E7 124 EG62
Orpington BR6 205 ET101
Sch **Broxbourne Sch, The**, Brox. EN10
off High Rd 49 DZ21
Broxburn Dr, S.Ock. RM15 149 FV73
Broxburn Par, S.Ock. RM15
off Broxburn Dr 149 FV73
Broxhill Rd, Hav.at.Bow. RM4 105 FH48
Broxholme Cl, SE25
off Whitehorse La 202 DR98
Broxholm Rd, SE27 181 DN90
Brox La, Ott. KT16 211 BD109
Brox Ms, Ott. KT16
off Brox Rd 211 BC107
Brox Rd, Ott. KT16 211 BC107
Broxted Ms, Hutt. CM13
off Bannister Dr 109 GC44
Broxted Rd, SE6 183 DZ89
Broxwood Way, NW8 274 D9
Bruce Av, Horn. RM12 128 FK61
Shepperton TW17 195 BQ100
★ **Bruce Castle Mus**, N17 100 DS53
Bruce Castle Rd, N17 100 DT53
Bruce Cl, W10 282 D6
Byfleet KT14 212 BK113
Slough SL1 131 AN74
Welling DA16 166 EV81
Bruce Dr, S.Croy. CR2 221 DX109
Bruce Gdns, N20 98 DF48
⊃ **Bruce Grove** 100 DT54
Jct **Bruce Gro**, N17 *off High Rd* 100 DT54
Bruce Gro, N17 100 DS53
Orpington BR6 206 EU102
Watford WD24 76 BW38
Sch **Bruce Gro Prim Sch**, N17
off Sperling Rd 100 DT54
Bruce Hall Ms, SW17 180 DG91
Bruce Rd, E3 290 C3
NW10 138 CR66
SE25 202 DR98
Barnet EN5 *off St. Albans Rd* 79 CY41
Harrow HA3 95 CE54
Mitcham CR4 180 DG94
Bruce's Wf Rd, Grays RM17 170 GA79
Bruce Wk, Wind. SL4 151 AK82
Bruce Way, Wal.Cr. EN8 67 DX33
Bruckner St, W10 282 F3
Brudenell, Wind. SL4 151 AM83
Brudenell Cl, Amer. HP6 72 AT38
Brudenell Rd, SW17 180 DF90
Bruffs Meadow, Nthlt. UB5 136 BY65
Bruford Ct, SE8 314 B3
Bruges Pl, NW1 275 M7
Brumana Cl, Wey. KT13 213 BP107
Brumfield Rd, Epsom KT19 216 CQ106
Brummel Cl, Bexh. DA7 167 FC83
★ **Brunei Gall**, WC1 285 P6
◆ **Brunel** 132 AT74
Brunel Cl, SE19 182 DT93
Hounslow TW5 155 BV80
Northolt UB5 136 BZ69
Romford RM1 127 FE56
Tilbury RM18 171 GH83

Brunel Est, W2 283 J7
Brunel Ho, N16
off Stamford Hill 122 DT60
Brwd. CM14 108 FW48
Brunel Ms, W10 282 D2
★ **Brunel Mus & Engine Ho**,
SE16 300 G4
Brunel Pl, Sthl. UB1 136 CB72
Brunel Rd, E17 123 DY58
SE16 300 G5
W3 138 CS71
Woodford Green IG8 103 EM50
Uni **Brunel Science Pk**,
Uxb. UB8 134 BL69
Brunel St, E16 291 L9
Uni **Brunel Uni**, Runnymede Campus,
Eng.Grn TW20
off Coopers Hill La 172 AW90
Uxbridge Campus, Uxb. UB8
off Kingston La 134 BK69
Brunel Wk, N15 122 DS56
Twickenham TW2
off Stephenson Rd 176 CA87
Brunel Way, Slou. SL1 132 AT74
Brune St, E1 288 A7
Brunlees Ho, SE1
off Bath Ter 299 J7
Brunner Cl, NW11 120 DB57
Brunner Ct, Ott. KT16 211 BC106
Brunner Rd, E17 123 DY57
W5 137 CK70
Bruno Pl, NW9 118 CQ61
Brunswick, WC1 286 A4
Brunswick Av, N11 98 DG48
Upminster RM14 129 FS59
Brunswick Cl, Bexh. DA6 166 EX84
Pinner HA5 116 BY58
Thames Ditton KT7 197 CF102
Twickenham TW2 177 CD90
Walton-on-Thames KT12 196 BW103
Brunswick Ct, EC1
off Tompion St 286 G3
SE1 299 P5
SW1 *off Regency St* 297 P9
Barnet EN4 80 DD43
Upminster RM14
off Waycross Rd 129 FS59
Brunswick Cres, N11 98 DG48
Brunswick Gdns, W5 138 CL69
W8 295 K3
Ilford IG6 103 EQ52
Brunswick Gro, N11 98 DG48
Cobham KT11 214 BW113
● **Brunswick Ind Pk**, N11 99 DH49
Brunswick Ms, SW16
off Potters La 181 DK93
W1 284 F8
BRUNSWICK PARK, N11 98 DF48
Brunswick Pk, SE5 311 M6
Brunswick Pk Gdns, N11 98 DG47
Sch **Brunswick Pk Prim Sch**, N14
off Osidge La 98 DG47
SE5 311 M5
Brunswick Pk Rd, N11 98 DG47
Brunswick Pl, N1 287 M3
NW1 285 H4
SE19 182 DU94
Brunswick Quay, SE16 301 K7
Brunswick Rd, E10 123 EC60
E14 *off Blackwall Tunnel
Northern App* 290 F9
N15 122 DS57
W5 137 CK70
Bexleyheath DA6 166 EX84
Enfield EN3 83 EA38
Kingston upon Thames KT2 198 CN95
Sutton SM1 218 DB105
Brunswick Sq, N17 100 DT51
WC1 286 B5
Brunswick St, E17 123 EC57
Brunswick Vil, SE5 311 N6
Brunswick Wk, Grav. DA12 191 GK87
Brunswick Way, N11 99 DH49
Brunton Pl, E14 289 M9
Brushfield St, E1 287 P6
Brushmakers Ct, Chesh. HP5
off Higham Rd 54 AP30
Brushrise, Wat. WD24 75 BU36
Brushwood Cl, E14 290 D6
Brushwood Dr, Chorl. WD3 73 BC42
Sch **Brushwood Jun Sch**, Chesh. HP5
off Brushwood Rd 54 AS29
Brushwood Rd, Chesh. HP5 54 AR29
Brussels Rd, SW11 160 DD84
Bruton Cl, Chis. BR7 185 EM94
Bruton La, W1 297 K1
Bruton Pl, W1 297 K1
Bruton Rd, Mord. SM4 200 DC99
Bruton St, W1 297 K1
Bruton Way, W13 137 CG71
Bryan Av, NW10 139 CV66
Bryan Cl, Sun. TW16 175 BU94
Bryan Rd, SE16 301 N4
Bryan's All, SW6 307 L8
Bryanston Av, Twick. TW2 176 CB88
Bryanston Cl, Sthl. UB2 156 BZ77
Bryanstone Av, Guil. GU2 242 AU131
Bryanstone Cl, Guil. GU2 242 AT131
Bryanstone Ct, Sutt. SM1
off Oakhill Rd 218 DC105
Bryanstone Gro, Guil. GU2 242 AT130
Bryanstone Rd, N8 121 DK57
Waltham Cross EN8 67 DZ34
Bryanston Ms E, W1 284 E7
Bryanston Ms W, W1 284 E7
Bryanston Pl, W1 284 E7
Bryanston Rd, Til. RM18 171 GJ82
Bryanston Sq, W1 284 E7
Bryanston St, W1 284 E9
Bryant Av, Rom. RM3 106 FK53
Slough SL2 131 AR71
Bryant Cl, Barn. EN5 79 CZ43
Bryant Ct, E2 278 A10
W3 138 CR74
Bryant Rd, Nthlt. UB5 136 BW69
Bryant Row, Noak Hill RM3
off Long Meadow 106 FJ47
Bryant St, E15 281 H7
Bryantwood Rd, N7 276 E2
Brycedale Cres, N14 99 DK49
Bryce Rd, Dag. RM8 126 EW63
Brydale Ho, SE16 301 J8
Bryden Cl, SE26 183 DY92
Brydges Pl, WC2 298 A1
Brydges Rd, E15 281 H2
Brydon Wk, N1 276 B8
Bryer Ct, EC2
off Bridgewater St 287 J6
Bryer Pl, Wind. SL4 151 AK83
Bryett Rd, N7 121 DL62
Brymay Cl, E3 290 B1
Brympton Cl, Dor. RH4 263 CG138
Brynford Cl, Wok. GU21 226 AY115
Brynmaer Rd, SW11 308 E7
Bryn-y-Mawr Rd, Enf. EN1 82 DT42
Bryony Cl, Loug. IG10 85 EP42
Uxbridge UB8 134 BM71
Bryony Rd, W12 139 CU73
Guildford GU1 243 BB131
Bryony Way, Sun. TW16 175 BT93
Coll **BSix, Brooke Ho 6th Form Coll**, E5
off Kenninghall Rd 122 DV62
Bubblestone Rd, Otford TN14 241 FH116
Buccleuch Rd, Datchet SL3 152 AU80
Buchanan Cl, N21 81 DM43
Aveley RM15 148 FQ74
Buchanan Ct, Borwd. WD6 78 CQ40
Buchanan Gdns, NW10 139 CV68
Buchan Cl, Uxb. UB8 134 BJ69
Buchan Rd, SE15 313 H10
Bucharest Rd, SW18 180 DC87
Buckbean Path, Rom. RM3
off Clematis Cl 106 FJ52
Buckden Cl, N2
off Southern Rd 120 DF56
SE12 184 EF86
Buckettsland La, Borwd. WD6 78 CR38
Buckfast Ct, W13
off Romsey Rd 137 CG73
Buckfast Rd, Mord. SM4 200 DB98
Buckfast St, E2 288 D3
Buckham Thorns Rd,
West. TN16 255 EQ126
Buck Hill Wk, W2 296 B1
Buckhold Rd, SW18 180 DA86
Buckhurst Av, Cars. SM5 200 DE102
Sevenoaks TN13 257 FJ125
Buckhurst Cl, Red. RH1 250 DE132
BUCKHURST HILL, IG9 102 EH45
⊖ **Buckhurst Hill** 102 EK47
Sch **Buckhurst Hill Comm Prim Sch**,
Buck.H. IG9
off Lower Queens Rd 102 EL47
Buckhurst La, Sev. TN13 257 FJ125
Buckhurst Rd, West. TN16 239 EN121
Buckhurst St, E1 288 F5
Buckhurst Way, Buck.H. IG9 102 EK49
Buckingham Arc, WC2 298 B1
Buckingham Av, N20 98 DC45
Feltham TW14 175 BV86
Perivale UB6 137 CG67
Slough SL1 131 AN72
Thornton Heath CR7 201 DN95
Welling DA16 165 ES84
West Molesey KT8 196 CB97
Buckingham Av E, Slou. SL1 131 AQ72
Buckingham Chambers, SW1
off Greencoat Pl 297 M8
Buckingham Cl, W5 137 CJ71
Enfield EN1 82 DS40
Guildford GU1 243 AZ133
Hampton TW12 176 BZ92
Hornchurch RM11 128 FK58
Petts Wood BR5 205 ES101
Sch **Buckingham Coll Prep Sch**, Pnr. HA5
off Rayners La 116 BZ59
Sch **Buckingham Coll Sch**, Har. HA1
off Hindes Rd 117 CE57
Buckingham Ct, NW4 119 CU55
Loughton IG10 85 EN40
Buckingham Dr, Chis. BR7 185 EP92
Buckingham Gdns, Edg. HA8 96 CM52
Slough SL1 152 AT75
Thornton Heath CR7 201 DN96
West Molesey KT8 196 CB96
Buckingham Gate, SW1 297 L5
London Gatwick Airport RH6 269 DJ152
Buckingham Gro, Uxb. UB10 134 BN68
Buckingham La, SE23 183 DY87
Buckingham Lo, N10 121 DJ56
Hoddesdon EN11
off Taverners Way 49 EA17
Buckingham Ms, N1 277 P5
NW10 139 CT68
SW1 297 L6
★ **Buckingham Palace**, SW1 297 K5
Buckingham Palace Rd, SW1 297 J9
Buckingham Pl, SW1 297 L6
Sch **Buckingham Prim Sch**, Hmptn.
TW12 *off Buckingham Rd* 176 BZ92
Buckingham Rd, E10 123 EB62
E11 124 EJ57
E15 281 L2
E18 102 EF53
N1 277 N5
N22 99 DL53
NW10 139 CT68
Borehamwood WD6 78 CR42
Edgware HA8 96 CM52
Gravesend DA11
off Dover Rd 190 GD87
Hampton TW12 176 BZ91
Harrow HA1 117 CD57
Ilford IG1 125 ER61
Kingston upon Thames KT1 198 CM98
Mitcham CR4 201 DL99
Richmond TW10 177 CK89
Watford WD24 76 BW37
Uni **Buckinghamshire Chilterns Uni Coll**,
Chalfont Campus, Ch.St.G. HP8
off Gorelands La 91 BA47
Buckingham St, WC2 298 B1
Buckingham Way, Wall. SM6 219 DJ109
BUCKLAND, Bet. RH3 249 CU133
Buckland Av, Slou. SL3 152 AV77
Buckland Cl, NW7 97 CU49
Buckland Ct Gdns, Bet. RH3 249 CU133
Buckland Cres, NW3 274 A6
Windsor SL4 151 AM81
Buckland Gate, Wexham SL3 132 AV68
Buckland La, Bet. RH3 249 CU130
Tadworth KT20 249 CT129
Sch **Buckland Prim Sch**, Laleham TW18
off Berryscroft Rd 174 BJ94
Buckland Ri, Pnr. HA5 94 BW53
Buckland Rd, E10 123 EC61
Chessington KT9 216 CM106
Lower Kingswood KT20 249 CZ128
Orpington BR6 223 ES105
Reigate RH2 249 CX133
Sutton SM2 217 CW110
Bucklands, The, Rick. WD3 92 BG45
Bucklands Rd, Tedd. TW11 177 CJ93
Buckland St, N1 287 M1
Buckland Wk, W3 138 CQ74
Morden SM4 200 DC98
Buckland Way, Wor.Pk. KT4 199 CW102
Buck La, NW9 118 CR57
Bucklebury, NW1 285 L4
Bucklebury Cl, Holy. SL6 150 AC78
Buckleigh Av, SW20 199 CY97
Buckleigh Rd, SW16 181 DK93
Buckleigh Way, SE19 202 DT95
Buckler Ct, N7
off Eden Gro 276 D3
Buckler Gdns, SE9
off Southold Ri 185 EM90
Bucklers All, SW6 307 H3
Bucklersbury, EC4 287 L9
Bucklersbury Pas, EC4 287 L9
Bucklers Cl, Brox. EN10 49 DZ22
Bucklers Ct, Warley CM14 108 FW50
Bucklers Way, Cars. SM5 200 DF104
Buckles Ct, Belv. DA17
off Fendyke Rd 166 EX76
Buckles La, S.Ock. RM15 149 FW71
Buckle St, E1 288 B8
Buckles Way, Bans. SM7 233 CY116
Buckley Cl, SE23 182 DV87
Dartford DA1 167 FF82
Buckley Rd, NW6 273 H7
Buckley St, SE1 298 E3
Buckmaster Cl, SW9 310 E10
Buckmaster Rd, SW11 160 DE84
Bucknalls Cl, Wat. WD25 60 BY32
Bucknalls Dr, Brick.Wd AL2 60 BZ31
Bucknalls La, Wat. WD25 60 BX32
Bucknall St, WC2 285 P8
Bucknall Way, Beck. BR3 203 EB98
Bucknell Cl, SW2 161 DM84
Buckner Rd, SW2 161 DM84
Bucknills Cl, Epsom KT18 216 CP114
Buckrell Rd, E4 101 ED47
Bucks All, Hert. SG13 47 DK19
Bucks Av, Wat. WD19 94 BY45
Bucks Cl, W.Byf. KT14 212 BH114
Bucks Cross Rd, Nthflt DA11 191 GF90
Orpington BR6 224 EY106
BUCKS HILL, Kings L. WD4 58 BK34
Bucks Hill, Kings L. WD4 58 BK34
Buckstone Cl, SE23 182 DW86
Buckstone Rd, N18 100 DU51
Buck St, NW1 275 K7
Buckters Rents, SE16 301 L3
Buckthorne Ho, Chig. IG7 104 EV49
Buckthorne Rd, SE4 183 DY86
Buckton Rd, Borwd. WD6 78 CM38
Buck Wk, E17
off Wood St 123 ED56
Buckwell Pl, Sev. TN13 257 FJ129
Budd Cl, N12 98 DB49
Buddcroft, Welw.G.C. AL7 30 DB08
Buddings Circle, Wem. HA9 118 CQ62
Budd's All, Twick. TW1 177 CJ85
Budebury Rd, Stai. TW18 174 BG92
Bude Cl, E17 123 DZ57
Budge La, Mitch. CR4 200 DF101
Budgen Dr, Red. RH1 250 DG131
Budge's Wk, W2 295 N2
Budgin's Hill, Orp. BR6 224 EW112
Budleigh Cres, Well. DA16 166 EW81
Budoch Ct, Ilf. IG3 126 EU61
Budoch Dr, Ilf. IG3 126 EU61
Buer Rd, SW6 306 F9
Buff Av, Bans. SM7 218 DB114
Buffers La, Lthd. KT22
off Kingston Rd 231 CG119
Buffins, Tap. SL6 130 AE69
Bug Hill, Wold. CR3 237 DX120
Bugsby's Way, SE7 303 P9
SE10 303 L8
Buick Ho, Kings.T. KT2 198 CN96
Building 22, SE18
off Carriage St 305 P7
Building 36, SE18
off Marlborough Rd 165 EQ76
Building 45, SE18
off Hopton Rd 305 P6
Building 47, SE18
off Marlborough Rd 165 EQ76
Building 48, SE18
off Marlborough Rd 165 EQ76
Building 49, SE18
off Argyll Rd 165 EQ76
Building 50, SE18
off Argyll Rd 165 EQ76
Coll **Building Crafts Coll**, E15 280 G7
Bulbourne Cl, Berk. HP4 38 AT17
Hemel Hempstead HP1 40 BG21
Bulganak Rd, Th.Hth. CR7 202 DQ98
Bulinga St, SW1 297 P9
Bulkeley Av, Wind. SL4 151 AP82
Bulkeley Cl, Eng.Grn TW20 172 AW91
Bullace Cl, Hem.H. HP1 40 BG19
Bullace La, Dart. DA1 188 FL86
Bullace Row, SE5 311 K6
Bull All, Well. DA16
off Welling High St 166 EV83
Bullards Pl, E2 289 J2
Bullbanks Rd, Belv. DA17 167 FC77
Bullbeggars La, Berk. HP4 39 AZ20
Godstone RH9 252 DW132
Woking GU21 226 AV116
Bull Cl, Grays RM16 170 FZ75
JCT **Bull Dog, The**, Ashf. TW15 174 BL89
Bullen Ho, E1 288 F5
Bullens Grn La, Coln.Hth AL4 44 CS23
BULLEN'S GREEN, St.Alb. AL4 44 CS22
Bullen St, SW11 308 C8
Buller Cl, SE15 312 C5
Buller Rd, N17 100 DU54
N22 99 DN54
NW10 282 D3
Barking IG11 145 ES66
Thornton Heath CR7 202 DR96
Bullers Cl, Sid. DA14 186 EY92
Bullers Wd Dr, Chis. BR7 184 EL94
Sch **Bullers Wd Sch**, Chis. BR7
off St. Nicolas La 204 EL95
Bullescroft Rd, Edg. HA8 96 CN48
Bullfinch Cl, Horl. RH6 268 DE147
Sevenoaks TN13 256 FD122
Bullfinch Dene, Sev. TN13 256 FD122
Bullfinch La, Sev. TN13 256 FD122
Bullfinch Rd, S.Croy. CR2 221 DX110
Bullhead Rd, Borwd. WD6 78 CQ41
Bull Hill, Hort.Kir. DA4 208 FQ98
Leatherhead KT22 231 CG121
Bullied Way, SW1 297 K9
Bull Inn Ct, WC2 298 B1
Bullivant Cl, Green. DA9 189 FU85
Bullivant St, E14 290 E9
Bull La, N18 100 DS50
Chislehurst BR7 185 ER94
Dagenham RM10 127 FB62
Gerrards Cross SL9 112 AX55
Sutton Green GU4 243 AZ126
Bullocks La, Hert. SG13 32 DQ11
Bull Plain, Hert. SG14 32 DR09
Bull Rd, E15 281 L10
Bullrush Cl, Cars. SM5 200 DE103
Croydon CR0 202 DS100
Hatfield AL10 45 CV19
Bullrush Gro, Uxb. UB8 134 BJ70
Bull's All, SW14 158 CR82
● **Bulls Br Centre**, Hayes UB3
off The Parkway 155 BV76
● **Bullsbridge Ind Est**,
Sthl. UB2 155 BV77
Bulls Br Rd, Sthl. UB2 155 BV76
Bullsbrook Rd, Hayes UB4 136 BW74
BULLS CROSS, Wal.Cr. EN7 82 DT35
Bulls Cross, Enf. EN2 82 DU37
Bulls Cross Ride, Wal.Cr. EN7 82 DU35
Bulls Gdns, SW3 296 D8
Bull's Head Pas, EC3 287 N9
Bullsland Gdns, Chorl. WD3 73 BB44
Bullsland La, Chorl. WD3 73 BB44
Gerrards Cross SL9 91 BB45
Bulls La, Hat. AL9 45 CZ24
BULLSMOOR, Enf. EN1 82 DV37
Bullsmoor Cl, Wal.Cr. EN8 82 DW35
Bullsmoor Gdns, Wal.Cr. EN8 82 DV35
Bullsmoor La, Enf. EN1, EN3 82 DW35
Waltham Cross EN7 82 DU35
Bullsmoor Ride, Wal.Cr. EN8 82 DW35
Bullsmoor Way, Wal.Cr. EN8 82 DV35
Bull Stag Grn, Hat. AL9 45 CW15
Bullwell Cres, Chsht EN8 67 DY29
Bull Yd, SE15 312 D7
Gravesend DA12
off High St 191 GH86
Bulmer Gdns, Har. HA3 117 CK59
Bulmer Ms, W11 295 J2
Bulmer Pl, W11 295 J2
Bulmer Wk, Rain. RM13 148 FJ68
Bulow Est, SW6 307 M7
Bulstrode Av, Houns. TW3 156 BZ82
Bulstrode Cl, Chipper. WD4 57 BE29
Bulstrode Ct, Ger.Cr. SL9 112 AX58
Bulstrode Gdns, Houns. TW3 156 BZ83
Bulstrode La, Chipper. WD4 57 BE29
Felden HP3 58 BG27
Bulstrode Pl, W1 285 H7
Slough SL1 152 AT76
Bulstrode Rd, Houns. TW3 156 CA83
Bulstrode St, W1 285 H8
Bulstrode Way, Ger.Cr. SL9 112 AX57
Bulwer Ct Rd, E11 123 ED60
Bulwer Gdns, Barn. EN5 80 DC42
Bulwer Rd, E11 123 ED59
N18 100 DS49
Barnet EN5 80 DB42
Bulwer St, W12 294 B3
Bumbles Grn La,
Naze.Gate EN9 68 EH25
BUMBLE'S GREEN,
Wal.Abb. EN9 50 EG24
Bunbury Way, Epsom KT17 233 CV116
Bunby Rd, Stoke P. SL2 132 AT66
BUNCE COMMON, Reig. RH2 264 CR141
Bunce Common Rd,
Leigh RH2 264 CR141
Bunce Dr, Cat. CR3 236 DR123
Buncefield La, Hem.H. HP2 41 BR20
● **Buncefield Terminal**,
Hem.H. HP2 41 BR18
Bunces Cl, Eton Wick SL4 151 AP78
Bunces La, Wdf.Grn. IG8 102 EF52
Bundys Way, Stai. TW18 173 BF93
Bungalow Rd, SE25 202 DS98
Woking GU23 229 BQ124
Bungalows, The, SW16 181 DH94
Wallington SM6 219 DH106
Bunhill Row, EC1 287 L4
Bunhouse Pl, SW1 296 G10
Bunkers Hill, NW11 120 DC59
Belvedere DA17 166 FA77
Sidcup DA14 186 EZ90
Bunkers La, Hem.H. HP3 58 BN25
Bunning Way, N7 276 B6
Bunnsfield, Welw.G.C. AL7 30 DC08
Bunns La, NW7 97 CT51
Bunn's La, Chesh. HP5 56 AU34
Bunsen St, E3 279 L10
Bunten Meade, Slou. SL1 131 AP74
Buntingbridge Rd, Ilf. IG2 125 ER57
Bunting Cl, N9
off Dunnock Cl 101 DX46
Mitcham CR4 200 DF99
Bunton St, SE18 305 M7
Bunyan Ct, EC2
off The Barbican 287 J6
Bunyan Rd, E17 123 DY55
Bunyard Dr, Wok. GU21 211 BC114
Bunyons Cl, Gt Warley CM13 107 FW51
Buonaparte Ms, SW1 297 N10
Burbage Cl, SE1 299 L7
Cheshunt EN8 67 DY31
Hayes UB3 135 BR72
Sch **Burbage Prim Sch**, N1 277 N10
Burbage Rd, SE21 182 DR86
SE24 182 DQ86
Burberry Cl, N.Mal. KT3 198 CS96
Harefield UB9 92 BJ54
Burbidge Rd, Shep. TW17 194 BN98
Burbridge Way, N17 100 DT54
Burcham St, E14 290 D8
Burcharbro Rd, SE2 166 EX79
Burchell Ct, Bushey WD23
off Catsey La 94 CC45
Burchell Rd, E10 123 EB60
SE15 312 F7
Burcher Gale Gro, SE15 311 P4
Burchets Hollow, Peasl. GU5 261 BR144
Burchetts Way, Shep. TW17 195 BP100
Burchett Way, Rom. RM6 126 EZ58
Burch Rd, Nthflt DA11 191 GF86
Burchwall Cl, Rom. RM5 105 FC52
Burcote, Wey. KT13 213 BR107
Burcote Rd, SW18 180 DD88
Burcott Gdns, Add. KT15 212 BJ107
Burcott Rd, Pur. CR8 219 DN114
Burden Cl, Brent. TW8 157 CJ78
Burdenshot Hill, Worp. GU3 242 AU125
Burdenshott Av, Rich. TW10 158 CP84
Burdenshott Rd, Wok. GU22 242 AU125
Worplesdon GU3 242 AU125
Burden Way, E11 124 EH61
Guildford GU2 242 AV129
Burder Cl, N1 277 P4
Burder Rd, N1 277 P4
Burdett Av, SW20 199 CU95
Burdett Cl, W7
off Cherington Rd 137 CF74
Sidcup DA14 186 EY92
Sch **Burdett Coutts C of E
Prim Sch**, SW1 297 N7
Burdett Ms, NW3 274 B4
W2 283 L8
Burdett Rd, E3 289 M4
E14 289 M4
Croydon CR0 202 DR100
Richmond TW9 158 CM82
Burdetts Rd, Dag. RM9 146 EZ67
Burdett St, SE1 298 E6
Burdock Cl, Croy. CR0 203 DX102
Burdock Rd, N17 122 DU55
Burdon La, Sutt. SM2 217 CY108
Burdon Pk, Sutt. SM2 217 CZ109
Burfield Cl, SW17 180 DD91
Hatfield AL10 45 CU16
Burfield Dr, Warl. CR6 236 DW119
Burfield Rd, Chorl. WD3 73 BB43
Old Windsor SL4 172 AU86
Burford Cl, Dag. RM8 126 EW62
Ilford IG6 125 EQ56
Uxbridge UB10 114 BL63
Burford Gdns, N13 99 DM48
Hoddesdon EN11 49 EB16
Slough SL1
off Buttermere Av 130 AJ71
Burford La, Epsom KT17 217 CW111
Burford Ms, Hodd. EN11
off Burford St 49 EA16
Burford Pl, Hodd. EN11 49 EA16
Burford Rd, E6 292 G2
E15 280 G7
SE6 183 DZ89
Brentford TW8 158 CL78
Bromley BR1 204 EL98
Sutton SM1 200 DA103
Worcester Park KT4 199 CT101
Burford St, Hodd. EN11 49 EA17
Burford Wk, SW6 307 M5
Burford Way, New Adgtn CR0 221 EC107
Burford Wf Apts, E15 280 G8
Burgage La, Ware SG12 33 DX06
Burgate Cl, Dart. DA1 167 FF83
Burges Cl, Horn. RM11 128 FM58
Burges Ct, E6 145 EN66
Burges Gro, SW13 159 CV80
Burges Rd, E6 144 EL66
Burgess Av, NW9 118 CR58
● **Burgess Business Pk**, SE5 311 M4
Burgess Cl, Chsht EN7 66 DQ25
Feltham TW13 176 BY91
Burgess Ct, Borwd. WD6
off Belford Rd 78 CM38
Burgess Hill, NW2 120 DA63
Burgess Ms, SW19 180 DB93
Burgess Rd, E15 281 J1
Sutton SM1 218 DB105
Burgess St, E14 290 A7
Burgess Wd Gro, Beac. HP9 88 AH53
Burgess Wd Rd, Beac. HP9 88 AH53
Burgess Wd Rd S, Beac. HP9 110 AH55
Burge St, SE1 299 M7
Burges Way, Stai. TW18 174 BG92
Burgett Rd, Slou. SL1 151 AP76
Burghfield, Epsom KT17 233 CT115
Burghfield Rd,
Istead Rise DA13 191 GF94
BURGH HEATH, Tad. KT20 233 CX119
Burgh Heath Rd, Epsom KT17 216 CS114
★ **Burgh Ho** (Hampstead Mus), NW3
off New End Sq 120 DD63
Burghill Rd, SE26 183 DY91
Burghley Av, Borwd. WD6 78 CQ43
New Malden KT3 198 CR95
Burghley Hall Cl, SW19 179 CY87
Burghley Ho, SW19 179 CY90
Burghley Pl, Mitch. CR4 200 DF99
Burghley Rd, E11 124 EE60
N8 121 DN55
NW5 275 K2
SW19 179 CX91
Chafford Hundred RM16 169 FW76
Burghley Twr, W3 139 CT73
Burgh Mt, Bans. SM7 233 CZ115
Burgh St, N1 277 H10
Burgh Wd, Bans. SM7 233 CY115
Burgon St, EC4 287 H9
Burgos Cl, Croy. CR0 219 DN107
Burgos Gro, SE10 314 C6
Burgoyne Hatch, Harl. CM20
off Momples Rd 36 EU14
Burgoyne Rd, N4 121 DP58
SE25 202 DT98
SW9 310 C10
Sunbury-on-Thames TW16 175 BT93
Burgundy Cft, Welw.G.C. AL7 29 CZ11
Burgundy Ho, Enf. EN2
off Bedale Rd 82 DQ38
Burgundy Pl, W12
off Bourbon La 294 C3
Burham Cl, SE20
off Maple Rd 182 DW94
Burhill Rd, Hersham KT12 213 BU109
Burhill Gro, Pnr. HA5 94 BY54
Sch **Burhill Prim Sch**, Hersham KT12
off Newberry La 214 BX107
Burhill Rd, Hersham KT12 214 BW107
Burke Cl, SW15 158 CS84
Burke Ho, SW11
off Maysoule Rd 160 DD84
Burkes Cl, Beac. HP9 110 AH55
Burkes Cres, Beac. HP9 89 AK53
Burkes Par, Beac. HP9
off Station Rd 89 AK52
Burkes Rd, Beac. HP9 88 AJ54
Burke St, E16 291 M7
Burket Cl, Sthl. UB2 156 BZ77
Burland Rd, SW11 180 DF85
Brentwood CM15 108 FX46
Romford RM5 105 FC51
Burlea Cl, Hersham KT12 213 BV106
Burleigh Av, Sid. DA15 185 ET85
Wallington SM6 200 DG104
Burleigh Cl, Add. KT15 212 BH106
Romford RM7 127 FB56
Burleigh Gdns, N14 99 DJ46
Ashford TW15 175 BQ92
Woking GU21 227 AZ116
Burleigh Ho, W10 282 D6
Burleigh Mead, Hat. AL9 45 CW16
Burleigh Pk, Cob. KT11 214 BY112
Burleigh Pl, SW15 179 CX85
Sch **Burleigh Prim Sch**, Chsht EN8
off Blindman's La 67 DX29

Burleigh Rd, Add. KT15 212 BH105
Cheshunt EN8 67 DY32
Enfield EN1 82 DS42
Hemel Hempstead HP2 41 BQ21
Hertford SG13 32 DU08
St. Albans AL1 43 CH20
Sutton SM3 199 CY102
Uxbridge UB10 135 BP67
Burleigh St, WC2 286 C10
Burleigh Wk, SE6 183 EC88
Burleigh Way, Cuffley EN6 65 DL30
Enfield EN2 off Church St 82 DR41
Burley Cl, E4 101 EA50
SW16 201 DK96
Burley Hill, Harl. CM17 52 EX16
Burley Orchard, Cher. KT16 194 BG100
Burley Rd, E16 292 C7
Burlingham Cl, Guil. GU4
off Gilliat Dr 243 BD132
Burlings La, Knock. TN14 239 ET118
Burlington Arc, W1 297 L1
Burlington Av, Rich. TW9 158 CN81
Romford RM7 127 FB58
Slough SL1 152 AS75
Burlington Cl, E6 293 H8
W9 283 H5
Feltham TW14 175 BR87
Orpington BR6 205 EP103
Pinner HA5 115 BV55
Sch Burlington Danes Acad, W12
off Wood La 139 CV72
Burlington Gdns, W1 297 L1
W3 138 CQ74
W4 158 CQ78
Romford RM6 126 EY59
Sch Burlington Inf & Nurs Sch,
N.Mal. KT3 off Burlington Rd 199 CT98
Sch Burlington Jun Sch, N.Mal. KT3
off Burlington Rd 199 CT98
Burlington La, W4 158 CS80
Burlington Ms, SW15 179 CZ85
W3 138 CQ74
Burlington Pl, SW6 306 F9
Reigate RH2 250 DA134
Woodford Green IG8 102 EG48
Burlington Ri, E.Barn. EN4 98 DE46
Burlington Rd, N10
off Tetherdown 120 DG55
N17 100 DU53
SW6 306 F8
W4 158 CQ78
Burnham SL1 130 AH70
Enfield EN2 82 DR39
Isleworth TW7 157 CD81
New Malden KT3 199 CU98
Slough SL1 152 AS75
Thornton Heath CR7 202 DQ96
Burman Cl, Dart. DA2 188 FQ87
Burma Rd, N16 122 DR63
Longcross KT16 192 AT104
Burmester Rd, SW17 180 DC90
Burnaby Cres, W4 158 CP79
Burnaby Gdns, W4 158 CQ79
Burnaby Rd, Nthflt DA11 190 GE87
Burnaby St, SW10 307 N5
Burnbrae Cl, N12 98 DB51
Burnbury Rd, SW12 181 DJ88
Burn Cl, Add. KT15 212 BK105
Oxshott KT22 230 CC115
Burncroft Av, Enf. EN3 82 DW40
Burndell Way, Hayes UB4 136 BX71
Burne Jones Ho, W14 294 G9
Burnell Av, Rich. TW10 177 CJ92
Welling DA16 166 EU82
Burnell Gdns, Stan. HA7 95 CK53
Burnell Rd, Sutt. SM1 218 DB105
Burnell Wk, SE1 300 B10
Great Warley CM13 107 FW51
Burnels Av, E6 293 L3
Burness Cl, N7 276 C4
Uxbridge UB8 134 BK68
Burne St, NW1 284 C6
Burnet Av, Guil. GU1 243 BB131
Burnet Cl, Hem.H. HP3 40 BL21
Burnet Gro, Epsom KT19 216 CQ113
Burnett Cl, E9 279 H3
Burnett Ho, SE13 314 F9
Burnett Pk, Harl. CM19 51 EP20
Burnett Rd, Erith DA8 168 FK79
Ilford IG6 103 EP52
Burnett Sq, Hert. SG14 31 DM08
Burnetts Rd, Wind. SL4 151 AL81
Burney Av, Surb. KT5 198 CM99
Burney Cl, Fetch. KT22 246 CC125
Burney Dr, Loug. IG10 85 EP40
Burney Ho, Lthd. KT22
off Highbury Dr 231 CG121
Burney Rd, Westh. RH5 247 CG131
Burney St, SE10 314 F4
Burnfoot Av, SW6 306 F7
Burnfoot Ct, SE22 182 DV88
BURNHAM, Slou. SL1 130 AJ68
Burnham 131 AK72
Burnham, NW3 274 C6
Burnham Av, Beac. HP9 111 AN55
Uxbridge UB10 115 BQ63
Burnham Cl, NW7 97 CU52
SE1 300 B9
Enfield EN1 82 DS38
Wealdstone HA3 117 CG56
Windsor SL4 151 AK82
Burnham Ct, NW4 119 CW56
Burnham Cres, E11 124 EJ56
Dartford DA1 168 FJ84
Burnham Dr, Reig. RH2 250 DA133
Worcester Park KT4 199 CX103
Burnham Gdns, Croy. CR0 202 DT101
Hayes UB3 155 BR76
Hounslow TW4 155 BV81
Sch Burnham Gram Sch, Burn. SL1
off Hogfair La 131 AK70
Burnham Hts, Slou. SL1
off Goldsworthy Way 130 AJ72
Burnham La, Slou. SL1 131 AL72
Burnham Rd, E4 101 DZ50
Beaconsfield HP9 111 AL58
Dagenham RM9 146 EV66
Dartford DA1 168 FJ84
Morden SM4 200 DB99
Romford RM7 127 FD55
St. Albans AL1 43 CG20
Sidcup DA14 186 EY89
Burnhams Gro, Epsom KT19 216 CP111
Burnhams Rd, Bkhm KT23 230 BY124
Burnham St, E2 288 G2
Kingston upon Thames KT2 198 CN95
Sch Burnham Upr Sch, Burn. SL1
off Opendale Rd 130 AH71
Burnham Wk, Slou. SL2 111 AN64
Burnham Way, SE26 183 DZ92
W13 157 CH77
Burnhill Cl, SE15 312 F4
Burnhill Rd, Beck. BR3 203 EA96
Burnley Cl, Wat. WD19 94 BW50
Burnley Rd, NW10 119 CU64
SW9 310 C8
Grays RM20 169 FT81
Burnsall St, SW3 296 D10
Burns Av, Chad.Hth RM6 126 EW59
Feltham TW14 175 BU86
Sidcup DA15 186 EV86
Southall UB1 136 CA73
Burns Cl, E17 123 EC56
SW19 180 DD93
Carshalton SM5 218 DG109
Erith DA8 167 FF81
Hayes UB4 135 BT71
Welling DA16 165 ET81
Burns Dr, Bans. SM7 217 CY114
Burnside, Ashtd. KT21 232 CM118
Hertford SG14 31 DN10
Hoddesdon EN11 49 DZ17
St. Albans AL1 43 CH22
Sawbridgeworth CM21 36 EX05
Burnside Av, E4 101 DZ51
Burnside Cl, SE16 301 K2
Barnet EN5 80 DA41
Hatfield AL10
off Homestead Rd 45 CU15
Twickenham TW1 177 CG86
Burnside Cres, Wem. HA0 137 CK67
Burnside Rd, Dag. RM8 126 EW61
Burnside Ter, Harl. CM17 36 EZ12
Burns Pl, Til. RM18 171 GH81
Burns Rd, NW10 139 CT67
SW11 308 E8
W13 157 CH75
Wembley HA0 137 CK68
Burns Ter, Esher KT10
off Farm Rd 196 CB103
Burns Way, Houns. TW5 156 BX82
Hutton CM13 109 GD45
Burnt Ash Hts, Brom. BR1 184 EH92
Burnt Ash Hill, SE12 184 EF86
Burnt Ash La, Brom. BR1 184 EG93
Sch Burnt Ash Prim Sch, Brom. BR1
off Rangefield Rd 184 EG92
Burnt Ash Rd, SE12 184 EF85
Burnt Common Cl,
Ripley GU23 243 BF125
Burnt Common La,
Ripley GU23 244 BG125
Burnt Fm Ride, Enf. EN2 65 DP34
Waltham Cross EN7 65 DP31
Burnt Ho La, Hawley DA2 188 FL91
Burnthwaite Rd, SW6 307 H5
Burnt Mill, Harl. CM20 35 EQ13
Burnt Mill Cl, Harl. CM20
off Burnt Mill La 35 EQ12
● Burnt Mill Ind Est, Harl. CM20 35 EQ12
Burnt Mill La, Harl. CM20 35 EQ12
Jct Burnt Mill Rbt, Harl. CM20 35 ER12
Sch Burnt Mill Sch, Harl. CM20
off First Av 35 ES13
BURNT OAK, Edg. HA8 96 CQ52
Burnt Oak 96 CQ53
Burnt Oak Bdy, Edg. HA8 96 CN52
Burnt Oak Flds, Edg. HA8 96 CQ53
Sch Burnt Oak Jun Sch, Sid. DA15
off Burnt Oak La 186 EU88
Burnt Oak La, Sid. DA15 186 EU86
Burntwood, Brwd. CM14 108 FW48
Burntwood Av, Horn. RM11 128 FK58
Burntwood Cl, SW18 180 DD88
Caterham CR3 236 DU121
Burntwood Dr, Oxt. RH8 254 EE131
Burntwood Gra Rd, SW18 180 DD88
Burntwood Gro, Sev. TN13 257 FH127
Burntwood La, SW17 180 DE89
Caterham CR3 236 DU121
Burntwood Rd, Sev. TN13 257 FH128
Sch Burntwood Sch, SW17
off Burntwood La 180 DD89
Burntwood Vw, SE19
off Bowley La 182 DT92
Burn Wk, Burn. SL1 130 AH70
Burnway, Horn. RM11 128 FL59
Buross St, E1 288 F9
BURPHAM, Guil. GU1 243 BB130
Jct Burpham, Guil. GU4 243 BC129
Burpham Cl, Hayes UB4 136 BX71
★ Burpham Court Fm Pk,
Guil. GU4 243 AZ128
Burpham La, Guil. GU4 243 BA129
Sch Burpham Prim Sch, Burpham GU4
off Burpham La 243 BA130
Burrage Gro, SE18 165 EQ77
Burrage Pl, SE18 165 EP78
Burrage Rd, SE18 165 EQ79
Redhill RH1 250 DG132
Burrard Rd, E16 292 A8
NW6 273 J2
Burr Cl, E1 300 C2
Bexleyheath DA7 166 EZ83
London Colney AL2
off Waterside 62 CL27
Burrell, The, Westc. RH4 262 CC137
Burrell Cl, Croy. CR0 203 DY100
Edgware HA8 96 CP47
Burrell Row, Beck. BR3
off High St 203 EA96
Burrell St, SE1 298 G2
Burrells Wf Sq, E14 302 C10
Burrell Twrs, E10 123 EA59
Burren Ct, N18
off Baxter Rd 100 DV49
Burrfield Dr, Orp. BR5 206 EX99
Burr Hill La, Chobham GU24 210 AS109
Burritt Rd, Kings.T. KT1 198 CN96
Burroughs, The, NW4 119 CV57
Burroughs Gdns, NW4 119 CV56
Burroughs Par, NW4
off The Burroughs 119 CV56
Burroway Rd, Slou. SL3 153 BB76
Burrow Cl, Chigwell IG7
off Burrow Rd 103 ET50
Watford WD17 75 BS36
Burrowfield, Welw.G.C. AL7 29 CX11
Burrow Grn, Chig. IG7 103 ET50
BURROWHILL, Wok. GU24 210 AS108
Burrow Rd, SE22 162 DS84
Chigwell IG7 103 ET50
Burrows Chase, Wal.Abb. EN9 83 ED36
Burrows Cl, Bkhm KT23 230 BZ124
Guildford GU2 242 AT133
Penn HP10 88 AC45
Burrows Cross, Shere GU5 261 BQ141
Burrows La, Goms. GU5 261 BQ140
Burrows Ms, SE1 298 G4
Burrows Rd, NW10 282 A2
Burrow Wk, SE21 182 DQ87
Burr Rd, SW18 180 DA87
Bursdon Cl, Sid. DA15 185 ET89
Burses Way, Hutt. CM13 109 GB45
Bursland Rd, Enf. EN3 83 DX42
Burslem Av, Ilf. IG6 104 EU51
Burslem St, E1 288 D9
Burstead Cl, Cob. KT11 214 BX113
Sch Bursted Wd Prim Sch, Bexh. DA7
off Swanbridge Rd 167 FB82
Burstock Rd, SW15 159 CY84
Burston Dr, Park St AL2 60 CC28
Burston Rd, SW15 179 CX85
Burston Vil, SW15
off St. John's Av 179 CX85
BURSTOW, Horl. RH6 269 DN152
● Burstow Business Cen,
Horl. RH6 269 DP146
Sch Burstow Prim Sch, Smallfield RH6
off Wheelers La 269 DP148
Burstow Rd, SW20 199 CY95
Burtenshaw Rd, T.Ditt. KT7 197 CG101
Burtley Cl, N4 122 DQ60
Burton Av, Wat. WD18 75 BU42
Burton Cl, Chess. KT9 215 CK108
Horley RH6 268 DG149
Thornton Heath CR7 202 DR97
Burton Ct, SW3
off Franklin's Row 296 F10
Burton Dr, Enf. EN3 83 EA37
Burton Gdns, Houns. TW5 156 BZ81
Burton Gro, SE17 311 L1
Burtonhole Cl, NW7 97 CX49
Burtonhole La, NW7 97 CY49
Burton La, SW9 310 F8
Goffs Oak EN7 66 DS29
Burton Ms, SW1 297 H9
Burton Pl, WC1 285 P3
Burton Rd, E18 124 EH55
NW6 273 H7
SW9 310 G8
Kingston upon Thames KT2 178 CL94
Loughton IG10 85 EQ42
Burtons La, Ch.St.G. HP8 73 AZ43
Rickmansworth WD3 73 AZ43
Burtons Rd, Hmptn H. TW12 176 CB91
Burton St, WC1 285 P3
Burtons Way, Ch.St.G. HP8 72 AW40
Burton Way, Wind. SL4 151 AL83
Burtwell La, SE27 182 DR91
Burwash Ct, Orp. BR5
off Rookery Gdns 206 EW99
Burwash Ho, SE1 299 M5
Burwash Rd, SE18 165 ER78
Burway Cl, S.Croy. CR2 220 DS107
Burway Cres, Cher. KT16 194 BG97
Burwell Av, Grnf. UB6 137 CE65
Burwell Cl, E1 288 F9
Burwell Rd, E10 123 DY60
Burwell Wk, E3 290 B4
Burwood Av, Brom. BR2 204 EH103
Kenley CR8 219 DP114
Pinner HA5 116 BW57
Burwood Cl, Guil. GU1 243 BD133
Hersham KT12 214 BW107
Reigate RH2 250 DD134
Surbiton KT6 198 CN102
Burwood Gdns, Rain. RM13 147 FF69
BURWOOD PARK, Walt. KT12 213 BT106
Burwood Pk, Cob. KT11 213 BS112
Burwood Pk Rd,
Hersham KT12 213 BV105
Burwood Pl, W2 284 D8
Barnet EN4 80 DC39
Burwood Rd, Hersham KT12 213 BV107
Sch Burwood Sch, Orp. BR6
off Avalon Rd 206 EX103
Bury, The, Chesh. HP5 54 AP31
Hemel Hempstead HP1 40 BJ19
Bury Av, Hayes UB4 135 BS68
Ruislip HA4 115 BQ58
Bury Cl, SE16 301 K2
Woking GU21 226 AX116
Bury Ct, EC3 287 P8
Burycroft, Welw.G.C. AL8 29 CY06
Burydell La, Park St AL2 61 CD27
Bury Fm, Amer. HP7
off Gore Hill 55 AQ40
Bury Flds, Guil. GU2 258 AW136
Buryfield Ter, Ware SG12
off Priory St 32 DW06
Buryfield Way, Ware SG12 32 DW05
BURY GREEN, Wal.Cr. EN7 66 DV31
Bury Grn, Hem.H. HP1 40 BJ19
Bury Grn Rd, Chsht EN7 66 DU31
Bury Gro, Mord. SM4 200 DB99
Bury Hill, Hem.H. HP1 40 BH19
Bury Hill Cl, Hem.H. HP1 40 BJ19
Buryholme, Brox. EN10 49 DZ23
Bury La, Chesh. HP5 54 AP31
Epping CM16 69 ES31
Rickmansworth WD3 92 BK46
Woking GU21 226 AW116
Bury Meadows, Rick. WD3 92 BK46
Bury Ms, Rick. WD3 off Bury La 92 BK46
Bury Pl, WC1 286 A7
Bury Ri, Hem.H. HP3 57 BD25
Bury Rd, E4 84 EE43
N22 121 DN55
Dagenham RM10 127 FB64
Epping CM16 69 ES31
Harlow CM17 36 EW11
Hatfield AL10 45 CW17
Hemel Hempstead HP1 40 BJ19
Sch Burys Ct Sch, Leigh RH2
off Flanchford Rd 265 CX140
Buryside Cl, Ilf. IG2 125 ET56
Bury St, EC3 287 P9
N9 100 DU46
SW1 297 M2
Guildford GU2 258 AW136
Ruislip HA4 115 BQ57
Bury St W, N9 100 DR45
Bury Wk, SW3 296 C9
Busbridge Ho, E14 290 B7
Busby Ms, NW5
off Busby Pl 275 N4
Busby Pl, NW5 275 N4
Busch Cl, Islw. TW7 157 CH81
Bushbaby Cl, SE1 299 N7
Bushbarns, Chsht EN7 66 DU29
Bushberry Rd, E9 279 M4
Bushbury La, Bet. RH3 264 CN139
Bushby Av, Brox. EN10 49 DZ22
Bush Cl, Add. KT15 212 BJ106
Ilford IG2 125 ER57
Bush Cotts, SW18
off Putney Br Rd 180 DA85
Bush Ct, W12 294 D4
Bushell Cl, SW2 181 DM89
Bushell Grn, Bushey Hth WD23 95 CD47
Bushell St, E1 300 D3
Bushell Way, Chis. BR7 185 EN92
Bush Elms Rd, Horn. RM11 127 FG59
Bushetts Gro, Merst. RH1 251 DH129
BUSHEY, WD23 94 CA45
Bushey 76 BX44
Sch Bushey Acad, The, Bushey WD23
off London Rd 76 BZ44
Sch Bushey & Oxhey Inf Sch, Bushey
WD23 off Aldenham Rd 76 BY43
Bushey Av, E18 124 EF55
Petts Wood BR5 205 ER101
Bushey Cl, E4 101 EC48
Kenley CR8 236 DS116
Uxbridge UB10 115 BP61
Welwyn Garden City AL7 30 DB10
Bushey Ct, SW20 199 CV96
Bushey Cft, Harl. CM18 51 ES17
Oxted RH8 253 EC130
Bushey Down, SW12
off Bedford Hill 181 DH89
Bushey Grn, Welw.G.C. AL7 30 DB10
Bushey Gro Rd, Bushey WD23 76 BX42
Bushey Hall Dr, Bushey WD23 76 BY42
Bushey Hall Pk, Bushey WD23 76 BY42
Bushey Hall Rd, Bushey WD23 76 BX42
BUSHEY HEATH, Bushey WD23 95 CE46
Sch Bushey Heath Prim Sch,
Bushey WD23 off The Rutts 95 CD46
Bushey Hill Rd, SE5 311 P7
Bushey La, Sutt. SM1 218 DA105
Bushey Lees, Sid. DA15
off Fen Gro 185 ET86
Bushey Ley, Welw.G.C. AL7 30 DB10
Sch Bushey Manor Jun Sch, Bushey
WD23 off Grange Rd 76 BY44
BUSHEY MEAD, SW20 199 CX97
Sch Bushey Meads Sch, Bushey WD23
off Coldharbour La 76 CC43
Bushey Mill Cres, Wat. WD24 76 BW37
Bushey Mill La, Bushey WD23 76 BZ40
Watford WD24 76 BW37
Bushey Rd, E13 292 C1
N15 122 DS58
SW20 199 CV97
Croydon CR0 203 EA103
Hayes UB3 155 BS77
Sutton SM1 218 DB105
Uxbridge UB10 114 BN61
Bushey Shaw, Ashtd. KT21 231 CH117
Bushey Vw Wk, Wat. WD24 76 BX40
Bushey Way, Beck. BR3 203 ED100
Bush Fair, Harl. CM18 51 ET17
Bushfield Cl, Edg. HA8 96 CP47
Bushfield Cres, Edg. HA8 96 CP47
Bushfield Dr, Red. RH1 266 DG139
Bushfield Rd, Bov. HP3 57 BC25
Bushfields, Loug. IG10 85 EN43
Bushfield Wk, Swans. DA10 190 FY86
Bush Gro, NW9 118 CQ59
Stanmore HA7 95 CK53
Bushgrove Rd, Dag. RM8 126 EX63
Bush Hall La, Hat. AL9 45 CX15
Bush Hill, N21 100 DQ45
BUSH HILL PARK, Enf. EN1 82 DS43
Bush Hill Park 82 DT44
Sch Bush Hill Pk Prim Sch, Enf. EN1
off Main Av 82 DU43
Bush Hill Rd, N21 82 DR44
Harrow HA3 118 CM58
Bush Ho, SE18
off Berber Par 164 EL80
Harlow CM18 off Bush Fair 51 ET17
● Bush Ind Est, N19 121 DJ62
NW10 138 CR70
Bush La, EC4 287 L10
Send GU23 227 BD124
Bushmead Cl, N15
off Duffield Dr 122 DT56
Bushmoor Cres, SE18 165 EQ80
Bushnell Rd, SW17 181 DH89
Bush Rd, E8 278 E9
E11 124 EF59
SE8 301 K8
Buckhurst Hill IG9 102 EK49
Richmond TW9 158 CM79
Shepperton TW17 194 BM99
Bushway, Dag. RM8 126 EX63
Bushwood, E11 124 EF60
Bushwood Cl, N.Mymms AL9
off Dellsome La 45 CV23
Bushwood Dr, SE1 300 B9
Bushwood Rd, Rich. TW9 158 CN79
Bushy Cl, Rom. RM1 105 FD51
BUSHY HILL, Guil. GU1 243 BC132
Bushy Hill Dr, Guil. GU1 243 BB132
Sch Bushy Hill Jun Sch, Guil. GU1
off Sheeplands Av 243 BD133
★ Bushy Park, Tedd. TW11 197 CF95
Bushy Pk, Hmptn H. TW12 197 CF95
Teddington TW11 197 CF95
Bushy Pk Gdns, Tedd. TW11 177 CD92
Bushy Pk Rd, Tedd. TW11 177 CH94
Bushy Rd, Fetch. KT22 230 CB122
Teddington TW11 177 CF93
Sch Business Acad Bexley, The,
Prim Sch, Erith DA18
off Yarnton Way 166 EY75
Sec Sch, Erith DA18
off Yarnton Way 166 EY75
● Business Centre, Rom. RM3
off Faringdon Ave 106 FK52
★ Business Design Cen, N1 276 F9
● Business Pk 8, Lthd. KT22
off Barnett Wd La 231 CH119
● Business Village, The,
Slou. SL2 132 AV74
Buslins La, Chesh. HP5 54 AL28
Butcher Row, E1 289 K10
E14 289 K10
Butchers La, Sev. TN15 209 FX103
Butchers Ms, Hayes UB3
off Hemmen La 135 BT73
Butchers Rd, E16 291 P8
Butcher Wk, Swans. DA10 190 FY87
Bute Av, Rich. TW10 178 CL89
Bute Ct, Wall. SM6 219 DJ106
Bute Gdns, W6 294 C9
Wallington SM6 219 DJ106
Bute Gdns W, Wall. SM6 219 DJ106
Sch Bute Ho Prep Sch
for Girls, W6 294 C8
Bute Ms, NW11
off Northway 120 DB57
Bute Rd, Croy. CR0 201 DN102
Ilford IG6 125 EP57
Wallington SM6 219 DJ105
Bute St, SW7 296 A8
Bute Wk, N1 277 L5
Butler Av, Har. HA1 117 CD59
Butler Cl, Edg. HA8
off Scott Rd 96 CP54
Butler Ct, Wem. HA0
off Harrow Rd 117 CG63
Butler Fm Cl, Rich. TW10 177 CK91
Butler Ho, Grays RM17
off Argent St 170 GB79
Butler Pl, SW1 297 N6
Butler Rd, NW10 139 CT66
Dagenham RM8 126 EV63
Harrow HA1 116 CC59
Butlers & Colonial Wf, SE1 300 B4
Butlers Cl, Amer. HP6 55 AN37
Hounslow TW4 156 BZ83
Windsor SL4 151 AK82
Butlers Ct, Wal.Cr. EN8 67 DY32
Butlers Ct Rd, Beac. HP9 89 AK54
Sch Butlers Ct Sch, Beac. HP9
off Wattleton Rd 89 AK54
BUTLERS CROSS, Beac. HP9 90 AT49
Butlers Dene Rd, Wold. CR3 237 DZ120
Butlers Dr, E4 83 EC38
Butlers Hill, W.Hors. KT24 245 BP130
Butler St, E2 289 H2
Uxbridge UB10 135 BP70
Butlers Wf, SE1 300 A3
Butler Wk, Grays RM17
off Palmers Dr 170 GD77
Buttell Cl, Grays RM17 170 GD78
Buttercross La, Epp. CM16 70 EU30
Buttercup Cl, Hat. AL10 29 CT14
Northolt UB5 136 BY65
Romford RM3
off Copperfields Way 106 FK53
Buttercup Sq, Stanw. TW19
off Diamedes Av 174 BK88
Butterfield, Woob.Grn HP10 110 AD59
Butterfield Cl, N17 100 DQ51
SE16 300 E5
Twickenham TW1 177 CF86
Butterfield Ho, SE18
off Berber Par 164 EL80
Butterfield La, St.Alb. AL1 43 CE24
Butterfields, E17 123 EC57
Butterfield Sq, E6 293 J9
Butterfly Cres, Hem.H. HP3 58 BN25
Butterfly La, SE9 185 EP86
Elstree WD6 77 CG41
Butterfly Wk, Warl. CR6 236 DW120
Butterfly Wk Shop Cen,
SE5 311 K7
Butter Hill, Cars. SM5 200 DG104
Dorking RH4 off South St 263 CG136
Wallington SM6 200 DG104
Butteridges Cl, Dag. RM9 146 EZ67
Butterly Av, Dart. DA1 188 FM89
Buttermere Av, Slou. SL1 130 AJ71
Buttermere Cl, E15 281 H1
SE1 300 A9
Feltham TW14 175 BT88
Morden SM4 199 CX100
St. Albans AL1 43 CH21
Buttermere Dr, SW15 179 CY85
Buttermere Gdns, Pur. CR8 220 DR113
Buttermere Pl, Wat. WD25
off Linden Lea 59 BU33
Buttermere Rd, Orp. BR5 206 EX98
Buttermere Wk, E8 278 B5
Buttermere Way, Egh. TW20
off Keswick Rd 173 BB94
Buttersweet Ri, Saw. CM21 36 EY06
Butterwick, W6 294 B9
Watford WD25 76 BY36
Butterwick La, St.Alb. AL4 44 CN22
Butterworth Gdns,
Wdf.Grn. IG8 102 EG51
Buttery Ms, N14 99 DL48
Buttesland St, N1 287 M2
Buttfield Cl, Dag. RM10 147 FB65
Butt Fld Vw, St.Alb. AL1 42 CC24
Buttlehide, Map.Cr. WD3 91 BD50
Buttmarsh Cl, SE18 305 P10
Buttondene Cres, Brox. EN10 49 EB22
Button Rd, Grays RM17 170 FZ77
Buttonscroft Cl, Th.Hth. CR7 202 DQ97
Button St, Swan. BR8 208 FJ96
Butts, The, Brent. TW8 157 CK79
Broxbourne EN10 49 DY24
Otford TN14 241 FH116
Sunbury-on-Thames TW16
off Elizabeth Gdns 196 BW97
Buttsbury Rd, Ilf. IG1 125 EQ64
Butts Cotts, Felt. TW13 176 BZ90
Butts Cres, Han. TW13 176 CA90
Butts End, Hem.H. HP1 40 BG18
Butts Grn Rd, Horn. RM11 128 FK58
Buttsmead, Nthwd. HA6 93 BQ52
Butts Piece, Nthlt. UB5
off Longhook Gdns 135 BV68
Butts Rd, Brom. BR1 184 EE92
Woking GU21 226 AY117
Buxhall Cres, E9 279 N4
Sch Buxlow Prep Sch, Wem. HA9
off Castleton Gdns 118 CL62
Buxted Rd, E8 278 A6
N12 98 DE50
SE22 162 DS84
Buxton Av, Cat. CR3 236 DS121
Buxton Cl, N9 100 DW47
Epsom KT19 216 CP111
St. Albans AL4 43 CK17
Woodford Green IG8 102 EK51
Buxton Ct, N1 287 K2
Buxton Cres, Sutt. SM3 217 CY105
Buxton Dr, E11 124 EE56
New Malden KT3 198 CR96
Buxton Gdns, W3 138 CP73
Buxton Ho, SW11
off Maysoule Rd 160 DD84
Buxton La, Cat. CR3 236 DR120
Buxton Ms, SW4 309 P8
Buxton Path, Wat. WD19 94 BW48
Buxton Pl, Cat. CR3 236 DR120
Buxton Rd, E4 101 ED45
E6 292 G2
E15 281 J3
E17 123 DY56
N19 121 DK60
NW2 139 CV65

Buxton Rd, SW14 158 CS83
Ashford TW15 174 BK92
Erith DA8 167 FD80
Grays RM16 170 GE75
Ilford IG2 125 ES58
Theydon Bois CM16 85 ES36
Thornton Heath CR7 201 DP99
Waltham Abbey EN9 68 EG32
Buxton St, E1 288 B5
● Buzzard Creek Ind Est, Bark. IG11 145 ET71
Byam St, SW6 307 N9
Byards Cft, SW16 201 DK95
Byatt Wk, Hmptn. TW12 off Victors Dr 176 BY93
Bybend Cl, Farn.Royal SL2 131 AP67
Bychurch End, Tedd. TW11 177 CF92
Bycliffe Ter, Grav. DA11 191 GF87
Bycroft Rd, Sthl. UB1 136 CA70
Bycroft St, SE20 off Penge La 183 DX94
Bycullah Av, Enf. EN2 81 DP41
Bycullah Rd, Enf. EN2 81 DP41
Byde St, Hert. SG14 32 DQ08
Bye, The, W3 138 CS72
Byegrove Ct, SW19 off Byegrove Rd 180 DD94
Byegrove Rd, SW19 180 DD93
Byers Cl, Pot.B. EN6 64 DC34
Byewaters, Wat. WD18 75 BQ44
Bye Way, The, Har. HA3 95 CE53
Byeway, The, SW14 158 CQ83
Rickmansworth WD3 92 BL47
Byeways, Twick. TW2 176 CB90
Byeways, The, Surb. KT5 198 CN99
Byfeld Gdns, SW13 159 CU81
Byfield, Welw.G.C. AL8 29 CY06
Byfield Cl, SE16 301 M4
Byfield Pas, Islw. TW7 157 CG83
Byfield Rd, Islw. TW7 157 CG83
BYFLEET, W.Byf. KT14 212 BM113
⇌ Byfleet & New Haw 212 BK110
● Byfleet Ind Est, Wat. WD18 93 BP46
Byfleet Prim Sch, Byfleet KT14 off Kings Head La 212 BK111
Byfleet Rd, Byfleet KT14 212 BN112
Cobham KT11 213 BS113
New Haw KT15 212 BK108
● Byfleet Tech Cen, Byfleet KT14 212 BK111
Byford Cl, E15 281 K7
Bygrove, New Adgtn CR0 221 EB107
Bygrove Prim Sch, E14 290 C9
Bygrove St, E14 290 C9
Byland Cl, N21 99 DM45
Morden SM4 off Bolton Dr 200 DD101
Bylands, Wok. GU22 227 BA119
Bylands Cl, SE2 166 EV76
SE16 301 K2
Byne Rd, SE26 182 DW93
Carshalton SM5 200 DE103
Bynes Rd, S.Croy. CR2 220 DR108
Byng Dr, Pot.B. EN6 64 DA31
Bynghams, Harl. CM19 51 EM17
Byng Pl, WC1 285 N5
Byng Rd, Barn. EN5 79 CX41
Byng St, E14 302 A4
Bynon Av, Bexh. DA7 166 EY83
Bypass Rd, Lthd. KT22 231 CH120
Byre, The, N14 81 DH44
Byrefield Rd, Guil. GU2 242 AT131
Byre Rd, N14 80 DG44
Byrne Cl, Croy. CR0 201 DP100
Byrne Ho, SW2 off Kett Gdns 181 DM85
Byrne Rd, SW12 181 DH88
Byron Av, E12 144 EL65
E18 124 EF55
NW9 118 CP56
Borehamwood WD6 78 CN43
Coulsdon CR5 235 DL115
Hounslow TW4 155 BU82
New Malden KT3 199 CU99
Sutton SM1 218 DD105
Watford WD24 76 BX39
Byron Av E, Sutt. SM1 218 DD105
Byron Cl, E8 278 C8
SE26 183 DY91
SE28 146 EW74
SW16 181 DL93
Bookham KT23 230 CA124
Hampton TW12 176 BZ91
Knaphill GU21 226 AS117
Waltham Cross EN7 off Allard Cl 66 DT27
Walton-on-Thames KT12 196 BY102
Byron Ct, W9 283 K4
Enfield EN2 81 DP40
Harrow HA1 117 CE58
Windsor SL4 151 AN83
Byron Ct Prim Sch, Wem. HA0 off Spencer Rd 117 CJ61
Byron Dr, N2 120 DD58
Erith DA8 167 FB80
Byron Gdns, Sutt. SM1 218 DD105
Tilbury RM18 171 GJ81
Byron Hill Rd, Har. HA2 117 CD60
Byron Ho, Beck. BR3 183 EA93
Slough SL3 153 BB78
Byron Ms, NW3 274 D2
W9 283 K4
Byron Pl, Lthd. KT22 231 CH122
Byron Prim Sch, Couls. CR5 off St. Davids 235 DM117
Byron Rd, E10 123 EB60
E17 123 EA55
NW2 119 CV61
NW7 97 CU50
W5 138 CM74
Addlestone KT15 212 BL105
Dartford DA1 168 FP84
Harrow HA1 117 CE58
Hutton CM13 109 GD45
South Croydon CR2 220 DV110
Wealdstone HA3 95 CF54
Wembley HA0 117 CJ62
Byron St, E14 290 E8
Byron Ter, N9 82 DW44
SE7 164 EJ80
Byron Way, Hayes UB4 135 BS70
Northolt UB5 136 BY69
Romford RM3 106 FJ53
West Drayton UB7 154 BM77
Bysouth Cl, N15 122 DR56
Ilford IG5 103 EP53
By the Mt, Welw.G.C. AL7 29 CX10
By the Wd, Wat. WD19 94 BX47
Bythorn St, SW9 161 DM83
Byton Rd, SW17 180 DF93
Bytham Hill, Mick. RH5 247 CJ127
Byward Av, Felt. TW14 176 BW86
Byward St, EC3 299 P1
Bywater Pl, SE16 301 M2
Bywater St, SW3 296 E10
Byway, The, Epsom KT19 217 CT105
Potters Bar EN6 64 DA33
Sutton SM2 218 DD109
Byways, Berk. HP4 38 AY18
Burnham SL1 130 AG71
Byways, The, Ashtd. KT21 off Skinners La 231 CK118
Bywell Pl, W1 285 L7
Bywood Av, Croy. CR0 202 DW100
Bywood Cl, Bans. SM7 233 CZ117
Kenley CR8 235 DP115
By-Wood End, Chal.St.P. SL9 91 AZ50
Byworth Wk, N19 off Courtauld Rd 121 DL60

C

Cabbell Pl, Add. KT15 212 BJ105
Cabbell St, NW1 284 C7
Cabell Rd, Guil. GU2 242 AS133
Caberfeigh Cl, Red. RH1 250 DD134
Cabinet Way, E4 101 DZ51
Cable Ho Ct, Wok. GU21 226 AY115
Cable Pl, SE10 314 F6
Cable St, E1 288 C10
● Cable Trade Pk, SE7 304 C9
Cabot Pl, E14 302 B2
Cabot Sq, E14 302 B2
Cabot Way, E6 off Parr Rd 144 EK67
Cabrera Av, Vir.W. GU25 192 AW100
Cabrera Cl, Vir.W. GU25 192 AX100
Cabul Rd, SW11 308 C9
Cacket's Cotts, Cudham TN14 239 ES115
Cackets La, Cudham TN14 239 ER115
Cactus Cl, SE15 311 P8
Cactus Wk, W12 off Du Cane Rd 139 CT72
Cadbury Cl, Islw. TW7 157 CG81
Sunbury-on-Thames TW16 175 BS94
Cadbury Rd, Sun. TW16 175 BS94
Cadbury Way, SE16 300 B7
Caddington Cl, Barn. EN4 80 DE43
Caddington Rd, NW2 119 CY62
Caddis Cl, Stan. HA7 95 CF52
Caddy Cl, Egh. TW20 173 BA92
Cade La, Sev. TN13 257 FJ128
Cadell Cl, E2 288 B1
Cade Rd, SE10 314 G6
Cader Rd, SW18 180 DC86
Cadet Dr, SE1 300 B10
Cadet Pl, SE10 303 J10
Cadiz Rd, Dag. RM10 147 FC66
Cadiz St, SE17 311 K1
Cadley Ter, SE23 182 DW89
Cadlocks Hill, Halst. TN14 224 EZ110
Cadman Cl, SW9 off Langton Rd 310 G5
Cadmer Cl, N.Mal. KT3 198 CS98
Cadmore Ct, Hert. SG14 off The Ridgeway 31 DM07
Cadmore La, Chsht EN8 67 DX28
Cadmus Cl, SW4 off Aristotle Rd 161 DK83
Cadnam Pt, SW15 off Dilton Gdns 179 CV88
Cadogan Av, Dart. DA2 189 FR87
Cadogan Cl, E9 279 P6
Beckenham BR3 off Albemarle Rd 203 ED95
Harrow HA2 116 CB63
Teddington TW11 177 CE92
Cadogan Ct, Sutt. SM2 218 DB107
Cadogan Gdns, E18 124 EH55
N3 98 DB53
N21 81 DN43
SW3 296 F8
Cadogan Gate, SW1 296 F8
Cadogan La, SW1 296 G7
Cadogan Pier 308 D3
Cadogan Pl, SW1 296 F6
Kenley CR8 236 DQ117
Cadogan Rd, SE18 305 P6
Surbiton KT6 197 CK99
Cadogan Sq, SW1 296 F7
Cadogan St, SW3 296 E9
Cadogan Ter, E9 279 N5
Cadoxton Av, N15 122 DT58
Cadwallon Rd, SE9 185 EP89
Caedmon Rd, N7 121 DM63
Caenshill Pl, Wey. KT13 212 BN108
Caenshill Rd, Wey. KT13 212 BN108
Caenwood Cl, Wey. KT13 212 BN107
Caen Wd Rd, Ashtd. KT21 231 CJ118
Caerleon Cl, Clay. KT10 215 CH108
Sidcup DA14 186 EW92
Caerleon Ter, SE2 off Blithdale Rd 166 EV77
Caernarvon Cl, Hem.H. HP2 40 BK20
Hornchurch RM11 128 FN60
Mitcham CR4 201 DL97
Caernarvon Dr, Ilf. IG5 103 EN53
Caesars Wk, Mitch. CR4 200 DF99
Caesars Way, Shep. TW17 195 BR100
Cage Pond Rd, Shenley WD7 62 CM33
Cages Wd Dr, Farn.Com. SL2 111 AP63
Cage Yd, Reig. RH2 off High St 250 DA134
Cahill St, EC1 287 K5
Cahir St, E14 302 C9
Caillard Rd, Byfleet KT14 212 BL111
Cain Cl, St.Alb. AL1 43 CF22
Cains La, Felt. TW14 175 BS85
Caird St, W10 282 F3
Cairn Av, W5 137 CK74
Cairncross Ms, N8 off Felix Av 121 DL58
Cairndale Cl, Brom. BR1 184 EF94
Cairnfield Av, NW2 118 CS62
Cairngorm Cl, Tedd. TW11 off Vicarage Rd 177 CG92
Cairngorm Pl, Slou. SL2 131 AR70
Cairns Av, Wdf.Grn. IG8 102 EL51
Cairns Cl, Dart. DA1 188 FK85
St. Albans AL4 43 CK21
Cairns Ms, SE18 off Bell St 164 EL81
Cairns Rd, SW11 180 DE85
Cairn Way, Stan. HA7 95 CF51
Cairo New Rd, Croy. CR0 201 DP103
Cairo Rd, E17 123 EA56
Caishowe Rd, Borwd. WD6 78 CP39
Caister Cl, Hem.H. HP2 40 BL21
Caistor Ms, SW12 off Caistor Rd 181 DH87
Caistor Pk Rd, E15 281 M9
Caistor Rd, SW12 181 DH87
Caithness Dr, Epsom KT18 216 CR114
Caithness Gdns, Sid. DA15 185 ET86
Caithness Rd, W14 294 C8
Mitcham CR4 181 DH94
Calabria Rd, N5 276 G4
Calais Cl, Chsht EN7 66 DR26
Calais Gate, SE5 off Cormont St 310 G6
Calais St, SE5 311 H6
Calbourne Av, Horn. RM12 127 FH64
Calbourne Rd, SW12 180 DF87
Calbroke Ct, Slou. SL2 off Calbroke Rd 131 AM69
Calbroke Rd, Slou. SL2 131 AM70
Calcott Cl, Brwd. CM14 108 FV46
Calcott Wk, SE9 184 EK91
Calcroft Av, Green. DA9 189 FW85
Calcutta Rd, Til. RM18 171 GF82
Caldbeck, Wal.Abb. EN9 67 ED34
Caldbeck Av, Wor.Pk. KT4 199 CU103
Caldecot Av, Chsht EN7 66 DT29
Caldecote Gdns, Bushey WD23 77 CE44
Caldecote La, Bushey WD23 95 CF45
Caldecot Rd, SE5 311 K8
Caldecott Way, E5 123 DX62
Caldecot Way, Brox. EN10 49 DZ22
Calder Av, Brook.Pk AL9 64 DB26
Perivale UB6 137 CF68
Calder Cl, Enf. EN1 82 DS41
Calder Ct, Rom. RM1 127 FD56
Slough SL3 153 AZ78
Calder Gdns, Edg. HA8 118 CN55
Calderon Pl, W10 282 A7
Calderon Rd, E11 123 EC63
Calder Rd, Mord. SM4 200 DC99
Caldervale Rd, SW4 181 DK85
Calder Way, Colnbr. SL3 153 BF83
Calderwood, Grav. DA12 191 GL92
Calderwood Pl, Barn. EN4 80 DB39
Calderwood St, SE18 305 M8
Caldicot Grn, NW9 118 CS58
Caldicott Sch, Farn.Royal SL2 off Crown La 131 AP66
Caldon Ho, Nthlt. UB5 off Waxlow Way 136 BZ70
Caldwell Gdns Est, SW9 310 E6
Caldwell Rd, Wat. WD19 94 BX49
Caldwell St, SW9 310 D5
Caldy Rd, Belv. DA17 167 FB76
Caldy Wk, N1 277 J6
Caleb St, SE1 299 J4
Caledon Cl, Beac. HP9 89 AK52
Caledonian Cl, Ilf. IG3 126 EV60
Caledonian Ct, Nthlt. UB5 off Taywood Rd 136 BY70
⊖ Caledonian Road 276 B4
Caledonian Rd, N1 286 B1
N7 276 C4
Caledonian Road & Barnsbury 276 D6
Caledonian Sq, NW1 275 N4
Caledonian Way, Gat. RH6 off Queen's Gate 269 DH151
Caledonian Wf, E14 302 G9
Caledonia Rd, Stai. TW19 174 BL88
Caledonia St, N1 286 B1
Caledon Pl, Guil. GU4 off Darfield Rd 243 BA131
Caledon Rd, E6 144 EL67
Beaconsfield HP9 89 AL52
London Colney AL2 61 CK26
Wallington SM6 218 DG105
Cale St, SW3 296 C10
Caletock Way, SE10 303 L10
Calfstock La, Fnghm DA4 208 FL98
Calico Row, SW11 307 P10
Calidore Cl, SW2 181 DM86
California Bldg, SE13 off Deals Gateway 314 C6
California Cl, Sutt. SM2 218 DA110
California La, Bushey Hth WD23 95 CD46
California Rd, N.Mal. KT3 198 CP98
Caliph Cl, Grav. DA12 191 GM90
Callaby Ter, N1 277 M5
Callaghan Cl, SE13 164 EE84
Callander Rd, SE6 183 EB89
Callan Gro, S.Ock. RM15 149 FV73
Callard Av, N13 99 DP50
Callcott Rd, NW6 272 G7
Callcott St, W8 295 J2
Callendar Rd, SW7 296 A6
Callender Ct, Croy. CR0 off Harry Cl 202 DQ100
Calley Down Cres, New Adgtn CR0 221 ED110
Callingham Cl, E14 289 P7
Callingham Pl, Beac. HP9 89 AL52
Callis Fm Cl, Stanw. TW19 off Bedfont Rd 174 BL86
Callisons Pl, SE10 303 K10
Callis Rd, E17 123 DZ58
Callisto Ct, Hem.H. HP2 off Jupiter Dr 40 BM17
Callow Fld, Pur. CR8 219 DN113
Callow Hill, Vir.W. GU25 192 AW97
Callowland Pl, Wat. WD24 75 BV38
Callow St, SW3 307 P2
Calluna Ct, Wok. GU22 off Heathside Rd 227 AZ118
Calmont Rd, Brom. BR1 183 ED93
Calmore Cl, Horn. RM12 128 FJ64
Calne Av, Ilf. IG5 103 EP53
Calonne Rd, SW19 179 CX91
Calshot Av, Chaff.Hun. RM16 170 FZ75
Calshot Rd, Lon.Hthrw Air. TW6 154 BN82
Calshot St, N1 276 C10
Calshot Way, Enf. EN2 81 DP41
London Heathrow Airport TW6 off Calshot Rd 155 BP82
Calthorpe Gdns, Edg. HA8 96 CL50
Sutton SM1 200 DC104
Calthorpe St, WC1 286 D4
Calton Av, SE21 182 DS85
Hertford SG14 31 DM08
Calton Ct, Hert. SG14 off Calton Av 31 DM09
Calton Rd, New Barn. EN5 80 DC44
Calverley Cl, Beck. BR3 183 EB93
Calverley Ct, Epsom KT19 off Kingston Rd 216 CR105
Calverley Cres, Dag. RM10 126 FA61
Calverley Gdns, Har. HA3 117 CK59
Calverley Gro, N19 121 DK60
Calverley Rd, Epsom KT17 217 CU107
Calvert Av, E2 287 P3
Calvert Cl, Belv. DA17 166 FA77
Epsom KT19 216 CP110
Sidcup DA14 186 EY93
Calvert Cres, Dor. RH4 off Calvert Rd 247 CH134
Calvert Dr, Dart. DA2 187 FD89
Calverton, SE5 311 M2
Calverton Prim Sch, E16 292 F9
Calverton Rd, E6 145 EN67
Calvert Rd, SE10 315 L1
Barnet EN5 79 CX40
Dorking RH4 247 CH134
Effingham KT24 245 BV128
Calvert's Bldgs, SE1 299 L3
Calvert St, NW1 274 G8
Calvin Cl, Orp. BR5 206 EX97
Calvin St, E1 288 A5
Calydon Rd, SE7 164 EH78
Calypso Cres, SE15 312 A4
Calypso Way, SE16 301 N7
Camac Rd, Twick. TW2 177 CD88
Camarthen Grn, NW9 118 CS57
Cambalt Rd, SW15 179 CX85
Cambell Inf Sch, Dag. RM9 off Langley Cres 146 EX66
Cambell Jun Sch, Dag. RM9 off Langley Cres 146 EX66
Camberley Av, SW20 199 CV96
Enfield EN1 82 DS42
Camberley Cl, Sutt. SM3 199 CX104
Camberley Rd, Lon.Hthrw Air. TW6 154 BN83
Cambert Way, SE3 164 EH84
CAMBERWELL, SE5 311 K5
● Camberwell Business Cen, SE5 311 L5
Camberwell Ch St, SE5 311 L7
Camberwell Coll of Arts, Peckham Rd, SE5 311 P6
Wilson Rd, SE5 311 N7
Camberwell Grn, SE5 311 K6
Camberwell Grn, SE5 311 L6
Camberwell Gro, SE5 311 M7
Camberwell New Rd, SE5 310 E3
Camberwell Pas, SE5 311 K6
Camberwell Rd, SE5 311 K3
Camberwell Sta Rd, SE5 311 J7
Cambeys Rd, Dag. RM10 127 FB64
Camborne Av, W13 157 CH75
Romford RM3 106 FL52
Camborne Cl, Lon.Hthrw Air. TW6 off Camborne Rd 154 BN83
Camborne Dr, Hem.H. HP2 40 BL16
Camborne Ms, SW18 off Camborne Rd 180 DA87
W11 282 E9
Camborne Rd, SW18 180 DA87
Croydon CR0 202 DU101
London Heathrow Airport TW6 154 BN83
Morden SM4 199 CX99
Sidcup DA14 186 EW90
Sutton SM2 218 DA108
Welling DA16 165 ET82
Camborne Way, Houns. TW5 156 CA81
London Heathrow Airport TW6 off Camborne Rd 154 BN83
Romford RM3 106 FL52
Cambourne Av, N9 101 DX45
Cambray Rd, SW12 181 DJ88
Orpington BR6 205 ET101
Cambria Cl, Houns. TW3 156 CA84
Sidcup DA15 185 ER88
Cambria Ct, Felt. TW14 175 BV87
Cambria Cres, Grav. DA12 191 GL91
Cambria Gdns, Stai. TW19 174 BL87
Cambria Ho, SE26 off High Level Dr 182 DU91
Erith DA8 off Larner Rd 167 FE80
Cambrian Av, Ilf. IG2 125 ES57
Cambrian Cl, SE27 181 DP90
Cambrian Grn, NW9 118 CS57
Cambrian Gro, Grav. DA11 191 GG87
Cambrian Rd, E10 123 EA59
Richmond TW10 178 CM86
Cambrian Way, Hem.H. HP2 40 BL17
Cambria Rd, SE5 311 J10
Cambria St, SW6 307 M5
Cambridge Av, NW6 273 K10
Burnham SL1 130 AH68
Greenford UB6 117 CF64
New Malden KT3 199 CT96
Romford RM2 128 FJ55
Slough SL1 131 AM72
Welling DA16 165 ET84
Cambridge Barracks Rd, SE18 305 K9
Cambridge Circ, WC2 285 P9
Cambridge Cl, E17 123 DZ58
N22 99 DN53
NW10 off Lawrence Way 118 CQ62
SW20 199 CV95
Cheshunt EN8 66 DW29
East Barnet EN4 98 DG46
Harmondsworth UB7 154 BK79
Hounslow TW4 156 BY84
Woking GU21 226 AT118
Cambridge Cotts, Rich. TW9 158 CN79
Cambridge Cres, E2 288 E1
Teddington TW11 177 CG92
Cambridge Dr, SE12 184 EG85
Potters Bar EN6 63 CX31
Ruislip HA4 116 BW61
Cambridge Gdns, N10 98 DG53
N13 99 DN50
N17 100 DR52
N21 100 DR45
NW6 273 K10
W10 282 F8
Enfield EN1 82 DU40
Grays RM16 171 GG77
Kingston upon Thames KT1 198 CN96
Cambridge Gate, NW1 285 K3
Cambridge Gate Ms, NW1 285 K3
Cambridge Grn, SE9 185 EP88
Cambridge Gro, SE20 202 DV95
W6 159 CV77
Cambridge Gro Rd, Kings.T. KT1 198 CN96
Cambridge Heath 278 E10
Cambridge Heath Rd, E1 288 F6
E2 288 F6
Cambridge Ho, Wind. SL4 off Ward Royal 151 AQ81
Cambridge Lo Mobile Home Pk, Horl. RH6 268 DG145
Cambridge Mans, SW11 308 E7
Cambridge Par, Enf. EN1 off Great Cambridge Rd 82 DU39
Cambridge Pk, E11 124 EG59
Twickenham TW1 177 CK87
Cambridge Pk Rd, E11 off Cambridge Pk 124 EG59
Cambridge Pl, W8 295 M5
Cambridge Rd, E4 101 ED46
E11 124 EF58
NW6 283 J2
SE20 202 DV97
SW11 308 E7
SW13 159 CT82
SW20 199 CU95
W7 157 CF75
Ashford TW15 175 BQ94
Barking IG11 145 EQ66
Beaconsfield HP9 88 AJ53
Bromley BR1 184 EG94
Carshalton SM5 218 DE107
Hampton TW12 176 BZ94
Harlow CM20 36 EW09
Harrow HA2 116 CA57
Hounslow TW4 156 BY84
Ilford IG3 125 ES60
Kingston upon Thames KT1, KT2 198 CM96
Mitcham CR4 201 DJ97
New Malden KT3 198 CS98
Richmond TW9 158 CN80
St. Albans AL1 43 CH21
Sidcup DA14 185 ES91
Southall UB1 136 BZ74
Teddington TW11 177 CF91
Twickenham TW1 177 CK86
Uxbridge UB8 134 BK65
Walton-on-Thames KT12 195 BV100
Watford WD18 76 BW42
West Molesey KT8 196 BZ98
Cambridge Rd N, W4 158 CP78
Cambridge Rd S, W4 158 CP78
Cambridge Row, SE18 165 EP78
Cambridge Sch, W6 off Cambridge Gro 159 CV77
Cambridge Sq, W2 284 C8
Redhill RH1 266 DG137
Cambridge St, SW1 297 K9
Cambridge Ter, N13 99 DN50
NW1 285 K3
Berkhamsted HP4 38 AX19
Cambridge Ter Ms, NW1 285 K3
Cambridge Tutors Coll, Croy. CR0 off Water Twr Hill 220 DS105
Cambstone Cl, N11 98 DG47
Cambus Cl, Hayes UB4 136 BY71
Cambus Rd, E16 291 P6
Camdale Rd, SE18 165 ET80
★ Camden Arts Cen, NW3 273 N3
Camden Av, Felt. TW13 176 BW89
Hayes UB4 136 BW73
Camden Cen for Learning, NW1 275 J6
Camden Cl, Chad.St.M. RM16 171 GH77
Chislehurst BR7 185 EQ94
Gravesend DA11 190 GC88
Camden Gdns, NW1 275 K7
Sutton SM1 218 DB106
Thornton Heath CR7 201 DP97
Camden Gro, Chis. BR7 185 EP93
Camden High St, NW1 275 K8
Camden Hill Rd, SE19 182 DS93
Camdenhurst St, E14 289 M8
Camden Jun Sch, Cars. SM5 off Camden Rd 218 DF105
Camden La, N7 275 P3
★ Camden Lock Mkt & Waterbuses, NW1 275 J7
Camden Lock Pl, NW1 275 J7
Camden Ms, NW1 275 M6
Camden Pk Rd, NW1 275 N4
Chislehurst BR7 185 EM94
Camden Pas, N1 276 G10
Camden Road 275 L7
Camden Rd, E11 124 EH58
E17 123 DZ58
N7 275 L7
NW1 275 N4
Bexley DA5 186 EZ88
Carshalton SM5 218 DF105
Grays RM16 170 FY76
Sevenoaks TN13 257 FH122
Sutton SM1 218 DA106
Camden Row, SE3 315 K9
Camden Sch for Girls, NW5 275 M5
Camden Sq, NW1 275 N6
SE15 312 A6
Camden St, NW1 275 L8
Camden Ter, NW1 275 N5
CAMDEN TOWN, NW1 275 L9
⊖ Camden Town 275 K8
Camden Wk, N1 276 G9
Camden Way, Chis. BR7 185 EM94
Thornton Heath CR7 201 DP97
Camelford Wk, W11 282 E9
Camel Gro, Kings.T. KT2 177 CK92
Camellia Cl, Rom. RM3 106 FL53
Camellia Ct, Wdf.Grn. IG8 off The Bridle Path 102 EE52
Camellia Ho, Felt. TW13 off Tilley Rd 175 BV88
Camellia La, Surb. KT5 off Chiltern Dr 198 CP99
Camellia Pl, Twick. TW2 176 CB87
Camellia St, SW8 310 A5
Camelot Cl, SE28 165 ER75
SW19 180 DA91
Biggin Hill TN16 238 EJ116
Camelot Ct, Bushey WD23 off Hartswood Cl 76 CA40
Camelot Ho, NW1 275 P4
Camelot Prim Sch, SE15 312 E3
Camelot St, SE15 312 E3
Camel Rd, E16 304 F2
Camera Pl, SW10 308 A3
Cameron Cl, N18 100 DV49
N20 off Myddelton Pk 98 DE47
N22 99 DM52
Bexley DA5 187 FD90
Warley CM14 108 FW49
Cameron Ct, Ware SG12 33 DX05
Cameron Cres, Edg. HA8 96 CP53
Cameron Dr, Dart. DA1 168 FN82
Wal.Cr. EN8 67 DX34
Cameron Ho, SE5 off Comber Gro 311 J5
Cameron Ho Sch, SW3 308 B2
Cameron Pl, E1 288 F8
SW16 181 DN89

Cameron Rd, SE6 183 DZ89
Bromley BR2 204 EG98
Chesham HP5 54 AQ30
Croydon CR0 201 DP100
Ilford IG3 125 ES60
Cameron Sq, Mitch. CR4 200 DE95
Camerton Cl, E8 278 B5
Camfield, Welw.G.C. AL7 29 CZ13
Camfield Pl, Essen. AL9 46 DD21
● **Camgate Cen**, Stanw. TW19 174 BM86
Cam Grn, S.Ock. RM15 149 FV72
Camilla Cl, Bkhm KT23 246 CB125
Sunbury-on-Thames TW16 175 BT93
Camilla Dr, Westh. RH5 247 CG130
Camilla Rd, SE16 300 E9
Camille Cl, SE25 202 DU97
Camlan Rd, Brom. BR1 184 EF91
Camlet St, E2 288 A4
Camlet Way, Barn. EN4 80 DA40
St. Albans AL3 42 CB19
Camley St, NW1 275 P10
★ **Camley St Natural Pk**, NW1 275 P10
Camm Av, Wind. SL4 151 AL83
Camm Gdns, Kings.T. KT1
off Church Rd 198 CM96
Thames Ditton KT7 197 CE101
Camms Ter, Dag. RM10 127 FC64
Camomile Av, Mitch. CR4 200 DF95
Camomile Rd, Rush Grn RM7 127 FD61
Camomile St, EC3 287 N8
Camomile Way, West Dr. UB7 134 BL72
CAMP, THE, St.Alb. AL1 43 CH21
Campana Rd, SW6 307 J6
Campbell Av, Ilf. IG6 125 EQ56
Woking GU22 227 AZ121
Campbell Cl, SE18
off Moordown 165 EN81
SW16 181 DK91
Byfleet KT14 212 BK112
Harlow CM17
off Carters Mead 52 EV16
Romford RM1 105 FE51
Ruislip HA4 115 BU58
Twickenham TW2 177 CD89
Campbell Ct, N17 100 DT53
SE22 *off Lordship La* 182 DU87
Campbell Cft, Edg. HA8 96 CN50
Campbell Dr, Beac. HP9 88 AJ51
Campbell Gordon Way, NW2 119 CV63
Campbell Rd, E3 290 B2
E6 144 EL67
E15 281 L1
E17 123 DZ56
N17 100 DU53
W7 137 CE73
Caterham CR3 236 DR121
Croydon CR0 201 DP101
East Molesey KT8
off Hampton Ct Rd 197 CF97
Gravesend DA11 191 GF88
Twickenham TW2 177 CD89
Weybridge KT13 212 BN108
Campbell Wk, N1 276 B8
Campdale Rd, N7 121 DK62
Campden Cres, Dag. RM8 126 EV63
Wembley HA0 117 CH61
Campden Gro, W8 295 K4
Campden Hill, W8 295 J4
Campden Hill Ct, W8 295 K4
Campden Hill Gdns, W8 295 H2
Campden Hill Gate, W8 295 J4
Campden Hill Pl, W11 295 H2
Campden Hill Rd, W8 295 K5
Campden Hill Sq, W8 295 H2
Campden Hill Twrs, W11 295 J2
Campden Ho Cl, W8 295 J4
Campden Rd, S.Croy. CR2 220 DS106
Uxbridge UB10 114 BM62
Campden St, W8 295 J3
Campden Way, Dag. RM8 126 EV63
Campen Cl, SW19 179 CY89
Camp End Rd, Wey. KT13 213 BR110
Camperdown St, E1 288 B9
Campfield Rd, SE9 184 EK87
Hertford SG14 31 DP09
St. Albans AL1 43 CG21
Camphill Ct, W.Byf. KT14 212 BG112
● **Camphill Ind Est**,
W.Byf. KT14 212 BH111
Camphill Rd, W.Byf. KT14 212 BG112
Campine Cl, Chsht EN8
off Welsummer Way 67 DX28
Campion Cl, E6 293 K10
Croydon CR0 220 DS105
Denham UB9 114 BG62
Harrow HA3 118 CM58
Hillingdon UB8 134 BM71
Northfleet DA11 190 GE91
Rush Green RM7 127 FD61
Watford WD25 59 BU33
Campion Ct, Grays RM17 170 GD79
Wembley HA0 *off Elmore Cl* 138 CL68
Campion Dr, Tad. KT20 233 CV120
Campion Gdns, Wdf.Grn. IG8 102 EG50
Campion Pl, SE28 146 EV74
Campion Rd, E10 123 EB59
SW15 159 CW84
Hatfield AL10 45 CT15
Hemel Hempstead HP1 39 BE21
Isleworth TW7 157 CF81
Campions, Epp. CM16 70 EU28
Loughton IG10 85 EN38
Campions, The, Borwd. WD6 78 CN38
Sch **Campion Sch, The**, Horn. RM11
off Wingletye La 128 FM56
Campions Cl, Borwd. WD6 78 CP37
Campions Ct, Berk. HP4 38 AU20
Campion Ter, NW2 119 CX62
Campion Way, Edg. HA8 96 CQ49
Camplea La, S.Ock. RM15 149 FU73
Camplin Rd, Har. HA3 118 CL57
Camplin St, SE14 313 K4
Sch **Camp Prim & Nurs Sch**, St.Alb. AL1
off Camp Rd 43 CH21
Camp Rd, SW19 179 CV92
Gerrards Cross SL9 112 AX59
St. Albans AL1 43 CJ21
Woldingham CR3 237 DY120
Campsbourne, The, N8
off High St 121 DL56
Campsbourne Rd, N8 121 DL55
Sch **Campsbourne Sch & Children's Cen**, N8
off Nightingale La 121 DL55
Campsey Gdns, Dag. RM9 146 EV66
Campsey Rd, Dag. RM9 146 EV66
Campsfield Rd, N8 121 DL55
Campshill Pl, SE13
off Campshill Rd 183 EC85
Campshill Rd, SE13 183 EC85
Campus, The, Loug. IG10 85 EP42
Welw.G.C. AL8 29 CX08
Campus Ave, Dag. RM9 126 EU63
Campus Rd, E17 123 DZ58
Campus Way, NW4 119 CV56
Camp Vw, SW19 179 CV92
Camp Vw Rd, St.Alb. AL1 43 CH21
Cam Rd, E15 280 G8
Camrose Av, Edg. HA8 96 CM53
Erith DA8 167 FB79
Feltham TW13 175 BV91
Camrose Cl, Croy. CR0 203 DY101
Morden SM4 200 DA98
Sch **Camrose Prim Sch**, Edg. HA8
off St. Davids Dr 96 CM53
Camrose St, SE2 166 EU78
Canada Av, N18 100 DQ51
Redhill RH1 266 DG138
Canada Cres, W3 138 CQ71
Canada Dr, Red. RH1 266 DG138
Canada Est, SE16 301 H6
Canada Fm Rd, Long. DA3 209 FU99
South Darenth DA4 209 FU98
Canada Gdns, SE13 183 EC85
Canada La, Brox. EN10 67 DY25
Canada Rd, W3 138 CQ70
Byfleet KT14 212 BK111
Cobham KT11 214 BW113
Erith DA8 167 FH80
Slough SL1 152 AV75
Canadas, The, Brox. EN10 67 DY25
Canada Sq, E14 302 C2
Canada St, SE16 301 J5
Canada Water 301 H5
⊖ **Canada Water** 301 H5
Canada Way, W12 139 CV73
Canadian Av, SE6 183 EB88
Canadian Mem Av, Egh. TW20 192 AT96
Canal App, SE8 313 L1
Canal Basin, Grav. DA12 191 GK86
Canal Boul, NW1 275 N4
Canal Bldg, N1
off Shepherdess Wk 277 K10
Canal Cl, E1 289 L4
W10 282 D4
Canal Ct, Berk. HP4 38 AY20
● **Canal Est**, Langley SL3 153 BA75
Canal Gro, SE15 312 D2
● **Canal Ind Pk**, Grav. DA12 191 GK86
Canal Path, E2 278 A9
Canal Reach, N1 276 A8
Canal Rd, Grav. DA12 191 GJ86
Canal Side, Hare. UB9 92 BG52
● **Canalside**, Berk. HP4 38 AT17
Redhill RH1 251 DH131
Canalside Gdns, Sthl. UB2 156 BY77
Canal Wk, N1 277 M8
NW10 *off West End Cl* 138 CQ66
SE26 182 DW92
Croydon CR0 202 DS100
Canal Way, N1 277 K10
NW1 284 D2
NW8 284 C3
NW10 139 CT70
W2 283 M6
W9 283 H6
W10 283 H6
Harefield UB9 92 BG51
Canal Way Wk, W10 282 C4
Canal Wf, Slou. SL3 153 BA75
⊖ **Canary Wharf** 302 C3
DLR **Canary Wharf** 302 B2
RB **Canary Wharf Pier** 301 P2
Canberra Cl, NW4 119 CU55
Dagenham RM10 147 FD66
Hornchurch RM12 128 FJ63
St. Albans AL3 43 CF16
Canberra Cres, Dag. RM10 147 FD66
Canberra Dr, Hayes UB4 136 BW69
Northolt UB5 136 BW69
Canberra Path, E10 123 EB59
Canberra Pl, Rich. TW9 158 CN83
Canberra Rd, E6
off Barking Rd 145 EM67
SE7 164 EJ79
W13 137 CG74
Bexleyheath DA7 166 EX79
London Heathrow Airport TW6 154 BN83
Canberra Sq, Til. RM18 171 GG82
Canbury Av, Kings.T. KT2 198 CM95
● **Canbury Business Pk**, Kings.T. KT2
off Elm Cres 198 CL95
Canbury Ms, SE26
off Wells Pk Rd 182 DU90
Canbury Pk Rd, Kings.T. KT2 198 CL95
Canbury Pas, Kings.T. KT2 197 CK95
Canbury Path, Orp. BR5 206 EU98
Sch **Canbury Sch**, Kings.T. KT2
off Kingston Hill 178 CP93
Cancell Rd, SW9 310 F6
Candahar Rd, SW11 308 C9
Cander Way, S.Ock. RM15 149 FV73
Candlefield Cl, Hem.H. HP3
off Candlefield Rd 40 BN23
Candlefield Rd, Hem.H. HP3 40 BN23
Candlefield Wk, Hem.H. HP3
off Candlefield Rd 40 BN23
Candle Gro, SE15 162 DV83
Candlemakers Apts, SW11 308 A10
Candlemas La, Beac. HP9 89 AL53
Candlemas Mead, Beac. HP9 89 AL53
Candlemas Oaks, Beac. HP9 89 AL53
Candler Ms, Twick. TW1 177 CG87
Candler St, N15 122 DR58
Candlerush Cl, Wok. GU22 227 BB117
Candlestick La, Wal.Cr. EN7
off Park La 66 DV27
Candle St, E1 289 L6
Candover Cl, Harm. UB7 154 BK80
Candover Rd, Horn. RM12 127 FH60
Candover St, W1 285 L7
Candy Cft, Bkhm KT23 246 CB125
Candy St, E3 279 P8
Cane Hill, Harold Wd RM3
off Bennison Dr 106 FK54
Caneland Ct, Wal.Abb. EN9 68 EF34
Canes La, Hast. CM17 52 EX21
North Weald Bassett CM16 52 FA23
Canewdon Cl, Wok. GU22 226 AY119
Caney Ms, NW2 119 CX61
Canfield Dr, Ruis. HA4 115 BV64
Canfield Gdns, NW6 273 N5
Canfield Pl, NW6 273 N5
Canfield Rd, Rain. RM13 147 FF67
Woodford Green IG8 102 EL52
Canford Av, Nthlt. UB5 136 BY67
Canford Cl, Enf. EN2 81 DN40
Canford Dr, Add. KT15 194 BH103
Canford Gdns, N.Mal. KT3 198 CR100
Canford Pl, Tedd. TW11 177 CH93
Canford Rd, SW11 180 DG85
Cangels Cl, Hem.H. HP1 39 BF22
Canham Rd, SE25 202 DS97
W3 158 CS75
Can Hatch, Tad. KT20 233 CY118
Canmore Gdns, SW16 181 DJ94
Sch **Cann Hall Prim Sch**, E11
off Cann Hall Rd 124 EF62
Cann Hall Rd, E11 281 J1
Canning Cres, N22 99 DM53
Canning Cross, SE5 311 N9
Canning Pas, W8 295 N6
Canning Pl, W8 295 N6
Canning Pl Ms, W8 295 N5
Canning Rd, E15 291 J1
E17 123 DY56
N5 121 DP62
Croydon CR0 202 DT103
Harrow HA3 117 CF55
Cannington Rd, Dag. RM9 146 EW65
CANNING TOWN, E16 291 N8
⊖ **Canning Town** 291 K8
DLR **Canning Town** 291 K8
Canning Town 291 K8
Canning Town, E16 291 K8
Cannizaro Rd, SW19 179 CW93
Cannock Ct, E17 101 EC54
Cannonbury Av, Pnr. HA5 116 BX58
Cannon Cl, SW20 199 CW97
Hampton TW12 176 CB93
Cannon Ct, EC1
off Brewhouse Yd 287 H4
Cannon Cres, Chobham GU24 210 AS111
Cannon Dr, E14 302 A1
Cannon Gate, Slou. SL2
off Uxbridge Rd 132 AW73
Cannon Gro, Fetch. KT22 231 CE121
Cannon Hill, N14 99 DK48
NW6 273 K2
Cannon Hill Cl, Bray SL6 150 AC77
Cannon Hill La, SW20 199 CY97
Cannon La, NW3 120 DD62
Pinner HA5 116 BY60
Sch **Cannon La First & Jun Schs**, Pnr. HA5
off Cannonbury Av 116 BX58
Cannon Ms, Wal.Abb. EN9 67 EB33
Cannon Mill Av, Chesh. HP5 54 AR33
Cannon Pl, NW3 120 DD62
SE7 305 H10
Cannon Rd, N14 99 DL48
Bexleyheath DA7 166 EY81
Watford WD18 76 BW43
Cannonside, Fetch. KT22 231 CE122
Cannons Meadow, Tewin AL6 30 DE06
⇌ **Cannon Street** 299 L1
⊖ **Cannon Street** 299 L1
Cannon St, EC4 287 J9
St. Albans AL3 43 CD19
Cannon St Rd, E1 288 E8
● **Cannon Trd Est**, Wem. HA9 118 CP63
Cannon Way, Fetch. KT22 231 CE121
West Molesey KT8 196 CA98
● **Cannon Wf Business Cen**, SE8 301 L9
● **Cannon Workshops**, E14 302 A1
Canon All, EC4
off St. Paul's Chyd 287 H9
Canon Av, Rom. RM6 126 EW57
Sch **Canon Barnett Prim Sch**, E1 288 B8
Canon Beck Rd, SE16 301 H4
Canonbie Rd, SE23 182 DW87
CANONBURY, N1 277 H5
Canonbury 277 J3
Canonbury Cres, N1 277 J6
Canonbury Gro, N1 277 J6
Canonbury La, N1 276 G6
Canonbury Pk N, N1 277 J5
Canonbury Pk S, N1 277 J5
Canonbury Pl, N1 277 H5
Sch **Canonbury Prim Sch**, N1 277 H5
Canonbury Rd, N1 276 G5
Enfield EN1 82 DS39
Canonbury Sq, N1 277 H6
Canonbury St, N1 277 J6
Canonbury Vil, N1 277 H6
Canonbury Yd, N1 277 K8
Canonbury Yd W, N1 277 H5
Canon Mohan Cl, N14
off Farm La 81 DH44
Canon Rd, Brom. BR1 204 EJ97
Canon Row, SW1 298 A5
Canons Brook, Harl. CM19 51 EN15
Canons Cl, N2 120 DD59
Edgware HA8 96 CM51
Radlett WD7 77 CH35
Reigate RH2 249 CZ133
Sch **Canons Cor**, Edg. HA8 96 CL49
Canons Ct, Edg. HA8 96 CM51
Canons Dr, Edg. HA8 96 CL51
Canons Gate, Chsht EN8 67 DZ26
Harlow CM20 35 EN14
Sch **Canons High Sch**, Edg. HA8
off Shaldon Rd 96 CM54
Canon's Hill, Couls. CR5 235 DN117
Canons La, Tad. KT20 233 CY118
Canonsleigh Rd, Dag. RM9 146 EV66
CANONS PARK, Edg. HA8 96 CL52
⊖ **Canons Park** 96 CL52
Canons Pk Cl, Edg. HA8
off Donnefield Av 96 CL52
Canons Rd, Ware SG12 32 DW05
Canon St, N1 277 J9
Canons Wk, Croy. CR0 203 DX104
Canopus Way, Nthwd. HA6 93 BU49
Staines-upon-Thames TW19 174 BL87
Canopy La, Harl. CM17 36 EW14
Canrobert St, E2 288 E2
Cantelowes Rd, NW1 275 P5
Canterbury Av, Ilf. IG1 124 EL59
Sidcup DA15 186 EW89
Slough SL2 131 AQ70
Upminster RM14 129 FT60
Canterbury Cl, E6 293 J8
Amersham HP7 55 AS39
Beckenham BR3 203 EB95
Chigwell IG7 103 ET48
Dartford DA1 188 FN87
Greenford UB6 136 CB72
Northwood HA6 93 BT51
Worcester Park KT4 199 CX103
Canterbury Ct, Dor. RH4
off Station Rd 263 CG135
Canterbury Cres, SW9 161 DN83
Canterbury Gro, SE27 181 DP90
Canterbury Ho, E3
off Bow Rd 290 C2
SE1 298 D6
Borehamwood WD6 78 CN40
Erith DA8 *off Arthur St* 167 FF80
Canterbury Ms, Oxshott KT22 214 CC113
Windsor SL4 151 AN82
Canterbury Par, S.Ock. RM15 149 FW69
Canterbury Pl, SE17 299 H9
Canterbury Rd, E10 123 EC59
NW6 283 J1
Borehamwood WD6 78 CN40
Croydon CR0 201 DM101
Feltham TW13 176 BY90
Gravesend DA12 191 GJ89
Guildford GU2 242 AT132
Harrow HA1, HA2 116 CB57
Morden SM4 200 DC99
Watford WD17 75 BV40
Canterbury Ter, NW6 273 J10
Canterbury Way,
Crox.Grn WD3 75 BQ41
Great Warley CM13 107 FW51
Purfleet RM19 169 FS80
Cantium Retail Pk, SE1 312 C2
Cantley Gdns, SE19 202 DT95
Ilford IG2 125 EQ58
Cantley Rd, W7 157 CG76
Canto Ct, EC1
off Old St 287 K4
Canton St, E14 290 A9
Cantrell Rd, E3
off Bow Common La 289 P5
Cantwell Rd, SE18 165 EP80
Canute Gdns, SE16 301 J8
Canvey St, SE1 299 H2
Capability Way, Green. DA9 169 FW84
Cape Cl, Bark. IG11 145 EP65
Capel Av, Wall. SM6 219 DM106
Capel Cl, N20 98 DC48
Bromley BR2 204 EL102
Capel Ct, EC2 287 M9
SE20 202 DW95
Capel Cres, Stan. HA7 95 CG47
Capel Gdns, Ilf. IG3 125 ET63
Pinner HA5 116 BZ56
Capella Rd, Nthwd. HA6 93 BT50
Capell Av, Chorl. WD3 73 BC43
Capell Rd, Chorl. WD3 73 BC43
Capell Way, Chorl. WD3 73 BD43
Coll **Capel Manor Coll**,
Regent's Pk, NW1 285 H3
Coll **Capel Manor Coll & Gdns**, Enf. EN1
off Bullsmoor La 82 DU35
Sch **Capel Manor Prim Sch**, Enf. EN1
off Bullsmoor La 82 DV35
Capel Pl, Dart. DA2 188 FJ91
Capel Pt, E7 124 EH63
Capel Rd, E7 124 EH63
E12 124 EJ63
Barnet EN4 80 DE44
Enfield EN1 82 DV36
Watford WD19 76 BY44
Capel Vere Wk, Wat. WD17 75 BS39
Capener's Cl, SW1 296 G5
Capern Rd, SW18
off Cargill Rd 180 DC88
Cape Rd, N17
off High Cross Rd 122 DU55
St. Albans AL1 43 CH20
Cape Yd, E1 300 D2
H **Capio Nightingale Hosp**,
NW1 284 D6
● **Capital Business Cen**,
Mitch. CR4 200 DF99
S.Croy. CR2 220 DR108
Wembley HA0 137 CK68
● **Capital Business Pk**,
Borwd. WD6 78 CQ41
Sch **Capital City Acad**, NW10
off Doyle Gdns 139 CV67
Coll **Capital Coll (CIFE) London Sch of Insurance**, WC1 286 C6
Capital E Apts, E16
off Western Gateway 303 P1
Capital Interchange Way,
Brent. TW8 158 CN78
● **Capital Pk**, Old Wok. GU22 227 BB121
● **Capital Pl**, Harl. CM19
off Lovet Rd 51 EN16
● **Capitol Ind Pk**, NW9 118 CQ55
Capitol Sq, Epsom KT17
off Church St 216 CS113
Capitol Way, NW9 118 CQ55
Capland St, NW8 284 B4
Caple Par, NW10
off Harley Rd 138 CS68
Caple Rd, NW10 139 CT68
Capon Cl, Brwd. CM14 108 FV46
Caponfield, Welw.G.C. AL7 30 DB11
Cappell La, Stans.Abb. SG12 33 ED10
Capper St, WC1 285 M5
Caprea Cl, Hayes UB4
off Triandra Way 136 BX71
Capri Rd, Croy. CR0 202 DT102
● **Capstan Cen**, Til. RM18 170 GD80
Capstan Cl, Rom. RM6 126 EV58
Capstan Ct, Dart. DA2 168 FQ84
Capstan Dr, Rain. RM13 147 FG70
Capstan Ms, Grav. DA11 190 GE87
Capstan Ride, Enf. EN2 81 DN40
Capstan Rd, SE8 301 N8
Capstan Sq, E14 302 F5
Capstan's Wf, Wok. GU21 226 AT118
Capstan Way, SE16 301 M3
Capstone Rd, Brom. BR1 184 EF91
● **Capswood Business Cen**,
Denh. UB9 113 BB60
Captain Cook Cl, Ch.St.G. HP8 90 AU49
Captains Cl, Chesh. HP5 54 AN27
Captains Wk, Berk. HP4 38 AX20
Capthorne Av, Har. HA2 116 BY60
Capuchin Cl, Stan. HA7 95 CH51
Capulet Ms, E16 303 P2
Capulet Sq, E3 290 D3
Capworth St, E10 123 EA60
Caractacus Cottage Vw,
Wat. WD18 93 BU45
Caractacus Grn, Wat. WD18 75 BT44
Caradoc Cl, W2 283 J8
Caradoc St, SE10 303 J10
Caradon Cl, E11 124 EE60
Woking GU21 226 AV118
Caradon Way, N15 122 DR56
Caravan La, Rick. WD3 92 BL45
Caravel Cl, E14 302 A6
Grays RM16 170 FZ76
Caravelle Gdns, Nthlt. UB5
off Javelin Way 136 BX69
Caravel Ms, SE8 314 A2
Caraway Cl, E13 292 A6
Caraway Pl, Guil. GU2 242 AU129
Wallington SM6 201 DH104
Carberry Rd, SE19 182 DS93
Carbery Av, W3 158 CM75
Carbis Cl, E4 101 ED46
Carbis Rd, E14 289 N8
Carbone Hill, Newgate St SG13 65 DK26
Northaw EN6 65 DJ27
Carbuncle Pas Way, N17 100 DU54
Carburton St, W1 285 K6
Carbury Cl, Horn. RM12 148 FJ65
Cardale St, E14 302 E5
Cardamom Cl, Guil. GU2 242 AU130
Carde Cl, Hert. SG14 31 DM08
Carden Rd, SE15 162 DV83
Cardiff Cl, Rom. RM5 105 FD52
Cardiff Rd, W7 157 CG76
Enfield EN3 82 DV42
Watford WD18 75 BV44
Cardiff St, SE18 165 ES80
Cardiff Way, Abb.L. WD5 59 BU32
Cardigan Cl, Slou. SL1 131 AM73
Woking GU21 226 AS118
Cardigan Gdns, Ilf. IG3 126 EU61
Cardigan Rd, E3 279 P10
SW13 159 CU82
SW19 *off Haydons Rd* 180 DC93
Richmond TW10 178 CL86
Cardigan St, SE11 298 E10
Cardigan Wk, N1 *off Ashby Gro* 277 K6
Cardinal Av, Borwd. WD6 78 CP41
Kingston upon Thames KT2 178 CL92
Morden SM4 199 CY100
Cardinal Bourne St, SE1 299 M7
Cardinal Bldg, Hayes UB3
off Station Rd 155 BT76
Cardinal Cap All, SE1
off New Globe Wk 299 J1
Cardinal Cl, Chsht EN7 66 DT26
Chislehurst BR7 205 ER95
Edgware HA8 96 CR52
Morden SM4 199 CY101
South Croydon CR2 220 DU113
Worcester Park KT4 217 CU105
Cardinal Ct, Borwd. WD6 78 CP41
Cardinal Cres, N.Mal. KT3 198 CQ96
Cardinal Dr, Ilf. IG6 103 EQ51
Walton-on-Thames KT12 196 BX102
Cardinal Gro, St.Alb. AL3 42 CB22
Cardinal Hinsley Cl, NW10 139 CU68
Sch **Cardinal Hinsley Mathematics & Computing Coll**, NW10
off Harlesden Rd 139 CU67
Sch **Cardinal Newman Catholic Prim Sch**, Hersham KT12
off Arch Rd 196 BX104
Cardinal Pl, SW15 159 CX84
Park St. AL2 61 CD25
Cardinal Rd, Chaff.Hun. RM16 170 FY76
Feltham TW13 175 BV88
Ruislip HA4 116 BX60
Sch **Cardinal Rd Inf & Nurs Sch**, Felt. TW13
off Cardinal Rd 175 BV88
Cardinals Wk, Hmptn. TW12 176 CC94
Sunbury-on-Thames TW16 175 BS93
Taplow SL6 130 AJ72
Cardinals Way, N19 121 DK60
Sch **Cardinal Vaughan Mem Sch**, W14 294 E4
Cardinal Wk, SW1
off Palace St 297 L6
Cardinal Way, Har. HA3 117 CE55
Rainham RM13 148 FK68
Sch **Cardinal Wiseman Sch, The**,
Grnf. UB6 *off Greenford Rd* 136 CC71
Cardine Ms, SE15 312 E4
Cardingham, Wok. GU21 226 AU117
Cardington Sq, Houns. TW4 156 BX84
Cardington St, NW1 285 L2
Cardinham Rd, Orp. BR6 223 ET105
Cardozo Rd, N7 276 B2
Cardrew Av, N12 98 DD50
Cardrew Cl, N12 98 DD50
Cardross St, W6 159 CV76
Sch **Cardwell Prim Sch**, SE18 305 J8
Cardwell Rd, N7 121 DL63
Cardwells Keep, Guil. GU2 242 AU131
Cardy Rd, Hem.H. HP1 40 BH21
Carew Cl, N7 121 DM61
Chafford Hundred RM16 170 FY76
Coulsdon CR5 235 DP119
Carew Ct, Sutt. SM2 218 DB109
Sch **Carew Manor Sch**, Wall. SM6
off Church Rd 201 DK104
Carew Rd, N17 100 DU54
W13 157 CJ75
Ashford TW15 175 BQ93
Mitcham CR4 200 DG96
Northwood HA6 93 BS51
Thornton Heath CR7 201 DP97
Wallington SM6 219 DJ107
Carew St, SE5 311 H8
Carew Way, Orp. BR5 206 EW102
Watford WD19 94 BZ48
Carey Cl, Wind. SL4 151 AP83
Carey Ct, Bexh. DA6 187 FB85
Carey Gdns, SW8 309 N7
Carey La, EC2 287 J8
Carey Pl, SW1 297 N9
Carey Rd, Dag. RM9 126 EY63
Careys Cft, Berk. HP4 38 AU16
Carey's Fld, Dunt.Grn TN13 241 FE120
Carey St, WC2 286 D9
Careys Wd, Smallfield RH6 269 DP148
Carey Way, Wem. HA9 118 CP63
Carfax Pl, SW4 161 DK84
Carfax Rd, Hayes UB3 155 BT78
Hornchurch RM12 127 FF63
Carfree Cl, N1 276 F6
Cargill Rd, SW18 180 DB88
Cargo Forecourt Rd, Gat. RH6 268 DD152
Cargo Rd, Gat. RH6 268 DD152
Cargreen Pl, SE25
off Cargreen Rd 202 DT98
Cargreen Rd, SE25 202 DT98
Carholme Rd, SE23 183 DZ88
Carisbrook Cl, Enf. EN1 82 DT39
Carisbrooke, N10 98 DG54
Carisbrooke Av, Bex. DA5 186 EX88
Watford WD24 76 BX39
Carisbrooke Cl, Horn. RM11 128 FN60
Hounslow TW4 176 BY87
Stanmore HA7 95 CK54

Carisbrooke Ct, Slou. SL1 132 AT73
Carisbrooke Gdns, SE15 312 B4
Carisbrooke Ho, Kings.T. KT2
off Kingsgate Rd 198 CL95
Carisbrooke Rd, E17 123 DY56
Bromley BR2 204 EJ98
Mitcham CR4 201 DK98
St. Albans AL2 60 CB26
Carisbrook Rd, Pilg.Hat. CM15 108 FV44
Carker's La, NW5 275 J2
Carlbury Cl, St.Alb. AL1 43 CH21
Carlcott Cl, Wal. KT12 195 BV101
Carl Ekman Ho, Grav. DA11 190 GD87
Carleton Av, Wall. SM6 219 DK109
Carleton Cl, Esher KT10 197 CD102
Carleton Pl, Hort.Kir. DA4 208 FQ98
Carleton Rd, N7 275 N2
Cheshunt EN8 67 DX28
Dartford DA1 188 FN87
Carlile Cl, E3 289 P1
Carlina Gdns, Wdf.Grn. IG8 102 EH50
Carlingford Gdns, Mitch. CR4 180 DF94
Carlingford Rd, N15 121 DP55
NW3 120 DD63
Morden SM4 199 CX100
Carlisle Av, EC3 287 P9
W3 138 CS72
St. Albans AL1, AL3 43 CD18
Carlisle Cl, Kings.T. KT2 198 CN95
Pinner HA5 116 BY59
Carlisle Gdns, Har. HA3 117 CK59
Ilford IG1 124 EL58
Sch Carlisle Inf Sch, Hmptn. TW12
off Broad La 176 CB93
Carlisle La, SE1 298 D7
Carlisle Ms, NW8 284 B6
Carlisle Pl, N11 99 DH49
SW1 297 L7
Carlisle Rd, E10 123 EA61
N4 121 DN59
NW6 272 E8
NW9 118 CQ55
Dartford DA1 188 FN86
Hampton TW12 176 CB94
Romford RM1 127 FF57
Slough SL1 131 AR73
Sutton SM1 217 CZ106
Carlisle St, W1 285 N9
Carlisle Wk, E8 278 A5
Carlisle Way, SW17 180 DG92
Carlos Pl, W1 297 H1
Carlow St, NW1 275 L10
Carlton Av, N14 81 DK43
Feltham TW14 176 BW86
Greenhithe DA9 189 FS86
Harrow HA3 117 CH57
Hayes UB3 155 BS77
South Croydon CR2 220 DS108
Carlton Av E, Wem. HA9 118 CL60
Carlton Av W, Wem. HA0 117 CH61
Carlton Cl, NW3 120 DA61
Borehamwood WD6 78 CR42
Chessington KT9 215 CK107
Edgware HA8 96 CN50
Northolt UB5
off Whitton Av W 116 CC64
Upminster RM14 128 FP61
Woking GU21 211 AZ114
Carlton Ct, Ilford IG6 125 ER55
Uxbridge UB8 134 BK71
Carlton Cres, Sutt. SM3 217 CY105
Carlton Dr, SW15 179 CY85
Ilford IG6 125 ER55
Carlton Gdns, SW1 297 N3
W5 137 CJ72
Carlton Grn, Red. RH1 250 DE131
Carlton Gro, SE15 312 E6
Carlton Hill, NW8 273 N9
Carlton Ho, Felt. TW14 175 BT87
Carlton Ho Ter, SW1 297 N3
Carlton Par, Orp. BR6 206 EV101
Sevenoaks TN13
off St. John's Hill 257 FJ122
Carlton Pk Av, SW20 199 CW96
Carlton Pl, Nthwd. HA6 93 BP50
Weybridge KT13
off Castle Vw Rd 213 BP105
Sch Carlton Prim Sch, NW5 275 H3
Carlton Rd, E11 124 EF60
E12 124 EK63
E17 101 DY53
N4 121 DN59
N11 98 DG50
SW14 158 CQ83
W4 158 CR75
W5 137 CJ73
Erith DA8 167 FB79
Grays RM16 171 GF75
New Malden KT3 198 CS96
Redhill RH1 250 DF131
Reigate RH2 250 DD132
Romford RM2 127 FG57
Sidcup DA14 185 ET92
Slough SL2 132 AV73
South Croydon CR2 220 DR107
Sunbury-on-Thames TW16 175 BT94
Walton-on-Thames KT12 195 BV101
Welling DA16 166 EV83
Woking GU21 211 BA114
Carlton Sq, E1 289 J4
Carlton St, SW1 297 N1
Carlton Ter, E11 124 EH57
N18 100 DR48
SE26 182 DW90
Carlton Twr Pl, SW1 296 F6
Carlton Twrs, Cars. SM5 200 DF104
Carlton Tye, Horl. RH6 269 DJ148
Carlton Vale, NW6 283 K1
Sch Carlton Vale Inf Sch, NW6 283 H2
Carlton Vil, SW15
off St. John's Av 179 CX85
Carlwell St, SW17 180 DE92
Carlyle Av, Brom. BR1 204 EK97
Southall UB1 136 BZ73
Carlyle Cl, N2 120 DC58
West Molesey KT8 196 CB96
Carlyle Ct, SW10
off Chelsea Harbour 307 P6
Carlyle Gdns, Sthl. UB1 136 BZ73
Carlyle Lo, New Barn. EN5
off Richmond Rd 80 DC43
Carlyle Ms, E1 289 K4
Carlyle Pl, SW15 159 CX84
Carlyle Rd, E12 124 EL63
NW10 138 CR67
SE28 146 EV73
W5 157 CJ78
Croydon CR0 202 DU103
Staines-upon-Thames TW18 173 BF94
★ Carlyle's Ho, SW3 308 C3
Carlyle Sq, SW3 308 B1
Carly Ms, E2 288 C3
Carlyon Av, Har. HA2 116 BZ63
Carlyon Cl, Wem. HA0 138 CL67
Carlyon Rd, Hayes UB4 136 BW72
Wembley HA0 138 CL68
Carlys Cl, Beck. BR3 203 DX96
Carmalt Gdns, SW15 159 CW84
Hersham KT12 214 BW106
Carmarthen Pl, SE1 299 N4
Carmarthen Rd, Slou. SL1 132 AS73
Carmel Cl, Wok. GU22 226 AY118
Carmel Ct, W8 295 L4
Wembley HA9 118 CP61
Carmelite Cl, Har. HA3 94 CC53
Carmelite Rd, Har. HA3 94 CC53
Carmelite St, EC4 286 F10
Carmelite Wk, Har. HA3 94 CC53
Carmelite Way, Har. HA3 94 CC54
Carmel Way, Rich. TW9 158 CP82
Carmen Ct, Borwd. WD6
off Belford Rd 78 CM38
Carmen St, E14 290 C8
Carmichael Av, Green. DA9 169 FW84
Carmichael Cl, SW11
off Darien Rd 160 DD83
Ruislip HA4 115 BU63
Carmichael Ms, SW18 180 DD87
Carmichael Rd, SE25 202 DU99
Carminia Rd, SW17 181 DH89
Carnaby Rd, Brox. EN10 49 DY20
Carnaby St, W1 285 L9
Carnach Grn, S.Ock. RM15 149 FV73
Carnac St, SE27 182 DR91
Carnanton Rd, E17 101 ED53
Carnarvon Av, Enf. EN1 82 DT41
Carnarvon Dr, Hayes UB3 155 BQ76
Carnarvon Rd, E10 123 EC58
E15 281 L4
E18 102 EF53
Barnet EN5 79 CY41
Carnation Cl, Rush Grn RM7 127 FE61
Carnation St, SE2 166 EV78
Carnbrook Ms, SE3
off Carnbrook Rd 164 EK83
Carnbrook Rd, SE3 164 EK83
Carnecke Gdns, SE9 184 EL85
Carnegie Cl, Enf. EN3 83 EB38
Surbiton KT6 off Fullers Av 198 CM103
Carnegie Pl, SW19 179 CX90
Carnegie Rd, St.Alb. AL3 43 CD16
Carnegie St, N1 276 C9
CARNELES GREEN, Brox. EN10 48 DV22
Carnet Cl, Dart. DA1 187 FE87
Carnforth Cl, Epsom KT19 216 CP107
Carnforth Gdns, Horn. RM12 127 FG64
Carnforth Rd, SW16 181 DK94
Carnie Lo, SW17
off Manville Rd 181 DH90
Carnoustie Cl, SE28 146 EX72
Carnoustie Dr, N1 276 C7
Carnwath Rd, SW6 160 DA83
Caro La, Hem.H. HP3 40 BN22
Carol Cl, NW4 119 CX56
Carolina Cl, E15 281 J3
Carolina Rd, Th.Hth. CR7 201 DP96
Caroline Cl, N10 99 DH54
SW16 181 DM90
W2 295 M1
Croydon CR0 220 DS105
Isleworth TW7 157 CD80
West Drayton UB7 154 BK75
Caroline Ct, Ashf. TW15 175 BP93
Stanmore HA7 95 CG51
Caroline Gdns, E2
off Kingsland Rd 287 P2
SE15 312 E4
Caroline Pl, SW11 309 H9
W2 283 M10
Harlington UB3 155 BS80
Watford WD19 76 BY44
Caroline Pl Ms, W2 295 M1
Caroline Rd, SW19 179 CZ94
Caroline St, E1 289 K9
Caroline Ter, SW1 296 G9
Caroline Wk, W6 306 E3
Carol St, NW1 275 L8
Carolyn Cl, Wok. GU21 226 AT119
Carolyn Dr, Orp. BR6 206 EU104
Caroon Dr, Sarratt WD3 74 BH36
Caro Pl, New Maldon KT3 199 CT98
Carpenders Av, Wat. WD19 94 BY48
CARPENDERS PARK,
Wat. WD19 94 BZ47
⊖ Carpenders Park 94 BX48
Carpenter Cl, Epsom KT17 217 CT109
Carpenter Gdns, N21 99 DP47
Carpenter Path, Hutt. CM13 109 GD43
Carpenters Arms La,
Thnwd CM16 70 EV25
Carpenters Arms Path, SE9
off Eltham High St 185 EM86
Carpenters Cl, Barn. EN5 80 DB44
Carpenters Ct, Twick. TW2 177 CE89
Carpenters Ms, N7 276 B3
Carpenters Pl, SW4 161 DK84
Sch Carpenters Prim Sch, E15 280 F8
Carpenters Rd, E15 280 F7
Enfield EN1 82 DW36
Carpenter St, W1 297 J1
Carpenters Wd Dr, Chorl. WD3 73 BB42
Carpenter Way, Pot.B. EN6 64 DC33
Carrack Ho, Erith DA8
off Saltford Cl 167 FE78
Carrara Cl, SW9 161 DP84
Carrara Ms, E8 278 C3
Carrara Wf, SW6 306 F10
Carr Cl, Stan. HA7 95 CG51
Carre Ms, SE5 311 H7
Carr Gro, SE18 305 H8
Carriage Dr E, SW11 308 G4
Carriage Dr N, SW11 309 H3
Carriage Dr S, SW11 308 E6
Carriage Dr W, SW11 308 E5
Carriage Ms, Ilf. IG1 125 EQ61
Carriage Pl, N16 122 DR62
SW16 181 DJ92
Carriages, The, Ware SG12
off Station Rd 33 DY07
Carriage St, SE18 305 P7
Carriageway, The,
Brasted TN16 240 EX124
Carrick Cl, Islw. TW7 157 CG83
Carrick Dr, Ilf. IG6 103 EQ53
Sevenoaks TN13 257 FH123
Carrick Gdns, N17 100 DS52
Carrick Gate, Esher KT10 196 CC104
Carrick Ms, SE8 314 A2
Carriden Ct, Hert. SG14
off The Ridgeway 31 DM07
Carrill Way, Belv. DA17 166 EX77
Carrington Av, Borwd. WD6 78 CP43
Hounslow TW3 176 CB85
Carrington Cl, Arkley EN5 79 CU43
Borehamwood WD6 78 CQ43
Croydon CR0 203 DY101
Kingston upon Thames KT2 178 CQ92
Redhill RH1 250 DF133
Carrington Gdns, E7
off Woodford Rd 124 EG63
Carrington Pl, Esher KT10 214 CB105
Carrington Rd, Dart. DA1 188 FM86
Richmond TW10 158 CN84
Slough SL1 132 AS73
Carrington Sq, Har. HA3 94 CC52
Carrington St, W1 297 J3
Carrol Cl, NW5 275 J1
Carroll Av, Guil. GU1 243 BB134
Carroll Cl, E15 281 K3
Carroll Hill, Loug. IG10 85 EM41
Carronade Ct, N7
off Eden Gro 276 D3
Carronade Pl, SE28 165 EQ76
Carron Cl, E14 290 D8
Carroun Rd, SW8 310 C4
Carroway La, Grnf. UB6 137 CD69
Carrow Rd, Dag. RM9 146 EV66
Walton-on-Thames KT12 196 BX104
Carr Rd, E17 101 DZ54
Northolt UB5 136 CA65
Carrs La, N21 82 DQ43
Carr St, E14 289 M7
CARSHALTON, SM5 218 DD105
⇌ Carshalton 218 DF105
CARSHALTON BEECHES,
Cars. SM5 218 DD109
⇌ Carshalton Beeches 218 DF107
Sch Carshalton Boys Sports Coll,
Cars. SM5
off Winchcombe Rd 200 DE103
Coll Carshalton Coll, Cars. SM5
off Nightingale Rd 200 DF104
Carshalton Gro, Sutt. SM1 218 DD105
Sch Carshalton High Sch for Girls, Cars.
SM5
off West St 200 DF104
CARSHALTON ON THE HILL,
Cars. SM5 218 DG109
Carshalton Pk Rd, Cars. SM5 218 DF106
Carshalton Pl, Cars. SM5 218 DG105
Carshalton Rd, Bans. SM7 218 DF114
Carshalton SM5 218 DC106
Mitcham CR4 200 DG98
Sutton SM1 218 DC106
Carsington Gdns, Dart. DA1 188 FK89
Carslake Rd, SW15 179 CW86
Carson Rd, E16 291 P5
SE21 182 DQ89
Cockfosters EN4 80 DF42
Carson Ter, W11 294 E2
Carstairs Rd, SE6 183 EC90
Carston Cl, SE12 184 EF85
Carswell Cl, Hutt. CM13 109 GD44
Ilford IG4 124 EK56
Carswell Rd, SE6 183 EC87
Cartbridge Cl, Send GU23
off Send Rd 227 BB123
Cartel Cl, Purf. RM19 169 FR77
Carter Cl, NW9 118 CR58
Romford RM5 105 FB52
Windsor SL4 151 AN82
Carter Dr, Rom. RM5 105 FB52
Carteret St, SW1 297 N5
Carteret Way, SE8 301 M9
Sch Carterhatch Inf Sch, Enf. EN1
off Carterhatch La 82 DV39
Sch Carterhatch Jun Sch, Enf. EN1
off Carterhatch La 82 DV39
Carterhatch La, Enf. EN1 82 DU40
Carterhatch Rd, Enf. EN3 82 DW40
Carter Ho, SW11
off Petergate 160 DC84
Carter La, EC4 287 H9
Carter Pl, SE17 311 K1
Carter Rd, E13 144 EH67
SW19 180 DD93
Carters Cl, Guil. GU1 242 AY130
Worcester Park KT4 199 CX103
Carters Cotts, Red. RH1 266 DE136
Cartersfield Rd, Wal.Abb. EN9 67 EC34
CARTERS GREEN, Harl. CM17 37 FD13
Carters Hill, Undrvr TN15 257 FP127
Carters Hill Cl, SE9 184 EJ88
Carters La, SE23 183 DY89
Epping Green CM16 51 EP24
Woking GU22 227 BC120
Carters Mead, Harl. CM17 52 EV16
Cartersmead Cl, Horl. RH6 269 DH147
Carters Rd, Epsom KT17 233 CT115
Carters Row, Nthflt DA11 191 GF88
Carter St, SE17 311 J2
Carters Yd, SW18 180 DA85
Carter Wk, Penn HP10 88 AC47
Carthagena Est, Brox. EN10 49 EC20
Carthew Rd, W6 159 CV76
Carthew Vil, W6 159 CV76
Carthouse La, Wok. GU21 210 AS114
Carthusian St, EC1 287 J6
Cartier Circle, E14 302 D3
Carting La, WC2 298 B1
Cart La, E4 101 ED45
Cart Lodge Ms, Croy. CR0 202 DS102
Cartmel, NW1 285 L2
Cartmel Cl, N17
off Heybourne Rd 100 DV52
Reigate RH2 250 DE133
Cartmel Ct, Nthlt. UB5 136 BY65
Cartmel Gdns, Mord. SM4 200 DC99
Cartmel Rd, Bexh. DA7 166 FA81
Carton St, W1 284 F8
Cart Path, Wat. WD25 60 BW33
Cartridge Pl, SE18 305 P7
Cartwright Gdns, WC1 286 A3
Cartwright Rd, Dag. RM9 146 EZ66
Cartwright St, E1 288 B10
Cartwright Way, SW13 159 CV80
Carve Ley, Welw.G.C. AL7 30 DB10
Carver Cl, W4 158 CQ76
Carver Rd, SE24 182 DQ86
Carville Cres, Brent. TW8 158 CL77
Carville St, N4 121 DN61
Cary Rd, E11 124 EE63
Carysfort Rd, N8 121 DK57
N16 122 DR62
Cary Wk, Rad. WD7 61 CH34
Casby Ho, SE16 300 C6
Cascade Av, N10 121 DJ56
Cascade Cl, Buck.H. IG9
off Cascade Rd 102 EK47
Orpington BR5 206 EW97
Cascade Rd, Buck.H. IG9 102 EK47
Cascades, Croy. CR0 221 DZ110
Cascades Twr, E14 301 P3
Caselden Cl, Add. KT15 212 BJ106
Casella Rd, SE14 313 J5
Casewick Rd, SE27 181 DP91
Casey Cl, NW8 284 C3
Casimir Rd, E5 122 DV62
Casino Av, SE24 182 DQ85
Caspian Cl, Purf. RM19 168 FN77
Caspian Ct, E3 off Violet Rd 290 C6
Caspian St, SE5 311 L4
Caspian Wk, E16 292 E9
Caspian Way, Purf. RM19 168 FN78
Swanscombe DA10 190 FY85
Caspian Wf, E3
off Violet Rd 290 C6
Cassander Pl, Pnr. HA5
off Holly Gro 94 BY53
Cassandra Cl, Nthlt. UB5 117 CD63
Cassandra Gate, Chsht EN8 67 DZ27
Cassel Ct, Stan. HA7
off Brightwen Gro 95 CG47
Casselden Rd, NW10 138 CR66
H Cassel Hosp, The,
Ham TW10 177 CK91
Cassidy Rd, SW6 307 J5
Cassilda Rd, SE2 166 EU77
Cassilis Rd, E14 302 B5
Twickenham TW1 177 CH85
Cassini Apts, E16
off Fords Pk Rd 291 N8
Cassiobridge, Wat. WD18 75 BR42
Cassiobridge Rd, Wat. WD18 75 BS42
Cassiobury Av, Felt. TW14 175 BT86
Cassiobury Ct, Wat. WD17 75 BS40
Cassiobury Dr, Wat. WD17 75 BT40
Sch Cassiobury Inf & Nurs Sch, Wat.
WD17 off Bellmount Wd Av 75 BS39
Sch Cassiobury Jun Sch, Wat. WD17
off Bellmount Wd Av 75 BS39
★ Cassiobury Park, Wat. WD18 75 BS41
Cassiobury Pk, Wat. WD18 75 BS41
Cassiobury Pk Av, Wat. WD18 75 BS41
Cassiobury Rd, E17 123 DX57
Cassio Pl, Wat. WD18 75 BS42
Cassio Rd, Wat. WD18 75 BV41
Cassis Ct, Loug. IG10 85 EQ42
Cassius Dr, St.Alb. AL3 42 CB22
Cassland Rd, E9 279 H6
Thornton Heath CR7 202 DR98
Casslee Rd, SE6 183 DZ87
Cassocks Sq, Shep. TW17 195 BR101
Casson St, E1 288 C7
Casstine Cl, Swan. BR8 187 FF94
Castalia Sq, E14
off Roserton St 302 E5
Castano Ct, Abb.L. WD5 59 BS31
Castellain Rd, W9 283 N5
Castellan Av, Rom. RM2 127 FH55
Castellane Cl, Stan. HA7 95 CF52
Castello Av, SW15 179 CW85
Castell Rd, Loug. IG10 85 EQ39
CASTELNAU, SW13 159 CU79
Castelnau, SW13 159 CV79
Castelnau Gdns, SW13
off Arundel Ter 159 CV79
Castelnau Pl, SW13
off Castelnau 159 CV79
Castelnau Row, SW13
off Lonsdale Rd 159 CV79
Casterbridge, NW6 273 M8
Casterbridge Rd, SE3 164 EG83
Casterton St, E8 278 F5
Castile Gdns, Kings L. WD4 58 BM29
Castile Rd, SE18 305 M8
Sch Castilion Prim Sch, SE28
off Copperfield Rd 146 EW72
Castille Ct, Wal.Cr. EN8 67 DZ34
Castillon Rd, SE6 184 EE89
Castlands Rd, SE6 183 DZ89
Castle Av, E4 101 ED50
Datchet SL3 152 AU79
Epsom KT17 217 CU109
Rainham RM13 147 FE66
West Drayton UB7 134 BL73
Castlebar Hill, W5 137 CH71
Castlebar Ms, W5 137 CJ71
⇌ Castle Bar Park 137 CF71
Castlebar Pk, W5 137 CH70
Castlebar Rd, W5 137 CJ71
Sch Castlebar Sch, W13
off Hathaway Gdns 137 CF71
Castle Baynard St, EC4 287 H10
Castlebrook Cl, SE11 298 G8
Castle Cl, E9 279 L3
SW19 179 CX90
W3 158 CP75
Bletchingley RH1 252 DQ133
Bromley BR2 204 EE97
Bushey WD23 76 CB44
Hoddesdon EN11 33 EC14
Reigate RH2 266 DB138
Romford RM3 106 FJ48
Sunbury-on-Thames TW16
off Percy Bryant Rd 175 BS94
Castlecombe Dr, SW19 179 CX87
Sch Castlecombe Prim Sch, SE9
off Castlecombe Rd 184 EL92
Castlecombe Rd, SE9 184 EL91
Castle Cor, Bletch. RH1
off Overdale 252 DQ133
Castle Ct, EC3 287 M9
SE26 183 DY91
SW15 159 CY83
Castledine Rd, SE20 182 DV94
Castle Dr, Horl. RH6 269 DJ150
Ilford IG4 124 EL58
Reigate RH2 266 DA138
Castle Fm, Wind. SL4 151 AK82
Castle Fm Rd, Shore. TN14 225 FF109
Castlefield Rd, Reig. RH2 250 DA133
Castleford Av, SE9 185 EP88
Castleford Cl, N17 100 DT51
Borehamwood WD6 78 CM38
Castle Gdns, Dor. RH4 248 CM134
Castlegate, Rich. TW9 158 CM83
Castle Gateway, Berk. HP4 38 AW17
Castle Grn, Wey. KT13 195 BS104
Castle Gro Rd, Chobham
GU24 210 AS113
Castlehaven Rd, NW1 275 J7
Castle Hill, Berk. HP4 38 AW17
Guildford GU1 258 AX136
Longfield DA3 209 FX99
Windsor SL4 151 AR81
Castle Hill Av, Berk. HP4 38 AW18
New Addington CR0 221 EB109
Castle Hill Cl, Berk. HP4 38 AV18
Sch Castle Hill Prim Sch, Chess. KT9
off Buckland Rd 216 CM105
Chessington KT9 off Moor La 216 CM106
New Addington CR0
off Dunley Dr 221 EC107
Castle Hill Rd, Egh. TW20 172 AV91
Castle La, SW1 297 M6
Castleleigh Ct, Enf. EN2 82 DR43
Castlemaine Av, Epsom KT17 217 CV109
South Croydon CR2 220 DT106
Castlemaine Twr, SW11 308 F8
Castlemain St, E1 288 E6
Castlemead, SE5 311 K5
Castle Mead, Hem.H. HP1 40 BH22
Castle Ms, N12
off Castle Rd 98 DC50
NW1 275 J5
SW17 180 DE91
Hampton TW12
off Station Rd 196 CB95
Weybridge KT13 195 BS104
Castle Par, Epsom KT17
off Ewell Bypass 217 CU108
Castle Pl, NW1 275 K5
W4 off Windmill Rd 158 CS77
Castle Pt, E13 292 D1
Castlereagh St, W1 284 D8
Castle Rd, N12 98 DC50
NW1 275 J5
Chipstead CR5 234 DE120
Dagenham RM9 146 EV67
Enfield EN3 83 DY39
Epsom KT18 232 CP115
Eynsford DA4 225 FH107
Grays RM17 170 FZ79
Hoddesdon EN11 33 EB14
Isleworth TW7 157 CF82
Northolt UB5 136 CB65
St. Albans AL1 43 CH20
Shoreham TN14 225 FG108
Southall UB2 156 BZ76
Swanscombe DA10 190 FZ86
Weybridge KT13 195 BS104
Woking GU21 211 AZ114
Castle Sq, Bletch. RH1 252 DQ133
Guildford GU1 258 AX136
Castle St, E6 144 EJ68
Berkhamsted HP4 38 AW19
Bletchingley RH1 251 DP133
Greenhithe DA9 189 FU85
Guildford GU1 258 AX136
Hertford SG14 32 DQ10
Kingston upon Thames KT1 198 CL96
Slough SL1 152 AT76
Swanscombe DA10 190 FZ86
Castleton Av, Bexh. DA7 167 FD81
Wembley HA9 118 CL63
Castleton Cl, Bans. SM7 234 DA115
Croydon CR0 203 DY100
Castleton Dr, Bans. SM7 234 DA115
Castleton Gdns, Wem. HA9 118 CL62
Castleton Rd, E17 101 ED54
SE9 184 EK91
Ilford IG3 126 EU60
Mitcham CR4 201 DK98
Ruislip HA4 116 BX60
Castletown Rd, W14 306 F1
Castle Vw, Epsom KT18 216 CP114
Castleview Cl, N4 122 DQ60
Castleview Gdns, Ilf. IG1 124 EL58
Castleview Rd, Slou. SL3 152 AW77
Castle Vw Rd, Wey. KT13 213 BP105
Sch Castleview Sch, Slou. SL3
off Woodstock Av 152 AX77
Castle Wk, Reig. RH2
off London Rd 250 DA134
Sunbury-on-Thames TW16
off Elizabeth Gdns 196 BW97
Castle Way, SW19 179 CX90
Epsom KT17 off Castle Av 217 CU109
Feltham TW13 176 BW91
Castlewood Dr, SE9 165 EM82
Castlewood Rd, N15 122 DU58
N16 122 DU59
Cockfosters EN4 80 DD41
Castle Yd, N6 off North Rd 120 DG59
SE1 299 H2
Richmond TW10 off Hill St 177 CK85
Castor La, E14 302 C1
Catalina Av, Chaff.Hun. RM16 170 FZ75
Catalina Rd, Lon.Hthrw Air. TW6
off Cromer Rd 154 BN82
Catalin Ct, Wal.Abb. EN9
off Howard Cl 67 ED33
Catalonia Apts, Wat. WD18
off Linden Av 75 BT42
Catalpa Cl, Guil. GU1
off Cedar Way 242 AW132
Catalpa Ct, SE13
off Hither Grn La 183 ED86
Cater Gdns, Guil. GU3 242 AT132
CATERHAM, CR3 236 DU123
⇌ Caterham 236 DU124
Caterham Av, Ilf. IG5 103 EM54
Caterham Bypass, Cat. CR3 236 DV120
Caterham Cl, Cat. CR3 236 DS120
Caterham Ct, Wal.Abb. EN9 68 EF34
H Caterham Dene Hosp,
Cat. CR3 236 DT123
Caterham Dr, Couls. CR5 235 DP118
Sch Caterham High Sch, Ilf. IG5
off Caterham Av 103 EM54
CATERHAM-ON-THE-HILL,
Cat. CR3 236 DT122
Caterham Rd, SE13 163 EC83
Sch Caterham Sch, Cat. CR3
off Harestone Valley Rd 252 DT126
Catesby St, SE17 299 M9
CATFORD, SE6 183 EB88
⇌ Catford 183 EA87
⇌ Catford Bridge 183 EA87
Catford Bdy, SE6 183 EB87
Jct Catford Gyratory, SE6 183 EB87
Catford Hill, SE6 183 DZ89
Catford Ms, SE6
off Holbeach Rd 183 EB87
Catford Rd, SE6 183 EA88
Cathall Rd, E11 123 ED62
Catham Cl, St.Alb. AL1 43 CH22
Catharine Cl, Chaff.Hun. RM16 170 FZ75
Cathay St, SE16 300 F5

Cathay Wk, Nthlt. UB5
off Brabazon Rd 136 CA68
Cathcart Dr, Orp. BR6 205 ES103
Cathcart Hill, N19 121 DJ62
Cathcart Rd, SW10 307 M2
Cathcart St, NW5 275 J4
Cathedral Cl, Guil. GU2 258 AV135
Cathedral Ct, St.Alb. AL3 42 CB22
Cathedral Hill, Guil. GU2 242 AU133
● **Cathedral Hill Ind Est**, Guil. GU2
off Cathedral Hill 242 AU133
★ **Cathedral of the Holy Spirit Guildford**,
Guil. GU2 242 AV134
Cathedral Piazza, SW1 297 L7
Cathedral Pl, Brwd. CM14 108 FX47
Cathedral Sch of St. Saviour & St. Mary Overie, The, SE1 299 K4
Cathedral St, SE1 299 L2
Cathedral Vw, Guil. GU2 242 AT134
Cathedral Wk, SW1 297 L6
Catherall Rd, N5 122 DQ62
Catherine Cl, Byfleet KT14 212 BL114
Hemel Hempstead HP2
off Parr Cres 41 BQ15
Loughton IG10
off Roding Gdns 85 EM44
Pilgrim's Hatch CM15 108 FU43
Catherine Ct, N14
off Conisbee Ct 81 DJ43
Catherine Dr, Rich. TW9 158 CL84
Sunbury-on-Thames TW16 175 BT93
Catherine Gdns, Houns. TW3 157 CD84
Catherine Griffiths Ct, EC1 286 F4
Catherine Gro, SE10 314 C6
Catherine Ho, N1 *off Phillipp St* 277 P9
Catherine Howard Ct, SE9
off Avery Hill Rd 185 ER86
Weybridge KT13
off Old Palace Rd 195 BP104
Catherine of Aragon Ct, SE9
off Avery Hill Rd 185 EQ86
Catherine Parr Ct, SE9
off Avery Hill Rd 185 ER86
Catherine Pl, SW1 297 L6
Harrow HA1 117 CF57
Catherine Rd, Enf. EN3 83 DY36
Romford RM2 127 FH57
Surbiton KT6 197 CK99
Catherine's Cl, West Dr. UB7
off Money La 154 BK76
Catherine St, WC2 286 C10
St. Albans AL3 43 CD19
Catherine Wheel All, E1 287 P7
Catherine Wheel Rd,
Brent. TW8 157 CK80
Catherine Wheel Yd, SW1 297 L3
Catherwood Ct, N1
off Murray Gro 287 L1
Cat Hill, Barn. EN4 80 DE44
Cathles Rd, SW12 181 DH86
Cathnor Rd, W12 159 CV75
Cathrow Ms, Hodd. EN11 33 EA14
Catisfield Rd, Enf. EN3 83 DY37
Catkin Cl, Hem.H. HP1 40 BH19
Catlin Cres, Shep. TW17 195 BR99
Catlin Gdns, Gdse. RH9 252 DV130
Catling Cl, SE23 182 DW90
Catlins La, Pnr. HA5 115 BV55
Catlin St, SE16 312 D1
Hemel Hempstead HP3 40 BH23
Cator Cl, New Adgtn CR0 222 EE111
Cator Cres, New Adgtn CR0 221 ED111
Cator La, Beck. BR3 203 DZ96
Cato Rd, SW4 161 DK83
Cator Pk Sch, Beck. BR3
off Lennard Rd 183 DY94
Cator Rd, SE26 183 DX93
Carshalton SM5 218 DF106
Cator St, SE15 312 A3
Cato St, W1 284 D7
Catsey La, Bushey WD23 94 CC45
Catsey Wds, Bushey WD23 94 CC45
Catterick Cl, N11 98 DG51
Catterick Way, Borwd. WD6 78 CM39
Cattistock Rd, SE9 184 EL92
CATTLEGATE, Enf. EN2 65 DL33
Cattlegate Hill, Northaw EN6 65 DK31
Cattlegate Rd, Enf. EN2 65 DL34
Northaw EN6 65 DK31
Cattley Cl, Barn. EN5 79 CY42
Cattlins Cl, Chsht EN7 66 DS29
Catton St, WC1 286 C7
Cattsdell, Hem.H. HP2 40 BL18
Caughley Ho, SE11
off Lambeth Wk 298 E7
Caulfield Rd, E6 145 EM66
SE15 312 F8
W3 158 CQ76
Causeway, The, N2 120 DE56
SW18 160 DB84
SW19 179 CX92
Bray SL6 150 AC75
Carshalton SM5 200 DG104
Chessington KT9 216 CL105
Claygate KT10 215 CF108
Feltham TW14 155 BU84
Hounslow TW4 155 BU84
Potters Bar EN6 64 DC31
Staines-upon-Thames TW18 173 BC91
Sutton SM2 218 DC109
Teddington TW11
off Broad St 177 CF93
Causeway Cl, Pot.B. EN6 64 DD31
● **Causeway Corporate Cen**,
Stai. TW18 173 BB91
Causeway Ct, Wok. GU21
off Bingham Dr 226 AT118
Causeyware Rd, N9 100 DV45
Causton Rd, N6 121 DH59
Causton Sq, Dag. RM10 146 FA66
Causton St, SW1 297 P9
Cautherly La, Gt Amwell SG12 33 DZ10
Cautley Av, SW4 181 DJ85
Cavalier Cl, Rom. RM6 126 EX56
Cavalier Gdns, Hayes UB3 135 BR72
Cavalier Ho, W5
off Uxbridge Rd 137 CJ73
Cavalry Barracks, Houns. TW4 156 BX83
Cavalry Cres, Houns. TW4 156 BX84
Windsor SL4 151 AQ83
Cavalry Gdns, SW15 179 CY85
Cavalry Sq, SW3 296 F10
Cavan Dr, St.Alb. AL3 43 CD15
Cavan Pl, Pnr. HA5 94 BZ53
Cavaye Pl, SW10 307 P1
Cavell Cres, Dart. DA1 168 FN84
Harold Wood RM3 106 FL54
Cavell Dr, Enf. EN2 81 DN40
Cavell Rd, N17 100 DR52
Cheshunt EN7 66 DT27
Cavell St, E1 288 F6
Cavell Way, Epsom KT19 216 CN111
Cavendish Av, N3 98 DA54
NW8 284 B1
W13 137 CG71
Erith DA8 167 FC79
Harrow HA1 117 CD63
Hornchurch RM12 147 FH65
New Malden KT3 199 CV99
Ruislip HA4 115 BV64
Sevenoaks TN13 256 FG122
Sidcup DA15 186 EU87
Welling DA16 165 ET83
Woodford Green IG8 102 EH53
Cavendish Cl, N18 100 DV50
NW6 272 G5
NW8 284 B2
Amersham HP6 72 AV39
Hayes UB4 135 BS71
Sunbury-on-Thames TW16 175 BT93
Taplow SL6 130 AG72
Cavendish Coll, WC1 285 N6
Cavendish Ct, EC3 287 P8
Croxley Green WD3
off Mayfare 75 BR43
Sunbury-on-Thames TW16 175 BT93
Cavendish Cres, Els. WD6 78 CN42
Hornchurch RM12 147 FH65
Cavendish Dr, E11 123 ED60
Claygate KT10 215 CE106
Edgware HA8 96 CM51
Cavendish Gdns, SW4 181 DJ86
Aveley RM15 168 FQ75
Barking IG11 125 ES64
Ilford IG1 125 EN60
Redhill RH1 250 DG133
Romford RM6 126 EY57
Cavendish Ms N, W1 285 K6
Cavendish Ms S, W1 285 K7
Cavendish Par, SW4
off Clapham Common S Side 181 DH86
Cavendish Pl, NW2 272 D5
W1 285 K8
Bromley BR1 205 EM97
Cavendish Prim Sch, W4
off Edensor Rd 158 CS80
Cavendish Rd, E4 101 EC51
N4 121 DN58
N18 100 DV50
NW6 272 F7
SW12 181 DH86
SW19 180 DD94
W4 158 CQ81
Barnet EN5 79 CW41
Chesham HP5 54 AR32
Croydon CR0 201 DP102
New Malden KT3 199 CT99
Redhill RH1 250 DG134
Saint Albans AL1 43 CF20
Sunbury-on-Thames TW16 175 BT93
Sutton SM2 218 DC108
Weybridge KT13 213 BQ108
Woking GU22 226 AX119
Cavendish Sch, The, NW1 275 K8
Hemel Hempstead HP1
off Warners End Rd 40 BH19
Cavendish Sq, W1 285 K8
Longfield DA3 209 FX97
Cavendish St, N1 287 L1
Cavendish Ter, Felt. TW13 175 BU89
Cavendish Wk, Epsom KT19 216 CP111
Cavendish Way, Hat. AL10 45 CT18
West Wickham BR4 203 EB102
Cavenham Cl, Wok. GU22 226 AY119
Cavenham Gdns, Horn. RM11 128 FJ57
Ilford IG1 125 ER62
Caverleigh Way, Wor.Pk. KT4 199 CU102
Cave Rd, E13 292 B1
Richmond TW10 177 CJ91
Caversham Av, N13 99 DN48
Sutton SM3 199 CY103
Caversham Ct, N11 98 DG48
Caversham Flats, SW3 308 E2
Caversham Rd, N15 122 DQ56
NW5 275 L4
Kingston upon Thames KT1 198 CM96
Caversham St, SW3 308 E2
Caverswall St, W12 282 A8
Caveside Cl, Chis. BR7 205 EN95
Cavill's Wk, Chig. IG7 104 EW47
Romford RM4 104 EX47
Cawcott Dr, Wind. SL4 151 AL81
Cawdor Av, S.Ock. RM15 149 FU73
Cawdor Cres, W7 157 CG77
Cawley Hatch, Harl. CM19 51 EM15
Cawnpore St, SE19 182 DS92
Cawsey Way, Wok. GU21 226 AY117
Caxton Av, Add. KT15 212 BG107
● **Caxton Cen**, St.Alb. AL3 43 CF15
Caxton Dr, Uxb. UB8 134 BK68
Caxton Gdns, Guil. GU2 242 AV133
Caxton Gro, E3 290 A2
Caxton Hill, Hert. SG13 32 DT09
Caxton Hill Ext Rd, Hert. SG13 32 DT09
Caxton La, Oxt. RH8 254 EL131
Caxton Ms, Brent. TW8
off The Butts 157 CK79
● **Caxton Pt Trading Est**,
Hayes UB3 155 BS75
Caxton Ri, Red. RH1 250 DG133
Caxton Rd, N22 99 DM54
SW19 180 DC92
W12 294 C4
Hoddesdon EN11 33 EB13
Southall UB2 156 BX76
Caxtons Ct, Guil. GU1 243 BA132
Caxton St, SW1 297 M6
Caxton St N, E16 291 L9
Caxton Way, Rom. RM1 127 FE56
Watford WD18 75 BR44
Cayenne Ct, SE1 300 B3
Cayford Ho, NW3 274 D2
Caygill Cl, Brom. BR2 204 EF98
Cayley Prim Sch, E14 289 L8
Cayley Rd, Sthl. UB2
off McNair Rd 156 CB76
Cayton Pl, EC1 287 L3
Cayton Rd, Couls. CR5 235 DJ122
Greenford UB6 137 CE68
Cayton St, EC1 287 L3
Cazenove Mans, N16
off Cazenove Rd 122 DU61
Cazenove Rd, E17 101 EA53
N16 122 DT61
Cearns Ho, E6 144 EK67
Cearn Way, Couls. CR5 235 DM115
Cecil Av, Bark. IG11 145 ER66
Enfield EN1 82 DT42
Grays RM16 170 FZ75
Hornchurch RM11 128 FL55
Wembley HA9 118 CM64
Cecil Cl, W5 137 CK71
Ashford TW15 175 BQ93
Chessington KT9 215 CK105
Cecil Ct, WC2 297 P1
Barnet EN5 79 CX41
Cecil Cres, Hat. AL10 45 CV16
Cecile Pk, N8 121 DL58
Cecilia Cl, N2 120 DC55
★ **Cecilia Colman Gall**, NW8 274 B10
Cecilia Rd, E8 278 C2
Cecil Manning Cl,
Perivale UB6 137 CG67
Cecil Pk, Pnr. HA5 116 BY56
Cecil Pl, Mitch. CR4 200 DF99
Cecil Rd, E11 124 EE62
E13 281 P8
E17 101 EA53
N10 99 DH54
N14 99 DJ46
NW9 118 CS55
NW10 138 CS67
SW19 180 DB94
W3 138 CQ71
Ashford TW15 175 BQ94
Cheshunt EN8 67 DX32
Croydon CR0 201 DM100
Enfield EN2 82 DR42
Gravesend DA11 191 GF88
Harrow HA3 117 CE55
Hertford SG13 32 DQ12
Hoddesdon EN11 49 EC15
Hounslow TW3 156 CC82
Ilford IG1 125 EP63
Iver SL0 133 BE72
Potters Bar EN6 63 CU32
Romford RM6 126 EX59
St. Albans AL1 43 CF20
Sutton SM1 217 CZ107
Cecil Rd Prim & Nurs Sch,
Grav. DA11
off Cecil Rd 191 GF88
★ **Cecil Sharp Ho**, NW1 275 H8
Cecil St, Wat. WD24 75 BV38
Cecil Way, Brom. BR2 204 EG102
Slough SL2 131 AM70
Cedar Av, Barn. EN4 98 DE45
Cobham KT11 230 BW115
Enfield EN3 82 DW40
Gravesend DA12 191 GJ91
Hayes UB3 135 BU72
Romford RM6 126 EY57
Ruislip HA4 136 BW65
Sidcup DA15 186 EU87
Twickenham TW2 176 CB86
Upminster RM14 128 FN63
Waltham Cross EN8 67 DX33
West Drayton UB7 134 BM74
Cedar Chase, Tap. SL6 130 AD70
Cedar Cl, E3 279 P8
SE21 182 DQ88
SW15 178 CR91
Borehamwood WD6 78 CP42
Bromley BR2 204 EL104
Buckhurst Hill IG9 102 EK47
Carshalton SM5 218 DF107
Chesham HP5 54 AS30
Dorking RH4 263 CH136
East Molesey KT8
off Cedar Rd 197 CE98
Epsom KT17 217 CT114
Esher KT10 214 BZ108
Hertford SG14 31 DP09
Hutton CM13 109 GD45
Ilford IG1 125 ER64
Iver SL0
off Thornbridge Rd 133 BC66
Potters Bar EN6 64 DA30
Reigate RH2 266 DC136
Romford RM7 127 FC56
Sawbridgeworth CM21 36 EY06
Staines-upon-Thames TW18 194 BJ97
Swanley BR8 207 FC96
Ware SG12 33 DX07
Warlingham CR6 237 DY119
Cedar Copse, Brom. BR1 205 EM96
Cedar Ct, E11
off Grosvenor Rd 124 EH57
N1 277 K6
SE7
off Fairlawn 164 EJ79
SE9 184 EL86
SW19 179 CX90
Egham TW20 173 BA91
Epping CM16 70 EU31
St. Albans AL4 43 CK20
Cedar Cres, Brom. BR2 204 EL104
Cedarcroft Rd, Chess. KT9 216 CM105
Cedar Dr, N2 120 DE56
Chesham HP5 54 AN30
Fetcham KT22 231 CE123
Loughton IG10 85 EP40
Pinner HA5 94 CA51
Sutton at Hone DA4 208 FP96
Cedar Gdns, Chobham GU24 210 AT110
Sutton SM2 218 DC107
Upminster RM14 128 FQ62
Woking GU21
off St. John's Rd 226 AV118
Cedar Grn, Hodd. EN11 49 EA18
Cedar Gro, W5 158 CL76
Amersham HP7 72 AR39
Bexley DA5 186 EW86
Southall UB1 136 CA71
Weybridge KT13 213 BQ105
Cedar Hts, Rich. TW10 178 CL88
Cedar Hill, Epsom KT18 232 CQ116
Cedar Ho, SW6
off Lensbury Ave 307 P8
Croy. CR0 221 EB107
Sunbury-on-Thames TW16 175 BT94
Cedarhurst, Brom. BR1 184 EE94
Cedarhurst Dr, SE9 184 EJ85
Cedar Lawn Av, Barn. EN5 79 CY43
Cedar Ms, SW15
off Cambalt Rd 179 CX85
Cedar Mt, SE9 184 EK88
Cedarne Rd, SW6 307 L5
Cedar Pk, Cat. CR3 236 DS121
Chigwell IG7
off High Rd 103 EP49
Cedar Pk Gdns, SW19 179 CV93
Rom. RM6 126 EX59
Cedar Pk Rd, Enf. EN2 82 DQ38
Cedar Pl, SE7 304 C10
Northwood HA6 93 BQ51
Cedar Ri, N14 98 DG45
South Ockendon RM15
off Sycamore Way 149 FX70
Cedar Rd, N17 100 DT53
NW2 119 CW63
Berkhamsted HP4 38 AX20
Bromley BR1 204 EJ96
Cobham KT11 213 BV114
Croydon CR0 202 DS103
Dartford DA1 188 FK88
East Molesey KT8 197 CE98
Enfield EN2 81 DP38
Erith DA8 167 FG81
Feltham TW14 175 BR88
Grays RM16 171 GG76
Hatfield AL10 45 CU19
Hornchurch RM12 128 FJ62
Hounslow TW4 156 BW82
Hutton CM13 109 GD44
Romford RM7 127 FC56
Sutton SM2 218 DC107
Teddington TW11 177 CG92
Watford WD19 76 BW44
Weybridge KT13 212 BN105
Woking GU22 226 AV120
Cedars, Bans. SM7 218 DF114
Cedars, The, E15 281 M8
W13 137 CJ72
Bookham KT23 246 CC126
Brockham RH3 248 CN134
Buckhurst Hill IG9 102 EG46
Byfleet KT14 212 BM112
Guildford GU1 243 BA131
Leatherhead KT22 232 CL121
Reigate RH2 250 DD134
Slough SL2 131 AM69
Teddington TW11
off Adelaide Rd 177 CF93
Cedars Av, E17 123 EA57
Mitcham CR4 200 DG98
Rickmansworth WD3 92 BJ46
Cedars Cl, NW4 119 CX55
SE13 163 ED83
Chalfont St. Peter SL9 90 AY50
Cedars Ct, N9 100 DT47
Cedars Dr, Uxb. UB10 134 BM68
Cedars Manor Sch, Har. HA3
off Whittlesea Rd 94 CC53
Cedars Ms, SW4 161 DH84
Cedars Prim Sch, The, Cran. TW5
off High St 155 BV80
Cedars Rd, E15 281 K4
N21 99 DP47
SW4 161 DH83
SW13 159 CT82
W4 158 CQ78
Beckenham BR3 203 DY96
Croydon CR0 201 DL104
Hampton Wick KT1 197 CJ95
Morden SM4 200 DA98
Cedars Wk, Chorl. WD3
off Badgers Wk 73 BF42
Cedar Ter, Rich. TW9 158 CL84
Cedar Ter Rd, Sev. TN13 257 FJ123
Cedar Tree Gro, SE27 181 DP92
Cedarville Gdns, SW16 181 DM93
Cedar Vista, Kew TW9 158 CL82
Cedar Wk, Clay. KT10 215 CF107
Hemel Hempstead HP3 40 BK22
Kenley CR8 236 DQ116
Kingswood KT20 233 CY120
Waltham Abbey EN9 67 ED34
Welwyn Garden City AL7 30 DB10
Cedar Way, NW1 275 N7
Berkhamsted HP4 38 AX20
Guildford GU1 242 AW132
Slough SL3 152 AY78
Sunbury-on-Thames TW16 175 BS94
● **Cedar Way Ind Est**, N1
off Cedar Way 275 N7
Cedarwood Dr, St.Alb. AL4 43 CK20
Cedar Wd Dr, Wat. WD25 75 BV35
Cedra Ct, N16 122 DU60
Cedric Av, Rom. RM1 127 FE55
Cedric Rd, SE9 185 EQ90
Celadon Cl, Enf. EN3 83 DY41
Celandine Cl, E14 290 A7
South Ockendon RM15 149 FW70
Celandine Dr, E8 278 B6
SE28 146 EV74
Celandine Gro, N14 81 DJ43
Celandine Rd, Hersham KT12 214 BY105
Celandine Way, E15 291 K2
Celbridge Ms, W2 283 M8
Celebration Av, E20 280 E3
Celebration Way, E4 101 EC51
Celedon Cl, Grays RM16 170 FY75
Celestial Gdns, SE13 163 ED84
Celia Cres, Ashf. TW15 174 BK93
Celia Rd, N19 275 M1
Cell Barnes Cl, St.Alb. AL1 43 CH22
Cell Barnes La, St.Alb. AL1 43 CH23
Cell Fm Av, Old Wind. SL4 172 AV85
Celtic Av, Brom. BR2 204 EE97
Celtic Rd, Byfleet KT14 212 BL114
Celtic St, E14 290 D6
Cement Block Cotts,
Grays RM17 170 GC79
Cemetery Hill, Hem.H. HP1 40 BJ21
Cemetery La, SE7 164 EL79
Lower Nazeing EN9 68 EF25
Shepperton TW17 195 BP101
Cemetery Rd, E7 281 L2
N17 100 DS52
SE2 166 EV80
Cemetery Way, E4 101 EA/
EB48
Cemmaes Ct Rd, Hem.H. HP1 40 BJ20
Cemmaes Meadow,
Hem.H. HP1 40 BJ20
Cenacle Cl, NW3 120 DA62
★ **Cenotaph, The**, SW1 298 A4
● **Centaurs Business Cen**,
Islw. TW7 157 CG79
Centaur St, SE1 298 D6
Centaurus Sq, Frog. AL2 61 CE27
Centaury Ct, Grays RM17 170 GD79
● **Centenary Ind Est**, Enf. EN3 83 DZ42
Centenary Rd, Enf. EN3 83 DZ42
Centenary Wk, Loug. IG10 84 EH41
Centenary Way, Amer. HP6 72 AT38
Centennial Av, Els. WD6 95 CH45
Centennial Ct, Els. WD6 95 CJ45
● **Centennial Pk**, Els. WD6 95 CJ45
Central Av, E11 123 ED61
N2 98 DD54
N9 100 DS48
SW11 308 E5
Aveley RM15 168 FQ75
Enfield EN1 82 DV40
Gravesend DA12 191 GH89
Grays RM20 169 FT77
Harlow CM20 35 ER14
Hayes UB3 135 BU73
Hounslow TW3 156 CC84
Pinner HA5 116 BZ58
Tilbury RM18 171 GG81
Wallington SM6 219 DL106
Waltham Cross EN8 67 DY33
Welling DA16 165 ET82
West Molesey KT8 196 BZ98
● **Central Business Cen**, NW10
off Great Cen Way 118 CS64
Central Circ, NW4
off Hendon Way 119 CV57
★ **Central Criminal Ct**,
(Old Bailey), EC4 287 H8
Central Dr, Horn. RM12 128 FL62
St. Albans AL4 43 CJ19
Slough SL1 131 AM73
Welwyn Garden City AL7 29 CZ07
Centrale 202 DQ103
Centrale Shop Cen,
Croy. CR0 202 DQ103
Central Foundation Boys' Sch, EC2 287 M4
Central Foundation Girls' Sch,
Lwr Sch, E3 289 M2
Upr Sch, E3 289 P3
Central Gdns, Mord. SM4 200 DB99
Central Hill, SE19 182 DR92
Central Ho, E15 280 D10
Barking IG11
off Cambridge Rd 145 EQ66
Central Middlesex Hosp,
NW10 138 CQ69
Central Par, E17
off Hoe St 123 EA56
Feltham TW14 176 BW87
Hounslow TW5
off Heston Rd 156 CA80
New Addington CR0 221 EC110
Perivale UB6 137 CG69
Surbiton KT6 198 CL100
Central Pk Av, Dag. RM10 127 FB62
● **Central Pk Est**, Houns. TW4 176 BX85
Central Pk Prim Sch, E6 292 F1
Central Pk Rd, E6 292 D1
Central Pl, SE25
off Portland Rd 202 DV98
Central Prim Sch, Wat. WD17
off Derby Rd 76 BW42
Central Rd, Dart. DA1 188 FL85
Harlow CM20 36 EU11
Morden SM4 200 DA100
Wembley HA0 117 CH64
Worcester Park KT4 199 CU103
Central St. Martins Coll of Art & Design, Back Hill Site, EC1 286 F5
Byam Shaw Sch of Art, N19
off Elthorne Rd 121 DK61
King's Cross, N1 276 A9
Central Sch Footpath, SW14 158 CQ83
Central Sch of Ballet, EC1 286 F5
Central Sch of Speech & Drama, NW3 274 A6
Central Sq, NW11 120 DB58
Wembley HA9
off Station Gro 118 CL64
West Molesey KT8 196 BZ98
Central St, EC1 287 J3
Central Wk, Epsom KT19
off Station App 216 CR113
Central Way, NW10 138 CQ69
SE28 146 EU74
Carshalton SM5 218 DE108
Feltham TW14 175 BU85
Oxted RH8 253 ED127
Central West, Grnf. UB6 136 CC70
● **Centrapark**, Welw.G.C. AL7 29 CY08
Centre, The, Felt. TW13
off High St 175 BV88
Centre, The, Walt. KT12 195 BT102
Centre Av, W3 138 CR74
W10 282 B3
Epping CM16 69 ET32
Centre Cl, Epp. CM16 69 ET32
Centre Common Rd, Chis. BR7 185 EQ93
Centre Ct Shop Cen, SW19 179 CZ93
Centre Dr, Epp. CM16 69 ET32
Centre Grn, Epp. CM16
off Centre Av 69 ET32
● **Centrepoint**, WC1 285 P8
Centre Pt, SE1 300 C10
Centre Rd, E7 124 EG61
E11 124 EG61
Dagenham RM10 147 FB68
Windsor SL4 150 AJ80
Centre St, E2 288 E1
Centre Way, E17 101 EC52
N9 100 DW47
Centreway Apts, Ilf. IG1
off High Rd 125 EQ61
Centric Cl, NW1 275 J8
Centrillion Pt, Croy. CR0
off Masons Av 220 DQ105
Centrium, Wok. GU22 226 AY117
Centurion Bldg, SW8 309 J3
Centurion Cl, N7 276 C6
Centurion Ct, SE18 305 K9
Hackbridge SM6
off Wandle Rd 201 DH104
Romford RM1 127 FD55
St. Albans AL1 *off Camp Rd* 43 CG21
Centurion La, E3 279 P10
Centurion Sq, SE18 164 EL81
Centurion Way, Erith DA18 166 FA76
Purfleet RM19 168 FM77
Century Cl, NW4 119 CX57
St. Albans AL3 42 CC19
Century Ct, Wok. GU21 227 AZ116
Century Gdns, S.Croy. CR2 220 DU113
Century Ms, E5 278 G1
N5 121 DP62
Century Pk, Wat. WD17 76 BW43
Century Rd, E17 123 DY55
Hoddesdon EN11 49 EA16
Staines-upon-Thames TW18 173 BC92
Ware SG12 33 DX05
Century Yd, SE23 182 DW89
Cephas Av, E1 289 H4
Cephas St, E1 288 G5
Ceres Rd, SE18 165 ET77

Cerise Rd, SE15 312 D7
Cerne Cl, Hayes UB4 136 BW73
Cerne Rd, Grav. DA12 191 GL91
Morden SM4 200 DC100
Cerney Ms, W2 284 A10
Cerotus Pl, Cher. KT16 193 BF101
Cervantes Ct, W2 283 M9
Northwood HA6
off Green La 93 BT52
Cervia Way, Grav. DA12 191 GM90
Cester St, E2 278 C9
Cestreham Cres, Chesh. HP5 54 AR29
Ceylon Rd, W14 294 D7
Cezanne Rd, Wat. WD25 76 BW36
Chabot Dr, SE15 162 DV83
Chace Av, Pot.B. EN6 64 DD32
Sch Chace Comm Sch, Enf. EN1
off Churchbury La 82 DS39
Chacombe Pl, Beac. HP9 89 AK50
Chadacre Av, Ilf. IG5 125 EM55
Chadacre Rd, Epsom KT17 217 CV107
Chadbourn St, E14 290 D7
Chad Cres, N9 100 DW48
Chadd Dr, Brom. BR1 204 EL97
Chadd Grn, E13 281 N9
Chadfields, Til. RM18 171 GG80
Chadhurst Cl, N.Holm. RH5
off Wildcroft Dr 263 CK139
Chadview Ct, Chad.Hth RM6 126 EX59
Chadville Gdns, Rom. RM6 126 EX57
Chadway, Dag. RM8 126 EW60
Chadwell, Ware SG12 32 DW07
Chadwell Av, Chsht EN8 66 DW28
Romford RM6 126 EV59
Chadwell Bypass, Grays RM16 171 GF78
CHADWELL HEATH,
Rom. RM6 126 EX58
⇌ Chadwell Heath 126 EX59
Sch Chadwell Heath Foundation Sch, The,
Chad.Hth RM6
off Christie Gdns 126 EV58
● Chadwell Heath Ind Pk,
Dag. RM8 126 EY60
Chadwell Heath La, Rom. RM6 126 EV57
Chadwell Hill, Grays RM16 171 GH78
Chadwell La, N8 121 DM55
Sch Chadwell Prim Sch, Chad.Hth RM6
off High Rd 126 EW59
Chadwell Ri, Ware SG12 32 DW07
Chadwell Rd, Grays RM17 170 GC77
Sch Chadwell St. Mary Prim Sch,
Chad.St.M. RM16
off River Vw 171 GH77
CHADWELL ST. MARY,
Grays RM16 171 GJ76
Chadwell St, EC1 286 F2
Chadwick Av, E4 101 ED49
N21 81 DM42
SW19 180 DA93
Chadwick Cl, SW15 179 CT87
W7 off Westcott Cres 137 CF71
Northfleet DA11 190 GE89
Teddington TW11 177 CG93
Chadwick Dr, Harold Wd RM3 106 FK54
Chadwick Ms, W4
off Thames Rd 158 CP79
Chadwick Pl, Long Dit. KT6 197 CJ101
Chadwick Rd, E11 124 EE59
NW10 139 CT67
SE15 312 A9
Ilford IG1 125 EP62
Slough SL3 152 AX75
Chadwick St, SW1 297 P7
Chadwick Way, SE28 146 EX73
Chadwin Rd, E13 292 A6
Chadworth Way, Clay. KT10 215 CD106
Chaffers Mead, Ashtd. KT21 232 CM116
Chaffinch Av, Croy. CR0 203 DX100
● Chaffinch Business Pk,
Beck. BR3 203 DX98
Chaffinch Cl, N9 101 DX46
Croydon CR0 203 DX99
Surbiton KT6 198 CN104
Chaffinches Grn, Hem.H. HP3 40 BN24
Chaffinch La, Wat. WD18 93 BT45
Chaffinch Rd, Beck. BR3 203 DY95
Chaffinch Way, Horl. RH6 268 DE147
CHAFFORD HUNDRED,
Grays RM16 169 FX76
⇌ Chafford Hundred 169 FV77
Sch Chafford Hundred Prim Sch,
Grays RM16
off Mayflower Rd 169 FW78
Sch Chafford Sch, The, Rain. RM13
off Lambs La S 148 FJ71
Chafford Wk, Rain. RM13 148 FJ68
Chafford Way, Rom. RM6 126 EW56
Chagford St, NW1 284 E5
Chailey Av, Enf. EN1 82 DT40
Chailey Cl, Houns. TW5
off Springwell Rd 156 BX81
Chailey Pl, Hersham KT12 214 BY105
Chailey St, E5 122 DW62
Chalbury Wk, N1 276 D10
Chalcombe Rd, SE2 166 EV76
Chalcot Cl, Sutt. SM2 218 DA108
Chalcot Cres, NW1 274 F8
Chalcot Gdns, NW3 274 E5
Chalcot Ms, SW16 181 DL90
Chalcot Rd, NW1 274 G7
Chalcot Sq, NW1 274 G7
Chalcott Gdns, Long Dit. KT6 197 CJ102
Chalcroft Rd, SE13 184 EE85
CHALDON, Cat. CR3 235 DN124
Chaldon Cl, Red. RH1 266 DE136
Chaldon Common Rd,
Chaldon CR3 236 DQ124
Chaldon Path, Th.Hth. CR7 201 DP98
Chaldon Rd, SW6 306 E4
Caterham CR3 236 DR124
Chaldon Way, Couls. CR5 235 DL117
Chale Rd, SW2 181 DL86
Chalet Cl, Berk. HP4 38 AT19
Bexley DA5 187 FD91
Chalet Est, NW7 97 CU49
Chale Wk, Sutt. SM2
off Hulverston Cl 218 DB109
⇌ Chalfont & Latimer 72 AW39
⊖ Chalfont & Latimer 72 AW39
Chalfont Av, Amer. HP6 72 AX39
Wembley HA9 138 CP65
Chalfont Cen for Epilepsy,
Chal.St.P. SL9 90 AY49
Chalfont Cl, Hem.H. HP2 41 BP15
CHALFONT COMMON,
Ger.Cr. SL9 91 AZ49
Chalfont Ct, NW9 119 CT55
Chalfont Grn, N9 100 DS48
● Chalfont Gro, Chal.St.P. SL9 90 AV51

Chalfont La, Chorl. WD3 73 BB43
Gerrards Cross SL9 91 BC51
West Hyde WD3 91 BC51
Chalfont Ms, SW19
off Augustus Rd 179 CZ88
Uxb. UB10 135 BP66
● Chalfont Pk, Chal.St.P. SL9 113 AZ55
Chalfont Rd, N9 100 DS48
SE25 202 DT97
Chalfont St. Giles HP8 91 BB48
Gerrards Cross SL9 91 BB48
Hayes UB3 155 BU75
Maple Cross WD3 91 BD49
Seer Green HP9 89 AR50
Sch Chalfont St. Giles Inf Sch & Nurs,
Ch.St.G. HP8 off School La 90 AV48
Sch Chalfont St. Giles Jun Sch,
Ch.St.G. HP8
off Parsonage Rd 90 AV48
Sch Chalfont St. Peter C of E Sch,
Chal.St.P. SL9
off Penn Rd 90 AX53
Sch Chalfont St. Peter Inf Sch,
Chal.St.P. SL9
off Lovel End 90 AW52
H Chalfonts & Gerrards Cross Hosp,
Chal.St.P. SL9 90 AX53
Sch Chalfonts Comm Coll,
Chal.St.P. SL9 off Narcot La 90 AW52
Chalfont Sta Rd, Amer. HP7 72 AW40
CHALFONT ST. GILES, HP8 90 AV47
CHALFONT ST. PETER,
Ger.Cr. SL9 91 AZ53
Chalfont Wk, Pnr. HA5
off Willows Cl 94 BW54
Chalfont Way, W13 157 CH76
Chalford Cl, W.Mol. KT8 196 CA98
Chalforde Gdns, Rom. RM2 127 FH56
Chalford Flats,
Woob.Grn HP10 110 AE57
Chalford Rd, SE21 182 DR91
Chalford Wk, Wdf.Grn. IG8 102 EK53
Chalgrove, Welw.G.C. AL7 30 DD08
Chalgrove Av, Mord. SM4 200 DA99
Chalgrove Cres, Ilf. IG5 102 EL54
Chalgrove Gdns, N3 119 CY55
Sch Chalgrove Prim Sch, N3
off Chalgrove Gdns 119 CY55
Chalgrove Rd, N17 100 DV53
Sutton SM2 218 DD108
Chalice Cl, Wall. SM6
off Lavender Vale 219 DK107
Chalice Way, Green. DA9 189 FS85
Chalk Ct, Grays RM17 170 GA79
Chalk Dale, Welw.G.C. AL7 30 DB08
Chalk Dell, Rick. WD3
off Orchard Way 92 BG45
Chalkdell Flds, St.Alb. AL4 43 CG16
Chalkdell Hill, Hem.H. HP2 40 BL20
Chalkenden Cl, SE20 182 DV94
Jct Chalkers Cor, SW14 158 CP83
⊖ Chalk Farm 274 F6
Chalk Fm Rd, NW1 274 G6
Chalk Hill, Chesh. HP5 54 AP29
Coleshill HP7 89 AM45
Watford WD19 76 BX44
Sch Chalkhill Prim Sch, Wem. HA9
off Barnhill Rd 118 CP62
Chalk Hill Rd, W6 294 C9
Chalkhill Rd, Wem. HA9 118 CP62
Chalklands, Wem. HA9 118 CQ62
Chalk La, Ashtd. KT21 232 CM119
Barnet EN4 80 DF42
East Horsley KT24 245 BT130
Epsom KT18 232 CR115
Harlow CM17 36 FA14
Chalkley Cl, Mitch. CR4 200 DF96
Chalkmill Dr, Enf. EN1 82 DV41
Chalk Paddock, Epsom KT18 232 CR115
Chalk Pit Av, Orp. BR5 206 EW97
Chalk Pit La, Burn. SL1 130 AH66
Chalkpit La, Bet. RH3 248 CP133
Bookham KT23 246 BZ128
Dorking RH4 263 CG135
Oxted RH8 253 EC125
Woldingham CR3 253 EC125
Chalk Pit Rd, Bans. SM7 234 DA117
Epsom KT18 232 CQ119
Chalkpit Ter, Dor. RH4 247 CG134
Chalk Pit Way, Sutt. SM1 218 DC106
Chalkpit Wd, Oxt. RH8 253 ED127
Chalk Rd, E13 292 B6
Chalkstone Cl, Well. DA16 166 EU81
Chalkstream Way, Woob.Grn HP10
off Glory Mill La 110 AE56
Chalkwell Pk Av, Enf. EN1 82 DS42
Chalky Bk, Grav. DA11 191 GG91
Chalky La, Chess. KT9 215 CK109
Challacombe Cl, Hutt. CM13 109 GB46
Challenge Cl, NW10 138 CS67
Gravesend DA12 191 GM91
Challenge Ct, Lthd. KT22 231 CH119
Twickenham TW2
off Langhorn Dr 177 CE87
Challenge Rd, Ashf. TW15 175 BQ90
Challice Way, SW2 181 DM88
Challinor, Harl. CM17 52 EY15
Challin St, SE20 202 DW95
Challis Rd, Brent. TW8 157 CK78
Challock Cl, Bigg.H. TN16 238 EJ116
Challoner Cl, N2 98 DD54
Challoner Cres, W14 306 G1
Challoners Cl, E.Mol. KT8 197 CD98
Challoner St, W14 294 G10
Chalmers Ct, Crox.Grn WD3 74 BM44
Chalmers Ho, SW11
off York Rd 160 DC83
Chalmers Rd, Ashf. TW15 175 BP91
Banstead SM7 234 DD115
Chalmers Rd E, Ashf. TW15 175 BP91
Chalmers Wk, SE17 311 H3
Chalmers Way, Felt. TW14 175 BV85
Twick. TW1 157 CH84
Chaloner Ct, SE1 299 L4
Chalsey Rd, SE4 163 DZ84
Chalton Dr, N2 120 DC58
Chalton St, NW1 285 P2
CHALVEY, Slou. SL1 151 AQ76
Chalvey Gdns, Slou. SL1 152 AS75
Chalvey Gro, Slou. SL1 151 AP75
Chalvey Pk, Slou. SL1 152 AS75
Chalvey Rd E, Slou. SL1 152 AS75
Chalvey Rd W, Slou. SL1 151 AR75
Chamberlain Cl, SE28
off Broadwater Rd 165 ER76
Harlow CM17 52 EW15
Hayes UB3 135 BT73
Ilford IG1 off Richmond Rd 125 EQ62
Chamberlain Cotts, SE5 311 M7

Chamberlain Cres,
W.Wick. BR4 203 EB102
Chamberlain Gdns,
Houns. TW3 156 CC81
Chamberlain La, Pnr. HA5 115 BU56
Chamberlain Pl, E17 123 DY55
Chamberlain Rd, N2 98 DC54
W13 off Midhurst Rd 157 CG75
Chamberlain St, NW1 274 F7
Chamberlain Wk, Felt. TW13
off Burgess Cl 176 BY91
Chamberlain Way, Pnr. HA5 115 BV55
Surbiton KT6 198 CL101
Chamberlayne Av, Wem. HA9 118 CL61
Chamberlayne Rd, NW10 282 C2
Chambers Av, Sid. DA14 186 EY93
Chambersbury La, Hem.H. HP3 58 BN25
Sch Chambersbury Prim Sch, Hem.H. HP3
off Hill Common 40 BN23
● Chambers Business Pk,
West Dr. UB7 154 BN79
Chambers Cl, Green. DA9 189 FU85
Chambers Gdns, N2 98 DD53
Chambers Gro, Welw.G.C. AL7 29 CY12
Chambers Ho, SW16
off Pringle Gdns 181 DJ91
Chambers La, NW10 139 CV66
Chambers Manor Ms,
Epp.Upl. CM16 69 EP26
Chambers Pl, S.Croy. CR2
off Rolleston Rd 220 DR108
Chambers Rd, N7 121 DL63
Chambers St, SE16 300 C4
Hertford SG14 32 DQ09
Chamber St, E1 288 B10
Chambers Wk, Stan. HA7 95 CH50
Chambon Pl, W6 off Beavor La 159 CU77
Chambord St, E2 288 B3
Chamers Ct, W12
off Heathstan Rd 139 CU72
Champa Cl, N17 100 DT54
Champion Cres, SE26 183 DY91
Champion Down, Eff. KT24
off Norwood Cl 246 BY128
Champion Gro, SE5 311 M10
Champion Hill, SE5 311 M10
Champion Hill Est, SE5 162 DS83
Champion Pk, SE5 311 L9
Champion Pk Est, SE5 311 M10
Champion Rd, SE26 183 DY91
Upminster RM14 128 FP61
Champions Grn, Hodd. EN11 33 EA14
Champions Way, NW4 97 CV53
NW7 97 CV53
Hoddesdon EN11 33 EA14
Champness Cl, SE27 182 DR91
Champness Rd, Bark. IG11 145 ET65
Champney Cl, Horton SL3 153 BA83
Champneys Cl, Sutt. SM2 217 CZ108
Chance Cl, Grays RM16 170 FZ76
Chancellor Gdns, S.Croy. CR2 219 DP109
Chancellor Gro, SE21 182 DQ89
Chancellor Pas, E14 302 B3
Chancellor Pl, NW9 97 CT54
Chancellors Ct, WC1
off Orde Hall St 286 C6
Chancellors Rd, W6 306 A1
Sch Chancellor's Sch, Brook.Pk AL9
off Pine Gro 64 DB25
Chancellors St, W6 306 A1
Chancellors Wf, W6 306 A1
Chancellor Way, Dag. RM8 126 EU63
Sevenoaks TN13 256 FG122
Chancelot Rd, SE2 166 EV77
Chancel St, SE1 298 G2
Chancery Cl, St.Alb. AL4 43 CK15
Chancery Ct, Dart. DA1 188 FN87
Egham TW20
off The Chantries 173 BA92
● Chancerygate Business Cen,
Slou. SL3 152 AY75
● Chancery Gate Business Cen,
Sthl. UB2 156 BW76
Chancerygate Cl, Ruis. HA4 116 BY64
Chancerygate Way, Ruis. HA4 116 BY63
⊖ Chancery Lane 286 E7
Chancery La, WC2 286 E8
Beckenham BR3 203 EB96
Chancery Ms, SW17 180 DE89
Chance St, E1 288 A4
E2 288 A4
Chanctonbury Chase,
Red. RH1 251 DH134
Chanctonbury Cl, SE9 185 EP90
Chanctonbury Gdns,
Sutt. SM2 218 DB108
Chanctonbury Way, N12 97 CZ49
Chandler Av, E16 291 N6
Chandler Cl, Hmptn. TW12 196 CA95
Chandler Rd, Loug. IG10 85 EP39
Chandlers Av, SE10 303 M6
Chandlers Cl, Felt. TW14 175 BT87
CHANDLERS CROSS,
Rick. WD3 74 BM38
Chandlers Dr, Erith DA8 167 FD77
Sch Chandlers Fld Prim Sch, W.Mol. KT8
off High St 196 CA99
Chandler's La, Chan.Cr. WD3 74 BL37
Chandlers Ms, E14 302 A4
Greenhithe DA9 169 FW84
Chandlers Rd, St.Alb. AL4 43 CJ17
Chandler St, E1 300 F2
Chandlers Way, SW2 181 DN87
Hertford SG14 31 DN09
Romford RM1 127 FE57
Chandler Way, SE15 311 P3
Dorking RH5 263 CJ138
Chandon Lo, Sutt. SM2
off Devonshire Rd 218 DC108
Chandos Av, E17 101 EA54
N14 99 DJ48
N20 98 DC46
W5 157 CJ77
Chandos Cl, Amer. HP6 72 AW38
Buckhurst Hill IG9 102 EH47
Chandos Ct, N14 99 DK47
Stan. HA7 95 CH51
Chandos Cres, Edg. HA8 96 CM52
Chandos Gdns, Couls. CR5 235 DP119
Chandos Pl, WC2 298 A1
Chandos Rd, E15 280 G2
N2 98 DD54
N17 100 DS54
NW2 272 A3
NW10 138 CS70
Borehamwood WD6 78 CM40
Harrow HA1 116 CC57
Pinner HA5 116 BW59
Staines-upon-Thames TW18 173 BD92

Chandos St, W1 285 K7
Chandos Way, NW11 120 DB60
Change All, EC3 287 M9
Chanlock Path, S.Ock. RM15
off Carnach Grn 149 FV73
Channel Cl, Houns. TW5 156 CA81
Channel Gate Rd, NW10
off Old Oak La 139 CT69
Channel Ho, E14 289 L7
SE16 off Canada St 301 J5
Channel Islands Est, N1 277 K5
● Channelsea Ho Business Cen,
E15 291 H1
Channelsea Rd, E15 280 G8
Channing Cl, Horn. RM11 128 FM59
Channings, Horsell GU21 226 AY115
Sch Channing Sch for Girls, Jun Sch, N6
off Highgate High St 121 DH60
Sen Sch, N6
off Highgate High St 121 DH60
Chantilly Way, Epsom KT19 216 CP110
Chanton Dr, Epsom KT17 217 CW110
Sutton SM2 217 CW110
Chantress Cl, Dag. RM10 147 FC67
Chantrey Cl, Ashtd. KT21 231 CJ119
Chantrey Rd, SW9 161 DM83
Chantreywood, Brwd. CM13 109 GA48
Chantries, The, Egh. TW20 173 BA92
Chantry, The, E4
off The Ridgeway 101 EC46
Harlow CM20 36 EU13
Uxbridge UB8 134 BM69
Chantry Cl, NW7
off Hendon Wd La 79 CT44
SE2 off Felixstowe Rd 166 EW76
W9 283 H5
Enfield EN2 82 DQ38
Harrow HA3 118 CM57
Horley RH6 268 DF147
Kings Langley WD4 58 BN29
Sidcup DA14
off Ellenborough Rd 186 EY92
Sunbury-on-Thames TW16 175 BU94
West Drayton UB7 134 BK73
Windsor SL4 151 AN81
Chantry Cotts, Chilw. GU4 259 BB140
Chantry Ct, Cars. SM5 200 DE104
Hatfield AL10 45 CT19
Chantry Cres, NW10 139 CT65
Chantry Hurst, Epsom KT18 232 CR115
Chantry La, Brom. BR2
off Bromley Common 204 EK99
Hatfield AL10 45 CT19
London Colney AL2 61 CK26
Shere GU5 260 BM139
Chantry Pl, Har. HA3 94 CB53
Sch Chantry Prim Sch, Grav. DA12
off Ordnance Rd 191 GJ86
Chantry Rd, Cher. KT16 194 BJ101
Chessington KT9 216 CM106
Chilworth GU4 259 BB140
Harrow HA3 94 CB53
Sch Chantry Sch, The, Yiew. UB7
off Falling La 134 BL73
Chantry Sq, W8
off St. Mary's Pl 295 L7
Chantry St, N1 277 H9
Chantry Vw Rd, Guil. GU1 258 AX137
Chantry Way, Mitch. CR4
off Church Rd 200 DD97
Chant Sq, E15 281 H7
Chant St, E15 281 H7
Chapel Av, Add. KT15 212 BH105
Chapel Cl, NW10 119 CT64
Brookmans Park AL9 64 DD27
Dartford DA1 187 FE85
Grays RM20 169 FV79
Watford WD25 59 BT34
Chapel Cotts, Hem.H. HP2 40 BK18
Chapel Ct, N2 120 DE55
SE1 299 L4
SE18 165 ET79
Dorking RH4 263 CG135
Chapel Cft, Chipper. WD4 58 BG31
Chapel Cfts, Nthch HP4 38 AS17
Chapel End, Chal.St.P. SL9 90 AX54
Hoddesdon EN11 49 EA18
Sch Chapel End Inf & Jun Schs, E17
off Beresford Rd 101 EB53
Chapel Fm Rd, SE9 185 EM90
Chapel Fld, Harl. CM17 52 EW17
Chapelfields, Stans.Abb. SG12 33 ED10
Chapel Gate Ms, SW4
off Bedford Rd 161 DL83
Chapel Gro, Add. KT15 212 BH105
Epsom KT18 233 CW119
Chapel Hill, Dart. DA1 187 FE85
Effingham KT24
off The Street 246 BX127
Chapelhouse Cl, Guil. GU2 242 AS134
Chapel Ho St, E14 302 D10
Chapelier Ho, SW18
off Eastfields Av 160 DA84
Chapel La, Bkhm KT23 246 CC128
Chigwell IG7 103 ET48
Harlow CM17 52 EW17
Letty Green SG14 31 DH13
Pinner HA5 116 BX55
Romford RM6 126 EX59
Stoke Poges SL2 132 AV66
Uxbridge UB8 134 BN72
Westcott RH4 262 CC137
Westhumble RH5 247 CD130
Chapel Mkt, N1 276 E10
Chapel Ms, Wdf.Grn. IG8 103 EN51
Chapel Mill Rd, Kings.T. KT1 198 CM97
Chapelmount Rd,
Wdf.Grn. IG8 103 EM51
Chapel Pk Rd, Add. KT15 212 BH105
Chapel Path, E11 124 EG58
Chapel Pl, EC2 287 N3
N1 276 F10
N17 off White Hart La 100 DT52
W1 285 J9
St. Albans AL1 43 CD23
Chapel Rd, SE27 181 DP91
W13 137 CH74
Bexleyheath DA7 166 FA84
Epping CM16 69 ET30
Hounslow TW3 156 CB83
Ilford IG1 125 EN62
Oxted RH8 254
EJ130 Redhill RH1 250 DF134
Smallfield RH6 269 DP148
Tadworth KT20 233 CW123
Twickenham TW1 177 CH87
Warlingham CR6 237 DX118
Chapel Row, Hare. UB9 92 BJ53
Chapels Cl, Slou. SL1 131 AL74

Chapel Side, W2 283 L10
Chapel Sq, Vir.W. GU25 192 AY98
Chapel Stones, N17 100 DT53
Chapel St, NW1 284 C7
SW1 297 H6
Berkhamsted HP4 38 AW19
Enfield EN2 82 DQ41
Guildford GU1 off Castle St 258 AX136
Hemel Hempstead HP2 40 BK19
Slough SL1 152 AT75
Uxbridge UB8
off Trumper Way 134 BJ67
Woking GU21 227 AZ117
Chapel Ter, Loug. IG10
off Forest Rd 84 EL42
Chapel Vw, S.Croy. CR2 220 DV107
Chapel Wk, Croy. CR0
off Whitgift Cen 202 DQ103
Chapel Wk, NW4 119 CV56
Bexley DA5 187 FE89
Coulsdon CR5 235 DK122
Dartford DA2 187 FE89
Chapel Way, N7
off Sussex Way 121 DM62
Bedmond WD5 59 BT27
Epsom KT18 233 CW119
Chapel Yd, SW18
off Wandsworth High St 180 DA85
Chaplaincy Gdns, Horn. RM11 128 FL60
Chaplin Cl, SE1 298 F4
Chaplin Ct, Sutt.H. DA4 188 FN93
Chaplin Cres, Sun. TW16 175 BS93
Chaplin Ms, Slou. SL3 153 AZ78
Chaplin Rd, E15 281 K10
N17 122 DT55
NW2 139 CU65
Dagenham RM9 146 EY66
Wembley HA0 137 CJ65
Chaplin Sq, N12 98 DD52
Chapman Cl, West Dr. UB7 154 BM76
Chapman Ct, Dart. DA1 168 FM82
Chapman Ctyd, Chsht EN8 67 DX30
Chapman Cres, Har. HA3 118 CL57
● Chapman Pk Ind Est, NW10 139 CT65
Chapman Pl, N4 121 DP61
Chapman Rd, E9 279 P5
Belvedere DA17 166 FA78
Croydon CR0 201 DN102
Chapmans Cl, Sund. TN14 240 EY124
Chapmans Cres, Chesh. HP5 54 AN29
Chapmans La, Orp. BR5 206 EX96
Chapman's La, SE2 166 EW77
Belvedere DA17 166 EX77
Chapman Sq, SW19 179 CX89
Chapmans Rd, Sund. TN14 240 EY124
Chapman St, E1 288 E10
Chapone Pl, W1 285 N9
Chapter Chambers, SW1
off Chapter St 297 N9
Chapter Cl, W4 158 CQ76
Uxbridge UB10 134 BM66
Chapter Ct, Egh. TW20
off The Chantries 173 BA92
Chapter Ho Ct, EC4 287 J9
Chapter Ms, Wind. SL4 151 AR80
Chapter Rd, NW2 119 CU64
SE17 311 H1
Chapter St, SW1 297 N9
Chapter Way, SW19 200 DC95
Hampton TW12 176 CA91
Chara Pl, W4 158 CR79
Charcot Ho, SW15
off Highcliffe Dr 179 CT86
Charcot Rd, NW9 96 CS54
Charcroft Gdns, Enf. EN3 83 DX42
Chardin Rd, W4
off Elliott Rd 158 CS77
Chardins Cl, Hem.H. HP1 39 BF19
Chardmore Rd, N16 122 DU60
Chard Rd, Lon.Hthrw Air. TW6
off Heathrow Tunnel App 155 BP82
Chardwell Cl, E6 293 J8
Charecroft Way, W12 294 C5
W14 294 C5
Charfield Ct, W9 283 L5
Charford Rd, E16 291 P7
Chargate Cl, Hersham KT12 213 BT107
Chargeable La, E13 291 M4
Chargeable St, E16 291 M4
Chargrove Cl, SE16 301 K4
Charing Cl, Orp. BR6 223 ET105
⇌ Charing Cross 298 A2
⊖ Charing Cross 298 A2
Charing Cross, SW1 297 P2
H Charing Cross Hosp, W6 306 C2
Charing Cross Rd, WC2 285 P8
Chariot Cl, E3 280 A9
Chariotts Pl, Wind. SL4
off Victoria St 151 AR81
Charkham Ms, N.Mymms AL9 45 CW24
Charlbert St, NW8 274 C10
Charlbury Av, Stan. HA7 95 CK50
Charlbury Cl, Rom. RM3 106 FJ51
Charlbury Cres, Rom. RM3 106 FJ51
Charlbury Gdns, Ilf. IG3 125 ET61
Charlbury Gro, W5 137 CJ72
Charlbury Ho, E12
off Grantham Rd 125 EN62
Charlbury Rd, Uxb. UB10 114 BM62
Charlcot Ms, Slou. SL1 131 AL73
Charldane Rd, SE9 185 EP90
Charlecote Gro, SE26 182 DV90
Charlecote Rd, Dag. RM8 126 EY62
Charlemont Rd, E6 293 K4
Charles Babbage Cl,
Chess. KT9 215 CJ108
Charles Barry Cl, SW4 309 M10
Charles Burton Ct, E5 279 L1
Charles Ch Wk, Ilf. IG1 125 EM58
Charles Cl, Sid. DA14 186 EV91
Charles Cobb Gdns, Croy. CR0 219 DN106
Charles Coveney Rd, SE15 312 A6
Charles Cres, Har. HA1 117 CD59
Sch Charles Darwin Sch, Bigg.H. TN16
off Jail La 239 EM116
Charles Dickens Ho, E2 288 E3
★ Charles Dickens Mus, WC1 286 D4
Sch Charles Dickens Prim Sch, SE1 299 J5
Charles Dickens Ter, SE20
off Maple Rd 182 DW94
Sch Charles Edward Brooke C of E
Girls' Sch, Lwr Sch, SE5 310 G7
Upr Sch, SW9 311 H6
Charlesfield, SE9 184 EJ90

C

C

Charlesfield Rd, Horl. RH6 268 DF147
Charles Flemwell Ms, E16 303 P3
Charles Gdns, Slou. SL2 132 AV72
Charles Gardner Ct, N1 287 M2
Charles Grinling Wk, SE18 305 L8
Charles Gro, N14 99 DJ46
Charles Haller St, SW2
off Tulse Hill 181 DN87
Charles Hocking Ho, W3
off Bollo Br Rd 158 CQ75
Charles Ho, N17
off Love La 100 DT52
Chertsey KT16
off Guildford St 193 BF102
Windsor SL4
off Ward Royal 151 AQ81
Charles La, NW8 284 B1
Charles Mackenzie Ho, SE16
off Linsey St 300 C8
Charlesmere Gdns, SE28
off Battery Rd 165 ES75
Charles Nex Ms, SE21 182 DQ89
Charles Pl, E4 101 ED45
NW1 285 M3
Charles Rd, E7
off Lens Rd 144 EJ66
SW19 200 DA95
W13 137 CG72
Badgers Mount TN14 225 FB110
Dagenham RM10 147 FD65
Romford RM6 126 EX59
Staines-upon-Thames TW18 174 BK93
Charles Rowan Ho, WC1 286 E3
Charles II Pl, SW3
off King's Rd 308 E1
Charles II St, SW1 297 N2
Charles Sevright Dr, NW7 97 CX50
Charles Sq, N1 287 M3
Charles Sq Est, N1 287 M3
Charles St, N19 121 DL60
SW13 158 CS82
W1 297 J2
Berkhamsted HP4 38 AV19
Chertsey KT16 193 BF102
Croydon CR0 202 DQ104
Enfield EN1 82 DT43
Epping CM16 70 EU32
Grays RM17 170 GB79
Greenhithe DA9 189 FT85
Hemel Hempstead HP1 40 BJ21
Hounslow TW3 156 BZ82
Uxbridge UB10 135 BP70
Windsor SL4 151 AQ81
Charleston Cl, Felt. TW13 175 BU90
Charleston St, SE17 299 K9
Charles Townsend Ho, EC1 286 F4
Charles Whincup Rd, E16 304 A2
Charlesworth Cl, Hem.H. HP3 40 BK22
Charlesworth Pl, SW13
off Eleanor Gro 159 CT83
Charleville Circ, SE26 182 DU92
Charleville Ms, Islw. TW7
off Railshead Rd 157 CH84
Charleville Rd, W14 306 F1
Jct Charlie Brown's Rbt, E18 102 EJ54
Charlie Chaplin Wk, SE1
off Waterloo Br 298 D3
Charlieville Rd, Erith DA8
off Northumberland Pk 167 FC80
Charlmont Rd, SW17 180 DF93
Charlock Way, Guil. GU1 243 BB131
Watford WD18 75 BT44
Charlotte Av, Slou. SL2 132 AT73
Charlotte Cl, Wat. WD19 94 BW45
Ashtd. KT21 232 CL118
Bexleyheath DA6 186 EY85
Ilford IG6
off Connor Cl 103 EQ53
St. Albans AL4 44 CL20
Charlotte Ct, N8 121 DK58
W6 off Invermead Cl 159 CU77
Esher KT10 214 CC106
Charlotte Despard Av, SW11 309 H7
Charlotte Gdns, Rom. RM5 105 FB51
Charlotte Gro, Smallfield RH6 269 DN147
Charlotte Ms, W1 285 M6
W10 282 C9
W14 294 E8
Rain. RM13 148 FJ68
Charlotte Pk Av, Brom. BR1 204 EL97
Charlotte Pl, NW9
off Uphill Dr 118 CQ57
SW1 297 L9
W1 285 M7
Grays RM20 169 FV79
Charlotte Rd, EC2 287 N4
SW13 159 CT81
Dagenham RM10 147 FB65
Wallington SM6 219 DJ107
Charlotte Row, SW4 161 DJ83
Sch Charlotte Sharman Prim Sch,
SE11 298 G7
Charlotte Sq, Rich. TW10
off Greville Rd 178 CM86
Charlotte St, W1 285 M6
Charlotte Ter, N1 276 D9
CHARLOTTEVILLE, Guil. GU1 258 AY137
Charlow Cl, SW6 307 N9
CHARLTON, SE7 164 EJ79
⇌ Charlton 304 B10
Charlton, Wind. SL4 150 AJ82
★ Charlton Athletic FC, SE7 304 D10
Charlton Av, Hersham KT12 213 BV105
Charlton Ch La, SE7 304 C10
Charlton Cl, Hodd. EN11 49 EA17
Slough SL1 151 AP75
Uxbridge UB10 115 BP6
Charlton Cres, Bark. IG11 145 ET68
Charlton Dene, SE7 164 EJ80
Charlton Dr, Bigg.H. TN16 238 EK117
Charlton Gdns, Couls. CR5 235 DJ118
● Charlton Gate, SE7
off Anchor And Hope La 304 C9
Charlton Kings, Wey. KT13 195 BS104
Charlton Kings Rd, NW5 275 N2
Charlton La, SE7 304 E10
Shepperton TW17 195 BS98
Sch Charlton Manor Prim Sch,
SE7 off Indus Rd 164 EK80
Charlton Mead La, Hodd. EN11 49 EC18
Charlton Mead La S, Hodd. EN11
off Charlton Mead La 49 ED18
Charlton Pk La, SE7 164 EK80
Charlton Pk Rd, SE7 164 EK79
Charlton Pl, N1 276 G10
Windsor SL4 off Charlton 150 AJ82
Charlton Rd, N9 101 DX46
NW10 138 CS67
SE3 164 EG80
SE7 164 EH80
Harrow HA3 117 CK56
Shepperton TW17 195 BQ97
Wembley HA9 118 CM60
Charlton Row, Wind. SL4
off Charlton 150 AJ82
Sch Charlton Sch, SE7
off Charlton Pk Rd 164 EL79
Charlton Sq, Wind. SL4
off Charlton 150 AJ82
Charlton St, Grays RM20 169 FX79
Charlton Wk, Wind. SL4
off Charlton 150 AJ82
Charlton Way, SE3 315 J7
Hoddesdon EN11 49 EA17
Windsor SL4 150 AJ82
Charlwood, Croy. CR0 221 DZ109
Charlwood Cl, Bkhm KT23 230 CB124
Harrow HA3 off Kelvin Cres 95 CE51
Charlwood Dr, Oxshott KT22 231 CD115
Charlwood Ho, SW1
off Vauxhall Br Rd 297 N9
Richmond TW9 158 CP80
Charlwood Pl, SW1 297 M9
Reigate RH2 249 CZ134
Charlwood Rd, SW15 159 CX83
Horley RH6 268 DB152
Charlwood St, SW1 297 M9
Charlwood Ter, SW15 159 CX84
Charman Ho, SW8
off Hemans St 310 A4
Charman Rd, Red. RH1 250 DE134
Charm Cl, Horl. RH6 268 DE147
Charmian Av, Stan. HA7 117 CK55
Charminster Av, SW19 200 DA96
Charminster Ct, Surb. KT6
off Lovelace Gdns 197 CK101
Charminster Rd, SE9 184 EK91
Worcester Park KT4 199 CX102
Charmouth Ct, St.Alb. AL1 43 CG17
Charmouth Ho, SW8
off Dorset Rd 310 C4
Charmouth Rd, St.Alb. AL1 43 CG18
Welling DA16 166 EW81
Charmwood La, Orp. BR6 224 EV109
Charne, The, Otford TN14 241 FG117
Charnock, Swan. BR8 207 FE98
Charnock Rd, E5 122 DV62
Charnwood Av, SW19 200 DA96
Charnwood Cl, N.Mal. KT3 198 CS98
Charnwood Dr, E18 124 EH55
Charnwood Gdns, E14 302 B8
Charnwood Pl, N20 98 DC48
Charnwood Rd, SE25 202 DR99
Enfield EN1 82 DV36
Uxbridge UB10 134 BN68
Charnwood St, E5 122 DU61
Charrington Court Rom,
Rom. RM1 127 FE58
Charrington Pl, St.Alb. AL1 43 CF21
Charrington Rd, Croy. CR0
off Drayton Rd 201 DP103
Charrington St, NW1 275 N10
Charsley Cl, Amer. HP6 72 AW39
Charsley Rd, SE6 183 EB89
Charta Rd, Egh. TW20 173 BC92
Chart Cl, Brom. BR2 204 EE95
Croydon CR0 202 DW100
Dorking RH5 263 CK138
Mitcham CR4 200 DF98
Chart Downs, Dor. RH5 263 CJ138
Charter Av, Ilf. IG2 125 ER60
Charter Cl, St.Alb. AL1
off Bricket Rd 43 CE20
Slough SL1 152 AT76
Charter Ct, N.Mal. KT3 198 CS97
Charter Cres, Houns. TW4 156 BY84
Charter Dr, Amer. HP6 72 AT38
Bexley DA5 186 EY87
★ Charterhouse, EC1 287 H5
Charterhouse Av, Wem. HA0 117 CJ63
Charterhouse Bldgs, EC1 287 H5
Charterhouse Dr, Sev. TN13 256 FG123
Charterhouse Ms, EC1 287 H6
Charterhouse Rd, E8 278 C1
Orpington BR6 206 EU104
Charterhouse Sq, EC1 287 H6
Sch Charterhouse Sq Sch, EC1 287 J6
Charterhouse St, EC1 286 F7
Charteris Rd, N4 121 DN60
NW6 273 H9
Woodford Green IG8 102 EH52
● Charter Pl, Uxb. UB8 134 BK66
● Charter Pl, Wat. WD17 76 BW42
Charter Pl, Stai. TW18 174 BG93
Charter Rd, Kings.T. KT1 198 CP97
Slough SL1 131 AL73
Charter Rd, The, Wdf.Grn. IG8 102 EE51
Sch Charter Sch, The, SE24
off Red Post Hill 182 DR85
Charters Cl, SE19 182 DS92
Charters Cross, Harl. CM18 51 ER18
Charter Sq, Kings.T. KT1 198 CP96
Charter Way, N3 119 CZ56
N14 81 DJ44
Chartfield Av, SW15 179 CV85
Chartfield Pl, Wey. KT13 213 BP106
Chartfield Rd, Reig. RH2 266 DC135
Chartfield Sq, SW15 179 CX85
Chart Gdns, Dor. RH5 263 CJ139
Chartham Ct, SW9 161 DN83
Chartham Gro, SE27
off Royal Circ 181 DP90
Chartham Rd, SE25 202 DV97
Chart Hills Cl, SE28
off Fairway Dr 146 EY72
Chart La, Dor. RH4 263 CH136
Reigate RH2 250 DB134
Chart La S, Dor. RH5 263 CJ138
Chartley Av, NW2 118 CS62
Stanmore HA7 95 CF51
Charton Cl, Belv. DA17 166 EZ79
Chartridge Cl, Barn. EN5 79 CU43
Bushey WD23 76 CC44
Chartridge La, Chesh. HP5 54 AM29
Chartridge Way, Hem.H. HP2 41 BQ20
Chart St, N1 287 M2
Chartway, Reig. RH2 250 DB133
Sevenoaks TN13 257 FJ124
★ Chartwell, West. TN16 255 ET131
Chartwell Cl, SE9 185 EQ89
Croydon CR0 202 DR102
Greenford UB6 136 CB67
Waltham Abbey EN9 68 EE33
Chartwell Ct, NW2 119 CU62
Chartwell Dr, Orp. BR6 223 ER106
Chartwell Gdns, Sutt. SM3 217 CY105
Chartwell Gate, Beac. HP9 89 AK53
Chartwell Pl, Epsom KT18 216 CS114
Harrow HA2 117 CD61
Sutton SM3 217 CZ105
Chartwell Rd, Nthwd. HA6 93 BT51
Chartwell Way, SE20 202 DV95
Charwood Pl, Dor. RH4
off South St 263 CG136
Charville La, Hayes UB4 135 BS68
Charville La W, Uxb. UB10 135 BP69
Sch Charville Prim Sch,
Hayes UB4 off Bury Av 135 BS68
Charwood, SW16 181 DN91
Charwood Cl, Shenley WD7 62 CL33
Chasden Rd, Hem.H. HP1 39 BF17
Chase, The, E12 124 EK63
SW4 309 J10
SW16 181 DM94
SW20 199 CY95
Ashtead KT21 231 CJ118
Bexleyheath DA7 167 FB83
Brentwood
(Cromwell Rd) CM14 108 FV49
Brentwood
(Seven Arches Rd) CM14 108 FX48
Brentwood
(Woodman Rd) CM14 108 FX50
Bromley BR1 204 EH97
Chadwell Heath RM6 126 EY58
Chesham HP5 54 AP29
Chigwell IG7 103 EQ49
Coulsdon CR5 219 DJ114
East Horsley KT24 245 BT126
Eastcote HA5 116 BW58
Edgware HA8 96 CP53
Goffs Oak EN7 65 DP28
Grays RM20 169 FX79
Great Amwell SG12 33 EA09
Guildford GU2 258 AU135
Harlow CM17 36 EW14
Hemel Hempstead HP2
off Turners Hill 40 BL21
Hornchurch RM12 127 FE62
Ingrave CM13 109 GC50
Kingswood KT20 234 DA122
Loughton IG10 102 EJ45
Oxshott KT22 230 CC115
Penn HP10 88 AC46
Pinner HA5 116 BZ56
Radlett WD7 77 CF35
Reigate RH2 266 DD135
Romford RM1 127 FE55
Rush Green RM7 127 FD62
Stanmore HA7 95 CG50
Sunbury-on-Thames TW16 195 BV95
Upminster RM14 129 FS62
Uxbridge UB10 114 BN64
Wallington SM6 219 DL106
Watford WD18 75 BS42
Wooburn Green HP10 110 AF59
Sch Chase Br Prim Sch,
Twick. TW2
off Kneller Rd 177 CE86
Chase Cl, Colesh. HP7 55 AN43
Penn HP10 88 AC46
Chase Ct Gdns, Enf. EN2 82 DQ41
CHASE CROSS, Rom. RM1 105 FE51
Chase Cross Rd, Rom. RM5 105 FC52
Chase End, Epsom KT19 216 CR112
H Chase Fm Hosp, Enf. EN2 81 DN38
Chasefield Cl, Guil. GU4 243 BA131
Chasefield Rd, SW17 180 DF91
Chase Gdns, E4 101 EA49
Twickenham TW2 177 CD86
Chase Grn, Enf. EN2 82 DQ41
Pot.B. EN6 65 DL29
Chase Grn Av, Enf. EN2 81 DP40
Chase Hill, Enf. EN2 82 DQ41
Chase Ho Gdns, Horn. RM11
off Great Nelmes Chase 128 FM57
Chase La, Chig. IG7 104 EU48
Ilford IG6 125 ER57
Sch Chase La Prim Sch, E4
off York Rd 101 DZ50
Chaseley Dr, W4 158 CP78
South Croydon CR2 220 DR110
Chaseley St, E14 289 L9
Chasemore Cl, Mitch. CR4 200 DF101
Chasemore Gdns, Croy. CR0 219 DN106
Chase Ridings, Enf. EN2 81 DN40
Chase Rd, N14 81 DJ44
NW10 138 CR70
W3 138 CR70
Brentwood CM14 108 FW48
Epsom KT19 216 CR112
Chase Side, N14 80 DG44
Enfield EN2 82 DQ41
Chase Side Av, SW20 199 CY95
Enfield EN2 82 DQ40
Chaseside Cl, Rom. RM1 105 FE51
Chase Side Cres, Enf. EN2 82 DQ39
Chaseside Gdns, Cher. KT16 194 BH101
Chase Side Pl, Enf. EN2
off Chase Side 82 DQ40
Sch Chase Side Prim Sch,
Enf. EN2 off Trinity St 82 DQ40
Chase Sq, Grav. DA11
off High St 191 GH86
Chaseville Par, N21 81 DM43
Chaseville Pk Rd, N21 81 DL43
Chase Way, N14 99 DH47
Chaseways, Saw. CM21 36 EW07
Chasewood Av, Enf. EN2 81 DP40
Chasewood Pk, Har. HA1 117 CE62
Chastilian Rd, Dart. DA1 187 FF87
Chaston Pl, NW5
off Grafton Ter 274 G3
Chatelet Cl, Horl. RH6 269 DH147
Chater Ho, E2
off Roman Rd 289 J2
Sch Chater Infants' Sch,
Wat. WD18 off Southsea Av 75 BU42
Sch Chater Jun Sch, Wat. WD18
off Addiscombe Rd 75 BV42
Chatfield, Slou. SL2 131 AN71
Chatfield Ct, Cat. CR3 236 DR122
Chatfield Dr, Guil. GU4 243 BC132
Chatfield Rd, SW11 160 DC83
Croydon CR0 201 DP102
Chatham Av, Brom. BR2 204 EF101
Chatham Cl, NW11 120 DA57
SE18 305 P6
Sutton SM3 199 CZ101
Chatham Hill Rd, Sev. TN14 257 FJ121
Chatham Ms, Guil. GU2 242 AU131
Chatham Pl, E9 278 G4
Chatham Rd, E17 123 DY55
E18 off Grove Hill 102 EF54
SW11 180 DF86
Kingston upon Thames KT1 198 CN96
Orpington BR6
off Gladstone Rd 223 EQ106
Chatham St, SE17 299 L8
Chatham Way, Brwd. CM14 108 FW47
Chatsfield, Epsom KT17 217 CU110
Chatsfield Pl, W5 138 CL72
Chatsworth Av, NW4 97 CW54
SW20 199 CY95
Bromley BR1 184 EH91
Sidcup DA15 186 EU88
Wembley HA9 118 CM64
Chatsworth Cl, NW4 97 CW54
Borehamwood WD6 78 CN41
West Wickham BR4 204 EF103
Chatsworth Ct, W8 295 J8
Stanmore HA7 off Marsh La 95 CJ50
Chatsworth Cres, Houns. TW3 157 CD84
Chatsworth Dr, Enf. EN1 100 DU45
Chatsworth Est, E5
off Elderfield Rd 123 DX63
Chatsworth Gdns, W3 138 CP73
Harrow HA2 116 CB60
New Malden KT3 199 CT99
Sch Chatsworth Inf & Nurs Sch,
Houns. TW3 off Heath Rd 156 CC84
Sch Chatsworth Inf Sch,
Sid. DA15 off Burnt Oak La 186 EU88
Sch Chatsworth Jun Sch,
Houns. TW3 off Heath Rd 156 CC84
Chatsworth Ms, Wat. WD24 75 BU38
Chatsworth Par, Petts Wd BR5
off Queensway 205 EQ99
Chatsworth Pl, Mitch. CR4 200 DF97
Oxshott KT22 215 CD112
Teddington TW11 177 CG91
Chatsworth Ri, W5 138 CM70
Chatsworth Rd, E5 122 DW62
E15 281 L3
NW2 272 E5
W4 158 CQ79
W5 138 CM70
Croydon CR0 220 DR105
Dartford DA1 188 FJ85
Hayes UB4 135 BV70
Sutton SM3 217 CX106
Chatsworth Way, SE27 181 DP90
Chatteris Av, Rom. RM3 106 FJ51
Chattern Hill, Ashf. TW15 175 BP91
Chattern Rd, Ashf. TW15 175 BQ91
Chatterton Ms, N4
off Chatterton Rd 121 DP62
Chatterton Rd, N4 121 DP62
Bromley BR2 204 EK98
Chatto Rd, SW11 180 DF85
Chaucer Av, Hayes UB4 135 BU71
Hounslow TW4 155 BV82
Richmond TW9 158 CN82
Weybridge KT13 212 BN108
Chaucer Cl, N11 99 DJ50
Banstead SM7 217 CY114
Berkhamsted HP4 38 AT18
Saint Albans AL1 43 CF18
Tilbury RM18 171 GJ82
Windsor SL4 151 AR83
Chaucer Ct, N16 277 N1
Guildford GU2 off Lawn Rd 258 AW137
Chaucer Dr, SE1 300 B9
Chaucer Gdns, Sutt. SM1 200 DA104
Chaucer Grn, Croy. CR0 202 DV101
Chaucer Gro, Borwd. WD6 78 CN42
Chaucer Ho, SW1 309 L1
Sutton SM1 200 DA104
Chaucer Pk, Dart. DA1 188 FM87
Chaucer Rd, E7 281 P5
E11 124 EG58
E17 101 EC54
SE24 181 DN85
W3 138 CQ74
Ashford TW15 174 BL91
Northfleet DA11 190 GD90
Romford RM3 105 FH52
Sidcup DA15 186 EW88
Sutton SM1 218 DA105
Welling DA16 165 ES81
Chaucer Way, SW19 180 DD93
Addlestone KT15 212 BG107
Dartford DA1 168 FN84
Hoddesdon EN11 33 EA13
Slough SL1 132 AT74
CHAULDEN, Hem.H. HP1 39 BE21
Chaulden Ho Gdns, Hem.H. HP1 39 BF21
Sch Chaulden Inf & Nurs Sch,
Hem.H. HP1 off School Row 39 BF21
Sch Chaulden Jun Sch,
Hem.H. HP1 off School Row 39 BF21
Chaulden La, Hem.H. HP1 39 BD22
Chaulden Ter, Hem.H. HP1 39 BF21
Chauncey Cl, N9 100 DU48
Chauncy Av, Pot.B. EN6 64 DC33
Chauncy Ct, Hert. SG14
off Bluecoats Av 32 DR09
Sch Chauncy Sch, The,
Ware SG12 off Park Rd 32 DV05
Chaundrye Cl, SE9 185 EM86
Chauntler Cl, E16 292 B10
Chauntry Cl, Maid. SL6 130 AC73
Chavecroft Ter, Epsom KT18 233 CW119
Chave Rd, Dart. DA2 188 FL90
Chaville Way, N3 98 DA53
Chaworth Cl, Ott. KT16 211 BC107
Chaworth Rd, Ott. KT16 211 BC107
CHEAM, Sutt. SM3 217 CX107
⇌ Cheam 217 CY108
Cheam Cl, Tad. KT20
off Waterfield 233 CW121
Sch Cheam Common Infants' Sch,
Wor.Pk. KT4 off Balmoral Rd 199 CV103
Sch Cheam Common Jun Sch,
Wor.Pk. KT4 off Kingsmead Av 199 CV103
Cheam Common Rd,
Wor.Pk. KT4 199 CV103
Sch Cheam Flds Prim Sch,
Cheam SM3 off Stoughton Av 217 CY106
Sch Cheam High Sch, Cheam
SM3 off Chatsworth Rd 217 CY105
Cheam Mans, Sutt. SM3 217 CY108
Sch Cheam Pk Fm Infants' Sch,
Sutt. SM3 off Molesey Dr 199 CY104
Sch Cheam Pk Fm Jun Sch,
Sutt. SM3 off Kingston Av 199 CY104
Cheam Pk Way, Sutt. SM3 217 CY107
Cheam Rd, E.Ewell SM2 217 CX110
Epsom KT17 217 CU109
Sutton SM1 217 CZ107
Cheam St, SE15 312 F10
Jct Cheam Village, Sutt. SM3 217 CY107
Cheapside, EC2 287 K9
N13 off Taplow Rd 100 DQ49
Woking GU21 210 AX114
Cheapside La, Denh. UB9 113 BF61
Cheapside Pas, EC4 287 J9
Chearsley, SE17 off Deacon Way 299 K8
Chedburgh, Welw.G.C. AL7 30 DD08
Cheddar Cl, N11 98 DF51
Cheddar Rd, Lon.Hthrw Air. TW6
off Cromer Rd 154 BN82
Cheddar Waye, Hayes UB4 135 BV72
Cheddington Rd, N18 100 DS48
Chedworth Cl, E16 291 L8
Cheelson Rd, S.Ock. RM15 149 FW68
Cheering La, E20 280 F3
Cheeseman Cl, Hmptn. TW12 176 BY93
Cheesemans Ter, W14 306 G1
Cheffins Rd, Hodd. EN11 33 DZ14
Cheldon Av, NW7 97 CX52
Chelford Rd, Brom. BR1 183 ED92
Chelmer Cres, Bark. IG11 146 EV68
Chelmer Dr, Hutt. CM13 109 GE44
South Ockendon RM15 149 FW73
Chelmer Rd, E9 279 K2
Grays RM16 171 GG78
Upminster RM14 129 FR58
Chelmsford Av, Rom. RM5 105 FD52
Chelmsford Cl, E6 293 J9
W6 306 D2
Sutton SM2 218 DA109
Chelmsford Dr, Upmin. RM14 128 FM62
Chelmsford Gdns, Ilf. IG1 124 EL59
Chelmsford Rd, E11 123 ED60
E17 123 EA58
E18 102 EF53
N14 99 DJ45
Hatfield Heath CM22 37 FH05
Hertford SG14 31 DN10
Shenfield CM15 109 FZ44
Chelmsford Sq, NW10 272 A9
CHELSEA, SW3 308 A2
Sch Chelsea Acad, SW10 307 P5
H Chelsea & Westminster Hosp,
SW10 307 P3
★ Chelsea Antique Mkt, SW3 308 B2
Chelsea Br, SW1 309 J2
SW8 309 J2
Chelsea Br Rd, SW1 296 G10
Chelsea Cloisters, SW3 296 D9
Chelsea Cl, NW10
off Winchelsea Rd 138 CR67
Edgware HA8 96 CN54
Hampton Hill TW12 176 CC93
Worcester Park KT4 199 CU101
Uni Chelsea Coll of Art & Design,
SW1 298 A10
Chelsea Cres, SW10 307 P7
Chelsea Embk, SW3 308 D3
Chelsea Flds, Hodd. EN11 33 EB13
★ Chelsea FC, SW6 307 L4
Chelsea Gdns, SW1
off Chelsea Br Rd 309 H1
W13 off Hathaway Gdns 137 CF71
Harlow CM17 52 EY16
Sutton SM3 217 CY105
Chelsea Harbour, SW10 307 P7
● Chelsea Harbour Design Cen,
SW10 off Harbour Av 307 P6
Chelsea Harbour Dr, SW10 307 P6
Pier Chelsea Harbour Pier 308 A7
Chelsea Manor Ct, SW3 308 D2
Chelsea Manor Gdns, SW3 308 D2
Chelsea Manor St, SW3 308 C1
Chelsea Ms, E11 124 EG58
Horn. RM11
off St. Leonards Way 127 FH60
Chelsea Pk Gdns, SW3 308 A2
★ Chelsea Physic Gdn, SW3 308 E2
Chelsea Reach Twr, SW10 308 A4
Chelsea Sq, SW3 296 B10
Chelsea Twrs, SW3 308 D1
Chelsea Village, SW6 307 M4
Chelsea Vista, SW6 307 P7
Chelsea Way, Brwd. CM14 108 FW46
Chelsea Wf, SW10 308 A5
CHELSFIELD, Orp. BR6 224 EW106
⇌ Chelsfield 224 EV106
Chelsfield Av, N9 101 DX45
Chelsfield Gdns, SE26 182 DW90
Chelsfield Hill, Orp. BR6 224 EW109
Chelsfield La, Maypole BR6 224 FA108
Orpington BR5, BR6 206 EX101
Sevenoaks TN14 225 FC109
H Chelsfield Pk Hosp,
Chels. BR6 224 EZ106
Sch Chelsfield Prim Sch,
Chels. BR6 off Warren Rd 224 EY106
Chelsfield Rd, Orp. BR5 206 EW100
CHELSHAM, Warl. CR6 237 EA117
Chelsham Cl, Warl. CR6 237 DY118
Chelsham Common, Warl. CR6 237 EA116
Chelsham Common Rd,
Warl. CR6 237 EA117
Chelsham Ct Rd, Warl. CR6 237 ED118
Chelsham Rd, SW4 309 P10
South Croydon CR2 220 DR107
Warlingham CR6 237 EA117
Chelsing Ri, Hem.H. HP2 41 BQ21
Chelston App, Ruis. HA4 115 BU61
Chelston Rd, Ruis. HA4 115 BU60
Chelsworth Cl, Rom. RM3
off Chelsworth Dr 106 FM53
Chelsworth Dr, SE18 165 ER79
Romford RM3 106 FL53
Cheltenham Av, Twick. TW1 177 CG87
Cheltenham Cl, Grav. DA12 191 GJ92
New Malden KT3
off Northcote Rd 198 CQ97
Northolt UB5 136 CB65
Cheltenham Gdns, E6 292 G1
Loughton IG10 84 EL44
Cheltenham Pl, W3 138 CP74
Harrow HA3 118 CL56
Cheltenham Rd, E10 123 EC58
SE15 162 DW84
Orpington BR6 206 EU104
Cheltenham Ter, SW3 296 F10
Cheltenham Vil, Stai. TW19 173 BF86
Chelverton Rd, SW15 159 CX84
Chelveston, Welw.G.C. AL7 30 DD08
Chelwood, N20
off Oakleigh Rd N 98 DD47
Chelwood Av, Hat. AL10 45 CU16
Chelwood Cl, E4 83 EB44
Coulsdon CR5 235 DJ119
Epsom KT17 217 CT112
Northwood HA6 93 BQ52
Chelwood Gdns, Rich. TW9 158 CN82

Chelwood Gdns Pas, Rich. TW9
off Chelwood Gdns 158 CN82
Chelwood Wk, SE4 163 DY84
Chenappa Cl, E13 291 M3
Chenduit Way, Stan. HA7 95 CF50
Chene Dr, St.Alb. AL3 43 CD18
Chene Ms, St.Alb. AL3 43 CD18
Cheney Row, E17 101 DZ53
Cheneys Rd, E11 124 EE62
Cheney St, Pnr. HA5 116 BW57
CHENIES, Rick. WD3 73 BB38
Chenies, The, Dart. DA2 187 FE91
Petts Wood BR6 205 ES100
Chenies Av, Amer. HP6 72 AW39
Chenies Bottom, Chenies WD3 73 BA37
Chenies Ct, Hem.H. HP2
off Datchet Cl 41 BP15
Chenies Hill, Flaun. HP3 57 BB34
★ **Chenies Manor**, Rick. WD3 73 BA38
Chenies Ms, WC1 285 N5
Chenies Par, Amer. HP7 72 AW40
Chenies Pl, NW1 275 N10
Barn. EN5 79 CU43
Chenies Rd, Chorl. WD3 73 BD40
Sch **Chenies Sch**, Chenies WD3
off Latimer Rd 73 BB38
Chenies St, WC1 285 N6
Chenies Way, Wat. WD18 93 BS45
Cheniston Cl, W.Byf. KT14 212 BG113
Cheniston Gdns, W8 295 L6
Chennells, Hat. AL10 45 CT19
Sch **Chennestone Prim Sch**,
Sun. TW16 *off Manor La* 195 BV96
Chepstow Av, Horn. RM12 128 FL62
Chepstow Cl, SW15 179 CY86
Chepstow Cres, W11 283 J10
Ilford IG3 125 ES58
Chepstow Gdns, Sthl. UB1 136 BZ72
Chepstow Pl, W2 283 K10
Chepstow Ri, Croy. CR0 202 DS104
Chepstow Rd, W2 283 K8
W7 157 CG76
Croydon CR0 202 DS104
Chepstow Vil, W11 283 H10
Chequers, Buck.H. IG9 102 EH46
Hatfield AL9 29 CX13
Welwyn Garden City AL7 29 CX11
Chequers Cl, NW9 118 CS55
Horley RH6 268 DG147
Orpington BR5 205 ET98
Walton on the Hill KT20 249 CU125
Chequers Dr, Horl. RH6 268 DG147
Chequers Fld, Welw.G.C. AL7 29 CX12
Chequers Gdns, N13 99 DP50
Chequers Hill, Amer. HP7 55 AR40
Chequers La, Dag. RM9 146 EZ70
Walton on the Hill KT20 249 CU125
Watford WD25 60 BW30
Chequers Orchard, Iver SL0 133 BF72
Chequers Par, SE9
off Eltham High St 185 EM86
Chequers Pl, Dor. RH4 263 CH136
Chequers Rd, Brwd. CM14 106 FM46
Loughton IG10 85 EN43
Romford RM3 106 FL47
🔒 **Chequers Sq**, Uxb. UB8
off The Mall Pavilions 134 BJ66
Chequer St, EC1 287 K5
St. Albans AL1 43 CD20
Chequers Wk, Wal.Abb. EN9 68 EF33
Chequers Way, N13 100 DQ50
Chequers Yd, Dor. RH4
off Chequers Pl 263 CH136
Chequer Tree Cl, Knap. GU21 226 AS116
Cherbury Cl, SE28 146 EX72
Cherbury Ct, N1 287 M1
Cherbury St, N1 287 M1
Cherchefelle Ms, Stan. HA7 95 CH50
Cherimoya Gdns, W.Mol. KT8
off Kelvinbrook 196 CB97
Cherington Rd, W7 137 CF74
Cheriton Av, Brom. BR2 204 EF99
Ilford IG5 103 EM54
Cheriton Cl, W5 137 CJ71
Barnet EN4 80 DF41
St. Albans AL4 43 CK16
Cheriton Ct, Walt. KT12 196 BW102
Cheriton Dr, SE18 165 ER80
Cheriton Ho, E5
off Pembury Rd 278 E2
Cheriton Lo, Ruis. HA4
off Pembroke Rd 115 BT60
Cheriton Sq, SW17 180 DG89
Cherkley Hill, Lthd. KT22 247 CJ126
Cherries, The, Slou. SL2 132 AV72
Cherry Acre, Chal.St.P. SL9 90 AX49
Cherry Av, Brwd. CM13 109 FZ48
Slough SL3 152 AX75
Southall UB1 136 BX74
Swanley BR8 207 FD97
Cherry Blossom Cl, N13 99 DP50
Harlow CM17 36 EW11
Cherry Bounce, Hem.H. HP1 40 BK18
Cherry Cl, E17 123 EB57
NW9 97 CT54
SW2 181 DN87
W5 157 CK76
Banstead SM7 217 CX114
Carshalton SM5 200 DF103
Morden SM4 199 CY98
Ruislip HA4 115 BT62
Cherrycot Hill, Orp. BR6 223 ER105
Cherrycot Ri, Orp. BR6 223 EQ105
Cherry Cres, Brent. TW8 157 CH80
Cherry Cft, Crox.Grn WD3 74 BN44
Welwyn Garden City AL8 29 CX05
Cherrycroft Gdns, Pnr. HA5
off Westfield Pk 94 BZ52
Cherrydale, Wat. WD18 75 BT42
Cherrydown Av, E4 101 DZ48
Cherrydown Cl, E4 101 DZ48
Cherrydown Rd, Sid. DA14 186 EX89
Cherrydown Wk, Rom. RM7 105 FB54
Cherry Dr, Forty Grn HP9 88 AH51
Cherry Gdns, Dag. RM9 126 EZ64
Northolt UB5 136 CB66
Sch **Cherry Gdn Sch**, SE16 300 D8
Cherry Gdn St, SE16 300 E5
Cherry Garth, Brent. TW8 157 CK77
Cherry Grn Cl, Red. RH1 267 DH136
Cherry Gro, Hayes UB3 135 BV74
Uxbridge UB8 135 BP71
Cherry Hill, Har. HA3 95 CE51
Loudwater WD3 74 BH41
New Barnet EN5 80 DB44
St. Albans AL2 60 CA25
Cherry Hill Gdns, Croy. CR0 219 DM105
Cherry Hills, Wat. WD19 94 BY50
Cherry Hollow, Abb.L. WD5 59 BT31
Cherrylands Cl, NW9 118 CQ61
Cherry La, Amer. HP7 55 AN40
West Drayton UB7 154 BM77
Sch **Cherry La Prim Sch**,
West Dr. UB7 *off Sipson Rd* 154 BM77
Jct **Cherry La Rbt**, West Dr. UB7 155 BP77
Cherry Laurel Wk, SW2
off Beechdale Rd 181 DM86
Cherry Orchard, SE7
off Charlton Rd 164 EJ79
Amer. HP6 55 AS37
Ashtead KT21 232 CP118
Hemel Hempstead HP1 40 BG18
Staines-upon-Thames TW18 174 BG92
Stoke Poges SL2 132 AV66
West Drayton UB7 154 BL75
Cherry Orchard Cl, Orp. BR5 206 EW99
Cherry Orchard Est, SE7 164 EJ80
Cherry Orchard Gdns,
Croy. CR0 *off Oval Rd* 202 DR103
West Molesey KT8 196 BZ97
Sch **Cherry Orchard Prim Sch**,
SE7 *off Rectory Fld Cres* 164 EJ80
Cherry Orchard Rd, Brom. BR2 204 EL103
Croydon CR0 202 DR103
West Molesey KT8 196 CA97
Cherry Ri, Ch.St.G. HP8 90 AX47
Cherry Rd, Enf. EN3 82 DW38
Cherry St, Rom. RM7 127 FD57
Woking GU21 226 AY118
Cherry Tree Av, Guil. GU2 242 AT134
London Colney AL2 61 CK26
Staines-upon-Thames TW18 174 BH93
West Drayton UB7 134 BM72
Cherry Tree Cl, E9 279 H8
Grays RM17 170 GC79
Rainham RM13 147 FG68
Wembley HA0 117 CG63
Cherry Tree Ct, NW9
off Boakes Cl 118 CQ56
SE7 *off Fairlawn* 164 EJ79
Coulsdon CR5 235 DM118
Cherry Tree Dr, SW16 181 DL90
South Ockendon RM15 149 FX70
Cherry Tree Grn, Hert. SG14 31 DM07
South Croydon CR2 220 DV114
Cherrytree La, Chal.St.P. SL9 90 AX54
Cherry Tree La, Dart. DA2 187 FF90
Epsom KT19 *off Christ Ch Rd* 216 CN112
Fulmer SL3 133 AZ65
Harlow CM20 35 EP14
Hemel Hempstead HP2 41 BQ17
Heronsgate WD3 91 BC46
Iver SL0 134 BG67
Potters Bar EN6 64 DB34
Rainham RM13 147 FF69
Cherry Tree Ms, Hodd. EN11
off Cherry Tree Rd 49 EA16
Sch **Cherry Tree Prim Sch**,
Wat. WD24 *off Berry Av* 75 BU36
Cherry Tree Ri, Buck.H. IG9 102 EJ49
Cherry Tree Rd, E15 281 J2
N2 120 DF56
Beaconsfield HP9 88 AH54
Farnham Royal SL2 131 AQ66
Hoddesdon EN11 49 EA16
Watford WD24 75 BV36
Cherrytrees, Couls. CR5 235 DK121
Sch **Cherry Trees Sch, The**, E3 290 B3
Cherry Tree Wk, EC1 287 K5
Beckenham BR3 203 DZ98
Chesham HP5 54 AR29
West Wickham BR4 222 EF105
Cherry Tree Way, E13 292 E4
Penn HP10 88 AC46
Stanmore HA7 95 CH51
Cherry Wk, Brom. BR2 204 EG102
Grays RM16 171 GG76
Kew. TW9 158 CM81
Loudwater WD3 74 BJ40
Rainham RM13 147 FF68
Cherry Way, Epsom KT19 216 CR107
Hatfield AL10 45 CU21
Horton SL3 153 BC83
Shepperton TW17 195 BR98
Cherrywood Av, Eng.Grn TW20 172 AV93
Cherrywood Cl, E3 289 M2
Kingston upon Thames KT2 178 CN94
Cherry Wd Cl, Seer Grn HP9 89 AR50
Cherrywood Dr, SW15 179 CX85
Northfleet DA11 190 GE90
Cherrywood La, Mord. SM4 199 CY98
Cherrywood Lo, SE13
off Oakwood Cl 183 ED86
Cherry Wd Way, W5
off Hanger Vale La 138 CN71
Cherston Gdns, Loug. IG10 85 EN42
Cherston Rd, Loug. IG10 85 EN42
CHERTSEY, KT16 194 BG102
⇌ **Chertsey** 193 BF102
Chertsey Br Rd, Cher. KT16 194 BK101
Chertsey Cl, Ken. CR8 235 DP115
Chertsey Cres, New Adgtn CR0 221 EC110
Chertsey Dr, Sutt. SM3 199 CY103
Chertsey La, Cher. KT16 193 BE95
Epsom KT19 216 CN112
Staines-upon-Thames TW18 173 BE92
Chertsey Meads, Cher. KT16 194 BK102
★ **Chertsey Mus**, Cher. KT16
off Windsor St 194 BG100
Chertsey Rd, E11 123 ED61
Addlestone KT15 194 BH103
Ashford TW15 175 BR94
Byfleet KT14 212 BK111
Chobham GU24 210 AY110
Feltham TW13 175 BS92
Ilford IG1 125 ER63
Shepperton TW17 194 BN101
Sunbury-on-Thames TW16 175 BR94
Twickenham TW1, TW2 177 CF86
Woking GU21 211 BA113
Chertsey St, SW17 180 DG92
Guildford GU1 258 AX135
Cherubs, The, Farn.Com. SL2 131 AQ65
Chervil Cl, Felt. TW13 175 BU90
Chervil Ms, SE28 146 EV74
Cherwell Cl, Crox.Grn WD3 74 BN43
Slough SL3 *off Tweed Rd* 153 BB79
Cherwell Ct, Epsom KT19 216 CQ105
Teddington TW11 177 CK94
Cherwell Gro, S.Ock. RM15 149 FV73
Cherwell Ho, NW8
off Church St Est 284 B5
Cherwell Way, Ruis. HA4 115 BQ58
Cherryls Cl, SW6 307 M6
Cheselden Rd, Guil. GU1 258 AY135
Cheseman St, SE26 182 DV90
Chesfield Rd, Kings.T. KT2 178 CL94
CHESHAM, HP5 54 AQ31
⊖ **Chesham** 54 AQ31
Chesham Av, Petts Wd BR5 205 EP100
CHESHAM BOIS, Amer. HP6 55 AQ36
Sch **Chesham Bois C of E Comb Sch**,
Amer. HP6 *off Bois La* 55 AS35
Chesham Cl, SW1 296 G7
Romford RM7 127 FD56
Sutton SM2 217 CY110
Chesham Ct, Nthwd. HA6
off Frithwood Av 93 BT51
Chesham Cres, SE20 202 DW96
Chesham Hts, Kgswd KT20 233 CZ121
Sch **Chesham High Sch**,
Chesh. HP5 *off White Hill* 54 AR30
H **Chesham Hosp**, Chesh. HP5 54 AQ32
Chesham La, Ch.St.G. HP8 90 AY48
Chalfont St. Peter SL9 90 AY49
Chesham Ms, SW1 296 G6
Guildford GU1
off Chesham Rd 259 AZ135
Chesham Pl, SW1 296 G7
Sch **Chesham Prep Sch**,
Chesh. HP5 *off Orchard Leigh* 56 AU27
Chesham Rd, SE20 202 DW96
SW19 180 DD92
Amersham HP6 55 AQ38
Ashley Green HP5 38 AT24
Berkhamsted HP4 38 AV21
Bovingdon HP3 56 AY27
Guildford GU1 258 AY135
Kingston upon Thames KT1 198 CN95
Chesham St, NW10 118 CR62
SW1 296 G7
Chesham Ter, W13 157 CH75
Chesham Way, Wat. WD18 75 BS44
Cheshire Cl, E17 101 EB53
SE4 313 N8
Hornchurch RM11 128 FN57
Mitcham CR4 201 DL97
Ottershaw KT16 211 BC107
Cheshire Ct, EC4 286 F9
Slough SL1 *off Sussex Pl* 152 AV75
Cheshire Dr, Lvsdn WD25 59 BT34
Cheshire Gdns, Chess. KT9 215 CK107
Cheshire Ho, N18 100 DV49
Cheshire Rd, N22 99 DM52
Cheshire St, E2 288 B4
Chesholm Rd, N16 122 DS62
CHESHUNT, Wal.Cr. EN8 67 DX31
⇌ **Cheshunt** 67 DZ30
⊖ **Cheshunt** 67 DZ30
H **Cheshunt Comm Hosp**,
Chsht EN8 67 DY31
Cheshunt Pk, Chsht EN7 66 DV26
Cheshunt Rd, E7 144 EH65
Belvedere DA17 166 FA78
Sch **Cheshunt Sch**, Chsht EN8
off College Rd 66 DW30
Cheshunt Wash, Chsht EN8 67 DY27
Chesil Ct, E2 278 G10
Chesilton Rd, SW6 306 G6
Chesil Way, Hayes UB4 135 BT69
Chesley Gdns, E6 292 F1
Chesney Cres, New Adgtn CR0 221 EC108
Chesney St, SW11 308 G7
Chesnut Est, N17 122 DT55
Chesnut Gro, N17 122 DT55
Chesnut Rd, N17 122 DT55
Chessbury Cl, Chesh. HP5
off Missenden Rd 54 AP32
Chessbury Rd, Chesh. HP5 54 AN32
● **Chess Business Pk**,
Chesh. HP5 54 AQ33
Chess Cl, Latimer HP5 72 AX36
Loudwater WD3 74 BK42
Chessell Cl, Th.Hth. CR7 201 DP98
Chessfield Pk, Amer. HP6 72 AY39
Chess Hill, Loud. WD3 74 BK42
Chessholme Ct, Sun. TW16 175 BS94
Chessholme Rd, Ashf. TW15 175 BQ93
CHESSINGTON, KT9 216 CL107
Chessington Av, N3 119 CY55
Bexleyheath DA7 166 EY80
Chessington Cl, Epsom KT19 216 CQ107
Sch **Chessington Comm Coll**,
Chess. KT9 *off Garrison La* 215 CK108
Chessington Ct, N3
off Charter Way 119 CZ55
Pinner HA5 116 BZ56
Chessington Hall Gdns,
Chess. KT9 215 CK108
Chessington Hill Pk,
Chess. KT9 216 CN106
Chessington Lo, N3 119 CZ55
Chessington Mans, E10
off Albany Rd 123 EA59
⇌ **Chessington North** 216 CL106
Chessington Rd,
Epsom KT17, KT19 217 CT109
⇌ **Chessington South** 215 CK108
● **Chessington Trade Pk**,
Chess. KT9 216 CN105
Chessington Way, W.Wick. BR4 203 EB103
★ **Chessington World of Adventures**,
Chess. KT9 215 CJ110
Chess La, Loud. WD3 74 BK42
CHESSMOUNT, Chesh. HP5 54 AR33
Chessmount Ri, Chesh. HP5 54 AR33
Chesson Rd, W14 306 G2
Chess Vale Ri, Crox.Grn WD3 74 BM44
Chess Valley Wk, Chesh. HP5 72 AU35
Rickmansworth WD3 74 BL44
Chess Way, Chorl. WD3 74 BG41
Chesswood Way, Pnr. HA5 94 BX54
Chester Av, Rich. TW10 178 CM86
Twickenham TW2 176 BZ88
Upminster RM14 129 FS61
Chester Cl, SW1 297 H5
SW13 159 CV83
Ashford TW15 175 BR92
Chafford Hundred RM16 170 FY76
Dorking RH4 247 CJ134
Guildford GU2 242 AT132
Loughton IG10 85 EQ39
Potters Bar EN6 64 DB29
Richmond TW10 178 CM86
Sutton SM1 200 DA103
Uxbridge UB8 135 BP72
Chester Cl N, NW1 285 K2
Chester Cl S, NW1 285 K3
Chester Cotts, SW1 296 G9
Chester Ct, NW1 *off Albany St* 285 K3
SE5 311 L5
Chester Cres, E8 278 B3
Chester Dr, Har. HA2 116 BZ58
Chesterfield Cl, Orp. BR5 206 EX98
Chesterfield Dr, Dart. DA1 187 FH85
Esher KT10 197 CG103
Sevenoaks TN13 256 FD122
Chesterfield Gdns, N4 121 DP57
SE10 314 G5
W1 297 J2
Chesterfield Gro, SE22 182 DT85
Chesterfield Hill, W1 297 J1
Chesterfield Ms, N4 121 DP57
Ashford TW15 174 BL91
Chesterfield Rd, E10 123 EC58
N3 98 DA51
W4 158 CQ79
Ashford TW15 174 BL91
Barnet EN5 79 CX43
Enfield EN3 83 DY37
Epsom KT19 216 CR108
Sch **Chesterfield Sch**, Enf. EN3
off Chesterfield Rd 83 DY37
Chesterfield St, W1 297 J2
Chesterfield Wk, SE10 315 H6
Chesterfield Way, SE15 312 G5
Hayes UB3 155 BU75
Chesterford Gdns, NW3 273 M1
Chesterford Ho, SE18
off Shooters Hill Rd 164 EK81
Chesterford Rd, E12 125 EM64
Chester Gdns, W13 137 CH72
Enfield EN3 82 DV44
Morden SM4 200 DC100
Chester Gate, NW1 285 J3
Chester Gibbons Grn,
Lon.Col. AL2 61 CK26
Chester Grn, Loug. IG10 85 EQ39
Chester Ms, E17
off Chingford Rd 101 EA54
SW1 297 J6
Chester Path, Loug. IG10 85 EQ39
Chester Pl, NW1 285 J2
Chester Rd, E7 144 EK66
E11 124 EH58
E16 291 K5
E17 123 DX57
N9 100 DV46
N17 122 DR55
N19 121 DH61
NW1 285 H3
SW19 179 CW93
Borehamwood WD6 78 CQ41
Chigwell IG7 103 EN48
Effingham KT24 245 BV128
Hounslow TW4 155 BV83
Ilford IG3 125 ET60
London Heathrow Airport TW6 154 BN83
Loughton IG10 85 EP40
Northwood HA6 93 BS52
Sidcup DA15 185 ES85
Slough SL1 131 AR72
Watford WD18 75 BU43
Chester Row, SW1 296 G9
Chesters, Horl. RH6 268 DE146
Chesters, The, N.Mal. KT3 198 CS95
Chester Sq, SW1 297 J8
Chester Sq Ms, SW1 297 J7
Chester St, E2 288 D4
SW1 297 H6
Chester Ter, NW1 285 J2
Chesterton Cl, SW18 180 DA85
Chesham HP5 *off Milton Rd* 54 AP29
Greenford UB6 136 CB68
Chesterton Dr, Merst. RH1 251 DL128
Staines-upon-Thames TW19 174 BM88
Chesterton Grn, Beac. HP9 89 AL52
Chesterton Ho, SW11
off Ingrave St 308 B10
Sch **Chesterton Prim Sch**, SW11 308 G7
Chesterton Rd, E13 291 P2
W10 282 D7
Chesterton Sq, W8 295 H8
Chesterton Ter, E13 291 N2
Kingston upon Thames KT1 198 CN96
Chesterton Way, Til. RM18 171 GJ82
Chester Way, SE11 298 F9
Chesthunte Rd, N17 100 DQ53
Chestnut All, SW6 307 H3
Chestnut Av, E7 124 EH63
N8 121 DL57
SW14 *off Thornton Rd* 158 CR83
SW17 181 DJ90
Bluewater DA9 189 FT87
Brentford TW8 157 CK77
Brentwood CM14 108 FS45
Buckhurst Hill IG9 102 EK48
Chesham HP5 54 AR29
East Molesey KT8 197 CF97
Edgware HA8 96 CL51
Epsom KT19 216 CS105
Esher KT10 197 CD101
Grays RM16 170 GB75
Guildford GU2 258 AW138
Hampton TW12 176 CA94
Hornchurch RM12 127 FF61
Northwood HA6 93 BT54
Rickmansworth WD3 74 BG43
Slough SL3 152 AY75
Teddington TW11 197 CF96
Virginia Water GU25 192 AT98
Wembley HA0 117 CH64
West Drayton UB7 134 BM73
West Wickham BR4 222 EE106
Westerham TN16 238 EK122
Weybridge KT13 213 BQ108
Whiteley Village KT12 213 BS109
Chestnut Av N, E17 123 EC56
Chestnut Av S, E17 123 EC56
Chestnut Cl, N14 81 DJ43
N16 122 DR61
SE6 183 EC92
SE14 313 N6
SW16 181 DN91
Addlestone KT15 212 BK106
Amersham HP6 55 AR37
Ashford TW15 175 BP91
Buckhurst Hill IG9 102 EK48
Carshalton SM5 200 DF102
Chalfont St. Peter SL9 91 AZ52
Englefield Green TW20 172 AW93
Hayes UB3 135 BS73
Hornchurch RM12
off Lancaster Dr 128 FJ63
Hunsdon SG12 34 EK06
Kingswood KT20 234 DA123
Northfleet DA11
off Burch Rd 191 GF86
Orpington BR6 224 EU106
Potten End HP4 39 BB17
Redhill RH1 *off Haigh Cres* 267 DH136
Ripley GU23 228 BG124
Sidcup DA15 186 EU88
Sunbury-on-Thames TW16 175 BT93
West Drayton UB7 155 BP80
Chestnut Copse, Oxt. RH8 254 EG132
Chestnut Ct, SW6 307 H3
Amersham HP6 55 AS37
Surbiton KT6
off Penners Gdns 198 CL101
Chestnut Cres, Whiteley Vill.
KT12 *off Chestnut Av* 213 BS109
Chestnut Dr, E11 124 EG58
Berkhamsted HP4 38 AX20
Bexleyheath DA7 166 EX83
Englefield Green TW20 172 AX93
Harrow HA3 95 CF52
Pinner HA5 116 BX58
St. Albans AL4 43 CH18
Windsor SL4 151 AL84
Chestnut Glen, Horn. RM12 127 FF61
Chestnut Gro, SE20 182 DV94
SW12 180 DG87
W5 157 CK76
Barnet EN4 80 DF43
Brentwood CM14 108 FW47
Dartford DA2 187 FD91
Hoddesdon EN11 33 EB13
Ilford IG6 103 ES51
Isleworth TW7 157 CG84
Mitcham CR4 201 DK98
New Malden KT3 198 CR97
South Croydon CR2 220 DV108
Staines-upon-Thames TW18 174 BJ93
Wembley HA0 117 CH64
Woking GU22 226 AY120
Sch **Chestnut Gro Sch**, SW12
off Chestnut Gro 180 DG88
Chestnut Ho, NW3
off Maitland Pk Vil 274 F4
Chestnut La, N20 97 CY46
Amersham HP6 55 AR36
Harlow CM20 35 EP14
Sevenoaks TN13 257 FH124
Weybridge KT13 213 BP106
Sch **Chestnut La Sch**, Amer. HP6
off Chestnut La 55 AS36
Chestnut Manor Cl, Stai. TW18 174 BH92
Chestnut Mead, Red. RH1
off Oxford Rd 250 DE133
Chestnut Ms, Chal.St.P. SL9
off Gold Hill E 90 AX54
Chestnut Pk, Bray SL6 150 AE77
Chestnut Pl, SE26 182 DT91
Ashtead KT21 232 CL119
Epsom KT17 217 CU111
Weybridge KT13 213 BP106
Chestnut Ri, SE18 165 ER79
Bushey WD23 94 CB45
Chestnut Rd, SE27 181 DP90
SW20 199 CX96
Ashford TW15 175 BP91
Beaconsfield HP9 88 AH54
Dartford DA1 188 FK88
Enfield EN3 83 DY36
Guildford GU1 242 AX134
Horley RH6 268 DG146
Kingston upon Thames KT2 178 CL94
Twickenham TW2 177 CE89
Chestnut Row, N3
off Nether St 98 DA52
Chestnuts, Hutt. CM13 109 GB46
Chestnuts, The, Abridge RM4 86 EV41
Hemel Hempstead HP3 39 BF24
Hertford SG13 32 DR10
Horley RH6 269 DH146
Walton-on-Thames KT12 195 BU103
Sch **Chestnuts Prim Sch**, N15
off Black Boy La 122 DQ57
Chestnut Wk, Byfleet KT14
off Royston Rd 212 BL112
Chalfont St. Peter SL9 90 AY52
Epping Green CM16
off Epping Rd 51 EP24
Sevenoaks TN15 257 FL129
Shepperton TW17 195 BS99
Watford WD24 75 BU37
Whiteley Village KT12
off Octagon Rd 213 BS109
Woodford Green IG8 102 EG50
Chestnut Way, Felt. TW13 175 BV90
Cheston Av, Croy. CR0 203 DY103
Chestwood Gro, Uxb. UB10 134 BM66
Cheswick Cl, Dart. DA1 167 FF84
Chesworth Cl, Erith DA8 167 FE81
Chettle Cl, SE1 299 L6
Chettle Ct, N8 121 DN58
Chetwode Dr, Epsom KT18 233 CX118
Chetwode Rd, SW17 180 DF90
Tadworth KT20 233 CW119
Chetwood Wk, E6 293 H7
Chetwynd Av, E.Barn. EN4 98 DF46
Chetwynd Dr, Uxb. UB10 134 BM68
Chetwynd Rd, NW5 121 DH63
Chevalier Cl, Stan. HA7 96 CL49
Cheval Pl, SW7 296 D6
Cheval St, E14 302 A6
Cheveley Cl, Rom. RM3
off Chelsworth Dr 106 FM53
Cheveley Gdns, Burn. SL1 130 AJ68
Chevely Cl, Cooper. CM16 70 EX29
Cheveney Wk, Brom. BR2
off Marina Cl 204 EG97
CHEVENING, Sev. TN14 240 EZ119
Jct **Chevening Cross**,
Chev. TN14 240 FA120
Chevening Cross Rd,
Chev. TN14 240 FA120
Chevening La, Knock.P. TN14 240 EY115
Chevening Rd, NW6 272 E9
SE10 315 M1
SE19 182 DR93
Chevening TN14 240 EZ119
Chipstead TN13 256 FB121
Sundridge TN14 240 EY123
Chevenings, The, Sid. DA14 186 EW90
Sch **Chevening St. Botolph's C of E
Prim Sch**, Sev. TN13
off Chevening Rd 256 FB122
Cheverton Rd, N19 121 DK60
Chevet St, E9 279 L3
Chevington Pl, Horn. RM12
off Chevington Way 128 FK64
Chevington Way, Horn. RM12 128 FK63
Cheviot Cl, Bans. SM7 234 DB115
Bexleyheath DA7 167 FE82
Bushey WD23 76 CC44
Enfield EN1 82 DR40
Harlington UB3 155 BR80
Sutton SM2 218 DD109

Cheviot Gdns, NW2 119 CX61
SE27 181 DP91
Cheviot Gate, NW2 119 CY61
Cheviot Rd, SE27 181 DN92
Hornchurch RM11 127 FG60
Slough SL3 153 BA78
Cheviots, Hat. AL10 45 CU21
Hemel Hempstead HP2 40 BM17
Cheviot Way, Ilf. IG2 125 ES56
Chevron Cl, E16 291 P8
Chevy Rd, Sthl. UB2 156 CC75
Chewton Rd, E17 123 DY56
Cheyham Gdns, Sutt. SM2 217 CX110
Cheyham Way, Sutt. SM2 217 CY110
Cheyne Av, E18 124 EF55
Twickenham TW2 176 BZ88
Cheyne Cl, NW4 119 CW57
Amersham HP6 55 AR36
Bromley BR2 204 EL104
Gerrards Cross SL9 112 AY60
Ware SG12 33 DX05
Cheyne Ct, SW3 308 E2
Banstead SM7 *off Park Rd* 234 DB115
Cheyne Gdns, SW3 308 D2
Cheyne Hill, Surb. KT5 198 CM98
Cheyne Ms, SW3 308 D2
Chesham HP5 54 AR30
Cheyne Pk Dr, W.Wick. BR4 203 EC104
Cheyne Path, W7 137 CF71
Cheyne Pl, SW3 308 E2
Cheyne Rd, Ashf. TW15 175 BR93
Cheyne Row, SW3 308 C3
Cheyne Wk, N21 81 DP43
NW4 119 CW58
SW3 308 D3
SW10 308 A4
Chesham HP5 54 AR31
Croydon CR0 202 DU103
Horley RH6 268 DG149
Longfield DA3
off Cavendish Sq 209 FX97
Cheyneys Av, Edg. HA8 95 CK51
Chichele Gdns, Croy. CR0 220 DS105
Chichele Rd, NW2 272 C2
Oxted RH8 254 EE128
Chicheley Gdns, Har. HA3 94 CC52
Chicheley Rd, Har. HA3 94 CC52
Chicheley St, SE1 298 D4
Chichester Av, Ruis. HA4 115 BR61
Chichester Cl, E6 293 H9
SE3 164 EJ80
Aveley RM15 148 FQ74
Chafford Hundred RM16 169 FX77
Dorking RH4 247 CH134
Hampton TW12 *off Maple Cl* 176 BZ93
Chichester Ct, NW1 275 L6
Epsom KT17 217 CT109
Slough SL1 152 AV75
Stanmore HA7 118 CL55
Chichester Dr, Pur. CR8 219 DM112
Sevenoaks TN13 256 FF125
Chichester Gdns, Ilf. IG1 124 EL59
Chichester Ms, SE27 181 DN91
Chichester Rents, WC2 286 E8
Chichester Ri, Grav. DA12 191 GK91
Chichester Rd, E11 124 EE62
N9 100 DU46
NW6 283 J1
W2 283 M6
Croydon CR0 202 DS104
Dorking RH4 247 CH133
Greenhithe DA9 189 FT85
Chichester Row, Amer. HP6 55 AR38
Chichester St, SW1 309 M1
Chichester Way, E14 302 G8
Feltham TW14 175 BV87
Watford WD25 60 BY33
Chichester Wf, Erith DA8 167 FE78
Chicksand St, E1 288 B7
Chiddingfold, N12 98 DA48
Chiddingstone Av, Bexh. DA7 166 EZ80
Chiddingstone Cl, Sutt. SM2 218 DA110
Chiddingstone St, SW6 307 K8
Chieftan Dr, Purf. RM19 168 FM77
Chieveley Rd, Bexh. DA7 167 FB84
Chiffinch Gdns, Nthflt DA11 190 GE90
Chignell Pl, W13
off Broadway 137 CG74
CHIGWELL, IG7 103 EP48
⊖ **Chigwell** 103 EP49
Chigwell Gra, Chig. IG7 103 EQ46
Chigwell Hill, E1 300 E1
Chigwell Hurst Ct, Pnr. HA5 116 BX55
Chigwell La, Loug. IG10 85 EQ43
Chigwell Pk, Chig. IG7 103 EP49
Chigwell Pk Dr, Chig. IG7 103 EN48
Chigwell Prim Sch, Chig. IG7
off High Rd 103 EQ47
Chigwell Ri, Chig. IG7 103 EN47
Chigwell Rd, E18 124 EH55
Woodford Green IG8 102 EJ54
CHIGWELL ROW, Chig. IG7 104 EU47
Chigwell Row Inf Sch, Chig. IG7
off Lambourne Rd 104 EV47
Chigwell Sch, Chig. IG7
off High Rd 103 EQ47
Chigwell Vw, Rom. RM5
off Lodge La 104 FA51
Chilberton Dr, S.Merst. RH1 251 DJ130
Chilbrook Rd, Down. KT11 229 BU118
Chilcombe Ho, SW15
off Fontley Way 179 CU87
Chilcot Cl, E14 290 D9
Chilcote La, Lt.Chal. HP7 72 AV39
Chilcott Cl, Wem. HA0 117 CJ63
Chilcott Rd, Wat. WD24 75 BS36
Childebert Rd, SW17 181 DH89
Childeric Prim Sch, SE14 313 M5
Childeric Rd, SE14 313 M5
Childerley, Kings.T. KT1
off Burritt Rd 198 CN97
Childerley St, SW6 306 E6
Childers, The, Wdf.Grn. IG8 103 EM50
Childers St, SE8 313 M2
Child La, SE10 303 M7
Children's Ho Upr Sch, The, N1 277 N3
Children's Trust, The, Tad. KT20 233 CX121
Childs Av, Hare. UB9 92 BJ54
Childs Cl, Horn. RM11 128 FJ58
Childs Cres, Swans. DA10 189 FX86
Childs Hall Cl, Bkhm KT23
off Childs Hall Rd 246 BZ125
Childs Hall Dr, Bkhm KT23 246 BZ125
Childs Hall Rd, Bkhm KT23 246 BZ125
CHILDS HILL, NW2 120 DA61
Childs Hill Prim Sch, NW2
off Dersingham Rd 119 CY62
Childs Hill Wk, NW2 119 CZ62
Childs La, SE19 *off Westow St* 182 DS93
Child's Ms, SW5 *off Child's Pl* 295 L9
Child's Pl, SW5 295 K9
Child's St, SW5 295 K9
Child's Wk, SW5 295 K9
Childs Way, NW11 119 CZ57
Childwick Ct, Hem.H. HP3
off Rumballs Rd 40 BN23
Chilham Cl, Bex. DA5 186 EZ87
Hemel Hempstead HP2 40 BL21
Perivale UB6 137 CG68
Chilham Rd, SE9 184 EL91
Chilham Way, Brom. BR2 204 EG101
Chillerton Rd, SW17 180 DG92
Chillingford Ho, SW17
off Blackshaw Rd 180 DC91
Chillington Dr, SW11 160 DC84
Chillingworth Gdns, Twick. TW1
off Tower Rd 177 CF90
Chillingworth Rd, N7 276 E3
Chilmans Dr, Bkhm KT23 246 CB125
Chilmark Gdns, Merst. RH1 251 DL129
New Malden KT3 199 CT101
Chilmark Rd, SW16 201 DK96
Chilmead La, Nutfld RH1 251 DK132
Chilsey Grn Rd, Cher. KT16 193 BE100
Chiltern Av, Amer. HP6 55 AR38
Bushey WD23 76 CC44
Twickenham TW2 176 CA88
● **Chiltern Business Village**, Uxb. UB8 134 BH68
Chiltern Cl, Berk. HP4 38 AT18
Bexleyheath DA7 167 FE81
Borehamwood WD6 78 CM40
Bushey WD23 76 CB44
Croydon CR0 202 DS104
Goffs Oak EN7 65 DP27
Ickenham UB10 115 BP61
Staines-upon-Thames TW18 174 BG92
Watford WD18 75 BT42
Woking GU22 226 AW122
Worcester Park KT4
off Cotswold Way 199 CW103
● **Chiltern Commerce Cen**, Chesh. HP5 *off Asheridge Rd* 54 AN29
Chiltern Cor, Berk. HP4
off Durrants Rd 38 AU18
● **Chiltern Ct**, Chesh. HP5
off Asheridge Rd 54 AN29
Chiltern Ct, N10 98 DG54
Uxb. UB8 135 BP70
Chiltern Dene, Enf. EN2 81 DM42
Chiltern Dr, Mill End WD3 91 BF45
Surbiton KT5 198 CP99
Chiltern Gdns, NW2 119 CX62
Bromley BR2 204 EF98
Hornchurch RM12 128 FJ62
Chiltern Hts, Amer. HP7 72 AU39
Chiltern Hill, Chal.St.P. SL9 90 AY53
Chiltern Hills Acad, Chesh. HP5 *off Chartridge La* 54 AN30
Chiltern Hills Rd, Beac. HP9 88 AJ53
★ **Chiltern Open Air Mus**, Ch.St.G. HP8 91 AZ47
Chiltern Par, Amer. HP6 55 AQ37
Chiltern Pk, Chal.St.P. SL9 90 AY53
Chiltern Pk Av, Berk. HP4 38 AU17
Chiltern Pl, E5 122 DV61
Chiltern Rd, E3 290 B5
Amersham HP6 55 AP35
Burnham SL1 130 AH71
Ilford IG2 125 ES56
Northfleet DA11 190 GE90
Pinner HA5 116 BW57
St. Albans AL4 43 CJ16
Sutton SM2 218 DB109
Chilterns, Hat. AL10 45 CU21
Hemel Hempstead HP2 40 BL18
Chilterns, The, Nthch HP4 38 AT17
off Stoney Cl
Sutton SM2 *off Gatton Cl* 218 DB109
Chiltern St, W1 284 G6
Chiltern Vw Rd, Uxb. UB8 134 BJ68
Chiltern Way, Wdf.Grn. IG8 102 EG48
Chilthorne Cl, SE6
off Ravensbourne Pk Cres 183 DZ87
Chilton Av, W5 157 CK77
Chilton Cl, Penn HP10 88 AC45
Chilton Ct, Hert. SG14 31 DM07
off The Ridgeway
Walton-on-Thames KT12 213 BU105
Chilton Grn, Welw.G.C. AL7 30 DC09
Chilton Gro, SE8 301 K9
● **Chiltonian Ind Est**, SE12 184 EF86
Chilton Rd, Chesh. HP5 54 AQ29
Edgware HA8 96 CN51
Grays RM16 171 GG76
Richmond TW9 158 CN83
Chiltons, The, E18
off Grove Hill 102 EG54
Chiltons Cl, Bans. SM7
off High St 234 DB115
Chilton St, E2 288 B4
Chilvers Cl, Twick. TW2 177 CE89
Chilver St, SE10 303 M10
Chilwell Gdns, Wat. WD19 94 BW49
Chilwick Rd, Slou. SL2 131 AM69
CHILWORTH, Guil. GU4 259 BC140
⇌ **Chilworth** 259 BE140
Chilworth C of E Inf Sch, Chilw. GU4 *off Dorking Rd* 259 BD140
Chilworth Ct, SW19 179 CX88
Chilworth Gdns, Sutt. SM1 200 DC104
Chilworth Gate, Brox. EN10
off Silverfield 49 DZ22
Cheshunt EN8 *off Davison Dr* 67 DX28
Chilworth Ms, W2 283 P9
Chilworth Pl, Bark. IG11 146 EU70
Chilworth Rd, Albury GU5 260 BG139
Chilworth St, W2 283 P9
Chimes Av, N13 99 DN50
Chime Sq, St.Alb. AL3 43 CE19
Chimney La, Woob.Grn HP10
off Glory Mill La 110 AE56
China Hall Ms, SE16 301 H7
China Ms, SW2 181 DM87
★ **Chinatown**, W1
off Gerrard St 285 P10
Chinbrook Cres, SE12 184 EH90
Chinbrook Est, SE9 184 EK90
Chinbrook Rd, SE12 184 EH90
Chinchilla Dr, Houns. TW4 156 BW82
Chindit Cl, Brox. EN10 49 DY20
Chindits La, Warley CM14 108 FW50
Chine, The, N10 121 DJ56
N21 81 DP44
Dorking RH4 *off High St* 263 CH135
Wembley HA0 117 CH64
Chine Fm Pl, Knock.P. TN14 240 EX116
Ching Ct, WC2 286 A9
Chingdale Rd, E4 102 EE48
CHINGFORD, E4 101 EB46
⇌ **Chingford** 102 EE45
⊖ **Chingford** 102 EE45
Chingford Av, E4 101 EB48
Chingford C of E Inf Sch, E4
off Kings Rd 101 ED46
Chingford C of E (VC) Jun Sch, E4 *off Cambridge Rd* 101 ED46
Chingford Foundation Sch, E4
off Nevin Dr 101 EC46
CHINGFORD GREEN, E4 102 EF46
Chingford Hall Comm Prim Sch, E4 *off Burnside Av* 101 DZ51
CHINGFORD HATCH, E4 101 EC49
● **Chingford Ind Cen**, E4 101 DY50
Chingford La, Wdf.Grn. IG8 102 EE49
Chingford Mt Rd, E4 101 EA49
Chingford Rd, E4 101 EA51
E17 101 EB53
Chingley Cl, Brom. BR1 184 EE93
Ching Way, E4 101 DZ51
Chinnery Cl, Enf. EN1 82 DT39
Chinnor Cres, Grnf. UB6 136 CB68
Chinthurst La, Guil. GU4, GU5 258 AY141
Chinthurst Ms, Couls. CR5 234 DG116
Chinthurst Pk, Shalf. GU4 258 AY142
Chinthurst Sch, Tad. KT20
off Tadworth St 233 CW123
Chipka St, E14 302 E5
Chipley St, SE14 313 L3
Chipmunk Chase, Hat. AL10 44 CR16
Chipmunk Gro, Nthlt. UB5
off Argus Way 136 BY69
Chippendale All, Uxb. UB8
off Chippendale Waye 134 BK66
Chippendale Ho, SW1 309 K1
Chippendale St, E5 123 DX62
Chippendale Waye, Uxb. UB8 134 BK66
Chippenham Av, Wem. HA9 118 CP64
Chippenham Cl, Pnr. HA5 115 BT56
Romford RM3 106 FK50
Chippenham Gdns, NW6 283 J3
Romford RM3 106 FK50
Chippenham Ms, W9 283 J5
Chippenham Rd, W9 283 J5
Romford RM3 106 FK51
Chippenham Wk, Rom. RM3
off Chippenham Rd 106 FK51
CHIPPERFIELD, Kings L. WD4 58 BG31
Chipperfield Cl, Upmin. RM14 129 FS60
Chipperfield Rd, Bov. HP3 57 BB27
Hemel Hempstead HP3 40 BJ24
Kings Langley WD4 58 BK30
Orpington BR5 206 EU95
CHIPPING BARNET, Barn. EN5 79 CY42
Chipping Cl, Barn. EN5
off St. Albans Rd 79 CY41
Chippingfield, Harl. CM17 36 EW12
CHIPSTEAD, Couls. CR5 234 DF118
CHIPSTEAD, Sev. TN13 256 FC122
⇌ **Chipstead** 234 DF118
Chipstead, Chal.St.P. SL9 90 AW53
Chipstead Av, Th.Hth. CR7 201 DP98
CHIPSTEAD BOTTOM, Couls. CR5 234 DE121
Chipstead Cl, SE19 182 DT94
Coulsdon CR5 234 DG116
Redhill RH1 266 DF136
Sutton SM2 218 DB109
Chipstead Ct, Knap. GU21
off Creston Av 226 AS117
Chipstead Gdns, NW2 119 CV61
Chipstead La, Chipstead CR5 234 DB124
Lower Kingswood KT20 249 CZ125
Sevenoaks TN13 256 FC122
Chipstead Pk, Sev. TN13 256 FD122
Chipstead Pk Cl, Sev. TN13 256 FC122
Chipstead Pl Gdns, Sev. TN13 256 FC122
Chipstead Rd, Bans. SM7 233 CZ117
Erith DA8 167 FE80
Lon.Hthrw Air. TW6 154 BN83
Chipstead Sta Par, Chipstead CR5 *off Station App* 234 DF118
Chipstead St, SW6 307 K7
Chipstead Valley Prim Sch, Couls. CR5
off Chipstead Valley Rd 234 DG116
Chipstead Valley Rd, Couls. CR5 235 DH116
Chipstead Way, Bans. SM7 234 DF115
Chip St, SW4 161 DK83
Chirk Cl, Hayes UB4 136 BY70
Chirton Wk, Wok. GU21 226 AU118
Chisenhale Prim Sch, E3 279 L10
Chisenhale Rd, E3 279 L10
Chisholm Rd, Croy. CR0 202 DS103
Richmond TW10 178 CM86
Chisledon Wk, E9 279 P4
CHISLEHURST, BR7 185 EN94
⇌ **Chislehurst** 205 EN96
Chislehurst & Sidcup Gram Sch, Sid. DA15 *off Hurst Rd* 186 EV89
Chislehurst Av, N12 98 DC52
★ **Chislehurst Caves**, Chis. BR7
off Caveside Cl 205 EN95
Chislehurst C of E Prim Sch, Chis. BR7 *off School Rd* 185 EQ94
Chislehurst Rd, Brom. BR1 204 EK96
Chislehurst BR7 204 EK96
Orpington BR5, BR6 205 ES98
Richmond TW10 178 CL86
Sidcup DA14 186 EU92
CHISLEHURST WEST, Chis. BR7 185 EM92
Chislet Cl, Beck. BR3 183 EA94
Chisley Rd, N15 122 DS58
Chiswell Ct, Wat. WD24 76 BW38
CHISWELL GREEN, St.Alb. AL2 60 CA26
Chiswell Grn La, St.Alb. AL2 60 BX25
Chiswell Sq, SE3
off Brook La 164 EH82
Chiswell St, EC1 287 K6
SE5 311 M4
CHISWICK, W4 158 CR79
⇌ **Chiswick** 158 CQ80
Chiswick & Bedford Pk Prep Sch, W4 *off Priory Av* 158 CS77
Chiswick Br, SW14 158 CQ82
W4 158 CQ82
Chiswick Cl, Croy. CR0 201 DM104
Chiswick Common Rd, W4 158 CR77
Chiswick Ct, Pnr. HA5 116 BZ55
Chiswick Grn Studios, W4
off Evershed Wk 158 CQ77
Chiswick High Rd, W4 158 CQ77
Brentford TW8 158 CM78
★ **Chiswick Ho**, W4 158 CS79
Chiswick Ho Grds, W4 158 CR79
Chiswick La, W4 158 CS78
Chiswick La S, W4 159 CT78
Chiswick Mall, W4 159 CT79
W6 159 CT79
⊖ **Chiswick Park** 158 CQ77
● **Chiswick Pk**, W4 158 CP77
Chiswick Pier, W4 159 CT80
Chiswick Quay, W4 158 CQ81
Chiswick Rd, N9 100 DU47
W4 158 CQ77
Chiswick Rbt, W4 158 CN78
Chiswick Sch, W4
off Burlington La 158 CR80
Chiswick Sq, W4
off Hogarth Rbt 158 CS79
Chiswick Staithe, W4 158 CQ81
Chiswick Ter, W4
off Acton La 158 CQ77
Chiswick Village, W4 158 CP78
Chiswick War Mem Homes, W4
off Burlington La 158 CR80
Chiswick Wf, W4 159 CT79
Chittenden Cl, Hodd. EN11
off Founders Rd 33 EB14
Chittenden Cotts, Wisley GU23 228 BL116
Chitterfield Gate, Sipson UB7 154 BN80
Chitty's Common, Guil. GU2 242 AT130
Chitty's La, Dag. RM8 126 EX61
Chitty St, W1 285 M6
Chittys Wk, Guil. GU3 242 AT130
Chivalry Rd, SW11 180 DE85
Chivenor Gro, Kings.T. KT2 177 CK92
Chivenor Pl, St.Alb. AL4 43 CJ22
Chivers Rd, E4 101 EB48
Choats Manor Way, Dag. RM9 146 EZ69
Choats Rd, Bark. IG11 146 EW68
Dagenham RM9 146 EW68
CHOBHAM, Wok. GU24 210 AT111
Chobham Academy Sec Sch, E20 280 F3
● **Chobham Business Cen**, Chobham GU24 210 AX110
Chobham Cl, Ott. KT16 211 BB107
★ **Chobham Common National Nature Reserve**, Wok. GU24 210 AS105
Chobham Gdns, SW19 179 CX89
Chobham La, Longcr. KT16 192 AV102
Chobham Pk La, Chobham GU24 210 AU110
Chobham Rd, E15 280 G3
Horsell GU21 210 AW113
Ottershaw KT16 211 BA108
Woking GU21 226 AY116
Chobham St. Lawrence C of E Prim Sch, Chobham GU24
off Bagshot Rd 210 AS111
Choice Vw, Ilf. IG1
off Axon Pl 125 EQ61
Choir Grn, Knap. GU21 226 AS117
Cholmeley Cres, N6 121 DH59
Cholmeley Pk, N6 121 DH60
Cholmley Gdns, NW6 273 J2
Cholmley Rd, T.Ditt. KT7 197 CH100
Cholmondeley Av, NW10 139 CU68
Cholmondeley Wk, Rich. TW9 177 CJ85
Choppins Ct, E1 300 F2
Chopwell Cl, E15 281 H7
CHORLEYWOOD, Rick. WD3 73 BE43
⇌ **Chorleywood** 73 BD42
⊖ **Chorleywood** 73 BD42
CHORLEYWOOD BOTTOM, Rick. WD3 73 BD44
Chorleywood Bottom, Chorl. WD3 73 BD43
Chorleywood Cl, Rick. WD3 92 BK45
Chorleywood Common, Chorl. WD3 73 BE42
Chorleywood Cres, Orp. BR5 205 ET96
Chorleywood Ho Dr, Chorl. WD3 73 BE41
Chorleywood Lo La, Chorl. WD3 73 BF41
Chorleywood Prim Sch, Chorl. WD3 *off Stag La* 73 BC44
Chorleywood Rd, Rick. WD3 74 BG42
Choumert Gro, SE15 312 C9
Choumert Ms, SE15 312 C9
Choumert Rd, SE15 312 A10
Choumert Sq, SE15 312 C9
Chow Sq, E8 278 A2
Chrislaine Cl, Stanw. TW19 174 BK86
Chrisp St, E14 290 C7
Chris Pullen Way, N7 276 A4
Christabel Cl, Islw. TW7 157 CE83
Christchurch Av, N12 98 DC51
NW6 272 F6
Erith DA8 167 FD79
Harrow HA3 117 CH56
Rainham RM13 147 FF68
Teddington TW11 177 CG92
Wembley HA0 138 CL65
Christ Ch Bentinck C of E Prim Sch, NW1 284 D6
Christchurch (Brixton) C of E Prim Sch, SW9 310 F6
Christchurch C of E Prim Sch, SW11 308 D10
Christ Ch C of E Inf Sch, Vir.W. GU25 *off Christchurch Rd* 192 AV97
Christ Ch C of E Jun Sch, W5
off New Bdy 137 CK73
Ottershaw KT16
off Fletcher Rd 211 BD107
Christ Ch C of E Prim Sch, Regent's Pk, NW1 285 K2
Hampstead, NW3
off Christchurch Hill 120 DD62
SE23 *off Perry Vale* 183 DX89
SW3 308 E2
Barnet EN5
off Byng Rd 79 CX40
Surbiton KT5 *off Pine Gdns* 198 CN100
Christ Ch C of E Prim Sch & Nurs, Ware SG12
off New Rd 33 DY06
Christ Ch C of E Prim Sch, Purley, Pur. CR8
off Montpelier Rd 219 DP110
Christ Ch C of E Sch, E1 288 B6
Chorleywood WD3
off Rickmansworth Rd 73 BF41
Christchurch Cl, N12
off Summers La 98 DD52
Christchurch Cl, SW19 180 DD94
Enfield EN2 82 DQ40
St. Albans AL3 42 CC19
Christchurch Ct, NW6 272 E6
Christchurch Cres, Grav. DA12
off Christchurch Rd 191 GJ87
Radlett WD7 77 CG36
Christ Ch Erith C of E Prim Sch, Erith DA8 *off Lesney Pk Rd* 167 FD79
Christchurch Gdns, Epsom KT19 216 CP111
Harrow HA3 117 CG56
Christchurch Grn, Wem. HA0 138 CL65
Christchurch Hill, NW3 120 DD62
Christchurch La, Barn. EN5 79 CY40
Christ Ch Mt, Epsom KT19 216 CP112
Christ Ch New Malden Prim Sch, N.Mal. KT3 *off Elm Rd* 198 CR97
New Malden KT3
off Lime Gro 198 CS97
Christchurch Pk, Sutt. SM2 218 DC108
Christ Ch Pas, EC1 287 H8
Christchurch Pas, NW3 120 DC62
Barnet EN5 79 CY41
Christ Ch Path, Hayes UB3 155 BQ76
Christchurch Pl, Epsom KT19 216 CP111
Hertford SG14 *off Port Vale* 32 DQ09
Christ Ch Prim Sch, NW6 272 G7
SE10 303 K10
SE18 *off Shooters Hill* 165 EN81
Christchurch Prim Sch, Ilf. IG1
off Wellesley Rd 125 EQ60
Christ Ch Rd, Beck. BR3
off Fairfield Rd 203 EA96
Epsom KT19 216 CL112
Surbiton KT5 198 CM100
Christchurch Rd, N8 121 DL58
SW2 181 DM88
SW14 178 CP85
SW19 200 DD95
Dartford DA1 188 FJ87
Gravesend DA12 191 GJ88
Hemel Hempstead HP2 40 BK19
Ilford IG1 125 EP60
Purley CR8 219 DP110
Sidcup DA15 185 ET91
Tilbury RM18 171 GG81
Virginia Water GU25 192 AU97
Christchurch Sq, E9 278 G9
Christ Ch (Streatham) C of E Prim Sch, SW2
off Cotherstone Rd 181 DM88
Christchurch St, SW3 308 E2
Christchurch Ter, SW3 308 E2
Christchurch Way, SE10 303 K9
Woking GU21 *off Church St E* 227 AZ117
Christian Cl, Hodd. EN11 33 DZ13
Christian Ct, SE16 301 N3
Christian Flds, SW16 181 DN94
Christian Flds Av, Grav. DA12 191 GJ91
Christian Sq, Wind. SL4
off Ward Royal 151 AQ81
Christian St, E1 288 D8
Christie Cl, Bkhm KT23 246 BZ125
Broxbourne EN10 49 DZ21
Guildford GU1
off Waterside Rd 242 AX131
Christie Ct, N19
off Hornsey Rd 121 DL61
Watford WD18 75 BU43
Christie Dr, Croy. CR0 202 DU99
Christie Gdns, Rom. RM6 126 EV58
Christie Ho, W12
off Du Cane Rd 139 CV72
Christie Rd, E9 279 L5
Waltham Abbey EN9
off Deer Pk Way 83 EB35
Christies Av, Bad.Mt TN14 224 FA110
Christie's Ed, W1 285 K6
Christie Wk, Cat. CR3 236 DR122
Christina Sq, N4 121 DP60
Christina St, EC2 287 N4
Christine Worsley Cl, N21
off Highfield Rd 99 DP47
Christmas Hill, Guil. GU4, GU5 259 AZ141
Christmas La, Farn.Com. SL2 111 AQ62
Christopher Av, W7 157 CG76
Christopher Cl, SE16 301 J4
Hornchurch RM12
off Chevington Way 128 FK63
Sidcup DA15 185 ET85
Christopher Ct, Hem.H. HP3
off Seaton Rd 40 BK23
Tadworth KT20 *off High St* 233 CW123
Christopher Gdns, Dag. RM9
off Wren Rd 126 EX64
Christopher Hatton Prim Sch, EC1 286 E5
Christopher Pl, NW1 285 P3
Christopher Pl Shop Cen, St.Alb. AL3 *off Market Pl* 43 CD20
Christopher Rd, Sthl. UB2 155 BV77
Christopher's Ms, W11 294 F2
Christopher St, EC2 287 M5
Christ's Coll Finchley, N2
off East End Rd 120 DB55
Christ's Coll, Guildford, Guil. GU1 *off Larch Av* 242 AW131
Christ's Sch, Rich. TW10
off Queens Rd 178 CN85
Christ the King 6th Form Coll, SE13 315 H10
Christ the King RC Prim Sch, N4 *off Tollington Pk* 121 DM61
Christy Rd, Bigg.H. TN16 238 EJ115
Chryssell Rd, SW9 310 F5
Chrystie La, Bkhm KT23 246 CB126
Chubworthy St, SE14 313 L3
Chucks La, Walt.Hill KT20 233 CV124
Chudleigh Cres, Ilf. IG3 125 ES63
Chudleigh Gdns, Sutt. SM1 200 DC104
Chudleigh Rd, NW6 272 B7
SE4 183 DZ85
Romford RM3 106 FL49
Twickenham TW2 177 CF87
Chudleigh St, E1 289 J8
Chudleigh Way, Ruis. HA4 115 BU60
Chulsa Rd, SE26 182 DV92
Chumleigh Gdns, SE5
off Chumleigh St 311 N2
Chumleigh St, SE5 311 N2
Chumleigh Wk, Surb. KT5 198 CM98
Church All, Ald. WD25 76 CC38
Croydon CR0 201 DN102
Gravesend DA11 *off High St* 191 GH86
Church App, SE21 182 DR90
Cudham TN14 239 EQ115
Egham TW20 193 BC97
Stanwell TW19 174 BK86

Church Av, E4 101 ED51
NW1 275 K5
SW14 158 CR83
Beckenham BR3 203 EA95
Northolt UB5 136 BZ66
Pinner HA5 116 BY58
Ruislip HA4 115 BR60
Sidcup DA14 186 EU92
Southall UB2 156 BY76
Churchbury Cl, Enf. EN1 82 DS40
Churchbury La, Enf. EN1 82 DR41
Churchbury Rd, SE9 184 EK87
Enfield EN1 82 DR40
Church Cl, N20 98 DE48
W8 295 L4
Addlestone KT15 212 BH105
Cuffley EN6 65 DL29
Edgware HA8 96 CQ50
Eton SL4 151 AR79
Fetcham KT22 231 CD124
Hayes UB4 135 BR71
Horsell GU21 226 AX116
Hounslow TW3 *off Bath Rd* 156 BZ83
Little Berkhamsted SG13 *off Church Rd* 47 DJ19
Loughton IG10 85 EM40
Lower Kingswood KT20 *off Buckland Rd* 249 CZ127
Northwood HA6 93 BT52
Radlett WD7 77 CG36
Staines-upon-Thames TW18 *off The Broadway* 194 BJ97
Uxbridge UB8 134 BH68
West Drayton UB7 154 BL76
Church Cor, SW17 *off Mitcham Rd* 180 DF92
Church Ct, Reig. RH2 250 DB134
Richmond TW9 *off George St* 177 CK85
Church Cres, E9 279 J6
N3 97 CZ53
N10 121 DH56
N20 98 DE48
St. Albans AL3 42 CC19
Sawbridgeworth CM21 36 EZ05
South Ockendon RM15 149 FW69
Church Cft, St.Alb. AL4 43 CJ22
Churchcroft Cl, SW12 180 DG87
Churchdown, Brom. BR1 184 EE91
Church Dr, NW9 118 CR60
Bray SL6 150 AC75
Harrow HA2 116 BZ58
West Wickham BR4 204 EE104
Church Elm La, Dag. RM10 146 FA65
CHURCH END, N3 97 CZ53
NW10 138 CS65
Church End, E17 123 EB56
NW4 119 CV55
Harlow CM19 51 EN17
Church Entry, EC4 287 H9
Church Est Almshouses, Rich. TW9 *off St. Mary's Gro* 158 CM84
Church Fm Cl, Swan. BR8 207 FC100
Church Fm La, Sutt. SM3 217 CY107
Church Fm Way, Ald. WD25 76 CB38
Church Fld, Dart. DA2 188 FK89
Epping CM16 70 EU29
Radlett WD7 77 CG36
Sevenoaks TN13 256 FE122
Churchfield, Harl. CM20 36 EU13
Churchfield Av, N12 98 DC51
Churchfield Cl, Har. HA2 116 CC56
Hayes UB3 135 BT73
Churchfield Ms, Slou. SL2 132 AU72
Churchfield Path, Chsht EN8 66 DW29
Churchfield Pl, Shep. TW17 *off Chertsey Rd* 195 BP101
Weybridge KT13 212 BN105
Sch **Churchfield Prim Sch**, N9 *off Latymer Rd* 100 DT46
Churchfield Rd, W3 138 CQ74
W7 157 CE75
W13 137 CH74
Chalfont St. Peter SL9 90 AX53
Reigate RH2 249 CZ133
Tewin AL6 30 DC06
Walton-on-Thames KT12 195 BU102
Welling DA16 166 EU83
Weybridge KT13 212 BN105
Churchfields, E18 102 EG53
SE10 314 E4
Broxbourne EN10 49 EA21
Guildford GU4 *off Burpham La* 243 BA129
Hertford SG13 32 DR10
Horsell GU21 226 AY116
Loughton IG10 84 EL42
West Molesey KT8 196 CA97
Churchfields Av, Felt. TW13 176 BZ90
Weybridge KT13 213 BP105
Sch **Churchfields Infants' Sch**, E18 *off Churchfields* 102 EG53
Sch **Churchfields Jun Sch**, E18 *off Churchfields* 102 EG53
Churchfields La, Brox. EN10 *off Station Rd* 49 EA20
Sch **Churchfields Prim Sch**, Beck. BR3 *off Churchfields Rd* 203 DX96
Churchfields Rd, Beck. BR3 203 DX96
Watford WD24 75 BT36
Church Gdns, W5 157 CK75
Dorking RH4 263 CG135
Wembley HA0 117 CG63
Church Garth, N19 *off Pemberton Gdns* 121 DK61
Church Gate, SW6 306 F10
Churchgate, Chsht EN8 66 DV30
Sch **Churchgate C of E Prim Sch**, Harl. CM17 *off Hobbs Cross Rd* 36 EZ12
Churchgate Gdns, Harl. CM17 *off Sheering Rd* 36 EZ11
Churchgate Rd, Chsht EN8 66 DV29
Churchgate St, Harl. CM17 36 EY11
Church Grn, SW9 310 F8
Hayes UB3 135 BT72
Hersham KT12 214 BW107
St. Albans AL1 *off Hatfield Rd* 43 CD19
Church Gro, SE13 163 EB84
Amersham HP6 72 AY39
Kingston upon Thames KT1 197 CJ95
Wexham SL3 132 AW71
Church Hill, E17 123 EA56
N21 99 DM45
SE18 305 K7
SW19 179 CZ92
Bedmond WD5 59 BT26
Carshalton SM5 218 DF106
Caterham CR3 236 DT124
Crayford DA2 167 FE84
Church Hill, Cudham TN14 239 EQ115
Dartford DA2 188 FK90
Epping CM16 70 EU29
Greenhithe DA9 189 FS85
Harefield UB9 114 BJ55
Harrow HA1 117 CE60
Hertford Heath SG13 32 DV11
Horsell GU21 226 AX116
Lemsford AL8 29 CU10
Loughton IG10 84 EL41
Merstham RH1 251 DH126
Nutfield RH1 251 DM133
Orpington BR6 206 EU101
Purley CR8 219 DL110
Pyrford GU22 227 BF117
Shere GU5 260 BN139
Tatsfield TN16 238 EK122
Sch **Church Hill Prim Sch**, Barn. EN4 *off Burlington Ri* 98 DF45
Church Hill Rd, E17 123 EB56
Barnet EN4 98 DF45
Surbiton KT6 198 CL99
Sutton SM3 217 CX105
Church Hill Wd, Orp. BR5 205 ET99
Church Hollow, Purf. RM19 168 FN78
Church Hyde, SE18 *off Old Mill Rd* 165 ES79
Churchill Av, Har. HA3 117 CH58
Uxbridge UB10 135 BP69
Churchill Cl, Dart. DA1 188 FP88
Feltham TW14 175 BT88
Fetcham KT22 231 CE123
Uxbridge UB10 135 BP69
Warlingham CR6 236 DW117
Sch **Churchill C of E Prim Sch**, West. TN16 *off Rysted La* 255 EQ125
Churchill Ct, SE18 *off Rushgrove St* 305 K9
W5 138 CM70
Northolt UB5 116 CA64
Staines-upon-Thames TW18 *off Chestnut Gro* 174 BH93
Churchill Cres, N.Mymms AL9 *off Dixons Hill Rd* 45 CW23
Churchill Dr, Knot.Grn HP9 88 AJ50
Weybridge KT13 195 BQ104
Churchill Gdns, SW1 309 L1
W3 138 CN72
Sch **Churchill Gdns Prim Sch**, SW1 309 M1
Churchill Gdns Rd, SW1 309 K1
Churchill Ms, Wdf.Grn. IG8 *off High Rd Woodford Grn* 102 EF51
★ **Churchill Mus & Cabinet War Rooms**, SW1 297 P4
Churchill Pl, E14 302 D2
Harrow HA1 *off Sandridge Cl* 117 CE56
Churchill Rd, E16 292 C9
NW2 139 CV65
NW5 121 DH63
Edgware HA8 96 CM51
Epsom KT19 216 CN111
Gravesend DA11 191 GF88
Grays RM17 170 GD79
Guildford GU1 258 AY135
Horton Kirby DA4 208 FQ98
St. Albans AL1 43 CG18
Slough SL3 153 AZ77
Smallfield RH6 269 DP148
South Croydon CR2 220 DQ109
Churchill Ter, E4 101 EA49
Churchill Wk, E9 279 H2
Churchill Way, Bigg.H. TN16 222 EK113
Bromley BR1 *off Ethelbert Rd* 204 EG97
Sunbury-on-Thames TW16 175 BU92
Church Island, Stai. TW18 173 BD91
Churchlands Way, Wor.Pk. KT4 199 CX103
Church La, E11 124 EE60
E17 123 EB56
N2 120 DD55
N8 121 DM56
N9 100 DU47
N17 100 DS53
NW9 118 CQ61
SW17 181 DH91
SW19 199 CZ95
W5 157 CJ75
Abridge RM4 86 EY40
Albury GU5 260 BH139
Aldenham WD25 76 CB38
Bayford SG13 47 DM17
Berkhamsted HP4 38 AW19
Bletchingley RH1 252 DR133
Bovingdon HP3 57 BB27
Bray SL6 150 AC75
Bromley BR2 204 EL102
Broxbourne EN10 48 DW22
Burstow RH6 269 DL153
Chaldon CR3 235 DN123
Chalfont St. Peter SL9 90 AX53
Chelsham CR6 237 EC116
Cheshunt EN8 66 DV29
Chessington KT9 216 CM107
Chislehurst BR7 205 EQ95
Colney Heath AL4 44 CP22
Coulsdon CR5 234 DG122
Dagenham RM10 147 FB65
Enfield EN1 82 DR41
Godstone RH9 253 DX132
Great Warley CM13 129 FW58
Harrow HA3 95 CF53
Hatfield AL9 45 CW18
Headley KT18 232 CQ124
Hutton CM13 109 GE46
Kings Langley WD4 58 BN29
Loughton IG10 85 EM41
Mill End WD3 92 BG46
Nork SM7 233 CX117
North Ockendon RM14 129 FV64
North Weald Bassett CM16 71 FB26
Northaw EN6 64 DG30
Oxted RH8 254 EE129
Pinner HA5 116 BY55
Purfleet RM19 168 FN78
Richmond TW10 178 CL88
Romford RM1 127 FE56
Sarratt WD3 73 BF38
Send GU23 243 BB126
Sheering CM22 37 FD07
Shere GU5 260 BN139
Stapleford Abbotts RM4 87 FC42
Stoke Poges SL2 132 AT69
Teddington TW11 177 CF92
Thames Ditton KT7 197 CF100
Twickenham TW1 177 CG88
Uxbridge UB8 134 BH68
Wallington SM6 201 DK104
Warlingham CR6 237 DX117
Wennington RM13 148 FK72
Westerham TN16 238 EK122
Church La, Wexham SL3 132 AW71
Weybridge KT13 212 BN105
Windsor SL4 151 AR81
Worplesdon GU3 242 AS127
Church La Av, Couls. CR5 235 DH122
Church La Dr, Couls. CR5 235 DH122
CHURCH LANGLEY, Harl. CM17 36 EY14
Sch **Church Langley Comm Prim Sch**, Ch.Lang. CM17 *off Church Langley Way* 52 EW15
Jct **Church Langley Rbt**, Harl. CM17 52 EV15
Church Langley Way, Harl. CM17 52 EW15
Churchley Rd, SE26 182 DV91
Church Leys, Harl. CM18 51 ET16
Church Manor Est, SW9 310 F5
Church Manorway, SE2 165 ET77
Erith DA8 167 FD76
Church Manorway Ind Est, Erith DA8 167 FC76
Churchmead, SE5 *off Camberwell Rd* 311 K5
Church Mead, Roydon CM19 34 EH14
Churchmead Cl, E.Barn. EN4 80 DE44
Sch **Churchmead C of E Sch**, Datchet SL3 *off Priory Way* 152 AV80
Church Meadow, Long Dit. KT6 197 CJ103
Churchmead Rd, NW10 139 CU65
Church Ms, Add. KT15 212 BJ105
Church Mill Gra, Harl. CM17 36 EY12
Churchmore Rd, SW16 201 DJ95
Church Mt, N2 120 DD57
Church Paddock Ct, Wall. SM6 201 DK104
● **Church Pk Ind Est**, Craw. RH11 268 DE154
Church Pas, EC2 *off Gresham St* 287 K8
Barnet EN5 *off Wood St* 79 CZ42
Surbiton KT6 198 CL99
Church Path, E11 124 EG57
E17 *off St. Mary Rd* 123 EB56
N5 277 H2
N12 98 DC50
N17 *off White Hart La* 100 DS52
N20 98 DC49
NW10 138 CS66
SW14 158 CR83
SW19 200 DA96
W4 158 CQ76
W7 137 CE74
Bray SL6 150 AC75
Cobham KT11 213 BV114
Coulsdon CR5 235 DN118
Grays RM17 170 GA79
Great Amwell SG12 33 DZ09
Greenhithe DA9 189 FT85
Mitcham CR4 200 DE97
Northfleet DA11 190 GC86
Southall UB1 136 CA74
Southall Green UB2 156 BZ76
Swanley BR8 *off School La* 207 FH95
Woking GU21 *off High St* 227 AZ117
Church Pl, SW1 297 M1
W5 *off Church Gdns* 157 CK75
Ickenham UB10 115 BQ62
Mitcham CR4 200 DE97
Twickenham TW1 *off Church St* 177 CG88
Church Ri, SE23 183 DX88
Chessington KT9 216 CM107
Church Rd, E10 123 EB61
E12 124 EL64
E17 101 DY54
N1 277 K5
N6 120 DG58
N17 100 DS53
NW4 119 CV56
NW10 138 CS65
SE19 202 DS95
SW13 159 CT82
SW19 (Wimbledon) 179 CY90
W3 158 CQ75
W7 137 CF74
Addlestone KT15 212 BG106
Ashford TW15 174 BM90
Ashtead KT21 231 CK117
Barking IG11 145 EQ65
Bexleyheath DA7 166 EZ82
Biggin Hill TN16 238 EK117
Bookham KT23 230 BZ123
Bourne End SL8 110 AD62
Brasted TN16 240 EV124
Bromley BR2 204 EG96
Buckhurst Hill IG9 102 EH46
Burstow RH6 269 DN151
Byfleet KT14 212 BM113
Caterham CR3 236 DT123
Chelsfield BR6 224 EY106
Claygate KT10 215 CF107
Cowley UB8 134 BK70
Cranford TW5 155 BV78
Crockenhill BR8 207 FD101
Croydon CR0 201 DP104
East Molesey KT8 197 CD98
Egham TW20 173 BA92
Enfield EN3 82 DW44
Epsom KT17 216 CS112
Erith DA8 167 FC78
Farnborough BR6 223 EQ106
Farnham Royal SL2 131 AQ69
Feltham TW13 176 BX92
Gravesend DA12, DA13 191 GJ94
Greenhithe DA9 189 FS85
Guildford GU1 258 AX135
Halstead TN14 224 EY111
Ham TW10 178 CM92
Harefield UB9 114 BJ55
Harlow CM17 52 EW18
Harold Wood RM3 106 FN53
Hayes UB3 135 BT72
Hemel Hempstead HP3 41 BQ21
Hertford SG14 31 DP08
Heston TW5 156 CA80
High Beach IG10 84 EH40
High Wycombe HP10 88 AD47
Horley RH6 268 DF149
Horsell GU21 226 AY116
Ilford IG2 125 ER58
Isleworth TW7 157 CD81
Iver SL0 133 BC69
Kenley CR8 236 DR115
Keston BR2 222 EK108
Kingston upon Thames KT1 198 CM96
Leatherhead KT22 231 CH122
Leigh RH2 265 CU141
Little Berkhamsted SG13 47 DJ19
Long Ditton KT6 197 CJ103
Lowfield Heath RH11 268 DE154
Church Rd, Mitcham CR4 200 DD96
Noak Hill RM4 106 FK46
Northolt UB5 136 BZ66
Northwood HA6 93 BT52
Old Windsor SL4 172 AV85
Penn HP10 88 AC47
Potten End HP4 39 BB16
Potters Bar EN6 64 DB30
Purley CR8 219 DL110
Redhill RH1 266 DE136
Reigate RH2 266 DA136
Richmond TW9, TW10 178 CL85
St. John's GU21 226 AU119
Seal TN15 257 FM121
Seer Green HP9 89 AR51
Shepperton TW17 195 BP101
Shortlands BR2 204 EE97
Sidcup DA14 186 EU91
Southall UB2 156 BZ76
Stanmore HA7 95 CH50
Sutton SM3 217 CY107
Sutton at Hone DA4 188 FL94
Swanley BR8 208 FK95
Swanscombe DA10 190 FZ86
Teddington TW11 177 CE91
Tilbury RM18 171 GF81
Wallington SM6 201 DJ104
Warlingham CR6 236 DW117
Watford WD17 75 BU39
Welling DA16 166 EV82
Welwyn Garden City AL8 29 CX09
West Drayton UB7 154 BK76
West Ewell KT19 216 CR108
West Tilbury RM18 171 GL79
Whyteleafe CR3 236 DT118
Woldingham CR3 237 DX122
Worcester Park KT4 198 CS102
Church Rd Merton, SW19 200 DD95
Church Row, NW3 273 N1
Chislehurst BR7 185 EQ94
Church Row Ms, Ware SG12 *off Church St* 33 DX06
Church Side, Epsom KT18 216 CP113
Churchside Cl, Bigg.H. TN16 238 EJ117
Church Sq, Shep. TW17 195 BP101
Trm **Church Street** 201 DP103
Church Street, E15 281 K8
E16 305 N3
N9 100 DS47
NW8 284 B6
W2 284 B6
W4 158 CS79
Amersham HP7 55 AP40
Betchworth RH3 264 CS135
Bovingdon HP3 57 BB27
Burnham SL1 130 AJ70
Chalvey SL1 151 AQ75
Chesham HP5 54 AP31
Cobham KT11 229 BV115
Croydon CR0 202 DQ103
Dagenham RM10 147 FB65
Dorking RH4 263 CG136
Effingham KT24 246 BX127
Enfield EN2 82 DR41
Epsom KT17 216 CS113
Esher KT10 214 CB105
Essendon AL9 46 DE17
Ewell KT17 217 CU109
Gravesend DA11 191 GH86
Grays RM17 170 GC79
Hampton TW12 196 CC95
Hatfield AL9 45 CW17
Hemel Hempstead HP2 40 BK18
Hertford SG14 32 DR09
Isleworth TW7 157 CH83
Kingston upon Thames KT1 197 CK96
Leatherhead KT22 231 CH122
Old Woking GU22 227 BC121
Reigate RH2 250 DA134
Rickmansworth WD3 92 BL46
St. Albans AL3 43 CD19
Sawbridgeworth CM21 36 EY05
Seal TN15 257 FN121
Shoreham TN14 225 FF111
Slough SL1 152 AT76
Southfleet DA13 190 GA92
Staines-upon-Thames TW18 173 BE91
Sunbury-on-Thames TW16 195 BV97
Sutton SM1 *off High St* 218 DB106
Twickenham TW1 177 CG88
Waltham Abbey EN9 67 EC33
Walton-on-Thames KT12 195 BU102
Ware SG12 33 DX06
Watford WD18 76 BW42
Weybridge KT13 212 BN105
Windsor SL4 *off Castle Hill* 151 AR81
Church St E, Wok. GU21 227 AZ117
Church St Est, NW8 284 B5
Church St N, E15 281 K8
Church St Pas, E15 281 K8
Church St W, Wok. GU21 226 AY117
Church Stretton Rd, Houns. TW3 176 CC85
Church Ter, NW4 119 CV55
SE13 164 EE83
SW8 309 P8
Richmond TW10 177 CK85
Windsor SL4 151 AL82
CHURCH TOWN, Gdse. RH9 253 DX131
● **Church Trd Est**, Erith DA8 167 FG80
Church Vale, N2 120 DF55
SE23 182 DW89
Church Vw, Aveley RM15 168 FQ75
Broxbourne EN10 49 DZ20
Swanley BR8 *off Lime Rd* 207 FD97
Upminster RM14 128 FN61
Church Vw Cl, Horl. RH6 268 DF149
Church Vw Gro, SE26 183 DX93
Churchview Rd, Twick. TW2 177 CD88
Church Vil, Sev. TN13 *off Maidstone Rd* 256 FE122
Church Wk, N6 120 DG62
N16 277 M2
NW2 119 CZ62
NW4 119 CW55
NW9 118 CR61
SW13 159 CU81
SW15 179 CV85
SW16 201 DJ96
SW20 199 CW97
Bletchingley RH1 252 DR133
Brentford TW8 157 CJ79
Burnham SL1 130 AH70
Bushey WD23 *off High St* 76 CA44
Caterham CR3 236 DU124
Chertsey KT16 194 BG101
Church Wk, Dartford DA2 188 FK90
Enfield EN2 82 DR41
Eynsford DA4 208 FL104
Gravesend DA12 191 GK88
Hayes UB3 135 BT72
Horley RH6 *off Woodroyd Av* 268 DF149
Leatherhead KT22 231 CH122
Outwood RH1 267 DP142
Reigate RH2 *off Reigate Rd* 250 DC134
Richmond TW9 *off Red Lion St* 177 CK85
Sawbridgeworth CM21 36 EZ05
Thames Ditton KT7 197 CF100
Walton-on-Thames KT12 195 BU102
Weybridge KT13 *off Beales La* 194 BN104
🔒 **Church Wk Shop Cen**, Cat. CR3 *off Church Wk* 236 DU124
Churchward Ho, W14 *off Ivatt Pl* 307 H1
Church Way, N20 98 DD48
Barnet EN4 80 DF42
Edgware HA8 96 CN51
Oxted RH8 254 EF132
South Croydon CR2 220 DT110
Churchway, NW1 285 P2
Churchwell Path, E9 278 G4
Churchwood Gdns, Wdf.Grn. IG8 102 EG49
Churchyard, The, Bray SL6 *off Church Dr* 150 AC75
Churchyard Row, SE11 299 H8
Church Yd Wk, W2 284 A6
Churston Av, E13 144 EH67
Churston Cl, SW2 *off Tulse Hill* 181 DP88
Churston Dr, Mord. SM4 199 CX99
Churston Gdns, N11 99 DJ51
Churton Pl, SW1 297 M9
Churton St, SW1 297 M9
Chuters Cl, Byfleet KT14 212 BL112
Chuters Gro, Epsom KT17 217 CT112
Chyne, The, Ger.Cr. SL9 113 AZ57
Chyngton Cl, Sid. DA15 185 ET90
Chynham Pl, S.Croy. CR2 220 DS110
Cibber Rd, SE23 183 DX89
Cicada Rd, SW18 180 DC85
Cicely Rd, SE15 312 D7
Cillocks Cl, Hodd. EN11 49 EA16
Cimba Wd, Grav. DA12 191 GL91
Cinderella Path, NW11 *off North End Rd* 120 DB60
Cinderford Way, Brom. BR1 184 EE91
Cinder Path, Wok. GU22 226 AW119
Cinnabar Wf, E1 300 D3
Cinnamon Cl, SE15 312 A4
Croydon CR0 201 DL101
Windsor SL4 151 AM81
Cinnamon Gdns, Guil. GU2 242 AU129
Cinnamon Row, SW11 307 P10
Cinnamon St, E1 300 F3
Cintra Pk, SE19 182 DT94
CIPPENHAM, Slou. SL1 151 AM75
Cippenham Cl, Slou. SL1 131 AM73
Sch **Cippenham Inf Sch**, Slou. SL1 *off Dennis Way* 131 AK73
Sch **Cippenham Jun Sch**, Cipp. SL1 *off Elmshott La* 131 AL73
Cippenham La, Slou. SL1 131 AM73
Circle, The, NW2 118 CS62
NW7 96 CR50
SE1 300 A4
Tilbury RM18 *off Toronto Rd* 171 GG81
Circle Gdns, SW19 200 DA96
Byfleet KT14 212 BM113
Circle Rd, Whiteley Vill. KT12 213 BS110
Circuits, The, Pnr. HA5 116 BW56
Circular Rd, N17 122 DT55
Circular Way, SE18 165 EM79
Circus Lo, NW8 284 A2
Circus Ms, W1 284 E6
Circus Pl, EC2 287 M7
Circus Rd, NW8 284 A2
Circus St, SE10 314 E5
Cirencester St, W2 283 L6
Cirrus Cl, Wall. SM6 219 DL108
Cirrus Cres, Grav. DA12 191 GL92
Cissbury Ring N, N12 97 CZ50
Cissbury Ring S, N12 97 CZ50
Cissbury Rd, N15 122 DR57
Citadel Pl, SE11 298 C10
Citizen Rd, N7 121 DN63
● **C.I. Twr**, N.Mal. KT3 198 CS97
Citron Ter, SE15 *off Nunhead La* 162 DV83
Coll **City & Guilds of London Art Sch**, SE11 310 F1
Coll **City & Islington 6th Form Coll**, EC1 286 G2
Coll **City & Islington Coll**, Adult Learning Cen, N19 *off Junction Rd* 121 DJ61
Cen for Applied Sciences, EC1 286 G2
Cen for Business, Arts & Tech, N7 276 B1
Cen for Health, Social & Child Care, N7 *off Holloway Rd* 121 DL63
Cen for Lifelong Learning, N4 *off Blackstock Rd* 121 DP61
● **City Business Cen**, SE16 *off Lower Rd* 300 G5
Coll **City Business Coll**, EC1 287 H3
Coll **City Coll, The**, N1 287 L2
● **City Cross Business Pk**, SE10 303 K8
● **City Forum**, EC1 287 J2
City Gdn Row, N1 287 H1
City Gate Ho, Ilf. IG2 125 EN58
City House, Croy. CR0 201 DP101
Coll **City Learning Cen**, NW10 272 C9
Coll **City Lit**, Keeley Ho, WC2 286 C9
Stukeley St, WC2 286 B8
City Mill River Towpath, E15 *off Blaker Rd* 280 E9
Sch **City of London Acad (Islington)**, N1 277 J9
Sch **City of London Acad (Southwark)**, SE1 300 D10
Sch **City of London Freemen's Sch**, Ashtd. KT21 *off Park La* 232 CN119
Sch **City of London Sch**, EC4 287 J10

C

Sch City of London Sch for Girls, EC2 287 K6
★ City of Westminster Archives Cen, SW1 297 P6
Coll City of Westminster Coll, Cockpit Thea, NW8 284 C5
Cosway St Cen, NW1 284 D6
Maida Vale Cen, W9 283 L3
Paddington Grn Cen, W2 284 A6
Queens Pk Cen, W9 283 J3
● City Pk, Welw.G.C. AL7 30 DA08
● City Pt, EC2 287 L6
City Rd, EC1 286 G1
⇌ City Thameslink 286 G9
City Twr, E14 302 D6
Uni City Uni, Cass Business Sch, EC1 287 L5
Halls of Res & Saddlers Sports Cen, EC1 287 J4
Northampton Sq Campus, EC1 286 G3
Walter Sickert Hall, N1 287 J2
Uni City Uni - Inns of Ct Sch of Law, Atkin Bldg, WC1 286 D6
Gray's Inn Pl, WC1 286 D7
Princeton St, WC1 286 D6
Uni City Uni - St. Bartholomew Sch of Nursing & Midwifery, E1 288 F7
City Vw, Ilf. IG1 off Axon Pl 125 EQ61
City Vw Apts, N1 277 J7
Cityview Ct, SE22 182 DU87
City Wk, SE1 299 N5
Civic Cl, St.Alb. AL1 43 CD20
Civic Offices, St.Alb. AL1 43 CD20
Civic Sq, Harl. CM20 off South Gate 51 ER15
Tilbury RM18 171 GG82
Civic Way, Ilf. IG6 125 EQ56
Ruislip HA4 116 BX64
Clabon Ms, SW1 296 E7
Clacket La, West. TN16 238 EL124
Clack La, Ruis. HA4 115 BQ60
Clack St, SE16 301 H5
Clacton Rd, E6 292 E2
E17 123 DY58
N17 off Sperling Rd 100 DT54
Claddagh Ct, N18 off Baxter Rd 100 DV49
Claigmar Gdns, N3 98 DB53
Claire Causeway, Dart. DA2 169 FS84
Claire Ct, N12 98 DC48
Bushey Heath WD23 95 CD46
Pinner HA5 off Westfield Pk 94 BZ52
Claire Gdns, Stan. HA7 95 CJ50
Claire Pl, E14 302 B6
Clairvale, Horn. RM11 128 FL59
Clairvale Rd, Houns. TW5 156 BX81
Clairview Rd, SW16 181 DH92
Clairville Ct, Reig. RH2 250 DD134
Clairville Gdns, W7 137 CE74
Clairville Pt, SE23 183 DX90
Clammas Way, Uxb. UB8 134 BJ71
Clamp Hill, Stan. HA7 95 CD49
Clancarty Rd, SW6 307 K9
⇌ Clandon 244 BH129
Clandon Av, Egh. TW20 173 BC94
Clandon Cl, W3 158 CP75
Epsom KT17 217 CT107
Sch Clandon C of E Inf Sch, W.Clan. GU4 off The Street 244 BG131
Clandon Gdns, N3 120 DA55
★ Clandon Park, Guil. GU4 244 BG132
Clandon Pk, W.Clan. GU4 244 BG132
Clandon Rd, Guil. GU1 258 AY135
Ilford IG3 125 ES61
Send GU23 243 BF125
West Clandon GU4 243 BF125
Clandon St, SE8 314 B8
Clanricarde Gdns, W2 295 K1
Clapgate Rd, Bushey WD23 76 CB44
CLAPHAM, SW4 161 DH83
★ Clapham Common, SW4 160 DG84
⊖ Clapham Common 161 DJ84
Jct Clapham Common, SW4 161 DJ84
Clapham Common N Side, SW4 161 DH84
Clapham Common S Side, SW4 181 DH85
Clapham Common W Side, SW4 160 DG84
Clapham Cres, SW4 161 DK84
Clapham Est, SW11 160 DE84
Clapham High Street 161 DK83
Clapham High St, SW4 161 DK84
⇌ Clapham Junction 160 DD84
Clapham Junction 160 DD84
Sch Clapham Manor Prim Sch, SW4 off Belmont Rd 161 DJ83
Clapham Manor St, SW4 309 M10
⊖ Clapham North 161 DL83
CLAPHAM PARK, SW4 181 DK86
Clapham Pk Est, SW4 181 DK86
Clapham Pk Rd, SW4 161 DK84
Clapham Rd, SW9 310 D6
Clapham Rd Est, SW4 309 P10
⊖ Clapham South 181 DH86
Clap La, Dag. RM10 127 FB62
Claps Gate La, E6 293 N4
Clapton 122 DV61
Clapton App, Woob.Grn HP10 110 AD55
Clapton Common, E5 122 DT59
Sch Clapton Girls' Tech Coll, E5 278 G1
CLAPTON PARK, E5 123 DY63
Clapton Pk Est, E5 off Blackwell Cl 123 DX63
Clapton Pas, E5 278 G2
Clapton Sq, E5 278 F2
Clapton Ter, E5 off Clapton Common 122 DU60
Clapton Way, E5 122 DU63
Sch Clara Grant Sch, E3 290 B5
Clara Pl, SE18 305 M8
Clare Cl, N2 120 DC55
Elstree WD6 78 CM44
West Byfleet KT14 212 BG113
Clare Cor, SE9 185 EP87
Clare Cotts, Bletch. RH1 251 DP133
Clare Ct, Aveley RM15 168 FQ75
Northwood HA6 93 BS50
Woldingham CR3 237 EA123
Clare Cres, Lthd. KT22 231 CG118
Claredale, Wok. GU22 226 AY119
Claredale St, E2 288 D1
Clare Dr, Farn.Com. SL2 111 AP63
Clare Gdns, E7 281 N1
W11 282 F9
Barking IG11 145 ET65
Egham TW20 off Mowbray Cres 173 BA92
Clare Hill, Esher KT10 214 CB107
Clare Ho, E3 279 N8
Sch Clare Ho Prim Sch, Beck. BR3 off Oakwood Av 203 EC96
Clare La, N1 277 K7
Clare Lawn Av, SW14 178 CR85
Clare Mkt, WC2 286 C9
Clare Ms, SW6 307 L5
Claremont, Brick.Wd AL2 60 CA31
Cheshunt EN7 66 DT29
Claremont Av, Esher KT10 214 BZ107
Harrow HA3 118 CL57
Hersham KT12 214 BX105
New Malden KT3 199 CU99
Sunbury-on-Thames TW16 195 BV95
Woking GU22 226 AY119
Claremont Cl, E16 305 M3
N1 286 F1
SW2 off Christchurch Rd 181 DM88
Grays RM16 off Premier Av 170 GC76
Hersham KT12 214 BW106
Orpington BR6 223 EN105
South Croydon CR2 236 DU115
Claremont Ct, Dor. RH4 263 CH137
Surbiton KT6 off St. James Rd 197 CK100
Claremont Cres, Crox.Grn WD3 75 BQ43
Dartford DA1 167 FE84
Claremont Dr, Esher KT10 214 CB108
Shepperton TW17 195 BP100
Woking GU22 226 AY119
Claremont End, Esher KT10 214 CB107
Sch Claremont Fan Ct Sch, Esher KT10 off Claremont Dr 214 CB108
Claremont Gdns, Ilf. IG3 125 ES61
Surbiton KT6 198 CL99
Upminster RM14 129 FR60
Claremont Gro, W4 off Edensor Gdns 158 CS80
Woodford Green IG8 102 EJ51
Sch Claremont High Sch, Kenton HA3 off Claremont Av 118 CL57
★ Claremont Landscape Gdn, Esher KT10 214 BZ108
Claremont La, Esher KT10 214 CB105
CLAREMONT PARK, Esher KT10 214 CB108
Claremont Pk, N3 97 CY53
Claremont Pk Rd, Esher KT10 214 CB107
Claremont Pl, Grav. DA11 off Cutmore St 191 GH87
Sch Claremont Prim Sch, NW2 off Claremont Rd 119 CX61
Claremont Rd, E7 124 EH64
E11 off Grove Grn Rd 123 ED62
E17 101 DY54
N6 121 DJ59
NW2 119 CX62
W9 282 F1
W13 137 CG71
Barnet EN4 80 DD37
Bromley BR1 204 EL98
Claygate KT10 215 CE108
Croydon CR0 202 DU102
Harrow HA3 95 CE54
Hornchurch RM11 127 FG58
Redhill RH1 250 DG131
Staines-upon-Thames TW18 173 BD92
Surbiton KT6 198 CL100
Swanley BR8 187 FE94
Teddington TW11 177 CF92
Twickenham TW1 177 CH86
West Byfleet KT14 212 BG112
Windsor SL4 151 AQ82
Claremont Sq, N1 286 E1
Claremont St, E16 305 M3
N18 100 DU51
SE10 314 D4
Claremont Way, NW2 119 CW60
● Claremont Way Ind Est, NW2 119 CW60
Claremount Cl, Epsom KT18 233 CW117
Claremount Gdns, Epsom KT18 233 CW117
Clarence Av, SW4 181 DK86
Bromley BR1 204 EL98
Ilford IG2 125 EN58
New Malden KT3 198 CQ96
Upminster RM14 128 FN61
Clarence Cl, Barn. EN4 80 DD43
Bushey Heath WD23 95 CF45
Hersham KT12 214 BW105
Clarence Ct, Egh. TW20 off Clarence St 173 AZ93
Horley RH6 269 DK147
Clarence Cres, SW4 181 DK86
Sidcup DA14 186 EV90
Windsor SL4 151 AQ81
Clarence Dr, Eng.Grn TW20 172 AW91
Clarence Gdns, NW1 285 K3
Clarence Gate, Wdf.Grn. IG8 103 EN51
Clarence Gate Gdns, NW1 off Glentworth St 284 F5
★ Clarence Ho, SW1 297 M4
Clarence La, SW15 178 CS86
Clarence Lo, Hodd. EN11 off Taverners Way 49 EA17
Clarence Ms, E5 278 F2
SE16 301 J3
SW12 181 DH87
Clarence Pk Ms, St.Alb. AL1 43 CF20
Clarence Pl, E5 278 F2
Gravesend DA12 191 GH87
Clarence Rd, E5 122 DV63
E12 124 EK64
E16 291 K5
E17 101 DX54
N15 122 DQ57
N22 99 DL52
NW6 272 G7
SE8 314 C3
SE9 184 EL89
SW19 180 DB93
W4 158 CN78
Berkhamsted HP4 38 AW19
Bexleyheath DA6 166 EY84
Biggin Hill TN16 239 EM118
Bromley BR1 204 EK97
Croydon CR0 202 DR101
Enfield EN3 82 DV43
Grays RM17 170 GA79
Hersham KT12 213 BV105
Pilgrim's Hatch CM15 108 FV44
Redhill RH1 266 DD137
Clarence Rd, Richmond TW9 158 CM81
St. Albans AL1 43 CF20
Sidcup DA14 186 EV90
Sutton SM1 218 DB105
Teddington TW11 177 CF93
Wallington SM6 219 DH106
Windsor SL4 151 AP81
Clarence Row, Grav. DA12 191 GH87
Clarence St, Egh. TW20 173 AZ93
Kingston upon Thames KT1 198 CL96
Richmond TW9 158 CL84
Southall UB2 156 BX76
Staines-upon-Thames TW18 173 BE91
Clarence Ter, NW1 284 F4
Hounslow TW3 156 CB84
Clarence Wk, SW4 310 A8
Redhill RH1 266 DD137
Clarence Way, NW1 275 J6
Horley RH6 269 DK147
South Ockendon RM15 149 FX72
Clarence Way Est, NW1 275 K6
Clarenden Pl, Dart. DA2 187 FD92
Clarendon Cl, E9 279 H7
W2 284 C10
Hemel Hempstead HP2 40 BK19
Orpington BR5 206 EU97
Clarendon Ct, Slou. SL2 132 AV73
Clarendon Cres, Twick. TW2 177 CD90
Clarendon Cross, W11 294 F1
Clarendon Dr, SW15 159 CW84
Clarendon Flds, Chan.Cr. WD3 74 BM38
Clarendon Gdns, NW4 119 CU55
W9 283 P5
Dartford DA2 189 FR87
Ilford IG1 125 EM60
Wembley HA9 118 CL63
Clarendon Gate, Ott. KT16 211 BD107
Clarendon Grn, Orp. BR5 206 EU98
Clarendon Gro, NW1 285 N2
Mitcham CR4 200 DF97
Orpington BR5 206 EU97
Clarendon Ho, Kings.T. KT2 off Cowleaze Rd 198 CL95
Clarendon Ms, W2 284 C9
Ashtead KT21 232 CL119
Bexley DA5 187 FB88
Borehamwood WD6 off Clarendon Rd 78 CN41
Clarendon Path, Orp. BR5 206 EU97
Clarendon Pl, W2 284 C10
Sevenoaks TN13 off Clarendon Rd 256 FG125
Sch Clarendon Prim Sch, Ashf. TW15 off Knapp Rd 174 BM91
Clarendon Ri, SE13 163 EC83
Clarendon Rd, E11 123 ED60
E17 123 EB58
E18 124 EG55
N8 121 DM55
N15 121 DP56
N18 100 DU51
N22 99 DM54
SW19 180 DE94
W5 138 CL69
W11 282 E10
Ashford TW15 174 BM91
Borehamwood WD6 78 CN41
Cheshunt EN8 67 DX29
Croydon CR0 201 DP103
Gravesend DA12 191 GJ86
Harrow HA1 117 CE58
Hayes UB3 155 BT75
Redhill RH1 250 DF133
Sevenoaks TN13 256 FG124
Wallington SM6 219 DJ107
Watford WD17 75 BV40
Sch Clarendon Sch, Hmptn. TW12 off Hanworth Rd 176 CB93
Clarendon St, SW1 309 K1
Clarendon Ter, W9 283 P4
Clarendon Wk, W11 282 E9
Clarendon Way, N21 82 DQ44
Chislehurst BR7 205 ET97
Orpington BR5 205 ET97
Clarens St, SE6 183 DZ89
Clare Pk, Amer. HP7 55 AS40
Clare Pl, SW15 off Minstead Gdns 179 CT87
Clare Pt, NW2 off Claremont Rd 119 CX60
Clare Rd, E11 123 ED58
NW10 139 CU66
SE14 313 N7
Greenford UB6 137 CD65
Hounslow TW4 156 BZ83
Stanwell TW19 174 BL87
Taplow SL6 130 AJ72
Clares, The, Cat. CR3 236 DU124
Clare St, E2 288 F1
Claret Gdns, SE25 202 DS98
Clareville Gro, SW7 295 P9
Clareville Gro Ms, SW7 off Clareville St 295 P9
Clareville Rd, Cat. CR3 236 DU124
Orpington BR5 205 EQ103
Clareville St, SW7 295 P9
Clare Way, Bexh. DA7 166 EY81
Sevenoaks TN13 257 FJ127
Clare Wd, Lthd. KT22 231 CH118
Clarewood Wk, SW9 161 DP84
Clarges Ms, W1 297 J2
Clarges St, W1 297 K2
Claribel Rd, SW9 310 G8
Clarice Way, Wall. SM6 219 DL109
Claridge Rd, Dag. RM8 126 EX60
Clarinda Ho, Green. DA9 169 FW84
Clarissa Rd, Rom. RM6 126 EX59
Clarissa St, E8 278 A9
Clark Cl, Erith DA8 167 FG81
Clarkebourne Dr, Grays RM17 170 GD79
Clarke Cl, Croy. CR0 202 DQ100
Clarke Ct, W6 off Great W Rd 159 CU78
Clarke Grn, Wat. WD25 75 BU35
Clarke Ms, N9 off Plevna Rd 100 DV48
Clarke Path, N16 122 DU60
Clarkes Av, Wor.Pk. KT4 199 CX102
Clarkes Dr, Uxb. UB8 134 BL71
Clarke's Ms, W1 285 H6
Clarkes Rd, Hat. AL10 45 CV17
Clarke Way, Wat. WD25 75 BU35
Clarkfield, Mill End WD3 92 BH46
Clark Gro, Ilf. IG3 125 ES63
Clark Lawrence Ct, SW11 off Winstanley Rd 160 DD83
Clarks La, Epp. CM16 69 ET31
Halstead TN14 224 EZ112
Warlingham CR6 238 EF123
Westerham TN16 238 EK123
Clarks Mead, Bushey WD23 94 CC45
Clarkson Ct, Hat. AL10 44 CS17
Clarkson Rd, E16 291 L8
Clarkson Row, NW1 285 L1
Clarksons, The, Bark. IG11 145 EQ68
Clarkson St, E2 288 E2
Clarks Pl, EC2 287 N8
Clarks Rd, Ilf. IG1 125 ER61
Clark St, E1 288 F7
Clark Way, Houns. TW5 156 BX80
Clarnico La, E20 280 B5
Classon Cl, West Dr. UB7 154 BL75
Claston Cl, Dart. DA1 167 FE84
CLATTERFORD END, Ong. CM5 71 FG30
Claude Rd, E10 123 EC61
E13 144 EH67
SE15 312 E9
Claude St, E14 302 A8
Claudia Jones Way, SW2 181 DL86
Claudian Pl, St.Alb. AL3 42 CA22
Claudian Way, Grays RM16 171 GH76
Claudia Pl, SW19 179 CY88
Claudius Cl, Stan. HA7 95 CK48
Claughton Rd, E13 292 D1
Claughton Way, Hutt. CM13 109 GD44
Clauson Av, Nthlt. UB5 116 CB64
Clavell St, SE10 314 E2
Claverdale Rd, SW2 181 DM87
Claverhambury Rd, Wal.Abb. EN9 68 EF29
Clavering Av, SW13 159 CV79
Clavering Cl, Twick. TW1 177 CG91
Clavering Pl, SW12 180 DG86
Clavering Rd, E12 124 EK60
● Claverings Ind Est, N9 101 DX47
Clavering Way, Hutt. CM13 off Poplar Dr 109 GC44
Claverley Gro, N3 98 DA52
Claverley Vil, N3 98 DB52
Claverton Cl, Bov. HP3 57 BA28
Claverton St, SW1 309 M1
Clave St, E1 300 G3
Claxton Gro, W6 306 D1
Claxton Path, SE4 off Hainford Cl 163 DX84
Clay Acre, Chesh. HP5 54 AR30
Clay Av, Mitch. CR4 201 DH96
Claybank Gro, SE13 314 C10
Claybourne Ms, SE19 off Church Rd 182 DS94
Claybridge Rd, SE12 184 EJ91
Claybrook Cl, N2 120 DD55
Claybrook Rd, W6 306 D2
Clayburn Gdns, S.Ock. RM15 149 FV73
Claybury, Bushey WD23 94 CB45
Claybury Bdy, Ilf. IG5 124 EL55
Claybury Hall, Wdf.Grn. IG8 103 EM52
Claybury Rd, Wdf.Grn. IG8 102 EL52
Clay Cor, Cher. KT16 off Eastworth Rd 194 BH102
Sch Claycots Prim Sch, Britwell Campus, Slou. SL2 off Monksfield Way 131 AN70
Town Hall Campus, Slou. SL1 off Bath Rd 131 AR74
Claycroft, Welw.G.C. AL7 30 DB08
Claydon, SE17 off Deacon Way 299 J8
Claydon Dr, Croy. CR0 219 DL105
Claydon End, Chal.St.P. SL9 112 AY55
Claydon La, Chal.St.P. SL9 112 AY55
Claydon Rd, Wok. GU21 226 AU116
Claydown Ms, SE18 305 M10
Clayfarm Rd, SE9 185 EQ89
Clayfields, Penn HP10 88 AC45
CLAYGATE, Esher KT10 215 CE108
⇌ Claygate 215 CD107
Claygate Cl, Horn. RM12 127 FG63
Claygate Cres, New Adgtn CR0 221 EC107
Claygate La, Esher KT10 197 CG103
Thames Ditton KT7 197 CG102
Waltham Abbey EN9 67 ED30
Claygate Lo Cl, Clay. KT10 215 CE108
Sch Claygate Prim Sch, Clay. KT10 off Foley Rd 215 CE108
Claygate Rd, W13 157 CH76
Dorking RH4 263 CH138
CLAYHALL, Ilf. IG5 103 EM54
Clayhall Av, Ilf. IG5 124 EL55
Clayhall La, Old Wind. SL4 172 AT85
Reigate RH2 265 CX138
Clayhanger, Guil. GU4 243 BC132
CLAY HILL, Enf. EN2 82 DQ37
Clay Hill, Enf. EN2 82 DQ37
Clayhill, Surb. KT5 198 CN99
Clayhill Cl, Leigh RH2 265 CU141
Clayhill Cres, SE9 184 EK91
Clayhill Rd, Leigh RH2 265 CT142
Claylands Pl, SW8 310 E4
Claylands Rd, SW8 310 D3
Clay La, Bushey Hth WD23 95 CE45
Edgware HA8 96 CN46
Guildford GU4 242 AY128
Harlow CM17 36 EW14
Headley KT18 232 CP124
South Nutfield RH1 267 DJ135
Stanwell TW19 174 BM87
Claymill Ho, SE18 165 EQ78
Claymills Ms, Hem.H. HP3 40 BN23
Claymore, Hem.H. HP2 40 BL16
Claymore Cl, Mord. SM4 200 DA101
Claymore Ct, E17 off Billet Rd 101 DY53
Clay Path, E17 off Bedford Rd 101 EA54
Claypit Hill, Wal.Abb. EN9 84 EJ36
Claypole Dr, Houns. TW5 156 BY81
Claypole Rd, E15 280 F10
Clayponds Av, Brent. TW8 158 CL77
Clayponds Gdns, W5 157 CK77
H Clayponds Hosp, W5 158 CL77
Clayponds La, Brent. TW8 158 CL78
Clay Rd, The, Loug. IG10 84 EL39
Clayside, Chig. IG7 103 EQ51
Clay's La, Loug. IG10 85 EN39
Clay St, W1 284 F7
Beaconsfield HP9 88 AJ48
Clayton Av, Upmin. RM14 128 FP64
Wembley HA0 138 CL66
● Clayton Business Cen, Hayes UB3 155 BS75
Clayton Cl, E6 293 K8
Clayton Cres, N1 276 B9
Brentford TW8 157 CK78
Clayton Cft Rd, Dart. DA2 187 FG89
Clayton Dr, SE8 301 L10
Guildford GU2 242 AT131
Hemel Hempstead HP3 41 BR22
Clayton Fld, NW9 96 CS52
Clayton Mead, Gdse. RH9 252 DV130
Clayton Ms, SE10 314 G6
Clayton Rd, SE15 312 D7
Chessington KT9 215 CJ105
Epsom KT17 216 CS113
Hayes UB3 155 BS75
Isleworth TW7 157 CE83
Romford RM7 127 FC60
Clayton St, SE11 310 E2
Clayton Ter, Hayes UB4 off Jollys La 136 BX71
Clayton Wk, Amer. HP7 72 AW39
Clayton Way, Uxb. UB8 134 BK70
Clay Tye Rd, Upmin. RM14 129 FW63
Claywood Cl, Orp. BR6 205 ES101
Claywood La, Bean DA2 189 FX90
Clayworth Cl, Sid. DA15 186 EV86
Cleall Av, Wal.Abb. EN9 off Quaker La 67 EC34
Cleanthus Cl, SE18 165 EP81
Cleanthus Rd, SE18 165 EP81
Clearbrook Way, E1 289 H8
Cleardene, Dor. RH4 263 CH136
Cleardown, Wok. GU22 227 BB118
Cleares Pasture, Burn. SL1 130 AH69
Clearmount, Chobham GU24 210 AS107
Clears, The, Reig. RH2 249 CY132
Clearwater Pl, Long Dit. KT6 197 CJ100
Clearwater Ter, W11 294 D4
Clearwell Dr, W9 283 L5
Cleave Av, Hayes UB3 155 BS77
Orpington BR6 223 ES107
Cleaveland Rd, Surb. KT6 197 CK99
Cleave Prior, Chipstead CR5 234 DE119
Cleaverholme Cl, SE25 202 DV100
Cleaver Sq, SE11 298 F10
Cleaver St, SE11 298 F10
Cleeve, The, Guil. GU1 243 BA134
Cleeve Ct, Felt. TW14 off Kilross Rd 175 BS88
Cleeve Hill, SE23 182 DV88
Cleeve Pk Gdns, Sid. DA14 186 EV89
Sch Cleeve Pk Sch, Sid. DA14 off Bexley La 186 EW90
Cleeve Rd, Lthd. KT22 231 CF120
● Cleeve Studios, E2 off Boundary St 288 A3
Cleeve Way, SW15 179 CT86
Sutton SM1 200 DB102
Clegg St, E1 300 F2
E13 281 P10
Cleland Path, Loug. IG10 85 EP39
Cleland Rd, Chal.St.P. SL9 90 AX54
Clematis Cl, Rom. RM3 106 FJ52
Clematis Gdns, Wdf.Grn. IG8 102 EG50
Clematis St, W12 139 CT73
Clem Attlee Ct, SW6 306 G3
Clem Attlee Par, SW6 off North End Rd 307 H3
Clemence Rd, Dag. RM10 147 FC67
Clemence St, E14 289 N7
Clement Av, SW4 161 DK84
Clement Cl, NW6 272 B7
W4 158 CR76
Purley CR8 off Croftleigh Av 235 DP116
Clement Danes Ho, W12 off Du Cane Rd 139 CV72
Clement Gdns, Hayes UB3 155 BS77
Clementhorpe Rd, Dag. RM9 146 EW65
Clementina Rd, E10 123 DZ60
H Clementine Churchill Hosp, Har. HA1 117 CF62
Clementine Cl, W13 off Balfour Rd 157 CH75
Clementine Wk, Wdf.Grn. IG8 off Salway Cl 102 EG52
Clementine Way, Hem.H. HP1 40 BH22
Clement Rd, SW19 179 CY92
Beckenham BR3 203 DX96
Cheshunt EN8 67 DY27
Clements Av, E16 291 N10
Clements Cl, N12 98 DB49
Slough SL1 152 AV75
Clements Ct, Houns. TW4 156 BX84
Ilford IG1 off Clements La 125 EP62
Watford WD25 76 BW35
Clements Ho, Lthd. KT22 231 CG119
Clement's Inn, WC2 286 D9
Clement's Inn Pas, WC2 286 D9
Clements La, EC4 287 M10
Ilford IG1 125 EP62
Clements Mead, Lthd. KT22 231 CG119
Clements Pl, Brent. TW8 157 CK78
Clements Rd, E6 145 EM66
SE16 300 D7
Chorleywood WD3 73 BD43
Ilford IG1 125 EP62
Walton-on-Thames KT12 195 BV103
Clements St, Ware SG12 33 DY06
Clement St, Swan. BR8 188 FK93
Clement Way, Upmin. RM14 128 FM62
Clemson Ms, Epsom KT17 217 CT112
Clenches Fm La, Sev. TN13 256 FG126
Clenches Fm Rd, Sev. TN13 256 FG126
Clendon Way, SE18 off Polthorne Gro 165 ER77
Clennam St, SE1 299 K4
Clensham Ct, Sutt. SM1 off Sutton Common Rd 200 DA103
Clensham La, Sutt. SM1 200 DA103
Clenston Ms, W1 284 E8
Cleopatra Cl, Stan. HA7 95 CK48
★ Cleopatra's Needle, WC2 298 C2
Clephane Rd, N1 277 L5
Clere St, EC2 287 M4
Clerics Wk, Shep. TW17 off Gordon Rd 195 BR100
CLERKENWELL, EC1 286 G5
Clerkenwell Cl, EC1 286 F4
Clerkenwell Grn, EC1 286 F5
Sch Clerkenwell Parochial C of E Prim Sch, EC1 286 E2
Clerkenwell Rd, EC1 286 E5
Clerks Cft, Bletch. RH1 252 DR133
Clerks Piece, Loug. IG10 85 EM41
Clermont Rd, E9 278 G8
Clevedon, Wey. KT13 213 BQ106
Clevedon Cl, N16 off Smalley Cl 122 DT62
Clevedon Gdns, Hayes UB3 155 BR76
Hounslow TW5 155 BV81
Clevedon Rd, SE20 203 DX95
Kingston upon Thames KT1 198 CN96
Twickenham TW1 177 CK86
Clevehurst Cl, Stoke P. SL2 132 AT65
Cleveland Av, SW20 199 CZ96
W4 159 CT77
Hampton TW12 176 BZ94
Cleveland Cl, Walt. KT12 195 BV104
Wooburn Green HP10 110 AE55
Cleveland Ct, Westh. RH5 247 CH131

Cleveland Cres, Borwd. WD6 78 CQ43
Cleveland Dr, Stai. TW18 194 BH96
Cleveland Gdns, N4 122 DQ57
NW2 119 CX61
SW13 159 CT82
W2 283 N9
Worcester Park KT4 198 CS103
Cleveland Gro, E1 288 G5
Sch Cleveland Inf & Jun Schs, Ilf. IG1 off Cleveland Rd 125 EP63
Cleveland Ms, W1 285 L6
Cleveland Pk, Stai. TW19 174 BL86
Cleveland Pk Av, E17 123 EA56
Cleveland Pk Cres, E17 123 EA56
Cleveland Pl, SW1 297 M2
Cleveland Ri, Mord. SM4 199 CX101
Cleveland Rd, E18 124 EG55
N1 277 M7
N9 100 DV45
SW13 159 CT82
W4 off Antrobus Rd 158 CQ76
W13 137 CH71
Hemel Hempstead HP2 41 BP18
Ilford IG1 125 EP62
Isleworth TW7 157 CG84
New Malden KT3 198 CS98
Uxbridge UB8 134 BK68
Welling DA16 165 ET82
Worcester Park KT4 198 CS103
Cleveland Row, SW1 297 L3
Cleveland Sq, W2 283 N9
Cleveland St, W1 285 L5
Cleveland Ter, W2 283 P8
Cleveland Way, E1 288 G5
Hemel Hempstead HP2 41 BP18
Cleveley Cl, SE7 304 F8
Cleveley Cres, W5 138 CL68
Cleveleys Rd, E5 122 DV62
Cleverly Est, W12 139 CU74
Cleve Rd, NW6 273 K6
Sidcup DA14 186 EX90
Cleves Av, Brwd. CM14 108 FV46
Epsom KT17 217 CV109
Cleves Cl, Cob. KT11 213 BV114
Loughton IG10 84 EL44
Cleves Ct, Wind. SL4 151 AM83
Cleves Cres, New Adgtn CR0 221 EC111
Sch Cleves Prim Sch, E6 off Arragon Rd 144 EK67
Cleves Rd, E6 144 EK67
Hemel Hempstead HP2 41 BP15
Richmond TW10 177 CJ90
Sch Cleves Sch, Wey. KT13 off Oatlands Av 213 BT105
Cleves Wk, Ilf. IG6 103 EQ52
Cleves Way, Hmptn. TW12 176 BZ94
Ruislip HA4 116 BX60
Sunbury-on-Thames TW16 175 BT93
Cleves Wd, Wey. KT13 213 BS105
Clewer Av, Wind. SL4 151 AN82
Clewer Ct Rd, Wind. SL4 151 AP80
Clewer Cres, Har. HA3 95 CD53
Clewer Flds, Wind. SL4 151 AQ81
CLEWER GREEN, Wind. SL4 151 AM82
Sch Clewer Grn C of E First Sch, Wind. SL4 off Hatch La 151 AN83
Clewer Hill Rd, Wind. SL4 151 AL82
Clewer Ho, SE2 off Wolvercote Rd 166 EX75
CLEWER NEW TOWN, Wind. SL4 151 AN82
Clewer New Town, Wind. SL4 151 AN82
Clewer Pk, Wind. SL4 151 AN80
CLEWER VILLAGE, Wind. SL4 151 AM80
Clichy Est, E1 289 H7
Clifden Ms, E5 279 K1
Clifden Rd, E5 279 H2
Brentford TW8 157 CK79
Twickenham TW1 177 CF88
Cliff End, Pur. CR8 219 DP112
Cliffe Rd, S.Croy. CR2 220 DR106
Cliffe Wk, Sutt. SM1 off Turnpike La 218 DC106
Clifford Av, SW14 158 CP83
Chislehurst BR7 185 EM93
Ilford IG5 103 EP53
Wallington SM6 219 DJ105
Clifford Cl, Nthlt. UB5 136 BY67
Clifford Dr, SW9 161 DP84
Clifford Gdns, NW10 282 A1
Hayes UB3 155 BR77
Clifford Gro, Ashf. TW15 174 BN91
Clifford Haigh Ho, SW6 off Fulham Palace Rd 159 CX80
Clifford Manor Rd, Guil. GU4 258 AY138
Clifford Rd, E16 291 L5
E17 101 EC54
N9 82 DW44
SE25 202 DU98
Barnet EN5 80 DB41
Chafford Hundred RM16 170 FZ75
Hounslow TW4 156 BX83
Richmond TW10 177 CK89
Wembley HA0 137 CK67
Clifford's Inn Pas, EC4 286 E9
Clifford St, W1 297 L1
Clifford Way, NW10 119 CT63
Cliff Pl, S.Ock. RM15 149 FX69
Cliff Reach, Bluewater DA9 189 FS87
Cliff Richard Ct, Chsht EN8 off High St 67 DX28
Cliff Rd, NW1 275 P4
Cliff Ter, SE8 314 B8
Cliffview Rd, SE13 163 EA83
Cliff Vil, NW1 275 P4
Cliff Wk, E16 291 M6
Clifton Av, E17 123 DX55
N3 97 CZ53
W12 139 CT74
Feltham TW13 176 BW90
Stanmore HA7 95 CH54
Sutton SM2 218 DB111
Wembley HA9 138 CM65
Clifton Cl, Add. KT15 194 BH103
Caterham CR3 236 DR123
Cheshunt EN8 67 DY29
Horley RH6 269 DK148
Orpington BR6 223 EQ106
Clifton Ct, N4 off Biggerstaff St 121 DN61
NW8 284 A4
Woodford Green IG8 off Snakes La W 102 EG51
Clifton Cres, SE15 312 F5
Clifton Est, SE15 312 D7
Clifton Gdns, N15 122 DT58
NW11 119 CZ58
W4 off Dolman Rd 158 CR77
W9 283 N5
Enfield EN2 81 DL42
Uxbridge UB10 135 BP68
Clifton Gro, E8 278 C4
Gravesend DA11 191 GH87
Clifton Hatch, Harl. CM18 off Trotters Rd 52 EU18
Clifton Hill, NW8 273 N9
Sch Clifton Hill Sch, Cat. CR3 off Chaldon Rd 236 DR123
Clifton Lawns, Amer. HP6 55 AQ35
Sch Clifton Lo Boys' Prep Sch, W5 off Mattock La 137 CK73
Clifton Marine Par, Grav. DA11 191 GF86
Clifton Pk Av, SW20 199 CW96
Clifton Pl, SE16 301 H4
W2 284 B10
Banstead SM7 234 DA115
Sch Clifton Prim Sch, Sthl. UB2 off Clifton Rd 156 BY77
Clifton Ri, SE14 313 M5
Windsor SL4 151 AK81
Clifton Rd, E7 144 EK65
E16 291 K6
N1 277 K5
N3 98 DC53
N8 121 DK58
N22 99 DJ53
NW10 139 CU68
SE25 202 DS98
SW19 179 CX93
W9 283 P4
Amersham HP6 55 AP35
Coulsdon CR5 235 DH115
Gravesend DA11 191 GG86
Greenford UB6 136 CC70
Harrow HA3 118 CM57
Hornchurch RM11 127 FG58
Ilford IG2 125 ER58
Isleworth TW7 157 CD82
Kingston upon Thames KT2 178 CM94
London Heathrow Airport TW6 off Inner Ring E 155 BP83
Loughton IG10 84 EL42
Sidcup DA14 185 ES91
Slough SL1 152 AV75
Southall UB2 156 BY77
Teddington TW11 177 CE91
Wallington SM6 219 DH106
Watford WD18 75 BV43
Welling DA16 166 EW83
Cliftons La, Reig. RH2 249 CX131
Jct Clifton's Rbt, SE12 184 EH86
Clifton St, EC2 287 N6
St. Albans AL1 43 CE19
Clifton Ter, N4 121 DN61
Clifton Vil, W9 283 M6
Cliftonville, Dor. RH4 263 CH137
Clifton Wk, E6 293 H8
W6 off Galena Rd 159 CV77
Dartford DA2 off Osbourne Rd 188 FP86
Clifton Way, SE15 312 F5
Borehamwood WD6 78 CN39
Hutton CM13 109 GD46
Wembley HA0 138 CL67
Woking GU21 226 AT117
★ Climate Change (DECC), SW1 298 A3
Climb, The, Rick. WD3 74 BH44
Cline Rd, N11 99 DJ51
Guildford GU1 259 AZ136
Clinger Ct, N1 277 N9
★ Clink Prison Mus, SE1 299 L2
Clink St, SE1 299 K2
Clinton Av, E.Mol. KT8 196 CC98
Welling DA16 165 ET84
Clinton Cl, Wey. KT13 195 BP104
Clinton Cres, Ilf. IG6 103 ES51
Clinton End, Hem.H. HP2 41 BQ20
Clinton Rd, E3 289 L3
E7 281 P1
N15 122 DR56
Leatherhead KT22 231 CJ123
Clinton Ter, Sutt. SM1 off Manor La 218 DC105
Clipper Boul, Dart. DA2 169 FS83
Clipper Boul W, Dart. DA2 169 FR83
Clipper Cl, SE16 301 J4
Clipper Cres, Grav. DA12 191 GM91
Clipper Pk, Til. RM18 170 GD80
Clipper Way, SE13 163 EC84
Clippesby Cl, Chess. KT9 216 CM108
Clipstone Ms, W1 285 L5
Clipstone Rd, Houns. TW3 156 CA83
Clipstone St, W1 285 K6
Clissold Cl, N2 120 DF55
Clissold Ct, N4 122 DQ61
Clissold Cres, N16 122 DR62
Clissold Rd, N16 122 DR62
Clitheroe Av, Har. HA2 116 CA60
Clitheroe Gdns, Wat. WD19 94 BX48
Clitheroe Rd, SW9 310 B9
Romford RM5 105 FC50
Clitherow Av, W7 157 CG76
Clitherow Pas, Brent. TW8 157 CJ78
Clitherow Rd, Brent. TW8 157 CH78
Clitterhouse Cres, NW2 119 CW60
Clitterhouse Rd, NW2 119 CW60
Clive Av, N18 off Claremont St 100 DU51
Dartford DA1 187 FF86
Clive Cl, Pot.B. EN6 63 CZ31
Clive Ct, W9 283 P4
Slough SL1 151 AR75
★ Cliveden, Maid. SL6 110 AD64
Cliveden Cl, N12 98 DC49
Shenfield CM15 109 FZ45
Cliveden Gages, Tap. SL6 130 AE65
Cliveden Pl, SW1 296 G8
Shepperton TW17 195 BP100
Cliveden Rd, SW19 199 CZ95
Burnham SL1 130 AE65
Taplow SL6 130 AE65
Clivedon Ct, W13 137 CH71
Clivedon Rd, E4 102 EE50
Clive Par, Nthwd. HA6 off Maxwell Rd 93 BS52
Clive Pas, SE21 off Clive Rd 182 DR90
Clive Rd, SE21 182 DR90
SW19 180 DE93
Belvedere DA17 166 FA77
Enfield EN1 82 DU42
Esher KT10 214 CB105
Feltham TW14 175 BU86
Gravesend DA11 191 GH86
Great Warley CM13 107 FW52
Romford RM2 127 FH57
Twickenham TW1 177 CF91
Clivesdale Dr, Hayes UB3 135 BV74
Clive Way, Enf. EN1 82 DU42
Watford WD24 76 BW39
Cloak La, EC4 287 K10
⇌ Clock House 203 DY96
Clockhouse Av, Bark. IG11 145 EQ67
Clockhouse Cl, SW19 179 CW90
Clock Ho Cl, Byfleet KT14 212 BM112
Clockhouse Ct, Guil. GU1 242 AW130
Jct Clockhouse Junct, N13 99 DM50
Clockhouse La, Ashf. TW15 174 BN91
Feltham TW14 175 BP89
Grays RM16 149 FX74
Romford RM5 105 FB52
Clock Ho La, Sev. TN13 256 FG123
Clockhouse La E, Egh. TW20 173 BB94
Clockhouse La W, Egh. TW20 173 BA94
Clock Ho Mead, Oxshott KT22 214 CB114
Clockhouse Ms, Chorl. WD3 off Chorleywood Ho Dr 73 BE41
● Clockhouse Pl, Felt. TW14 175 BQ88
Clockhouse Pl, SW15 179 CY85
Sch Clockhouse Prim Sch, Coll.Row RM5 off Clockhouse La 105 FB51
Clock Ho Rd, Beck. BR3 203 DY97
Jct Clockhouse Rbt, Felt. TW14 175 BP88
★ Clockmakers' Museum, The, (Guildhall Lib), EC2 287 K8
Clock Twr Ind Est, Islw. TW7 157 CF83
Clock Twr Ms, N1 277 K9
SE28 146 EV73
W7 off Uxbridge Rd 137 CE74
Clock Twr Rd, Islw. TW7 157 CF83
Jct Clock Twr Rbt, Harl. CM17 52 EV16
Clock Vw Cres, N7 276 A4
Cloister Cl, Rain. RM13 147 FH70
Teddington TW11 177 CH92
Cloister Gdns, SE25 202 DV100
Edgware HA8 96 CQ50
Cloister Garth, Berk. HP4 38 AW19
St. Albans AL1 43 CE24
Cloister Rd, NW2 119 CZ62
W3 138 CQ71
Cloisters, The, Bushey WD23 76 CB44
Guildford GU1 off London Rd 243 BA131
Rickmansworth WD3 92 BL45
Welwyn Garden City AL8 29 CX09
Windsor SL4 151 AN82
Woking GU22 227 BB121
Cloisters Av, Brom. BR2 205 EM99
● Cloisters Business Cen, SW8 off Battersea Pk Rd 309 K5
Cloisters Ct, Rick. WD3 off The Cloisters 92 BL45
Cloisters Mall, Kings.T. KT1 off Union St 197 CK96
Cloister Wk, Hem.H. HP2 off Townsend 40 BK18
Clonard Way, Pnr. HA5 94 CA51
Clonbrock Rd, N16 122 DS63
Cloncurry St, SW6 306 D8
Clonmel Cl, Har. HA2 117 CD61
Clonmell Rd, N17 122 DR55
Clonmel Rd, SW6 307 H5
Teddington TW11 177 CD91
Clonmel Way, Burn. SL1 130 AH69
Clonmore St, SW18 179 CZ88
Cloonmore Av, Orp. BR6 223 ET105
Clorane Gdns, NW3 120 DA62
Sch Clore Shalom Sch, Shenley WD7 off Hugo Gryn Way 62 CL30
Sch Clore Tikva Sch, Ilf. IG6 off Fullwell Av 103 EQ54
Close, The, E4 off Beech Hall Rd 101 EC52
N14 99 DK47
N20 97 CZ47
SE3 315 H9
Beckenham BR3 203 DY98
Berry's Green TN16 239 EP116
Bexley DA5 186 FA86
Brentwood CM14 108 FW48
Brookmans Park AL9 63 CY26
Bushey WD23 76 CB43
Carshalton SM5 218 DE109
Dartford DA2 188 FJ90
East Barnet EN4 80 DF44
Eastcote HA5 116 BW59
Grays RM16 170 GC75
Harrow HA2 94 CC54
Hillingdon UB10 134 BN67
Horley RH6 269 DJ150
Isleworth TW7 157 CD82
Iver SL0 133 BC69
Mitcham CR4 200 DF98
New Malden KT3 198 CQ96
Petts Wood BR5 205 ES100
Potters Bar EN6 64 DA32
Purley (Pampisford Rd) CR8 219 DP110
Purley (Russ.Hill) CR8 219 DM110
Radlett WD7 61 CF33
Rayners Lane HA5 116 BZ59
Reigate RH2 266 DB135
Richmond TW9 158 CP83
Rickmansworth WD3 92 BJ46
Romford RM6 126 EY58
Sevenoaks TN13 256 FE124
Sidcup DA14 186 EV91
Slough SL1 off St. George's Cres 131 AK73
Strood Green RH3 264 CP138
Sutton SM3 199 CZ101
Uxbridge UB10 134 BL66
Virginia Water GU25 192 AW99
Ware SG12 33 DY06
Wembley (Barnhill Rd) HA9 118 CQ62
Wembley (Lyon Pk Av) HA0 138 CL65
West Byfleet KT14 212 BG113
Wonersh GU5 259 BB144
Closemead Cl, Nthwd. HA6 93 BQ51
Cloth Ct, EC1 287 H7
Cloth Fair, EC1 287 H7
Clothier St, E1 287 P8
Cloth St, EC1 287 J6
Clothworkers Rd, SE18 165 ER80
Cloudberry Rd, Rom. RM3 106 FK51
Cloudesdale Rd, SW17 181 DH89
Cloudeseley Cl, Sid. DA14 185 ET92
Cloudesley Pl, N1 276 E9
Cloudesley Rd, N1 276 E8
Bexleyheath DA7 166 EZ81
Erith DA8 167 FF81
Cloudesley Sq, N1 276 E9
Cloudesley St, N1 276 F9
Clouston Cl, Wall. SM6 219 DL106
Clova Rd, E7 281 M4
Clove Cres, E14 290 F10
Clove Hitch Quay, SW11 307 P10
Clovelly Av, NW9 119 CT56
Uxbridge UB10 115 BQ63
Warlingham CR6 236 DV118
Clovelly Cl, Pnr. HA5 115 BV55
Uxbridge UB10 115 BQ63
Clovelly Ct, Horn. RM11 128 FM61
Clovelly Gdns, SE19 202 DT95
Enfield EN1 100 DS45
Romford RM7 105 FB53
Clovelly Pl, Green. DA9 off Carmichael Ave 169 FW84
Clovelly Rd, N8 121 DK56
W4 158 CQ75
W5 157 CJ75
Bexleyheath DA7 166 EY79
Hounslow TW3 156 CA82
Clovelly Way, E1 289 H8
Harrow HA2 116 BZ61
Orpington BR6 205 ET100
Clover Cl, E11 off Norman Rd 123 ED61
Clover Ct, Edg. HA8 off Springwood Cres 96 CQ47
Grays RM17 off Churchill Rd 170 GD79
Woking GU22 226 AX118
Cloverdale Gdns, Sid. DA15 185 ET86
Clover Fld, Harl. CM18 52 EU18
Cloverfield, Welw.G.C. AL7 29 CZ06
Clover Fld, The, Bushey WD23 76 BZ44
Cloverfields, Horl. RH6 269 DH147
Clover Hill, Couls. CR5 235 DH121
Cloverland, Hat. AL10 45 CT21
Clover Lea, Gdmg. GU7 258 AS143
Clover Leas, Epp. CM16 69 ET30
Cloverleys, Loug. IG10 84 EK43
Clover Ms, SW3 308 E2
Clover Rd, Guil. GU2 242 AS132
Clovers, The, Nthflt DA11 190 GE91
Clover Way, Hat. AL10 45 CT15
Hemel Hempstead HP1 40 BH19
Wallington SM6 200 DG102
Clove St, E13 291 N5
Clowders Rd, SE6 183 DZ90
Clowser Cl, Sutt. SM1 off Turnpike La 218 DC106
Cloysters Grn, E1 300 C2
Cloyster Wd, Edg. HA8 95 CK52
Club Gdns Rd, Brom. BR2 204 EG101
Club Row, E1 288 A4
E2 288 A4
Clump, The, Rick. WD3 74 BG43
Clump Av, Box H. KT20 248 CQ131
Clumps, The, Ashf. TW15 175 BR91
Clunas Gdns, Rom. RM2 106 FK54
Clunbury Av, Sthl. UB2 156 BZ78
Clunbury Ct, Berk. HP4 off Manor St 38 AX19
Clunbury St, N1 287 M1
Cluny Est, SE1 299 N6
Cluny Ms, SW5 295 J9
Cluny Pl, SE1 299 N6
Cluse Ct, N1 277 J10
Clutterbucks, Sarratt WD3 74 BG36
Clutton St, E14 290 D7
Clydach Rd, Enf. EN1 82 DT42
Clyde Av, S.Croy. CR2 236 DV115
Clyde Circ, N15 122 DS56
Clyde Cl, Red. RH1 250 DG133
Clyde Cres, Upmin. RM14 129 FS58
Clyde Pl, E10 123 EB59
Clyde Rd, N15 122 DS56
N22 99 DK53
Croydon CR0 202 DT102
Hoddesdon EN11 49 ED19
Stanwell TW19 174 BK88
Sutton SM1 218 DA106
Wallington SM6 219 DJ106
Clydesdale, Enf. EN3 83 DX42
Clydesdale Av, Stan. HA7 117 CK55
Clydesdale Cl, Borwd. WD6 78 CR43
Isleworth TW7 157 CF83
Clydesdale Gdns, Rich. TW10 158 CP84
Clydesdale Ho, Erith DA18 off Kale Rd 166 EY75
Clydesdale Rd, W11 282 G8
Hornchurch RM11 127 FF59
Clydesdale Wk, Brox. EN10 off Tarpan Way 67 DZ25
Clyde Sq, Hem.H. HP2 40 BM15
Clyde St, SE8 313 P3
Clyde Ter, SE23 182 DW89
Hertford SG13 32 DU09
Clyde Vale, SE23 182 DW89
Clyde Way, Rom. RM1 105 FE53
Clydon Cl, Erith DA8 167 FE79
Clyfford Rd, Ruis. HA4 115 BT63
Clyfton Cl, Brox. EN10 49 DZ23
Clymping Dene, Felt. TW14 175 BV87
Clyston Rd, Wat. WD18 75 BT44
Clyston St, SW8 309 N8
Clyve Way, Stai. TW18 193 BE95
Coach All, Woob.Grn HP10 110 AF60
Coach & Horses Yd, W1 285 K10
Coach Ho La, N5 276 G1
SW19 179 CX91
Coach Ho Ms, SE14 313 J8
Coachhouse Ms, SE20 182 DV94
Coach Ho Ms, SE23 183 DX86
Redhill RH1 off Mill St 266 DF135
Whiteley Vill. KT12 213 BS109
Coach Ho Yd, SW18 off Ebner St 160 DB84
Coachlads Av, Guil. GU2 242 AT134
Coachmaker Ms, SW4 off Fenwick Pl 161 DL83
W4 off Berrymede Rd 158 CR76
Coach Ms, St.Alb. AL1 43 CH20
Coach Rd, Brock. RH3 248 CL134
Ottershaw KT16 211 BC107
Coach Yd Ms, N19 121 DL60
Coade Ct, SW4 off Paradise Rd 310 A8
Coal Ct, Grays RM17 off Columbia Wf Rd 170 GA79
Coaldale Wk, SE21 off Lairdale Cl 182 DQ87
Coalecroft Rd, SW15 159 CW84
Coalmans Way, Burn. SL1 130 AH72
Coalport Cl, Harl. CM17 52 EW16
Coalport Ho, SE11 off Walnut Tree Wk 298 E8
Coal Post Cl, Grn St Grn BR6 off Lynne Cl 223 ET107
Coal Rd, Til. RM18 171 GL77
Coast Hill, Westc. RH4 262 BZ139
Coast Hill La, Westc. RH4 262 CA138
Coaters La, Woob.Grn HP10 110 AE56
Coates Av, SW18 180 DE86
Coates Cl, Th.Hth. CR7 202 DQ97
Coates Dell, Wat. WD25 60 BY33
Coates Hill Rd, Brom. BR1 205 EN96
Coates Rd, Els. WD6 95 CK45
Coate St, E2 288 D1
Coates Wk, Brent. TW8 158 CL78
Coates Way, Wat. WD25 60 BX33
Sch Coates Way JMI & Nurs Sch, Wat. WD25 off Coates Way 60 BY33
Coat Wicks, Seer Grn HP9 89 AQ51
Cobalt Cl, Beck. BR3 203 DX98
Cobb Cl, Borwd. WD6 78 CQ43
Datchet SL3 152 AX81
Cobbett Cl, Enf. EN3 82 DW36
Cobbett Rd, SE9 164 EL83
Guildford GU2 242 AS133
Twickenham TW2 176 CA88
Cobbetts Av, Ilf. IG4 124 EK57
Cobbetts Cl, Wok. GU21 226 AV117
Cobbetts Hill, Wey. KT13 213 BP107
Cobbett St, SW8 310 D5
Cobb Grn, Wat. WD25 59 BV32
Cobbins, The, Wal.Abb. EN9 68 EE33
Cobbinsbank, Wal.Abb. EN9 off Farm Hill Rd 67 ED33
Cobbinsend Rd, Wal.Abb. EN9 68 EK29
Cobbins Way, Harl. CM17 36 EY11
Cobble La, N1 276 G6
Cobble Ms, N5 122 DQ62
N6 off Highgate W Hill 120 DG60
Cobble Path, E17 123 EA57
Cobblers Cl, Farn.Royal SL2 131 AP68
Cobblers Wk, E.Mol. KT8 197 CG95
Hampton TW12 176 CC94
Kingston upon Thames KT2 197 CG95
Teddington TW11 197 CG95
Cobbles, The, Brwd. CM15 108 FY47
Upminster RM14 129 FT59
Cobblestone Pl, Croy. CR0 off Oakfield Rd 202 DQ102
Cobblestone Sq, E1 300 F2
● Cobbold Est, NW10 139 CT65
Cobbold Ms, W12 off Cobbold Rd 159 CT75
Cobbold Rd, E11 124 EF62
NW10 139 CT65
W12 158 CS75
Cobb Rd, Berk. HP4 38 AT19
Cobb's Ct, EC4 off Pilgrim St 287 H9
Cobb's Rd, Houns. TW4 156 BZ84
Cobb St, E1 288 A7
Cobb Terr Ms, E6 off Sandford Rd 293 J2
Cobden Cl, Uxb. UB8 134 BJ67
Cobden Hill, Rad. WD7 77 CH36
Cobden Ms, SE26 182 DV92
Cobden Rd, E11 124 EE62
SE25 202 DU99
Orpington BR6 223 ER105
Sevenoaks TN13 257 FJ123
COBHAM, KT11 229 BV115
Cobham, Grays RM16 170 GB75
⇌ Cobham & Stoke D'Abernon 230 BY117
Cobham Av, N.Mal. KT3 199 CU99
Cobham Cl, SW11 180 DE86
Bromley BR2 204 EL101
Edgware HA8 96 CP54
Enfield EN1 82 DU41
Greenhithe DA9 189 FV86
Sidcup DA15 off Park Mead 186 EV86
Slough SL1 151 AM75
Wallington SM6 219 DL107
H Cobham Comm Hosp, Cob. KT11 213 BV113
Cobham Gate, Cob. KT11 213 BV114
Cobham Gra, Cob. KT11 off Between Sts 213 BV114
Cobham Ho, Bark. IG11 off St. Margarets 145 EQ67
Erith DA8 off Boundary St 167 FF80
Cobham Ms, NW1 275 N6
Cobham Pk, Cob. KT11 229 BV116
Cobham Pk Rd, Cob. KT11 229 BV117
Cobham Pl, Bexh. DA6 186 EX85
Cobham Rd, E17 101 EC53
N22 121 DP55
Fetcham KT22 231 CE122
Hounslow TW5 156 BW80
Ilford IG3 125 ES61
Kingston upon Thames KT1 198 CN95
Stoke D'Abernon KT11 230 CA118
Ware SG12 33 DZ05
Cobham St, Grav. DA11 191 GG87
Cobham Ter, Green. DA9 off Bean Rd 189 FV85
Cobham Way, E.Hors. KT24 245 BS126
Cobill Cl, Horn. RM11 128 FJ56
Cobland Rd, SE12 184 EJ91
Cobmead, Hat. AL10 45 CV16
Coborn Rd, E3 289 N1
Coborn St, E3 289 P2
Sch Cobourg Prim Sch, SE5 312 A2
Cobourg Rd, SE5 312 A2
Cobourg St, NW1 285 M3
Cobsdene, Grav. DA12 191 GK93
Cobs Way, New Haw KT15 212 BJ110
Cobtree Ct, Sthl. UB1 136 CC72
Coburg Cl, SW1 297 M8
Coburg Cres, SW2 181 DM88
Coburg Gdns, Ilf. IG5 102 EK54
Coburg Rd, N22 121 DM55
Cochrane Dr, Dart, DA1 188 FK86
Cochrane Ms, NW8 284 B1
Cochrane Rd, SW19 179 CZ94
Cochrane St, NW8 284 B1
Cockayne Way, SE8 301 M10
Cockbush Av, Hert. SG13 32 DU08
Cockerell Rd, E17 123 DY59
Cockerhurst Rd, Shore. TN14 225 FD107
Cocker Rd, Enf. EN1 82 DV36
Cockett Rd, Slou. SL3 152 AY76
COCKFOSTERS, Barn. EN4 80 DE42
⊖ Cockfosters 80 DG42
Cockfosters Par, Barn. EN4 off Cockfosters Rd 80 DG42
Cockfosters Rd, Barn. EN4 80 DF40
Cock Grn, Harl. CM19 51 EP17
Cock Hill, E1 287 P7
Cock La, EC1 286 G7
Broxbourne EN10 48 DU20
Fetcham KT22 230 CC122
Hoddesdon EN11 49 DY19
Cockle Way, Shenley WD7 62 CL33
Cockmannings La, Orp. BR5 206 EX102
Cockmannings Rd, Orp. BR5 206 EX101

Cockpit Steps, SW1 297 P5
Cockpit Yd, WC1 286 D6
Cockrobin La, Harl. CM20 35 EN08
Ware SG12 35 EN05
Cocks Cres, N.Mal. KT3 199 CT98
Cocksett Av, Orp. BR6 223 ES107
Cockshot Hill, Reig. RH2 266 DB136
Cockshot Rd, Reig. RH2 266 DB135
Cockspur Ct, SW1 297 P2
Cockspur St, SW1 297 P2
Cocksure La, Sid. DA14 186 FA90
Cock's Yd, Uxb. UB8
off Bakers Rd 134 BK66
● **Coda Studios**, SW6 306 E5
Code St, E1 288 B5
Codham Hall La,
Gt Warley CM13 129 FV56
Codicote Dr, Wat. WD25 60 BX34
Codicote Rd, Welw. AL6 28 CL05
Wheathampstead AL4 28 CL05
Codling Cl, E1 300 D2
Codling Way, Wem. HA0 117 CK63
CODMORE, Chesh. HP5 54 AS29
Codmore Cres, Chesh. HP5 54 AS30
Codmore Wd Rd, Chesh. HP5 56 AW33
Codrington Ct, Wok. GU21
off Raglan Rd 226 AT118
Codrington Cres, Grav. DA12 191 GJ92
Codrington Gdns, Grav. DA12 191 GK92
Codrington Hill, SE23 183 DY87
Codrington Ms, W11 282 F9
Cody Cl, Har. HA3 117 CK55
Wallington SM6 *off Alcock Cl* 219 DK108
Cody Rd, E16 291 H5
● **Cody Rd Business Cen**, E16 291 H5
Coe Av, SE25 202 DU100
Coe's All, Barn. EN5
off Wood St 79 CY42
Coe Spur, Slou. SL1 151 AP75
Coffey St, SE8 314 B4
Coftards, Slou. SL2 132 AW72
Cogan Av, E17 101 DY53
Cohen Cl, Chsht EN8 67 DY31
Coin St, SE1 298 E2
Coity Rd, NW5 275 H4
Cokers La, SE21
off Perifield 182 DQ88
Coke's Fm La, Ch.St.G. HP8 72 AV41
Coke's La, Amer. HP7 72 AW41
Chalfont St. Giles HP8 72 AU42
Coke St, E1 288 C8
Colas Ms, NW6 273 K8
Colbeck Ms, SW7 295 M9
Colbeck Rd, Har. HA1 116 CC59
Colberg Pl, N16 122 DS59
Colborne Way, Wor.Pk. KT4 199 CW104
Colbrook Av, Hayes UB3 155 BR76
Colbrook Cl, Hayes UB3 155 BR76
Colburn Av, Cat. CR3 236 DT124
Pinner HA5 94 BY51
Colburn Cres, Guil. GU4
off Sutherland Dr 243 BA131
Colburn Way, Sutt. SM1 200 DD104
Colby Ms, SE19 182 DS92
Colby Rd, SE19 182 DS92
Walton-on-Thames KT12
off Winchester Rd 195 BU102
Colchester Av, E12 125 EM62
Colchester Dr, Pnr. HA5 116 BX57
Colchester Rd, E10 123 EC59
E17 123 EA58
Edgware HA8 96 CQ52
Northwood HA6 93 BU54
Romford RM3 106 FK53
Colchester St, E1 288 B8
Colclough Ct, Croy. CR0
off Simpson Cl 202 DQ100
Colcokes Rd, Bans. SM7 234 DA116
Cold Arbor Rd, Sev. TN13 256 FD124
Coldbath Sq, EC1 286 E4
Coldbath St, SE13 314 D7
COLDBLOW, Bex. DA5 187 FC89
Cold Blow Cres, Bex. DA5 187 FD88
Cold Blow La, SE14 313 K3
Cold Blows, Mitch. CR4 200 DF97
Coldershaw Rd, W13 137 CG74
Coldfall Av, N10 98 DF54
Sch **Coldfall Prim Sch**, N10
off Coldfall Av 98 DF54
Coldham Gro, Enf. EN3 83 DY37
Cold Harbour, E14 302 F3
Coldharbour Cl, Egh. TW20 193 BC97
Coldharbour Crest, SE9
off Great Harry Dr 185 EN90
Coldharbour La, SE5 161 DN84
SW9 161 DN84
Bletchingley RH1 252 DT134
Bushey WD23 76 CB44
Dorking RH4, RH5 263 CG138
Egham TW20 193 BC97
Hayes UB3 135 BU73
Purley CR8 219 DN110
Rainham RM13 147 FE72
Woking GU22 227 BF115
● **Coldharbour La Ind Est**, SE5
off Coldharbour La 311 K9
● **Coldharbour Pinnacles Est**,
Harl. CM19 51 EM16
Coldharbour Pl, SE5 311 L8
Coldharbour Rd, Croy. CR0 219 DN106
Harlow CM19 51 EM16
Northfleet DA11 190 GE89
West Byfleet KT14 211 BF114
Woking GU22 227 BF115
Coldharbour Way, Croy. CR0 219 DN106
Coldmoreham Yd, Amer. HP7 55 AM39
Coldshott, Oxt. RH8 254 EG133
Coldstream Gdns, SW18 179 CZ86
Coldstream Rd, Cat. CR3 236 DQ121
Cole Av, Chad.St.M. RM16 171 GJ77
Colebeck Ms, N1 277 H5
Colebert Av, E1 288 G4
Colebrook, Ott. KT16 211 BD107
Colebrook Cl, NW7 97 CX52
SW15 179 CX87
Colebrooke Av, W13 137 CH72
Colebrooke Dr, E11 124 EH59
Colebrooke Pl, N1 277 H9
Colebrooke Rd, Red. RH1 250 DE132
Colebrooke Row, N1 286 G1
Colebrook Gdns, Loug. IG10 85 EP40
Colebrook Ho, E14 290 B8
Colebrook La, Loug. IG10 85 EP40
Colebrook Path, Loug. IG10 85 EP40
Colebrook Pl, Ott. KT16 211 BB108
Colebrook Ri, Brom. BR2 204 EE96
Colebrook Rd, SW16 201 DL95
Colebrook St, Erith DA8 167 FF78
Colebrook Way, N11 99 DH50
Coleby Path, SE5 311 M5
Colechurch Ho, SE1
off Avondale Sq 312 C1
Cole Cl, SE28 146 EV74
Coledale Dr, Stan. HA7 95 CJ53
Coleford Rd, SW18 180 DC85
Cole Gdns, Houns. TW5 155 BU80
Sch **Colegrave Prim Sch**, E15 281 H3
Colegrave Rd, E15 280 G2
COLE GREEN, Hert. SG14 30 DG12
Cole Grn Bypass, Hert. SG14 30 DF12
Cole Grn La, Welw.G.C. AL7 30 DB11
Cole Grn Way, Hert. SG14 31 DK12
Colegrove Rd, SE15 312 B3
Coleherne Ct, SW5 307 M1
Coleherne Ms, SW10 307 L1
Coleherne Rd, SW10 307 L1
Colehill Gdns, SW6 306 E7
Colehill La, SW6 306 E7
Colekitchen La, Goms. GU5 261 BR136
Coleman Cl, SE25 202 DU96
Coleman Flds, N1 277 K8
COLEMAN GREEN, St.Alb. AL4 28 CM10
Coleman Grn La, Wheat. AL4 28 CM10
Coleman Rd, SE5 311 N4
Belvedere DA17 166 FA77
Dagenham RM9 146 EY65
Colemans Heath, SE9 185 EP90
Colemans La, Ong. CM5 71 FH30
Coleman's La, Lwr Naze. EN9 67 ED26
Coleman St, EC2 287 L8
Colenorton Cres,
Eton Wick SL4 151 AL77
Colenso Dr, NW7 97 CU52
Colenso Rd, E5 122 DW63
Ilford IG2 125 ES60
Cole Pk Gdns, Twick. TW1 177 CG86
Cole Pk Rd, Twick. TW1 177 CG86
Cole Pk Vw, Twick. TW1
off Hill Vw Rd 177 CG86
Colepits Wd Rd, SE9 185 EQ85
Sch **Coleraine Pk Prim Sch**, N17
off Glendish Rd 100 DV53
Coleraine Rd, N8 121 DN55
SE3 315 L3
Coleridge Av, E12 144 EL65
Sutton SM1 218 DE105
Coleridge Cl, SW8 309 K9
Cheshunt EN7 66 DT27
Coleridge Cres, Colnbr. SL3 153 BE81
Coleridge Dr, Ruis HA4 115 BV58
Coleridge Gdns, NW6 273 N7
SW10 307 M4
Coleridge Ho, SW1 309 L1
Coleridge La, N8 121 DL58
Sch **Coleridge Prim Sch**, N8
off Crouch End Hill 121 DK59
Coleridge Rd, E17 123 DZ56
N4 121 DN61
N8 121 DK58
N12 98 DC50
Ashford TW15 174 BL91
Croydon CR0 202 DW101
Dartford DA1 168 FN84
Romford RM3 105 FH52
Tilbury RM18 171 GJ82
Coleridge Sq, SW10 307 N4
W13 137 CG72
Coleridge Wk, NW11 120 DA56
Hutton CM13 109 GC45
Coleridge Way, Borwd. WD6 78 CN42
Hayes UB4 135 BU72
Orpington BR6 206 EU100
West Drayton UB7 154 BM77
Cole Rd, Twick. TW1 177 CG86
Watford WD17 75 BV39
Colesburg Rd, Beck. BR3 203 DZ97
Coles Cres, Har. HA2 116 CB61
Colescroft Hill, Pur. CR8 235 DN115
Colesdale, Cuffley EN6 65 DL30
Coles Grn, Bushey Hth WD23 94 CC46
Loughton IG10 85 EN39
Coles Grn Ct, NW2 119 CU61
Coles Grn Rd, NW2 119 CU60
COLESHILL, Amer. HP7 55 AM43
Coles Hill, Hem.H. HP1 40 BG18
Sch **Coleshill C of E Inf Sch**,
Colesh. HP7 *off Village Rd* 55 AM44
Coleshill Flats, SW1
off Pimlico Rd 297 H9
Coleshill La, Winch.Hill HP7 88 AJ45
Coleshill Rd, Tedd. TW11 177 CE93
Coles La, Brasted TN16 240 EW123
Colesmead Rd, Red. RH1 250 DF131
COLES MEADS, Red. RH1 250 DF131
Colestown St, SW11 308 D8
Cole St, SE1 299 K5
Colet Cl, N13 99 DP51
Colet Gdns, W14 294 D10
Colet Rd, Hutt. CM13 109 GC43
Colets Orchard, Otford TN14 241 FH116
Coley Av, Wok. GU22 227 BA118
Coley St, WC1 286 D5
Colfe Rd, SE23 183 DY88
Sch **Colfe's Sch**, SE12
off Horn Pk La 184 EH86
Colgate Pl, Enf. EN3 83 EA37
Colgrove, Welw.G.C. AL8 29 CW10
Colham Av, West Dr. UB7 134 BL74
Colham Grn Rd, Uxb. UB8 134 BN71
Sch **Colham Manor Prim Sch**,
Hlgdn UB8 *off Violet Av* 134 BN72
Colham Mill Rd, West Dr. UB7 154 BK75
Colham Rd, Uxb. UB8 134 BM70
Jct **Colham Rbt**, Uxb. UB8 134 BN73
Colina Ms, N15 121 DP56
Colina Rd, N15 121 DP57
Colin Cl, NW9 118 CS56
Croydon CR0 203 DZ104
Dartford DA2 188 FP86
West Wickham BR4 204 EF104
Colin Cres, NW9 119 CT56
⊖ **Colindale** 118 CS55
Colindale Av, NW9 118 CR55
St. Albans AL1 43 CF22
● **Colindale Business Pk**, NW9 118 CQ55
Sch **Colindale Prim Sch**, NW9
off Clovelly Ave 119 CT56
Colindeep Gdns, NW4 119 CU57
Colindeep La, NW4 118 CS55
NW9 118 CS55
Colin Dr, NW9 119 CT57
Colinette Rd, SW15 159 CW84
Colin Gdns, NW9 119 CT57
Colin Par, NW9 *off Edgware Rd* 118 CS56
Colin Pk Rd, NW9 118 CS56
Colin Rd, NW10 139 CU65
Caterham CR3 236 DU123
Colinsdale, N1 276 G9
Colinton Rd, Ilf. IG3 126 EV61
Colin Way, Slou. SL1 151 AP76
Coliston Pas, SW18
off Coliston Rd 180 DA87
Coliston Rd, SW18 180 DA87
Collamore Av, SW18 180 DE88
Collapit Cl, Har. HA1 116 CB57
Collard Av, Loug. IG10 85 EQ40
Collard Cl, Ken. CR8 236 DS120
Collard Grn, Loug. IG10 85 EQ40
Collard Pl, NW1 275 J6
College App, SE10 314 F3
College Av, Egh. TW20 173 BB93
Epsom KT17 217 CT114
Grays RM17 170 GB77
Harrow HA3 95 CE53
Slough SL1 152 AS76
College Cl, E9 278 G2
N18 100 DT50
Grays RM17 170 GC78
Harrow HA3 95 CE52
Loug. IG10 85 EP42
North Mymms AL9 63 CX28
Twickenham TW2 177 CD88
Ware SG12 33 DX07
College Ct, Chsht EN8 66 DW30
College Cres, NW3 274 A5
Redhill RH1 250 DG131
Windsor SL4 151 AP82
College Cross, N1 276 F7
College Dr, Ruis. HA4 115 BU59
Thames Ditton KT7 197 CE101
College Gdns, E4 101 EB45
N18 100 DT50
SE21 182 DS88
SW17 180 DE89
Enfield EN2 82 DR39
Ilford IG4 124 EL57
New Malden KT3 199 CT99
College Gate, Harl. CM20 51 EQ15
College Grn, SE19 182 DS94
College Gro, NW1 275 N9
College Hill, EC4 287 K10
College Hill Rd, Har. HA3 95 CF53
College La, NW5 121 DH63
Hatfield AL10 44 CS20
Woking GU22 226 AW119
College Ms, SW1 298 A6
SW18 *off St. Ann's Hill* 180 DB85
★ **College of Arms**, EC4 287 H10
Coll **College of Haringey, Enfield &**
North East London (Enfield Cen),
Enf. EN *off Hertford Rd* 82 DW41
Coll **College of Haringey, Enfield &**
North East London (Tottenham Cen),
Tottenham N15
off Town Hall App. Rd 122 DT56
Coll **College of Law, The**,
Bloomsbury Cen, WC1 285 N6
Moorgate Cen, EC1 287 L5
Guildford GU3
off Portsmouth Rd 258 AW138
Coll **College of N W London**,
Wembley Pk Cen, Wem. HA9
off North End Rd 118 CN62
Willesden Cen, NW10
off Dudden Hill La 119 CT64
College Pk Cl, SE13 163 ED84
College Pk Rd, N17 100 DT51
Sch **College Pk Sch**, W2 283 L9
College Pl, E17 124 EE56
NW1 275 M9
SW10 307 N4
Greenhithe DA9 169 FW84
St. Albans AL3 42 CC20
College Pt, E15 281 L4
College Rd, E17 123 EC57
N17 100 DT51
N21 99 DN47
NW10 282 A1
SE19 182 DT92
SE21 182 DS87
SW19 180 DD93
W13 137 CH72
Abbots Langley WD5 59 BT31
Bromley BR1 184 EG94
Cheshunt EN8 66 DV30
Croydon CR0 202 DR103
Enfield EN2 82 DR40
Epsom KT17 217 CU114
Grays RM17 170 GC77
Guildford GU1 258 AX135
Harrow on the Hill HA1 117 CE58
Harrow Weald HA3 95 CE53
Hertford Heath SG13 32 DW13
Hoddesdon EN11 49 DZ15
Isleworth TW7 157 CF81
Northfleet DA11 190 GB85
St. Albans AL1 43 CH21
Slough SL1 131 AM74
Swanley BR8 207 FE95
Wembley HA9 117 CK60
Woking GU22 227 BB116
College Row, E9 279 J3
College Slip, Brom. BR1 204 EG95
College Sq, Harl. CM20
off College Gate 51 ER15
College St, EC4 287 K10
St. Albans AL3 43 CD20
College Ter, E3 289 N2
N3 *off Hendon La* 97 CZ54
College Vw, SE9 184 EK88
College Wk, Kings.T. KT1
off Grange Rd 198 CL97
College Way, Ashf. TW15 174 BM91
Hayes UB3 135 BU73
Northwood HA6 93 BR51
Welwyn Garden City AL8 29 CX08
College Yd, NW5 275 K1
Watford WD24
off Gammons La 75 BV38
Collent St, E9 279 H5
Coller Cres, Lane End DA2 189 FS91
Colless Rd, N15 122 DT57
Collet Cl, Chsht EN8 67 DX28
Collet Gdns, Chsht EN8
off Collet Cl 67 DX28
Collett Ho, N16
off Stamford Hill 122 DT60
Collett Rd, SE16 300 D7
Hemel Hempstead HP1 40 BJ20
Ware SG12 33 DX05
Sch **Collett Sch, The**, Hem.H. HP1
off Lockers Pk La 40 BH19
Collett Way, Sthl. UB2 136 CB74
Colley Hill La, Hedg. SL2 112 AT62
Colley Ho, Uxb. UB8 134 BK67
Colleyland, Chorl. WD3 73 BD42
Colley La, Reig. RH2 249 CY132
Colley Manor Dr, Reig. RH2 249 CX133
Colley Way, Reig. RH2 249 CY131
Collier Cl, E6 293 N10
Epsom KT19 216 CN107
Slough SL1 151 AM75
Collier Dr, Edg. HA8 96 CN54
COLLIER ROW, Rom. RM5 104 FA53
Collier Row La, Rom. RM5 105 FB52
Collier Row Rd, Rom. RM5 104 EZ53
Colliers, Cat. CR3 252 DU125
Colliers Cl, Wok. GU21 226 AV117
COLLIER'S WOOD, SW19 180 DD94
Colliers Shaw, Kes. BR2 222 EK105
Collier St, N1 286 C1
Colliers Water La, Th.Hth. CR7 201 DN99
⊖ **Colliers Wood** 180 DD94
Collier Way, Guil. GU4 243 BD132
Collindale Av, Erith DA8 167 FB79
Sidcup DA15 186 EU88
Collingbourne Rd, W12 139 CV74
Collingham Gdns, SW5 295 M9
Collingham Pl, SW5 295 L9
Collingham Rd, SW5 295 M8
Sch **Collingham Sch**, SW5 295 M9
Collings Cl, N22 99 DM51
Collington Cl, Nthflt DA11
off Beresford Rd 190 GE87
Collington St, SE10 315 H1
Collingtree Rd, SE26 182 DW91
Collingwood Av, N10 120 DG55
Surbiton KT5 198 CQ102
Collingwood Cl, SE20 202 DV95
Horley RH6 269 DH147
Twickenham TW2 176 CA86
Collingwood Cres, Guil. GU1 243 BA133
Collingwood Dr, Lon.Col. AL2 61 CK25
Collingwood Pl, Walt. KT12 195 BU104
Collingwood Rd, E17 123 EA58
N15 122 DS56
Mitcham CR4 200 DE96
Rainham RM13 147 FF68
Sutton SM1 200 DA104
Uxbridge UB8 135 BP70
Sch **Collingwood Sch**,
Jun Dept, Wall. SM6
off Maldon Rd 219 DH106
Sen Dept, Wall. SM6
off Springfield Rd 219 DH106
Collingwood St, E1 288 F4
Collins Av, Stan. HA7 96 CL54
Collins Dr, Ruis. HA4 116 BW61
Collins Meadow, Harl. CM19 51 EP15
Collinson Ct, Enf. EN3
off The Generals Wk 83 DY37
Collinson St, SE1 299 J5
Collinson Wk, SE1 299 J5
Collins Rd, N5 122 DQ63
Collins Sq, SE3 315 L9
Collins St, SE3 315 K9
Collins Way, Hutt. CM13 109 GE43
Collinswood Rd, Farn.Com. SL2 111 AN60
Collin's Yd, N1 276 G9
Collinwood Av, Enf. EN3 82 DW41
Collinwood Gdns, Ilf. IG5 125 EM57
Collis All, Twick. TW2
off The Green 177 CE88
Collison Pl, N16 122 DS61
Sch **Collis Prim Sch**, Tedd. TW11
off Fairfax Rd 177 CH93
Colls Rd, SE15 312 G6
Collum Grn Rd, Slou. SL2 111 AR62
Collyer Av, Croy. CR0 219 DL105
Collyer Pl, SE15 312 C7
Collyer Rd, Croy. CR0 219 DL105
London Colney AL2 61 CJ27
Colman Cl, Epsom KT18 233 CW117
Colman Rd, E16 292 C7
Colmans Hill, Peasl. GU5 261 BS144
Colman Way, Red. RH1 250 DE132
Colmar Cl, E1 289 J4
Colmer Pl, Har. HA3 95 CD52
Colmer Rd, SW16 201 DL95
Colmore Ms, SE15 312 F7
Colmore Rd, Enf. EN3 82 DW42
COLNBROOK, Slou. SL3 153 BD80
Colnbrook Bypass, Slou. SL3 153 BF80
West Drayton UB7 153 BF80
Colnbrook Cl, Lon.Col. AL2 62 CL27
Sch **Colnbrook C of E Prim Sch**,
Colnbr. SL3 *off High St* 153 BD80
Colnbrook Ct, Slou. SL3 153 BF81
Sch **Colnbrook Sch**, S.Oxhey
WD19 *off Hayling Rd* 94 BW48
Colnbrook St, SE1 298 G7
Colndale Rd, Colnbr. SL3 153 BE82
Colne Av, Mill End WD3 92 BG47
Watford WD19 75 BV44
West Drayton UB7 154 BJ75
Colne Bk, Horton SL3 153 BC83
Colnebridge Cl, Stai. TW18
off Clarence St 173 BE91
🔒 **Colne Br Retail Pk**, Wat. WD17
off Lower High St 76 BX43
Colne Cl, S.Ock. RM15 149 FW73
Colne Ct, Epsom KT19 216 CQ105
Colnedale Rd, Uxb. UB8 114 BK64
Colne Dr, Rom. RM3 106 FM51
Walton-on-Thames KT12 196 BX104
Colne Gdns, Lon.Col. AL2 62 CL27
Colne Ho, Bark. IG11 145 EP65
Colne Mead, Mill End WD3
off Uxbridge Rd 92 BG47
Colne Orchard, Iver SL0 133 BF72
Colne Pk Caravan Site,
West Dr. UB7 154 BJ77
Colne Reach, Stai. TW19 173 BF85
Colne Rd, E5 279 L1
N21 100 DR45
Twickenham TW1, TW2 177 CE88
Colne St, E13 291 N3
Colne Valley, Upmin. RM14 129 FS58
🔒 **Colne Valley Retail Pk**,
Wat. WD17 76 BX43
Colne Way, Hem.H. HP2 40 BM15
Staines-upon-Thames TW19 173 BB90
Watford WD24, WD25 76 BW36
Colne Way Ct, Wat. WD24
off North Western Ave 76 BX36
🔒 **Colney Flds Shop Pk**,
Lon.Col. AL2 62 CM28
Colney Hatch La, N10 98 DG52
N11 98 DF51
COLNEY HEATH, St.Alb. AL4 44 CR22
Colney Heath La, St.Alb. AL4 44 CL20
Sch **Colney Heath Sch**,
Coln.Hth AL4 *off High St* 44 CQ22
Colney Rd, Dart. DA1 188 FM86
COLNEY STREET, St.Alb. AL2 61 CE31
Colnhurst Rd, Wat. WD17 75 BU38
● **Coln Ind Est**, Colnbr. SL3 153 BF81
Cologne Rd, SW11 160 DD84
Sch **Coloma Conv Girls' Sch**, Croy.
CR0 *off Upper Shirley Rd* 203 DX104
Colombo Rd, Ilf. IG1 125 EQ60
Colombo St, SE1 298 G3
Colomb St, SE10 315 K1
Colonels La, Cher. KT16 194 BG100
Colonels Wk, Enf. EN2 81 DP40
Colonial Av, Twick. TW2 176 CC85
● **Colonial Business Pk**,
Wat. WD24 *off Colonial Way* 76 BW39
Colonial Dr, W4 158 CQ77
Colonial Rd, Felt. TW14 175 BS87
Slough SL1 152 AU75
Colonial Way, Wat. WD24 76 BX39
Colonnade, WC1 286 A5
Colonnade, The, SE8 301 N9
🔒 **Colonnade Wk**, SW1 297 J9
Colonsay, Hem.H. HP3 41 BQ22
Colony Ms, N1
off Mildmay Gro N 277 M3
Colorado Apts, N8
off Great Amwell La 121 DM55
Colorado Bldg, SE13
off Deals Gateway 314 C7
Colosseum Ter, NW1
off Albany St 285 K4
Colson Gdns, Loug. IG10 85 EN42
Colson Grn, Loug. IG10
off Colson Rd 85 EP42
Colson Path, Loug. IG10 85 EN42
Colson Rd, Croy. CR0 202 DS103
Loughton IG10 85 EP42
Colson Way, SW16 181 DJ91
Colsterworth Rd, N15 122 DT56
Colston Av, Cars. SM5 218 DE105
Colston Cl, Cars. SM5
off West St 218 DF105
Colston Cres, Goffs Oak EN7 65 DP27
Colston Rd, E7 144 EK65
SW14 158 CQ84
Colt Hatch, Harl. CM20 35 EP13
Colthurst Cres, N4 122 DQ61
Colthurst Dr, N9 100 DV48
Colthurst Gdns, Hodd. EN11 49 ED15
Coltishall Rd, Horn. RM12 148 FJ65
Coltman St, E14 289 M7
Colt Ms, Enf. EN3 83 EA37
Coltness Cres, SE2 166 EV78
Colton Gdns, N17 122 DQ55
Colton Rd, Har. HA1 117 CE57
Coltsfoot, Welw.G.C. AL7 30 DB11
Coltsfoot, The, Hem.H. HP1 39 BE21
Coltsfoot Ct, Grays RM17 170 GD79
Coltsfoot Dr, Guil. GU1 243 BA131
West Drayton UB7 134 BL72
Coltsfoot La, Oxt. RH8 254 EF133
Coltsfoot Path, Rom. RM3 106 FJ52
Columbas Dr, NW3 120 DD60
Columbia Av, Edg. HA8 96 CP53
Ruislip HA4 115 BV60
Worcester Park KT4 199 CT101
Columbia Pt, SE16 301 H6
Sch **Columbia Prim Sch**, E2 288 B2
Columbia Rd, E2 288 A2
E13 291 M6
Broxbourne EN10 67 DY26
Columbia Sq, SW14
off Upper Richmond Rd W 158 CQ84
Columbia Wf Rd, Grays RM17 170 GA79
Columbine Av, E6 292 G7
South Croydon CR2 219 DP108
Columbine Way, SE13 314 E9
Romford RM3 106 FL53
Columbus Ct, SE16
off Rotherhithe St 301 H3
Columbus Ctyd, E14 302 A2
Columbus Gdns, Nthwd. HA6 93 BU53
Columbus Sq, Erith DA8 167 FF79
Colva Wk, N19
off Chester Rd 121 DH61
Colvestone Cres, E8 278 A3
Sch **Colvestone Prim Sch**, E8 278 A3
Colview Ct, SE9
off Mottingham La 184 EK88
Colville Est, N1 277 N9
Colville Gdns, W11 283 H9
Colville Hos, W11 282 G8
Colville Ms, W11 283 H9
Colville Pl, W1 285 M7
Sch **Colville Prim Sch**, W11 283 H9
Colville Rd, E11 123 EC62
E17 101 DY54
N9 100 DV46
W3 158 CP76
W11 283 H9
Colville Sq, W11 282 G9
Colville Ter, W11 282 G9
Colvin Cl, SE26 182 DW92
Colvin Gdns, E4 101 EC48
E11 124 EH56
Ilford IG6 103 EQ53
Waltham Cross EN8 83 DX35
Colvin Rd, E6 144 EL66
Thornton Heath CR7 201 DN99
Colwall Gdns, Wdf.Grn. IG8 102 EG50
Colwell Rd, SE22 182 DT85
Colwick Cl, N6 121 DK59
Colwith Rd, W6 306 B3
Colwood Gdns, SW19 180 DD94
Colworth Gro, SE17 299 K9
Colworth Rd, E11 124 EE58
Croydon CR0 202 DU102
Colwyn Av, Perivale UB6 137 CF68
Colwyn Cl, SW16 181 DJ92
Colwyn Cres, Houns. TW3 156 CC81
Colwyn Grn, NW9
off Snowdon Dr 118 CS58
Colwyn Ho, SE1
off Briant Est 298 E7
Colwyn Rd, NW2 119 CV62
Colyer Cl, N1 276 D10
SE9 185 EP89
Colyer Rd, Nthflt DA11 190 GC89
Colyers Cl, Erith DA8 167 FD81
Colyers La, Erith DA8 167 FC81
Colyers Wk, Erith DA8
off Colyers La 167 FE81
Colyton Cl, Well. DA16 166 EX81
Wembley HA0 137 CJ65
Woking GU21 226 AW118
Colyton La, SW16 181 DN92
Colyton Rd, SE22 182 DV85

Colyton Way, N18 100 DU50
Combe, The, NW1 285 K3
Combe Av, SE3 315 M4
Combe Bk Dr, Sund. TN14 240 EY122
Combe Bk Sch, Sund. TN14
off Combe Bk Dr 240 EY123
Combe Bottom, Guil. GU5 260 BM137
Combedale Rd, SE10 303 N10
Combe La, Guil. GU5 261 BP135
Combemartin Rd, SW18 179 CY87
Combe Ms, SE3 315 L4
Comber Cl, NW2 119 CV62
Comber Gro, SE5 311 J6
Comber Gro Prim Sch, SE5 311 J5
Comber Ho, SE5
off Comber Gro 311 K5
Combermere Cl, Wind. SL4 151 AP82
Combermere Rd, SW9 310 C10
Morden SM4 200 DB100
Combe Rd, Gdmg. GU7 258 AS143
Watford WD18 75 BT44
Comberton Rd, E5 122 DV61
Combeside, SE18 165 ET80
Combe St, Hem.H. HP1 40 BJ20
Combwell Cres, SE2 166 EU76
Comely Bk Rd, E17 123 EC57
Comeragh Cl, Wok. GU22 226 AU119
Comeragh Ms, W14 294 F10
Comeragh Rd, W14 306 E1
Comer Cres, Sthl. UB2
off Windmill Av 156 CC75
Comerford Rd, SE4 163 DY84
Comer Ho, Barn. EN5
off Station Rd 80 DC42
Comet Cl, E12 124 EK63
Purfleet RM19 168 FN77
Watford WD25 59 BT34
Comet Pl, SE8 314 A5
Comet Rd, Hat. AL10 45 CT18
Stanwell TW19 174 BK87
Comet St, SE8 314 A5
Comet Way, Hat. AL9, AL10 44 CS19
Comforts Fm Av, Oxt. RH8 254 EF133
Comfort St, SE15 311 N3
Comfrey Ct, Grays RM17 170 GD79
Commander Ave, NW9 119 CU55
● Commerce Pk Croydon,
Croy. CR0 201 DM103
Commerce Rd, N22 99 DM53
Brentford TW8 157 CJ80
● Commerce Trade Pk,
Croy. CR0 201 DM104
Commerce Way, Croy. CR0 201 DM103
Commercial Pl, Grav. DA12 191 GJ86
Commercial Rd, E1 288 C8
E14 289 M9
N17 100 DS51
N18 100 DS50
Guildford GU1 258 AX135
Staines-upon-Thames TW18 174 BG93
Commercial St, E1 288 A5
Commercial Way, NW10 138 CP68
SE15 312 A5
Woking GU21 227 AZ117
Commerell Pl, SE10 303 L10
Commerell St, SE10 303 K10
Commodity Quay, E1 300 B1
Commodore Ho, SW18 160 DC84
Commodore St, E1 289 L5
Common, The, E15 281 L4
W5 138 CL73
Ashtead KT21 231 CK116
Berkhamsted HP4 39 AZ17
Chipperfield WD4 58 BG32
Hatfield AL10 45 CU17
Kings Langley WD4 58 BN28
Penn HP10 88 AC46
Richmond TW10 177 CK90
Shalford GU4 258 AY141
Southall UB2 156 BW77
Stanmore HA7 95 CE47
West Drayton UB7 154 BJ77
Wonersh GU5 259 BB143
Common Cl, Wok. GU21 210 AX114
Commondale, SW15 306 A9
Commonfield Rd, Bans. SM7 218 DA114
Commonfields, Harl. CM20 35 ES13
Common Gdns, Pott.End HP4 39 BB17
Common Gate Rd, Chorl. WD3 73 BD43
Common La, Burn. SL1 111 AK62
Claygate KT10 215 CG108
Dartford DA2 187 FG89
Eton SL4 151 AQ78
Kings Langley WD4 58 BM28
Letchmore Heath WD25 77 CE39
New Haw KT15 212 BJ109
Radlett WD7 77 CE39
Commonmeadow La,
Ald. WD25 60 CB33
Common Mile Cl, SW4 181 DK85
Common Rd, SW13 159 CU83
Chorleywood WD3 73 BD42
Claygate KT10 215 CG107
Dorney SL4 150 AJ79
Eton Wick SL4 151 AM78
Ingrave CM13 109 GC50
Langley SL3 153 BA77
Leatherhead KT23 230 BY121
Redhill RH1 266 DF136
Stanmore HA7 95 CD49
Waltham Abbey EN9 50 EK22
Commons, The, Welw.G.C. AL7 30 DA12
Commonside, Bkhm KT23 230 CA122
Epsom KT18 232 CN115
Keston BR2 222 EJ105
Commonside Cl, Couls. CR5 235 DP120
Sutton SM2 218 DB111
Commonside E, Mitch. CR4 200 DF97
Commonside Rd, Harl. CM18 51 ES19
Commonside W, Mitch. CR4 200 DF97
Commons La, Hem.H. HP2 40 BL19
Commons Wd Caravan Club,
Welw.G.C. AL7 30 DA13
Commonswood Sch, Welw.G.C.
AL7 off The Commons 30 DB12
Commonwealth Av, W12 139 CV73
Hayes UB3 135 BR72
Commonwealth Rd, N17 100 DU52
Caterham CR3 236 DU123
Commonwealth Way, SE2 166 EV78
COMMONWOOD, Kings L. WD4 58 BH34
Common Wd, Farn.Com. SL2 111 AQ63
Commonwood La, Kings L. WD4 74 BH35
Common Wd La, Penn HP10 88 AD46
Community Cl, Houns. TW5 155 BV81
Uxbridge UB10 115 BQ62
Community Coll Hackney,
London Flds, E8 278 F7
Shoreditch Campus, N1 287 P2
Community Ed Lewisham,
Brockley Cen, SE23
off Brockley Ri 183 DY88
Granville Pk Adult Learning Cen,
SE13 314 F10
Grove Pk Cen, SE12
off Pragnell Rd 184 EH89
Holbeach Cen, SE6
off Doggett Rd 183 EA87
Community La, N7 275 N2
Community Learning & Skills
Service Friday Hill Cen, E4
off Simmons La 102 EE47
Community Rd, E15 281 H3
Greenford UB6 136 CC67
Community Wk, Esher KT10
off High St 214 CC105
Community Way, Crox.Grn WD3
off Barton Way 75 BP43
Como Rd, SE23 183 DY89
Como St, Rom. RM7 127 FD57
Compass Bldg, Hayes UB3
off Station Rd 155 BT76
Compass Cl, Ashf. TW15 175 BQ94
Edgware HA8 96 CM49
Compass Hill, Rich. TW10 177 CK86
Compass Ho, SW18
off Smugglers Way 160 DB84
Compass La, Brom. BR1
off North St 204 EG95
Compass Pt, Nthch HP4
off Chapel Cfts 38 AS17
Compayne Gdns, NW6 273 L6
Comport Grn, New Adgtn CR0 222 EE112
Compter Pas, EC2
off Wood St 287 K8
Compton Av, E6 144 EK68
N1 276 G5
N6 120 DE59
Hutton CM13 109 GC46
Romford RM2 127 FH55
Wembley HA0 117 CJ63
Compton Cl, E3 290 B6
NW1 285 K3
NW11 119 CX62
SE15 312 C5
W13 137 CG72
Edgware HA8 96 CQ52
Esher KT10 214 CC106
Compton Ct, SE19 182 DS92
Slough SL1 off Brook Cres 131 AL72
Compton Cres, N17 100 DQ52
W4 158 CQ79
Chessington KT9 216 CL107
Northolt UB5 136 BX67
Compton Gdns, Add. KT15
off Monks Cres 212 BH106
St. Albans AL2 60 CB26
Compton Ho, SW11
off Parkham St 308 C6
Compton Pas, EC1 287 H4
Compton Pl, WC1 286 A4
Erith DA8 167 FF79
Watford WD19 94 BY48
Compton Ri, Pnr. HA5 116 BY57
Compton Rd, N1 277 H5
N21 99 DN46
NW10 282 C3
SW19 179 CZ93
Croydon CR0 202 DV102
Hayes UB3 135 BS73
Compton Sch, The, N12
off Summers La 98 DE51
Compton St, EC1 286 G4
Compton Ter, N1 276 G5
Comreddy Cl, Enf. EN2 81 DP39
Comus Pl, SE17 299 N9
Comyne Rd, Wat. WD24 75 BT36
Comyn Rd, SW11 160 DE84
Comyns, The,
Bushey Hth WD23 94 CC46
Comyns Cl, E16 291 L6
Comyns Rd, Dag. RM9 146 FA66
Conant Ms, E1 288 C10
Conaways Cl, Epsom KT17 217 CU110
Concanon Rd, SW2 161 DM84
Concert Hall App, SE1 298 D3
● Concord Business Cen, W3
off Concord Rd 138 CP71
Concord Cl, Nthlt. UB5 136 BY69
Concorde Cl, Houns. TW3 156 CB82
Uxbridge UB10 134 BL68
Concorde Ct, Wind. SL4
off Green La 151 AN82
Concorde Dr, E6 293 J7
Hemel Hempstead HP2 40 BK20
Concorde Way, SE16 301 J9
Slough SL1 151 AQ75
Concord Rd, W3 138 CP70
Enfield EN3 82 DW43
Concord Ter, Har. HA2
off Coles Cres 116 CB61
Concourse, The, N9
off Edmonton Grn Shop Cen 100 DU47
NW9 97 CT53
Concrete Cotts, Wisley GU23
off Wisley La 228 BL116
Condell Rd, SW8 309 M7
Conder St, E14 289 L8
Condor Ct, Guil. GU2
off Millmead Ter 258 AW136
Condor Path, Nthlt. UB5
off Brabazon Rd 136 CA68
Condor Rd, Stai. TW18 194 BH97
Condor Wk, Horn. RM12
off Heron Flight Av 147 FH66
Condover Cres, SE18 165 EP80
Condray Pl, SW11 308 C5
Conductive Ed Cen, N10
off Muswell Hill 121 DH55
Conduit, The, Bletch. RH1 252 DS129
Conduit Av, SE10 315 H6
Conduit Ct, WC2 286 A10
Conduit La, N18 100 DW50
Croydon CR0 220 DU106
Enfield EN3
off Morson Rd 83 DY44
Hoddesdon EN11 49 EA17
South Croydon CR2 220 DU106
Conduit La E, Hodd. EN11 49 EB17
Conduit Ms, SE18 305 P10
W2 284 A9
Conduit Pas, W2 284 A9
Conduit Pl, W2 284 A9
Conduit Rd, SE18 305 P10
Conduit St, W1 285 K10
Conduit Way, NW10 138 CQ66
Conegar Ct, Slou. SL1 132 AS74
Conewood St, N5 121 DP62
Coney Acre, SE21 182 DQ88
Coneyberry, Reig. RH2 266 DC138
Coney Burrows, E4 102 EE47
Coneybury, Bletch. RH1 252 DS134
Coneybury Cl, Warl. CR6 236 DV119
Coney Cl, Hat. AL10 45 CV19
Coneydale, Welw.G.C. AL8 29 CX07
Coney Gro, Uxb. UB8 134 BN69
Coneygrove Path, Nthlt. UB5
off Arnold Rd 136 BY65
CONEY HALL, W.Wick. BR4 204 EF104
Coney Hill Rd, W.Wick. BR4 204 EE103
Coney Way, SW8 310 D3
Conference Cl, E4
off Greenbank Cl 101 EC47
Conference Rd, SE2 166 EW77
Conford Dr, Shalf. GU4 258 AY141
Congleton Gro, SE18 165 EQ78
Congo Dr, N9 100 DW48
Congo Rd, SE18 165 ER78
Congress Ho, Har. HA1
off Lyon Rd 117 CF58
Congress Rd, SE2 166 EW77
Congreve Rd, SE9 165 EM83
Waltham Abbey EN9 68 EE33
Congreve St, SE17 299 N8
Congreve Wk, E16 292 E7
Conical Cor, Enf. EN2 82 DQ40
Coniers Way, Guil. GU4 243 BB131
Conifer Av, Rom. RM5 105 FB50
Conifer Cl, Orp. BR6 223 ER105
Reigate RH2 250 DA132
Waltham Cross EN7 66 DT29
Conifer Dr, Warley CM14 108 FX50
Conifer Gdns, SW16 181 DL90
Enfield EN1 82 DS44
Sutton SM1 200 DB103
Conifer La, Egh. TW20 173 BC92
Conifer Pk, Epsom KT17 216 CS111
Conifers, Wey. KT13 213 BS105
Conifers, The, Hem.H. HP3 39 BF23
Watford WD25 76 BW35
Conifers Cl, Tedd. TW11 177 CH94
Conifer Way, Hayes UB3 135 BU73
Swanley BR8 207 FC95
Wembley HA0 117 CJ62
Coniger Rd, SW6 307 J8
Coningesby Dr, Wat. WD17 75 BS39
Coningham Ms, W12 139 CU74
Coningham Rd, W12 159 CV75
Coningsby Av, NW9 96 CS54
Coningsby Bk, St.Alb. AL1 42 CC24
Coningsby Cl, N.Mymms AL9 45 CX24
Coningsby Cotts, W5
off Coningsby Rd 157 CK75
Coningsby Dr, Pot.B. EN6 64 DD33
Coningsby Gdns, E4 101 EB51
Coningsby La, Fifield SL6 150 AC81
Coningsby Rd, N4 121 DP59
W5 157 CJ75
South Croydon CR2 220 DQ109
Conington Rd, SE13 314 D8
Conisbee Ct, N14 81 DJ43
Conisborough Coll, SE6
off Bellingham Rd 183 EC90
Conisborough Cres, SE6 183 EC90
Coniscliffe Cl, Chis. BR7 205 EN95
Coniscliffe Rd, N13 100 DQ48
Conista Ct, Wok. GU21
off Roundthorn Way 226 AT116
Coniston Av, Bark. IG11 145 ES66
Perivale UB6 137 CH69
Purfleet RM19 168 FQ79
Upminster RM14 128 FQ63
Welling DA16 165 ES83
Coniston Cl, N20 98 DC48
SW13 159 CT80
SW20 199 CX100
W4 158 CQ81
Barking IG11
off Coniston Av 145 ES66
Bexleyheath DA7 167 FC81
Dartford DA1 187 FH88
Erith DA8 167 FE80
Hemel Hempstead HP3 41 BQ21
Coniston Ct, NW7
off Langstone Way 97 CY52
Wallington SM6 219 DH105
Weybridge KT13 213 BP107
Coniston Cres, Slou. SL1 130 AJ71
Conistone Way, N7 276 B6
Coniston Gdns, N9 100 DW46
NW9 118 CR57
Ilford IG4 124 EL56
Pinner HA5 115 BU56
Sutton SM2 218 DD107
Wembley HA9 117 CJ60
Coniston Ho, SE5 311 J4
Coniston Rd, N10 99 DH54
N17 100 DU51
Bexleyheath DA7 167 FC81
Bromley BR1 184 EE93
Coulsdon CR5 235 DJ116
Croydon CR0 202 DU101
Kings Langley WD4 58 BM28
Twickenham TW2 176 CB86
Woking GU22 227 BB120
Coniston Wk, E9 279 H2
Coniston Way, Chess. KT9 198 CL104
Egham TW20 173 BB94
Hornchurch RM12 127 FG64
Reigate RH2 250 DE133
Conlan St, W10 282 E4
Conley Rd, NW10 138 CS65
Conley St, SE10 303 K10
Connaught Av, E4 101 ED45
SW14 158 CQ83
Ashford TW15 174 BL91
East Barnet EN4 98 DF46
Enfield EN1 82 DS40
Grays RM16 170 GB75
Hounslow TW4 176 BY85
Loughton IG10 84 EK42
Connaught Br, E16 304 E3
● Connaught Business Cen,
NW9 off Hyde Est Rd 119 CT57
Mitcham CR4 200 DF99
Connaught Cl, E10 123 DY61
W2 284 C9
Enfield EN1 82 DS40
Hemel Hempstead HP2 40 BN18
Sutton SM1 200 DD103
Uxbridge UB8 135 BQ70
Connaught Ct, E17
off Orford Rd 123 EB56
Buckhurst Hill IG9
off Chequers 102 EH46
Connaught Dr, NW11 120 DA56
Weybridge KT13 212 BN111
Connaught Gdns, N10 121 DH57
N13 99 DP49
Berkhamsted HP4 38 AT16
Morden SM4 200 DC98
Connaught Hts, Uxb. UB10
off Uxbridge Rd 135 BQ70
Connaught Hill, Loug. IG10 84 EK42
Connaught Ho Sch, W2 284 E9
Connaught La, Ilf. IG1 125 EQ61
Connaught Ms, NW3 274 C1
SE18 305 M10
Ilford IG1 off Connaught Rd 125 ER61
Connaught Pl, W2 284 E10
Connaught Rd, E4 102 EE45
E11 123 ED60
E16 304 F2
E17 123 EA57
N4 121 DN59
NW10 138 CS67
SE18 305 M10
W13 137 CH73
Barnet EN5 79 CX44
Harrow HA3 95 CF53
Hornchurch RM12 128 FK62
Ilford IG1 125 ER61
New Malden KT3 198 CS98
Richmond TW10
off Albert Rd 178 CM85
St. Albans AL3 42 CC18
Slough SL1 152 AV75
Sutton SM1 200 DD103
Teddington TW11 177 CD92
Connaught Rbt, E16 292 E10
Connaught Sch for Girls, E11
off Connaught Rd 124 EE60
Annexe, E11 off Madeira Rd 124 EE61
Connaught Sq, W2 284 E9
Connaught St, W2 284 C9
Connaught Way, N13 99 DP49
Connect La, Barkingside IG6 103 EQ54
Connell Cres, W5 138 CM70
Connemara Cl, Borwd. WD6 78 CQ44
Connicut La, Lthd. KT23 246 CB128
Connington Cres, E4 101 ED48
Connop Rd, Enf. EN3 83 DX38
Connor Cl, E11 124 EE60
Ilford IG6 103 EP53
Connor Ct, SW11
off Alfreda St 309 J7
Connor Rd, Dag. RM9 126 EZ63
Connor St, E9 279 J8
Conolly Rd, W7 137 CE74
Conquerors Hill, Wheat. AL4 28 CL07
Conquest Rd, Add. KT15 212 BG106
Conrad Cl, Grays RM16 170 GB75
Conrad Dr, Wor.Pk. KT4 199 CW102
Conrad Gdns, Grays RM16 170 GA75
Conrad Ho, N16 277 N2
Consfield Av, N.Mal. KT3 199 CU98
Consort Cl, Warley CM14 108 FW50
Consort Ms, Islw. TW7 177 CD85
Consort Rd, SE15 312 E8
Consort Way, Horl. RH6 268 DG148
Consort Way E, Horl. RH6 269 DH149
Cons St, SE1 298 F4
Constable Av, E16 304 A2
Constable Cl, N11
off Friern Barnet La 98 DF50
NW11 120 DB58
Hayes UB4 135 BQ68
Constable Cres, N15 122 DU57
Constable Gdns, Edg. HA8 96 CN53
Isleworth TW7 177 CD85
Constable Ho, E14
off Cassilis Rd 302 B5
NW3 274 F6
Enf. EN1 off Ayley Cft 82 DU43
Constable Ms, Brom. BR1 204 EH96
Dagenham RM8
off Stonard Rd 126 EV63
Constable Rd, Nthflt DA11 190 GE90
Constable Wk, SE21 182 DS90
Constance Cl, SW15 178 CR91
Constance Cres, Brom. BR2 204 EF101
Constance Gro, Dart. DA1 188 FK86
Constance Rd, Croy. CR0 201 DP101
Enfield EN1 82 DS44
Sutton SM1 218 DC105
Twickenham TW2 176 CB87
Constance St, E16 304 G3
Constantine Pl, Hlgdn UB10 134 BM67
Constantine Rd, NW3 274 D1
Constitution Cres, Grav. DA12
off South Hill Rd 191 GJ88
Constitution Hill, SW1 297 J4
Gravesend DA12 191 GJ88
Woking GU22 226 AY119
Constitution Ri, SE18 165 EN81
Consul Av, Dag. RM9 147 FC69
Rain. RM13 147 FD69
Consul Gdns, Swan. BR8 187 FG94
Content St, SE17 299 K9
Contessa Cl, Orp. BR6 223 ES106
Control Twr Rd,
Lon.Hthrw Air. TW6 154 BN83
Convair Wk, Nthlt. UB5
off Kittiwake Rd 136 BX69
Convent Cl, Barn. EN5 79 CZ40
Beck. BR3 183 EC94
Convent Ct, Wind. SL4 151 AN82
Convent Gdns, W5 157 CJ77
W11 282 F9
Convent Hill, SE19 182 DQ93
Convent La, Cob. KT11 213 BS111
Convent of Jesus & Mary
Language Coll, NW10
off Crownhill Rd 139 CT67
Convent of Jesus &
Mary RC Inf Sch, NW2 272 A5
Convent Rd, Ashf. TW15 174 BN92
Windsor SL4 151 AN82
Convent Way, Sthl. UB2 156 BW77
Conway Cl, Beck. BR3 203 DY95
Loudwater HP10 88 AC53
Rainham RM13 147 FG66
Stanmore HA7 95 CG51
Conway Cres, Perivale UB6 137 CE68
Romford RM6 126 EW59
Conway Dr, Ashf. TW15 175 BQ93
Hayes UB3 155 BQ76
Sutton SM2 218 DB107
Conway Gdns, Enf. EN2 82 DS38
Grays RM17 170 GB80
Mitcham CR4 201 DK98
Wembley HA9 117 CJ59
Conway Gro, W3 138 CR71
Conway Ms, W1 285 L6
Conway Prim Sch, SE18
off Gallosson Rd 165 ES77
Conway Rd, N14 99 DL48
N15 121 DP57
NW2 119 CW61
SE18 165 ER77
SW20 199 CW95
Feltham TW13 176 BX92
Hounslow TW4 176 BZ87
London Heathrow Airport TW6
off Inner Ring E 155 BP83
Taplow SL6 130 AH72
Conway St, E13 291 N5
W1 285 L5
Conway Wk, Hmptn. TW12
off Fearnley Cres 176 BZ93
Conybeare, NW3 274 D6
Conybury Cl, Wal.Abb. EN9 68 EG32
Cony Cl, Chsht EN7 66 DS26
Conyers, Harl. CM20 35 EQ13
Conyers Cl, Hersham KT12 214 BX106
Woodford Green IG8 102 EE51
Conyers Rd, SW16 181 DK92
Conyer St, E3 289 L1
Conyers Way, Loug. IG10 85 EP41
Cooden Cl, Brom. BR1 184 EH94
Cook Ct, SE16
off Rotherhithe St 301 H3
Cooke Cl, Chaff.Hun. RM16 170 FY76
Cookes Cl, E11 124 EF61
Cookes La, Sutt. SM3 217 CY107
Cooke St, Bark. IG11 145 EQ67
Cookham Cl, Sthl. UB2 156 CB75
Cookham Cres, SE16 301 J4
Cookham Dene Cl, Chis. BR7 205 ER95
Cookham Hill, Orp. BR6 206 FA104
Cookham Rd, Sid. DA14 186 FA94
Swanley BR8 206 FA95
Cookhill Rd, SE2 166 EV75
Cook Rd, Dag. RM9 146 EX67
Cooks Cl, E14
off Cabot Sq 302 B2
Chalfont St. Peter SL9 90 AY51
Romford RM5 105 FC53
Cooks Ferry, N18 101 DY50
Cooks Ferry Rbt, N18
off Advent Way 101 DX50
Cook's Hole Rd, Enf. EN2 81 DP38
Cooks Mead, Bushey WD23 76 CB44
Cookson Gro, Erith DA8 167 FB80
Cook Sq, Erith DA8 167 FF80
Cooks Rd, SE17 310 G2
Cook's Rd, E15 280 C10
Cooks Spinney, Harl. CM20 36 EU13
Cooks Vennel, Hem.H. HP1 40 BG18
Cooks Way, Hat. AL10 45 CV20
Coolfin Rd, E16 291 P9
Coolgardie Av, E4 101 EC50
Chigwell IG7 103 EN48
Coolgardie Rd, Ashf. TW15 175 BQ92
Coolhurst Rd, N8 121 DK58
Cool Oak La, NW9 118 CS59
Coomassie Rd, W9 282 G4
COOMBE, Kings.T. KT2 178 CQ94
Coombe, The, Bet. RH3 248 CR131
Coombe Av, Croy. CR0 220 DS105
Sevenoaks TN14 241 FH120
Coombe Bk, Kings.T. KT2 198 CS95
Coombe Boys' Sch,
N.Mal. KT3 off College Gdns 199 CU99
Coombe Cliff CETS Cen,
Croy. CR0 off Coombe Rd 220 DR105
Coombe Cl, Edg. HA8 96 CM54
Hounslow TW3 156 CA84
Coombe Cor, N21 99 DP46
Coombe Cres, Hmptn. TW12 176 BY94
Coombe Dr, Add. KT15 211 BF107
Kingston upon Thames KT2 178 CR94
Ruislip HA4 115 BV60
Coombe End, Kings.T. KT2 178 CR94
Coombefield Cl, N.Mal. KT3 198 CS99
Coombe Gdns, SW20 199 CU96
Berkhamsted HP4 38 AT18
New Malden KT3 199 CT98
Coombe Girls' Sch,
N.Mal. KT3 off Clarence Av 198 CR96
Coombe Hts, Kings.T. KT2 178 CS94
Coombe Hill Ct, Wind. SL4 151 AK84
Coombe Hill Glade, Kings.T. KT2 178 CS94
Coombe Hill Inf & Jun Schs,
Kings.T. KT2
off Coombe La W 198 CR95
Coombe Hill Rd, Kings.T. KT2 178 CS94
Mill End WD3 92 BG45
Coombe Ho Chase, N.Mal. KT3 198 CR95
Coombehurst Cl, Barn. EN4 80 DF40
Coombe La, SW20 199 CT95
Coombe La, SW20 199 CU95
Croydon CR0 220 DV106
Whiteley Village KT12 213 BT109
Coombelands La, Add. KT15 212 BG107
Coombe Lane 220 DW106
Coombe La W, Kings.T. KT2 178 CS94
Coombe Lea, Brom. BR1 204 EL97
Coombe Lo, SE7 164 EJ79
Coombe Neville, Kings.T. KT2 178 CR94
Coombe Pk, Kings.T. KT2 178 CR92
Coombe Ridings, Kings.T. KT2 178 CQ92
Coombe Ri, Kings.T. KT2 198 CQ95
Shenfield CM15 109 FZ46
Coombe Rd, N22 99 DN53
NW10 118 CR62
SE26 182 DV91
W4 158 CS78
W13 off Northcroft Rd 157 CH76
Bushey WD23 94 CC45
Croydon CR0 220 DR105
Gravesend DA12 191 GJ89
Hampton TW12 176 BZ93
Kingston upon Thames KT2 198 CN95
New Malden KT3 198 CS96
Romford RM3 128 FM55
Coomber Way, Croy. CR0 201 DK101
Coombes Rd, Dag. RM9 146 EZ67
London Colney AL2 61 CH26
Coombe Vale, Ger.Cr. SL9 112 AY60
Coombe Wk, Sutt. SM1 200 DB104
Coombe Way, Byfleet KT14 212 BM112
Coombewood Dr, Rom. RM6 126 EZ58
Coombe Wd Hill, Pur. CR8 220 DQ112
Coombe Wd Rd, Kings.T. KT2 178 CQ92
Coombfield Dr, Lane End DA2 189 FR91
Coombs St, N1 287 H1
Coomer Ms, SW6 307 H3
Coomer Pl, SW6 307 H3
Coomer Rd, SW6 307 H3

Cooms Wk, Edg. HA8
off East Rd 96 CQ53
Cooperage Cl, N17 100 DT51
Cooper Av, E17 101 DX53
Cooper Cl, SE1 298 F5
Greenhithe DA9 189 FS85
Smallfield RH6 269 DN148
Cooper Cres, Cars. SM5 200 DF104
Cooper Rd, NW4 119 CX58
NW10 119 CT64
Croydon CR0 219 DN105
Guildford GU1 258 AY136
COOPERSALE, Epp. CM16 70 EX29
Sch Coopersale & Theydon Garnon C of E Prim Sch, Epp. CM16
off Brickfield Rd 70 EX29
Coopersale Cl, Wdf.Grn. IG8
off Navestock Cres 102 EJ52
Coopersale Common, Cooper. CM16 70 EX28
Sch Coopersale Hall Sch, Epp. CM16
off Flux's La 70 EV34
Coopersale La, Epp. CM16 86 EU37
Coopersale Rd, E9 279 K2
Coopersale St, Epp. CM16 70 EW32
Coopers Cl, E1 288 G5
Chigwell IG7 104 EV47
Dagenham RM10 147 FB65
South Darenth DA4 209 FR95
Staines-upon-Thames TW18 173 BE92
Sch Coopers' Company & Coborn Sch, Upmin. RM14
off St. Mary's La 129 FR61
Coopers Ct, Gidea Pk RM2
off Kidman Cl 128 FJ55
Hertford SG14 off The Folly 32 DR09
Cooper's Ct, Ware SG12 33 DY06
Coopers Cres, Borwd. WD6 78 CQ39
Coopers Dr, Dart. DA2 187 FE89
Coopers Gate, Coln.Hth AL4 44 CP22
Coopers Grn La, Hat. AL10 28 CS13
St. Albans AL4 44 CL17
Welwyn Garden City AL8 28 CQ14
Coopers Hill La, Egh. TW20 172 AY91
Coopers Hill Rd, Red. RH1 251 DM133
Coopers La, E10 123 EB60
NW1 275 P10
Pot.B. EN6 64 DD31
Staines-upon-Thames TW18 173 BF91
Cooper's La, SE12 184 EH89
Sch Cooper's La Prim Sch, SE12
off Pragnell Rd 184 EH89
Coopers La Rd, Pot.B. EN6 64 DE31
Coopers Ms, Beck. BR3 203 EA96
Watford WD25
off High Elms La 60 BW31
Coopers Rd, SE1 312 B1
Northfleet DA11 190 GE88
Potters Bar EN6 64 DC30
Swanscombe DA10 190 FZ86
Coopers Row, Iver SL0 133 BC70
Cooper's Row, EC3 288 A10
Coopers Shaw Rd, Til. RM18 171 GK80
Sch Coopers Tech Coll, Chis. BR7
off Hawkwood La 205 EQ95
Cooper St, E16 291 M7
Coopers Wk, E15 281 J3
Cheshunt EN8 67 DX28
Coopers Yd, N1 276 G6
Cooper's Yd, SE19 182 DS93
Cooper Way, Berk. HP4
off Robertson Rd 38 AX19
Slough SL1 151 AP76
Coote Gdns, Dag. RM8 126 EZ62
Coote Rd, Bexh. DA7 166 EZ81
Dagenham RM8 126 EZ62
Copeland Dr, E14 302 B8
Copeland Ho, SE11 298 D7
Copeland Rd, E17 123 EB57
SE15 312 D9
Copeman Cl, SE26 182 DW92
Copeman Rd, Hutt. CM13 109 GD45
Copenhagen Gdns, W4 158 CQ75
Copenhagen Pl, E14 289 N9
Sch Copenhagen Prim Sch, N1 276 C9
Copenhagen St, N1 276 B9
Copenhagen Way, Walt. KT12 195 BV104
Cope Pl, W8 295 J7
Copers Cope Rd, Beck. BR3 183 DZ93
Cope St, SE16 301 J8
Copford Cl, Wdf.Grn. IG8 102 EL51
Copford Wk, N1 277 J8
Copgate Path, SW16 181 DM93
Copinger Wk, Edg. HA8
off North Rd 96 CP53
Copland Av, Wem. HA0 117 CK64
Copland Cl, Wem. HA0 117 CJ64
Sch Copland Comm Sch & Tech Cen, Wem. HA9 off Cecil Av 118 CM64
Copland Ms, Wem. HA0 138 CL65
Copland Rd, Wem. HA0 138 CL65
Copleigh Dr, Kgswd KT20 233 CY120
Copleston Ms, SE15 312 A10
Copleston Pas, SE15 312 A10
Copleston Rd, SE15 162 DT83
Copley Cl, SE17 311 H3
W7 137 CF71
Redhill RH1 250 DE132
Woking GU21 226 AS119
Copley Dene, Brom. BR1 204 EK95
Copley Pk, SW16 181 DM93
Copley Rd, Stan. HA7 95 CJ50
Copley St, E1 289 J7
Copley Way, Tad. KT20 233 CX120
Copmans Wick, Chorl. WD3 73 BD43
Coppard Gdns, Chess. KT9 215 CJ107
Copped Hall, SE21
off Glazebrook Cl 182 DR89
Epping CM16 69 EN32
Coppelia Rd, SE3 164 EF84
Coppen Rd, Dag. RM8 126 EZ59
Copperas St, SE8 314 C3
Copper Beech Cl, Grav. DA12 191 GK87
Hemel Hempstead HP3 39 BF23
Ilford IG5 103 EN53
Orpington BR5 206 EW99
Windsor SL4 151 AK81
Woking GU22 226 AV121
Copperbeech Cl, NW3
off Akenside Rd 274 A3
Copper Beech Ct, Loug. IG10 85 EN39
Copper Beeches, Islw. TW7 157 CD81
Copper Beech Rd, S.Ock. RM15 149 FW69
★ Copper Box, E20 280 B5
Copper Cl, N17 100 DV52
SE19 off Auckland Rd 182 DT94
Copperdale Rd, Hayes UB3 155 BU75
Copperfield, Chig. IG7 103 ER51
Sch Copperfield Acad, Nthflt DA11
off Dover Rd E 190 GE88
Copperfield Av, Uxb. UB8 134 BN71
Copperfield Cl, S.Croy. CR2 220 DQ111
Copperfield Ct, Lthd. KT22
off Kingston Rd 231 CG121
Pinner HA5
off Copperfield Way 116 BZ56
Copperfield Dr, N15 122 DT56
Copperfield Gdns, Brwd. CM14 108 FV46
Copperfield Ms, N18 100 DS50
Copperfield Ri, Add. KT15 211 BF106
Copperfield Rd, E3 289 M5
SE28 146 EW72
Copperfields, Beac. HP9 89 AL50
Dartford DA1 off Spital St 188 FL86
Fetcham KT22 230 CC122
Welwyn Garden City AL7
off Forresters Dr 30 DC10
Copperfield St, SE1 299 H4
Copperfields Way, Rom. RM3 106 FK53
Copperfield Ter, Slou. SL2
off Mirador Cres 132 AV73
Copperfield Way, Chis. BR7 185 EQ93
Pinner HA5 116 BZ56
Coppergate Cl, Brom. BR1 204 EH95
Coppergate Ct, Wal.Abb. EN9
off Farthingale La 68 EG34
Coppergate Ms, Surb. KT6 197 CJ100
Copperkins Gro, Amer. HP6 55 AP36
Copperkins La, Amer. HP6 55 AM35
Copper Mead Cl, NW2 119 CW62
Copper Ms, W4 158 CQ76
Copper Mill Dr, Islw. TW7 157 CF82
Copper Mill La, SW17 180 DC91
Coppermill La, E17 122 DW58
Harefield UB9 91 BE52
Rickmansworth WD3 91 BE52
Sch Coppermill Prim Sch, E17
off Edward Rd 123 DX57
Coppermill Rd, Wrays. TW19 153 BC84
Copper Ridge, Chal.St.P. SL9 91 AZ50
Copper Row, SE1 300 A3
Copperwood, Hert. SG13 32 DT09
Coppetts Centre, N12 98 DF52
Coppetts Cl, N12 98 DE52
Coppetts Rd, N10 98 DG54
H Coppetts Wd Hosp, N10 98 DF53
Sch Coppetts Wd Prim Sch, N10
off Coppetts Rd 98 DG53
Coppice, The, Ashf. TW15
off School Rd 175 BP93
Bexley DA5 187 FD90
Enfield EN2 81 DP42
Hemel Hempstead HP2 41 BP19
Seer Green HP9 89 AR51
Watford WD19 76 BW44
West Drayton UB7 134 BL72
Coppice Ave, Cob. KT11 214 BZ114
Coppice Cl, SW20 199 CW97
Beckenham BR3 203 EB98
Hatfield AL10 45 CT22
Ruislip HA4 115 BR58
Stanmore HA7 95 CF51
Coppice Dr, SW15 179 CV86
Wraysbury TW19 172 AX87
Coppice End, Wok. GU22 227 BE116
Coppice Fm Rd, Penn HP10 88 AC45
Coppice Hatch, Harl. CM18 51 ER17
Coppice La, Reig. RH2 249 CZ132
Coppice Path, Chig. IG7 104 EV49
Sch Coppice Prim Sch, Chig. IG7
off Manford Way 104 EU50
Coppice Row, They.B. CM16 85 EM36
Coppice Wk, N20 98 DA48
Coppice Way, E18 124 EF56
Hedgerley SL2 111 AR61
Coppies Gro, N11 98 DG49
Copping Cl, Croy. CR0 220 DS105
Coppings, The, Hodd. EN11
off Danemead 33 EA14
Coppins, The, Har. HA3 95 CE51
New Addington CR0 221 EB107
Welwyn Garden City AL8 29 CU11
Coppins Cl, Berk. HP4 38 AS19
Coppins La, Iver SL0 133 BF71
Coppock Cl, SW11 308 C9
Coppsfield, W.Mol. KT8
off Hurst Rd 196 CA97
Copse, The, E4 102 EF46
Amersham HP7 55 AQ38
Beaconsfield HP9 88 AJ51
Bushey WD23 76 BY41
Caterham CR3 252 DU126
Fetcham KT22 230 CB123
Hemel Hempstead HP1 39 BE18
Hertford SG13 32 DU09
Send Marsh GU23 227 BF124
South Nutfield RH1 267 DL136
Tatsfield TN16 238 EJ120
Warlingham CR6 237 DY117
Copse Av, W.Wick. BR4 203 EB104
Copse Cl, SE7 164 EH79
Chilworth GU4 259 BC140
Northwood HA6 93 BQ54
Slough SL1 131 AM74
West Drayton UB7 154 BK76
Copse Edge Av, Epsom KT17 217 CT113
Copse Glade, Surb. KT6 197 CK102
COPSE HILL, SW20 179 CV94
Copse Hill, SW20 179 CV94
Harlow CM19 51 EP18
Purley CR8 219 DL113
Sutton SM2 218 DB108
Copse La, Horl. RH6 269 DJ147
Jordans HP9 90 AS52
Copsem Dr, Esher KT10 214 CB107
Copsem La, Esher KT10 214 CB107
Oxshott KT22 214 CC111
Copsem Way, Esher KT10 214 CC107
Copsen Wd, Oxshott KT22 214 CC111
Copse Rd, Cob. KT11 213 BV113
Redhill RH1 266 DC136
Woking GU21 226 AT118
Copse Vw, S.Croy. CR2 221 DX109
Copse Way, Chesh. HP5 54 AN27
Copse Wd, Iver SL0 133 BD67
Copsewood Cl, Sid. DA15 185 ES86
Copse Wd Ct, Reig. RH2
off Green La 250 DE132
Copsewood Rd, Wat. WD24 75 BV39
Copse Wd Way, Nthwd. HA6 93 BQ52
Copshall Cl, Harl. CM18 51 ES19
Copsleigh Av, Red. RH1 266 DG141
Copsleigh Cl, Salf. RH1 266 DG140
Copsleigh Way, Red. RH1 266 DG140
Coptain Ho, SW18
off Eastfields Av 160 DA84
Coptefield Dr, Belv. DA17 166 EX76
Coptfold Rd, Brwd. CM14 108 FW47
Copthall Av, EC2 287 M8
Copthall Bldgs, EC2 287 L8
Copthall Cl, EC2 287 L8
Chalfont St. Peter SL9 91 AZ52
Copthall Cor, Chal.St.P. SL9 90 AY52
Copthall Ct, EC2 287 L8
Copthall Dr, NW7 97 CU52
Copthall Gdns, NW7 97 CU52
Twickenham TW1 177 CF88
COPTHALL GREEN, Wal.Abb. EN9 68 EK33
Copthall La, Chal.St.P. SL9 90 AY52
Copthall Rd E, Uxb. UB10 114 BN61
Copthall Rd W, Uxb. UB10 114 BN61
Sch Copthall Sch, NW7
off Pursley Rd 97 CV52
Copthall Way, New Haw KT15 211 BF110
Copt Hill La, Kgswd KT20 233 CY120
Copthorn Av, Brox. EN10 49 DZ21
Copthorne Av, SW12 181 DK87
Bromley BR2 205 EM103
Ilford IG6 103 EP51
Copthorne Chase, Ashf. TW15 174 BM91
Copthorne Cl, Crox.Grn WD3 74 BM43
Shepperton TW17 195 BQ100
Copthorne Gdns, Horn. RM11 128 FN57
Copthorne Ms, Hayes UB3 155 BS77
Copthorne Pl, Eff.Junct. KT24 229 BU122
Copthorne Ri, S.Croy. CR2 220 DR113
Copthorne Rd, Crox.Grn WD3 74 BM44
Leatherhead KT22 231 CH120
Coptic St, WC1 286 A7
Copwood Cl, N12 98 DD49
Coral Apts, E16
off Western Gateway 303 P1
Coral Cl, Rom. RM6 126 EW56
Coral Gdns, Hem.H. HP2 40 BM19
Coraline Cl, Sthl. UB1 136 BZ69
Coralline Wk, SE2 166 EW75
Coral Row, SW11 307 P10
Corals Mead, Welw.G.C. AL7 29 CX10
Coral St, SE1 298 F5
Coram Cl, Berk. HP4 38 AW20
Coram Grn, Hutt. CM13 109 GD44
★ Coram's Flds, WC1 286 B5
Coram St, WC1 286 A5
Coran Cl, N9 101 DX45
Corban Rd, Houns. TW3 156 CA83
Corbar Cl, Barn. EN4 80 DD38
Corbden Cl, SE15 312 B6
Corben Ms, SW8
off Clyston St 309 M8
Corbet Cl, Wall. SM6 200 DG102
Corbet Ct, EC3 287 M9
Corbet Pl, E1 288 A6
Corbet Rd, Epsom KT17 216 CS110
Corbets Av, Upmin. RM14 128 FP64
CORBETS TEY, Upmin. RM14 148 FQ65
Corbets Tey Rd, Upmin. RM14 128 FP63
Sch Corbets Tey Sch, Upmin. RM14 off Harwood Hall La 128 FQ64
Corbett Cl, Croy. CR0 221 ED112
Corbett Gro, N22 99 DL52
Corbett Rd, E11 124 EJ58
E17 123 EC55
Corbetts La, SE16 300 G9
Corbetts Pas, SE16 300 G9
Corbicum, E11 124 EE59
Corbidge Ct, SE8 314 C2
Corbiere Ct, SW19
off Thornton Rd 179 CX93
Corbiere Ho, N1 277 N8
Corbin Ho, E3 290 D2
Corbins La, Har. HA2 116 CB62
Corbould Cl, Cars. SM5 218 DF107
Corbridge Cres, E2 278 E10
Corbridge Ms, Rom. RM1 127 FF57
Corby Cl, Eng.Grn TW20 172 AW93
St. Albans AL2 60 CA25
Corby Cres, Enf. EN2 81 DL42
Corby Dr, Eng.Grn TW20 172 AV93
Corbylands Rd, Sid. DA15 185 ES87
Corbyn St, N4 121 DL60
Corby Rd, NW10 138 CR68
Corby Way, E3 290 A5
Corcorans, Pilg.Hat. CM15 108 FV44
Cordelia Cl, SE24 161 DP84
Cordelia Ct, NW7
off Marchant Cl 96 CS51
Cordelia Gdns, Stai. TW19 174 BL87
Cordelia Rd, Stai. TW19 174 BL87
Cordelia St, E14 290 C8
Cordell Cl, Chsht EN8 67 DY28
Cordell Ho, N15 122 DU57
Corder Cl, St.Alb. AL3 42 CA23
Corderoy Pl, Cher. KT16 193 BE100
Cordingley Rd, Ruis. HA4 115 BR61
Cording St, E14 290 D7
Cordons Cl, Chal.St.P. SL9 90 AX53
Cordrey Gdns, Couls. CR5 235 DL115
Uni Cordwainers at London Coll of Fashion, EC1 287 J5
Cordwainers Wk, E13 281 P10
Cord Way, E14 302 B6
Cordwell Rd, SE13 184 EE85
Corefield Cl, N11
off Benfleet Way 98 DG47
Corelli Rd, SE3 164 EL82
Corfe Av, Har. HA2 116 CA63
Corfe Cl, Ashtd. KT21 231 CJ118
Borehamwood WD6 78 CR41
Hayes UB4 136 BW72
Hemel Hempstead HP2 40 BL21
Hounslow TW4 176 BY87
Corfe Gdns, Slou. SL1
off Avebury 131 AN74
Corfe Ho, SW8
off Dorset Rd 310 C4
Corfe Twr, W3 158 CP75
Corfield Rd, N21 81 DM43
Corfield St, E2 288 F3
Corfton Rd, W5 138 CL72
Coriander Av, E14 290 G9
Coriander Cres, Guil. GU2 242 AU129
Cories Cl, Dag. RM8 126 EX61
Corinium Cl, Wem. HA9 118 CM63
Corinium Gate, St.Alb. AL3 42 CA22
● Corinium Ind Est, Amer. HP6 72 AT38
Corinne Rd, N19 275 M1
Corinthian Manorway, Erith DA8 167 FD77
Corinthian Rd, Erith DA8 167 FD77
Corinthian Way, Stanw. TW19
off Clare Rd 174 BK87
Corker Wk, N7 121 DM61
Cork Ho, SW19 off Plough La 180 DB92
Corkran Rd, Surb. KT6 197 CK101
Corkscrew Hill, W.Wick. BR4 203 ED103
Cork Sq, E1 300 E2
Cork St, W1 297 L1
Cork St Ms, W1 297 L1
Cork Tree Retail Pk, E4 101 DY50
Cork Tree Way, E4 101 DY50
Corlett St, NW1 284 C6
Cormongers La, Nutfld RH1 251 DK131
Cormont Rd, SE5 310 G7
Cormorant Cl, E17 101 DX53
Cormorant Ct, SE21
off Elmworth Gro 182 DR89
Cormorant Ho, Enf. EN3
off Alma Rd 83 DX43
Cormorant Pl, Sutt. SM1
off Sandpiper Rd 217 CZ106
Cormorant Rd, E7 281 M2
Cormorant Wk, Horn. RM12
off Heron Flight Av 147 FH65
Cornbury Ho, SE8 off Evelyn St 313 P2
Cornbury Rd, Edg. HA8 95 CK52
Corncroft, Hat. AL10 45 CV16
Cornelia Dr, Hayes UB4 136 BW70
Cornelia Pl, Erith DA8
off Queen St 167 FE79
Cornelia St, N7 276 D5
Cornell Cl, Sid. DA14 186 EY93
Cornell Ct, Enf. EN3 83 DY41
Cornell Way, Rom. RM5 104 FA50
Corner, The, W.Byf. KT14 212 BG113
Corner Fm Cl, Tad. KT20 233 CW122
Cornerfield, Hat. AL10 45 CV15
Corner Fielde, SW2
off Streatham Hill 181 DL88
Corner Grn, SE3 315 N9
Corner Hall, Hem.H. HP3 40 BJ22
Corner Hall Av, Hem.H. HP3 40 BK22
Corner Ho St, WC2 298 A2
Corner Mead, NW9 97 CT52
Corner Meadow, Harl. CM18 52 EU19
Corners, Welw.G.C. AL7 30 DA07
Cornerside, Ashf. TW15 175 BQ94
Corner Vw, N.Mymms AL9 45 CW24
Corney Reach Way, W4 158 CS80
Corney Rd, W4 158 CS79
Cornfield Cl, Uxb. UB8 134 BK68
Cornfield Rd, Bushey WD23 76 CB42
Reigate RH2 266 DC135
Cornfields, Gdmg. GU7 258 AT143
Cornfields, The, Hem.H. HP1 40 BH21
Cornflower La, Croy. CR0 203 DX102
Cornflower Ter, SE22 182 DV86
Cornflower Way, Hat. AL10 44 CS15
Romford RM3 106 FL53
Cornford Cl, Brom. BR2 204 EG99
Cornford Gro, SW12 181 DH89
Cornhill, EC3 287 M9
Cornhill Cl, Add. KT15 194 BH103
Cornhill Dr, Enf. EN3 83 DY37
Corn Ho, NW7
off Peacock Cl 97 CY50
Cornish Ct, N9 100 DV45
Cornish Gro, SE20 182 DV94
Cornish Ho, SE17 310 G3
Brentford TW8
off Green Dragon La 158 CM78
Corn Mead, Welw.G.C. AL8 29 CW06
Cornmill, Wal.Abb. EN9 67 EB33
Corn Mill Dr, Orp. BR6 205 ET101
Cornmill Ms, Wal.Abb. EN9
off Highbridge St 67 EB33
Cornmow Dr, NW10 119 CT64
Cornshaw Rd, Dag. RM8 126 EX60
Cornsland, Brwd. CM14 108 FX48
Cornsland Cl, Upmin. RM14 128 FQ55
Cornsland Ct, Brwd. CM14 108 FW48
Cornthwaite Rd, E5 122 DW62
Cornwall Av, E2 288 G3
N3 98 DA52
N22 99 DL53
Byfleet KT14 212 BM114
Claygate KT10 215 CF108
Slough SL2 131 AQ70
Southall UB1 136 BZ71
Welling DA16 165 ES83
Cornwall Cl, Bark. IG11 145 ET65
Eton Wick SL4 151 AL78
Hornchurch RM11 128 FN56
Waltham Cross EN8 67 DY33
Cornwall Cres, W11 282 E10
Cornwall Dr, Orp. BR5 186 EW94
Cornwall Gdns, NW10 139 CV65
SW7 295 M7
Cornwall Gdns Wk, SW7 295 M7
Cornwall Gate, Purf. RM19
off Fanns Ri 168 FN77
Cornwall Gro, W4 158 CS78
Cornwallis Av, N9 100 DV47
SE9 185 ER89
Cornwallis Cl, Cat. CR3 236 DQ122
Erith DA8 167 FF79
Cornwallis Ct, SW8 310 A6
Cornwallis Gro, N9 100 DV47
Cornwallis Rd, E17 123 DX56
N9 100 DV47
N19 121 DL61
SE18 165 EQ77
Dagenham RM9 126 EX63
Cornwallis Sq, N19 121 DL61
Cornwallis Wk, SE9 165 EM83
Cornwall Ms S, SW7 295 N7
Cornwall Ms W, SW7 295 M7
Cornwall Pl, E4 83 EB42
Cornwall Rd, N4 121 DN59
N15 122 DR57
N18 100 DU50
SE1 298 E2
Croydon CR0 201 DP103
Dartford DA1 168 FM83
Harrow HA1 116 CC58
Pilgrim's Hatch CM15 108 FV43
Pinner HA5 94 BZ52
Ruislip HA4 115 BT62
St. Albans AL1 43 CE22
Sutton SM2 217 CZ108
Twickenham TW1 177 CG87
Uxbridge UB8 134 BK65
Cornwall Sq, SE11 298 F10
Cornwall St, E1 288 F10
Cornwall Ter, NW1 284 F5
Cornwall Ter Ms, NW1 284 F5
Cornwall Way, Stai. TW18 173 BE93
Corn Way, E11 123 ED62
Cornwell Av, Grav. DA12 191 GJ90
Cornwell Rd, Old Wind. SL4 172 AU86
Cornwood Cl, N2 120 DD57
Cornwood Dr, E1 288 G8
Cornworthy Rd, Dag. RM8 126 EW64
Corona Rd, SE12 184 EG87
Coronation Av, N16
off Victorian Rd 122 DT62
George Green SL3 132 AY72
Windsor SL4 152 AT81
Coronation Cl, Bex. DA5 186 EX86
Ilford IG6 125 EQ56
Coronation Dr, Horn. RM12 127 FH63
Coronation Hill, Epp. CM16 69 ET30
Coronation Rd, E13 292 D3
NW10 138 CN70
Hayes UB3 155 BT77
Ware SG12 33 DX05
Coronation Wk, Twick. TW2 176 CA88
Coronet, The, Horl. RH6 269 DJ150
Coronet St, N1 287 N3
★ Coronet Thea, SE1 299 H7
Corporation Av, Houns. TW4 156 BY84
Corporation Row, EC1 286 F4
Corporation St, E15 291 K1
N7 276 A3
Sch Corpus Christi Prim Sch, N.Mal. KT3 off Chestnut Gro 198 CQ97
Sch Corpus Christi RC Prim Sch, SW2 off Trent Rd 181 DM85
Annexe, SW2 off Trent Rd 181 DM85
Corrance Rd, SW2 161 DL84
Corran Way, S.Ock. RM15 149 FV73
Corri Av, N14 99 DK49
Corrib Dr, Sutt. SM1 218 DE106
Corrie Gdns, Vir.W. GU25 192 AW101
Corrie Rd, Add. KT15 212 BK105
Woking GU22 227 BC120
Corrigan Av, Couls. CR5 218 DG114
Corrigan Cl, NW4 119 CW55
Corringham Ct, NW11
off Corringham Rd 120 DA59
St. Albans AL1
off Lemsford Rd 43 CF19
Corringham Rd, NW11 120 DA59
Wembley HA9 118 CN61
Corringway, NW11 120 DB59
W5 138 CN70
Corris Grn, NW9 118 CS58
Corry Dr, SW9 161 DP84
Corsair Cl, Stai. TW19 174 BK87
Corsair Rd, Stai. TW19 174 BL87
Corscombe Cl, Kings.T. KT2 178 CQ92
Corsehill St, SW16 181 DJ93
Corsellis Sq, Twick. TW1 157 CH84
Corsham St, N1 287 M3
Corsica St, N5 276 G4
Corsley Way, E9
off Silk Mills Sq 279 P4
Cortayne Rd, SW6 307 H8
Cortina Dr, Dag. RM9 147 FC69
Cortis Rd, SW15 179 CV86
Cortis Ter, SW15 179 CV86
Cortland Cl, Dart. DA1 187 FE86
Woodford Green IG8 102 EJ53
Corunna Rd, SW8 309 M6
Corunna Ter, SW8 309 L6
Corve La, S.Ock. RM15 149 FV73
Corvette Sq, SE10 315 H2
Corwell Gdns, Uxb. UB8 135 BQ72
Corwell La, Uxb. UB8 135 BQ72
Cory Dr, Hutt. CM13 109 GB45
Coryton Path, W9 283 H4
Cory Wright Way, Wheat. AL4 28 CL06
Cosbycote Av, SE24 182 DQ85
Cosdach Av, Wall. SM6 219 DK108
Cosedge Cres, Croy. CR0 219 DN106
Cosgrove Cl, N21 100 DQ47
Hayes UB4 off Kingsash Dr 136 BY70
Cosmo Pl, WC1 286 B6
Cosmopolitan Ct, Enf. EN1
off Main Ave 82 DU43
Cosmur Cl, W12 159 CT76
Cossall Wk, SE15 312 E8
Cossar Ms, SW2 181 DN86
Cosser St, SE1 298 E6
Costa St, SE15 312 C9
Costead Manor Rd, Brwd. CM14 108 FV46
Costell's Meadow, West. TN16 255 ER126
Costins Wk, Berk. HP4
off Robertson Rd 38 AX19
Sch Coston Prim Sch, Grnf. UB6
off Oldfield La S 136 CC69
Costons Av, Grnf. UB6 137 CD69
Costons La, Grnf. UB6 137 CD69
Coston Wk, SE4
off Hainford Cl 163 DX84
Cosway St, NW1 284 D6
Cotall St, E14 290 B8
Coteford Cl, Loug. IG10 85 EP40
Pinner HA5 115 BU57
Sch Coteford Inf Sch, Eastcote HA5 off Fore St 115 BU58
Sch Coteford Jun Sch, Eastcote HA5 off Fore St 115 BT57
Coteford St, SW17 180 DF91
Cotelands, Croy. CR0 202 DS104
Cotesbach Rd, E5 122 DW62
Cotesmore Gdns, Dag. RM8 126 EW63
Cotesmore Rd, Hem.H. HP1 39 BE21
Cotford Rd, Th.Hth. CR7 202 DQ98
Cotham St, SE17 299 K9
Cotherstone, Epsom KT19 216 CR110
Cotherstone Rd, SW2 181 DM88
Cotland Acres, Red. RH1 266 DD136
Cotlandswick, Lon.Col. AL2 61 CJ26
Cotleigh Av, Bex. DA5 186 EX89
Cotleigh Rd, NW6 273 J6
Romford RM7 127 FD58
Cotman Cl, NW11 120 DC58
SW15 179 CX86
Cotmandene, Dor. RH4 263 CH136
Cotmandene Cres, Orp. BR5 206 EU96
Cotman Gdns, Edg. HA8 96 CN54
Cotman Ms, Dag. RM8 126 EW64
Cotmans Cl, Hayes UB3 135 BU74
Coton Dr, Uxb. UB10 114 BQ61
Coton Rd, Well. DA16 166 EU83
Cotsford Av, N.Mal. KT3 198 CQ99
Cotsmoor, St.Alb. AL1
off Granville Rd 43 CF20
Cotswold, Hem.H. HP2
off Mendip Way 40 BL17
Cotswold Av, Bushey WD23 76 CC44
Cotswold Cl, Bexh. DA7 167 FE82
Hinchley Wood KT10 197 CF104
Kingston upon Thames KT2 178 CP93
St. Albans AL4 off Chiltern Rd 43 CJ15
Slough SL1 151 AP76
Staines-upon-Thames TW18 174 BG92
Uxbridge UB8 134 BJ67

Cotswold Ct, EC1 287 J4
N11 98 DG49
Cotswold Gdns, E6 292 F2
NW2 119 CX61
Hutton CM13 109 GE45
Ilford IG2 125 ER59
Cotswold Gate, NW2 119 CY60
Cotswold Grn, Enf. EN2
off Cotswold Way 81 DM42
Cotswold Ms, SW11 308 B7
Cotswold Ri, Orp. BR6 205 ET100
Cotswold Rd, Hmptn. TW12 176 CA93
Northfleet DA11 190 GE90
Romford RM3 106 FM54
Sutton SM2 218 DB110
Cotswolds, Hat. AL10 45 CU20
Cotswold St, SE27
off Norwood High St 181 DP91
Cotswold Way, Enf. EN2 81 DM42
Worcester Park KT4 199 CW103
Cottage Av, Brom. BR2 204 EL102
Cottage Cl, Crox.Grn WD3 74 BM44
Harrow HA2 117 CE61
Ottershaw KT16 211 BC107
Ruislip HA4 115 BR60
Watford WD17 75 BT40
Cottage Fm Way, Egh. TW20
off Green Rd 193 BC97
Cottage Fld Cl, Sid. DA14 186 EW88
Cottage Gdns, Chsht EN8 66 DW29
Cottage Grn, SE5 311 M4
Cottage Gro, SW9 161 DL83
Surbiton KT6 197 CK100
Cottage Pk Rd, Hedg. SL2 111 AR61
Cottage Pl, SW3 296 C6
Cottage Rd, N7 276 C3
Epsom KT19 216 CR108
Cotts Cl, W7 *off Westcott Cres* 137 CF72
Cottage St, E14 290 D10
Cotts Wd Dr, Guil. GU4 243 BA129
Cottage Wk, N16
off Brooke Rd 122 DT62
Cottenham Dr, NW9 119 CT55
SW20 179 CV94
Cottenham Par, SW20
off Durham Rd 199 CV96
COTTENHAM PARK, SW20 199 CV95
Cottenham Pk Rd, SW20 179 CV94
Cottenham Pl, SW20 179 CV94
Cottenham Rd, E17 123 DZ56
Cotterells, Hem.H. HP1 40 BJ21
Cotterells Hill, Hem.H. HP1 40 BJ20
Cotterill Rd, Surb. KT6 198 CL103
Cottesbrooke Cl, Colnbr. SL3 153 BD81
Cottesbrook St, SE14 313 L4
Cottesloe Ms, SE1 298 F6
Cottesmore Av, Ilf. IG5 103 EN54
Cottesmore Gdns, W8 295 M6
Cottimore Av, Walt. KT12 195 BV102
Cottimore Cres, Walt. KT12 195 BV101
Cottimore La, Walt. KT12 196 BW102
Cottimore Ter, Walt. KT12 195 BV101
Cottingham Chase, Ruis. HA4 115 BU62
Cottingham Rd, SE20 183 DX94
SW8 310 D3
Cottington Rd, Felt. TW13 176 BX91
Cottington St, SE11 298 F10
Cottle Way, SE16 300 F5
Cotton Av, W3 138 CR72
Cotton Cl, E11 124 EE61
Dagenham RM9
off Flamstead Rd 146 EW66
Cotton Dr, Hert. SG13 32 DV08
Cotton Fld, Hat. AL10 45 CV16
Cottongrass Cl, Croy. CR0
off Cornflower La 203 DX102
Cottonham Cl, N12
off Fenstanton Ave 98 DD50
Cotton Hill, Brom. BR1 183 ED91
Cotton La, Dart. DA2 188 FQ86
Greenhithe DA9 188 FQ85
Cottonmill Cres, St.Alb. AL1 43 CD21
Cottonmill La, St.Alb. AL1 43 CE23
Cotton Rd, Pot.B. EN6 64 DC31
Cotton Row, SW11 307 P10
Cottons App, Rom. RM7 127 FD57
Cottons Ct, Rom. RM7 127 FD57
Cottons Gdns, E2 287 P2
Cottons La, SE1 299 M2
Cotton St, E14 290 E10
Cottrell Ct, SE10
off Greenroof Way 303 M8
Cottrill Gdns, E8 278 E4
Couchmore Av, Esher KT10 197 CE103
Ilford IG5 103 EM54
Coulgate St, SE4 163 DY83
COULSDON, CR5 235 DJ116
Coulsdon C of E Prim Sch,
Couls. CR5 *off Bradmore Grn* 235 DM118
Coulsdon Coll, Couls. CR5
off Placehouse La 235 DN119
Coulsdon Common, Cat. CR3 236 DQ121
Coulsdon Ct Rd, Couls. CR5 236 DM116
Coulsdon La, Chipstead CR5 234 DF119
● **Coulsdon N Ind Est**,
Couls. CR5 235 DK116
Coulsdon Pl, Cat. CR3 236 DR122
Coulsdon Ri, Couls. CR5 235 DL117
Coulsdon Rd, Cat. CR3 236 DQ121
Coulsdon CR5 235 DM115
Coulsdon South 235 DK116
Coulsdon Town 235 DL115
Coulser Cl, Hem.H. HP1 40 BG17
Coulson Cl, Dag. RM8 126 EW59
Coulson Ct, Lon.Col. AL2 61 CK27
Coulson St, SW3 296 E10
Coulson Way, Burn. SL1 130 AH71
Coulter Cl, Cuffley EN6 65 DK27
Hayes UB4 *off Berrydale Rd* 136 BY70
Coulter Rd, W6 159 CV76
Coulton Av, Nthflt DA11 190 GE87
Council Av, Nthflt DA11 190 GC86
Council Cotts, Wisley GU23
off Wisley La 228 BK115
Councillor St, SE5 311 J5
Counter Ct, SE1
off Borough High St 299 L3
Counters Cl, Hem.H. HP1 40 BG20
Counter St, SE1
off Tooley St 299 N2
Countess Anne C of E Prim Sch,
Hat. AL10
off School La 45 CW17
Countess Cl, Hare. UB9 92 BJ54
Countess Rd, NW5 275 L2
Countisbury Av, Enf. EN1 100 DT45
Countisbury Gdns, Add. KT15 212 BH106
Country Way, Han. TW13 175 BV94
Sunbury-on-Thames TW16 175 BV94
County Gate, SE9 185 EQ90
New Barnet EN5 80 DB44
County Gro, SE5 311 J6
★ **County Hall**, SE1 298 C4
Co-operative Ho, SE15 312 D10
County Rd, E6 293 N7
Thornton Heath CR7 201 DP96
County St, SE1 299 K7
Coupland Pl, SE18 165 EQ78
Courage Cl, Horn. RM11 128 FJ58
Courage Wk, Hutt. CM13 109 GD44
Courcy Rd, N8 121 DN55
Courier Rd, Dag. RM9 147 FC70
Courland Gro, SW8 309 P7
Courland Gro Hall, SW8 309 P8
Courland Rd, Add. KT15 194 BH104
Courland St, SW8 309 P7
Course, The, SE9 185 EN90
Coursers Rd, Coln.Hth AL4 62 CN27
Court, The, Ruis. HA4 116 BY63
Warlingham CR6 237 DY118
Courtauld Cl, SE28 146 EU74
★ **Courtauld Inst of Art**, WC2 286 C10
Courtauld Rd, N19 121 DK60
Courtaulds, Chipper. WD4 58 BH30
Court Av, Belv. DA17 166 EZ78
Coulsdon CR5 235 DN118
Romford RM3 106 FN52
Court Bushes Rd, Whyt. CR3 236 DU120
Court Cl, Har. HA3 117 CK55
Maidenhead SL6 150 AC77
Twickenham TW2 176 CB90
Wallington SM6 219 DK108
Court Cl Av, Twick. TW2 176 CB90
Court Cres, Chess. KT9 215 CK106
Slough SL1 131 AR72
Swanley BR8 207 FE98
Court Downs Rd, Beck. BR3 203 EB96
Court Dr, Croy. CR0 219 DM105
Maidenhead SL6 130 AC68
Stanmore HA7 96 CL49
Sutton SM1 218 DE105
Uxbridge UB10 134 BM67
Courtenay Av, N6 120 DE58
Harrow HA3 94 CC53
Sutton SM2 218 DA109
Courtenay Dr, Beck. BR3 203 ED96
Chafford Hundred RM16
off Clifford Rd 170 FZ76
Courtenay Gdns, Har. HA3 94 CC54
Upminster RM14 128 FQ60
Courtenay Ms, E17
off Cranbrook Ms 123 DY57
Courtenay Pl, E17 123 DY57
Courtenay Rd, E11 124 EF62
E17 123 DX56
SE20 183 DX94
Wembley HA9 117 CK62
Woking GU21 227 BA116
Worcester Park KT4 199 CW104
Courtenay Sq, SE11 310 E1
Courtenay St, SE11 298 E10
Courtens Ms, Stan. HA7 95 CJ52
Court Fm Av, Epsom KT19 216 CR106
Court Fm Cl, Slou. SL1
off Weekes Dr 131 AP74
Court Fm La, Oxt. RH8 254 EE128
Court Fm Pk, Warl. CR6 236 DU116
Court Fm Rd, SE9 184 EK89
Northolt UB5 136 CA66
Warlingham CR6 236 DU118
Courtfield, W5
off Castlebar Hill 137 CJ71
Courtfield Av, Har. HA1 117 CF57
Courtfield Cl, Brox. EN10 49 EA20
Courtfield Cres, Har. HA1 117 CF57
Courtfield Gdns, SW5 295 M8
W13 137 CG72
Denham UB9 114 BG62
Ruislip HA4 115 BT61
Courtfield Ms, SW5 295 N9
Courtfield Ri, W.Wick. BR4 203 ED104
Courtfield Rd, SW7 295 M9
Ashford TW15 175 BP93
Court Gdns, N7 276 F5
Courtgate Cl, NW7 97 CT51
Court Grn Hts, Wok. GU22 226 AW120
Court Haw, Bans. SM7 234 DE115
Court Hill, Chipstead CR5 234 DE118
South Croydon CR2 220 DS112
Courthill Rd, SE13 163 EC84
Courthope Rd, NW3 274 F1
SW19 179 CY92
Greenford UB6 137 CD68
Courthope Vil, SW19 179 CY94
Court Ho Gdns, N3 98 DA51
Courthouse Rd, N12 98 DB51
Courtland Av, E4 102 EF47
NW7 96 CR48
SW16 181 DM94
Ilford IG1 125 EM61
Courtland Dr, Chig. IG7 103 EP48
Courtland Gro, SE28 146 EX73
Courtland Prim Sch, NW7
off Courtland Av 96 CS47
Courtland Rd, E6
off Harrow Rd 144 EL67
Courtlands, Rich. TW10 158 CN84
Courtlands Av, SE12 184 EH85
Bromley BR2 204 EF102
Esher KT10 214 BZ107
Hampton TW12 176 BZ93
Richmond TW9 158 CP82
Slough SL3 152 AX77
Courtlands Cl, Ruis. HA4 115 BT59
South Croydon CR2 220 DT110
Watford WD24 75 BS35
Courtlands Cres, Bans. SM7 234 DA115
Courtlands Dr, Epsom KT19 216 CS107
Watford WD17, WD24 75 BS37
Courtlands Rd, Surb. KT5 198 CN101
Court La, SE21 182 DS86
Burnham SL1 131 AK69
Dorney SL4 150 AG76
Epsom KT19 216 CQ113
Iver SL0 134 BG74
Court La Gdns, SE21 182 DS87
Court Lawns, Penn HP10 88 AC46
Courtleas, Cob. KT11 214 CA113
Courtleet Dr, Erith DA8 167 FB81
Courtleigh Av, Barn. EN4 80 DD38
Courtleigh Gdns, NW11 119 CY56
Court Lo Rd, Horl. RH6 268 DE147
Courtman Rd, N17 100 DQ52
Court Mead, Nthlt. UB5 136 BZ69
Courtmead Cl, SE24 182 DQ86
Courtnell St, W2 283 J8
Courtney Cl, SE19 182 DS93
Courtney Cres, Cars. SM5 218 DF108
Courtney Pl, Cob. KT11 214 BZ112
Croydon CR0 201 DN104
Courtney Rd, N7 276 E2
SW19 180 DE94
Croydon CR0 201 DN104
Grays RM16 171 GJ75
London Heathrow Airport
TW6 154 BN83
Courtney Way,
Lon.Hthrw Air. TW6 154 BN83
Court Par, Wem. HA0 117 CH62
Courtrai Rd, SE23 183 DY86
Court Rd, SE9 184 EL89
SE25 202 DT96
Banstead SM7 234 DA116
Caterham CR3 236 DR123
Godstone RH9 252 DW131
Lane End DA2 189 FS92
Maidenhead SL6 130 AC69
Orpington BR6 206 EV101
Southall UB2 156 BZ77
Uxbridge UB10 115 BP64
Courtside, N8 121 DK58
Court St, E1 288 E6
Bromley BR1 204 EG96
Court Way, NW9 118 CS56
W3 138 CQ71
Ilford IG6 125 EQ55
Romford RM3 106 FL54
Twickenham TW2 177 CF87
Courtway, Wdf.Grn. IG8 102 EJ50
Courtway, The, Wat. WD19 94 BY47
Courtwood Dr, Sev. TN13 256 FG124
Court Wd Gro, Croy. CR0 221 DZ111
Courtwood La, Croy. CR0 221 DZ110
Courtwood Prim Sch,
Croy. CR0 *off Courtwood La* 221 DZ110
Court Yd, SE9 184 EL86
Courtyard, The, N1 276 D6
Brentwood CM15 108 FV45
Hertingfordbury SG14 31 DM10
Keston BR2 222 EL107
Shendish HP3 58 BK26
Courtyard Ho, SW6
off Lensbury Av 307 P8
Courtyard Ms, Green. DA9 189 FU86
Orp. BR5 *off Dorchester Cl* 186 EU94
Rain. RM13 147 FF67
● **Courtyards, The**, Wat. WD18 93 BR45
Courtyards, The, Slou. SL3
off Waterside Dr 153 BA75
Cousin La, EC4 299 L1
Cousins Cl, West Dr. UB7 134 BL73
Couthurst Rd, SE3 164 EH79
Coutts Av, Chess. KT9 216 CL106
Coutts Cres, NW5 120 DG62
Couzins Wk, Dart. DA1 168 FN82
Coval Gdns, SW14 158 CP84
Coval La, SW14 158 CP84
Coval Pas, SW14
off Coval Rd 158 CQ84
Coval Rd, SW14 158 CP84
Coveham Cres, Cob. KT11 213 BU113
Covelees Wall, E6 293 M8
Covell Ct, SE8
off Reginald Sq 314 B5
Covenbrook, Brwd. CM13 109 GB48
★ **Covent Garden**, WC2 286 B10
Covent Garden 286 A10
Covent Gdn Mkt, WC2 286 B10
Coventry Cl, E6 293 J9
NW6 273 K9
Coventry Rd, E1 288 F4
E2 288 F4
SE25 202 DU98
Ilford IG1 125 EP60
Coventry St, W1 297 N1
Coverack Cl, N14 81 DJ44
Croydon CR0 203 DY101
Coverdale, Hem.H. HP2
off Wharfedale 40 BL17
Coverdale Cl, Stan. HA7 95 CH50
Coverdale Ct, Enf. EN3
off Raynton Rd 83 DY37
Coverdale Gdns, Croy. CR0
off Park Hill Ri 202 DT104
Coverdale Rd, N11 98 DG51
NW2 272 D6
W12 139 CV74
Coverdales, The, Bark. IG11 145 EQ68
Coverdale Way, Slou. SL2 131 AL70
Coverley Cl, E1 288 D6
Great Warley CM13
off Wilmot Grn 107 FW51
Covert, The, Nthwd. HA6 93 BQ53
Petts Wood BR6 205 ES100
Coverton Rd, SW17 180 DE92
Covert Rd, Ilf. IG6 103 ET51
Coverts, The, Hutt. CM13 109 GA46
Coverts Rd, Clay. KT10 215 CF109
Covert Way, Barn. EN4 80 DC40
Covesfield, Grav. DA11 191 GF87
Covet Wd Cl, Orp. BR5 205 ET100
Covey Cl, SW19 200 DB96
Covey Rd, Wor.Pk. KT4 199 CX103
Covington Gdns, SW16 181 DP94
Covington Way, SW16 181 DM93
Cowan Cl, E6 293 H7
Cowbridge, Hert. SG14 32 DQ09
Cowbridge La, Bark. IG11 145 EP66
Cowbridge Rd, Har. HA3 118 CM56
Cowcross St, EC1 286 G6
Cowdenbeath Path, N1 276 C8
Cowden Rd, Orp. BR6 205 ET101
Cowden St, SE6 183 EA91
Cowdray Rd, Uxb. UB10 135 BQ67
Cowdray Way, Horn. RM12 127 FF63
Cowdrey Cl, Enf. EN1 82 DS40
Cowdrey Ct, Dart. DA1 187 FH87
Cowdrey Rd, SW19 180 DB92
Cowdry Rd, E9
off East Cross Route 279 N5
Cowen Av, Har. HA2 116 CC61
Cowgate Rd, Grnf. UB6 137 CD68
Cowick Rd, SW17 180 DF91
Cowings Mead, Nthlt. UB5 136 BY66
Cowland Av, Enf. EN3 82 DW42
Cow La, Bushey WD23 76 CA44
Greenford UB6 137 CD68
Watford WD25 76 BW36
Cow Leaze, E6 293 M8
Cowleaze Rd, Kings.T. KT2 198 CL95
Cowles, Chsht EN7 66 DT27
COWLEY, Uxb. UB8 134 BJ70
Cowley Av, Cher. KT16 193 BF101
Greenhithe DA9 189 FT85
● **Cowley Business Pk**,
Cowley UB8 134 BJ69
Cowley Cl, S.Croy. CR2 220 DW109
Cowley Cres, Hersham KT12 214 BW105
Uxbridge UB8 134 BJ71
Cowley Est, SW9 310 E6
Cowley Hill, Borwd. WD6 78 CP37
Cowley Hill Prim Sch,
Borwd. WD6 *off Winstre Rd* 78 CP39
Cowley La, Cher. KT16 193 BF101
Cowley Mill Rd, Uxb. UB8 134 BH68
Cowley Pl, NW4 119 CW57
Cowley Retail Pk,
Cowley UB8 134 BK73
Cowley Rd, E11 124 EH57
SW9 310 F7
SW14 158 CS83
W3 139 CT74
Ilford IG1 125 EM59
Romford RM3 105 FH52
Uxbridge UB8 134 BJ68
Cowley St. Laurence C of E Prim Sch, Cowley UB8
off Worcester Rd 134 BK71
Cowley St, SW1 298 A6
Cowling Cl, W11 294 E2
Cowlins, Harl. CM17 36 EX11
Cowper Av, E6 144 EL66
Sutton SM1 218 DD105
Tilbury RM18 171 GH81
Cowper Cl, Brom. BR2 204 EK98
Chertsey KT16 193 BF100
Welling DA16 186 EU85
Cowper Ct, Wat. WD24 75 BU37
Cowper Cres, Hert. SG14 31 DP07
Cowper Gdns, N14 81 DJ44
Wallington SM6 219 DJ107
Cowper Rd, N14 99 DH46
N16 277 N2
N18 100 DU50
SW19 180 DC93
W3 138 CR74
W7 137 CF73
Belvedere DA17 166 FA77
Berkhamsted HP4 38 AV19
Bromley BR2 204 EK98
Chesham HP5 54 AP29
Hemel Hempstead HP1 40 BH21
Kingston upon Thames KT2 178 CM92
Rainham RM13 147 FG70
Slough SL2 131 AN70
Welwyn Garden City AL7 29 CZ11
Cowpers Ct, EC3
off Birchin La 287 M9
Cowper St, EC2 287 M4
Cowper Ter, W10 282 C7
Cowslip Cl, Uxb. UB10 134 BL66
Cowslip La, Mick. RH5 247 CG129
Woking GU21 226 AV115
Cowslip Meadow, Berk. HP4 38 AT16
Cowslip Rd, E18 102 EH54
Cowslips, Welw.G.C. AL7 30 DC10
Cowthorpe Rd, SW8 309 P6
Cox Cl, Shenley WD7 62 CM32
Coxdean, Epsom KT18 233 CW119
Coxe Pl, Wealds. HA3 117 CG56
Coxfield Cl, Hem.H. HP2 40 BL21
Cox La, Chess. KT9 216 CM105
Epsom KT19 216 CP106
Coxley Ri, Pur. CR8 220 DQ113
Coxmount Rd, SE7 304 E10
Coxon Dr, Chaff.Hun. RM16 170 FY76
Coxson Way, SE1 300 A5
Cox's Wk, SE21 182 DU88
Coxwell Rd, SE18 165 ER78
SE19 182 DS94
Coxwold Path, Chess. KT9
off Garrison La 216 CL108
Coyle Dr, Uxb. UB10 115 BQ61
Cozens La E, Brox. EN10 49 DZ23
Cozens La W, Brox. EN10 49 DY22
Cozens Rd, Ware SG12 33 DZ06
Crabbe Cres, Chesh. HP5 54 AR29
Crabbs Cft Cl, Orp. BR6
off Ladycroft Way 223 EQ106
Crab Hill, Beck. BR3 183 ED94
Crab Hill La, S.Nutfld RH1 267 DM138
Crab La, Ald. WD25 76 CB35
Crabtree Av, Rom. RM6 126 EX56
Wembley HA0 138 CL68
Crabtree Cl, E2 288 A1
Beaconsfield HP9 88 AH54
Bookham KT23 246 CC126
Bushey WD23 76 CB43
Hemel Hempstead HP3 40 BK22
Crabtree Cor, Egh. TW20 193 BB95
Crabtree Ct, Hem.H. HP3
off Crabtree La 40 BL22
Crabtree Dr, Lthd. KT22 231 CJ124
Crabtree Hill, Lamb.End RM4 104 EZ45
Crabtree La, SW6 306 C4
Bookham KT23 246 CC126
Headley KT18 248 CQ126
Hemel Hempstead HP3 40 BK22
Westhumble RH5 247 CF130
● **Crabtree Manorway Ind Est**,
Belv. DA17 167 FB76
Crabtree Manorway N,
Belv. DA17 167 FC75
Crabtree Manorway S,
Belv. DA17 167 FC76
● **Crabtree Office Village**, Egh. TW20
off Eversley Way 193 BC96
Crabtree Rd, Egh. TW20 193 BC96
Crabtree Wk, Brox. EN10 49 DY19
Crace St, NW1
off Drummond Cres 285 N2
Crackley Meadow, Hem.H. HP2 41 BP15
Cracknell Cl, Enf. EN1 82 DV37
Craddock Rd, Enf. EN1 82 DT41
Craddocks Av, Ashtd. KT21 232 CL117
Craddocks Cl, Ashtd. KT21 232 CN116
Craddocks Par, Ashtd. KT21 232 CL117
Craddock St, NW5 274 G5
Cradhurst Cl, Westc. RH4 262 CC137
Cradley Rd, SE9 185 ER88
Cragg Av, Rad. WD7 77 CF36
Craigavon Rd, Hem.H. HP2 40 BM16
Craigdale Rd, Horn. RM11 127 FF58
Craig Dr, Uxb. UB8 135 BP72
Craigen Av, Croy. CR0 202 DV102
Craigen Gdns, Ilf. IG3 125 ES63
Craigerne Rd, SE3 164 EH80
Craig Gdns, E18 102 EF54
Craigholm, SE18 165 EN82
Craiglands, St.Alb. AL4 43 CK16
Craigmore Twr, Wok. GU22
off Guildford Rd 226 AY119
Craig Mt, Rad. WD7 77 CH35
Craigmuir Pk, Wem. HA0 138 CM67
Craignair Rd, SW2 181 DN87
Craignish Av, SW16 201 DM96
Craig Pk Rd, N18 100 DV50
Craig Rd, Rich. TW10 177 CJ91
Craigs Ct, SW1 298 A2
Craigs Wk, Chsht EN8
off Davison Dr 67 DX28
Craigton Rd, SE9 165 EM84
Craigweil Av, Rad. WD7 77 CH35
Craigweil Cl, Stan. HA7 95 CK50
Craigweil Dr, Stan. HA7 95 CK50
Craigwell Av, Felt. TW13 175 BU90
Craigwell Cl, Stai. TW18 193 BE95
Craik Ct, NW6 283 H1
Crail Row, SE17 299 M9
Crakell Rd, Reig. RH2 266 DC135
Cramer Ct, N.Mal. KT3
off Warwick Rd 198 CQ97
Cramer St, W1 285 H7
Crammerville Wk, Rain. RM13 147 FH70
Crammond Cl, W6 306 E2
● **Crammond Pk**, Harl. CM19 51 EN16
Cramond Ct, Felt. TW14 175 BS88
Crampshaw La, Ashtd. KT21 232 CM119
Crampton Prim Sch, SE17 299 H10
Crampton Rd, SE20 182 DW93
Cramptons Rd, Sev. TN14 241 FH120
Crampton St, SE17 299 J9
Cranberry Cl, Nthlt. UB5
off Parkfield Av 136 BX68
Cranberry La, E16 291 J5
Cranborne Av, Sthl. UB2 156 CA77
Surbiton KT6 198 CN104
Cranborne Cl, Hert. SG13 32 DQ12
Potters Bar EN6 63 CY31
Cranborne Cres, Pot.B. EN6 63 CY31
Cranborne Gdns,
Upmin. RM14 128 FP61
Welwyn Garden City AL7 29 CZ10
● **Cranborne Ind Est**,
Pot.B. EN6 63 CY30
Cranborne Prim Sch,
Pot.B. EN6 *off Laurel Flds* 63 CZ31
Cranborne Rd, Bark. IG11 145 ER67
Cheshunt EN8 67 DX32
Hatfield AL10 45 CV17
Hoddesdon EN11 49 EB16
Potters Bar EN6 63 CY31
Cranborne Waye, Hayes UB4 136 BW73
Cranbourn All, WC2
off Cranbourn St 285 P10
Cranbourne Av, E11 124 EH56
Windsor SL4 151 AM82
Cranbourne Cl, SW16 201 DL97
Hersham KT12 214 BW107
Horley RH6 269 DH146
Slough SL1 131 AQ74
Cranbourne Dr, Hodd. EN11 33 EB13
Pinner HA5 116 BX57
Cranbourne Gdns, NW11 119 CY57
Ilford IG6 125 EQ55
Cranbourne Pas, SE16 300 E5
Cranbourne Prim Sch,
Hodd. EN11 *off Bridle Way N* 33 EB13
Cranbourne Rd, E12
off High St N 124 EL64
E15 280 F1
N10 99 DH54
Northwood HA6 115 BT55
Slough SL1 131 AQ74
Cranbourn St, WC2 285 P10
CRANBROOK, Ilf. IG1 125 EM60
Cranbrook Cl, Brom. BR2 204 EG100
Cranbrook Coll, Ilf. IG1
off Mansfield Rd 125 EN61
Cranbrook Dr, Esher KT10 196 CC102
Romford RM2 127 FH56
St. Albans AL4 44 CL20
Twickenham TW2 176 CB88
Cranbrook Ho, E5
off Pembury Rd 278 E2
Erith DA8
off Boundary St 167 FF80
Cranbrook La, N11 99 DH49
Cranbrook Ms, E17 123 DY57
Cranbrook Pk, N22 99 DM53
Cranbrook Prim Sch, Ilf. IG1
off The Drive 125 EM59
Cranbrook Ri, Ilf. IG1 125 EM59
Cranbrook Rd, SE8 314 B7
SW19 179 CY94
W4 158 CS78
Barnet EN4 80 DD44
Bexleyheath DA7 166 EZ81
Hounslow TW4 156 BZ84
Ilford IG1, IG2, IG6 125 EN59
Thornton Heath CR7 202 DQ96
Cranbrook St, E2 289 K1
Cranbury Rd, SW6 307 M8
Crandale Ho, E5
off Pembury Rd 278 E2
Crandon Wk, S.Darenth DA4
off Gorringe Av 209 FS96
Crane Av, W3 138 CQ73
Isleworth TW7 177 CG85
Cranebank Ms, Twick. TW1 157 CG84
Cranebrook, Twick. TW2
off Manor Rd 176 CC89
Crane Cl, Dag. RM10 146 FA65
Harrow HA2 116 CC62
Crane Ct, EC4 286 F9
W13 *off Gurnell Gro* 137 CF70
Epsom KT19 216 CQ105
Cranefield Dr, Wat. WD25 60 BY32
Craneford Cl, Twick. TW2 177 CF87
Craneford Way, Twick. TW2 177 CE87
Crane Gdns, Hayes UB3 155 BT77
Crane Gro, N7 276 F4
Crane Ho, SE15 312 A7
Cranell Grn, S.Ock. RM15 149 FV74
Crane Lo Rd, Houns. TW5 155 BV79
Crane Mead, SE16 301 H10
Ware SG12 33 DY07
● **Crane Mead Business Pk**,
Ware SG12 33 DY07
Crane Pk Prim Sch,
Han. TW13 *off Norman Av* 176 BZ89
Crane Pk Rd, Twick. TW2 176 CB89
Crane Rd, Twick. TW2 177 CE88
Cranesbill Cl, NW9
off Annesley Av 118 CR55
SW16 201 DK96
Cranes Dr, Surb. KT5 198 CL98
Cranes Pk, Surb. KT5 198 CL98
Cranes Pk Av, Surb. KT5 198 CL97
Cranes Pk Cres, Surb. KT5 198 CM98

Crane St, SE10 314 G1
SE15 312 A6
Craneswater, Hayes UB3 155 BT80
Craneswater Pk, Sthl. UB2 156 BZ78
Cranes Way, Borwd. WD6 78 CQ43
Crane Way, Twick. TW2 176 CC87
Cranfield Cl, SE27
off Norwood High St 182 DQ90
Cranfield Ct, Wok. GU21
off Martindale Rd 226 AU118
Cranfield Cres, Cuffley EN6 65 DL29
Cranfield Dr, NW9 96 CS52
Cranfield Rd, SE4 313 N10
Cranfield Rd E, Cars. SM5 218 DG109
Cranfield Rd W, Cars. SM5 218 DF109
Cranfield Row, SE1 298 F6
CRANFORD, Houns. TW5 155 BU80
Cranford Av, N13 99 DL50
Staines-upon-Thames TW19 174 BL87
Cranford Cl, SW20 199 CV95
Purley CR8 220 DQ113
Staines-upon-Thames TW19 174 BL87
Sch **Cranford Comm Coll**,
Cran. TW5 *off High St* 155 BV79
Cranford Cotts, E1
off Cranford St 289 K10
Cranford Ct, Hert. SG14
off The Ridgeway 31 DM08
Cranford Dr, Hayes UB3 155 BT77
Slough SL1 151 AM75
Sch **Cranford Inf & Nurs Sch**,
Cran. TW4 *off Berkeley Av* 155 BV82
Sch **Cranford Jun Sch**, Cran. TW4
off Woodfield Rd 155 BV82
Cranford La, Hayes UB3 155 BR79
Heston TW5 156 BX80
London Heathrow Airport
TW6 155 BT83
London Heathrow Airport
N TW6 155 BT81
Cranford Ms, Brom. BR2 204 EL99
Sch **Cranford Pk Prim Sch**,
Harling. UB3
off Phelps Way 155 BT77
Cranford Pk Rd, Hayes UB3 155 BT77
Cranford Ri, Esher KT10 214 CC106
Cranford Rd, Dart. DA1 188 FL88
Cranford St, E1 289 K10
Cranford Way, N8 121 DM57
CRANHAM, Upmin. RM14 129 FS59
Cranham Gdns, Upmin. RM14 129 FS60
Cranham Hall Ms,
Upmin. RM14 129 FS62
Cranham Rd, Horn. RM11 127 FH58
Cranhurst Rd, NW2 272 B4
Cranleigh Cl, SE20 202 DV96
Bexley DA5 187 FB86
Cheshunt EN7 66 DU28
Orpington BR6 206 EU104
South Croydon CR2 220 DU112
Cranleigh Ct, Mitch. CR4
off Phipps Br Rd 200 DD97
Cranleigh Dr, Swan. BR8 207 FE98
Cranleigh Gdns, N21 81 DN43
SE25 202 DS97
Barking IG11 145 ER66
Harrow HA3 118 CL57
Kingston upon Thames KT2 178 CM93
Loughton IG10 85 EM44
South Croydon CR2 220 DU112
Southall UB1 136 BZ72
Sutton SM1 200 DB103
● **Cranleigh Gdns Ind Est**, Sthl. UB1
off Cranleigh Gdns 136 BZ71
Cranleigh Ms, SW11 308 D9
Cranleigh Rd, N15 122 DQ57
SW19 200 DA97
Esher KT10 196 CC102
Feltham TW13 175 BT91
Wonersh GU5 259 BB144
Cranleigh St, NW1 285 M1
Cranley Cl, Guil. GU1 243 BA134
Cranley Dene, Guil. GU1 243 BA134
Cranley Dene Ct, N10 120 DG56
Cranley Dr, Ilf. IG2 125 EQ59
Ruislip HA4 115 BT61
Cranley Gdns, N10 121 DJ56
N13 99 DM48
SW7 295 P10
Wallington SM6 219 DJ108
Cranley Ms, SW7 295 P10
Cranley Par, SE9
off Beaconsfield Rd 184 EL91
Cranley Pl, SW7 296 A9
Cranley Rd, E13 292 A6
Guildford GU1 243 AZ134
Hersham KT12 213 BS106
Ilford IG2 125 EQ58
Cranmer Av, W13 157 CH76
Cranmer Cl, Mord. SM4 199 CX100
Potters Bar EN6 64 DB30
Ruislip HA4 116 BX60
Stanmore HA7 95 CJ52
Warlingham CR6 237 DY117
Weybridge KT13 212 BN108
Cranmer Ct, SW3 296 D9
SW4 161 DK83
Hampton Hill TW12
off Cranmer Rd 176 CB92
Sch **Cranmere Prim Sch**, Esher KT10
off The Drive 196 CC102
Cranmer Fm Cl, Mitch. CR4 200 DF98
Cranmer Gdns, Dag. RM10 127 FC63
Warlingham CR6 237 DY117
Cranmer Ho, SW11
off Surrey La 308 C6
Sch **Cranmer Prim Sch**, Mitch. CR4
off Cranmer Rd 200 DF98
Cranmer Rd, E7 124 EH63
SW9 310 F4
Croydon CR0 201 DP104
Edgware HA8 96 CP48
Hampton Hill TW12 176 CB92
Hayes UB3 135 BR72
Kingston upon Thames KT2 178 CL92
Mitcham CR4 200 DF98
Sevenoaks TN13 256 FE123
Cranmer Ter, SW17 180 DD92
Cranmore Av, Islw. TW7 156 CC80
Cranmore Cotts, Lthd. KT24 245 BP129
Cranmore Ct, St.Alb. AL1 43 CF19
Cranmore La, W.Hors. KT24 245 BP129
Cranmore Rd, Brom. BR1 184 EE90
Chislehurst BR7 185 EM92
Sch **Cranmore Sch**, W.Hors. KT24
off Epsom Rd 245 BQ130
Cranmore Way, N10 121 DJ56
Cranston Cl, Houns. TW3 156 BY82
Reigate RH2 266 DB135
Uxbridge UB10 115 BR61
Cranston Est, N1 287 M1
Cranston Gdns, E4 101 EB50
Cranston Pk Av, Upmin. RM14 128 FP63
Cranston Rd, SE23 183 DY88
Cranstoun Cl, Guil. GU3 242 AT130
Cranswick Rd, SE16 300 F10
Crantock Rd, SE6 183 EB89
Cranwell Cl, E3 290 C5
St. Albans AL4 43 CJ22
Cranwell Gro, Shep. TW17 194 BM98
Cranwells La, Farn.Com. SL2 111 AQ62
Cranwich Av, N21 100 DR45
Cranwich Rd, N16 122 DR59
Cranwood St, EC1 287 L3
Cranworth Cres, E4 101 ED46
Cranworth Gdns, SW9 310 E7
Craster Rd, SW2 181 DM87
Crathie Rd, SE12 184 EH86
Cravan Av, Felt. TW13 175 BU89
Craven Av, W5 137 CJ73
Southall UB1 136 BZ71
Craven Cl, N16 122 DU59
Hayes UB4 135 BU72
Craven Gdns, SW19 180 DA92
Barking IG11 145 ES68
Collier Row RM5 104 FA50
Harold Wood RM3 106 FQ51
Ilford IG6 103 ER54
Craven Hill, W2 283 P10
Craven Hill Gdns, W2 283 N10
Craven Hill Ms, W2 283 P10
Craven Ms, SW11
off Taybridge Rd 160 DG83
Craven Pk, NW10 138 CS67
Craven Pk Ms, NW10 138 CS66
Craven Pk Rd, N15 122 DT58
NW10 138 CS67
Craven Pas, WC2 298 A2
Craven Rd, NW10 138 CR67
W2 283 P10
W5 137 CJ73
Croydon CR0 202 DV102
Kingston upon Thames KT2 198 CM95
Orpington BR6 206 EX104
Cravens, The, Smallfield RH6 269 DN148
Craven St, WC2 298 A2
Craven Ter, W2 283 P10
Craven Wk, N16 122 DU59
Crawford Av, Dart. DA1 188 FK86
Wem. HA0 117 CK64
Crawford Cl, Islw. TW7 157 CE82
Crawford Compton Cl,
Horn. RM12 148 FJ65
Crawford Est, SE5 311 K8
Crawford Gdns, N13 99 DP48
Northolt UB5 136 BZ69
Crawford Ms, W1 284 E7
Crawford Pas, EC1 286 E5
Crawford Pl, W1 284 D8
Sch **Crawford Prim Sch**, SE5 311 K7
Crawford Rd, SE5 311 K7
Hatfield AL10 45 CU16
Crawfords, Swan. BR8 187 FE94
Crawford St, NW10 138 CR66
W1 284 E7
Crawley Dr, Hem.H. HP2 40 BM16
Crawley Rd, E10 123 EB60
N22 100 DQ54
Enfield EN1 100 DS45
Crawshaw Rd, Ott. KT16 211 BD107
Crawshay Cl, Sev. TN13 256 FG123
Crawshay Rd, SW9 310 F7
Crawthew Gro, SE22 162 DT84
Cray Av, Ashtd. KT21 232 CL116
Orpington BR5 206 EV99
Craybrooke Rd, Sid. DA14 186 EV91
Crayburne, Sthflt DA13 190 FZ92
Craybury End, SE9 185 EQ89
Cray Cl, Dart. DA1 167 FG84
Craydene Rd, Erith DA8 167 FF81
● **Crayfields Business Pk**,
Orp. BR5 206 EW95
● **Crayfields Ind Pk**, Orp. BR5 206 EW96
CRAYFORD, Dart. DA1 187 FD85
⇌ **Crayford** 187 FE86
Crayford Cl, E6 292 G8
● **Crayford Creek**, Dart. DA1
off Thames Rd 167 FH83
Crayford High St, Dart. DA1 167 FE84
● **Crayford Ind Est**, Dart. DA1 187 FF85
Crayford Rd, N7 121 DK63
Dartford DA1 187 FF85
Crayford Way, Dart. DA1 187 FF85
Crayke Hill, Chess. KT9 216 CL108
Craylands, Orp. BR5 206 EW97
Craylands La, Swans. DA10 189 FX85
Sch **Craylands Sch, The**, Swans. DA10
off Craylands La 189 FX85
Craylands Sq, Swans. DA10 189 FX85
Crayle St, Slou. SL2 131 AN69
Craymill Sq, Dart. DA1 167 FF82
Crayonne Cl, Sun. TW16 195 BS95
Cray Riverway, Dart. DA1 187 FF85
Sid. DA14 186 EX92
Cray Rd, Belv. DA17 166 FA79
Sidcup DA14 186 EW94
Swanley BR8 207 FB100
● **Crayside Ind Est**, Cray. DA1 167 FH84
Cray Valley Rd, Orp. BR5 206 EU99
Cray Vw Cl, Orp. BR5
off Mill Brook Rd 206 EW98
Crealock Gro, Wdf.Grn. IG8 102 EF50
Crealock St, SW18 180 DB86
Creasey Cl, Horn. RM11 127 FH61
Creasy Cl, Abb.L. WD5 59 BT31
Creasy Est, SE1 299 N7
Crebor St, SE22 182 DU86
Crecy Ct, SE11
off Hotspur St 298 E10
Credenhill Dr, Brom. BR2 205 EM102
Credenhill St, SW16 181 DJ93
Crediton Hill, NW6 273 L2
Crediton Rd, E16 291 N8
NW10 272 C9
Crediton Way, Clay. KT10 215 CG106
Credon Rd, E13 144 EJ68
SE16 300 F10
Credo Way, Grays RM20 169 FV79
Creechurch La, EC3 287 P9
Creechurch Pl, EC3 287 P9
Creed Ct, EC4
off Ludgate Sq 287 H9
Creed La, EC4 287 H9
Creed's Fm Yd, Epp. CM16 69 ES32
Creek, The, Grav. DA11 190 GB85
Sunbury-on-Thames TW16 195 BU99
CREEKMOUTH, Bark. IG11 146 EU70
Creek Rd, SE8 314 A3
SE10 314 A3
Barking IG11 145 ET69
East Molesey KT8 197 CE98
Creekside, SE8 314 C5
Rainham RM13 147 FF70
Creek Way, Rain. RM13 147 FE71
Creeland Gro, SE6 183 DZ88
Cree Way, Rom. RM1 105 FE52
Crefeld Cl, W6 306 D3
Creffield Rd, W3 138 CM73
W5 138 CM73
Creighton Av, E6 144 EK68
N2 120 DE55
N10 98 DG54
St. Albans AL1 43 CD24
Creighton Cl, W12 139 CU73
Creighton Rd, N17 100 DS52
NW6 272 D10
W5 157 CK76
Cremer St, E2 288 A1
Cremorne Br, SW6
off Townmead Rd 307 P7
SW11 *off Lombard Rd* 160 DD82
Cremorne Est, SW10 308 A4
Cremorne Gdns, Epsom KT19 216 CR109
Cremorne Rd, SW10 307 P5
Northfleet DA11 191 GF87
Crescent, EC3 288 A10
Crescent, The, E17 123 DY57
N11 98 DF49
NW2 119 CV62
SW13 159 CT82
SW19 180 DA90
W3 138 CS72
Abbots Langley WD5 59 BT30
Aldenham WD25 76 CB37
Ashford TW15 174 BM92
Barnet EN5 80 DB41
Beckenham BR3 203 EA95
Belmont SM2 218 DA111
Bexley DA5 186 EW87
Bricket Wood AL2 60 CA30
Caterham CR3 237 EA123
Chertsey KT16
off Western Av 194 BG97
Croxley Green WD3 75 BP44
Croydon CR0 202 DR99
Egham TW20 172 AY93
Epping CM16 69 ET32
Epsom KT18 216 CN114
Greenhithe DA9 189 FW85
Guildford GU2 242 AU132
Harlington UB3 155 BQ80
Harlow CM17 36 EW09
Harrow HA2 117 CD60
Horley RH6 269 DH150
Ilford IG2 125 EN58
Leatherhead KT22 231 CH122
Loughton IG10 84 EK43
New Malden KT3 198 CQ96
Northfleet DA11 191 GF89
Reigate RH2
off Chartway 250 DB134
Sevenoaks TN13 257 FK121
Shepperton TW17 195 BT101
Sidcup DA14 185 ET91
Slough SL1 152 AS75
Southall UB1 156 BZ75
Surbiton KT6 198 CL99
Sutton SM1 218 DD105
Upminster RM14 129 FS59
Watford WD18 76 BW42
Wembley HA0 117 CH61
West Molesey KT8 196 CA98
West Wickham BR4 204 EE100
Weybridge KT13 194 BN104
Crescent Arc, SE10 314 E3
Crescent Av, Grays RM17 170 GD78
Hornchurch RM12 127 FF61
Crescent Cotts, Sev. TN13 241 FE120
Crescent Ct, Grays RM17 170 GD78
Surb. KT6 197 CK99
Crescent Dr, Petts Wd BR5 205 EP100
Shenfield CM15 108 FY46
Crescent E, Barn. EN4 80 DC38
Crescent Gdns, SW19 180 DA90
Ruislip HA4 115 BV58
Swanley BR8 207 FC96
Crescent Gro, SW4 161 DJ84
Mitcham CR4 200 DE98
Crescent Ho, SE13
off Ravensbourne Pl 314 C8
Crescent La, SW4 181 DK85
Crescent Ms, N22 99 DL53
Crescent Par, Uxb. UB10
off Uxbridge Rd 134 BN69
Crescent Pl, SW3 296 C8
Sch **Crescent Prim Sch, The**,
Croy. CR0 202 DR99
Crescent Ri, N22 99 DK53
Barnet EN4 80 DE43
Crescent Rd, E4 102 EE45
E6 144 EJ67
E10 123 EB61
E13 281 P8
E18 102 EJ54
N3 97 CZ53
N8 121 DK59
N9 100 DU46
N11 98 DF49
N15 *off Carlingford Rd* 121 DP55
N22 99 DK53
SE18 305 N10
SW20 199 CX95
Aveley RM15 168 FQ75
Barnet EN4 80 DE43
Beckenham BR3 203 EB96
Bletchingley RH1 252 DQ133
Bromley BR1 184 EG94
Caterham CR3 236 DU124
Dagenham RM10 127 FB63
Enfield EN2 81 DP41
Erith DA8 167 FF79
Hemel Hempstead HP2 40 BK20
Kingston upon Thames KT2 178 CN94
Reigate RH2 266 DA136
Shepperton TW17 195 BQ99
Sidcup DA15 185 ET90
Warley CM14 108 FV49
Crescent Row, EC1 287 J5
Crescent Stables, SW15 179 CY85
Crescent St, N1 276 D6
Crescent Vw, Loug. IG10 84 EK44
Crescent Wk, Aveley RM15 168 FQ75
Crescent Way, N12 98 DE51
SE4 163 EA83
SW16 181 DM94
Aveley RM15 149 FR74
Horley RH6 268 DG150
Orpington BR6 223 ES106
Crescent W, Barn. EN4 80 DC38
Crescent Wd Rd, SE26 182 DU90
Cresford Rd, SW6 307 L7
Crespigny Rd, NW4 119 CV58
Cressage Cl, Sthl. UB1 136 CA70
Cressall Cl, Lthd. KT22 231 CH120
Cressall Mead, Lthd. KT22 231 CH120
Cress End, Rick. WD3 92 BG47
Cresset Cl, Stans.Abb. SG12 33 EC12
Cresset Rd, E9 279 H5
Cresset St, SW4 161 DK83
Cressfield Cl, NW5 275 H2
Cressida Rd, N19 121 DJ60
Cressingham Gro, Sutt. SM1 218 DC105
Cressingham Rd, SE13 314 F10
Edgware HA8 96 CR51
Cressinghams, The,
Epsom KT18 216 CR113
Cressington Cl, N16 277 P2
Cress Ms, Brom. BR1 183 ED92
Cress Rd, Slou. SL1 151 AP75
Cresswell Gdns, SW5 295 N10
Cresswell Pk, SE3 315 L10
Cresswell Pl, SW10 295 N10
Cresswell Rd, SE25 202 DU98
Chesham HP5 54 AR34
Feltham TW13 176 BY91
Twickenham TW1 177 CK86
Cresswell Way, N21 99 DN45
Cressy Ct, E1 289 H6
W6 159 CV76
Cressy Ho, E1
off Hannibal Rd 289 H6
Cressy Pl, E1 289 H6
Cressy Rd, NW3 274 E2
Crest, The, N13 99 DN49
NW4 119 CW57
Beaconsfield HP9 88 AG54
Goffs Oak EN7
off Orchard Way 65 DP27
Sawbridgeworth CM21 36 EX05
Surbiton KT5 198 CN99
Cresta Dr, Wdhm KT15 211 BF110
Crest Av, Grays RM17 170 GB80
Crestbrook Av, N13 99 DP48
Crestbrook Pl, N13 99 DP48
Crest Cl, Bad.Mt TN14 225 FB111
Crest Dr, Enf. EN3 82 DW38
Crestfield St, WC1 286 B2
Crest Gdns, Ruis. HA4 116 BW62
Crest Hill, Peasl. GU5 261 BR142
Cresthill Av, Grays RM17 170 GC77
Creston Av, Knap. GU21 226 AS116
Creston Way, Wor.Pk. KT4 199 CX102
Crest Pk, Hem.H. HP2 41 BQ19
Crest Rd, NW2 119 CT62
Bromley BR2 204 EF101
South Croydon CR2 220 DV108
Crest Vw, Green. DA9
off Woodland Way 169 FU84
Pinner HA5 116 BX56
Crest Vw Dr, Petts Wd BR5 205 EP99
Crestway, SW15 179 CV86
Crestwood Way, Houns. TW4 176 BZ85
Creswell Dr, Beck. BR3 203 EB99
Creswick Ct, Welw.G.C. AL7 29 CX10
Sch **Creswick Prim & Nurs Sch**,
Welw.G.C. AL7 *off Chequers* 29 CY12
Creswick Rd, W3 138 CP73
Creswick Wk, E3 290 A2
NW11 119 CZ56
Crete Hall Rd, Grav. DA11 190 GD86
Creton St, SE18 305 M7
Creukhorne Rd, NW10 138 CS66
Crewdson Rd, SW9 310 E5
Horley RH6 269 DH148
Crewe Curve, Berk. HP4 38 AT16
Crewe Pl, NW10 139 CT69
Crewe's Av, Warl. CR6 236 DW116
Crewe's Cl, Warl. CR6 236 DW116
Crewe's Fm La, Warl. CR6 237 DX116
Crewe's La, Warl. CR6 237 DX116
CREWS HILL, Enf. EN2 81 DP35
⇌ **Crews Hill** 65 DM34
Crews St, E14 302 A8
Crewys Rd, NW2 119 CZ61
SE15 312 F9
Crib St, Ware SG12 33 DX05
Crichton Av, Wall. SM6 219 DK106
Crichton Rd, Cars. SM5 218 DF107
Crichton St, SW8 309 L8
Crick Ct, Bark. IG11
off Spring Pl 145 EQ68
Cricketers Arms Rd, Enf. EN2 82 DQ40
Cricketers Cl, N14 99 DJ45
Chessington KT9 215 CK105
Erith DA8 167 FE78
St. Albans AL3
off Stonecross 43 CE19
Cricketers Ct, SE11 298 G9
Cricketers Ms, SW18
off East Hill 180 DB85
Cricketers Ter, Cars. SM5
off Wrythe La 200 DE104
Cricketers Wk, SE26
off Doctors Cl 182 DW92
Cricket Fld Rd, Uxb. UB8 134 BK67
Cricketfield Rd, E5 278 F1
West Drayton UB7 154 BJ77
Cricket Grn, Mitch. CR4 200 DF97
Sch **Cricket Grn Sch**, Mitch. CR4
off Lower Grn W 200 DE97
Cricket Grd Rd, Chis. BR7 205 EP95
Cricket Hill, S.Nutfld RH1 267 DM136
Cricket La, Beck. BR3 183 DY93
Crickett's Hill, Shere GU5 260 BN139
Cricket Way, Wey. KT13 195 BS103
Cricklade Av, SW2 181 DL89
Romford RM3 106 FK51
CRICKLEWOOD, NW2 119 CX62
⇌ **Cricklewood** 119 CX63
Cricklewood Bdy, NW2 119 CW62
Cricklewood La, NW2 272 D1
Cridland St, E15 281 L9
Crieff Ct, Tedd. TW11 177 CJ94
Crieff Rd, SW18 180 DC86
Criffel Av, SW2 181 DK89
Crimp Hill, Eng.Grn TW20 172 AU90
Crimp Hill Rd, Old Wind. SL4 172 AU88
Crimscott St, SE1 299 P7
Crimsworth Rd, SW8 309 P6
Crinan St, N1 276 B10
Cringle St, SW8 309 L4
Cripplegate St, EC2 287 J6
Cripps Grn, Hayes UB4
off Stratford Rd 135 BV70
Crispe Ho, Bark. IG11
off Dovehouse Mead 145 ER68
Crispen Rd, Felt. TW13 176 BY91
Crispian Cl, NW10 118 CS63
Crispin Cl, Ashtd. KT21 232 CM118
Beaconsfield HP9 88 AJ51
Croydon CR0
off Harrington Cl 201 DL103
Crispin Cres, Croy. CR0 201 DK104
Crispin Ms, NW11 119 CZ57
Crispin Pl, E1 288 A6
Crispin Rd, Edg. HA8 96 CQ51
Crispin St, E1 288 A7
Crispin Way, Farn.Com. SL2 111 AR63
Uxbridge UB8 134 BM70
Crisp Rd, W6 306 A1
Criss Cres, Chal.St.P. SL9 90 AW54
Criss Gro, Chal.St.P. SL9 90 AW54
Cristowe Rd, SW6 307 H8
Critchley Ave, Dart. DA1 188 FK86
Criterion Ms, N19 121 DK61
SE24 *off Shakespeare Rd* 181 DP85
Jct **Crittall's Cor**, Sid. DA14 186 EV94
Critten La, Dor. RH5 246 BX132
Crockenhall Way,
Istead Rise DA13 190 GE94
CROCKENHILL, Swan. BR8 207 FD101
Crockenhill La, Eyns. DA4 207 FG101
Sch **Crockenhill Prim Sch**, Crock.
BR8 *off Stones Cross Rd* 207 FC100
Crockenhill Rd, Orp. BR5 206 EX99
Swanley BR8 206 EZ100
Crockerton Rd, SW17 180 DF89
Crockery La, E.Clan. GU4 244 BL129
Crockford Cl, Add. KT15 212 BJ105
Crockford Pk Rd, Add. KT15 212 BJ106
CROCKHAM HILL, Eden. TN8 255 EQ133
Sch **Crockham Hill C of E Prim Sch**,
Crock.H. TN8 *off Main Rd* 255 EQ133
Crockham Way, SE9 185 EN91
Crocknorth Rd, Dor. RH5 245 BU133
East Horsley KT24 245 BT132
Crocus Cl, Croy. CR0
off Cornflower La 203 DX102
Crocus Fld, Barn. EN5 79 CZ44
Croffets, Tad. KT20 233 CX121
Croft, The, E4 102 EE47
NW10 139 CT68
W5 138 CL71
Barnet EN5 79 CX42
Broxbourne EN10 49 DY23
Fetcham KT22 231 CE123
Hounslow TW5 156 BY79
Loughton IG10 85 EN40
Pinner HA5 116 BZ59
Ruislip HA4 116 BW63
St. Albans AL2 60 CA25
Swanley BR8 207 FC97
Welwyn Garden City AL7 29 CZ12
Wembley HA0 117 CJ64
Croft Av, Dor. RH4 247 CH134
West Wickham BR4 203 EC102
Croft Cl, NW7 96 CS48
Belvedere DA17 166 EZ78
Chalfont St. Peter SL9 90 AX54
Chipperfield WD4 58 BG30
Chislehurst BR7 185 EM91
Harlington UB3 155 BQ80
Uxbridge UB10 134 BN66
Croft Cor, Old Wind. SL4 172 AV85
Croft Ct, Borwd. WD6 78 CR41
Croftdown Rd, NW5 120 DG62
Croft End Cl, Chess. KT9
off Ashcroft Rd 198 CM104
Croft End Rd, Chipper. WD4 58 BG30
Crofters, The, Wind. SL4 172 AU86
Crofters Cl, Islw. TW7
off Ploughmans End 177 CD85
Redhill RH1 267 DH136
Stanwell TW19 *off Park Rd* 174 BK86
Crofters Ct, SE8
off Croft St 301 L9
Crofters Mead, Croy. CR0 221 DZ109
Crofters Rd, Nthwd. HA6 93 BS49
Crofters Way, NW1 275 N8
Croft Fld, Chipper. WD4 58 BG30
Hatfield AL10 45 CU18
Croft Gdns, W7 157 CG75
Ruislip HA4 115 BS60
Crofthill Rd, Slou. SL2 131 AP70
Croft La, Chipper. WD4 58 BG30
Croftleigh Av, Pur. CR8 235 DN116
Croft Lo Cl, Wdf.Grn. IG8 102 EH51
Croft Meadow, Chipper. WD4 58 BG30
Croft Ms, N12 98 DC48
Crofton, Ashtd. KT21 232 CL118
Crofton Av, W4 158 CR80
Bexley DA5 186 EX87
Orpington BR6 205 EQ103
Walton-on-Thames KT12 196 BW104
Crofton Cl, Ott. KT16 211 BC108
Croftongate Way, SE4 183 DY85
Crofton Gro, E4 101 ED49
Sch **Crofton Inf Sch**, Orp. BR5
off Towncourt La 205 ER101
Sch **Crofton Jun Sch**, Orp. BR5
off Towncourt La 205 ER101
Crofton La, Orp. BR5, BR6 205 ER101
⇌ **Crofton Park** 183 DZ85
Crofton Pk Rd, SE4 183 DZ86
Crofton Rd, E13 292 A4
SE5 311 P7
Grays RM16 170 GE76
Orpington BR6 205 EN104
Crofton Ter, E5
off Studley Cl 279 L2
Richmond TW9 158 CM84
Crofton Way, Barn. EN5
off Wycherley Cres 80 DB44
Enfield EN2 81 DN40
Croft Rd, SW16 201 DN95
SW19 180 DC94
Bromley BR1 184 EG93
Chalfont St. Peter SL9 90 AY54
Enfield EN3 83 DY39
Sutton SM1 218 DE106
Ware SG12 32 DW05
Westerham TN16 255 EP126
Woldingham CR3 237 DZ122
Crofts, The, Hem.H. HP3 41 BP21
Shepperton TW17 195 BS98
Croftside, SE25 *off Sunny Bk* 202 DU97
Crofts La, N22 99 DN52
Crofts Path, Hem.H. HP3 41 BP22
Crofts Rd, Har. HA1 117 CG58
Crofts St, E1 300 C1

C

Croft St, SE8 301 L9
Croft Wk, Brox. EN10 49 DY23
Croftway, NW3 273 K1
Richmond TW10 177 CH90
Croft Way, Sev. TN13 256 FF125
Sidcup DA15 185 ES90
Crogsland Rd, NW1 274 G6
Croham Cl, S.Croy. CR2 220 DS108
Croham Manor Rd,
S.Croy. CR2 220 DS106
Croham Mt, S.Croy. CR2 220 DS108
Croham Pk Av, S.Croy. CR2 220 DT106
Croham Rd, S.Croy. CR2 220 DR106
Croham Valley Rd,
S.Croy. CR2 220 DT107
Croindene Rd, SW16 201 DL95
Cromartie Rd, N19 121 DK59
Cromarty Rd, Edg. HA8 96 CP47
Crombie Cl, Ilf. IG4 125 EM57
Crombie Rd, Sid. DA15 185 ER88
Cromer Cl, Uxb. UB8 135 BQ72
CROMER HYDE,
Welw.G.C. AL8 28 CS10
Cromer Hyde La, Lmsfd AL8 28 CR10
Crome Rd, NW10 138 CS65
Cromer Pl, Orp. BR6
off Andover Rd 205 ER102
Cromer Rd, E10 123 ED59
N17 100 DU54
SE25 202 DV97
SW17 180 DG93
Chadwell Heath RM6 126 EY58
Hornchurch RM11 128 FK59
London Heathrow Airport
TW6 154 BN83
New Barnet EN5 80 DC42
Romford RM7 127 FC58
Watford WD24 76 BW38
Woodford Green IG8 102 EG49
Sch Cromer Rd Prim Sch,
New Barn. EN5 off Cromer Rd 80 DC41
Cromer St, WC1 286 B3
Cromer Ter, E8 278 C2
Cromer Vil Rd, SW18 179 CZ86
Cromford Cl, Orp. BR6 205 ES104
Cromford Path, E5
off Overbury St 123 DX63
Cromford Rd, SW18 180 DA85
Cromford Way, N.Mal. KT3 198 CR95
Cromlix Cl, Chis. BR7 205 EP96
Crompton Pl, Enf. EN3
off Brunswick Rd 83 EA38
Crompton St, W2 284 A5
Cromwell Av, N6 121 DH60
W6 159 CV78
Bromley BR2 204 EH98
Cheshunt EN7 66 DU30
New Malden KT3 199 CT99
Cromwell Cl, N2 120 DD56
W3 off High St 138 CQ74
Bromley BR2 204 EH98
Chalfont St. Giles HP8 90 AW48
St. Albans AL4 43 CK15
Walton-on-Thames KT12 195 BV102
Cromwell Cres, SW5 295 J8
Cromwell Dr, Slou. SL1 132 AS72
Cromwell Gdns, SW7 296 B7
Cromwell Gro, W6 294 B6
Caterham CR3 236 DQ121
Cromwell Highwalk, EC2
off Silk St 287 K6
H Cromwell Hosp, The, SW5 295 L8
● Cromwell Ind Est, E10 123 DY60
Cromwell Ms, SW7 296 B8
Cromwell Pl, N6 121 DH60
SW7 296 B8
SW14 158 CQ83
W3 off Grove Pl 138 CQ74
◆ Cromwell Road 198 CL95
Cromwell Rd, E7 144 EJ66
E17 123 EC57
N3 98 DC54
N10 98 DG52
SW5 295 K8
SW7 296 A8
SW9 310 G6
SW19 180 DA92
Beckenham BR3 203 DY96
Borehamwood WD6 78 CL39
Caterham CR3 236 DQ121
Cheshunt EN7 66 DV28
Croydon CR0 202 DR101
Feltham TW13 175 BV88
Grays RM17 170 GA77
Hayes UB3 135 BR72
Hertford SG13 32 DT08
Hounslow TW3 156 CA84
Kingston upon Thames KT2 198 CL95
Redhill RH1 250 DF133
Teddington TW11 177 CG93
Walton-on-Thames KT12 195 BV102
Ware SG12 33 DZ06
Warley CM14 108 FV49
Wembley HA0 138 CL68
Worcester Park KT4 198 CR104
Cromwells Ct, Slou. SL3 133 AZ74
Cromwells Mere, Rom. RM1
off Havering Rd 105 FD51
Cromwell St, Houns. TW3 156 CA84
Cromwell Twr, EC2 287 K6
Cromwell Wk, Red. RH1 250 DF134
Crondace Rd, SW6 307 K7
Crondall Ct, N1 287 N1
Crondall Ho, SW15
off Fontley Way 179 CU88
Crondall St, N1 287 M1
Cronin St, SE15 312 A5
Cronks Hill, Red. RH1 266 DC135
Reigate RH2 266 DC135
Cronks Hill Cl, Red. RH1 266 DD136
Cronks Hill Rd, Red. RH1 266 DD136
Jct Crooked Billet, E17 101 EB52
Crooked Billet, SW19 179 CW93
Jct Crooked Billet Rbt,
Stai. TW18 174 BG91
Crooked Billet Yd, E2 287 P2
Crooked La, Grav. DA12 191 GH86
Crooked Mile, Wal.Abb. EN9 67 EC33
Jct Crooked Mile Rbt,
Wal.Abb. EN9 67 EC33
Crooked Usage, N3 119 CY55
Crooked Way, Lwr Naze. EN9 50 EE22
Crooke Rd, SE8 301 L10
Crookham Rd, SW6 306 G7
Crookhams, Welw.G.C. AL7 30 DA07
Crook Log, Bexh. DA6 166 EX83
Sch Crook Log Prim Sch, Bexh. DA6
off Crook Log 166 EX84
Crookston Rd, SE9 165 EN83
Croombs Rd, E16 292 C7
Crooms Hill, SE10 314 F4
Crooms Hill Gro, SE10 314 F4
Crop Common, Hat. AL10
off Stonecross Rd 45 CV16
Cropley Ct, N1 277 L10
Cropley St, N1 277 L10
Croppath Rd, Dag. RM10 126 FA63
Cropthorne Ct, W9 283 P3
Crosby Cl, Beac. HP9 111 AM55
Feltham TW13 176 BY91
St. Albans AL4 43 CJ23
Crosby Ct, SE1 299 L4
Crosby Rd, E7 281 N4
Dagenham RM10 147 FB68
Crosby Row, SE1 299 L5
Crosby Sq, EC3 287 N9
Crosby Wk, E8 278 A5
SW2 181 DN87
Crosier Cl, SE3 164 EL81
Crosier Rd, Ickhm UB10 115 BQ63
Crosier Way, Ruis. HA4 115 BS62
Crosland Pl, SW11
off Taybridge Rd 160 DG83
Crossacres, Wok. GU22 227 BE115
Cross Av, SE10 315 H3
Crossbow Rd, Chig. IG7 103 ET50
Crossbrook, Hat. AL10 44 CS19
Crossbrook Rd, SE3 164 EL82
Crossbrook St, Chsht EN8 67 DX31
Cross Cl, SE15 312 E8
Cross Deep, Twick. TW1 177 CF89
Cross Deep Gdns, Twick. TW1 177 CF89
Crossett Grn, Hem.H. HP3 41 BQ22
Crossfell Rd, Hem.H. HP3 41 BQ22
Crossfield Cl, Berk. HP4 38 AT19
Crossfield Pl, Wey. KT13 213 BP108
Crossfield Rd, N17 122 DQ55
NW3 274 B5
Hoddesdon EN11 49 EB15
Crossfields, Loug. IG10 85 EP43
St. Albans AL3 42 CB23
Crossfield St, SE8 314 A4
Crossford St, SW9 310 B9
Crossgate, Edg. HA8 96 CN48
Greenford UB6 137 CH65
DLR Crossharbour 302 D6
Crossing Rd, Epp. CM16 70 EU32
Cross Keys Cl, N9
off Balham Rd 100 DU47
W1 285 H7
Sevenoaks TN13 256 FG127
Cross Keys Sq, EC1 287 J7
Cross Lances Rd, Houns. TW3 156 CB84
Crossland Rd, Red. RH1 250 DG134
Thornton Heath CR7 201 DP100
Crosslands Av, W5 138 CM74
Southall UB2 156 BZ78
Crosslands, Cher. KT16 193 BE104
Crosslands, Map.Cr. WD3 91 BE49
Crosslands Rd, Epsom KT19 216 CR107
Cross La, EC3
off Great Tower St 299 N1
N8 121 DM56
Beaconsfield HP9 111 AM55
Bexley DA5 186 EZ87
Hertford SG14 31 DP09
Ottershaw KT16 211 BB107
Cross La E, Grav. DA12 191 GH89
Cross Las, Chal.St.P. SL9 90 AY50
Guildford GU1 259 AZ135
Cross Las Cl, Chal.St.P. SL9
off Cross Las 91 AZ50
Cross La W, Grav. DA11 191 GH89
Crosslet St, SE17 299 M8
Crosslet Vale, SE10 314 C7
Crossley Cl, Bigg.H. TN16 238 EK115
Crossleys, Ch.St.G. HP8 90 AW49
Crossley St, N7 276 E4
Crossmead, SE9 185 EM88
Watford WD19 75 BV44
Crossmead Av, Grnf. UB6 136 CA69
Cross Meadow, Chesh. HP5 54 AM29
Crossmount Ho, SE5 311 J4
Crossness La, SE28 146 EX73
★ Crossness Pumping Sta,
SE2 146 EY72
Crossness Rd, Bark. IG11 145 ET69
Cross Oak, Wind. SL4 151 AN82
Crossoak La, Red. RH1 267 DH144
Cross Oak Rd, Berk. HP4 38 AU20
Crossoaks La, Borwd. WD6 78 CR35
South Mimms EN6 62 CS34
Crosspath, The, Rad. WD7 77 CG35
Cross Rd, E4 101 ED46
N11 99 DH50
N22 99 DN52
SE5 311 P8
SW19 180 DA94
Belmont SM2 218 DA110
Bromley BR2 204 EL103
Chadwell Heath RM6 126 EW59
Croydon CR0 202 DR102
Dartford DA1 188 FJ86
Enfield EN1 82 DS42
Feltham TW13 176 BY91
Harrow HA1 117 CD56
Hawley DA2 188 FM91
Hertford SG14 32 DQ08
Kingston upon Thames KT2 178 CM94
Northfleet DA11 191 GF86
Orpington BR5 206 EV99
Purley CR8 219 DP113
Romford RM7 126 FA55
Sidcup DA14 off Sidcup Hill 186 EV91
South Harrow HA2 116 CB62
Sutton SM2 218 DD106
Tadworth KT20 233 CW122
Uxbridge UB8 134 BJ66
Waltham Cross EN8 67 DY33
Watford WD19 76 BY44
Wealdstone HA3 95 CG54
Weybridge KT13 195 BR104
Woodford Green IG8 103 EM51
Cross Rds, High Beach IG10 84 EH40
Crossroads, The, Eff. KT24 246 BX128
Cross St, N1 276 G8
SW13 158 CS82
Erith DA8 off Bexley Rd 167 FE78
Hampton Hill TW12 176 CC92
Harlow CM20 51 ER15
St. Albans AL3
off Spencer St 43 CD20
Uxbridge UB8 134 BJ66
Ware SG12 33 DY06
Watford WD17 76 BW41
Cross Ter, Wal.Abb. EN9
off Stonyshotts 68 EE34
Crossthwaite Av, SE5 162 DR84
Crosstrees Ho, E14
off Cassilis Rd 302 B6
Crosswall, EC3 288 A10
Crossway, N12 98 DD51
N16 277 P3
NW9 119 CT56
SE28 146 EW72
SW20 199 CW98
W13 137 CG70
Chesham HP5 54 AS30
Dagenham RM8 126 EW62
Enfield EN1 100 DS45
Harlow CM17 36 EX14
Hayes UB3 135 BU74
Petts Wood BR5 205 ER98
Pinner HA5 93 BV54
Ruislip HA4 116 BW63
Walton-on-Thames KT12 195 BV103
Welwyn Garden City AL8 29 CW05
Woodford Green IG8 102 EJ49
Cross Way, NW10 139 CU66
Crossway, The, N22 99 DP52
SE9 184 EK89
Uxbridge UB10 134 BM68
Cross Way, The, Har. HA3 95 CE54
CROSSWAYS, Dart. DA2 169 FR84
Crossways, N21 82 DQ44
Beaconsfield HP9 89 AM54
Berkhamstead HP4 38 AT20
Effingham KT24 246 BX127
Egham TW20 173 BD93
Hemel Hempstead HP3 41 BP20
Romford RM2 127 FH55
Shenfield CM15 109 GA44
South Croydon CR2 221 DY108
Sunbury-on-Thames TW16 175 BT94
Sutton SM2 218 DD109
Tatsfield TN16 238 EJ120
Crossways, The, Couls. CR5 235 DM119
Guildford GU2 258 AU135
Hounslow TW5 156 BZ80
South Merstham RH1 251 DJ130
Wembley HA9 118 CN61
Crossways Boul, Dart. DA2 168 FQ84
Greenhithe DA9 169 FT84
● Crossways Business Pk,
Dart. DA2 168 FQ84
Crossways La, Reig. RH2 250 DC128
Crossways Rd, Beck. BR3 203 EA98
Mitcham CR4 201 DH97
Coll Crossways Sixth Form, SE4 313 L9
Crosswell Cl, Shep. TW17 195 BQ96
Crosthwaite Way, Slou. SL1 131 AK71
Croston St, E8 278 D8
Crothall Cl, N13 99 DM48
Crouch Av, Bark. IG11 146 EV68
Crouch Cl, Beck. BR3 183 EA93
Crouch Ct, Harl. CM20 35 EQ13
Crouch Cft, SE9 185 EN90
CROUCH END, N8 121 DJ58
Crouch End Hill, N8 121 DK59
Crouchfield, Hem.H. HP1 40 BH21
Hertford SG14 32 DQ06
Crouch Hall Rd, N8 121 DK58
⊖ Crouch Hill 121 DM59
Crouch Hill, N4 121 DL58
N8 121 DL58
Crouch La, Goffs Oak EN7 66 DQ28
Crouchman Cl, Grays RM16 170 GB75
Crouchman's Cl, SE26 182 DT90
Crouch Oak La, Add. KT15 212 BJ105
Crouch Rd, NW10 138 CR66
Grays RM16 171 GG78
Crouch Valley, Upmin. RM14 129 FS59
Crowborough Cl, Warl. CR6 237 DY117
Crowborough Dr, Warl. CR6 237 DY118
Crowborough Path,
Wat. WD19 94 BX49
Crowborough Rd, SW17 180 DG93
Crowcroft Cl, Guil. GU2
off Henderson Av 242 AV130
Crowden Way, SE28 146 EW73
Crowder Cl, N12 98 DC53
Crowder St, E1 288 E10
Crow Dr, Halst. TN14 241 FC115
Crowfoot Cl, E9 279 P3
SE28 145 ES74
CROW GREEN, Brwd. CM15 108 FT41
Crow Grn La, Pilg.Hat. CM15 108 FU43
Crow Grn Rd, Pilg.Hat. CM15 108 FT43
Crowhurst Cl, SW9 310 F8
Crowhurst Mead, Gdse. RH9 252 DW130
Crowhurst Way, Orp. BR5 206 EW99
Crowland Av, Hayes UB3 155 BS77
Crowland Gdns, N14 99 DL45
Sch Crowland Prim Sch, N15
off Crowland Rd 122 DU57
Crowland Rd, N15 122 DT57
Thornton Heath CR7 202 DR98
Crowlands Av, Rom. RM7 127 FB58
Sch Crowlands Inf & Jun Schs,
Rom. RM7 off London Rd 127 FC58
Crowland Ter, N1 277 L6
Crowland Wk, Mord. SM4 200 DB100
Crow La, Rom. RM7 126 EZ59
Crowley Cres, Croy. CR0 219 DN106
Crowline Wk, N1
off Clephane Rd 277 K4
Crowmarsh Gdns, SE23
off Tyson Rd 182 DW87
Crown Arc, Kings.T. KT1
off Union St 197 CK96
Crown Ash Hill, West. TN16 222 EH114
Crown Ash La, Warl. CR6 238 EG116
Westerham TN16 238 EG116
Crownbourne Ct, Sutt. SM1
off St. Nicholas Way 218 DB105
● Crown Business Est, Chesh.
HP5 off Berkhampstead Rd 54 AQ30
Crown Cl, E3 280 A8
N22 off Winkfield Rd 99 DN53
NW6 273 L4
NW7 97 CT47
Buckhurst Hill IG9 102 EH46
Colnbrook SL3 153 BC80
Hayes UB3 155 BT75
Orpington BR6 224 EU105
Sheering CM22 37 FC07
Walton-on-Thames KT12 196 BW101
● Crown Cl Business Cen, E3 280 A9
Crown Ct, EC2 287 K9
SE12 184 EH86
WC2 286 B9
Crown Dale, SE19 181 DP93
Crowndale Rd, NW1 275 L10
Crownfield, Brox. EN10 49 EA21
Crownfield Av, Ilf. IG2 125 ES57
Sch Crownfield Inf Sch, Coll.Row
RM7 off White Hart La 104 FA54
Sch Crownfield Jun Sch, Coll.Row RM7
off White Hart La 104 FA54
Crownfield Rd, E15 280 G2
Crownfields, Sev. TN13 257 FH125
Crown Gate, Harl. CM20 51 ER15
Crowngate Ho, E3 289 P1
Jct Crown Gate Rbt,
Harl. CM18 51 ER15
Crown Grn Ms, Wem. HA9 118 CL61
Crown Hts, Guil. GU1 258 AY137
Crown Hill, Croy. CR0
off Church St 202 DQ103
Epping CM16 69 EM33
Waltham Abbey EN9 69 EM33
Crownhill Rd, NW10 139 CT67
Woodford Green IG8 102 EL52
Crown Ho, N.Mal. KT3
off Kingston Rd 198 CQ98
Crown La, N14 99 DJ46
SW16 181 DN92
Bromley BR2 204 EK99
Chislehurst BR7 205 EQ95
Farnham Royal SL2 131 AN68
High Wycombe HP11 88 AF48
Morden SM4 200 DB97
Virginia Water GU25 192 AX100
Crown La Gdns, SW16 181 DN92
Sch Crown La Prim Sch, SW16
off Crown La 181 DP92
Crown La Spur, Brom. BR2 204 EK100
Crown Meadow, Colnbr. SL3 153 BB80
Crownmead Way, Rom. RM7 127 FB56
Crown Ms, E13
off Waghorn Rd 144 EJ67
W6 159 CU77
Crown Mill, Mitch. CR4 200 DE99
Crown Office Row, EC4 286 E10
Crown Pas, SW1 297 M3
Kingston upon Thames KT1
off Church St 197 CK96
Watford WD18
off The Crescent 76 BW42
Crown Pl, EC2 287 N6
NW5 275 K4
SE16 312 F1
Crown Pt Par, SE19
off Beulah Hill 181 DP93
Crown Reach, SW1 309 P1
Crown Ri, Cher. KT16 193 BF102
Watford WD25 60 BW34
Crown Rd, N10 98 DG52
Borehamwood WD6 78 CN39
Enfield EN1 82 DV42
Grays RM17 170 GA79
Ilford IG6 125 ER56
Morden SM4 200 DB98
New Malden KT3 198 CQ95
Orpington BR6 224 EU106
Ruislip HA4 116 BX64
Shoreham TN14 225 FF110
Sutton SM1 218 DB105
Twickenham TW1 177 CH86
Virginia Water GU25 192 AW100
Crown Sq, Wok. GU21
off Commercial Way 227 AZ117
Crownstone Rd, SW2 181 DN85
Crown St, SE5 311 K4
W3 138 CP74
Brentwood CM14 108 FW47
Dagenham RM10 147 FC65
Egham TW20 173 BA92
Harrow HA2 117 CD60
Crown Ter, Rich. TW9 158 CM84
Crown Trading Est, Hayes UB3 155 BS75
Crowntree Cl, Islw. TW7 157 CF79
Crown Wk, Uxb. UB8
off The Mall Pavilions 134 BJ66
Crown Wk, Hem.H. HP3 40 BL24
Wembley HA9 118 CM62
Crown Wks, E2 288 E1
Crown Way, West Dr. UB7 134 BM74
Crown Wds La, SE9 165 EP82
SE18 165 EP82
Crown Wds Way, SE9 185 ER85
Crown Yd, Houns. TW3
off High St 156 CC83
Crow Piece La, Farn.Royal SL2 131 AM66
Crowshott Av, Stan. HA7 95 CJ53
Crows Rd, E15 291 H2
Barking IG11 145 EP65
Epping CM16 69 ET30
Crowstone Rd, Grays RM16 170 GC75
Crowther Av, Brent. TW8 158 CL77
Crowther Cl, SW6 307 H3
Crowther Rd, SE25 202 DU98
Crowthorne Cl, SW18 179 CZ88
Crowthorne Rd, W10 282 C9
Croxdale Rd, Borwd. WD6 78 CM40
Croxden Cl, Edg. HA8 118 CM55
Croxden Wk, Mord. SM4 200 DC100
Croxford Gdns, N22 99 DP52
Croxford Way, Rom. RM7
off Horace Av 127 FD60
⊖ Croxley 75 BP44
Croxley Cl, Orp. BR5 206 EV96
CROXLEY GREEN, Rick. WD3 74 BN43
Croxley Grn, Orp. BR5 206 EV95
● Croxley Green Business Pk,
Wat. WD18 75 BR44
Croxley Hall Wds,
Crox.Grn WD3 92 BM45
Croxley Rd, W9 283 H3
Hemel Hempstead HP3 58 BN25
Croxley Vw, Wat. WD18 75 BS44
Croxted Cl, SE21 182 DQ87
Croxted Ms, SE24 182 DQ86
Croxted Rd, SE21 182 DQ87
SE24 182 DQ87
Croxteth Ho, SW8 309 N8
Croxton, Kings.T. KT1
off Burritt Rd 198 CN96
Croyde Av, Grnf. UB6 136 CC69
Hayes UB3 155 BS77
Croyde Cl, Sid. DA15 185 ER87
CROYDON, CR0 202 DR102
Coll Croydon Coll, Croy. CR0
off College Rd 202 DR103
Croydon Gro, Croy. CR0 201 DP102
Sch Croydon High Sch, S.Croy.
CR2 off Old Farleigh Rd 220 DW110
Croydon La, Bans. SM7 218 DB114
Croydon La S, Bans. SM7 218 DB114
Croydon Rd, E13 291 M5
SE20 202 DV96
Beckenham BR3 203 DY98
Beddington CR0 219 DL105
Bromley BR2 204 EF104
Caterham CR3 236 DU122
Keston BR2 204 EJ104
Croydon Rd,
London Heathrow Airport TW6 155 BP82
Mitcham CR4 200 DG98
Mitcham Common CR0 200 DG98
Reigate RH2 250 DB134
Wallington SM6 219 DH105
Warlingham CR6 237 ED122
West Wickham BR4 204 EE104
Westerham TN16 239 EM123
● Croydon Rd Ind Est,
Beck. BR3 203 DX98
● Croydon Valley Trade Pk, Croy.
CR0 off Beddington Fm Rd 201 DL101
Croyland Rd, N9 100 DU46
Croylands Dr, Surb. KT6 198 CL101
Croysdale Av, Sun. TW16 195 BU97
Crozier Dr, S.Croy. CR2 220 DV110
Crozier Ho, SE3
off Ebdon Way 164 EH83
Crozier Ter, E9 279 K3
Crucible Cl, Rom. RM6 126 EV58
Crucifix La, SE1 299 N4
Cruden Ho, SE17 310 G3
Cruden Rd, Grav. DA12 191 GM90
Cruden St, N1 277 H9
Cruick Av, S.Ock. RM15 149 FW73
Cruikshank Rd, E15 281 K1
Cruikshank St, WC1 286 E2
Crummock Cl, Slou. SL1 130 AJ72
Crummock Gdns, NW9 118 CS57
Crumpsall St, SE2 166 EW77
Crundale Av, NW9 118 CN57
Crundal Twr, Orp. BR5 206 EW102
Crunden Rd, S.Croy. CR2 220 DR108
Crusader Cl, Purf. RM19
off Centurion Way 168 FN77
Crusader Gdns, Croy. CR0
off Cotelands 202 DS104
● Crusader Industral Est, N4
off Hermitage Rd 122 DQ58
Crusader Way, Wat. WD18 75 BT44
Crushes Cl, Hutt. CM13 109 GE44
Crusoe Ms, N16 122 DR61
Crusoe Rd, Erith DA8 167 FD78
Mitcham CR4 180 DF94
Crutched Friars, EC3 287 P10
Crutches La, Jordans HP9 90 AS51
Crutchfield La, Hkwd RH6 268 DA145
Walton-on-Thames KT12 195 BV103
Crutchley Rd, SE6 184 EE89
★ Crystal, The, E16 303 N1
Crystal Av, Horn. RM12 128 FL63
Crystal Ct, SE19
off College Rd 182 DT92
Crystal Ho, SE18
off Spinel Cl 165 ET78
⇌ Crystal Palace 182 DU93
⊖ Crystal Palace 182 DU93
★ Crystal Palace FC, SE25 202 DS98
★ Crystal Palace Nat Sports Cen,
SE19 182 DU93
Crystal Palace Par, SE19 182 DT93
★ Crystal Palace Pk, SE19 182 DT92
Crystal Palace Pk Rd, SE26 182 DU92
Crystal Palace Rd, SE22 162 DU84
Crystal Palace Sta Rd, SE19 182 DU93
Crystal Ter, SE19 182 DR93
Crystal Vw Ct, Brom. BR1 183 ED91
Crystal Way, Dag. RM8 126 EW60
Harrow HA1 117 CF57
Crystal Wf, N1 287 H1
Cuba Dr, Enf. EN3 82 DW40
Cuba St, E14 302 A4
Cubitt Bldg, SW1 309 J1
Cubitt Sq, Sthl. UB2
off Windmill Av 136 CC74
Cubitt Steps, E14 302 B2
Cubitt St, WC1 286 D3
Cubitts Yd, WC2 286 B10
Cubitt Ter, SW4 309 M10
CUBITT TOWN, E14 302 F6
Sch Cubitt Town Inf & Jun Schs,
E14 302 F7
Cublands, Hert. SG13 32 DV09
Cuckmans Dr, St.Alb. AL2 60 CA25
Cuckmere Way, Orp. BR5 206 EX102
Cuckoo Av, W7 137 CE70
Cuckoo Dene, W7 137 CD71
Cuckoo Hall La, N9 100 DW45
Sch Cuckoo Hall Prim Sch, N9
off Cuckoo Hall La 101 DX45
Cuckoo Hill, Pnr. HA5 116 BW55
Cuckoo Hill Dr, Pnr. HA5 116 BW55
Cuckoo Hill Rd, Pnr. HA5 116 BW56
Cuckoo La, W7 137 CE73
Cuckoo Pound, Shep. TW17 195 BS99
Cucumber La, Essen. AL9 46 DF20
Hertford SG13 46 DF20
Cudas Cl, Epsom KT19 217 CT105
Cuddington, SE17 299 J8
Cuddington Av, Wor.Pk. KT4 199 CT104
Cuddington Cl, Tad. KT20 233 CW120
Sch Cuddington Comm Prim Sch,
Wor.Pk. KT4 off Salisbury Rd 199 CT104
Sch Cuddington Cft Prim Sch,
Cheam SM2 off West Dr 217 CX109
Cuddington Glade, Epsom KT19 216 CN112
Cuddington Pk Cl, Bans. SM7 217 CZ113
Cuddington Way, Sutt. SM2 217 CX112
CUDHAM, Sev. TN14 239 ER115
Cudham Cl, Belmont SM2 218 DA110
Sch Cudham C of E Prim Sch,
Bigg.H. TN16 off Jail La 239 EN116
Cudham Dr, New Adgtn CR0 221 EC110
Cudham La N, Cudham TN14 223 ER112
Orpington BR6 223 ES110
Cudham La S, Sev. TN14 239 EQ115
Cudham Pk Rd, Cudham TN14 223 ES110
Cudham Rd, Downe BR6 223 EN111
Tatsfield TN16 238 EL120
Cudham St, SE6 183 EC87
Cudworth St, E1 288 F4
Cuff Cres, SE9 184 EK86
CUFFLEY, Pot.B. EN6 65 DM29
⇌ Cuffley 65 DM29
Cuffley Av, Wat. WD25 60 BX34
Cuffley Ct, Hem.H. HP2 41 BQ15
Cuffley Hill, Goffs Oak EN7 65 DN29
Sch Cuffley Sch, Cuffley EN6
off Theobalds Rd 65 DM30
Cuff Pt, E2 288 A2
Cugley Rd, Dart. DA2 188 FQ87
Culford Gdns, SW3 296 F9
Culford Gro, N1 277 N5

Culford Ms, N1 277 N4
Culford Rd, N1 277 N6
Grays RM16 170 GC75
Culgaith Gdns, Enf. EN2 81 DL42
Cullen Sq, S.Ock. RM15 149 FW73
Cullen Way, NW10 138 CQ70
Cullera Cl, Nthwd. HA6 93 BT51
Cullerne Cl, Ewell KT17 217 CT110
Cullesden Rd, Ken. CR8 235 DP115
Culling Rd, SE16 300 G6
Cullings Ct, Wal.Abb. EN9 68 EF33
Cullington Cl, Har. HA3 117 CG56
Cullingworth Rd, NW10 119 CU64
Culloden Cl, SE7 164 EJ79
SE16 312 D1
Sch Culloden Prim Sch, E14 290 F9
Culloden Rd, Enf. EN2 81 DP40
Culloden St, E14 290 F8
Cullum St, EC3 287 N10
Culmington Rd, W13 157 CJ75
South Croydon CR2 220 DQ109
Culmore Rd, SE15 312 F5
Culmstock Rd, SW11 180 DG85
Culpeper Cl, Ilf. IG6 103 EP51
Culpepper Cl, N18 100 DV50
Culross Cl, N15 122 DQ56
Culross St, W1 296 G1
Culsac Rd, Surb. KT6 198 CL103
Culverden Rd, SW12 181 DJ89
Watford WD19 93 BV48
Culver Dr, Oxt. RH8 254 EE130
Culver Gro, Stan. HA7 95 CJ54
Culverhay, Ashtd. KT21 232 CL116
Culverhouse Gdns, SW16 181 DM90
Culverlands Cl, Stan. HA7 95 CH49
Culverley Rd, SE6 183 EB88
Culver Rd, St.Alb. AL1 43 CE19
Culvers Av, Cars. SM5 200 DF103
Culvers Ct, Grav. DA12 191 GM88
Culvers Cft, Seer Grn HP9 89 AQ51
Sch Culvers Ho Prim Sch, Mitch. CR4 off Orchard Av 200 DG102
Culvers Retreat, Cars. SM5 200 DF102
Culverstone Cl, Brom. BR2 204 EF100
Culvers Way, Cars. SM5 200 DF103
Culvert La, Uxb. UB8 134 BH68
Culvert Pl, SW11 308 G9
Culvert Rd, N15 122 DS57
SW11 308 F7
Culworth St, NW8 284 C1
Culzean Cl, SE27
off Chatsworth Way 181 DP90
Cumberland Av, NW10 138 CP69
Gravesend DA12 191 GJ87
Guildford GU2 242 AU129
Hornchurch RM12 128 FL62
Slough SL2 131 AQ70
Welling DA16 165 ES83
● Cumberland Business Pk, NW10 138 CN69
Cumberland Cl, E8 278 A5
SW20 off Lansdowne Rd 179 CX94
Amersham HP7 72 AV39
Epsom KT19 216 CS110
Hemel Hempstead HP3 41 BS24
Hertford SG14 31 DP06
Hornchurch RM12 128 FL62
Ilford IG6 103 EQ53
Twickenham TW1
off Westmorland Cl 177 CH86
Cumberland Ct, Hodd. EN11 49 EA16
Welling DA16
off Bellegrove Rd 165 ES82
Cumberland Cres, W14 294 F8
Cumberland Dr, Bexh. DA7 166 EY80
Chessington KT9 198 CM104
Dartford DA1 188 FM87
Esher KT10 197 CG103
Cumberland Gdns, NW4 97 CX54
WC1 286 D2
Cumberland Gate, W1 284 E10
Cumberland Ho, NW10 139 CU70
SE28 165 EQ75
Cumberland Mkt, NW1 285 K2
Cumberland Mkt Est, NW1 285 K2
Cumberland Ms, SE11 310 F1
Cumberland Mills Sq, E14 302 G10
● Cumberland Pk, NW10 139 CU69
Cumberland Pk, W3 138 CQ73
Cumberland Pl, NW1 285 J2
SE6 184 EF88
Sunbury-on-Thames TW16 195 BU98
Cumberland Rd, E12 124 EK63
E13 292 A6
E17 101 DY54
N9 100 DW46
N22 99 DM54
SE25 202 DV100
SW13 159 CT81
W3 138 CQ73
W7 157 CF75
Ashford TW15 174 BK90
Bromley BR2 204 EE98
Chafford Hundred RM16 170 FY75
Harrow HA1 116 CB57
Richmond TW9 158 CN80
Stanmore HA7 118 CM55
Cumberlands, Ken. CR8 236 DR115
Sch Cumberland Sch, E13 292 C4
Cumberland St, SW1 297 K10
Staines-upon-Thames TW18 173 BD92
Cumberland Ter, NW1 285 J1
Cumberland Ter Ms, NW1 285 J1
Cumberland Vil, W3
off Cumberland Rd 138 CQ73
Cumberlow Av, SE25 202 DU97
Cumberlow Pl, Hem.H. HP2 41 BQ21
Cumbernauld Gdns, Sun. TW16 175 BT92
Cumberton Rd, N17 100 DR53
Cumbrae Cl, Slou. SL2
off St. Pauls Av 132 AU74
Cumbrae Gdns, Long Dit. KT6 197 CK103
Cumbrian Av, Bexh. DA7 167 FE81
Cumbrian Gdns, NW2 119 CX61
Cumbrian Way, Uxb. UB8 134 BK67
Cum Cum Hill, Hat. AL9 46 DD21
★ Cuming Mus, SE17
off Walworth Rd 299 J9
Cumley Rd, Toot Hill CM5 71 FE30
Cummings Hall La, Noak Hill RM3 106 FJ48
Cumming St, N1 286 C1
Cumnor Gdns, Epsom KT17 217 CU107
Sch Cumnor Ho Sch, S.Croy. CR2
off Pampisford Rd 219 DP109
Cumnor Ri, Ken. CR8 236 DQ117
Cumnor Rd, Sutt. SM2 218 DC107
Cunard Ct, Stan. HA7
off Brightwen Gro 95 CG47
Cunard Cres, N21 82 DR44
Cunard Pl, EC3 287 P9
Cunard Rd, NW10 138 CR69
Cunard Wk, SE16 301 K8
Cundalls Rd, Ware SG12 33 DY05
Cundy Rd, E16 292 C9
Cundy St, SW1 297 H9
Cundy St Est, SW1 297 H9
Cunliffe Cl, Headley KT18 232 CP124
Cunliffe Rd, Epsom KT19 217 CT105
Cunliffe St, SW16 181 DJ93
Cunningham Av, Enf. EN3 83 DY36
Guildford GU1 243 BA133
Hatfield AL10 44 CR17
St. Albans AL1 43 CF22
Cunningham Cl, Rom. RM6 126 EW57
West Wickham BR4 203 EB103
Cunningham Ct, E10
off Oliver Rd 123 EB62
Sch Cunningham Hill Inf Sch, St.Alb. AL1 off Cell Barnes La 43 CG21
Sch Cunningham Hill Jun Sch, St.Alb. AL1 off Cell Barnes La 43 CG22
Cunningham Hill Rd, St.Alb. AL1 43 CF22
Cunningham Pk, Har. HA1 116 CC57
Cunningham Pl, NW8 284 A4
Cunningham Ri, N.Wld Bas. CM16 71 FC25
Cunningham Rd, N15 122 DU56
Banstead SM7 234 DD115
Cheshunt EN8 67 DY27
Cunnington St, W4 158 CQ76
Cupar Rd, SW11 309 H6
CUPID GREEN, Hem.H. HP2 40 BN16
Cupid Grn La, Hem.H. HP2 40 BN15
Cupola Cl, Brom. BR1 184 EH92
Curates Wk, Dart. DA2 188 FK90
Curchin Cl, Bigg.H. TN16 222 EJ112
Cureton St, SW1 297 P9
Curfew Bell Rd, Cher. KT16 193 BF101
Curfew Yd, Wind. SL4
off Thames St 151 AR81
Curie Gdns, NW9 96 CS54
Curlew Cl, SE28 146 EX73
Berkhamsted HP4 38 AW20
South Croydon CR2 221 DX111
Curlew Ct, W13
off Gurnell Gro 137 CF70
Brox. EN10 49 DZ23
Surbiton KT6 198 CM104
Curlew Gdns, Guil. GU4 243 BD132
Curlew Ho, Enf. EN3
off Allington Ct 83 DX43
Curlews, The, Grav. DA12 191 GK89
Curlew St, SE1 300 A4
Curlew Ter, Ilf. IG5
off Tiptree Cres 125 EN55
Curlew Way, Hayes UB4 136 BX71
Curling Cl, Couls. CR5 235 DM120
Curling La, Bad.Dene RM17 170 FZ78
Curling Vale, Guil. GU2 258 AU136
Curness St, SE13 163 EC84
Curnick's La, SE27
off Chapel Rd 182 DQ91
Curnock Est, NW1 275 L9
● Curo Pk, Frog. AL2 61 CE27
Curran Av, Sid. DA15 185 ET85
Wallington SM6 200 DG104
Curran Cl, Uxb. UB8 134 BJ70
Currey Rd, Grnf. UB6 137 CD65
Curricle St, W3 138 CS74
Currie Hill Cl, SW19 179 CZ91
Curries La, Slou. SL1 111 AK64
Currie St, Hert. SG13 32 DS09
Curry Ri, NW7 97 CX51
Cursitor St, EC4 286 E8
Curtain Pl, EC2 287 P4
Curtain Rd, EC2 287 N5
Curteys, Harl. CM17 36 EX10
Curthwaite Gdns, Enf. EN2 81 DK42
Curtis Cl, Mill End WD3 92 BG46
Curtis Dr, W3 138 CR72
Curtis Fld Rd, SW16 181 DM91
Curtis Gdns, Dor. RH4 263 CG135
Curtis Ho, N11 99 DH50
Curtis La, Wem. HA0
off Station Gro 118 CL64
Curtismill Cl, Orp. BR5 206 EV97
Curtis Mill Grn, Nave. RM4 87 FF42
Curtis Mill La, Nave. RM4 87 FF42
Curtismill Way, Orp. BR5 206 EV97
Curtis Rd, Dor. RH4 263 CF135
Epsom KT19 216 CQ105
Hemel Hempstead HP3 41 BQ21
Hornchurch RM11 128 FM60
Hounslow TW4 176 BZ87
Curtiss Dr, Lvsdn WD25 59 BT34
Curtis St, SE1 300 A8
Curtis Way, SE1 300 A8
SE28 off Tawney Rd 146 EV73
Berkhamsted HP4 38 AX20
Curvan Cl, Epsom KT17 217 CT110
Curve, The, W12 139 CU73
Curwen Av, E7
off Woodford Rd 124 EH63
Sch Curwen Prim Sch, E13 291 N1
Curwen Rd, W12 159 CU75
Curzon Av, Beac. HP9 89 AK51
Enfield EN3 83 DX43
Hazlemere HP15 88 AC45
Stanmore HA7 95 CG53
Curzon Cl, Haz. HP15 88 AC45
Orpington BR6 223 ER105
Weybridge KT13
off Curzon Rd 212 BN105
Curzon Cres, NW10 139 CT66
Barking IG11 145 ET68
Curzon Dr, Grays RM17 170 GC80
Curzon Gate, W1 296 G3
Curzon Pl, Pnr. HA5 116 BW57
Curzon Rd, N10 99 DH54
W5 137 CH70
Thornton Heath CR7 201 DN100
Weybridge KT13 212 BN105
Curzon Sq, W1 297 H3
Curzon St, W1 297 H3
Cusack Cl, Twick. TW1
off Waldegrave Rd 177 CF91
Cussons Cl, Chsht EN7 66 DU29
CUSTOM HOUSE, E16 292 F8
DLR Custom House for ExCeL 292 B10
Custom Ho Reach, SE16 301 N5
Custom Ho Wk, EC3 299 N1
Cut, The, SE1 298 F4
Slough SL2 131 AN70
Cutcombe Rd, SE5 311 K9
Cuthberga Cl, Bark. IG11
off George St 145 EQ66
Cuthbert Ct, Whyt. CR3
off Godstone Rd 236 DU119
Cuthbert Gdns, SE25 202 DS97
Cuthbert Rd, E17 123 EC55
N18 off Fairfield Rd 100 DU50
Croydon CR0 201 DP103
Cuthberts Cl, Chsht EN7 66 DT29
Cuthbert St, W2 284 A6
Cut Hills, Egh. TW20 192 AV95
Virginia Water GU25 192 AU96
Cuthill Wk, SE5 311 L7
Cutlers Gdns, E1 287 P8
Cutlers Gdns Arc, EC2
off Devonshire Sq 287 P8
Cutlers Sq, E14 302 B9
Cutlers Ter, N1 277 N4
Cutler St, E1 287 P8
Cutmore, Bark. IG11
off Ripple Rd 145 EQ66
Cutmore Dr, Coln.Hth AL4 44 CP22
Cutmore St, Grav. DA11 191 GH87
Cutter La, SE10 303 K4
Cutthroat All, Rich. TW10
off Ham St 177 CJ89
Cutthroat La, Hodd. EN11 49 DZ15
Cutting, The, Red. RH1 266 DF136
Cuttsfield Ter, Hem.H. HP1 39 BF21
★ Cutty Sark, SE10 314 E2
Cutty Sark Ct, Green. DA9
off Low Cl 189 FU85
DLR Cutty Sark for Maritime Greenwich 314 E3
Cutty Sark Gdns, SE10 314 F2
Cuxton Cl, Bexh. DA6 186 EY85
Cwmbran Ct, Hem.H. HP2 40 BM16
Cyclamen Cl, Hmptn. TW12
off Gresham Rd 176 CA93
Cyclamen Rd, Swan. BR8 207 FD98
Cyclamen Way, Epsom KT19 216 CP106
Cyclops Ms, E14 302 A8
Cygnet Av, Felt. TW14 176 BW87
Cygnet Cl, NW10 118 CR64
Borehamwood WD6 78 CQ39
Northwood HA6 93 BQ52
Woking GU21 226 AV116
Cygnet Gdns, Nthflt DA11 191 GF89
Cygnets, The, Felt. TW13 176 BY91
Staines-upon-Thames TW18
off Edgell Rd 173 BF92
Cygnets Cl, Red. RH1 250 DG132
Cygnet St, E1 288 B4
Cygnet Vw, Grays RM20 169 FT77
Cygnet Way, Hayes UB4 136 BX71
● Cygnus Business Cen, NW10 139 CT65
Cygnus Ct, Pur. CR8
off Brighton Rd 219 DN111
Cymbeline Ct, Har. HA1
off Gayton Rd 117 CF58
Cynthia St, N1 286 D1
Cyntra Pl, E8 278 F7
Cypress Av, Enf. EN2 81 DN35
Twickenham TW2 176 CC87
Welwyn Garden City AL7 30 DC10
Cypress Cl, E5 122 DU61
Waltham Abbey EN9 67 ED34
Cypress Ct, Vir.W. GU25 192 AY98
Cypress Gdns, SE4 183 DY85
Cypress Gro, Ilf. IG6 103 ES51
Sch Cypress Inf Sch, SE25
off Cypress Rd 202 DS96
Sch Cypress Jun Sch, SE25
off Cypress Rd 202 DS96
Cypress Path, Rom. RM3 106 FK52
Cypress Pl, W1 285 M5
Cypress Rd, SE25 202 DS96
Guildford GU1 242 AW132
Harrow HA3 95 CD54
Cypress Tree Cl, Sid. DA15 185 ET88
Cypress Wk, Eng.Grn TW20 172 AV93
Watford WD25
off Cedar Wd Dr 75 BV35
Cypress Way, Bans. SM7 217 CX114
DLR Cyprus 293 M10
Cyprus Av, N3 97 CY54
Cyprus Cl, Epsom KT19 216 CR109
N4 off Atterbury Rd 121 DP58
Cyprus Gdns, N3 97 CY54
Cyprus Pl, E2 289 H1
E6 293 M10
Cyprus Rd, N3 97 CZ54
N9 100 DT47
Cyprus Rbt, E16 293 M10
Cyprus St, E2 288 G1
Cyrena Rd, SE22 182 DT86
Sch Cyril Jackson Prim Sch,
N Bldg, E14 289 P10
S Bldg, E14 301 P1
Cyril Mans, SW11 308 F7
Cyril Rd, Bexh. DA7 166 EY82
Orpington BR6 206 EU101
Cyrus St, EC1 287 H4
Czar St, SE8 314 A2

D

Dabbling Cl, Erith DA8 167 FH80
Dabbs Hill La, Nthlt. UB5 116 CB64
D'Abernon Chase, Lthd. KT22 215 CG114
D'Abernon Cl, Esher KT10 214 CA105
D'Abernon Dr, Stoke D'Ab. KT11 230 BY116
Dabin Cres, SE10 314 E6
Dacca St, SE8 313 P2
Dace Rd, E3 280 A8
Dacorum Way, Hem.H. HP1 40 BJ20
Dacre Av, Aveley RM15 149 FR74
Ilford IG5 103 EN54
Dacre Cl, Chig. IG7 103 EQ49
Greenford UB6 136 CB68
Dacre Cres, Aveley RM15 149 FR74
Dacre Gdns, SE13 164 EE84
Borehamwood WD6 78 CR43
Chigwell IG7 103 EQ49
● Dacre Ind Est, Chsht EN8
off Fieldings Rd 67 DZ29
Dacre Pk, SE13 164 EE83
Dacre Pl, SE13 164 EE83
Dacre Rd, E11 124 EF60
E13 144 EH67
Croydon CR0 201 DL101
Dacres Est, SE23 183 DX90
Dacres Rd, SE23 183 DX90
Dacre St, SW1 297 N6
Dade Way, Sthl. UB2 156 BZ78
Dads Wd, Harl. CM20 51 EQ15
Daerwood Cl, Brom. BR2 205 EM102
Daffodil Av, Pilg.Hat. CM15 108 FV43
Daffodil Cl, Croy. CR0 203 DX102
Hatfield AL10 29 CT14
Daffodil Gdns, Ilf. IG1 125 EP64
Daffodil Pl, Hmptn. TW12
off Gresham Rd 176 CA93
Daffodil St, W12 139 CT73
Dafforne Rd, SW17 180 DG90
Dagden Rd, Shalf. GU4 258 AY140
DAGENHAM, RM8 - RM10 146 FA65
Dagenham Av, Dag. RM9
off Cook Rd 146 EY67
⇌ Dagenham Dock 146 EZ68
⊖ Dagenham East 127 FC64
⊖ Dagenham Heathway 146 EZ65
Dagenham Leisure Pk, Dag. RM9 146 EY67
Sch Dagenham Pk Comm Sch, Dag. RM10 off School Rd 147 FB67
Dagenham Rd, E10 123 DZ60
Dagenham RM10 127 FC63
Rainham RM13 147 FD66
Romford RM7 127 FD62
Dagger La, Els. WD6 77 CG44
Daggs Dell Rd, Hem.H. HP1 39 BE18
Dagley Fm Pk Homes, Shalf. GU4 258 AX140
Dagley La, Shalf. GU4 258 AY140
Dagmar Av, Wem. HA9 118 CM63
Dagmar Ct, E14
off New Union Cl 302 F6
Dagmar Gdns, NW10 282 C1
Dagmar Ms, Sthl. UB2
off Dagmar Rd 156 BY76
Dagmar Pas, N1 277 H8
Dagmar Rd, N4 121 DN59
N15 off Cornwall Rd 122 DR56
N22 99 DK53
SE5 311 N7
SE25 202 DS99
Dagenham RM10 147 FC66
Kingston upon Thames KT2 198 CM95
Southall UB2 156 BY76
Windsor SL4 151 AR82
Dagmar Ter, N1 277 H8
Dagnall Cres, Uxb. UB8 134 BJ71
Dagnall Pk, SE25 202 DS100
Dagnall Rd, SE25 202 DS99
Dagnall St, SW11 308 F8
Dagnam Pk Cl, Rom. RM3 106 FN50
Dagnam Pk Dr, Rom. RM3 106 FL50
Dagnam Pk Gdns, Rom. RM3 106 FN51
Dagnam Pk Sq, Rom. RM3 106 FP51
Dagnan Rd, SW12 181 DH87
Dagonet Gdns, Brom. BR1 184 EG90
Dagonet Rd, Brom. BR1 184 EG90
Dahlia Cl, Chsht EN7 66 DQ25
Dahlia Dr, Swan. BR8 207 FF96
Dahlia Gdns, Ilf. IG1 145 EP65
Mitcham CR4 201 DK98
Dahlia Rd, SE2 166 EV77
Dahomey Rd, SW16 181 DJ93
Daiglen Dr, S.Ock. RM15 149 FU73
Sch Daiglen Sch, The, Buck.H. IG9
off Palmerston Rd 102 EJ47
Daimler Way, Wall. SM6 219 DL108
Daines Cl, E12 125 EM62
South Ockendon RM15 149 FU70
Dainford Cl, Brom. BR1 183 ED92
Dainton Cl, Brom. BR1 204 EH95
Daintry Cl, Har. HA3 117 CG56
Daintry Lo, Nthwd. HA6 93 BT52
Daintry Way, E9 279 N4
Sch Dair Ho Sch, Farn.Royal SL2
off Beaconsfield Rd 131 AQ67
Dairsie Rd, SE9 165 EN83
Dairy Cl, NW10 139 CU67
SW6 307 H7
Bromley BR1
off Plaistow La 184 EH94
Enfield EN3 82 DW37
Greenford UB6 137 CD68
Sutton at Hone DA4 188 FP94
Thornton Heath CR7 202 DQ96
Westcott RH4 262 CC137
Dairy Fm La, Hare. UB9 92 BJ54
Dairy Fm Pl, SE15 312 G7
Dairyglen Av, Chsht EN8 67 DY31
Dairy La, SE18 305 J9
Crockham Hill TN8 255 EN134
Dairyman Cl, NW2 119 CY62
Dairyman's Wk, Guil. GU4 243 BB129
Sch Dairy Meadow Prim Sch, Sthl. UB2 off Swift Rd 156 BZ76
Dairy Ms, N2
off East End Rd 120 DE56
SW9 161 DL83
Rom. RM6 126 EX59
Dairy Wk, SW19 179 CY91
Dairy Way, Abb.L. WD5 59 BT29
Daisy Cl, NW9 118 CQ61
Croydon CR0 203 DX102
Daisy Dobbins Wk, N19
off Hillrise Rd 121 DL59
Daisy Dr, Hat. AL10 45 CT15
Daisy La, SW6 307 J10
Daisy Meadow, Egh. TW20 173 BA92
Daisy Rd, E16 291 J4
E18 102 EH54
Dakin Pl, E1 289 L7
Dakota Bldg, SE13
off Deals Gateway 314 B7
Dakota Cl, Wall. SM6 219 DM108
Dakota Gdns, E6 293 H5
Northolt UB5 off Argus Way 136 BY69
Dalberg Rd, SW2 161 DN84
Dalberg Way, SE2
off Lanridge Rd 166 EX76
Dalby Rd, SW18 160 DC84
Dalbys Cres, N17 100 DS51
Dalby St, NW5 275 J5
Dalcross Rd, Houns. TW4 156 BY82
Dale, The, Kes. BR2 222 EK105
Waltham Abbey EN9 68 EE34
Dale Av, Edg. HA8 96 CM53
Hounslow TW4 156 BY83
Dalebury Rd, SW17 180 DE89
Dale Cl, SE3 315 N10
Addlestone KT15 212 BH106
Bookham KT23 246 CC125
Dartford DA1 187 FF86
New Barnet EN5 80 DB44
Pinner HA5 93 BV53
South Ockendon RM15 149 FU72
Dale Ct, Saw. CM21
off The Crest 36 EX06
Slough SL1 151 AQ75
Wat. WD25 off High Rd 59 BU33
Dale Dr, Hayes UB4 135 BT70
Dale End, Dart. DA1
off Dale Rd 187 FF86
Dale Gdns, Wdf.Grn. IG8 102 EH49
Dalegarth Gdns, Pur. CR8 220 DR113
Dale Grn Rd, N11 99 DH48
Dale Gro, N12 98 DC50
Daleham Av, Egh. TW20 173 BA93
Daleham Dr, Uxb. UB8 135 BP72
Daleham Gdns, NW3 274 A3
Daleham Ms, NW3 274 B4
Dalehead, NW1 285 L1
Dalemain Ms, E16 303 P2
Dale Pk Av, Cars. SM5 200 DF103
Dale Pk Rd, SE19 202 DQ95
Dale Rd, NW5 275 H2
SE17 311 H3
Dartford DA1 187 FF86
Greenford UB6 136 CB71
Purley CR8 219 DN112
Southfleet DA13 190 GA91
Sunbury-on-Thames TW16 175 BT94
Sutton SM1 217 CZ105
Swanley BR8 207 FC96
Walton-on-Thames KT12 195 BT101
Dale Row, W11 282 F9
Daleside, Ger.Cr. SL9 112 AY60
Orpington BR6 224 EU106
Daleside Cl, Orp. BR6 224 EU107
Daleside Dr, Pot.B. EN6 63 CZ32
Daleside Gdns, Chig. IG7 103 EQ48
Daleside Rd, SW16 181 DH92
Epsom KT19 216 CR107
Dales Path, Borwd. WD6
off Farriers Way 78 CR43
Dales Rd, Borwd. WD6 78 CR43
Dalestone Ms, Rom. RM3 105 FH51
Dale St, W4 158 CS78
Dale Vw, Erith DA8 167 FF82
Headley KT18 232 CP123
Woking GU21 226 AU118
Dale Vw Av, E4 101 EC47
Dale Vw Cres, E4 101 EC47
Dale Vw Gdns, E4 101 ED48
Daleview Rd, N15 122 DS58
Dale Wk, Dart. DA2 188 FQ88
Dalewood, Welw.G.C. AL7 30 DD10
Dalewood Cl, Horn. RM11 128 FM59
Dalewood Gdns, Wor.Pk. KT4 199 CV103
Dale Wd Rd, Orp. BR6 205 ES101
Daley St, E9 279 K4
Daley Thompson Way, SW8 309 J9
Dalgarno Gdns, W10 282 A6
Dalgarno Way, W10 282 A5
Dalgleish St, E14 289 M9
Daling Way, E3 279 M9
Dalkeith Gro, Stan. HA7 95 CK50
Dalkeith Rd, SE21 182 DQ88
Ilford IG1 125 EQ62
Dallas Rd, NW4 119 CU59
SE26 182 DV90
W5 138 CM71
Sutton SM3 217 CY107
Dallas Ter, Hayes UB3 155 BT76
Dallega Cl, Hayes UB3 135 BR73
Dallinger Rd, SE12 184 EF86
Dalling Rd, W6 159 CV76
Dallington Cl, Hersham KT12 214 BW107
Sch Dallington Sch, EC1 287 H4
Dallington Sq, EC1
off Dallington St 287 H4
Dallington St, EC1 287 H4
Dallin Rd, SE18 165 EP80
Bexleyheath DA6 166 EX84
Sch Dalmain Prim Sch, SE23
off Grove Cl 183 DY88
Dalmain Rd, SE23 183 DX88
Dalmally Pas, Croy. CR0
off Morland Rd 202 DT101
Dalmally Rd, Croy. CR0 202 DT101
Dalmeny Av, N7 276 A2
SW16 201 DN96
Dalmeny Cl, Wem. HA0 137 CJ65
Dalmeny Cres, Houns. TW3 157 CD84
Dalmeny Rd, N7 275 P1
Carshalton SM5 218 DG108
Erith DA8 167 FB81
New Barnet EN5 80 DC44
Worcester Park KT4 199 CV104
Dalmeny Way, Epsom KT18 216 CQ113
Dalmeyer Rd, NW10 139 CT65
Dalmore Av, Clay. KT10 215 CF107
Dalmore Rd, SE21 182 DQ89
Dalroy Cl, S.Ock. RM15 149 FU72
Dalrymple Cl, N14 99 DK45
Dalrymple Rd, SE4 163 DY84
DALSTON, E8 278 C6
Dalston Gdns, Stan. HA7 96 CL53
Dalston Junction 278 A5
Dalston Kingsland 277 P4
Dalston La, E8 278 A4
Dalston Sq, E8 278 A5
Dalton Av, Mitch. CR4 200 DE96
Dalton Cl, Hayes UB4 135 BR70
Orpington BR6 205 ES104
Purley CR8 220 DQ112
Dalton Grn, Slou. SL3 153 AZ79
Dalton Rd, Har.Wld HA3 95 CD54
Daltons Rd, Chels. BR6 207 FB104
Swanley BR8 207 FC102
Dalton St, SE27 181 DP89
St. Albans AL3 43 CD19
Dalton Way, Wat. WD17 76 BX43
Dalwood St, SE5 311 N6
Daly Dr, Brom. BR1 205 EN97
Dalyell Rd, SW9 310 C10
Damascene Wk, SE21
off Lovelace Rd 182 DQ88
Damask Ct, Sutt. SM1
off Cleeve Way 200 DB102
Damask Cres, E16 291 J4
Damask Grn, Hem.H. HP1 39 BE21
Sch Dame Alice Owen's Sch, Pot.B. EN6 off Dugdale Hill La 63 CY33
Damer Ter, SW10 307 P5
Dames Rd, E7 124 EG62
Dame St, N1 277 J10
Sch Dame Tipping C of E Prim Sch, Hav.at.Bow. RM4
off North Road 105 FE48
Damien St, E1 288 F8
Damigos Rd, Grav. DA12 191 GM88
Damon Cl, Sid. DA14 186 EV90
Damory Ho, SE16
off Abbeyfield Rd 300 G8

Damphurst La, Dor. RH5 262 BZ139
Damson Ct, Swan. BR8 207 FD98
Damson Dr, Hayes UB3 135 BU73
Damson Gro, Slou. SL1 151 AQ75
Damson Ho, SW16
off Hemlock Cl 201 DK96
Damson Way, Cars. SM5 218 DF110
St. Albans AL4 43 CJ18
Damsonwood Rd, Sthl. UB2 156 CA76
Danbrook Rd, SW16 201 DL95
Danbury Cl, Pilg.Hat. CM15 108 FT43
Romford RM6 126 EX55
Danbury Cres, S.Ock. RM15 149 FV72
Danbury Ms, Wall. SM6 219 DH105
Danbury Rd, Loug. IG10 102 EL45
Rainham RM13 147 FF67
Danbury St, N1 277 H10
Danbury Way, Wdf.Grn. IG8 102 EJ51
Danby St, SE15 312 A10
Dancer Rd, SW6 306 G7
Richmond TW9 158 CN83
DANCERS HILL, Barn. EN5 79 CW35
Dancers Hill Rd, Barn. EN5 79 CY36
Dancers La, Barn. EN5 79 CW35
Dance Sq, EC1 287 J3
Dandelion Cl, Rush Grn RM7 127 FE61
Dando Cres, SE3 164 EH83
Dandridge Cl, SE10 303 M10
Slough SL3 152 AX77
Dandridge Dr, B.End SL8
off Millside 110 AC60
Danebury, New Adgtn CR0 221 EB107
Danebury Av, SW15 178 CS86
Daneby Rd, SE6 183 EB90
Dane Cl, Amer. HP7 72 AT41
Bexley DA5 186 FA87
Orpington BR6 223 ER106
Dane Ct, Wok. GU22 227 BF115
Danecourt Gdns, Croy. CR0 202 DT104
Danecroft Rd, SE24 182 DQ85
Sch Danegrove Prim Sch, Years 2-6,
Barn. EN4 *off Windsor Dr* 80 DE44
Reception & Year 1, E.Barn. EN4
off Ridgeway Av 80 DF44
Danehill Wk, Sid. DA14
off Hatherley Rd 186 EU90
Jct Daneholes Rbt,
Grays RM16 170 GD76
Danehurst Cl, Egh. TW20 172 AY93
Danehurst Gdns, Ilf. IG4 124 EL57
Danehurst St, SW6 306 E6
Daneland, Barn. EN4 80 DF44
Danemead, Hodd. EN11 33 EA14
Danemead Gro, Nthlt. UB5 116 CB64
Danemere St, SW15 306 B10
Dane Pl, E3 279 N10
Dane Rd, N18 100 DW49
SW19 200 DC95
W13 137 CJ74
Ashford TW15 175 BQ93
Ilford IG1 125 EQ64
Otford TN14 241 FE117
Southall UB1 136 BY73
Warlingham CR6 237 DX117
Danes, The, Park St AL2 60 CC28
Danesbury Pk, Hert. SG14 32 DR08
Danesbury Rd, Felt. TW13 175 BV88
Danes Cl, Nthflt DA11 190 GC90
Oxshott KT22 214 CC114
Danescombe, SE12 184 EG88
Danes Ct, Wem. HA9
off North End Rd 118 CP62
Danescourt Cres, Sutt. SM1 200 DC103
Danescroft, NW4 119 CX57
Danescroft Av, NW4 119 CX57
Danescroft Gdns, NW4 119 CX57
Danesdale Rd, E9 279 L5
Danesfield, SE5 311 N2
Ripley GU23 227 BF123
Danesfield Cl, Walt. KT12 195 BV104
Sch Danesfield Manor Sch,
Walt. KT12 *off Rydens Av* 196 BW103
Danes Gate, Har. HA1 117 CE55
Daneshill, Red. RH1 250 DE133
Danes Hill, Wok. GU22 227 BA118
Daneshill Cl, Red. RH1 250 DE133
Sch Danes Hill Sch,
Main Sch, Oxshott KT22
off Leatherhead Rd 215 CD114
Pre-Prep Dept, Oxshott KT22
off Steels La 214 CC113
Danes Rd, Rom. RM7 127 FC59
Danesrood, Guil. GU1
off Lower Edgeborough Rd 259 AZ135
Dane St, WC1 286 C7
Danes Way, Oxshott KT22 215 CD114
Pilgrim's Hatch CM15 108 FU43
Daneswood Av, SE6 183 EC90
Daneswood Cl, Wey. KT13 213 BP106
Danethorpe Rd, Wem. HA0 137 CK65
Danetree Cl, Epsom KT19 216 CQ108
Sch Danetree Jun Sch, W.Ewell
KT19 *off Danetree Rd* 216 CQ108
Danetree Rd, Epsom KT19 216 CQ108
Danette Gdns, Dag. RM10 126 EZ61
Daneville Rd, SE5 311 L7
Dangan Rd, E11 124 EG58
Daniel Bolt Cl, E14 290 D6
Daniel Cl, N18 100 DW49
SW17 180 DE93
Chafford Hundred RM16 170 FY75
Grays RM16 171 GH76
Hounslow TW4 176 BZ87
Daniel Gdns, SE15 312 A4
Daniells, Welw.G.C. AL7 30 DA08
Daniell Way, Croy. CR0 201 DL102
Daniel Pl, NW4 119 CV58
Daniel Rd, W5 138 CM73
Daniels La, Warl. CR6 237 DZ116
Daniels Rd, SE15 162 DW83
Daniel Way, Bans. SM7 218 DB114
Dan Leno Wk, SW6 307 L5
Dan Mason Dr, W4 158 CR82
Danses Cl, Guil. GU4 243 BD132
Dansey Pl, W1 285 N10
Dansington Rd, Well. DA16 166 EU84
Danson Cres, Well. DA16 166 EV83
Jct Danson Interchange,
Sid. DA15 186 EW86
Danson La, Well. DA16 166 EU84
Danson Mead, Well. DA16 166 EW83
★ Danson Park, Well. DA16 166 EW84
Danson Pk, Bexh. DA6 166 EW84
Sch Danson Prim Sch,
Well. DA16 *off Danson La* 166 EU84
Danson Rd, Bex. DA5 186 EX85
Bexleyheath DA6 186 EX85
Danson Underpass, Sid. DA15
off Danson Rd 186 EW85
Dante Pl, SE11 299 H8
Dante Rd, SE11 298 G8
Danube Apts, N8
off Great Amwell La 121 DM55
Danube Cl, N9 100 DW48
Danube St, SW3 296 D10
Danvers Rd, N8 121 DK56
Danvers St, SW3 308 B3
Danvers Way, Cat. CR3 236 DQ123
Danyon Cl, Rain. RM13 148 FJ68
Danziger Way, Borwd. WD6 78 CQ39
Dapdune Cl, Guil. GU1 242 AW134
Dapdune Rd, Guil. GU1 242 AX134
Dapdune Wf, Guil. GU1 242 AW134
Daphne Gdns, E4
off Gunners Gro 101 EC48
Daphne Jackson Rd,
Guil. GU2 258 AS135
Daphne St, SW18 180 DC86
Daplyn St, E1 288 C6
Darblay Cl, Sand. AL4 28 CM10
D'Arblay St, W1 285 M9
Darby Cl, Cat. CR3 236 DQ122
Darby Cres, Sun. TW16 196 BW96
Darby Dr, Wal.Abb. EN9 67 EC33
Darby Gdns, Sun. TW16 196 BW96
Darcy Av, Wall. SM6 219 DJ105
Darcy Cl, N20 98 DD47
Cheshunt EN8 67 DY31
Coulsdon CR5 235 DP119
D'Arcy Cl, Hutt. CM13 109 GB45
D'Arcy Dr, Har. HA3 117 CK56
Darcy Gdns, Dag. RM9 146 EZ67
D'Arcy Gdns, Har. HA3 118 CL56
Darcy Ho, E8 278 E8
D'Arcy Pl, Ashtd. KT21 232 CM117
Bromley BR2 204 EG98
Darcy Rd, SW16 201 DL96
Islw. TW7 *off London Rd* 157 CG81
D'Arcy Rd, Ashtd. KT21 232 CM117
Sutt. SM3 217 CX105
Dare Gdns, Dag. RM8 126 EY62
Sch Darell Prim Sch, Rich. TW9
off Darell Rd 158 CN83
Darell Rd, Rich. TW9 158 CN83
Darent Cl, Chipstead TN13 256 FC122
DARENTH, Dart. DA2 188 FQ91
Sch Darenth Comm Prim Sch, Dart.
DA2 *off Green St Grn Rd* 189 FT93
Darenth Gdns, West. TN16 255 ER126
Darenth Hill, Dart. DA2 188 FQ92
Jct Darenth Interchange,
Dart. DA2 188 FP90
Darenth La, Dunt.Grn TN13 256 FE121
South Ockendon RM15 149 FU72
Darenth Pk Av, Dart. DA2 189 FR89
Darenth Rd, N16 122 DT59
Darenth DA2 188 FP91
Dartford DA1 188 FM87
Welling DA16 166 EU81
Darenth Way, Horl. RH6 268 DF145
Shoreham TN14 225 FG111
Darenth Wd Rd, Dart. DA2 189 FS89
● Darent Ind Pk, Erith DA8 168 FJ79
Darent Mead, Sutt.H. DA4 208 FP95
H Darent Valley Hosp,
Dart. DA2 189 FS88
Darent Valley Path,
Dart. DA1, DA2, DA4 188 FM89
Sevenoaks TN13, TN14 241 FG115
Darfield Rd, SE4 183 DZ85
Guildford GU4 243 BA131
Darfield Way, W10 282 C10
Darfur St, SW15 159 CX83
Dargate Cl, SE19
off Chipstead Cl 182 DT94
Dariel Cl, Slou. SL1 151 AM75
Darien Rd, SW11 160 DD83
Darkes La, Pot.B. EN6 64 DA32
Darkhole Ride, Wind. SL4 150 AH84
Dark Ho Wk, EC3
off Grant's Quay Wf 299 M1
Dark La, Chsht EN7 66 DU31
Great Warley CM14 107 FU52
Puttenham GU3 260 BM139
Ware (Musley La) SG12 33 DY05
Darlands Dr, Barn. EN5 79 CX43
Darlan Rd, SW6 307 H5
Darlaston Rd, SW19 179 CX94
Darley Cl, Add. KT15 212 BJ106
Croydon CR0 203 DY100
Darley Cft, Park St AL2 60 CB28
Sch Darley Dene Inf Sch,
Add. KT15 *off Garfield Rd* 212 BJ106
Darley Dr, N.Mal. KT3 198 CR96
Darley Gdns, Mord. SM4 200 DB100
Darley Rd, N9 100 DT46
SW11 180 DF86
Darling Rd, SE4 314 A10
Darling Row, E1 288 F5
Darlington Cl, Amer. HP6
off King George V Rd 55 AR38
Darlington Gdns, Rom. RM3 106 FK50
Darlington Path, Rom. RM3
off Darlington Gdns 106 FK50
Darlington Rd, SE27 181 DP92
Darlton Cl, Dart. DA1 167 FF83
Darmaine Cl, S.Croy. CR2 220 DQ108
Darnaway Pl, E14 290 F7
Darndale Cl, E17 101 DZ54
Darnets Fld, Otford TN14 241 FF117
Darnhills, Rad. WD7 77 CG35
Darnicle Hill, Chsht EN7 65 DM25
Darnley Ho, E14 289 M8
Darnley Pk, Wey. KT13 195 BP104
Darnley Rd, E9 278 F5
Gravesend DA11 191 GG88
Grays RM17 *off Stanley Rd* 170 GB79
Woodford Green IG8 102 EG53
Darnley St, Grav. DA11 191 GG87
Darnley Ter, W11 294 D2
Darns Hill, Swan. BR8 207 FC101
Darrell Cl, Slou. SL3 153 AZ77
Darrell Rd, SE22 182 DU85
Darren Cl, N4 121 DM59
Sch Darrick Wd Inf Sch, Orp. BR6
off Lovibonds Av 223 EP105
Sch Darrick Wd Jun Sch, Orp. BR6
off Lovibonds Av 223 EP105
Darrick Wd Rd, Orp. BR6 205 ER103
Sch Darrick Wd Sch, Orp. BR6
off Lovibonds Av 205 EP104
Darrington Rd, Borwd. WD6 78 CL39
Darris Cl, Hayes UB4 136 BY70
Darsley Dr, SW8 309 P6
Dart, The, Hem.H. HP2 40 BN15
Dart Cl, Slou. SL3 153 BB79
Upminster RM14 129 FR58
Dartfields, Rom. RM3 106 FK51
DARTFORD, DA1 & DA2; DA4 188 FJ87
⇌ Dartford 188 FL86
Coll Dartford Adult Ed Cen,
Dart. DA1 *off Highfield Rd* 188 FK87
Dartford Av, N9 82 DW44
Dartford Bridge Comm Prim Sch,
Dart. DA1 168 FM82
Dartford Bypass, Bex. DA5 187 FE88
Dartford DA2 187 FH89
Dartford Gdns, Chad.Hth RM6
off Heathfield Pk Dr 126 EV57
Sch Dartford Gram Sch, Dart. DA1
off West Hill 188 FJ86
Sch Dartford Gram Sch for Girls,
Dart. DA1 *off Shepherds La* 188 FJ87
★ Dartford Heath, Dart. DA1 187 FG88
Dartford Heath, Bex. DA5 187 FF88
Dartford Heath Retail Pk,
Dart, DA1 188 FJ88
Dartford Ho, SE1
off Longfield Est 300 B9
★ Dartford Mus, Dart. DA1 188 FL87
Dartford Rd, Bex. DA5 187 FC88
Dartford DA1 187 FG86
Farningham DA4 208 FP95
Sevenoaks TN13 257 FJ124
Dartford St, SE17 311 K2
Coll Dartford Tech Coll, Dart. DA1
off Heath La 188 FJ87
Dartford Tunnel, Dart. DA1 169 FR83
Purfleet RM19 169 FR83
Dartford Tunnel App Rd,
Dart. DA1 188 FN86
Dart Grn, S.Ock. RM15 149 FV72
Dartmoor Wk, E14 302 B8
Dartmouth Av, Wok. GU21 211 BC114
Dartmouth Cl, W11 283 H8
Dartmouth Grn, Wok. GU21 211 BD114
Dartmouth Gro, SE10 314 F7
Dartmouth Hill, SE10 314 F7
Dartmouth Ho, Kings.T. KT2
off Kingsgate Rd 198 CL95
DARTMOUTH PARK, NW5 121 DH62
Dartmouth Pk Av, NW5 121 DH62
Dartmouth Pk Hill, N19 121 DH60
NW5 121 DH60
Dartmouth Pk Rd, NW5 121 DH63
Dartmouth Path, Wok. GU21 211 BD114
Dartmouth Pl, SE23
off Dartmouth Rd 182 DW89
W4 158 CS79
Dartmouth Rd, E16 291 N8
NW2 272 C4
NW4 119 CU58
SE23 182 DW90
SE26 182 DW90
Bromley BR2 204 EG101
Ruislip HA4 115 BU62
Dartmouth Row, SE10 314 F8
Dartmouth St, SW1 297 N5
Dartmouth Ter, SE10 314 G7
Dartnell Av, W.Byf. KT14 212 BH112
Dartnell Cl, W.Byf. KT14 212 BH112
Dartnell Ct, W.Byf. KT14 212 BJ112
Dartnell Cres, W.Byf. KT14 212 BH112
Dartnell Pk Rd, W.Byf. KT14 212 BJ111
Dartnell Pl, W.Byf. KT14 212 BH112
Dartnell Rd, Croy. CR0 202 DT101
Dartrey Twr, SW10
off Blantyre St 308 A4
Dartrey Wk, SW10
off Blantyre St 308 A4
Dart St, W10 282 F2
Dartview Cl, Grays RM17 170 GE77
Darvel Cl, Wok. GU21 226 AU116
Darvell Dr, Chesh. HP5 54 AN29
Darvells Yd, Chorl. WD3 73 BD41
Darville Rd, N16 122 DT62
Darvills La, Slou. SL1 151 AR75
Darwell Cl, E6 293 L1
Darwen Pl, E2 278 E9
Darwin Cl, N11 99 DH48
Orpington BR6 223 ER106
St. Albans AL3 43 CE16
Darwin Ct, SE17 299 M9
Guildford GU1 242 AX130
Darwin Dr, Sthl. UB1 136 CB72
Darwin Gdns, Wat. WD19 94 BW50
Darwin Ri, Nthflt. DA11 190 GB88
Darwin Rd, N22 99 DP53
W5 157 CJ78
Slough SL3 153 AZ75
Tilbury RM18 171 GF81
Welling DA16 165 ET83
Darwin St, SE17 299 M8
Daryngton Dr, Grnf. UB6 137 CD68
Guildford GU1 243 BB134
Dashes, The, Harl. CM20 35 ES14
Dashwood Cl, Bexh. DA6 186 FA85
Slough SL3 152 AW77
West Byfleet KT14 212 BJ112
Dashwood Lang Rd, Add. KT15 212 BK105
Dashwood Rd, N8 121 DM58
Gravesend DA11 191 GG89
Dassett Rd, SE27 181 DP92
Datchelor Pl, SE5
off Camberwell Church St 311 M7
DATCHET, Slou. SL3 152 AW81
⇌ Datchet 152 AV81
Datchet Cl, Hem.H. HP2 41 BP15
Datchet Pl, Datchet SL3 152 AV81
Datchet Rd, SE6 183 DZ90
Horton SL3 153 AZ83
Old Windsor SL4 152 AU84
Slough SL3 152 AT77
Windsor SL4 151 AR80
Sch Datchet St. Mary's C of E
Prim Sch, Datchet SL3
off The Green 152 AV81
Datchworth Ct, N4
off Queens Dr 122 DQ62
Datchworth Turn, Hem.H. HP2 41 BQ20
Date St, SE17 311 L1
Daubeney Gdns, N17 100 DQ52
Daubeney Pl, Hmptn. TW12
off High St 196 CC95
Sch Daubeney Prim Sch, E5 279 L1
Daubeney Rd, E5 279 L1
N17 100 DQ52
Daubeney Twr, SE8 301 N9
Dault Rd, SW18 180 DC86
Davall Ho, Grays RM17
off Argent St 170 GB79
Davema Cl, Chis. BR7 205 EN95
Sch Davenant Foundation Sch,
Loug. IG10 *off Chester Rd* 85 EQ38
Davenant Rd, N19 121 DK61
Croydon CR0
off Duppas Hill Rd 219 DP105
Davenant St, E1 288 D7
Davenham Av, Nthwd. HA6 93 BT49
Sch Davenies Sch, Beac. HP9
off Station Rd 89 AL53
Davenport, Ch.Lang. CM17 52 EY16
Davenport Cl, Tedd. TW11 177 CG93
Davenport Ho, SE11
off Walnut Tree Wk 298 E8
Davenport Rd, SE6 183 EB86
Sidcup DA14 186 EX89
Daventer Dr, Stan. HA7 95 CF52
Daventry Av, E17 123 EA58
Daventry Cl, Colnbr. SL3 153 BF81
Daventry Gdns, Rom. RM3 106 FJ50
Daventry Grn, Rom. RM3
off Hailsham Rd 106 FJ50
Daventry Rd, Rom. RM3 106 FJ50
Daventry St, NW1 284 C6
Davern Cl, SE10 303 L9
Davey Cl, N7 276 D5
N13 99 DM50
Davey Gdns, Bark. IG11 146 EU70
Davey Rd, E9 280 A6
Davey St, SE15 312 B3
David Av, Grnf. UB6 137 CE69
David Cl, Harling. UB3 155 BR80
David Dr, Rom. RM3 106 FN51
Davidge Pl, Knot.Grn HP9 88 AJ50
Davidge St, SE1 298 G5
David Lee Pt, E15 281 K9
Sch David Livingstone Prim Sch,
Th.Hth. CR7
off Northwood Rd 202 DQ95
David Ms, SE10 314 E4
W1 284 F6
David Rd, Colnbr. SL3 153 BF82
Dagenham RM8 126 EY61
Davidson Gdns, SW8 310 A5
Davidson La, Har. HA1
off Grove Hill 117 CF59
Sch Davidson Prim Sch,
Croy. CR0 *off Dartnell Rd* 202 DT101
Davidson Rd, Croy. CR0 202 DT100
Davidson Terraces, E7
off Windsor Rd 124 EH64
Davidson Way, Rom. RM7 127 FE58
Davids Rd, SE23 182 DW88
David St, E15 281 H4
David's Way, Ilf. IG6 103 ES52
David Twigg Cl, Kings.T. KT2 198 CL95
Davies Cl, Croy. CR0 202 DU100
Rainham RM13 148 FJ69
Coll Davies Laing & Dick
Indep Coll, W1 285 H8
Davies La, E11 124 EE61
Sch Davies La Prim Sch, E11
off Davies La 124 EF61
Davies Ms, W1 285 J10
Davies St, W1 285 J10
Hertford SG13 32 DS09
Davies Wk, Islw. TW7 157 CD81
Davies Way, Loud. HP10 88 AC54
Da Vinci Lo, SE10 303 M7
Davington Gdns, Dag. RM8 126 EV64
Davington Rd, Dag. RM8 146 EV65
Davinia Cl, Wdf.Grn. IG8
off Deacon Way 103 EM51
Davis Av, Nthflt DA11 190 GE88
Davis Cl, Sev. TN13 257 FJ122
Davis Ct, St.Alb. AL1 43 CE20
Davison Cl, Chsht EN8 67 DX28
Epsom KT19 216 CP111
Davison Dr, Chsht EN8 67 DX28
Davison Rd, Slou. SL3 153 AZ78
Davis Rd, W3 139 CT74
Aveley RM15 149 FR74
Chafford Hundred RM16 170 FZ76
Chessington KT9 216 CN105
Weybridge KT13 212 BM110
● Davis Rd Ind Pk, Chess. KT9 216 CN105
Davis St, E13 292 B1
Davisville Rd, W12 159 CU75
Davis Way, Sid. DA14 186 EY93
Davos Cl, Wok. GU22 226 AY119
Davys Cl, Wheat. AL4 28 CL08
Davys Pl, Grav. DA12 191 GL93
Dawell Dr, Bigg.H. TN16 238 EJ117
Dawes Av, Horn. RM12 128 FK62
Isleworth TW7 177 CG85
Dawes Cl, Chesh. HP5 54 AP32
Greenhithe DA9 189 FT85
Dawes Ct, Esher KT10 214 CB105
Dawes E Rd, Burn. SL1 130 AJ70
DAWESGREEN, Reig. RH2 265 CT140
Dawes Ho, SE17 299 L9
Dawes La, Sarratt WD3 73 BE37
Dawes Moor Cl, Slou. SL2 132 AW72
Dawes Rd, SW6 306 E4
Uxbridge UB10 134 BL68
Dawes St, SE17 299 M10
Dawley, Welw.G.C. AL7 29 CZ06
Dawley Av, Uxb. UB8 135 BQ71
Dawley Ct, Hem.H. HP2 40 BM16
Dawley Grn, S.Ock. RM15 149 FU72
Dawley Par, Hayes UB3 135 BQ73
Dawley Ride, Colnbr. SL3 153 BE81
Dawley Rd, Hayes UB3 135 BR73
Uxbridge UB8 135 BQ73
Dawlish Av, N13 99 DL49
SW18 180 DB89
Perivale UB6 137 CG68
Dawlish Dr, Ilf. IG3 125 ES63
Pinner HA5 116 BY57
Ruislip HA4 115 BU61
Sch Dawlish Prim Sch, E10
off Jesse Rd 123 EC60
Dawlish Rd, E10 123 EC61
N17 122 DU55
NW2 272 D4
Dawlish Wk, Rom. RM3 106 FJ53
Dawnay Gdns, SW18 180 DD89
Dawnay Rd, SW18 180 DC89
Bookham KT23 246 CB126
Sch Dawnay Sch, The, Bkhm KT23
off Griffin Way 246 CA126
Dawn Cl, Houns. TW4 156 BY83
Dawn Cres, E15 281 H8
Dawn Redwood Cl,
Horton SL3 153 BA83
Dawpool Rd, NW2 119 CT61
Daws Hill, E4 83 EC41
Daws La, NW7 97 CT50
Dawson Av, Bark. IG11 145 ES66
Orpington BR5 206 EV96
Dawson Cl, SE18 165 EQ77
Hayes UB3 135 BR71
Windsor SL4 151 AN82
Dawson Dr, Rain. RM13 147 FH66
Swanley BR8 187 FE94
Dawson Gdns, Bark. IG11 145 ET66
Dawson Hts Est, SE22 182 DU87
Dawson Pl, W2 283 J10
Dawson Rd, NW2 272 B2
Byfleet KT14 212 BK111
Kingston upon Thames KT1 198 CM97
Dawson St, E2 288 B1
Dawson Ter, N9 100 DW45
Daws Pl, Red. RH1 251 DJ131
Dax Ct, Sun. TW16
off Thames St 196 BW97
Daybrook Rd, SW19 200 DB96
Day Dr, Dag. RM8 126 EX60
Daye Mead, Welw.G.C. AL7 30 DB12
Daylesford Av, SW15 159 CU84
Daylesford Gro, Slou. SL1 151 AM75
Daylop Dr, Chig. IG7 104 EV48
Daymer Gdns, Pnr. HA5 115 BV56
Daymerslea Ridge, Lthd. KT22 231 CJ121
Days Acre, S.Croy. CR2 220 DT110
Daysbrook Rd, SW2 181 DM89
Days Cl, Hat. AL10 45 CT18
Dayseys Hill, Outwood RH1 267 DN143
Days La, Pilg.Hat. CM15 108 FU42
Sidcup DA15 185 ES87
Sch Days La Prim Sch, Sid. DA15
off Days La 185 ET86
Days Mead, Hat. AL10 45 CT18
Dayspring, Guil. GU2 242 AV130
Dayton Dr, Erith DA8 168 FK78
Dayton Gro, SE15 312 G6
Deacon Cl, Down. KT11 229 BV119
Purley CR8 219 DL109
St. Albans AL1
off Creighton Av 43 CD24
Deacon Fld, Guil. GU2
off Cathedral Hill 242 AU133
Deacon Ms, N1 277 M7
Deacon Pl, Cat. CR3 236 DQ123
Deacon Rd, NW2 119 CU64
Kingston upon Thames KT2 198 CM95
Deacons Cl, Els. WD6 78 CN42
Pinner HA5 93 BV54
Deaconsfield Rd, Hem.H. HP3 40 BK23
Deacons Hts, Els. WD6 78 CN44
Deacons Hill, Wat. WD19 76 BW44
Deacons Hill Rd, Els. WD6 78 CM42
Deacons Leas, Orp. BR6 223 ER105
Deacons Ri, N2 120 DD57
Deacons Wk, Hmptn. TW12
off Bishops Gro 176 BZ91
● Deacon Trd Est, E4
off Cabinet Way 101 DZ51
Deacon Way, SE17 299 J8
Woodford Green IG8 103 EM52
Deadfield La, Hert. SG14 30 DF13
Deadhearn La, Ch.St.G. HP8 90 AY46
Deadman's Ash La,
Sarratt WD3 74 BH36
Deakin Cl, Wat. WD18
off Chenies Way 93 BS45
Deal Av, Slou. SL1 131 AM72
Deal Ms, W5 157 CK77
Deal Porters Wk, SE16 301 J4
Deal Porters Way, SE16 301 H6
Deal Rd, SW17 180 DG93
Deals Gateway, SE13 314 B6
Deal St, E1 288 C6
Dealtry Rd, SW15 159 CW84
Deal Wk, SW9 310 E5
Deanacre Cl, Chal.St.P. SL9 90 AY51
Dean Av, Hodd. EN11 49 DX17
DEAN BOTTOM, Dart. DA4 209 FV97
Dean Bradley St, SW1 298 A7
Dean Cl, E9 279 H2
SE16 301 K3
Uxbridge UB10 134 BM66
Windsor SL4 151 AK83
Woking GU22 227 BE115
Dean Ct, SW8 *off Thorncroft St* 310 A5
Wembley HA0 117 CH62
Deancroft Rd, Chal.St.P. SL9 90 AY51
Deancross St, E1 288 G9
Dean Dr, Stan. HA7 96 CL54
Deane Av, Ruis. HA4 116 BW64
Deane Cft Rd, Pnr. HA5 115 BV58
Deanery Cl, N2 120 DE56
Deanery Ms, W1 297 H2
Deanery Rd, E15 281 J5
Crockham Hill TN8 255 EQ134
Deanery St, W1 297 H2
Sch Deanesfield Prim Sch,
Ruis. HA4 *off Queens Wk* 116 BX63
Deane Way, Ruis. HA4 115 BV58
Dean Farrar St, SW1 297 N6
Dean Fld, Bov. HP3 57 BA27
Dean Gdns, E17 123 ED56
W13 *off Northfield Av* 137 CH74
Deanhill Ct, SW14 158 CP84
Deanhill Rd, SW14 158 CP84
Dean Ho, E1 *off Tarling St* 288 G9
N16 *off Stamford Hill* 122 DT60
Dean La, EC4
off New Fetter La 286 F8
Redhill RH1 235 DH123
Dean Moore Cl, St.Alb. AL1 43 CD21
Dean Oak La, Leigh RH2 265 CW144
Dean Rd, NW2 272 A5
SE28 146 EU73
Croydon CR0 220 DR105
Hampton TW12 176 CA92
Hounslow TW3 176 CB85
Dean Ryle St, SW1 298 A8
Deansbrook Cl, Edg. HA8 96 CQ51
Sch Deansbrook Inf Sch, NW7
off Hale Dr 96 CQ51
Sch Deansbrook Jun Sch, NW7
off Hale Dr 96 CQ51
Deansbrook Rd, Edg. HA8 96 CQ52
Deans Bldgs, SE17 299 L9
Deans Cl, W4 158 CP79
Abbots Langley WD5 59 BR32
Amersham HP6 72 AT37
Edg. HA8 96 CQ51
Stoke Poges SL2 132 AV67
Walton on the Hill KT20 233 CV124
Dean's Cl, Croy. CR0 202 DT104
Deans Ct, EC4 287 H9
Deanscroft Av, NW9 118 CQ61
Deans Dr, N13 99 DP51
Edgware HA8 96 CR50
● Deans Factory Est,
Rain. RM13 *off Lambs La N* 148 FK70
Deansfield, Cat. CR3 252 DT125

Deansfield Prim Sch, SE9
off Dairsie Rd 165 EN83
Deans Gdns, St.Alb. AL4 43 CG16
Dean's Gate Cl, SE23 183 DX90
Deans La, W4 off Deans Cl 158 CP79
Edgware HA8 96 CQ51
Nutfield RH1 251 DN133
Walton on the Hill KT20 233 CV124
Deans Ms, W1 285 K8
Deans Rd, W7 137 CF74
South Merstham RH1 251 DJ130
Sutton SM1 200 DB104
Warley CM14 108 FV49
Dean Stanley St, SW1 298 A7
Dean St, E7 281 N2
W1 285 N8
Deans Wk, Couls. CR5 235 DN118
Deans Way, Edg. HA8 96 CQ50
Deansway, N2 120 DD56
N9 100 DS48
Chesham HP5 54 AP29
Hemel Hempstead HP3 40 BM23
Dean's Yd, SW1 297 P6
Dean Trench St, SW1 298 A7
Dean Wk, Bkhm KT23 246 CB126
Edgware HA8
off Deansbrook Rd 96 CQ51
Deanway, Ch.St.G. HP8 90 AU48
Dean Way, Sthl. UB2 156 CB75
Dean Wd Rd, Jordans HP9 89 AR52
Dearne Cl, Stan. HA7 95 CG50
De'Arn Gdns, Mitch. CR4 200 DE97
Dearsley Rd, Enf. EN1 82 DU41
Deason St, E15 280 F9
De Barowe Ms, N5 277 H1
DEBDEN, Loug. IG10 85 ER41
Debden 85 EQ42
Debden Cl, NW9
off Kenley Av 96 CS54
Kingston upon Thames KT2 177 CK92
Woodford Green IG8 102 EJ52
DEBDEN GREEN, Loug. IG10 85 EQ38
Debden Grn, Loug. IG10 85 EP38
Debden La, Loug. IG10 85 EP38
Debden Pk High Sch,
Loug. IG10 off Willingale Rd 85 ER40
Debden Rd, Loug. IG10 85 EP38
Debden Wk, Horn. RM12 147 FH65
De Beauvoir, N1
off Tottenham Rd 277 P5
De Beauvoir Cres, N1 277 N8
De Beauvoir Est, N1 277 M8
De Beauvoir Prim Sch, N1 277 P5
De Beauvoir Rd, N1 277 N6
De Beauvoir Sq, N1 277 P7
DE BEAUVOIR TOWN, N1 277 M8
Debenham Rd, Chsht EN7 66 DV27
Debnams Rd, SE16 300 G9
De Bohun Av, N14 81 DH44
De Bohun Prim Sch, N14
off Green Rd 81 DH43
Deborah Cl, Islw. TW7 157 CE81
Deborah Cres, Ruis. HA4 115 BR59
Debrabant Cl, Erith DA8 167 FD79
De Brome Rd, Felt. TW13 176 BW88
De Burgh Gdns, Tad. KT20 233 CX119
De Burgh Pk, Bans. SM7 234 DB115
Deburgh Rd, SW19 180 DC94
Decies Way, Stoke P. SL2 132 AU67
Decima St, SE1 299 N6
Deck Cl, SE16 301 K4
De Coubertin St, E20 280 F4
Decoy Av, NW11 119 CY57
De Crespigny Pk, SE5 311 L8
Dedswell Dr, W.Clan. GU4 244 BG128
DEDWORTH, Wind. SL4 151 AL81
Dedworth Dr, Wind. SL4 151 AL81
Dedworth Grn First Sch,
Wind. SL4 off Smiths La 151 AL82
Dedworth Mid Sch,
Wind. SL4 off Smiths La 151 AL82
Dedworth Rd, Wind. SL4 151 AL82
Dee, The, Hem.H. HP2 40 BM15
Dee Cl, Upmin. RM14 129 FS58
Deeley Rd, SW8 309 N6
Deena Cl, W3 138 CM72
Slough SL1 131 AL73
Deep Acres, Amer. HP6 55 AN36
Deepdale, SW19 179 CX91
Deepdale Av, Brom. BR2 204 EF98
Deepdale Cl, N11 98 DG51
Deepdene, W5 138 CM70
Potters Bar EN6 63 CX31
Deepdene Av, Croy. CR0 202 DT104
Dorking RH4, RH5 247 CJ134
Deepdene Av Rd, Dor. RH4 247 CJ134
Deepdene Cl, E11 124 EG56
Deepdene Ct, N21 81 DP44
Bromley BR2 204 EE97
Deepdene Dr, Dor. RH5 263 CJ135
Deepdene Gdns, SW2 181 DM87
Dorking RH4 263 CH135
Deepdene Pk Rd, Dor. RH5 263 CJ135
Deepdene Path, Loug. IG10 85 EN42
Deepdene Rd, SE5 162 DR84
Loughton IG10 85 EN42
Welling DA16 166 EU83
Deepdene Vale, Dor. RH4 263 CJ135
Deepdene Wd, Dor. RH5 263 CJ136
Deep Fld, Datchet SL3 152 AV80
Deepfields, Horl. RH6 268 DF146
Deepfield Way, Couls. CR5 235 DL116
Deep Pool La, Chobham GU24 210 AV114
Deeprose Cl, Guil. GU2 242 AV130
Deepwell Cl, Islw. TW7 157 CG81
Deepwood La, Grnf. UB6 137 CD69
Deerbarn Rd, Guil. GU2 242 AV133
Deerbrook Rd, SE24 181 DP88
Deer Cl, Hert. SG13 32 DT09
Deercote Ct, Chsht EN8
off Glen Luce 67 DX31
Deerdale Rd, SE24 162 DQ84
Deere Av, Rain. RM13 147 FG65
Deerfield Cl, NW9 119 CT57
Ware SG12 33 DX05
Deerhurst Cl, Felt. TW13 175 BU91
Deerhurst Cres,
Hmptn H. TW12 176 CC92
Deerhurst Rd, NW2 272 D5
SW16 181 DM92
Deerings Dr, Pnr. HA5 115 BU57
Deerings Rd, Reig. RH2 250 DB134
Deerleap Gro, E4 83 EB43
Deerleap La, Sev. TN14 224 EX113
Deerleap Rd, Westc. RH4 262 CB137
Deer Mead Ct, Rom. RM1
off Junction Rd 127 FF57
Dee Rd, Rich. TW9 158 CM84
Windsor SL4 150 AJ80
Deer Pk, Harl. CM19 51 EN18
Deer Pk Cl, Kings.T. KT2 178 CP94
Deer Pk Gdns, Mitch. CR4 200 DD97
Deer Pk Rd, SW19 200 DB96
Deer Pk Wk, Chesh. HP5 54 AS28
Deer Pk Way, Wal.Abb. EN9 83 EB36
West Wickham BR4 204 EF103
Deers Fm Cl, Wisley GU23 228 BL116
Deerswood Av, Hat. AL10 45 CV20
Deerswood Cl, Cat. CR3 236 DU124
Deeside Rd, SW17 180 DD90
Dee St, E14 290 F8
Deeves Hall La, Pot.B. EN6 62 CS33
Dee Way, Epsom KT19 216 CS110
Romford RM1 105 FE53
Defence Cl, SE28 145 ES74
Defence Medical Rehab Cen
Headley Ct, Epsom KT18 232 CP123
Defence Sch of Languages,
Seer Grn HP9
off Wilton Pk 89 AP54
Defiance Wk, SE18 305 J7
Defiant Way, Wall. SM6 219 DL108
Defoe Av, Rich. TW9 158 CN80
Defoe Cl, SE16 301 N5
SW17 180 DE93
Erith DA8 off Selkirk Dr 167 FF81
Defoe Ho, EC2
off The Barbican 287 J6
Defoe Par, Grays RM16 171 GH76
Defoe Pl, EC2
off The Barbican 287 K6
SW17 off Lessingham Av 180 DF91
Defoe Rd, N16 122 DS61
Defoe Way, Rom. RM5 104 FA51
De Frene Rd, SE26 183 DX91
De Gama Pl, E14
off Maritime Quay 302 B10
Degema Rd, Chis. BR7 185 EP92
Dehar Cres, NW9 119 CU59
★ De Havilland Aircraft Heritage
Cen, St.Alb. AL2 62 CP29
De Havilland Cl, Hat. AL10 45 CT17
Dehavilland Cl, Nthlt. UB5 136 BX69
De Havilland Cl, Ilf. IG1
off Piper Way 125 ER60
Shenley WD7
off Armstrong Gdns 62 CL32
De Havilland Dr, SE18 165 EP79
Weybridge KT13 212 BL111
De Havilland Prim Sch,
Hat. AL10 off Travellers La 45 CU20
De Havilland Rd, Edg. HA8 96 CP54
Hounslow TW5 156 BW80
De Havilland Way, Abb.L. WD5 59 BT32
Stanwell TW19 174 BK86
Deimos Dr, Hem.H. HP2 40 BN17
Dekker Rd, SE21 182 DS86
Delabole Rd, Merst. RH1 251 DL129
Delacourt Rd, SE3
off Old Dover Rd 164 EH80
Delafield Ho, E1 288 D9
Delafield Rd, SE7 304 B10
Grays RM17 170 GD78
Delaford Cl, Iver SL0 133 BF72
Delaford Rd, SE16 300 F10
Delaford St, SW6 306 F4
Delagarde Rd, West. TN16 255 EQ126
Delahay Ri, Berk. HP4 38 AV17
Delamare Cres, Croy. CR0 202 DW100
Delamare Rd, Chsht EN8 67 DZ30
Delamere Ct, E17
off Hawker Pl 101 EC54
Delamere Gdns, NW7 96 CR51
Delamere Rd, SW20 199 CX95
W5 138 CL74
Borehamwood WD6 78 CP39
Hayes UB4 136 BX73
Reigate RH2 266 DB138
Delamere St, W2 283 N6
Delamere Ter, W2 283 M6
Delancey Pas, NW1 275 K9
Delancey St, NW1 275 J9
Delaporte Cl, Epsom KT17 216 CS112
De Lapre Cl, Orp. BR5 206 EX101
De Lara Way, Wok. GU21 226 AX118
Delargy Cl, Grays RM16 171 GH76
De Laune St, SE17 310 G1
Delaware Rd, W9 283 L4
Delawyk Cres, SE24 182 DQ86
Delcombe Av, Wor.Pk. KT4 199 CW102
Delderfield, Lthd. KT22 231 CK120
Delft Way, SE22
off East Dulwich Gro 182 DS85
Delhi Rd, Enf. EN1 100 DT45
Delhi St, N1 276 B9
Delia St, SW18 180 DB87
Delisle Rd, SE28 145 ES74
Delius Cl, Els. WD6 77 CJ44
Delius Gro, E15 280 G10
Dell, The, SE2 166 EU78
SE19 202 DT95
Bexley DA5 187 FE88
Brentford TW8 157 CJ79
Chalfont St. Peter SL9 90 AY51
Feltham TW14 175 BV87
Great Warley CM13 107 FV51
Greenhithe DA9 189 FV85
Hertford SG13 32 DQ12
Horley RH6 269 DH147
Northwood HA6 93 BS47
Penn HP10 88 AC46
Pinner HA5 94 BX54
Radlett WD7 77 CG36
Reigate RH2 250 DA133
St. Albans AL1 43 CG18
Tadworth KT20 233 CW121
Waltham Abbey EN9
off Greenwich Way 83 EC36
Wembley HA0 117 CH64
Woking GU21 226 AW118
Woodford Green IG8 102 EH48
Della Path, E5 122 DV62
Dellbow Rd, Felt. TW14 175 BV85
Dell Cl, E15 281 H8
Chesham HP5 54 AM29
Farnham Common SL2 111 AQ64
Fetcham KT22 231 CE123
Mickleham RH5 247 CJ127
Wallington SM6 219 DJ105
Woodford Green IG8 102 EH48
Dellcott Cl, Welw.G.C. AL8 29 CV08
Dellcut Rd, Hem.H. HP2 40 BN18
Dell Fm Rd, Ruis. HA4 115 BR57
Dellfield, Chesh. HP5 54 AN29
St. Albans AL1 43 CF21
Dellfield Av, Berk. HP4 38 AV17
Dellfield Cl, Beck. BR3 203 EC95
Berkhamsted HP4 38 AU17
Radlett WD7 77 CE35
Watford WD17 75 BU40
Dellfield Cres, Uxb. UB8 134 BJ70
Dellfield Par, Cowley UB8 134 BJ70
Dellfield Rd, Hat. AL10 45 CU18
Dell La, Epsom KT17 217 CU106
Dell Lees, Seer Grn HP9 89 AQ51
Dellmeadow, Abb.L. WD5 59 BS30
Dell Meadow, Hem.H. HP3 40 BL24
Dell Orchard, Winch.Hill HP7
off Fagnall La 88 AJ45
Dellors Cl, Barn. EN5 79 CX43
Dellow Cl, Ilf. IG2 125 ER59
Dellow St, E1 288 F10
Dell Ri, Park St AL2 60 CB26
Dell Rd, Enf. EN3 82 DW38
Epsom KT17 217 CU107
Grays RM17 170 GB77
Watford WD24 75 BU37
West Drayton UB7 154 BM76
Dells, The, Hem.H. HP3 41 BP21
Dells Cl, E4 101 EB45
Teddington TW11
off Middle La 177 CF93
Dellside, Hare. UB9 114 BJ57
Dell Side, Wat. WD24 75 BU37
Dell's Ms, SW1 297 M9
Dellsome La, Coln.Hth AL4 44 CS23
North Mymms AL9 45 CV23
Dellswood Cl, Hert. SG13 32 DS10
Dells Wd Cl, Hodd. EN11 33 DZ14
Dell Wk, N.Mal. KT3 198 CS96
Dell Way, W13 137 CJ72
Dellwood, Rick. WD3 92 BH46
Dellwood Gdns, Ilf. IG5 125 EN55
Delmar Av, Hem.H. HP2 41 BR21
Delmare Cl, SW9 161 DM84
Delmeade Rd, Chesh. HP5 54 AN32
Delme Cres, SE3 164 EH82
Delmey Cl, Croy. CR0 202 DT104
Deloraine St, SE8 314 A7
Delorme St, W6 306 C3
Delta Bungalows, Horl. RH6
off Michael Cres 268 DG150
● Delta Cen, Wem. HA0
off Mount Pleasant 138 CM67
Delta Cl, Chobham GU24 210 AT110
Worcester Park KT4 198 CS104
Delta Ct, NW2 119 CU61
Delta Dr, Horl. RH6
off Cheyne Wk 268 DG150
Delta Gain, Wat. WD19 94 BX47
Delta Gro, Nthlt. UB5 136 BX69
Delta Ho, N1 off Nile St 287 L2
● Delta Pk Ind Est, Enf. EN3 83 DZ40
Delta Rd, Chobham GU24 210 AT110
Hutton CM13 109 GD44
Woking GU21 227 BA116
Worcester Park KT4 198 CS104
Delta St, E2 288 C2
Delta Way, Egh. TW20 193 BC95
De Luci Rd, Erith DA8 167 FC78
De Lucy Prim Sch, SE2
off Cookhill Rd 166 EV75
De Lucy St, SE2 166 EV77
Delvan Cl, SE18
off Ordnance Rd 165 EN80
Delvers Mead, Dag. RM10 127 FC63
Delverton Rd, SE17 311 H1
Delves, Tad. KT20 233 CX121
Delvino Rd, SW6 307 J7
De Mandeville Gate, Enf. EN1
off Southbury Rd 82 DU42
De Mel Cl, Epsom KT19 216 CP112
Demesne Rd, Wall. SM6 219 DK106
Demeta Cl, Wem. HA9 118 CQ62
De Montfort Par, SW16
off Streatham High Rd 181 DL90
De Montfort Rd, SW16 181 DL90
De Morgan Rd, SW6 307 M10
Dempster Cl, Long Dit. KT6 197 CJ102
Dempster Rd, SW18 180 DC85
Denbar Par, Rom. RM7
off Mawney Rd 127 FC56
Denberry Dr, Sid. DA14 186 EV90
Denbigh Cl, W11 283 H10
Chislehurst BR7 185 EM93
Hemel Hempstead HP2 40 BL21
Hornchurch RM11 128 FN56
Ruislip HA4 115 BT61
Southall UB1 136 BZ72
Sutton SM1 217 CZ106
Denbigh Dr, Hayes UB3 155 BQ75
Denbigh Gdns, Rich. TW10 178 CM85
Denbigh Ms, SW1 297 L9
Denbigh Pl, SW1 297 L10
Denbigh Rd, E6 292 E3
W11 283 H10
W13 137 CH73
Hounslow TW3 156 CB82
Southall UB1 136 BZ72
Denbigh St, SW1 297 L9
Denbigh Ter, W11 283 H10
Denbridge Rd, Brom. BR1 205 EM96
Denby Gra, Harl. CM17 52 EY15
Denby Rd, Cob. KT11 214 BW113
Den Cl, Beck. BR3 203 ED97
Dendridge Cl, Enf. EN1 82 DV37
Dene, The, W13 137 CH71
Abinger Hammer RH5 261 BV141
Croydon CR0 221 DX105
Sevenoaks TN13 257 FH126
Sutton SM2 217 CZ111
Wembley HA9 118 CL63
West Molesey KT8 196 BZ99
Dene Av, Houns. TW3 156 BZ83
Sidcup DA15 186 EV87
Dene Cl, E10 123 EB61
SE4 163 DY83
Bromley BR2 204 EF102
Coulsdon CR5 234 DE119
Dartford DA2 187 FE91
Guildford GU1 243 BB132
Horley RH6 268 DE146
Worcester Park KT4 199 CT103
Dene Ct, Stan. HA7 95 CJ50
Denecroft Cres, Uxb. UB10 135 BP67
Denecroft Gdns, Grays RM17 170 GD76
Dene Dr, Orp. BR6 206 EV104
Denefield Dr, Ken. CR8 236 DR115
Dene Gdns, Stan. HA7 95 CJ50
Thames Ditton KT7 197 CG103
Deneholm Prim Sch,
Grays RM16 off Culford Rd 170 GC75
Dene Holm Rd, Nthflt DA11 190 GD90
Denehurst Gdns, NW4 119 CW58
W3 138 CP74
Richmond TW10 158 CN84
Twickenham TW2 177 CD87
Woodford Green IG8 102 EH49
Dene Path, S.Ock. RM15 149 FU72
Dene Pl, Wok. GU21 226 AV118
Dene Rd, N11 98 DF46
Ashtead KT21 232 CM119
Buckhurst Hill IG9 102 EK46
Dartford DA1 188 FM87
Guildford GU1 258 AY135
Northwood HA6 93 BS51
Denes, The, Hem.H. HP3
off Barnacres Rd 40 BM24
Dene St, Dor. RH4 263 CH136
Dene St Gdns, Dor. RH4 263 CH136
Denewood, New Barn. EN5 80 DC43
Denewood Cl, Wat. WD17 75 BT37
Denewood Ms, Wat. WD17 75 BT37
Denewood Rd, N6 120 DF58
Denfield, Dor. RH4 263 CH138
Denford St, SE10 303 L10
Dengie Wk, N1 277 J8
DENHAM, Uxb. UB9 114 BG62
⇌ Denham 114 BG59
★ Denham Aerodrome,
Uxb. UB9 113 BD57
Denham Av, Denh. UB9 113 BF61
Denham Cl, Denh. UB9 114 BG62
Hemel Hempstead HP2 40 BN15
Welling DA16 166 EW83
Denham Ct Dr, Denh. UB9 114 BH63
Denham Cres, Mitch. CR4 200 DF98
Denham Dr, Ilf. IG2 125 EQ58
Denham Gdn Village,
Denh. UB9 113 BF58
⇌ Denham Golf Club 113 BD59
DENHAM GREEN, Uxb. UB9 113 BE58
Denham Grn Cl, Denh. UB9 114 BG59
Denham Grn La, Denh. UB9 113 BE57
Denham La, Chal.St.P. SL9 91 BA53
Denham Lo, Denh. UB9 134 BJ65
● Denham Media Pk,
Denh. UB9 114 BG57
Denham Rd, N20 98 DF48
Denham UB9 133 BE65
Egham TW20 173 BA91
Epsom KT17 217 CT112
Feltham TW14 176 BW86
Iver SL0 133 BD67
Denham Rbt, Uxb. UB9 114 BG63
Denham St, SE10 303 N10
Denham Village Inf Sch, Denh. UB9
off Cheapside La 113 BF61
Denham Wk, Chal.St.P. SL9 91 AZ51
Denham Way, Bark. IG11 145 ES67
Borehamwood WD6 78 CR39
Denham UB9 114 BG62
Maple Cross WD3 91 BE50
Denholme Rd, W9 283 H2
Denholme Wk, Rain. RM13
off Ryder Gdns 147 FF65
Denholm Gdns, Guil. GU4 243 BA131
Denison Cl, N2 120 DC55
Denison Rd, SW19 180 DD93
W5 137 CJ70
Feltham TW13 175 BT91
Deniston Av, Bex. DA5 186 EY88
Denis Way, SW4 309 P10
Denleigh Gdns, N21 99 DN46
Thames Ditton KT7 197 CE100
Denman Dr, NW11 120 DA57
Ashford TW15 175 BP93
Claygate KT10 215 CG106
Denman Dr N, NW11 120 DA57
Denman Dr S, NW11 120 DA57
Denman Pl, W1
off Great Windmill St 297 N1
Denman Rd, SE15 312 A7
Denman St, W1 297 N1
Denmark Av, SW19 179 CY94
Denmark Ct, Mord. SM4 200 DA99
Denmark Gdns, Cars. SM5 200 DF104
Denmark Gro, N1 276 E10
⇌ Denmark Hill 311 L9
⊖ Denmark Hill 311 L9
Denmark Hill, SE5 311 L7
Denmark Hill Dr, NW9 119 CT56
Denmark Hill Est, SE5 162 DR84
Denmark Pl, E3 290 B2
WC2 285 P8
Denmark Rd, N8 121 DN56
NW6 283 H1
SE5 311 J7
SE25 202 DU99
SW19 179 CX93
W13 137 CH73
Bromley BR1 204 EH95
Carshalton SM5 200 DF104
Guildford GU1 258 AY135
Kingston upon Thames KT1 198 CL97
Twickenham TW2 177 CD90
Denmark St, E11
off High Rd Leytonstone 124 EE62
E13 292 A6
N17 100 DV53
WC2 285 P9
Watford WD17 75 BV40
Denmark Ter, N2
off Fortis Grn 120 DF55
Denmead Cl, Ger.Cr. SL9 112 AY59
Denmead Ho, SW15
off Highcliffe Dr 179 CT86
Denmead Rd, Croy. CR0 201 DP102
Denmead Sch, Hmptn.
TW12 off Wensleydale Rd 176 CB94
Dennan Rd, Surb. KT6 198 CM102
Dennard Way, Farnboro. BR6 223 EP105
Denner Rd, E4 101 EA47
Denne Ter, E8 278 B9
Dennett Rd, Croy. CR0 201 DN102
Dennetts Gro, SE14 313 J8
Dennettsland Rd, Crock.H. TN8 255 EQ134
Dennetts Rd, SE14 313 H7
Denning Av, Croy. CR0 219 DN105
Denning Cl, NW8 283 P2
Hampton TW12 176 BZ93
Denning Ms, SW12 180 DG86
Denning Pt, E1 288 A8
Denning Rd, NW3 120 DD63
Dennington Cl, E5
off Detmold Rd 122 DV61
Dennington Pk Rd, NW6 273 K4
Denningtons, The, Wor.Pk. KT4 198 CS103
Dennis Av, Wem. HA9 118 CM64
Dennis Cl, Ashf. TW15 175 BR94
Redhill RH1 250 DE132
Dennises La, S.Ock. RM15 149 FU66
Upminster RM14 149 FS67
Dennis Gdns, Stan. HA7 95 CJ50
Dennis La, Stan. HA7 95 CH48
Dennison Pt, E15 280 F7
Dennis Pk Cres, SW20 199 CY95
Dennis Reeve Cl, Mitch. CR4 200 DF95
Dennis Rd, E.Mol. KT8 196 CC98
Gravesend DA11 191 GG90
Dennis Way, Guil. GU1 242 AY129
Slough SL1 131 AK73
Denny Av, Wal.Abb. EN9 67 ED34
Denny Cl, E6 292 G7
Denny Cres, SE11 298 F9
Denny Gdns, Dag. RM9
off Canonsleigh Rd 146 EV66
Denny Gate, Chsht EN8 67 DZ27
Denny Rd, N9 100 DV46
Slough SL3 153 AZ77
Dennys La, Berk. HP4 38 AT21
Denny St, SE11 298 F10
De Novo Pl, St.Alb. AL1
off Granville Rd 43 CF20
Den Rd, Brom. BR2 203 ED97
Densham Dr, Pur. CR8 219 DN114
Densham Rd, E15 281 K8
Densley Cl, Welw.G.C. AL8 29 CX07
Densole Cl, Beck. BR3 203 DY95
Densworth Gro, N9 100 DW47
Dent Cl, S.Ock. RM15 149 FU72
DENTON, Grav. DA12 191 GL87
Denton, NW1 275 H5
Denton Cl, Barn. EN5 79 CW43
Redhill RH1 266 DG139
Denton Ct Rd, Grav. DA12 191 GL87
Denton Gro, Walt. KT12 196 BX103
Denton Rd, N8 121 DM57
N18 100 DS49
Bexley DA5 187 FE89
Dartford DA1 187 FE88
Twickenham TW1 177 CK86
Welling DA16 166 EW80
Denton St, SW18 180 DB86
Gravesend DA12 191 GL87
Denton Ter, Bex. DA5
off Denton Rd 187 FE89
Denton Way, E5 123 DX62
Woking GU21 226 AT118
Dents Gro, Lwr Kgswd KT20 249 CZ128
Dents Rd, SW11 180 DF86
Denvale Wk, Wok. GU21 226 AU118
Denver Cl, Petts Wd BR6 205 ES100
● Denver Ind Est, Rain. RM13 147 FF71
Denver Rd, N16 122 DS59
Dartford DA1 187 FG87
Denyer St, SW3 296 D9
Denziloe Av, Uxb. UB10 135 BP69
Denzil Rd, NW10 119 CT64
Guildford GU2 258 AV135
Deodar Rd, SW15 159 CY84
Deodora Cl, N20 98 DE48
★ Department for Environment, Food
& Rural Affairs (Defra), SW1 298 A7
★ Department for Transport
(DfT), SW1 297 P8
★ Department of Energy &
Climate Change (DECC), SW1 298 A3
★ Department of Health, SW1 298 A4
De Pass Gdns, Bark. IG11 146 EU70
De Paul Way, Brwd. CM14 108 FV46
Depot App, NW2 119 CX63
Depot Rd, W12 282 B10
Epsom KT17 216 CS113
Hounslow TW3 157 CD83
DEPTFORD, SE8 313 P1
⇌ Deptford 314 A4
Deptford Bridge 314 B6
Deptford Br, SE8 314 B6
Deptford Bdy, SE8 314 A6
Deptford Ch St, SE8 314 B3
Deptford Ferry Rd, E14 302 B9
Deptford Grn, SE8 314 B3
Deptford Grn Sch, SE14 313 M4
Deptford High St, SE8 314 A3
Deptford Pk Prim Sch, SE8 301 M10
Deptford Strand, SE8 301 P9
● Deptford Trd Est, SE8 313 L2
Deptford Wf, SE8 301 N8
De Quincey Ho, SW1
off Lupus St 309 L1
De Quincey Ms, E16 303 P2
De Quincey Rd, N17 100 DR53
Derby Arms Rd, Epsom KT18 233 CT117
Derby Av, N12 98 DC50
Harrow HA3 95 CD53
Romford RM7 127 FC58
Upminster RM14 128 FM62
Derby Cl, Epsom KT18 233 CV119
Derby Ct, E5
off Overbury St 123 DX63
Derby Gate, SW1 298 A4
Derby Hill, SE23 182 DW89
Derby Hill Cres, SE23 182 DW89
Derby Ho, SE11
off Walnut Tree Wk 298 E8
Derby Rd, E7 144 EJ66
E9 279 J8
E18 102 EF53
N18 100 DW50
SW14 158 CP84
SW19 180 DA94
Croydon CR0 201 DP103
Enfield EN3 82 DV43
Grays RM17 170 GB78
Greenford UB6 136 CB67
Guildford GU2 242 AT134
Hoddesdon EN11 49 ED19
Hounslow TW3 156 CB84
Surbiton KT5 198 CN102
Sutton SM1 217 CZ107
Uxbridge UB8 134 BJ68
Watford WD17 76 BW41
Derby Rd Br, Grays RM17 170 GB79
● Derby Rd Ind Est,
Houns. TW3 off Derby Rd 156 CB84
Derbyshire St, E2 288 D3
Derby Sq, The, Epsom KT19
off High St 216 CR113
Derby Stables Rd,
Epsom KT18 232 CS117
Derby St, W1 297 H3
Dereham Pl, EC2 287 P3
Romford RM5 105 FB51
Dereham Rd, Bark. IG11 145 ET65
Derehams Av, Loud. HP10 88 AC52
Derehams La, Loud. HP10 88 AC53
Derek Av, Epsom KT19 216 CN106
Wallington SM6 219 DH105
Wembley HA9 138 CP66

Derek Cl, Ewell KT19 216 CP106
Derek Walcott Cl, SE24
off Shakespeare Rd 161 DP84
Derham Gdns, Upmin. RM14 128 FQ62
Deri Av, Rain. RM13 147 FH70
Dericote St, E8 278 D8
Deridene Cl, Stanw. TW19 174 BL86
Derifall Cl, E6 293 K6
Dering Pl, Croy. CR0 220 DQ105
Dering Rd, Croy. CR0 220 DQ105
Dering St, W1 285 J9
Dering Way, Grav. DA12 191 GM87
Derinton Rd, SW17 180 DF91
Derley Rd, Sthl. UB2 156 BW76
Dermody Gdns, SE13 183 ED85
Dermody Rd, SE13 183 ED85
Deronda Rd, SE24 181 DP88
De Ros Pl, Egh. TW20 173 BA93
Deroy Cl, Cars. SM5 218 DF107
Derrick Av, S.Croy. CR2 220 DQ110
Derrick Gdns, SE7
off Anchor And Hope La 304 C7
Derrick Rd, Beck. BR3 203 DZ97
Derry Av, S.Ock. RM15 149 FU72
Derrydown, Wok. GU22 226 AW121
DERRY DOWNS, Orp. BR5 206 EX100
Derry Downs, Orp. BR5 206 EW100
Derry Leys, Hat. AL10 44 CS16
Derry Rd, Croy. CR0 201 DL104
Derry St, W8 295 L5
Dersingham Av, E12 125 EN64
[Sch] Dersingham Inf Sch, E12
off Dersingham Av 125 EN64
Dersingham Rd, NW2 119 CY62
Derwent Av, N18 100 DR50
NW7 96 CR50
NW9 118 CS57
SW15 178 CS91
Barnet EN4 98 DF46
Pinner HA5 94 BY51
Uxbridge UB10 114 BN62
Derwent Cl, Add. KT15 212 BK106
Amersham HP7 72 AV39
Claygate KT10 215 CE107
Dartford DA1 187 FH88
Feltham TW14 175 BT88
Watford WD25 60 BW34
Derwent Cres, N20 98 DC48
Bexleyheath DA7 166 FA82
Stanmore HA7 95 CJ54
Derwent Dr, Hayes UB4 135 BS71
Petts Wood BR5 205 ER101
Purley CR8 220 DR113
Slough SL1 130 AJ71
Derwent Gdns, Ilf. IG4 124 EL56
Wembley HA9 117 CJ59
Derwent Gro, SE22 162 DT84
Derwent Par, S.Ock. RM15 149 FU72
Derwent Ri, NW9 118 CS58
Derwent Rd, N13 99 DM49
SE20 202 DU96
SW20 199 CX100
W5 157 CJ76
Egham TW20 173 BB94
Hemel Hempstead HP3 41 BQ21
Southall UB1 136 BZ72
Twickenham TW2 176 CB86
Derwent St, SE10 303 J10
Derwent Wk, Wall. SM6 219 DH108
[Sch] Derwentwater Prim Sch, W3
off Shakespeare Rd 138 CQ74
Derwentwater Rd, W3 138 CQ74
Derwent Way, Horn. RM12 127 FH64
Derwent Yd, W5
off Northfield Av 157 CJ76
De Salis Rd, Uxb. UB10 135 BQ70
Desborough Cl, W2 283 M6
Hertford SG14 31 DP06
Shepperton TW17 194 BN101
Welwyn Garden City AL7 30 DB12
Desborough Ho, W14
off North End Rd 307 H2
Desborough St, W2 283 L6
Desenfans Rd, SE21 182 DS86
● Deseronto Trd Est, Slou. SL3 152 AY75
Desford Ct, Ashf. TW15
off Desford Way 174 BM89
Desford Ms, E16 291 K5
Desford Rd, E16 291 K5
Desford Way, Ashf. TW15 174 BM89
★ Design Mus, SE1 300 B3
Desmond Rd, Wat. WD24 75 BT36
Desmond St, SE14 313 M3
Desmond Tutu Dr, SE23
off St. Germans Rd 183 DY88
De Soissons Cl, Welw.G.C. AL8 29 CV11
Despard Rd, N19 121 DJ60
[Sch] De Stafford Sch, Cat. CR3
off Burntwood La 236 DT121
Desvignes Dr, SE13 183 ED86
De Tany Ct, St.Alb. AL1 43 CD21
Detillens La, Oxt. RH8 254 EG129
Detling Cl, Horn. RM12 128 FJ64
Detling Rd, Brom. BR1 184 EG92
Erith DA8 167 FD80
Northfleet DA11 190 GD88
Detmold Rd, E5 122 DW61
Dettingen Pl, Bark. IG11 146 EV68
Deva Cl, St.Alb. AL3 42 CA22
Devalls Cl, E6 293 M10
Devana End, Cars. SM5 200 DF104
Devane Way, SE27 181 DP90
Devas Rd, SW20 199 CW95
Devas St, E3 290 D4
Devenay Rd, E15 281 L7
Devenish Rd, SE2 166 EU75
Deventer Cres, SE22 182 DS85
Deveraux Cl, Beck. BR3 203 EC99
De Vere Cl, Wall. SM6 219 DL108
De Vere Gdns, W8 295 N5
Ilford IG1 125 EM61
Deverell St, SE1 299 L7
De Vere Ms, W8 295 N6
Devereux Ct, WC2 286 E9
Devereux Dr, Wat. WD17 75 BS38
Devereux La, SW13 159 CV80
Devereux Rd, SW11 180 DF86
Grays RM16 170 FZ76
Windsor SL4 151 AR82
De Vere Wk, Wat. WD17 75 BS40
Deverill Ct, SE20 202 DW95
Deverills Way, Slou. SL3 153 BC77
Deveron Gdns, S.Ock. RM15 149 FU71
Deveron Way, Rom. RM1 105 FE53
Devey Cl, Kings.T. KT2 178 CS94
Devils La, Egh. TW20 173 BD94
Devil's La, Hert. SG13 47 DP21
Devitt Cl, Ashtd. KT21 232 CN116
Devizes St, N1 277 M9
Devoil Cl, Guil. GU4 243 BB130
Devoke Way, Walt. KT12 196 BX103
Devon Av, Slou. SL1 131 AQ72
Twickenham TW2 176 CC88
Devon Bk, Guil. GU2
off Portsmouth Rd 258 AW137
Devon Cl, N17 122 DT55
Buckhurst Hill IG9 102 EH47
Kenley CR8 236 DT116
Perivale UB6 137 CJ67
Devon Ct, Buck.H. IG9
off Chequers 102 EH46
St. Albans AL1 43 CE21
Sutton at Hone DA4 208 FP95
Devon Cres, Red. RH1 250 DD134
Devoncroft Gdns, Twick. TW1 177 CG87
Devon Gdns, N4 121 DP58
Devonhurst Pl, W4
off Heathfield Ter 158 CR78
Devonia Gdns, N18 100 DQ51
Devonia Rd, N1 277 H10
Devon Mans, SE1
off Tooley St 300 A4
Devon Mead, Hat. AL10
off Chipmunk Chase 44 CR16
Devonport Gdns, Ilf. IG1 125 EM58
Devonport Ms, W12
off Devonport Rd 139 CV74
Devonport Rd, W12 159 CV75
Devonport St, E1 289 J9
Devon Ri, N2 120 DD56
Devon Rd, Bark. IG11 145 ES67
Hersham KT12 214 BW105
South Merstham RH1 251 DJ130
Sutton SM2 217 CY109
Sutton at Hone DA4 208 FP95
Watford WD24 76 BX39
Devons Est, E3 290 D3
Devonshire Av, Amer. HP6 55 AP37
Box Hill KT20 248 CQ131
Dartford DA1 187 FH86
Sutton SM2 218 DC108
Woking GU21 211 BC114
● Devonshire Business Cen, Pot.B. EN6 63 CY30
● Devonshire Business Pk, Borwd. WD6 78 CR41
Devonshire Cl, E15 281 K1
N13 99 DN49
W1 285 J6
Amersham HP6 55 AQ37
Farnham Royal SL2 131 AP68
Devonshire Cres, NW7 97 CX52
Devonshire Dr, SE10 314 C5
Long Ditton KT6 197 CK102
Devonshire Gdns, N17 100 DQ51
N21 100 DQ45
W4 158 CQ80
Devonshire Grn, Farn.Royal SL2 131 AP68
Devonshire Gro, SE15 312 F3
Devonshire Hill La, N17 100 DQ51
[Sch] Devonshire Hill Prim Sch, N17 off Weir Hall Rd 100 DR51
Devonshire Ho, SE1
off Bath Ter 299 J6
Sutton SM2
off Devonshire Av 218 DC108
[Sch] Devonshire Ho Prep Sch, NW3 273 P2
Devonshire Ms, SW10
off Park Wk 308 A2
W4 158 CS78
Devonshire Ms N, W1 285 J6
Devonshire Ms S, W1 285 J6
Devonshire Ms W, W1 285 J5
Devonshire Pas, W4 158 CS78
Devonshire Pl, NW2 120 DA62
W1 285 H5
W8 295 L7
Devonshire Pl Ms, W1 285 H5
[Sch] Devonshire Prim Sch, Sutt. SM2 off Devonshire Av 218 DC108
Devonshire Rd, E16 292 B8
E17 123 EA58
N9 100 DW46
N13 99 DM49
N17 100 DQ51
NW7 97 CX52
SE9 184 EL89
SE23 182 DW88
SW19 180 DE94
W4 158 CS78
W5 157 CJ76
Bexleyheath DA6 166 EY84
Carshalton SM5 218 DG105
Croydon CR0 202 DR101
Eastcote HA5 116 BW58
Feltham TW13 176 BY90
Gravesend DA12 191 GH88
Grays RM16 170 FY77
Harrow HA1 117 CD58
Hatch End HA5 94 BZ53
Hornchurch RM12 128 FJ61
Ilford IG2 125 ER59
Orpington BR6 206 EU101
Southall UB1 136 CA71
Sutton SM2 218 DC108
Weybridge KT13 212 BN105
Devonshire Row, EC2 287 P7
Devonshire Row Ms, W1 285 K5
Devonshire Sq, EC2 287 P8
Bromley BR2 204 EH98
Devonshire St, W1 285 H6
W4 158 CS78
Devonshire Ter, W2 283 P9
Devonshire Way, Croy. CR0 203 DY103
Hayes UB4 135 BV72
[DLR] Devons Road 290 C4
Devons Rd, E3 290 B6
Devon St, SE15 312 F3
Devon Way, Chess. KT9 215 CJ106
Epsom KT19 216 CP106
Uxbridge UB10 134 BM68
Devon Waye, Houns. TW5 156 BZ80
De Walden St, W1 285 H7
Dewar Spur, Slou. SL3 153 AZ79
Dewar St, SE15 162 DU83
Dewberry Gdns, E6 292 G6
Dewberry St, E14 290 E7
Dewey La, SW2
off Tulse Hill 181 DN86
Dewey Path, Horn. RM12 148 FJ65
Dewey Rd, N1 276 E10
Dagenham RM10 147 FB65
Dewey St, SW17 180 DF92
Dewgrass Gro, Wal.Cr. EN8 83 DX35
Dewhurst Rd, W14 294 C6
Cheshunt EN8 66 DW29
[Sch] Dewhurst St. Mary C of E Prim Sch, Chsht EN8 off Churchgate 66 DW29
Dewlands, Gdse. RH9 252 DW131
Dewlands Av, Dart. DA2 188 FP87
Dewlands Ct, NW4 97 CX54
Dewsbury Cl, Pnr. HA5 116 BY58
Romford RM3 106 FL51
Dewsbury Ct, W4
off Chiswick Rd 158 CQ77
Dewsbury Gdns, Rom. RM3 106 FK51
Worcester Park KT4 199 CU104
Dewsbury Rd, NW10 119 CU64
Romford RM3 106 FK51
Dewsbury Ter, NW1 275 K8
Dexter Cl, Grays RM17 170 GA76
St. Albans AL1 43 CG21
Dexter Ct, SW6
off Parsons Grn La 307 J7
Dexter Ho, Erith DA18
off Kale Rd 166 EY76
Dexter Rd, Barn. EN5 79 CX44
Harefield UB9 92 BJ54
Deyncourt Gdns, Upmin. RM14 128 FQ61
Deyncourt Rd, N17 100 DQ53
Deynecourt Gdns, E11 124 EJ56
D'Eynsford Rd, SE5 311 L6
Dhonan Ho, SE1
off Longfield Est 300 B8
Diadem Ct, W1 285 N9
Dial Cl, Green. DA9 189 FW85
Dialmead, Ridge EN6
off Crossoaks La 63 CT34
Dial Wk, The, W8 295 M4
Diamedes Av, Stanw. TW19 174 BK87
Diameter Rd, Petts Wd BR5 205 EP101
Diamond Cl, Dag. RM8 126 EW60
Grays RM16 170 FZ76
Diamond Rd, Ruis. HA4 116 BX63
Slough SL1 152 AU75
Watford WD24 75 BU38
Diamond St, NW10 138 CR66
SE15 311 P5
Diamond Ter, SE10 314 F6
Diamond Way, SE8 314 B4
Diana Cl, E18 102 EH53
SE8 313 P2
Chafford Hundred RM16 170 FZ76
George Green SL3 132 AY72
Sidcup DA14 186 EY89
Diana Gdns, Surb. KT6 198 CM103
Diana Ho, SW13 159 CT81
★ Diana Princess of Wales Mem, W2 296 C4
Diana Rd, E17 123 DZ55
Diana Wk, Horl. RH6
off High St 269 DH148
Dianne Way, Barn. EN4 80 DE43
Dianthus Cl, SE2
off Carnation St 166 EV78
Chertsey KT16 193 BE101
Dianthus Ct, Wok. GU22 226 AX118
Diban Av, Horn. RM12 127 FH63
Diban Ct, Horn. RM12 127 FH63
Dibden Hill, Ch.St.G. HP8 90 AW49
Dibden La, Ide Hill TN14 256 FE126
Dibden St, N1 277 H8
Dibdin Cl, Sutt. SM1 200 DA104
Dibdin Ho, W9 273 L10
Dibdin Rd, Sutt. SM1 200 DA104
Diceland Rd, Bans. SM7 233 CZ116
Dicey Av, NW2 272 A2
Dickens Av, N3 98 DC53
Dartford DA1 168 FN84
Tilbury RM18 171 GH81
Uxbridge UB8 135 BP72
Dickens Cl, Chsht EN7 66 DU26
Erith DA8 167 FB80
Hayes UB3 off Croyde Av 155 BS77
Richmond TW10 178 CL89
St. Albans AL3 43 CD19
Dickens Ct, Hat. AL10 45 CV16
Dickens Dr, Add. KT15 211 BF107
Chislehurst BR7 185 EQ93
Dickens Est, SE1 300 C5
SE16 300 C5
Dickens Ho, NW6 283 J2
Dickens La, N18 100 DS50
Dickens Ms, EC1 286 G6
Dickenson Cl, N9 100 DU46
Dickenson Rd, N8 121 DL59
Feltham TW13 176 BW92
Dickensons La, SE25 202 DU99
Dickensons Pl, SE25 202 DU100
Dickenson Way, Ware SG12 33 DX05
Dickens Pl, Colnbr. SL3 153 BE81
Dickens Ri, Chig. IG7 103 EN48
Dickens Rd, E6 144 EK68
Gravesend DA12 191 GL88
Dickens Sq, SE1 299 K6
Dickens St, SW8 309 K8
Dickens Way, Rom. RM1 127 FE56
Dickenswood Cl, SE19 181 DP94
Dickerage La, N.Mal. KT3 198 CQ97
Dickerage Rd, Kings.T. KT1 198 CQ95
New Malden KT3 198 CQ95
● Dicker Mill Est, Hert. SG13 32 DR08
Dickinson Av, Crox.Grn WD3 74 BN44
Dickinson Ct, EC1
off Brewhouse Yd 287 H5
Dickinson Quay, Hem.H. HP3 58 BL25
Dickinson Sq, Crox.Grn WD3 74 BN44
Dickson, Chsht EN7 66 DT27
Dickson Fold, Pnr. HA5 116 BX56
Dickson Rd, SE9 164 EL83
Dick Turpin Way, Felt. TW14 155 BT84
Didsbury Cl, E6 off Barking Rd 145 EM67
Dieppe Cl, W14 295 H10
Digby Cres, N4 122 DQ61
Digby Gdns, Dag. RM10 146 FA67
Digby Pl, Croy. CR0 202 DT104
Digby Rd, E9 279 J3
Barking IG11 145 ET66
Digby St, E2 289 H3
Digby Wk, Horn. RM12
off Pembrey Way 148 FJ65
Digby Way, Byfleet KT14
off High Rd 212 BM112
Dig Dag Hill, Chsht EN7 66 DT27
Digdens Ri, Epsom KT18 232 CQ115
Diggon St, E1 289 J7
Dighton Ct, SE5 311 J3
Dighton Rd, SW18 180 DC85
Dignum St, N1 276 E10
Digswell Cl, Borwd. WD6 78 CN38
Digswell Hill, Welw. AL6 29 CU06
Digswell Ho, Welw.G.C. AL8 29 CX05
Digswell Ho Ms, Welw.G.C. AL8 29 CX05
Digswell La, Welw. AL6 29 CZ05
Digswell Pl, Welw.G.C. AL8 29 CW06
Digswell Ri, Welw.G.C. AL8 29 CX07
Digswell Rd, Welw.G.C. AL8 29 CY06
Digswell St, N7 276 F4
Dilhorne Cl, SE12 184 EH90
[Sch] Dilkes Prim Sch, S.Ock. RM15
off Garron La 149 FT72
Dilke St, SW3 308 F2
Dillon Cl, Epsom KT19 216 CM112
● Dilloway Yd, Sthl. UB2
off The Green 156 BY75
Dillwyn Cl, SE26 183 DY91
Dilston Cl, Nthlt. UB5
off Yeading La 136 BW69
Dilston Gro, SE16 300 G8
Dilston Rd, Lthd. KT22 231 CG119
Dilton Gdns, SW15 179 CU88
Dilwyn Ct, E17
off Hillyfield 101 DY54
Dimes Pl, W6
off King St 159 CV77
Dimmock Dr, Grnf. UB6 117 CD64
Dimmocks La, Sarratt WD3 74 BH36
Dimond Cl, E7 281 P1
Dimsdale Dr, NW9 118 CQ60
Enfield EN1 82 DU44
Slough SL2 111 AM63
Dimsdale St, Hert. SG14 32 DQ09
Dimsdale Wk, E13 281 P9
Dimson Cres, E3 290 A4
Dinant Link Rd, Hodd. EN11 49 EA16
Dingle, The, Uxb. UB10 135 BP68
Dingle Cl, Barn. EN5 79 CT44
Dingle Gdns, E14 302 B1
Dingle Rd, Ashf. TW15 175 BP92
Dingley La, SW16 181 DK89
Dingley Pl, EC1 287 K3
Dingley Rd, EC1 287 J3
Dingwall Av, Croy. CR0 202 DQ103
Dingwall Gdns, NW11 120 DA58
Dingwall Rd, SW18 180 DC87
Carshalton SM5 218 DF109
Croydon CR0 202 DR103
Dinmont St, E2 278 E10
Dinmore, Bov. HP3 57 AZ28
Dinsdale Cl, Wok. GU22 227 AZ118
Dinsdale Gdns, SE25 202 DS98
New Barnet EN5 80 DB43
Dinsdale Rd, SE3 315 L2
Dinsmore Rd, SW12 181 DH87
Dinton Rd, SW19 180 DD93
Kingston upon Thames KT2 178 CM94
Dione Rd, Hem.H. HP2
off Saturn Way 40 BM17
Diploma Av, N2 120 DE56
Diploma Ct, N2
off Diploma Av 120 DE56
Dirdene Cl, Epsom KT17 217 CT112
Dirdene Gdns, Epsom KT17 217 CT112
Dirdene Gro, Epsom KT17 216 CS112
Dirleton Rd, E15 281 L8
Dirtham La, Eff. KT24 245 BU127
Disbrowe Rd, W6 306 E3
● Discovery Business Pk, SE16 off St. James's Rd 300 D7
Discovery Dock Apts E, E14 302 C4
Discovery Dock Apts W, E14 302 C4
[Sch] Discovery Prim Sch & Children's Cen, SE28
off Battery Rd 145 ET74
Discovery Wk, E1 300 E1
Dishforth La, NW9 96 CS53
Disney Ms, N4 121 DP57
Disney Pl, SE1 299 K4
Disney St, SE1 299 K4
Dison Cl, Enf. EN3 83 DX39
Disraeli Cl, SE28 146 EW74
W4 off Acton La 158 CR76
Disraeli Ct, Slou. SL3
off Sutton Pl 153 BB79
Disraeli Gdns, SW15
off Fawe Pk Rd 159 CZ84
Disraeli Pk, Beac. HP9 89 AK50
Disraeli Rd, E7 281 P4
NW10 138 CQ68
SW15 159 CY84
W5 137 CK74
Diss St, E2 288 A2
Distaff La, EC4 287 J10
Distillery La, W6 306 B1
Distillery Rd, W6 306 B1
Distillery Twr, SE8 313 B6
Distillery Wk, Brent. TW8 158 CL79
Distin St, SE11 298 E9
District Rd, Wem. HA0 117 CH64
Ditch All, SE10 314 D7
Ditchburn St, E14 302 F1
Ditches La, Cat. CR3 235 DM122
Coulsdon CR5 235 DL120
Ditches Ride, The, Loug. IG10 85 EN37
Ditchfield Rd, Hayes UB4 136 BY70
Hoddesdon EN11 33 EA14
Dittisham Rd, SE9 184 EL91
Ditton Cl, T.Ditt. KT7 197 CG101
Dittoncroft Cl, Croy. CR0 220 DS105
Ditton Gra Cl, Long Dit. KT6 197 CK102
Ditton Gra Dr, Long Dit. KT6 197 CK102
Ditton Hill, Long Dit. KT6 197 CJ102
Ditton Hill Rd, Long Dit. KT6 197 CJ102
Ditton Lawn, T.Ditt. KT7 197 CG102
Ditton Pk, Slou. SL3 152 AX78
Ditton Pk Rd, Slou. SL3 152 AY79
Ditton Pl, SE20 202 DV95
Ditton Reach, T.Ditt. KT7 197 CH100
Ditton Rd, Bexh. DA6 186 EX85
Datchet SL3 152 AX81
Slough SL3 153 AZ79
Southall UB2 156 BZ78
Surbiton KT6 198 CL102
[Sch] Divine Saviour RC Prim Sch, The, Abb.L. WD5 off Broomfield Ri 59 BR32
Divine Way, Hayes UB3 135 BR72
Divis Way, SW15
off Dover Pk Dr 179 CV86
Divot Pl, Hert. SG13 32 DV08
Dixon Clark Ct, N1 276 G5
Dixon Cl, E6 293 K8
Dixon Dr, Wey. KT13 212 BM110
Dixon Ho, W10 282 C9
Dixon Pl, W.Wick. BR4 203 EB102
Dixon Rd, SE14 313 M6
SE25 202 DS97
Dixon's All, SE16 300 E5
Dixon's Ct, Ware SG12
off Crane Mead 33 DY06
Dixons Hill Cl, N.Mymms AL9 63 CV25
Dixons Hill Rd, N.Mymms AL9 63 CU25
Dixon Way, NW10
off Church Rd 138 CS66
Dobbin Cl, Har. HA3 95 CG54
Dobb's Weir, Hodd. EN11 49 EC18
Dobb's Weir Rd, Hodd. EN11 49 ED18
Roydon CM19 49 ED18
Dobell Path, SE9
off Dobell Rd 185 EM85
Dobell Rd, SE9 185 EM85
Doble Ct, S.Croy. CR2 220 DU111
Dobree Av, NW10 139 CV66
Dobson Cl, NW6 274 A7
Dobson Rd, Grav. DA12 191 GL92
Doby Ct, EC4 287 K10
Dockers Tanner Rd, E14 302 A7
Dockett Eddy, Cher. KT16 194 BL102
Dockett Eddy La, Shep. TW17 194 BM102
Dockhead, SE1 300 B5
Dock Hill Av, SE16 301 K4
Dockland St, E16 305 L3
Dockley Rd, SE16 300 C7
● Dockley Rd Ind Est, SE16
off Rouel Rd 300 C7
Dock Rd, E16 303 M1
Barking IG11 145 EQ68
Brentford TW8 157 CK80
Grays RM17 170 GD79
Tilbury RM18 171 GF82
Dockside Rd, E16 292 F10
Dock St, E1 288 C10
Dockwell Cl, Felt. TW14 155 BU84
[Sch] Doctor Challoner's Gram Sch, Amer. HP6 off Chesham Rd 55 AQ38
[Sch] Doctor Challoner's High Sch, Lt.Chal. HP7 off Coke's La 72 AV40
Doctor Johnson Av, SW17 181 DH90
★ Doctor Johnson's Ho, EC4 286 F9
Doctors Cl, SE26 182 DW92
Doctors Commons Rd, Berk. HP4 38 AV20
Doctors La, Chaldon CR3 235 DN123
[Sch] Doctor Triplett's C of E Prim Sch, Hayes UB3 off Hemmen La 135 BT72
Docwra's Bldgs, N1 277 N4
Dodbrooke Rd, SE27 181 DN90
Dodd Ho, SE16
off Rennie Est 300 F9
Doddinghurst Rd, Brwd. CM15 108 FW44
Doddington Gro, SE17 310 G2
Doddington Pl, SE17 310 G2
Dodd Rd, Wat. WD24 75 BU36
Dodd's Cres, W.Byf. KT14 212 BH114
Doddsfield Rd, Slou. SL2 131 AN69
Dodds La, Ch.St.G. HP8 90 AU47
Piccotts End HP2 40 BJ16
Dodd's La, Wok. GU22 212 BG114
Dodds Pk, Brock. RH3 264 CP136
Dodsley Pl, N9 100 DW48
Dodson St, SE1 298 F5
Dod St, E14 289 P8
Dodwood, Welw.G.C. AL7 30 DB10
Doebury Wk, SE18
off Prestwood Cl 166 EU79
Doel Cl, SW19 180 DC94
Doggett Rd, SE6 183 EA87
Doggetts Cl, E.Barn. EN4 80 DE43
Doggetts Fm Rd, Denh. UB9 113 BC59
Doggetts Way, St.Alb. AL1 42 CC22
Doggetts Wd Cl, Ch.St.G. HP8 72 AV42
Doggetts Wd La, Ch.St.G. HP8 72 AV41
Doghurst Av, Harling. UB3 155 BP80
Doghurst Dr, West Dr. UB7 155 BP80
Doghurst La, Chipstead CR5 234 DF120
Dog Kennel Grn, Ran.Com. RH5 246 BX133
Dog Kennel Hill, SE22 162 DS83
Dog Kennel Hill Est, SE22 162 DS83
[Sch] Dog Kennel Hill Prim Sch, SE22 311 P10
Dog Kennel La, Chorl. WD3 73 BF42
Hatfield AL10 45 CU17
Dog La, NW10 118 CS63
Dognell Grn, Welw.G.C. AL8 29 CV08
Dogwood Cl, Nthflt DA11 190 GE91
Doherty Rd, E13 291 P4
● Dokal Ind Est, Sthl. UB2
off Hartington Rd 156 BY76
Dolben St, SE1 298 G3
Dolby Rd, SW6 306 G9
Dolland St, SE11 310 D1
Dollis Av, N3 97 CZ53
Dollis Brook Wk, Barn. EN5 79 CY44
Dollis Cres, Ruis. HA4 116 BW60
DOLLIS HILL, NW2 119 CV62
⊖ Dollis Hill 119 CU64
Dollis Hill Av, NW2 119 CV62
Dollis Hill La, NW2 119 CV62
[Sch] Dollis Inf Sch, NW7
off Pursley Rd 97 CW52
[Sch] Dollis Jun Sch, NW7
off Pursley Rd 97 CW52
● Dollis Ms, N3 98 DA53
Dollis Pk, N3 97 CZ53
Dollis Rd, N3 97 CY52
NW7 97 CY52
Dollis Valley Dr, Barn. EN5 79 CZ44
Dollis Valley Grn Wk, N20
off Totteridge La 98 DC47
Barnet EN5 79 CY44
Dollis Valley Way, Barn. EN5 79 CZ44
Dolman Cl, N3
off Avondale Rd 98 DC54
Dolman Rd, W4 158 CR77
Dolman St, SW4 161 DM84
Dolphin App, Rom. RM1 127 FF56
Dolphin Cl, SE16 301 J4
SE28 146 EX72
Surbiton KT6 197 CK100
Dolphin Ct, NW11 119 CY58
Slough SL1 152 AV75
Staines-upon-Thames TW18 174 BG90
Dolphin Ct N, Stai. TW18 174 BG90
● Dolphin Est, Sun. TW16 195 BS95
Dolphin Ho, SW6
off Lensbury Ave 307 P8
SW18 off Smugglers Way 160 DB84
Dolphin La, E14 302 C1
Dolphin Pt, Purf. RM19 169 FS78
Dolphin Rd, Nthlt. UB5 136 BZ68
Slough SL1 152 AV75
Sunbury-on-Thames TW16 195 BS95
Dolphin Rd N, Sun. TW16 195 BS95
Dolphin Rd S, Sun. TW16 195 BR95
Dolphin Rd W, Sun. TW16 195 BR95
Dolphin Sq, SW1 309 M1
W4 158 CS80
Dolphin St, Kings.T. KT1 198 CL95

D

Dolphin Twr, SE8 313 P3
Dolphin Way, Purf. RM19 169 FS78
Dolphin Yd, St.Alb. AL1 43 CD20
Ware SG12 off East St 33 DX06
Dombey St, WC1 286 C6
Jct Dome, The, Wat. WD25 76 BW36
Dome Hill, Cat. CR3 252 DS127
Dome Hill Pk, SE26 182 DT91
Dome Hill Peak, Cat. CR3 252 DS126
Domett Cl, SE5 162 DR84
Dome Way, Red. RH1 250 DF133
Domfe Pl, E5
off Rushmore Rd 122 DW63
Domingo St, EC1 287 J4
Dominica Cl, E13 292 D1
Dominic Ct, Wal.Abb. EN9 67 EB33
● Dominion Business Pk, N9
off Goodwin Rd 101 DX47
Dominion Cl, Houns. TW3 157 CD82
Dominion Dr, SE16 301 J5
Rom. RM5 105 FB51
Dominion Ho, W13 137 CH73
Dominion Rd, Croy. CR0 202 DT101
Southall UB2 156 BY76
Dominion St, EC2 287 M6
★ Dominion Thea, W1 285 P8
Dominion Way, Rain. RM13 147 FG69
Domonic Dr, SE9 185 EP91
Domus Ct, Edg. HA8
off Fortune Ave 96 CP52
Domville Cl, N20 98 DD47
Donald Biggs Dr, Grav. DA12 191 GK87
Donald Dr, Rom. RM6 126 EW57
Donald Rd, E13 144 EH67
Croydon CR0 201 DM100
Donaldson Rd, NW6 273 H9
SE18 165 EN81
Donald Wds Gdns, Surb. KT5 198 CP103
Donato Dr, SE15 311 N3
Doncaster Dr, Nthlt. UB5 116 BZ64
Doncaster Gdns, N4 122 DQ58
Northolt UB5 116 BZ64
Doncaster Grn, Wat. WD19 94 BW50
Doncaster Rd, N9 100 DV45
Doncaster Way, Upmin. RM14 128 FM62
Doncel Ct, E4 101 ED45
Doncella Cl, Chaff.Hun. RM16 169 FX76
Donegal St, N1 286 D1
Doneraile St, SW6 306 D8
Dongola Rd, E1 289 L6
E13 292 A3
N17 122 DS55
Dongola Rd W, E13 292 A3
Sch Donhead Wimbledon Coll
Prep Sch, SW19 off Edge Hill 179 CX94
Donington Av, Ilf. IG6 125 EQ57
Donkey All, SE22 182 DU87
Donkey La, Abin.Com. RH5 262 BX143
Enfield EN1 82 DU40
Farningham DA4 208 FP103
Horley RH6 269 DK152
West Drayton UB7 154 BJ77
Donkin Ho, SE16
off Rennie Est 300 F9
Donnay Cl, Ger.Cr. SL9 112 AX58
Donne Ct, SE24 182 DQ86
Donnefield Av, Edg. HA8 96 CL52
Donne Gdns, Wok. GU22 227 BE115
Donne Pl, SW3 296 D8
Mitcham CR4 201 DH98
Donne Rd, Dag. RM8 126 EW61
Donnington Ct, NW10 139 CV66
Sch Donnington Prim Sch,
NW10 off Uffington Rd 139 CV66
Donnington Rd, NW10 139 CV66
Dunton Green TN13 241 FD120
Harrow HA3 117 CK57
Worcester Park KT4 199 CU103
Donnybrook Rd, SW16 181 DJ94
Donovan Av, N10 99 DH54
Donovan Cl, Epsom KT19 216 CR110
Donovan Ct, SW10
off Drayton Gdns 308 A1
Donovan Pl, N21 81 DM43
Don Phelan Cl, SE5 311 M6
Don Way, Rom. RM1 105 FE52
Doods Pk Rd, Reig. RH2 250 DC133
Doods Pl, Reig. RH2 250 DC133
Doods Rd, Reig. RH2 250 DC133
Doods Way, Reig. RH2 250 DD133
Doone Cl, Tedd. TW11 177 CG93
Doon St, SE1 298 E3
Dorado Gdns, Orp. BR6 206 EX104
Doral Way, Cars. SM5 218 DF106
Dorando Cl, W12 139 CV73
Doran Dr, Red. RH1 250 DD134
Doran Gdns, Red. RH1 250 DD134
Doran Gro, SE18 165 ES80
Doran Wk, E15 280 F7
Dora Rd, SW19 180 DA92
Dora St, E14 289 N8
Dora Way, SW9 310 F9
Dorcas Ct, St.Alb. AL1 43 CE21
Dorchester Av, N13 100 DQ49
Bexley DA5 186 EX88
Harrow HA2 116 CC58
Hoddesdon EN11 49 EA15
Dorchester Cl, Dart. DA1 188 FM87
Northolt UB5 116 CB64
Orpington BR5 186 EU94
Dorchester Ct, N14 99 DH45
SE24 182 DQ85
Croxley Green WD3
off Mayfare 75 BQ43
Woking GU22 227 BA116
Dorchester Dr, SE24 182 DQ85
Feltham TW14 175 BS86
Dorchester Gdns, E4 101 EA49
NW11 120 DA56
Dorchester Gro, W4 158 CS78
Dorchester Ho, Rich. TW9 158 CP80
Dorchester Ms, N.Mal. KT3
off Elm Rd 198 CR98
Twickenham TW1 177 CJ87
Sch Dorchester Prim Sch, Wor.Pk. KT4
off Dorchester Rd 199 CW102
Dorchester Rd, Grav. DA12 191 GK90
Morden SM4 200 DB101
Northolt UB5 116 CB64
Weybridge KT13 195 BP104
Worcester Park KT4 199 CW102
Dorchester Way, Har. HA3 118 CM58
Dorchester Waye, Hayes UB4 136 BW72
Dorcis Av, Bexh. DA7 166 EY82
Dordrecht Rd, W3 138 CS74
Dore Av, E12 125 EN64
Doreen Av, NW9 118 CR60
Dore Gdns, Mord. SM4 200 DB101
Dorell Cl, Sthl. UB1 136 BZ71
Dorey Ho, Brent. TW8
off London Rd 157 CJ80
Doria Dr, Grav. DA12 191 GL90
Dorian Rd, Horn. RM12 127 FG60
Doria Rd, SW6 307 H8
Doric Dr, Kgswd KT20 233 CZ120
Doric Way, NW1 285 N2
Dorie Ms, N12 98 DB49
Dorien Rd, SW20 199 CX96
Dorin Ct, Warl. CR6 236 DV119
Dorincourt, Wok. GU22 227 BE115
Doris Ashby Cl, Perivale UB6 137 CG67
Doris Av, Erith DA8 167 FC81
Doris Rd, E7 281 P6
Ashford TW15 175 BR93
DORKING, RH4 & RH5 263 CH137
⇌ Dorking 247 CJ134
Coll Dorking Adult Learning Cen,
Dor. RH4 off Dene St 263 CH136
★ Dorking & District Mus,
Dor. RH4 263 CG136
● Dorking Business Pk,
Dor. RH4 263 CG135
Dorking Cl, SE8 313 N2
Worcester Park KT4 199 CX103
⇌ Dorking Deepdene 247 CJ134
Dorking Gdns, Rom. RM3 106 FK50
H Dorking Gen Hosp, Dor. RH4 263 CG137
Dorking Glen, Rom. RM3 106 FK49
Dorking Ri, Rom. RM3 106 FK49
Dorking Rd, Abin.Ham. RH5 261 BS139
Bookham KT23 246 CB126
Chilworth GU4, GU5 259 BF139
Epsom KT18 232 CN116
Gomshall GU5 261 BR139
Leatherhead KT22 231 CH122
Romford RM3 106 FK49
Tadworth KT20 233 CX123
Dorking Wk, Rom. RM3 106 FK49
⇌ Dorking West 263 CG135
Dorkins Way, Upmin. RM14 129 FS59
Dorlcote Rd, SW18 180 DD87
Dorling Dr, Epsom KT17 217 CT112
Dorly Cl, Shep. TW17 195 BS99
Dorman Pl, N9 100 DU47
Dormans Cl, Nthwd. HA6 93 BR52
Dorman Wk, NW10 118 CQ64
Dorman Way, NW8 274 A8
● Dorma Trd Pk, E10 123 DX60
Dormay St, SW18 180 DB85
Dormer Cl, E15 281 L4
Barnet EN5 79 CX43
Dormers Av, Sthl. UB1 136 CA72
DORMER'S WELLS, Sthl. UB1 136 CB73
Dormers Ri, Sthl. UB1 136 CB72
Sch Dormers Wells High Sch, Sthl.
UB1 off Dormers Wells La 136 CA72
Sch Dormers Wells Inf & Jun Schs,
Sthl. UB1
off Dormers Wells La 136 CB73
Dormers Wells La, Sthl. UB1 136 CA72
Dormie Cl, St.Alb. AL3 42 CC18
Dormywood, Ruis. HA4 115 BT57
Dornberg Cl, SE3 315 P4
Dornberg Rd, SE3
off Banchory Rd 164 EH80
Dorncliffe Rd, SW6 306 F8
Dornels, Slou. SL2 132 AW72
DORNEY, Wind. SL4 150 AH76
Dorney, NW3 274 D6
★ Dorney Ct, Wind. SL4 150 AG77
Dorney End, Chesh. HP5 54 AN30
Dorney Gro, Wey. KT13 195 BP103
DORNEY REACH, Maid. SL6 150 AF76
Dorney Reach Rd,
Dorney R. SL6 150 AF76
Dorney Ri, Orp. BR5 205 ET98
Sch Dorney Sch, Dorney R. SL6
off Harcourt Cl 150 AF76
Dorney Way, Houns. TW4 176 BY85
Dorney Wd Rd, Burn. SL1 111 AK63
Dornfell St, NW6 273 H3
Dornford Gdns, Couls. CR5 236 DQ119
Dornton Rd, SW12 181 DH89
South Croydon CR2 220 DR106
Dorothy Av, Wem. HA0 138 CL66
Sch Dorothy Barley Inf Sch,
Dag. RM8 off Davington Rd 126 EV64
Sch Dorothy Barley Jun Sch,
Dag. RM8 off Ivinghoe Rd 126 EV64
Dorothy Evans Cl, Bexh. DA7 167 FB84
Dorothy Gdns, Dag. RM8 126 EV63
Dorothy Rd, SW11 160 DF83
Dorrell Pl, SW9 off Brixton Rd 161 DN84
Dorriens Cft, Berk. HP4 38 AT16
Dorrien Wk, SW16 181 DK89
Dorrington Ct, SE25 202 DS96
Dorrington Gdns, Horn. RM12 128 FK60
Dorrington Pt, E3 290 C2
Dorrington St, EC1 286 E6
Dorrington Way, Beck. BR3 203 EC99
Dorrit Cres, Guil. GU3 242 AS132
Dorrit Ms, N18 100 DS49
Dorrit St, SE1 299 K4
Dorrit Way, Chis. BR7 185 EQ93
Dorrofield Cl, Crox.Grn WD3 75 BQ43
Dors Cl, NW9 118 CR60
Dorset Av, Hayes UB4 135 BS69
Romford RM1 127 FD55
Southall UB2 156 CA77
Welling DA16 165 ET84
Dorset Bldgs, EC4 286 G9
Dorset Cl, NW1 284 E6
Berkhamsted HP4 38 AT18
Hayes UB4 135 BS69
Dorset Ct, Nthlt. UB5
off Taywood Rd 136 BY70
Dorset Cres, Grav. DA12 191 GL91
Dorset Dr, Edg. HA8 96 CM51
Woking GU22 227 BB117
Dorset Est, E2 288 B2
Dorset Gdns, Mitch. CR4 201 DM98
Dorset Ho, Enf. EN3 83 DX37
Dorset Ms, N3 98 DA53
SW1 297 J6
Dorset Ri, EC4 286 G9
Dorset Rd, E7 144 EJ66
N15 122 DR56
N22 99 DL53
SE9 184 EL89
SW8 310 B4
SW19 200 DA95
W5 157 CJ76
Ashford TW15 174 BK90
Dorset Rd, Beckenham BR3 203 DX97
Harrow HA1 116 CC58
Mitcham CR4 200 DE96
Sutton SM2 218 DA110
Windsor SL4 151 AQ82
Sch Dorset Rd Inf Sch, SE9
off Dorset Rd 184 EL89
Dorset Sq, NW1 284 E5
Epsom KT19 216 CR110
Dorset St, W1 284 F7
Sevenoaks TN13 off High St 257 FJ125
Dorset Way, Byfleet KT14 212 BK110
Twickenham TW2 177 CD88
Uxbridge UB10 134 BM68
Dorset Waye, Houns. TW5 156 BZ80
Dorton Cl, SE15 311 P5
Coll Dorton Coll of Further Ed,
Seal TN15 off Seal Dr 257 FM122
Dorton Dr, Sev. TN15 257 FM122
Sch Dorton Ho Sch, Seal TN15
off Wildernesse Av 257 FM122
Dorton Way, Ripley GU23 228 BH121
Dorville Cres, W6 159 CV76
Dorville Rd, SE12 184 EF85
Dothill Rd, SE18 165 ER80
Douai Gro, Hmptn. TW12 196 CC95
Sch Douay Martyrs Sch, The,
Ickhm UB10 off Edinburgh Dr 115 BP63
Doubleday Rd, Loug. IG10 85 EQ41
Doughty Ms, WC1 286 C5
Doughty St, WC1 286 C4
Douglas Av, E17 101 EA53
New Malden KT3 199 CV98
Romford RM3 106 FL54
Watford WD24 76 BX37
Wembley HA0 138 CL66
Douglas Cl, Barn. EN4 80 DD38
Chaff.Hun. RM16 170 FY76
Ilford IG6 103 EP52
Jacobs Well GU4 242 AX128
Stanmore HA7 95 CG50
Wallington SM6 219 DL108
Douglas Ct, Cat. CR3 236 DQ122
Westerham TN16 238 EL117
Douglas Cres, Hayes UB4 136 BW70
Douglas Dr, Croy. CR0 203 EA104
Douglas Gdns, Berk. HP4 38 AT18
Douglas Ho, Chsht EN8
off Coopers Wk 67 DX28
Douglas La, Wrays. TW19 173 AZ85
Douglas Ms, NW2 119 CY62
Banstead SM7 off North Acre 233 CZ116
Douglas Path, E14 302 F10
Douglas Rd, E4 102 EE45
E16 291 P7
N1 277 J6
N22 99 DN53
NW6 272 G8
Addlestone KT15 194 BH104
Esher KT10 196 CB103
Hornchurch RM11 127 FF58
Hounslow TW3 156 CB83
Ilford IG3 126 EU58
Kingston upon Thames KT1 198 CP96
Reigate RH2 250 DA133
Slough SL2 131 AR71
Stanwell TW19 174 BK86
Surbiton KT6 198 CM103
Welling DA16 166 EV81
Douglas Sq, Mord. SM4 200 DA100
Douglas St, SW1 297 N9
Douglas Ter, E17
off Penrhyn Av 101 DZ53
Douglas Way, SE8 313 P5
Welwyn Garden City AL7 30 DC09
Doug Siddons Ct, Grays RM17
off Elm Rd 170 GC79
Doulton Cl, Harl. CM17 52 EY16
Doulton Ho, SE11
off Lambeth Wk 298 D7
Doulton Ms, NW6 273 M4
Doultons, The, Stai. TW18 174 BG94
Dounesforth Gdns, SW18 180 DB88
Dounsell Ct, Pilg.Hat. CM15
off Ongar Rd 108 FU44
Douro Pl, W8 295 M6
Douro St, E3 280 A10
Douthwaite Sq, E1 300 D2
Dove App, E6 292 G7
Dove Cl, NW7 97 CT52
Chafford Hundred RM16 170 FY76
Northolt UB5 off Wayfarer Rd 136 BX70
South Croydon CR2 221 DX111
Wallington SM6 219 DM108
Dovecot Cl, Pnr. HA5 115 BV57
Dovecote Av, N22 121 DN55
Dovecote Barns, Purf. RM19 169 FR79
Dovecote Cl, Wey. KT13 195 BP104
Dovecote Gdns, SW14
off Avondale Rd 158 CR83
Dovecote Ho, SE16
off Canada St 301 J5
Dove Ct, EC2 287 L9
Beaconsfield HP9 89 AK52
Hatfield AL10 45 CU20
Dovedale Av, Har. HA3 117 CJ58
Ilford IG5 103 EN54
Dovedale Cl, Guil. GU4
off Weylea Av 243 BA131
Harefield UB9 92 BJ54
Welling DA16 166 EU81
Dovedale Ri, Mitch. CR4 180 DF94
Dovedale Rd, SE22 182 DV85
Dartford DA2 188 FQ88
Dovedon Cl, N14 99 DL47
Dove Ho Cres, Slou. SL2 131 AL69
Dovehouse Cft, Harl. CM20 36 EU13
Dove Ho Gdns, E4 101 EA47
Dovehouse Grn, Wey. KT13
off Rosslyn Pk 213 BR105
Dovehouse Mead, Bark. IG11 145 ER68
Dovehouse St, SW3 296 C10
Dove La, Pot.B. EN6 64 DB34
Dove Ms, SW5 295 N9
Doveney Cl, Orp. BR5 206 EW97
Dove Pk, Chorl. WD3 73 BB44
Pinner HA5 94 CA52
Dover Cl, NW2
off Brent Ter 119 CX61
Romford RM5 105 FC54
Dovercourt Av, Th.Hth. CR7 201 DN98
Dovercourt Est, N1 277 M5
Dovercourt Gdns, Stan. HA7 96 CL50
Dovercourt La, Sutt. SM1 200 DC104
Dovercourt Rd, SE22 182 DS86
Doverfield, Goffs Oak EN7 66 DQ29
Doverfield Rd, SW2 181 DL86
Guildford GU4 243 BA131
Dover Flats, SE1 299 P9
Dover Gdns, Cars. SM5 200 DF104
Dover Ho, SE5
off Cormont Rd 310 G7
Dover Ho Rd, SW15 159 CU84
Doveridge Gdns, N13 99 DP49
Dove Rd, N1 277 L4
Dove Row, E2 278 C9
Dover Pk Dr, SW15 179 CV86
Dover Patrol, SE3
off Kidbrooke Way 164 EH82
Dover Rd, E12 124 EJ61
N9 100 DW47
SE19 182 DR93
Northfleet DA11 190 GD87
Romford RM6 126 EY58
Slough SL1 131 AM72
Dover Rd E, Grav. DA11 190 GE87
Jct Dovers Cor, Rain. RM13 147 FG69
● Dovers Cor Ind Est,
Rain. RM13 147 FF70
DOVERSGREEN, Reig. RH2 266 DB139
Dovers Grn Rd, Reig. RH2 266 DB139
Sch Dovers Grn Sch, Reig. RH2
off Rushetts Rd 266 DC138
Doversmead, Knap. GU21 226 AS116
Dover St, W1 297 K1
Dovers West, Reig. RH2 266 DB138
Dover Way, Crox.Grn WD3 75 BQ42
Dover Yd, W1 297 K2
Doves Cl, Brom. BR2 204 EL103
Doves Yd, N1 276 F9
Dovet Ct, SW8 310 C6
Doveton Rd, S.Croy. CR2 220 DR106
Doveton St, E1 288 G4
Dove Tree Ct,, Epsom KT19 216 CR109
Dove Wk, SW1 296 G10
Hornchurch RM12
off Heron Flight Av 147 FH65
Dowanhill Rd, SE6 183 ED88
Dowdeswell Cl, SW15 158 CS84
Dowding Dr, SE9 184 EJ85
Dowding Pl, Stan. HA7 95 CG51
Dowding Rd, Bigg.H. TN16 238 EK115
Uxbridge UB10 134 BM66
Dowding Wk, Nthflt DA11 190 GE90
Dowding Way, Horn. RM12 147 FH66
Leavesden WD25 59 BT34
Waltham Abbey EN9 83 ED36
Dowdney Cl, NW5 275 M3
Dowells St, SE10 314 D2
Dower Av, Wall. SM6 219 DH109
Dower Cl, Knot.Grn HP9 88 AJ50
Dower Ct, Edg. HA8
off Penniwell Cl 96 CM49
Dower Pk, Wind. SL4 151 AL84
Dowgate Hill, EC4 287 L10
Dowland St, W10 282 F2
Dowlans Cl, Bkhm KT23 246 CA127
Dowlans Rd, Bkhm KT23 246 CB127
Dowlas Est, SE5 311 N4
Dowlas St, SE5 311 N4
Dowlerville Rd, Orp. BR6 223 ET107
Dowley Wd, Welw.G.C. AL7 30 DB10
Dowling Ct, Hem.H. HP3 40 BK23
Dowman Cl, SW19
off Nelson Gro Rd 200 DB95
Downage, NW4 119 CW55
Downage, The, Grav. DA11 191 GG89
Downalong, Bushey Hth WD23 95 CD46
Downbank Av, Bexh. DA7 167 FD81
Downbarns Rd, Ruis. HA4 116 BX62
Downbury Ms, SW18
off Merton Rd 180 DA86
Down Cl, Nthlt. UB5 135 BV68
Sch Downderry Prim Sch,
Brom. BR1 off Downderry Rd 184 EE91
Downderry Rd, Brom. BR1 183 ED90
DOWNE, Orp. BR6 223 EM111
Downe Av, Cudham TN14 223 EQ112
Downe Cl, Horl. RH6 268 DE146
Welling DA16 166 EW80
Downedge, St.Alb. AL3 42 CB19
Downe Ho, SE7
off Springfield Gro 164 EJ79
Sch Downe Manor Prim Sch,
Nthlt. UB5 off Down Way 135 BV69
Downend, SE18
off Moordown 165 EP80
Sch Downe Prim Sch, Downe
BR6 off High Elms Rd 223 EN111
Downer Dr, Sarratt WD3 74 BG36
Downer Meadow, Gdmg. GU7 258 AS143
Downe Rd, Cudham TN14 223 EQ114
Keston BR2 222 EK109
Mitcham CR4 200 DF96
Downes Cl, Twick. TW1
off St. Margarets Rd 177 CH86
Downes Ct, N21 99 DN46
Downes Rd, St.Alb. AL4 43 CH16
Downfield, Wor.Pk. KT4 199 CT102
Downfield Cl, W9 283 L5
Hertford Heath SG13 32 DW11
Sch Downfield JMI Sch,
Chsht EN8 off Downfield Rd 67 DY31
Downfield Rd, Chsht EN8 67 DY31
Hertford Heath SG13 32 DW09
Downfields, Welw.G.C. AL8 29 CV11
Down Hall Rd, Kings.T. KT2 197 CK95
Downhall Rd,
Matching Green CM17 37 FH08
Hatfield Heath CM22 37 FH08
DOWNHAM, Brom. BR1 184 EF92
Downham Cl, Rom. RM5 104 FA52
Downham La, Brom. BR1 183 ED92
Downham Rd, N1 277 L7
Downham Way, Brom. BR1 183 ED92
Downhills Av, N17 122 DR55
Downhills Pk Rd, N17 122 DQ55
Sch Downhills Prim Sch, N15
off Philip La 122 DR56
Downhills Way, N17 122 DQ55
★ Down Ho - Darwin Mus,
Orp. BR6 223 EN112
Downhurst Av, NW7 96 CR50
Downing Av, Guil. GU2 258 AT135
Downing Cl, Har. HA2 116 CC55
Downing Ct, Borwd. WD6
off Bennington Dr 78 CM39
Downing Dr, Grnf. UB6 137 CD67
Downing Path, Slou. SL2 131 AL70
Downing Rd, Dag. RM9 146 EZ67
Downings, E6 293 M8
Downings Rds Moorings, SE1
off Mill St 300 C4
Downing St, SW1 298 A4
Downings Wd, Map.Cr. WD3 91 BD50
Downland Cl, N20 98 DC46
Coulsdon CR5 219 DH114
Epsom KT18 233 CV118
Downland Gdns, Epsom KT18 233 CV118
Downlands, Wal.Abb. EN9 68 EE34
Downlands Rd, Pur. CR8 219 DL113
Downland Way, Epsom KT18 233 CV118
Downleys Cl, SE9 184 EL89
Downman Rd, SE9 164 EL83
Down Pl, W6 159 CV77
Water Oakley SL4 150 AG79
Down Rd, Guil. GU1 243 BB134
Teddington TW11 177 CH93
Downs, The, SW20 179 CX94
Harlow CM20 51 ES15
Hatfield AL10 45 CU20
Leatherhead KT22 247 CJ125
Downs Av, Chis. BR7 185 EM92
Dartford DA1 188 FN87
Epsom KT18 216 CS114
Pinner HA5 116 BZ58
Downs Br Rd, Beck. BR3 203 ED95
Downsbury Ms, SW18
off Merton Rd 180 DA85
Downs Ct, Sutt. SM2 218 DB111
Downs Ct Rd, Pur. CR8 219 DP112
Downsedge Ter, Guil. GU1
off Uplands Rd 243 BB134
Sch Downsell Prim Sch, E15
off Downsell Rd 123 ED63
Downsell Rd, E15 280 F1
Sch Downsend Sch, Lthd. KT22
off Leatherhead Rd 231 CK120
Downsfield, Hat. AL10
off Sandifield 45 CV21
Downsfield Rd, E17 123 DY58
Downshall Av, Ilf. IG3 125 ES58
Sch Downshall Prim Sch,
Seven Kings IG3 off Meads La 125 ES59
Downs Hill, Beck. BR3 183 ED94
Southfleet DA13 190 GC94
Downs Hill Rd, Epsom KT18 216 CS114
Downshire Hill, NW3 274 B1
Downs Ho Rd, Epsom KT18 233 CT118
DOWNSIDE, Cob. KT11 229 BV118
Downside, Cher. KT16 193 BF102
Epsom KT18 216 CS114
Hemel Hempstead HP2 40 BL19
Sunbury-on-Thames TW16 195 BU95
Twickenham TW1 177 CF90
Downside Br Rd, Cob. KT11 229 BV115
Downside Cl, SW19 180 DC93
Downside Common,
Down. KT11 229 BV118
Downside Common Rd,
Down. KT11 229 BV118
Downside Cres, NW3 274 D3
W13 137 CG70
Downside Orchard,
Wok. GU22 off Park Rd 227 BA117
Downside Rd, Down. KT11 229 BV116
Guildford GU4 259 BB135
Sutton SM2 218 DD107
Downside Wk, Brent. TW8
off Sidney Gdns 157 CJ79
Northolt UB5 136 BZ69
Downsland Dr, Brwd. CM14 108 FW48
Downs La, E5
off Downs Rd 122 DV63
Hatfield AL10 45 CU20
Leatherhead KT22 231 CH123
Downs Pk Rd, E5 278 D2
E8 278 B2
Sch Downs Prim Sch & Nurs,
The, Harl. CM20 off The Hides 51 ES15
Downs Rd, E5 122 DU63
Beckenham BR3 203 EB96
Coulsdon CR5 235 DK118
Dorking RH5 247 CJ128
Enfield EN1 82 DS42
Epsom KT18 232 CS115
Istead Rise DA13 190 GD91
Purley CR8 219 DP111
Slough SL3 152 AX75
Sutton SM2 218 DB110
Thornton Heath CR7 202 DQ95
Downs Side, Sutt. SM2 217 CZ111
Down St, W1 297 J3
West Molesey KT8 196 CA99
Down St Ms, W1 297 J3
Downs Vw, Dor. RH4 247 CJ134
Isleworth TW7 157 CF81
Tadworth KT20 233 CV121
Downsview Av, Wok. GU22 227 AZ121
Downs Vw Cl, Orp. BR6 224 EW110
Downsview Cl, Downside KT11 229 BV119
Swanley BR8 207 FF97
Downsview Ct, Guil. GU1
off Hazel Av 242 AW130
Downsview Gdns, SE19 181 DP94
Dorking RH4 263 CH137
Sch Downsview Prim Sch, SE19
off Biggin Way 182 DQ94
Swanley BR8 off Beech Av 207 FG97
Downs Vw Rd, Bkhm KT23 246 CC126
Downsview Rd, SE19 182 DQ94
Sevenoaks TN13 256 FF125
Sch Downsview Sch, E5
off Downs Rd 122 DV63
Downs Way, Bkhm KT23 246 CC126
Epsom KT18 233 CT116
Oxted RH8 254 EE127
Tadworth KT20 233 CV121
Downsway, Guil. GU1 243 BD134
Orpington BR6 223 ES106
South Croydon CR2 220 DS111
Whyteleafe CR3 236 DT116
Downsway, The, Sutt. SM2 218 DC109
Downsway Cl, Tad. KT20 233 CU121
Sch Downs Way Sch, Oxt. RH8
off Downs Way 254 EE128
Downs Wd, Epsom KT18 233 CV117
Downswood, Reig. RH2 250 DE131
Downton Av, SW2 181 DL89
Downtown Rd, SE16 301 M4
Down Way, Nthlt. UB5 135 BV69
Dowrey St, N1 276 E8
Dowry Wk, Wat. WD17 75 BT38
Dowsett Rd, N17 100 DT54
Dowson Cl, SE5 162 DR84
Doyce St, SE1 299 J4
Doyle Cl, Erith DA8 167 FE81
Doyle Gdns, NW10 139 CU67
Doyle Rd, SE25 202 DU98
Doyle Way, Til. RM18
off Coleridge Rd 171 GJ82
D'Oyley St, SW1 296 G8
D'Oyly Carte Island, Wey. KT13 195 BP102
Doynton St, N19 121 DH61
Draco Gate, SW15 306 A10
Draco St, SE17 311 J2
Dragmore St, SW4 181 DK86

Dragonfly Cl, E13 292 B2
Surbiton KT5 198 CQ102
Dragon La, Wey. KT13 212 BN110
Dragon Rd, SE15 311 N3
Hatfield AL10 44 CS17
Dragoon Rd, SE8 313 N1
Dragor Rd, NW10 138 CQ70
Drake Av, Cat. CR3 236 DQ122
Slough SL3 152 AX77
Staines-upon-Thames TW18 173 BF92
Drake Cl, SE16 301 K4
Barking IG11 146 EU70
Warley CM14 108 FX50
Drake Ct, SE19 182 DT92
W12 294 A5
Harrow HA2 116 BZ60
Drake Cres, SE28 146 EW72
Drakefell Rd, SE4 313 J9
SE14 313 J9
Drakefield Rd, SW17 180 DG90
Drake Ho, SW8
off St. George Wf 310 A1
Drakeley Ct, N5 121 DP63
Drake Ms, Brom. BR2 204 EJ98
Hornchurch RM12
off Fulmar Rd 147 FG66
Drake Rd, SE4 314 A10
Chafford Hundred RM16 170 FY76
Chessington KT9 216 CN106
Croydon CR0 201 DM101
Harrow HA2 116 BZ61
Horley RH6 268 DE148
Mitcham CR4 200 DG100
Drakes,The, Denh. UB9
off Patrons Way E 113 BF58
Drakes Cl, Chsht EN8 67 DX28
Esher KT10 214 CA106
Drakes Ctyd, NW6 273 H6
Drakes Dr, Nthwd. HA6 93 BP53
St. Albans AL1 43 CH23
Drakes Dr Mobile Home Pk,
St.Alb. AL1 *off Drakes Dr* 43 CH22
Drakes Meadow, Harl. CM17 36 EY11
Drakes Rd, Amer. HP7 55 AR39
Drake St, WC1 286 C7
Enfield EN2 82 DR39
Drakes Wk, E6 145 EM67
Drakes Way, Hat. AL10 45 CV20
Woking GU22 226 AX122
Drakewood Rd, SW16 181 DK94
Draper Cl, Belv. DA17 166 EZ77
Isleworth TW7 157 CD82
Draper Ct, Horn. RM12 128 FL61
Draper Ho, SE1 299 H8
Draper Pl, N1
off Dagmar Ter 277 H8
Sch **Drapers' Acad**,
Harold Hill RM3 *off Settle Rd* 106 FN49
Drapers' Ct, SW11 309 H6
Drapers' Cres, Whiteley Vill.
KT12 *off Octagon Rd* 213 BT110
Drapers Rd, E15 280 F1
N17 122 DT55
Enfield EN2 81 DP40
Drappers Way, SE16 300 D8
Draven Cl, Brom. BR2 204 EF101
Drawdock Rd, SE10 303 H3
Drawell Cl, SE18 165 ES78
Drax Av, SW20 179 CV94
Draxmont, SW19 179 CY93
Draycot Rd, E11 124 EH58
Surbiton KT6 198 CN102
Draycott Av, SW3 296 D8
Harrow HA3 117 CH58
Draycott Cl, NW2 119 CX62
SE5 311 L5
Harrow HA3 117 CH58
Draycott Ms, SW6 307 H8
Draycott Pl, SW3 296 E9
Draycott Ter, SW3 296 F8
Dray Ct, Guil. GU2
off The Chase 258 AV135
Drayford Cl, W9 283 H4
Dray Gdns, SW2 181 DM85
Draymans Ms, SE15 312 A9
Draymans Way, Islw. TW7 157 CF83
Drayside Ms, Sthl. UB2 156 BZ75
Drayson Cl, Wal.Abb. EN9 68 EE32
Drayson Ms, W8 295 K5
Drayton Av, W13 137 CG73
Loughton IG10 85 EM44
Orpington BR6 205 EP102
Potters Bar EN6 63 CY32
Drayton Br Rd, W7 137 CF73
W13 137 CF73
Drayton Cl, Fetch. KT22 231 CE124
Hounslow TW4 176 BZ85
Ilford IG1 125 ER60
Drayton Ford, Rick. WD3 92 BG48
Drayton Gdns, N21 99 DP45
SW10 295 P10
W13 137 CG73
West Drayton UB7 154 BL75
≠ **Drayton Green** 137 CF72
Drayton Grn, W13 137 CG73
Sch **Drayton Grn Prim Sch**,
W13 *off Drayton Gro* 137 CG73
Drayton Grn Rd, W13 137 CH73
Drayton Gro, W13 137 CG73
Sch **Drayton Ho Sch**, Guil. GU1
off Austen Rd 259 AZ135
Sch **Drayton Manor High Sch**,
W7 *off Drayton Br Rd* 137 CF73
≠ **Drayton Park** 276 F2
Drayton Pk, N5 276 E3
Drayton Pk Ms, N5 276 E2
Sch **Drayton Pk Prim Sch**, N5 276 F2
Drayton Rd, E11 123 ED60
N17 100 DS54
NW10 139 CT67
W13 137 CG73
Borehamwood WD6 78 CN42
Croydon CR0 201 DP103
Drayton Waye, Har. HA3 117 CH58
Dreadnought Cl, SW19 200 DD96
Dreadnought St, SE10
off Boord St 303 K6
Dreadnought Wk, SE10 314 D2
Drenon Sq, Hayes UB3 135 BT73
Dresden Cl, NW6 273 M4
Dresden Rd, N19 121 DJ60
Dresden Way, Wey. KT13 213 BQ106
Dressington Av, SE4 183 EA86
Drew Av, NW7 97 CY51
Drew Gdns, Grnf. UB6 137 CF65
Drew Meadow, Farn.Com. SL2 111 AQ63
Drew Pl, Cat. CR3 236 DR123
Sch **Drew Prim Sch**, E16 304 G3
Drew Rd, E16 304 G3

Drews Pk, Knot.Grn HP9 88 AH49
Drewstead Rd, SW16 181 DK89
Drey,The, Chal.St.P. SL9 90 AY50
Driffield Rd, E3 279 M10
Drift,The, Brom. BR2 204 EK104
Jct **Drift Br**, Epsom KT17 233 CW115
Drift La, Cob. KT11 230 BZ117
Drift Rd, Lthd. KT24 229 BT124
Winkfield SL4 150 AD84
Drift Way, Colnbr. SL3 153 BC81
Richmond TW10 178 CM88
Driftway,The, Bans. SM7 233 CW115
Hemel Hempstead HP2 40 BM20
Leatherhead KT22
off Downs La 231 CH123
Mitcham CR4 200 DG95
Driftwood Av, St.Alb. AL2 60 CA26
Driftwood Dr, Ken. CR8 235 DP117
Drill Hall Rd, Cher. KT16 194 BG101
Dorking RH4 263 CG136
Drinkwater Rd, Har. HA2 116 CB61
Drive,The, E4 101 ED45
E17 123 EB56
E18 124 EG56
N3 98 DA52
N6 120 DF57
N11 99 DJ51
NW10 *off Longstone Av* 139 CT67
NW11 119 CY59
SW6 306 F8
SW16 201 DM97
SW20 179 CW94
W3 138 CQ72
Amersham HP7 55 AR38
Artington GU3 258 AV138
Ashford TW15 175 BR94
Banstead SM7 233 CY117
Barking IG11 145 ET66
Beckenham BR3 203 EA96
Bexley DA5 186 EW86
Brookmans Park AL9 64 DA25
Buckhurst Hill IG9 102 EJ45
Chalfont St. Peter SL9 90 AY52
Chislehurst BR7 205 ET97
Cobham KT11 214 BY114
Collier Row RM5 105 FC53
Coulsdon CR5 219 DL114
Datchet SL3 152 AV81
Edgware HA8 96 CN50
Enfield EN2 82 DR39
Epsom KT19 217 CT107
Erith DA8 167 FB80
Esher KT10 196 CC102
Feltham TW14 176 BW87
Fetcham KT22 231 CE122
Goffs Oak EN7 65 DP28
Gravesend DA12 191 GK91
Great Warley CM13 108 FW50
Guildford GU2 *off Beech Gro* 242 AT134
Harlow CM20 35 ES14
Harold Wood RM3 106 FL53
Harrow HA2 116 CA59
Headley KT18 232 CN124
Hertford SG14 32 DQ07
High Barnet EN5 79 CY41
Hoddesdon EN11 49 EA15
Horley RH6 269 DH149
Hounslow TW3 157 CD82
Ilford IG1 125 EM60
Isleworth TW7 157 CD82
Kingston upon Thames KT2 178 CQ94
Loughton IG10 84 EL41
Morden SM4 200 DD99
New Barnet EN5 80 DC44
Newgate Street SG13 47 DL24
Northwood HA6 93 BS54
Onslow Village GU2 258 AT136
Orpington BR6 205 ET103
Potters Bar EN6 63 CZ33
Radlett WD7 61 CG34
Rickmansworth WD3 74 BJ44
Sawbridgeworth CM21 36 EY05
Scadbury Park BR7 205 ES95
Sevenoaks TN13 257 FH124
Sidcup DA14 186 EV90
Slough SL3 152 AY75
Surbiton KT6 198 CL101
Sutton SM2 217 CZ112
Thornton Heath CR7 202 DR98
Tyrrell's Wood KT22 232 CN124
Uxbridge UB10 114 BL63
Virginia Water GU25 193 AZ99
Wallington SM6 219 DJ110
Watford WD17 75 BR37
Wembley HA9 118 CQ61
West Wickham BR4 203 ED101
Woking GU22 226 AV120
Wraysbury TW19 172 AX85
Drive Mead, Couls. CR5 219 DL114
Drive Rd, Couls. CR5 235 DM119
Drive Spur, Kgswd KT20 234 DB121
Driveway,The, E17 123 EA58
Cuffley EN6 65 DL28
Drodges Cl, Bramley GU5 259 AZ143
Droitwich Cl, SE26 182 DU90
Dromey Gdns, Har. HA3 95 CF52
Dromore Rd, SW15 179 CY86
Dronfield Gdns, Dag. RM8 126 EW64
Droop St, W10 282 E4
Drop La, Brick.Wd AL2 60 CB30
Sch **Dropmore Inf Sch**, Burn. SL1
off Littleworth Rd 110 AJ62
Dropmore Pk, Burn. SL1 110 AH62
Dropmore Rd, Burn. SL1 130 AJ67
Drove Rd, Dor. RH5 262 BW135
Guildford GU4 260 BG136
Drovers Mead, Warley CM14 108 FV49
Drovers Pl, SE15 312 F4
Drovers Rd, S.Croy. CR2 220 DR106
Drovers Way, N7 276 A4
Hatfield AL10 45 CV15
St. Albans AL3 43 CD20
Seer Green HP9 89 AQ51
Droveway, Loug. IG10 85 EP40
Drove Way,The,
Istead Rise DA13 190 GE94
Druce Rd, SE21 182 DS86
Drudgeon Way, Bean DA2 189 FV90
Druids Cl, Ashtd. KT21 232 CM120
Druid St, SE1 299 P4
Druids Way, Brom. BR2 203 ED98
Drumaline Ridge, Wor.Pk. KT4 198 CS103
Sch **Drumbeat Sch**, Downham BR1
off Roundtable Rd 184 EG90
Drummond Av, Rom. RM7 127 FD56
Drummond Cl, Erith DA8 167 FE81
Drummond Cres, NW1 285 N2
Drummond Dr, Stan. HA7 95 CF52
Drummond Gdns, Epsom KT19 216 CP111

Drummond Gate, SW1 297 P10
Drummond Ho, Wind. SL4
off Balmoral Gdns 151 AR83
Drummond Pl, Twick. TW1 177 CH86
Drummond Rd, E11 124 EH58
SE16 300 E6
Croydon CR0 202 DQ103
Guildford GU1 242 AX134
Romford RM7 127 FD56
Drummonds,The, Buck.H. IG9 102 EH47
Epping CM16 70 EU30
Drummonds Pl, Rich. TW9 158 CL84
Drummond St, NW1 285 L4
Drum St, E1 288 B8
Drury Cres, Croy. CR0 201 DN103
Drury La, WC2 286 B9
Hunsdon SG12 34 EK06
Drury Rd, Har. HA1 116 CC59
Drury Way, NW10 118 CR64
● **Drury Way Ind Est**, NW10 118 CQ64
Dryad St, SW15 159 CX83
Dryburgh Gdns, NW9 118 CN55
Dryburgh Rd, SW15 159 CV83
Drycroft, Welw.G.C. AL7 29 CY13
Drydell La, Chesh. HP5 54 AM31
Dryden Av, W7 137 CF72
Dryden Cl, SW4 181 DK85
Ilford IG6 103 ET51
Dryden Ct, SE11 298 F9
Dryden Pl, Til. RM18
off Fielding Av 171 GH81
Dryden Rd, SW19 180 DC93
Enfield EN1 82 DS44
Harrow HA3 95 CF53
Welling DA16 165 ES81
Dryden St, WC2 286 B9
Dryden Twrs, Rom. RM3 105 FH52
Dryden Way, Orp. BR6 206 EU102
Dryfield Cl, NW10 138 CQ65
Dryfield Rd, Edg. HA8 96 CQ51
Dryfield Wk, SE8 314 A2
Dryhill La, Sund. TN14 256 FB123
Dryhill Rd, Belv. DA17 166 EZ79
Dryland Av, Orp. BR6 223 ET105
Drylands Rd, N8 121 DL58
Drynham Pk, Wey. KT13 195 BS104
Drysdale Av, E4 101 EB45
Drysdale Cl, Nthwd. HA6
off Northbrook Dr 93 BS52
Drysdale Pl, N1 287 P2
Drysdale St, N1 287 P3
Duarte Pl, Grays RM16 170 FZ76
Dublin Av, E8 278 D8
Dubrae Cl, St.Alb. AL3 42 CA22
Du Burstow Ter, W7 157 CE75
Ducal St, E2 288 B3
Du Cane Ct, SW17 180 DG88
Du Cane Rd, W12 139 CT72
Duchess Cl, N11 99 DH50
Sutton SM1 218 DC105
Duchess Ct, Wey. KT13 195 BR104
Duchess Gro, Buck.H. IG9 102 EH47
Duchess Ms, W1 285 K7
Duchess of Bedford's Wk, W8 295 J5
Duchess of Kent Cl, Guil. GU2 242 AV130
Duchess St, W1 285 K7
Slough SL1 131 AL74
Duchess Wk, Sev. TN15 257 FL125
Duchy Pl, SE1 298 F2
Duchy Rd, Barn. EN4 80 DD38
Duchy St, SE1 298 F2
Ducie Ho, SE7
off Springfield Gro 164 EJ79
Ducie St, SW4 161 DM84
Duckett Ms, N4 121 DP58
Duckett Rd, N4 121 DP58
Ducketts Mead, Roydon CM19 34 EH14
Ducketts Rd, Dart. DA1 187 FF85
Duckett St, E1 289 L6
Ducking Stool Ct, Rom. RM1 127 FE56
Duck La, W1 285 N9
Thornwood CM16 70 EW26
Duck Lees La, Enf. EN3 83 DY42
Duckling La, Saw. CM21
off Vantorts Rd 36 EY05
Ducks Hill, Nthwd. HA6 92 BN54
Ducks Hill Rd, Nthwd. HA6 93 BP54
Ruislip HA4 93 BP54
DUCKS ISLAND, Barn. EN5 79 CX44
Ducks Wk, Twick. TW1 177 CJ85
Duckworth Dr, Lthd. KT22 231 CK120
Du Cros Dr, Stan. HA7 95 CK51
Du Cros Rd, W3 *off The Vale* 138 CS74
Dudden Hill La, NW10 119 CT63
Duddington Cl, SE9 184 EK91
Dudley Av, Har. HA3 117 CJ55
Waltham Cross EN8 67 DX32
Dudley Cl, Add. KT15 194 BJ104
Bovingdon HP3 57 BA27
Chafford Hundred RM16 170 FY75
Dudley Ct, NW11 119 CZ56
Slough SL1 *off Upton Rd* 152 AU76
Dudley Dr, Mord. SM4 199 CY101
Ruislip HA4 115 BV64
Dudley Gdns, W13 157 CH75
Harrow HA2 117 CD60
Romford RM3 106 FK51
Dudley Gro, Epsom KT18 216 CQ114
Dudley Ho, W2
off North Wf Rd 284 A7
Dudley Ms, SW2
off Bascombe St 181 DN86
Dudley Pl, Hayes UB3 155 BR77
Stanw. TW19 174 BM86
Dudley Rd, E17 101 EA54
N3 98 DB54
NW6 272 F10
SW19 180 DA93
Ashford TW15 174 BM92
Feltham TW14 175 BQ88
Harrow HA2 116 CC61
Ilford IG1 125 EP63
Kingston upon Thames KT1 198 CM97
Northfleet DA11 190 GE87
Richmond TW9 158 CM82
Romford RM3 106 FK51
Southall UB2 156 BX75
Walton-on-Thames KT12 195 BU100
Dudley St, W2 284 A7
Dudlington Rd, E5 122 DW61
Dudmaston Ms, SW3 296 B10
Dudrich Cl, N11 98 DF51
Dudrich Ms, SE22 182 DT85
Dudsbury Rd, Dart. DA1 187 FG86
Sidcup DA14 186 EV93
Dudset La, Houns. TW5 155 BU81
Duffell Ho, SE11 298 D10
Dufferin Av, EC1 287 L5
Dufferin St, EC1 287 K5

Duffield Cl,
Grays (Daniel Cl) RM16 170 FY75
Grays (Davis Rd) RM16 170 FZ76
Harrow HA1 117 CF57
Duffield Dr, N15 122 DT56
Duffield La, Stoke P. SL2 132 AT65
Duffield Pk, Stoke P. SL2 132 AU69
Duffield Rd, Walt.Hill KT20 233 CV124
Duffins Orchard, Ott. KT16 211 BC108
Duff St, E14 290 C9
Dufour's Pl, W1 285 M9
Dugard Way, SE11 298 G8
Dugdale Hill La, Pot.B. EN6 63 CY33
Dugdales, Crox.Grn WD3 74 BN42
Duggan Dr, Chis. BR7 184 EL92
Dugolly Av, Wem. HA9 118 CP62
Duke Ct, Har. HA2
off Station Rd 116 CB57
Duke Gdns, Ilf. IG6
off Duke Rd 125 ER56
Duke Humphrey Rd, SE3 315 K6
Duke of Cambridge Cl,
Twick. TW2 177 CD86
Duke of Edinburgh Rd,
Sutt. SM1 200 DD103
Duke of Wellington Av, SE18 305 P7
Duke of Wellington Pl, SW1 297 H4
Duke of York Sq, SW3 296 F9
Duke of York St, SW1 297 M2
Duke Pl, Slou. SL1
off Montague Rd 132 AT73
Duke Rd, W4 158 CR78
Ilford IG6 125 ER56
Dukes Av, N3 98 DB53
N10 121 DJ55
W4 158 CR78
Edgware HA8 96 CM51
Grays RM17 170 GA75
Harrow HA1 117 CE56
Hounslow TW4 156 BY84
Kingston upon Thames KT2 177 CJ91
New Malden KT3 199 CT97
North Harrow HA2 116 BZ58
Northolt UB5 136 BY66
Richmond TW10 177 CJ91
Theydon Bois CM16 85 ES35
Dukes Cl, Ashf. TW15 175 BQ91
Gerrards Cross SL9 112 AX60
Hampton TW12 176 BZ92
North Weald Bassett CM16 71 FB27
● **Dukes Ct**, Wok. GU21 227 AZ117
Dukes Ct, E6 145 EN67
Dukes Dr, Slou. SL2 111 AM64
Dukes Gate, W4 158 CQ77
Dukes Grn Av, Felt. TW14 175 BU85
Dukes Head Yd, N6
off Highgate High St 121 DH60
Dukes Hill, Wold. CR3 237 DY120
Duke Shore Pl, E14 301 N1
Duke Shore Wf, E14 301 M1
Dukes Kiln Dr, Ger.Cr. SL9 112 AW60
Dukes La, W8 295 K4
Gerrards Cross SL9 112 AY59
Dukes Lo, Nthwd. HA6 93 BS50
Duke's Meadows, W4 158 CR81
Dukes Ms, N10 121 DH55
Duke's Ms, W1 285 H8
Dukes Orchard, Bex. DA5 187 FC88
● **Dukes Pk**, Harl. CM20 35 ET12
Duke's Pas, E17 123 EC56
Dukes Pl, EC3 287 P9
Dukes Ride, Ger.Cr. SL9 112 AY60
North Holmwood RH5 263 CK139
Uxbridge UB10 114 BL63
Dukes Rd, E6 145 EN67
W3 138 CN71
Hersham KT12 214 BX106
Duke's Rd, WC1 285 P3
Dukesthorpe Rd, SE26 183 DX91
Duke St, SW1 297 M2
W1 285 H8
Hoddesdon EN11 49 EA16
Richmond TW9 157 CK84
Sutton SM1 218 DD105
Watford WD17 76 BW41
Windsor SL4 151 AP80
Woking GU21 227 AZ117
Duke St Hill, SE1 299 M2
Dukes Valley, Ger.Cr. SL9 112 AV61
Dukes Way, Berk. HP4 38 AU17
Uxbridge UB8
off Waterloo Rd 134 BJ67
West Wickham BR4 204 EE104
Dukes Wd Av, Ger.Cr. SL9 112 AY60
Dukes Wd Dr, Ger.Cr. SL9 112 AW60
Duke's Yd, W1 285 H10
Dulas St, N4 121 DM60
Dulcie Cl, Green. DA9 189 FT86
Dulford St, W11 282 E10
Dulka Rd, SW11 180 DF85
Dulshott Grn, Epsom KT17
off Church St 216 CS113
Sch **Dulverton Prim Sch**, SE9
off Dulverton Rd 185 ER89
Dulverton Rd, SE9 185 EQ89
Romford RM3 106 FK51
Ruislip HA4 115 BU60
South Croydon CR2 220 DW110
DULWICH, SE21 182 DS87
Sch **Dulwich Coll**, SE21
off College Rd 182 DS89
★ **Dulwich Coll Picture Gall**,
SE21 182 DS87
Sch **Dulwich Coll Prep Sch**,
SE21 *off Alleyn Pk* 182 DS90
Dulwich Common, SE21 182 DS88
SE22 182 DS88
H **Dulwich Comm Hosp**, SE22 162 DS84
Sch **Dulwich Hamlet Jun Sch**,
SE21 *off Dulwich Village* 182 DS86
Dulwich Lawn Cl, SE22
off Colwell Rd 182 DT85
Dulwich Oaks,The, SE21 182 DS90
Dulwich Ri Gdns, SE22
off Lordship La 182 DT85
Dulwich Rd, SE24 181 DN85
Dulwich Village, SE21 182 DS86
Sch **Dulwich Village C of E Inf Sch**, SE21 *off Dulwich Village* 182 DS86
Dulwich Way, Crox.Grn WD3 74 BN43
Dulwich Wd Av, SE19 182 DS91
Dulwich Wd Pk, SE19 182 DS91
Dumas Way, Wat. WD18 75 BS42
Dumbarton Av, Wal.Cr. EN8 67 DX34
Dumbarton Rd, SW2 181 DL86
Dumbleton Cl, Kings.T. KT1 198 CP95
Dumbletons,The, Map.Cr. WD3 91 BE49
Dumbreck Rd, SE9 165 EM84
Dumfries Cl, Wat. WD19 93 BT48

Dumont Rd, N16 122 DS62
Dumpton Pl, NW1 274 G7
Dumsey Eyot, Cher. KT16 194 BK101
Dumville Dr, Gdse. RH9 252 DV131
Dunally Pk, Shep. TW17 195 BR101
Dunbar Av, SW16 201 DN96
Beckenham BR3 203 DY98
Dagenham RM10 126 FA62
Dunbar Cl, Hayes UB4 135 BU71
Slough SL2 132 AU72
Dunbar Ct, Sutt. SM1 218 DD106
Walton-on-Thames KT12 196 BW103
Dunbar Gdns, Dag. RM10 126 FA64
Dunbar Rd, E7 281 P5
N22 99 DN53
New Malden KT3 198 CQ98
Dunbar St, SE27 182 DQ90
Dunblane Cl, Edg. HA8 96 CP47
Dunblane Rd, SE9 164 EL83
Dunboe Pl, Shep. TW17 195 BQ101
Dunboyne Pl, Old Wind. SL4 152 AU84
Dunboyne Rd, NW3 274 E2
Dunbridge Ho, SW15
off Highcliffe Dr 179 CT86
Dunbridge St, E2 288 D4
Duncan Cl, Barn. EN5 80 DC42
Welwyn Garden City AL7 29 CY10
Duncan Dr, Guil. GU1 243 BA133
Duncan Gdns, Stai. TW18 174 BG93
Duncan Gro, W3 138 CS72
Duncannon Cres, Wind. SL4 151 AK83
Duncannon Pl, Green. DA9 169 FW84
Duncannon St, WC2 298 A1
Duncan Rd, E8 278 E8
Richmond TW9 158 CL84
Tadworth KT20 233 CY119
Duncan St, N1 276 G10
Duncan Ter, N1 286 G1
Duncan Way, Bushey WD23 76 BZ40
Dunch St, E1 288 F9
Duncombe Cl, Amer. HP6 55 AS38
Hertford SG14 32 DQ07
Duncombe Ct, Stai. TW18 173 BF94
Duncombe Hill, SE23 183 DY87
Sch **Duncombe Prim Sch**, N19
off Sussex Way 121 DL60
Duncombe Rd, N19 121 DK60
Hertford SG14 32 DQ08
Northchurch HP4 38 AS17
Sch **Duncombe Sch**, Hert. SG14
off Warren Pk Rd 32 DQ08
Duncrievie Rd, SE13 183 ED86
Duncroft, SE18 165 ES80
Windsor SL4 151 AM83
Duncroft Cl, Reig. RH2 249 CZ133
Dundalk Rd, SE4 163 DY83
Dundas Gdns, W.Mol. KT8 196 CB97
Dundas Ms, Enf. EN3 83 EA37
Dundas Rd, SE15 312 G8
SW9 310 F7
Dundee Ho, W9 283 N2
Dundee Rd, E13 292 A1
SE25 202 DV99
Slough SL1 131 AM72
Dundee St, E1 300 E3
Dundee Way, Enf. EN3 83 DY41
Dundee Wf, E14 301 N1
Dundela Gdns, Wor.Pk. KT4 217 CV105
Dundonald Cl, E6 293 H8
Sch **Dundonald Prim Sch**,
SW19 *off Dundonald Rd* 179 CZ94
Tram **Dundonald Road** 179 CZ94
Dundonald Rd, NW10 272 C9
SW19 179 CY94
Dundrey Cres, Merst. RH1 251 DL129
Dunedin Dr, Cat. CR3 252 DS125
Dunedin Ho, E16
off Manwood St 305 K3
Dunedin Rd, E10 123 EB62
Ilford IG1 125 EQ60
Rainham RM13 147 FF69
Dunedin Way, Hayes UB4 136 BW70
Dunelm Gro, SE27 182 DQ91
Dunelm St, E1 289 J8
Dunfee Way, W.Byf. KT14 212 BL112
Dunfield Gdns, SE6 183 EB91
Dunfield Rd, SE6 183 EB92
Dunford Ct, Pnr. HA5
off Cornwall Rd 94 BZ52
Dunford Rd, N7 276 D1
Dungarvan Av, SW15 159 CU84
Dungates La, Buckland RH3 249 CU133
Dunham Ms, Hat. AL10 45 CW17
Dunheved Cl, Th.Hth. CR7 201 DN100
Dunheved Rd N, Th.Hth. CR7 201 DN100
Dunheved Rd S, Th.Hth. CR7 201 DN100
Dunheved Rd W, Th.Hth. CR7 201 DN100
Dunhill Pt, SW15
off Dilton Gdns 179 CV88
Dunholme Grn, N9 100 DT48
Dunholme La, N9 100 DT48
Dunholme Rd, N9 100 DT48
Dunkeld Rd, SE25 202 DR98
Dagenham RM8 126 EV61
Dunkellin Gro, S.Ock. RM15 149 FU71
Dunkellin Way, S.Ock. RM15 149 FU72
Dunkery Rd, SE9 184 EK91
Dunkin Rd, Dart. DA1 168 FN84
Dunkirk Cl, Grav. DA12 191 GJ92
Dunkirks Ms, Hert. SG13
off Queens Rd 32 DR11
Dunkirk St, SE27 182 DQ91
Dunlace Rd, E5 279 H2
Dunleary Cl, Houns. TW4 176 BZ87
Dunley Dr, New Adgtn CR0 221 EB108
Dunlin Cl, Red. RH1 266 DE139
Dunlin Ct, Enf. EN3 *off Teal Cl* 82 DW36
Dunlin Ho, W13 137 CF70
Dunlin Ri, Guil. GU4 243 BD132
Dunlin Rd, Hem.H. HP2 40 BL15
Dunloe Av, N17 122 DR55
Dunloe St, E2 288 A1
Dunlop Cl, Dart. DA1 168 FL83
Tilbury RM18 *off Dunlop Rd* 171 GF82
Dunlop Pl, SE16 300 B7
Dunlop Rd, Til. RM18 171 GF81
Dunmail Dr, Pur. CR8 220 DS114
Dunmore Pt, E2 288 A3
Dunmore Rd, NW6 272 E9
SW20 199 CW95
Dunmow Cl, Felt. TW13 176 BX91
Loughton IG10 84 EL44
Romford RM6 126 EW57
Dunmow Dr, Rain. RM13 147 FF67

D

D
E

Dunmow Rd, E15 281 H1
Dunmow Wk, N1 277 J8
Dunnage Cres, SE16 301 M8
Dunnets, Knap. GU21 226 AS117
Dunning Cl, S.Ock. RM15 149 FU72
Dunningford Cl, Horn. RM12 127 FF64
Sch Dunningford Prim Sch, Elm Pk RM12 off Upper Rainham Rd 127 FF64
Dunn Mead, NW9 97 CT52
Dunnock Cl, N9 101 DX46
Borehamwood WD6 78 CN42
Dunnock Ct, SE21 off Elmworth Gro 182 DR89
Dunnock Rd, E6 293 H8
Dunns Pas, WC1 286 B8
Dunn St, E8 278 A2
Dunny La, Chipper. WD4 57 BE32
Dunnymans Rd, Bans. SM7 233 CZ115
Dunollie Pl, NW5 275 M2
Dunollie Rd, NW5 275 L2
Dunoon Rd, SE23 182 DW87
Dunottar Cl, Red. RH1 266 DD136
Sch Dunottar Sch, Reig. RH2 off High Trees Rd 266 DD135
Dunraven Av, Red. RH1 267 DH141
Dunraven Dr, Enf. EN2 81 DN40
Dunraven Rd, W12 139 CU74
Sch Dunraven Sch, Lwr Sch, SW16 off Mount Nod Rd 181 DM90
Upr Sch, SW16 off Leigham Ct Rd 181 DM90
Dunraven St, W1 284 F10
Dunsany Rd, W14 294 C7
Dunsborough Pk, Ripley GU23 228 BJ120
Dunsbury Cl, Sutt. SM2 off Nettlecombe Cl 218 DB109
Dunsdon Av, Guil. GU2 258 AV135
Dunsfold Ri, Couls. CR5 219 DK113
Dunsfold Way, New Adgtn CR0 221 EB108
Dunsford Way, SW15 179 CV86
Dunsmore Cl, Bushey WD23 77 CD44
Hayes UB4 136 BX70
Dunsmore Rd, Walt. KT12 195 BV100
Dunsmore Way, Bushey WD23 77 CD44
Dunsmure Rd, N16 122 DS60
Dunspring La, Ilf. IG5 103 EP54
Dunstable Cl, Rom. RM3 off Dunstable Rd 106 FK51
Dunstable Ms, W1 285 H6
Dunstable Rd, Rich. TW9 158 CL84
Romford RM3 106 FK51
West Molesey KT8 196 BZ98
Dunstall Grn, Chobham GU24 210 AW109
Dunstall Rd, SW20 179 CV93
Dunstalls, Harl. CM19 51 EN19
Dunstall Way, W.Mol. KT8 196 CB97
● Dunstall Welling Est, Well. DA16 off Leigh Pl 166 EV82
Dunstan Cl, N2 120 DC55
Dunstan Ct, Whyt. CR3 off Godstone Rd 236 DU119
Dunstan Ho, E1 off Stepney Grn 289 H6
Dunstan Rd, NW11 119 CZ60
Coulsdon CR5 235 DK117
Dunstans Gro, SE22 182 DV86
Dunstans Rd, SE22 182 DU87
Dunster Av, Mord. SM4 199 CX102
Dunster Cl, Barn. EN5 79 CX42
Harefield UB9 92 BH53
Romford RM5 105 FC54
Dunster Ct, EC3 287 N10
Borehamwood WD6 off Kensington Way 78 CR41
Dunster Cres, Horn. RM11 128 FN61
Dunster Dr, NW9 118 CQ60
Dunster Gdns, NW6 273 H6
Slough SL1 off Avebury 131 AN73
Dunsters Mead, Welw.G.C. AL7 30 DA11
Dunsterville Way, SE1 299 M5
Dunster Way, Har. HA2 116 BY62
Wallington SM6 off Helios Rd 200 DG102
Dunston Rd, E8 278 A9
SW11 309 H9
Dunston St, E8 278 A8
Dunton Cl, Surb. KT6 198 CL102
DUNTON GREEN, Sev. TN13 241 FC119
⇌ Dunton Green 241 FF119
Sch Dunton Grn Prim Sch, Dunt.Grn TN13 off London Rd 241 FE120
Dunton Rd, E10 123 EB59
SE1 300 A10
Romford RM1 127 FE56
Duntshill Rd, SW18 180 DB88
Dunvegan Cl, W.Mol. KT8 196 CB98
Dunvegan Rd, SE9 165 EM84
Dunwich Rd, Bexh. DA7 166 EZ81
Dunworth Ms, W11 282 G8
Duplex Ride, SW1 296 F5
Dupont Rd, SW20 199 CX96
Duppas Av, Croy. CR0 off Violet La 219 DP105
Duppas Cl, Shep. TW17 195 BR99
Duppas Hill La, Croy. CR0 off Duppas Hill Rd 219 DP105
Duppas Hill Rd, Croy. CR0 219 DP105
Duppas Hill Ter, Croy. CR0 201 DP104
Duppas Rd, Croy. CR0 201 DN104
Dupre Cl, Chaff.Hun. RM16 170 FY76
Slough SL1 151 AL75
Dupre Cres, Beac. HP9 89 AP54
Dupree Rd, SE7 304 A10
Du Pre Wk, Woob.Grn HP10 off Stratford Dr 110 AD59
Dura Den Cl, Beck. BR3 183 EB94
Durand Cl, Cars. SM5 200 DF102
Durand Gdns, SW9 310 D6
Sch Durand Prim Sch, SW9 310 D6
Cowley Rd Annexe, SW9 310 F7
Durands Wk, SE16 301 M4
Durand Way, NW10 138 CQ66
Durant Rd, Swan. BR8 187 FG93
Durants Pk Av, Enf. EN3 83 DX42
Durants Rd, Enf. EN3 82 DW42
Sch Durants Sch, Enf. EN3 off Pitfield Way 82 DW39
Durant St, E2 288 C2
Durban Gdns, Dag. RM10 147 FC66
Durban Rd, E15 291 J2
E17 101 DZ53
N17 100 DS51
SE27 182 DQ91
Beckenham BR3 203 DZ96
Ilford IG2 125 ES60
Durban Rd E, Wat. WD18 75 BU42
Durban Rd W, Wat. WD18 75 BU42
Durbin Rd, Chess. KT9 216 CL105
Sch Durdans Pk Prim Sch, Sthl. UB1 off King Georges Dr 136 BZ71
Durdans Rd, Sthl. UB1 136 BZ72
Durell Gdns, Dag. RM9 126 EX64
Durell Rd, Dag. RM9 126 EX64
Durfey Pl, SE5 311 M4
Durfold Dr, Reig. RH2 250 DC134
Durford Cres, SW15 179 CU88
Durham Av, Brom. BR2 204 EF98
Hounslow TW5 156 BZ78
Romford RM2 128 FJ56
Woodford Green IG8 102 EK50
Durham Cl, SW20 off Durham Rd 199 CV96
Guildford GU2 242 AT132
Sawbridgeworth CM21 36 EW06
Stanstead Abbotts SG12 33 EB10
Durham Hill, Brom. BR1 184 EF91
Durham Ho St, WC2 298 B1
Durham Pl, SW3 308 E1
Ilford IG1 off Eton Rd 125 EQ63
Durham Ri, SE18 165 EQ78
Durham Rd, E12 124 EK63
E16 291 K5
N2 120 DE55
N7 121 DM61
N9 100 DU47
SW20 199 CV95
W5 157 CK76
Borehamwood WD6 78 CQ41
Bromley BR2 204 EF97
Dagenham RM10 127 FC64
Feltham TW14 176 BW87
Harrow HA1 116 CB57
Sidcup DA14 186 EV92
Durham Row, E1 289 K7
Durham St, SE11 310 C1
Durham Ter, W2 283 L8
Durham Wf Dr, Brent. TW8 157 CJ80
Durham Yd, E2 288 E2
Duriun Way, Erith DA8 167 FH80
Durleston Pk Dr, Bkhm KT23 246 CC125
Durley Av, Pnr. HA5 116 BY59
Durley Gdns, Orp. BR6 224 EV105
Durley Rd, N16 122 DS59
Durlston Rd, E5 122 DU61
Kingston upon Thames KT2 178 CL93
Durndale La, Nthflt DA11 191 GF91
Durnell Way, Loug. IG10 85 EN41
Durnford St, N15 122 DS57
SE10 314 F3
Durning Rd, SE19 182 DR92
Durnsford Av, SW19 180 DA89
Durnsford Ct, Enf. EN3 off Enstone Rd 83 DY41
Durnsford Rd, N11 99 DK53
SW19 180 DA89
Durrants Cl, Rain. RM13 148 FJ68
Durrants Dr, Crox.Grn WD3 75 BQ42
Durrants Hill Rd, Hem.H. HP3 40 BK23
Durrants La, Berk. HP4 38 AT18
Durrants Path, Chesh. HP5 54 AN27
Durrants Rd, Berk. HP4 38 AT18
Durrant Way, Orp. BR6 223 ER106
Swanscombe DA10 190 FY87
Durrell Rd, SW6 306 G7
Durrell Way, Shep. TW17 195 BR100
Durrington Av, SW20 199 CW95
Durrington Pk Rd, SW20 179 CW94
Durrington Rd, E5 279 L1
Durrington Twr, SW8 309 M8
Dursley Cl, SE3 164 EJ82
Dursley Gdns, SE3 164 EK81
Dursley Rd, SE3 164 EJ82
Sch Durston Ho Sch, W5 off Castlebar Rd 137 CK72
Durward St, E1 288 E6
Durweston Ms, W1 284 F6
Durweston St, W1 284 F6
Dury Falls Cl, Horn. RM11 128 FM60
Dury Rd, Barn. EN5 79 CZ39
Dutch Barn Cl, Stanw. TW19 174 BK86
Dutch Elm Av, Wind. SL4 152 AT80
Dutch Gdns, Kings.T. KT2 178 CP93
Dutch Yd, SW18 off Wandsworth High St 180 DA85
Dutton St, SE10 314 E6
Dutton Way, Iver SL0 133 BE72
Duxberry Cl, Brom. BR2 off Southborough La 204 EL99
Duxford Cl, Horn. RM12 147 FH65
Duxford Ho, SE2 off Wolvercote Rd 166 EX75
Duxhurst La, Reig. RH2 266 DB144
Duxons Turn, Hem.H. HP2 off Maylands Av 41 BP19
Dwight Ct, SW6 306 F8
Dwight Rd, Wat. WD18 93 BR45
Sch Dycorts Sch, Harold Hill RM3 off Settle Rd 106 FN49
Dye Ho La, E3 280 B9
Dyer Ct, Enf. EN3 off Manton Rd 83 EA37
Dyer's Bldgs, EC1 286 E7
Dyers Fld, Smallfield RH6 269 DP148
Dyers Hall Rd, E11 124 EE60
Dyers La, SW15 159 CV84
Dyers Way, Rom. RM3 105 FH52
Dyke Dr, Orp. BR5 206 EW102
Dykes Path, Wok. GU21 off Bentham Av 227 BC115
Dykes Way, Brom. BR2 204 EF97
Dykewood Cl, Bex. DA5 187 FE90
Dylan Cl, Els. WD6 95 CK45
Dylan Rd, SE24 161 DP84
Belvedere DA17 166 FA76
Dylways, SE5 162 DR84
Dymchurch Cl, Ilf. IG5 103 EN54
Orpington BR6 223 ES105
Dymes Path, SW19 off Queensmere Rd 179 CX89
Dymock St, SW6 307 L10
Dymoke Grn, St.Alb. AL4 43 CG16
Dymoke Rd, Horn. RM11 127 FF59
Dymokes Way, Hodd. EN11 33 EA14
Dymond Est, SW17 off Glenburnie Rd 180 DE90
Dyneley Rd, SE12 184 EJ91
Dyne Rd, NW6 272 F7
Dynevor Rd, N16 122 DS62
Richmond TW10 178 CL85
Dynham Rd, NW6 273 J6
Dyott St, WC1 286 A8
Dyrham La, Barn. EN5 79 CU36
Dysart Av, Kings.T. KT2 177 CJ92
Sch Dysart Sch, Surb. KT6 off Ewell Rd 198 CM101
Dysart St, EC2 287 M5
Dyson Cl, Wind. SL4 151 AP83
Dyson Rd, E11 124 EE58
E15 281 M5
Dysons Cl, Wal.Cr. EN8 67 DX33
Dysons Rd, N18 100 DV50

E

Eade Rd, N4 122 DQ59
Eagans Cl, N2 120 DD55
Eagle Av, Rom. RM6 126 EY58
Eagle Cl, SE16 312 G1
Amersham HP6 72 AT37
Enfield EN3 82 DW42
Hornchurch RM12 147 FH65
Wallington SM6 219 DL107
Waltham Abbey EN9 68 EG34
Eagle Ct, EC1 286 G6
N18 100 DT51
Hertford SG13 32 DV08
Eagle Dr, NW9 96 CS54
Eagle Hts, SW11 off Bramlands Cl 308 C10
Eagle Hill, SE19 182 DR93
Eagle Ho Ms, SW4 off Narbonne Av 181 DJ85
Sch Eagle Ho Sch, Mitch. CR4 off London Rd 200 DF96
Eagle La, E11 124 EG56
Eagle Lo, NW11 119 CZ59
Eagle Ms, N1 277 N5
Eagle Pl, SW1 297 M1
SW7 295 P10
Eagle Rd, Guil. GU1 258 AX135
Lon.Hthrw Air. TW6 155 BT83
Slough SL1 131 AM73
Wembley HA0 137 CK66
Eagles, The, Denh. UB9 off Patrons Way E 113 BF58
Eagles Dr, Tats. TN16 238 EK118
Eaglesfield Rd, SE18 165 EP80
Eagles Rd, Green. DA9 169 FV84
Eagle St, WC1 286 C7
Eagle Ter, Wdf.Grn. IG8 102 EH52
● Eagle Trd Est, Mitch. CR4 200 DF100
Eagle Way, Gt Warley CM13 107 FV51
Hatfield AL10 45 CU20
Northfleet DA11 190 GA85
Eagle Wf Rd, N1 277 K10
Eagling Cl, E3 290 B3
Sch Ealdham Prim Sch, SE9 off Eldham Sq 164 EJ84
Eldham Sq, SE9 164 EJ84
EALING, W5 137 CJ73
Coll Ealing & W London Coll, W5 off Ealing Grn 137 CK74
⇌ Ealing Broadway 137 CK73
⊖ Ealing Broadway 137 CK73
● Ealing Bdy Shop Cen, W5 137 CK73
Coll Ealing City Learning Cen, W3 off Gunnersbury La 158 CN75
Ealing Cl, Borwd. WD6 78 CR39
Sch Ealing Coll Upr Sch, W13 off The Avenue 137 CH72
★ Ealing Common, W5 138 CL74
⊖ Ealing Common 138 CM74
Jct Ealing Common, W5 138 CM73
Ealing Grn, W5 137 CK74
H Ealing Hosp NHS Trust, Sthl. UB1 157 CD75
Coll Ealing Indep Coll, W5 off New Bdy 137 CJ73
Ealing Pk Gdns, W5 157 CJ77
Ealing Rd, Brent. TW8 157 CK78
Northolt UB5 136 CA66
Wembley HA0 137 CK67
Ealing Village, W5 138 CL72
Eamont Cl, Ruis. HA4 115 BP59
Eamont St, NW8 274 C10
Eardemont Cl, Dart. DA1 167 FF84
Eardley Cres, SW5 307 K1
Eardley Pt, SE18 305 P9
Sch Eardley Prim Sch, SW16 off Cunliffe St 181 DJ93
Eardley Rd, SW16 181 DJ92
Belvedere DA17 166 FA78
Sevenoaks TN13 257 FH124
Earhart Way, Houns. TW4 155 BU83
Earl Cl, N11 99 DH50
Earldom Rd, SW15 159 CW84
Earle Gdns, Kings.T. KT2 178 CL93
Earleswood, Cob. KT11 214 BX112
Earlham Gro, E7 281 L3
N22 99 DM52
Sch Earlham Prim Sch, E7 281 M3
N22 off Earlham Gro 99 DN52
Earlham St, WC2 285 P9
Earl Ri, SE18 165 ER77
Earl Rd, SW14 158 CQ84
Northfleet DA11 190 GE89
Earlsbrook Rd, Red. RH1 266 DF136
Earlsbury Gdns, Edg. HA8 96 CN49
EARLS COURT, SW5 295 H10
⊖ Earl's Court 295 K9
Earls Ct Gdns, SW5 295 L9
Earls Ct Rd, SW5 295 K8
W8 295 K8
Earls Ct Sq, SW5 295 L10
Earls Cres, Har. HA1 117 CE56
Earlsdown Ho, Bark. IG11 off Wheelers Cross 145 ER68
Earlsferry Way, N1 276 B7
EARLSFIELD, SW18 180 DC88
⇌ Earlsfield 180 DC88
Earlsfield Ho, Kings.T. KT2 off Kingsgate Rd 197 CK95
Sch Earlsfield Prim Sch, SW18 off Tranmere Rd 180 DC89
Earlsfield Rd, SW18 180 DC88
Earlshall Rd, SE9 165 EM84
Earls Ho, Rich. TW9 158 CP80
Earls La, Slou. SL1 131 AM74
South Mimms EN6 62 CS32
Earlsmead, Har. HA2 116 BZ63
Sch Earlsmead Prim Sch, N15 off Broad La 122 DT57
South Harrow HA2 off Arundel Dr 116 BZ63
Earlsmead Rd, N15 122 DT57
NW10 282 A2
Earl's Path, Loug. IG10 84 EJ40
Earls Ter, W8 295 H7
Earlsthorpe Ms, SW12 180 DG86
Earlsthorpe Rd, SE26 183 DX91
Earlstoke St, EC1 286 G2
Earlston Gro, E9 278 F9
Earl St, EC2 287 N6
Watford WD17 76 BW41
Earls Wk, W8 295 J7
Dagenham RM8 126 EV63
EARLSWOOD, Red. RH1 266 DF136
⇌ Earlswood 266 DF136
Earlswood Av, Th.Hth. CR7 201 DN99
Earlswood Gdns, Ilf. IG5 125 EN55
Sch Earlswood Inf & Nurs Sch, Red. RH1 off St. John's Rd 266 DG135
Earlswood Rd, Red. RH1 266 DF135
Earlswood St, SE10 315 K1
Early Ms, NW1 275 K8
Earnshaw St, WC2 285 P8
Earsby St, W14 294 F8
Easby Cres, Mord. SM4 200 DB100
Easebourne Rd, Dag. RM8 126 EW64
Easedale Dr, Horn. RM12 127 FG64
Easedale Ho, Islw. TW7 off Summerwood Rd 177 CF85
Eashing Pt, SW15 off Wanborough Dr 179 CV88
Easington Pl, Guil. GU1 off Maori Rd 259 AZ135
Easington Way, S.Ock. RM15 149 FU71
Easley's Ms, W1 285 H8
EASNEYE, Ware SG12 33 EC06
● East 10 Enterprise Pk, E10 off Argall Way 123 DY60
Coll East 15 Acting Sch, Loug. IG10 off Rectory La 85 EP41
EAST ACTON, W3 138 CR74
⊖ East Acton 139 CT72
East Acton La, W3 138 CS73
Sch East Acton Prim Sch, W3 off East Acton La 138 CS73
East Arbour St, E1 289 J8
East Av, E12 144 EL66
E17 123 EB56
Hayes UB3 155 BT75
Southall UB1 136 BZ73
Wallington SM6 219 DM106
Whiteley Village KT12 off Octagon Rd 213 BT110
East Bk, N16 122 DS59
Eastbank Cl, E17 off Grosvenor Pk Rd 123 EB57
Eastbank Rd, Hmptn H. TW12 176 CC92
EAST BARNET, Barn. EN4 80 DE44
East Barnet Rd, Barn. EN4 80 DE44
Sch East Barnet Sch, Barn. EN4 off Chestnut Gro 80 DF44
EAST BEDFONT, Felt. TW14 175 BS88
Coll East Berkshire Coll, Langley Campus, Langley SL3 off Station Rd 153 BA76
Windsor Campus, Wind. SL4 off St. Leonards Rd 151 AQ82
Eastbourne Av, W3 138 CR72
Eastbourne Gdns, SW14 158 CQ83
Eastbourne Ms, W2 283 P8
Eastbourne Rd, E6 293 M2
E15 281 K9
N15 122 DS58
SW17 180 DG93
W4 158 CQ79
Brentford TW8 157 CJ78
Feltham TW13 176 BX89
Godstone RH9 252 DW132
Slough SL1 131 AM72
Eastbourne Ter, W2 283 P8
Eastbournia Av, N9 100 DV48
Eastbridge, Slou. SL2 152 AV75
Eastbrook Av, N9 100 DW45
Dagenham RM10 127 FC63
Eastbrook Cl, Dag. RM10 127 FC63
Wok. GU21 227 BA116
Sch Eastbrook Comp Sch, Dag. RM10 off Dagenham Rd 127 FC63
Eastbrook Dr, Rom. RM7 127 FE62
Sch Eastbrook Prim Sch, Hem.H. HP2 off St. Agnells La 40 BN15
Eastbrook Rd, SE3 164 EH80
Waltham Abbey EN9 68 EE33
Eastbrook Way, Hem.H. HP2 40 BL20
EAST BURNHAM, Slou. SL2 131 AN67
East Burnham La, Farn.Royal SL2 131 AN67
East Burrowfield, Welw.G.C. AL7 29 CX11
EASTBURY, Nthwd. HA6 93 BS49
Eastbury Av, Bark. IG11 145 ES67
Enfield EN1 82 DS39
Northwood HA6 93 BS50
Sch Eastbury Comp Sch, Bark. IG11 off Rosslyn Rd 145 ES65
Eastbury Ct, Bark. IG11 145 ES67
St. Albans AL1 43 CF19
Eastbury Fm Cl, Nthwd. HA6 93 BS49
Eastbury Gro, W4 158 CS78
★ Eastbury Manor Ho, Bark. IG11 145 ET67
Eastbury Pl, Nthwd. HA6 93 BT50
Sch Eastbury Prim Sch, Bark. IG11 off Dawson Av 145 ET66
Northwood HA6 off Bishops Ave 93 BT49
Eastbury Rd, E6 293 L5
Kingston upon Thames KT2 178 CL94
Northwood HA6 93 BS51
Petts Wood BR5 205 ER100
Romford RM7 127 FD58
Watford WD19 93 BV45
Eastbury Sq, Bark. IG11 145 ET67
Eastbury Ter, E1 289 J5
Eastcastle St, W1 285 L8
Eastcheap, EC3 287 M10
East Churchfield Rd, W3 138 CR74
East Ch Rd, Lon.Hthrw Air. TW6 155 BS82
EAST CLANDON, Guil. GU4 244 BL131
East Cl, W5 138 CN70
Barnet EN4 80 DG42
Greenford UB6 136 CC68
Rainham RM13 147 FH70
St. Albans AL2 60 CB25
Eastcombe Av, SE7 164 EH79
East Common, Ger.Cr. SL9 112 AY58
EASTCOTE, Pnr. HA5 116 BW58
⊖ Eastcote 116 BW59
Eastcote, Orp. BR6 205 ET102
Eastcote Av, Grnf. UB6 117 CG64
Harrow HA2 116 CB61
West Molesey KT8 196 BZ99
Eastcote High Rd, Eastcote Vill. HA5 115 BU58
● Eastcote Ind Est, Ruis. HA4 116 BW59
Eastcote La, Har. HA2 116 CA62
Northolt UB5 136 CA66
Eastcote La N, Nthlt. UB5 136 BZ65
Eastcote Pl, Pnr. HA5 115 BV58
Sch Eastcote Prim Sch, Well. DA16 off Eastcote Rd 165 ER83
Eastcote Rd, Harrow HA2 116 CC62
Pinner HA5 116 BX57
Ruislip HA4 115 BS59
Welling DA16 165 ER82
Eastcote St, SW9 310 C9
Eastcote Vw, Pnr. HA5 116 BW56
EASTCOTE VILLAGE, Pnr. HA5 115 BV57
Eastcott Cl, Kings.T. KT2 178 CQ92
Eastcourt, Sun. TW16 196 BW96
East Ct, Wem. HA0 117 CJ61
Sch Eastcourt Sch, Ilf. IG3 off Eastwood Rd 126 EU60
East Cres, N11 98 DF49
Enfield EN1 82 DT43
Windsor SL4 151 AM81
East Cres Rd, Grav. DA12 191 GJ86
Eastcroft, Slou. SL2 131 AP70
Eastcroft Rd, Epsom KT19 216 CS108
East Cross Route, E3 279 P6
E9 279 M5
⇌ East Croydon 202 DR103
Tram East Croydon 202 DR103
Eastdean Av, Epsom KT18 216 CP113
East Dene Dr, Harold Hill RM3 106 FK50
Eastdown Pk, SE13 163 ED84
East Dr, NW9 119 CU55
Carshalton SM5 218 DE109
Oaklands AL4 44 CL19
Orpington BR5 206 EV100
Sawbridgeworth CM21 36 EY06
Stoke Poges SL2 132 AS69
Virginia Water GU25 192 AU101
Watford WD25 75 BV35
East Duck Lees La, Enf. EN3 83 DY42
EAST DULWICH, SE22 182 DU86
⇌ East Dulwich 162 DS84
East Dulwich Gro, SE22 182 DS86
East Dulwich Rd, SE15 162 DT84
SE22 162 DT84
EAST END GREEN, Hert. SG14 31 DK13
East End Rd, N2 120 DC55
N3 98 DA54
East End Way, Pnr. HA5 116 BY55
East Entrance, Dag. RM10 147 FB68
Eastergate, Beac. HP9 88 AJ51
Eastern Av, E11 124 EJ58
Aveley RM15 148 FQ74
Chertsey KT16 194 BG97
Ilford IG2, IG4 124 EL58
Pinner HA5 116 BX59
Romford RM6 126 EW56
Waltham Cross EN8 67 DY33
West Thurrock RM20 169 FT79
Eastern Av E, Rom. RM1, RM2, RM3 127 FD55
● Eastern Av Retail Pk, Rom. RM7 127 FC56
Eastern Av W, Rom. RM1, RM5, RM6, RM7 126 EY56
Eastern Dr, B.End SL8 110 AC59
Eastern Gateway, E16 304 D1
● Eastern Ind Est, Erith DA18 166 FA75
Eastern Pathway, Horn. RM12 148 FJ67
Eastern Perimeter Rd, Lon.Hthrw Air. TW6 155 BT83
Eastern Quay Apts, E16 off Rayleigh Rd 304 B2
Eastern Rd, E13 144 EH68
E17 123 EC57
N2 120 DF55
N22 99 DL53
SE4 163 EA84
Grays RM17 170 GD77
Romford RM1 127 FE57
Jct Eastern Rbt, Ilf. IG1 125 EQ61
Eastern Vw, Bigg.H. TN16 238 EJ117
Easternville Gdns, Ilf. IG2 125 EQ58
Eastern Way, SE2 146 EX74
SE28 166 EU75
Belvedere DA17 167 FB75
Erith DA18 146 EX74
Grays RM17 170 GA79
● Easter Pk, Rain. RM13 147 FE73
EAST EWELL, Sutt. SM2 217 CX110
East Ferry Rd, E14 302 D8
Eastfield Av, Wat. WD24 76 BX39
Eastfield Cl, Slou. SL1 off St. Laurence Way 152 AU76
Eastfield Cotts, Hayes UB3 155 BR78
Eastfield Ct, St.Alb. AL4 off Southfield Way 43 CK17
Eastfield Gdns, Dag. RM10 126 FA63
Eastfield Par, Pot.B. EN6 64 DD32
Sch Eastfield Prim Sch, Enf. EN3 off Eastfield Rd 83 DX38
Eastfield Rd, E17 123 EA56
N8 121 DL55
Brentwood CM14 108 FX47
Burnham SL1 130 AG71
Dagenham RM9, RM10 126 FA63
Enfield EN3 83 DX38
Redhill RH1 267 DJ135
Waltham Cross EN8 67 DY32
Eastfields, Pnr. HA5 116 BW57
Eastfields Av, SW18 160 DA84
Eastfields Rd, W3 138 CQ71
Mitcham CR4 200 DG96
Eastfield St, E14 289 M7
EAST FINCHLEY, N2 120 DD56
⊖ East Finchley 120 DE56
East Flint, Hem.H. HP1 39 BF19
East Gdns, SW17 180 DE93
Woking GU22 227 BC117
Eastgate, Bans. SM7 217 CY114
East Gate, Harl. CM20 35 EQ14
● Eastgate Business Pk, E10 123 DY60
Eastgate Cl, SE28 146 EX72
Eastgate Gdns, Guil. GU1 258 AY135
Eastglade, Nthwd. HA6 93 BS50
Pinner HA5 116 BY55
East Gorse, Croy. CR0 221 DY112
East Grn, Hem.H. HP3 58 BM25
East Hall La, Wenn. RM13 148 FK72
East Hall Rd, Orp. BR5 206 EY101
EAST HAM, E6 292 F1
⊖ East Ham 144 EL66
Eastham Cl, Barn. EN5 79 CY43
Eastham Cres, Brwd. CM13 109 GA49
● East Ham Ind Est, E6 292 G5
East Ham Manor Way, E6 293 L8

East Ham Mkt Hall, E6
off Myrtle Rd 144 EL67
East Ham Nature Reserve &
Visitor Cen, E6 293 K4
East Harding St, EC4 286 F8
East Heath Rd, NW3 120 DD62
East Hill, SW18 180 DB85
Biggin Hill TN16 238 EH118
Dartford DA1 188 FM87
Oxted RH8 254 EE129
South Croydon CR2 220 DS110
South Darenth DA4 208 FQ95
Wembley HA9 118 CN61
Woking GU22 227 BC116
East Hill Dr, Dart. DA1 188 FM87
East Hill Rd, Oxt. RH8 254 EE129
Eastholm, NW11 120 DB56
East Holme, Erith DA8 167 FD81
Eastholme, Hayes UB3 135 BU74
EAST HORSLEY, Lthd. KT24 245 BS127
East India 291 H10
East India Dock Rd, E14 289 P9
East India Way, Croy. CR0 202 DT102
East Kent Av, Nthflt DA11 190 GC86
Eastlake Ho, NW8
off Frampton St 284 B5
Eastlake Rd, SE5 311 H9
Eastlands Cl, Oxt. RH8 253 ED127
Eastlands Cres, SE21 182 DT86
Eastlands Way, Oxt. RH8 253 ED127
East La, SE16 300 C5
Abbots Langley WD5 59 BU29
Kingston upon Thames KT1
off High St 197 CK97
South Darenth DA4 209 FR96
Watford WD25 59 BU29
Wembley HA0, HA9 117 CK62
West Horsley KT24 245 BQ125
East La Business Pk,
Wem. HA9 117 CK62
Eastlea Av, Wat. WD25 76 BY37
Eastlea Comm Sch, E16 291 K4
Eastlea Ms, E16 291 K5
Eastleigh Av, Har. HA2 116 CB61
Eastleigh Cl, NW2 118 CS62
Sutton SM2 218 DB108
Eastleigh Rd, E17 101 DZ54
Bexleyheath DA7 167 FC82
Eastleigh Wk, SW15 179 CU87
Eastleigh Way, Felt. TW14 175 BU88
East Lo La, Enf. EN2 81 DK36
East Mall, Rom. RM1
off Mercury Gdns 127 FE57
Eastman Dental Hosp, WC1 286 C3
Eastman Rd, W3 138 CR74
Eastman Way, Epsom KT19 216 CP110
Hemel Hempstead HP2 40 BN17
East Mascalls, SE7
off Mascalls Rd 164 EJ79
East Mead, Ruis. HA4 116 BX62
Welwyn Garden City AL7 30 DB12
Eastmead, Wok. GU21 226 AV117
Eastmead Av, Grnf. UB6 136 CB69
Eastmead Cl, Brom. BR1 204 EL96
East Meads, Guil. GU2 258 AT135
Eastmearn Rd, SE21 182 DQ89
East Ms, E15
off East Rd 281 N9
East Mill, Grav. DA11 191 GF86
East Milton Rd, Grav. DA12 191 GK87
East Mimms, Hem.H. HP2 40 BL19
EAST MOLESEY, KT8 197 CD98
Eastmont Rd, Esher KT10 197 CE103
Eastmoor Pl, SE7 304 E7
Eastmoor St, SE7 304 E7
East Mt St, E1 288 F7
Eastney Rd, Croy. CR0 201 DP102
Eastney St, SE10 314 G1
Eastnor, Bov. HP3 57 BA28
Eastnor Cl, Reig. RH2 265 CZ137
Eastnor Rd, SE9 185 EQ88
Reigate RH2 266 DA136
Easton Gdns, Borwd. WD6 78 CR42
Easton St, WC1 286 E3
Eastor, Welw.G.C. AL7 30 DA06
East Pk, Harl. CM17 36 EV12
Sawbridgeworth CM21 36 EY06
East Pk Cl, Rom. RM6 126 EX57
East Parkside, SE10 303 L5
Warlingham CR6 237 EA116
East Pas, EC1 287 H6
East Pier, E1 300 E3
East Pl, SE27
off Pilgrim Hill 182 DQ91
East Pt, SE1 300 C10
East Poultry Av, EC1 286 G7
East Putney 179 CY85
East Ramp,
Lon.Hthrw Air. TW6 155 BP81
East Ridgeway, Cuffley EN6 65 DK29
East Rd, E15 281 N9
N1 287 L3
SW3 308 G1
SW19 180 DC93
Barnet EN4 98 DG46
Chadwell Heath RM6 126 EY57
Edgware HA8 96 CP53
Enfield EN3 82 DW38
Feltham TW14 175 BR87
Harlow CM20 36 EV11
Kingston upon Thames KT2 198 CL95
Reigate RH2 249 CZ133
Rush Green RM7 127 FD59
Welling DA16 166 EV82
West Drayton UB7 154 BM77
Weybridge KT13 213 BR108
East Rochester Way, SE9 165 ES84
Bexley DA5 186 EX86
Sidcup DA15 165 ES84
East Row, E11 124 EG58
W10 282 E5
Eastry Av, Brom. BR2 204 EF100
Eastry Rd, Erith DA8 166 FA80
East Shalford La, Guil. GU4 258 AY139
EAST SHEEN, SW14 158 CR84
East Sheen Av, SW14 158 CR84
East Sheen Prim Sch, SW14
off Upper Richmond Rd W 158 CS84
Eastside Ms, E3 290 A1
Eastside Rd, NW11 119 CZ56
East Smithfield, E1 300 B1
Eaststand Apts, N5 121 DP62
East St, SE17 299 K10
Barking IG11 145 EQ66
Bexleyheath DA7 166 FA84
Bookham KT23 246 CB125
Brentford TW8 157 CJ80
Bromley BR1 204 EG96
Chertsey KT16 194 BG101
East St, Chesham HP5 54 AP32
Epsom KT17 216 CS113
Grays RM17 170 GC79
Hemel Hempstead HP2 40 BK20
South Stifford RM20 170 FY79
Ware SG12 33 DX06
East Surrey College,
Gatton Pt N, Red. RH1
off Claremont Rd 250 DG130
Gatton Pt S, Red. RH1
off College Cres 250 DG131
East Surrey Gro, SE15 312 A5
East Surrey Hosp, Red. RH1 266 DG138
East Surrey Mus, Cat. CR3 236 DU124
East Tenter St, E1 288 B9
East Ter, Grav. DA12 191 GJ86
East Thurrock Rd, Grays RM17 170 GB79
East Twrs, Pnr. HA5 116 BX57
East Vale, W3
off The Vale 139 CT74
East Vw, E4 101 EC50
Barnet EN5 79 CZ41
Essendon AL9 46
DF17 Eastview Av, SE18 165 ES80
East Village London, E20 280 E3
Eastville Av, NW11 119 CZ58
East Wk, E.Barn. EN4 98 DG45
Harlow CM20 35 ER14
Hayes UB3 135 BU74
Reigate RH2 250 DB134
Eastway, E9 279 N4
East Way, E11 124 EH57
Bromley BR2 204 EG101
Croydon CR0 203 DY103
Guildford GU2 242 AT134
Hayes UB3 135 BU74
Ruislip HA4 115 BU60
Eastway, Beac. HP9 88 AG54
Epsom KT19 216 CQ112
Gatwick RH6 269 DH152
Morden SM4 199 CX99
Wallington SM6 219 DJ105
Eastway Cres, Har. HA2
off Eliot Dr 116 CB61
Eastwell Cl, Beck. BR3 203 DY95
EASTWICK, Harl. CM20 35 EP11
Eastwick Ct, SW19
off Victoria Dr 179 CX88
Eastwick Cres, Mill End WD3 91 BF47
Eastwick Dr, Bkhm KT23 230 CA123
Eastwick Hall La, Harl. CM20 35 EN09
EAST WICKHAM, Well. DA16 166 EU80
East Wickham Inf Sch,
Well. DA16 off Wickham St 165 ET81
East Wickham Jun Sch,
Well. DA16 off Wickham St 166 EU81
Eastwick Inf Sch,
Bkhm KT23 off Eastwick Dr 230 CB124
Eastwick Jun Sch,
Bkhm KT23 off Eastwick Dr 230 CB124
Eastwick Lo Rbt,
Harl. CM20 35 EQ11
Eastwick Pk Av, Bkhm KT23 230 CB124
Eastwick Rd, Bkhm KT23 246 CB125
Harlow CM20 35 EM11
Hersham KT12 213 BV106
Hunsdon SG12 34 EK08
Stanstead Abbotts SG12 34 EF12
Eastwick Row, Hem.H. HP2 40 BN21
East Wood Apts, Ald.WD25
off Wall Hall Dr 76 CB36
Eastwood Cl, E18
off George La 102 EG54
N7 276 D2
N17 100 DV52
Eastwood Ct, Hem.H. HP2 40 BN19
Eastwood Dr, Rain. RM13 147 FH72
Eastwood Rd, E18 102 EG54
N10 98 DG54
Bramley GU5 259 AZ144
Ilford IG3 126 EU59
West Drayton UB7 154 BN75
East Woodside, Bex. DA5 186 EY88
Eastwood St, SW16 181 DJ93
Eastworth Rd, Cher. KT16 194 BG102
Eatington Rd, E10 123 ED57
Eaton Av, Slou. SL1 130 AJ73
Eaton Cl, SW1 296 G9
Stanmore HA7 95 CH49
Eaton Ct, Guil. GU1 243 BA132
Eaton Dr, SW9 161 DP84
Kingston upon Thames KT2 178 CN94
Romford RM5 105 FB52
Eaton Gdns, Brox. EN10 49 DY22
Dagenham RM9 146 EY66
Eaton Gate, SW1 296 G8
Northwood HA6 93 BQ51
Eaton Ho, E14 301 P1
Eaton La, SW1 297 K7
Eaton Ms N, SW1 296 G8
Eaton Ms S, SW1 297 H8
Eaton Ms W, SW1 297 H8
Eaton Pk, Cob. KT11 214 BY114
Eaton Pk Rd, N13 99 DN47
Cobham KT11 214 BY114
Eaton Pl, SW1 296 G7
Eaton Ri, E11 124 EJ57
W5 137 CK72
Eaton Rd, NW4 119 CW57
Enfield EN1 82 DS41
Hemel Hempstead HP2 41 BP17
Hounslow TW3 157 CD84
St. Albans AL1 43 CH20
Sidcup DA14 186 EX89
Sutton SM2 218 DD107
Eaton Row, SW1 297 J6
Eatons Mead, E4 101 EA47
Eaton Sq, SW1 297 J6
Longfield DA3
off Bramblefield Cl 209 FX97
Eaton Ter, SW1 296 G8
Eaton Ter Ms, SW1 296 G8
Eatonville Rd, SW17 180 DF89
Eatonville Vil, SW17
off Eatonville Rd 180 DF89
Eaton Way, Borwd. WD6 78 CM39
Eaves Cl, Add. KT15 212 BJ107
Ebbas Way, Epsom KT18 232 CP115
Ebb Ct, E16
off Albert Basin Way 145 EQ73
Ebberns Rd, Hem.H. HP3 40 BK23
Ebbett Ct, W3
off Victoria Rd 138 CR71
Ebbisham Cl, Dor. RH4
off Nower Rd 263 CG136
Ebbisham Dr, SW8 310 C2
Ebbisham La, Walt.Hill KT20 233 CT121
Ebbisham Rd, Epsom KT18 216 CP114
Worcester Park KT4 199 CW103
Ebbsfleet Business Pk,
Nthflt. DA11 190 GA85
Ebbsfleet Gateway,
Swans. DA11 190 GA88
Ebbsfleet International 190 GA86
Ebbsfleet Rd, NW2 272 E2
Ebbsfleet Wk, Nthflt DA11 190 GB86
Ebdon Way, SE3 164 EH83
Ebenezer Ho, SE11 298 F9
Ebenezer St, N1 287 L2
Ebenezer Wk, SW16 201 DJ95
Ebley Cl, SE15 312 A3
Ebner St, SW18 180 DB85
Ebor Cotts, SW15 178 CS90
Ebor St, E1 288 A4
Ebrington Rd, Har. HA3 117 CK58
Ebsworth Cl, Maid. SL6 130 AC68
Ebsworth St, SE23 183 DX87
Eburne Rd, N7 121 DL62
Ebury App, Rick. WD3
off Ebury Rd 92 BK46
Ebury Br, SW1 297 J10
Ebury Br Est, SW1 297 J10
Ebury Br Rd, SW1 309 H1
Ebury Cl, Kes. BR2 204 EL104
Northwood HA6 93 BQ50
Ebury Ms, SE27 181 DP90
SW1 297 H8
Ebury Ms E, SW1 297 J8
Ebury Rd, Rick. WD3 92 BK46
Watford WD17 76 BW41
Ebury Sq, SW1 297 H9
Ebury St, SW1 297 J8
Ebury Way Cycle Path, The,
Rick. WD3 93 BP45
Watford WD18 93 BP45
Ecclesbourne Cl, N13 99 DN50
Ecclesbourne Gdns, N13 99 DN50
Ecclesbourne Prim Sch,
Th.Hth. CR7 off Bensham La 202 DQ99
Ecclesbourne Rd, N1 277 K7
Thornton Heath CR7 202 DQ99
Eccles Hill, N.Holm. RH5 263 CJ140
Eccles Rd, SW11 160 DF84
Eccleston Br, SW1 297 K8
Eccleston Cl, Cockfos. EN4 80 DF42
Orpington BR6 205 ER102
Eccleston Cres, Rom. RM6 126 EU59
Ecclestone Ct, Wem. HA9
off St. John's Rd 118 CL64
Ecclestone Pl, Wem. HA9 118 CM64
Eccleston Ms, SW1 297 H7
Eccleston Pl, SW1 297 J8
Eccleston Rd, W13 137 CG73
Eccleston Sq, SW1 297 K9
Eccleston Sq Ms, SW1 297 L9
Eccleston St, SW1 297 J7
Echelforde Dr, Ashf. TW15 174 BN91
Echelford Prim Sch, The,
Ashf. TW15 off Park Rd 175 BP92
Echo Hts, E4 101 EB46
Echo Pit Rd, Guil. GU1 258 AY138
Echo Sq, Grav. DA12
off Old Rd E 191 GJ89
Eckford St, N1 276 E10
Eckington Ho, N15 122 DR58
Eckstein Rd, SW11 160 DE84
Eclipse Ho, N22
off Station Rd 99 DM54
Eclipse Rd, E13 292 A6
Ecob Cl, Guil. GU3 242 AT130
Ecole Française de Londres,
W6 294 D8
Ecton Rd, Add. KT15 212 BH105
Ector Rd, SE6 184 EE89
Edbrooke Rd, W9 283 J4
Eddington Cres,
Welw.G.C. AL7 29 CX12
Eddinton Cl, New Adgtn. CR0 221 EC107
Eddiscombe Rd, SW6 307 H8
Eddy Cl, Rom. RM7 127 FB58
Eddystone Rd, SE4 183 DY85
Eddystone Twr, SE8 301 M9
Eddystone Wk, Stai. TW19 174 BL87
Eddy St, Berk. HP4 38 AU18
Ede Cl, Houns. TW3 156 BZ83
Edenbridge Cl, SE16 312 F1
Orpington BR5 206 EX98
Edenbridge Rd, E9 279 K7
Enfield EN1 82 DS44
Eden Cl, NW3 120 DA61
W8 295 K6
Bexley DA5 187 FD91
Enfield EN3 83 EA38
New Haw KT15 212 BH110
Slough SL3 153 BA78
Wembley HA0 137 CK67
Edencourt Rd, SW16 181 DH93
Edencroft, Bramley GU5 259 AZ144
Edendale Rd, Bexh. DA7 167 FD81
Edenfield Gdns, Wor.Pk. KT4 199 CT104
Eden Grn, S.Ock. RM15 149 FV71
Eden Gro, E17 123 EB57
N7 276 D3
NW10 off St. Andrews Rd 139 CV65
Eden Gro Rd, Byfleet KT14 212 BL113
Edenhall Cl, Hem.H. HP2 41 BR21
Romford RM3 106 FJ50
Edenhall Glen, Rom. RM3 106 FJ50
Edenhall Rd, Rom. RM3 106 FJ50
Edenham High Sch,
Croy. CR0 off Orchard Way 203 DZ101
Edenham Way, W10 282 G6
Eden Ho, SE16
off Canada St 301 J5
Edenhurst Av, SW6 306 G10
Eden Ms, SW17
off Huntspill St 180 DC90
EDEN PARK, Beck. BR3 203 EA99
Eden Park 203 EA99
Eden Pk Av, Beck. BR3 203 DY98
Eden Pl, Grav. DA12
off Lord St 191 GH87
Eden Rd, E17 123 EB57
SE27 181 DP92
Beckenham BR3 203 DY98
Bexley DA5 187 FC91
Croydon CR0 220 DR105
Edenside Rd, Bkhm KT23 230 BZ124
Edensor Gdns, W4 158 CS80
Edensor Rd, W4 158 CS80
Eden St, Kings.T. KT1 197 CK96
Edenvale, Goffs Oak EN7 66 DV29
Edenvale Cl, Mitch. CR4
off Edenvale Rd 180 DG94
Edenvale Rd, Mitch. CR4 180 DG94
Edenvale St, SW6 307 M9
Eden Wk, Kings.T. KT1
off Eden Wk Shop Cen 198 CL96
Eden Wk Shop Cen,
Kings.T. KT1 198 CL96
Eden Way, E3
off Old Ford Rd 279 P9
Beckenham BR3 203 DZ99
Warlingham CR6 237 DY118
Ederline Av, SW16 201 DM97
Edes Flds, Reig. RH2 265 CY136
EDF Energy London Eye,
SE1 298 C4
Edgar Cl, Swan. BR8 207 FF97
Edgar Ho, E11 124 EG59
NW7 off Morphou Rd 97 CY50
Edgar Kail Way, SE22 162 DS84
Edgarley Ter, SW6 306 E7
Edgar Myles Ho, E16
off Malmesbury Rd 291 L6
Edgar Rd, E3 290 D2
Hounslow TW4 176 BZ87
Romford RM6 126 EX59
South Croydon CR2 220 DR109
Tatsfield TN16 238 EK121
West Drayton UB7 134 BL73
Edgars Ct, Welw.G.C. AL7 29 CY10
Edgar Wallace Cl, SE15 311 P4
Edgbaston Dr, Shenley WD7 62 CL32
Edgbaston Rd, Wat. WD19 93 BV48
Edgeborough Way, Brom. BR1 184 EK94
Edgebury, Chis. BR7 185 EP91
Edgebury Prim Sch,
Chis. BR7 off Belmont La 185 EQ91
Edgebury Wk, Chis. BR7 185 EQ91
Edge Business Cen, NW2 119 CV61
Edge Cl, Wey. KT13 212 BN108
Edgecombe Ho, SW19 179 CY88
Edgecoombe, S.Croy. CR2 220 DW108
Edgecoombe Cl, Kings.T. KT2 178 CR94
Edgecote Cl, W3
off Cheltenham Pl 138 CQ74
Edgecot Gro, N15 122 DS57
Edgefield Av, Bark. IG11 145 ET66
Edgefield Cl, Dart. DA1 188 FP88
Redhill RH1 266 DG139
Edge Gro Sch, Ald. WD25
off High Cross 76 CC37
Edge Hill, SE18 165 EP79
SW19 179 CX94
Edge Hill Av, N3 120 DA56
Edge Hill Ct, SW19 179 CX94
Edgehill Ct, Walt. KT12
off St. Johns Dr 196 BW102
Edgehill Gdns, Dag. RM10 126 FA63
Edgehill Rd, W13 137 CJ71
Chislehurst BR7 185 EQ90
Mitcham CR4 201 DH95
Purley CR8 219 DN110
Edgeley, Bkhm KT23 230 BY124
Edgeley Caravan Pk,
Far.Grn GU5 260 BL143
Edgeley La, SW4
off Edgeley Rd 161 DK83
Edgeley Rd, SW4 309 N10
Edgell Cl, Vir.W. GU25 193 AZ97
Edgell Rd, Stai. TW18 173 BF92
Edgel St, SW18
off Ferrier St 160 DB84
Edge Pt Cl, SE27 181 DP92
Edge St, W8 295 K2
Edgewood Dr, Orp. BR6 223 ET106
Edgewood Grn, Croy. CR0 203 DX102
Edgeworth Av, NW4 119 CU57
Edgeworth Cl, NW4 119 CU57
Slough SL3 152 AX75
Whyteleafe CR3 236 DU118
Edgeworth Cres, NW4 119 CU57
Edgeworth Rd, SE9 164 EJ84
Cockfosters EN4 80 DE42
Edgington Rd, SW16 181 DK93
Edgington Way, Sid. DA14 186 EW94
Edgson Ho, SW1
off Ebury Br Rd 297 J10
EDGWARE, HA8 96 CP50
Edgware 96 CP51
Edgware 96 CN51
Edgwarebury Gdns, Edg. HA8 96 CN50
Edgwarebury La, Edg. HA8 96 CN49
Elstree WD6 96 CL45
Edgware Comm Hosp,
Edg. HA8 96 CP52
Edgware Ct, Edg. HA8
off High St 96 CN51
Edgware Inf Sch, Edg. HA8
off High St 96 CN51
Edgware Jun Sch, Edg. HA8
off Heming Rd 96 CN51
Edgware Road 284 C7
Edgware Rd, NW2 119 CV60
NW9 118 CR55
W2 284 D8
Edgware Rd Sub, W2
off Edgware Rd 284 C7
Edgware Way, Edg. HA8 96 CM49
Edinburgh Av, Mill End WD3 74 BG44
Slough SL1 131 AN71
Edinburgh Cl, E2 288 G1
Pinner HA5 116 BX59
Uxbridge UB10 115 BP63
Edinburgh Ct, SW20 199 CX99
Kingston upon Thames KT1
off Watersplash Cl 198 CL97
Edinburgh Cres, Wal.Cr. EN8 67 DY33
Edinburgh Dr, Abb.L. WD5 59 BU32
Ickenham UB10 115 BP63
Staines-upon-Thames TW18 174 BK93
Edinburgh Gdns, Wind. SL4 151 AR83
Edinburgh Gate, SW1 296 E4
Denham UB9 113 BF58
Harlow CM20 35 ER12
Edinburgh Ho, W9 283 M2
Edinburgh Ms, Til. RM18 171 GH82
Edinburgh Pl, Harl. CM20 36 EU11
Edinburgh Prim Sch, E17 123 DZ58
Edinburgh Rd, E13 144 EH68
E17 123 EA57
N18 100 DU50
W7 157 CF75
Sutton SM1 200 DC103
Edinburgh Way, Harl. CM20 35 ER12
Edington Rd, SE2 166 EV76
Enfield EN3 82 DW40
Edison Av, Horn. RM12 127 FF61
Edison Cl, E17
off Exeter Rd 123 EA57
Hornchurch RM12
off Edison Av 127 FF60
St. Albans AL4 43 CJ21
West Drayton UB7 154 BM75
Edison Ct, SE10 303 M8
Watford WD18 75 BU44
Edison Dr, Sthl. UB1 136 CB72
Wembley HA9 118 CL62
Edison Gro, SE18 165 ET80
Edison Rd, N8 121 DK58
Bromley BR2 204 EG96
Enfield EN3 83 DZ40
Welling DA16 165 ET81
Edis St, NW1 274 G8
Edith Cavell Cl, N19
off Hillrise Rd 121 DL59
Edith Cavell Way, SE18 164 EL81
Edith Gdns, Surb. KT5 198 CP101
Edith Gro, SW10 307 N3
Edithna St, SW9 310 B10
Edith Nesbit Wk, SE9 184 EL85
Edith Neville Prim Sch,
NW1 285 N1
Edith Rd, E6 144 EK66
E15 281 H2
N11 99 DK52
SE25 202 DR99
SW19 180 DB93
W14 294 E9
Orpington BR6 224 EU106
Romford RM6 126 EX58
Edith Row, SW6 307 M6
Edith St, E2 278 C10
Edith Summerskill Ho, SW6 307 H3
Edith Ter, SW10 307 N4
Edith Vil, SW15 off Bective Rd 159 CY84
W14 294 G9
Edith Yd, SW10 307 P4
Edlyn Cl, Berk. HP4 38 AT18
Edmansons Cl, N17 100 DS53
Edmeston Cl, E9 279 M4
Edmond Beaufort Dr,
St.Alb. AL3 43 CD18
Edmonds Ct, W.Mol. KT8
off Avern Rd 196 CB99
EDMONTON, N9 100 DU49
Edmonton Co Sch,
Lwr Sch, N9 off Little Bury St 100 DS46
Upr Sch, Enf. EN1
off Great Cambridge Rd 100 DT45
Edmonton Green 100 DU47
Edmonton Green 100 DU47
Edmonton Green 100 DU47
Edmonton Grn, N9
off The Green 100 DU47
Edmonton Grn Mkt, N9
off Edmonton Grn Shop Cen 100 DV47
Edmonton Grn Shop Cen, N9 100 DV47
Edmonton Trade Pk, N18
off Eley Rd 100 DW50
Edmund Ct, Beac. HP9
off North Dr 110 AG55
Edmund Gro, Felt. TW13 176 BZ89
Edmund Halley Way, SE10 303 J5
Edmund Hurst Dr, E6 293 N7
Edmund Rd, Chaff.Hun. RM16 169 FX75
Mitcham CR4 200 DE97
Orpington BR5 206 EW100
Rainham RM13 147 FE68
Welling DA16 166 EU83
Edmunds Av, Orp. BR5 206 EX97
Edmunds Cl, Hayes UB4 136 BW71
Edmunds Ms, Kings L. WD4 58 BN29
Edmunds Rd, Hert. SG14 31 DM08
Edmunds Twr, Harl. CM19 51 EQ15
Edmund St, SE5 311 L4
Edmunds Wk, N2 120 DE56
Edmunds Way, Slou. SL2 132 AV71
Edmund Waller Prim Sch,
SE14 313 J8
Edna Rd, SW20 199 CX96
Edna St, SW11 308 C7
Edrich Ho, SW4 310 A7
Edric Ho, SW1 off Page St 297 P8
Edrick Rd, Edg. HA8 96 CQ51
Edrick Wk, Edg. HA8 96 CQ51
Edric Rd, SE14 313 J4
Edridge Cl, Bushey WD23 76 CC43
Hornchurch RM12 128 FK64
Edridge Rd, Croy. CR0 202 DQ104
Edson Cl, Wat. WD25 59 BT33
Edulf Rd, Borwd. WD6 78 CP39
Edward Amey Cl, Wat. WD25 76 BW36
Edward Av, E4 101 EB51
Morden SM4 200 DD99
Edward Betham C of E Prim Sch,
Grnf. UB6 off Oldfield La S 136 CC68
Edward Cl, N9 100 DT45
NW2 272 D1
Abbots Langley WD5 59 BT32
Chafford Hundred RM16 169 FX76
Hampton Hill TW12
off Edward Rd 176 CC92
Romford RM2 128 FJ55
St. Albans AL1 43 CF21
Edward Ct, E16 291 N6
Hemel Hempstead HP3 40 BK24
Staines-upon-Thames TW18 174 BJ93
Waltham Abbey EN9 68 EF33
Edwardes Pl, W8 295 H7
Edwardes Sq, W8 295 J6
Edward Gro, Barn. EN4 80 DD43
Edward Ho, Red. RH1
off Royal Earlswood Pk 266 DG137
Edward Ms, NW1 285 K1
Edward Pauling Ho, Felt.
TW14 off Westmacott Dr 175 BT87
Edward Pauling Prim Sch,
Felt. TW13 off Redford Cl 175 BS89
Edward Pl, SE8 313 P3
Edward Rd, E17 123 DX56
SE20 183 DX94
Barnet EN4 80 DD43
Biggin Hill TN16 238 EL118
Bromley BR1 184 EH94
Chislehurst BR7 185 EP92
Coulsdon CR5 235 DK115
Croydon CR0 202 DS101
Feltham TW14 175 BR85
Hampton Hill TW12 176 CC92
Harrow HA2 116 CC55
Northolt UB5 136 BW68
Romford RM6 126 EY58
Edward's Av, Ruis. HA4 135 BV65
Edwards Cl, Hutt. CM13 109 GE44
Worcester Park KT4 199 CX103
Edwards Cotts, N1 276 G5
Edwards Ct, Slou. SL1 152 AS75
Waltham Cross EN8
off Turners Hill 67 DX31

E

Edwards Dr, N11
off Gordon Rd 99 DK52
Edward II Av, Byfleet KT14 212 BM114
Edwards Gdns, Swan. BR8 207 FD98
Edwards La, N16 122 DR61
Edwards Ms, N1 276 F6
W1 284 G9
Edward Sq, N1 276 C9
SE16 301 M2
Edwards Rd, Belv. DA17 166 FA77
Edward St, E16 291 N5
SE8 313 N4
SE14 313 M4
Edwards Way, Hutt. CM13 109 GE44
Edward's Way, SE4
off Adelaide Av 183 EA85
Edwards Yd, Wem. HA0
off Mount Pleasant 138 CL67
Edward Temme Av, E15 281 L7
Edward Tyler Rd, SE12 184 EH89
Edward Way, Ashf. TW15 174 BM89
Sch Edward Wilson Prim Sch,
W2 283 L6
Edwina Gdns, Ilf. IG4 124 EL57
Edwin Av, E6 293 L1
Edwin Cl, Bexh. DA7 166 EZ79
Rainham RM13 147 FF69
West Horsley KT24 245 BR125
Edwin Hall Pl, SE13
off Hither Grn La 183 ED86
Sch Edwin Lambert Sch,
Horn. RM11 off Malvern Rd 127 FG59
Edwin Pl, Croy. CR0
off Cross Rd 202 DR102
Edwin Rd, Dart. DA2 187 FH90
Edgware HA8 96 CR51
Twickenham TW1, TW2 177 CF88
West Horsley KT24 245 BQ125
Edwin's Mead, E9
off Lindisfarne Way 123 DY63
Edwin St, E1 289 H4
E16 291 N7
Gravesend DA12 191 GH87
Edwin Ware Ct, Pnr. HA5
off Crossway 94 BW54
Edwyn Cl, Barn. EN5 79 CW44
Edwyn Ho, SW18
off Neville Gill Cl 180 DB86
Eel Brook Cl, SW6 307 L6
Eel Brook Studios, SW6 307 K5
Eel Pie Island, Twick. TW1 177 CG88
Effie Pl, SW6 307 K5
Effie Rd, SW6 307 K5
EFFINGHAM, Lthd. KT24 246 BY127
Effingham Cl, Sutt. SM2 218 DB108
Effingham Common, Eff. KT24 229 BU123
Effingham Common Rd,
Eff. KT24 229 BU123
Effingham Ct, Wok. GU22
off Constitution Hill 226 AY119
Effingham Hill, Dor. RH5 246 BX132
⇌ Effingham Junction 229 BU123
Effingham Pl, Eff. KT24 246 BX127
Effingham Rd, N8 121 DN57
SE12 184 EE85
Croydon CR0 201 DM101
Long Ditton KT6 197 CH101
Reigate RH2 266 DB135
Effort St, SW17 180 DE92
Effra Par, SW2 181 DN85
Effra Rd, SW2 161 DN84
SW19 180 DB93
Egan Cl, Ken. CR8 236 DR120
Egan Way, Hayes UB3 135 BS73
Egbert St, NW1 274 G8
Egbury Ho, SW15
off Tangley Gro 179 CT86
Egdean Wk, Sev. TN13 257 FJ123
Egeremont Rd, SE13 314 D8
Egerton Av, Swan. BR8 187 FF94
Egerton Cl, Dart. DA1 187 FH88
Pinner HA5 115 BU56
Egerton Ct, Guil. GU2
off Egerton Rd 242 AS134
Egerton Cres, SW3 296 D8
Egerton Dr, SE10 314 C6
Egerton Gdns, NW4 119 CV56
NW10 272 A9
SW3 296 C7
W13 137 CH72
Ilford IG3 125 ET62
Egerton Gdns Ms, SW3 296 D7
Egerton Pl, SW3 296 D7
Weybridge KT13 213 BQ107
Egerton Rd, N16 122 DT59
SE25 202 DS97
Berkhamsted HP4 38 AU17
Guildford GU2 242 AS134
New Malden KT3 199 CT98
Slough SL2 131 AL70
Twickenham TW2 177 CE87
Wembley HA0 138 CM66
Weybridge KT13 213 BQ107
Sch Egerton-Rothesay Nurs & Pre-Prep
Sch, Berk. HP4 off Charles St 38 AV19
Sch Egerton-Rothesay Sch,
Berk. HP4 off Durrants La 38 AT19
Egerton Ter, SW3 296 D7
Egerton Way, Hayes UB3 155
BP80 Eggardon Ct, Nthlt. UB5
off Lancaster Rd 136 CC65
Egg Fm La, Kings L. WD4 59 BP30
Egg Hall, Epp. CM16 70 EU29
Egglesfield Cl, Berk. HP4 38 AS17
EGHAM, TW20 173 BA93
⇌ Egham 173 BA92
● Egham Business Village,
Egh. TW20 193 BC96
Egham Bypass, Egh. TW20 173 AZ92
Egham Cl, SW19 179 CY89
Sutton SM3 199 CY103
Egham Cres, Sutt. SM3 199 CX104
Egham Hill, Egh. TW20 172 AX93
EGHAM HYTHE, Stai. TW18 173 BE93
★ Egham Mus, Egh. TW20 173 BA92
Egham Rd, E13 292 B6
Eghams Cl, Knot.Grn HP9 88 AJ51
Eghams Wd Rd, Beac. HP9 88 AH51
EGHAM WICK, Egh. TW20 172 AU94
Eglantine La, Dart. DA4 208 FN101
Eglantine Rd, SW18 180 DC85
Egleston Rd, Mord. SM4 200 DB100
Egley Dr, Wok. GU22 226 AX122
Egley Rd, Wok. GU22 226 AX122
Eglington Ct, SE17 311 J2
Eglington Rd, E4 101 ED45
Eglinton Hill, SE18 165 EP79
Sch Eglinton Prim Sch & Early
Years Cen, SE18 off Paget Ri 165 EN80
Eglinton Rd, SE18 165 EN79
Swanscombe DA10 190 FZ86
Eglise Rd, Warl. CR6 237 DY117
Egliston Ms, SW15 159 CW83
Egliston Rd, SW15 159 CW83
Eglon Ms, NW1 274 F7
Egmont Av, Surb. KT6 198 CM102
Egmont Ms, Epsom KT19 216 CR105
Egmont Pk Rd, Walt.Hill KT20 249 CU125
Egmont Rd, N.Mal. KT3 199 CT98
Surbiton KT6 198 CM102
Sutton SM2 218 DC108
Walton-on-Thames KT12 195 BV101
Egmont St, SE14 313 K5
Egmont Way, Tad. KT20 233 CY119
Egremont Gdns, Slou. SL1 131 AN74
Egremont Ho, SE13 314 D8
Egremont Rd, SE27 181 DN90
Egret Ct, Enf. EN3 off Teal Cl 82 DW36
Egret Way, Hayes UB4 136 BX71
EGYPT, Slou. SL2 111 AQ63
Egypt La, Farn.Com. SL2 111 AP61
Eider Cl, E7 281 L2
Hayes UB4 off Cygnet Way 136 BX71
Eight Acres, Burn. SL1 130 AH70
Eighteenth Rd, Mitch. CR4 201 DL98
Eighth Av, E12 125 EM63
Hayes UB3 135 BU74
Eileen Rd, SE25 202 DR99
Eindhoven Cl, Cars. SM5 200 DG102
Eisenhower Dr, E6 293 H7
Elaine Gro, NW5 274 G2
Elam Cl, SE5 311 H9
Elam St, SE5 311 H8
Eland Pl, Croy. CR0
off Eland Rd 201 DP104
Eland Rd, SW11 308 F10
Croydon CR0 201 DP104
Sch Elangeni Sch, Amer. HP6
off Woodside Av 55 AS36
Elan Rd, S.Ock. RM15 149 FU71
Elba Pl, SE17 299 K8
Elberon Av, Croy. CR0 201 DJ100
Elbe St, SW6 307 N8
Elborough Rd, SE25 202 DU99
Elborough St, SW18 180 DA88
Elbow La, Hert.Hth SG13 48 DV17
Elbow Meadow, Colnbr. SL3 153 BF81
Elbury Dr, E16 291 P9
Elcho St, SW11 308 C5
Elcot Av, SE15 312 E4
● Eldenwall Est, Dag. RM8 126 EZ60
Elder Av, N8 121 DL57
Elderbek Cl, Chsht EN7 66 DU28
Elderberry Cl, Ilf. IG6
off Hazel La 103 EP52
Elderberry Gro, SE27
off Linton Gro 182 DQ91
Elderberry Rd, W5 158 CL75
Elderberry Way, E6 293 K2
Watford WD25 75 BV35
Elder Cl, N20 98 DB47
Guildford GU4 243 BA131
Sidcup DA15 185 ET88
West Drayton UB7 134 BL73
Elder Ct, Bushey Hth WD23 95 CE47
Hertford SG13 32 DR09
Elderfield, Harl. CM17 36 EX11
Welwyn Garden City AL7 30 DB10
Elderfield Pl, SW17 181 DH91
Elderfield Rd, E5 279 H1
Stoke Poges SL2 132 AT65
Elderfield Wk, E11 124 EH57
Elderflower Way, E15 281 J6
Elder Gdns, SE27 182 DQ91
Elder Oak Cl, SE20 202 DV95
Elder Pl, S.Croy. CR2 219 DP107
Elder Rd, SE27 182 DQ92
Eldersley Cl, Red. RH1 250 DF132
Elderslie Cl, Beck. BR3 203 EB99
Elderslie Rd, SE9 185 EN85
Elder St, E1 288 A6
Elderton Rd, SE26 183 DY91
Eldertree Pl, Mitch. CR4
off Eldertree Way 201 DJ95
Eldertree Way, Mitch. CR4 201 DH95
Elder Wk, N1 277 H8
SE13 off Bankside Av 163 EC83
Elder Way, Langley SL3 153 AZ75
North Holmwood RH5 263 CJ140
Rainham RM13 148 FK69
Elderwood Pl, SE27 182 DQ92
Eldon Av, Borwd. WD6 78 CN40
Croydon CR0 202 DW103
Hounslow TW5 156 CA80
Eldon Ct, Rom. RM1
off Slaney Rd 127 FE57
Eldon Gro, NW3 274 B2
Sch Eldon Inf Sch, N9
off Eldon Rd 100 DW46
Sch Eldon Jun Sch, N9
off Eldon Rd 100 DW46
Eldon Pk, SE25 202 DV98
Eldon Rd, E17 123 DZ56
N9 100 DW47
N22 99 DP53
W8 295 M7
Caterham CR3 236 DR121
Hoddesdon EN11 49 ED19
Eldon St, EC2 287 M7
Eldon Way, NW10 138 CP68
Eldred Dr, Orp. BR5 206 EW103
Eldred Gdns, Upmin. RM14 129 FS59
Eldred Rd, Bark. IG11 145 ES67
Eldrick Ct, Felt. TW14 175 BR88
Eldridge Cl, Felt. TW14 175 BU88
Eldridge Ct, Dag. RM10
off St. Mark's Pl 147 FB65
Eleanor Av, Epsom KT19 216 CR110
St. Albans AL3 43 CD18
Eleanor Cl, N15 122 DT55
SE16 301 J4
Eleanor Cres, NW7 97 CX49
Eleanor Cross Rd, Wal.Cr. EN8 67 DY34
Eleanor Pl, St.Alb. AL3 43 CD18
Eleanor Gdns, Barn. EN5 79 CX43
Dagenham RM8 126 EZ62
Eleanor Gro, SW13 158 CS83
Ickenham UB10 115 BP62
Sch Eleanor Palmer Prim Sch,
NW5 275 L1
Eleanor Rd, E8 278 E5
E15 281 M5
N11 99 DL51
Eleanor Rd, SW9 310 F7
Chalfont St. Peter SL9 90 AW53
Hertford SG14 32 DQ08
Waltham Cross EN8 67 DY33
Sch Eleanor Smith Sch, E13 292 A1
Eleanor St, E3 290 A3
Eleanor Wk, SE18 305 J9
Greenhithe DA9 169 FW84
Eleanor Way, Wal.Cr. EN8 67 DZ34
Warley CM14 108 FX50
Electra Av, Lon.Hthrw Air. TW6 155 BT83
● Electra Business Pk, E16 291 H6
Electric Av, SW9 161 DN84
Enfield EN3 83 DZ36
Electric La, SW9 161 DN84
Electric Par, E18 off George La 102 EG54
Surbiton KT6 197 CK100
Elektron Ho, E14 291 H10
Element Ho, Enf. EN3
off Tysoe Av 83 DZ36
⇌ Elephant & Castle 299 J8
⊖ Elephant & Castle 299 J8
Elephant & Castle, SE1 299 H7
● Elephant & Castle Shop Cen,
SE1 off Elephant & Castle 299 J8
Elephant La, SE16 300 G4
Elephant Rd, SE17 299 J8
Elers Rd, W13 157 CJ75
Hayes UB3 155 BR77
Eleven Acre Ri, Loug. IG10 85 EM41
● Eley Est, N18 100 DW50
Eley Pl, Wat. WD19 94 BX45
Eley Rd, N18 101 DX50
● Eley Rd Retail Pk, N18 101 DX50
Elfindale Rd, SE24 182 DQ85
Elford Cl, SE3 164 EH84
Elfort Rd, N5 121 DN63
Elfrida Cres, SE6 183 EA91
Sch Elfrida Prim Sch, SE6
off Elfrida Cres 183 EB91
Elfrida Rd, Wat. WD18 76 BW43
Elf Row, E1 289 H10
Elfwine Rd, W7 137 CE71
Elgal Cl, Orp. BR6 223 EP106
Elgar Av, NW10 138 CR65
SW16 201 DL97
W5 158 CL75
Surbiton KT5 198 CP101
Elgar Cl, E13 off Bushey Rd 144 EJ68
SE8 314 A5
Buckhurst Hill IG9 102 EK47
Elstree WD6 95 CJ45
Uxbridge UB10 114 BN61
Elgar Gdns, Til. RM18 171 GH81
Elgar St, SE16 301 M6
Elgin Av, W9 283 L3
W12 159 CU75
Ashford TW15 175 BQ93
Harrow HA3 95 CH54
Romford RM3 106 FP52
Elgin Cl, W12 159 CV75
Elgin Cres, W11 282 G9
Caterham CR3 236 DU122
London Heathrow Airport TW6
off Eastern Perimeter Rd 155 BS82
Elgin Dr, Nthwd. HA6 93 BS52
Elgin Gdns, Guil. GU1 243 BA133
Elgin Ho, Rom. RM6 126 EZ58
Elgin Ms, W11 282 F9
Elgin Ms N, W9 283 M2
Elgin Ms S, W9 283 M2
Elgin Pl, Wey. KT13 213 BQ107
Elgin Rd, N22 99 DJ54
Broxbourne EN10 49 DZ24
Cheshunt EN8 66 DW30
Croydon CR0 202 DT102
Ilford IG3 125 ES60
Sutton SM1 200 DC104
Wallington SM6 219 DJ107
Weybridge KT13 212 BN106
Elgiva La, Chesh. HP5 54 AP31
Elgood Av, Nthwd. HA6 93 BU51
Elgood Cl, W11 294 E1
Elham Cl, Brom. BR1 184 EK94
Elham Ho, E5
off Pembury Rd 278 E3
Elia Ms, N1 286 G1
Elias Pl, SW8 310 E3
Elia St, N1 286 G1
Elibank Rd, SE9 165 EN84
Elim Est, SE1 299 N6
Elim St, SE1 299 M6
Elim Way, E13 291 M3
Eliot Bk, SE23 182 DV89
Sch Eliot Bk Prim Sch, SE26
off Thorpewood Av 182 DV89
Eliot Cotts, SE3 315 K9
Eliot Ct, N15
off Tynemouth Rd 122 DT56
Eliot Dr, Har. HA2 116 CB61
Eliot Gdns, SW15 159 CU84
Eliot Hill, SE13 314 F9
Eliot Ms, NW8 283 P1
Eliot Pk, SE13 314 F9
Eliot Pl, SE3 315 J9
Eliot Rd, Dag. RM9 126 EX63
Dartford DA1 188 FP85
Eliot Vale, SE3 315 H9
Elis Way, E20 280 F3
Elizabethan Cl, Stanw. TW19 174 BK87
Elizabethan Way, Stanw. TW19 174 BK87
Elizabeth Av, N1 277 K8
Amersham HP6 72 AV39
Enfield EN2 81 DP41
Ilford IG1 125 ER61
Staines-upon-Thames TW18 174 BJ93
Elizabeth Br, SW1 297 J9
Elizabeth Cl, E14 290 C9
W9 283 P4
Barnet EN5 79 CX41
Hertford SG14 off Welwyn Rd 31 DM09
Lower Nazeing EN9 49 ED23
Romford RM7 105 FB53
Sutton SM1 217 CZ105
Tilbury RM18 171 GH82
Welwyn Garden City AL7 30 DC09
Elizabeth Clyde Cl, N15 122 DS56
Elizabeth Cotts, Kew TW9 158 CM81
Elizabeth Ct, SW1 297 P7
Godalming GU7 258 AS144
Gravesend DA11
off St. James's Rd 191 GG86
Horley RH6 268 DG148
Kingston upon Thames KT2
off Lower Kings Rd 198 CL95
St. Albans AL4 off Villiers Cres 43 CK17
Watford WD17 75 BT38
Woodford Green IG8
off Navestock Cres 102 EJ52
Elizabeth Dr, Bans. SM7 234 DC118
Theydon Bois CM16 85 ES36
Elizabeth Est, SE17 311 L2
Elizabeth Fry Pl, SE18 164 EL81
Elizabeth Fry Rd, E8 278 F7
Elizabeth Gdns, W3 139 CT74
Isleworth TW7 157 CG84
Stanmore HA7 95 CJ51
Sunbury-on-Thames TW16 196 BW97
Sch Elizabeth Garrett Anderson
Language Coll, N1 276 D10
Elizabeth Ho, Bans. SM7 234 DC118
Rom. RM2 128 FJ56
Wem. SW9 118 CM64
Elizabeth Huggins Cotts,
Grav. DA11 191 GG89
Elizabeth Ms, NW3 274 D5
Elizabeth Pl, N15 122 DR56
Elizabeth Ride, N9 100 DV45
Elizabeth Rd, E6 144 EK67
N15 122 DS57
Godalming GU7 258 AS144
Grays RM16 170 FZ76
Pilgrim's Hatch CM15 108 FV44
Rainham RM13 147 FH71
Sch Elizabeth Selby Inf Sch, E2 288 D2
Elizabeth Sq, SE16 301 L1
Elizabeth St, SW1 297 H8
Greenhithe DA9 189 FS85
Elizabeth Ter, SE9 185 EM86
Elizabeth Way, SE19 182 DR94
Feltham TW13 176 BW91
Harlow CM19, CM20 51 EM16
Orpington BR5 206 EW99
Stoke Poges SL2 132 AT67
Eliza Cook Cl, Green. DA9
off Watermans Way 169 FV84
Elkanette Ms, N20 98 DC47
Elkington Pt, SE11 298 E9
Elkington Rd, E13 292 A5
Elkins, The, Rom. RM1 105 FE54
Elkins Gdns, Guil. GU4 243 BA131
Elkins Rd, Hedg. SL2 112 AS61
Elkstone Rd, W10 282 G6
Ella Cl, Beck. BR3 203 EA96
Ellacott Ms, SW16 181 DK89
Ellaline Rd, W6 306 C3
Ella Ms, NW3 274 E1
Ellanby Cres, N18 100 DV49
Elland Cl, Barn. EN5 80 DD43
Elland Rd, SE15 162 DW84
Walton-on-Thames KT12 196 BX103
Ella Rd, N8 121 DL59
Ellement Cl, Pnr. HA5 116 BX57
Ellenborough Pl, SW15 159 CU84
Ellenborough Rd, N22 100 DQ53
Sidcup DA14 186 EX92
Ellenbridge Way, S.Croy. CR2 220 DS109
ELLENBROOK, Hat. AL10 44 CR19
Ellenbrook Cl, Wat. WD24
off Hatfield Rd 75 BV39
Ellenbrook Cres, Hat. AL10
off Ellenbrook La 44 CR18
Ellenbrook La, Hat. AL10 44 CS19
Ellen Cl, Brom. BR1 204 EK97
Hemel Hempstead HP2 40 BM19
Ellen Ct, N9 100 DW47
Ellen St, E1 288 D9
Ellen Webb Dr, Wealds. HA3 117 CE55
Ellen Wilkinson Ho, E2
off Usk St 289 J2
Sch Ellen Wilkinson Prim Sch,
E6 292 G7
Sch Ellen Wilkinson Sch for Girls,
The, W3 off Queens Dr 138 CM72
Elleray Rd, Tedd. TW11 177 CF93
Ellerby St, SW6 306 D7
Ellerdale Cl, NW3 273 N1
Ellerdale Rd, NW3 273 P1
Ellerdale St, SE13 163 EB84
Ellerdine Rd, Houns. TW3 156 CC84
Ellerker Gdns, Rich. TW10 178 CL86
Ellerman Av, Twick. TW2 176 BZ88
Ellerman Rd, Til. RM18 171 GF82
Ellerslie, Grav. DA12 191 GK87
Ellerslie Gdns, NW10 139 CU67
Ellerslie Rd, W12 139 CV74
● Ellerslie Sq Ind Est, SW2 181 DL85
Ellerton, NW6 273 H3
Ellerton Gdns, Dag. RM9 146 EW66
Ellerton Rd, SW13 159 CU81
SW18 180 DD88
SW20 179 CU94
Dagenham RM9 146 EW66
Surbiton KT6 198 CM103
Ellery Rd, SE19 182 DR94
Ellery St, SE15 312 E9
Elles Av, Guil. GU1 243 BB134
Ellesborough Cl, Wat. WD19 94 BW50
Ellesmere Av, NW7 96 CR48
Beckenham BR3 203 EB96
Ellesmere Cl, E11 124 EF57
Datchet SL3 152 AU79
Ruislip HA4 115 BQ59
Ellesmere Dr, S.Croy. CR2 220 DV114
Ellesmere Gdns, Ilf. IG4 124 EL57
Ellesmere Gro, Barn. EN5 79 CZ43
Ellesmere Pl, Walt. KT12 213 BS106
Ellesmere Rd, E3 279 L10
NW10 119 CU64
W4 158 CR79
Berkhamsted HP4 38 AX19
Greenford UB6 136 CC70
Twickenham TW1 177 CJ86
Weybridge KT13 213 BR107
Ellesmere St, E14 290 C8
Ellice Rd, Oxt. RH8 254 EF129
Ellies Ms, Ashf. TW15 174 BL89
Elliman Av, Slou. SL2 132 AS73
Ellingfort Rd, E8 278 F6
Ellingham Cl, Hem.H. HP2 40 BN18
Sch Ellingham Prim Sch,
Chess. KT9
off Ellingham Rd 215 CK108
Ellingham Rd, E15 123 ED63
W12 159 CU75
Chessington KT9 215 CK107
Hemel Hempstead HP2 40 BM19
Ellington Ct, N14 99 DK47
Tap. SL6 off Ellington Rd 130 AC72
Ellington Gdns, Tap. SL6 130 AC72
Ellington Ho, SE1 299 K6
Ellington Rd, N10 121 DH56
Feltham TW13 175 BT91
Hounslow TW3 156 CB82
Taplow SL6 130 AC72
Ellington St, N7 276 E5
Ellington Way, Epsom KT18 233 CV117
Elliot Cl, E15 281 J7
Elliot Rd, NW4 119 CV58
Stanmore HA7 95 CG51
Watford WD17 75 BU38
Elliott Av, Ruis. HA4 115 BV61
Elliott Cl, Welw.G.C. AL7 29 CX12
Wembley HA9 118 CM62
Elliott Gdns, Rom. RM3 105 FH53
Shepperton TW17 194 BN98
Elliott Rd, SW9 310 G5
W4 158 CS77
Bromley BR2 204 EK98
Thornton Heath CR7 201 DP98
Elliotts Cl, Cowley UB8 134 BJ71
Elliotts La, Brasted TN16 240 EW124
Elliott's Pl, N1 277 H9
Elliott Sq, NW3 274 D6
Elliotts Row, SE11 298 G8
Elliott St, Grav. DA12 191 GK87
Ellis Av, Chal.St.P. SL9 91 AZ53
Onslow Village GU2 258 AT136
Rainham RM13 147 FG71
Slough SL1 152 AS75
Ellis Cl, NW10
off High Rd 139 CV65
SE9 185 EQ89
Coulsdon CR5 235 DM120
Edgware HA8 96 CS51
Hoddesdon EN11 33 DZ13
Ruislip HA4 115 BU58
Swanley BR8 207 FD98
Elliscombe Rd, SE7 164 EJ78
Ellis Ct, W7 137 CF71
Ellis Fm Cl, Wok. GU22 226 AX122
Ellisfield Dr, SW15 179 CT87
Ellis Flds, St.Alb. AL3 43 CE17
Ellis Ho, St.Alb. AL1 43 CF21
Ellison Cl, Wind. SL4 151 AM83
Ellison Gdns, Sthl. UB2 156 BZ77
Ellison Ho, SE13 314 E8
Ellison Rd, SW13 159 CT82
SW16 181 DK94
Sidcup DA15 185 ER88
Ellis Rd, Couls. CR5 235 DM120
Mitcham CR4 200 DF100
Southall UB2 136 CC74
Ellis St, SW1 296 F8
Elliston Ho, SE18 305 L9
Elliston Way, Ashtd. KT21 232 CL119
Ellis Way, Dart. DA1 188 FM89
Ellmore Cl, Rom. RM3 105 FH53
Ellora Rd, SW16 181 DK92
Ellsworth St, E2 288 E2
Ellwood Ct, W9 283 L5
Ellwood Gdns, Wat. WD25 59 BV34
Ellwood Ri, Ch.St.G. HP8 90 AW47
Ellwood Rd, Beac. HP9 88 AH54
Elmar Grn, Slou. SL2 131 AN69
Elmar Rd, N15 122 DR56
Elm Av, W5 138 CL74
Carshalton SM5 218 DF110
Ruislip HA4 115 BU60
Upminster RM14 128 FP62
Watford WD19 94 BY45
Elmbank, N14 99 DL45
Elmbank Av, Barn. EN5 79 CW42
Englefield Green TW20 172 AV93
Guildford GU2 258 AU135
Elm Bk Dr, Brom. BR1 204 EK96
Elm Bk Gdns, SW13 158 CS82
Elmbank Way, W7 137 CD71
Elmbourne Dr, Belv. DA17 167 FB77
Elmbourne Rd, SW17 180 DG90
Elmbridge, Harl. CM17 36 EZ12
Elmbridge Av, Surb. KT5 198 CP99
Elmbridge Cl, Ruis. HA4 115 BU58
Elmbridge Dr, Ruis. HA4 115 BT57
Elmbridge La, Wok. GU22 227 AZ119
★ Elmbridge Mus, Wey. KT13 212 BN105
Elmbridge Rd, Ilf. IG6 104 EU51
Elmbridge Wk, E8 278 D6
Elmbrook Cl, Sun. TW16 195 BV95
Elmbrook Gdns, SE9 164 EL84
Elmbrook Rd, Sutt. SM1 217 CZ105
Elm Cl, E11 124 EH58
N19 121 DJ61
NW4 119 CX57
SW20 199 CW98
Amersham HP6 55 AQ38
Box Hill KT20 248 CQ130
Buckhurst Hill IG9 102 EK47
Carshalton SM5 200 DF102
Dartford DA1 188 FJ88
Epping Green CM16 51 EP24
Farnham Common SL2 131 AQ65
Harrow HA2 116 CB58
Hayes UB3 135 BU72
Leatherhead KT22 231 CH122
Ripley GU23 228 BG124
Romford RM7 105 FB54
South Croydon CR2 220 DS107
Stanwell TW19 174 BK88
Surbiton KT5 198 CQ101
Twickenham TW2 176 CB89
Waltham Abbey EN9 67 ED34
Warlingham CR6 237 DX117
Woking GU21 226 AX115
ELM CORNER, Wok. GU23 228 BN119
Elmcote Way, Crox.Grn WD3 74 BM44
Elm Ct, EC4 286 E10
Mitcham CR4
off Armfield Cres 200 DF96
Sunbury-on-Thames TW16 175 BT94
Elmcourt Rd, SE27 181 DP89
Sch Elm Ct Sch, SE27
off Elmcourt Rd 182 DQ89
Elm Cres, W5 138 CL74
Kingston upon Thames KT2 198 CL95
Elm Cft, Datchet SL3 152 AW81
Elmcroft, N8 121 DM57
Leatherhead KT23 230 CA124
Elmcroft Av, E11 124 EH57
N9 82 DV44
NW11 119 CZ59
Sidcup DA15 185 ET86
Elmcroft Cl, E11 124 EH56
W5 137 CK72
Chessington KT9 198 CL104
Feltham TW14 175 BT86
Elmcroft Cres, NW11 119 CY59
Harrow HA2 116 CA55
Elmcroft Dr, Ashf. TW15 174 BN92
Chessington KT9 198 CL104
Elmcroft Gdns, NW9 118 CN57
Elmcroft Rd, Orp. BR6 206 EU101
Elmcroft St, E5 122 DW63
Elmdale Rd, N13 99 DM50
Elmdene, Surb. KT5 198 CQ102
Elmdene Av, Horn. RM11 128 FM57
Elmdene Cl, Beck. BR3 203 DZ99

Elmdene Ct, Wok. GU22
off Constitution Hill 226 AY118
Elmdene Ms, Nthwd. HA6 93 BQ51
Elmdene Rd, SE18 165 EP78
Elmdon Pl, Guil. GU1
off Buckingham Cl 243 AZ133
Elmdon Rd, Houns. TW4 156 BX82
London Heathrow Airport TW6 155 BT83
South Ockendon RM15 149 FU71
Elm Dr, Chsht EN8 67 DY28
Chobham GU24 210 AT110
Harrow HA2 116 CB58
Hatfield AL10 45 CU19
Leatherhead KT22 231 CH122
St. Albans AL4 43 CJ20
Sunbury-on-Thames TW16 196 BW96
Swanley BR8 207 FD96
Elmer Av, Hav.at.Bow. RM4 105 FE48
Elmer Cl, Enf. EN2 81 DM41
Rainham RM13 147 FG66
Elmer Cotts, Fetch. KT22 231 CG123
Elmer Gdns, Edg. HA8 96 CP52
Isleworth TW7 157 CD83
Rainham RM13 147 FG66
Elmer Ms, Fetch. KT22 231 CG123
Elmer Rd, SE6 183 EC87
Elmers Ct, Beac. HP9
off Post Office La 89 AK52
Elmers Dr, Tedd. TW11
off Kingston Rd 177 CH93
ELMERS END, Beck. BR3 203 DY97
⇌ **Elmers End** 203 DX98
Tra **Elmers End** 203 DX98
Elmers End Rd, SE20 202 DW96
Beckenham BR3 202 DW96
Elmerside Rd, Beck. BR3 203 DY98
Elmers Rd, SE25 202 DU101
Elm Fm Caravan Pk, Lyne KT16 193 BC101
Elmfield, Bkhm KT23 230 CA123
Elmfield Av, N8 121 DL57
Mitcham CR4 200 DG95
Teddington TW11 177 CF92
Elmfield Cl, Grav. DA11 191 GH88
Harrow HA1 117 CE61
Potters Bar EN6 63 CY33
Elmfield Pk, Brom. BR1 204 EG97
Elmfield Rd, E4 101 EC47
E17 123 DX58
N2 120 DD55
SW17 180 DG89
Bromley BR1 204 EG97
Potters Bar EN6 63 CY33
Southall UB2 156 BY76
Elmfield Way, W9 283 J6
South Croydon CR2 220 DT109
Elm Friars Wk, NW1 275 P7
Elm Gdns, N2 120 DC55
Claygate KT10 215 CF107
Enfield EN2 82 DR38
Epsom KT18 233 CW119
Mitcham CR4 201 DK98
North Weald Bassett CM16 71 FB26
Welwyn Garden City AL8 29 CV09
Elmgate Av, Felt. TW13 175 BV90
Elmgate Gdns, Edg. HA8 96 CR50
Elm Grn, W3 138 CS72
Hemel Hempstead HP1 39 BE18
Elmgreen Cl, E15 281 K8
Sch **Elmgreen Sch** (Former), SE27 182 DQ91
Elm Gro, N8 121 DL58
NW2 119 CX63
SE15 312 B8
SW19 179 CY94
Berkhamsted HP4 38 AV19
Caterham CR3 236 DS122
Epsom KT18 216 CQ114
Erith DA8 167 FD80
Harrow HA2 116 CA59
Hornchurch RM11 128 FL58
Kingston upon Thames KT2 198 CL95
Orpington BR6 205 ET102
Sutton SM1 218 DB105
Watford WD24 75 BU37
West Drayton UB7 134 BM73
Woodford Green IG8 102 EF50
Elmgrove Cres, Har. HA1 117 CF57
Elmgrove Gdns, Har. HA1 117 CG57
Elm Gro Par, Wall. SM6
off Butter Hill 200 DG104
Sch **Elmgrove Prim Sch**, Kenton HA3 *off Kenmore Av* 117 CG56
Elm Gro Rd, SW13 159 CU82
W5 158 CL75
Cobham KT11 230 BX116
Elmgrove Rd, Croy. CR0 202 DV101
Harrow HA1 117 CF57
Weybridge KT13 212 BN105
Elm Hall Gdns, E11 124 EH58
Elm Hatch, Harl. CM18
off St. Andrews Meadow 51 ET16
Elmhurst, Belv. DA17 166 EY79
Elmhurst Av, N2 120 DD55
Mitcham CR4 181 DH94
Elmhurst Cl, Bushey WD23 76 BY42
Elmhurst Ct, Guil. GU1
off Lower Edgeborough Rd 259 AZ135
Elmhurst Dr, E18 102 EG54
Dorking RH4 263 CH138
Hornchurch RM11 128 FJ60
Elmhurst Mans, SW4 309 N10
Sch **Elmhurst Prim Sch**, E7
off Upton Pk Rd 144 EH66
Elmhurst Rd, E7 144 EH66
N17 100 DS54
SE9 184 EL89
Enfield EN3 82 DW37
Slough SL3 153 BA76
Sch **Elmhurst Sch**, S.Croy. CR2
off South Pk Hill Rd 220 DR106
Elmhurst St, SW4 309 N10
Elmhurst Vil, SE15
off Cheltenham Rd 162 DW84
Elmhurst Way, Loug. IG10 103 EM45
Elmington Cl, Bex. DA5 187 FB86
Elmington Est, SE5 311 M4
Elmington Rd, SE5 311 L6
Elmira St, SE13 163 EB83
Elm La, SE6 183 DZ89
Woking GU23 229 BP118
Elm Lawn Cl, Uxb. UB8 134 BL66
Elm Lawns Cl, St.Alb. AL1
off Avenue Rd 43 CE19
Elmlea Dr, Hayes UB3 135 BS72
Elmlee Cl, Chis. BR7 185 EM93
Elmley Cl, E6 293 H7
Elmley St, SE18 165 ER77

Elm Ms, Rich. TW10 178 CM86
Elmore Cl, Wem. HA0 138 CL68
Elmore Rd, E11 123 EC62
Chipstead CR5 234 DF121
Enfield EN3 83 DX39
Elmores, Loug. IG10 85 EN41
Elmore St, N1 277 K6
Elm Par, Horn. RM12 127 FH63
Sidcup DA14 *off Main Rd* 186 EU91
ELM PARK, Horn. RM12 127 FH64
⊖ **Elm Park** 127 FH63
Elm Pk, SW2 181 DM86
Stanmore HA7 95 CH50
Elm Pk Av, N15 122 DT57
Hornchurch RM12 127 FG63
Elm Pk Ct, Pnr. HA5 116 BW55
Elm Pk Gdns, NW4 119 CX57
SW10 308 A1
South Croydon CR2 220 DW110
Elm Pk La, SW3 308 A1
Elm Pk Mans, SW10 307 P2
Elm Pk Rd, E10 123 DY60
N3 97 CZ52
N21 100 DQ45
SE25 202 DT97
SW3 308 A2
Pinner HA5 94 BW54
Elm Pl, SW7 296 A10
Ashford TW15 *off Limes Cl* 174 BN92
Elm Quay Ct, SW8 309 N2
Elm Rd, E7 281 M4
E11 123 ED61
E17 123 EC57
N22 99 DP53
SW14 158 CQ83
Aveley RM15 148 FQ74
Barnet EN5 79 CZ42
Beckenham BR3 203 DZ96
Chessington KT9 216 CL105
Claygate KT10 215 CF107
Dartford DA1 188 FK88
Epsom KT17 217 CT107
Erith DA8 167 FG81
Feltham TW14 175 BR88
Godalming GU7 258 AT143
Gravesend DA12 191 GJ90
Grays RM17 170 GC79
Greenhithe DA9 189 FS86
Horsell GU21 227 AZ115
Kingston upon Thames KT2 198 CM95
Leatherhead KT22 231 CH122
New Malden KT3 198 CR98
Orpington BR6 224 EU108
Penn HP10 88 AD46
Purley CR8 219 DP113
Redhill RH1 250 DE134
Romford RM7 105 FB54
Sidcup DA14 186 EU91
Thornton Heath CR7 202 DR98
Wallington SM6 200 DG102
Warlingham CR6 237 DX117
Wembley HA9 118 CL64
Westerham TN16 255 ES125
Windsor SL4 151 AP83
Woking GU21 226 AX118
Elm Rd W, Sutt. SM3 199 CZ101
Elm Row, NW3 120 DC62
Elmroyd Av, Pot.B. EN6 63 CZ33
Elmroyd Cl, Pot.B. EN6 63 CZ33
Elms, The, SW13 159 CT83
Hertford SG13 32 DU09
Loughton IG10 84 EF40
Warlingham CR6 236 DW115
Elms Av, N10 121 DH55
NW4 119 CX57
Elms Cl, Horn. RM11 127 FH59
Elmscott Gdns, N21 82 DQ44
Elmscott Rd, Brom. BR1 184 EE92
Elms Ct, Wem. HA0 117 CF63
Elms Cres, SW4 181 DJ86
Elmscroft Gdns, Pot.B. EN6 63 CZ32
Elmsdale Rd, E17 123 DZ56
Elms Fm Rd, Horn. RM12 128 FJ64
Elms Gdns, Dag. RM9 126 EZ63
Wembley HA0 117 CG63
Elmshaw Rd, SW15 179 CU85
Elmshorn, Epsom KT17 233 CW116
Elmshott La, Slou. SL1 131 AL73
Elmshurst Cres, N2 120 DD56
Elmside, Guil. GU2 258 AU135
New Addington CR0 221 EB107
Elmside Rd, Wem. HA9 118 CN62
Elms La, Wem. HA0 117 CG63
Elmsleigh Av, Har. HA3 117 CH56
Elmsleigh Cen, The, Stai. TW18 195 BF91
Elmsleigh Ct, Sutt. SM1 200 DB104
Elmsleigh Rd, Stai. TW18 173 BF92
Twickenham TW2 177 CD89
Elmslie Cl, Epsom KT18 216 CQ114
Woodford Green IG8 103 EM51
Elmslie Pt, E3 289 P7
Elms Ms, W2 284 A10
Elms Pk Av, Wem. HA0 117 CG63
Elms Rd, SW4 181 DJ85
Chalfont St. Peter SL9 90 AY52
Harrow HA3 95 CE52
Ware SG12 33 EA05
ELMSTEAD, Chis. BR7 184 EK92
Elmstead Av, Chis. BR7 185 EM92
Wembley HA9 118 CL60
Elmstead Cl, N20 98 DA47
Epsom KT19 216 CS106
Sevenoaks TN13 256 FE122
Elmstead Cres, Well. DA16 166 EW79
Elmstead Gdns, Wor.Pk. KT4 199 CU104
Elmstead Glade, Chis. BR7 185 EM93
Elmstead La, Chis. BR7 185 EM92
Elmstead Rd, Erith DA8 167 FE81
Ilford IG3 125 ES61
West Byfleet KT14 212 BG113
⇌ **Elmstead Woods** 184 EL93
Elmstone Rd, SW6 307 J6
Elm St, WC1 286 D5
Elmsway, Ashf. TW15 174 BM92
Elmswell Ct, Hert. SG14
off The Ridgeway 31 DM08
Elmswood, Bkhm KT23 230 BZ124
Chigwell IG7 *off Copperfield* 103 ER51
Elmsworth Av, Houns. TW3 156 CB82
Elm Ter, NW2 120 DA62
SE9 185 EN86
Grays RM20 169 FV79
Harrow HA3 95 CD52
Elm Tree Av, Esher KT10 197 CD101
Elm Tree Cl, NW8 284 A2
Ashford TW15 *off Convent Rd* 175 BP92
Chertsey KT16 193 BE103
Horley RH6 268 DG147
Northolt UB5 136 BZ68

Elmtree Cl, Byfleet KT14 212 BL113
Elm Tree Ct, SE7 *off Fairlawn* 164 EJ79
Elmtree Hill, Chesh. HP5 54 AP30
Elm Tree Rd, NW8 284 A2
Elmtree Rd, Tedd. TW11 177 CE91
Sch **Elmtree Sch**, Chesh. HP5
off Elmtree Hill 54 AP30
Elm Tree Wk, Chorl. WD3 73 BF42
Elm Wk, NW3 120 DA61
SW20 199 CW98
Orpington BR6 205 EM104
Radlett WD7 77 CF36
Romford RM2 127 FG55
Elm Way, N11 98 DG51
NW10 118 CS63
Brentwood CM14 108 FU48
Epsom KT19 216 CR106
Rickmansworth WD3 92 BH46
Worcester Park KT4 199 CW104
Elmwood, Saw. CM21 36 EZ06
Welwyn Garden City AL8 29 CV10
Elmwood Av, N13 99 DL50
Borehamwood WD6 78 CP42
Feltham TW13 175 BU89
Harrow HA3 117 CG57
Elmwood Cl, Ashtd. KT21 231 CK117
Epsom KT17 217 CU108
Wallington SM6 200 DG103
Elmwood Ct, SW11 309 J6
Ashtead KT21 *off Elmwood Cl* 253 CK117
Wembley HA0 117 CG62
Elmwood Cres, NW9 118 CQ56
Elmwood Dr, Bex. DA5 186 EY87
Epsom KT17 217 CU107
Elmwood Gdns, W7 137 CE72
Elmwood Gro, Hem.H. HP3 40 BM23
Sch **Elmwood Inf Sch**, Croy. CR0 *off Lodge Rd* 201 DP100
Sch **Elmwood Jun Sch**, Croy. CR0 *off Lodge Rd* 201 DP101
Elmwood Pk, Ger.Cr. SL9 112 AY60
Sch **Elm Wd Prim Sch**, SE27
off Carnac St 182 DR90
Elmwood Rd, SE24 182 DR85
W4 158 CQ79
Croydon CR0 201 DP101
Mitcham CR4 200 DF97
Redhill RH1 250 DG130
Slough SL2 132 AV73
Elmworth Gro, SE21 182 DR89
Elnathan Ms, W9 283 M5
Elphinstone Rd, E17 101 DZ54
Elphinstone St, N5 121 DP63
Elppin Ct, Brox. EN10 49 DZ20
Elrick Cl, Erith DA8
off Queen St 167 FE79
Elrington Rd, E8 278 C5
Woodford Green IG8 102 EG50
Elruge Cl, West Dr. UB7 154 BK76
Elsa Rd, Well. DA16 166 EV82
Elsa St, E1 289 L7
Elsdale St, E9 279 H5
Elsden Ms, E2 289 H1
Elsden Rd, N17 100 DT53
Elsdon Rd, Wok. GU21 226 AU117
Elsenham, The, Chsht EN8 66 DW28
Elsenham Rd, E12 125 EM64
Elsenham St, SW18 179 CZ88
Elsham Rd, E11 124 EE62
W14 294 E5
Elsham Ter, W14 294 E5
Elsiedene Rd, N21 100 DQ45
Elsiemaud Rd, SE4 183 DZ85
Elsie Rd, SE22 162 DT84
Elsinge Rd, Enf. EN1 82 DV36
Elsinore Av, Stai. TW19 174 BL87
Elsinore Gdns, NW2 119 CY62
Elsinore Rd, SE23 183 DY88
Elsinore Way, Rich. TW9 158 CP83
Sch **Elsley Prim Sch**, Wem. HA9
off Tokyngton Av 138 CM65
Elsley Rd, SW11 308 F10
Sch **Elsley Sch**, SW11 308 G10
Elsons Ms, Welw.G.C. AL7 30 DB09
Elspeth Rd, SW11 160 DF84
Wembley HA0 118 CL64
Elsrick Av, Mord. SM4 200 DA99
Elstan Way, Croy. CR0 203 DY101
Elstead Ct, Sutt. SM3
off Stonecot Hill 199 CY102
Elstead Ho, Mord. SM4
off Green La 200 DA100
Elsted St, SE17 299 M9
Elstow Cl, SE9 185 EN85
Ruislip HA4 116 BX59
Elstow Gdns, Dag. RM9 146 EY67
Elstow Rd, Dag. RM9 146 EY66
ELSTREE, Borwd. WD6 77 CK43
★ **Elstree Aerodrome**, Borwd. WD6 77 CF41
⇌ **Elstree & Borehamwood** 78 CM42
● **Elstree Business Cen**, Borwd. WD6 78 CR41
Elstree Cl, Horn. RM12 147 FH66
Elstree Gdns, N9 100 DV46
Belvedere DA17 166 EY77
Ilford IG1 125 EQ64
Elstree Hill, Brom. BR1 184 EE94
Elstree Hill N, Els. WD6 77 CK44
Elstree Hill S, Els. WD6 95 CJ45
Elstree Pk, Borwd. WD6 78 CR44
Elstree Rd, Bushey Hth WD23 95 CD45
Elstree WD6 77 CG44
Elstree Way, Borwd. WD6 78 CP41
Elswick Rd, SE13 314 C10
Elswick St, SW6 307 N8
Elsworth Cl, Felt. TW14 175 BS88
Elsworthy, T.Ditt. KT7 197 CE100
Elsworthy Ri, NW3 274 D6
Elsworthy Rd, NW3 274 D7
Elsworthy Ter, NW3 274 D7
Elsynge Rd, SW18 180 DD85
ELTHAM, SE9 184 EK86
⇌ **Eltham** 185 EM85
Eltham 185 EM85
Eltham Av, Slou. SL1 151 AL75
Slough (east section) SL1 151 AM75
Sch **Eltham C of E Prim Sch**, SE9 *off Roper St* 185 EM85
Sch **Eltham Coll Jun Sch**, SE9
off Mottingham La 184 EK88
Sch **Eltham Coll Sen Sch**, SE9
off Grove Pk Rd 184 EK89
Eltham Grn, SE9 184 EJ85
Eltham Grn Rd, SE9 164 EJ84
Eltham High St, SE9 185 EM86
Eltham Hill, SE9 184 EK85
Sch **Eltham Hill Tech Coll for Girls**, SE9 *off Eltham Hill* 184 EL86

★ **Eltham Palace**, SE9 184 EL87
Eltham Palace Rd, SE9 184 EJ86
Eltham Pk Gdns, SE9 165 EN84
Eltham Rd, SE9 184 EJ85
SE12 184 EF85
Elthiron Rd, SW6 307 K7
Elthorne Av, W7 157 CF75
Elthorne Ct, Felt. TW13 176 BW88
Sch **Elthorne Pk High Sch**, W7
off Westlea Rd 157 CF76
Elthorne Pk Rd, W7 157 CF75
Elthorne Rd, N19 121 DK61
NW9 118 CR59
Uxbridge UB8 134 BK68
Elthorne Way, NW9 118 CR58
Elthruda Rd, SE13 183 ED86
Eltisley Rd, Ilf. IG1 125 EP63
Elton Av, Barn. EN5 79 CZ43
Greenford UB6 137 CF65
Wembley HA0 117 CH64
Elton Cl, Kings.T. KT1 177 CJ94
Elton Ho, E3 279 P8
Elton Pk, Wat. WD17 75 BV40
Elton Pl, N16 277 N2
Elton Rd, Hert. SG14 32 DQ08
Kingston upon Thames KT2 198 CM95
Purley CR8 219 DJ112
Elton Way, Wat. WD25 76 CB40
Eltringham St, SW18 160 DC84
Eluna Apts, E1
off Wapping La 300 F1
Elvaston Ms, SW7 295 P6
Elvaston Pl, SW7 295 N7
Elveden Cl, Wok. GU22 228 BH117
Elveden Pl, NW10 138 CN68
Elveden Rd, NW10 138 CN68
Elvedon Rd, Cob. KT11 213 BV111
Feltham TW13 175 BT90
Elvendon Rd, N13 99 DL51
Elver Gdns, E2 288 D2
Elverson Ms, SE8 314 C9
DLR **Elverson Road** 314 D9
Elverson Rd, SE8 314 D8
Elverton St, SW1 297 N8
Elvet Av, Rom. RM2 128 FJ56
Elvin Dr, N.Stfd RM16 149 FX74
Elvington Grn, Brom. BR2 204 EF99
Elvington La, NW9 96 CS53
Elvino Rd, SE26 183 DY92
Elvis Rd, NW2 272 A4
Elwell Cl, Egh. TW20
off Mowbray Cres 173 BA92
Elwick Rd, S.Ock. RM15 149 FW72
Elwill Way, Beck. BR3 203 EC98
Elwin St, E2 288 C2
Elwood, Harl. CM17 52 EY16
Elwood Cl, Barn. EN5 80 DC42
Elwood Ct, N9 100 DV46
Elwood St, N5 121 DP62
Elwyn Gdns, SE12 184 EG87
Ely Av, Slou. SL1 131 AQ71
Ely Cl, Amer. HP7 55 AS39
Erith DA8 167 FF82
Hatfield AL10 45 CT17
New Malden KT3 199 CT96
Ely Ct, EC1 286 F7
Ely Gdns, Borwd. WD6 78 CR43
Dagenham RM10 127 FC62
Ilford IG1 124 EL59
Elyne Rd, N4 121 DN58
Ely Pl, EC1 286 F7
Guildford GU2
off Canterbury Rd 242 AT132
Woodford Green IG8 103 EN51
Ely Rd, E10 123 EC58
Croydon CR0 202 DR99
Hounslow West TW4 156 BW83
London Heathrow Airport TW6
off Eastern Perimeter Rd 155 BT82
St. Albans AL1 43 CH21
Elysian Av, Orp. BR5 205 ES100
Elysian Ms, N7 276 D4
Elysian Pl, S.Croy. CR2 220 DQ108
Elysium Bldg, The, SE8 301 K10
Elysium Pl, SW6 306 G9
Elysium St, SW6 306 G9
Elystan Cl, Wall. SM6 219 DH109
Elystan Pl, SW3 296 D10
Elystan St, SW3 296 C9
Elystan Wk, N1 276 E9
Emanuel Av, W3 138 CQ72
Emanuel Dr, Hmptn. TW12 176 BZ92
Sch **Emanuel Sch**, SW11
off Battersea Ri 180 DE85
⊖ **Embankment** 298 B2
Embankment, SW15 306 C9
Embankment, The, Twick. TW1 177 CG88
Wraysbury TW19 172 AW87
Embankment Gdns, SW3 308 F2
Pier **Embankment Pier** 298 C2
Embankment Pl, WC2 298 B2
Embassy Ct, Sid. DA14 186 EV90
Welling DA16
off Welling High St 166 EV83
Embassy Gdns, Beck. BR3
off Blakeney Rd 203 DZ95
Emba St, SE16 300 D5
● **Ember Cen**, Walt. KT12 196 BY103
Ember Cl, Add. KT15 212 BK106
Petts Wood BR5 205 EQ101
Embercourt Rd, T.Ditt. KT7 197 CE100
Ember Fm Av, E.Mol. KT8 197 CD100
Ember Fm Way, E.Mol. KT8 197 CD100
Ember Gdns, T.Ditt. KT7 197 CE101
Ember La, E.Mol. KT8 197 CD101
Esher KT10 197 CD101
Ember Rd, Slou. SL3 153 BB76
Emberson Way, N.Wld Bas. CM16 71 FC26
Emberton, SE5 311 N2
Emberton Ct, EC1
off Tompion St 286 G3
Embleton Rd, SE13 163 EB83
Watford WD19 93 BU48
Embleton Wk, Hmptn. TW12
off Fearnley Cres 176 BZ93
Embry Cl, Stan. HA7 95 CG49
Embry Dr, Stan. HA7 95 CG51
Embry Way, Stan. HA7 95 CG50
Emden Cl, West Dr. UB7 154 BN75
Emden St, SW6 307 M6
Emerald Cl, E16 292 G9
Emerald Ct, Slou. SL1 152 AS75
Emerald Gdns, Dag. RM8 126 FA60
Emerald Rd, NW10 138 CR67
Emerald Sq, Sthl. UB2 156 BX76
Emerald St, WC1 286 C6
Emerson Apts, N8
off Chadwell La 121 DM55

Emerson Ct, Woob.Grn HP10 110 AE57
Emerson Dr, Horn. RM11 128 FK59
Emerson Gdns, Har. HA3 118 CM58
EMERSON PARK, Horn. RM11 128 FL58
⊖ **Emerson Park** 128 FL59
Sch **Emerson Pk Sch**, Horn. RM11
off Wych Elm Rd 128 FP59
Emerson Rd, Ilf. IG1 125 EN59
Emersons Av, Swan. BR8 187 FF94
Emerson St, SE1 299 J2
Emerton Cl, Bexh. DA6 166 EY84
Emerton Ct, Nthch HP4
off Emerton Garth 38 AS16
Emerton Garth, Nthch HP4 38 AS16
Emerton Rd, Lthd. KT22 230 CC120
Emery Hill St, SW1 297 M7
Emery St, SE1 298 F6
Emes Rd, Erith DA8 167 FC80
Emilia Cl, Enf. EN3 82 DV43
Emily Davison Dr, Epsom KT18 255 CV118
Emily Duncan Pl, E7 124 EH63
Emily Jackson Cl, Sev. TN13 257 FH124
★ **Emirates Air Line**, E16/SE10 303 L3
Emley Rd, Add. KT15 194 BG104
Emlyn Gdns, W12 158 CS75
Emlyn La, Lthd. KT22 231 CG122
Emlyn Rd, W12 158 CS75
Horley RH6 268 DE147
Redhill RH1 266 DG136
Emma Ho, Rom. RM1
off Market Link 127 FE56
Emmanuel Cl, Guil. GU2 242 AU131
Sch **Emmanuel C of E Prim Sch**, NW6 273 K2
Emmanuel Lo, Chsht EN8 66 DW30
Emmanuel Rd, SW12 181 DJ88
Northwood HA6 93 BT52
Emma Rd, E13 291 M1
Emma's Cres, Stans.Abb. SG12 33 EB11
Emma St, E2 278 E10
Emmaus Way, Chig. IG7 103 EN50
Emmett Cl, Shenley WD7 62 CL33
Emmetts Cl, Wok. GU21 226 AW117
Emminster, NW6 *off Abbey Rd* 273 L8
Emmott Av, Ilf. IG6 125 EQ57
Emmott Cl, E1 289 M5
NW11 120 DC58
Emms Pas, Kings.T. KT1 197 CK96
Emperor Cl, Berk. HP4 38 AT16
Emperor's Gate, SW7 295 M7
Empire Av, N18 100 DQ50
Empire Centre, Wat. WD24 76 BW39
Empire Cl, SE7 164 EH79
Empire Ct, Wem. HA9 118 CP62
Empire Ms, SW16 181 DL92
Empire Par, N18 *off Empire Av* 100 DR51
Empire Rd, Perivale UB6 137 CJ67
Empire Sq, N7 121 DL62
SE1 299 L5
SE20 *off High St* 183 DX94
Empire Sq E, SE1
off Empire Sq 299 L5
Empire Sq S, SE1
off Empire Sq 299 L5
Empire Sq W, SE1
off Empire Sq 299 L5
Empire Vil, Red. RH1 266 DG144
Empire Wk, Green. DA9 169 FW84
Empire Way, Wem. HA9 118 CM63
Empire Wf Rd, E14 302 G9
Empress App, SW6 307 J1
Empress Approach Bus Terminus 307 J1
Empress Av, E4 101 EB52
E12 124 EJ61
Ilford IG1 125 EM61
Woodford Green IG8 102 EF52
Empress Dr, Chis. BR7 185 EP93
Empress Ms, SE5 311 J8
Empress Pl, SW6 307 J1
Empress Rd, Grav. DA12 191 GL87
Empress St, SE17 311 K2
Empson St, E3 290 D4
Emsworth Cl, N9 100 DW46
Emsworth Rd, Ilf. IG6 103 EP54
Emsworth St, SW2 181 DM89
Emu Rd, SW8 309 H9
Ena Rd, SW16 201 DL97
Enborne Grn, S.Ock. RM15 149 FU71
Enbrook St, W10 282 F3
Endale Cl, Cars. SM5 200 DF103
Endeavour Rd, Chsht EN8 67 DY27
Sch **Endeavour Sch, The**, Brwd. CM15 *off Hogarth Av* 109 FZ48
Endeavour Way, SW19 180 DB91
Barking IG11 146 EU68
Croydon CR0 201 DK101
Endell St, WC2 286 A8
Enderby St, SE10 315 H1
Enderley Cl, Har. HA3 95 CE53
Enderley Rd, Har. HA3 95 CE53
Endersby Rd, Barn. EN5 79 CW43
Enders Cl, Enf. EN2 81 DN39
Endersleigh Gdns, NW4 119 CU56
Endlebury Rd, E4 101 EB47
Endlesham Rd, SW12 180 DG87
Endsleigh Cl, S.Croy. CR2 220 DW110
Endsleigh Gdns, WC1 285 N4
Hersham KT12 214 BW106
Ilford IG1 125 EM61
Surbiton KT6 197 CJ100
● **Endsleigh Ind Est**, Sthl. UB2 156 BZ77
Endsleigh Pl, WC1 285 P4
Endsleigh Rd, W13 137 CG73
South Merstham RH1 251 DJ129
Southall UB2 156 BY77
Endsleigh St, WC1 285 N4
Endway, Surb. KT5 198 CN101
Endwell Rd, SE4 313 M9
Endymion Ct, Hat. AL10
off Endymion Rd 45 CW17
Endymion Ms, Hat. AL10
off Endymion Rd 45 CW17
Endymion Rd, N4 121 DN59
SW2 181 DM86
Hatfield AL10 45 CW17
Energen Cl, NW10 138 CS65
ENFIELD, EN1 - EN3 82 DT41
⇌ **Enfield Chase** 82 DQ41
Enfield Cl, Uxb. UB8 134 BK68
Sch **Enfield Co Sch**, Lwr Sch, Enf. EN2 *off Rosemary Av* 82 DS39
Upr Sch, Enf. EN2
off Holly Wk 82 DR41

E

● Enfield Enterprise Cen, Enf. EN3 off Queensway 82 DW43
Sch Enfield Gram Sch,
Lwr Sch, Enf. EN1 off Baker St 82 DR40
Upr Sch, Enf. EN2 off Market Pl 82 DR41
ENFIELD HIGHWAY, Enf. EN3 83 DW41
ENFIELD LOCK, Enf. EN3 83 DZ37
⇌ Enfield Lock 83 DY37
Enfield Lock, Enf. EN3 83 EA38
Enfield Retail Pk, Enf. EN1 82 DV41
Enfield Rd, N1 277 P7
W3 158 CP75
Brentford TW8 157 CK78
Enfield EN2 81 DK42
Lon.Hthrw Air. TW6 off Eastern Perimeter Rd 155 BS82
Jct Enfield Rd Rbt, Lon.Hthrw Air. TW6 155 BS82
ENFIELD TOWN, Enf. EN2 82 DR40
Enfield Town 82 DS42
Enfield Wk, Brent. TW8 157 CK78
ENFIELD WASH, Enf. EN3 83 DX38
Enford St, W1 284 E6
Engadine Cl, Croy. CR0 202 DT104
Engadine St, SW18 179 CZ88
Engate St, SE13 163 EC84
Engayne Gdns, Upmin. RM14 128 FP60
Sch Engayne Prim Sch, Upmin. RM14 off Severn Dr 129 FS58
Engel Pk, NW7 97 CW51
Engineer Cl, SE18 165 EN79
Engineers Way, Wem. HA9 118 CN63
Engineer's Wf, Nthlt. UB5 136 BZ70
Englands La, NW3 274 E5
Loughton IG10 85 EN40
England Way, N.Mal. KT3 198 CP98
Englefield Cl, Croy. CR0 202 DQ100
Enfield EN2 81 DN40
Englefield Green TW20 off Alexandra Rd 172 AW93
Orpington BR5 205 ET99
Englefield Cres, Orp. BR5 205 ET98
ENGLEFIELD GREEN, Egh. TW20 172 AV92
Englefield Grn, Eng.Grn TW20 172 AW91
Sch Englefield Grn Inf Sch, Eng.Grn TW20 off Barley Mow Rd 172 AW92
Englefield Path, Orp. BR5 205 ET98
Englefield Rd, N1 277 L5
Orpington BR5 206 EU98
Engleheart Dr, Felt. TW14 175 BT86
Engleheart Rd, SE6 183 EB87
Englehurst, Eng.Grn TW20 172 AW93
Englemere Pk, Oxshott KT22 214 CB114
Englewood Rd, SW12 181 DH86
Engliff La, Wok. GU22 227 BF116
English Gdns, Wrays. TW19 152 AX84
English Grds, SE1 off Tooley St 299 N3
Sch English Martyrs' Cath Prim Sch, SE17 299 M9
Sch English Martyrs RC Prim Sch, E1 288 B9
English St, E3 289 N4
Enid Cl, Brick.Wd AL2 60 BZ31
Enid St, SE16 300 B6
Enmore Av, SE25 202 DU99
Enmore Gdns, SW14 178 CR85
Enmore Rd, SE25 202 DU99
SW15 159 CW84
Southall UB1 136 CA70
Ennerdale Av, Horn. RM12 127 FG64
Stanmore HA7 117 CJ55
Ennerdale Cl, Felt. TW14 175 BT88
St. Albans AL1 43 CH22
Sutton SM1 217 CZ105
Ennerdale Cres, Slou. SL1 130 AJ71
Ennerdale Dr, NW9 118 CS57
Watford WD25 60 BW33
Ennerdale Gdns, Wem. HA9 117 CJ60
Ennerdale Ho, E3 289 N4
Ennerdale Rd, Bexh. DA7 166 FA81
Richmond TW9 158 CM82
Ennersdale Rd, SE13 183 ED85
Ennismore Av, W4 159 CT77
Greenford UB6 137 CE65
Guildford GU1 243 AZ134
Ennismore Gdns, SW7 296 C5
Thames Ditton KT7 197 CE100
Ennismore Gdns Ms, SW7 296 C6
Ennismore Ms, SW7 296 C6
Ennismore St, SW7 296 C6
Ennis Rd, N4 121 DN60
SE18 165 EQ79
Ensign Cl, Lon.Hthrw Air. TW6 155 BS83
Purley CR8 219 DN110
Stanwell TW19 174 BK88
Ensign Dr, N13 100 DQ48
Ensign Ho, SW8 off St. George Wf 310 A2
SW18 160 DC83
Ensign St, E1 288 C10
Ensign Way, Stanw. TW19 174 BK88
Wallington SM6 219 DL108
Enslin Rd, SE9 185 EN86
Ensor Ms, SW7 296 A10
Enstone Rd, Enf. EN3 83 DY41
Uxbridge UB10 114 BM62
Enterdent, The, Gdse. RH9 253 DX133
Enterdent Rd, Gdse. RH9 252 DW134
● Enterprise Cen, The, Pot.B. EN6 63 CY30
Enterprise Cl, Croy. CR0 201 DN102
● Enterprise Distribution Cen, Til. RM18 171 GG84
● Enterprise Est, Guil. GU1 242 AY130
Enterprise Ho, E9 278 G7
● Enterprise Ind Est, SE16 300 G10
Enterprise Way, NW10 139 CU69
SW18 160 DA84
Hemel Hempstead HP2 41 BQ18
Teddington TW11 177 CF92
Enterprize Way, SE8 301 N8
Entertainment Av, SE10 off Millennium Way 303 J3
Envoy Av, Lon.Hthrw Air. TW6 155 BT83
Jct Envoy Av Rbt, Lon.Hthrw Air. TW6 155 BT83
Eothen Cl, Cat. CR3 236 DU124
Epirus Ms, SW6 307 J4
Epirus Rd, SW6 307 H4
EPPING, CM16 69 ES31
⊖ Epping 70 EU31
Epping Cl, E14 302 B8
Romford RM7 127 FB55
★ Epping Forest, Epp. CM16 & Loug. IG10 84 EJ39
Coll Epping Forest Coll, Loug. IG10 off Borders La 85 EP42
★ Epping Forest District Mus, Wal.Abb. EN9 off Sun St 67 EC33
Coll Epping Forest Fld Cen, High Beach IG10 off Wake Rd 84 EJ38
Epping Glade, E4 83 EC44
EPPING GREEN, Epp. CM16 51 EN24
Hert. SG13 47 DK21
Epping Grn, Hem.H. HP2 40 BN15
Epping Grn Rd, Epp.Grn CM16 51 EN21
Epping La, Stap.Taw. RM4 86 EV40
Epping Long Grn, Epp.Grn CM16 51 EM24
Epping New Rd, Buck.H. IG9 102 EH47
Loughton IG10 84 EH43
Epping Pl, N1 276 F5
Epping Rd, Epp. CM16 85 EM36
Epping Green CM16 69 ER27
North Weald Bassett CM16 70 EW28
North Weald Bassett North CM16 75 FD24
Ongar CM5 53 FF24
Roydon CM19 50 EK18
Toot Hill CM5 71 FC30
Waltham Abbey EN9 50 EK18
Sch Epping St. John's C of E Sch, Epp. CM16 69 ES31
EPPING UPLAND, Epp. CM16 69 EQ25
Sch Epping Upland C of E Prim Sch, Epp.Grn CM16 off Carters La 51 EP24
Epping Way, E4 83 EB44
Epple Rd, SW6 307 H6
EPSOM, KT17 - KT19 216 CQ114
⇌ Epsom 216 CR113
Coll Epsom Adult Ed Cen, Epsom KT17 off Church St 216 CS113
Sch Epsom & Ewell High Sch, W.Ewell KT19 off Ruxley La 216 CQ106
● Epsom Business Pk, Epsom KT17 216 CS111
Epsom Cl, Bexh. DA7 167 FB83
Northolt UB5 116 BZ64
Sch Epsom Coll, Epsom KT17 off College Rd 217 CU114
⇌ Epsom Downs 233 CV115
Epsom Downs, Epsom KT18 233 CT118
● Epsom Downs Metro Cen, Tad. KT20 off Waterfield 233 CV120
★ Epsom Downs Racecourse, Epsom KT18 233 CT118
Epsom Gap, Lthd. KT22 231 CH115
H Epsom Gen Hosp, Epsom KT18 232 CQ115
Epsom La N, Epsom KT18 233 CV118
Tadworth KT20 233 CV118
Epsom La S, Tad. KT20 233 CW121
Sch Epsom Prim Sch, Epsom KT19 off Pound La 216 CR111
Epsom Rd, E10 123 EC58
Ashtead KT21 232 CM118
Croydon CR0 219 DN105
Epsom KT17 217 CT110
Guildford GU1, GU4 243 BE133
Ilford IG3 125 ET58
Leatherhead KT22 231 CH121
Morden SM4 199 CZ101
Sutton SM3 199 CZ101
West Horsley KT24 245 BP130
Epsom Sq, Lon.Hthrw Air. TW6 off Eastern Perimeter Rd 155 BT82
● Epsom Trade Pk, Epsom KT19 216 CR111
Epsom Way, Horn. RM12 128 FM63
Epstein Rd, SE28 146 EU74
Epworth Rd, Islw. TW7 157 CH80
Epworth St, EC2 287 M5
Equana Apts, SE8 301 L10
Equinox Ho, Bark. IG11 145 EQ65
Equity Ms, W5 137 CK74
Equity Sq, E2 288 B3
Erasmus St, SW1 297 P9
Erbin Ct, N9 off Galahad Rd 100 DU47
Erconwald St, W12 139 CT72
Erebus Dr, SE28 165 EQ76
Eresby Dr, Beck. BR3 203 EA102
Eresby Pl, NW6 273 J7
Erica Cl, Slou. SL1 131 AL73
Erica Ct, Swan. BR8 off Azalea Dr 207 FE98
Woking GU22 226 AX118
Erica Gdns, Croy. CR0 221 EB105
Erica St, W12 139 CU73
Eric Clarke La, Bark. IG11 293 P4
Eric Cl, E7 281 N1
Ericcson Cl, SW18 180 DA85
Eric Fletcher Ct, N1 off Essex Rd 277 K6
Eric Rd, E7 281 N1
NW10 139 CT65
Romford RM6 126 EX59
Ericson Ho, N16 off Stamford Hill 122 DS60
Eric Steele Ho, St.Alb. AL2 60 CB27
Eric St, E3 289 N4
Eridge Grn Cl, Orp. BR5 206 EW102
Eridge Rd, W4 158 CR76
Erin Cl, Brom. BR1 184 EE94
Ilford IG3 126 EU58
Erin Ct, NW2 272 B4
Erindale, SE18 165 ER79
Erindale Ter, SE18 165 ER79
Eriswell Cres, Hersham KT12 213 BS107
Eriswell Rd, Hersham KT12 213 BT105
ERITH, DA8; DA18 167 FD79
⇌ Erith 167 FE78
H Erith & District Hosp, Erith DA8 167 FD79
Erith Ct, Purf. RM19 168 FN77
Erith Cres, Rom. RM5 105 FC53
Erith High St, Erith DA8 167 FE78
★ Erith Lib & Mus, Erith DA8 off Walnut Tree Rd 167 FE78
Erith Riverside, Erith DA8 167 FE79
Erith Rd, Belv. DA17 166 FA78
Bexleyheath DA7 167 FB84
Erith DA8 167 FB84
Sch Erith Sch, Erith DA8 off Avenue Rd 167 FD80
Erkenwald Cl, Cher. KT16 193 BE101
Erlanger Rd, SE14 313 K8
Erlesmere Gdns, W13 157 CG76
Ermine Cl, Chsht EN7 66 DV31
Hounslow TW4 156 BW82
St. Albans AL3 42 CA21
Ermine Ho, N17 off Moselle St 100 DT52
Ermine Ms, E2 278 A9
Ermine Rd, N15 122 DT58
SE13 163 EB83
Ermine Side, Enf. EN1 82 DU43
Ermington Rd, SE9 185 EQ89
Ermyn Cl, Lthd. KT22 231 CK121
Ermyn Way, Lthd. KT22 231 CK121
Ernald Av, E6 144 EL68
Ernan Cl, S.Ock. RM15 149 FU71
Ernan Rd, S.Ock. RM15 149 FU71
Erncroft Way, Twick. TW1 177 CF86
Ernest Av, SE27 181 DP91
Sch Ernest Bevin Coll, SW17 off Beechcroft Rd 180 DE89
Ernest Cl, Beck. BR3 203 EA99
Ernest Gdns, W4 158 CP79
Ernest Gro, Beck. BR3 203 DZ99
Ernest Rd, Horn. RM11 128 FL58
Kingston upon Thames KT1 198 CP96
Ernest Sq, Kings.T. KT1 198 CP96
Ernest St, E1 289 K5
Ernle Rd, SW20 179 CV94
Ernshaw Pl, SW15 off Carlton Dr 179 CY85
Ernst Chain Rd, Guil. GU2 258 AR135
★ Eros, W1 297 N1
Eros Ho, SE6 off Brownhill Rd 183 EB87
Erpingham Rd, SW15 159 CW83
Erridge Rd, SW19 200 DA96
Erriff Dr, S.Ock. RM15 149 FT71
Errington Cl, Grays RM16 off Cedar Rd 171 GH76
Hatfield AL10 44 CS17
Errington Dr, Wind. SL4 151 AN81
Errington Rd, W9 283 H4
Errol Gdns, Hayes UB4 135 BV70
New Malden KT3 199 CU98
Erroll Rd, Rom. RM1 127 FF56
Errol St, EC1 287 K5
Erskine Cl, Sutt. SM1 200 DE104
Erskine Cres, N17 122 DV56
Erskine Hill, NW11 120 DA57
Erskine Ho, SE7 off Springfield Gro 164 EJ79
Erskine Ms, NW3 274 F7
Erskine Rd, E17 123 DZ56
NW3 274 F7
Sutton SM1 218 DD105
Watford WD19 94 BW48
Erwood Rd, SE7 305 H10
Esam Way, SW16 181 DN92
Esbies Est, Saw. CM21 36 EZ05
Escombe Ct, Whyt. CR3 off Godstone Rd 236 DU119
Escombe Dr, Guil. GU2 242 AV129
Escott Gdns, SE9 184 EL91
Escott Pl, Ott. KT16 211 BC107
Escot Way, Barn. EN5 79 CW43
Coll ESCP-EAP European Sch of Management, NW3 273 K1
Escreet Gro, SE18 305 L8
Esdaile Gdns, Upmin. RM14 129 FR59
Esdaile La, Hodd. EN11 49 EA18
ESHER, KT10 214 CB105
⇌ Esher 197 CD103
Esher Av, Rom. RM7 127 FC58
Sutton SM3 199 CX104
Walton-on-Thames KT12 195 BU101
Esher Bypass, Chess. KT9 215 CH108
Cobham KT11 213 BU112
Esher KT10 215 CH108
Sch Esher Ch Sch, Esher KT10 off Milbourne La 214 CC106
Esher Cl, Bex. DA5 186 EY88
Esher KT10 214 CB106
Sch Esher C of E High Sch, Esher KT10 off More La 196 CA104
Coll Esher Coll, T.Ditt. KT7 off Weston Grn Rd 197 CE101
Jct Esher Common, Esher KT10 214 CC110
Esher Cres, Lon.Hthrw Air. TW6 off Eastern Perimeter Rd 155 BS82
Esher Gdns, SW19 179 CX89
Esher Grn, Esher KT10 214 CB105
Coll Esher Grn Adult Learning Cen, Esher KT10 off Esher Grn 214 CB105
Esher Grn Dr, Esher KT10 196 CB104
Esher Ms, Mitch. CR4 200 DF97
Esher Pk Av, Esher KT10 214 CC105
Esher Pl Av, Esher KT10 214 CB105
Esher Rd, E.Mol. KT8 197 CD100
Hersham KT12 214 BX106
Ilford IG3 125 ES62
Eskdale, NW1 285 L1
London Colney AL2 62 CM27
Eskdale Av, Chesh. HP5 54 AQ30
Northolt UB5 136 BZ67
Eskdale Cl, Dart. DA2 188 FQ89
Wembley HA9 117 CK61
Eskdale Ct, Hem.H. HP2 off Lonsdale 40 BL17
Eskdale Gdns, Pur. CR8 220 DR114
Eskdale Rd, Bexh. DA7 166 FA82
Uxbridge UB8 134 BH68
Eskley Gdns, S.Ock. RM15 149 FV70
Eskmont Ridge, SE19 182 DS94
Esk Rd, E13 291 P4
Esk Way, Rom. RM1 105 FD52
Esmar Cres, NW9 119 CU59
Esme Ho, SW15 159 CT84
Esmeralda Rd, SE1 300 D9
Esmond Cl, Rain. RM13 off Dawson Dr 147 FH66
Esmond Gdns, W4 off South Par 158 CR77
Esmond Rd, NW6 273 H9
W4 158 CR77
Esmond St, SW15 159 CY84
Esparto St, SW18 180 DB87
Esparto Way, S.Darenth DA4 208 FQ95
Essendene Cl, Cat. CR3 236 DS123
Sch Essendene Lo Sch, Cat. CR3 off Essendene Rd 236 DS123
Essendene Rd, Cat. CR3 236 DS123
Essenden Rd, Belv. DA17 166 FA78
South Croydon CR2 220 DS108
Sch Essendine Prim Sch, W9 283 K3
Essendine Rd, W9 283 K4
ESSENDON, Hat. AL9 46 DE17
Sch Essendon C of E Prim Sch, Essen. AL9 off School La 46 DF17
Essendon Gdns, Welw.G.C. AL7 29 CZ09
Essendon Hill, Essen. AL9 46 DE17
Essendon Pl, Essen. AL9 46 DE19
Essendon Rd, Hert. SG13 46 DG15
Essex Av, Islw. TW7 157 CE83
Slough SL2 131 AQ71
Essex Cl, E17 123 DY56
Addlestone KT15 212 BJ105
Morden SM4 199 CX101
Romford RM7 127 FB56
Ruislip HA4 116 BX60
Essex Ct, EC4 286 E9
SW13 159 CT82
Essex Gdns, N4 121 DP58
Hornchurch RM11 128 FM57
Essex Gro, SE19 182 DR93
Essex Ho, E14 290 C8
Essex La, Kings L. WD4 59 BS33
Essex Lo, N10 98 DG54
Essex Ms, SE19 182 DS93
Essex Pk, N3 98 DB51
Essex Pk Ms, W3 138 CS74
Essex Pl, W4 158 CQ77
Essex Pl Sq, W4 off Chiswick High Rd 158 CR77
Sch Essex Prim Sch, E12 off Sheridan Rd 125 EM64
⇌ Essex Road 277 J7
Essex Rd, E4 102 EE46
E10 123 EC58
E12 124 EL64
E17 123 DY58
E18 102 EH54
N1 277 J7
NW10 138 CS66
W3 138 CQ73
W4 off Belmont Ter 158 CR77
Barking IG11 145 ER66
Borehamwood WD6 78 CN41
Chadwell Heath RM6 126 EW59
Chesham HP5 54 AQ29
Dagenham RM10 127 FC64
Dartford DA1 188 FK86
Enfield EN2 82 DR42
Gravesend DA11 191 GG88
Grays RM20 169 FU79
Hoddesdon EN11 49 EC18
Longfield DA3 209 FX96
Romford RM7 127 FB56
Watford WD17 75 BU40
Essex Rd S, E11 123 ED59
Essex St, E7 281 N2
WC2 286 E10
St. Albans AL1 43 CE19
Essex Twr, SE20 202 DV95
Essex Vil, W8 295 J5
Essex Way, Epp. CM16 70 EV32
Great Warley CM13 107 FW51
Hoddesdon EN11 49 EC17
Ongar CM5 71 FF29
Essex Wf, E5 122 DW61
Essian St, E1 289 L6
Essoldo Way, Edg. HA8 118 CM55
Estate Way, E10 123 DZ60
Estcourt Rd, SE25 202 DV100
SW6 306 G4
Watford WD17 76 BW41
Estella Av, N.Mal. KT3 199 CV98
Estelle Rd, NW3 274 F1
Esterbrooke St, SW1 297 N9
Este Rd, SW11 308 C10
Estfeld Cl, Hodd. EN11 33 EB14
Esther Cl, N21 99 DN45
Esther Ms, Brom. BR1 204 EH95
Esther Rd, E11 124 EE59
Estoria Cl, SW2 181 DN87
★ Estorick Collection of Modern Italian Art, N1 277 H5
Estreham Rd, SW16 181 DK93
Estridge Cl, Houns. TW3 156 CA84
Estuary Cl, Bark. IG11 146 EV69
Eswyn Rd, SW17 180 DF91
Etchingham Pk Rd, N3 98 DB52
Etchingham Rd, E15 123 EC63
Eternit Wk, SW6 306 B6
Etfield Gro, Sid. DA14 186 EV92
Ethel Bailey Cl, Epsom KT19 216 CN112
Ethelbert Cl, Brom. BR1 204 EG97
Ethelbert Gdns, Ilf. IG2 125 EM57
Ethelbert Rd, SW20 199 CX95
Bromley BR1 204 EG97
Erith DA8 167 FC80
Hawley DA2 188 FL91
Orpington BR5 206 EX97
Ethelbert St, SW12 181 DH88
Ethelburga Rd, Rom. RM3 106 FM53
Ethelburga St, SW11 308 D6
Ethelburga Twr, SW11 308 D6
Etheldene Av, N10 121 DJ56
Ethelden Rd, W12 139 CV74
Ethelred Cl, Welw.G.C. AL7 29 CZ10
Ethelred Ct, Whyt. CR3 off Godstone Rd 236 DU119
Ethelred Est, SE11 298 D9
Ethel Rd, E16 292 A9
Ashford TW15 174 BL92
Ethel St, SE17 299 J9
Ethel Ter, Orp. BR6 224 EW109
Ethelwine Pl, Abb.L. WD5 off The Crescent 59 BT30
Etheridge Grn, Loug. IG10 85 EQ41
Etheridge Rd, NW4 119 CW59
Loughton IG10 85 EP40
Etherley Rd, N15 122 DQ57
Etherow St, SE22 182 DU86
Etherstone Grn, SW16 181 DN91
Etherstone Rd, SW16 181 DN91
Ethnard Rd, SE15 312 E3
Ethorpe Cl, Ger.Cr. SL9 112 AY57
Ethorpe Cres, Ger.Cr. SL9 112 AY57
Ethronvi Rd, Bexh. DA7 166 EY83
Etloe Rd, E10 123 EA61
Etna Rd, St.Alb. AL3 43 CD19
ETON, Wind. SL4 151 AQ80
Eton Av, N12 98 DC52
NW3 274 C6
Barnet EN4 80 DE44
Hounslow TW5 156 BZ79
New Malden KT3 198 CR99
Wembley HA0 117 CH63
Eton Cl, SW18 180 DB87
Datchet SL3 152 AU79
Sch Eton Coll, Eton SL4 off High St 151 AR79
Eton Coll Rd, NW3 274 F5
Eton Ct, NW3 274 B6
Eton SL4 151 AR80
Staines-upon-Thames TW18 173 BF92
Wembley HA0 117 CJ63
Sch Eton End PNEU Sch, Datchet SL3 off Eton Rd 152 AU79
Eton Garages, NW3 274 D5
Eton Gro, NW9 118 CN55
SE13 164 EE83
Eton Hall, NW3 274 F5
Sch Eton Ho The Manor Sch, SW4 off Clapham Common N Side 183 DH84
Eton Pl, NW3 274 G6
Sch Eton Porny C of E First Sch, Eton SL4 off High St 151 AR79
Eton Ri, NW3 274 F5
Eton Rd, NW3 274 E6
Datchet SL3 152 AT78
Hayes UB3 155 BT80
Ilford IG1 125 EQ64
Orpington BR6 224 EV105
Eton Sq, Eton SL4 151 AR80
Eton St, Rich. TW9 178 CL85
Eton Vil, NW3 274 F5
Eton Way, Dart. DA1 168 FJ84
ETON WICK, Wind. SL4 151 AM77
Sch Eton Wick C of E First Sch, Eton Wick SL4 off Sheepcote Rd 173 AN78
Eton Wick Rd, Wind. SL4 151 AL77
Etta St, SE8 313 M2
Etton Cl, Horn. RM12 128 FL61
Ettrick St, E14 290 F8
Etwell Pl, Surb. KT5 198 CM100
Sch Etz Chaim Jewish Prim Sch, NW7 97 CT50
Eucalyptus Ms, SW16 off Estreham Rd 181 DK93
Euclid Way, Grays RM20 169 FT78
Euesden Cl, N9 100 DV48
Eugene Cl, Rom. RM2 128 FJ56
Eugenia Rd, SE16 301 H9
Eugenie Ms, Chis. BR7 205 EP95
Eunice Gro, Chesh. HP5 54 AR32
Eureka Gdns, Epp.Grn CM16 51 EN21
Eureka Rd, Kings.T. KT1 off Washington Rd 198 CN96
Coll Eurocentres, Lee Grn, SE3 off Meadowcourt Rd 164 EF84
London Cen, SW1 297 K9
Euro Cl, NW10 139 CU65
Coll Europa Cen for Modern Languages, Horn. RM11 off The Walk 128 FM61
Europa Pk Rd, Guil. GU1 242 AW133
Europa Pl, EC1 287 J3
Europa Rd, Hem.H. HP2 off Jupiter Dr 40 BM17
● Europa Trade Est, Erith DA8 167 FD78
● Europa Trade Pk, E16 291 J5
Europe Rd, SE18 305 K7
Eustace Bldg, SW8 309 J3
Eustace Pl, SE18 305 J8
Eustace Rd, E6 292 G2
SW6 307 J4
Guildford GU4 243 BD132
Romford RM6 126 EX59
⇌ Euston 285 M2
Euston 285 M2
⊖ Euston 285 M2
Euston 285 N3
Euston Av, Wat. WD18 75 BT43
Euston Cen, NW1 off Triton Sq 285 L4
Euston Gro, NW1 285 N3
Euston Rd, N1 286 A2
NW1 285 K5
Croydon CR0 201 DN102
⊖ Euston Square 285 M4
Euston Sq, NW1 285 N3
Euston Sta Colonnade, NW1 285 N3
Euston St, NW1 285 M4
● Euston Twr, NW1 285 L4
Evan Cook Cl, SE15 312 G7
Evandale Rd, SW9 310 F8
Evangelist Rd, NW5 275 K1
Evans Av, Wat. WD25 75 BT35
● Evans Business Cen, NW2 119 CU62
Evans Cl, E8 278 B5
Croxley Green WD3 74 BN43
Greenhithe DA9 189 FU85
Evansdale, Rain. RM13 off New Zealand Way 147 FF69
Evans Gro, Felt. TW13 176 CA89
St. Albans AL4 43 CJ16
Evans Rd, SE6 184 EE89
Evanston Av, E4 101 EC52
Evanston Gdns, Ilf. IG4 124 EL58
Evans Wf, Hem.H. HP3 40 BL24
Eva Rd, Rom. RM6 126 EW59
H Evelina Children's Hosp, SE1 298 C6
Evelina Rd, SE15 312 G10
SE20 183 DX94
Eveline Lowe Est, SE16 300 C7
Eveline Rd, Mitch. CR4 200 DF95
Evelyn Av, NW9 118 CR56
Ruislip HA4 115 BT58
Titsey RH8 238 EJ124
Evelyn Cl, Twick. TW2 176 CB87
Woking GU22 226 AX120
Evelyn Cotts, Dor. RH5 262 BX143
Evelyn Ct, N1 287 L1
Evelyn Cres, Sun. TW16 195 BT95
Evelyn Denington Rd, E6 293 H5
Evelyn Dr, Pnr. HA5 94 BX52
Evelyn Fox Ct, W10 282 B7
Evelyn Gdns, SW7 308 A1
Godstone RH9 252 DW130
Richmond TW9 158 CL84
Sch Evelyn Grace Acad, SE24 161 DP84
Evelyn Gro, W5 138 CM74
Southall UB1 136 BZ72
Evelyn Rd, E16 303 P2
E17 123 EC56
SW19 180 DB92
W4 158 CR76
Cockfosters EN4 80 DF42
Ham TW10 177 CJ90
Richmond TW9 158 CL83
Evelyns Cl, Uxb. UB8 134 BN72
Evelyn Sharp Cl, Rom. RM2 off Amery Gdns 128 FK55
Evelyn St, SE8 301 L9
Evelyn Ter, Rich. TW9 158 CL83
Evelyn Wk, N1 287 L1
Great Warley CM13 off Essex Way 107 FW51
Evelyn Way, Epsom KT19 216 CN111
Stoke D'Abernon KT11 230 BZ116
Sunbury-on-Thames TW16 195 BT95
Wallington SM6 219 DK105
Evelyn Yd, W1 285 N8
Evening Hill, Beck. BR3 183 EC94
Evensyde, Wat. WD18 75 BR44
Evenwood Cl, SW15 179 CY85
Everard Av, Brom. BR2 204 EG102
Slough SL1 152 AS75
Everard Cl, St.Alb. AL1 43 CD22
Everard La, Cat. CR3 off Tillingdown Hill 236 DU122
Everard Way, Wem. HA9 118 CL62

Everatt Cl, SW18 off Amerland Rd 179 CZ86
Everdon Rd, SW13 159 CU79
Everest Cl, Nthflt DA11 190 GE90
Everest Ct, Wok. GU21 off Langmans Way 226 AS116
Everest Pl, E14 290 E6
Swanley BR8 207 FD98
Everest Rd, SE9 184 EL85
Stanwell TW19 174 BK87
Everest Way, Hem.H. HP2 40 BN19
Everett Cl, Bushey Hth WD23 95 CE46
Cheshunt EN7 66 DQ25
Pinner HA5 115 BT55
Everett Wk, Belv. DA17 off Osborne Rd 166 EZ78
Everglade, Bigg.H. TN16 238 EK118
Everglade Strand, NW9 97 CT53
Evergreen Cl, SE20 182 DW94
Evergreen Ct, Stanw. TW19 off Evergreen Way 174 BK87
Evergreen Oak Av, Wind. SL4 152 AU83
Evergreen Sq, E8 278 A6
Evergreen Wk, Hem.H. HP3 40 BL22
Evergreen Way, Hayes UB3 135 BT73
Stanwell TW19 174 BK87
Everilda St, N1 276 D9
Evering Rd, E5 122 DT62
N16 122 DT62
Everington Rd, N10 98 DF54
Everington St, W6 306 D2
Everitt Rd, NW10 138 CR69
Everlands Cl, Wok. GU22 226 AY118
Everlasting La, St.Alb. AL3 42 CC19
Everleigh St, N4 121 DM60
Eve Rd, E11 281 J1
E15 291 K1
N17 122 DS55
Isleworth TW7 157 CG84
Woking GU21 227 BB115
Eversfield Gdns, NW7 96 CS51
Eversfield Rd, Reig. RH2 250 DB134
Richmond TW9 158 CM82
Evershed Wk, W4 158 CQ76
Eversholt Ct, Barn. EN5 off Lyonsdown Rd 80 DC43
Eversholt St, NW1 275 M10
Evershot Rd, N4 121 DM60
Eversleigh Gdns, Upmin. RM14 151 FR60
Eversleigh Rd, E6 144 EK67
N3 97 CZ52
SW11 308 G9
Barnet EN5 80 DC43
Eversley Av, Bexh. DA7 167 FD82
Wembley HA9 118 CN61
Eversley Cl, N21 81 DM44
Loughton IG10 85 EQ41
Eversley Cres, N21 81 DM44
Isleworth TW7 157 CD81
Ruislip HA4 115 BS61
Eversley Cross, Bexh. DA7 167 FE82
Eversley Mt, N21 81 DM44
Eversley Pk, SW19 179 CV92
Eversley Pk Rd, N21 81 DM44
Sch Eversley Prim Sch, N21 off Chaseville Pk Rd 81 DM43
Eversley Rd, SE7 164 EH79
SE19 182 DR94
Surbiton KT5 198 CM98
Eversley Way, Croy. CR0 221 EA105
Egham TW20 193 BC96
Everthorpe Rd, SE15 162 DT83
Everton Bldgs, NW1 285 L3
Everton Dr, Stan. HA7 118 CM55
Everton Rd, Croy. CR0 202 DU102
Evesham Av, E17 101 EA54
Evesham Cl, Grnf. UB6 136 CB68
Reigate RH2 249 CZ133
Sutton SM2 218 DA108
Evesham Ct, W13 off Tewkesbury Rd 137 CG74
Evesham Grn, Mord. SM4 200 DB100
Evesham Rd, E15 281 L8
N11 99 DJ50
Gravesend DA12 191 GK89
Morden SM4 200 DB100
Reigate RH2 249 CZ134
Evesham Rd N, Reig. RH2 249 CZ133
Evesham St, W11 294 C1
Evesham Wk, SE5 311 L8
SW9 310 E7
Evesham Way, SW11 309 H10
Ilford IG5 125 EN55
Evette Ms, Ilf. IG5 103 EN53
Evreham Rd, Iver SL0 133 BE72
Evron Pl, Hert. SG14 off Fore St 54 DR09
Evry Rd, Sid. DA14 186 EW93
Ewald Rd, SW6 306 G9
Ewanrigg Ter, Wdf.Grn. IG8 102 EJ50
Ewan Rd, Harold Wd RM3 106 FK54
Ewart Gro, N22 99 DN53
Ewart Pl, E3 279 N10
Ewart Rd, SE23 183 DX87
Ewe Cl, N7 276 B4
Ewelands, Horl. RH6 269 DJ147
EWELL, Epsom KT17 217 CU110
Ewell Bypass, Epsom KT17 217 CU108
Sch Ewell Castle Sch, Ewell KT17 off Church St 217 CU109
Ewell Ct Av, Epsom KT19 216 CS106
Ewell Downs Rd, Epsom KT17 217 CU111
⇌ Ewell East 217 CV110
Sch Ewell Gro Inf & Nurs Sch, Ewell KT17 off West St 217 CT109
Ewell Ho Gro, Epsom KT17 217 CT110
Ewellhurst Rd, Ilf. IG5 102 EL54
Ewell Pk Gdns, Epsom KT17 217 CU108
Ewell Pk Way, Ewell KT17 217 CU107
Ewell Rd, Long Dit. KT6 197 CH101
Surbiton KT6 198 CL100
Sutton SM3 217 CY107
⇌ Ewell West 216 CS109
Ewelme Rd, SE23 182 DW88
Ewen Cres, SW2 181 DN87
Ewer St, SE1 299 J3
Ewhurst Av, S.Croy. CR2 220 DT109
Ewhurst Cl, E1 289 H7
Sutton SM2 217 CW109
Ewhurst Ct, Mitch. CR4 off Phipps Br Rd 200 DD97
Ewhurst Rd, SE4 183 DZ86
Exbury Rd, SE6 183 EA89
Excalibur Ct, N9 off Galahad Rd 100 DU48
Excel Ct, WC2 297 P1
★ ExCeL London, E16 304 B1
ExCeL Marina, E16 304 A1
Excelsior Cl, Kings.T. KT1 off Washington Rd 198 CN96
Excelsior Gdns, SE13 314 E9
ExCeL Waterfront, E16 304 B1
Exchange, The, E1 off Commercial St 288 A5
Croy. CR0 off Scarbrook Rd 202 DQ104
Exchange Arc, EC2 287 P6
Exchange Cl, N11 off Benfleet Way 98 DG47
Exchange Ct, WC2 298 B1
Exchange Ho, N8 121 DL58
Exchange Pl, EC2 287 N6
Exchange Rd, Wat. WD18 75 BV42
Exchange Shop cen, SW15 159 CX84
Exchange Sq, EC2 287 N6
Exchange St, Rom. RM1 127 FE57
Exchange Wk, Pnr. HA5 116 BY59
Exeforde Av, Ashf. TW15 174 BN91
Exeter Cl, E6 293 J8
Watford WD24 76 BW40
Exeter Ct, Surb. KT6 off Maple Rd 198 CL99
Exeter Gdns, Ilf. IG1 124 EL60
Exeter Ho, SW15 off Putney Heath 179 CW86
Exeter Ms, NW6 273 L5
SW6 307 J4
Exeter Pl, Guil. GU2 242 AT132
Exeter Rd, E16 291 P7
E17 123 EA57
N9 100 DW47
N14 99 DH46
NW2 272 F5
Croydon CR0 202 DS101
Dagenham RM10 147 FB65
Enfield EN3 83 DX41
Feltham TW13 176 BZ90
Gravesend DA12 191 GK90
Harrow HA2 116 BY61
London Heathrow Airport TW6 177 BS83
Welling DA16 165 ET82
Exeter St, WC2 286 B10
Exeter Way, SE14 313 N5
London Heathrow Airp. TW6 155 BS82
Exford Gdns, SE12 184 EH88
Exford Rd, SE12 184 EH89
Exhibition Cl, W12 294 A1
Exhibition Rd, SW7 296 B5
Exmoor Cl, Ilf. IG6 103 EQ53
Exmoor St, W10 282 D5
Exmouth Mkt, EC1 286 E4
Exmouth Ms, NW1 285 M3
Exmouth Pl, E8 278 E7
Exmouth Rd, E17 123 DZ57
Grays RM17 170 GB79
Hayes UB4 135 BS69
Ruislip HA4 116 BW62
Welling DA16 166 EW81
Exmouth St, E1 289 H8
Exning Rd, E16 291 L5
Exon Apts, Rom. RM1 off Mercury Gdns 127 FE56
Exon St, SE17 299 N9
Explorer Av, Stai. TW19 174 BL88
Explorer Dr, Wat. WD18 75 BT44
Express Dr, Ilf. IG3 126 EV60
Exton Gdns, Dag. RM8 126 EW64
Exton Rd, NW10 138 CQ66
Exton St, SE1 298 E3
Eyebright Cl, Croy. CR0 off Primrose La 203 DX102
Eyhurst Av, Horn. RM12 127 FG62
Eyhurst Cl, NW2 119 CU61
Kingswood KT20 233 CZ123
Eyhurst Pk, Tad. KT20 234 DC123
Eyhurst Spur, Kgswd KT20 233 CZ124
Eylewood Rd, SE27 182 DQ92
Eynella Rd, SE22 182 DT87
Eynham Rd, W12 282 A7
EYNSFORD, Dart. DA4 208 FL103
★ Eynsford Castle, Dart. DA4 208 FL103
Eynsford Cl, Petts Wd BR5 205 EQ101
Eynsford Cres, Bex. DA5 186 EW88
Eynsford Rd, Fnghm DA4 208 FM102
Greenhithe DA9 189 FW85
Ilford IG3 125 ES61
Swanley BR8 207 FD100
Eynsham Dr, SE2 166 EU77
Eynswood Dr, Sid. DA14 186 EV92
Eyot Gdns, W6 159 CT78
Eyot Grn, W4 159 CT78
Eyre Cl, Rom. RM2 127 FH56
Eyre Ct, NW8 274 A10
Eyre Grn, Slou. SL2 131 AN69
Eyre St Hill, EC1 286 E5
Eyston Dr, Wey. KT13 212 BN110
Eythorne Ct, Epsom KT17 off Windmill La 217 CT112
Eywood Rd, St.Alb. AL1 42 CC22
Ezra St, E2 288 B2

F

Faber Gdns, NW4 119 CU57
Fabian Rd, SW6 307 H4
Fabian St, E6 293 H5
Fackenden La, Shore. TN14 225 FH113
Factory La, N17 100 DT54
Croydon CR0 201 DN102
Factory Rd, E16 304 G3
Northfleet DA11 190 GC86
Factory Sq, SW16 181 DL93
Factory Yd, W7 137 CE74
Faesten Way, Bex. DA5 187 FE90
Faggotters La, High Laver CM5 53 FF15
Matching Tye CM17 37 FE13
Faggotts Cl, Rad. WD7 77 CJ35
Faggs Rd, Felt. TW14 175 BU85
Fagnall La, Winch.Hill HP7 88 AJ45
Fagus Av, Rain. RM13 148 FK69
Faints Cl, Chsht EN7 66 DS29
Fairacre, Hem.H. HP3 40 BM24
New Malden KT3 198 CS97
Fair Acres, Brom. BR2 204 EG99
Fairacres, SW15 159 CU84
Cobham KT11 214 BX112
Croydon CR0 221 DZ109
Redhill RH1 267 DJ142
Ruislip HA4 115 BT59
Tadworth KT20 233 CW121
Windsor SL4 151 AK82
Fairacres Cl, Pot.B. EN6 63 CZ33
● Fairacres Ind Est, Wind. SL4 150 AJ82
Fairbairn Cl, Pur. CR8 219 DN113
Fairbairn Grn, SW9 310 F6
SW9 310 G6
Fairbank Av, Orp. BR6 205 EP103
Fairbank Est, N1 287 M1
Fairbanks Rd, N17 122 DT55
Fairborne Way, Guil. GU2 242 AU131
Fairbourne, Cob. KT11 214 BX113
Fairbourne Cl, Wok. GU21 226 AU118
Fairbourne La, Cat. CR3 236 DQ122
Fairbourne Rd, N17 122 DS55
SW4 181 DK86
Fairbridge Rd, N19 121 DK61
Fairbrook Cl, N13 99 DN50
Fairbrook Rd, N13 99 DN51
Fairburn Cl, Borwd. WD6 78 CN39
Fairburn Ct, SW15 179 CY85
Fairburn Ho, N16 off Stamford Hill 122 DS60
W14 off Ivatt Pl 307 H1
Fairby Ho, SE1 300 B8
Fairby Rd, SE12 184 EH85
● Faircharm Trd Est, SE8 314 C4
Fairchild Cl, SW11 308 B9
Fairchildes Av, New Adgtn CR0 221 ED112
Fairchildes La, Warl. CR6 221 ED114
Sch Fairchildes Prim Sch, New Adgtn CR0 off Fairchildes Av 222 EE112
Fairchild Pl, EC2 287 P5
Fairchild St, EC2 287 P5
Fair Cl, Bushey WD23 off Claybury 94 CB45
Fairclough Cl, Nthlt. UB5 136 BZ70
Fairclough St, E1 288 D9
Faircroft, Slou. SL2 131 AP70
Faircross Av, Bark. IG11 145 EQ65
Romford RM5 105 FD52
Faircross Par, Bark. IG11 145 ES65
Faircross Way, St.Alb. AL1 43 CG18
Fairdale Gdns, SW15 159 CV84
Hayes UB3 135 BU74
Fairdene Rd, Couls. CR5 235 DK117
Fairey Av, Hayes UB3 155 BT77
Fairfax Av, Epsom KT17 217 CV109
Redhill RH1 250 DE133
Fairfax Cl, Oxt. RH8 253 ED130
Walton-on-Thames KT12 195 BV102
Fairfax Ct, Dart. DA1 188 FN86
Fairfax Gdns, SE3 164 EK81
Fairfax Ms, E16 304 A2
SW15 159 CW84
Amersham HP7 55 AN40
Fairfax Pl, NW6 273 P7
W14 294 F7
Fairfax Rd, N8 121 DN56
NW6 273 P7
W4 158 CS76
Grays RM17 170 GB78
Hertford SG13 32 DT08
Teddington TW11 177 CG93
Tilbury RM18 171 GF81
Woking GU22 227 BB120
Fairfield 198 CL96
Fairfield App, Wrays. TW19 172 AX86
Fairfield Av, NW4 119 CV58
Datchet SL3 152 AW80
Edgware HA8 96 CP51
Horley RH6 268 DG149
Ruislip HA4 115 BQ59
Staines-upon-Thames TW18 173 BF91
Twickenham TW2 176 CB88
Upminster RM14 128 FQ62
Watford WD19 94 BW48
Fairfield Cl, N12 98 DC49
Datchet SL3 152 AX80
Dorking RH4 off Fairfield Dr 247 CH134
Enfield EN3 off Scotland Grn Rd N 83 DY42
Ewell KT19 216 CS106
Guildford GU2 242 AU133
Hatfield AL10 45 CW15
Hornchurch RM12 127 FG60
Mitcham CR4 180 DE94
Northwood HA6 off Thirlmere Gdns 93 BP50
Radlett WD7 77 CE37
Sidcup DA15 185 ET86
Fairfield Cotts, Lthd. KT23 246 CB125
Fairfield Ct, NW10 139 CU67
Northwood HA6 off Windsor Cl 115 BU54
Fairfield Cres, Edg. HA8 96 CP51
Fairfield Dr, SW18 180 DB85
Broxbourne EN10 49 DZ24
Dorking RH4 247 CH134
Harrow HA2 116 CC55
Perivale UB6 137 CJ67
Fairfield E, Kings.T. KT1 198 CL96
Fairfield Gdns, N8 121 DL57
Fairfield Gro, SE7 164 EK78
★ Fairfield Halls, Croy. CR0 202 DR104
Sch Fair Fld Jun Sch, Rad. WD7 off Watford Rd 77 CE36
Fairfield La, Farn.Royal SL2 131 AP68
Fairfield N, Kings.T. KT1 198 CL96
Fairfield Pk, Cob. KT11 214 BX114
Fairfield Path, Croy. CR0 202 DR104
Fairfield Pathway, Horn. RM12 148 FJ66
Fairfield Pl, Kings.T. KT1 198 CL97
Fairfield Ri, Guil. GU2 242 AT133
Fairfield Rd, E3 280 A10
E17 101 DY54
N8 121 DL57
N18 100 DU49
W7 157 CG76
Beckenham BR3 203 EA96
Bexleyheath DA7 166 EZ82
Brentwood CM14 108 FW48
Bromley BR1 184 EG94
Burnham SL1 130 AJ69
Croydon CR0 202 DS104
Epping CM16 70 EV29
Hoddesdon EN11 49 EA15
Ilford IG1 145 EP65
Kingston upon Thames KT1 198 CL96
Leatherhead KT22 231 CH121
Petts Wood BR5 205 ER100
Southall UB1 136 BZ72
Uxbridge UB8 134 BK65
West Drayton UB7 134 BL74
Woodford Green IG8 102 EG51
Wraysbury TW19 172 AX86
Fairfields, Cher. KT16 194 BG102
Gravesend DA12 191 GL92
Fairfields Cl, NW9 118 CQ57
Fairfields Cres, NW9 118 CQ56
Fairfield S, Kings.T. KT1 198 CL97
Sch Fairfields Prim Sch, Chsht EN7 off Rosedale Way 66 DU27
Fairfield Sq, Grav. DA11 191 GG86
Fairfields Rd, Houns. TW3 156 CC83
Fairfield St, SW18 180 DB85
● Fairfield Trade Pk, Kings.T. KT1 220 CM97
Fairfield Wk, Chsht EN8 67 DY28
Leatherhead KT22 off Fairfield Rd 231 CH121
Fairfield Way, Barn. EN5 80 DA43
Coulsdon CR5 219 DK114
Epsom KT19 216 CS106
Fairfield W, Kings.T. KT1 198 CL96
Fairfolds, Wat. WD25 76 BY36
Fairfoot Rd, E3 290 A5
Fairford Av, Bexh. DA7 167 FD81
Croydon CR0 203 DX99
Fairford Cl, Croy. CR0 203 DY99
Reigate RH2 250 DC132
Romford RM3 106 FP51
West Byfleet KT14 211 BF114
Fairford Ct, Sutt. SM2 off Grange Rd 218 DB108
Fairford Gdns, Wor.Pk. KT4 199 CT104
Fairford Ho, SE11 298 F9
Fairford Way, Rom. RM3 106 FP51
Fairgreen, Barn. EN4 80 DF41
Fair Grn, Saw. CM21 off The Square 36 EY05
Fairgreen E, Barn. EN4 80 DF41
Fairgreen Par, Mitch. CR4 off London Rd 200 DF97
Fairgreen Rd, Th.Hth. CR7 201 DP99
Fairham Av, S.Ock. RM15 149 FU73
Fairhaven, Egh. TW20 173 AZ92
Fairhaven Av, Croy. CR0 203 DX100
Fairhaven Cres, Wat. WD19 93 BU48
Fairhaven Rd, Red. RH1 250 DG130
Fairhazel Gdns, NW6 273 M5
Fairhill, Hem.H. HP3 40 BM24
Fairholme, Felt. TW14 175 BR87
Fairholme Av, Rom. RM2 127 FG57
Fairholme Cl, N3 119 CY56
Fairholme Cres, Ashtd. KT21 231 CJ117
Hayes UB4 135 BT70
Fairholme Gdns, N3 119 CY55
Upminster RM14 129 FT59
Sch Fairholme Prim Sch, Felt. TW14 off Peacock Av 175 BR88
Fairholme Rd, W14 306 F1
Ashford TW15 174 BL92
Croydon CR0 201 DN101
Harrow HA1 117 CF57
Ilford IG1 125 EM59
Sutton SM1 217 CZ107
Fairholt Cl, N16 122 DS60
Fairholt Rd, N16 122 DR60
Fairholt St, SW7 296 D6
Fairkytes Av, Horn. RM11 128 FK60
Fairland Rd, E15 281 L5
Fairlands Av, Buck.H. IG9 102 EG47
Sutton SM1 200 DA103
Thornton Heath CR7 201 DM98
Fairlands Ct, SE9 off North Pk 185 EN86
Fair La, Chipstead CR5 250 DC125
Fairlawn, SE7 164 EJ79
Bookham KT23 230 BZ124
Weybridge KT13 213 BS106
Fairlawn Av, N2 120 DE56
W4 158 CQ77
Bexleyheath DA7 166 EX82
Fairlawn Cl, N14 81 DJ44
Claygate KT10 215 CF107
Feltham TW13 176 BZ91
Kingston upon Thames KT2 178 CQ93
Fairlawn Ct, SE7 off Fairlawn 164 EJ80
Fairlawn Dr, Red. RH1 266 DE136
Woodford Green IG8 102 EG52
● Fairlawn Enterprise Pk, Salf. RH1 266 DG143
Fairlawnes, Wall. SM6 off Maldon Rd 219 DH106
Fairlawn Gdns, Sthl. UB1 136 BZ73
Fairlawn Gro, W4 158 CQ77
Banstead SM7 218 DD113
Fairlawn Pk, SE26 183 DY92
Windsor SL4 151 AL84
Woking GU21 210 AY114
Sch Fairlawn Prim Sch, SE23 off Honor Oak Rd 182 DW87
Fairlawn Rd, SW19 179 CZ94
Banstead SM7 218 DD112
Carshalton SM5 218 DC111
Fairlawns, Brwd. CM14 108 FU48
Horley RH6 269 DH149
Pinner HA5 94 BW54
Sunbury-on-Thames TW16 195 BU97
Twickenham TW1 177 CJ86
Watford WD17 75 BT38
Woodham KT15 211 BF111
Fairlawns Cl, Horn. RM11 128 FM59
Staines-upon-Thames TW18 174 BH93
Fairlead Ho, E14 off Cassilis Rd 302 B6
Fairlea Pl, W5 137 CK70
Fair Leas, Chesh. HP5 54 AN29
Fairley Way, Chsht EN7 66 DV28
Fairlie Ct, E3 off Stroudley Wk 290 C2
Fairlie Gdns, SE23 182 DW87
Fairlie Rd, Slou. SL1 131 AN72
Fairlight Av, E4 101 ED47
NW10 138 CS68
Windsor SL4 151 AR82
Woodford Green IG8 102 EG51
Fairlight Cl, E4 101 ED47
Worcester Park KT4 217 CW105
Fairlight Dr, Uxb. UB8 134 BK65
Fairlight Rd, SW17 180 DD91
⊖ Fairlop 103 ER53
Fairlop Cl, Horn. RM12 147 FH65
Fairlop Gdns, Ilf. IG6 103 EQ52
Sch Fairlop Prim Sch, Ilf. IG6 off Colvin Gdns 103 EQ53
Fairlop Rd, E11 123 ED59
Ilford IG6 103 EQ54
Fairmark Dr, Uxb. UB10 134 BN65
Fairmead, Brom. BR1 205 EM98
Surbiton KT5 198 CP102
Woking GU21 226 AW118
Fairmead Cl, Brom. BR1 205 EM98
Hounslow TW5 156 BX80
New Malden KT3 198 CR97
Fairmead Cres, Edg. HA8 96 CQ48
Fairmead Gdns, Ilf. IG4 124 EL57
Fairmead Ho, E9 off Kingsmead Way 279 M1
Fairmead Rd, N19 121 DK62
Croydon CR0 201 DM102
Loughton IG10 84 EH42
Fairmeads, Cob. KT11 214 BZ113
Loughton IG10 85 EP40
Fairmeadside, Loug. IG10 84 EJ43
FAIRMILE, Cob. KT11 214 BZ112
Fairmile Av, SW16 181 DK92
Cobham KT11 214 BY114
Fairmile Ct, Cob. KT11 214 BY112
Fairmile Ho, Tedd. TW11 off Twickenham Rd 177 CG91
Fairmile La, Cob. KT11 214 BX112
Fairmile Pk Copse, Cob. KT11 214 BZ112
Fairmile Pk Rd, Cob. KT11 214 BZ113
Fairmont Av, E14 302 G2
Fairmont Cl, Belv. DA17 166 EZ78
Fairmount Rd, SW2 181 DM86
Fairoak Cl, Ken. CR8 235 DP115
Oxshott KT22 215 CD112
Petts Wood BR5 205 EP101
Fairoak Dr, SE9 185 ER85
Fairoak Gdns, Rom. RM1 105 FE54
Fairoak Gro, Enf. EN3 83 DX37
Fair Oak La, Chess. KT9 215 CF111
Oxshott KT22 215 CF111
Fair Oak Pl, Ilf. IG6 103 EQ54
Fairseat Cl, Bushey Hth WD23 95 CE47
Fairs Rd, Lthd. KT22 231 CG119
Fairstead Wk, N1 277 J8
Fairstone Ct, Horl. RH6 off Tanyard Way 269 DH147
Fair St, SE1 299 P4
Hounslow TW3 off High St 156 CC83
Fairthorn Rd, SE7 303 P10
Fairtrough Rd, Orp. BR6 224 EV112
Fairview, Epsom KT17 217 CW111
Erith DA8 off Guild Rd 167 FF80
Potters Bar EN6 off Hawkshead Rd 64 DB29
Ruislip HA4 off The Fairway 116 BW63
Fairview Av, Hutt. CM13 109 GE45
Rainham RM13 148 FK68
Wembley HA0 137 CK65
Woking GU22 226 AY118
● Fairview Business Cen, Hayes UB3 off Clayton Rd 155 BT75
Fairview Cl, E17 101 DY53
Chigwell IG7 103 ES49
Woking GU22 off Fairview Av 227 AZ118
Fairview Ct, NW4 97 CX54
Ashford TW15 174 BN92
Fairview Cres, Har. HA2 116 CA60
Fairview Dr, Chig. IG7 103 ES49
Orpington BR6 223 ER105
Shepperton TW17 194 BM99
Watford WD17 75 BS36
Fairview Gdns, Wdf.Grn. IG8 102 EH53
● Fairview Ind Est, Amer. HP6 72 AT38
● Fairview Ind Pk, Rain. RM13 147 FD71
Fairview Pl, SW2 181 DM87
Fairview Rd, N15 122 DT57
SW16 201 DM95
Chigwell IG7 103 ES49
Enfield EN2 81 DN39
Epsom KT17 217 CT111
Istead Rise DA13 190 GD94
Slough SL2 131 AM70
Sutton SM1 218 DD106
Taplow SL6 130 AG72
Fairview Way, Edg. HA8 96 CN49
Fairwater Av, Well. DA16 166 EU84
Fairwater Dr, New Haw KT15 212 BK109
Fairway, SW20 199 CW97
Bexleyheath DA6 186 EY85
Carshalton SM5 218 DC111
Chertsey KT16 194 BH102
Guildford GU1 243 BD133
Hemel Hempstead HP3 40 BM24
Petts Wood BR5 205 ER99
Sawbridgeworth CM21 36 EY05
Virginia Water GU25 192 AV100
Ware SG12 32 DW07
Woodford Green IG8 102 EJ50
Fairway, The, N13 100 DQ48
N14 81 DH44
NW7 96 CR48
W3 138 CS72
Abbots Langley WD5 59 BR32
Bromley BR1 205 EM99
Burnham SL1 130 AJ68
Flackwell Heath HP10 110 AC56
Gravesend DA11 191 GG89
Harlow CM18 51 ET17
Leatherhead KT22 231 CG118
New Barnet EN5 80 DB44
New Malden KT3 198 CR95
Northolt UB5 136 CC65
Northwood HA6 93 BS49
Ruislip HA4 116 BX62
Upminster RM14 128 FQ59
Uxbridge UB10 134 BM68
Wembley HA0 117 CH62
West Molesey KT8 196 CB97
Weybridge KT13 212 BN111
Fairway Av, NW9 118 CP55
Borehamwood WD6 78 CP40
West Drayton UB7 134 BJ74
Fairway Cl, NW11 120 DC59
Croydon CR0 203 DY99
Epsom KT19 216 CQ105
Esher KT10 197 CH104
Hounslow TW4 176 BW85
Park Street AL2 60 CC27
West Drayton UB7 off Fairway Av 134 BK74
Woking GU22 226 AU119
Fairway Ct, NW7 96 CR48
Hemel Hempstead HP3 off Fairway 40 BM24
Fairway Dr, SE28 146 EX72
Dartford DA2 188 FP87
Greenford UB6 136 CB66
Fairway Gdns, Beck. BR3 203 ED100
Ilford IG1 125 EQ64
Sch Fairway Prim Sch & Northway Sch, NW7 off The Fairway 96 CR47
Fairways, Ashf. TW15 175 BP93
Cheshunt EN8 67 DX26
Effingham Junction KT24 229 BU123
Kenley CR8 236 DQ117
Stanmore HA7 96 CL54
Teddington TW11 177 CK94
Waltham Abbey EN9 68 EE34
Fairways, The, Red. RH1 266 DD137
● Fairways Business Pk, E10 off Lammas Rd 123 DY61
Fairweather Cl, N15 122 DS56
Fairweather Rd, N16 122 DU58
Fairwell La, W.Hors. KT24 245 BP128
Fairwyn Rd, SE26 183 DY91
Faithfield, Bushey WD23 off Aldenham Rd 76 BY44

E
F

Faithorn Cl, Chesh. HP5 54 AN30
Fakenham Cl, NW7 97 CU52
Northolt UB5
off Goodwood Dr 136 CA65
Fakruddin St, E1 288 D5
Falaise, Egh. TW20 172 AY92
Falcon Av, Brom. BR1 204 EL98
Grays RM17 170 GB79
Falconberg Ct, W1 285 P8
Falconberg Ms, W1 285 N8
Falconbrook Prim Sch, SW11 40 B10
● Falcon Business Cen,
Mitch. CR4 200 DF99
Romford RM3 106 FL52
Falcon Cl, W4
off Sutton La S 158 CQ79
Dartford DA1 188 FM85
Hatfield AL10 45 CU20
Northwood HA6 93 BS52
Sawbridgeworth CM21 36 EW06
Waltham Abbey EN9
off Kestrel Rd 68 EG34
Falcon Ct, EC4 286 E9
SE21 off Elmwood Gro 182 DR89
Woking GU21 211 BC113
Falcon Cres, Enf. EN3 83 DX43
Falcon Dr, Stanw. TW19 174 BK86
Falconer Ct, N17
off Compton Cres 100 DQ52
Falconer Rd, Bushey WD23 76 BZ44
Ilford IG6 104 EV50
Falconer Sch, Bushey
WD23 off Falconer Rd 76 BZ43
Falconers Pk, Saw. CM21 36 EX06
Falconer Wk, N7
off Newington Barrow Way 121 DM61
● Falcon Est, Felt. TW14 175 BV85
Falcon Gro, SW11 308 C10
Falcon Ho, W13 137 CF70
Falconhurst, Oxshott KT22 231 CD115
Falcon La, SW11 160 DE83
Falcon Ms, Grav. DA11 190 GE88
● Falcon Pk Ind Est, NW10 118 CS64
Falcon Ridge, Berk. HP4 38 AW20
Falcon Rd, SW11 308 C9
Enfield EN3 83 DX43
Guildford GU1 258 AX135
Hampton TW12 176 BZ94
Falcons Cl, Bigg.H. TN16 238 EK117
Falcons Cft, Woob.Moor HP10 110 AE55
Falcons Sch for Boys, The,
W4 off Burnaby Gdns 158 CQ79
Falcons Sch for Girls, The,
W5 off Gunnersbury Av 138 CM74
Falcon St, E13 291 N4
Falcon Ter, SW11 160 DE83
Falcon Way, E11 124 EG56
E14 302 D8
NW9 96 CS54
Feltham TW14 175 BV85
Harrow HA3 118 CL57
Hornchurch RM12 147 FG66
Sunbury-on-Thames TW16 195 BS96
Watford WD25 60 BY34
Welwyn Garden City AL7 29 CY07
Falcon Wf, SW11 308 A9
FALCONWOOD, Well. DA16 165 ER83
⇌ Falconwood 165 EQ84
Falconwood, SE9 165 EQ84
Falconwood, Bushey WD23 76 BZ44
East Horsley KT24 229 BT124
Egham TW20 172 AY92
Falcon Wd, Lthd. KT22 231 CF120
Falconwood Av, Well. DA16 165 ER82
Falconwood Par, Well. DA16 165 ES84
Falconwood Rd, Croy. CR0 221 EA108
Falcourt Cl, Sutt. SM1 218 DB106
Falkirk Cl, Horn. RM11 128 FN60
Falkirk Gdns, Wat. WD19 94 BX50
Falkirk Ho, W9 283 M2
Falkirk St, N1 287 P1
Falkland Av, N3 98 DA52
N11 98 DG49
Falkland Gdns, Dor. RH4
off Harrow Rd W 263 CG137
Falkland Gro, Dor. RH4 263 CG137
Falkland Ho, SE6
off Bromley Rd 183 EC91
Falkland Pk Av, SE25 202 DS97
Falkland Pl, NW5 275 L2
Falkland Rd, N8 121 DN56
NW5 275 L2
Barnet EN5 79 CY40
Dorking RH4 263 CG137
Falkner Ho Sch, SW7 295 P9
Fallaize Av, Ilf. IG1
off Riverdene Rd 125 EP63
Falling La, West Dr. UB7 134 BL73
Falloden Way, NW11 120 DA56
Fallow Cl, Chig. IG7 103 ET50
Fallow Ct, SE16 312 D1
Fallow Ct Av, N12 98 DC52
Fallowfield, N4
off Six Acres Est 121 DM61
Bean DA2 189 FV90
Stanmore HA7 95 CG48
Welwyn Garden City AL7 29 CZ06
Fallowfield Cl, Hare. UB9 92 BJ53
Fallowfield Ct, Stan. HA7 95 CG48
Fallow Flds, Loug. IG10 102 EJ45
Fallowfields Dr, N12 98 DE51
Fallowfield Wk, Hem.H. HP1
off Tollpit End 40 BG17
Fallowfield Way, Horl. RH6 269 DH147
Fallow Ri, Hert. SG13 32 DS09
Fallows Cl, N2 98 DC54
Fallsbrook Rd, SW16 181 DJ94
Falman Cl, N9 100 DU46
Falmer Rd, E17 123 EB55
N15 122 DQ57
Enfield EN1 82 DS42
Falmouth Av, E4 101 ED50
Falmouth Cl, N22 99 DM52
SE12 184 EF85
Falmouth Ct, St.Alb. AL3 43 CD18
Falmouth Gdns, Ilf. IG4 124 EL57
Falmouth Ho, SE11
off Seaton Cl 298 F10
Kingston upon Thames KT2
off Kingsgate Rd 197 CK95
Falmouth Rd, SE1 299 K6
Hersham KT12 214 BW105
Slough SL1 131 AN72
Falmouth St, E15 281 H3
Falmouth Way, E17
off Gosport Rd 123 DZ57
Falstaff Cl, Cray. DA1 187 FE87
Falstaff Gdns, St.Alb. AL1 42 CB23
Falstaff Ms, Hmptn H. TW12
off Hampton Rd 177 CD92
Falstone, Wok. GU21 226 AV118
Fambridge Cl, SE26 183 DZ91
Fambridge Ct, Rom. RM7 127 FD57
Fambridge Rd, Dag. RM8 126 FA60
Famet Av, Pur. CR8 220 DQ113
Famet Cl, Pur. CR8 220 DQ113
Famet Gdns, Ken. CR8
off Godstone Rd 220 DQ113
Famet Wk, Pur. CR8 220 DQ113
Fancourt Ms, Brom. BR1 205 EN97
Fane St, W14 307 H2
Fangrove Pk, Lyne KT16 193 BB102
Fanhams Rd, Ware SG12 33 DY05
★ Fan Mus, SE10 314 F4
Fanns Ri, Purf. RM19 168 FN77
Fann St, EC1 287 J5
EC2 287 J5
Fanshawe, The, Dag. RM9
off Gale St 146 EX66
Fanshawe Av, Bark. IG11 145 EQ65
Fanshawe Ct, Hert. SG14
off Byde St 32 DQ08
Fanshawe Cres, Dag. RM9 126 EY64
Hornchurch RM11 128 FK58
Ware SG12 32 DW05
Fanshawe Rd, Grays RM16 171 GG76
Richmond TW10 177 CJ91
Fanshawe St, Hert. SG14 31 DP08
Fanshaws La, Brickendon SG13 48 DQ18
Fanshaw St, N1 287 N2
Fantail, The, Orp. BR6 223 EM105
Fantail Cl, SE28
off Greenhaven Dr 146 EW72
Fantasia Ct, Warley CM14 108 FV50
Fanthorpe St, SW15 306 B10
Faraday Av, Sid. DA14 186 EU89
Faraday Cl, N7 276 D5
Slough SL2 131 AP71
Watford WD18 75 BR44
Faraday Ct, Wat. WD18 75 BU44
Faraday Ho, Enf. EN3
off Innova Science Pk 83 DZ37
Faraday Lo, SE10
off Renaissance Wk 303 M6
★ Faraday Mus, W1 297 L1
Faraday Pl, W.Mol. KT8 196 CA98
Faraday Rd, E15 281 L5
SW19 180 DA93
W3 138 CQ73
W10 282 E6
Guildford GU1 242 AW133
Slough SL2 131 AP71
Southall UB1 136 CB73
Welling DA16 166 EU83
West Molesey KT8 196 CA98
Faraday Way, SE18 304 E7
Croydon CR0
off Ampere Way 201 DM102
Orpington BR5 206 EV98
Fareham Rd, Felt. TW14 176 BW87
Fareham St, W1 285 N8
Far End, Hat. AL10 45 CV21
Farewell Pl, Mitch. CR4 200 DE95
Faringdon Av, Brom. BR2 205 EP100
Romford RM3 106 FJ53
Faringford Cl, Pot.B. EN6 64 DD31
Faringford Rd, E15 281 J7
Farington Acres, Wey. KT13 195 BR104
Faris Barn Dr, Wdhm KT15 211 BF112
Faris La, Wdhm KT15 211 BF111
Farjeon Rd, SE3 164 EK81
Farland Rd, Hem.H. HP2 40 BN21
FARLEIGH, Warl. CR6 221 DZ114
Farleigh Av, Brom. BR2 204 EF100
Farleigh Border, Croy. CR0 221 DY112
Farleigh Ct, Guil. GU2
off Chapelhouse Cl 242 AS134
Farleigh Ct Rd, Warl. CR6 221 DZ114
Farleigh Dean Cres, Croy. CR0 221 EB111
Farleigh Pl, N16 122 DT63
Farleigh Prim Sch, Warl. CR6
off Farleigh Rd 237 DY117
Farleigh Rd, N16 122 DT63
New Haw KT15 212 BG111
Warlingham CR6 237 DX118
Farleton Cl, Wey. KT13 213 BR107
Farley Common, West. TN16 255 EP126
Farleycroft, West. TN16 255 EQ126
Farley Dr, Ilf. IG3 125 ES60
FARLEY GREEN, Guil. GU5 260 BK144
Farley Heath, Albury GU5 260 BJ144
Farley La, West. TN16 255 EP127
Farley Ms, SE6 183 EC87
Farley Nurs, West. TN16 255 EQ127
Farley Pk, Oxt. RH8 253 ED130
Farley Pl, SE25 202 DU98
Farley Rd, SE6 183 EB87
Gravesend DA12 191 GM88
South Croydon CR2 220 DV108
Farleys Cl, W.Hors. KT24 245 BQ126
Farlington Pl, SW15
off Roehampton La 179 CV87
Farlow Cl, Nthflt DA11 191 GF90
Farlow Rd, SW15 159 CX83
Farlton Rd, SW18 180 DB87
Farman Gro, Nthlt. UB5
off Wayfarer Rd 136 BX69
Farm Av, NW2 119 CY62
SW16 181 DL91
Harrow HA2 116 BZ59
Swanley BR8 207 FC97
Wembley HA0 137 CJ65
Farmborough Cl, Har. HA1 117 CD59
Farm Cl, SW6 307 K4
Amersham HP6 72 AX39
Barnet EN5 79 CW43
Borehamwood WD6 77 CK38
Buckhurst Hill IG9 102 EJ48
Byfleet KT14 212 BM112
Cheshunt EN8 66 DW30
Chipstead CR5 234 DF120
Cuffley EN6 65 DK27
Dagenham RM10 147 FC66
East Horsley KT24 245 BT128
Fetcham KT22 231 CD124
Guildford GU1 242 AX131
Hertford SG14 31 DN09
Holyport SL6 150 AC78
Hutton CM13 109 GC45
Lyne KT16 193 BA100
Roydon CM19 34 EH14
Shenley WD7 62 CL30
Shepperton TW17 194 BN101
Farm Cl, Southall UB1 136 CB73
Staines-upon-Thames TW18 173 BE92
Sutton SM2 218 DD108
Uxbridge UB10 115 BP61
Wallington SM6 219 DJ110
Welwyn Garden City AL8 29 CW09
West Wickham BR4 204 EE104
Farmcote Rd, SE12 184 EG88
Farm Ct, NW4 119 CU55
Farm Cres, Lon.Col. AL2 61 CG26
Slough SL2 132 AV71
Farmcroft, Grav. DA11 191 GG89
Farmdale Rd, SE10 303 P10
Carshalton SM5 218 DE108
Farm Dr, Croy. CR0 203 DZ103
Purley CR8 219 DK112
Farm End, E4 84 EE43
Northwood HA6 off Drakes Dr 93 BP53
Farmer Rd, E10 123 EB60
Farmers Cl, Wat. WD25 59 BV33
Farmers Ct, Wal.Abb. EN9
off Winters Way 68 EG33
Farmers Pl, Chal.St.P. SL9 90 AW54
Farmers Rd, SE5 311 H4
Staines-upon-Thames TW18 173 BE92
Farmer St, W8 295 J2
Farmers Way, Seer Grn HP9 89 AQ51
Farmery Ct, Berk. HP4 38 AY17
Farm Fld, Wat. WD17 75 BS38
Farmfield Dr, Charl. RH6 268 DB150
Farmfield Hosp, Horl. RH6 268 DB150
Farmfield Rd, Brom. BR1 184 EE92
Farm Flds, S.Croy. CR2 220 DS111
Farm Gro, Knot.Grn HP9 88 AJ50
Farm Hill Rd, Wal.Abb. EN9 67 ED33
Farm Ho Cl, Brox. EN10 67 DZ25
Farmhouse Cl, Wok. GU22 227 BD115
Farmhouse La, Hem.H. HP2 40 BN18
Farmhouse Rd, SW16 181 DJ94
Farmilo Rd, E17 123 DZ59
Farmington Av, Sutt. SM1 200 DD104
Farmlands, Enf. EN2 81 DN39
Pinner HA5 115 BU56
Farmlands, The, Nthlt. UB5 136 BZ65
Farmland Wk, Chis. BR7 185 EP92
Farm La, N14 80 DG44
SW6 307 K3
Addlestone KT15 212 BG107
Ashtead KT21 232 CN116
Carshalton SM5 218 DF110
Croydon CR0 203 DZ103
East Horsley KT24 245 BT128
Epsom KT18 232 CP119
Hoddesdon EN11 49 EC15
Jordans HP9 89 AR52
Loudwater WD3 74 BH41
Purley CR8 219 DJ110
Send GU23 227 BC123
Slough SL1 131 AR73
Farm Lea, Woob.Grn HP10 110 AF56
Farmleigh, N14 99 DJ45
Farmleigh Gro, Hersham KT12 213 BT106
Farm Pl, W8 295 J2
Berkhamsted HP4 38 AT18
Dartford DA1 167 FG84
Farm Rd, N21 99 DP46
NW10 138 CR67
Chorleywood WD3 73 BA42
Edgware HA8 96 CP51
Esher KT10 196 CB102
Hoddesdon EN11 49 EC16
Hounslow TW4 176 BY88
Morden SM4 200 DB99
Northwood HA6 93 BQ50
Orsett RM16 171 GF75
Rainham RM13 148 FJ69
St. Albans AL1 43 CH19
Sevenoaks TN14 257 FJ121
Staines-upon-Thames TW18 174 BH93
Sutton SM2 218 DD108
Taplow SL6 130 AG72
Warlingham CR6 237 DY119
Woking GU22 227 BB120
Farmside Pl, Epsom KT19 216 CM112
Farmstead Rd, SE6 183 EB91
Harrow HA3 95 CD53
Farm St, W1 297 J1
Farm Vale, Bex. DA5 187 FB86
Farm Vw, Cob. KT11 230 BX116
Lower Kingswood KT20 249 CZ127
Farm Wk, NW11 119 CZ57
Guildford GU2
off Wilderness Rd 258 AT136
Horley RH6 off Court Lo Rd 268 DF148
Farm Way, Buck.H. IG9 102 EJ49
Bushey WD23 76 CB42
Farmway, Dag. RM8 126 EW63
Farm Way, Hat. AL10 45 CV15
Hemel Hempstead HP2 40 BM19
Hornchurch RM12 127 FH63
Northwood HA6 93 BS49
Staines-upon-Thames TW19 173 BF86
Worcester Park KT4 199 CW104
Farm Yd, Wind. SL4 151 AR80
Farnaby Dr, Sev. TN13 256 FF126
Farnaby Rd, SE9 164 EJ84
Bromley BR1, BR2 183 ED94
Farnan Av, E17 101 EA54
Farnan Rd, SW16 181 DL92
FARNBOROUGH, Orp. BR6 223 EP106
Farnborough Av, E17 123 DY55
South Croydon CR2 221 DX108
Farnborough Cl, Wem. HA9 118 CP61
Farnborough Common,
Orp. BR6 205 EM104
Farnborough Cres, Brom. BR2
off Saville Row 204 EF102
South Croydon CR2 221 DY109
Farnborough Hill, Orp. BR6 223 ER106
Farnborough Ho, SW15
off Fontley Way 179 CU88
Farnborough Prim Sch, Farnboro.
BR6 off Farnborough Hill 223 EQ106
Farnborough Way, Orp. BR6 223 EQ105
Farnburn Av, Slou. SL1 131 AP71
⇌ Farncombe 258 AT144
Farncombe C of E Inf Sch,
Farnc. GU7 off Grays Rd 258 AS144
Farncombe St, SE16 300 D5
Godalming GU7 258 AS144
Farndale Av, N13 99 DP48
Farndale Ct, SE18 164 EL80
Farndale Cres, Grnf. UB6 136 CC69
Farnell Ms, SW5 295 L10
Weybridge KT13 off Thames St 217 BP104
Farnell Pl, W3 138 CP73
Farnell Rd, Islw. TW7 157 CD83
Staines-upon-Thames TW18 174 BG90
Farnes Dr, Rom. RM2 106 FJ54
Farney Fld, Peasl. GU5 261 BR142
Farnham Cl, N20 98 DC45
Bovingdon HP3 57 BA28
Sawbridgeworth CM21 36 EW06
FARNHAM COMMON,
Slou. SL2 131 AQ65
Farnham Common Inf Sch,
Farn.Com. SL2
off Beaconsfield Rd 111 AQ63
Farnham Common Jun Sch,
Farn.Com. SL2
off Sherbourne Wk 111 AQ63
Farnham Gdns, SW20 199 CV96
Farnham Grn Prim Sch,
Seven Kings IG3 off Royal Cl 126 EU58
Farnham La, Slou. SL2 131 AN68
Farnham Pk La, Farn.Royal SL2 131 AQ66
Farnham Pl, SE1 299 H3
Farnham Rd, Guil. GU1, GU2 258 AT137
Ilford IG3 125 ET59
Romford RM3 106 FK50
Slough SL1, SL2 131 AQ71
Welling DA16 166 EW82
Farnham Rd Hosp, Guil. GU2 280 AV136
FARNHAM ROYAL, Slou. SL2 131 AQ68
Farnham Royal, SE11 310 D1
FARNINGHAM, Dart. DA4 208 FN100
Farningham Cres, Cat. CR3
off Commonwealth Rd 236 DU123
Farningham Hill Rd, Fnghm DA4 230 FJ99
⇌ Farningham Road 208 FP96
Farningham Rd, N17 100 DU52
Caterham CR3 236 DU123
Farnley, Wok. GU21 226 AT117
Farnley Rd, E4 102 EE45
SE25 202 DR98
Farnol Rd, Dart. DA1 168 FN84
Farnsworth Ct, SE10
off West Parkside 303 M7
Farnworth Ho, E14
off Manchester Rd 302 F8
Faro Cl, Brom. BR1 205 EN96
Faroe Rd, W14 294 D7
Farorna Wk, Enf. EN2 81 DN39
Farquhar Rd, SE19 182 DT92
SW19 180 DA90
Farquharson Rd, Croy. CR0 202 DQ102
Farquhar St, Hert. SG14 32 DQ08
Farraline Rd, Wat. WD18 75 BV42
Farrance Rd, Rom. RM6 126 EY58
Farrance St, E14 289 P9
Farrans Ct, Har. HA3 117 CH59
Farrant Av, N22 99 DN54
Farrant Cl, Orp. BR6 224 EU108
Farrant Way, Borwd. WD6 78 CL39
Farr Av, Bark. IG11 146 EU68
Farrell Ho, E1 289 H9
Farren Rd, SE23 183 DY89
Farrer Ms, N8
off Farrer Rd 121 DJ56
Farrer Rd, N8 121 DJ56
Harrow HA3 118 CL57
Farrer's Pl, Croy. CR0 221 DX105
Farriday Cl, St.Alb. AL3 43 CE16
Farrier Cl, Brom. BR1 204 EK97
Sunbury-on-Thames TW16 195 BU98
Uxbridge UB8 134 BN72
Farrier Pl, Sutt. SM1 200 DA104
Farrier Rd, Nthlt. UB5 136 CA68
Farriers, Gt Amwell SG12 33 EA09
Farriers Cl, Bov. HP3 57 BB28
Epsom KT17 216 CS111
Gravesend DA12 191 GM88
Farriers Ct, Sutt. SM3
off Forge La 217 CY108
Watford WD25 59 BV32
Farriers End, Brox. EN10 67 DZ26
Farriers Ms, SE15 312 G10
Farriers Rd, Epsom KT17 216 CS112
Farrier St, NW1 275 K6
Farriers Way, Borwd. WD6 78 CQ44
Chesham HP5 54 AN28
Farrier Wk, SW10 307 N2
⇌ Farringdon 286 F6
⊖ Farringdon 286 F6
Farringdon Ho, Rich. TW9 158 CP80
Farringdon La, EC1 286 F5
Farringdon Rd, EC1 286 E4
Farringdon St, EC4 286 G8
Farringford Cl, St.Alb. AL2 60 CA26
Farrington Ave, Bushey WD23 76 CB43
Orpington BR5 206 EV97
Farrington Pl, Chis. BR7 185 ER94
Northwood HA6 93 BT49
Farringtons Sch, Chis. BR7
off Perry St 185 ER94
Farrins Rents, SE16 301 L3
Farrow La, SE14 313 H4
Farrow Pl, SE16 301 L6
Farr Rd, Enf. EN2 82 DR39
Farrs All, Rick. WD3
off High St 92 BK46
Farthingale Ct, Wal.Abb. EN9 68 EG34
Farthingale La, Wal.Abb. EN9 68 EG34
Farthingale Wk, E15 280 G7
Farthing All, SE1 300 C5
Farthing Cl, Dart. DA1 168 FM84
Watford WD18 76 BW43
Farthing Ct, NW7 97 CY52
Farthing Flds, E1 300 F2
Farthing Grn La, Stoke P. SL2 132 AU68
Farthings, Knap. GU21 226 AS116
Farthings, The, Amer. HP6
off Milton Lawns 55 AR36
Hemel Hempstead HP1 40 BH20
Kingston upon Thames KT2 198 CN95
Farthings Cl, E4 102 EE48
Pinner HA5 115 BV58
Farthing St, Downe BR6 223 EM108
Farthing Way, Couls. CR5 235 DK117
Farwell Rd, Sid. DA14 186 EV90
Farwig La, Brom. BR1 204 EF95
Fashion St, E1 288 A7
Fashoda Rd, Brom. BR2 204 EK98
Fassett Rd, E8 278 D4
Kingston upon Thames KT1 198 CL98
Fassett Sq, E8 278 C4
Fassnidge Way, Uxb. UB8
off Oxford Rd 134 BJ66
Fauconberg Rd, W4 158 CQ79
Faulkner Cl, Dag. RM8 126 EX59
Faulkner Ms, E17 101 DY53
Faulkner's All, EC1 286 G6
Faulkners Rd, Hersham KT12 214 BW106
Faulkner St, SE14 313 H6
Fauna Cl, Rom. RM6 126 EW59
Stanmore HA7 95 CK49
Faunce St, SE17 310 G2
Favart Rd, SW6 307 K6
Faverolle Grn, Chsht EN8 67 DX28
Faversham Av, E4 102 EE46
Enfield EN1 82 DR44
Faversham Cl, Chig. IG7 104 EV47
Faversham Rd, SE6 183 DZ87
Beckenham BR3 203 DZ96
Morden SM4 200 DB100
Fawbert & Barnard Infants'
Sch, Saw. CM21 off Knight St 36 EY05
Fawbert & Barnard's Prim
Sch, Harl. CM17 off London Rd 36 EW12
Fawcett Cl, SW11 308 B9
SW16 181 DN91
Fawcett Est, E5 122 DU60
Fawcett Rd, NW10 139 CT67
Croydon CR0 202 DQ104
Windsor SL4 151 AP81
Fawcett St, SW10 307 N2
Fawcus Cl, Clay. KT10 215 CE107
Fawe Pk Rd, SW15 159 CZ84
Fawe St, E14 290 D7
Fawke Common, Undrvr TN15 257 FP127
Fawke Common Rd, Sev. TN15 257 FP126
Fawkes Av, Dart. DA1 188 FM89
Fawkham C of E Prim Sch,
Long. DA3 off Valley Rd 209 FV102
FAWKHAM GREEN, Long. DA3 209 FV104
Fawkham Grn Rd,
Fawk.Grn DA3 209 FV104
Fawkham Ho, SE1
off Longfield Est 300 B9
Fawkham Manor Hosp,
Fawk. DA3 209 FW102
Fawkham Rd, Long. DA3 209 FX97
Fawkon Wk, Hodd. EN11 49 EA17
Fawley Rd, NW6 273 L3
Fawnbrake Av, SE24 181 DP85
Fawn Ct, Hat. AL9 45 CW16
Fawn Rd, E13 144 EJ68
Chigwell IG7 103 ET50
Fawns Manor Cl, Felt. TW14 175 BQ88
Fawns Manor Rd, Felt. TW14 175 BR88
Fawood Av, NW10 138 CR66
Fawsley Cl, Colnbr. SL3 153 BE80
Fawters Cl, Hutt. CM13 109 GD44
Fayerfield, Pot.B. EN6 64 DD31
Faygate Cres, Bexh. DA6 186 FA85
Faygate Rd, SW2 181 DM89
Fay Grn, Abb.L. WD5 59 BR33
Fayland Av, SW16 181 DJ92
Fayland Est, SW16 181 DJ92
Faymore Gdns, S.Ock. RM15 149 FU72
Feacey Down, Hem.H. HP1 40 BG18
Fearn Cl, E.Hors. KT24 245 BS129
Fearney Mead, Mill End WD3 92 BG46
Fearnley Cres, Hmptn. TW12 176 BY92
Fearnley Rd, Welw.G.C. AL8 29 CW10
Fearnley St, Wat. WD18 75 BV42
Fearns Mead, Warley CM14
off Bucklers Ct 108 FW50
Fearon St, SE10 303 N10
Featherbed La, Croy. CR0 221 DZ108
Hemel Hempstead HP3 40 BJ24
Romford RM4 104 EY45
Warlingham CR6 221 ED113
Feather Dell, Hat. AL10 45 CT18
Feathers La, Wrays. TW19 173 BA89
Feathers Pl, SE10 315 H2
Featherstone Av, SE23 182 DV89
Featherstone Gdns,
Borwd. WD6 78 CQ42
Featherstone High Sch, Sthl.
UB2 off Montague Waye 156 BY76
● Featherstone Ind Est, Sthl. UB2 156 BY75
Featherstone Prim Sch,
Sthl. UB2 off Western Rd 156 BW77
Featherstone Rd, NW7 97 CV51
Southall UB2 156 BY76
Featherstone St, EC1 287 L4
Featherstone Ter, Sthl. UB2 156 BY76
Featley Rd, SW9 310 G10
Federal Rd, Perivale UB6 137 CJ68
Federal Way, Wat. WD24 76 BW38
Federation Rd, SE2 166 EV77
Fee Fm Rd, Clay. KT10 215 CF108
Feenan Highway, Til. RM18 171 GH80
Feeny Cl, NW10 119 CT63
Felbridge Av, Stan. HA7 95 CG53
Felbridge Cl, SW16 181 DN91
Sutton SM2 218 DB109
Felbridge Ho, SE22
off Pytchley Rd 162 DS83
Felbrigge Rd, Ilf. IG3 125 ET61
Felcott Cl, Hersham KT12 196 BW104
Felcott Rd, Hersham KT12 196 BW104
Felday Hos, Holm.St.M. RH5 261 BV144
Felday Rd, SE13 183 EB86
Abinger Hammer RH5 261 BT140
FELDEN, Hem.H. HP3 40 BG24
Felden Cl, Pnr. HA5 94 BY52
Watford WD25 60 BX34
Felden Dr, Felden HP3 40 BG24
Felden La, Felden HP3 40 BG24
Felden St, SW6 306 G6
Feldman Cl, N16 122 DU60
Feldspar Ct, Enf. EN3
off Enstone Rd 83 DY41
Felgate Ms, W6 159 CV77
Felhampton Rd, SE9 185 EP89
Felhurst Cres, Dag. RM10 127 FB63
Felicia Way, Grays RM16 171 GH77
Felipe Rd, Chaff.Hun. RM16 169 FW76
Felix Av, N8 121 DL58
Felix Dr, W.Clan. GU4 244 BG128
Felix La, Shep. TW17 195 BS100
Felix Pl, SW2 off Talma Rd 181 DN85
Felix Rd, W13 137 CG73
Walton-on-Thames KT12 195 BU100
Felixstowe Ct, E16 305 P3
Felixstowe Rd, N9 100 DU49
N17 122 DT55
NW10 139 CV69
SE2 166 EV76
Felland Way, Reig. RH2 266 DC138
Fellbrigg Rd, SE22 182 DT85
Fellbrook, Rich. TW10 177 CH90
Fellmongers Path, SE1 299 P5
Fellmongers Yd, Croy. CR0
off Surrey St 202 DQ104
Fellowes Cl, Hayes UB4
off Paddington Cl 136 BX70
Fellowes La, Coln.Hth AL4 44 CS23
Fellowes Rd, Cars. SM5 200 DE104
Fellows Ct, E2 288 A1
Croy. CR0 202 DT101
Fellowship Cl, Dag. RM8 126 EU63
Fellows Rd, NW3 274 B6
Fell Rd, Croy. CR0 202 DQ104
Felltram Ms, SE7 303 P10

F

Felltram Way, SE7 303 P10
Fell Wk, Edg. HA8 *off East Rd* 96 CQ53
Felmersham Cl, SW4 161 DK84
Felmingham Rd, SE20 202 DW96
Felmongers, Harl. CM20 36 EV13
● **Felnex Trd Est**, Wall. SM6 200 DG103
Felsberg Rd, SW2 181 DL86
Fels Cl, Dag. RM10 127 FB62
Fels Fm Av, Dag. RM10 127 FC62
Felsham Rd, SW15 159 CX83
Felspar Cl, SE18 165 ET78
Felstead Av, Ilf. IG5 103 EN53
Felstead Cl, N13 99 DN50
Hutton CM13 109 GC44
Felstead Gdns, E14 314 E1
Felstead Rd, E11 124 EG59
Epsom KT19 216 CR111
Loughton IG10 102 EL45
Orpington BR6 206 EU103
Romford RM5 105 FC51
Waltham Cross EN8 67 DY32
Felstead St, E9 279 P5
Felsted Rd, E16 292 E9
FELTHAM, TW13 & TW14 175 BV89
≠ **Feltham** 175 BV88
Feltham Av, E.Mol. KT8 197 CE98
Felthambrook Way, Felt. TW13 175 BV90
● **Feltham Business Complex**, Felt. TW13 175 BV89
Coll **Feltham City Learning Cen**, Felt. TW13 *off Browells La* 176 BW89
Sch **Feltham Comm Coll**, Felt. TW13 *off Browells La* 176 BW89
FELTHAMHILL, Felt. TW13 175 BU92
Sch **Feltham Hill Inf & Nurs Sch**, Felt. TW13 *off Bedfont Rd* 175 BT90
Sch **Feltham Hill Jun Sch**, Felt. TW13 *off Ashford Rd* 175 BT90
Feltham Hill Rd, Ashf. TW15 175 BP92
Feltham Rd, Ashf. TW15 175 BP91
Mitcham CR4 200 DF96
Redhill RH1 266 DF139
Feltham Wk, Red. RH1 266 DF139
● **Feltimores Pk**, Harl. CM17 36 FA12
Felton Cl, Borwd. WD6 78 CL38
Broxbourne EN10 67 DZ25
Petts Wood BR5 205 EP100
Sch **Feltonfleet Sch**, Cob. KT11 *off Byfleet Rd* 213 BS113
Felton Gdns, Bark. IG11 *off Sutton Rd* 145 ES67
Felton Lea, Sid. DA14 185 ET92
Felton Rd, W13 *off Camborne Av* 157 CJ75
Barking IG11 *off Sutton Rd* 145 ES68
Felton St, N1 277 M9
Fencepiece Rd, Chig. IG7 103 EQ50
Ilford IG6 103 EQ50
Fenchurch Av, EC3 287 N9
Fenchurch Bldgs, EC3 287 P9
Fenchurch Pl, EC3 287 P10
≠ **Fenchurch Street** 287 P10
Fenchurch St, EC3 287 N10
Fen Cl, Shenf. CM15 109 GC42
Fen Ct, EC3 287 N9
Fendall Rd, Epsom KT19 216 CQ106
Fendall St, SE1 299 P7
Fendt Cl, E16 291 M9
Fendyke Rd, Belv. DA17 166 EX76
Fenelon Pl, W14 295 H9
Fenemore Rd, Ken. CR8 236 DR119
Fengate Cl, Chess. KT9 215 CK107
Fengates Rd, Red. RH1 250 DE134
Fen Gro, Sid. DA15 185 ET86
Fenham Rd, SE15 312 D5
Fenland Ho, E5 *off Mount Pleasant Hill* 122 DW61
Fen La, SW13 159 CV81
North Ockendon RM14 129 FW64
Fenman Ct, N17 100 DV53
Fenman Gdns, Ilf. IG3 126 EV60
Fenn Cl, Brom. BR1 184 EG93
Fennel Cl, E16 291 K4
Croydon CR0 *off Primrose La* 203 DX102
Guildford GU1 243 BB131
Fennells, Harl. CM19 51 EQ20
Fennells Mead, Epsom KT17 217 CT109
Fennel St, SE18 165 EN79
Fenner Cl, SE16 300 F8
Fenner Ho, Walt. KT12 213 BU105
Fenner Rd, Grays RM16 169 FW77
Fenners Marsh, Grav. DA12 191 GM88
Fenner Sq, SW11 *off Thomas Baines Rd* 160 DD83
Fennings, The, Amer. HP6 55 AR36
Fennings Rd, SW4 181 DK86
Fenning St, SE1 299 N4
Fenn St, E9 279 H3
Fenns Way, Wok. GU21 226 AY115
Fennycroft Rd, Hem.H. HP1 40 BG17
Fensomes All, Hem.H. HP2 *off Queensway* 40 BK19
Fensomes Cl, Hem.H. HP2 *off Broad St* 40 BK19
Fenstanton Av, N12 98 DD50
Sch **Fenstanton Prim Sch**, SW2 *off Abbots Pk* 181 DN88
Fen St, E16 291 M10
Fens Way, Swan. BR8 187 FG93
Fenswood Cl, Bex. DA5 186 FA85
Fentiman Rd, SW8 310 B3
Fentiman Way, Har. HA2 116 CB61
Hornchurch RM11 128 FL60
Fenton Av, Stai. TW18 174 BJ93
Fenton Cl, E8 278 B4
SW9 310 C8
Chislehurst BR7 185 EM92
Redhill RH1 250 DG134
Fenton Gra, Harl. CM17 52 EW16
★ **Fenton Ho**, NW3 120 DC62
Fenton Ho, Houns. TW5 156 CA79
Fenton Rd, N17 100 DQ52
Chafford Hundred RM16 170 FY76
Redhill RH1 250 DG134
Fentons Av, E13 292 A1
Fenton St, E1 *off Commercial Rd* 288 F8
Fentum Rd, Guil. GU2 242 AU132
Fenwick Cl, SE18 165 EN79
Woking GU21 226 AV118
Fenwick Gro, SE15 162 DU83
Fenwick Path, Borwd. WD6 78 CM38
Fenwick Pl, SW9 161 DL83
South Croydon CR2 219 DP108
Fenwick Rd, SE15 162 DU83
Ferdinand Dr, SE15 311 P5
Ferdinand Pl, NW1 275 H6
Ferdinand St, NW1 275 H5
Ferguson Av, Grav. DA12 191 GJ91
Romford RM2 106 FJ54
Surbiton KT5 198 CM99
Ferguson Cl, E14 302 A9
Bromley BR2 203 ED97
Ferguson Ct, Rom. RM2 106 FK54
Ferguson Dr, W3 138 CR72
Fergus Rd, N5 277 H3
Ferme Pk Rd, N4 121 DL57
N8 121 DL57
Fermor Rd, SE23 183 DY88
Fermoy Rd, W9 282 G5
Greenford UB6 136 CB70
Fern Av, Mitch. CR4 201 DK98
Fernbank, Buck.H. IG9 102 EH46
Fernbank Av, Horn. RM12 128 FJ63
Walton-on-Thames KT12 196 BY101
Wembley HA0 117 CF63
Fernbank Ms, SW12 181 DH86
Fernbank Rd, Add. KT15 212 BG106
Fernbrook Av, Sid. DA15 *off Blackfen Rd* 185 ES85
Fernbrook Cres, SE13 184 EE86
Fernbrook Dr, Har. HA2 116 CB59
Fernbrook Rd, SE13 184 EE86
Ferncliff Rd, E8 278 C2
Fern Cl, N1 277 N10
Broxbourne EN10 49 DZ23
Erith DA8 *off Hollywood Way* 167 FH81
Warlingham CR6 237 DY118
Fern Ct, Rom. RM7 *off Cottons App* 127 FD57
Ferncroft Av, N12 98 DE51
NW3 120 DA62
Ruislip HA4 116 BW61
Ferndale, Brom. BR1 204 EJ96
Guildford GU3 242 AS132
Ferndale Av, E17 123 ED57
Chertsey KT16 193 BE104
Hounslow TW4 156 BY83
Ferndale Cl, Bexh. DA7 166 EY81
Ferndale Ct, SE3 315 M4
Ferndale Cres, Uxb. UB8 134 BJ69
Ferndale Pk, Harl. SL6 150 AE79
Ferndale Rd, E7 144 EH66
E11 124 EE61
N15 122 DT58
SE25 202 DV99
SW4 161 DL84
SW9 161 DM83
Ashford TW15 174 BK92
Banstead SM7 233 CZ116
Enfield EN3 83 DY37
Gravesend DA12 191 GH89
Romford RM5 105 FC54
Woking GU21 227 AZ116
Ferndale St, E6 293 N10
Ferndale Ter, Har. HA1 117 CF56
Ferndale Way, Orp. BR6 223 ER106
Ferndell Av, Bex. DA5 187 FD90
Fern Dells, Hat. AL10 45 CT19
Fern Dene, W13 *off Templewood* 137 CH71
Ferndene, Brick.Wd AL2 60 BZ31
Ferndene Rd, SE24 162 DQ84
Fernden Ri, Gdmg. GU7 258 AS144
Ferndown Way, Rom. RM7 127 FB58
Ferndown, Horl. RH6 268 DF146
Hornchurch RM11 128 FM58
Northwood HA6 93 BU54
Ferndown Av, Orp. BR6 205 ER102
Ferndown Cl, Guil. GU1 259 BA135
Pinner HA5 94 BY52
Sutton SM2 218 DD107
Ferndown Ct, Guil. GU1 242 AW133
Ferndown Gdns, Cob. KT11 214 BW113
Ferndown Lo, E14 *off Manchester Rd* 302 F7
Ferndown Rd, SE9 184 EK87
Watford WD19 94 BW48
Fern Dr, Hem.H. HP3 40 BL21
Taplow SL6 130 AH72
Fernecroft, St.Alb. AL1 43 CD23
Fernery, The, Stai. TW18 173 BE92
Fernes Cl, Uxb. UB8 134 BJ72
Ferney Ct, Byfleet KT14 *off Ferney Rd* 212 BK112
Ferney Meade Way, Islw. TW7 157 CG82
Ferney Rd, Byfleet KT14 212 BK112
Cheshunt EN7 66 DR26
East Barnet EN4 98 DG45
Fern Gro, Felt. TW14 175 BV87
Welwyn Garden City AL8 29 CX05
Ferngrove Cl, Fetch. KT22 231 CE122
Fernhall Dr, Ilf. IG4 124 EK57
Fernhall La, Wal.Abb. EN9 68 EK31
Fernham Rd, Th.Hth. CR7 202 DQ97
Fernhead Rd, W9 283 H2
Fernheath Way, Dart. DA2 187 FD92
Fernhill, Oxshott KT22 215 CD114
Fernhill Cl, Wok. GU22 226 AW120
Fernhill Ct, E17 101 ED54
Fernhill Gdns, Kings.T. KT2 177 CK92
Fern Hill La, Harl. CM18 51 ES19
Fernhill La, Wok. GU22 226 AW120
Fernhill Pk, Wok. GU22 226 AW120
Sch **Fern Hill Prim Sch**, Kings.T. KT2 *off Richmond Rd* 178 CL93
Fernhill Rd, Horl. RH6 269 DK152
Fernhills, Hunt.Br. WD4 59 BR33
Fernhill St, E16 305 K3
Fernholme Rd, SE15 183 DX85
Fernhurst Cl, Beac. HP9 89 AM53
Fernhurst Gdns, Edg. HA8 96 CN51
Fernhurst Rd, SW6 306 F6
Ashford TW15 175 BQ91
Croydon CR0 202 DU101
Fernie Cl, Chig. IG7 104 EU50
Fernihough Cl, Wey. KT13 212 BN111
Fernlands Cl, Cher. KT16 193 BE104
Fern La, Houns. TW5 156 BZ78
Fernlea, Bkhm KT23 230 CB124
Fernlea Pl, Cob. KT11 214 BX112
Fernlea Rd, SW12 181 DH88
Mitcham CR4 200 DG96
Fernleigh Cl, W9 283 H2
Croydon CR0 219 DN105
Walton-on-Thames KT12 195 BV104
Fernleigh Ct, Har. HA2 94 CB54
Wembley HA9 118 CL61
Fernleigh Rd, N21 99 DN47
Fernley Cl, Eastcote HA5 115 BU56
Fernleys, St.Alb. AL4 43 CJ17
Ferns, The, Beac. HP9 89 AM54
Hatfield AL10 *off Campion Rd* 45 CT15
St. Albans AL3 43 CD16
Fernsbury St, WC1 286 E3
Ferns Cl, Enf. EN3 83 DY36
South Croydon CR2 220 DV110
Fernshaw Rd, SW10 307 N3
Fernside, NW11 120 DA61
Buckhurst Hill IG9 102 EH46
Slough SL3 132 AV73
Fernside Av, NW7 96 CR48
Feltham TW13 175 BV91
Fernside La, Sev. TN13 257 FJ129
Fernside Rd, SW12 180 DF88
Fernsleigh Cl, Chal.St.P. SL9 90 AY51
Ferns Rd, E15 281 L5
Fern St, E3 290 B5
Fernthorpe Rd, SW16 181 DJ93
Ferntower Rd, N5 277 L2
Fern Twrs, Cat. CR3 252 DU125
Fernville La, Hem.H. HP2 40 BK20
Fern Wk, SE16 312 D1
Ashford TW15 *off Ferndale Rd* 174 BK92
Fern Way, Wat. WD25 75 BU35
Fernways, Ilf. IG1 *off Cecil Rd* 125 EP63
Fernwood, SW19 *off Albert Dr* 179 CZ88
Fernwood Av, SW16 181 DK91
Wembley HA0 117 CJ64
Fernwood Cl, Brom. BR1 204 EJ96
Fernwood Cres, N20 98 DF48
Ferny Hill, Barn. EN4 80 DF38
Ferranti Cl, SE18 304 F7
Ferraro Cl, Houns. TW5 156 CA79
Ferrers Av, Wall. SM6 219 DK105
West Drayton UB7 154 BK75
Ferrers Cl, Slou. SL1 131 AL74
Ferrers Rd, SW16 181 DK92
Ferrestone Rd, N8 121 DM56
Ferrey Ms, SW9 310 F9
Ferriby Cl, N1 276 E6
● **Ferrier Ind Est**, SW18 160 DB84
Ferrier Pt, E16 291 N7
Ferrier St, SW18 160 DB84
Ferriers Way, Epsom KT18 233 CW119
Ferring Cl, Har. HA2 116 CC60
Ferrings, SE21 182 DS89
Ferris Av, Croy. CR0 203 DZ104
Ferris Rd, SE22 162 DU84
Ferron Rd, E5 122 DV62
Ferro Rd, Rain. RM13 147 FG70
Ferrour Ct, N2 120 DD55
Ferry Av, Stai. TW18 173 BE94
Ferrybridge Ho, SE11 298 D7
Ferryhills Cl, Wat. WD19 94 BW48
Ferry Ho, E5 *off Harrington Hill* 122 DW60
Ferry La, N17 122 DU56
SW13 159 CT79
Brentford TW8 158 CL79
Chertsey KT16 194 BH98
Guildford GU2 *off Portsmouth Rd* 258 AW138
Laleham TW18 194 BJ97
Rainham RM13 147 FE72
Richmond TW9 158 CM79
Shepperton TW17 194 BN102
Wraysbury TW19 173 BB89
● **Ferry La Ind Est**, E17 123 DX55
Sch **Ferry La Prim Sch**, N17 *off Jarrow Rd* 122 DV56
Ferryman's Quay, SW6 307 N9
Ferrymead Av, Grnf. UB6 136 CA69
Ferrymead Dr, Grnf. UB6 136 CA68
Ferrymead Gdns, Grnf. UB6 136 CC68
Ferrymoor, Rich. TW10 177 CH90
Ferry Pl, SE18 305 M7
Ferry Quays, Brent. TW8 *off Ferry La* 158 CL79
Ferry Rd, SW13 159 CU80
Bray SL6 150 AC75
Teddington TW11 177 CH92
Thames Ditton KT7 197 CH100
Tilbury RM18 171 GG83
Twickenham TW1 177 CH88
West Molesey KT8 196 CA97
Ferry Sq, Brent. TW8 157 CK79
Shepperton TW17 195 BP101
Ferry St, E14 302 E10
Feryby Rd, Grays RM16 171 GH76
Feryngs Cl, Harl. CM17 *off Watlington Rd* 36 EX11
Fesants Cft, Harl. CM20 36 EV12
Festing Rd, SW15 306 C10
Festival Cl, Bex. DA5 186 EX88
Erith DA8 *off Betsham Rd* 167 FF80
Uxbridge UB10 135 BP67
Festival Ct, Sutt. SM1 *off Cleeve Way* 200 DB101
Festival Path, Wok. GU21 226 AT119
Riv **Festival Pier** 298 C2
Festival Wk, Cars. SM5 218 DF106
Festoon Way, E16 292 E10
FETCHAM, Lthd. KT22 231 CD123
Fetcham Common La, Fetch. KT22 230 CB121
Fetcham Downs, Fetch. KT22 247 CE126
Fetcham Pk Dr, Fetch. KT22 231 CE123
Sch **Fetcham Village Inf Sch**, Fetch. KT22 *off School La* 231 CD122
Fetherstone Cl, Pot.B. EN6 64 DD32
Fetherton Ct, Bark. IG11 *off Spring Pl* 145 EQ68
Fetter La, EC4 286 F9
Ffinch St, SE8 314 A4
Fiddicroft Av, Bans. SM7 218 DB114
● **Fiddlebridge Ind Cen**, Hat. AL10 *off Lemsford Rd* 45 CT17
Fiddlebridge La, Hat. AL10 45 CT17
Fiddlers Cl, Green. DA9 169 FV84
FIDDLERS HAMLET, Epp. CM16 70 EW32
Fidgeon Cl, Brom. BR1 205 EN97
Field Bk, Horl. RH6 269 DH146
Field Cl, E4 101 EB51
NW2 119 CU61
Abridge RM4 86 EV41
Bromley BR1 204 EJ96
Buckhurst Hill IG9 102 EJ48
Chesham HP5 54 AS28
Chessington KT9 215 CJ106
Guildford GU4 243 BD132
Harlington UB3 155 BQ80
Hounslow TW4 155 BV81
Horl. RH6 269 DJ146
Ruislip HA4 115 BQ60
Sandridge AL4 43 CG16
South Croydon CR2 220 DV114
West Molesey KT8 196 CB99
Fieldcommon La, Walt. KT12 196 BZ101
Field Ct, WC1 286 D7
Gravesend DA11 191 GF89
Oxted RH8 254 EE127
Field End, Barn. EN5 79 CV42
Coulsdon CR5 219 DK114
Northolt UB5 136 BX65
Ruislip HA4 136 BW65
Fieldend, Twick. TW1 177 CF91
Field End Cl, Wat. WD19 94 BY45
Sch **Field End Inf & Jun Schs**, Ruis. HA4 *off Field End Rd* 116 BX61
Field End Ms, Wat. WD19 *off Field End Cl* 94 BY45
Fieldend Rd, SW16 201 DJ95
Field End Rd, Pnr. HA5 115 BV58
Ruislip HA4 116 BY63
Fielden Ter, Nthflt. DA11 190 GC88
Fielders Cl, Enf. EN1 *off Woodfield Cl* 82 DS42
Harrow HA2 116 CC60
Fielders Grn, Guil. GU1 243 AZ134
Fielders Way, Shenley WD7 62 CL33
Fieldfare Rd, SE28 146 EW73
Fieldgate La, Mitch. CR4 200 DE97
Fieldgate St, E1 288 D7
Fieldhouse Cl, E18 102 EG53
Fieldhouse Rd, SW12 181 DJ88
Fieldhurst, Slou. SL3 153 AZ78
Fieldhurst Cl, Add. KT15 212 BH106
Sch **Field Inf Sch**, Wat. WD18 *off Neal St* 76 BW43
Fielding Av, Til. RM18 171 GH81
Twickenham TW2 176 CC90
Sch **Fielding Co Prim Sch**, W13 *off Wyndham Rd* 157 CH76
Fielding Gdns, Slou. SL3 152 AW75
Fielding Ho, NW6 283 K2
Fielding La, Brom. BR2 204 EJ98
Fielding Ms, SW13 *off Castelnau* 159 CV79
Fielding Rd, W4 158 CR76
W14 294 D6
Fieldings, The, SE23 182 DW88
Banstead SM7 233 CZ117
Horley RH6 269 DJ147
Woking GU21 226 AT116
Fieldings Rd, Chsht EN8 67 DZ29
Fielding St, SE17 311 J2
Fielding Wk, W13 157 CH76
Fielding Way, Hutt. CM13 109 GC44
Sch **Field Jun Sch**, Wat. WD18 *off Watford Fld Rd* 76 BW43
Field La, Brent. TW8 157 CJ80
Godalming GU7 *off The Oval* 258 AT144
Teddington TW11 177 CG92
Field Mead, NW7 96 CS52
NW9 96 CS52
Fieldpark Gdns, Croy. CR0 203 DY102
Field Pl, Gdmg. GU7 258 AS144
New Malden KT3 199 CT100
Field Pt, E7 *off Station Rd* 124 EG63
Field Rd, E7 124 EF63
N17 122 DR55
W6 306 E1
Aveley RM15 148 FQ74
Denham UB9 113 BE63
Feltham TW14 175 BV86
Hemel Hempstead HP2 40 BN21
Watford WD19 76 BY44
Fields, The, Slou. SL1 151 AR75
Fields Ct, Pot.B. EN6 64 DD33
Fields End La, Hem.H. HP1 39 BE18
Fieldsend Rd, Sutt. SM3 217 CY106
Fields Est, E8 278 D7
Fieldside Cl, Orp. BR6 *off State Fm Av* 223 EQ105
Fieldside Rd, Brom. BR1 183 ED92
Fields Pk Cres, Rom. RM6 126 EX57
Field St, WC1 286 C2
Field Vw, Egh. TW20 173 BC92
Feltham TW13 175 BR91
Fieldview, SW18 180 DD88
Horley RH6 *off Stockfield* 269 DH147
Field Vw Cl, Rom. RM7 126 FA55
Fieldview Ct, Slou. SL1 131 AQ71
Staines-upon-Thames TW18 *off Burges Way* 174 BG93
Field Vw Ri, Brick.Wd AL2 60 BY29
Field Vw Rd, Pot.B. EN6 64 DA33
Field Way, NW10 138 CQ66
Bovingdon HP3 57 BA27
Chalfont St. Peter SL9 90 AX52
Greenford UB6 136 CB67
Hoddesdon EN11 33 EC13
Rickmansworth WD3 92 BH46
Ripley GU23 243 BF125
Ruislip HA4 115 BQ60
Uxbridge UB8 134 BK70
Tr **Fieldway** 221 EB108
Fieldway, Amerersham HP7 55 AP41
Berkhamsted HP4 38 AY21
Dagenham RM8 126 EV63
New Addington CR0 221 EB107
Petts Wood BR5 205 ER100
Stanstead Abbotts SG12 33 EB11
Fieldway Cres, N5 276 F3
Fiennes Cl, Dag. RM8 126 EW60
Fiennes Way, Sev. TN13 257 FJ127
Fiesta Dr, Dag. RM9 147 FC70
Fifehead Cl, Ashf. TW15 174 BL93
Fife Rd, E16 291 N7
N22 99 DP52
SW14 178 CQ85
Kingston upon Thames KT1 198 CL96
Fife Ter, N1 276 D10
Fife Way, Lthd. KT23 246 CA125
FIFIELD, Maid. SL6 150 AD81
Fifield La, Wink. SL4 150 AD84
Fifield Path, SE23 *off Bampton Rd* 183 DX90
Fifield Rd, Maid. SL6 150 AD80
Fifth Av, E12 125 EM63
W10 282 E3
Grays RM20 169 FU79
Harlow CM20 35 ER13
Hayes UB3 135 BT74
Watford WD25 76 BX35
Fifth Cross Rd, Twick. TW2 177 CD89
Fifth Way, Wem. HA9 118 CP63
Figges Rd, Mitch. CR4 180 DG94
Figgswood, Couls. CR5 235 DJ122
Fig St, Sev. TN14 256 FF129
Fig Tree Cl, NW10 *off Craven Pk* 138 CS67
Figtree Hill, Hem.H. HP2 40 BK19
Filbert Cl, Hat. AL10 45 CT21
Filby Rd, Chess. KT9 216 CM107
Filey Av, N16 122 DU60
Filey Cl, Bigg.H. TN16 238 EH119
Sutton SM2 218 DC108
Filey Spur, Slou. SL1 151 AP75
Filey Waye, Ruis. HA4 115 BU61
Filigree Ct, SE16 301 M3
Fillebrook Av, Enf. EN1 82 DS40
Fillebrook Rd, E11 123 ED60
Fillingham Way, Hat. AL10 44 CS16
Filmer La, Sev. TN14 257 FL121
Filmer Rd, SW6 306 G6
Windsor SL4 151 AK82
Filston La, Sev. TN14 225 FE113
Filston Rd, Erith DA8 *off Riverdale Rd* 167 FC78
Filton Cl, NW9 96 CS54
Finborough Rd, SW10 307 L2
SW17 180 DF93
Finchale Rd, SE2 166 EU76
Fincham Cl, Uxb. UB10 115 BQ62
Finch Av, SE27 182 DR91
Finch Cl, NW10 118 CR64
Barnet EN5 80 DA43
Hatfield AL10 *off Eagle Way* 45 CU20
Finchdale, Hem.H. HP1 40 BG20
Finchdean Ho, SW15 *off Tangley Gro* 179 CT87
Finch Dr, Felt. TW14 176 BX87
Finch End, Penn HP10 88 AC47
Finches, The, Hert. SG13 32 DV09
Finches Av, Crox.Grn WD3 74 BM41
Finches Ri, Guil. GU1 243 BC132
Finch Gdns, E4 101 EA50
Finch Grn, Chorl. WD3 73 BF42
Finchingfield Av, Wdf.Grn. IG8 102 EJ52
Finch La, EC3 287 M9
Amersham HP7 72 AV40
Bushey WD23 76 CA43
Knotty Green HP9 88 AJ50
FINCHLEY, N3 98 DB53
Sch **Finchley Catholic High Sch**, N12 *off Woodside La* 98 DB48
⊖ **Finchley Central** 98 DA53
Finchley Cl, Dart. DA1 188 FN86
Finchley Ct, N3 98 DB51
Finchley La, NW4 119 CW56
H **Finchley Mem Hosp**, N12 98 DC52
Finchley Pk, N12 98 DC49
Finchley Pl, NW8 274 A10
⊖ **Finchley Road** 273 N4
Finchley Rd, NW2 120 DA62
NW3 273 N4
NW8 274 A9
NW11 119 CZ58
Grays RM17 170 GB79
Finchley Road & Frognal 273 N3
Finchley Way, N3 98 DA52
Finch Ms, SE15 312 A6
Finchmoor, Harl. CM18 51 ER18
Finch Rd, Berk. HP4 38 AU19
Guildford GU1 242 AX134
Finden Rd, E7 124 EH64
Findhorn Av, Hayes UB4 135 BV71
Findhorn St, E14 290 F8
Findlay Dr, Guil. GU3 242 AT130
Findon Cl, SW18 180 DA86
Harrow HA2 116 CB62
Findon Ct, Add. KT15 211 BF106
Findon Gdns, Rain. RM13 147 FG71
Findon Rd, N9 100 DV46
W12 159 CU75
Fine Bush La, Hare. UB9 115 BP58
Fingal St, SE10 303 M10
Finglesham Cl, Orp. BR5 *off Westwell Cl* 206 EX102
Finians Cl, Uxb. UB10 134 BM66
Finland Quay, SE16 301 L7
Finland Rd, SE4 163 DY83
Finland St, SE16 301 M6
Finlay Gdns, Add. KT15 212 BJ105
Finlays Cl, Chess. KT9 216 CN106
Finlay St, SW6 306 C7
Finnart Cl, Wey. KT13 213 BQ105
Finnart Ho Dr, Wey. KT13 *off Vaillant Rd* 213 BQ105
Finney La, Islw. TW7 157 CG81
Finnis St, E2 288 F3
Finnymore Rd, Dag. RM9 146 EY66
FINSBURY, EC1 286 F2
Finsbury Av, EC2 287 M7
Finsbury Av Sq, EC2 *off Eldon St* 287 M7
Finsbury Circ, EC2 287 M7
Finsbury Cotts, N22 99 DL52
Finsbury Ct, Wal.Cr. EN8 *off Parkside* 67 DY34
Finsbury Est, EC1 286 F3
Finsbury Ho, N22 99 DL53
Finsbury Mkt, EC2 287 N5
FINSBURY PARK, N4 121 DN60
★ **Finsbury Park**, N4 121 DP59
≠ **Finsbury Park** 121 DN61
⊖ **Finsbury Park** 121 DN61
Finsbury Park 121 DN61
Finsbury Pk Av, N4 122 DQ58
Finsbury Pk Rd, N4 121 DP61
Finsbury Pavement, EC2 287 M6
Finsbury Rd, N22 99 DM53
Finsbury Sq, EC2 287 M6
Finsbury St, EC2 287 L6
● **Finsbury Twr**, EC1 287 L5
Finsbury Way, Bex. DA5 186 EZ86
Finsen Rd, SE5 162 DQ83
Finstock Rd, W10 282 C8
Sch **Finton Ho Sch**, SW17 *off Trinity Rd* 180 DF89
Finucane Dr, Orp. BR5 206 EW101
Finucane Gdns, Rain. RM13 147 FG65
Finucane Ri, Bushey Hth WD23 94 CC47
Finway Ct, Wat. WD18 *off Whippendell Rd* 75 BT43
Finway Rd, Hem.H. HP2 41 BP16
Fiona Cl, Bkhm KT23 230 CA124
Firbank Cl, E16 292 E6
Enfield EN2 *off Gladbeck Way* 82 DQ42
Firbank Dr, Wat. WD19 94 BY45
Woking GU21 226 AV119
Firbank La, Wok. GU21 226 AV119
Firbank Pl, Eng.Grn TW20 172 AV93
Firbank Rd, SE15 312 F8
Romford RM5 105 FB50
St. Albans AL3 43 CF16
Fir Cl, Walt. KT12 195 BU101
Fircroft Cl, Stoke P. SL2 132 AU65
Woking GU22 227 AZ118
Fircroft Ct, Wok. GU22 *off Fircroft Cl* 227 AZ118

F

Fircroft Gdns, Har. HA1 117 CE62
Sch Fircroft Prim Sch, SW17
off Fircroft Rd 180 DF90
Fircroft Rd, SW17 180 DF89
Chessington KT9 216 CM105
Englefield Green TW20 172 AW94
Fir Dene, Orp. BR6 205 EM104
Firdene, Surb. KT5 198 CQ102
Fire Bell All, Surb. KT6 198 CL100
Firecrest Dr, NW3 120 DB62
Firefly Cl, Hayes UB3 135 BT73
Firefly Gdns, E6 292 G5
Firemans Run, S.Darenth DA4
off East Hill 208 FQ95
★ Firepower, SE18 305 P6
Fire Sta All, Barn. EN5
off Christchurch La 79 CY40
Firethorn Cl, Edg. HA8
off Larkspur Gro 96 CQ49
Firfield Rd, Add. KT15 212 BG105
Firfields, Wey. KT13 213 BP107
Fir Gra Av, Wey. KT13 213 BP106
Fir Gro, N.Mal. KT3 199 CT100
Firgrove, St.John's GU21 226 AU119
Fir Gro Rd, SW9 310 F8
Firham Pk Av, Rom. RM3 106 FN52
Firhill Rd, SE6 183 EA91
Firlands, Horl. RH6
off Stockfield 269 DH147
Weybridge KT13 213 BS107
Firle Ct, Epsom KT17
off Dirdene Gdns 217 CT112
Firman Cl, New Maldon KT3 199 CT98
Firmans Ct, E17 123 ED56
Firmingers Rd, Orp. BR6 225 FB106
Firmin Rd, Dart. DA1 188 FJ85
Fir Pk, Harl. CM19 51 EP18
Fir Rd, Felt. TW13 176 BX92
Sutton SM3 199 CZ102
Firs, The, E6 144 EL66
E17 off Leucha Rd 123 DY57
N20 98 DD46
W5 137 CK71
Artington GU3 258 AV138
Bexley DA5 187 FD88
Bookham KT23 230 CC124
Caterham CR3 off Chatfield Ct 258 DR122
Cheshunt EN7 66 DS27
Pilgrim's Hatch CM15 108 FU44
St. Albans AL1 43 CH24
Tadworth KT20 249 CZ126
Welwyn Garden City AL8 29 CW05
Firs Av, N10 120 DG55
N11 98 DG51
SW14 158 CQ84
Windsor SL4 151 AM83
Firsby Av, Croy. CR0 203 DX102
Firsby Rd, N16 122 DT60
Firs Cl, N10 120 DG55
SE23 183 DX87
Claygate KT10 215 CE107
Dorking RH4 263 CG138
Hatfield AL10 45 CV19
Iver SL0 off Thornbridge Rd 133 BC67
Mitcham CR4 201 DH96
Firscroft, N13 100 DQ48
Firsdene Cl, Ott. KT16
off Slade Rd 211 BD107
Firs Dr, Houns. TW5 155 BV80
Loughton IG10 85 EN39
Slough SL3 133 AZ74
Firs End, Chal.St.P. SL9 112 AY55
Sch Firs Fm Prim Sch, N13
off Rayleigh Rd 100 DR48
Firsgrove Cres, Warley CM14 108 FV49
Firsgrove Rd, Warley CM14 108 FV49
Firside Gro, Sid. DA15 185 ET88
Firs La, N13 100 DQ48
N21 100 DQ47
Potters Bar EN6 64 DB33
Firs Pk, The, Hat. AL9 46 DA23
Firs Pk Av, N21 100 DR46
Firs Pk Gdns, N21 100 DQ46
Firs Rd, Ken. CR8 235 DP115
First Av, E12 124 EL63
E13 291 N2
E17 123 EA57
N18 100 DW49
NW4 119 CW56
SW14 158 CS83
W3 139 CT74
W10 282 G4
Amersham HP7 55 AQ40
Bexleyheath DA7 166 EW80
Dagenham RM10 147 FB68
Enfield EN1 82 DT44
Epsom KT19 216 CS109
Grays RM20 169 FU79
Harlow CM17, CM20 35 ER14
Hayes UB3 135 BT74
Lower Kingswood KT20 249 CY125
Northfleet DA11 190 GE88
Romford RM6 126 EW57
Waltham Abbey EN9 off Breach Barn
Mobile Home Pk 68 EH30
Walton-on-Thames KT12 195 BV100
Watford WD25 76 BW35
Wembley HA9 117 CK61
West Molesey KT8 196 BZ98
First Cl, W.Mol. KT8 196 CC97
First Cres, Slou. SL1 131 AQ71
First Cross Rd, Twick. TW2 177 CE89
First Dr, NW10 138 CQ66
● First Quarter, Epsom KT19 216 CS110
First Slip, Lthd. KT22 231 CG118
First St, SW3 296 D8
Firstway, SW20 199 CW96
First Way, Wem. HA9 118 CP63
Firs Wk, Nthwd. HA6 93 BR51
Woodford Green IG8 102 EG50
Firsway, Guil. GU2 242 AT133
Firswood Av, Epsom KT19 217 CT106
Firs Wd Cl, Pot.B. EN6 64 DF32
Firth Gdns, SW6 306 E7
Fir Tree Av, Mitch. CR4 200 DG96
Stoke Poges SL2 132 AT70
West Drayton UB7 154 BN76
Fir Tree Cl, SW16 181 DJ92
W5 138 CL72
Epsom KT17 233 CW115
Esher KT10 214 CC106
Ewell KT19 217 CT105
Grays RM17 170 GD79
Hemel Hempstead HP3 40 BN21
Fir Tree Cl, Leatherhead KT22 231 CJ123
Orpington BR6 223 ET106
Romford RM1 127 FD55
Firtree Ct, Els. WD6 78 CM42
Fir Tree Gdns, Croy. CR0 221 EA105
Fir Tree Gro, Cars. SM5 218 DF108
Fir Tree Hill, Chan.Cr. WD3 74 BM38
Fir Tree Pl, Ashf. TW15
off Percy Av 174 BN92
Fir Tree Rd, Bans. SM7 217 CW114
Epsom KT17 233 CV116
Guildford GU1 242 AX131
Hounslow TW4 156 BY84
Leatherhead KT22 231 CJ123
Fir Trees, Abridge RM4 86 EV41
Fir Trees Cl, SE16 301 M3
Fir Tree Wk, Dag. RM10
off Wheel Fm Dr 127 FC62
Enfield EN1 82 DR41
Reigate RH2 250 DD134
Firwood Av, St.Alb. AL4 44 CL20
Firwood Cl, Wok. GU21 226 AS119
Firwood Rd, Vir.W. GU25 192 AS100
Fisgard Ct, Grav. DA12
off Admirals Way 191 GK86
Fisher Cl, E9 279 K2
Croydon CR0 202 DT102
Enfield EN3 83 EB37
Greenford UB6 136 CA69
Hersham KT12 213 BV105
Kings Langley WD4 58 BN29
Fisher Ct, Warley CM14 108 FV50
Fisher Ho, N1 276 E9
Fisherman Cl, Rich. TW10 177 CJ91
Fishermans Dr, SE16 301 K4
Fishermans Hill, Nthflt DA11 190 GB85
Fishermans Wk, SE28
off Tugboat St 165 ES75
Fisherman's Wk, E14 302 A2
Fishermans Way, Hodd. EN11 49 ED15
Fisher Rd, Har. HA3 95 CF54
Fishers, Horl. RH6
off Ewelands 269 DJ147
Fishers Cl, SW16 181 DK90
Bushey WD23 76 BY41
Waltham Cross EN8 67 EA34
Fishers Ct, SE14 313 J6
Fishersdene, Clay. KT10 215 CG108
Fishers Grn La, Wal.Abb. EN9 67 EB29
Fishers Hatch, Harl. CM20 35 ES14
● Fisher's Ind Est, Wat. WD18 76 BW43
Fishers La, W4 158 CR77
Epping CM16 69 ES32
Fisher St, E16 291 N6
WC1 286 B7
Fishers Way, Belv. DA17 147 FC74
Fisherton St, NW8 284 A5
Fishery Pas, Hem.H. HP1
off Fishery Rd 40 BG22
Fishery Rd, Hem.H. HP1 40 BG22
Maidenhead SL6 130 AC74
Fishguard Spur, Slou. SL1 152 AV75
Fishguard Way, E16 305 P4
Fishing Temple, Stai. TW18 193 BF95
Fishlock Ct, SW4
off Paradise Rd 310 A8
Fishponds Rd, SW17 180 DE91
Keston BR2 222 EK106
Fishpool St, St.Alb. AL3 42 CB20
Fish St Hill, EC3 287 M10
Fisk Cl, Sun. TW16 175 BT93
Fiske Ct, N17 100 DU53
Bark. IG11 145 ER68
Fitzalan Rd, N3 119 CY55
Claygate KT10 215 CE108
Fitzalan St, SE11 298 E8
Fitzgeorge Av, W14 294 E9
New Malden KT3 198 CR95
Fitzgerald Av, SW14 158 CS83
Fitzgerald Ho, E14 290 D9
SW9 310 E9
Hayes UB3 135 BV74
Fitzgerald Rd, E11 124 EG57
SW14 158 CR83
Thames Ditton KT7 197 CG100
Fitzhardinge St, W1 284 G8
Fitzherbert Ho, Rich. TW10
off Kingsmead 178 CM86
Fitzhugh Gro, SW18 180 DD86
Fitzilian Av, Rom. RM3 106 FM53
Fitzjames Av, W14 294 F9
Croydon CR0 202 DU103
Fitzjohn Av, Barn. EN5 79 CY43
Fitzjohn Cl, Guil. GU4 243 BC131
Fitzjohn's Av, NW3 274 A3
Sch Fitzjohn's Prim Sch, NW3 274 A2
Fitzmaurice Ho, SE16
off Rennie Est 300 F9
Fitzmaurice Pl, W1 297 K2
Fitzneal St, W12 139 CT72
Fitzpatrick Rd, SW9 310 G6
Fitzrobert Pl, Egh. TW20 173 BA93
Fitzroy Cl, N6 120 DF60
Fitzroy Ct, W1 285 M5
Fitzroy Cres, W4 158 CR80
Fitzroy Gdns, SE19 182 DS94
Fitzroy Ms, W1 285 L5
Fitzroy Pk, N6 120 DF60
Fitzroy Pl, Reig. RH2 250 DD134
Fitzroy Rd, NW1 274 F8
Fitzroy Sq, W1 285 L5
Fitzroy St, W1 285 L5
Fitzroy Yd, NW1 274 G8
Fitzsimmons Ct, NW10
off Knatchbull Rd 138 CR67
Fitzstephen Rd, Dag. RM8 126 EV64
Fitzwarren Gdns, N19 121 DJ60
Fitzwilliam Av, Rich. TW9 158 CM82
Fitzwilliam Cl, N20 98 DG46
Fitzwilliam Ct, Borwd. WD6
off Eaton Way 78 CM39
Harl. CM17 36 EY11
Fitzwilliam Ms, E16 303 N2
Fitzwilliam Rd, SW4 309 L10
Fitzwygram Cl, Hmptn H. TW12 198 CC92
Five Acre, NW9 97 CT53
Fiveacre Cl, Th.Hth. CR7 201 DN100
Five Acres, Chesh. HP5 54 AR33
Harlow CM18 51 ES18
Kings Langley WD4 58 BM29
London Colney AL2 61 CK25
Wooburn Green HP10 110 AF56
Five Acres Av, Brick.Wd AL2 60 BZ29
Five Ash Rd, Grav. DA11 191 GF87
Five Bell All, E14 289 P9
Sch Five Elms Prim Sch, Dag. RM9
off Wood La 126 EZ62
Five Elms Rd, Brom. BR2 204 EH104
Dagenham RM9 126 EZ62
Five Flds Cl, Wat. WD19 94 BZ48
Five Oaks, Add. KT15 211 BF107
Five Oaks La, Chig. IG7 104 EY51
Five Oaks Ms, Brom. BR1 184 EG90
Jct Five Points, Iver SL0 133 BB69
Fives Ct, SE11 298 G8
Jct Fiveways, Croy. CR0 219 DN105
Jct Five Ways Cor, NW4 97 CV53
Fiveways Rd, SW9 310 F8
Five Wents, Swan. BR8 207 FG96
Fladbury Rd, N15 122 DR58
Fladgate Rd, E11 124 EE58
Flag Cl, Croy. CR0 203 DX102
Flagon Ct, Croy. CR0
off Lower Coombe St 220 DQ105
Flags, The, Hem.H. HP2 41 BP20
Flagstaff Cl, Wal.Abb. EN9 67 EB33
Flagstaff Ho, SW8
off St. George Wf 310 A2
Flagstaff Rd, Wal.Abb. EN9 67 EB33
Flag Wk, Pnr. HA5 115 BU58
Flambard Rd, Har. HA1 117 CG58
Flamborough Cl, Bigg.H. TN16 238 EH119
Flamborough Rd, Ruis. HA4 115 BU62
Flamborough Spur, Slou. SL1 151 AN75
Flamborough St, E14 289 L8
Flamborough Wk, E14 289 L9
Flamingo Cl, Hat. AL10 44 CR17
Flamingo Gdns, Nthlt. UB5
off Jetstar Way 136 BY69
Flamingo Wk, Horn. RM12 147 FG65
FLAMSTEAD END, Wal.Cr. EN7 66 DU28
Sch Flamstead End Prim Sch,
Chsht EN7 off Longfield La 66 DU27
Flamstead End Rd, Chsht EN8 66 DV28
Flamstead Gdns, Dag. RM9
off Flamstead Rd 146 EW66
Flamstead Rd, Dag. RM9 146 EW66
Flamsted Av, Wem. HA9 138 CN65
Flamsteed Rd, SE7 164 EL78
Flanchford Rd, W12 159 CT76
Reigate RH2 249 CX134
Flanders Ct, Egh. TW20 173 BC92
Flanders Cres, SW17 180 DF94
Flanders Rd, E6 293 K1
W4 158 CS77
Flanders Way, E9 279 J4
Flandrian Cl, Enf. EN3 83 EA38
Flank St, E1 288 C10
Flannery Ct, SE16
off Drummond Rd 300 E6
Flash La, Enf. EN2 81 DP37
Flask Cotts, NW3
off New End Sq 120 DD63
Flask Wk, NW3 273 P1
Flatfield Rd, Hem.H. HP3 40 BN22
Flather Cl, SW16
off Blegborough Rd 181 DJ92
Flat Iron Sq, SE1 off Union St 299 K3
FLAUNDEN, Hem.H. HP3 57 BB33
Flaunden Bottom, Chesh. HP5 72 AY36
Flaunden HP3 72 AY35
Flaunden Hill, Flaun. HP3 57 AZ33
Flaunden La, Hem.H. HP3 57 BB32
Rickmansworth WD3 57 BD33
Flaunden Pk, Flaun. HP3 57 BA32
Flavell Ms, SE10 303 K10
Flavian Cl, St.Alb. AL3 42 BZ22
Flaxen Cl, E4
off Flaxen Rd 101 EB48
Flaxen Rd, E4 101 EB48
Flaxley Rd, Mord. SM4 200 DB100
Flaxman Ct, W1 285 N9
Flaxman Rd, SE5 311 H9
Flaxman Ter, WC1 285 P3
Flaxton Rd, SE18 165 ER81
Flecker Cl, Stan. HA7 95 CF50
Fleece Dr, N9 100 DU49
Sch Fleecefield Prim Sch, N18
off Brettenham Rd 100 DU49
Fleece Rd, Long Dit. KT6 197 CJ102
Fleece Wk, N7 276 B4
Fleeming Cl, E17
off Pennant Ter 101 DZ54
Fleeming Rd, E17 101 DZ54
Fleet Av, Dart. DA2 188 FQ88
Upminster RM14 129 FR58
Fleet Cl, Ruis. HA4 115 BQ58
Upminster RM14 129 FR58
West Molesey KT8 196 BZ99
Fleetdale Par, Dart. DA2
off Fleet Av 188 FQ88
Sch Fleetdown Inf Sch, Dart. DA2
off Lunedale Rd 188 FQ89
Sch Fleetdown Jun Sch, Darenth DA2
off Lunedale Rd 188 FQ89
Fleet La, W.Mol. KT8 196 BZ100
Fleet Pl, EC4
off Limeburner La 286 G8
Sch Fleet Prim Sch, NW3 274 E2
Fleet Rd, NW3 274 D2
Barking IG11 145 EP68
Dartford DA2 188 FQ88
Northfleet DA11 190 GC90
Fleetside, W.Mol. KT8 196 BZ100
Fleet Sq, WC1 286 D3
Fleet St, EC4 286 E9
Fleet St Hill, E1 288 C5
FLEETVILLE, St.Alb. AL1 43 CG20
Sch Fleetville Inf & Nurs Sch,
St.Alb. AL1 off Woodstock Rd S 43 CH20
Sch Fleetville Jun Sch, St.Alb. AL1
off Hatfield Rd 43 CG20
Fleetway, Egh. TW20 193 BC97
● Fleetway Business Pk,
Perivale UB6 137 CH68
Fleetwood Cl, E16 292 E6
Chalfont St. Giles HP8 90 AU49
Chessington KT9 215 CK108
Croydon CR0 202 DT104
Tadworth KT20 233 CW120
Fleetwood Ct, E6 293 J6
West Byfleet KT14 212 BG113
Fleetwood Gro, W3
off East Acton La 138 CS73
Fleetwood Rd, NW10 119 CU64
Kingston upon Thames KT1 198 CP97
Slough SL2 132 AT74
Fleetwood Sq, Kings.T. KT1 198 CP97
Fleetwood St, N16
off Stoke Newington Ch St 122 DS61
Fleetwood Way, Wat. WD19 94 BW49
Fleming Cl, W9 283 J5
Cheshunt EN7 66 DU26
Fleming Ct, W2 284 A6
Croydon CR0 219 DN106
Nthflt. DA11 190 GC88
Fleming Cres, Hert. SG14
off Tudor Way 31 DN09
Fleming Dr, N21 81 DM43
Fleming Gdns, Harold Wd RM3
off Bartholomew Dr 106 FK54
Tilbury RM18 off Fielding Av 171 GJ81
Fleming Mead, Mitch. CR4 180 DE94
Fleming Rd, SE17 311 H2
Chafford Hundred RM16 169 FW77
Southall UB1 136 CB72
Waltham Abbey EN9 83 EB35
Flemings, Gt Warley CM13 107 FW51
Fleming Wk, NW9
off Pasteur Cl 96 CS54
Fleming Way, SE28 146 EX73
Isleworth TW7 157 CF83
Flemish Flds, Cher. KT16 194 BG101
Flemming Av, Ruis. HA4 115 BV60
Flempton Rd, E10 123 DY59
Fletcher Cl, E6 293 N10
Ottershaw KT16 211 BE107
St. John's GU21 226 AT118
Fletcher La, E10 123 EC59
Fletcher Path, SE8 314 B5
Fletcher Rd, W4 158 CQ76
Chigwell IG7 103 ET50
Ottershaw KT16 211 BD107
Fletchers Cl, Brom. BR2 204 EH98
Fletcher St, E1 288 D10
Fletcher Way, Hem.H. HP2 40 BJ18
Fletching Rd, E5 122 DW62
SE7 164 EJ79
Fletton Rd, N11 99 DL52
Fleur de Lis St, E1 287 P5
Fleur Gates, SW19 179 CX87
Flexley Wd, Welw.G.C. AL7 29 CZ06
Flex Meadow, Harl. CM19 50 EL16
Flexmere Gdns, N17 100 DR53
Flexmere Rd, N17 100 DR53
Flight App, NW9 97 CT54
Flimwell Cl, Brom. BR1 184 EE92
Flinders Cl, St.Alb. AL1 43 CG22
Flint Cl, E15 281 L6
Banstead SM7 218 DB114
Bookham KT23 246 CC126
Green Street Green BR6
off Lynne Cl 223 ET107
Horl. RH6 269 DJ146
Redhill RH1 250 DF133
Flint Down Cl, Orp. BR5 206 EU95
Flint Hill, Dor. RH4 263 CH138
Flint Hill Cl, Dor. RH4 263 CH139
Flint La, Harl. CM17 36 EW14
Flintlock Cl, Stai. TW19 154 BG84
Flintmill Cres, SE3 164 EL82
Flinton St, SE17 299 P10
Flint St, SE17 299 M9
Grays RM20 169 FV79
Flint Way, St.Alb. AL3 42 CC15
Flitcroft St, WC2 285 P8
Floathaven Cl, SE28 146 EU74
Floats, The, Rvrhd TN13 256 FE121
Flock Mill Pl, SW18 180 DB88
Flockton St, SE16 300 C5
Flodden Rd, SE5 311 J7
Flood La, Twick. TW1
off Church La 177 CG88
Flood Pas, SE18 305 J7
Flood St, SW3 308 D1
Flood Wk, SW3 308 D2
Flora Cl, E14 290 C9
Stanmore HA7 96 CL48
Flora Gdns, W6 159 CV77
Croydon CR0 221 EC111
Romford RM6 126 EW58
Sch Flora Gdns Prim Sch, W6
off Dalling Rd 159 CV77
Flora Gro, St.Alb. AL1 43 CF21
Flora Ho, E3 off Garrison Rd 280 A9
Floral Ct, Ashtd. KT21
off Rosedale 231 CJ118
Floral Dr, Lon.Col. AL2 61 CK26
Floral Pl, N1
off Northampton Gro 277 L3
Floral St, WC2 286 A10
Flora St, Belv. DA17 166 EZ78
Florence Av, Enf. EN2 82 DQ41
Morden SM4 200 DC99
New Haw KT15 212 BG111
Florence Cantwell Wk, N19
off Hillrise Rd 121 DL59
Florence Cl, Grays RM20 170 FY79
Harlow CM17 52 EW17
Hornchurch RM12 128 FL61
Walton-on-Thames KT12
off Florence Rd 195 BV101
Watford WD25 75 BU35
Florence Ct, W9 off Maida Vale 283 P3
Hertford SG14 31 DP09
Florence Dr, Enf. EN2 82 DQ41
Florence Elson Cl, E12 125 EN63
Florence Gdns, W4 158 CQ79
Romford RM6 off Roxy Av 126 EW59
Staines-upon-Thames TW18 174 BH94
Florence Nightingale Ho, N1
off Nightingale Rd 277 K5
★ Florence Nightingale Mus,
SE1 298 C5
Florence Rd, E6 144 EJ67
E13 291 N1
N4 121 DN60
SE2 166 EW76
SE14 313 P7
SW19 180 DB93
W4 158 CR76
W5 138 CL73
Beckenham BR3 203 DX96
Bromley BR1 204 EG95
Feltham TW13 175 BV88
Kingston upon Thames KT2 178 CM94
South Croydon CR2 220 DR109
Southall UB2 156 BX77
Walton-on-Thames KT12 195 BV101
Florence St, E16 291 M4
N1 276 G7
NW4 119 CW56
Florence Ter, SE14 313 P6
SW15 off Roehampton Vale 178 CS90
Florence Way, SW12 180 DF88
Uxbridge UB8 134 BJ66
Florence White Ct, N9
off Colthurst Dr 100 DV48
Florey Sq, N21
off Highlands Av 81 DM43
Florfield Pas, E8 278 F5
Florfield Rd, E8 278 F5
Florian Av, Sutt. SM1 218 DD105
Florian Rd, SW15 159 CY84
Florida Cl, Bushey Hth WD23 95 CD47
Florida Ct, Brom. BR2
off Westmoreland Rd 204 EF98
Florida Rd, Shalf. GU4 258 AY140
Thornton Heath CR7 201 DP95
Florida St, E2 288 C3
Florin Ct, EC1 287 J6
SE1 off Tanner St 300 A5
Floris Pl, SW4 309 L10
Floriston Av, Uxb. UB10 135 BQ66
Floriston Cl, Stan. HA7 95 CH53
Floriston Ct, Nthlt. UB5 116 CB64
Floriston Gdns, Stan. HA7 95 CH53
Floss St, SW15 306 B9
Flower & Dean Wk, E1 288 B7
Flower Cres, Ott. KT16 211 BB107
Flowerfield, Otford TN14 241 FF117
Flowerhill Way,
Istead Rise DA13 190 GE94
Flower La, NW7 97 CT50
Godstone RH9 253 DY128
Flower Ms, NW11 119 CY58
Flower Pot Cl, N15
off St. Ann's Rd 122 DT58
Flowers Av, Ruis HA4 115 BU58
Flowers Cl, NW2 119 CU62
Flowersmead, SW17 180 DG89
Flowers Ms, N19
off Archway Rd 121 DJ61
Flower Wk, Guil. GU2 258 AW137
Flower Wk, The, SW7 295 N5
Floyd Rd, SE7 304 C10
Floyds La, Wok. GU22 228 BG116
Floyer Cl, Rich. TW10 178 CM85
Fludyer St, SE13 164 EE84
Flux's La, Epp. CM16 70 EU33
Flyer's Way, The, West. TN16 255 ER126
● Flyers Way Ind Est, West. TN16
off The Flyer's Way 255 ER126
Fogerty Cl, Enf. EN3 83 EB37
Fold Cft, Harl. CM20 35 EN14
Foley Cl, Beac. HP9 88 AJ51
Foley Ho, E1
off Tarling St 288 G9
Foley Ms, Clay. KT10 215 CE108
Foley Rd, Bigg.H. TN16 238 EK118
Claygate KT10 215 CE108
Foley St, W1 285 L7
Foley Wd, Clay. KT10 215 CF108
Folgate St, E1 287 P6
Foliot Ho, N1
off Priory Grn Est 276 C10
Foliot St, W12 139 CT72
Folkes La, Upmin. RM14 129 FT57
Folkestone Ct, Slou. SL3 153 BA78
Folkestone Rd, E6 293 M1
E17 123 EB56
N18 100 DU49
Folkingham La, NW9 96 CR53
Folkington Cor, N12 97 CZ50
Follet Dr, Abb.L. WD5 59 BT31
Follett Cl, Old Wind. SL4 172 AV86
Follett St, E14 290 E9
Folly, The, Hert. SG14 32 DR09
Folly Av, St.Alb. AL3 42 CC19
Folly Cl, Rad. WD7 77 CF36
Follyfield Rd, Bans. SM7 218 DA114
Folly La, E4 101 DZ52
E17 101 DY53
St. Albans AL3 42 CC19
South Holmwood RH5 263 CH144
Folly Ms, W11 282 G9
Folly Pathway, Rad. WD7 77 CF35
Folly Vw, Stans.Abb. SG12 33 EB10
Folly Wall, E14 302 F5
Fontaine Rd, SW16 181 DM94
Fontarabia Rd, SW11 160 DG84
Fontayne Av, Chig. IG7 103 EQ49
Rainham RM13 147 FE66
Romford RM1 105 FE54
Fontenelle, SE5 311 N6
Fontenoy Rd, SW12 181 DH89
Fonteyne Gdns, Wdf.Grn. IG8 102 EJ54
Fonthill Cl, SE20
off Selby Rd 202 DU96
Fonthill Ms, N4 121 DM61
Fonthill Rd, N4 121 DM60
Font Hills, N2 98 DC54
● Fontigarry Fm Business Pk,
Reig. RH2 266 DC143
Fontley Way, SW15 179 CU87
Fontmell Cl, Ashf. TW15 174 BN92
St. Albans AL3 43 CE18
Fontmell Pk, Ashf. TW15 174 BM92
Fontwell Cl, Har. HA3 95 CE52
Northolt UB5 136 CA65
Fontwell Dr, Brom. BR2 205 EN99
Fontwell Pk Gdns, Horn. RM12 128 FL63
Foord Cl, Dart. DA2 189 FS89
Football La, Har. HA1 117 CE60
Footbury Hill Rd, Orp. BR6 206 EU101
Footpath, The, SW15 179 CU85
FOOTS CRAY, Sid. DA14 186 EV93
Foots Cray High St, Sid. DA14 186 EW93
Foots Cray La, Sid. DA14 186 EW88
Footscray Rd, SE9 185 EN86
Forbench Cl, Ripley GU23 228 BH122
Forbes Av, Pot.B. EN6 64 DD33
Forbes Cl, NW2 119 CU62
Hornchurch RM11
off St. Leonards Way 127 FH60
Forbes Ct, SE19 182 DS92
Forbe's Ride, Wind. SL4 150 AG84
Forbes St, E1 288 D9
Forbes Way, Ruis. HA4 115 BV61
Forburg Rd, N16 122 DU60
FORCE GREEN, West. TN16 239 ER124
Force Grn La, West. TN16 239 ER124
Fordbridge Cl, Cher. KT16 194 BH102
Fordbridge Pk, Sun. TW16 195 BT100
Fordbridge Rd, Ashf. TW15 194 BM92
Shepperton TW17 195 BS100
Sunbury-on-Thames TW16 195 BS100
Jct Fordbridge Rbt, Ashf. TW15 174 BL93
Ford Cl, E3 279 M10
Ashford TW15 174 BL93
Bushey WD23 76 CC42
Harrow HA1 117 CD59
Rainham RM13 147 FF66
Shepperton TW17 194 BN98
Thornton Heath CR7 201 DP100
Fordcroft Rd, Orp. BR5 206 EV99
Forde Av, Brom. BR1 204 EJ97
Fordel Rd, SE6 183 ED88
Ford End, Denh. UB9 113 BF61
Woodford Green IG8 102 EH51
Fordham Cl, Barn. EN4 80 DE41
Hornchurch RM11 128 FN59
Worcester Park KT4 199 CV102
Fordham Rd, Barn. EN4 80 DD41
Fordham St, E1 288 D8
Fordhook Av, W5 138 CM73

Fordingley Rd, W9 283 H3
Fordington Ho, SE26
off Sydenham Hill Est 182 DV90
Fordington Rd, N6 120 DF57
Ford La, Iver SL0 134 BG72
Rainham RM13 147 FF66
Fordmill Rd, SE6 183 EA89
Ford Rd, E3 279 N10
Ashford TW15 174 BM91
Chertsey KT16 194 BH102
Dagenham RM9, RM10 146 EZ66
Northfleet DA11 190 GB85
Old Woking GU22 227 BB120
Fords Gro, N21 100 DQ46
Fords Pk Rd, E16 291 N8
Ford Sq, E1 288 F7
Ford St, E3 279 M9
E16 291 L8
Fordwater Rd, Cher. KT16 194 BH102
● **Fordwater Trd Est**, Cher. KT16 216 BJ102
Fordwich Cl, Hert. SG14 31 DN09
Orpington BR6 205 ET101
Fordwich Hill, Hert. SG14 31 DN09
Fordwich Ri, Hert. SG14 31 DN09
Fordwich Rd, Welw.G.C. AL8 29 CW10
Fordwych Rd, NW2 272 G3
Fordyce Cl, Horn. RM11 128 FM59
Fordyce Ho, SW16
off Colson Way 181 DJ91
Fordyce Rd, SE13 183 EC86
Fordyke Rd, Dag. RM8 126 EZ61
Forebury, The, Saw. CM21 36 EY05
Forebury Av, Saw. CM21 36 EZ05
Forebury Cres, Saw. CM21 36 EZ05
Forefield, St.Alb. AL2 60 CA27
★ **Foreign & Commonwealth Office**, SW1 297 P4
Foreign St, SE5 311 H8
Foreland Ct, NW4 97 CY53
Forelands Pl, Saw. CM21
off Bell St 36 EY05
Forelands Way, Chesh. HP5 54 AQ32
Foremark Cl, Ilf. IG6 103 ET50
Foreshore, SE8 301 P9
Forest, The, E11 124 EE56
Forest App, E4 102 EE45
Woodford Green IG8 102 EF52
Forest Av, E4 102 EE45
Chigwell IG7 103 EN50
Hemel Hempstead HP3 40 BK22
● **Forest Business Pk**, E10 123 DX59
Forest Cl, E11 124 EF57
NW6 272 E7
Chislehurst BR7 205 EN95
East Horsley KT24 245 BT125
Slough SL2 132 AV71
Waltham Abbey EN9 84 EH37
Woking GU22 227 BD115
Woodford Green IG8 102 EH48
Forest Ct, E4 102 EF46
E11 124 EE56
Forest Cres, Ashtd. KT21 232 CN116
Forest Cft, SE23 182 DV89
FORESTDALE, Croy. CR0 221 EA109
Forestdale, N14 99 DK49
Forestdale Cen, The, Croy. CR0
off Holmbury Gro 221 DZ108
Sch **Forestdale Prim Sch**, Croy. CR0
off Pixton Way 221 DZ109
Forest Dr, E12 124 EK62
Keston BR2 222 EL105
Kingswood KT20 233 CZ121
Sunbury-on-Thames TW16 175 BT94
Theydon Bois CM16 85 ES36
Woodford Green IG8 101 ED52
Forest Dr E, E11 123 ED59
Forest Dr W, E11 123 EC59
Forest Edge, Buck.H. IG9 102 EJ49
Forester Rd, SE15 162 DV84
Foresters Cl, Chsht EN7 66 DS27
Wallington SM6 219 DK108
Woking GU21 226 AT118
Foresters Cres, Bexh. DA7 167 FB84
Foresters Dr, E17 123 ED56
Wallington SM6 219 DK108
Sch **Foresters Prim Sch**, Wall. SM6
off Redford Av 219 DK107
Forest Gdns, N17 100 DT54
FOREST GATE, E7 281 N3
⇌ **Forest Gate** 281 P2
Forest Gate, NW9 118 CS56
Sch **Forest Gate Comm Sch**, E7 281 P2
Forest Glade, E4 102 EE49
E11 124 EE58
North Weald Bassett CM16 70 EY27
Forest Gro, E8 278 A5
Thnwd. CM16 70 EW26
Forest Hts, Buck.H. IG9 102 EG47
FOREST HILL, SE23 183 DX88
⇌ **Forest Hill** 182 DW89
⊖ **Forest Hill** 182 DW89
Jct **Forest Hill**, SE23 182 DW89
● **Forest Hill Business Cen**, SE23
off Clyde Vale 182 DW89
● **Forest Hill Ind Est**, SE23
off Perry Vale 182 DW89
Forest Hill Rd, SE22 182 DV85
SE23 182 DV85
Sch **Forest Hill Sch**, SE23
off Dacres Rd 183 DX90
Forestholme Cl, SE23 182 DW89
● **Forest Ind Pk**, Ilf. IG6 103 ES53
Forest La, E7 281 N3
E15 281 K4
Chigwell IG7 103 EN50
Leatherhead KT24 229 BT124
Forest Mt Rd, Wdf.Grn. IG8 101 ED52
Forest Pt, E7
off Windsor Rd 124 EH64
Fore St, EC2 287 K7
N9 100 DU50
N18 100 DT51
Harlow CM17 36 EW11
Hatfield AL9 45 CW17
Hertford SG14 32 DR09
Pinner HA5 115 BU57
Fore St Av, EC2 287 L7
Forest Ridge, Beck. BR3 203 EA97
Keston BR2 222 EL105
Forest Ri, E17 123 ED57
Forest Rd, E7 124 EG63
E8 278 A5
E11 123 ED59
E17 122 DW56
N9 100 DV46
N17 122 DW56
Cheshunt EN8 67 DX29
Enfield EN3 83 DY36
Erith DA8 167 FG81
Forest Rd, Feltham TW13 176 BW89
Ilford IG6 103 ES53
Leatherhead KT24 229 BU123
Loughton IG10 84 EK41
Richmond TW9 158 CN80
Romford RM7 127 FB55
Sutton SM3 200 DA102
Watford WD25 59 BV33
Windsor SL4 151 AK82
Woking GU22 227 BD115
Woodford Green IG8 102 EG48
Sch **Forest Sch**, E17
off College Pl 124 EE56
Forest Side, E4 102 EF45
E7 124 EH63
Buckhurst Hill IG9 102 EJ46
Epping CM16 69 ER33
Waltham Abbey EN9 84 EJ36
Worcester Park KT4 199 CT102
Forest St, E7 281 N2
● **Forest Trd Est**, E17 123 DX55
Forest Vw, E4 101 ED45
E11 124 EF59
Forest Vw Av, E10 123 ED57
Forest Vw Rd, E12 124 EL63
E17 101 EC53
Loughton IG10 84 EK42
Forest Wk, N10 99 DH53
Bushey WD23 *off Millbrook Rd* 98 BZ39
● **Forest Wks**, E17
off Forest Rd 123 DX55
Forest Way, N19
off Hargrave Pk 121 DJ61
Ashtead KT21 232 CM117
Loughton IG10 84 EL41
Orpington BR5 205 ET99
Sidcup DA15 185 ER87
Waltham Abbey EN9 84 EK35
Woodford Green IG8 102 EH49
Forfar Rd, N22 99 DP53
SW11 309 H6
Forge, The, Northaw EN6 64 DE30
Forge Av, Couls. CR5 235 DN120
Forge Br La, Couls. CR5 235 DH121
Forge Cl, Brom. BR2 204 EG102
Chipperfield WD4 58 BG31
Harlington UB3 155 BR79
Forge Dr, Clay. KT10 215 CG108
Farnham Common SL2 131 AQ65
Forge End, Amer. HP7 55 AP40
St. Albans AL2 60 CA26
Woking GU21 226 AY117
Forgefield, Bigg.H. TN16
off Main Rd 238 EK116
Forge La, Felt. TW13 176 BY92
Gravesend DA12 191 GM89
Horton Kirby DA4 208 FQ98
Northwood HA6 93 BS52
Richmond TW10
off Petersham Rd 178 CL88
Sunbury-on-Thames TW16 195 BU97
Sutton SM3 217 CY108
Sch **Forge La Prim Sch**, Han. TW13
off Forge La 176 BY92
Forge Ms, Croy. CR0
off Addington Village Rd 221 EA106
Forge Pl, NW1 275 H5
Horley RH6 268 DE150
Forge Sq, E14 *off Westferry Rd* 302 C9
Forge Steading, Bans. SM7
off Salisbury Rd 234 DB115
Forge Way, Shore. TN14 225 FF111
Forlong Path, Nthlt. UB5
off Cowings Mead 136 BY65
Forman Pl, N16
off Farleigh Rd 122 DT63
Formation, The, E16 305 N4
Formby Av, Stan. HA7 117 CJ55
Formby Cl, Slou. SL3 153 BC77
Formosa St, W9 283 N5
Formunt Cl, E16 291 M7
Forres Cl, Hodd. EN11 49 EA15
Forres Gdns, NW11 120 DA58
Sch **Forres Prim Sch**, Hodd. EN11
off Stanstead Rd 33 EB14
Forrester Path, SE26 182 DW91
Forresters Dr, Welw.G.C. AL7 30 DC10
Forrest Gdns, SW16 201 DM97
Forrest Pl, Shere GU5
off Wellers Ct 260 BN139
Forris Av, Hayes UB3 135 BT74
Forset St, W1 284 D8
Forstal Cl, Brom. BR2
off Ridley Rd 204 EG97
Forster Cl, Wdf.Grn. IG8 101 ED52
Sch **Forster Pk Prim Sch**, SE6
off Boundfield Rd 184 EE90
Forster Rd, E17 123 DY58
N17 122 DT55
SW2 181 DL87
Beckenham BR3 203 DY97
Croydon CR0 *off Windmill Rd* 224 DQ101
Guildford GU2 242 AU130
Forsters Cl, Rom. RM6 126 EZ58
Forsters Way, Hayes UB4 135 BV72
Forster's Way, SW18 180 DB88
Forston St, N1 277 L10
Forsyte Cres, SE19 202 DS95
Forsyth Ct, Dag. RM10
off St. Mark's Pl 147 FB65
Forsyth Gdns, SE17 311 H2
Forsyth Ho, SW1
off Tachbrook St 297 M10
Forsythia Cl, Ilf. IG1 125 EP64
Forsythia Gdns, Slou. SL3 152 AY76
Forsythia Pl, Guil. GU1
off Larch Av 242 AW132
Forsyth Path, Wok. GU21 211 BD113
Forsyth Pl, Enf. EN1 82 DS43
Forsyth Rd, Wok. GU21 211 BC114
Forterie Gdns, Ilf. IG3 126 EU62
Fortescue Av, E8 278 F7
Twickenham TW2 176 CC90
Fortescue Rd, SW19 180 DD94
Edgware HA8 96 CR53
Weybridge KT13 212 BM105
Fortess Gro, NW5 275 L2
Fortess Rd, NW5 275 K2
Fortess Wk, NW5 275 K2
Fortess Yd, NW5 275 K1
Forthbridge Rd, SW11 160 DG84
Forth Rd, Upmin. RM14 129 FR58
Fortin Cl, S.Ock. RM15 149 FU73
Fortin Path, S.Ock. RM15 149 FU73
Fortin Way, S.Ock. RM15 149 FU73
Fortis Cl, E16 292 C9
FORTIS GREEN, N2 120 DF56
Fortis Grn, N2 120 DE56
N10 120 DE56
Fortis Grn Av, N2 120 DF55
Fortis Grn Rd, N10 120 DG55
Fortismere Av, N10 120 DG55
Sch **Fortismere Sch**, N10
off Tetherdown 120 DG55
Coll **Fortismere Sch 6th Form Cen**, N10
off Tetherdown 120 DG55
Fort La, Reig. RH2 250 DB130
Fortnam Rd, N19 121 DK61
★ **Fortnum & Mason**, W1 297 L2
Fortnums Acre, Stan. HA7 95 CF51
● **Fortress Distribution Pk**, Til. RM18 171 GG84
Fort Rd, SE1 300 B9
Box Hill KT20 248 CP131
Guildford GU1 258 AY137
Halstead TN14 241 FC115
Northolt UB5 136 CA66
Tilbury RM18 171 GH84
Fortrose Cl, E14 291 H8
Fortrose Gdns, SW2 181 DL88
Fortrye Cl, Nthflt DA11 190 GE89
Fort St, E1 287 P7
E16 304 B3
Fortuna Cl, N7 276 D4
Fortune Ave, Edg. HA8 96 CP52
Fortune Gate Rd, NW10 138 CS67
Fortune Grn Rd, NW6 273 J1
Fortune La, Els. WD6 77 CK44
Fortune Pl, SE1 312 B1
Fortunes, The, Harl. CM18 51 ET17
Fortunes Mead, Nthlt. UB5 136 BY65
Fortune St, EC1 287 K5
Fortunes Wk, E20 280 E3
Fortune Wk, SE28
off Broadwater Rd 165 ER76
Fortune Way, NW10 139 CU69
Forty Acre La, E16 291 N7
Forty Av, Wem. HA9 118 CM62
Forty Cl, Wem. HA9 118 CM61
Forty Footpath, SW14 158 CQ83
Fortyfoot Rd, Lthd. KT22 231 CJ121
FORTY GREEN, Beac. HP9 88 AH50
Forty Grn Rd, Knot.Grn HP9 88 AH51
★ **Forty Hall & Mus**, Enf. EN2 82 DT38
FORTY HILL, Enf. EN2 82 DS37
Forty Hill, Enf. EN2 82 DT38
Sch **Forty Hill C of E Prim Sch**, Enf. EN2 *off Forty Hill* 82 DU37
Forty La, Wem. HA9 118 CP61
★ **Forum, The**, NW5 275 K2
Forum, The, W.Mol. KT8 196 CB98
Forum Cl, E3 280 A9
Forum Ho, Wem. HA9 118 CN63
Forum Magnum Sq, SE1 298 C4
Forum Pl, Hat. AL10 45 CU17
Forumside, Edg. HA8
off Station Rd 96 CN51
Forum Way, Edg. HA8 96 CN51
Forval Cl, Mitch. CR4 200 DF99
Forward Dr, Har. HA3 117 CF56
Fosbery Ct, Enf. EN3
off Sten Cl 83 EA37
Fosbury Ms, W2 295 M1
Foscote Ms, W9 283 K5
Foscote Rd, NW4 119 CV58
Foskett Ms, E8 278 B2
Foskett Rd, SW6 306 G9
Foss Av, Croy. CR0 219 DN106
Sch **Fossdene Prim Sch**, SE7
off Victoria Way 164 EH78
Fossdene Rd, SE7 164 EH78
Fossdyke Cl, Hayes UB4 136 BY71
Fosse Way, W13 137 CG71
West Byfleet KT14
off Brantwood Dr 211 BF113
Fossil Rd, SE13 163 EA83
Fossington Rd, Belv. DA17 166 EX77
Foss Rd, SW17 180 DD91
Fossway, Dag. RM8 126 EW61
Foster Av, Wind. SL4 151 AL83
Foster Cl, Chsht EN8 67 DX30
Fosterdown, Gdse. RH9 252 DV129
Foster La, EC2 287 J8
Foster Rd, E13 291 N4
W3 138 CS73
W4 158 CR78
Hemel Hempstead HP1 40 BG22
Fosters Cl, E18 102 EH53
Chislehurst BR7 185 EM92
Fosters Path, Slou. SL2 131 AM70
Sch **Foster's Prim Sch**, Well. DA16
off Westbrooke Rd 166 EW83
Foster St, NW4 119 CW56
Harlow CM17 52 EY17
Foster Wk, NW4
off Foster St 119 CW56
Fothergill Cl, E13 281 N10
Fothergill Dr, N21 81 DL43
Fotheringay Gdns, Slou. SL1 131 AN73
Fotheringham Rd, Enf. EN1 82 DT42
Fotherley Rd, Mill End WD3 91 BF47
Foubert's Pl, W1 285 L9
Foulden Rd, N16 122 DT63
Sch **Foulds Prim Sch**, Barn. EN5
off Byng Rd 79 CX41
Foulis Ter, SW7 296 B10
Foulser Rd, SW17 180 DF90
Foulsham Rd, Th.Hth. CR7 202 DQ97
● **Foundation Units**, Guil. GU1 242 AY130
Founder Cl, E6 293 N9
Founders Cl, Nthlt. UB5 136 BZ69
Founders Ct, EC2 287 L8
Founders Gdns, SE19 182 DQ94
Founders Rd, Hodd. EN11 33 EB14
★ **Foundling Mus**, WC1 286 B4
Foundry Cl, SE16 301 L2
Foundry Ct, Slou. SL2 132 AT74
Foundry Gate, Wal.Cr. EN8
off York Rd 67 DY33
Foundry La, Horton SL3 153 BB83
Foundry Ms, NW1 285 M4
Hounslow TW3 *off New Rd* 156 CB84
Foundry Pl, E1 288 G6
Founes Dr, Chaff.Hun. RM16 170 FY76
Fountain Cl, E5
off Lower Clapton Rd 122 DV62
SE18 305 N10
Uxbridge UB8 135 BQ71
Fountain Ct, EC4 286 E10
Borwd. WD6 78 CN40
Eynsford DA4
off Pollyhaugh 208 FL103
Fountain Dr, SE19 182 DT91
Carshalton SM5 218 DF109
Hertford SG13 32 DT08
Fountain Fm, Harl. CM18 51 ET17
Fountain Gdns, Wind. SL4 151 AR83
Fountain Grn Sq, SE16 300 D5
Fountain Ho, SW6
off The Boulevard 307 P8
SW8 *off St. George Wf* 310 B1
Fountain La, Sev. TN15 257 FP122
Fountain Ms, N5
off Highbury Gra 277 J1
NW3 274 E4
Fountain Pl, SW9 310 F7
Waltham Abbey EN9 67 EC34
Fountain Rd, SW17 180 DD92
Redhill RH1 266 DE136
Thornton Heath CR7 202 DQ96
Fountains, The, Loug. IG10
off Fallow Flds 102 EK45
Fountains Av, Felt. TW13 176 BZ90
Fountains Cl, Felt. TW13 176 BZ89
Fountains Cres, N14 99 DL45
Fountain Sq, SW1 297 J8
Fountain Wk, Nthflt DA11 190 GE86
Fountayne Rd, N15 122 DU56
N16 122 DU61
Fount St, SW8 309 P5
Fouracre Path, SE25 202 DS100
Fouracres, SW12
off Little Dimocks 181 DH89
Enfield EN3 83 DY39
Four Acres, Cobham KT11 214 BY113
Guildford GU1 243 BC132
Welwyn Garden City AL7 29 CZ11
Four Acres, The, Saw. CM21 36 EZ06
Fouracres Dr, Hem.H. HP3 40 BM22
Fouracres Wk, Hem.H. HP3 40 BM22
Fourdinier Way, Hem.H. HP3 40 BK23
Four Hills Est, Enf. EN2 82 DQ38
Fourland Wk, Edg. HA8 96 CQ51
Fournier St, E1 288 A6
Four Oaks, Chesh. HP5 54 AN27
Four Seasons Cl, E3 280 A10
● **Four Seasons Cres**, Sutt. SM3 199 CZ103
Sch **Four Swannes Prim Sch**, Wal.Cr. EN8 *off King Edward Rd* 67 DY33
Fourth Av, E12 125 EM63
W10 282 E3
Grays RM20 169 FU79
Harlow CM19, CM20 51 EM15
Hayes UB3 135 BT74
Romford RM7 127 FD60
Watford WD25 76 BX35
Fourth Cross Rd, Twick. TW2 177 CD89
Fourth Dr, Couls. CR5 235 DK116
Fourth Way, Wem. HA9 118 CQ63
Four Trees, St.Alb. AL2 42 CB24
Four Tubs, The, Bushey WD23 95 CD45
Fourways, Bayford SG13 47 DN18
St. Albans AL4 *off Hatfield Rd* 44 CM20
Fourways Mkt, N.Mymms AL9
off Dixons Hill Rd 45 CW24
Four Wents, Cob. KT11 213 BV113
Four Wents, The, E4
off Kings Rd 101 ED47
Fowey Av, Ilf. IG4 124 EK57
Fowey Cl, E1 300 E2
Fowler Cl, SW11 160 DD83
Fowler Rd, E7 124 EG63
N1 277 H7
Ilford IG6 104 EV51
Mitcham CR4 200 DG96
Fowlers Cl, Sid. DA14
off Thursland Rd 186 EY92
Fowlers Mead, Chobham GU24
off Windsor Rd 210 AS110
Fowlers Wk, W5 137 CK70
Fowley Cl, Wal.Cr. EN8 67 DZ34
Fowley Mead Pk, Wal.Cr. EN8 67 EA34
Fownes St, SW11 308 D10
Foxacre, Cat. CR3
off Town End Cl 236 DS122
Fox All, Wat. WD18
off Lower High St 76 BW43
Fox & Knot St, EC1 287 H6
Foxberry Rd, SE4 163 DY83
Foxberry Wk, Nthflt DA11
off Rowmarsh Cl 190 GD91
Foxboro Rd, Red. RH1 250 DG132
Foxborough Cl, Slou. SL3 153 BA78
Foxborough Gdns, SE4 183 EA86
Sch **Foxborough Sch**, Langley SL3
off Common Rd 153 BA78
Foxbourne Rd, SW17 180 DG89
Fox Burrow Rd, Chig. IG7 104 EX50
Foxburrows Av, Guil. GU2 242 AT134
Foxbury Av, Chis. BR7 185 ER93
Foxbury Cl, Brom. BR1 184 EH93
Orpington BR6 224 EU106
Foxbury Dr, Orp. BR6 224 EU107
Foxbury Rd, Brom. BR1 184 EG93
Fox Cl, E1 289 H4
E16 291 N7
Bushey WD23 76 CB42
Elstree WD6 77 CK44
Orpington BR6 224 EU106
Romford RM5 105 FB50
Weybridge KT13 213 BR106
Woking GU22 227 BD115
Foxcombe, New Adgtn CR0 221 EB107
Foxcombe Cl, E6 *off Boleyn Rd* 166 EK68
Foxcombe Rd, SW15
off Alton Rd 179 CU88
Foxcote, SE5 311 P1
Fox Covert, Fetch. KT22 231 CD124
Foxcroft, St.Alb. AL1 43 CG22
Foxcroft Rd, SE18 165 EP81
Foxdell, Nthwd. HA6 93 BR51
Foxdells, Birch Grn SG14 31 DJ12
Foxdell Way, Chal.St.P. SL9 90 AY50
Foxdene Cl, E18 124 EH55
Foxearth Cl, Bigg.H. TN16 238 EL118
Foxearth Rd, S.Croy. CR2 220 DW110
Foxearth Spur, S.Croy. CR2 220 DW109
Foxenden Rd, Guil. GU1 258 AY135
Foxes Cl, Hert. SG13 32 DV09
Foxes Dale, SE3 315 N10
Bromley BR2 203 ED97
Foxes Dr, Wal.Cr. EN7 66 DU29
Foxes Grn, Orsett RM16 171 GG75
Foxes La, Cuffley EN6 65 DL28
North Mymms AL9 45 CY23
Foxes Path, Sutt.Grn GU4 243 AZ126
Foxfield Cl, Nthwd. HA6 93 BT51
Sch **Foxfield Prim Sch**, SE18
off Sandbach Pl 165 EQ78
Foxfield Rd, Orp. BR6 205 ER103
Foxglove Cl, N9 100 DW46
Hatfield AL10 45 CV19
Hoddesdon EN11 *off Castle Cl* 33 EC14
Sidcup DA15 186 EU86
Southall UB1 136 BY73
Stanwell TW19 174 BK88
Foxglove Gdns, E11 124 EJ56
Guildford GU4 243 BC132
Purley CR8 219 DL111
Foxglove La, Chess. KT9 216 CN105
Foxglove Path, SE28
off Crowfoot Cl 145 ES74
Foxglove Rd, Rush Grn RM7 127 FE61
South Ockendon RM15 149 FW71
Foxgloves, The, Hem.H. HP1 39 BE21
Foxglove St, W12 139 CT73
Foxglove Way, Wall. SM6 201 DH102
Foxgrove, N14 99 DL48
Fox Gro, Walt. KT12 195 BV101
Foxgrove Av, Beck. BR3 183 EB94
Foxgrove Dr, Wok. GU21 227 BA115
Foxgrove Path, Wat. WD19 94 BX50
Foxgrove Rd, Beck. BR3 183 EB94
Foxhall Rd, Upmin. RM14 128 FQ64
Foxham Rd, N19 121 DK62
Foxhanger Gdns, Wok. GU22
off Oriental Rd 227 BA116
Foxherne, Slou. SL3 152 AW75
Fox Hill, SE19 182 DT94
Foxhill, Wat. WD24 75 BU36
Fox Hill Gdns, SE19 182 DT94
Foxhills, Wok. GU21 226 AW117
Foxhills Cl, Ott. KT16 211 BB107
Foxhills Ms, Cher. KT16 193 BB104
Foxhills Rd, Ott. KT16 211 BA105
Foxhole Rd, SE9 184 EL85
Foxholes, Wey. KT13 213 BR106
Foxholes Av, Hert. SG13 32 DT09
● **Foxholes Business Pk**, Hert. SG13 32 DT09
Foxholes Rbt, Hert. SG13 32 DT10
Fox Hollow Cl, SE18 165 ES78
Fox Hollow Dr, Bexh. DA7 166 EX83
Foxhollow Dr, Farn.Com. SL2 111 AQ64
Foxhollows, Hat. AL10 45 CV16
London Colney AL2 61 CJ26
Foxholt Gdns, NW10 138 CQ66
Foxhome Cl, Chis. BR7 185 EN93
Foxhounds La, Grav. DA13 190 GA90
Fox Ho, SW11
off Maysoule Rd 160 DD84
Chertsey KT16 *off Fox La N* 193 BF102
Fox Ho Rd, Belv. DA17 167 FB77
Foxlake Rd, Byfleet KT14 212 BM112
Foxlands Cl, Wat. WD25 59 BU34
Foxlands Cres, Dag. RM10 127 FC64
Foxlands La, Dag. RM10 127 FC64
Foxlands Rd, Dag. RM10 127 FC64
Fox La, N13 99 DM48
W5 138 CL70
Bookham KT23 230 BY124
Caterham CR3 235 DP121
Keston BR2 222 EJ106
Reigate RH2 250 DB131
Fox La N, Cher. KT16 193 BF102
Fox La S, Cher. KT16
off Guildford St 193 BF102
Foxlees, Wem. HA0 117 CG63
Foxley Cl, E8 278 C2
Loughton IG10 85 EP40
Redhill RH1 266 DG139
Foxley Ct, Sutt. SM2 218 DC108
Foxley Gdns, Pur. CR8 219 DP113
Foxley Hill Rd, Pur. CR8 219 DN112
Foxley Ho, E3
off Bromley High St 290 D2
Foxley La, Pur. CR8 219 DK111
Foxley Rd, SW9 310 F4
Kenley CR8 219 DP114
Thornton Heath CR7 201 DP98
Foxleys, Wat. WD19 94 BY48
Foxley Sq, SW9 310 G6
Foxmead Cl, Enf. EN2 81 DM41
Foxmoor Ct, Denh. UB9
off Broadway E 114 BG58
Foxmore St, SW11 308 E7
Foxon Cl, Cat. CR3 236 DS121
Foxon La, Cat. CR3 236 DR121
Foxon La Gdns, Cat. CR3 236 DS121
Sch **Fox Prim Sch**, W8 295 J2
Fox Rd, E16 291 L7
Slough SL3 152 AX77
Fox's Path, Mitch. CR4 200 DE96
Foxton Gro, Mitch. CR4 200 DD96
Foxton Rd, Grays RM20 169 FX79
Hoddesdon EN11 49 DZ17
Foxwarren, Clay. KT10 215 CF109
Foxwell Ms, SE4 313 M10
Foxwell St, SE4 313 M10
Fox Wd, Walt. KT12 213 BT108
Foxwood Chase, Wal.Abb. EN9 83 EC35
Foxwood Cl, NW7 96 CS49
Feltham TW13 175 BV90
Foxwood Grn Cl, Enf. EN1 82 DS44
Foxwood Gro, Nthflt DA11 190 GE88
Pratt's Bottom BR6 224 EW110
Foxwood Rd, SE3 164 EF84
Bean DA2 189 FV90
Foyle Dr, S.Ock. RM15 149 FU71
Foyle Rd, N17 100 DU53
SE3 315 L3
Frailey Cl, Wok. GU22 227 BB116
Frailey Hill, Wok. GU22 227 BB116
Framewood Rd, Slou. SL2, SL3 132 AW66
Framfield Cl, N12 98 DA48
Framfield Ct, Enf. EN1 82 DS44
Framfield Rd, N5 276 G2
W7 137 CE72
Mitcham CR4 180 DG94
Framlingham Cl, E5
off Detmold Rd 122 DW61
Framlingham Cres, SE9 184 EL91
Frampton Cl, Sutt. SM2 218 DA108
Frampton Ct, Denh. UB9
off Denham Grn La 113 BF58
Frampton Pk Est, E9 278 G6
Frampton Pk Rd, E9 278 G5
Frampton Rd, Epp. CM16 70 EU28
Hounslow TW4 176 BY85
Potters Bar EN6 64 DC30
Frampton St, NW8 284 A5
Hertford SG14 32 DR09
Francemary Rd, SE4 183 EA85
Frances & Dick James Ct, NW7
off Langstone Way 97 CY52
Frances Av, Chaff.Hun. RM16 169 FW77
Maidenhead SL6 130 AC70
Sch **Frances Bardsley Sch for Girls**, Rom. RM1 *off Brentwood Rd* 127 FH58
Frances Gdns, S.Ock. RM15 149 FT72

F

Sch Frances King Sch of English,
South Kensington, SW7 295 P8
Victoria, SW1 297 K6
Frances Ms, Hem.H. HP3 58 BN25
Frances Rd, E4 101 EA51
Windsor SL4 151 AR82
Frances St, SE18 305 J8
Chesham HP5 54 AQ30
Franche Ct Rd, SW17 180 DC90
Franchise St, Chesh. HP5 54 AQ30
Francis Av, Bexh. DA7 166 FA82
Feltham TW13 175 BU90
Ilford IG1 125 ER61
St. Albans AL3 42 CC17
Francis Barber Cl, SW16
off Well Cl 181 DM91
Francis Bentley Ms, SW4
off Old Town 161 DJ83
Sch Franciscan Prim Sch, SW17
off Franciscan Rd 180 DG92
Franciscan Rd, SW17 180 DF92
Francis Chichester Way, SW11 309 H7
Francis Cl, E14 302 G8
Epsom KT19 216 CR105
Shepperton TW17 194 BN98
Francisco Cl, Chaff.Hun. RM16 169 FW77
Sch Francis Combe Acad, Wat. WD25
off Horseshoe La 60 BW32
Francis Ct, Guil. GU2 242 AV132
Francis Gro, SW19 179 CZ93
Sch Francis Holland Sch,
Marylebone, NW1 284 E4
Belgravia, SW1 297 H9
Francis Pl, N6
off Holmesdale Rd 121 DH59
Francis Rd, E10 123 EC60
N2 120 DF56
Caterham CR3 236 DR122
Croydon CR0 201 DP101
Dartford DA1 188 FK85
Harrow HA1 117 CG57
Hounslow TW4 156 BX82
Ilford IG1 125 ER61
Orpington BR5 206 EX97
Perivale UB6 137 CH68
Pinner HA5 116 BW57
Wallington SM6 219 DJ107
Ware SG12 33 DX05
Watford WD18 75 BV42
Francis St, E15 281 J3
SW1 297 L8
Ilford IG1 125 ER61
Francis Ter, N19 121 DJ62
Francis Ter Ms, N19
off Francis Ter 121 DJ62
Francis Wk, N1 276 C8
Francis Way, Slou. SL1 131 AK73
Francklyn Gdns, Edg. HA8 96 CN48
Francombe Gdns, Rom. RM1 127 FG58
Franconia Rd, SW4 181 DJ85
Frank Bailey Wk, E12
off Gainsborough Av 125 EN64
Frank Burton Cl, SE7
off Victoria Way 164 EH78
Frank Dixon Cl, SE21 182 DS88
Frank Dixon Way, SE21 182 DS88
Frankfurt Rd, SE24 182 DQ85
Frankham St, SE8 314 A5
Frankland Cl, SE16 300 F7
Croxley Green WD3 92 BN45
Woodford Green IG8 102 EJ50
Frankland Rd, E4 101 EA50
SW7 296 A7
Croxley Green WD3 75 BP44
Franklands Dr, Add. KT15 211 BF108
Franklin Av, Chsht EN7 66 DV30
Slough SL2 131 AP70
Watford WD18 75 BU44
Franklin Cl, N20 98 DC45
SE13 314 C7
SE27 181 DP90
Colney Heath AL4 44 CS22
Hemel Hempstead HP3 40 BL23
Kingston upon Thames KT1 198 CN97
Franklin Ct, Guil. GU2
off Humbolt Cl 242 AT134
Franklin Cres, Mitch. CR4 201 DJ98
Franklin Ho, NW9 119 CT59
Enf. EN3
off Innova Science Pk 83 DZ37
Franklin Pas, SE9 164 EL83
Franklin Pl, SE13 314 C7
Franklin Rd, SE20 182 DW94
Bexleyheath DA7 166 EY81
Dartford DA2 187 FE89
Gravesend DA12 191 GK92
Hornchurch RM12 148 FJ65
Watford WD17 75 BV40
Franklins, Map.Cr. WD3 91 BE49
Franklins Ms, Har. HA2 116 CC61
Franklin Sq, W14 307 H1
Franklin's Row, SW3 296 F10
Franklin St, E3 290 D2
N15 122 DS58
Frank Lunnon Cl, B.End SL8 110 AC60
Franklyn Cres, Wind. SL4 151 AK83
Franklyn Gdns, Ilf. IG6 103 ER51
Franklyn Rd, NW10 139 CT66
Walton-on-Thames KT12 195 BU100
Frank Martin Ct, Wal.Cr. EN7 66 DU30
Frank Ms, SE16 300 E9
Franks Av, N.Mal. KT3 198 CQ98
Franksfield, Peasl. GU5 261 BS144
Franks La, Hort.Kir. DA4 208 FN98
Franks Rd, Guil. GU2 242 AU131
Frank St, E13 291 P5
Frank Sutton Way, Slou. SL1 131 AR73
Frankswood Av,
Petts Wd BR5 205 EP99
West Drayton UB7 134 BM72
Frank Towell Ct, Felt. TW14 175 BU87
Franlaw Cres, N13 100 DQ49
Franmil Rd, Horn. RM12 127 FG60
Fransfield Gro, SE26 182 DV90
Frant Cl, SE20 182 DW94
Franthorne Way, SE6 183 EB89
Frant Rd, Th.Hth. CR7 201 DP99
Fraser Cl, E6 292 G8
Bexley DA5 187 FC88
Fraser Ct, W12
off Heathstan Rd 139 CU72
Fraser Gdns, Dor. RH4 263 CG135
Fraser Ho, Brent. TW8
off Green Dragon La 158 CM78
Fraser Rd, E17 123 EB57
N9 100 DV48
Cheshunt EN8 67 DY28
Erith DA8 167 FC78
Perivale UB6 137 CH67
Fraser St, W4 158 CS78
Frating Cres, Wdf.Grn. IG8 102 EG51
Frays Av, West Dr. UB7 154 BK75
Frays Cl, West Dr. UB7 154 BK76
Frayslea, Uxb. UB8 134 BJ68
Frays Waye, Uxb. UB8 134 BJ67
Frazer Av, Ruis. HA4 116 BW64
Frazer Cl, Rom. RM1 127 FF59
Frazier St, SE1 298 E5
Frean St, SE16 300 C6
Freda Corbett Cl, SE15 312 C4
Frederica Rd, E4 101 ED45
Frederica St, N7 276 C6
Frederick Andrews Ct,
Grays RM17 170 GD79
Sch Frederick Bremer Sch, E17
off Fulbourne Rd 101 EC54
Frederick Cl, W2 284 D10
Sutton SM1 217 CZ105
Frederick Ct, NW2 119 CY62
Frederick Cres, SW9 310 G5
Enfield EN3 82 DW40
Frederick Gdns, Croy. CR0 201 DP100
Sutton SM1 217 CZ106
Frederick Pl, N8
off Crouch Hall Rd 121 DL58
SE18 305 N10
Frog. AL2 off Curo Pk 61 CE28
Frederick Rd, SE17 311 H2
Rainham RM13 147 FD68
Sutton SM1 217 CZ106
Fredericks Pl, N12 98 DC49
Frederick's Pl, EC2 287 L9
Frederick Sq, SE16 301 L1
Frederick's Row, EC1 286 G2
Frederick St, WC1 286 C3
Frederick Ter, E8 278 A7
Frederick Vil, W7
off Lower Boston Rd 137 CE74
Frederic Ms, SW1 296 F5
Frederic St, E17 123 DY57
Fredley Pk, Mick. RH5 247 CJ129
Fredora Av, Hayes UB4 135 BT70
Fred White Wk, N7 276 B4
Fred Wigg Twr, E11 124 EF61
Freeborne Gdns, Rain. RM13 147 FG65
Freedom Cl, E17 123 DY56
Freedom Rd, N17 100 DR54
Freedom St, SW11 308 F8
Freedown La, Sutt. SM2 218 DC113
Freegrove Rd, N7 276 B3
Freehold Ind Centre, Houns. TW4
off Amberley Way 176 BW85
Freeland Pk, NW4 97 CY54
Freeland Rd, W5 138 CM73
Freelands Av, S.Croy. CR2 221 DX109
Freelands Gro, Brom. BR1 204 EH95
Freelands Rd, Brom. BR1 204 EH95
Cobham KT11 213 BV114
Freeland Way, Erith DA8
off Slade Grn Rd 167 FG81
Freeling St, N1 276 C7
Freeman Cl, Nthlt. UB5 136 BY66
Shepperton TW17 195 BS98
Freeman Ct, N7
off Tollington Way 121 DL62
SW16 201 DL96
Chesham HP5 off Barnes Av 54 AQ30
Freeman Dr, W.Mol. KT8 196 BZ97
Freeman Rd, Grav. DA12 191 GL90
Morden SM4 200 DD99
Freemans Acre, Hat. AL10
off Cunningham Av 44 CR17
Freemans Cl, Stoke P. SL2 132 AT65
Freemans La, Hayes UB3 135 BS73
Freemantle Av, Enf. EN3 83 DX43
Sch Freemantles Sch, Wok. GU22
off Smarts Heath Rd 226 AW122
Freemantle St, SE17 299 N10
Freeman Wk, SE9 184 EJ85
Freeman Way, Horn. RM11 128 FL58
★ Freemason's Hall (United Grand Lo
of England), WC2 286 B8
Freemasons Pl, Croy. CR0
off Freemasons Rd 202 DS102
Freemasons Rd, E16 292 A7
Croydon CR0 202 DS102
Free Prae Rd, Cher. KT16 194 BG102
Freesia Cl, Orp. BR6 223 ET106
Freethorpe Cl, SE19 202 DR95
Free Trade Wf, E1 289 J10
Freezeland Way, Hlgdn UB10 135 BP65
FREEZYWATER, Wal.Cr. EN8 83 DY35
Sch Freezywater St. George's Prim Sch,
Enf. EN3 off Hertford Rd 83 DX36
Freight La, N1 275 P7
★ Freightliners Fm, N7 276 D4
● Freightmaster Est,
Rain. RM13 167 FG76
Freke Rd, SW11 160 DG83
Frelford Cl, Wat. WD25 60 BW34
Fremantle Ho, Til. RM18 171 GF81
Fremantle Rd, Belv. DA17 166 FA77
Ilford IG6 103 EQ54
Fremantle Way, Hayes UB3 135 BT73
Fremont St, E9 278 G8
French Apts, The, Pur. CR8
off Lansdowne Rd 219 DN112
Frenchaye, Add. KT15 212 BJ106
Frenches, The, Red. RH1 250 DG132
Frenches Ct, Red. RH1
off Frenches Rd 250 DG132
Frenches Rd, Red. RH1 250 DG132
French Gdns, Cob. KT11 214 BW114
French Horn La, Hat. AL10 45 CV17
Frenchlands Gate,
E.Hors. KT24 245 BS127
French Ordinary Ct, EC3 287 P10
French Pl, E1 287 P4
French Row, St.Alb. AL3
off Market Pl 43 CD20
French's Cl, Stans.Abb. SG12 33 EB11
French St, Sun. TW16 196 BW96
Westerham TN16 255 ES128
French's Wells, Wok. GU21 226 AV117
Frenchum Gdns, Slou. SL1 131 AL74
Frendsbury Rd, SE4 163 DY84
Frensham, Chsht EN7 66 DT27
Frensham Cl, Sthl. UB1 136 BZ70
Frensham Ct, Mitch. CR4 200 DD97
Frensham Dr, SW15 179 CU89
New Addington CR0 221 EC108
Frensham Rd, SE9 185 ER89
Kenley CR8 219 DP114
Frensham St, SE15 312 D3
Frensham Wk, Farn.Com. SL2 111 AQ64
Frensham Way, Epsom KT17 233 CW116
Frere St, SW11 308 D8
Freshborough Ct, Guil. GU1
off Lower Edgeborough Rd 259 AZ135
Freshfield Av, E8 278 A7
Freshfield Cl, SE13
off Mercator Rd 163 ED84
Freshfield Dr, N14 99 DH45
Freshfields, Croy. CR0 203 DZ101
Freshfields Av, Upmin. RM14 128 FP64
Freshford St, SW18 180 DC90
Freshmount Gdns, Epsom KT19 238 CP111
Freshwater Cl, SW17 180 DG93
Freshwater Rd, SW17 180 DG93
Dagenham RM8 126 EX60
Freshwaters, Harl. CM20
off School La 35 ES14
Freshwell Av, Rom. RM6 126 EW56
Fresh Wf, Bark. IG11 145 EP67
● Fresh Wf Est, Bark. IG11
off Fresh Wf 145 EP67
Freshwood Cl, Beck. BR3 203 EB95
Freshwood Way, Wall. SM6 219 DH109
Freston Gdns, Barn. EN4 80 DG43
Freston Pk, N3 97 CZ54
Freston Rd, W10 282 C10
W11 294 D1
Freta Rd, Bexh. DA6 186 EZ85
Fretherne Rd, Welw.G.C. AL8 29 CX09
Fretwell Ho, N14
off Chase Side 99 DK46
★ Freud Mus, NW3 274 A4
Frewin Rd, SW18 180 DD88
Frithe, The, Slou. SL2 132 AV72
Friar Ms, SE27 181 DP90
Friar Rd, Hayes UB4 136 BX70
Orpington BR5 206 EU99
Friars, The, Chig. IG7 103 ES49
Harlow CM19 51 EN17
Friars Av, N20 98 DE48
SW15 179 CT90
Shenfield CM15 109 GA46
Friars Cl, E4 101 EC48
SE1 298 G3
Ilford IG1 125 ER60
Northolt UB5
off Broomcroft Av 136 BX69
Shenfield CM15 109 FZ45
Friarscroft, Brox. EN10 49 EA20
Friars Croft, Guil. GU4 243 BC131
Friars Fld, Nthch HP4
off Herons Elm 38 AS16
Friars Gdns, W3
off St. Dunstans Av 138 CR72
Friars Gate, Guil. GU2 258 AU136
Friars Gate Cl, Wdf.Grn. IG8 102 EG49
Friars La, Hat.Hth CM22 37 FH06
Richmond TW9 177 CK85
Friars Mead, E14 302 E7
Friars Ms, SE9 185 EN85
Friars Orchard, Fetch. KT22 231 CD121
Friars Pl La, W3 138 CR73
Sch Friars Prim Sch, SE1 299 H4
Friars Ri, Wok. GU22 227 BA118
Friars Rd, E6 144 EK67
Virginia Water GU25 192 AX98
Friars Stile Pl, Rich. TW10
off Friars Stile Rd 178 CL86
Friars Stile Rd, Rich. TW10 178 CL86
Friar St, EC4 287 H9
Friars Wk, N14 99 DH46
SE2 166 EX78
Friars Way, W3 138 CR72
Bushey WD23 76 BZ39
Chertsey KT16 194 BG100
Kings Langley WD4 58 BN30
Friars Wd, Croy. CR0 221 DY109
Friary, The, Old Wind. SL4 172 AW86
Waltham Cross EN8 67 DZ33
Friary Br, Guil. GU1 258 AW135
Friary Cl, N12 98 DE50
Friary Ct, SW1 297 M3
Woking GU21 226 AT118
Friary Est, SE15 312 D3
Friary Island, Wrays. TW19 172 AW86
Friary La, Wdf.Grn. IG8 102 EG49
Friary Pk Est, W3 off Friary Rd 138 CR72
Friary Pas, Guil. GU1
off Friary St 258 AW136
Friary Rd, N12 98 DD49
SE15 312 D3
W3 138 CR72
Wraysbury TW19 172 AW86
Friary Shop Cen, The, Guil. GU1
off Onslow St 258 AW135
Friary St, Guil. GU1 258 AW136
Friary Way, N12 98 DE49
FRIDAY HILL, E4 101 ED47
Friday Hill, E4 102 EE47
Friday Hill E, E4 102 EE48
Friday Hill W, E4 102 EE47
Friday Rd, Erith DA8 167 FD78
Mitcham CR4 180 DF94
FRIDAY STREET, Dor. RH5 262 BZ143
Friday St, EC4 287 J9
Abinger Common RH5 262 BZ143
Frideswide Pl, NW5 275 L3
Friendly Pl, SE13 314 D7
Friendly St, SE8 314 A8
Friendly St Ms, SE8 314 A8
Friends Av, Chsht EN8 67 DX31
Friendship Wk, Nthlt. UB5
off Wayfarer Rd 136 BX69
Friendship Way, E15 280 F8
Friends Rd, Croy. CR0 202 DR104
Purley CR8 219 DP112
Friend St, EC1 286 G2
Friends Wk, Stai. TW18 173 BF92
Uxbridge UB8 off Bakers Rd 134 BK66
FRIERN BARNET, N11 98 DE49
Friern Barnet La, N11 98 DE49
N20 98 DE49
Friern Barnet Rd, N11 98 DF50
Sch Friern Barnet Sch, N11
off Hemington Av 98 DF50
Friern Br Retail Pk, N11 99 DH51
Friern Cl, Chsht EN7 66 DS26
Friern Ct, N20 98 DD48
Friern Mt Dr, N20 98 DC45
Friern Pk, N12 98 DC50
Friern Rd, SE22 182 DU86
Friern Watch Av, N12 98 DC49
Frigate Ms, SE8 314 A2
Frimley Av, Horn. RM11 128 FN60
Wallington SM6 219 DL106
Frimley Cl, SW19 179 CY89
New Addington CR0 221 EC108
Frimley Ct, Sid. DA14 186 EV92
Frimley Cres, New Adgtn CR0 221 EC108
Frimley Dr, Slou. SL1 151 AM75
Frimley Gdns, Mitch. CR4 200 DE97
Frimley Rd, Chess. KT9 216 CL106
Hemel Hempstead HP1 39 BE19
Ilford IG3 125 ES62
Frimley Way, E1 289 J4
Fringewood Cl, Nthwd. HA6 93 BP53
Frinstead Gro, Orp. BR5 206 EX98
Frinstead Ho, W10 282 C10
Frinsted Rd, Erith DA8 167 FD80
Frinton Cl, Wat. WD19 93 BV47
Frinton Dr, Wdf.Grn. IG8 101 ED52
Frinton Ms, Ilf. IG2 125 EN58
Frinton Rd, E6 292 E3
N15 122 DS58
SW17 180 DG93
Romford RM5 104 EZ52
Sidcup DA14 186 EY89
Friston Path, Chig. IG7 103 ES50
Friston St, SW6 307 L9
Friswell Pl, Bexh. DA6 166 FA84
Fritham Cl, N.Mal. KT3 198 CS100
Frith Ct, NW7 97 CY52
Frith Knowle, Hersham KT12 213 BV106
Frith La, NW7 97 CY52
Sch Frith Manor Prim Sch, N12
off Lullington Garth 97 CZ50
Frith Rd, E11 123 EC63
Croydon CR0 202 DQ103
Frithsden Copse, Pott.End HP4 39 AZ15
Frithsden Rd, Berk. HP4 38 AY17
Friths Dr, Reig. RH2 250 DB131
Frith St, W1 285 N9
Frithville Gdns, W12 294 A2
Frithwald Rd, Cher. KT16 193 BF101
Frithwood Av, Nthwd. HA6 93 BS51
Sch Frithwood Prim Sch, Nthwd. HA6
off Carew Rd 93 BT51
Frizlands La, Dag. RM10 127 FB63
Frobisher Cl, Bushey WD23 76 CA44
Kenley CR8 off Hayes La 236 DQ117
Pinner HA5 116 BX59
Frobisher Cres, EC2
off The Barbican 287 K6
Staines-upon-Thames TW19 174 BL87
Frobisher Gdns,
Chaff.Hun. RM16 170 FY76
Guildford GU1 243 BA133
Staines-upon-Thames TW19 174 BL87
Frobisher Ms, Enf. EN2 82 DR42
Frobisher Pas, E14 302 B2
Frobisher Pl, SE15 312 G7
Frobisher Rd, E6 293 K8
N8 121 DN56
Erith DA8 167 FF80
St. Albans AL1 43 CJ22
Frobisher St, SE10 315 K2
Frobisher Way, Grav. DA12 191 GL92
Greenhithe DA9 169 FV84
Hatfield AL10 44 CR15
Froggy La, Denh. UB9 113 BD62
Froghall La, Chig. IG7 103 ER49
FROGHOLE, Eden. TN8 255 ER133
Froghole La, Eden. TN8 255 ER132
Frog La, Sutt.Grn GU4 242 AY125
Frogley Rd, SE22 162 DT84
Frogmoor La, Rick. WD3 92 BK47
FROGMORE, St.Alb. AL2 61 CE28
Frogmore, SW18 180 DA85
St. Albans AL2 61 CD27
Frogmore Av, Hayes UB4 135 BS69
Frogmore Cl, Slou. SL1 151 AN75
Sutton SM3 199 CX104
Frogmore Dr, Wind. SL4 152 AS81
● Frogmore Est, Grays RM20 169 FU78
Frogmore Gdns, Hayes UB4 135 BS70
Sutton SM3 217 CY105
Frogmore Home Pk, St.Alb. AL2 83 CD27
● Frogmore Ind Est, N5 277 J1
NW10 138 CQ69
Frogmore Rd, Hem.H. HP3 40 BK23
Frognal, NW3 273 N4
Frognal Av, Har. HA1 117 CF56
Sidcup DA14 186 EU92
Frognal Cl, NW3 273 N2
Jct Frognal Cor, Sid. DA14 185 ET93
Frognal Ct, NW3 273 P4
Frognal Gdns, NW3 273 N1
Frognal La, NW3 273 L2
Frognal Par, NW3
off Frognal Ct 273 P4
Frognal Pl, Sid. DA14 186 EU93
Frognal Ri, NW3 120 DC63
Frognal Way, NW3 273 N1
Froissart Rd, SE9 184 EK85
Frome Rd, N22 121 DP55
Fromer Rd, Woob.Grn HP10 110 AD59
Frome Sq, Hem.H. HP2
off Waveney 40 BM15
Frome St, N1 277 J10
Fromondes Rd, Sutt. SM3 217 CY106
Front, The, Pott.End HP4 39 BB16
Front La, Upmin. RM14 129 FS59
Frostic Wk, E1 288 B7
Froude St, SW8 309 K9
Frowick Cl, N.Mymms AL9 45 CW23
Frowyke Cres, S.Mimms EN6 63 CU32
Fruen Rd, Felt. TW14 175 BT87
Fruiterers Pas, EC4
off Southwark Br 299 K1
Fryatt Rd, N17 100 DR52
Fry Cl, Rom. RM5 104 FA50
Fryday Gro Ms, SW12 181 DJ87
Fryent Cl, NW9 118 CN58
Fryent Cres, NW9 118 CS58
Fryent Flds, NW9 118 CS58
Fryent Gro, NW9 118 CS58
Sch Fryent Prim Sch, NW9
off Church La 118 CQ59
Fryent Way, NW9 118 CN57
Fryer Cl, Chesh. HP5 54 AR33
Fryern Wd, Chaldon CR3 236 DQ124
Frying Pan All, E1 288 A7
Frymley Vw, Wind. SL4 151 AK81
Fry Rd, E6 144 EK66
NW10 139 CT67
Fryston Av, Couls. CR5 219 DH114
Croydon CR0 202 DU103
Fryth Mead, St.Alb. AL3 42 CB19
Fuchsia Cl, Rush Grn RM7 127 FE61
Fuchsia St, SE2 166 EV78
Fulbeck Dr, NW9 96 CS53
Fulbeck Wk, Edg. HA8
off Burrell Cl 96 CP47
Fulbeck Way, Har. HA2 94 CC54
Fulbourne Cl, Red. RH1
off Dennis Cl 250 DE132
Fulbourne Rd, E17 101 EC53
Fulbourne St, E1 288 E6
Fulbrook Av, New Haw KT15 212 BG111
Fulbrook La, S.Ock. RM15 149 FT73
Fulbrook Ms, N19
off Junction Rd 121 DJ63
Fulbrook Rd, N19
off Junction Rd 121 DJ63
Fulford Gro, Wat. WD19 93 BV47
Fulford Rd, Cat. CR3 236 DR121
Epsom KT19 216 CR108
Fulford St, SE16 300 F5
FULHAM, SW6 306 E8
Fulham Br, SW15 159 CY83
⊖ Fulham Broadway 307 K4
Fulham Bdy, SW6 307 K4
Fulham Bdy Retail Cen, SW6
off Fulham Bdy 307 K4
Fulham Cl, Uxb. UB10 135 BQ71
Fulham Ct, SW6 307 J6
Sch Fulham Cross Girls' Sch, SW6 38 E4
★ Fulham FC, SW6 306 C7
Fulham High St, SW6 306 F9
★ Fulham Palace, SW6 306 E9
Fulham Palace Rd, SW6 306 D4
W6 294 B10
Fulham Pk Gdns, SW6 306 G9
Fulham Pk Rd, SW6 306 G8
Sch Fulham Prep Sch,
Pre-Prep, SW6 306 F9
Prep, W14 306 F2
Sch Fulham Prim Sch, SW6 307 J3
Fulham Rd, SW3 308 A1
SW6 307 L5
SW10 308 A1
Fulkes Cotts, Lthd. KT24 245 BP128
Fullarton Cres, S.Ock. RM15 149 FT72
Fullbrooks Av, Wor.Pk. KT4 199 CT102
Sch Fullbrook Sch, New Haw KT15
off Selsdon Rd 212 BG111
Fuller Cl, E2 288 C4
Bushey WD23 95 CD45
Orpington BR6 223 ET106
Fuller Gdns, Wat. WD24 75 BV37
Fullerian Cres, Wat. WD18 75 BT42
Fuller Rd, Dag. RM8 126 EV62
Watford WD24 75 BV37
Fullers Av, Surb. KT6 198 CM103
Woodford Green IG8 102 EF52
Fullers Cl, Chesh. HP5 54 AP32
Romford RM5 105 FC52
Waltham Abbey EN9 68 EG33
Fullers Fm Rd, W.Hors. KT24 245 BP134
★ Fuller's Griffin Brewery, W4 159 CT79
Fullers Hill, Chesh. HP5 54 AM34
Hyde Heath HP6 54 AM34
Westerham TN16
off Market Sq 255 ER126
Fullers La, Rom. RM5 105 FC52
Fullers Mead, Harl. CM17 52 EW16
Fullers Rd, E18 102 EF53
Fuller St, NW4 119 CW56
Fullers Way N, Surb. KT6 198 CM104
Fullers Way S, Chess. KT9 216 CL105
Fullers Wd, Croy. CR0 221 EA106
Fullers Wd La, S.Nutfld RH1 251 DJ134
Fuller Ter, Ilf. IG1
off Oaktree Gro 125 ER64
Fullerton Cl, Byfleet KT14 212 BM114
Fullerton Dr, Byfleet KT14 212 BL114
Fullerton Rd, SW18 180 DC85
Byfleet KT14 212 BM114
Carshalton SM5 218 DE109
Croydon CR0 202 DT101
Fullerton Way, Byfleet KT14 212 BL114
Fuller Way, Crox.Grn WD3 74 BN43
Hayes UB3 155 BT78
Fullmer Way, Wdhm KT15 211 BF110
Fullwell Av, Ilf. IG5, IG6 103 EM53
FULLWELL CROSS, Ilf. IG6 103 ER53
Fullwell Cross Rbt, Ilf. IG6
off High St 103 ER54
Sch Fullwood Prim Sch, Barkingside IG6
off Burford Cl 125 EQ56
Fullwoods Ms, N1 287 M2
Fulmar Cl, Surb. KT5 198 CM100
Fulmar Cres, Hem.H. HP1 40 BG21
Fulmar Rd, Horn. RM12 147 FG66
Fulmead St, SW6 307 M7
FULMER, Slou. SL3 112 AX63
Fulmer Cl, Hmptn. TW12 176 BY92
Fulmer Common Rd,
Fulmer SL3 133 AZ65
Iver SL0 133 AZ65
Fulmer Dr, Ger.Cr. SL9 112 AY61
Sch Fulmer Inf Sch, Fulmer SL3
off Alderbourne La 112 AY63
Fulmer La, Fulmer SL3 112 AY62
Gerrards Cross SL9 113 BB60
Fulmer Ri, Fulmer SL3 133 AZ65
Fulmer Rd, E16 292 E7
Fulmer SL3 112 AY63
Gerrards Cross SL9 112 AY59
Fulmer Way, W13 157 CH76
Gerrards Cross SL9 112 AY58
Fulready Rd, E10 123 ED57
Fulstone Cl, Houns. TW4 156 BZ84
Fulthorp Rd, SE3 315 M8
Fulton Ct, Borwd. WD6 78 CM38
Enfield EN3 off Harston Dr 83 EA38
Fulton Ms, W2 283 N10
Fulton Rd, Wem. HA9 118 CN62
Fulvens, Peasl. GU5 261 BS143
Fulvens Cotts, Peasl. GU5 261 BS142
⇌ Fulwell 177 CD91
Fulwell Pk Av, Twick. TW2 176 CB89
Fulwell Rd, Tedd. TW11 177 CD91
Fulwich Rd, Dart. DA1 188 FM86
Fulwood Av, Wem. HA0 138 CM67
Fulwood Cl, Hayes UB3 135 BT72
Fulwood Gdns, Twick. TW1 177 CF86
Fulwood Pl, WC1 286 D7
Fulwood Wk, SW19 179 CY88
Furber St, W6 159 CV76
Furham Feild, Pnr. HA5 94 CA52
Furley Rd, SE15 312 D5
Furlong Cl, Wall. SM6 201 DH102
Furlong Rd, N7 276 F4
Westcott RH4 262 CC137
Furlongs, Hem.H. HP1 40 BG19
Furlongs, The, Esher KT10 196 CB104
Furlong Way, Gat. RH6
off Racecourse Way 268 DF151
Great Amwell SG12 33 DZ09
Furlough, The, Wok. GU22
off Pembroke Rd 227 BA117
Furmage St, SW18 180 DB87
Furneaux Av, SE27 181 DP92
Furner Cl, Dart. DA1 167 FF83

F

Furness, Wind. SL4 150 AJ82
Furness Cl, Grays RM16 171 GH78
Furness Pl, Wind. SL4
off Furness 150 AJ82
Sch Furness Prim Sch, NW10
off Palermo Rd 139 CU68
Furness Rd, NW10 139 CU68
SW6 307 M8
Harrow HA2 116 CB59
Morden SM4 200 DB101
Furness Row, Wind. SL4
off Furness 150 AJ82
Sch Furness Sch, Hext. BR8
off Rowhill Rd 187 FF93
Furness Sq, Wind. SL4
off Furness 150 AJ82
Furness Wk, Wind. SL4
off Furness 150 AJ82
Furness Way, Horn. RM12 127 FG64
Windsor SL4 150 AJ82
Furnival Av, Slou. SL2 131 AP71
Furnival Cl, Vir.W. GU25 192 AX100
Furnival St, EC4 286 E8
Furrowfield, Hat. AL10
off Stonecross Rd 45 CV16
Furrow La, E9 279 H3
Furrows, The, Hare. UB9 114 BJ57
Walton-on-Thames KT12 196 BW103
Furrows Pl, Cat. CR3 236 DT123
Fursby Av, N3 98 DA51
Furse Av, St.Alb. AL4 43 CG17
Further Acre, NW9 97 CT54
Furtherfield, Abb.L. WD5 59 BS32
Furtherfield Cl, Croy. CR0 201 DN100
Further Grn Rd, SE6 184 EE87
Furtherground, Hem.H. HP2 40 BL21
Furzebushes La, St.Alb. AL2 60 BY25
Furze Cl, Horl. RH6 269 DK148
Redhill RH1 250 DF133
Watford WD19 94 BW50
FURZEDOWN, SW17 180 DG92
Furzedown Cl, Egh. TW20 172 AY93
Furzedown Dr, SW17 181 DH92
Furzedown Hall, SW17
off Spalding Rd 181 DH92
Sch Furzedown Prim Sch, SW17
off Beclands Rd 180 DG93
Furzedown Rd, SW17 181 DH92
Sutton SM2 218 DC111
Furze Fm Cl, Rom. RM6 104 EY54
Furzefield, Chsht EN8 66 DV28
Furze Fld, Oxshott KT22 215 CD113
Furzefield Cl, Chis. BR7 185 EP93
Furzefield Ct, Pot.B. EN6 63 CY31
Furzefield Cres, Reig. RH2 266 DC136
Sch Furzefield Prim Comm Sch,
Merst. RH1 off Delabole Rd 251 DK128
Furzefield Rd, SE3 164 EH79
Beaconsfield HP9 88 AJ53
Reigate RH2 266 DC136
Welwyn Garden City AL7 29 CY10
Furzeground Way, Uxb. UB11 135 BQ74
Furze Gro, Kgswd KT20 233 CZ121
Furzeham Rd, West Dr. UB7 154 BL75
Furze Hill, Kgswd KT20 233 CZ120
Purley CR8 219 DL111
Redhill RH1 off Linkfield La 250 DE133
Furzehill Par, Borwd. WD6
off Shenley Rd 78 CN41
Furzehill Rd, Borwd. WD6 78 CN42
Furzehill Sq, St.M.Cray BR5 206 EV98
Sch Furze Inf Sch, Chad.Hth RM6
off Bennett Rd 126 EY58
Furze La, Gdmg. GU7 258 AT143
Purley CR8 219 DL111
Furzen Cl, Slou. SL2 131 AN69
Furzen Cres, Hat. AL10 45 CT21
Furze Rd, Add. KT15 211 BF107
Hemel Hempstead HP1 39 BE21
Thornton Heath CR7 202 DQ97
Furze St, E3 290 B6
Furze Vw, Chorl. WD3 73 BC44
Furzewood, Sun. TW16 195 BU95
Fuschia Ct, Wdf.Grn. IG8
off The Bridle Path 102 EE52
Fusedale Way, S.Ock. RM15 149 FT73
Fusiliers Way, Houns. TW4 156 BW83
Fuzzens Wk, Wind. SL4 151 AL82
Fyefoot La, EC4
off Queen Victoria St 287 J10
Fyfe Apts, N8 off Chadwell La 121 DM55
Fyfe Way, Brom. BR1
off Widmore Rd 204 EG96
Fyfield, N4 off Six Acres Est 121 DN61
Fyfield Cl, Bromley BR2 203 ED98
Epsom KT17 217 CT114
Fyfield Ct, E7 281 N4
Fyfield Dr, S.Ock. RM15 149 FT73
Fyfield Rd, E17 123 ED55
SW9 310 F10
Enfield EN1 82 DS41
Rainham RM13 147 FF67
Woodford Green IG8 102 EJ52
Fynes St, SW1 297 N8

G

Gabion Av, Purf. RM19 169 FR77
Gable Cl, Abb.L. WD5 59 BS32
Dartford DA1 187 FG85
Pinner HA5 94 CA52
Gable Ct, SE26
off Lawrie Pk Av 182 DV91
Gables, The, Bans. SM7 233 CZ117
Guildford GU2 242 AV131
Hemel Hempstead HP2
off Chapel St 40 BK19
Oxshott KT22 214 CC112
Wembley HA9 118 CN62
Weybridge KT13 213 BQ106
Gables Av, Ashf. TW15 174 BM92
Borehamwood WD6 78 CM41
Gables Cl, SE5 311 N6
SE12 184 EG88
Chalfont St. Peter SL9 90 AY49
Datchet SL3 152 AU79
Kingfield GU22
off Kingfield Rd 227 AZ120
Gables Ct, Kgfld GU22
off Kingfield Rd 227 AZ120
Pur. CR8 off Godstone Rd 219 DP112
Gables Way, Bans. SM7 233 CZ117
Gabriel Cl, Chaff.Hun. RM16 169 FW76
Feltham TW13 176 BX91
Romford RM5 105 FC52
Gabriel Gdns, Grav. DA12 191 GL92
Gabrielle Cl, Wem. HA9 118 CM62
Gabrielle Ct, NW3 274 B5
Gabrielle Ho, Ilf. IG2
off Perth Rd 125 EN58
Gabriel Ms, NW2 119 CZ61
Gabriel's Ms, Beck. BR3 203 DX95
Gabriel Spring Rd,
Fawk.Grn DA3 209 FR103
Gabriel Spring Rd (East),
Fawk.Grn DA3 209 FS103
Gabriel St, SE23 183 DX87
Gabriel's Wf, SE1 298 E2
Gadbrook Rd, Bet. RH3 264 CS139
Gad Cl, E13 292 A2
Gaddesden Av, Wem. HA9 138 CM65
Gaddesden Cres, Wat. WD25 60 BX34
Gaddesden Gro, Welw.G.C. AL7
off Widford Rd 30 DC09
Gade Av, Wat. WD18 75 BS42
Gade Bk, Crox.Grn WD3 75 BR42
GADEBRIDGE, Hem.H. HP1 39 BF18
Gadebridge La, Hem.H. HP1 40 BJ18
Gadebridge Rd, Hem.H. HP1 40 BG18
Gadebury Hts, Hem.H. HP1 40 BJ20
Gade Cl, Hayes UB3 135 BV74
Hemel Hempstead HP1 40 BH17
Watford WD18 75 BS42
Gadesden Rd, Epsom KT19 216 CQ107
Gadeside, Wat. WD25 75 BS35
Gade Twr, Hem.H. HP3 58 BN25
Gade Valley Cl, Kings L. WD4 58 BN28
Sch Gade Valley JMI Sch, Hem.H. HP1
off Gadebridge Rd 40 BH19
Gade Vw Gdns, Kings L. WD4 59 BQ32
Gadeview Rd, Hem.H. HP3 40 BK24
Gadsbury Cl, NW9 119 CT58
Gadsden Cl, Upmin. RM14 129 FS58
Gadswell Cl, Wat. WD25 76 BX36
Gadwall Cl, E16 292 A8
Gadwall Way, SE28 165 ER75
Gage Ms, S.Croy. CR2 220 DQ106
Gage Rd, E16 291 K6
Gage St, WC1 286 B6
Gainford St, N1 276 E8
Gainsboro Gdns, Grnf. UB6 117 CE64
Gainsborough Av, E12 125 EN64
Dartford DA1 188 FJ85
St. Albans AL1 43 CF19
Tilbury RM18 171 GG81
Gainsborough Cl, Beck. BR3 183 EA94
Esher KT10 197 CE102
Sch Gainsborough Comm Sch, E9 280 A4
Gainsborough Ct, N12 98 DB50
W12 294 A5
Bromley BR2 204 EJ98
Walton-on-Thames KT12 213 BU105
Gainsborough Dr, Nthflt DA11 190 GD90
South Croydon CR2 220 DU113
Gainsborough Gdns, NW3 120 DD62
NW11 119 CZ59
Edgware HA8 96 CM54
Isleworth TW7 177 CD85
Gainsborough Ho, E14 302 B5
Enfield EN1 off Ayley Cft 82 DU43
Gainsborough Ms, SE26
off Panmure Rd 182 DV90
Gainsborough Pl, Chig. IG7 103 ET48
Cobham KT11 230 BY115
Sch Gainsborough Prim Sch, E15 291 K3
Gainsborough Rd, E11 124 EE59
E15 291 J3
N12 98 DB50
W4 159 CT77
Dagenham RM8 126 EV63
Epsom KT19 216 CQ110
Hayes UB4 135 BQ68
New Malden KT3 198 CR101
Rainham RM13 147 FG67
Richmond TW9 158 CM83
Woodford Green IG8 102 EL51
Gainsborough Sq, Bexh. DA6
off Regency Way 166 EX83
Gainsborough Studios, N1 277 L9
Gainsford Rd, E17 123 DZ56
Gainsford St, SE1 300 A4
Gainswood, Welw.G.C. AL7 29 CY10
Gairloch Rd, SE5 311 P8
Gaisford St, NW5 275 L4
Gaist Av, Cat. CR3 236 DU122
Gaitskell Ct, SW11 308 B8
Gaitskell Ho, Borwd. WD6 78 CR42
Gaitskell Rd, SE9 185 EQ88
Gaitskell Way, SE1 off Weller St 31 J4
Galahad Cl, Slou. SL1 151 AN75
Galahad Rd, N9 100 DU48
Bromley BR1 184 EG90
Galata Rd, SW13 159 CU80
Galatea Sq, SE15 312 E10
Galaxy, E14
off Crews St 302 A8
Galba Ct, Brent. TW8
off Augustus Cl 157 CK80
Galbraith St, E14 302 E6
Galdana Av, Barn. EN5 80 DC41
Galeborough Av, Wdf.Grn. IG8 101 ED52
Gale Cl, Hmptn. TW12 176 BY93
Mitcham CR4 200 DD97
Gale Cres, Bans. SM7 234 DA117
Galena Ho, SE18
off Grosmont Rd 165 ET78
Galena Rd, W6 159 CV77
Galen Cl, Epsom KT19 216 CN111
Galen Pl, WC1 286 B7
Galesbury Rd, SW18 180 DC86
Gales Cl, Guil. GU4
off Gilliat Dr 243 BD132
Gales Gdns, E2 288 F3
Gale St, E3 290 B6
Dagenham RM9 146 EX67
Gales Way, Wdf.Grn. IG8 102 EL52
Galey Grn, S.Ock. RM15
off Bovey Way 149 FV71
Galgate Cl, SW19 179 CY88
Gallants Fm Rd, E.Barn. EN4 98 DE45
Galleon Boul, Dart. DA2 169 FR84
Galleon Cl, SE16 301 H4
Erith DA8 167 FD77
Galleon Ho, SW8
off St. George Wf 310 A2
Galleon Ms, Grav. DA11
off Maritime Gate 190 GE87
Galleon Rd, Chaff.Hun. RM16 169 FW77
Galleons Dr, Bark. IG11 146 EU69
Galleons La, Geo.Grn SL3 132 AX71
Galleons Vw, E14
off Stewart St 302 F5
Galleria, The, Hat. AL10 44 CS18
Galleries, The, Brwd. CM14 108 FV50
Gallery Ct, Egh. TW20
off The Chantries 173 BA92
Gallery Gdns, Nthlt. UB5 136 BX68
Gallery Rd, SE21 182 DR88
Galley, The, E16 305 P1
Galley Grn, Hailey SG13 33 EA13
Galley Hill, Hem.H. HP1 39 BF18
Waltham Abbey EN9 68 EF30
Galley Hill Rd, Nthflt DA11 190 FZ85
Swanscombe DA10 190 FZ85
● Galley Hill Trade Pk,
Swans. DA10 190 FY85
Galley La, Barn. EN5 79 CV41
Galleymead Rd, Colnbr. SL3 153 BF81
Galleywall Rd, SE16 300 E9
Galleywood Cres, Rom. RM5 105 FD51
Galliard Cl, N9 82 DW44
Sch Galliard Prim Sch, N9
off Galliard Rd 82 DU44
Galliard Rd, N9 100 DU46
Gallia Rd, N5 277 H3
Gallica Ct, Sutt. SM1
off Cleeve Way 200 DB102
Gallions Cl, Bark. IG11 146 EU69
Sch Gallions Mt Prim Sch, SE18
off Purrett Rd 165 ET78
Sch Gallions Prim Sch, E6 293 N8
DLR Gallions Reach 293 P10
Gallions Reach Shop Pk, E6 145 EQ71
Gallions Rd, E16 305 P1
SE7 304 B9
Jct Gallions Rbt, E16 293 N10
Gallions Vw Rd, SE28
off Goldfinch Rd 165 ES75
Gallipoli Pl, Dag. RM9 146 EV67
Gallon Cl, SE7 304 D9
Gallop, The, S.Croy. CR2 220 DV108
Sutton SM2 218 DC108
Gallops, The, Esher KT10 196 CB104
Tadworth KT20 249 CV126
Gallosson Rd, SE18 165 ES77
Galloway Chase, Slou. SL2 132 AU73
Galloway Cl, Brox. EN10 67 DZ26
Galloway Dr, Dart. DA1 187 FE87
Galloway Path, Croy. CR0 220 DR105
Galloway Rd, W12 139 CU74
Jct Gallows Cor,
Harold Wd RM3 106 FK53
Gallows Hill, Kings L. WD4 59 BQ31
Gallows Hill La, Abb.L. WD5 59 BQ32
Gallus Cl, N21 81 DM44
Gallus Sq, SE3 164 EH83
Gallys Rd, Wind. SL4 151 AK82
Galpins Rd, Th.Hth. CR7 201 DM98
Galsworthy Av, E14 289 M7
Romford RM6 126 EV59
Galsworthy Cl, SE28 146 EV74
Galsworthy Cres, SE3
off Merriman Rd 164 EJ81
Galsworthy Rd, NW2 119 CY63
Chertsey KT16 194 BG101
Kingston upon Thames KT2 178 CP94
Tilbury RM18 171 GJ81
Galsworthy Ter, N16 122 DS62
Galton St, W10 282 E4
Galva Cl, Barn. EN4 80 DG42
Galvani Way, Croy. CR0
off Ampere Way 201 DM102
Galveston Rd, SW15 179 CZ85
Galvin Rd, Slou. SL1 131 AQ74
Galvins Cl, Guil. GU2 242 AU131
Galway Cl, SE16 312 F1
Galway Ho, EC1 287 K3
Galway St, EC1 287 K3
Gambetta St, SW8 309 K9
Gambia St, SE1 299 H3
Gambier Ho, EC1 287 K2
Gambles La, Ripley GU23 228 BJ124
Gambole Rd, SW17 180 DE91
Games Ho, SE7
off Springfield Gro 164 EJ79
Games Rd, Barn. EN4 80 DF41
Gamlen Rd, SW15 159 CX84
Gammon Cl, Hem.H. HP3 40 BN21
Gammons Fm Cl, Wat. WD24 75 BT36
Gammons La, Brox. EN10 66 DT25
Watford WD24 75 BV38
Gamuel Cl, E17 123 EA58
Gander Grn Cres,
Hmptn. TW12 196 CA95
Gander Grn La,
Sutt. SM1, SM3 199 CY103
Ganders Ash, Wat. WD25 59 BU33
Gandhi Cl, E17 123 EA58
Gandolfi St, SE15 311 N3
Gangers Hill, Gdse. RH9 253 EA127
Woldingham CR3 253 EA127
Ganghill, Guil. GU1 243 BA132
Ganley Ct, SW11
off Newcomen Rd 160 DD83
Ganley Rd, SW11 308 B10
Gant Ct, Wal.Abb. EN9 68 EF34
Ganton St, W1 285 L10
Ganton Wk, Wat. WD19 94 BX49
GANTS HILL, Ilf. IG2 125 EN57
⊖ Gants Hill 125 EN58
Jct Gants Hill, Ilf. IG2
off Eastern Av 125 EN58
Gantshill Cres, Ilf. IG2 125 EN57
Ganwick, Barn. EN5 80 DA36
GANWICK CORNER, Barn. EN5 80 DB35
Ganymede Pl, Hem.H. HP2
off Jupiter Dr 40 BM18
Gap Rd, SW19 180 DA92
Garage Rd, W3 138 CN72
Garand Ct, N7 276 D2
Garbrand Wk, Epsom KT17 217 CT109
Garbutt Pl, W1 285 H6
Garbutt Rd, Upmin. RM14 128 FQ61
Sch Garden, The, N16 277 P1
Garden Av, Bexh. DA7 166 FA83
Hatfield AL10 45 CU22
Mitcham CR4 181 DH94
Garden City, Edg. HA8 96 CN51
Garden Cl, E4 101 EA50
SE12 184 EH90
SW15 179 CV87
Addlestone KT15 212 BK105
Arkley EN5 79 CW42
Ashford TW15 175 BQ93
Banstead SM7 234 DA115
Hampton TW12 176 BZ92
Leatherhead KT22 231 CJ124
New Malden KT3 198 CS98
Northolt UB5 136 BY67
Ruislip HA4 115 BS61
St. Albans AL1 43 CH19
Wallington SM6 219 DL106
Watford WD17 75 BT40
Garden Cotts, Orp. BR5
off Main Rd 206 EW96
Garden Ct, EC4 286 E10
N12 98 DB50
Richmond TW9 158 CM81
Stanmore HA7 95 CJ50
Welwyn Garden City AL7 29 CY08
West Molesey KT8
off Avern Rd 196 CB98
● Garden Ct Business Cen,
Welw.G.C. AL7 off Garden Ct 29 CZ08
Garden End, Amer. HP6 55 AS37
Gardeners Cl, N11 98 DG47
SE9 184 EL90
Gardeners Rd, Croy. CR0 201 DP102
Gardeners Wk, Bkhm KT23 246 CB126
Garden Fld La, Berk. HP4 43 AZ21
Sch Garden Flds JMI Sch, St.Alb. AL3
off Townsend Dr 43 CD17
Sch Garden Ho Sch, SW3 296 F10
Gardenia Rd, Brom. BR1 205 EN97
Enfield EN1 82 DS44
Gardenia Way, Wdf.Grn. IG8 102 EG50
Garden La, SW2
off Christchurch Rd 181 DM88
Bromley BR1 184 EH93
Garden Ms, W2 295 K1
Slough SL1 off Littledown Rd 132 AT74
★ Garden Museum, SE1 298 C7
Garden Pl, E8 278 B8
Dartford DA2 188 FK90
Sch Garden Prim Sch, Mitch. CR4
off Abbotts Rd 201 DK97
Garden Reach, Ch.St.G. HP8 72 AX41
Garden Rd, NW8 283 P2
SE20 202 DW95
Abbots Langley WD5 59 BS31
Bromley BR1 184 EH94
Richmond TW9 158 CN83
Sevenoaks TN13 257 FK122
Walton-on-Thames KT12 195 BV100
Garden Row, SE1 298 G7
Northfleet DA11 191 GF90
Gardens, The, E5 122 DT59
SE22 162 DU84
Beckenham BR3 203 EC96
Brookmans Park AL9 63 CY27
Esher KT10 214 CA105
Feltham TW14 175 BR85
Harrow HA1 116 CC58
Pinner HA5 116 BZ58
Watford WD17 75 BT40
Garden St, E1 289 K7
Sch Garden Suburb Inf Sch, NW11
off Childs Way 119 CZ57
Sch Garden Suburb Jun Sch, NW11
off Childs Way 119 CZ57
Garden Ter, SW1 297 N10
Garden Ter Rd, Harl. CM17 36 EW11
Garden Wk, EC2 287 N3
Beckenham BR3 203 DZ95
Coulsdon CR5 235 DH123
Garden Way, NW10 138 CQ65
Loughton IG10 85 EN38
Gardiner Av, NW2 272 A2
Gardiner Cl, Dag. RM8 126 EX63
Enfield EN3 83 DX44
Orpington BR5 206 EW96
Gardiners, The, Harl. CM17 52 EV15
Gardner Cl, E11 124 EH58
Gardner Ct, EC1 off Brewery Sq 18 G4
N5 277 J1
Gardner Gro, Felt. TW13 176 BZ89
● Gardner Ind Est, Beck. BR3 183 DY92
Gardner Pl, Felt. TW14 175 BV86
Gardner Rd, E13 292 A4
Guildford GU1 242 AW134
Gardners La, EC4 287 J10
Gardnor Rd, NW3 off Flask Wk 120 DD63
Gard St, EC1 287 H2
Garendon Gdns, Mord. SM4 200 DB101
Garendon Rd, Mord. SM4 200 DB101
Gareth Cl, Wor.Pk. KT4 199 CX103
Gareth Dr, N9 100 DU47
Gareth Gro, Brom. BR1 184 EG91
Garfield Ms, SW11
off Garfield Rd 161 DH83
Garfield Pl, Wind. SL4
off Russell St 151 AR81
Sch Garfield Prim Sch, N11
off Springfield Rd 99 DJ50
SW19 off Garfield Rd 180 DC93
Garfield Rd, E4 101 ED46
E13 291 M5
SW11 160 DG83
SW19 180 DC92
Addlestone KT15 212 BJ106
Enfield EN3 82 DW42
Twickenham TW1 177 CG88
Garfield St, Wat. WD24 75 BV38
Garford St, E14 302 A1
Garganey Wk, SE28 146 EX73
Garibaldi Rd, Red. RH1 266 DF135
Garibaldi St, SE18 165 ES77
Garland Cl, Chsht EN8 67 DY31
Hemel Hempstead HP2 40 BK19
Garland Ct, SE17
off Wansey St 299 K9
Garland Dr, Houns. TW3 156 CC82
Garland Ho, N16 122 DR62
Kingston upon Thames KT2
off Kingsgate Rd 198 CL95
Garland Rd, SE18 165 ER80
Bromley BR1 205 EP97
Stanmore HA7 96 CL53
Ware SG12 33 DY06
Garlands Ct, Croy. CR0 220 DR105
Garlands Rd, Lthd. KT22 231 CH121
Redhill RH1 266 DF135
Garland Way, Cat. CR3 236 DR122
Hornchurch RM11 128 FL56
Garlichill Rd, Epsom KT18 233 CV117
Garlick Hill, EC4 287 K10
Garlic St, Dor. RH5 246 BZ133
Garlies Rd, SE23 183 DY90
Garlinge Rd, NW2 272 G5
Garman Cl, N18 100 DR50
Garman Rd, N17 100 DW52
Garnault Ms, EC1 286 F3
Garnault Pl, EC1 286 F3
Garnault Rd, Enf. EN1 82 DT38
Garner Cl, Dag. RM8 126 EX60
Garner Dr, Brox. EN10 67 DY26
Garner Rd, E17 101 EC53
Garners Cl, Chal.St.P. SL9 90 AY51
Garners End, Chal.St.P. SL9 90 AY51
Garners Rd, Chal.St.P. SL9 90 AY51
Garner St, E2 288 D1
Garnet Cl, Slou. SL1 151 AN75
Garnet Rd, NW10 138 CS65
Thornton Heath CR7 202 DR98
Garnet St, E1 300 G1
Garnett Cl, SE9 165 EM83
Watford WD24 76 BX37
Garnett Dr, Brick.Wd AL2 60 BZ29
Garnett Rd, NW3 274 E2
Garnett Way, E17
off McEntee Av 101 DY53
Garnet Wk, E6 293 H6
Garnham Cl, N16
off Garnham St 122 DT61
Garnham St, N16 122 DT61
Garnies Cl, SE15 312 A4
Garnon Mead, Cooper. CM16 70 EX28
Garrad's Rd, SW16 181 DK90
Garrard Cl, Bexh. DA7 166 FA83
Chislehurst BR7 185 EP92
Garrard Rd, Bans. SM7 234 DA116
Slough SL2 131 AL70
Garrard Wk, NW10
off Garnet Rd 138 CS65
Garratt Cl, Croy. CR0 219 DL105
Garratt Ho, N16
off Stamford Hill 122 DS60
Garratt La, SW17 180 DD91
SW18 180 DB85
Sch Garratt Pk Sch, SW18
off Waldron Rd 180 DC90
Garratt Rd, Edg. HA8 96 CN52
Garratts Cl, Hert. SG14 32 DQ09
Garratts La, Bans. SM7 233 CZ116
Garratts Rd, Bushey WD23 94 CC45
Garratt Ter, SW17 180 DE91
Garrett Cl, W3 138 CR71
Chesham HP5 54 AQ33
Garrett St, EC1 287 K4
Garrick Av, NW11 119 CY58
Garrick Cl, SW18 160 DC84
W5 138 CL70
Hersham KT12 213 BV105
Richmond TW9
off Old Palace La 177 CK85
Staines-upon-Thames TW18 174 BG94
Garrick Cres, Croy. CR0 202 DS103
Garrick Dr, NW4 97 CW54
SE28 165 ER76
Garrick Gdns, W.Mol. KT8 196 CA97
Garrick Pk, NW4 97 CX54
Garrick Rd, NW9 119 CT58
Greenford UB6 136 CB70
Richmond TW9 158 CN82
● Garrick Rd Ind Est, NW9 119 CT57
Garricks Ho, Kings.T. KT1 197 CK96
Garrick St, WC2 286 A10
Gravesend DA11
off Barrack Row 191 GH86
Garrick Way, NW4 119 CX56
Garrick Yd, WC2
off St. Martin's La 286 A10
Garrison Cl, SE18
off Red Lion La 165 EN80
Hounslow TW4 176 BZ85
Garrison La, Chess. KT9 215 CK108
Garrison Par, Purf. RM19
off Comet Cl 168 FN77
Garrison Rd, E3 279 P9
Garrolds Cl, Swan. BR8 207 FD96
Garron La, S.Ock. RM15 149 FT72
Garrowsfield, Barn. EN5 79 CZ43
Garry Cl, Rom. RM1 105 FE52
Garry Way, Rom. RM1 105 FE52
Garsdale Cl, N11 98 DG51
Garside Cl, SE28 165 ER76
Hampton TW12 176 CB93
Garsington Ms, SE4 163 DZ83
Garsmouth Way, Wat. WD25 76 BX36
Garson Cl, Esher KT10
off Garson Rd 214 BZ107
Garson Gro, Chesh. HP5 54 AN29
Garson La, Wrays. TW19 172 AX87
Garson Mead, Esher KT10 214 BZ106
Garson Rd, Esher KT10 214 BZ107
GARSTON, Wat. WD25 76 BW35
⇌ Garston 76 BX35
Garston Cres, Wat. WD25 60 BW34
Garston Dr, Wat. WD25 60 BW34
Garston Gdns, Ken. CR8
off Godstone Rd 236 DR115
Garston La, Ken. CR8 220 DR114
Watford WD25 60 BX34
Sch Garston Manor Sch, Wat. WD25
off Horseshoe La 60 BW32
Garston Pk Par, Wat. WD25 60 BX34
Garstons, The, Bkhm KT23 246 CA125
Garter Way, SE16 301 J5
Garth, The, N12 98 DB50
Abbots Langley WD5 59 BR33
Cobham KT11 214 BY113
Hampton Hill TW12 176 CB93
Harrow HA3 118 CM58
Garth Cl, W4 158 CR78
Kingston upon Thames KT2 178 CM92
Morden SM4 199 CX101
Ruislip HA4 116 BX60
Garth Ct, W4 158 CR78
Garth Ho, NW2
off Granville Rd 119 CZ61
Garthland Dr, Barn. EN5 79 CV43
Garth Ms, W5
off Greystoke Gdns 138 CL70
Garthorne Rd, SE23 183 DX87
Garth Rd, NW2 119 CZ61
W4 158 CR79
Kingston upon Thames KT2 178 CM92
Morden SM4 199 CW100
Sevenoaks TN13 257 FJ128
South Ockendon RM15 149 FW70
● Garth Rd Ind Cen,
Mord. SM4 199 CX101
Garthside, Ham TW10 178 CL92
Garthway, N12 98 DE51
Gartlet Rd, Wat. WD17 76 BW41
Gartmoor Gdns, SW19 179 CZ88
Gartmore Rd, Ilf. IG3 125 ET60
Garton Bk, Bans. SM7 234 DA117
Garton Pl, SW18 180 DC86
Gartons Cl, Enf. EN3 82 DW43
Gartons Way, SW11 160 DC83
Garvary Rd, E16 292 B9
Garvin Av, Beac. HP9 89 AL52
Garvin Ms, Beac. HP9 89 AL53
Garvock Dr, Sev. TN13 256 FG126
Garway Rd, W2 283 L9
Garwood Cl, N17 100 DV53
Gary Ct, Croy. CR0 201 DP101

F
G

Gascoigne Gdns, Wdf.Grn. IG8 102 EE52
Gascoigne Pl, E2 288 A3
Gascoigne Prim Sch, Bark. IG11
off Gascoigne Rd 145 EQ67
Gascoigne Rd, Bark. IG11 145 EQ67
New Addington CR0 221 EC110
Weybridge KT13 195 BP104
Gascons Gro, Slou. SL2 131 AN70
Gascony Av, NW6 273 J7
Gascony Pl, W12 off Bourbon La 294 C3
Gascoyne Cl, Rom. RM3 106 FK52
South Mimms EN6 63 CU32
Gascoyne Dr, Dart. DA1 167 FF82
Gascoyne Rd, E9 279 K6
Gascoyne Way,
Hert. SG13, SG14 32 DQ09
Gaselee St, E14 302 F1
Gaskarth Rd, SW12 181 DH86
Edgware HA8 96 CQ53
Gaskell Rd, N6 120 DF58
Gaskell St, SW4 310 A8
Gaskin St, N1 276 G8
Gaspar Cl, SW5 295 M8
Gaspar Ms, SW5 295 M8
Gassiot Rd, SW17 180 DF91
Gassiot Way, Sutt. SM1 200 DD104
Gasson Rd, Swans. DA10 190 FY86
Gastein Rd, W6 306 D2
Gaston Bell Cl, Rich. TW9 158 CM83
Gaston Br Rd, Shep. TW17 195 BS99
Gaston Rd, Mitch. CR4 200 DG97
Gaston Way, Shep. TW17 195 BR99
Gas Wks La, Brox. EN10 49 EA19
★ Gasworks Gall, SE11 310 D2
Gataker St, SE16 300 F6
Gatcombe Ho, SE22
off Pytchley Rd 162 DS83
Gatcombe Ms, W5 138 CM73
Gatcombe Rd, E16 303 P2
N19 121 DK62
Gatcombe Way, Barn. EN4 80 DF41
Gate Cl, Borwd. WD6 78 CQ39
Gatecroft, Hem.H. HP3 40 BM22
Gate End, Nthwd. HA6 93 BU52
Gateforth St, NW8 284 C5
Gatehill Rd, Nthwd. HA6 93 BT52
Gatehope Dr, S.Ock. RM15 149 FT72
Gatehouse, The, Rom. RM1 127 FE57
Gatehouse Cl, Kings.T. KT2 178 CQ94
Windsor SL4
off St. Leonards Rd 151 AP83
Gate Ho Pl, Wat. WD18 75 BU41
Gatehouse Sch, E2 279 J10
Gate Ho Sq, SE1 299 K2
Gateley Rd, SW9 161 DM83
Gate Lo, Har. HA3
off Weston Dr 95 CH53
Gate Ms, SW7 296 D5
Gater Dr, Enf. EN2 82 DR39
Gatesborough St, EC2 287 N4
Gatesden Cl, Fetch. KT22 230 CC123
Gatesden Rd, Fetch. KT22 230 CC123
Gates Grn Rd, Kes. BR2 222 EG105
West Wickham BR4 204 EF104
Gateshead Rd, Borwd. WD6 78 CM39
Gateside Rd, SW17 180 DF90
Gatestone Rd, SE19 182 DS93
Gate St, WC2 286 C8
Gate Studios, Borwd. WD6 78 CN42
Gateway, SE17 311 K2
Gate Way, Wey. KT13
off Palace Dr 195 BP104
Gateway, The, Wat. WD18 75 BS43
Woking GU21 211 BB114
Gateway Acad, The, Grays RM16
off Marshfoot Rd 171 GG79
● Gateway Business Cen,
SE26 183 DY93
SE28 off Tom Cribb Rd 165 ER76
Gateway Cl, Nthwd. HA6 93 BQ51
Gateway Ct, Ilf. IG2 125 EN58
● Gateway Ind Est, NW10 139 CT69
Gateway Ms, E8 278 A2
N11 off Ringway 99 DJ51
Gateway Prim Sch, NW8 284 B4
Gateway Prim Sch, The, Dart. DA2
off Milestone Rd 188 FP86
Gateway Retail Pk, E6 293 P5
Gateway Rd, E10 123 EB62
Gateways, Guil. GU1 243 BA134
Gateways, The, SW3 296 D9
Goffs Oak EN7 66 DR28
Gatewick Cl, Slou. SL1 132 AS74
Gatfield Gro, Felt. TW13 176 CA89
Gathorne Rd, N22 99 DN54
Gathorne St, E2 289 K1
Gatley Av, Epsom KT19 216 CP106
Gatley Dr, Guil. GU4 243 AZ131
Gatliff Cl, SW1
off Ebury Br Rd 309 J1
Gatliff Rd, SW1 309 H1
Gatling Rd, SE2 166 EU78
Gatonby St, SE15 312 B6
Gatting Cl, Edg. HA8 96 CQ52
Gatting Way, Uxb. UB8 134 BL65
GATTON, Reig. RH2 250 DF128
Gatton Bottom, Merst. RH1 251 DH127
Reigate RH2 250 DE128
Gatton Cl, Reig. RH2 250 DC131
Sutton SM2 218 DB109
Gatton Pk, Reig. RH2 250 DF129
Gatton Pk Rd, Red. RH1 250 DD132
Reigate RH2 250 DD132
Gatton Prim Sch, SW17
off Gatton Rd 180 DE91
Gatton Rd, SW17 180 DE91
Reigate RH2 250 DC131
Gattons Way, Sid. DA14 186 EZ91
Gatward Cl, N21 81 DP44
Gatward Grn, N9 100 DT47
Gatward Pl, Bark. IG11 145 ET69
⇌ Gatwick Airport 269 DH152
★ Gatwick Airport (London),
Gat. RH6 268 DD153
● Gatwick Business Pk,
Hkwd RH6 268 DC149
Gatwick Gate, Craw. RH11 268 DD154
● Gatwick Gate Ind Est,
Lwfld Hth RH11 268 DE154
● Gatwick Metro Cen,
Horl. RH6 269 DH147
Gatwick Rd, SW18 179 CZ87
Gatwick RH6 268 DG154
Gravesend DA12 191 GH90
Gatwick Rd Rbt, Horl. RH6 268 DG154
Gatwick Way, Gat. RH6 268 DF151
Hornchurch RM12
off Haydock Cl 128 FM63
Gauden Cl, SW4 309 N10
Gauden Rd, SW4 309 N9
Gaumont App, Wat. WD17 75 BV41
Gaumont Ter, W12
off Lime Gro 294 A4
Gauntlet Cl, Nthlt. UB5 136 BY66
Gauntlett Ct, Wem. HA0 117 CH64
Gauntlett Rd, Sutt. SM1 218 DD106
Gaunt St, SE1 299 H6
Gautrey Rd, SE15 313 H8
Gautrey Sq, E6 293 K9
● Gavel Cen, The, St.Alb. AL3
off Porters Wd 43 CF16
Gavell Rd, Cob. KT11 213 BU113
Gavel St, SE17 299 M8
Gavenny Path, S.Ock. RM15 149 FT72
Gaverick Ms, E14 302 A8
Gaveston Cl, Byfleet KT14 212 BM113
Gaveston Dr, Berk. HP4 38 AV17
Gavestone Cres, SE12 184 EH87
Gavestone Rd, SE12 184 EH87
Gaveston Rd, Lthd. KT22 231 CG120
Slough SL2 131 AL69
Gaviller Pl, E5
off Clarence Rd 122 DV63
Gavina Cl, Mord. SM4 200 DE99
Gavin St, SE18 165 ES77
Gaviots Cl, Ger.Cr. SL9 113 AZ60
Gaviots Grn, Ger.Cr. SL9 112 AY60
Gaviots Way, Ger.Cr. SL9 112 AY59
Gawain Wk, N9 off Galahad Rd 122 DU48
Gawber St, E2 289 H2
Gawdrey Cl, Chesh. HP5
off Five Acres 54 AR33
Gawsworth Cl, E15 281 K2
Gawthorne Ct, E3
off Mostyn Gro 290 A1
Gawton Cres, Couls. CR5 235 DJ121
Gay Cl, NW2 119 CV64
Gaydon Ho, W2 283 M6
Gaydon La, NW9 96 CS53
Gayfere Rd, Epsom KT17 217 CU106
Ilford IG5 125 EM55
Gayfere St, SW1 298 A7
Gayford Rd, W12 159 CT75
Gay Gdns, Dag. RM10 127 FC63
Gayhurst, SE17 311 M2
Gayhurst Comm Sch, E8 278 D6
Gayhurst Rd, E8 278 C6
Gayhurst Sch,
Jun Sch, Ger.Cr. SL9
off Maltmans La 112 AW56
Sen Sch, Chal.St.P. SL9
off Bull La 112 AW56
Gayler Cl, Bletch. RH1 252 DT133
Gaylor Rd, Nthlt. UB5 116 BZ64
Tilbury RM18 170 GE81
Gaynes Ct, Upmin. RM14 128 FP63
Gaynesford Rd, SE23 183 DX89
Carshalton SM5 218 DF108
Gaynes Hill Rd, Wdf.Grn. IG8 102 EL51
Gaynes Pk, Cooper. CM16 70 EY31
Gaynes Pk Rd, Upmin. RM14 128 FN63
Gaynes Rd, Upmin. RM14 128 FP61
Gaynes Sch, Upmin. RM14
off Brackendale Gdns 128 FQ64
Gay Rd, E15 280 G10
Gaysham Av, Ilf. IG2 125 EN57
Gaysham Hall, Ilf. IG5 125 EP55
Gay St, SW15 159 CX83
Gayton Cl, Amer. HP6 55 AS35
Ashtead KT21 232 CL118
Gayton Ct, Har. HA1 117 CF58
Gayton Cres, NW3 120 DD63
Gayton Ho, E3 290 B5
Gayton Rd, NW3 274 A1
SE2 off Florence Rd 166 EW76
Harrow HA1 117 CF58
Gayville Rd, SW11 180 DF86
Gaywood Av, Chsht EN8 67 DX30
Gaywood Cl, SW2 181 DM88
Gaywood Est, SE1 298 G7
Gaywood Rd, E17 123 EA55
Ashtead KT21 232 CM118
Gaywood St, SE1 299 H7
Gaza St, SE17 310 G1
Gazelle Glade, Grav. DA12 191 GM92
Gazelle Ho, E15 281 J4
Gean Ct, N11
off Cline Rd 99 DJ51
Gean Wk, Hat. AL10 45 CU21
Gearies Infants' Sch, Ilf. IG2
off Waremead Rd 125 EP57
Gearies Jun Sch, Ilf. IG2
off Gantshill Cres 125 EP57
Geariesville Gdns, Ilf. IG6 125 EP56
Gearing Cl, SW17 180 DG91
Geary Cl, Smallfield RH6 269 DP150
Geary Ct, N9
off The Broadway 100 DU47
Geary Dr, Brwd. CM14, CM15 108 FW46
Geary Rd, NW10 119 CU64
Geary St, N7 276 D3
Geddes Pl, Bexh. DA6
off Market Pl 166 FA84
Geddes Rd, Bushey WD23 76 CC42
Geddings Rd, Hodd. EN11 49 EB17
Geddington Ct, Wal.Cr. EN8
off Eleanor Way 67 EA34
Gedeney Rd, N17 100 DQ53
Gedling Ho, SE22
off Quorn Rd 162 DT83
Gedling Pl, SE1 300 B6
Geere Rd, E15 281 M9
Gees Ct, W1 285 H9
Gee St, EC1 287 J4
Geffrye Ct, N1 287 P1
Geffrye Est, N1 287 P1
★ Geffrye Mus, E2 287 P1
Geffrye St, E2 278 A10
Geisthorp Ct, Wal.Abb. EN9 68 EG33
Geldart Rd, SE15 312 E5
Geldeston Rd, E5 122 DU61
Gellatly Rd, SE14 313 H8
Gell Cl, Uxb. UB10 114 BM62
Gelsthorpe Rd, Rom. RM5 105 FB52
● Gemini Business Pk, E6 145 ER71
Gemini Ct, Pur. CR8
off Brighton Rd 219 DN111
Gemini Gro, Nthlt. UB5
off Javelin Way 136 BY69
Gemini Ho, E3
off Garrison Rd 280 A9
● Gemini Project, SE14 313 K1
Gemmell Cl, Pur. CR8 219 DM114
Genas Cl, Ilf. IG6 103 EP53
General Gordon Pl, SE18 305 N8
Generals Wk, The, Enf. EN3 83 DY37
General Wolfe Rd, SE10 315 H6
● Genesis Business Pk, NW10 138 CP68
Wok. GU21 227 BC115
Genesis Cl, Stanw. TW19 174 BM88
Genesta Rd, SE18 165 EP79
Geneva Cl, Shep. TW17 195 BS96
Geneva Dr, SW9 161 DN84
Geneva Gdns, Rom. RM6 126 EY57
Geneva Rd, Kings.T. KT1 198 CL98
Thornton Heath CR7 202 DQ99
Genever Cl, E4 101 EA50
Genista Rd, N18 100 DV50
Genoa Av, SW15 179 CW85
Genoa Rd, SE20 202 DW95
Genotin Ms, Horn. RM12 128 FJ64
Genotin Rd, Enf. EN1 82 DR41
Genotin Ter, Enf. EN1
off Genotin Rd 82 DR41
Gentlemans Row, Enf. EN2 82 DQ41
Gentry Gdns, E13 291 P4
Genyn Rd, Guil. GU2 258 AV136
Geoff Cade Way, E3 290 A6
Geoffrey Av, Rom. RM3 106 FN51
Geoffrey Cl, SE5 311 J9
Geoffrey Gdns, E6 292 G1
Geoffrey Rd, SE4 313 N10
George Abbot Sch, Guil. GU1
off Woodruff Av 243 BB132
George Avey Cft,
N.Wld Bas. CM16 71 FB26
George Beard Rd, SE8 301 N9
George Belt Ho, E2 289 J2
George Carey C of E Prim Sch,
Bark. IG11 146 EU70
George Comberton Wk, E12
off Gainsborough Av 125 EN64
George Ct, WC2 298 B1
George Cres, N10 98 DG52
George Crook's Ho, Grays RM17
off New Rd 170 GB79
George Downing Est, N16 122 DT61
George Eliot Ho, SW1
off Vauxhall Br Rd 297 M9
George Eliot Inf Sch, NW8 274 A8
George Eliot Jun Sch, NW8 274 A8
George Elliston Ho, SE1
off Old Kent Rd 312 C1
George V Av, Pnr. HA5 116 CA55
George V Cl, Pnr. HA5 116 CA55
Watford WD18 75 BT42
George V Way, Perivale UB6 137 CH67
Sarratt WD3 74 BG36
George Gange Way,
Wealds. HA3 117 CE55
GEORGE GREEN, Slou. SL3 132 AX72
George Grn Dr, Geo.Grn SL3 133 AZ71
George Grn Rd, Geo.Grn SL3 132 AX72
George Green's Sch, E14 302 F10
George Gros Rd, SE20 202 DU95
George Hudson Twr, E15
off High St 290 D1
★ George Inn, SE1 299 L3
George Inn Yd, SE1 299 L3
Georgelands, Ripley GU23 228 BH121
George La, E18 102 EG54
SE13 183 EC86
Bromley BR2 204 EH102
George La Rbt, E18 102 EG54
George Lansbury Ho, N22
off Progress Way 99 DN53
George Loveless Ho, E2 288 B2
George Lovell Dr, Enf. EN3 83 EA37
George Lowe Ct, W2 283 L6
George Mathers Rd, SE11 298 G8
George Ms, NW1 285 L3
SW9 310 E9
Enfield EN2
off Church St 82 DR41
George Mitchell Sch, E10
off Farmer Rd 123 EB60
George Rd, E4 101 EA51
Godalming GU7 258 AS144
Guildford GU1 242 AX134
Kingston upon Thames KT2 178 CP94
New Malden KT3 199 CT98
George Row, SE16 300 C5
Georges Cl, Orp. BR5 206 EW97
Georges Dr, Flack.Hth HP10 110 AC56
Pilgrim's Hatch CM15 108 FT43
Georges Mead, Els. WD6 77 CK44
George Spicer Prim Sch, Enf. EN1
off Southbury Rd 82 DT41
George Sq, SW19
off Mostyn Rd 199 CZ97
Georges Rd, Tats. TN16 238 EK120
George's Rd, N7 276 D3
Georges Sq, SW6 307 H2
Georges Ter, Cat. CR3
off Coulsdon Rd 236 DR122
George Street 202 DQ103
George St, E16 291 L9
W1 284 F8
W7 off Uxbridge Rd 137 CE74
Barking IG11 145 EQ66
Berkhamsted HP4 38 AY19
Chesham HP5 54 AQ30
Croydon CR0 202 DR103
Grays RM17 170 GA79
Hemel Hempstead HP2 40 BK19
Hertford SG14 32 DQ09
Hounslow TW3 156 BZ82
Richmond TW9 177 CK85
Romford RM1 127 FF58
St. Albans AL3 42 CC20
Southall UB2 156 BY77
Staines-upon-Thames TW18 173 BF91
Uxbridge UB8 134 BK66
Watford WD18 76 BW42
George St Prim Sch, Hem.H. HP2
off George St 40 BK19
George's Wd Rd, Brook.Pk AL9 64 DA26
George Taylor Ct, N9
off Colthurst Dr 100 DV48
George Tilbury Ho,
Grays RM16 171 GH75
George Tomlinson Prim Sch, E11
off Vernon Rd 124 EE60
Georgetown Cl, SE19 182 DS92
Georgette Pl, SE10 314 F5
Georgeville Gdns, Ilf. IG6 125 EP56
Georgewood Rd, Hem.H. HP3 58 BM25
George Wyver Cl, SW19
off Beaumont Rd 179 CY87
George Yd, EC3 287 M9
W1 285 H10
Georgiana St, NW1 275 L8
Georgian Cl, Brom. BR2 204 EH101
Staines-upon-Thames TW18 174 BH91
Stanmore HA7 95 CG52
Uxbridge UB10 114 BL63
Georgian Ct, SW16
off Gleneldon Rd 181 DL91
Wembley HA9 138 CN65
Georgian Way, Har. HA1 117 CD61
Georgia Rd, N.Mal. KT3 198 CQ98
Thornton Heath CR7 201 DP95
Georgina Gdns, E2 288 B2
Geraint Rd, Brom. BR1 184 EG91
Gerald Game Br, Hodd. EN11 49 EC17
Geraldine Rd, SW18 180 DC85
W4 158 CN79
Geraldine St, SE11 298 G7
Gerald Ms, SW1 297 H8
Gerald Rd, E16 291 L4
SW1 297 H8
Dagenham RM8 126 EZ61
Gravesend DA12 191 GL87
Geralds Gro, Bans. SM7 217 CX114
Gerard Av, Houns. TW4 176 CA87
Gerard Ct, NW2 272 C2
Gerard Gdns, Rain. RM13 147 FE68
Gerard Pl, E9 279 J6
Gerard Rd, SW13 159 CT81
Harrow HA1 117 CG58
Gerards Cl, SE16 312 G1
Gerards Pl, SW4
off Clapham Pk Rd 161 DK84
Gerda Rd, SE9 185 EQ89
Gerdview Dr, Dart. DA2 188 FJ91
Gerrains Cl, Chesh. HP5 54 AP32
Germain St, Chesh. HP5 54 AP32
Germander Way, E15 291 K3
German Sch, The, Rich. TW10
off Petersham Rd 177 CK88
Gernigan Ho, SW18 180 DD86
Gernon Cl, Rain. RM13
off Jordans Way 148 FK68
Gernon Rd, E3 289 L1
Geron Way, NW2 119 CV60
Gerpins La, Upmin. RM14 148 FM68
Gerrard Cres, Brwd. CM14 108 FV48
Gerrard Gdns, Pnr. HA5 115 BU57
Gerrard Ho, SE14 313 H5
Gerrard Pl, W1 285 P10
Gerrard Rd, N1 277 H10
Gerrards Cl, N14 81 DJ43
GERRARDS CROSS, SL9 112 AX58
⇌ Gerrards Cross 112 AY57
Gerrards Cross C of E Sch, The,
Ger.Cr. SL9 off Moreland Dr 113 AZ59
Gerrards Cross Rd, Stoke P. SL2 132 AU66
Gerrards Mead, Bans. SM7 233 CZ116
Gerrard St, W1 285 N10
Gerrard Way, SE3 164 EJ84
Gerridge St, SE1 298 F5
Gerry Raffles Sq, E15 281 H5
Gertrude Rd, Belv. DA17 166 FA77
Gertrude St, SW10 307 P3
Gervaise Cl, Slou. SL1 131 AM74
Gervase Cl, Wem. HA9 118 CQ62
Gervase Rd, Edg. HA8 96 CQ53
Gervase St, SE15 312 F4
Gews Cor, Chsht EN8 67 DX29
Ghent St, SE6 183 EA89
Ghent Way, E8 278 B4
Giant Arches Rd, SE24 182 DQ87
Giant Tree Hill,
Bushey Hth WD23 95 CD46
Gibbard Ms, SW19 179 CX92
Gibb Cft, Harl. CM18 51 ES19
Gibbfield Cl, Rom. RM6 126 EY55
Gibbins Rd, E15 280 F7
Gibbon Rd, SE15 313 H9
W3 138 CS73
Kingston upon Thames KT2 198 CL95
Gibbons Cl, Borwd. WD6 78 CL39
Gibbons La, Dart. DA1 188 FK86
Gibbons Ms, NW11 119 CZ57
Gibbons Rents, SE1
off Bermondsey St 299 N3
Gibbons Rd, NW10 138 CR65
Gibbon Wk, SW15 159 CU84
Gibbs Av, SE19 182 DR92
Gibbs Brook La, Oxt. RH8 253 ED133
Gibbs Cl, SE19 182 DR92
Cheshunt EN8 67 DX29
Gibbs Couch, Wat. WD19 94 BX48
Gibbs Grn, W14 295 H10
Edgware HA8 96 CQ50
Gibbs Grn Sch, W14 295 H10
Gibbs Rd, N18 100 DW49
Gibbs Sq, SE19 182 DR92
Gibney Ter, Brom. BR1
off Durham Hill 184 EF91
Gibraltar Cl, Gt Warley CM13 107 FW51
Gibraltar Cres, Epsom KT19 216 CS110
Gibraltar Ho, Brwd. CM13 107 FW51
Gibraltar Wk, E2 288 B3
● Gibson Business Cen, N17
off High Rd 100 DT52
Gibson Cl, E1 289 H4
N21 81 DN44
Chessington KT9 215 CJ107
Isleworth TW7 157 CD83
North Weald Bassett CM16
off Beamish Cl 71 FC25
Northfleet DA11 191 GF90
Gibson Ct, Rom. RM1
off Regarth Av 127 FE58
Slough SL3 153 AZ78
Gibson Gdns, N16 122 DT61
Gibson Ms, Twick. TW1
off Richmond Rd 177 CJ87
Gibson Pl, Stanw. TW19 174 BJ86
Gibson Rd, SE11 298 D9
Dagenham RM8 126 EW60
Sutton SM1 218 DB106
Uxbridge UB10 114 BM63
Gibson's Hill, SW16 181 DN93
Gibsons Pl, Eyns. DA4 208 FL103
Gibson Sq, N1 276 F8
Gibson St, SE10 315 J1
Gidd Hill, Couls. CR5 234 DG116
Gidea Av, Rom. RM2 127 FG55
Gidea Cl, Rom. RM2 127 FG55
South Ockendon RM15
off Tyssen Pl 149 FW69
GIDEA PARK, Rom. RM2 127 FG55
⇌ Gidea Park 128 FJ56
Gidea Pk Coll, Gidea Pk RM2
off Balgores La 127 FG55
Gidea Pk Prim Sch, Gidea Pk RM2
off Lodge Av 127 FG55
Gideon Cl, Belv. DA17 167 FB77
Gideon Ms, W5 157 CK75
Gideon Rd, SW11 308 G10
Gidian Ct, Park St AL2 61 CD27
Giesbach Rd, N19 121 DJ61
Giffard Rd, N18 100 DS50
Giffard Way, Guil. GU2 242 AU131
Giffin St, SE8 314 A4
Gifford Gdns, W7 137 CD71
Gifford Pl, Warley CM14 108 FX50
Gifford Prim Sch, Nthlt. UB5
off Greenhill Gdns 136 BZ68
Gifford Rd, NW10 138 CS66
Giffordside, Grays RM16 171 GH78
Gifford St, N1 276 B7
Gift La, E15 281 L8
Giggs Hill, Orp. BR5 206 EU96
Giggs Hill Gdns, T.Ditt. KT7 197 CG102
Giggs Hill Rd, T.Ditt. KT7 197 CG101
Gilbert Cl, SE18 165 EM81
Swanscombe DA10 189 FX86
Gilbert Colvin Prim Sch, Ilf. IG5
off Strafford Av 103 EN54
Gilbert Gro, Edg. HA8 96 CR53
Gilbert Ho, EC2
off The Barbican 287 K6
SE8 314 B3
SW1 309 K1
Gilbert Pl, WC1 286 A7
Gilbert Rd, SE11 298 F9
SW19 180 DC94
Belvedere DA17 166 FA76
Bromley BR1 184 EG94
Chafford Hundred RM16 169 FW76
Harefield UB9 92 BK54
Pinner HA5 116 BX56
Romford RM1 127 FF56
Gilbert Scott Ct, Amer. HP7 55 AP40
Gilbert Scott Prim Sch, S.Croy. CR2
off Farnborough Av 221 DY108
Gilbert Sq, Har. HA2
off Station Rd 116 CB57
Gilbert St, E15 281 J1
W1 285 H9
Enfield EN3 82 DW37
Hounslow TW3 off High St 156 CC83
Gilbert Way, Berk. HP4 38 AU19
Croydon CR0
off Beddington Fm Rd 201 DL102
Slough SL3 153 AZ78
Gilbert White Cl, Perivale UB6 137 CG67
Gilbey Cl, Uxb. UB10 115 BP63
Gilbey Rd, SW17 180 DE91
Gilbeys Yd, NW1 275 H7
Gilbey Wk, Woob.Grn HP10
off Stratford Dr 110 AD59
Gilbourne Rd, SE18 165 ET79
Gilda Av, Enf. EN3 83 DY43
Gilda Cres, N16 122 DU60
Gildea Cl, Pnr. HA5 94 CA52
Gildea St, W1 285 K7
Gilden Cl, Harl. CM17 36 EY11
Gilden Cres, NW5 274 G3
Gildenhill Rd, Swan. BR8 188 FJ94
Gilden Way, Harl. CM17 36 EW12
Gildens, Saw. CM21 36 EX05
Gildersome St, SE18
off Nightingale Vale 165 EN79
Gilders Rd, Chess. KT9 216 CM107
Giles Cl, Rain. RM13 148 FK68
Giles Coppice, SE19 182 DT91
Giles Fld, Grav. DA12 191 GM88
Giles Travers Cl, Egh. TW20 193 BC97
Gilfrid Cl, Uxb. UB8 135 BP72
Gilhams Av, Bans. SM7 217 CX112
Gilkes Cres, SE21 182 DS86
Gilkes Pl, SE21 182 DS86
Gillam Way, Rain. RM13 147 FG65
Gillan Grn, Bushey Hth WD23 94 CC47
Gillards Ms, E17 off Gillards Way 123 EA56
Gillards Way, E17 123 EA56
Gill Av, E16 291 P9
Guildford GU2 258 AS135
Gill Cl, Wat. WD18 75 BQ44
Gill Cres, Nthflt DA11 191 GF90
Gillender St, E3 290 E4
E14 290 E4
Gillespie Prim Sch, N5
off Gillespie Rd 121 DP62
Gillespie Rd, N5 121 DN62
Gillett Av, E6 144 EL68
Gillette Cor, Islw. TW7 157 CG80
Gillett Pl, N16 277 P3
Gillett Rd, Th.Hth. CR7 202 DR98
Gillett Sq, N16 277 P3
Gillett St, N16 277 P3
Gillfoot, NW1 285 L1
Gillham Ter, N17 100 DU51
Gilliam Gro, Pur. CR8 219 DN110
Gillian Av, St.Alb. AL1 42 CC24
Gillian Cres, Rom. RM2 106 FJ54
Gillian Pk Rd, Sutt. SM3 199 CZ102
Gillian St, SE13 183 EB85
Gilliat Cl, Iver SL0
off Grange Way 133 BF72
Gilliat Dr, Guil. GU4 243 BD132
Gilliat Rd, Slou. SL1 132 AS73
Gilliat's Grn, Chorl. WD3 73 BD42
Gillies St, NW5 275 H3
Gilling Ct, NW3 274 D4
Gillingham Rd, NW2 119 CY62
Gillingham Row, SW1 297 L8
Gillingham St, SW1 297 K8
Gillison Wk, SE16
off Tranton Rd 300 D6
Gillman Dr, E15 281 L9
Gillmans Rd, Orp. BR5 206 EV102
Gills Hill, Rad. WD7 77 CF35
Gills Hill La, Rad. WD7 77 CF36
Gills Hollow, Rad. WD7 77 CF36
Gill's Rd, S.Darenth DA2, DA4 209 FS95
Gillsted Ct, St.Alb. AL3
off Repton Grn 43 CD17
Gill St, E14 289 P10
Gillum Cl, E.Barn. EN4 98 DF46
Gilmais, Bkhm KT23 246 CC125
Gilman Cres, Wind. SL4 151 AK83
Gilmore Cl, Slou. SL3 152 AW75
Uxbridge UB10 114 BQ62
Gilmore Cres, Ashf. TW15 174 BN92
Gilmore Rd, SE13 163 ED84
Gilmour Cl, Wal.Cr. EN7 82 DU35
Gilpin Av, SW14 158 CR84
Gilpin Cl, W2 284 A6
Mitcham CR4 200 DE96
Gilpin Cres, N18 100 DT50
Twickenham TW2 176 CB87
Gilpin Rd, E5 123 DY63
Ware SG12 33 DY07
Gilpin's Gallop, Stans.Abb. SG12 33 EB11
Gilpins Ride, Berk. HP4 38 AX18

Gilpin Way, Harling. UB3 155 BR80
Gilroy Cl, Rain. RM13 147 FF65
Gilroy Rd, Hem.H. HP2 40 BK19
Gilroy Way, Orp. BR5 206 EV101
Gilsland, Wal.Abb. EN9 84 EE35
Gilsland Pl, Th.Hth. CR7
off Gilsland Rd 202 DR98
Gilsland Rd, Th.Hth. CR7 202 DR98
Gilson Pl, N10 98 DF52
Gilstead Rd, SW6 307 M8
Gilston La, Gilston Pk CM20 35 EQ09
GILSTON PARK, Harl. CM20 35 EP08
Gilston Rd, SW10 307 P1
Gilton Rd, SE6 184 EE90
Giltspur St, EC1 287 H8
Gilwell Cl, E4
off Antlers Hill 83 EB42
Gilwell La, E4 83 EC42
Gilwell Pk, E4 83 EC41
Gimcrack Hill, Lthd. KT22
off Dorking Rd 231 CH123
Ginsburg Yd, NW3
off Heath St 120 DC63
Gippeswyck Cl, Pnr. HA5
off Uxbridge Rd 94 BX53
⇌ Gipsy Hill 182 DS92
Gipsy Hill, SE19 182 DS91
Gipsy La, SW15 159 CU83
Grays RM17 170 GC79
Gipsy Rd, SE27 182 DQ91
Welling DA16 166 EX81
Gipsy Rd Gdns, SE27 182 DQ91
Giralda Cl, E16 292 E7
Giraud St, E14 290 C8
Girdlers Rd, W14 294 D8
Girdlestone Wk, N19 121 DJ61
Girdwood Rd, SW18 179 CY87
Girling Way, Felt. TW14 155 BU83
Girona Cl, Chaff.Hun. RM16 169 FW76
Gironde Rd, SW6 307 H5
Girton Av, NW9 118 CN55
Girton Cl, Nthlt. UB5 136 CC65
Girton Ct, Chsht EN8 67 DY30
Girton Gdns, Croy. CR0 203 EA104
Girton Rd, SE26 183 DX92
Northolt UB5 136 CC65
Girton Vil, W10 282 D8
Girton Way, Crox.Grn WD3 75 BQ43
Gisborne Gdns, Rain. RM13 147 FF69
Gisbourne Cl, Wall. SM6 201 DK104
Gisburne Way, Wat. WD24 75 BU37
Gisburn Rd, N8 121 DM56
Gissing Wk, N1 276 F7
Gittens Cl, Brom. BR1 184 EF91
Given Wilson Wk, E13 291 M1
Giverny Ho, SE16
off Canada St 301 J5
GIVONS GROVE, Lthd. KT22 247 CJ126
Givons Gro, Lthd. KT22 247 CH125
Jct Givons Gro Rbt,
Lthd. KT22 247 CH125
Glacier Way, Wem. HA0 137 CK68
Gladbeck Way, Enf. EN2 81 DP42
Gladding Rd, E12 124 EK63
Cheshunt EN7 65 DP25
Glade, The, N21 81 DM44
SE7 164 EJ80
Bromley BR1 204 EK96
Coulsdon CR5 235 DN119
Croydon CR0 203 DX99
Enfield EN2 81 DN41
Epsom KT17 217 CU106
Fetcham KT22 230 CA122
Gerrards Cross SL9 112 AX60
Hutton CM13 109 GA46
Ilford IG5 103 EM53
Kingswood KT20 234 DA121
Penn HP10 88 AC46
Sevenoaks TN13 257 FH123
Staines-upon-Thames TW18 174 BH94
Sutton SM2 217 CY109
Upminster RM14 128 FQ64
Welwyn Garden City AL8 29 CW07
West Byfleet KT14 211 BE113
West Wickham BR4 203 EB104
Woodford Green IG8 102 EH48
● Glade Business Cen,
Grays RM20 169 FT78
Glade Cl, Long Dit. KT6 197 CK103
Glade Ct, Ilf. IG5 103 EM53
Uxbridge UB8 134 BJ65
Glade Gdns, Croy. CR0 203 DY101
Glade La, Sthl. UB2 156 CB75
Glade Ms, Guil. GU1 259 AZ135
Sch Glade Prim Sch, Ilf. IG5
off Atherton Rd 103 EM54
Glades, The, Grav. DA12 191 GK93
Hemel Hempstead HP1 39 BE19
Gladeside, N21 81 DM44
Croydon CR0 203 DX100
St. Albans AL4 43 CK17
Gladeside Cl, Chess. KT9 215 CK108
Gladeside Ct, Warl. CR6 236 DV120
Gladesmere Ct, Wat. WD24 75 BV36
Sch Gladesmore Comm Sch, N15
off Crowland Rd 122 DU57
Gladesmore Rd, N15 122 DT58
Glade Spur, Kgswd KT20 234 DB121
Gladeswood Rd, Belv. DA17 167 FB77
Glade Wk, E20 280 D4
Gladeway, The, Wal.Abb. EN9 67 ED33
Gladiator St, SE23 183 DY86
Glading Ter, N16 122 DT62
Gladioli Cl, Hmptn. TW12
off Gresham Rd 176 CA93
Gladsdale Dr, Pnr. HA5 115 BU56
Gladsmuir Cl, Walt. KT12 196 BW103
Gladsmuir Rd, N19 121 DJ60
Barnet EN5 79 CY40
Gladstone Av, E12 144 EL66
N22 99 DN54
Feltham TW14 175 BU86
Twickenham TW2 177 CD87
Gladstone Ct, SW1
off Regency St 297 P9
SW8 off Havelock Ter 309 K6
SW19 180 DA94
Gladstone Gdns, Houns. TW3 156 CC81
Gladstone Ms, N22
off Pelham Rd 99 DN54
NW6 272 G6
SE20 182 DW94
Gladstone Par, NW2
off Edgware Rd 119 CV60
Gladstone Pk Gdns, NW2 119 CV62
Sch Gladstone Pk Prim Sch, NW10
off Sherrick Grn Rd 119 CV64
Gladstone Pl, E3 279 P10
Barnet EN5 79 CX42
Gladstone Rd, SW19 180 DA94
W4 off Acton La 158 CR76
Ashtead KT21 231 CK118
Buckhurst Hill IG9 102 EH46
Chesham HP5 54 AQ31
Croydon CR0 202 DR101
Dartford DA1 188 FM86
Hoddesdon EN11 49 EB16
Kingston upon Thames KT1 198 CN97
Orpington BR6 223 EQ106
Southall UB2 156 BY75
Surbiton KT6 197 CK103
Ware SG12 32 DW05
Watford WD17 76 BW41
Gladstone St, SE1 298 G6
Gladstone Ter, SE27
off Bentons La 182 DQ91
Gladstone Way, Slou. SL1 151 AN75
Wealdstone HA3 117 CE55
Gladwell Rd, N8 121 DM58
Bromley BR1 184 EG93
Gladwin Way, Harl. CM20 35 ER13
Gladwyn Rd, SW15 306 C10
Gladys Rd, NW6 273 K6
Glaisher St, SE8 314 B2
Glaisyer Way, Iver SL0 133 BC68
Glamis Cl, Chsht EN7 66 DU29
Glamis Cres, Hayes UB3 155 BQ76
Glamis Dr, Horn. RM11 128 FL60
Glamis Pl, E1 289 H10
Hemel Hempstead HP2 40 BL19
Glamis Rd, E1 289 H10
Glamis Way, Nthlt. UB5 136 CC65
Glamorgan Cl, Mitch. CR4 201 DL97
Glamorgan Rd, Kings.T. KT1 177 CJ94
Glan Avon Ms, Harl. CM17 52 EW16
Glandford Way, Chad.Hth RM6 126 EV57
Glanfield, Hem.H. HP2
off Bathurst Rd 40 BL17
Glanfield Rd, Beck. BR3 203 DZ98
Glanleam Rd, Stan. HA7 95 CK49
Glanmead, Shenf. CM15 108 FY46
Glanmor Rd, Slou. SL2 132 AV73
Glanthams Cl, Shenf. CM15 108 FY47
Glanthams Rd, Shenf. CM15 109 FZ47
Glanty, The, Egh. TW20 173 BB91
Glanville Dr, Horn. RM11 128 FM60
Glanville Ms, Stan. HA7 95 CG50
Glanville Rd, SW2 181 DL85
Bromley BR2 204 EH97
Glanville Way, Epsom KT19 216 CL112
Glasbrook Av, Twick. TW2 176 BZ88
Glasbrook Rd, SE9 184 EK87
Glaserton Rd, N16 122 DS59
Glasford St, SW17 180 DF93
Glasgow Ho, W9 283 M1
Glasgow Rd, E13 292 A1
N18 100 DV50
Glasgow Ter, SW1 309 L1
Glasier Ct, E15 281 K6
Glaskin Ms, E9 279 M5
Glasse Cl, W13 137 CG73
Glasshill St, SE1 299 H4
Glasshouse Cl, Uxb. UB8 135 BP71
Glasshouse Flds, E1 289 J10
Glasshouse St, W1 297 M1
Glasshouse Wk, SE11 298 B10
Glasshouse Yd, EC1 287 J5
Glasslyn Rd, N8 121 DK57
Glassmill La, Brom. BR2 204 EF96
Glass St, E2 288 F4
Glass Yd, SE18 305 M6
Glastonbury Av, Wdf.Grn. IG8 102 EK52
Glastonbury Cl, Orp. BR5 206 EW102
Glastonbury Ho, SW1 297 J10
Glastonbury Pl, E1 288 G9
Glastonbury Rd, N9 100 DU46
Morden SM4 200 DA101
Glastonbury St, NW6 273 H3
Glaucus St, E3 290 C6
Glazbury Rd, W14 294 F9
Glazebrook Cl, SE21 182 DR89
Glazebrook Rd, Tedd. TW11 177 CF94
Gleave Cl, St.Alb. AL1 43 CH19
Glebe, The, SE3 315 J10
SW16 181 DK91
Chislehurst BR7 205 EQ95
Harlow CM20 off School La 35 ES14
Horley RH6 268 DF148
Kings Langley WD4 58 BN29
Leigh RH2 265 CU141
Magdalen Laver CM5 53 FD18
Watford WD25 60 BW33
West Drayton UB7 154 BM77
Worcester Park KT4 199 CT102
Glebe Av, Enf. EN2 81 DP41
Harrow HA3 118 CL55
Mitcham CR4 200 DE96
Ruislip HA4 135 BV65
Uxbridge UB10 115 BQ63
Woodford Green IG8 102 EG51
Glebe Cl, W4 158 CS78
Bookham KT23 246 CA126
Chalfont St. Peter SL9 90 AX52
Essendon AL9 46 DF17
Hemel Hempstead HP3 40 BL24
Hertford SG14 32 DR07
South Croydon CR2 220 DT111
Taplow SL6 150 AF75
Uxbridge UB10 115 BQ63
Glebe Cotts, Brasted TN16 240 EV123
Essendon AL9 46 DF17
Sutton SM1 off Vale Rd 218 DB105
West Clandon GU4 244 BH132
Glebe Ct, W7 137 CD73
Coulsdon CR5 235 DH115
Guildford GU1 243 AZ134
Mitcham CR4 200 DF97
Sevenoaks TN13 off Oak La 257 FH126
Stanmore HA7 95 CJ50
Glebe Cres, NW4 119 CW56
Harrow HA3 118 CL55
Glebefield, The, Sev. TN13 256 FF123
Glebe Gdns, Byfleet KT14 212 BK114
New Malden KT3 198 CS101
Glebe Ho Dr, Brom. BR2 204 EH102
Glebe Hyrst, SE19 182 DS91
South Croydon CR2 220 DT112
Glebeland, Hat. AL10
off St. Etheldredas Dr 45 CW18
Glebeland Gdns, Shep. TW17 195 BQ100
Glebelands, Chig. IG7 104 EV48
Claygate KT10 215 CF109
Dartford DA1 167 FF84
Harlow CM20 35 ET12
Penn HP10 88 AC47
West Molesey KT8 196 CB99
Glebelands Av, E18 102 EG54
Ilford IG2 125 ER59
Glebelands Cl, N12 98 DD53
Glebelands Rd, Felt. TW14 175 BU87
Glebe La, Abin.Com. RH5 262 BX143
Barnet EN5 79 CU43
Harrow HA3 118 CL56
Sevenoaks TN13 257 FH126
Glebe Ms, Sid. DA15 185 ET85
Glebe Path, Mitch. CR4 200 DE97
Glebe Pl, SW3 308 C2
Horton Kirby DA4 208 FQ98
Sch Glebe Prim Sch, Ickenham UB10
off Sussex Rd 115 BQ63
Kenton HA3 off D'Arcy Gdns 118 CL56
Glebe Rd, E8 278 A7
N3 98 DC53
N8 121 DM56
NW10 139 CT65
SW13 159 CU82
Ashtead KT21 231 CK118
Bromley BR1 204 EG95
Carshalton SM5 218 DF107
Chalfont St. Peter SL9 90 AW53
Dagenham RM10 147 FB65
Dorking RH4 263 CF136
Egham TW20 173 BC93
Gravesend DA11 191 GF88
Hayes UB3 135 BT74
Hertford SG14 32 DR07
Merstham RH1 235 DH124
Old Windsor SL4 172 AV85
Rainham RM13 148 FJ69
Staines-upon-Thames TW18 174 BH93
Stanmore HA7 95 CJ50
Sutton SM2 217 CY109
Uxbridge UB8 134 BJ68
Warlingham CR6 237 DX117
Sch Glebe Sch, W.Wick. BR4
off Hawes La 203 ED103
Glebe Side, Twick. TW1 177 CF86
Glebe Sq, Mitch. CR4 200 DF97
Glebe St, W4 158 CS78
Glebe Ter, W4
off Glebe St 158 CS78
Glebe Way, Amer. HP6 55 AR36
Erith DA8 167 FE79
Hanworth TW13 176 CA90
Hornchurch RM11 128 FL59
South Croydon CR2 220 DT112
West Wickham BR4 203 EC103
Glebeway, Wdf.Grn. IG8 102 EJ50
Gledhow Gdns, SW5 295 N9
Gledhow Wd, Kgswd KT20 234 DB121
Gledstanes Rd, W14 306 F1
Gledwood Av, Hayes UB4 135 BT71
Gledwood Cres, Hayes UB4 135 BT71
Gledwood Dr, Hayes UB4 135 BT71
Gledwood Gdns, Hayes UB4 135 BT71
Gleed Av, Bushey Hth WD23 95 CD47
Gleeson Dr, Orp. BR6 223 ET106
Gleeson Ms, Add. KT15 212 BJ105
Glegg Pl, SW15 159 CX84
Glen, The, Add. KT15 211 BF106
Bromley BR2 204 EE96
Croydon CR0 203 DX104
Eastcote HA5 115 BV57
Enfield EN2 81 DP42
Hemel Hempstead HP2 40 BM15
Northwood HA6 93 BR52
Orpington BR6 205 EM104
Pinner HA5 116 BY59
Rainham RM13 148 FJ70
Slough SL3 152 AW77
Southall UB2 156 BZ78
Wembley HA9 117 CK63
Glenaffric Av, E14 302 F9
Glen Albyn Rd, SW19 179 CX89
Glenalla Rd, Ruis. HA4 115 BT59
Glenalmond Rd, Har. HA3 118 CL56
Glenalvon Way, SE18 304 G8
Glena Mt, Sutt. SM1 218 DC105
Sch Glenarm Coll, Ilf. IG1
off Coventry Rd 125 EP61
Glenarm Rd, E5 278 G2
Glen Av, Ashf. TW15 174 BN91
Glenavon Cl, Clay. KT10 215 CG108
Glenavon Gdns, Slou. SL3 152 AW77
Glenavon Rd, E15 281 K6
Glenbarr Cl, SE9 165 EP83
Glenbow Rd, Brom. BR1 184 EE93
Glenbrook N, Enf. EN2 81 DM42
Sch Glenbrook Prim Sch, SW4
off Clarence Av 181 DK86
Glenbrook Rd, NW6 273 J3
Glenbrook S, Enf. EN2 81 DM42
Glenbuck Ct, Surb. KT6
off Glenbuck Rd 198 CL100
Glenbuck Rd, Surb. KT6 197 CK100
Glenburnie Rd, SW17 180 DF90
Glencairn Dr, W5 137 CH70
Glencairne Cl, E16 292 E6
Glencairn Rd, SW16 201 DL95
Glen Cl, Kgswd KT20 233 CY123
Shepperton TW17 194 BN98
Glencoe Av, Ilf. IG2 125 ER59
Glencoe Dr, Dag. RM10 126 FA63
Glencoe Rd, Bushey WD23 76 CA44
Hayes UB4 136 BY71
Weybridge KT13 194 BN104
Glencorse Grn, Wat. WD19 94 BX49
Glen Ct, Stai. TW18 173 BF94
Glen Cres, Wdf.Grn. IG8 102 EH51
Glendale, Hem.H. HP1 40 BH20
Swanley BR8 207 FF99
Glendale Av, N22 99 DN52
Edgware HA8 96 CM49
Romford RM6 126 EW59
Glendale Cl, SE9 165 EN83
Shenfield CM15 108 FY45
Woking GU21 226 AW118
Glendale Dr, SW19 179 CZ92
Guildford GU4 243 BB130
Glendale Gdns, Wem. HA9 117 CK60
Glendale Ms, Beck. BR3 203 EB95
Glendale Ri, Ken. CR8 235 DP115
Glendale Rd, Erith DA8 167 FC77
Northfleet DA11 190 GE91
Glendale Wk, Chsht EN8 67 DY30
Glendale Way, SE28 146 EW73
Glendall St, SW9 161 DM84
Glendarvon St, SW15 306 D10
Glendean Ct, Enf. EN3
off Tysoe Av 83 DZ36
Glendene Av, E.Hors. KT24 245 BS126
Glendevon Cl, Edg. HA8 96 CP48
Glendish Rd, N17 100 DU53
Glendor Gdns, NW7 96 CR49
Glendower Cres, Orp. BR6 206 EU100
Glendower Gdns, SW14
off Glendower Rd 158 CR83
Glendower Pl, SW7 296 A8
Sch Glendower Prep Sch, SW7 296 A8
Glendower Rd, E4 101 ED46
SW14 158 CR83
Glendown Rd, SE2 166 EU78
Glendun Rd, W3 138 CS73
Gleneagle Ms, SW16
off Ambleside Av 181 DK92
Gleneagle Rd, SW16 181 DK92
Gleneagles, Stan. HA7 95 CH51
Gleneagles Cl, SE16 312 E1
Orpington BR6 205 ER102
Romford RM3 106 FM52
Stanwell TW19 174 BK86
Watford WD19 94 BX49
Gleneagles Grn, Orp. BR6
off Tandridge Dr 205 ER102
Gleneagles Twr, Sthl. UB1 136 CC72
Gleneldon Ms, SW16 181 DL91
Gleneldon Rd, SW16 181 DL91
Glenelg Rd, SW2 181 DL85
Glenesk Rd, SE9 165 EN83
Sch Glenesk Sch, E.Hors. KT24
off Ockham Rd N 245 BR125
Glenester Cl, Hodd. EN11 33 EA14
Glen Faba, Roydon CM19 50 EE16
Glen Faba Rd, Roydon CM19 50 EF17
Glenfarg Rd, SE6 183 ED88
Glenferrie Rd, St.Alb. AL1 43 CG20
Glenfield Cl, Brock. RH3 264 CP138
Glenfield Cres, Ruis. HA4 115 BR59
Glenfield Rd, SW12 181 DJ88
W13 157 CH75
Ashford TW15 175 BP93
Banstead SM7 234 DB115
Brockham RH3 264 CP138
Glenfields, Stoke P. SL2 132 AT67
Glenfield Ter, W13 157 CH75
Glenfinlas Way, SE5 311 H4
Glenforth St, SE10 303 M10
Glengall Gro, E14 302 E6
Glengall Rd, NW6 273 H9
SE15 312 B2
Bexleyheath DA7 166 EY83
Edgware HA8 96 CP48
Woodford Green IG8 102 EG51
Glengall Ter, SE15 312 B2
Glen Gdns, Croy. CR0 201 DP104
Glengarnock Av, E14 302 F9
Glengarry Rd, SE22 182 DS85
Glenham Dr, Ilf. IG2 125 EP57
Glenhaven Av, Borwd. WD6 78 CN41
Glenhead Cl, SE9 165 EP83
Glenheadon Cl, Lthd. KT22
off Glenheadon Ri 231 CK123
Glenheadon Ri, Lthd. KT22 231 CK123
Glenhill Cl, N3 98 DA54
Glen Ho, E16
off Storey St 305 M3
Glenhouse Rd, SE9 185 EN85
Glenhurst Av, NW5 120 DG63
Bexley DA5 186 EZ88
Ruislip HA4 115 BQ59
Glenhurst Ct, SE19 182 DT92
Glenhurst Ri, SE19 182 DQ94
Glenhurst Rd, N12 98 DD50
Brentford TW8 157 CJ79
Glenilla Rd, NW3 274 C4
Glenister Gdns, Hayes UB3 155 BV75
Glenister Ho, Hayes UB3 135 BV74
Glenister Pk Rd, SW16 181 DK94
Glenister Rd, SE10 303 L10
Chesham HP5 54 AQ28
Glenister St, E16 305 M3
Glenkerry Ho, E14 290 E8
Glenlea Path, SE9
off Well Hall Rd 185 EM85
Glenlea Rd, SE9 185 EM85
Glenlion Ct, Wey. KT13 195 BR104
Glenloch Rd, NW3 274 C4
Enfield EN3 82 DW40
Glen Luce, Chsht EN8 67 DX31
Glenluce Rd, SE3 315 N3
Glenlyn Av, St.Alb. AL1 43 CH21
Glenlyon Rd, SE9 185 EN85
Glenmere Av, NW7 97 CU52
Glenmere Row, SE12 184 EG86
Glen Ms, E17
off Glen Rd 123 DZ57
Glenmill, Hmptn. TW12 176 BZ92
Glenmire Ter, Stans.Abb. SG12 33 ED11
Glenmore Cl, Add. KT15 194 BH104
Glenmore Gdns, Abb.L. WD5
off Stewart Cl 59 BU32
Glenmore Rd, NW3 274 C4
Welling DA16 165 ET81
Glenmore Way, Bark. IG11 146 EU69
Glenmount Path, SE18
off Raglan Rd 165 EQ78
Glenn Av, Pur. CR8 219 DP111
Glennie Rd, SE27 181 DN90
Glenny Rd, Bark. IG11 145 EQ65
Glenorchy Cl, Hayes UB4 136 BY71
Glenparke Rd, E7 144 EH65
Glen Ri, Wdf.Grn. IG8 102 EH51
Glen Rd, E13 292 C4
E17 123 DZ57
Chessington KT9 198 CL104
Glen Rd End, Wall. SM6 219 DH109
Glenrosa Gdns, Grav. DA12 191 GM92
Glenrosa St, SW6 307 N8
Glenrose Cl, Slou. SL2 132 AW72
Glenrose Ct, Sid. DA14 186 EV92
Glenroy St, W12 282 A8
Glensdale Rd, SE4 163 DZ83
Glenshee Cl, Nthwd. HA6
off Rickmansworth Rd 93 BQ51
Glenshiel Rd, SE9 185 EN85
Glenside, Chig. IG7 103 EP51
Glenside Cl, Ken. CR8 236 DR115
Glenside Cotts, Slou. SL1 152 AT76
Glentanner Way, SW17 180 DD90
Glen Ter, E14 302 E4
Glentham Gdns, SW13 159 CV79
Glentham Rd, SW13 159 CU79
Glenthorne Av, Croy. CR0 202 DV102
Glenthorne Cl, Sutt. SM3 200 DA102
Uxbridge UB10 134 BN69
Glenthorne Gdns, Ilf. IG6 125 EN55
Sutton SM3 200 DA102
Sch Glenthorne High Sch, Sutt. SM3
off Sutton Common Rd 200 DA102
Glenthorne Ms, W6
off Glenthorne Rd 159 CV77
Glenthorne Rd, E17 123 DY57
N11 98 DF50
W6 294 A8
Kingston upon Thames KT1 198 CM98
Glenthorpe Rd, Mord. SM4 199 CX99
Glenton Cl, Rom. RM1 105 FE51
Glenton Ms, SE15 312 G9
Glenton Rd, SE13 164 EE84
Glenton Way, Rom. RM1 105 FE52
Glentrammon Av, Orp. BR6 223 ET107
Glentrammon Cl, Orp. BR6 223 ET107
Glentrammon Gdns, Orp. BR6 223 ET107
Glentrammon Rd, Orp. BR6 223 ET107
Glentworth Pl, Slou. SL1 131 AQ74
Glentworth St, NW1 284 F5
Glenure Rd, SE9 185 EN85
Glenview, SE2 166 EX79
Glen Vw, Grav. DA12 191 GJ88
Glenview Gdns, Hem.H. HP1
off Glenview Rd 40 BH20
Glenview Rd, Brom. BR1 204 EK96
Hemel Hempstead HP1 40 BH20
Glenville Av, Enf. EN2 82 DQ38
Glenville Gro, SE8 313 P5
Glenville Ms, SW18 180 DB87
Glenville Rd, Kings.T. KT2 198 CN95
Glen Wk, Islw. TW7 177 CD85
Glen Way, Wat. WD17 75 BS38
Glenwood, Brox. EN10 49 DZ19
Dorking RH5 263 CJ138
Welwyn Garden City AL7 30 DD10
Glenwood Av, NW9 118 CS60
Rainham RM13 147 FG70
Glenwood Cl, Har. HA1 117 CF57
Glenwood Ct, E18
off Clarendon Rd 124 EG55
Glenwood Dr, Rom. RM2 127 FG56
Glenwood Gdns, Ilf. IG2 125 EN57
Glenwood Gro, NW9 118 CQ60
Glenwood Rd, N15 121 DP57
NW7 96 CS48
SE6 183 DZ88
Epsom KT17 217 CU107
Hounslow TW3 157 CD83
Glenwood Way, Croy. CR0 203 DX100
Glenworth Av, E14 302 G9
Glevum Cl, St.Alb. AL3 42 BZ22
Gliddon Dr, E5 122 DU63
Gliddon Rd, W14 294 E9
Glimpsing Grn, Erith DA18 166 EY76
Glisson Rd, Uxb. UB10 134 BN68
Gload Cres, Orp. BR5 206 EX103
Global App, E3 290 D1
Sch Globe Acad, SE1 299 M7
Globe Ct, Hert. SG14
off Bengeo St 32 DQ07
● Globe Ind Est, Grays RM17 170 GC78
Globe Pond Rd, SE16 301 L3
Sch Globe Prim Sch, E2 289 H2
Globe Rd, E1 289 H2
E2 288 G1
E15 281 L3
Hornchurch RM11 127 FG58
Woodford Green IG8 102 EJ51
Globe Rope Wk, E14 302 E9
Globe St, SE1 299 K6
Globe Ter, E2 288 G2
Globe Town, E2 289 J1
Globe Vw, EC4
off High Timber St 287 J10
Globe Wf, SE16 301 K1
Globe Yd, W1 285 J9
Glory Cl, Woob.Grn HP10 110 AF56
Glory Hill La, Beac. HP9 110 AF55
Glory Mead, Dor. RH4 263 CH139
Glory Mill La, Woob.Grn HP10 110 AE56
Glossop Rd, S.Croy. CR2 220 DR109
Gloster Rd, N.Mal. KT3 198 CS98
Woking GU22 227 BA120
Gloucester Arc, SW7 295 N8
Gloucester Av, NW1 275 H8
Grays RM16 170 GC75
Hornchurch RM11 128 FN56
Sidcup DA15 185 ES89
Slough SL1 131 AQ71
Waltham Cross EN8 67 DY33
Welling DA16 165 ET84
Gloucester Circ, SE10 314 F4
Gloucester Cl, NW10 138 CR66
Thames Ditton KT7 197 CG102
Gloucester Ct, EC3
off Byward St 299 P1
Croxley Green WD3 75 BP41
Denham UB9 114 BG59
Hatfield AL10
off De Havilland Cl 45 CT17
Richmond TW9 158 CN80
Tilbury RM18 off Dock Rd 171 GF82
Gloucester Cres, NW1 275 J8
Staines-upon-Thames TW18 174 BK93
Gloucester Dr, N4 121 DP61
NW11 120 DA56
Staines-upon-Thames TW18 173 BC90
Gloucester Gdns, NW11 119 CZ59
W2 283 M8
Cockfosters EN4 80 DG42
Ilford IG1 124 EL59
Sutton SM1 200 DB103
Gloucester Gate, NW1 275 J10
Gloucester Gate Ms, NW1 275 J10
Gloucester Gro, Edg. HA8 96 CR53
Gloucester Ho, NW6 283 K1
Gloucester Ms, E10
off Gloucester Rd 123 EA59
W2 283 P9
Gloucester Ms W, W2 283 N9
Gloucester Par, Sid. DA15 186 EU85
Gloucester Pl, NW1 284 E4
W1 284 F6
Windsor SL4 151 AR82
Gloucester Pl Ms, W1 284 F7
Sch Gloucester Prim Sch, SE15 312 A4
⊖ Gloucester Road 295 P8
Gloucester Rd, E10 123 EA59
E11 124 EH57
E12 125 EM62
E17 101 DX54
N17 100 DR54
N18 100 DT50
SW7 295 N6
W3 158 CQ75
W5 157 CJ75
Barnet EN5 80 DC43
Belvedere DA17 166 EZ78
Croydon CR0 202 DR100
Dartford DA1 187 FH87
Enfield EN2 82 DQ38
Feltham TW13 176 BW88
Gravesend DA12 191 GJ91

Gloucester Rd, Guildford GU2 242 AT132
Hampton TW12 176 CB94
Harrow HA1 116 CB57
Hounslow TW4 156 BY84
Kingston upon Thames KT1 198 CP96
Pilgrim's Hatch CM15 108 FV43
Redhill RH1 250 DF133
Richmond TW9 158 CN80
Romford RM1 127 FE58
Teddington TW11 177 CE92
Twickenham TW2 176 CC88
Gloucester Sq, E2 278 C9
W2 284 B9
Woking GU21, GU22
off Church St E 227 AZ117
Gloucester St, SW1 309 L1
Gloucester Ter, W2 283 N8
Gloucester Wk, W8 295 K4
Woking GU21 227 AZ117
Gloucester Way, EC1 286 F3
Glover Cl, SE2 166 EW77
Cheshunt EN7 *off Allwood Rd* 66 DT27
Glover Dr, N18 100 DW51
Glover Rd, Pnr. HA5 116 BX58
Glovers Cl, Bigg.H. TN16 238 EH116
Hertford SG13 32 DQ11
Glovers Gro, Ruis. HA4 115 BP59
Glovers La, Hast. CM17 52 EY20
Glovers Rd, Reig. RH2 266 DB135
Gloxinia Rd, Sthflt DA13 190 GB93
Gloxinia Wk, Hmptn. TW12 176 CA93
Glycena Rd, SW11 308 F10
Glyn Av, Barn. EN4 80 DD42
Glyn Cl, SE25 202 DS96
Epsom KT17 217 CU109
Glyn Ct, SW16 181 DN90
Stanmore HA7 95 CH51
Glyncroft, Slou. SL1 151 AM75
Glyn Davies Cl, Dunt.Grn TN13 241 FE120
Glyndebourne Pk, Orp. BR6 205 EP103
Glynde Ms, SW3 296 D7
Glynde Rd, Bexh. DA7 166 EX83
Glynde St, SE4 183 DZ86
Glyndon Rd, SE18 165 EQ77
Glyn Dr, Sid. DA14 186 EV91
Glynfield Rd, NW10 138 CS66
Glynne Rd, N22 99 DN54
Glyn Rd, E5 279 K2
Enfield EN3 82 DW42
Worcester Park KT4 199 CX103
Glyn St, SE11 310 C1
Glynswood, Chal.St.P. SL9 91 AZ52
Glynswood Pl, Nthwd. HA6 93 BP52
Glyn Tech Sch, Ewell KT17
off The Kingsway 217 CT111
Glynwood Ct, SE23 182 DW89
Goaters All, SW6 306 G5
GOATHURST COMMON,
Sev. TN14 256 FB130
Goat La, Enf. EN1 82 DT38
Surbiton KT6 197 CJ103
Goat Rd, Mitch. CR4 200 DG101
Goatsfield Rd, Tats. TN16 238 EJ120
Goatswood La, Nave. RM4 105 FH45
Goat Wf, Brent. TW8 158 CL79
Gobions Av, Rom. RM5 105 FD52
Gobions Way, Pot.B. EN6
off Swanley Bar La 64 DB28
Goblins Grn, Welw.G.C. AL7 29 CX10
Godalming Av, Wall. SM6 219 DL106
Godalming Rd, E14 290 C7
Godbold Rd, E15 291 J3
Goddard Cl, Guil. GU2 242 AU130
Shepperton TW17
off Magdalene Rd 194 BM97
Goddard Dr, Bushey WD23 76 CC43
Goddard Pl, N19 121 DJ62
Goddard Rd, Beck. BR3 203 DX98
Goddards Cl, Lt.Berk. SG13 47 DJ19
Goddards Way, Ilf. IG1 125 ER60
GODDEN GREEN, Sev. TN15 257 FN125
Godden Grn Clinic,
Godden Grn TN15 257 FP125
GODDINGTON, Orp. BR6 206 EW104
Goddington Chase, Orp. BR6 224 EV105
Goddington La, Orp. BR6 206 EU104
Godfrey Av, Nthlt. UB5 136 BY67
Twickenham TW2 177 CD87
Godfrey Hill, SE18 305 H9
Godfrey Ho, EC1 287 L3
Godfrey Pl, E2
off Austin St 288 A3
Godfrey Rd, SE18 305 J9
Godfrey St, E15 280 F10
SW3 296 D10
Godfrey Way, Houns. TW4 176 BY87
Goding St, SE11 310 B1
Godley Cl, SE14 313 H6
Godley Rd, SW18 180 DD88
Byfleet KT14 212 BM113
Godliman St, EC4 287 J9
Godman Rd, SE15 312 E9
Grays RM16 171 GG76
Godolphin & Latymer Sch, The,
W6 *off Iffley Rd* 159 CV77
Godolphin Cl, N13 99 DP51
Sutton SM2 217 CZ111
Godolphin Inf Sch, Slou. SL1
off Warrington Av 131 AQ72
Godolphin Jun Sch, Slou. SL1
off Oatlands Dr 131 AR72
Godolphin Pl, W3 138 CR73
Godolphin Rd, W12 159 CV75
Seer Green HP9 89 AQ51
Slough SL1 131 AR73
Weybridge KT13 213 BR107
Godric Cres, New Adgtn CR0 221 ED110
Godson Rd, Croy. CR0 201 DN104
Godson St, N1 276 E10
Godson Yd, NW6
off Kilburn Pk Rd 283 J3
GODSTONE, RH9 252 DV131
Godstone Bypass, Gdse. RH9 252 DW129
Godstone Grn, Gdse. RH9 252 DV131
Godstone Grn Rd, Gdse. RH9 252 DV131
Godstone Hill, Gdse. RH9 252 DV127
Godstone Interchange,
Gdse. RH9 252 DW128
Godstone Rd, Bletch. RH1 252 DR133
Caterham CR3 236 DU124
Kenley CR8 220 DR114
Oxted RH8 253 EA131
Purley CR8 219 DN112
Sutton SM1 218 DC105
Godstone Rd,
Twickenham TW1 177 CG86
Whyteleafe CR3 236 DT116
Godstone Village Sch, Gdse. RH9
off Ivy Mill La 252 DV132
Godstow Rd, SE2 166 EW75
Godwin Cl, E4 83 EC38
N1 277 K10
Epsom KT19 216 CQ107
Godwin Ct, NW1 275 M10
Godwin Ho, NW6
off Tollgate Gdns 273 L10
Godwin Jun Sch, E7
off Cranmer Rd 124 EH63
Godwin Prim Sch, Dag. RM9
off Finnymore Rd 146 EY66
Godwin Rd, E7 124 EH63
Bromley BR2 204 EJ97
Goethe Institut, SW7 296 B6
Goffers Rd, SE3 315 J7
Goffs Cres, Goffs Oak EN7 65 DP29
Goffs La, Goffs Oak EN7 66 DU29
GOFFS OAK, Wal.Cr. EN7 66 DQ29
Goffs Oak Av, Goffs Oak EN7 65 DP28
Goffs Oak Prim Sch, Goffs Oak EN7
off Millcrest Rd 65 DP28
Goffs Rd, Ashf. TW15 175 BR93
Goffs Sch, Chsht EN7
off Goffs La 66 DU29
Gogmore Fm Cl, Cher. KT16 193 BF101
Gogmore La, Cher. KT16 194 BG101
Goidel Cl, Wall. SM6 219 DK105
Golborne Gdns, W10 282 F5
Golborne Ms, W10 282 E7
Golborne Rd, W10 282 F7
Goldace, Grays RM17 170 FZ79
Golda Cl, Barn. EN5 79 CX44
Goldbeaters Gro, Edg. HA8 96 CS51
Goldbeaters Prim Sch, Edg. HA8
off Thirleby Rd 96 CR53
Goldcliff Cl, Mord. SM4 200 DA101
Gold Cl, Brox. EN10 49 DY20
Goldcrest Cl, E16 292 E6
SE28 146 EW73
Horley RH6 268 DD147
Goldcrest Ms, W5 137 CK71
Goldcrest Way, Bushey WD23 94 CC46
New Addington CR0 221 ED109
Purley CR8 219 DK110
Goldcroft, Hem.H. HP3 40 BN22
Golden Ct, Islw. TW7 157 CD82
Richmond TW9 *off George St* 177 CK85
Golden Cres, Hayes UB3 135 BT74
Golden Cross Ms, W11 282 G8
Golden Dell, Welw.G.C. AL7 29 CZ13
★ **Golden Hinde**, SE1 299 L2
Golden Jubilee Br, SE1 298 C3
WC2 298 B2
Golden La, EC1 287 J5
W.Wick. BR4 203 EC104
Golden La Est, EC1 287 J5
Golden Lion Ct, N9 *off The Grn* 100 DU47
Golden Manor, W7 137 CE73
Golden Oak Cl, Farn.Com. SL2 131 AQ65
Golden Plover Cl, E16 292 A8
Golden Sq, W1 285 M10
Golden Yd, NW3 *off Heath St* 120 DC63
Golders Cl, Edg. HA8 96 CP50
Golders Gdns, NW11 119 CY59
GOLDERS GREEN, NW11 120 DA59
Golders Green 120 DA59
Golders Green 120 DA60
Golders Grn Cres, NW11 119 CZ59
Golders Grn Rd, NW11 119 CY58
Golders Hill Sch, NW11
off Finchley Rd 120 DA59
Golders Manor Dr, NW11 119 CX58
Golders Pk Cl, NW11 120 DA60
Golders Ri, NW4 119 CX57
Golders Way, NW11 119 CZ59
Goldfinch Cl, Orp. BR6 224 EU106
Goldfinch Gdns, Guil. GU4 243 BD133
Goldfinch Rd, SE28 165 ER76
South Croydon CR2 221 DY110
Goldfinch Way, Borwd. WD6 78 CN42
Goldfort Wk, Wok. GU21
off Langmans Way 226 AS116
Goldhawk Ms, W12
off Devonport Rd 159 CV75
Goldhawk Road 294 A5
Goldhawk Rd, W6 159 CT77
W12 159 CU76
Goldhaze Cl, Wdf.Grn. IG8 102 EK52
Gold Hill, Edg. HA8 96 CR51
Gold Hill E, Chal.St.P. SL9 90 AX54
Gold Hill N, Chal.St.P. SL9 90 AW53
Gold Hill W, Chal.St.P. SL9 90 AW53
Goldhurst Ter, NW6 273 N7
Goldie Leigh Hosp, SE2 166 EW79
Golding Cl, N18 100 DR51
Chess. KT9 *off Coppard Gdns* 215 CJ107
Golding Ct, Ilf. IG1 125 EN62
Goldingham Av, Loug. IG10 85 EQ40
Golding Rd, Sev. TN13 257 FJ122
Goldings, Hert. SG14 31 DN06
Goldings, The, Wok. GU21 226 AT116
Goldings Cres, Hat. AL10 45 CV17
Goldings Hill, Loug. IG10 85 EN39
Goldings Ho, Hat. AL10 45 CV17
Goldings La, Waterf. SG14 31 DN06
Goldings Ri, Loug. IG10 85 EN39
Goldings Rd, Loug. IG10 85 EN39
Golding St, E1 288 D9
Golding Ter, SW11
off Longhedge St 309 H8
Goldington Cl, Hodd. EN11 33 DZ14
Goldington Cres, NW1 275 N10
Goldington St, NW1 275 N10
Gold La, Edg. HA8 96 CR51
Goldman Cl, E2 288 C4
Goldmark Ho, SE3
off Lebrun Sq 164 EH83
Goldney Rd, W9 283 J5
Goldrill Dr, N11 98 DG47
Goldrings Rd, Oxshott KT22 214 CC113
Goldring Way, Lon.Col. AL2 61 CH27
Goldsboro Rd, SW8 309 P6
Goldsborough Cres, E4 101 EC47
Goldsborough Indep Hosp,
Red. RH1 266 DG138
Goldsdown Cl, Enf. EN3 83 DY40
Goldsdown Rd, Enf. EN3 83 DX40
Goldsel Rd, Swan. BR8 207 FD99
Goldsmid St, SE18 165 ES78
Goldsmith, Grays RM17 170 FZ79
Goldsmith Av, E12 144 EL65
NW9 119 CT58
W3 138 CR73
Romford RM7 126 FA59
Goldsmith Cl, W3 138 CR74
Biggin Hill TN16 238 EL117
Harrow HA2 116 CB60
Goldsmith La, NW9 118 CP56
Goldsmith Rd, E10 123 EA60
E17 101 DX54
N11 98 DF50
SE15 312 C6
W3 138 CR74
Goldsmiths Bottom,
Sev. TN14 256 FE127
Goldsmiths Cl, Wok. GU21 226 AW118
Goldsmiths Coll, SE14 313 M6
★ **Goldsmiths' Hall**, EC2 287 J8
Goldsmith's Pl, NW6 273 L9
Goldsmith's Row, E2 288 C1
Goldsmith's Sq, E2 278 D10
Goldsmith St, EC2 287 K8
Goldsmith Way, St.Alb. AL3 42 CC19
Goldstone Cl, Ware SG12
off High Oak Rd 33 DX05
Goldstone Fm Vw, Lthd. KT23 246 CA127
Goldsworth Orchard, Wok. GU21
off St. John's Rd 226 AU118
GOLDSWORTH PARK,
Wok. GU21 226 AU117
Goldsworth Pk, Wok. GU21 226 AU117
● **Goldsworth Pk Trd Est**,
Wok. GU21 226 AU116
Goldsworth Prim Sch, Wok. GU21
off Bridge Barn La 226 AW118
Goldsworth Rd, Wok. GU21 226 AW118
● **Goldsworth Rd Ind Est**, Wok. GU21
off Goldsworth Rd 226 AX117
Goldsworthy Gdns, SE16 301 H9
Goldsworthy Way, Slou. SL1 130 AJ72
Goldwell Ho, SE22
off Quorn Rd 162 DS83
Goldwell Rd, Th.Hth. CR7 201 DM98
Goldwin Cl, SE14 313 H6
Goldwing Cl, E16 291 P9
Golf Cl, Bushey WD23 76 BX41
Stanmore HA7 95 CJ52
Thornton Heath CR7
off Kensington Av 201 DN95
Woking GU22 211 BE114
Golf Club Dr, Kings.T. KT2 178 CR94
Golf Club Rd, Brook.Pk AL9 64 DA26
Weybridge KT13 213 BP109
Woking GU22 226 AU120
Golfe Rd, Ilf. IG1 125 ER62
Golf Ho Rd, Oxt. RH8 254 EJ129
Golf Links Av, Grav. DA11 191 GH92
Golf Ride, Enf. EN2 81 DN35
Golf Rd, W5 138 CM72
Bromley BR1 205 EN97
Kenley CR8 236 DR118
Golf Side, Sutt. SM2 217 CY111
Twickenham TW2 177 CD90
Golfside Cl, N20 98 DE48
New Malden KT3 198 CS96
Gollogly Ter, SE7 164 EJ78
Gombards, St.Alb. AL3 43 CD19
Gombards All, St.Alb. AL3
off Worley Rd 43 CD19
Gomer Gdns, Tedd. TW11 177 CG93
Gomer Pl, Tedd. TW11 177 CG93
Gomm Rd, SE16 300 G7
Gomms Wd Cl, Forty Grn HP9 88 AH51
GOMSHALL, Guil. GU5 261 BR139
Gomshall 261 BR139
Gomshall Av, Wall. SM6 219 DL106
Gomshall Gdns, Ken. CR8 236 DS115
Gomshall La, Shere GU5 260 BN139
Gomshall Rd, Sutt. SM2 217 CW110
Gondar Gdns, NW6 272 G2
Gonnerston, St.Alb. AL3 42 CB19
Gonson St, SE8 314 C3
Gonston Cl, SW19 179 CY89
Gonville Av, Crox.Grn WD3 75 BP44
Gonville Cres, Nthlt. UB5 136 CB65
Gonville Prim Sch, Th.Hth. CR7
off Gonville Rd 201 DM99
Gonville Rd, Th.Hth. CR7 201 DM99
Gonville St, SW6 306 F10
Gooch Ho, E5 122 DV62
Goodacre Cl, Pot.B. EN6 64 DB32
Goodall Rd, E11 123 EC62
Goodchild Rd, N4 122 DQ60
Gooden Ct, Har. HA1 117 CE62
Goodenough Cl, Couls. CR5 235 DN120
Goodenough Rd, SW19 179 CZ94
Goodenough Way, Couls. CR5 235 DM120
Gooderham Ho, Grays RM16 171 GH75
Goodey Rd, Bark. IG11 145 ET66
Goodge Pl, W1 285 M7
Goodge Street 285 M6
Goodge St, W1 285 M7
Goodhall Cl, Stan. HA7 95 CG51
Goodhall St, NW10 138 CS69
Goodhart Pl, E14 289 M10
Goodhart Way, W.Wick. BR4 204 EE101
Goodhew Rd, Croy. CR0 202 DU100
Gooding Cl, N.Mal. KT3 198 CQ98
Goodinge Cl, N7 276 A4
Goodison Cl, Bushey WD23 76 CC43
Goodlake Ct, Denh. UB9 113 BF59
GOODLEY STOCK, West. TN16 255 EP130
Goodley Stock, West. TN16 255 EP129
Goodley Stock Rd,
Crock.H. TN8 255 EP131
Westerham TN16 255 EP128
Goodman Cres, SW2 181 DK89
Croy. CR0 201 DP100
Goodman Pk, Slou. SL2 132 AW74
Goodman Pl, Stai. TW18 173 BF91
Goodman Rd, E10 123 EC59
Goodmans Ct, E1 288 A10
Wembley HA0 117 CK63
Goodman's Stile, E1 288 C8
Goodman's Yd, E1 288 A10
GOODMAYES, Ilf. IG3 126 EV61
Goodmayes 126 EU60
Goodmayes Av, Ilf. IG3 126 EU60
Goodmayes Hosp, Ilf. IG3 126 EU57
Goodmayes La, Ilf. IG3 126 EU63
Goodmayes Prim Sch, Ilf. IG3
off Airthrie Rd 126 EV60
Goodmayes Retail Pk,
Rom. RM6 126 EV60
Goodmayes Rd, Ilf. IG3 126 EU60
Goodmead Rd, Orp. BR6 206 EU101
Goodrich Cl, Wat. WD25 75 BU35
Goodrich Prim Sch, SE22
off Dunstans Rd 182 DU86
Goodrich Rd, SE22 182 DT86
Good Shepherd Prim Sch,
Downham BR1
off Moorside Rd 184 EF91
Good Shepherd RC Prim Sch,
New Adgtn CR0 *off Dunley Dr* 243 EB108
Good Shepherd RC Prim Sch, The,
W12 *off Gayford Rd* 159 CT75
Goodson Rd, NW10 138 CS66
Goods Way, NW1 276 A10
Goodway Gdns, E14 290 G8
Goodwill Dr, Har. HA2 116 CA60
Goodwin Cl, SE16 300 B7
Mitcham CR4 200 DD97
Goodwin Ct, Barn. EN4 80 DE44
Waltham Cross EN8 67 DY28
Goodwin Dr, Sid. DA14 186 EX90
Goodwin Gdns, Croy. CR0 219 DP107
Goodwin Meadows,
Woob.Grn HP10 110 AE57
Goodwin Rd, N9 100 DW46
W12 159 CU75
Croydon CR0 219 DP106
Slough SL2 131 AM69
Goodwins Ct, WC2 286 A10
Goodwin St, N4
off Fonthill Rd 121 DN61
Goodwood Av, Enf. EN3 82 DW37
Hornchurch RM12 128 FL63
Hutton CM13 109 GE44
Watford WD24 75 BS35
Goodwood Cl, Hodd. EN11 49 DZ16
Morden SM4 200 DA98
Stanmore HA7 95 CJ50
Goodwood Cres, Grav. DA12 191 GJ93
Goodwood Dr, Nthlt. UB5 136 CA65
Goodwood Path, Borwd. WD6 78 CN40
Goodwood Rd, SE14 313 L5
Redhill RH1 250 DF132
Goodworth Rd, Red. RH1 251 DH132
Goodwyn Av, NW7 96 CS50
Goodwyn Sch, NW7
off Hammers La 97 CU50
Goodwyns Pl, Dor. RH4 263 CH138
Goodwyns Rd, Dor. RH4 263 CH139
Goodwyns Vale, N10 98 DG53
Goodyers Av, Rad. WD7 61 CF33
Goodyers Gdns, NW4 119 CX57
Goosander Way, SE28 165 ER76
Goose Acre, Chesh. HP5 56 AT30
Gooseacre, Welw.G.C. AL7 29 CZ11
Gooseacre La, Har. HA3 117 CK57
Goosecroft, Hem.H. HP1 39 BF19
Goosefields, Rick. WD3 74 BJ44
GOOSE GREEN, Hodd. EN11 48 DW17
Goose Grn, Cob. KT11 229 BU119
Farnham Royal SL2 131 AP68
Gomshall GU5 261 BQ139
Goose Grn Cl, Orp. BR5 206 EU96
Goose Grn Prim Sch, SE22
off Tintagel Cres 162 DT84
Goose La, Wok. GU22 226 AV122
Gooseley La, E6 293 L2
Goosens Cl, Sutt. SM1
off Turnpike La 218 DC106
Goose Rye Rd, Worp. GU3 242 AT125
Goose Sq, E6 293 J9
Gooshays Dr, Rom. RM3 106 FL50
Gooshays Gdns, Rom. RM3 106 FL51
Gophir La, EC4 287 L10
Gopsall St, N1 277 M9
Goral Mead, Rick. WD3 92 BK46
Goran Ct, N9
off Bedevere Rd 100 DU48
Gordon Av, E4 102 EE51
SW14 158 CS84
Hornchurch RM12 127 FF61
South Croydon CR2 220 DQ110
Stanmore HA7 95 CH51
Twickenham TW1 177 CG85
Gordonbrock Prim Sch, SE4
off Gordonbrock Rd 183 EA85
Gordonbrock Rd, SE4 183 EA85
Gordon Cl, E17 123 EA58
N19 121 DJ61
Chertsey KT16 193 BE104
St. Albans AL1
off Kitchener Cl 43 CH21
Staines-upon-Thames TW18 174 BH93
Gordon Cres, Croy. CR0 202 DS102
Hayes UB3 155 BU76
Gordondale Rd, SW19 180 DA89
Gordon Dr, Cher. KT16 193 BE104
Shepperton TW17 195 BR100
Gordon Gdns, Edg. HA8 96 CP54
Gordon Gro, SE5 311 H9
Gordon Hill 81 DP39
Gordon Hill, Enf. EN2 82 DQ39
Gordon Hosp, SW1 297 N9
Gordon Ho, E1 288 G10
Gordon Ho Rd, NW5 275 H1
Gordon Infants' Sch, Ilf. IG1
off Golfe Rd 125 ER62
Gordon Pl, W8 295 K4
Gravesend DA12 *off East Ter* 191 GJ86
Gordon Prim Sch, SE9
off Craigton Rd 165 EM84
Gordon Prom, Grav. DA12 191 GJ86
Gordon Prom E, Grav. DA12 191 GJ86
Gordon Rd, E4 102 EE45
E11 124 EG58
E15 280 F1
E18 102 EH53
N3 97 CZ52
N9 100 DV47
N11 99 DK52
SE15 312 E7
W4 158 CP79
W5 137 CJ73
W13 137 CH73
Ashford TW15 174 BL90
Barking IG11 145 ES67
Beckenham BR3 203 DZ97
Belvedere DA17 167 FC77
Carshalton SM5 218 DF107
Caterham CR3 236 DR121
Chesham HP5 54 AQ32
Claygate KT10 215 CE107
Dartford DA1 188 FK87
Enfield EN2 82 DQ39
Grays RM16 171 GF75
Harrow HA3 117 CE55
Hounslow TW3 156 CC84
Ilford IG1 125 ER62
Kingston upon Thames KT2 198 CM95
Northfleet DA11 190 GE87
Redhill RH1 250 DG131
Richmond TW9 158 CM82
Romford RM6 126 EZ58
Sevenoaks TN13 257 FH125
Shenfield CM15 109 GA46
Shepperton TW17 195 BR100
Sidcup DA15 185 ES85
Gordon Rd, Southall UB2 156 BY77
Staines-upon-Thames TW18 173 BC91
Surbiton KT5 198 CM101
Waltham Abbey EN9 67 EA34
West Drayton UB7 134 BL73
Windsor SL4 151 AM82
Gordon Sq, WC1 285 P5
Gordon St, E13 291 P3
WC1 285 N4
Gordons Way, Oxt. RH8 253 ED128
Gordon Way, Barn. EN5 79 CZ42
Bromley BR1 204 EG95
Chalfont St. Giles HP8 90 AV48
Gore, The, Burn. SL1 130 AG69
Gore Cl, Hare. UB9 114 BH56
Gore Ct, NW9 118 CN57
Gorefield Pl, NW6 273 J10
Gore Hill, Amer. HP7 55 AP43
Gorelands La, Ch.St.G. HP8 91 AZ47
Gorell Rd, Beac. HP9 89 AP54
Gore Rd, E9 279 H9
SW20 199 CW96
Burnham SL1 130 AH69
Dartford DA2 188 FQ90
Goresbrook Rd, Dag. RM9 146 EV67
Goresbrook Village, Dag. RM9
off Goresbrook Rd 146 EV67
Gore St, SW7 295 P6
GORHAMBURY, St.Alb. AL3 42 BY18
★ **Gorhambury**, St.Alb. AL3 42 BW19
Gorhambury Dr, St.Alb. AL3 42 BW19
Gorham Dr, St.Alb. AL1 43 CE23
Gorham Pl, W11 294 E1
Goring Cl, Rom. RM5 105 FC53
Goring Gdns, Dag. RM8 126 EW63
Goring Rd, N11 99 DL51
Dagenham RM10 147 FD65
Staines-upon-Thames TW18 173 BD92
Gorings Sq, Stai. TW18 173 BE91
Goring St, EC3 287 P8
Goring Way, Grnf. UB6 136 CC68
Gorle Cl, Wat. WD25 59 BU34
Gorleston Rd, N15 122 DR57
Gorleston St, W14 294 F8
Gorman Rd, SE18 305 K8
Gorringe Av, S.Darenth DA4 209 FR96
Gorringe Pk Av, Mitch. CR4 180 DF94
Gorringe Pk Prim Sch,
Mitch. CR4 *off Sandy La* 200 DG95
Gorse Cl, E16 291 N9
Hatfield AL10 45 CT21
Tadworth KT20 233 CV120
Gorse Ct, Guil. GU4 243 BC132
Gorse Hill, Fnghm DA4 208 FL100
Gorse Hill La, Vir.W. GU25 192 AX98
Gorse Hill Rd, Vir.W. GU25 192 AX98
Gorselands Cl, W.Byf. KT14 212 BJ111
Gorse La, Chobham GU24 210 AS108
Gorse Meade, Slou. SL1 131 AN74
Gorse Ri, SW17 180 DG92
Gorse Rd, Croy. CR0 221 EA105
Orpington BR5 206 FA103
Gorse Wk, West Dr. UB7 134 BL72
Gorseway, Hat. AL10 29 CT14
Romford RM7 127 FD61
Gorst Rd, NW10 138 CQ70
SW11 180 DF86
Gorsuch Pl, E2 288 A2
Gorsuch St, E2 288 A2
Gosberton Rd, SW12 180 DG88
Gosbury Hill, Chess. KT9 216 CL105
Gosden Cl, Bramley GU5 258 AY143
Gosden Common,
Bramley GU5 258 AY143
Gosden Hill Rd, Guil. GU4 243 BC130
Gosden Ho Sch, Bramley GU5
off Gosden Common 258 AY143
Gosfield Rd, Dag. RM8 126 FA61
Epsom KT19 216 CR112
Gosfield St, W1 285 L6
Gosford Gdns, Ilf. IG4 125 EM57
Gosforth La, Wat. WD19 94 BW48
Gosforth Path, Wat. WD19 93 BU48
Goshawk Gdns, Hayes UB4 135 BS69
Goshawk Way, Felt. TW14 175 BV85
Goslar Way, Wind. SL4 151 AP82
Goslett Ct, Bushey WD23
off Bournehall Av 76 CA43
Goslett Yd, WC2 285 P9
Gosling Cl, Grnf. UB6 136 CA69
Gosling Grn, Slou. SL3 152 AY76
Gosling Rd, Slou. SL3 152 AY76
Gosling Way, SW9 310 F7
Gospatrick Rd, N17 100 DQ52
GOSPEL OAK, NW5 275 H1
Gospel Oak 275 H1
Gospel Oak Prim Sch, NW3 274 G1
Gosport Dr, Horn. RM12 148 FJ65
Gosport Rd, E17 123 DZ57
Gosport Wk, N17
off Yarmouth Cres 122 DV57
Gossage Rd, SE18 165 ER78
Uxbridge UB10 134 BM66
Gossamers, The, Wat. WD25 76 BY36
Gosse Cl, Hodd. EN11 33 DZ14
Gosselin Rd, Hert. SG14 32 DQ07
Gosset St, E2 288 B2
Goss Hill, Dart. DA2 188 FJ93
Swanley BR8 188 FJ93
Gosshill Rd, Chis. BR7 205 EN96
Gossington Cl, Chis. BR7
off Beechwood Ri 185 EP91
Gossoms End, Berk. HP4 38 AU18
Gossoms Ryde, Berk. HP4 38 AU18
Gosterwood St, SE8 313 M2
Gostling Rd, Twick. TW2 176 CA88
Goston Gdns, Th.Hth. CR7 201 DN97
Goswell Arches, Wind. SL4
off Goswell Rd 151 AR81
Goswell Hill, Wind. SL4
off Peascod St 151 AR81
Goswell Rd, EC1 287 J5
Windsor SL4 151 AR81
Gothic Cl, Dart. DA1 188 FK90
Gothic Ct, Hayes UB3
off Sipson La 155 BR79
Gothic Rd, Twick. TW2 177 CD89
Gottfried Ms, NW5
off Fortess Rd 121 DJ63
Goudhurst Rd, Brom. BR1 184 EE92
Gouge Av, Nthflt DA11 190 GE88
Gough Rd, E15 281 L1
Enfield EN1 82 DV40
Gough Sq, EC4 286 F8
Gough St, WC1 286 D4
Gough Wk, E14 290 A9
Gould Cl, N.Mymms AL9 45 CV24
Gould Ct, SE19 182 DS92
Guildford GU4 243 BD132

G

Goulden Ho App, SW11 308 C8
Goulding Gdns, Th.Hth. CR7 201 DP96
Gould Rd, Felt. TW14 175 BS87
Twickenham TW2 177 CE88
Goulds Grn, Uxb. UB8 135 BP72
Gould Ter, E8 278 F3
Goulston St, E1 288 A8
Goulton Rd, E5 278 F2
Gourley Pl, N15 122 DS57
Gourley St, N15 122 DS57
Gourock Rd, SE9 185 EN85
Govan St, E2 278 D9
Gover Ct, SW4 off Paradise Rd 310 B8
Government Row, Enf. EN3 83 EA38
Governors Av, Denh. UB9 113 BF57
Governors Cl, Amer. HP6 72 AT37
Govett Av, Shep. TW17 195 BQ99
Govier Cl, E15 281 K7
Gowan Av, SW6 306 E7
Gowan Rd, NW10 139 CV65
Gowar Fld, S.Mimms EN6 63 CU32
Gower, The, Egh. TW20 193 BB97
Gower Cl, SW4 181 DJ86
Gower Ct, WC1 285 N4
Sch Gower Ho Sch, NW9
off Blackbird Hill 118 CQ61
Gower Ms, WC1 285 N7
Gower Pl, WC1 285 M4
Gower Rd, E7 281 P5
Horley RH6 268 DE148
Isleworth TW7 157 CF79
Weybridge KT13 213 BR107
Gowers, The, Amer. HP6 55 AS36
Harlow CM20 36 EU13
Gowers La, Orsett RM16 171 GF75
Gower St, WC1 285 M4
Gower's Wk, E1 288 C8
Gowings Grn, Slou. SL1 151 AL75
Gowland Pl, Beck. BR3 203 DZ96
Gowlett Rd, SE15 162 DU83
Gowlland Cl, Croy. CR0 202 DU101
Gowrie Pl, Cat. CR3 236 DQ122
Gowrie Rd, SW11 160 DG83
Graburn Way, E.Mol. KT8 197 CD97
Grace Av, Bexh. DA7 166 EZ82
Shenley WD7 61 CK33
● Grace Business Cen,
Mitch. CR4 200 DF100
Gracechurch St, EC3 287 M10
Grace Cl, SE9 184 EK90
Borehamwood WD6 78 CR39
Edgware HA8 96 CQ52
Ilford IG6 103 ET51
Grace Ct, Slou. SL1 131 AQ74
Gracedale Rd, SW16 181 DH92
Gracefield Gdns, SW16 181 DL90
Grace Jones Cl, E8 278 C5
Grace Ms, Beck. BR3 183 EA93
Grace Path, SE26 182 DW91
Grace Pl, E3 290 D3
Grace Rd, Croy. CR0 202 DQ100
Grace's All, E1 288 C10
Graces Ms, SE5 311 M8
Graces Rd, SE5 311 N8
Grace St, E3 290 D3
Gracious La, Sev. TN13 256 FG130
Gracious La End, Sev. TN14 256 FF130
Gracious Pond Rd,
Chobham GU24 210 AT108
Gradient, The, SE26 182 DU91
Graduate Pl, SE1
off Long La 299 N6
Graeme Rd, Enf. EN1 82 DR40
Graemesdyke Av, SW14 158 CP83
Graemesdyke Rd, Berk. HP4 38 AU20
Grafton Cl, W13 137 CG72
George Green SL3 132 AY72
Hounslow TW4 176 BY88
St. Albans AL4
off Princess Diana Dr 43 CK21
West Byfleet KT14
off Madeira Rd 211 BF113
Worcester Park KT4 198 CS104
Grafton Ct, Felt. TW14 175 BR88
Grafton Cres, NW1 275 J5
Grafton Gdns, N4 122 DQ58
Dagenham RM8 126 EY61
Grafton Ho, E3 290 A3
Sch Grafton Inf & Jun Schs, Dag. RM8
off Grafton Rd 126 EZ61
Grafton Ms, W1 285 L5
Grafton Pk Rd, Wor.Pk. KT4 198 CS103
Grafton Pl, NW1 285 N3
Sch Grafton Prim Sch, N7
off Eburne Rd 121 DL62
Grafton Rd, NW5 275 J4
W3 138 CQ73
Croydon CR0 201 DN102
Dagenham RM8 126 EY61
Enfield EN2 81 DM41
Harrow HA1 116 CC57
New Malden KT3 198 CS97
Worcester Park KT4 198 CR104
Graftons, The, NW2
off Hermitage La 120 DA62
Grafton Sq, SW4 161 DJ83
Grafton St, W1 297 K1
Grafton Ter, NW5 274 F3
Grafton Way, W1 285 L5
WC1 285 L5
West Molesey KT8 196 BZ98
Grafton Yd, NW5 275 K5
Graham Av, W13 157 CH75
Broxbourne EN10 49 DY20
Mitcham CR4 200 DG95
Graham Cl, Croy. CR0 203 EA103
Hutton CM13 109 GC43
St. Albans AL1 43 CD23
Grahame Pk Est, NW9 96 CS53
Grahame Pk Way, NW7 97 CT52
NW9 97 CT54
Graham Gdns, Surb. KT6 198 CL102
Graham Rd, E8 278 C4
E13 291 N4
N15 121 DP55
NW4 119 CV58
SW19 179 CZ94
W4 158 CR76
Bexleyheath DA6 166 FA84
Hampton TW12 176 CA91
Harrow HA3 117 CE55
Mitcham CR4 200 DG95
Purley CR8 219 DN113
Graham St, N1 287 H1
Graham Ter, SW1 296 G9
Grainger Cl, Nthlt. UB5
off Lancaster Rd 116 CC64
Grainger Rd, N22 100 DQ53
Isleworth TW7 157 CF82
Grainge's Yd, Uxb. UB8
off Cross St 134 BJ66
Grainstore, The, E16 292 A10
Gramer Cl, E11
off Norman Rd 123 ED61
Sch Grammar Sch for Girls Wilmington,
The, Dart. DA2 off Parsons La 187 FH90
Grampian Cl, Harling. UB3 155 BR80
Orpington BR6
off Clovelly Way 205 ET100
Sutton SM2 218 DC108
Grampian Gdns, NW2 119 CY60
Grampian Ho, N9
off Edmonton Grn Shop Cen 100 DV47
Grampian Way, Slou. SL3 153 BA78
Gramsci Way, SE6 183 EB90
Granard Av, SW15 179 CV85
● Granard Business Cen, NW7
off Bunns La 96 CS51
Sch Granard Prim Sch, SW15
off Cortis Rd 179 CV86
Granard Rd, SW12 180 DF87
Granaries, The, Wal.Abb. EN9 68 EE34
Granary, The, Roydon CM19 34 EH14
Stanstead Abbotts SG12 33 EC12
Granary Cl, N9 100 DW45
Horley RH6 off Waterside 268 DG146
Granary Ct, E15 281 H4
Granary Mans, SE28 165 EQ75
Granary Rd, E1 288 E5
Granary Sq, N1 276 A10
Granary St, NW1 275 N9
Granby Pk Rd, Chsht EN7 66 DT28
Granby Pl, SE1 298 E5
Granby Rd, SE9 165 EM82
Gravesend DA11 190 GD85
Granby St, E2 288 B4
Granby Ter, NW1 285 L1
Grand Av, EC1 287 H6
N10 120 DG56
Surbiton KT5 198 CP99
Wembley HA9 118 CN64
Grand Av E, Wem. HA9 118 CP64
Sch Grand Av Prim & Nurs Sch,
Surb. KT5 off Grand Av 198 CQ100
Grand Dep Rd, SE18 165 EN78
Grand Dr, SW20 199 CW96
Southall UB2 156 CC75
Granden Rd, SW16 201 DL96
Grandfield Av, Wat. WD17 75 BT39
Grandis Cotts, Ripley GU23 228 BH122
Grandison Rd, SW11 180 DF85
Worcester Park KT4 199 CW103
Grand Junct Isle, Sun. TW16
off Lower Hampton Rd 196 BY96
Grand Junct Wf, N1 287 J1
Grand Par, N4 off Green Las 121 DP58
Wembley HA9 off Forty Av 118 CN61
Grand Par Ms, SW15 179 CY85
Grand Stand Rd, Epsom KT18 233 CT117
Grand Union Canal Wk, W7 157 CE76
Grand Union Centre, W10
off West Row 282 D4
Grand Union Cres, E8 278 D7
Grand Union Enterprise Pk, Sthl. UB2
off Bridge Rd 156 CA75
Grand Union Hts, Wem. HA0 137 CK67
● Grand Union Ind Est, NW10 138 CP68
Grand Union Wk, NW1 275 K7
Wembley HA0 off Water Rd 138 CM67
Grand Union Way,
Kings L. WD4 59 BP29
Southall UB2 156 CA75
Grand Vw Av, Bigg.H. TN16 238 EJ117
Grand Wk, E1 289 M4
Granfield St, SW11 308 B7
Grange, The, N20 98 DC46
SE1 300 A6
SW19 179 CX93
W14 off Lisgar Ter 294 G9
Abbots Langley WD5 59 BS31
Chobham GU24 210 AS110
Croydon CR0 203 DZ103
Old Windsor SL4 172 AV85
South Darenth DA4 209 FR95
Walton-on-Thames KT12 195 BV103
Wembley HA0 138 CN66
Worcester Park KT4 198 CR104
Grange Av, N12 98 DC50
N20 97 CY45
SE25 202 DS96
East Barnet EN4 98 DE46
Stanmore HA7 95 CH54
Twickenham TW2 177 CE89
Woodford Green IG8 102 EG51
Grangecliffe Gdns, SE25 202 DS96
Grange Cl, Bletch. RH1 252 DR133
Chalfont St. Peter SL9 90 AY53
Edgware HA8 96 CQ50
Guildford GU2 242 AV130
Hayes UB3 135 BS71
Hemel Hempstead HP2 40 BN21
Hertford SG14 31 DP09
Hounslow TW5 156 BZ79
Ingrave CM13 109 GC50
Leatherhead KT22 231 CK120
Merstham RH1 251 DH128
Sidcup DA15 186 EU90
Watford WD17 75 BU39
West Molesey KT8 196 CB98
Westerham TN16 255 EQ126
Woodford Green IG8 102 EG52
Wraysbury TW19 172 AY86
Sch Grange Comm Inf Sch, The,
New Haw KT15
off The Avenue 212 BG110
Grange Ct, WC2 286 D9
Chigwell IG7 103 EQ47
Loughton IG10 84 EK43
Northolt UB5 136 BW68
Staines-upon-Thames TW18
off Gresham Rd 174 BG92
Waltham Abbey EN9 67 EC34
Walton-on-Thames KT12 195 BU103
Grangecourt Rd, N16 122 DS60
Grange Cres, SE28 146 EW72
Chigwell IG7 103 ER50
Dartford DA2 188 FP86
Grangedale Cl, Nthwd. HA6 93 BS53
Grange Dr, Chis. BR7 184 EL93
Merstham RH1 251 DH128
Orpington BR6
off Rushmore Hill 224 EW109
Woking GU21 210 AY114
Wooburn Green HP10 110 AD60
Grange End, Smallfield RH6 269 DN148
Grange Est, The, N2 98 DD54
Grange Farm Cl, Har. HA2 116 CC61
Grange Farm La, Chig. IG7 103 EQ46
Grange Flds, Chal.St.P. SL9 90 AY53
Grangefields Rd,
Jacobs Well GU4 242 AX128
Grange Gdns, N14 99 DK46
NW3 120 DB62
SE25 202 DS96
Banstead SM7 218 DB113
Farnham Common SL2 111 AR64
Pinner HA5 116 BZ56
Ware SG12 33 DY07
Grange Gro, N1 277 H4
GRANGE HILL, Chig. IG7 103 ER51
⊖ Grange Hill 103 ER49
Grange Hill, SE25 202 DS96
Edgware HA8 96 CQ50
Grangehill Pl, SE9
off Westmount Rd 165 EM83
Grangehill Rd, SE9 165 EM84
Grange Ho, Erith DA8 167 FG82
Grange La, SE21 182 DT89
Letchmore Heath WD25 77 CD39
Roydon CM19 50 EJ15
Grange Mans, Epsom KT17 217 CT108
Grange Meadow, Bans. SM7 218 DB113
Grangemill Rd, SE6 183 EA90
Grangemill Way, SE6 183 EA89
Grangemount, Lthd. KT22 231 CK120
GRANGE PARK, N21 81 DP43
⇌ Grange Park 81 DP43
Grange Pk, W5 138 CL74
Woking GU21 226 AY115
Grange Pk Av, N21 81 DP44
Sch Grange Pk Inf & Jun Schs,
Hayes UB4 off Lansbury Dr 135 BT70
Grange Pk Pl, SW20 179 CV94
Sch Grange Pk Prep Sch, N21
off The Chine 81 DP44
Sch Grange Pk Prim Sch, N21
off Worlds End La 81 DN42
Grange Pk Rd, E10 123 EB60
Thornton Heath CR7 202 DR98
Grange Pl, NW6 273 J7
Staines-upon-Thames TW18 194 BJ96
Walton-on-Thames KT12 195 BU103
Sch Grange Prim Sch, E13 291 M3
SE1 299 N7
W5 off Church Pl 157 CK75
South Harrow HA2
off Welbeck Rd 116 CB60
Grange Rd, E10 123 EA60
E13 291 L3
E17 123 DY57
N6 120 DG58
N17 100 DU51
N18 100 DU51
NW10 139 CV65
SE1 299 P6
SE19 202 DR98
SE25 202 DR98
SW13 159 CU81
W4 158 CP78
W5 137 CK74
Aveley RM15 148 FQ74
Bushey WD23 76 BY43
Caterham CR3 252 DU125
Chalfont St. Peter SL9 90 AY53
Chessington KT9 216 CL105
Edgware HA8 96 CR51
Egham TW20 173 AZ92
Elstree WD6 78 CM43
Gravesend DA11 191 GG87
Grays RM17 170 GB79
Guildford GU2 242 AV129
Harrow HA1 117 CG58
Hayes UB3 135 BS72
Hersham KT12 214 BY105
Ilford IG1 125 EP63
Kingston upon Thames KT1 198 CL97
Leatherhead KT22 231 CK120
New Haw KT15 212 BG110
Orpington BR6 205 EQ103
Romford RM3 105 FH51
Sevenoaks TN13 256 FG127
South Croydon CR2 220 DQ110
South Harrow HA2 117 CD61
Southall UB1 156 BY75
Sutton SM2 218 DA108
Thornton Heath CR7 202 DR98
West Molesey KT8 196 CB98
Woking GU21 210 AY114
Granger Way, Rom. RM1 127 FG58
Grange St, N1 277 M9
St. Albans AL3 43 CD19
Grange Vale, Sutt. SM2 218 DB108
Grange Vw Rd, N20 98 DC46
Grange Wk, SE1 299 P6
Grange Wk Ms, SE1 299 P7
Grangeway, N12 98 DB49
NW6 273 J7
Smallfield RH6 269 DN148
Woodford Green IG8 102 EJ49
Grange Way, Erith DA8 167 FH80
Iver SL0 133 BF72
Grangeway, The, N21 81 DP44
Grangeway Gdns, Ilf. IG4 124 EL57
Grangeways Cl, Nthflt DA11 191 GF91
Grangewood, Bex. DA5 186 EZ88
Potters Bar EN6 64 DB30
Wexham SL3 132 AW71
Grangewood Av, Grays RM16 170 GE76
Rainham RM13 148 FJ70
Grangewood Cl, Brwd. CM13
off Knight's Way 109 GA48
Pinner HA5 115 BU57
Grangewood Dr, Sun. TW16
off Spelthorne Gro 175 BT94
Sch Grangewood Indep Sch, E7
off Chester Rd 144 EK66
Grangewood La, Beck. BR3 183 DZ93
Sch Grangewood Sch, Eastcote HA5
off Fore St 115 BT57
Grangewood St, E6 144 EJ67
Grangewood Ter, SE25
off Grange Rd 202 DR96
Grange Yd, SE1 300 A7
Granham Gdns, N9 100 DT47
Granite Apts, E15 281 H4
Granite St, SE18 165 ET78
Granleigh Rd, E11 124 EE61
Gransden Av, E8 278 F7
Gransden Rd, W12
off Wendell Rd 159 CT75
Grant Av, Slou. SL1 132 AS72
Grantbridge St, N1 277 H10
Grantchester Cl, Har. HA1 117 CF62
Grant Cl, N14 99 DJ45
N17 100 DS54
Shepperton TW17 195 BP100
Grant Ct, E4 off The Ridgeway 101 EC46
Grantham Cl, Edg. HA8 96 CL48
Grantham Gdns, Rom. RM6 126 EZ58
Ware SG12 33 DY05
Grantham Grn, Borwd. WD6 78 CQ43
Grantham Ms, Berk. HP4 38 AX19
Grantham Pl, W1 297 J3
Grantham Rd, E12 125 EN63
SW9 310 B9
W4 158 CS80
Grantley Cl, Shalf. GU4 258 AY141
Grantley Gdns, Guil. GU2 242 AU133
Grantley Pl, Esher KT10 214 CB106
Grantley Rd, Guil. GU2 242 AU133
Hounslow TW4 156 BW82
Grantley St, E1 289 J3
Grantock Rd, E17 101 ED53
Granton Av, Upmin. RM14 128 FM61
Sch Granton Prim Sch, SW16
off Granton Rd 181 DJ94
Granton Rd, SW16 201 DJ95
Ilford IG3 126 EU60
Sidcup DA14 186 EW93
Grant Pl, Croy. CR0 202 DT102
Grant Rd, SW11 160 DD84
Croydon CR0 202 DT102
Harrow HA3 117 CF55
Grants Cl, NW7 97 CW52
Grants La, Oxt. RH8 254 EJ132
Grant's Quay Wf, EC3 299 M1
Grant St, E13 291 N3
N1 276 E10
Grantully Rd, W9 283 L3
Grant Way, Islw. TW7 157 CG79
Grantwood Cl, Red. RH1
off Bushfield Dr 267 DH139
Granville Av, N9 100 DW48
Feltham TW13 175 BU89
Hounslow TW3 176 CA85
Slough SL2 131 AR71
Granville Cl, Byfleet KT14
off Church Rd 212 BM113
Croydon CR0 202 DS103
Weybridge KT13 213 BQ107
Granville Ct, N1 277 M8
Granville Dene, Bov. HP3 57 BA27
Granville Gdns, SW16 201 DM95
W5 138 CM74
Hoddesdon EN11 33 EA13
Granville Gro, SE13 163 EC83
Granville Ms, Sid. DA14 186 EU91
Granville Pk, SE13 314 F10
Granville Pl, N12 98 DC52
SW6 307 L5
W1 284 G9
Pinner HA5 116 BX55
Granville Pt, NW2 119 CZ61
Granville Rd, E17 123 EB58
E18 102 EH54
N4 121 DM58
N12 98 DB52
N13 99 DM51
N22 99 DP53
NW2 119 CZ61
NW6 283 J1
SW18 180 DA87
SW19 off Russell Rd 180 DA94
Barnet EN5 79 CW42
Epping CM16 70 EV29
Gravesend DA11 191 GF87
Hayes UB3 155 BT77
Ilford IG1 125 EP60
Northchurch HP4 38 AS17
Oxted RH8 254 EF129
St. Albans AL1 43 CF20
Sevenoaks TN13 256 FG124
Sidcup DA14 186 EU91
Uxbridge UB10 135 BP65
Watford WD18 76 BW42
Welling DA16 166 EW83
Westerham TN16 255 EQ126
Weybridge KT13 213 BQ107
Woking GU22 227 AZ120
Sch Granville Sch, The, Sev. TN13
off Bradbourne Pk Rd 256 FG123
Granville Sq, SE15 311 P4
WC1 286 D3
Granville St, WC1 286 D3
Grape St, WC2 286 A8
Graphite Apts, N1
off Provost St 287 L1
Graphite Sq, SE11 298 C10
Grapsome Cl, Chess. KT9
off Nigel Fisher Way 215 CJ108
Grasdene Rd, SE18 166 EU80
Grasgarth Cl, W3 138 CQ73
Grasholm Way, Slou. SL3 153 BC77
Grasmere Av, SW15 178 CR91
SW19 200 DA97
W3 138 CQ73
Hounslow TW3 176 CB86
Orpington BR6 205 EP104
Ruislip HA4 115 BQ59
Slough SL2 132 AU73
Wembley HA9 117 CK59
Grasmere Cl, Egh. TW20
off Keswick Rd 173 BB94
Feltham TW14 175 BT88
Guildford GU1 243 BB133
Hemel Hempstead HP3 41 BP22
Loughton IG10 85 EM40
Watford WD25 59 BV32
Grasmere Ct, N22 99 DM51
Grasmere Gdns, Har. HA3 95 CG54
Ilford IG4 125 EM57
Orpington BR6 205 EP104
Grasmere Pt, SE15 312 G4
Sch Grasmere Prim Sch, N16 277 M1
Grasmere Rd, E13 281 N10
N10 99 DH53
N17 100 DU51
SE25 202 DV100
SW16 181 DM92
Bexleyheath DA7 167 FC81
Bromley BR1 204 EF95
Orpington BR6 205 EP104
Purley CR8 219 DP111
St. Albans AL1 43 CH22
Grasmere Way, Byfleet KT14 212 BM112
Grassbanks, Dart. DA1 188 FM88
Grassfield Cl, Couls. CR5 235 DH119
Grasshaven Way, SE28 145 ET74
Grassingham End,
Chal.St.P. SL9 90 AY52
Grassingham Rd,
Chal.St.P. SL9 90 AY52
Grassington Cl, N11 98 DG50
Bricket Wood AL2 60 CA30
Grassington Rd, Sid. DA14 186 EU91
Grasslands, Smallfield RH6 269 DN148
Grassmere, Horl. RH6 269 DH147
Grassmere Rd, Horn. RM11 128 FM56
Grassmount, SE23 182 DV89
Purley CR8 219 DJ110
Grass Pk, N3 97 CZ53
Grass Warren, Tewin AL6 30 DE06
Grassway, Wall. SM6 219 DJ105
Grassy Cl, Hem.H. HP1 40 BG19
Grassy La, Sev. TN13 257 FH126
Grasvenor Av, Barn. EN5 80 DA44
Sch Grasvenor Av Inf Sch, Barn. EN5
off Grasvenor Av 80 DA44
Gratton Dr, Wind. SL4 151 AL84
Gratton Rd, W14 294 E7
Gratton Ter, NW2 119 CX62
Gravel Cl, Chig. IG7 104 EU47
Graveley, Kings.T. KT1
off Willingham Way 198 CN96
Graveley Av, Borwd. WD6 78 CQ42
Graveley Ct, Hem.H. HP2 41 BQ21
Graveley Dell, Welw.G.C. AL7 30 DB10
Tra Gravel Hill 221 DY108
Gravel Hill, N3 97 CZ54
Bexleyheath DA6 187 FB85
Chalfont St. Peter SL9 90 AY53
Croydon CR0 221 DX107
Hemel Hempstead HP1 40 BH20
High Beach IG10 84 EG38
Leatherhead KT22
off North St 231 CH121
Uxbridge UB8 114 BK64
Gravel Hill Cl, Bexh. DA6 187 FB85
Sch Gravel Hill Prim Sch, Bexh. DA6
off Watling St 167 FB84
Gravelhill Ter, Hem.H. HP1 40 BG21
Gravel La, E1 288 A8
Chigwell IG7 104 EU46
Hemel Hempstead HP1 40 BG21
Gravelly Hill, Cat. CR3 252 DS128
Gravelly Ride, SW19 179 CV91
Gravel Path, Berk. HP4 38 AX19
Hemel Hempstead HP1 40 BG20
Gravel Pit La, SE9 185 EQ85
Gravelpits La, Goms. GU5 261 BQ139
Gravel Pit Way, Orp. BR6 206 EU103
Gravel Rd, Brom. BR2 204 EL103
Sutton at Hone DA4 188 FP94
Twickenham TW2 177 CE88
Gravelwood Cl, Chis. BR7 185 EQ90
Gravely Way, Penn HP10 88 AF45
Gravenel Gdns, SW17
off Nutwell St 180 DE92
Graveney Gro, SE20 182 DW94
Graveney Rd, SW17 180 DE91
Sch Graveney Sch, SW17
off Welham Rd 181 DH92
GRAVESEND, DA11 - DA13 191 GJ85
⇌ Gravesend 191 GG87
Coll Gravesend Adult Ed Cen,
Grav. DA11 off Darnley Rd 191 GG86
Sch Gravesend Gram Sch,
Grav. DA12 off Church Wk 191 GK87
Gravesend Rd, W12 139 CU73
H Gravesham Comm Hosp, The,
Grav. DA11 191 GG86
Gravesham Ct, Grav. DA12
off Clarence Row 191 GH87
★ Gravesham Mus, Grav. DA11 191 GH86
● Graves Yd Ind Est, Well. DA16
off Upper Wickham La 166 EV82
Gravetts La, Guil. GU3 242 AS131
Gray Av, Dag. RM8 126 EZ60
Grayburn Cl, Ch.St.G. HP8 90 AU47
Gray Cl, Add. KT15
off Monks Cres 212 BH106
Gray Gdns, Rain. RM13 147 FG65
Grayham Cres, N.Mal. KT3 198 CR98
Grayham Rd, N.Mal. KT3 198 CR98
Grayland Cl, Brom. BR1 204 EK95
Graylands, They.B. CM16 85 ER37
Woking GU21 226 AY116
Graylands Cl, Slou. SL1 131 AM74
Woking GU21 226 AY116
Grayling Cl, E16 291 K4
Grayling Ct, Berk. HP4
off Admiral Way 38 AT17
Grayling Rd, N16 122 DR61
Graylings, The, Abb.L. WD5 59 BR33
Grayling Sq, E2 288 D2
Gray Pl, Ott. KT16
off Clarendon Gate 211 BD107
GRAYS, RM16 & RM17; RM20 170 GA78
⇌ Grays 170 GA79
Sch Grays Conv High Sch, Grays RM17
off College Av 170 GB77
Grayscroft Rd, SW16 181 DK94
Grays End Cl, Grays RM17 170 GA76
Sch Gray's Fm Prim Sch, Orp. BR5
off Grays Fm Rd 206 EV95
Grays Fm Rd, Orp. BR5 206 EV95
Graysfield, Welw.G.C. AL7 30 DA12
Grayshott Rd, SW11 308 G9
★ Gray's Inn, WC1 286 D6
Gray's Inn Pl, WC1 286 D7
Gray's Inn Rd, WC1 286 C3
Gray's Inn Sq, WC1 286 E6
Grays La, Ashf. TW15 175 BP91
Gray's La, Ashtd. KT21 232 CM119
Epsom KT18 232 CN120
Grayson Ho, EC1 287 K3
Grays Pk Rd, Stoke P. SL2 132 AU68
Grays Pl, Slou. SL2 132 AT74
Grays Rd, Gdmg. GU7 258 AT144
Slough SL1 132 AT74
Uxbridge UB10 134 BL67
Westerham TN16 239 EP121
🔒 Grays Shop Cen, Grays RM17
off High St 170 GA79
Gray St, SE1 298 F5
Grays Wk, Chesh. HP5 54 AP29
Hutton CM13 109 GD45
Grays Wd, Horl. RH6 269 DJ148
Grayswood Gdns, SW20
off Farnham Gdns 199 CV96
Grayswood Pt, SW15
off Norley Vale 179 CU88
Gray's Yd, W1 285 H9
Graywood Ct, N12 98 DC52
Sch Grazebrook Prim Sch, N16
off Lordship Rd 122 DR61
Grazebrook Rd, N16 122 DR61
Grazeley Cl, Bexh. DA6 187 FC85
Grazeley Ct, SE19
off Gipsy Hill 182 DS92

Grazings, The, Hem.H. HP2 40 BM18
Greatacre, Chesh. HP5 54 AR30
Great Acre Ct, SW4
off Clapham Pk Rd 161 DK84
GREAT AMWELL, Ware SG12 33 DZ10
Great Amwell La, N8 121 DM55
Great Arthur Ho, EC1 287 J5
Great Auger St, Harl. CM17 36 EX14
Great Bell All, EC2 287 L8
Great Benty, West Dr. UB7 154 BL77
Great Bois Wd, Amer. HP6
off Manor Dr 55 AQ36
GREAT BOOKHAM, Lthd. KT23 246 CB125
★ Great Bookham Common, Lthd. KT23 230 BZ121
Great Braitch La, Hat. AL10 29 CT14
Great Brays, Harl. CM18 52 EU16
Great Break, Welw.G.C. AL7 30 DB10
Great Brownings, SE21 182 DT91
Great Bushey Dr, N20 98 DB46
Great Cambridge Ind Est, Enf. EN1 82 DU43
Jct Great Cambridge Junct, N18 122 DR49
Great Cambridge Rd, N9 100 DS46
N17 100 DR50
N18 100 DR50
Cheshunt EN8 66 DW34
Enfield EN1 82 DU42
Turnford EN10 67 DY26
Great Castle St, W1 285 K8
Great Cen Av, Ruis. HA4 116 BW64
Great Cen St, NW1 284 E6
Great Cen Way, NW10 118 CS64
Wembley HA9 118 CQ63
Great Chapel St, W1 285 N8
Great Chart St, SW11 160 DD84
Great Chertsey Rd, W4 158 CQ82
Feltham TW13 176 CA90
Great Ch La, W6 294 D10
Great Coll St, SW1 298 A6
Great Conduit, Welw.G.C. AL7 30 DC08
Great Cross Av, SE10 315 J5
Great Cullings, Rom. RM7 127 FE61
Great Cumberland Ms, W1 284 E9
Great Cumberland Pl, W1 284 E8
Great Dell, Welw.G.C. AL8 29 CX07
Great Dover St, SE1 299 K5
Greatdown Rd, W7 137 CF70
● Great Eastern Enterprise Cen, E14 302 C5
Great Eastern Rd, E15 280 G6
Waltham Cross EN8
off Great Cambridge Rd 66 DW33
Warley CM14 108 FW49
Great Eastern St, EC2 287 N3
Great Eastern Wk, EC2 287 P7
Great Ellshams, Bans. SM7 234 DA116
Great Elms Rd, Brom. BR2 204 EJ98
Hemel Hempstead HP3 40 BM24
Great Fld, NW9 96 CS53
Greatfield Av, E6 293 J4
Greatfield Cl, N19
off Warrender Rd 121 DJ63
SE4 163 EA84
Greatfields Dr, Uxb. UB8 134 BN71
Greatfields Rd, Bark. IG11 145 ER67
Great Fleete Way, Bark. IG11
off Choats Rd 146 EW68
Greatford Dr, Guil. GU1 243 BD134
Great Galley Cl, Bark. IG11 146 EV69
Great Ganett, Welw.G.C. AL7 30 DB11
Great Gdns Rd, Horn. RM11 127 FH58
Great Gatton Cl, Croy. CR0 203 DY101
Great George St, SW1 297 P5
Great Goodwin Dr, Guil. GU1 243 BB132
Great Gregories La, Epp. CM16 69 ES33
Great Gro, Bushey WD23 76 CB42
Great Gros, Goffs Oak EN7 66 DS28
Great Guildford St, SE1 299 J2
Great Hall, SW11
off Battersea Pk Rd 309 H6
Greatham Rd, Bushey WD23 76 BX41
● Greatham Rd Ind Est, Bushey WD23 76 BX41
Greatham Wk, SW15 179 CU88
Great Harry Dr, SE9 185 EN90
Great Heart, Hem.H. HP2 40 BL18
Great Heath, Hat. AL10 45 CV15
GREAT HIVINGS, Chesh. HP5 54 AP27
Great Hivings, Chesh. HP5 54 AN27
Greathurst End, Bkhm KT23 230 BZ124
Great James St, WC1 286 C5
Great Julians, Rick. WD3 74 BN42
Great Lake Ct, Horl. RH6
off Tanyard Way 269 DH147
Great Ley, Welw.G.C. AL7 29 CY11
Great Leylands, Harl. CM18 52 EU16
Great Marlborough St, W1 285 L9
Great Maze Pond, SE1 299 M4
Great Meadow, Brox. EN10 49 EA22
Great Molewood, Hert. SG14 31 DP06
Great Nelmes Chase, Horn. RM11 128 FM57
Greatness La, Sev. TN14 257 FJ121
Greatness Rd, Sev. TN14 257 FJ121
Great Newport St, WC2
off Charing Cross Rd 285 P10
Great New St, EC4
off New Fetter La 286 F8
Great N Leisure Pk, N12 98 DD52
Great N Rd, N2 120 DE56
N6 120 DE56
Barnet EN5 79 CZ38
Hatfield AL9, AL10 45 CZ23
New Barnet EN5 80 DA43
Potters Bar EN6 64 DB27
Welwyn Garden City AL8 29 CU10
Great N Way, NW4 97 CW54
Great Oak Ct, Hunsdon SG12 34 EK08
Great Oaks, Chig. IG7 103 EQ49
Hutton CM13 109 GB44
Great Oaks Pk, Guil. GU4 243 BB129
Greatorex St, E1 288 C6
Great Ormond St, WC1 286 B6
H Great Ormond St Hosp for Children, The, WC1 286 B5
Great Owl Rd, Chig. IG7 103 EN48
Great Palmers, Hem.H. HP2 40 BM15
Great Pk, Kings L. WD4 58 BM30
Great Pk Cl, Uxb. UB10 134 BN66
GREAT PARNDON, Harl. CM19 51 EP17
Great Percy St, WC1 286 D2
Great Peter St, SW1 297 N7
Great Pettits Ct, Rom. RM1 105 FE54
Great Plumtree, Harl. CM20 35 ET13
⊖ Great Portland Street 285 K5
Great Portland St, W1 285 K6
Great Pulteney St, W1 285 M10
Great Quarry, Guil. GU1 258 AX137
Great Queen St, WC2 286 B9
Dartford DA1 188 FM87
Great Rd, Hem.H. HP2 40 BM19
Great Ropers La, Gt Warley CM13 107 FU51
Great Russell St, WC1 285 P8
Great St. Helens, EC3 287 N8
Great St. Thomas Apostle, EC4 287 K10
Great Scotland Yd, SW1 298 A3
Great Slades, Pot.B. EN6 63 CZ33
Great Smith St, SW1 297 P6
Great South-West Rd, Felt. TW14 175 BQ87
Hounslow TW4 155 BT84
Great Spilmans, SE22 182 DS85
Great Stockwood Rd, Chsht EN7 66 DR26
Great Strand, NW9 97 CT53
Great Sturgess Rd, Hem.H. HP1 39 BF20
Great Suffolk St, SE1 299 H3
Great Sutton St, EC1 287 H5
Great Swan All, EC2 287 L8
Great Tattenhams, Epsom KT18 233 CV118
Great Thrift, Petts Wd BR5 205 EQ98
Great Till Cl, Otford TN14 241 FE116
Great Titchfield St, W1 285 L8
Great Twr St, EC3 287 N10
Great Trinity La, EC4 287 K10
Great Turnstile, WC1 286 D7
GREAT WARLEY, Brwd. CM14 107 FV53
Great Warley St, Gt Warley CM13 107 FU53
Great Western Rd, W2 283 J7
W9 283 H5
W11 283 J7
● Great W Ho, Brent. TW8 157 CJ79
Great W Rd, W4 158 CP78
W6 159 CT78
Brentford TW8 158 CP78
Hounslow TW5 156 BX82
Isleworth TW7 157 CF80
Great Whites Rd, Hem.H. HP3 40 BM22
Great Winchester St, EC2 287 M8
Great Windmill St, W1 285 N10
Greatwood, Chis. BR7 185 EN94
Greatwood Cl, Ott. KT16 211 BC109
Great Woodcote Dr, Pur. CR8 219 DK110
Great Woodcote Pk, Pur. CR8 219 DK110
Great Yd, SE1 299 P4
Greaves Cl, Bark. IG11 145 ER66
Greaves Pl, SW17 180 DE91
Greaves Twr, SW10 307 P4
Grebe Av, Hayes UB4
off Cygnet Way 136 BX72
Grebe Cl, E7 281 M2
E17 101 DY52
Barking IG11 146 EU70
Grebe Ct, Sutt. SM1 217 CZ106
Grebe Crest, Grays RM20 169 FU77
Grecian Cres, SE19 181 DP93
Greding Wk, Hutt. CM13 109 GB47
Greek Ct, W1 285 P9
★ Greek Orthodox Cath of the Divine Wisdom (St. Sophia), W2 283 K10
Greek St, W1 285 P9
Greek Yd, WC2 286 A10
Green, The, E4 101 EC46
E11 124 EH58
E15 281 K5
N9 100 DU47
N14 99 DK48
N17 100 DQ51
N21 99 DN45
SW14 158 CQ83
SW19 179 CX92
W3 138 CS72
W5 off High St 137 CK73
Amersham HP7 55 AR38
Bexleyheath DA7 166 FA81
Bovingdon HP3 57 BA29
Bromley BR1
off Downham Way 184 EG90
Burgh Heath KT20 233 CY119
Burnham SL1 130 AH70
Carshalton SM5 off High St 218 DG105
Chalfont St. Giles HP8
off High St 90 AW47
Chalvey SL1 151 AR75
Cheshunt EN8 66 DW28
Claygate KT10 215 CF107
Croxley Green WD3 74 BN44
Croydon CR0 221 DZ109
Dartford DA2 189 FR89
Datchet SL3 152 AV80
Englefield Green TW20 172 AW91
Epsom KT17 217 CU111
Feltham TW13 175 BV89
Fetcham KT22 231 CD124
Harefield UB9 92 BJ53
Havering-atte-Bower RM4 105 FE48
Hayes UB3 off Wood End 135 BS72
Hayes BR2 204 EG101
Hounslow TW5 156 CA79
Ickenham UB10 115 BQ61
Letchmore Heath WD25 77 CE39
London Colney AL2 61 CK27
Matching Tye CM17 37 FE12
Morden SM4 199 CY98
New Malden KT3 198 CQ97
Otford TN14 241 FH116
Potten End HP4 39 BB17
Pratt's Bottom BR6
off Rushmore Hill 224 EW110
Richmond TW9 177 CK85
Ripley GU23 228 BH121
St. Albans AL3 42 CB22
St. Paul's Cray BR5
off The Avenue 186 EV94
Sarratt WD3 74 BG35
Seal TN15 off Church Rd 257 FM121
Sevenoaks TN13 257 FK122
Shepperton TW17 195 BS98
Sidcup DA14 186 EU91
South Ockendon RM15 149 FW69
Southall UB2 156 BY76
Sutton SM1 200 DB104
Theydon Bois CM16 85 ES37
Twickenham TW2 177 CE88
Waltham Abbey EN9 67 EC34
Warlingham CR6 237 DX117
Welling DA16 165 ES84
Welwyn Garden City AL7 30 DA11
Wembley HA0 117 CG61
Green, The, Wennington RM13 148 FL73
West Drayton UB7 154 BK76
West Tilbury RM18 171 GL79
Westerham TN16 255 ER126
Whiteley Village KT12
off Octagon Rd 213 BS110
Woldingham CR3 237 EA123
Wooburn Green HP10 110 AE58
Woodford Green IG8 102 EG50
Wraysbury TW19 172 AY86
Greenacre, Dart. DA1 188 FK89
Knaphill GU21 off Mead Ct 226 AS116
Windsor SL4 151 AL82
Greenacre Cl, Barn. EN5 79 CZ38
Northolt UB5 116 BZ64
Swanley BR8 207 FE98
Greenacre Ct, Eng.Grn TW20 172 AW93
Greenacre Gdns, E17 123 EC56
Greenacre Pl, Hackbr. SM6
off Park Rd 201 DH103
Greenacres, N3 97 CY54
SE9 185 EN86
Barnet EN4 80 DD42
Bookham KT23 230 CB124
Bushey Heath WD23 95 CD47
Dartford DA2 188 FP86
Epping CM16 69 ET29
Lower Kingswood KT20 249 CZ128
Oxted RH8 254 EE127
Green Acres, Croydon CR0 202 DT104
Hemel Hempstead HP2 41 BR21
Welwyn Garden City AL7 29 CZ12
Greenacres Av, Uxb. UB10 114 BM62
Sch Greenacre Sch, Bans. SM7
off Sutton La 218 DB113
Greenacres Cl, Orp. BR6 223 EQ105
Rainham RM13 148 FL69
Greenacres Dr, Stan. HA7 95 CH52
Sch Greenacres Prim Sch, SE9
off Witherston Way 185 EN89
Greenacre Sq, SE16 301 K4
Greenacre Wk, N14 99 DK48
Greenall Cl, Chsht EN8 67 DY30
Green Arbour Ct, EC1 286 G8
Green Av, NW7 96 CR49
W13 157 CH76
Greenaway Av, N18 101 DX51
Greenaway Gdns, NW3 273 L1
Green Bk, E1 300 E3
N12 98 DB49
Greenbank, Chsht EN8 66 DV28
Greenbank Av, Wem. HA0 117 CG64
Greenbank Cl, E4 101 EC47
Romford RM3 106 FK48
Greenbank Ct, Islw. TW7
off Lanadron Cl 157 CF82
Greenbank Cres, NW4 119 CY56
Greenbank Rd, Wat. WD17 75 BR36
Greenbanks, Dart. DA1 188 FL89
St. Albans AL1 43 CF22
Upminster RM14 129 FS60
Greenbanks Cl, SE13
off Algernon Rd 163 EB83
Greenbay Rd, SE7 164 EK80
Greenberry St, NW8 284 C1
Greenbrook Av, Barn. EN4 80 DC39
Greenbury Cl, Chorl. WD3 73 BC41
● Green Business Cen, Stai. TW18
off The Glanty 173 BC91
Green Cl, NW9 118 CQ58
NW11 120 DC59
Bromley BR2 204 EE97
Brookmans Park AL9 63 CY26
Carshalton SM5 200 DF103
Cheshunt EN8 67 DY32
Epping Green CM16 51 EP24
Feltham TW13 176 BY92
Taplow SL6 130 AG72
Greencoates, Hert. SG13 32 DS10
Greencoat Pl, SW1 297 M8
Greencoat Row, SW1 297 M7
Sch Green C of E Prim Sch, The, N17 off Somerset Rd 122 DT55
Green Common La, Woob.Grn HP10 110 AG59
Greencourt Av, Croy. CR0 202 DV103
Edgware HA8 96 CP53
Greencourt Gdns, Croy. CR0 202 DV102
Greencourt Rd, Petts Wd BR5 205 ER99
Green Ct Rd, Swan. BR8 207 FD99
Green Cres, Flack.Hth HP10 110 AC56
Greencrest Pl, NW2
off Dollis Hill La 119 CU62
Greencroft, Edg. HA8 96 CQ50
Guildford GU1 243 BB134
Green Cft, Hat. AL10
off Talbot Rd 45 CU15
Greencroft Av, Ruis. HA4 116 BW61
Greencroft Cl, E6 292 G7
Greencroft Gdns, NW6 273 L7
Enfield EN1 82 DS41
Greencroft Rd, Houns. TW5 156 BZ81
Green Curve, Bans. SM7 217 CZ114
Green Dale, SE5 162 DR84
SE22 182 DS85
Green Dale Cl, SE22
off Green Dale 182 DS85
Greendale Ms, Slou. SL2 132 AU73
Greendale Wk, Nthflt DA11 190 GE90
Green Dell Way, Hem.H. HP3 41 BP20
Green Dene, E.Hors. KT24 245 BT131
Green Dragon Ct, SE1 299 L2
Green Dragon La, N21 81 DP44
Brentford TW8 158 CL78
Sch Green Dragon Prim Sch, Brent. TW8 off North Rd 158 CL79
Green Dragon Yd, E1 288 C7
Green Dr, Maid. SL6 130 AE65
Ripley GU23 227 BF123
Slough SL3 152 AY77
Southall UB1 136 CA74
Green E Rd, Jordans HP9 90 AS52
Greene Fielde End, Stai. TW18 174 BK94
Greene Fld Rd, Berk. HP4 38 AW19
Green End, N21 99 DP47
Chessington KT9 216 CL105
● Green End Business Cen, Sarratt WD3 74 BG37
Green End Gdns, Hem.H. HP1 40 BG21
Green End La, Hem.H. HP1 39 BF20
Greenend Rd, W4 158 CS75
Green End Rd, Hem.H. HP1 40 BG21
Greener Ct, Enf. EN3
off Martini Dr 83 EA37
Greenes Ct, Berk. HP4
off Lower Kings Rd 38 AW18
Greene Wk, Berk. HP4 38 AX20
Green Fm Cl, Orp. BR6 223 ET106
Greenfell Mans, SE8 314 C2
Greenfern Av, Slou. SL1 130 AJ72
Green Ferry Way, E17 123 DX56
Greenfield, Hat. AL9 45 CX15
Welwyn Garden City AL8 29 CX06
Greenfield Av, Surb. KT5 198 CP101
Watford WD19 94 BX47
Greenfield Dr, N2 120 DF56
Bromley BR1 204 EJ96
Greenfield End, Chal.St.P. SL9 90 AY51
Greenfield Gdns, NW2 119 CY61
Dagenham RM9 146 EX67
Petts Wood BR5 205 ER101
Greenfield Link, Couls. CR5 235 DL115
Greenfield Rd, E1 288 D7
N15 122 DS57
Dagenham RM9 146 EW67
Dartford DA2 187 FD92
Greenfields, Cuffley EN6
off South Dr 65 DL30
Loughton IG10 85 EN42
Sch Greenfield Sch, Wok. GU22
off Brooklyn Rd 226 AY119
Greenfields Cl, Gt Warley CM13 107 FW51
Horley RH6 268 DE146
Loughton IG10 85 EN42
Sch Greenfields Prim Sch, S.Oxhey WD19
off Ellesborough Cl 94 BW50
Greenfields Rd, Horl. RH6 268 DE146
Greenfield St, Wal.Abb. EN9 67 EC34
Greenfield Way, Har. HA2 116 CB55
GREENFORD, UB6 136 CB69
⇌ Greenford 137 CD67
⊖ Greenford 137 CD67
Greenford Av, W7 137 CE70
Southall UB1 136 BZ73
Greenford Gdns, Grnf. UB6 136 CB69
● Greenford Grn Business Pk, Grnf. UB6 137 CE67
Sch Greenford High Sch, Sthl. UB1
off Lady Margaret Rd 136 CA69
Greenford Pk, Grnf. UB6 137 CD66
Greenford Rd, Grnf. UB6 136 CC71
Harrow HA1 117 CE64
Southall UB1 136 CC74
Sutton SM1 218 DB105
Jct Greenford Rbt, Grnf. UB6 137 CD68
Green Gdns, Orp. BR6 223 EQ106
Greengate, Grnf. UB6 137 CH65
Greengate St, E13 292 A1
Green Glade, They.B. CM16 85 ES37
Green Glades, Horn. RM11 128 FM58
Greenhalgh Wk, N2 120 DC56
Greenham Cl, SE1 298 E5
Greenham Cres, E4 101 DZ51
Greenham Rd, N10 98 DG54
Greenham Wk, Wok. GU21 226 AW118
Greenhaven Dr, SE28 146 EV72
Greenhayes Av, Bans. SM7 218 DA114
Greenhayes Cl, Reig. RH2 250 DC134
Greenhayes Gdns, Bans. SM7 234 DA115
● Greenheath Business Cen, E2
off Three Colts La 288 F4
Greenheys Cl, Nthwd. HA6 93 BS53
Greenheys Dr, E18 124 EF55
Greenheys Pl, Wok. GU22
off White Rose La 227 AZ118
Greenhill, NW3 274 A1
Sutton SM1 200 DC103
Wembley HA9 118 CP61
Green Hill, SE18 165 EM78
Buckhurst Hill IG9 102 EJ46
Downe BR6 222 EL112
Greenhill Av, Cat. CR3 236 DV121
Greenhill Cres, Wat. WD18 75 BS44
Greenhill Gdns, Guil. GU4 243 BC131
Northolt UB5 136 BZ68
Greenhill Gro, E12 124 EL63
Green Hill La, Warl. CR6 237 DY117
Greenhill Par, New Barn. EN5
off Great N Rd 80 DB43
Greenhill Pk, NW10 138 CS67
New Barnet EN5 80 DB43
Greenhill Rd, NW10 138 CS67
Harrow HA1 117 CE58
Northfleet DA11 191 GF89
Greenhills, Harl. CM20 51 ES15
Greenhills Cl, Rick. WD3 74 BH43
Greenhill's Rents, EC1 286 G6
Greenhills Ter, N1 277 M5
Greenhill Ter, SE18 305 K10
Northolt UB5 136 BZ68
Greenhill Way, Croy. CR0 221 DX111
Harrow HA1 117 CE58
Wembley HA9 118 CP61
GREENHITHE, DA9 189 FV85
Greenhithe Cl, Sid. DA15 185 ES87
⇌ Greenhithe for Bluewater 189 FU85
Greenholm Rd, SE9 185 EP85
Green Hundred Rd, SE15 312 D3
Greenhurst La, Oxt. RH8 254 EG132
Greenhurst Rd, SE27 181 DN92
Greening St, SE2 166 EW77
Green Knight Ct, N9
off Galahad Rd 100 DU48
Greenlake Ter, Stai. TW18 173 BF94
Greenland Cres, Sthl. UB2 156 BW76
Greenland Ms, SE8 313 K1
Riv Greenland Pier 301 N7
Greenland Pl, NW1 275 K8
Greenland Quay, SE16 301 K8
Greenland Rd, NW1 275 K8
Barnet EN5 79 CW44
Greenlands, Ott. KT16 193 BC104
Greenlands La, NW4 97 CV53
Greenlands Rd, Stai. TW18 174 BG91
Weybridge KT13 195 BP104
Greenland St, NW1 275 K8
Greenland Way, Croy. CR0 201 DK101
Green La, E4 84 EE41
NW4 119 CX57
SE9 185 EN89
SE20 183 DX94
SW16 181 DM94
W7 157 CE75
Addlestone KT15 194 BG104
Amersham HP6 55 AS38
Ashtead KT21 231 CJ117
Bletchingley RH1 252 DS131
Bovingdon HP3 57 AZ28
Broxbourne EN10 49 EB23
Burnham SL1 131 AK66
Byfleet KT14 212 BM112
Caterham CR3 236 DQ122
Chertsey KT16 193 BE103
Chesham HP5 56 AV33
Chesham Bois HP6 55 AR35
Chessington KT9 216 CL109
Chigwell IG7 103 ER47
Green La, Chipstead CR5 250 DA125
Chislehurst BR7 185 EP91
Chobham GU24 210 AT110
Cobham KT11 214 BY112
Croxley Green WD3 74 BM43
Dagenham RM8 126 EU60
Datchet SL3 152 AV81
Edgware HA8 96 CN50
Egham TW20 173 BB91
Farnham Common SL2 111 AP64
Feltham TW13 176 BY92
Fifield SL6 150 AC81
Godalming GU7 258 AS142
Guildford GU1 243 BB134
Harrow HA1 117 CE62
Hemel Hempstead HP2 41 BQ21
Hersham KT12 213 BV107
Hounslow TW4 155 BV83
Ilford IG1, IG3 125 EQ61
Leatherhead KT22 231 CK121
Lower Kingswood KT20 249 CZ126
Mayford GU24
off Copper Beech Cl 226 AV121
Morden SM4 200 DB100
New Malden KT3 198 CQ99
Northwood HA6 93 BT52
Ockham GU23 229 BP124
Outwood RH1 267 DL141
Panshanger AL7 30 DD10
Pilgrim's Hatch CM15 108 FV43
Purley CR8 219 DJ111
Redhill RH1 250 DE132
Reigate RH2 249 CZ134
St. Albans AL3 43 CD16
Shamley Green GU5 260 BG144
Shepperton TW17 195 BQ100
Shipley Bridge RH6 269 DM152
South Ockendon RM15 149 FR69
Staines-upon-Thames TW18 193 BE95
Stanmore HA7 95 CH49
Sunbury-on-Thames TW16 175 BT94
Thornton Heath CR7 201 DN95
Thorpe TW20 193 BD95
Threshers Bush CM17 52 FA16
Upminster RM14 149 FR68
Uxbridge UB8 135 BQ71
Waltham Abbey EN9 68 EJ34
Warley CM14 107 FU52
Warlingham CR6 237 DY116
Watford WD19 94 BW46
West Clandon GU4 244 BG127
West Molesey KT8 196 CB99
White Bushes RH1 266 DG139
Windsor SL4 151 AP82
Worcester Park KT4 199 CU102
Green La Av, Hersham KT12 214 BW106
Green La Cl, Amer. HP6 55 AR36
Byfleet KT14 212 BM112
Chertsey KT16 193 BE103
Green La Gdns, Th.Hth. CR7 202 DQ96
Sch Green La Prim & Nurs Sch, Wor.Pk. KT4 off Green La 199 CV101
Green Las, N4 122 DQ60
N8 121 DP55
N13 99 DM51
N15 121 DP55
N16 122 DQ62
N21 99 DP46
Epsom KT19 216 CS109
Hatfield AL10 29 CT13
Lemsford AL8 29 CT11
Sch Green Las Prim Sch, Hat. AL10
off Green Las 29 CT14
Green La W, Wok. GU23 244 BN125
Greenlaw Ct, W5 137 CK72
Greenlaw Gdns, N.Mal. KT3 199 CT101
Greenlawn La, Brent. TW8 157 CK77
Green Lawns, Ruis. HA4 116 BW60
Greenlaw St, SE18 305 L7
Green Leaf Av, Wall. SM6 219 DK105
Greenleaf Cl, SW2 181 DN87
Greenleafe Dr, Ilf. IG6 125 EP55
Sch Greenleaf Prim Sch, E17
off Greenleaf Rd 123 DZ55
Greenleaf Rd, E6
off Redclyffe Rd 144 EJ67
E17 123 DZ55
Greenleaf Way, Har. HA3 117 CF55
● Greenlea Pk, SW19 180 DD94
Green Leas, Sun. TW16 175 BT93
Greenleas, Wal.Abb. EN9 83 ED35
Green Leas Cl, Sun. TW16 175 BT94
Greenleaves Ct, Ashf. TW15
off Redleaves Av 175 BP93
Greenleigh Av, St.P.Cray BR5 206 EV98
Greenlink Wk, Rich. TW9 158 CP81
Green Man Ct, Eastwick CM20
off Eastwick Hall La 35 EN11
Green Man Gdns, W13 137 CG73
Green Man La, W13 137 CG74
Feltham TW14 155 BU84
Green Manor Way, Grav. DA11 170 FZ84
Green Man Pas, W13 137 CH73
Green Man Rd, Ong. CM5 53 FD19
Jct Green Man Rbt, E11 124 EF59
Greenman St, N1 277 J7
Green Mead, Esher KT10
off Winterdown Gdns 214 BZ107
Greenmead Cl, SE25 202 DU99
Green Meadow, Pot.B. EN6 64 DA30
Greenmeads, Wok. GU22 226 AY122
Sch Greenmead Sch, SW15
off St. Margaret's Cres 179 CV85
Green Moor Link, N21 99 DP45
Greenmoor Rd, Enf. EN3 82 DW40
Green N Rd, Jordans HP9 90 AS51
Greenoak Pl, Cockfos. EN4 80 DF40
Greenoak Ri, Bigg.H. TN16 238 EJ118
Greenoak Way, SW19 179 CX91
Greenock Rd, SW16 201 DK95
W3 158 CP76
Slough SL1 131 AN72
Greenock Way, Rom. RM1 105 FE52
Greeno Cres, Shep. TW17 194 BN99
⊖ Green Park 297 L3
Green Pk, Harl. CM20 51 ES15
Staines-upon-Thames TW18 173 BE90
★ Green Park, The, SW1 297 K3
Green Pk Ct, Rom. RM1
off Kew Cl 105 FE51
Greenpark Ct, Wem. HA0 137 CJ66
Green Pk Way, Grnf. UB6 137 CE67
Green Pl, SE10 303 J4
Dartford DA1 187 FE85
Green Pt, E15 281 K5
Green Pond Cl, E17 123 DZ55
Green Pond Rd, E17 123 DY55
Green Ride, Epp. CM16 85 EP35
Loughton IG10 84 EG43

Green Rd, N14 81 DH44
N20 98 DC48
Thorpe TW20 193 BB98
Greenroof Way, SE10 303 M7
Greensand Cl, S.Merst. RH1 251 DK128
Green Sand Rd, Red. RH1 250 DG133
Greensand Way, Bet. RH3 264 CM136
Dorking RH5 264 CM136
Godstone RH9 252 DV134
South Nutfield RH1 267 DP135
Sch **Green Sch, The**, Islw. TW7
off London Rd 157 CG81
Greens Cl, The, Loug. IG10 85 EN40
Green's Ct, W1 285 N10
Green's End, SE18 305 N8
Greenshank Cl, E17
off Banbury Rd 101 DY52
Greenshaw, Brwd. CM14 108 FV46
Sch **Greenshaw High Sch**, Sutt. SM1
off Grennell Rd 200 DD103
● **Greenshields Ind Est**, E16 303 P3
Greenside, Bex. DA5 186 EY88
Borehamwood WD6 78 CN38
Dagenham RM8 126 EW60
Slough SL2 131 AN71
Swanley BR8 207 FD96
Greenside Cl, N20 98 DD47
SE6 183 ED89
Guildford GU4 243 BC131
Ilf. IG6 103 EQ51
Greenside Dr, Ashtd. KT21 231 CH118
Sch **Greenside Prim Sch**, W12
off Westville Rd 159 CU75
Greenside Rd, W12 159 CU75
Croydon CR0 201 DN101
Greenside Wk, Bigg.H. TN16
off Kings Rd 238 EH118
Greenslade Av, Ashtd. KT21 232 CP119
Sch **Greenslade Prim Sch**, SE18
off Erindale 165 ER79
Greenslade Rd, Bark. IG11 145 ER66
Greensleeves Cl, St.Alb. AL4 43 CJ21
Greensleeves Dr, Warley CM14 108 FV50
Greenstead, Saw. CM21 36 EY06
Greenstead Av, Wdf.Grn. IG8 102 EJ52
Greenstead Cl, Hutt. CM13 109 GE45
Woodford Green IG8
off Greenstead Gdns 102 EJ51
Greenstead Gdns, SW15 179 CU85
Woodford Green IG8 102 EJ51
Greensted Ct, Whyt. CR3
off Godstone Rd 236 DU119
GREENSTED GREEN, Ong. CM5 93 FH28
Greensted Rd, Loug. IG10 102 EL45
Ongar CM5 71 FG28
Greenstone Ms, E11 124 EG58
GREEN STREET, Borwd. WD6 78 CP37
Green St, E7 144 EH65
E13 144 EJ67
W1 284 F10
Borehamwood WD6 78 CN36
Enfield EN3 82 DW40
Harlow CM17 36 EX14
Hatfield AL9 45 CZ21
Hertford SG14 32 DR09
Rickmansworth WD3 73 BC40
Shenley WD7 78 CN36
Sunbury-on-Thames TW16 195 BU95
GREEN STREET GREEN,
Dart. DA2 189 FU93
Orp. BR6 223 ES107
Sch **Green St Grn Prim Sch**,
Grn St Grn BR6 *off Vine Rd* 223 ET107
Green St Grn Rd,
Dart. DA1, DA2 188 FP88
Greensward, Bushey WD23 76 CB44
Green Ter, EC1 286 F3
Green Tiles La, Denh. UB9 113 BF58
Green Trees, Epp. CM16 70 EU31
Green Vale, W5 138 CM72
Bexleyheath DA6 186 EX85
Greenvale, Welw.G.C. AL7 30 DA10
Sch **Greenvale Prim Sch**, S.Croy. CR2
off Sandpiper Rd 221 DX111
Greenvale Rd, SE9 165 EM84
Sch **Greenvale Sch**, SE6
off Waters Rd 184 EE90
Green Valley, Woob.Grn HP10 88 AE54
Green Verges, Stan. HA7 95 CK52
Green Vw, Chess. KT9 216 CM108
Greenview Av, Beck. BR3 203 DY100
Croydon CR0 203 DY100
Greenview Cl, W3 138 CS74
Green Vw Cl, Bov. HP3 57 BA29
Greenview Ct, Ashf. TW15
off Church Rd 174 BM91
Greenview Dr, SW20 199 CW97
Green Wk, NW4 119 CX57
SE1 299 N7
Buckhurst Hill IG9 102 EL45
Dartford DA1 167 FF84
Hampton TW12
off Orpwood Cl 176 BZ93
Ruislip HA4 115 BT60
Southall UB2 156 CA78
Woodford Green IG8 102 EL51
Green Wk, The, E4 101 EC46
Greenwatt Way, Slou. SL1 151 AR76
Greenway, N14 99 DL47
N20 98 DA47
Greenway, SW20 199 CW98
Berkhamsted HP4 38 AU19
Greenway, Chesham HP5 54 AP28
Chislehurst BR7 185 EN92
Dagenham RM8 126 EW61
Harlow CM19 50 EL15
Hayes UB4 135 BV70
Hemel Hempstead HP2 41 BP20
Hutton CM13 109 GA45
Kenton HA3 118 CL57
Pinner HA5 93 BV54
Rom. RM3 106 FP51
Tatsfield TN16 238 EJ120
Wallington SM6 219 DJ105
Woodford Green IG8 102 EJ50
Green Way, SE9 184 EK85
Bookham KT23 230 CB123
Bromley BR2 204 EL100
Burnham SL1 130 AH69
Redhill RH1 250 DE132
Sunbury-on-Thames TW16 195 BU98
Greenway, The, NW9 96 CR54
Chalfont St. Peter SL9 112 AX55
Enfield EN3 83 DX35
Epsom KT18 232 CN115
Harrow Weald HA3 95 CE53
Hounslow TW4 156 BZ84
Ickenham UB10 115 BQ61
Mill End WD3 92 BG45
Greenway, The,
Orpington BR5 206 EV100
Oxted RH8 254 EH133
Pinner HA5 116 BZ58
Potters Bar EN6 64 DA33
Slough SL1 131 AK74
Uxbridge UB8 134 BJ68
Greenway Av, E17 123 ED56
● **Greenway Business Cen**,
Harl. CM19 50 EL15
Greenway Cl, N4 122 DQ61
N11 98 DG51
N15 *off Copperfield Dr* 122 DT56
N20 98 DA47
NW9 96 CR54
West Byfleet KT14 212 BG113
Greenway Dr, Stai. TW18 194 BK95
Sch **Greenway First & Nurs Sch**,
Berk. HP4 *off Crossways* 38 AU19
Greenway Gdns, NW9 96 CR54
Croydon CR0 203 DZ104
Greenford UB6 136 CA69
Harrow HA3 95 CE54
Greenway Par, Chesh. HP5 54 AP28
Greenways, Abb.L. WD5 59 BS32
Beckenham BR3 203 EA96
Egham TW20 172 AY92
Esher KT10 215 CE105
Goffs Oak EN7 65 DP29
Hertford SG14 31 DN09
Walton on the Hill KT20 249 CV125
Woking GU22
off Pembroke Rd 227 BA117
Greenways, The, Twick. TW1
off South Western Rd 177 CG86
Greenways Ct, Horn. RM11 128 FK58
Greenwell Cl, Gdse. RH9 252 DV130
Greenwell St, W1 285 K5
Green W Rd, Jordans HP9 90 AS52
GREENWICH, SE10 314 G4
⇌ **Greenwich** 314 D4
DLR **Greenwich** 314 D4
Greenwich Av, Brwd. CM14 108 FV45
● **Greenwich Cen Business Pk**,
SE10 314 D4
Greenwich Ch St, SE10 314 F3
Coll **Greenwich Comm Coll**,
Burrage Cen, SE18
off Burrage Gro 165 EQ77
Haimo Cen, SE9
off Haimo Rd 184 EK85
London Leisure Coll, SE7 304 E10
New Horizon Cen, SE3
off Telemann Sq 164 EH83
Plumstead Cen, SE18
off Plumstead Rd 165 EQ77
Greenwich Ct, Wal.Cr. EN8
off Parkside 67 DY34
Greenwich Cres, E6 292 G7
Greenwich Foot Tunnel, E14 314 F1
SE10 314 F1
Greenwich Hts, SE18 164 EL80
★ **Greenwich Heritage Cen**,
SE18 305 N6
Greenwich High Rd, SE10 314 C6
Greenwich Ho, SE13
off Hither Grn La 183 ED86
🛍 **Greenwich Mkt**, SE10 314 F3
★ **Greenwich Pk**, SE10 315 J4
Greenwich Pk St, SE10 315 H1
GREENWICH PENINSULA 303 J5
Pier **Greenwich Pier** 314 E2
Greenwich Quay, SE8 314 C3
Coll **Greenwich Sch of Management**,
SE10 314 E4
🛍 **Greenwich Shop Pk**, SE7 303 P9
Greenwich S St, SE10 314 D6
Greenwich Vw Pl, E14 302 C7
Greenwich Way, Wal.Abb. EN9 83 EC36
Greenwood, The, Guil. GU1 243 BA134
Greenwood Av, Chsht EN7 66 DV31
Dagenham RM10 127 FB63
Enfield EN3 83 DY40
Greenwood Cl, Amer. HP6 55 AS37
Bushey Heath WD23
off Langmead Dr 95 CE45
Cheshunt EN7 66 DV31
Morden SM4 199 CY98
Petts Wood BR5 205 ES100
Seer Green HP9
off Farmers Way 89 AR51
Sidcup DA15 186 EU89
Thames Ditton KT7 197 CG102
Woodham KT15 211 BF111
Greenwood Ct, SW1 297 L10
Greenwood Dr, E4
off Avril Way 101 EC50
Redhill RH1 266 DG139
Watford WD25 59 BV34
Greenwood Gdns, N13 99 DP48
Caterham CR3 252 DU125
Ilford IG6 103 EQ52
Oxted RH8 254 EG134
Shenley WD7 62 CL33
Greenwood Ho, Grays RM17
off Argent St 170 GB79
Greenwood La, Hmptn H. TW12 198 CB92
Greenwood Pk, Kings.T. KT2 178 CS94
Greenwood Pl, NW5 275 K2
Sch **Greenwood Prim Sch**, Nthlt. UB5
off Wood End Way 117 CD64
Greenwood Rd, E8 278 D5
E13 281 M10
Bexley DA5 187 FD91
Chigwell IG7 104 EV49
Croydon CR0 201 DP101
Isleworth TW7 157 CE83
Mitcham CR4 201 DK97
Thames Ditton KT7 197 CG102
Woking GU21 226 AS120
Greenwoods, The, S.Har. HA2 116 CC62
Greenwood Ter, NW10 138 CR67
Greenwood Way, Sev. TN13 256 FF125
Green Wrythe Cres, Cars. SM5 200 DE102
Green Wrythe La, Cars. SM5 200 DD100
Sch **Green Wrythe Prim Sch**, Cars. SM5
off Green Wrythe La 200 DD100
Greenyard, Wal.Abb. EN9 67 EC33
Greer Rd, Har. HA3 94 CC53
Greet St, SE1 298 F3
Greg Cl, E10 123 EC58
Gregories Fm La, Beac. HP9 89 AK53
Gregories Rd, Beac. HP9 88 AH53
Gregor Ms, SE3 315 P5
Gregory Av, Pot.B. EN6 64 DC33
Gregory Cl, Brom. BR2 204 EE98
Woking GU21 226 AW117
Gregory Cres, SE9 184 EK87
Gregory Dr, Old Wind. SL4 172 AV86
Gregory Ms, Wal.Abb. EN9
off Beaulieu Dr 67 EB32
Gregory Pl, W8 295 L4
Gregory Rd, Hedg. SL2 111 AR61
Romford RM6 126 EX56
Southall UB2 156 CB76
Gregson Cl, Borwd. WD6 78 CQ39
Gregson's Ride, Loug. IG10 85 EN38
Sch **Greig City Acad**, N8
off High St 121 DL56
Greig Cl, N8 121 DL57
Greig Ter, SE17 311 H2
Grenaby Av, Croy. CR0 202 DR101
Grenaby Rd, Croy. CR0 202 DR101
Grenada Rd, SE7 164 EJ80
Grenade St, E14 289 P10
Grenadier Cl, St.Alb. AL4 43 CJ21
Grenadier Pl, Cat. CR3 236 DQ122
Grenadier St, E16 305 L3
Grenadine Cl, Chsht EN7 66 DT27
Grena Gdns, Rich. TW9 158 CM84
Grenard Cl, SE15 312 C5
Grena Rd, Rich. TW9 158 CM84
Grendon Cl, Horl. RH6 268 DF146
Grendon Gdns, Wem. HA9 118 CN61
Grendon Ho, N1
off Priory Grn Est 286 C1
Grendon St, NW8 284 C4
Grenfell Av, Horn. RM12 127 FF60
Grenfell Cl, Borwd. WD6 78 CQ39
Grenfell Gdns, Har. HA3 118 CL59
Grenfell Ho, SE5
off Comber Gro 311 J5
Grenfell Rd, W11 282 D10
Beaconsfield HP9 89 AL52
Mitcham CR4 180 DF93
Grenfell Twr, W11 282 D10
Grenfell Wk, W11 282 D10
Grennell Cl, Sutt. SM1 200 DD103
Grennell Rd, Sutt. SM1 200 DC103
Grenoble Gdns, N13 99 DN51
Grenside Rd, Wey. KT13 195 BP104
Grenville Av, Brox. EN10 49 DZ21
Grenville Cl, N3 97 CZ53
Burnham SL1 130 AH68
Cobham KT11 214 BX113
Surbiton KT5 198 CQ102
Waltham Cross EN8 67 DX32
Grenville Ct, SE19
off Lymer Av 182 DT92
Grenville Gdns, Wdf.Grn. IG8 102 EJ53
Grenville Ms, N19 121 DL60
Hampton TW12 176 CB92
Grenville Pl, NW7 96 CR50
SW7 295 N7
Grenville Rd, N19 121 DL60
Chafford Hundred RM16 169 FV78
New Addington CR0 221 EC109
Grenville St, WC1 286 B5
Gresford Cl, St.Alb. AL4 43 CK20
Gresham Av, N20 98 DF49
Warlingham CR6 237 DY118
Gresham Cl, Bex. DA5 186 EY86
Brentwood CM14 108 FW48
Enfield EN2 82 DQ41
Oxted RH8 254 EF128
Gresham Ct, Berk. HP4 38 AV20
Gresham Dr, Rom. RM6 126 EV57
Gresham Gdns, NW11 119 CY60
Gresham Pl, N19 121 DK61
Sch **Gresham Prim Sch**, S.Croy. CR2
off Limpsfield Rd 220 DU112
Gresham Rd, E6 293 K1
E16 292 B9
NW10 118 CR64
SE25 202 DU98
SW9 161 DN83
Beckenham BR3 203 DY96
Brentwood CM14 108 FW48
Edgware HA8 96 CM51
Hampton TW12 176 CA93
Hounslow TW3 156 CC81
Oxted RH8 254 EF128
Slough SL1 131 AN72
Staines-upon-Thames TW18 173 BF92
Uxbridge UB10 134 BN68
Gresham St, EC2 287 J8
Gresham Way, SW19 180 DA90
Gresley Cl, E17 123 DY58
N15 122 DR56
Welwyn Garden City AL8 29 CY08
Gresley Ct, Pot.B. EN6 64 DC30
Gresley Rd, N19 121 DJ60
Gressenhall Rd, SW18 179 CZ86
Gresse St, W1 285 N7
Gresswell Cl, Sid. DA14 186 EU90
Greswell St, SW6 306 C7
Greta Bk, W.Hors. KT24 245 BQ126
Gretton Rd, N17 100 DS52
Greville Av, S.Croy. CR2 221 DX110
Greville Cl, Ashtd. KT21 232 CL119
Guildford GU2 242 AS134
North Mymms AL9 45 CV24
Twickenham TW1 177 CH87
Greville Ct, E5
off Napoleon Rd 122 DV62
Bookham KT23 246 CC125
Greville Hall, NW6 273 L10
Greville Ms, NW6 273 L9
Greville Pk Av, Ashtd. KT21 232 CL118
Greville Pk Rd, Ashtd. KT21 232 CL118
Greville Pl, NW6 273 M10
Sch **Greville Prim Sch, The**, Ashtd. KT21
off Stonny Cft 232 CM117
Greville Rd, E17 123 EC56
NW6 273 L10
Richmond TW10 178 CM86
Greville St, EC1 286 F7
Grey Alders, Bans. SM7 217 CW114
Greycaine Rd, Wat. WD24 76 BX37
Grey Cl, NW11 120 DC58
Greycoat Gdns, SW1
off Greycoat St 297 N7
Sch **Grey Coat Hosp Sch**,
Lwr Sch, SW1 297 N7
Upr Sch, SW1 297 N9
Greycoat Pl, SW1 297 N7
Greycoat St, SW1 297 N7
Greycot Rd, Beck. BR3 183 EA92
Sch **Grey Ct Sch**, Rich. TW10
off Ham St 177 CJ90
Grey Eagle St, E1 288 A6
Greyfell Cl, Stan. HA7
off Coverdale Cl 95 CH50
Greyfields Cl, Pur. CR8 219 DP113
Greyford Cl, Lthd. KT22 231 CJ122
Greyfriars, Hutt. CM13 109 GB45
Greyfriars Pas, EC1 287 H8
Greyfriars Rd, Ripley GU23 228 BG124
Greygoose Pk, Harl. CM19 51 EN18
Greyhound Hill, NW4 119 CU55
Greyhound La, SW16 181 DK93
Orsett RM16 171 GG75
South Mimms EN6 63 CU33
Greyhound Rd, N17 122 DS55
NW10 139 CV69
W6 306 D2
W14 306 D2
Sutton SM1 218 DC106
Greyhound Ter, SW16 201 DJ95
Greyhound Way, Dart. DA1 187 FE86
Greyladies Gdns, SE10 314 F7
Greys Pk Cl, Kes. BR2 222 EJ106
Greystead Rd, SE23 182 DW87
Greystoke Av, Pnr. HA5 116 CA55
Greystoke Cl, Berk. HP4 38 AU20
Greystoke Dr, Ruis. HA4 115 BP58
Greystoke Gdns, W5 138 CL70
Enfield EN2 81 DK42
Greystoke Pk Ter, W5 137 CK69
Greystoke Pl, EC4 286 E8
Greystoke Rd, Slou. SL2 131 AM71
Greystone Cl, S.Croy. CR2 220 DW111
Greystone Gdns, Har. HA3 117 CJ58
Ilford IG6 103 EQ54
Greystone Path, E11
off Grove Rd 124 EF59
Greystones Cl, Red. RH1 266 DD136
Greystones Dr, Reig. RH2 250 DC132
Greyswood Av, N18 101 DX51
Greyswood St, SW16 181 DH93
Greythorne Rd, Wok. GU21 226 AU118
Grey Twrs Av, Horn. RM11 128 FK60
Grey Twrs Gdns, Horn. RM11
off Grey Twrs Av 128 FK60
Grice Av, Bigg.H. TN16 222 EH113
Gridiron Pl, Upmin. RM14 128 FP62
Grierson Rd, SE23 183 DX87
Grieves Rd, Nthflt DA11 191 GF90
Griffetts Yd, Chesh. HP5
off Bellingdon Rd 54 AP30
Griffin Av, Upmin. RM14 129 FS58
● **Griffin Cen**, Felt. TW14 175 BV86
Griffin Cl, NW10 119 CV64
Slough SL1 151 AQ75
Griffin Ct, Ashtd. KT21
off The Warren 232 CL119
Bookham KT23
off Griffin Way 246 CB126
Northfleet DA11 190 GA85
Griffin Manor Way, SE28 165 ER76
Sch **Griffin Prim Sch**, SW8 309 M7
Griffin Rd, N17 100 DS54
SE18 165 ER78
Griffins, The, Grays RM16 170 GB75
Griffins Cl, N21 100 DR45
Griffin Wk, Green. DA9
off Church Rd 189 FT85
Griffin Way, Bkhm KT23 246 CA126
Sunbury-on-Thames TW16 195 BU96
Griffith Cl, Dag. RM8
off Gibson Rd 126 EW60
Griffiths Cl, Wor.Pk. KT4 199 CV103
Griffiths Rd, SW19 180 DA94
Griffiths Way, St.Alb. AL1 42 CC22
Griffon Way, Lvsdn WD25 59 BT34
Grifon Rd, Chaff.Hun. RM16 169 FW76
Griggs App, Ilf. IG1 125 EQ61
Griggs Cl, Ilf. IG3 125 ES63
Griggs Gdns, Horn. RM12
off Tylers Cres 128 FJ64
Griggs Pl, SE1 299 P7
Griggs Rd, E10 123 EC58
Grilse Cl, N9 100 DV49
Grimsby Gro, E16 305 P4
Grimsby Rd, Slou. SL1 151 AM75
Grimsby St, E2 288 B5
Grimsdells La, Amer. HP6 55 AR37
Grimsdyke Cres, Barn. EN5 79 CW41
Grimsdyke Rd, Pnr. HA5 94 BY52
Sch **Grimsdyke Sch**, Hatch End HA5
off Sylvia Av 94 BZ51
Grimsel Path, SE5 311 H4
Grimshaw Cl, N6 120 DG59
Grimshaw Way, Rom. RM1 127 FF57
Grimstone Cl, Rom. RM5 105 FB51
Grimston Rd, SW6 306 G9
St. Albans AL1 43 CF21
Grimthorpe Cl, St.Alb. AL3 43 CD17
Grimthorpe Ho, EC1 286 G4
Grimwade Av, Croy. CR0 202 DU104
Grimwade Cl, SE15 312 G10
Grimwood Rd, Twick. TW1 177 CF87
Grindall Cl, Croy. CR0 219 DP105
Grindal St, SE1 298 E5
Grindcobbe, St.Alb. AL1 43 CD23
Grindleford Av, N11 98 DG47
Grindley Gdns, Croy. CR0 202 DT100
Sch **Grinling Gibbons Prim Sch**,
SE8 313 P3
Grinling Pl, SE8 314 A3
Grinstead Rd, SE8 313 L1
Grisedale Cl, Pur. CR8 220 DS114
Grisedale Gdns, Pur. CR8 220 DS114
Grittleton Av, Wem. HA9 138 CP65
Grittleton Rd, W9 283 J4
Grizedale Ter, SE23 182 DV89
Grobars Av, Wok. GU21 226 AW115
Grocer's Hall Ct, EC2 287 L9
Grogan Cl, Hmptn. TW12 176 BZ93
Groombridge Cl,
Hersham KT12 213 BV106
Welling DA16 186 EU85
Groombridge Rd, E9 279 J7
Groom Cl, Brom. BR2 204 EH98
Groom Cres, SW18 180 DD87
Groomfield Cl, SW17 180 DG91
Groom Pl, SW1 297 H6
Groom Rd, Brox. EN10 67 DZ26
Grooms Cotts, Chesh. HP5 56 AV30
Grooms Dr, Pnr. HA5 115 BU57
Groom Wk, Guil. GU1 242 AY131
Grosmont Rd, SE18 165 ET78
Grosse Way, SW15 179 CV86
Grosvenor Av, N5 277 J3
SW14 158 CS83
Carshalton SM5 218 DF107
Harrow HA2 116 CB58
Hayes UB4 135 BS68
Kings Langley WD4 59 BQ28
Richmond TW10 178 CL85
Grosvenor Br, SW1 309 K2
Grosvenor Cl, Horl. RH6 268 DG150
Iver SL0 133 BD69
Loughton IG10 85 EP39
Grosvenor Cotts, SW1 296 G8
Grosvenor Ct, N14 99 DJ45
NW6 272 D8
Grosvenor Ct, Croxley Green WD3
off Mayfare 75 BR43
Guildford GU4 243 BB130
Slough SL1 132 AS72
Sutton SM2
off Brighton Rd 218 DC107
Grosvenor Cres, NW9 118 CN56
SW1 297 H5
Dartford DA1 188 FK85
Uxbridge UB10 135 BP66
Grosvenor Cres Ms, SW1 296 G5
Grosvenor Dr, Horn. RM11 128 FJ60
Loughton IG10 85 EP39
Maidenhead SL6 130 AC71
Grosvenor Est, SW1 297 P8
Grosvenor Gdns, E6 292 E2
N10 121 DJ55
N14 81 DK43
NW2 272 B3
NW11 119 CZ58
SW1 297 J6
SW14 158 CS83
Kingston upon Thames KT2 177 CK93
Upminster RM14 129 FR60
Wallington SM6 219 DJ108
Woodford Green IG8 102 EG51
Grosvenor Gdns Ms E, SW1 297 K6
Grosvenor Gdns Ms N, SW1 297 J7
Grosvenor Gdns Ms S, SW1 297 K7
Grosvenor Gate, W1 296 F1
Grosvenor Hill, SW19 179 CY93
W1 285 J10
Grosvenor Ms, Epsom KT18 232 CR119
Reigate RH2 266 DB137
Grosvenor Pk, SE5 311 J3
Grosvenor Pk Rd, E17 123 EA57
Grosvenor Path, Loug. IG10 85 EP39
Grosvenor Pl, SW1 297 H5
Weybridge KT13
off Vale Rd 195 BR104
Woking GU21
off Burleigh Gdns 227 AZ116
Grosvenor Ri E, E17 123 EB57
Grosvenor Rd, E6 144 EK67
E7 144 EJ65
E10 123 EC60
E11 124 EG57
N3 97 CZ52
N9 100 DV46
N10 99 DH53
SE25 202 DU98
SW1 309 J2
W4 158 CP78
W7 137 CG74
Belvedere DA17 166 FA79
Bexleyheath DA6 186 EX85
Borehamwood WD6 78 CN41
Brentford TW8 157 CK79
Broxbourne EN10 49 DZ20
Dagenham RM8 126 EZ60
Epsom KT18 232 CR119
Hounslow TW3 156 BZ83
Ilford IG1 125 EQ62
Northwood HA6 93 BT50
Petts Wood BR5 205 ES100
Richmond TW10 178 CL85
Romford RM7 127 FD59
St. Albans AL1 43 CE21
Southall UB2 156 BZ76
Staines-upon-Thames TW18 174 BG94
Twickenham TW1 177 CG87
Wallington SM6 219 DH107
Watford WD17 76 BW42
West Wickham BR4 203 EB102
Grosvenor Sq, W1 285 H10
Kings Langley WD4
off Grosvenor Av 59 BQ28
Grosvenor St, W1 285 J10
Grosvenor Ter, SE5 311 H4
Hemel Hempstead HP1 40 BG21
Grosvenor Vale, Ruis. HA4 115 BT61
Grosvenor Way, E5 122 DW61
Grosvenor Wf Rd, E14 302 G9
Grote's Bldgs, SE3 315 K9
Grote's Pl, SE3 315 J9
Groton Rd, SW18 180 DB89
Grotto, The, Ware SG12 33 DX07
Grotto Pas, W1 285 H6
Grotto Rd, Twick. TW1 177 CF89
Weybridge KT13 195 BP104
Ground La, Hat. AL10 45 CV16
Jct **Grove, The**, SE22 182 DU88
Grove, The, E15 281 J4
N3 98 DA53
N4 121 DM59
N6 120 DG60
N8 121 DK57
N13 99 DN50
N14 81 DJ43
NW9 118 CR57
NW11 119 CY59
W5 137 CK74
Addlestone KT15 212 BH106
Amersham HP6 55 AR36
Bexleyheath DA6 166 EX84
Biggin Hill TN16 238 EK118
Brentwood CM14 108 FT49
Brookmans Park AL9 64 DA27
Caterham CR3 235 DP121
Chipperfield WD4 58 BJ30
Coulsdon CR5 235 DK115
Edgware HA8 96 CP49
Effingham KT24 246 BX128
Egham TW20 173 BA92
Enfield EN2 81 DN40
Epsom KT17 216 CS113
Esher KT10 196 CB102
Ewell KT17 217 CT110
Gravesend DA12 191 GH87
Greenford UB6 136 CC72
Horley RH6 269 DH149
Isleworth TW7 157 CE81
Latimer HP5 72 AX36
Potters Bar EN6 64 DC32
Radlett WD7 61 CG34
Sidcup DA14 186 EY91
Slough SL1 152 AU75
Stanmore HA7 95 CG47
Swanley BR8 207 FF97
Swanscombe DA10 190 FZ85
Teddington TW11 177 CG91
Twickenham TW1 *off Bridge Rd* 177 CH86
Upminster RM14 128 FP63
Uxbridge UB10 114 BN64

G

Grove, The,
Walton-on-Thames KT12 195 BV101
Watford WD17 75 BQ37
West Wickham BR4 203 EB104
Woking GU21 227 AZ116
Grove Av, N3 98 DA52
N10 99 DJ54
W7 137 CE72
Epsom KT17 216 CS113
Pinner HA5 116 BY56
Sutton SM1 218 DA107
Twickenham TW1 177 CF88
Grove Bk, Wat. WD19 94 BX46
Grovebarns, Stai. TW18 174 BG93
Grovebury Cl, Erith DA8 167 FD79
Grovebury Gdns, Park St AL2 60 CC27
Grovebury Rd, SE2 166 EV75
Grove Cl, N14 99 DJ45
SE23 183 DX88
Bromley BR2 204 EG103
Chalfont St. Peter SL9
off Grove La 90 AW53
Epsom KT19 216 CP110
Feltham TW13 176 BY91
Kingston upon Thames KT1 198 CM98
Old Windsor SL4 172 AV87
Slough SL1 *off Alpha St S* 152 AU76
Uxbridge UB10 114 BN64
Grove Cor, Bkhm KT23
off Lower Shott 246 CA126
Grove Cotts, SW3 308 D2
Grove Ct, Barn. EN5
off High St 79 CZ41
Beaconsfield HP9
off Station Rd 89 AK53
East Molesey KT8
off Walton Rd 197 CD99
Egham TW20 173 BA92
Send GU23 *off Send Rd* 227 BD123
Waltham Abbey EN9 67 EB33
Grove Cres, E18 102 EF54
NW9 118 CQ56
Croxley Green WD3 74 BN42
Feltham TW13 176 BY91
Kingston upon Thames KT1 198 CL97
Walton-on-Thames KT12 195 BV101
Grove Cres Rd, E15 281 H5
Grovedale Cl, Chsht EN7 66 DT30
Grovedale Rd, N19 121 DK61
Grove Dws, E1 288 G6
Grove End, E18 *off Grove Hill* 102 EF54
NW5 *off Chetwynd Rd* 121 DH63
Chalfont St. Peter SL9 90 AW53
Grove End Gdns, NW8
off Grove End Rd 284 A1
Grove End La, Esher KT10 197 CD102
Grove End Rd, NW8 284 A1
Grove Fm Ct, Mitch. CR4
off Brookfields Av 200 DF98
Grove Fm Pk, Nthwd. HA6 93 BR50
Grove Fm Retail Pk,
Chad.Hth RM6 126 EW59
Grove Footpath, Surb. KT5 198 CL98
Grove Gdns, NW4 119 CU56
NW8 284 D3
Dagenham RM10 127 FC62
Enfield EN3 83 DX39
Teddington TW11 177 CG91
Grove Grn Rd, E11 123 EC62
Grove Hall Ct, NW8 283 P2
Grove Hall Rd, Bushey WD23 76 BY42
Grove Heath, Ripley GU23 228 BJ124
Grove Heath Ct, Ripley GU23 228 BJ124
Grove Heath N, Ripley GU23 228 BH122
Grove Heath Rd, Ripley GU23 228 BJ123
Groveherst Rd, Dart. DA1 168 FM83
GROVEHILL, Hem.H. HP2 40 BL16
Grove Hill, E18 102 EF54
Chalfont St. Peter SL9 90 AW52
Harrow HA1 117 CE59
Grove Hill Rd, SE5 311 N10
Harrow HA1 117 CE59
Grovehill Rd, Red. RH1 250 DE134
Grove Ho, Chsht EN8 66 DW30
Grove Ho Rd, N8 121 DL56
Groveland Av, SW16 181 DM94
Groveland Ct, EC4 287 K9
Groveland Rd, Beck. BR3 203 DZ97
Grovelands, Horl. RH6
off The Grove 269 DH149
Park Street AL2 60 CB27
West Molesey KT8 196 CA98
Grovelands Business Cen,
Hem.H. HP2 41 BQ18
Grovelands Cl, SE5 311 N9
Harrow HA2 116 CB62
Grovelands Ct, N14 99 DK45
Grovelands Rd, N13 99 DM49
N15 122 DU58
Orpington BR5 186 EU94
Purley CR8 219 DL112
Grovelands Sch, Walt. KT12
off Terrace Rd 195 BV100
Grovelands Way, Grays RM17 170 FZ78
Groveland Way, N.Mal. KT3 198 CQ99
Grove La, SE5 311 L7
Chalfont St. Peter SL9 90 AW53
Chesham HP5 56 AV27
Chigwell IG7 103 ET48
Coulsdon CR5 218 DG113
Epping CM16 *off High St* 70 EU30
Kingston upon Thames KT1 198 CL98
Uxbridge UB8 134 BM70
Grove La Ter, SE5 *off Grove La* 311 N10
Grove Lea, Hat. AL10 45 CU21
Groveley Rd, Sun. TW16 175 BT92
Grove Mkt Pl, SE9 185 EM86
Grove Mead, Hat. AL10 45 CT18
Grove Meadow, Welw.G.C. AL7 30 DC09
Grove Ms, W6 294 A6
W11 282 G9
Grove Mill, Mitch. CR4 200 DE99
Grove Mill La, Wat. WD17 75 BP37
Grove Mill Pl, Cars. SM5 200 DG104
GROVE PARK, SE12 184 EG89
W4 158 CP80
Grove Park 184 EG90
Grove Park 184 EH90
Grove Pk, E11 124 EH58
NW4 119 CV56
NW9 118 CQ56
SE5 311 N9
Grove Pk Av, E4 101 EB52
Grove Pk Br, W4 158 CQ80
Grove Pk Gdns, W4 158 CP79
Grove Pk Ms, W4 158 CQ80
Grove Pk Prim Sch, W4
off Nightingale Cl 158 CQ79
Grove Pk Rd, N15 122 DS56
SE9 184 EJ90
W4 158 CP80
Rainham RM13 147 FG67
Grove Pk Sch, NW9
off Grove Pk 118 CQ56
Grove Pk Ter, W4 158 CP79
Grove Pas, E2 278 E10
Teddington TW11 177 CG92
Grove Path, Chsht EN7 66 DU31
Grove Pl, NW3
off Christchurch Hill 120 DD62
SW12 181 DH86
W3 138 CQ74
Banstead SM7 218 DF112
Barking IG11
off Clockhouse Av 145 EQ67
North Mymms AL9
off Dixons Hill Rd 45 CW24
Watford WD25 76 CB39
Weybridge KT13 213 BQ106
Grove Prim Sch, Chad.Hth RM6
off Chadwell Heath La 126 EW57
Grover Cl, Hem.H. HP2 40 BK19
Grove Rd, E3 279 K10
E4 101 EB49
E11 124 EF59
E17 123 EB58
E18 102 EF54
N11 99 DH50
N12 98 DD50
N15 122 DS57
NW2 272 A4
SW13 159 CT82
SW19 180 DC94
W3 138 CQ74
W5 137 CK73
Amersham HP6 72 AT37
Ashtead KT21 232 CM118
Beaconsfield HP9 89 AK53
Belvedere DA17 166 EZ79
Bexleyheath DA7 167 FC84
Borehamwood WD6 78 CN39
Brentford TW8 157 CJ78
Burnham SL1 131 AL67
Chertsey KT16 193 BF100
Cockfosters EN4 80 DE41
East Molesey KT8 197 CD98
Edgware HA8 96 CN51
Epsom KT17 216 CS113
Grays RM17 170 GC79
Guildford GU1 243 BC134
Hemel Hempstead HP1 40 BG22
Horley RH6 268 DE147
Hounslow TW3 156 CB84
Isleworth TW7 157 CE81
Mill End WD3 92 BG47
Mitcham CR4 201 DH96
Northfleet DA11 190 GB85
Northwood HA6 93 BR50
Oxted RH8 *off Southlands La* 253 EC134
Pinner HA5 116 BZ57
Redhill RH1 *off Lower Br Rd* 250 DF134
Richmond TW10 178 CM86
Romford RM6 126 EV59
St. Albans AL1 43 CD21
Seal TN15 257 FN122
Sevenoaks TN14 257 FJ121
Shepperton TW17 195 BQ100
Surbiton KT6 197 CK99
Sutton SM1 218 DB107
Tatsfield TN16 238 EJ120
Thornton Heath CR7 201 DN98
Twickenham TW2 177 CD90
Uxbridge UB8 134 BK66
Ware SG12 33 DZ05
Windsor SL4 151 AQ82
Woking GU21 227 AZ116
Grove Rd Prim Sch, Houns. TW3
off Cromwell Rd 156 CA84
Grove Rd W, Enf. EN3 82 DW37
Grover Rd, Wat. WD19 94 BX45
Groves Cl, B.End SL8 110 AC60
South Ockendon RM15 149 FT73
Grove Shaw, Kgswd KT20 233 CY124
Groveside, Bkhm KT23 246 CA127
Groveside Cl, W3 138 CN72
Bookham KT23 246 CA127
Carshalton SM5 200 DE103
Groveside Rd, E4 102 EE47
Grovestile Waye, Felt. TW14 175 BR87
Grove St, N18 100 DT51
SE8 301 N8
Groves Way, Chesh. HP5 54 AM29
Grove Ter, NW5 121 DH62
Teddington TW11 177 CG91
Grove Ter Ms, NW5
off Grove Ter 121 DH62
Grove Vale, SE22 162 DS84
Chislehurst BR7 185 EN93
Grove Vil, E14 290 D10
Grove Wk, Hert. SG14 32 DQ07
Groveway, SW9 310 D7
Dagenham RM8 126 EX63
Grove Way, Chorleywood WD3 73 BB42
Esher KT10 196 CC101
Uxbridge UB8 134 BK66
Wembley HA9 118 CP64
Grovewood, Rich. TW9 158 CN81
Grove Wd Cl, Brom. BR1 205 EN97
Grovewood Cl, Chorl. WD3 73 BB43
Grove Wd Hill, Couls. CR5 219 DK114
Grovewood Pl, Wdf.Grn. IG8 103 EM51
Grubbs La, Hat. AL9 46 DA22
Grub St, Oxt. RH8 254 EJ128
Grummant Rd, SE15 312 A6
Grundy St, E14 290 C9
Gruneisen Rd, N3 98 DB52
Gryphon Ind Pk, The,
Port.Wd AL3 43 CF15
GSA Conservatoire, Guil. GU2
off Millmead Ter 258 AW136
Guardian Angels RC Prim Sch,
E3 289 M4
Guardian Av, N.Stfd RM16 169 FX75
Guardian Business Cen, Rom. RM3
off Faringdon Ave 106 FK52
Guardian Cl, Horn. RM11 127 FH60
Guards Av, Cat. CR3 236 DQ122
Guards Club Rd, Maid. SL6 130 AC72
Guardsman Cl, Warley CM14 108 FX50
Guards Mus, SW1 297 M5
Guards Rd, Wind. SL4 150 AJ82
Guards Wk, Wind. SL4
off Guards Rd 150 AJ82
Gubbins La, Rom. RM3 106 FM52
Gubyon Av, SE24 181 DP85
Guerin Sq, E3 289 N2
Guernsey Cl, Guil. GU4
off Cotts Wd Dr 243 BA129
Hounslow TW5 156 CA81
Guernsey Fm Dr, Wok. GU21 226 AX115
Guernsey Gro, SE24 182 DQ87
Guernsey Ho, N1 277 K5
Enfield EN3 *off Eastfield Rd* 83 DX38
Guernsey Rd, E11 123 ED60
Guessens Ct, Welw.G.C. AL8 29 CW09
Guessens Gro, Welw.G.C. AL8 29 CW09
Guessens Rd, Welw.G.C. AL8 29 CW09
Guessens Wk, Welw.G.C. AL8 29 CW08
Guibal Rd, SE12 184 EH87
Guildcroft, Guil. GU1 243 BA134
Guildersfield Rd, SW16 181 DL94
GUILDFORD, GU1 - GU5 258 AU137
Guildford 258 AW135
Guildford 258 AX135
Guildford Adult Learning Cen,
Guil. GU1 *off Sydenham Rd* 258 AY135
Guildford & Godalming Bypass, Guil.
GU2, GU3 258 AS136
Guildford Av, Felt. TW13 175 BT89
Guildford Business Pk,
Guil. GU2 242 AV133
Guildford Bypass,
Guil. GU1, GU2, GU4 243 AZ131
Guildford Castle, Guil. GU1 258 AX136
Guildford Coll,
Stoke Pk Campus, Guil. GU1
off Stoke Rd 242 AX133
Guildford Co Sch, Guil. GU2
off Farnham Rd 258 AV136
Guildford Gdns, Rom. RM3 106 FL51
Guildford Gro, SE10 314 D6
Guildford Gro Prim Sch, Guil. GU2
off Southway 242 AS134
Guildford High Sch, Guil. GU1
off London Rd 242 AY134
Guildford House Gall, Guil. GU1
off High St 258 AX135
Guildford Ind Est, Guil. GU2 242 AU133
Guildford La, Albury GU5 260 BH139
Woking GU22 226 AX120
Guildford Lo Dr, E.Hors. KT24 245 BT129
Guildford Mus, Guil. GU1 258 AX136
Guildford Nuffield Hosp,
Guil. GU2 242 AS134
GUILDFORD PARK, Guil. GU2 258 AV135
Guildford Pk Av, Guil. GU2 258 AV135
Guildford Pk Rd, Guil. GU2 258 AV135
Guildford Rd, E6 293 J9
E17 101 EC53
SW8 310 B6
Bookham KT23 246 BZ127
Chertsey KT16 193 BE102
Croydon CR0 202 DR100
Dorking RH5 262 BW140
Fetcham KT22 231 CG122
Godalming GU7 258 AU144
Guildford GU3, GU4 242 AX127
Ilford IG3 125 ES61
Leatherhead KT24 246 BW129
Mayford GU22 226 AX122
Romford RM3 106 FL51
St. Albans AL1 43 CH21
Westcott RH4 262 CA138
Woking GU22 226 AY119
Guildford St, Cher. KT16 194 BG101
Staines-upon-Thames TW18 174 BG93
Guildford Way, Wall. SM6 219 DL106
Guildhall, The, EC2 287 L8
Guildhall Art Gall,
(Guildhall Lib), EC2 287 K8
Guildhall Bldgs, EC2 287 L8
Guildhall Sch of Music & Drama,
EC2 287 K6
Hall of Res, EC1 287 L6
Milton Ct EC2 287 L6
Guildhall Yd, EC2 287 K8
Guildhouse St, SW1 297 L8
Guildown Av, N12 98 DB49
Guildford GU2 258 AV137
Guildown Rd, Guil. GU2 258 AV137
Guild Rd, SE7 164 EK78
Erith DA8 167 FF80
Guildsway, E17 101 DZ53
Guildway, The, Guil. GU3 258 AW140
Guileshill La, Ock. GU23 228 BL123
Guilford Av, Surb. KT5 198 CM99
Guilford Pl, WC1 286 C5
Guilfords, Harl. CM17 36 EX10
Guilford St, WC1 286 B5
Guinery Gro, Hem.H. HP3 40 BM24
Guinevere Gdns, Wal.Cr. EN8 67 DY31
Guinness Cl, E9 279 L7
Hayes UB3 155 BR76
Guinness Ct, E1 288 B9
Woking GU21 *off Iveagh Rd* 226 AT118
Guinness Sq, SE1 299 N8
Guinness Trust Bldgs, SE1
off Snowsfields 299 N4
SE11 298 G10
SW3 296 E9
SW9 161 DP84
W6 *off Fulham Palace Rd* 294 B10
Guinness Trust Est, N16 122 DS60
Guion Rd, SW6 307 H8
Gulland Wk, N1
off Nightingale Rd 277 K5
Gullbrook, Hem.H. HP1 40 BG20
Gullet Wd Rd, Wat. WD25 75 BU35
Gulliver Cl, Nthlt. UB5 136 BZ67
Gulliver Rd, Sid. DA15 185 ES89
Gulliver St, SE16 301 N6
Gull Wk, Horn. RM12
off Heron Flight Av 147 FH66
Gulphs, The, Hert. SG13 32 DR10
Gulston Wk, SW3 296 F9
Gumbrell Ms, Red. RH1 251 DH132
Gumleigh Rd, W5 157 CJ77
Gumley Gdns, Islw. TW7 157 CG83
Gumley Ho RC Conv Sch, Islw. TW7
off St. John's Rd 157 CG83
Gumley Rd, Grays RM20 169 FX79
Gumping Rd, Orp. BR5 205 EQ103
Gundulph Rd, Brom. BR2 204 EJ97
Gunfleet Cl, Grav. DA12 191 GL87
Gun Hill, W.Til. RM18 171 GK79
Gunmakers La, E3 279 M9
Gunnell Cl, SE26 182 DU92
Croydon CR0 202 DU100
Gunner Dr, Enf. EN3 83 EA37
Gunner La, SE18 165 EN78
GUNNERSBURY, W4 158 CP77
Gunnersbury 158 CP78
Gunnersbury 158 CP78
Gunnersbury Av, W3 158 CN76
W4 158 CN76
W5 138 CM74
Gunnersbury Catholic Sch for Boys,
Brent. TW8 *off The Ride* 157 CJ78
Gunnersbury Cl, W4
off Grange Rd 158 CP78
Gunnersbury Ct, W3 158 CP75
Gunnersbury Cres, W3 158 CN75
Gunnersbury Dr, W5 158 CN75
Gunnersbury Gdns, W3 158 CN75
Gunnersbury La, W3 158 CN76
Gunnersbury Ms, W4
off Chiswick High Rd 158 CP78
Gunnersbury Park, W3 158 CM77
Gunnersbury Pk, W3 158 CM76
Gunnersbury Pk, W3 158 CM77
W5 158 CM77
Gunnersbury Park Mus, W3 158 CN76
Gunners Gro, E4 101 EC48
Gunners Rd, SW18 180 DD89
Gunnery Ter, SE18 165 EQ77
Gunning Rd, Grays RM17 170 GD78
Gunning St, SE18 165 ES77
Gunn Rd, Swans. DA10 190 FY86
Gunpowder Sq, EC4 286 F8
Gunstor Rd, N16 122 DS63
Gun St, E1 288 A7
Gunter Gro, SW10 307 N3
Edgware HA8 96 CR53
Gunters Mead, Esher KT10 214 CC110
Gunterstone Rd, W14 294 E9
Gunthorpe St, E1 288 B7
Gunton Rd, E5 122 DV62
SW17 180 DG93
Gunwhale Cl, SE16 301 K3
Gunyard Ms, SE18 164 EL80
Gurdon Rd, SE7 315 P1
Gurnard Cl, West Dr. UB7 134 BK73
Gurnell Gro, W13 137 CF70
Gurnells Rd, Seer Grn HP9 89 AQ50
Gurney Cl, E15 281 K2
E17 101 DX53
Barking IG11 145 EP65
Beaconsfield HP9 88 AJ53
Gurney Ct Rd, St.Alb. AL1 43 CF18
Gurney Cres, Croy. CR0 201 DM102
Gurney Dr, N2 120 DC57
Gurney Rd, E15 281 J2
SW6 307 N10
Carshalton SM5 218 DG105
Northolt UB5 135 BV69
Gurney's Cl, Red. RH1 266 DF135
Guru Gobind Singh Khalsa Coll,
Chig. IG7 *off Roding La* 103 EM46
Guru Nanak Marg, Grav. DA12 191 GJ87
Guru Nanak Prim Sch, Hayes UB4
off Springfield Rd 136 BW74
Guru Nanak Sec Sch, Hayes UB4
off Springfield Rd 136 BW74
Guthrie St, SW3 296 C10
Gutteridge La, Stap.Abb. RM4 87 FC44
Gutter La, EC2 287 K8
Guyatt Gdns, Mitch. CR4
off Ormerod Gdns 200 DG96
Guy Barnett Gro, SE3
off Casterbridge Rd 164 EG83
Guy Rd, Wall. SM6 201 DK104
Guyscliff Rd, SE13 183 EC85
Guysfield Cl, Rain. RM13 147 FG67
Guysfield Dr, Rain. RM13 147 FG67
Guy's Hosp, SE1 299 M4
Guy St, SE1 299 M4
Gwalior Rd, SW15
off Felsham Rd 159 CX83
Gwendolen Av, SW15 179 CX85
Gwendolen Cl, SW15 179 CW85
Gwendolen Ho, Stai. TW19
off Yeoman Dr 174 BL88
Gwendoline Av, E13 144 EH67
Gwendoline Ct, Wal.Cr. EN8 67 DZ34
Gwendwr Rd, W14 294 F10
Gwen Morris Ho, SE5 311 K5
Gwent Cl, Wat. WD25 60 BX34
Gwillim Cl, Sid. DA15 186 EU85
Gwydor Rd, Beck. BR3 203 DX98
Gwydyr Rd, Brom. BR2 204 EF97
Gwyn Cl, SW6 307 N5
Gwyn Jones Prim Sch, E11
off Hainault Rd 123 ED59
Gwynne Av, Croy. CR0 203 DX101
Gwynne Cl, W4
off Pumping Sta Rd 159 CT79
Windsor SL4 151 AL81
Gwynne Ct, Guil. GU2
off Railton Rd 242 AV130
Gwynne Pk Av, Wdf.Grn. IG8 103 EM51
Gwynne Pl, WC1 286 D3
Gwynne Rd, SW11 308 A8
Caterham CR3 236 DR123
Gwynn Rd, Nthflt DA11 190 GC89
Gwynns Wk, Hert. SG13 32 DS09
Gyfford Wk, Chsht EN7 66 DV31
Gylcote Cl, SE5 162 DR84
Gyles Pk, Stan. HA7 95 CJ53
Gyllyngdune Gdns, Ilf. IG3 125 ET61
Gypsy Cl, Gt Amwell SG12 33 DZ11
Gypsy Cor, W3 138 CQ71
Gypsy La, Gt Amwell SG12 33 DZ11
Hunton Bridge WD4 75 BR35
Stoke Poges SL2 112 AS63
Welwyn Garden City AL7 29 CZ13
Gypsy Moth Av, Hat. AL10 44 CS16

H

Haarlem Rd, W14 294 C7
Haberdasher Est, N1
off Haberdasher St 287 M2
Haberdasher Pl, N1 287 M2
Haberdashers' Aske's Boys' Sch,
Els. WD6 *off Butterfly La* 77 CH41
Haberdashers' Aske's Hatcham Coll,
SE14 313 L6
Pepys Rd, SE14 313 L9
Haberdashers' Aske's Knights Acad,
Brom. BR1 *off Launcelot Rd* 184 EG91
Haberdashers' Aske's Sch for Girls,
Els. WD6 *off Aldenham Rd* 77 CH42
Haberdashers' Askes's Crayford Temple
Gro, South Campus, Cray. DA1
off Iron Mill La 167 FG84
North Campus, Erith DA8
off Slade Grn Rd 167 FG80
Haberdasher St, N1 287 M2
Habgood Rd, Loug. IG10 84 EL41
Habitat Cl, SE15 312 F9
Haccombe Rd, SW19
off Haydons Rd 180 DC93
HACKBRIDGE, Wall. SM6 201 DH103
Hackbridge 201 DH103
Hackbridge Grn, Wall. SM6 200 DG103
Hackbridge Pk Gdns,
Cars. SM5 200 DG103
Hackbridge Prim Sch, Wall. SM6
off Hackbridge Rd 200 DG103
Hackbridge Rd, Wall. SM6 200 DG103
Hackett La, Saw. CM21 35 ET05
Hacketts La, Wok. GU22 211 BF114
Hackford Rd, SW9 310 E5
Hackford Wk, SW9 310 D7
Hackforth Cl, Barn. EN5 79 CV43
Hackhurst La, Abin.Ham. RH5 261 BT138
Hackington Cres, Beck. BR3 183 EA93
HACKNEY, E8 278 E5
Hackney Central 278 E4
Hackney City Fm, E2 288 C1
Hackney Cl, Borwd. WD6 78 CR43
Hackney Downs 278 E3
Hackney Downs 278 E3
Hackney Gro, E8
off Reading La 278 F5
Hackney Marsh, E9 123 DY62
Hackney Mus, E8 278 F5
Hackney Rd, E2 288 A3
HACKNEY WICK, E9 280 A4
Hackney Wick 280 A5
Hackworth Ho, N16
off Stamford Hill 122 DS60
Hackworth Pt, E3 290 B3
Hacon Sq, E8 278 F6
HACTON, Rain. RM13 128 FM64
Hacton Dr, Horn. RM12 128 FK63
Hacton La, Horn. RM12 128 FM62
Upminster RM14 128 FM64
Hacton Prim Sch, Horn. RM12
off Chepstow Av 128 FL63
Hadar Cl, N20 98 DA46
Hadden Rd, SE28 165 ES76
Hadden Way, Grnf. UB6 137 CD65
Haddestoke Gate, Chsht EN8 67 DZ26
Haddington Rd, Brom. BR1 183 ED90
Haddo Ho, SE10
off Haddo St 314 D3
Haddon Cl, Borwd. WD6 78 CN40
Enfield EN1 82 DU44
Hemel Hempstead HP3 40 BN21
New Malden KT3 199 CT99
Weybridge KT13 195 BR104
Haddonfield, SE8 301 K9
Haddon Gro, Sid. DA15 186 EU87
Haddon Rd, Chorl. WD3 73 BC43
Orpington BR5 206 EW99
Sutton SM1 218 DB105
Haddo St, SE10 314 E3
Haden Ct, N4
off Lennox Rd 121 DN61
Haden La, N11 99 DJ49
Hadfield Cl, Sthl. UB1
off Adrienne Av 136 BZ69
Hadfield Rd, Stanw. TW19 174 BK86
Hadlands Cl, Bov. HP3 57 AZ26
Hadleigh Cl, E1 288 G4
SW20 199 CZ96
Shenley WD7 61 CK30
Hadleigh Ct, Brox. EN10 49 DZ22
Hadleigh Dr, Sutt. SM2 218 DA109
Hadleigh Rd, N9 100 DV45
Hadleigh St, E2 289 H3
Hadleigh Wk, E6 293 H8
HADLEY, Barn. EN5 79 CZ40
Hadley Cl, N21 81 DN44
Elstree WD6 78 CM43
Hadley Common, Barn. EN5 80 DA40
Hadley Ct, N16 122 DU60
Hadley Gdns, W4 158 CR78
Southall UB2 156 BZ78
Hadley Gra, Harl. CM17 52 EW16
Hadley Grn, Barn. EN5 79 CZ40
Hadley Grn Rd, Barn. EN5 79 CZ40
Hadley Grn W, Barn. EN5 79 CZ40
Hadley Gro, Barn. EN5 79 CY40
Hadley Hts, Barn. EN5
off Hadley Rd 80 DB40
Hadley Highstone, Barn. EN5 79 CZ39
Hadley Pl, Wey. KT13 212 BN108
Hadley Ridge, Barn. EN5 79 CZ41
Hadley Rd, Belv. DA17 166 EZ77
Enfield EN2 81 DL38
Hadley Wood EN4 81 DH38
Mitcham CR4 201 DK98
New Barnet EN5 80 DB42
Hadley St, NW1 275 J5
Hadley Way, N21 81 DN44
HADLEY WOOD, Barn. EN4 80 DE38
Hadley Wood 80 DC38
Hadley Wd Prim Sch, Had.Wd EN4
off Courtleigh Av 80 DC38
Hadley Wd Ri, Ken. CR8 235 DP115
Hadlow Coll Mottingham Cen,
SE12 *off Mottingham La* 184 EJ88
Hadlow Ct, Slou. SL1 131 AQ73
Hadlow Pl, SE19 182 DU94
Hadlow Rd, Sid. DA14 186 EU91
Welling DA16 166 EW80
Hadlow Way, Istead Rise DA13 190 GE94
Hadrian Cl, E3 280 A9
St. Albans AL3 42 BZ22
Staines-upon-Thames TW19 174 BL87
Hadrian Ct, Sutt. SM2
off Stanley Rd 218 DB108
Hadrian Est, E2 288 D1
Hadrian Ms, N7 276 D6
Hadrians Ride, Enf. EN1 82 DT43
Hadrian St, SE10 303 J10
Hadrian Way, Stanw. TW19 174 BL87
Hadyn Pk Rd, W12 159 CU75
Hafer Rd, SW11 160 DF84
Hafton Rd, SE6 184 EE88
Hagden La, Wat. WD18 75 BT43
Haggard Rd, Twick. TW1 177 CH87
HAGGERSTON, E2 278 B10
Haggerston 278 A8
Haggerston Rd, E8 278 A7
Borehamwood WD6 78 CL38
Haggerston Sch, E2 278 B10
Haggerston Studios, E8
off Kingsland Rd 278 A8
Hag Hill La, Tap. SL6 130 AG72
Hag Hill Ri, Tap. SL6 130 AG72
Hagsdell La, Hert. SG13 32 DR10
Hagsdell Rd, Hert. SG13 32 DR10
Hague Prim Sch, E2 288 F4
Hague St, E2 288 D3
Ha-Ha Rd, SE18 165 EM79
Haig Cl, St.Alb. AL1 43 CH21

Haig Dr, Slou. SL1 151 AP75
Haig Gdns, Grav. DA12 191 GJ87
Haigh Cres, Red. RH1 267 DH136
Haig Pl, Mord. SM4
off Green La 200 DA100
Haig Rd, Bigg.H. TN16 238 EL117
Grays RM16 171 GG76
Stanmore HA7 95 CJ50
Uxbridge UB8 135 BP71
Haig Rd E, E13 292 C2
Haig Rd W, E13 292 C2
Haigville Gdns, Ilf. IG6 125 EP56
Hailes Cl, SW19 180 DC93
HAILEY, Hert. SG13 33 DZ13
Hailey Av, Hodd. EN11 33 EA13
Sch Haileybury, Hert. SG13
off College Rd 33 DX13
Haileybury Av, Enf. EN1 82 DT44
Haileybury Rd, Orp. BR6 224 EU105
Hailey Cl, Hailey SG13 33 DY13
Sch Hailey Hall Sch, Hert. SG13
off Hailey La 33 DZ13
Hailey La, Hailey SG13 33 DX14
Hailey Rd, Erith DA18 166 FA75
Hailsham Av, SW2 181 DM89
Hailsham Cl, Rom. RM3 106 FJ50
Surbiton KT6 197 CK101
Hailsham Dr, Har. HA1 117 CD55
Hailsham Gdns, Rom. RM3 106 FJ50
Hailsham Rd, SW17 180 DG93
Romford RM3 106 FJ50
Hailsham Ter, N18 100 DQ50
Sch Haimo Prim Sch, SE9
off Haimo Rd 184 EK85
Haimo Rd, SE9 184 EK85
HAINAULT, Ilf. IG6 103 ES52
⊖ Hainault 103 ES52
● Hainault Business Pk,
Ilf. IG6 104 EW50
Hainault Ct, E17 123 ED56
★ Hainault Forest Country Pk,
Chig. IG7 104 EW47
Sch Hainault Forest High Sch, Ilf. IG6
off Harbourer Rd 104 EV50
Hainault Gore, Rom. RM6 126 EY57
Hainault Gro, Chig. IG7 103 EQ49
Hainault Rd, E11 123 EC60
Chadwell Heath RM6 126 EZ58
Chigwell IG7 103 EP48
Little Heath RM6 126 EV55
Romford RM5 105 FC54
Hainault St, SE9 185 EP88
Ilford IG1 125 EP61
Haines Cl, N1 277 N7
Haines Ct, Wey. KT13 213 BR106
Haines Wk, Mord. SM4
off Dorchester Rd 200 DB101
Haines Way, Wat. WD25 59 BU34
Hainford Cl, SE4 163 DX84
Haining Cl, W4
off Wellesley Rd 158 CN78
Hainthorpe Rd, SE27 181 DP90
Hainton Cl, E1 288 F9
Halberd Ms, E5 122 DV61
Halbutt Gdns, Dag. RM9 126 EZ62
Halbutt St, Dag. RM9 126 EZ63
Halcomb St, N1 277 N9
Halcot Av, Bexh. DA6 187 FB85
Halcrow St, E1 288 F7
Halcyon Way, Horn. RM11 128 FM60
Haldane Cl, N10 99 DH52
Enfield EN3 83 EB38
Haldane Gdns, Grav. DA11 190 GC88
Haldane Pl, SW18 180 DB88
Haldane Rd, E6 292 G2
SE28 146 EX73
SW6 307 H4
Southall UB1 136 CC73
Haldan Rd, E4 101 EC51
Haldens, Welw.G.C. AL7 29 CZ06
Haldon Cl, Chig. IG7
off Arrowsmith Rd 103 ES50
Haldon Rd, SW18 179 CZ85
Hale, The, E4 101 ED52
N17 122 DU55
Hale Cl, E4 101 EC48
Edgware HA8 96 CQ50
Orpington BR6 223 EQ105
Hale Dr, NW7 96 CQ51
HALE END, E4 101 ED51
Hale End, Rom. RM3 105 FH51
Woking GU22 226 AV121
Hale End Cl, Ruis. HA4 115 BU58
Hale End Rd, E4 101 ED51
E17 101 ED53
Woodford Green IG8 101 ED52
Halefield Rd, N17 100 DU53
Hale Gdns, N17 122 DU55
W3 138 CN74
Hale Gro Gdns, NW7 96 CR50
Hale La, NW7 96 CR50
Edgware HA8 96 CP50
Otford TN14 241 FE117
Hale Path, SE27 181 DP91
Hale Pit Rd, Bkhm KT23 246 CC126
Hale Rd, E6 293 H5
N17 122 DU55
Hertford SG13 32 DR10
Hales Oak, Bkhm KT23 246 CC126
Halesowen Rd, Mord. SM4 200 DB101
Hales Pk, Hem.H. HP2 41 BQ19
Hales Pk Cl, Hem.H. HP2 41 BQ19
Hales Prior, N1 off Calshot St 286 C1
Hales St, SE8 314 A5
Hale St, E14 290 C10
Staines-upon-Thames TW18 173 BE91
Haleswood, Cob. KT11 213 BV114
Halesworth Cl, E5
off Theydon Rd 122 DW61
Romford RM3 106 FL52
Halesworth Rd, SE13 314 C10
Romford RM3 106 FL51
Hale Wk, W7 137 CE71
Haley Rd, NW4 119 CW58
Half Acre, Brent. TW8 157 CK79
Halfacre Hill, Chal.St.P. SL9 90 AY53
Half Acre Rd, W7 137 CE74
Halfhide La, Chsht EN8 67 DX27
Turnford EN10 67 DY26
Halfhides, Wal.Abb. EN9 67 ED33
Half Moon Ct, EC1 287 J7
Half Moon Cres, N1 276 D10
Half Moon La, SE24 182 DQ86
Epping CM16 69 ET31
Half Moon Meadow,
Hem.H. HP2 41 BQ15
Half Moon Ms, St.Alb. AL1
off London Rd 43 CD20
Half Moon Pas, E1 off Alie St 288 B9
Half Moon St, W1 297 K2
Half Moon Yd, St.Alb. AL1
off London Rd 43 CD20
Halford Cl, Edg. HA8 96 CP54
Halford Ct, Hat. AL10 44 CS17
Halford Rd, E10 123 ED57
SW6 307 K3
Richmond TW10 178 CL85
Uxbridge UB10 114 BN64
Halfpenny Cl, Chilw. GU4 259 BD140
Halfpenny La, Chilw. GU4 259 BC136
Halfway Ct, Purf. RM19 168 FN77
Halfway Grn, Walt. KT12 195 BV104
Halfway Ho La, Amer. HP6 54 AL33
Halfway St, Sid. DA15 185 ER87
Haliburton Rd, Twick. TW1 177 CG85
Haliday Wk, N1 277 M4
Halidon Cl, E9 278 G2
Halidon Ri, Rom. RM3 106 FP51
Halifax Cl, Brick.Wd AL2 60 BZ30
Leavesden WD25 59 BT34
Teddington TW11 177 CE93
Halifax Rd, Enf. EN2 82 DQ40
Greenford UB6 136 CB67
Heronsgate WD3 91 BC45
Halifax St, SE26 182 DV91
Halifax Way, Welw.G.C. AL7 30 DE09
Halifield Dr, Belv. DA17 166 EY76
Haling Down Pas, S.Croy. CR2 220 DQ109
Haling Gro, S.Croy. CR2 220 DQ108
Haling Pk, S.Croy. CR2 220 DQ107
Haling Pk Gdns, S.Croy. CR2 219 DP107
Haling Pk Rd, S.Croy. CR2 219 DP106
Haling Rd, S.Croy. CR2 220 DR107
Halings La, Denh. UB9 113 BE56
Halkin Arc, SW1 296 G6
Halkingcroft, Slou. SL3 152 AW75
Halkin Ms, SW1 296 G6
Halkin Pl, SW1 296 G6
Halkin St, SW1 297 H5
Hall, The, SE3 315 N10
Hallam Cl, Chis. BR7 185 EM92
Watford WD24 76 BW40
Hallam Gdns, Pnr. HA5 94 BY52
Hallam Ms, W1 285 K6
Hallam Rd, N15 121 DP56
SW13 159 CV83
Hallam St, W1 285 K5
Halland Way, Nthwd. HA6 93 BR51
Hallane Ho, SE27 off Elder Rd 182 DQ92
Hall Av, N18 100 DR51
Aveley RM15 148 FQ74
Hall Cl, W5 138 CL71
Godalming GU7 258 AS144
Mill End WD3 92 BG46
Hall Ct, Datchet SL3 152 AV80
Teddington TW11 177 CF92
Hall Cres, Aveley RM15 168 FQ75
Hall Dene Cl, Guil. GU1 243 BC133
Hall Dr, SE26 182 DW92
W7 137 CE72
Harefield UB9 92 BJ53
Halley Gdns, SE13 163 ED84
Sch Halley Prim Sch, E14 289 M7
Halley Rd, E7 144 EJ65
E12 144 EK65
Waltham Abbey EN9 83 EB36
Halleys App, Wok. GU21 226 AU118
Halleys Ct, Wok. GU21
off Halleys App 226 AU118
Halleys Ridge, Hert. SG14 31 DN10
Halley St, E14 289 L7
Halleys Wk, Add. KT15 212 BJ108
Hall Fm Cl, Stan. HA7 95 CH49
Hall Fm Dr, Twick. TW2 177 CD87
Hallfield Est, W2 283 N8
Sch Hallfield Inf & Jun Schs, W2 283 M9
Hallford Way, Dart. DA1 188 FJ85
Hall Gdns, E4 101 DZ49
Colney Heath AL4 44 CR23
Hall Gate, NW8 283 P2
Hall Grn La, Hutt. CM13 109 GC45
HALL GROVE, Welw.G.C. AL7 30 DB11
Hall Gro, Welw.G.C. AL7 30 DB11
Hall Heath Cl, St.Alb. AL1 43 CH18
Hall Hill, Oxt. RH8 253 ED131
Seal TN15 257 FP123
Halliards, The, Walt. KT12
off Felix Rd 195 BU100
Halliday Cl, Shenley WD7 62 CL32
Halliday Ho, E1
off Christian St 288 D9
Halliday Sq, Sthl. UB2 137 CD74
Halliford Cl, Shep. TW17 195 BR98
Halliford Rd, Shep. TW17 195 BS99
Sunbury-on-Thames TW16 195 BS99
Sch Halliford Sch, Shep. TW17
off Russell Rd 195 BQ101
Halliford St, N1 277 K6
Halliloo Valley Rd, Wold. CR3 237 DZ119
Hallingbury Ct, E17 123 EB55
Halling Hill, Harl. CM20 35 ET13
Hallings Wf Studios, E15 280 G8
Hallington Cl, Wok. GU21 226 AV117
Halliwell Rd, SW2 181 DM86
Halliwick Rd, N10 98 DG53
Jct Hall La, E4 101 DY50
Hall La, E4 101 DY50
NW4 97 CU53
Harlington UB3 155 BR80
Shenfield CM15 109 FZ44
South Ockendon RM15 149 FX68
Upminster RM14 128 FQ60
● Hallmark Trd Cen, Wem. HA9 118 CQ63
Hall Meadow, Burn. SL1 130 AJ68
Hallmead Rd, Sutt. SM1 200 DB104
Sch Hall Mead Sch, Upmin. RM14
off Marlborough Gdns 129 FR60
Hallmores, Brox. EN10 49 EA19
Hall Oak Wk, NW6 273 H4
Hallowell Av, Croy. CR0 219 DL105
Hallowell Cl, Mitch. CR4 200 DG97
Hallowell Gdns, Th.Hth. CR7 202 DQ96
Hallowell Rd, Nthwd. HA6 93 BS52
Hallowes Cl, Guil. GU2 242 AV129
Hallowes Cres, Wat. WD19 93 BU48
Hallowfield Way, Mitch. CR4 200 DD97
Hallows Gro, Sun. TW16 175 BT92
Hall Pk, Berk. HP4 38 AY20
Hall Pk Gate, Berk. HP4 38 AY21
Hall Pk Hill, Berk. HP4 38 AY21
Hall Pk Rd, Upmin. RM14 128 FQ64
★ Hall Pl, Bex. DA5 187 FC86
Hall Pl, W2 284 A5
Woking GU21 227 BA116
Hall Pl Cl, St.Alb. AL1 43 CE19
Hall Pl Cres, Bex. DA5 187 FC85
Hall Pl Dr, Wey. KT13 213 BS106
Hall Pl Gdns, St.Alb. AL1 43 CE19
Hall Rd, E6 145 EM67
E15 123 ED63
NW8 283 P3
Aveley RM15 168 FQ75
Chadwell Heath RM6 126 EW58
Dartford DA1 168 FM84
Gidea Park RM2 127 FH55
Hemel Hempstead HP2 41 BP18
Isleworth TW7 177 CD85
Northfleet DA11 190 GC90
Wallington SM6 219 DH109
Sch Hall Sch, The, Jun Sch, NW3 274 B5
Sen Sch, NW3 274 B5
Sch Hall Sch Wimbledon,
Jun Sch, SW15
off Stroud Cres 179 CU90
Sen Sch, SW20
off The Downs 199 CX95
HALLS GREEN, Harl. CM19 50 EJ18
Hallside Rd, Enf. EN1 82 DT38
Hallsland Way, Oxt. RH8 254 EF133
Hall St, EC1 287 H2
N12 98 DC50
Sch Hallsville Prim Sch, E16 291 N9
Hallsville Rd, E16 291 L9
Hallswelle Par, NW11
off Finchley Rd 119 CZ57
Hallswelle Rd, NW11 119 CZ57
Hall Ter, Aveley RM15 169 FR75
Romford RM3 106 FN52
Hall Twr, W2 284 B6
Hall Vw, SE9 184 EK89
Hall Way, Pur. CR8 219 DP113
Hallwood Cres, Shenf. CM15 108 FY45
Hallywell Cres, E6 293 K7
Halo, E15 280 F9
Halons Rd, SE9 185 EN87
Halpin Pl, SE17 299 M9
Halsbrook Rd, SE3 164 EK83
Halsbury Cl, Stan. HA7 95 CH49
Halsbury Rd, W12 139 CV74
Halsbury Rd E, Nthlt. UB5 116 CC63
Halsbury Rd W, Nthlt. UB5 116 CB64
Halse Dr, Slou. SL2 111 AM64
Halsend, Hayes UB3 135 BV74
Halsey Dr, Hem.H. HP1 39 BF18
Halsey Ms, SW3 296 E8
Halsey Pk, Lon.Col. AL2 62 CM27
Halsey Pl, Wat. WD24 75 BV38
Halsey Rd, Wat. WD18 75 BV41
Halsey St, SW3 296 E8
Halsham Cres, Bark. IG11 145 ET65
Halsmere Rd, SE5 311 H6
HALSTEAD, Sev. TN14 224 EZ113
Halstead Cl, Croy. CR0
off Charles St 202 DQ104
Sch Halstead Comm Prim Sch,
Halst. TN14 off Otford La 224 EZ112
Halstead Ct, N1 287 L1
Halstead Gdns, N21 100 DR46
Halstead Hill, Goffs Oak EN7 66 DS29
Halstead La, Knock.P. TN14 224 EZ114
Halstead Pl, Halst. TN14 240 EY112
Sch Halstead Prep Sch, Wok. GU21
off Woodham Ri 211 BA114
Halstead Rd, E11 124 EG57
N21 100 DQ46
Enfield EN1 82 DS42
Erith DA8 167 FE81
Halstead Way, Hutt. CM13 109 GC44
Halston Cl, SW11 180 DF86
Sch Halstow Prim Sch, SE10 315 N1
Halstow Rd, NW10 282 C3
SE10 303 N10
Halsway, Hayes UB3 135 BU74
Halter Cl, Borwd. WD6 78 CR43
Halton Cl, N11 98 DF51
Park Street AL2 60 CC28
Halton Cross St, N1 277 H8
Halton Pl, N1 277 J8
Halton Rd, N1 277 H6
Grays RM16 171 GH76
Kenley CR8 236 DS120
Halt Robin La, Belv. DA17
off Halt Robin Rd 167 FB77
Halt Robin Rd, Belv. DA17 166 FA77
Haltside, Hat. AL10 44 CS19
Halwick Cl, Hem.H. HP1 40 BH21
Halyard Ct, Rom. RM1
off Western Rd 127 FE57
Halyard Ho, E14
off New Union Cl 302 F6
HAM, Rich. TW10 177 CK90
Ham, The, Brent. TW8 157 CJ80
Hamara Ghar, E13 144 EJ67
Hambalt Rd, SW4 181 DJ85
Hamble Cl, Ruis. HA4 115 BS61
Woking GU21 226 AU117
Hamble Ct, Tedd. TW11 177 CK94
Hambledon Cl, Uxb. UB8 135 BP70
Hambledon Gdns, SE25 202 DT97
Hambledon Hill, Epsom KT18 232 CQ116
Hambledon Ho, Mord. SM4
off Yenston Cl 200 DA100
Hambledon Pl, SE21 182 DS88
Bookham KT23 230 CA123
Hambledon Rd, SW18 179 CZ87
Caterham CR3 236 DR123
Hambledon Vale, Epsom KT18 232 CQ116
Hambledown Rd, Sid. DA15 185 ER87
Hamble Dr, Hayes UB3 135 BT73
Hamble La, S.Ock. RM15 149 FT71
Hamble St, SW6 307 M10
Hambleton Cl, Wor.Pk. KT4 199 CW103
Hamble Wk, Nthlt. UB5
off Brabazon Rd 136 CA68
Woking GU21 226 AU118
Hambley Ho, SE16 off Manor Est 32 E9
Hamblings Cl, Shenley WD7 61 CK33
Hambridge Way, SW2 181 DN87
Hambro Av, Brom. BR2 204 EG102
Hambrook Rd, SE25 202 DV97
Hambro Rd, SW16 181 DK93
Sch Hambrough Prim Sch, Sthl. UB1
off South Rd 136 BZ74
Hambrough Rd, Sthl. UB1 136 BY74
Hamburgh Ct, Chsht EN8 67 DX28
Ham Cl, Rich. TW10 177 CJ90
Ham Common, Rich. TW10 178 CL91
Ham Cft Cl, Felt. TW13 175 BU90
Hamden Cres, Dag. RM10 127 FB62
Hamel Cl, Har. HA3 117 CK55
Hamelin St, E14 290 F9
Hamels Dr, Hert. SG13 32 DV08
Hamels Ms, Bov. HP3 57 BA28
Hamerton Rd, Nthflt DA11 190 GB85
Hameway, E6 293 L4
Ham Fm Rd, Rich. TW10 177 CK91
Hamfield Cl, Oxt. RH8 253 EC127
Ham Flds, Rich. TW10 177 CG90
Hamfrith Rd, E15 281 L4
Ham Gate Av, Rich. TW10 177 CK90
Hamhaugh Island, Shep. TW17 194 BN103
★ Ham Ho, Rich. TW10 177 CJ88
Hamilton Av, N9 100 DU45
Cobham KT11 213 BU113
Hoddesdon EN11 49 EA15
Ilford IG6 125 EP56
Romford RM1 105 FD54
Surbiton KT6 198 CP102
Sutton SM3 199 CY103
Woking GU22 227 BE115
Hamilton Cl, N17 122 DT55
NW8 284 A3
SE16 301 M5
Bricket Wood AL2 60 CA30
Chertsey KT16 193 BF102
Cockfosters EN4 80 DE42
Epsom KT19 216 CQ112
Feltham TW13 175 BT92
Guildford GU2 242 AU129
Horley RH6 268 DG149
Purley CR8 219 DP112
South Mimms EN6 63 CU33
Teddington TW11 177 CH93
Hamilton Ct, W5 138 CM73
W9 283 N2
Bookham KT23
off Eastwick Pk Av 246 CB125
Hatfield AL10 off Cooks Way 45 CV20
Hounslow TW3
off Hanworth Rd 156 CB84
Hamilton Cres, N13 99 DN49
Harrow HA2 116 BZ62
Hounslow TW3 176 CB85
Warley CM14 108 FW49
Hamilton Dr, Guil. GU2 242 AU129
Romford RM3 106 FL54
Hamilton Gdns, NW8 283 P2
Burnham SL1 130 AH69
Hamilton Gordon Ct, Guil. GU1
off Langley Cl 242 AW133
Hamilton Ho, SW8
off St. George Wf 310 A2
Hamilton La, N5 277 H1
Hamilton Mead, Bov. HP3 57 BA27
Hamilton Ms, SW18
off Merton Rd 180 DA88
W1 297 J4
Hamilton Pk, N5 277 H1
Hamilton Pk W, N5 276 G1
Hamilton Pl, N19 121 DK62
W1 297 H3
Guildford GU2 242 AU129
Kingswood KT20 233 CZ122
Sunbury-on-Thames TW16 175 BV94
Hamilton Rd, E15 291 K3
E17 101 DY54
N2 120 DC55
N9 100 DU45
NW10 119 CU64
NW11 119 CX59
SE27 182 DR91
SW19 180 DB94
W4 158 CS75
W5 138 CL73
Berkhamsted HP4 38 AV19
Bexleyheath DA7 166 EY82
Brentford TW8 157 CK79
Cockfosters EN4 80 DE42
Feltham TW13 175 BT91
Harrow HA1 117 CE57
Hayes UB3 135 BV73
Hunton Bridge WD4 59 BQ33
Ilford IG1 125 EP63
Romford RM2 127 FH57
St. Albans AL1 43 CG19
Sidcup DA15 186 EU91
Slough SL1 131 AN72
Southall UB1 136 BZ74
Thornton Heath CR7 202 DR97
Twickenham TW2 177 CE88
Uxbridge UB8 134 BK71
Watford WD19 93 BV48
● Hamilton Rd Ind Est, SE27 182 DR91
Hamilton Rd Ms, SW19
off Hamilton Rd 180 DB94
Hamilton Sq, N12 98 DD51
SE1 299 M4
Hamilton St, SE8 314 A4
Watford WD18 76 BW43
Hamilton Ter, NW8 283 P2
Hamilton Wk, Erith DA8 167 FF80
Hamilton Way, N3 98 DA51
N13 99 DP49
Farnham Common SL2 111 AQ64
Wallington SM6 219 DK109
Ham Island, Old Wind. SL4 152 AX84
Ham La, Eng.Grn TW20 172 AV91
Old Windsor SL4 152 AX84
Hamlea Cl, SE12 184 EG85
Hamlet, The, SE5 162 DR83
Potten End HP4 39 BA16
Hamlet Cl, SE13 164 EE84
Bricket Wood AL2 60 BZ30
Romford RM5 104 FA52
Hamlet Est, Erith DA8 167 FD78
Hamlet Gdns, W6 159 CU77
Hamlet Hill, Roydon CM19 50 EG19
Hamlet Ms, SE21
off Thurlow Pk Rd 182 DR88
Hamleton Ter, Dag. RM9
off Flamstead Rd 146 EW66
Hamlet Rd, SE19 182 DT94
Romford RM5 104 FA52
Hamlet Sq, NW2 119 CY62
Hamlets Way, E3 289 N4
Hamlet Way, SE1 299 M4
★ Hamleys, W1 285 L10
Hamlin Cres, Pnr. HA5 116 BW57
Hamlin Rd, Sev. TN13 256 FE121
Hamlyn Cl, Edg. HA8 96 CL48
Hamlyn Gdns, SE19 182 DS94
Hamlyn Ho, Felt. TW13
off High St 175 BV88
Hammarskjold Rd, Harl. CM20 35 EQ14
Hamm Ct, Wey. KT13 194 BL103
Hammelton Rd, Brom. BR1 204 EF95
HAMMERFIELD, Hem.H. HP1 40 BG20
Hammerfield Dr,
Abin.Ham. RH5 261 BT140
Hammer La, Hem.H. HP2 40 BM19
Hammer Par, Wat. WD25 59 BU33
Hammers Gate, St.Alb. AL2 60 CA25
Hammers La, NW7 97 CU50
Hammersley La,
Penn HP10, HP13 88 AC49
Hammersley Rd, E16 291 P7
HAMMERSMITH, W6 294 B10
⊖ Hammersmith 294 B9
⊖ Hammersmith 294 B9
Sch Hammersmith Acad, W12 159 CV75
Coll Hammersmith & W London Coll,
W14 294 E10
Hammersmith Br, SW13 159 CV79
W6 159 CV79
Hammersmith Br Rd, W6 306 A1
Jct Hammersmith Bdy, W6 294 B9
Hammersmith Bdy, W6 294 B9
Hammersmith Flyover, W6 294 B10
Hammersmith Gro, W6 294 A7
H Hammersmith Hosp, W12 139 CV72
Hammersmith Rd, W6 294 C9
W14 294 C9
Hammersmith Ter, W6 159 CU78
Hammerton Cl, Bex. DA5 187 FE90
Hammet Cl, Hayes UB4 136 BX71
Hammett St, EC3 288 A10
Hamm Moor La, Add. KT15 212 BL106
Hammond Av, Mitch. CR4 201 DH96
Hammond Cl, Barn. EN5 79 CY43
Cheshunt EN7 66 DS26
Greenford UB6
off Lilian Board Way 117 CD64
Hampton TW12 196 CA95
Woking GU21 226 AW115
Hammond Ct, SE11
off Hotspur St 298 E10
Chsht EN7
off Stocksbridge Cl 66 DS26
Hammond End, Farn.Com. SL2 111 AP63
Hammond Ho, SE14
off Lubbock St 313 H5
Sch Hammond JMI & Nurs Sch, Hem.H.
HP2 off Cambrian Way 40 BM17
Hammond Rd, Enf. EN1 82 DV40
Southall UB2 156 BY76
Woking GU21 226 AW115
Hammonds Cl, Dag. RM8 126 EW62
Hammonds La,
Gt Warley CM13 107 FV51
Hammond's La, Hat. AL10 28 CQ13
Sandridge AL4 28 CN12
HAMMOND STREET,
Wal.Cr. EN7 66 DR26
Hammond St, NW5 275 L4
Hammondstreet Rd, Chsht EN7 66 DR26
Hammond Way, SE28
off Oriole Way 146 EV73
Hamond Cl, S.Croy. CR2 219 DP109
Hamonde Cl, Edg. HA8 96 CP47
Hamond Sq, N1 277 N10
Ham Pk Rd, E7 281 L6
E15 281 L6
Hampden Av, Beck. BR3 203 DY96
Chesham HP5 54 AN30
Hampden Cl, NW1 285 P1
North Weald Bassett CM16 70 FA27
Stoke Poges SL2 132 AU69
Hampden Cres, Chsht EN7 66 DV31
Warley CM14 108 FW49
Sch Hampden Gurney C of E Prim Sch,
W1 284 D8
Hampden Gurney St, W1 284 E9
Hampden Hill, Beac. HP9 88 AH53
Ware SG12 33 DZ06
Hampden Hill Cl, Ware SG12 33 DZ05
Hampden La, N17 100 DT53
Hampden Pl, Frog. AL2 61 CE29
Hampden Rd, N8 121 DN56
N10 98 DG52
N17 100 DU53
N19 off Holloway Rd 121 DK61
Beckenham BR3 203 DY96
Chalfont St. Peter SL9 90 AX53
Grays RM17 170 GB78
Harrow HA3 94 CC53
Kingston upon Thames KT1 198 CN97
Romford RM5 105 FB52
Slough SL3 153 AZ76
Hampden Sq, N14
off Osidge La 99 DH46
Hampden Way, N14 99 DH47
Watford WD17 75 BS36
Hampermill La, Wat. WD19 93 BT47
Hampshire Av, Slou. SL1 131 AQ71
Hampshire Cl, N18 100 DV50
Hampshire Ct, Add. KT15
off Garfield Rd 212 BJ106
Hampshire Hog La, W6
off King St 159 CV77
Hampshire Rd, N22 99 DM52
Hornchurch RM11 128 FN56
Sch Hampshire Sch, The,
Pre-Prep, SW7 296 C5
Prep, W2 283 N10
Hampshire St, NW5 275 N4
Hampson Way, SW8 310 C6
HAMPSTEAD, NW3 120 DD63
⊖ Hampstead 120 DC63
Hampstead Av, Wdf.Grn. IG8 103 EN52
Hampstead Cl, SE28 146 EV74
Bricket Wood AL2 60 BZ31
Hampstead Gdns, NW11 120 DA58
Chadwell Heath RM6 126 EV57
HAMPSTEAD GARDEN SUBURB,
N2 120 DC57
Hampstead Grn, NW3 274 C2
Hampstead Gro, NW3 120 DC62
★ Hampstead Heath, NW3 120 DD61
⊖ Hampstead Heath 274 D1
Hampstead Hts, N2 120 DC56
Hampstead High St, NW3 120 DC63
Hampstead Hill Gdns, NW3 274 B1
Hampstead La, N6 120 DD59
NW3 120 DD59
Dorking RH4 263 CG137
Hampstead Ms, Beck. BR3 203 EB98
Sch Hampstead Parochial C of E Prim Sch,
NW3 273 P1
Hampstead Rd, NW1 275 L10
Dorking RH4 263 CG137
Sch Hampstead Sch, NW2 272 F1
Hampstead Sq, NW3 120 DC62
Hampstead Wk, E3
off Waterside Cl 279 P8
Hampstead Way, NW11 120 DC60
HAMPTON, TW12 196 CB95
⇌ Hampton 196 CA95
Sch Hampton Acad, Hmptn. TW12
off Hanworth Rd 176 CA92

H

● Hampton Business Pk,
Felt. TW13 176 BY90
Hampton Cl, N11 99 DH50
NW6 283 J3
SW20 179 CW94
Borehamwood WD6 78 CQ43
Chafford Hundred RM16 169 FW76
⇌ Hampton Court 197 CE98
Hampton Ct, N1 276 G5
Hampton Ct Av, E.Mol. KT8 197 CD99
Hampton Ct Cres, E.Mol. KT8 197 CD97
★ Hampton Court Palace & Pk,
E.Mol. KT8 197 CE97
Hampton Ct Par, E.Mol. KT8
off Creek Rd 197 CE98
Hampton Ct Pk,
E.Mol. (Home Pk) KT8 197 CG98
Kingston upon Thames
(Home Pk) KT1 197 CG98
Hampton Ct Rd, E.Mol. KT8 197 CF97
Hampton TW12 196 CC96
Kingston upon Thames KT1 197 CF97
Hampton Ct Way, E.Mol. KT8 197 CE100
Esher KT10 197 CE103
Thames Ditton KT7 197 CE103
Hampton Cres, Grav. DA12 191 GL89
Hampton Gdns, Saw. CM21 36 EV08
Hampton Gro, Epsom KT17 217 CT111
HAMPTON HILL, Hmptn. TW12 176 CC93
● Hampton Hill Business Pk,
Hmptn. TW12
off Wellington Rd 176 CC92
Sch Hampton Hill Jun Sch,
Hmptn H. TW12
off St. James's Av 176 CC92
Hampton Ho, SW8
off Ascalon St 309 L5
Sch Hampton Inf Sch, Hmptn. TW12
off Ripley Rd 176 CA94
Sch Hampton Jun Sch, Hmptn. TW12
off Percy Rd 196 CA95
Hampton La, Felt. TW13 176 BY91
Hampton Lo, Sutt. SM2
off Cavendish Rd 218 DC107
Hampton Mead, Loug. IG10 85 EP41
Hampton Ms, NW10
off Minerva Rd 138 CR69
Enfield EN3 82 DW41
Hampton Ri, Har. HA3 118 CL58
Hampton Rd, E4 101 DZ50
E7 124 EH64
E11 123 ED60
Croydon CR0 202 DQ100
Hampton Hill TW12 177 CD92
Ilford IG1 125 EP63
Redhill RH1 266 DF139
Teddington TW11 177 CD92
Twickenham TW2 177 CD90
Worcester Park KT4 199 CU103
Hampton Rd E, Han. TW13 176 BZ90
Hampton Rd W, Felt. TW13 176 BY89
Sch Hampton Sch, Hmptn. TW12
off Hanworth Rd 176 CA92
Hampton St, SE1 299 H9
SE17 299 H9
HAMPTON WICK, Kings.T. KT1 197 CH95
⇌ Hampton Wick 197 CJ95
Sch Hampton Wick Inf & Nurs Sch,
Hmptn W. TW11
off Normansfield Av 177 CK94
Ham Ridings, Rich. TW10 178 CM92
HAMSEY GREEN, Warl. CR6 236 DW116
Hamsey Grn Gdns, Warl. CR6 236 DV116
Sch Hamsey Grn Inf Sch, Warl. CR6
off Tithepit Shaw La 236 DV116
Sch Hamsey Grn Jun Sch, Warl. CR6
off Tithepit Shaw La 236 DV116
Hamsey Way, S.Croy. CR2 236 DV115
Hamshades Cl, Sid. DA15 185 ET90
Hamstel Rd, Harl. CM20 35 EP14
Ham St, Rich. TW10 177 CJ89
Ham Vw, Croy. CR0 203 DY100
Ham Yd, W1 285 N10
Hanah Ct, SW19 179 CX94
Hanameel St, E16 303 P2
Hana Ms, E5 278 F1
Hanbury Cl, NW4 119 CW55
Burnham SL1 130 AG71
Cheshunt EN8 67 DX29
Ware SG12 33 DY06
Hanbury Ct, Har. HA1 117 CF58
Hanbury Dr, E11
off High Rd Leytonstone 124 EF59
N21 81 DM43
Biggin Hill TN16 222 EH113
Hanbury La, Essen. AL9 46 DE17
Hanbury Ms, N1 277 K9
Hanbury Path, Wok. GU21 211 BD114
Hanbury Rd, N17 100 DV54
W3 158 CP75
Hanbury St, E1 288 A6
Hanbury Wk, Bex. DA5 187 FE90
Hancock Ct, Borwd. WD6 78 CQ39
Hancock Rd, E3 290 E3
SE19 182 DR93
Hancroft Rd, Hem.H. HP3 40 BM22
Hancross Cl, Brick.Wd AL2 60 BY30
Handa Cl, Hem.H. HP3 41 BP23
Handa Wk, N1 277 K4
Hand Ct, WC1 286 D7
Handcroft Rd, Croy. CR0 201 DP101
Handel Cl, Edg. HA8 96 CM51
Handel Cres, Til. RM18 171 GG80
Handel Pl, NW10 138 CR65
Handel St, WC1 286 A4
Handel Way, Edg. HA8 96 CN52
Handen Rd, SE12 184 EE85
Handford Ct, Wat. WD25 60 BX34
Handforth Rd, SW9 310 E4
Ilford IG1 off Winston Way 125 EP62
Handinhand La, Tad. KT20 248 CQ130
Hand La, Saw. CM21 36 EW06
Handley Gate, Brick.Wd AL2 60 BZ29
Handley Gro, NW2 119 CX62
Handley Page Rd, Wall. SM6 219 DM108
Handley Page Way, Coln.St AL2 61 CF30
Handley Rd, E9 279 H8
Handowe Cl, NW4 119 CU56
Handpost Hill, Northaw EN6 65 DH28
Handpost Lo Gdns,
Hem.H. HP2 41 BR21
HANDSIDE, Welw.G.C. AL8 29 CV10
Handside Cl, Welw.G.C. AL8 29 CW09
Worcester Park KT4 199 CX102
Handside Grn, Welw.G.C. AL8 29 CW08
Handside La, Welw.G.C. AL8 29 CV11
Hands Wk, E16 291 P8
Handsworth Av, E4 101 ED51
Sch Handsworth Prim Sch, E4
off Handsworth Av 101 ED51
Handsworth Rd, N17 122 DR55
Handsworth Way, Wat. WD19 93 BU48
Handtrough Way, Bark. IG11
off Fresh Wf 145 EP68
Handyside St, N1 276 A9
Hanford Cl, SW18 180 DA88
Hanford Rd, Aveley RM15 148 FQ74
Hanford Row, SW19 179 CW93
Hangar Ruding, Wat. WD19 94 BZ48
Hanger Cl, Hem.H. HP1 40 BH21
Hanger Ct, Knap. GU21 226 AS117
Hanger Grn, W5 138 CN70
Hanger Hill, Wey. KT13 213 BP107
⊖ Hanger Lane 138 CM69
Jct Hanger La, W5 138 CL69
Hanger La, W5 138 CM70
Hanger Vale La, W5 138 CM72
Hanger Vw Way, W3 138 CN72
Hanging Hill La, Hutt. CM13 109 GB48
Hanging Sword All, EC4 286 F9
Hangrove Hill, Downe BR6 223 EP113
Hankey Pl, SE1 299 M5
Hankins La, NW7 96 CS48
Hanley Cl, Wind. SL4 151 AK81
Hanley Gdns, N4 121 DL60
Hanley Pl, Beck. BR3 183 EA94
Hanley Rd, N4 121 DL60
Hanmer Wk, N7
off Newington Barrow Way 121 DM62
Hannaford Wk, E3 290 D4
Hannah Cl, NW10 118 CQ63
Beckenham BR3 203 EC97
Hannah Ct, N13 99 DM47
Hannah Mary Way, SE1 300 D9
Hannah Ms, Wall. SM6 219 DJ108
Hannards Way, Ilf. IG6 104 EV50
Hannay La, N8 121 DK59
Hannay Wk, SW16 181 DK89
Hannell Rd, SW6 306 E4
Hannen Rd, SE27
off Norwood High St 181 DP90
Hannibal Rd, E1 289 H6
Stanwell TW19 174 BK87
Hannibal Way, Croy. CR0 219 DM107
Hannington Rd, SW4 161 DH83
Hanno Cl, Wall. SM6 219 DK108
Hanover Av, E16 303 N2
Feltham TW13 175 BU88
Hanover Circle, Hayes UB3 135 BQ72
Hanover Cl, Eng.Grn TW20 172 AV93
Merstham RH1 251 DJ128
Richmond TW9 158 CN80
Slough SL1 152 AU76
Sutton SM3 217 CZ105
Windsor SL4 off Hanover Way 173 AM81
Hanover Ct, SE19
off Anerley Rd 182 DT94
W12 off Uxbridge Rd 139 CU74
Dorking RH4 263 CF136
Guildford GU1 off Riverside 242 AX132
Hoddesdon EN11
off Jersey Cl 49 EA16
Waltham Abbey EN9
off Quaker La 67 EC34
Woking GU22
off Midhope Rd 226 AY119
Hanover Dr, Chis. BR7 185 EQ91
Hanover Gdns, SE11 310 E3
Abbots Langley WD5 59 BT30
Ilford IG6 103 EQ52
Hanover Gate, NW1 284 D3
Slough SL1
off Cippenham La 131 AN74
Hanover Gate Mans, NW1 284 D4
Hanover Grn, Hem.H. HP1 40 BG22
Hanover Ho, Surb. KT6
off Lenelby Rd 198 CN102
Hanover Mead, Bray SL6 150 AC76
Hanover Pk, SE15 312 C7
Hanover Pl, E3 289 N3
WC2 286 B9
Warley CM14 108 FV50
Sch Hanover Prim Sch, N1 277 H10
Hanover Rd, N15 122 DT56
NW10 272 B8
SW19 180 DC94
Hanover Sq, W1 285 K9
Hanover Steps, W2
off St. Georges Flds 284 D9
Hanover St, W1 285 K9
Croydon CR0 off Abbey Rd 201 DP104
Hanover Ter, Islw. TW7
off London Rd 157 CG81
NW1 284 D3
Hanover Ter Ms, NW1 284 D3
Hanover Wk, Hat. AL10 45 CT21
Weybridge KT13 195 BS104
Hanover Way, Bexh. DA6 166 EX83
Windsor SL4 151 AM82
● Hanover W Ind Est, NW10 138 CR68
Hanover Yd, N1 277 H10
Hansa Cl, Sthl. UB2 156 BW76
Hansard Ms, W14 294 D4
Hansart Way, Enf. EN2
off The Ridgeway 81 DN39
Hanscomb Ms, SW4
off Bromell's Rd 161 DJ84
Hans Cres, SW1 296 E6
Hanselin Cl, Stan. HA7 95 CF50
Hansells Mead, Roydon CM19 50 EG15
Hansen Dr, N21 81 DM43
Hanshaw Dr, Edg. HA8 96 CR53
Hansler Gro, E.Mol. KT8 197 CD98
Hansler Rd, SE22 182 DT85
Hansol Rd, Bexh. DA6 186 EY85
Hanson Cl, SW12 181 DH87
SW14 158 CQ83
Beckenham BR3 183 EB93
Guildford GU4 243 AZ131
Loughton IG10 85 EQ40
West Drayton UB7 154 BM76
Hanson Dr, Loug. IG10 85 EQ40
Hanson Gdns, Sthl. UB1 156 BY75
Hanson Grn, Loug. IG10 85 EQ40
Hanson St, W1 285 L6
Hans Pl, SW1 296 F6
Hans Rd, SW3 296 E6
Hans St, SW1 296 F7
Hanway Pl, W1 285 N8
Hanway Rd, W7 137 CD72
Hanway St, W1 285 N8
HANWELL, W7 137 CF74
⇌ Hanwell 137 CE73
HANWORTH, Felt. TW13 176 BX91
Hanworth Ho, SE5
off John Ruskin St 310 G4
Hanworth La, Cher. KT16 193 BF102
Hanworth Rd, Felt. TW13 175 BV88
Hampton TW12 176 CB93
Hounslow TW3, TW4 156 CB83
Redhill RH1 266 DF139
Sunbury-on-Thames TW16 175 BU94
Hanworth Ter, Houns. TW3 156 CB84
● Hanworth Trd Est,
Felt. TW13 176 BY90
Hanyards End, Cuffley EN6 65 DL28
Hanyards La, Cuffley EN6 65 DK28
Hapgood Cl, Grnf. UB6 117 CD64
Harads Pl, E1 300 D1
Harbans Ct, Colnbr. SL3
off Old Bath Rd 153 BE81
Harben Rd, NW6 273 P6
Harberson Rd, E15 281 L8
SW12 181 DH88
Harberton Rd, N19 121 DJ60
Harberts Rd, Harl. CM19 51 EP16
Harbet Rd, E4 101 DX50
N18 101 DX50
W2 284 B7
Harbex Cl, Bex. DA5 187 FB87
Sch Harbinger Prim Sch, E14 302 C9
Harbinger Rd, E14 302 C9
Harbledown Pl, Orp. BR5
off Okemore Gdns 206 EW98
Harbledown Rd, SW6 307 J6
South Croydon CR2 220 DU111
Harbord Cl, SE5 311 L8
Harbord St, SW6 306 C6
Harborne Cl, Wat. WD19 94 BW50
Harborough Av, Sid. DA15 185 ES87
Harborough Cl, Slou. SL1 131 AK74
Harborough Rd, SW16 181 DM91
Harbour Av, SW10 307 P6
Harbour Cl, Mitch. CR4 200 DG95
Harbourer Cl, Ilf. IG6 104 EV50
Harbourer Rd, Ilf. IG6 104 EV50
Harbour Ex Sq, E14 302 D5
Harbourfield Rd, Bans. SM7 234 DB115
Harbour Reach, SW6
off The Boulevard 307 P7
Harbour Rd, SE5 311 J10
Harbour Yd, SW10 307 P7
Harbridge Av, SW15 179 CT87
Harbury Rd, Cars. SM5 218 DE109
Harbut Rd, SW11 160 DD84
Harcamlow Way, Ware SG12 34 EH10
Harcombe Rd, N16 122 DS62
Harcourt, Wrays. TW19 172 AY86
Harcourt Av, E12 125 EM63
Edgware HA8 96 CQ48
Sidcup DA15 186 EW86
Wallington SM6 219 DH105
Harcourt Cl, Dorney R. SL6 150 AF76
Egham TW20 173 BC93
Isleworth TW7 157 CG83
Harcourt Fld, Wall. SM6 219 DH105
Harcourt Lo, Wall. SM6
off Croydon Rd 219 DH105
Harcourt Ms, Rom. RM2 127 FF57
Harcourt Rd, E15 291 L1
N22 99 DK53
SE4 163 DY84
SW19 off Russell Rd 180 DA94
Bexleyheath DA6 166 EY84
Bushey WD23 76 CC43
Dorney Reach SL6 150 AF76
Thornton Heath CR7 201 DM100
Wallington SM6 219 DH105
Windsor SL4 151 AL81
Harcourt St, W1 284 D7
Harcourt Ter, SW10 307 M1
Hardcastle Cl, Croy. CR0 202 DU100
Hardcourts Cl, W.Wick. BR4 203 EB104
Hardell Cl, Egh. TW20 173 BA92
Hardel Ri, SW2 181 DP89
Hardel Wk, SW2
off Papworth Way 181 DN87
Harden Fm Cl, Couls. CR5 235 DJ121
Harden Rd, Nthflt DA11 191 GF90
Hardens Manorway, SE7 304 E7
Harders Rd, SE15 312 E8
Hardess St, SE24
off Herne Hill Rd 162 DQ83
Hardie Cl, NW10 118 CR64
Hardie Rd, Dag. RM10 127 FC62
Harding Cl, SE17 311 J2
Croydon CR0 202 DT104
Watford WD25 60 BW33
Harding Dr, Dag. RM8 126 EY60
Hardinge Cl, Uxb. UB8 135 BP72
Hardinge Cres, SE18 165 EQ76
Hardinge Rd, N18 100 DS50
NW10 139 CV67
Hardinge St, E1 289 H9
Harding Ho, Hayes UB3 135 BU72
Harding Rd, Bexh. DA7 166 EZ82
Chesham HP5 54 AR30
Epsom KT18 232 CS119
Grays RM16 171 GG76
Hardings, Welw.G.C. AL7 30 DC08
Hardings Cl, Hem.H. HP3 40 BH23
Iver SL0 133 BD69
Harding's Cl, Kings.T. KT2 198 CM95
Hardings La, SE20 183 DX93
Harding Spur, Slou. SL3
off Shaw Gdns 153 AZ78
Hardings Row, Iver SL0 133 BC69
Hardingstone Ct, Wal.Cr. EN8
off Eleanor Way 67 DZ34
Hardley Cres, Horn. RM11 128 FK56
Hardman Rd, SE7 304 A10
Kingston upon Thames KT2 198 CL96
Hardwick Cl, Oxshott KT22 230 CC115
Stanmore HA7 95 CJ50
Hardwick Cres, Dart. DA2 188 FP86
Hardwicke Av, Houns. TW5 156 CA81
Hardwicke Gdns, Amer. HP6 55 AS38
Hardwicke Ho, E3
off Bromley High St 290 C2
Hardwicke Ms, WC1 286 D3
Hardwicke Pl, Lon.Col. AL2 61 CK27
Hardwicke Rd, N13 99 DL51
W4 158 CQ77
Reigate RH2 250 DA133
Richmond TW10 177 CJ91
Hardwicke St, Bark. IG11 145 EQ67
Hardwick Grn, W13 137 CH71
Hardwick Ho, Brom. BR2
off Masons Hill 204 EH98
Hardwick La, Lyne KT16 193 BC101
Hardwick Pl, SW16
off Farmhouse Rd 181 DJ94
Hardwick Rd, Red. RH1 266 DD136
Hardwick's Sq, SW18 180 DA85
Hardwick St, EC1 286 F3
Hardwidge St, SE1 299 N4
Hardy Av, E16 303 P2
Northfleet DA11 190 GE89
Ruislip HA4 115 BV64
Hardy Cl, SE16 301 K5
Barnet EN5 79 CY44
Horley RH6 268 DE148
North Holmwood RH5 263 CH141
Pinner HA5 116 BX59
Slough SL1 131 AN74
Hardy Ct, SW18
off Furmage St 180 DB87
Borhamwood WD6
off Chaucer Gro 78 CN42
Hardy Gro, Dart. DA1 168 FN84
Hardy Ms, Uxb. UB8 134 BJ67
Hardy Pas, N22
off Berners Rd 99 DN54
Hardy Rd, E4 101 DZ51
SE3 315 M3
SW19 180 DB94
Hemel Hempstead HP2 40 BM19
Hardy's Ms, E.Mol. KT8 197 CE98
Hardy Way, Enf. EN2 81 DN39
Hare & Billet Rd, SE3 314 G7
Harebell, Welw.G.C. AL7 29 CY13
Harebell Cl, Hert. SG13 32 DV09
Harebell Dr, E6 293 M7
Harebell Hill, Cob. KT11 214 BX114
Harebell Way, Rom. RM3 106 FK52
Harebreaks, The, Wat. WD24 75 BV38
Harecastle Cl, Hayes UB4 136 BY70
Hare Ct, EC4 286 E9
Harecourt Rd, N1 277 J4
Hare Cres, Wat. WD25 59 BU32
Harecroft, Dor. RH4 263 CJ139
Fetcham KT22 230 CB123
Harecroft La, Uxb. UB10 115 BQ62
Haredale Rd, SE24 162 DQ84
Haredon Cl, SE23 182 DW87
HAREFIELD, Uxb. UB9 92 BL53
Harefield, Esher KT10 215 CE105
Harlow CM20 36 EU14
Sch Harefield Acad, The, Hare. UB9
off Northwood Way 92 BK53
Harefield Av, Sutt. SM2 217 CY109
Harefield Cl, Enf. EN2 81 DN39
H Harefield Hosp, Hare. UB9 92 BJ53
Sch Harefield Inf Sch, Hare. UB9
off High St 92 BJ53
Sch Harefield Jun Sch, Hare. UB9
off Park La 92 BJ53
Harefield Ms, SE4 313 N10
Harefield Pl, St.Alb. AL4 43 CK17
Harefield Rd, N8 121 DK57
SE4 163 DZ83
SW16 181 DM94
Rickmansworth WD3 92 BK50
Sidcup DA14 186 EX89
Uxbridge UB8 134 BK65
Hare Hall La, Rom. RM2 127 FH56
Harehatch La, Slou. SL2 111 AL60
Hare Hill, Add. KT15 211 BF107
Hare Hill Cl, Pyrford GU22 228 BG115
Harelands Cl, Wok. GU21 226 AW117
Harelands La, Wok. GU21 226 AW117
Hare La, Clay. KT10 215 CE107
Hatfield AL10 45 CU20
Hare Marsh, E2 288 C4
Harendon, Tad. KT20 233 CW121
Harepark Cl, Hem.H. HP1 39 BF19
Harepit Cl, S.Croy. CR2 219 DP108
Hare Pl, EC4 286 F9
Hare Row, E2 278 F10
Hares Bk, New Adgtn CR0 221 ED110
Haresfield Rd, Dag. RM10 146 FA65
Sch Haresfoot Sch, Berk. HP4
off Chesham Rd 38 AV22
Harestone Dr, Cat. CR3 236 DT124
Harestone Hill, Cat. CR3 252 DT126
Harestone La, Cat. CR3 252 DS125
H Harestone Marie Curie Cen,
Cat. CR3 252 DT125
Harestone Valley Rd, Cat. CR3 252 DT126
HARE STREET, Harl. CM19 51 EP16
Hare St, SE18 305 M7
Harlow CM19 51 EP15
Sch Hare St Comm Prim Sch & Nurs,
Harl. CM19 off Little Gro Fld 51 EQ15
Hare St Springs, Harl. CM19 51 EP15
Hare Ter, Grays RM20
off Mill La 169 FX78
Hare Wk, N1 287 P1
Hareward Rd, Guil. GU4 243 BC132
Harewood, Rick. WD3 74 BH43
Harewood Av, NW1 284 D5
Northolt UB5 136 BY66
Harewood Cl, Nthlt. UB5 136 BZ66
Reigate RH2 250 DC132
Harewood Ct, Warl. CR6 237 DY118
Harewood Dr, Ilf. IG5 103 EM54
Harewood Gdns, S.Croy. CR2 236 DV115
Harewood Hill, They.B. CM16 85 ES35
Harewood Pl, W1 285 K9
Slough SL1 152 AU76
Harewood Rd, SW19 180 DE93
Chalfont St. Giles HP8 72 AW41
Isleworth TW7 157 CF80
Pilgrim's Hatch CM15 108 FV44
South Croydon CR2 220 DS107
Watford WD19 93 BV48
Harewood Row, NW1 284 D6
Harewood Ter, Sthl. UB2 156 BZ77
Harfield Gdns, SE5 311 N10
Harfield Rd, Sun. TW16 196 BX96
Harford Cl, E4 101 EB45
Harford Dr, Wat. WD17 75 BS38
Harford Ms, N19 121 DK62
Harford Rd, E4 101 EB45
Harford St, E1 289 L5
Harford Wk, N2 120 DD57
Harfst Way, Swan. BR8 207 FC95
Hargood Cl, Har. HA3 118 CL58
Hargood Rd, SE3 164 EJ81
Hargrave Pk, N19 121 DJ61
Sch Hargrave Pk Prim Sch, N19
off Hargrave Pk 121 DJ61
Hargrave Pl, N7 275 N3
Hargrave Rd, N19 121 DJ61
Hargreaves Av, Chsht EN7 66 DV30
Hargreaves Cl, Chsht EN7 66 DV31
Hargwyne St, SW9 161 DM83
Hari Cl, Nthlt. UB5 116 CB64
Coll Haringey 6th Form Cen, N17
off College Rd 100 DT51
Haringey Pk, N8 121 DL58
Haringey Pas, N4 121 DP58
N8 121 DN56
Haringey Rd, N8 121 DL56
Harington Ter, N9 100 DR48
N18 100 DR48
Harkett Cl, Har. HA3
off Byron Rd 95 CF54
Harkett Ct, Har. HA3 95 CF54
Harkness, Chsht EN7 66 DU29
Harkness Cl, Epsom KT17 233 CW116
Romford RM3 106 FM50
Harkness Ct, Sutt. SM1
off Cleeve Way 200 DC102
Harkness Ho, E1
off Christian St 288 D9
Harkness Rd, Burn. SL1 130 AH71
Hemel Hempstead HP2 40 BK19
Harland Av, Croy. CR0 202 DT104
Sidcup DA15 185 ER90
Harland Cl, SW19 200 DB97
Harland Rd, SE12 184 EG88
Harlands Gro, Orp. BR6 223 EP105
Harlech Gdns, Houns. TW5 156 BW79
Pinner HA5 116 BX59
Harlech Rd, N14 99 DL48
Abbots Langley WD5 59 BU31
Harlech Twr, W3 158 CP75
Harlequin Av, Brent. TW8 157 CG79
Harlequin Cl, Bark. IG11 146 EU70
Hayes UB4 off Cygnet Way 136 BX71
Isleworth TW7 177 CE85
Harlequin Ho, Erith DA18
off Kale Rd 166 EY76
Harlequin Rd, Tedd. TW11 177 CH94
★ Harlequins RL, Twick. TW2 177 CE87
Harlescott Rd, SE15 163 DX84
HARLESDEN, NW10 138 CS68
◯ Harlesden 138 CR68
⊖ Harlesden 138 CR68
Harlesden Cl, Rom. RM3 106 FM52
Harlesden Gdns, NW10 139 CT67
Harlesden La, NW10 139 CU67
Sch Harlesden Prim Sch, NW10
off Acton La 138 CS68
Harlesden Rd, NW10 139 CU67
Romford RM3 106 FM51
St. Albans AL1 43 CG20
Harlesden Wk, Rom. RM3 106 FM52
Harleston Cl, E5
off Theydon Rd 122 DW61
Harley Cl, Wem. HA0 137 CK65
Harley Ct, E11
off Blake Hall Rd 124 EG59
St. Albans AL4 off Villiers Cres 43 CK16
Harley Cres, Har. HA1 117 CD56
Harleyford, Brom. BR1 204 EH95
Harleyford Rd, SE11 310 C2
Harleyford St, SE11 310 E3
Harley Gdns, SW10 307 P1
Orpington BR6 223 ES105
Harley Gro, E3 289 P2
Harley Pl, W1 285 J7
Harley Rd, NW3 274 B7
NW10 138 CS68
Harrow HA1 117 CD56
Harley St, W1 285 J7
H Harley St Clinic, The, W1 285 J6
Harling Ct, SW11 308 E8
Harlinger St, SE18 304 G6
Harlings, Hert.Hth SG13 32 DW13
HARLINGTON, Hayes UB3 155 BQ79
Harlington Cl, Harling. UB3 155 BQ80
Sch Harlington Comm Sch,
Harling. UB3 off Pinkwell La 155 BR77
Jct Harlington Cor, Hayes UB3
off Bath Rd 155 BR81
Harlington Rd, Bexh. DA7 166 EY83
Uxbridge UB8 135 BP71
Harlington Rd E,
Felt. TW13, TW14 175 BV87
Harlington Rd W, Felt. TW14 175 BV86
HARLOW, CM17 - CM20 51 ER15
⇌ Harlow 35 ER14
Sch Harlowbury Prim Sch,
Old Harl. CM17
off Watlington Rd 36 EX11
● Harlow Business Cen,
Harl. CM19 51 EN16
● Harlow Business Pk,
Harl. CM19 50 EL15
Coll Harlow Coll, Harl. CM20
off Velizy Av 35 ES14
Harlow Common, Harl. CM17 52 EW18
Harlow Ct, Hem.H. HP2 40 BN16
Sch Harlow Flds Sch, Harl. CM18
off Tendring Rd 51 ES17
Harlow Gdns, Rom. RM5 105 FC51
● Harlow Ind Cen, Harl. CM20 36 EV10
Harlow Mkt, Harl. CM20
off East Gate 35 ER14
⇌ Harlow Mill 36 EW10
Harlow Potter St Bypass,
Harl. CM17, CM20 52 EV15
Sch Harlow PRU, Harl. CM20
off Mowbray Rd 36 EU12
Harlow Retail Pk, Harl. CM20 35 ET11
Harlow Rd, N13 100 DR48
Harlow CM20 36 EW08
Matching Tye CM17 37 FC12
Old Harlow CM17 36 FA09
Rainham RM13 147 FF67
Roydon CM19 50 EJ15
Sawbridgeworth CM21 36 EW08
Sheering CM22 36 FA09
⇌ Harlow Town 35 ER12
HARLOW TYE, Harl. CM17 37 FC12
Harlton Ct, Wal.Abb. EN9 68 EF34
Harlyn Dr, Pnr. HA5 115 BV55
Sch Harlyn Prim Sch, Pnr. HA5
off Tolcarne Dr 115 BV55
Harman Av, Grav. DA11 191 GH92
Woodford Green IG8 102 EF52
Harman Cl, E4 101 ED49
NW2 119 CY62
SE1 off Avondale Sq 312 C1
Harman Dr, NW2 119 CY62
Sidcup DA15 185 ET86
Harman Pl, Pur. CR8 219 DP111
Harman Ri, Ilf. IG3 125 ES63
Harman Rd, Enf. EN1 82 DT43
Harmer Rd, Swans. DA10 190 FZ86
Harmer St, Grav. DA12 191 GJ86
Harmonds Wd Cl, Brox. EN10 49 DY19
HARMONDSWORTH,
West Dr. UB7 154 BK79
Harmondsworth La,
West Dr. UB7 154 BL79
Sch Harmondsworth Prim Sch,
Harm. UB7 off School Rd 154 BK79

H

Harmondsworth Rd,
West Dr. UB7 154 BL78
Harmonia Ct, Wat. WD17 75 BU38
Harmony Cl, NW11 119 CY57
Hatfield AL10 45 CU16
Wallington SM6 219 DL109
Harmony Pl, SE1 300 B10
Harmony Ter, Har. HA2
off Goldsmith Cl 116 CB60
Harmony Way, NW4 119 CW56
Harmood Gro, NW1 275 J6
Harmood Pl, NW1 275 J6
Harmood St, NW1 275 J5
Harms Gro, Guil. GU4 243 BC131
Harmsworth Ms, SE11 298 G7
Harmsworth St, SE17 310 G1
Harmsworth Way, N20 97 CZ46
Harness Way, St.Alb. AL4 43 CK17
Harnetts Cl, Swan. BR8 207 FD100
Harold Av, Belv. DA17 166 EZ78
Hayes UB3 155 BT76
Harold Cl, Harl. CM19 51 EM16
Harold Ct, Wal.Cr. EN8
off Alexandra Way 67 DZ34
Sch Harold Ct Prim Sch, Harold Wd RM3
off Church Rd 106 FN52
Harold Ct Rd, Rom. RM3 106 FP51
Harold Cres, Wal.Abb. EN9 67 EC32
Harold Est, SE1 299 P7
Harold Gibbons Ct, SE7 164 EJ79
HAROLD HILL, Rom. RM3 106 FL50
● Harold Hill Ind Est,
Rom. RM3 106 FK52
Harold Laski Ho, EC1 286 G3
HAROLD PARK, Rom. RM3 106 FN52
Harold Pl, SE11 off Kennington La 42 E1
Harold Rd, E4 101 EC49
E11 124 EE60
E13 144 EH67
N8 121 DM57
N15 122 DT57
NW10 138 CR69
SE19 182 DS93
Hawley DA2 188 FM91
Sutton SM1 218 DD105
Woodford Green IG8 102 EG53
Haroldslea, Horl. RH6 269 DK150
Haroldslea Cl, Horl. RH6 269 DJ150
Haroldslea Dr, Horl. RH6 269 DJ150
Harolds Rd, Harl. CM19 50 EL16
Haroldstone Rd, E17 123 DX57
Harold Vw, Rom. RM3 106 FM54
HAROLD WOOD, Rom. RM3 106 FL54
⇌ Harold Wood 106 FM53
Harold Wd Hall, Rom. RM3 106 FK53
Sch Harold Wd Prim Sch, Harold Wd RM3
off Recreation Av 128 FN55
Harp All, EC4 286 G8
● Harp Business Cen, NW2 119 CT61
Harpenden Rd, E12 124 EJ61
SE27 181 DP90
St. Albans AL3 43 CD17
Harpenmead Pt, NW2 119 CZ61
H Harperbury Hosp,
Shenley WD7 61 CJ31
Harper Cl, N14 off Alexandra Ct 103 DJ43
Chafford Hundred RM16 169 FW78
Harper La, Rad. WD7 61 CG32
Harper Ms, SW17 180 DC90
Harper Rd, E6 293 J9
SE1 299 J6
Harpers Yd, N17 100 DT53
Harpesford Av, Vir.W. GU25 192 AV99
Harp Island Cl, NW10 118 CR61
Harp La, EC3 299 N1
Sch Harpley Sch, E1 289 J4
Harpley Sq, E1 289 H3
Harpour Rd, Bark. IG11 145 EQ65
Harp Rd, W7 137 CF70
Harpsden St, SW11 308 G7
Harpsfield Bdy, Hat. AL10 45 CT17
Harps Oak La, Merst. RH1 250 DF125
Harpswood Cl, Couls. CR5 235 DJ122
Harptree Way, St.Alb. AL1 43 CG18
Harpur Ms, WC1 286 C6
Harpurs, Tad. KT20 233 CX122
Harpur St, WC1 286 C6
Harraden Rd, SE3 164 EJ81
Harrap Chase, Bad.Dene RM17 170 FZ78
Harrap St, E14 290 F10
Harrier Av, E11 off Eastern Av 124 EH58
Harrier Cl, Horn. RM12 147 FH65
Harrier Ms, SE28 165 ER76
Harrier Rd, NW9 96 CS54
Harriers Cl, W5 138 CL73
Harrier Way, E6 293 K7
Waltham Abbey EN9 68 EG34
Harries Cl, Chesh. HP5
off Deansway 54 AP30
Harriescourt, Wal.Abb. EN9 68 EG32
Harries Rd, Hayes UB4 136 BW70
Harriet Cl, E8 278 C8
Harriet Gdns, Croy. CR0 202 DU103
Harriet St, SW1 296 F5
Harriet Tubman Cl, SW2 181 DN87
Harriet Wk, SW1 296 F5
Harriet Walker Way, Rick. WD3 91 BF45
Harriet Way, Bushey WD23 95 CD45
HARRINGAY, N8 121 DN57
⇌ Harringay 121 DN58
Harringay Gdns, N8 121 DP56
⊖ Harringay Green Lanes 121 DP58
Harringay Rd, N15 121 DP57
Harrington Cl, NW10 118 CR62
Croydon CR0 201 DL103
Leigh RH2 265 CU141
Windsor SL4 151 AM84
Harrington Ct, W10
off Dart St 282 G2
Croydon CR0 off Altyre Rd 202 DR103
Hertford Heath SG13
off Trinity Rd 32 DW12
Harrington Cres, N.Stfd RM16 149 FX74
Harrington Gdns, SW7 295 M9
Harrington Hill, E5 122 DV60
Sch Harrington Hill Prim Sch, E5
off Harrington Hill 122 DV60
Harrington Ho, NW1 285 L2
Tram Harrington Road 202 DW97
Harrington Rd, E11 124 EE60
SE25 202 DU98
SW7 296 A8
Harrington Sq, NW1 285 L1
Harrington St, NW1 285 L2
Harrington Way, SE18 304 F6
Harriott Cl, SE10 303 L9
Harriotts Cl, Ashtd. KT21
off Harriotts La 231 CJ120
Harriotts La, Ashtd. KT21 231 CJ119
Sch Harris Acad Bermondsey,
SE16 300 B8
Sch Harris Acad Chafford Hundred,
Chaff.Hun. RM16
off Mayflower Rd 169 FW78
Sch Harris Acad Crystal Palace, SE19
off Maberley Rd 202 DT95
Sch Harris Acad Falconwood,
Well. DA16 off The Green 165 ES84
Sch Harris Acad Greenwich, SE9
off Queenscroft Rd 184 EK86
Sch Harris Acad Merton, Mitch. CR4
off Wide Way 201 DK97
Sch Harris Acad Peckham, SE15 312 B7
Sch Harris Acad Purley, S.Croy. CR2
off Kendra Hall Rd 219 DP108
Sch Harris Acad S Norwood, SE25
off South Norwood Hill 202 DT97
Sch Harris Boys' Acad E Dulwich, SE22
off Peckham Rye 182 DV85
Harris Cl, Enf. EN2 81 DP39
Hounslow TW3 156 CA81
Northfleet DA11 190 GE90
Romford RM3 106 FL52
Harris Gdns, Slou. SL1 151 AQ75
Sch Harris Girls' Acad E Dulwich, SE22
off Homestall Rd 182 DW85
Harris La, Shenley WD7 62 CN34
Harrison Cl, N20 98 DE46
Hutton CM13 109 GD43
Northwood HA6 93 BQ51
Reigate RH2 266 DB135
Harrison Dr, Brom. BR1 205 EP98
North Weald Bassett CM16 71 FB26
Harrison Rd, NW10 138 CR67
Dagenham RM10 147 FB65
Waltham Abbey EN9 83 EC35
Harrisons Ri, Croy. CR0 201 DP104
Harrison St, WC1 286 B3
Harrisons Wf, Purf. RM19 168 FN78
Harrison Wk, Chsht EN8 67 DX30
Harrison Way, Sev. TN13 256 FG122
Shepperton TW17 195 BP99
Slough SL1 131 AK74
Sch Harris Prim Acad (Kenley), Ken. CR8
off Little Roke Rd 220 DQ114
Harris Rd, Bexh. DA7 166 EY81
Dagenham RM9 126 EZ64
Watford WD25 75 BU35
Harris's La, Ware SG12 32 DW05
Harris St, E17 123 DZ59
SE5 311 M5
Harris Way, Sun. TW16 195 BS95
Harrod Ct, NW9 118 CQ56
Sch Harrodian Sch, The, SW13
off Lonsdale Rd 159 CT80
★ Harrods, SW1 296 E6
Harrogate Ct, Slou. SL3 153 BA78
Harrogate Rd, Wat. WD19 94 BW48
Harrold Rd, Dag. RM8 126 EV64
● Harrovian Business Village, Har. HA1
off Bessborough Rd 117 CD59
HARROW, HA1 - HA3 117 CD59
⊖ Harrow 117 CE58
⇌ Harrow & Wealdstone 117 CE56
⊖ Harrow & Wealdstone 117 CE56
⊖ Harrow & Wealdstone 117 CE56
★ Harrow Arts Cen, Pnr. HA5 94 CB52
Harrow Av, Enf. EN1 82 DT44
Harroway Manor, Fetch. KT22 231 CF122
Harroway Rd, SW11 308 B9
Harrowbond Rd, Harl. CM17 36 EW14
Harrow Bottom Rd,
Vir.W. GU25 193 AZ100
Harrowby Gdns, Nthflt DA11 190 GE89
Harrowby St, W1 284 D8
Harrow Cl, Add. KT15 194 BH103
Chessington KT9 215 CK108
Dorking RH4 263 CG137
Hornchurch RM11 127 FH60
Coll Harrow Coll,
Harrow-on-the-Hill Campus, Har. HA1
off Lowlands Rd 117 CE59
Harrow Weald Campus, Har.Wld HA3
off Brookshill 95 CE51
Harrow Cres, Rom. RM3 105 FH52
Harrowdene Cl, Wem. HA0 117 CK63
Harrowdene Gdns,
Tedd. TW11 177 CG93
Harrowdene Rd, Wem. HA0 117 CK62
Harrow Dr, N9 100 DT46
Hornchurch RM11 127 FH60
Harrowes Meade, Edg. HA8 96 CN48
Harrow Flds Gdns, Har. HA1 117 CE62
Coll Harrow Fire Training Cen, Pnr. HA5
off Pinner Rd 116 CA56
Harrow Gdns, Orp. BR6 224 EV105
Warlingham CR6 237 DZ115
Harrow Gate Gdns, Dor. RH4
off Horsham Rd 263 CH138
Harrowgate Rd, E9 279 L5
Harrow Grn, E11 124 EE62
Sch Harrow High Sch, Har. HA1
off Gayton Rd 117 CG58
Harrowlands Pk, Dor. RH4 263 CH137
Harrow La, E14 302 E1
Godalming GU7 258 AS144
Harrow Manorway, SE2 146 EW74
🔒 Harrow Mkt, Slou. SL3 153 BA76
★ Harrow Mus, Har. HA2 116 CB55
HARROW ON THE HILL,
Har. HA1 117 CE61
⇌ Harrow on the Hill 117 CE58
⊖ Harrow on the Hill 117 CE58
Harrow Pk, Har. HA1 117 CE61
Harrow Pas, Kings.T. KT1
off Market Pl 197 CK96
Harrow Pl, E1 287 P8
Harrow Rd, E6 144 EL67
E11 124 EE62
NW10 282 C3
W2 283 L7
W9 283 J5
W10 282 F4
Barking IG11 145 ES67
Cars. SM5 218 DE106
Feltham TW14 174 BN88
Ilford IG1 125 EQ63
Knockholt Pound TN14 240 EY115
Slough SL3 153 AZ76
Tokyngton HA9 118 CM64
Warlingham CR6 237 DZ115
Wembley HA0 117 CJ64
Harrow Rd E, Dor. RH4 263 CH138
Harrow Rd W, Dor. RH4 263 CG138
Sch Harrow Sch, Har.Hill HA1
off High St 117 CE60
Harrowsley Ct, Horl. RH6
off Tanyard Way 269 DH147
Harrowsley Grn La, Horl. RH6 269 DJ149
Harrow Vw, Har. HA1, HA2 117 CD56
Hayes UB3 135 BU72
Uxbridge UB10 135 BQ69
Harrow Vw Rd, W5 137 CH70
Harrow Way, Shep. TW17 195 BQ96
Watford WD19 94 BY48
HARROW WEALD, Har. HA3 95 CD53
Harrow Weald Pk, Har. HA3 95 CD51
Harry Cl, Croy. CR0 202 DQ100
Harry Day Ms, SE27 182 DQ90
Sch Harry Gosling Prim Sch, E1 288 D9
Harry's Pl, S.Ock. RM15 149 FX71
Harry Zeital Way, E5
off Mount Pleasant Hill 122 DW61
Harston Dr, Enf. EN3 83 EA38
Harston Wk, E3 290 E4
Hart Cl, Bletch. RH1 252 DT134
Croydon CR0 201 DP104
Hart Cor, Grays RM20 169 FX78
Hart Cres, Chig. IG7 103 ET50
Hartcroft Cl, Hem.H. HP3 41 BP21
Hart Dyke Cres, Swan. BR8
off Hart Dyke Rd 207 FD97
Hart Dyke Rd, Orp. BR5 206 EW102
Swanley BR8 207 FD97
Harte Rd, Houns. TW3 156 BZ82
Hartfield Av, Els. WD6 78 CN43
Northolt UB5 135 BV68
Hartfield Cl, Els. WD6 78 CN43
Hartfield Ct, Ware SG12 33 DX05
Hartfield Cres, SW19 179 CZ94
West Wickham BR4 204 EG104
Hartfield Gro, SE20 202 DV95
Hartfield Pl, Nthflt DA11 190 GD87
Hartfield Rd, SW19 179 CZ94
Chessington KT9 215 CK106
West Wickham BR4 222 EG105
Hartfield Ter, E3 290 B1
Hartford Av, Har. HA3 117 CG55
Hartforde Rd, Borwd. WD6 78 CN40
Hartford Rd, Bex. DA5 186 FA86
Epsom KT19 216 CN107
Hart Gdns, Dor. RH4 off Hart Rd 263 CH135
Hart Gro, W5 138 CN74
Southall UB1 136 CA71
Harthall La, Hem.H. HP3 59 BS26
Kings Langley WD4 59 BP28
Hartham Cl, N7 276 B3
Isleworth TW7 157 CG81
Hartham La, Hert. SG14 32 DQ09
Hartham Rd, N7 276 A2
N17 100 DT54
Isleworth TW7 157 CF81
Harting Rd, SE9 184 EL91
Hartington Cl, Farnboro. BR6 223 EQ106
Harrow HA1 117 CE63
Reigate RH2 250 DA132
Hartington Ct, W4 158 CP80
Hartington Rd, E16 292 A9
E17 123 DY58
SW8 310 A5
W4 158 CP80
W13 137 CH73
Southall UB2 156 BY76
Twickenham TW1 177 CH87
Hartismere Rd, SW6 307 H4
Hartlake Rd, E9 279 K5
Hartland Cl, N21
off Elmscott Gdns 82 DQ44
Edgware HA8 96 CN47
New Haw KT15 212 BJ110
Slough SL1 131 AR74
Hartland Dr, Edg. HA8 96 CN47
Ruislip HA4 115 BV62
Hartland Rd, E15 281 L7
N11 98 DF50
NW1 275 J6
NW6 272 G10
Addlestone KT15 212 BG108
Cheshunt EN8 67 DX30
Epping CM16 70 EU31
Hampton Hill TW12 176 CB91
Hornchurch RM12 127 FG61
Isleworth TW7 157 CG83
Morden SM4 200 DA101
Hartlands Cl, Bex. DA5 186 EZ86
Hartland Way, Croy. CR0 203 DY103
Morden SM4 199 CZ101
Hartlepool Ct, E16 305 P3
Hartley Av, E6 144 EL67
NW7 97 CT50
Hartley Cl, NW7 97 CT50
Bromley BR1 205 EM96
Stoke Poges SL3 132 AW67
Hartley Copse, Old Wind. SL4 172 AU86
Hartley Down, Pur. CR8 219 DM114
Hartley Fm Est, Pur. CR8 235 DM115
HARTLEY GREEN, Long. DA3 209 FX99
Hartley Hill, Pur. CR8 235 DM115
Hartley Ho, SE1
off Longfield Est 300 B8
Hartley Old Rd, Pur. CR8 219 DM114
Sch Hartley Prim Sch, E6
off Hartley Av 144 EL67
Hartley Rd, E11 124 EF60
Croydon CR0 201 DP101
Welling DA16 166 EW80
Westerham TN16 255 ER125
Hartley St, E2 289 H2
Hartley Way, Pur. CR8 235 DM115
Hartmann Rd, E16 304 F2
Hartmoor Ms, Enf. EN3 83 DX37
Hartnoll St, N7 276 D2
Harton Cl, Brom. BR1 204 EK95
Harton Rd, N9 100 DV47
Harton St, SE8 314 A6
Hartopp Pt, SW6
off Pellant Rd 306 F4
Hart Rd, Byfleet KT14 212 BL113
Dorking RH4 263 CH135
Harlow CM17 36 EW10
St. Albans AL1 43 CD21
Hartsbourne Av,
Bushey Hth WD23 94 CC47
Hartsbourne Cl,
Bushey Hth WD23 95 CD47
Sch Hartsbourne Prim Sch,
Bushey WD23
off Hartsbourne Rd 95 CD47
Hartsbourne Rd,
Bushey Hth WD23 95 CD47
Hartsbourne Way, Hem.H. HP2 41 BQ21
Harts Cl, Bushey WD23 76 CA40
Hartscroft, Croy. CR0 221 DY109
Harts Gdns, Guil. GU2 242 AV131
Harts Gro, Wdf.Grn. IG8 102 EG50
Hartshill Cl, Uxb. UB10 134 BN65
Hartshill Rd, Nthflt DA11 191 GF89
Hartshill Wk, Wok. GU21 226 AV116
Hartshorn All, EC3 287 P9
Hartshorn Gdns, E6 293 L4
Hartslands Rd, Sev. TN13 257 FJ123
Harts La, SE14 313 L5
Barking IG11 145 EP65
Hartslock Dr, SE2 166 EX75
Hartsmead Rd, SE9 185 EM89
Hartspiece Rd, Red. RH1 266 DG136
Hartspring La, Bushey WD23 76 CA40
Watford WD25 76 CA39
Hart Sq, Mord. SM4 200 DA100
Hart St, EC3 287 P10
Brentwood CM14 108 FW47
Hartsway, Enf. EN3 82 DW42
Jct Hartswood, Wat. WD25 76 CA39
Hartswood, N.Holm. RH5
off Wildcroft Dr 263 CK139
Hartswood Av, Reig. RH2 266 DA138
Hartswood Cl, Bushey WD23 76 CA40
Warley CM14 108 FY49
Hartswood Gdns, W12 159 CT76
Hartswood Grn,
Bushey Hth WD23 95 CD47
Hartswood Rd, W12 159 CT75
Warley CM14 108 FY49
Hartsworth Cl, E13 291 M1
Hartville Rd, SE18 165 ES77
Hartwell Cl, SW2
off Challice Way 181 DM88
Penn HP10 88 AC45
Hartwell Dr, E4 101 EC51
Beaconsfield HP9 89 AK52
Hartwell St, E8 278 A4
Harvard Hill, W4 158 CP79
Harvard La, W4 158 CQ78
Harvard Rd, SE13 183 EC85
W4 158 CP78
Isleworth TW7 157 CE81
Harvard Wk, Horn. RM12 127 FG63
Harvel Cl, Orp. BR5 206 EU97
Harvel Cres, SE2 166 EX78
Harvest Bk Rd, W.Wick. BR4 204 EF104
Harvest Ct, St.Alb. AL4
off Harvesters 43 CJ16
Shepperton TW17 194 BN98
Harvest End, Wat. WD25 76 BX36
Harvester Rd, Epsom KT19 216 CR110
Harvesters, St.Alb. AL4 43 CK16
Harvesters Cl, Islw. TW7 177 CD85
Harvest Hill, B.End SL8 110 AD61
Harvest La, Loug. IG10 102 EK45
Thames Ditton KT7 197 CG100
Harvest Mead, Hat. AL10 45 CV17
Harvest Rd, Bushey WD23 76 CB42
Englefield Green TW20 172 AX92
Feltham TW13 175 BU91
Harvestside, Horl. RH6 269 DJ147
Harvest Way, Swan. BR8 207 FD101
Harvey, Grays RM16 170 GB75
Harvey Cen App, Harl. CM20 51 ER15
🔒 Harvey Cen, Harl. CM20 51 EQ15
Harvey Dr, Hmptn. TW12 196 CB95
Harveyfields, Wal.Abb. EN9 67 EC34
Harvey Gdns, E11 124 EF60
SE7 304 D10
Loughton IG10 85 EP41
Harvey Ho, Brent. TW8
off Green Dragon La 158 CL78
Harvey Orchard, Beac. HP9 88 AJ52
Harvey Rd, E11 124 EE60
N8 121 DM57
SE5 311 L6
Croxley Green WD3 74 BN44
Guildford GU1 258 AY136
Hounslow TW4 176 BZ87
Ilford IG1 125 EP64
London Colney AL2 61 CJ26
Northolt UB5 136 BW66
Slough SL3 153 BB76
Uxbridge UB10 134 BN68
Walton-on-Thames KT12 195 BT101
Sch Harvey Rd Prim Sch,
Crox.Grn WD3 off Harvey Rd 74 BN44
Harveys La, Rom. RM7 127 FD61
Harvey St, N1 277 M9
Harvill Rd, Sid. DA14 186 EX92
Harvil Rd, Hare. UB9 114 BK58
Ickenham UB10 114 BL60
Sch Harvington Sch, W5
off Castlebar Rd 137 CK72
Harvington Wk, E8 278 D6
Harvist Est, N7 121 DM63
Harvist Rd, NW6 282 D2
Harwater Dr, Loug. IG10 85 EM40
Harwell Cl, Ruis. HA4 115 BR60
Harwell Pas, N2 120 DF56
Harwich Rd, Slou. SL1 131 AN72
Harwood Av, Brom. BR1 204 EH96
Hornchurch RM11 128 FL55
Mitcham CR4 200 DE97
Harwood Cl, N12 98 DE51
Tewin AL6 30 DE05
Welwyn Garden City AL8 29 CY05
Wembley HA0 117 CK62
Harwood Dr, Uxb. UB10 134 BM67
Harwood Gdns, Old Wind. SL4 172 AV87
Harwood Hall La,
Upmin. RM14 148 FP65
Harwood Hill, Welw.G.C. AL8 29 CY06
Harwood Hill JMI & Nurs Sch,
Welw.G.C. AL8
off Harwood Hill 29 CY05
Harwood Pk, Red. RH1 266 DG143
Harwood Rd, SW6 307 K5
Harwoods, The, Ware SG12 32 DV05
Harwoods Rd, Wat. WD18 75 BU42
Harwoods Yd, N21
off Wades Hill 99 DN45
Harwood Ter, SW6 307 L6
Hascombe Ter, SE5 311 L8
Hasedines Rd, Hem.H. HP1 40 BG19
Haselbury Rd, N9 100 DS49
N18 100 DS49
Haseldine Meadows, Hat. AL10 45 CT19
Haseldine Rd, Lon.Col. AL2 61 CK26
Haseley End, SE23 off Tyson Rd 182 DW87
Haselrigge Rd, SW4 161 DK84
Sch Haseltine Prim Sch, SE26
off Haseltine Rd 183 DZ91
Haseltine Rd, SE26 183 DZ91
Haselwood Dr, Enf. EN2 81 DP42
Haskard Rd, Dag. RM9 126 EX63
Hasker St, SW3 296 D8
Haslam Av, Sutt. SM3 199 CY102
Haslam Cl, N1 276 F6
Uxbridge UB10 115 BQ61
Haslam Ct, N11
off Waterfall Rd 99 DH49
Haslam St, SE15 312 B5
Haslemere Av, NW4 119 CX58
SW18 180 DB89
W7 157 CG76
W13 157 CG76
Barnet EN4 98 DF46
Hounslow TW5 156 BW82
Mitcham CR4 200 DD96
● Haslemere Business Cen,
Enf. EN1 82 DV43
Haslemere Cl, Hmptn. TW12 176 BZ92
Wallington SM6 219 DL106
Haslemere Gdns, N3 119 CZ55
● Haslemere Heathrow Est,
Houns. TW4 155 BU82
● Haslemere Ind Est, SW18 180 DB89
Sch Haslemere Prim Sch, Mitch. CR4
off Haslemere Av 200 DD96
Haslemere Rd, N8 121 DK59
N21 99 DP47
Bexleyheath DA7 166 EZ82
Ilford IG3 125 ET61
Thornton Heath CR7 201 DP99
Windsor SL4 151 AN81
Hasler Cl, SE28 146 EV73
Haslett Rd, Shep. TW17 195 BS96
Haslewood Av, Hodd. EN11 49 EA17
Hasluck Gdns, New Barn. EN5 80 DC44
Sch Hasmonean High Sch,
Boys, NW4 off Holders Hill Rd 119 CX54
Girls, NW7 off Page St 97 CU53
Sch Hasmonean Prim Sch,
NW4 off Shirehall La 119 CX57
Hassard St, E2 288 B1
Hassendean Rd, SE3 164 EH79
Hassett Rd, E9 279 K4
Hassocks Cl, SE26 182 DV90
Hassocks Rd, SW16 201 DK95
Hassock Wd, Kes. BR2 222 EK105
Hassop Rd, NW2 119 CX63
Hassop Wk, SE9 184 EL91
Hasted Cl, Green. DA9 189 FW86
Hasted Rd, SE7 304 E10
Hastings Av, Ilf. IG6 125 EQ56
Hastings Cl, SE15 312 C5
Barnet EN5 80 DC42
Grays RM17 170 FY79
Wembley HA0 117 CJ63
Hastings Dr, Surb. KT6 197 CJ100
Hastings Ho, SE18 305 K9
Hastings Pl, Croy. CR0
off Hastings Rd 202 DT102
Hastings Rd, E16 291 P7
N11 99 DJ50
N17 122 DR55
W13 137 CH73
Bromley BR2 204 EL102
Croydon CR0 202 DT102
Romford RM2 127 FH57
Hastings St, SE18 165 EQ76
WC1 286 A3
Hastings Way, Bushey WD23 76 BY42
Croxley Green WD3 75 BP42
HASTINGWOOD, Harl. CM17 52 EZ19
● Hastingwood Business Cen,
Hast. CM17 52 EZ18
Jct Hastingwood Interchange,
Harl. CM17 52 EW20
Hastingwood Rd, Hast. CM17 52 EX20
Magdalen Laver CM5 53 FB19
● Hastingwood Trd Est, N18 101 DX51
Hastoe Cl, Hayes UB4 136 BY70
Hasty Cl, Mitch. CR4
off Slade Way 200 DG95
Haswell Cres, Slou. SL1 151 AM75
Hat & Mitre Ct, EC1 287 H5
Hatch, The, Enf. EN3 83 DX39
Windsor SL4 150 AJ80
● Hatcham Ms Business Cen,
SE14 313 K6
Hatcham Pk Ms, SE14 313 K6
Hatcham Pk Rd, SE14 313 K6
Hatcham Rd, SE15 312 G3
Sch Hatcham Temple Gro Free Sch,
SE14 313 J4
Hatchard Rd, N19 121 DK61
Hatch Cl, Add. KT15 194 BH104
Hatchcroft, NW4 119 CV55
HATCH END, Pnr. HA5 94 BY52
⊖ Hatch End 94 BZ52
Sch Hatch End High Sch, Har. HA3
off Headstone La 94 CB53
Hatchers Ms, SE1 299 P5
Hatchett Rd, Felt. TW14 175 BQ88
Hatch Fm Ms, Add. KT15 194 BJ103
Hatch Gdns, Tad. KT20 233 CX120
Hatchgate, Horl. RH6 268 DF149
Hatchgate Gdns, Burn. SL1 131 AK69
Hatch Gro, Rom. RM6 126 EY56
Hatchingtan, The, Worp. GU3 242 AW126
★ Hatchlands Ho & Pk,
Guil. GU4 244 BM131
Hatchlands Rd, Red. RH1 250 DE134
Hatch La, E4 101 ED49
Cobham KT11 229 BP119
Coulsdon CR5 234 DG115
Harmondsworth UB7 154 BK80
Ockham GU23 229 BP120
Redhill RH1 267 DM142
Windsor SL4 151 AN83
Hatch Pl, Kings.T. KT2 178 CM92
Hatch Rd, SW16 201 DL96
Pilgrim's Hatch CM15 108 FU43
Hatch Side, Chig. IG7 103 EN50
Hatchwood Cl, Wdf.Grn. IG8
off Sunset Av 102 EF49
Hatcliffe Cl, SE3 315 L10
Hatcliffe St, SE10 303 L10
Hatfeild Cl, Mitch. CR4 200 DD98
Hatfeild Mead, Mord. SM4 200 DA99
Sch Hatfeild Prim Sch, Mord. SM4
off Lower Morden La 199 CY100
HATFIELD, AL9 & AL10 45 CV17
⇌ Hatfield 45 CW17
Hatfield Av, Hat. AL10 44 CS15
● Hatfield Business Pk,
Hat. AL10 44 CR15
Hatfield Cl, SE14 313 J5
Hornchurch RM12 128 FK64
Hutton CM13 109 GD45
Ilford IG6 125 EP55
Sutton SM2 218 DA109
West Byfleet KT14 212 BH112
Hatfield Cres, Hem.H. HP2 40 BM16

H

HATFIELD GARDEN VILLAGE, Hat. AL10 29 CU14
★ Hatfield Ho & Pk, Hat. AL9 45 CX18
HATFIELD HYDE, Welw.G.C. AL7 29 CZ12
Hatfield Ms, Dag. RM9 146 EY66
Hatfield Pk, Hat. AL9 45 CX18
Hatfield Rd, E15 281 K2
W4 158 CR75
W13 137 CG74
Ashtead KT21 232 CM119
Chafford Hundred RM16 169 FX77
Dagenham RM9 146 EY65
Hatfield AL9 30 DE14
Potters Bar EN6 64 DC30
St. Albans AL1, AL4 43 CF20
Slough SL1 152 AU75
Watford WD24 75 BV39
Hatfields, SE1 298 F2
Loughton IG10 85 EP41
Hatfield Tunnel, Hat. AL10 45 CT17
Sch Hathaway Acad, The, Grays RM17 off Hathaway Rd 170 GB76
Hathaway Cl, Brom. BR2 205 EM102
Ilford IG6 103 EP51
Ruislip HA4 off Stafford Rd 115 BT63
Stanmore HA7 95 CG50
Hathaway Ct, St.Alb. AL4 44 CL20
Hathaway Cres, E12 145 EM65
Hathaway Gdns, W13 137 CF71
Grays RM17 off Hathaway Rd 170 GA76
Romford RM6 126 EX57
Sch Hathaway Prim Sch, W13 off Hathaway Gdns 137 CF71
Hathaway Rd, Croy. CR0 201 DP101
Grays RM17 170 GB77
Hatherleigh Cl, NW7 97 CX52
Chessington KT9 215 CK106
Morden SM4 200 DA98
Hatherleigh Gdns, Pot.B. EN6 64 DD32
Hatherleigh Rd, Ruis. HA4 115 BU61
Hatherleigh Way, Rom. RM3 106 FK53
Hatherley Cres, Sid. DA14 186 EU89
Hatherley Gdns, E6 292 F4
N8 121 DL58
Hatherley Gro, W2 283 L8
Hatherley Ms, E17 123 EA56
Hatherley Rd, E17 123 DZ56
Richmond TW9 158 CM81
Sidcup DA14 186 EU91
Hatherley St, SW1 297 M9
Hathern Gdns, SE9 185 EN91
Hatherop Rd, Hmptn. TW12 176 BZ94
Hathersage Ct, N1 277 M2
Hathersham Cl, Smallfield RH6 269 DN147
Hathersham La, Smallfield RH6 267 DK144
Hatherwood, Lthd. KT22 231 CK121
Hathorne Cl, SE15 312 F8
Hathway St, SE15 313 H9
Hathway Ter, SE14 off Hathway St 313 J9
Hatley Av, Ilf. IG6 125 EQ56
Hatley Cl, N11 98 DF50
Hatley Rd, N4 121 DM61
Hatteraick St, SE16 301 H4
Hattersfield Cl, Belv. DA17 166 EZ77
Hatters La, Wat. WD18 75 BR44
HATTON, Felt. TW14 155 BT84
Hatton Av, Slou. SL2 131 AR70
Hatton Cl, SE18 165 ER80
Chafford Hundred RM16 169 FX76
Northfleet DA11 190 GE90
⊖ Hatton Cross 155 BT84
Hatton Cross 155 BT84
Hatton Cross, Felt. TW14 155 BT84
Hatton Cross Rbt, Lon.Hthrw Air. TW6 155 BS83
Hatton Gdn, EC1 286 F6
Hatton Gdns, Mitch. CR4 200 DF99
Hatton Grn, Felt. TW14 155 BU84
Hatton Gro, West Dr. UB7 154 BK75
Hatton Ho, E1 288 D10
Hatton Ms, Green. DA9 169 FW84
Hatton Pl, EC1 286 F5
Hatton Rd, Chsht EN8 67 DX29
Croydon CR0 201 DN102
Feltham TW14 175 BS85
London Heathrow Airport TW6 155 BT84
Hatton Row, NW8 284 B5
Sch Hatton Sch, Wdf.Grn. IG8 off Roding La S 124 EK55
Hatton St, NW8 284 B5
Hatton Wk, Enf. EN2 off London Rd 82 DR42
Hatton Wall, EC1 286 E6
Haunch of Venison Yd, W1 285 J9
Hauteville Ct Gdns, W6 off Stamford Brook Av 159 CT76
Havana Cl, Rom. RM1 off Exchange St 127 FE57
Havana Rd, SW19 180 DA89
Havannah St, E14 302 B5
Havant Rd, E17 123 EC55
Havelock Cl, W12 off India Way 139 CV73
Havelock Pl, Har. HA1 117 CE58
Sch Havelock Prim Sch, Sthl. UB2 off Havelock Rd 156 BZ76
Havelock Rd, N17 100 DU54
SW19 180 DC92
Belvedere DA17 166 EZ77
Bromley BR2 204 EJ98
Croydon CR0 202 DT102
Dartford DA1 187 FH87
Gravesend DA11 191 GF88
Harrow HA3 117 CE55
Kings Langley WD4 58 BN28
Southall UB2 156 BZ76
Havelock St, N1 276 B8
Ilford IG1 125 EP61
Havelock Ter, SW8 309 K5
Havelock Wk, SE23 182 DW88
Haven, The, SE26 182 DV92
Grays RM16 171 GF78
Richmond TW9 158 CN83
Sunbury-on-Thames TW16 175 BU94
● Havenbury Ind Est, Dor. RH4 off Station Rd 263 CG135
Haven Cl, SE9 185 EM90
SW19 179 CX90
Esher KT10 197 CE103
Hatfield AL10 45 CT17
Haven Cl, Hayes UB4 135 BS71
Istead Rise DA13 191 GF94
Sidcup DA14 186 EW93
Swanley BR8 207 FF96
Haven Ct, Esher KT10 off Portsmouth Rd 197 CE103
Haven Dr, Epsom KT19 216 CP110
Havengore Av, Grav. DA12 191 GL87
Haven Grn, W5 137 CK72
Haven Grn Ct, W5 137 CK72
Havenhurst Ri, Enf. EN2 81 DN40
Haven La, W5 138 CL72
Haven Ms, N1 276 F7
Haven Pl, W5 137 CK73
Esher KT10 197 CE103
Grays RM16 170 GC75
Haven Rd, Ashf. TW15 175 BP91
Havensfield, Chipper. WD4 58 BH31
Haven St, NW1 275 J7
Haven Way, SE1 300 A6
Epsom KT19 216 CP111
Havenwood, Wem. HA9 118 CP62
Havenwood Cl, Gt Warley CM13 off Wilmot Grn 107 FW51
Havercroft Cl, St.Alb. AL3 42 CB22
Haverfield Gdns, Rich. TW9 158 CN80
Haverfield Rd, E3 289 L2
Haverford Way, Edg. HA8 96 CM53
Haverhill Rd, E4 101 EC46
SW12 181 DJ88
Sch Havering 6th Form Coll, Horn. RM11 off Wingletye La 128 FM60
HAVERING-ATTE-BOWER, Rom. RM4 105 FE48
Sch Havering Coll of Further & Higher Ed, Ardleigh Grn Campus, Horn. RM11 off Ardleigh Grn Rd 128 FL56
Quarles Campus, Harold Hill RM3 off Tring Gdns 106 FL49
Havering Dr, Rom. RM1 127 FE56
Havering Gdns, Rom. RM6 126 EW57
Sch Havering Music Sch, Horn. RM11 off The Walk 128 FM61
HAVERING PARK, Rom. RM5 104 FA50
Havering Rd, Rom. RM1 127 FD55
Havering St, E1 289 J9
Havering Way, Bark. IG11 146 EV69
Havers Av, Hersham KT12 214 BX106
Haversfield Est, Brent. TW8 158 CL78
Haversham Cl, Twick. TW1 177 CK86
Haversham Pl, N6 120 DF61
Haverstock Ct, Orp. BR5 206 EU96
Haverstock Hill, NW3 274 D3
Haverstock Pl, N1 off Haverstock St 287 H2
Haverstock Rd, NW5 274 G3
Sch Haverstock Sch, NW3 274 G5
Haverstock St, N1 287 H1
Haverthwaite Rd, Orp. BR6 205 ER103
Havil St, SE5 311 N5
Havisham Pl, SE19 181 DP93
Hawarden Gro, SE24 182 DQ87
Hawarden Hill, NW2 119 CU62
Hawarden Rd, E17 123 DX56
Caterham CR3 236 DQ121
Haward Rd, Hodd. EN11 49 EC15
Hawbridge Rd, E11 123 ED60
Hawes Cl, Nthwd. HA6 93 BT52
Sch Hawes Down Inf Sch, W.Wick. BR4 off The Mead 203 ED102
Sch Hawes Down Jun Sch, W.Wick. BR4 off The Mead 203 ED102
Hawes La, E4 83 EC38
West Wickham BR4 203 EC102
Hawes Rd, N18 100 DV51
Bromley BR1 204 EH95
Tadworth KT20 off Hatch Gdns 233 CX120
Hawes St, N1 277 H7
Haweswater Dr, Wat. WD25 60 BW33
Haweswater Ho, Islw. TW7 off Summerwood Rd 177 CF85
Hawfield Bk, Orp. BR6 206 EX104
Hawfield Gdns, Park St AL2 61 CD26
Hawgood St, E3 290 B7
Hawk Cl, Wal.Abb. EN9 68 EG34
Hawkdene, E4 83 EB44
Sch Hawkedale Inf - A Foundation Sch, Sun. TW16 off Stratton Rd 195 BT97
Hawkenbury, Harl. CM19 51 EN17
Hawke Pk Rd, N22 121 DP55
Hawke Pl, SE16 301 K4
Hawke Rd, SE19 182 DS93
Hawker Pl, E17 101 EC54
Hawker Rd, Croy. CR0 219 DN107
Hawkesbury Cl, Ilf. IG6 104 EV49
Hawkesbury Rd, SW15 179 CV85
Hawkes Cl, Grays RM17 off New Rd 170 GB79
Langley SL3 153 BB76
Hawkes Ct, Chesh. HP5 54 AQ30
Hawkesfield Rd, SE23 183 DY89
Hawkesley Cl, Twick. TW1 177 CG91
Hawke's Pl, Sev. TN13 256 FG127
Hawkes Rd, Felt. TW14 175 BU87
Mitcham CR4 200 DE95
Hawkesworth Cl, Nthwd. HA6 93 BS52
Hawke Twr, SE14 313 L3
Hawkewood Rd, Sun. TW16 195 BU97
Hawkhirst Rd, Ken. CR8 236 DR115
Hawkhurst, Cob. KT11 214 CA114
Hawkhurst Gdns, Chess. KT9 216 CL105
Romford RM5 105 FD51
Hawkhurst Rd, SW16 201 DK95
Hawkhurst Way, N.Mal. KT3 198 CR99
West Wickham BR4 203 EB103
Hawkinge Wk, Orp. BR5 206 EV97
Hawkinge Way, Horn. RM12 148 FJ65
Hawkins Av, Grav. DA12 191 GJ91
Hawkins Cl, NW7 off Hale La 96 CR50
Borehamwood WD6 off Banks Rd 78 CQ40
Harrow HA1 117 CD59
Hawkins Dr, Chaff.Hun. RM16 169 FX75
Hawkins Rd, NW10 138 CS66
Teddington TW11 177 CH93
Hawkins Ter, SE7 305 H10
Hawkins Way, SE6 183 EA92
Bovingdon HP3 57 BA26
Hawkley Gdns, SE27 181 DP89
Hawkridge, NW5 275 H4
Hawkridge Cl, Rom. RM6 126 EW59
Hawkridge Dr, Grays RM17 170 GD78
Hawksbrook La, Beck. BR3 203 EB100
Hawkshaw Cl, SW2 off Tierney Rd 181 DL87
Hawkshead, NW1 285 L2
Hawkshead Cl, Brom. BR1 184 EE94
Hawkshead La, N.Mymms AL9 63 CW28
Hawkshead Rd, NW10 139 CT66
W4 158 CS75
Potters Bar EN6 64 DB29
Hawks Hill, B.End SL8 110 AC61
N.Wld Bas. CM16 70 FA27
Hawkshill, St.Alb. AL1 43 CG21
Hawk's Hill, Lthd. KT22 231 CF123
Hawkshill Cl, Esher KT10 214 CA107
Hawks Hill Cl, Fetch. KT22 231 CF123
Hawkshill Dr, Felden HP3 39 BE23
Hawkshill Rd, Slou. SL2 131 AN69
Hawkshill Way, Esher KT10 214 BZ107
Hawkslade Rd, SE15 183 DX85
Hawksley Rd, N16 122 DS62
Hawksmead Cl, Enf. EN3 83 DX35
Hawks Ms, SE10 314 F5
Hawksmoor, Shenley WD7 62 CN33
Hawksmoor Cl, E6 292 G8
SE18 165 ES78
Hawksmoor Grn, Hutt. CM13 109 GD43
Hawksmoor Ms, E1 288 E10
Sch Hawksmoor Prim Sch, SE28 off Bentham Rd 146 EV74
Hawksmoor St, W6 306 D3
Hawksmouth, E4 101 EB45
Hawks Rd, Kings.T. KT1 198 CM96
Hawkstone Est, SE16 301 H9
Hawkstone Rd, SE16 301 H9
Hawksview, Cob. KT11 214 BZ113
Hawksway, Stai. TW18 173 BF90
Hawkswell Cl, Wok. GU21 226 AT117
Hawkswell Wk, Wok. GU21 off Lockfield Dr 226 AS117
Hawkswood Gro, Fulmer SL3 133 AZ65
Hawkswood La, Ger.Cr. SL9 113 AZ64
Hawk Ter, Ilf. IG5 off Tiptree Cres 125 EN55
Hawkwell Ct, E4 off Colvin Gdns 101 EC48
Hawkwell Ho, Dag. RM8 126 FA60
Hawkwell Wk, N1 277 K8
Hawkwood Cres, E4 83 EB44
Hawkwood Dell, Bkhm KT23 246 CA126
Hawkwood La, Chis. BR7 205 EQ95
Hawkwood Mt, E5 122 DV60
Hawkwood Ri, Bkhm KT23 246 CA126
Hawlands Dr, Pnr. HA5 116 BY59
HAWLEY, Dart. DA2 188 FM92
Hawley Cl, Hmptn. TW12 176 BZ93
Hawley Cres, NW1 275 K7
Sch Hawley Inf Sch, NW1 275 K7
Hawley Ms, NW1 275 J6
Hawley Mill, Dart. DA2 188 FN91
Hawley Rd, N18 101 DX50
NW1 275 K6
Dartford DA1, DA2 188 FL89
HAWLEY'S CORNER, West. TN16 239 EN121
Hawley St, NW1 275 J7
Hawley Ter, Dart. DA2 188 FN92
Hawley Vale, Dart. DA2 188 FN92
Hawley Way, Ashf. TW15 174 BN92
Haws La, Stai. TW19 174 BG86
Hawstead La, Orp. BR6 224 EZ106
Hawstead Rd, SE6 183 EB86
Hawsted, Buck.H. IG9 102 EH45
Hawthorn Av, E3 279 N8
N13 99 DL50
Brentwood CM13 109 FZ48
Kew TW9 158 CL82
Rainham RM13 147 FH70
Thornton Heath CR7 201 DP95
● Hawthorn Cen, The, Har. HA1 off Elmgrove Rd 117 CF56
Hawthorn Cl, Abb.L. WD5 59 BU32
Banstead SM7 217 CY114
Gravesend DA12 191 GH91
Hampton TW12 176 CA92
Hertford SG14 31 DN08
Hounslow TW5 155 BV80
Iver SL0 133 BD68
Petts Wood BR5 205 ER100
Redhill RH1 off Bushfield Dr 266 DG139
Watford WD17 75 BT38
Woking GU22 226 AY120
Hawthorn Cres, SW17 180 DG92
South Croydon CR2 220 DW111
Hawthornden Cl, N12 off Fallowfields Dr 98 DE51
Hawthorndene Cl, Brom. BR2 204 EF103
Hawthorndene Rd, Brom. BR2 204 EF103
Hawthorn Dr, Denh. UB9 134 BJ65
Harrow HA2 116 BZ58
West Wickham BR4 222 EE105
Hawthorne Av, Bigg.H. TN16 238 EK115
Carshalton SM5 218 DG108
Cheshunt EN7 66 DV31
Harrow HA3 117 CG58
Mitcham CR4 200 DD96
Ruislip HA4 115 BV58
Hawthorne Cl, N1 277 N4
Bromley BR1 205 EM97
Cheshunt EN7 66 DV31
Sutton SM1 off Aultone Way 200 DC103
Hawthorne Ct, Nthwd. HA6 off Ryefield Cres 93 BU54
Walton-on-Thames KT12 off Ambleside Av 196 BX103
Hawthorne Cres, Slou. SL1 132 AS71
West Drayton UB7 154 BM75
Hawthorne Fm Av, Nthlt. UB5 136 BY67
Hawthorne Gro, NW9 118 CQ59
Hawthorne La, Hem.H. HP1 39 BF19
Hawthorne Ms, Grnf. UB6 136 CC72
Hawthorne Pl, Epsom KT17 216 CS112
Hayes UB3 135 BT73
Hawthorne Rd, E17 123 EA55
Bromley BR1 204 EL97
Radlett WD7 61 CG34
Staines-upon-Thames TW18 173 BC92
Hawthornes, Hat. AL10 45 CT20
Hawthorne Way, N9 100 DS47
Guildford GU4 243 BB130
Stanwell TW19 174 BK87
Hawthorn Gdns, W5 157 CK76
Hawthorn Gro, SE20 182 DV94
Barnet EN5 79 CT44
Enfield EN2 82 DR38
Hawthorn Hatch, Brent. TW8 157 CH80
Hawthorn La, Farn.Com. SL2 131 AP65
Sevenoaks TN13 256 FF122
Hawthorn Ms, NW7 off Holders Hill Rd 97 CY53
Hawthorn Pl, Erith DA8 167 FC78
Guildford GU4 off Merrow St 243 BD132
Penn HP10 88 AC47
Hawthorn Rd, N8 121 DK55
N18 100 DT51
NW10 139 CU66
Bexleyheath DA6 166 EZ84
Brentford TW8 157 CH80
Buckhurst Hill IG9 102 EK49
Dartford DA1 188 FK88
Feltham TW13 175 BU88
Hoddesdon EN11 49 EB15
Ripley GU23 228 BG124
Sutton SM1 218 DE107
Wallington SM6 219 DH108
Woking GU22 226 AX120
Hawthorns, Harl. CM18 51 ET19
Welwyn Garden City AL8 29 CX07
Woodford Green IG8 102 EG48
Hawthorns, The, Berk. HP4 38 AU18
Chalfont St. Giles HP8 72 AW40
Colnbrook SL3 153 BF81
Epsom KT17 off Kingston Rd 217 CT107
Hemel Hempstead HP3 39 BF24
Loughton IG10 85 EN42
Maple Cross WD3 91 BD50
Oxted RH8 254 EG133
Ridge EN6 62 CS33
Sch Hawthorns Sch, The, Bletch. RH1 off Pendell Rd 251 DP131
Hawthorn Wk, W10 282 E4
Hawthorn Way, Chesh. HP5 54 AR29
New Haw KT15 212 BJ110
Redhill RH1 267 DH136
St. Albans AL2 42 CA24
Shepperton TW17 195 BR98
Hawtrees, Rad. WD7 77 CF35
Hawtrey Av, Nthlt. UB5 136 BX68
Hawtrey Cl, Slou. SL1 152 AV75
Hawtrey Dr, Ruis. HA4 115 BU59
Hawtrey Rd, NW3 274 C7
Windsor SL4 151 AQ82
Haxted Rd, Brom. BR1 off North Rd 204 EH95
Hayburn Mead, Hem.H. HP1 40 BH21
Hayburn Way, Horn. RM12 127 FF60
Hay Cl, E15 281 K6
Borehamwood WD6 78 CQ40
Haycroft Cl, Couls. CR5 off Caterham Dr 235 DP118
Haycroft Gdns, NW10 139 CU67
Haycroft Rd, SW2 181 DL85
Surbiton KT6 198 CL104
Hay Currie St, E14 290 D8
Hayday Rd, E16 291 N6
Hayden Ct, Felt. TW13 175 BS91
New Haw KT15 212 BH111
Hayden Rd, Wal.Abb. EN9 83 EC35
Haydens Cl, Orp. BR5 206 EV100
Haydens Pl, W11 282 G8
Haydens Rd, Harl. CM20 51 EQ15
Hayden Way, Rom. RM5 105 FC54
Haydn Av, Pur. CR8 219 DN114
Haydns Ms, W3 138 CQ72
Haydock Av, Nthlt. UB5 136 CA65
Haydock Cl, Horn. RM12 128 FM63
Haydock Grn, Nthlt. UB5 off Haydock Av 136 CA65
Haydon Cl, NW9 118 CQ56
Enfield EN1 off Mortimer Dr 82 DS44
Romford RM3 105 FH52
Haydon Dell, Bushey WD23 76 BZ44
Haydon Dr, Pnr. HA5 115 BU56
Haydon Pk Rd, SW19 180 DB92
Haydon Pl, Guil. GU1 258 AX135
Haydon Rd, Dag. RM8 126 EW61
Watford WD19 76 BY44
Sch Haydon Sch, Eastcote HA5 off Wiltshire La 115 BT55
⇌ Haydons Road 180 DC92
Haydons Rd, SW19 180 DB92
Haydon St, EC3 288 A10
Haydon Wk, E1 288 B9
Haydon Way, SW11 160 DD84
HAYES, UB3 & UB4 135 BS72
Brom. BR2 204 EG103
⇌ Hayes 204 EF102
Hayes, The, Epsom KT18 232 CR119
⇌ Hayes & Harlington 155 BT76
Hayes Barton, Wok. GU22 227 BD116
🛍 Hayes Br Retail Pk, Hayes UB4 136 BW73
Hayes Bypass, Hayes UB3, UB4 136 BX70
Hayes Chase, W.Wick. BR4 204 EE99
Hayes Cl, Brom. BR2 204 EG103
Grays RM20 169 FW79
Hayes Ct, SW2 181 DL88
Hayes Cres, NW11 119 CZ57
Sutton SM3 217 CX105
Hayes Dr, Rain. RM13 147 FH66
HAYES END, Hayes UB3 135 BQ71
Hayes End Cl, Hayes UB4 135 BR70
Hayes End Dr, Hayes UB4 135 BR70
Hayesend Ho, SW17 off Blackshaw Rd 180 DC91
Hayes End Rd, Hayes UB4 135 BR70
Hayesford Pk Dr, Brom. BR2 204 EF99
Hayes Gdn, Brom. BR2 204 EG103
Hayes Gro, SE22 162 DT84
Hayes Hill, Brom. BR2 204 EE102
Hayes Hill Rd, Brom. BR2 204 EF102
Hayes La, Beck. BR3 203 EC97
Bromley BR2 204 EG99
Kenley CR8 220 DQ114
Hayes Mead Rd, Brom. BR2 204 EE102
● Hayes Metro Cen, Hayes UB4 136 BW73
Hayes Pk, Hayes UB4 135 BS70
Sch Hayes Pk Sch, Hayes UB4 off Raynton Dr 135 BT70
Hayes Pl, NW1 284 D5
Sch Hayes Prim Sch, Hayes BR2 off George La 204 EH102
Sch Hayes Prim Sch, The, Ken. CR8 off Hayes La 235 DP116
Hayes Rd, Brom. BR2 204 EG98
Greenhithe DA9 189 FS87
Southall UB2 155 BV77
Sch Hayes Sch, Hayes BR2 off West Common Rd 204 EH103
Hayes St, Brom. BR2 204 EH102
HAYES TOWN, Hayes UB3 155 BS75
Hayes Wk, Brox. EN10 off Landau Way 67 DZ25
Potters Bar EN6 64 DB33
Smallfield RH6 269 DN147
Hayes Way, Beck. BR3 203 EC98
Hayes Wd Av, Brom. BR2 204 EH102
Hayfield Cl, Bushey WD23 76 CB42
Hayfield Pas, E1 289 H5
Hayfield Rd, Orp. BR5 206 EU99
Hayfields, Horl. RH6 off Ryelands 269 DJ147
Hayfield Yd, E1 289 H5
Haygarth Pl, SW19 179 CX92
Hay Grn, Horn. RM11 128 FN58
Haygreen Cl, Kings.T. KT2 178 CP93
Hay Hill, W1 297 K1
Hayland Cl, NW9 118 CR56
Hay La, NW9 118 CR56
Fulmer SL3 112 AX63
Sch Hay La Sch, NW9 off Grove Pk 118 CQ56
Haylard St, Dag. RM9 146 EY69
Hayles St, SE11 298 G8
Haylett Gdns, Kings.T. KT1 off Anglesea Rd 197 CK98
Hayley Cl, Chaff.Hun. RM16 169 FW76
Hayling Av, Felt. TW13 175 BU90
Hayling Cl, N16 277 P2
Slough SL1 131 AP74
Hayling Rd, Wat. WD19 93 BV47
Haymaker Cl, Uxb. UB10 134 BM66
Hayman Cres, Hayes UB4 135 BR68
Hayman St, N1 277 H7
Haymarket, SW1 297 N1
Haymarket Arc, SW1 297 N1
Haymeads, Welw.G.C. AL8 29 CY06
Haymeads Dr, Esher KT10 214 CC107
Haymer Gdns, Wor.Pk. KT4 199 CU104
Haymerle Rd, SE15 312 C3
Sch Haymerle Sch, SE15 312 C3
Hay Ms, NW3 274 F5
Haymill Cl, Perivale UB6 137 CF69
Haymill Rd, Slou. SL1, SL2 131 AK70
Hayne Rd, Beck. BR3 203 DZ96
Haynes Cl, N11 98 DG48
N17 100 DV52
SE3 164 EE83
Ripley GU23 228 BH122
Slough SL3 153 AZ78
Welwyn Garden City AL7 30 DA10
Haynes Dr, N9 100 DV48
Haynes La, SE19 182 DS93
Haynes Mead, Berk. HP4 38 AU17
Haynes Pk Ct, Horn. RM11 128 FJ57
Haynes Rd, Horn. RM11 128 FK57
Northfleet DA11 191 GF90
Wembley HA0 138 CL66
Hayne St, EC1 287 H6
Haynt Wk, SW20 199 CY97
Hayre Dr, Sthl. UB2 156 BX78
Hayse Hill, Wind. SL4 151 AK81
🛍 Hay's Galleria, SE1 299 N2
Hay's La, SE1 299 N3
Haysleigh Gdns, SE20 202 DU96
Hay's Ms, W1 297 J1
Haysoms Cl, Rom. RM1 127 FE56
Haystall Cl, Hayes UB4 135 BS68
Hay St, E2 278 D9
Hays Wk, Sutt. SM2 217 CX110
Hayter Ct, E11 124 EH61
Hayter Rd, SW2 181 DL85
Hayton Cl, E8 278 B5
Haywain, Oxt. RH8 253 ED130
Hayward Cl, SW19 200 DB95
Dartford DA1 187 FD85
Hayward Copse, Loud. WD3 74 BK42
Hayward Dr, Dart. DA1 188 FM89
★ Hayward Gall, SE1 298 D2
Hayward Gdns, SW15 179 CW86
Hayward Rd, N20 98 DC47
Thames Ditton KT7 197 CG102
Haywards Cl, Chad.Hth RM6 126 EV57
Hutton CM13 109 GE44
Haywards Mead, Eton Wick SL4 151 AM78
Hayward's Pl, EC1 286 G5
Haywood Cl, Pnr. HA5 94 BX54
Haywood Ct, Wal.Abb. EN9 68 EF34
Haywood Dr, Chorl. WD3 73 BF43
Hemel Hempstead HP3 39 BF23
Haywood Pk, Chorl. WD3 73 BF43
Haywood Ri, Orp. BR6 223 ES105
Haywood Rd, Brom. BR2 204 EK98
Hazel Av, Guil. GU1 242 AW130
West Drayton UB7 154 BN76
Hazelbank, Crox.Grn WD3 75 BQ44
Surbiton KT5 198 CQ102
Hazelbank Ct, Cher. KT16 194 BJ102
Hazelbank Rd, SE6 183 ED89
Chertsey KT16 194 BJ102
Hazelbourne Rd, SW12 181 DH86
Hazelbrouck Gdns, Ilf. IG6 103 ER52
Hazelbury Av, Abb.L. WD5 59 BQ32
Hazelbury Cl, SW19 200 DA96
Hazelbury Grn, N9 100 DS48
Sch Hazelbury Inf Sch, N9 off Haselbury Rd 100 DS48
Sch Hazelbury Jun Sch, N9 off Haselbury Rd 100 DS48
Hazelbury La, N9 100 DS48
Hazel Cl, N13 100 DR48
N19 121 DJ61
NW9 96 CS54
SE15 312 D9
Brentford TW8 157 CH80
Croydon CR0 203 DX101
Englefield Green TW20 172 AV93
Epsom KT19 216 CR110
Hornchurch RM12 127 FH62
Mitcham CR4 201 DK98
Reigate RH2 266 DC136
Twickenham TW2 176 CC87
Waltham Cross EN7 66 DS26
Hazel Ct, Shenley WD7 62 CM33
Hazelcroft, Pnr. HA5 94 CA51
Hazelcroft Cl, Uxb. UB10 134 BM66
Hazeldean Rd, NW10 138 CR66
Hazeldell Link, Hem.H. HP1 39 BF21
Hazeldell Rd, Hem.H. HP1 39 BE21
Hazeldene, Add. KT15 212 BJ106
Waltham Cross EN8 67 DY32
Hazeldene Ct, Ken. CR8 236 DR115
Hazeldene Dr, Pnr. HA5 116 BW55
Hazeldene Gdns, Uxb. UB10 135 BQ67
Hazeldene Rd, Ilf. IG3 126 EV61
Welling DA16 166 EW82
Hazeldon Rd, SE4 183 DY85
Hazel Dr, Erith DA8 167 FH81
Ripley GU23 243 BF125
South Ockendon RM15 149 FW69
Hazeleigh, Brwd. CM13 109 GB48
Hazeleigh Gdns, Wdf.Grn. IG8 102 EL50
Hazel End, Swan. BR8 207 FE99
Hazel Gdns, Edg. HA8 96 CP49
Grays RM16 170 GE76
Sawbridgeworth CM21 36 EZ06
Hazelgreen Cl, N21 99 DP46

H

Hazel Gro, SE26 183 DX91
Enfield EN1 off Dimsdale Dr 82 DU44
Feltham TW13 175 BU88
Hatfield AL10 45 CT21
Orpington BR6 205 EP103
Romford RM6 126 EY55
Staines-upon-Thames TW18 174 BH93
Watford WD25
off Cedar Wd Dr 75 BV35
Welwyn Garden City AL7 30 DB08
Wembley HA0 off Carlyon Rd 138 CL67
Hazel Gro Est, SE26 183 DX91
Hazel Ho, NW3
off Maitland Pk Rd 274 F4
Hazelhurst, Beck. BR3 203 ED95
Horley RH6 269 DJ147
Hazelhurst Cl, Guil. GU4
off Weybrook Dr 243 BB129
Hazelhurst Rd, SW17 180 DC91
Burnham SL1 130 AJ68
Hazel La, Ilf. IG6 103 EP52
Richmond TW10 178 CL89
Hazell Cres, Rom. RM5 105 FB53
Hazell Pk, Amer. HP7 55 AR39
Hazells Rd, Grav. DA13 190 GD92
Hazellville Rd, N19 121 DK59
Hazell Way, Stoke P. SL2 132 AT65
Hazel Mead, Barn. EN5 79 CV43
Epsom KT17 217 CU110
Hazelmere Cl, Felt. TW14 175 BR86
Leatherhead KT22 231 CH119
Northolt UB5 136 BZ68
Hazelmere Dr, Nthlt. UB5 136 BZ68
Hazelmere Gdns, Horn. RM11 127 FH57
Hazelmere Rd, NW6 273 H8
Northolt UB5 136 BZ68
Petts Wood BR5 205 EQ98
St. Albans AL4 43 CJ17
Hazelmere Wk, Nthlt. UB5 136 BZ68
Hazelmere Way, Brom. BR2 204 EG100
Hazel Ms, N8 121 DN55
Hazel Ri, Horn. RM11 128 FJ58
Hazel Rd, E15 281 J2
NW10 282 A2
Berkhamsted HP4 38 AX20
Dartford DA1 188 FK89
Erith DA8 167 FG81
Park Street AL2 60 CB28
Reigate RH2 266 DC136
West Byfleet KT14 212 BG114
Hazels, The, Welw. AL6 30 DE05
Hazeltree La, Nthlt. UB5 136 BY69
Hazel Tree Rd, Wat. WD24 75 BV37
Hazel Wk, Brom. BR2 205 EN100
North Holmwood RH5
off Lake Vw 263 CJ139
Hazel Way, E4 101 DZ51
SE1 300 A8
Chipstead CR5 234 DF119
Fetcham KT22 230 CC122
Hazelway Cl, Fetch. KT22 230 CC123
HAZELWOOD, Sev. TN14 223 ER111
Hazelwood, Dor. RH4 263 CH137
Loughton IG10 84 EK43
Hazelwood Av, Mord. SM4 200 DB98
Hazelwood Cl, W5 158 CL75
Chesham HP5 54 AR29
Harrow HA2 116 CB56
Hazelwood Ct, NW10
off Neasden La N 118 CS62
Hazelwood Cres, N13 99 DN49
Hazelwood Cft, Surb. KT6 198 CL100
Hazelwood Dr, Pnr. HA5 93 BV54
St. Albans AL4 43 CJ19
Hazelwood Gdns,
Pilg.Hat. CM15 108 FU44
Hazelwood Gro, S.Croy. CR2 220 DV113
Hazelwood Hts, Oxt. RH8 254 EG131
Sch Hazelwood Inf Sch, N13
off Hazelwood La 99 DN49
Sch Hazelwood Jun Sch, N13
off Hazelwood La 99 DN49
Hazelwood La, N13 99 DN49
Abbots Langley WD5 59 BQ32
Chipstead CR5 234 DF119
Hazelwood Pk Cl, Chig. IG7 103 ES50
Hazelwood Rd, E17 123 DY57
Croxley Green WD3 75 BQ44
Cudham TN14 223 ER112
Enfield EN1 82 DT44
Knaphill GU21 226 AS118
Oxted RH8 254 EH132
Sch Hazelwood Sch, Lmpfld RH8
off Wolfs Hill 254 EG131
Hazlebury Rd, SW6 307 L8
Hazledean Rd, Croy. CR0 202 DR103
Hazledene Rd, W4 158 CQ79
Hazlemere Gdns, Wor.Pk. KT4 199 CV102
Hazlemere Rd, Penn HP10 88 AC45
Slough SL2 132 AW74
Hazlewell Rd, SW15 179 CV85
Hazlewood Cl, E5 123 DY62
Hazlewood Cres, W10 282 F5
Hazlewood Ms, SW9 310 A10
Hazlewood Twr, W10 282 F5
Hazlitt Cl, Felt. TW13 176 BY91
Hazlitt Ms, W14 294 E7
Hazlitt Rd, W14 294 E7
Hazon Way, Epsom KT19 216 CQ112
Heacham Av, Uxb. UB10 115 BQ62
Headcorn Pl, Th.Hth. CR7
off Headcorn Rd 201 DM98
Headcorn Rd, N17 100 DT52
Bromley BR1 184 EF92
Thornton Heath CR7 201 DM98
Headfort Pl, SW1 297 H5
Headingley Cl, Chsht EN7 66 DT26
Ilford IG6 103 ET51
Shenley WD7 62 CL32
Headingley Dr, Beck. BR3 183 EA93
Headington Pl, Slou. SL2 132 AT74
Headington Rd, SW18 180 DC88
Headlam Rd, SW4 181 DK86
Headlam St, E1 288 F5
Headlands Dr, Berk. HP4 38 AX18
HEADLEY, Epsom KT18 248 CQ125
Headley App, Ilf. IG2 125 EN57
Headley Av, Wall. SM6 219 DM106
Headley Chase, Warley CM14 108 FW49
Headley Cl, Epsom KT19 216 CN107
Headley Common, Gt Warley
CM13 off Warley Gap 107 FV52
Headley Common Rd,
Headley KT18 248 CR127
Tadworth KT20 248 CR127
Headley Ct, SE26 182 DV92
Headley Dr, Epsom KT18 233 CV119
Ilford IG2 125 EP58
New Addington CR0 221 EB108
Headley Gro, Tad. KT20 233 CV120
★ Headley Heath,
Epsom KT18 248 CP128
Headley Heath App,
Box H. KT20 248 CP130
Mickleham RH5 248 CP130
Headley La, Mick. RH5 247 CJ129
Headley Rd, Lthd. KT22 231 CK123
Tyrrell's Wood KT18 232 CN123
Woodcote KT18 232 CP118
Head's Ms, W11 283 J9
HEADSTONE, Har. HA2 116 CC56
Headstone Dr, Har. HA1, HA3 117 CE55
Headstone Gdns, Har. HA2 116 CC56
Headstone Lane 94 CB53
Headstone La, Har. HA2, HA3 116 CB56
Headstone Rd, Har. HA1 117 CE57
Head St, E1 289 J9
Headway, The, Epsom KT17 217 CT109
Headway Cl, Rich. TW10
off Locksmeade Rd 177 CJ91
Headway Gdns, E17 101 EA53
Heald St, SE14 314 A6
Healey Rd, Wat. WD18 75 BT44
Healey St, NW1 275 J5
Healy Dr, Orp. BR6 223 ET105
Heanor Ct, E5
off Pedro St 123 DX63
Heards La, Shenf. CM15 109 FZ41
Hearle Way, Hat. AL10 44 CS16
Hearne Ct, Ch.St.G. HP8
off Gordon Way 90 AV48
Hearne Rd, W4 158 CN79
Hearnes Cl, Seer Grn HP9 89 AR50
Hearnes Meadow,
Seer Grn HP9 89 AR50
Hearn Ri, Nthlt. UB5 136 BX67
Hearn Rd, Rom. RM1 127 FF58
Hearn's Bldgs, SE17 299 M9
Hearnshaw St, E14 289 M7
Hearn's Rd, Orp. BR5 206 EW98
Hearn St, EC2 287 P5
Hearnville Rd, SW12 180 DG88
Heart, The, Walt. KT12
off New Zealand Av 195 BU102
H Heart Hosp, The, W1 285 H7
Sch Heartlands High Sch, N22 99 DL54
Heath, The, W7
off Lower Boston Rd 137 CE74
Chaldon CR3 236 DQ124
Hatfield Heath CM22 37 FG05
Radlett WD7 61 CG33
Heathacre, Colnbr. SL3
off Park St 153 BE81
Heatham Pk, Twick. TW2 177 CF87
Heath Av, Bexh. DA7 166 EX79
St. Albans AL3 43 CD18
Heathbourne Rd,
Bushey Hth WD23 95 CE47
Stanmore HA7 95 CE47
Heathbridge, Wey. KT13 212 BN108
Sch Heathbrook Prim Sch, SW8 309 L9
Heath Brow, NW3
off North End Way 120 DC62
Hemel Hempstead HP1 40 BJ22
● Heath Business Cen, The,
Salf. RH1 266 DG143
Heath Cl, NW11 120 DB59
W5 138 CM70
Banstead SM7 218 DB114
Harlington UB3 155 BR80
Hemel Hempstead HP1 40 BJ21
Orpington BR5 off Sussex Rd 206 EW100
Potters Bar EN6 64 DB30
Romford RM2 127 FG55
South Croydon CR2 219 DP107
Stanwell TW19 174 BJ86
Virginia Water GU25 192 AX98
Heathclose, Swan. BR8
off Moreton Cl 207 FE96
Heathclose Av, Dart. DA1 187 FH87
Heathclose Rd, Dart. DA1 187 FG88
Heathcock Ct, WC2
off Exchange Ct 298 B1
Heathcote, Tad. KT20 233 CX121
Heathcote Av, Hat. AL10 45 CU16
Ilford IG5 103 EM54
Heathcote Ct, Ilf. IG5
off Heathcote Av 103 EM54
Heathcote Gdns, Harl. CM17 52 EY15
Heathcote Gro, E4 101 EC48
Heathcote Pt, E9 279 J5
Heathcote Rd, Epsom KT18 216 CR114
Twickenham TW1 177 CH86
Sch Heathcote Sch, E4
off Normanton Pk 102 EE47
Heathcote St, WC1 286 C4
Heathcote Way, West Dr. UB7 134 BK74
Heath Cotts, Pot.B. EN6
off Heath Rd 64 DB30
Heath Ct, SE9 185 EQ88
Hertford SG14 31 DM08
Hounslow TW4 156 BZ84
Uxbridge UB8 134 BL66
Heathcroft, NW11 120 DB60
W5 138 CM70
Welwyn Garden City AL7 30 DC09
Heathcroft Av, Sun. TW16 175 BT94
Heathcroft Gdns, E17 101 ED53
Heathdale Av, Houns. TW4 156 BY83
Heathdene, Tad. KT20
off Brighton Rd 233 CY119
Heathdene Dr, Belv. DA17 167 FB77
Heathdene Manor, Wat. WD17
off Grandfield Ave 75 BT39
Heathdene Rd, SW16 181 DM94
Wallington SM6 219 DH108
Heathdown Rd, Wok. GU22 227 BD115
Heath Dr, NW3 273 L1
SW20 199 CW98
Potters Bar EN6 64 DA30
Romford RM2 105 FG53
Send GU23 227 BB123
Sutton SM2 218 DC109
Theydon Bois CM16 85 ES35
Walton on the Hill KT20 249 CU125
Heathedge, SE26 182 DV89
Heath End Rd, Bex. DA5 187 FE88
Heather Av, Rom. RM1 105 FD54
Heatherbank, SE9 165 EM82
Chislehurst BR7 205 EN96
Heatherbank Cl, Cob. KT11 214 BX111
Dartford DA1 187 FE86
Heather Cl, E6 293 N9
N7 121 DM62
SE13 183 ED86
SW8 309 J10
Abbots Langley WD5 59 BU32
Guildford GU2 242 AV132
Heather Cl, Hampton TW12 196 BZ95
Isleworth TW7
off Harvesters Cl 177 CD85
Kingswood KT20 233 CY122
New Haw KT15 212 BH110
Pilgrim's Hatch CM15 108 FV43
Redhill RH1 251 DH130
Romford RM1 105 FD53
Uxbridge UB8 134 BM71
Woking GU21 226 AW115
Heatherdale Cl, Kings.T. KT2 178 CN93
Heatherdene, W.Hors. KT24 245 BR125
Heatherdene Cl, N12 98 DC53
Mitcham CR4 200 DE98
Heatherden Grn, Iver SL0 133 BC67
Heather Dr, Dart. DA1 187 FG87
Enfield EN2 81 DP40
Romford RM1 105 FD54
Heather End, Swan. BR8 207 FD98
Heatherfield La, Wey. KT13 213 BS106
Heatherfields, New Haw KT15 212 BH110
Heatherfold Way, Pnr. HA5 115 BT55
Heather Gdns, NW11 119 CY58
Romford RM1 105 FD54
Sutton SM2 218 DA107
Waltham Abbey EN9 83 EC36
Heather Glen, Rom. RM1 105 FD54
Heatherlands, Horl. RH6
off Stockfield 269 DH147
Sunbury-on-Thames TW16 175 BU93
Heather La, Wat. WD24 75 BT35
West Drayton UB7 134 BL72
Heatherlea Gro, Wor.Pk. KT4 199 CV102
Heatherley Dr, Ilf. IG5 124 EL55
Coll Heatherley's Sch of Fine Art,
SW10 307 P5
Heathermount, Guil. GU3
off Broad St 242 AS132
Heather Pk Dr, Wem. HA0 138 CN66
Heather Pl, Esher KT10
off Park Rd 214 CB105
Heather Ri, Bushey WD23 76 BZ40
Heather Rd, E4 101 DZ51
NW2 119 CT61
SE12 184 EG89
Welwyn Garden City AL8 29 CW11
Heathers, The, Stai. TW19 174 BM87
Heatherset Cl, Esher KT10 214 CC106
Heatherset Gdns, SW16 181 DM94
Heatherside Cl, Bkhm KT23 246 BZ125
Heatherside Dr, Vir.W. GU25 192 AU100
Heatherside Gdns,
Farn.Com. SL2 111 AR62
Heatherside Rd, Epsom KT19 216 CR108
Sidcup DA14 off Wren Rd 186 EW90
Heathersland, Dor. RH4
off Goodwyns Rd 263 CJ139
Sch Heatherton Ho Sch,
Amer. HP6 off Copperkins La 55 AQ36
Heatherton Pk, Amer. HP6 55 AP36
Heatherton Ter, N3 98 DB54
Heathervale Caravan Pk,
New Haw KT15 212 BJ110
Heathervale Rd, New Haw KT15 212 BH110
Heathervale Way,
New Haw KT15 212 BJ110
Heather Wk, W10 282 F4
Edgware HA8 96 CP50
Twickenham TW2
off Hedley Rd 176 CA87
Whiteley Village KT12
off Octagon Rd 213 BT110
Heather Way, Chobham GU24 210 AS108
Hemel Hempstead HP2 40 BK19
Potters Bar EN6 63 CZ32
Romford RM1 105 FD54
South Croydon CR2 221 DX109
Stanmore HA7 95 CF51
Heatherwood Cl, E12 124 EJ61
Heatherwood Dr, Hayes UB4 135 BR68
Heath Fm Ct, Wat. WD17 75 BR37
Heath Fm La, St.Alb. AL3 43 CE18
Heathfield, E4 101 EC48
Chislehurst BR7 185 EQ93
Cobham KT11 214 CA114
Heathfield Av, SW18
off Heathfield Rd 180 DD87
South Croydon CR2 221 DY109
Heathfield Cl, E16 292 E6
Keston BR2 222 EJ106
Potters Bar EN6 64 DB30
Watford WD19 94 BW45
Woking GU22 227 BA118
Heathfield Ct, SE14 313 H4
St. Albans AL1 off Avenue Rd 43 CE19
Heathfield Dr, Mitch. CR4 200 DE95
Redhill RH1 266 DE139
Heathfield Gdns, NW11 119 CX58
SE3 315 J9
SW18 180 DD86
W4 158 CQ78
Croydon CR0 off Coombe Rd 220 DQ105
Heathfield La, Chis. BR7 185 EP93
Heathfield N, Twick. TW2 177 CF87
Sch Heathfield Nurs & Inf & Jun Schs,
Twick. TW2 off Cobbett Rd 176 CA88
Heathfield Pk, NW2 272 A5
Heathfield Pk Dr,
Chad.Hth RM6 126 EV57
Heathfield Ri, Ruis. HA4 115 BQ59
Heathfield Rd, SW18 180 DC86
W3 158 CP75
Bexleyheath DA6 166 EZ84
Bromley BR1 184 EF94
Burnham SL1 110 AG62
Bushey WD23 76 BY42
Croydon CR0 220 DR105
Hersham KT12 214 BY105
Keston BR2 222 EJ106
Sevenoaks TN13 256 FF122
Woking GU22 227 BA118
Sch Heathfield Sch, Pnr. HA5
off Beaulieu Dr 116 BX59
Heathfields Cl, Ashtd. KT21 231 CJ118
Heathfields Ct, Houns. TW4
off Heathlands Way 176 BY85
Heathfield S, Twick. TW2 177 CF87
Heathfield Sq, SW18 180 DD87
Heathfield St, W11 294 E1
Heathfield Ter, SE18 165 ET79
W4 158 CQ78
Heathfield Vale, S.Croy. CR2 221 DX109
Heath Gdns, Twick. TW1 177 CF88
Heathgate, NW11 120 DB58
Hertford Heath SG13 32 DV13
Heathgate Pl, NW3
off Agincourt Rd 274 F2
Heath Gro, SE20 off Maple Rd 182 DW94
Sunbury-on-Thames TW16 175 BT94
Heath Hill, Dor. RH4 263 CH136
Heath Hurst Rd, NW3 274 C1
Heathhurst Rd, S.Croy. CR2 220 DS109
Heathland Rd, N16 122 DS60
Heathlands, Tad. KT20 233 CX122
Sch Heathland Sch, The, Houns. TW4
off Wellington Rd S 176 BZ86
Sch Heathland Sch, S.Har. HA2
off Eastcote La 116 CA62
Heathlands Cl, Sun. TW16 195 BT96
Twickenham TW1 177 CF89
Woking GU21 210 AY114
Heathlands Dr, St.Alb. AL3 43 CE18
Heathlands Ri, Dart. DA1 187 FH86
Sch Heathlands Sch, St.Alb. AL3
off Heathlands Dr 43 CE17
Heathlands Way,
Houns. TW4 176 BY85
Heath La, SE3 315 H9
Albury GU5 260 BL141
Dartford (Lower) DA1 188 FJ88
Dartford (Upper) DA1 187 FG89
Hemel Hempstead HP1 40 BJ22
Hertford Heath SG13 32 DW13
Heathlee Rd, SE3 164 EF84
Dartford DA1 187 FE86
Heathley End, Chis. BR7 185 EQ93
Heathmans Rd, SW6 307 H7
Heath Mead, SW19 179 CX90
Sch Heathmere Prim Sch, SW15
off Alton Rd 179 CU88
Heath Ms, Ripley GU23 228 BH123
Heath Pk Ct, Rom. RM2
off Heath Pk Rd 127 FG57
Heath Pk Dr, Brom. BR1 204 EL97
Heath Pk Rd, Rom. RM2 127 FG57
Heath Pas, NW3 120 DB61
Heath Ridge Grn, Cob. KT11 214 CA113
Heath Ri, SW15 179 CX86
Bromley BR2 204 EF100
Ripley GU23 228 BH123
Virginia Water GU25 192 AX98
Westcott RH4 262 CC138
Heath Rd, SW8 309 K9
Beaconsfield HP9 110 AG55
Bexley DA5 187 FC88
Caterham CR3 236 DR123
Dartford DA1 187 FF86
Grays RM16 171 GG75
Harrow HA1 116 CC59
Hounslow TW3 156 CB84
Oxshott KT22 214 CC112
Potters Bar EN6 64 DA30
Romford RM6 126 EX59
St. Albans AL1 43 CE19
Thornton Heath CR7 202 DQ97
Twickenham TW1, TW2 177 CF88
Uxbridge UB10 135 BQ70
Watford WD19 94 BX45
Weybridge KT13 212 BN106
Woking GU21 227 AZ115
Heathrow, Goms. GU5 261 BQ139
★ Heathrow Airport (London),
Houns. TW6 155 BP81
⇌ Heathrow Airport
Terminal 4 175 BP85
⊖ Heathrow Airport
Terminal 4 175 BP85
⇌ Heathrow Airport
Terminal 5 154 BJ83
⊖ Heathrow Airport
Terminal 5 154 BJ83
⇌ Heathrow Airport
Terminals 2-3 155 BP83
⊖ Heathrow Airport
Terminals 2-3 155 BP83
● Heathrow Causeway Centre,
Houns. TW4 155 BV83
Heathrow Cl, West Dr. UB7 154 BH81
● Heathrow Int Trd Est,
Houns. TW4 155 BV83
Sch Heathrow Prim Sch, Sipson
UB7 off Harmondsworth La 154 BM79
Heathrow Tunnel App,
Lon.Hthrw Air. TW6 155 BP83
Heathrow Vehicle Tunnel,
Lon.Hthrw Air. TW6 155 BP81
Heaths Cl, Enf. EN1 82 DS40
Heath Side, NW3 120 DD63
Petts Wood BR5 205 EQ102
Heathside, NW11 120 DA60
Colney Heath AL4 44 CP23
Esher KT10 197 CE104
Hounslow TW4 176 BZ87
Saint Albans AL1 43 CE18
Weybridge KT13 213 BP106
Heathside Av, Bexh. DA7 166 EY81
Heathside Cl, Esher KT10 197 CE104
Ilford IG2 125 ER57
Northwood HA6 93 BR50
Heathside Ct, Tad. KT20 233 CV123
Heathside Cres, Wok. GU22 227 AZ117
Heathside Gdns, Wok. GU22 227 BA117
Heathside Pk Rd, Wok. GU22 227 AZ118
Heathside Pl, Epsom KT18 233 CX118
Sch Heathside Prep Sch,
Lwr Sch, NW3 off Heath St 120 DC63
Upr Sch, NW3 off New End 120 DD63
Heathside Rd, Nthwd. HA6 93 BR49
Woking GU22 227 AZ118
Sch Heathside Sch, Wey. KT13
off Brooklands La 212 BM106
Heathstan Rd, W12 139 CU72
Heath St, NW3 120 DC62
Dartford DA1 188 FK87
Heath Vw, N2 120 DC56
East Horsley KT24 245 BT125
Heathview Av, Dart. DA1 187 FE86
Heath Vw Cl, N2 120 DC56
Heathview Ct, SW19 179 CX89
Heathview Cres, Dart. DA1 187 FG88
Heathview Dr, SE2 166 EX79
Heathview Gdns, SW15 179 CW87
Grays RM16 170 GC75
Heathview Rd, Grays RM16 170 GC75
Thornton Heath CR7 201 DN98
Heath Vil, SE18 165 ET78
SW18 off Cargill Rd 180 DC88
Heathville Rd, N19 121 DL59
Heathwall St, SW11 308 F10
Heathway, SE3 315 N5
Chaldon CR3 252 DQ125
Croydon CR0 203 DZ104
Dagenham RM9, RM10 146 FA66
East Horsley KT24 229 BT124
Iver SL0 133 BD68
Southall UB2 156 BW77
Woodford Green IG8 102 EJ49
Heath Way, Erith DA8 167 FC81
● Heathway Ind Est, Dag. RM10
off Manchester Way 127 FB63
Heathwood Gdns, SE7 304 G9
Swanley BR8 207 FC96
Heathwood Pt, SE23
off Dacres Rd 183 DX90
Heathwood Wk, Bex. DA5 187 FE88
Heaton Av, Rom. RM3 105 FH52
Heaton Cl, E4 101 EC48
Romford RM3 106 FJ52
Heaton Ct, Chsht EN8 67 DX29
Heaton Gra Rd, Rom. RM2 105 FF54
Heaton Rd, SE15 312 D10
Mitcham CR4 180 DG94
Heaton Way, Rom. RM3 106 FJ52
Heavens Lea, B.End SL8 110 AC61
Heaven Tree Cl, N1 277 K3
Heaver Rd, SW11 308 B10
Sch Heavers Fm Prim Sch, SE25
off Dinsdale Gdns 202 DT99
Heavitree Cl, SE18 165 ER78
Heavitree Rd, SE18 165 ER78
Heayfield, Welw.G.C. AL7 30 DC08
Hebden Ct, E2 278 A9
Hebden Ter, N17 100 DS51
Hebdon Rd, SW17 180 DE90
Sch Heber Prim Sch, SE22
off Heber Rd 182 DT86
Heber Rd, NW2 272 C2
SE22 182 DT86
Hebron Rd, W6 159 CV76
Hecham Cl, E17 101 DY54
Heckets Ct, Esher KT10 214 CC111
Heckfield Pl, SW6 307 J5
Heckford Cl, Wat. WD18 75 BQ44
Heckford St, E1 289 K10
Hector Cl, N9 100 DU47
Hector St, SE18 165 ES77
Heddington Gro, N7 276 C2
Heddon Cl, Islw. TW7 157 CG84
Heddon Ct Av, Barn. EN4 80 DF43
Heddon Ct Par, Barn. EN4
off Cockfosters Rd 80 DG43
Heddon Rd, Cockfos. EN4 80 DF43
Heddon St, W1 285 L10
Hedgebrooms, Welw.G.C. AL7 30 DC08
Hedge Hill, Enf. EN2 81 DP39
Hedge La, N13 99 DP48
Hedge Lea, Woob.Grn HP10 110 AD55
Hedgeley, Ilf. IG4 125 EM56
Hedgemans Rd, Dag. RM9 146 EX66
Hedgemans Way, Dag. RM9 146 EY65
Hedge Pl Rd, Green. DA9 189 FT86
HEDGERLEY, Slou. SL2 111 AR62
Hedgerley Ct, Wok. GU21 226 AW117
Hedgerley Gdns, Grnf. UB6 136 CC68
Hedgerley Grn, Hedg. SL2 112 AT58
Hedgerley Hill, Hedg. SL2 111 AR62
Hedgerley La, Beac. HP9 111 AN56
Gerrards Cross SL9 112 AV59
Hedgerley SL2 112 AS58
Hedgerow, Chal.St.P. SL9 90 AY51
Hedge Row, Hem.H. HP1 40 BG18
Hedgerow La, Arkley EN5 79 CV43
Hedgerows, Hutt. CM13 109 GE44
Sawbridgeworth CM21 36 EZ05
Hedgerows, The, Nthflt DA11 190 GE89
Hedgerow Wk, Chsht EN8 67 DX30
Hedgers Cl, Loug. IG10
off Newmans La 85 EN42
Hedgers Gro, E9 279 L5
Hedger St, SE11 298 G8
Hedges, The, St.Alb. AL3 42 CC16
Hedges Cl, Hat. AL10 45 CV17
Hedgeside, Pott.End HP4 39 BA16
Hedgeside Rd, Nthwd. HA6 93 BQ50
Hedges Way, Crox.Grn WD3 74 BM44
Hedge Wk, SE6 183 EB92
Hedgeway, Guil. GU2 258 AU136
Hedgewood Gdns, Ilf. IG5 125 EN56
Sch Hedgewood Sch, Hayes UB4
off Weymouth Rd 135 BS69
Hedgley St, SE12 184 EF85
Hedingham Cl, N1 277 J7
Horley RH6 269 DJ147
Hedingham Ho, Kings.T. KT2
off Kingsgate Rd 198 CL95
Hedingham Rd,
Chaff.Hun. RM16 169 FW78
Dagenham RM8 126 EV64
Hornchurch RM11 128 FN60
Hedley Av, Grays RM20 169 FW80
Hedley Cl, Rom. RM1
off High St 127 FE57
Hedley Ho, E14
off Stewart St 302 F6
Hedley Rd, St.Alb. AL1 43 CH20
Twickenham TW2 176 CA87
Hedley Row, N5 277 M2
Hedley Vw, Loud. HP10 88 AD54
Hedsor Hill, B.End SL8 110 AC62
Hedsor La, Burn. SL1 110 AG61
Wooburn Green HP10 110 AG61
Hedsor Pk, Tap. SL6 110 AD63
Hedsor Wf, B.End SL8 110 AC62
Hedworth Av, Wal.Cr. EN8 67 DX33
Heenan Cl, Bark. IG11
off Glenny Rd 145 EQ65
Heene Rd, Enf. EN2 82 DR39
Heideck Gdns, Hutt. CM13
off Victors Cres 109 GB47
Heidegger Cres, SW13
off Wyatt Dr 159 CV80
Heigham Rd, E6 144 EK66
Heighams, Harl. CM19 51 EM18
Heighton Gdns, Croy. CR0 219 DP106
Heights, The, SE7 164 EJ78
Beckenham BR3 183 EC94
Hemel Hempstead HP2
off Saturn Way 40 BM18
Loughton IG10 85 EM40
Nazeing EN9 68 EH25
Northolt UB5 116 BZ64
Weybridge KT13 212 BN110
Heights Cl, SW20 179 CV94
Banstead SM7 233 CY116
Heiron St, SE17 311 H3
Helby Rd, SW4 181 DK86
Helder Gro, SE12 184 EF87
Helder St, S.Croy. CR2 220 DR107
Heldmann Cl, Houns. TW3 157 CD84
Helegan Cl, Orp. BR6 223 ET105
Helena Cl, Barn. EN4 80 DD38
Helena Ho, Red. RH1 266 DG137

H

Helena Pl, E9 278 F9
Helena Rd, E13 291 M1
E17 123 EA57
NW10 119 CV64
W5 137 CK71
Windsor SL4 151 AR82
Helena Sq, SE16 301 L1
Helen Av, Felt. TW14 175 BV87
Helen Cl, N2 120 DC55
Dartford DA1 187 FH87
West Molesey KT8 196 CB98
Helen Rd, Horn. RM11 128 FK55
Helens Gate, Chsht EN8 67 DZ26
Helenslea Av, NW11 119 CZ60
Helen's Pl, E2 288 G2
Helen St, SE18 305 P8
Helford Cl, Ruis. HA4 115 BS61
Helford Wk, Wok. GU21 226 AU118
Helford Way, Upmin. RM14 129 FR58
Helgiford Gdns, Sun. TW16 175 BS94
Heligan Ho, SE16
off Canada St 301 J5
Helions Rd, Harl. CM19 51 EP15
Helios Rd, Wall. SM6 200 DG102
● **Heliport Ind Est**, SW11
off Bridges Ct 307 P9
Helix Gdns, SW2 181 DM86
Helix Rd, SW2 181 DM86
Helleborine, Bad.Dene RM17 170 FZ78
Hellen Way, Wat. WD19 94 BW49
Hellings St, E1 300 D3
Hellyer Way, B.End SL8 110 AC60
Helm, The, E16
off Albert Basin Way 305 P1
Helm Cl, Epsom KT19 216 CN112
Helme Cl, SW19 179 CZ92
Helmet Row, EC1 287 K4
Helmore Rd, Bark. IG11 145 ET66
Helmsdale, Wok. GU21
off Winnington Way 226 AV118
Helmsdale Cl, Hayes UB4 136 BY70
Romford RM1 105 FE52
Helmsdale Rd, SW16 201 DJ95
Romford RM1 105 FE52
Helmsley Pl, E8 278 E7
Helperby Rd, NW10 138 CS66
Helsinki Sq, SE16 301 M6
Helston Cl, Pnr. HA5 94 BZ52
Helston Gro, Hem.H. HP2 40 BK16
Helston La, Wind. SL4 151 AN81
Helston Pl, Abb.L. WD5
off Shirley Rd 59 BT32
Helvellyn Cl, Egh. TW20 173 BB94
Helvetia St, SE6 183 DZ89
Hemans Est, SW8 309 P5
Hemans St, SW8 309 P4
Hemberton Rd, SW9 310 A10
HEMEL HEMPSTEAD,
HP1 - HP3 40 BK21
⇌ **Hemel Hempstead** 40 BG23
Hemel Hempstead 40 BJ20
H **Hemel Hempstead Gen Hosp**,
Hem.H. HP2 40 BK21
● **Hemel Hempstead Ind Est**,
Hem.H. HP2 41 BP17
Hemel Hempstead Rd,
Hem.H. HP3 41 BR22
Redbourn AL3 41 BQ15
St. Albans AL3 42 CA21
Sch **Hemel Hempstead Sch, The**,
Hem.H. HP1 *off Heath La* 40 BJ21
Hemery Rd, Grnf. UB6 117 CD64
Hemingford Cl, N12 98 DD50
Hemingford Rd, N1 276 D9
Sutton SM3 217 CW105
Watford WD17 75 BS36
Heming Rd, Edg. HA8 96 CP52
Hemington Av, N11 98 DF50
Hemingway Cl, NW5 275 H1
Hemlock Cl, SW16 201 DK96
Kgswd KT20 233 CY123
Hemlock Rd, W12 139 CT73
Hemmen La, Hayes UB3 135 BT72
Hemming Cl, Hmptn. TW12 196 CA95
Hemmings, The, Berk. HP4 38 AT20
Hemmings Cl, Sid. DA14 186 EV89
Hemmings Mead,
Epsom KT19 238 CP107
Hemming St, E1 288 D5
Hemming Way, Slou. SL2 131 AP69
Watford WD25 75 BU35
Hemnall Ms, Epp. CM16
off Hemnall St 70 EU30
Hemnall St, Epp. CM16 69 ET31
Hempshaw Av, Bans. SM7 234 DF116
Hempson Av, Slou. SL3 152 AW76
Hempstall, Welw.G.C. AL7 30 DB11
Hempstead Cl, Buck.H. IG9 102 EJ47
Hempstead La, Pott.End HP4 39 BC17
Hempstead Rd, E17 101 ED54
Bovingdon HP3 57 BA27
Kings Langley WD4 58 BM26
Watford WD17 75 BT39
Hemp Wk, SE17 299 M8
Hemsby Rd, Chess. KT9 216 CM107
Hemsley Rd, Kings L. WD4 59 BP29
Hemstal Rd, NW6 273 J6
Hemsted Rd, Erith DA8 167 FE80
Hemswell Dr, NW9 96 CS53
Hemsworth Ct, N1 277 N9
Hemsworth St, N1 277 N10
Hemus Pl, SW3 308 D1
Hemwood Rd, Wind. SL4 151 AK83
Henage La, Wok. GU22 227 BC120
Hen & Chicken Ct, EC4 286 E9
Henbane Path, Rom. RM3
off Clematis Cl 106 FK52
Henbit Cl, Tad. KT20 233 CV119
Henbury Way, Wat. WD19 94 BX48
Henchley Dene, Guil. GU4 243 BD131
Henchman St, W12 139 CT72
Hencroft St N, Slou. SL1 152 AT75
Hencroft St S, Slou. SL1 152 AT76
Hendale Av, NW4 119 CU55
Henderson Av, Guil. GU2 242 AV130
Henderson Cl, NW10 138 CQ65
Hornchurch RM11 127 FH61
St. Albans AL3 42 CC16
Henderson Dr, NW8 284 A4
Dartford DA1 168 FM84
Henderson Gro, Bigg.H. TN16 222 EJ112
Henderson Pl,
Bedmond WD5 59 BT27
Epping Green SG13 47 DJ21
Henderson Rd, E7 144 EJ65
N9 100 DV46
SW18 180 DE87
Croydon CR0 202 DR100
Hayes UB4 135 BU69
Hendham Rd, SW17 180 DE89
HENDON, NW4 119 CV56
⇌ **Hendon** 119 CU58
Hendon Av, N3 97 CY53
⊖ **Hendon Central** 119 CW57
Hendon Gdns, Rom. RM5 105 FC51
Hendon Gro, Epsom KT19 216 CN109
Hendon Hall Ct, NW4
off Parson St 119 CX55
Hendon La, N3 119 CY55
Hendon Pk Row, NW11 119 CZ58
Sch **Hendon Prep Sch**, NW4
off Tenterden Gro 119 CX55
Hendon Rd, N9 100 DU47
Sch **Hendon Sch**, NW4
off Golders Ri 119 CX57
Hendon Way, NW2 119 CZ62
NW4 119 CV58
Stanwell TW19 174 BK86
Hendon Wd La, NW7 97 CT45
Hendren Cl, Grnf. UB6 117 CD64
Hendre Rd, SE1 299 P9
Hendrick Av, SW12 180 DF86
Heneage Cres,
New Adgtn CR0 221 EC110
Heneage La, EC3 287 P9
Heneage St, E1 288 B6
Henfield Cl, N19 121 DJ60
Bexley DA5 186 FA86
Henfield Rd, SW19 199 CZ95
Henfold La, Dor. RH5 264 CL144
Hengelo Gdns, Mitch. CR4 200 DD98
Hengest Ave, Esher KT10 197 CG104
Hengist Rd, SE12 184 EH87
Erith DA8 167 FB80
Hengist Way, Brom. BR2 204 EE98
Wallington SM6 219 DK108
Hengrave Rd, SE23 183 DX87
Hengrove Ct, Bex. DA5 186 EY88
Hengrove Cres, Ashf. TW15 174 BK90
Henhurst Rd, Cobham DA12 191 GK94
Henley Av, Sutt. SM3 199 CY104
Henley Bk, Guil. GU2 258 AU136
Henley Cl, SE16
off St. Marychurch St 300 G4
Greenford UB6 136 CC68
Isleworth TW7 157 CF81
Henley Ct, N14 99 DJ45
Woking GU22 227 BA120
Henley Cross, SE3 164 EH83
Henley Deane, Nthflt DA11 190 GE91
Henley Dr, SE1 300 B8
Kingston upon Thames KT2 179 CT94
Henley Gdns, Pnr. HA5 115 BV55
Romford RM6 126 EY57
Henley Prior, N1 *off Collier St* 286 C1
Henley Rd, E16 305 K4
N18 100 DS49
NW10 272 B8
Ilford IG1 125 EQ63
Slough SL1 131 AL72
Henley St, SW11 309 H8
Henley Way, Felt. TW13 176 BX92
Henlow Pl, Rich. TW10 177 CK89
Henlys Cor, N3 119 CZ56
Henlys Rbt, Houns. TW5 156 BW81
Henman Way, Brwd. CM14 108 FV46
Henmarsh Ct, Hert. SG13 32 DS10
Henneker Cl, Rom. RM5 105 FC51
Hennel Cl, SE23 182 DW90
Hennessy Ct, Wok. GU21 211 BC113
Hennessy Rd, N9 100 DW47
Henniker Gdns, E6 292 F2
Henniker Ms, SW3 308 A2
Henniker Pt, E15 281 J3
Henniker Rd, E15 280 G3
Henningham Rd, N17 100 DR53
Henning St, SW11 308 C7
Sch **Henrietta Barnett Sch, The**,
NW11 *off Central Sq* 120 DB57
Henrietta Barnett Wk, NW11 120 DA58
Henrietta Cl, SE8 314 B2
Henrietta Gdns, N21 99 DP46
Henrietta Ms, WC1 286 B4
Henrietta Pl, W1 285 J9
Henrietta St, E15 280 F2
WC2 286 B10
Henriques St, E1 288 D8
Henry Addlington Cl, E6 293 N7
Sch **Henry Cavendish Prim Sch Balham**,
SW12 *off Hydethorpe Rd* 181 DJ88
Streatham SW16 181 DK89
Henry Cl, Enf. EN2 82 DS38
Sch **Henry Compton Sch**, SW6 306 E6
Henry Cooper Way, SE9 184 EK90
Henry Darlot Dr, NW7 97 CX50
Henry DeGrey Cl, Grays RM17 170 FZ77
Henry Dent Cl, SE5 162 DR83
Henry Dickens Ct, W11 294 D2
Henry Doulton Dr, SW17 181 DH91
Sch **Henry Fawcett Prim Sch**,
SE11 310 E2
Sch **Henry Grn Prim Sch**,
Dag. RM8 *off Green La* 126 EX61
Henry Jackson Rd, SW15 159 CX83
Henry Macaulay Av,
Kings.T. KT2 197 CK95
Sch **Henry Maynard Infants' Sch**,
E17 *off Maynard Rd* 123 EC57
Sch **Henry Maynard Jun Sch**,
E17 *off Addison Rd* 123 EC57
Sch **Henry Moore Prim Sch**,
Harl. CM17 *off Kiln La* 52 EX17
Henry Peters Dr, Tedd. TW11
off Somerset Gdns 177 CE92
Henry Rd, E6 144 EL68
N4 122 DQ60
Barnet EN4 80 DD43
Slough SL1 151 AR75
Henry's Av, Wdf.Grn. IG8 102 EF50
Henryson Rd, SE4 183 EA85
Henry St, Brom. BR1 204 EH95
Grays RM17
off East Thurrock Rd 170 GC79
Hemel Hempstead HP3 40 BK24
Henry's Wk, Ilf. IG6 103 ER52
Henry Tate Ms, SW16 181 DN92
Henry Wells Sq, Hem.H. HP2
off Aycliffe Dr 40 BL16
Henry Wise Ho, SW1
off Vauxhall Br Rd 297 M9
Hensby Ms, Wat. WD19 76 BY44
Hensford Gdns, SE26
off Wells Pk Rd 182 DV91
Henshall Pt, E3 290 C2
Henshall St, N1 277 M5
Henshawe Rd, Dag. RM8 126 EX62
Henshaw St, SE17 299 L8
Hensley Pt, E9 279 K5
Henslowe Rd, SE22 182 DU85
Henslow Way, Wok. GU21 211 BD114
Henson Av, NW2 272 A2
Henson Cl, Orp. BR6 205 EP103
Henson Path, Har. HA3 117 CK55
Henson Pl, Nthlt. UB5 136 BW67
Henstridge Pl, NW8 274 C10
Hensworth Rd, Ashf. TW15 174 BK92
Henty Cl, SW11 308 D5
Henty Wk, SW15 179 CV85
Henville Rd, Brom. BR1 204 EH95
Sch **Henwick Prim Sch**, SE9
off Henwick Rd 164 EK83
Henwick Rd, SE9 164 EK83
Henwood Side, Wdf.Grn. IG8
off Love La 103 EM51
Hepburn Cl, Chaff.Hun. RM16 169 FX77
Hepburn Ct, S.Mimms EN6 63 CU32
Hepburn Gdns, Brom. BR2 204 EE102
Hepburn Ms, SW11
off Webbs Rd 180 DF85
Hepple Cl, Islw. TW7 157 CH82
Hepplestone Cl, SW15 179 CV86
Hepscott Rd, E9 280 A5
Hepworth Ct, SW1 309 H1
Barking IG11 126 EU64
Hepworth Gdns, Bark. IG11 126 EU64
Hepworth Rd, SW16 181 DL94
Hepworth Wk, NW3 274 D3
Hepworth Way, Walt. KT12 195 BT102
Heracles Cl, Park St AL2 60 CC28
Herald Gdns, Wall. SM6 201 DH104
Herald's Pl, SE11 298 G8
Herald St, E2 288 F4
Herald Wk, Dart. DA1
off Temple Hill Sq 188 FM85
Herbal Hill, EC1 286 F5
Herbert Cres, SW1 296 F6
Knaphill GU21 226 AS118
Herbert Gdns, NW10 139 CV68
W4 158 CP79
Romford RM6 126 EX59
St. Albans AL2 60 CB29
Herbert Ms, SW2
off Bascombe St 181 DN86
Herbert Morrison Ho, SW6 306 G3
Sch **Herbert Morrison Prim Sch**,
SW8 310 A5
Herbert Pl, SE18
off Plumstead Common Rd 165 EP79
Isleworth TW7 157 CD81
Herbert Rd, E12 124 EL63
E17 123 DZ59
N11 99 DL52
N15 122 DT57
NW9 119 CU58
SE18 165 EN80
SW19 179 CZ94
Bexleyheath DA7 166 EY82
Bromley BR2 204 EK99
Hornchurch RM11 128 FL59
Ilford IG3 125 ES61
Kingston upon Thames KT1 198 CM97
Southall UB1 136 BZ74
Swanley BR8 187 FH93
Swanscombe DA10 190 FZ86
Herbert St, E13 291 P1
NW5 274 G4
Hemel Hempstead HP2
off St. Mary's Rd 40 BK19
Herbert Ter, SE18 165 EP80
Herbrand St, WC1 286 A4
Hercies Rd, Uxb. UB10 134 BM66
Hercules Pl, N7 121 DL62
Hercules Rd, SE1 298 D7
Hercules St, N7 121 DL62
Hercules Way, Lvsdn WD25 59 BT34
Hereford Av, Barn. EN4 98 DF46
Hereford Cl, Epsom KT18 216 CR113
Guildford GU2 242 AT132
Staines-upon-Thames TW18 194 BH95
Hereford Copse, Wok. GU22 226 AV119
Hereford Ct, Sutt. SM2
off Worcester Rd 218 DA108
Hereford Gdns, SE13
off Longhurst Rd 184 EE85
Ilford IG1 124 EL59
Pinner HA5 116 BY57
Twickenham TW2 176 CC88
Hereford Ho, NW6 283 K1
Hereford Ms, W2 283 K9
Hereford Pl, SE14 313 N4
Hereford Retreat, SE15 312 C3
Hereford Rd, E3 289 P1
E11 124 EH57
W2 283 K8
W3 138 CP73
W5 157 CJ76
Feltham TW13 176 BW88
Hereford Sq, SW7 295 P9
Hereford St, E2 288 C4
Hereford Way, Chess. KT9 215 CJ106
Herent Dr, Ilf. IG5 124 EL56
Hereward Av, Pur. CR8 219 DN111
Hereward Cl, Wal.Abb. EN9 67 ED32
Hereward Gdns, N13 99 DN50
Hereward Grn, Loug. IG10 85 EQ39
Sch **Hereward Ho Sch**, NW3 274 C6
Sch **Hereward Prim Sch**,
Loug. IG10 *off Colebrook La* 85 EQ39
Hereward Rd, SW17 180 DF91
Herga Ct, Har. HA1 117 CE62
Watford WD17 75 BU40
Herga Rd, Har. HA3 117 CF56
Herington Gro, Hutt. CM13 109 GA45
Sch **Herington Ho Sch**,
Hutt. CM13 *off Mount Av* 109 GB44
Heriot Av, E4 101 EA47
Heriot Rd, NW4 119 CW57
Chertsey KT16 194 BG101
Heriots Cl, Stan. HA7 95 CG49
Heritage Av, NW9 97 CT54
Heritage Cl, SW9 161 DP83
Sunbury-on-Thames TW16 195 BU95
Uxbridge UB8 134 BJ70
Heritage Hill, Kes. BR2 222 EJ106
Heritage Ho, N14
off Chase Side 99 DK46
Sch **Heritage Ho Sch**, Chesh. HP5
off Cameron Rd 54 AR30
Heritage Lawn, Horl. RH6 269 DJ147
Heritage Pl, SW18
off Earlsfield Rd 180 DC88
Heritage Vw, Har. HA1 117 CF62
Heritage Wk, Chorl. WD3
off Chenies Rd 73 BE41
Herkomer Cl, Bushey WD23 76 CB44
Herkomer Rd, Bushey WD23 76 CA43
Herlwyn Av, Ruis. HA4 115 BS62
Herlwyn Gdns, SW17 180 DF91
Herm Cl, Islw. TW7 156 CC80
Hermes Cl, W9 283 J5
Hermes St, N1 286 E1
Hermes Wk, Nthlt. UB5
off Hotspur Rd 136 CA68
Herm Ho, Enf. EN3
off Eastfield Rd 83 DX38
Hermiston Av, N8 121 DL57
Hermitage, The, SE13 314 F8
SE23 182 DW88
SW13 159 CT81
Feltham TW13 175 BT90
Richmond TW10 177 CK85
Uxbridge UB8 134 BL65
Hermitage Cl, E18 124 EF56
SE2 *off Felixstowe Rd* 166 EW76
Claygate KT10 215 CG107
Enfield EN2 81 DP40
Shepperton TW17 194 BN98
Slough SL3 152 AW76
Hermitage Ct, E18 124 EG56
NW2 *off Hermitage La* 120 DA62
Potters Bar EN6
off Southgate Rd 64 DC33
Hermitage Gdns, NW2 120 DA62
SE19 182 DQ93
Hermitage La, N18 100 DR50
NW2 120 DA62
SE25 202 DU100
SW16 181 DM94
Croydon CR0 202 DU100
Windsor SL4 151 AN83
Hermitage Path, SW16 201 DL95
Sch **Hermitage Prim Sch**, E1 300 D3
Uxbridge UB8
off Belmont Rd 134 BK66
Hermitage Rd, N4 121 DP59
N15 121 DP59
SE19 182 DQ94
Kenley CR8 236 DQ116
Woking GU21 226 AT119
Hermitage Row, E8 278 D3
Sch **Hermitage Sch, The**, St.John's
GU21 *off Oakwood Rd* 226 AS119
Hermitage St, W2 284 A7
Hermitage Wk, E18 124 EF56
Hermitage Wall, E1 300 D3
Hermitage Waterside, E1 300 C2
Hermitage Way, Stan. HA7 95 CG53
Hermitage Wds Cres,
Wok. GU21 226 AS119
Hermit Pl, NW6 273 L9
Hermit Rd, E16 291 L6
Hermit St, EC1 286 G2
Hermon Gro, Hayes UB3 135 BU74
Hermon Hill, E11 124 EG57
E18 124 EG57
Herndon Cl, Egh. TW20 173 BA91
Herndon Rd, SW18 180 DC85
Herne Cl, NW10
off North Circular Rd 118 CR64
Hayes UB3 135 BT72
Herne Ct, Bushey WD23
off Richfield Rd 94 CC45
HERNE HILL, SE24 182 DQ85
⇌ **Herne Hill** 181 DP86
Herne Hill, SE24 182 DQ86
Herne Hill Ho, SE24
off Railton Rd 181 DP86
Herne Hill Rd, SE24 311 H10
Sch **Herne Hill Sch**, SE24
off Herne Hill Rd 182 DQ85
Herne Ms, N18 100 DU49
Herne Pl, SE24 181 DP85
Herne Rd, Bushey WD23 76 CB44
Surbiton KT6 197 CK103
Hernes Cl, Stai. TW18
off Staines Rd 194 BH95
Herneshaw, Hat. AL10 45 CT20
Herns La, Welw.G.C. AL7 30 DB08
Herns Way, Welw.G.C. AL7 30 DA07
Herold Ct, Rain. RM13 147 FG67
Heron Cl, E17 101 DZ54
NW10 138 CS65
Buckhurst Hill IG9 102 EG46
Guildford GU2 242 AV131
Hemel Hempstead HP3 58 BM25
Rickmansworth WD3 92 BK47
Sawbridgeworth CM21 36 EX06
Sutton SM1
off Sandpiper Rd 217 CZ106
Uxbridge UB8 134 BK65
Heron Ct, E5
off Big Hill 122 DV60
Bromley BR2 204 EJ98
Heron Cres, Sid. DA14 185 ES90
Heron Dale, Add. KT15 212 BK106
Herondale, S.Croy. CR2 221 DX109
Herondale Av, SW18 180 DD88
Heron Dr, N4 122 DQ61
Slough SL3 153 BB77
Stanstead Abbotts SG12 33 EC12
Heronfield, Eng.Grn TW20 172 AV93
Potters Bar EN6 64 DC30
Heron Flight Av, Horn. RM12 147 FG66
Herongate Rd, E12 124 EJ61
Cheshunt EN8 67 DY27
Swanley BR8 187 FE93
Heron Hill, Belv. DA17 166 EZ77
Heron Ho, W13
off Gurnell Gro 137 CF70
Heron Mead, Enf. EN3 83 EA38
Heron Ms, Ilf. IG1
off Balfour Rd 125 EP61
Heron Pl, SE16 301 M2
Harefield UB9 92 BG51
Heron Quay, E14 302 A3
DLR **Heron Quays** 302 B3
Heron Rd, SE24 162 DQ84
Croydon CR0 *off Tunstall Rd* 202 DS103
Twickenham TW1 157 CG84
Heronry, The, Hersham KT12 213 BU107
Herons, The, E11 124 EF58
Herons Cft, Wey. KT13 213 BQ107
Herons Elm, Nthch HP4 38 AS16
Heronsforde, W13 137 CJ72
HERONSGATE, Rick. WD3 91 BD45
Heronsgate, Edg. HA8 96 CN50
Sch **Heronsgate Prim Sch**, SE28
off Whinchat Rd 165 ER76
Heronsgate Rd, Chorl. WD3 73 BB44
Heronslea, Wat. WD25 76 BW36
Heronslea Dr, Stan. HA7 96 CL50
Heron's Pl, Islw. TW7 157 CH83
Heron Sq, Rich. TW9
off Bridge St 177 CK85
Herons Ri, New Barn. EN4 80 DE42
Herons Way, St.Alb. AL1 43 CH23
Herons Wd, Harl. CM20 35 EP13
Heronswood, Wal.Abb. EN9 68 EE34
Heronswood Ct, Horl. RH6
off Tanyard Way 269 DH147
Heronswood Pl, Welw.G.C. AL7 29 CZ10
Heronswood Rd, Welw.G.C. AL7 52 DA09
● **Heron Trd Est**, W3
off Alliance Rd 138 CP70
Heron Wk, Nthwd. HA6 93 BS49
Woking GU21
off Blackmore Cres 211 BC114
Heron Way, Felt. TW14 155 BU84
Grays RM20 169 FV78
Hatfield AL10 45 CU19
Upminster RM14 129 FS60
Wallington SM6 219 DK108
Heronway, Hutt. CM13 109 GA46
Woodford Green IG8 102 EJ49
Herrick Rd, N5 122 DQ62
Herrick St, SW1 297 P8
Herries St, W10 282 F1
Sch **Herringham Prim Sch**,
Chad.St.M. RM16
off St. Mary's Rd 171 GH77
Herringham Rd, SE7 304 D7
Herrings La, Cher. KT16 194 BG100
Herrongate Cl, Enf. EN1 82 DT40
H **Her Royal Highness Princess
Christian's Hosp**, Wind. SL4 151 AQ81
Hersant Cl, NW10 139 CU67
Sch **Herschel Gram Sch**, Slou. SL1
off Northampton Av 131 AQ73
Herschell Ms, SE5
off Bicknell Rd 162 DQ83
Herschell Rd, SE23 183 DX87
Herschel Pk Dr, Slou. SL1 152 AT75
Herschel St, Slou. SL1 152 AT75
HERSHAM, Walt. KT12 214 BX107
⇌ **Hersham** 196 BY104
Hersham Bypass, Walt. KT12 213 BV106
Hersham Cen, The, Walt. KT12 214 BX106
Hersham Cl, SW15 179 CU87
Hersham Gdns,
Hersham KT12 214 BW105
Hersham Rd, Walt. KT12 214 BW105
HERTFORD, SG13 & SG14 31 DP10
Hertford Av, SW14 178 CR85
Hertford Cl, Barn. EN4 80 DD41
Croxley Green WD3 75 BP42
H **Hertford Co Hosp**,
Hert. SG14 31 DP09
Hertford Ct, N13
off Green Las 99 DN48
⇌ **Hertford East** 32 DS09
HERTFORD HEATH, Hert. SG13 32 DV12
Sch **Hertford Heath Prim Sch**,
Hert.Hth SG13
off Woodland Rd 32 DW12
Hertford Ho, Nthlt. UB5
off Taywood Rd 136 BZ70
★ **Hertford Mus**, Hert. SG14 32 DR09
⇌ **Hertford North** 31 DP09
● **Hertford Pl**, Rick. WD3 91 BF48
Coll **Hertford Regional Coll**,
Broxbourne Cen, Turnf. EN10
off High Rd 67 DZ25
Ware Cen, Ware SG12
off Scotts Rd 33 DX07
Hertford Rd, N1 277 P8
N2 120 DE55
N9 100 DV47
Barking IG11 145 EP66
Barnet EN4 80 DC41
Enfield EN3 82 DW41
Great Amwell SG12 33 DZ11
Hatfield AL9 45 CW16
Hertford SG14 30 DB06
Hertford Heath SG13 32 DW13
Hoddesdon EN11 49 DY15
Ilford IG2 125 ES58
Marden Hill SG14 30 DG06
Tewin AL6 30 DE05
Waltham Cross EN8 83 DX37
Ware SG12 32 DW07
Welwyn AL6 30 DB06
Sch **Hertford St. Andrew's C of E
Prim Sch**, Hert. SG14
off Calton Av 31 DM08
Hertfordshire Co Hall,
Hert. SG13 32 DQ10
Hertford Sq, Mitch. CR4
off Hertford Way 201 DL98
Hertford St, W1 297 J2
Hertford Wk, Belv. DA17
off Hoddesdon Rd 166 FA78
Hertford Way, Mitch. CR4 201 DL98
HERTINGFORDBURY,
Hert. SG14 31 DL10
Sch **Hertingfordbury Cowper Prim
Sch**, Hert. SG14 *off Birch Grn* 31 DJ11
Hertingfordbury Rd, Hert. SG14 31 DL11
Hertslet Rd, N7 121 DM62
● **Hertsmere Ind Pk**,
Borwd. WD6 78 CR41
Sch **Hertsmere Jewish Prim Sch**,
Rad. WD7 *off Watling St* 77 CJ38
Hertsmere Rd, E14 302 A1
Hertswood Ct, Barn. EN5
off Hillside Gdns 79 CY42
Sch **Hertswood Sch**,
Lwr Sch, Borwd. WD6
off Cowley Hill 78 CQ39
Upr Sch, Borwd. WD6
off Thrift Fm La 78 CQ40
Hervey Cl, N3 98 DA53
Hervey Pk Rd, E17 123 DY56
Hervey Rd, SE3 164 EH81
Hervines Ct, Amer. HP6 55 AQ37
Hervines Rd, Amer. HP6 55 AP37
Hesa Rd, Hayes UB3 135 BU72
Hesewall Cl, SW4 309 M9
Hesiers Hill, Warl. CR6 238 EE117
Hesiers Rd, Warl. CR6 238 EE117
Hesketh Av, Dart. DA2 188 FP88
Hesketh Pl, W11 294 E1
Hesketh Rd, E7 124 EG62
Heslop Rd, SW12 180 DF88
Hesper Ms, SW5 295 L10
Hesperus Cres, E14 302 C9
Hessel Rd, W13 157 CG75
Hessel St, E1 288 E9
Hesselyn Dr, Rain. RM13 147 FH66
Hessle Gro, Epsom KT17 217 CT111
Hestercombe Av, SW6 306 F8

Hester Ct, Dag. RM10
off St. Mark's Pl 146 FA65
Hesterman Way, Croy. CR0 201 DL102
Hester Rd, N18 100 DU50
SW11 308 C5
Hester Ter, Rich. TW9
off Chilton Rd 158 CN83
Hestia Ho, SE1
off Royal Oak Yd 299 N5
HESTON, Houns. TW5 156 BZ80
Heston Av, Houns. TW5 156 BY80
● Heston Centre, The, Houns.
TW5 off International Ave 156 BW78
Sch Heston Comm Sch,
Heston TW5 off Heston Rd 156 CA80
Heston Gra, Houns. TW5 156 BZ79
Heston Gra La, Houns. TW5 156 BZ79
● Heston Ind Mall,
Houns. TW5 156 BZ80
Sch Heston Inf & Nurs Sch,
Heston TW5 off Heston Rd 156 CA80
Sch Heston Jun Sch, Heston TW5
off Heston Rd 156 CA80
Heston Rd, Houns. TW5 156 CA80
Redhill RH1 266 DF138
Heston St, SE14 314 A6
Heston Wk, Red. RH1 266 DF138
Heswell Grn, Wat. WD19
off Fairhaven Cres 93 BU48
Hetchleys, Hem.H. HP1 40 BG17
Hetherington Cl, Slou. SL2 131 AM69
Hetherington Rd, SW4 161 DL84
Shepperton TW17 195 BQ96
Hetherington Way, Uxb. UB10 114 BL63
Hethersett Cl, Reig. RH2 250 DC131
Hetley Gdns, SE19 182 DT94
Hetley Rd, W12 139 CV74
Heton Gdns, NW4 119 CU56
Heusden Way, Ger.Cr. SL9 113 AZ60
Hevelius Cl, SE10 303 L10
Hever Ct Rd, Grav. DA12 191 GH93
Hever Cft, SE9 185 EN91
Hever Gdns, Brom. BR1 205 EN96
Heverham Rd, SE18 165 ES77
Hevers Av, Horl. RH6 268 DF147
Hevers Cor, Horl. RH6
off Horley Row 268 DF147
Heversham Rd, Bexh. DA7 166 FA82
Hevingham Dr, Chad.Hth RM6 126 EW57
Hewens Coll, Hayes End UB4
off Hewens Rd 135 BQ70
Hewens Rd, Uxb. UB10 135 BQ70
Hewer St, W10 282 D6
Hewers Way, Tad. KT20 233 CV120
Hewett Cl, Stan. HA7 95 CH49
Hewett Pl, Swan. BR8 207 FD98
Hewett Rd, Dag. RM8 126 EX64
Hewetts Quay, Bark. IG11 145 EP67
Hewett St, EC2 287 P5
Hewins Cl, Wal.Abb. EN9
off Broomstick Hall Rd 68 EE32
Hewish Rd, N18 100 DS49
Hewison St, E3 279 P10
Hewitt Av, N22 99 DP54
Hewitt Cl, Croy. CR0 203 EA104
Hewitt Rd, N8 121 DN57
Hewitts Rd, Orp. BR6 224 EZ108
Hewlett Rd, E3 279 M10
Hexagon, The, N6 120 DF60
● Hexagon Business Cen,
Hayes UB4 136 BW73
Hexal Rd, SE6 184 EE90
Hexham Gdns, Islw. TW7 157 CG80
Northolt UB5 116 BZ64
Hexham Rd, SE27 182 DQ89
Barnet EN5 80 DB42
Morden SM4 200 DB102
HEXTABLE, Swan. BR8 187 FG94
Sch Hextable Inf Sch, Hext. BR8
off St. Davids Rd 187 FF93
Sch Hextable Jun Sch, Hext. BR8
off Rowhill Rd 187 FF93
Sch Hextable Sch, Hext. BR8
off Egerton Av 207 FF95
Hextalls La, Bletch. RH1 252 DR128
Hexton Ct, N4
off Brownswood Rd 122 DQ61
Heybourne Cres, NW9 96 CS53
Heybourne Rd, N17 100 DV52
Heybridge Av, SW16 181 DL94
Heybridge Ct, Hert. SG14
off The Ridgeway 31 DM08
Heybridge Dr, Ilf. IG6 103 ER54
Heybridge Way, E10 123 DY59
Heydons Cl, St.Alb. AL3 43 CD18
Heyford Av, SW8 310 B4
SW20 199 CZ97
Heyford Rd, Mitch. CR4 200 DE96
Radlett WD7 77 CF37
Heyford Ter, SW8
off Heyford Av 310 B4
Heyford Way, Hat. AL10 45 CW16
Heygate St, SE17 299 J9
Heylyn Sq, E3 289 P2
Heymede, Lthd. KT22 231 CJ123
Heynes Rd, Dag. RM8 126 EW63
Heysham Dr, Wat. WD19 94 BW50
Heysham La, NW3 120 DB62
Heysham Rd, N15 122 DR58
Heythorp Cl, Wok. GU21 226 AT117
Heythorp St, SW18 179 CZ88
Uni Heythrop Coll, W8 295 L6
Heythrop Dr, Ickhm UB10 114 BM63
Heywood Av, NW9 96 CS53
Heyworth Rd, E5 122 DV63
E15 281 L2
Hibbert Av, Wat. WD24 76 BX38
Hibbert Lo, Chal.St.P. SL9
off Gold Hill E 90 AX54
Hibbert Rd, E17 123 DZ59
Harrow HA3 95 CF54
Hibberts All, Wind. SL4
off Bachelors Acre 151 AR81
Hibbert St, SW11 160 DC83
Hibberts Way, Ger.Cr. SL9 112 AY55
Hibbs Cl, Swan. BR8 207 FD96
Hibernia Dr, Grav. DA12 191 GM90
Hibernia Gdns, Houns. TW3 156 CA84
Hibernia Pt, SE2
off Wolvercote Rd 166 EX75
Hibernia Rd, Houns. TW3 156 CA84
Hibiscus Cl, Edg. HA8
off Campion Way 96 CQ49
Hibiscus Ho, Felt. TW13
off High St 175 BV88
Hichisson Rd, SE15 182 DW85
Hicken Rd, SW2 181 DM85
Hickeys Almshouses, Rich. TW9
off St. Mary's Gro 158 CM84
Hickin Cl, SE7 304 E9
Hickin St, E14 302 E6
Hickling Rd, Ilf. IG1 125 EP64
Hickman Av, E4 101 EC51
Hickman Cl, E16 292 E7
Broxbourne EN10 49 DX20
Hickman Rd, Rom. RM6 126 EW59
Hickmans Cl, Gdse. RH9 252 DW132
Hickmore Wk, SW4 309 M10
Hickory Cl, N9 100 DU45
Hicks Av, Grnf. UB6 137 CD68
Hicks Cl, SW11 308 C10
Hicks St, SE8 301 L10
Hidalgo Ct, Hem.H. HP2 40 BM18
Hidcote Cl, Wok. GU22 227 BB116
Hidcote Gdns, SW20 199 CV97
Hide, E6 293 M8
Hideaway, The, Abb.L. WD5 59 BU31
Hide Pl, SW1 297 N9
Hide Rd, Har. HA1 117 CD56
Hides, The, Harl. CM20 35 ER14
Hides St, N7 276 D4
Hide Twr, SW1 297 N9
Higgins Rd, Chsht EN7 66 DR27
Higgins Wk, Hmptn. TW12
off Abbott Cl 176 BY93
High, The, Harl. CM20 51 ER15
Highacre, Dor. RH4 263 CH139
High Acres, Abb.L. WD5 59 BR32
Enfield EN2 off Old Pk Vw 81 DN41
HIGHAM HILL, E17 101 DY54
Higham Hill Rd, E17 101 DY54
Higham Mead, Chesh. HP5 54 AQ30
Higham Ms, Nthlt. UB5
off Taywood Rd 136 BZ70
Higham Pl, E17 123 DY55
Higham Rd, N17 122 DR55
Chesham HP5 54 AP30
Woodford Green IG8 102 EG51
Highams Ct, E4 off Friars Cl 101 ED48
● Highams Lo Business Cen, E17 123 DX55
HIGHAMS PARK, E4 101 ED50
⟳ Highams Park 101 ED51
● Highams Pk Ind Est, E4 101 EC51
Sch Highams Pk Sch, E4
off Handsworth Av 101 ED51
Higham Sta Av, E4 101 EB51
Higham St, E17 123 DY55
Higham Vw, N.Wld Bas. CM16 71 FB26
Highbanks Cl, Well. DA16 166 EV80
Highbanks Rd, Pnr. HA5 94 CB50
Highbank Way, N8 121 DN58
HIGH BARNET, Barn. EN5 79 CX40
⊖ High Barnet 80 DA42
High Barn Rd, Dor. RH5 246 BX134
Effingham KT24 246 BX129
Highbarns, Hem.H. HP3 58 BN25
Highbarrow Cl, Pur. CR8 219 DM110
Highbarrow Rd, Croy. CR0 202 DU101
HIGH BEACH, Loug. IG10 84 EG39
High Beech, S.Croy. CR2 220 DS108
Sch High Beech C of E Prim Sch,
Loug. IG10 off Mott St 84 EG39
High Beeches, Bans. SM7 217 CW114
Gerrards Cross SL9 112 AX60
Orpington BR6 224 EU107
Sidcup DA14 186 EY92
Weybridge KT13 213 BS107
High Beeches Cl, Pur. CR8 219 DK110
High Beech Rd, Loug. IG10 84 EL42
High Bois La, Amer. HP6 55 AR35
High Br, SE10 315 H1
Highbridge Cl, Rad. WD7 61 CF33
● Highbridge Est, Uxb. UB8 134 BJ66
Highbridge Rd, Bark. IG11 145 EP67
Highbridge St, Wal.Abb. EN9 67 EA33
High Br Wf, SE10 314 G1
Highbrook Rd, SE3 164 EK83
High Broom Cres, W.Wick. BR4 203 EB101
HIGHBURY, N5 277 J3
⇌ Highbury & Islington 276 F5
⟳ Highbury & Islington 276 F5
⊖ Highbury & Islington 276 F5
Highbury Av, Hodd. EN11 49 EA15
Thornton Heath CR7 201 DN96
Highbury Cl, N.Mal. KT3 198 CQ98
West Wickham BR4 203 EB103
Highbury Cor, N5 276 G4
Highbury Cres, N5 276 F3
Highbury Dr, Lthd. KT22 231 CG121
Highbury Est, N5 277 K3
Sch Highbury Flds Sch, N5 276 G2
Annexe, N5 277 J2
Highbury Gdns, Ilf. IG3 125 ES61
Highbury Gra, N5 277 H1
Highbury Gro, N5 277 H4
Sch Highbury Gro Sch, N5 277 J3
Highbury Hill, N5 277 H2
Highbury New Pk, N5 277 H4
Highbury Pk, N5 277 H1
Highbury Pl, N5 276 G4
Highbury Quad, N5 121 DP62
Sch Highbury Quad Prim Sch,
N5 277 K1
Highbury Rd, SW19 179 CY92
Highbury Sq, N14
off Burleigh Gdns 99 DJ46
Highbury Stadium Sq, N5 121 DP62
Highbury Sta Rd, N1 276 F5
Highbury Ter, N5 276 G3
Highbury Ter Ms, N5 276 G3
High Canons, Borwd. WD6 78 CQ37
High Cedar Dr, SW20 179 CV94
High Clandon, E.Clan. GU4 244 BL133
Highclere, Guil. GU1 243 BA132
Highclere Cl, Ken. CR8 236 DQ115
Highclere Ct, St.Alb. AL1
off Avenue Rd 43 CE19
Highclere Dr, Hem.H. HP3 40 BN24
Highclere Rd, N.Mal. KT3 198 CR97
Highclere St, SE26 183 DY91
Highcliffe Dr, SW15 179 CT86
Highcliffe Gdns, Ilf. IG4 124 EL57
High Cl, Rick. WD3 74 BJ43
Highcombe, SE7 164 EH79
Highcombe Cl, SE9 184 EK88
High Coombe Pl, Kings.T. KT2 178 CR94
High Coppice, Amer. HP7 55 AQ39
Highcotts La, Guil. GU4 243 BF126
Highcroft, NW9 118 CS57
Highcroft Av, Wem. HA0 138 CN66
Highcroft Ct, Bkhm KT23 230 CA123
Highcroft Gdns, NW11 119 CZ58
Highcroft Rd, N19 121 DL59
Felden HP3 58 BG25
High Cross, Ald. WD25 77 CD37
● High Cross Cen, The, N15 122 DU56
High Cross Rd, N17 122 DU55
Highcross Rd, Sthflt DA13 189 FX92
Highcross Way, SW15 179 CU88
Highdaun Dr, SW16 201 DM98
High Dells, Hat. AL10 45 CT19
Highdown, Wor.Pk. KT4 198 CS103
Highdown Cl, Bans. SM7 233 CZ116
Highdown La, Sutt. SM2 218 DB111
Highdown Rd, SW15 179 CV86
High Dr, N.Mal. KT3 198 CQ95
Oxshott KT22 215 CD114
Woldingham CR3 237 DZ122
High Elms, Chig. IG7 103 ES49
Upminster RM14 129 FS60
Woodford Green IG8 102 EG50
High Elms Cl, Nthwd. HA6 93 BR51
High Elms La, Wat. WD25 59 BV31
High Elms Rd, Downe BR6 223 EP110
HIGHER DENHAM, Uxb. UB9 113 BB59
Higher Dr, Bans. SM7 217 CX112
Leatherhead KT24 245 BS127
Purley CR8 219 DN113
Higher Grn, Epsom KT17 217 CU113
HIGHFIELD, Hem.H. HP2 40 BL18
Highfield, Bans. SM7 234 DE117
Bushey Heath WD23 95 CE47
Chalfont St. Giles HP8 90 AX47
Harlow CM18 52 EU16
Kings Langley WD4 58 BL28
Shalford GU4 258 AY142
Watford WD19 94 BZ48
Highfield Av, NW9 118 CQ57
NW11 119 CX59
Erith DA8 167 FB79
Greenford UB6 117 CE64
Orpington BR6 223 ET106
Pinner HA5 116 BZ57
Wembley HA9 118 CL62
Highfield Cl, N22 99 DN53
NW9 118 CQ57
SE13 183 ED86
Amersham HP6 55 AR37
Englefield Green TW20
off Highfield Rd 172 AW93
Long Ditton KT6 197 CJ102
Northwood HA6 93 BS53
Oxshott KT22 215 CD111
Romford RM5 105 FC51
West Byfleet KT14 212 BG113
Highfield Ct, N14 81 DJ44
Highfield Cres, Horn. RM12 128 FM61
Northwood HA6 93 BS53
Highfield Dr, Brom. BR2 204 EE98
Broxbourne EN10 49 DY21
Caterham CR3 236 DU122
Epsom KT19 217 CT108
Ickenham UB10 114 BL63
West Wickham BR4 203 EB103
Highfield Gdns, NW11 119 CY58
Grays RM16 170 GD75
Highfield Grn, Epp. CM16 69 ES31
Highfield Hill, SE19 182 DR94
Sch Highfield Inf Sch, Short. BR2
off Highfield Dr 204 EE98
Sch Highfield Jun Sch, Short. BR2
off South Hill Rd 204 EE98
Highfield La, Hem.H. HP2 40 BM18
Tyttenhanger AL4 44 CL23
Highfield Link, Rom. RM5 105 FC51
Highfield Manor, St.Alb. AL4 44 CL24
Highfield Ms, NW6 273 L6
Highfield Pk Dr,
St.Alb. AL1, AL4 43 CH23
Highfield Pl, Epp. CM16 69 ES31
Sch Highfield Prim Sch, N21
off Highfield Rd 100 DQ46
Hillingdon UB10
off Charville La W 135 BP69
Highfield Rd, N21 99 DP47
NW11 119 CY58
W3 138 CP71
Berkhamsted HP4 38 AX20
Bexleyheath DA6 186 EZ85
Biggin Hill TN16 238 EJ117
Bromley BR1 205 EM98
Bushey WD23 76 BY43
Caterham CR3 236 DU122
Chertsey KT16 194 BG102
Chesham HP5 54 AP29
Cheshunt EN7 66 DS26
Chislehurst BR7 205 ET97
Dartford DA1 188 FK87
Englefield Green TW20 172 AX93
Feltham TW13 175 BU89
Hertford SG13 32 DR11
Hornchurch RM12 128 FM61
Isleworth TW7 157 CF81
Northwood HA6 93 BS53
Purley CR8 219 DM110
Romford RM5 105 FC52
Sunbury-on-Thames TW16 195 BT98
Surbiton KT5 198 CQ101
Sutton SM1 218 DE106
Walton-on-Thames KT12 195 BU102
West Byfleet KT14 212 BG113
Windsor SL4 151 AM83
Woodford Green IG8 102 EL52
Highfield Rd N, Dart. DA1 188 FK86
Highfields, Ashtd. KT21 231 CK119
Cuffley EN6 65 DL28
East Horsley KT24 245 BS128
Fetcham KT22 231 CD124
Radlett WD7 77 CF35
Highfields Gro, N6 120 DF60
Highfield Twr, Rom. RM5 105 FD50
Highfield Way, Horn. RM12 128 FM61
Potters Bar EN6 64 DB32
Rickmansworth WD3 74 BH44
High Firs, Rad. WD7 77 CF35
Swanley BR8 207 FE98
Sch High Firs Prim Sch,
Swan. BR8 off Court Cres 207 FF98
High Foleys, Clay. KT10 215 CH108
High Gables, Loug. IG10 84 EK43
High Garth, Esher KT10 214 CC107
HIGHGATE, N6 120 DG61
⊖ Highgate 121 DH58
H Highgate Acute Mental
Health Cen, N19 121 DH61
Highgate Av, N6 121 DH58
★ Highgate Cem, N6 120 DG60
Highgate Cl, N6 120 DG59
Highgate Edge, N2 120 DE57
Highgate Gro, Saw. CM21 36 EX05
Highgate High St, N6 120 DG60
Highgate Hill, N6 121 DH60
N19 121 DH60
Highgate Ho, SE26
off Sydenham Hill Est 182 DU90
Sch Highgate Jun Sch, N6
off Bishopswood Rd 120 DF59
Sch Highgate Prim Sch, N6
off North Hill 120 DF58
Highgate Rd, NW5 121 DH63
Sch Highgate Sch, N6
off North Rd 120 DG59
Highgate Spinney, N8
off Crescent Rd 121 DK58
Highgate Wk, SE23 182 DW89
Highgate W Hill, N6 120 DG61
Sch Highgate Wd Sch, N8
off Montenotte Rd 121 DJ57
High Gro, SE18 165 ER80
Bromley BR1 204 EJ95
Saint Albans AL3 43 CD18
Highgrove, Pilg.Hat. CM15 108 FV44
Welwyn Garden City AL8 29 CW08
Highgrove Cl, N11
off Balmoral Av 98 DG50
Chislehurst BR7 204 EL95
Highgrove Ms, Cars. SM5 200 DF104
Grays RM17 170 GC78
Highgrove Rd, Dag. RM8 126 EW64
Highgrove Way, Ruis. HA4 115 BU58
High Hill, E5
off Mount Pleasant La 122 DV60
High Hill Ferry, E5 off Big Hill 122 DV60
High Hill Rd, Warl. CR6 237 EC115
High Holborn, WC1 286 B8
High Ho Est, Harl. CM17 36 EZ11
High Ho La, Orsett RM16 171 GJ75
West Tilbury RM18 171 GK77
Highland Av, W7 137 CE72
Brentwood CM15 108 FW46
Dagenham RM10 127 FC62
Loughton IG10 84 EL44
Highland Cotts, Wall. SM6 219 DH105
Highland Ct, E18 102 EH53
Highland Cft, Beck. BR3 183 EB92
Highland Dr, Bushey WD23 94 CC45
Hemel Hempstead HP3 41 BP20
Highland Pk, Felt. TW13 175 BT91
Highland Rd, SE19 182 DS93
Amersham HP7 55 AR39
Badgers Mount TN14 225 FB111
Bexleyheath DA6 186 FA85
Bromley BR1, BR2 204 EF95
Lower Nazeing EN9 50 EE22
Northwood HA6 93 BT54
Purley CR8 219 DN114
Highlands, Ashtd. KT21 231 CJ119
Farnham Common SL2 111 AP64
Hatfield AL9 45 CW15
Watford WD19 94 BW46
Highlands, The, Barn. EN5 80 DB43
East Horsley KT24 245 BS125
Edgware HA8 96 CP54
Potters Bar EN6 64 DC30
Rickmansworth WD3 92 BH45
Highlands Av, N21 81 DM43
W3 138 CQ73
Leatherhead KT22 231 CJ122
Highlands Cl, N4
off Mount Vw Rd 121 DL59
Chalfont St. Peter SL9 91 AZ52
Hounslow TW3 156 CB81
Leatherhead KT22 231 CH122
Highlands End, Chal.St.P. SL9 91 AZ52
Highlands Gdns, Ilf. IG1 125 EM60
Highlands Heath, SW15 179 CW87
Highlands Hill, Swan. BR8 207 FG96
Highlands La, Chal.St.P. SL9 91 AZ51
Woking GU22 226 AY122
Highlands Pk, Lthd. KT22 231 CK123
Seal TN15 257 FL121
Sch Highlands Prim Sch, Ilf. IG1
off Lennox Gdns 125 EM60
Highlands Rd, Barn. EN5 80 DA43
Leatherhead KT22 231 CH122
Orpington BR5 206 EV101
Reigate RH2 250 DD133
Seer Green HP9 89 AQ50
Sch Highlands Sch, N21
off Worlds End La 81 DN42
High La, W7 137 CD72
Caterham CR3 237 DZ119
Sheering CM22 37 FE09
Warlingham CR6 237 DZ118
HIGH LAVER, Ong. CM5 53 FH17
High Lawns, Har. HA1 117 CE62
Highlea Cl, NW9 96 CS53
High Leigh Barns, Hodd. EN11 49 DY17
High Level Dr, SE26 182 DU91
Highlever Rd, W10 282 B7
Sch High March Sch, Beac. HP9
off Ledborough La 89 AK51
Highmead, SE18 165 ET80
High Mead, Chig. IG7 103 EQ47
Harrow HA1 117 CE57
West Wickham BR4 203 ED103
Highmead Cres, Wem. HA0 138 CM66
High Meadow Cl, Dor. RH4 263 CH137
Pinner HA5 116 BW56
Highmeadow Cres, NW9 118 CR57
High Meadow Pl, Cher. KT16 193 BF100
High Meadows, Chig. IG7 103 ER50
High Meads Rd, E16 292 E8
High Molewood, Hert. SG14 31 DP07
Highmoor, Amer. HP7 55 AR39
Highmore Rd, SE3 315 K4
High Mt, NW4 119 CU58
High Oak Rd, Ware SG12 33 DX05
High Oaks, Enf. EN2 81 DM38
St. Albans AL3 42 CC15
High Oaks Rd, Welw.G.C. AL8 29 CV08
Highover Pk, Amer. HP7 55 AR40
High Pk Av, E.Hors. KT24 245 BT126
Richmond TW9 158 CN81
High Pk Rd, Rich. TW9 158 CN81
High Pastures, Sheering CM22 37 FD06
High Path, SW19 200 DB95
High Path Rd, Guil. GU1 243 BC134
High Pewley, Guil. GU1 258 AY136
High Pine Cl, Wey. KT13 213 BQ106
High Pines, Warl. CR6 236 DW119
High Pt, N6 120 DG59
SE9 185 EP90
Weybridge KT13 212 BN106
High Ridge, Cuffley EN6 65 DL27
Highridge Cl, Epsom KT18 232 CS115
High Ridge Cl, Hem.H. HP3 58 BK25
Highridge La, Bet. RH3 264 CP140
High Ridge Rd, Hem.H. HP3 58 BK25
High Rd, N2 120 DE56
N11 99 DH50
N12 98 DC51
N15 122 DT58
N17 100 DT53
N20 98 DC45
N22 121 DN55
High Rd, NW10 (Willesden) 139 CV65
Broxbourne EN10 49 DZ20
Buckhurst Hill IG9 102 EH47
Bushey Heath WD23 95 CD46
Byfleet KT14 212 BM112
Chadwell Heath RM6 126 EV60
Chigwell IG7 103 EM50
Chipstead CR5 234 DF121
Cowley UB8 134 BJ71
Eastcote HA5 115 BV56
Epping CM16 69 ER32
Essendon AL9 46 DE17
Harrow Weald HA3 95 CE52
Ilford IG1 125 EP62
Leavesden WD25 75 BT35
Loughton IG10 102 EJ45
North Weald Bassett CM16 71 FB27
Reigate RH2 250 DD126
Seven Kings IG3 125 ET60
Thornwood CM16 70 EV28
Wembley HA0, HA9 117 CK64
Wilmington DA2 188 FJ90
High Rd Ickenham, Uxb. UB10 115 BP62
High Rd Leyton, E10 123 EB60
E15 123 EC62
High Rd Leytonstone, E11 281 J1
E15 124 EE63
High Rd Turnford, Brox. EN10 67 DY25
High Rd Woodford Grn, E18 102 EF52
Woodford Green IG8 102 EF52
High Rd Wormley, Turnf. EN10 49 DY24
Highshore Rd, SE15 312 B8
Sch Highshore Sch, SE15 312 B7
High Silver, Loug. IG10 84 EK42
High Standing, Chaldon CR3 252 DQ125
Highstead Cres, Erith DA8 167 FE81
Highstone Av, E11 124 EG58
High St, E11 124 EG57
E13 281 N10
E15 280 E10
E17 123 DZ57
N8 121 DL56
N14 99 DK46
NW7 97 CV49
NW10 (Harlesden) 139 CT68
SE20 182 DV93
SE25 (S.Norwood) 202 DT98
W3 138 CP74
W5 137 CK73
Abbots Langley WD5 59 BS31
Addlestone KT15 212 BH105
Amersham HP7 55 AM38
Aveley RM15 149 FR74
Banstead SM7 234 DA115
Barkingside IG6 103 EQ54
Barnet EN5 79 CY41
Bean DA2 189 FV90
Beckenham BR3 203 EA96
Bedmond WD5 59 BT27
Berkhamsted HP4 38 AW19
Bletchingley RH1 252 DQ133
Bookham KT23 246 CB125
Bovingdon HP3 57 BA27
Brasted TN16 240 EV124
Bray SL6 150 AC75
Brentford TW8 157 CJ80
Brentwood CM14 108 FW47
Bromley BR1 204 EG96
Burnham SL1 130 AJ69
Bushey WD23 76 CA44
Carshalton SM5 218 DG105
Caterham CR3 236 DS123
Chalfont St. Giles HP8 90 AW48
Chalfont St. Peter SL9 90 AY53
Chalvey SL1 151 AQ76
Cheam SM3 217 CY107
Chesham HP5 54 AQ31
Cheshunt EN8 67 DX29
Chipstead TN13 256 FC122
Chislehurst BR7 185 EP93
Chobham GU24 210 AS111
Claygate KT10 215 CF107
Cobham KT11 213 BV114
Colnbrook SL3 153 BC80
Colney Heath AL4 44 CP22
Cowley UB8 134 BJ70
Cranford TW5 155 BV80
Croydon CR0 202 DQ103
Dartford DA1 188 FL86
Datchet SL3 152 AV81
Dorking RH4 263 CH136
Downe BR6 223 EN111
Edgware HA8 96 CN51
Egham TW20 173 BA92
Elstree WD6 77 CK44
Epping CM16 69 ET31
Epsom KT19 216 CR113
Esher KT10 214 CB105
Eton SL4 151 AR79
Ewell KT17 217 CT109
Eynsford DA4 208 FL103
Farnborough BR6 223 EP106
Farningham DA4 208 FM100
Feltham TW13 175 BT90
Godstone RH9 252 DV131
Gravesend DA11 191 GH86
Grays RM17 170 GA79
Green Street Green BR6 223 ET108
Greenhithe DA9 169 FV84
Guildford GU1, GU2 258 AX135
Hampton TW12 176 CC93
Hampton Wick KT1 197 CJ95
Harefield UB9 92 BJ54
Harlington UB3 155 BS78
Harlow CM17 36 EW11
Harmondsworth UB7 154 BK79
Harrow HA1, HA2 117 CE60
Hemel Hempstead HP1 40 BJ18
Hoddesdon EN11 49 EA19
Horley RH6 269 DH148
Hornchurch RM11, RM12 128 FK60
Horsell GU21 226 AV115
Hounslow TW3 156 CC83
Hunsdon SG12 34 EK06
Iver SL0 133 BE72
Kings Langley WD4 58 BN29
Kingston upon Thames KT1 197 CK96
Langley SL3 153 AZ78
Leatherhead KT22 231 CH122
Limpsfield RH8 254 EG128
London Colney AL2 61 CJ25
Merstham RH1 251 DH128
New Malden KT3 198 CS97
Northchurch HP4 38 AS17

High St, Northfleet DA11 190 GB86
Northwood HA6 93 BT53
Nutfield RH1 251 DM133
Old Woking GU22 227 BB121
Orpington BR6 206 EU102
Otford TN14 241 FF116
Oxshott KT22 215 CD113
Oxted RH8 253 ED130
Pinner HA5 116 BY55
Ponders End EN3 82 DW43
Potters Bar EN6 64 DC33
Purfleet RM19 168 FN78
Purley CR8 219 DN111
Redhill RH1 250 DF134
Reigate RH2 250 DA134
Rickmansworth WD3 92 BK46
Ripley GU23 228 BJ121
Romford RM1 127 FE57
Roydon CM19 34 EH14
Ruislip HA4 115 BS59
St. Albans AL3 43 CD20
St. Mary Cray BR5 206 EW98
Seal TN15 257 FL121
Sevenoaks TN13 257 FJ125
Shepperton TW17 195 BP100
Shoreham TN14 225 FF110
Slough SL1 152 AU75
Southall UB1 136 BZ74
Staines-upon-Thames TW18 173 BF91
Stanstead Abbotts SG12 33 EC11
Stanwell TW19 174 BK86
Sutton SM1 218 DB105
Swanley BR8 207 FF98
Swanscombe DA10 190 FZ85
Tadworth KT20 233 CW123
Taplow SL6 130 AE70
Teddington TW11 177 CG92
Thames Ditton KT7 197 CG101
Thornton Heath CR7 202 DQ98
Uxbridge UB8 134 BK67
Waltham Cross EN8 67 DY34
Walton-on-Thames KT12 195 BU102
Ware SG12 33 DX06
Watford WD17 75 BV41
Wealdstone HA3 117 CE55
Wembley HA9 118 CM63
West Molesey KT8 196 CA98
West Wickham BR4 203 EB102
Westerham TN16 255 EQ127
Weybridge KT13 212 BN105
Whitton TW2 176 CC87
Windsor SL4 151 AR81
Woking GU21 226 AY117
Wraysbury TW19 172 AY86
Yiewsley UB7 134 BK74
High St Colliers Wd, SW19 180 DD94
High St Grn, Hem.H. HP2 40 BN18
⊖ **High Street Kensington** 295 L5
High St Ms, SW19 179 CY92
High St N, E6 144 EL67
E12 124 EL64
High St S, E6 145 EM68
High St Wimbledon, SW19 179 CX92
High Timber St, EC4 287 J10
High Tor Cl, Brom. BR1 184 EH94
High Tor Vw, SE28 145 ES74
High Tree Cl, Add. KT15 211 BF106
Purley CR8 219 DM110
Sawbridgeworth CM21 36 EX06
High Tree Ct, W7 137 CE73
High Trees, SW2 181 DN88
Barnet EN4 80 DE43
Croydon CR0 203 DY102
Dartford DA2 188 FP86
High Trees Cl, Cat. CR3 236 DT123
High Trees Ct, Brwd. CM14
off Warley Mt 108 FW49
High Trees Rd, Reig. RH2 266 DD135
Highview, Cat. CR3 236 DS124
High Vw, Ch.St.G. HP8 90 AX47
Chorleywood WD3 74 BG42
Gomshall GU5 261 BQ139
Hatfield AL10 45 CT20
Highview, Knap. GU21
off Mulgrave Way 226 AS117
Northolt UB5 136 BY69
Tadworth KT20 233 CU121
High Vw, Pnr. HA5 116 BW56
Sutton SM2 217 CZ111
Watford WD18 75 BT44
Highview Av, Edgware HA8 96 CQ49
Wallington SM6 219 DM106
High Vw Av, Grays RM17 170 GC78
High Vw Cl, SE19 202 DT96
Loughton IG10 84 EJ43
Highview Cl, Pot.B. EN6 64 DC33
Highview Cres, Hutt. CM13 109 GC44
Highview Gdns, N3 119 CY56
N11 99 DJ50
Edgware HA8 96 CQ49
Potters Bar EN6 64 DC33
St. Albans AL4 43 CJ15
Upminster RM14 128 FP61
High Vw Gdns, Grays RM17 170 GC78
Highview Ho, Rom. RM6 126 EY56
High Vw Mobile Home Pk,
Kings L. WD4 59 BR28
Highview Path, Bans. SM7 234 DA115
High View Pl, Amer. HP7 77 AQ40
Sch **High Vw Prim Sch**, SW11
off Plough Rd 160 DD84
Wallington SM6
off The Chase 219 DL106
High Vw Rd, E18 124 EF55
SE19 182 DR93
Guildford GU2 258 AS137
Highview Rd, W13 137 CG71
Sidcup DA14 186 EV91
Highway, The, E1 300 D1
E14 300 D1
Beaconsfield HP9
off Station Rd 89 AK52
Orpington BR6 224 EW106
Stanmore HA7 95 CF53
Sutton SM2 218 DC109
Highway Ct, Beac. HP9
off Station Rd 89 AK52
Sch **Highway Prim Sch, The**,
Orp. BR6 *off The Highway* 224 EW106
High Wickfield, Welw.G.C. AL7 30 DC10
Highwold, Chipstead CR5 234 DG118
Highwood, Brom. BR2 203 ED97
Highwood Av, N12 98 DC49
Bushey WD23 76 BZ39
Highwood Cl, SE22 182 DU88
Brentwood CM14 108 FV45
Kenley CR8 236 DQ117
Orpington BR6 205 EQ103
Highwood Dr, Orp. BR6 205 EQ103
Highwood Gdns, Ilf. IG5 125 EM57
Highwood Gro, NW7 96 CR50
High Woodhall La, Hem.H. HP3 58 BN25
HIGHWOOD HILL, NW7 97 CU47
Highwood Hill, NW7 97 CT47
Highwood La, Loug. IG10 85 EN43
Sch **Highwood Prim Sch**, Bushey
WD23 *off Bushey Mill La* 76 BY39
Highwood Rd, N19 121 DL62
High Wd Rd, Hodd. EN11 49 DZ15
Highwoods, Cat. CR3 252 DS125
Leatherhead KT22 231 CJ121
High Worple, Har. HA2 116 BZ59
Highworth Rd, N11 99 DK51
HIGH WYCH, Saw. CM21 36 EV06
Sch **High Wych C of E Prim Sch**,
High Wych CM21
off High Wych Rd 36 EU06
High Wych Rd,
High Wych. CM21 36 EV06
Hilary Av, Mitch. CR4 200 DG97
Hilary Cl, SW6 307 L4
Erith DA8 167 FC81
Hornchurch RM12 128 FK64
Hilary Rd, W12 139 CT72
Hilbert Rd, Sutt. SM3 199 CX104
Hilborough Way, Orp. BR6 223 ER106
Hilbury, Hat. AL10 45 CT19
Hilbury Cl, Amer. HP6 55 AQ35
Hilda Lockert Wk, SW9
off Fiveways Rd 310 G9
Hilda May Av, Swan. BR8 207 FE97
Hilda Rd, E6 144 EK66
E16 291 K5
Hilda Ter, SW9 310 F8
Hilda Vale Cl, Orp. BR6 223 EN105
Hilda Vale Rd, Orp. BR6 223 EN105
Hildenborough Gdns,
Brom. BR1 184 EE93
Hilden Dr, Erith DA8 167 FH80
Hildenlea Pl, Brom. BR2 204 EE96
Hildenley Cl, Merst. RH1
off Malmstone Av 251 DK128
Hildens, The, Westc. RH4 262 CB138
Hilders, The, Ashtd. KT21 232 CP117
Hildreth St, SW12 181 DH88
Hildreth St Ms, SW12
off Hildreth St 181 DH88
Hildyard Rd, SW6 307 K2
Hiley Rd, NW10 282 A1
Hilfield La, Ald. WD25 77 CD41
Hilfield La S, Bushey WD23 77 CF44
Hilgay, Guil. GU1 243 AZ134
Hilgay Cl, Guil. GU1 243 AZ134
Hilgrove Rd, NW6 273 P7
Hiliary Gdns, Stan. HA7 95 CJ54
Hiljon Cres, Chal.St.P. SL9 90 AY53
Hill, The, Cat. CR3 236 DT124
Harlow CM17 36 EW11
Northfleet DA11 190 GC86
Hillars Heath Rd, Couls. CR5 235 DL115
Hillary Av, Nthflt DA11 190 GE90
Hillary Cres, Walt. KT12 196 BW102
Hillary Dr, Islw. TW7 157 CF84
Hillary Ri, Barn. EN5 80 DA42
Hillary Rd, Hem.H. HP2 40 BN19
Slough SL3 152 AY75
Southall UB2 156 CA76
Hill Av, Amer. HP6 55 AQ38
Hill Barn, S.Croy. CR2 220 DS111
Hillbeck Cl, SE15 312 G4
Hillbeck Way, Grnf. UB6 137 CD67
Hillborne Cl, Hayes UB3 155 BU78
Hillborough Av, Sev. TN13 257 FK122
Hillborough Cl, SW19 180 DC94
Hillbrook Gdns, Wey. KT13 212 BN108
Sch **Hillbrook Prim Sch**, SW17
off Hillbrook Rd 180 DG91
Hillbrook Rd, SW17 180 DF90
Hill Brow, Brom. BR1 204 EK95
Dartford DA1 187 FF86
Hillbrow, N.Mal. KT3 199 CT97
Hillbrow Cl, Bex. DA5 187 FD91
Hillbrow Cotts, Gdse. RH9 252 DW132
Hillbrow Ct, Gdse. RH9 252 DW132
Hillbrow Rd, Brom. BR1 184 EE94
Esher KT10 214 CC105
Hillbury Av, Har. HA3 117 CH57
Hillbury Cl, Warl. CR6 236 DV118
Hillbury Cres, Warl. CR6 236 DW118
Hillbury Gdns, Warl. CR6 236 DW118
Hillbury Rd, SW17 181 DH90
Warlingham CR6 236 DU117
Whyteleafe CR3 236 DU117
Hill Cl, NW2 119 CV62
NW11 120 DA58
Barnet EN5 79 CW43
Chislehurst BR7 185 EP92
Cobham KT11 214 CA112
Harrow HA1 117 CE62
Istead Rise DA13 190 GE94
Purley CR8 220 DQ113
Stanmore HA7 95 CH49
Woking GU21 226 AX116
Wooburn Green HP10 110 AF56
Hill Common, Hem.H. HP3 40 BN24
Hillcote Av, SW16 181 DN94
Hill Ct, Gdmg. GU7 258 AS144
Northolt UB5 116 CA64
Hillcourt Av, N12 98 DB51
Hillcourt Est, N16 122 DR60
Hillcourt Rd, SE22 182 DV86
Hill Cres, N20 98 DB47
Bexley DA5 187 FC88
Harrow HA1 117 CG57
Hornchurch RM11 128 FJ58
Surbiton KT5 198 CM99
Worcester Park KT4 199 CW103
Hill Crest, Pot.B. EN6 64 DC34
Sevenoaks TN13 256 FG122
Sidcup DA15 186 EU87
Hillcrest, N6 120 DG59
N21 99 DP45
SE24 162 DR84
Hatfield AL10 45 CU18
St. Albans AL3 42 CB22
Weybridge KT13 213 BP105
Hillcrest Av, NW11 119 CY57
Chertsey KT16 211 BE105
Edgware HA8 96 CP49
Grays RM20 169 FU79
Pinner HA5 116 BX56
Hillcrest Caravan Pk,
Box H. KT20 248 CP131
Hillcrest Cl, SE26 182 DU91
Beckenham BR3 203 DZ99
Epsom KT18 233 CT115
Goffs Oak EN7 66 DQ29
Hillcrest Ct, Sutt. SM2
off Eaton Rd 218 DD107
Hillcrest Dr, Green. DA9
off Riverview Rd 189 FU85
Hillcrest Gdns, N3 119 CY56
NW2 119 CU62
Esher KT10 197 CF104
Hillcrest Par, Couls. CR5 219 DH114
Hillcrest Rd, E17 101 ED54
E18 102 EF54
W3 138 CN74
W5 138 CL71
Biggin Hill TN16 238 EK116
Bromley BR1 184 EG92
Dartford DA1 187 FF87
Guildford GU2 242 AT133
Hornchurch RM11 127 FG59
Loughton IG10 84 EK44
Orpington BR6 206 EU103
Purley CR8 219 DM110
Shenley WD7 62 CN33
Toot Hill CM5 71 FE30
Whyteleafe CR3 236 DT117
Hillcrest Vw, Beck. BR3 203 DZ100
Hillcrest Way, Epp. CM16 70 EU31
Hillcrest Waye, Ger.Cr. SL9 113 AZ59
Hillcroft, Loug. IG10 85 EN40
Hill Cft, Rad. WD7 61 CG33
Hillcroft Av, Pnr. HA5 116 BZ58
Purley CR8 219 DJ113
Coll **Hillcroft Coll**, Surb. KT6
off South Bk 198 CL100
Hillcroft Cres, W5 138 CL72
Ruislip HA4 116 BX62
Watford WD19 93 BV46
Wembley HA9 118 CM63
Sch **Hillcroft Prim Sch**, Cat. CR3
off Chaldon Rd 236 DS123
Hillcroft Rd, E6 293 N6
Chesham HP5 54 AR29
Penn HP10 88 AC46
Hillcroome Rd, Sutt. SM2 218 DD107
Hillcross Av, Mord. SM4 199 CZ99
Sch **Hillcross Prim Sch**,
Mord. SM4 *off Ashridge Way* 199 CZ98
Hilldale Rd, Sutt. SM1 217 CZ105
Hilldeane Rd, Pur. CR8 219 DN109
Hilldene Av, Rom. RM3 106 FJ51
Hilldene Cl, Rom. RM3 106 FK50
Sch **Hilldene Prim Sch**, Rom. RM3
off Grange Rd 106 FJ51
Hilldown Rd, SW16 181 DL94
Bromley BR2 204 EE102
Hemel Hempstead HP1 40 BG18
Hill Dr, NW9 118 CQ60
SW16 201 DM97
Leatherhead KT22 231 CF119
Hilldrop Cres, N7 275 P3
Hilldrop Est, N7 275 N2
Hilldrop La, N7 275 P3
Hilldrop Rd, N7 275 N2
Bromley BR1 184 EG93
HILL END, Uxb. UB9 92 BH51
Hillend, SE18 165 EN81
Hill End, Orp. BR6
off The Approach 205 ET103
Hill End La, St.Alb. AL4 43 CJ23
Hill End Rd, Hare. UB9 92 BH51
Hillersdon, Slou. SL2 132 AV71
Hillersdon Av, SW13 159 CU82
Edgware HA8 96 CM50
Hillery Cl, SE17 299 M9
Hilley Fld La, Fetch. KT22 230 CC122
Hill Fm App, Woob.Grn HP10 110 AE55
Hill Fm Av, Wat. WD25 59 BU33
Hill Fm Cl, Wat. WD25 59 BU33
● **Hill Fm Ind Est**, Wat. WD25 59 BT33
Hill Fm La, Ch.St.G. HP8 90 AT46
Hill Fm Rd, W10 282 B6
Chalfont St. Peter SL9 90 AY52
Chesham HP5 54 AR34
Taplow SL6 130 AE68
Uxbridge UB10
off Austin's La 115 BR63
Hillfield, Hat. AL10 45 CV15
Hillfield Av, N8 121 DL57
NW9 118 CS57
Morden SM4 200 DE100
Wembley HA0 138 CL66
Hillfield Cl, Guil. GU1 243 BC132
Harrow HA2 116 CC56
Redhill RH1 250 DG134
Hillfield Ct, NW3 274 C3
Hemel Hempstead HP2 40 BL20
Hillfield Ms, N8 121 DM56
Hillfield Pk, N10 121 DH56
N21 99 DN47
Hillfield Pk Ms, N10 121 DH56
Hillfield Pl, Dunt.Grn TN13 241 FE120
Hillfield Rd, NW6 273 H3
Chalfont St. Peter SL9 90 AY52
Dunton Green TN13 241 FE120
Hampton TW12 176 BZ94
Hemel Hempstead HP2 40 BK20
Redhill RH1 250 DG134
Hillfield Sq, Chal.St.P. SL9 90 AY52
Hillfoot Av, Rom. RM5 105 FC53
Hillfoot Rd, Rom. RM5 105 FC53
Hillford Pl, Red. RH1 266 DG140
Hillgate Pl, SW12 181 DH87
W8 295 J2
Hillgate St, W8 295 J2
Hill Gate Wk, N6 121 DJ58
Hillground Gdns, S.Croy. CR2 219 DP110
Hillgrove, Chal.St.P. SL9 91 AZ53
Hill Gro, Felt. TW13
off Watermill Way 176 BZ89
Romford RM1 127 FE55
● **Hillgrove Business Pk**,
Lwr Naze. EN9 49 EC22
Hill Hall, They.Mt CM16 86 EZ35
Hill Ho, E5 122 DV60
Hillhouse, Wal.Abb. EN9 68 EF33
Hill Ho Av, Stan. HA7 95 CF52
Hill Ho Cl, N21 99 DN45
Chalfont St. Peter SL9
off Rickmansworth La 90 AY52
Sch **Hillhouse C of E Prim Sch**,
Wal.Abb. EN9 *off Ninefields* 68 EF33
Hill Ho Dr, Chad.St.M. RM16 171 GH78
Hampton TW12 196 CA95
Weybridge KT13 212 BN111
Hillhouse Dr, Reig. RH2 266 DB136
Sch **Hill Ho Int Jun Sch**, SW1 296 F7
Hill Ho Ms, Brom. BR2 204 EF96
Hill Ho Rd, SW16 181 DM92
Hillhouse Rd, Dart. DA2 188 FQ87
Hillhurst Gdns, Cat. CR3 236 DS120
Hilliard Rd, Nthwd. HA6 93 BT53
Hilliards Ct, E1 300 F2
Hilliards Rd, Uxb. UB8 134 BK72
Hillier Cl, New Barn. EN5 80 DB44
Hillier Gdns, Croy. CR0 219 DN106
Hillier Pl, Chess. KT9 215 CK107
Hillier Rd, SW11 180 DF86
Guildford GU1 243 BA134
Hilliers Av, Uxb. UB8 134 BN69
Hilliers La, Croy. CR0 201 DL104
Hillier Way, Slou. SL3 153 BA77
Hillingdale, Bigg.H. TN16 238 EH118
HILLINGDON, Uxb. UB8 134 BN69
⊖ **Hillingdon** 114 BN64
Hillingdon Av, Sev. TN13 257 FJ121
Staines-upon-Thames TW19 174 BL88
Jct **Hillingdon Circ**, Uxb. UB10 114 BM64
Hillingdon Hill, Uxb. UB10 134 BL69
H **Hillingdon Hosp**, Uxb. UB8 134 BM71
Sch **Hillingdon Manor Sch**,
Lwr & Mid Schs, Hayes End
UB8 *off Harlington Rd* 135 BP71
Sch **Hillingdon Prim Sch**, Hlgdn
UB10 *off Uxbridge Rd* 135 BP69
Hillingdon Ri, Sev. TN13 257 FK122
Hillingdon Rd, Bexh. DA7 167 FC82
Gravesend DA11 191 GG89
Uxbridge UB10 134 BL67
Watford WD25 59 BU34
Hillingdon St, SE17 311 H3
Hillington Gdns, Wdf.Grn. IG8 102 EK54
Hill La, Kgswd KT20 233 CY121
Ruislip HA4 115 BQ60
Hill Ley, Hat. AL10 45 CT18
Hill Leys, Cuffley EN6 65 DL28
Hillman Cl, Horn. RM11 128 FK55
Uxbridge UB8 114 BL64
Hillman Dr, W10 282 B5
Hillman St, E8 278 F5
Hillmarton Rd, N7 276 A2
Hillmead, Berk. HP4 38 AU20
Hillmead Ct, Tap. SL6 130 AF71
Hillmead Dr, SW9 161 DP84
Hill Meadow, Colesh. HP7 55 AM43
Sch **Hill Mead Prim Sch**, SW9
off Hillmead Dr 161 DP84
Hillmont Rd, Esher KT10 197 CE104
Hillmore Gro, SE26 183 DX92
Hillmount, Wok. GU22
off Constitution Hill 226 AY119
Hill Path, SW16
off Valley Rd 181 DM92
Hill Pl, Farn.Com. SL2 131 AP66
Hillpoint, Loud. WD3 74 BJ43
Hillreach, SE18 305 J10
Hill Ri, N9 82 DV44
NW11 120 DB56
SE23 182 DV88
Chalfont St. Peter SL9 90 AX54
Cuffley EN6 65 DK27
Dorking RH4 247 CG134
Esher KT10 197 CH103
Greenford UB6 136 CC66
Lane End DA2 189 FR92
Potters Bar EN6 64 DC34
Richmond TW10 177 CK85
Rickmansworth WD3 74 BH44
Ruislip HA4 115 BQ60
Slough SL3 153 BA79
Upminster RM14 128 FN61
Hillrise, Walt. KT12 195 BT101
Hillrise Av, Wat. WD24 76 BX38
Hill Ri Cres, Chal.St.P. SL9 90 AY54
Hillrise Rd, N19 121 DL59
Romford RM5 105 FC51
Hill Rd, N10 98 DF53
NW8 283 P1
Brentwood CM14 108 FU48
Carshalton SM5 218 DE107
Dartford DA2 188 FL89
Fetcham KT22 230 CB122
Harrow HA1 117 CG57
Mitcham CR4 201 DH95
Northwood HA6 93 BR51
Pinner HA5 116 BY57
Purley CR8 219 DM112
Sutton SM1 218 DB106
Theydon Bois CM16 85 ES37
Wembley HA0 117 CH62
Hillsboro Rd, SE22 182 DS85
Hillsborough Grn, Wat. WD19 93 BU48
Hills Chace, Warley CM14 108 FW49
Hillsgrove Cl, Well. DA16 166 EW80
Sch **Hillsgrove Prim Sch**,
Well. DA16 *off Sidmouth Rd* 166 EW80
Hillside, NW9 118 CR56
NW10 138 CQ67
SW19 179 CX93
Banstead SM7 233 CY115
Chesham HP5 54 AN28
Erith DA8 167 FD77
Farningham DA4 208 FM101
Grays RM17 170 GD77
Harefield UB9 114 BJ57
Harlow CM17 52 EW17
Hatfield AL10 45 CU18
Hoddesdon EN11 49 DZ16
Lane End DA2 189 FS92
New Barnet EN5 80 DC43
Slough SL1 152 AS75
Virginia Water GU25 192 AW100
Ware SG12 32 DW07
Welwyn Garden City AL7 30 DB12
Woking GU22 226 AX120
Hillside, The, Orp. BR6 224 EV109
Hillside Av, N11 98 DF51
Borehamwood WD6 78 CP42
Cheshunt EN8 67 DX31
Gravesend DA12 191 GK89
Purley CR8 219 DP113
Wembley HA9 118 CM63
Woodford Green IG8 102 EJ50
Hillside Cl, NW8 273 M10
Abbots Langley WD5 59 BS32
Banstead SM7 233 CY116
Brockham RH3 264 CN135
Chalfont St. Giles HP8 90 AV48
Chalfont St. Peter SL9 90 AY51
Morden SM4 199 CY98
Woodford Green IG8 102 EJ50
Hillside Ct, St.Alb. AL1
off Hillside Rd 43 CE19
Swanley BR8 207 FG98
Hillside Cres, Chsht EN8 67 DX31
Enfield EN2 82 DR38
Harrow HA2 116 CC60
Hillside Cres, Northwood HA6 93 BU53
Stanstead Abbotts SG12 33 EB11
Watford WD19 76 BY44
Hillside Dr, Edg. HA8 96 CN51
Gravesend DA12 191 GK89
Hillside Gdns, E17 123 ED55
N6 120 DG58
SW2 181 DN89
Addlestone KT15 211 BF106
Amersham HP7 55 AS40
Barnet EN5 79 CY42
Berkhamsted HP4 38 AX20
Brockham RH3 248 CN134
Edgware HA8 96 CM49
Harrow HA3 118 CL59
Northwood HA6 93 BU52
Wallington SM6 219 DJ108
Hillside Gate, St.Alb. AL1 43 CE19
Hillside Gro, N14 99 DK45
NW7 97 CU52
Sch **Hillside Inf & Jun Schs**,
Nthwd. HA6
off Northwood Way 93 BU52
Hillside La, Brom. BR2 204 EG103
Great Amwell SG12 33 EA10
Hillside Pas, SW2 181 DM89
Sch **Hillside Prim Sch**, Orp. BR5
off Dyke Dr 206 EW101
Hillside Ri, Nthwd. HA6 93 BU52
Hillside Rd, N15 122 DS59
SW2 181 DN89
W5 138 CL71
Ashtead KT21 232 CM117
Bromley BR2 204 EF97
Bushey WD23 76 BY43
Chorleywood WD3 73 BC43
Coulsdon CR5 235 DM118
Croydon CR0 219 DP106
Dartford DA1 187 FG86
Epsom KT17 217 CV110
Northwood HA6 93 BU52
Pinner HA5 93 BV52
Radlett WD7 77 CH35
St. Albans AL1 43 CE19
Sevenoaks TN13 257 FK123
Southall UB1 136 CA70
Surbiton KT5 198 CM99
Sutton SM2 217 CZ108
Tatsfield TN16 238 EL119
Whyteleafe CR3 236 DU118
Hillside Ter, Hert. SG13 32 DQ11
Hillside Wk, Brwd. CM14 108 FU48
Hills La, Nthwd. HA6 93 BS53
Hillsleigh Rd, W8 295 H2
Hillsmead Way, S.Croy. CR2 220 DU113
Hills Ms, W5 138 CL73
Hills Pl, W1 285 L9
Hillspur Cl, Guil. GU2 242 AT133
Hillspur Rd, Guil. GU2 242 AT133
Hills Rd, Buck.H. IG9 102 EH46
Hillstowe St, E5 122
DW61 **Hill St**, W1 297 H2
Richmond TW9 177 CK85
St. Albans AL3 42 CC20
● **Hillswood Business Pk**,
Cher. KT16 211 BC105
Hillswood Dr, Cher. KT16 211 BC105
Hillthorpe Cl, Pur. CR8 219 DM110
HILLTOP, Chesh. HP5 54 AR28
Hilltop, Loug. IG10 85 EN40
Hill Top, NW11 120 DB56
Morden SM4 200 DA100
Sutton SM3 199 CZ101
Hilltop Av, NW10 138 CQ66
Hilltop Cl, Chsht EN7 66 DT26
Guildford GU3 242 AT130
Leatherhead KT22 231 CJ123
Hill Top Cl, Loug. IG10 85 EN41
Sch **Hilltop First Sch**, Wind. SL4
off Clewer Hill Rd 151 AL83
Hilltop Gdns, NW4 97 CV54
Dartford DA1 188 FM85
Orpington BR6 205 ES103
Hilltop La, Chaldon CR3 251 DN126
Redhill RH1 251 DN126
Hill Top Pl, Loug. IG10 85 EN41
Hilltop Ri, Bkhm KT23 246 CC126
Hilltop Rd, NW6 273 K6
Berkhamsted HP4 38 AW20
Grays RM20 169 FV79
Kings Langley WD4 59 BR27
Reigate RH2 266 DB136
Whyteleafe CR3 236 DS117
Hill Top Vw, Wdf.Grn. IG8 103 EM51
Hilltop Wk, Wold. CR3 237 DY120
Hilltop Way, Stan. HA7 95 CG48
Hillview, SW20 179 CV94
Mitcham CR4 201 DL98
Whyteleafe CR3 236 DT117
Hill Vw, Berk. HP4 38 AU17
Dorking RH4 263 CJ135
Hillview Av, Har. HA3 118 CL57
Hornchurch RM11 128 FJ58
Hillview Cl, Pnr. HA5 94 BZ51
Purley CR8 219 DP111
Wembley HA9 118 CM61
Hill Vw Cl, Tad. KT20 233 CW121
Hillview Ct, Wok. GU22 227 AZ118
Hillview Cres, Guil. GU2 242 AT132
Ilford IG1 125 EM58
Orpington BR6 205 ES102
Hill Vw Dr, SE28 145 ES74
Welling DA16 165 ES82
Hillview Dr, Red. RH1 266 DG135
Hillview Gdns, NW4 119 CX56
Cheshunt EN8 67 DX27
Harrow HA2 116 CA55
Hill Vw Gdns, NW9 118 CR57
Hillview Rd, NW7 97 CX49
Chislehurst BR7 185 EN92
Orpington BR6 205 ET102
Pinner HA5 94 BZ52
Sutton SM1 200 DC104
Hill Vw Rd, Clay. KT10 215 CG108
Twickenham TW1 177 CG86
Woking GU22 227 AZ118
Wraysbury TW19 172 AX86
Hillway, N6 120 DG61
NW9 118 CS60
Amersham HP7 55 AP41
Hill Waye, Ger.Cr. SL9 113 AZ58
Hillwood Cl, Hutt. CM13 109 GB46
Hillwood Gro, Hutt. CM13 109 GB46
Hillworth Rd, SW2 181 DN87
Hillyard Rd, W7 137 CE71
Hillyard St, SW9 310 D7
Hillyfield, E17 101 DY54
Hilly Fld, Harl. CM18 51 ET19
Hillyfield Cl, E9 279 M3

H

Sch Hillyfield Prim Sch, E17
off Higham Hill Rd 123 DY55
N16 101 EA53
Hillyfields, Loug. IG10 85 EN40
Hilly Flds, Welw.G.C. AL7 30 DC08
Hilly Flds Cres, SE4 163 EA83
Hilmay Dr, Hem.H. HP1 40 BH21
Hilperton Rd, Slou. SL1 152 AS75
Hilsea Pt, SW15
off Wanborough Dr 179 CV88
Hilsea St, E5 122 DW63
Hilton Av, N12 98 DD50
Hilton Cl, Uxb. UB8 134 BH68
Hilton Ct, Horl. RH6
off Clarence Way 269 DK147
Riv Hilton Docklands Nelson Dock Pier 301 N2
Hilton Way, S.Croy. CR2 236 DV115
Hilversum Cres, SE22
off East Dulwich Gro 182 DS85
Himalayan Way, Wat. WD18 75 BT43
Himley Rd, SW17 180 DE92
Hinchley Cl, Esher KT10 197 CF104
Hinchley Dr, Esher KT10 197 CF104
Hinchley Manor, Esher KT10 197 CF104
Hinchley Way, Esher KT10 197 CG104
HINCHLEY WOOD, Esher KT10 197 CF104
⇌ Hinchley Wood 197 CF104
Sch Hinchley Wd Prim Sch, Hinch.Wd KT10
off Claygate La 197 CG103
Sch Hinchley Wd Sch & 6th Form Cen, Hinch.Wd KT10
off Claygate La 197 CG103
Hinckley Rd, SE15 162 DU84
Hind Cl, Chig. IG7 103 ET50
Hind Ct, EC4 286 F9
Hind Cres, Erith DA8 167 FD79
Hinde Ms, W1
off Marylebone La 285 H8
Hindes Rd, Har. HA1 117 CD57
Hinde St, W1 285 H8
Hind Gro, E14 290 A9
Hindhead Cl, N16 122 DS60
Uxbridge UB8 135 BP71
Hindhead Gdns, Nthlt. UB5 136 BY67
Hindhead Grn, Wat. WD19 94 BW50
Hindhead Pt, SW15
off Wanborough Dr 179 CV88
Hindhead Way, Wall. SM6 219 DL106
Hind Ho, N7
off Harvist Est 121 DN63
Hindle Ho, E8 278 A1
Hindmans Rd, SE22 182 DU85
Hindmans Way, Dag. RM9 146 EZ70
Hindmarsh Cl, E1 288 D10
Hindmarsh Cres, Nthflt. DA11 190 GC89
Hindon Ct, SW1 297 L8
Hindrey Rd, E5 278 E2
Hindsley's Pl, SE23 182 DW89
Hind Ter, Grays RM20
off Mill La 169 FX78
Hine Cl, Couls. CR5 235 DJ122
Epsom KT19 216 CP111
Hinkler Rd, Har. HA3 117 CK55
Hinkley Cl, Hare. UB9 114 BJ56
Hinksey Cl, Slou. SL3 153 BB76
Hinksey Path, SE2 166 EX76
Hinstock Rd, SE18 165 EQ79
Hinton Av, Houns. TW4 156 BX84
Hinton Cl, SE9 184 EL88
Hinton Rd, N18 100 DS49
SE24 161 DP83
Slough SL1 131 AL73
Uxbridge UB8 134 BJ67
Wallington SM6 219 DJ107
Hintons, Harl. CM19 51 EM19
Hipkins Pl, Brox. EN10 49 DY20
Hipley Ct, Guil. GU1 259 BA135
Hipley St, Wok. GU22 227 BB121
Hippodrome Ms, W11 294 E1
Hippodrome Pl, W11 294 F1
Hirst Ct, SW1 309 J1
Hirst Cres, Wem. HA9 118 CL62
Hispano Ms, Enf. EN3 83 EA37
Hitcham La, Burn. SL1 130 AG69
Taplow SL6 130 AG69
Hitcham Rd, E17 123 DZ59
Burnham SL1 130 AF70
Taplow SL6 130 AF72
Hitchcock Cl, Shep. TW17 194 BM97
Hitchcock La, E20 280 F5
Hitchen Hatch La, Sev. TN13 256 FG124
Hitchens Cl, Hem.H. HP1 39 BF19
Hitchin Cl, Rom. RM3 106 FJ49
Hitchings Way, Reig. RH2 266 DA138
Hitchin La, Stan. HA7 96 CL52
Hitchin Sq, E3 279 M10
Hitch St, Dag. RM9 146 EY69
Hithe Gro, SE16 301 H7
Hitherbaulk, Welw.G.C. AL7 29 CY11
Hitherbroom Rd, Hayes UB3 135 BU74
Hitherbury Cl, Guil. GU2 258 AW137
Hither Fm Rd, SE3 164 EJ83
Sch Hitherfield Prim Sch, SW16
off Hitherfield Rd 181 DN90
Hitherfield Rd, SW16 181 DM89
Dagenham RM8 126 EY61
HITHER GREEN, SE13 184 EE86
⇌ Hither Green 184 EE86
Hither Grn La, SE13 183 EC85
Sch Hither Grn Prim Sch, SE13
off Beacon Rd 183 ED86
Hitherlands, SW12 181 DH89
Hither Meadow, Chal.St.P. SL9
off Lower Rd 90 AY54
Hithermoor Rd, Stai. TW19 174 BG85
Hitherway, Welw.G.C. AL8 29 CY05
Hitherwell Dr, Har. HA3 95 CD53
Hitherwood Cl, Horn. RM12
off Swanbourne Dr 128 FK63
Reigate RH2 250 DD132
Hitherwood Dr, SE19 182 DT91
Hive, The, Nthflt DA11
off Fishermans Hill 190 GB85
Hive Cl, Brwd. CM14 108 FU47
Bushey Heath WD23 95 CD47
Hive La, Nthflt DA11 190 GB86
Hive Rd, Bushey Hth WD23 95 CD47
Hivings Hill, Chesh. HP5 54 AN28
Hivings Pk, Chesh. HP5 54 AP28
Hixberry La, St.Alb. AL4 43 CK21
★ H.M.S. Belfast, SE1 299 P2
★ H.M.S. President, EC4 298 F1
★ H.M. Treasury, SW1 298 A4
Hoadly Rd, SW16 181 DK90
Hobart Cl, N20
off Oakleigh Rd N 98 DE47
Hayes UB4 136 BX70
Hobart Dr, Hayes UB4 136 BX70
Hobart Gdns, Th.Hth. CR7 202 DR97
Hobart La, Hayes UB4 136 BX70
Hobart Pl, SW1 297 J6
Richmond TW10
off Chisholm Rd 178 CM86
Hobart Rd, Dag. RM9 126 EX63
Hayes UB4 136 BX70
Ilford IG6 103 EQ54
Tilbury RM18 171 GG81
Worcester Park KT4 199 CV104
Hobart Wk, St.Alb. AL3
off Valley Rd 43 CF16
Hobbans Fm Chase, Ong. CM5 53 FH23
Sch Hobbayne Prim Sch, W7
off Greenford Av 137 CF72
Hobbayne Rd, W7 137 CD72
Hobbes Wk, SW15 179 CV85
Hobbs Cl, Chsht EN8 67 DX29
St. Albans AL4 44 CL21
West Byfleet KT14 212 BH113
Hobbs Cross, Harl. CM17 36 FA14
● Hobbs Cross Business Cen, They.Gar. CM16 86 EX36
Hobbs Cross Rd, Harl. CM17 36 EY12
Theydon Garnon CM16 86 EW35
Hobbs Grn, N2 120 DC55
Hobbs Hill Rd, Hem.H. HP3 40 BL24
Sch Hobbs Hill Wd Prim Sch, Hem.H. HP3 off Peascroft Rd 41 BP22
Hobbs Ms, Ilf. IG3
off Ripley Rd 125 ET61
Hobbs Pl Est, N1 277 N9
Hobbs Rd, SE27 182 DQ91
Hobbs Way, Welw.G.C. AL8 29 CW10
Hobby Horse Cl, Chsht EN7
off Great Stockwood Rd 66 DR26
Hobby St, Enf. EN3 83 DX43
Hobday St, E14 290 C8
Hobill Wk, Surb. KT5 198 CM100
Hoblands End, Chis. BR7 185 ES93
Sch Hobletts Manor Inf & Nurs Sch, Hem.H. HP2 off Adeyfield Rd 40 BN19
Sch Hobletts Manor Jun Sch, Hem.H. HP2 off Adeyfield Rd 40 BN19
Hobletts Rd, Hem.H. HP2 40 BM19
Hobsons Cl, Hodd. EN11 33 DZ14
Hobsons Pl, E1 288 C6
Hobtoe Rd, Harl. CM20 35 EN14
Hobury St, SW10 307 P3
Hockenden La, Swan. BR8 207 FB96
Hockeridge Bottom, Berk. HP4 38 AT21
Hockering Gdns, Wok. GU22 227 BA117
Hockering Rd, Wok. GU22 227 BA118
Hocker St, E2 288 A3
Hocklands, Welw.G.C. AL7 30 DC08
Hockley Av, E6 144 EL68
Hockley Ct, E18
off Churchfields 102 EG53
Hockley Dr, Rom. RM2 105 FH54
Hockley La, Stoke P. SL2 132 AV67
Hockley Ms, Bark. IG11 145 ES68
Hocroft Av, NW2 119 CZ62
Hocroft Rd, NW2 119 CZ63
Hocroft Wk, NW2 119 CZ62
Hodder Dr, Perivale UB6 137 CF68
HODDESDON, EN11 49 DZ18
Jct Hoddesdon, Hodd. EN11 49 DX16
Hoddesdon Bypass, Brox. EN10 49 DX19
Hertford SG13 33 DY14
Hoddesdon EN11 33 DY14
● Hoddesdon Ind Cen, Hodd. EN11 49 EC15
Hoddesdon Rd, Belv. DA17 166 FA78
Broxbourne EN10 67 DX27
Stanstead Abbotts SG12 33 EC11
Hodds Wd Rd, Chesh. HP5 54 AQ33
Hodes Row, NW3 274 F1
Hodford Rd, NW11 119 CZ61
Hodgemoor Vw, Ch.St.G. HP8 90 AT48
Hodges Cl, Chaff.Hun. RM16 169 FX78
Hodges Way, Wat. WD18 75 BU44
Hodgkin Cl, SE28
off Fleming Way 146 EX73
Hodgkins Ms, Stan. HA7 95 CH50
Hodgson Gdns, Guil. GU4
off Sutherland Dr 243 BA131
Hodings Rd, Harl. CM20 35 EP14
Hodister Cl, SE5 311 K5
Hodnet Gro, SE16 301 J8
Hodsoll Ct, Orp. BR5 206 EX100
Hodson Cl, Har. HA2 116 BZ62
Hodson Cres, Orp. BR5 206 EX100
Hodson Pl, Enf. EN3 83 EA38
HOE, Guil. GU5 261 BS143
Hoe, The, Wat. WD19 94 BX47
Sch Hoe Br Sch, Old Wok. GU22
off Old Woking Rd 227 BC119
Hoebrook Cl, Wok. GU22 226 AX121
Hoecroft, Lwr Naze. EN9 50 EF22
Hoe La, Abin.Ham. RH5 261 BT143
Abridge RM4 86 EV43
Enfield EN1, EN3 82 DU38
Nazeing EN9 50 EF22
Peaslake GU5 261 BR144
Ware SG12 33 DX09
Hoe Meadow, Beac. HP9 88 AJ51
Hoestock Rd, Saw. CM21 36 EX05
Hoe St, E17 123 EA56
Hoffmann Gdns, S.Croy. CR2 220 DU108
Hoffman Sq, N1 off Chart St 287 M2
Hofland Rd, W14 294 D6
Hoford Rd, Grays RM16 171 GK76
Linford SS17 171 GL75
West Tilbury RM18 171 GK77
Hogan Ms, W2 284 A6
Hogan Way, E5 122 DU61
Hogarth Av, Ashf. TW15 175 BQ93
Brentwood CM15 108 FY48
● Hogarth Business Pk, W4 158 CS79
Hogarth Cl, E16 292 E6
W5 138 CL71
Slough SL1 131 AL73
Uxbridge UB8 134 BJ69
Hogarth Ct, EC3 287 P10
SE19 off Fountain Dr 182 DT91
Bushey WD23
off Steeplands 94 CB45
Hogarth Cres, SW19 200 DD95
Croydon CR0 202 DQ101
Hogarth Gdns, Houns. TW5 156 CA80
Hogarth Hill, NW11 119 CZ56
Hogarth Ho, Enf. EN1
off Ayley Cft 82 DU43
Hogarth La, W4 158 CS79
Hogarth Pl, SW5 295 L9
Sch Hogarth Prim Sch, Brwd. CM15 off Riseway 109 FZ48
Hogarth Reach, Loug. IG10 85 EM43
Hogarth Rd, SW5 295 L9
Dagenham RM8 126 EV64
Edgware HA8 96 CN54
Jct Hogarth Rbt, W4 159 CT79
Hogarth Rbt Flyover, W4
off Burlington La 158 CS79
★ Hogarth's Ho, W4
off Hogarth La 158 CS79
Hogarth Way, Hmptn. TW12 196 CC95
Hogback Wd Rd, Beac. HP9 88 AH51
Hogden La, Lthd. KT23 246 CA129
Ranmore Common RH5 246 BZ132
Hogfair La, Burn. SL1 130 AJ69
Hogg End La, Hem.H. HP2 41 BR17
St. Albans AL3 41 BT17
Hogges Cl, Hodd. EN11
off Conduit La 49 EA17
Hogg La, Els. WD6 77 CG42
Grays RM16, RM17 170 GA76
Hog Hill Rd, Rom. RM5 104 EZ52
Hog Pits, Flaun. HP3 57 BB32
HOGPITS BOTTOM, Hem.H. HP3 57 BA31
Hogpits Bottom, Flaun. HP3 57 BA32
Hogs Back, Guil. GU3 258 AS137
Hogscross La, Chipstead CR5 234 DF123
Hogsdell La, Hert.Hth SG13 32 DV11
Hogshead Pas, E1 300 F1
Hogshill La, Cob. KT11 213 BV114
Hogs La, Grav. DA11 190 GD90
Hogsmill La, Kings.T. KT1 198 CM97
Hogsmill Way, Epsom KT19 216 CQ106
Hogs Orchard, Swan. BR8 207 FH95
Hogtrough Hill, Brasted TN16 239 ET120
Hogtrough La, Gdse. RH9 253 EA128
Oxted RH8 253 EB128
Redhill RH1 267 DJ135
Holbeach Cl, NW9 96 CS53
Holbeach Gdns, Sid. DA15 185 ES86
Holbeach Ms, SW12 181 DH88
Sch Holbeach Prim Sch, SE6
off Doggett Rd 183 EA87
Holbeach Rd, SE6 183 EA87
Holbeck La, Chsht EN7 66 DT26
Holbeck Row, SE15 312 D5
Holbein Gate, Nthwd. HA6 93 BS50
Holbein Ms, SW1 296 G10
Holbein Pl, SW1 296 G9
Holbein Ter, Barn. EN5
off Ivere Dr 80 DB44
Dag. RM8
off Marlborough Rd 126 EW63
Holberton Gdns, NW10 139 CV69
HOLBORN, WC2 286 C8
⊖ Holborn 286 B8
Holborn, EC1 286 E7
Holborn Circ, EC1 286 F7
Holborn Cl, St.Alb. AL4 43 CK15
Holborn Pl, WC1 286 C7
Holborn Rd, E13 292 A5
Holborn Viaduct, EC1 286 F7
Holborn Way, Mitch. CR4 200 DF96
Holbreck Pl, Wok. GU22
off Heathside Rd 227 AZ118
Holbrook Cl, N19
off Dartmouth Pk Hill 121 DH60
Enfield EN1 82 DT39
Shalford GU4 258 AY142
Holbrooke Ct, N7 121 DL63
Holbrooke Pl, Rich. TW10 177 CK85
Holbrook Gdns, Ald. WD25 76 CB36
Holbrook La, Chis. BR7 185 ER94
Holbrook Meadow, Egh. TW20 173 BC93
Holbrook Rd, E15 291 L1
Holbrook Way, Brom. BR2 205 EM100
Holburne Cl, SE3 164 EJ81
Holburne Gdns, SE3 164 EK81
Holburne Rd, SE3 164 EJ81
Holcombe Cl, West. TN16 255 ER126
Holcombe Hill, NW7 97 CU48
Holcombe Rd, N17 122 DT55
Ilford IG1 125 EN59
Holcombe St, W6 159 CV78
Holcon Ct, Red. RH1 250 DG131
Holcote Cl, Belv. DA17
off Blakemore Way 166 EY76
Holcroft Rd, E9 279 H6
HOLDBROOK, Wal.Cr. EN8 67 EA34
Holdbrook Ct, Wal.Cr. EN8
off Queens Way 67 DZ34
Holdbrook N, Wal.Cr. EN8 67 DZ33
Sch Holdbrook Prim Sch, Wal.Cr. EN8 off Longcroft Dr 67 DZ34
Holdbrook S, Wal.Cr. EN8
off Queens Way 67 DZ34
Holdbrook Way, Rom. RM3 106 FM54
Holden Av, N12 98 DB50
NW9 118 CQ60
Holdenby Rd, SE4 183 DY85
Holden Cl, Dag. RM8 126 EV62
Hertford SG13 32 DS09
Holden Gdns, Warley CM14 108 FX50
Holdenhurst Av, N12 98 DB52
Holden Pl, Cob. KT11 213 BV114
Holden Pt, E15 281 H4
Holden Rd, N12 98 DB50
HOLDENS, Welw.G.C. AL7 30 DA06
Holden St, SW11 308 G9
Holden Way, Upmin. RM14 129 FR59
Holder Cl, N3 98 DB52
Holdernesse Cl, Islw. TW7 157 CG81
Holdernesse Rd, SW17 180 DF90
Holderness Way, SE27 181 DP92
HOLDERS HILL, NW4 97 CX54
Holders Hill Av, NW4 97 CX54
Holders Hill Circ, NW7
off Dollis Rd 97 CY52
Holders Hill Cres, NW4 97 CX54
Holders Hill Dr, NW4 119 CX55
Holders Hill Gdns, NW4 97 CY54
Holders Hill Rd, NW4 97 CX54
NW7 97 CX54
Holdings, The, Hat. AL9 45 CW16
Holecroft, Wal.Abb. EN9 68 EE34
Hole Fm La, Gt Warley CM13 129 FV55
Holegate St, SE7 304 E7
Hole Hill, Westc. RH4 262 CA136
Holford Ho, SE16 300 E9
off Manor Est
Holford Ms, WC1 286 E1
Holford Pl, WC1 286 D2
Holford Rd, NW3 120 DC62
Guildford GU1 243 BC134
Holford St, WC1 286 E2
Holford Way, SW15 179 CU86
Holford Yd, WC1 286 D1
Holgate Av, SW11 160 DD83
Holgate Gdns, Dag. RM10 126 FA64
Holgate Rd, Dag. RM10 126 FA64
HOLLAND, Oxt. RH8 254 EG134
Holland Av, SW20 199 CT95
Sutton SM2 218 DA109
Holland Cl, Brom. BR2 204 EF103
Epsom KT19 216 CQ111
New Barnet EN5 98 DD45
Redhill RH1 250 DF134
Romford RM7 127 FC57
Stanmore HA7 95 CH50
Holland Ct, E17
off Evelyn Rd 123 EC56
NW7 97 CU51
Borhamwood WD6
off Chaucer Gro 78 CN42
Holland Cres, Oxt. RH8 254 EG133
Holland Dr, SE23 183 DY90
Holland Gdns, W14 294 F6
Brentford TW8 158 CL79
Egham TW20 193 BF96
Watford WD25 76 BW35
Holland Gro, SW9 310 F5
Sch Holland Ho Sch, Edg. HA8
off Broadhurst Av 96 CP49
Sch Holland Jun Sch, Oxt. RH8
off Holland Rd 254 EG134
Holland La, Oxt. RH8 254 EG133
★ Holland Pk, W8 294 G4
W11 294 F3
⊖ Holland Park 294 G3
Holland Pk Av, W11 294 D4
Ilford IG3 125 ES58
Holland Pk Gdns, W14 294 E3
Holland Pk Ms, W11 294 F3
Holland Pk Rd, W14 294 G7
Jct Holland Pk Rbt, W11 294 D4
Sch Holland Pk Sch, W8 295 H4
Holland Pas, N1 277 J8
Holland Pl, W8 295 L4
Holland Ri Ho, SW9 310 D5
Holland Rd, E6 145 EM67
E15 291 K2
NW10 139 CU67
SE25 202 DU99
W14 294 D4
Oxted RH8 254 EG133
Wembley HA0 137 CK65
Hollands, The, Felt. TW13 176 BX91
Woking GU22
off Montgomery Rd 226 AY118
Worcester Park KT4 199 CT102
Hollands Cft, Hunsdon SG12 34 EK06
Holland St, SE1 299 H2
W8 295 K5
Holland Town Est, SW9
off Mandela St 310 F5
Holland Vil Rd, W14 294 E4
Holland Wk, N19
off Duncombe Rd 121 DK60
W8 295 H3
Stanmore HA7 95 CG50
Holland Way, Bromley BR2 204 EF103
Harlow CM17
off Harrowbond Rd 36 EX14
Hollar Rd, N16
off Stoke Newington High St 122 DT62
Hollen St, W1 285 N8
Holles Cl, Hmptn. TW12 176 CA93
Holles St, W1 285 K8
Holley Rd, W3 158 CS75
Hollickwood Av, N12 98 DF51
Sch Hollickwood Prim Sch, N10
off Sydney Rd 99 DH52
Holliday Sq, SW11
off Fowler Cl 160 DD83
Holliday St, Berk. HP4 38 AX19
Hollidge Way, Dag. RM10 147 FB65
Hollie Cl, Smallfield RH6 269 DP149
Hollier Ct, Hat. AL10
off Cranborne Rd 45 CV17
Holliers Way, Hat. AL10 45 CU18
Hollies, The, E11 124 EG57
N20 off Oakleigh Pk N 98 DD46
Bovingdon HP3 57 BA29
Gravesend DA12 191 GK93
Harrow HA3 117 CG56
Oxted RH8 254 EH133
Welwyn Garden City AL8 29 CV13
Hollies Av, Sid. DA15 185 ET89
West Byfleet KT14 211 BF113
Hollies Cl, SW16 181 DN93
Twickenham TW1 177 CF89
Hollies Ct, Add. KT15 212 BJ106
Hollies End, NW7 97 CV50
Hollies Rd, W5 157 CJ77
Hollies Way, SW12
off Bracken Av 180 DG87
Potters Bar EN6 64 DC31
Holligrave Rd, Brom. BR1 204 EG95
Hollingbourne Av, Bexh. DA7 166 EZ80
Hollingbourne Gdns, W13 137 CH71
Hollingbourne Rd, SE24 182 DQ85
Hollingbourne Twr, Orp. BR5 206 EX102
Hollingsworth Ms, Wat. WD25
off Bramble Cl 59 BU34
Hollingsworth Rd, Croy. CR0 220 DV107
Hollington Cres, N.Mal. KT3 199 CT100
Hollington Rd, E6 293 J3
N17 100 DU54
Hollingworth Cl, W.Mol. KT8 196 BZ98
Hollingworth Rd, Petts Wd BR5 205 EP100
Hollingworth Way, West. TN16 255 ER126
Hollins Ho, N7
off Tufnell Pk Rd 121 DL63
Hollis Pl, Grays RM17
off Ward Av 170 GA77
Hollman Gdns, SW16 181 DP93
Hollow, The, Wdf.Grn. IG8 102 EF49
HOLLOWAY, N7 276 B2
Holloway Cl, West Dr. UB7 154 BL78
Holloway Dr, Vir.W. GU25 192 AY98
Holloway Hill, Cher. KT16 193 BC104
Holloway La, Chenies WD3 73 BD36
West Drayton UB7 154 BL79
⊖ Holloway Road 276 D2
Holloway Rd, E6 293 K3
E11 124 EE62
N7 276 F4
N19 121 DK61
Sch Holloway Sch, N7 275 P2
Holloways La, N.Mymms AL9 45 CX23
Holloway St, Houns. TW3 156 CB83
Hollow Cl, Guil. GU2
off Lynwood 258 AV135
Hollow Cotts, Purf. RM19 168 FN78
Hollowfield Av, Grays RM17 170 GD77
Hollowfield Wk, Nthlt. UB5 136 BY65
Hollow Hill La, Iver SL0 133 BB73
Hollow La, Vir.W. GU25 192 AY97
Wotton RH5 262 BX140
Hollows, The, Brent. TW8 158 CM79
Hollow Wk, Kew TW9
off Royal Botanic Gdns 158 CL80
Hollow Way La, Amer. HP6 55 AS35
Chesham HP5 55 AS35
Holly Av, New Haw KT15 212 BG110
Stanmore HA7 96 CL54
Walton-on-Thames KT12 196 BX102
Hollybank Cl, Hmptn. TW12 176 CA92
Hollybank Rd, W.Byf. KT14 212 BG114
Holly Bk Rd, Wok. GU22 226 AV121
Hollyberry La, NW3
off Holly Wk 120 DC63
Hollybrake Cl, Chis. BR7 185 ER94
Hollybush Av, St.Alb. AL2 42 CA24
Hollybush Cl, E11 124 EG57
Harrow HA3 95 CE53
Potten End HP4 39 BD16
Sevenoaks TN13 257 FJ124
Watford WD19 94 BW45
Hollybush Ct, Sev. TN13 257 FJ124
Hollybush Gdns, E2 288 F2
Hollybush Hill, E11 124 EF58
Stoke Poges SL2 132 AU66
Holly Bush Hill, NW3 120 DC63
Hollybush La, Amer. HP6 55 AR37
Denham UB9 113 BE63
Hemel Hempstead HP1 39 BF19
Iver SL0 133 BB73
Orpington BR6 224 FA107
Ripley GU23 228 BK119
Welwyn Garden City AL7 29 CZ13
Holly Bush La, Hmptn. TW12 176 BZ94
Sevenoaks TN13 257 FJ123
Hollybush Pl, E2 288 F2
Sch Hollybush Prim Sch, Hert. SG14
off Fordwich Ri 31 DN09
Hollybush Rd, Chesh. HP5 54 AN27
Gravesend DA12 191 GJ89
Kingston upon Thames KT2 178 CL92
Holly Bush Steps, NW3
off Heath St 120 DC63
Hollybush St, E13 292 B2
Holly Bush Vale, NW3
off Heath St 120 DC63
Hollybush Way, Chsht EN7 66 DU28
Holly Cl, Beck. BR3 203 EC98
Buckhurst Hill IG9 102 EK48
Englefield Green TW20 172 AV93
Epsom KT19 216 CR109
Farnham Common SL2 111 AQ63
Feltham TW13 176 BY92
Hatfield AL10 45 CT19
Longcross KT16 192 AU104
Sunbury-on-Thames TW16 195 BV97
Wallington SM6 219 DH108
Woking GU21 226 AV119
Hollycombe, Eng.Grn TW20 172 AW91
Holly Cottage Ms, Uxb. UB8
off Pield Heath Rd 134 BN71
Holly Ct, SE10 303 M7
Romford RM1
off Dolphin App 127 FF56
Sutton SM2
off Worcester Rd 218 DA108
Holly Cres, Beck. BR3 203 DZ99
Windsor SL4 151 AK82
Woodford Green IG8 101 ED52
Holly Cft, Hert. SG14 31 DN08
Hollycroft Av, NW3 120 DA62
Wembley HA9 118 CM61
Hollycroft Cl, Sipson UB7 154 BN79
South Croydon CR2 220 DS106
Hollycroft Gdns, Sipson UB7 154 BN79
Hollycross Rd, Ware SG12 33 DZ07
Hollydale Dr, Brom. BR2 205 EM104
Sch Hollydale Prim Sch, SE15 313 H9
Hollydale Rd, SE15 312 G7
Hollydell, Hert. SG13 32 DQ11
Hollydene, SE15 312 E6
Hollydown Way, E11 123 ED62
Holly Dr, E4 101 EB45
Berkhamsted HP4 38 AX20
Brentford TW8 157 CG79
Potters Bar EN6 64 DB33
South Ockendon RM15 149 FX70
Windsor SL4 172 AS85
Holly Fm Rd, Sthl. UB2 156 BY78
Holly Fld, Harl. CM19 51 EQ18
Hollyfield, Hat. AL10 45 CU21
Hollyfield Av, N11 98 DF50
Hollyfield Rd, Surb. KT5 198 CM101
Hollyfields, Brox. EN10 67 DY26
Sch Hollyfield Sch & 6th Form Cen, The, Surb. KT6
off Surbiton Hill Rd 198 CL99
Holly Gdns, Bexh. DA7 167 FC84
West Drayton UB7 154 BM75
Holly Gate, Add. KT15 212 BH105
Holly Grn, Wey. KT13 195 BR104
Holly Gro, NW9 118 CQ59
SE15 312 B8
Bushey WD23 95 CD45
Pinner HA5 94 BY53
Hollygrove Cl, Houns. TW3 156 BZ84
Holly Gro Rd, Bramfld SG14 31 DH07
Hollyhedge Rd, Cob. KT11 213 BV114
Holly Hedges La, Bov. HP3 57 BC30
Rickmansworth WD3 57 BC30
Holly Hedge Ter, SE13 183 ED85
Holly Hill, N21 81 DM44
NW3 120 DC63
Holly Hill Dr, Bans. SM7 234 DA117
Holly Hill Pk, Bans. SM7 234 DA117
Holly Hill Rd, Belv. DA17 167 FB78
Erith DA8 167 FB78
Hollyhock Cl, Hem.H. HP1 39 BE18
Holly Ho, Brwd. CM15
off Sawyers Hall La 108 FX46
H Holly Ho Hosp, Buck.H. IG9 102 EH47
● Holly Ind Pk, Wat. WD24 76 BW39
Holly La, Bans. SM7 234 DA116
Ilford IG3
off Goodmayes La 126 EU61
Holly La E, Bans. SM7 234 DA116
Holly La W, Bans. SM7 234 DA117
Holly Lea, Jacobs Well GU4 242 AX128
Holly Lo, Lwr Kgswd KT20 249 CY126
Holly Lo Gdns, N6 120 DG61
Hollymead, Cars. SM5 200 DF104
Hollymead Rd, Chipstead CR5 234 DG118
Hollymeoak Rd, Couls. CR5 235 DH119
Holly Ms, SW10 307 P1
Hollymoor La, Epsom KT19 216 CR110

H

Holly Mt, NW3
off Holly Bush Hill 120 DC63
Hollymount Cl, SE10 314 E6
Sch Hollymount Prim Sch, SW20
off Cambridge Rd 199 CW95
Holly Pk, N3 119 CZ55
N4 121 DM59
Holly Pk Est, N4
off Blythwood Rd 121 DL59
Holly Pk Gdns, N3 120 DA55
Sch Holly Pk Prim Sch, N11
off Bellevue Rd 98 DG50
Holly Pk Rd, N11 98 DG50
W7 137 CF74
Holly Pl, NW3 off Holly Wk 120 DC63
Holly Rd, E11
off Green Man Rbt 124 EF59
W4 off Dolman Rd 158 CR77
Dartford DA1 188 FK88
Enfield EN3 83 DX36
Hampton Hill TW12 176 CC93
Hounslow TW3 156 CB84
Orpington BR6 224 EU108
Reigate RH2 266 DB136
Twickenham TW1 177 CG88
Holly St, E8 278 B6
Holly Ter, N6
off Highgate W Hill 120 DG60
N20 off Swan La 98 DC47
Hollytree Av, Swan. BR8 207 FE96
Hollytree Cl, SW19 179 CX88
Chalfont St. Peter SL9 90 AY50
Holly Tree Cl, Ley Hill HP5 56 AV31
Holly Tree Rd, Cat. CR3
off Elm Gro 236 DS122
Sch Holly Trees Prim Sch, Warley CM14
off Vaughan Williams Way 108 FV49
Hollyview Cl, NW4 119 CU58
Holly Village, N6
off Swains La 121 DH61
Holly Wk, NW3 273 N1
Enfield EN2 82 DQ41
Richmond TW9 158 CL82
Welwyn Garden City AL8 29 CW05
Holly Way, Mitch. CR4 201 DK98
Hollywood Ct, Els. WD6
off Deacons Hill Rd 78 CM42
Hollywood Gdns, Hayes UB4 135 BV72
Hollywood Ms, SW10 307 N2
Hollywood Rd, E4 101 DY50
SW10 307 N1
Hollywoods, Croy. CR0 221 DZ109
Hollywood Way, Erith DA8 167 FH81
Woodford Green IG8 101 ED52
Holman Ho, E2
off Roman Rd 289 J2
Holman Rd, SW11 308 A9
Epsom KT19 216 CQ106
Holmbank Dr, Shep. TW17 195 BS98
Holmbridge Gdns, Enf. EN3 83 DX42
Holmbrook Dr, NW4 119 CX57
Holmbury Ct, SW17 180 DF90
SW19 180 DE94
Holmbury Dr, N.Holm. RH5 263 CJ139
Holmbury Gdns, Hayes UB3 135 BT74
Holmbury Gro, Croy. CR0 221 DZ108
Holmbury Keep, Horl. RH6
off Langshott La 269 DJ147
Holmbury Pk, Brom. BR1 184 EL94
Holmbury Vw, E5 122 DV60
Holmbush Rd, SW15 179 CY86
Holm Cl, Wdhm KT15 211 BE112
Holmcote Gdns, N5 277 J3
Holmcroft, Walt.Hill KT20 249 CV125
Holmcroft Way, Brom. BR2 205 EM99
Holmdale Cl, Borwd. WD6 78 CM40
Holmdale Gdns, NW4 119 CX57
Holmdale Rd, NW6 273 J3
Chislehurst BR7 185 EQ92
Holmdale Ter, N15 122 DS59
Holmdene Av, NW7 97 CU51
SE24 182 DQ85
Harrow HA2 116 CB55
Holmdene Cl, Beck. BR3 203 EC96
Holmead Rd, SW6 307 M5
Holmebury Cl,
Bushey Hth WD23 95 CE47
Holme Chase, Wey. KT13 213 BQ107
Holme Cl, Chsht EN8 67 DY31
Hatfield AL10 45 CT15
Holme Ct, Islw. TW7
off Twickenham Rd 157 CG83
Holmedale, Slou. SL2 132 AW73
Holmefield Ct, NW3 274 D4
Holme Lacey Rd, SE12 184 EF86
Holme Lea, Wat. WD25 60 BW34
Holme Oak Av, Rain. RM13 147 FG68
Holme Pk, Borwd. WD6 78 CM40
Holme Pl, Hem.H. HP2
off Crest Pk 41 BQ19
Holme Rd, E6 144 EL67
Hatfield AL10 45 CT15
Hornchurch RM11 128 FN60
Holmes Av, E17 123 DZ55
NW7 97 CY50
Holmes Cl, SE22 162 DU84
Purley CR8 219 DM113
Woking GU22 227 AZ121
Holmes Ct, SW4
off Paradise Rd 310 A8
Gravesend DA12 191 GM88
Holmesdale, Wal.Cr. EN8 83 DX35
Holmesdale Av, SW14 158 CP83
Redhill RH1 251 DJ131
Holmesdale Cl, SE25 202 DT97
Guildford GU1 243 BB133
Sch Holmesdale Comm Inf Sch,
Reig. RH2 off Alma Rd 250 DB132
Holmesdale Hill, S.Darenth DA4 208 FQ95
Holmesdale Manor, Red. RH1 250 DG132
Holmesdale Pk, Nutfld RH1 251 DM134
Holmesdale Rd, N6 121 DH59
SE25 202 DR99
Bexleyheath DA7 166 EX82
Croydon CR0 202 DR99
North Holmwood RH5 263 CH140
Reigate RH2 250 DA133
Richmond TW9 158 CM81
Sevenoaks TN13 257 FJ123
South Darenth DA4 208 FQ95
South Nutfield RH1 267 DM136
Teddington TW11 177 CJ94
Holmesdale Ter, N.Holm. RH5 263 CH140
Holmesley Rd, SE23 183 DY86
Holmes Meadow, Harl. CM19 51 EP21
Holmes Pl, SW10 307 P2
Holmes Rd, NW5 275 J4
SW19 180 DC94
Twickenham TW1 177 CF89
Holmes Ter, SE1 298 E4
HOLMETHORPE, Red. RH1 251 DH132
Holmethorpe Av, Red. RH1 251 DH131
● Holmethorpe Ind Est,
Red. RH1 251 DH131
Holme Way, Stan. HA7 95 CF51
Holmewood Gdns, SW2 181 DM87
Holmewood Rd, SE25 202 DS97
SW2 181 DL87
Holmfield Av, NW4 119 CX57
Holm Gro, Uxb. UB10 134 BN66
Holmhurst Rd, Belv. DA17 167 FB78
Holmlea Rd, Datchet SL3 152 AX81
Holmlea Wk, Datchet SL3 152 AW81
Holmleigh Av, Dart. DA1 168 FJ84
Sch Holmleigh Prim Sch, N16
off Dunsmure Rd 122 DT60
Holmleigh Rd, N16 122 DS60
Holmleigh Rd Est, N16
off Holmleigh Rd 122 DS60
Holmoak Cl, Pur. CR8 219 DM110
Holm Oak Cl, SW15 179 CZ86
Holm Oak Ms, SW4 181 DL85
Holm Oak Pk, Wat. WD18 75 BT43
Holmsdale Cl, Iver SL0 133 BF72
Holmsdale Gro, Bexh. DA7 167 FE82
Holmshaw Cl, SE26 183 DY91
Holmshill La, Borwd. WD6 78 CS36
Holmside Ri, Wat. WD19 93 BV48
Holmside Rd, SW12 180 DG86
Holmsley Cl, N.Mal. KT3 199 CT100
Holmsley Ho, SW15
off Tangley Gro 179 CT87
Holms St, E2 278 C10
Holmstall Av, Edg. HA8 118 CQ55
Holm Wk, SE3 315 P9
Holmwood Av, Shenf. CM15 109 GA44
South Croydon CR2 220 DT113
Holmwood Cl, Add. KT15 212 BG106
East Horsley KT24 245 BS128
Harrow HA2 116 CC55
Northolt UB5 136 CB65
Sutton SM2 217 CX109
Holmwood Gdns, N3 98 DA54
Wallington SM6 219 DH107
Holmwood Gro, NW7 96 CR50
Holmwood Rd, Chess. KT9 215 CK106
Enfield EN3 83 DX36
Ilford IG3 125 ES61
Sutton SM2 217 CW110
Holmwood Vw Rd, Mid Holm.
RH5 off Horsham Rd 263 CH142
Holmwood Vil, SE7 303 P10
Holne Chase, N2 120 DC58
Morden SM4 199 CZ100
Holness Rd, E15 281 L5
Holroyd Cl, Clay. KT10 215 CF109
Holroyd Rd, SW15 159 CW84
Claygate KT10 215 CF109
Holsart Cl, Tad. KT20 233 CV122
Holstein Av, Wey. KT13 212 BN105
Holstein Way, Erith DA18 166 EY76
Holst Ho, W12
off Du Cane Rd 139 CV72
Holstock Rd, Ilf. IG1 125 EQ61
Holsworth Cl, Har. HA2 116 CC57
Holsworthy Sq, WC1 286 D5
Holsworthy Way, Chess. KT9 215 CJ106
Holt, The, Hem.H. HP2
off Turners Hill 40 BL21
Ilford IG6 103 EQ51
Morden SM4 off London Rd 200 DA98
Wallington SM6 219 DJ105
Welwyn Garden City AL7 30 DD10
Holt Cl, N10 120 DG56
SE28 146 EV73
Chigwell IG7 103 ET50
Elstree WD6 78 CM42
Holton St, E1 289 J4
Holt Rd, E16 305 H3
Romford RM3 106 FL52
Wembley HA0 117 CH62
Holtsmere Cl, Wat. WD25 76 BW35
Sch Holtsmere End Inf & Nurs Sch,
Hem.H. HP2 off Shenley Rd 41 BP15
Sch Holtsmere End Jun Sch,
Hem.H. HP2 off Shenley Rd 41 BP15
HOLTSPUR, Beac. HP9 88 AF54
Holtspur Av, Woob.Grn HP10 110 AE56
Holtspur Cl, Beac. HP9 88 AG54
Holtspur La, Woob.Grn HP10 110 AE57
Sch Holtspur Sch, Holt. HP9
off Cherry Tree Rd 88 AG54
Holtspur Top La, Beac. HP9 88 AG54
Holtspur Way, Beac. HP9 88 AG54
Holt Way, Chig. IG7 103 ET50
Holtwhite Av, Enf. EN2 82 DQ40
Holtwhites Hill, Enf. EN2 81 DP39
Holtwood Rd, Oxshott KT22 214 CC113
Holwell Caravan Site, Hat. AL9 30 DE14
Holwell Hyde, Welw.G.C. AL7 30 DC11
Holwell Hyde La, Welw.G.C. AL7 30 DC12
Holwell La, Hat. AL9 30 DE14
Holwell Pl, Pnr. HA5 116 BY56
Sch Holwell Prim Sch,
Welw.G.C. AL7 off Holwell Rd 29 CZ10
Holwell Rd, Welw.G.C. AL7 29 CY10
Holwood Cl, Walt. KT12 196 BW103
Holwood Pk Av, Orp. BR6 223 EM105
Holwood Pl, SW4 161 DK84
Holy Acre, Roydon CM19
off Roydon Mill Pk 34 EG14
Holybourne Av, SW15 179 CU87
Sch Holy Cross Cath Prim Sch,
SE6 off Culverley Rd 183 EC88
SW6 307 J6
Harlow CM18 off Tracyes Rd 52 EU17
South Ockendon RM15
off Daiglen Dr 149 FV72
Sch Holy Cross Conv Sch,
Chal.St.P. SL9 off Gold Hill E 90 AX53
Holy Cross Hill, Brox. EN10 48 DU24
Sch Holy Cross Prep Sch,
Kings.T. KT2 off George Rd 178 CQ94
Sch Holy Cross Sch, The,
N.Mal. KT3 off Sandal Rd 198 CS99
Sch Holy Family Catholic Prim Sch,
Add. KT15 off Ongar Hill 212 BG106
Langley SL3 off High St 153 AZ78
Sch Holy Family RC Prim Sch,
E14 290 C10
SE3 off Tudway Rd 164 EJ84
Welwyn Garden City AL7
off Crookhams 30 DA06
Sch Holy Family Tech Coll, E17
off Shernhall St 123 EC55
Wiseman Ho Site, E17
off Shernhall St 123 EC56
HOLYFIELD, Wal.Abb. EN9 67 ED28
Holyfield, Wal.Abb. EN9 67 EC29
Sch Holy Ghost RC Prim Sch,
SW12 off Nightingale Sq 180 DG87
Holyhead Cl, E6 293 J6
Holyhead Ms, Slou. SL1 131 AL72
Sch Holy Innocents Cath Prim Sch,
Orp. BR6 off Mitchell Rd 205 ET104
Holyoake Av, Wok. GU21 226 AW117
Holyoake Ct, SE16 301 M4
Holyoake Cres, Wok. GU21 226 AW117
Holyoake Ter, Sev. TN13 256 FG124
Holyoake Wk, N2 120 DC55
W5 137 CJ70
Holyoak Rd, SE11 298 G8
HOLYPORT, Maid. SL6 150 AC78
Holyport Rd, SW6 306 B4
Holyrood Av, Har. HA2 116 BY63
Holyrood Cres, St.Alb. AL1 43 CD24
Holyrood Gdns, Edg. HA8 118 CP55
Grays RM16 171 GJ77
Holyrood Ms, E16 303 P2
Holyrood Rd, New Barn. EN5 80 DC44
Sch Holy Rood RC Prim Sch,
Wat. WD17 off Greenbank Rd 75 BR36
Holyrood St, SE1
off Bermondsey St 299 N3
Sch Holy Trinity & St. Silas C of E
Prim Sch, NW1 275 J6
Sch Holy Trinity C of E Jun Sch,
Wall. SM6 off Bute Rd 219 DJ105
Sch Holy Trinity C of E Jun Sch Guildford,
Guil. GU1 off Addison Rd 259 AZ136
Sch Holy Trinity C of E
Prim Sch, E8 278 A5
N2 off Eagans Cl 120 DD55
NW3 273 P5
SE23 off Dartmouth Rd 182 DW89
Jun, SW1 296 G8
SW2 off Upper Tulse Hill 181 DM87
Inf, SW3 296 F8
SW19 off Effra Rd 180 DB93
Dartford DA1
off Chatsworth Rd 188 FJ85
Gravesend DA12 off Trinity Rd 213 GJ87
Northwood HA6
off Rickmansworth Rd 93 BQ51
Richmond TW10
off Carrington Rd 158 CN84
Waltham Cross EN8
off Crossbrook St 67 DX32
Sch Holy Trinity Lamorbey C of E
Prim Sch, Sid. DA15
off Burnt Oak La 186 EU88
Holy Wk, Brox. EN10
off St. Catharines Rd 49 EA19
Hoddesdon EN11 off High St 49 EA18
HOLYWELL, Wat. WD18 75 BS44
Holywell Cl, SE3 315 P2
SE16 300 F10
Orpington BR6 224 EU105
Staines-upon-Thames TW19 174 BL88
Holywell Hill, St.Alb. AL1 42 CC21
● Holywell Ind Est, Wat. WD18 93 BR45
Holywell La, EC2 287 P4
Sch Holywell Prim Sch,
Wat. WD18 off Tolpits La 75 BT44
Holywell Rd, Wat. WD18 75 BU43
Holywell Row, EC2 287 N5
Holywell Way, Stai. TW19 174 BL88
Homan Ct, N12 98 DC49
Home Barn Ct, Eff. KT24
off The Street 246 BX127
Home Cl, Brox. EN10 49 DZ24
Carshalton SM5 200 DF103
Fetcham KT22 231 CD121
Harlow CM20 51 ET15
Northolt UB5 136 BZ69
Virginia Water GU25 192 AX100
Homecroft Gdns, Loug. IG10 85 EP42
Homecroft Rd, N22 99 DP53
SE26 182 DW92
Homedean Rd,
Chipstead TN13 256 FC122
Home Fm, Orp. BR6 224 FA106
Home Fm Cl, Bet. RH3 264 CS135
Esher KT10 214 CB107
Ottershaw KT16 211 BA108
Shepperton TW17 195 BS98
Tadworth KT20 233 CX117
Thames Ditton KT7 197 CF101
Home Fm Gdns, Walt. KT12 196 BW103
● Home Fm Ind Est,
Stans.Abb. SG12 34 EF10
Homefarm Rd, W7 137 CE72
Home Fm Rd, N.Mymms AL9 63 CV26
Rickmansworth WD3 92 BN49
Home Fm Way, Stoke P. SL3 132 AW67
Homefield, Bov. HP3 57 BB28
Waltham Abbey EN9 68 EG32
Walton-on-Thames KT12 214 BX105
Home Fld, Pott.End HP4 39 BB16
Homefield Av, Ilf. IG2 125 ES57
Homefield Cl, NW10 138 CQ65
Epping CM16 70 EU30
Hayes UB4 136 BW70
Horley RH6 off Tanyard Way 269 DH147
Leatherhead KT22 231 CJ121
St. Paul's Cray BR5 206 EV98
Swanley BR8 207 FF97
Woodham KT15 211 BE112
Homefield Fm Rd, Sutt.H. DA4 208 FM96
Homefield Gdns, N2 120 DD55
Mitcham CR4 200 DC96
Tadworth KT20 233 CW120
Homefield Ms, Beck. BR3 203 EA95
Homefield Pk, Sutt. SM1 218 DB107
Homefield Pl, Croy. CR0 202 DT103
Sch Homefield Prep Sch,
Sutt. SM1 off Western Rd 218 DA106
Homefield Ri, Orp. BR6 206 EU102
Homefield Rd, SW19 179 CX93
W4 159 CT77
Bromley BR1 204 EJ95
Bushey WD23 76 CA43
Chorleywood WD3 73 BC42
Coulsdon CR5 235 DP119
Edgware HA8 96 CR51
Hemel Hempstead HP2 40 BN20
Radlett WD7 77 CF37
Sevenoaks TN13 256 FE122
Walton-on-Thames KT12 196 BY101
Ware SG12 33 DY05
Warlingham CR6 236 DW119
Wembley HA0 117 CG63
Homefield St, N1 287 N1
Homefirs Ho, Wem. HA9 118 CM62
Home Gdns, Dag. RM10 127 FC62
Dartford DA1 188 FL86
Home Hill, Swan. BR8 187 FF94
Homeland Dr, Sutt. SM2 218 DB109
Homelands, Lthd. KT22 231 CJ121
Homelands Dr, SE19 182 DS94
Home Lea, Orp. BR6 223 ET106
Homeleigh Ct, Chsht EN8 66 DV29
Homeleigh Rd, SE15 183 DX85
Home Ley, Welw.G.C. AL7 29 CY10
Homemead, SW12 181 DH89
Home Mead, Stan. HA7 95 CJ53
Homemead Cl, Grav. DA12 191 GH87
Homemead Ct, Grav. DA12
off Homemead Cl 191 GH87
Home Meadow, Bans. SM7 234 DA116
Farnham Royal SL2 131 AQ68
Welwyn Garden City AL7 29 CZ09
Home Meadow Ms, SE22 182 DU85
Homemead Rd, Brom. BR2 205 EM99
Croydon CR0 201 DJ100
★ Home Office, SW1 297 P7
Home Orchard, Dart. DA1 188 FL86
Home Pk,
E.Mol (Hampton Ct Pk) KT8 197 CH98
Kingston upon Thames
(Hampton Ct Pk) KT1 197 CH98
Oxted RH8 254 EG131
● Home Pk Ind Est,
Kings L. WD4 59 BP30
Home Pk Mill Link Rd,
Kings L. WD4 59 BP31
Home Pk Par, Kings.T. KT1
off High St 197 CK96
Home Pk Rd, SW19 180 DA90
Home Pk Wk, Kings.T. KT1 197 CK98
Homer Cl, Bexh. DA7 167 FC81
Homer Dr, E14 302 A9
Homerfield, Welw.G.C. AL8 29 CW08
Sch Homer First Sch, Wind. SL4
off Testwood Rd 151 AK81
Home Rd, SW11 308 C8
Homer Rd, E9 279 M5
Croydon CR0 203 DX100
Homer Row, W1 284 D7
Homersham Rd, Kings.T. KT1 198 CN96
Homers Rd, Wind. SL4 151 AK81
Homer St, W1 284 D7
Homerswood La, Welw. AL6 29 CU05
Sch Homerswood Prim Sch,
Welw.G.C. AL8 off Kirklands 29 CX05
HOMERTON, E9 279 M3
⇌ Homerton 279 J4
Homerton Gro, E9 279 J3
Homerton High St, E9 279 H3
Homerton Rd, E9 279 M2
Homerton Row, E9 279 H3
Homerton Ter, E9 279 H4
H Homerton Uni Hosp, E9 279 J2
Homesdale Cl, E11 124 EG57
Homesdale Rd,
Brom. BR1, BR2 204 EJ98
Caterham CR3 236 DR123
Petts Wood BR5 205 ES101
Homesfield, NW11 120 DA57
Homestall Rd, SE22 182 DW85
Homestead, The, N11 99 DH49
Dartford DA1 188 FJ86
Homestead Cl, Park St AL2 60 CC27
Homestead Ct, Welw.G.C. AL7 29 CZ11
Homestead Gdns, Clay. KT10 215 CE106
Homestead La, Welw.G.C. AL7 29 CZ12
Homestead Paddock, N14 81 DH43
Homestead Pk, NW2 119 CT62
Homestead Rd, SW6 306 G5
Caterham CR3 236 DR123
Dagenham RM8 126 EZ61
Hatfield AL10 45 CU15
Orpington BR6 224 EV108
Rickmansworth WD3 92 BK45
Staines-upon-Thames TW18 174 BH93
Homesteads, The, Hunsdon
SG12 off Hunsdon Rd 34 EK07
Homestead Way,
New Adgtn CR0 221 EC111
Homewaters Av, Sun. TW16 195 BT95
Home Way, Mill End WD3 91 BF46
Homeway, Rom. RM3 106 FP51
Homewillow Cl, N21 81 DP44
Homewood, Geo.Grn SL3 132 AX72
Homewood Av, Cuffley EN6 65 DL27
Homewood Cl, Hmptn. TW12 176 BZ93
Homewood Cres, Chis. BR7 185 ES93
Sch Homewood Indep Sch,
Park St AL2 off Hazel Rd 60 CB28
Homewood La, Northaw EN6 65 DJ27
Homewood Rd, St.Alb. AL1 43 CH17
Homildon Ho, SE26
off Sydenham Hill Est 182 DU90
Honduras St, EC1 287 J4
Honeybourne Rd, NW6 273 L2
Honeybourne Way,
Petts Wd BR5 205 ER102
Honey Brook, Wal.Abb. EN9 68 EE33
Honeybrook Rd, SW12 181 DJ87
Honey Cl, Dag. RM10 147 FB65
Honeycrock La, Red. RH1 266 DG141
Honeycroft, Loug. IG10 85 EN42
Welwyn Garden City AL8 29 CW10
Honeycroft Dr, St.Alb. AL4 43 CJ22
Honeycroft Hill, Uxb. UB10 134 BL66
Honeycross Rd, Hem.H. HP1 39 BE21
Honeyden Rd, Sid. DA14 186 EY93
Honey Hill, Uxb. UB10 134 BM66
Honey La, EC2 287 K9
Hertford SG14 off Fore St 32 DR09
Waltham Abbey EN9 84 EG35
Honeyman Cl, NW6 272 C6
Honeymeade, Saw. CM21 36 EW08
Honey Ms, SE27
off Chapel Rd 182 DQ91
● Honeypot Business Cen,
Stan. HA7 96 CL53
Honeypot Cl, NW9 118 CM56
Honeypot La, NW9 118 CM55
Brentwood CM14 108 FU48
Stanmore HA7 118 CM55
Waltham Abbey EN9 68 EJ34
Honeypots Rd, Wok. GU22 226 AX122
Honeysett Rd, N17
off Reform Row 100 DT54
Honeysuckle Bottom,
E.Hors. KT24 245 BS134
Honeysuckle Cl, Hert. SG13 32 DU09
Horley RH6 269 DJ147
Iver SL0 133 BC72
Pilgrim's Hatch CM15 108 FV43
Honeysuckle Cl, Romford RM3 106 FJ51
Southall UB1 136 BY73
Honeysuckle Fld, Chesh. HP5 54 AQ30
Honeysuckle Gdns, Croy. CR0 203 DX101
Hatfield AL10 45 CV19
Honeysuckle La, N.Holm. RH5
off Treelands 263 CJ139
Sch Honeywell Inf & Jun Schs,
SW11 off Honeywell Rd 180 DF86
Honeywell Rd, SW11 180 DF86
Honeywood Cl, Pot.B. EN6 64 DE33
★ Honeywood Heritage Cen,
Cars. SM5 218 DF106
Honeywood Rd, NW10 139 CT68
Isleworth TW7 157 CG84
Honeywood Wk, Cars. SM5 218 DF105
Sch Honilands Prim Sch,
Enf. EN1 off Lovell Rd 82 DV36
Honister Cl, Stan. HA7 95 CH53
Honister Gdns, Stan. HA7 95 CH52
Honister Hts, Pur. CR8 220 DR114
Honister Pl, Stan. HA7 95 CH53
Honiton Gdns, NW7 97 CX52
SE15 off Gibbon Rd 313 H9
Honiton Ho, Enf. EN3
off Exeter Rd 83 DX41
Honiton Rd, NW6 272 G10
Romford RM7 127 FD58
Welling DA16 165 ET82
Honley Rd, SE6 183 EB87
Honnor Gdns, Islw. TW7 157 CD82
Honnor Rd, Stai. TW18 174 BK94
HONOR OAK, SE23 182 DW86
HONOR OAK PARK, SE4 183 DY86
⇌ Honor Oak Park 183 DX86
⊖ Honor Oak Park 183 DX86
Honor Oak Pk, SE23 182 DW86
Honor Oak Ri, SE23 182 DW86
Honor Oak Rd, SE23 182 DW88
Honor St, Harl. CM17 36 EX14
Honour Lea Ave, E20 280 D3
Hoo, The, Harl. CM17 36 EW10
Hood Av, N14 81 DH44
SW14 178 CQ85
Orpington BR5 206 EV99
Hood Cl, Croy. CR0 201 DP102
Hoodcote Gdns, N21 99 DP45
Hood Ct, EC4 286 F9
Hood Rd, SW20 179 CT94
Rainham RM13 147 FE67
Hood Wk, Rom. RM7 105 FB53
HOOK, Chess. KT9 216 CL105
Hook, The, New Barn. EN5 80 DD44
Hooke Rd, E.Hors. KT24 245 BT125
Hookers Rd, E17 123 DX55
Hook Fm Rd, Brom. BR2 204 EK99
Hookfield, Epsom KT18 216 CQ113
Harlow CM18 51 ES17
Hookfields, Nthflt DA11 190 GE90
Hook Gate, Enf. EN1 82 DV36
HOOK GREEN, Dart. DA2 187 FG91
Grav. DA13 190 FZ93
Hook Grn La, Dart. DA2 187 FF90
Hook Grn Rd, Sthflt DA13 190 FY94
HOOK HEATH, Wok. GU22 226 AV120
Hook Heath Av, Wok. GU22 226 AV119
Hook Heath Gdns, Wok. GU22 226 AT121
Hook Heath Rd, Wok. GU22 226 AW121
Hook Hill, S.Croy. CR2 220 DS110
Hook Hill La, Wok. GU22 226 AV121
Hook Hill Pk, Wok. GU22 226 AV121
Hooking Grn, Har. HA2 116 CB57
Jct Hook Junct, Surb. KT6 197 CK104
Hook La, Northaw EN6 64 DF32
Romford RM4 86 EZ44
Shere GU5 260 BN141
Welling DA16 185 ET85
Sch Hook La Prim Sch,
Well. DA16 off Faraday Rd 166 EU83
Hook Ri N, Surb. KT6 198 CN104
Hook Ri S, Surb. KT6 198 CN104
● Hook Ri S Business Cen,
Surb. KT6 198 CN104
● Hook Ri S Ind Pk, Surb. KT6 198 CM104
Hook Rd, Chess. KT9 215 CK106
Epsom KT19 216 CR111
Surbiton KT6 198 CL104
Hooks Cl, SE15 312 F7
Hooks Hall Dr, Dag. RM10 127 FC62
Hookstone Way, Wdf.Grn. IG8 102 EK52
Hook Wk, Edg. HA8 96 CQ51
HOOKWOOD, Horl. RH6 268 DC150
Hookwood Cor, Oxt. RH8
off Hookwood Pk 254 EH128
Hookwood Cotts,
Headley KT18 232 CQ123
Hookwood Pk, Oxt. RH8 254 EH128
Hookwood Rd, Orp. BR6 224 EW111
Hool Cl, NW9 118 CQ57
HOOLEY, Couls. CR5 234 DG122
Hooley La, Red. RH1 266 DF135
Hooper Dr, Uxb. UB8 135 BP71
Hooper Rd, E16 291 P9
Hooper's Ct, SW3 296 E5
Hoopers Ms, W3 138 CQ74
Hooper's Ms, Bushey WD23 94 CB46
Hooper St, E1 288 C10
Hoopers Yd, NW6 272 G8
Sevenoaks TN13 257 FJ126
Hoop La, NW11 119 CZ59
Hope Cl, N1 277 K4
SE12 184 EH90
Brentford TW8 158 CL78
Chadwell Heath RM6 126 EW56
Sutton SM1 218 DC106
Woodford Green IG8
Honeysuckle Cl, off West Gro 102 EJ51
Sch Hope Comm Sch, Sid. DA14
off Rectory La 186 EW92
Hopedale Rd, SE7 164 EH79
Hopefield Av, NW6 272 F10
Hope Gdns, W3
off Park Rd N 158 CP75
Hope Grn, Wat. WD25 59 BU33
Hope La, SE9 185 EP89
Hope Pk, Brom. BR1 184 EF94
Hope Rd, Swans. DA10 190 FZ86
Hopes Cl, Houns. TW5
off Old Cote Dr 156 CA79
Hope St, SW11 160 DD83
Hope Ter, Grays RM20 169 FX78
Hopetown St, E1 288 B7
Hopewell Cl, Chaff.Hun. RM16 169 FX78
Hopewell Dr, Grav. DA12 191 GM92
Hopewell St, SE5 311 M5
Hopewell Yd, SE5 311 M5
Hope Wf, SE16
off St. Marychurch St 300 G4
Hopfield, Horsell GU21 226 AY116

Hopfield Av, Byfleet KT14 212 BL112
Hopfield Cl, Otford TN14 241 FH116
Hopgarden La, Sev. TN13 256 FG128
Hop Gdns, WC2 298 A1
Hop Gdn Way, Wat. WD25 60 BW31
Hopgood St, W12 294 B4
Hopground Cl, St.Alb. AL1 43 CG22
Hopkin Cl, Guil. GU2 242 AV130
Hopkins Cl, N10 98 DG52
Romford RM2 128 FJ55
Hopkins Ms, E15 281 M9
Hopkinsons Pl, NW1 274 F8
Hopkins Rd, E10 123 EB59
Hopkins St, W1 285 M9
Hoppers Rd, N13 99 DN47
N21 99 DN47
Hoppett Rd, E4 102 EE48
Hoppety, The, Tad. KT20 233 CX122
Hopping La, N1 277 H5
Hoppingwood Av, N.Mal. KT3 198 CS97
Hoppit Rd, Wal.Abb. EN9 67 EB32
Hoppner Rd, Hayes UB4 135 BQ68
Hop St, SE10 303 M8
Hopton Ct, Guil. GU2 242 AS134
off Chapelhouse Cl
Hopton Gdns, N.Mal. KT3 199 CU100
Hopton Rd, SE18 305 P6
SW16 181 DL92
Hopton's Gdns, SE1 299 H2
Hopton St, SE1 299 H2
Hoptree Cl, N12
off Woodside Pk Rd 98 DB49
Hopwood Cl, SW17 180 DC90
Watford WD17 75 BR36
Hopwood Rd, SE17 311 M2
Hopwood Wk, E8 278 D6
Horace Av, Rom. RM7 127 FC60
Horace Bldg, SW8
off Queenstown Rd 309 J4
Horace Rd, E7 124 EH63
Ilford IG6 125 EQ55
Kingston upon Thames KT1 198 CM97
Horatio Ct, SE16
off Rotherhithe St 301 H3
Horatio Pl, E14 302 F4
SW19 200 DA95
Horatio St, E2 288 B1
Horatius Way, Croy. CR0 219 DM107
Horbury Cres, W11 295 J1
Horbury Ms, W11 295 H1
Horder Rd, SW6 306 F7
Hordle Gdns, St.Alb. AL1 43 CF21
● **Horizon Business Cen**, N9
off Goodwin Rd 101 DX46
● **Horizon Business Village**,
Wey. KT13 212 BN112
Horizon Cl, West. TN16 240 EU124
Horizon Ho, Enf. EN3
off Tysoe Av 83 DZ36
● **Horizon Trade Pk**, N11
off Ringway 99 DJ51
Horksley Gdns, Hutt. CM13
off Bannister Dr 109 GC44
Horle Wk, SE5 310 G8
HORLEY, RH6 268 DG148
⇌ **Horley** 269 DH149
Horley Cl, Bexh. DA6 186 FA85
Horley Inf Sch, Horl. RH6
off Lumley Rd 268 DG148
Horley Lo La, Red. RH1 266 DF143
Horley Rd, SE9 184 EL91
Redhill RH1 266 DF136
Horley Row, Horl. RH6 268 DF147
Hormead Rd, W9 282 G5
Hornbeam Av, Upmin. RM14 128 FN63
Hornbeam Chase, S.Ock. RM15 149 FX69
Hornbeam Cl, NW7 97 CT48
SE11 298 E8
Barking IG11 146 EU69
Borehamwood WD6 78 CN39
Brentwood CM13 109 GB48
Buckhurst Hill IG9
off Hornbeam Rd 102 EK48
Hertford SG14 31 DP08
Ilford IG1 125 ER64
Northolt UB5 116 BZ64
Theydon Bois CM16 85 ES37
Hornbeam Cres, Brent. TW8 157 CH80
Hornbeam Gdns, N.Mal. KT3 199 CU100
Slough SL1 *off Upton Rd* 152 AU76
Hornbeam Gro, E4 102 EE48
Hornbeam Ho, NW3 274 F4
Hornbeam La, E4 84 EE43
Bexleyheath DA7 167 FC82
Essendon AL9 46 DE22
Hornbeam Rd, Buck.H. IG9 102 EK48
Guildford GU1 242 AW131
Hayes UB4 136 BW71
Reigate RH2 266 DB137
Theydon Bois CM16 85 ER37
Hornbeams, Brick.Wd AL2 60 BZ30
Hornbeams, The, Harl. CM20 35 EP13
Hornbeams Av, Enf. EN1 82 DW35
Hornbeam Sq, E3 279 N8
Hornbeams Ri, N11 98 DG51
Hornbeam Ter, Cars. SM5 200 DE102
Hornbeam Wk, Rich. TW10 178 CM90
Whiteley Village KT12
off Octagon Rd 213 BT109
Hornbeam Way, Brom. BR2 205 EN100
Waltham Cross EN7 66 DT29
Hornbill Cl, Uxb. UB8 134 BK72
Hornblower Cl, SE16 301 L8
Hornbuckle Cl, Har. HA2 117 CD61
Hornby Cl, NW3 274 B6
Horncastle Cl, SE12 184 EG87
Horncastle Rd, SE12 184 EG87
HORNCHURCH, RM11 & RM12 128 FJ61
⊖ **Hornchurch** 128 FK62
Hornchurch Cl, Kings.T. KT2 177 CK91
Hornchurch Hill, Whyt. CR3 236 DT117
Hornchurch Rd,
Horn. RM11, RM12 127 FG60
Horndean Cl, SW15
off Bessborough Rd 179 CU88
Horndon Cl, Rom. RM5 105 FC53
Horndon Grn, Rom. RM5 105 FC53
Horndon Rd, Rom. RM5 105 FC53
Horner La, Mitch. CR4 200 DD96
Horne Rd, Shep. TW17 194 BN98
Horner Sq, E1
off Commercial St 288 A6
Hornets, The, Wat. WD18 75 BV42
Hornet Way, E6 145 ER71
Horne Way, SW15 306 A9
Hornfair Rd, SE7 164 EJ79
Hornford Way, Rom. RM7 127 FE59
Hornhatch, Chilw. GU4 259 BB140
Hornhatch Cl, Chilw. GU4 259 BB140
Hornhatch La, Guil. GU4 259 BA140
Hornhill Rd, Ger.Cr. SL9 91 BB50
Maple Cross WD3 91 BD50
Horniman Dr, SE23 182 DV88
★ **Horniman Mus**, SE23 182 DV88
Horniman Prim Sch, SE23
off Horniman Dr 182 DV88
Horning Cl, SE9 184 EL91
Horn La, SE10 303 N9
W3 138 CQ73
Woodford Green IG8 102 EG51
Horn Link Way, SE10 303 N8
Hornminster Glen, Horn. RM11 128 FN61
Horn Pk Cl, SE12 184 EH85
Horn Pk La, SE12 184 EH85
Horn Pk Prim Sch, SE12
off Alnwick Rd 184 EH87
Hornsby Ho Sch, SW12
off Hearnville Rd 180 DG88
Hornsby La, Orsett RM16 171 GG75
Horns Cl, Hert. SG13 32 DQ11
Horns Cft Cl, Bark. IG11
off Thornhill Gdns 145 ES66
Horns End Pl, Pnr. HA5 116 BW56
HORNSEY, N8 121 DM55
⇌ **Hornsey** 121 DM56
Hornsey La, N6 121 DH60
Hornsey La Est, N19 121 DK59
Hornsey La Gdns, N6 121 DJ59
Hornsey Pk Rd, N8 121 DM55
Hornsey Ri, N19 121 DK59
Hornsey Ri Gdns, N19 121 DK59
Hornsey Rd, N7 121 DM61
N19 121 DL60
Hornsey Sch for Girls, N8
off Inderwick Rd 121 DM57
Hornsey St, N7 276 D2
Hornsfield, Welw.G.C. AL7 30 DC08
HORNS GREEN, Sev. TN14 239 ES117
Hornshay St, SE15 313 H3
Horns Mill Rd, Hert. SG13 32 DQ12
Horns Rd, Hert. SG13 32 DQ10
Ilford IG2, IG6 125 EQ57
Hornton Pl, W8 295 K5
Hornton St, W8 295 K4
Horsa Gdns, Hat. AL10 44 CR16
Horsa Rd, SE12 184 EJ87
Erith DA8 167 FC80
Horse & Dolphin Yd, W1 285 P10
Horsebridges Cl, Dag. RM9 146 EY67
Horsecroft, Bans. SM7
off Lyme Regis Rd 233 CZ117
Horsecroft Cl, Orp. BR6 206 EV102
Horsecroft Pl, Harl. CM19 50 EL16
Horsecroft Rd, Edg. HA8 96 CR52
Harlow CM19 50 EL16
Hemel Hempstead HP1 40 BG22
Horse Fair, Kings.T. KT1 197 CK96
Horseferry Pl, SE10 314 E3
Horseferry Rd, E14 289 L10
SW1 297 N7
Horse Guards Av, SW1 298 A3
★ **Horse Guards Par**, SW1 297 P3
Horse Guards Rd, SW1 297 P3
Horse Hill, Chesh. HP5 56 AX32
Horsehill, Horl. RH6 268 DA146
Horse La, Ware SG12 33 DX05
Horse Leaze, E6 293 M8
Horselers, Hem.H. HP3 40 BN23
HORSELL, Wok. GU21 226 AW116
Horsell Birch, Wok. GU21 226 AV115
Horsell C of E Jun Sch,
Horsell GU21 *off Meadway Dr* 248 AW116
Horsell Common, Wok. GU21 210 AX114
Horsell Common Rd,
Wok. GU21 210 AW114
Horsell Ct, Cher. KT16
off Stepgates 194 BH101
Horsell Moor, Wok. GU21 226 AX117
Horsell Pk, Wok. GU21 226 AX116
Horsell Pk Cl, Wok. GU21 226 AX116
Horsell Ri, Wok. GU21 226 AX115
Horsell Ri Cl, Wok. GU21 226 AX115
Horsell Rd, N5 276 E3
Orpington BR5 206 EV95
Horsell Vale, Wok. GU21 226 AY115
Horsell Village Sch, The,
Horsell GU21 *off Church Hill* 226 AX116
Horsell Way, Wok. GU21 226 AW116
Horselydown La, SE1 300 A4
Horseman Side,
Nave.S. CM14 105 FH45
Horsemans Ride, St.Alb. AL2 60 CA26
Horsemongers Ms, SE1 299 K5
Horsemoor Cl, Slou. SL3 153 BA77
Horsenden Av, Grnf. UB6 117 CE64
Horsenden Cres, Grnf. UB6 117 CF64
Horsenden La N, Grnf. UB6 137 CF65
Horsenden La S,
Perivale UB6 137 CG67
Horsenden Prim Sch, Grnf.
UB6 *off Horsenden La N* 137 CF65
Horse Ride, SW1 297 N3
Dorking RH5 263 CD144
Leatherhead KT24 245 BR130
Tadworth KT20 249 CY125
Horse Rd, E7
off Centre Rd 124 EH62
Horseshoe, The, Bans. SM7 233 CZ115
Coulsdon CR5 219 DK113
Hemel Hempstead HP3 41 BQ22
● **Horseshoe Business Pk**,
Brick.Wd AL2 60 CA30
Horseshoe Cl, E14 302 E10
NW2 119 CV61
Waltham Abbey EN9 68 EG34
Horse Shoe Ct, EC1
off Brewhouse Yd 287 H4
Horseshoe Cres, Beac. HP9 89 AL54
Horse Shoe Cres, Nthlt. UB5 136 CA68
Horseshoe Dr, Uxb. UB8 134 BN72
Horse Shoe Grn, Sutt. SM1
off Aultone Way 200 DB103
Horseshoe Hill, Burn. SL1 110 AJ63
Waltham Abbey EN9 68 EJ33
Horseshoe La, N20 97 CX46
Enfield EN2 *off Chase Side* 82 DQ41
Watford WD25 59 BV32
Horseshoe La E, Guil. GU1 243 BB133
Horseshoe La W, Guil. GU1 243 BB133
Horseshoe Ms, SW2
off Acre La 161 DL84
Horseshoe Ridge, Wey. KT13 213 BQ111
Horse Yd, N1 277 H8
Horsfeld Gdns, SE9 184 EL85
Horsfeld Rd, SE9 184 EK85
Horsfield Cl, Dart. DA2 188 FQ87
Horsford Rd, SW2 181 DM85
Horsham Av, N12 98 DE50
Horsham Rd, Abin.Ham. RH5 261 BT142
Bexleyheath DA6 186 FA85
Dorking RH4 263 CG137
Feltham TW14 175 BQ86
Guildford GU4, GU5 258 AY142
Holmwood RH5 263 CH140
Horshams, Harl. CM19
off Little Gro Fld 51 EQ15
⇌ **Horsley** 245 BS125
Horsley Cl, Epsom KT19 216 CR113
Horsleydown Old Stairs, SE1 300 A3
Horsley Dr, Kings.T. KT2 177 CK92
New Addington CR0 221 EC108
Horsley Rd, E4 101 EC47
Bromley BR1 *off Palace Rd* 204 EH95
Cobham KT11 229 BV119
Horsleys, Map.Cr. WD3 91 BD50
Horsley St, SE17 311 L2
Horsmonden Cl, Orp. BR6 205 ES101
Horsmonden Rd, SE4 183 DZ85
Hortensia Rd, SW10 307 N3
Horticultural Pl, W4 158 CR78
HORTON, Epsom KT19 216 CP110
Slou. SL3 153 BA83
Horton Av, NW2 272 F1
Horton Br Rd, West Dr. UB7 134 BM74
Horton Cl, Maid. SL6 130 AC70
West Drayton UB7 134 BM74
★ **Horton Country Pk**,
Epsom KT19 216 CM110
Horton Cres, Epsom KT19 216 CP110
Horton Footpath, Epsom KT19 216 CQ111
Horton Gdns, Epsom KT19 216 CQ111
Horton Hill, Epsom KT19 216 CQ111
Horton Ho, SW8 310 C4
● **Horton Ind Pk**, West Dr. UB7 134 BM74
HORTON KIRBY, Dart. DA4 209 FR98
Horton Kirby C of E Prim Sch,
Hort.Kir. DA4 *off Horton Rd* 208 FQ97
Horton La, Epsom KT19 216 CP110
Horton Par, West Dr. UB7
off Horton Rd 134 BL74
★ **Horton Park Children's Fm**,
Epsom KT19 216 CN110
● **Horton Pl**, West. TN16
off Hortons Way 255 ER126
Horton Rd, E8 278 E4
Colnbrook SL3 153 BA81
Dartford DA4 208 FQ97
Datchet SL3 152 AV80
Poyle SL3 153 BE83
Staines-upon-Thames TW19 174 BG85
West Drayton UB7 134 BN74
Hortons Way, West. TN16 255 ER126
Horton Way, Croy. CR0 203 DX99
Farningham DA4 208 FM101
Hortus Rd, E4 101 EC47
Southall UB2 156 BZ75
Horvath Cl, Wey. KT13 213 BR105
Horwood Cl, Rick. WD3
off Thellusson Way 92 BG45
Horwood Ct, Wat. WD24 76 BX37
Hosack Rd, SW17 180 DF89
Hoser Av, SE12 184 EG89
Hosey Common La, West. TN16 255 ES130
Hosey Common Rd, Eden. TN8 255 EQ133
Westerham TN16 255 ER130
HOSEY HILL, West. TN16 255 EC127
Hosey Hill, West. TN16 255 ER127
Hosier La, EC1 286 G7
Hoskins Cl, E16 292 D8
Hayes UB3 155 BT78
Hoskins Rd, Oxt. RH8 254 EE129
Hoskins St, SE10 315 H1
Hoskins Wk, Oxt. RH8 254 EE129
Hospital Br Rd, Twick. TW2 176 CB87
Hospital Hill, Chesh. HP5 54 AQ32
Hospital of St. John &
St. Elizabeth, NW8 284 A1
Hospital Rd, E9 279 H2
Hounslow TW3 156 CA83
Sevenoaks TN13 257 FJ121
Hospital Way, SE13 183 ED87
Hotham Cl, Sutt.H. DA4 188 FP94
Swanley BR8 207 FH95
West Molesey KT8
off Garrick Gdns 196 CA97
Hotham Prim Sch, SW15
off Charlwood Rd 159 CX84
Hotham Rd, SW15 159 CW83
SW19 180 DC94
Hotham Rd Ms, SW19
off Haydons Rd 180 DC94
Hotham St, E15 281 J8
Hothfield Pl, SE16 301 H7
● **Hotspur Ind Est**, N17 100 DV51
Hotspur Rd, Nthlt. UB5 136 CA68
Hotspur St, SE11 298 E10
Hotspur Way, Enf. EN2 82 DU35
Houblon Rd, Rich. TW10 178 CL85
Houblons Hill, Cooper. CM16 70 EW31
Houghton Cl, E8 278 B5
Hampton TW12 176 BY93
Houghton Rd, N15 122 DT56
off West Grn Rd
Houghton Sq, SW9 310 A9
Houghton St, WC2 286 D9
Houlder Cres, Croy. CR0 219 DP107
Hound Ho Rd, Shere GU5 260 BN141
Houndsden Rd, N21 81 DM44
Houndsditch, EC3 287 P8
Houndsfield Prim Sch, N9
off Ripon Rd 100 DV45
Houndsfield Rd, N9 100 DV45
HOUNSLOW, TW3 - TW6 156 BZ84
⇌ **Hounslow** 176 CB85
Hounslow Av, Houns. TW3 176 CB85
● **Hounslow Business Pk**,
Houns. TW3 *off Alice Way* 156 CB84
⊖ **Hounslow Central** 156 CA83
⊖ **Hounslow East** 156 CC82
Hounslow Gdns, Houns. TW3 176 CB85
★ **Hounslow Heath**, TW4 176 BY86
Hounslow Heath Inf & Nurs Sch,
Houns. TW4 *off Martindale Rd* 156 BY83
Hounslow Heath Jun Sch,
Houns. TW4 *off Selwyn Cl* 156 BY83
Hounslow Manor Sch, Houns.
TW3 *off Prince Regent Rd* 156 CC83
Hounslow Rd, Feltham TW14 175 BV88
Hanworth TW13 176 BX90
Twickenham TW2 176 CC86
Hounslow Town Prim Sch,
Houns. TW3 *off Pears Rd* 156 CC83
HOUNSLOW WEST, Houns. TW4 156 BX83
⊖ **Hounslow West** 156 BY82
Housden Cl, Wheat. AL4 28 CL08
Housefield Way, St.Alb. AL4 43 CJ23
House La, Sand. AL4 43 CK16
Houseman Way, SE5 311 M5
★ **Houses of Parliament**, SW1 298 B5
Housewood End, Hem.H. HP1 40 BH17
HOUSHAM TYE, Harl. CM17 37 FD13
Houston Pl, Esher KT10
off Lime Tree Av 197 CE102
Houston Rd, SE23 183 DY89
Long Ditton KT6 197 CH100
Hove Av, E17 123 DZ57
Hove Cl, Grays RM17 170 GA79
Hutton CM13 109 GC47
Hoveden Rd, NW2 272 E2
Hove Gdns, Sutt. SM1 200 DB102
Hoveton Rd, SE28 146 EW72
Hoveton Way, Ilf. IG6 103 EP52
Howard Agne Cl, Bov. HP3 57 BA27
Howard Av, Bex. DA5 186 EW88
Epsom KT17 217 CU110
Slough SL2 131 AR71
Howard Bldg, SW8 309 J3
Howard Business Pk,
Wal.Abb. EN9 *off Howard Cl* 67 ED34
Howard Cen, The,
Welw.G.C. AL8 29 CX09
Howard Cl, N11 98 DG47
NW2 119 CY63
W3 138 CP72
Ashtead KT21 232 CM118
Bushey Heath WD23 95 CE45
Hampton TW12 176 CC93
Leatherhead KT22 231 CJ123
Loughton IG10 84 EL44
St. Albans AL1 43 CJ22
Sunbury-on-Thames TW16 175 BT93
Waltham Abbey EN9 67 ED34
Walton on the Hill KT20 249 CT125
Watford WD24 75 BU37
West Horsley KT24 245 BR125
Howard Ct, Reig. RH2 250 DC133
Howard Cres, Seer Grn HP9 89 AQ50
Howard Dr, Borwd. WD6 78 CR42
Howard Gdns, Guil. GU1 243 BA133
● **Howard Ind Est**, Chesh. HP5 54 AQ29
Howard Ms, N5 277 H1
Slough SL3 *off Laburnum Gro* 153 BB79
Howard of Effingham Sch,
Eff. KT24 *off Lower Rd* 246 BX127
Howard Pl, Reig. RH2 250 DA132
Howard Prim Sch, Croy. CR0
off Dering Pl 220 DQ105
Howard Ridge, Burpham GU4 243 BA130
Howard Rd, E6 145 EM68
E11 124 EE62
E17 123 EA55
N15 122 DS58
N16 277 M1
NW2 272 C1
SE20 202 DW95
SE25 202 DU99
Barking IG11 145 ER67
Bookham KT23 246 CB127
Bromley BR1 184 EG94
Chafford Hundred RM16 169 FW76
Chesham HP5 54 AP28
Coulsdon CR5 235 DJ115
Dartford DA1 188 FN86
Dorking RH4 263 CG136
Effingham Junction KT24 229 BU122
Ilford IG1 125 EP63
Isleworth TW7 157 CF83
New Malden KT3 198 CS97
North Holmwood RH5
off Holmesdale Rd 263 CJ140
Reigate RH2 266 DB135
Seer Green HP9 89 AQ50
Stanmore HA7 96 CL52
Southall UB1 136 CB72
Surbiton KT5 198 CM100
Upminster RM14 128 FQ61
Howards Cl, Pnr. HA5 93 BV54
Woking GU22 227 BA120
Howards Crest Cl, Beck. BR3 203 EC96
Howards Dr, Hem.H. HP1 39 BF17
Howards Gate, Farn.Royal SL2
off Farnham Rd 131 AQ69
Howardsgate, Welw.G.C. AL8 29 CX08
Howards La, SW15 179 CV85
Addlestone KT15 211 BE107
Howards Rd, E13 291 N2
Woking GU22 227 AZ120
Howards Thicket, Ger.Cr. SL9 112 AW61
Howard St, T.Ditt. KT7 197 CH101
Howards Wd Dr, Ger.Cr. SL9 112 AX61
Howard Wk, N2 120 DC56
Howard Way, Barn. EN5 79 CX43
Harlow CM20 52 EU15
Howarth Rd, SE2 166 EU78
Howberry Cl, Edg. HA8 95 CK51
Howberry Rd, Edg. HA8 95 CK51
Stanmore HA7 95 CK51
Thornton Heath CR7 202 DR95
Howbury La, Erith DA8 167 FG82
Howbury Rd, SE15 312 G10
Howcroft Cres, N3 98 DA52
Howcroft La, Grnf. UB6 137 CD69
Howden Cl, SE28 146 EX73
Howden Rd, SE25 202 DT96
Howden St, SE15 312 C10
Howe Cl, Rom. RM7 104 FA53
Shenley WD7 62 CL32
Howe Dell, Hat. AL10 45 CV18
Howe Dell Prim Sch,
Hat. AL10 *off The Runway* 44 CS16
Howe Dell Sch, Hat. AL10
off The Runway 44 CS16
Howe Dr, Beac. HP9 89 AK50
Caterham CR3 236 DR122
Howell Cl, Rom. RM6 126 EX57
Howell Hill Cl, Epsom KT17 217 CW111
Howell Hill Gro, Epsom KT17 217 CW110
Howell Wk, SE1 299 H9
Howerd Way, SE18 164 EL81
Howe Rd, Hem.H. HP3 40 BN22
Howes Cl, N3 120 DA55
Howfield Grn, Hodd. EN11 33 DZ14
Howfield Pl, N17 122 DT55
Howgate Rd, SW14 158 CR83
Howick Pl, SW1 297 M7
Howicks Grn, Welw.G.C. AL7 30 DA12
Howie St, SW11 308 C5
Howitt Cl, N16 *off Allen Rd* 122 DS63
NW3 274 D4
Howitt Rd, NW3 274 C4
Howitts Cl, Esher KT10 214 CA107
Howland Est, SE16 301 H6
Howland Garth, St.Alb. AL1 42 CC24
Howland Ms E, W1 285 M6
Howlands, Welw.G.C. AL7 30 DB12
Howlands Ho, Welw.G.C. AL7 30 DA12
Howland St, W1 285 L6
Howland Way, SE16 301 M5
How La, Chipstead CR5 234 DG117
Howletts La, Ruis. HA4 115 BQ57
Howletts Rd, SE24 182 DQ86
Howley Pl, W2 283 P6
Howley Rd, Croy. CR0 201 DP104
Hows Cl, Uxb. UB8 134 BJ67
Howse Rd, Wal.Abb. EN9
off Deer Pk Way 83 EB35
Howsman Rd, SW13 159 CU79
Hows Mead, N.Wld Bas. CM16 53 FD24
Howson Rd, SE4 163 DY84
Howson Ter, Rich. TW10 178 CL86
Hows Rd, Uxb. UB8 134 BJ67
Hows St, E2 278 A10
Howton Pl, Bushey Hth WD23 95 CD46
HOW WOOD, St.Alb. AL2 60 CC27
⇌ **How Wood** 60 CC28
How Wd, Park St AL2 60 CB28
How Wd Prim Sch,
Park St AL2 *off Spooners Dr* 60 CC27
HOXTON, N1 287 N1
⊖ **Hoxton** 287 P1
Hoxton Mkt, N1 287 N3
Hoxton Sq, N1 287 N3
Hoxton St, N1 287 P3
Hoylake Cl, Slou. SL1 151 AL75
Hoylake Cres, Ickhm UB10 114 BN60
Hoylake Gdns, Mitch. CR4 201 DJ97
Romford RM3 106 FN53
Ruislip HA4 115 BV60
Watford WD19 94 BX49
Hoylake Rd, W3 138 CS72
Hoyland Cl, SE15 312 E4
Hoyle Rd, SW17 180 DE92
Hoy St, E16 291 L9
Hoy Ter, Grays RM20 169 FX78
★ **H.Q.S. Wellington, Master**
Mariners' Hall, WC2 286 E10
Hubbard Dr, Chess. KT9 215 CJ107
Hubbard Rd, SE27 182 DQ91
Hubbards Chase, Horn. RM11 128 FN57
Hubbards Cl, Horn. RM11 128 FN57
Uxbridge UB8 135 BP72
Hubbard's Hall Est, Harl. CM17 36 EY14
Hubbards Rd, Chorl. WD3 73 BD43
Hubbard St, E15 281 J9
● **Hubbinet Ind Est**, Rom. RM7 127 FC55
Hubert Day Cl, Beac. HP9
off Seeleys Rd 89 AK52
Hubert Gro, SW9 161 DL83
Hubert Rd, E6 292 E2
Brentwood CM14 108 FV48
Rainham RM13 147 FF69
Slough SL3 152 AX76
Hucknall Cl, Rom. RM3 106 FM51
Huddart St, E3 289 P6
Huddleston Cl, E2 278 G10
Huddlestone Cres, Merst. RH1 251 DK128
Huddlestone Rd, E7 124 EF63
NW2 139 CV65
Huddleston Rd, N7 275 N1
Hudson Apts, N8
off Chadwell La 121 DM55
Hudson Av, Denh. UB9 113 BF58
Hudson Cl, E15 281 N8
W12 *off Canada Way* 139 CV73
St. Albans AL1 43 CD23
Watford WD24 75 BT36
Hudson Ct, E14
off Maritime Quay 302 B10
SW19 180 DB94
Guildford GU2 *off Cobbett Rd* 264 AT133
Hudson Gdns, Grn St Grn BR6
off Superior Dr 223 ET107
Hudson Ho, Epsom KT19 216 CR113
Hudson Pl, SE18 165 EQ78
Slough SL3 153 AZ78
Hudson Rd, Bexh. DA7 166 EZ82
Harlington UB3 155 BR79
Hudsons, Tad. KT20 233 CX121
Hudsons Ct, Pot.B. EN6 64 DA31
Hudson's Pl, SW1 297 K8
Hudson Way, N9 100 DW48
NW2 *off Gratton Ter* 119 CX62
Huggens College, Nthflt. DA11 190 GB85
Huggin Ct, EC4 287 K10
Huggin Hill, EC4 287 K10
Huggins La, N.Mymms AL9 45 CV23
Huggins Pl, SW2 181 DM88
Hughan Rd, E15 281 H2
Hugh Dalton Av, SW6 306 G3
Hughenden Av, Har. HA3 117 CH57
Hughenden Gdns, Nthlt. UB5 136 BW69
Hughenden Rd, St.Alb. AL4 43 CH17
Slough SL1 131 AR72
Worcester Park KT4 199 CU101
Hughenden Ter, E15
off Westdown Rd 123 EC63
Hughes Cl, N12 98 DC50
Hughes Rd, Ashf. TW15 175 BQ94
Grays RM16 171 GG76
Hayes UB3 135 BV73
Hughes Ter, SW9
off Styles Gdns 311 H10
Hughes Wk, Croy. CR0
off St. Saviours Rd 202 DQ101
Hugh Gaitskell Cl, SW6 306 G3
Hugh Herland Ho, Kings.T. KT1 198 CL97
Hugh Ms, SW1 297 K9
Hugh Myddelton Prim Sch,
EC1 286 F3
Hugh's Twr, Harl. CM20 35 ER14
Hugh St, SW1 297 K9
Hugo Cl, Wat. WD18
off Malkin Way 75 BS42
Hugo Gdns, Rain. RM13 147 FF65
Hugo Gryn Way, Shenley WD7 62 CL31
Hugon Rd, SW6 307 L10
Hugo Rd, N19 121 DJ63
Huguenot Pl, E1 288 B6
SW18 180 DC85
Huguenot Sq, SE15 312 E10
HULBERRY, Dart. DA4 207 FG103
Hullbridge Ms, N1 277 L8
Hull Cl, SE16 301 K4
Cheshunt EN7 66 DR26
Slough SL1 151 AQ75
Sutton SM2 *off Yarbridge Cl* 218 DB110
Hulletts La, Pilg.Hat. CM15 108 FT43
Hull Gro, Harl. CM19 51 EN20
Hull Pl, E16 *off Fishguard Way* 145 EQ74
Hull St, EC1 287 J3

H

Hulme Pl, SE1 299 K5
Hulse Av, Bark. IG11 145 ER65
Romford RM7 105 FB53
Hulse Ter, Ilf. IG1
off Buttsbury Rd 125 EQ64
Hulsewood Cl, Dart. DA2 187 FH90
Hulton Cl, Lthd. KT22 231 CJ123
Hulverston Cl, Sutt. SM2 218 DB110
Humber Av, S.Ock. RM15 149 FT72
Humber Cl, West Dr. UB7 134 BK74
Humber Dr, W10 282 C5
Upminster RM14 129 FR58
Humber Rd, NW2 119 CV61
SE3 315 L2
Dartford DA1 188 FK85
Humberstone Rd, E13 292 C3
Humberton Cl, E9 279 L3
Humber Way, Slou. SL3 153 BA77
Humbolt Cl, Guil. GU2 242 AS134
Humbolt Rd, W6 306 E3
Hume Av, Til. RM18 171 GG83
Hume Cl, Til. RM18 171 GG83
Hume Ms, Til. RM18
off Hume Cl 171 GG83
Humes Av, W7 157 CE76
Hume Ter, E16 292 C7
Hume Way, Ruis. HA4 115 BU58
Hummer Rd, Egh. TW20 173 BA91
Humphrey Cl, Fetch. KT22 230 CC122
Ilford IG5 103 EM53
Humphrey St, SE1 300 A10
Humphries Cl, Dag. RM9 126 EZ63
Hundred Acre, NW9 97 CT54
Hundred Acres La, Amer. HP7 55 AR40
Hungerdown, E4 101 EC46
Hungerford Av, Slou. SL2 132 AS71
Hungerford Br, SE1 298 B2
WC2 298 B2
Hungerford La, WC2 298 A2
Sch Hungerford Prim Sch, N7 275 P4
Hungerford Rd, N7 275 P4
Hungerford Sq, Wey. KT13
off Rosslyn Pk 213 BR105
Hungerford St, E1 288 F8
Hungry Hill, Ripley GU23 228 BK124
Hungry Hill La, Send GU23 228 BK124
HUNSDON, Ware SG12 34 EJ06
Hunsdon, Welw.G.C. AL7 30 DD09
HUNSDONBURY, Ware SG12 34 EJ08
Hunsdon Cl, Dag. RM9 146 EY65
Hunsdon Dr, Sev. TN13 257 FH123
Sch Hunsdon JMI Sch,
Hunsdon SG12 off High St 34 EK06
Hunsdon Pound,
Stans.Abb. SG12 34 EL12
Hunsdon Rd, SE14 313 J4
Stanstead Abbotts SG12 34 EE11
Hunslett St, E2 289 H1
Hunstanton Cl, Colnbr. SL3 153 BC80
Hunston Rd, Mord. SM4 200 DB102
Hunt Cl, W11 294 D2
St. Albans AL4 off Villiers Cres 43 CK17
Hunter Av, Shenf. CM15 109 GA44
Hunter Cl, SE1 299 M7
SW12 180 DG88
Borehamwood WD6 78 CQ43
Potters Bar EN6 64 DB33
Wallington SM6 219 DL108
Huntercombe Cl, Tap. SL6 130 AH72
Huntercombe La N, Slou. SL1 130 AJ71
Taplow SL6 130 AJ71
Huntercombe La S, Tap. SL6 130 AH74
H Huntercombe Manor,
Tap. SL6 130 AJ73
Huntercombe Spur, Slou. SL1 130 AJ73
Huntercrombe Gdns,
Wat. WD19 94 BW50
Hunter Dr, Horn. RM12 128 FJ63
Hunter Ho, Felt. TW13 175 BU88
Hunter Rd, SW20 199 CW95
Guildford GU1 258 AY135
Ilford IG1 125 EP64
Thornton Heath CR7 202 DR97
Hunters, The, Beck. BR3 203 EC95
Hunters Cl, Bex. DA5 187 FE90
Bovingdon HP3 57 BA29
Chesham HP5 54 AN30
Epsom KT19 off Marshalls Cl 216 CQ113
Hunters Ct, Rich. TW9 177 CK85
Huntersfield Cl, Reig. RH2 250 DB131
Hunters Gate, Nutfld RH1 251 DM133
Watford WD25 off Hunters La 59 BU33
Hunters Gro, Har. HA3 117 CJ56
Hayes UB3 135 BU74
Orpington BR6 223 EP105
Romford RM5 105 FB50
Sch Hunters Hall Prim Sch,
Dag. RM10 off Alibon Rd 127 FB64
Hunters Hall Rd, Dag. RM10 126 FA63
Hunters Hill, Ruis. HA4 116 BW62
Hunters La, Wat. WD25 59 BT33
Hunters Meadow, SE19
off Dulwich Wd Av 182 DS91
Hunters Oak, Hem.H. HP2 41 BP15
Hunters Pk, Berk. HP4 38 AY18
Hunters Reach, Wal.Cr. EN7 66 DT29
Hunters Ride, Brick.Wd AL2 60 CA31
Hunters Rd, Chess. KT9 198 CL104
Hunters Sq, Dag. RM10 126 FA63
Hunter St, WC1 286 B4
Hunters Wk, Knock.P. TN14 224 EY114
Hunters Way, Croy. CR0 220 DS105
Enfield EN2 81 DN39
Slough SL1 151 AL75
Welwyn Garden City AL7 29 CZ12
Hunter Wk, E13 281 N10
Borehamwood WD6
off Hunter Cl 78 CQ43
Hunting Cl, Esher KT10 214 CA105
Huntingdon Cl, Brox. EN10 49 DY24
Mitcham CR4 201 DL97
Northolt UB5 136 CA65
Huntingdon Gdns, W4 158 CQ80
Worcester Park KT4 199 CW104
Huntingdon Rd, N2 120 DE55
N9 100 DW46
Redhill RH1 250 DF134
Woking GU21 226 AT117
Huntingdon St, E16 291 M9
N1 276 C7
Huntingfield, Croy. CR0 221 DZ108
Huntingfield Rd, SW15 159 CU84
Huntingfield Way, Egh. TW20 173 BD94
Hunting Gate, Hem.H. HP2 40 BL16
Hunting Gate Cl, Enf. EN2 81 DN41
Hunting Gate Dr, Chess. KT9 216 CL108
Hunting Gate Ms, Sutt. SM1 200 DB104
Twickenham TW2 off Colne Rd 199 CE88
Huntings Rd, Dag. RM10 146 FA65
Huntington Pl, Langley SL3 153 BB76
Huntland Cl, Rain. RM13 147 FH71
Huntley Av, Nthflt DA11 190 GB86
Huntley Cl, Stanw. TW19
off Cambria Gdns 174 BL87
Huntley Ho, Walt. KT12
off Octagon Rd 213 BT109
Huntley St, WC1 285 M5
Huntley Way, SW20 199 CU96
Huntly Dr, N3 98 DA51
Huntly Rd, SE25 202 DS98
HUNTON BRIDGE,
Kings L. WD4 59 BP33
Hunton Br Hill, Hunt.Br. WD4 59 BQ33
Jct Hunton Br Interchange,
Wat. WD17 75 BQ35
Hunton Cl, Abb.L. WD4 59 BR33
Hunton St, E1 288 C5
Hunt Rd, Nthflt DA11 190 GE90
Southall UB2 156 CA76
Hunt's Cl, SE3 315 P8
Hunt's Ct, WC2 297 P1
Hunts La, E15 290 E1
Taplow SL6 130 AE68
Huntsman Rd, Ilf. IG6 104 EU51
Huntsmans Cl, Felt. TW13 175 BV91
Fetcham KT22
off The Green 231 CD124
Warlingham CR6 236 DW119
Huntsmans Dr, Upmin. RM14 128 FQ64
Huntsman St, SE17 299 M9
Hunts Mead, Enf. EN3 83 DX41
Hunts Mead Cl, Chis. BR7 185 EM94
Huntsmill Rd, Hem.H. HP1 39 BE21
Huntsmoor Rd, Epsom KT19 216 CR106
Huntspill St, SW17 180 DC90
Hunts Slip Rd, SE21 182 DS90
Huntswood La, Slou. SL1 130 AE66
Taplow SL6 130 AE66
Huntsworth Ms, NW1 284 E5
Hurdwick Pl, NW1
off Harrington Sq 275 L10
Hurley Cl, Bans. SM7 233 CZ116
Walton-on-Thames KT12 195 BV103
Hurley Ct, SW17
off Mitcham Rd 180 DG93
Hurley Cres, SE16 301 K4
Hurley Gdns, Guil. GU4 243 AZ130
Hurley Ho, SE11 298 F9
Hurley Rd, Grnf. UB6 136 CB72
Hurlfield, Dart. DA2 188 FJ90
Hurlford, Wok. GU21 226 AU117
Sch Hurlingham & Chelsea Sch,
SW6 307 K10
● Hurlingham Business Pk,
SW6 160 DA83
★ Hurlingham Club, SW6 159 CZ83
Hurlingham Ct, SW6 306 G10
Hurlingham Gdns, SW6 306 G10
★ Hurlingham Park, SW6 307 H10
Hurlingham Retail Pk, SW6
off Carnwath Rd 160 DB83
Hurlingham Rd, SW6 306 G9
Bexleyheath DA7 166 EZ80
Sch Hurlingham Sch, SW15
off Putney Br Rd 159 CZ84
Hurlingham Sq, SW6 160 DA83
Hurlock St, N5 121 DP62
Hurlstone Rd, SE25 202 DR99
Hurn Ct Rd, Houns. TW4 156 BX82
Hurnford Cl, S.Croy. CR2 220 DS110
Huron Cl, Grn St Grn BR6
off Winnipeg Dr 223 ET107
Huron Rd, SW17 180 DG89
Broxbourne EN10 67 DY26
Uni Huron Uni USA in London,
WC1 286 A6
Hurren Cl, SE3 315 J10
Hurricane Rd, Wall. SM6 219 DL108
● Hurricane Trd Cen, NW9 97 CU53
Hurricane Way, Abb.L. WD5
off Abbey Dr 59 BU32
North Weald Bassett CM16 70 EZ27
Slough SL3 153 BB78
Hurry Cl, E15 281 K7
Hursley Rd, Chig. IG7 103 ET50
Hurst Av, E4 101 EA49
N6 121 DJ58
Hurstbourne, Clay. KT10 215 CF107
Hurstbourne Gdns, Bark. IG11 145 ES65
Hurstbourne Ho, SW15
off Tangley Gro 179 CT86
Hurstbourne Rd, SE23 183 DY88
Hurst Cl, E4 101 EA48
NW11 120 DB58
Bromley BR2 204 EF102
Chessington KT9 216 CN106
Headley KT18 232 CQ124
Northolt UB5 136 BZ65
Welwyn Garden City AL7 30 DC10
Woking GU22 226 AW120
Hurstcourt Rd, Sutt. SM1 200 DB103
Hurst Cft, Guil. GU1 258 AY137
Hurstdene Av, Brom. BR2 204 EF102
Staines-upon-Thames TW18 174 BH93
Hurstdene Gdns, N15 122 DS59
Hurst Dr, Wal.Cr. EN8 67 DX34
Walton on the Hill KT20 249 CU126
Sch Hurst Dr Prim Sch,
Wal.Cr. EN8 off Hurst Dr 67 DX34
Hurst Est, SE2 166 EX78
Hurstfield, Brom. BR2 204 EG99
Hurstfield Cres, Hayes UB4 135 BS70
Hurstfield Dr, Tap. SL6 130 AH72
Hurstfield Rd, W.Mol. KT8 196 CA97
HURST GREEN, Oxt. RH8 254 EG132
⇌ Hurst Green 254 EF132
Hurst Grn Cl, Oxt. RH8 254 EG132
Hurst Grn Rd, Oxt. RH8 254 EF132
Sch Hurst Grn Sch, Oxt. RH8
off Wolfs Wd 254 EG132
Hurst Gro, Walt. KT12 195 BT102
Hurstlands, Oxt. RH8 254 EG132
Hurstlands Cl, Horn. RM11 128 FJ59
Hurstlands Dr, Orp. BR6 206 EW104
Hurst La, SE2 166 EX78
East Molesey KT8 196 CC98
Egham TW20 193 BA96
Headley KT18 232 CQ124
Hurstleigh Cl, Red. RH1 250 DF132
Hurstleigh Dr, Red. RH1 250 DF132
Hurstleigh Gdns, Ilf. IG5 103 EM53
Hurstlings, Welw.G.C. AL7 30 DB10
Hurstmead Ct, Edg. HA8 96 CP49
Sch Hurstmere Sch, Sid. DA15
off Hurst Rd 186 EW88
Hurst Pk Av, Horn. RM12
off Crystal Av 128 FL63
Sch Hurst Pk Prim Sch,
W.Mol. KT8 off Hurst Rd 196 CA97
Hurst Pl, Nthwd. HA6 93 BP53
Sch Hurst Prim Sch, Bex. DA5
off Dorchester Av 186 EX87
Hurst Ri, Barn. EN5 80 DA41
Hurst Rd, E17 123 EB55
N21 99 DN46
Bexley DA5 186 EX88
Buckhurst Hill IG9 102 EK46
Croydon CR0 220 DR106
East Molesey KT8 196 CA97
Epsom KT19 216 CR111
Erith DA8 167 FC80
Headley KT18 232 CR123
Horley RH6 268 DE147
Sidcup DA15 186 EU89
Slough SL1 131 AK71
Walton on the Hill KT20 232 CR123
Walton-on-Thames KT12 196 BW99
West Molesey KT8 196 BY97
Hurst Springs, Bex. DA5 186 EY88
Hurst St, SE24 181 DP86
Hurst Vw Rd, S.Croy. CR2 220 DS108
Hurst Way, Pyrford GU22 211 BE114
Sevenoaks TN13 257 FJ127
South Croydon CR2 220 DS107
Hurstway Wk, W11 282 D10
Hurstwood Av, E18 124 EH56
Bexley DA5 186 EY88
Bexleyheath DA7 167 FE81
Erith DA8 167 FE81
Pilgrim's Hatch CM15 108 FV45
Hurstwood Ct, Upmin. RM14 128 FP60
Hurstwood Dr, Brom. BR1 205 EM97
Hurstwood Rd, NW11 119 CY56
Hurtwood Rd, Walt. KT12 196 BZ101
Hurworth Av, Slou. SL3 152 AW76
Huskards, Upmin. RM14 128 FP61
Huson Cl, NW3 274 C6
Hussain Cl, Har. HA1 117 CF63
Hussars Cl, Houns. TW4 156 BY83
Husseywell Cres, Brom. BR2 204 EG102
Hutchingsons Rd,
New Adgtn CR0 221 EC111
Hutchings Rd, Beac. HP9 89 AK50
Hutchings St, E14 302 A5
Hutchings Wk, NW11 120 DB56
Hutchins Cl, E15 280 F7
Hornchurch RM12 128 FL62
Hutchinson Ter, Wem. HA9 117 CK62
Hutchins Rd, SE28 146 EU73
Hutchins Way, Horl. RH6 268 DF146
Hutson Ter, Purf. RM19
off London Rd Purfleet 169 FR79
HUTTON, Brwd. CM13 109 GD44
Sch Hutton All Saints' C of E Prim Sch,
Hutt. CM13 off Claughton Way 131 GD44
Hutton Cl, Grnf. UB6
off Mary Peters Dr 117 CD64
Hertford SG14 31 DN09
Walton-on-Thames KT12 213 BV106
Woodford Green IG8 102 EH51
Hutton Dr, Hutt. CM13 109 GD45
Hutton Gdns, Har. HA3 94 CC52
Hutton Gate, Hutt. CM13 109 GB45
Hutton Gro, N12 98 DB50
Hutton La, Har. HA3 94 CC52
Hutton Ms, SW15 179 CV85
HUTTON MOUNT, Brwd. CM13 109 GB46
Hutton Pl, Hutt. CM13 109 GB44
Hutton Rd, Shenf. CM15 109 FZ45
Hutton Row, Edg. HA8 96 CQ52
Hutton St, EC4 286 F9
Hutton Village, Hutt. CM13 109 GE45
Hutton Wk, Har. HA3 94 CC52
Huxbear St, SE4 183 DZ85
Huxley Cl, Nthlt. UB5 136 BY67
Uxbridge UB8 134 BK70
Wexham SL3 132 AV70
Huxley Dr, Rom. RM6 126 EV59
Huxley Gdns, NW10 138 CM69
Huxley Par, N18 100 DR50
Huxley Pl, N13 99 DP49
Huxley Rd, E10 123 EC61
N18 100 DR49
Welling DA16 165 ET83
Huxley Sayze, N18 100 DR50
Huxley St, W10 282 E3
Huxtable Gdns, Maid. SL6 150 AD79
Hythe, The, Stai. TW18 173 BE92
Hyacinth Cl, Hmptn. TW12
off Gresham Rd 176 CA93
Ilford IG1 145 EP65
Hyacinth Ct, Pnr. HA5
off Tulip Ct 116 BW55
Hyacinth Dr, Uxb. UB10 134 BL66
Hyacinth Rd, SW15 179 CU88
Hyburn Cl, Brick.Wd AL2 60 BZ30
Hemel Hempstead HP3 41 BP21
Hycliffe Gdns, Chig. IG7 103 EQ49
HYDE, THE, NW9 119 CT56
Hyde, The, NW9 118 CS57
Ware SG12 32 DV05
Hyde Av, Pot.B. EN6 64 DB33
Hyde Cl, E13 281 P10
Ashford TW15 off Hyde Ter 175 BS93
Barnet EN5 79 CZ41
Chafford Hundred RM16 169 FX76
Romford RM1 105 FD51
Hyde Ct, N20 98 DD48
Waltham Cross EN8
off Parkside 67 DY34
Hyde Cres, NW9 118 CS57
Hyde Dr, St.P.Cray BR5 206 EV98
Hyde Est Rd, NW9 119 CT57
Hyde Fm Ms, SW12 181 DK88
Hydefield Cl, N21 100 DR46
Hydefield Ct, N9 100 DS47
Hyde Grn, Beac. HP9 89 AM52
Hyde Gro, Dart, DA1 168 FN82
● Hyde Ho, NW9 118 CS57
Hyde La, SW11 308 C6
Bovingdon HP3 57 BA27
Frogmore AL2 61 CE28
Hemel Hempstead HP3 59 BR26
Ockham GU23 228 BN120
Park Street AL2 60 CC28
Hyde Mead, Lwr Naze. EN9 50 EE23
Hyde Meadows, Bov. HP3 57 BA28
Hyde Ms, Rom. RM1
off Hyde Cl 105 FE51
★ Hyde Park, W2 296 C2
Hyde Pk, SW7 296 C2
W1 296 C2
Hyde Pk Av, N21 100 DQ47
⊖ Hyde Park Corner 296 G4
Hyde Pk Cor, W1 297 H4
Hyde Pk Cres, W2 284 C9
Hyde Pk Gdns, N21 100 DQ46
W2 284 B10
Hyde Pk Gdns Ms, W2 284 B10
Hyde Pk Gate, SW7 295 P5
Hyde Pk Gate Ms, SW7 295 P5
Hyde Pk Pl, W2 284 D10
Hyde Pk Sq, W2 284 C9
Hyde Pk Sq Ms, W2 284 C9
Hyde Pk St, W2 284 C9
Sch Hyde Prim Sch, The, NW9
off Hyde Cres 119 CT57
Hyderabad Way, E15 281 J6
Hyde Rd, N1 277 M9
Bexleyheath DA7 166 EZ82
Richmond TW10 off Albert Rd 200 CM85
South Croydon CR2 220 DS113
Watford WD17 75 BU40
Hyder Rd, Grays RM16 171 GJ76
Hydeside Gdns, N9 100 DT47
Hydes Pl, N1 276 G6
Hyde St, SE8 314 A3
Hyde Ter, Ashf. TW15 175 BS93
Hydethorpe Av, N9 100 DT47
Hydethorpe Rd, SW12 181 DJ88
Hyde Vale, SE10 314 F5
Hyde Valley, Welw.G.C. AL7 29 CZ11
Hyde Wk, Mord. SM4 200 DA101
Hyde Way, N9 100 DT47
Hayes UB3 155 BT77
Welwyn Garden City AL7 29 CY09
Hydro Ho, Cher. KT16
off Bridge Wf 194 BJ101
Hyland Cl, Horn. RM11 127 FH59
Sch Hyland Ho Sch, E17
off Forest Rd 101 ED54
Hylands Cl, Epsom KT18 232 CQ115
Hylands Ms, Epsom KT18 232 CQ115
Hylands Rd, E17 101 ED54
Epsom KT18 232 CQ115
Hyland Way, Horn. RM11 127 FH59
Hylle Cl, Wind. SL4 151 AL81
Hylton Pl, S.Merst. RH1 251 DJ131
Hylton St, SE18 165 ET77
Hyndewood, SE23 183 DX90
Hyndford Cres, Green. DA9
off Ingress Pk Av 189 FW85
Hyndman St, SE15 312 E3
Hynton Rd, Dag. RM8 126 EW61
Hyperion Ct, Hem.H. HP2 40 BM17
Hyperion Ho, E3 289 L1
Hyperion Pl, Epsom KT19 216 CR109
Hyperion Wk, Horl. RH6 269 DH150
Hyrons Cl, Amer. HP6 55 AS38
Hyrons La, Amer. HP6 55 AR38
Hyrstdene, S.Croy. CR2 219 DP105
Hyson Rd, SE16 300 F10
Hythe Av, Bexh. DA7 166 EZ80
Hythe Cl, N18 100 DU49
Orpington BR5
off Sandway Rd 206 EW98
HYTHE END, Stai. TW19 173 BB90
Hythe End Rd, Wrays. TW19 173 BA89
Hythe Fld Av, Egh. TW20 173 BD93
Hythe Pk Rd, Egh. TW20 173 BC92
Hythe Path, Th.Hth. CR7 202 DR97
Hythe Rd, NW10 139 CU70
Staines-upon-Thames TW18 173 BD92
Thornton Heath CR7 202 DR96
● Hythe Rd Ind Est, NW10 139 CU69
Sch Hythe Sch, The, Stai. TW18
off Thorpe Rd 173 BD92
Hythe St, Dart. DA1 188 FL86
Hythe St Lwr, Dart. DA1 188 FL85
Hyver Hill, NW7 78 CR44

I

Sch Ian Mikardo High Sch, E3 290 D3
Ian Sq, Enf. EN3
off Lansbury Rd 83 DX39
Ibbetson Path, Loug. IG10 85 EP41
Ibbotson Av, E16 291 M8
Ibbott St, E1 289 H4
Iberian Av, Wall. SM6 219 DK105
Ibex Ho, E15 281 K4
Ibis La, W4 158 CQ81
Ibis Way, Hayes UB4
off Cygnet Way 136 BX72
Ibscott Cl, Dag. RM10 147 FC65
Ibsley Gdns, SW15 179 CU88
Ibsley Way, Cockfos. EN4 80 DE43
Sch Ibstock Pl Sch, SW15
off Clarence La 178 CS86
★ ICC London, E16 304 B1
Icehouse Wd, Oxt. RH8 254 EE131
Iceland Rd, E3 280 B9
Iceland Wf, SE16 301 L8
Iceni Ct, E3 279 P9
Ice Wf, N1 276 B10
Ice Wf Marina, N1
off New Wf Rd 276 B10
Ickburgh Est, E5 122 DV61
Ickburgh Rd, E5 122 DV62
Sch Ickburgh Sch, E5
off Ickburgh Rd 122 DV62
ICKENHAM, Uxb. UB10 115 BQ62
⊖ Ickenham 115 BQ63
Ickenham Cl, Ruis. HA4 115 BR61
Ickenham Rd, Ickhm UB10 115 BQ61
Ruislip HA4 115 BR60
Ickleton Rd, SE9 184 EL91
Icklingham Gate, Cob. KT11 214 BW112
Icklingham Rd, Cob. KT11 214 BW112
Icknield Cl, St.Alb. AL3 42 BZ22
Icknield Dr, Ilf. IG2 125 EP57
Ickworth Pk Rd, E17 123 DY56
Icona Pt, E15 off Warton Rd 280 E8
Idaho Bldg, SE13
off Deals Gateway 314 C7
Ida Rd, N15 122 DR57
Ida St, E14 290 E9
Iden Cl, Brom. BR2 204 EE97
Idlecombe Rd, SW17 180 DG93
Idmiston Rd, E15 281 L3
SE27 182 DQ90
Worcester Park KT4 199 CT101
Idmiston Sq, Wor.Pk. KT4 199 CT101
Idol La, EC3 299 N1
Idonia St, SE8 313 P4
Idris Ct, N9
off Galahad Rd 100 DU48
Iffley Cl, Uxb. UB8 134 BK66
Iffley Rd, W6 159 CV76
IFIELD, Grav. DA13 191 GH94
Ifield Cl, Red. RH1 266 DE137
Ifield Rd, SW10 307 M2
Sch Ifield Sch, Grav. DA12
off Cedar Av 191 GJ92
Ifield Way, Grav. DA12 191 GK93
Ifold Rd, Red. RH1 266 DG136
Ifor Evans Pl, E1 289 K5
Ightham Rd, Erith DA8 166 FA80
Igraine Ct, N9
off Galahad Rd 100 DU48
Ikona Ct, Wey. KT13 213 BQ106
Ilbert St, W10 282 D3
Ilchester Gdns, W2 283 L10
Ilchester Pl, W14 294 G6
Ilchester Rd, Dag. RM8 126 EV64
Ildersly Gro, SE21 182 DR89
Sch Ilderton Prim Sch, SE16 312 G1
Ilderton Rd, SE15 312 G2
SE16 300 F10
Ilex Cl, Eng.Grn TW20 172 AV94
Sunbury-on-Thames TW16
off Oakington Dr 196 BW96
Ilex Ct, Berk. HP4 38 AV19
Ilex Ho, N4 121 DM59
Ilex Rd, NW10 139 CT65
Ilex Way, SW16 181 DN92
ILFORD, IG1 - IG6 125 EQ62
⇌ Ilford 125 EN62
Sch Ilford Co High Sch, Ilf. IG6
off Fremantle Rd 103 EP54
Ilford Hill, Ilf. IG1 125 EN62
Ilford La, Ilf. IG1 125 EP62
Sch Ilford Ursuline High Sch,
Ilf. IG1 off Morland Rd 125 EP61
Sch Ilford Ursuline Prep Sch,
Ilf. IG1 off Coventry Rd 125 EN61
Ilfracombe Cres, Horn. RM12 128 FJ63
Ilfracombe Gdns, Rom. RM6 126 EV59
Ilfracombe Rd, Brom. BR1 184 EF90
Iliffe St, SE17 299 H10
Iliffe Yd, SE17 299 H10
Ilkeston Ct, E5
off Overbury St 123 DX63
Ilkley Cl, SE19 182 DR93
Ilkley Rd, E16 292 C7
Watford WD19 94 BX50
Illingworth, Wind. SL4 151 AL84
Illingworth Cl, Mitch. CR4 200 DD97
Illingworth Way, Enf. EN1 82 DS42
Ilmington Rd, Har. HA3 117 CK58
Ilminster Gdns, SW11 160 DE84
Imber Cl, N14 99 DJ45
Esher KT10 197 CD102
● Imber Ct Trd Est, E.Mol. KT8 197 CD100
Imber Gro, Esher KT10 197 CD101
Imber Pk Rd, Esher KT10 197 CD102
Imber St, N1 277 L9
Imer Pl, T.Ditt. KT7 197 CF101
Sch Immanuel & St. Andrew
C of E Prim Sch, SW16
off Buckleigh Rd 181 DL93
Sch Immanuel Coll,
Bushey WD23 off Elstree Rd 95 CE45
Sch Immanuel Sch, Rom. RM1
off Havering Rd 105 FD50
Imperial Av, N16 122 DT62
● Imperial Business Est,
Grav. DA11 191 GF86
Imperial Cl, NW2 119 CV64
Harrow HA2 116 CA58
Uni Imperial Coll London,
Charing Cross Campus, W6 306 C1
Hammersmith Campus, W12
off Du Cane Rd 139 CU72
St. Mary's Campus, W2 284 B8
S. Kensington Campus, SW7 296 A6
Imperial Coll Rd, SW7 296 A7
Imperial Ct, NW8 274 D10
Chislehurst BR7 205 EN95
Imperial Cres, SW6 307 N8
Weybridge KT13 195 BQ104
Imperial Dr, Grav. DA12 191 GM92
Harrow HA2 116 CA59
Imperial Gdns, Mitch. CR4 201 DH97
Imperial Gro, Barn. EN4 80 DB39
Imperial Ms, E6 292 E1
Imperial Pk, Ruis. HA4 116 BY64
● Imperial Pk, Wat. WD24 76 BW39
Imperial Pl, Chis. BR7
off Forest Cl 205 EN95
Imperial Retail Pk,
Grav. DA11 191 GG86
Imperial Rd, N22 99 DL53
SW6 307 M6
Feltham TW14 175 BS87
Windsor SL4 151 AN83
Imperial Sq, SW6 307 M6
Imperial St, E3 290 E3
● Imperial Trd Est, Rain. RM13 148 FJ70
★ Imperial War Mus, SE1 298 F7
Imperial Way, Chis. BR7 185 EQ90
Croxley Green WD3 93 BP45
Croydon CR0 219 DM107
Harrow HA3 118 CL58
Hemel Hempstead HP3 40 BL24
Watford WD24 76 BW39
Imperial Wf 307 P7
Imperial Wf, SW6 307 N8
Impington, Kings.T. KT1
off Willingham Way 198 CN96
● Impresa Pk, Hodd. EN11 49 EC16
● Imprimo Pk, Loug. IG10 85 EQ42
Imre Cl, W12 139 CV74
Inca Dr, SE9 185 EP87
Inca Ter, N15
off Milton Rd 121 DP55
Ince Rd, Hersham KT12 213 BS107
Coll Inchbald Sch of Design,
Garden Design Faculty, SW1 297 K9
Interior Design Faculty, SW1 296 G8
Inchmery Rd, SE6 183 EB89
Inchwood, Croy. CR0 221 EB105
Indells, Hat. AL10 45 CT19
Independence Ho, SW19
off Chapter Way 200 DD95
Sch Independent Jewish Day Sch,
The, NW4 off Green La 119 CX57
Independent Pl, E8 278 B2
Independents Rd, SE3 315 L10
Inderwick Rd, N8 121 DM57
Indescon Ct, E14 302 B5
Index Apts, Rom. RM1
off Mercury Gdns 127 FF56
Indiana Bldg, SE13
off Deals Gateway 314 B7
India Pl, WC2 286 C10
India Rd, Slou. SL1 152 AV75
India St, EC3 288 A9
India Way, W12 139 CV73

Indigo Ms, E14 290 F9
N16 122 DR62
Indigo Wk, N2 120 DF56
N6 120 DF56
Indus Rd, SE7 164 EJ80
Industry Ter, SW9
off Canterbury Cres 161 DN83
Inforum Ms, SE15 312 D4
Ingal Rd, E13 291 N5
Ingate Pl, SW8 309 K7
Ingatestone Rd, E12 124 EJ60
SE25 202 DV98
Woodford Green IG8 102 EG52
Ingelow Rd, SW8 309 J9
Ingels Mead, Epp. CM16 69 ET29
Ingersoll Rd, W12 139 CV74
Enfield EN3 82 DW38
Ingestre Ct, W1 *off Ingestre Pl* 285 M10
Ingestre Pl, W1 285 M9
Ingestre Rd, E7 124 EG63
NW5 121 DH63
Ingham Cl, S.Croy. CR2 221 DX109
Ingham Rd, NW6 273 J1
South Croydon CR2 220 DW109
Inglebert St, EC1 286 E2
Ingleboro Dr, Pur. CR8 220 DR113
Ingleborough St, SW9 310 E8
Ingleby Dr, Har. HA1 117 CD62
Ingleby Gdns, Chig. IG7 104 EV48
Ingleby Rd, N7 *off Bryett Rd* 121 DL62
Dagenham RM10 147 FB65
Grays RM16 171 GH76
Ilford IG1 125 EP60
Ingleby Way, Chis. BR7 185 EN92
Wallington SM6 219 DK109
Ingle Cl, Pnr. HA5 116 BY55
Ingledew Rd, SE18 165 ER78
Inglefield, Pot.B. EN6 64 DA30
Ingleglen, Farn.Com. SL2 111 AP64
Hornchurch RM11 128 FN59
Inglehurst, New Haw KT15 212 BH110
Inglehurst Gdns, Ilf. IG4 125 EM57
Inglemere Rd, SE23 183 DX90
Mitcham CR4 180 DF94
Ingle Ms, EC1 286 E2
Ingles, Welw.G.C. AL8 29 CX06
Inglesham Wk, E9 279 P4
Ingleside, Colnbr. SL3 153 BE81
Ingleside Cl, Beck. BR3 183 EA94
Ingleside Gro, SE3 315 M3
Inglethorpe St, SW6 306 C6
Ingleton Av, Well. DA16 186 EU85
Ingleton Rd, N18 100 DU51
Carshalton SM5 218 DE109
Ingleton St, SW9 310 E8
Ingleway, N12 98 DD51
Inglewood, Cher. KT16 193 BF104
Croydon CR0 221 DY109
Woking GU21 226 AV118
Inglewood Cl, E14 302 B8
Hornchurch RM12 128 FK63
Ilford IG6 103 ET51
Inglewood Copse, Brom. BR1 204 EL96
Inglewood Gdns, St.Alb. AL2
off North Orbital Rd 61 CE25
Inglewood Ms, SE27 182 DQ92
Surbiton KT6 198 CN102
Inglewood Rd, NW6 273 K3
Bexleyheath DA7 167 FD84
Inglis Barracks, NW7 97 CX50
Inglis Rd, W5 138 CM73
Croydon CR0 202 DT102
Inglis St, SE5 311 H7
Ingoldsby Rd, Grav. DA12 191 GL88
Ingram Av, NW11 120 DC59
Ingram Cl, SE11 298 D8
Stanmore HA7 95 CJ50
Ingram Ho, E3 279 L10
Ingram Rd, N2 120 DE56
Dartford DA1 188 FL88
Grays RM17 170 GD77
Thornton Heath CR7 202 DQ95
Ingrams Cl, Hersham KT12 214 BW106
Ingram Way, Grnf. UB6 137 CD67
Ingrave Rd,
Brwd. CM13, CM14, CM15 108 FX47
Romford RM1 127 FD56
Ingrave St, SW11 308 B10
Ingrebourne Ave, Rom. RM3 106 FK49
Ingrebourne Gdns,
Upmin. RM14 128 FQ60
Sch **Ingrebourne Prim Sch**,
Harold Hill RM3 *off Taunton Rd* 128 FJ49
Ingrebourne Rd, Rain. RM13 147 FH70
Ingrebourne Valley Grn Way,
Horn. RM12 128 FK64
Ingress Gdns, Green. DA9 189 FX85
Ingress Pk, Green. DA9
off Ingress Pk Av 169 FW84
Ingress Pk Av, Green. DA9 169 FV84
Ingress St, W4
off Devonshire Rd 158 CS78
Ingreway, Rom. RM3 106 FP52
Inholms La, Dor. RH5 263 CH140
Inigo Jones Rd, SE7 164 EL80
Inigo Pl, WC2 286 A10
Inkerman Rd, NW5 275 J4
Eton Wick SL4 151 AM77
Knaphill GU21 226 AS118
St. Albans AL1 43 CE21
Inkerman Ter, W8 *off Allen St* 295 K7
Chesham HP5 54 AQ33
Inkerman Way, Wok. GU21 226 AS118
Inks Grn, E4 101 EC50
Inkster Ho, SW11
off Ingrave St 308 C10
Inkwell Cl, N12 98 DC48
Inman Rd, NW10 138 CS67
SW18 180 DC87
Inmans Row, Wdf.Grn. IG8 102 EG49
Inner Circle, NW1 284 G3
Innerd Ct, Croy. CR0
off Pawson's Rd 202 DQ100
Inner Pk Rd, SW19 179 CX88
Inner Ring E,
Lon.Hthrw Air. TW6 155 BP83
Inner Ring W,
Lon.Hthrw Air. TW6 154 BN83
Inner Temple, EC4
off Fleet St 286 F9
Inner Temple La, EC4 286 E9
Innes Cl, SW20 199 CY96
Innes Ct, Hem.H. HP3 40 BK22
Innes Gdns, SW15 179 CV86
Innes St, SE15 311 P4
Innes Yd, Croy. CR0
off Whitgift St 202 DQ104
Inniskilling Rd, E13 292 D1
● **Innova Business Pk**, Enf. EN3 105 DZ36
Innovation Cl, Wem. HA0 138 CL67
Innova Way, Enf. EN3 83 DZ36
Inskip Cl, E10 123 EB61
Inskip Dr, Horn. RM11 128 FL60
Inskip Rd, Dag. RM8 126 EX60
Insley Ho, E3
off Bow Rd 290 C2
Uni **Institute of Cancer Research**,
The, Sutton Site, Sutt. SM2
off Cotswold Rd 218 DC110
★ **Institute of Contemporary**
Arts (I.C.A.), SW1 297 P3
Uni **Institute of Ed**, WC1 285 P5
Institute Pl, E8 278 E3
Institute Rd, Cooper. CM16 70 EX29
Taplow SL6 130 AF72
Westcott RH4 *off Guildford Rd* 284 CC137
Instone Rd, Dart. DA1 188 FK87
Integer Gdns, E11 123 ED59
● **Interchange E Ind Est**, E5
off Grosvenor Way 122 DW61
International Av, Houns. TW5 156 BW78
Sch **International Comm Sch**,
NW1 285 H5
Sch **International Sch of London**,
W3 *off Gunnersbury Av* 158 CN77
● **International Trd Est**,
Southall. UB2 155 BV76
International Way, E20 280 E4
Swanscombe DA10, DA11 190 GA87
🔒 **Intu Bromley**, Brom. BR1 204 EG96
🔒 **Intu Lakeside**, Grays RM20 169 FU77
🔒 **Intu Uxbridge**, Uxb. UB8 134 BK66
🔒 **Intu Watford**, Wat. WD17 76 BW42
Inveraray Pl, SE18
off Old Mill Rd 165 ER79
Inver Cl, E5 *off Theydon Rd* 122 DW61
Inverclyde Gdns, Rom. RM6 126 EX56
Inver Ct, W2 283 M9
W6 *off Invermead Cl* 159 CU76
Inveresk Gdns, Wor.Pk. KT4 199 CT104
Inverforth Cl, NW3
off North End Way 120 DC61
Inverforth Rd, N11 99 DH50
Inverine Rd, SE7 164 EH78
Invermead Cl, W6 159 CU77
Invermore Pl, SE18 165 EQ77
Inverness Av, Enf. EN1 82 DS39
Inverness Dr, Ilf. IG6 103 ES51
Inverness Gdns, W8 295 L3
Inverness Ms, E16 145 EQ74
W2 283 M10
Inverness Pl, W2 283 M10
Inverness Rd, N18 100 DV50
Hounslow TW3 156 BZ84
Southall UB2 156 BY77
Worcester Park KT4 199 CX102
Inverness St, NW1 275 J8
Inverness Ter, W2 283 M10
Inverton Rd, SE15 163 DX84
Invicta Cl, E3 290 B7
Chislehurst BR7 185 EN92
Feltham TW14 175 BT88
Invicta Gro, Nthlt. UB5 136 BZ69
Invicta Plaza, SE1 298 G2
Sch **Invicta Prim Sch**, SE3 315 P3
Invicta Rd, SE3 315 P4
Dartford DA2 188 FP86
Inville Rd, SE17 311 M1
Invito Ho, Ilf. IG2 125 EN58
Inwen Ct, SE8 313 M1
Inwood Av, Couls. CR5 235 DN120
Hounslow TW3 156 CC83
● **Inwood Business Pk**,
Houns. TW3 *off Whitton Rd* 156 CB84
Inwood Cl, Croy. CR0 203 DY103
Inwood Ct, Walt. KT12 196 BW103
Inwood Ho, SE22
off Pytchley Rd 162 DS83
Inwood Rd, Houns. TW3 156 CB84
Inworth St, SW11 308 D8
Inworth Wk, N1 277 J8
● **IO Cen**, SE18
off Armstrong Rd 165 EQ76
Barking IG11 145 ET70
Hatfield AL10 44 CS16
Sutton SM3 199 CY103
Waltham Abbey EN9 83 EA35
Iona Cl, SE6 183 EA87
Morden SM4 200 DB101
Iona Cres, Slou. SL1 131 AL72
Ionian Bldg, E14 289 L10
Ionian Way, Hem.H. HP2
off Jupiter Dr 40 BM18
Ionia Wk, Grav. DA12 191 GM90
Ion Sq, E2 288 C1
● **IO Trade Centre Croydon**,
Bedd. CR0 219 DM105
Ipswich Rd, SW17 180 DG93
Slough SL1 131 AN73
Sch **Iqua Slough Islamic Prim Sch**,
Slough SL3 132 AV73
Ira Ct, SE27 *off Norwood Rd* 181 DP89
Ireland Cl, E6 293 J7
Ireland Pl, N22 99 DL52
Ireland Yd, EC4 287 H9
Irene Rd, SW6 307 J7
Orpington BR6 205 ET101
Stoke D'Abernon KT11 214 CA114
Ireton Av, Walt. KT12 195 BS103
Ireton Cl, N10 98 DG52
Ireton Pl, Grays RM17
off Russell Rd 170 GA77
Ireton St, E3 290 A4
Iris Av, Bex. DA5 186 EY85
Iris Cl, E6 293 H6
N14 99 DK45
Croydon CR0 203 DX102
Pilgrim's Hatch CM15 108 FV43
Surbiton KT6 198 CM101
Iris Ct, Pnr. HA5 116 BW55
Iris Cres, Bexh. DA7 166 EZ79
Iris Ms, Houns. TW4 176 CA86
Iris Path, Rom. RM3
off Clematis Cl 106 FJ52
Iris Rd, W.Ewell KT19 216 CP106
Iris Wk, Edg. HA8
off Ash Cl 96 CQ49
Irkdale Av, Enf. EN1 82 DT39
Iron Br Cl, NW10 118 CS64
Southall UB2 136 CC74
Ironbridge Rd N, Uxb. UB11 154 BN75
Ironbridge Rd S, West Dr. UB7 154 BN75
Iron Dr, Hert. SG13 32 DV08
Iron Mill La, Dart. DA1 167 FE84
Iron Mill Pl, SW18
off Garratt La 180 DB86
Dartford DA1 167 FF84
Iron Mill Rd, SW18 180 DB86
Ironmonger La, EC2 287 L9
Ironmonger Pas, EC1 287 K4
Ironmonger Row, EC1 287 K3
Ironmongers Pl, E14 302 B9
IRONS BOTTOM, Reig. RH2 266 DA142
Ironsbottom, Horl. RH6 268 DA146
Sidlow RH2 266 DB141
Ironside Cl, SE16 301 J4
Ironside Rd, Brent. TW8 157 CJ80
Irons Way, Rom. RM5 105 FC52
Iron Wks, E3 280 A8
Irvine Av, Har. HA3 117 CG55
Irvine Cl, E14 290 D6
N20 98 DE47
Irvine Gdns, S.Ock. RM15 149 FT72
Irvine Pl, Vir.W. GU25 192 AY99
Irvine Way, Orp. BR6 205 ET101
Irving Av, Nthlt. UB5 136 BX67
Irving Gro, SW9 310 C9
Irving Ms, N1 277 J5
Irving Rd, W14 294 D6
Irving St, WC2 297 P1
Irving Wk, Swans. DA10 190 FY87
Irving Way, NW9 119 CT57
Swanley BR8 207 FD96
Irwell Est, SE16
off Neptune St 300 G5
Irwin Av, SE18 165 ES80
Irwin Cl, Uxb. UB10 114 BN62
Irwin Gdns, NW10 139 CV67
Irwin Rd, Guil. GU2 258 AU135
Isaac Way, SE1 299 K4
Isabel Ct, Hodd. EN11 49 EB15
Isabel Gate, Chsht EN8 67 DZ26
Isabel Hill Cl, Hmptn. TW12
off Upper Sunbury Rd 196 CB95
Isabella Cl, N14 99 DJ45
Isabella Ct, Rich. TW10
off Grove Rd 178 CM86
Isabella Dr, Orp. BR6 223 EQ105
Isabella Ms, N1 277 N4
Isabella Pl, Kings.T. KT2 178 CM92
Isabella Rd, E9 279 H3
Isabella St, SE1 298 G3
Isabelle Cl, Goffs Oak EN7 66 DQ29
Isambard Cl, Uxb. UB8
off Station Rd 134 BK70
Isambard Ms, E14 302 F7
Isambard Pl, SE16 301 H3
Isbell Gdns, Rom. RM1 105 FE52
Isbells Dr, Reig. RH2 266 DB135
Isel Way, SE22
off East Dulwich Gro 182 DS85
Isenburg Way, Hem.H. HP2 40 BK15
Isham Rd, SW16 201 DL96
Isis Cl, SW15 159 CW84
Ruislip HA4 115 BQ58
Isis Dr, Upmin. RM14 129 FS58
Isis Ho, N18 100 DT51
Cher. KT16 *off Bridge Wf* 194 BJ101
● **Isis Reach**, Belv. DA17 147 FB74
Isis St, SW18 180 DC89
Sch **Islamia Prim Sch**, NW6 272 F8
Coll **Islamic Coll for Advanced**
Studies, NW10 *off High Rd* 139 CV65
Island, The, West Dr. UB7 154 BH81
Island Apts, N1
off Coleman Flds 277 K8
Island Cen Way, Enf. EN3 83 EA37
Island Cl, Stai. TW18 173 BE91
Island Fm Av, W.Mol. KT8 196 BZ99
Island Fm Rd, W.Mol. KT8 196 BZ99
DLR **Island Gardens** 302 E9
Island Ho, E3 290 E2
Island Rd, SE16 301 J9
Mitcham CR4 180 DF94
Island Row, E14 289 N9
Isla Rd, SE18 165 EQ79
Islay Gdns, Houns. TW4 176 BX85
Islay Wk, N1 277 K5
Isledon Rd, N7 121 DN62
Islehurst Cl, Chis. BR7 205 EN95
Islet Pk, Maid. SL6 130 AC68
Islet Pk Dr, Maid. SL6 130 AC68
ISLEWORTH, TW7 157 CF83
⇌ **Isleworth** 157 CF82
Sch **Isleworth & Syon Sch for Boys**,
Islw. TW7 *off Ridgeway Rd* 157 CE80
● **Isleworth Business Complex**,
Islw. TW7 *off St. John's Rd* 157 CF82
Isleworth Prom, Twick. TW1 157 CH84
Sch **Isleworth Town Prim Sch**,
Islw. TW7 *off Twickenham Rd* 157 CG82
ISLINGTON, N1 276 E9
Sch **Islington Arts & Media Sch**,
N4 *off Turle Rd* 121 DM60
Coll **Islington City Learning Cen**,
N5 277 J3
Islington Grn, N1 276 G9
Islington High St, N1 286 F1
Islington Pk Ms, N1 276 G6
Islington Pk St, N1 276 F6
Islip Gdns, Edg. HA8 96 CR52
Northolt UB5 136 BY66
Islip Manor Rd, Nthlt. UB5 136 BY66
Islip St, NW5 275 L3
Ismailia Rd, E7 144 EH66
★ **Ismaili Cen**, SW7 296 B8
Isom Cl, E13 292 B3
Issa Rd, Houns. TW3 156 BZ84
Issigonis Ho, W3 *off Cowley Rd* 139 CT74
ISTEAD RISE, Grav. DA13 190 GE94
Istead Ri, Grav. DA13 191 GF94
Sch **Italia Conti Acad of Thea Arts**,
EC1 287 J5
Coll **Italia Conti Arts Cen**,
Guil. GU1 *off Epsom Rd* 243 BD133
Itchingwood Common Rd,
Oxt. RH8 254 EJ133
Ivanhoe Cl, Uxb. UB8 134 BK71
Ivanhoe Dr, Har. HA3 117 CG55
Ivanhoe Rd, SE5 162 DT83
Hounslow TW4 156 BX83
Ivatt Pl, W14 307 H1
Ivatt Way, N17 121 DP55
Iveagh Av, NW10 138 CN68
Iveagh Cl, E9 279 K8
NW10 138 CN68
Northwood HA6 93 BP53
Iveagh Ct, Hem.H. HP2 40 BK19
Iveagh Rd, Guil. GU2 258 AV135
Woking GU21 226 AT118
Iveagh Ter, NW10
off Iveagh Av 138 CN68
Ivedon Rd, Well. DA16 166 EW82
Ive Fm Cl, E10 123 EA61
Ive Fm La, E10 123 EA61
Iveley Rd, SW4 309 L9
IVER, SL0 133 BF72
⇌ **Iver** 153 BF75
Iverdale Cl, Iver SL0 133 BC73
Ivere Dr, New Barn. EN5 80 DB44
IVER HEATH, Iver SL0 133 BD69
Sch **Iver Heath Inf Sch & Nurs**,
Iver SL0 *off Slough Rd* 133 BD69
Sch **Iver Heath Jun Sch**, Iver SL0
off St. Margarets Cl 133 BD68
Iverhurst Cl, Bexh. DA6 186 EX85
Iver La, Iver SL0 134 BH71
Uxbridge UB8 134 BH71
Iver Lo, Iver SL0 133 BF71
Iverna Ct, W8 295 K6
Iverna Gdns, W8 295 K6
Feltham TW14 175 BR85
Iver Rd, Iver SL0 134 BG72
Pilgrim's Hatch CM15 108 FV44
Iverson Rd, NW6 273 H5
Ivers Way, New Adgtn CR0 221 EB108
Sch **Iver Village Inf Sch**,
Iver SL0 *off West Sq* 133 BF72
Sch **Iver Village Jun Sch**,
Iver SL0 *off High St* 133 BE72
Ives Gdns, Rom. RM1
off Sims Cl 127 FF56
Ives Rd, E16 291 J7
Hertford SG14 31 DP08
Slough SL3 153 AZ76
Ives St, SW3 296 D8
Ivestor Ter, SE23 182 DW87
Ivimey St, E2 288 D2
Ivinghoe Cl, Enf. EN1 82 DS40
St. Albans AL4
off Highview Gdns 43 CJ15
Watford WD25 76 BX35
Ivinghoe Rd, Bushey WD23 95 CD45
Dagenham RM8 126 EV64
Mill End WD3 92 BG45
Ivins Rd, Beac. HP9 88 AG54
Ivo Pl, N19 121 DK62
Ivor Cl, Guil. GU1 259 AZ135
Ivor Gro, SE9 185 EP88
Ivor Pl, NW1 284 E5
Ivor St, NW1 275 L7
Ivory Cl, St.Alb. AL4 43 CJ22
Ivory Ct, Felt. TW13 175 BU88
Hemel Hempstead HP3 40 BL23
Ivorydown, Brom. BR1 184 EG91
Ivory Sq, SW11
off Gartons Way 160 DC83
Ivy Bower Cl, Green. DA9
off Riverview Rd 189 FV85
Ivybridge, Brox. EN10 49 EA19
Ivybridge Cl, Twick. TW1 177 CG86
Uxbridge UB8 134 BL69
Ivybridge Est, Islw. TW7 177 CF85
Ivybridge Ho, SE22
off Pytchley Rd 162 DS83
Ivybridge La, WC2 298 B1
Sch **Ivybridge Prim Sch**, Islw.
TW7 *off Summerwood Rd* 177 CF86
IVY CHIMNEYS, Epp. CM16 69 ES32
Sch **Ivy Chimneys Prim Sch**, Epp.
CM16 *off Ivy Chimneys Rd* 69 ET32
Ivy Chimneys Rd, Epp. CM16 69 ES32
Ivychurch Cl, SE20 182 DW94
Ivychurch La, SE17 300 A10
Ivy Cl, Chesh. HP5 54 AP30
Dartford DA1 188 FN87
Gravesend DA12 191 GJ90
Harrow HA2 116 BZ63
Pinner HA5 116 BW59
Sunbury-on-Thames TW16 196 BW96
Ivy Cotts, E14 290 D10
Ivy Ct, SE16 312 D1
Ivy Cres, W4 158 CQ77
Slough SL1 131 AM73
Sch **Ivydale Prim Sch**, SE15
off Ivydale Rd 163 DX84
Ivydale Rd, SE15 163 DX83
Carshalton SM5 200 DF103
Ivyday Gro, SW16 181 DM90
Ivydene, W.Mol. KT8 196 BZ99
Ivydene Cl, Red. RH1 267 DH139
Sutton SM1 218 DC105
Ivy Gdns, N8 121 DL58
Mitcham CR4 201 DK97
Ivy Ho La, Berk. HP4 38 AY19
Sevenoaks TN14 241 FD118
Ivyhouse Rd, Dag. RM9 146 EX65
Ivy Ho Rd, Uxb. UB10 115 BP62
Ivy La, Houns. TW4 156 BZ84
Knockholt Pound TN14 240 EY116
Woking GU22 227 BB118
Ivy Lea, Rick. WD3
off Springwell Av 92 BG46
Ivy Lo La, Rom. RM3 106 FP53
Ivy Mill Cl, Gdse. RH9 252 DV132
Ivy Mill La, Gdse. RH9 252 DU132
Ivymount Rd, SE27 181 DN90
Ivy Rd, E16 291 N8
E17 123 EA58
N14 99 DJ45
NW2 119 CW63
SE4 163 DZ84
SW17 *off Tooting High St* 180 DE92
Hounslow TW3 156 CB84
Surbiton KT6 198 CN102
Ivy St, N1 277 N10
Ivy Ter, Hodd. EN11 49 EC15
Ivy Wk, Dag. RM9 146 EY65
Hatfield AL10 44 CS15
Ixworth Pl, SW3 296 C10
Izane Rd, Bexh. DA6 166 EZ84

J

J31 Pk, Grays RM20 169 FU78
Jacaranda Cl, N.Mal. KT3 198 CS97
Jacaranda Gro, E8 278 B7
Sch **Jack & Jill Sch**, Hmptn.
TW12 *off Nightingale Rd* 176 CA93
Jackass La, Kes. BR2 222 EH107
Tandridge RH8 253 DZ131
Jack Barnett Way, N22 99 DM54
Jack Clow Rd, E15 291 K1
Jack Cornwell St, E12 125 EN63
Jack Dash Way, E6 292 G5
Jackdaws, Welw.G.C. AL7 30 DC09
Jackets La, Hare. UB9 92 BN52
Northwood HA6 93 BP53
Jacketts Fld, Abb.L. WD5 59 BT31
Jack Goodchild Way,
Kings.T. KT1 *off Kingston Rd* 198 CP97
Jack Jones Way, Dag. RM9 146 EZ67
Jacklin Grn, Wdf.Grn. IG8 102 EG49
Jackman Ms, NW2 118 CS62
Jackmans La, Wok. GU21 226 AU119
Jackman St, E8 278 E9
Jack's Fm Way, E4 101 EC51
JACKS HATCH, Epp. CM16 51 EN21
Jacks La, Hare. UB9 92 BG53
Jackson Cl, E9 279 H7
Epsom KT18 216 CR114
Greenhithe DA9
off Cowley Av 189 FU85
Hornchurch RM11 128 FM56
Slough SL3 152 AY76
Jackson Ct, E11
off Brading Cres 124 EH60
Dagenham RM10
off St. Mark's Pl 146 FA65
Jackson Rd, N7 276 D1
Barking IG11 145 ER67
Barnet EN4 80 DE44
Bromley BR2 204 EL103
Jacksons Dr, Chsht EN7 66 DU28
Jacksons La, N6 120 DG59
Jacksons Pl, Croy. CR0
off Cross Rd 202 DR102
Jackson St, SE18 165 EN79
Jacksons Way, Croy. CR0 203 EA104
Jackson Way, Epsom KT19
off Lady Harewood Way 216 CN109
Southall UB2 156 CB75
Jack Stevens Cl, Harl. CM17
off Potter St 52 EW17
Sch **Jack Taylor Sch**, NW8 273 N8
Sch **Jack Tizard Sch**, W12
off South Africa Rd 139 CV74
Jack Walker Ct, N5 277 H1
Jacob Cl, Wind. SL4 151 AL81
Jacob Ct, Enf. EN3
off Baddeley Cl 83 EA37
Jacob Ho, Erith DA18
off Kale Rd 166 EX75
Jacob Ms, Stan. HA7 95 CG47
Jacobs Av, Harold Wd RM3 106 FL54
Jacobs Cl, Dag. RM10 127 FB62
Jacobs Ho, E13 292 C2
Jacobs Ladder, Hat. AL9
off The Broadway 45 CW18
Jacobs La, Hort.Kir. DA4 208 FQ97
Jacob St, SE1 300 B4
JACOBS WELL, Guil. GU4 242 AY129
Jacob's Well Ms, W1 285 H8
Jacob's Well Rd,
Jacobs Well GU4 242 AX129
Jacqueline Cl, Nthlt. UB5 136 BY67
Jade Cl, E16 292 F9
NW2 119 CX59
Dagenham RM8 126 EW60
Jaffe Rd, Ilf. IG1 125 EQ60
Jaffray Rd, Brom. BR2 204 EK98
Jaggard Way, SW12 180 DF87
Jagger Cl, Dart. DA2 188 FQ87
Jago Cl, SE18 165 EQ79
Jago Wk, SE5 311 L5
Jail La, Bigg.H. TN16 238 EK116
Jake's Vw, Park St AL2 60 CC27
Jamaica Rd, SE1 300 B5
SE16 300 E6
Thornton Heath CR7 201 DP100
Jamaica St, E1 289 H8
Sch **James Allen's Girls' Sch**,
SE22 *off East Dulwich Gro* 182 DS85
Sch **James Allen's Prep Sch**,
Pre-Prep Sch, SE21
off Dulwich Village 182 DR86
Mid Sch, SE22
off East Dulwich Gro 182 DS85
James Av, NW2 272 B2
Dagenham RM8 126 EZ60
James Bedford Cl, Pnr. HA5 94 BW54
James Boswell Cl, SW16
off Samuel Johnson Cl 181 DN91
James Clavell Sq, SE18 305 P6
James Cl, E13 281 P10
NW11 *off Woodlands* 119 CY58
Bushey WD23 76 BY43
Romford RM2 127 FG57
James Collins Cl, W9 282 G5
James Ct, N1 277 K7
Sch **James Dixon Prim Sch**,
SE20 *off William Booth Rd* 202 DU95
James Dudson Ct, NW10 138 CQ66
Sch **James Elliman Prim Sch**,
Slou. SL2 *off Elliman Av* 132 AT73
James Gdns, N22 99 DP52
James Hammett Ho, E2 288 B1
James Ho, W10
off Appleford Rd 282 F5
James Joyce Wk, SE24
off Shakespeare Rd 161 DP84
James La, E10 123 ED59
E11 123 ED58
James Lee Sq, Enf. EN3
off Harston Dr 83 EA38
James Martin Cl, Denh. UB9 114 BG58
James Meadow, Slou. SL3 153 AZ79
James Newman Ct, SE9
off Great Harry Dr 185 EN90
Sch **James Oglethorpe**
Prim Sch, The, Upmin. RM14
off Ashvale Gdns 129 FT61
Jameson Cl, W3
off Acton La 158 CQ75
Jameson Ct, E2 288 G1
St. Albans AL1 *off Avenue Rd* 43 CF19
Jameson Ho, SE11
off Glasshouse Wk 298 C10
Jameson St, W8 295 K2
James Pl, N17 100 DT53
James Riley Pt, E15 280 F8
James Rd, Dart. DA1 187 FG87
Peasmarsh GU3 258 AW142
James's Cotts, Rich. TW9 158 CN80
James St, W1 285 H8
WC2 286 B10
Barking IG11 145 EQ66
Enfield EN1 82 DT43
Epping CM16 69 ET28
Hounslow TW3 157 CD83
Windsor SL4 151 AR81
James Ter, SW14
off Mullins Path 158 CR83
Jameston Lo, Ruis. HA4
off Pembroke Rd 115 BT60
Jamestown Rd, NW1 275 J8
Jamestown Way, E14 303 H1
James Voller Way, E1 288 G9
James Watt Way, Erith DA8 167 FE79

James Way, Wat. WD19 94 BX49
Sch James Wolfe Prim Sch (Randall Pl Campus), SE10 314 E4
James Yd, E4 101 ED51
Jamieson Ho, Houns. TW4 176 BZ87
Jamnagar Cl, Stai. TW18 173 BF93
Jamuna Cl, E14 289 M7
Jane Cl, Hem.H. HP2 41 BP15
Jane Seymour Ct, SE9 off Avery Hill Rd 185 ER87
Jane St, E1 288 E8
Janet St, E14 302 B6
Janeway Pl, SE16 300 E5
Janeway St, SE16 300 D5
Janice Ms, Ilf. IG1 off Oakfield Rd 125 EP62
Janmead, Hutt. CM13 109 GB45
Janoway Hill La, Wok. GU21 226 AW119
Jansen Wk, SW11 off Hope St 160 DD84
Janson Cl, E15 281 J2
NW10 118 CR62
Janson Rd, E15 281 J2
Jansons Rd, N15 122 DS55
Japan Cres, N4 121 DM60
Sch Japanese Sch, The, W3 off Creffield Rd 138 CN73
Japan Rd, Rom. RM6 126 EX58
Japonica Cl, Wok. GU21 226 AW118
Jardine Rd, E1 289 K10
Jarman Cl, Hem.H. HP3 40 BL22
Jarman Ho, E1 288 G7
Jarman Pk, Hem.H. HP2 40 BM21
Jarman Way, Hem.H. HP2 40 BM21
Jarrah Cotts, Purf. RM19 169 FR79
Jarrett Cl, SW2 181 DP88
Jarrow Cl, Mord. SM4 200 DB99
Jarrow Rd, N17 122 DV56
SE16 300 G9
Romford RM6 126 EW58
Jarrow Way, E9 279 M1
Jarvis Cleys, Chsht EN7 66 DT26
Jarvis Cl, Bark. IG11 off Westbury Rd 145 ER67
Barnet EN5 79 CX43
Jarvis Rd, SE22 off Melbourne Gro 162 DS84
South Croydon CR2 220 DR107
Jarvis Way, Harold Wd RM3 106 FL54
Jasmin Cl, Nthwd. HA6 93 BT53
Jasmine Cl, Ilf. IG1 125 EP64
Orpington BR6 205 EP103
Redhill RH1 off Spencer Way 266 DG139
Southall UB1 136 BY73
Woking GU21 226 AT116
Jasmine Dr, Hert. SG13 32 DU09
Jasmine Gdns, Croy. CR0 203 EB104
Harrow HA2 116 CA61
Hatfield AL10 45 CU16
Jasmine Gro, SE20 202 DV95
Jasmine Rd, Rush Grn RM7 127 FE61
Jasmine Sq, E3 279 N9
Jasmine Ter, West Dr. UB7 154 BN75
Jasmine Wk, Chesh. HP5 54 AN30
Jasmine Way, E.Mol. KT8 off Hampton Ct Way 197 CE98
Jasmin Ho, Ilf. IG2 off Perth Rd 125 EN58
Jasmin Rd, Epsom KT19 216 CP106
Jasmin Way, Hem.H. HP1 off Larkspur Cl 39 BE19
Jason Cl, Brwd. CM14 108 FT49
Redhill RH1 266 DE139
Weybridge KT13 213 BQ106
Jason Ct, W1 off Marylebone La 285 H8
Jasons Dr, Guil. GU4 243 BC131
Jasons Hill, Chesh. HP5 56 AV30
Jason Wk, SE9 185 EN91
Jasper Ave, W7 157 CF75
Jasper Cl, Enf. EN3 82 DW38
Jasper Pas, SE19 182 DT93
Jasper Rd, E16 292 F9
SE19 182 DT92
Jasper Wk, N1 287 L2
Javelin Way, Nthlt. UB5 136 BX69
Jaycroft, Enf. EN2 off The Ridgeway 81 DN39
Jay Gdns, Chis. BR7 185 EM91
Jay Ms, SW7 295 P5
Jays Cl, Brick.Wd AL2 60 CA31
Jays Covert, Couls. CR5 234 DG119
Jazzfern Ter, Wem. HA0 off Maybank Av 117 CG64
Jean Batten Cl, Wall. SM6 219 DM108
Jebb Av, SW2 181 DL86
Jebb Cl, Wind. SL4 151 AK82
Jebb St, E3 290 B1
Jedburgh Rd, E13 292 C2
Jedburgh St, SW11 160 DG84
Jeddo Rd, W12 159 CT75
Jeeva Mans, N16 off Shacklewell La 278 B1
Jefferson Cl, W13 157 CH76
Ilford IG2 125 EP57
Slough SL3 153 BA77
Jefferson Plaza, E3 290 E4
Jefferson Wk, SE18 off Kempt St 165 EN79
Jeffreys Pl, NW1 275 L6
Jeffreys Rd, SW4 310 A8
Enfield EN3 83 DZ41
Jeffreys St, NW1 275 K6
Jeffreys Wk, SW4 310 A8
Jeffries Pas, Guil. GU1 off High St 258 AX135
Jeffries Rd, Ware SG12 33 DY06
West Horsley KT24 245 BQ130
Jeffs Cl, Hmptn. TW12 176 CB93
Jeffs Rd, Sutt. SM1 217 CZ105
Jeger Av, E2 278 A9
Jeken Rd, SE9 164 EJ84
Jelf Rd, SW2 181 DN85
Jellicoe Av, Grav. DA12 191 GJ90
Jellicoe Av W, Grav. DA12 off Kitchener Av 191 GJ90
Jellicoe Cl, Slou. SL1 151 AP75
Jellicoe Gdns, Stan. HA7 95 CF51
Jellicoe Ho, SW8 off St. George Wf 310 A2
Jellicoe Rd, E13 291 P5
N17 100 DR52
Watford WD18 75 BU44
Jemma Knowles Cl, SW2 off Neil Wates Cres 181 DN88
Jemmett Cl, Kings.T. KT2 198 CP95
Jengar Cl, Sutt. SM1 218 DB105
Jenkins Av, Brick.Wd AL2 60 BY30
Jenkins Cl, Nthflt DA11 191 GF90
Jenkins La, E6 293 M1
Barking IG11 293 P1
Jenkinson Ho, E2 off Usk St 289 J2
Jenkins Rd, E13 292 B5
Jenner Av, W3 138 CR71
Jenner Cl, Sid. DA14 186 EU91
Jenner Pl, SW13 159 CV79
Jenner Rd, N16 122 DT61
Guildford GU1 258 AY135
Jenner Way, Epsom KT19 off Monro Pl 216 CN109
Jennery La, Burn. SL1 130 AJ69
Jennett Rd, Croy. CR0 201 DN104
Jennifer Rd, Brom. BR1 184 EF90
Jennings Cl, RM8 126 EY60
Long Ditton KT6 197 CJ101
New Haw KT15 off Woodham La 212 BJ109
Jennings Fld, Flack.Hth HP10 110 AC56
Jennings Rd, SE22 182 DT86
St. Albans AL1 43 CG19
Jennings Way, Barn. EN5 79 CW41
Hemel Hempstead HP3 40 BL22
Horley RH6 269 DK148
Jenningtree Rd, Erith DA8 167 FH80
Jenningtree Way, Belv. DA17 167 FC75
Jenny Hammond Cl, E11 off Newcomen Rd 124 EF62
Sch Jenny Hammond Prim Sch, E11 off Worsley Rd 124 EE63
Jenny Path, Rom. RM3 106 FK52
Jennys Way, Couls. CR5 235 DJ122
Jenson Way, SE19 182 DT94
Jenton Av, Bexh. DA7 166 EY81
Jephson Rd, E7 144 EJ66
Jephson St, SE5 311 L7
Jephtha Rd, SW18 180 DA86
Jeppos La, Mitch. CR4 200 DF98
Jepps Cl, Chsht EN7 66 DS27
Jepson Ho, SW6 off Pearscroft Rd 307 M7
Jerdan Pl, SW6 307 K4
Jeremiah Ct, Red. RH1 251 DJ131
Jeremiah St, E14 290 C9
Jeremys Grn, N18 100 DV49
Jermyn St, SW1 297 L2
Jerningham Av, Ilf. IG5 103 EP54
Jerningham Rd, SE14 313 L6
Jerome Cres, NW8 284 C4
Jerome Dr, St.Alb. AL3 42 CA22
Jerome Pl, Kings.T. KT1 off Wadbrook St 197 CK96
Jerome St, E1 288 A6
Jerome Twr, W3 158 CP75
Jerounds, Harl. CM19 51 EP17
Sch Jerounds Comm Inf Sch, Harl. CM19 off Pyenest Rd 51 EP18
Sch Jerounds Comm Jun Sch, Harl. CM19 off Pyenest Rd 51 EP18
Jerrard St, N1 287 P1
SE13 314 D10
Jersey Av, Stan. HA7 95 CH54
Jersey Cl, Cher. KT16 193 BF104
Guildford GU4 off Weybrook Dr 243 BB129
Hoddesdon EN11 49 EA16
Jersey Ct, SW6 off Dairy Cl 307 H7
Jersey Dr, Petts Wd BR5 205 ER100
JERSEY FARM, St.Alb. AL4 43 CJ15
Jersey Ho, N1 277 K5
Enfield EN3 off Eastfield Rd 83 DX38
Jersey La, St.Alb. AL4 43 CH18
Jersey Par, Houns. TW5 156 CB81
Jersey Rd, E11 123 ED60
E16 292 C8
SW17 181 DH93
W7 157 CG75
Hounslow TW3, TW5 156 CB81
Ilford IG1 125 EP63
Isleworth TW7 157 CE79
Rainham RM13 147 FG66
Jersey St, E2 288 F3
Jerusalem Pas, EC1 286 G5
Jervis Av, Enf. EN3 83 DY35
Jervis Ct, W1 285 K9
Jervis Rd, SW6 307 H3
Jerviston Gdns, SW16 181 DN93
Jesmond Av, Wem. HA9 138 CM65
Jesmond Cl, Mitch. CR4 201 DH97
Jesmond Rd, Croy. CR0 202 DT101
Jesmond Way, Stan. HA7 96 CL50
Jessam Av, E5 122 DV60
Jessamine Pl, Dart. DA2 188 FQ87
Jessamine Rd, W7 137 CE74
Jessamy Rd, Wey. KT13 195 BP103
Jessel Dr, Loug. IG10 85 EQ39
Jessel Ho, SW1 off Page St 297 P8
Jesse Rd, E10 123 EC60
Jesses La, Peasl. GU5 261 BQ144
Jessett Cl, Erith DA8 off West St 167 FD77
Jessica Rd, SW18 180 DC86
Jessie Blythe La, N19 121 DL59
Jessiman Ter, Shep. TW17 194 BN99
Jessop Av, Sthl. UB2 156 BZ77
Jessop Ct, N1 off Graham St 287 H1
Sch Jessop Prim Sch, SE24 off Lowden Rd 162 DQ84
Jessop Rd, SE24 off Milkwood Rd 161 DP84
Jessops Way, Croy. CR0 201 DJ100
Jessup Cl, SE18 165 EQ77
Jethou Ho, N1 off Nightingale Rd 277 K5
Jetstar Way, Nthlt. UB5 136 BY69
Jetty Wk, Grays RM17 170 GA79
Jevington Way, SE12 184 EH88
Jewel Rd, E17 123 EA55
Jewels Hill, Bigg.H. TN16 222 EG112
★ Jewel Twr (Hos of Parliament), SW1 298 A6
★ Jewish Mus, NW1 275 J9
Jewry St, EC3 288 A9
Jew's Row, SW18 160 DB84
Jews Wk, SE26 182 DV91
Jeymer Av, NW2 119 CV64
Jeymer Dr, Grnf. UB6 136 CC67
Jeypore Pas, SW18 off Jeypore Rd 180 DC86
Jeypore Rd, SW18 180 DC87
JFK Ho, Bushey WD23 off Royal Connaught Dr 76 BZ42
Sch JFS, Har. HA3 off The Mall 118 CN58
Jigger Mast Ho, SE18 305 K6
Jillian Cl, Hmptn. TW12 176 CA94
Jim Bradley Cl, SE18 305 M8
Jim Desormeaux Bungalows, Harl. CM20 off School La 35 ES13
Jim Griffiths Ho, SW6 off Clem Attlee Ct 307 H3
Jim O'Neill Wk, Ruis. HA4 off Sidmouth Dr 115 BU62
Jim Veal Dr, N7 276 B4
Jinnings, The, Welw.G.C. AL7 30 DA12
Joan Cres, SE9 184 EK87
Joan Gdns, Dag. RM8 126 EY61
Joan Rd, Dag. RM8 126 EY61
Joan St, SE1 298 G3
Jocelyn Rd, Rich. TW9 158 CL83
Jocelyns, Harl. CM17 36 EW11
Jocelyn St, SE15 312 C6
Jocketts Hill, Hem.H. HP1 39 BF20
Jocketts Rd, Hem.H. HP1 39 BF21
Jockey's Flds, WC1 286 D6
Jodane St, SE8 301 N9
Jodies Ct, St.Alb. AL4 43 CJ18
Jodrell Cl, Islw. TW7 157 CG81
Jodrell Rd, E3 279 P8
Jodrell Way, W.Thur. RM20 169 FT78
Joel St, Nthwd. HA6 115 BU55
Pinner HA5 115 BU55
Johanna St, SE1 298 E5
John Adam St, WC2 298 B2
John Aird Ct, W2 283 P6
John Archer Way, SW18 180 DD86
John Ashby Cl, SW2 181 DL86
John Austin Cl, Kings.T. KT2 off Queen Elizabeth Rd 198 CM95
Sch John Ball Prim Sch, SE3 315 K9
John Barnes Wk, E15 281 L4
Sch John Betts Prim Sch, W6 off Paddenswick Rd 159 CV76
John Bradshaw Rd, N14 99 DK46
Sch John Bramston Prim Sch, Ilf. IG6 off Newcastle Av 104 EU51
John Burns Dr, Bark. IG11 145 ES66
Sch John Burns Prim Sch, SW11 309 H9
Johnby Cl, Enf. EN3 83 DY37
John Campbell Rd, N16 277 P3
John Carpenter St, EC4 286 G10
John Cobb Rd, Wey. KT13 212 BN108
John Cornwell VC Ho, E12 125 EN63
John Ct, Hodd. EN11 off Molesworth 33 EA14
Sch John Donne Prim Sch, SE15 312 E7
John Drinkwater Cl, E11 off Browning Rd 124 EF59
John Eliot Cl, Lwr Naze. EN9 50 EE21
John Fearon Wk, W10 282 F2
John Felton Rd, SE16 300 C5
Sch John Fisher Sch, The, Pur. CR8 off Peaks Hill 219 DL110
John Fisher St, E1 288 C10
Sch John F. Kennedy Post 16 (Beckton) Annexe, E16 292 E6
Sch John F. Kennedy RC Sch, Hem.H. HP1 off Hollybush La 39 BF19
Sch John F. Kennedy Sch, E15 281 H8
John Gale Ct, Ewell KT17 off West St 217 CT109
John Gooch Dr, Enf. EN2 81 DP39
John Harrison Ho, E1 off Philpot St 288 F8
John Harrison Way, SE10 303 L7
John Horner Ms, N1 277 J10
H John Howard Cen, E9 279 K3
John Islip St, SW1 298 A9
John Keats Ho, N22 99 DM52
Sch John Keble C of E Prim Sch, NW10 off Crownhill Rd 139 CT67
Sch John Kelly Boys' Tech Coll, NW2 off Crest Rd 119 CU62
Sch John Kelly Girls' Tech Coll, NW2 off Crest Rd 119 CU62
John Kennedy Ct, N1 off Newington Grn Rd 277 M4
John Kennedy Ho, SE16 301 H8
Jct John Lyon Rbt, Har. HA1 117 CG61
Sch John Lyon Sch, The, Har. HA2 off Middle Rd 117 CD60
John Maurice Cl, SE17 299 L8
John McKenna Wk, SE16 300 D6
John Mills Ct, Denh. UB9 113 BF58
John Milton Pas, EC4 off Bread St 287 K9
John Newton Ct, Well. DA16 166 EV83
John Parker Cl, Dag. RM10 147 FB66
John Parker Sq, SW11 off Thomas Baines Rd 160 DD83
Sch John Paul II RC Sch, SW19 off Princes Way 179 CX87
John Penn St, SE13 314 D7
John Perrin Pl, Har. HA3 118 CL59
Sch John Perryn Prim Sch, W3 off Long Dr 138 CS72
Sch John Perry Prim Sch, Dag. RM10 off Charles Rd 147 FD65
John Princes St, W1 285 K8
John Rennie Wk, E1 300 F2
Sch John Roan Sch, The, SE3 315 K4
John Roll Way, SE16 300 D6
Coll John Ruskin 6th Form Coll, S.Croy. CR2 off Selsdon Pk Rd 221 DY108
Sch John Ruskin Prim Sch, SE5 311 J3
John Ruskin St, SE5 310 G4
John Russell Cl, Guil. GU2 242 AU131
Johns Av, NW4 119 CW56
Johns Cl, Ashf. TW15 175 BQ91
Sch John Scurr Prim Sch, E1 288 G5
Johnsdale, Oxt. RH8 254 EF129
John Silkin La, SE8 301 K9
Johns La, Mord. SM4 200 DC99
John's Ms, WC1 286 D5
John Smith Av, SW6 306 G4
John Smith Ms, E14 290 G10
Johnson Cl, E8 278 C8
Northfleet DA11 190 GD90
Johnson Ct, Hem.H. HP3 40 BL22
Johnson Ho, E2 288 D2
Johnson Rd, NW10 138 CR67
Bromley BR2 204 EK99
Croydon CR0 202 DR101
Hounslow TW5 156 BW80
Johnsons Av, Bad.Mt TN14 225 FB110
Johnsons Cl, Cars. SM5 200 DF104
Johnsons Ct, Seal TN15 off School La 257 FM121
Johnson's Ct, EC4 off Fleet St 286 F9
Johnsons Dr, Hmptn. TW12 196 CC95
Johnson's Pl, SW1 309 L1
Johnson St, E1 289 H9
Southall UB2 156 BW76
Johnsons Way, NW10 138 CP70
Greenhithe DA9 189 FW86
Johnsons Yd, Uxb. UB8 off Redford Way 134 BJ66
John Spencer Sq, N1 277 H5
John's Pl, E1 288 F8
Johns Rd, Tats. TN16 238 EK120
Sch John Stainer Prim Sch, SE4 off St. Asaph Rd 163 DY83
John's Ter, Croy. CR0 202 DR102
Romford RM3 106 FP51
Johnston Cl, SW9 310 D7
Johnston Ct, E10 off Oliver Rd 123 EB62
Johnstone Cl, Wat. WD19 94 BX48
Johnstone Rd, E6 293 K3
Johnston Grn, Guil. GU2 242 AU130
Johnston Rd, Wdf.Grn. IG8 102 EG50
Johnston Ter, NW2 off Kara Way 119 CX62
Johnston Wk, Guil. GU2 242 AU130
John St, E15 281 L9
SE25 202 DU98
WC1 286 D5
Enfield EN1 82 DT43
Grays RM17 170 GC79
Hounslow TW3 156 BY82
Johns Wk, Whyt. CR3 236 DU119
John's Way, S.Ock. RM15 149 FX72
John Tate Rd, Hert. SG13 32 DT10
John Trundle Ct, EC2 off The Barbican 287 J6
John Walsh Twr, E11 124 EF61
Sch John Warner Sch, The, Hodd. EN11 off Stanstead Rd 33 EB14
John Watkin Cl, Epsom KT19 216 CP109
John Wesley Cl, E6 293 K2
John William Cl, Chaff.Hun. RM16 169 FX78
John Williams Cl, SE14 313 J3
Kingston upon Thames KT2 off Henry Macaulay Av 197 CK95
John Wilson St, SE18 305 L7
John Woolley Cl, SE13 164 EE84
Joiner's Arms Yd, SE5 311 L7
Joiners Cl, Chal.St.P. SL9 91 AZ52
Ley Hill HP5 56 AV30
Joiners La, Chal.St.P. SL9 90 AY53
Joiners Pl, N5 277 L1
Joiner St, SE1 299 M2
Joiners Way, Chal.St.P. SL9 90 AY52
Joiners Yd, N1 off Caledonia St 286 B1
Joinville Pl, Add. KT15 212 BK105
Jolles Ho, E3 off Bromley High St 290 D2
Jolliffe Rd, Red. RH1 251 DJ126
Jollys La, Har. HA2 117 CD60
Hayes UB4 136 BX71
Jonathan Ct, W4 off Windmill Rd 158 CS77
Jonathan St, SE11 298 C10
Jones Ho, N16 off Stamford Hill 122 DS60
Jones Rd, E13 292 B5
Goffs Oak EN7 65 DP30
Jones St, W1 297 J1
Jones Wk, Rich. TW10 off Lower Gro Rd 178 CM86
Jones Way, Hedg. SL2 111 AR61
Jonquil Cl, Welw.G.C. AL7 30 DB11
Jonquil Gdns, Hmptn. TW12 off Partridge Rd 176 CA93
Jonson Cl, Hayes UB4 135 BU71
Mitcham CR4 201 DH98
Jordan Cl, Har. HA2 116 BZ62
South Croydon CR2 220 DT111
Watford WD25 75 BT35
Jordan Ct, SW15 off Charlwood Rd 159 CX84
Jordan Rd, Perivale UB6 137 CH67
JORDANS, Beac. HP9 90 AT52
Jordans Cl, Dag. RM10 127 FB63
Guildford GU1 off Beatty Av 243 BA133
Isleworth TW7 157 CE81
Redhill RH1 266 DG139
Stanwell TW19 174 BJ87
Jordans La, Jordans HP9 90 AS53
Jordans Ms, Twick. TW2 177 CE89
Jordans Rd, Rick. WD3 92 BG45
Sch Jordans Sch, Jordans HP9 off Puers La 90 AT51
Jordans Way, Brick.Wd AL2 60 BZ30
Jordans HP9 90 AT51
Rainham RM13 148 FK68
Sch Jo Richardson Comm Sch, The, Dag. RM9 off Gale St 146 EX67
Joseph Av, W3 138 CR72
Sch Joseph Clarke Sch, E4 off Vincent Rd 101 ED51
Joseph Conrad Ho, SW1 off Tachbrook St 297 M9
Joseph Hardcastle Cl, SE14 313 K4
Sch Joseph Hood Prim Sch, SW20 off Whatley Av 199 CY97
Josephine Av, SW2 181 DM85
Lower Kingswood KT20 249 CZ126
Josephine Cl, Lwr Kgswd KT20 249 CZ127
Joseph Locke Way, Esher KT10 196 CA103
Joseph Ms, N7 276 E5
Joseph Powell Cl, SW12 181 DJ86
Joseph Ray Rd, E11 124 EE61
Joseph's Rd, Guil. GU1 242 AX133
Joseph St, E3 289 P5
Joseph Trotter Cl, EC1 off Myddelton St 286 F3
Joshua Cl, N10 99 DH52
South Croydon CR2 219 DP108
Joshua St, E14 290 E8
Joshua Wk, Wal.Cr. EN8 off Longcroft Dr 67 EA34
Josiah Dr, Uxb. UB10 115 BQ61
Josling Cl, Grays RM17 170 FZ79
Joslings Cl, W12 139 CV73
Joslin Rd, Purf. RM19 168 FQ78
Joslyn Cl, Enf. EN3 83 EA38
Joubert St, SW11 308 E8
Journeys End, Stoke P. SL2 132 AS71
Jowett St, SE15 312 B5
Joyce Av, N18 100 DT50
Joyce Ct, Wal.Abb. EN9 67 ED34
Joyce Dawson Way, SE28 off Thamesmere Dr 146 EU73
Joyce Dawson Way Shop Arc, SE28 off Thamesmere Dr 146 EU73
Joyce Grn La, Dart. DA1 168 FL81
Joyce Grn Wk, Dart. DA1 168 FM84
Joyce Lattimore Ct, N9 off Colthurst Dr 100 DV48
Joyce Page Cl, SE7 164 EK79
Joyce Wk, SW2 181 DN86
JOYDENS WOOD, Bex. DA5 187 FC92
Sch Joydens Wd Inf Sch, Bex. DA5 off Park Way 187 FE90
Sch Joydens Wd Jun Sch, Wilm. DA2 off Birchwood Dr 187 FE91
Joydens Wd Rd, Bex. DA5 187 FD91
Joydon Dr, Rom. RM6 126 EV58
Joyes Cl, Rom. RM3 106 FK49
Joyners Cl, Dag. RM9 126 EZ63
Joyners Fld, Harl. CM18 51 EQ19
Joy Rd, Grav. DA12 191 GJ88
Jubb Powell Ho, N15 122 DS58
Jubilee Arch, Wind. SL4 off High St 151 AR81
Jubilee Av, E4 101 EC51
London Colney AL2 61 CK26
Romford RM7 127 FB57
Twickenham TW2 176 CC88
Ware SG12 33 DZ05
Jubilee Cl, NW9 118 CR58
NW10 138 CS68
Greenhithe DA9 189 FW86
Kingston upon Thames KT1 off High St 197 CJ95
Pinner HA5 94 BW54
Romford RM7 127 FB57
Stanwell TW19 174 BJ87
Jubilee Ct, Hat. AL10 45 CV15
Staines-upon-Thames TW18 174 BG91
Waltham Abbey EN9 68 EF33
Jubilee Cres, N9 100 DU46
Addlestone KT15 212 BK106
Gravesend DA12 191 GL89
Jubilee Dr, Ruis. HA4 116 BX63
★ Jubilee Gdns, SE1 298 C3
Jubilee Gdns, Sthl. UB1 136 CA72
Sch Jubilee International High Sch, Add. KT15 off School La 212 BG106
Jubilee La, W5 off Haven La 138 CL72
Jubilee Mkt Hall, WC2 286 B10
Jubilee Par, Wdf.Grn. IG8 off Snakes La E 102 EJ51
Jubilee Pl, SW3 296 D10
Sch Jubilee Prim Sch, N16 off Filey Av 122 DU60
SE28 off Crossway 146 EW73
SW2 off Tulse Hill 181 DN86
Jubilee Ri, Seal TN15 257 FM121
Jubilee Rd, Grays RM20 169 FV79
Orpington BR6 224 FA107
Perivale UB6 137 CH67
Sutton SM3 217 CX108
Watford WD24 75 BU38
Jubilee St, E1 288 G8
Jubilee Ter, Bet. RH3 264 CP138
Dorking RH4 263 CH135
Jubilee Trust, SE10 off Egerton Dr 314 D5
Jubilee Wk, Kings L. WD4 58 BN30
Watford WD19 93 BV49
Jubilee Way, SW19 200 DB95
Chessington KT9 216 CN105
Coulsdon CR5 235 DM118
Datchet SL3 152 AW80
Feltham TW14 175 BT88
Sidcup DA14 186 EU89
Judd Apts, N8 off Great Amwell La 121 DM55
Judd St, WC1 286 A3
Jude St, E16 291 L9
Judeth Gdns, Grav. DA12 191 GL92
Judge Heath La, Hayes UB3 135 BQ72
Uxbridge UB8 135 BQ72
Judges Hill, Northaw EN6 64 DE29
Judge St, Wat. WD24 75 BV38
Judge Wk, Clay. KT10 215 CE107
Judith Av, Rom. RM5 105 FB51
Juer St, SW11 308 D5
Jug Hill, Bigg.H. TN16 off Hillcrest Rd 238 EK116
Juglans Rd, Orp. BR6 206 EU102
Jules Thorn Av, Enf. EN1 82 DT41
Julia Gdns, Bark. IG11 146 EX68
Julia Garfield Ms, E16 304 B2
Juliana Cl, N2 120 DC55
Julian Av, W3 138 CP73
Julian Cl, New Barn. EN5 80 DB41
Woking GU21 226 AW118
Julian Hill, Har. HA1 117 CE61
Weybridge KT13 212 BN108
Julian Ho, SE21 off Kingswood Est 182 DS91
Julian Pl, E14 302 D10
Julian Rd, Orp. BR6 224 EU107
Julians Cl, Sev. TN13 256 FG127
Sch Julian's Prim Sch, SW16 off Leigham Ct Rd 181 DN91
Julians Way, Sev. TN13 256 FG127
Julian Tayler Path, SE23 182 DV89
Julia St, NW5 274 G1
Julien Rd, W5 157 CJ76
Coulsdon CR5 235 DK115
Juliet Ct, NW7 off Marchant Cl 96 CS51
Juliette Cl, Aveley RM15 168 FN75
Juliette Rd, E13 291 M1
Juliette Way, Aveley RM15 168 FM75
Julius Caesar Way, Stan. HA7 95 CK49
Julius Nyerere Cl, N1 276 C9
Junction, The, Grays RM20 169 FT77
Junction App, SE13 314 E10
SW11 160 DE83
Junction Av, W10 282 B3
Junction Ms, W2 284 C8
Junction Pl, W2 284 B8
Junction Rd, E13 144 EH68
N9 100 DU46
N17 122 DU55
N19 121 DJ63
W5 157 CJ77
Ashford TW15 175 BQ92
Brentford TW8 157 CJ77
Dartford DA1 188 FK86
Dorking RH4 263 CG136
Harrow HA1 117 CE58
Romford RM1 127 FF56
South Croydon CR2 220 DR106
Warley CM14 108 FW49
Junction Rd E, Rom. RM6 off Kenneth Rd 126 EY59
Junction Rd W, Rom. RM6 126 EY59
Junction Shop Cen, The, SW11 off St. John's Hill 160 DE84
June Cl, Couls. CR5 219 DH114

June La, Red. RH1 267 DH141
Junewood Cl, Wdhm KT15 211 BF111
Juniper Av, Brick.Wd AL2 60 CA31
Juniper Cl, Barn. EN5 79 CX43
Biggin Hill TN16 238 EL117
Broxbourne EN10 67 DZ25
Chesham HP5 54 AN30
Chessington KT9 216 CM107
Epsom KT19 216 CQ109
Feltham TW13 175 BV90
Guildford GU1 242 AV129
Harrow HA2 116 CB61
Oxted RH8 254 EH133
Reigate RH2 266 DC136
Rickmansworth WD3 92 BK48
Wembley HA9 118 CM64
Juniper Ct, Nthwd. HA6
off Neal Cl 93 BU53
Slou. SL1 *off Nixey Cl* 152 AU75
Juniper Cres, NW1 275 H7
Juniper Dr, SW18 160 DC84
Juniper Gdns, SW16
off Leonard Rd 201 DJ95
Shenley WD7 62 CL33
Sunbury-on-Thames TW16 175 BT93
Juniper Gate, Rick. WD3 92 BK47
Juniper Grn, Hem.H. HP1 39 BE20
Juniper Gro, Wat. WD17 75 BU38
Juniper La, E6 293 H7
High Wycombe HP10 110 AD56
Juniper Pl, Shalf. GU4 258 AX141
Juniper Rd, Ilf. IG1 125 EN63
Reigate RH2 266 DC136
Juniper St, E1 288 G10
Juniper Ter, Shalf. GU4 258 AX141
Juniper Wk, Brock. RH3 264 CQ136
Swanley BR8 207 FD96
Juniper Way, Hayes UB3 135 BR73
Romford RM3 106 FL53
Juno Ho, E3
off Garrison Rd 280 A9
Juno Rd, Hem.H. HP2
off Saturn Way 40 BM17
Juno Way, SE14 313 K2
Jupiter Ct, Slou. SL1 131 AL73
Jupiter Dr, Hem.H. HP2 40 BM18
Jupiter Dr Prim Sch,
Hem.H. HP2 *off Jupiter Dr* 40 BM18
Jupiter Way, N7 276 D4
Jupp Rd, E15 280 G7
Jupp Rd W, E15 280 F8
Jury St, Grav. DA11
off Princes St 191 GH86
Justice Wk, SW3 308 C3
Justin Cl, Brent. TW8 157 CK80
Justines Pl, E2 289 K2
Justin Pl, N22 99 DM52
Justin Rd, E4 101 DZ51
Jute La, Enf. EN3 83 DY40
Jutland Cl, N19 121 DL60
Jutland Gdns, Couls. CR5 235 DM120
Jutland Pl, Egh. TW20 173 BC92
Jutland Rd, E13 291 P5
SE6 183 EC87
Jutsums Av, Rom. RM7 127 FB58
Jutsums La, Rom. RM7 127 FB58
Juxon Cl, Har. HA3 94 CB53
Juxon St, SE11 298 D8

K

Kaduna Cl, Pnr. HA5 115 BU57
Kaine Pl, Croy. CR0 203 DY101
Kaizen Prim Sch, E13 292 A5
Kale Rd, Erith DA18 166 EY75
Kambala Rd, SW11 308 B9
Kandlewood, Hutt. CM13 109 GB45
Kangley Br Rd, SE26 183 DZ93
Kaplan Dr, N21 81 DL43
Kapuvar Cl, SE15 312 D9
Kara Way, NW2 119 CX63
Karen Cl, Brwd. CM15 108 FW45
Rainham RM13 147 FE68
Karen Ct, SE4 313 P10
Bromley BR1 204 EF95
Karen Ter, E11
off Montague Rd 124 EF61
Karenza Ct, Wem. HA9
off Lulworth Av 117 CJ59
Kariba Cl, N9 100 DW48
Karim Ms, E17
off Warner Rd 123 DY56
Karina Cl, Chig. IG7 103 ES50
Karma Way, Har. HA2 116 CA60
Karoline Gdns, Grnf. UB6
off Oldfield La N 137 CD68
Kashgar Rd, SE18 165 ET78
Kashmir Cl, New Haw KT15 212 BK109
Kashmir Rd, SE7 164 EK80
Kassala Rd, SW11 308 F7
● **Katella Trd Est**, Bark. IG11 145 ES69
Kates Cl, Barn. EN5 79 CU43
Katescroft, Welw.G.C. AL7 29 CY13
Katharine St, Croy. CR0 202 DQ104
Katherine Cl, N4 122 DQ59
SE16 301 J3
Addlestone KT15 212 BG107
Hemel Hempstead HP3 40 BL23
Penn HP10 88 AC47
Katherine Gdns, SE9 164 EK84
Ilford IG6 103 EQ52
Katherine Ms, Whyt. CR3 236 DT117
Katherine Pl, Abb.L. WD5 59 BU32
Katherine Rd, E6 144 EK66
E7 124 EJ64
Twickenham TW1
off London Rd 177 CG88
KATHERINES, Harl. CM19 51 EM18
Katherines Hatch, Harl. CM19
off Brookside 51 EN17
Katherines Prim Sch,
Harl. CM19 *off Brookside* 51 EN17
Katherine Sq, W11 294 E2
Katherines Way, Harl. CM19 51 EN18
Kathleen Av, W3 138 CQ71
Wembley HA0 138 CL66
Kathleen Rd, SW11 160 DF83
Katrine Sq, Hem.H. HP2 40 BK16
Kavanaghs Rd, Brwd. CM14 108 FU48
Kavanaghs Ter, Brwd. CM14 108 FV48
Kavsan Pl, Houns. TW5 155 BU80
Kayani Av, N4 122 DQ59
Kaye Ct, Guil. GU1 242 AW131
Kaye Don Way, Wey. KT13 212 BN111
Kayemoor Rd, Sutt. SM2 218 DE108
Kay Rd, SW9 310 B9
Kays Ter, E18
off Walpole Rd 102 EF53
Kay St, E2 278 D10
Welling DA16 166 EV81
Kay Wk, St.Alb. AL4 43 CK20
Kay Way, SE10 314 D4
Kaywood Cl, Slou. SL3 152 AW76
Kean Cres, Dag. RM8 126 EY60
Kean St, WC2 286 C9
Kearton Cl, Ken. CR8 236 DQ117
Keary Rd, Swans. DA10 190 FY87
Keate's La, Eton SL4 151 AR79
Keatley Grn, E4 101 DZ51
Keats Av, E16 304 A2
Redhill RH1 250 DG132
Romford RM3 105 FH52
Keats Cl, E11
off Nightingale La 124 EH57
NW3 274 C1
SE1 300 A9
SE7 164 EJ80
SW19 180 DD93
Borhamwood WD6 78 CN42
Chigwell IG7 103 EQ51
Enfield EN3 83 DX43
Hayes UB4 135 BU71
Keats Gdns, Til. RM18 171 GH82
Keats Gro, NW3 274 B1
★ **Keats Ho**, NW3 274 C1
Keats Ho, SW1 309 M2
Beckenham BR3 183 EA93
Keats Pl, EC2 287 L7
Keats Rd, E10 123 EB59
Belvedere DA17 167 FC76
Welling DA16 165 ES81
Keats Wk, Hutt. CM13
off Byron Rd 109 GD45
Keats Way, Croy. CR0 202 DW100
Greenford UB6 136 CB71
West Drayton UB7 154 BM77
Kebbell Ter, E7 124 EH64
Keble Cl, Nthlt. UB5 116 CC64
Worcester Park KT4 199 CT102
Keble Ct, Borwd. WD6
off Gateshead Rd 78 CM39
Keble Pl, SW13
off Somerville Av 159 CV79
Keble Sch, N21
off Wades Hill 99 DN45
Keble St, SW17 180 DC91
Keble Ter, Abb.L. WD5 59 BT32
Kebony Cl, West Dr. UB7 154 BN75
Kechill Gdns, Brom. BR2 204 EG101
Kedelston Ct, E5
off Redwald Rd 123 DY63
Kedeston Ct, Sutt. SM1
off Hurstcourt Rd 200 DB102
Kedleston Dr, Orp. BR5 205 ET100
Kedleston Wk, E2 288 F2
Keedonwood Rd, Brom. BR1 184 EE92
Keefield, Harl. CM19 51 EP20
Keel Cl, N18
off Amersham Ave 100 DS51
SE16 301 K3
Barking IG11 146 EW68
Keel Ct, E14
off Newport Av 291 H10
Keel Dr, Slou. SL1 151 AQ75
Keele Cl, Wat. WD24 76 BW40
Keeler Cl, Wind. SL4 151 AL83
Keeley Rd, Croy. CR0 202 DQ103
Keeley St, WC2 286 C9
Keeling Ho, E2 288 F1
Keeling Rd, SE9 184 EK85
Keely Cl, Barn. EN4 80 DE43
Keemor Cl, SE18 165 EN80
Keensacre, Iver SL0 133 BD68
Keens Cl, SW16 181 DK92
Keens La, Guil. GU3 242 AT130
Keens Pk Rd, Guil. GU3 242 AT130
Keens Rd, Croy. CR0 220 DQ105
Keen Students Sch, E1 288 D6
Keens Yd, N1 277 H5
Keep, The, SE3 315 N9
Kingston upon Thames KT2 178 CM93
Keepers Cl, Guil. GU4 243 BD131
Keepers Fm Cl, Wind. SL4 151 AL82
Keepers Ms, Tedd. TW11 177 CJ93
Keepers Wk, Vir.W. GU25 192 AX99
Keep La, N11 *off Gardeners Cl* 98 DG47
Keetons Rd, SE16 300 E6
Keevil Dr, SW19 179 CX87
Keighley Cl, N7 276 B1
Keighley Rd, Rom. RM3 106 FL52
Keightley Dr, SE9 185 EQ88
Keilder Cl, Uxb. UB10 134 BN68
Keildon Rd, SW11 160 DF84
Keir, The, SW19 179 CW92
Keir Hardie Est, E5
off Springfield 122 DV60
Keir Hardie Ho, W6 306 B2
Keir Hardie Prim Sch, E16 291 N7
Keir Hardie Way, Bark. IG11 146 EU66
Hayes UB4 135 BU69
Keith Av, Sutt.H. DA4 188 FP93
Keith Connor Cl, SW8 309 J10
Keith Gro, W12 159 CU75
Keith Pk Cres, Bigg.H. TN16 222 EH112
Keith Pk Rd, Uxb. UB10 134 BM66
Keith Rd, E17 101 DZ53
Barking IG11 145 ER68
Hayes UB3 155 BS76
Keiths Rd, Hem.H. HP3 40 BN21
Keith Way, Horn. RM11 128 FL59
Kelbrook Rd, SE3 164 EL83
Kelburn Way, Rain. RM13
off Dominion Way 147 FG69
Kelby Path, SE9 185 EP90
Kelbys, Welw.G.C. AL7 30 DC08
Kelceda Cl, NW2 119 CU61
Kelday Hts, E1 288 F9
Kelf Gro, Hayes UB3 135 BT72
Kelfield Gdns, W10 282 B8
Kelfield Ms, W10 282 C7
Kelland Cl, N8 121 DK57
Kelland Rd, E13 291 P4
Kellaway Rd, SE3 164 EJ82
Keller Cres, E12 124 EK63
Kellerton Rd, SE13 184 EE85
Kellett Rd, SW2 161 DN84
Kelling Gdns, Croy. CR0 201 DP101
Kellino St, SW17 180 DF91
Kellner Rd, SE28 165 ET76
Kell St, SE1 299 H6
Kelly Av, SE15 312 A5
Kelly Cl, NW10 118 CR62
Shepperton TW17 195 BS96
Kelly Ct, Borwd. WD6 78 CQ40
Kelly Ms, W9 283 H5
Kelly Rd, NW7 97 CY51
Kelly St, NW1 275 K5
Kelly Way, Rom. RM6 126 EY57
Kelman Cl, SW4 309 P9
Waltham Cross EN8 67 DX31
Kelmore Gro, SE22 162 DU84
Kelmscott Cl, E17 101 DZ54
Watford WD18 75 BU43
Kelmscott Cres, Wat. WD18 75 BU43
Kelmscott Gdns, W12 159 CU76
Kelmscott Pl, Ashtd. KT21 231 CJ117
Kelmscott Rd, SW11 180 DE85
Kelmscott Sch, E17
off Markhouse Rd 123 DZ58
Kelpatrick Rd, Slou. SL1 131 AK72
Kelross Pas, N5
off Kelross Rd 122 DQ63
Kelross Rd, N5 121 DP63
Kelsall Cl, SE3 164 EH82
Kelsall Ms, Rich. TW9 158 CP81
Kelsey Cl, Chess. KT9 215 CK108
Horley RH6 *off Court Lo Rd* 268 DF148
Kelsey Gate, Beck. BR3 203 EB96
Kelsey La, Beck. BR3 203 EA97
Kelsey Pk Av, Beck. BR3 203 EB96
Kelsey Pk Rd, Beck. BR3 203 EA96
Kelsey Pk Sports Coll,
Beck. BR3 *off Manor Way* 203 EA97
Kelsey Rd, Orp. BR5 206 EV96
Kelsey Sq, Beck. BR3 203 EA96
Kelsey St, E2 288 D4
Kelsey Way, Beck. BR3 203 EA97
Kelshall, Wat. WD25 76 BY36
Kelshall Ct, N4
off Brownswood Rd 122 DQ61
Kelsie Way, Ilf. IG6 103 ES52
Kelso Dr, Grav. DA12 191 GM91
Kelson Ho, E14 302 F6
Kelso Pl, W8 295 M6
Kelso Rd, Cars. SM5 200 DC101
Kelston Rd, Ilf. IG6 103 EP54
Kelvedon Av, Hersham KT12 213 BS108
Kelvedon Cl, Hutt. CM13 109 GE44
Kingston upon Thames KT2 178 CM93
Kelvedon Ho, SW8 310 B6
Kelvedon Rd, SW6 307 H5
Kelvedon Wk, Rain. RM13
off Ongar Way 147 FE66
Kelvedon Way, Wdf.Grn. IG8 103 EM51
Kelvin Av, N13 99 DM51
Leatherhead KT22 231 CF119
Teddington TW11 177 CE93
Kelvinbrook, W.Mol. KT8 196 CB97
Kelvin Cl, Epsom KT19 216 CN107
Kelvin Cres, Har. HA3 95 CE52
Kelvin Dr, Twick. TW1 177 CH86
Kelvin Gdns, Croy. CR0 201 DL101
Southall UB1 136 CA72
Kelvin Gro, SE26 182 DV90
Chessington KT9 197 CK104
Kelvin Gro Prim Sch, SE26
off Kirkdale 182 DV90
Kelvington Cl, Croy. CR0 203 DY101
Kelvington Rd, SE15 183 DX85
● **Kelvin Ind Est**, Grnf. UB6 136 CB66
Kelvin Par, Orp. BR6 205 ES102
Kelvin Rd, N5 277 H1
Tilbury RM18 171 GG82
Welling DA16 166 EU83
Kember St, N1 276 C7
Kemble Cl, Pot.B. EN6 64 DD33
Weybridge KT13 213 BR105
Kemble Cotts, Add. KT15
off Emley Rd 212 BG105
Kemble Dr, Brom. BR2 204 EL104
Kemble Par, Pot.B. EN6
off High St 64 DC32
Kemble Rd, N17 100 DU53
SE23 183 DX88
Croydon CR0 201 DN104
Kembleside Rd, Bigg.H. TN16 238 EJ118
Kemble St, WC2 286 C9
Kemerton Rd, SE5 162 DQ83
Beckenham BR3 203 EB96
Croydon CR0 202 DT101
Kemeys St, E9 279 L3
Kemishford, Wok. GU22 226 AU123
Kemmel Pl, Dag. RM9 146 EV67
Kemnal Rd, Chis. BR7 185 ER91
Kemnal Tech Coll, Sid.
DA14 *off Sevenoaks Way* 186 EV94
Kemp Ct, SW8 310 A5
Kempe Cl, St.Alb. AL1 42 CC24
Slough SL3 153 BC77
Kempe Rd, NW6 282 C1
Enfield EN1 82 DV36
Kemp Gdns, Croy. CR0 202 DQ100
Kemp Ho, W1 *off Berwick St* 285 N10
Kempis Way, SE22
off East Dulwich Gro 182 DS85
Kemplay Rd, NW3 274 A1
Kemp Pl, Bushey WD23 76 CA44
Kemp Rd, Dag. RM8 126 EX60
Kemprow, Ald. WD25 77 CD36
Kemp's Ct, W1 285 M9
Kemps Dr, E14 290 B10
Northwood HA6 93 BT52
Kempsford Gdns, SW5 307 K1
Kempsford Rd, SE11 298 F9
Kemps Gdns, SE13
off Thornford Rd 183 EC85
Kempshott Rd, SW16 181 DK94
Kempson Rd, SW6 307 K6
Kempthorne Rd, SE8 301 M8
Kempton Av, Horn. RM12 128 FM63
Northolt UB5 136 CA65
Sunbury-on-Thames TW16 195 BV95
Kempton Cl, Erith DA8 167 FC79
Uxbridge UB10 115 BQ63
Kempton Ct, E1 288 E6
Sunbury-on-Thames TW16 195 BV95
⇌ **Kempton Park** 175 BV94
★ **Kempton Park Racecourse**,
Sun. TW16 176 BW94
Kempton Rd, E6 145 EM67
Hampton TW12 196 BZ96
Kempton Wk, Croy. CR0 203 DY100
Kempt St, SE18 165 EN79
Kemsing Cl, Bex. DA5 186 EY87
Bromley BR2 204 EF103
Thornton Heath CR7 202 DQ98
Kemsing Rd, SE10 303 N10
Kemsley, SE13 183 EC85
Kemsley Chase,
Farn.Royal SL2 131 AR67
Kemsley Cl, Green. DA9 189 FV86
Northfleet DA11 191 GF91
Kemsley Rd, Tats. TN16 238 EK119
Kenbury Cl, Uxb. UB10 114 BN62
Kenbury Dr, Slou. SL1 151 AM75
Kenbury Gdns, SE5 311 J8
Kenbury St, SE5 311 J8
Kenchester Cl, SW8 310 B5
Kencot Cl, Erith DA18 166 EZ75
● **Kencot Cl Business Pk**,
Erith DA18 166 EZ75
Kendal, Purf. RM19 168 FQ78
Kendal Av, N18 100 DR49
W3 138 CN70
Barking IG11 145 ES66
Epping CM16 70 EU30
Kendal Cl, N20 98 DE47
SW9 310 G4
Feltham TW14
off Ambleside Dr 175 BT88
Hayes UB4 135 BS68
Reigate RH2 250 DD133
Slough SL2 132 AU73
Woodford Green IG8 102 EF47
Kendal Cft, Horn. RM12 127 FG64
Kendal Dr, Slou. SL2 132 AU73
Kendale, Grays RM16 171 GH76
Hemel Hempstead HP3 41 BP21
Kendale Rd, Brom. BR1 184 EE92
Kendal Gdns, N18 100 DR49
Sutton SM1 200 DC103
Kendal Ho, N1 276 D10
Kendall Av, Beck. BR3 203 DY96
South Croydon CR2 220 DR109
Kendall Av S, S.Croy. CR2 220 DQ110
Kendall Cl, Welw.G.C. AL7 29 CY13
Kendall Ct, SW19 180 DD93
Borehamwood WD6
off Gregson Cl 78 CQ39
Kendall Gdns, Grav. DA11 191 GF87
Kendall Pl, W1 284 G7
Kendall Rd, SE18 164 EL81
Beckenham BR3 203 DY96
Isleworth TW7 157 CG82
Kendalmere Cl, N10 99 DH53
Kendal Par, N18
off Great Cambridge Rd 100 DR49
Kendal Pl, SW15 179 CZ85
Kendal Rd, NW10 119 CU63
Waltham Abbey EN9 83 EC35
Kendals Cl, Rad. WD7 77 CE36
Kendal Steps, W2
off St. Georges Flds 284 D9
Kendal St, W2 284 D9
Kender Prim Sch, SE14 313 H6
Kender St, SE14 313 H5
Kendoa Rd, SW4 161 DK84
Kendon Cl, E11 124 EH57
Kendor Av, Epsom KT19 216 CQ111
Kendra Hall Rd, S.Croy. CR2 219 DP108
Kendrey Gdns, Twick. TW2 177 CE86
Kendrick Ms, SW7 296 A8
Kendrick Pl, SW7 296 A9
Kendrick Rd, Slou. SL3 152 AV76
Kenelm Cl, Har. HA1 117 CG62
Kenerne Dr, Barn. EN5 79 CY43
Kenford Cl, Wat. WD25 59 BV32
Kenia Wk, Grav. DA12 191 GM90
Kenilford Rd, SW12 181 DH87
Kenilworth Av, E17 101 EA54
SW19 180 DA92
Harrow HA2 116 BZ63
Romford RM3 106 FP50
Stoke D'Abernon KT11 214 CB114
Kenilworth Cl, Bans. SM7 234 DB116
Borehamwood WD6 78 CQ41
Hemel Hempstead HP2 40 BL21
Slough SL1 152 AT76
Kenilworth Ct, SW15
off Lower Richmond Rd 159 CY83
Watford WD17 75 BU39
Kenilworth Cres, Enf. EN1 82 DS39
Kenilworth Dr, Borwd. WD6 78 CQ41
Croxley Green WD3 75 BP42
Walton-on-Thames KT12 196 BX104
Kenilworth Gdns, SE18 165 EP82
Hayes UB4 135 BT71
Hornchurch RM12 128 FJ62
Ilford IG3 125 ET61
Loughton IG10 85 EM44
Southall UB1 136 BZ69
Staines-upon-Thames TW18 174 BJ92
Watford WD19 94 BW50
Kenilworth Prim Sch, Borwd.
WD6 *off Kenilworth Dr* 78 CR41
Kenilworth Rd, E3 279 L10
NW6 273 H8
SE20 203 DX95
W5 138 CL74
Ashford TW15 174 BK90
Edgware HA8 96 CQ48
Epsom KT17 217 CU107
Petts Wood BR5 205 EQ100
KENLEY, CR8 236 DQ116
⇌ **Kenley** 220 DQ114
Kenley, N17 100 DR54
Kenley Av, NW9 96 CS54
Kenley Cl, Barn. EN4 80 DE42
Bexley DA5 186 FA87
Caterham CR3 236 DR120
Chislehurst BR7 205 ES97
Kenley Gdns, Horn. RM12 128 FM61
Thornton Heath CR7 201 DP98
Kenley La, Ken. CR8 220 DQ114
Kenley Prim Sch, Whyt. CR3
off New Barn La 236 DS116
Kenley Rd, SW19 199 CZ96
Kingston upon Thames KT1 198 CP96
Twickenham TW1 177 CG86
Kenley Wk, W11 294 E1
Sutton SM3 217 CX105
Kenlor Rd, SW17 180 DD92
Kenmare Dr, N17 100 DT54
Mitcham CR4 180 DF94
Kenmare Gdns, N13 99 DP49
Kenmare Rd, Th.Hth. CR7 201 DN100
Kenmere Gdns, Wem. HA0 138 CN67
Kenmere Rd, Well. DA16 166 EW82
Kenmont Gdns, NW10 139 CV69
Kenmont Prim Sch, NW10
off Valliere Rd 139 CV69
Kenmore Av, Har. HA3 117 CG56
Kenmore Cl, Richmond TW9
off Kent Rd 158 CN80
Uxbridge UB10 115 BR61
Kenmore Cres, Hayes UB4 135 BT69
Kenmore Gdns, Edg. HA8 96 CP54
Kenmore Pk Inf & Jun Schs,
Kenton HA3
off Moorhouse Rd 118 CL55
Kenmore Rd, Har. HA3 117 CK55
Kenley CR8 219 DP114
Kenmure Rd, E8 278 F3
Kenmure Yd, E8 278 F3
Kennacraig Cl, E16 303 P3
Kennard Rd, E15 280 G7
N11 98 DF50
Kennards Ct, Amer. HP6 55 AS38
Kennard St, E16 305 J3
SW11 308 G7
Kenneally, Wind. SL4 150 AJ82
Kenneally Cl, Wind. SL4
off Kenneally 150 AJ82
Kenneally Pl, Wind. SL4
off Kenneally 150 AJ82
Kenneally Row, Wind. SL4
off Kenneally 150 AJ82
Kenneally Wk, Wind. SL4
off Kenneally 150 AJ82
Kennedy Av, Enf. EN3 82 DW44
Hoddesdon EN11 49 DZ17
Kennedy Cl, E13 291 P1
Cheshunt EN8 67 DX28
Farnham Common SL2 131 AQ65
London Colney AL2 61 CK26
Mitcham CR4 200 DG96
Petts Wood BR5 205 ER102
Pinner HA5 94 BZ51
Kennedy Gdns, Sev. TN13 257 FJ123
Kennedy Ho, SE11
off Vauxhall Wk 298 C10
Kennedy Path, W7
off Harp Rd 137 CF70
Kennedy Rd, W7 137 CE71
Barking IG11 145 ES67
Kennedy Wk, SE17
off Flint St 299 M9
Kennel Cl, Fetch. KT22 230 CC124
Kennel La, Fetch. KT22 230 CC122
Hookwood RH6 268 DD149
Kennelwood Cres,
New Adgtn CR0 221 ED111
Kennelwood La, Hat. AL10 45 CV17
Kennet Cl, SW11
off Maysoule Rd 160 DD84
Upminster RM14 129 FS58
Kennet Grn, S.Ock. RM15 149 FV73
Kenneth Av, Ilf. IG1 125 EP63
Kenneth Cres, NW2 119 CV64
Kenneth Gdns, Stan. HA7 95 CG51
Kenneth More Rd, Ilf. IG1
off Oakfield Rd 125 EP62
Kennet Ho, NW8 284 B6
Kenneth Rd, Bans. SM7 234 DD115
Romford RM6 126 EX59
Kenneth Robbins Ho, N17 100 DV52
Kennet Rd, W9 283 H4
Dartford DA1 167 FG83
Isleworth TW7 157 CF83
Kennet Sq, Mitch. CR4 200 DE95
Kennet St, E1 300 D2
Kennett Ct, Swan. BR8 207 FE97
Kennett Dr, Hayes UB4 136 BY71
Kennett Rd, Slou. SL3 153 BB76
Kennet Wf La, EC4 287 K10
Kenninghall, N18 100 DV50
Kenninghall Rd, E5 122 DU62
N18 100 DW50
Kenning Rd, Hodd. EN11 49 EA15
Kenning St, SE16 301 H4
Kennings Way, SE11 298 F10
Kenning Ter, N1 277 N8
KENNINGTON, SE11 310 E3
⊖ **Kennington** 298 G10
Kennington Grn, SE11 310 E1
Kennington La, SE11 298 F10
Kennington Oval, SE11 310 D2
● **Kennington Pk**, SW9 310 F4
Kennington Pk Est, SE11 310 E3
Kennington Pk Gdns, SE11 310 G2
Kennington Pk Pl, SE11 310 F1
Kennington Pk Rd, SE11 310 F2
Kennington Rd, SE1 298 E6
SE11 298 E7
Kenningtons Prim Sch,
Aveley RM15 *off Tamar Dr* 148 FQ72
Kennoldes, SE21 182 DR89
Kenny Dr, Cars. SM5 218 DF109
Kenrick Pl, W1 284 G6
Kenrick Sq, Bletch. RH1 252 DS133
KENSAL GREEN, NW10 282 B2
⊖ **Kensal Green** 282 B2
⊖ **Kensal Green** 282 B2
★ **Kensal Green Cem**, W10 282 A3
KENSAL RISE, NW6 282 C1
⊖ **Kensal Rise** 282 B1
Kensal Rd, W10 282 F4
KENSAL TOWN, W10 282 E4
Kensal Wf, W10 282 D4
KENSINGTON, W8 295 H3
Kensington & Chelsea Coll,
Hortensia Cen, SW10 307 N4
Marlborough Cen, SW3 296 D9
Wornington Cen, W10 282 F6
Kensington Av, E12 144 EL65
Thornton Heath CR7 201 DN95
Watford WD18 75 BT42
Kensington Av Prim Sch,
Th.Hth. CR7
off Kensington Av 201 DN95
Kensington Ch Ct, W8 295 L5
Kensington Ch St, W8 295 K2
Kensington Ch Wk, W8 295 L4
Kensington Cl, N11 98 DG50
St. Albans AL1 43 CG22
Kensington Coll of Business,
WC2 286 C8
Kensington Ct, NW7
off Grenville Pl 96 CR50
W8 295 M5
Kensington Ct Gdns, W8
off Kensington Ct Pl 295 M6
Kensington Ct Ms, W8 295 M5
Kensington Ct Pl, W8 295 M6
Kensington Dr, Wdf.Grn. IG8 102 EK53
★ **Kensington Gdns**, W2 295 P3
Kensington Gdns, Ilf. IG1 125 EM61
Kingston upon Thames KT1
off Portsmouth Rd 197 CK97
Kensington Gdns Sq, W2 283 L9
Kensington Gate, W8 295 N6
Kensington Gore, SW7 296 A5
Kensington Grn, W8 295 L7
Kensington Hall Gdns, W14 294 G10
Kensington High St, W8 295 J6
W14 294 G7
Kensington Ho, West Dr. UB7
off Park Lo Ave 154 BM75

Kensington Mall, W8 295 K2
⇌ Kensington (Olympia) 294 E6
⊂ Kensington (Olympia) 294 E6
⊖ Kensington (Olympia) 294 E6
★ Kensington Palace, W8 295 M3
Kensington Palace Gdns, W8 295 L2
Kensington Pk, Stap.Abb. RM4 105 FE45
Kensington Pk Gdns, W11 294 G1
Kensington Pk Ms, W11 282 G9
Kensington Pk Rd, W11 282 G10
Kensington Path, E10 off Balmoral Rd 123 EB61
Kensington Pl, W8 295 J3
Sch Kensington Prim Sch, E12 off Kensington Av 145 EM65
Kensington Rd, SW7 296 B5
W8 295 M5
Northolt UB5 136 CA69
Pilgrim's Hatch CM15 108 FU44
Romford RM7 127 FC58
Kensington Sq, W8 295 L5
Kensington Ter, S.Croy. CR2 220 DR108
Kensington Village, W14 295 H9
Kensington Way, Borwd. WD6 78 CR41
Brentwood CM14 108 FW46
Kent Av, W13 137 CH71
Dagenham RM9 146 FA70
Slough SL1 131 AQ71
Welling DA16 185 ET85
Kent Cl, Borwd. WD6 78 CR38
Mitcham CR4 201 DL98
Orpington BR6 223 ES107
Staines-upon-Thames TW18 174 BK93
Uxbridge UB8 134 BJ65
Kent Dr, Cockfos. EN4 80 DG42
Hornchurch RM12 128 FK63
Teddington TW11 177 CE92
Kentford Way, Nthlt. UB5 136 BY67
Kent Gdns, W13 137 CH71
Ruislip HA4 115 BV58
Kent Gate Way, Croy. CR0 221 EA106
KENT HATCH, Eden. TN8 255 EP131
Kent Hatch Rd, Crock.H. TN8 255 EM131
Oxted RH8 254 EJ129
⇌ Kent House 203 DY95
Kent Ho La, Beck. BR3 183 DY92
Kent Ho Rd, SE26 203 DX95
Beckenham BR3 183 DY92
Kentish Bldgs, SE1 299 L3
Kentish La, Hat. AL9 64 DC25
Kentish Rd, Belv. DA17 166 FA77
KENTISH TOWN, NW5 275 L4
⇌ Kentish Town 275 L3
⊖ Kentish Town 275 L3
Sch Kentish Town C of E Prim Sch, NW5 275 L3
Kentish Town Rd, NW1 275 K7
NW5 275 K7
⊂ Kentish Town West 275 H5
Kentish Way, Brom. BR1 204 EG96
● Kent Kraft Ind Est, Nthflt DA11 190 FZ85
Kentlea Rd, SE28 165 ES75
Kentmere Rd, SE18 165 ES77
KENTON, Har. HA3 117 CH57
⊂ Kenton 117 CH58
⊖ Kenton 117 CH58
Kenton Av, Har. HA1 117 CF59
Southall UB1 136 CA73
Sunbury-on-Thames TW16 196 BY96
Kenton Ct, W14 294 G7
Kenton Gdns, Har. HA3 117 CJ57
St. Albans AL1 43 CF21
Kenton La, Har. HA3 117 CJ55
Kenton Pk Av, Har. HA3 117 CK56
Kenton Pk Cl, Har. HA3 117 CJ56
Kenton Pk Cres, Har. HA3 117 CK56
Kenton Pk Par, Har. HA3 117 CJ57
Kenton Pk Rd, Har. HA3 117 CJ56
Kenton Rd, E9 279 J5
Harrow HA1, HA3 117 CK57
Kentons La, Wind. SL4 151 AL82
Kenton St, WC1 286 A4
Kenton Way, Hayes UB4 off Exmouth Rd 135 BS69
Woking GU21 226 AT117
● Kent Pk Ind Est, SE15 312 E2
Kent Pas, NW1 284 E4
Kent Rd, N21 100 DR46
W4 158 CQ76
Dagenham RM10 127 FB64
Dartford DA1 188 FK86
East Molesey KT8 196 CC98
Gravesend DA11 191 GG88
Grays RM17 170 GC79
Kingston upon Thames KT1 off The Bittoms 197 CK97
Longfield DA3 209 FX96
Orpington BR5 206 EV100
Richmond TW9 158 CN80
West Wickham BR4 203 EB102
Woking GU22 227 BB116
Kents Av, Hem.H. HP3 40 BK24
Kents La, N.Wld Bas. CM16 53 FD21
Kents Pas, Hmptn. TW12 196 BZ95
Kent St, E2 278 B10
E13 292 B3
Kent Ter, NW1 284 D3
Kent Vw, Aveley RM15 168 FQ75
Kent Vw Gdns, Ilf. IG3 125 ES61
Kent Way, Surb. KT6 198 CL104
Kentwell Cl, SE4 163 DY84
Kentwode Grn, SW13 159 CU80
Kentwyns Ri, S.Nutfld RH1 267 DM135
Kent Yd, SW7 296 D5
Kenver Av, N12 98 DD51
Kenward Rd, SE9 184 EJ85
Kenway, Rain. RM13 148 FJ69
Romford RM5 105 FC54
Ken Way, Wem. HA9 118 CQ61
Kenway Cl, Rain. RM13 148 FJ69
Kenway Dr, Amer. HP7 72 AV39
Kenway Rd, SW5 295 L9
Kenway Wk, Rain. RM13 148 FK69
Kenwood Av, N14 81 DK43
Kenwood Cl, NW3 120 DD60
Sipson UB7 154 BN79
Kenwood Dr, Beck. BR3 203 EC97
Hersham KT12 213 BV107
Mill End WD3 91 BF47
Kenwood Gdns, E18 124 EH55
Ilford IG2 125 EN56
★ Kenwood Ho, NW3 120 DE60
Kenwood Pk, Wey. KT13 213 BR107
Kenwood Ridge, Ken. CR8 235 DP117
Kenwood Rd, N6 120 DF58
N9 100 DU46
Kenworth Cl, Wal.Cr. EN8 67 DX33
Kenworth Ho, Enf. EN1 off Great Cambridge Rd 82 DU43
Kenworthy Rd, E9 279 L3
Kenwyn Dr, NW2 118 CS62
Kenwyn Rd, SW4 161 DK84
SW20 199 CW95
Dartford DA1 188 FK85
Kenya Rd, SE7 164 EK80
Kenyngton Dr, Sun. TW16 175 BU92
Sch Kenyngton Manor Prim Sch, Sun. TW16 off Bryony Way 175 BU93
Kenyngton Pl, Har. HA3 117 CJ57
Kenyon Pl, Welw.G.C. AL7 off Twelve Acres 29 CY12
Kenyons, W.Hors. KT24 245 BP128
Kenyon St, SW6 306 C6
Keogh Rd, E15 281 K4
Kepler Rd, SW4 161 DL84
Keppel Rd, E6 145 EM66
Dagenham RM9 126 EY63
Dorking RH4 247 CH134
Keppel Row, SE1 299 J3
Keppel Spur, Old Wind. SL4 172 AV87
Keppel St, WC1 285 P6
Windsor SL4 151 AR82
Kerbela St, E2 288 C4
Kerbey St, E14 290 D8
Kerdistone Cl, Pot.B. EN6 64 DB30
Sch Kerem Sch, N2 off Norrice Lea 120 DD57
Kerfield Cres, SE5 311 L7
Kerfield Pl, SE5 311 L7
Kernow Cl, Horn. RM12 128 FL61
Kerr Cl, S.Croy. CR2 221 DY108
Kerri Cl, Barn. EN5 79 CW42
Kerridge Ct, N1 277 P4
Kerril Cft, Harl. CM20 35 EN14
Kerrill Av, Couls. CR5 235 DN119
Kerrison Pl, W5 137 CK74
Kerrison Rd, E15 280 G8
SW11 308 C10
W5 137 CK74
Kerrison Vil, W5 off Kerrison Pl 137 CK74
Kerry Av, Aveley RM15 168 FM75
Stanmore HA7 95 CK49
Kerry Av N, Stan. HA7 95 CK49
Kerry Cl, E16 292 A9
N13 99 DM47
Upminster RM14 129 FT59
Kerry Ct, SW6 off Dairy Cl 307 H7
Stanmore HA7 95 CK49
Kerry Dr, Upmin. RM14 129 FT59
Kerry Ho, E1 off Sidney St 288 G8
Kerry Path, SE14 313 N3
Kerry Rd, SE14 313 N3
Kerry Ter, Wok. GU21 227 BB116
Kersey Dr, S.Croy. CR2 220 DW112
Kersey Gdns, SE9 184 EL91
Romford RM3 106 FL52
Kersfield Rd, SW15 179 CX86
Kershaw Cl, SW18 180 DC86
Chafford Hundred RM16 169 FW77
Hornchurch RM11 128 FK59
Kershaw Rd, Dag. RM10 126 FA62
Kersley Ms, SW11 308 E7
Kersley Rd, N16 122 DS62
Kersley St, SW11 308 E8
Kerstin Cl, Hayes UB3 135 BT73
Kerswell Cl, N15 122 DS57
Kerwick Cl, N7 276 B6
Keslake Rd, NW6 282 C1
Kessock Cl, N17 122 DV57
Kesters Rd, Chesh. HP5 54 AR32
Kesteven Cl, Ilf. IG6 103 ET51
Kestlake Rd, Bex. DA5 off East Rochester Way 186 EW86
KESTON, BR2 222 EJ106
Keston Av, Couls. CR5 235 DN119
Keston BR2 222 EJ106
New Haw KT15 212 BG111
Keston Cl, N18 100 DR48
Welling DA16 166 EW80
Sch Keston C of E Prim Sch, Kes. BR2 off Lakes Rd 222 EK106
Keston Gdns, Kes. BR2 222 EJ105
Jct Keston Mark, Kes. BR2 204 EL104
Keston Ms, Wat. WD17 off Nascot Rd 75 BV40
Keston Pk Cl, Kes. BR2 205 EM104
Sch Keston Prim Sch, Couls. CR5 off Keston Av 235 DN119
Keston Rd, N17 122 DR55
SE15 162 DU83
Thornton Heath CR7 201 DN100
Kestral Ct, Wall. SM6 off Carew Rd 219 DJ106
Kestrel Av, E6 292 G7
SE24 181 DP85
Staines-upon-Thames TW18 173 BF90
Kestrel Cl, NW9 96 CS54
NW10 118 CR64
Berkhamsted HP4 38 AW20
Epsom KT19 216 CN111
Guildford GU4 243 BD132
Hornchurch RM12 147 FH66
Ilford IG6 104 EW49
Kingston upon Thames KT2 177 CK91
Watford WD25 60 BY34
Kestrel Grn, Hat. AL10 45 CU19
Kestrel Ho, EC1 287 J2
SW8 off St. George Wf 310 A2
W13 137 CF70
Enfield EN3 off Alma Rd 83 DY43
Kestrel Path, Slou. SL2 131 AL70
Kestrel Pl, SE14 off Milton Ct Rd 313 M3
Kestrel Rd, Wal.Abb. EN9 68 EG34
Kestrels, The, Brick.Wd AL2 60 BZ31
Denh. UB9 off Patrons Way E 113 BF57
Kestrel Way, Felt. TW14 175 BV85
Hayes UB3 155 BR75
New Addington CR0 221 ED109
Welwyn Garden City AL7 29 CZ07
Woking GU21 226 AV115
Keswick Av, SW15 178 CS92
SW19 200 DA96
Hornchurch RM11 128 FK60
Keswick Bdy, SW15 off Upper Richmond Rd 179 CZ85
Keswick Cl, St.Alb. AL1 43 CH21
Sutton SM1 218 DC105
Keswick Ct, Slou. SL2 off Stoke Rd 132 AT73
Keswick Dr, Enf. EN3 82 DW36
Keswick Gdns, Ilf. IG4 124 EL57
Purfleet RM19 168 FQ79
Ruislip HA4 115 BR58
Wembley HA9 118 CL63
Keswick Ms, W5 138 CL74
Keswick Rd, SW15 179 CY85
Bexleyheath DA7 166 FA82
Egham TW20 173 BB94
Leatherhead KT22, KT23 246 CC125
Orpington BR6 205 ET102
Twickenham TW2 176 CC86
West Wickham BR4 204 EE103
Kettering Rd, Enf. EN3 off Beaconsfield Rd 83 DX37
Romford RM3 106 FL52
Kettering St, SW16 181 DJ93
Kett Gdns, SW2 181 DM85
Kettlebaston Rd, E10 123 DZ60
Kettlewell Cl, N11 98 DG51
Woking GU21 210 AX114
Kettlewell Ct, Swan. BR8 207 FF96
Kettlewell Dr, Wok. GU21 210 AY114
Kettlewell Hill, Wok. GU21 210 AY114
Ketton Grn, Merst. RH1 off Malmstone Av 251 DK128
Kevan Dr, Send GU23 227 BE124
Kevan Ho, SE5 311 J5
Kevelioc Rd, N17 100 DQ53
Kevin Cl, Houns. TW4 156 BX82
Kevington Cl, Orp. BR5 205 ET98
Kevington Dr, Chis. BR7 205 ET98
Orpington BR5 205 ET98
KEW, Rich. TW9 158 CN79
⇌ Kew Bridge 158 CM78
Jct Kew Br, Brent. TW8 158 CM78
Kew Br, Brent. TW8 158 CM79
Richmond TW9 158 CM79
Kew Br Arches, Rich. TW9 off Kew Br 158 CM79
Kew Br Ct, W4 158 CN78
● Kew Br Distribution Cen, Brent. TW8 158 CM78
Kew Br Rd, Brent. TW8 158 CM79
Kew Cl, Rom. RM1 105 FE51
Uxbridge UB8 134 BK68
Sch Kew Coll, Kew TW9 off Cumberland Rd 158 CN80
Kew Cres, Sutt. SM3 199 CY104
Kewferry Dr, Nthwd. HA6 93 BP50
Kewferry Rd, Nthwd. HA6 93 BQ51
Kew Foot Rd, Rich. TW9 158 CL84
⊂ Kew Gardens 158 CM81
⊖ Kew Gardens 158 CM81
Kew Gdns Rd, Rich. TW9 158 CM80
Jct Kew Grn, Rich. TW9 158 CM80
Kew Grn, Rich. TW9 158 CN80
Kew Meadows Path, Rich. TW9 158 CP82
★ Kew Observatory, Rich. TW9 157 CH83
★ Kew Palace (Royal Botanic Gdns), Rich. TW9 158 CL80
Kew Retail Pk, Rich. TW9 158 CP81
Sch Kew Riverside Prim Sch, Rich. TW9 off Courtlands Av 158 CP82
Kew Rd, Rich. TW9 158 CN79
Key Cl, E1 288 F5
Keyes Rd, NW2 272 D2
Dartford DA1 168 FM84
Keyfield Ter, St.Alb. AL1 43 CD21
Keyham Ho, W2 283 J7
Keymer Cl, Bigg.H. TN16 238 EK116
Keymer Rd, SW2 181 DM89
Keynes Cl, N2 120 DF55
Keynsham Av, Wdf.Grn. IG8 102 EE49
Keynsham Gdns, SE9 184 EL85
Keynsham Rd, SE9 184 EK85
Morden SM4 200 DB102
Keynsham Wk, Mord. SM4 200 DB102
Keynton Cl, Hert. SG14 31 DM08
Keys, The, Gt Warley CM13 off Eagle Way 107 FW51
Keyse Rd, SE1 300 A7
Keysers Est, Brox. EN10 49 EB21
Keysers Rd, Brox. EN10 49 EA22
Keysham Av, Houns. TW5 off The Avenue 155 BU81
Keys Ho, Enf. EN3 off Beaconsfield Rd 83 DX37
Sch Keys Meadow Prim Sch, Enf. EN3 off Tysoe Av 83 DZ36
Keystone Cres, N1 286 B1
Keywood Dr, Sun. TW16 175 BU93
Keyworth Cl, E5 123 DY63
Keyworth Pl, SE1 299 H6
Sch Keyworth Prim Sch, SE17 310 G1
Keyworth St, SE1 299 H6
Kezia Ms, SE8 301 L10
Kezia St, SE8 313 L1
Khalsa Av, Grav. DA12 191 GJ87
Khalsa Ct, N22 99 DP53
Sch Khalsa Prim Sch, Slou. SL2 off Wexham Rd 132 AU72
Khama Rd, SW17 180 DE91
Khartoum Pl, Grav. DA12 191 GJ86
Khartoum Rd, E13 292 A3
SW17 180 DD91
Ilford IG1 125 EP64
Khyber Rd, SW11 308 C9
★ Kia Oval, The (Surrey CCC), SE11 310 D2
★ Kibes La, Ware SG12 33 DX06
Kibworth St, SW8 310 C5
Kidborough Down, Bkhm KT23 246 CA127
KIDBROOKE, SE3 164 EH83
⇌ Kidbrooke 164 EH83
Kidbrooke Gdns, SE3 315 N8
Kidbrooke Gro, SE3 315 P6
Jct Kidbrooke Interchange, SE3 164 EJ83
Kidbrooke La, SE9 164 EL84
Kidbrooke Pk Cl, SE3 164 EH81
Sch Kidbrooke Pk Prim Sch, SE3 off Hargood Rd 164 EJ81
Kidbrooke Pk Rd, SE3 164 EH81
Sch Kidbrooke Sch, SE3 off Corelli Rd 164 EK82
Kidbrooke Way, SE3 164 EH82
Kidderminster Pl, Croy. CR0 off Kidderminster Rd 201 DP102
Kidderminster Rd, Croy. CR0 201 DP102
Slough SL2 131 AN69
Kidderpore Av, NW3 120 DA63
Kidderpore Gdns, NW3 120 DA63
Kidd Pl, SE7 305 H10
Kidman Cl, Gidea Pk RM2 128 FJ55
Kidworth Cl, Horl. RH6 268 DF147
Kielder Cl, Ilf. IG6 103 ET51
Kiffen St, EC2 287 M4
Kilberry Cl, Islw. TW7 157 CD81
Kilbride Ct, Hem.H. HP2 off Aycliffe Dr 40 BM16
KILBURN, NW6 273 J10
⊖ Kilburn 272 F5
Kilburn Br, NW6 273 K9
Kilburn Gate, NW6 273 L10
⊂ Kilburn High Road 273 K9
Kilburn High Rd, NW6 273 H6
Kilburn La, W9 282 D3
W10 282 D3
⊖ Kilburn Park 273 J10
Sch Kilburn Pk Jun Sch, NW6 283 H1
Kilburn Pk Rd, NW6 283 J3
Kilburn Pl, NW6 273 K9
Kilburn Priory, NW6 273 L9
Kilburn Sq, NW6 273 J8
Kilburn Vale, NW6 273 L9
Kilby Cl, Wat. WD25 76 BX35
Kilby Ct, SE10 off Child La 303 M7
Kilcorral Cl, Epsom KT17 217 CU114
Kildare Cl, Ruis. HA4 116 BW60
Kildare Gdns, W2 283 K8
Kildare Rd, E16 291 N6
Kildare Ter, W2 283 K8
Kildare Wk, E14 290 A9
Kildonan Cl, Wat. WD17 75 BT39
Kildoran Rd, SW2 181 DL85
Kildowan Rd, Ilf. IG3 126 EU60
Kilfillan Gdns, Berk. HP4 38 AU20
Kilgour Rd, SE23 183 DY86
Kilkie St, SW6 307 N9
Killarney Rd, SW18 180 DC86
Killasser Ct, Tad. KT20 233 CW123
Killburns Mill Cl, Wall. SM6 off London Rd 201 DH103
Killearn Rd, SE6 183 ED88
Killester Gdns, Wor.Pk. KT4 217 CV105
Killewarren Way, Orp. BR5 206 EW100
Killick Cl, Dunt.Grn TN13 256 FE121
Killick Ms, Sutt. SM3 217 CY107
Killick St, N1 276 C10
Killick Way, E1 289 K6
Killieser Av, SW2 181 DL89
Sch Killigrew Inf & Nurs Sch, St.Alb. AL2 off West Av 60 CB25
Sch Killigrew Jun Sch, St.Alb. AL2 off West Av 60 CB25
Killip Cl, E16 291 M8
Killowen Av, Nthlt. UB5 116 CC64
Killowen Cl, Tad. KT20 233 CX122
Killowen Rd, E9 279 J5
Killy Hill, Chobham GU24 210 AS108
Killyon Rd, SW8 309 M8
Killyon Ter, SW8 309 M9
Kilmaine Rd, SW6 306 F5
Kilmarnock Gdns, Dag. RM8 off Lindsey Rd 126 EW62
Kilmarnock Pk, Reig. RH2 250 DB133
Kilmarnock Rd, Wat. WD19 94 BX49
Kilmarsh Rd, W6 294 A8
Kilmartin Av, SW16 201 DM97
Kilmartin Rd, Ilf. IG3 126 EU61
Kilmartin Way, Horn. RM12 127 FH64
Kilmington Cl, Hutt. CM13 109 GB47
Kilmington Rd, SW13 159 CU79
Kilmiston Av, Shep. TW17 195 BQ100
Kilmorey Gdns, Twick. TW1 177 CH85
Kilmorey Rd, Twick. TW1 157 CH84
Sch Kilmorie Prim Sch, SE23 off Kilmorie Rd 183 DY89
Kilmorie Rd, SE23 183 DY88
Kiln Av, Amer. HP6 72 AW38
Kiln Cl, Harling. UB3 155 BR79
Potten End HP4 39 BB17
Kiln Ct, Beac. HP9 110 AG55
Kilncroft, Hem.H. HP3 41 BP22
Kilndown, Grav. DA12 191 GK93
Kilner St, E14 290 A7
Kilnfield, Welw.G.C. AL7 29 CZ06
Kiln Flds, Woob.Grn HP10 110 AE61
Kiln Grd, Hem.H. HP3 40 BN22
Kiln Ho Cl, Ware SG12 33 DY05
Kiln La, B.End SL8 110 AC60
Brockham RH3 264 CP135
Church Langley CM17 52 EW16
Epsom KT17 216 CS111
Hedgerley SL2 111 AQ60
Horley RH6 268 DG146
Ley Hill HP5 56 AV31
Ripley GU23 228 BH124
Wooburn Green HP10 110 AC60
Kiln Ms, SW17 180 DD92
Kiln Pl, NW5 275 H2
Kiln Rd, N.Wld Bas. CM16 70 FA27
Kilnside, Clay. KT10 215 CG108
Kiln Wk, Red. RH1 266 DG139
Kiln Way, Bad.Dene RM17 170 FZ78
Northwood HA6 93 BS51
Kilnwood, Halst. TN14 224 EZ113
Kiln Wd La, Hav.at.Bow. RM4 105 FD50
Kilpatrick Way, Hayes UB4 136 BY71
Kilravock St, W10 282 E3
Kilross Rd, Felt. TW14 175 BR88
Kilrue La, Hersham KT12 213 BT105
Kilrush Ter, Wok. GU21 227 BA116
Kilsby Wk, Dag. RM9 off Rugby Rd 146 EV65
Kilsha Rd, Walt. KT12 195 BV100
Kilsmore La, Chsht EN8 67 DX28
Kilvinton Dr, Enf. EN2 82 DR38
Kilworth Av, Shenf. CM15 109 GA44
Kilworth Cl, Welw.G.C. AL7 30 DB11
Kimbell Gdns, SW6 306 E7
Kimbell Pl, SE3 164 EJ84
Kimber Cl, Wind. SL4 151 AM83
Kimber Ct, Guil. GU4 off Gilliat Dr 243 BD132
Kimberley Av, E6 144 EL68
SE15 312 F9
Ilford IG2 125 ER59
Romford RM7 127 FC58
Kimberley Cl, Horl. RH6 268 DE148
Slough SL3 153 AZ77
Kimberley Dr, Sid. DA14 186 EX89
Kimberley Gdns, N4 121 DP57
Enfield EN1 82 DT41
Kimberley Pl, Pur. CR8 off Brighton Rd 219 DN111
Kimberley Ride, Cob. KT11 214 CB113
Kimberley Rd, E4 102 EE46
E11 123 ED61
E16 291 L4
E17 101 DZ53
N17 100 DU54
N18 100 DV51
NW6 272 F8
Kimberley Rd, SW9 310 B9
Beckenham BR3 203 DX96
Croydon CR0 201 DP100
St. Albans AL3 42 CC19
Kimberley Wk, Walt. KT12 off Cottimore La 195 BV101
Kimberley Way, E4 102 EE46
Kimber Pl, Houns. TW4 off Meadow Cl 176 CA87
Kimber Rd, SW18 180 DA87
Kimbers Dr, Burn. SL1 131 AK69
Kimble Cl, Wat. WD18 75 BS44
Kimble Cres, Bushey WD23 94 CC45
Kimble Rd, SW19 180 DD93
Kimbolton Cl, SE12 184 EF86
Kimbolton Grn, Borwd. WD6 78 CQ42
Kimbolton Row, SW3 296 C9
Kimmeridge Gdns, SE9 184 EL91
Kimmeridge Rd, SE9 184 EL91
Kimps Way, Hem.H. HP3 40 BN23
Kimpton Av, Brwd. CM15 108 FV45
Kimpton Cl, Hem.H. HP2 41 BP15
Kimpton Ho, SW15 off Fontley Way 179 CU87
● Kimpton Link Business Cen, Sutt. SM3 off Kimpton Rd 199 CZ103
Kimpton Pk Way, Sutt. SM3 199 CZ103
Kimpton Pl, Wat. WD25 60 BX34
Kimpton Rd, SE5 311 L6
Sutton SM3 199 CZ103
Kimptons Cl, Pot.B. EN6 63 CX33
Kimptons Mead, Pot.B. EN6 63 CX32
● Kimpton Trade & Business Cen, Sutt. SM3 199 CZ103
Kinburn Dr, Egh. TW20 172 AY92
Kinburn St, SE16 301 J4
Kincaid Rd, SE15 312 E5
Kincardine Gdns, W9 283 J5
Kinch Gro, Wem. HA9 118 CM59
Kincraig Dr, Sev. TN13 256 FG124
Kinder Cl, SE28 146 EX73
Kinderscout, Hem.H. HP3 40 BN22
Kindersley Way, Abb.L. WD5 59 BQ31
Kinder St, E1 288 E9
Kinderton Cl, N14 99 DJ46
Kinefold Ho, N7 276 A4
● Kinetic Business Cen, Borwd. WD6 78 CM41
Kinetic Cres, Enf. EN3 83 DZ36
Kinfauns Av, Horn. RM11 128 FJ58
Kinfauns Rd, SW2 181 DN89
Ilford IG3 126 EU60
Kingaby Gdns, Rain. RM13 147 FG66
King Acre Ct, Stai. TW18 173 BE90
King Alfred Av, SE6 183 EA90
King Alfred Rd, Rom. RM3 106 FM54
Sch King Alfred Sch, The, NW11 off North End Rd 120 DB60
King & Queen Cl, SE9 off St. Keverne Rd 184 EL91
King & Queen St, SE17 299 K9
King & Queen Wf, SE16 301 J2
King Arthur Cl, SE15 312 G5
King Arthur Ct, Chsht EN8 67 DX31
Sch King Athelstan Prim Sch, Kings.T. KT1 off Villiers Rd 198 CM97
Coll King Charles Cen, Surb. KT5 off Hollyfield Rd 198 CM101
King Charles Cl, Ware SG12 33 DZ05
King Charles Cres, Surb. KT5 198 CM101
King Charles Rd, Shenley WD7 62 CL32
Surbiton KT5 198 CM99
King Charles St, SW1 297 P4
King Charles Ter, E1 off Sovereign Cl 300 F1
King Charles Wk, SW19 off Princes Way 179 CY88
Kingcup Cl, Croy. CR0 203 DX101
King David La, E1 288 G10
Kingdom St, W2 283 N7
Kingdon Rd, NW6 273 K4
King Edward Av, Dart. DA1 188 FK86
Rainham RM13 148 FK68
King Edward Ct, Wem. HA9 off Elm Rd 118 CL64
Windsor SL4 151 AR81
King Edward Dr, Chess. KT9 off Kelvin Gro 198 CL104
Grays RM16 170 GE75
King Edward Ms, SW13 159 CU81
King Edward Rd, E10 123 EC60
E17 123 DY55
Barnet EN5 80 DA42
Brentwood CM14 108 FW48
Greenhithe DA9 189 FU85
Romford RM1 127 FF58
Shenley WD7 62 CM33
Waltham Cross EN8 67 DY33
Watford WD19 76 BY44
King Edward VII Av, Wind. SL4 152 AS80
H King Edward VII Hosp, Wind. SL4 151 AQ83
H King Edward VII's Hosp for Officers, W1 285 H6
King Edward's Gdns, W3 138 CN74
King Edwards Gro, Tedd. TW11 177 CH93
King Edward's Pl, W3 138 CN74
King Edwards Rd, E9 278 F8
N9 100 DV45
Barking IG11 145 ER67
Ruis. HA4 115 BR60
Ware SG12 33 DY05
King Edward's Rd, Enf. EN3 83 DX42
King Edward St, EC1 287 J8
Hemel Hempstead HP3 40 BJ24
Slough SL1 151 AR75
King Edward III Ms, SE16 300 F5
King Edward Wk, SE1 298 F6
Sch King Fahad Acad, The, W3 off Bromyard Av 138 CS73
Girls Upr Sch, W5 off Little Ealing La 157 CJ77
Kingfield Cl, Wok. GU22 227 AZ120
Kingfield Dr, Wok. GU22 227 AZ120
Kingfield Gdns, Wok. GU22 227 AZ120
Kingfield Grn, Wok. GU22 227 AZ120
Kingfield Rd, W5 137 CK70
Woking GU22 226 AY120
Sch Kingfield Sch, Wok. GU22 off Kingfield Rd 227 BA120
Kingfield St, E14 302 F9
Kingfisher Av, E11 off Eastern Av 124 EH58
Kingfisher Cl, SE28 146 EW73
Broxbourne EN10 49 EA20
Harrow Weald HA3 95 CF52
Hersham KT12 214 BY106
Hutton CM13 109 GA45
Lthd. KT22 231 CK120

Kingfisher Cl, Northwood HA6 93 BP53
Orpington BR5 206 EX98
Stanstead Abbotts SG12
off Lawrence Av 33 EC12
Kingfisher Ct, SW19
off Queensmere Rd 179 CY89
Enfield EN2 off Mount Vw 81 DM38
Sheerwater GU21
off Blackmore Cres 211 BC114
Surbiton KT6 off Ewell Rd 198 CM101
Sutton SM1
off Sandpiper Rd 217 CZ106
Woking GU21 off Vale Fm Rd 226 AX117
Kingfisher Dr, Green. DA9 189 FU85
Guildford GU4 243 BC132
Hemel Hempstead HP3 58 BM25
Redhill RH1 250 DG131
Richmond TW10 177 CH91
Staines-upon-Thames TW18 173 BF91
Kingfisher Gdns, S.Croy. CR2 221 DX111
Kingfisher Height, Grays RM17 170 GA78
Kingfisher Ho, SW18 160 DC83
Kingfisher Lure, Kings L. WD4 59 BP29
Loudwater WD3 74 BH42
Kingfisher Ms, SE13 163 EB84
Kingfisher Pl, N22
off Clarendon Rd 99 DM54
Kingfisher Rd, Upmin. RM14 129 FT60
Kingfishers, Denh. UB9
off Patrons Way E 113 BF58
Kingfisher Sq, SE8 313 P3
Kingfisher St, E6 293 H6
Kingfisher Wk, NW9 96 CS54
Kingfisher Way, NW10 118 CR64
Beckenham BR3 203 DX99
King Frederik IX Twr, SE16 301 N6
King Gdns, Croy. CR0 219 DP106
King George Av, E16 292 E8
Bushey WD23 76 CB44
Ilford IG2 125 ER57
Walton-on-Thames KT12 196 BX102
King George Cl, Rom. RM7 127 FC55
Sunbury-on-Thames TW16 175 BS92
King George Cres, Wem. HA0 117 CK64
DLR King George V 305 M3
King George V Dock, E16 305 J2
King George V Rd, Amer. HP6 55 AR38
H King George Hosp, Ilf. IG3 126 EV57
King George Rd, Wal.Abb. EN9 67 EC34
Ware SG12 33 DY05
King Georges Av, Wat. WD18 75 BS43
King Georges Dr,
New Haw KT15 212 BG110
Southall UB1 136 BZ71
King George VI Av, Mitch. CR4 200 DF98
Westerham TN16 238 EK116
King George Sq, Rich. TW10 178 CM86
King Georges Rd,
Pilg.Hat. CM15 108 FV44
● King George's Trd Est,
Chess. KT9 216 CN105
King George St, SE10 314 F5
Kingham Cl, SW18 180 DC87
W11 294 E4
King Harold Ct, Wal.Abb. EN9
off Sun St 67 EC33
Sch King Harold Sch, Wal.Abb. EN9
off Broomstick Hall Rd 68 EE33
King Harolds Way, Bexh. DA7 166 EX80
King Harry La, St.Alb. AL3 42 CA21
King Harry St, Hem.H. HP2 40 BK21
King Henry Ms, Har. HA2 117 CE60
Orpington BR6
off Osgood Av 223 ET106
King Henrys Ct, Wal.Abb.
EN9 off Deer Pk Way 83 EC36
Tra King Henry's Drive 221 EB109
King Henry's Dr,
New Adgtn CR0 221 EC109
King Henry's Ms, Enf. EN3 83 EA37
King Henry's Reach, W6 306 B2
King Henry's Rd, NW3 274 D7
Kingston upon Thames KT1 198 CP97
King Henry St, N16 277 N2
King Henry's Wk, N1 277 N4
Epp. CM16 off Boleyn Row 70 EV29
King Henry Ter, E1 300 F1
Kinghorn St, EC1 287 J7
King James Av, Cuffley EN6 65 DL29
King James Ct, SE1 299 H5
King James St, SE1 299 H5
King John Ct, EC2 287 P4
King Johns Cl, Wrays. TW19 172 AW86
King Johns Pl, Eng.Grn TW20 172 AY92
King John St, E1 289 K7
King Johns Wk, SE9 184 EK88
Kinglake Ct, Wok. GU21
off Raglan Rd 226 AS118
Kinglake Est, SE17 299 P10
Kinglake St, SE17 311 N1
Kinglet Cl, E7 281 N4
● Kingley Pk, Kings L. WD4 59 BP29
Kingly Ct, W1 285 M10
Kingly St, W1 285 L9
Kingsand Rd, SE12 184 EG89
Kings Arbour, Sthl. UB2 156 BY78
Kings Arms Ct, E1 288 C7
Kings Arms Yd, EC2 287 L8
Kingsash Dr, Hayes UB4 136 BY70
Kings Av, N10 120 DG55
N21 99 DP46
W5 137 CK72
Bromley BR1 184 EF93
Buckhurst Hill IG9 102 EK47
Byfleet KT14 212 BK112
Carshalton SM5 218 DE108
Greenford UB6 136 CB72
Hemel Hempstead HP3 40 BM24
Hounslow TW3 156 CB81
New Malden KT3 198 CS98
Redhill RH1 266 DE136
Romford RM6 126 EZ58
Sunbury-on-Thames TW16 175 BT92
Watford WD18 75 BT42
Woodford Green IG8 102 EH51
King's Av, SW4 181 DK87
SW12 181 DK88
Sch King's Av Prim Sch, SW4
off King's Av 181 DL85
Sch King's Av Sch Early Years Cen,
SW4 off Park Hill 181 DL85
Kings Bench St, SE1 299 H4
Kings Bench Wk, EC4 286 F9
Kingsbridge Av, W3 158 CM75
Kingsbridge Circ, Rom. RM3 106 FL51
Kingsbridge Cl, Rom. RM3 106 FL51
Kingsbridge Ct, E14
off Dockers Tanner Rd 302 B7
Kingsbridge Cres, Sthl. UB1 136 BZ71
Kingsbridge Dr, NW7 97 CX52
Kingsbridge Rd, W10 282 B8
Barking IG11 145 ER68
Morden SM4 199 CX101
Romford RM3 106 FL51
Southall UB2 156 BZ77
Walton-on-Thames KT12 195 BV101
Kingsbridge Way, Hayes UB4 135 BS69
Kingsbrook, Lthd. KT22
off Ryebrook Rd 231 CG118
KINGSBURY, NW9 118 CP58
⊖ Kingsbury 118 CN57
Kingsbury Av, St.Alb. AL3 42 CC19
Kingsbury Circle, NW9 118 CN57
Kingsbury Cres, Stai. TW18 173 BD91
Kingsbury Dr, Old Wind. SL4 172 AV86
Sch Kingsbury Grn Prim Sch, NW9
off Old Kenton La 118 CQ57
Sch Kingsbury High Sch,
Lwr Sch, NW9 off Bacon La 118 CQ56
Upr Sch, NW9 off Princes Av 118 CP56
Kingsbury Ms, St.Alb. AL3 42 CB19
Kingsbury Rd, N1 277 P4
NW9 118 CP57
Kingsbury Ter, N1 277 P4
● Kingsbury Trd Est, NW9 118 CQ58
★ Kingsbury Watermill,
St.Alb. AL3 42 CB19
Kings Butts, SE9
off Strongbow Cres 185 EM85
Kings Chace Vw, Enf. EN2
off Crofton Way 81 DN40
Kings Chase, Brwd. CM14 108 FW48
East Molesey KT8 196 CC97
Kingsclere Cl, SW15 179 CU87
Kingsclere Ct, Barn. EN5
off Gloucester Rd 80 DC43
Kingsclere Pl, Enf. EN2 82 DQ40
Kingscliffe Gdns, SW19 179 CZ88
Kings Cl, E10 123 EB59
NW4 119 CX56
Beaconsfield HP9 110 AG55
Chalfont St. Giles HP8 90 AX47
Chipperfield WD4 58 BH31
Dartford DA1 167 FE84
Northwood HA6 93 BT51
Staines-upon-Thames TW18 174 BK94
Thames Ditton KT7 197 CG100
Walton-on-Thames KT12 195 BV102
King's Cl, Wat. WD18
off Lady's Cl 76 BW42
Sch Kings Coll, Guil. GU2
off Southway 242 AS134
Uni King's Coll - Denmark Hill Campus,
SE5 off Champion Hill 162 DR83
Uni King's Coll - Guy's Campus,
SE1 299 L6
Uni King's Coll - Hampstead Campus,
NW3 off Kidderpore Av 120 DA63
H King's Coll Hosp, SE5 311 L9
Uni King's Coll - Maughan Lib &
Information Services Cen, WC2 286 E8
Kings Coll Rd, NW3 274 C6
Ruislip HA4 115 BT58
Sch King's Coll Sch, SW19
off Southside Common 179 CW93
Uni King's Coll - Strand Campus,
WC2 286 D10
Uni King's Coll - Waterloo
Campus, SE1 298 E3
Kingscote Rd, W4 158 CR76
Croydon CR0 202 DV101
New Malden KT3 198 CR97
Sch Kingscote Sch, Ger.Cr. SL9
off Oval Way 112 AY55
Kingscote St, EC4 286 G10
Kings Ct, E13 144 EH67
W6 off Hamlet Gdns 159 CU77
Berkhamsted HP4 off
Lower Kings Rd 38 AW18
Borhamwood WD6
off Bennington Dr 78 CM39
Tadworth KT20 233 CW122
Wembley HA9 118 CP61
Sch Kings Ct First Sch, Old Wind.
SL4 off Ashbrook Rd 172 AV87
Kingscourt Rd, SW16 181 DK90
Kings Ct S, SW3
off Chelsea Manor Gdns 308 D1
Kings Cres, N4 122 DQ62
Kings Cres Est, N4 122 DQ61
Kingscroft, Welw.G.C. AL7 30 DB08
Sch Kingscroft Jun Sch,
Stai. TW18 off Park Av 174 BG93
Kingscroft Rd, NW2 272 F4
Banstead SM7 234 DD115
Leatherhead KT22 231 CH120
KING'S CROSS, N1 275 P8
⇌ King's Cross 286 A1
King's Cross Br, N1 286 B2
Kings Cross La, S.Nutfld RH1 267 DL136
King's Cross Rd, WC1 286 D2
⊖ King's Cross St. Pancras 286 A1
Kingsdale Ct, Wal.Abb. EN9
off Lamplighters Cl 68 EG34
Sch Kingsdale Foundation Sch,
SE21 off Alleyn Pk 182 DS90
Kingsdale Gdns, W11 294 D3
Kingsdale Rd, SE18 165 ET80
SE20 183 DX94
Berkhamsted HP4 38 AU20
Kingsdene, Tad. KT20 233 CV121
Kingsdon La, Harl. CM17 52 EW16
Kingsdown Av, W3 138 CS73
W13 157 CH75
South Croydon CR2 219 DP109
Kingsdown Cl, SE16 312 F1
W10 282 D9
Gravesend DA12
off Farley Rd 191 GM88
Kingsdowne Rd, Surb. KT6 198 CL101
Kingsdown Rd, E11 124 EE62
N19 121 DL61
Epsom KT17 217 CU113
Sutton SM3 217 CY106
Kingsdown Way, Brom. BR2 204 EG101
Kings Dr, Edg. HA8 96 CM49
Gravesend DA12 191 GH90
Surbiton KT5 198 CN101
Teddington TW11 177 CD92
Thames Ditton KT7 197 CH100
Wembley HA9 118 CP61
Kings Dr, The, Hersham KT12 213 BT110
Kingsend, Ruis. HA4 115 BR60
KINGS FARM, Grav. DA12 191 GJ90
Kings Fm Av, Rich. TW10 158 CN84
Sch King's Fm Prim Sch,
Grav. DA12 off Cedar Av 191 GJ91
Kings Fm Rd, Chorl. WD3 73 BD44
Kingsfield, Albury GU5 260 BL144
Hoddesdon EN11 49 EA15
Windsor SL4 151 AK81
Kingsfield Av, Har. HA2 116 CB56
● Kingsfield Business Cen,
Red. RH1 266 DG135
Kingsfield Ct, Wat. WD19 94 BX45
Kingsfield Dr, Enf. EN3 83 DX35
Kingsfield Ho, SE9 184 EK90
Kingsfield Rd, Har. HA1 117 CD59
Watford WD19 94 BX45
Kingsfield Ter, Dart. DA1 188 FK85
Kingsfield Way, Enf. EN3 83 DX35
Redhill RH1 266 DG135
Sch Kingsford Comm Sch, E6 293 J8
Kingsford St, NW5 274 E3
Kingsford Way, E6 293 K7
Kings Gdns, NW6 273 K7
Ilford IG1 125 ER60
Upminster RM14 129 FS59
Walton-on-Thames KT12 195 BV102
King's Garth Ms, SE23
off London Rd 182 DW89
Kings Gate, Add. KT15 212 BH105
Kingsgate, St.Alb. AL3
off King Harry La 42 CB22
Wembley HA9 118 CQ62
Kingsgate Av, N3 120 DA55
Kingsgate Cl, Bexh. DA7 166 EY81
Orpington BR5 off Main Rd 206 EW97
Kingsgate Est, N1 277 P5
Kingsgate Pl, NW6 273 J7
Sch Kingsgate Prim Sch, NW6 273 J6
Kingsgate Rd, NW6 273 J6
Kingston upon Thames KT2 198 CL95
Kings Grn, Loug. IG10 84 EL41
Kingsground, SE9 184 EL87
Kings Gro, SE15 312 F5
Romford RM1 127 FG57
Kings Hall Ms, SE13 314 F10
Kings Hall Rd, Beck. BR3 183 DY94
Kings Head Hill, E4 101 EB45
Kings Head La, Byfleet KT14 212 BK111
Kings Head Yd, SE1 299 L3
Kings Highway, SE18 165 ES79
Kings Hill, Loug. IG10 84 EL40
Kingshill Av, Har. HA3 117 CH56
Hayes UB4 135 BS69
Northolt UB5 135 BU69
Romford RM5 105 FC51
St. Albans AL4 43 CG17
Worcester Park KT4 199 CU101
Kingshill Cl, Hayes UB4 135 BU69
Kingshill Dr, Har. HA3 117 CH55
Kingshill Way, Berk. HP4 38 AU21
Kingshold Est, E9 278 G8
Kingshold Rd, E9 279 H7
Kingsholm Gdns, SE9 164 EK84
King's Ho, SW8 310 B4
Sch King's Ho Sch,
Jun Dept, Rich. TW10
off Kings Rd 178 CM85
Sen Dept, Rich. TW10
off Kings Rd 178 CM85
Kingshurst Rd, SE12 184 EG87
● Kingside, SE18 304 G7
Kings Keep, Kings.T. KT1
off Beaufort Rd 198 CL98
King's Keep, SW15
off Westleigh Av 179 CX85
KINGSLAND, N1 277 N5
Kingsland, NW8 274 D9
Harlow CM18 51 EQ17
Potters Bar EN6 63 CZ33
Kingsland Basin, N1 277 P8
Kingsland Grn, E8 277 P4
Kingsland High St, E8 278 A4
Kingsland Pas, E8 277 P4
Kingsland Rd, E2 287 P2
E8 277 P8
E13 292 C3
Hemel Hempstead HP1 40 BG22
Kingsland Shop Cen, E8 278 A4
Kings La, Chipper. WD4 58 BG31
Englefield Green TW20 172 AU92
Sutton SM1 218 DD107
KINGS LANGLEY, WD4 58 BM30
⇌ Kings Langley 59 BQ30
Kings Langley Bypass,
Hem.H. HP1, HP3 40 BG23
Kings Langley WD4 58 BK28
Sch Kings Langley Prim Sch,
Kings L. WD4 off Common La 58 BM28
Sch Kings Langley Sch,
Kings L. WD4 off Love La 58 BL28
Kingslawn Cl, SW15 179 CV85
Kingslea, Lthd. KT22 231 CG120
Kingsleigh Cl, Brent. TW8 157 CK79
Kingsleigh Pl, Mitch. CR4 200 DF97
Kingsleigh Wk, Brom. BR2
off Stamford Dr 204 EF98
Kingsley Av, W13 137 CG72
Banstead SM7 234 DA115
Borehamwood WD6 78 CM40
Cheshunt EN8 66 DV29
Dartford DA1 188 FN85
Englefield Green TW20 172 AV93
Hounslow TW3 156 CC82
Southall UB1 136 CA73
Sutton SM1 218 DD105
Kingsley Cl, N2 120 DC57
Dagenham RM10 127 FB63
Horley RH6 268 DF146
Kingsley Ct, Edg. HA8 96 CP47
Welwyn Garden City AL7 29 CZ13
Kingsley Dr, Wor.Pk. KT4
off Badgers Copse 199 CT103
Kingsley Flats, SE1 299 N8
Kingsley Gdns, E4 101 EA50
Hornchurch RM11 128 FK56
Ottershaw KT16 211 BD107
Kingsley Grn, St.Alb. WD7 61 CJ31
Kingsley Gro, Reig. RH2 266 DA137
Sch Kingsley High Sch, Har. HA3
off Whittlesea Rd 94 CC52
Kingsley Ms, E1 300 F1
W8 295 M7
Chislehurst BR7 185 EP93
Kingsley Path, Slou. SL2 131 AK70
Kingsley Pl, N6 120 DG59
Sch Kingsley Prim Sch, Croy. CR0
off Thomson Cres 201 DN102
Kingsley Rd, E7 281 P6
E17 101 EC54
N13 99 DN49
NW6 273 H8
SW19 180 DB92
Croydon CR0 201 DN102
Harrow HA2 116 CC63
Kingsley Rd, Horley RH6 268 DF146
Hounslow TW3 156 CC82
Hutton CM13 109 GD45
Ilford IG6 103 EQ53
Loughton IG10 85 ER41
Orpington BR6 223 ET107
Pinner HA5 116 BZ56
Kingsley St, SW11 308 F10
Kingsley Wk, Grays RM16 171 GG77
Kingsley Way, N2 120 DC58
Kingsley Wd Dr, SE9 185 EM90
Kings Lo, Ruis. HA4
off Pembroke Rd 115 BS60
Kingslyn Cres, SE19 202 DS95
Kings Lynn Cl, Rom. RM3
off Kings Lynn Dr 106 FK51
Kings Lynn Dr, Rom. RM3 106 FK51
Kings Lynn Path, Rom. RM3
off Kings Lynn Dr 106 FK51
Kings Mall, W6 294 A9
Kingsman Par, SE18 305 K7
Kingsman St, SE18 305 K7
Kingsmead, Barn. EN5 80 DA42
Biggin Hill TN16 238 EK116
Cuffley EN6 65 DL28
Richmond TW10 178 CM86
St. Albans AL4 43 CK17
Sawbridgeworth CM21 36 EY06
Waltham Cross EN8 67 DX28
Kings Mead, Smallfield RH6 269 DP148
South Nutfield RH1 267 DL136
Kingsmead Av, N9 100 DV46
NW9 118 CR59
Mitcham CR4 201 DJ97
Romford RM1 127 FE58
Sunbury-on-Thames TW16 196 BW97
Surbiton KT6 198 CN103
Worcester Park KT4 199 CV104
Kingsmead Cl, Epsom KT19 216 CR108
Roydon CM19 50 EH16
Sidcup DA15 186 EU89
Teddington TW11 177 CH93
Kingsmead Dr, Nthlt. UB5 136 BZ66
Kingsmead Est, E9 279 M2
Kingsmead Hill,
Roydon CM19 50 EH16
Kingsmead Ho, E9
off Kingsmead Way 279 M1
Kings Meadow, Kings L. WD4 58 BN28
Kings Mead Pk, Clay. KT10 215 CE108
Sch Kingsmead Prim Sch, E9 279 M1
Kingsmead Rd, SW2 181 DN89
Sch Kingsmead Sch, Enf. EN1
off Southbury Rd 82 DU41
Kingsmead Way, E9 279 M1
Kingsmere Cl, SW15
off Felsham Rd 159 CX83
Kingsmere Pk, NW9 118 CP60
Kingsmere Pl, N16 122 DR60
Kingsmere Rd, SW19 179 CX89
Kings Ms, SW4
off King's Av 181 DL85
Chig. IG7 103 EQ47
King's Ms, WC1 286 D5
● Kingsmill Business Pk,
Kings.T. KT1 198 CM97
Kingsmill Ct, Hat. AL10
off Drakes Way 45 CV20
Kingsmill Gdns, Dag. RM9 126 EZ64
Kings Mill La, Red. RH1 267 DK138
Kingsmill Rd, Dag. RM9 126 EZ64
Kingsmill Ter, NW8 274 B10
Kingsmill Way, Denh. UB9 134 BJ65
KINGSMOOR, Harl. CM19 51 EQ20
Sch Kingsmoor Inf Sch,
Harl. CM18 off Ployters Rd 51 EQ19
Sch Kingsmoor Jun Sch,
Harl. CM18 off Ployters Rd 51 EQ19
Kingsmoor Rd, Harl. CM19 51 EP18
Kingsnympton Pk,
Kings.T. KT2 178 CP93
Kings Oak, Rom. RM7 126 FA55
H Kings Oak Hosp, The,
Enf. EN2 81 DN38
Sch Kings Oak Prim Sch,
N.Mal. KT3 off Dickerage La 198 CP97
Sch King Solomon Acad, NW1 284 C6
Sch King Solomon High Sch,
Ilf. IG6 off Forest Rd 103 ER54
King's Orchard, SE9 184 EL86
Kings Paddock, Hmptn. TW12 196 CC95
Kings Par, Cars. SM5
off Wrythe La 200 DE104
Kings Pk, Colnbr. SL3 153 BD80
Kingspark Ct, E18 124 EG55
● Kings Pk Ind Est,
Kings L. WD4 59 BP29
Kings Pas, Kings.T. KT1
off Market Pl 197 CK96
King's Pas, E11 124 EE59
★ Kings Pl, N1 276 B10
Kings Pl, SE1 299 J5
W4 158 CQ78
Buckhurst Hill IG9 102 EJ47
Loughton IG10 102 EK45
King Sq, EC1 287 J3
Kings Quarter Apts, N1
off Copenhagen St 276 B9
King's Quay, SW10 307 P6
Kings Ride Gate, Rich. TW10 158 CN84
Kingsridge, SW19 179 CY89
Kingsridge Gdns, Dart. DA1 188 FK86
Kings Rd, E4 101 ED46
E6 144 EJ67
E11 124 EE59
N18 100 DU50
N22 99 DM53
NW10 139 CV66
SE25 202 DU97
SW14 158 CR83
SW19 180 DA93
W5 137 CK71
Barking IG11 145 EQ66
Barnet EN5 79 CW41
Berkhamsted HP4 38 AU20
Biggin Hill TN16 238 EJ116
Brentwood CM14 108 FW48
Chalfont St. Giles HP8 90 AX47
Egham TW20 173 BA91
Feltham TW13 176 BW88
Guildford GU1 242 AX134
Harrow HA2 116 BZ61
Horl. RH6 268 DG148
Kingston upon Thames KT2 178 CL94
London Colney AL2 61 CJ26
Long Ditton KT6 197 CJ102
Mitcham CR4 200 DG97
New Haw KT15 212 BH110
Orpington BR6 223 ET105
Kings Rd, Richmond TW10 178 CM85
Romford RM1 127 FG57
St. Albans AL3 42 CB19
Shalford GU4 258 AY141
Slough SL1 152 AS76
Sutton SM2 218 DA110
Teddington TW11 177 CD92
Twickenham TW1 177 CH86
Wal.Cr. EN8 67 DY34
Walton-on-Thames KT12 195 BV103
West Drayton UB7 154 BM75
Wok. GU21 227 BA116
King's Rd, N17 100 DT53
SW3 296 D10
SW6 307 M5
SW10 307 M5
Hert. SG13 32 DU08
Uxb. UB8 134 BK68
Wind. SL4 151 AR82
Kings Rd Bungalows,
Har. HA2 off Kings Rd 116 BZ62
King's Scholars' Pas, SW1 297 L7
King Stable Ct, Wind. SL4
off King Stable St 151 AR80
King Stable St, Eton SL4 151 AR80
King Stairs Cl, SE16 300 F4
Kings Ter, Islw. TW7 off South St 179 CG83
King's Ter, NW1 275 L9
Kingsthorpe Rd, SE26 183 DX91
⇌ Kingston 198 CL95
Sch Kingston Acad, The, Kings.T.
KT2 off Richmond Rd 178 CL93
Kingston Av, E.Hors. KT24 245 BS126
Feltham TW14 175 BS86
Leatherhead KT22 231 CH121
Sutton SM3 199 CY104
West Drayton UB7 134 BM73
Kingston Br, Kings.T. KT1 197 CK96
● Kingston Business Cen,
Chess. KT9 198 CL104
Kingston Bypass, SW15 178 CS93
SW20 178 CS93
Esher KT10 197 CG104
New Malden KT3 199 CU96
Surbiton KT5 198 CL104
Kingston Cl, Nthlt. UB5 136 BZ66
Romford RM6 126 EY55
Teddington TW11 177 CH93
Coll Kingston Coll, Kings.T. KT1
off Kingston Hall Rd 197 CK97
Sch of Art & Design, Kings.T.
KT2 off Richmond Rd 198 CL95
Kingston Ct, Nthflt DA11 190 GB85
Kingston Cres, Ashf. TW15 174 BJ92
Beckenham BR3 203 DZ95
Kingston Gdns, Croy. CR0 201 DL104
Sch Kingston Gram Sch,
Kings.T. KT2 off London Rd 198 CM96
Kingston Hall Rd, Kings.T. KT1 197 CK97
Kingston Hill, Kings.T. KT2 178 CQ93
Kingston Hill Av, Rom. RM6 104 EY54
Kingston Hill Pl, Kings.T. KT2 178 CQ91
H Kingston Hosp, Kings.T. KT2 198 CP95
● Kingston Ho Est,
Long Dit. KT6 197 CH100
Kingston Ho Gdns, Lthd. KT22
off Upper Fairfield Rd 231 CH121
Kingston La, Lthd. KT24 244 BM127
Teddington TW11 177 CG92
Uxbridge UB8 134 BL69
West Drayton UB7 154 BM75
Kingston Lo, N.Mal. KT3
off Kingston Rd 198 CS98
★ Kingston Mus & Heritage Cen,
Kings.T. KT1 198 CL96
Kingston Pk Est, Kings.T. KT2 178 CP93
Kingston Pl, Har. HA3
off Richmond Gdns 95 CF52
Kingston Ri, New Haw KT15 212 BG110
Kingston Rd, N9 100 DU47
SW15 179 CU88
SW19 199 CZ95
SW20 199 CW96
Ashford TW15 174 BL93
Barnet EN4 80 DD43
Epsom KT17, KT19 216 CS106
Ilford IG1 125 EP63
Kingston upon Thames KT1 198 CP97
Leatherhead KT22 231 CG117
New Malden KT3 198 CR98
Romford RM1 127 FF56
Southall UB2 156 BZ75
Staines-upon-Thames TW18 174 BJ93
Surbiton KT5 198 CP103
Teddington TW11 177 CH92
Worcester Park KT4 198 CP103
Kingston Sq, SE19 182 DR92
Leatherhead KT22
off Kingston Rd 231 CG119
Uni Kingston Uni,
Clayhills Halls of Res, Surb. KT5
off Clayhill 198 CN99
Kingston Hill, Kings.T. KT2
off Kingston Hill 178 CR92
Kingston Vale, SW15
off Kingston Vale 178 CR91
Knights Pk, Kings.T. KT1
off Grange Rd 198 CL97
Penrhyn Rd, Kings.T. KT1
off Penrhyn Rd 198 CL98
Roehampton Vale, SW15
off Friars Av 179 CT90
Seething Wells Halls of Res,
Surb. KT6 off Portsmouth Rd 197 CJ100
KINGSTON UPON THAMES,
KT1 & KT2 198 CL96
KINGSTON VALE, SW15 178 CS91
Kingston Vale, SW15 178 CR91
Kingstown St, NW1 274 G8
King St, E13 291 N5
EC2 287 K9
N2 120 DD55
N17 100 DT53
SW1 297 M3
W3 138 CP74
W6 159 CU77
WC2 286 A10
Chertsey KT16 194 BG102
Chesham HP5 54 AP32
Gravesend DA12 191 GH86
Richmond TW9 177 CK85
Southall UB2 156 BY76
Twickenham TW1 177 CG88
Watford WD18 76 BW42

King St Ms, N2
off King St 120 DD55
Kings Wk, Grays RM17 170 GA79
S.Croy. CR2 220 DV114
King's Wk, Kings.T. KT2 197 CK95
Kings Wk Shop Mall, SW3
off King's Rd 296 E10
Kings Wardrobe Apts, EC4
off Carter La 287 H9
Kings Warren, Oxshott KT22 214 CC111
Kingswater Pl, SW11
off Battersea Ch Rd 308 C5
Kingsway, N12 98 DC51
SW14 158 CP83
WC2 286 C8
Chalfont St. Peter SL9 112 AY55
Cuffley EN6 65 DL30
Enfield EN3 82 DV43
Farnham Common SL2 131 AP65
Hayes UB3 135 BQ71
Iver SL0 133 BE72
New Malden KT3 199 CW98
Petts Wood BR5 205 ES99
Staines-upon-Thames TW19 174 BK88
Watford WD25 60 BW34
Wembley HA9 118 CL63
West Wickham BR4 204 EE104
Woking GU21 226 AX118
Woodford Green IG8 102 EJ50
Kings Way, Croy. CR0 219 DM106
Harrow HA1 117 CE56
Kingsway, The, Epsom KT17 217 CT111
Kingsway Av, S.Croy. CR2 220 DW109
Woking GU21 226 AX118
● Kingsway Business Pk, Hmptn. TW12 196 BZ95
Kingsway Cres, Har. HA2 116 CC56
Sch Kingsway Infants' Sch, Wat. WD25 off North App 59 BU34
Sch Kingsway Jun Sch, Wat. WD25
off Briar Rd 59 BU34
Kingsway Ms, Farn.Com. SL2 131 AQ65
Kingsway Pl, EC1 286 F4
Kingsway Rd, Sutt. SM3 217 CY108
Kingswear Rd, NW5 121 DH62
Ruislip HA4 115 BU61
Kingswell Ride, Cuffley EN6 65 DL30
● Kingswey Business Pk, Wok. GU21 211 BC114
Kings Wf, E8 277 P8
KINGSWOOD, Tad. KT20 233 CY123
Wat. WD25 59 BV34
⇌ Kingswood 233 CZ121
Kingswood Av, NW6 272 E9
Belvedere DA17 166 EZ77
Bromley BR2 204 EE97
Hampton TW12 176 CB93
Hounslow TW3 156 BZ81
South Croydon CR2 236 DV115
Swanley BR8 207 FF98
Thornton Heath CR7 201 DN99
H Kingswood Cen, The, NW9 118 CN56
Kingswood Cl, N20 80 DC44
SW8 310 B5
Ashford TW15 175 BQ91
Dartford DA1 188 FJ85
Enfield EN1 82 DS43
Englefield Green TW20 172 AX91
Guildford GU1 243 BC133
New Malden KT3 199 CT100
Orpington BR6 205 ER101
Surbiton KT6 198 CL101
Weybridge KT13 213 BP108
Kingswood Ct, SE13
off Hither Grn La 183 ED86
Kingswood Creek, Wrays. TW19 172 AX85
Kingswood Dr, SE19 182 DS91
Carshalton SM5 200 DF102
Sutton SM2 218 DB109
Kingswood Est, SE21 182 DS91
Kingswood Gra, Lwr Kgswd KT20 250 DA128
Sch Kingswood Ho Sch, Epsom KT19 off West Hill 216 CQ113
Kingswood La, S.Croy. CR2 220 DW113
Warlingham CR6 236 DW115
Kingswood Ms, N15
off Harringay Rd 121 DP57
Kingswood Pk, N3 97 CZ54
Kings Wood Pk, Epp. CM16 70 EV29
Kingswood Pl, SE13 164 EE84
Sch Kingswood Prim Sch, Upper site, SE27
off Gipsy Rd 182 DR92
Lower site, SE27 182 DQ91
Lower Kingswood KT20
off Buckland Rd 249 CZ128
Kingswood Ri, Eng.Grn TW20 172 AX92
Kingswood Rd, E11 124 EE59
SE20 182 DW93
SW2 181 DL86
SW19 179 CZ94
W4 158 CQ76
Bromley BR2 203 ED98
Dunton Green TN13 241 FE120
Ilford IG3 126 EU60
Tadworth KT20 233 CV121
Watford WD25 59 BV34
Wembley HA9 118 CN62
Kingswood Ter, W4
off Kingswood Rd 158 CQ76
Kingswood Way, S.Croy. CR2 220 DW113
Wallington SM6 219 DL106
Kingsworth Cl, Beck. BR3 203 DY99
Kingsworthy Cl, Kings.T. KT1 198 CM97
Kings Yard, Guil. GU2 242 AT131
King's Yd, SW15
off Stanbridge Rd 306 B10
Kingthorpe Rd, NW10 138 CR66
Kingthorpe Ter, NW10 138 CR65
Kingwell Rd, Barn. EN4 80 DD38
Kingweston Cl, NW2 119 CY62
King William Ct, Wal.Abb. EN9
off Kendal Rd 83 EC35
King William IV Gdns, SE20
off St. John's Rd 182 DW93
King William La, SE10 315 J1
King William St, EC4 299 M1
King William Wk, SE10 314 F2
Coll Kingwood City Learning Cen, The, SW6 306 E6
Kingwood Rd, SW6 306 D6
Kinlet Rd, SE18 165 EQ81
Kinloch Dr, NW9 118 CS59
Kinloch St, N7 121 DM62
Kinloss Ct, N3
off Kinloss Gdns 119 CZ56
Kinloss Gdns, N3 119 CZ56
Kinloss Rd, Cars. SM5 200 DC101
Kinnaird Av, W4 158 CQ80
Bromley BR1 184 EF93
Kinnaird Cl, Brom. BR1 184 EF93
Slough SL1 130 AJ72
Kinnaird Ho, N6 121 DK59
Kinnaird Way, Wdf.Grn. IG8 103 EM51
Kinnear Apts, N8
off Chadwell La 121 DM55
Kinnear Rd, W12 159 CT75
Kinnersley Manor, Reig. RH2 266 DC142
Kinnersley Wk, Reig. RH2 266 DB139
Kinnerton Pl N, SW1 296 F5
Kinnerton Pl S, SW1 296 F5
Kinnerton St, SW1 296 G5
Kinnerton Yd, SW1 296 F5
Kinnoul Rd, W6 306 E2
Kinross Av, Wor.Pk. KT4 199 CU103
Kinross Cl, Edg. HA8 96 CP47
Harrow HA3 118 CM57
Sunbury-on-Thames TW16 175 BT92
Kinross Dr, Sun. TW16 175 BT92
Kinross Ter, E17 101 DZ54
Kinsale Rd, SE15 162 DU83
Kinsella Gdns, SW19 179 CV92
Kinsey Ho, SE21
off Kingswood Est 182 DS91
Kintore Way, SE1 300 A8
Kintyre Cl, SW16 201 DM96
Kinveachy Gdns, SE7 304 G9
Kinver Ho, N19
off Elthorne Rd 121 DK61
Kinver Rd, SE26 182 DW91
Kipings, Tad. KT20 233 CX122
Kipling Av, Til. RM18 171 GH81
Kipling Cl, Warley CM14 108 FV50
Kipling Dr, SW19 180 DD93
Kipling Est, SE1 299 M5
Kipling Pl, Stan. HA7 95 CF51
Kipling Rd, Bexh. DA7 166 EY81
Dartford DA1 188 FP85
Woking GU21 226 AW117
Kipling St, SE1 299 M5
Kipling Ter, N9 100 DR48
Kipling Twrs, Rom. RM3 105 FH52
KIPPINGTON, Sev. TN13 256 FG126
Kippington Cl, Sev. TN13 256 FF124
Kippington Dr, SE9 184 EK88
Kippington Ho, Sev. TN13
off Kippington Rd 256 FG126
Kippington Rd, Sev. TN13 256 FG124
Kirby Cl, Epsom KT19 217 CT106
Ilford IG6 103 ES51
Loughton IG10 102 EL45
Northwood HA6 93 BT51
Romford RM3 106 FN50
Kirby Est, SE16 300 E6
West Dr. UB7 off Trout Rd 134 BK73
Kirby Gro, SE1 299 N4
Kirby Rd, Dart. DA2 188 FQ87
Woking GU21 226 AW117
Kirby St, EC1 286 F6
Kirby Way, Uxb. UB8 134 BM70
Walton-on-Thames KT12 196 BW100
Kirchen Rd, W13 137 CH73
Kirkby Cl, N11
off Coverdale Rd 98 DG51
Kirkcaldy Grn, Wat. WD19
off Trevose Way 94 BW48
Kirk Ct, Sev. TN13 256 FG123
Kirkdale, SE26 182 DV89
Kirkdale Rd, E11 124 EE60
Kirkefields, Guil. GU2 242 AU131
Kirkfield Cl, W13
off Broomfield Rd 137 CH74
Kirkham Rd, E6 293 H8
Kirkham St, SE18 165 ES79
Kirkland Av, Ilf. IG5 103 EN54
Woking GU21 226 AS116
Kirkland Cl, Sid. DA15 185 ES86
Kirkland Dr, Enf. EN2 81 DP39
Kirklands, Welw.G.C. AL8 29 CX05
Kirkland Wk, E8 278 A5
Kirk La, SE18 165 EQ79
Kirkleas Rd, Surb. KT6 198 CL102
Kirklees Rd, Dag. RM8 126 EW64
Thornton Heath CR7 201 DN99
Kirkley Rd, SW19 200 DA95
Kirkly Cl, S.Croy. CR2 220 DS109
Kirkman Pl, W1 285 N7
Kirkmichael Rd, E14 290 F8
Kirk Ri, Sutt. SM1 200 DB104
Kirk Rd, E17 123 DZ58
Kirkside Rd, SE3 315 N2
Kirkstall Av, N17 122 DR56
Kirkstall Gdns, SW2 181 DK88
Kirkstall Rd, SW2 181 DK88
Kirkstead Ct, E5
off Mandeville St 123 DY63
Kirksted Rd, Mord. SM4 200 DB102
Kirkstone Lo, Islw. TW7
off Summerwood Rd 177 CF85
Kirkstone Way, Brom. BR1 184 EE94
Kirk St, WC1 286 C5
Kirkton Rd, N15 122 DS56
Kirkwall Pl, E2 289 H2
Kirkwall Spur, Slou. SL1 132 AS71
Kirkwood Rd, SE15 312 F8
Kirn Rd, W13 off Kirchen Rd 137 CH73
Kirrane Cl, N.Mal. KT3 199 CT99
Kirsty Cl, Dor. RH5 263 CJ138
Kirtle Rd, Chesh. HP5 54 AQ31
Kirtley Ho, N16
off Stamford Hill 122 DS60
Kirtley Rd, SE26 183 DY91
Kirtling St, SW8 309 L4
Kirton Cl, W4 158 CR77
Hornchurch RM12 148 FJ65
Kirton Gdns, E2 288 B3
Kirton Rd, E13 144 EJ68
Kirton Wk, Edg. HA8 96 CQ52
Kirwyn Way, SE5 311 H4
Sch Kisharon Day Sch, NW11
off Finchley Rd 119 CZ58
Kitcat Ter, E3 290 B2
Kitchen Ct, E10
off Brisbane Rd 123 EB61
Kitchener Av, Grav. DA12 191 GJ90
Kitchener Cl, St.Alb. AL1 43 CH21
Kitchener Rd, E7 144 EH65
E17 101 EB53
N2 120 DE55
N17 122 DR55
Dagenham RM10 147 FB65
Thornton Heath CR7 202 DR97
Kitcheners Mead, St.Alb. AL3 42 CC20
Jct Kitchenride Cor, Cher. KT16 211 BA105
Kite Fld, Nthch HP4 38 AS16
Kite Pl, E2 288 D2
Kite Yd, SW11 308 E7
Kitley Gdns, SE19 202 DT95
Kitsbury Rd, Berk. HP4 38 AV19
Kitsbury Ter, Berk. HP4 38 AV19
Kitsmead La, Longcr. KT16 192 AX103
Kitson Rd, SE5 311 K4
SW13 159 CU81
Kitson Way, Harl. CM20 35 EQ14
Kitswell Way, Rad. WD7 61 CF33
Kitten La, Stans.Abb. SG12 34 EE11
Kitters Grn, Abb.L. WD5
off High St 59 BS31
Kittiwake Cl, S.Croy. CR2 221 DY110
Kittiwake Pl, Sutt. SM1
off Sandpiper Rd 217 CZ106
Kittiwake Rd, Nthlt. UB5 136 BX69
Kittiwake Way, Hayes UB4 136 BX71
Kitto Rd, SE14 313 J9
Kitt's End Rd, Barn. EN5 79 CX36
KITT'S END, Barn. EN5 79 CY37
Kittywake Ho, Slou. SL1 132 AS74
Kiver Rd, N19 121 DK61
Klea Av, SW4 181 DJ86
Kleine Wf, N1 277 P9
Knapdale Cl, SE23 182 DV89
Knapmill Rd, SE6 183 EA89
Knapmill Way, SE6 183 EB89
Knapp Cl, NW10 138 CS65
Knapp Rd, E3 290 A5
Ashford TW15 174 BM91
Knapton Ms, SW17
off Seely Rd 180 DG93
Knaresborough Dr, SW18 180 DB88
Knaresborough Pl, SW5 295 L8
Knatchbull Rd, NW10 138 CR67
SE5 311 J7
Knaves Beech, Loud. HP10 88 AD53
● Knaves Beech Business Cen, H.Wyc. HP10
off Boundary Rd 88 AC54
● Knaves Beech Ind Est, Loud. HP10 88 AC54
Knaves Beech Way, Loud. HP10 88 AC54
Knaves Hollow, Woob.Moor HP10 88 AD54
Knebworth Av, E17 101 EA53
Knebworth Cl, Barn. EN5 80 DB42
Knebworth Path, Borwd. WD6 78 CR42
Knebworth Rd, N16 122 DS63
Knee Hill, SE2 166 EW77
Knee Hill Cres, SE2 166 EW77
Knella Grn, Welw.G.C. AL7 30 DA09
Knella Rd, Welw.G.C. AL7 29 CY10
Kneller Gdns, Islw. TW7 177 CD85
Kneller Rd, SE4 163 DY84
New Malden KT3 198 CS101
Twickenham TW2 176 CC86
Knevett Ter, Houns. TW3 156 CA84
Knight Cl, Dag. RM8 126 EW61
Knight Ct, E4
off The Ridgeway 101 EC46
Knighten St, E1 300 E3
Knighthead Pt, E14 302 A6
Knightland Rd, E5 122 DV61
Knighton Cl, Rom. RM7 127 FD58
South Croydon CR2 219 DP108
Woodford Green IG8 102 EH49
Knighton Dr, Wdf.Grn. IG8 102 EG49
Knighton Grn, Buck.H. IG9
off High Rd 102 EH47
Knighton La, Buck.H. IG9 102 EH47
Knighton Pk Rd, SE26 183 DX92
Knighton Rd, E7 124 EG62
Otford TN14 241 FF116
Redhill RH1 266 DG136
Romford RM7 127 FC58
Knighton Way La, Denh. UB9 134 BH65
Knightrider Ct, EC4
off Knightrider St 287 J10
Knightrider St, EC4 287 J10
Knights Av, W5 158 CL75
⊖ Knightsbridge 296 E5
Knightsbridge, SW1 296 F5
SW7 296 D5
Knightsbridge Apts, The, SW7
off Knightsbridge 296 E5
Knightsbridge Ct, Langley SL3
off High St 153 BA77
Knightsbridge Cres, Stai. TW18 174 BH93
Knightsbridge Gdns, Rom. RM7 127 FD57
Knightsbridge Grn, SW1 296 E5
Knightsbridge Way, Hem.H. HP2 40 BL20
Knights Cl, E9 279 H3
Egham TW20 173 BD93
West Molesey KT8 196 BZ99
Windsor SL4 151 AK81
Knightscote Cl, Hare. UB9 92 BK54
Knights Ct, Kings.T. KT1 198 CL97
Romford RM6 126 EY58
Knights Fld, Eyns. DA4 208 FL104
Knightsfield, Welw.G.C. AL8 29 CY06
Knights Hill, SE27 181 DP92
Knights Hill Sq, SE27 181 DP91
Knights La, N9 100 DU48
Knights Manor Way, Dart. DA1 188 FM86
Knights Ms, Sutt. SM2
off York Rd 218 DA108
Knights Orchard, Hem.H. HP1 39 BF18
Knights Pk, Kings.T. KT1 198 CL97
Knights Pl, Red. RH1
off Noke Dr 250 DG133
Wind. SL4 off Frances Rd 151 AQ82
Knight's Pl, Twick. TW2
off May Rd 177 CE88
Knights Ridge, Orp. BR6
off Stirling Dr 224 EV106
Knights Rd, E16 303 P4
Stanmore HA7 95 CJ49
Knights Twr, SE8 163 EA78
Knight St, Saw. CM21 36 EY05
Knights Wk, SE11 298 G9
Abridge RM4 86 EV41
Knights Way, Ilf. IG6 103 EQ51
Knight's Way, Brwd. CM13 109 GA48
Knightswood, Wok. GU21 226 AT118
Knightswood Cl, Edg. HA8 96 CQ47
Knightswood Rd, Rain. RM13 147 FG68
Knightwood Cl, Reig. RH2 266 DA136
Knightwood Cres, N.Mal. KT3 198 CS100
Knipp Hill, Cob. KT11 214 BZ113
Knivet Rd, SW6 307 J3
Knobfield, Abin.Ham. RH5 261 BT143
KNOCKHALL, Green. DA9 189 FW85
Knockhall Chase, Green. DA9 189 FV85
Sch Knockhall Comm Prim Sch, Green. DA9
off Eynsford Rd 189 FW85
Knockhall Rd, Green. DA9 189 FW86
KNOCKHOLT, Sev. TN14 240 EU116
⇌ Knockholt 224 EY109
Knockholt Cl, Sutt. SM2 218 DB110
Knockholt Main Rd, Knock.P. TN14 240 EY115
KNOCKHOLT POUND, Sev. TN14 240 EX115
Knockholt Rd, SE9 184 EK85
Halstead TN14 224 EZ113
Knole, The, SE9 185 EN91
Istead Rise DA13 190 GE94
Sch Knole Acad, (Knole East), Sev. TN13
off Seal Hollow Rd 257 FL121
(Knole West), Sev. TN13
off Bradbourne Vale Rd 256 FG121
Knole Cl, Croy. CR0 202 DW100
Knole Gate, Sid. DA15
off Woodside Cres 185 ES90
★ Knole Ho & Pk, Sev. TN15 257 FL126
Knole La, Sev. TN13 257 FJ126
Knole Rd, Dart. DA1 187 FG87
Sevenoaks TN13 257 FK123
Knole Way, Sev. TN13 257 FJ125
Knoll, The, W13 137 CJ71
Beckenham BR3 203 EB95
Bromley BR2 204 EG103
Chertsey KT16 193 BF102
Cobham KT11 214 CA113
Hertford SG13 32 DV08
Leatherhead KT22 231 CJ121
Knoll Ct, SE19 182 DS92
Knoll Cres, Nthwd. HA6 93 BS53
Knoll Dr, N14 98 DG45
Knolles Cres, N.Mymms AL9 45 CV24
Knollmead, Surb. KT5 198 CQ102
Sch Knollmead Prim Sch, Surb. KT5 off Knollmead 198 CQ103
Knoll Pk Rd, Cher. KT16 193 BF102
Knoll Ri, Orp. BR6 205 ET102
Knoll Rd, SW18 180 DC85
Bexley DA5 186 FA87
Dorking RH4 263 CG138
Sidcup DA14 186 EV92
Jct Knoll Rbt, Lthd. KT22 231 CJ121
Knolls, The, Epsom KT17 233 CW116
Knolls Cl, Wor.Pk. KT4 199 CV104
Knollys Cl, SW16 181 DN90
Knollys Rd, SW16 181 DN90
Knolton Way, Slou. SL2 132 AW72
Knotley Way, W.Wick. BR4 203 EB103
Knottisford St, E2 289 H2
Knottocks Cl, Beac. HP9 88 AJ50
Knottocks Dr, Beac. HP9 88 AJ50
Knottocks End, Beac. HP9 89 AK50
Knotts Grn Ms, E10 123 EB58
Knotts Grn Rd, E10 123 EB58
Knotts Pl, Sev. TN13 256 FG124
KNOTTY GREEN, Beac. HP9 88 AJ49
Knowle, The, Hodd. EN11 49 EA18
Tadworth KT20 233 CW121
Knowle Av, Bexh. DA7 166 EY80
Knowle Cl, SW9 310 E10
Knowle Gdns, W.Byf. KT14
off Madeira Rd 211 BF113
Knowle Grn, Stai. TW18 174 BG92
Knowle Gro, Vir.W. GU25 192 AW101
Knowle Gro Cl, Vir.W. GU25 192 AW101
Knowle Hill, Vir.W. GU25 192 AV101
Knowle Pk, Cob. KT11 230 BY115
Knowle Pk Av, Stai. TW18 174 BH93
Sch Knowle Pk Inf Sch, Stai. TW18
off Knowle Grn 174 BG92
Knowle Rd, Brom. BR2 204 EL103
Twickenham TW2 177 CE88
Knowles Cl, West Dr. UB7 134 BL74
Knowles Ct, Har. HA1 117 CF58
Knowles Hill Cres, SE13 183 ED85
Knowles Ho, SW18
off Neville Gill Cl 180 DB86
Knowles Wk, SW4 309 M10
Knowl Hill, Wok. GU22 227 BB119
Knowl Pk, Els. WD6 78 CL43
Knowlton Grn, Brom. BR2 204 EF99
Knowl Way, Els. WD6 78 CL42
Knowsley Av, Sthl. UB1 136 CA74
Knowsley Rd, SW11 308 E9
Knoxfield Caravan Pk, Dart. DA2 189 FS90
Knox Rd, E7 281 M5
Guildford GU2 242 AU129
Knox St, W1 284 E6
Knoyle St, SE14 313 L3
Knutsford Av, Wat. WD24 76 BX38
Sch Knutsford Prim Sch, Wat. WD24 off Knutsford Av 76 BX38
Sch Kobi Nazrul Prim Sch, E1 288 D8
Kohat Rd, SW19 180 DB92
Koh-i-noor Av, Bushey WD23 76 CA44
Koonowla Cl, Bigg.H. TN16 238 EK115
Kooringa, Warl. CR6 236 DV119
Korda Cl, Shep. TW17 194 BM97
Kossuth St, SE10 303 J10
Kotan Dr, Stai. TW18 173 BC90
Kotree Way, SE1 300 D9
Kramer Ms, SW5 307 K1
Kreedman Wk, E8 278 C3
Kreisel Wk, Rich. TW9 158 CM79
Sch Krishna Avanti Prim Sch, Edg. HA8 96 CN53
Krithia Rd, Dag. RM9 146 EV67
Kuala Gdns, SW16 201 DM95
● Kubrick Business Est, E7
off Woodgrange Rd 124 EH63
Kuhn Way, E7 281 P2
Kwesi Ms, SE27 181 DN92
Kydbrook Cl, Petts Wd BR5 205 EQ101
Kylemore Cl, E6
off Parr Rd 144 EK68
Kylemore Rd, NW6 273 J6
Kymberley Rd, Har. HA1 117 CE58
Kyme Rd, Horn. RM11 127 FF58
Kynance Cl, Rom. RM3 106 FJ48
Kynance Gdns, Stan. HA7 95 CJ53
Kynance Ms, SW7 295 N7
Kynance Pl, SW7 295 N7
Kynaston Av, N16
off Dynevor Rd 122 DT62
Thornton Heath CR7 202 DQ99
Kynaston Cl, Har. HA3 95 CD52
Kynaston Cres, Th.Hth. CR7 202 DQ99
Kynaston Rd, N16 122 DS62
Bromley BR1 184 EG92
Enfield EN2 82 DR39
Orpington BR5 206 EV101
Thornton Heath CR7 202 DQ99
Kynaston Wd, Har. HA3 95 CD52
Kynersley Cl, Cars. SM5
off William St 200 DF104
Kyngeshene Gdns, Guil. GU1 259 BA135
Kynoch Rd, N18 100 DW49
Kyrle Rd, SW11 180 DG85
Kytes Dr, Wat. WD25 60 BX33
Kytes Est, Wat. WD25 60 BX33
Kyverdale Rd, N16 122 DT61

L

Laburnham Cl, Barn. EN5 79 CZ41
Upminster RM14 129 FU59
Laburnham Gdns, Upmin. RM14 129 FT59
Laburnum Av, N9 100 DS47
N17 100 DR52
Dartford DA1 188 FJ88
Hornchurch RM12 127 FF62
Sutton SM1 200 DE104
Swanley BR8 207 FC97
West Drayton UB7 134 BM73
Laburnum Cl, E4 101 DZ51
N11 98 DG51
SE15 312 G5
Cheshunt EN8 67 DX31
Guildford GU1 242 AW131
Sheering CM22 37 FC07
Wembley HA0 138 CN66
Laburnum Ct, E2 278 A9
Stanmore HA7 95 CJ49
Laburnum Cres, Sun. TW16
off Batavia Rd 195 BV95
Laburnum Gdns, N21 100 DQ47
Croydon CR0 203 DX101
Laburnum Gro, N21 100 DQ47
NW9 118 CQ59
Hounslow TW3 156 BZ84
New Malden KT3 198 CR96
Northfleet DA11 190 GD87
Ruislip HA4 115 BR58
St. Albans AL2 60 CB25
Slough SL3 153 BB79
South Ockendon RM15 149 FW69
Southall UB1 136 BZ70
Laburnum Ho, Dag. RM10
off Bradwell Av 126 FA61
Laburnum Pl, Eng.Grn TW20 172 AV93
Laburnum Rd, SW19 180 DC94
Chertsey KT16 194 BG102
Coopersale CM16 70 EW29
Epsom KT18 216 CS113
Hayes UB3 155 BT77
Hoddesdon EN11 49 EB15
Mitcham CR4 200 DG96
Woking GU22 226 AX120
Laburnum St, E2 278 A9
Laburnum Wk, Horn. RM12 128 FJ64
Laburnum Way, Brom. BR2 205 EN101
Goffs Oak EN7 off Millcrest Rd 65 DP28
Staines-upon-Thames TW19 174 BM88
Lacebark Cl, Sid. DA15 185 ET87
Lacewing Cl, E13 291 P2
Lacey Av, Couls. CR5 235 DN120
Lacey Cl, N9 100 DU47
Egham TW20 173 BD94
Lacey Dr, Couls. CR5 235 DN120
Dagenham RM8 126 EV63
Edgware HA8 96 CL49
Hampton TW12 196 BZ95
Lacey Grn, Couls. CR5 235 DN120
Lacey Ms, E3 280 A10
Lackford Rd, Chipstead CR5 234 DF118
Lackington St, EC2 287 M6
Lackmore Rd, Enf. EN1 82 DW35
Lacock Cl, SW19 180 DC93
Lacock Ct, W13
off Singapore Rd 137 CG74
Lacon Rd, SE22 162 DU84
Lacrosse Way, SW16 201 DK95
Lacy Rd, SW15 159 CX84
Ladas Rd, SE27 182 DQ91
Ladbroke Ct, Red. RH1 250 DG132
Ladbroke Cres, W11 282 F9
Ladbroke Gdns, W11 282 G10
⊖ Ladbroke Grove 282 F8
Ladbroke Gro, W10 282 D4
W11 282 F9
Redhill RH1 250 DG133
Ladbroke Ms, W11 294 F3
Ladbroke Rd, W11 294 F2
Enfield EN1 82 DT44
Epsom KT18 216 CR114
Horley RH6 268 DG146
Redhill RH1 250 DG133
Ladbroke Sq, W11 294 G1
Ladbroke Ter, W11 295 H1
Ladbroke Wk, W11 295 H2
Ladbrook Cl, Pnr. HA5 116 BZ57
Ladbrooke Cl, Pot.B. EN6 64 DA32
Ladbrooke Cres, Sid. DA14 186 EX90
Ladbrooke Dr, Pot.B. EN6 64 DA32
Sch Ladbrooke JMI Sch, Pot.B. EN6 off Watkins Ri 64 DB32
Ladbrooke Rd, Slou. SL1 151 AQ76
Ladbrook Rd, SE25 202 DR97
Ladderstile Ride, Kings.T. KT2 178 CP92
Ladderswood Way, N11 99 DJ50
Ladds Way, Swan. BR8 207 FD98
Ladies Gro, St.Alb. AL3 42 CB18
Ladlands, SE22 182 DU87
Lady Aylesford Av, Stan. HA7 95 CH50
Sch Lady Bankes Inf & Jun Schs, Hlgdn HA4 off Dawlish Dr 115 BU61
Lady Booth Rd, Kings.T. KT1 198 CL96
Sch Lady Boswell's C of E Prim Sch, Sev. TN13
off Plymouth Dr 257 FJ125
Lady Cooper Ct, Berk. HP4
off Benningfield Gdns 38 AY17
Lady Craig Ct, Uxb. UB8
off Harlington Rd 135 BP71
Ladycroft Gdns, Orp. BR6 223 EQ106
Ladycroft Rd, SE13 163 EB83
Ladycroft Wk, Stan. HA7 95 CK53
Ladycroft Way, Orp. BR6 223 EQ106
Ladyday Pl, Slou. SL1
off Glentworth Pl 131 AQ74
Lady Dock Path, SE16 301 L5
Ladyegate Cl, Dor. RH5 263 CK135
Ladyegate Rd, Dor. RH5 263 CJ136

Lady Eleanor Holles Sch,
The, Hmptn. TW12
off Hanworth Rd 176 CB92
Jun Dept, Hmptn. TW12
off Uxbridge Rd 176 CB92
Ladyfield Cl, Loug. IG10 85 EP42
Ladyfields, Loug. IG10 85 EP42
Northfleet DA11 191 GF91
Lady Forsdyke Way,
Epsom KT19 216 CN109
Ladygate La, Ruis. HA4 115 BP58
Ladygrove, Croy. CR0 221 DY109
Lady Gro, Welw.G.C. AL7 29 CY12
Ladygrove Dr, Guil. GU4 243 BA129
Lady Harewood Way,
Epsom KT19 216 CN109
Lady Hay, Wor.Pk. KT4 199 CT103
Lady Margaret Prim Sch,
Sthl. UB1
off Lady Margaret Rd 136 BZ71
Lady Margaret Rd, N19 275 M1
NW5 275 L2
Southall UB1 136 BZ71
Lady Margaret Sch, SW6 307 J7
Ladymead, Guil. GU1 242 AW133
Lady Meadow, Kings L. WD4 58 BK27
Ladymead Retail Pk,
Guil. GU1 242 AW133
Lady's Cl, Wat. WD18 75 BV42
Ladyshot, Harl. CM20 36 EU14
Ladysmith Av, E6 144 EL68
Ilford IG2 125 ER59
Ladysmith Cl, NW7 97 CU52
Ladysmith Rd, E16 291 L3
N17 100 DU54
N18 100 DV50
SE9 185 EN86
Enfield EN1 82 DS41
Harrow HA3 95 CE54
St. Albans AL3 43 CD19
Lady Somerset Rd, NW5 275 K1
Ladythorpe Cl, Add. KT15
off Church Rd 212 BH105
Ladywalk, Map.Cr. WD3 91 BE50
LADYWELL, SE13 183 EA85
⇌ **Ladywell** 183 EB85
Ladywell Cl, SE4
off Adelaide Av 163 EA84
Ladywell Hts, SE4 183 DZ86
Ladywell Prospect, Saw. CM21 36 FA06
Ladywell Rd, SE13 183 EA85
Ladywell St, E15 281 L9
Ladywood Av, Petts Wd BR5 205 ES99
Ladywood Cl, Rick. WD3 74 BH41
Ladywood Rd, Hert. SG14 31 DM09
Lane End DA2 189 FS92
Surbiton KT6 198 CN103
Lady Yorke Pk, Iver SL0 133 BD65
Lafone Av, Felt. TW13
off Alfred Rd 176 BW88
Lafone St, SE1 300 A4
Lagado Ms, SE16 301 K3
Lagger, The, Ch.St.G. HP8 90 AW48
Lagger Cl, Ch.St.G. HP8 90 AW48
Laglands Cl, Reig. RH2 250 DC132
Lagonda Av, Ilf. IG6 103 ET51
Lagonda Way, Dart. DA1 168 FJ84
Lagoon Rd, Orp. BR5 206 EV99
Laidlaw Dr, N21 81 DM42
Laidon Sq, Hem.H. HP2 40 BK16
Laing Cl, Ilf. IG6 103 ER51
Laing Dean, Nthlt. UB5 136 BW67
Laing Ho, SE5 *off Comber Gro* 311 J5
Laings Av, Mitch. CR4 200 DF96
Lainlock Pl, Houns. TW3 156 CB81
Lainson St, SW18 180 DA87
Lairdale Cl, SE21 182 DQ88
Laird Av, Grays RM16 170 GD75
Laird Ho, SE5 311 J5
Lairs Cl, N7 276 B4
Lait Ho, Beck. BR3 203 EA95
Laitwood Rd, SW12 181 DH88
Lakanal, SE5 *off Sceaux Gdns* 311 P6
Lake, The, Bushey Hth WD23 94 CC46
Lake Av, Brom. BR1 184 EG93
Rainham RM13 148 FK68
Slough SL1 131 AR73
● **Lake Business Cen**, N17
off Tariff Rd 100 DU52
Lake Cl, SW19
off Lake Rd 179 CZ92
Byfleet KT14 212 BK112
Dagenham RM8 126 EW62
Lakedale Rd, SE18 165 ES79
Lake Dr, Bushey Hth WD23 94 CC47
Lake End Ct, Tap. SL6
off Taplow Rd 130 AH72
Lake End Rd, Dorney SL4 150 AH76
Taplow SL6 130 AH73
Lakefield Cl, SE20
off Limes Av 182 DV94
Lakefield Rd, N22 99 DP54
Lakefields Cl, Rain. RM13 148 FK68
Lake Gdns, Dag. RM10 126 FA64
Richmond TW10 177 CH89
Wallington SM6 201 DH104
Lakehall Gdns, Th.Hth. CR7 201 DP99
Lakehall Rd, Th.Hth. CR7 201 DP99
Lake Ho Rd, E11 124 EG62
Lakehurst Rd, Epsom KT19 216 CS106
Lakeland Cl, Chig. IG7 104 EV49
Harrow HA3 95 CD51
Lake La, Horl. RH6 267 DJ144
Lakenheath, N14 81 DK44
Lake Ri, Grays RM20 169 FU77
Romford RM1 127 FF55
Lake Rd, E10 123 EB59
SW19 179 CZ92
Croydon CR0 203 DZ103
Lower Nazeing EN9 50 EE21
Romford RM6 126 EX56
Virginia Water GU25 192 AV98
Laker Pl, SW15 179 CY86
Lakers Ri, Bans. SM7 234 DE116
Lakes Cl, Chilw. GU4 259 BB140
Lakes Ct, Stans.Abb. SG12 33 EB11
Lakeside 169 FV76
Lakeside, Grays RM20 169 FV77
Lakeside, W13
off Edgehill Rd 137 CJ72
Beckenham BR3 203 EB97
Enfield EN2 81 DK42
Rainham RM13 148 FL68
Redhill RH1 250 DG132
Wallington SM6 *off Derek Av* 201 DH104
Weybridge KT13 195 BS103
Woking GU21 226 AS119
Lakeside Av, SE28 146 EU74
Ilford IG4 124 EK56
Lakeside Cl, SE25 202 DU96
Chigwell IG7 103 ET49
Ruislip HA4 115 BR56
Sidcup DA15 186 EW85
Woking GU21 226 AS119
Lakeside Ct, N4 121 DP61
Elstree WD6 78 CN43
Lakeside Cres, Barn. EN4 80 DF43
Brentwood CM14 108 FX48
Weybridge KT13
off Churchill Dr 195 BQ104
Lakeside Dr, NW10 138 CM69
Bromley BR2 204 EL104
Chobham GU24 210 AS113
Esher KT10 214 CC107
Stoke Poges SL2 132 AS67
Lakeside Gra, Wey. KT13 195 BQ104
● **Lakeside Ind Est**,
Colnbr. SL3 154 BG79
Lakeside Pl, Lon.Col. AL2 61 CK27
Lakeside Rd, N13 99 DM49
W14 294 C6
Cheshunt EN8 66 DW28
Slough SL3 153 BF80
Lakeside Sch, Welw.G.C.
AL8 *off Lemsford La* 29 CV11
Lakeside Way, Wem. HA9 118 CM63
Lakes La, Beac. HP9 89 AM54
Lakes Rd, Kes. BR2 222 EJ106
Lakeswood Rd, Petts Wd BR5 205 EP100
Lake Vw, Edg. HA8 96 CM50
Kings Langley WD4 59 BP28
North Holmwood RH5 263 CJ139
Potters Bar EN6 64 DC33
Lakeview Ct, SW19
off Victoria Dr 179 CY89
Lakeview Est, E3 279 K10
Lakeview Rd, SE27 181 DN92
Welling DA16 166 EV84
Lake Vw Rd, Sev. TN13 256 FG122
Lakis Cl, NW3
off Flask Wk 120 DC63
LALEHAM, Stai. TW18 194 BJ97
Laleham Av, NW7 96 CR48
Laleham Cl, Stai. TW18
off Worple Rd 194 BH95
Laleham C of E Prim Sch,
Laleham TW18
off The Broadway 194 BJ96
Laleham Ct, Wok. GU21 226 AY116
Laleham Lea Prep Sch,
Pur. CR8 *off Peaks Hill* 219 DL110
Laleham Pk, Stai. TW18 194 BJ98
Laleham Reach, Cher. KT16 194 BH96
Laleham Rd, SE6 183 EC86
Shepperton TW17 194 BM98
Staines-upon-Thames TW18 173 BF92
Lalor St, SW6 306 E8
Lamb All, St.Alb. AL3
off Market Pl 43 CD20
Lambarde Av, SE9 185 EN91
Lambarde Dr, Sev. TN13 256 FG123
Lambarde Rd, Sev. TN13 256 FG122
Lambardes Cl, Pr.Bot. BR6 224 EW110
Lamb Cl, Hat. AL10 45 CV19
Northolt UB5 136 BY69
Tilbury RM18
off Coleridge Rd 171 GJ82
Watford WD25 60 BW34
Lamberhurst Cl, Orp. BR5 206 EX102
Lamberhurst Rd, SE27 181 DN91
Dagenham RM8 126 EZ60
Lambert Av, Rich. TW9 158 CP83
Slough SL3 152 AY75
Lambert Cl, Bigg.H. TN16 238 EK116
Lambert Ct, Bushey WD23 76 BX42
Lambert Jones Ms, EC2
off The Barbican 287 J6
Lamberton Ct, Borwd. WD6
off Blyth Cl 78 CN39
Lambert Rd, E16 292 A8
N12 98 DC50
SW2 181 DL85
Banstead SM7 218 DA114
Lamberts Pl, Croy. CR0 202 DR102
Lamberts Rd, Surb. KT5 198 CL99
Lambert St, N1 276 E7
Lambert Wk, Wem. HA9 117 CK62
Lambert Way, N12 98 DC50
LAMBETH, SE1 298 C6
Lambeth Acad, SW4
off Elms Rd 181 DJ85
Lambeth Br, SE1 298 B8
SW1 298 B8
Lambeth Coll, Brixton Cen,
SW2 *off Brixton Hill* 181 DM85
Clapham Cen, SW4
off Clapham Common S Side 203 DJ85
Vauxhall Cen, SW8 309 P6
Lambeth High St, SE1 298 C9
Lambeth Hill, EC4 287 J10
Lambeth Hosp, SW9 310 B10
⊖ **Lambeth North** 298 E5
★ **Lambeth Palace**, SE1 298 C7
Lambeth Palace Rd, SE1 298 C7
Lambeth Pier, SE1 298 B7
Lambeth Rd, SE1 298 D7
SE11 298 D7
Croydon CR0 201 DN101
Lambeth Twrs, SE11 298 E7
Lambeth Wk, SE1 298 D8
SE11 298 D8
Lambfold Ho, N7 276 A4
Lambkins Ms, E17 123 EC56
Lamb La, E8 278 E7
Lamble St, NW5 274 G2
Lambley Rd, Dag. RM9 146 EV65
Lambly Hill, Vir.W. GU25 192 AY97
Lambolle Pl, NW3 274 D5
Lambolle Rd, NW3 274 C5
Lambourn Chase, Rad. WD7 77 CF36
Lambourn Cl, W7 157 CF75
South Croydon CR2 219 DP109
Lambourne Av, SW19 179 CZ91
Lambourne Cl, Chig. IG7 104 EV48
Lambourne Ct, Wdf.Grn. IG8
off Navestock Cres 102 EJ53
Lambourne Cres, Chig. IG7 104 EV47
Woking GU21 211 BD113
Lambourne Dr, Cob. KT11 230 BX115
Hutton CM13 109 GE45
LAMBOURNE END, Rom. RM4 86 EX44
Lambourne Gdns, E4 101 EA47
Barking IG11 145 ET66
Enfield EN1 82 DT40
Hornchurch RM12 128 FK61
Lambourne Gro, SE16 301 J9
Lambourne Pl, SE3
off Shooters Hill Rd 164 EH81
Lambourne Prim Sch,
Abridge RM4 *off Hoe La* 86 EV42
Lambourne Rd, E11 123 EC59
Barking IG11 145 ES66
Chigwell IG7 103 ES49
Ilford IG3 125 ES61
Lambourne Sq,
Lamb.End RM4 104 EW46
Lambourn Gro, Kings.T. KT1 198 CP96
Lambourn Rd, SW4 309 K10
Lambrook Ter, SW6 306 E6
Lambs Bldgs, EC1 287 L5
Lambs Cl, N9
off Winchester Rd 100 DU47
Cuffley EN6 65 DM29
Lambs Conduit Pas, WC1 286 C6
Lamb's Conduit St, WC1 286 C5
Lambscroft Av, SE9 184 EJ90
Lambscroft Way, Chal.St.P. SL9 112 AY54
Lambs La N, Rain. RM13 148 FJ70
Lambs La S, Rain. RM13 147 FH71
Lambs Meadow, Wdf.Grn. IG8 102 EK54
Lambs Ms, N1 276 G9
Lambs Pas, EC1 287 L6
Lambs Ter, N9 100 DR47
Lamb St, E1 288 A6
Lambs Wk, Enf. EN2 82 DQ40
Lambton Av, Wal.Cr. EN8 67 DX32
Lambton Ms, N19
off Lambton Rd 121 DL60
Lambton Pl, W11 283 H10
Lambton Rd, N19 121 DL60
SW20 199 CW95
Lamb Wk, SE1 299 N5
Lambyn Cft, Horl. RH6 269 DJ147
Lamerock Rd, Brom. BR1 184 EF91
Lamerton Rd, Ilf. IG6 103 EP54
Lamerton St, SE8 314 A3
Lamford Cl, N17 100 DR52
Lamington St, W6 159 CV77
Lamlash St, SE11 298 G8
Lammas Av, Mitch. CR4 200 DG96
Lammas Cl, Stai. TW18 173 BE90
Lammas Ct, Stai. TW19 173 BD89
Windsor SL4 151 AQ82
Lammas Dr, Stai. TW18 173 BD90
Lammas Grn, SE26 182 DV90
Lammas La, Esher KT10 214 CA106
Lammasmead, Brox. EN10 49 DZ23
Lammas Pk, W5 157 CJ75
Lammas Pk Gdns, W5 157 CJ75
Lammas Pk Rd, W5 137 CJ74
Lammas Rd, E9 279 K7
E10 123 DY61
Richmond TW10 177 CJ91
Slough SL1 131 AK71
Watford WD18 76 BW43
Lammas Sch, The,
E10 *off Seymour Rd* 123 DZ60
Lammas Way, Loud. HP10 88 AC54
Lammermoor Rd, SW12 181 DH87
Lammtarra Pl, Epsom KT17
off Windmill La 217 CT112
Lamont Rd, SW10 307 P3
Lamont Rd Pas, SW10
off Lamont Rd 308 A3
LAMORBEY, Sid. DA15 185 ET88
Lamorbey Cl, Sid. DA15 185 ET88
Lamorna Av, Grav. DA12 191 GJ90
Lamorna Cl, E17 101 EC54
Orpington BR6 206 EU101
Radlett WD7 61 CH34
Lamorna Gro, Stan. HA7 95 CK53
Lampard Gro, N16 122 DT60
Lampern Sq, E2 288 D2
Lampeter Cl, NW9 118 CS58
Woking GU22 226 AY118
Lampeter Sq, W6 306 E3
Lampits, Hodd. EN11 49 EB17
Lamplighter Cl, E1 288 G5
Lamplighters Cl, Dart. DA1 188 FM86
Waltham Abbey EN9 68 EG34
Lampmead Rd, SE12 184 EE85
Lamp Office Ct, WC1 286 C5
Lamport Cl, SE18 305 K8
LAMPTON, Houns. TW3 156 CB81
Lampton Av, Houns. TW3 156 CB81
Lampton Ho Cl, SW19 179 CX91
Lampton Pk Rd, Houns. TW3 156 CB82
Lampton Rd, Houns. TW3 156 CB82
Lampton Sch, Houns. TW3
off Lampton Av 156 CA81
Lamsey Rd, Hem.H. HP3 40 BK22
Lamson Rd, Rain. RM13 147 FF70
Lanacre Av, NW9 97 CT53
Lanadron Cl, Islw. TW7 157 CF82
Lanark Cl, W5 137 CJ71
Lanark Ms, W9 283 N3
Lanark Pl, W9 283 P4
Lanark Rd, W9 283 N3
Lanark Sq, E14 302 D6
Lanata Wk, Hayes UB4
off Ramulis Dr 136 BX70
Lanbury Rd, SE15 163 DX84
Lancashire Ct, W1 285 K10
Lancaster Av, E18 124 EH56
SE27 181 DP89
SW19 179 CX92
Barking IG11 145 ES66
Barnet EN4 80 DD38
Guildford GU1 259 AZ136
Mitcham CR4 201 DL99
Slough SL2 131 AQ70
Lancaster Cl, N1 277 P7
N17 100 DU52
NW9 97 CT52
Ashford TW15 174 BL91
Bromley BR2 204 EF98
Egham TW20 172 AX92
Kingston upon Thames KT2 177 CK92
Pilgrim's Hatch CM15 108 FU43
Stanwell TW19 174 BL86
Woking GU21 227 BA116
Lancaster Cotts, Rich. TW10
off Lancaster Pk 178 CL86
Lancaster Ct, SE27 181 DP89
SW6 307 J5
W2 295 P1
Banstead SM7 217 CZ114
Walton-on-Thames KT12 195 BU101
Lancaster Dr, E14 302 F3
NW3 274 C5
Bovingdon HP3 57 AZ27
Hornchurch RM12 127 FH64
Loughton IG10 84 EL44
Lancaster Gdns, SW19 179 CY92
W13 157 CH75
Bromley BR1 204 EL99
Kingston upon Thames KT2 177 CK92
⊖ **Lancaster Gate** 284 A10
Lancaster Gate, W2 295 P1
Lancaster Gro, NW3 274 B5
Lancaster Ho, Islw. TW7 157 CF80
★ **Lancaster Ho**, SW1 297 L4
Lancasterian Prim Sch,
N17 *off King's Rd* 100 DT53
Lancaster Ms, SW18 180 DB85
off East Hill
W2 283 P10
Richmond TW10
off Richmond Hill 178 CL86
Lancaster Pk, Rich. TW10 178 CL85
Lancaster Pl, SW19 179 CX92
WC2 286 C10
Hounslow TW4 156 BW82
Ilford IG1 *off Staines Rd* 125 EQ63
Twickenham TW1 177 CG86
Lancaster Rd, E7 281 P6
E11 124 EE61
E17 101 DX54
N4 121 DN59
N11 99 DK51
N18 100 DT50
NW10 119 CT64
SE25 202 DT96
SW19 179 CX92
W11 282 E9
Barnet EN4 80 DD43
Chafford Hundred RM16 169 FX78
Enfield EN2 82 DR39
Harrow HA2 116 CA57
North Weald Bassett CM16 70 FA26
Northolt UB5 136 CC65
St. Albans AL1 43 CF18
Southall UB1 136 BY73
Uxbridge UB8 134 BK65
Lancaster St, SE1 299 H5
Lancaster Ter, W2 284 A10
Lancaster Wk, W2 296 A4
Hayes UB3 135 BQ72
Lancaster Way, Abb.L. WD5 59 BT31
Worcester Park KT4 199 CV101
Lancaster W, W11
off Grenfell Rd 282 D10
Lancastrian Rd, Wall. SM6 219 DL108
Lancefield St, W10 282 G2
Lancell St, N16 122 DS62
Lancelot Av, Wem. HA0 117 CK63
Lancelot Ct, Slou. SL1 151 AN75
Lancelot Cl, Bushey WD23
off Hartswood Cl 76 CA40
Lancelot Cres, Wem. HA0 117 CK63
Lancelot Gdns, E.Barn. EN4 98 DG45
Lancelot Pl, SW7 296 E5
Lancelot Rd, Ilf. IG6 103 ES51
Welling DA16 166 EU84
Wembley HA0 117 CK64
Lance Rd, Har. HA1 116 CC59
Lancer Sq, W8 295 L4
Lancey Cl, SE7 304 F8
Lanchester Rd, N6 120 DF57
Lanchester Way, SE14 313 H6
Lancing Gdns, N9 100 DT46
Lancing Rd, W13
off Drayton Grn Rd 137 CH73
Croydon CR0 201 DM100
Feltham TW13 175 BT89
Ilford IG2 125 ER58
Orpington BR6 206 EU103
Romford RM3 106 FL52
Lancing St, NW1 285 N3
Lancing Way, Crox.Grn WD3 75 BP43
Lancresse Cl, Uxb. UB8 134 BK65
Lancresse Ct, N1 277 N8
Landale Gdns, Dart. DA1 188 FJ87
Landau Way, Brox. EN10 67 DZ26
Erith DA8 168 FK78
Landcroft Rd, SE22 182 DT86
Landells Rd, SE22 182 DT86
Landen Pk, Horl. RH6 268 DE146
Lander Rd, Grays RM17 170 GD78
Landford Cl, Rick. WD3 92 BL47
Landford Rd, SW15 159 CW83
Landgrove Rd, SW19 180 DA92
Landmann Ho, SE16 300 F9
Landmann Way, SE14 313 K2
● **Landmark Commercial Cen**,
N18 100 DS51
Landmark East Twr, E14 302 A4
Landmark Hts, E5 279 L1
Landmark Row, Red. SL3
off Sutton La 153 BB79
Landmark West Twr, E14 302 A3
Landmead Rd, Chsht EN8 67 DY29
Landon Pl, SW1 296 E6
Landons Cl, E14 302 F2
Landon Wk, E14 290 D10
Landon Way, Ashf. TW15
off Courtfield Rd 175 BP93
Landor Rd, SW9 161 DL83
Landor Wk, W12 159 CU75
Landra Gdns, N21 81 DP44
● **Land Registry**, Croy. CR0 202 DQ102
Landridge Dr, Enf. EN1 82 DV38
Landridge Rd, SW6 306 F8
Landrock Rd, N8 121 DL58
Landscape Rd, Warl. CR6 236 DV119
Woodford Green IG8 102 EH52
Landsdown Cl, New Barn. EN5 80 DC42
Landseer Av, E12 125 EN64
Northfleet DA11 190 GD90
Landseer Cl, SW19
off Thorburn Way 200 DD95
Edgware HA8 96 CN54
Hornchurch RM11 127 FH60
Landseer Rd, N19 121 DL62
Enfield EN1 82 DU43
New Malden KT3 198 CR101
Sutton SM1 218 DA107
Lands End, Els. WD6 77 CK44
Landstead Rd, SE18 165 ER80
Landway, The, Orp. BR5 206 EW97
Lane, The, NW8 273 N10
SE3 315 P10
Chertsey KT16 194 BG97
Virginia Water GU25 192 AY97
Lane Av, Green. DA9 189 FW86
Lane Cl, NW2 119 CV62
Addlestone KT15 212 BG106
LANE END, Dart. DA2 189 FR92
Lane End, Berk. HP4 38 AT19
Bexleyheath DA7 167 FB83
Epsom KT18 216 CP114
Harlow CM17 52 EY15
Hatfield AL10 45 CT21
Lanefield Wk, Welw.G.C. AL8 29 CW09
Lane Gdns, Bushey Hth WD23 95 CE45
Claygate KT10 215 CF108
Lane Ms, E12
off Colchester Av 125 EM62
La Plata Gro, Brwd. CM14 108 FV48
Lanercost Cl, SW2 181 DN89
Lanercost Gdns, N14 99 DL45
Lanercost Rd, SW2 181 DN89
La Retraite RC Girls' Sch,
SW12 *off Atkins Rd* 181 DJ87
La Roche Cl, Slou. SL3 152 AW76
La Sainte Union Cath Sch,
NW5 *off Highgate Rd* 120 DG62
La Salette Cath Prim Sch,
Rain. RM13 *off Dunedin Rd* 147 FF69
Lanes Av, Nthflt DA11 191 GG90
Lanesborough Pl, SW1 297 H4
Lanesborough Sch,
Guil. GU1 *off Maori Rd* 243 AZ134
Laneside, Chis. BR7 185 EP92
Edgware HA8 96 CQ50
Laneside Av, Dag. RM8 126 EZ59
Las Palmas Est, Shep. TW17 195 BQ101
La Tourne Gdns, Orp. BR6 205 EQ104
Laneway, SW15 179 CV85
Lane Wd Cl, Amer. HP7 72 AT39
Lanfranc Rd, E3 289 L1
Lanfrey Pl, W14 306 G1
Langaller La, Fetch. KT22 230 CB122
Langbourne Av, N6 120 DG61
Langbourne Pl, E14 302 C10
Langbourne Prim Sch, SE21
off Lyall Av 182 DS90
Langbourne Way, Clay. KT10 215 CG107
Langbrook Rd, SE3 164 EK83
Lang Cl, Fetch. KT22 230 CB123
Langcroft Cl, Cars. SM5 200 DF104
Langdale, NW1 285 L2
Langdale Av, Mitch. CR4 200 DF97
Langdale Cl, SE17 311 J2
SW14 158 CP84
Dagenham RM8 126 EW60
Orpington BR6
off Grasmere Rd 205 EP104
Woking GU21 226 AW116
Langdale Ct, Hem.H. HP2
off Wharfedale 40 BL17
Langdale Cres, Bexh. DA7 166 FA80
Langdale Dr, Hayes UB4 135 BS68
Langdale Gdns, Horn. RM12 127 FG64
Perivale UB6 137 CH69
Waltham Cross EN8 83 DX35
Langdale Rd, SE10 314 E5
Thornton Heath CR7 201 DN98
Langdale St, E1 288 E9
Harlow CM17 36 EW14
Langdale Wk, Nthflt DA11
off Landseer Av 190 GE90
Langdon Ct, EC1
off City Rd 287 H1
NW10 138 CS67
Langdon Cres, E6 145 EN68
Langdon Dr, NW9 118 CQ60
Langdon Park 290 D7
Langdon Pk, Tedd. TW11 177 CJ94
Langdon Pk Rd, N6 121 DJ59
Langdon Pk Sch, E14 290 D8
Langdon Pl, SW14 158 CQ83
Langdon Rd, E6 145 EN67
Bromley BR2 204 EH97
Morden SM4 200 DC99
Langdon Sch, E6
off Sussex Rd 145 EP67
Langdons Ct, Sthl. UB2 156 CA76
Langdon Shaw, Sid. DA14 185 ET92
Langdon Wk, Mord. SM4 200 DC99
Langdon Way, SE1 300 D9
Langfield Cl, Lwr Naze. EN9 50 EE22
Langford Cl, E8 278 C2
N15 122 DS58
NW8 273 P10
W3 158 CP75
St. Albans AL4 43 CJ18
Langford Ct, NW8 283 N1
Langford Cres, Cockfos. EN4 80 DF42
Langford Grn, SE5 162 DS83
Hutton CM13 109 GC44
Langford Ho, SE8
off Evelyn St 314 A2
Langford Ms, N1 276 F6
SW11 *off St. John's Hill* 160 DD84
Langford Pl, NW8 283 P1
Sidcup DA14 186 EU90
Langford Prim Sch, SW6 307 M8
Langford Rd, SW6 307 M8
Cockfosters EN4 80 DE42
Woodford Green IG8 102 EJ51
Langfords, Buck.H. IG9 102 EK47
Langfords Way, Croy. CR0 221 DY111
Langham Cl, N15
off Langham Rd 121 DP55
Bromley BR2 204 EL103
St. Albans AL4 43 CK15
Langham Ct, Horn. RM11 128 FK59
Langham Dene, Ken. CR8 235 DP115
Langham Dr, Rom. RM6 126 EV58
Langham Gdns, N21 81 DN43
W13 137 CH73
Edgware HA8 96 CQ52
Richmond TW10 177 CJ91
Wembley HA0 117 CJ61
Langham Ho Cl, Rich. TW10 177 CK91
Langham Pk Pl, Brom. BR2 204 EF98
Langham Pl, N15 121 DP55
W1 285 K7
W4 158 CS79
Egham TW20 173 AZ92
Langham Rd, N15 121 DP55
SW20 199 CW95
Edgware HA8 96 CQ51
Teddington TW11 177 CH92
Langham St, W1 285 K7
Langhedge Cl, N18 100 DT51
Langhedge La, N18 100 DT50
● **Langhedge La Ind Est**, N18 100 DT51
Langholm Cl, SW12 181 DK87
Langholme, Bushey WD23 94 CC46
Langhorn Dr, Twick. TW2 177 CE87
Langhorne Ho, SE7
off Springfield Gro 164 EJ79
Langhorne Rd, Dag. RM10 146 FA66
Langland Ct, Nthwd. HA6 93 BQ52
Langland Cres, Stan. HA7 118 CL55
Langland Dr, Pnr. HA5 94 BY52
Langland Gdns, NW3 273 M2
Croydon CR0 203 DZ103

L

Langlands Dr, Lane End DA2 189 FS92
Langlands Ri, Epsom KT19 216 CQ113
Langler Rd, NW10 282 B1
LANGLEY, Slou. SL3 153 BA76
≠ Langley 153 BA75
Sch Langley Acad, Langley SL3 off Langley Rd 152 AY76
Langley Av, Hem.H. HP3 40 BL23
Ruislip HA4 115 BV60
Surbiton KT6 197 CK102
Worcester Park KT4 199 CX103
Langley Broom, Slou. SL3 153 AZ78
LANGLEYBURY, Kings L. WD4 59 BP34
Langleybury Flds, Kings L. WD4 58 BM34
Langleybury La, Kings L. WD4 75 BP37
● Langley Business Cen, Langley SL3 153 BA75
Langley Cl, Epsom KT18 232 CR119
Guildford GU1 242 AW133
Romford RM3 106 FK52
Jct Langley Cor, Fulmer SL3 133 AZ65
● Langley Ct, Beck. BR3 203 EB99
Langley Ct, WC2 286 A10
Langley Cres, E11 124 EJ59
Dagenham RM9 146 EW66
Edgware HA8 96 CQ48
Hayes UB3 155 BT80
Kings Langley WD4 58 BN30
St. Albans AL3 42 CC18
Langley Dr, E11 124 EH59
W3 138 CP74
Brentwood CM14 108 FU48
Langley Gdns, Brom. BR2 off Great Elms Rd 204 EJ98
Dagenham RM9 146 EW66
Petts Wood BR5 205 EP100
Sch Langley Gram Sch, Langley SL3 off Reddington Dr 153 AZ77
Langley Gro, N.Mal. KT3 198 CS96
Langley Hill, Kings L. WD4 58 BM29
Langley Hill Cl, Kings L. WD4 58 BN29
Langley La, SW8 310 B2
Abbots Langley WD5 59 BT31
Headley KT18 248 CP125
Langley Lo La, Kings L. WD4 58 BN31
Sch Langley Manor Sch, Langley SL3 off St. Mary's Rd 132 AY74
Langley Meadow, Loug. IG10 85 ER40
Langley Oaks Av, S.Croy. CR2 220 DU110
Langley Pk, NW7 96 CS51
★ Langley Park Country Pk, Slou. SL3 133 BA70
Langley Pk Rd, Iver SL0 133 BC72
Slough SL3 153 BA75
Sutton SM1, SM2 218 DC106
Sch Langley Pk Sch for Boys, Beck. BR3 off Hawksbrook La 203 EB100
Sch Langley Pk Sch for Girls, Beck. BR3 off Hawksbrook La 203 EC100
Langley Pl, Wat. WD17 off Langley Rd 75 BU39
Langley Quay, Langley SL3 153 BA75
Langley Rd, SW19 199 CZ95
Abbots Langley WD5 59 BS31
Beckenham BR3 203 DY98
Chipperfield WD4 58 BH30
Isleworth TW7 157 CF82
Slough SL3 152 AW75
South Croydon CR2 221 DX109
Staines-upon-Thames TW18 173 BF93
Surbiton KT6 198 CL101
Watford WD17 75 BU39
Welling DA16 166 EW79
Langley Row, Barn. EN5 79 CZ39
Langley St, WC2 286 A9
LANGLEY VALE, Epsom KT18 232 CR120
Langley Vale Rd, Epsom KT18 232 CR118
Langley Wk, Wok. GU22 226 AY119
Langley Way, Wat. WD17 75 BS40
West Wickham BR4 203 ED102
Langmans La, Wok. GU21 226 AV118
Langmans Way, Wok. GU21 226 AS116
Langmead Dr, Bushey Hth WD23 95 CD46
Langmead St, SE27 off Beadman St 181 DP91
Langmore Ct, Bexh. DA6 off Regency Way 166 EX83
Langport Ct, Walt. KT12 196 BW102
Langridge Ms, Hmptn. TW12 off Oak Av 176 BZ93
Langroyd Rd, SW17 180 DF89
Langshott, Horl. RH6 269 DH146
Langshott Cl, Wdhm KT15 211 BE111
Sch Langshott Inf Sch, Horl. RH6 off Smallfield Rd 269 DJ148
Langshott La, Horl. RH6 269 DJ147
Langside Av, SW15 159 CU84
Langside Cres, N14 99 DK48
Langstone Ley, Welw.G.C. AL7 30 DB09
Langstone Way, NW7 97 CX52
Langston Hughes Cl, SE24 off Shakespeare Rd 161 DP84
Langston Rd, Loug. IG10 85 EQ43
Lang St, E1 288 G4
Langthorn Ct, EC2 287 L8
Langthorne Ct, Brom. BR1 183 EC91
Langthorne Cres, Grays RM17 170 GC77
Langthorne Rd, E11 123 ED62
Langthorne St, SW6 306 C5
Langton Av, E6 293 L2
N20 98 DC45
Epsom KT17 217 CT111
Langton Cl, WC1 286 D3
Addlestone KT15 194 BH104
Slough SL1 131 AK74
Woking GU21 226 AT117
Langton Gro, Nthwd. HA6 93 BQ50
Langton Ho, SW16 off Colson Way 181 DJ91
Langton Pl, SW18 off Merton Rd 180 DA88
Langton Ri, SE23 182 DV87
Langton Rd, NW2 119 CW62
SW9 311 H5
Harrow HA3 94 CC52
Hoddesdon EN11 49 DZ17
West Molesey KT8 196 CC98
Sch Langtons Inf & Jun Schs, Horn. RM11 off Westland Av 128 FL60
Langton's Meadow, Farn.Com. SL2 131 AQ65
Langton St, SW10 307 P3
Langton Way, SE3 315 M6
Croydon CR0 220 DS105
Egham TW20 173 BC93
Grays RM16 171 GJ77
Langtree Ave, Slou. SL1 151 AM75
Langtry Ct, Islw. TW7 off Lanadron Cl 157 CF82
Langtry Pl, SW6 307 K2
Langtry Rd, NW8 273 L9
Northolt UB5 136 BX68
Langtry Wk, NW8 273 N8
Langwood Chase, Tedd. TW11 177 CJ93
Langwood Cl, Ashtd. KT21 232 CN117
Langwood Gdns, Wat. WD17 75 BU39
Langworth Cl, Dart. DA2 188 FK90
Langworth Dr, Hayes UB4 135 BU72
Lanherne Ho, SW20 179 CX94
Lanhill Rd, W9 283 J4
Lanier Rd, SE13 183 EC86
Lanigan Dr, Houns. TW3 176 CB85
Lankaster Gdns, N2 98 DD53
Lankers Dr, Har. HA2 116 BZ58
Lankester Sq, Oxt. RH8 253 ED128
Lankton Cl, Beck. BR3 203 EC95
Lannock Rd, Hayes UB3 135 BS74
Lannoy Pt, SW6 off Pellant Rd 306 F4
Lannoy Rd, SE9 185 EQ88
Lanrick Copse, Berk. HP4 38 AY18
Lanrick Rd, E14 291 H8
Lanridge Rd, SE2 166 EX76
Lansbury Av, N18 100 DR50
Barking IG11 146 EU66
Feltham TW14 175 BV86
Romford RM6 126 EY57
Lansbury Cl, NW10 118 CQ64
Lansbury Cres, Dart. DA1 188 FN85
Lansbury Dr, Hayes UB4 135 BT71
Lansbury Est, E14 290 C8
Lansbury Gdns, E14 290 G8
Tilbury RM18 171 GG81
Sch Lansbury Lawrence Prim Sch, E14 290 C9
Lansbury Rd, Enf. EN3 83 DX39
Lansbury Way, N18 100 DS50
Lanscombe Wk, SW8 310 A6
Lansdell Rd, Mitch. CR4 200 DG96
Lansdown, Guil. GU1 243 BA134
Lansdown Cl, Walt. KT12 196 BW102
Woking GU21 226 AT119
Lansdowne Av, Bexh. DA7 166 EX80
Orpington BR6 205 EP102
Slough SL1 132 AS74
Lansdowne Cl, SW20 179 CX94
Surbiton KT5 198 CP103
Twickenham TW1 177 CF88
Watford WD25 76 BX35
Coll Lansdowne Coll, W2 295 L1
Lansdowne Copse, Wor.Pk. KT4 199 CU103
Lansdowne Ct, Pur. CR8 219 DP110
Slough SL1 132 AS74
Worcester Park KT4 199 CU103
Lansdowne Cres, W11 294 F1
Lansdowne Dr, E8 278 D5
Lansdowne Gdns, SW8 310 A6
Lansdowne Grn, SW8 309 P5
Lansdowne Gro, NW10 118 CS63
Lansdowne Hill, SE27 181 DP90
Lansdowne La, SE7 164 EK79
Lansdowne Ms, SE7 164 EK78
W11 294 G2
Lansdowne Pl, SE1 299 M6
SE19 182 DT94
Sch Lansdowne Prim Sch, Til. RM18 off Alexandra Rd 171 GF82
Lansdowne Ri, W11 294 F1
Lansdowne Rd, E4 101 EA47
E11 124 EF61
E17 123 EA57
E18 124 EG55
N3 97 CZ52
N10 99 DJ54
N17 100 DT53
SW20 179 CW94
W11 282 F10
Bromley BR1 184 EG94
Chesham HP5 54 AQ29
Croydon CR0 202 DR103
Epsom KT19 216 CQ108
Harrow HA1 117 CE59
Hounslow TW3 156 CB83
Ilford IG3 125 ET60
Purley CR8 219 DN112
Sevenoaks TN13 257 FK122
Staines-upon-Thames TW18 174 BH94
Stanmore HA7 95 CJ51
Tilbury RM18 171 GF82
Uxbridge UB8 135 BP72
Lansdowne Row, W1 297 K2
Sch Lansdowne Sch, SW9 310 C10
Lansdowne Sq, Nthflt DA11 191 GF86
Lansdowne Ter, WC1 286 B5
Lansdowne Wk, W11 294 F2
Lansdowne Way, SW8 309 P6
Lansdowne Wd Cl, SE27 181 DP90
Lansdown Pl, Nthflt DA11 191 GF88
Lansdown Rd, E7 144 EJ66
Chalfont St. Peter SL9 90 AX53
Sidcup DA14 186 EV90
Lansfield Av, N18 100 DU49
Lanson Bldg, SW8 309 J4
Lantern Cl, SW15 159 CU84
Orpington BR6 223 EP105
Wembley HA0 117 CK64
Lantern Way, West Dr. UB7 154 BL75
Lantern Cl, Brox. EN10 49 DY19
Lant St, SE1 299 J4
Lanvanor Rd, SE15 312 G8
Lapford Cl, W9 283 H4
Lapis Cl, NW10 138 CN69
Lapis Ms, E15 280 F9
Lapponum Wk, Hayes UB4 off Lochan Cl 136 BY70
Lapraik Gro, Ch.St.G. HP8 90 AW48
Lapse Wd Wk, SE26 182 DV89
Lapstone Gdns, Har. HA3 117 CJ58
Lapwing Cl, Erith DA8 167 FH80
Hemel Hempstead HP2 40 BL16
South Croydon CR2 221 DY110
Lapwing Ct, Surb. KT6 off Chaffinch Cl 198 CN104
Lapwing Gro, Guil. GU4 243 BD132
Lapwing Pl, Wat. WD25 60 BW32
Lapwings, The, Grav. DA12 191 GK89
Lapwing Ter, E7 off Hampton Rd 124 EK64
Lapwing Twr, SE8 313 N2
Lapwing Way, Abb.L. WD5 59 BU31
Hayes UB4 136 BX72
Lapworth Cl, Orp. BR6 206 EW103
Lara Cl, SE13 183 EC86
Chessington KT9 216 CL108
Larbert Rd, SW16 201 DJ95
Larby Pl, Epsom KT17 216 CS110
Larch Av, W3 138 CS74
Bricket Wood AL2 60 BY30
Guildford GU1 242 AW132
Larch Cl, E13 292 C4
N11 98 DG52
N19 off Bredgar Rd 121 DJ61
SE8 313 P3
SW12 181 DH89
Cheshunt EN7 off The Firs 66 DS27
Kingswood KT20 234 DC121
Penn HP10 88 AC45
Redhill RH1 266 DC136
Slough SL2 131 AP71
Warlingham CR6 237 DY119
Larch Cres, Epsom KT19 216 CP107
Hayes UB4 136 BW70
Larch Dene, Orp. BR6 205 EN103
Larch Dr, W4 off Gunnersbury Av 158 CN78
Larches, The, N13 100 DQ48
Amersham HP6 72 AV38
Bushey WD23 76 BY43
Northwood HA6 off Rickmansworth Rd 93 BQ51
St. Albans AL4 43 CK16
Uxbridge UB10 135 BP69
Woking GU21 226 AY116
Larches Av, SW14 158 CR84
Enfield EN1 82 DW35
Larchfield Cl, Wey. KT13 195 BT104
Larch Grn, NW9 off Clayton Fld 96 CS53
Larch Gro, Sid. DA15 185 ET88
Larchlands, The, Penn HP10 88 AD46
Larchmoor Pk, Stoke P. SL2 112 AU64
Larch Ri, Berk. HP4 38 AU18
Larch Rd, E10 123 EA61
NW2 119 CW63
Dartford DA1 188 FK87
Larch Tree Way, Croy. CR0 203 EA104
Larch Wk, Swan. BR8 207 FD96
Larch Way, Brom. BR2 205 EN101
Larchwood Av, Rom. RM5 105 FB51
Larchwood Cl, Bans. SM7 233 CY116
Romford RM5 105 FC51
Larchwood Dr, Eng.Grn TW20 172 AV93
Larchwood Gdns, Pilg.Hat. CM15 108 FU44
Larchwood Ho, Chig. IG7 104 EV49
Sch Larchwood Prim Sch, Pilg.Hat. CM15 off Larchwood Gdns 108 FU44
Larchwood Rd, SE9 185 EP89
Hemel Hempstead HP2 40 BM18
Larcombe Cl, Croy. CR0 220 DT105
Larcom St, SE17 299 K9
Larden Rd, W3 138 CS74
Largewood Av, Surb. KT6 198 CN103
Largo Wk, Erith DA8 off Selkirk Dr 167 FE81
Larissa St, SE17 299 M10
Lark Av, Stai. TW18 173 BF90
Larkbere Rd, SE26 183 DY91
Lark Cl, Warley CM14 108 FV49
Larken Cl, Bushey WD23 off Larken Dr 94 CC46
Larken Dr, Bushey WD23 94 CC46
Larkfield, Cob. KT11 213 BU113
Larkfield Av, Har. HA3 117 CH55
Larkfield Cl, Brom. BR2 204 EF103
Larkfield Ct, Smallfield RH6 off Cooper Cl 269 DN148
Larkfield Rd, Rich. TW9 158 CL84
Sevenoaks TN13 256 FC123
Sidcup DA14 185 ET90
Larkfields, Nthflt DA11 190 GE90
Larkhall Cl, Hersham KT12 214 BW107
Larkhall La, SW4 309 N9
Sch Larkhall Prim Sch, SW4 309 P9
Larkhall Ri, SW4 309 M10
Larkham Cl, Felt. TW13 175 BS90
Larkhill Ter, SE18 off Prince Imperial Rd 165 EN80
Larkin Cl, Couls. CR5 235 DM117
Hutton CM13 109 GC45
Larkings La, Stoke P. SL2 132 AV67
Larkins Rd, Lon.Gat.Air. RH6 268 DD152
Lark Ri, E.Hors. KT24 245 BS131
Hatfield AL10 45 CU20
Lark Row, E2 278 G9
Larksfield, Eng.Grn TW20 172 AW94
Horley RH6 269 DH147
Larksfield Gro, Enf. EN1 82 DV39
Larks Gro, Bark. IG11 145 ES66
Larkshall Ct, Rom. RM7 105 FC54
Larkshall Cres, E4 101 EC49
Larkshall Rd, E4 101 EC50
Larkspur Cl, E6 292 G6
N17 100 DR52
NW9 118 CP57
Hemel Hempstead HP1 39 BE19
Orpington BR6 206 EW103
Ruislip HA4 115 BQ59
South Ockendon RM15 149 FW69
Larkspur Gro, Edg. HA8 96 CQ49
Larkspur Way, Epsom KT19 216 CQ106
North Holmwood RH5 263 CK139
Larks Ridge, St.Alb. AL2 60 CA27
Larks Ri, Chesh. HP5 54 AR33
Larkswood, Harl. CM17 52 EW17
Larkswood Cl, Erith DA8 167 FG81
Larkswood Ct, E4 101 ED50
🔒 Larkswood Leisure Pk, E4 off New Rd 101 EC49
Sch Larkswood Prim Sch, E4 off New Rd 101 EB49
Larkswood Ri, Pnr. HA5 116 BW56
St. Albans AL4 43 CJ15
Larkswood Rd, E4 101 EA49
Lark Way, Cars. SM5 200 DE101
Larkway Cl, NW9 118 CR56
Larmans Rd, Enf. EN3 82 DW36
Sch Larmenier & Sacred Heart Prim Sch, W6 294 D9
Larnach Rd, W6 306 C3
Larner Ct, W12 off Heathstan Rd 139 CU72
Larne Rd, Ruis. HA4 115 BT59
Larner Rd, Erith DA8 167 FE80
Larpent Av, SW15 179 CW85
Larsen Dr, Wal.Abb. EN9 67 ED34
Larwood Cl, Grnf. UB6 117 CD64
Lascar Cl, Houns. TW3 156 BZ83
Lascelles Av, Har. HA1 117 CD59
Lascelles Cl, E11 123 ED61
Pilgrim's Hatch CM15 108 FU43
Lascelles Rd, Slou. SL3 152 AV76
Lascotts Rd, N22 99 DM51
Lassa Rd, SE9 184 EL85
Lassell St, SE10 315 H1
Lasseter Pl, SE3 315 K2
Lasswade Rd, Cher. KT16 193 BF101
Latchett Rd, E18 102 EH53
Latchford Pl, Chig. IG7 104 EV49
Hemel Hempstead HP1 40 BG21
Latching Cl, Rom. RM3 off Troopers Dr 106 FK49
Latchingdon Ct, E17 123 DX56
Latchingdon Gdns, Wdf.Grn. IG8 102 EL51
Latchmere Cl, Rich. TW10 178 CL92
Sch Latchmere Inf Sch, Kings.T. KT2 off Latchmere Rd 178 CM93
Sch Latchmere Jun Sch, Kings.T. KT2 off Latchmere Rd 178 CM93
Latchmere La, Kings.T. KT2 178 CM93
Latchmere Pas, SW11 308 D9
Latchmere Pl, Ashf. TW15 174 BL89
Latchmere Rd, SW11 308 E8
Kingston upon Thames KT2 178 CL94
Latchmere St, SW11 308 E8
Latchmoor Av, Chal.St.P. SL9 112 AX56
Latchmoor Gro, Chal.St.P. SL9 112 AX56
Latchmoor Way, Chal.St.P. SL9 112 AX56
Lateward Rd, Brent. TW8 157 CK79
Latham Cl, E6 293 H8
Biggin Hill TN16 238 EJ116
Dartford DA2 189 FS89
Twickenham TW1 177 CG87
Latham Grn, Upmin. RM14 128 FQ61
Latham Ho, E1 289 K8
Latham Rd, Bexh. DA6 186 FA85
Twickenham TW1 177 CF87
Lathams Way, Croy. CR0 201 DM102
Lathkill Cl, Enf. EN1 100 DU45
Sch Lathom Jun Sch, E6 off Lathom Rd 144 EL66
Lathom Rd, E6 145 EM66
LATIMER, Chesh. HP5 72 AY36
Latimer, SE17 311 N1
Latimer Av, E6 145 EM67
Latimer Cl, Amer. HP6 72 AW39
Hemel Hempstead HP2 40 BN15
Pinner HA5 94 BW53
Watford WD18 93 BS45
Woking GU22 227 BB116
Worcester Park KT4 217 CV105
Latimer Ct, Earls. RH1 266 DF136
Waltham Cross EN8 67 DZ34
Latimer Dr, Horn. RM12 128 FK62
Latimer Gdns, Pnr. HA5 94 BW53
Welwyn Garden City AL7 30 DB09
● Latimer Ind Est, W10 282 B8
Latimer Pl, W10 282 B8
⊖ Latimer Road 282 D10
Latimer Rd, E7 124 EH63
N15 122 DS58
SW19 180 DB93
W10 282 A7
Barnet EN5 80 DB41
Chenies WD3 73 BB38
Chesham HP5 72 AU36
Croydon CR0 off Abbey Rd 201 DP104
Teddington TW11 177 CF92
Latimer Way, Knot.Grn HP9 88 AJ49
Latitude Apts, N16 122 DS60
Latitude Ct, E16 off Albert Basin Way 145 EQ73
Latium Cl, St.Alb. AL1 43 CD21
Latona Dr, Grav. DA12 191 GM92
Latona Rd, SE15 312 C3
Lattimer Pl, W4 158 CS79
Lattimore Rd, St.Alb. AL1 43 CE21
LATTON BUSH, Harl. CM18 52 EU18
Latton Cl, Esher KT10 214 CB105
Walton-on-Thames KT12 196 BY101
Latton Common, Harl. CM17 52 EV18
Latton Common Rd, Harl. CM18 52 EU18
Latton Grn, Harl. CM18 51 ET19
Sch Latton Grn Prim Sch, Harl. CM18 off Riddings La 51 ET19
Latton Hall Cl, Harl. CM20 36 EU14
Latton Ho, Harl. CM18 52 EV18
Latton St, Harl. CM20 36 EU14
Potter Street CM17 52 EW18
Sch Latymer All Saints C of E Prim Sch, N9 off Hydethorpe Av 100 DT47
Latymer Cl, Wey. KT13 213 BQ105
Latymer Ct, W6 294 D9
Latymer Rd, N9 100 DT46
Sch Latymer Sch, The, N9 off Haselbury Rd 100 DS47
Sch Latymer Upr Sch, W6 off King St 159 CU77
Latymer Way, N9 100 DR47
Laubin Cl, Twick. TW1 157 CH84
Lauder Cl, Nthlt. UB5 136 BX68
Lauderdale Dr, Rich. TW10 177 CK90
Lauderdale Pl, EC2 off The Barbican 287 J6
Lauderdale Rd, W9 283 L3
Hunton Bridge WD4 59 BQ33
Lauderdale Twr, EC2 287 J6
Laud St, SE11 298 C10
Croydon CR0 202 DQ104
Laugan Wk, SE17 off East St 299 K10
Laughton Ct, Borwd. WD6 off Banks Rd 78 CR40
Laughton Rd, Nthlt. UB5 136 BX67
Sch Launcelot Prim Sch, Downham BR1 off Launcelot Rd 184 EG91
Launcelot Rd, Brom. BR1 184 EG91
Launcelot St, SE1 298 E5
Launceston, Chorl. WD3 73 BB44
Launceston Cl, Rom. RM3 106 FJ53
Launceston Gdns, Perivale UB6 137 CJ67
Launceston Pl, W8 295 N6
Launceston Rd, Perivale UB6 137 CJ67
Launch St, E14 302 E6
Launders Gate, W3 158 CP75
Launders La, Rain. RM13 148 FM69
Laundress La, N16 122 DU62
Laundry La, N1 277 J7
Lower Nazeing EN9 68 EE25
Laundry Ms, SE23 183 DY87
Laundry Rd, W6 306 E3
Guildford GU1 258 AW135
Launton Dr, Bexh. DA6 166 EX84
Laura Cl, E11 124 EJ57
Enfield EN1 82 DS43
Lauradale Rd, N2 120 DF56
Laura Dr, Swan. BR8 187 FG94
Sch Laurance Haines Prim & Nurs Sch, Wat. WD18 off Vicarage Rd 75 BU44
Laura Pl, E5 278 G1
Laureate Way, Hem.H. HP1 40 BG18
Laurel Apts, SE17 off Townsend St 299 N8
Laurel Av, Eng.Grn TW20 172 AV92
Gravesend DA12 191 GJ89
Potters Bar EN6 63 CZ32
Slough SL3 152 AY75
Twickenham TW1 177 CF88
Laurel Bk, Felden HP3 39 BF23
Laurel Bk Gdns, SW6 307 H8
Laurel Bk Rd, Enf. EN2 82 DQ39
Laurel Bk Vil, W7 off Lower Boston Rd 137 CE74
Laurel Cl, N19 off Hargrave Pk 121 DJ61
SW17 180 DE92
Colnbrook SL3 153 BE80
Dartford DA1 off Willow Rd 188 FJ88
Hemel Hempstead HP2 40 BM19
Hutton CM13 109 GB43
Ilford IG6 103 EQ51
Sidcup DA14 186 EU90
Watford WD19 94 BX45
Woking GU21 211 BD113
Laurel Ct, Amer. HP6 55 AQ36
Cuffley EN6 off Station Rd 65 DM29
Laurel Cres, Croy. CR0 203 EA104
Romford RM7 127 FE60
Woking GU21 211 BC113
Laurel Dr, N21 99 DN45
Oxted RH8 254 EF131
South Ockendon RM15 149 FX70
Laurel Flds, Pot.B. EN6 63 CZ31
Laurel Gdns, E4 101 EB45
NW7 96 CR48
W7 137 CE74
Ashford TW15 175 BQ92
Bromley BR1 204 EL98
Hounslow TW4 156 BY84
New Haw KT15 212 BH110
Laurel Gro, SE20 182 DV94
SE26 183 DX91
Laurel La, Horn. RM12 off Station La 128 FL61
West Drayton UB7 154 BL77
Sch Laurel La Prim Sch, West Dr. UB7 154 BL77
Laurel Lo La, Barn. EN5 79 CW36
Laurel Manor, Sutt. SM2 218 DC108
Laurel Ms, SE5 311 J10
Laurel Pk, Har. HA3 95 CF52
Laurel Rd, SW13 159 CU82
SW20 199 CV95
Chalfont St. Peter SL9 90 AX53
Hampton Hill TW12 177 CD92
St. Albans AL1 43 CF20
Laurels, Brom. BR1 204 EH95
Saint Albans AL2 60 CA28
Laurels, The, Bans. SM7 233 CZ117
Cobham KT11 230 BY115
Dartford DA2 188 FJ90
Fetcham KT22 231 CD124
Potten End HP4 39 BB17
Waltham Cross EN7 66 DS27
Weybridge KT13 195 BR104
Laurelsfield, St.Alb. AL3 42 CB23
Laurels Rd, Iver SL0 133 BD68
Laurel St, E8 278 B5
Laurel Vw, N12 98 DB48
Laurel Way, E18 124 EF56
N20 98 DA48
Laurence Ms, W12 off Askew Rd 159 CU75
Laurence Pountney Hill, EC4 287 L10
Laurence Pountney La, EC4 287 L10
Laurie Gro, SE14 313 M6
Laurie Rd, W7 137 CE71
Laurier Rd, NW5 121 DH62
Croydon CR0 202 DT101
Lauries Cl, Hem.H. HP1 39 BB22
🔒 Laurie Wk, Rom. RM1 off Market Pl 127 FE56
Laurimel Cl, Stan. HA7 95 CH51
Laurino Pl, Bushey Hth WD23 94 CC47
Sch Lauriston Prim Sch, E9 279 J8
Lauriston Rd, E9 279 J8
SW19 179 CX93
Lausanne Rd, N8 121 DN56
SE15 313 H7
Lauser Rd, Stanw. TW19 174 BJ87
Laustan Cl, Guil. GU1 243 BC134
Lavell St, N16 277 M1
Lavender Av, NW9 118 CQ60
Mitcham CR4 200 DE95
Pilgrim's Hatch CM15 108 FV43
Worcester Park KT4 199 CW104
Lavender Cl, E4 101 EA49
SW3 308 B3
Bromley BR2 204 EL100
Carshalton SM5 218 DG105
Chaldon CR3 252 DQ125
Cheshunt EN7 66 DT27
Coulsdon CR5 235 DJ119
Harlow CM20 35 ES14
Hatfield AL10 44 CS15
Leatherhead KT22 231 CJ122
Redhill RH1 267 DH139
Romford RM3 106 FK52
Lavender Ct, W.Mol. KT8 off Molesham Way 196 CB97
Lavender Cres, St.Alb. AL3 42 CC18
Lavender Dr, Uxb. UB8 134 BM71
Lavender Gdns, SW11 160 DF84
Enfield EN2 81 DP39
Harrow Weald HA3 95 CE51
Lavender Gate, Oxshott KT22 214 CB113
Lavender Gro, E8 278 B7
Mitcham CR4 200 DE95
Lavender Hill, SW11 160 DE84
Enfield EN2 81 DN39
Swanley BR8 207 FD97
Lavender Pk Rd, W.Byf. KT14 212 BG112
Lavender Pl, Ilf. IG1 125 EP64
Sch Lavender Prim Sch, Enf. EN2 off Lavender Rd 82 DS39
Lavender Ri, West Dr. UB7 154 BN75
Lavender Rd, SE16 301 L2
SW11 308 B10
Carshalton SM5 218 DG105
Croydon CR0 201 DM100
Enfield EN2 82 DR39
Epsom KT19 216 CP106
Sutton SM1 218 DD105
Uxbridge UB8 134 BM71
Woking GU22 227 BB116

Lavender Sq, SW9 310 D6
Lavender St, E15 281 J4
Lavender Sweep, SW11 160 DF84
Lavender Ter, SW11 308 D10
Lavender Vale, Wall. SM6 219 DK107
Lavender Wk, SW11 160 DF84
Hemel Hempstead HP2 40 BK18
Mitcham CR4 200 DG97
Lavender Way, Croy. CR0 203 DX100
Lavengro Rd, SE27 182 DQ89
Lavenham Rd, SW18 179 CZ89
Lavernock Rd, Bexh. DA7 166 FA82
Sch Laverock Sch, Oxt. RH8 off Bluehouse La 254 EE128
Lavers Rd, N16 122 DS62
Laverstoke Gdns, SW15 179 CU87
Laverton Ms, SW5 295 M9
Laverton Pl, SW5 295 M9
Lavidge Rd, SE9 184 EL89
Lavina Gro, N1 276 C10
Lavington Cl, E9 279 N4
Lavington Rd, W13 137 CH74
Croydon CR0 201 DM104
Lavington St, SE1 299 H3
Lavinia Av, Wat. WD25 60 BX34
Lavinia Rd, Dart. DA1 188 FM86
Lavrock La, Rick. WD3 92 BM45
Lawbrook La, Guil. GU5 261 BQ144
Sch Lawdale Jun Sch, E2 288 D2
Lawdons Gdns, Croy. CR0 219 DP105
Lawes Way, Bark. IG11 146 EU69
Lawford Av, Chorl. WD3 73 BC44
Lawford Cl, Chorl. WD3 73 BC44
Hornchurch RM12 128 FJ63
Lawford Gdns, Dart. DA1 188 FJ85
Kenley CR8 236 DQ116
Lawford Rd, N1 277 N7
NW5 275 L5
W4 158 CQ80
Law Ho, Bark. IG11 146 EU68
Lawkland, Farn.Royal SL2 131 AQ69
Lawless St, E14 290 D10
Lawley Rd, N14 99 DH45
Lawley St, E5 122 DW63
Lawn, The, Harl. CM20 36 EV12
Southall UB2 156 CA78
Lawn Av, West Dr. UB7 154 BJ75
Lawn Cl, N9 100 DT45
Bromley BR1 184 EH93
Datchet SL3 152 AW80
New Malden KT3 198 CS96
Ruislip HA4 115 BT62
Swanley BR8 207 FC96
Lawn Cres, Rich. TW9 158 CM82
Lawn Fm Gro, Rom. RM6 126 EY56
Lawn Gdns, W7 137 CE74
Lawn Ho Cl, E14 302 E4
Lawn La, SW8 310 B2
Hemel Hempstead HP3 40 BK22
Lawn Pk, Sev. TN13 257 FH127
Sch Lawn Prim Sch, Nthflt DA11 off High St 190 GC86
Lawn Rd, NW3 274 E2
Beckenham BR3 183 DZ94
Gravesend DA11 190 GC86
Guildford GU2 258 AW137
Uxbridge UB8 134 BJ66
Lawns, Brwd. CM14 off Uplands Rd 108 FY50
Lawns, The, E4 101 EA50
SE3 315 K10
SE19 202 DR95
Colnbrook SL3 153 BE81
Hemel Hempstead HP1 39 BE19
Pinner HA5 94 CB52
St. Albans AL3 42 CC19
Shenley WD7 62 CL33
Sidcup DA14 186 EV91
Sutton SM2 217 CY108
Welwyn Garden City AL8 29 CX06
Lawns Ct, Wem. HA9 off The Avenue 118 CM61
Lawns Cres, Grays RM17 170 GD79
Lawns Dr, The, Brox. EN10 49 DZ21
Lawnside, SE3 164 EF84
Lawnsmead, Won. GU5 259 BB144
Lawns Way, Rom. RM5 105 FC52
Lawn Ter, SE3 315 K10
Lawn Vale, Pnr. HA5 94 BX54
Lawrance Gdns, Chsht EN8 67 DX28
Lawrance Rd, St.Alb. AL3 42 CC16
Lawrance Sq, Nthflt DA11 191 GF90
Lawrence Av, E12 125 EN63
E17 101 DX53
N13 99 DP49
NW7 96 CS49
NW10 138 CR67
New Malden KT3 198 CR100
Stanstead Abbotts SG12 33 EC11
Lawrence Bldgs, N16 122 DT62
Lawrence Campe Cl, N20 98 DD48
Lawrence Cl, E3 290 A1
N15 122 DS55
W12 off Australia Rd 139 CV73
Guildford GU4 off Ladygrove Dr 243 BB129
Hertford SG14 31 DL08
Lawrence Ct, NW7 96 CS50
Lawrence Cres, Dag. RM10 127 FB62
Edgware HA8 96 CN54
Lawrence Dr, Uxb. UB10 115 BQ63
Lawrence Gdns, NW7 97 CT48
Tilbury RM18 171 GH80
Lawrence Hall, E13 292 A4
Lawrence Hall End, Welw.G.C. AL7 29 CY12
Lawrence Hill, E4 101 EA47
Lawrence Hill Gdns, Dart. DA1 188 FJ86
Lawrence Hill Rd, Dart. DA1 188 FJ86
Lawrence La, EC2 287 K9
Buckland RH3 249 CV131
Lawrence Moorings, Saw. CM21 36 EZ06
Lawrence Orchard, Chorl. WD3 73 BD43
Lawrence Pl, N1 276 B8
Lawrence Rd, E6 144 EK67
E13 144 EH67
N15 122 DS56
N18 100 DV49
SE25 202 DT98
W5 157 CJ77
Erith DA8 167 FB80
Hampton TW12 176 BZ94
Hayes UB4 135 BQ68
Hounslow TW4 156 BW84
Pinner HA5 116 BX57
Richmond TW10 177 CJ91
Romford RM2 127 FH57
West Wickham BR4 222 EG105
Lawrence St, E16 291 M7
NW7 97 CT49
SW3 308 C3
● Lawrence Trading Est, Grays RM17 off Askew Fm La 170 FY79
Lawrence Way, NW10 118 CQ62
Slough SL1 131 AK71
Lawrence Weaver Cl, Mord. SM4 off Green La 200 DA100
Lawrie Ho, SW19 off Plough La 180 DB92
Lawrie Pk Av, SE26 182 DV92
Lawrie Pk Cres, SE26 182 DV92
Lawrie Pk Gdns, SE26 182 DV91
Lawrie Pk Rd, SE26 182 DV93
Laws Cl, SE25 202 DR98
Lawson Cl, E16 292 D7
SW19 179 CX90
Ilford IG1 125 ER64
Lawson Ct, N11 off Ringway 99 DJ51
Lawson Est, SE1 299 L7
Lawson Gdns, Dart. DA1 188 FK85
Pinner HA5 115 BV55
Lawson Rd, Dart. DA1 168 FK84
Enfield EN3 82 DW39
Southall UB1 136 BZ70
Lawson Wk, Cars. SM5 218 DF110
Law St, SE1 299 M6
Lawton Rd, E3 289 M3
E10 123 EC60
Cockfosters EN4 80 DD41
Loughton IG10 85 EP41
Laxcon Cl, NW10 118 CQ64
Laxey Rd, Orp. BR6 223 ET107
Laxley Cl, SE5 311 H4
Laxton Gdns, Merst. RH1 251 DK128
Shenley WD7 62 CL32
Laxton Pl, NW1 285 K4
Layard Rd, SE16 300 F8
Enfield EN1 82 DT39
Thornton Heath CR7 202 DR96
Layard Sq, SE16 300 F8
Layborne Av, Noak Hill RM3 off North End 106 FJ47
Laybrook, St.Alb. AL4 43 CG16
Layburn Cres, Slou. SL3 153 BB79
Sch Laycock Prim Sch, N1 276 G5
Laycock St, N1 276 F5
Layer Gdns, W3 138 CN73
Layfield Cl, NW4 119 CV59
Layfield Cres, NW4 119 CV59
Layfield Rd, NW4 119 CV59
Layhams Rd, Kes. BR2 222 EF106
West Wickham BR4 203 ED104
Layhill, Hem.H. HP2 40 BK18
Laymarsh Cl, Belv. DA17 166 EZ76
Laymead Cl, Nthlt. UB5 136 BY65
Laystall St, EC1 286 E5
Layters Av, Chal.St.P. SL9 90 AW54
Layters Av S, Chal.St.P. SL9 90 AW54
Layters Cl, Chal.St.P. SL9 90 AW54
Layters End, Chal.St.P. SL9 90 AW54
Layters Grn La, Chal.St.P. SL9 112 AU55
Layter's Grn Mobile Home Pk, Chal.St.P. SL9 off Layters Grn La 90 AV54
LAYTER'S GREEN, Ger.Cr. SL9 90 AV54
Layters Way, Ger.Cr. SL9 112 AX56
Layton Ct, Wey. KT13 213 BP105
Layton Cres, Croy. CR0 219 DN106
Layton Pl, Kew TW9 158 CN81
Layton Rd, Brent. TW8 157 CK78
Hounslow TW3 156 CB84
Laytons Bldgs, SE1 299 K4
Laytons La, Sun. TW16 195 BT96
Layton St, Welw.G.C. AL7 29 CY12
Layzell Wk, SE9 off Mottingham La 184 EK88
Lazar Wk, N7 off Briset Way 121 DM61
Lazell Gdns, Bet. RH3 264 CQ140
Lazenby Ct, WC2 286 A10
Lea, The, Egh. TW20 193 BB95
Leabank Cl, Har. HA1 117 CE62
Leabank Sq, E9 280 A4
Leabank Vw, N15 122 DU58
Leabourne Rd, N16 122 DU58
LEA BRIDGE, E5 123 DX62
⇌ Lea Bridge 123 DY10
Lea Br Rd, E5 122 DW62
E10 123 DY60
E17 123 ED56
Lea Bushes, Wat. WD25 76 BY35
Leachcroft, Chal.St.P. SL9 90 AV53
Leach Gro, Lthd. KT22 231 CJ122
Lea Cl, Bushey WD23 76 CB43
Twickenham TW2 176 BZ87
Lea Ct, N15 off Broad La 122 DU56
Lea Cres, Ruis. HA4 115 BT63
Leacroft, Slou. SL1 151 AM75
Staines-upon-Thames TW18 174 BH91
Leacroft Av, SW12 180 DF87
Leacroft Cl, N21 99 DP47
Kenley CR8 236 DQ116
Staines-upon-Thames TW18 174 BH91
West Drayton UB7 134 BL72
Leacroft Rd, Iver SL0 133 BD72
Leadale Av, E4 101 EA47
Leadale Rd, N15 122 DU58
N16 122 DU58
Leadbeaters Cl, N11 off Goldsmith Rd 98 DF50
Leadbetter Dr, Wat. WD25 75 BR36
Leaden Cl, Loug. IG10 85 EP41
Leadenhall Bldg, The, EC3 287 N9
🔒 Leadenhall Mkt, EC3 287 N9
Leadenhall Pl, EC3 287 N9
Leadenhall St, EC3 287 N9
Leadenham Ct, E3 290 A5
Leaden Hill, Couls. CR5 235 DL115
● Leaden Hill Ind Est, Couls. CR5 235 DL115
Leader Av, E12 125 EN64
Leadings, The, Wem. HA9 118 CQ62
Leadmill La, E20 123 EB63
Leaf Cl, Nthwd. HA6 93 BR52
Thames Ditton KT7 197 CE99
Leaf Gro, SE27 181 DN92
Leafield Cl, SW16 181 DP93
Woking GU21 off Winnington Way 226 AV118
Leafield La, Sid. DA14 186 EZ91
Leafield Rd, SW20 199 CZ97
Sutton SM1 200 DA103
Leaford Cres, Wat. WD24 75 BT37
Leaforis Rd, Wal.Cr. EN7 66 DU28
Leaf Way, St.Alb. AL1 43 CD23
Leafy Gro, Croy. CR0 221 DY111
Keston BR2 222 EJ106
Leafy Oak Rd, SE12 184 EJ90
Leafy Way, Croy. CR0 202 DT103
Hutton CM13 109 GD46
Lea Gdns, Wem. HA9 118 CL63
Leagrave St, E5 122 DW62
Lea Hall Gdns, E10 off Lea Hall Rd 123 EA60
Lea Hall Rd, E10 123 EA60
Leahoe Gdns, Hert. SG13 32 DQ10
Leaholme Gdns, Slou. SL1 130 AJ71
Leaholme Way, Ruis. HA4 115 BP58
Leahurst Rd, SE13 183 ED85
DLR Lea Interchange, E9 280 B2
Leake St, SE1 298 D4
Lealand Rd, N15 122 DT58
Leamington Av, E17 123 EA57
Bromley BR1 184 EJ92
Morden SM4 199 CZ98
Orpington BR6 223 ES105
Leamington Cl, E12 124 EL64
Bromley BR1 184 EJ91
Hounslow TW3 176 CC85
Romford RM3 106 FM51
Leamington Ct, SE3 315 K2
Leamington Cres, Har. HA2 116 BY62
Leamington Gdns, Ilf. IG3 125 ET61
Leamington Pk, W3 138 CR71
Leamington Pl, Hayes UB4 135 BT70
Leamington Rd, Rom. RM3 106 FN50
Southall UB2 156 BX77
Leamington Rd Vil, W11 283 H7
Leamore St, W6 159 CV77
Lea Mt, Goffs Oak EN7 66 DS28
Leamouth Rd, E6 292 G8
E14 291 H9
Leander Ct, SE8 314 A7
Leander Dr, Grav. DA12 191 GM91
Leander Gdns, Wat. WD25 76 BY37
Leander Rd, SW2 181 DM86
Northolt UB5 136 CA68
Thornton Heath CR7 201 DM98
Leapale La, Guil. GU1 258 AX135
Leapale Rd, Guil. GU1 258 AX135
● Lea Pk Trd Estates, E10 off Warley Cl 123 DZ60
Learner Dr, Har. HA2 116 CA61
Lea Rd, Beck. BR3 off Fairfield Rd 203 EA96
Enfield EN2 82 DR39
Grays RM16 171 GG78
Hoddesdon EN11 49 EC15
Sevenoaks TN13 257 FJ127
Southall UB2 156 BY77
Waltham Abbey EN9 67 EA34
Watford WD24 75 BV38
Learoyd Gdns, E6 293 L10
Leas, The, Bushey WD23 76 BZ39
Hemel Hempstead HP3 40 BN24
Staines-upon-Thames TW18 off Raleigh Ct 174 BG91
Upminster RM14 129 FR59
Leas Cl, Chess. KT9 216 CM108
Leas Dale, SE9 185 EN90
Leas Dr, Iver SL0 133 BE72
Leas Grn, Chis. BR7 185 ET93
Leaside, Bkhm KT23 230 CA123
Hemel Hempstead HP2 41 BQ21
Leaside Av, N10 120 DG55
Leaside Ct, Uxb. UB10 135 BP69
Leaside Rd, E5 122 DW60
Leaside Wk, Ware SG12 off East St 33 DX06
Leas La, Warl. CR6 237 DX118
Leasowes Rd, E10 123 EA60
Lea Sq, E3 279 P9
Leas Rd, Guil. GU1 258 AW135
Warlingham CR6 237 DX118
Leasway, Brwd. CM14 108 FX48
Upminster RM14 128 FQ62
Leathart Cl, Horn. RM12 off Dowding Way 147 FH66
Leatherbottle Grn, Erith DA18 166 EZ76
Leather Bottle La, Belv. DA17 166 EY77
Leather Cl, Mitch. CR4 200 DG96
Leatherdale St, E1 289 J3
Leather Gdns, E15 281 K9
LEATHERHEAD, KT22 - KT24 231 CF121
⇌ Leatherhead 231 CG121
Leatherhead Bypass Rd, Lthd. KT22 231 CJ120
Leatherhead Cl, N16 122 DT60
LEATHERHEAD COMMON, Lthd. KT22 231 CF119
H Leatherhead Hosp, Lthd. KT22 231 CJ122
★ Leatherhead Mus of Local History, Lthd. KT22 231 CH122
Leatherhead Rd, Ashtd. KT21 231 CK121
Bookham KT22, KT23 246 CB126
Chessington KT9 215 CJ111
Leatherhead KT22 231 CK121
Oxshott KT22 215 CD114
● Leatherhead Trade Pk, Lthd. KT22 231 CG121
Sch Leatherhead Trinity Sch, Lthd. KT22 off Woodvill Rd 231 CH120
Leatherhead KT22 off Fortyfoot Rd 231 CJ122
Leather La, EC1 286 F7
Gomshall GU5 261 BQ139
Hornchurch RM11 off North St 128 FK60
Leather Mkt, The, SE1 299 N5
Leathermarket Ct, SE1 299 N5
Leathermarket St, SE1 299 N5
Leather Rd, SE16 301 J9
Leathersellers Cl, Barn. EN5 off The Avenue 79 CY42
Leathsail Rd, Har. HA2 116 CB62
Leathwaite Rd, SW11 160 DF84
Leathwell Rd, SE8 314 D8
Lea Vale, Dart. DA1 167 FD84
● Lea Valley Business Pk, E10 off Lammas Rd 123 DY61
Sch Lea Valley High Sch, Enf. EN3 off Bullsmoor La 82 DW35
Sch Lea Valley Prim Sch, N17 off Somerford Gro 100 DU52
Lea Valley Rd, E4 83 DY43
Enfield EN3 83 DY43
● Lea Valley Trd Est, N18 101 DX50
Lea Valley Viaduct, E4 101 DX50
N18 101 DX50
Lea Valley Wk, E3 290 E1
E5 123 DY62
E9 279 P2
E10 123 DY62
E14 290 A8
E15 280 B8
Lea Valley Wk, E17 100 DW53
N9 101 DY46
N15 122 DU58
N16 122 DU58
N17 100 DW53
N18 100 DW53
Broxbourne EN10 49 EB21
Enfield EN3 83 DZ41
Hatfield AL9 46 DA15
Hertford SG13, SG14 31 DP11
Hoddesdon EN11 49 ED18
Waltham Abbey EN9 67 DZ30
Waltham Cross EN8 67 DZ30
Ware SG12 32 DW06
Welwyn Garden City AL7, AL8 29 CW13
Leaveland Cl, Beck. BR3 203 EA98
Leaver Gdns, Grnf. UB6 137 CD68
Leavesden Ct, Abb.L. WD5 59 BU31
LEAVESDEN GREEN, Wat. WD25 59 BS34
Sch Leavesden Grn, Wat. WD25 75 BT35
Sch Leavesden Grn JMI Sch, Lvsdn WD25 off High Rd 59 BU34
Leavesden Rd, Stan. HA7 95 CG51
Watford WD24 75 BV38
Weybridge KT13 213 BP106
LEAVES GREEN, Kes. BR2 222 EK109
Leaves Grn Cres, Kes. BR2 222 EJ111
Leaves Grn Rd, Kes. BR2 222 EK111
Leaview, Wal.Abb. EN9 67 EB33
Lea Vw Ho, E5 off Springfield 122 DV60
Leaway, E10 123 DX60
Leazes Av, Chaldon CR3 235 DN123
Leazes La, Cat. CR3 235 DN123
Lebanon Av, Felt. TW13 176 BX92
Lebanon Cl, Wat. WD17 75 BR36
Lebanon Ct, Twick. TW1 177 CH87
Lebanon Dr, Cob. KT11 214 CA113
Lebanon Gdns, SW18 180 DA86
Biggin Hill TN16 238 EK117
Lebanon Pk, Twick. TW1 177 CH87
Tram Lebanon Road 202 DS103
Lebanon Rd, SW18 180 DA85
Croydon CR0 202 DS102
Lebrun Sq, SE3 164 EH83
Lechford Rd, Horl. RH6 268 DG149
Lechmere App, Wdf.Grn. IG8 102 EJ54
Lechmere Av, Chig. IG7 103 EQ49
Woodford Green IG8 102 EK54
Lechmere Rd, NW2 139 CV65
Leckford Rd, SW18 180 DC89
Leckhampton Pl, SW2 off Scotia Rd 181 DN87
Leckwith Av, Bexh. DA7 166 EY79
Lecky St, SW7 296 A10
Leclair Ho, SE3 off Gallus Sq 164 EH83
Leconfield Av, SW13 159 CT83
Leconfield Rd, N5 277 L1
Leconfield Wk, Horn. RM12 off Airfield Way 148 FJ65
Le Corte Cl, Kings L. WD4 58 BM29
Lectern La, St.Alb. AL1 43 CD24
Leda Av, Enf. EN3 83 DX39
Leda Rd, SE18 305 J7
Ledborough Gate, Beac. HP9 89 AM51
Ledborough La, Beac. HP9 89 AK52
Ledborough Wd, Beac. HP9 89 AL51
Ledbury Est, SE15 312 E4
Ledbury Ho, SE22 off Pytchley Rd 162 DS83
Ledbury Ms N, W11 283 J10
Ledbury Ms W, W11 283 J10
Ledbury Pl, Croy. CR0 220 DR105
Ledbury Rd, W11 283 H8
Croydon CR0 220 DQ105
Reigate RH2 249 CZ133
Ledbury St, SE15 312 D4
Ledger Cl, Guil. GU1 243 BB132
Ledger Dr, Add. KT15 211 BF106
Ledger La, Fifield SL6 150 AD82
Ledgers Rd, Slou. SL1 151 AR75
Warlingham CR6 237 EA116
Ledrington Rd, SE19 182 DU93
Ledway Dr, Wem. HA9 118 CM59
LEE, SE12 164 EE84
⇌ Lee 184 EG86
Lee, The, Nthwd. HA6 93 BT50
Lee Av, Rom. RM6 126 EY58
Lee Br, SE13 163 EC83
Leechcroft Av, Sid. DA15 185 ET85
Swanley BR8 207 FF97
Leechcroft Rd, Wall. SM6 200 DG104
Leech La, Headley KT18 248 CQ126
Leatherhead KT22 248 CQ126
Lee Ch St, SE13 164 EE84
Lee Cl, E17 101 DX53
Barnet EN5 80 DC42
Hertford SG13 32 DQ11
Stanstead Abbotts SG12 33 EC11
Lee Conservancy Rd, E9 279 P3
Leecroft Rd, Barn. EN5 79 CY43
Leeds Cl, Orp. BR6 206 EX103
Leeds Pl, N4 121 DM60
Leeds Rd, Ilf. IG1 125 ER60
Slough SL1 132 AS73
Leeds St, N18 100 DU50
Lee Fm Cl, Chesh. HP5 56 AU30
Leefern Rd, W12 159 CU75
Leefe Way, Cuffley EN6 65 DK28
Lee Gdns Av, Horn. RM11 128 FN60
Leegate, SE12 184 EF85
Leegate Cl, Wok. GU21 off Sythwood 226 AV116
Sch Lee Grn, SE12 off Lee High Rd 184 EF85
Lee Grn, Orp. BR5 206 EU99
Lee Grn La, Epsom KT18 232 CP124
Lee Gro, Chig. IG7 103 EN47
Lee High Rd, SE12 163 ED83
SE13 163 ED83
Leeke St, WC1 286 C2
Leeland Rd, W13 137 CG74
Leeland Ter, W13 137 CG74
Leeland Way, NW10 118 CS63
Sch Lee Manor Prim Sch, SE13 off Leahurst Rd 184 EE86
Leeming Rd, Borwd. WD6 78 CM39
Lee Pk, SE3 164 EF84
Lee Pk Way, N9 101 DX49
N18 101 DX49
Leerdam Dr, E14 302 F7
Lee Rd, NW7 97 CX52
SE3 315 L10
SW19 200 DB95
Enfield EN1 82 DU44
Perivale UB6 137 CJ67
Lees, The, Croy. CR0 203 DZ103
Lees Av, Nthwd. HA6 93 BT53
Leeside, Barn. EN5 79 CY43
Potters Bar EN6 off Wayside 64 DD32
● Leeside Business Cen, Enf. EN3 83 DZ40
Leeside Ct, SE16 301 J2
Leeside Cres, NW11 119 CZ58
● Leeside Ind Est, N17 off Garman Rd 100 DW52
Leeside Rd, N17 100 DV51
Leeson Gdns, Eton Wick SL4 off Victoria Rd 151 AL77
Leeson Rd, SE24 161 DN84
Leesons Hill, Chis. BR7 205 ES97
Orpington BR5 206 EU97
Sch Leesons Prim Sch, St.P.Cray BR5 off Leesons Hill 206 EV97
Leesons Way, Orp. BR5 205 ET96
Lees Pl, W1 284 G10
Lees Rd, Uxb. UB8 135 BP70
Lee St, E8 278 A8
Horley RH6 268 DE148
Lee Ter, SE3 164 EE83
SE13 164 EE83
Lee Valley Cycle Route, Harl. CM19 50 EF15
Hoddesdon EN11 34 EE13
Waltham Abbey EN9 49 ED20
Ware SG12 33 EB09
★ Lee Valley Hockey & Tennis Cen, E20 280 C1
★ Lee Valley Pk, E10 67 DZ31
Lee Valley Pathway, E9 123 DZ62
E10 122 DW59
E17 122 DW59
Waltham Abbey EN9 67 DZ30
● Lee Valley Technopark, N17 122 DU55
★ Lee Valley VeloPark, E20 280 D2
★ Lee Valley White Water Cen, Waltham Cross EN9 67 EA33
★ Lee Vw, Enf. EN2 81 DP39
Leeward Gdns, SW19 179 CZ93
Leeway, SE8 301 N10
Leeway Cl, Hatch End HA5 94 BZ52
Leewood Cl, SE12 off Upwood Rd 184 EF86
Leewood Pl, Swan. BR8 207 FD98
Leewood Way, Eff. KT24 246 BW127
Le Fay Ct, N9 off Galahad Rd 100 DU48
Lefevre Wk, E3 280 A10
Lefroy Rd, W12 159 CT75
Legard Rd, N5 121 DP63
Legatt Rd, SE9 184 EK85
Leggatt Rd, E15 280 F10
Leggatts Cl, Wat. WD24 75 BT36
Leggatts Pk, Pot.B. EN6 64 DD29
Leggatts Ri, Wat. WD25 75 BU35
Leggatts Way, Wat. WD24 75 BT36
Leggatts Wd Av, Wat. WD24 75 BV36
Legge St, SE13 183 EC85
Leggfield Ter, Hem.H. HP1 39 BF20
Leghorn Rd, NW10 139 CT68
SE18 165 ER78
Legion Cl, N1 276 F5
Legion Ct, Mord. SM4 200 DA100
Legion Rd, Grnf. UB6 136 CC67
Legion Ter, E3 279 P9
Legion Way, N12 98 DE52
Legon Av, Rom. RM7 127 FC60
Legra Av, Hodd. EN11 49 EA17
Legrace Av, Houns. TW4 156 BX82
Leicester Av, Mitch. CR4 201 DL98
Leicester Cl, Wor.Pk. KT4 217 CW105
Leicester Ct, WC2 285 P10
Leicester Gdns, Ilf. IG3 125 ES59
Leicester Ms, N2 120 DE55
Leicester Pl, WC2 285 P10
Leicester Rd, E11 124 EH57
N2 120 DE55
Barnet EN5 80 DB43
Croydon CR0 202 DS101
Tilbury RM18 171 GF81
⊖ Leicester Square 285 P10
Leicester Sq, WC2 297 P1
Leicester St, WC2 285 P10
LEIGH, Reig. RH2 265 CU141
Leigh, The, Kings.T. KT2 178 CS93
Leigham Av, SW16 181 DL90
Leigham Cl, SW16 181 DM90
Leigham Ct, Wall. SM6 off Clyde Rd 219 DJ107
Leigham Ct Rd, SW16 181 DL89
Leigham Dr, Islw. TW7 157 CE80
Leigham Vale, SW2 181 DN90
SW16 181 DM90
Leigh Av, Ilf. IG4 124 EK56
Leigh Cl, Add. KT15 211 BF108
New Malden KT3 198 CQ98
● Leigh Cl Ind Est, N.Mal. KT3 off Leigh Cl 198 CR98
Leigh Common, Welw.G.C. AL7 29 CY11
Leigh Cor, Cob. KT11 off Leigh Hill Rd 230 BW115
Leigh Ct, SE4 off Lewisham Way 314 A8
Borehamwood WD6 off Banks Rd 78 CR40
Harrow HA2 117 CE60
Leigh Ct Cl, Cob. KT11 214 BW114
Leigh Cres, New Adgtn CR0 221 EB108
Leigh Dr, Rom. RM3 106 FK49
Leigh Gdns, NW10 282 A1
Leigh Hill Rd, Cob. KT11 214 BW114
Leigh Hunt Dr, N14 99 DK46
Leigh Hunt St, SE1 299 J4
Leigh Orchard Cl, SW16 181 DM90
Leigh Pk, Datchet SL3 152 AV80
Leigh Pl, EC1 286 E6
Cobham KT11 230 BW115
Dartford DA2 188 FN92
Feltham TW13 176 BW88
Welling DA16 166 EU82
Leigh Pl La, Gdse. RH9 253 DY132
Leigh Pl Rd, Reig. RH2 265 CU140
Leigh Rd, E6 145 EN65
E10 123 EC59
N5 276 G1
Betchworth RH3 264 CQ140
Cobham KT11 213 BV113
Gravesend DA11 191 GH89
Hounslow TW3 157 CD84
Slough SL1 131 AP73

L

Leigh Rodd, Wat. WD19 94 BZ48
Leigh Sq, Wind. SL4 151 AK82
Leigh St, WC1 286 A4
Sch Leigh Tech Acad, The, Dart. DA1 off Green St Grn Rd 188 FP88
Leigh Ter, Orp. BR5 off Saxville Rd 206 EV97
Leighton Av, E12 125 EN64
Pinner HA5 116 BY55
Leighton Buzzard Rd, Hem.H. HP1 40 BJ19
Leighton Cl, Edg. HA8 96 CN54
Leighton Cres, NW5 275 M2
Leighton Gdns, NW10 139 CV68
South Croydon CR2 220 DV113
Tilbury RM18 171 GG80
Leighton Gro, NW5 275 M3
★ Leighton Ho Mus, W14 295 H6
Leighton Pl, NW5 275 L3
Leighton Rd, NW5 275 N3
W13 157 CG75
Enfield EN1 82 DT43
Harrow Weald HA3 95 CD54
Leighton St, Croy. CR0 201 DP102
Leighton Way, Epsom KT18 216 CR114
Leila Parnell Pl, SE7 164 EJ79
Leinster Av, SW14 158 CQ83
Leinster Gdns, W2 283 N9
Leinster Ms, W2 283 N10
Barnet EN5 79 CY41
Leinster Pl, W2 283 N9
Leinster Rd, N10 121 DH56
Leinster Sq, W2 283 K10
Leinster Ter, W2 283 N10
Leirum St, N1 141 DM67
Leiston Spur, Slou. SL1 132 AS72
Leisure La, W.Byf. KT14 212 BH112
Leisure Way, N12 98 DD52
Leith Cl, NW9 118 CR60
Slough SL1 132 AU74
Leithcote Gdns, SW16 181 DM91
Leithcote Path, SW16 181 DM90
Leith Hill, Orp. BR5 206 EU95
Leith Hill Grn, Orp. BR5 off Leith Hill 206 EU95
Leith Hill Rd, Abin.Com. RH5 262 BY144
Leith Pk Rd, Grav. DA12 191 GH88
Leith Rd, N22 99 DP53
Epsom KT17 216 CS112
Leith Twrs, Sutt. SM2 218 DB108
Leith Vw, N.Holm. RH5 263 CJ140
Leith Yd, NW6 273 J8
Lela Av, Houns. TW4 156 BW82
Lelitia Cl, E8 278 C9
Leman St, E1 288 B9
Lemark Cl, Stan. HA7 95 CJ50
Le May Av, SE12 184 EH90
Le May Cl, Horl. RH6 268 DG147
Lemmon Rd, SE10 315 J2
Lemna Rd, E11 124 EE59
Lemonfield Dr, Wat. WD25 60 BY32
Lemon Gro, Felt. TW13 175 BU88
Lemonwell Ct, SE9 off Lemonwell Dr 185 EQ85
Lemonwell Dr, SE9 185 EQ85
LEMSFORD, Welw.G.C. AL8 29 CT10
Lemsford Cl, N15 122 DU57
Lemsford Ct, N4 off Brownswood Rd 122 DQ61
Borehamwood WD6 78 CQ42
Lemsford La, Welw.G.C. AL8 29 CV10
Lemsford Rd, Hat. AL10 45 CT17
Lemsford AL8 29 CT10
St. Albans AL1 43 CF20
Lemsford Village, Lmsfd AL8 29 CU10
Lemuel St, SW18 180 DB86
Lena Cres, N9 100 DW47
Lena Gdns, W6 294 B7
Sch Lena Gdns Prim Sch, W6 294 B6
Lena Kennedy Cl, E4 101 EB51
Lenanton Steps, E14 302 B4
Lendal Ter, SW4 161 DK83
Lenelby Rd, Surb. KT6 198 CN102
Len Freeman Pl, SW6 306 G3
Lenham Rd, SE12 164 EF84
Bexleyheath DA7 166 EZ79
Sutton SM1 218 DB105
Thornton Heath CR7 202 DR96
Lenmore Av, Grays RM17 170 GC76
Lennard Av, W.Wick. BR4 204 EE103
Lennard Cl, W.Wick. BR4 204 EE103
Lennard Rd, SE20 182 DW93
Beckenham BR3 183 DX93
Bromley BR2 205 EM102
Croydon CR0 202 DQ102
Dunton Green TN13 241 FE120
Lennard Row, Aveley RM15 149 FR74
Lennon Rd, NW2 272 A3
Lennox Av, Grav. DA11 191 GF86
Lennox Cl, Chaff.Hun. RM16 169 FW77
Romford RM1 127 FF58
Lennox Gdns, NW10 119 CT63
SW1 296 E7
Croydon CR0 219 DP105
Ilford IG1 125 EM60
Lennox Gdns Ms, SW1 296 E7
Lennox Rd, E17 123 DZ58
N4 121 DM61
Gravesend DA11 191 GF86
Lennox Rd E, Grav. DA11 191 GG87
Lenor Cl, Bexh. DA6 166 EY84
Lensbury Av, SW6 307 P8
Lensbury Cl, Chsht EN8 67 DY28
Lensbury Way, SE2 166 EW76
Lens Rd, E7 144 EJ66
Len Taylor Cl, Hayes UB4 off Welwyn Way 135 BS70
Lenten Cl, Peasl. GU5 261 BR142
Lent Grn, Burn. SL1 130 AH70
Lent Grn La, Burn. SL1 130 AH70
Lenthall Av, Grays RM17 170 GA75
Lenthall Ho, SW1 309 M1
Lenthall Rd, E8 278 B6
Loughton IG10 85 ER42
Lenthorp Rd, SE10 303 L10
Lentmead Rd, Brom. BR1 184 EF90
Lenton Path, SE18 165 ER79
Lenton Ri, Rich. TW9 158 CL83
Lenton St, SE18 165 ER77
Lenton Ter, N4 off Fonthill Rd 121 DN61
LENT RISE, Slou. SL1 130 AH72
Sch Lent Ri Comb Sch, Burn. SL1 off Coulson Way 130 AH71
Lent Ri Rd, Burn. SL1 130 AH72
Taplow SL6 130 AH72
Coll Leo Baeck Coll, N3 off East End Rd 98 DA54
Leof Cres, SE6 183 EB92
Leominster Rd, Mord. SM4 200 DC100
Leominster Wk, Mord. SM4 200 DC100
Leonard Av, Mord. SM4 200 DC99
Otford TN14 241 FH116
Romford RM7 127 FD60
Swanscombe DA10 190 FY87
Leonard Pl, N16 off Allen Rd 122 DS63
Leonard Rd, E4 101 EA51
E7 281 N1
N9 100 DT48
SW16 201 DJ95
Southall UB2 156 BX76
Leonard Robbins Path, SE28 off Tawney Rd 146 EV73
Leonard St, E16 305 H3
EC2 287 M4
Leonard Way, Brwd. CM14 108 FS49
Leonora Tyson Ms, SE21 182 DR89
Leontine Cl, SE15 312 D5
Leopards Ct, EC1 286 E6
Leopold Av, SW19 179 CZ92
Leopold Ms, E9 278 G8
Sch Leopold Prim Sch, NW10 off Hawkshead Rd 139 CT66
Leopold Rd, E17 123 EA57
N2 120 DD55
N18 100 DV50
NW10 138 CS66
SW19 179 CZ91
W5 138 CM74
Leopold St, E3 289 P6
Leopold Ter, SW19 179 CZ92
Leo St, SE15 312 F4
Leo Yd, EC1 287 H5
Le Personne Rd, Cat. CR3 236 DR122
Leppoc Rd, SW4 181 DK85
Leret Way, Lthd. KT22 231 CH121
Leroy St, SE1 299 N8
Lerry Cl, W14 307 H2
Lerwick Dr, Slou. SL1 132 AS71
Lesbourne Rd, Reig. RH2 266 DB135
Lescombe Cl, SE23 183 DY90
Lescombe Rd, SE23 183 DY90
Lesley Cl, Bex. DA5 187 FB87
Istead Rise DA13 191 GF94
Swanley BR8 207 FD97
Leslie Gdns, Sutt. SM2 218 DA108
Leslie Gro, Croy. CR0 202 DS102
Leslie Gro Pl, Croy. CR0 off Leslie Gro 202 DS102
Leslie Pk Rd, Croy. CR0 202 DS102
Leslie Rd, E11 280 F1
E16 292 A9
N2 120 DD55
Chobham GU24 210 AS110
Dorking RH4 247 CK134
Leslie Smith Sq, SE18 off Nightingale Vale 165 EN79
★ Lesnes Abbey (ruins), Erith DA18 166 EX77
Lesney Fm Est, Erith DA8 167 FD80
Lesney Pk, Erith DA8 167 FD79
Lesney Pk Rd, Erith DA8 167 FD79
Lessar Av, SW4 181 DJ85
Lessingham Av, SW17 180 DF91
Ilford IG5 125 EN55
Lessing St, SE23 183 DY87
Lessington Av, Rom. RM7 127 FC58
Lessness Av, Bexh. DA7 166 EX80
LESSNESS HEATH, Belv. DA17 167 FB78
Sch Lessness Heath Prim Sch, Belv. DA17 off Erith Rd 166 FA78
Lessness Pk, Belv. DA17 166 EZ78
Lessness Rd, Belv. DA17 off Stapley Rd 166 FA78
Morden SM4 200 DC100
Lester Av, E15 291 K3
Lestock Cl, SE25 202 DU97
Leston Cl, Rain. RM13 147 FH69
Leswin Pl, N16 122 DT62
Leswin Rd, N16 122 DT62
Letchfield, Ley Hill HP5 56 AV31
Letchford Gdns, NW10 139 CU69
Letchford Ms, NW10 off Letchford Gdns 139 CU69
Letchford Ter, Har. HA3 94 CB53
LETCHMORE HEATH, Wat. WD25 77 CD38
Letchmore Rd, Rad. WD7 77 CG36
Letchworth Av, Felt. TW14 175 BT87
Letchworth Cl, Brom. BR2 204 EG99
Watford WD19 94 BX50
Letchworth Dr, Brom. BR2 204 EG99
Letchworth Rd, Stan. HA7 96 CL52
Letchworth St, SW17 180 DF91
Lethbridge Cl, SE13 314 F7
Letter Box La, Sev. TN13 257 FJ129
Letterstone Rd, SW6 306 G5
Lettice St, SW6 306 G7
Lett Rd, E15 280 G7
SW9 310 D6
Lettsom St, SE5 311 N8
Lettsom Wk, E13 281 N10
LETTY GREEN, Hert. SG14 31 DH13
Leucha Rd, E17 123 DY57
Levana Cl, SW19 179 CY88
Levehurst Ho, SE27 off Elder Rd 182 DQ92
Levehurst Way, SW4 310 B8
Leven Cl, Wal.Cr. EN8 67 DX33
Watford WD19 94 BX50
Levendale Rd, SE23 183 DY89
Leven Dr, Wal.Cr. EN8 67 DX33
Leven Rd, E14 290 F7
Leven Way, Hayes UB3 135 BS72
Hemel Hempstead HP2 40 BK16
Leveret Cl, New Adgtn CR0 221 ED111
Watford WD25 59 BU34
Leverett St, SW3 296 D8
Leverholme Gdns, SE9 185 EN90
Leverson St, SW16 181 DJ93
Lever Sq, Grays RM16 171 GG77
LEVERSTOCK GREEN, Hem.H. HP3 41 BQ21
Sch Leverstock Grn C of E Prim Sch, Hem.H. HP2 off Green La 41 BR21
Leverstock Grn Rd, Hem.H. HP2, HP3 41 BQ21
Leverstock Grn Way, Hem.H. HP3 41 BQ20
Lever St, EC1 287 H3
Sch Leverton Inf & Nurs Sch, Wal.Abb. EN9 off Honey La 68 EF34
Sch Leverton Jun Sch, Wal.Abb. EN9 off Honey La 68 EF34
Leverton Pl, NW5 275 K3
Leverton St, NW5 275 L3
Leverton Way, Wal.Abb. EN9 67 EC33
Leveson Rd, Grays RM16 171 GH76
Levett Gdns, Ilf. IG3 125 ET63
Levett Rd, Bark. IG11 145 ES65
Leatherhead KT22 231 CH120
Levine Gdns, Bark. IG11 146 EX68
Levison Way, N19 off Grovedale Rd 121 DK61
Levylsdene, Guil. GU1 243 BD134
Lewen Cl, Croy. CR0 202 DR102
Lewes Cl, Grays RM17 170 GA79
Northolt UB5 136 CA65
Lewes Ct, Slou. SL1 off Chalvey Gro 151 AQ75
Lewesdon Cl, SW19 179 CX88
Lewes Rd, N12 98 DE50
Bromley BR1 204 EK96
Romford RM3 106 FJ49
Leweston Pl, N16 122 DT59
Lewes Way, Crox.Grn WD3 75 BQ42
Lewey Ho, E3 289 P5
Lewgars Av, NW9 118 CQ58
Lewing Cl, Orp. BR6 off Place Fm Av 205 ES102
Lewington Ct, Enf. EN3 off Hertford Rd 83 DX37
Lewin Rd, SW14 158 CR83
SW16 181 DK93
Bexleyheath DA6 166 EY84
Lewins Rd, Chal.St.P. SL9 112 AX55
Epsom KT18 216 CP114
Lewins Way, Slou. SL1 131 AM73
Lewin Ter, Felt. TW14 175 BR87
Lewis Av, E17 101 EA53
Lewis Cl, N14 99 DJ45
Addlestone KT15 212 BJ105
Harefield UB9 92 BJ54
Shenfield CM15 109 FZ45
Lewis Cres, NW10 118 CQ64
Lewis Gdns, N2 98 DD54
N16 122 DT58
Lewis Gro, SE13 163 EC83
LEWISHAM, SE13 163 EB84
⇌ Lewisham 314 D10
DLR Lewisham 314 E10
Lewisham 314 E10
Sch Lewisham Br Prim Sch, SE13 off Elmira St 163 EB83
Lewisham Cen, SE13 163 EC83
Coll Lewisham City Learning Cen, SE23 off Mayow Rd 183 DX90
Lewisham Ct, Enf. EN3 off Hodson Pl 83 EA38
Lewisham High St, SE13 314 F10
Lewisham Hill, SE13 314 F9
Lewisham Pk, SE13 183 EB86
Lewisham Rd, SE13 314 D7
Coll Lewisham Southwark College,
(Camberwell Campus), SE5 311 N5
(Deptford Campus), SE8 314 B6
(Lewisham Way Campus), SE4 314 A9
(Waterloo Campus), SE1 298 G4
Lewisham St, SW1 297 P5
Lewisham Way, SE4 313 N6
SE14 313 N6
Lewis La, Chal.St.P. SL9 90 AY53
Lewis Pl, E8 278 C3
Lewis Rd, Horn. RM11 128 FJ58
Mitcham CR4 200 DD96
Richmond TW10 off Red Lion St 177 CK85
Sidcup DA14 186 EW90
Southall UB1 156 BY75
Sutton SM1 218 DB105
Swanscombe DA10 190 FY86
Welling DA16 166 EW83
Lewis St, NW1 275 K5
Lewiston Cl, Wor.Pk. KT4 199 CV101
Lewis Way, Dag. RM10 147 FB65
Leworth Pl, Wind. SL4 off Bachelors Acre 151 AR81
Lexden Dr, Rom. RM6 126 EV58
Lexden Rd, W3 138 CP73
Mitcham CR4 201 DK98
Lexham Ct, Grnf. UB6 off Oldfield La N 137 CD67
Lexham Gdns, W8 295 L8
Amersham HP6 55 AQ37
Lexham Gdns Ms, W8 295 M7
Lexham Ho, Bark. IG11 off St. Margarets 145 ER67
Lexham Ms, W8 295 K8
Lexham Wk, W8 295 M7
Lexicon Apts, Rom. RM1 off Mercury Gdns 127 FE56
Lexington Apts, EC1 287 L4
Lexington Bldg, E3 off Fairfield Rd 290 B1
Lexington Cl, Borwd. WD6 78 CM41
Lexington Ct, Pur. CR8 220 DQ110
Lexington Ho, West Dr. UB7 off Park Lo Ave 154 BM75
Lexington Pl, Kings.T. KT1 177 CK94
Lexington St, W1 285 M9
Lexington Way, Barn. EN5 79 CX42
Upminster RM14 129 FT58
Lexton Gdns, SW12 181 DK88
Leybourne Av, W13 157 CH75
Leybourne Pk, Rich. TW9 158 CN81
Leybourne Av, Byfleet KT14 212 BM113
Leybourne Cl, Brom. BR2 204 EG100
Byfleet KT14 212 BM113
Leybourne Rd, E11 124 EF60
NW1 275 K7
NW9 118 CN57
Uxbridge UB10 135 BQ67
Leybourne St, NW1 275 J7
Leybridge Ct, SE12 184 EG85
Leyburn Cl, E17 123 EB56
Leyburn Cres, Rom. RM3 106 FL52
Leyburn Gdns, Croy. CR0 202 DS103
Leyburn Gro, N18 100 DU51
Leyburn Rd, N18 100 DU51
Romford RM3 106 FL52
Leycroft Cl, Loug. IG10 85 EN43
Leycroft Gdns, Erith DA8 167 FH81
Leydenhatch La, Swan. BR8 207 FC95
Leyden St, E1 288 A7
Leydon Cl, SE16 301 K3
Ley Fm Cl, Wat. WD25 76 BW36
Leyfield, Wor.Pk. KT4 198 CS102
Leyhill Cl, Swan. BR8 207 FE99
Ley Hill Rd, Bov. HP3 56 AX30
Sch Ley Hill Sch, Ley Hill HP5 off Jasons Hill 56 AV30
Leyland Av, Enf. EN3 83 DY40
St. Albans AL1 43 CD22
Leyland Cl, Chsht EN8 66 DW28
Leyland Ct, N11 off Oakleigh Rd S 99 DH49
Leyland Gdns, Wdf.Grn. IG8 102 EJ50
Leyland Rd, SE12 184 EG85
Leylands La, Stai. TW19 173 BF85
Leylang Rd, SE14 313 K4
Leys, The, N2 120 DC56
Amersham HP6 55 AP35
Harrow HA3 118 CM58
St. Albans AL4 43 CK17
Leys Av, Dag. RM10 147 FC66
Leys Cl, Dag. RM10 147 FC66
Harefield UB9 92 BK53
Harrow HA1 117 CD57
Leysdown, Welw.G.C. AL7 30 DD09
Leysdown Av, Bexh. DA7 167 FC84
Leysdown Rd, SE9 184 EL89
Leysfield Rd, W12 159 CU75
Leys Gdns, Barn. EN4 80 DG43
Sch Leys Prim Sch, The, Dag. RM10 off Leys Av 147 FC66
Leyspring Rd, E11 124 EF60
Leys Rd, Hem.H. HP3 40 BL22
Oxshott KT22 215 CD112
Leys Rd E, Enf. EN3 83 DY39
Leys Rd W, Enf. EN3 83 DY39
Ley St, Ilf. IG1, IG2 125 EP61
Leyswood Dr, Ilf. IG2 125 ES57
Leythe Rd, W3 158 CQ75
LEYTON, E11 123 EB60
⊖ Leyton 123 EC62
Coll Leyton 6th Form Coll, E10 off Essex Rd 123 ED58
● Leyton Business Cen, E10 123 EA61
Leyton Cross Rd, Dart. DA2 187 FF90
Leyton Gra, E10 123 EA61
Leyton Gra Est, E10 off Leyton Gra 123 EA61
Leyton Grn Rd, E10 123 EC58
● Leyton Ind Village, E10 123 DX59
Leyton Midland Road 123 EC60
★ Leyton Orient FC, E10 123 EB62
Leyton Pk Rd, E10 123 EC62
Leyton Rd, E15 280 G3
SW19 180 DC94
LEYTONSTONE, E11 123 ED59
⊖ Leytonstone 124 EE60
Leytonstone High Road 124 EE61
Leytonstone Rd, E15 281 J3
Sch Leytonstone Sch, E11 off Colworth Rd 124 EE58
Ley Wk, Welw.G.C. AL7 30 DC09
Leywick St, E15 281 J10
Leywood Cl, Amer. HP7 55 AR40
Lezayre Rd, Orp. BR6 223 ET107
Lianne Gro, SE9 184 EJ90
Liardet St, SE14 313 M3
Liberia Rd, N5 277 H4
★ Liberty, W1 285 L9
Liberty, The, Rom. RM1 127 FE57
Liberty Av, SW19 200 DD95
Liberty Br Rd, E20 280 F3
● Liberty Cen, Wem. HA0 off Mount Pleasant 138 CM67
Liberty Cl, N18 100 DT49
Hertford SG13 32 DQ11
Worcester Park KT4 199 CW102
Liberty Hall Rd, Add. KT15 212 BG106
Liberty Ho, Cher. KT16 off Guildford St 193 BF102
Liberty La, Add. KT15 212 BG106
Liberty Ms, SW12 181 DH86
Sch Liberty Prim Sch, Mitch. CR4 off Western Rd 200 DE96
Liberty Ri, Add. KT15 212 BG107
Liberty St, SW9 310 D7
Liberty Wk, St.Alb. AL1 43 CJ21
Libra Rd, E3 279 P9
E13 281 N10
Library Ct, N17 off High Rd 122 DT55
Library Hill, Brwd. CM14 off Coptfold Rd 108 FX47
Library Ms, Hmptn H. TW12 176 CC93
Library Pl, E1 288 F10
Library St, SE1 298 G5
Lichfield Cl, Barn. EN4 80 DF41
Lichfield Ct, Rich. TW9 off Sheen Rd 178 CL85
Lichfield Gdns, Rich. TW9 158 CL84
Lichfield Gro, N3 98 DA53
Lichfield Pl, St.Alb. AL1 off Avenue Rd 43 CF19
Lichfield Rd, E3 289 M2
E6 292 E3
N9 100 DU47
NW2 119 CY63
Dagenham RM8 126 EV63
Hounslow TW4 156 BW83
Northwood HA6 115 BU55
Richmond TW9 158 CM81
Woodford Green IG8 102 EE49
Lichfield Ter, Upmin. RM14 129 FS61
Lichfield Way, Brox. EN10 49 DZ22
South Croydon CR2 221 DX110
Lichlade Cl, Orp. BR6 223 ET105
Lickey Ho, W14 off North End Rd 307 H2
Lidbury Rd, NW7 97 CY51
Lidcote Gdns, SW9 310 E9
Liddall Way, West Dr. UB7 134 BM74
Liddell, Wind. SL4 150 AJ83
Liddell Cl, Har. HA3 117 CK55
Liddell Gdns, NW10 272 A10
Liddell Pl, Wind. SL4 off Liddell 150 AJ82
Liddell Rd, NW6 273 J4
Liddell Sq, Wind. SL4 off Liddell 150 AJ82
Liddell Way, Wind. SL4 off Liddell 150 AJ83
Lidding Rd, Har. HA3 117 CK57
Liddington Hall Dr, Rydes. GU3 242 AS131
Liddington New Rd, Rydes. GU3 242 AS131
Liddington Rd, E15 281 L8
Liddon Rd, E13 292 A3
Bromley BR1 204 EJ97
Liden Cl, E17 123 DZ59
Lidfield Rd, N16 277 L1
Lidgate Rd, SE15 312 A5
Lidgould Gr, Ruis. HA4 115 BU58
Lidiard Rd, SW18 180 DC89
Lidlington Pl, NW1 285 L1
Lido Ho, W13 off Northfield Av 137 CH74
Lido Sq, N17 100 DR53
Lidstone Cl, Wok. GU21 226 AV117
Lidstone Ct, Geo.Grn SL3 132 AX72
Lidyard Rd, N19 121 DJ60
Lieutenant Ellis Way, Wal.Cr. EN7, EN8 66 DT31
Coll Lifelong Learning, The Shadwell Cen, E1 289 J10
★ Lifetimes Mus (Croydon Cen Lib), Croy. CR0 202 DQ104
★ Liffler Rd, SE18 165 ES78
Liffords Pl, SW13 159 CT82
Lifford St, SW15 159 CX84
Lightcliffe Rd, N13 99 DN49
Lighter Cl, SE16 301 M8
Lighterman Ms, E1 289 K8
Lighterman's Ms, Grav. DA11 190 GE87
Lightermans Rd, E14 302 B5
Lightermans Way, Green. DA9 169 FW84
Lightfoot Rd, N8 121 DL57
Lightley Cl, Wem. HA0 138 CM67
Lightswood Cl, Chsht EN7 66 DR27
Ligonier St, E2 288 A4
Lilac Av, Enf. EN1 82 DW36
Woking GU22 226 AX120
Lilac Cl, E4 101 DZ51
Cheshunt EN7 66 DV31
Guildford GU1 242 AW130
Pilgrim's Hatch CM15 off Magnolia Way 108 FV43
Lilac Ct, Slou. SL2 131 AM69
Lilac Gdns, W5 157 CK76
Croydon CR0 203 EA104
Hayes UB3 135 BS72
Romford RM7 127 FE60
Swanley BR8 207 FD97
Lilac Ms, N8 off Courcy Rd 121 DN55
Lilac Pl, SE11 298 C9
West Drayton UB7 134 BM73
Lilac Rd, Hodd. EN11 49 EB15
Lilac St, W12 139 CU73
Lilah Ms, Brom. BR2 off Beckenham La 204 EE96
Lila Pl, Swan. BR8 207 FE98
Lilbourne Dr, Hert. SG13 32 DU08
Lilburne Gdns, SE9 184 EL85
Lilburne Rd, SE9 184 EL85
Lilburne Wk, NW10 138 CQ65
Lile Cres, W7 137 CE71
Lilestone St, NW8 284 C4
Lilford Rd, SE5 310 G8
Lilian Barker Cl, SE12 184 EG85
Sch Lilian Baylis Tech Sch, SE11 310 D1
Lilian Board Way, Grnf. UB6 117 CD64
Lilian Cl, N16 122 DS62
Lilian Cres, Hutt. CM13 109 GC47
Lilian Gdns, Wdf.Grn. IG8 102 EH53
Lilian Rd, SW16 201 DJ95
Lillechurch Rd, Dag. RM8 146 EV65
Lilleshall Rd, Mord. SM4 200 DD100
Lilley Cl, E1 300 D3
Brentwood CM14 108 FT49
Lilley Dr, Kgswd KT20 234 DB122
Lilley La, NW7 96 CR50
Lilley Mead, Red. RH1 251 DJ131
Lilley Way, Slou. SL1 131 AL74
Lillian Av, W3 158 CN75
Lillian Rd, SW13 159 CU79
Lilliards Cl, Hodd. EN11 33 EB13
Lillie Rd, SW6 306 D3
Biggin Hill TN16 238 EK118
Lillieshall Rd, SW4 161 DH83
Lillie Yd, SW6 307 J2
Lillingston Ho, N7 off Harvist Est 121 DN63
Lillington Gdns Est, SW1 297 M9
Lilliots La, Lthd. KT22 off Kingston Rd 231 CG119
Lilliput Av, Nthlt. UB5 136 BZ67
Lilliput Rd, Rom. RM7 127 FD59
Lillyfee Fm La, Woob.Grn HP10 110 AG57
Lilly La, Hem.H. HP2 41 BR16
Lily Cl, W14 294 E9
Lily Dr, West Dr. UB7 154 BK77
Lily Gdns, Wem. HA0 137 CJ68
Lily Pl, EC1 286 F6
Lily Rd, E17 123 EA58
Lilyville Rd, SW6 306 G6
Limbourne Av, Dag. RM8 126 EZ59
Limburg Rd, SW11 160 DF84
Lime Av, Brwd. CM13 109 FZ48
Northfleet DA11 190 GD87
Upminster RM14 128 FN63
West Drayton UB7 134 BM73
Windsor SL4 152 AT80
Limeburner La, EC4 286 G9
Limebush Cl, New Haw KT15 212 BJ109
Lime Cl, E1 300 D2
Bromley BR1 204 EL98
Buckhurst Hill IG9 102 EK48
Carshalton SM5 200 DF103
Harrow HA3 95 CF54
Pinner HA5 115 BT55
Reigate RH2 266 DB137
Romford RM7 127 FC56
South Ockendon RM15 149 FW69
Ware SG12 33 DY05
Watford WD19 94 BX45
West Clandon GU4 244 BH128
Lime Ct, Mitch. CR4 200 DD96
Lime Cres, Sun. TW16 196 BW96
Limecroft Cl, Epsom KT19 216 CR108
Limedene Cl, Pnr. HA5 94 BX53
Lime Gro, E4 101 DZ51
N20 97 CZ46
W12 294 A4
Addlestone KT15 212 BG105
Guildford GU1 242 AV130
Hayes UB3 135 BR73
Ilford IG6 103 ET51
New Malden KT3 198 CR97
Orpington BR6 205 EP103
Ruislip HA4 115 BV59
Sidcup DA15 185 ET86
Twickenham TW1 177 CF86
Warlingham CR6 237 DY118
West Clandon GU4 244 BG128
Woking GU22 226 AY121
Limeharbour, E14 302 D5
LIMEHOUSE, E14 289 M10
⇌ Limehouse 289 L9
DLR Limehouse 289 L9
Limehouse Causeway, E14 289 P10
Limehouse Link, E14 301 P1
Limehouse Lo, E5 off Mount Pleasant Hill 122 DW61
Limekiln Dr, SE7 164 EH79
Limekiln Pl, SE19 182 DT94

L

Lime Meadow Av,
S.Croy. CR2 220 DU113
Lime Pit La, Dunt.Grn TN13 241 FC117
Lime Quarry Ms, Guil. GU1 243 BD133
Limerick Cl, SW12 181 DJ87
Limerick Gdns, Upmin. RM14 129 FT59
Limerick Ms, N2 120 DE55
Lime Rd, Epp. CM16 69 ET31
Richmond TW9 158 CM84
Swanley BR8 207 FD97
Lime Row, Erith DA18
off Northwood Pl 166 EZ76
Limerston St, SW10 307 P2
Limes, The, SW18 180 DA86
W2 295 K1
Amersham HP6 55 AP35
Brentwood CM13 109 FZ48
Bromley BR2 204 EL103
Hornchurch RM11 128 FK55
Horsell GU21 226 AX115
Purfleet RM19
off Tank Hill Rd 168 FN78
St. Albans AL1 43 CE18
Welwyn Garden City AL7 30 DA11
Windsor SL4 150 AJ82
Limes Av, E11 124 EH56
N12 98 DC49
NW7 96 CS51
NW11 119 CY59
SE20 182 DV94
SW13 159 CT82
Carshalton SM5 200 DF102
Chigwell IG7 103 EQ50
Croydon CR0 201 DN104
Horley RH6 269 DH150
Limes Av, The, N11 99 DH50
Limes Cl, Ashf. TW15 174 BN92
Leatherhead KT22
off Linden Gdns 231 CJ120
Limes Ct, Brwd. CM15
off Sawyers Hall La 108 FX46
Hoddesdon EN11
off Conduit La 49 EA17
Limesdale Gdns, Edg. HA8 96 CQ54
Sch Limes Fm Inf & Nurs & Jun Schs, Chig. IG7 off Limes Av 103 ER50
Limes Fld Rd, SW14
off First Av 158 CS83
Limesford Rd, SE15 163 DX84
Limes Gdns, SW18 180 DA86
Limes Gro, SE13 163 EC84
Limes Ms, Egh. TW20
off Limes Rd 173 AZ92
Limes Pl, Croy. CR0 202 DR101
Limes Rd, Beck. BR3 203 EB96
Cheshunt EN8 67 DX32
Croydon CR0 202 DR100
Egham TW20 173 AZ92
Weybridge KT13 212 BN105
Limes Row, Farnboro. BR6 223 EP106
Limestone Wk, Erith DA18 166 EX76
Lime St, E17 123 DY56
EC3 287 N10
Lime St Pas, EC3 287 N9
Limes Wk, SE15 162 DV84
W5 157 CK75
Lime Ter, W7
off Manor Ct Rd 137 CE73
Lime Tree Av, Bluewater DA9 189 FU88
Esher KT10 197 CD102
Thames Ditton KT7 197 CD102
Lime Tree Cl, E18 124 EJ56
Bookham KT23 230 CA124
Limetree Cl, SW2 181 DM88
Lime Tree Ct, Ashtd. KT21
off Greville Pk Rd 232 CL118
London Colney AL2 61 CH26
Lime Tree Gro, Croy. CR0 203 DZ104
Lime Tree Pl, Mitch. CR4 201 DH95
St. Albans AL1 43 CF21
Sch Lime Tree Prim Sch,
Surb. KT6 198 CL100
Lime Tree Rd, Houns. TW5 156 CB81
Limetree Wk, SW17
off Hawthorn Cres 180 DG92
Lime Tree Wk, Amer. HP7 72 AT39
Bushey Heath WD23 95 CE46
Enfield EN2 82 DQ38
Rickmansworth WD3 74 BH43
Sevenoaks TN13 257 FH125
Virginia Water GU25 192 AY98
West Wickham BR4 222 EF105
Lime Wk, E15 281 K8
Denham UB9 114 BJ64
Hemel Hempstead HP3 40 BM22
Shere GU5 260 BM139
Sch Lime Wk Prim Sch,
Hem.H. HP3 off Lime Wk 40 BM22
Lime Wks Rd, Merst. RH1 251 DJ126
Limeway Ter, Dor. RH4 247 CG134
Limewood Cl, E17 123 DZ56
W13 137 CH72
Beckenham BR3 203 EC99
Limewood Ct, Ilf. IG4 125 EM57
Limewood Ms, SE20
off Lullington Road 182 DU94
Limewood Rd, Erith DA8 167 FC80
LIMPSFIELD, Oxt. RH8 254 EG128
Limpsfield Av, SW19 179 CX89
Thornton Heath CR7 201 DM99
LIMPSFIELD CHART, Oxt. RH8 254 EL130
Sch Limpsfield C of E Inf Sch,
Oxt. RH8 off Westerham Rd 254 EJ129
Sch Limpsfield Gra Sch,
Oxt. RH8 off Bluehouse La 254 EG127
Limpsfield Rd, S.Croy. CR2 220 DU112
Warlingham CR6 236 DW116
Linacre Cl, SE15 312 F10
Linacre Ct, W6 294 D10
Linacre Rd, NW2 139 CV65
Linale Ho, N1
off Murray Gro 287 L1
Linberry Wk, SE8 301 M9
Lince La, Westc. RH4 263 CD136
Linces Way, Welw.G.C. AL7 30 DB11
Linchfield Rd, Datchet SL3 152 AW81
Linchmere Rd, SE12 184 EF87
Lincoln Av, N14 99 DJ48
SW19 179 CX90
Romford RM7 127 FD60
Twickenham TW2 176 CB89
Lincoln Cl, SE25
off Woodside Grn 202 DV100
Erith DA8 167 FF82
Greenford UB6 136 CC67
Harrow HA2 116 BZ57
Horley RH6 268 DF149
Hornchurch RM11 128 FN57
Welwyn Garden City AL7 30 DD08
Lincoln Ct, N16 122 DR59
Berkhamsted HP4 38 AV19
Borehamwood WD6 78 CR43
Denham UB9 113 BF58
Lincoln Cres, Enf. EN1 82 DS43
Lincoln Dr, Crox.Grn WD3 75 BP42
Watford WD19 94 BW48
Woking GU22 227 BE115
Lincoln Gdns, Ilf. IG1 124 EL59
Lincoln Grn Rd, Orp. BR5 205 ET99
Lincoln Gro, Wey. KT13 195 BP104
Lincoln Hatch La, Burn. SL1 130 AJ70
Lincoln Ms, N15 122 DQ56
NW6 272 G8
SE21 182 DR88
Lincoln Pk, Amer. HP7 55 AS39
Lincoln Rd, E7 144 EK65
E13 292 A5
E18 off Grove Rd 102 EG53
N2 120 DE55
SE25 202 DV97
Chalfont St. Peter SL9 90 AY53
Dorking RH4 247 CJ134
Enfield EN1, EN3 82 DU43
Erith DA8 167 FF82
Feltham TW13 176 BZ90
Guildford GU2 242 AT132
Harrow HA2 116 BZ57
Mitcham CR4 201 DL99
New Malden KT3 198 CQ97
Northwood HA6 115 BT55
Sidcup DA14 186 EV92
Wembley HA0 137 CK65
Worcester Park KT4 199 CV102
Lincolns, The, NW7 97 CT48
Lincolns Cl, St.Alb. AL4 43 CJ15
Lincolns Fld, Epp. CM16 69 ET29
Lincolnshott, Sthflt DA13 190 GB92
★ Lincoln's Inn, WC2 286 D8
Lincoln's Inn Flds, WC2 286 C8
Lincoln St, E11 124 EE61
SW3 296 E9
Lincoln Wk, Epsom KT19 216 CR110
Lincoln Way, Crox.Grn WD3 75 BP42
Enfield EN1 82 DV43
Slough SL1 131 AK73
Sunbury-on-Thames TW16 195 BS95
Lincombe Rd, Brom. BR1 184 EF90
Lindal Cres, Enf. EN2 81 DL42
Lindale Cl, Vir.W. GU25 192 AT98
Lindales, The, N17
off Brantwood Rd 100 DT51
Lindal Rd, SE4 183 DZ85
Lindbergh, Welw.G.C. AL7 30 DC09
Lindbergh Rd, Wall. SM6 219 DL108
Linden Av, NW10 282 C1
Coulsdon CR5 235 DH116
Dartford DA1 188 FJ88
Enfield EN1 82 DU39
Hounslow TW3 176 CB85
Ruislip HA4 115 BU60
Thornton Heath CR7 201 DP98
Watford WD18 75 BS42
Wembley HA9 118 CM64
Sch Linden Br Sch, Wor.Pk.
KT4 off Grafton Rd 198 CS104
Linden Chase, Sev. TN13 257 FH122
Linden Cl, N14 81 DJ44
Iver SL0 133 BD68
New Haw KT15 212 BG111
Orpington BR6 224 EU106
Purfleet RM19 168 FQ79
Ruislip HA4 115 BU60
Stanmore HA7 95 CH50
Tadworth KT20 233 CX120
Thames Ditton KT7 197 CF101
Waltham Cross EN7 66 DV30
Linden Ct, W12 294 A2
Englefield Green TW20 172 AV93
Leatherhead KT22 231 CH121
Linden Cres, Grnf. UB6 137 CF65
Kingston upon Thames KT1 198 CM96
St. Albans AL1 43 CJ20
Woodford Green IG8 102 EH51
Linden Dr, Chaldon CR3 236 DQ124
Chalfont St. Peter SL9 90 AY53
Farnham Royal SL2 131 AQ66
Lindenfield, Chis. BR7 205 EP96
Linden Gdns, W2 295 K1
W4 158 CR78
Enfield EN1 82 DU39
Leatherhead KT22 231 CJ121
Linden Glade, Hem.H. HP1 40 BG21
Linden Gro, SE15 162 DV83
SE26 182 DW93
New Malden KT3 198 CS97
Teddington TW11
off Waldegrave Rd 177 CF92
Walton-on-Thames KT12 195 BT103
Warlingham CR6 237 DY118
Linden Ho, Slou. SL3 153 BB78
Linden Lawns, Wem. HA9 118 CM63
Linden Lea, N2 120 DC57
Dorking RH4 263 CJ138
Watford WD25 59 BU33
Linden Leas, W.Wick. BR4 203 ED103
Sch Linden Lo Sch, SW19
off Princes Way 179 CY88
Linden Mans, N6
off Hornsey La 121 DH60
Linden Ms, N1 277 M3
W2 295 K1
Linden Pas, W4
off Linden Gdns 158 CR78
Linden Pit Path, Lthd. KT22 231 CH121
Linden Pl, Epsom KT17
off East St 216 CS112
Leatherhead KT24
off Station App 245 BS126
Mitcham CR4 200 DE98
Linden Ri, Warley CM14 108 FX50
Linden Rd, E17
off High St 123 DZ57
N10 121 DH56
N11 98 DF47
N15 122 DQ56
Guildford GU1 242 AX134
Hampton TW12 176 CA94
Leatherhead KT22 231 CH121
Weybridge KT13 213 BQ109
Lindens, The, N12 98 DD50
W4 158 CQ81
Hemel Hempstead HP3 39 BF23
Loughton IG10 85 EM43
New Addington CR0 221 EC107
Lindens Cl, Eff. KT24 246 BY128
Linden Sq, Hare. UB9 92 BG51
Sevenoaks TN13
off London Rd 256 FE122
Linden St, Rom. RM7 127 FD56
Linden Wk, N19
off Hargrave Pk 121 DJ61
Linden Way, N14 81 DJ44
Purley CR8 219 DJ110
Ripley GU23 227 BF124
Shepperton TW17 195 BQ99
Woking GU22 227 AZ121
Lindeth Cl, Stan. HA7 95 CH51
Lindfield Gdns, NW3 273 M2
Guildford GU1 243 AZ133
Lindfield Rd, W5 137 CJ70
Croydon CR0 202 DT100
Romford RM3 106 FL50
Lindfield St, E14 290 A8
Lindhill Cl, Enf. EN3 83 DX39
Lindie Gdns, Uxb. UB10 134 BL66
Lindisfarne Cl, Grav. DA12 191 GL89
Lindisfarne Rd, SW20 179 CU94
Dagenham RM8 126 EW62
Lindisfarne Way, E9 279 M1
Lindley Est, SE15 312 C4
Lindley Pl, Kew TW9 158 CN81
Lindley Rd, E10 123 EB61
Godstone RH9 252 DW130
Walton-on-Thames KT12 196 BX104
Lindley St, E1 288 G6
Lindlings, Hem.H. HP1 39 BE21
Lindo Cl, Chesh. HP5 54 AP30
Sch Lindon Bennett Sch,
Han. TW13 off Main St 176 BX92
Lindore Rd, SW11 160 DF84
Lindores Rd, Cars. SM5 200 DC101
Lindo St, SE15 313 H9
Lind Rd, Sutt. SM1 218 DC106
Lindrop St, SW6 307 N8
Lindsay Cl,
Chessington KT9 216 CL108
Epsom KT18 216 CQ113
Stanwell TW19 174 BK85
Lindsay Ct, SW11 308 B7
Lindsay Dr, Har. HA3 118 CL58
Shepperton TW17 195 BR100
Lindsay Pl, Wal.Cr. EN7 66 DV30
Lindsay Rd, Hmptn H. TW12 176 CB91
New Haw KT15 212 BG110
Worcester Park KT4 199 CV103
Lindsay Sq, SW1 297 P10
Lindsell St, SE10 314 E6
Lindsey Cl, Brwd. CM14 108 FU49
Bromley BR1 204 EK97
Mitcham CR4 201 DL98
Lindsey Gdns, Felt. TW14 175 BR87
Lindsey Ms, N1 277 K6
Lindsey Rd, Dag. RM8 126 EW63
Denham UB9 114 BG62
Lindsey St, EC1 287 H6
Epping CM16 69 ER28
Lindsey Way, Horn. RM11 128 FJ57
Lind St, SE8 314 B8
Lindum Pl, St.Alb. AL3 42 BZ22
Lindum Rd, Tedd. TW11 177 CJ94
Lindvale, Wok. GU21 226 AY115
Lindway, SE27 181 DP92
Lindwood Cl, E6 293 H7
Linfield Cl, NW4 119 CW55
Hersham KT12 213 BV106
Linfield Ct, Hert. SG14 31 DM08
Linfields, Amer. HP7 72 AW40
LINFORD, S.le H. SS17 171 GM75
Linford Cl, Harl. CM19 51 EP17
Linford End, Harl. CM19 51 EQ17
Linford Rd, E17 123 EC55
Grays RM16 171 GH78
West Tilbury RM18 171 GJ77
Linford St, SW8 309 L6
Lingards Rd, SE13 163 EC84
Lingey Cl, Sid. DA15 185 ET89
Lingfield Av, Dart. DA2 188 FP87
Kingston upon Thames KT1 198 CL98
Upminster RM14 128 FM62
Lingfield Cl, Enf. EN1 82 DS44
Northwood HA6 93 BS52
Lingfield Cres, SE9 165 ER84
Lingfield Gdns, N9 100 DV45
Coulsdon CR5 235 DP119
Lingfield Rd, SW19 179 CX92
Gravesend DA12 191 GH89
Worcester Park KT4 199 CW104
Lingfield Way, Wat. WD17 75 BT38
Lingham St, SW9 310 B8
Lingholm Way, Barn. EN5 79 CX43
Lingmere Cl, Chig. IG7 103 EQ47
Lingmoor Dr, Wat. WD25 60 BW33
Ling Rd, E16 291 P6
Erith DA8 167 FC79
Lingrove Gdns, Buck.H. IG9 102 EH48
Lings Coppice, SE21 182 DR89
Lingwell Rd, SW17 180 DE90
Lingwood Gdns, Islw. TW7 157 CE80
Lingwood Rd, E5 122 DU59
Linhope St, NW1 284 E4
Linington Av, Chesh. HP5 56 AU30
Link, The, SE9 185 EN90
W3 138 CP72
Eastcote HA5 116 BW59
Enfield EN3 83 DY39
Northolt UB5
off Eastcote La 116 BZ64
Slough SL2 132 AV72
Wembley HA0
off Nathans Rd 117 CJ60
Link Av, Wok. GU22 227 BD115
Link Cl, Hat. AL10 45 CV18
Link Dr, Hat. AL10 45 CV18
Linkfield, Brom. BR2 204 EG100
Welwyn Garden City AL7 29 CY13
West Molesey KT8 196 CA97
Linkfield Cor, Red. RH1
off Hatchlands Rd 250 DE133
Linkfield Gdns, Red. RH1
off Hatchlands Rd 250 DE134
Linkfield La, Red. RH1 250 DE133
Linkfield Rd, Islw. TW7 157 CF82
Linkfield St, Red. RH1 250 DE134
Link La, Wall. SM6 219 DK107
Linklea Cl, NW9 96 CS52
Sch Link Prim Sch, The, Croy. CR0
off Croydon Rd 219 DL105
Link Rd, N11 98 DG49
Addlestone KT15
off Weybridge Rd 212 BL105
Chenies WD3 73 BA37
Dagenham RM9 147 FB68
Datchet SL3 152 AW80
Feltham TW14 175 BT87
Hemel Hempstead HP1, HP2 40 BJ17
Wallington SM6 200 DG102
Watford WD24 76 BX40
Links, The, E17 123 DY56
Cheshunt EN8 67 DX26
Walton-on-Thames KT12 195 BU103
Welwyn Garden City AL8
off Applecroft Rd 29 CV09
Links Av, Hert. SG13 32 DV08
Morden SM4 200 DA98
Romford RM2 105 FH54
Links Brow, Fetch. KT22 231 CE124
Links Cl, Ashtd. KT21 231 CJ117
Linkscroft Av, Ashf. TW15 175 BP93
Links Dr, N20 98 DA46
Elstree WD6 78 CM41
Radlett WD7 61 CF33
Sch Link Sec Sch, The,
Bedd. CR0 off Croydon Rd 219 DM105
Links Gdns, SW16 181 DN94
Links Grn Way, Cob. KT11 214 CA114
Linkside, N12 97 CZ51
Chigwell IG7 103 EQ50
New Malden KT3 198 CS96
Linkside Cl, Enf. EN2 81 DM41
Linkside Gdns, Enf. EN2 81 DM41
Links Pl, Ashtd. KT21 231 CK117
Sch Links Prim Sch, SW17
off Frinton Rd 180 DG93
Links Rd, NW2 119 CT61
SW17 180 DF93
W3 138 CN72
Ashford TW15 174 BL92
Ashtead KT21 231 CJ118
Bramley GU5 258 AY144
Epsom KT17 217 CU113
Flackwell Heath HP10 110 AC56
West Wickham BR4 203 EC102
Woodford Green IG8 102 EG50
Links Side, Enf. EN2 81 DN41
Link St, E9 279 H4
Links Vw, N3 97 CZ52
Dartford DA1 188 FJ88
St. Albans AL3 42 CB18
Links Vw Av, Brock. RH3 248 CN134
Links Vw Cl, Stan. HA7 95 CG51
Links Vw Rd, Croy. CR0 203 EA104
Hampton Hill TW12 176 CC92
Linksway, NW4 97 CX54
Northwood HA6 93 BQ53
Links Way, Beck. BR3 203 EA100
Bookham KT23 246 BY128
Croxley Green WD3 75 BQ41
Linkswood Rd, Burn. SL1 130 AJ68
Links Yd, E1 288 C6
Link Wk, Hat. AL10 45 CV17
Linkway, N4 122 DQ59
SW20 199 CV97
Link Way, Brom. BR2 204 EL101
Denham UB9 114 BG58
Hornchurch RM11 128 FL60
Pinner HA5 94 BX53
Staines-upon-Thames TW18 174 BH93
Linkway, Dag. RM8 126 EW63
Guil. GU2 242 AT133
Harlow CM20 off North Gate 35 EQ14
Rich. TW10 177 CH89
Wok. GU22 227 BC117
Linkway, The, Barn. EN5 80 DB44
Sutton SM2 218 DC109
Linkway Rd, Brwd. CM14 108 FT48
Linkwood Wk, NW1 275 P6
Linley Cres, Rom. RM7 127 FB55
Linley Rd, N17 100 DS54
★ Linley Sambourne Ho, W8 295 K5
Linnell Cl, NW11 120 DB58
Linnell Dr, NW11 120 DB58
Linnell Rd, N18 100 DU50
SE5 311 P8
Redhill RH1 266 DG135
Linnet Cl, N9 101 DX46
SE28 146 EW73
Bushey WD23 94 CC45
South Croydon CR2 221 DX110
Linnet Gro, Guil. GU4
off Partridge Way 243 BD132
Linnet Ms, SW12 180 DG87
Linnet Rd, Abb.L. WD5 59 BU31
Linnett Cl, E4 101 EC49
Linnet Ter, Ilf. IG5
off Tiptree Cres 125 EN55
Linnet Wk, Hat. AL10
off Lark Ri 45 CU20
Linnet Way, Purf. RM19 168 FP78
Linom Rd, SW4 161 DL84
Linscott Rd, E5 278 G1
Linsdell Rd, Bark. IG11 145 EQ67
Linsey Cl, Hem.H. HP3 40 BN24
Linsey St, SE16 300 C8
Linslade Cl, Houns. TW4
off Heathlands Way 176 BY85
Pinner HA5 115 BV55
Linslade Rd, Orp. BR6 224 EU107
Linstead St, NW6 273 J6
Linstead Way, SW18 179 CY87
Linsted Ct, SE9 185 ES86
Linster Gro, Borwd. WD6 78 CQ43
Lintaine Cl, W6 306 F3
Linthorpe Av, Wem. HA0 137 CJ65
Linthorpe Rd, N16 122 DS59
Cockfosters EN4 80 DE41
Linton Av, Borwd. WD6 78 CM39
Linton Cl, Mitch. CR4 200 DF101
Welling DA16 166 EV81
Linton Ct, Rom. RM1 105 FE54
Linton Gdns, E6 292 G8
Linton Glade, Croy. CR0 221 DY109
Linton Gro, SE27 181 DP92
Sch Linton Mead Prim Sch,
SE28 off Central Way 146 EV73
Linton Rd, Bark. IG11 145 EQ66
Lintons Cl, Hodd. EN11
off Essex Rd 49 EB16
Lintons La, Epsom KT17 216 CS112
Linton St, N1 277 K9
Lintott Ct, Stanw. TW19 174 BK86
Linver Rd, SW6 307 H8
Linwood, Saw. CM21 36 EY05
Linwood Cl, SE5 312 A9
Linwood Cres, Enf. EN1 82 DU39
Linzee Rd, N8 121 DL56
Lion Av, Twick. TW1 off Lion Rd 177 CF88
● Lion Business Pk,
Grav. DA12 191 GM87
Lion Cl, SE4 183 EA86
Shepperton TW17 194 BL97
Lion Ct, Borwd. WD6 78 CQ39
Hemel Hempstead HP3 58 BN25
Lionel Gdns, SE9 184 EK85
Lionel Ms, W10 282 E6
Lionel Oxley Ho, Grays RM17
off New Rd 170 GB79
Sch Lionel Prim Sch, Brent.
TW8 off Lionel Rd N 158 CL77
Lionel Rd, SE9 184 EK85
Lionel Rd N, Brent. TW8 158 CL77
Lionel Rd S, Brent. TW8 158 CM78
● Liongate Enterprise Pk,
Mitch. CR4 200 DD98
Lion Gate Gdns, Rich. TW9 158 CM83
Lion Gate Ms, SW18 180 DA87
Lion Grn Rd, Couls. CR5 235 DK115
Lion La, Red. RH1 250 DF133
Lion Mills, E2 288 D1
Lion Pk Av, Chess. KT9 216 CN105
Lion Plaza, EC2 off Lothbury 287 L8
Lion Rd, E6 293 K7
N9 100 DU47
Bexleyheath DA6 166 EZ84
Croydon CR0 202 DQ99
Twickenham TW1 177 CF88
Lions Cl, SE9 184 EJ90
Lion Way, Brent. TW8 157 CK80
Lion Wf Rd, Islw. TW7 157 CH83
Lion Yd, SW4
off Tremadoc Rd 161 DK84
Liphook Cl, Horn. RM12
off Petworth Way 127 FF63
Liphook Cres, SE23 182 DW87
Liphook Rd, Wat. WD19 94 BX49
Lippitts Hill, High Beach IG10 84 EE39
Lipsham Cl, Bans. SM7 218 DD113
Lipton Cl, SE28 off Aisher Rd 146 EW73
Lipton Rd, E1 289 J9
Lisbon Av, Twick. TW2 176 CC89
Lisbon Cl, E17 101 DZ54
Lisburne Rd, NW3 274 E1
Lisford St, SE15 312 B6
Lisgar Ter, W14 294 G8
Liskeard Cl, Chis. BR7 185 EQ93
Liskeard Gdns, SE3 315 P7
Liskeard Lo, Cat. CR3 252 DU126
Lisle Cl, SW17 181 DH91
Lisle Pl, Grays RM17 170 GA76
Lisle St, WC2 285 P10
● Lismirrane Ind Pk, Els. WD6 77 CG44
Lismore, Hem.H. HP3 41 BQ22
Lismore Circ, NW5
off Wellesley Rd 274 G2
Lismore Cl, Islw. TW7 157 CG82
Lismore Pk, Slou. SL2 132 AT72
Lismore Rd, N17 122 DR55
South Croydon CR2 220 DS107
Lismore Wk, N1 277 K4
Lissant Cl, Long Dit. KT6 197 CK101
Lissenden Gdns, NW5 120 DG63
Lissoms Rd, Chipstead CR5 234 DG118
Lisson Grn Est, NW8 284 C3
LISSON GROVE, NW8 284 B4
Lisson Gro, NW1 284 C4
NW8 284 B3
Lisson St, NW1 284 C6
Lister Av, Rom. RM3 106 FK54
Lister Cl, W3 138 CR71
Mitcham CR4 200 DE95
Sch Lister Comm Sch, E13
off St. Marys Rd 144 EH68
Lister Ct, NW9 96 CS54
Lister Dr, Nthflt. DA11 190 GC88
Lister Gdns, N18 100 DQ50
H Lister Hosp, The, SW1 309 J1
Lister Rd, E11 124 EE60
Tilbury RM18 171 GG82
Lister Wk, SE28
off Haldane Rd 146 EX73
Liston Rd, N17 100 DU53
SW4 161 DJ83
Liston Way, Wdf.Grn. IG8
off Navestock Cres 102 EJ52
Listowel Cl, SW9 310 F4
Listowel Rd, Dag. RM10 126 FA62
Listria Pk, N16 122 DS61
Litcham Spur, Slou. SL1 131 AR72
Litchfield Av, E15 281 J5
Morden SM4 199 CZ101
Litchfield Gdns, NW10 139 CU65
Cobham KT11 213 BU114
Litchfield Rd, Sutt. SM1 218 DC105
Litchfield St, WC2 285 P10
Litchfield Way, NW11 120 DB57
Guildford GU2 258 AT136
Lithos Rd, NW3 273 M4
Litten Cl, Col.Row. RM5 104 FA51
Little Acre, Beck. BR3 203 EA97
Bookham KT23 230 BZ124
St. Albans AL3 43 CD17
Little Acres, Ware SG12 33 DX07
Little Albany St, NW1 285 K4
Little Argyll St, W1 285 L9
Little Aston Rd, Rom. RM3 106 FM52
Little Belhus Cl, S.Ock. RM15 149 FU70
Little Benty, West Dr. UB7 154 BK78
LITTLE BERKHAMSTED,
Hert. SG13 47 DH18
Little Berkhamsted La,
Lt.Berk. SG13 47 DH20
Little Birch Cl, New Haw KT15 212 BK109
Little Birches, Sid. DA15 185 ES89
Little Boltons, The, SW5 295 M10
SW10 295 M10
LITTLE BOOKHAM,
Lthd. KT23 246 BY125
Little Bookham Common,
Bkhm KT23 230 BY122
Little Bookham St,
Bkhm KT23 230 BZ124
Little Bornes, SE21 182 DS91
Little Borough, Brock. RH3 264 CN135
Little Brays, Harl. CM18 52 EU16
Little Br Rd, Berk. HP4 38 AX19
Little Britain, EC1 287 J8
Littlebrook Av, Slou. SL2 131 AL70
Littlebrook Cl, Croy. CR0 203 DX100
Littlebrook Gdns, Chsht EN8 66 DW30
Jct Littlebrook Interchange,
Dart. DA1 168 FP84
Littlebrook Manor Way,
Dart. DA1 188 FN85
Little Brook Rd, Roydon CM19 50 EJ15
Little Brownings, SE23 182 DV89
Little Buntings, Wind. SL4 151 AM83
Little Burrow, Welw.G.C. AL7 29 CX11
Littlebury Rd, SW4 309 N10
Little Bury St, N9 100 DR46
Little Bushey La,
Bushey WD23 77 CD44

Little Bushey La Footpath, Bushey WD23 off Little Bushey La 95 CD45
Little Catherells, Hem.H. HP1 39 BE18
Little Cattins, Harl. CM19 51 EM19
Little Cedars, N12 98 DC49
LITTLE CHALFONT, Amer. HP7 72 AW40
Sch Little Chalfont Prim Sch, Lt.Chal. HP6 off Oakington Av 72 AY39
Little Chapels Way, Slou. SL1 131 AN74
Little Chester St, SW1 297 H6
Little Cloisters, SW1 off College Ms 298 A6
Little Coll La, EC4 off College St 287 L10
Little Coll St, SW1 298 A6
Little Collins, Outwood RH1 267 DP144
Littlecombe, SE7 164 EH79
Littlecombe Cl, SW15 179 CX86
Little Common, Stan. HA7 95 CG48
Little Common La, Bletch. RH1 251 DP132
Littlecote Cl, SW19 179 CX87
Littlecote Pl, Pnr. HA5 94 BY53
Little Cottage Pl, SE10 314 D4
Little Ct, W.Wick. BR4 204 EE103
Littlecourt Rd, Sev. TN13 256 FG124
Little Cranmore La, W.Hors. KT24 245 BP128
Littlecroft, SE9 165 EN83
Istead Rise DA13 190 GE94
Littlecroft Rd, Egh. TW20 173 AZ92
Littledale, SE2 166 EU79
Dartford DA2 188 FQ90
Little Dean's Yd, SW1 298 A6
Little Dell, Welw.G.C. AL8 29 CX07
Little Dimocks, SW12 181 DH89
Little Dormers, Ger.Cr. SL9 113 AZ56
Little Dorrit Ct, SE1 299 K4
Littledown Rd, Slou. SL1 132 AT74
Little Dragons, Loug. IG10 84 EK42
LITTLE EALING, W5 157 CJ77
Little Ealing La, W5 157 CJ77
Sch Little Ealing Prim Sch, W5 off Weymouth Av 157 CJ76
Little E Fld, Couls. CR5 235 DK121
Little Edward St, NW1 285 K2
Little Elms, Harling. UB3 155 BR80
Little Essex St, WC2 286 E10
Little Ferry Rd, Twick. TW1 off Ferry Rd 177 CH88
Littlefield Cl, N19 off Tufnell Pk Rd 121 DJ63
Kingston upon Thames KT1 off Fairfield W 198 CL96
Littlefield Rd, Edg. HA8 96 CQ52
Littleford La, Guil. GU4, GU5 259 BE142
Little Friday Rd, E4 102 EE47
Little Ganett, Welw.G.C. AL7 30 DB11
Little Gaynes Gdns, Upmin. RM14 128 FP63
Little Gaynes La, Upmin. RM14 128 FM63
Little Gearies, Ilf. IG6 125 EP56
Little George St, SW1 298 A5
Little Gerpins La, Upmin. RM14 148 FM67
Little Gra, Grnf. UB6 off Perivale La 137 CG69
Little Graylings, Abb.L. WD5 59 BS33
Little Grn, Rich. TW9 157 CK84
Little Greencroft, Chesh. HP5 54 AN27
Sch Little Grn Jun Sch, Crox.Grn WD3 off Lincoln Dr 75 BP41
Little Grn La, Cher. KT16 193 BE104
Croxley Green WD3 75 BP41
Little Grn St, NW5 275 J1
Little Gregories La, They.B. CM16 85 ER35
Little Gro, Bushey WD23 76 CB42
Littlegrove, E.Barn. EN4 80 DE44
Little Gro Av, Chsht EN7 66 DS27
Little Gro Fld, Harl. CM19 51 EQ15
Little Halliards, Walt. KT12 off Felix Rd 195 BU100
Little Hardings, Welw.G.C. AL7 30 DC08
Little Hayes, Kings L. WD4 58 BN29
Jct Little Heath, Rom. RM6 126 EV56
Little Heath, SE7 164 EL79
Chadwell Heath RM6 126 EV56
Little Heath La, Berk. HP4 39 BB21
Chobham GU24 210 AS109
Littleheath La, Cob. KT11 214 CA114
Sch Little Heath Prim Sch, Pot.B. EN6 off School Rd 64 DC30
Little Heath Rd, Bexh. DA7 166 EZ81
Chobham GU24 210 AS109
Littleheath Rd, S.Croy. CR2 220 DV108
Sch Little Heath Sch, Rom. RM6 off Hainault Rd 126 EV56
Little Henleys, Hunsdon SG12 34 EK06
Little Hide, Guil. GU1 243 BB132
Little Highwood Way, Borehamwood. CM14 108 FV46
Little Hill, Herons. WD3 73 BC44
Little Hivings, Chesh. HP5 54 AN27
★ Little Holland Ho, Cars. SM5 218 DE108
Little How Cft, Abb.L. WD5 59 BQ31
LITTLE ILFORD, E12 124 EL64
Little Ilford La, E12 125 EM63
Sch Little Ilford Sch, E12 off Browning Rd 125 EM64
Littlejohn Rd, W7 137 CF72
Orpington BR5 206 EU100
Little Julians Hill, Sev. TN13 256 FG128
Little Kiln, Gdmg. GU7 258 AS143
Little Lake, Welw.G.C. AL7 30 DB12
Little Ley, Welw.G.C. AL7 29 CY12
Jct Little London, Chig. IG7 85 ET42
Little London, Albury GU5 260 BL141
Little London Cl, Uxb. UB8 135 BP71
Little London Ct, SE1 off Mill St 300 B5
Little Marlborough St, W1 off Foubert's Pl 285 L9
Little Martins, Bushey WD23 76 CB43
Littlemead, Esher KT10 215 CD105
Little Mead, Hat. AL10 45 CV15
Woking GU21 226 AT116
Littlemede, SE9 185 EM90
Little Mimms, Hem.H. HP2 40 BK19
Littlemoor Rd, Ilf. IG1 125 ER62
Littlemore Rd, SE2 166 EU75
Little Moreton Cl, W.Byf. KT14 212 BH112
Little Moss La, Pnr. HA5 94 BY54
Little Mundells, Welw.G.C. AL7 29 CZ07
Little Newport St, WC2 285 P10
Little New St, EC4 286 F8
Little Oaks Cl, Shep. TW17 194 BM98
Little Orchard, Hem.H. HP2 40 BN18
Woking GU21 211 BA114
Woodham KT15 211 BF111
Little Orchard Cl, Abb.L. WD5 59 BR32
Pinner HA5 off Barrow Pt La 94 BY54
Little Orchard Way, Shalf. GU4 258 AY141
Little Oxhey La, Wat. WD19 94 BX50
Little Pk, Bov. HP3 57 BA28
Little Pk Dr, Felt. TW13 176 BX89
Little Pk Gdns, Enf. EN2 82 DQ41
LITTLE PARNDON, Harl. CM20 35 EP14
Sch Little Parndon Prim Sch, Harl. CM20 off Park Mead 35 EP14
Little Pipers Cl, Goffs Oak EN7 65 DP29
Little Plucketts Way, Buck.H. IG9 102 EJ46
Little Portland St, W1 285 L8
Littleport Spur, Slou. SL1 132 AS72
Little Potters, Bushey WD23 95 CD45
Little Pynchons, Harl. CM18 51 ET18
Little Queens Rd, Tedd. TW11 177 CF93
Little Queen St, Dart. DA1 188 FM87
Sch Little Reddings Prim Sch, Bushey WD23 off Harcourt Rd 76 CB43
Little Redlands, Brom. BR1 204 EL96
Little Reeves Av, Amer. HP7 72 AT39
Little Ridge, Welw.G.C. AL7 30 DA09
Little Riding, Wok. GU22 227 BB116
Little Rivers, Welw.G.C. AL7 30 DA08
Little Rd, Croy. CR0 off Lower Addiscombe Rd 202 DS102
Hayes UB3 155 BT75
Hemel Hempstead HP2 40 BM19
Little Roke Av, Ken. CR8 219 DP114
Little Roke Rd, Ken. CR8 220 DQ114
Littlers Cl, SW19 off Runnymede 200 DD95
Little Russell St, WC1 286 A7
Little Russets, Hutt. CM13 off Hutton Village 109 GE45
Little St. James's St, SW1 297 L3
Little St. Leonards, SW14 158 CQ83
Little Sanctuary, SW1 297 P5
Little Shardeloes, Amer. HP7 55 AN39
Little Smith St, SW1 297 P6
Little Somerset St, E1 288 A9
Little Spring, Chesh. HP5 54 AP28
Sch Little Spring Prim Sch, Chesh. HP5 off Greenway 54 AP28
Little Stock Rd, Chsht EN7 66 DR26
Littlestone Cl, Beck. BR3 183 EA93
Little Strand, NW9 97 CT54
Little Stream Cl, Nthwd. HA6 93 BS50
Little St, Guil. GU2 242 AV130
Waltham Abbey EN9 off Greenwich Way 83 EC36
Little Sutton La, Slou. SL3 153 BC78
Little Thistle, Welw.G.C. AL7 30 DC12
Little Thrift, Petts Wd BR5 205 EQ98
LITTLE THURROCK, Grays RM17 170 GD76
Sch Little Thurrock Prim Sch, Grays RM17 off Rectory Rd 170 GD76
Little Titchfield St, W1 285 L7
LITTLETON, Guil. GU3 258 AU140
Shep. TW17 195 BP97
Littleton Av, E4 102 EF46
Sch Littleton C of E Inf Sch, Littleton TW17 off Rectory Cl 194 BN97
Littleton Cres, Har. HA1 117 CF61
Littleton Ho, SW1 off Lupus St 309 L1
Littleton La, Littleton GU3 258 AU139
Reigate RH2 265 CX136
Shepperton TW17 194 BK101
Littleton Rd, Ashf. TW15 175 BQ94
Harrow HA1 117 CF61
Littleton St, SW18 180 DC89
Little Trinity La, EC4 287 K10
Little Tumners Ct, Gdmg. GU7 258 AS144
Little Turnstile, WC1 286 C8
★ Little Venice (Waterbuses), W2 283 N6
Little Wade, Welw.G.C. AL7 29 CZ12
Little Wk, Harl. CM20 51 EQ15
Little Warren Cl, Guil. GU4 259 BB136
Littlewick Common, Knap. GU21 226 AS115
Littlewick Rd, Wok. GU21 210 AW114
Little Widbury, Ware SG12 33 DZ06
Little Widbury La, Ware SG12 33 DZ06
Little Windmill Hill, Chipper. WD4 57 BE32
Littlewood, SE13 183 EC85
Little Wd, Sev. TN13 257 FJ122
Littlewood Cl, W13 157 CH76
Little Wd Cl, Orp. BR5 206 EU95
LITTLE WOODCOTE, Cars. SM5 218 DG111
Little Woodcote Est, Cars. SM5 218 DG111
Wallington SM6 218 DG111
Little Woodcote La, Cars. SM5 219 DH112
Purley CR8 219 DH112
Wallington SM6 219 DH112
Little Woodlands, Wind. SL4 151 AM83
Littleworth Av, Esher KT10 215 CD106
Littleworth Common Rd, Esher KT10 197 CD104
Littleworth La, Esher KT10 215 CD105
Littleworth Pl, Esher KT10 215 CD105
Littleworth Rd, Burn. SL1 111 AK61
Esher KT10 215 CE105
Little Youngs, Welw.G.C. AL8 29 CW09
Litton Ct, Loud. HP10 88 AC53
Livermere Rd, E8 278 A8
Liverpool Gro, SE17 311 K1
Liverpool Rd, E10 123 EC58
E16 291 K6
N1 276 F7
N7 276 E4
W5 157 CK75
Kingston upon Thames KT2 178 CN94
St. Albans AL1 43 CE20
Slough SL1 131 AP72
Thornton Heath CR7 202 DQ97
Watford WD18 75 BV43
⇌ Liverpool Street 287 N7
⊖ Liverpool Street 287 N7
⊖ Liverpool Street 287 N7
Liverpool St, EC2 287 N7
Liveryman Wk, Green. DA9 off Capability Way 169 FW84
Livesey Cl, SE28 165 EQ76
Kingston upon Thames KT1 198 CM97
Livesey Pl, SE15 312 D2
Livingstone Ct, E10 off Matlock Rd 123 EC58
Barnet EN5 off Christchurch La 79 CY40
Livingstone Gdns, Grav. DA12 191 GK92
H Livingstone Hosp, Dart. DA1 188 FM87
Livingstone Pl, E14 314 E1
Sch Livingstone Prim Sch, New Barn. EN4 off Baring Rd 80 DD41
Livingstone Rd, E17 123 EB58
N13 99 DL51
SW11 off Winstanley Rd 160 DD83
Caterham CR3 236 DR122
Gravesend DA12 191 GK92
Hounslow TW3 156 CC84
Southall UB1 136 BX73
Thornton Heath CR7 202 DQ96
Livingstone Ter, Rain. RM13 147 FE67
Livingstone Wk, SW11 160 DD83
Hemel Hempstead HP2 40 BM16
Sch Livity School, The, SW16 181 DM89
Livonia St, W1 285 M9
Lizard St, EC1 287 K3
Lizban St, SE3 164 EH80
Llanbury Cl, Chal.St.P. SL9 90 AY52
Llanelly Rd, NW2 119 CZ61
Llanover Rd, SE18 165 EN79
Wembley HA9 117 CK62
Llanthony Rd, Mord. SM4 200 DD100
Llanvanor Rd, NW2 119 CZ61
Llewellyn St, SE16 300 D5
Lloyd Av, SW16 201 DL95
Coulsdon CR5 218 DG114
Lloyd Baker St, WC1 286 D3
Lloyd Ct, Pnr. HA5 116 BX57
Lloyd Ms, Enf. EN3 83 EA38
Tram Lloyd Park 220 DT105
Lloyd Pk, E17 101 EA54
Lloyd Pk Av, Croy. CR0 220 DT105
Lloyd Rd, E6 145 EM67
E17 123 DX56
Dagenham RM9 146 EZ65
Worcester Park KT4 199 CW104
Lloyd's Av, EC3 287 P9
★ Lloyd's of London, EC3 287 N9
Lloyds Pl, SE3 315 K9
Lloyd Sq, WC1 286 E2
Lloyd's Row, EC1 286 F3
Lloyd St, WC1 286 E2
Lloyds Way, Beck. BR3 203 DY99
Lloyd Vil, SE4 314 A8
Sch Lloyd Williamson Sch, W10 282 E6
Loampit Hill, SE13 314 B9
Jct Loampit Vale, SE13 314 E10
Loampit Vale, SE13 314 D10
Loanda Cl, E8 278 A8
Loates La, Wat. WD17 76 BW41
Loats Rd, SW2 181 DL86
Lobelia Cl, E6 292 G6
Local Board Rd, Wat. WD17 76 BX43
Locarno Rd, W3 138 CQ74
Greenford UB6 136 CC70
Lochaber Rd, SE13 164 EE84
Lochaline St, W6 306 B2
Lochan Cl, Hayes UB4 136 BY70
Loch Cres, Edg. HA8 96 CM49
Lochinvar Cl, Slou. SL1 151 AP75
Lochinvar St, SW12 181 DH87
Sch Lochinver Ho Sch, Pot.B. EN6 off Heath Rd 64 DB30
Lochmere Cl, Erith DA8 167 FB79
Lochnagar St, E14 290 F7
Lochnell Rd, Berk. HP4 38 AT17
Lock Av, Maid. SL6 130 AC69
Lock Bldg, The, E15 280 E10
Lock Chase, SE3 164 EE83
Lock Cl, Sthl. UB2 off Navigator Dr 156 CC75
Woodham KT15 211 BE113
Locke Cl, Rain. RM13 147 FF65
Locke Gdns, Slou. SL3 152 AW75
Locke Ho, N16 off Stamford Hill 122 DS60
Locke King Cl, Wey. KT13 212 BN108
Locke King Rd, Wey. KT13 212 BN108
Lockers Pk La, Hem.H. HP1 40 BH20
Sch Lockers Pk Sch, Hem.H. HP1 off Lockers Pk La 40 BH20
Lockesfield Pl, E14 302 D10
Lockesley Dr, Orp. BR5 205 ET100
Lockesley Sq, Surb. KT6 off Lovelace Gdns 197 CK100
Lockestone, Wey. KT13 212 BM107
Lockestone Cl, Wey. KT13 212 BM107
Locket Rd, Har. HA3 117 CE55
Locket Rd Ms, Har. HA3 117 CE55
Lockets Cl, Wind. SL4 151 AL81
Locke Way, Wok. GU21 off The Broadway 227 AZ117
Lockfield Av, Enf. EN3 83 DY40
Lockfield Dr, Wok. GU21 226 AT118
Lockgate Cl, E9 279 N2
Lockhart Cl, N7 276 C4
Enfield EN3 82 DV43
Lockhart Rd, Cob. KT11 214 BW113
Watford WD17 off Church Rd 75 BU39
Lockhart St, E3 289 P5
Lock Ho, NW1 off Oval Rd 275 H7
● Lock Ho Ind Est, Hert. SG13 32 DS08
Lockhursthatch La, Far.Grn GU5 260 BM144
Lockhurst St, E5 123 DX63
Lockie Pl, SE25 202 DU97
Lockier Wk, Wem. HA9 117 CK62
Lockington Rd, SW8 309 K6
Lock Island, Shep. TW17 194 BN103
Lock La, Wok. GU22 228 BH116
Lockley Cres, Hat. AL10 45 CV16
Lock Mead, Maid. SL6 130 AC69
Lockmead Rd, N15 122 DU58
SE13 314 F10
Lock Ms, NW1 275 N4
Lockner Holt, Chilw. GU4 259 BF141
Lock Path, Dorney SL4 151 AL79
Lock Rd, Guil. GU1 242 AX131
Richmond TW10 177 CJ91
Lockside, E14 off Northey St 289 M10
Locks La, Mitch. CR4 200 DF95
Locksley Dr, Wok. GU21 off Robin Hood Rd 226 AT118
Locksley Est, E14 289 N8
Locksley St, E14 289 N7
Locksmeade Rd, Rich. TW10 177 CJ91
Locksons Cl, E14 290 C7
Lockswood Cl, Barn. EN4 80 DF42
Lockton St, W10 282 C10
Lockwell Rd, Dag. RM10 126 EZ62
Lockwood Cl, SE26 183 DX91
Lockwood Ho, E5 off Mount Pleasant Hill 122 DW61
SE11 off Kennington Oval 310 E3
● Lockwood Ind Pk, N17 122 DV55
Lockwood Path, Wok. GU21 211 BD113
Lockwood Pl, E4 101 EA51
Lockwood Sq, SE16 300 E6
Lockwood Wk, Rom. RM1 off Western Rd 127 FE57
Lockwood Way, E17 101 DX54
Chessington KT9 216 CN106
Lockyer Est, SE1 299 M4
Lockyer Ms, Enf. EN3 83 EB38
Lockyer Rd, Purf. RM19 168 FQ79
Lockyer St, SE1 299 M5
Locomotive Dr, Felt. TW14 175 BU88
Locton Grn, E3 279 P8
Loddiges Rd, E9 278 G6
Loddon Spur, Slou. SL1 132 AS73
Loder Cl, Wok. GU21 211 BD113
Loder St, SE15 312 G6
Lodge Av, SW14 158 CS83
Croydon CR0 201 DN104
Dagenham RM8, RM9 146 EU67
Dartford DA1 188 FJ86
Elstree WD6 78 CM43
Harrow HA3 118 CL56
Romford RM2 127 FG56
Jct Lodge Av Junct, Bark. IG11 146 EU67
Lodgebottom Rd, Lthd. KT22 248 CM127
Lodge Cl, N18 100 DQ50
Chigwell IG7 104 EU48
Edgware HA8 96 CM51
Englefield Green TW20 172 AX92
Epsom KT17 off Howell Hill Gro 217 CW110
Fetcham KT22 231 CD122
Hertford SG14 32 DQ07
Hutton CM13 109 GE45
Isleworth TW7 157 CH81
North Holmwood RH5 263 CJ140
Orpington BR6 206 EV102
Slough SL1 151 AQ75
Stoke D'Abernon KT11 230 BZ115
Uxbridge UB8 134 BJ70
Wallington SM6 200 DG102
Lodge Ct, Horn. RM12 128 FL61
Wembley HA0 118 CL64
Lodge Cres, Orp. BR6 206 EV102
Waltham Cross EN8 67 DX34
Lodge Dr, N13 99 DN49
Hatfield AL9 45 CX15
Loudwater WD3 74 BJ42
Lodge End, Crox.Grn WD3 75 BR42
Radlett WD7 61 CH34
Lodgefield, Welw.G.C. AL7 29 CY06
Lodge Gdns, Beck. BR3 203 DZ99
Lodge Hall, Harl. CM18 51 ES19
Lodge Hill, SE2 166 EV80
Ilford IG4 124 EL56
Purley CR8 235 DN115
Welling DA16 166 EV80
Lodgehill Pk Cl, Har. HA2 116 CB61
Lodge La, N12 98 DC50
Bexley DA5 186 EX86
Chalfont St. Giles HP8 73 AZ41
Grays RM16, RM17 170 GA75
New Addington CR0 221 EA107
Redhill RH1 266 DE143
Romford RM5 104 FA52
South Holmwood RH5 264 CL144
Waltham Abbey EN9 83 ED35
Westerham TN16 255 EQ127
Lodge Pl, Sutt. SM1 218 DB106
Lodge Rd, NW4 119 CW56
NW8 284 B3
Bromley BR1 184 EH94
Croydon CR0 201 DP100
Epping CM16 off Crown Hill 69 EN34
Fetcham KT22 230 CC122
Wallington SM6 219 DH106
Sch Lodge Sch, Commonweal Lo, Pur. CR8 off Woodcote La 219 DK112
Downside Lo, Pur. CR8 off Woodcote La 219 DK111
Lodge Vil, Wdf.Grn. IG8 102 EF52
Lodge Wk, Warl. CR6 237 EA116
Lodge Way, Ashf. TW15 174 BL89
Shepperton TW17 195 BQ96
Windsor SL4 151 AL83
Lodore Gdns, NW9 118 CS57
Lodore Grn, Uxb. UB10 114 BL62
Lodore St, E14 290 E9
Loewen Rd, Grays RM16 171 GG76
Lofthouse Pl, Chess. KT9 215 CJ107
Loftie St, SE16 300 D5
Lofting Rd, N1 276 E7
Loftus Rd, W12 139 CV74
Barking IG11 145 EQ65
Logan Cl, E20 280 D3
Enfield EN3 83 DX39
Hounslow TW4 156 BZ83
Logan Ct, Rom. RM1 off Logan Ms 127 FE57
Logan Ms, W8 295 J8
Romford RM1 127 FE57
Logan Pl, W8 295 J8
Logan Rd, N9 100 DV47
Wembley HA9 118 CL61
Loggetts, The, SE21 182 DS90
Logmore La, Dor. RH4 262 CB138
Logs Hill, Brom. BR1 184 EL94
Chislehurst BR7 184 EL94
Logs Hill Cl, Chis. BR7 204 EL95
Lohmann Ho, SE11 off Kennington Oval 310 E2
Lois Dr, Shep. TW17 195 BP99
Lolesworth Cl, E1 288 A7
Lollards Cl, Amer. HP6 55 AQ37
Lollard St, SE11 298 D8
Lollesworth La, W.Hors. KT24 245 BQ126
Loman Path, S.Ock. RM15 149 FT72
Loman St, SE1 299 H4
Lomas Cl, Croy. CR0 221 EC108
Lomas Dr, E8 278 B6
Lomas St, E1 288 D6
Lombard Av, Enf. EN3 82 DW39
Ilford IG3 125 ES60
● Lombard Business Pk, SW19 200 DB96
Lombard Ct, EC3 287 M10
W3 off Crown St 138 CP74
Lombard La, EC4 286 F9
Lombard Rd, N11 99 DH50
SW11 308 A9
SW19 200 DB96
Jct Lombard Rbt, Croy. CR0 201 DM101
Lombards, The, Horn. RM11 128 FM59
Lombard St, EC3 287 M9
Horton Kirby DA4 208 FQ99
Lombard Wall, SE7 304 A7
Lombardy Cl, Hem.H. HP2 41 BR21
Ilford IG6 off Hazel La 103 EP52
Woking GU21 off Nethercote Av 226 AT117
Lombardy Dr, Berk. HP4 38 AX20
Lombardy Pl, W2 295 L1
Lombardy Retail Pk, Hayes UB3 135 BV73
Lombardy Way, Borwd. WD6 78 CL39
Lomond Cl, N15 122 DS56
Wembley HA0 138 CM66
Lomond Gdns, S.Croy. CR2 221 DY108
Lomond Gro, SE5 311 L4
Lomond Rd, Hem.H. HP2 40 BK16
Loncin Mead Av, New Haw KT15 212 BJ109
Loncroft Rd, SE5 311 P2
Londesborough Rd, N16 122 DS63
Londinium Twr, E1 off Mansell St 288 B10
Sch London Acad, Edg. HA8 off Spur Rd 96 CM49
Coll London Acad of Computing & Electronics, SW17 off Upper Tooting Rd 180 DF90
Coll London Acad of Management Sciences, Ilf. IG1 off Cranbrook Rd 125 EN61
Coll London Acad of Music & Dramatic Art, W14 294 D10
★ London Aquatics Cen, E20 280 E7
★ London Biggin Hill Airport, West. TN16 222 EK113
★ London Brass Rubbing Cen (St. Martin-in-the-Fields Ch), WC2 298 A1
⇌ London Bridge 299 N3
⊖ London Bridge 299 N3
London Br, EC4 299 M2
SE1 299 M2
Riv London Bridge City Pier 299 N2
★ London Bridge Experience & The London Tombs, The, SE1 299 M2
H London Br Hosp, SE1 299 M2
London Br St, SE1 299 L3
Coll London Business Sch, NW1 284 E4
★ London Canal Mus, The, N1 off New Wf Rd 276 B10
London Cen Mkts, EC1 286 G6
★ London Cen Mosque, NW8 284 D2
★ London City Airport, E16 304 G2
DLR London City Airport 304 G2
Coll London City Coll, SE1 298 E3
H London Clinic, The, W1 285 H5
★ London Coliseum, WC2 298 A1
Coll London Coll of Beauty Therapy, W1 285 L9
Uni London Coll of Communication, SE1 299 H7
Uni London Coll of Fashion, Curtain Rd, EC2 287 P4
John Princes St, W1 285 K8
Lime Gro, W12 294 A4
Mare St, E8 278 F6
LONDON COLNEY, St.Alb. AL2 62 CL26
London Colney Bypass, Lon.Col. AL2 61 CK25
Sch London Colney JMI Sch, Lon.Col. AL2 off Alexander Rd 61 CK26
Jct London Colney Rbt, St.Alb. AL2 43 CJ24
London Designer Outlet, Wem. HA9 118 CN63
★ London Dungeon, The, SE1 299 M3
Coll London Electronics Coll, SW5 295 L10
London End, Beac. HP9 89 AM54
Riv London Eye Pier 298 C4
London Fields 278 E7
London Flds, E8 278 E6
London Flds E Side, E8 278 E7
Sch London Flds Prim Sch, E8 278 E8
London Flds W Side, E8 278 D6
★ London Fire Brigade Mus, SE1 299 J4
★ London Gatwick Airport, Gat. RH6 268 DD153
London Gatwick Airport 269 DH152
★ London Heathrow Airport, Houns. TW6 155 BP81
London Heathrow Airport Central 155 BP83
London Heathrow Airport Terminal 4 175 BQ85
H London Indep Hosp, E1 289 J6
● London Ind Est, E6 293 M6
London La, E8 278 F6
Bromley BR1 184 EF94
East Horsley KT24 245 BU131
Shere GU5 260 BN138
London Master Bakers Almshouses, E10 off Lea Br Rd 123 EB58
★ London Met Archives, EC1 286 F4
Uni London Met Uni - London City Campus, Calcutta Ho, E1 288 B8
Central Ho, E1 288 C8
Commercial Rd, E1 288 D8
Goulston St, E1 288 A8
Jewry St, EC3 288 A9
Moorgate, EC2 287 M7
Students Union, E1 288 B8
Tower Hill, EC3 288 A10
Whitechapel High St, E1 288 B8
Uni London Met Uni - London N Campus, Carleton Gra Hall of Res, N7 275 P1
Dept of Architecture, N7 276 F4
Eden Gro, N7 276 D2
Harglenis, N7 276 E2
Ladbroke Ho, N5 277 H2
Learning Cen, N7 276 D1
Science Cen, N7 276 E1
Stapleton Ho, N7 276 D2
The Arc Hall of Res, N7 off Holloway Rd 121 DL63
Tower Bldg, N7 276 E2
Tufnell Pk Hall of Res, N7 off Huddleston Rd 121 DJ62
London Ms, W2 284 B9
★ London Motor Mus, Hayes UB3 155 BT76
★ London Mus of Water & Steam, Brent. TW8 158 CM78
Sch London Nautical Sch, SE1 298 F2

L

Sch London Oratory Sch, The, SW6 307 L4
★ London Palladium, W1 285 L9
★ London Peace Pagoda, SW11 308 F4
★ London Regatta Cen, E16 304 F1
London Rd, E13 281 N10
SE1 298 G6
SE23 182 DV88
SW16 201 DM95
SW17 200 DF96
Abridge RM4 85 ET42
Amersham HP7 55 AQ40
Ashford TW15 174 BH90
Aveley RM15 148 FM74
Barking IG11 145 EP66
Beaconsfield HP9 89 AM54
Beddington Corner CR4 200 DG101
Berkhamsted HP4 38 AY20
Borehamwood WD6 62 CN34
Brentwood CM14 108 FS49
Bromley BR1 184 EF94
Bushey WD23 76 BY44
Caterham CR3 236 DR123
Chadwell Heath RM6, RM7 126 FA58
Chalfont St. Giles HP8 90 AW47
Crayford DA1 187 FD85
Croydon CR0 201 DP101
Datchet SL3 152 AV80
Dorking RH4, RH5 247 CJ133
Dunton Green TN13 241 FD118
Enfield EN2 82 DR41
Englefield Green TW20 192 AV95
Ewell KT17 217 CT109
Farningham DA4 208 FL100
Feltham TW14 174 BH90
Gatwick RH6 268 DF150
Grays RM17, RM20 169 FW79
Greenhithe DA9 189 FS86
Guildford GU1, GU4 243 BB129
Halstead TN14 225 FB112
Harrow HA1 117 CE61
Hemel Hempstead HP1, HP3 40 BK24
Hertford SG13 32 DT10
High Wycombe HP10 88 AD54
Hounslow TW3 156 CC83
Isleworth TW7 157 CF82
Kingston upon Thames KT2 198 CM96
Mitcham CR4 200 DF96
Morden SM4 200 DA99
Northfleet DA11 190 GD86
Old Harlow CM17 52 EV16
Potter Street CM17 52 EW18
Redhill RH1 250 DG132
Reigate RH2 250 DA134
Rickmansworth WD3 92 BM47
St. Albans AL1 43 CH24
Sawbridgeworth CM21 52 EW15
Send GU23 243 BC128
Sevenoaks TN13 256 FF123
Shenley WD7 62 CM33
Slough SL3 153 AZ78
Staines-upon-Thames TW18 173 BF91
Stanford Rivers CM5 87 FH36
Stanmore HA7 95 CJ50
Stapleford Tawney RM4 87 FC40
Stone DA2 188 FP87
Sutton SM3 199 CX104
Swanley BR8 207 FC95
Swanscombe DA10 189 FV85
Thornton Heath CR7 201 DN99
Thornwood CM17 52 EV23
Tilbury RM18 171 GG82
Twickenham TW1 177 CG85
Virginia Water GU25 192 AU97
Wallington SM6 219 DH105
Ware SG12 33 DY07
Wembley HA9 138 CL65
Westerham TN16 239 EQ123
● London Rd Business Pk, St.Alb. AL1 43 CF22
London Rd E, Amer. HP7 72 AT42
⇌ London Road (Guildford) 242 AY134
London Rd N, Merst. RH1 251 DH125
London Rd Purfleet, Purf. RM19 168 FN78
Jct London Rd Rbt, Twick. TW1 177 CG86
London Rd S, Merst. RH1 250 DG130
London Rd W, Amer. HP7 55 AQ40
London Rd W Thurrock, Grays RM20 169 FS79
Uni London Sch of Economics & Political Science, WC2 286 D9
Coll London Sch of Flying, Borwd. WD6 *off Hogg La* 77 CF42
Uni London Sch of Hygiene & Tropical Medicine, WC1 285 P6
Coll London Sch of Jewish Studies, NW4 *off Albert Rd* 119 CX56
Coll London Sch of Theology, Nthwd. HA6 *off Green La* 93 BR51
Londons Cl, Upmin. RM14 128 FQ64
London Silver Vaults, WC2 286 E7
Uni London S Bk Uni, SE1 299 H6
Caxton Ho, SE1 298 G6
● London Sq, Guil. GU1 242 AY134
London Stile, W4 *off Wellesley Rd* 158 CN78
★ London Stone, EC4 287 L10
London St, EC3 287 P10
W2 284 A9
Chertsey KT16 194 BG101
★ London Television Cen, SE1 298 E2
London Ter, E2 288 C1
Coll London Theological Seminary, N3 *off Hendon La* 97 CY54
★ London Tombs, The, SE1 299 M2
★ London Transport Mus, WC2 286 B10
London Trocadero, The, W1 297 N1
London Wall, EC2 287 K7
London Wall Bldgs, EC2 287 M7
Londrina Ct, Berk. HP4 38 AX19
Londrina Ter, Berk. HP4 38 AX19
Lone Oak, Smallfield RH6 269 DP150
Lonesome La, Reig. RH2 266 DB138
Sch Lonesome Prim Sch, Mitch. CR4 *off Grove Rd* 201 DH96
Lonesome Way, SW16 201 DH95
Long Acre, WC2 286 A10
Orpington BR6 206 EX103
Longacre, Harl. CM17 36 EV11
Longacre Pl, Cars. SM5 *off Beddington Gdns* 218 DG107
Longacre Rd, E17 101 ED53
Longacres, St.Alb. AL4 43 CK20
Longaford Way, Hutt. CM13 109 GC46
Long Arrotts, Hem.H. HP1 40 BH18
Long Banks, Harl. CM18 51 ER19
Long Barn Cl, Wat. WD25 59 BU32
Longbeach Rd, SW11 160 DF83
Longberrys, NW2 119 CZ62
Longboat Row, Sthl. UB1 136 BZ72
Long Bottom La, Beac. HP9 89 AR52
Longbourn, Wind. SL4 151 AN83
Longbourne Grn, Gdmg. GU7 258 AS143
Longbourne Way, Cher. KT16 193 BF100
Longboyds, Cob. KT11 213 BV114
Longbridge Ho, E16 305 N1
Longbridge Rd, Bark. IG11 145 EQ66
Dagenham RM8 126 EU63
Horley RH6 268 DF150
Jct Longbridge Rbt, Horl. RH6 268 DE149
Longbridge Vw, Chipstead CR5 234 DF120
Longbridge Wk, Horl. RH6 268 DF150
Longbridge Way, SE13 183 EC85
Cowley UB8 134 BH68
London Gatwick Airport RH6 268 DF150
Longbury Cl, Orp. BR5 206 EV97
Longbury Dr, Orp. BR5 206 EV97
Longchamp Cl, Horl. RH6 269 DJ148
Long Chaulden, Hem.H. HP1 39 BE20
Longcliffe Path, Wat. WD19 93 BU48
Long Cl, Farn.Com. SL2 131 AP66
Sch Long Cl Sch, Slou. SL3 *off Upton Ct Rd* 152 AU76
Long Copse Cl, Bkhm KT23 230 CB123
Long Ct, Purf. RM19 168 FN77
Longcourt Ms, E11 124 EJ56
Longcroft, SE9 185 EM90
Watford WD19 93 BV45
Longcroft Av, Bans. SM7 218 DC114
Longcroft Dr, Wal.Cr. EN8 67 DZ34
Longcrofte Rd, Edg. HA8 95 CK52
Longcroft Gdns, Welw.G.C. AL8 29 CX10
Longcroft Grn, Welw.G.C. AL8 *off Stanborough Rd* 29 CX10
Longcroft La, Hem.H. HP3 57 BC28
Welwyn Garden City AL8 29 CX10
Longcroft Ri, Loug. IG10 85 EN43
Longcroft Rd, SE5 312 A2
Map.Cr. WD3 91 BD50
Longcrofts, Wal.Abb. EN9 *off Roundhills* 68 EE34
LONGCROSS, Cher. KT16 192 AU104
⇌ Longcross 192 AT102
Longcross Rd, Longcr. KT16 192 AY104
Long Deacon Rd, E4 102 EE46
Longdean Pk, Hem.H. HP3 40 BN24
Sch Longdean Sch, Hem.H. HP3 *off Rumballs Rd* 41 BP23
LONG DITTON, Surb. KT6 197 CJ102
Sch Long Ditton Inf & Nurs Sch, Long Dit. KT6 *off Ditton Hill Rd* 197 CJ102
Sch Long Ditton St. Mary's C of E Jun Sch, Long Dit. KT7 *off Sugden Rd* 197 CH102
Longdon Ct, Rom. RM1 127 FF57
Longdon Wd, Kes. BR2 222 EL105
Longdown La N, Epsom KT17 217 CU114
Longdown La S, Epsom KT17 217 CU114
Longdown Rd, SE6 183 EA91
Epsom KT17 217 CU114
Guildford GU4 259 BB137
Long Dr, W3 138 CS72
Burnham SL1 130 AJ69
Greenford UB6 136 CB67
Ruislip HA4 116 BX63
Long Dyke, Guil. GU1 243 BB132
Long Elmes, Har. HA3 94 CB53
Long Elms, Abb.L. WD5 59 BR33
Long Elms Cl, Abb.L. WD5 59 BR33
Long Fallow, St.Alb. AL2 60 CA27
Longfellow Dr, Hutt. CM13 109 GC45
Longfellow Rd, E17 123 DZ58
Worcester Park KT4 199 CU103
Longfellow Way, SE1 300 B9
Long Fld, NW9 96 CS52
Longfield, Brom. BR1 204 EF95
Harlow CM18 52 EU17
Hedgerley SL2 111 AR61
Hemel Hempstead HP3 41 BP22
Loughton IG10 84 EJ43
Longfield Av, E17 123 DY56
NW7 97 CU52
W5 137 CJ73
Enfield EN3 82 DW37
Hornchurch RM11 127 FF59
Wallington SM6 200 DG102
Wembley HA9 118 CL60
Longfield Cres, SE26 182 DW90
Tadworth KT20 233 CW120
Longfield Dr, SW14 178 CP85
Amersham HP6 55 AP38
Mitcham CR4 180 DE94
Longfield Est, SE1 300 B9
Longfield La, Chsht EN7 66 DU27
Sch Longfield Prim Sch, Har. HA2 *off Dukes Av* 116 CA58
Longfield Rd, W5 137 CJ73
Chesham HP5 54 AM29
Dorking RH4 263 CF137
Longfield St, SW18 180 DA87
Longfield Wk, W5 137 CJ72
LONGFORD, Sev. TN13 241 FD120
West Dr. UB7 154 BH81
Longford Av, Felt. TW14 175 BS86
Southall UB1 136 CA73
Staines-upon-Thames TW19 174 BL88
Longford Cl, Hmptn H. TW12 176 CA91
Hanworth TW13 176 BY90
Hayes UB4 136 BX73
Sch Longford Comm Sch, Felt. TW14 *off Tachbrook Rd* 175 BT87
Longford Ct, E5 *off Pedro St* 123 DX63
NW4 119 CX56
Epsom KT19 216 CQ105
Longford Gdns, Hayes UB4 136 BX73
Sutton SM1 200 DC104
Longford Ho, E1 *off Jubilee St* 288 G8
Longford Rd, Twick. TW2 176 CA88
Jct Longford Rbt, Stai. TW19 154 BG81
Longford St, NW1 285 K4
Longford Wk, SW2 *off Papworth Way* 181 DN87
Longford Way, Stai. TW19 174 BL88
Long Furlong Dr, Slou. SL2 131 AN70
Long Gore, Gdmg. GU7 258 AS142
Long Grn, Chig. IG7 103 ES49
Nazeing Gate EN9 68 EH25
Long Gro, Harold Wd RM3 106 FL54
Seer Green HP9 89 AQ51
Long Gro Cl, Brox. EN10 49 DY19
Long Gro Rd, Epsom KT19 216 CQ111
Longhayes Av, Rom. RM6 126 EX56
Longhayes Ct, Rom. RM6 *off Longhayes Av* 126 EX56
Longheath Dr, Bkhm KT23 230 BY124
Longheath Gdns, Croy. CR0 202 DW99
Longhedge Ho, SE26 182 DT91
Long Hedges, Houns. TW3 156 CA81
Longhedge St, SW11 309 H8
Long Hill, Wold. CR3 237 DX121
Longhill Rd, SE6 183 ED89
Longhook Gdns, Nthlt. UB5 135 BU68
Longhope Cl, SE15 312 A3
Long Ho, Harl. CM18 *off Bush Fair* 51 ET17
Longhouse Rd, Grays RM16 171 GH76
Longhurst Rd, SE13 183 ED85
Croydon CR0 202 DV100
East Horsley KT24 245 BS129
Long John, Hem.H. HP3 40 BM22
Longland Br, Sheering CM22 37 FC07
Longland Ct, SE1 300 C10
Longland Dr, N20 98 DB48
Longland Pl, Epsom KT19 216 CL112
LONGLANDS, Chis. BR7 185 EQ90
Longlands, Hem.H. HP2 40 BN20
Longlands Av, Couls. CR5 218 DG114
Longlands Cl, Chsht EN8 67 DX32
Longlands Ct, W11 283 H10
Mitcham CR4 *off Summerhill Way* 200 DG95
Longlands Pk Cres, Sid. DA15 185 ES90
Sch Longlands Prim Sch, Sid. DA15 *off Woodside Rd* 185 ES90
Sch Longlands Prim Sch & Nurs, Turnf. EN10 *off Nunsbury Dr* 67 DZ25
Longlands Rd, Sid. DA15 185 ES90
Welwyn Garden City AL7 29 CY11
Long La, EC1 287 H6
N2 98 DC54
N3 98 DB52
SE1 299 L5
Bexleyheath DA7 166 EX80
Bovingdon HP3 57 AZ31
Croydon CR0 202 DW99
Grays RM16 170 GA75
Heronsgate WD3 73 BC44
Mill End WD3 91 BF47
Stanwell TW19 174 BM87
Uxbridge UB10 134 BN69
Longleat Ho, SW1 *off Rampayne St* 297 N10
Longleat Ms, Orp. BR5 *off High St* 206 EW98
Longleat Rd, Enf. EN1 82 DS43
Longleat Way, Felt. TW14 175 BR87
Longlees, Map.Cr. WD3 91 BC50
Longleigh La, SE2 166 EW79
Bexleyheath DA7 166 EW79
Long Ley, Harl. CM20 51 ET15
Welwyn Garden City AL7 30 DC09
Longley Av, Wem. HA0 138 CM67
Longley Ct, SW8 310 A6
Longley Ms, Grays RM16 171 GF75
Longley Rd, SW17 180 DE93
Croydon CR0 201 DP101
Harrow HA1 116 CC57
Long Leys, E4 101 EB51
Longley St, SE1 300 C9
Longley Way, NW2 119 CW62
Long Lo Dr, Walt. KT12 196 BW104
Longman Ct, Hem.H. HP3 58 BL25
Longmans Cl, Wat. WD18 75 BQ44
Long Mark Rd, E16 292 E7
Longmarsh La, SE28 145 ES74
Longmarsh Vw, Sutt.H. DA4 208 FP95
Long Mead, NW9 97 CT53
Longmead, Chis. BR7 205 EN96
Guildford GU1 243 BC134
Hatfield AL10 45 CV15
Windsor SL4 151 AL81
● Longmead Business Cen, Epsom KT19 216 CR111
● Longmead Business Pk, Epsom KT19 216 CR111
Longmead Cl, Cat. CR3 236 DS122
Shenfield CM15 108 FY46
Longmead Dr, Sid. DA14 186 EX89
Longmeade, Grav. DA12 191 GM88
Longmead Ho, SE27 *off Elder Rd* 182 DQ92
● Longmead Ind Est, Epsom KT19 216 CS111
Longmead La, Slou. SL1 131 AK66
Long Meadow, NW5 275 N3
Chesham HP5 54 AQ28
Hutton CM13 109 GC47
Noak Hill RM3 106 FJ48
Riverhead TN13 256 FD121
Longmeadow, Bkhm KT23 246 BZ125
Long Meadow Cl, W.Wick. BR4 203 EC101
Longmeadow Rd, Sid. DA15 185 ES88
Longmead Rd, SW17 180 DF92
Epsom KT19 216 CR111
Hayes UB3 135 BT73
Thames Ditton KT7 197 CE101
Longmere Gdns, Tad. KT20 233 CW119
Long Mimms, Hem.H. HP2 40 BL19
Long Moor, Chsht EN8 67 DY29
Longmoore St, SW1 297 L9
Longmoor Pt, SW15 *off Norley Vale* 179 CU88
Longmore Av, Barn. EN4, EN5 80 DC44
Longmore Cl, Map.Cr. WD3 91 BF49
Longmore Gdns, Welw.G.C. AL7 29 CZ09
Longmore Rd, Hersham KT12 214 BY105
Longnor Rd, E1 289 K3
Long Orchard Dr, Penn HP10 88 AC47
Long Pk, Amer. HP6 55 AQ36
Long Pk Cl, Amer. HP6 55 AQ36
Long Pk Way, Amer. HP6 55 AQ35
Long Pond Rd, SE3 315 K7
Longport Cl, Ilf. IG6 104 EU51
Long Reach, Ock. GU23 228 BN123
West Horsley KT24 245 BP125
Long Reach Ct, Bark. IG11 145 ER68
Longreach Rd, Bark. IG11 145 ET70
Erith DA8 167 FH80
Long Readings La, Slou. SL2 131 AP70
Long Ride, The, Hat. AL9 45 CZ18
Longridge, Rad. WD7 61 CH34
Longridge Gro, Wok. GU22 211 BF114
Longridge Ho, SE1 299 K7
Longridge La, Sthl. UB1 136 CB73
Longridge Rd, SW5 295 J9
Long Ridings Av, Hutt. CM13 109 GB43
Sch Long Ridings Prim Sch, Hutt. CM13 *off Long Ridings Av* 109 GB43
Long Rd, SW4 161 DH84
Longs Cl, Wok. GU22 228 BG116
Longs Ct, Rich. TW9 *off Crown Ter* 158 CM84
Long's Ct, WC2 285 N10
Longsdon Way, Cat. CR3 236 DU124
Longshaw, Lthd. KT22 231 CG119
Sch Longshaw Prim Sch, E4 *off Longshaw Rd* 101 ED48
Longshaw Rd, E4 101 ED48
Longshore, SE8 301 N9
Longside Cl, Egh. TW20 193 BC95
Long Spring, Port.Wd AL3 43 CF16
Longspring, Wat. WD24 75 BV38
Longspring Wd, Sev. TN14 256 FF130
Longstaff Cres, SW18 180 DA86
Longstaff Rd, SW18 180 DA86
Longstone Av, NW10 139 CT66
Longstone Ct, SE1 299 K5
Longstone Rd, SW17 181 DH92
Iver SL0 133 BC68
Long St, E2 288 A2
Waltham Abbey EN9 68 EL32
Longthornton Rd, SW16 201 DJ96
Longthorpe Ct, W6 *off Invermead Cl* 159 CU76
Longton Av, SE26 182 DU91
Longton Gro, SE26 182 DV91
Longton Ho, SE11 *off Lambeth Wk* 298 D8
Longtown Cl, Rom. RM3 106 FJ50
Longtown Rd, Rom. RM3 106 FJ50
Longview, Beac. HP9 110 AF55
Long Vw, Berk. HP4 38 AU17
Longview Way, Rom. RM5 105 FD53
Longville Rd, SE11 298 G8
Long Wk, SE1 299 P6
SE18 165 EP79
SW13 158 CS82
Chalfont St. Giles HP8 72 AX41
Epsom KT18 233 CX119
New Malden KT3 198 CQ97
Waltham Abbey EN9 67 EA30
West Byfleet KT14 212 BJ114
West Horsley KT24 244 BN128
Long Wk, The, Wind. SL4 151 AR83
Longwalk Rd, Uxb. UB11 135 BP74
Longwood, Harl. CM18 51 ER20
Longwood Av, Slou. SL3 153 BB78
● Longwood Business Pk, Sun. TW16 195 BT99
Longwood Cl, Upmin. RM14 128 FQ64
Longwood Ct, Wor.Pk. KT4 199 CU103
Longwood Dr, SW15 179 CU86
Long Wd Dr, Jordans HP9 90 AT51
Longwood Gdns, Ilf. IG5, IG6 125 EM56
Longwood La, Amer. HP7 55 AR39
Longwood Rd, Hert. SG14 31 DM08
Kenley CR8 236 DR116
Sch Longwood Sch, Bushey WD23 *off Bushey Hall Dr* 76 BZ42
Longworth Cl, SE28 146 EX72
Longworth Dr, Maid. SL6 130 AC70
Long Yd, WC1 286 C5
Loning, The, NW9 118 CS56
Enfield EN3 82 DW38
Lonsdale, Hem.H. HP2 40 BL17
Lonsdale Av, E6 292 E3
Hutton CM13 109 GD44
Romford RM7 127 FC58
Wembley HA9 118 CL64
Lonsdale Cl, E6 292 G4
SE9 184 EK90
Edgware HA8 96 CM50
Pinner HA5 94 BY52
Uxbridge UB8 135 BQ71
Lonsdale Cres, Dart. DA2 188 FQ88
Ilford IG2 125 EP58
Lonsdale Dr, Enf. EN2 81 DL43
Lonsdale Gdns, Th.Hth. CR7 201 DM98
Lonsdale Ms, W11 283 H9
Richmond TW9 *off Elizabeth Cotts* 158 CN81
Lonsdale Pl, N1 276 F7
Dorking RH4 *off Lonsdale Rd* 263 CH135
Lonsdale Rd, E11 124 EF59
NW6 272 G10
SE25 202 DV98
SW13 159 CU79
W4 159 CT77
W11 283 H9
Bexleyheath DA7 166 EZ82
Dorking RH4 263 CH135
Southall UB2 156 BX76
Weybridge KT13 212 BN108
Lonsdale Sq, N1 276 F7
Lonsdale Way, Maid. SL6 150 AC78
Loobert Rd, N15 122 DS55
Looe Gdns, Ilf. IG6 125 EP55
Loom La, Rad. WD7 77 CG37
Loom Pl, Rad. WD7 77 CG36
Loop Rd, Chis. BR7 185 EQ93
Epsom KT18 *off Woodcote Side* 232 CQ116
Waltham Abbey EN9 67 EB32
Woking GU22 227 AZ121
Lopen Rd, N18 100 DS49
Loraine Cl, Enf. EN3 82 DW43
Loraine Gdns, Ashtd. KT21 232 CL117
Loraine Rd, N7 121 DM63
W4 158 CP79
Lorane Ct, Wat. WD17 75 BU40
Lord Amory Way, E14 302 E4
Lord Av, Ilf. IG5 125 EM56
Lord Chancellor Wk, Kings.T. KT2 198 CQ95
Lord Chatham's Ride, Sev. TN14 240 EX117
Lord Darby Ms, Cudham TN14 239 ER115
Lordell Pl, SW19 179 CW93
Lorden Wk, E2 288 C3
Lord Gdns, Ilf. IG5 124 EL56
Lord Hills Br, W2 283 M7
Lord Hills Rd, W2 283 M6
Lord Holland La, SW9 310 F8
Lord Knyvett Cl, Stanw. TW19 174 BK86
Lord Knyvetts Ct, Stanw. TW19 *off De Havilland Way* 174 BL86
Lord Mayors Dr, Farn.Com. SL2 111 AN64
Lord Napier Pl, W6 *off Oil Mill La* 159 CU78
Lord N St, SW1 298 A7
Lord Reith Pl, Beac. HP9 111 AM55
Lord Roberts Ms, SW6 307 L5
Lord Roberts Ter, SE18 165 EN78
★ Lord's (Marylebone CC & Mus, Middlesex CCC), NW8 284 B2
★ Lordsbury Fld, Wall. SM6 219 DJ110
Lords Cl, Felt. TW13 176 BY89
Shenley WD7 62 CL32
Lord's Cl, SE21 182 DQ89
Lordsgrove Cl, Tad. KT20 *off Whitegate Way* 233 CV120
Lordship Cl, Hutt. CM13 109 GD46
Lordship Gro, N16 122 DR61
Lordship La, N17 100 DQ53
N22 99 DN54
SE22 182 DT86
Lordship La Est, SE22 182 DU88
Sch Lordship La Prim Sch, N22 *off Lordship La* 100 DQ53
Lordship Pk, N16 122 DQ61
Lordship Pk Ms, N16 122 DQ61
Lordship Pl, SW3 308 C3
Lordship Rd, N16 122 DR61
Cheshunt EN7 66 DV30
Northolt UB5 136 BY66
Lordship Ter, N16 122 DR61
Lordsmead Rd, N17 100 DS53
Lord St, E16 305 H3
Gravesend DA12 191 GH87
Hoddesdon EN11 48 DV17
Watford WD17 76 BW41
Lord's Vw, NW8 284 B3
Lords Wd, Welw.G.C. AL7 30 DC09
Lordswood Cl, Bexh. DA6 186 EY85
Lane End DA2 189 FS91
Lord Warwick St, SE18 305 J7
Lorenzo Ho, Ilf. IG3 126 EU58
Lorenzo St, WC1 286 C2
Coll Loreto Coll, St.Alb. AL1 *off Hatfield Rd* 43 CE20
Loretto Gdns, Har. HA3 118 CL56
Lorian Cl, N12 98 DB49
Lorian Dr, Reig. RH2 250 DC133
Loriners Cl, Cob. KT11 213 BU114
Loring Rd, N20 98 DE47
SE14 313 M6
Berkhamsted HP4 38 AW20
Isleworth TW7 157 CF82
Windsor SL4 151 AM81
Loris Rd, W6 294 B7
Lorn Ct, SW9 310 E8
Lorne, The, Bkhm KT23 246 CA126
Lorne Av, Croy. CR0 203 DX101
Lorne Cl, NW8 284 D3
Slough SL1 151 AP76
Lorne Gdns, E11 124 EJ56
W11 294 D4
Croydon CR0 203 DX101
Lorne Rd, E7 124 EH63
E17 123 EA57
N4 121 DM60
Harrow HA3 95 CF54
Richmond TW10 *off Albert Rd* 178 CM85
Warley CM14 108 FW49
Lorn Rd, SW9 310 D8
Lorraine Pk, Har. HA3 95 CE52
Lorrimore Rd, SE17 311 H2
Lorrimore Sq, SE17 311 H2
Lorton Cl, Grav. DA12 191 GL89
Loseberry Rd, Clay. KT10 215 CD106
Sch Loseley Flds Prim Sch, Farnc. GU7 *off Green La* 258 AS143
★ Loseley Ho & Pk, Guil. GU3 258 AS140
Loseley Pk, Littleton GU3 258 AS140
Loseley Rd, Gdmg. GU7 258 AS143
Losfield Rd, Wind. SL4 151 AL81
Lossie Dr, Iver SL0 133 BB73
Lothair Rd, W5 157 CK75
Lothair Rd N, N4 121 DP58
Lothair Rd S, N4 121 DN59
Lothair St, SW11 *off Grant Rd* 160 DE83
Lothbury, EC2 287 L8
Lothian Av, Hayes UB4 135 BV71
Lothian Cl, Wem. HA0 117 CG63
Lothian Rd, SW9 311 H6
Lothian Wd, Tad. KT20 233 CV122
Lothrop St, W10 282 E2
Lots Rd, SW10 307 N5
Lotus Cl, SE21 182 DQ90
Lotus Rd, Bigg.H. TN16 239 EM118
Loubet St, SW17 180 DF93
Loudhams Rd, Amer. HP7 72 AW39
Loudhams Wd La, Ch.St.G. HP8 72 AX40
Loudoun Av, Ilf. IG6 125 EP57
Loudoun Rd, NW8 273 P10
LOUDWATER, H.Wyc. HP10 88 AD53
Rick. WD3 74 BK41
Loudwater Cl, Sun. TW16 195 BU98
Loudwater Dr, Loud. WD3 74 BJ42
Loudwater Hts, Loud. WD3 74 BH41
Loudwater La, Rick. WD3 74 BK42
Loudwater Ridge, Loud. WD3 74 BJ42
Loudwater Rd, Sun. TW16 195 BU98
Loughborough Est, SW9 310 F9
⇌ Loughborough Junction 311 H10
Loughborough Pk, SW9 161 DP84
Sch Loughborough Prim Sch, SW9 310 G9
Loughborough Rd, SW9 310 E8
Loughborough St, SE11 298 D10
Lough Rd, N7 276 D4
LOUGHTON, IG10 85 EM43
⊖ Loughton 84 EL43
Loughton Business Cen, Loug. IG10 85 EQ42
Loughton Ct, Wal.Abb. EN9 68 EH33
Loughton La, They.B. CM16 85 ER38
● Loughton Seedbed Cen, Loug. IG10 *off Langston Rd* 85 ER42
Loughton Way, Buck.H. IG9 102 EK46
Louisa Cl, E9 279 K8
Louisa Gdns, E1 289 J5
Louisa Ho, SW15 158 CS84
Ilford IG3 126 EU58
Louisa St, E1 289 J5
Louise Aumonier Wk, N19 *off Hillrise Rd* 121 DL59
Louise Bennett Cl, SE24 *off Shakespeare Rd* 161 DP84
Louise Ct, E11 124 EH57
Louise Gdns, Rain. RM13 147 FE69
Louise Rd, E15 281 K4
Louise Wk, Bov. HP3 57 BA28
Louis Gdns, Chis. BR7 185 EM91
Louis Ms, N10 99 DH53
Louisville Cl, Stans.Abb. SG12 33 EC11
Louisville Rd, SW17 180 DG90
Louvaine Rd, SW11 160 DD84
Louvain Rd, Green. DA9 189 FS87

Louvain Way, Wat. WD25 59 BV32
Lovage App, E6 293 H7
Lovat Cl, NW2 119 CT62
Lovat La, EC3 299 N1
Lovatt Cl, Edg. HA8 96 CP51
Lovatt Dr, Ruis. HA4 115 BT57
Lovatts, Crox.Grn WD3 74 BN42
Lovat Wk, Houns. TW5
off Cranford La 156 BY80
Loveday Rd, W13 137 CH74
Love Grn La, Iver SL0 133 BD71
Lovegrove Cl, S.Croy. CR2 220 DR110
Lovegrove Dr, Slou. SL2 131 AM70
Lovegrove St, SE1 312 D1
Lovegrove Wk, E14 302 E3
Love Hill La, Slou. SL3 133 BA73
Lovejoy La, Wind. SL4 151 AK83
Lovekyn Cl, Kings.T. KT2
off Queen Elizabeth Rd 198 CM96
Lovelace Av, Brom. BR2 205 EN100
Lovelace Cl, Eff.Junct. KT24 229 BU123
Lovelace Dr, Wok. GU22 227 BF115
Lovelace Gdns, Bark. IG11 126 EU63
Hersham KT12 214 BW106
Surbiton KT6 197 CK101
Lovelace Grn, SE9 165 EM83
Lovelace Ho, W13 137 CH73
Sch Lovelace Prim Sch,
Chess. KT9 *off Mansfield Rd* 215 CJ106
Lovelace Rd, SE21 182 DQ89
Barnet EN4 98 DE45
Surbiton KT6 197 CJ101
Lovelands La,
Lwr Kgswd KT20 250 DB127
Love La, EC2 287 K8
N17 100 DT52
SE18 305 M9
SE25 202 DV97
Abbots Langley WD5 59 BT30
Aveley RM15 168 FQ75
Bexley DA5 186 EZ86
Godstone RH9 252 DW132
Gravesend DA12 191 GJ87
Iver SL0 133 BD72
Kings Langley WD4 58 BL29
Mitcham CR4 200 DE97
Morden SM4 200 DA101
Pinner HA5 116 BY55
Surbiton KT6 197 CK103
Sutton SM3 217 CY107
Walton on the Hill KT20 249 CT126
Woodford Green IG8 103 EM51
Lovel Av, Well. DA16 166 EU82
Lovel Cl, Hem.H. HP1 40 BG20
Lovel End, Chal.St.P. SL9 90 AW52
Lovelinch Cl, SE15 313 H3
Lovell Ho, E8 278 C8
Lovell Pl, SE16 301 M6
Lovell Rd, Enf. EN1 82 DV35
Richmond TW10 177 CJ90
Southall UB1 136 CB72
Lovell Wk, Rain. RM13 147 FG65
Lovel Mead, Chal.St.P. SL9 90 AW52
Lovelock Cl, Ken. CR8 236 DQ117
Lovel Rd, Chal.St.P. SL9 90 AW52
Loveridge Ms, NW6 273 H5
Loveridge Rd, NW6 273 H5
Lovering Rd, Chsht EN7 66 DQ26
Lovers La, Green. DA9 169 FX84
Lovers Wk, N3 98 DA52
NW7 97 CZ51
SE10 315 J3
Lover's Wk, W1 296 G2
Lovet Rd, Harl. CM19 51 EN16
Lovett Dr, Cars. SM5 200 DC101
Lovett Rd, Hare. UB9 114 BJ55
London Colney AL2 61 CG26
Staines-upon-Thames TW18 173 BB91
Lovett's Pl, SW18
off Old York Rd 160 DB84
Lovett Way, NW10 118 CQ64
Love Wk, SE5 311 L8
Lovibonds Av, Orp. BR6 223 EP105
West Drayton UB7 134 BM72
Lowbell La, Lon.Col. AL2 62 CL27
Lowbrook Rd, Ilf. IG1 125 EP64
Lowburys, Dor. RH4 263 CH139
Low Cl, Green. DA9 189 FU85
Low Cross Wd La, SE21 182 DT90
Lowdell Cl, West Dr. UB7 134 BL72
Lowden Rd, N9 100 DV46
SE24 161 DP84
Southall UB1 136 BY73
Lowe, The, Chig. IG7 104 EU50
Lowe Av, E16 291 P7
Lowe Cl, Chig. IG7 104 EU50
Lowell St, E14 289 M9
Lowen Rd, Rain. RM13 147 FD68
Lower Addiscombe Rd,
Croy. CR0 202 DS102
Lower Addison Gdns, W14 294 D5
Lower Adeyfield Rd,
Hem.H. HP2 40 BK19
Lower Alderton Hall La,
Loug. IG10 85 EN43
LOWER ASHTEAD,
Ashtd. KT21 231 CJ119
Lower Barn, Hem.H. HP3 40 BM23
Lower Barn Rd, Pur. CR8 220 DR112
Lower Bedfords Rd, Rom. RM1 105 FE51
Lower Belgrave St, SW1 297 J7
Lower Bobbingworth Grn,
Ong. CM5 53 FG24
LOWER BOIS, Chesh. HP5 54 AR34
Lower Boston Rd, W7 137 CE74
Lower Br Rd, Red. RH1 250 DF134
Lower Britwell Rd, Slou. SL2 131 AK70
Lower Broad St, Dag. RM10 146 FA67
Lower Bury La, Epp. CM16 69 ES31
Lower Camden, Chis. BR7 185 EM94
Lower Ch Hill, Green. DA9 189 FS85
Lower Ch St, Croy. CR0
off Waddon New Rd 201 DP103
Lower Cippenham La,
Slou. SL1 131 AN74
Lower Clabdens, Ware SG12 33 DZ06
LOWER CLAPTON, E5 279 H1
Lower Clapton Rd, E5 278 G3
Lower Clarendon Wk, W11
off Lancaster Rd 282 E9
Lower Common S, SW15 159 CV83
Lower Coombe St, Croy. CR0 220 DQ105
Lower Ct Rd, Epsom KT19 216 CQ111
Lower Cft, Swan. BR8 207 FF98
Lower Dagnall St, St.Alb. AL3 42 CC20
Lower Derby Rd, Wat. WD17
off Water La 76 BW42
Lower Downs Rd, SW20 199 CX95
Lower Drayton Pl, Croy. CR0
off Drayton Rd 201 DP103
Lower Dr, Beac. HP9 89 AK50
Lower Dunnymans, Bans. SM7
off Upper Sawley Wd 217 CZ114
Lower Edgeborough Rd,
Guil. GU1 259 AZ135
LOWER EDMONTON, N9 100 DU46
Lower Emms, Hem.H. HP2
off Hunters Oak 41 BQ15
Lower Fm Rd, Eff. KT24 229 BV124
LOWER FELTHAM, Felt. TW13 175 BS90
Lowerfield, Welw.G.C. AL7 30 DA10
Lower George St, Rich. TW9 177 CK85
Lower Gravel Rd, Brom. BR2 204 EL102
LOWER GREEN, Esher KT10 196 CA103
Lower Grn, Tewin AL6 30 DE05
Lower Grn Gdns, Wor.Pk. KT4 199 CU102
Lower Grn Rd, Esher KT10 196 CB103
Lower Grn W, Mitch. CR4 200 DE97
Lower Grosvenor Pl, SW1 297 J6
Lower Gro Rd, Rich. TW10 178 CM86
Lower Guild Hall, Bluewater
DA9 *off Bluewater Shop Cen* 189 FT87
Lower Hall La, E4 101 DY50
Lower Hampton Rd,
Sun. TW16 196 BW97
Lower Ham Rd, Kings.T. KT2 177 CK93
Lower Hatfield Rd, Hert. SG13 47 DK15
Lower Higham Rd, Grav. DA12 191 GM88
Lower High St, Wat. WD17 76 BX43
Lower Hill Rd, Epsom KT19 216 CP112
LOWER HOLLOWAY, N7 276 C2
● Lower Hook Business Pk,
Orp. BR6 223 EM108
Lower James St, W1 285 M10
Lower John St, W1 285 M10
Lower Kenwood Av, Enf. EN2 81 DK43
Lower Kings Rd, Berk. HP4 38 AW19
Kingston upon Thames KT2 198 CL95
LOWER KINGSWOOD,
Tad. KT20 250 DA127
Lower Lea Crossing, E14 291 J10
E16 291 J10
Lower Lees Rd, Slou. SL2 131 AN69
Lower Maidstone Rd, N11
off Telford Rd 99 DJ51
Lower Mall, W6 159 CV78
Lower Mardyke Av,
Rain. RM13 147 FC68
Lower Marsh, SE1 298 E5
Lower Marsh La, Kings.T. KT1 198 CM98
Lower Mast Ho, SE18 305 K6
Lower Mead, Iver SL0 133 BD69
Lowermead, Red. RH1 250 DF132
Lower Meadow, Chsht EN8 67 DX27
Harlow CM18 51 ES19
Lower Merton Ri, NW3 274 D6
Lower Morden La, Mord. SM4 199 CW100
Lower Mortlake Rd, Rich. TW9 158 CL84
LOWER NAZEING,
Wal.Abb. EN9 50 EE23
Lower Noke Cl, Brwd. CM14 106 FL47
Lower Northfield, Bans. SM7 217 CZ114
Lower Paddock Rd, Wat. WD19 76 BY44
Lower Pk Rd, N11 99 DJ50
Belvedere DA17 166 FA76
Chipstead CR5 234 DE118
Loughton IG10 84 EK43
Lower Paxton Rd, St.Alb. AL1 43 CE21
Lower Peryers, E.Hors. KT24 245 BS128
Lower Pillory Down,
Cars. SM5 218 DG113
● Lower Pl Business Cen,
NW10 *off Steele Rd* 138 CQ68
Lower Plantation, Loud. WD3 74 BJ41
Lower Queens Rd, Buck.H. IG9 102 EK47
Lower Range Rd, Grav. DA12 191 GL87
Lower Richmond Rd, SW14 158 CP83
SW15 159 CW83
Richmond TW9 158 CN83
Lower Riding, Beac. HP9 88 AH53
Lower Rd, SE1 298 E4
SE8 300 G6
SE16 301 J8
Belvedere DA17 166 FA76
Chorleywood WD3 73 BC42
Denham UB9 113 BC59
Erith DA8 167 FD77
Gerrards Cross SL9 90 AY53
Great Amwell SG12 33 DZ08
Harrow HA2 117 CD61
Hemel Hempstead HP3 58 BN25
Kenley CR8 219 DP113
Leatherhead
KT22, KT23, KT24 231 CD123
Loughton IG10 85 EN40
Mountnessing CM13, CM15 109 GD41
Northfleet DA11 170 FY84
Orpington BR5 206 EV101
Redhill RH1 266 DD136
Sutton SM1 218 DC105
Swanley BR8 187 FF94
Lower Robert St, WC2
off John Adam St 298 B1
Lower Rose Gall, Bluewater
DA9 *off Bluewater Shop Cen* 189 FU87
Lower Sales, Hem.H. HP1 39 BF21
Lower Sandfields,
Send GU23 227 BD124
Lower Sand Hills,
Long Dit. KT6 197 CJ101
Lower Sawley Wd, Bans. SM7
off Upper Sawley Wd 217 CZ114
Lower Shott, Bkhm KT23 246 CA126
Cheshunt EN7 66 DT26
Lower Sloane St, SW1 296 G9
Lower Sq, Islw. TW7 157 CH83
Lower Sta Rd, Cray. DA1 187 FE86
Lower Strand, NW9 97 CT54
Lower St, Shere GU5 260 BN139
Lower Sunbury Rd,
Hmptn. TW12 196 BZ96
Lower Swaines, Epp. CM16 69 ES30
LOWER SYDENHAM, SE26 183 DX91
⇌ Lower Sydenham 183 DZ92
● Lower Sydenham Ind Est,
SE26 *off Kangley Br Rd* 183 DZ92
Lower Tail, Wat. WD19 94 BY48
Lower Talbot Wk, W11
off Talbot Wk 139 CY72
Lower Teddington Rd,
Kings.T. KT1 197 CK95
Lower Ter, NW3 120 DC62
Lower Thames St, EC3 299 M1
Lower Thames Wk, Bluewater
DA9 *off Bluewater Shop Cen* 189 FT88
Lower Tub, Bushey WD23 95 CD45
Lower Wd Rd, Clay. KT10 215 CG107
Lower Woodside, Hat. AL9 45 CZ22
Lower Yott, Hem.H. HP2 40 BM21
Lowestoft Cl, E5
off Theydon Rd 122 DW61
Lowestoft Dr, Slou. SL1 130 AJ72
Lowestoft Ms, E16 305 P4
Lowestoft Rd, Wat. WD24 75 BV39
Loweswater Cl, Wat. WD25 60 BW33
Wembley HA9 117 CK61
★ Lowewood Mus, Hodd. EN11 49 EA18
Lowfield, Saw. CM21 36 EX06
● Lowfield Heath Ind Est,
Craw. RH11 268 DE154
Lowfield La, Hodd. EN11 49 EA17
Lowfield Rd, NW6 273 J6
W3 138 CQ72
Lowfield St, Dart. DA1 188 FL89
Low Hall Cl, E4 101 EA45
Low Hall La, E17 123 DY58
Low Hill Rd, Roydon CM19 50 EF17
Lowick Rd, Har. HA1 117 CE56
Lowlands, Hat. AL9 45 CW15
Lowlands Dr, Stanw. TW19 174 BK85
Lowlands Gdns, Rom. RM7 127 FB58
Lowlands Rd, Aveley RM15 148 FP74
Harrow HA1 117 CE59
Pinner HA5 116 BW59
Lowman Rd, N7 276 D1
Lowndes Av, Chesh. HP5 54 AP30
Lowndes Cl, SW1 297 H7
Lowndes Ct, W1 285 L9
Bromley BR1 *off Queens Rd* 204 EG96
Lowndes Ms, SW16
off Broadlands Ave 181 DL89
Lowndes Pl, SW1 296 G7
Lowndes Sq, SW1 296 F5
Lowndes St, SW1 296 F6
Lowood Ct, SE19 182 DT92
Lowood St, E1 288 F10
Low Rd, Hat. AL9 46 DF15
Lowry Cl, Erith DA8 167 FD77
Lowry Cres, Mitch. CR4 200 DE96
Lowry Ho, E14
off Cassilis Rd 302 B5
Lowry Rd, Dag. RM8 126 EV63
Lowshoe La, Rom. RM5 105 FB53
Lowson Gro, Wat. WD19 94 BY45
LOW STREET, Til. RM18 171 GM79
Low St La, E.Til. RM18 171 GM78
Lowswood Cl, Nthwd. HA6 93 BQ53
Lowther Cl, Els. WD6 78 CM43
Lowther Dr, Enf. EN2 81 DL42
Lowther Gdns, SW7 296 A6
Lowther Hill, SE23 183 DY87
Sch Lowther Prim Sch, SW13
off Stillingfleet Rd 159 CU79
Lowther Rd, E17 101 DY54
N7 276 E3
SW13 159 CT81
Kingston upon Thames KT2 198 CM95
Stanmore HA7 118 CM55
Lowthorpe, Wok. GU21
off Shilburn Way 226 AU118
Lowth Rd, SE5 311 J7
LOXFORD, Ilf. IG1 125 EQ64
Loxford Av, E6 144 EK68
Loxford Cl, Cat. CR3 252 DT125
Loxford Gdns, N5 121 DP63
Loxford La, Ilf. IG1, IG3 125 EQ64
Loxford Rd, Bark. IG11 145 EP65
Caterham CR3 252 DT125
Sch Loxford Sch of Science &
Tech, Ilf. IG1 *off Loxford La* 125 ER64
Loxford Ter, Bark. IG11
off Fanshawe Av 145 EQ65
Loxford Way, Cat. CR3 252 DT125
Loxham Rd, E4 101 EA52
Loxham St, WC1 286 B3
Loxley Cl, SE26 183 DX92
Byfleet KT14 212 BL114
Loxley Ct, Ware SG12 33 DY06
Loxley Rd, SW18 180 DD88
Berkhamsted HP4 38 AS17
Hampton TW12 176 BZ91
Loxton Rd, SE23 183 DX88
Loxwood Cl, Felt. TW14 175 BR88
Hemel Hempstead HP3 39 BF23
Orpington BR5 206 EX103
Loxwood Rd, N17 122 DS55
Sch Loyola Prep Sch, Buck.H.
IG9 *off Palmerston Rd* 102 EJ46
Coll L.S.O. St. Luke's, EC1 287 K4
Sch Lubavitch Girls Prim Sch,
N16 *off Stamford Hill* 122 DT59
Sch Lubavitch Ho Boys' Sch,
E5 *off Clapton Common* 122 DT59
Lubbock Rd, Chis. BR7 185 EM94
Lubbock St, SE14 313 H5
Lucan Dr, Stai. TW18 174 BK94
Lucan Pl, SW3 296 C9
Lucan Rd, Barn. EN5 79 CY41
Lucas Av, E13 144 EH67
Harrow HA2 116 CA61
Lucas Cl, NW10
off Pound La 139 CU66
Lucas Ct, SW11 309 H7
Harrow HA2 116 CA60
Waltham Abbey EN9 68 EF33
Lucas Cres, Green. DA9
off Ingress Pk Av 189 FW85
Lucas Gdns, N2 98 DC54
Lucas Rd, SE20 182 DW93
Grays RM17 170 GA76
Lucas Sq, NW11
off Hampstead Way 120 DA58
Lucas St, SE8 314 A8
Sch Lucas Vale Prim Sch, SE8 314 A7
Lucern Cl, Chsht EN7 66 DS27
Lucerne Cl, N13 99 DL49
Woking GU22 226 AY119
Lucerne Ct, Erith DA18
off Middle Way 166 EY76
Lucerne Gro, E17 123 ED56
Lucerne Ms, W8 295 K2
Lucerne Rd, N5 121 DP63
Orpington BR6 205 ET102
Thornton Heath CR7 201 DP99
Lucerne Way, Rom. RM3 106 FK51
Lucey Rd, SE16 300 C7
Lucey Way, SE16 300 D7
Lucida Ct, Wat. WD18
off Whippendell Rd 75 BS43
Lucie Av, Ashf. TW15 175 BP93
Lucien Rd, SW17 180 DG91
SW19 180 DB89
Lucknow St, SE18 165 ES80
Lucks Hill, Hem.H. HP1 39 BE20
Lucorn Cl, SE12 184 EF86
Lucton Ms, Loug. IG10 85 EP42
Luctons Av, Buck.H. IG9 102 EJ46
Lucy Cres, W3 138 CQ71
Lucy Gdns, Dag. RM8 126 EY62
Luddesdon Rd, Erith DA8 166 FA80
Luddington Av, Vir.W. GU25 193 AZ96
Ludford Cl, Croy. CR0
off Warrington Rd 219 DP105
Ludgate Bdy, EC4 286 G9
Ludgate Circ, EC4 286 G9
Ludgate Hill, EC4 286 G9
Ludgate Sq, EC4 287 H9
Ludham Cl, SE28
off Rollesby Way 146 EW72
Ilford IG6 103 EQ53
Ludlow Cl, Brom. BR2
off Aylesbury Rd 204 EG97
Harrow HA2 116 BZ63
Ludlow Ct, Dag. RM10
off St. Mark's Pl 146 FA65
Ludlow Mead, Wat. WD19 93 BV48
Ludlow Pl, Grays RM17 170 GB76
Ludlow Rd, W5 137 CJ70
Feltham TW13 175 BU91
Guildford GU2 258 AV135
Ludlow St, EC1 287 J4
Ludlow Way, N2 120 DC56
Croxley Green WD3 75 BQ42
Ludovick Wk, SW15 158 CS84
Ludwick Cl, Welw.G.C. AL7 29 CZ11
Ludwick Grn, Welw.G.C. AL7 29 CZ10
Ludwick Ms, SE14 313 M4
Ludwick Way, Welw.G.C. AL7 29 CZ09
Luff Cl, Wind. SL4 151 AL83
Luffield Rd, SE2 166 EV76
Luffman Rd, SE12 184 EH90
Lugard Rd, SE15 312 F8
Lugg App, E12 125 EN62
Luke Allsop Sq, Dag. RM10 127 FB62
Luke Ho, E1 288 E9
Luke St, EC2 287 N4
Lukin Cres, E4 101 ED48
Lukin St, E1 289 H9
Lukintone Cl, Loug. IG10 84 EL44
Lullarook Cl, Bigg.H. TN16 238 EJ116
Lullingstone Av, Swan. BR8 207 FF97
Lullingstone Cl, Orp. BR5 186 EV94
Lullingstone Cres, Orp. BR5 186 EU94
Lullingstone La, SE13 183 ED86
Eynsford DA4 208 FJ104
★ Lullingstone Park Visitor
Cen, Dart. DA4 225 FG107
Lullingstone Rd, Belv. DA17 166 EZ79
★ Lullingstone Roman Vil,
Dart. DA4 207 FH104
Lullington Garth, N12 97 CZ50
Borehamwood WD6 78 CP43
Bromley BR1 184 EE94
Lullington Rd, SE20 182 DU94
Dagenham RM9 146 EY66
Lulot Gdns, N19 121 DH61
Lulworth, NW1 275 M7
SE17 299 L10
Lulworth Av, Goffs Oak EN7 65 DP29
Hounslow TW5 156 CB80
Wembley HA9 117 CJ59
Lulworth Cl, Har. HA2 116 BZ62
Lulworth Cres, Mitch. CR4 200 DE96
Lulworth Dr, Pnr. HA5 116 BX59
Romford RM5 105 FB50
Lulworth Gdns, Har. HA2 116 BY61
Lulworth Ho, SW8 310 C4
Lulworth Pl, Epsom KT19 216 CL112
Lulworth Rd, SE9 184 EL89
SE15 312 F8
Welling DA16 165 ET82
Lulworth Waye, Hayes UB4 136 BW72
Lumbards, Welw.G.C. AL7 30 DA06
Lumen Rd, Wem. HA9 117 CK61
Lumiere Ct, SW17 180 DG89
Lumina Way, Enf. EN1 82 DU43
Luminoscity Ct, W13
off Drayton Grn Rd 137 CH73
Lumley Cl, Belv. DA17 166 FA79
Lumley Ct, WC2 298 B1
Horley RH6 268 DG147
Lumley Flats, SW1
off Holbein Pl 296 G10
Lumley Gdns, Sutt. SM3 217 CY106
Lumley Rd, Horl. RH6 268 DG147
Sutton SM3 217 CY107
Lumley St, W1 285 H9
Luna Ho, SE16 300 D4
Luna Pl, St.Alb. AL1 43 CG20
Lunar Cl, Bigg.H. TN16 238 EK116
Luna Rd, Th.Hth. CR7 202 DQ97
Lundin Wk, Wat. WD19 94 BX49
Lund Pt, E15 280 E8
Lundy Dr, Hayes UB3 155 BS77
Lundy Wk, N1 277 K5
Lunedale Rd, Dart. DA2 188 FQ88
Lunedale Wk, Dart. DA2
off Lunedale Rd 188 FQ88
Lunghurst Rd, Wold. CR3 237 DZ120
Lunham Rd, SE19 182 DS93
Lupin Cl, SW2
off Palace Rd 181 DP89
Croydon CR0
off Primrose La 203 DX102
Rush Green RM7 127 FD61
West Drayton UB7
off Magnolia St 154 BK78
Lupin Cres, Ilf. IG1
off Bluebell Way 145 EP65
Lupino Ct, SE11 298 D9
Lupin Pt, SE1 300 B5
Luppit Cl, Hutt. CM13 109 GA46
Lupton Cl, SE12 184 EH91
Lupton St, NW5 275 L1
Lupus St, SW1 309 M1
Luralda Gdns, E14 302 F10
Lurgan Av, W6 306 D2
Lurline Gdns, SW11 309 H6
Luscombe Ct, Brom. BR2 204 EE96
Luscombe Way, SW8 310 A4
Lushes Ct, Loug. IG10
off Lushes Rd 85 EP43
Lushes Rd, Loug. IG10 85 EP43
Lushington Dr, Cob. KT11 213 BV114
Lushington Rd, NW10 139 CV68
SE6 183 EB92
Lushington Ter, E8 278 D3
Lusted Hall La, Tats. TN16 238 EJ120
Lusted Rd, Sev. TN13 241 FE120
Lusteds Cl, Dor. RH4
off Glory Mead 263 CJ139
Luther Cl, Edg. HA8 96 CQ47
Luther King Cl, E17 123 DY58
Luther Ms, Tedd. TW11
off Luther Rd 177 CF92
Luther Rd, Tedd. TW11 177 CF92
Luton Pl, SE10 314 F5
Luton Rd, E13 291 N5
E17 123 DZ55
Sidcup DA14 186 EW90
Luton St, NW8 284 B5
Lutton Ter, NW3 120 DC63
Luttrell Av, SW15 179 CV85
Lutwyche Rd, SE6 183 DZ89
Lutyens Cl, Eff. KT24 246 BX127
Lutyens Ho, SW1
off Churchill Gdns 309 L1
Luxborough La, Chig. IG7 102 EL48
Luxborough St, W1 284 G6
Luxborough Twr, W1
off Luxborough St 284 G6
Luxembourg Ms, E15 281 J3
Luxemburg Gdns, W6 294 C8
Luxfield Rd, SE9 184 EL88
Luxford Pl, Saw. CM21 36 EZ06
Luxford St, SE16 301 J9
Luxmore St, SE4 313 P7
Luxor St, SE5 311 H9
Luxted Rd, Downe BR6 223 EN112
Lyall Av, SE21 182 DS90
Lyall Ms, SW1 296 G7
Lyall Ms W, SW1 296 G7
Lyall St, SW1 296 G7
Lyal Rd, E3 289 M1
Lycaste Cl, St.Alb. AL1 43 CF21
Lycée, The, SE11 310 F1
Sch Lycée Français Charles
de Gaulle, SW7 296 A8
Lycett Pl, W12
off Becklow Rd 159 CU75
Lych Gate, Wat. WD25 60 BX33
Lych Gate Rd, Orp. BR6 206 EU102
Lych Gate Wk, Hayes UB3 135 BT73
Lych Way, Wok. GU21 226 AX116
Lyconby Gdns, Croy. CR0 203 DY101
Lycrome La, Chesh. HP5 54 AR28
Lycrome Rd, Chesh. HP5 54 AS28
Lydd Cl, Sid. DA14 185 ES90
Lydden Ct, SE9 185 ES86
Lydden Gro, SW18 180 DB87
Lydden Rd, SW18 180 DB87
Lydd Rd, Bexh. DA7 166 EZ80
Lydeard Rd, E6 145 EM66
Lydele Cl, Wok. GU21 227 AZ115
Lydford Av, Slou. SL2 131 AR71
Lydford Cl, N16 277 P2
Lydford Rd, N15 122 DR57
NW2 272 B5
W9 283 H4
Lydger Cl, Wok. GU22 227 BB120
Lydhurst Av, SW2 181 DM89
Lydia Ms, N.Mymms AL9 45 CW24
Lydia Rd, Erith DA8 167 FF79
Lydney Cl, SW19
off Princes Way 179 CY89
Lydon Rd, SW4 161 DJ83
Lydsey Cl, Slou. SL2 131 AN69
Lydstep Rd, Chis. BR7 185 EN91
Lye, The, Tad. KT20 233 CW122
LYE GREEN, Chesh. HP5 56 AT27
Lye Grn Rd, Chesh. HP5 54 AR30
Lye La, Brick.Wd AL2 60 CA30
Lyell Pl E, Wind. SL4
off Lyell Rd 150 AJ83
Lyell Pl W, Wind. SL4
off Lyell Rd 150 AJ83
Lyell Rd, Wind. SL4 150 AJ83
Lyell Wk E, Wind. SL4
off Lyell Rd 150 AJ83
Lyell Wk W, Wind. SL4
off Lyell Rd 150 AJ83
Lyfield, Oxshott KT22 214 CB114
Lyford Rd, SW18 180 DD87
Lyford St, SE18 305 H9
Lygean Av, Ware SG12 33 DY06
Lygon Ho, SW6 306 E6
Lygon Pl, SW1 297 J7
Lyham Cl, SW2 181 DL86
Lyham Rd, SW2 181 DL85
Lyle Cl, Mitch. CR4 200 DG101
Lyle Pk, Sev. TN13 257 FH123
Lymbourne Cl, Sutt. SM2 218 DA110
Lymden Gdns, Reig. RH2 266 DB135
Lyme Fm Rd, SE12 164 EG84
Lyme Gro, E9 278 G6
Lymer Av, SE19 182 DT92
Lyme Regis Rd, Bans. SM7 233 CZ117
Lyme Rd, Well. DA16 166 EV81
Lymescote Gdns, Sutt. SM1 200 DA103
Lyme St, NW1 275 L7
Lyme Ter, NW1 275 L7
Lyminge Cl, Sid. DA14 185 ET91
Lyminge Gdns, SW18 180 DE88
Lymington Av, N22 99 DN54
Lymington Cl, E6 293 J6
SW16 201 DK96
Lymington Ct, Sutt. SM1
off All Saints Rd 200 DC104
Lymington Dr, Ruis. HA4 115 BR61
Lymington Gdns,
Epsom KT19 217 CT106
Lymington Rd, NW6 273 L4
Dagenham RM8 126 EX60
Lyminster Cl, Hayes UB4
off West Quay Dr 136 BY71
Lympstone Gdns, SE15 312 D4
Lynbridge Gdns, N13 99 DP49
Lynbrook Cl, Rain. RM13 147 FD68
Lynbrook Gro, SE15 311 P4
Lynceley Gra, Epp. CM16 70 EU29
Lynch, The, Hodd. EN11 49 EB17
Uxbridge UB8 134 BJ66
Lynch Cl, SE3 315 L9
Uxbridge UB8 *off Cross Rd* 134 BJ66
Lynchen Cl, Houns. TW5
off The Avenue 155 BU81
Lynch Hill La, Slou. SL2 131 AL70
Sch Lynch Hill Prim Sch,
Slou. SL2 *off Garrard Rd* 131 AM69
Lynchmere Pl, Guil. GU2
off Peak Rd 242 AU131
Lynch Wk, SE8 313 P2
Lyncott Cres, SW4 161 DH84
Lyncroft Av, Pnr. HA5 116 BY57
Lyncroft Gdns, NW6 273 K2
W13 157 CJ75
Epsom KT17 217 CT109
Hounslow TW3 156 CC84
Lyndale, NW2 119 CZ63
Lyndale Av, NW2 119 CZ62

L

Lyndale Cl, SE3 315 L3
Lyndale Ct, W.Byf. KT14
off Parvis Rd 212 BG113
● **Lyndale Est**, Grays RM20 169 FV79
Lyndale Rd, Red. RH1 250 DF131
Lynden Hyrst, Croy. CR0 202 DT103
Lynden Way, Swan. BR8 207 FC97
Lyndhurst Av, N12 98 DF51
NW7 96 CS51
SW16 201 DK96
Pinner HA5 93 BV53
Southall UB1 136 CB74
Sunbury-on-Thames TW16 195 BU97
Surbiton KT5 198 CP102
Twickenham TW2 176 BZ88
Lyndhurst Cl, NW10 118 CR62
Bexleyheath DA7 167 FB83
Croydon CR0 202 DT104
Orpington BR6 223 EP105
Woking GU21 226 AX115
Lyndhurst Ct, E18
off Churchfields 102 EG53
Sutton SM2 *off Overton Rd* 218 DA108
Lyndhurst Dr, E10 123 EC59
Hornchurch RM11 128 FJ60
New Malden KT3 198 CS100
Sevenoaks TN13 256 FE124
Lyndhurst Gdns, N3 97 CY53
NW3 274 B2
Barking IG11 145 ES65
Enfield EN1 82 DS42
Ilford IG2 125 ER58
Pinner HA5 93 BV53
Lyndhurst Gro, SE15 311 P8
Lyndhurst Ho, SW15
off Ellisfield Dr 179 CU87
Sch **Lyndhurst Ho Prep Sch**,
NW3 274 B2
Sch **Lyndhurst Prim Sch**, SE5 311 M8
Lyndhurst Ri, Chig. IG7 103 EN49
Lyndhurst Rd, E4 101 EC52
N18 100 DU49
N22 99 DM51
NW3 274 B2
Bexleyheath DA7 167 FB83
Chesham HP5 54 AP28
Coulsdon CR5 234 DG116
Greenford UB6 136 CB70
Reigate RH2 266 DA137
Thornton Heath CR7 201 DN98
Lyndhurst Sq, SE15 312 B7
Lyndhurst Ter, NW3 274 A2
Lyndhurst Wk, Borwd. WD6 78 CM39
Lyndhurst Way, SE15 312 B6
Chertsey KT16 193 BE104
Hutton CM13 109 GC46
Sutton SM2 218 DA108
Lyndon Av, Pnr. HA5 94 BY51
Sidcup DA15 185 ET85
Wallington SM6 200 DG104
Lyndon Rd, Belv. DA17 166 FA77
Lyndon Yd, SW17 180 DB91
Lyndwood Dr, Old Wind. SL4 172 AU86
LYNE, Cher. KT16 193 BA102
Sch **Lyne & Long Cross C of E Inf Sch**, Lyne KT16 *off Lyne La* 193 BB103
Lyne Cl, Vir.W. GU25 193 AZ100
Lyne Cres, E17 101 DZ53
Lyne Crossing Rd, Lyne KT16 193 BA100
Lyne Gdns, Bigg.H. TN16 238 EL118
Lynegrove Av, Ashf. TW15 175 BQ92
Lyneham Dr, NW9 96 CS53
Lyneham Wk, E5
off Boscombe Cl 279 L2
Pinner HA5 115 BT55
Lyne La, Egh. TW20 193 BA99
Lyne KT16 193 BA100
Virginia Water GU25 193 BA100
Lyne Rd, Vir.W. GU25 192 AX100
Lynette Av, SW4 181 DH86
Lynett Rd, Dag. RM8 126 EX61
Lyne Way, Hem.H. HP1 39 BF18
Lynford Cl, Barn. EN5 79 CT43
Edgware HA8 96 CQ52
Lynford Gdns, Edg. HA8 96 CP48
Ilford IG3 125 ET61
Lyngarth Cl, Bkhm KT23 246 CC125
Lyngfield Pk, Maid. SL6 150 AD79
Lynhurst Cres, Uxb. UB10 135 BQ66
Lynhurst Rd, Uxb. UB10 135 BQ66
Lynmere Rd, Well. DA16 166 EV82
Lyn Ms, E3 289 N3
N16 277 P1
Lynmouth Av, Enf. EN1 82 DT44
Morden SM4 199 CX101
Lynmouth Dr, Ruis. HA4 115 BV61
Lynmouth Gdns, Houns. TW5 156 BX81
Perivale UB6 137 CH67
Lynmouth Ri, Orp. BR5 206 EV98
Lynmouth Rd, E17 123 DY58
N2 120 DF55
N16 122 DT60
Perivale UB6 137 CH67
Welwyn Garden City AL7 29 CZ09
Lynn Cl, Ashf. TW15 175 BR92
Harrow HA3 95 CD54
Lynne Cl, Grn St Grn BR6 223 ET107
South Croydon CR2 220 DW111
Lynne Wk, Esher KT10 214 CC106
Lynne Way, Nthlt. UB5 136 BX68
Lynn Ms, E11 *off Lynn Rd* 124 EE61
Lynn Rd, E11 124 EE61
SW12 181 DH87
Ilford IG2 125 ER59
Lynn St, Enf. EN2 82 DR39
Lynn Wk, Reig. RH2 266 DB137
Lynross Cl, Rom. RM3 106 FM54
Lynscott Way, S.Croy. CR2 219 DP109
Lynsted Cl, Bexh. DA6 187 FB85
Bromley BR1 204 EJ96
Lynsted Ct, Beck. BR3
off Churchfields Rd 203 DY96
Lynsted Gdns, SE9 164 EK83
Lynton Av, N12 98 DD49
NW9 119 CT56
W13 137 CG72
Orpington BR5 206 EV98
Romford RM7 104 FA53
St. Albans AL1 43 CJ21
Lynton Cl, NW10 118 CS64
Chessington KT9 216 CL105
Isleworth TW7 157 CF84
Lynton Cres, Ilf. IG2 125 EP58
Lynton Crest, Pot.B. EN6
off Strafford Gate 64 DA32
Lynton Est, SE1 300 C9
Lynton Gdns, N11 99 DK51
Enfield EN1 100 DS45
Lynton Mead, N20 98 DA48
Lynton Par, Chsht EN8
off Turners Hill 67 DX30
Lynton Rd, E4 101 EB50
N8 121 DK57
NW6 273 H9
SE1 300 B9
W3 138 CN73
Chesham HP5 54 AP28
Croydon CR0 201 DN100
Gravesend DA11 191 GG88
Harrow HA2 116 BY61
New Malden KT3 198 CR99
Lynton Rd S, Grav. DA11 191 GG88
Lynton Ter, W3 138 CP72
Lynton Wk, Hayes UB4 135 BS69
Lynwood, Guil. GU2 258 AV135
Lynwood Av, Couls. CR5 235 DH115
Egham TW20 172 AY93
Epsom KT17 217 CT114
Slough SL3 152 AX76
Lynwood Cl, E18 102 EJ53
Harrow HA2 116 BY62
Romford RM5 105 FB51
Woking GU21 211 BD113
Lynwood Dr, Nthwd. HA6 93 BS53
Romford RM5 105 FB51
Worcester Park KT4 199 CU103
Lynwood Gdns, Croy. CR0 219 DM105
Southall UB1 136 BZ72
Lynwood Gro, N21 99 DN46
Orpington BR6 205 ES101
Lynwood Hts, Rick. WD3 74 BH43
Lynwood Rd, SW17 180 DF90
W5 138 CL70
Epsom KT17 217 CT114
Redhill RH1 250 DG132
Thames Ditton KT7 197 CF103
Lynx Hill, E.Hors. KT24 245 BT128
Lynx Way, E16 292 E10
● **Lyon Business Pk**,
Bark. IG11 145 ES68
Lyon Ho, Har. HA1
off Lyon Rd 117 CF58
Lyon Meade, Stan. HA7 95 CJ53
Lyon Pk Av, Wem. HA0 138 CL65
Sch **Lyon Pk Inf & Jun Schs**,
Wem. HA0 *off Vincent Rd* 138 CM66
Lyon Rd, SW19 200 DC95
Harrow HA1 117 CF58
Romford RM1 127 FF59
Walton-on-Thames KT12 196 BY103
Lyons Ct, Dor. RH4 263 CH136
Lyonsdene, Lwr Kgswd KT20 249 CZ127
Lyonsdown Av,
New Barn. EN5 80 DC44
Lyonsdown Rd,
New Barn. EN5 80 DC44
Sch **Lyonsdown Sch**, New Barn.
EN5 *off Richmond Rd* 80 DC43
Lyons Dr, Guil. GU2 242 AU129
Lyons Pl, NW8 284 A4
Lyon St, N1 276 C7
Lyons Wk, W14 294 E8
Lyon Way, Grnf. UB6 137 CE67
St. Albans AL4 44 CN20
Lyoth Rd, Orp. BR5 205 EQ103
Lyra Ct, W3 138 CR71
Lyrical Way, Hem.H. HP1 40 BH18
Lyric Dr, Grnf. UB6 136 CB70
★ **Lyric Hammersmith**, W6 294 A9
Lyric Ms, SE26 182 DW91
Lyric Rd, SW13 159 CT81
Lyric Sq, W6
off King St 294 A9
Lysander Cl, Bov. HP3 57 AZ27
Lysander Ct, N.Wld Bas. CM16 71 FB26
Lysander Gdns, Surb. KT6
off Ewell Rd 198 CM100
Lysander Gro, N19 121 DK60
Lysander Ho, E2 288 E1
Lysander Ms, N19 121 DJ60
Lysander Rd, Croy. CR0 219 DM107
Ruislip HA4 115 BR61
Lysander Way, Abb.L. WD5 59 BU32
Orpington BR6 205 EQ104
Welwyn Garden City AL7 30 DD08
Lys Hill Gdns, Hert. SG14 31 DP07
Lysias Rd, SW12 180 DG86
Lysia St, SW6 306 C5
Lysley Pl, Brook.Pk AL9 64 DC27
Lysons Wk, SW15 179 CU85
Lyster Ms, Cob. KT11 213 BV113
Lytchet Rd, Brom. BR1 184 EH94
Lytchet Way, Enf. EN3 82 DW39
Lytchgate Cl, S.Croy. CR2 220 DS108
Lytcott Dr, W.Mol. KT8
off Freeman Dr 196 BZ98
Lytcott Gro, SE22 182 DT85
Lyte St, E2 278 G10
Lytham Av, Wat. WD19 94 BX50
Lytham Cl, SE28 146 EY72
Lytham Gro, W5 138 CM69
Lytham St, SE17 311 L1
Lyttelton Cl, NW3 274 C7
Lyttelton Rd, E10 123 EB62
N2 120 DC57
Lyttleton Rd, N8 121 DN55
Lytton Av, N13 99 DN47
Enfield EN3 83 DY38
Lytton Cl, N2 120 DD58
Loughton IG10 85 ER41
Northolt UB5 136 BZ66
Lytton Gdns, Wall. SM6 219 DK105
Welwyn Garden City AL8 29 CX09
Lytton Gro, SW15 179 CX85
Lytton Pk, Cob. KT11 214 BZ112
Lytton Rd, E11 124 EE59
Barnet EN5 80 DC42
Grays RM16 171 GG77
Pinner HA5 94 BY52
Romford RM2 127 FH57
Woking GU22 227 BB116
Lytton Strachey Path, SE28
off Titmuss Av 146 EV73
Lyttons Way, Hodd. EN11 33 EA14
Lyveden Rd, SE3 164 EH80
SW17 180 DE93
Lywood Cl, Tad. KT20 233 CW122

M

Mabbotts, Tad. KT20 233 CX121
Mabbutt Cl, Brick.Wd AL2 60 BY30
Mabel Rd, Swan. BR8 187 FG93
Mabel St, Wok. GU21 226 AX117
Maberley Cres, SE19 182 DU94
Maberley Rd, SE19 202 DT95
Beckenham BR3 203 DX97
Mabeys Wk, High Wych CM21 36 EV06
Mabledon Pl, WC1 285 P3
Mablethorpe Rd, SW6 306 E5
Mabley St, E9 279 L4
Macaret Cl, N20 98 DB45
MacArthur Cl, E7 281 P5
Erith DA8 167 FE78
Wembley HA9 138 CP65
MacArthur Ter, SE7 164 EK79
Macaulay Av, Esher KT10 197 CE103
Sch **Macaulay C of E Prim Sch**,
SW4 *off Victoria Ri* 161 DH83
Macaulay Ct, SW4 161 DH83
Macaulay Rd, E6 144 EK68
SW4 161 DH83
Caterham CR3 236 DS122
Macaulay Sq, SW4 161 DJ84
Macaulay Way, SE28
off Booth Cl 146 EV73
Macauley Ms, SE13 314 F7
Macbean St, SE18 305 M7
Macbeth St, W6 159 CV78
Macclesfield Br, NW1 274 D10
Macclesfield Rd, EC1 287 J2
SE25 202 DV99
Macclesfield St, W1 285 P10
Macdonald Av, Dag. RM10 127 FB62
Hornchurch RM11 128 FL56
Macdonald Cl, Amer. HP6 55 AR35
Macdonald Rd, E7 281 N1
E17 101 EC54
N11 98 DF50
N19 121 DJ61
Macdonald Way, Horn. RM11 128 FL56
Macdonnell Gdns, Wat. WD25 75 BT35
Macdowall Rd, Guil. GU2 242 AV129
Macduff Rd, SW11 309 H6
Mace Cl, E1 300 E2
Mace Ct, Grays RM17 170 GE79
Mace La, Cudham TN14 223 ER113
Macers Ct, Brox. EN10 49 DZ24
Macers La, Brox. EN10 49 DZ24
Mace St, E2 289 J1
Macey Ho, SW11
off Surrey La 308 D7
Macfarland Gro, SE15 311 P4
MacFarlane La, Islw. TW7 157 CF79
Macfarlane Rd, W12 294 A2
Macfarren Pl, NW1 285 H5
Macgregor Rd, E16 292 D6
Machell Rd, SE15 312 G10
Macintosh Cl, Chsht EN7 66 DR26
Mackay Rd, SW4 309 K10
Mackennal St, NW8 284 D1
Mackenzie Cl, W12
off Australia Rd 139 CV73
Mackenzie Rd, N7 276 C4
Beckenham BR3 202 DW96
Mackenzie St, Slou. SL1 132 AT74
Mackenzie Wk, E14 302 B3
Mackenzie Way, Grav. DA12 191 GK93
Mackeson Rd, NW3 274 E1
Mackie Rd, SW2 181 DN87
Mackies Hill, Peasl. GU5 261 BR144
Mackintosh La, E9 279 K3
Macklin St, WC2 286 B8
Mackrells, Red. RH1 266 DC137
Mackrow Wk, E14 290 E10
Macks Rd, SE16 300 D8
Mackworth St, NW1 285 L2
Maclaren Ms, SW15 159 CW84
Maclean Rd, SE23 183 DY86
Maclennan Av, Rain. RM13 148 FK69
Macleod Cl, Grays RM17 170 GD77
Macleod Rd, N21 81 DL43
Macleod St, SE17 311 K1
Maclise Rd, W14 294 E7
Macmahon Cl,
Chobham GU24 210 AS110
Macmillan Ct, Grnf. UB6
off Ruislip Rd E 136 CC70
Macmillan Gdns, Dart. DA1 168 FN84
Macmillan Way, SW17 181 DH91
Macoma Rd, SE18 165 ER79
Macoma Ter, SE18 165 ER79
Maconochies Rd, E14 302 C10
Macon Way, Upmin. RM14 129 FT59
Macquarie Way, E14 302 D9
Macroom Rd, W9 283 H2
Mac's Pl, EC4 286 F8
★ **Madame Tussauds**, NW1 284 G5
Madan Cl, West. TN16 255 ES125
Sch **Madani Girls Sch**, E1 288 E8
Madan Rd, West. TN16 255 ER125
Madans Wk, Epsom KT18 216 CR114
Mada Rd, Orp. BR6 205 EP104
Maddams St, E3 290 C5
Madden Cl, Swans. DA10 189 FX86
Maddison Cl, N2 *off Long La* 98 DC54
Teddington TW11 177 CF93
Maddocks Cl, Sid. DA14 186 EY92
Maddock Way, SE17 311 H3
Maddox La, Bkhm KT23 230 BY123
Maddox Pk, Bkhm KT23 230 BY123
Maddox Rd, Harl. CM20 35 ES14
Hemel Hempstead HP2 41 BP20
Maddox St, W1 285 K10
Madeira Av, Brom. BR1 184 EE94
Madeira Cl, W.Byf. KT14
off Brantwood Gdns 212 BG113
Madeira Cres, W.Byf. KT14
off Brantwood Gdns 212 BG113
Madeira Gro, Wdf.Grn. IG8 102 EJ51
Madeira Rd, E11 123 ED60
N13 99 DP49
SW16 181 DL92
Mitcham CR4 200 DF98
West Byfleet KT14 211 BF113
Madeira Wk, Brwd. CM15 108 FY48
Reigate RH2 250 DD133
Windsor SL4 151 AR81
Madeleine Cl, Rom. RM6 126 EW58
Madeleine Terr, SE5 312 A7
Madeley Cl, Amer. HP6 55 AR36
Madeley Rd, W5 138 CL72
Madeline Gro, Ilf. IG1 125 ER64
Madeline Rd, SE20 202 DU95
Madells, Epp. CM16 69 ET31
🛍 **Madford Retail Pk**,
Hert. SG13 32 DS09
Madge Gill Way, E6
off Ron Leighton Way 144 EL67
Madgeways Cl,
Gt Amwell SG12 33 DZ09
Madgeways La,
Gt Amwell SG12 33 DZ10
Madinah Rd, E8 278 C3
Madingley, Kings.T. KT1
off St. Peters Rd 198 CN96
Madison Bldg, SE10
off Blackheath Rd 314 C6
Madison Cl, Sutt. SM2 218 DD108
Madison Ct, Dag. RM10
off St. Mark's Pl 147 FB65
Madison Cres, Bexh. DA7 166 EW80
Madison Gdns, Bexh. DA7 166 EW80
Bromley BR2 204 EF97
Madison Hts, Houns. TW3 156 CC83
Madison Way, Sev. TN13 256 FF123
Madoc Cl, NW2 119 CZ61
Madras Pl, N7 276 E4
Madras Rd, Ilf. IG1 125 EP63
Madresfield Ct, Shenley WD7
off Russet Dr 62 CL32
Madrid Rd, SW13 159 CU81
Guildford GU2 258 AV135
Madrigal La, SE5 311 H5
Madron St, SE17 299 P10
Maesmaur Rd, Tats. TN16 238 EK121
Mafeking Av, E6 144 EK68
Brentford TW8 158 CL79
Ilford IG2 125 ER59
Mafeking Rd, E16 291 L4
N17 100 DU54
Enfield EN1 82 DT41
Wraysbury TW19 173 BB89
Magazine Pl, Lthd. KT22 231 CH122
Magazine Rd, Cat. CR3 235 DP122
Magdala Av, N19 121 DH61
Magdala Rd, Islw. TW7 157 CG83
South Croydon CR2
off Napier Rd 220 DR108
Magdalen Cl, Byfleet KT14 212 BL114
Magdalen Cres, Byfleet KT14 212 BL114
Magdalene Cl, SE15 312 E9
Magdalene Gdns, E6 293 L4
N20 98 DF46
Magdalene Rd, Shep. TW17 194 BM98
Magdalen Gdns, Hutt. CM13 109 GE44
Magdalen Gro, Orp. BR6 224 EV105
MAGDALEN LAVER,
Ong. CM5 53 FE17
Magdalen Ms, NW3 273 N4
Magdalen Pas, E1 288 B10
Magdalen Rd, SW18 180 DC88
Magdalen St, SE1
off Bermondsey St 299 N3
Magee St, SE11 310 E2
Magellan Boul, E16 145 EQ73
Magellan Pl, E14
off Maritime Quay 302 B9
Magellan Blakes Causeway, SE1
off Shad Thames 300 A3
Magna Carta La, Wrays. TW19 172 AX88
★ **Magna Carta Monument**,
Egh. TW20 172 AX89
Sch **Magna Carta Sch, The**,
Stai. TW18 *off Thorpe Rd* 173 BD93
Magna Rd, Eng.Grn TW20 172 AV93
Magnaville Rd,
Bushey Hth WD23 95 CE45
● **Magnet Est**, Grays RM20 169 FW78
Magnetic Cres, Enf. EN3 83 DZ37
Magnet Rd, Wem. HA9 117 CK61
West Thurrock RM20 169 FW79
Magnin Cl, E8 278 D8
Magnolia Av, Abb.L. WD5 59 BU32
Magnolia Cl, E10 123 EA61
Hertford SG13 32 DU09
Kingston upon Thames KT2 178 CP93
Park Street AL2 61 CD27
Magnolia Ct, Felt. TW13
off Highfield Rd 175 BU88
Harrow HA3 118 CM59
Horley RH6 268 DG148
Uxbridge UB10 135 BP65
Wallington SM6
off Parkgate Rd 219 DH106
Magnolia Dr, Bans. SM7 233 CZ116
Biggin Hill TN16 238 EK116
Magnolia Gdns, Edg. HA8 96 CQ49
Slough SL3 152 AW76
Magnolia Pl, SW4 181 DK85
W5 137 CK71
Magnolia Rd, W4 158 CP79
Magnolia St, West Dr. UB7 154 BK77
Magnolia Way, Epsom KT19 216 CQ106
North Holmwood RH5 263 CK139
Pilgrim's Hatch CM15 108 FV43
Wooburn Green HP10
off Glory Mill La 110 AE56
Magnum Cl, Rain. RM13 148 FJ70
Magnum Ho, Kings.T. KT2
off London Rd 198 CN95
Magnus Ct, N9
off Bedevere Rd 100 DU48
Magpie All, EC4 286 F9
Magpie Cl, E7 281 M2
NW9 *off Eagle Dr* 96 CS54
Coulsdon CR5
off Ashbourne Cl 235 DJ118
Enfield EN1 82 DU39
Magpie Hall Cl, Brom. BR2 204 EL100
Magpie Hall La, Brom. BR2 205 EM99
Magpie Hall Rd,
Bushey Hth WD23 95 CE47
Magpie La, Colesh. HP7 89 AM45
Little Warley CM13 107 FW54
Magpie Pl, SE14
off Milton Ct Rd 313 M3
Watford WD25 60 BW32
Magpies, The,
Epp.Grn CM16 51 EN24
Magpie Wk, Hat. AL10
off Lark Ri 45 CU20
Magpie Way, Slou. SL2
off Pemberton Rd 131 AL70
Magri Wk, E1 288 G7
Maguire Dr, Rich. TW10 177 CJ91
Maguire St, SE1 300 B4
● **Mahatma Gandhi Ind Est**, SE24
off Milkwood Rd 161 DP84
Mahlon Av, Ruis. HA4 115 BV64
Mahogany Cl, SE16 301 M3
Mahon Cl, Enf. EN1 82 DT39
Maibeth Gdns, Beck. BR3 203 DY98
Maida Av, E4 101 EB45
W2 283 P6
MAIDA HILL, W9 283 J4
Maida Rd, Belv. DA17 166 FA76
MAIDA VALE, W9 283 M4
⊖ **Maida Vale** 283 M2
Maida Vale, W9 283 N3
Maida Vale Rd, Dart. DA1 187 FG85
Maida Way, E4 101 EB45
Maiden Erlegh Av, Bex. DA5 186 EY88
Maidenhead Rd, Wind. SL4 151 AK80
Maidenhead St, Hert. SG14 32 DR09
Maiden La, NW1 275 P6
SE1 299 K2
WC2 298 B1
Dartford DA1 167 FG83
Maiden Pl, NW5 121 DJ62
Maiden Rd, E15 281 K6
Maiden's Br, Enf. EN2 82 DU37
Maidensfield, Welw.G.C. AL8 29 CX06
Maidenshaw Rd,
Epsom KT19 216 CR112
Maidenstone Hill, SE10 314 E6
Maids of Honour Row,
Rich. TW9 *off The Green* 177 CK85
Maidstone Av, Rom. RM5 105 FC54
Maidstone Bldgs Ms, SE1 299 K3
Maidstone Ho, E14 290 C8
Maidstone Rd, N11 99 DJ51
Grays RM17 170 GA79
Seal TN15 257 FN121
Sevenoaks TN13 256 FE122
Sidcup DA14 186 EX93
Swanley BR8 207 FB95
Main Av, Enf. EN1 82 DT43
Northwood HA6 93 BQ48
Main Dr, Ger.Cr. SL9 112 AW57
Iver SL0 153 BE76
Wembley HA9 117 CK62
Main Par, Chorl. WD3
off Whitelands Av 73 BC42
Main Par Flats, Chorl. WD3
off Whitelands Av 73 BC42
Main Ride, Egh. TW20 172 AS93
Mainridge Rd, Chis. BR7 185 EN91
Main Rd, Crock. BR8 207 FD100
Crockham Hill TN8 255 EQ134
Farningham DA4 208 FL100
Hextable BR8 187 FF94
Knockholt TN14 240 EV117
Longfield DA3 209 FX96
Orpington BR5 206 EW95
Romford RM1, RM2, RM7 127 FF56
Sidcup DA14 185 ES90
Sundridge TN14 240 EX124
Sutton at Hone DA4 188 FP93
Westerham TN16 222 EJ113
Windsor SL4 150 AJ80
Main St, Felt. TW13 176 BX92
Maisie Webster Cl, Stanw.
TW19 *off Lauser Rd* 174 BK87
Maismore St, SE15 312 D3
Maisonettes, The, Sutt. SM1 217 CZ106
Maitland Cl, SE10 314 D5
Hounslow TW4 156 BZ83
Walton-on-Thames KT12 196 BY103
West Byfleet KT14 212 BG113
Maitland Cl Est, SE10 314 D5
Maitland Pk Est, NW3 274 F4
Maitland Pk Rd, NW3 274 F5
Maitland Pk Vil, NW3 274 F4
Maitland Pl, E5 278 G1
Maitland Rd, E15 281 L5
SE26 183 DX93
Maize Cft, Horl. RH6 269 DJ147
Maizey Ct, Pilg.Hat. CM15
off Danes Way 108 FU43
Majendie Rd, SE18 165 ER78
Majestic Way, Mitch. CR4 200 DF96
Major Cl, SW9 311 H10
Major Draper St, SE18 305 P7
Sch **Majorie McClure Sch**,
Chis. BR7 *off Hawkwood La* 205 EQ96
Major Rd, E15 280 F2
SE16 300 D6
Majors Fm Rd, Slou. SL3 152 AX80
Makepeace Av, N6 120 DG61
Makepeace Rd, E11 124 EG56
Northolt UB5 136 BY68
Makins St, SW3 296 D9
Malabar St, E14 302 A5
Malacca Fm, W.Clan. GU4 244 BH127
Malam Ct, SE11 298 E9
Malam Gdns, E14 290 C10
Malan Cl, Bigg.H. TN16 238 EL117
Malan Sq, Rain. RM13 147 FH65
Malbrook Rd, SW15 159 CV84
Malcolm Cl, SE20
off Oakfield Rd 182 DW94
Malcolm Ct, Stan. HA7 95 CJ50
Malcolm Cres, NW4 119 CU58
Malcolm Dr, Surb. KT6 198 CL102
Malcolm Gdns, Hkwd RH6 268 DD150
Malcolm Pl, E2 288 G4
Sch **Malcolm Prim Sch**, SE20
off Malcolm Rd 182 DW94
Malcolm Rd, E1 288 G4
SE20 182 DW94
SE25 202 DU100
SW19 179 CY93
Coulsdon CR5 235 DK115
Uxbridge UB10 114 BM63
Malcolms Way, N14 81 DJ43
Malcolm Way, E11 124 EG57
Malden Av, SE25 202 DV98
Greenford UB6 117 CE64
Malden Cl, Amer. HP6 72 AT38
Malden Ct, N.Mal. KT3 199 CV97
Malden Cres, NW1 275 H5
Malden Flds, Bushey WD23 76 BX42
Malden Grn Av, Wor.Pk. KT4 199 CT102
Malden Grn Ms, Wor.Pk. KT4
off Malden Rd 199 CU102
Malden Hill, N.Mal. KT3 199 CT97
Malden Hill Gdns,
N.Mal. KT3 199 CT97
⇌ **Malden Junct**,
N.Mal. KT3 199 CT99
⇌ **Malden Manor** 198 CS101
Sch **Malden Manor Prim & Nurs Sch**, N.Mal. KT3
off Lawrence Av 198 CS101
Malden Pk, N.Mal. KT3 199 CT100
Sch **Malden Parochial C of E Prim Sch**, Wor.Pk. KT4
off The Manor Drive 198 CS102
Malden Pl, NW5 274 G3
Malden Rd, NW5 274 F3
Borehamwood WD6 78 CN41
New Malden KT3 198 CS99
Sutton SM3 217 CX105
Watford WD17 75 BU40
Worcester Park KT4 199 CT101
MALDEN RUSHETT,
Chess. KT9 215 CH111
Malden Way, N.Mal. KT3 199 CT99

Maldon Cl, E15 281 J3
N1 277 J8
SE5 311 N10
Maldon Ct, Wall. SM6 219 DJ106
Maldon Rd, N9 100 DT48
W3 138 CQ73
Romford RM7 127 FC59
Wallington SM6 219 DH106
Maldon Wk, Wdf.Grn. IG8 102 EJ51
Malet Cl, Egh. TW20 173 BD93
Malet Pl, WC1 285 N5
Malet St, WC1 285 N5
Maley Av, SE27 181 DP89
Malford Ct, E18 102 EG54
Malford Gro, E18 124 EF56
Malfort Rd, SE5 311 P10
Malham Cl, N11
off Catterick Cl 98 DG51
Malham Rd, SE23 183 DX88
Malham Ter, N18
off Dysons Rd 100 DV51
Malin Ct, Hem.H. HP3 40 BJ23
Malins Cl, Barn. EN5 79 CV43
Malkin Dr, Beac. HP9 88 AJ52
Church Langley CM17 52 EY16
Malkin Way, Wat. WD18 75 BS42
Mall, The, Brom. BR1 204 EG97
Croydon CR0 202 DQ103
Romford RM1 127 FF56
Mall, The, N14 99 DL48
SW1 297 M4
SW14 178 CQ85
W5 138 CL73
Harrow HA3 118 CM58
Hornchurch RM11 127 FH60
Park Street AL2 60 CC27
Surbiton KT6 197 CK99
Swanley BR8 off London Rd 207 FE97
Mallams Ms, SW9 310 F10
Mallard Cl, E9 279 P4
NW6 273 K9
W7 157 CE75
Burnham SL1 130 AH68
Dartford DA1 188 FM85
Horley RH6 268 DG146
New Barnet EN5
off The Hook 80 DD44
Redhill RH1 250 DG131
Twickenham TW2
off Stephenson Rd 176 CA87
Upminster RM14 129 FT59
Mallard Dr, Slou. SL1 131 AM73
Mallard Path, SE28
off Goosander Way 165 ER76
Mallard Pl, Twick. TW1 177 CG90
Mallard Pt, E3 290 C3
Mallard Rd, Abb.L. WD5 59 BU31
South Croydon CR2 221 DX110
Mallards, E11 124 EG59
Mallards, The, Denh. UB9
off Patrons Way E 113 BF58
Hem.H. HP3 58 BM25
Staines-upon-Thames TW18 194 BH96
Mallards Reach, Wey. KT13 195 BR103
Mallards Ri, Harl. CM17 52 EX15
Mallards Rd, Bark. IG11 146 EU69
Woodford Green IG8 102 EH52
Mallard Wk, Beck. BR3 203 DX99
Sidcup DA14 186 EW92
Mallard Way, NW9 118 CQ59
Hutton CM13 109 GB45
Northwood HA6 93 BQ52
Wallington SM6 219 DJ109
Watford WD25 76 BY37
Mall Bexleyheath, The,
Bexleyheath DA6 166 FA84
Mall Chambers, W8
off Kensington Mall 295 K2
Mallet Dr, Nthlt. UB5 116 BZ64
Mallet Rd, SE13 183 ED86
Mall Ex, The, Ilf. IG1 125 EP61
★ Mall Galleries, SW1 297 P2
Malling, SE13 183 EC85
Malling Cl, Croy. CR0 202 DW100
Malling Gdns, Mord. SM4 200 DC100
Malling Way, Brom. BR2 204 EF101
Mallinson Cl, Horn. RM12 128 FJ64
Mallinson Rd, SW11 180 DE85
Croydon CR0 201 DK104
Mallion Ct, Wal.Abb. EN9 68 EF33
Mallord St, SW3 308 B2
Mallory Cl, E14 290 D6
SE4 163 DY84
Mallory Gdns, E.Barn. EN4 98 DG45
Mallory St, NW8 284 D4
Mallow Cl, Croy. CR0
off Marigold Way 203 DX102
Northfleet DA11 190 GE91
Tadworth KT20 233 CV119
● Mallow Ct, Welw.G.C. AL7 30 DA08
Mallow Ct, Grays RM17 170 GD79
Mallow Cres, Guil. GU4 243 BB131
Mallow Cft, Hat. AL10
off Oxlease Dr 45 CV19
Mallow Mead, NW7 97 CY52
Mallows, The, Uxb. UB10 115 BP62
Mallows Grn, Harl. CM19 51 EN19
Mallow St, EC1 287 L4
Mallow Wk, Goffs Oak EN7 66 DR28
Mall Pavilions, The,
Uxb. UB8 134 BJ66
Mall Rd, W6 159 CV78
Sch Mall Sch, The, Twick. TW2
off Hampton Rd 177 CD90
Mall Shop, Dag. RM10
off Heathway 146 FA65
Mall Walthamstow, The, E17 123 DZ56
Mall Wood Green, The, N22 99 DN54
Mallys Pl, S.Darenth DA4 208 FQ95
Malmains Cl, Beck. BR3 203 ED99
Malmains Way, Beck. BR3 203 EC98
Malm Cl, Rick. WD3 92 BK47
Malmesbury, E2 288 G1
Malmesbury Cl, Pnr. HA5 115 BT56
Sch Malmesbury Prim Sch, E3 289 P2
Morden SM4
off Malmesbury Rd 200 DC100
Malmesbury Rd, E3 289 N2
E16 291 K6
E18 102 EF53
Morden SM4 200 DC101
Malmesbury Ter, E16 291 L6
Malmes Cft, Hem.H. HP3 41 BQ22
Malmsdale, Welw.G.C. AL8 29 CX05
Malmsmead Ho, E9
off Kingsmead Way 279 M2
Malmstone Av, Merst. RH1 251 DJ128
Sch Malorees Inf & Jun Schs,
NW6 272 D7
Malory Cl, Beck. BR3 203 DY96
Malory Ct, N9
off Galahad Rd 100 DU48
Malpas Dr, Pnr. HA5 116 BX57
Malpas Rd, E8 278 E4
SE4 313 N9
Dagenham RM9 146 EX65
Grays RM16 171 GJ76
Slough SL2 132 AV73
Malta Rd, E10 123 EA60
Tilbury RM18 171 GF82
Malta St, EC1 287 H4
Maltby Cl, Orp. BR6 206 EU102
Maltby Dr, Enf. EN1 82 DV38
Maltby Rd, Chess. KT9 216 CN107
Maltby St, SE1 300 A5
Malt Hill, Egh. TW20 172 AY92
Malt Ho Cl, Old Wind. SL4 172 AV87
Malthouse Dr, W4 158 CS79
Feltham TW13 176 BX92
Malthouse Pas, SW13
off The Terrace 158 CS82
Malthouse Pl, Rad. WD7 61 CG34
Malt Ho Pl, Rom. RM1
off Exchange St 127 FE57
Malthouse Sq, Beac. HP9 111 AM55
Malthus Path, SE28
off Byron Cl 146 EW74
Malting Ho, E14 289 N10
Malting Mead, Hat. AL10
off Endymion Rd 45 CW17
● Maltings, The,
Sawbridgeworth CM21 36 FA5
Stanstead Abbotts SG12 33 ED11
Maltings, The, St.Alb. AL1 43 CD20
Maltings, The, Byfleet KT14 212 BM113
Hunton Bridge WD4 59 BQ33
Orpington BR6 205 ET102
Oxted RH8 254 EF131
Romford RM1 127 FF59
Staines-upon-Thames TW18
off Church St 173 BE91
Worcester Park KT4
off Sherbrooke Way 199 CV101
Maltings Cl, E3 290 E3
SW13 off Cleveland Gdns 158 CS82
Maltings Dr, Epp. CM16 70 EU29
Maltings La, Epp. CM16 70 EU29
Maltings Ms, Amer. HP7 55 AP40
Sidcup DA15 off Station Rd 186 EU90
Maltings Pl, SE1 299 P5
SW6 307 M7
Malting Way, Islw. TW7 157 CF83
Malt La, Rad. WD7 77 CG35
Sch Maltman's Grn Sch,
Chal.St.P. SL9
off Maltmans La 112 AW55
Maltmans La, Chal.St.P. SL9 112 AW55
Malton Av, Slou. SL1 131 AP72
Malton Ms, SE18
off Malton St 165 ES79
W10 off Malton Rd 282 E8
Malton Rd, W10 282 E8
Malton St, SE18 165 ES79
Maltravers St, WC2 286 D10
Malt St, SE1 312 C2
Malus Cl, Add. KT15 211 BF108
Hemel Hempstead HP2 40 BN19
Malus Dr, Add. KT15 211 BF107
Malva Cl, SW18
off St. Ann's Hill 180 DB85
Malvern Av, E4 101 ED52
Bexleyheath DA7 166 EY80
Harrow HA2 116 BY62
Malvern Cl, SE20
off Derwent Rd 202 DU96
W10 282 G7
Bushey WD23 76 CC44
Hatfield AL10 45 CT17
Mitcham CR4 201 DJ97
Ottershaw KT16 211 BC107
St. Albans AL4 43 CH16
Surbiton KT6 198 CL102
Uxbridge UB10 115 BP61
Malvern Ct, SE14 313 H4
SW7 296 B9
Slough SL3 off Hill Ri 153 BA79
Sutton SM2
off Overton Rd 218 DA108
Malvern Dr, Felt. TW13 176 BX92
Ilford IG3 125 ET63
Woodford Green IG8 102 EJ50
Malvern Gdns, NW2 119 CY61
NW6 283 H1
Harrow HA3 118 CL55
Loughton IG10 85 EM44
Malvern Ms, NW6 283 J3
Malvern Pl, NW6 283 H2
Malvern Rd, E6 144 EL67
E8 278 C7
E11 124 EE61
N8 121 DM55
N17 122 DU55
NW6 283 J2
Enfield EN3 83 DY37
Grays RM17 170 GD77
Hampton TW12 176 CA94
Hayes UB3 155 BS80
Hornchurch RM11 127 FG58
Orpington BR6 224 EV105
Surbiton KT6 198 CL103
Thornton Heath CR7 201 DN98
Malvern Ter, N1 276 E8
N9 100 DT46
Malvern Way, W13
off Templewood 137 CH71
Croxley Green WD3 75 BP43
Hemel Hempstead HP2 40 BM18
Sch Malvern Way Inf & Nurs
Sch, Crox.Grn WD3
off Malvern Way 75 BQ43
Malvina Av, Grav. DA12 191 GH89
Malwood Rd, SW12 181 DH86
Malyons, The, Shep. TW17
off Gordon Rd 195 BR100
Malyons Rd, SE13 183 EB85
Swanley BR8 187 FF94
Malyons Ter, SE13 183 EB85
Managers St, E14 302 F3
Manan Cl, Hem.H. HP3 41 BQ22
Manatee Pl, Wall. SM6
off Croydon Rd 201 DK104
Manaton Cl, SE15 312 E10
Manaton Cres, Sthl. UB1 136 CA72
Manbey Gro, E15 281 J4
Manbey Pk Rd, E15 281 J4
Manbey Rd, E15 281 J4
Manbey St, E15 281 J5
Manbre Rd, W6 306 B2
Manbrough Av, E6 293 K3
Sch Manby Lo Inf Sch,
Wey. KT13 off Princes Rd 213 BQ105
Manchester Ct, E16 292 B9
Manchester Dr, W10 282 E5
Manchester Gro, E14 302 E10
Manchester Ms, W1 284 G7
Manchester Rd, E14 302 E10
N15 122 DR58
Thornton Heath CR7 202 DQ97
Manchester Sq, W1 284 G8
Manchester St, W1 284 G7
Manchester Way, Dag. RM10 127 FB63
Manchuria Rd, SW11 180 DG86
Manciple St, SE1 299 L5
Mandalay Rd, SW4 181 DJ85
Mandarin St, E14 290 A10
Mandarin Way, Hayes UB4 136 BX72
Mandela Av, Harl. CM20 35 ES13
Mandela Cl, NW10 138 CQ66
Mandela Rd, E16 291 P9
Mandela St, NW1 275 M8
SW9 310 E5
Mandela Way, SE1 299 P8
Mandel Ho, SW18
off Eastfields Av 160 DA84
Mandelyns, Nthch HP4 38 AS16
Coll Mander Portman Woodward
6th Form Tutorial Coll, SW7 296 A9
Mandeville Cl, SE3 315 M5
SW20 199 CY95
Broxbourne EN10 49 DZ20
Guildford GU2 242 AU131
Harlow CM17 52 EW17
Hertford SG13 32 DQ12
Watford WD17 75 BT38
Mandeville Ct, E4 101 DY49
Egham TW20 173 BA91
Mandeville Dr, St.Alb. AL1 43 CD23
Surbiton KT6 197 CK102
Mandeville Ho, SE1 300 B10
Mandeville Ms, SW4
off Clapham Pk Rd 161 DL84
Mandeville Pl, W1 285 H8
Sch Mandeville Prim Sch, E5
off Oswald St 123 DX62
St. Albans AL1
off Mandeville Dr 43 CD23
Mandeville Ri, Welw.G.C. AL8 29 CX07
Mandeville Rd, N14 99 DH47
Enfield EN3 83 DX36
Hertford SG13 32 DQ12
Isleworth TW7 157 CG82
Northolt UB5 136 CA66
Potters Bar EN6 64 DC32
Shepperton TW17 194 BN99
Sch Mandeville Sch, Grnf. UB6
off Horsenden La N 137 CE65
Mandeville St, E5 123 DY62
Mandeville Wk, Hutt. CM13 109 GE44
Mandrake Rd, SW17 180 DF90
Mandrake Way, E15 281 J6
Mandrell Rd, SW2 181 DL85
Manette St, W1 285 P9
Manfield Cl, Slou. SL2 131 AN69
Manford Cl, Chig. IG7 104 EU49
Manford Ct, Chig. IG7
off Manford Way 104 EU50
Manford Cross, Chig. IG7 104 EU50
● Manford Ind Est, Erith DA8 167 FG79
Sch Manford Prim Sch,
Chig. IG7 off Manford Way 103 ET50
Manford Way, Chig. IG7 103 ES49
Manfred Rd, SW15 179 CZ85
Manger Rd, N7 276 B4
Mangles Rd, Guil. GU1 242 AX132
Mangold Way, Erith DA18 166 EY76
Mangrove Dr, Hert. SG13 32 DS11
Mangrove La, Hert. SG13 48 DT16
Mangrove Rd, Hert. SG13 32 DS10
Manhattan Av, Wat. WD18 75 BT42
Manhattan Bldg, E3 280 B10
Manhattan Wf, E16 303 N4
Manilla St, E14 302 A4
Manister Rd, SE2 166 EU76
Manitoba Ct, SE16 301 H5
Manitoba Gdns, Grn St Grn
BR6 off Superior Dr 223 ET107
Manley Ct, N16 122 DT62
Manley Rd, Hem.H. HP2
off Knightsbridge Way 40 BL19
Manley St, NW1 274 G8
Manly Dixon Dr, Enf. EN3 83 DY37
Mannamead, Epsom KT18 232 CS119
Mannamead Cl, Epsom KT18
off Mannamead 232 CS119
Mann Cl, Croy. CR0
off Scarbrook Rd 202 DQ104
Manneby Prior, N1
off Cumming St 286 D1
Mannicotts, Welw.G.C. AL8 29 CV09
Manningford Cl, EC1 286 G2
Manning Gdns, Croy. CR0 202 DV101
Harrow HA3 117 CK59
Manning Pl, Rich. TW10
off Grove Rd 178 CM86
Manning Rd, E17
off Southcote Rd 123 DY57
Dagenham RM10 146 FA65
Orpington BR5 206 EX99
Manning St, Aveley RM15 148 FQ74
Manningtree Cl, SW19 179 CY88
Manningtree Rd, Ruis. HA4 115 BV63
Manningtree St, E1 288 C8
Mannin Rd, Rom. RM6 126 EV59
Mannock Cl, NW9 118 CR55
Mannock Dr, Loug. IG10 85 EQ40
Mannock Ms, E18 102 EH53
Mannock Rd, N22 121 DP55
Dartford DA1
off Barnwell Rd 168 FM83
Manns Cl, Islw. TW7 177 CF85
Manns Rd, Edg. HA8 96 CN51
Manns Ter, SE27 181 DP90
Manoel Rd, Twick. TW2 176 CC89
Manor Av, SE4 313 P9
Caterham CR3 236 DS124
Hemel Hempstead HP3 40 BK23
Hornchurch RM11 128 FJ57
Hounslow TW4 156 BX83
Northolt UB5 136 BZ66
Manorbrook, SE3 164 EG84
Manor Chase, Wey. KT13 213 BP106
Jun Manor Circ, Rich. TW9 158 CN83
Manor Cl, E17 off Manor Rd 101 DY54
NW7 off Manor Dr 96 CR50
NW9 118 CP57
SE28 146 EW72
Aveley RM15 148 FQ74
Barnet EN5 79 CY42
Berkhamsted HP4 38 AW19
Crayford DA1 167 FD84
Dagenham RM10 147 FD65
East Horsley KT24 245 BS128
Hatfield AL10 45 CT15
Hertford SG14 32 DR07
Horley RH6 268 DF148
Romford RM1 off Manor Rd 127 FG57
Ruislip HA4 115 BT60
Warlingham CR6 237 DY117
Wilmington DA2 187 FG90
Woking GU22 227 BF116
Worcester Park KT4 198 CS102
Manor Cl S, Aveley RM15
off Manor Cl 148 FQ74
Sch Manor Comm Prim Sch,
Swans. DA10 off Keary Rd 190 FZ87
Manor Cotts, Nthwd. HA6 93 BT53
Manor Cotts App, N2 98 DC54
Manor Ct, E10
off Grange Pk Rd 123 EB60
N2 120 DF57
SW2 off St. Matthew's Rd 181 DM85
SW6 307 M7
Enfield EN1 82 DV36
Harefield UB9 92 BJ54
Radlett WD7 77 CF38
Slough SL1 off Richards Way 131 AM74
Twickenham TW2 176 CC89
Wembley HA9 118 CL64
Weybridge KT13 213 BP105
Manor Ct Rd, W7 137 CE73
Manor Cres, Byfleet KT14 212 BM113
Epsom KT19 216 CN112
Guildford GU2 242 AV132
Hornchurch RM11 128 FJ57
Seer Green HP9 89 AR51
Surbiton KT5 198 CN100
Sch Manorcroft Prim Sch,
Egh. TW20 off Wesley Dr 173 BA93
Manorcrofts Rd, Egh. TW20 173 BA93
Manordene Cl, T.Ditt. KT7 197 CG102
Manordene Rd, SE28 146 EW72
Manor Dr, N14 99 DH45
N20 98 DE48
NW7 96 CR50
Amersham HP6 55 AP36
Epsom KT19 216 CS107
Esher KT10 197 CF103
Feltham TW13
off Lebanon Av 176 BX92
Horley RH6 268 DF148
New Haw KT15 212 BG110
St. Albans AL2 60 CA27
Sunbury-on-Thames TW16 195 BU96
Surbiton KT5 198 CM100
Wembley HA9 118 CM63
Manor Dr, The, Wor.Pk. KT4 198 CS102
Manor Dr N, N.Mal. KT3 198 CR101
Worcester Park KT4 198 CS102
Manor Est, SE16 300 E9
Manor Fm, Fnghm DA4 208 FM101
Manor Fm Av, Shep. TW17 195 BP100
Manor Fm Cl, Wind. SL4 151 AM83
Worcester Park KT4 198 CS102
Manor Fm Ct, Egh. TW20
off Manor Fm La 173 BA92
Manor Fm Dr, E4 102 EE48
Manor Fm La, Egh. TW20 173 BA92
Manor Fm Rd, Enf. EN1 82 DV35
Thornton Heath CR7 201 DN96
Wembley HA0 137 CK68
Manor Fm Way, Seer Grn HP9
off Orchard Rd 89 AR51
Manorfield Cl, N19
off Junction Rd 121 DJ63
Sch Manorfield Prim & Nurs
Sch, Horl. RH6 off Sangers Dr 268 DF148
Sch Manorfield Prim Sch, E14 290 D6
Manor Flds, SW15 179 CX86
Manorfields Cl, Chis. BR7 205 ET97
Manor Gdns, N7 121 DL62
SW20 199 CZ96
W3 158 CN77
W4 off Devonshire Rd 158 CS78
Effingham KT24 246 BX128
Godalming GU7
off Farncombe St 258 AS144
Guildford GU2 242 AV132
Hampton TW12 176 CB94
Richmond TW9 158 CM84
Ruislip HA4 116 BW64
South Croydon CR2 220 DT107
Sunbury-on-Thames TW16 195 BU96
Wooburn Green HP10 110 AE58
Manor Gate, Nthlt. UB5 136 BY66
Manorgate Rd, Kings.T. KT2 198 CN95
Manor Grn Rd, Epsom KT19 216 CP113
Manor Gro, SE15 312 G3
Beckenham BR3 203 EB96
Fifield SL6 150 AD80
Richmond TW9 158 CN84
Manor Hall Av, NW4 97 CW54
Manor Hall Dr, NW4 97 CX54
Manorhall Gdns, E10 123 EA60
Manor Hatch Cl, Harl. CM18 52 EV16
⊖ Manor House 121 DP59
Manor Ho Ct, Epsom KT18 216 CQ113
Shepperton TW17 195 BP101
Manor Ho Dr, NW6 272 D7
Hersham KT12 213 BT107
Northwood HA6 93 BP52
Manor Ho Est, Stan. HA7 95 CH51
Manor Ho Gdns, Abb.L. WD5 59 BR31
Manor Ho La, Bkhm KT23 246 BY126
Datchet SL3 152 AV81
Sch Manor Ho Sch, Bkhm KT23
off Manor Ho La 246 BY127
Manor Ho Way, Islw. TW7 157 CH83
Sch Manor Inf & Nurs Sch,
Til. RM18 off Dickens Av 171 GH80
Sch Manor Inf Sch, Bark. IG11
off Sandringham Rd 145 ET65
(Longbridge Rd) Dag. RM9 126 EV63
Sch Manor Jun Sch, Bark. IG11
off Sandringham Rd 145 ET65
Manor La, SE12 184 EE86
SE13 164 EE84
Fawkham Green DA3 209 FW101
Feltham TW13 175 BU89
Gerrards Cross SL9 112 AX59
Harlington UB3 155 BR79
Lower Kingswood KT20 250 DA129
Manor La, Sevenoaks TN15 209 FW103
Sunbury-on-Thames TW16 195 BU96
Sutton SM1 218 DC106
Manor La Ter, SE13 164 EE84
Manor Leaze, Egh. TW20 173 BB92
Manor Lo, Guil. GU2 242 AV132
Sch Manor Lo Sch, Shenley
WD7 off Rectory La 62 CQ30
Sch Manor Mead Sch,
Shep. TW17 off Laleham Rd 195 BP99
Manor Ms, NW6 273 K10
SE4 313 P8
Manor Mt, SE23 182 DW88
Sch Manor Oak Prim Sch,
Orp. BR5 off Sweeps La 206 EX99
Manor Par, NW10
off Station Rd 139 CT68
Hatfield AL10 45 CT15
MANOR PARK, E12 124 EL63
Slou. SL2 131 AQ70
⇌ Manor Park 124 EK63
Manor Pk, SE13 163 ED84
Chislehurst BR7 205 ER96
Richmond TW9 158 CM84
Staines-upon-Thames TW18 173 BD90
Manor Pk Cl, W.Wick. BR4 203 EB102
Manor Pk Cres, Edg. HA8 96 CN51
Manor Pk Dr, Har. HA2 116 CB55
Manor Pk Gdns, Edg. HA8 96 CN50
Manor Pk Par, SE13
off Lee High Rd 163 ED84
Sch Manor Pk Prim Sch,
Sutt. SM1 off Greyhound Rd 218 DC106
Manor Pk Rd, E12 124 EK63
N2 120 DC55
NW10 139 CT67
Chislehurst BR7 205 EQ95
Sutton SM1 218 DC106
West Wickham BR4 203 EB102
Manor Pl, SE17 311 H1
Bookham KT23 246 CA126
Chislehurst BR7 205 ER95
Feltham TW14 175 BU88
Mitcham CR4 201 DJ97
Staines-upon-Thames TW18 174 BH92
Sutton SM1 218 DB105
Walton-on-Thames KT12 195 BT101
Sch Manor Prim Sch, E15 281 J10
Sch Manor Prim Sch, The,
Rom. RM1 off Shaftesbury Rd 127 FF57
Manor Rd, E10 123 EA59
E15 291 J1
E16 291 J4
E17 101 DY54
N16 122 DR61
N17 100 DU53
N22 99 DL51
SE25 202 DU98
SW20 199 CZ96
W13 137 CG73
Ashford TW15 174 BM92
Barking IG11 145 ET65
Barnet EN5 79 CY43
Beckenham BR3 203 EB96
Bexley DA5 187 FB88
Chadwell Heath RM6 126 EX58
Chesham HP5
off Lansdowne Rd 54 AQ29
Chigwell IG7 103 EP50
Dagenham RM10 147 FC65
Dartford DA1 167 FE84
East Molesey KT8 197 CD98
Enfield EN2 82 DR40
Erith DA8 167 FF79
Gravesend DA12 191 GH86
Grays RM17 170 GC79
Guildford GU2 242 AV132
Harlow CM17 36 EW10
Harrow HA1 117 CG58
Hatfield AL10 45 CT15
Hayes UB3 135 BU72
High Beach IG10 84 EH38
Hoddesdon EN11 49 EA16
Lambourne End RM4 104 EW47
London Colney AL2 61 CJ26
Loughton IG10 84 EH44
Mitcham CR4 201 DJ98
Potters Bar EN6 63 CZ31
Reigate RH2 249 CZ132
Richmond TW9 158 CM83
Ripley GU23 227 BF123
Romford RM1 127 FG57
Ruislip HA4 115 BR60
St. Albans AL1 43 CE19
Seer Green HP9 89 AR50
Sidcup DA15 185 ET90
South Merstham RH1 251 DJ129
Sundridge TN14 240 EX124
Sutton SM2 217 CZ108
Swanscombe DA10 189 FX86
Tatsfield TN16 238 EL120
Teddington TW11 177 CH92
Tilbury RM18 171 GG82
Twickenham TW2 176 CC89
Wallington SM6 219 DH105
Waltham Abbey EN9 67 ED33
Walton-on-Thames KT12 195 BT101
Watford WD17 75 BV39
West Thurrock RM20 169 FW79
West Wickham BR4 203 EB103
Windsor SL4 151 AL82
Woking GU21 226 AW116
Woodford Green IG8 103 EM51
Manor Rd N, Esher KT10 197 CF104
Thames Ditton KT7 197 CG103
Wallington SM6 219 DH105
Manor Rd S, Esher KT10 215 CE105
Sch Manor Sch, NW10 272 B9
Manorside, Barn. EN5 79 CY42
Manorside Cl, SE2 166 EW77
Sch Manorside Prim Sch, N3
off Squires La 98 DC53
Manor Sq, Dag. RM8 126 EX61
Manor St, Berk. HP4 38 AX19
Manor Vale, Brent. TW8 157 CJ78
Manor Vw, N3 98 DB54
Manorville Rd, Hem.H. HP3 40 BJ24
Manor Wk, Wey. KT13 213 BP106
Manor Way, E4 101 ED49
NW9 118 CS55
SE3 164 EF84
SE23 182 DW87
SE28 146 EW74
Banstead SM7 234 DF116
Beckenham BR3 203 EA96
Bexley DA5 186 FA88
Bexleyheath DA7 167 FD83
Borehamwood WD6 78 CQ42
Brentwood CM14 108 FU48

Manor Way, Bromley BR2 204 EL100
Chesham HP5 54 AR30
Cheshunt EN8
off Russells Ride 67 DY31
Coleshill HP7 55 AM44
Croxley Green WD3 74 BN42
Egham TW20 173 AZ93
Grays RM17 170 GB80
Guildford GU2 258 AS137
Harrow HA2 116 CB56
Mitcham CR4 201 DJ97
Oxshott KT22 230 CC115
Petts Wood BR5 205 EQ98
Potters Bar EN6 64 DA30
Purley CR8 219 DL112
Rainham RM13 147 FE70
Ruislip HA4 115 BS59
South Croydon CR2 220 DS107
Southall UB2 156 BX77
Swanscombe DA10 170 FY84
Woking GU22 227 BB121
Worcester Park KT4 198 CS102
Manorway, Enf. EN1 100 DS45
Woodford Green IG8 102 EJ50
Manor Way, The, Wall. SM6 219 DH105
● Manor Way Business Cen, Rain. RM13 off Marsh Way 147 FD71
● Manor Way Business Pk, Swans. DA10 170 FY84
Manor Waye, Uxb. UB8 134 BK67
● Manor Way Ind Est, Grays RM17 170 GC80
Manor Wd Rd, Pur. CR8 219 DL113
Manpreet Ct, E12 125 EM64
Manresa Rd, SW3 308 C1
Mansard Beeches, SW17 180 DG92
Mansard Cl, Horn. RM12 127 FG61
Pinner HA5 116 BX55
Mansards, The, St.Alb. AL1 off Avenue Rd 43 CE19
Manscroft Rd, Hem.H. HP1 40 BH17
Manse Cl, Harling. UB3 155 BR79
Mansel Cl, Guil. GU2 242 AV129
Slough SL2 132 AV71
Mansel Gro, E17 101 EA53
Mansell Cl, Wind. SL4 151 AL82
Mansell Rd, W3 158 CR75
Greenford UB6 136 CB71
Mansell St, E1 300 B1
Mansell Way, Cat. CR3 236 DQ122
Mansel Rd, SW19 179 CY93
Mansergh Cl, SE18 164 EL80
Manse Rd, N16 122 DT62
Manser Rd, Rain. RM13 147 FE69
Manse Way, Swan. BR8 207 FG98
Mansfield, High Wych CM21 36 EU06
Mansfield Av, N15 122 DR56
Barnet EN4 80 DF44
Ruislip HA4 115 BV60
Mansfield Cl, N9 82 DU44
Orpington BR5 206 EX101
Weybridge KT13 213 BP106
Mansfield Dr, Hayes UB4 135 BS70
Merstham RH1 251 DK128
Mansfield Gdns, Hert. SG14 32 DQ07
Hornchurch RM12 128 FK61
Mansfield Hill, E4 101 EB46
Mansfield Ms, W1 285 J7
Mansfield Pl, NW3 off New End 142 DC63
South Croydon CR2 220 DR107
Mansfield Rd, E11 124 EH58
E17 123 DZ56
NW3 274 F2
W3 138 CP70
Chessington KT9 215 CJ106
Ilford IG1 125 EN61
South Croydon CR2 220 DR107
Swanley BR8 187 FE93
Mansfield St, W1 285 J7
Mansford St, E2 288 D1
Manship Rd, Mitch. CR4 180 DG94
Mansion, The, Albury GU5 260 BL139
Berkhamsted HP4 38 AY17
Mansion Cl, SW9 310 F6
Mansion Gdns, NW3 120 DB62
★ Mansion Ho, EC4 287 L9
⊖ Mansion House 287 K10
Mansion Ho Pl, EC4 287 L9
Mansion Ho St, EC4 287 L9
Mansion La, Iver SL0 133 BC74
Mansion La Caravan Site, Iver SL0 133 BC74
Mansions, The, SW5 off Earls Ct Rd 295 L10
Manson Ms, SW7 295 P9
Manson Pl, SW7 296 A9
Manstead Gdns, Rain. RM13 147 FH72
Mansted Gdns, Rom. RM6 126 EW59
Manston Av, Sthl. UB2 156 CA77
Manston Cl, SE20 off Garden Rd 202 DW95
Cheshunt EN8 66 DW30
Manstone Rd, NW2 272 E2
Manston Gro, Kings.T. KT2 177 CK92
Manston Rd, Guil. GU4 243 BA130
Harlow CM20 51 ES15
Manston Way, Horn. RM12 147 FH65
St. Albans AL4 43 CK21
Manthorp Rd, SE18 165 EQ78
Mantilla Rd, SW17 180 DG91
Mantle Rd, SE4 163 DY83
Mantlet Cl, SW16 181 DJ94
Mantle Way, E15 281 J6
Manton Av, W7 157 CF75
Manton Cl, Hayes UB3 135 BS73
Manton Rd, SE2 166 EU77
Enfield EN3 83 EA37
Mantua St, SW11 308 B10
Mantus Cl, E1 289 H4
Mantus Rd, E1 288 G4
Manuka Cl, W7 137 CG74
Manville Gdns, SW17 181 DH90
Manville Rd, SW17 180 DG89
Manwood Rd, SE4 183 DZ85
Manwood St, E16 305 K3
Manygate La, Shep. TW17 195 BQ101
Manygates, SW12 181 DH89
Maori Rd, Guil. GU1 243 AZ134
Mapesbury Ms, NW4 off Station Rd 119 CU58
Mapesbury Rd, NW2 272 E4
Mapeshill Pl, NW2 272 B5
Mape St, E2 288 E4
Maple Av, E4 101 DZ50
W3 138 CS74
Harrow HA2 116 CB61
St. Albans AL3 42 CC16
Upminster RM14 128 FP62
West Drayton UB7 134 BL73
Maple Cl, N3 98 DA51
N16 122 DU58
SW4 181 DK86
Brentwood CM13 off Cherry Av 109 FZ48
Buckhurst Hill IG9 102 EK48
Bushey WD23 76 BY40
Epsom KT19 216 CR109
Hampton TW12 176 BZ93
Hatfield AL10 off Elm Dr 45 CU19
Hayes UB4 136 BX69
Hornchurch RM12 127 FH62
Ilford IG6 103 ES50
Mitcham CR4 201 DH95
Petts Wood BR5 205 ER99
Ruislip HA4 115 BV58
Swanley BR8 207 FE96
Theydon Bois CM16 off Loughton La 85 ER36
Whyteleafe CR3 236 DT117
Maple Ct, Eng.Grn TW20 off Ashwood Rd 172 AV93
Erith DA8 167 FF80
New Malden KT3 198 CR97
Stanstead Abbotts SG12 33 ED11
Maplecourt Wk, Wind. SL4 off Common Rd 151 AN78
Maple Cres, Sid. DA15 186 EU86
Slough SL2 132 AV73
Maplecroft Cl, E6 292 G8
Maplecroft La, Lwr Naze. EN9 50 EE21
MAPLE CROSS, Rick. WD3 91 BD49
Sch Maple Cross JMI Sch, Rick. WD3 off Denham Way 91 BE50
Maple Cross Rbt, Rick. WD3 91 BE48
Mapledale Av, Croy. CR0 202 DU103
Mapledene, Chis. BR7 185 EQ92
Mapledene Est, E8 278 C6
Mapledene Rd, E8 278 B6
Sch Mapledown Spec Sch, NW2 off Claremont Rd 119 CW59
Maple Dr, Bkhm KT23 246 CB125
South Ockendon RM15 149 FX70
Maplefield, Park St AL2 60 CB29
Maplefield La, Ch.St.G. HP8 72 AV41
Maple Gdns, Edg. HA8 96 CS52
Staines-upon-Thames TW19 174 BL89
Maple Gate, Loug. IG10 85 EN40
Maple Grn, Hem.H. HP1 39 BE18
Maple Gro, NW9 118 CQ59
W5 157 CK76
Bookham KT23 246 CA127
Brentford TW8 157 CH80
Guildford GU1 242 AX132
Southall UB1 136 BZ71
Watford WD17 75 BU39
Welwyn Garden City AL7 29 CZ06
Woking GU22 226 AY121
Maple Gro Business Cen, Houns. TW4 off Lawrence Rd 156 BW84
Maple Ho, NW3 off Maitland Pk Vil 274 F4
Maplehurst, Lthd. KT22 231 CD123
Maplehurst Cl, Dart. DA2 off Sandringham Dr 187 FE89
Kingston upon Thames KT1 198 CL98
● Maple Ind Est, Felt. TW13 off Maple Way 175 BV90
Sch Maple Inf Sch, Surb. KT6 off Maple Rd 197 CK99
Maple Leaf Cl, Abb.L. WD5 59 BU32
Biggin Hill TN16 off Main Rd 238 EK116
Stanstead Abbotts SG12 33 ED12
Mapleleaf Cl, S.Croy. CR2 221 DX111
Maple Leaf Dr, Sid. DA15 185 ET88
Mapleleafe Gdns, Ilf. IG6 125 EP55
Maple Leaf Sq, SE16 301 K5
Maple Lo Cl, Map.Cr. WD3 91 BE49
Maple Ms, NW6 273 L10
SW16 181 DM92
● Maple Pk, Hodd. EN11 49 EC17
Maple Pl, N17 off Park La 100 DU52
W1 285 M5
Banstead SM7 217 CX114
West Drayton UB7 134 BL73
● Maple River Ind Est, Harl. CM20 36 EV09
Maple Rd, E11 124 EE58
SE20 202 DV95
Ashtead KT21 231 CK119
Dartford DA1 188 FJ88
Gravesend DA12 191 GJ91
Grays RM17 170 GC79
Hayes UB4 136 BW69
Redhill RH1 266 DF138
Ripley GU23 228 BG124
Surbiton KT6 198 CL99
Whyteleafe CR3 236 DT117
Maples, The, Bans. SM7 218 DB114
Claygate KT10 215 CG108
Goffs Oak EN7 66 DS28
Harlow CM19 51 EP19
Ottershaw KT16 211 BB107
St. Albans AL1 off Granville Rd 43 CF20
Sch Maple Sch, St.Alb. AL1 off Hall Pl Gdns 43 CE19
Maplescombe La, Fnghm DA4 208 FN104
Maples Pl, E1 288 F6
Maple Springs, Wal.Abb. EN9 68 EG33
Maplestead Rd, SW2 181 DM87
Dagenham RM9 146 EV67
Maple St, E2 288 D1
W1 285 L6
Romford RM7 127 FC56
Maplethorpe Rd, Th.Hth. CR7 201 DN98
Mapleton Cl, Brom. BR2 204 EG100
Mapleton Cres, SW18 180 DB86
Enfield EN3 82 DW38
Mapleton Rd, E4 101 EC48
SW18 180 DB86
Edenbridge TN8 255 ET133
Enfield EN1 82 DV40
Westerham TN16 255 ES130
Maple Wk, W10 282 D4
Sutton SM2 218 DB110
Maple Way, Couls. CR5 235 DH121
Feltham TW13 175 BU90
Waltham Abbey EN9 off Breach Barn Mobile Home Pk 68 EH29
Maplewood Gdns, Beac. HP9 88 AH54
Maplin Cl, N21 81 DM44
Maplin Ho, SE2 off Wolvercote Rd 166 EX75
Maplin Pk, Slou. SL3 153 BC75
Maplin Rd, E16 292 A8
Maplin St, E3 289 N3
Mapperley Dr, Wdf.Grn. IG8 off Forest Dr 102 EE52
Marabou Cl, E12 124 EL64
Maran Way, Erith DA18 166 EX75
Marathon Ho, NW1 284 E6
Marathon Way, SE28 165 ET75
Marbaix Gdns, Islw. TW7 157 CD81
Marban Rd, W9 282 G2
Marbeck Cl, Wind. SL4 151 AK81
★ Marble Arch, W1 284 F10
⊖ Marble Arch 284 F10
Marble Arch Apts, W1 off Harrowby St 284 D8
Marble Cl, W3 138 CP74
Marble Dr, NW2 119 CX60
Marble Hill Cl, Twick. TW1 177 CH87
Marble Hill Gdns, Twick. TW1 177 CH87
★ Marble Hill Ho, Twick. TW1 177 CJ87
Marble Ho, SE18 off Felspar Cl 165 ET78
Marble Quay, E1 300 C2
Marbles Way, Tad. KT20 233 CX119
Marbrook Ct, SE12 184 EJ90
Marcella Rd, SW9 310 F9
Marcellina Way, Orp. BR6 205 ES104
Marcet Rd, Dart. DA1 188 FJ85
Marchant Cl, NW7 96 CS51
Marchant Rd, E11 123 ED61
Marchant St, SE14 313 L3
Marchbank Rd, W14 307 H2
Marchmant Cl, Horn. RM12 128 FJ62
Marchmont Gdns, Rich. TW10 off Marchmont Rd 178 CM85
Marchmont Grn, Hem.H. HP2 off Paston Rd 40 BK18
Marchmont Rd, Rich. TW10 178 CM85
Wallington SM6 219 DJ108
Marchmont St, WC1 286 A4
March Rd, Twick. TW1 177 CG87
Weybridge KT13 212 BN106
Marchside Cl, Houns. TW5 156 BX81
Marchwood Cl, SE5 311 P5
Marchwood Cres, W5 137 CJ72
Marcia Ct, Slou. SL1 131 AM74
Marcia Rd, SE1 299 P9
Marcilly Rd, SW18 180 DD85
Marco Dr, Pnr. HA5 94 BZ52
Marconi Gdns, Pilg.Hat. CM15 108 FW43
Marconi Pl, N11 99 DH49
Marconi Rd, E10 123 EA60
Northfleet DA11 190 GD90
Marconi Way, St.Alb. AL4 43 CK20
Southall UB1 136 CB72
Marcon Pl, E8 278 E3
Marco Rd, W6 159 CW76
Marcourt Lawns, W5 138 CL70
Marcus Ct, E15 281 K8
Marcuse Rd, Cat. CR3 236 DR123
Marcus Garvey Ms, SE22 off St. Aidan's Rd 182 DV85
Marcus Garvey Way, SE24 161 DN84
Marcus Rd, Dart. DA1 187 FG87
Marcus St, E15 281 K8
SW18 180 DB86
Marcus Ter, SW18 180 DB86
Mardale Dr, NW9 118 CR57
Mardell Rd, Croy. CR0 203 DX99
Marden Av, Brom. BR2 204 EG100
Marden Cl, Chig. IG7 104 EV47
Marden Cres, Bex. DA5 187 FC85
Croydon CR0 201 DM100
Marden Ho, E8 278 E2
Sch Marden Lo Prim Sch, Cat. CR3 off Croydon Rd 236 DV121
Marden Pk, Wold. CR3 253 DZ125
Marden Rd, N17 122 DS55
Croydon CR0 201 DM100
Romford RM1 127 FE58
Marden Sq, SE16 300 E7
Marder Rd, W13 157 CG75
Mardyke Cl, Rain. RM13 147 FC68
Mardyke Ho, SE17 off Crosslet St 299 M8
Mardyke Rd, Harl. CM20 36 EU13
Marechal Niel Av, Sid. DA15 185 ER90
Mareschal Rd, Guil. GU2 258 AW136
Marescroft Rd, Slou. SL2 131 AL70
Maresfield, Croy. CR0 202 DS104
Maresfield Gdns, NW3 273 P3
Mare St, E8 278 F9
Marfleet Cl, Cars. SM5 200 DE103
Marford Rd, Welw.G.C. AL8 28 CS10
Wheathampstead AL4 28 CN07
Margaret Av, E4 83 EB44
St. Albans AL3 43 CD18
Shenfield CM15 109 FZ45
Margaret Bondfield Av, Bark. IG11 146 EU66
Margaret Bldgs, N16 off Margaret Rd 122 DT60
Margaret Cl, Abb.L. WD5 59 BT32
Epping CM16 off Margaret Rd 70 EU29
Potters Bar EN6 64 DC33
Romford RM2 off Margaret Rd 127 FH57
Staines-upon-Thames TW18 off Charles Rd 174 BK93
Waltham Abbey EN9 67 ED33
Margaret Ct, W1 285 L8
Margaret Dr, Horn. RM11 128 FM60
Margaret Gardner Dr, SE9 185 EM89
Margaret Ingram Cl, SW6 306 G3
Margaret Lockwood Cl, Kings.T. KT1 198 CM98
Margaret McMillan Ho, E16 292 C9
Margaret Rd, N16 122 DT60
Barnet EN4 80 DD43
Bexley DA5 186 EX86
Epping CM16 70 EU29
Guildford GU1 258 AW135
Romford RM2 127 FH57
Sch Margaret Roper Cath Prim Sch, Pur. CR8 off Russell Hill Rd 219 DN110
Margaret Rutherford Pl, SW12 181 DJ88
Margaret Sq, Uxb. UB8 134 BJ67
Margaret St, W1 285 K8
Margaretta Ter, SW3 308 C2
Margaretting Rd, E12 124 EJ61
Margaret Way, Couls. CR5 235 DP118
Ilford IG4 124 EL58
Sch Margaret Wix Prim Sch, St.Alb. AL3 off High Oaks 42 CC16
Margate Rd, SW2 181 DL85
Margeholes, Wat. WD19 94 BY47
MARGERY, Tad. KT20 250 DA129
Margery Fry Ct, N7 121 DL62
Margery Gro, Lwr Kgswd KT20 249 CY129
Margery La, Lwr Kgswd KT20 249 CZ129
Tewin AL6 30 DD05
Margery Pk Rd, E7 281 N6
Margery Rd, Dag. RM8 126 EX62
Margery St, WC1 286 E3
Margery Wd, Welw.G.C. AL7 30 DA06
Margery Wd La, Lwr Kgswd KT20 249 CZ129
Margherita Pl, Wal.Abb. EN9 68 EF34
Margherita Rd, Wal.Abb. EN9 68 EG34
Margin Dr, SW19 179 CX92
Margravine Gdns, W6 294 D10
Margravine Rd, W6 306 D1
Marham Dr, NW9 off Kenley Av 96 CS53
Marham Gdns, SW18 180 DE88
Morden SM4 200 DC100
Mar Ho, SE7 off Springfield Gro 164 EJ79
Maria Cl, SE1 300 D8
Sch Maria Fidelis Conv Sch, Lwr Sch, NW1 285 M3
Upr Sch, NW1 285 N2
Mariam Gdns, Horn. RM12 128 FM61
Marian Cl, Hayes UB4 136 BX70
Marian Ct, Sutt. SM1 218 DB106
Marian Lawson Ct, Chig. IG7 off Manford Way 104 EU50
Marian Pl, E2 278 E10
Marian Rd, SW16 201 DJ95
Marian St, E2 278 E10
Sch Marian Vian Prim Sch, Beck. BR3 off Shirley Cres 203 DY99
Marian Way, NW10 139 CT66
Maria Ter, E1 289 J6
Maria Theresa Cl, N.Mal. KT3 198 CR99
Maricas Av, Har. HA3 95 CD53
Marie Curie, SE5 off Sceaux Gdns 311 P6
Marie Lloyd Gdns, N19 121 DL59
Marie Lloyd Ho, N1 287 L1
Marie Lloyd Wk, E8 278 B5
Marie Manor Way, Dart. DA2 169 FS84
Mariette Way, Wall. SM6 219 DL109
Marigold All, SE1 298 G1
Marigold Cl, Sthl. UB1 off Lancaster Rd 136 BY73
Marigold Ct, Guil. GU1 242 AY131
Marigold Pl, Harl. CM17 36 EV11
Marigold Rd, N17 100 DW52
Marigold St, SE16 300 E5
Marigold Way, Croydon CR0 203 DX102
H Marillac Hosp, Warley CM13 107 FX51
Marina App, Hayes UB4 136 BY71
Marina Av, N.Mal. KT3 199 CV99
Marina Cl, Brom. BR2 204 EG97
Chertsey KT16 194 BH102
Marina Dr, Dart. DA1 188 FN88
Northfleet DA11 191 GF87
Welling DA16 165 ES82
Marina Gdns, Chsht EN8 66 DW30
Romford RM7 127 FC58
Marina Pl, Hmptn W. KT1 197 CK95
Marina Pt, SW6 off Lensbury Ave 307 P8
Marina Way, Iver SL0 133 BF73
Slough SL1 131 AK73
Teddington TW11 off Fairways 177 CK94
Marine Dr, SE18 305 K9
Barking IG11 146 EV70
Marinefield Rd, SW6 307 M8
● Mariner Business Cen, Croy. CR0 219 DM106
Mariner Gdns, Rich. TW10 177 CJ90
Mariner Rd, E12 off Dersingham Av 125 EN63
Mariners Cl, Barn. EN4 80 DD43
Mariners Ct, Green. DA9 off High St 169 FV84
Mariners Ms, E14 302 G8
Mariners Wk, Erith DA8 off Cornwallis Cl 167 FF79
Mariner's Way, Grav. DA11 190 GE87
Mariner Way, Hem.H. HP2 40 BN21
Marine St, SE16 300 C6
Marine Twr, SE8 313 N2
Marion Av, Shep. TW17 195 BP99
Marion Cl, Bushey WD23 76 BZ39
Ilford IG6 103 ER52
Marion Cres, Orp. BR5 206 EU99
Marion Gro, Wdf.Grn. IG8 102 EE50
Marion Ms, SE21 182 DR90
Sch Marion Richardson Prim Sch, E1 289 J9
Marion Rd, NW7 97 CU50
Thornton Heath CR7 202 DQ99
Marion Wk, Hem.H. HP2 off Washington Av 40 BM15
Marischal Rd, SE13 163 ED83
Marisco Cl, Grays RM16 171 GH77
Marish La, Denh. UB9 113 BC56
Sch Marish Prim Sch, Langley SL3 off Swabey Rd 153 BA76
Marish Wf, Mdgrn SL3 152 AY75
Sch Marist Catholic Prim Sch, The, W.Byf. KT14 off Old Woking Rd 211 BF113
Maritime Cl, Green. DA9 189 FV85
Maritime Gate, Grav. DA11 190 GE87
Maritime Ho, SE18 305 N8
Maritime Quay, E14 302 B10
Maritime St, E3 289 P5
Marius Pas, SW17 off Marius Rd 180 DG89
Marius Rd, SW17 180 DG89
Marjoram Cl, Guil. GU2 242 AU130
Marjorams Av, Loug. IG10 85 EM40
Marjorie Gro, SW11 160 DF84
Marjorie Ms, E1 289 J9
Sch Marjory Kinnon Sch, Felt. TW14 off Hatton Rd 175 BS85
Markab Rd, Nthwd. HA6 93 BT50
Mark Av, E4 83 EB44
Mark Cl, Bexh. DA7 166 EY81
Southall UB1 off Longford Av 136 CB74
Mark Dr, Chal.St.P. SL9 90 AX49
Marke Cl, Kes. BR2 222 EL105
Markedge La, Chipstead CR5 234 DE124
Merstham RH1 250 DF126
Markenfield Rd, Guil. GU1 242 AX134
Markeston Grn, Wat. WD19 94 BX49
Market, The, Cars. SM5 off Wrythe La 200 DC102
Sutton SM1 off Rose Hill 200 DC102
Market App, W12 294 A4
Market Ct, W1 285 L8
Market Dr, W4 158 CS80
Market Est, N7 276 A4
Marketfield Rd, Red. RH1 250 DF134
Marketfield Way, Red. RH1 250 DF134
Market Hill, SE18 305 M7
Market Ho, Harl. CM20 off Birdcage Wk 35 ER14
Market La, W12 294 A5
Edgware HA8 96 CQ53
Iver SL0 153 BC75
Slough SL3 153 BC76
Market Link, Rom. RM1 127 FE56
Market Meadow, Orp. BR5 206 EW98
Market Ms, W1 297 J3
Market Oak La, Hem.H. HP3 40 BN24
Market Pl, N2 120 DE55
SE16 300 D8
W1 285 L8
W3 138 CQ74
Abridge RM4 86 EV41
Beaconsfield HP9 off London End 89 AM54
Bexleyheath DA6 166 FA84
Brentford TW8 157 CJ80
Chalfont St. Peter SL9 90 AX53
Dartford DA1 off Market St 188 FL87
Enfield EN2 off The Town 82 DR41
Hatfield AL10 off Kennelwood La 45 CV17
Hertford SG14 off Fore St 32 DR09
Kingston upon Thames KT1 197 CK96
Romford RM1 127 FE57
St. Albans AL3 43 CD20
Tilbury RM18 171 GF82
Market Pl, The, NW11 120 DB56
Market Rd, N7 276 A5
Richmond TW9 158 CN83
Market Row, SW9 off Atlantic Rd 161 DN84
Market Service Rd, The, Sutt. SM1 off Rosehill Av 200 DC102
Market Sq, N9 off Edmonton Grn Shop Cen 100 DV47
Uxbridge UB8 off The Mall Pavilions 134 BJ66
Market Sq, E14 290 D9
Amersham HP7 off High St 55 AP40
Bromley BR1 204 EG96
Chesham HP5 off High St 54 AP31
Harlow CM20 off East Gate 35 ER14
Staines-upon-Thames TW18 off Clarence St 173 BE91
Waltham Abbey EN9 off Church St 67 EC33
Westerham TN16 255 EQ127
Woking GU21 off Cawsey Way 226 AY117
Market St, E1 288 A6
E6 145 EM68
SE18 305 M8
Dartford DA1 188 FL87
Guildford GU1 258 AX135
Harlow CM17 36 EW11
Hertford SG14 32 DR09
Watford WD18 75 BV42
Windsor SL4 151 AR81
● Market Trading Est, Sthl. UB2 155 BV77
Market Way, E14 290 D9
Wembley HA0 off Turton Rd 118 CL64
Westerham TN16 off Costell's Meadow 255 ER126
Market Yd Ms, SE1 299 N6
Markfield, Croy. CR0 221 DZ110
Markfield Gdns, E4 101 EB45
Markfield Rd, N15 122 DU56
Caterham CR3 252 DV126
Sch Mark Hall Comm Sch & Sports Coll, Harl. CM17 off First Av 36 EW12
Mark Hall Moors, Harl. CM20 36 EV12
MARK HALL NORTH, Harl. CM20 36 EU12
MARK HALL SOUTH, Harl. CM20 36 EV14
Markham Cl, Borwd. WD6 78 CM41
Markham Pl, SW3 296 E10
Markham Rd, Chsht EN7 66 DQ26
Markham Sq, SW3 296 E10
Markham St, SW3 296 D10
Markhole Cl, Hmptn. TW12 176 BZ94
Markhouse Av, E17 123 DY58
Markhouse Rd, E17 123 DZ57
Markland Ho, W10 282 C10
Mark La, EC3 299 P1
Gravesend DA12 191 GL86
Markmanor Av, E17 123 DY59
Mark Oak La, Lthd. KT22 230 CA122
Mark Rd, N22 99 DP54
Hemel Hempstead HP2 40 BN18
Marksbury Av, Rich. TW9 158 CN83
Sch Marks Gate Inf Sch, Chad.Hth RM6 off Lawn Fm Gro 126 EY55
Sch Marks Gate Jun Sch, Chad.Hth RM6 off Rose La 126 EY55
MARK'S GATE, Rom. RM6 104 EY54
Mark Sq, EC2 287 N4
Marks Rd, Rom. RM7 127 FC57
Warlingham CR6 237 DY118
Marks Sq, Nthflt DA11 191 GF91
Mark St, E15 281 J7
EC2 287 N4
Reigate RH2 250 DB133
Markville Gdns, Cat. CR3 252 DU125
Mark Wade Cl, E12 124 EK60
Markway, Sun. TW16 196 BW96
Mark Way, Swan. BR8 207 FG99
Markwell Cl, SE26 182 DV91
Markwell Wd, Harl. CM19 51 EP21
Markyate Rd, Dag. RM8 126 EV64
Marlands Rd, Ilf. IG5 124 EL55
Marlborough, SW3 296 D8
Marlborough Av, E8 278 C9
N14 99 DJ48
Edgware HA8 96 CP48
Ruislip HA4 115 BQ58
Marlborough Cl, N20 98 DF48
SE17 299 H9
SW19 180 DE93
Grays RM16 170 GC75
Hersham KT12 196 BX104
Orpington BR6 off Aylesham Rd 205 ET100
Upminster RM14 129 FS60

Marlborough Ct, W1 285 L9
W8 295 J8
Dorking RH4
off Marlborough Hill 263 CH136
Wallington SM6
off Cranley Gdns 219 DJ108
Marlborough Cres, W4 158 CR76
Harlington UB3 155 BR80
Sevenoaks TN13 256 FE124
Marlborough Dr, Ilf. IG5 124 EL55
Weybridge KT13 195 BQ104
Marlborough Gdns, N20 98 DF48
Upminster RM14 129 FR60
Marlborough Gate, St.Alb. AL1 43 CE20
Marlborough Gate Ho, W2 284 A10
Marlborough Gro, SE1 312 C1
Marlborough Hill, NW8 273 P9
Dorking RH4 263 CH136
Harrow HA1 117 CF56
★ Marlborough Ho, SW1 297 M3
Marlborough La, SE7 164 EJ79
Marlborough Ms, SW2
off Acre La 161 DM84
Banstead SM7 234 DA115
Marlborough Par, Uxb. UB10
off Uxbridge Rd 135 BP70
Marlborough Pk Av, Sid. DA15 186 EU87
Marlborough Pl, NW8 283 N1
Sch Marlborough Prim Sch,
SW3 296 D9
Harrow HA1
off Marlborough Hill 117 CE56
Isleworth TW7 *off London Rd* 157 CG81
Marlborough Ri, Hem.H. HP2 40 BL17
Marlborough Rd, E4 101 EA51
E7 144 EJ66
E15 281 K1
E18 124 EG55
N9 100 DT46
N19 121 DK61
N22 99 DL52
SE18 305 P6
SW1 297 M3
SW19 180 DE93
W4 158 CQ78
W5 157 CK75
Ashford TW15 174 BK92
Bexleyheath DA7 166 EX83
Bromley BR2 204 EJ98
Dagenham RM8 126 EV63
Dartford DA1 188 FJ86
Dorking RH4 263 CH136
Feltham TW13 176 BX89
Hampton TW12 176 CA93
Isleworth TW7 157 CH81
Pilgrim's Hatch CM15 108 FU44
Richmond TW10 178 CL86
Romford RM7 126 FA56
St. Albans AL1 43 CE20
Slough SL3 152 AX77
South Croydon CR2 220 DQ108
Southall UB2 156 BW76
Sutton SM1 200 DA104
Uxbridge UB10 135 BP70
Watford WD18 75 BV42
Woking GU21 227 BA116
Sch Marlborough Sch,
St.Alb. AL1 *off Watling St* 42 CC23
Sidcup DA15
off Marlborough Pk Av 186 EU87
Marlborough St, SW3 296 C9
Marlborough Yd, N19 121 DK61
Marld, The, Ashtd. KT21 232 CM118
Marle Gdns, Wal.Abb. EN9 67 EC32
Marler Rd, SE23 183 DY88
Marlescroft Way, Loug. IG10 85 EP43
Marley Av, Bexh. DA7 166 EX79
Marley Cl, N15 121 DP56
Addlestone KT15 211 BF107
Greenford UB6 136 CA69
Marley Ct, Brox. EN10 49 DZ23
Marley Ho, E16
off University Way 305 N1
Marley Mead, Dor. RH4 263 CG139
Marley Ri, Dor. RH4 263 CG139
Marley Rd, Welw.G.C. AL7 30 DA11
Marley St, SE16 301 J9
Marley Wk, NW2 272 A3
Marl Fld Cl, Wor.Pk. KT4 199 CU102
Marlin Cl, Berk. HP4 38 AT18
Sunbury-on-Thames TW16 175 BS93
Marlin Copse, Berk. HP4 38 AU20
Marlin End, Berk. HP4 38 AT20
Marlingdene Cl, Hmptn. TW12 176 CA93
Marlings Cl, Chis. BR7 205 ES98
Whyteleafe CR3 236 DS117
Marlings Pk Av, Chis. BR7 205 ES98
Marling Way, Grav. DA12 191 GL92
Marlin Pk, Felt. TW14 175 BV85
Marlins, The, Nthwd. HA6 93 BT51
Marlins Cl, Chorl. WD3 73 BE40
Sutton SM1 *off Turnpike La* 218 DC106
Marlins Meadow, Wat. WD18 75 BR44
Marlin Sq, Abb.L. WD5 59 BT31
Marlins Turn, Hem.H. HP1 40 BH17
Marloes Cl, Wem. HA0 117 CK63
Marloes Rd, W8 295 L7
Marlow Av, Purf. RM19 168 FN77
Marlow Cl, SE20 202 DV97
Marlow Ct, NW6 272 D6
NW9 119 CT55
Marlow Cres, Twick. TW1 177 CF86
Marlow Dr, Sutt. SM3 199 CX103
Marlowe Cl, Chis. BR7 185 ER93
Ilford IG6 103 EQ53
Marlowe Ct, SE19
off Lymer Av 182 DT92
Marlowe Gdns, SE9 185 EN86
Romford RM3 106 FJ53
Marlowe Path, SE8 314 C2
Marlowe Rd, E17 123 EC56
Marlowes, Hem.H. HP1 40 BK21
Marlowes, The, NW8 274 A9
Dartford DA1 167 FD84
Marlowes Cen, The,
Hem.H. HP1 40 BK21
Marlowe Sq, Mitch. CR4 201 DJ98
Marlowe Way, Croy. CR0 201 DL103
Marlow Gdns, Hayes UB3 155 BR76
Marlow Rd, E6 293 J3
SE20 202 DV97
Southall UB2 156 BZ76
Marlow Way, SE16 301 J4
Marlpit Av, Couls. CR5 235 DL117
Marlpit La, Couls. CR5 235 DK116
Marl Rd, SW18 160 DB84
Marlton St, SE10 303 M10
Marlwood Cl, Sid. DA15 185 ES89
Marlyns Cl, Guil. GU4 243 BA130
Marlyns Dr, Guil. GU4 243 BA130
Marlyon Rd, Ilf. IG6 104 EV50
Marmadon Rd, SE18 165 ET77
Marmara Apts, E16
off Western Gateway 303 P1
Marmion App, E4 101 EA49
Marmion Av, E4 101 DZ49
Marmion Cl, E4 101 DZ49
Marmion Ms, SW11
off Taybridge Rd 160 DG83
Marmion Rd, SW11 160 DG84
Marmont Rd, SE15 312 D6
Marmora Rd, SE22 182 DW86
Marmot Rd, Houns. TW4 156 BX83
Marne Av, N11 99 DH49
Welling DA16 166 EU83
Marnell Way, Houns. TW4 156 BX83
Marne Rd, Dag. RM9 146 EV67
Sch Marner Prim Sch, E3 290 D4
Marne St, W10 282 E2
Marney Rd, SW11 160 DG84
Marneys Cl, Epsom KT18 232 CN115
Marnfield Cres, SW2 181 DM88
Marnham Av, NW2 119 CY63
Marnham Cres, Grnf. UB6 136 CB69
Marnham Pl, Add. KT15 212 BJ105
Marnham Ri, Hem.H. HP1 40 BG18
Marnock Rd, SE4 183 DY85
Maroon St, E14 289 L7
Maroons Way, SE6 183 EA92
Marquess Est, N1 277 K4
Marquess Rd, N1 277 L5
Marquis Cl, Wem. HA0 138 CM66
Marquis Rd, N4 121 DM60
N22 99 DM51
NW1 275 P5
Marrabon Cl, Sid. DA15 186 EU88
Marram Ct, Grays RM17
off Medlar Rd 170 GE79
Marrick Cl, SW15 159 CU84
Marrilyne Av, Enf. EN3 83 DZ38
Marriott Cl, Felt. TW14 175 BR86
Marriott Ter, Chorl. WD3 73 BF42
Marriott Lo Cl, Add. KT15 212 BJ105
Marriott Rd, E15 281 J8
N4 121 DM60
N10 98 DF53
Barnet EN5 79 CX41
Dartford DA1 188 FN87
Marriotts, Harl. CM17 36 EW10
Marriotts Cl, NW9 119 CT58
Marriotts Way, Hem.H. HP3 40 BK22
Mar Rd, S.Ock. RM15 149 FW70
Marrods Bottom, Beac. HP9 88 AJ47
Marrowells, Wey. KT13 195 BS104
Marryat Cl, Houns. TW4 156 BZ84
Marryat Pl, SW19 179 CY91
Marryat Rd, SW19 179 CX92
Enfield EN1 82 DV35
Marryat Sq, SW6 306 E6
Marsala Rd, SE13 163 EB84
Marsden Cl, Welw.G.C. AL8 29 CV11
Marsden Gdns, Dart. DA1 168 FM82
Marsden Grn, Welw.G.C. AL8 29 CV10
Marsden Rd, N9 100 DV47
SE15 162 DT83
Welwyn Garden City AL8 29 CV10
Marsden St, NW5 274 G5
Marsden Way, Orp. BR6 223 ET105
Marshall, W2
off Hermitage St 284 A7
Marshall Av, St.Alb. AL3 43 CE17
Marshall Cl, SW18
off Allfarthing La 180 DC86
Harrow HA1 *off Bowen Rd* 117 CD59
Hounslow TW4 176 BZ85
South Croydon CR2 220 DU113
Marshall Ct, SE20
off Anerley Pk 182 DV94
Marshall Dr, Hayes UB4 135 BT71
Marshall Est, NW7 97 CU49
Marshall Path, SE28
off Attlee Rd 146 EV73
Marshall Pl, New Haw KT15 212 BJ109
Marshall Rd, E10 123 EB62
N17 100 DR53
Marshalls Cl, N11 99 DH49
Epsom KT19 216 CQ113
Marshalls Dr, Rom. RM1 127 FE55
Marshall's Gro, SE18 305 H8
Sch Marshalls Pk Sch,
Rom. RM1 *off Pettits La* 105 FE54
Marshalls Pl, SE16 300 B7
Marshalls Rd, Rom. RM7 127 FD56
Marshall's Rd, Sutt. SM1 218 DB105
Marshall St, NW10 138 CR66
W1 285 M9
Marshals Dr, St.Alb. AL1 43 CG17
Marshalsea Rd, SE1 299 K4
MARSHALSWICK, St.Alb. AL1 43 CG17
Marshalswick La, St.Alb. AL1 43 CH17
Marsham Cl, Chis. BR7 185 EP92
Marsham La, Ger.Cr. SL9 112 AY58
Marsham Lo, Ger.Cr. SL9 112 AY58
Marsham St, SW1 297 P7
Marsham Way, Ger.Cr. SL9 112 AY57
Marsh Av, Epsom KT19 216 CS110
Mitcham CR4 200 DF96
Marshbrook Cl, SE3 164 EK83
Marsh Cl, NW7 97 CT48
Waltham Cross EN8 67 DZ33
Marsh Ct, SW19 200 DC95
Uxb. UB3 *off Uxbridge Rd* 135 BS71
Marshcroft Dr, Chsht EN8 67 DY30
Marsh Dr, NW9 119 CT58
Marshe Cl, Pot.B. EN6 64 DD32
Marsh Fm Rd, Twick. TW2 177 CF88
Marshfield, Datchet SL3 152 AW81
Sch Marshfields C of E Inf Sch,
Ott. KT16 *off Fletcher Cl* 211 BE107
Marshfield St, E14 302 E6
Marshfoot Interchange,
Grays RM16, RM17 170 GE79
Marshfoot Rd,
Grays RM16, RM17 170 GE78
Marshgate, Harl. CM20
off School La 35 ES12
● Marshgate Cen, Harl. CM19 50 EK15
Marshgate Dr, Hert. SG13 32 DS08
Marshgate La, E15 280 E10
Marshgate Path, SE28
off Tom Cribb Rd 165 EQ76
Sch Marshgate Prim Sch,
Rich. TW10 *off Queens Rd* 158 CM84
● Marshgate Trd Est, Tap. SL6 130 AG72
Sch Marsh Grn Prim Sch,
Dag. RM10 *off South Cl* 146 FA67
Marsh Grn Rd, Dag. RM10 146 FA67
Marsh Hill, E9 279 L3
Marsh La, E10 123 EA61
N17 100 DV52
NW7 96 CS49
Addlestone KT15 212 BH105
Dorney SL4 150 AF75
Harlow CM17 36 EY10
Maidenhead SL6 150 AF75
Stanmore HA7 95 CJ50
Stanstead Abbotts SG12 33 ED12
Ware SG12 33 DY07
Marshmoor Cres,
N.Mymms AL9 45 CW22
Marshmoor La, N.Mymms AL9 45 CW22
Marsh Rd, Pnr. HA5 116 BY56
Wembley HA0 137 CK68
Marshside Cl, N9 100 DW46
Marsh St, E14 302 C9
Dartford DA1 168 FN84
Marsh St N, Dart. DA1 168 FN82
Marsh Ter, Orp. BR5
off Buttermere Rd 206 EX98
Marsh Vw, Grav. DA12 191 GM88
Marsh Wall, E14 302 A3
Marsh Way, Rain. RM13 147 FD70
Marsland Cl, SE17 311 H1
Marston, SE17
off Deacon Way 299 K8
Epsom KT19 216 CQ111
Marston Av, Chess. KT9 216 CL107
Dagenham RM10 126 FA61
Marston Cl, NW6 273 P6
Chesham HP5 54 AN27
Dagenham RM10 126 FA62
Hemel Hempstead HP3 40 BN21
Marston Ct, Green. DA9 169 FU84
Walton-on-Thames KT12
off St. Johns Dr 196 BW102
Marston Dr, Warl. CR6 237 DY118
Marston Rd, Hodd. EN11 49 EB16
Ilford IG5 102 EL53
Teddington TW11 177 CH92
Woking GU21 226 AV117
Marston Way, SE19 181 DP94
Marsworth Av, Pnr. HA5 94 BX53
Marsworth Cl, Hayes UB4 136 BY71
Watford WD18 75 BS44
Marsworth Ho, E2 278 C9
Martaban Rd, N16 122 DS61
Martara Ms, SE17 311 J1
Martello St, E8 278 E6
Martello Ter, E8 278 E6
Martell Rd, SE21 182 DR90
Martel Pl, E8 278 B4
Marten Gate, St.Alb. AL4 43 CG16
Marten Rd, E17 101 EA54
Martens Av, Bexh. DA7 167 FC84
Martens Cl, Bexh. DA7 167 FC84
Martha Ct, E2 278 F10
Martham Cl, SE28 146 EX73
Ilford IG6 103 EP53
Martha Rd, E15 281 K4
Martha's Bldgs, EC1 287 L4
Martha St, E1 288 F9
Marthorne Cres, Har. HA3 95 CD54
Martian Av, Hem.H. HP2 40 BM17
Martina Ter, Chig. IG7
off Manford Way 103 ES50
Martin Bowes Rd, SE9 165 EM83
● Martinbridge Trd Est,
Enf. EN1 82 DU43
Martin Cl, N9 101 DX46
Hatfield AL10 45 CU20
South Croydon CR2 221 DX111
Uxbridge UB10 134 BL68
Warlingham CR6 236 DV116
Windsor SL4 150 AJ81
Martin Cres, Croy. CR0 201 DN102
Martindale, SW14 178 CQ85
Iver SL0 133 BD70
Martindale Av, E16 291 P10
Orpington BR6 224 EU106
Martindale Cl, Guil. GU4
off Gilliat Dr 243 BD132
Sch Martindale Prim & Nurs Sch,
Hem.H. HP1 *off Boxted Rd* 39 BF19
Martindale Rd, SW12 181 DH87
Hemel Hempstead HP1 39 BF19
Hounslow TW4 156 BY83
Woking GU21 226 AT118
Martin Dene, Bexh. DA6 186 EZ85
Martin Dr, Nthlt. UB5 116 BZ64
Rainham RM13 147 FH70
Stone DA2 188 FQ86
Martineau Cl, Esher KT10 215 CD105
Martineau Dr, Dor. RH4 263 CH138
Twickenham TW1 157 CH84
Martineau Ms, N5 276 G1
Martineau Rd, N5 276 F1
Martineau St, E1 288 G9
Martinfield, Welw.G.C. AL7 29 CZ08
● Martinfield Business Pk,
Welw.G.C. AL7 *off Martinfield* 29 CZ08
Martingale Cl, Sun. TW16 195 BU98
Martingales Cl, Rich. TW10 177 CK90
Martin Gdns, Dag. RM8 126 EW63
Martin Gro, Mord. SM4 200 DA97
Martin Ho, SE1 299 K7
Martini Dr, Enf. EN3 83 EA37
Martin Kinggett Gdns,
Dag. RM9 146 EY67
Martin La, EC4 287 M10
Sch Martin Prim Sch, N2
off Plane Tree Wk 98 DE54
Martin Ri, Bexh. DA6 186 EZ85
Martin Rd, Aveley RM15 149 FR73
Dagenham RM8 126 EW63
Dartford DA2 188 FJ90
Guildford GU2 242 AU132
Slough SL1 152 AS76
Martins, The, Wem. HA9 118 CM62
Martins Cl, Guil. GU1 243 BC133
Orpington BR5 206 EX97
Radlett WD7 77 CE36
West Wickham BR4 203 ED102
Martins Ct, St.Alb. AL1
off Swallow La 43 CJ23
Martins Dr, Chsht EN8 67 DY28
Hertford SG13 32 DV09
Martinsfield Cl, Chig. IG7 103 ES49
Martins Mt, New Barn. EN5 80 DA42
Martins Pl, SE28
off Martin St 145 ES74
Martin's Plain, Stoke P. SL2 132 AT69
Martins Rd, Brom. BR2 204 EE96
Martins Shaw,
Chipstead TN13 256 FC122
Martinstown Cl, Horn. RM11 128 FN58
Martin St, SE28 145 ES74
Martins Wk, N8
off Alexandra Rd 121 DN55
N10 98 DG53
SE28 145 ES74
Borehamwood WD6
off Siskin Cl 78 CN42
Martinsyde, Wok. GU22 227 BC117
Martin Way, SW20 199 CY97
Morden SM4 199 CY97
Woking GU21 226 AU118
● Martlands Ind Est,
Wok. GU22 226 AU123
Martlesham, Welw.G.C. AL7 30 DE09
Martlesham Cl, Horn. RM12 128 FJ64
Martlesham Wk, NW9
off Kenley Av 96 CS54
Martlet Gro, Nthlt. UB5 136 BX69
Martlett Ct, WC2 286 B9
Martley Dr, Ilf. IG2 125 EP57
Martock Cl, Har. HA3 117 CG56
Martock Gdns, N11 98 DF50
Marton Cl, SE6 183 EA90
Marton Rd, N16 122 DS61
Martyr Cl, St.Alb. AL1
off Creighton Av 43 CD24
Martyr Rd, Guil. GU1 258 AX135
Martyrs La, Wok. GU21 211 BB112
MARTYR'S GREEN,
Wok. GU23 229 BR120
Martys Yd, NW3 274 A1
Marunden Grn, Slou. SL2 131 AM69
Marvell Av, Hayes UB4 135 BU71
Marvels Cl, SE12 184 EH89
Marvels La, SE12 184 EH89
Sch Marvels La Prim Sch,
SE12 *off Riddons Rd* 184 EJ91
Marville Rd, SW6 306 G5
Marvin St, E8 278 F4
Marwell, West. TN16 255 EP126
Marwell Cl, Rom. RM1 127 FG57
West Wickham BR4
off Deer Pk Way 204 EF103
Marwood Cl, Kings L. WD4 58 BN29
Welling DA16 166 EV83
Marwood Dr, NW7 97 CX52
Mary Adelaide Cl, SW15 178 CS91
Mary Ann Gdns, SE8 314 A3
Maryatt Av, Har. HA2 116 CB61
Marybank, SE18 305 J8
Mary Cl, Stan. HA7 118 CM56
Mary Datchelor Cl, SE5 311 M6
Maryfield Cl, Bex. DA5 187 FE90
Marygold Wk, Amer. HP6 72 AV39
Mary Grn, NW8 273 M9
Maryhill Cl, Ken. CR8 236 DQ117
⇌ Maryland 281 J4
Maryland, Hat. AL10 45 CT19
Maryland Conv, St.Alb. AL3
off Townsend Dr 43 CD18
● Maryland Ind Est, E15
off Maryland Rd 281 H3
Maryland Pk, E15 281 K3
Maryland Pt, E15 *off The Grove* 281 J4
Sch Maryland Prim Sch, E15 281 K2
Maryland Rd, E15 281 H3
N22 99 DM51
Thornton Heath CR7 201 DP95
Maryland Sq, E15 281 K3
Marylands Rd, W9 283 K5
Maryland St, E15 281 H3
Maryland Wk, N1 277 J8
Maryland Way, Sun. TW16 195 BU96
Mary Lawrenson Pl, SE3 315 N5
MARYLEBONE, NW1 284 E8
⇌ Marylebone 284 E5
⊖ Marylebone 284 E5
Marylebone Flyover, NW1 284 B7
W2 284 B7
Marylebone Gdns, Rich. TW9
off Manor Rd 158 CM84
Marylebone High St, W1 285 H6
Marylebone La, W1 285 J9
Marylebone Ms, W1 285 J7
Marylebone Pas, W1 285 M8
Marylebone Rd, NW1 284 D6
Marylebone St, W1 285 H7
Marylee Way, SE11 298 D10
Mary Macarthur Ho, E2 289 J2
W6 306 E2
Mary Morgan Ct, Slou. SL2
off Douglas Rd 131 AR71
Sch Marymount Int Sch,
Kings.T. KT2 *off George Rd* 178 CQ94
Mary Neuner Rd, N8 121 DM55
Maryon Gro, SE7 305 H9
Maryon Ms, NW3 274 C1
Maryon Rd, SE7 304 G8
SE18 304 G8
Mary Peters Dr, Grnf. UB6 117 CD64
Mary Pl, W11 294 E1
Mary Rd, Guil. GU1 258 AW135
Mary Rose Cl,
Chaff.Hun. RM16 169 FW77
Hampton TW12
off Ashley Rd 196 CA95
Mary Rose Mall, E6 293 K7
Maryrose Way, N20 98 DD46
Mary Seacole Cl, E8 278 A8
Mary Seacole Ho, W6
off Invermead Cl 159 CU76
Maryside, Slou. SL3 152 AY75
Mary's Ter, Twick. TW1 177 CG87
Mary St, E16 291 L6
N1 277 K9
Mary Ter, NW1 275 K9
Coll Mary Ward Adult Ed Cen, The, WC1 286 B6
Mary Way, Wat. WD19 94 BW49
Masbro Rd, W14 294 D7
Mascalls Ct, SE7 164 EJ79
Mascalls Gdns, Brwd. CM14 108 FT49
Mascalls La, Brwd. CM14 108 FT49
Mascalls Rd, SE7 164 EJ79
Mascoll Path, Slou. SL2 131 AM69
Mascotte Rd, SW15 159 CX84
Mascotts Cl, NW2 119 CV62
Masefield Av, Borwd. WD6 78 CP43
Southall UB1 136 CA73
Stanmore HA7 95 CF50
Masefield Cl, Chesh. HP5 54 AP28
Erith DA8 167 FF81
Romford RM3 106 FJ53
Masefield Ct, Brwd. CM14 108 FW49
Masefield Cres, N14 81 DJ44
Romford RM3 106 FJ53
Masefield Dr, Upmin. RM14 128 FQ59
Masefield Gdns, E6 293 L4
Masefield La, Hayes UB4 135 BV70
Masefield Rd, Dart. DA1 188 FP85
Grays RM16 170 GE75
Hampton TW12
off Wordsworth Rd 176 BZ91
Northfleet DA11 190 GD90
Masefield Vw, Orp. BR6 205 EQ104
Masefield Way, Stai. TW19 174 BM88
Masham Ho, Erith DA18
off Kale Rd 166 EX75
Mashie Rd, W3 138 CS72
Mashiters Hill, Rom. RM1 105 FD53
Mashiters Wk, Rom. RM1 127 FE55
Maskall Cl, SW2 181 DN88
Maskani Wk, SW16
off Bates Cres 181 DJ94
Maskell Rd, SW17 180 DC90
Maskelyne Cl, SW11 308 D6
Maslen Rd, St.Alb. AL4 43 CJ23
Mason Cl, E16 291 N10
SE16 300 D10
SW20 199 CX95
Bexleyheath DA7 167 FB83
Borehamwood WD6 78 CQ40
Hampton TW12 196 BZ95
Waltham Abbey EN9 68 EF34
Mason Ct, Wem. HA9
off The Avenue 118 CN61
Mason Dr, Harold Wd RM3
off Whitmore Av 106 FL54
Masonic Hall Rd, Cher. KT16 193 BF100
Mason Rd, Sutt. SM1
off Manor Pl 218 DB106
Woodford Green IG8 102 EE49
Masons Arms Ms, W1 285 K9
Masons Av, EC2 287 L8
Croydon CR0 202 DQ104
Harrow HA3 117 CF56
Masons Br Rd, Red. RH1 267 DH139
Masons Ct, Slou. SL1 131 AL73
Masons Grn La, W3 138 CN71
Masons Hill, SE18 305 P9
Bromley BR1, BR2 204 EG97
Masons Paddock, Dor. RH4 247 CG134
Masons Pl, EC1 287 H2
Mitcham CR4 200 DF95
Masons Rd, Enf. EN1 82 DW36
Hemel Hempstead HP2 41 BP19
Slough SL1 131 AL73
Mason St, SE17 299 M9
Masons Yd, EC1 287 H2
Mason's Yd, SW1 297 M2
SW19 *off High St Wimbledon* 179 CX92
Mason Way, Wal.Abb. EN9 68 EF34
Massetts Rd, Horl. RH6 268 DF149
Massey Cl, N11 99 DH50
Massey Ct, E6 144 EJ67
Massey Ms, SW2 181 DN85
Massie Rd, E8 278 C5
Massingberd Way, SW17 181 DH91
Massinger St, SE17 299 N9
Massingham St, E1 289 J4
Masson Av, Ruis. HA4 136 BW65
Mast, The, E16 305 P1
Master Cl, Oxt. RH8
off Church La 254 EE129
Master Gunner Pl, SE18 164 EL80
Masterman Ho, SE5 311 K4
Masterman Rd, E6 292 G3
Masters Cl, SW16 181 DJ93
Masters Dr, SE16 312 E1
Masters St, E1 289 K6
Masthead Cl, Dart. DA2 168 FQ84
Mast House Terrace, E14 302 B9
Riv Masthouse Terrace Pier 302 B10
Mastin Ms, Grav. DA12 191 GK86
Mast Leisure Pk, SE16 301 K7
Mastmaker Rd, E14 302 B5
Mast Quay, SE18
off Woolwich Ch St 305 K6
Maswell Pk Cres, Houns. TW3 176 CC85
Maswell Pk Rd, Houns. TW3 176 CB85
Matcham Rd, E11 124 EE62
Matching Rd, Hat.Hth CM22 37 FH06
Old Harlow CM17 37 FB11
Ongar CM5 53 FH18
MATCHING TYE, Harl. CM17 37 FF12
Matchless Dr, SE18 165 EN80
Matfield Cl, Brom. BR2 204 EG99
Matfield Rd, Belv. DA17 166 FA79
Matham Gro, SE22 162 DT84
Matham Rd, E.Mol. KT8 197 CD99
Mathecombe Rd, Slou. SL1 151 AM74
Matheson Lang Gdns, SE1
off Baylis Rd 298 E5
Matheson Rd, W14 294 G9
Mathews Av, E6 293 M1
Mathews Pk Av, E15 281 M5
Mathews Yd, Croy. CR0
off Surrey St 202 DQ104
Mathias Cl, Epsom KT18 216 CQ113
Sch Mathilda Marks-Kennedy
Prim Sch, NW7 *off Hale La* 96 CR50
Mathisen Way, Colnbr. SL3 153 BE81
Mathon Ct, Guil. GU1 243 AZ134
Matilda Cl, SE19
off Elizabeth Way 182 DR94
Matilda Gdns, E3 290 A1
Matilda St, N1 276 D9
Matisse Rd, Houns. TW3 156 CB83
Matlock Cl, SE24 162 DQ84
Barnet EN5 79 CX43
Matlock Ct, SE5
off Denmark Hill Est 162 DR84
Matlock Cres, Sutt. SM3 217 CY105
Watford WD19 94 BW48
Matlock Gdns, Horn. RM12 128 FL62
Sutton SM3 217 CY105
Matlock Pl, Sutt. SM3 217 CY105
Matlock Rd, E10 123 EC58
Caterham CR3 236 DS121
Matlock St, E14 289 L8
Matlock Way, N.Mal. KT3 198 CR95
Matrimony Pl, SW8 309 L9
Matson Ct, Wdf.Grn. IG8
off The Bridle Path 102 EE52
Matson Ho, SE16 300 F6
Matthew Arnold Cl, Cob. KT11 213 BU114
Staines-upon-Thames TW18
off Elizabeth Av 174 BJ93
Sch Matthew Arnold Sch, The,
Stai. TW18 *off Kingston Rd* 174 BJ93
Matthew Cl, W10 282 C5
Matthew Ct, Mitch. CR4 201 DK99
Matthew Parker St, SW1 297 P5
Matthews Cl, Rom. RM3
off Oak Rd 106 FM53

Matthews Gdns, New Adgtn CR0 221 ED111
Matthews La, Stai. TW18 off Kingston Rd 174 BG91
Matthews Lo, Add. KT15 194 BK104
Matthews Rd, Grnf. UB6 117 CD64
Matthews St, SW11 308 E8
Reigate RH2 266 DA138
Matthews Yd, WC2 286 A9
Matthias Rd, N16 277 M2
Mattingley Way, SE15 312 A4
Mattison Rd, N4 121 DN58
Mattock La, W5 137 CH74
W13 137 CH74
Maud Cashmore Way, SE18 305 K7
Maud Chadburn Pl, SW4 off Balham Hill 181 DH86
Maude Cres, Wat. WD24 75 BV37
Maude Rd, E17 123 DY57
SE5 311 N7
Beaconsfield HP9 89 AN54
Swanley BR8 187 FG93
Maudesville Cotts, W7 137 CE74
Maude Ter, E17 123 DY56
Maud Gdns, E13 281 M10
Barking IG11 145 ET68
Maudlin's Grn, E1 300 C2
Maud Rd, E10 123 EC62
E13 281 M10
Maudslay Rd, SE9 165 EM83
H Maudsley Hosp, SE5 311 M8
Maudsley Ho, Brent. TW8 off Green Dragon La 158 CL78
Maud St, E16 291 L7
Maud Wilkes Cl, NW5 275 L3
Maugham Way, W3 158 CQ76
Mauleverer Rd, SW2 181 DL85
Maundeby Wk, NW10 off Neasden La 138 CS65
Maunder Cl, Chaff.Hun. RM16 169 FX77
Maunder Rd, W7 137 CF74
Maunds Fm, Harl. CM18 51 ER20
Maunds Hatch, Harl. CM18 51 ER19
Maunsel St, SW1 297 N8
Maurer Ct, SE10 303 M6
Maurice Av, N22 99 DP54
Caterham CR3 236 DR122
Maurice Brown Cl, NW7 97 CX50
Maurice St, W12 139 CV72
Maurice Wk, NW11 120 DC56
Maurier Cl, Nthlt. UB5 136 BW67
Mauritius Rd, SE10 303 K9
Maury Rd, N16 122 DU61
Mauveine Gdns, Houns. TW3 156 CA84
Mavelstone Cl, Brom. BR1 204 EL95
Mavelstone Rd, Brom. BR1 204 EL95
Maverton Rd, E3 280 A9
Mavis Av, Epsom KT19 216 CS106
Mavis Cl, Epsom KT19 216 CS106
Mavis Gro, Horn. RM12 128 FL61
Mavis Wk, E6 292 G7
Mawbey Est, SE1 312 C1
Mawbey Ho, SE1 off Old Kent Rd 312 B1
Mawbey Pl, SE1 312 B1
Mawbey Rd, SE1 312 B1
Ottershaw KT16 211 BD107
Mawbey St, SW8 310 A5
Mawney Cl, Rom. RM7 105 FB54
Sch Mawney Prim Sch, The, Rom. RM7 off Mawney Rd 127 FD57
Mawney Rd, Rom. RM7 127 FC56
Mawson Cl, SW20 199 CY96
Mawson La, W4 off Great W Rd 159 CT79
Maxey Gdns, Dag. RM9 126 EY63
Maxey Rd, SE18 165 EQ77
Dagenham RM9 126 EY63
Maxfield Cl, N20 98 DC45
Maxilla Gdns, W10 282 D8
Maxilla Wk, W10 282 D9
Maximfeldt Rd, Erith DA8 167 FE78
Maxim Rd, N21 81 DN44
Dartford DA1 187 FE85
Erith DA8 off West St 167 FE78
Maxim Twr, Rom. RM1 off Mercury Gdns 127 FE56
Maxted Cl, Hem.H. HP2 41 BQ18
Maxted Pk, Har. HA1 117 CE59
Maxted Rd, SE15 312 B10
Hemel Hempstead HP2 41 BP17
Maxwell Cl, Croy. CR0 201 DL102
Hayes UB3 135 BU73
Mill End WD3 92 BG47
Maxwell Dr, W.Byf. KT14 212 BJ111
Maxwell Gdns, Orp. BR6 205 ET104
Maxwell Ri, Wat. WD19 94 BY45
Maxwell Rd, SW6 307 L5
Ashford TW15 175 BQ93
Beaconsfield HP9 89 AK52
Borehamwood WD6 78 CP41
Northwood HA6 93 BR52
St. Albans AL1 43 CH21
Welling DA16 165 ET83
West Drayton UB7 154 BM77
● Maxwells W, Chsht EN8 66 DW31
Maxwelton Av, NW7 96 CR50
Maxwelton Cl, NW7 96 CR50
Maya Angelou Ct, E4 off Bailey Cl 101 EC49
Maya Cl, SE15 312 E8
Mayall Cl, Enf. EN3 83 EA38
Mayall Rd, SE24 181 DP85
Maya Pl, N11 99 DK52
Maya Rd, N2 120 DC56
May Av, Nthflt DA11 191 GF88
Orpington BR5 206 EV99
● May Av Ind Est, Nthflt DA11 off May Av 191 GF88
Maybank Av, E18 102 EH54
Hornchurch RM12 127 FH64
Wembley HA0 117 CF64
Maybank Gdns, Pnr. HA5 115 BU57
Maybank Lo, Horn. RM12 off Maybank Av 128 FJ64
Maybank Rd, E18 102 EH53
May Bate Av, Kings.T. KT2 197 CK95
● Maybells Commercial Est, Bark. IG11 146 EX68
Mayberry Pl, Surb. KT5 198 CM101
Maybourne Cl, SE26 182 DV92
Maybourne Ri, Wok. GU22 226 AX124
Maybrick Rd, Horn. RM11 128 FJ58
Maybrook Meadow Est, Bark. IG11 146 EU66
MAYBURY, Wok. GU22 227 BB117
Maybury Av, Chsht EN8 66 DV28
Dartford DA2 188 FQ88
Maybury Cl, Enf. EN1 82 DV38
Loughton IG10 85 EP42
Petts Wood BR5 205 EP99
Slough SL1 131 AK72
Tadworth KT20 off Ballards Grn 233 CY119
Maybury Gdns, NW10 139 CV65
Maybury Hill, Wok. GU22 227 BB116
Sch Maybury Inf Sch, Wok. GU21 off Walton Rd 227 BA116
Maybury Ms, N6 121 DJ59
Maybury Rd, E13 292 C5
Barking IG11 145 ET68
Woking GU21 227 AZ117
Maybury St, SW17 180 DE92
Maybush Rd, Horn. RM11 128 FL59
Maychurch Cl, Stan. HA7 95 CK52
May Cl, Chess. KT9 216 CM107
St. Albans AL3 43 CD18
Maycock Gro, Nthwd. HA6 93 BT51
May Cotts, Wat. WD18 76 BW43
May Ct, SW19 200 DB95
Grays RM17 off Medlar Rd 170 GE79
Maycroft, Pnr. HA5 93 BV54
Maycroft Av, Grays RM17 170 GD78
Maycroft Gdns, Grays RM17 170 GD78
Maycroft Rd, Chsht EN7 66 DS26
Maycross Av, Mord. SM4 199 CZ97
Mayday Gdns, SE3 164 EL82
Mayday Rd, Th.Hth. CR7 201 DP100
H Mayday Uni Hosp, Th.Hth. CR7 201 DP100
Maydew Ho, SE16 300 G8
Maydwell Lo, Borwd. WD6 78 CM40
Mayell Cl, Lthd. KT22 231 CJ123
Mayerne Rd, SE9 184 EK85
Mayer Rd, Wal.Abb. EN9 off Deer Pk Way 83 EB36
Mayesbrook Rd, Bark. IG11 145 ET67
Dagenham RM8 126 EU62
Ilford IG3 126 EU62
Mayes Cl, New Adgtn CR0 221 ED108
Swanley BR8 207 FG98
Warlingham CR6 237 DX118
Mayesford Rd, Rom. RM6 126 EW59
Sch Mayespark Prim Sch, Ilf. IG3 off Goodmayes La 126 EU62
Mayes Rd, N22 99 DN54
Mayeswood Rd, SE12 184 EJ90
MAYFAIR, W1 297 J1
Mayfair Av, Bexh. DA7 166 EX81
Ilford IG1 125 EM61
Romford RM6 126 EX58
Twickenham TW2 176 CC87
Worcester Park KT4 199 CU102
Mayfair Cl, Beck. BR3 203 EB95
St. Albans AL4 43 CJ15
Surbiton KT6 198 CL102
Mayfair Gdns, N17 100 DR51
Woodford Green IG8 102 EG52
Mayfair Ms, NW1 274 F7
Mayfair Pl, W1 297 K2
Mayfair Rd, Dart. DA1 188 FK85
Mayfair Ter, N14 99 DK45
Mayfare, Crox.Grn WD3 75 BR43
Mayfield, Bexh. DA7 166 EZ83
Leatherhead KT22 231 CJ121
Waltham Abbey EN9 67 ED34
Welwyn Garden City AL8 29 CW05
Mayfield Av, N12 98 DC49
N14 99 DJ47
W4 158 CS77
W13 157 CH76
Gerrards Cross SL9 112 AX56
Harrow HA3 117 CH57
New Haw KT15 212 BH110
Orpington BR6 205 ET102
Woodford Green IG8 102 EG52
Mayfield Cl, E8 278 A5
SW4 181 DK85
Ashford TW15 175 BP93
Harlow CM17 36 EZ11
Hersham KT12 213 BU105
New Haw KT15 212 BJ110
Redhill RH1 266 DG140
Thames Ditton KT7 197 CH102
Uxbridge UB10 135 BP69
Mayfield Cres, N9 82 DV44
Thornton Heath CR7 201 DM98
Mayfield Dr, Pnr. HA5 116 BZ56
Windsor SL4 151 AN83
Mayfield Gdns, NW4 119 CX58
W7 137 CD72
Brentwood CM14 108 FV46
Hersham KT12 213 BU105
New Haw KT15 212 BH110
Staines-upon-Thames TW18 173 BF93
Sch Mayfield Gram Sch, Grav. DA11 off Pelham Rd 191 GG88
Mayfield Grn, Bkhm KT23 246 CA126
Mayfield Gro, Rain. RM13 148 FJ69
Sch Mayfield Inf & Nurs Sch, Wal.Cr. EN8 off Cheshunt Wash 89 DY27
Mayfield Mans, SW15 off West Hill 179 CX87
Mayfield Pk, West Dr. UB7 154 BJ76
Sch Mayfield Prim Sch, W7 off High La 137 CD72
Mayfield Rd, E4 101 EC47
E8 278 A7
E13 291 M5
E17 101 DY54
N8 121 DM58
SW19 199 CZ95
W3 138 CP73
W12 158 CS75
Belvedere DA17 167 FC77
Bromley BR1 204 EL99
Dagenham RM8 126 EW60
Enfield EN3 83 DX40
Gravesend DA11 191 GF87
Hersham KT12 213 BU105
South Croydon CR2 220 DR109
Sutton SM2 218 DD107
Thornton Heath CR7 201 DM98
Weybridge KT13 212 BM106
Wooburn Green HP10 110 AE57
Mayfields, Grays RM16 170 GC75
Swanscombe DA10 189 FX86
Wembley HA9 118 CN61
Sch Mayfield Sch & Coll, Dag. RM8 off Pedley Rd 126 EW60
Mayfields Cl, Wem. HA9 118 CN61
Mayflower Cl, SE16 301 K8
Hertingfordbury SG14 31 DL11
Lower Nazeing EN9 50 EE22
Ruislip HA4 115 BQ58
South Ockendon RM15 149 FW70
Mayflower Ct, SE16 off St. Marychurch St 300 G5
Harlow CM19 51 EP19
Sch Mayflower Prim Sch, E14 290 C9
Mayflower Rd, SW9 310 A10
Chafford Hundred RM16 169 FW78
Park Street AL2 60 CB27
Mayflower St, SE16 300 G5
Mayflower Way, Beac. HP9 110 AG55
Farnham Common SL2 111 AQ64
Mayfly Cl, Eastcote HA5 116 BW59
Orpington BR5 206 EX98
Mayfly Gdns, Nthlt. UB5 off Seasprite Cl 136 BX69
MAYFORD, Wok. GU22 226 AW122
Mayford Cl, SW12 180 DF87
Beckenham BR3 203 DX97
Woking GU22 226 AX122
Mayford Grn, Wok. GU22 off Smarts Heath Rd 226 AX122
Mayford Rd, SW12 180 DF87
May Gdns, Els. WD6 77 CK44
Wembley HA0 137 CJ68
Maygoods Cl, Uxb. UB8 134 BK71
Maygoods Grn, Uxb. UB8 134 BK71
Maygoods La, Uxb. UB8 134 BK71
Maygood St, N1 276 D10
Maygoods Vw, Cowley UB8 134 BJ71
Maygreen Cres, Horn. RM11 127 FG59
Maygrove Rd, NW6 272 G5
Mayhall La, Amer. HP6 55 AP35
Mayhew Cl, E4 101 EA48
Mayhill Rd, SE7 164 EH79
Barnet EN5 79 CY44
Mayhurst Av, Wok. GU22 227 BC116
Mayhurst Cl, Wok. GU22 227 BC116
Mayhurst Cres, Wok. GU22 227 BC116
Maylands Av, Hem.H. HP2 41 BP17
Hornchurch RM12 127 FH63
Maylands Dr, Sid. DA14 186 EX90
Uxbridge UB8 134 BK65
Maylands Rd, Wat. WD19 94 BW49
Maylands Way, Rom. RM3 106 FQ51
Maylins Dr, Saw. CM21 36 EX05
Maynard Cl, N15 off Brunswick Rd 122 DS57
SW6 307 M5
Erith DA8 167 FF80
Maynard Ct, Enf. EN3 off Harston Dr 83 EA38
Waltham Abbey EN9 68 EF34
Maynard Dr, St.Alb. AL1 43 CD23
Maynard Path, E17 123 EC57
Maynard Pl, Cuffley EN6 65 DL29
Maynard Rd, E17 123 EC57
Hemel Hempstead HP2 40 BK21
Maynards, Horn. RM11 128 FL59
Maynards Quay, E1 300 G1
Mayne Av, St.Alb. AL3 42 BZ22
Maynooth Gdns, Cars. SM5 200 DF101
Mayo Cl, Chsht EN8 66 DW28
Mayo Gdns, Hem.H. HP1 40 BH21
Mayola Rd, E5 122 DW63
Mayo Rd, NW10 138 CS65
Croydon CR0 202 DR99
Walton-on-Thames KT12 195 BT101
Mayor's La, Dart. DA2 188 FJ92
Mayow Rd, SE23 183 DX90
SE26 183 DX91
Mayplace Av, Dart. DA1 167 FG84
Mayplace Cl, Bexh. DA7 167 FB83
Mayplace La, SE18 165 EP80
Sch Mayplace Prim Sch, Barne. DA7 off Woodside Rd 167 FD84
Mayplace Rd E, Bexh. DA7 167 FB83
Dartford DA1 167 FC83
Mayplace Rd W, Bexh. DA7 166 FA84
MAYPOLE, Orp. BR6 224 EZ106
Maypole Cres, Erith DA8 168 FK79
Ilford IG6 103 ER52
Maypole Dr, Chig. IG7 104 EU48
Sch Maypole Prim Sch, Dart. DA2 off Franklin Rd 187 FE90
Maypole Rd, Grav. DA12 191 GM88
Orpington BR6 224 EZ106
Taplow SL6 130 AG71
Maypole St, Harl. CM17 36 EW14
May Rd, E4 101 EA51
E13 281 P10
Hawley DA2 188 FM91
Twickenham TW2 177 CE88
Mayroyd Av, Surb. KT6 198 CN103
May's Bldgs Ms, SE10 314 F5
Mays Cl, Wey. KT13 212 BM110
Mays Ct, WC2 298 A1
Maysfield Rd, Send GU23 227 BD123
Mays Gro, Send GU23 227 BD124
Mays Hill Rd, Brom. BR2 204 EE96
Mays La, E4 101 ED47
Barnet EN5 79 CY43
Maysoule Rd, SW11 160 DD84
MAY'S GREEN, Cob. KT11 229 BT121
Mays Rd, Tedd. TW11 177 CD92
Mayston Ms, SE10 off Westcombe Hill 315 P1
May St, W14 307 H1
Mayswood Gdns, Dag. RM10 147 FC65
Maythorne Cl, Wat. WD18 75 BS42
Mayton St, N7 121 DM62
Maytree Cl, Edg. HA8 96 CQ48
Guildford GU1 242 AV131
Rainham RM13 147 FE68
Maytree Cres, Wat. WD24 75 BT35
Maytree Gdns, W5 157 CK76
May Tree La, Stan. HA7 95 CF52
Maytrees, Rad. WD7 77 CG37
Maytree Wk, SW2 181 DN89
Mayville Est, N16 277 N2
Sch Mayville Prim Sch, E11 off Lincoln St 124 EE62
Mayville Rd, E11 124 EE61
Ilford IG1 125 EP64
May Wk, E13 144 EH68
Maywater Cl, S.Croy. CR2 220 DR111
Maywin Dr, Horn. RM11 128 FM60
Maywood Cl, Beck. BR3 183 EB94
⇌ Maze Hill 315 J2
Maze Hill, SE3 315 J3
SE10 315 J2
Mazenod Av, NW6 273 K7
Maze Rd, Rich. TW9 158 CN80
McAdam Cl, Hodd. EN11 49 EA15
McAdam Dr, Enf. EN2 81 DP40
McAllister Gro, Bark. IG11 146 EU69
McAuley Cl, SE1 298 E6
SE9 185 EP85
McAuliffe Dr, Slou. SL2 111 AM63
McCabe Ct, E16 291 L7
McCall Cl, SW4 310 A8
McCall Cres, SE7 164 EL78
McCall Ho, N7 off Tufnell Pk Rd 121 DL62
McCarthy Rd, Felt. TW13 176 BX92
McClintock Pl, Enf. EN3 83 EB37
McCoid Way, SE1 299 J5
McCrone Ms, NW3 274 B4
McCudden Rd, Dart. DA1 off Cornwall Rd 168 FM83
McCullum Rd, E3 279 N9
McDermott Cl, SW11 308 C10
McDermott Rd, SE15 312 C10
● McDonald Business Pk, Hem.H. HP2 41 BP17
McDonald Ct, Hat. AL10 45 CU20
McDonough Cl, Chess. KT9 216 CL105
McDougall Rd, Berk. HP4 38 AX19
McDowall Cl, E16 291 M7
McDowall Rd, SE5 311 J7
McEntee Av, E17 101 DY53
McEwen Way, E15 281 H8
McGrath Rd, E15 281 L3
McGredy, Chsht EN7 66 DV29
McGregor Rd, W11 282 G8
McIntosh Cl, Rom. RM1 127 FE55
Wallington SM6 219 DL108
McIntosh Rd, Rom. RM1 127 FE55
McKay Rd, SW20 179 CV94
● McKay Trd Est, Colnbr. SL3 153 BE82
McKellar Cl, Bushey Hth WD23 94 CC47
McKenzie Rd, Brox. EN10 49 DZ20
McKenzie Way, Epsom KT19 216 CN110
McKerrell Rd, SE15 312 D7
McLeod Rd, SE2 166 EV77
McLeod's Ms, SW7 295 M7
McMillan Cl, Grav. DA12 191 GJ91
McMillan St, SE8 314 A3
McMillan Student Village, SE8 314 B3
McNair Rd, Sthl. UB2 156 CB75
McNeil Rd, SE5 311 N9
McNicol Dr, NW10 138 CQ68
McRae La, Mitch. CR4 200 DF101
Mead, The, N2 98 DC54
W13 137 CH71
Ashtead KT21 232 CL119
Beaconsfield HP9 89 AL53
Beckenham BR3 203 EC95
Cheshunt EN8 66 DW29
Uxbridge UB10 114 BN61
Wallington SM6 219 DK107
Watford WD19 94 BY48
West Wickham BR4 203 ED102
Mead Av, Red. RH1 266 DG142
Slough SL3 153 BB75
● Mead Business Cen, Hert. SG13 32 DS08
● Mead Business Pk, Chesh. HP5 off Berkhampstead Rd 54 AQ30
Mead Cl, NW1 275 H6
Denham UB9 114 BG61
Egham TW20 173 BB93
Grays RM16 170 GB75
Harrow HA3 95 CD53
Loughton IG10 85 EP40
Redhill RH1 250 DG131
Romford RM2 105 FG54
Slough SL3 153 BB75
Swanley BR8 207 FG99
Mead Ct, NW9 118 CQ57
Addlestone KT15 194 BK104
Egham TW20 off Holbrook Meadow 173 BC93
Knaphill GU21 226 AS116
Waltham Abbey EN9 67 EB34
Mead Cres, E4 101 EC49
Bookham KT23 246 CA125
Dartford DA1 off Beech Rd 188 FK88
Sutton SM1 218 DE105
Meadcroft Rd, SE11 310 G3
Meade Cl, W4 158 CN79
Meade Ct, Walt.Hill KT20 233 CU124
Mead End, Ashtd. KT21 232 CM116
Meades, The, Wey. KT13 213 BQ107
Meades La, Chesh. HP5 54 AP32
Meadfield, Edg. HA8 96 CP47
Mead Fld, Har. HA2 off Kings Rd 116 BZ62
Meadfield Av, Slou. SL3 153 BA76
Meadfield Grn, Edg. HA8 96 CP47
Meadfield Rd, Slou. SL3 153 BA76
Meadfoot Rd, SW16 181 DJ94
Meadgate Av, Wdf.Grn. IG8 102 EL50
Meadgate Rd, Lwr Naze. EN9 49 ED20
Roydon CM19 49 ED20
Mead Gro, Rom. RM6 126 EX55
Mead Ho La, Hayes UB4 135 BR70
Meadhurst Pk, Sun. TW16 175 BS93
Meadhurst Rd, Cher. KT16 194 BH102
Sch Mead Inf Sch, The, Ewell KT19 off Newbury Gdns 217 CT105
Meadlands Dr, Rich. TW10 177 CK89
Sch Meadlands Prim Sch, Rich. TW10 off Broughton Av 177 CJ91
Mead La, Cher. KT16 194 BH102
Hertford SG13 32 DR08
● Mead La Ind Est, Hert. SG13 32 DT08
Meadow, The, Chis. BR7 185 EQ93
Hailey SG13 33 DY13
Meadow Av, Croy. CR0 203 DX100
Meadow Bk, N21 81 DM44
East Horsley KT24 245 BT128
Guildford GU1 off Stoughton Rd 242 AW132
Meadowbank, NW3 274 E7
SE3 164 EF83
Kings Langley WD4 58 BN30
Surbiton KT5 198 CM100
Watford WD19 94 BW45
Meadowbank Cl, SW6 306 B5
Bovingdon HP3 57 BB28
Isleworth TW7 157 CE81
Meadow Bk Cl, Amer. HP7 55 AS38
Meadowbank Gdns, Houns. TW5 155 BU82
Meadowbank Rd, NW9 118 CR59
Meadowbanks, Barn. EN5 79 CT43
Meadowbrook, Oxt. RH8 253 EC130
Meadowbrook Cl, Colnbr. SL3 153 BF82
Meadowbrook Rd, Dor. RH4 263 CG135
Meadow Bungalows, Chilw. GU4 259 BB140
Meadow Cl, E4 101 EB46
E9 279 P3
SE6 183 EA92
SW20 199 CW98
Barking IG11 145 ET67
Barnet EN5 79 CZ44
Bexleyheath DA6 186 EZ85
Bricket Wood AL2 60 CA29
Meadow Cl, Chesham HP5 off Little Hivings 54 AN27
Chislehurst BR7 185 EP92
Enfield EN3 83 DY38
Esher KT10 197 CF104
Godalming GU7 258 AS144
Hersham KT12 214 BZ105
Hertford SG13 32 DT08
Hounslow TW4 176 CA86
London Colney AL2 61 CK27
North Mymms AL9 45 CX24
Northolt UB5 136 CA68
Old Windsor SL4 172 AV86
Purley CR8 219 DK113
Richmond TW10 178 CL88
Ruislip HA4 115 BT58
St. Albans AL4 43 CJ17
Sevenoaks TN13 256 FG123
Sutton SM1 off Aultone Way 200 DC103
Meadowcot La, Colesh. HP7 55 AM44
Meadow Cotts, Beac. HP9 89 AL54
Meadow Ct, Epsom KT18 216 CQ113
Harlow CM18 off Lodge Hall 51 ES19
Redhill RH1 251 DJ130
Staines-upon-Thames TW18 173 BE90
Meadowcourt Rd, SE3 164 EF84
Meadowcroft, Brom. BR1 205 EM97
Bushey WD23 76 CB44
Chalfont St. Peter SL9 90 AX54
St. Albans AL1 43 CG23
Meadow Cft, Hat. AL10 45 CT18
Meadowcroft Cl, Horl. RH6 269 DJ151
Sch Meadowcroft Comm Inf Sch, Cher. KT16 off Little Grn La 193 BF104
Meadowcroft Rd, N13 99 DN47
Meadowcross, Wal.Abb. EN9 68 EE34
Meadow Dell, Hat. AL10 45 CT18
Meadow Dr, N10 121 DH55
NW4 97 CW54
Amersham HP6 55 AS37
Ripley GU23 227 BF123
Meadow Fm, Hemel Hempstead HP3 59 BR26
Meadowford Cl, SE28 146 EU73
Meadow Gdns, Edg. HA8 96 CP51
Staines-upon-Thames TW18 173 BD92
Meadow Garth, NW10 138 CQ66
Meadow Gate, Ashtd. KT21 232 CL117
Meadowgate Cl, NW7 97 CT50
Sch Meadowgate Sch, SE4 off Revelon Rd 163 DY83
Meadow Grn, Welw.G.C. AL8 29 CW09
Sch Meadow High Sch, Hlgdn UB8 off Royal La 134 BM71
Meadow Hill, New Malden KT3 198 CS100
Purley CR8 219 DJ113
Meadowlands, Cob. KT11 213 BU113
Hornchurch RM11 128 FL59
Oxted RH8 254 EG134
West Clandon GU4 244 BH130
Meadowlands Pk, Add. KT15 194 BL104
Meadow La, SE12 184 EH90
Beaconsfield HP9 89 AM53
Eton SL4 151 AQ80
Fetcham KT22 230 CC121
Meadowlea Cl, Harm. UB7 154 BK79
Meadow Ms, SW8 310 C3
Meadow Pl, SW8 310 B4
W4 off Edensor Rd 158 CS80
Sch Meadow Prim Sch, Epsom KT17 off Sparrow Fm Rd 217 CV105
Meadow Ri, Couls. CR5 219 DK113
Meadow Rd, SW8 310 C4
SW19 180 DC94
Ashford TW15 175 BR92
Ashtead KT21 232 CL117
Barking IG11 145 ET66
Berkhamsted HP4 38 AU17
Borehamwood WD6 78 CP40
Bromley BR2 204 EE95
Bushey WD23 76 CB43
Claygate KT10 215 CE107
Dagenham RM9 146 EZ65
Epping CM16 69 ET29
Feltham TW13 176 BY89
Gravesend DA11 191 GG89
Guildford GU4 243 BA130
Hemel Hempstead HP3 40 BN24
Loughton IG10 84 EL43
Pinner HA5 116 BX57
Romford RM7 127 FC60
Slough SL3 152 AY76
Southall UB1 136 BZ73
Sutton SM1 218 DE106
Virginia Water GU25 192 AS99
Watford WD25 59 BU34
Meadow Row, SE1 299 J7
Meadows, The, Amer. HP7 55 AS39
Guildford GU2 258 AW137
Halstead TN14 224 EZ113
Hemel Hempstead HP1 39 BE19
Orpington BR6 224 EW107
Sawbridgeworth CM21 36 FA05
Warlingham CR6 237 DX117
Watford WD25 76 BX36
Welwyn Garden City AL7 30 DC09
Meadows Cl, E10 123 EA61
Meadows End, Sun. TW16 195 BU95
Meadows Est, SE6 off Chestnut Cl 183 EC92
Meadowside, SE9 164 EK84
Bookham KT23 230 CA123
Dartford DA1 188 FK88
Horley RH6 off Stockfield 269 DH147
Jordans HP9 90 AT52
Walton-on-Thames KT12 196 BW103
Meadow Side, Wat. WD25 59 BV31
Meadowside Rd, Sutt. SM2 217 CY109
Upminster RM14 128 FQ64
Meadows Leigh Cl, Wey. KT13 195 BQ104
Sch Meadows Sch, The, Woob.Grn HP10 off School Rd 110 AE57
Meadow Stile, Croy. CR0 off High St 202 DQ104
Meadowsweet Cl, E16 292 E7
SW20 199 CW98
Meadow Vw, Ch.St.G. HP8 90 AU48
Chertsey KT16 194 BJ102
Harrow HA1 117 CE60
Orpington BR5 206 EW97
Sidcup DA15 186 EV87
Staines-upon-Thames TW19 173 BF85

M

Meadowview Rd, SE6 183 DZ92
Bexley DA5 186 EY86
Epsom KT19 216 CS109
Meadow Vw Rd, Hayes UB4 135 BQ70
Thornton Heath CR7 201 DP99
Meadow Wk, E18 124 EG56
Dagenham RM9 146 EZ65
Dartford DA2 188 FJ91
Epsom KT17, KT19 216 CS107
Penn HP10 88 AC46
Wallington SM6 201 DH104
Walton on the Hill KT20 233 CV124
Meadow Way, NW9 118 CR57
Addlestone KT15 212 BH105
Bedmond WD5 59 BT27
Bookham KT23 230 CB123
Chessington KT9 216 CL106
Chigwell IG7 103 EQ48
Dartford DA2 188 FQ87
Dorney Reach SL6 150 AF75
Fifield SL6 150 AD81
Hemel Hempstead HP3 39 BF23
Horl. RH6 269 DJ146
Kings Langley WD4 58 BN30
Old Windsor SL4 172 AV86
Orpington BR6 205 EN104
Potters Bar EN6 64 DA34
Reigate RH2 266 DB138
Rickmansworth WD3 92 BJ45
Ruislip HA4 115 BV58
Sawbridgeworth CM21 36 FA06
Tadworth KT20 233 CY118
Upminster RM14 128 FQ62
Wembley HA9 117 CK63
West Horsley KT24 245 BR125
Meadow Way, The, Har. HA3 95 CE53
Meadow Waye, Houns. TW5 156 BY79
Sch Meadow Wd Sch, Bushey WD23 off Coldharbour La 76 CC43
● Mead Pk, Harl. CM20 35 ET11
Mead Path, SW17 180 DC92
Mead Pl, E9 279 H5
Croydon CR0 201 DP102
Rickmansworth WD3 92 BH46
Mead Plat, NW10 138 CQ65
Sch Mead Prim Sch, Harold Hill RM3 off Amersham Rd 106 FM51
Mead Rd, Cat. CR3 236 DT123
Chislehurst BR7 185 EQ93
Dartford DA1 188 FK88
Edgware HA8 96 CN51
Gravesend DA11 191 GH89
Hersham KT12 214 BY105
Richmond TW10 177 CJ90
Shenley WD7 62 CN33
Uxbridge UB8 134 BK65
Sch Mead Rd Inf Sch, Chis. BR7 off Mead Rd 185 EQ93
Mead Row, SE1 298 E6
Meads, The, Brick.Wd AL2 60 BZ29
Edgware HA8 96 CR51
Northchurch HP4 38 AS17
Sutton SM3 199 CY104
Upminster RM14 129 FS61
Uxbridge UB8 134 BL70
Jct Meads Cor, Purf. RM19 168 FP77
Meadside Cl, Beck. BR3 203 DY95
Meads La, Ilf. IG3 125 ES59
Meads Rd, N22 99 DP54
Enfield EN3 83 DY39
Guildford GU1 243 BA134
Meadsway, Gt Warley CM13 107 FV51
MEAD VALE, Red. RH1 266 DD136
Meadvale Rd, W5 137 CH70
Croydon CR0 202 DT101
Meadview Rd, Ware SG12 33 DX07
Mead Wk, Slou. SL3 153 BB75
Meadway, N14 99 DK47
NW11 120 DB58
SW20 199 CW98
Ashford TW15 174 BN91
Barnet EN5 80 DA42
Beckenham BR3 203 EC95
Berkhamsted HP4 38 AY18
Colney Heath AL4 44 CR23
Effingham KT24 246 BY128
Enfield EN3 82 DW36
Epsom KT19 216 CQ112
Esher KT10 214 CB109
Grays RM17 170 GD77
Halstead TN14 224 EZ113
Hoddesdon EN11 49 EA19
Ilford IG3 125 ES63
Oxshott KT22 215 CD114
Romford RM2 105 FG54
Ruislip HA4 115 BR58
Staines-upon-Thames TW18 174 BG94
Surbiton KT5 198 CQ102
Twickenham TW2 177 CD88
Warlingham CR6 236 DW115
Welwyn Garden City AL7 29 CZ11
Woodford Green IG8 102 EJ50
Mead Way, Brom. BR2 204 EF100
Bushey WD23 76 BY40
Coulsdon CR5 235 DL118
Croydon CR0 203 DY103
Guildford GU4 243 BC129
Slough SL1 131 AK71
Meadway, The, SE3 315 H9
Buckhurst Hill IG9 102 EK46
Cuffley EN6 65 DM28
Horley RH6 269 DJ148
Loughton IG10 85 EM44
Orpington BR6 224 EV106
Sevenoaks TN13 256 FF122
Meadway Cl, NW11 120 DB58
Barnet EN5 80 DA42
Pinner HA5 off Highbanks Rd 94 CB51
Staines-upon-Thames TW18 173 BF94
Meadway Ct, NW11 120 DB58
Meadway Dr, Add. KT15 212 BJ108
Woking GU21 226 AW116
Meadway Gdns, Ruis. HA4 115 BR58
Meadway Gate, NW11 120 DA58
Meadway Pk, Ger.Cr. SL9 112 AX60
Meaford Way, SE20 182 DV94
Meakin Est, SE1 299 N6
Meanley Rd, E12 124 EL63
Meard St, W1 285 N9
Meare Cl, Tad. KT20 233 CW123
Meare Est, Woob.Grn HP10 110 AD55
Mears Cl, E1
off Settles St 288 D7
Meath Cl, Orp. BR5 206 EV99
Meath Cres, E2 289 J3
Meath Gdns, Horl. RH6 268 DE146
MEATH GREEN, Horl. RH6 268 DE146
Meath Grn Av, Horl. RH6 268 DF146
Sch Meath Grn Inf Sch, Horl. RH6 off Kiln La 268 DF146
Sch Meath Grn Jun Sch, Horl. RH6 off Greenfields Rd 268 DF146
Meath Grn La, Horl. RH6 266 DE143
Meath Rd, E15 281 L10
Ilford IG1 125 EQ62
Sch Meath Sch, Ott. KT16 off Brox Rd 211 BD108
Meath St, SW11 309 J6
Meautys, St.Alb. AL3 42 BZ22
Sch Mechinah Liyeshiva Zichron Moshe Sch, N16 off Amhurst Pk 122 DR59
Mecklenburgh Pl, WC1 286 C4
Mecklenburgh Sq, WC1 286 C4
Mecklenburgh St, WC1 286 C4
Medals Way, E20 280 F5
Medbury Rd, Grav. DA12 191 GM88
Medcalf Rd, Enf. EN3 83 DZ37
Medcroft Gdns, SW14 158 CQ84
Medebourne Cl, SE3 315 P10
Mede Cl, Wrays. TW19 172 AX88
Mede Fld, Fetch. KT22 231 CD124
Medesenge Way, N13 99 DP51
Medfield St, SW15 179 CV87
Medhurst Cl, E3 289 M1
Chobham GU24 210 AT109
Medhurst Cres, Grav. DA12 191 GM90
Medhurst Dr, Brom. BR1 183 ED92
Medhurst Gdns, Grav. DA12 191 GM90
Median Rd, E5 278 G2
Medici Cl, Ilf. IG3
off Barley La 126 EU58
★ Medici Galleries, W1 297 L1
Medick Ct, Grays RM17 170 GE79
Medina Av, Esher KT10 197 CE104
Medina Gro, N7 121 DN62
Medina Rd, N7 121 DN62
Grays RM17 170 GD77
Medina Sq, Epsom KT19 216 CN109
Medlake Rd, Egh. TW20 173 BC93
Medland Cl, Wall. SM6 200 DG102
Medland Ho, E14 289 L10
Medlar Cl, Guil. GU1 242 AW132
Northolt UB5
off Parkfield Av 136 BY68
Medlar Ct, Slou. SL2 132 AW74
Medlar Ho, SW16
off Hemlock Cl 201 DK96
Medlar Rd, Grays RM17 170 GD79
Medlar St, SE5 311 K6
Medley Rd, NW6 273 K5
Medman Cl, Uxb. UB8 134 BJ68
Medora Rd, SW2 181 DM87
Romford RM7 127 FD56
Medow Mead, Rad. WD7 61 CF33
Medusa Rd, SE6 183 EB86
Medway Bldgs, E3 289 M1
Medway Cl, Croy. CR0 202 DW100
Ilford IG1 125 EQ64
Watford WD25 60 BW34
Medway Dr, Perivale UB6 137 CF68
Medway Gdns, Wem. HA0 117 CG63
Medway Ms, E3 289 M1
Medway Par, Perivale UB6 137 CF68
Medway Rd, E3 289 M1
Dartford DA1 167 FG83
Hemel Hempstead HP2 40 BM15
Medway St, SW1 297 P7
Medwick Ms, Hem.H. HP2
off Hunters Oak 41 BP15
Medwin St, SW4 161 DM84
Meecham Ct, SW11 308 B8
Meerbrook Rd, SE3 164 EJ83
Meeson Rd, E15 281 L8
Meesons La, Grays RM17 170 FZ77
Meeson St, E5 279 L1
Meeting Fld Path, E9 279 H4
Meeting Ho All, E1 300 F2
Meeting Ho La, SE15 312 E6
Megg La, Chipper. WD4 58 BH29
Mehetabel Rd, E9 278 G4
Meister Cl, Ilf. IG1 125 ER60
Melancholy Wk, Rich. TW10 177 CJ89
Melanda Cl, Chis. BR7 185 EM92
Melanie Cl, Bexh. DA7 166 EY81
Melba Gdns, Til. RM18 171 GG80
Melba Way, SE13 314 D7
Melbourne Av, N13 99 DM51
W13 137 CG74
Pinner HA5 116 CB55
Slough SL1 131 AQ72
Melbourne Cl, Orp. BR6 205 ES101
St. Albans AL3 43 CF16
Uxbridge UB10 114 BN63
Wallington SM6
off Melbourne Rd 219 DJ106
Melbourne Ct, E5
off Daubeney Rd 123 DY63
SE20 182 DU94
Waltham Cross EN8
off Alexandra Way 67 DZ34
Welwyn Garden City AL8 29 CV10
Melbourne Gdns, Rom. RM6 126 EY57
Melbourne Gro, SE22 162 DS84
Melbourne Ho, Hayes UB4 136 BW70
Melbourne Ms, SE6 183 EC87
SW9 310 E7
Melbourne Pl, WC2 286 D10
Melbourne Rd, E6 145 EM67
E10 123 EB59
E17 123 DY56
SW19 200 DA95
Bushey WD23 76 CB44
Ilford IG1 125 EP60
Teddington TW11 177 CJ93
Tilbury RM18 170 GE81
Wallington SM6 219 DH106
Melbourne Sq, SW9 310 E7
Melbourne Ter, SW6
off Moore Pk Rd 307 L5
Melbourne Way, Enf. EN1 82 DT44
Melbourne Yd, SE19
off Westow St 182 DS93
Melbray Ms, SW6 306 G9
Melbreak Ho, SE22
off Pytchley Rd 162 DS83
Melbury Av, Sthl. UB2 156 CB76
Melbury Cl, Cher. KT16 194 BG101
Chislehurst BR7 184 EL93
Claygate KT10 215 CH107
West Byfleet KT14 212 BG114
Melbury Ct, W8 295 H6
Melbury Dr, SE5 311 N5
Melbury Gdns, SW20 199 CV95
South Croydon CR2 220 DS111
Melbury Rd, W14 294 G6
Harrow HA3 118 CM57
Melchester Ho, N19
off Wedmore St 121 DK62
Melcombe Gdns, Har. HA3 118 CM58
Melcombe Ho, SW8
off Dorset Rd 310 C5
Melcombe Pl, NW1 284 E6
Sch Melcombe Prim Sch, W6 306 C2
Melcombe St, NW1 284 F5
Meldex Cl, NW7 97 CW51
Meldon Cl, SW6 307 M7
Meldone Cl, Surb. KT5 198 CP100
Meldrum Cl, Orp. BR5
off Killewarren Way 206 EW100
Oxted RH8 254 EF132
Meldrum Rd, Ilf. IG3 126 EU61
Melfield Gdns, SE6 183 EB91
Melford Av, Bark. IG11 145 ES65
Melford Cl, Chess. KT9 216 CM106
Melford Rd, E6 293 J4
E11 124 EE61
E17 123 DY56
SE22 182 DU87
Ilford IG1 125 ER61
Melfort Av, Th.Hth. CR7 201 DP97
Melfort Rd, Th.Hth. CR7 201 DP97
Melgund Rd, N5 276 F3
Melia Cl, Wat. WD25 76 BW35
Melina Cl, Hayes UB3 135 BR71
Melina Pl, NW8 284 A3
Melina Rd, W12 159 CV75
Melings, The, Hem.H. HP2 41 BP15
Melior Pl, SE1 299 N4
Melior St, SE1 299 M4
Meliot Rd, SE6 183 ED89
Melksham Cl, Rom. RM3 106 FL52
Melksham Dr, Rom. RM3
off Melksham Gdns 106 FM52
Melksham Gdns, Rom. RM3 106 FL52
Melksham Grn, Rom. RM3
off Melksham Gdns 106 FM52
Meller Cl, Croy. CR0 201 DL104
Mellersh Hill Rd, Won. GU5 259 BB144
Mellifont Cl, Cars. SM5 200 DD101
Melling Dr, Enf. EN1 82 DU39
Melling St, SE18 165 ES79
Mellish Cl, Bark. IG11 145 ET67
Mellish Gdns, Wdf.Grn. IG8 102 EG50
● Mellish Ind Est, SE18 304 F6
Mellish St, E14 302 A6
Mellish Way, Horn. RM11 128 FJ57
Mellison Rd, SW17 180 DE92
Melliss Av, Rich. TW9 158 CP81
Mellitus St, W12 139 CT72
Mellor Cl, Walt. KT12 196 BZ101
Mellor Wk, Wind. SL4 151 AR81
Mellow Cl, Bans. SM7 218 DB114
Mellow La E, Hayes UB4 135 BQ69
Sch Mellow La Sch, Hayes End UB4 off Hewens Rd 135 BQ70
Mellow La W, Uxb. UB10 135 BQ69
Mellows Rd, Ilf. IG5 125 EM55
Wallington SM6 219 DK106
Mells Cres, SE9 185 EM91
Mell St, SE10 315 J1
Melody Ct, W4
off Wellesley Rd 158 CN78
Melody La, N5 277 H2
Melody Rd, SW18 180 DC85
Biggin Hill TN16 238 EJ118
Melon Pl, W8 295 L4
Melon Rd, E11 124 EE62
SE15 312 C6
Melrose Av, N22 99 DP53
NW2 272 B2
SW16 201 DM97
SW19 180 DA89
Borehamwood WD6 78 CP43
Dartford DA1 187 FE87
Greenford UB6 136 CB68
Mitcham CR4 181 DH94
Potters Bar EN6 64 DB32
Twickenham TW2 176 CB87
Melrose Cl, SE12 184 EG88
Greenford UB6 136 CB68
Hayes UB4 135 BU71
Melrose Ct, W13
off Williams Rd 137 CG74
Melrose Cres, Orp. BR6 223 ER105
Melrose Dr, Sthl. UB1 136 CA74
Melrose Gdns, W6 294 B6
Edgware HA8 96 CP54
Hersham KT12 214 BW106
New Malden KT3 198 CR97
Melrose Pl, Wat. WD17 75 BT38
Melrose Rd, SW13 159 CT82
SW18 179 CZ86
SW19 200 DA96
W3 off Stanley Rd 158 CQ76
Biggin Hill TN16 238 EJ116
Coulsdon CR5 235 DH115
Pinner HA5 116 BZ56
Weybridge KT13 212 BN106
Sch Melrose Sch, Mitch. CR4
off Church Rd 200 DE97
Melrose Ter, W6 294 B5
Melsa Rd, Mord. SM4 200 DC100
Melsted Rd, Hem.H. HP1 40 BH20
Melstock Av, Upmin. RM14 128 FQ63
Melthorne Dr, Ruis. HA4 116 BW62
Melthorpe Gdns, SE3 164 EL81
Melton Cl, Ruis. HA4 116 BW60
Melton Ct, SW7 296 B9
Sutton SM2 218 DC108
Melton Flds, Epsom KT19 216 CR109
Melton Gdns, Rom. RM1 127 FF59
Melton Pl, Epsom KT19 216 CR109
Melton Rd, S.Merst. RH1 251 DJ130
Melton St, NW1 285 M3
Melville Av, SW20 179 CU94
Greenford UB6 117 CF64
South Croydon CR2 220 DT106
Melville Cl, Uxb. UB10 115 BR62
Melville Ct, W4
off Stonehill Rd 158 CN78
W12 off Goldhawk Rd 159 CV76
Melville Gdns, N13 99 DP50
Melville Pl, N1 277 J7
Melville Rd, E17 123 DZ55
NW10 138 CR66
SW13 159 CU81
Rainham RM13 147 FG70
Romford RM5 105 FB52
Sidcup DA14 186 EW89
Melville Vil Rd, W3
off High St 138 CR74
Melvin Rd, SE20 202 DW95
Melvinshaw, Lthd. KT22 231 CJ121
Melvyn Cl, Goffs Oak EN7 65 DP28
Melwas Ct, N9
off Galahad Rd 100 DU48
Melyn Cl, N7 275 M1
Memel Ct, EC1 287 J5
Memel St, EC1 287 J5
Memess Path, SE18 165 EN79
Memorial Av, E15 291 J2
Memorial Cl, Houns. TW5 156 BZ79
Oxted RH8 253 ED127
Memorial Hts, Ilf. IG2 125 ER58
H Memorial Hosp, SE18 165 EN82
Menai Pl, E3 280 A10
Mendez Way, SW15 179 CU86
Mendip Cl, SE26 182 DW91
Harlington UB3 155 BR80
St. Albans AL4 43 CJ15
Slough SL3 153 BA78
Worcester Park KT4 199 CW102
Mendip Dr, NW2 119 CX61
Mendip Ho, N9
off Edmonton Grn Shop Cen 100 DU47
Mendip Hos, E2 289 H2
Mendip Rd, SW11 160 DC83
Bexleyheath DA7 167 FE81
Bushey WD23 76 CC44
Hornchurch RM11 127 FG59
Ilford IG2 125 ES57
Mendip Way, Hem.H. HP2 40 BL17
Mendlesham, Welw.G.C. AL7 30 DE09
Mendora Rd, SW6 306 F4
Mendoza Cl, Horn. RM11 128 FL57
Menelik Rd, NW2 272 F2
★ Menier Chocolate Factory, SE1 off Southwark St 299 K3
Menlo Gdns, SE19 182 DR94
Menon Dr, N9 100 DV48
Sch Menorah Foundation Sch, Edg. HA8 off Abbots Rd 96 CQ52
Sch Menorah Gram Sch, Edg. HA8 off Abbots Rd 96 CQ52
Sch Menorah Prim Sch, NW11
off Woodstock Av 119 CY59
Menotti St, E2 288 D4
Menthone Pl, Horn. RM11 128 FK59
Mentmore Cl, Har. HA3 117 CJ58
Mentmore Rd, St.Alb. AL1 43 CD22
Mentmore Ter, E8 278 F7
Meon Cl, Tad. KT20 233 CV122
Meon Ct, Islw. TW7 157 CE82
Meon Rd, W3 158 CQ75
Meopham Rd, Mitch. CR4 201 DJ95
Mepham Cres, Har. HA3 94 CC52
Mepham Gdns, Har. HA3 94 CC52
Mepham St, SE1 298 D3
Mera Dr, Bexh. DA7 166 FA84
Merantun Way, SW19 200 DC95
Merbury Cl, SE13 183 EC85
SE28 145 ER74
Merbury Rd, SE28 165 ES75
Mercator Pl, E14 302 B10
Mercator Rd, SE13 163 ED84
Mercer Cl, T.Ditt. KT7 197 CF101
Merceron Hos, E2
off Globe Rd 288 G2
Merceron St, E1 288 E5
Mercer Pl, Pnr. HA5 94 BW54
Mercers, Harl. CM19 51 EN18
Hemel Hempstead HP2 40 BL18
Mercers Cl, SE10 303 L9
Mercers Ms, N19 121 DK62
Mercers Pl, W6 294 B8
Mercers Rd, N19 121 DK62
Mercers Row, St.Alb. AL1 42 CC22
Mercer St, WC2 286 A9
Mercer Wk, Uxb. UB8
off The Mall Pavilions 134 BJ66
Merchant Cl, Epsom KT19 216 CR106
Merchant Dr, Hert. SG13 32 DT08
Merchants Cl, SE25
off Clifford Rd 202 DU98
Merchants Ho, SE10
off Collington St 315 H1
Merchants Row, SE10
off Hoskins St 315 H1
Merchant St, E3 289 P3
Sch Merchant Taylors' Sch, Nthwd. HA6 off Sandy Lo La 93 BS46
Merchiston Rd, SE6 183 ED89
Merchland Rd, SE9 185 EQ88
Mercia Gro, SE13 163 EC84
Mercian Way, Slou. SL1 131 AK74
Mercia Wk, Wok. GU21
off Commercial Way 227 AZ117
Mercier Rd, SW15 179 CY85
● Mercury Cen, Felt. TW14 175 BU85
Mercury Gdns, Rom. RM1 127 FE56
Mercury Ho, E3
off Garrison Rd 280 A9
● Mercury Pk, Woob.Grn HP10 110 AE56
Mercury Wk, Hem.H. HP2 40 BM17
Mercury Way, SE14 313 J2
Mercy Ter, SE13 163 EB84
Merebank Cl, Gdse. RH9 252 DW130
Merebank La, Croy. CR0 219 DM106
Mere Cl, SW15 179 CX87
Orpington BR6 205 EP103
Meredith Av, NW2 272 B2
Meredith Cl, Pnr. HA5 94 BX52
Meredith Ms, SE4 163 DZ84
Meredith Rd, Grays RM16 171 GG77
Meredith St, E13 291 P3
EC1 286 G3
Meredyth Rd, SW13 159 CU82
Mere End, Croy. CR0 203 DX101
Merefield, Saw. CM21 36 EY06
Merefield Gdns, Tad. KT20 233 CX119
Mere Rd, SE2 166 EX75
Shepperton TW17 195 BP100
Slough SL1 152 AT76
Tadworth KT20 233 CV124
Weybridge KT13 195 BR104
Mereside, Orp. BR6 205 EN103
Mereside Pl, Vir.W. GU25 192 AX100
Meretone Cl, SE4 163 DY84
Mereton Mans, SE8 314 B6
Merevale Cres, Mord. SM4 200 DC100
Mereway Rd, Twick. TW2 177 CD88
Merewood Cl, Brom. BR1 205 EN96
Merewood Gdns, Croy. CR0 203 DX101
Merewood Rd, Bexh. DA7 167 FC82
Mereworth Cl, Brom. BR2 204 EF99
Mereworth Dr, SE18 165 EP80
Merganser Gdns, SE28
off Avocet Ms 165 ER76
MERIDEN, Wat. WD25 76 BY35
Meriden Cl, Brom. BR1 184 EK94
Ilford IG6 103 EQ53
Meriden Way, Wat. WD25 76 BY36
Meridia Ct, E15
off Biggerstaff Rd 280 F8
● Meridian Business Pk, Wal.Abb. EN9 83 EB35
Meridian Cl, NW7 96 CR49
Meridian Ct, SE16
off East La 300 C4
Meridian Gate, E14 302 E4
Meridian Gro, Horl. RH6 269 DJ147
Meridian Pl, E14 302 D4
Sch Meridian Prim Sch, SE10 315 H1
Meridian Rd, SE7 164 EK80
Meridian Sq, E15 280 G6
● Meridian Trd Est, SE7 304 B8
Meridian Wk, N17
off Commercial Rd 100 DS51
Meridian Way, N9 100 DW50
N18 100 DW51
Enfield EN3 83 DX44
Stanstead Abbotts SG12 33 EB10
Waltham Abbey EN9 83 EB35
Meriel Wk, Green. DA9
off The Avenue 169 FV84
Merifield Rd, SE9 164 EJ84
Merino Cl, E11 124 EJ56
Merino Pl, Sid. DA15
off Blackfen Rd 186 EU86
Merivale Rd, SW15 159 CY84
Harrow HA1 116 CC59
Merland Cl, Tad. KT20 233 CW120
Merland Grn, Tad. KT20 233 CW120
Merland Ri, Epsom KT18 233 CW119
Tadworth KT20 233 CW119
Sch Merland Ri Comm Prim Sch, Epsom KT18 off Merland Ri 233 CW119
Merle Av, Hare. UB9 92 BH54
Merlewood, Sev. TN13 257 FH123
Merlewood Cl, Cat. CR3 236 DR120
Merlewood Dr, Chis. BR7 205 EM95
Merley Ct, NW9 118 CQ60
Merlin Cl, Chaff.Hun. RM16 170 FY76
Croydon CR0 220 DS105
Ilford IG6 104 EW50
Mitcham CR4 200 DE97
Northolt UB5 136 BW69
Romford RM5 105 FD51
Slough SL3 153 BB79
Wallington SM6 219 DM107
Waltham Abbey EN9 68 EG34
Merlin Ct, Brom. BR2
off Durham Av 204 EF98
Woking GU21
off Blackmore Cres 211 BC114
Merlin Cres, Edg. HA8 96 CM53
Merlin Gdns, Brom. BR1 184 EG90
Romford RM5 105 FD51
Merling Cl, Chess. KT9
off Coppard Gdns 215 CK106
Merling Cft, Nthch HP4 38 AS17
Merlin Gro, Beck. BR3 203 DZ98
Ilford IG6 103 EP52
Merlin Ho, Enf. EN3
off Allington Ct 83 DX43
Sch Merlin Prim Sch, Downham BR1 off Ballamore Rd 184 EG90
Merlin Rd, E12 124 EJ61
Romford RM5 105 FD51
Welling DA16 166 EU84
Merlin Rd N, Well. DA16 166 EU84
Merlins Av, Har. HA2 116 BZ62
Sch Merlin Sch, SW15
off Carlton Dr 179 CX85
Merlin St, WC1 286 E3
Merlin Way, Lvsdn WD25 59 BT34
North Weald Bassett CM16 70 FA27
Merlot Ms, St.Alb. AL3 43 CD16
Mermagen Dr, Rain. RM13 147 FH66
Mermaid Cl, Grav. DA11 190 GD87
Mermaid Ct, SE1 299 L4
SE16 301 N3
Mermaid Twr, SE8 313 N3
Mermerus Gdns, Grav. DA12 191 GM91
Merredene St, SW2 181 DM86
Merriam Av, E9 279 P4
Merriam Cl, E4 101 EC50
Merrick Rd, Sthl. UB2 156 BZ75
Merrick Sq, SE1 299 K6
Merridale, SE12 184 EG85
Merridene, N21 81 DP44
Merrielands Cres, Dag. RM9 146 EZ67
Merrifield Ct, Welw.G.C. AL7 29 CX12
Merrilands Rd, Wor.Pk. KT4 199 CW102
Merrilees Rd, Sid. DA15 185 ES88
Merrilyn Cl, Clay. KT10 215 CG107
Merriman Rd, SE3 164 EJ81
Merrington Rd, SW6 307 K2
Merrin Hill, S.Croy. CR2 220 DS111
Merrion Av, Stan. HA7 95 CK50
Merrion Ct, Ruis. HA4
off Pembroke Rd 115 BT60
Merritt Gdns, Chess. KT9 215 CJ107
Merritt Rd, SE4 183 DZ85
Merritt Wk, N.Mymms AL9 45 CV23
Merrivale, N14 81 DK44
Merrivale Av, Ilf. IG4 124 EK56
Merrivale Gdns, Wok. GU21 226 AW117
Merrivale Ms, West Dr. UB7 134 BK74
MERROW, Guil. GU1 243 BB133
● Merrow Business Cen, Guil. GU4 243 BD131
Merrow Chase, Guil. GU1 243 BC134
Sch Merrow C of E Inf Sch, Guil. GU4 off Kingfisher Dr 243 BD132
Merrow Common Rd, Guil. GU4 243 BC131
Merrow Copse, Guil. GU1 243 BB133
Merrow Ct, Guil. GU1 243 BD134
Merrow Cft, Guil. GU1 243 BC133
Merrow Downs, Guil. GU1 259 BD135
Merrow Dr, Hem.H. HP1 39 BE19
● Merrow Ind Est, Guil. GU4 243 BD131
Merrow La, Guil. GU4 243 BC129
Merrow Pl, Guil. GU4 243 BD132
Merrow Rd, Sutt. SM2 217 CX109
Merrows Cl, Nthwd. HA6
off Rickmansworth Rd 93 BQ51
Merrow St, SE17 311 L2
Guildford GU4 243 BD132
Merrow Wk, SE17 299 M10
Merrow Way, Guil. GU1 243 BD133
New Addington CR0 221 EC107
Merrow Wds, Guil. GU1 243 BB132
Merrydown Way, Chis. BR7 204 EL95
Merryfield, SE3 315 M9
Merryfield Gdns, Stan. HA7 95 CJ50
Merryfield Ho, SE9
off Grove Pk Rd 184 EJ90

M

Merryfields, St.Alb. AL4
off Firwood Av 44 CL20
Uxbridge UB8 134 BK68
Merryfields Way, SE6 183 EB87
MERRY HILL, Bushey WD23 94 CA46
Merryhill Cl, E4 101 EB45
Sch Merry Hill Inf Sch & Nurs,
Bushey WD23 off School La 94 CB45
Merry Hill Mt, Bushey WD23 94 CB46
Merry Hill Rd, Bushey WD23 94 CB46
Merryhills Cl, Bigg.H. TN16 238 EK116
Merryhills Ct, N14 81 DJ43
Merryhills Dr, Enf. EN2 81 DK42
Sch Merryhills Prim Sch,
Enf. EN2 off Bincote Rd 81 DM41
Merrylands, Cher. KT16 193 BE104
Merrylands Rd, Bkhm KT23 230 BZ123
Merrymeade Chase,
Brwd. CM15 108 FX46
Merrymeet, Bans. SM7 218 DF114
Merryweather Cl, Dart. DA1 188 FM86
Merryweather Ct, N.Mal. KT3
off Rodney Cl 198 CS99
Merrywood Gro,
Lwr Kgswd KT20 249 CX130
Merrywood Pk, Box H. KT20 248 CP130
Reigate RH2 250 DB132
Mersea Ho, Bark. IG11 145 EP65
Mersey Av, Upmin. RM14 129 FR58
Mersey Pl, Hem.H. HP2
off Colne Way 40 BM15
Mersey Rd, E17 123 DZ55
Mersey Wk, Nthlt. UB5
off Brabazon Rd 136 CA68
Mersham Dr, NW9 118 CN57
Mersham Pl, SE20 202 DV95
Mersham Rd, Th.Hth. CR7 202 DR97
MERSTHAM, Red. RH1 251 DJ128
⇌ Merstham 251 DJ128
Sch Merstham Prim Sch,
Merst. RH1
off London Rd S 251 DJ129
Merstham Rd, Red. RH1 251 DN129
Merten Rd, Rom. RM6 126 EY59
Merthyr Ter, SW13 159 CV79
MERTON, SW19 200 DA95
Merton Abbey Mills, SW19
off Watermill Way 200 DC95
Sch Merton Abbey Prim Sch,
SW19 off High Path 200 DB95
Coll Merton Adult Ed, SW20
off Whatley Av 199 CY97
Merton Av, W4 159 CT77
Northolt UB5 116 CC64
Uxbridge UB10 135 BP66
Merton Ct, Borwd. WD6
off Bennington Dr 78 CM39
Ilford IG1
off Castleview Gdns 124 EL58
Sch Merton Ct Sch, Sid. DA14
off Knoll Rd 186 EW91
Merton Gdns, Petts Wd BR5 205 EP99
Tadworth KT20 233 CX119
Merton Hall Gdns, SW20 199 CY95
Merton Hall Rd, SW19 199 CY95
Merton High St, SW19 180 DB94
● Merton Ind Pk, SW19 200 DC95
Merton La, N6 120 DF61
Merton Mans, SW20 199 CX96
MERTON PARK, SW19 200 DA96
Tra Merton Park 200 DA95
Merton Pk Par, SW19
off Kingston Rd 199 CZ95
Sch Merton Pk Prim Sch,
SW19 off Church La 200 DA96
Merton Pl, Grays RM16 171 GG77
Merton Ri, NW3 274 D7
Merton Rd, E17 123 EC57
SE25 202 DU99
SW18 180 DA85
SW19 180 DB94
Barking IG11 145 ET66
Enfield EN2 82 DR38
Harrow HA2 116 CC60
Ilford IG3 125 ET59
Slough SL1 152 AU76
Watford WD18 75 BV42
Merton Wk, Lthd. KT22 231 CG118
Merton Way, Lthd. KT22 231 CG119
Uxbridge UB10 135 BP66
West Molesey KT8 196 CB98
Merttins Rd, SE15 183 DX85
Meru Cl, NW5 275 H2
Mervan Rd, SW2 161 DN84
Mervyn Av, SE9 185 EQ90
Mervyn Rd, W13 157 CG76
Shepperton TW17 195 BQ101
Merwin Way, Wind. SL4 151 AK83
Meryfield Cl, Borwd. WD6 78 CM40
Sch Meryfield Comm Prim Sch,
Borwd. WD6 off Theobald St 78 CM39
Mesne Way, Shore. TN14 225 FF112
Messaline Av, W3 138 CQ72
Messant Cl, Harold Wd RM3 106 FK54
Messent Rd, SE9 184 EJ85
Messeter Pl, SE9 185 EN86
Messina Av, NW6 273 J7
Messon Ms, Twick. TW1 177 CG88
Metcalfe Ct, SE10 303 M6
Metcalf Rd, Ashf. TW15 175 BP92
Metcalf Wk, Felt. TW13
off Cresswell Rd 176 BY91
Meteor St, SW11 160 DG84
Meteor Way, Wall. SM6 219 DL108
Metford Cres, Enf. EN3 83 EA38
Methley St, SE11 310 F1
★ Methodist Cen Hall, SW1 297 P5
Methuen Cl, Edg. HA8 96 CN52
Methuen Pk, N10 99 DH54
Methuen Rd, Belv. DA17 167 FB77
Bexleyheath DA6 166 EZ84
Edgware HA8 96 CN52
Methven Ct, N9
off The Broadway 100 DU48
Methwold Rd, W10 282 C6
Metro Apts, The, Wok. GU21
off Goldsworth Rd 226 AY117
● Metro Business Cen, SE26 183 DZ92
Metro Cen Hts, SE1 299 J7
● Metro Cen, St.Alb. AL4 43 CF16
● Metro Ind Cen, Islw. TW7 157 CE82
● Metropolitan Cen, The,
Grnf. UB6 136 CB67
Metropolitan Cl, E14 290 B7
★ Met Collection, The, SW6 307 J2
Metropolitan Ms, Wat. WD18 75 BS42
Coll Metropolitan Pol Cadet
Training Cen, Loug. IG10
off Lippitts Hill 84 EF40
Coll Metropolitan Pol Mounted
Branch Training Sch, E.Mol.
KT8 off Ember La 197 CD100
Metropolitan Sta App,
Wat. WD18 75 BT41
Meux Cl, Chsht EN7 66 DU31
Mews, Islw. TW7
off Worton Rd 157 CD84
Mews, The, N1 277 K8
N8 off Turnpike La 121 DN55
Grays RM17 170 GC77
Guil. GU1 off Walnut Tree Cl 258 AW135
Harlow CM18 off Lodge Hall 51 ES19
Ilford IG4 124 EK57
Rom. RM1 off Market Link 127 FE56
Sevenoaks TN13 256 FG123
Twick. TW1 off Bridge Rd 177 CH86
Mews Deck, E1 300 F1
Mews End, Bigg.H. TN16 238 EK118
Mews Pl, Wdf.Grn. IG8 102 EG49
Mews St, E1 300 C2
Mexfield Rd, SW15 179 CZ85
Meyer Grn, Enf. EN1 82 DU38
Meyer Rd, Erith DA8 167 FC79
Meymott St, SE1 298 G3
Meynell Cres, E9 279 J6
Meynell Gdns, E9 279 J6
Meynell Rd, E9 279 J6
Romford RM3 105 FH52
Meyrick Cl, Knap. GU21 226 AS116
Meyrick Rd, NW10 139 CU65
SW11 308 B10
Mezen Cl, Nthwd. HA6 93 BR50
★ MI5 (Security Service)
Thames Ho, SW1 298 A8
Miah Ter, E1 300 D3
Miall Wk, SE26 183 DY91
Micawber Av, Uxb. UB8 134 BN70
Micawber St, N1 287 K2
Michael Cliffe Ho, EC1 286 F3
Michael Cres, Horl. RH6 268 DG150
Michael Faraday Ho, SE17 311 M1
Sch Michael Faraday Prim Sch,
SE17 311 M2
Michael Gdns, Grav. DA12 191 GL92
Hornchurch RM11 128 FK56
Michael Gaynor Cl, W7 137 CF74
Michael La, Guil. GU2 242 AV129
Michaelmas Cl, SW20 199 CW97
Michael Rd, E11 124 EE60
SE25 202 DS97
SW6 307 M6
Michaels Cl, SE13 164 EE84
Michaels La, Ash TN15 209 FV103
Fawkham Green DA3 209 FV103
Sch Michael Sobell Sinai Sch,
Har. HA3 off Shakespeare Dr 118 CN58
Michael Stewart Ho, SW6
off Clem Attlee Ct 307 H3
Sch Michael Tippett Sch, SE24
off Heron Rd 162 DQ84
Micheldever Rd, SE12 184 EE86
Michelham Gdns, Tad. KT20
off Waterfield 233 CW120
Twickenham TW1 177 CF90
Michelsdale Dr, Rich. TW9
off Rosedale Rd 158 CL84
Michels Row, Rich. TW9
off Kew Foot Rd 158 CL84
Michel Wk, SE18 165 EP78
Michigan Av, E12 124 EL63
Michigan Bldg, E14 302 F1
Michigan Cl, Brox. EN10 67 DY26
Michleham Down, N12 97 CZ49
Micholls Av, Ger.Cr. SL9 90 AY49
Micklefield Rd, Hem.H. HP2 41 BQ20
Sch Micklefield Sch, Reig. RH2
off Somers Rd 250 DA133
Micklefield Way, Borwd. WD6 78 CL38
MICKLEHAM, Dor. RH5 247 CJ128
Mickleham Bypass,
Mick. RH5 247 CH127
Mickleham Cl, Orp. BR5 205 ET96
Mickleham Downs, Mick. RH5 247 CK127
Mickleham Dr, Lthd. KT22 247 CJ126
Mickleham Gdns, Sutt. SM3 217 CY107
Mickleham Rd, Orp. BR5 205 ET95
Mickleham Way,
New Adgtn CR0 221 ED108
Micklem Dr, Hem.H. HP1 39 BF19
Sch Micklem Prim Sch,
Hem.H. HP1 off Boxted Rd 40 BG19
Micklethwaite Rd, SW6 307 K3
● Midas Ind Est, Cowley UB8 134 BH68
Midcot Way, Berk. HP4 38 AT17
Midcroft, Ruis. HA4 115 BS60
Slough SL2 131 AP70
Middle Boy, Abridge RM4 86 EW41
Middle Cl, Amer. HP6 72 AT37
Coulsdon CR5 235 DN120
Epsom KT17 216 CS112
Middle Cres, Denh. UB9 113 BD59
Mid Cross La, Chal.St.P. SL9 90 AY50
Middle Dartrey Wk, SW10
off Blantyre St 308 A4
Middle Dene, NW7 96 CR48
Middle Down, Ald. WD25 76 CB36
Middle Dr, Beac. HP9 89 AK50
Coll Mid Essex Adult Comm Coll,
Bishops Hill, Hutt. CM13
off Rayleigh Rd 109 GB44
Warley Cen, Warley CM13
off Essex Way 107 FW51
Middle Fm Cl, Eff. KT24 246 BX127
Middle Fm Pl, Eff. KT24 246 BW127
Middle Fld, NW8 274 A8
Middlefield, Hat. AL10 45 CU17
Horley RH6 269 DJ147
Welwyn Garden City AL7 29 CY13
Middlefield Av, Hodd. EN11 49 EA15
Middlefield Cl, Hodd. EN11 49 EA15
St. Albans AL4 43 CJ17
Middlefielde, W13 137 CH71
Middlefield Gdns, Ilf. IG2 125 EP58
Middlefield Rd, Hodd. EN11 49 EA15
Middlefields, Croy. CR0 221 DY109
Middle Furlong, Bushey WD23 76 CB42
Middle Gorse, Croy. CR0 221 DY112
MIDDLE GREEN, Slou. SL3 132 AY73
Middle Grn, Brock. RH3 264 CP136
Slough SL3 132 AY74
Staines-upon-Thames TW18 174 BK94
Middle Grn Cl, Surb. KT5
off Alpha Rd 198 CM100
Middle Grn Rd, Slou. SL3 152 AX75
Middleham Gdns, N18 100 DU51
Middleham Rd, N18 100 DU51
Coll Mid Herts Music Cen,
Hat. AL10 off Birchwood Av 45 CV16
Middle Hill, Egh. TW20 172 AW91
Hemel Hempstead HP1 39 BE20
Mid Holmwood La,
Mid Holm. RH5 263 CJ142
Middleknights Hill,
Hem.H. HP1 40 BG17
Middle La, N8 121 DL57
Bovingdon HP3 57 BA29
Epsom KT17 216 CS112
Seal TN15 off Church Rd 257 FM121
Teddington TW11 177 CF93
Middle La Ms, N8
off Middle La 121 DL57
Middlemead Cl, Bkhm KT23 246 CA125
Middle Meadow, Ch.St.G. HP8 90 AW48
Middlemead Rd, Bkhm KT23 246 BZ125
Middle Ope, Wat. WD24 75 BV37
Middle Pk Av, SE9 184 EK86
Sch Middle Pk Prim Sch, SE9
off Middle Pk Av 184 EK87
Middle Path, Har. HA2
off Middle Rd 117 CD60
Middle Rd, E13 291 N1
SW16 201 DK96
Berkhamsted HP4 38 AV19
Denham UB9 113 BC59
East Barnet EN4 80 DE44
Harrow HA2 117 CD61
Ingrave CM13 109 GC50
Leatherhead KT22 231 CH121
Waltham Abbey EN9 67 EB32
Middle Row, W10 282 E5
Middlesborough Rd, N18 100 DU51
● Middlesex Business Cen,
Sthl. UB2 156 BZ75
Middlesex Cl, Sthl. UB1 136 CB70
Middlesex Ct, W4 159 CT78
Addlestone KT15
off Garfield Rd 212 BJ105
Middlesex Ho, Uxb. UB8
off High St 134 BJ66
Middlesex Pas, EC1 287 H7
Middlesex Rd, Mitch. CR4 201 DL99
Middlesex St, E1 287 P7
Uni Middlesex Uni,
Grove Campus, NW4 119 CV56
Hendon Campus, NW4
off The Burroughs 119 CV56
New Southgate Campus, N11
off Oakleigh Rd S 98 DG48
Middlesex Wf, E5 122 DW61
Middle St, EC1 287 J6
Betchworth RH3 264 CP136
Croydon CR0 off Surrey St 202 DQ103
Lower Nazeing EN9 50 EG23
Shere GU5 260 BN139
Mid St, S.Nutfld RH1 251 DM134
Middle Temple, EC4 286 E10
Middle Temple La, EC4 286 E9
Middleton Av, E4 101 DZ49
Greenford UB6 137 CD68
Sidcup DA14 186 EW93
Middleton Cl, E4 101 DZ48
Middleton Dr, SE16 301 K5
Pinner HA5 115 BU55
Middleton Gdns, Ilf. IG2 125 EP58
Middleton Gro, N7 276 A2
Barking IG11 146 EU69
Middleton Hall La,
Brwd. CM15 108 FY47
Middleton Ms, N7 276 A2
Middleton Pl, W1 285 L7
Middleton Rd, E8 278 B7
NW11 120 DA59
Carshalton SM5 200 DE101
Downside KT11 229 BV119
Epsom KT19 216 CR110
Hayes UB3 135 BR71
Mill End WD3 92 BG46
Morden SM4 200 DC100
Shenfield CM15 108 FY46
Middleton St, E2 288 E2
Middleton Way, SE13 163 ED84
Middle Wk, Burn. SL1 130 AH69
Woking GU21
off Commercial Way 226 AY117
Middleway, NW11 120 DB57
Middle Way, SW16 201 DK96
Erith DA18 166 EY76
Hayes UB4 136 BW70
Watford WD24 75 BV37
Middle Way, The, Har. HA3 95 CF54
Middlewich Ho, Nthlt. UB5
off Taywood Rd 136 BZ69
Middle Yd, SE1 299 M2
Middlings, The, Sev. TN13 256 FF125
Middlings Ri, Sev. TN13 256 FF126
Middlings Wd, Sev. TN13 256 FF125
Midfield Av, Bexh. DA7 167 FC83
Swanley BR8 187 FH93
Midfield Par, Bexh. DA7 167 FC83
Sch Midfield Prim Sch, St.P.Cray
BR5 off Grovelands Rd 186 EU94
Midfield Way, Orp. BR5 206 EV95
Midford Pl, W1 285 M5
Midgarth Cl, Oxshott KT22 214 CC114
Midholm, NW11 120 DB56
Wembley HA9 118 CN60
Midholm Cl, NW11 120 DB56
Midholm Rd, Croy. CR0 203 DY103
MID HOLMWOOD, Dor. RH5 263 CJ142
Midhope Cl, Wok. GU22 226 AY119
Midhope Gdns, Wok. GU22
off Midhope Rd 226 AY119
Midhope Rd, Wok. GU22 226 AY119
Midhope St, WC1 286 B3
Midhurst Av, N10 120 DG55
Croydon CR0 201 DN101
Midhurst Cl, Horn. RM12 127 FG63
Midhurst Gdns, Uxb. UB10 135 BQ66
Midhurst Hill, Bexh. DA6 186 FA86
Midhurst Rd, W13 157 CG75
Midhurst Way, E5 122 DU63
Midland Cres, NW3 273 N4
Midland Pl, E14 302 E10
Midland Rd, E10 123 EC59
NW1 285 P1
Hemel Hempstead HP2 40 BK20
Midland Ter, NW2 119 CX62
NW10 138 CS70
● Midleton Ind Est, Guil. GU2 242 AV133
Midleton Rd, Guil. GU2 242 AV133
New Malden KT3 198 CQ97
Midlothian Rd, E3 289 N5
Midmoor Rd, SW12 181 DJ88
SW19 199 CX95
Midnight Ave, SE5 310 G4
Midship Cl, SE16 301 K3
Midship Pt, E14 302 A5
Midstrath Rd, NW10 118 CS63
Midsummer Av, Houns. TW4 156 BZ84
Midsummer Wk, Wok. GU21 226 AX116
Midway, St.Alb. AL3 42 CB23
Sutton SM3 199 CZ101
Walton-on-Thames KT12 195 BV103
Midway Av, Cher. KT16 194 BG97
Egham TW20 193 BB97
Midway Cl, Stai. TW18 174 BH90
Midwinter Cl, Well. DA16 166 EU83
Midwood Cl, NW2 119 CV62
Miena Way, Ashtd. KT21 231 CK117
Miers Cl, E6 145 EN67
Mighell Av, Ilf. IG4 124 EK57
Mikado Cl, Hare. UB9 92 BK54
Mike Spring Ct, Grav. DA12 191 GK91
Milan Rd, Sthl. UB1 156 BZ75
Milan Wk, Brwd. CM14 108 FV46
Milborne Gro, SW10 307 P1
Milborne St, E9 279 H5
Milborough Cres, SE12 184 EE86
Milbourne La, Esher KT10 214 CC107
Sch Milbourne Lo Jun Sch,
Esher KT10
off Milbourne La 214 CC107
Sch Milbourne Lo Sch,
Esher KT10 off Arbrook La 215 CD107
Milbourne Pl, Epsom KT19 216 CR105
Milbrook, Esher KT10 214 CC107
Milburn Dr, West Dr. UB7 134 BL73
Milburn Wk, Epsom KT18 232 CS115
Milby Ct, Borwd. WD6
off Blyth Cl 78 CM39
Milcombe Cl, Wok. GU21
off Inglewood 226 AV118
Milcote St, SE1 298 G5
Mildenhall Rd, E5 122 DW63
Slough SL1 132 AS72
Mildmay Av, N1 277 M4
Mildmay Gro N, N1 277 M3
Mildmay Gro S, N1 277 M3
Mildmay Pk, N1 277 M2
Mildmay Pl, N16 277 P3
Shoreham TN14 225 FF111
Mildmay Rd, N1 277 M2
Ilford IG1 off Albert Rd 125 EP62
Romford RM7 127 FC57
Mildmay St, N1 277 M4
Mildred Av, Borwd. WD6 78 CN42
Hayes UB3 155 BR77
Northolt UB5 116 CB64
Watford WD18 75 BT42
Mildred Cl, Dart. DA1 188 FN86
Mildred Ct, Croy. CR0 202 DU102
Mildred Rd, Erith DA8 167 FE78
Mile Cl, Wal.Abb. EN9 67 EC33
MILE END, E1 289 L3
⊖ Mile End 289 N4
Mile End, The, E17 101 DX53
MILE END GREEN, Dart. DA2 209 FW96
H Mile End Hosp, E1 289 K4
Mile End Pl, E1 289 J4
Mile End Rd, E1 288 F6
E3 288 F6
Mile Ho Cl, St.Alb. AL1 43 CG23
Mile Ho La, St.Alb. AL1 43 CG23
Mile Path, Wok. GU22 226 AV120
Mile Rd, Wall. SM6 200 DG102
Miles Cl, SE28 145 ER74
Harlow CM19 51 EP16
Sch Miles Coverdale Prim Sch,
W12 294 A4
Miles Dr, SE28 145 ER74
Miles La, Cob. KT11 214 BY113
Milespit Hill, NW7 97 CV50
Miles Pl, NW1 284 B6
Surbiton KT5 off Villiers Av 198 CM98
Miles Rd, N8 121 DL55
Epsom KT19 216 CR112
Mitcham CR4 200 DE97
Miles St, SW8 310 A3
Milestone Cl, N9 100 DU47
Ripley GU23 228 BG122
Sutton SM2 218 DD107
Milestone Dr, Pur. CR8 219 DM114
Jct Milestone Grn, SW14 158 CQ84
Milestone Rd, SE19 182 DT93
Dartford DA2 188 FP86
Harlow CM17 36 EW13
Miles Way, N20 98 DE47
Milfoil St, W12 139 CU73
Milford Cl, SE2 166 EY79
St. Albans AL4 43 CK16
Milford Gdns, Croy. CR0 203 DX99
Edgware HA8 96 CN52
Wembley HA0 117 CK64
Milford Gro, Sutt. SM1 218 DC105
Milford La, WC2 286 D10
Milford Ms, SW16 181 DM90
Milford Rd, W13 137 CH74
Southall UB1 136 CA73
Milford Twrs, SE6
off Thomas La 183 EB87
Milkhouse Gate, Guil. GU1
off High St 258 AX136
Milking La, Downe BR6 222 EL112
Keston BR2 222 EK111
Milk St, E16 305 N3
EC2 287 K9
Bromley BR1 184 EH93
Milkwell Gdns, Wdf.Grn. IG8 102 EH52
Milkwell Yd, SE5 311 K7
Milkwood Rd, SE24 181 DP85
Milk Yd, E1 300 G1
Mill, The,
Hertingfordbury SG14 31 DM10
Millacres, Ware SG12 33 DX06
Millais Av, E12 125 EN64
Millais Cres, Epsom KT19 216 CS106
Millais Gdns, Edg. HA8 96 CN54
Millais Pl, Til. RM18 171 GG80
Millais Rd, E11 123 EC63
Enfield EN1 82 DT43
New Malden KT3 198 CS101
Millais Way, Epsom KT19 216 CQ105
Millan Cl, New Haw KT15 212 BH110
Milland Ct, Borwd. WD6 78 CR39
Millard Cl, N16 277 P2
Millard Rd, SE8 301 N10
Millard Ter, Dag. RM10
off Church Elm La 146 FA65
Mill Av, Uxb. UB8 134 BJ68
Millbank, SW1 298 A7
Hemel Hempstead HP3 40 BK24
Millbank Ct, SW1 298 A8
Pier Millbank Pier 298 B9
Sch Millbank Prim Sch, SW1 297 P9
● Millbank Twr, SW1 298 A9
Millbank Way, SE12 184 EG85
Mill Bottom, S.Holm. RH5 263 CK144
Millbourne Rd, Felt. TW13 176 BY91
Mill Br, Barn. EN5 79 CZ44
Millbridge, Hert. SG14 32 DQ09
Millbridge Ms, Hert. SG14
off Millbridge 32 DQ09
Mill Br Pl, Uxb. UB8 134 BH68
Millbro, Swan. BR8 187 FG94
Millbrook, Guil. GU1 258 AX136
Weybridge KT13 213 BS105
Millbrook Av, Well. DA16 165 ER84
Millbrook Ct, Ware SG12 33 DX05
Millbrook Gdns,
Chad.Hth RM6 126 EZ58
Gidea Park RM2 105 FE54
Millbrook Pl, NW1
off Hampstead Rd 275 L10
Sch Millbrook Prim Sch,
Chsht EN8 off Gews Cor 67 DX29
Millbrook Rd, N9 100 DV46
SW9 161 DP83
Bushey WD23 76 BZ39
Mill Brook Rd, St.M.Cray BR5 206 EW98
Millbrook Way, Colnbr. SL3 153 BE82
Mill Cl, Bkhm KT23 230 CA124
Carshalton SM5 200 DG103
Chesham HP5 54 AS34
Hemel Hempstead HP3 58 BN25
Horley RH6 268 DE147
Lemsford AL8 29 CU10
Piccotts End HP1 40 BH16
Ware SG12 33 DX06
West Drayton UB7 154 BK76
Mill Cor, Barn. EN5 79 CZ39
Mill Ct, E10 123 EC62
Harlow CM20 35 ER12
Millcrest Rd, Goffs Oak EN7 65 DP28
Millcroft Ho, SE6 183 EC91
Mill Dr, Ruis. HA4 115 BR59
Millen Ct, Hort.Kir. DA4 208 FP98
MILL END, Rick. WD3 91 BF46
Millender Wk, SE16 301 H9
Millennium Br, EC4 287 J10
SE1 287 J10
● Millennium Business Cen,
NW2 119 CV61
Millennium Cl, E16 291 P8
Uxbridge UB8 134 BH68
Millennium Dr, E14 302 G8
Millennium Harbour, E14 301 P4
Millennium Pl, E2 288 F1
Sch Millennium Prim Sch, SE10 303 L7
Millennium Sq, SE1 300 A4
Millennium Way, SE10 303 J4
Millennium Wf, Rick. WD3
off Wharf La 92 BL45
Miller Av, Enf. EN3 83 EA38
Miller Cl, Brom. BR1 184 EG92
Collier Row RM5 104 FA51
Mitcham CR4 200 DF101
Pinner HA5 94 BW54
Miller Pl, Epsom KT19 216 CL112
Gerrards Cross SL9 112 AX57
Miller Rd, SW19 180 DD93
Croydon CR0 201 DM102
Guildford GU4 243 BC131
Miller's Av, E8 278 A2
Millers Cl, NW7 97 CU49
Chigwell IG7 104 EV47
Chorleywood WD3 73 BE41
Dartford DA1 188 FK87
Hersham KT12 214 BW105
Staines-upon-Thames TW18 174 BH92
Millers Copse, Epsom KT18 232 CR119
Redhill RH1 267 DP144
Millers Ct, W4
off Chiswick Mall 159 CT78
Hertford SG14
off Parliament Sq 32 DR10
Millersdale, Harl. CM19 51 EP19
Millers Grn Cl, Enf. EN2 81 DP41
Millers La, Stans.Abb. SG12 33 EC11
Windsor SL4 172 AT86
Miller's La, Chig. IG7 104 EV46
Millers Meadow Cl, SE3 184 EF85
Millers Ri, St.Alb. AL1 43 CE21
Miller's Ter, E8 278 A2
Miller St, NW1 275 L10
Millers Way, W6 294 B5
Miller Wk, SE1 298 F3
Millet Rd, Grnf. UB6 136 CB69
Mill Fm Av, Sun. TW16 175 BS94
● Mill Fm Business Pk,
Houns. TW4 176 BY87
Mill Fm Cl, Pnr. HA5 94 BW54
Mill Fm Cres, Houns. TW4 176 BY88
Millfield, N4
off Six Acres Est 121 DN61
Berkhamsted HP4 38 AX18
Sunbury-on-Thames TW16 195 BR95
Welwyn Garden City AL7 30 DC08
Mill Fld, Harl. CM17 36 EW11
Millfield Av, E17 101 DY53
Millfield Cl, Lon.Col. AL2 61 CK26
Millfield Dr, Nthflt DA11 190 GE89
Millfield La, N6 120 DF61
Lower Kingswood KT20 249 CZ125
Millfield Pl, N6 120 DG61
Millfield Rd, Edg. HA8 96 CQ54
Hounslow TW4 176 BY88
Millfields, Chesh. HP5 54 AQ33
Millfields Cl, Orp. BR5 206 EV97
Sch Millfields Comm Sch, E5
off Hilsea St 122 DW63
Millfields Cotts, Orp. BR5
off Millfields Cl 206 EV98
Millfields Est, E5 123 DX62
Millfields Rd, E5 122 DW63
Millfield Wk, Hem.H. HP3 40 BN22
Millford, Wok. GU21 226 AV117
Mill Gdns, SE26 182 DV91
MILL GREEN, Hat. AL9 45 CY15
Mill Grn, Mitch. CR4 200 DG101
● Mill Grn Business Pk,
Mitch. CR4 off Mill Grn Rd 200 DG101
Mill Grn La, Hat. AL9 45 CY15
★ Mill Green Mus, Hat. AL9 45 CX15
Mill Grn Rd, Mitch. CR4 200 DF101
Welwyn Garden City AL7 29 CY10
Millgrove St, SW11 308 G8
Millharbour, E14 302 C6
Millhaven Cl, Rom. RM6 126 EV58
Millhedge Cl, Cob. KT11 230 BY116
MILL HILL, NW7 97 CU50

M

Mill Hill, SW13 159 CU83
Shenfield CM15 108 FY45
≠ Mill Hill Broadway 96 CS51
Jct Mill Hill Circ, NW7 97 CT50
Sch Mill Hill Co High Sch, NW7
off Worcester Cres 96 CS47
Oakhill Campus, Barn. EN4
off Church Hill Rd 98 DF46
⊖ Mill Hill East 97 CX52
Mill Hill Gro, W3 138 CP74
● Mill Hill Ind Est, NW7 97 CT51
Mill Hill La, Brock. RH3 248 CP134
Mill Hill Rd, SW13 159 CU82
W3 158 CP75
Sch Mill Hill Sch, NW7
off The Ridgeway 97 CV49
Millhoo Ct, Wal.Abb. EN9 68 EF34
Mill Ho Cl, Eyns. DA4
off Mill La 208 FL102
Millhouse La, Bedmond WD5 59 BT27
Mill Ho La, Cher. KT16 193 BB98
Egham TW20 193 BB98
Millhouse Pl, SE27 181 DP91
Millhurst Ms, Harl. CM17 36 EY11
Millicent Gro, N13 99 DP50
Millicent Rd, E10 123 DZ60
Milligan St, E14 301 P1
Milliners Ct, Loug. IG10
off The Croft 85 EN40
Milliner's Ct, St.Alb. AL1 43 CE20
Milliners Ho, SW18
off Eastfields Av 160 DA84
Milling Rd, Edg. HA8 96 CR52
Millington Cl, Slou. SL1 131 AM74
Millington Rd, Hayes UB3 155 BS76
Mill La, E4 83 EB41
NW6 273 H3
SE18 305 M10
Albury GU5 259 BF139
Amersham HP7 55 AN39
Beaconsfield HP9 89 AL54
Broxbourne EN10 49 DZ21
Byfleet KT14 212 BM113
Carshalton SM5 218 DF105
Chadwell Heath RM6 126 EY58
Chafford Hundred RM16 169 FX77
Chalfont St. Giles HP8 90 AU47
Cheshunt EN8 67 DY28
Chilworth GU4 259 BF139
Croxley Green WD3 75 BQ44
Croydon CR0 201 DM104
Dorking RH4 263 CH135
Downe BR6 223 EN110
Egham TW20 193 BC98
Epsom KT17 217 CT109
Eynsford DA4 208 FL102
Fetcham KT22 231 CG122
Gerrards Cross SL9 113 AZ58
Grays RM20 169 FX78
Guildford GU1 off Quarry St 258 AX136
Harlow CM17 36 EY11
Hookwood RH6 268 DD148
Horton SL3 153 BB83
Kings Langley WD4 58 BN29
Limpsfield Chart RH8 255 EM131
Navestock RM4 87 FH40
Oxted RH8 254 EF132
Ripley GU23 228 BK119
Sevenoaks TN14 257 FJ121
Shoreham TN14 225 FF110
South Merstham RH1 251 DJ131
Taplow SL6 130 AC71
Toot Hill CM5 71 FF29
Westerham TN16 255 EQ127
Windsor SL4 151 AN80
Woodford Green IG8 102 EF50
Mill La Cl, Brox. EN10 49 DZ21
● Mill La Trd Est, Croy. CR0 201 DM104
Millman Ms, WC1 286 C5
Millman Pl, WC1
off Millman St 286 C5
Millman Rd, E16 293 K10
Millman St, WC1 286 C5
Millmark Gro, SE14 313 M9
Millmarsh La, Enf. EN3 83 DY40
Millmead, Byfleet KT14 212 BM112
Guildford GU1, GU2 258 AW136
Mill Mead, Stai. TW18 173 BF91
Mill Mead Rd, N17 122 DV56
Sch Mill Mead Sch, Hert. SG14
off Port Vale 32 DQ09
Millmead Ter, Guil. GU2 258 AW136
Millmead Way, Hert. SG14 31 DP08
Mill Pk Av, Horn. RM12 128 FL61
Mill Pl, E14 289 M9
Chislehurst BR7 off Old Hill 205 EP95
Dartford DA1 167 FG84
Datchet SL3 152 AX82
Kingston upon Thames KT1 198 CM97
Mill Pl Caravan Pk,
Datchet SL3 152 AW82
Mill Plat, Islw. TW7 157 CG82
Mill Plat Av, Islw. TW7 157 CG82
Mill Pond Cl, SW8 309 P5
Sevenoaks TN14 257 FK121
Millpond Ct, Add. KT15 212 BL106
Millpond Est, SE16 300 E5
Millpond Pl, Cars. SM5 200 DG104
Mill Pond Rd, Dart. DA1 188 FL86
Mill Race, Stans.Abb. SG12 33 ED11
Mill Ridge, Edg. HA8 96 CM50
Mill Rd, E16 304 B2
SW19 180 DC94
Aveley RM15 148 FQ73
Cobham KT11 230 BW115
Dunton Green TN13 256 FE121
Epsom KT17 217 CT112
Erith DA8 167 FC80
Esher KT10 196 CA103
Hawley DA2 188 FM91
Hertford SG14 32 DR08
Ilford IG1 125 EN62
Northfleet DA11 190 GE87
Purfleet RM19 168 FP79
South Holmwood RH5 263 CJ144
Tadworth KT20 233 CX123
Twickenham TW2 176 CC89
West Drayton UB7 154 BJ76
Mill Row, N1 277 P9
Mills Cl, Uxb. UB10 134 BN68
Mills Ct, EC2 287 P3
Mills Gro, E14 290 E7
NW4 119 CX55
Mill Shaw, Oxt. RH8 254 EF132
Millshot Dr, Amer. HP7 55 AR40
Millshott Cl, SW6 306 B6
Millside, B.End SL8 110 AC60
Carshalton SM5 200 DF103
Millside Ct, Iver SL0 154 BH75
● Millside Ind Est, Dart. DA1 168 FK84
Millside Pl, Islw. TW7 157 CH82
Millsmead Way, Loug. IG10 85 EM40
Millson Cl, N20 98 DD47
Mills Rd, Hersham KT12 214 BW106
Mills Row, W4 158 CR77
Mills Spur, Old Wind. SL4 172 AV87
Millstead Cl, Tad. KT20 233 CV122
Millstone Cl, E15 281 H4
South Darenth DA4 208 FQ96
Millstone Ms, S.Darenth DA4 208 FQ95
Millstream Cl, N13 99 DN50
Hertford SG14 31 DP09
Millstream La, Slou. SL1 131 AL74
Millstream Rd, SE1 300 A5
Millstream Way,
Woob.Moor HP10 110 AD55
Mill St, SE1 300 B5
W1 285 K10
Berkhamsted HP4 38 AW19
Colnbrook SL3 153 BD80
Harlow CM17 52 EY17
Hemel Hempstead HP3
off Fourdinier Way 40 BK23
Kingston upon Thames KT1 198 CL97
Redhill RH1 266 DE135
Slough SL2 132 AT74
Westerham TN16 255 ER127
Mills Way, Hutt. CM13 109 GC46
Mills Yd, SW6 307 L10
Millthorne Cl, Crox.Grn WD3 74 BM43
Mill Vale, Brom. BR2 204 EF96
Mill Vw, Park St AL2
off Park St 61 CD27
Mill Vw Cl, Ewell KT17 217 CT108
Millview Cl, Reig. RH2 250 DD132
Mill Vw Gdns, Croy. CR0 203 DX104
MILLWALL, E14 302 C8
Millwall Dock Rd, E14 302 A6
★ Millwall FC, SE16 313 H1
Millwards, Hat. AL10 45 CV21
Millway, NW7 96 CS50
Reigate RH2 250 DD134
Mill Way, Bushey WD23 76 BY40
Feltham TW14 175 BV85
Leatherhead KT22 232 CM124
Mill End WD3 91 BF46
Millway Gdns, Nthlt. UB5 136 BZ65
Millwell Cres, Chig. IG7 103 ER50
Millwood Rd, Houns. TW3 176 CC85
Orpington BR5 206 EW97
Millwood St, W10 282 E7
Millwrights Wk, Hem.H. HP3
off Stephenson Wf 58 BM25
Mill Yd, E1 288 C10
● Mill Yd Indusrial Est,
Edg. HA8 96 CP53
Milman Cl, Pnr. HA5 116 BX55
Milman Rd, NW6 272 D10
Milman's St, SW10 308 A3
● Milmead Ind Cen, N17 100 DV54
Milne Ct, E18
off Churchfields 102 EG53
Milne Feild, Pnr. HA5 94 CA52
Milne Gdns, SE9 184 EL85
Milne Pk E, New Adgtn CR0 221 ED111
Milne Pk W, New Adgtn CR0 221 ED111
Milner App, Cat. CR3 236 DU121
Milner Cl, Cat. CR3 236 DT121
Watford WD25 59 BV34
Milner Ct, Bushey WD23 76 CB44
Milner Dr, Cob. KT11 214 BZ112
Twickenham TW2 177 CD87
Milner Pl, N1 276 F8
Carshalton SM5 off High St 218 DG105
Milner Rd, E15 291 J3
SW19 200 DB95
Burnham SL1 130 AJ69
Caterham CR3 236 DU122
Dagenham RM8 126 EW61
Kingston upon Thames KT1 197 CK97
Morden SM4 200 DD99
Thornton Heath CR7 202 DR97
Milner Sq, N1 276 G7
Milner St, SW3 296 E8
Milner Wk, SE9 185 ER89
Milne Way, Hare. UB9 92 BH53
Milnthorpe Rd, W4 158 CR79
Milo Gdns, SE22
off Milo Rd 182 DT86
Milo Rd, SE22 182 DT86
Milroy Av, Nthflt DA11 190 GE89
Milroy Wk, SE1 298 G2
Milson Rd, W14 294 D6
Milstead Ho, E5 278 F2
MILTON, Grav. DA12 191 GK86
Milton Av, E6 144 EK66
N6 121 DJ59
NW9 118 CQ55
NW10 138 CQ67
Badgers Mount TN14 225 FB110
Barnet EN5 79 CZ43
Chalfont St. Peter SL9 112 AX55
Croydon CR0 202 DR101
Gravesend DA12 191 GJ88
Hornchurch RM12 127 FF61
Sutton SM1 200 DD104
Westcott RH4 263 CD137
Milton Cl, N2 120 DC58
SE1 300 A9
Hayes UB4 135 BU72
Horton SL3 153 BA83
Sutton SM1 200 DD104
Milton Ct, EC2 287 L6
Chadwell Heath RM6
off Cross Rd 126 EW59
Hemel Hempstead HP2
off Milton Dene 41 BP15
Uxbridge UB10 115 BP62
Waltham Abbey EN9 67 EC34
Milton Ct La, Dor. RH4 263 CF136
Milton Ct Rd, SE14 313 M3
Milton Cres, Ilf. IG2 125 EQ59
Milton Dene, Hem.H. HP2 41 BP15
Milton Dr, Borwd. WD6 78 CP43
Shepperton TW17 194 BL98
Milton Flds, Ch.St.G. HP8 90 AV48
Milton Gdn Est, N16 277 N1
Milton Gdns, Epsom KT18 216 CS114
Staines-upon-Thames TW19
off Chesterton Dr 174 BM88
Tilbury RM18 171 GH81
Milton Gro, N11 99 DJ50
N16 277 M1
Milton Hall Rd, Grav. DA12 191 GK88
Milton Hill, Ch.St.G. HP8 90 AV48
Milton Lawns, Amer. HP6 55 AR36
● Milton Pk, Egh. TW20 173 BA94
Milton Pk, N6 121 DJ59
Milton Pl, N7 276 E2
Gravesend DA12 191 GJ86
Milton Rd, E17 123 EA56
N6 121 DJ59
N15 121 DP56
NW7 97 CU50
NW9
off West Hendon Bdy 119 CU59
SE24 181 DP85
SW14 158 CR83
SW19 180 DC93
W3 138 CR74
W7 137 CF73
Addlestone KT15 212 BG107
Belvedere DA17 166 FA77
Caterham CR3 236 DR121
Chesham HP5 54 AP29
Croydon CR0 202 DR102
Dunton Green TN13 256 FE121
Egham TW20 173 AZ92
Gravesend DA12 191 GJ86
Grays RM17 170 GB78
Hampton TW12 176 CA94
Harrow HA1 117 CE56
Mitcham CR4 180 DG94
Romford RM1 127 FG58
Slough SL2 131 AR70
Sutton SM1 200 DA104
Swanscombe DA10 190 FY86
Uxbridge UB10 114 BN63
Wallington SM6 219 DJ107
Walton-on-Thames KT12 196 BX104
Ware SG12 33 DX05
Warley CM14 108 FV49
Welling DA16 165 ET81
● Milton Rd Business Pk,
Grav. DA12 off Milton Rd 191 GJ87
★ Milton's Cottage,
Ch.St.G. HP8 90 AV48
Milton St, EC2 287 L6
Swanscombe DA10 189 FX86
Waltham Abbey EN9 67 EC34
Watford WD24 75 BV38
Westcott RH4 263 CD137
Milton Way, Fetch. KT22 246 CC125
West Drayton UB7 154 BM77
Milverton Dr, Uxb. UB10 115 BQ63
Milverton Gdns, Ilf. IG3 125 ET61
Milverton Ho, SE23 183 DY90
Milverton Rd, NW6 272 B7
Milverton St, SE11 310 F1
Milverton Way, SE9 185 EN91
Milwards, Harl. CM19 51 EP19
Sch Milwards Prim Sch & Nurs,
Harl. CM19 off Paringdon Rd 51 EP19
Milward St, E1 288 F7
Milward Wk, SE18
off Spearman St 165 EN79
Mimas Rd, Hem.H. HP2 40 BM17
MIMBRIDGE, Wok. GU24 210 AV113
Mimms Hall Rd, Pot.B. EN6 63 CX31
Mimms La, Ridge EN6 62 CQ33
Shenley WD7 62 CN33
Mimosa Cl, Orp. BR6 206 EW103
Pilgrim's Hatch CM15 108 FV43
Romford RM3 106 FL53
Mimosa Rd, Hayes UB4 136 BW71
Mimosa St, SW6 306 G7
Mimram Rd, Hert. SG14 31 DP10
Mina Av, Slou. SL3 152 AX75
Minard Rd, SE6 184 EE87
Mina Rd, SE17 311 P1
SW19 200 DA95
Minchenden Cres, N14 99 DJ48
Minchen Rd, Harl. CM20 35 ET13
Minchin Cl, Lthd. KT22 231 CG122
Mincing La, EC3 287 N10
Chobham GU24 210 AT108
Minden Gdns, Bark. IG11 146 EV69
Minden Rd, SE20 202 DV95
Sutton SM3 199 CZ103
Minehead Rd, SW16 181 DM92
Harrow HA2 116 CA62
Mineral Cl, Barn. EN5 79 CW44
Mineral La, Chesh. HP5 54 AQ32
Mineral St, SE18 165 ES77
Minera Ms, SW1 297 H8
Minerva Cl, SW9 310 F5
Sidcup DA14 185 ES90
Staines-upon-Thames TW19 174 BG85
Minerva Dr, Wat. WD24 75 BS36
Minerva Est, E2
off Minerva St 288 E1
Minerva Rd, E4 101 EB52
NW10 138 CQ70
Kingston upon Thames KT1 198 CM96
Minerva St, E2 288 E1
Minerva Way, Beac. HP9 89 AP54
Minet Av, NW10 138 CS68
Minet Dr, Hayes UB3 135 BU74
Minet Gdns, NW10 138 CS68
Hayes UB3 135 BU74
Sch Minet Inf Sch, Hayes UB3
off Avondale Dr 135 BV74
Sch Minet Jun Sch, Hayes UB3
off Avondale Dr 135 BV74
Minet Rd, SW9 310 G8
Minford Gdns, W14 294 C5
Mingard Wk, N7
off Hornsey Rd 121 DM62
Ming St, E14 290 B10
Minims, The, Hat. AL10 45 CU17
Minister Ct, Frog. AL2 61 CE28
Ministers Gdns, St.Alb. AL2
off Frogmore 61 CE28
★ Ministry of Defence, SW1 298 A4
★ Ministry of Justice, SW1 297 M6
Ministry Way, SE9 185 EM89
Miniver Pl, EC4
off Garlick Hill 287 K10
Mink Ct, Houns. TW4 156 BW83
Minniecroft Rd, Burn. SL1 130 AH69
Minniedale, Surb. KT5 198 CM99
Minnow St, SE17 299 P9
Minnow Wk, SE17
off Minnow St 299 P9
Minoan Dr, Hem.H. HP3 40 BL24
Minorca Rd, Wey. KT13 212 BN105
Minories, EC3 288 A10
Minshull Pl, Beck. BR3 183 EA94
Minshull St, SW8 309 N7
Minson Rd, E9 279 K8
Minstead Gdns, SW15 179 CT87
Minstead Way, N.Mal. KT3 198 CS100
Minster Av, Sutt. SM1
off Leafield Rd 200 DA103
Minster Cl, Hat. AL10 45 CU20
● Minster Ct, EC3 287 N10
Minster Ct, Horn. RM11 128 FN61
Minster Dr, Croy. CR0 220 DS105
Minster Gdns, W.Mol. KT8 196 BZ98
Minsterley Av, Shep. TW17 195 BS98
Minster Pavement, EC3
off Mincing La 287 N10
Minster Rd, NW2 272 F3
Bromley BR1 184 EH94
Minster Wk, N8
off Lightfoot Rd 121 DL56
Minster Way, Horn. RM11 128 FM60
Slough SL3 153 AZ75
Minstrel Cl, Hem.H. HP1 40 BH19
Minstrel Gdns, Surb. KT5 198 CM98
● Mint Business Pk, E16 291 P7
Mint Cl, Hlgdn UB10 135 BP69
Mintern Cl, N13 99 DP48
Minterne Av, Sthl. UB2 156 CA77
Minterne Rd, Har. HA3 118 CM57
Minterne Waye, Hayes UB4 136 BW72
Mintern St, N1 277 M10
Minter Rd, Bark. IG11 146 EU70
Mint Gdns, Dor. RH4
off Church St 263 CG136
Mint La, Lwr Kgswd KT20 250 DA129
Minton Ho, SE11
off Walnut Tree Wk 298 E8
Minton La, Harl. CM17 52 EW15
Minton Ms, NW6 273 M4
Minton Ri, Tap. SL6 130 AH72
Mint Rd, Bans. SM7 234 DC116
Wallington SM6 219 DH105
Mint St, SE1 299 J4
Mint Wk, Croy. CR0
off High St 202 DQ104
Knaphill GU21 226 AS117
Warlingham CR6 237 DX118
Mintwater Cl, Ewell KT17 217 CU110
Mirabelle Gdns, E20 280 F4
Mirabel Rd, SW6 307 H4
Mirador Cres, Slou. SL2 132 AV73
Miramar Way, Horn. RM12 128 FK64
Miranda Cl, E1 288 G7
Miranda Ct, W3
off Queens Dr 138 CM72
Miranda Rd, N19 121 DJ60
Mirfield St, SE7 304 E8
Miriam Rd, SE18 165 ES78
● Mirravale Trd Est, Dag. RM8 126 EZ59
Mirren Cl, Har. HA2 116 BZ63
Mirrie La, Denh. UB9 113 BC57
Mirror Path, SE9
off Lambscroft Av 184 EJ90
Misbourne Av, Chal.St.P. SL9 90 AY50
Misbourne Cl, Chal.St.P. SL9 90 AY50
Misbourne Ct, Slou. SL3
off High St 153 BA77
Misbourne Meadows,
Denh. UB9 113 BC60
Misbourne Rd, Uxb. UB10 134 BN67
Misbourne Vale, Chal.St.P. SL9 90 AX50
Miskin Rd, Dart. DA1 188 FJ87
Miskin Way, Grav. DA12 191 GK93
Missden Dr, Hem.H. HP3 41 BQ22
Missenden Cl, Felt. TW14 175 BT88
Missenden Gdns, Burn. SL1 130 AH72
Morden SM4 200 DC100
Missenden Rd, Amer. HP7 55 AL39
Chesham HP5 54 AL32
Mission Gro, E17 123 DY57
Sch Mission Gro Prim Sch, E17
off Buxton Rd 123 DZ56
E17 off Edinburgh Rd 123 DZ58
Mission Pl, SE15 312 D6
Mission Sq, Brent. TW8 158 CL79
Mistletoe Cl, Croy. CR0
off Marigold Way 203 DX102
Mistley Gdns, Hkwd RH6 268 DD149
Mistley Rd, Harl. CM20 36 EU13
Misty's Fld, Walt. KT12 196 BW102
Mitali Pas, E1 288 C9
MITCHAM, CR4 200 DG97
Tram Mitcham 200 DE98
≠ Mitcham Eastfields 200 DG96
Mitcham Gdn Village,
Mitch. CR4 200 DG99
● Mitcham Ind Est,
Mitch. CR4 200 DG95
≠ Mitcham Junction 200 DG99
Tram Mitcham Junction 200 DG99
Mitcham La, SW16 181 DJ93
Mitcham Pk, Mitch. CR4 200 DF98
Mitcham Rd, E6 293 H2
SW17 180 DF92
Croydon CR0 201 DL100
Ilford IG3 125 ET59
Mitchell Av, Nthflt DA11 190 GD89
Sch Mitchell Brook Prim Sch,
NW10 off Bridge Rd 138 CR65
Mitchellbrook Way, NW10 138 CR65
Mitchell Cl, SE2 166 EW77
Abbots Langley WD5 59 BU32
Belvedere DA17 167 FC76
Bovingdon HP3 57 AZ27
Dartford DA1 188 FL89
Rainham RM13 148 FJ68
St. Albans AL1 43 CD24
Slough SL1 151 AN75
Welwyn Garden City AL7 30 DC09
Mitchell Rd, N13 99 DP50
Orpington BR6 223 ET105
Mitchells Cl, Shalf. GU4
off Station Rd 258 AY140
Mitchell's Pl, SE21
off Dulwich Village 182 DS87
Mitchells Row, Shalf. GU4 258 AY141
Mitchell St, EC1 287 J4
Mitchell Wk, E6 292 G7
Amersham HP6 55 AS38
Swanscombe DA10 190 FY87
Mitchell Way, NW10 138 CQ65
Bromley BR1 204 EG95
Mitchison Rd, N1 277 L5
Mitchley Av, Pur. CR8 220 DQ113
South Croydon CR2 220 DQ113
Mitchley Gro, S.Croy. CR2 220 DU113
Mitchley Hill, S.Croy. CR2 220 DT113
Mitchley Rd, N17 122 DU55
Mitchley Vw, S.Croy. CR2 220 DU113
Mitford Cl, Chess. KT9
off Merritt Gdns 215 CJ107
Mitford Rd, N19 121 DL61
Mitre, The, E14 289 N10
Mitre Av, E17
off Greenleaf Rd 123 DZ55
● Mitre Br Ind Est, W10 139 CV70
Mitre Cl, Brom. BR2
off Beckenham La 204 EF96
Shepperton TW17 195 BR100
Sutton SM2 218 DC108
Mitre Ct, EC2 287 K8
Hertford SG14 32 DR09
Mitre Rd, E15 281 J10
SE1 298 F4
Mitre Sq, EC3 287 P9
Mitre St, EC3 287 P9
Mitre Way, W10 139 CV70
Mitre Wf, NW10 139 CV70
Mixbury Gro, Wey. KT13 213 BR107
Mixnams La, Cher. KT16 194 BG97
Mizen Cl, Cob. KT11 214 BX114
Mizen Way, Cob. KT11 230 BW115
Mizzen Mast Ho, SE18 305 L6
Moat, The, N.Mal. KT3 198 CS95
Toot Hill CM5 71 FF29
Sch Moatbridge Sch, SE9
off Eltham Palace Rd 184 EK86
Moat Cl, Bushey WD23 76 CB43
Chipstead TN13 256 FB123
Orpington BR6 223 ET107
Moat Ct, Ashtd. KT21 232 CL117
Moat Cres, N3 120 DB55
Moat Cft, Well. DA16 166 EW83
Moat Dr, E13 292 D1
Harrow HA1 116 CC56
Ruislip HA4 115 BS59
Slough SL2 132 AW71
Moated Fm Dr, Add. KT15 212 BJ108
Moat Fm Rd, Nthlt. UB5 136 BZ65
Moatfield Rd, Bushey WD23 76 CB43
Moat La, Erith DA8 167 FG81
Moat Pl, SW9 310 D10
W3 138 CP72
Denham UB9 114 BH63
Moatside, Enf. EN3 83 DX42
Feltham TW13 176 BW91
Moats La, S.Nutfld RH1 267 DN140
Moatview Ct, Bushey WD23 76 CB43
Moatwood Grn,
Welw.G.C. AL7 29 CY10
Moberly Rd, SW4 181 DK87
Moberly Way, Ken. CR8 236 DR120
Jct Moby Dick, Rom. RM6 126 EZ56
Mocatta Ms, Red. RH1 251 DJ131
Mockford Ms, Red. RH1 251 DJ131
Modbury Gdns, NW5 274 F5
Modder Pl, SW15 159 CX84
Model Cotts, SW14 158 CQ83
Model Fm Cl, SE9 184 EL90
Modena Ms, Wat. WD18 75 BS42
Modling Ho, E2 289 J1
Moelwyn Hughes Ct, N7 275 P3
Moelyn Ms, Har. HA1 117 CG57
Moffat Ho, SE5
off Comber Gro 311 J5
Moffat Rd, N13 99 DL51
SW17 180 DE91
Thornton Heath CR7 202 DQ96
Moffats Cl, Brook.Pk AL9 64 DA26
Moffats La, Brook.Pk AL9 63 CZ27
MOGADOR, Tad. KT20 249 CY129
Mogador Cotts, Tad. KT20
off Mogador Rd 249 CX128
Mogador Rd, Lwr Kgswd KT20 249 CX128
Mogden La, Islw. TW7 177 CE85
Mohmmad Khan Rd, E11
off Harvey Rd 124 EF60
Moira Cl, N17 100 DS54
Moira Ct, SW17 180 DG89
Moira Rd, SE9 165 EM84
Moir Cl, S.Croy. CR2 220 DU109
Molash Rd, Orp. BR5 206 EX98
Molasses Row, SW11 307 P10
Mole Abbey Gdns, W.Mol. KT8 196 CA97
● Mole Business Pk,
Lthd. KT22 231 CG121
Mole Ct, Epsom KT19 216 CQ105
Mole Hill Pl, Dor. RH4 247 CK134
Molember Ct, E.Mol. KT8 197 CE99
Molember Rd, E.Mol. KT8 197 CE99
Mole Rd, Fetch. KT22 231 CD121
Hersham KT12 214 BX106
Molescroft, SE9 185 EQ90
Coll Molesey Adult Learning
Cen, W.Mol. KT8 off Ray Rd 196 CB99
Molesey Av, W.Mol. KT8 196 BZ98
Molesey Cl, Hersham KT12 214 BY105
Molesey Dr, Sutt. SM3 199 CY103
H Molesey Hosp, W.Mol. KT8 196 CA99
Molesey Pk Av, W.Mol. KT8 196 CB99
Molesey Pk Cl, E.Mol. KT8 196 CC99
Molesey Pk Rd, E.Mol. KT8 197 CD99
West Molesey KT8 196 CB99
Molesey Rd, Walt. KT12 214 BX106
West Molesey KT8 196 BY99
Molesford Rd, SW6 307 J7
Molesham Cl, W.Mol. KT8 196 CB97
Molesham Way, W.Mol. KT8 196 CB97
Moles Hill, Oxshott KT22 215 CD111
Molesworth, Hodd. EN11 33 EA13
Molesworth Rd, Cob. KT11 213 BU113
Molesworth St, SE13 163 EC83
Mole Valley Pl, Ashtd. KT21 231 CK119
Molewood Rd, Hert. SG14 31 DP08
Mollands La, S.Ock. RM15 149 FW70
Mollison Av, Enf. EN3 83 DY43
Mollison Dr, Wall. SM6 219 DL107
Mollison Ri, Grav. DA12 191 GL92
Mollison Sq, Wall. SM6
off Mollison Dr 219 DL108
Mollison Way, Edg. HA8 96 CN54
Molloy Ct, Wok. GU21
off Courtenay Rd 227 BA116
Molly Huggins Cl, SW12 181 DJ87
Molteno Rd, Wat. WD17 75 BU39
Molyneaux Av, Bov. HP3 57 AZ27
Molyneux Dr, SW17 181 DH91
Molyneux Rd, Gdmg. GU7 258 AT144
Weybridge KT13 212 BN106
Molyneux St, W1 284 D7
Molyns Ms, Slou. SL1
off Nicholas Gdns 131 AL74
Momples Rd, Harl. CM20 36 EV13
Monaco Wks, Kings L. WD4 59 BP30
Monahan Av, Pur. CR8 219 DM112
Monarch Cl, Felt. TW14 175 BS87
Rainham RM13
off Wymark Cl 147 FG68
Tilbury RM18 171 GH82
West Wickham BR4 222 EF105
Monarch Dr, E16 292 E7
Hayes UB3 135 BT73
Monarch Ms, E17 123 EB57
SW16 181 DN92

M

Monarch Par, Mitch. CR4 *off London Rd* 200 DF96
Monarch Pl, Buck.H. IG9 102 EJ47
Monarch Rd, Belv. DA17 166 FA76
Monarchs Ct, NW7 *off Grenville Pl* 96 CR50
Monarchs Way, Ruis. HA4 115 BR60
Waltham Cross EN8 67 DY34
Monarch Way, Ilf. IG2 125 ER58
Mona Rd, SE15 313 H8
Monastery Gdns, Enf. EN2 82 DR40
Mona St, E16 291 M7
Monaveen Gdns, W.Mol. KT8 196 CA97
Monck St, SW1 297 P7
Monclar Rd, SE5 162 DR84
Moncorvo Cl, SW7 296 C5
Moncrieff Cl, E6 292 G8
Moncrieff Pl, SE15 312 C8
Moncrieff St, SE15 312 D8
Mondial Way, Harling. UB3 155 BQ80
Sch **Monega Prim Sch**, E12 *off Monega Rd* 144 EK65
Monega Rd, E7 144 EJ65
E12 144 EK65
Money Av, Cat. CR3 236 DR122
MONEYHILL, Rick. WD3 92 BH46
Moneyhill Ct, Rick. WD3 *off Dellwood* 92 BH46
Moneyhill Par, Rick. WD3 *off Uxbridge Rd* 92 BH46
Money Hill Rd, Rick. WD3 92 BJ46
Money Hole La, Tewin AL6 30 DE08
Money La, West Dr. UB7 154 BK76
Money Rd, Cat. CR3 236 DR122
Mongers La, Epsom KT17 217 CT110
Monica Cl, Wat. WD24 76 BW40
Monier Rd, E3 280 A7
Monivea Rd, Beck. BR3 183 DZ94
Monkchester Cl, Loug. IG10 85 EN39
Monk Dr, E16 291 N9
MONKEN HADLEY, Barn. EN5 79 CZ39
Sch **Monken Hadley C of E Prim Sch**, Barn. EN4 *off Camlet Way* 80 DA39
Monkey Island La, Bray SL6 150 AE78
Monkfrith Av, N14 81 DH44
Monkfrith Cl, N14 99 DH45
Sch **Monkfrith Prim Sch**, N14 *off Knoll Dr* 98 DG45
Monkfrith Way, N14 98 DG45
Monkhams, Wal.Abb. EN9 67 EC29
Monkhams Av, Wdf.Grn. IG8 102 EG50
Monkhams Dr, Wdf.Grn. IG8 102 EH49
Monkhams La, Buck.H. IG9 102 EH48
Woodford Green IG8 102 EG50
Monkleigh Rd, Mord. SM4 199 CY97
Monk Pas, E16 291 N10
Monks Av, Barn. EN5 80 DC44
West Molesey KT8 196 BZ99
Monksbury, Harl. CM18 52 EU18
Monks Chase, Ingrave CM13 109 GC50
Monks Cl, SE2 166 EX77
Broxbourne EN10 49 EA20
Enfield EN2 82 DQ40
Harrow HA2 116 CB61
Ruislip HA4 116 BX63
St. Albans AL1 43 CE22
Monks Cres, Add. KT15 212 BH106
Walton-on-Thames KT12 195 BV102
Monksdene Gdns, Sutt. SM1 200 DB104
Monks Dr, W3 138 CN71
Monksfield Way, Slou. SL2 131 AN69
Monksgate, St.Alb. AL1 *off Monks Cl* 43 CE22
Monks Grn, Fetch. KT22 230 CC121
Monksgrove, Loug. IG10 85 EN43
Monks Horton Way, St.Alb. AL1 43 CH18
Monksmead, Borwd. WD6 78 CQ42
Sch **Monksmead Sch**, Borwd. WD6 *off Hillside Av* 78 CQ41
MONKS ORCHARD, Croy. CR0 203 DZ101
Monks Orchard, Dart. DA1 188 FJ89
Sch **Monks Orchard Prim Sch**, Croy. CR0 *off The Glade* 203 DX99
Monks Orchard Rd, Beck. BR3 203 EA102
Monks Pk, Wem. HA9 138 CQ65
Monks Pk Gdns, Wem. HA9 138 CP65
Monks Pl, Cat. CR3 *off Tillingdown Hill* 236 DV122
Monk's Ridge, N20 97 CV46
Monks Ri, Welw.G.C. AL8 29 CX05
Monks Rd, Bans. SM7 234 DA116
Enfield EN2 82 DQ40
Virginia Water GU25 192 AX98
Windsor SL4 151 AK82
Monk St, SE18 305 M8
Monks Wk, Cher. KT16 193 BE98
Sthflt DA13 190 GA93
Monk's Wk, Reig. RH2 250 DB134
Monks Way, NW11 119 CZ56
Beckenham BR3 203 EA100
Harmondsworth UB7 154 BL79
Orpington BR5 205 EQ102
Staines-upon-Thames TW18 174 BK94
Monks Well, Green. DA9 169 FV84
Monkswell Ct, N10 98 DG53
Monkswell La, Chipstead CR5 234 DB124
Monkswick Rd, Harl. CM20 35 ET13
Monkswood, Welw.G.C. AL8 29 CW05
Monkswood Av, Wal.Abb. EN9 67 ED33
Monkswood Gdns, Borwd. WD6 78 CR43
Ilford IG5 125 EN55
Monkton Ho, E5 *off Pembury Rd* 278 E2
Monkton Rd, Well. DA16 165 ET82
Monkton St, SE11 298 F8
Monkville Av, NW11 119 CZ56
Monkwell Sq, EC2 287 K7
Monkwood Cl, Rom. RM1 127 FG57
Monmouth Av, E18 124 EH56
Kingston upon Thames KT1 177 CJ94
Monmouth Cl, W4 158 CR76
Mitcham CR4 *off Recreation Way* 201 DL98
Welling DA16 166 EU84
Monmouth Gro, Brent. TW8 *off Sterling Pl* 158 CL77
Monmouth Ho, NW5 275 K4
Monmouth Pl, W2 283 K9
Monmouth Rd, E6 293 J3
N9 100 DV47
W2 283 K9
Dagenham RM9 126 EZ64
Hayes UB3 155 BS77
Watford WD17 75 BV41
Monmouth St, WC2 286 A9
Monnery Rd, N19 121 DJ62
Monnow Grn, Aveley RM15 *off Monnow Rd* 148 FQ73
Monnow Rd, SE1 300 C10
Aveley RM15 148 FQ73
Mono La, Felt. TW13 175 BV89
Monoux Gro, E17 101 EA53
Monro Dr, Guil. GU2 242 AU131
Monroe Cres, Enf. EN1 82 DV39
Monroe Dr, SW14 178 CP85
Monro Gdns, Har. HA3 95 CE52
● **Monro Ind Est**, Wal.Cr. EN8 67 DY34
Monro Pl, Epsom KT19 216 CN109
Monro Way, E5 122 DU63
Monsal Ct, E5 *off Redwald Rd* 123 DY63
Monsell Ct, N4 *off Monsell Rd* 121 DP62
Monsell Gdns, Stai. TW18 173 BE92
Monsell Rd, N4 121 DP62
Sch **Monson Prim Sch**, SE14 313 J4
Monson Rd, NW10 139 CU68
SE14 313 J5
Broxbourne EN10 49 DZ20
Redhill RH1 250 DF130
Mons Wk, Egh. TW20 173 BC92
Mons Way, Brom. BR2 204 EL100
Montacute Rd, SE6 183 DZ87
Bushey Heath WD23 95 CE45
Morden SM4 200 DD100
New Addington CR0 221 EC109
Montagu Cres, N18 100 DV49
Montague Av, SE4 163 DZ84
W7 137 CF74
South Croydon CR2 220 DS112
Montague Cl, SE1 299 L2
Barnet EN5 79 CZ42
Farnham Royal SL2 131 AP68
Walton-on-Thames KT12 195 BU101
Montague Dr, Cat. CR3 236 DQ122
Montague Gdns, W3 138 CN73
Montague Hall Pl, Bushey WD23 76 CA44
Montague Pl, WC1 285 P6
Montague Rd, E8 278 C3
E11 124 EF61
N8 121 DM57
N15 122 DU56
SW19 180 DB94
W7 137 CF74
W13 137 CH72
Berkhamsted HP4 38 AV19
Croydon CR0 201 DP102
Hounslow TW3 156 CB83
Richmond TW10 178 CL86
Slough SL1 132 AT73
Southall UB2 156 BY77
Uxbridge UB8 134 BK66
Montague Sq, SE15 313 H5
Montague St, EC1 287 J7
WC1 286 A6
Montague Waye, Sthl. UB2 156 BY76
Montagu Gdns, N18 100 DW49
Wallington SM6 219 DJ105
Montagu Mans, W1 284 F6
Montagu Ms N, W1 284 F7
Montagu Ms S, W1 284 F8
Montagu Ms W, W1 284 F8
Montagu Pl, W1 284 E7
Montagu Rd, N9 100 DW49
N18 100 DV50
NW4 119 CU58
Datchet SL3 152 AV81
● **Montagu Rd Ind Est**, N18 100 DW49
Montagu Row, W1 284 F7
Montagu Sq, W1 284 F7
Montagu St, W1 284 F8
Montaigne Cl, SW1 297 P9
Montalt Rd, Wdf.Grn. IG8 102 EF50
Montana Bldg, SE13 *off Deals Gateway* 314 C6
Montana Cl, S.Croy. CR2 220 DR110
Montana Gdns, SE26 183 DZ92
Sutton SM1 *off Lind Rd* 218 DC106
Montana Rd, SW17 180 DG91
SW20 199 CW95
Montayne Rd, Chsht EN8 67 DX32
Sch **Montbelle Prim Sch**, SE9 *off Milverton Way* 185 EN91
Montbelle Rd, SE9 185 EP90
Montbretia Cl, Orp. BR5 206 EW98
Montcalm Cl, Brom. BR2 204 EG100
Hayes UB4 135 BV69
Montcalm Rd, SE7 164 EK80
Montclare St, E2 288 A3
Monteagle Av, Bark. IG11 145 EQ65
Sch **Monteagle Prim Sch**, Dag. RM9 *off Burnham Rd* 146 EV67
Monteagle Way, E5 122 DU62
SE15 312 F10
Montefiore St, SW8 309 K9
Montego Cl, SE24 *off Railton Rd* 161 DN84
Montem La, Slou. SL1 131 AR74
Sch **Montem Prim Sch**, N7 *off Hornsey Rd* 121 DM62
Slough SL1 *off Chalvey Gro* 151 AP75
Montem Rd, SE23 183 DZ87
New Malden KT3 198 CS98
Montem St, N4 *off Thorpedale Rd* 121 DM60
Montenotte Rd, N8 121 DJ57
Monterey Cl, NW7 *off The Broadway* 96 CS50
Bexley DA5 187 FC89
Uxbridge UB10 134 BN66
Montesole Ct, Pnr. HA5 94 BW54
Montevetro, SW11 308 A6
Montfichet Rd, E20 280 E7
Montford Pl, SE11 310 E1
Montford Rd, Sun. TW16 195 BU98
Montfort Gdns, Ilf. IG6 103 EQ51
Montfort Pl, SW19 179 CX88
Montfort Ri, Red. RH1 266 DF142
Montgolfier Wk, Nthlt. UB5 *off Wayfarer Rd* 136 BY69
Montgomerie Cl, Berk. HP4 *off Mortain Dr* 38 AU17
Montgomerie Dr, Guil. GU2 242 AU129
Montgomerie Ms, SE23 182 DW87
Montgomery Av, Esher KT10 197 CE104
Hemel Hempstead HP2 40 BN19
Montgomery Cl, Grays RM16 170 GC75
Mitcham CR4 201 DL98
Sidcup DA15 185 ET86
Montgomery Ct, W2 *off Harrow Rd* 284 A7
W4 *off St. Thomas' Rd* 158 CQ79
Dagenham RM10 *off St. Mark's Pl* 146 FA65
Montgomery Cres, Rom. RM3 106 FJ50
Montgomery Dr, Chsht EN8 67 DY28
Montgomery Gdns, Sutt. SM2 218 DD108
Montgomery Pl, Slou. SL2 132 AW72
Montgomery Rd, W4 158 CQ77
Edgware HA8 96 CM51
South Darenth DA4 209 FR95
Woking GU22 226 AY118
Montgomery St, E14 302 D3
Montgomery Way, Ken. CR8 236 DR120
Montholme Rd, SW11 180 DF86
Monthope Rd, E1 288 C7
Montolieu Gdns, SW15 179 CV85
Montpelier Av, W5 137 CJ71
Bexley DA5 186 EX87
Montpelier Cl, Uxb. UB10 134 BN67
Montpelier Ct, Wind. SL4 *off St. Leonards Rd* 151 AQ82
Montpelier Gdns, E6 292 F2
Romford RM6 126 EW59
Montpelier Gro, NW5 275 M2
Montpelier Ms, SW7 296 D6
Montpelier Pl, E1 288 G9
SW7 296 D6
Sch **Montpelier Prim Sch**, W5 *off Montpelier Rd* 137 CK71
Montpelier Ri, NW11 119 CY59
Wembley HA9 117 CK60
Montpelier Rd, N3 98 DC53
SE15 312 F6
W5 137 CK71
Purley CR8 219 DP110
Sutton SM1 218 DC105
Montpelier Row, SE3 315 L9
Twickenham TW1 177 CH87
Montpelier Sq, SW7 296 D5
Montpelier St, SW7 296 D5
Montpelier Ter, SW7 296 D5
Montpelier Vale, SE3 315 L9
Montpelier Wk, SW7 296 D6
Montpelier Way, NW11 119 CY59
Montrave Rd, SE20 182 DW93
Montreal Ho, SE16 301 J5
Montreal Pl, WC2 286 C10
Montreal Rd, Ilf. IG1 125 EQ59
Sevenoaks TN13 256 FE123
Tilbury RM18 171 GG83
Montrell Rd, SW2 181 DL88
Montrose Av, NW6 272 F10
Datchet SL3 152 AW80
Edgware HA8 96 CQ54
Romford RM2 106 FJ54
Sidcup DA15 186 EU87
Slough SL1 131 AP72
Twickenham TW2 176 CB87
Welling DA16 165 ER83
Montrose Cl, Ashf. TW15 175 BQ93
Welling DA16 165 ET83
Woodford Green IG8 102 EG49
Montrose Ct, SW7 296 B5
Montrose Cres, N12 98 DC51
Wembley HA0 138 CL65
Montrose Gdns, Mitch. CR4 200 DF97
Oxshott KT22 215 CD112
Sutton SM1 200 DB103
Montrose Pl, SW1 297 H5
Montrose Rd, Felt. TW14 175 BR86
Harrow HA3 95 CE54
Montrose Wk, Wey. KT13 195 BP104
Montrose Way, SE23 183 DX88
Datchet SL3 152 AX81
Montrouge Cres, Epsom KT17 233 CW116
Montserrat Av, Wdf.Grn. IG8 101 ED52
Montserrat Cl, SE19 182 DR92
Montserrat Rd, SW15 159 CY84
⊖ **Monument** 287 M10
★ **Monument, The**, EC3 287 M10
● **Monument Business Cen**, Wok. GU21 *off Monument Way E* 227 BB115
Monument Gdns, SE13 183 EC85
Monument Grn, Wey. KT13 195 BP104
Monument Hill, Wey. KT13 213 BP105
Monument La, Chal.St.P. SL9 90 AY51
Monument Rd, Wey. KT13 213 BP105
Woking GU21 211 BA114
Monument St, EC3 299 M1
Monument Way, N17 122 DT55
Monument Way E, Wok. GU21 227 BB115
Monument Way W, Wok. GU21 227 BA115
Monza St, E1 300 G1
Moodkee St, SE16 300 G6
Moody Rd, SE15 312 A5
Moody St, E1 289 K3
Moon La, Barn. EN5 79 CZ41
Moon St, N1 276 G8
Moorcroft Gdns, Brom. BR2 *off Southborough Rd* 204 EL99
Moorcroft La, Uxb. UB8 134 BN71
Moorcroft Rd, SW16 181 DL90
Sch **Moorcroft Sch**, Hlgdn UB8 *off Bramble Cl* 134 BM72
Moorcroft Way, Pnr. HA5 116 BY57
Moordown, SE18 165 EP81
Moore Av, Grays RM20 170 FY78
Tilbury RM18 171 GH82
Moore Cl, SW14 158 CQ83
Addlestone KT15 212 BH106
Dartford DA2 189 FR89
Mitcham CR4 201 DH96
Slough SL1 151 AP75
Moore Ct, Wem. HA0 *off Station Gro* 138 CL65
Moore Cres, Dag. RM9 146 EV67
Moorefield Rd, N17 100 DT54
Moore Gro Cres, Egh. TW20 172 AY94
Moorehead Way, SE3 164 EH83
Moore Ho, E14 302 B5
Mooreland Rd, Brom. BR1 184 EF94
Moor End, Maid. SL6 150 AC78
Moorend, Welw.G.C. AL7 30 DA12
Moor End Rd, Hem.H. HP1 40 BJ21
Moore Pk Rd, SW6 307 L5
Moore Rd, SE19 182 DQ93
Berkhamsted HP4 38 AT17
Swanscombe DA10 190 FY86
Moores La, Eton Wick SL4 151 AM77
Moores Pl, Brwd. CM14 108 FX47
Moores Rd, Dor. RH4 263 CH135
Moore St, SW3 296 E8
Moore Wk, E7 281 P2
Moore Way, Sutt. SM2 218 DA109
Moorey Cl, E15 281 L9
Moorfield, Harl. CM18 51 EQ20
South Holmwood RH5 263 CK144
Moorfield Av, W5 137 CK70
● **Moorfield Pt**, Guil. GU1 242 AY130
Moorfield Rd, Chess. KT9 216 CL106
Denham UB9 114 BG59
Enfield EN3 82 DW39
Guildford GU1 242 AX130
Moorfield Rd, Orpington BR6 206 EU101
Uxbridge UB8 134 BK72
Moorfields, EC2 287 L7
Moorfields Cl, Stai. TW18 193 BE95
H **Moorfields Eye Hosp**, EC1 287 L3
Moorfields Highwalk, EC2 287 L7
Moor Furlong, Slou. SL1 131 AL74
⇌ **Moorgate** 287 L7
⊖ **Moorgate** 287 L7
Moorgate, EC2 287 L8
Moorgate Pl, EC2 287 L8
Moorhall Rd, Hare. UB9 114 BH58
Moor Hall Rd, Harl. CM17 36 EZ11
Moorhayes Dr, Stai. TW18 194 BJ97
Moorhen Cl, Erith DA8 167 FH80
Moorhen Wk, Green. DA9 *off Waterstone Way* 189 FU86
Moorholme, Wok. GU22 *off Oakbank* 226 AY119
MOORHOUSE, West. TN16 255 EM127
MOORHOUSE BANK, West. TN16 255 EM128
Moorhouse Rd, W2 283 J8
Harrow HA3 117 CK55
Oxted RH8 255 EM131
Westerham TN16 255 EM128
Sch **Moor Ho Sch**, Oxt. RH8 *off Mill La* 254 EF132
Moorhurst Av, Goffs Oak EN7 65 DN29
Moorings, SE28 146 EV73
Moorings, The, E16 *off Prince Regent La* 292 C7
Bookham KT23 246 CA125
Windsor SL4 *off Straight Rd* 172 AW87
Moorings Ho, Brent. TW8 *off Tallow Rd* 157 CJ80
Moorland Cl, Rom. RM5 105 FB52
Twickenham TW2 176 CA87
Moorland Rd, SW9 161 DP84
Harmondsworth UB7 154 BJ79
Hemel Hempstead HP1 40 BG22
Moorlands, Frog. AL2 61 CD28
Welwyn Garden City AL7 30 DA12
Moorlands, The, Wok. GU22 227 AZ121
Moorlands Av, NW7 97 CV51
Moorlands Est, SW9 161 DN84
Moorlands Reach, Saw. CM21 36 EZ06
Moor La, EC2 287 L7
Chessington KT9 216 CL105
Harmondsworth UB7 154 BJ79
Rickmansworth WD3 92 BM47
Sarratt WD3 73 BE36
Staines-upon-Thames TW18, TW19 173 BE90
Upminster RM14 129 FS60
Woking GU22 226 AY122
Moor La Crossing, Wat. WD18 93 BQ46
Moormead Dr, Epsom KT19 216 CS106
Moor Mead Rd, Twick. TW1 177 CG86
Moormede Cres, Stai. TW18 173 BF91
Moor Mill La, Coln.St AL2 61 CE29
MOOR PARK, Nthwd. HA6 93 BQ49
★ **Moor Park**, Rick. WD3 92 BN48
⊖ **Moor Park** 93 BR48
Moor Pk Est, Nthwd. HA6 93 BQ49
Moor Pk Gdns, Kings.T. KT2 178 CS94
● **Moor Pk Ind Cen**, Wat. WD18 93 BQ45
Moor Pk Rd, Nthwd. HA6 93 BR50
Moor Pl, EC2 287 L7
Moor Rd, Chesh. HP5 54 AQ32
Sevenoaks TN14 241 FH120
Moors, The, S.Merst. RH1 251 DJ131
Welwyn Garden City AL7 30 DA08
Moorside, Hem.H. HP3 40 BH23
Welwyn Garden City AL7 30 DA12
Wooburn Green HP10 110 AE55
Moorside Rd, Brom. BR1 184 EE90
Moors La, Orch.L. HP5 56 AV28
Moorsom Way, Couls. CR5 235 DK117
Moorstown Ct, Slou. SL1 152 AS75
Moor St, W1 285 P9
Moors Wk, Welw.G.C. AL7 30 DC09
Moor Twr, Harl. CM18 51 ET16
Moortown Rd, Wat. WD19 94 BW49
Moor Vw, Wat. WD18 93 BU45
Moot Ct, NW9 118 CN57
Moran Cl, Brick.Wd AL2 60 BZ31
Morant Gdns, Rom. RM5 105 FB50
Morant Pl, N22 99 DM53
Morant Rd, Grays RM16 171 GH76
Jct **Morants Ct Cross**, Dunt.Grn TN14 241 FB118
Morants Ct Rd, Dunt.Grn TN13 241 FC118
Morant St, E14 290 B10
Sch **Mora Prim Sch**, NW2 *off Mora Rd* 119 CW63
Mora Rd, NW2 119 CW63
Mora St, EC1 287 K3
Morat St, SW9 310 D6
Moravian Pl, SW10 308 B3
Moravian St, E2 288 G1
Moray Av, Hayes UB3 135 BT74
Moray Cl, Edg. HA8 *off Pentland Av* 96 CP47
Romford RM1 105 FE52
Moray Dr, Slou. SL2 132 AU72
Moray Ms, N7 121 DM61
Moray Rd, N4 121 DM61
Moray Way, Rom. RM1 105 FD52
Morcote Cl, Shalf. GU4 258 AY141
Mordaunt Gdns, Dag. RM9 146 EY66
Mordaunt Rd, NW10 138 CR67
Mordaunt St, SW9 310 C10
MORDEN, SM4 200 DA97
⊖ **Morden** 200 DB97
Morden Cl, Tad. KT20 233 CX120
Morden Ct, Mord. SM4 200 DB98
Morden Gdns, Grnf. UB6 117 CF64
Mitcham CR4 200 DD98
★ **Morden Hall Pk NT**, Mord. SM4 200 DB97
Morden Hall Rd, Mord. SM4 200 DB97
Morden Hill, SE13 314 E8
Morden La, SE13 314 F7
Sch **Morden Mt Prim Sch**, SE13 314 D8
MORDEN PARK, Mord. SM4 199 CY99
Sch **Morden Prim Sch**, Mord. SM4 *off London Rd* 200 DA99
Tra **Morden Road** 200 DB96
Morden Rd, SE3 315 N8
SW19 180 DB94
Mitcham CR4 200 DC98
Romford RM6 126 EY59
Morden Rd Ms, SE3 315 N9
⇌ **Morden South** 200 DA99
Morden St, SE13 314 D7
Morden Way, Sutt. SM3 200 DA101
Morden Wf Rd, SE10 303 J7
Mordon Rd, Ilf. IG3 125 ET59
Mordred Ct, N9 *off Galahad Rd* 100 DU47
Mordred Rd, SE6 184 EE89
Moreau Wk, Geo.Grn SL3 *off Alan Way* 132 AY72
Morecambe Cl, E1 289 J6
Hornchurch RM12 127 FH64
Morecambe Gdns, Stan. HA7 95 CK49
Morecambe St, SE17 299 K9
Morecambe Ter, N18 100 DR49
More Circle, Gdmg. GU7 258 AS144
More Cl, E16 291 M8
W14 294 D9
Purley CR8 219 DN111
Morecoombe Cl, Kings.T. KT2 178 CP94
Moree Way, N18 100 DU49
Sch **More Ho Sch**, SW1 296 F7
Moreland Av, Colnbr. SL3 153 BC80
Grays RM16 170 GC75
Moreland Cl, Colnbr. SL3 *off Moreland Av* 153 BC80
Moreland Dr, Ger.Cr. SL9 113 AZ59
Sch **Moreland Prim Sch**, EC1 287 H2
Moreland St, EC1 287 H2
Moreland Way, E4 101 EB48
More La, Esher KT10 196 CB103
Morel Ct, Sev. TN13 257 FH122
Morella Cl, Vir.W. GU25 192 AW98
Morella Rd, SW12 180 DF87
Morell Cl, Barn. EN5 80 DC41
Morello Av, Uxb. UB8 135 BP71
Morello Cl, Swan. BR8 207 FD98
Morello Dr, Slou. SL3 133 AZ74
Morel Ms, Dag. RM8 *off Ager Ave* 126 EX60
More London Pl, SE1 *off Tooley St* 299 N3
More London Riverside, SE1 *off Tooley St* 299 P3
Moremead, Wal.Abb. EN9 67 ED33
Moremead Rd, SE6 183 DZ91
Morena St, SE6 183 EB87
More Rd, Gdmg. GU7 258 AS144
Moresby Av, Surb. KT5 198 CP101
Moresby Rd, E5 122 DV60
Moresby Wk, SW8 309 L9
Moretaine Rd, Ashf. TW15 *off Hengrove Cres* 174 BK90
MORETON, Ong. CM5 53 FH20
Moreton Av, Islw. TW7 157 CE81
Moreton Cl, E5 122 DW61
N15 122 DR58
NW7 97 CW51
SW1 297 M10
Cheshunt EN7 66 DV27
Swanley BR8 207 FE96
Moreton Gdns, Wdf.Grn. IG8 102 EL50
Moreton Ho, SE16 300 F6
● **Moreton Ind Est**, Swan. BR8 207 FG98
Moreton Pl, SW1 297 M10
Moreton Rd, N15 122 DR58
Moreton CM5 53 FG24
South Croydon CR2 220 DR106
Worcester Park KT4 199 CU103
Moreton St, SW1 297 M10
Moreton Ter, SW1 297 M10
Moreton Ter Ms N, SW1 297 M10
Moreton Ter Ms S, SW1 297 M10
Moreton Twr, W3 138 CP74
Moreton Way, Slou. SL1 131 AK74
Morewood Cl, Sev. TN13 256 FF123
● **Morewood Cl Ind Pk**, Sev. TN13 *off Morewood Cl* 256 FF123
Morford Cl, Ruis. HA4 115 BV59
Morford Way, Ruis. HA4 115 BV59
Morgan Av, E17 123 ED56
Morgan Cl, Dag. RM10 146 FA66
Northwood HA6 93 BT51
Morgan Ct, N9 *off Galahad Rd* 100 DU48
SW11 *off Battersea High St* 308 B7
Morgan Cres, They.B. CM16 85 ER36
Morgan Dr, Green. DA9 189 FS87
Morgan Gdns, Ald. WD25 76 CB38
Morgan Ho, SW1 *off Vauxhall Br Rd* 297 M9
Morgan Rd, N7 276 E3
W10 282 G6
Bromley BR1 184 EG94
Morgans Cl, Hert. SG13 32 DR11
Sch **Morgans JMI Sch**, Hert. SG13 *off Morgans Rd* 32 DR11
Morgans La, SE1 299 N3
Hayes UB3 135 BR71
Morgans Rd, Hert. SG13 32 DR11
Morgan St, E3 289 M3
E16 291 M6
Morgans Wk, Hert. SG13 32 DR12
Morgan Way, Rain. RM13 148 FJ69
Woodford Green IG8 102 EL51
Sch **Moriah Jewish Day Sch**, Pnr. HA5 *off Cannon La* 116 BY60
Moriarty Cl, Brom. BR1 205 EP98
Moriatry Cl, N7 121 DL63
Morice Rd, Hodd. EN11 49 DZ15
Morie St, SW18 160 DB84
Morieux Rd, E10 123 DZ60
Moring Rd, SW17 180 DG91
Morkyns Wk, SE21 182 DS90
Morland Av, Croy. CR0 202 DS102
Dartford DA1 187 FH85
Morland Cl, NW11 120 DB60
Hampton TW12 176 BZ92
Mitcham CR4 200 DE97
Morland Est, E8 278 D6
Morland Gdns, NW10 138 CR66
Southall UB1 136 CB74
Morland Ms, N1 276 F7
Morland Pl, N15 122 DS56
Morland Rd, E17 123 DX57
SE20 183 DX93
Croydon CR0 202 DS102
Dagenham RM10 146 FA66
Harrow HA3 118 CL57
Ilford IG1 125 EP61
Sutton SM1 218 DC106
Morland Way, Chsht EN8 67 DY28
Morley Av, E4 101 ED52
N18 100 DU49
N22 99 DN54

M

Morley Cl, Orp. BR6 205 EP103
Slough SL3 153 AZ75
Coll Morley Coll, SE1 298 F6
Morley Cres, Edg. HA8 96 CQ47
Ruislip HA4 116 BW61
Morley Cres E, Stan. HA7 95 CJ54
Morley Cres W, Stan. HA7 95 CJ54
Morley Gro, Harl. CM20 35 EQ13
Morley Hill, Enf. EN2 82 DR38
Morley Rd, E10 123 EC60
E15 281 L10
SE13 163 EC84
Barking IG11 145 ER67
Chislehurst BR7 205 EQ95
Romford RM6 126 EY57
South Croydon CR2 220 DT110
Sutton SM3 199 CZ102
Twickenham TW1 177 CK86
Morley Sq, Grays RM16 171 GG77
Morley St, SE1 298 F6
Morna Rd, SE5 311 K8
Morning La, E9 278 G4
Morning Ri, Loud. WD3 74 BK41
Sch Morningside Prim Sch, E9 279 H4
Morningside Rd, Wor.Pk. KT4 199 CV103
Mornington Av, W14 294 G9
Bromley BR1 204 EJ97
Ilford IG1 125 EN59
Mornington Cl, Bigg.H. TN16 238 EK117
Woodford Green IG8 102 EG49
Mornington Ct, Bex. DA5 187 FC88
⊖ Mornington Crescent 275 L10
Mornington Cres, NW1 275 L10
Hounslow TW5 155 BV81
Mornington Gro, E3 290 A3
Mornington Ms, SE5 311 J6
Mornington Pl, NW1 275 K10
Mornington Rd, E4 101 ED45
E11 124 EF60
SE8 313 P5
Ashford TW15 175 BQ92
Greenford UB6 136 CB71
Loughton IG10 85 EQ41
Radlett WD7 61 CG34
Woodford Green IG8 102 EF49
Morningtons, Harl. CM19 51 EQ19
Mornington St, NW1 275 K10
Mornington Ter, NW1 275 K9
Mornington Wk, Rich. TW10 177 CJ91
Morocco St, SE1 299 N5
Morpeth Av, Borwd. WD6 78 CM38
Morpeth Cl, Hem.H. HP2
off York Way 40 BL21
Morpeth Gro, E9 279 J8
Morpeth Rd, E9 279 H9
Sch Morpeth Sch, E2 289 H3
Annexe, E2 288 G3
Morpeth St, E2 289 J2
Morpeth Ter, SW1 297 L7
Morpeth Wk, N17
off West Rd 100 DV52
Morphou Rd, NW7 97 CY51
Morrab Gdns, Ilf. IG3 125 ET62
Morrell Ct, Welw.G.C. AL7 29 CZ08
Morrells Yd, SE11 298 F10
Morrice Cl, Slou. SL3 153 AZ77
Morris Ave, E12 125 EM64
Uxbridge UB10 134 BL65
Morris Cl, Chal.St.P. SL9 91 AZ53
Croydon CR0 203 DY100
Orpington BR6 205 ES104
Morris Ct, E4 101 EB48
E5 off Mount Pleasant Hill 122 DW61
Enfield EN3 off Rigby Pl 83 EA37
Waltham Abbey EN9 68 EF34
Morris Gdns, SW18 180 DA87
Dartford DA1 188 FN85
Morris Ho, W3
off Swainson Rd 159 CT75
Harlow CM18 51 EQ18
Morrish Rd, SW2 181 DL87
Morrison Av, E4 101 EA51
N17 122 DS55
Morrison Rd, SW9 310 F9
Barking IG11 146 EY68
Hayes UB4 135 BV69
Morrison St, SW11 308 G10
Morris Pl, N4 121 DN61
Morris Rd, E14 290 C6
E15 124 EE63
Dagenham RM8 126 EZ61
Isleworth TW7 157 CF83
Romford RM3 105 FH52
South Nutfield RH1 267 DL136
Morris St, E1 288 F9
Morriston Cl, Wat. WD19 94 BW50
Morris Wk, Dart. DA1
off Birdwood Ave 168 FN82
Morris Way, Lon.Col. AL2 61 CK26
Morse Cl, E13 291 N3
Harefield UB9 92 BJ54
Morshead Mans, W9
off Morshead Rd 283 K3
Morshead Rd, W9 283 K3
Morson Rd, Enf. EN3 83 DY44
Morston Cl, Tad. KT20
off Waterfield 233 CV120
Morston Gdns, SE9 185 EM91
Mortain Dr, Berk. HP4 38 AT17
Morten Cl, SW4 181 DK86
Morten Gdns, Denh. UB9 114 BG59
Mortens Wd, Amer. HP7 55 AR40
Morteyne Rd, N17 100 DR53
Mortham St, E15 281 J9
Mortimer Cl, NW2 119 CZ62
SW16 181 DK89
Bushey WD23 76 CB44
Mortimer Cres, NW6 273 L9
Saint Albans AL3 42 CA22
Worcester Park KT4 198 CR104
Mortimer Dr, Bigg.H. TN16 222 EJ112
Enf. EN1 82 DR43
Mortimer Est, NW6 273 L9
Mortimer Gate, Chsht EN8 67 DZ27
Mortimer Ho, W11
off St. Anns Rd 294 D2
Mortimer Mkt, WC1 285 M5
Mortimer Pl, NW6 273 L9
Mortimer Rd, E6 293 J3
N1 277 P7
NW10 282 A2
W13 137 CJ72
Erith DA8 167 FD79
Mitcham CR4 200 DF95
Mortimer Rd, Orpington BR6 206 EU103
Slough SL3 152 AX76
Mortimer Sq, W11 294 D1
Mortimer St, W1 285 L8
Mortimer Ter, NW5
off Gordon Ho Rd 121 DH63
MORTLAKE, SW14 158 CQ83
⇌ Mortlake 158 CQ83
Mortlake Cl, Croy. CR0 201 DL104
Mortlake Dr, Mitch. CR4 200 DE95
Mortlake High St, SW14 158 CR83
Mortlake Rd, E16 292 B8
Ilford IG1 125 EQ63
Richmond TW9 158 CN80
Mortlake Sta Pas, SW14
off Sheen La 158 CQ83
Mortlake Ter, Rich. TW9
off Kew Rd 158 CN80
Mortlock Cl, SE15 312 E7
Morton, Tad. KT20 233 CX121
Morton Cl, E1 288 G9
Uxbridge UB8 134 BM70
Wallington SM6 219 DM108
Woking GU21 226 AW115
Morton Ct, Nthlt. UB5 116 CC64
Morton Cres, N14 99 DK49
Morton Dr, Slou. SL2 111 AL64
Morton Gdns, Wall. SM6 219 DJ106
Morton Ms, SW5 295 L9
Morton Pl, SE1 298 E7
Morton Rd, E15 281 L7
N1 277 K7
Morden SM4 200 DD99
Woking GU21 226 AW115
Morton Way, N14 99 DJ48
Morvale Cl, Belv. DA17 166 EZ77
Morval Rd, SW2 181 DN85
Morven Cl, Pot.B. EN6 64 DC31
Morven Rd, SW17 180 DF90
Morville Ho, SW18
off Fitzhugh Gro 180 DD86
Morville St, E3 280 A10
Morwell St, WC1 285 P7
Mosbach Gdns, Hutt. CM13 109 GB47
Moscow Pl, W2 283 L10
Moscow Rd, W2 283 L10
Moseley Row, SE10 303 M8
Moselle Av, N22 99 DN54
Moselle Cl, N8
off Miles Rd 121 DL55
Moselle Ho, N17
off William St 100 DT52
Moselle Pl, N17 100 DT52
Moselle Rd, Bigg.H. TN16 238 EL118
Sch Moselle Sch, Main Site,
N17 off Adams Rd 100 DS54
Sch Moselle Spec Sch, Upr Sch,
N17 off Downhills Pk Rd 122 DQ55
Moselle St, N17 100 DT52
Mosford Cl, Horl. RH6 268 DF146
Mospey Cres, Epsom KT17 233 CT115
Mosquito Cl, Wall. SM6 219 DL108
Mosquito Way, Hat. AL10 44 CS17
Moss Bk, Grays RM17 170 FZ78
Mossborough Cl, N12 98 DB51
Sch Mossbourne Comm Acad, E5 278 D2
Mossbury Rd, SW11 160 DE83
Moss Cl, E1 288 D6
N9 100 DU46
Pinner HA5 94 BZ54
Rickmansworth WD3 92 BK47
Moss Ct, Seer Grn HP9
off Orchard Rd 89 AR51
Mossdown Cl, Belv. DA17 166 FA77
Mossendew Cl, Hare. UB9 92 BK53
Mossfield, Cob. KT11 213 BU113
Mossford Ct, Ilf. IG6 125 EP55
Mossford Grn, Ilf. IG6 125 EP55
Sch Mossford Grn Prim Sch,
Barkingside IG6
off Fairlop Rd 103 EQ54
Mossford La, Ilf. IG6 103 EP54
Mossford St, E3 289 N4
Moss Gdns, Felt. TW13 175 BU89
South Croydon CR2
off Warren Av 221 DX108
Moss Grn, Welw.G.C. AL7 29 CY11
Moss Hall Ct, N12 98 DB51
Moss Hall Cres, N12 98 DB51
Moss Hall Gro, N12 98 DB51
Sch Moss Hall Inf Sch, N12
off Moss Hall Gro 98 DB51
Sch Moss Hall Jun Sch, N3
off Nether St 98 DB51
Mossington Gdns, SE16 300 G9
Moss La, Harlow CM17 36 EW14
Pinner HA5 116 BZ55
Romford RM1 off Albert Rd 127 FF58
Mosslea Rd, SE20 182 DW94
Bromley BR2 204 EK99
Orpington BR6 205 EQ104
Whyteleafe CR3 236 DT116
Mossop St, SW3 296 D8
Moss Rd, Dag. RM10 146 FA66
South Ockendon RM15 149 FW71
Watford WD25 59 BV34
Moss Side, Brick.Wd AL2 60 BZ30
Mossville Gdns, Mord. SM4 199 CZ97
Moss Way, Beac. HP9 88 AJ51
Lane End DA2 189 FR91
Moston Cl, Hayes UB3 155 BT78
Mostyn Av, Wem. HA9 118 CM64
Mostyn Gdns, NW10 282 C2
Mostyn Gro, E3 289 P1
Mostyn Rd, SW9 310 E7
SW19 199 CZ95
Bushey WD23 76 CC43
Edgware HA8 96 CR52
Mostyn Ter, Red. RH1 266 DG135
Mosul Way, Brom. BR2 204 EL100
Mosyer Dr, Orp. BR5 206 EX103
Motcomb St, SW1 296 F6
Moth Cl, Wall. SM6 219 DL108
Mothers' Sq, E5 278 F1
Motherwell Way, Grays RM20 169 FU78
Motley Av, EC2 287 N4
MOTSPUR PARK, N.Mal. KT3 199 CV100
⇌ Motspur Park 199 CV99
Motspur Pk, N.Mal. KT3 199 CT100
MOTTINGHAM, SE9 184 EJ89
⇌ Mottingham 184 EL88
Mottingham Gdns, SE9 184 EK88
Mottingham La, SE9 184 EJ88
SE12 184 EJ88
Sch Mottingham Prim Sch, SE9
off Ravensworth Rd 185 EM90
Mottingham Rd, N9 83 DX44
SE9 184 EL89
Mottisfont Rd, SE2 166 EU76
Motts Hill La, Tad. KT20 233 CU123
Motts La, Dag. RM8
off Becontree Av 126 EZ61
Mott St, E4 83 ED38
High Beach IG10 84 EF39
Mouchotte Cl, Bigg.H. TN16 222 EH112
Moulins Rd, E9 279 H7
Moulsford Ho, N7 275 P3
Moultain Hill, Swan. BR8 207 FG98
Moulton Av, Houns. TW3 156 BY82
Moultrie Way, Upmin. RM14 129 FS59
Mound, The, SE9 185 EN90
Moundfield Rd, N16 122 DU58
Moundsfield Way, Slou. SL1 151 AL75
Mount, The, E5 122 DV61
N20 98 DC47
NW3 off Heath St 120 DC63
W3 138 CP74
Brentwood CM14 108 FW48
Cheshunt EN7 66 DR26
Coulsdon CR5 234 DG115
Esher KT10 214 CA107
Ewell KT17 217 CT110
Fetcham KT22 231 CE123
Guildford GU1, GU2 258 AV137
Lower Kingswood KT20 249 CZ126
New Malden KT3 199 CT97
Potters Bar EN6 64 DB30
Rickmansworth WD3 74 BJ44
Romford RM3 106 FJ48
St. John's GU21 226 AU119
Virginia Water GU25 192 AX100
Warlingham CR6 236 DU119
Wembley HA9 118 CP61
Weybridge KT13 195 BS103
Woking GU21 226 AX118
Worcester Park KT4 217 CV105
Mountacre Cl, SE26 182 DT91
Mount Adon Pk, SE22 182 DU87
Mountague Pl, E14 290 E10
Mountain Ho, SE11 298 C10
H Mount Alvernia Hosp,
Guil. GU1 258 AY136
Mount Angelus Rd, SW15 179 CT87
Mount Ararat Rd, Rich. TW10 178 CL85
Mount Ash Rd, SE26 182 DV90
Mount Av, E4 101 EA48
W5 137 CK71
Brentwood CM13 109 GA44
Chaldon CR3 236 DQ124
Romford RM3 106 FQ51
Southall UB1 136 CA72
Mountbatten Cl, SE18 165 ES79
SE19 182 DS92
St. Albans AL1 43 CH23
Slough SL1 152 AU76
Mountbatten Ct, SE16
off Rotherhithe St 301 H3
Buckhurst Hill IG9 102 EK47
Mountbatten Gdns, Beck. BR3
off Balmoral Av 203 DY98
Mountbatten Ms, SW18
off Inman Rd 180 DC88
Mountbatten Sq, Wind. SL4
off Ward Royal 151 AQ81
Mountbel Rd, Stan. HA7 95 CG53
Sch Mount Carmel RC Prim
Sch, W5 off Little Ealing La 157 CJ77
Sch Mount Carmel RC Tech
Coll for Girls, N19
off Holland Wk 121 DK60
Mount Cl, W5 137 CJ71
Bromley BR1 204 EL95
Carshalton SM5 218 DG109
Cockfosters EN4 80 DG42
Farnham Common SL2 111 AQ63
Fetcham KT22 231 CE123
Hemel Hempstead HP1 39 BF20
Kenley CR8 236 DQ116
Sevenoaks TN13 256 FF123
Woking GU22 226 AV121
Mount Cl, The, Vir.W. GU25 192 AX100
Mountcombe Cl, Surb. KT6 198 CL101
Mount Cor, Felt. TW13 176 BX89
Mount Ct, SW15
off Weimar St 159 CY83
Guildford GU2
off The Mount 258 AW136
West Wickham BR4 204 EE103
Mount Cres, Warley CM14 108 FX49
Mount Culver Av, Sid. DA14 186 EX93
Mount Dr, Bexh. DA6 186 EY85
Harrow HA2 116 BZ57
Park Street AL2 61 CD25
Wembley HA9 118 CQ61
Mount Dr, The, Reig. RH2 250 DC132
Mountearl Gdns, SW16 181 DM90
Mount Echo Av, E4 101 EB47
Mount Echo Dr, E4 101 EB46
MOUNT END, Epp. CM16 70 EZ32
Mount Ephraim La, SW16 181 DK90
Mount Ephraim Rd, SW16 181 DK90
Mount Felix, Walt. KT12 195 BT102
Mountfield Cl, SE6 183 ED87
Mountfield Rd, E6 293 L1
N3 120 DA55
W5 137 CK72
Hemel Hempstead HP2 40 BL20
Mountfield Ter, SE6
off Mountfield Cl 183 ED87
Mountfield Way, Orp. BR5 206 EW98
Mountford Mans, SW11 309 H7
Mountfort Cres, N1 276 E6
Mountfort Ter, N1 276 E7
Mount Gdns, SE26 182 DV90
Mount Grace Rd, Pot.B. EN6 64 DA31
Sch Mount Grace Sch, Pot.B.
EN6 off Church Rd 64 DB30
Mount Gro, Edg. HA8 96 CQ48
Mountgrove Rd, N5 121 DP62
Mount Harry Rd, Sev. TN13 256 FG123
MOUNT HERMON, Wok. GU22 226 AX118
Mount Hermon Cl, Wok. GU22 226 AX118
Mount Hermon Rd, Wok. GU22 226 AX119
Mount Hill La, Ger.Cr. SL9 112 AV60
Mount Holme, T.Ditt. KT7 197 CH101
Mounthurst Rd, Brom. BR2 204 EF101
Mountington Pk Cl, Har. HA3 117 CK58
Mountjoy Cl, SE2 166 EV75
Mountjoy Ho, EC2
off The Barbican 287 K7
Mount La, Denh. UB9 113 BD61
Mount Lee, Egh. TW20 172 AY92
Mount Ms, Hmptn. TW12 196 CB95
Mount Mills, EC1 287 H3
Mountnessing Bypass,
Brwd. CM15 109 GD41
Jct Mountnessing Rbt,
Brwd. CM15 109 GC41
Mount Nod Rd, SW16 181 DM90
Mount Nugent, Chesh. HP5 54 AN27
Mount Pk, Cars. SM5 218 DG109
Mount Pk Av, Har. HA1 117 CD61
South Croydon CR2 219 DP109
Mount Pk Cres, W5 137 CK72
Mount Pk Rd, W5 137 CK71
Harrow HA1 117 CD62
Pinner HA5 115 BU57
Mount Pl, W3 off High St 138 CP74
Guildford GU2
off The Mount 258 AW136
Mount Pleasant, SE27 182 DQ91
WC1 286 D5
Barnet EN4 80 DE42
Biggin Hill TN16 238 EK117
Effingham KT24 246 BY128
Epsom KT17 217 CT110
Guildford GU2 258 AW136
Harefield UB9 92 BG53
Hertford Heath SG13 32 DW11
Ruislip HA4 116 BW61
St. Albans AL3 42 CB19
Wembley HA0 138 CL67
West Horsley KT24 245 BP129
Weybridge KT13 194 BN104
Mount Pleasant Av,
Hutt. CM13 109 GE44
Mount Pleasant Cl, Hat. AL9 45 CW15
Mount Pleasant Cres, N4 121 DM59
Mount Pleasant Est, Ilf. IG1
off Ilford La 125 EQ64
Mount Pleasant Hill, E5 122 DV61
Mount Pleasant La, E5 122 DV61
Bricket Wood AL2 60 BY30
Hatfield AL9 29 CW14
Sch Mount Pleasant La JMI
Sch, Brick.Wd AL2
off Mount Pleasant La 60 BY30
Mount Pleasant Pl, SE18 165 ER77
Mount Pleasant Rd, E17 101 DY54
N17 100 DS54
NW10 272 B7
SE13 183 EB86
W5 137 CJ70
Caterham CR3 236 DU123
Chigwell IG7 103 ER49
Dartford DA1 188 FM86
New Malden KT3 198 CQ97
Romford RM5 105 FD51
Mount Pleasant Vil, N4 121 DM59
Mount Pleasant Wk, Bex. DA5 187 FC85
Mount Ri, Red. RH1 266 DD136
Mount Rd, NW2 119 CV62
NW4 119 CU58
SE19 182 DR93
SW19 180 DA89
Barnet EN4 80 DE43
Bexleyheath DA6 186 EX85
Chessington KT9 216 CM106
Chobham GU24 210 AV112
Dagenham RM8 126 EZ60
Dartford DA1 187 FF86
Epping CM16 70 EW32
Feltham TW13 176 BY90
Hayes UB3 155 BT75
Hertford SG14 31 DN10
Ilford IG1 125 EP64
Mitcham CR4 200 DE96
New Malden KT3 198 CR97
Woking GU22 226 AV121
Mount Row, W1 297 J1
Sch Mount Sch, The, NW7
off Milespit Hill 97 CV50
Mountsfield Cl, Stai. TW19 174 BG86
Mountsfield Ct, SE13 183 ED86
Mountside, Felt. TW13 176 BY90
Guildford GU2 258 AV136
Stanmore HA7 95 CF53
Mountsorrel, Hert. SG13 32 DT08
Mounts Pond Rd, SE3 314 G8
Mount Sq, The, NW3
off Heath St 120 DC62
Mounts Rd, Green. DA9 189 FV85
Mount Stewart Av, Har. HA3 117 CK58
Sch Mount Stewart Inf Sch,
Kenton HA3 off Carlisle Gdns 117 CK59
Sch Mount Stewart Jun Sch,
Kenton HA3
off Mount Stewart Av 117 CK59
Mount St, W1 297 H1
Dorking RH4 263 CG136
Mount St Ms, W1 297 J1
Mount Ter, E1 288 E7
Mount Vernon, NW3 120 DC63
H Mount Vernon Hosp,
Nthwd. HA6 93 BP51
Mount Vw, NW7 96 CR48
W5 137 CK70
Enfield EN2 81 DM38
London Colney AL2 62 CL27
Rickmansworth WD3 92 BH46
Mountview, Nthwd. HA6 93 BT51
Coll Mountview Acad of Thea
Arts, Crouch End, N8
off Crouch Hill 121 DL58
Wood Grn, N22
off Kingfisher Pl 99 DM54
Mountview Cl, NW11 120 DB60
Redhill RH1 266 DE136
Mountview Ct, N8
off Green Las 121 DP56
Mountview Dr, Red. RH1 266 DD136
Mount Vw Rd, E4 101 EC45
N4 121 DL59
NW9 118 CR56
Mountview Rd, Chsht EN7 66 DS26
Claygate KT10 215 CH108
Orpington BR6 206 EU101
Mount Vil, SE27 181 DP90
Mount Way, Cars. SM5 218 DG109
Mountway, Pot.B. EN6 64 DA30
Welwyn Garden City AL7 29 CZ12
Mountway Cl, Welw.G.C. AL7 29 CZ12
Mountwood, W.Mol. KT8 196 CA97
Mountwood Cl, S.Croy. CR2 220 DV110
Jct Movers La, Bark. IG11 145 ES68
Movers La, Bark. IG11 145 ER67
● Mowat Ind Est, Wat. WD24 76 BW38
Mowatt Cl, N19 121 DK60
Mowbray Av, Byfleet KT14 212 BL113
Mowbray Cres, Egh. TW20 173 BA92
Mowbray Gdns, Dor. RH4 247 CH134
Mowbray Rd, NW6 272 E6
SE19 202 DT95
Edgware HA8 96 CN49
Harlow CM20 35 ET13
New Barnet EN5 80 DC42
Richmond TW10 177 CJ90
Mowbrays Cl, Rom. RM5 105 FC53
Mowbrays Rd, Rom. RM5 105 FC54
Mowbrey Gdns, Loug. IG10 85 EQ40
Sch Mowlem Prim Sch, E2 278 G10
Mowlem St, E2 278 F10
● Mowlem Trd Est, N17 100 DW52
Mowll St, SW9 310 E5
Moxey Cl, Bigg.H. TN16 222 EJ113
Moxom Av, Chsht EN8 67 DY30
Moxon Cl, E13 291 M1
Moxon St, W1 284 G7
Barnet EN5 79 CZ41
Moye Cl, E2 278 D10
Moyers Rd, E10 123 EC59
Moylan Rd, W6 306 F3
Moyne Ct, Wok. GU21
off Iveagh Rd 226 AT118
Moyne Pl, NW10 138 CN68
Moynihan Dr, N21 81 DL43
Moys Cl, Croy. CR0 201 DL100
Moyser Rd, SW16 181 DH92
Mozart St, W10 282 G3
Mozart Ter, SW1 297 H9
Muchelney Rd, Mord. SM4 200 DC100
Muckhatch La, Egh. TW20 193 BB97
MUCKINGFORD, S.le H. SS17 171 GM76
Muckingford Rd, Linford SS17 171 GM77
West Tilbury RM18 171 GL77
DLR Mudchute 302 D9
Muddy La, Slou. SL2 132 AS71
● Mudlands Ind Est,
Rain. RM13 147 FE69
Mud La, W5 137 CK71
Mudlarks Boul, SE10
off John Harrison Way 303 M6
Muggeridge Cl, S.Croy. CR2 220 DR106
Muggeridge Rd, Dag. RM10 127 FB63
MUGSWELL, Couls. CR5 250 DB125
Muirdown Av, SW14 158 CQ84
Muir Dr, SW18 180 DE86
Muirfield, W3 138 CS72
Muirfield Cl, SE16 312 F1
Watford WD19 94 BW49
Muirfield Cres, E14 302 C6
Muirfield Grn, Wat. WD19 94 BW49
Muirfield Rd, Wat. WD19 94 BX49
Woking GU21 226 AU118
Muirkirk Rd, SE6 183 EC88
Muir Rd, E5 122 DU62
Muir St, E16 305 J3
Mulberry Av, Stai. TW19 174 BL88
Windsor SL4 152 AT82
Mulberry Cl, E4 101 EA47
N8 121 DL57
NW3 274 A1
NW4 119 CW55
SE7 164 EK79
SE22 182 DU85
SW3 off Beaufort St 308 B3
SW16 181 DJ91
Amersham HP7 72 AT39
Barnet EN4 80 DD42
Broxbourne EN10 49 DZ24
Epsom KT17 216 CQ109
Feltham TW13 175 BV90
Northolt UB5 off Parkfield Av 136 BY68
Park Street AL2 60 CB28
Romford RM2 127 FH56
Watford WD17 75 BS36
Weybridge KT13 195 BP104
Woking GU21 210 AY114
● Mulberry Ct, Dart. DA1
off Bourne Ind Pk 187 FE85
Mulberry Ct, EC1
off Tompion St 287 H3
N2 off Great N Rd 120 DE55
Barking IG11 145 ET65
Beaconsfield HP9 111 AM55
Guildford GU4 off Gilliat Dr 243 BD132
Surbiton KT6 197 CK101
Mulberry Cres, Brent. TW8 157 CH80
West Drayton UB7 154 BN75
Mulberry Dr, Purf. RM19 168 FM77
Slough SL3 152 AY78
Mulberry Gdns, Harl. CM17 36 EX11
Shenley WD7 62 CL33
Mulberry Gate, Bans. SM7 233 CZ116
Mulberry Grn, Harl. CM17 36 EX11
Mulberry Hill, Shenf. CM15 109 FZ45
Sch Mulberry Ho Sch, The, NW2 272 F3
Mulberry La, Croy. CR0 202 DT102
Mulberry Mead, Hat. AL10 29 CT14
Mulberry Ms, SE14 313 N6
Wallington SM6 219 DJ107
Mulberry Par, West Dr. UB7 154 BN76
Mulberry Pl, SE9 164 EK84
W6 off Chiswick Mall 159 CU78
Brasted TN16 240 EW124
Sch Mulberry Prim Sch, N17
off Parkhurst Rd 100 DU54
Mulberry Rd, E8 278 A6
Northfleet DA11 190 GE90
Sch Mulberry Sch for Girls, E1 288 E9
Coll Mulberry Sch for Girls -
St. George's, E1 288 E10
Mulberry St, E1 288 C8
Mulberry Tree Ms, W4
off Clovelly Rd 158 CQ75
Mulberry Trees, Shep. TW17 195 BQ101
Mulberry Wk, SW3 308 B2
Mulberry Way, E18 102 EH54
Ashtead KT21 232 CL119
Belvedere DA17 167 FC75
Ilford IG6 125 EQ56
Mulgrave Rd, NW10 119 CT63
SE18 305 K9
SW6 306 G2
W5 137 CK69
Croydon CR0 202 DR104
Harrow HA1 117 CG61
Sutton SM2 218 DA107
Sch Mulgrave Sch & Early Years
Cen, SE18 305 N7
Mulgrave Way, Knap. GU21 226 AS118
Mulholland Cl, Mitch. CR4 201 DH96
Mulkern Rd, N19 121 DK60
Mullards Cl, Mitch. CR4 200 DF102
Mullein Ct, Grays RM17 170 GD79
Mullens Rd, Egh. TW20 173 BB92
Muller Ho, SE18 305 M10
Muller Rd, SW4 181 DK86
Mullet Gdns, E2 288 D2
Mullins Path, SW14 158 CR83
Mullins Pl, SW4 181 DK87
Mullion Cl, Har. HA3 94 CB53
Mullion Wk, Wat. WD19
off Ormskirk Rd 94 BX49
Mull Wk, N1 277 K5
Mulready St, NW8 284 C5

M

Mulready Wk, Hem.H. HP3 40 BL24
Multi Way, W3 158 CS75
Multon Rd, SW18 180 DD87
Mulvaney Way, SE1 299 M5
Mumford Mills, SE10 314 C6
Mumford Rd, SE24 181 DP85
Mumfords La, Chal.St.P. SL9 112 AU55
Muncaster Cl, Ashf. TW15 174 BN91
Muncaster Rd, SW11 180 DF85
Ashford TW15 175 BP92
Muncies Ms, SE6 183 EC89
Mundania Rd, SE22 182 DV86
Munday Rd, E16 291 N9
Mundells, Chsht EN7 66 DU27
Welwyn Garden City AL7 29 CZ07
Mundells Ct, Welw.G.C. AL7 29 CZ07
MUNDEN, Wat. WD25 60 CB34
Munden Dr, Wat. WD25 76 BY37
Munden Gro, Wat. WD24 76 BW38
Munden Ho, E3
off Bromley High St 290 D2
Munden St, W14 294 E8
Munden Vw, Wat. WD25 76 BX36
Mundesley Cl, Wat. WD19 94 BW49
Mundesley Spur, Slou. SL1 132 AS72
Mundford Rd, E5 122 DW61
Mundon Gdns, Ilf. IG1 125 ER60
Mund St, W14 307 H1
Mundy Ct, Eton SL4
off Eton Ct 151 AR80
Mundy St, N1 287 N2
Munford Dr, Swans. DA10 190 FY87
Mungo Pk Cl,
Bushey Hth WD23 94 CC47
Mungo Pk Rd, Grav. DA12 191 GK92
Rainham RM13 147 FG65
Mungo Pk Way, Orp. BR5 206 EW101
Munkenbeck Building, W2
off Hermitage St 284 A7
Munnery Way, Orp. BR6 205 EN104
Munnings Gdns, Islw. TW7 177 CD85
Munro Dr, N11 99 DJ51
Munro Ho, SE1 off Murphy St 298 E5
Munro Ms, W10 282 F6
Munro Ter, SW10 308 A3
Munslow Gdns, Sutt. SM1 218 DD105
Munstead Vw, Art. GU3 258 AV138
Munster Av, Houns. TW4 156 BZ84
Munster Ct, Tedd. TW11 177 CJ93
Munster Gdns, N13 99 DP49
Munster Ms, SW6 306 E4
Munster Rd, SW6 306 E4
Teddington TW11 177 CH93
Munster Sq, NW1 285 K3
Munton Rd, SE17 299 K8
Murchison Av, Bex. DA5 186 EX88
Murchison Rd, E10 123 EC61
Hoddesdon EN11 33 EB14
Murdoch Cl, Stai. TW18 174 BG92
Murdock Cl, E16 291 M8
Murdock St, SE15 312 E3
Murfett Cl, SW19 179 CY89
Murfitt Way, Upmin. RM14 128 FN63
Muriel Av, Wat. WD18 76 BW43
Muriel St, N1 276 D10
Murillo Rd, SE13 163 ED84
Murphy St, SE1 298 E5
Murray Av, Brom. BR1 204 EH96
Hounslow TW3 176 CB85
● Murray Business Cen,
Orp. BR5 206 EV97
Murray Cl, SE28 145 ES74
Murray Ct, W7 157 CE76
Murray Cres, Pnr. HA5 94 BX53
Murray Grn, Wok. GU21
off Bunyard Dr 211 BC114
Murray Gro, N1 287 K1
Murray Ms, NW1 275 N6
Murray Rd, SW19 179 CX93
W5 157 CJ77
Berkhamsted HP4 38 AV18
Northwood HA6 93 BS53
Orpington BR5 206 EV97
Ottershaw KT16 211 BC107
Richmond TW10 177 CH89
Murrays La, Byfleet KT14 212 BK114
Murray Sq, E16 291 P9
Murray St, NW1 275 M6
Murrays Yd, SE18 305 N8
Murray Ter, NW3 off Flask Wk 120 DD63
W5 off Murray Rd 157 CK77
Murrells Wk, Bkhm KT23 230 CA123
Murreys, The, Ashtd. KT21 231 CK118
Mursell Est, SW8 310 C6
Murthering La, Rom. RM4 87 FG43
Murton Ct, St.Alb. AL1 43 CE19
Murtwell Dr, Chig. IG7 103 EQ51
Musard Rd, W6 306 F2
W14 306 F2
Musbury St, E1 288 G8
Muscal, W6 306 E2
Muscatel Pl, SE5 311 P5
Sch Muschamp Prim Sch,
Cars. SM5 off Muschamp Rd 200 DE103
Muschamp Rd, SE15 162 DT83
Carshalton SM5 200 DE103
Muscovy Ho, Erith DA18
off Kale Rd 166 EY75
Muscovy St, EC3 299 P1
Museum La, SW7 296 B7
★ Museum of Childhood at
Bethnal Grn, E2 288 F2
★ Museum of Croydon,
Croy. CR0 202 DQ104
★ Museum of Harlow,
Harl. CM20 36 EV12
★ Museum of Instruments
(Royal Coll of Music), SW7 296 A6
★ Museum of London, EC2 287 J7
★ Museum of London
Docklands, E14 302 B1
★ Museum of Richmond,
Rich. TW9 177 CK85
★ Museum of St. Albans,
St.Alb. AL1 43 CE19
Museum Pas, E2 288 G2
Museum St, WC1 286 A7
Museum Way, W3 158 CN75
Musgrave Cl, Barn. EN4 80 DC39
Cheshunt EN7
off Allwood Rd 66 DT27
Musgrave Cres, SW6 307 K5
Musgrave Rd, Islw. TW7 157 CF81
Musgrove Cl, Ken. CR8 219 DM113
Musgrove Rd, SE14 313 K7
Musjid Rd, SW11 308 B9
Muskalls Cl, Chsht EN7 66 DU27
Musket Cl, E.Barn. EN4
off East Barnet Rd 80 DD43
Muskham Rd, Harl. CM20 36 EU12
Musk Hill, Hem.H. HP1 39 BE21
Musleigh Manor, Ware SG12 33 DZ06
Musley Hill, Ware SG12 33 DY05
Musley La, Ware SG12 33 DY05
Musquash Way, Houns. TW4 156 BW82
Mussenden La, Fawk.Grn DA3 209 FS101
Horton Kirby DA4 208 FQ99
Mustard Mill Rd, Stai. TW18 173 BF91
Muston Rd, E5 122 DV61
Mustow Pl, SW6 307 H8
Muswell Av, N10 99 DH54
MUSWELL HILL, N10 121 DH55
Muswell Hill, N10 121 DH55
Muswell Hill Bdy, N10 121 DH55
Muswell Hill Pl, N10 121 DH56
Sch Muswell Hill Prim Sch, N10
off Muswell Hill 121 DH55
Muswell Hill Rd, N6 120 DG58
N10 120 DG56
Muswell Ms, N10 121 DH55
Muswell Rd, N10 121 DH55
Mutchetts Cl, Wat. WD25 60 BY33
Mutrix Rd, NW6 273 K8
Mutton La, Pot.B. EN6 63 CY31
Mutton Pl, NW1 275 H5
Muybridge Rd, N.Mal. KT3 198 CQ96
Sch Myatt Gdn Prim Sch, SE4 313 P8
Myatt Rd, SW9 310 G6
Myatts Flds S, SW9
off St. Lawrence Way 310 F8
Myatts N, SW9
off Fairbairn Grn 310 F6
Mycenae Rd, SE3 315 N4
Myddelton Av, Enf. EN1 82 DS38
Myddelton Cl, Enf. EN1 82 DT39
Myddelton Gdns, N21 99 DP45
Myddelton Pk, N20 98 DD48
Myddelton Pas, EC1 286 F2
Myddelton Rd, N8 121 DL56
Myddelton Sq, EC1 286 F2
Myddelton St, EC1 286 F3
Myddleton Av, N4 122 DQ61
Myddleton Cl, Stan. HA7 95 CG47
Myddleton Ct, Horn. RM11 127 FF59
Myddleton Ms, N22 99 DL52
Myddleton Path, Chsht EN7 66 DV31
Myddleton Rd, N22 99 DL52
Uxbridge UB8 134 BJ67
Ware SG12 33 DX07
Myers Cl, Shenley WD7 62 CL32
Myers Dr, Slou. SL2 111 AP64
Myers La, SE14 313 J2
Mygrove Cl, Rain. RM13 148 FK68
Mygrove Gdns, Rain. RM13 148 FK68
Mygrove Rd, Rain. RM13 148 FK68
Myles Ct, Goffs Oak EN7 66 DQ29
Mylis Cl, SE26 182 DV91
Mylius Cl, SE14 313 H6
Mylne Cl, W6 159 CU78
Cheshunt EN8 66 DW27
Mylner Ct, Hodd. EN11
off Ditchfield Rd 49 EA15
Mylne St, EC1 286 E1
Mylor Cl, Wok. GU21 210 AY114
Mymms Dr, Brook.Pk AL9 64 DA26
Mynchen Cl, Beac. HP9 89 AK49
Mynchen End, Beac. HP9 89 AK49
Mynchen Rd, Beac. HP9 89 AK50
Mynns Cl, Epsom KT18 216 CP114
Mynterne Ct, SW19
off Swanton Gdns 179 CX88
MYNTHURST, Reig. RH2 265 CV144
Myra St, SE2 166 EU78
Myrdle St, E1 288 D7
Myrke, The, Datchet SL3 152 AT77
Myrna Cl, SW19 180 DE94
Myron Pl, SE13 163 EC83
Myrtle All, SE18 305 M7
Myrtle Av, Felt. TW14 155 BS84
Ruislip HA4 115 BU59
Myrtleberry Cl, E8 278 A5
Myrtle Cl, Colnbr. SL3 153 BE81
East Barnet EN4 98 DF46
Erith DA8 167 FE81
Uxbridge UB8 134 BM71
West Drayton UB7 154 BM76
Myrtle Cres, Slou. SL2 132 AT73
Myrtledene Rd, SE2 166 EU78
Myrtle Gdns, W7 137 CE74
Myrtle Grn, Hem.H. HP1
off Newlands Rd 39 BE19
Myrtle Gro, Aveley RM15 168 FQ75
Enfield EN2 82 DR38
New Malden KT3 198 CQ96
Myrtle Pl, Dart. DA2 189 FR87
Myrtle Rd, E6 144 EL67
E17 123 DY58
N13 100 DQ48
W3 138 CQ74
Croydon CR0 203 EA104
Dartford DA1 188 FK88
Dorking RH4 263 CG135
Hampton Hill TW12 176 CC93
Hounslow TW3 156 CC82
Ilford IG1 125 EP61
Romford RM3 106 FJ51
Sutton SM1 218 DC106
Warley CM14 108 FW49
Myrtleside Cl, Nthwd. HA6 93 BR52
Myrtle Wk, N1 287 N1
Mysore Rd, SW11 160 DF83
Myton Rd, SE21 182 DR90

N

● N17 Studios, N17 100 DT52
Nacovia Ho, SW6
off Townmead Rd 307 P8
Nadine Ct, Wall. SM6
off Woodcote Rd 219 DJ109
Nadine St, SE7 164 EJ78
Nafferton Ri, Loug. IG10 84 EK43
Nagle Cl, E17 101 ED54
Jct Nags Head, N7 121 DM63
● Nags Head Cen, N7 121 DM63
Nags Head Cl, Hert. SG13 32 DV08
Nag's Head Ct, EC1 287 J5
Nags Head La, Brwd. CM14 107 FR51
Upminster RM14 106 FQ53
Welling DA16 166 EV83
Nags Head Rd, Enf. EN3 82 DW42
Nailsworth Cres, Merst. RH1 251 DK129
Nailzee Cl, Ger.Cr. SL9 112 AY59
Nairn Ct, Til. RM18
off Dock Rd 171 GF82
Nairne Gro, SE24 182 DR85
Nairn Grn, Wat. WD19 93 BU48
Nairn Rd, Ruis. HA4 136 BW65
Nairn St, E14 290 F7
Nalders Rd, Chesh. HP5 54 AR29
NALDERSWOOD, Reig. RH2 265 CW144
Nallhead Rd, Felt. TW13 176 BW92
Namba Roy Cl, SW16 181 DM91
Namton Dr, Th.Hth. CR7 201 DM98
Nan Clark's La, NW7 97 CT47
Nancy Downs, Wat. WD19 94 BW45
Nankin St, E14 290 B9
Nansen Rd, SW11 160 DG84
Gravesend DA12 191 GK92
Nansen Village, N12 98 DB49
Nant Ct, NW2
off Granville Rd 119 CZ61
Nanterre Ct, Wat. WD17 75 BU40
Nantes Cl, SW18 160 DC84
Nantes Pas, E1 288 A6
Nant Rd, NW2 119 CZ61
Nant St, E2 288 F2
Naoroji St, WC1 286 E3
Nap, The, Kings L. WD4 58 BN29
Napa Cl, E20 280 E3
Napier Av, E14 302 B10
SW6 306 G10
Napier Cl, SE8 313 P4
W14 294 G6
Hornchurch RM11 127 FH60
London Colney AL2 61 CK25
West Drayton UB7 154 BM76
Napier Ct, SE12 184 EH90
SW6 off Ranelagh Gdns 306 G10
Cheshunt EN8
off Flamstead End Rd 66 DV28
Surbiton KT6 197 CK100
Napier Dr, Bushey WD23 76 BY42
Napier Gdns, Guil. GU1 243 BB133
Napier Gro, N1 287 K1
Napier Ho, Rain. RM13 147 FF69
Napier Pl, W14 294 G7
Napier Rd, E6 145 EN67
E11 124 EE63
E15 291 K1
N17 122 DS55
NW10 139 CV69
SE25 202 DV98
W14 294 G7
Ashford TW15 175 BR94
Belvedere DA17 166 EZ77
Bromley BR2 204 EH98
Enfield EN3 83 DX43
Isleworth TW7 157 CG84
London Heathrow Airport
TW6 154 BK81
Northfleet DA11 191 GF88
South Croydon CR2 220 DR108
Wembley HA0 117 CK64
Napier Ter, N1 276 G7
Napier Wk, Ashf. TW15 175 BR94
Napoleon Rd, E5 122 DV62
Twickenham TW1 177 CH87
Napsbury Av, Lon.Col. AL2 61 CJ26
Napsbury La, St.Alb. AL1 43 CG23
Napton Cl, Hayes UB4 136 BY70
Narbonne Av, SW4 181 DJ85
Narboro Ct, Rom. RM1 127 FG58
Narborough Cl, Uxb. UB10 115 BQ61
Narborough St, SW6 307 L9
Narcissus Rd, NW6 273 J3
Narcot La, Ch.St.G. HP8 90 AU48
Chalfont St. Peter SL9 90 AV52
Narcot Rd, Ch.St.G. HP8 90 AU48
Narcot Way, Ch.St.G. HP8 90 AU49
Nare Rd, Aveley RM15 148 FQ73
Naresby Fold, Stan. HA7 95 CJ51
Narford Rd, E5 122 DU62
Narrow Boat Cl, SE28
off Ridge Cl 165 ER75
Narrow La, Warl. CR6 236 DV119
Narrow St, E14 289 L10
Narrow Way, Brom. BR2 204 EL100
Nascot Pl, Wat. WD17 75 BV39
Nascot Rd, Wat. WD17 75 BV40
Nascot St, W12 282 A8
Watford WD17 75 BV40
Sch Nascot Wd Inf & Nurs Sch,
Wat. WD17 off Nascot Wd Rd 75 BU38
Sch Nascot Wd Jun Sch, Wat.
WD17 off Nascot Wd Rd 75 BU38
Nascot Wd Rd, Wat. WD17 75 BT37
Naseberry Ct, E4
off Merriam Cl 101 EC50
Naseby Cl, NW6 273 P6
Isleworth TW7 157 CE81
Naseby Ct, Walt. KT12
off Clements Rd 196 BW103
Naseby Rd, SE19 182 DR93
Dagenham RM10 126 FA62
Ilford IG5 103 EM53
Nash Cl, Berk. HP4 38 AU18
Elstree WD6 78 CM42
North Mymms AL9 45 CX23
Sutton SM1 200 DD104
Coll Nash Coll, Brom. BR2
off Croydon Rd 204 EF104
Nash Cft, Nthflt DA11 190 GE91
Nashdom La, Burn. SL1 130 AG66
Nash Dr, Red. RH1 250 DF132
Nashes Farm La, St.Alb. AL4 44 CL15
Nash Gdns, Red. RH1 250 DF132
Nash Grn, Brom. BR1 184 EG93
Hemel Hempstead HP3 58 BM25
Nash Ho, SW1 309 K1
Nash La, Kes. BR2 222 EG106
Nashleigh Hill, Chesh. HP5 54 AQ29
Sch Nash Mills C of E Prim Sch,
Hem.H. HP3 off Belswains La 58 BM25
Nash Mills La, Hem.H. HP3 58 BM26
Nash Rd, N9 100 DW47
SE4 163 DX84
Romford RM6 126 EX56
Slough SL3 153 AZ77
Nash St, NW1 285 K3
Nash's Yd, Uxb. UB8
off George St 134 BK66
Nash Way, Kenton HA3 117 CH58
Nasmyth St, W6 159 CV76
Nassau Path, SE28
off Disraeli Cl 146 EW74
Nassau Rd, SW13 159 CT81
Nassau St, W1 285 L7
Nassington Rd, NW3 120 DE63
Natalie Cl, Felt. TW14 175 BR87
Natalie Ms, Twick. TW2
off Sixth Cross Rd 177 CD90
Natal Rd, N11 99 DL51
SW16 181 DK93
Ilford IG1 125 EP63
Thornton Heath CR7 202 DR97
Nathan Cl, Upmin. RM14 129 FS60
Nathaniel Cl, E1 288 B7
Nathans Rd, Wem. HA0 117 CJ61
Nathan Way, SE28 165 ES77
★ National Archives, The,
Rich. TW9 158 CP80
★ National Army Mus, SW3 308 F2
H National Blood Service,
Brentwood Transfusion Cen,
Brwd. CM15 109 FZ46
N London Blood Transfusion
Cen, NW9 96 CR54
S Thames Blood Transfusion
Cen, SW17 180 DD92
Coll National Centre for Circus
Arts, The, N1 287 N3
Coll National Film & Television
Sch Beaconsfield Studios,
Beac. HP9 off Station Rd 89 AL54
H National Gall, WC2 297 P1
H National Hosp for Neurology
& Neurosurgery, The, WC1 286 B5
★ National Maritime Mus, SE10 314 G3
★ National Portrait Gall, WC2 297 P1
Coll National Sch of Govt, SW1 297 L9
National Ter, SE16
off Bermondsey Wall E 300 E5
★ National Thea, SE1 298 D2
National Wks, Houns. TW4
off Bath Rd 156 BZ83
Nation Way, E4 101 EC46
★ Natural History Mus, SW7 296 A7
Natwoke Cl, Beac. HP9 89 AK50
Naunton Way, Horn. RM12 128 FK62
Naval Row, E14 290 F10
Naval Wk, Brom. BR1
off High St 204 EG96
Navarino Gro, E8 278 D4
Navarino Mansions, E8
off Dalston La 278 D3
Navarino Rd, E8 278 D4
Navarre Ct, Kings L. WD4
off Primrose Hill 59 BP28
Navarre Gdns, Rom. RM5 105 FB51
Navarre Rd, E6 144 EL68
SW9 310 G6
Navarre St, E2 288 A4
Navenby Wk, E3 290 B4
Navestock Cl, E4
off Mapleton Rd 101 EC48
Navestock Cres, Wdf.Grn. IG8 102 EJ53
Navigation Bldg, Hayes UB3
off Station Rd 155 BT76
Navigation Ct, E16
off Albert Basin Way 145 EQ73
Navigation Dr, Enf. EN3 83 EA38
Navigator Dr, Sthl. UB2 156 CC75
Navy St, SW4 309 N10
Naxos Bldg, E14 302 A5
Nayim Pl, E8 278 E3
Nayland Ct, Rom. RM1
off Market Pl 127 FE56
Naylor Gro, Enf. EN3
off South St 83 DX43
Naylor Rd, N20 98 DC47
SE15 312 E4
Naylor Ter, Colnbr. SL3
off Vicarage Way 153 BC80
Nazareth Gdns, SE15 312 E8
NAZEING, Wal.Abb. EN9 50 EJ22
Nazeingbury Cl, Lwr Naze. EN9 49 ED22
Nazeingbury Par, Wal.Abb.
EN9 off Nazeing Rd 49 ED22
Nazeing Common, Naze. EN9 50 EH24
NAZEING GATE, Wal.Abb. EN9 68 EJ25
Nazeing New Rd, Brox. EN10 49 EA21
Sch Nazeing Prim Sch, Naze.
EN9 off Hyde Mead 50 EE23
Nazeing Rd, Lwr Naze. EN9 49 EC22
Nazeing Wk, Rain. RM13
off Ongar Way 147 FF67
Nazrul St, E2 288 A2
● NCR Business Cen, NW10
off Great Cen Way 118 CS64
Neagle Cl, Borwd. WD6
off Balcon Way 78 CQ39
Neal Av, Sthl. UB1 136 BZ70
Neal Cl, Ger.Cr. SL9 113 BB60
Northwood HA6 93 BU53
Neal Ct, Hert. SG14 32 DQ09
Waltham Abbey EN9 68 EF33
Nealden St, SW9 310 C10
Neale Cl, N2 120 DC55
Neal St, WC2 286 A9
Watford WD18 76 BW43
Neal's Yd, WC2 286 A9
Near Acre, NW9 97 CT53
NEASDEN, NW2 118 CS62
⊖ Neasden 118 CS64
Neasden Cl, NW10 118 CS64
Jct Neasden Junct, NW10
off North Circular Rd 118 CS63
Neasden La, NW10 118 CS63
Neasden La N, NW10 118 CR62
Neasham Rd, Dag. RM8 126 EV64
Neatby Ct, Chsht EN8
off Coopers Wk 67 DX28
Neate St, SE5 312 A2
Neath Gdns, Mord. SM4 200 DC100
Neathouse Pl, SW1 297 L8
Neats Acre, Ruis. HA4 115 BR59
Neatscourt Rd, E6 292 F7
Neave Cres, Rom. RM3 106 FJ53
Neb La, Oxt. RH8 253 EC131
Nebraska Bldg, SE13
off Deals Gateway 314 C7
Nebraska St, SE1 299 L5
★ NEC Harlequins RFC,
Twick. TW2 177 CE87
Neckinger, SE16 300 B6
Neckinger Est, SE16 300 B6
Neckinger St, SE1 300 B5
Nectarine Way, SE13 314 D8
Necton Rd, Wheat. AL4 28 CL07
Needham Cl, Wind. SL4 151 AL81
Needham Ct, Enf. EN3
off Manton Rd 83 EA37
Needham Rd, W11 283 J9
Needham Ter, NW2
off Kara Way 119 CX62
Needleman St, SE16 301 J5
Needles Bk, Gdse. RH9 252 DV131
Neela Cl, Uxb. UB10 115 BP63
Neeld Cres, NW4 119 CV57
Wembley HA9 118 CN64
Neeld Par, Wem. HA9
off Harrow Rd 118 CN64
Neil Cl, Ashf. TW15 175 BQ92
Neild Way, Rick. WD3 91 BF45
Neil Wates Cres, SW2 181 DN88
Nelgarde Rd, SE6 183 EA87
Nella Rd, W6 306 C3
Nelldale Rd, SE16 300 G8
Nellgrove Rd, Uxb. UB10 135 BP70
Nell Gwynn Cl, Shenley WD7 62 CL32
Nell Gwynne Av, Shep. TW17 195 BR100
Nell Gwynne Cl, Epsom KT19 216 CN111
Nello James Gdns, SE27 182 DR91
Nelmes Cl, Horn. RM11 128 FM57
Nelmes Cres, Horn. RM11 128 FL57
Sch Nelmes Prim Sch, Horn.
RM11 off Wingletye La 128 FM56
Nelmes Rd, Horn. RM11 128 FL59
Nelmes Way, Horn. RM11 128 FL56
Nelson Av, St.Alb. AL1 43 CH23
Nelson Cl, NW6 283 J2
Biggin Hill TN16 238 EL117
Croydon CR0 201 DP102
Feltham TW14 175 BT88
Romford RM7 105 FB53
Slough SL3 152 AX77
Uxbridge UB10 135 BP69
Walton-on-Thames KT12 195 BV102
Warley CM14 108 FX50
Nelson Ct, SE16
off Brunel Rd 301 H3
Gravesend DA12 191 GJ88
Nelson Gdns, E2 288 D2
Guildford GU1 243 BA133
Hounslow TW3 176 CA86
Nelson Gro Rd, SW19 200 DB95
Nelson Ho, Green. DA9 189 FW85
Nelson La, Uxb. UB10 135 BP69
Nelson Mandela Cl, N10 98 DG54
Nelson Mandela Ho, N16
off Cazenove Rd 122 DU61
Nelson Mandela Rd, SE3 164 EJ83
Nelson Pas, EC1 287 K3
Nelson Pl, N1 287 H1
Sidcup DA14
off Sidcup High St 186 EU91
Sch Nelson Prim Sch, E6
off Napier Rd 145 EN68
Whitton TW2 off Nelson Rd 176 CB87
Nelson Rd, E4 101 EB51
E11 124 EG56
N8 121 DM57
N9 100 DV47
N15 122 DS56
SE10 314 F3
SW19 180 DB94
Ashford TW15 174 BL92
Belvedere DA17 166 EZ78
Bromley BR2 204 EJ98
Caterham CR3 236 DR123
Dartford DA1 188 FJ86
Enfield EN3 83 DX44
Harrow HA1 117 CD60
Hounslow TW3, TW4 176 CA86
London Heathrow Airport
TW6 154 BM81
New Malden KT3 198 CR99
Northfleet DA11 191 GF89
Rainham RM13 147 FF68
Sidcup DA14
off Sidcup High St 186 EU91
South Ockendon RM15 149 FW68
Stanmore HA7 95 CJ51
Twickenham TW2 176 CC86
Uxbridge UB10 135 BP69
Windsor SL4 151 AM83
★ Nelson's Column, WC2 298 A2
Nelson Sq, SE1 298 G4
Nelson's Row, SW4 161 DK84
Nelson St, E1 288 E8
E6 145 EM68
E16 291 L10
Hertford SG14 31 DP08
Nelsons Yd, NW1 275 L10
Nelson Ter, N1 287 H1
● Nelson Trd Est, SW19 200 DB95
Nelson Wk, E3 290 D4
SE16 301 M3
Epsom KT19 216 CN109
Nelwyn Av, Horn. RM11 128 FM57
Nemor Ct, Edg. HA8
off Atlas Cres 96 CQ47
Nemoure Rd, W3 138 CQ73
Nene Gdns, Felt. TW13 176 BZ89
Nene Rd, Lon.Hthrw Air. TW6 155 BP81
Nepaul Rd, SW11 308 C9
Nepean St, SW15 179 CU86
Neptune Cl, Rain. RM13 147 FF68
Neptune Ct, Borwd. WD6
off Clarendon Rd 78 CN41
Neptune Dr, Hem.H. HP2 40 BL18
Neptune Ho, E3
off Garrison Rd 280 A9
Neptune Rd, Har. HA1 117 CD58
London Heathrow Airport
TW6 155 BR81
Neptune St, SE16 300 G6
Neptune Wk, Erith DA8 167 FD77
Neptune Way, Slou. SL1
off Hunters Way 151 AL75
Nero Ct, Brent. TW8
off Justin Cl 157 CK80
Nesbit Rd, SE9 164 EK84
Nesbitt Cl, SE3 315 J9
Nesbitts All, Barn. EN5
off Bath Pl 79 CZ41
Nesbitt Sq, SE19
off Coxwell Rd 182 DS94
Coll Nescot, Ewell KT17
off Reigate Rd 217 CU111
Nesham St, E1 300 C2
Ness Rd, Erith DA8 168 FK79
Ness St, SE16 300 C6
Nesta Rd, Wdf.Grn. IG8 102 EE51
Nestles Av, Hayes UB3 155 BT76
Neston Rd, Wat. WD24 76 BW37
Nestor Av, N21 81 DP44
Nethan Dr, Aveley RM15 148 FQ73
Netheravon Rd, W4 159 CT77
W7 137 CF74
Netheravon Rd S, W4 159 CT78
Netherbury Rd, W5 157 CK76
Netherby Gdns, Enf. EN2 81 DL42
Netherby Pk, Wey. KT13 213 BS106
Netherby Rd, SE23 182 DW87
Nether Cl, N3 98 DA52
Nethercote Av, Wok. GU21 226 AT117
Nethercourt Av, N3 98 DA51

M
N

Netherfield Ct,
Stans.Abb. SG12 33 ED12
Netherfield Gdns, Bark. IG11 145 ER65
Netherfield La,
Stans.Abb. SG12 34 EE12
Netherfield Rd, N12 98 DB50
SW17 180 DG90
Netherford Rd, SW4 309 M9
Netherhall Gdns, NW3 273 P4
Netherhall Rd, Roydon CM19 50 EF17
Netherhall Way, NW3 273 P3
Netherheys Dr, S.Croy. CR2 219 DP108
Netherlands, The, Couls. CR5 235 DJ119
Netherlands Rd,
New Barn. EN5 80 DD44
Netherleigh Cl, N6 121 DH60
Netherleigh Pk, Red. RH1 267 DL137
Nether Mt, Guil. GU2 258 AV136
Nethern Ct Rd, Wold. CR3 237 EA123
Netherne Dr, Couls. CR5 235 DH121
Netherne La, Couls. CR5 235 DK121
Merstham RH1 235 DJ123
Netherpark Dr, Rom. RM2 105 FF54
Nether St, N3 98 DA53
N12 98 DB50
Netherton Gro, SW10 307 P3
Netherton Rd, N15 122 DR58
Twickenham TW1 177 CG85
Netherway, St.Alb. AL3 42 CA23
Netherwood, N2 98 DD54
Netherwood Pl, W14 294 C6
Netherwood Rd, W14 294 C6
Beaconsfield HP9 89 AK50
Netherwood St, NW6 273 H6
Netley Cl, Goms. GU5 261 BQ138
New Addington CR0 221 EC108
Sutton SM3 217 CX106
Netley Dr, Walt. KT12 196 BZ101
Netley Gdns, Mord. SM4 200 DC101
Sch Netley Prim Sch, NW1 285 L3
Netley Rd, E17 123 DZ57
Brentford TW8 158 CL79
Ilford IG2 125 ER57
London Heathrow Airport
TW6 155 BR81
Morden SM4 200 DC101
Netley St, NW1 285 L3
NETTESWELL, Harl. CM20 35 ET14
Netteswellbury Fm, Harl. CM18 51 ET16
Netteswell Orchard, Harl.
CM20 35 ER14
Netteswell Rd, Harl. CM20 35 ES12
Netteswell Twr, Harl. CM20 35 ER14
Nettlecombe Cl, Sutt. SM2 218 DB109
Nettlecroft, Hem.H. HP1 40 BH21
Welwyn Garden City AL7 30 DB08
Nettleden Av, Wem. HA9 138 CN65
Nettleden Rd, Hem.H. HP1 39 BB15
Potten End HP4 39 BA16
Nettlefold Pl, SE27 181 DP90
Nettlestead Cl, Beck. BR3 203 DZ95
Nettles Ter, Guil. GU1 242 AX134
Nettleton Rd, SE14 313 K6
London Heathrow Airport
TW6 155 BP81
Uxbridge UB10 114 BM63
Nettlewood Rd, SW16 181 DK94
Neuchatel Rd, SE6 183 DZ89
Nevada Bldg, SE10
off Blackheath Rd 314 C6
Nevada Cl, N.Mal. KT3 198 CQ98
Nevada St, SE10 314 F4
Nevell Rd, Grays RM16 171 GH76
Nevern Pl, SW5 295 K9
Nevern Rd, SW5 295 J9
Nevern Sq, SW5 295 K9
Nevil Cl, Nthwd. HA6 93 BQ50
Neville Av, N.Mal. KT3 198 CR95
Neville Cl, E11 124 EF62
NW1 285 P1
NW6 283 H1
SE15 312 C5
W3 off Acton La 158 CQ75
Banstead SM7 218 DB114
Esher KT10 214 BZ107
Hounslow TW3 156 CB82
Potters Bar EN6 63 CZ31
Sidcup DA15 185 ET91
Stoke Poges SL2 132 AT65
Neville Ct, Slou. SL1
off Dropmore Rd 130 AJ69
Uxb. UB3 off Uxbridge Rd 135 BS71
Neville Dr, N2 120 DC58
Neville Gdns, Dag. RM8 126 EX62
Neville Gill Cl, SW18 180 DA86
Neville Pl, N22 99 DM53
Neville Rd, E7 281 P7
NW6 283 H1
W5 137 CK70
Croydon CR0 202 DR101
Dagenham RM8 126 EX61
Ilford IG6 103 EQ53
Kingston upon Thames KT1 198 CN96
Richmond TW10 177 CJ90
Nevilles Ct, NW2 119 CU62
Neville St, SW7 296 A10
Neville Ter, SW7 296 A10
Neville Wk, Cars. SM5 200 DE101
Nevill Gro, Wat. WD24 75 BV39
Nevill Rd, N16 122 DS63
Nevill Way, Loug. IG10
off Valley Hill 84 EL44
Nevin Dr, E4 101 EB46
Nevinson Cl, SW18 180 DD86
Nevis Cl, E13 292 B1
Rom. RM1 105 FE51
Nevis Rd, SW17 180 DG89
New Acres Rd, SE28 165 ES75
NEW ADDINGTON, Croy. CR0 221 ED109
Tra New Addington 221 EC110
Newall Ct, W12
off Heathstan Rd 139 CU72
Newall Ho, SE1 299 K6
Newall Rd,
Lon.Hthrw Air. TW6 155 BQ81
New Arc, Uxb. UB8
off High St 134 BK67
Newark Cl, Guil. GU4
off Dairyman's Wk 243 BB129
Ripley GU23 228 BG121
Newark Cotts, Ripley GU23 228 BG121
Newark Ct, Walt. KT12 196 BW102
Newark Cres, NW10 138 CR69
Newark Grn, Borwd. WD6 78 CR41
Newark Knok, E6 293 L8
Newark La,
Ripley GU22, GU23 227 BF118
Newark Rd, S.Croy. CR2 220 DR107
Newark St, E1 288 E7
Newark Way, NW4 119 CU56
New Ash Cl, N2 120 DD55
New Atlas Wf, E14 301 P7
New Barn Cl, Wall. SM6 219 DM107
New Barnes Av, St.Alb. AL1 43 CG23
NEW BARNET, Barn. EN5 80 DB42
⇌ New Barnet 80 DD43
New Barn La, Cudham TN14 239 EQ116
Westerham TN16 239 EQ118
Whyteleafe CR3 236 DS117
Newbarn La, Seer Grn HP9 90 AS49
New Barn Rd, Sthflt DA13 190 GC90
Swanley BR8 207 FE95
New Barns Av, Mitch. CR4 201 DK98
New Barn St, E13 291 P4
New Barns Way, Chig. IG7 103 EP48
New Battlebridge La,
Red. RH1 251 DH130
Sch New Beacon Sch, The,
Sev. TN13 off Brittains La 256 FG127
NEW BECKENHAM,
Beck. BR3 183 DZ93
⇌ New Beckenham 183 DZ94
New Bell Yd, EC4
off Carter La 287 H9
Newberries Av, Rad. WD7 77 CJ35
Sch Newberries Prim Sch,
Rad. WD7 off Newberries Av 77 CJ36
Newberry Cres, Wind. SL4 151 AK82
New Berry La, Hersham KT12 214 BX106
Newbery Cl, Cat. CR3 252 DS125
Newbery Rd, Erith DA8 167 FF81
Newbery Way, Slou. SL1 151 AR75
Newbiggin Path, Wat. WD19 94 BW49
Newbolt Av, Sutt. SM3 217 CW106
Newbolt Rd, Stan. HA7 95 CF51
New Bond St, W1 285 J9
Newborough Grn, N.Mal. KT3 198 CR98
New Brent St, NW4 119 CW57
Newbridge Pt, SE23
off Windrush La 183 DX90
Sch Newbridge Sch,
Barley La Campus, Ilf. IG3
off Barley La 126 EV57
Loxford La Campus, Ilf. IG3
off Loxford La 125 ES63
New Br St, EC4 286 G9
New Broad St, EC2 287 N7
New Bdy, W5 137 CJ73
Hampton Hill TW12
off Hampton Rd 177 CD92
Uxb. UB10 off Uxbridge Rd 135 BP69
New Bdy Bldgs, W5
off New Bdy 137 CK73
Newburgh Rd, W3 138 CQ74
Grays RM17 170 GD78
Newburgh St, W1 285 L9
New Burlington Ms, W1 285 L10
New Burlington Pl, W1 285 L10
New Burlington St, W1 285 L10
Newburn St, SE11 310 D1
Newbury Av, Enf. EN3 83 DZ38
Newbury Cl, Dart. DA2
off Lingfield Av 188 FP87
Northolt UB5 136 BZ65
Romford RM3 106 FK51
Newbury Gdns, Epsom KT19 217 CT105
Romford RM3 106 FK51
Upminster RM14 128 FM62
Newbury Ho, N22 99 DL53
Newbury Ms, NW5 275 H5
NEWBURY PARK, Ilf. IG2 125 ER57
⊖ Newbury Park 125 ER58
Sch Newbury Pk Prim Sch,
Barkingside IG2
off Perrymans Fm Rd 125 ER58
Newbury Rd, E4 101 EC51
Bromley BR2 204 EG97
Ilford IG2 125 ES58
London Heathrow Airport
TW6 154 BM81
Romford RM3 106 FK50
Newbury St, EC1 287 J7
Newbury Wk, Rom. RM3 106 FK50
Newbury Way, Nthlt. UB5 136 BY65
New Butt La, SE8 314 B5
New Butt La N, SE8 314 B5
Newby Cl, Enf. EN1 82 DS40
Newby Pl, E14 290 E10
Newby St, SW8 309 K10
New Caledonian Wf, SE16 301 N6
Newcastle Av, Ilf. IG6 104 EU51
Newcastle Cl, EC4 286 G8
Newcastle Pl, W2 284 B7
Newcastle Row, EC1 286 F4
New Causeway, Reig. RH2 266 DB137
New Cavendish St, W1 285 K6
New Change, EC4 287 J9
New Change Pas, EC4 287 J9
New Chapel Rd, Felt. TW13
off High St 175 BV88
New Chapel Sq, Felt. TW13 175 BV88
New Charles St, EC1 287 H2
NEW CHARLTON, SE7 304 C8
New Ch Ct, SE19
off Waldegrave Rd 182 DU94
New Ch Rd, SE5 311 K4
Newchurch Rd, Slou. SL2 131 AM71
Sch New City Prim Sch, E13 292 D3
New City Rd, E13 292 C2
New Clocktower Pl, N7 276 A4
New Cl, SW19 200 DC97
Feltham TW13 176 BY92
New Coll Ct, NW3
off Finchley Rd 273 P5
New Coll Ms, N1 276 F6
New Coll Par, NW3
off Finchley Rd 274 A5
Newcombe Gdns, SW16 181 DL91
Hounslow TW4 156 BZ84
Newcombe Pk, NW7 96 CS50
Wembley HA0 138 CM67
Newcombe Ri, West Dr. UB7 134 BL72
Newcombe St, W8 295 K2
Newcomen Rd, E11 124 EF62
SW11 160 DD83
Newcomen St, SE1 299 L4
Newcome Path, Shenley WD7
off Newcome Rd 62 CN34
Newcome Rd, Shenley WD7 62 CN34
New Compton St, WC2 285 P9
New Concordia Wf, SE1 300 B4
New Coppice, Wok. GU21 226 AT119
New Cotts, Wenn. RM13 148 FJ72
New Ct, EC4 286 E10
Addlestone KT15 194 BJ104
Northolt UB5 116 CB64
Newcourt, Uxb. UB8 134 BJ71
Newcourt St, NW8 284 C1
New Covent Gdn Flower
Mkt, SW8 309 P3
New Covent Gdn Mkt, SW8 309 N5
New Crane Pl, E1 300 G2
Newcroft Cl, Uxb. UB8 134 BM71
NEW CROSS, SE14 313 L6
⇌ New Cross 313 P5
⊖ New Cross 313 P5
Jct New Cross, SE14 313 N5
NEW CROSS GATE, SE14 313 J6
⇌ New Cross Gate 313 L5
⊖ New Cross Gate 313 L5
New Cross Rd, SE14 313 H5
Guildford GU2 242 AU132
New Cut, Slou. SL1 130 AG70
Newdales Cl, N9 100 DU47
Newdene Av, Nthlt. UB5 136 BX68
Newdigate Grn, Hare. UB9 92 BK53
Newdigate Rd, Hare. UB9 92 BJ53
Leigh RH2 264 CS141
Newdigate Rd E, Hare. UB9 92 BK53
New Ealing Bdy, W5
off Haven Grn 137 CK73
Newell Ri, Hem.H. HP3 40 BL23
Newell Rd, Hem.H. HP3 40 BL23
Newell St, E14 289 N9
NEW ELTHAM, SE9 185 EN89
⇌ New Eltham 185 EP88
New End, NW3 120 DC63
Sch New End Prim Sch, NW3
off Streatley Pl 120 DC63
New End Sq, NW3 120 DD63
● New England Ind Est,
Bark. IG11 145 EQ68
New England St, St.Alb. AL3 42 CC20
Newenham Rd, Bkhm KT23 246 CA126
Newent Cl, SE15 311 N4
Carshalton SM5 200 DF102
H New Epsom & Ewell
Cottage Hosp, Epsom KT19 216 CL111
New Era Est, N1
off Whitmore Rd 277 N9
New Fm Av, Brom. BR2 204 EG98
New Fm Cl, Stai. TW18 194 BJ95
New Fm Dr, Abridge RM4 86 EV41
New Fm La, Nthwd. HA6 93 BS53
New Ferry App, SE18 305 L6
New Fetter La, EC4 286 F8
Newfield Cl, Hmptn. TW12 196 CA95
Newfield La, Hem.H. HP2 40 BL20
Sch Newfield Prim Sch, NW10
off Longstone Av 139 CT66
Newfield Ri, NW2 119 CV62
Newfields, Welw.G.C. AL8 29 CV10
Newfield Way, St.Alb. AL4 43 CJ22
● New Ford Business Cen,
Wal.Cr. EN8 67 DZ34
Newford Cl, Hem.H. HP2 41 BP19
New Ford Rd, Wal.Cr. EN8 67 DZ34
New Forest La, Chig. IG7 103 EN51
● New Frontiers Science Pk,
Harl. CM19 51 EM16
Newgale Gdns, Edg. HA8 96 CM53
New Gdn Dr, West Dr. UB7
off Drayton Gdns 154 BL75
Newgate, Croy. CR0 202 DQ102
Newgate Cl, Felt. TW13 176 BY89
St. Albans AL4 43 CK17
NEWGATE STREET, Hert. SG13 47 DK24
Newgate St, E4 102 EF48
EC1 287 H8
Hertford SG13 47 DK22
Newgatestreet Rd,
Goffs Oak EN7 65 DP27
Newgate St Village, Hert. SG13 65 DL25
New Globe Wk, SE1 299 J2
New Goulston St, E1 288 A8
New Grn Pl, SE19 182 DS93
NEW GREENS, St.Alb. AL3 43 CD16
New Grns Av, St.Alb. AL3 43 CD15
New Hall Cl, Bov. HP3 57 BA27
Newhall Ct, Wal.Abb. EN9 68 EF33
New Hall Dr, Rom. RM3 106 FL53
Newhall Gdns, Walt. KT12 196 BW103
Newhall Ho, NW7
off Morphou Rd 97 CY50
Coll Newham 6th Form Coll,
Main Site, E13 292 B4
Stratford Site, E15 281 H7
Coll Newham Acad of Music,
E6 off Wakefield St 144 EL67
H Newham Cen for Mental
Health, E13 292 E5
Coll Newham Coll of Further
Ed, SE1 299 P4
East Ham Campus, E6
off High St S 145 EM68
Coll Newham Coll of Further
Ed, Little Ilford Cen, E12
off Browning Rd 125 EM64
Stratford Campus, E15 281 K7
Newham Collegiate Sixth
Form Cen, E6 145 EM67
● Newham Dockside, E16 304 G1
Newhams Row, SE1 299 P5
H Newham Uni Hosp, E13 292 D4
Gateway Surgical Cen, E13 292 E5
Newham Way, E6 293 P2
E16 291 N7
Newhaven Cl, Hayes UB3 155 BT77
Newhaven Cres, Ashf. TW15 175 BR92
Newhaven Gdns, SE9 164 EK84
Newhaven La, E16 291 M5
Newhaven Rd, SE25 202 DR99
Newhaven Spur, Slou. SL2 131 AP70
NEW HAW, Add. KT15 212 BK108
Sch New Haw Comm Jun Sch,
New Haw KT15
off The Avenue 212 BG110
New Haw Rd, Add. KT15 212 BJ106
New Heston Rd, Houns. TW5 156 BZ80
New Hope Ct, NW10 139 CV69
New Horizons, Borwd. WD6 78 CQ40
● New Horizons Ct, Brent. TW8 157 CG79
Newhouse Av, Rom. RM6 126 EX55
Newhouse Cl, N.Mal. KT3 198 CS101
Newhouse Cres, Wat. WD25 59 BV32
New Ho La, Grav. DA11 191 GF90
North Weald Bassett CM16 53 FC24
Redhill RH1 267 DK142
New Ho Pk, St.Alb. AL1 43 CG23
Newhouse Rd, Bov. HP3 57 BA26
Newhouse Wk, Mord. SM4 200 DC101
Newick Cl, Bex. DA5 187 FB86
Newick Rd, E5 122 DV62
Newing Grn, Brom. BR1 184 EK94
NEWINGTON, SE1 299 J8
Newington Barrow Way, N7 121 DM62
Newington Butts, SE1 299 H9
SE11 299 H9
Newington Causeway, SE1 299 H7
Newington Grn, N1 277 M2
N16 277 M2
Sch Newington Grn Prim Sch,
N16 277 M2
Newington Grn Rd, N1 277 L3
New Inn Bdy, EC2 287 P4
New Inn La, Guil. GU4 243 BB130
New Inn Pas, WC2 286 D9
New Inn Sq, EC2 287 P4
New Inn St, EC2 287 P4
New Inn Yd, EC2 287 P4
New James Ct, SE15
off Nunhead La 162 DV83
New Jersey Ter, SE15
off Nunhead La 162 DV83
New Jubilee Ct, Wdf.Grn. IG8
off Grange Av 102 EG52
New Kent Rd, SE1 299 J7
St. Albans AL1 43 CD20
New Kings Rd, SW6 306 F9
New King St, SE8 314 A2
Newland Cl, Pnr. HA5 94 BY51
St. Albans AL1 43 CG23
Newland Ct, EC1
off St. Luke's Est 287 L4
Wembley HA9 118 CN61
Newland Dr, Enf. EN1 82 DV39
Newland Gdns, W13 157 CG75
Hertford SG13 32 DS09
Sch Newland Ho Sch, Twick.
TW1 off Waldegrave Pk 177 CF91
Newland Rd, N8 121 DL55
Newlands, Hat. AL9 45 CW16
Newlands, The, Wall. SM6 219 DJ108
Newlands Av, Rad. WD7 61 CF34
Thames Ditton KT7 197 CE102
Woking GU22 227 AZ121
Newlands Cl, Edg. HA8 96 CL48
Hersham KT12 214 BY105
Horley RH6 268 DF146
Hutton CM13 109 GD45
Southall UB2 156 BY78
Wembley HA0 137 CJ65
Newlands Cor, Guil. GU4 260 BG136
Newlands Ct, SE9 185 EN86
Caterham CR3 236 DQ121
Newlands Cres, Guil. GU1 259 AZ136
Newlands Dr, Colnbr. SL3 153 BE83
Newlands Pk, SE26 183 DX92
Bedmond WD5 59 BT26
Newlands Pl, Barn. EN5 79 CX43
Newlands Quay, E1 300 G1
Newlands Rd, SW16 201 DL96
Hemel Hempstead HP1 39 BE19
Woodford Green IG8 102 EF47
Newland St, E16 305 H3
Newlands Wk, Wat. WD25 60 BX33
Newlands Way, Chess. KT9 215 CJ106
Potters Bar EN6 64 DB30
Newlands Wds, Croy. CR0 221 DZ109
New La, Sutt.Grn GU4 226 AY122
Newling Cl, E6 293 K8
New Lo Dr, Oxt. RH8 254 EF128
Sch New Lo Sch, Dor. RH4
off Chichester Rd 247 CH134
New London St, EC3 287 P10
● New Lydenburg
Commercial Est, SE7
off New Lydenburg St 304 D7
New Lydenburg St, SE7 304 D7
Newlyn Cl, Brick.Wd AL2 60 BY30
Orpington BR6 223 ET105
Uxbridge UB8 134 BN71
Newlyn Gdns, Har. HA2 116 BZ59
Newlyn Rd, N17 100 DT53
Barnet EN5 79 CZ42
Welling DA16 165 ET82
NEW MALDEN, KT3 198 CR97
⇌ New Malden 198 CS97
Newman Cl, Horn. RM11 128 FL57
Newman Pas, W1 285 M7
Newman Rd, E13 292 A3
E17 123 DX56
Bromley BR1 204 EG95
Croydon CR0 201 DM102
Hayes UB3 135 BV73
Horl. RH6 269 DJ146
Newmans Cl, Loug. IG10 85 EP41
Newman's Ct, EC3 287 M9
Newmans Dr, Hutt. CM13 109 GC45
Newmans Gate, Hutt.. CM13 109 GC45
Newmans La, Loug. IG10 85 EN41
Surbiton KT6 197 CK100
NEWMAN'S END, Harl. CM17 37 FE10
Newmans Rd, Nthflt DA11 191 GF89
Newman's Row, WC2 286 D7
Newman St, W1 285 M7
Newmans Way, Barn. EN4 80 DC39
Newman Yd, W1 285 M8
Newmarket Av, Nthlt. UB5 116 CA64
Newmarket Ct, St.Alb. AL3 42 CC19
Newmarket Grn, SE9
off Middle Pk Av 184 EK87
Newmarket Way, Horn. RM12 128 FL63
Newmarsh Rd, SE28 145 ET74
New Mill Rd, Orp. BR5 206 EW95
Newminster Rd, Mord. SM4 200 DC100
Sch New Monument Prim Sch,
Wok. GU22 off Alpha Rd 227 BC115
New Mt St, E15 281 H8
Newnes Path, SW15
off Putney Pk La 159 CV84
Newnham Av, Ruis. HA4 116 BW60
Newnham Cl, Loug. IG10 84 EK44
Northolt UB5 116 CC64
Slough SL2 132 AU74
Thornton Heath CR7 202 DQ96
Newnham Gdns, Nthlt. UB5 116 CC64
Sch Newnham Inf & Jun Schs,
Ruis. HA4 off Newnham Av 116 BW60
Newnham Ms, N22 99 DM53
Newnham Pl, Grays RM16 171 GG77
Newnham Rd, N22 99 DM53
Newnhams Cl, Brom. BR1 205 EM97
Newnham Ter, SE1 298 E6
Newnham Way, Har. HA3 118 CL57
Sch New N Comm Sch, N1 277 J8
New N Pl, EC2 287 N5
New N Rd, N1 287 M1
Ilford IG6 103 ER52
Reigate RH2 265 CZ137
New N St, WC1 286 C6
Newnton Cl, N4 122 DR59
New Oak Rd, N2 98 DC54
New Orleans Wk, N19 121 DK59
New Oxford St, WC1 285 P8
New Par, Ashf. TW15
off Church Rd 174 BM91
Chorleywood WD3
off Whitelands Av 73 BC42
Croxley Green WD3
off The Green 74 BM44
New Par Flats, Chorl. WD3
off Whitelands Av 73 BC42
New Pk Av, N13 100 DQ48
New Pk Cl, Nthlt. UB5 136 BY65
New Pk Ct, SW2 181 DL87
New Pk Dr, Hem.H. HP2 41 BP19
● New Pk Ind Est, N18 100 DW50
New Pk Par, SW2
off New Pk Rd 181 DL87
New Pk Rd, SW2 181 DK88
Ashford TW15 175 BQ92
Harefield UB9 92 BJ53
Newgate Street SG13 47 DK24
New Peachey La, Uxb. UB8 134 BK72
Newpiece, Loug. IG10 85 EP41
New Pl Gdns, Upmin. RM14 129 FR61
New Pl Sq, SE16 300 E6
New Plaistow Rd, E15 281 K8
New Plymouth Ho,
Rain. RM13 147 FF69
New Pond Par, Ruis. HA4
off West End Rd 115 BU62
New Pond St, Harl. CM17 36 EX13
Newport Av, E13 292 B5
E14 303 H1
Newport Cl, Enf. EN3 83 DY37
Newport Ct, WC2 285 P10
Newport Mead, Wat. WD19
off Kilmarnock Rd 94 BX49
Newport Pl, WC2 285 P10
Newport Rd, E10 123 EC61
E17 123 DY56
SW13 159 CU81
W3 158 CQ75
Hayes UB4 135 BR71
London Heathrow Airport
TW6 154 BN81
Slough SL2 131 AL70
Newports, Saw. CM21 36 EW06
Swanley BR8 207 FD101
Sch Newport Sch, E10
off Newport Rd 123 EC61
Newport St, SE11 298 C9
New Priory Ct, NW6 273 K7
New Providence Wf, E14 302 G2
New Provident Pl, Berk. HP4
off Holliday St 38 AX19
Newquay Cres, Har. HA2 116 BY61
Newquay Gdns, Wat. WD19
off Fulford Gro 93 BV47
Newquay Rd, SE6 183 EB89
New Quebec St, W1 284 F9
New Ride, SW7 296 E4
Jct New River Arms, Brox. EN10 67 DY25
New River Av, N8 121 DM55
Stanstead Abbotts SG12 33 EB11
New River Cl, Hodd. EN11 49 EB16
New River Ct, N5 277 L1
Cheshunt EN7 66 DV31
New River Cres, N13 99 DP49
New River Head, EC1 286 F2
● New River Trd Est,
Chsht EN8 67 DX26
New River Wk, N1 277 J5
New River Way, N4 122 DR59
New Rd, E1 288 E7
E4 101 EB49
N8 121 DL57
N9 100 DV47
N17 100 DT53
N22 100 DQ53
NW7 97 CY52
SE2 166 EX77
Albury GU5 260 BK139
Amersham HP6 55 AS37
Berkhamsted HP4 38 AX18
Brentford TW8 157 CK79
Brentwood CM14 108 FX47
Broxbourne EN10 49 DZ19
Chalfont St. Giles HP8 72 AY41
Chilworth GU4 259 BB141
Chipperfield WD4 57 BF30
Church End WD3 73 BF39
Claygate KT10 215 CF110
Coleshill HP7 55 AM42
Croxley Green WD3 74 BN43
Dagenham RM9, RM10 146 FA67
Datchet SL3 152 AX81
Dorking RH5 263 CK137
East Bedfont TW14 175 BR86
East Clandon GU4 244 BL131
Elstree WD6 77 CK44
Epping CM16 70 FA32
Esher KT10 196 CC104
Feltham TW14 175 BV88
Gomshall GU5 261 BQ139
Gravesend DA11 191 GH86
Grays RM17 170 GA79
Grays (Bridge Rd) RM17 170 GB79
Hanworth TW13 176 BY92
Harlington UB3 155 BQ80
Harlow CM17 36 EX11
Harrow HA1 117 CF63
Hertford SG14 32 DQ07
Hextable BR8 187 FF94
Hounslow TW3 156 CB84
Ilford IG3 125 ES61
Kingston upon Thames KT2 178 CN94
Lambourne End RM4 86 EX44
Langley SL3 153 BA76
Leatherhead KT22 215 CF110
Letchmore Heath WD25 77 CE39
Limpsfield RH8 254 EH130
Mitcham CR4 200 DF102
Northchurch HP4 38 AS17
Orpington BR6 206 EU101
Penn HP10 88 AC47
Radlett WD7 77 CE36
Rainham RM13 147 FG69
Richmond TW10 177 CJ91
Shenley WD7 62 CN34
Shepperton TW17 195 BP97
Smallfield RH6 269 DP148
South Darenth DA4 208 FQ96
South Mimms EN6 63 CU33
Staines-upon-Thames TW18 173 BC92
Stanborough AL8 29 CU12
Sundridge TN14 240 EX124
Swanley BR8 207 FF97

New Rd, Tadworth KT20 233 CW123
Uxbridge UB8 135 BQ70
Ware SG12 33 DX06
Watford WD17 76 BW42
Welling DA16 166 EV82
West Molesey KT8 196 CA97
Weybridge KT13 213 BQ106
Wonersh GU5 259 BB143
New Rd Hill, Downe BR6 222 EL109
Keston BR2 222 EL109
New Row, WC2 286 A10
Sch New Rush Hall Sch, Ilf. IG6
off Fencepiece Rd 103 EQ52
Newry Rd, Twick. TW1 157 CG84
Newsam Av, N15 122 DR57
● News Building, The, SE1 299 M3
Sch New Sch at W Heath, The,
Sev. TN13 off Ashgrove Rd 257 FH129
★ New Scotland Yd, SW1 297 N6
Newsham Rd, Wok. GU21 226 AT117
Newsholme Dr, N21 81 DM43
Newsom Pl, St.Alb. AL1 43 CE19
NEW SOUTHGATE, N11 99 DK49
⇌ New Southgate 99 DH50
● New Southgate Ind Est, N11 99 DJ50
🔒 New Spitalfields Mkt, E10 123 EA62
New Spring Gdns Wk, SE11 310 B1
● New Sq, Felt. TW14 175 BQ88
New Sq, WC2 286 D8
Slough SL1 152 AS75
Newstead, Hat. AL10 45 CT21
Newstead Av, Orp. BR6 205 ER104
Newstead Cl, N12 98 DE51
Newstead Ri, Cat. CR3 252 DV126
Newstead Rd, SE12 184 EE87
Newstead Wk, Cars. SM5 200 DC101
Newstead Way, SW19 179 CX91
Harlow CM20 35 EQ13
Sch Newstead Wd Sch for Girls,
Orp. BR6 off Avebury Rd 205 ER104
New St, EC2 287 P7
Berkhamsted HP4 38 AX19
Staines-upon-Thames TW18 174 BG91
Watford WD18 76 BW42
Westerham TN16 255 EQ127
New St Hill, Brom. BR1 184 EH92
New St Sq, EC4 286 F8
New Swan Yd, Grav. DA12
off Bank St 191 GH86
New Tank Hill Rd, Purf. RM19 168 FN76
Newteswell Dr, Wal.Abb. EN9 67 ED32
Newton Abbot Rd, Nthflt DA11 191 GF89
Newton Av, N10 98 DG53
W3 158 CQ75
Newton Cl, E17 123 DY58
Harrow HA2 116 CA61
Hoddesdon EN11 33 EB13
Slough SL3 153 AZ75
Newton Ct, Old Wind. SL4 172 AU86
Newton Cres, Borwd. WD6 78 CQ42
Newton Dr, Saw. CM21 36 EX06
Sch Newton Fm Inf & Jun Sch,
S.Har. HA2
off Ravenswood Cres 116 BZ61
Newton Gro, W4 158 CS77
Newton Ho, Enf. EN3
off Exeter Rd 83 DX41
● Newton Ind Est, Rom. RM6 126 EX56
Newton La, Old Wind. SL4 172 AV86
Newton Lo, SE10 303 M7
Newton Pk Pl, Chis. BR7 185 EM94
Newton Pl, E14 302 A8
Sch Newton Prep Sch, SW8 309 K6
Newton Rd, E15 281 H2
N15 122 DT57
NW2 119 CW62
SW19 179 CY94
W2 283 K9
Chigwell IG7 104 EV50
Harrow HA3 95 CE54
Isleworth TW7 157 CF82
Purley CR8 219 DJ112
Tilbury RM18 171 GG82
Welling DA16 166 EU83
Wembley HA0 138 CM66
Newtons Cl, Rain. RM13 147 FF66
Jct Newtons Cor, Rain. RM13 147 FE66
● Newtons Ct, Dart. DA2 169 FR84
Newtonside Orchard,
Wind. SL4 172 AU86
Sch Newtons Prim Sch,
Rain. RM13 off Lowen Rd 147 FD68
Newton St, WC2 286 B8
Newtons Yd, SW18
off Wandsworth High St 180 DA85
Newton Wk, Edg. HA8
off Roscoff Cl 96 CQ53
Newton Way, N18 100 DQ50
Newton Wd, Ashtd. KT21 216 CL114
Newton Wd Rd, Ashtd. KT21 232 CM116
NEWTOWN, Chesh. HP5 54 AP30
NEWTOWN, Dart. DA1 188 FN86
Sch Newtown Inf Sch & Nurs,
Chesh. HP5
off Berkhampstead Rd 54 AQ29
Newtown Rd, Denh. UB9 134 BH65
Newtown St, SW11 309 J6
New Trinity Rd, N2 120 DD55
New Turnstile, WC1 286 C7
New Union Cl, E14 302 F6
New Union St, EC2 287 L7
H New Victoria Hosp, The,
Kings.T. KT2 198 CS95
New Wanstead, E11 124 EF58
New Way La, Thres.B. CM17 53 FB16
New Way Rd, NW9 118 CS56
New Wf Rd, N1 276 B10
New Wickham La, Egh. TW20 173 BA94
New Windsor St, Uxb. UB8 134 BJ67
New Wd, Welw.G.C. AL7 30 DC08
Sch New Woodlands Sch,
Brom. BR1 off Shroffold Rd 184 EE91
NEWYEARS GREEN, Uxb. UB9 114 BN59
New Years Grn La, Hare. UB9 114 BL58
New Years La, Knock. TN14 239 ET116
New Zealand Av, Walt. KT12 195 BT102
New Zealand Way, W12 139 CV73
Rainham RM13 147 FF69
Nexus Ct, E11
off Kirkdale Rd 124 EE59
Niagara Av, W5 157 CJ77
Niagara Cl, N1
off Cropley St 277 K10
Cheshunt EN8 67 DX29
Nibthwaite Rd, Har. HA1 117 CE57
● Nice Business Pk, SE15 312 F3
Sch Nicholas Breakspear RC
Sch, St.Alb. AL4
off Colney Heath La 44 CL21
Nicholas Cl, Grnf. UB6 136 CB68
St. Albans AL3 43 CD17
South Ockendon RM15 149 FW69
Watford WD24 75 BV37
Nicholas Ct, E13 292 B3
N7 276 C3
Nicholas Gdns, W5 157 CK75
Slough SL1 131 AL74
Woking GU22 227 BE116
Nicholas La, EC4 287 M10
Hertford SG14 off Old Cross 32 DQ09
Nicholas Ms, W4
off Short Rd 158 CS79
Nicholas Pas, EC4 287 M10
Nicholas Rd, E1 289 H4
W11 294 C1
Croydon CR0 219 DL105
Dagenham RM8 126 EZ61
Elstree WD6 78 CM44
Nicholas Way, Hem.H. HP2 40 BM18
Northwood HA6 93 BQ53
Nicholay Rd, N19 121 DK61
Nichol Cl, N14 99 DK46
Nicholes Rd, Houns. TW3 156 CA84
Nichol La, Brom. BR1 184 EG94
Nicholl Rd, Epp. CM16 69 ET31
Nicholls, Wind. SL4 150 AJ83
Nicholls Av, Uxb. UB8 134 BN70
Nicholls Cl, Cat. CR3 236 DQ122
Nicholls Fld, Harl. CM18 52 EV16
Nichollsfield Wk, N7 276 C3
Nicholls Pt, E15 281 P8
Nicholls Twr, Harl. CM18 52 EU16
Nicholl St, E2 278 C9
Nichols Cl, N4
off Osborne Rd 121 DN60
Chessington KT9
off Merritt Gdns 215 CJ107
Nichols Ct, E2 288 A1
Nichols Grn, W5 138 CL71
● Nicholson Ct, Hodd. EN11 49 EB17
Nicholson Rd, Croy. CR0 202 DT102
Nicholson St, SE1 298 G3
Nicholson Wk, Egh. TW20 173 BA92
Nicholson Way, Sev. TN13 257 FK122
Nickelby Cl, SE28 146 EW72
Nickleby Cl, Uxb. UB8 135 BP72
Nickols Wk, SW18
off Jew's Row 160 DB84
Nicola Cl, Har. HA3 95 CD54
South Croydon CR2 220 DQ107
Nicola Ms, Ilf. IG6 103 EP52
Nicolas Wk, Grays RM16
off Godman Rd 171 GH75
Nicol Cl, Chal.St.P. SL9 90 AX53
Twickenham TW1
off Cassilis Rd 177 CH86
Nicol End, Chal.St.P. SL9 90 AW53
Nicoll Pl, NW4 119 CV58
Nicoll Rd, NW10 138 CS67
Nicoll Way, Borwd. WD6 78 CR43
Nicol Rd, Chal.St.P. SL9 90 AW53
Nicolson Dr,
Bushey Hth WD23 94 CC46
Nicolson Rd, Orp. BR5 206 EX101
Nicosia Rd, SW18 180 DE87
Nidderdale, Hem.H. HP2
off Wharfedale 40 BM17
Nido Twr, E1 288 A7
Niederwald Rd, SE26 183 DY91
Nield Rd, Hayes UB3 155 BT75
Nigel Cl, Nthlt. UB5 136 BY67
Nigel Fisher Way, Chess. KT9 215 CJ108
Nigel Ms, Ilf. IG1 125 EP63
Nigel Playfair Av, W6
off King St 159 CV77
Nigel Rd, E7 124 EJ64
SE15 312 C10
Nigeria Rd, SE7 164 EJ80
Nightingale Av, E4 102 EE50
Harrow HA1 117 CH59
Upminster RM14 129 FT60
West Horsley KT24 229 BR124
Nightingale Cl, E4 102 EE49
W4 158 CQ79
Abbots Langley WD5 59 BU31
Biggin Hill TN16 238 EJ115
Carshalton SM5 200 DG103
Cobham KT11 214 BX111
Epsom KT19 216 CN112
Northfleet DA11 190 GE91
Pinner HA5 116 BW57
Radlett WD7 77 CF36
Rickmansworth WD3 92 BK45
Nightingale Ct, E11
off Nightingale La 124 EH57
Hertford SG14 32 DQ09
Slough SL1
off St. Laurence Way 152 AU76
Sutton SM1 off Lind Rd 218 DC106
Woking GU21
off Inkerman Way 226 AT118
Nightingale Cres,
Harold Wd RM3 106 FL54
West Horsley KT24 229 BQ124
Nightingale Dr, Epsom KT19 216 CP107
Nightingale Est, E5 122 DU62
Nightingale Gro, SE13 183 ED85
Dartford DA1 168 FN84
Nightingale Hts, SE18
off Nightingale Vale 165 EP79
Nightingale Ho, E1
off Thomas More St 300 C2
W12 off Du Cane Rd 282 A9
Nightingale La, E11 124 EG57
N6 120 DE60
N8 121 DL56
SW4 180 DF87
SW12 180 DF87
Bromley BR1 204 EJ96
Ide Hill TN14 256 FB130
Richmond TW10 178 CL87
St. Albans AL1 43 CJ24
Nightingale Ms, E3 279 L10
E11 124 EG57
SE11 298 F8
Kingston upon Thames KT1
off South La 197 CK97
Nightingale Pk,
Farn.Com. SL2 131 AM66
Nightingale Pl, SE18 165 EN79
SW10 307 P2
Rickmansworth WD3
off Nightingale Rd 92 BK45
Sch Nightingale Prim Sch, E5
off Rendlesham Rd 122 DU63
E18 off Ashbourne Av 124 EJ56
N22 off Bounds Grn Rd 99 DM53
SE18 off Bloomfield Rd 165 EP78
Nightingale Rd, E5 122 DV62
N1 277 K5
N9 82 DW44
N22 99 DL53
NW10 139 CT68
W7 137 CF74
Bushey WD23 76 CA43
Carshalton SM5 200 DF104
Chesham HP5 54 AP29
Cheshunt EN7 66 DQ25
East Horsley KT24 245 BT125
Esher KT10 214 BZ106
Guildford GU1 242 AX134
Hampton TW12 176 CA92
Petts Wood BR5 205 EQ100
Rickmansworth WD3 92 BJ46
South Croydon CR2 221 DX111
Walton-on-Thames KT12 195 BV101
West Molesey KT8 196 CB99
Nightingales, Harl. CM17 52 EW17
Wal.Abb. EN9 off Roundhills 68 EE34
Nightingales, The, Stai. TW19 174 BM87
Sch Nightingale Sch, SW17
off Beechcroft Rd 180 DE89
Nightingales Cor, Amer. HP7
off Chalfont Sta Rd 72 AW40
Nightingale Shott, Egh. TW20 173 AZ93
Nightingales La, Ch.St.G. HP8 90 AX46
Nightingale Sq, SW12 180 DG87
Nightingale Vale, SE18 165 EN79
Nightingale Wk, SW4 181 DH86
Windsor SL4 151 AQ83
Nightingale Way, E6 293 H6
Bletchingley RH1 252 DS134
Denham UB9 113 BF59
Swanley BR8 207 FE97
Nile Cl, N16 122 DT62
Nile Dr, N9 100 DW47
Nile Path, SE18
off Jackson St 165 EN79
Nile Rd, E13 292 C1
Nile St, N1 287 K2
Nile Ter, SE15 312 A1
Nimbus Rd, Epsom KT19 216 CR110
Nimegen Way, SE22 182 DS85
Nimmo Dr, Bushey Hth WD23 95 CD45
Nimrod Cl, Nthlt. UB5 136 BX69
St. Albans AL4 43 CJ18
Nimrod Dr, Hat. AL10 44 CR17
Nimrod Pas, N1 277 P5
Nimrod Rd, SW16 181 DH93
Nina Mackay Cl, E15 281 J8
Nina Wk, N20
off Friern Barnet La 98 DC47
Nine Acre La, Hat. AL10 45 CT19
Nine Acres, Slou. SL1 131 AM74
Nine Acres Cl, E12 124 EL64
Hayes UB3 155 BQ76
Nineacres Way, Couls. CR5 235 DL116
Nine Ashes, Hunsdon SG12
off Acorn St 34 EK08
NINE ELMS, SW8 309 M4
Nine Elms Av, Uxb. UB8 134 BK71
Nine Elms Cl, Felt. TW14 175 BT88
Uxbridge UB8 134 BK72
Nine Elms Gro, Grav. DA11 191 GG87
Nine Elms La, SW8 309 M3
Ninefields, Wal.Abb. EN9 68 EF33
Ninehams Cl, Cat. CR3 236 DR120
Ninehams Gdns, Cat. CR3 236 DR120
Ninehams Rd, Cat. CR3 236 DR121
Tatsfield TN16 238 EJ121
Nine Stiles Cl, Denh. UB9 134 BH65
Nineteenth Rd, Mitch. CR4 201 DL98
Ninhams Wd, Orp. BR6 223 EN105
Ninian Rd, Hem.H. HP2 40 BL15
Ninnings Rd, Chal.St.P. SL9 91 AZ52
Ninnings Way, Chal.St.P. SL9 91 AZ52
Ninth Av, Hayes UB3 135 BU73
Nipper All, King.T. KT1 198 CL96
Nisbet Ho, E9 279 K3
Nisbett Wk, Sid. DA14
off Sidcup High St 186 EU91
Nita Rd, Warley CM14 108 FW50
Nithdale Rd, SE18 165 EP80
Nithsdale Gro, Uxb. UB10 115 BQ62
Niton Cl, Barn. EN5 79 CX44
Niton Rd, Rich. TW9 158 CN83
Niton St, SW6 306 C4
Niven Cl, Borwd. WD6 78 CQ39
Nixey Cl, Slou. SL1 152 AU75
No. 1 St, SE18 305 P7
Noah Cl, Enf. EN3 82 DW38
Noahs Ct Gdns, Hert. SG13 32 DS10
NOAK HILL, Rom. RM4 106 FK47
Noak Hill Rd, Rom. RM3 106 FJ49
Nobel Dr, Harling. UB3 155 BR80
Nobel Rd, N18 100 DW50
Noble Ct, Mitch. CR4 200 DD96
Slough SL2 132 AT74
Noble St, EC2 287 J8
Walton-on-Thames KT12 195 BV104
Nobles Way, Egh. TW20 172 AY93
Noel Coward Ho, SW1
off Vauxhall Br Rd 297 M9
NOEL PARK, N22 99 DN54
Sch Noel Pk Prim Sch, N22
off Gladstone Av 99 DN54
Noel Pk Rd, N22 99 DN54
Noel Rd, E6 292 G5
N1 276 G10
W3 138 CP72
Noel Sq, Dag. RM8 126 EW63
Noel St, W1 285 M9
Noel Ter, SE23
off Dartmouth Rd 182 DW89
Noke Dr, Red. RH1 250 DG133
Noke Fm Barns, Couls. CR5 234 DF122
Noke La, St.Alb. AL2 60 BY26
Nokes, The, Hem.H. HP1 40 BG18
Noke Side, St.Alb. AL2 60 CA27
Noko, W10 282 D2
Nolan Path, Borwd. WD6 78 CM39
Nolan Way, E5 122 DU63
Nolton Pl, Edg. HA8 96 CM53
Nonsuch Cl, Ilf. IG6 103 EP51
Nonsuch Ct Av, Epsom KT17 217 CV110
Sch Nonsuch High Sch for Girls,
Cheam SM3 off Ewell Rd 217 CX108
Nonsuch Ho, SW19
off Chapter Way 200 DD95
● Nonsuch Ind Est,
Epsom KT17 216 CS111
★ Nonsuch Mansion, Sutt. SM3 217 CW107
Sch Nonsuch Prim Sch,
Stoneleigh KT17
off Chadacre Rd 217 CV106
Nonsuch Wk, Sutt. SM2 217 CW110
Nook, The, Stans.Abb. SG12 33 EB11
Noons Cor Rd, Dor. RH5 262 BZ143
Nora Gdns, NW4 119 CX56
NORBITON, Kings.T. KT2 198 CP96
⇌ Norbiton 198 CN95
Norbiton Av, Kings.T. KT1 198 CN96
Norbiton Common Rd,
Kings.T. KT1 198 CP97
Norbiton Rd, E14 289 N8
Norbreck Gdns, NW10
off Lytham Gro 138 CM69
Norbreck Par, NW10
off Lytham Gro 138 CM69
Norbroke St, W12 139 CT73
Norburn St, W10 282 E7
NORBURY, SW16 201 DN95
⇌ Norbury 201 DM95
Norbury Av, SW16 201 DM95
Hounslow TW3 177 CD85
Thornton Heath CR7 201 DN96
Watford WD24 76 BW39
Norbury Cl, SW16 201 DN95
Norbury Ct Rd, SW16 201 DL97
Norbury Cres, SW16 201 DM95
Norbury Cross, SW16 201 DL97
Norbury Gdns, Rom. RM6 126 EX57
Norbury Gro, NW7 96 CS48
Norbury Hill, SW16 181 DN94
Sch Norbury Manor Business
& Enterprise Coll for Girls,
Th.Hth. CR7
off Kensington Av 201 DN95
Sch Norbury Manor Prim Sch,
SW16 off Abingdon Rd 201 DL95
Norbury Pk, Mick. RH5 247 CF127
Norbury Ri, SW16 201 DL97
Norbury Rd, E4 101 EA50
Feltham TW13 175 BT90
Reigate RH2 249 CZ134
Thornton Heath CR7 202 DQ96
Sch Norbury Sch, Har. HA1
off Welldon Cres 117 CE57
Norbury Way, Bkhm KT23 246 CC125
Norcombe Gdns, Har. HA3 117 CJ58
Norcombe Ho, N19
off Wedmore St 121 DK62
Norcott Cl, Hayes UB4 136 BW70
Norcott Rd, N16 122 DU61
Norcroft Gdns, SE22 182 DU87
Norcutt Rd, Twick. TW2 177 CE88
Nordenfeldt Rd, Erith DA8 167 FD78
Nordmann Pl, S.Ock. RM15 149 FX70
Norelands Dr, Burn. SL1 130 AJ68
Norfield Rd, Dart. DA2 187 FC91
Norfolk Av, N13 99 DP51
N15 122 DT58
Slough SL1 131 AQ71
South Croydon CR2 220 DU110
Watford WD24 76 BW38
Norfolk Cl, N2 120 DE55
N13 99 DP51
Barnet EN4 80 DG42
Dartford DA1 188 FN86
Horley RH6 268 DF149
Twick. TW1 off Cassilis Rd 177 CH86
Norfolk Ct, Dor. RH5 263 CK140
Norfolk Cres, W2 284 D8
Sidcup DA15 185 ES87
Norfolk Fm Cl, Wok. GU22 227 BD116
Norfolk Fm Rd, Wok. GU22 227 BD115
Norfolk Gdns, Bexh. DA7 166 EZ81
Borehamwood WD6 78 CR42
Norfolk Ho, SW1 off Regency St 297 P8
Norfolk Ho Rd, SW16 181 DK90
Norfolk La, Mid Holm. RH5 263 CH142
Norfolk Ms, W10 282 F7
Norfolk Pl, W2 284 B8
Chafford Hundred RM16 169 FW78
Welling DA16 166 EU82
Norfolk Rd, E6 145 EM67
E17 101 DX54
NW8 274 B9
NW10 138 CS66
SW19 180 DE94
Barking IG11 145 ES66
Barnet EN5 80 DA41
Claygate KT10 215 CE106
Dagenham RM10 127 FB64
Dorking RH4 263 CG136
Enfield EN3 82 DV44
Feltham TW13 176 BW88
Gravesend DA12 191 GK86
Harrow HA1 116 CB57
Ilford IG3 125 ES60
Rickmansworth WD3 92 BL46
Romford RM7 127 FC58
South Holmwood RH5 263 CJ144
Thornton Heath CR7 202 DQ97
Upminster RM14 128 FN62
Uxbridge UB8 134 BK65
Norfolk Row, SE1 298 C8
Norfolk Sq, W2 284 B9
Norfolk Sq Ms, W2 284 B9
Norfolk St, E7 281 N2
Norfolk Ter, W6 306 E1
Norgrove Pk, Ger.Cr. SL9 112 AY56
Norgrove St, SW12 180 DG87
Norheads La, Bigg.H. TN16 238 EJ116
Warlingham CR6 238 EG119
Norhyrst Av, SE25 202 DT97
NORK, Bans. SM7 233 CY115
Nork Gdns, Bans. SM7 217 CY114
Nork Ri, Bans. SM7 233 CX116
Nork Way, Bans. SM7 233 CY115
Norland Ho, W11 294 D3
Norland Pl, W11 294 F3
Sch Norland Pl Sch, W11 294 E3
Norland Rd, W11 294 D3
Norlands Cres, Chis. BR7 205 EP95
Norlands Gate, Chis. BR7 205 EP95
Norlands La, Egh. TW20 193 BE97
Norland Sq, W11 294 F3
Norley Vale, SW15 179 CU88
Norlington Rd, E10 123 EC60
E11 123 EC60
Sch Norlington Sch, E10
off Norlington Rd 123 ED60
Norman Av, N22 99 DP53
Epsom KT17 217 CT112
Feltham TW13 176 BY89
South Croydon CR2 220 DQ110
Southall UB1 136 BY73
Twickenham TW1 177 CH87
Normanby Cl, SW15 179 CZ85
Normanby Rd, NW10 119 CT63
Norman Cl, Epsom KT18 233 CV119
Orpington BR6 205 EQ104
Romford RM5 105 FB54
St. Albans AL1 43 CE23
Waltham Abbey EN9 67 ED33
Norman Colyer Ct, Epsom
KT19 off Hollymoor La 216 CR110
Norman Ct, Ilf. IG2 125 ER59
Potters Bar EN6 64 DC30
Woodford Green IG8
off Monkhams Av 102 EH50
Norman Cres, Brwd. CM13 109 GA48
Hounslow TW5 156 BX81
Pinner HA5 94 BW53
Sch Normand Cft Comm Sch for
Early Years & Prim Ed, W14 307 H2
Normand Gdns, W14
off Greyhound Rd 306 F2
Normand Ms, W14 306 F2
Normand Rd, W14 306 G2
Normandy Av, Barn. EN5 79 CZ43
Normandy Cl, SE26 183 DY90
Normandy Ct, Hem.H. HP2 40 BK19
Normandy Dr, Berk. HP4 38 AV17
Hayes UB3 135 BQ72
Normandy Ho, Enf. EN2
off Cedar Rd 82 DQ38
Normandy Pl, W12
off Bourbon La 294 C3
Sch Normandy Prim Sch,
Barne. DA7 off Fairford Av 167 FD81
Normandy Rd, SW9 310 E7
St. Albans AL3 43 CD18
Normandy Ter, E16 292 A9
Normandy Wk, Egh. TW20
off Mullens Rd 173 BC92
Normandy Way, Erith DA8 167 FE81
Hoddesdon EN11 49 EC16
Norman Gro, E3 289 M1
Normanhurst, Ashf. TW15 174 BN92
Hutton CM13 109 GC44
Normanhurst Av, Bexh. DA7 166 EX81
Normanhurst Dr, Twick. TW1
off St. Margarets Rd 177 CH85
Normanhurst Rd, SW2 181 DM89
Orpington BR5 206 EV96
Walton-on-Thames KT12 196 BX103
Sch Normanhurst Sch, E4
off Station Rd 101 ED45
Norman Rd, E6 293 K4
E11 123 ED61
N15 122 DT57
SE10 314 D4
SW19 180 DC94
Ashford TW15 175 BR93
Belvedere DA17 167 FB76
Dartford DA1 188 FL88
Hornchurch RM11 127 FG59
Ilford IG1 125 EP64
Sutton SM1 218 DA106
Thornton Heath CR7 201
DP99 Normans, The, Slou. SL2 132 AV72
Normans Cl, NW10 138 CR65
Gravesend DA11 191 GG87
Uxbridge UB8 134 BL71
Normansfield Av, Tedd. TW11 177 CJ94
Normansfield Cl,
Bushey WD23 94 CB45
Normanshire Av, E4 101 EA49
Normanshire Dr, E4 101 EA49
Normans Mead, NW10 138 CR65
Norman St, EC1 287 J3
Normanton Av, SW19 180 DA89
Normanton Pk, E4 102 EE48
Normanton Rd, S.Croy. CR2 220 DS107
Normanton St, SE23 183 DX89
Norman Way, N14 99 DL47
W3 138 CP71
Normington Cl, SW16 181 DN92
Norrels Dr, E.Hors. KT24 245 BT126
Norrels Ride, E.Hors. KT24 245 BT125
Norrice Lea, N2 120 DD57
Norris Cl, Epsom KT19 216 CP111
London Colney AL2 61 CH26
Norris Gro, Brox. EN10 49 DY20
Norris La, Hodd. EN11 49 EA16
Norris Ri, Hodd. EN11 49 DZ16
Norris Rd, Hodd. EN11 49 EA17
Staines-upon-Thames TW18 173 BF91
Norris St, SW1 297 N1
Norris Way, Dart. DA1 167 FF83
Norroy Rd, SW15 159 CX84
Norrys Cl, Cockfos. EN4 80 DF43
Norrys Rd, Cockfos. EN4 80 DF42
Norseman Cl, Ilf. IG3 126 EV60
Norseman Way, Grnf. UB6
off Olympic Way 136 CB67
Norstead Pl, SW15 179 CU89
Norsted La, Pr.Bot. BR6 224 EU110
North Access Rd, E17 123 DX58
North Acre, NW9 96 CS53
Banstead SM7 233 CZ116
NORTH ACTON, W3 138 CR70
⊖ North Acton 138 CR70
North Acton Rd, NW10 138 CR69
Northallerton Way, Rom. RM3 106 FK50
Northall Rd, Bexh. DA7 167 FC82
Northampton Av, Slou. SL1 131 AQ72
Northampton Gro, N1 277 L3
Northampton Pk, N1 277 K4
Northampton Rd, EC1 286 F4
Croydon CR0 202 DU103
Enfield EN3 83 DY42
Northampton Row, EC1 286 F3
Northampton Sq, EC1 286 G3
Northampton St, N1 277 J6
Coll North & W Essex Adult
Comm Coll, Northbrooks Ho,
Harl. CM19 off Northbrooks 51 EQ16
Rivermill Cen, Harl. CM20
off Hodings Rd 35 EQ13
Northanger Rd, SW16 181 DL93
North App, Nthwd. HA6 93 BQ47
Watford WD25 75 BT35
🔒 North Arc, Croy. CR0
off North End 202 DQ103
North Audley St, W1 284 G9
North Av, N18 100 DU49
W13 137 CH72
Brentwood CM14 107 FR45
Carshalton SM5 218 DG108
Harrow HA2 116 CB58
Hayes UB3 135 BU73
Richmond TW9
off Sandycombe Rd 158 CN81
Shenley WD7 62 CL32
Southall UB1 136 BZ73
Whiteley Village KT12 213 BS109
NORTHAW, Pot.B. EN6 64 DF30

Northaw Cl, Hem.H. HP2 41 BP15
Northaw C of E Prim Sch, Northaw EN6 off Vineyards Rd 86 DG30
Northaw Pl, Northaw EN6 64 DD30
Northaw Rd E, Cuffley EN6 65 DK31
Northaw Rd W, Northaw EN6 64 DG30
North Bk, NW8 284 B3
Northbank Rd, E17 101 EC54
North Barn, Brox. EN10 49 EA21
NORTH BECKTON, E6 293 H5
North Beckton Prim Sch, E6 293 K6
North Birkbeck Rd, E11 123 ED62
Northborough Rd, SW16 201 DK97
Slough SL2 131 AN70
Northbourne, Brom. BR2 204 EG101
Godalming GU7 258 AT143
Northbourne Ho, E5 off Pembury Rd 278 E2
Northbourne Rd, SW4 161 DK84
North Branch Av, W10 282 B3
North Br Ho Jun Sch, NW3 273 P3
North Br Ho Sen Sch, NW1 275 J9
Northbridge Rd, Berk. HP4 38 AT17
Northbrook Dr, Nthwd. HA6 93 BS53
Northbrook Rd, N22 99 DL52
SE13 183 ED85
Barnet EN5 79 CY44
Croydon CR0 202 DR99
Ilford IG1 125 EN61
Northbrooks, Harl. CM19 51 EQ16
Northburgh St, EC1 287 H4
North Burnham Cl, Burn. SL1 off Wyndham Cres 130 AH68
Northbury Inf & Jun Schs, Bark. IG11 off North St 145 EQ65
North Carriage Dr, W2 284 C10
NORTH CHEAM, Sutt. SM3 217 CW105
NORTHCHURCH, Berk. HP4 38 AT17
Northchurch, SE17 299 M10
Northchurch Rd, N1 277 L6
Wembley HA9 138 CM65
Northchurch Ter, N1 277 N7
North Circular Rd, E4 (A406) 101 DZ52
E6 (A406) 145 EP68
E11 (A406) 102 EJ54
E12 (A406) 125 EP64
E17 (A406) 101 DZ52
E18 (A406) 102 EJ54
N3 (A406) 120 DB55
N11 (A406) 98 DD53
N12 (A406) 98 DD53
N13 (A406) 99 DN50
N18 (A406) 100 DS50
NW2 (A406) 118 CS62
NW10 (A406) 138 CP66
NW11 (A406) 119 CY56
W3 (A406) 158 CM75
W4 (A406) 158 CM75
W5 (A406) 158 CM75
Barking (A406) IG11 145 EP68
Ilford (A406) IG1, IG4 124 EL60
Northcliffe Cl, Wor.Pk. KT4 198 CS104
Northcliffe Dr, N20 97 CZ46
North Cl, Barn. EN5 79 CW43
Beaconsfield HP9 110 AH55
Bexleyheath DA6 166 EX84
Chigwell IG7 104 EU50
Dagenham RM10 146 FA67
Feltham TW14 off North Rd 175 BR86
Morden SM4 199 CY98
North Holmwood RH5 263 CJ140
St. Albans AL2 60 CB25
Windsor SL4 151 AM81
North Colonnade, The, E14 302 B2
North Common, Wey. KT13 213 BP105
North Common Rd, W5 138 CL73
Uxbridge UB8 114 BK64
Northcote, Add. KT15 212 BK105
Oxshott KT22 214 CC114
Pinner HA5 94 BW54
Northcote Av, W5 138 CL73
Isleworth TW7 177 CG85
Southall UB1 136 BY73
Surbiton KT5 198 CN101
Northcote Cl, W.Hors. KT24 245 BQ125
Northcote Cres, W.Hors. KT24 245 BQ125
Northcote Lo Sch, SW11 off Bolingbroke Gro 180 DF86
Northcote Ms, SW11 off Northcote Rd 160 DE84
Northcote Rd, E17 123 DY56
NW10 138 CS66
SW11 160 DE84
Croydon CR0 202 DR100
Gravesend DA11 191 GF88
New Malden KT3 198 CQ97
Sidcup DA14 185 ES91
Twickenham TW1 177 CG85
West Horsley KT24 245 BQ125
North Cotts, Lon.Col. AL2 61 CG25
Northcott Av, N22 99 DL53
Northcotts, Abb.L. WD5 off Long Elms 59 BR33
Hatfield AL9 45 CW17
North Countess Rd, E17 101 DZ54
Northcourt, Mill End WD3 off Springwell Av 92 BG46
NORTH CRAY, Sid. DA14 186 FA90
North Cray Rd, Bex. DA5 186 EZ90
Sidcup DA14 186 EY93
North Cres, E16 291 H5
N3 97 CZ54
WC1 285 N6
Northcroft, Slou. SL2 131 AP70
Wooburn Green HP10 110 AE56
Northcroft Cl, Eng.Grn TW20 172 AV92
Northcroft Gdns, Eng.Grn TW20 172 AV92
Northcroft Rd, W13 157 CH75
Englefield Green TW20 172 AV92
Epsom KT19 216 CR108
Northcroft Ter, W13 off Northcroft Rd 157 CH75
Northcroft Vil, Eng.Grn TW20 172 AV92
North Cross Rd, SE22 182 DT85
Ilford IG6 125 EQ56
North Dene, NW7 96 CR48
Hounslow TW3 156 CB81
Northdene, Chig. IG7 103 ER50
Northdene Gdns, N15 122 DT58
North Down, S.Croy. CR2 220 DS111
Northdown Cl, Ruis. HA4 115 BT62
Northdown Gdns, Ilf. IG2 125 ES57
Northdown La, Guil. GU1 258 AY137
Northdown Rd, Chal.St.P. SL9 90 AY51
Hatfield AL10 45 CU21
Hornchurch RM11 127 FH59
Longfield DA3 209 FX96
Sutton SM2 218 DA110
Welling DA16 166 EV82
Woldingham CR3 237 EA123
North Downs Business Pk, Dunt.Grn TN13 241 FC117
North Downs Cres, New Adgtn CR0 221 EB110
North Downs Private Hosp, The, Cat. CR3 252 DT125
North Downs Rd, New Adgtn CR0 221 EB110
Northdown St, N1 276 B10
North Downs Way, Bet. RH3 249 CU130
Caterham CR3 251 DN126
Dorking RH5 247 CE133
Godstone RH9 253 DY128
Guildford GU3, GU4 258 AT138
Oxted RH8 254 EE126
Redhill RH1 250 DG128
Reigate RH2 250 DD130
Sevenoaks TN13, TN14 241 FD118
Tadworth KT20 249 CX130
Westerham TN16 239 ER121
North Dr, SW16 181 DJ91
Beaconsfield HP9 110 AG55
Beckenham BR3 203 EB98
Hatfield AL9 off Great N Rd 45 CW16
Hounslow TW3 156 CC82
Oaklands AL4 44 CL18
Orpington BR6 223 ES105
Romford RM2 128 FJ55
Ruislip HA4 115 BS59
Slough SL2 132 AS69
Virginia Water GU25 192 AS100
North Dulwich 182 DR85
North Ealing 138 CM72
North Ealing Prim Sch, W5 off Pitshanger La 137 CH70
North End, NW3 120 DC61
Buckhurst Hill IG9 102 EJ45
Croydon CR0 202 DQ103
Noak Hill RM3 106 FJ47
Northend, Hem.H. HP3 41 BP22
Warley CM14 108 FW50
North End Av, NW3 120 DC61
Northend Cl, Flack.Hth HP10 110 AC56
North End Cres, W14 294 G9
North End Ho, W14 294 F9
North End La, Downe BR6 223 EN110
North End Par, W14 294 F9
Northend Prim Sch, Erith DA8 off Peareswood Rd 167 FF81
North End Rd, NW11 120 DA60
SW6 307 H2
W14 294 G10
Wembley HA9 118 CN62
Northend Rd, Dart. DA1 167 FF80
Erith DA8 167 FF80
Northend Trd Est, Erith DA8 167 FE81
North End Way, NW3 120 DC61
Northern Av, N9 100 DT47
Northernhay Wk, Mord. SM4 199 CY98
Northern Perimeter Rd, Lon.Hthrw Air. TW6 155 BQ81
Northern Perimeter Rd W, Lon.Hthrw Air. TW6 154 BK81
Northern Relief Rd, Bark. IG11 145 EP66
Northern Rd, E13 144 EH67
Slough SL2 131 AR70
Northern Service Rd, Barn. EN5 79 CY41
Northern Wds, Flack.Hth HP10 110 AC56
Northey Av, Sutt. SM2 217 CZ110
North Eyot Gdns, W6 159 CU78
Northey St, E14 289 M10
North Feltham Trading Est, Felt. TW14 175 BV85
Northfield, Hat. AL10 off Longmead 45 CV15
Loughton IG10 84 EK42
Shalford GU4 258 AY142
Northfield Av, W5 157 CH75
W13 157 CH75
Orpington BR5 206 EW100
Pinner HA5 116 BX56
Northfield Cl, Brom. BR1 204 EL95
Hayes UB3 155 BS76
Northfield Ct, Stai. TW18 194 BH95
Northfield Cres, Sutt. SM3 217 CY105
Northfield Fm Ms, Cob. KT11 213 BU113
Northfield Gdns, Dag. RM9 off Northfield Rd 126 EZ63
Watford WD24 76 BW37
Northfield Pk, Hayes UB3 155 BT76
Northfield Path, Dag. RM9 126 EZ62
Northfield Pl, Wey. KT13 213 BP108
Northfield Rd, E6 145 EM66
N16 122 DS59
W13 157 CH75
Barnet EN4 80 DE41
Borehamwood WD6 78 CP39
Cobham KT11 213 BU113
Dagenham RM9 126 EZ63
Enfield EN3 82 DV43
Eton Wick SL4 151 AM77
Hounslow TW5 156 BX79
Staines-upon-Thames TW18 194 BH95
Waltham Cross EN8 67 DY32
Northfields 157 CH76
Northfields, SW18 160 DA84
Ashtead KT21 232 CL119
Grays RM17 170 GC77
Northfields Ind Est, Wem. HA0 138 CN67
Northfields Rd, W3 138 CP71
NORTH FINCHLEY, N12 98 DD50
NORTHFLEET, Grav. DA10 190 GD86
Northfleet 190 GA86
NORTHFLEET GREEN, Grav. DA13 190 GC92
Northfleet Grn Rd, Grav. DA13 190 GC93
Northfleet Ind Est, Nthflt DA11 170 GA84
Northfleet Sch for Girls, Grav. DA11 off Hall Rd 190 GD89
Northfleet Tech Coll, Nthflt DA11 off Colyer Rd 190 GD88
North Flockton St, SE16 300 C4
North Gdn, E14 off Westferry Circ 301 P2
North Gdns, SW19 180 DD94
North Gate, NW8 284 C1
Harl. CM20 35 EQ14
Northgate, Gat. RH6 268 DF151
Nthwd. HA6 93 BQ52
Northgate Ct, SW9 off Canterbury Cres 161 DN83
Northgate Dr, NW9 118 CS58
Northgate Ind Pk, Rom. RM5 104 EZ54
Northgate Path, Borwd. WD6 78 CM38
North Gates, N12 off High Rd 98 DC53
North Glade, The, Bex. DA5 186 EZ87
North Gower St, NW1 285 M3
North Grn, NW9 off Clayton Fld 96 CS52
Slough SL1 132 AS73
North Greenwich 303 J4
North Greenwich 303 J4
North Greenwich Uni Tech Coll, SE7 304 F8
North Gro, N6 120 DG59
N15 122 DR57
Chertsey KT16 193 BF100
Harlow CM18 52 EU16
North Harringay Prim Sch, N8 off Falkland Rd 121 DN56
NORTH HARROW, Har. HA2 116 CA58
North Harrow 116 CA57
North Hatton Rd, Lon.Hthrw Air. TW6 155 BR81
North Hill, N6 120 DF57
Rickmansworth WD3 73 BE40
North Hill Av, N6 120 DF58
North Hill Dr, Rom. RM3 106 FK48
North Hill Grn, Rom. RM3 106 FK49
NORTH HILLINGDON, Uxb. UB10 135 BQ66
North Hillingdon Adult Ed Cen, Uxb. UB10 off Long La 115 BP64
NORTH HOLMWOOD, Dor. RH5 263 CH141
North Ho, Harl. CM18 off Bush Fair 51 ET17
NORTH HYDE, Sthl. UB2 156 BY77
North Hyde Gdns, Hayes UB3 155 BU77
North Hyde La, Houns. TW5 156 BY78
Southall UB2 156 BY78
North Hyde Rd, Hayes UB3 155 BT76
Northiam, N12 98 DA48
Northiam St, E9 278 F9
Northington St, WC1 286 C5
NORTH KENSINGTON, W10 282 D7
North Kent Av, Nthflt DA11 190 GC86
Northlands, Pot.B. EN6 64 DD31
Northlands Av, Orp. BR6 223 ES105
Northlands St, SE5 311 J9
North La, Tedd. TW11 177 CF93
North Lo Cl, SW15 179 CX85
North London Business Pk, N11 98 DF47
North London Collegiate Sch, Edg. HA8 off Canons Dr 96 CL50
North London Int Sch, The, IB Diploma Cen, N11 off Friern Barnet La 98 DF50
Upr Sch, N11 off Friern Barnet Rd 98 DF50
Lwr Sch, N12 off Woodside Av 98 DC48
Lwr Sch, N12 off Woodside Pk Rd 98 DB49
NORTH LOOE, Epsom KT17 217 CW113
North Loop Rd, Uxb. UB8 134 BK69
North Mall, N9 off Edmonton Grn Shop Cen 100 DV47
North Mead, Red. RH1 250 DF131
Northmead Jun Sch, Guil. GU2 off Grange Rd 242 AV131
Northmead Rd, Slou. SL2 131 AM70
North Ms, WC1 286 D5
North Middlesex Uni Hosp, N18 100 DS50
North Moors, Guil. GU1 242 AY130
NORTH MYMMS, Hat. AL9 63 CU25
North Mymms Pk, N.Mymms AL9 63 CT25
NORTH OCKENDON, Upmin. RM14 129 FV64
Northolm, Edg. HA8 96 CR49
Northolme Cl, Grays RM16 off Premier Av 170 GC76
Northolme Gdns, Edg. HA8 96 CN53
Northolme Ri, Orp. BR6 205 ES103
Northolme Rd, N5 122 DQ63
NORTHOLT, UB5 136 BZ66
Northolt 136 CA66
Northolt, N17 100 DR54
Northolt Av, Ruis. HA4 115 BV64
Northolt Gdns, Grnf. UB6 117 CF64
Northolt High Sch, Nthlt. UB5 off Eastcote La 136 BZ65
Northolt Park 116 CB63
Northolt Rd, Har. HA2 116 CB63
London Heathrow Airport TW6 154 BK81
Northolt Trading Est, Nthlt. UB5 136 CB66
Northolt Way, Horn. RM12 148 FJ65
North Orbital Commercial Pk, St.Alb. AL1 43 CG24
North Orbital Rd, Denh. UB9 113 BF60
Hatfield AL10 29 CV14
Rickmansworth WD3 113 BF55
St. Albans AL1, AL2, AL4 61 CK25
Watford WD25 59 BU34
Northover, Brom. BR1 184 EF90
North Par, Chess. KT9 216 CL106
Edgware HA8 off Mollison Way 96 CN54
Southall UB1 off North Rd 136 CA72
North Pk, SE9 185 EM86
Chalfont St. Peter SL9 112 AY56
Iver SL0 153 BC76
North Pk La, Gdse. RH9 252 DU129
North Pas, SW18 180 DA85
North Perimeter Rd, Uxb. UB8 off Kingston La 134 BL69
North Pl, Guil. GU1 258 AX135
Mitcham CR4 180 DF94
Teddington TW11 177 CF93
Waltham Abbey EN9 off Highbridge St 67 EB33
North Pt, N8 121 DM57
Northpoint, Brom. BR1 off Sherman Rd 204 EG95
Northpoint Cl, Sutt. SM1 200 DC104
Northpoint Ho, N1 off Essex Rd 277 L5
Northpoint Sq, NW1 275 N4
North Pole La, Kes. BR2 222 EF107
North Pole Rd, W10 282 A7
Northport St, N1 277 M9
North Prim Sch, Sthl. UB1 off Meadow Rd 136 BZ73
North Ride, W2 296 C1
Northridge Rd, Grav. DA12 191 GJ90
Northridge Way, Hem.H. HP1 39 BF21
North Riding, Brick.Wd AL2 60 CA30
North Ri, W2 off St. Georges Flds 284 D9
North Rd, N6 120 DG59
N7 275 P4
N9 100 DV46
SE18 165 ES77
SW19 180 DC93
W5 157 CK76
Belvedere DA17 167 FB76
Berkhamsted HP4 38 AV19
Brentford TW8 158 CL79
Brentwood CM14 108 FW46
Bromley BR1 204 EH95
Chadwell Heath RM6 126 EY57
Chesham Bois HP6 55 AQ36
Chorleywood WD3 73 BD43
Dartford DA1 187 FF86
Edgware HA8 96 CP53
Feltham TW14 175 BR86
Guildford GU2 242 AV131
Havering-atte-Bower RM4 105 FE48
Hayes UB3 135 BR71
Hersham KT12 214 BW106
Hertford SG14 31 DP09
Hoddesdon EN11 49 EA16
Ilford IG3 125 ES61
Purfleet RM19 168 FQ77
Reigate RH2 265 CZ137
Richmond TW9 158 CN83
South Ockendon RM15 149 FW68
Southall UB1 136 CA73
Surbiton KT6 197 CK100
Waltham Cross EN8 67 DY33
West Drayton UB7 154 BM76
West Wickham BR4 203 EB102
Woking GU21 227 BA116
North Rd Av, Brwd. CM14 108 FW46
Hertford SG14 31 DN08
North Rd Gdns, Hert. SG14 31 DP09
Northrop Rd, Lon.Hthrw Air. TW6 155 BS81
North Row, W1 284 F10
North Several, SE3 315 H8
NORTH SHEEN, Rich. TW9 158 CN82
North Sheen 158 CN84
Northside Prim Sch, N12 off Albert St 98 DC50
Northside Rd, Brom. BR1 off Mitchell Way 204 EG95
North Side Wandsworth Common, SW18 180 DC85
Northspur Rd, Sutt. SM1 200 DA104
North Sq, N9 off Edmonton Grn Shop Cen 100 DV47
North Sq, NW11 120 DA57
Northstand Apts, N5 121 DP62
North Sta App, S.Nutfld RH1 267 DM136
Northstead Rd, SW2 181 DN89
North St, E13 292 A1
NW4 119 CW57
SW4 309 L10
Barking IG11 145 EP65
Bexleyheath DA7 166 FA84
Bromley BR1 204 EG95
Carshalton SM5 200 DF104
Dartford DA1 188 FK87
Dorking RH4 263 CG136
Egham TW20 173 AZ92
Godalming GU7 off Station Rd 258 AT144
Gravesend DA12 off South St 191 GH87
Guildford GU1 258 AX135
Hornchurch RM11 128 FK59
Isleworth TW7 157 CG83
Leatherhead KT22 231 CG121
Lower Nazeing EN9 50 EE22
Redhill RH1 250 DF133
Romford RM1, RM5 127 FD55
Westcott RH4 262 CC137
North St Pas, E13 144 EH68
North Tenter St, E1 288 B9
North Ter, SW3 296 C7
Windsor SL4 off Windsor Castle 152 AS80
Northumberland All, EC3 287 P9
Northumberland Av, E12 124 EJ60
WC2 298 A2
Enfield EN1 82 DV39
Hornchurch RM11 128 FJ57
Isleworth TW7 157 CF81
Welling DA16 165 ER84
Northumberland Cl, Erith DA8 167 FC80
Stanwell TW19 174 BL86
Northumberland Cres, Felt. TW14 175 BS86
Northumberland Gdns, N9 100 DT48
Bromley BR1 205 EN98
Isleworth TW7 157 CG80
Mitcham CR4 201 DK99
Northumberland Gro, N17 100 DV52
NORTHUMBERLAND HEATH, Erith DA8 167 FC80
Northumberland Heath Prim Sch, Erith DA8 off Byron Dr 167 FB80
Northumberland Park 100 DV53
Northumberland Pk, N17 100 DT52
Erith DA8 167 FC80
Northumberland Pk Comm Sch, N17 off Trulock Rd 100 DU52
Northumberland Pk Ind Est, N17 off Willoughby La 100 DV52
Northumberland Pl, W2 283 J8
Richmond TW10 177 CK85
Northumberland Rd, E6 293 H8
E17 123 EA59
Har. HA2 116 BZ57
Istead Rise DA13 191 GF94
New Barnet EN5 80 DC44
Northumberland Row, Twick. TW2 off Colne Rd 177 CE88
Northumberland St, WC2 298 A2
Northumberland Wk, Iver SL0 153 BE75
Northumberland Way, Erith DA8 167 FC81
Northumbria St, E14 290 B8
North Verbena Gdns, W6 off St. Peter's Sq 159 CU78
Northview, N7 121 DL62
Hemel Hempstead HP1 off Winkwell 39 BD22
Swanley BR8 207 FE96
North Vw, SW19 179 CV92
W5 137 CJ70
Ilford IG6 104 EU52
Pinner HA5 116 BW59
North Vw Av, Til. RM18 171 GG81
Northview Cres, NW10 119 CT63
North Vw Cres, Epsom KT18 233 CV117
North Vw Dr, Wdf.Grn. IG8 102 EK54
Northview Prim Sch, NW10 off Northview Cres 119 CT64
North Vw Rd, N8 121 DK55
Sevenoaks TN14 off Seal Rd 257 FJ121
North Vil, NW1 275 N5
North Wk, W2 295 N1
New Addington CR0 221 EB106
Northwall Rd, E20 280 C2
NORTH WATFORD, Wat. WD24 75 BV37
North Way, N9 100 DW47
N11 99 DJ51
NW9 118 CP55
Pinner HA5 116 BW55
Uxbridge UB10 134 BL66
Northway, NW11 120 DB57
Guildford GU2 242 AU132
Morden SM4 199 CY97
Rickmansworth WD3 92 BK45
Wallington SM6 219 DJ105
Welwyn Garden City AL7 off Nursery Hill 29 CZ06
Northway Circ, NW7 96 CR49
Northway Cres, NW7 96 CR49
Northway Ho, N20 98 DC46
Northway Rd, SE5 162 DQ83
Croydon CR0 202 DT100
Northways Par, NW3 off Finchley Rd 274 A6
North Weald Airfield, N.Wld Bas. CM16 70 EZ26
NORTH WEALD BASSETT, Epp. CM16 71 FB27
North Weald Cl, Horn. RM12 147 FH66
Northweald La, Kings.T. KT2 177 CK92
NORTH WEMBLEY, Wem. HA0 117 CH61
North Wembley 117 CK62
North Wembley 117 CK62
North Western Av, Wat. WD24, WD25 75 BU35
North Western Commercial Cen, NW1 off Broadfield La 276 A7
North W Kent Coll, Dartford Campus, Dart. DA1 off Oakfield La 188 FJ89
Gravesend Campus, Grav. DA12 off Dering Way 191 GM88
North W London Jewish Prim Sch, NW6 272 E6
Northwest Pl, N1 276 F10
North Wf Rd, W2 284 A7
Northwick Av, Har. HA3 117 CG58
Northwick Circle, Har. HA3 117 CJ58
Northwick Cl, NW8 284 A4
Harrow HA1 117 CH60
Northwick Park 117 CG59
Northwick Pk Hosp, Har. HA1 117 CG59
Northwick Pk Rd, Har. HA1 117 CF58
Northwick Rd, Wat. WD19 94 BW49
Wembley HA0 off Glacier Wy 137 CK67
Northwick Ter, NW8 284 A4
Northwick Wk, Har. HA1 117 CF59
Northwold Dr, Pnr. HA5 off Cuckoo Hill 116 BW55
Northwold Est, E5 122 DU61
Northwold Prim Sch, E5 off Northwold Rd 122 DU61
Northwold Rd, E5 122 DT61
N16 122 DT61
NORTHWOOD, HA6 93 BR51
Northwood 93 BS52
Northwood, Grays RM16 171 GH75
Welwyn Garden City AL7 30 DD09
Northwood Av, Horn. RM12 127 FG63
Purley CR8 219 DN113
Northwood Cl, Chsht EN7 66 DT27
Northwood Coll, Nthwd. HA6 off Maxwell Rd 93 BR52
North Wd Ct, SE25 off Regina Rd 202 DU97
Northwood Dr, Green. DA9 off Stone Castle Dr 189 FU86
Northwood Gdns, N12 98 DD50
Greenford UB6 117 CF64
Ilford IG5 125 EN56
Northwood Hall, N6 121 DJ59
NORTHWOOD HILLS, Nthwd. HA6 93 BT54
Northwood Hills 93 BU54
Northwood Ho, SE27 182 DR91
Northwood Pl, Erith DA18 166 EZ76
Northwood Prep Sch, Rick. WD3 off Sandy Lo Rd 93 BQ47
Northwood Prim Sch, Erith DA18 off Northwood Pl 166 EZ76
Northwood Rd, N6 121 DH59
SE23 183 DZ88
Carshalton SM5 218 DG107
Harefield UB9 92 BJ53
London Heathrow Airport TW6 154 BK81
Thornton Heath CR7 201 DP96
Northwood Sch, Nthwd. HA6 off Potter St 93 BU53
Northwood Twr, E17 123 EC56
Northwood Way, SE19 off Roman Ri 182 DR93
Harefield UB9 92 BK53
Northwood HA6 93 BU52
NORTH WOOLWICH, E16 305 H4
North Woolwich Rd, E16 303 M2
North Woolwich Rbt, E16 304 E3
North Worple Way, SW14 158 CR83
Nortoft Rd, Chal.St.P. SL9 91 AZ51
Norton Av, Surb. KT5 198 CP101
Norton Cl, E4 101 EA50
Borehamwood WD6 78 CN39
Enfield EN1 off Brick La 82 DV40
Norton Folgate, E1 287 P6
Norton Gdns, SW16 201 DL96
Norton La, Cob. KT11 229 BT119
Norton Rd, E10 123 DZ60
Dagenham RM10 147 FD65
Uxbridge UB8 134 BK69
Wembley HA0 137 CK65
Norval Rd, Wem. HA0 117 CH61
Norway Dr, Slou. SL2 132 AV71
Norway Gate, SE16 301 M6
Norway Pl, E14 289 N9
Norway St, SE10 314 D3

N

Norway Wk, Rain. RM13 off The Glen 148 FJ70
Norwegian Sch in London, The, SW20 off Arterberry Rd 179 CW94
Norwich Cres, Chad.Hth RM6 126 EV57
Norwich Ho, E14 290 D8
Norwich Ms, Ilf. IG3 126 EU60
Norwich Pl, Bexh. DA6 166 FA84
Norwich Rd, E7 281 N3
Dagenham RM9 146 FA68
Greenford UB6 136 CB67
Northwood HA6 115 BT55
Thornton Heath CR7 202 DQ97
Norwich St, EC4 286 E8
Norwich Wk, Edg. HA8 96 CQ52
Norwich Way, Crox.Grn WD3 75 BP41
NORWOOD, SE19 182 DR93
Norwood Av, Rom. RM7 127 FE59
Wembley HA0 138 CM67
Norwood Cl, NW2 119 CY62
Effingham KT24 246 BY128
Hertford SG14 31 DM08
Southall UB2 156 CA77
Twickenham TW2 off Fourth Cross Rd 177 CD89
Norwood Ct, Amer. HP7 55 AP40
Norwood Cres, Lon.Hthrw Air. TW6 155 BQ81
Norwood Dr, Har. HA2 116 BZ58
Norwood Fm La, Cob. KT11 213 BU111
Norwood Gdns, Hayes UB4 136 BW70
Southall UB2 156 BZ77
NORWOOD GREEN, Sthl. UB2 156 CA77
Norwood Grn Inf & Nurs Sch, Sthl. UB2 off Thorncliffe Rd 156 BZ78
Norwood Grn Jun Sch, Sthl. UB2 off Thorncliffe Rd 156 BY78
Norwood Grn Rd, Sthl. UB2 156 CA77
Norwood High St, SE27 181 DP90
Norwood Junction 202 DT98
Norwood Junction 202 DT98
Norwood La, Iver SL0 133 BD70
NORWOOD NEW TOWN, SE19 182 DQ93
Norwood Pk Rd, SE27 182 DQ92
Norwood Rd, SE24 181 DP88
SE27 181 DP89
Cheshunt EN8 67 DY30
Effingham KT24 246 BY128
Southall UB2 156 BZ77
Norwood Sch, The, SE19 off Crown Dale 182 DQ92
Norwood Ter, Sthl. UB2 off Tentelow La 156 CB77
Notley End, Eng.Grn TW20 172 AW93
Notley Pl, SW4 181 DL87
Notley St, SE5 311 L4
Notre Dame Est, SW4 161 DJ84
Notre Dame Prep Sch, Cob. KT11 off Burwood Pk 213 BT112
Notre Dame RC Prim Sch, SE18 off Eglinton Rd 165 EP79
Notre Dame Sch, SE1 298 G6
Notre Dame Sen Sch, Cob. KT11 off Burwood Pk 213 BT111
Notson Rd, SE25 202 DV98
Notting Barn Rd, W10 282 C5
Nottingdale Sq, W11 294 E1
Nottingham Av, E16 292 C7
Nottingham Cl, Wat. WD25 59 BU33
Woking GU21 226 AT118
Nottingham Ct, WC2 286 A9
St. John's GU21 off Nottingham Cl 226 AT118
Nottingham Pl, W1 284 G5
Nottingham Rd, E10 123 EC58
SW17 180 DF88
Heronsgate WD3 91 BC45
Isleworth TW7 157 CF82
South Croydon CR2 220 DQ105
Nottingham St, W1 284 G6
Nottingham Ter, NW1 284 G5
NOTTING HILL, W11 282 F10
Notting Hill & Ealing High Sch, Sen Sch & 6th Form, W13 off Cleveland Rd 137 CH71
Notting Hill Gate 295 J1
Notting Hill Gate, W11 295 J2
Nova, E14 302 A8
Nova Ms, Sutt. SM3 199 CY102
Novar Cl, Orp. BR6 205 ET101
Nova Rd, Croy. CR0 201 DP102
Novar Rd, SE9 185 EQ88
Novello St, SW6 307 J7
Novello Way, Borwd. WD6 78 CR39
Nowell Rd, SW13 159 CU79
Nower, The, Sev. TN14 239 ET119
Nower Ct, Dor. RH4 263 CF137
Nower Cl W, Dor. RH4 263 CF137
Nower Hill, Pnr. HA5 116 BZ56
Nower Hill High Sch, Pnr. HA5 off George V Av 116 CA56
Nower Rd, Dor. RH4 263 CG136
Noyna Rd, SW17 180 DF90
Nubia Way, Brom. BR1 184 EE90
Nuding Cl, SE13 163 EA83
Nuffield Hosp Brentwood, Brwd. CM15 108 FY46
Nuffield Hosp N London (Enfield), Enf. EN2 81 DN40
Nuffield Rd, Swan. BR8 187 FG93
Nuffield Speech & Language Unit, W5 137 CJ71
Nugent Ind Pk, Orp. BR5 206 EW99
Nugent Rd, N19 121 DL60
SE25 202 DT97
Nugents Ct, Pnr. HA5 94 BY53
Nugent Shop Pk, Orp. BR5 206 EW98
Nugents Pk, Pnr. HA5 94 BY53
Nugent Ter, NW8 283 P1
Numa Ct, Brent. TW8 off Justin Cl 157 CK80
Nunappleton Way, Oxt. RH8 254 EG132
Nun Ct, EC2 287 L8
Nuneaton Rd, Dag. RM9 146 EX66
Nuneham Est, SW16 181 DK91
Nunfield, Chipper. WD4 58 BH31
NUNHEAD, SE15 162 DW83
Nunhead 312 G9
Nunhead Cres, SE15 162 DV83
Nunhead Est, SE15 162 DV84
Nunhead Grn, SE15 312 F10
Nunhead Gro, SE15 162 DV83
Nunhead La, SE15 162 DV83
Nunhead Pas, SE15 off Peckham Rye 162 DU83
Nunnery Cl, St.Alb. AL1 43 CD22
Nunnery Stables, St.Alb. AL1 43 CD22
Nunnington Cl, SE9 184 EL90
Nunns Rd, Enf. EN2 82 DQ40
Nunns Way, Grays RM17 170 GD77
Nunsbury Dr, Brox. EN10 67 DY25
Nuns La, St.Alb. AL1 43 CE24
Nuns Wk, Vir.W. GU25 192 AX99
NUPER'S HATCH, Rom. RM4 105 FE45
Nupton Dr, Barn. EN5 79 CW44
Nurse Cl, Edg. HA8 off Gervase Rd 96 CQ53
Nurseries Rd, Wheat. AL4 28 CL08
Nursery, The, Erith DA8 167 FF80
Nursery Av, N3 98 DC54
Bexleyheath DA7 166 EZ83
Croydon CR0 203 DX103
Nursery Cl, SE4 313 N9
SW15 159 CX84
Amersham HP7 55 AS39
Croydon CR0 203 DX103
Dartford DA2 188 FQ87
Enfield EN3 83 DX39
Epsom KT17 216 CS110
Feltham TW14 175 BV87
Orpington BR6 205 ET101
Penn HP10 88 AC47
Romford RM6 126 EX58
Sevenoaks TN13 257 FJ122
South Ockendon RM15 149 FW70
Swanley BR8 207 FC96
Walton on the Hill KT20 249 CV125
Watford WD19 93 BV46
Woking GU21 226 AW116
Woodford Green IG8 102 EH50
Woodham KT15 211 BF110
Nursery Ct, N17 off Nursery St 122 DT52
Nursery Flds, Saw. CM21 36 EX05
Nursery Gdns, Chilw. GU4 259 BB140
Chislehurst BR7 185 EP93
Enfield EN3 83 DX39
Goffs Oak EN7 66 DR28
Hampton TW12 176 BZ91
Hounslow TW4 176 BZ85
Staines-upon-Thames TW18 174 BH94
Sunbury-on-Thames TW16 195 BT96
Ware SG12 33 DY06
Welwyn Garden City AL7 29 CY06
Nursery Hill, Welw.G.C. AL7 29 CY06
Nursery La, E2 278 A9
E7 281 P4
W10 282 A7
Hookwood RH6 268 DD149
Penn HP10 88 AC47
Slough SL3 132 AW74
Uxbridge UB8 134 BK70
Nurserymans Rd, N11 98 DG47
Nursery Pl, Old Wind. SL4 off Gregory Dr 172 AV86
Sevenoaks TN13 256 FD122
Nursery Rd, E9 278 G4
N2 98 DD53
N14 99 DJ45
SW9 161 DM84
Broxbourne EN10 67 DZ25
Godalming GU7 258 AT144
Hoddesdon EN11 33 EB14
Loughton IG10 84 EJ43
Lower Nazeing EN9 49 ED22
Pinner HA5 116 BW55
Sunbury-on-Thames TW16 195 BS96
Sutton SM1 218 DC105
Taplow SL6 130 AH72
Thornton Heath CR7 202 DR98
Walton on the Hill KT20 249 CU125
Nursery Rd Merton, SW19 200 DB96
Nursery Rd Mitcham, Mitch. CR4 200 DE97
Nursery Rd Wimbledon, SW19 off Worple Rd 179 CY94
Nursery Row, SE17 299 L9
Barnet EN5 off St. Albans Rd 79 CY41
Nursery St, N17 100 DT52
Nursery Ter, Pott.End HP4 off The Front 39 BB16
Nursery Wk, NW4 119 CV55
Romford RM7 127 FD59
Nursery Way, Wrays. TW19 172 AX86
Nursery Waye, Uxb. UB8 134 BK67
Nurstead Rd, Erith DA8 166 FA80
Nut Ash La, Epsom KT18 248 CQ126
Nutberry Av, Grays RM16 170 GA75
Nutberry Cl, Grays RM16 off Long La 170 GA75
Nutbourne St, W10 282 E2
Nutbrook St, SE15 162 DU83
Nutbrowne Rd, Dag. RM9 146 EZ67
Nutcombe La, Dor. RH4 263 CF136
Nutcroft Gro, Fetch. KT22 231 CE121
Nutcroft Rd, SE15 312 E4
NUTFIELD, Red. RH1 251 DM133
Nutfield 267 DL136
Nutfield, Welw.G.C. AL7 30 DA06
Nutfield Ch C of E Prim Sch, S.Nutfld RH1 off Mid St 267 DM135
Nutfield Cl, N18 100 DU51
Carshalton SM5 200 DE104
Nutfield Gdns, Ilf. IG3 125 ET61
Northolt UB5 136 BW68
Nutfield Marsh Rd, Nutfld RH1 251 DJ130
Nutfield Pk, S.Nutfld RH1 267 DN137
Nutfield Rd, E15 123 EC63
NW2 119 CU61
SE22 182 DT85
Coulsdon CR5 234 DG116
Redhill RH1 250 DG134
South Merstham RH1 251 DJ129
Thornton Heath CR7 201 DP98
Nutfield Way, Orp. BR6 205 EN103
Nutford Pl, W1 284 D8
Nut Gro, Welw.G.C. AL8 29 CX06
Nuthatch Cl, Stai. TW19 174 BM88
Nuthatch Gdns, SE28 165 ER75
Reigate RH2 266 DC138
Nuthurst Av, SW2 181 DM89
Nutkins Way, Chesh. HP5 54 AQ29
Nutkin Wk, Uxb. UB8 134 BL66
Nutley Cl, Swan. BR8 207 FF95
Nutley Ct, Reig. RH2 off Nutley La 249 CZ134
Nutley La, Reig. RH2 249 CZ133
Nutley Ter, NW3 273 P4
Nutmead Cl, Bex. DA5 187 FC88
Nutmeg Cl, E16 291 K4
Nutmeg La, E14 290 G9
Nuttall St, N1 277 P10
Nutter La, E11 124 EJ58
Nuttfield Cl, Crox.Grn WD3 75 BP44
Nutt Gro, Edg. HA8 95 CK47
Nut Tree Cl, Orp. BR6 206 EX104
Nutt St, SE15 312 B4
Nutty La, Shep. TW17 195 BQ98
Nutwell St, SW17 180 DE92
Nutwood Av, Brock. RH3 264 CQ135
Nutwood Cl, Brock. RH3 264 CQ135
Nutwood Gdns, Chsht EN7 off Great Stockwood Rd 66 DS26
Nuxley Rd, Belv. DA17 166 EZ79
Nyall Ct, Gidea Pk RM2 128 FJ56
Nyanza St, SE18 165 ER79
Nye Bevan Est, E5 123 DX62
Nyefield Pk, Walt.Hill KT20 249 CU126
Nye Way, Bov. HP3 57 BA28
Nylands Av, Rich. TW9 158 CN81
Nymans Gdns, SW20 off Hidcote Gdns 199 CV97
Nynehead St, SE14 313 L4
Nyon Gro, SE6 183 DZ89
Nyssa Cl, Wdf.Grn. IG8 off Gwynne Pk Av 103 EM51
Nyth Cl, Upmin. RM14 129 FR58
Nyton Cl, N19 off Courtauld Rd 121 DL60

O

O2, The, SE10 303 J3
O2 Academy Brixton, SW9 310 E10
O2 Shop Cen, NW3 273 N4
Oakapple Cl, S.Croy. CR2 220 DV114
Oak Apple Ct, SE12 184 EG89
Oak Av, N8 121 DL56
N10 99 DH52
N17 100 DR52
Bricket Wood AL2 60 CA30
Croydon CR0 203 EA103
Egham TW20 173 BC94
Enfield EN2 81 DM38
Hampton TW12 176 BY92
Hounslow TW5 156 BX80
Sevenoaks TN13 257 FH128
Upminster RM14 128 FP62
Uxbridge UB10 115 BP61
West Drayton UB7 154 BN76
Oakbank, Fetch. KT22 230 CC123
Hutton CM13 109 GE43
Woking GU22 226 AY119
Oak Bk, New Adgtn CR0 221 EC107
Oakbank Av, Walt. KT12 196 BZ101
Oakbank Gro, SE24 162 DQ84
Oakbark Ho, Brent. TW8 off High St 157 CJ80
Oakbrook Cl, Brom. BR1 184 EH91
Oakbury Rd, SW6 307 M9
Oak Cl, N14 99 DH45
Box Hill KT20 248 CP130
Dartford DA1 167 FE84
Godalming GU7 258 AS143
Hemel Hempstead HP3 40 BM24
Oxted RH8 254 EG132
Sutton SM1 200 DC103
Waltham Abbey EN9 67 ED34
Oakcombe Cl, N.Mal. KT3 198 CS95
Oak Cottage Cl, SE6 184 EE88
Oak Ct E, Stan. HA7 off Valencia Rd 95 CJ49
Oak Ct W, Stan. HA7 off Valencia Rd 95 CJ49
Oak Cres, E16 291 K7
Oakcroft Cl, Pnr. HA5 93 BV54
West Byfleet KT14 211 BF114
Oakcroft Rd, SE13 314 G9
Chessington KT9 216 CM105
West Byfleet KT14 211 BF114
Oakcroft Vil, Chess. KT9 216 CM105
Oakdale, N14 99 DH46
Welwyn Garden City AL8 29 CW05
Oakdale Av, Har. HA3 118 CL57
Northwood HA6 93 BU54
Oakdale Cl, Wat. WD19 94 BW49
Oakdale Gdns, E4 101 EC50
Oakdale Infants' Sch, E18 off Woodville Rd 102 EH54
Oakdale Jun Sch, E18 off Oakdale Rd 102 EH54
Oakdale La, Crock.H. TN8 255 EP133
Oakdale Rd, E7 144 EH66
E11 123 ED61
E18 102 EH54
N4 122 DQ58
SE15 313 H10
SW16 181 DL92
Epsom KT19 216 CR109
Watford WD19 94 BW48
Weybridge KT13 194 BN104
Oakdale Way, Mitch. CR4 200 DG101
Oakdene, SE15 312 E6
Beaconsfield HP9 89 AL52
Cheshunt EN8 67 DY30
Chobham GU24 210 AT110
Romford RM3 106 FM54
Tadworth KT20 233 CY120
Oak Dene, W13 off The Dene 137 CH71
Oakdene Av, Chis. BR7 185 EN92
Erith DA8 167 FC79
Thames Ditton KT7 197 CG102
Oakdene Cl, Bkhm KT23 246 CC127
Brockham RH3 264 CQ136
Hornchurch RM11 127 FH58
Pinner HA5 94 BZ52
Oakdene Ct, Walt. KT12 195 BV104
Oakdene Dr, Surb. KT5 198 CQ101
Oakdene Ms, Sutt. SM3 199 CZ102
Oakdene Par, Cob. KT11 off Anyards Rd 213 BV114
Oakdene Pk, N3 97 CZ52
Oakdene Pl, Peasm. GU3 258 AW142
Oakdene Rd, Bkhm KT23 230 BZ124
Brockham RH3 264 CQ136
Cobham KT11 213 BV114
Hemel Hempstead HP3 40 BM24
Hillingdon UB10 135 BP68
Orpington BR5 205 ET99
Peasmarsh GU3 258 AW142
Redhill RH1 250 DE134
Sevenoaks TN13 256 FG122
Watford WD24 75 BV36
Oakdene Way, St.Alb. AL1 43 CJ20
Oakden St, SE11 298 F8
Oak Dr, Berk. HP4 38 AX20
Box Hill KT20 248 CP130
Sawbridgeworth CM21 36 EW07
Oake Ct, SW15 off Portinscale Rd 179 CY85
Oaken Coppice, Ashtd. KT21 232 CN119
Oak End, Harl. CM18 51 ET17
Oak End Dr, Iver SL0 133 BC68
Oaken Dr, Clay. KT10 215 CF107
Oak End Way, Ger.Cr. SL9 113 AZ57
Woodham KT15 211 BE112
Oakengate Wd, Tad. KT20 248 CQ131
Oaken Gro, Welw.G.C. AL7 29 CY11
Oakenholt Ho, SE2 off Hartslock Dr 166 EX75
Oaken La, Clay. KT10 215 CE106
Oakenshaw Cl, Surb. KT6 198 CL101
Warlingham CR6 236 DW115
Oakes Cl, E6 293 K9
Oakeshott Av, N6 120 DG61
Oakey La, SE1 298 E6
Oak Fm, Borwd. WD6 78 CQ43
Oak Fm Inf & Jun Schs, Hlgdn UB10 off Windsor Av 135 BP67
Oakfield, E4 101 EB50
Mill End WD3 91 BF45
Woking GU21 226 AS116
Oak Fld, Chesh. HP5 54 AP30
Oakfield Av, Har. HA3 117 CH55
Slough SL1 131 AP74
Oakfield Cl, Amer. HP6 55 AQ37
New Malden KT3 off Blakes La 199 CT99
Potters Bar EN6 63 CZ31
Ruislip HA4 115 BT58
Weybridge KT13 213 BQ105
Oakfield Co Inf & Nurs Sch, Dart. DA1 off Oakfield La 188 FL89
Oakfield Ct, N8 121 DL59
NW2 off Hendon Way 119 CX59
Borehamwood WD6 78 CP41
Oakfield Dr, Reig. RH2 250 DA132
Oakfield First Sch, Wind. SL4 off Imperial Rd 151 AP82
Oakfield Gdns, N18 100 DS49
SE19 182 DS92
Beckenham BR3 203 EA99
Carshalton SM5 200 DE102
Greenford UB6 137 CD70
Oakfield Glade, Wey. KT13 213 BQ105
Oakfield Jun Sch, Dart. DA1 off Oakfield La 188 FK89
Fetcham KT22 off Bell La 231 CD123
Oakfield La, Bex. DA5 187 FF89
Dartford DA1, DA2 187 FG89
Keston BR2 222 EJ105
Oakfield Lo, Ilf. IG1 off Albert Rd 125 EP62
Oakfield Pk Rd, Dart. DA1 188 FK89
Oakfield Pl, Dart. DA1 188 FK89
Oakfield Prep Sch, SE21 off Thurlow Pk Rd 182 DR88
Oakfield Rd, E6 144 EL67
E17 101 DY54
N3 98 DB53
N4 121 DN58
N14 99 DL48
SE20 182 DV94
SW19 179 CX90
Ashford TW15 175 BP92
Ashtead KT21 231 CK117
Cobham KT11 213 BV113
Croydon CR0 202 DQ102
Ilford IG1 125 EP61
Oakfield Rd Ind Est, SE20 off Oakfield Rd 182 DV94
Oakfields, Guil. GU3 242 AS132
Sevenoaks TN13 257 FH126
Walton-on-Thames KT12 195 BU102
West Byfleet KT14 212 BH114
Oakfield Sch, Pyrford GU22 off Coldharbour Rd 227 BF115
Oakfields Rd, NW11 119 CY58
Oakfield St, SW10 307 N2
Oakford Ms, Shalf. GU4 258 AY140
Oakford Rd, NW5 275 L1
Oak Gdns, Croy. CR0 203 EA103
Edgware HA8 96 CQ54
Oak Glade, Cooper. CM16 off Coopersale Common 70 EX29
Epsom KT19 off Christ Ch Rd 216 CN112
Northwood HA6 93 BP53
Oak Glen, Horn. RM11 128 FL55
Oak Gra Rd, W.Clan. GU4 244 BH128
Oak Grn, Abb.L. WD5 59 BS32
Oak Grn Way, Abb.L. WD5 59 BS32
Oak Gro, NW2 119 CY63
Hatfield AL10 45 CT18
Hertford SG13 32 DS11
Ruislip HA4 115 BV59
Sunbury-on-Thames TW16 175 BV94
West Wickham BR4 203 EC103
Oak Gro Rd, SE20 202 DW95
Oakhall Ct, E11 124 EH58
Oak Hall Ct, Sun. TW16 175 BT92
Oakhall Dr, Sun. TW16 175 BT92
Oak Hall Rd, E11 124 EH58
Oakham Cl, SE6 off Rutland Wk 183 DZ89
Barnet EN4 80 DF41
Oakham Dr, Brom. BR2 204 EF98
Oakhampton Rd, NW7 97 CX52
Oak Hill, Burpham GU4 243 BC129
Epsom KT18 232 CR116
Surbiton KT6 198 CL101
Woodford Green IG8 101 ED52
Oakhill, Clay. KT10 215 CG107
Oakhill Av, NW3 273 L1
Pinner HA5 94 BY54
Oakhill Cl, Ashtd. KT21 231 CJ118
Maple Cross WD3 91 BE49
Oak Hill Cl, Wdf.Grn. IG8 101 ED52
Oak Hill Coll, N14 off Chase Side 80 DG44
Oakhill Ct, SW19 179 CX94
Oak Hill Cres, Surb. KT6 198 CL101
Woodford Green IG8 101 ED52
Oakhill Dr, Surb. KT6 198 CL101
Oakhill Gdns, Wey. KT13 195 BS103
Oak Hill Gdns, Wdf.Grn. IG8 102 EE53
Oak Hill Gro, Surb. KT6 198 CL100
Oak Hill Pk, NW3 120 DB63
Oak Hill Pk Ms, NW3 120 DC63
Oakhill Path, Surb. KT6 198 CL100
Oakhill Pl, SW15 off Oakhill Rd 180 DA85
Oakhill Prim Sch, Wdf.Grn. IG8 off Alders Av 102 EE51
Oakhill Rd, SW15 179 CZ85
SW16 201 DL95
Addlestone KT15 211 BF107
Ashtead KT21 231 CJ118
Beckenham BR3 203 EC96
Maple Cross WD3 91 BD49
Orpington BR6 205 ET102
Purfleet RM19 168 FP78
Reigate RH2 266 DB135
Sevenoaks TN13 256 FG124
Sutton SM1 200 DB104
Oak Hill Rd, Stap.Abb. RM4 105 FD45
Surbiton KT6 198 CL100
Oak Hill Way, NW3 120 DC63
Oak Ho, NW3 off Maitland Pk Vil 274 F4
Romford RM7 off Cottons App 127 FD57
Oakhouse Rd, Bexh. DA6 186 FA85
Oakhurst, Chobham GU24 210 AS109
Oakhurst Av, Bexh. DA7 166 EY80
East Barnet EN4 98 DE45
Oakhurst Cl, E17 124 EE56
Chislehurst BR7 205 EM95
Ilford IG6 103 EQ53
Kingston upon Thames KT2 178 CM93
Teddington TW11 177 CE92
Oakhurst Gdns, E4 102 EF46
E17 124 EE56
Bexleyheath DA7 166 EY80
Oakhurst Gro, SE22 162 DU84
Oakhurst Pl, Wat. WD18 off Cherrydale 75 BT42
Oakhurst Ri, Cars. SM5 218 DE110
Oakhurst Rd, Enf. EN3 83 DX36
Epsom KT19 216 CQ107
Oakhyrst Gra Sch, Cat. CR3 off Stanstead Rd 252 DR126
Oakington, Welw.G.C. AL7 30 DD08
Oakington Av, Amer. HP6 72 AY39
Harrow HA2 116 CA59
Hayes UB3 155 BR77
Wembley HA9 118 CM62
Oakington Cl, Sun. TW16 196 BW96
Oakington Dr, Sun. TW16 196 BW96
Oakington Manor Dr, Wem. HA9 118 CN64
Oakington Manor Prim Sch, Wem. HA9 off Oakington Manor Dr 118 CP64
Oakington Rd, W9 283 K4
Oakington Way, N8 121 DL58
Oakland Gdns, Hutt. CM13 109 GC43
Oakland Pl, Buck.H. IG9 102 EG47
Oakland Rd, E15 281 H1
Oaklands, N21 99 DM47
Berkhamsted HP4 38 AU19
Fetcham KT22 231 CD124
Horley RH6 269 DJ148
Kenley CR8 220 DQ114
Loughton IG10 84 EJ44
Twickenham TW2 176 CC87
Oaklands Av, N9 82 DV44
Brookmans Park AL9 63 CY27
Esher KT10 197 CD102
Isleworth TW7 157 CF79
Romford RM1 127 FE55
Sidcup DA15 185 ET87
Thornton Heath CR7 201 DN98
Watford WD19 93 BV46
West Wickham BR4 203 EB104
Oaklands Cl, Bexh. DA6 186 EZ85
Chessington KT9 215 CJ105
Petts Wood BR5 205 ES100
Shalford GU4 258 AY142
Oaklands Coll, St. Albans Campus, Saint Albans AL4 off Hatfield Rd 44 CL19
Welwyn Gdn City Campus, Welwyn Garden City AL8 off The Campus 29 CX08
Oaklands Ct, W12 off Uxbridge Rd 139 CV74
Addlestone KT15 194 BH104
Watford WD17 75 BU39
Wembley HA0 117 CK64
Oaklands Dr, Harl. CM17 52 EW16
Redhill RH1 267 DH136
South Ockendon RM15 149 FW71
Oaklands Est, SW4 181 DJ86
Oaklands Gdns, Ken. CR8 220 DQ114
Oaklands Gate, Nthwd. HA6 93 BS51
Oaklands Gro, W12 139 CU74
Broxbourne EN10 49 DY24
Oaklands Ho, NW6 off Belsize Rd 273 N7
Oaklands Inf Sch, Bigg.H. TN16 off Norheads La 238 EJ116
Oaklands Jun Sch, Bigg.H. TN16 off Oaklands La 238 EJ116
Oaklands La, Barn. EN5 79 CV42
Biggin Hill TN16 222 EH113
Smallford AL4 44 CL18
Oaklands Ms, NW2 272 C1
Oaklands Pk, Hutt. CM13 109 GB46
Oaklands Pk Av, Ilf. IG1 off High Rd 125 ER61
Oaklands Pl, SW4 off St. Alphonsus Rd 161 DJ84
Oaklands Prim Sch, W7 off Oaklands Rd 157 CF75
Oaklands Rd, N20 97 CZ45
NW2 272 C2
SW14 158 CR83
W7 157 CF75
Bexleyheath DA6 166 EZ84
Bromley BR1 184 EE94
Cheshunt EN7 66 DS26
Dartford DA2 188 FP88
Northfleet DA11 191 GF91
Oaklands Sch, E2 288 E2
Isleworth TW7 off Woodlands Rd 157 CD83
Loughton IG10 off Albion Hill 84 EK43
Oaklands Way, Tad. KT20 233 CW122
Wallington SM6 219 DK108
Oaklands Wd, Hat. AL10 45 CU18
Oakland Way, Epsom KT19 216 CR107
Oak La, E14 289 N10
N2 98 DD54
N11 99 DK51
Cuffley EN6 65 DM28
Englefield Green TW20 172 AW90
Isleworth TW7 157 CE84
Sevenoaks TN13 256 FG127
Twickenham TW1 177 CG87
Windsor SL4 151 AN81
Woking GU22 off Beaufort Rd 227 BC116
Woodford Green IG8 102 EF49
Oaklawn Rd, Lthd. KT22 231 CE118
Oak Leaf Cl, Epsom KT19 216 CQ112
Oakleafe Gdns, Ilf. IG6 125 EP55

N
O

O

Oaklea Pas, Kings.T. KT1 197 CK97
Oakleigh Av, N20 98 DD47
Edgware HA8 96 CP54
Surbiton KT6 198 CN102
Oakleigh Cl, N20 98 DF48
Swanley BR8 207 FE97
Oakleigh Ct, N1 287 L1
Barnet EN4 80 DE44
Edgware HA8 96 CQ54
Oakleigh Cres, N20 98 DE47
Oakleigh Dr, Crox.Grn WD3 75 BQ44
Oakleigh Gdns, N20 98 DC46
Edgware HA8 96 CM50
Orpington BR6 223 ES105
Oakleigh Ms, N20
off Oakleigh Rd N 98 DC47
OAKLEIGH PARK, N20 98 DD46
⇌ Oakleigh Park 98 DD45
Oakleigh Pk Av, Chis. BR7 205 EN95
Oakleigh Pk N, N20 98 DD46
Oakleigh Pk S, N20 98 DE47
Oakleigh Ri, Epp. CM16 70 EU32
Oakleigh Rd, Pnr. HA5 94 BZ51
Uxbridge UB10 135 BQ66
Oakleigh Rd N, N20 98 DD47
Oakleigh Rd S, N11 98 DG48
Sch Oakleigh Spec Sch, N20
off Oakleigh Rd N 98 DF48
Oakleigh Way, Mitch. CR4 201 DH95
Surbiton KT6 198 CN102
Oakley Av, W5 138 CN73
Barking IG11 145 ET66
Croydon CR0 219 DL105
Oakley Cl, E4 101 EC48
E6 293 H8
W7 137 CE73
Addlestone KT15 212 BK105
Grays RM20 169 FW79
Isleworth TW7 157 CD81
Oakley Ct, Loug. IG10
off Hillyfields 85 EN40
Mitcham CR4 200 DG101
Oakley Cres, EC1 287 H1
Slough SL1 132 AS73
Oakley Dell, Guil. GU4 243 BC132
Oakley Dr, SE9 185 ER88
SE13 183 ED86
Bromley BR2 204 EL104
Romford RM3 106 FN50
Oakley Gdns, N8 121 DM57
SW3 308 D2
Banstead SM7 234 DB115
Betchworth RH3 264 CQ140
OAKLEY GREEN, Wind. SL4 150 AH82
Oakley Grn Rd,
Oakley Grn SL4 150 AG82
Oakley Ho, SE11
off Hotspur St 298 E9
Oakley Pk, Bex. DA5 186 EW87
Oakley Pl, SE1 312 A1
Oakley Rd, N1 277 L6
SE25 202 DV99
Bromley BR2 204 EL104
Harrow HA1 117 CE58
Warlingham CR6 236 DU118
Oakley Sq, NW1 285 M1
Oakley St, SW3 308 C2
Oakley Wk, W6 306 D2
Oakley Yd, E2 288 B4
Oak Lock Ms, W4 158 CS78
Oak Lo Av, Chig. IG7 103 ER50
Oak Lo Cl, Hersham KT12 214 BW106
Stanmore HA7 *off Dennis La* 95 CJ50
Oak Lo Dr, Red. RH1 266 DG142
West Wickham BR4 203 EB101
Oak Lo La, West. TN16 255 ER125
Sch Oak Lo Prim Sch, W.Wick.
BR4 *off Chamberlain Cres* 203 EB101
Sch Oak Lo Sch, SW12
off Nightingale La 180 DG87
Sch Oak Lo Spec Sch, N2
off Heath Vw 120 DC56
Oaklodge Way, NW7 97 CT50
Oak Manor Dr, Wem. HA9
off Oakington Manor Dr 118 CM64
Oakmead Av, Brom. BR2 204 EG100
Oakmeade, Pnr. HA5 94 CA51
Oakmead Gdns, Edg. HA8 96 CR49
Oakmead Grn, Epsom KT18 232 CP115
Oakmead Pl, Mitch. CR4 200 DE95
Oakmead Rd, SW12 180 DG88
Croydon CR0 201 DK100
Oakmere Av, Pot.B. EN6 64 DC33
Oakmere Cl, Pot.B. EN6 64 DD31
Oakmere La, Pot.B. EN6 64 DC32
Oakmere Ms, Pot.B. EN6 64 DC32
Sch Oakmere Prim Sch,
Pot.B. EN6 *off Chace Av* 64 DD32
Oakmere Rd, SE2 166 EU79
Oakmont Pl, Orp. BR6 205 ER102
Oakmoor Way, Chig. IG7 103 ES50
Oak Pk, Hunsdon SG12 34 EH06
West Byfleet KT14 211 BE113
Oak Pk Gdns, SW19 179 CX87
Oak Pk Ms, N16 122 DT62
Oak Path, Bushey WD23
off Mortimer Cl 76 CB44
Oak Piece, N.Wld Bas. CM16 71 FC25
Oak Pl, SW18
off East Hill 180 DB85
Oakridge, Brick.Wd AL2 60 BZ29
Oak Ridge, Dor. RH4 263 CH139
Oakridge Av, Rad. WD7 61 CF34
Oakridge Dr, N2 120 DD55
Oakridge La, Ald. WD25 77 CD35
Bromley BR1 183 ED92
Radlett WD7 61 CF33
Oakridge Rd, Brom. BR1 183 ED91
Oak Ri, Buck.H. IG9 102 EK48
Oak Rd, W5 *off The Broadway* 137 CK73
Caterham CR3 236 DS122
Cobham KT11 230 BX115
Epping CM16 69 ET30
Gravesend DA12 191 GJ90
Grays RM17 170 GC79
Greenhithe DA9 189 FS86
Leatherhead KT22 231 CG118
New Malden KT3 198 CR96
Northumberland Heath DA8 167 FC80
Orpington BR6 224 EU108
Reigate RH2 250 DB133
Romford RM3 106 FM53
Slade Green DA8 167 FG81
Westerham TN16 255 ER125
Oak Row, SW16 201 DJ96
Oakroyd Av, Pot.B. EN6 63 CZ33
Oakroyd Cl, Pot.B. EN6 63 CZ34
Oaks, The, N12 98 DB49
SE18 165 EQ78
Berkhamsted HP4 38 AU19
Dartford DA2 188 FP86
Dorking RH4
off Oak Ridge 263 CH139
Epsom KT18 217 CT114
Fetcham KT22 230 CC123
Hayes UB4 135 BQ68
Morden SM4 199 CY98
Ruislip HA4 115 BS59
Staines-upon-Thames TW18
off Moormede Cres 173 BF91
Swanley BR8 207 FE96
Tadworth KT20 233 CW123
Watford WD19 94 BW46
West Byfleet KT14 212 BG113
Woodford Green IG8 102 EE51
Oaks Av, SE19 182 DS92
Feltham TW13 176 BY89
Romford RM5 105 FC54
Worcester Park KT4 199 CV104
Oaks Cl, Lthd. KT22 231 CG121
Radlett WD7 77 CF35
Oaksford Av, SE26 182 DV90
Oaks Gro, E4 102 EE47
Oakshade Rd, Brom. BR1 183 ED91
Oxshott KT22 214 CC114
Oakshaw, Oxt. RH8 253 ED127
Oakshaw Rd, SW18 180 DB87
Oakside, Denh. UB9 134 BH65
Oakside Ct, Horl. RH6
off Oakside La 269 DJ147
Ilford IG6 103 ER53
Oakside La, Horl. RH6 269 DJ147
Oaks La, Croy. CR0 202 DW104
Ilford IG2 125 ES57
Mid Holmwood RH5 263 CH143
Sch Oaks Pk High Sch, Ilf. IG2
off Oaks La 125 ES57
Oaks Pavilion Ms, SE19 182 DS91
Oak Sq, Sev. TN13
off High St 257 FJ126
SW9 310 C9
Oaks Retail Pk, The,
Harl. CM20 35 ET12
Oaks Rd, Croy. CR0 220 DV106
Kenley CR8 219 DP114
Reigate RH2 250 DC133
Stanwell TW19 174 BK86
Woking GU21 226 AY117
Oaks Shop Cen, W3
off High St 138 CQ74
Oaks Sq, The, Epsom KT19
off Waterloo Rd 216 CR113
Oaks Track, Cars. SM5 218 DF111
Wallington SM6 219 DH110
Oak St, Hem.H. HP3 40 BM24
Romford RM7 127 FC57
Oak Stubbs La, Dorney R. SL6 150 AF75
Oaks Way, Cars. SM5 218 DF108
Epsom KT18
off Epsom La N 233 CV119
Kenley CR8 220 DQ114
Long Ditton KT6 197 CK103
Ripley GU23 228 BG124
Sch Oakthorpe Prim Sch, N13
off Tile Kiln La 100 DQ50
Oakthorpe Rd, N13 99 DN50
Oaktree Av, N13 99 DP48
Oak Tree Av, Bluewater DA9 189 FT87
Oak Tree Cl, W5 137 CJ72
Abbots Langley WD5 59 BR32
Oaktree Cl, Brwd. CM13
off Hawthorn Av 109 FZ48
Oak Tree Cl, Burpham GU4 243 BB129
Epsom KT19 216 CP107
Oaktree Cl, Goffs Oak EN7 65 DP28
Oak Tree Cl, Hat. AL10 45 CU17
Hertford Heath SG13 32 DW12
Jacobs Well GU4 242 AW128
Loughton IG10 85 EQ39
Stanmore HA7 95 CJ52
Virginia Water GU25 192 AX101
Oak Tree Ct, Els. WD6 77 CK44
Oak Tree Dell, NW9 118 CQ57
Oak Tree Dr, N20 98 DB46
Englefield Green TW20 172 AW92
Guildford GU1 242 AW130
Slough SL3 153 BB78
Oak Tree Gdns, Brom. BR1 184 EH92
Guildford GU1 243 BB131
Oaktree Gdns, Ch.Lang. CM17
off Burley Hill 52 EX16
Oaktree Garth, Welw.G.C. AL7 29 CY10
Oaktree Gro, Ilf. IG1 125 ER64
Oak Tree Pl, Esher KT10 196 CB103
Oak Tree Rd, NW8 284 B3
Sch Oak Tree Sch, N14
off Chase Side 80 DG44
Sch Oaktree Sch, The, St.John's
GU21 *off Gorsewood Rd* 226 AS119
Oaktree Wk, Cat. CR3 236 DS122
Oak Vw, Wat. WD18 75 BS41
Oakview Cl, Chsht EN7 66 DV28
Watford WD19 76 BW44
Oakview Gdns, N2 120 DD56
Oak Vw Gdns, Slou. SL3 153 AZ77
Oakview Gro, Croy. CR0 203 DY102
Sch Oak Vw Prim & Nurs Sch,
Hat. AL10 *off Woods Av* 45 CV19
Oakview Rd, SE6 183 EB92
Sch Oak Vw Sch, Loug. IG10
off Whitehills Rd 85 EN42
Oak Village, NW5 275 H2
Oak Wk, Saw. CM21 36 EX07
Wallington SM6
off Helios Rd 200 DG102
Oak Warren, Sev. TN13 256 FG129
Oak Way, N14 99 DH45
Ashtead KT21 232 CN116
Croydon CR0 203 DX100
Feltham TW14 175 BS88
Reigate RH2 266 DD135
Oakway, SW20 199 CW98
W3 138 CS74
Amersham HP6 55 AP35
Bromley BR2 203 ED96
Woking GU21 226 AS119
Oakway Cl, Bex. DA5 186 EY86
Oakway Pl, Rad. WD7
off Watling St 61 CG34
Oakways, SE9 185 EP86
Oakwell Dr, Northaw EN6 65 DH32
OAKWOOD, N14 81 DK44
⊖ Oakwood 81 DJ43
Oakwood, Berk. HP4 38 AT20
Guildford GU2 242 AU129
Wallington SM6 219 DH109
Waltham Abbey EN9
off Fairways 68 EE34
Oakwood Av, N14 99 DK45
Beckenham BR3 203 EC96
Borehamwood WD6 78 CP42
Bromley BR2 204 EH97
Epsom KT19 216 CN109
Hutton CM13 109 GE44
Mitcham CR4 200 DD96
Purley CR8 219 DP112
Southall UB1 136 CA73
Oakwood Chase, Horn. RM11 128 FM58
Oakwood Cl, N14 81 DJ44
SE13 183 ED87
Chislehurst BR7 185 EM93
Dartford DA1 188 FP88
East Horsley KT24 245 BS127
Redhill RH1 250 DG134
South Nutfield RH1
off Mid St 267 DM136
Woodford Green IG8
off Green Wk 102 EL51
Oakwood Ct, W14 294 G6
Slough SL1 *off Oatlands Dr* 132 AS72
Oakwood Cres, N21 81 DL44
Greenford UB6 137 CG65
Oakwood Dr, SE19 182 DR93
Bexleyheath DA7 167 FD84
East Horsley KT24 245 BS127
Edgware HA8 96 CQ51
St. Albans AL4 43 CJ19
Sevenoaks TN13 257 FH123
● Oakwood Est, Harl. CM20 36 EV11
Oakwood Gdns, Ilf. IG3 125 ET61
Orpington BR6 205 EQ103
Sutton SM1 200 DA103
Oakwood Hill, Loug. IG10 85 EM44
● Oakwood Hill Ind Est,
Loug. IG10 85 EP43
Oakwood La, W14 294 G6
Oakwood Ms, Harl. CM17
off Station Rd 36 EW11
Oakwood Pk Rd, N14 99 DK45
Oakwood Pl, Croy. CR0 201 DN100
Sch Oakwood Prim Sch,
St.Alb. AL4 *off Oakwood Dr* 43 CJ19
Oakwood Ri, Cat. CR3 252 DS125
Oakwood Rd, NW11 120 DB57
SW20 199 CU95
Bricket Wood AL2 60 BY29
Croydon CR0 201 DN100
Horley RH6 268 DG147
Merstham RH1 251 DN129
Orpington BR6 205 EQ103
Pinner HA5 93 BV54
Virginia Water GU25 192 AW99
Woking GU21 226 AS119
Sch Oakwood Sch, Bexh. DA7
off Woodside Rd 167 FD84
Sch Oakwood Sch, Horley RH6
off Balcombe Rd 269 DJ148
Purley CR8 *off Godstone Rd* 219 DP113
Oakwood Vw, N14 81 DK44
Oakworth Rd, W10 282 B6
Oarsman Pl, E.Mol. KT8 197 CE98
Sch Oasis Acad Coulsdon,
Couls. CR5 *off Homefield Rd* 235 DP120
Sch Oasis Acad Enfield,
Enf. EN3 *off Kinetic Cres* 83 DZ37
Sch Oasis Acad Hadley,
Enf. EN3 *off Bell La* 83 DX38
Sch Oasis Acad Johanna, SE1 298 E5
Sch Oasis Acad Shirley Pk,
Croy. CR0 *off Shirley Rd* 202 DV101
Sch Oasis Acad Southbank, SE1 298 E6
Oast Ho Cl, Wrays. TW19 172 AY87
Oasthouse Way, Orp. BR5 206 EV98
Oast Rd, Oxt. RH8 254 EF131
Oates Cl, Brom. BR2 203 ED97
Oates Rd, Rom. RM5 105 FB50
Oatfield Ho, N15 122 DS58
Oatfield Rd, Orp. BR6 205 ET102
Tadworth KT20 233 CV120
Oatland Ri, E17 101 DY54
Oatlands, Horl. RH6 269 DH147
Oatlands Av, Wey. KT13 213 BR106
Oatlands Chase, Wey. KT13 195 BS104
Oatlands Cl, Wey. KT13 213 BQ105
Oatlands Dr, Slou. SL1 131 AR72
Weybridge KT13 195 BR104
Oatlands Grn, Wey. KT13 195 BR104
Sch Oatlands Inf Sch,
Wey. KT13 *off St. Marys Rd* 213 BR105
Oatlands Mere, Wey. KT13 195 BR104
OATLANDS PARK, Wey. KT13 213 BR105
Oatlands Rd, Enf. EN3 82 DW39
Tadworth KT20 233 CY119
Oat La, EC2 287 J8
Oatridge Gdns, Hem.H. HP2 41 BP19
Oban Cl, E13 292 C5
Oban Ct, Slou. SL1
off Montem La 151 AR75
Oban Ho, E14 291 H8
Barking IG11
off Wheelers Cross 145 ER68
Oban Rd, E13 292 D3
SE25 202 DR98
Oban St, E14 291 H8
Obelisk Ride, Egh. TW20 172 AS93
Oberon Cl, Borwd. WD6 78 CQ39
Oberon Ct, Denh. UB9
off Patrons Way E 113 BF58
Oberon Way, Shep. TW17 194 BL97
Oberstein Rd, SW11 160 DD84
Oborne Cl, SE24 181 DP85
O'Brien Ho, E2 289 K2
Observatory Gdns, W8 295 J4
Observatory Ms, E14 302 G9
Observatory Rd, SW14 158 CQ84
Observatory Shop Cen,
Slou. SL1 152 AU75
Observatory Wk, Red. RH1
off Lower Br Rd 250 DF134
Observer Dr, Wat. WD18 75 BS42
Occupation La, SE18 165 EP81
W5 157 CK77
Roydon CM19 50 EH15
Occupation Rd, SE17 299 J10
W13 157 CH75
Watford WD18 75 BV43
Ocean Est, E1 289 K5
Oceanis, E16 *off Seagull La* 291 N10
Ocean St, E1 289 K6
Ocean Wf, E14 302 A5
Ockenden Cl, Wok. GU22
off Ockenden Rd 227 AZ118
Ockenden Gdns, Wok. GU22
off Ockenden Rd 227 AZ118
Ockenden Rd, Wok. GU22 227 AZ118
⇌ Ockendon 149 FX69
Sch Ockendon Acad, The,
S.Ock. RM15 *off Erriff Dr* 149 FU71
Ockendon Ms, N1 277 L5
Ockendon Rd, N1 277 L5
Upminster RM14 128 FQ64
OCKHAM, Wok. GU23 228 BN121
Ockham Dr, Grnf. UB6 136 CC66
Orpington BR5 186 EU94
West Horsley KT24 229 BR124
Ockham La, Cob. KT11 229 BT118
Ockham GU23 229 BP120
Jct Ockham Pk, Wok. GU23 228 BL119
Ockham Rd N, Lthd. KT24 229 BQ124
Ockham GU23 228 BN121
Ockham Rd S, E.Hors. KT24 245 BS126
Ockley Ct, Guil. GU4
off Cotts Wd Dr 243 BB129
Sutton SM1 *off Oakhill Rd* 218 DC105
Ockley Rd, SW16 181 DL90
Croydon CR0 201 DM101
Ockleys Mead, Gdse. RH9 252 DW129
Octagon, The, Ware SG12 33 DX05
Octagon Arc, EC2 287 N7
Octagon Rd,
Whiteley Vill. KT12 213 BS109
Octavia Cl, Mitch. CR4 200 DE99
Octavia Ct, Wat. WD24 76 BW40
Octavia Ms, W9 282 G4
Octavia Rd, Islw. TW7 157 CF82
Octavia St, SW11 308 C7
Octavia Way, SE28
off Booth Cl 146 EV73
Staines-upon-Thames TW18 174 BG93
Octavius St, SE8 314 A4
Odard Rd, W.Mol. KT8
off Down St 196 CA98
Oddesey Rd, Borwd. WD6 78 CP39
Odds Fm Est, Woob.Grn HP10 110 AH59
Odelia Ct, E15
off Biggerstaff Rd 280 F8
Odell Cl, Bark. IG11 145 ET66
Odell Wk, SE13
off Bankside Av 163 EB83
Odencroft Rd, Slou. SL2 131 AN69
Odeon, The, Bark. IG11
off Longbridge Rd 145 ER66
Odeon Par, Grnf. UB6
off Allendale Rd 137 CH65
Sch Odessa Inf Sch, E7 281 N2
Odessa Rd, E7 281 M1
NW10 139 CU68
Odessa St, SE16 301 N5
Odger St, SW11 308 F8
● Odhams Trading Est,
Wat. WD24 76 BW37
Odhams Wk, WC2 286 B9
● Odyssey Business Pk,
Ruis. HA4 115 BV64
Offa Rd, St.Alb. AL3 42 CC20
Offa's Mead, E9 279 M1
Offenbach Ho, E2 289 J1
Offenham Rd, SE9 185 EM91
Offers Ct, Kings.T. KT1
off Winery La 198 CM97
Offerton Rd, SW4 161 DJ83
Offham Slope, N12 97 CZ50
Offley Pl, Islw. TW7 157 CD82
Offley Rd, SW9 310 E4
Offord Cl, N17 100 DU51
Offord Rd, N1 276 C6
Offord St, N1 276 C6
Ogard Rd, Hodd. EN11 49 EC15
Ogilby St, SE18 305 J9
Oglander Rd, SE15 162 DT84
Ogle St, W1 285 L6
Oglethorpe Rd, Dag. RM10 126 EZ62
Ohio Bldg, SE13
off Deals Gateway 314 C7
Ohio Rd, E13 291 M5
Oil Mill La, W6 159 CU78
Okeburn Rd, SW17 180 DG92
Okehampton Cl, N12 98 DD50
Okehampton Cres, Well. DA16 166 EV81
Okehampton Rd, NW10 272 B9
Romford RM3 106 FJ51
Okehampton Sq, Rom. RM3 106 FJ51
Okemore Gdns, Orp. BR5 206 EW98
Olaf St, W11 294 D1
Old Acre, Wok. GU22 212 BG114
Oldacre Ms, SW12
off Balham Gro 181 DH87
★ Old Admiralty Bldg (MOD),
SW1 297 P3
★ Old Amersham Rd,
Ger.Cr. SL9 113 BB60
Old Av, W.Byf. KT14 211 BE113
Weybridge KT13 213 BR107
Old Av Cl, W.Byf. KT14 211 BE113
Old Bailey, EC4 287 H9
Old Bakery Ms, Albury GU5 260 BH139
Old Barge Ho All, SE1
off Upper Grd 298 F2
Old Barn Cl, Sutt. SM2 217 CY108
Old Barn La, Crox.Grn WD3 74 BM43
Kenley CR8 236 DT116
Old Barn Ms, Crox.Grn WD3
off Old Barn La 74 BM43
Old Barn Rd, Epsom KT18 232 CQ117
Old Barn Way, Bexh. DA7 167 FD83
Old Barrack Yd, SW1 296 G4
Old Barrowfield, E15 281 K9
Old Bath Rd, Colnbr. SL3 153 BE81
Old Beaconsfield Rd,
Farn.Com. SL2 131 AQ65
Old Bell Ct, Hem.H. HP2
off George St 40 BK19
Old Bellgate Pl, E14 302 A7
Oldberry Rd, Edg. HA8 96 CR51
Old Bethnal Grn Rd, E2 288 D2
OLD BEXLEY, Bex. DA5 187 FB87
● Old Bexley Business Pk,
Bex. DA5 187 FB87
Sch Old Bexley C of E Prim Sch,
Bex. DA5 *off Hurst Rd* 186 EZ88
Old Bexley La, Bex. DA5 187 FD89
Dartford DA1 187 FF88
★ Old Billingsgate, EC3 299 N1
Old Billingsgate Wk, EC3
off Lower Thames St 299 N1
Old Bond St, W1 297 L1
Oldborough Rd, Wem. HA0 117 CJ61
Old Brewers Yd, WC2 286 A9
Old Brewery Ms, NW3 274 A1
Old Br Cl, Nthlt. UB5 136 CA68
Old Br La, Epsom KT17 217 CT112
Old Br St, Hmptn W. KT1 197 CK96
Old Broad St, EC2 287 M9
Old Bromley Rd, Brom. BR1 183 ED92
Old Brompton Rd, SW5 307 K1
SW7 307 K1
Old Bldgs, WC2 286 E8
Old Burlington St, W1 285 L10
Oldbury Cl, Cher. KT16
off Oldbury Rd 193 BE101
Orpington BR5 206 EX98
Oldbury Gro, Beac. HP9 89 AK50
Old Bury Hill, Westc. RH4 263 CE138
Oldbury Pl, W1 285 H6
Oldbury Rd, Cher. KT16 193 BE101
Enfield EN1 82 DU40
Old Canal Ms, SE15 312 B1
Old Carriageway, The,
Sev. TN13 256 FC123
Old Castle St, E1 288 A7
Old Cavendish St, W1 285 J8
Old Change Ct, EC4
off Carter La 287 J9
Old Chapel Rd, Swan. BR8 207 FC101
Old Charlton Rd, Shep. TW17 195 BQ99
● Old Char Wf, Dor. RH4 263 CF135
Old Chelsea Ms, SW3 308 B3
Old Chertsey Rd,
Chobham GU24 210 AV110
Old Chestnut Av, Esher KT10 214 CA107
Old Chorleywood Rd, Rick.
WD3 *off Chorleywood Rd* 74 BK44
Old Ch Cl, Orp. BR6 206 EV102
Oldchurch Gdns, Rom. RM7 127 FD59
Old Ch La, NW9 118 CQ61
Mountnessing CM13 109 GE42
Perivale UB6 *off Perivale La* 137 CG69
Stanmore HA7 95 CJ52
Old Ch Path, Esher KT10
off High St 214 CB105
Oldchurch Ri, Rom. RM7 127 FE58
Old Ch Rd, E1 289 J9
E4 101 EA49
Oldchurch Rd, Rom. RM7 127 FD59
Old Ch St, SW3 308 B1
Old Claygate La, Clay. KT10 215 CG107
Old Clem Sq, SE18
off Kempt St 165 EN79
Old Coach Rd, Cher. KT16 193 BD99
Old Coach Rd, The,
Cole Grn SG14 30 DF12
Old Coal Yd, SE28
off Pettman Cres 165 ER77
Old College Ct, Belv. DA17 167 FB78
Old Common Rd, Chorl. WD3
off Common Rd 73 BD42
Cobham KT11 213 BU112
Old Compton St, W1 285 N10
Old Cote Dr, Houns. TW5 156 CA79
OLD COULSDON, Couls. CR5 235 DN119
Old Ct, Ashtd. KT21 232 CL119
Old Ct Grn, Pott.End HP4
off Hempstead La 39 BC17
Old Ct Pl, W8 295 L4
Old Ct Rd, Guil. GU2 258 AU135
Old Crabtree La, Hem.H. HP2 40 BL21
Old Cross, Hert. SG14 32 DQ09
Old Cross Wf, Hert. SG14
off Old Cross 32 DQ09
★ Old Curiosity Shop, WC2 286 C8
Old Dairy, The, Wok. GU21
off Goldsworth Rd 226 AX117
Old Dairy Ms, SW4
off Tintern St 161 DL84
SW12 180 DG88
Old Dairy Sq, N21
off Wades Hill 99 DN45
Old Dartford Rd, Fnghm DA4 208 FM100
Old Dean, Bov. HP3 57 BA27
Old Deer Pk Gdns, Rich. TW9 158 CL83
Old Devonshire Rd, SW12 181 DH87
Old Dock App Rd, Grays RM17 170 GE77
Old Dock Cl, Rich. TW9 158 CN79
Old Dover Rd, SE3 315 P4
Old Dr, The, Welw.G.C. AL8 29 CV10
Olden La, Pur. CR8 219 DN112
Old Esher Cl, Hersham KT12 214 BX106
Old Esher Rd, Hersham KT12 214 BX106
Old Essex Rd, Hodd. EN11 49 EB16
Old Farleigh Rd, S.Croy. CR2 220 DW110
Warlingham CR6 221 DY113
Old Fm Av, N14 99 DJ45
Sidcup DA15 185 ER88
Old Fm Cl, Houns. TW4 156 BZ84
Knotty Green HP9 88 AJ50
Old Fm Gdns, Swan. BR8 207 FF97
Old Farmhouse Dr,
Oxshott KT22 231 CD115
Old Fm Pas, Hmptn. TW12 196 CC95
Old Fm Rd, N2 98 DD53
Guildford GU1 242 AX131
Hampton TW12 176 BZ93
West Drayton UB7 154 BK75
Old Fm Rd E, Sid. DA15 186 EU89
Old Fm Rd W, Sid. DA15 185 ET89
Old Fm Yd, The,
Sheering CM22 37 FC07
Old Ferry Dr, Wrays. TW19 172 AW86
Sch Oldfield Cen, Hmptn.
TW12 *off Oldfield Rd* 196 BZ95
Oldfield Circ, Nthlt. UB5 136 CC65
Old Fld Cl, Amer. HP6 72 AY39
Oldfield Cl, Brom. BR1 205 EM98
Cheshunt EN8 67 DY28
Greenford UB6 117 CE64
Horley RH6 *off Oldfield Rd* 268 DF150
Stanmore HA7 95 CG50
Oldfield Dr, Chsht EN8 67 DY28
Oldfield Fm Gdns, Grnf. UB6 137 CD67
Oldfield Gdns, Ashtd. KT21 231 CK119
Oldfield Gro, SE16 301 J9
Oldfield La N, Grnf. UB6 137 CE65
Oldfield La S, Grnf. UB6 136 CC70
Oldfield Ms, N6 121 DJ59
Sch Oldfield Prim Sch,
Grnf. UB6 *off Oldfield La N* 137 CD68
Oldfield Rd, N16 122 DS62
NW10 139 CT66
SW19 179 CY93
W3 *off Valetta Rd* 159 CT75
Bexleyheath DA7 166 EY82
Bromley BR1 205 EM98
Hampton TW12 196 BZ95
Hemel Hempstead HP1 39 BE21
Horley RH6 268 DF150
London Colney AL2 61 CK25
Oldfields Rd, Sutt. SM1 199 CZ104
● Oldfields Trd Est, Sutt. SM1 200 DA104
Oldfield Wd, Wok. GU22
off Maybury Hill 227 BB117

Old Fishery La, Hem.H. HP1 39 BF22
Old Fish St Hill, EC4 287 J10
Old Fives Ct, Burn. SL1 130 AH69
Old Fleet La, EC4 286 G8
Old Fold Cl, Barn. EN5
off Old Fold La 79 CZ39
Old Fold La, Barn. EN5 79 CZ39
Old Fold Vw, Barn. EN5 79 CW41
OLD FORD, E3 279 N7
Sch **Old Ford Prim Sch**, E3 279 N10
Old Ford Rd, E2 288 F2
E3 279 K10
Old Forge Cl, Stan. HA7 95 CG49
Watford WD25 59 BU33
Welwyn AL6 29 CZ05
Old Forge Cres, Shep. TW17 195 BP100
Old Forge Ms, W12
off Goodwin Rd 159 CV75
Old Forge Rd, N19 121 DK61
Enfield EN1 82 DT38
Loudwater HP10 88 AC53
Old Forge Way, Sid. DA14 186 EV91
Old Fox Cl, Cat. CR3 235 DP121
Old Fox Footpath, S.Croy.
CR2 *off Essenden Rd* 220 DS108
Old French Horn La, Hat. AL10 45 CV17
Old Gannon Cl, Nthwd. HA6 93 BQ50
Old Gdn, The, Sev. TN13 256 FD123
Old Gdn Ct, St.Alb. AL3 42 CC20
Old Gloucester St, WC1 286 B6
Old Gro Cl, Chsht EN7 66 DR26
Old Hall Cl, Pnr. HA5 94 BY53
Old Hall Dr, Pnr. HA5 94 BY53
Old Hall Ri, Harl. CM17 52 EY15
Old Hall St, Hert. SG14 32 DR09
Oldham Ter, W3 138 CQ74
OLD HARLOW, Harl. CM17 36 EX11
Old Harpenden Rd, St.Alb. AL3 43 CE17
Old Harrow La, West. TN16 239 EQ119
Old Hatch Manor, Ruis. HA4 115 BT59
OLD HATFIELD, Hat. AL9 45 CX17
Old Heath Rd, Wey. KT13 212 BN107
Old Herns La, Welw.G.C. AL7
off Herns La 30 DC07
Old Hertford Rd, Hat. AL9 45 CW16
Old Highway, Hodd. EN11 33 EB14
Old Hill, Chis. BR7 205 EN95
Orpington BR6 223 ER107
Woking GU22 226 AX120
Oldhill St, N16 122 DU60
Old Homesdale Rd,
Brom. BR2 204 EJ98
Old Hosp Cl, SW12 180 DF88
Old Ho Cl, SW19 179 CY92
Epsom KT17 217 CT110
Old Ho Ct, Hem.H. HP2 40 BM20
Oldhouse Cft, Harl. CM20 35 ES13
Old Ho Gdns, Twick. TW1 177 CJ85
Old Ho La, Kings L. WD4 74 BL35
Lower Nazeing EN9 50 EF23
Roydon CM19 50 EK18
Old Ho Rd, Hem.H. HP2 40 BM20
Old Howlett's La, Ruis. HA4 115 BQ58
Old Jamaica Rd, SE16 300 C6
Old James St, SE15 162 DV83
Old Jewry, EC2 287 L9
Old Kenton La, NW9 118 CP57
Old Kent Rd, SE1 299 M7
SE15 312 D2
Old Kiln La, Brock. RH3 264 CQ135
Old Kiln Rd, Penn HP10 88 AC45
Old Kingston Rd, Wor.Pk. KT4 198 CQ104
Old La, Cob. KT11 229 BP117
Oxted RH8 254 EF129
Tatsfield TN16 238 EK121
Old La Gdns, Cob. KT11 229 BT122
Old Leys, Hat. AL10 45 CU22
Old Lib La, Hert. SG14
off Old Cross 32 DQ09
Old Lo Dr, Beac. HP9 89 AL54
Old Lo La, Ken. CR8 235 DN115
Purley CR8 219 DM113
Old Lo Pl, Twick. TW1
off St. Margarets Rd 177 CH86
Old Lo Way, Stan. HA7 95 CG50
Old London Rd, Bad.Mt TN14 224 FA110
East Horsley KT24 245 BU126
Epsom KT18 233 CU118
Harlow CM17 52 EV16
Hertford SG13 32 DS09
Kingston upon Thames KT2 198 CL96
Knockholt Pound TN14 240 EY115
Mickleham RH5 247 CJ127
St. Albans AL1 43 CD21
Old Long Gro, Beac. HP9 89 AQ51
Old Maidstone Rd, Sid. DA14 186 EZ94
OLD MALDEN, Wor.Pk. KT4 198 CR102
Old Malden La, Wor.Pk. KT4 198 CR103
Old Malt Way, Wok. GU21 226 AX117
Old Manor Dr, Grav. DA12 191 GJ88
Isleworth TW7 176 CC86
Old Manor Gdns, Chilw. GU4 259 BD140
Old Manor Ho Ms, Shep.
TW17 *off Squires Br Rd* 194 BN97
Old Manor La, Chilw. GU4 259 BC140
Old Manor Rd, Sthl. UB2 156 BX77
Old Manor Way, Bexh. DA7 167 FD82
Chislehurst BR7 185 EM92
Old Manor Yd, SW5 295 K10
Old Mkt Sq, E2 288 A2
Old Marsh La, Tap. SL6 150 AF75
Old Marylebone Rd, NW1 284 D7
Old Mead, Chal.St.P. SL9 90 AY51
Old Meadow Cl, Berk. HP4 38 AU21
Old Merrow St, Guil. GU4 243 BC131
Old Ms, Har. HA1
off Hindes Rd 117 CE57
Old Mill Cl, Eyns. DA4 208 FL102
Old Mill Ct, E18 124 EJ55
Old Mill Gdns, Berk. HP4 38 AX19
Old Mill La, Bray SL6 150 AD75
Merstham RH1 251 DH128
Uxbridge UB8 134 BH72
Old Mill Pl, Rom. RM7 127 FD58
Wraysbury TW19 173 BB86
Old Mill Rd, SE18 165 ER79
Denham UB9 114 BG62
Hunton Bridge WD4 59 BQ33
Old Mitre Ct, EC4 286 F9
Old Montague St, E1 288 C7
Old Moor La,
Woob.Moor HP10 110 AE55
Old Nazeing Rd, Brox. EN10 49 EA21
Old Nichol St, E2 288 A4
Old N St, WC1 286 C6
Old Nurseries La, Cob. KT11 213 BV113
Old Nursery Ct, Hedg. SL2 111 AQ61
Old Nursery Pl, Ashf. TW15
off Park Rd 175 BP92
Old Oak, St.Alb. AL1 43 CE23
Old Oak Av, Chipstead CR5 234 DE119
Old Oak Cl, Chess. KT9 216 CM105
Cobham KT11 213 BV113
OLD OAK COMMON, NW10 139 CT71
Old Oak Common La, NW10 138 CS71
W3 138 CS71
Old Oak La, NW10 138 CS69
Sch **Old Oak Prim Sch**, W12
off Mellitus St 139 CT72
Old Oak Rd, W3 139 CT73
Old Oaks, Wal.Abb. EN9 68 EE32
★ **Old Operating Thea Mus &**
Herb Garret, SE1 299 M3
Old Orchard, Byfleet KT14 212 BM112
Harlow CM18 51 ER17
Park Street AL2 60 CC26
Sunbury-on-Thames TW16 196 BW96
Old Orchard, The, NW3
off Nassington Rd 120 DF63
Iver SL0 133 BF72
Old Orchard Cl, Barn. EN4 80 DD38
Uxbridge UB8 134 BN72
Old Orchard Ms, Berk. HP4 38 AW20
Old Otford Rd, Sev. TN14 241 FH117
Old Palace La, Rich. TW9 177 CJ85
Sch **Old Palace of John**
Whitgift Jun Sch,
S.Croy. CR2 *off Melville Av* 220 DT107
Sch **Old Palace of John**
Whitgift Sen Sch,
Croy. CR0 *off Old Palace Rd* 201 DP104
Sch **Old Palace Prim Sch**, E3 290 D2
Old Palace Rd, Croy. CR0 201 DP104
Guildford GU2 258 AU135
Weybridge KT13 195 BP104
Old Palace Ter, Rich. TW9
off King St 177 CK85
Old Palace Yd, SW1 298 A6
Richmond TW9 177 CJ85
Old Papermill Cl, Woob.Grn
HP10 *off Glory Mill La* 110 AE56
Old Paradise St, SE11 298 C8
Old Pk Av, SW12 180 DG86
Enfield EN2 82 DQ42
Old Parkbury La, Coln.St AL2 61 CF30
Old Pk Gro, Enf. EN2 82 DQ42
Old Pk La, W1 297 H3
Old Pk Ms, Houns. TW5 156 BZ80
Old Pk Ride, Wal.Cr. EN7 66 DT33
Old Pk Ridings, N21 81 DP44
Old Pk Rd, N13 99 DM49
SE2 166 EU78
Enfield EN2 81 DP41
Old Pk Rd S, Enf. EN2 81 DP42
Old Pk Vw, Enf. EN2 81 DN41
Old Parsonage Yd,
Hort.Kir. DA4 208 FQ97
Old Parvis Rd, W.Byf. KT14 212 BK112
Old Pearson St, SE10 314 D4
Old Perry St, Chis. BR7 185 ES94
Northfleet DA11 190 GE89
Old Polhill, Sev. TN14 241 FD115
Old Portsmouth Rd,
Gdmg. GU7 258 AV142
Guildford GU3 258 AV142
Old PO La, SE3 164 EH83
Old Post Office Wk, Surb.
KT6 *off St. Marys Rd* 197 CK100
Old Pottery Cl, Reig. RH2 266 DB136
Old Pound Cl, Islw. TW7 157 CG81
Old Priory, Hare. UB9 115 BP59
Old Priory Av, Orp. BR6 206 EV101
Old Quebec St, W1 284 F9
Old Queen St, SW1 297 P5
Old Rectory Cl, Walt.Hill KT20 233 CU124
Old Rectory Dr, Hat. AL10 45 CV18
Old Rectory Gdns, Cob. KT11 229 BV115
Edgware HA8 96 CN51
Old Rectory La, Denh. UB9 113 BE59
East Horsley KT24 245 BS126
Old Redding, Har. HA3 94 CC49
Old Redstone Dr, Red. RH1 266 DG135
Old Reigate Rd, Bet. RH3 248 CP134
Dorking RH4 248 CL134
Oldridge Rd, SW12 180 DG87
Old Rd, SE13 164 EE84
Addlestone KT15 211 BF108
Buckland RH3 248 CS134
Dartford DA1 167 FD84
Enfield EN3 82 DW39
Harlow CM17 36 EX11
Old Rd E, Grav. DA12 191 GH88
Old Rd W, Grav. DA11 191 GF88
Old Royal Free Pl, N1
off Old Royal Free Sq 276 F9
Old Royal Free Sq, N1 276 F9
Old Ruislip Rd, Nthlt. UB5 136 BX68
Old St. Mary's, W.Hors. KT24
off Ripley La 245 BP129
Olds App, Wat. WD18 93 BP46
Old Savill's Cotts, Chig. IG7
off The Chase 103 EQ49
Old Sch Cl, SE10 303 K7
SW19 200 DA96
Beckenham BR3 203 DX96
Guildford GU1
off Markenfield Rd 242 AX134
Redhill RH1 250 DG132
Old Sch Ct, Wrays. TW19 172 AY87
Old Sch Cres, E7 281 N5
Old Sch Ho,
Godden Grn TN15 257 FN124
Old Sch La, E5 123 DX61
Brockham RH3 264 CN138
Old Sch Ms, Stai. TW18 173 BD92
Weybridge KT13 213 BR105
Old Sch Pl, Croy. CR0 219 DN105
Woking GU22 226 AY121
Old Sch Rd, Uxb. UB8 134 BM70
Old Schs La, Epsom KT17 217 CT109
Old Sch Sq, E14 290 A9
Thames Ditton KT7 197 CF100
Old Sch Wk, Sev. TN13 257 FH125
Olds Cl, Wat. WD18 93 BP46
Old Seacoal La, EC4 286 G8
Old Shire La, Chorl. WD3 73 BB44
Gerrards Cross SL9 91 BA46
Waltham Abbey EN9 84 EG35
Old Slade La, Iver SL0 153 BE76
Old Solesbridge La,
Chorl. WD3 74 BG41
Old Sopwell Gdns, St.Alb. AL1 43 CE22
Old S Cl, Hatch End HA5 94 BX53
Old S Lambeth Rd, SW8 310 B4
Old Spitalfields Mkt, E1 288 A6
Old Sq, WC2 286 D8
Old Stable Ms, N5 122 DQ62
Old Sta App, Lthd. KT22 231 CG121
Old Sta Pas, Rich. TW9
off Little Grn 157 CK84
Old Sta Rd, Hayes UB3 155 BT76
Loughton IG10 84 EL43
Old Sta Way, SW4
off Voltaire Rd 161 DK83
Wooburn Green HP10 110 AE58
Old Sta Yd, Brom. BR2
off Bourne Way 204 EF102
Oldstead Rd, Brom. BR1 183 ED91
Old Stede Cl, Ashtd. KT21 232 CM117
Old Stockley Rd,
West Dr. UB7 155 BP75
⇌ **Old Street** 287 L3
⊖ **Old Street** 287 L3
Old St, E13 292 B1
EC1 287 J4
Old St, The, Fetch. KT22 231 CD123
Old Studio Cl, Croy. CR0 202 DR101
Old Swan Yd, Cars. SM5 218 DF105
Old Thea Ct, SE1
off Porter St 299 K2
Old Thieves La, Hertingfordbury
SG14 *off Thieves La* 31 DM10
Old Tilburstow Rd, Gdse. RH9 252 DW134
Old Town, SW4 161 DJ83
Croydon CR0 201 DP104
Old Town Cl, Beac. HP9 89 AL54
★ **Old Town Hall Arts Cen**,
Hem.H. HP1 40 BK19
Old Tram Yd, SE18
off Lakedale Rd 165 ES77
Old Twelve Cl, W7 137 CE70
Old Tye Av, Bigg.H. TN16 238 EL116
Old Uxbridge Rd, W.Hyde WD3 91 BE53
Sch **Old Vicarage Sch**, Rich.
TW10 *off Richmond Hill* 178 CL86
Old Vicarage Way,
Woob.Grn HP10 110 AE59
Old Wk, The, Otford TN14 241 FH117
Old Watermen's Wk, EC3 142 DR73
Old Watery La,
Woob.Grn HP10 110 AE55
Old Watford Rd, Brick.Wd AL2 60 BY30
Old Watling St, Grav. DA11 191 GG92
Oldway La, Slou. SL1 151 AK75
Old Westhall Cl, Warl. CR6 236 DW119
Old Wf Way, Wey. KT13
off Weybridge Rd 212 BM105
OLD WINDSOR, Wind. SL4 172 AU86
Old Windsor Lock,
Old Wind. SL4 172 AW85
OLD WOKING, Wok. GU22 227 BA121
Old Woking Rd, W.Byf. KT14 211 BF113
Woking GU22 227 BE116
Old Woolwich Rd, SE10 315 H2
Old Yd, The, West. TN16 240 EW124
Old York Rd, SW18 180 DB85
Oleander Cl, Orp. BR6 223 ER106
O'Leary Sq, E1 288 G6
Sch **Olga Prim Sch**, E3 289 M1
Olga St, E3 289 M1
Olinda Rd, N16 122 DT58
Oliphant St, W10 282 D2
Olive Cl, St.Alb. AL1 43 CH21
Olive Gro, N15 122 DQ56
Oliver Av, SE25 202 DT97
● **Oliver Business Pk**, NW10
off Oliver Rd 138 CQ68
Oliver Cl, W4 158 CP79
Addlestone KT15 212 BG105
Grays RM20 169 FT80
Hemel Hempstead HP3 40 BL24
Hoddesdon EN11 49 EB15
Park Street AL2 61 CD27
Oliver Cres, Fnghm DA4 208 FM101
Oliver Gdns, E6 293 H8
Oliver-Goldsmith Est, SE15 312 D6
Sch **Oliver Goldsmith Prim Sch**,
NW9 *off Coniston Gdns* 118 CR57
SE5 312 A6
Oliver Gro, SE25 202 DT98
Oliver Ms, SE15 312 C8
Olive Rd, E13 292 D3
NW2 119 CW63
SW19 *off Norman Rd* 180 DC94
W5 157 CK76
Dartford DA1 188 FK88
Oliver Ri, Hem.H. HP3 40 BL24
Oliver Rd, E10 123 EB61
E17 123 EC57
NW10 138 CQ68
Grays RM20 169 FU80
Hemel Hempstead HP3 40 BL24
New Malden KT3 198 CQ96
Rainham RM13 147 FF67
Shenfield CM15 109 GA43
Sutton SM1 218 DD105
Swanley BR8 207 FD97
Olivers Cl, Pott.End HP4 39 BC16
Olivers Yd, EC1 287 M4
Olive St, Rom. RM7 127 FD57
Olivette St, SW15 159 CX83
Olivia Dr, Slou. SL3 153 AZ78
Olivia Gdns, Hare. UB9 92 BJ53
Olivier Ct, Denh. UB9
off Patrons Way E 113 BF58
Olivier Cres, Dor. RH4
off Stubs Cl 263 CJ138
Ollards Gro, Loug. IG10 84 EK42
Olleberrie La, Sarratt WD3 57 BD32
Ollerton Grn, E3 279 P8
Ollerton Rd, N11 99 DK50
Olley Cl, Wall. SM6 219 DL108
Ollgar Cl, W12 139 CT74
Olliffe St, E14 302 F7
Olmar St, SE1 312 C2
Olney Rd, SE17 311 J2
Olron Cres, Bexh. DA6 186 EX85
Olven Rd, SE18 165 EQ80
Olveston Wk, Cars. SM5 200 DD100
Olwen Ms, Pnr. HA5 94 BX54
Olyffe Av, Well. DA16 166 EU82
Olyffe Dr, Beck. BR3 203 EC95
★ **Olympia**, W14 294 F7
Olympia Ms, W2 295 M1
Olympian Way, Stanw. TW19 174 BK86
Olympia Way, W14 294 F7
H **Olympic Med Inst**, Har. HA1 117 CH59
Olympic Pk Ave, E20 280 D4
Olympic Sq, Wem. HA9 118 CN62
★ **Olympic Stadium**, E20 280 C7
Olympic Way, Grnf. UB6 136 CB67
Wembley HA9 118 CN63
Olympus Gro, N22 99 DN53
Olympus Sq, E5
off Nolan Way 122 DU62
Oman Av, NW2 119 CW63
O'Meara St, SE1 299 K3
Omega Bldg, SW18
off Smugglers Way 160 DB84
Omega Cl, E14 302 C6
Omega Ct, Rom. RM7 127 FC58
Ware SG12 *off Crib St* 33 DX06
Omega Maltings, Ware SG12
off Star St 33 DY06
Omega Pl, N1 286 B1
Omega Rd, Wok. GU21 227 BA115
Omega St, SE14 313 P6
● **Omega Wks**, E3 280 B6
Omega Way, Egh. TW20 193 BC95
Ommaney Rd, SE14 313 L7
Omnibus Ho, N22
off Redvers Rd 99 DN54
Omnibus Way, E17 101 EA54
Ondine Rd, SE15 162 DT84
Onega Gate, SE16 301 L6
One Hyde Pk, SW1 296 E5
O'Neill Path, SE18
off Kempt St 165 EN79
● **One New Change**, EC4 287 J9
One Pin La, Farn.Com. SL2 111 AQ63
One Tree Cl, SE23 182 DW86
One Tree Hill Rd, Guil. GU4 259 BB135
One Tree La, Beac. HP9 89 AL52
Ongar Cl, Add. KT15 211 BF107
Romford RM6 126 EW57
Ongar Hill, Add. KT15 212 BG107
Ongar Par, Add. KT15
off Ongar Hill 212 BG107
Ongar Pl, Add. KT15 212 BG107
Sch **Ongar Pl Inf Sch**,
Add. KT15 *off Milton Rd* 212 BG107
Ongar Rd, SW6 307 J2
Addlestone KT15 212 BG106
Brentwood CM15 108 FV45
Romford RM4 86 EW40
Ongar Way, Rain. RM13 147 FE67
Onra Rd, E17 123 EA59
Onslow Av, Rich. TW10 178 CL85
Sutton SM2 217 CZ110
Onslow Cl, E4 101 EC47
W10 282 G2
Hatfield AL10 45 CV18
Thames Ditton KT7 197 CE102
Woking GU22 227 BA117
Onslow Cres, SW7 296 B9
Chislehurst BR7 205 EP95
Woking GU22 227 BA117
Onslow Dr, Sid. DA14 186 EX89
Onslow Gdns, E18 124 EH55
N10 121 DH57
N21 81 DN43
SW7 296 A9
South Croydon CR2 220 DU112
Thames Ditton KT7 197 CE102
Wallington SM6 219 DJ107
Sch **Onslow Inf Sch**,
Ons.Vill. GU2 *off Powell Cl* 258 AT136
Onslow Ms, Cher. KT16 194 BG100
Onslow Ms E, SW7 296 A9
Onslow Ms W, SW7 296 A9
Onslow Par, N14
off Osidge La 99 DH46
Onslow Rd, Croy. CR0 201 DM101
Guildford GU1 242 AX134
Hersham KT12 213 BT105
New Malden KT3 199 CU98
Richmond TW10 178 CL85
Sch **Onslow St. Audrey's Sch**,
Hat. AL10 *off Old Rectory Dr* 45 CV18
Onslow Sq, SW7 296 B8
Onslow St, EC1 286 F5
Guildford GU1 258 AW135
ONSLOW VILLAGE, Guil. GU2 258 AS136
Onslow Way, T.Ditt. KT7 197 CE102
Woking GU22 227 BF115
Ontario Cl, Brox. EN10 67 DY25
Smallfield RH6 269 DN149
Ontario St, SE1 299 H7
Ontario Twr, E14 302 F1
Ontario Way, E14 302 A1
On The Hill, Wat. WD19 94 BY47
Onyx Ms, E15
off Vicarage La 281 K5
Opal Cl, E16 292 F9
Opal Ct, Wexham SL3 132 AW70
Opal Ms, NW6 273 H8
Ilford IG1 125 EP61
Opal St, SE11 298 G10
Opecks Cl, Wexham SL2 132 AV70
Opendale Rd, Burn. SL1 130 AH71
Openshaw Rd, SE2 166 EV77
Uni **Open Uni in London, The**,
NW1 275 K6
Openview, SW18 180 DC88
Ophelia Gdns, NW2
off Hamlet Sq 119 CY62
Ophir Ter, SE15 312 C7
Opossum Way, Houns. TW4 156 BW82
Oppenheim Rd, SE13 314 E8
Oppidans Ms, NW3 274 E7
Oppidans Rd, NW3 274 E7
● **Optima Business Pk**,
Hodd. EN11 49 EC16
● **Optima Pk**, Cray. DA1 167 FG83
Opulens Pl, Nthwd. HA6 93 BP52
Oram Pl, Hem.H. HP3 40 BK23
Orange Ct, E1
off Hermitage Wall 300 D3
Orange Ct La, Downe BR6 223 EN109
Orange Gro, E11 123 ED62
Chigwell IG7 103 EQ51
Orange Hill Rd, Edg. HA8 96 CQ52
Orange Pl, SE16 301 H7
Orangery, The, Rich. TW10 177 CJ89
Orangery La, SE9 185 EM85
Orange Sq, SW1 297 H9
Orange St, WC2 297 N1
Orange Tree Hill,
Hav.at.Bow. RM4 105 FD50
Orange Yd, W1 285 P9
Oransay Rd, N1 277 K5
Oransay Wk, N1
off Oransay Rd 277 K5
Oratory La, SW3 296 B10
Sch **Oratory RC Prim Sch**, SW3 296 C10
Orbain Rd, SW6 306 F5
Orbel St, SW11 308 C7
★ **Orbis Wf**, SW11 308 A10
● **Orbital 25 Business Pk**,
Wat. WD18 93 BR45
Orbital Cres, Wat. WD25 75 BT35
Orbital One, Dart. DA1 188 FP89
Orb St, SE17 299 L9
Orchard, The, N14 81 DH43
N20 98 DB46
N21 82 DR44
Orchard, The, NW11 120 DA57
SE3 315 H8
W4 158 CR77
W5 *off Montpelier Rd* 137 CK71
Banstead SM7 234 DA115
Croxley Green WD3 74 BM43
Dunton Green TN13 241 FE120
Epsom KT17 217 CT108
Ewell KT17
off Tayles Hill Dr 217 CT110
Hertford SG14 32 DQ06
Hounslow TW3 156 CC82
Kings Langley WD4 58 BN29
North Holmwood RH5 263 CJ140
Swanley BR8 207 FD96
Virginia Water GU25 192 AY99
Welwyn Garden City AL8 29 CX07
Weybridge KT13 213 BP105
Woking GU22 226 AY122
Orchard Av, N3 120 DA55
N14 81 DJ44
N20 98 DD47
Ashford TW15 175 BQ93
Belvedere DA17 166 EY79
Berkhamsted HP4 38 AU19
Brentwood CM13 109 FZ48
Croydon CR0 203 DY101
Dartford DA1 187 FH87
Feltham TW14 175 BR85
Gravesend DA11 191 GH92
Hounslow TW5 156 BY80
Mitcham CR4 200 DG102
New Malden KT3 198 CS96
Rainham RM13 148 FJ70
Slough SL1 131 AK71
Southall UB1 136 BY74
Thames Ditton KT7 197 CG102
Watford WD25 59 BV32
Windsor SL4 151 AN81
Woodham KT15 211 BF111
Orchard Bungalow Caravan
Site, Slou. SL2 131 AM66
● **Orchard Business Cen**,
Red. RH1 267 DH143
Orchard Cl, E4
off Chingford Mt Rd 101 EA49
E11 124 EH56
N1 277 K7
NW2 119 CU62
SE23 182 DW86
SW20 199 CW98
W10 282 F6
Ashford TW15 175 BQ93
Banstead SM7 218 DB114
Beaconsfield HP9
off Seeleys Rd 89 AK52
Bexleyheath DA7 166 EY81
Bushey Heath WD23 95 CD46
Chorleywood WD3 73 BD42
Cuffley EN6 65 DL28
Denham UB9 134 BH65
East Horsley KT24 229 BT124
Edgware HA8 96 CL51
Egham TW20 173 BB92
Elstree WD6 78 CM42
Fetcham KT22 231 CD122
Guildford GU1 243 BB134
Hemel Hempstead HP2 40 BM18
Horley RH6 268 DF147
Leatherhead KT22 231 CF119
Little Berkhamsted SG13 47 DJ19
Long Ditton KT6 197 CH101
Northolt UB5 116 CC64
Radlett WD7 77 CE37
Ruislip HA4 115 BQ59
St. Albans AL1 43 CF21
Sheering CM22 37 FC07
South Ockendon RM15 149 FW70
Stanstead Abbotts SG12 33 EC11
Walton-on-Thames KT12 195 BV101
Ware SG12 33 DX05
Watford WD17 75 BT40
Wembley HA0 138 CL67
West Ewell KT19 216 CP107
Woking GU22 227 BB116
Orchard Ct, Bov. HP3 57 BA27
Twickenham TW2 177 CD89
Wallington SM6
off Parkgate Rd 219 DH106
Worcester Park KT4 199 CU102
Orchard Cres, Edg. HA8 96 CQ50
Enfield EN1 82 DT39
Orchard Cft, Harl. CM20 36 EU13
Orchard Dr, SE3 315 H8
Ashtead KT21 231 CK120
Chorleywood WD3 73 BC41
Edgware HA8 96 CM50
Grays RM17 170 GA75
Horl. RH6 269 DH145
Park Street AL2 60 CB27
Theydon Bois CM16 85 ES36
Uxbridge UB8 134 BK70
Watford WD17 75 BT39
Woking GU21 227 AZ115
Wooburn Green HP10 110 AD59
Orchard End, Cat. CR3 236 DS122
Fetcham KT22 230 CC124
Weybridge KT13 195 BS103
Orchard End Av, Amer. HP7 72 AT39
Orchard Est, Wdf.Grn. IG8 102 EJ52
Orchard Fm Pk, Red. RH1 267 DM143
Orchard Fld Rd, Gdmg. GU7 258 AT144
Orchard Gdns, Chess. KT9 216 CL105
Effingham KT24 246 BY128
Epsom KT18 216 CQ114
Sutton SM1 218 DA106
Waltham Abbey EN9 67 EC34
Orchard Gate, NW9 118 CS56
Esher KT10 197 CD102
Farnham Common SL2 111 AQ64
Greenford UB6 137 CH65
Orchard Grn, Orp. BR6 205 ES103
Orchard Gro, E5 278 F3
SE20 182 DU94
Chalfont St. Peter SL9 90 AW53
Croydon CR0 203 DY101
Edgware HA8 96 CN53
Harrow HA3 118 CM57
Orpington BR6 205 ET103
Orchard Hill, SE13 314 D8
Carshalton SM5 218 DF106
Dartford DA1 187 FE85
Coll **Orchard Hill Coll**,
Wall. SM6 *off Woodcote Rd* 219 DH107

O

Orchard Ho, Erith DA8 167 FF81
Sch Orchard Inf & Nurs & Jun Schs, The, Houns. TW4
off Orchard Rd 176 CA85
Orchard La, SW20 199 CV95
Amersham HP6 55 AR38
East Molesey KT8 197 CD100
Godstone RH9 252 DV130
Pilgrim's Hatch CM15 108 FT43
Woodford Green IG8 102 EJ49
Orchard Lea, Saw. CM21 36 EW06
Orchard Lea Cl, Wok. GU22 227 BE115
ORCHARD LEIGH, Chesh. HP5 56 AV28
Orchard Leigh, Chesh. HP5 56 AU28
Orchardleigh, Lthd. KT22 231 CH122
Orchardleigh Av, Enf. EN3 82 DW40
Orchard Mains, Wok. GU22 226 AW119
Orchard Mead Ho, NW11 119 CZ61
Orchardmede, N21 82 DR44
Orchard Ms, N1 277 M7
N6 off Orchard Rd 121 DH59
SW17 off Franche Ct Rd 180 DC90
Seer Green HP9
off Orchard Rd 89 AR51
Orchard Path, Slou. SL3 133 BA72
Orchard Pl, E14 291 J10
N17 100 DT52
Chsht EN8 off Turners Hill 67 DX30
Keston BR2 222 EJ109
Sundridge TN14 240 EY124
Sch Orchard Prim Sch, E9 279 H7
SW2 off Christchurch Rd 181 DM88
Sidcup DA14 off Oxford Rd 186 EV92
Sch Orchard Prim Sch, The,
Wat. WD24 off Gammons La 75 BT36
Orchard Ri, Croy. CR0 203 DY102
Kingston upon Thames KT2 198 CQ95
Pinner HA5 115 BT55
Richmond TW10 158 CP84
Orchard Ri E, Sid. DA15 185 ET85
Orchard Ri W, Sid. DA15 185 ES85
Orchard Rd, N6 121 DH59
SE3 315 J8
SE18 165 ER77
Barnet EN5 79 CZ42
Beaconsfield HP9 89 AM54
Belvedere DA17 166 FA77
Brentford TW8 157 CJ79
Bromley BR1 204 EJ95
Burpham GU4 243 BB130
Chalfont St. Giles HP8 90 AW47
Chessington KT9 216 CL105
Dagenham RM10 146 FA67
Dorking RH4 263 CH137
Enfield EN3 82 DW43
Farnborough BR6 223 EP106
Feltham TW13 175 BU88
Hampton TW12 176 BZ94
Hayes UB3 135 BT73
Hounslow TW4 176 BZ85
Kingston upon Thames KT1 198 CL96
Mitcham CR4 200 DG102
Northfleet DA11 190 GC89
Old Windsor SL4 172 AV86
Onslow Village GU2 258 AT136
Otford TN14 241 FF116
Pratt's Bottom BR6 224 EW110
Reigate RH2 250 DB134
Richmond TW9 158 CN83
Riverhead TN13 256 FE122
Romford RM7 105 FB53
Seer Green HP9 89 AQ50
Shalford GU4 258 AY140
Shere GU5 260 BN139
Sidcup DA14 185 ES91
Smallfield RH6 269 DP148
South Croydon CR2 220 DV114
South Ockendon RM15 149 FW70
Sunbury-on-Thames TW16
off Hanworth Rd 175 BV94
Sutton SM1 218 DA106
Swanscombe DA10 190 FY85
Twickenham TW1 177 CG85
Welling DA16 166 EV83
Orchards, The, Epp. CM16 70 EU32
Sawbridgeworth CM21 36 EY05
Sch Orchards Acad, Swan. BR8
off St. Marys Rd 207 FE97
Sch Orchard Sch, The,
E.Mol. KT8 off Bridge Rd 197 CD98
Orchards Cl, W.Byf. KT14 212 BG114
Orchardson Ho, NW8
off Orchardson St 284 B4
Orchardson St, NW8 284 A5
Orchard Sq, W14 306 G1
Broxbourne EN10 49 DZ24
Orchards Residential Pk, The,
Slou. SL3 133 AZ74
Orchards Shop Cen,
Dart. DA1 188 FL86
Orchard St, E17 123 DY56
W1 284 G9
Dartford DA1 188 FL86
Hemel Hempstead HP3 40 BK24
St. Albans AL3 42 CC21
Orchard Ter, Enf. EN1 82 DU44
Orchard Vw, Cher. KT16 194 BG100
Uxbridge UB8 134 BK70
Orchard Vil, Sid. DA14 186 EV93
Orchardville, Burn. SL1 130 AH70
Orchard Wk, Kings.T. KT2
off Clifton Rd 198 CN95
Orchard Way, Add. KT15 212 BH106
Ashford TW15 174 BM89
Beckenham BR3 203 DY99
Bovingdon HP3 57 BA28
Chigwell IG7 104 EU48
Croydon CR0 203 DY102
Dartford DA2 188 FK90
Dorking RH4 263 CH137
Enfield EN1 82 DS41
Esher KT10 214 CC107
Goffs Oak EN7 65 DP27
Lower Kingswood KT20 249 CZ126
Mill End WD3 92 BG45
Oxted RH8 254 EG133
Potters Bar EN6 64 DB28
Reigate RH2 266 DB138
Send GU23 243 BC125
Slough SL3 132 AY74
Sutton SM1 218 DD105
Orchard Waye, Uxb. UB8 134 BK68
Sch Orchard Way Prim Sch,
Croy. CR0 off Orchard Way 203 DY101
Orchehill Av, Ger.Cr. SL9 112 AX56
Orchehill Ct, Ger.Cr. SL9 112 AY57
Orchehill Ri, Ger.Cr. SL9 112 AY57
Orchestra Cl, Edg. HA8
off Symphony Cl 96 CP52
Orchid Cl, E6 292 G6
SE13 183 ED85
Abridge RM4 86 EV41
Chessington KT9 215 CJ108
Goffs Oak EN7 66 DQ30
Hatfield AL10 29 CT14
Southall UB1 136 BY72
Orchid Ct, Egh. TW20 173 BB91
Romford RM7 127 FE61
Orchid Gdns, Houns. TW3 156 BZ84
Orchid Rd, N14 99 DJ45
Orchid St, W12 139 CU73
Orchis Gro, Bad.Dene RM17 170 FZ78
Orchis Way, Rom. RM3 106 FM51
Orde Hall St, WC1 286 C5
Ordell Rd, E3 289 P1
Ordnance Cl, Felt. TW13 175 BU89
Ordnance Cres, SE10 303 H4
Ordnance Hill, NW8 274 B9
Ordnance Ms, NW8 274 B10
Ordnance Rd, E16 291 L6
SE18 165 EN79
Enfield EN3 83 DX37
Gravesend DA12 191 GJ86
Oregano Cl, West Dr. UB7 134 BL72
Oregano Dr, E14 291 H9
Oregano Way, Guil. GU2 242 AU129
Oregon Av, E12 125 EM63
Oregon Bldg, SE13
off Deals Gateway 314 C6
Oregon Cl, N.Mal. KT3
off Georgia Rd 198 CQ98
Oregon Sq, Orp. BR6 205 ER102
Orestan La, Eff. KT24 245 BV127
Orestes Ms, NW6 273 J2
Oreston Rd, Rain. RM13 148 FK69
Orewell Gdns, Reig. RH2 266 DB136
Orford Ct, SE27 181 DP89
Orford Gdns, Twick. TW1 177 CF89
Orford Rd, E17 123 EA57
E18 124 EH55
SE6 183 EB90
Jct Organ Crossroads,
Epsom KT17 217 CU108
Organ Hall Rd, Borwd. WD6 78 CL39
Organ La, E4 101 EC47
Oriel Cl, Mitch. CR4 201 DK98
Oriel Ct, NW3 273 P1
Oriel Dr, SW13 159 CV79
Oriel Gdns, Ilf. IG5 125 EM55
Oriel Pl, NW3 273 P1
Sch Oriel Prim Sch, Han. TW13
off Hounslow Rd 176 BY90
Oriel Rd, E9 279 K4
Oriel Way, Nthlt. UB5 136 CB66
Oriens Ms, E20 280 F4
Oriental Cl, Wok. GU22
off Oriental Rd 227 BA117
Oriental Rd, E16 304 F2
Woking GU22 227 BA117
Oriental St, E14 290 B10
Orient Cl, St.Alb. AL1 43 CE22
● Orient Ind Pk, E10 123 EA61
Orient St, SE11 298 G8
Orient Way, E5 123 DX62
E10 123 DY61
Oriole Cl, Abb.L. WD5 59 BU31
Oriole Way, SE28 146 EV73
● Orion Business Cen, SE14 313 J1
● Orion Cen, The, Croy. CR0 201 DL103
Orion Ho, E1 288 F5
Orion Pt, E14 302 A8
Sch Orion Prim Sch, The, NW9
off Lanacre Av 97 CT54
Orion Rd, N11 99 DH51
Orion Way, Nthwd. HA6 93 BT49
Orissa Rd, SE18 165 ES78
Orkney Ct, Tap. SL6 130 AE66
Orkney St, SW11 308 G8
Orlando Gdns, Epsom KT19 216 CR110
Orlando Rd, SW4 161 DJ83
Orleans Cl, Esher KT10 197 CD103
★ Orleans Ho Gall,
Twick. TW1 177 CH88
Sch Orleans Inf Sch, Twick.
TW1 off Hartington Rd 177 CH87
Sch Orleans Pk Sch, Twick.
TW1 off Richmond Rd 177 CH87
Orleans Rd, SE19 182 DR93
Twickenham TW1 177 CH87
Orlestone Gdns, Orp. BR6 224 EY106
Orleston Ms, N7 276 F4
Orleston Rd, N7 276 F4
Orley Fm Rd, Har. HA1 117 CE62
Sch Orley Fm Sch, Har.Hill
HA1 off South Hill Av 117 CD62
Orlop St, SE10 315 J1
Ormanton Rd, SE26 182 DU91
Orme Ct, W2 295 L1
Orme Ct Ms, W2 295 M1
Orme La, W2 295 L1
Ormeley Rd, SW12 181 DH88
Orme Rd, Kings.T. KT1 198 CP96
Sutton SM1 off Grove Rd 218 DB107
Ormerod Gdns, Mitch. CR4 200 DG96
Ormesby Cl, SE28
off Wroxham Rd 146 EX73
Ormesby Dr, Pot.B. EN6 63 CX32
Ormesby Way, Har. HA3 118 CM58
Orme Sq, W2 295 L1
Ormiston Gro, W12 139 CV74
Sch Ormiston Pk Acad,
Aveley RM15 off Nethan Dr 149 FR73
Ormiston Rd, SE10 315 N1
Ormond Av, Hmptn. TW12 196 CB95
Richmond TW10
off Ormond Rd 177 CK85
Ormond Cl, WC1 286 B6
Harold Wood RM3
off Chadwick Dr 106 FK54
Ormond Cres, Hmptn. TW12 196 CB95
Ormond Dr, Hmptn. TW12 176 CB94
Ormonde Av, Epsom KT19 216 CR109
Orpington BR6 205 EQ103
Ormonde Gate, SW3 308 F1
Ormonde Pl, SW1 296 G9
Ormonde Ri, Buck.H. IG9 102 EJ46
Ormonde Rd, SW14 158 CP83
Northwood HA6 93 BR49
Woking GU21 226 AW116
Ormonde Ter, NW8 274 E9
Ormond Ms, WC1 286 B5
Ormond Rd, N19 121 DL60
Richmond TW10 177 CK85
Ormond Yd, SW1 297 M2
Ormsby, Sutt. SM2
off Grange Rd 218 DB108
Ormsby Gdns, Grnf. UB6 136 CC68
Ormsby Pl, N16 122 DT62
Ormsby Pt, SE18 305 P9
Ormsby St, E2 278 A10
Ormside St, SE15 312 G3
Ormside Way, Red. RH1 251 DH130
Ormskirk Rd, Wat. WD19 94 BX49
Ornan Rd, NW3 274 C3
Oronsay, Hem.H. HP3
off Northend 41 BP22
Orpen Wk, N16 122 DS62
Orphanage Rd,
Wat. WD17, WD24 76 BW40
Coll Orpheus Cen, Gdse. RH9
off North Pk La 252 DU130
Orpheus St, SE5 311 L7
ORPINGTON, BR5 & BR6 205 ES102
⇌ Orpington 205 ET103
⊖ Orpington 205 ET103
Orpington Bypass, Orp. BR6 206 EV103
Sevenoaks TN14 224 FA109
Coll Orpington Coll, Orp. BR6
off The Walnuts 206 EU102
Orpington Gdns, N18 100 DS48
H Orpington Hosp, Orp. BR6 223 ET105
Orpington Rd, N21 99 DP46
Chislehurst BR7 205 ES97
Orpin Rd, S.Merst. RH1 251 DH130
Orpwood Cl, Hmptn. TW12 176 BZ92
ORSETT HEATH, Grays RM16 171 GG75
Orsett Heath Cres,
Grays RM16 171 GG76
Orsett Rd, Grays RM17 170 GA78
Orsett St, SE11 298 D10
Orsett Ter, W2 283 M8
Woodford Green IG8 102 EJ52
Orsman Rd, N1 277 N9
Orton Cl, St.Alb. AL4 43 CG16
Orton Gro, Enf. EN1 82 DU39
Orton Pl, SW19 180 DB94
Orton St, E1 300 C3
Orville Rd, SW11 308 B8
Orwell Cl, Hayes UB3 135 BS73
Rainham RM13 147 FD71
Windsor SL4 151 AR83
Orwell Ct, N5 277 K1
Orwell Rd, E13 144 EJ68
Osbaldeston Rd, N16 122 DU61
Osberton Rd, SE12 184 EG85
Osbert St, SW1 297 N9
Osborn Cl, E8 278 C8
Osborne Av, Stai. TW19 174 BL88
Osborne Cl, Barn. EN4 80 DF41
Beckenham BR3 203 DY98
Feltham TW13 176 BX92
Hornchurch RM11 127 FH58
Osborne Ct, Pot.B. EN6 64 DB29
Windsor SL4 off Osborne Rd 151 AQ82
Osborne Gdns, Pot.B. EN6 64 DB30
Thornton Heath CR7 202 DQ96
Osborne Gro, E17 123 DZ56
N4 121 DN60
Osborne Hts, Warley CM14 108 FV49
Osborne Ms, E17
off Osborne Gro 123 DZ56
Windsor SL4 151 AQ82
Osborne Pl, Sutt. SM1 218 DD106
Osborne Rd, E7 124 EH64
E9 279 P4
E10 123 EB62
N4 121 DM60
N13 99 DN48
NW2 139 CV65
W3 158 CP76
Belvedere DA17 166 EZ78
Broxbourne EN10 49 EA19
Buckhurst Hill IG9 102 EH46
Cheshunt EN8 67 DY27
Dagenham RM9 126 EZ64
Egham TW20 173 AZ93
Enfield EN3 83 DY40
Hornchurch RM11 127 FH58
Hounslow TW3 156 BZ83
Kingston upon Thames KT2 178 CL94
Pilgrim's Hatch CM15 108 FU44
Potters Bar EN6 64 DB30
Redhill RH1 250 DG131
Southall UB1 136 CC72
Thornton Heath CR7 202 DQ96
Uxbridge UB8 off Oxford Rd 134 BJ66
Walton-on-Thames KT12 195 BU102
Watford WD24 76 BW38
Windsor SL4 151 AQ82
Osborne Sq, Dag. RM9 126 EZ63
Osborne St, Slou. SL1 152 AT75
Osborne Ter, SW17
off Church La 180 DG92
Osborne Way, Chess. KT9
off Bridge Rd 216 CM106
Epsom KT19 216 CL112
Osborn Gdns, NW7 97 CX52
Osborn La, SE23 183 DY87
Osborn St, E1 288 B7
Osborn Ter, SE3
off Lee Rd 164 EF84
Osborn Way, Welw.G.C. AL8 29 CX10
Osborn Way Tunnel,
Welw.G.C. AL8 off Osborn Way 29 CX09
Osbourne Av, Kings L. WD4 58 BM28
Osbourne Ct, W5 138 CL71
Osbourne Rd, Dart. DA2 188 FP86
Oscar Cl, Pur. CR8 219 DN110
Oscar Faber Pl, N1 277 P7
Oscar St, SE8 314 A8
Oseney Cres, NW5 275 M4
Osgood Av, Orp. BR6 223 ET106
Osgood Gdns, Orp. BR6 223 ET106
OSIDGE, N14 99 DH46
Osidge La, N14 98 DG46
Sch Osidge Prim Sch, N14
off Chase Side 99 DJ46
Osier Cres, N10 98 DF53
Osier La, SE10 303 M7
Osier Ms, W4 159 CT79
Osier Pl, Egh. TW20 173 BC93
Osiers, The, Crox.Grn WD3 75 BQ44
Osiers Rd, SW18 160 DA84
Osier St, E1 289 H5
Osier Way, E10 123 EB62
Banstead SM7 217 CY114
Mitcham CR4 200 DE99
Oslac Rd, SE6 183 EB92
Oslo Ct, NW8 284 C1
Oslo Sq, SE16 301 M6
Osman Cl, N15
off Pulford Rd 122 DR58
Sch Osmani Prim Sch, E1 288 D6
Osman Rd, N9 100 DU48
W6 294 B6
Osmington Ho, SW8 310 C5
Osmond Cl, Har. HA2 116 CC61
Osmond Gdns, Wall. SM6 219 DJ106
Osmund St, W12
off Braybrook St 139 CT71
Osnaburgh St, NW1 285 K5
NW1 (north section) 285 K3
Osnaburgh Ter, NW1 285 K4
Osney Ho, SE2 off Hartslock Dr 166 EX75
Osney Wk, Cars. SM5 200 DD100
Osney Way, Grav. DA12 191 GM89
Osprey Cl, E6 292 G7
E11 124 EG56
E17 101 DY52
Bromley BR2 204 EL102
Fetcham KT22 230 CC122
Sutton SM1 off Sandpiper Rd 217 CZ106
Watford WD25 60 BY34
West Drayton UB7 154 BK75
Osprey Ct, Wal.Abb. EN9 68 EG34
Osprey Dr, Epsom KT18 233 CV117
Osprey Gdns, S.Croy. CR2 221 DX110
Osprey Hts, SW11
off Bramlands Cl 160 DE83
Osprey La, Har. HA2 116 CB61
Osprey Ms, Enf. EN3 82 DV43
Osprey Rd, Wal.Abb. EN9 68 EG34
Ospringe Cl, SE20 182 DW94
Ospringe Ct, SE9 185 ER86
Ospringe Rd, NW5 275 L1
Osram Ct, W6 294 B7
Osram Rd, Wem. HA9 117 CK62
Osric Path, N1 287 N1
Ossian Ms, N4 121 DM59
Ossian Rd, N4 121 DM59
Jct Ossie Garvin Rbt,
Hayes UB4 136 BW73
Ossington Bldgs, W1 284 G6
Ossington Cl, W2 295 K1
Ossington St, W2 295 K1
Ossory Rd, SE1 312 C1
Ossulston St, NW1 285 N1
Ossulton Pl, N2 120 DC55
Ossulton Way, N2 120 DC56
Ostade Rd, SW2 181 DM87
Ostell Cres, Enf. EN3 83 EA38
Osten Ms, SW7 295 M7
Osterberg Rd, Dart. DA1 168 FM84
OSTERLEY, Islw. TW7 156 CC80
⊖ Osterley 157 CD80
Osterley Av, Islw. TW7 157 CD80
Osterley Cl, Orp. BR5 206 EU95
Osterley Ct, Islw. TW7 157 CD81
Osterley Cres, Islw. TW7 157 CE81
Osterley Gdns, Sthl. UB2 156 CC75
Thornton Heath CR7 202 DQ96
Osterley Ho, E14 290 C8
Osterley La, Islw. TW7 156 CE78
Southall UB2 156 CA78
Osterley Pk, Islw. TW7 157 CD78
★ Osterley Park Ho, Islw. TW7 156 CC78
Osterley Pk Rd, Sthl. UB2 156 BZ76
Osterley Pk Vw Rd, W7 157 CE75
Osterley Rd, N16 122 DS63
Isleworth TW7 157 CE80
Osterley Views, Sthl. UB2 136 CC74
Oster St, St.Alb. AL3 42 CC19
Oster Ter, E17 off Southcote Rd 123 DX57
Ostlers Dr, Ashf. TW15 175 BQ92
Ostliffe Rd, N13 100 DQ50
Oswald Bldg, SW8 309 J3
Oswald Cl, Fetch. KT22 230 CC122
Oswald Rd, Fetch. KT22 230 CC122
St. Albans AL1 43 CE21
Southall UB1 136 BY74
Oswald's Mead, E9
off Lindisfarne Way 123 DY63
Oswald St, E5 123 DX62
Oswald Ter, NW2 off Temple Rd 119 CW62
Osward, Croy. CR0 221 DZ109
Osward Pl, N9 100 DV47
Osward Rd, SW17 180 DF89
Oswell Ho, E1 300 F2
Oswin St, SE11 299 H8
Oswyth Rd, SE5 311 P8
OTFORD, Sev. TN14 241 FH116
Otford Cl, SE20 202 DW95
Bexley DA5 off Southwold Rd 187 FB86
Bromley BR1 205 EN97
Otford Cres, SE4 183 DZ86
Otford La, Halst. TN14 224 EZ112
Sch Otford Prim Sch,
Otford TN14 off High St 241 FH116
Otford Rd, Sev. TN14 241 FH118
Othello Cl, SE11 298 G10
Otho Ct, Brent. TW8 157 CK80
Otis St, E3 290 E2
Otley App, Ilf. IG2 125 EP58
Otley Dr, Ilf. IG2 125 EP57
Otley Rd, E16 292 C8
Otley Ter, E5 123 DX61
Otley Way, Wat. WD19 94 BW48
Otlinge Rd, Orp. BR5 206 EX98
Ottawa Ct, Brox. EN10 67 DY25
Ottawa Gdns, Dag. RM10 147 FD66
Ottawa Rd, Til. RM18 171 GG82
Ottaway St, E5 122 DU62
Ottenden Cl, Orp. BR6
off Southfleet Rd 223 ES105
Otterbourne Rd, E4 101 ED48
Croydon CR0 202 DQ103
Otterburn Gdns, Islw. TW7 157 CG80
Otterburn Ho, SE5 311 J4
Otterburn St, SW17 180 DF93
Otter Cl, E15 280 E9
Ottershaw KT16 211 BB107
Otterden St, SE6 183 EA91
Otterfield Rd, West Dr. UB7 134 BL73
Otter Gdns, Hat. AL10 45 CV19
Ottermead La, Ott. KT16 211 BC107
Otter Meadow, Lthd. KT22 231 CF119
Otter Rd, Grnf. UB6 136 CC70
Otters Cl, Orp. BR5 206 EX98
OTTERSHAW, Cher. KT16 211 BC106
Ottershaw Pk, Ott. KT16 211 BA109
Otterspool La, Wat. WD25 76 BY38
Otterspool Service Rd,
Wat. WD25 76 BZ39
Otterspool Way, Wat. WD25 76 BY37
Otto Cl, SE26 182 DV90
Ottoman Ter, Wat. WD17
off Ebury Rd 76 BW41
Otto St, SE17 310 G3
Ottways Av, Ashtd. KT21 231 CK119
Ottways La, Ashtd. KT21 231 CK120
Otway Gdns, Bushey WD23 95 CE45
Otways Cl, Pot.B. EN6 64 DB32
Oulton Cl, E5
off Mundford Rd 122 DW61
SE28 off Rollesby Way 146 EW72
Oulton Cres, Bark. IG11 145 ET65
Potters Bar EN6 63 CX32
Oulton Rd, N15 122 DR57
Oulton Way, Wat. WD19 94 BY49
Oundle Av, Bushey WD23 76 CC44
Sch Our Lady & St. John's RC
Prim Sch, Brent. TW8
off Boston Pk Rd 157 CJ78
Sch Our Lady & St. Joseph RC
Prim Sch, N1 277 N5
Sch Our Lady & St. Philip Neri
Prim Sch, Annexe, SE23
off Mayow Rd 183 DX90
SE26 off Sydenham Rd 183 DY91
Sch Our Lady Immaculate Cath
Prim Sch, Surb. KT6
off Ewell Rd 198 CP102
Sch Our Lady of Dolours RC
Prim Sch, W2 283 L6
Sch Our Lady of Grace Inf Sch,
NW2 off Dollis Hill Av 119 CW61
Sch Our Lady of Grace Jun Sch,
NW2 off Dollis Hill La 119 CV62
Sch Our Lady of Grace RC Prim
Sch, SE7 off Charlton Rd 164 EH79
Sch Our Lady of Lourdes Cath
Prim Sch, E11
off Chestnut Dr 124 EG58
SE13 off Belmont Hill 163 ED83
Sch Our Lady of Lourdes Prim
Sch, NW10 off Wesley Rd 138 CQ67
Sch Our Lady of Lourdes RC
Prim Sch, N11
off The Limes Avenue 99 DJ50
N12 off Bow La 98 DC53
Sch Our Lady of Muswell Cath
Prim Sch, N10 off Pages La 120 DG55
Sch Our Lady of Peace Catholic
Inf & Nurs Sch, Slou. SL1
off Derwent Dr 130 AJ71
Sch Our Lady of Peace Catholic
Jun Sch, Slou. SL1
off Derwent Dr 130 AJ71
Sch Our Lady of the Rosary
RC Prim Sch, Sid. DA15
off Holbeach Gdns 185 ES86
Staines-upon-Thames TW18
off Park Av 174 BG93
Sch Our Lady of the Visitation
RC Prim Sch, Grnf. UB6
off Greenford Rd 136 CC70
Sch Our Lady of Victories RC
Prim Sch, SW7 295 P9
SW15 off Clarendon Dr 159 CX84
Sch Our Lady Queen of Heaven
RC Prim Sch, SW19
off Victoria Dr 179 CX87
Sch Our Lady's Catholic Prim
Sch, Chesh.B. HP6
off Amersham Rd 55 AP35
Dartford DA1
off King Edward Av 188 FK86
Sch Our Lady's Conv High Sch,
N16 off Amhurst Pk 122 DS59
Sch Our Lady's Prim Sch, E14 289 P9
Sch Our Lady's RC Prim Sch,
NW1 275 L8
Welwyn Garden City AL7
off Woodhall La 29 CY11
Ousden Cl, Chsht EN8 67 DY30
Ousden Dr, Chsht EN8 67 DY30
Ouseley Rd, SW12 180 DF88
Old Windsor SL4 172 AW87
Wraysbury TW19 172 AW87
Outdowns, Eff. KT24 245 BV129
Outer Circle, NW1 284 G5
Outfield Rd, Chal.St.P. SL9 90 AX52
Outgate Rd, NW10 139 CT66
Outlook Dr, Ch.St.G. HP8 90 AX48
Outlook Ho, Enf. EN3
off Tysoe Av 83 DZ36
Outlook Pl, Wat. WD17
off Langley Rd 75 BU39
Outram Pl, N1 276 B8
Weybridge KT13 213 BQ106
Outram Rd, E6 144 EL67
N22 99 DK53
Croydon CR0 202 DT102
Outwich St, EC3 287 P8
OUTWOOD, Red. RH1 267 DP143
Outwood La, Chipstead CR5 234 DF118
Kingswood KT20 234 DB122
⊖ Oval 310 E3
Oval, The, E2 278 E10
Banstead SM7 218 DA114
Broxbourne EN10 67 DY25
Godalming GU7 258 AT144
Guildford GU2 258 AU135
Sidcup DA15 186 EU87
Oval Gdns, Grays RM17 170 GC76
Oval Pl, SW8 310 C4
Sch Oval Prim Sch, Croy. CR0
off Cherry Orchard Rd 202 DS102
Oval Rd, NW1 275 J7
Croydon CR0 202 DS102
Oval Rd N, Dag. RM10 147 FB67
Oval Rd S, Dag. RM10 147 FB68
Ovaltine Ct, Kings L. WD4 59 BP29
Ovaltine Dr, Kings L. WD4 59 BP29
Oval Way, SE11 310 D1
Gerrards Cross SL9 112 AY56
Ovanna Ms, N1 277 P5
Ovenden Rd, Sund. TN14 240 EX120
Overbrae, Beck. BR3 183 EA93
Overbrook, W.Hors. KT24 245 BP129
Overbrook Wk, Edg. HA8 96 CN52
Overbury Av, Beck. BR3 203 EB97
Overbury Cres, New Adgtn CR0 221 EC110
Overbury Rd, N15 122 DR58
Overbury St, E5 123 DX63
Overchess Ridge, Chorl. WD3 73 BF41
Overcliffe, Grav. DA11 191 GG86
Overcliff Rd, SE13 163 EA83
Grays RM17 170 GD77
Overcourt Cl, Sid. DA15 186 EV86
Overdale, Ashtd. KT21 232 CL115
Bletchingley RH1 252 DQ133
Dorking RH5 263 CJ135
Overdale Av, N.Mal. KT3 198 CQ96
Overdale Rd, W5 157 CJ76
Chesham HP5 54 AP28
Overdown Rd, SE6 183 EA91
Overhill, Warl. CR6 236 DW119
Overhill Rd, SE22 182 DU87
Purley CR8 219 DN109

O

Overhill Way, Beck. BR3 203 ED99
Overlea Rd, E5 122 DU59
Overlord Cl, Brox. EN10 49 DY20
Overlord Ct, Lthd. KT22 231 CD121
Overmead, Sid. DA15 185 ER87
Swanley BR8 207 FE99
Oversley Ho, W2 283 J6
Overstand Cl, Beck. BR3 203 EA99
Overstone Gdns, Croy. CR0 203 DZ101
Overstone Rd, W6 294 A7
Overstrand Ho, Horn. RM12 127 FH61
Overstream, Loud. WD3 74 BH42
Over The Misbourne,
Denh. UB9 113 BC58
Gerrards Cross SL9 113 BA58
Overthorpe Cl, Knap. GU21 226 AS117
Overton Cl, NW10 138 CQ65
Isleworth TW7 157 CF81
Overton Ct, E11 124 EG59
Overton Dr, E11 124 EH59
Romford RM6 126 EW59
Sch Overton Gra Sch, Sutt.
SM2 off Stanley Rd 218 DB109
Overton Ho, SW15
off Tangley Gro 179 CT87
Overton Rd, E10 123 DY60
N14 81 DL43
SE2 166 EW76
SW9 310 F9
Sutton SM2 218 DA107
Overton Rd E, SE2 166 EX76
Overtons Yd, Croy. CR0 202 DQ104
Overy St, Dart. DA1 188 FL86
Ovesdon Av, Har. HA2 116 BZ60
Oveton Way, Bkhm KT23 246 CA126
Ovett Cl, SE19 182 DS93
Ovex Cl, E14 302 F5
Ovington Ct, Wok. GU21
off Roundthorn Way 226 AT116
Ovington Gdns, SW3 296 D7
Ovington Ms, SW3 296 D7
Ovington Sq, SW3 296 D7
Ovington St, SW3 296 D7
Owen Cl, SE28 146 EW74
Croydon CR0 202 DR100
Hayes UB4 135 BV69
Northolt UB5 136 BY65
Romford RM5 105 FB51
Slough SL3 off Parsons Rd 153 AZ78
Owen Gdns, Wdf.Grn. IG8 102 EL51
Owenite St, SE2 166 EV77
Owen Pl, Lthd. KT22
off Church Rd 231 CH122
Owen Rd, N13 100 DQ50
Hayes UB4 135 BV69
Owens Ms, E11
off Short Rd 124 EE61
Owen's Row, EC1 286 G2
Owen St, EC1 286 G1
Owens Vw, Hert. SG14 32 DR07
Owens Way, SE23 183 DY87
Croxley Green WD3 74 BN43
Owen Wk, SE20
off Sycamore Gro 202 DU95
Owen Waters Ho, Ilf. IG5 103 EM53
Owen Way, NW10 138 CQ65
Owgan Cl, SE5 311 M5
Owl, The, High Beach IG10 84 EF40
Owl Cl, S.Croy. CR2 221 DX110
Owlets Hall Cl, Horn. RM11
off Prospect Rd 128 FM55
Owlsears Cl, Beac. HP9 89 AK51
Ownstead Gdns, S.Croy. CR2 220 DT111
Ownsted Hill, New Adgtn CR0 221 EC110
Oxberry Av, SW6 306 F8
Oxdowne Cl,
Stoke D'Ab. KT11 214 CB114
Oxenden Dr, Hodd. EN11 49 EA18
Oxenden Wd Rd, Orp. BR6 224 EV107
Oxendon St, SW1 297 N1
Oxenford St, SE15 162 DT83
Oxenholme, NW1 285 M1
Oxenpark Av, Wem. HA9 118 CL59
Oxestalls Rd, SE8 301 M10
Oxfield Cl, Berk. HP4 38 AU20
Oxford Av, N14 99 DJ46
SW20 199 CY96
Burnham SL1 130 AG68
Grays RM16 171 GG77
Hayes UB3 155 BT80
Hornchurch RM11 128 FN56
Hounslow TW5 156 CA78
St. Albans AL1 43 CJ21
Slough SL1 131 AM71
⊖ Oxford Circus 285 L9
Oxford Circ Av, W1 285 L9
Oxford Cl, N9 100 DV47
Ashford TW15 175 BQ94
Cheshunt EN8 67 DX29
Gravesend DA12 191 GM89
Mitcham CR4 201 DJ97
Northwood HA6 93 BQ49
Romford RM2 127 FG57
Oxford Ct, EC4 287 L10
W3 138 CN72
Feltham TW13 off Oxford Way 176 BX91
Warley CM14 108 FX49
Oxford Cres, N.Mal. KT3 198 CR100
Oxford Dr, SE1 299 N3
Ruislip HA4 116 BW61
Oxford Gdns, N20 98 DD46
N21 100 DQ45
W4 158 CN78
W10 282 F7
Denham UB9 113 BF62
Sch Oxford Gdns Prim Sch,
W10 282 C8
Oxford Gate, W6 294 D8
Oxford Ms, Bex. DA5 186 FA88
Oxford Pl, NW10
off Press Rd 118 CR62
Hatfield AL10 44 CS16
Oxford Rd, E15 281 H5
N4 121 DN60
N9 100 DV47
NW6 283 K1
SE19 182 DR93
SW15 159 CY84
W5 137 CK73
Beaconsfield HP9 111 AP55
Carshalton SM5 218 DE107
Enfield EN3 82 DV43
Gerrards Cross SL9 113 BA60
Guildford GU1 258 AX136
Harrow HA1 116 CC58
High Wycombe HP10 88 AE54
Holtspur HP9 88 AE54
Ilford IG1 125 EQ63
Redhill RH1 250 DE133
Oxford Rd, Romford RM3 106 FM51
Sidcup DA14 186 EV92
Teddington TW11 177 CD92
Uxbridge UB8, UB9 134 BJ65
Wallington SM6 219 DJ106
Wealdstone HA3 117 CF55
Windsor SL4 151 AQ81
Woodford Green IG8 102 EJ50
Oxford Rd E, Wind. SL4 151 AQ81
Oxford Rd N, W4 158 CP78
Oxford Rd S, W4 158 CN78
Oxford Sq, W2 284 D9
Oxford St, W1 285 M8
Watford WD18 75 BV43
Oxford Ter, Guil. GU1
off Pewley Hill 258 AX136
Oxford Wk, Sthl. UB1 136 BZ74
Oxford Way, Felt. TW13 176 BX91
● Oxgate Cen Ind Est, The,
NW2 119 CV60
Oxgate Gdns, NW2 119 CV62
Oxgate La, NW2 119 CV61
Oxhawth Cres, Brom. BR2 205 EN99
OXHEY, Wat. WD19 76 BW44
Oxhey Av, Wat. WD19 94 BX45
Oxhey Dr, Nthwd. HA6 93 BV50
Watford WD19 94 BW48
Oxhey Dr S, Nthwd. HA6 93 BV50
Oxhey La, Har. HA3 94 CA50
Pinner HA5 94 CA50
Watford WD19 94 BZ47
Oxhey Ridge Cl, Nthwd. HA6 93 BU50
Oxhey Rd, Wat. WD19 76 BW44
Sch Oxhey Wd Prim Sch,
S.Oxhey WD19 off Oxhey Dr 94 BW48
Ox La, Epsom KT17 217 CU109
Oxleas, E6 293 N8
Oxleas Cl, Well. DA16 165 ER82
OXLEASE, Hat. AL10 45 CV19
Oxlease Dr, Hat. AL10 45 CV19
Oxleay Ct, Har. HA2 116 CA60
Oxleay Rd, Har. HA2 116 CA60
Oxleigh Cl, N.Mal. KT3 198 CS99
Oxley Cl, SE1 300 B10
Romford RM2 106 FJ54
Oxleys, The, Harl. CM17 36 EX11
Oxley Sq, E3 290 D4
Oxleys Rd, NW2 119 CV62
Waltham Abbey EN9 68 EG32
Oxlip Cl, Croy. CR0
off Marigold Way 203 DX102
Oxlow La, Dag. RM9, RM10 126 FA63
Oxonian St, SE22 162 DT84
Oxo Twr Wf, SE1 298 F1
OXSHOTT, Lthd. KT22 215 CD113
⇌ Oxshott 214 CC113
Oxshott Ri, Cob. KT11 214 BX113
Oxshott Rd, Lthd. KT22 231 CE115
Oxshott Way, Cob. KT11 230 BY115
OXTED, RH8 253 ED129
⇌ Oxted 254 EE129
Oxted Cl, Mitch. CR4 200 DD97
Oxted Rd, Gdse. RH9 252 DW130
Sch Oxted Sch, Oxt. RH8
off Bluehouse La 254 EF128
Oxtoby Way, SW16 201 DK96
Oxygen, E16 291 N10
● Oyo Business Units
Belvedere, Belv. DA17
off Crabtree Manorway N 167 FC75
Oyster Catchers Cl, E16 292 A8
Oyster Catcher Ter, Ilf. IG5
off Tiptree Cres 125 EN55
Oysterfields, St.Alb. AL3 42 CB19
Oystergate Wk, EC4
off Swan La 299 L1
Oyster La, Byfleet KT14 212 BK110
Oyster Row, E1 289 H9
Oyster Wf, SW11 308 A8
Ozolins Way, E16 291 N8

P

Pablo Neruda Cl, SE24
off Shakespeare Rd 161 DP84
Paceheath Cl, Rom. RM5 105 FD51
Pace Pl, E1 288 F9
PACHESHAM PARK,
Lthd. KT22 231 CF116
Pachesham Pk, Lthd. KT22 231 CG117
Pacific Cl, Felt. TW14 175 BT88
Swanscombe DA10 190 FY85
Pacific Ms, SW9
off Saltoun Rd 161 DN84
Pacific Rd, E16 291 N8
● Pacific Wf, Bark. IG11 145 EP66
Pacific Wf, SE16
off Rotherhithe St 301 J3
Packet Boat La, Uxb. UB8 134 BH72
Packham Cl, Orp. BR6 206 EV104
Packham Ct, Wor.Pk. KT4
off Lavender Av 199 CW104
Packham Rd, Nthflt DA11 191 GF90
Packhorse Cl, St.Alb. AL4 43 CJ17
Packhorse La, Borwd. WD6 78 CS37
Ridge EN6 62 CR31
Packhorse Rd, Ger.Cr. SL9 112 AY58
Sevenoaks TN13 256 FC123
Packington Rd, W3 158 CQ76
Packington Sq, N1 277 J9
Packington St, N1 277 H8
Packmores Rd, SE9 185 ER85
Padbrook, Oxt. RH8 254 EG129
Padbrook Cl, Oxt. RH8 254 EH128
Padbury, SE17 311 N1
Padbury Cl, Felt. TW14 175 BR88
Padbury Ct, E2 288 B3
Padcroft Rd, West Dr. UB7 134 BK74
Paddenswick Rd, W6 159 CU76
Paddick Cl, Hodd. EN11 49 DZ16
PADDINGTON, W2 283 N7
⇌ Paddington 284 A8
⊖ Paddington 284 A8
Sch Paddington Acad, W9 283 K5
Paddington Cl, Hayes UB4 136 BX70
Paddington Grn, W2 284 B6
Sch Paddington Grn Prim Sch,
W2 284 A5
Paddington St, W1 284 G6
Paddock, The, Brox. EN10 49 EA20
Chalfont St. Peter SL9 90 AY50
Dartford DA2 189 FS89
Datchet SL3 152 AV81
Guildford GU1 243 BD133
Hatfield AL10 45 CU16
Ickenham UB10 115 BP63
Westcott RH4 262 CB137
Westerham TN16 255 EQ126
Paddock Cl, SE3 315 P9
SE26 183 DX91
Farnboro. BR6
off State Fm Av 223 EP105
Hunsdon SG12 34 EK06
Northolt UB5 136 CA68
Oxted RH8 254 EF131
South Darenth DA4 208 FQ95
Watford WD19 76 BY44
Worcester Park KT4 198 CS102
Paddock Gdns, SE19
off Westow St 182 DS93
Paddock Mead, Harl. CM18 51 EQ20
Paddock Rd, NW2 119 CU62
Bexleyheath DA6 166 EY84
Ruislip HA4 116 BX62
Paddocks, The, NW7 97 CY51
Bookham KT23
off Leatherhead Rd 246 CB126
Chorleywood WD3 73 BF42
Cockfosters EN4 80 DF41
Hertford Heath SG13 32 DV12
New Haw KT15 212 BH110
Sevenoaks TN13 257 FK124
Stapleford Abbotts RM4 87 FF44
Virginia Water GU25 192 AY100
Welwyn Garden City AL7 30 DB08
Wembley HA9 118 CP61
Weybridge KT13 195 BS104
Sch Paddock Sch, SW15
off Priory La 159 CT84
Paddocks Cl, Ashtd. KT21 232 CL118
Cobham KT11 214 BW114
Harrow HA2 116 CB63
Orpington BR5 206 EX103
Paddocks End, Seer Grn HP9
off Orchard Rd 89 AR51
Paddocks Mead, Wok. GU21 226 AS116
Paddocks Retail Pk,
Wey. KT13 212 BL111
Paddocks Rd, Guil. GU4 243 BA130
Paddocks Way, Ashtd. KT21 232 CL118
Chertsey KT16 194 BH102
Paddock Wk, Warl. CR6 236 DV119
Paddock Way, SW15 179 CW87
Ashley Green HP5 56 AT25
Chislehurst BR7 185 ER94
Hemel Hempstead HP1 39 BE20
Oxted RH8 254 EF131
Woking GU21 211 BB114
Padelford La, Stan. HA7 95 CG47
Padfield Ct, Wem. HA9
off Forty Av 118 CM62
Padfield Rd, SE5 311 J10
Padgets, The, Wal.Abb. EN9 67 ED34
Padley Cl, Chess. KT9 216 CM106
Padnall Ct, Rom. RM6
off Padnall Rd 126 EX55
Padnall Rd, Rom. RM6 126 EX56
Padstow Cl, Orp. BR6 223 ET105
Slough SL3 152 AY76
Padstow Rd, Enf. EN2 81 DP40
Padstow Wk, Felt. TW14 175 BT88
Padua Rd, SE20 202 DW95
Pagden St, SW8 309 K6
Pageant Av, NW9 96 CR53
Pageant Cl, Til. RM18 171 GJ81
Pageant Cres, SE16 301 M2
Pageantmaster Ct, EC4 286 G9
Pageant Rd, St.Alb. AL1 43 CD21
Pageant Wk, Croy. CR0 202 DS104
Page Av, Wem. HA9 118 CQ62
Page Cl, Bean DA2 189 FW90
Dagenham RM9 126 EY64
Hampton TW12 176 BY93
Harrow HA3 118 CM58
Page Cres, Croy. CR0 219 DN106
Erith DA8 167 FF80
Page Grn Rd, N15 122 DU57
Page Grn Ter, N15 122 DT57
Page Heath La, Brom. BR1 204 EK97
Page Heath Vil, Brom. BR1 204 EK97
Page Hill, Ware SG12 32 DV05
Pagehurst Rd, Croy. CR0 202 DV101
Page Meadow, NW7 97 CU52
Page Pl, Frog. AL2
off Frogmore 61 CE27
Page Rd, Felt. TW14 175 BR86
Hertford SG13 32 DU09
Pages Cft, Berk. HP4 38 AU17
Pages Hill, N10 98 DG54
Pages La, N10 98 DG54
Romford RM3 106 FP54
Uxbridge UB8 134 BJ65
Page St, NW7 97 CU53
SW1 297 P8
Pages Wk, SE1 299 N8
Pages Yd, W4
off Church St 158 CS79
Paget Av, Sutt. SM1 200 DD104
Paget Cl, Hmptn. TW12 177 CD91
Paget Gdns, Chis. BR7 205 EP95
Paget La, Islw. TW7 157 CD83
Paget Pl, Kings.T. KT2 178 CQ93
Thames Ditton KT7
off Brooklands Rd 197 CG102
Paget Ri, SE18 165 EN80
Paget Rd, N16 122 DR60
Ilford IG1 125 EP63
Slough SL3 153 AZ77
Uxbridge UB10 135 BQ70
Paget St, EC1 286 G2
Paget Ter, SE18 165 EN79
Pagette Way, Bad.Dene RM17 170 GA77
Pagitts Gro, Barn. EN4 80 DB39
Paglesfield, Hutt. CM13 109 GC44
Pagnell St, SE14 313 N4
Pagoda Av, Rich. TW9 158 CM83
Pagoda Gdns, SE3 314 G9
Pagoda Gro, SE27 182 DQ89
Pagoda Vista, Rich. TW9 158 CM82
Paignton Cl, Rom. RM3 106 FK53
Paignton Rd, N15 122 DS58
Ruislip HA4 115 BU62
Paines Brook Rd, Rom. RM3
off Paines Brook Way 106 FM51
Paines Brook Way, Rom. RM3 106 FM51
Paines Cl, Pnr. HA5 116 BY55
Painesfield Dr, Cher. KT16 194 BG103
Paines La, Pnr. HA5 94 BY53
Pains Cl, Mitch. CR4 201 DH96
Jct Painshill, Cob. KT11 213 BT113
Pains Hill, Oxt. RH8 254 EJ132
★ Painshill Park, Cob. KT11 213 BS114
Painsthorpe Rd, N16
off Oldfield Rd 122 DS62
Painter Ho, E1
off Sidney St 288 F8
Painters Ash La, Nthflt DA11 190 GD90
Sch Painters Ash Prim Sch,
Nthflt DA11 off Masefield Rd 190 GD90
Painters La, Enf. EN3 83 DY35
Painters Ms, SE16
off Macks Rd 300 D8
Painters Rd, Ilf. IG2 125 ET55
Paisley Rd, N22 99 DP53
Carshalton SM5 200 DD102
Paisley Ter, Cars. SM5 200 DD101
Sch Pakeman Prim Sch, N7
off Hornsey Rd 121 DM62
Pakeman St, N7 121 DM62
Pakenham Cl, SW12
off Balham Pk Rd 180 DG88
Pakenham St, WC1 286 D3
Pakes Way, They.B. CM16 85 ES37
Palace Av, W8 295 M3
Palace Cl, E9 279 P5
Kings Langley WD4 58 BM30
Slough SL1 131 AM74
Palace Ct, NW3 273 M2
W2 283 L10
Harrow HA3 118 CL58
Palace Ct Gdns, N10 121 DJ55
Palace Dr, Wey. KT13 195 BP104
Palace Ex, Enf. EN2 82 DR42
Palace Gdns, Enf. EN2 82 DR42
Palace Gdns, Buck.H. IG9 102 EK46
Palace Gdns Ms, W8 295 K2
Palace Gdns Ter, W8 295 K2
Palace Gate, W8 295 N5
Palace Gates Rd, N22 99 DK53
Palace Grn, W8 295 M4
Croydon CR0 221 DZ108
Palace Gro, SE19 182 DT94
Bromley BR1 204 EH95
Palace Ms, E17 123 DZ56
SW1 297 H9
SW6 307 H5
● Palace of Industry,
Wem. HA9 off Fulton Rd 118 CN63
Palace Par, E17 123 DZ56
Palace Pl, SW1 297 L6
Palace Rd, N8 121 DK57
N11 99 DL52
SE19 182 DT94
SW2 181 DM88
Bromley BR1 204 EH95
East Molesey KT8 197 CD97
Kingston upon Thames KT1 197 CK98
Ruislip HA4 116 BY63
Westerham TN16 239 EN121
Palace Rd Est, SW2 181 DM88
Palace Sq, SE19 182 DT94
Palace St, SW1 297 L6
Palace Vw, SE12 184 EG89
Bromley BR1 204 EG97
Croydon CR0 221 DZ105
Palace Vw Rd, E4 101 EB50
Palace Way, Wey. KT13
off Palace Dr 195 BP104
Woking GU22 227 BB120
Palamos Rd, E10 123 EA60
Palatine Av, N16 277 P1
Palatine Rd, N16 277 P1
Palemead Cl, SW6 306 C6
Palermo Rd, NW10 139 CU68
Palestine Gro, SW19 200 DD95
Palewell Cl, Orp. BR5 206 EV96
Palewell Common Dr, SW14 178 CR85
Palewell Pk, SW14 178 CR85
Paley Gdns, Loug. IG10 85 EP41
Palfrey Cl, St.Alb. AL3 43 CD18
Palfrey Pl, SW8 310 D4
Palgrave Av, Sthl. UB1 136 CA73
Palgrave Gdns, NW1 284 D4
Palgrave Ho, NW3 274 E2
Palgrave Rd, W12 159 CT76
Palissy St, E2 288 A3
Palladian Circ, Green. DA9 169 FW84
Palladino Ho, SW17
off Laurel Cl 180 DE92
Palladio Ct, SW18
off Mapleton Rd 180 DB86
Pallant Way, Orp. BR6 205 EN104
Pallas Rd, Hem.H. HP2 40 BM18
Pallet Way, SE18 164 EL81
Palliser Dr, Rain. RM13 147 FG71
Palliser Rd, W14 294 E10
Chalfont St. Giles HP8 90 AU48
Pallister Ter, SW15
off Roehampton Vale 179 CT90
Pall Mall, SW1 297 M3
Pall Mall E, SW1 297 P2
Palmar Cres, Bexh. DA7 166 FA83
Palmar Rd, Bexh. DA7 166 FA82
Palmarsh Rd, Orp. BR5
off Wotton Grn 206 EX98
Palm Av, Sid. DA14 186 EX93
Palm Cl, E10 123 EB62
Palmeira Rd, Bexh. DA7 166 EX83
Palmer Av, Bushey WD23 76 CB43
Gravesend DA12 191 GK91
Sutton SM3 217 CW105
Sch Palmer Cath Sch, The,
Ilf. IG3 off Aldborough Rd S 125 ES60
Palmer Cl, Hert. SG14 32 DQ07
Horley RH6 268 DF145
Hounslow TW5 156 CA81
Northolt UB5 136 BY65
Redhill RH1 266 DG135
West Wickham BR4 203 ED104
Palmer Cres, Kings.T. KT1 198 CL97
Ottershaw KT16 211 BD107
Palmer Dr, Brom. BR1 205 EP98
Palmer Gdns, Barn. EN5 79 CX43
Palmer Ho, SE14
off Lubbock St 313 J5
Palmer Pl, N7 276 E3
Palmer Rd, E13 292 B5
Dagenham RM8 126 EX60
Hertford SG14 32 DR07
Palmers Av, Grays RM17 170 GC78
Coll Palmer's Coll, Grays RM17
off Chadwell Rd 170 GE77
Palmers Dr, Grays RM17 170 GC77
Palmersfield Rd, Bans. SM7 218 DA114
PALMERS GREEN, N13 99 DN48
⇌ Palmers Green 99 DM49
Sch Palmers Grn High Sch, N21
off Hoppers Rd 99 DN47
Palmers Gro, Lwr Naze. EN9 50 EF22
West Molesey KT8 196 CA98
Palmers Hill, Epp. CM16 70 EU29
Palmers La, Enf. EN1, EN3 82 DV39
Palmer's Lo, Guil. GU2
off Old Palace Rd 258 AV135
Palmers Moor La, Iver SL0 134 BG70
Palmers Orchard, Shore. TN14 225 FF111
Palmers Pas, SW14
off Palmers Rd 158 CQ83
Palmers Rd, E2 289 K1
N11 99 DJ50
SW14 158 CQ83
SW16 201 DM96
Borehamwood WD6 78 CP39
Palmerston Av, Slou. SL3 152 AV76
Palmerston Cl, Red. RH1
off Reed Dr 266 DG137
Welwyn Garden City AL8 29 CW09
Woking GU21 211 AZ114
Palmerston Cres, N13 99 DM50
SE18 165 EQ79
Palmerstone Ct, Vir.W. GU25
off Sandhills La 192 AY99
Palmerston Gdns,
Grays RM20 169 FX78
Palmerston Gro, SW19 180 DA94
Palmerston Ho, SW11
off Strasburg Rd 309 H7
W8 295 J3
Palmerston Rd, E7 124 EH64
E17 123 DZ56
N22 99 DM52
NW6 273 J6
SW14 158 CQ84
SW19 180 DA94
W3 158 CQ76
Buckhurst Hill IG9 102 EH47
Carshalton SM5 218 DF105
Croydon CR0 202 DR99
Grays RM20 169 FX78
Harrow HA3 117 CF55
Hounslow TW3 156 CC81
Orpington BR6 223 EQ105
Rainham RM13 148 FJ68
Sutton SM1 off Vernon Rd 218 DC106
Twickenham TW2 177 CE86
Palmerston Way, SW8 309 K5
Palmer St, SW1 297 N5
Palmers Way, Chsht EN8 67 DY29
Palm Gro, W5 158 CL76
Guildford GU1 242 AW129
Palm Rd, Rom. RM7 127 FC57
Pamela Av, Hem.H. HP3 40 BM23
Pamela Gdns, Pnr. HA5 115 BV57
Pamela Wk, E8 278 C8
Pampisford Rd, Pur. CR8 219 DN111
South Croydon CR2 219 DP108
Pams Way, Epsom KT19 216 CR106
Pancake La, Hem.H. HP2 41 BR21
Pancras La, EC4 287 K9
Pancras Rd, N1 276 A10
NW1 275 N10
Pancras Sq, N1 276 A10
Pancras Sq Lib, N1 276 A10
Pancras Way, E3 280 A10
Pancroft, Abridge RM4 86 EV41
Pandian Way, NW1 275 N4
Pandora Rd, NW6 273 J4
Panfield Ms, Ilf. IG2 125 EN58
Panfield Rd, SE2 166 EU76
Pangbourne Av, W10 282 B6
Pangbourne Dr, Stan. HA7 95 CK50
Pangbourne Ho, N7 275 P3
Panhard Pl, Sthl. UB1 136 CB73
Pank Av, Barn. EN5 80 DC43
Pankhurst Av, E16 304 B2
Pankhurst Cl, SE14 313 J5
Isleworth TW7 157 CF83
Pankhurst Ho, W12
off Du Cane Rd 282 A9
Pankhurst Pl, Wat. WD24 76 BW41
Pankhurst Rd, Walt. KT12 196 BW101
Panmuir Rd, SW20 199 CV95
Panmure Cl, N5 277 H1
Panmure Rd, SE26 182 DV90
Pannells Cl, Cher. KT16 193 BF102
Pannells Ct, Guil. GU1 258 AX135
Hounslow TW5 156 BZ79
Panoramic, The, NW3 274 D2
Pan Peninsula Sq, E14
off Millharbour 302 C5
PANSHANGER, Welw.G.C. AL7 30 DB09
Panshanger Dr, Welw.G.C. AL7 30 DB09
Panshanger La, Cole Grn SG14 30 DF10
Sch Panshanger Prim Sch,
Welw.G.C. AL7 off Daniells 30 DA08
Pansy Gdns, W12 139 CU73
Panters, Swan. BR8 187 FF94
Panther Dr, NW10 118 CR64
Pantile Rd, Wey. KT13 213 BR105
Pantile Row, Slou. SL3 153 BA77
Pantiles, The, NW11 119 CZ56
Bexleyheath DA7 166 EZ80
Bromley BR1 204 EL97
Bushey Heath WD23 95 CD45
Pantiles Cl, N13 99 DP50
Woking GU21 226 AV118
Pantile Wk, Uxb. UB8
off The Mall Pavilions 134 BJ66
Panton Cl, Croy. CR0 201 DP102
Panton St, SW1 297 N1
Panxworth Rd, Hem.H. HP3 40 BL22
Panyer All, EC4 287 J9
Panyers Gdns, Dag. RM10 127 FB62
Papercourt La, Ripley GU23 227 BF122
Paper Ms, Dor. RH4 263 CH135
Papermill Cl, Cars. SM5 218 DG105
Paper Mill La, Dart. DA1
off Lawson Rd 168 FK84
Sch Papillon Ho Sch,
Tad. KT20 off Pebble Cl 248 CS129
Papillons Wk, SE3 315 N9
Papworth Gdns, N7 276 D3
Papworth Way, SW2 181 DN87
Parade, The, SW11 308 F4
Aveley RM15 168 FQ75
Brentwood CM14
off Kings Rd 108 FW48
Burgh Heath KT20 233 CY119
Carpenders Park WD19 94 BY48
Carshalton SM5
off Beynon Rd 218 DF106
Claygate KT10 215 CE107
Dartford DA1
off Crayford Way 187 FF85
Epsom KT17, KT18 216 CR113
Epsom Common KT18
off Spa Dr 216 CN114
Hampton TW12
off Hampton Rd 177 CD92
Romford RM3 106 FP51

O
P

Parade, The, South Oxhey
WD19 off Prestwick Rd 94 BX48
Sunbury-on-Thames TW16 175 BT94
Virginia Water GU25 192 AX100
Watford WD17 75 BV41
Windsor SL4 151 AK81
Par Cl, Hert. SG13
off Birdie Way 32 DV08
Parade Ms, SE27 181 DP89
Paradise, Hem.H. HP2 40 BK21
Paradise Cl, Chsht EN7 66 DV28
Paradise Pk, E5 123 DX61
Paradise Pas, N7 276 E3
Paradise Path, SE28
off Birchdene Dr 146 EU74
Paradise Pl, SE18 305 H9
Paradise Rd, SW4 310 A8
Richmond TW9 177 CK85
Waltham Abbey EN9 67 EC34
Paradise Row, E2 288 F2
Paradise St, SE16 300 E5
Paradise Wk, SW3 308 E2
Paragon, The, SE3 315 M8
Paragon Cl, E16 291 N8
Paragon Gro, Surb. KT5 198 CM100
Paragon Ms, SE1 299 M8
Paragon Pl, SE3 315 M8
Surbiton KT5
off Berrylands Rd 198 CM100
Paragon Rd, E9 278 F5
● **Paramount Ind Est**,
Wat. WD24 76 BW38
Parbury Ri, Chess. KT9 216 CL107
Parbury Rd, SE23 183 DY86
Parchment Cl, Amer. HP6 55 AS37
Parchmore Rd, Th.Hth. CR7 201 DP96
Parchmore Way, Th.Hth. CR7 201 DP96
Sch **Pardes Ho Gram Sch**, N3
off Hendon La 97 CZ54
Sch **Pardes Ho Prim Sch**, N3
off Hendon La 97 CZ54
Pardoe Rd, E10 123 EB59
Pardoner St, SE1 299 M6
Pardon St, EC1 287 H4
Pares Cl, Wok. GU21 226 AX116
Parfett St, E1 288 D7
Parfitt Cl, NW3 off North End 120 DC61
Parfour Dr, Ken. CR8 236 DQ116
Parfrey St, W6 306 B2
Parham Dr, Ilf. IG2 125 EP58
Parham Way, N10 99 DJ54
Sch **Paringdon Jun Sch**,
Harl. CM18 off Paringdon Rd 51 ER19
Paringdon Rd,
Harl. CM18, CM19 51 EP19
Paris Gdn, SE1 298 G2
Sch **Parish Ch C of E Junior, Inf & Nurs Schs**, Croy. CR0
off Warrington Rd 201 DP104
Parish Cl, Horn. RM12 127 FH61
Watford WD25 off Crown Ri 60 BX34
Sch **Parish C of E Prim Sch**,
Brom. BR1 off London La 184 EG94
Parish Gate Dr, Sid. DA15 185 ES86
Parish La, SE20 183 DX93
Farnham Common SL2 111 AP61
Parish Ms, SE20 183 DX94
Parish Way, Harl. CM20 35 EQ13
Parish Wf, SE18 305 H8
Parison Cl, Rich. TW9 158 CN83
Park, The, N6 120 DG58
NW11 120 DB60
SE19 182 DS94
SE23 off Park Hill 182 DW88
W5 137 CK74
Bookham KT23 230 CA123
Carshalton SM5 218 DF106
St. Albans AL1 43 CG18
Sidcup DA14 186 EU92
Park App, Well. DA16 166 EV84
Park Av, E6 145 EN67
E15 281 J5
N3 98 DB53
N13 99 DN48
N18 100 DU49
N22 99 DL54
NW2 139 CV65
NW10 138 CM69
NW11 120 DB60
SW14 158 CR84
Barking IG11 145 EQ65
Bromley BR1 184 EF93
Bushey WD23 76 BZ40
Carshalton SM5 218 DG107
Caterham CR3 236 DS124
Chorleywood WD3 74 BG43
Egham TW20 173 BC93
Enfield EN1 82 DS44
Farnborough BR6 205 EM104
Gravesend DA12 191 GJ88
Grays RM20 169 FU79
Harlow CM17 52 EW18
Hounslow TW3 176 CB86
Hutton CM13 109 GC46
Ilford IG1 125 EN61
Mitcham CR4 181 DH94
Northfleet DA11 190 GE88
Orpington BR6 206 EU103
Potters Bar EN6 64 DC34
Radlett WD7 61 CH33
Redhill RH1 266 DF142
Ruislip HA4 115 BR58
St. Albans AL1 43 CG19
Southall UB1 136 CA74
Staines-upon-Thames TW18 173 BF93
Upminster RM14 129 FS59
Watford WD18 75 BU42
West Wickham BR4 203 EC103
Woodford Green IG8 102 EH50
Wraysbury TW19 172 AX85
Park Av E, Epsom KT17 217 CU107
Park Av Ms, Mitch. CR4
off Park Av 181 DH94
Park Av N, N8 121 DK55
NW10 119 CV64
Park Av Rd, N17 100 DV52
Park Av S, N8 121 DK56
Park Av W, Epsom KT17 217 CU107
PARK BARN, Guil. GU2 242 AS133
Park Barn Dr, Guil. GU2 242 AS132
Park Barn E, Guil. GU2 242 AT133
Park Boul, Rom. RM2 105 FF53
Park Cen Bldg, E3
off Fairfield Rd 280 B10
Park Chase, Guil. GU1 242 AY134
Wembley HA9 118 CM63
Park Cliff Rd, Green. DA9 169 FW84
Park Cl, E9 279 H8
NW2 119 CV62
NW10 138 CM69
SW1 296 E5
W4 158 CR78
W14 295 H6
Brookmans Park AL9 63 CZ26
Bushey WD23 76 BX41
Byfleet KT14 212 BK113
Carshalton SM5 218 DF107
Esher KT10 214 BZ107
Fetcham KT22 231 CD124
Hampton TW12 196 CC95
Harrow HA3 95 CE53
Hatfield AL9 45 CW17
Hounslow TW3 176 CC85
Kingston upon Thames KT2 198 CN95
New Haw KT15 212 BH110
North Weald Bassett CM16 70 FA27
Oxted RH8 254 EF128
Rickmansworth WD3 93 BP49
Strood Green RH3 264 CP139
Walton-on-Thames KT12 195 BT103
Windsor SL4 151 AR82
Park Copse, Dor. RH5 263 CK136
Park Cor, Coln.Hth AL4 44 CP23
Windsor SL4 151 AL83
Park Cor Dr, E.Hors. KT24 245 BS128
Park Cor Rd, Sthflt DA13 190 FZ91
Park Ct, SE21 182 DQ90
SE26 182 DV93
SW11 309 J6
Bookham KT23 246 CA125
Hampton Wick KT1 197 CJ95
Harlow CM20 35 ER14
New Malden KT3 198 CR98
Wembley HA9 118 CL64
West Byfleet KT14 212 BG113
Woking GU22 off Park Dr 227 AZ118
Park Cres, N3 98 DB52
W1 285 J5
Elstree WD6 78 CM41
Enfield EN2 82 DR42
Erith DA8 167 FC79
Harrow HA3 95 CE53
Hornchurch RM11 127 FG59
Twickenham TW2 177 CD88
Park Cres Ms E, W1 285 K5
Park Cres Ms W, W1 285 J6
Park Cres Rd, Erith DA8 167 FD79
Park Cft, Edg. HA8 96 CQ53
Parkcroft Rd, SE12 184 EF87
Park Dale, N11 99 DK51
Parkdale Cres, Wor.Pk. KT4 198 CR104
Parkdale Rd, SE18 165 ES78
Park Dr, N21 82 DQ44
NW11 120 DB60
SE7 164 EL79
SW14 158 CR84
W3 158 CN76
Ashtead KT21 232 CN118
Dagenham RM10 127 FC62
Harrow Weald HA3 95 CE51
Hatfield Heath CM22 37 FH05
North Harrow HA2 116 CA59
Potters Bar EN6 64 DA31
Romford RM1 127 FD56
Upminster RM14 128 FQ63
Weybridge KT13 213 BP106
Woking GU22 227 AZ118
Park Dr Cl, SE7 164 EL78
Park E Bldg, E3 off Fairfield Rd 280 B10
Park End, NW3 274 D1
Bromley BR1 204 EF95
Park End Rd, Rom. RM1 127 FE56
Parker Av, Hert. SG14 32 DR07
Tilbury RM18 171 GJ81
Parker Cl, E16 304 G3
Carshalton SM5 218 DF107
Parker Ms, WC2 286 B8
Parke Rd, SW13 159 CU81
Sunbury-on-Thames TW16 195 BU98
Parker Rd, Croy. CR0 220 DQ105
Grays RM17 170 FZ78
Parkers Cl, Ashtd. KT21 232 CL119
Parkers Hill, Ashtd. KT21 232 CL119
Parkers La, Ashtd. KT21 232 CL119
Parkers Row, SE1 300 B5
Parker St, E16 304 G3
WC2 286 B8
Watford WD24 75 BV39
Parkes Rd, Chig. IG7 103 ES50
Park Fm Cl, N2 120 DC55
Pinner HA5 115 BV57
Park Fm Rd, Brom. BR1 204 EK95
Kingston upon Thames KT2 178 CL94
Upminster RM14 128 FM64
Parkfield, Chorl. WD3 73 BF42
Sevenoaks TN15 257 FM123
Parkfield Av, SW14 158 CS84
Amersham HP6 55 AR37
Feltham TW13 175 BU90
Harrow HA2 94 CC54
Hillingdon UB10 135 BP69
Northolt UB5 136 BX68
Parkfield Cl, Edg. HA8 96 CP51
Northolt UB5 136 BY68
Parkfield Cres, Felt. TW13 175 BU90
Harrow HA2 94 CC54
Ruislip HA4 116 BY62
Parkfield Dr, Nthlt. UB5 136 BX68
Parkfield Gdns, Har. HA2 116 CB55
Sch **Parkfield Prim Sch**, NW4
off Park Rd 119 CV59
Parkfield Rd, NW10 139 CU66
SE14 313 N6
SW4 181 DK86
Feltham TW13 175 BU90
Harrow HA2 116 CC62
Ickenham UB10 115 BP61
Northolt UB5 136 BY68
Parkfields, SW15 159 CW84
Croydon CR0 203 DZ102
Oxshott KT22 215 CD111
Roydon CM19 50 EH16
Welwyn Garden City AL8 29 CX09
Parkfields Av, NW9 118 CR60
SW20 199 CV95
Parkfields Cl, Cars. SM5 218 DG105
Parkfields Rd, Kings.T. KT2 178 CM92
Parkfield St, N1 276 F10
Parkfield Vw, Pot.B. EN6 64 DB32
Parkfield Way, Brom. BR2 205 EM100
Park Gdns, NW9 118 CP55
Erith DA8 off Valley Rd 167 FD77
Kingston upon Thames KT2 178 CM92
Park Gate, N2 120 DD55
N21 99 DM45
W5 137 CK71
Parkgate, SE3 164 EF83
Burnham SL1 130 AJ70
Parkgate Av, Barn. EN4 80 DC39
Parkgate Cl, Kings.T. KT2
off Warboys App 178 CP93
Park Gate Ct, Wok. GU22
off Constitution Hill 226 AY118
Parkgate Cres, Barn. EN4 80 DC40
Parkgate Gdns, SW14 178 CR85
Sch **Parkgate Inf & Nurs Sch**,
Wat. WD24
off Northfield Gdns 76 BW37
Sch **Parkgate Jun Sch**, Wat.
WD24 off Southwold Rd 76 BW37
Parkgate Ms, N6 121 DJ59
Parkgate Rd, SW11 308 C5
Orpington BR6 225 FB105
Reigate RH2 266 DB135
Wallington SM6 218 DG106
Watford WD24 76 BW37
Park Gates, Har. HA2 116 CA63
Park Gra Gdns, Sev. TN13
off Solefields Rd 257 FJ127
Park Grn, Bkhm KT23 230 CA124
Park Gro, E15 281 N8
N11 99 DK52
Bexleyheath DA7 167 FC84
Bromley BR1 204 EH95
Chalfont St. Giles HP8 72 AX41
Edgware HA8 96 CM50
Knotty Green HP9 88 AJ48
Park Gro Rd, E11 124 EE61
Park Hall Rd, N2 120 DE56
SE21 182 DQ90
Reigate RH2 250 DA132
● **Park Hall Trd Est**, SE21 182 DQ90
Parkham Ct, Brom. BR2 204 EE96
Parkham St, SW11 308 B7
Park Hts, Wok. GU22
off Constitution Hill 226 AY118
Sch **Park High Sch**, Stan. HA7
off Thistlecroft Gdns 95 CK54
Park Hill, SE23 182 DV89
SW4 181 DK85
W5 137 CK71
Bromley BR1 204 EL98
Carshalton SM5 218 DE107
Harlow CM17 36 EV12
Loughton IG10 84 EK43
Richmond TW10 178 CM86
Park Hill Cl, Cars. SM5 218 DE106
Parkhill Cl, Horn. RM12 128 FJ62
Park Hill Ct, SW17
off Beeches Rd 180 DF90
Sch **Parkhill Inf & Jun Schs**,
Ilf. IG5 off Lord Av 125 EN55
Sch **Park Hill Inf Sch**,
Croy. CR0 off Stanhope Rd 202 DS104
Sch **Park Hill Jun Sch**,
Croy. CR0 off Stanhope Rd 202 DS104
Park Hill Ri, Croy. CR0 202 DS103
Parkhill Rd, E4 101 EC46
NW3 274 F4
Bexley DA5 186 EZ87
Hemel Hempstead HP1 40 BH20
Sidcup DA15 185 ER90
Park Hill Rd, Brom. BR2 204 EE96
Croydon CR0 202 DS103
Epsom KT17 217 CT111
Wallington SM6 219 DH108
Sch **Park Hill Sch**, Kings.T.
KT2 off Queens Rd 178 CN94
Parkhill Wk, NW3 274 F3
Parkholme Rd, E8 278 B4
Park Homes, Lon.Col. AL2
off Peters Av 61 CJ26
Park Horsley, E.Hors. KT24 245 BU129
Parkhouse 45 CT17
Park Ho, N21 99 DM45
Parkhouse Ct, Hat. AL10 44 CS17
Park Ho Dr, Reig. RH2 265 CZ136
Park Ho Gdns, Twick. TW1 177 CJ86
Parkhouse St, SE5 311 M4
Parkhurst, Epsom KT19 216 CQ110
Parkhurst Gdns, Bex. DA5 186 FA87
Parkhurst Gro, Horl. RH6 268 DE147
Parkhurst Ho, W12 282 A9
Parkhurst Rd, E12 125 EN63
E17 123 DY56
N7 276 A1
N11 98 DG49
N17 100 DU54
N22 99 DM52
Bexley DA5 186 FA87
Guildford GU2 242 AU133
Hertford SG14 31 DP08
Horley RH6 268 DE147
Sutton SM1 218 DD105
● **Park Ind Est**, Frog. AL2 61 CE27
Parkinson Ho, SW1
off Tachbrook St 297 N10
Parkland Av, Rom. RM1 127 FE55
Slough SL3 152 AX77
Upminster RM14 128 FP64
Parkland Cl, Chig. IG7 103 EQ48
Hoddesdon EN11 33 EB14
Sevenoaks TN13 257 FJ129
Parkland Dr, St.Alb. AL3 42 CA21
Parkland Gdns, SW19 179 CX88
Parkland Gro, Ashf. TW15 174 BN91
Parkland Mead, Brom. BR1
off Gardenia Rd 205 EP97
Parkland Ms, Chis. BR7 185 ER94
Parkland Rd, N22 99 DM54
Ashford TW15 174 BN91
Woodford Green IG8 102 EG52
Parklands, N6 121 DH59
Addlestone KT15 212 BJ106
Bookham KT23 230 CA123
Chigwell IG7 103 EQ48
Coopersale CM16 70 EX29
Guildford GU2 242 AU130
Hemel Hempstead HP1 39 BF18
North Holmwood RH5 263 CH140
Oxted RH8 254 EE131
Shere GU5 260 BN141
Surbiton KT5 198 CM99
Waltham Abbey EN9 67 ED32
Parklands Cl, SW14 178 CQ85
Barnet EN4 80 DD38
Ilford IG2 125 EQ59
Parklands Ct, Houns. TW5 156 BX82
Parklands Dr, N3 119 CY55
Parklands Gro, Islw. TW7 157 CF81
Sch **Parklands Inf Sch**,
Rom. RM1 off Havering Rd 105 FD54
Sch **Parklands Jun Sch**,
Rom. RM1 off Havering Rd 127 FD55
Parklands Pl, Guil. GU1 243 BB134
Parklands Rd, SW16 181 DH92
Parklands Way, Wor.Pk. KT4 198 CS104
Parkland Wk, N4 121 DM59
N6 121 DK59
N10 121 DH56
Park La, E15 280 G8
N9 100 DT48
N17 100 DU52
W1 297 H3
Ashtead KT21 232 CM118
Aveley RM15 149 FR74
Banstead SM7 234 DD118
Beaconsfield HP9 89 AM54
Broxbourne EN10 49 DY19
Burnham SL1 111 AL64
Carshalton SM5 218 DG105
Chadwell Heath RM6 126 EX58
Cheshunt EN7 66 DU26
Colney Heath AL4 44 CP23
Coulsdon CR5 235 DK121
Cranford TW5 155 BU80
Croydon CR0 202 DR104
Elm Pk RM12 147 FH65
Greenhithe DA9 189 FU86
Guildford GU4 243 BC131
Harefield UB9 92 BG53
Harlow CM20 35 ER13
Harrow HA2 116 CB62
Hayes UB4 135 BS71
Hemel Hempstead HP1, HP2 40 BK21
Hornchurch RM11 127 FG58
Horton SL3 153 BA83
Reigate RH2 265 CY135
Richmond TW9 157 CK84
Seal TN15 257 FN121
Sevenoaks TN13 257 FJ124
Slough SL3 152 AV76
Stanmore HA7 95 CG48
Sutton SM3 217 CY107
Swanley BR8 208 FJ96
Teddington TW11 177 CF93
Wallington SM6 218 DG105
Waltham Cross EN8 67 DX33
Wembley HA9 118 CL64
Wormley EN10 48 DV22
Park La Cl, N17 100 DU52
Park La E, Reig. RH2 266 DA136
Park La Paradise, Chsht EN7 48 DU24
Sch **Park La Prim Sch**,
Wem. HA9 off Park La 118 CL63
PARK LANGLEY, Beck. BR3 203 EC99
Park Lawn, Farn.Royal SL2 131 AQ69
Parklawn Av, Epsom KT18 216 CP113
Horley RH6 268 DF146
Park Lawn Rd, Wey. KT13 213 BQ105
Park Lawns, Wem. HA9 118 CM63
Parklea Cl, NW9 96 CS53
Parkleigh Rd, SW19 200 DB96
Park Ley Rd, Wold. CR3 237 DX120
Parkleys, Rich. TW10 177 CK91
Park Lo Av, West Dr. UB7 154 BM75
Park Mans, SW1
off Knightsbridge 296 E5
SW8 310 B2
Parkmead, SW15 179 CV86
Loughton IG10 85 EN43
Park Mead, Harl. CM20 35 EP14
Harrow HA2 116 CB62
Sidcup DA15 186 EV85
Parkmead Cl, Croy. CR0 203 DX100
Parkmead Gdns, NW7 97 CT51
Park Meadow, Hat. AL9 45 CW17
Park Ms, SE10 315 M1
SE24 off Croxted Rd 182 DQ86
Chislehurst BR7 185 EP93
East Molesey KT8 196 CC98
Hatfield AL9 45 CW16
Oxted RH8 254 EF128
Rainham RM13 147 FG65
Parkmore Cl, Wdf.Grn. IG8 102 EG49
Park Nook Gdns, Enf. EN2 82 DR37
Parkpale La, Bet. RH3 264 CN139
Park Par, NW10 139 CT68
Park Piazza, SE13
off Highfield Cl 183 ED86
Park Pl, E14 302 A2
N1 277 M8
SW1 297 L3
W3 158 CN77
W5 137 CK74
Amersham HP6 72 AT38
Gravesend DA12 191 GJ86
Hampton Hill TW12 176 CC93
Park Street AL2 61 CD27
Seer Green HP9 89 AR50
Sevenoaks TN13 256 FD123
Wembley HA9 118 CM63
Woking GU22 off Hill Vw Rd 227 AZ118
Park Pl Vil, W2 283 P6
Sch **Park Prim Sch**, E15 281 M6
Park Ridings, N8 121 DN55
Park Ri, SE23 183 DY88
Harrow HA3 95 CE53
Leatherhead KT22 231 CH121
Northchurch HP4 38 AS17
Park Ri Cl, Lthd. KT22 231 CH121
Park Ri Rd, SE23 183 DY88
Park Rd, E6 144 EJ67
E10 123 EA60
E12 124 EH60
E15 281 N8
E17 123 DZ57
N2 120 DD55
N8 121 DJ56
N11 99 DK52
N14 99 DK45
N15 121 DP56
N18 100 DT49
NW1 284 C2
NW4 119 CU59
NW8 284 C2
NW9 118 CR59
NW10 138 CS67
SE25 202 DS98
SW19 180 DD93
W4 158 CQ80
W7 137 CF73
Albury GU5 260 BL140
Amersham HP6 72 AT37
Ashford TW15 175 BP92
Ashtead KT21 232 CL118
Banstead SM7 234 DB115
Beckenham BR3 183 DZ94
Brentwood CM14 108 FV46
Bromley BR1 204 EH95
Bushey WD23 76 CA44
Park Rd, Caterham CR3 236 DS123
Chesham HP5 54 AP31
Chislehurst BR7 185 EP93
Dartford DA1 188 FN87
East Molesey KT8 196 CC98
Egham TW20 173 BA91
Enfield EN3 83 DY36
Esher KT10 214 CB105
Feltham TW13 176 BX91
Gravesend DA11 191 GH88
Grays RM17 170 GB78
Guildford GU1 242 AX134
Hackbridge SM6 201 DH103
Hampton Hill TW12 176 CB91
Hampton Wick KT1 197 CJ95
Hayes UB4 135 BS71
Hemel Hempstead HP1 40 BJ22
Hertford SG13 32 DS09
High Barnet EN5 79 CZ42
Hoddesdon EN11 49 EA17
Hounslow TW3 156 CC84
Ilford IG1 125 ER62
Isleworth TW7 157 CH81
Kenley CR8 235 DP115
Kingston upon Thames KT2 178 CM92
New Barnet EN4 80 DE42
New Malden KT3 198 CR98
Northaw EN6 64 DG30
Orpington BR5 206 EW99
Oxted RH8 254 EF128
Radlett WD7 77 CG35
Redhill RH1 250 DF132
Richmond TW10 178 CM86
Rickmansworth WD3 92 BK45
Shepperton TW17 194 BN102
Slough SL2 131 AQ68
Stanwell TW19 174 BH86
Sunbury-on-Thames TW16 175 BV94
Surbiton KT5 198 CM99
Sutton SM3 217 CY107
Swanley BR8 207 FF97
Swanscombe DA10 190 FY86
Teddington TW11 177 CF93
Twickenham TW1 177 CJ86
Uxbridge UB8 134 BL66
Wallington SM6 219 DH106
Waltham Cross EN8 67 DX33
Ware SG12 32 DV05
Warlingham CR6 222 EE114
Watford WD17 75 BU39
Wembley HA0 138 CL65
Woking GU22 227 BA117
Park Rd E, W3 158 CP75
Uxbridge UB10 134 BK68
Park Rd N, W3 158 CP75
W4 158 CR78
Park Row, SE10 314 G2
PARK ROYAL, NW10 138 CN69
⊖ **Park Royal** 138 CN70
H **Park Royal Cen for Mental Health**, NW10 138 CQ68
● **Park Royal Metro Cen**,
NW10 138 CP70
Park Royal Rd, NW10 138 CQ69
W3 138 CQ69
Sch **Park Sch, The**, Wok. GU22
off Onslow Cres 227 BA117
Sch **Park Sch for Girls**, Ilf. IG1
off Park Av 125 EP60
Parkshot, Rich. TW9 158 CL84
Parkside, N3 98 DB53
NW2 119 CU62
NW7 97 CU51
SE3 315 L4
SW19 179 CX91
Buckhurst Hill IG9 102 EH47
Chalfont St. Peter SL9
off Lower Rd 113 AZ56
Grays RM16 170 GE76
Halstead TN14 224 EZ113
Hampton Hill TW12 177 CD92
Matching Tye CM17 37 FE12
New Haw KT15 212 BH110
Potters Bar EN6 off High St 64 DC32
Sidcup DA14 186 EV89
Sutton SM3 217 CY107
Waltham Cross EN8 67 DY34
Watford WD19 76 BW44
Park Side, Epp. CM16 70 EV29
Parkside Av, SE10 314 E7
SW19 179 CX92
Bexleyheath DA7 167 FD82
Bromley BR1 204 EL98
Romford RM1 127 FD55
Tilbury RM18 171 GH82
● **Parkside Business Est**, SE8 313 M2
Parkside Cl, SE20 182 DW94
East Horsley KT24 245 BT125
Sch **Parkside Comm Prim Sch**,
Borwd. WD6
off Aycliffe Rd 78 CM38
Parkside Ct, Wey. KT13 212 BN105
Parkside Cres, N7 121 DN62
Surbiton KT5 198 CQ100
Parkside Cross, Bexh. DA7 167 FE82
Parkside Dr, Edg. HA8 96 CN48
Watford WD17 75 BS40
Parkside Est, E9 279 H8
Parkside Gdns, SW19 179 CX91
Coulsdon CR5 235 DH117
East Barnet EN4 98 DF46
H **Parkside Hosp**, SW19 179 CX90
Parkside Ho, Dag. RM10 127 FC62
Parkside Ms, Warl. CR6 237 EA116
H **Parkside Oncology Clinic**,
SW19 179 CX90
Parkside Pl, E.Hors. KT24 245 BS125
Staines-upon-Thames TW18 174 BG93
Parkside Prim Sch, E4
off Wellington Ave 101 EB47
Parkside Rd, SW11 308 G7
Belvedere DA17 167 FC77
Hounslow TW3 176 CB85
Northwood HA6 93 BT50
Sch **Parkside Sch**, Stoke D'Ab.
KT11 off Stoke Rd 230 CA118
Parkside Ter, N18
off Great Cambridge Rd 100 DR49
Orpington BR6
off Willow Wk 205 EP104
Parkside Wk, SE10 303 J7
Slough SL1 152 AU76
Parkside Way, Har. HA2 116 CB56
Park S, SW11 308 G7
Parkspring Ct, Erith DA8
off Erith High St 167 FF79
Park Sq, Esher KT10
off Park Rd 214 CB105
Lambourne End RM4 86 EY44

P

Street	Page	Grid
Park Sq E, NW1	285	J4
Park Sq Ms, NW1	285	J5
Park Sq W, NW1	285	J4
Parkstead Rd, SW15	179	CU85
Park Steps, W2 / off St. Georges Flds	284	D10
Parkstone Av, N18	100	DT50
Hornchurch RM11	128	FK58
Parkstone Rd, E17	123	EC55
SE15	312	D9
PARK STREET, St.Alb. AL2	61	CD26
⇌ Park Street	61	CD26
Park St, SE1	299	J2
W1	284	G10
Berkhamsted HP4	38	AV18
Colnbrook SL3	153	BD80
Croydon CR0	202	DQ103
Guildford GU1	258	AW136
Hatfield AL9	45	CW17
St. Albans AL2	61	CD26
Slough SL1	152	AT76
Teddington TW11	177	CE93
Windsor SL4	151	AR81
Sch Park St C of E Prim Sch & Nurs, Park St AL2 off Branch Rd	61	CD27
Park St La, Park St AL2	60	CB30
Jct Park St Rbt, St.Alb. AL2	42	CC24
Park Ter, Green. DA9	189	FV85
Sundridge TN14 off Main Rd	240	EX124
Worcester Park KT4	199	CU102
Parkthorne Cl, Har. HA2	116	CB58
Parkthorne Dr, Har. HA2	116	CA58
Parkthorne Rd, SW12	181	DK87
Park Twrs, W1 / off Brick St	297	J3
Park Vw, N21	99	DM45
W3	138	CQ71
Aveley RM15	149	FR74
Bookham KT23	246	CA125
Caterham CR3	252	DU125
Hatfield AL9	45	CW16
Hoddesdon EN11	49	EA18
Horley RH6 off Brighton Rd	268	DG148
New Malden KT3	199	CT97
Pinner HA5	94	BZ53
Potters Bar EN6	64	DC33
Wem. HA9	118	CP64
Sch Park Vw Acad, N15 / off Langham Rd	122	DQ56
Parkview Chase, Slou. SL1	131	AL72
Parkview Cl, Cars. SM5	218	DF108
Park Vw Cl, St.Alb. AL1	43	CG21
Parkview Ct, SW18 / off Broomhill Rd	180	DA86
Park Vw Ct, E3 off Devons Rd	290	B6
Ilf. IG2	125	ES58
Woking GU22	226	AY119
Parkview Cres, Wor.Pk. KT4	199	CW102
Park Vw Cres, N11	99	DH49
Parkview Dr, Mitch. CR4	200	DD96
Park Vw Est, E2	279	H10
N5	122	DQ63
Park Vw Gdns, NW4	119	CW57
Grays RM17	170	GB78
Ilford IG4	125	EM56
Parkview Ho, Horn. RM12	127	FH61
Park Vw Ms, SW9	310	D8
Parkview Ms, Rain. RM13	147	FH71
Park Vw Rd, N3	98	DB53
N17	122	DU55
NW10	119	CT63
W5	138	CL71
Berkhamsted HP4	38	AV19
Leatherhead KT22	231	CF120
Pinner HA5	93	BV52
Redhill RH1	266	DG141
Southall UB1	136	CA74
Uxbridge UB8	134	BN72
Welling DA16	166	EW83
Woldingham CR3	237	DY122
Parkview Rd, SE9	185	EP88
Croydon CR0	202	DU102
Park Vw Rd Est, N17	100	DV54
Parkview Vale, Guil. GU4	243	BC131
Parkview Way, Epsom KT19	216	CQ110
Park Vil, Rom. RM6	126	EX58
Park Village E, NW1	275	J9
Park Village W, NW1	275	J10
Parkville Rd, SW6	306	G5
Park Vista, SE10	315	H3
Park Wk, N6 / off North Rd	120	DG59
SE10	314	G5
SW10	307	P2
Ashtead KT21 off Rectory La	232	CM119
Sch Park Wk Prim Sch, SW10	308	A3
Park Wks Rd, Red. RH1	251	DM133
Parkway, N14	99	DL47
NW1	275	J9
SW20	199	CX98
Dorking RH4	263	CG135
Erith DA18	166	EY76
Guildford GU1	242	AY133
Harlow CM19	50	EL15
Ilford IG3	125	ET62
New Addington CR0	221	EC109
Porters Wood AL3	43	CF16
Rainham RM13 / off Upminster Rd S	147	FG70
Romford RM2	127	FF55
Sawbridgeworth CM21	36	EY06
Uxbridge UB10	134	BN66
Welwyn Garden City AL8	29	CW11
Weybridge KT13	213	BR105
Woodford Green IG8	102	EJ50
Park Way, N20	98	DF49
NW11	119	CY57
Bexley DA5	187	FE90
Bookham KT23	230	CA123
Edgware HA8	96	CP53
Enfield EN2	81	DN40
Feltham TW14	175	BV87
Horley RH6	268	DG148
Rickmansworth WD3	92	BJ46
Ruislip HA4	115	BU60
Shenfield CM15	109	FZ46
West Molesey KT8	196	CB97
Parkway, The, / Cran. TW4, TW5	155	BV82
Hayes UB3, UB4	136	BW72
Iver SL0	133	BC68
Northolt UB5	136	BX69
Southall UB2	155	BU78
Parkway Cl, Welw.G.C. AL8	29	CW09
Parkway Ct, St.Alb. AL1	43	CH23
Parkway Cres, E15	280	F2
Parkway Gdns, Welw.G.C. AL8	29	CW10
Sch Parkway Prim Sch, / Erith DA18 off Alsike Rd	166	EY76
● Parkway Trd Est, / Houns. TW5	156	BW79
Park W, W2	284	D9
Park W Bldg, E3 / off Fairfield Rd	280	B10
Park W Pl, W2	284	D8
Parkwood, N20	98	DF48
Beckenham BR3	203	EA95
Parkwood Av, Esher KT10	196	CC102
Parkwood Cl, Bans. SM7	233	CX115
Broxbourne EN10	49	DZ19
Parkwood Dr, Hem.H. HP1	39	BF20
Parkwood Gro, Sun. TW16	195	BU97
Sch Parkwood Hall Sch, / Swan. BR8 / off Beechenlea La	207	FH97
Parkwood Ms, N6	121	DH58
Park Wood Ms, Bans. SM7	233	CZ116
Sch Parkwood Prim Sch, N4 / off Queens Dr	121	DP61
Parkwood Rd, SW19	179	CZ92
Banstead SM7	233	CX115
Bexley DA5	186	EZ87
Isleworth TW7	157	CF81
Nutfield RH1	251	DL133
Tatsfield TN16	238	EL121
Parkwood Vw, Bans. SM7	233	CW116
Sch Parlaunt Pk Prim Sch, / Langley SL3 off Kennett Rd	153	BB76
Parlaunt Rd, Slou. SL3	153	BA77
Parley Dr, Wok. GU21	226	AW117
Parliament Ct, E1	287	P7
Parliament Hill, NW3	274	D1
Sch Parliament Hill Sch, NW5 / off Highgate Rd	120	DG63
Parliament La, Burn. SL1	130	AF66
Parliament Ms, SW14 / off Thames Bk	158	CQ82
Parliament Sq, SW1	298	A5
Hertford SG14	32	DR09
Parliament St, SW1	298	A5
Parliament Vw Apts, SE1	298	C8
Parma Cres, SW11	160	DF84
● Parmiter Ind Cen, E2	278	F10
Sch Parmiter's Sch, Wat. WD25 / off High Elms La	60	BW31
Parmiter St, E2	278	F10
Parmoor Ct, EC1	287	J4
Parnall Rd, Harl. CM18	51	ER18
Parndon Mill La, Harl. CM20	35	EP12
Parndon Wd Rd, Harl. CM19	51	EQ20
Parnell Cl, W12	159	CV76
Abbots Langley WD5	59	BT30
Chafford Hundred RM16	169	FW78
Edgware HA8	96	CP49
Parnell Gdns, Wey. KT13	212	BN111
Parnell Rd, E3	279	P9
Parnell Way, Har. HA3 / off Weston Dr	95	CH53
Parnel Rd, Ware SG12	33	DZ05
Parnham Cl, Brom. BR1 / off Stoneleigh Rd	205	EP97
Parnham St, E14	289	M8
Parolles Rd, N19	121	DJ60
Paroma Rd, Belv. DA17	166	FA76
Parr Av, Epsom KT17	217	CV109
Parr Cl, N9	100	DV49
N18	100	DV49
Chafford Hundred RM16	169	FW77
Leatherhead KT22	231	CF120
Parr Ct, N1	277	L10
Feltham TW13	176	BW91
Parr Cres, Hem.H. HP2	41	BP15
Parris Cft, Dor. RH4 / off Goodwyns Rd	263	CJ139
Parritt Rd, Red. RH1	251	DH132
Parrock, The, Grav. DA12	191	GJ88
Parrock Av, Grav. DA12	191	GJ88
PARROCK FARM, Grav. DA12	191	GK91
Parrock Rd, Grav. DA12	191	GJ88
Parrock St, Grav. DA12	191	GH87
Parrotts Cl, Crox.Grn WD3	74	BN42
Parrotts Fld, Hodd. EN11	49	EB16
Parr Pl, W4 / off Chiswick High Rd	159	CT77
Parr Rd, E6	144	EK67
Stanmore HA7	95	CK53
Parrs Cl, S.Croy. CR2	220	DR109
Parrs Pl, Hmptn. TW12	176	CA94
Parr St, N1	277	L10
Parry Av, E6	293	J9
Parry Cl, Epsom KT17	217	CU108
Parry Dr, Wey. KT13	212	BN110
Parry Grn N, Slou. SL3	153	AZ77
Parry Grn S, Slou. SL3	153	AZ77
Parry Pl, SE18	305	P8
Parry Rd, SE25	202	DS97
W10	282	F2
Parry St, SW8	310	A2
Parsifal Rd, NW6	273	K2
Parsley Gdns, Croy. CR0 / off Primrose La	203	DX102
Parsloe Rd, Epp.Grn CM16	51	EN21
Harlow CM19	51	EP20
Parsloes Av, Dag. RM9	126	EX63
Sch Parsloes Prim Sch, / Dag. RM9 off Spurling Rd	146	EZ65
Parsonage Bk, Eyns. DA4 / off Pollyhaugh	208	FL103
Parsonage Cl, Abb.L. WD5	59	BS30
Hayes UB3	135	BT72
Warlingham CR6	237	DY116
Westcott RH4	262	CC138
Parsonage Ct, Loug. IG10	85	EP41
Sch Parsonage Fm Prim Sch, / Rain. RM13 off Farm Rd	148	FJ69
Parsonage Gdns, Enf. EN2	82	DQ40
Parsonage La, Chesh. HP5 / off Blucher St	54	AP31
Enfield EN1, EN2	82	DR40
North Mymms AL9	45	CV23
Sidcup DA14	186	EZ91
Slough SL2	131	AQ68
Sutton at Hone DA4	188	FP93
Westcott RH4	262	CC137
Windsor SL4	151	AN81
Parsonage Leys, Harl. CM20	35	ET14
Parsonage Manorway, / Belv. DA17	166	FA79
Parsonage Rd, Ch.St.G. HP8	90	AW48
Englefield Green TW20	172	AX92
Grays RM20	169	FW79
North Mymms AL9	45	CV23
Rainham RM13	148	FJ69
Rickmansworth WD3	92	BK45
Parsonage Sq, Dor. RH4	263	CG135
Parsonage St, E14	302	F9
Parsons Cl, Horl. RH6	268	DE147
Sutton SM1	200	DB104
Parsons Ct, Borwd. WD6 / off Chaucer Gro	78	CN42
Parsons Cres, Edg. HA8	96	CN48
Parsonsfield Cl, Bans. SM7	233	CX115
Parsonsfield Rd, Bans. SM7	233	CX116
PARSONS GREEN, SW6	307	J6
⊖ Parsons Green	307	H7
Parsons Grn, SW6	307	J7
Guildford GU1 / off Bellfields Rd	242	AX132
Parsons Grn Ct, Guil. GU1 / off Bellfields Rd	242	AX132
Parsons Grn La, SW6	307	J6
Parsons Gro, Edg. HA8	96	CN48
Parsons Hill, SE18 / off John Wilson St	305	L7
Parsons Ho, SW2 / off New Pk Rd	181	DL87
Parson's Ho, W2	284	A5
Parsons La, Dart. DA2	187	FH90
Parsons Mead, E.Mol. KT8	196	CC97
Parson's Mead, Croy. CR0	201	DP102
Parsons Pightle, Couls. CR5	235	DN120
Parsons Rd, E13	292	C1
Slough SL3	153	AZ79
Parson St, NW4	119	CW56
Parsons Wd, Farn.Com. SL2	131	AQ65
Parthenia Rd, SW6	307	K7
Parthia Cl, Tad. KT20	233	CV119
Partingdale La, NW7	97	CX50
Partington Cl, N19	121	DK60
Partridge Cl, E16	292	E7
Barnet EN5	79	CW44
Bushey WD23	94	CB46
Chesham HP5	54	AS28
Stanmore HA7	96	CL49
Partridge Ct, Harl. CM18	51	ER17
Partridge Dr, Orp. BR6	205	EQ104
Partridge Grn, SE9	185	EN90
Partridge Knoll, Pur. CR8	219	DP112
Partridge Mead, Bans. SM7	233	CW116
Partridge Rd, Hmptn. TW12	176	BZ93
Harlow CM18	51	ER17
St. Albans AL3	43	CD16
Sidcup DA14	185	ES90
Partridges, Hem.H. HP3 / off Reddings	40	BN22
Partridge Sq, E6	293	H6
Partridge Way, N22	99	DL53
Guildford GU4	243	BD132
Parvills, Wal.Abb. EN9	67	ED32
Parvin St, SW8	309	N6
Parvis Rd, W.Byf. KT14	212	BG113
Pasadena Cl, Hayes UB3	155	BV75
● Pasadena Trd Est, / Hayes UB3	155	BU75
Pascal Ms, SE19 / off Anerley Hill	182	DU94
Pascal St, SW8	309	P4
Pascoe Rd, SE13	183	ED85
Pasfield, Wal.Abb. EN9	67	ED33
Pasgen Ct, N9 / off Galahad Rd	100	DU47
Pasley Cl, SE17	311	J1
Pasquier Rd, E17	123	DY55
Passey Pl, SE9	185	EM86
Passfield Dr, E14	290	D6
Passfield Path, SE28 / off Booth Cl	146	EV73
Passfields, SE6	183	EB90
Passing All, EC1	287	H5
Passmore Gdns, N11	99	DK51
PASSMORES, Harl. CM18	51	ER17
Sch Passmores Acad, / Harl. CM18	52	EV17
Sch Passmores Sch & Tech Coll, / Harl. CM18 off Tendring Rd	51	ER17
Passmore St, SW1	296	G9
★ Passport Office, SW1	297	K8
Pastens Rd, Oxt. RH8	254	EJ131
Pasteur Cl, NW9	96	CS54
Pasteur Dr, Harold Wd RM3	106	FK54
Pasteur Gdns, N18	99	DP50
Paston Cl, E5 / off Caldecott Way	123	DX62
Wallington SM6	201	DJ104
Paston Cres, SE12	184	EH87
Paston Rd, Hem.H. HP2	40	BK18
Pastoral Way, Warley CM14	108	FV50
Pastor St, SE11	299	H8
Pasture Cl, Bushey WD23	94	CC45
Wembley HA0	117	CH62
Pasture Rd, SE6	184	EF88
Dagenham RM9	126	EZ63
Wembley HA0	117	CH61
Pastures, The, N20	97	CZ46
Hatfield AL10	45	CV19
Hemel Hempstead HP1	39	BE19
St. Albans AL2	42	CA24
Watford WD19	94	BW45
Welwyn Garden City AL7	30	DA11
Pastures Mead, Uxb. UB10	134	BN65
Pastures Path, E11	124	EE61
Pasture Vw, St.Alb. AL4	44	CN18
Patch, The, Sev. TN13	256	FE122
Patcham Ct, Sutt. SM2	218	DC109
Patcham Ter, SW8	309	K6
Patch Cl, Uxb. UB10	134	BM67
PATCHETTS GREEN, / Wat. WD25	76	CC39
Patching Way, Hayes UB4	136	BY71
Paternoster Cl, Wal.Abb. EN9	68	EF33
Paternoster Hill, / Wal.Abb. EN9	68	EF32
Paternoster La, EC4 / off Warwick La	287	H9
Paternoster Row, EC4	287	J9
Noak Hill RM4	106	FJ47
Paternoster Sq, EC4	287	H9
Paterson Ct, EC1 / off St. Luke's Est	287	L3
Paterson Rd, Ashf. TW15	174	BK92
Pater St, W8	295	J7
Pates Manor Dr, Felt. TW14	175	BR87
Path, The, SW19	200	DB95
Pathfield Rd, SW16	181	DK93
Pathfields, Shere GU5	260	BN140
Pathway, The, Rad. WD7	77	CF36
Send GU23	243	BF125
Watford WD19 / off Anthony Cl	94	BX46
Patience Rd, SW11	308	C9
Patio Cl, SW4	181	DK86
Patmore Est, SW8	309	L6
Patmore La, Hersham KT12	213	BT107
Patmore Link Rd, Hem.H. HP2	41	BQ20
Patmore Rd, Wal.Abb. EN9	68	EE34
Patmore St, SW8	309	M6
Patmore Way, Rom. RM5	105	FB50
Patmos Rd, SW9	310	G5
Paton Cl, E3	290	B2
Paton St, EC1	287	J3
Patricia Cl, Slou. SL1	131	AL73
Patricia Ct, Chis. BR7 / off Manor Pk Rd	205	ER95
Welling DA16	166	EV80
Patricia Dr, Horn. RM11	128	FL60
Patricia Gdns, Sutt. SM2	218	DA111
Patrick Connolly Gdns, E3	290	D3
Patrick Gro, Wal.Abb. EN9 / off Beaulieu Dr	67	EB33
Patrick Rd, E13	292	D3
Patrington Cl, Uxb. UB8	134	BJ69
Patriot Sq, E2	288	F1
Patrol Pl, SE6	183	EB86
Patrons Way E, Denh. UB9	113	BF58
Patrons Way W, Denh. UB9	113	BF58
Patshull Pl, NW5	275	L5
Patshull Rd, NW5	275	K4
Patten All, Rich. TW10 / off The Hermitage	177	CK85
Pattenden Rd, SE6	183	DZ88
Patten Rd, SW18	180	DE87
Patterdale Cl, Brom. BR1	184	EF93
Patterdale Rd, SE15	312	G4
Dartford DA2	189	FR88
Patterson Ct, SE19	182	DT94
Dartford DA1	188	FN85
Wooburn Green HP10 / off Glory Mill La	110	AE56
Patterson Rd, SE19	182	DT93
Chesham HP5	54	AP28
Pattina Wk, SE16	301	M3
Pattison Rd, NW2	120	DA62
Pattison Wk, SE18	165	EQ78
Paul Cl, E15	281	J7
Cheshunt EN7 / off Gladding Rd	66	DQ25
Paulet Rd, SE5	311	H8
Paulet Way, NW10	138	CS66
Paul Gdns, Croy. CR0	202	DT103
Paulhan Rd, Har. HA3	117	CK56
Paulin Dr, N21	99	DN45
Pauline Cres, Twick. TW2	176	CC88
Pauline Ho, E1	288	D6
Paulinus Cl, Orp. BR5	206	EW96
Paul Julius Cl, E14	302	G1
Paul Robeson Cl, E6	293	M2
Pauls Grn, Wal.Cr. EN8	67	DY33
Pauls Hill, Penn HP10	88	AF48
Pauls La, Hodd. EN11 / off Taverners Way	49	EA17
Paul's Nurs Rd, / High Beach IG10	84	EH39
Paul's Pl, Ashtd. KT21	232	CP119
Paul St, E15	281	J8
EC2	287	M5
Paul's Wk, EC4	287	H10
Paultons Sq, SW3	308	B2
Paultons St, SW3	308	B3
Pauntley St, N19	121	DJ60
Paved Ct, Rich. TW9	177	CK85
Paveley Ct, NW7	97	CX52
Paveley Dr, SW11	308	C5
Paveley Ho, N1 / off Priory Grn Est	286	C1
Paveley St, NW8	284	D4
Pavement, The, SW4	161	DJ84
W5 off Popes La	158	CL76
Isleworth TW7 off South St	157	CG83
Pavement Ms, Rom. RM6 / off Clarissa Rd	126	EX59
Pavement Sq, Croy. CR0	202	DU102
Pavet Cl, Dag. RM10	147	FB65
Pavilion, The, Hodd. EN11	49	EA17
Pavilion End, Knot.Grn HP9	88	AJ50
Pavilion Gdns, Stai. TW18	174	BH94
Pavilion Ho, SE16 / off Canada St	301	J5
Pavilion La, SE10 / off Ordnance Cres	303	J5
Beck. BR3	183	DZ93
Pavilion Ms, N3 / off Windermere Av	98	DA54
Pavilion Par, W12	282	A8
Pavilion Rd, SW1	296	F7
Ilford IG1	125	EM59
Pavilions, Wind. SL4	151	AP81
Pavilions, The, Byfleet KT14	212	BK111
North Weald Bassett CM16	71	FC25
Pavilion Sq, SW17	180	DE90
Pavilions Shop Cen, / Wal.Cr. EN8	67	DX34
Pavilion St, SW1	296	F7
Pavilion Ter, W12	282	A8
East Molesey KT8	197	CF98
Ilford IG2 / off Southdown Cres	125	ES57
Pavilion Way, Amer. HP6	72	AW39
Edgware HA8	96	CP52
Ruislip HA4	116	BW61
Pavillion Ms, N4	121	DM61
Pawleyne Cl, SE20	182	DW94
Pawsey Cl, E13	281	P8
Pawson's Rd, Croy. CR0	202	DQ100
Paxford Rd, Wem. HA0	117	CH61
Paxton Av, Slou. SL1	151	AQ76
Paxton Cl, Rich. TW9	158	CM82
Walton-on-Thames KT12	196	BW101
Paxton Ct, SE12	184	EJ90
Borwd. WD6 / off Manor Way	78	CQ42
Paxton Gdns, Wok. GU21	211	BE112
Paxton Ms, SE19	182	DS93
Paxton Pl, SE27	182	DS91
Sch Paxton Prim Sch, SE19 / off Woodland Rd	182	DS93
Paxton Rd, N17	100	DT52
SE23	183	DY90
W4	158	CS79
Berkhamsted HP4	38	AX19
Bromley BR1	184	EG94
St. Albans AL1	43	CE21
Paxton Ter, SW1	309	K2
Paycock Rd, Harl. CM19	51	EN17
Payne Cl, Bark. IG11	145	ES66
Paynell Ct, SE3	315	K10
Payne Rd, E3	290	C1
Paynesfield Av, SW14	158	CR83
Paynesfield Rd, / Bushey Hth WD23	95	CF45
Tatsfield TN16	238	EK119
Paynes La, Lwr Naze. EN9	50	EC24
Payne St, SE8	313	P3
Paynes Wk, W6	306	E3
Paynetts Ct, Wey. KT13	213	BR106
Payzes Gdns, Wdf.Grn. IG8 / off Chingford La	102	EF50
Peabody Av, SW1	297	J10
Peabody Cl, SE10	314	D6
SW1	309	K2
Croydon CR0	202	DW102
Peabody Cotts, SE24 / off Rosendale Rd	182	DQ87
Peabody Ct, Enf. EN3 / off Martini Dr	83	EA37
Peabody Dws, WC1	286	A4
Peabody Est, EC1 (Clerkenwell) / off Farringdon La	286	F5
EC1 (St. Luke's)	287	K5
N1 (Islington)	277	J7
N17	100	DS53
SE1	298	F3
SE17	299	L9
SE24	181	DP87
SW1	297	L8
SW3	308	D2
SW6	307	J2
W6	306	B1
W10	282	B6
Peabody Hill, SE21	181	DP88
Peabody Hill Est, SE21	181	DP87
Peabody Sq, SE1	298	G5
Peabody Twr, EC1 / off Golden La	287	K5
Peabody Trust, SE1	299	J3
Peabody Trust Camberwell Grn Est, SE5	311	L6
Peabody Trust Old Pye St Est, / SW1 off Old Pye St	297	N7
Peabody Yd, N1	277	J8
Peace Cl, N14	81	DH43
SE25	202	DS98
Cheshunt EN7	66	DU29
Greenford UB6	137	CD67
Peace Dr, Wat. WD17	75	BU41
Peace Gro, Wem. HA9	118	CP62
Peace Prospect, Wat. WD17	75	BU41
Peace Rd, Iver SL0	133	BA67
Slough SL3	133	BA68
Peace St, SE18 / off Nightingale Vale	165	EP79
Peach Cft, Nthflt DA11	190	GE90
Peaches Cl, Sutt. SM2	217	CY108
Peachey Cl, Uxb. UB8	134	BK72
Peachey La, Uxb. UB8	134	BK71
Peach Gro, E11	123	ED62
Peach Rd, W10	282	D2
Feltham TW13	175	BU88
Peach Tree Av, West Dr. UB7 / off Pear Tree Av	134	BM72
Peachum Rd, SE3	315	M2
Peachwalk Ms, E3	279	K10
Peachy Cl, Edg. HA8 / off Manor Pk Cres	96	CN51
Peacock Av, Felt. TW14	175	BR88
Peacock Cl, E4	101	DZ52
NW7	97	CY50
Dagenham RM8	126	EW60
Epsom KT19	216	CM112
Hornchurch RM11	128	FL56
Peacock Gdns, S.Croy. CR2	221	DY110
● Peacock Ind Est, N17	100	DT52
Peacock Pl, N1 / off Laycock St	276	F5
Peacocks, Harl. CM19	51	EM17
Peacocks Cen, The, / Wok. GU21	226	AY117
Peacocks Cl, Berk. HP4	38	AT16
Peacock St, SE17	299	H9
Gravesend DA12	191	GJ87
Peacock Wk, E16	292	B8
Abbots Langley WD5	59	BU31
Dorking RH4 / off Rose Hill	263	CG137
Peacock Yd, SE17	299	H9
Peak, The, SE26	182	DW90
Peakes La, Chsht EN7	66	DT27
Peakes Pl, St.Alb. AL1 / off Granville Rd	43	CF20
Peakes Way, Chsht EN7	66	DT27
Peakeston Av, Ilf. IG4	124	EK56
Peak Hill, SE26	182	DW91
Peak Hill Av, SE26	182	DW91
Peak Hill Gdns, SE26	182	DW91
Peak Rd, Guil. GU2	242	AU131
Peaks Hill, Pur. CR8	219	DK110
Peaks Hill Ri, Pur. CR8	219	DL110
Pea La, Upmin. RM14	149	FU66
Peal Gdns, W13	137	CG70
Peall Rd, Croy. CR0	201	DM100
Pearce Cl, Mitch. CR4	200	DG96
Pearcefield Av, SE23	182	DW88
Pearce Rd, Chesh. HP5	54	AP29
Pearces Wk, St.Alb. AL1 / off Albert St	43	CD21
Pear Cl, NW9	118	CR56
SE14	313	M5
Pearcroft Rd, E11	123	ED61
Pearcy Cl, Harold Hill RM3	106	FL52
Peardon St, SW8	309	K9
Peareswood Gdns, Stan. HA7	95	CK53
Peareswood Rd, Erith DA8	167	FF81
Pearfield Rd, SE23	183	DY90
Pearing Cl, Wor.Pk. KT4	199	CX103
Pearl Cl, E6	293	L8
NW2	119	CX59
Pearl Gdns, Slou. SL1	131	AP74
Pearl Rd, E17	123	EA55
Pearl St, E1	300	F2
Pearmain Cl, Shep. TW17	195	BP99
Pearman St, SE1	298	F6
Pear Pl, SE1	298	E4
Pear Rd, E11	123	ED62
Pearscroft Ct, SW6	307	M7
Pearscroft Rd, SW6	307	L8
Pearse St, SE15	311	P3
Pearson Av, Hert. SG13	32	DQ11
Pearson Cl, SE5	311	K6
Barnet EN5	80	DB42
Hertford SG13 / off Pearson Av	32	DQ11
Purley CR8	219	DP111
Pearson Ms, SW4	161	DK83
Pearsons Av, SE14	314	A6
Pearson St, E2	277	P10
Pearson Way, Dart. DA1	188	FM89
Mitcham CR4	200	DG95
Pears Rd, Houns. TW3	156	CC83
PEARTREE, Welw.G.C. AL7	29	CZ09
Peartree Av, SW17	180	DC90
Pear Tree Av, West Dr. UB7	134	BM72

P

Pear Tree Cl, E2 278 A9
Add. KT15 *off Pear Tree Rd* 212 BG106
Amersham HP7
off Orchard End Av 72 AT39
Bromley BR2 204 EK99
Chessington KT9 216 CN106
Epsom KT19 216 CR109
Mitcham CR4 200 DE96
Seer Green HP9 89 AQ51
Slough SL1 131 AM74
Swanley BR8 207 FD96
Peartree Cl, Erith DA8 167 FD81
Hemel Hempstead HP1 40 BG19
South Croydon CR2 220 DV114
South Ockendon RM15 149 FW68
Welwyn Garden City AL7 29 CY09
Peartree Ct, E18
off Churchfields 102 EH53
Welwyn Garden City AL7 29 CY10
Pear Tree Ct, EC1 286 F5
Peartree Fm, Welw.G.C. AL7 29 CY09
Peartree Gdns, Dag. RM8 126 EV63
Romford RM7 105 FB54
Pear Tree Hill, Salf. RH1 266 DG143
Peartree La, E1 301 H1
Welwyn Garden City AL7 29 CY10
Pear Tree Mead, Harl. CM18 52 EU18
Sch Pear Tree Mead Prim & Nurs Sch, Harl. CM18
off Pear Tree Mead 52 EU18
Sch Peartree Prim Sch, Welw.G.C. AL7 *off Peartree La* 29 CY10
Pear Tree Rd, Add. KT15 212 BG106
Ashford TW15 175 BQ92
Peartree Rd, Enf. EN1 82 DS41
Hemel Hempstead HP1 40 BG19
Pear Tree St, EC1 287 H4
Pear Tree Wk, Chsht EN7 66 DR26
Peartree Way, SE10 303 N8
Peary Pl, E2 289 H2
Peascod Pl, Wind. SL4
off Peascod St 151 AR81
Peascod St, Wind. SL4 151 AR81
Peascroft Rd, Hem.H. HP3 40 BN23
Pease Cl, Horn. RM12
off Dowding Way 147 FH66
PEASMARSH, Guil. GU3 258 AW142
Peatfield Cl, Sid. DA15
off Woodside Rd 185 ES90
Peatmore Av, Wok. GU22 228 BG116
Peatmore Cl, Wok. GU22 228 BG116
Pebble Cl, Tad. KT20 248 CS128
PEBBLE COOMBE, Tad. KT20 248 CS128
Pebble Hill, Lthd. KT24 245 BQ133
Pebble Hill Rd, Bet. RH3 248 CS131
Tadworth KT20 248 CS131
Pebble La, Epsom KT18 232 CN121
Leatherhead KT22 248 CL125
Pebble Way, W3 138 CP74
Pebworth Rd, Har. HA1 117 CG61
Peckarmans Wd, SE26 182 DU90
Peckett Sq, N5 277 H1
Peckford Pl, SW9 310 F9
PECKHAM, SE15 312 A8
Peckham Gro, SE15 311 P4
Peckham High St, SE15 312 C7
Peckham Hill St, SE15 312 C4
Peckham Pk Rd, SE15 312 C4
Sch Peckham Pk Sch, SE15 312 D5
Peckham Rd, SE5 311 N7
SE15 311 N7
≠ Peckham Rye 312 C8
⊖ Peckham Rye 312 C8
Peckham Rye, SE15 312 D10
SE22 162 DU84
Pecks Hill, Lwr Naze. EN9 50 EE21
Pecks Yd, E1 288 A6
Peckwater St, NW5 275 L3
● Pedham Pl Ind Est, Swan. BR8 207 FG99
Pedlars End, Moreton CM5 53 FH21
Pedlars Wk, N7 276 B4
Pedley Rd, Dag. RM8 126 EW60
Pedley St, E1 288 B5
PEDNORMEAD END, Chesh. HP5 54 AN32
Pednormead End, Chesh. HP5 54 AP32
Pednor Rd, Chesh. HP5 54 AM30
Pedro St, E5 123 DX62
Pedworth Gdns, SE16 300 G9
Peek Cres, SW19 179 CX92
Peeks Brook La, Horl. RH6 269 DM150
Coll Peel Cen (Met Pol Training & Driving Sch), NW9 *off Aerodrome Rd* 119 CT55
Peel Cl, E4 101 EB47
N9 *off Plevna Rd* 100 DU48
Windsor SL4 151 AP83
Peel Ct, Slou. SL1 131 AP71
Peel Cres, Hert. SG14 31 DP07
Peel Dr, NW9 119 CT55
Ilford IG5 124 EL55
Peelers Pl, Ripley GU23 228 BJ121
Peel Gro, E2 288 G1
Peel Pas, W8 295 J3
Peel Pl, Ilf. IG5 102 EL54
Peel Prec, NW6 283 J1
Peel Rd, E18 102 EF53
Orpington BR6 223 EQ106
Wealdstone HA3 117 CF55
Wembley HA9 117 CK62
Peel St, W8 295 J3
Peel Way, Rom. RM3 106 FM54
Uxbridge UB8 134 BL71
Peerage Way, Horn. RM11 128 FL59
● Peerglow Cen, Ware SG12 33 DY07
● Peerglow Est, Enf. EN3 82 DW43
● Peerglow Ind Est, Wat. WD18 *off Olds App* 93 BP46
Peerless Dr, Hare. UB9 114 BJ57
Peerless St, EC1 287 L3
Pegamoid Rd, N18 100 DW48
Pegasus Cl, N16 277 L1
Pegasus Ct, W3
off Horn La 138 CQ72
Abbots Langley WD5
off Furtherfield 59 BT32
Gravesend DA12 191 GJ90
Harrow HA3 117 CK57
Pegasus Pl, SE11 310 E2
SW6 *off Ackmar Rd* 307 J7
St. Albans AL3 43 CD18
Pegasus Rd, Croy. CR0 219 DN107
Pegasus Way, N11 99 DH51
Pegelm Gdns, Horn. RM11 128 FM59
Peggotty Way, Uxb. UB8 135 BP72
Pegg Rd, Houns. TW5 156 BX80
Pegley Gdns, SE12 184 EG89
Pegmire La, Ald. WD25 76 CC39
Pegrams Rd, Harl. CM18 51 EQ18
Pegrum Dr, Lon.Col. AL2 61 CH26
Pegs La, Hert. SG13 32 DR11
Pegwell St, SE18 165 ES80
Peket Cl, Stai. TW18 193 BE95
Pekin Cl, E14 290 B9
Pekin St, E14 290 B9
Peldon Ct, Rich. TW9 158 CM84
Peldon Pas, Rich. TW10
off Worple Way 158 CM84
Peldon Rd, Harl. CM19 51 EN17
Peldon Wk, N1 277 H8
Pelham Av, Bark. IG11 145 ET67
Pelham Cl, SE5 311 P10
Pelham Ct, Hem.H. HP2 41 BQ20
Welwyn Garden City AL7 30 DC10
Pelham Cres, SW7 296 C9
Pelham Ho, W14 294 G9
Pelham La, Ald. WD25 76 CB36
Pelham Pl, SW7 296 C9
W13 *off Ruislip Rd E* 137 CF70
Sch Pelham Prim Sch, SW19
off Southey Rd 180 DA94
Bexleyheath DA7
off Pelham Rd 166 FA83
Pelham Rd, E18 124 EH55
N15 122 DT56
N22 99 DN54
SW19 180 DA94
Beckenham BR3 202 DW96
Bexleyheath DA7 166 FA83
Gravesend DA11 191 GF87
Ilford IG1 125 ER61
Pelham Rd S, Grav. DA11 191 GF88
Pelhams, The, Wat. WD25 76 BX35
Pelhams Cl, Esher KT10 214 CA105
Pelham St, SW7 296 B8
Pelhams Wk, Esher KT10 196 CA104
Pelham Ter, Grav. DA11
off Campbell Rd 191 GF87
Pelham Way, Bkhm KT23 246 CB126
Pelican Dr, Har. HA2 116 CB61
Pelican Est, SE15 312 A7
Pelican Ho, SE15
off Peckham Rd 312 A7
Pelican Pas, E1 288 G4
Pelier St, SE17 311 K2
Pelinore Rd, SE6 184 EE89
Pellant Rd, SW6 306 F3
Pellatt Gro, N22 99 DN53
Pellatt Rd, SE22 182 DT85
Wembley HA9 118 CL61
Pellerin Rd, N16 277 P2
Pelling Hill, Old Wind. SL4 172 AV87
Pellings Cl, Brom. BR2 204 EE97
Pelling St, E14 290 A8
Pellipar Cl, N13 99 DN48
Pellipar Gdns, SE18 305 J10
Pellow Cl, Barn. EN5 79 CZ44
Pelly Ct, Epp. CM16 69 ET31
Pelly Rd, E13 281 P10
Pelman Way, Epsom KT19 216 CP110
Pelter St, E2 288 A2
Pelton Av, Sutt. SM2 218 DB110
Pelton Rd, SE10 303 J10
Pembar Av, E17 123 DY55
Pemberley Chase, W.Ewell KT19 216 CP106
Pemberley Cl, W.Ewell KT19 216 CP106
Pember Rd, NW10 282 C3
Pemberton Av, Rom. RM2 127 FH55
Pemberton Cl, St.Alb. AL1 43 CD23
Stai. TW19 174 BL88
Pemberton Gdns, N19 121 DJ62
Romford RM6 126 EY57
Swanley BR8 207 FE97
Pemberton Ho, SE26
off High Level Dr 182 DU91
Pemberton Pl, E8 278 F7
Esher KT10
off Carrick Gate 196 CC104
Pemberton Rd, N4 121 DN57
East Molesey KT8 196 CC98
Slough SL2 131 AL70
Pemberton Row, EC4 286 F8
Pemberton Ter, N19 121 DJ62
Pembrey Way, Horn. RM12 148 FJ65
Pembridge Av, Twick. TW2 176 BZ88
Pembridge Chase, Bov. HP3 57 AZ28
Pembridge Cl, Bov. HP3 57 AZ28
Pembridge Cres, W11 283 J10
Pembridge Gdns, W2 295 J1
Coll Pembridge Hall, W2 295 K1
Sch Pembridge Hall Sch, W2 295 K1
Pembridge La, Brickendon SG13 48 DQ19
Broxbourne EN10 48 DR21
Pembridge Ms, W11 283 J10
Pembridge Pl, SW15 180 DA85
W2 283 K10
Pembridge Rd, W11 295 J1
Bovingdon HP3 57 BA28
Pembridge Sq, W2 295 J1
Pembridge Vil, W2 283 J10
W11 283 J10
Pembroke Av, N1 276 B8
Enfield EN1 82 DV38
Harrow HA3 117 CG55
Hersham KT12 214 BX105
Pinner HA5 116 BX60
Surbiton KT5 198 CP99
Pembroke Cl, SW1 297 H5
Banstead SM7 234 DB117
Broxbourne EN10 49 DY23
Erith DA8
off Pembroke Rd 167 FD77
Hornchurch RM11 128 FM56
Pembroke Cotts, W8
off Pembroke Sq 295 J7
Pembroke Dr, Aveley RM15 168 FP75
Goffs Oak EN7 65 DP29
Pembroke Gdns, W8 295 H8
Dagenham RM10 127 FB62
Woking GU22 227 BA118
Pembroke Gdns Cl, W8 295 H7
Pembroke Ms, E3 289 M2
N10 98 DG53
W8 295 J7
Sevenoaks TN13 257 FH125
Pembroke Pl, W8 295 J7
Edgware HA8 96 CN52
Isleworth TW7
off Thornbury Rd 157 CE82
Sutton at Hone DA4 208 FP95
Pembroke Rd, E6 293 J6
E17 123 EB57
N8 121 DL56
N10 98 DG53
N13 100 DQ48
N15 122 DT57
SE25 202 DS98
W8 295 J8
Bromley BR1 204 EJ96
Erith DA8 167 FC78
Greenford UB6 136 CB70
Ilford IG3 125 ET60
Mitcham CR4 200 DG96
Northwood HA6 93 BQ48
Ruislip HA4 115 BS60
Sevenoaks TN13 257 FH125
Wembley HA9 117 CK62
Woking GU22 227 BA118
Pembroke Sq, W8 295 J7
Pembroke St, N1 276 B7
Pembroke Studios, W8 295 H7
Pembroke Vil, W8 295 J8
Richmond TW9 157 CK84
Pembroke Wk, W8 295 J8
Pembroke Way, Hayes UB3 155 BQ76
Pembry Cl, SW9 310 E7
Pembury Av, Wor.Pk. KT4 199 CU101
Pembury Cl, E5 278 F2
Bromley BR2 204 EF101
Coulsdon CR5 218 DG114
Pembury Ct, Harling. UB3 155 BR79
Pembury Cres, Sid. DA14 186 EY89
Pembury Pl, E5 278 E3
Pembury Rd, E5 278 E3
N17 100 DT54
SE25 202 DU98
Bexleyheath DA7 166 EY80
Pemdevon Rd, Croy. CR0 201 DN101
Pemell Cl, E1 289 H4
Pemerich Cl, Hayes UB3 155 BT78
Pempath Pl, Wem. HA9 117 CK61
Pemsel Ct, Hem.H. HP3
off Crabtree La 40 BL22
Penally Pl, N1 277 M8
Penang St, E1 300 F2
Penard Rd, Sthl. UB2 156 CA76
Penarth St, SE15 312 G2
Penates, Esher KT10 215 CD105
Penberth Rd, SE6 183 EC89
Penbury Rd, Sthl. UB2 156 BZ77
Pencombe Ms, W11 283 H10
Pencraig Way, SE15 312 E3
Pencroft Dr, Dart. DA1
off Shepherds La 188 FJ87
Pendall Cl, Barn. EN4 80 DE42
Penda Rd, Erith DA8 167 FB80
Pendarves Rd, SW20 199 CW95
Penda's Mead, E9 279 M1
Pendell Av, Hayes UB3 155 BT80
Pendell Ct, Bletch. RH1 251 DP131
Pendell Rd, Bletch. RH1 251 DP131
Pendennis Cl, W.Byf. KT14 212 BG114
Pendennis Rd, N17 122 DR55
SW16 181 DL91
Orpington BR6 206 EW103
Sevenoaks TN13 257 FH123
Pendenza, Cob. KT11 230 BY116
Penderel Rd, Houns. TW3 176 CA85
Penderry Ri, SE6 183 ED89
Penderyn Way, N7 121 DK63
Pendle Ct, Uxb. UB10
off Sutton Ct Rd 135 BP67
Pendle Rd, SW16 181 DH93
Pendlestone Rd, E17 123 EB57
Pendleton Cl, Red. RH1 266 DF136
Pendleton Rd, Red. RH1 266 DE136
Reigate RH2 266 DC137
Pendlewood Cl, W5 137 CJ71
Pendolino Way, NW10 138 CN66
Pendragon Rd, Brom. BR1 184 EF90
Pendragon Wk, NW9 118 CS58
Pendrell Rd, SE4 313 L9
Pendrell St, SE18 165 ER80
Pendula Dr, Hayes UB4 136 BX70
Pendulum Ms, E8 278 A3
Penerley Rd, SE6 183 EB88
Rainham RM13 147 FH71
Penfields Ho, N7 276 A5
Penfold Cl, Croy. CR0 201 DN104
Penfold La, Bex. DA5 186 EX89
Penfold Pl, NW1 284 B6
Penfold Rd, N9 101 DX46
Penfold St, NW1 284 B5
NW8 284 B5
● Penfold Trading Est, Wat. WD24 76 BW39
Penford Gdns, SE9 164 EK83
Penford St, SE5 310 G8
Pengarth Rd, Bex. DA5 186 EX85
PENGE, SE20 182 DW94
≠ Penge East 182 DW93
Penge Ho, SW11 308 B10
Penge La, SE20 182 DW94
Pengelly Cl, Chsht EN7 66 DV30
Penge Rd, E13 144 EJ66
SE20 202 DU97
SE25 202 DU97
≠ Penge West 182 DV93
⊖ Penge West 182 DV93
Penhale Cl, Orp. BR6 224 EU105
Penhall Rd, SE7 304 E8
Penhill Rd, Bex. DA5 186 EW87
Penhurst, Wok. GU21 211 AZ114
Penhurst Pl, SE1 298 D7
Penhurst Rd, Ilf. IG6 103 EP52
Penifather La, Grnf. UB6 137 CD69
Penington Rd, Beac. HP9 110 AH55
Peninsula Apts, W2
off Praed St 284 C7
Peninsula Hts, SE1 298 B10
Peninsular Cl, Felt. TW14 175 BR86
Peninsular Pk Rd, SE7 303 P9
Penistone Rd, SW16 181 DL94
Penistone Wk, Rom. RM3
off Okehampton Rd 106 FJ51
Penketh Dr, Har. HA1 117 CD62
Penlow Rd, Harl. CM18 51 EQ18
Penman Cl, St.Alb. AL2 60 CA27
Penman's Grn, Kings L. WD4 57 BF32
Penmans Hill, Chipper. WD4 57 BF33
Penmon Rd, SE2 166 EU76
PENN, H.Wyc. HP10 88 AE48
Pennack Rd, SE15 312 B3
Pennant Ms, W8 295 L8
Pennant Ter, E17 101 DZ54
Pennard Mans, W12 294 A5
Pennard Rd, W12 294 A4
Pennards, The, Sun. TW16 196 BW96
Penn Av, Chesh. HP5 54 AN30
Penn Bottom, Penn HP10 88 AG47
Penn Cl, Chorl. WD3 73 BD44
Greenford UB6 136 CB68
Harrow HA3 117 CJ56
Uxbridge UB8 134 BK70
Penn Dr, Denh. UB9 113 BF58
Penne Cl, Rad. WD7 61 CF34
Penner Cl, SW19 179 CY89
Penners Gdns, Surb. KT6 198 CL101
Pennethorne Cl, E9 278 G9
Pennethorne Ho, SW11 308 B10
Pennethorne Rd, SE15 312 E5
Penney Cl, Dart. DA1 188 FK87
Penn Gdns, Chis. BR7 205 EP96
Romford RM5 104 FA52
Penn Gaskell La, Chal.St.P. SL9 91 AZ50
Penn Grn, Beac. HP9 89 AK51
Penn Ho, Burn. SL1 130 AJ69
Pennine Dr, NW2 119 CY61
Pennine Ho, N9
off Edmonton Grn Shop Cen 100 DU48
Pennine La, NW2 119 CY61
Pennine Rd, Slou. SL2 131 AN71
Pennine Way, Bexh. DA7 167 FE81
Harlington UB3 155 BR80
Hemel Hempstead HP2 40 BM17
Northfleet DA11 190 GE90
Pennings Av, Guil. GU2 242 AT132
Pennington Cl, SE27
off Hamilton Rd 182 DR91
Romford RM5 104 FA50
Pennington Dr, N21 81 DL43
Weybridge KT13 195 BS104
Pennington Rd, Chal.St.P. SL9 90 AX52
Penningtons, The, Amer. HP6 55 AS37
Pennington St, E1 300 D1
Pennington Way, SE12 184 EH89
Pennis La, Fawk.Grn DA3 209 FX100
Penniston Cl, N17 100 DQ54
Penniwell Cl, Edg. HA8 96 CM49
Penn La, Bex. DA5 186 EX85
Penn Meadow, Stoke P. SL2 132 AT67
Penn Pl, Rick. WD3
off Northway 92 BK45
Penn Rd, N7 276 B2
Beaconsfield HP9 88 AJ48
Chalfont St. Peter SL9 90 AX53
Datchet SL3 152 AX81
Mill End WD3 91 BF46
Park Street AL2 60 CC27
Slough SL2 131 AR70
Watford WD24 75 BV39
Sch Penn Sch, Penn HP10
off Church Rd 88 AD48
Penn St, N1 277 M9
Penn Way, Chorl. WD3 73 BD44
Penny Brookes St, E20 280 F4
Penny Cl, Rain. RM13 147 FH69
Pennycroft, Croy. CR0 221 DY109
Pennyfather La, Enf. EN2 82 DQ40
Pennyfield, Cob. KT11 213 BU113
Pennyfields, E14 290 A10
Warley CM14 108 FW49
Penny La, Shep. TW17 195 BS101
Pennylets Grn, Stoke P. SL2 132 AT66
Pennymead, Harl. CM20 52 EU15
Pennymead Dr, E.Hors. KT24 245 BT127
Pennymead Ri, E.Hors. KT24 245 BT127
Pennymead Twr, Harl. CM20 52 EU15
Penny Ms, SW12 181 DH87
Pennymoor Wk, W9 283 H4
Penny Rd, NW10 138 CP69
Pennyroyal Av, E6 293 L9
Pennys La, High Wych CM21 35 ER05
Penpoll Rd, E8 278 E4
Penpool La, Well. DA16 166 EV83
Penrhyn Av, E17 101 DZ53
Penrhyn Cl, Cat. CR3 236 DR120
Penrhyn Cres, E17 101 EA53
SW14 158 CQ84
Penrhyn Gdns, Kings.T. KT1
off Surbiton Rd 197 CK98
Penrhyn Gro, E17 101 EA53
Penrhyn Rd, Kings.T. KT1 198 CL97
Penrith Cl, SW15 179 CY85
Beckenham BR3 203 EB95
Reigate RH2 250 DE133
Uxbridge UB8 134 BK66
Penrith Cres, Rain. RM13 127 FG64
Penrith Pl, SE27 181 DP89
Penrith Rd, N15 122 DR57
Ilford IG6 103 ET51
New Malden KT3 198 CR98
Romford RM3 106 FN51
Thornton Heath CR7 202 DQ96
Penrith St, SW16 181 DJ93
Penrose Av, Wat. WD19 94 BX47
Penrose Ct, Eng.Grn TW20 172 AW93
Hemel Hempstead HP2 40 BL16
Penrose Dr, Epsom KT19 216 CN111
Penrose Gro, SE17 311 J1
Penrose Ho, SE17 311 J1
Penrose Rd, Fetch. KT22 230 CC122
Penrose St, SE17 311 J1
Penryn St, NW1 275 N10
Penry St, SE1 299 P9
Pensbury Pl, SW8 309 M8
Pensbury St, SW8 309 M8
Penscroft Gdns, Borwd. WD6 78 CR42
Pensford Av, Rich. TW9 158 CN82
Penshurst, Harl. CM17 36 EV12
Penshurst Av, Sid. DA15 186 EU86
Penshurst Cl, Chal.St.P. SL9 90 AX54
Penshurst Gdns, Edg. HA8 96 CP50
Penshurst Grn, Brom. BR2 204 EF99
Penshurst Rd, E9 279 J7
N17 100 DT52
Bexleyheath DA7 166 EZ81
Potters Bar EN6 64 DD31
Thornton Heath CR7 201 DP99
Penshurst Wk, Brom. BR2
off Penshurst Grn 204 EF99
Penshurst Way, Orp. BR5
off Star La 206 EW98
Sutton SM2 218 DA108
Pensilver Cl, Barn. EN4 80 DE42
Pensons La, Ong. CM5 71 FG28
Penstemon Cl, N3 98 DA52
Penstock Footpath, N22 121 DL55
🛍 Pentavia Retail Pk, NW7 97 CT52
Pentelow Gdns, Felt. TW14 175 BU86
Pentire Cl, Horsell GU21 210 AY114
Upminster RM14 129 FS58
Pentire Rd, E17 101 ED53
Pentland, Hem.H. HP2
off Mendip Way 40 BM17
Pentland Av, Edg. HA8 96 CP47
Shepperton TW17 194 BN99
Pentland Cl, N9 100 DW47
NW11 119 CY61
Pentland Gdns, SW18 180 DC86
Pentland Pl, Nthlt. UB5 136 BY67
Pentland Rd, NW6 283 J2
Bushey WD23 76 CC44
Slough SL2 131 AN71
Pentlands Cl, Mitch. CR4 201 DH97
Pentland St, SW18 180 DC86
Pentland Way, Uxb. UB10 115 BQ62
Pentley Cl, Welw.G.C. AL8 29 CX06
Pentley Pk, Welw.G.C. AL8 29 CX06
Pentlow St, SW15 306 B10
Pentlow Way, Buck.H. IG9 102 EL45
Pentney Rd, E4 101 ED46
SW12 181 DJ88
SW19 *off Midmoor Rd* 199 CY95
Penton Av, Stai. TW18 173 BF94
Penton Dr, Chsht EN8 67 DX29
Penton Gro, N1 286 E1
Penton Hall Dr, Stai. TW18 194 BG95
Penton Hook Rd, Stai. TW18 174 BG94
Penton Ho, SE2
off Hartslock Dr 166 EX75
Penton Pk, Cher. KT16 194 BG97
Penton Pl, SE17 299 H10
Penton Ri, WC1 286 D2
Penton Rd, Stai. TW18 173 BF94
Penton St, N1 276 E10
PENTONVILLE, N1 286 E1
Pentonville Rd, N1 286 C1
Pentreath Av, Guil. GU2 258 AT135
Pentrich Av, Enf. EN1 82 DU38
Pentridge St, SE15 312 A4
Pentstemon Dr, Swans. DA10 190 FY85
Pentyre Av, N18 100 DR50
Penwerris Av, Islw. TW7 156 CC80
Penwith Rd, SW18 180 DB89
Penwith Wk, Wok. GU22 226 AX119
Penwood End, Wok. GU22 226 AV121
Penwood Ho, SW15
off Tunworth Cres 179 CT86
Sch Penwortham Prim Sch, SW16 *off Penwortham Rd* 181 DH93
Penwortham Rd, SW16 181 DH93
South Croydon CR2 220 DQ110
Penylan Pl, Edg. HA8 96 CN52
Penywern Rd, SW5 295 K10
Penzance Cl, Hare. UB9 92 BK53
Penzance Gdns, Rom. RM3 106 FN51
Penzance Pl, W11 294 E2
Penzance Rd, Rom. RM3 106 FN51
Penzance Spur, Slou. SL2 131 AP70
Penzance St, W11 294 E2
Peony Cl, Pilg.Hat. CM15 108 FV44
Peony Ct, Wdf.Grn. IG8
off The Bridle Path 102 EE52
Peony Gdns, W12 139 CU73
● Peoplebuilding, Hem.H. HP2 41 BP19
Pepler Ms, SE5 312 A2
Pepler Way, Burn. SL1 130 AH69
Peplins Cl, Brook.Pk AL9 63 CY26
Peplins Way, Brook.Pk AL9 63 CY25
Peploe Rd, NW6 272 D10
Peplow Cl, West Dr. UB7 134 BK74
Pepper All, High Beach IG10 84 EG39
Pepper Cl, E6 293 K6
Caterham CR3 252 DS125
Peppercorn Cl, Th.Hth. CR7 202 DR96
Pepper Hill, Gt Amwell SG12 33 DZ10
Northfleet DA11 190 GC90
Pepperhill La, Nthflt DA11 190 GC90
Peppermead Sq, SE13 183 EA85
Peppermint Cl, Croy. CR0 201 DL101
Peppermint Hts, Wem. HA0 137 CK67
Peppermint Pl, E11
off Birch Gro 124 EE62
Pepper St, E14 302 C6
SE1 299 J4
Peppie Cl, N16 122 DS61
Pepys Cl, Ashtd. KT21 232 CN117
Dartford DA1 168 FN84
Northfleet DA11 190 GD90
Slough SL3 153 BB79
Tilbury RM18 171 GJ81
Uxbridge UB10 115 BP63
Pepys Cres, E16 303 P2
Barnet EN5 79 CW43
Pepys Ri, Orp. BR6 205 ET102
Pepys Rd, SE14 313 K7
SW20 199 CW95
Pepys St, EC3 287 P10
Perceval Av, NW3 274 C2
Percheron Cl, Islw. TW7 157 CG83
Percheron Rd, Borwd. WD6 78 CR44
Perch St, E8 278 B1
Percival Cl, Oxshott KT22 214 CB111
Percival Ct, N17 100 DT52
Northolt UB5 116 CA64
★ Percival David Foundation of Chinese Art, WC1
off Gordon Sq 285 P5
Percival Gdns, Rom. RM6 126 EW58
Percival Rd, SW14 158 CQ84
Enfield EN1 82 DT42
Feltham TW13 175 BT89
Hornchurch RM11 128 FJ58
Orpington BR6 205 EP103
Percival St, EC1 286 G4
Percival Way, Epsom KT19 216 CQ105
Percy Av, Ashf. TW15 174 BN92
Percy Bryant Rd, Sun. TW16 175 BS94
Percy Bush Rd, West Dr. UB7 154 BM76
Percy Circ, WC1 286 D2
Percy Gdns, Enf. EN3 83 DX43
Hayes UB4 135 BS69
Isleworth TW7 157 CG82
Worcester Park KT4 198 CR102
Percy Ho, SW16
off Pringle Gdns 181 DJ91
Percy Ms, W1 285 N7
Percy Pas, W1 285 M7
Percy Pl, Datchet SL3 152 AV81
Percy Rd, E11 124 EE59
E16 291 K6
N12 98 DC50
N21 100 DQ45
SE20 203 DX95
SE25 202 DU99
W12 159 CU75
Bexleyheath DA7 166 EY82
Guildford GU2 242 AV132
Hampton TW12 176 CA94
Ilford IG3 126 EU59
Isleworth TW7 157 CG84
Mitcham CR4 200 DG101
Romford RM7 127 FB55
Twickenham TW2 176 CB88
Watford WD18 75 BV42

Percy St, W1 285 N7
Grays RM17 170 GC79
Percy Ter, Brom. BR1 205 EP97
Percy Way, Twick. TW2 176 CC88
Percy Yd, WC1 286 D2
Peregrine Cl, NW10 118 CR64
Watford WD25 60 BY34
Peregrine Ct, SW16 181 DM91
Welling DA16 165 ET81
Peregrine Gdns, Croy. CR0 203 DY103
Peregrine Ho, EC1 287 H2
Peregrine Rd, N17 100 DQ52
Ilford IG6 104 EV50
Sunbury-on-Thames TW16 195 BT96
Waltham Abbey EN9 68 EG34
Peregrine Wk, Horn. RM12
off Heron Flight Av 147 FH65
Peregrine Way, SW19 179 CW94
Perendale Dr, Shep. TW17 195 BQ95
Perham Rd, W14 306 F1
Perham Way, Lon.Col. AL2 61 CK26
Peridot St, E6 293 H6
Perifield, SE21 182 DQ88
Perimeade Rd, Perivale UB6 137 CJ68
Perimeter Rd E,
Lon.Gat.Air. RH6 268 DG154
Perimeter Rd N,
Lon.Gat.Air. RH6 268 DF151
Perimeter Rd S,
Lon.Gat.Air. RH6 268 DC154
Periton Rd, SE9 164 EK84
PERIVALE, Grnf. UB6 137 CJ67
⊖ **Perivale** 137 CG68
Perivale, Grnf. UB6 137 CF69
Perivale Gdns, W13 137 CH70
Watford WD25 59 BV34
Perivale Gra, Perivale UB6 137 CG69
Perivale La, Perivale UB6 137 CG69
● **Perivale New Business Cen**,
Perivale UB6 137 CH68
● **Perivale Pk**, Perivale UB6 137 CG68
Perivale Prim Sch, Perivale UB6
off Federal Rd 137 CJ68
Periwood Cres, Perivale UB6 137 CG67
Perkin Cl, Houns. TW3 156 CB84
Wembley HA0 117 CH64
Perkins Cl, Green. DA9 189 FT85
Perkins Ct, Ashf. TW15 174 BM92
Perkins Gdns, Uxb. UB10 115 BQ61
Perkin's Rents, SW1 297 N6
Perkins Rd, Ilf. IG2 125 ER57
Perkins Sq, SE1 299 K2
Perks Cl, SE3 315 J9
Perleybrooke La, Wok. GU21
off Bampton Way 226 AU117
Permain Cl, Shenley WD7 61 CK33
Perpins Rd, SE9 185 ES86
Perram Cl, Brox. EN10 67 DY26
Perran Rd, SW2
off Christchurch Rd 181 DP89
Perran Wk, Brent. TW8 158 CL78
Perren St, NW5 275 J4
Perrers Rd, W6 159 CV77
Perrett Gdns, Hert. SG14 31 DL08
Perrin Cl, Ashf. TW15
off Fordbridge Rd 174 BM92
Perrin Ct, Wok. GU21
off Blackmore Cres 227 BB115
Perrin Rd, Wem. HA0 117 CG63
Perrins Ct, NW3 273 P1
Perrins La, NW3 273 P1
Perrin's Wk, NW3 273 P1
Perrior Rd, Gdmg. GU7 258 AS144
Perriors Cl, Chsht EN7 66 DU27
Perronet Ho, SE1
off Princess St 299 H7
Perrott St, SE18 165 EQ77
Perry Av, W3 138 CR72
Perry Cl, Rain. RM13
off Lowen Rd 147 FD68
Uxbridge UB8 135 BP72
Perry Ct, E14
off Maritime Quay 302 B10
N15 122 DS58
Perrycroft, Wind. SL4 151 AL83
Perryfields Way, Burn. SL1 130 AH70
Perryfield Way, NW9 119 CT58
Richmond TW10 177 CH89
Perry Gdns, N9 100 DS48
Perry Garth, Nthlt. UB5 136 BW67
Perry Gro, Dart. DA1 168 FN84
Perry Hall Cl, Orp. BR6 206 EU101
Perry Hall Prim Sch, Orp. BR6
off Perry Hall Rd 205 ET100
Perry Hall Rd, Orp. BR6 205 ET100
Perry Hill, SE6 183 DZ90
Lower Nazeing EN9 50 EF23
Worplesdon GU3 242 AS128
Perry Ho, SW2
off Tierney Rd 181 DL87
Perry How, Wor.Pk. KT4 199 CT102
Perrylands La, Smallfield RH6 269 DM149
Perryman Ho, Bark. IG11 145 EQ67
Perrymans Fm Rd, Ilf. IG2 125 ER58
Perryman Way, Slou. SL2 131 AM69
Perry Mead, Bushey WD23 94 CB45
Enfield EN2 81 DP40
Perrymead St, SW6 307 K7
Perrymount Prim Sch, SE23
off Sunderland Rd 183 DX89
Perryn Rd, SE16 300 E6
W3 138 CR73
Perry Ri, SE23 183 DY90
Perry Rd, Dag. RM9 146 EZ70
Harlow CM18 51 EQ18
Perrysfield Rd, Chsht EN8 67 DY27
Perrys La, Knock.P. TN14 224 EV113
Perrys Pl, W1 285 N8
Perry Spring, Harl. CM17 52 EW17
PERRY STREET, Grav. DA11 190 GE88
Perry St, Chis. BR7 185 ER93
Dartford DA1 167 FE84
Northfleet DA11 190 GE88
Perry St Gdns, Chis. BR7
off Old Perry St 185 ES93
Perrys Way, S.Ock. RM15 149 FW71
Perry Vale, SE23 182 DW89
Perry Way, Aveley RM15 148 FQ73
● **Perrywood Business Pk**,
Red. RH1 267 DH142
Perrywood Ho, E5
off Pembury Rd 278 E2
Persant Rd, SE6 184 EE89
Perseid Lwr Sch, W7
off Springfield Rd 137 CE74
Morden SM4
off Bordesley Rd 200 DB99
Perseverance Cotts,
Ripley GU23 228 BJ121
Perseverance Pl, SW9 310 F5
Rich. TW9 *off Shaftesbury Rd* 158 CL83
Persfield Cl, Epsom KT17 217 CT110
Pershore Cl, Ilf. IG2 125 EP57
Pershore Gro, Cars. SM5 200 DD100
Perspective Ho, Enf. EN3
off Tysoe Av 83 DY36
Pert Cl, N10 99 DH52
Perth Av, NW9 118 CR59
Hayes UB4 136 BW70
Slough SL1 131 AP72
Perth Cl, SW20 *off Huntley Way* 199 CU96
Northolt UB5 116 CA64
Perth Rd, E10 123 DY60
E13 292 A1
N4 121 DN60
N22 99 DP53
Barking IG11 145 ER68
Beckenham BR3 203 EC96
Ilford IG2 125 EN58
Perth Ter, Ilf. IG2 125 EQ59
● **Perth Trd Est**, Slou. SL1 131 AP71
Perwell Av, Har. HA2 116 BZ60
Perwell Ct, Har. HA2 116 BZ60
Pescot Hill, Hem.H. HP1 40 BH18
Petal La, Harl. CM17
off Harrowbond Rd 36 EX14
Petchey Acad, E8 278 B2
Peter Av, NW10 139 CV66
Oxted RH8 253 ED129
Peterboat Cl, SE10 303 K8
Peterborough &
St. Margaret's Sch,
Stan. HA7 *off Common Rd* 95 CE48
Peterborough Av,
Upmin. RM14 129 FS60
Peterborough Gdns, Ilf. IG1 124 EL59
Peterborough Ms, SW6 307 J8
Peterborough Prim Sch,
SW6 307 K9
Peterborough Rd, E10 123 EC57
SW6 307 J8
Carshalton SM5 200 DE100
Guildford GU2 242 AT132
Harrow HA1 117 CE60
Peterborough Vil, SW6 307 L6
Peterchurch Ho, SE15 312 E4
Peter Dwight Dr, Amer. HP6
off Woodside Rd 55 AS38
Petergate, SW11 160 DC84
Peterhead Ms, Slou. SL3 153 BA78
Peter Heathfield Ho, E15
off Wise Rd 280 G8
Peterhill Cl, Chal.St.P. SL9 90 AY50
Peter Hills with St. Mary's
& St. Paul's C of E Prim Sch,
SE16 301 K2
Peter Ho, E1
off Commercial Rd 288 F8
Peterhouse Gdns, SW6 307 M7
● **Peter James Business Cen**,
Hayes UB3 155 BU75
Peterlee Ct, Hem.H. HP2 40 BM16
● **Peterley Business Cen**, E2 288 E1
Peter Moore Ct, N9
off Menon Dr 100 DV48
★ **Peter Pan Statue**, W2 296 A2
Peters Av, Lon.Col. AL2 61 CJ26
Peters Cl, Dag. RM8 126 EX60
Stanmore HA7 95 CK51
Welling DA16 165 ES82
Petersfield, St.Alb. AL3 43 CE16
Petersfield Av, Rom. RM3 106 FL51
Slough SL2 132 AU74
Staines-upon-Thames TW18 174 BJ92
Petersfield Cl, N18 100 DQ50
Romford RM3 106 FN51
Petersfield Cres, Couls. CR5 235 DL115
Petersfield Ri, SW15 179 CV88
Petersfield Rd, W3 158 CQ75
Staines-upon-Thames TW18 174 BJ92
Petersgate, Kings.T. KT2 178 CQ93
PETERSHAM, Rich. TW10 178 CL88
Petersham Av, Byfleet KT14 212 BL112
Petersham Cl, Byfleet KT14 212 BL112
Richmond TW10 177 CK89
Sutton SM1 218 DA106
Petersham Dr, Orp. BR5 205 ET96
Petersham Gdns, Orp. BR5 205 ET96
Petersham La, SW7 295 N6
Petersham Ms, SW7 295 N7
Petersham Pl, SW7 295 N6
Petersham Rd, Rich. TW10 178 CL86
Peters Hill, EC4 287 J10
Peter's La, EC1 287 H6
Petersleа, Kings L. WD4 59 BP29
Petersmead Cl, Tad. KT20 233 CW123
Peters Path, SE26 182 DV91
Peterstone Rd, SE2 166 EV76
Peterstow Cl, SW19 179 CY89
Peter St, W1 285 M10
Gravesend DA12 191 GH87
Peterswood, Harl. CM18 51 ER19
Peters Wd Hill, Ware SG12 33 DX07
Peterswood Inf Sch & Nurs,
Harl. CM18 *off Paringdon Rd* 51 ER19
Peterwood Way, Croy. CR0 201 DM103
Petham Ct, Swan. BR8 207 FF100
Petherton Rd, N5 277 K3
Petiver Cl, E9 279 H6
Petley Rd, W6 306 B3
Peto Pl, NW1 285 K4
Peto St N, E16 291 L9
Petridge Rd, Red. RH1 266 DF139
Petridgewood Common,
Red. RH1 266 DF140
Petrie Cl, NW2 272 F4
★ **Petrie Mus of Egyptian**
Archaeology, WC1 *off Malet Pl* 285 N5
Petros Gdns, NW3 273 N3
Pettacre Cl, SE28 165 EQ76
Pett Cl, Horn. RM11 127 FH61
Petten Cl, Orp. BR5 206 EX102
Petten Gro, Orp. BR5 206 EW102
Petters Rd, Ashtd. KT21 232 CM116
Petticoat La, E1 287 P7
Petticoat Sq, E1 288 A8
Petticoat Twr, E1 288 A8
Pettits Boul, Rom. RM1 105 FE53
Pettits Cl, Rom. RM1 105 FE54
Pettits La, Rom. RM1 105 FE54
Pettits La N, Rom. RM1 105 FD53
Pettits Pl, Dag. RM10 126 FA64
Pettits Rd, Dag. RM10 126 FA64
Pettiward Cl, SW15 159 CW84
Pettley Gdns, Rom. RM7 127 FD57
Pettman Cres, SE28 165 ER76
Pettsgrove Av, Wem. HA0 117 CJ64
Petts Hill, Nthlt. UB5 116 CB64
Petts Hill Prim Sch, Nthlt.
UB5 *off Newmarket Av* 116 CB64
Petts La, Shep. TW17 194 BN98
Pett St, SE18 304 G8
PETTS WOOD, Orp. BR5 205 ER99
⇌ **Petts Wood** 205 EQ99
Petts Wd Rd, Petts Wd BR5 205 EQ99
Petty Cross, Slou. SL1 131 AL72
Petty France, SW1 297 M6
Pettys Cl, Chsht EN8 67 DX28
Petty Wales, EC3
off Lower Thames St 299 P1
Petworth Cl, Couls. CR5 235 DJ119
Northolt UB5 136 BZ66
Petworth Ct, Wind. SL4 151 AP81
Petworth Gdns, SW20
off Hidcote Gdns 199 CV97
Uxbridge UB10 135 BQ67
Petworth Ho, SE22
off Pytchley Rd 162 DS83
Petworth Rd, N12 98 DE50
Bexleyheath DA6 186 FA85
Petworth St, SW11 308 D6
Petworth Way, Horn. RM12 127 FF63
Petyt Pl, SW3 308 C3
Petyward, SW3 296 D9
Pevensey Av, N11 99 DK50
Enfield EN1 82 DR40
Pevensey Cl, Islw. TW7 156 CC80
Pevensey Rd, E7 124 EF63
SW17 180 DD91
Feltham TW13 176 BY88
Slough SL2 131 AN71
Pevensey Way, Crox.Grn WD3 75 BP42
Peverel, E6 293 L8
Peverel Ho, Dag. RM10 126 FA61
Peveret Cl, N11 99 DH50
Peveril Dr, Tedd. TW11 177 CD92
Pewley Bk, Guil. GU1 258 AY136
Pewley Down Inf Sch,
Guil. GU1 *off Semaphore Rd* 258 AY136
Pewley Hill, Guil. GU1 258 AX136
Pewley Pt, Guil. GU1 258 AY136
Pewley Way, Guil. GU1 258 AY136
Pewsey Cl, E4 101 EA50
Peyton Pl, SE10 314 E4
Peyton's Cotts, Red. RH1 251 DM132
Pharaoh Cl, Mitch. CR4 200 DF101
Pharaoh's Island, Shep. TW17 194 BM103
Pheasant Cl, E16 291 P8
Berkhamsted HP4 38 AW20
Purley CR8
off Partridge Knoll 219 DP113
Pheasant Ct, Wat. WD25 76 BW35
Pheasant Hill, Ch.St.G. HP8 90 AW47
Pheasant Ri, Chesh. HP5 54 AR33
Pheasants Way, Rick. WD3 92 BH45
Pheasant Wk, Chal.St.P. SL9 90 AX49
Phelips Rd, Harl. CM19 51 EN20
Phelp St, SE17 311 L2
Phelps Way, Hayes UB3 155 BT77
Phene St, SW3 308 D2
Philanthropic Rd, Red. RH1 266 DG135
Philan Way, Rom. RM5 105 FD51
Philbeach Gdns, SW5 295 H10
Phil Brown Pl, SW8 309 K10
Philbye Ms, Slou. SL1 151 AM75
Philchurch Pl, E1 288 D9
Philimore Cl, SE18 165 ES78
Philip Av, Rom. RM7 127 FD60
Swanley BR8 207 FD98
Philip Cl, Pilg.Hat. CM15 108 FV44
Romford RM7 *off Philip Av* 127 FD60
Philip Dr, Flack.Hth HP10 110 AC56
Philip Gdns, Croy. CR0 203 DZ103
Philip La, N15 122 DR56
Philipot Path, SE9 185 EM86
Philippa Gdns, SE9 184 EK85
Philippa Way, Grays RM16 171 GH77
Philip Rd, Rain. RM13 147 FE69
Staines-upon-Thames TW18 174 BK93
Philips Cl, Cars. SM5 200 DG102
Philip Sidney Ct,
Chaff.Hun. RM16 169 FX78
Philip Southcote Sch, Add.
KT15 *off Addlestone Moor* 194 BJ103
Philip St, E13 291 N4
Philip Sydney Rd, Grays RM16 169 FX78
Philip Wk, SE15 312 D10
Phillida Rd, Rom. RM3 106 FN54
Phillimore Ct, Rad. WD7
off Phillimore Pl 77 CE36
Phillimore Gdns, NW10 272 A8
W8 295 J5
Phillimore Gdns Cl, W8 295 J6
Phillimore Pl, W8 295 J5
Radlett WD7 77 CE36
Phillimore Wk, W8 295 J6
Phillipers, Wat. WD25 76 BY35
Phillipp St, N1 277 N9
Phillips Cl, Dart. DA1 187 FH86
Phillips Hatch, Won. GU5 259 BC143
Philpot La, EC3 287 N10
Chobham GU24 210 AV113
Philpot Path, Ilf. IG1
off Richmond Rd 125 EQ62
Philpots Cl, West Dr. UB7 134 BK73
Philpot Sq, SW6
off Peterborough Rd 160 DB83
Philpot St, E1 288 F8
Phineas Pett Rd, SE9 164 EL83
Phipps Bridge 200 DC97
Phipps Br Rd, SW19 200 DC96
Mitcham CR4 200 DC96
Phipps Hatch La, Enf. EN2 82 DQ38
Phipp's Ms, SW1 297 K7
Phipps Rd, Slou. SL1 131 AK71
Phipp St, EC2 287 N4
Phoebe Rd, Hem.H. HP2 40 BM17
Phoebeth Rd, SE4 183 EA85
Phoebe Wk, E16
off Garvary Rd 292 B9
Phoenix Arch Sch, NW10
off Drury Way 118 CR64
Phoenix Ave, SE10 303 K4
● **Phoenix Business Cen**,
Chesh. HP5 *off Higham Rd* 54 AP30
Phoenix Cl, E8 278 A8
E17 101 DZ54
W12 139 CV73
Epsom KT19 216 CN112
Northwood HA6 93 BT49
West Wickham BR4 204 EE103
Phoenix Ct, Felt. TW13 175 BS91
Guildford GU1
off High St 258 AX136
New Malden KT3 199 CT97
Northfleet DA11 190 GA85
Phoenix Dr, Kes. BR2 204 EK104
Phoenix High Sch, W12
off The Curve 139 CU73
● **Phoenix Ind Est**, Har. HA1 117 CF56
● **Phoenix Pk**, Brent. TW8 157 CK78
Phoenix Pl, WC1 286 D4
Dartford DA1 188 FK87
Phoenix Pt, SE28 146 EW74
Phoenix Prim Sch, SE1 312 D1
Phoenix Rd, NW1 285 N2
SE20 182 DW93
Phoenix Sch, E3 289 P2
Phoenix Sch, The, NW3 273 P5
Phoenix St, WC2 285 P9
● **Phoenix Trd Est**,
Perivale UB6 137 CJ67
Phoenix Wks, Pnr. HA5
off Cornwall Rd 94 BZ52
Phoenix Way, SW18
off North Side Wandsworth
Common 180 DC85
Hounslow TW5 156 BW79
Phoenix Wf, SE10 303 L4
Phoenix Wf Rd, SE1 300 B5
Phoenix Yd, WC1 286 D3
★ **Photographers' Gall**, W1 285 L9
Phygtle, The, Chal.St.P. SL9 90 AY51
Phyllis Av, N.Mal. KT3 199 CV99
★ **Physical Energy Statue**, W2 295 P3
Physic Pl, SW3 308 E2
Picardy Ho, Enf. EN2
off Cedar Rd 82 DQ38
Picardy Manorway,
Belv. DA17 167 FB76
Picardy Rd, Belv. DA17 166 FA78
Picardy St, Belv. DA17 166 FA76
Piccadilly, W1 297 K3
Piccadilly Arc, SW1 297 L2
⊖ **Piccadilly Circus** 297 M1
Piccadilly Circ, W1 297 N1
Piccadilly Ct, N7 276 C4
Piccadilly Pl, W1 297 M1
Piccards, The, Guil. GU2
off Chestnut Av 258 AW138
PICCOTTS END, Hem.H. HP2 40 BJ16
Piccotts End La, Hem.H. HP2 40 BJ17
Piccotts End Rd, Hem.H. HP1 40 BJ18
Pickard Cl, N14 99 DK46
Pickard St, EC1 287 H2
Pickering Av, E6 293 M1
Pickering Cl, E9 279 J6
Pickering Gdns, N11 98 DG51
Croydon CR0 202 DT100
Pickering Ms, W2 283 M8
Pickering Pl, SW1 297 M3
Guildford GU2 242 AU132
Pickering Rd, Bark. IG11 145 EQ65
Pickering St, N1 277 H8
Pickets Cl, Bushey Hth WD23 95 CD46
Pickets St, SW12 181 DH87
Pickett Cft, Stan. HA7 95 CK53
Picketts, Welw.G.C. AL8 29 CX06
Picketts La, Red. RH1 267 DJ144
Picketts Lock La, N9 100 DW47
Pickford Cl, Bexh. DA7 166 EY82
Pickford Dr, Slou. SL3 133 AZ74
Pickford La, Bexh. DA7 166 EY82
Pickford Rd, Bexh. DA7 166 EY83
St. Albans AL1 43 CH20
Pickfords Gdns, Slou. SL1 131 AR73
Pickfords Wf, N1 287 J1
Pick Hill, Wal.Abb. EN9 68 EF32
Pickhurst Grn, Brom. BR2 204 EF101
Pickhurst Inf Sch,
W.Wick. BR4 *off Pickhurst La* 204 EF100
Pickhurst Jun Sch,
W.Wick. BR4 *off Pickhurst La* 204 EF100
Pickhurst La, Brom. BR2 204 EF102
West Wickham BR4 204 EE100
Pickhurst Mead, Brom. BR2 204 EF101
Pickhurst Pk, Brom. BR2 204 EE99
Pickhurst Ri, W.Wick. BR4 203 EC101
Pickins Piece, Horton SL3 153 BA82
Pickmoss La, Otford TN14 241 FH116
Pickwick Cl, Houns. TW4
off Dorney Way 176 BY85
Pickwick Ct, SE9 184 EL88
Pickwick Gdns, Nthflt DA11 190 GD90
Pickwick Ms, N18 100 DS50
Pickwick Pl, Har. HA1 117 CE59
Pickwick Rd, SE21 182 DR87
Pickwick St, SE1 299 J5
Pickwick Ter, Slou. SL2
off Maple Cres 132 AV73
Pickwick Way, Chis. BR7 185 EQ93
Pickworth Cl, SW8 310 B5
Picquets Way, Bans. SM7 233 CY116
Picton Pl, W1 285 H9
Surbiton KT6 198 CN102
Picton St, SE5 311 L5
Picture Ho, SW16 181 DL89
Pied Bull Yd, N1
off Theberton St 276 G8
Piedmont Rd, SE18 165 ER78
Pield Heath Av, Uxb. UB8 134 BN70
Pield Heath Ho Sch,
Uxb. UB8 *off Pield Heath Rd* 134 BL70
Pield Heath Rd, Uxb. UB8 134 BM71
Piercing Hill, They.B. CM16 85 ER35
Pier Head, E1 300 E3
Pierian Spring, Hem.H. HP1 40 BH18
Pieris Ho, Felt. TW13
off High St 175 BU89
Piermont Grn, SE22 182 DV85
Piermont Pl, Brom. BR1 204 EL96
Piermont Rd, SE22 182 DV85
Pier Par, E16 305 L3
Pierrepoint Arc, N1 276 G10
Pierrepoint Rd, W3 138 CP73
Pierrepoint Row, N1 276 G10
Pier Rd, E16 305 L5
Erith DA8 167 FE79
Feltham TW14 175 BV85
Greenhithe DA9 169 FV84
Northfleet DA11 191 GF86
Pierson Rd, Wind. SL4 151 AK82
Pier St, E14 302 F8
Pier Ter, SW18
off Jew's Row 160 DB84
Pier Wk, Grays RM17 170 GA80
Pier Way, SE28 165 ER76
Pigeonhouse La,
Chipstead CR5 250 DC125
Pigeon La, Hmptn. TW12 176 CA91
Piggotts End, Amer. HP7 55 AP40
Piggotts Orchard, Amer. HP7 55 AP40
Piggs Cor, Grays RM17 170 GC76
Piggy La, Chorl. WD3 73 BB44
Pigott St, E14 290 A9
Pigsty All, SE10 314 F6
Pike Cl, Brom. BR1 184 EH92
Uxbridge UB10 134 BM67
Pike La, Upmin. RM14 129 FT64
Pike Rd, NW7
off Ellesmere Av 96 CR49
Pikes End, Pnr. HA5 115 BV56
Pikes Hill, Epsom KT17 216 CS113
Pikestone Cl, Hayes UB4
off Berrydale Rd 136 BY70
Pike Way, N.Wld Bas. CM16 70 FA27
Pilgrimage St, SE1 299 L5
Pilgrim Cl, Mord. SM4 200 DB101
Park Street AL2 60 CC27
Pilgrim Hill, SE27 182 DQ91
Orpington BR5 206 EY96
Pilgrims Cl, N13 99 DM49
Northolt UB5 116 CC64
Pilgrim's Hatch CM15 108 FT43
Shere GU5 260 BN139
Watford WD25 *off Kytes Dr* 60 BX33
Westhumble RH5 247 CG131
Pilgrims Ct, SE3 315 P6
Dartford DA1 188 FN85
Pilgrims La, Chaldon CR3 251 DM125
North Stifford RM16 149 FW74
Titsey RH8 254 EH125
Westerham TN16 238 EL123
Pilgrim's La, NW3 274 B1
Pilgrims Ms, E14 291 H10
PILGRIM'S HATCH,
Brwd. CM15 108 FU42
Pilgrims Pl, NW3 274 A1
Reigate RH2 250 DA132
Pilgrims Ri, Barn. EN4 80 DE43
Pilgrim St, EC4 286 G9
Pilgrims Vw, Green. DA9 189 FW86
Pilgrims Way, E6
off High St N 144 EL67
N19 121 DK60
Chev. TN14 240 EV121
Dartford DA1 188 FN88
Guil. GU4 258 AX138
Reig. RH2 250 DA131
Shere GU5 260 BN139
South Croydon CR2 220 DT106
West. TN16 239 EM123
Westhumble RH5 247 CH131
Pilgrims' Way, Albury GU5 260 BL138
Betchworth RH3 249 CY131
Caterham CR3 251 DP126
Dor. RH4 247 CE134
Red. RH1 251 DJ127
Pilgrim's Way, Wem. HA9 118 CP60
Pilgrims' Way Prim Sch,
SE15 312 G3
Pilgrims Way W, Otford TN14 241 FD116
Pilkington Rd, SE15 312 E9
Orpington BR6 205 EQ103
Pilkingtons, Harl. CM17 52 EX15
Pillions La, Hayes UB4 135 BR70
Pilot Busway, SE10 303 K5
Pilot Cl, SE8 313 N2
Pilots Pl, Grav. DA12 191 GJ86
Pilsdon Cl, SW19 179 CX88
Piltdown Rd, Wat. WD19 94 BX49
● **Pilton Ind Est**, Croy. CR0 201 DP103
Pilton Pl, SE17 299 K10
PIMLICO, SW1 297 L10
⊖ **Pimlico** 297 N10
Pimlico Acad, SW1 309 M1
Pimlico Rd, SW1 296 G10
Pimlico Wk, N1 287 N2
Pimms Cl, Guil. GU4 243 BA130
Pimpernel Way, Rom. RM3 106 FK51
Pinceybrook Rd, Harl. CM18 51 EQ19
Pinchbeck Rd, Orp. BR6 223 ET107
Pinchfield, Map.Cr. WD3 91 BE50
Pinchin St, E1 288 D10
Pincott La, W.Hors. KT24 245 BP129
Pincott Pl, SE4 313 K10
Pincott Rd, SW19 180 DC94
Bexleyheath DA6 186 FA85
Pindar Rd, Hodd. EN11 49 EC16
Pindar St, EC2 287 N6
PINDEN, Dart. DA2 209 FW96
Pindock Ms, W9 283 M5
Pineapple Ct, SW1 297 L6
Pineapple Rd, Amer. HP7 72 AT39
Pine Av, E15 281 H2
Gravesend DA12 191 GK88
West Wickham BR4 203 EB102
Pine Cl, E10 123 EA61
N14 99 DJ45
N19 121 DJ61
SE20 202 DW95
Berkhamsted HP4 38 AV19
Cheshunt EN8 67 DX28
Epsom KT19 216 CQ109
Kenley CR8 236 DR117
New Haw KT15 212 BH111
Stanmore HA7 95 CH49
Swanley BR8 207 FF98
Woking GU21 226 AW117
Pine Coombe, Croy. CR0 221 DX105
Pine Ct, Addlestone KT15 212 BH105
Upminster RM14 128 FN63
Pine Cres, Cars. SM5 218 DD111
Hutton CM13 109 GD43
Pinecrest Gdns, Orp. BR6 223 EP105
Pinecroft, Gidea Pk RM2 128 FJ56
Hemel Hempstead HP3 40 BM24
Hutton CM13 109 GB45
Pinecroft Cres, Barn. EN5 79 CY42
Pine Dean, Bkhm KT23 246 CB125
Pinedene, SE15 312 E6
Pinefield Cl, E14 290 A10
Pine Gdns, Horl. RH6 268 DG149
Ruislip HA4 115 BV60
Surbiton KT5 198 CN100
Pine Glade, Orp. BR6 223 EM105
Pine Gro, N4 121 DL61
N20 97 CZ46
SW19 179 CZ92
Bricket Wood AL2 60 BZ30
Brookmans Park AL9 64 DB25
Bushey WD23 76 BZ40
Weybridge KT13 213 BP106
Pine Gro Ms, Wey. KT13 213 BQ106
Pine Hill, Epsom KT18 232 CR115
Pinehurst, Sev. TN14 257 FL121
Pinehurst Cl, Abb.L. WD5 59 BS32
Kingswood KT20 234 DA122
Pinehurst Gdns, W.Byf. KT14 212 BJ112
Pinehurst Wk, Orp. BR6 205 ES102

P

Pinelands Cl, SE3 315 M5
Pinel Cl, Vir.W. GU25 192 AY98
Pinemartin Cl, NW2 119 CW62
Pine Ms, NW10 272 C10
Pineneedle La, Sev. TN13 257 FH123
Pine Pl, Bans. SM7 217 CX114
Hayes UB4 135 BT70
Pine Ridge, Cars. SM5 218 DG109
Pineridge Cl, Wey. KT13 213 BS105
Pine Rd, N11 98 DG47
NW2 119 CW63
Woking GU22 226 AW120
Pines, The, N14 81 DJ43
Borehamwood WD6
off Anthony Rd 78 CM40
Coulsdon CR5 235 DH118
Dorking RH4 *off South Ter* 263 CH137
Hemel Hempstead HP3 39 BF24
Purley CR8 219 DP113
Slough SL3 133 AZ74
Sunbury-on-Thames TW16 195 BU97
Woking GU21 211 AZ114
Woodford Green IG8 102 EG48
Pines Av, Enf. EN1 82 DV36
Pines Cl, Amer. HP6 55 AP36
Northwood HA6 93 BS51
Pines Rd, Brom. BR1 204 EL96
● **Pines Trd Est, The**,
Guil. GU3 242 AS132
Pine St, EC1 286 E4
Pinetree Cl, Chal.St.P. SL9 90 AW52
Pine Tree Cl, Hem.H. HP2 40 BK19
Hounslow TW5 155 BV81
Pinetree Gdns, Hem.H. HP3 40 BL22
Pine Tree Hill, Wok. GU22 227 BD116
Pine Trees Dr, Uxb. UB10 114 BL63
Pine Tree Way, SE13
off Elmira St 163 EB83
Pine Vw Cl, Chilw. GU4 259 BF140
Pine Vw Manor, Epp. CM16 70 EU30
Pine Wk, Bans. SM7 234 DF117
Bromley BR1 204 EJ95
Carshalton SM5 218 DD110
Caterham CR3 236 DS122
Cobham KT11 214 BX114
East Horsley KT24 245 BT128
Surbiton KT5 198 CN100
Pinewalk, Bkhm KT23 246 CB125
Pine Way, Eng.Grn TW20
off Ashwood Rd 172 AV93
Pine Wd, Sun. TW16 195 BU95
Pinewood, Welw.G.C. AL7 29 CY11
Pinewood Av, New Haw KT15 212 BJ109
Pinner HA5 94 CB51
Rainham RM13 147 FH70
Sevenoaks TN14 257 FK121
Sidcup DA15 185 ES88
Uxbridge UB8 134 BM72
Pinewood Cl, Borwd. WD6 78 CR39
Croydon CR0 203 DY104
Gerrards Cross SL9
off Oxford Rd 112 AY59
Harlow CM17 52 EW16
Iver SL0 133 BC66
Northwood HA6 93 BV50
Orpington BR6 205 ER103
Pinner HA5 94 CB51
St. Albans AL4 43 CJ20
Watford WD17 75 BU39
Woking GU21 211 BA114
Pinewood Dr, Orp. BR6 223 ES106
Potters Bar EN6 63 CZ31
Staines-upon-Thames TW18 174 BG92
Pinewood Gdns, Hem.H. HP1 40 BH20
Pinewood Grn, Iver SL0 133 BC66
Pinewood Gro, W5 137 CJ72
New Haw KT15 212 BH110
Pinewood Ms, Stanw. TW19 174 BK86
Pinewood Pk, New Haw KT15 212 BH111
Pinewood Pl, Dart. DA2 187 FE89
Epsom KT19 216 CR105
Sch **Pinewood Prim Sch**,
Coll.Row RM5 105 FB50
off Thistledene Av
Pinewood Ride, Iver SL0 133 BA68
Slough SL3 133 BA68
Pinewood Rd, SE2 166 EX79
Bromley BR2 204 EG98
Feltham TW13 175 BV90
Havering-atte-Bower RM4 105 FC49
Iver SL0 133 BB67
Virginia Water GU25 192 AU98
Sch **Pinewood Sch**, Ware SG12
off Hoe La 33 DX08
Pinewood Way, Hutt. CM13 109 GD43
Pinfold Rd, SW16 181 DL91
Bushey WD23 76 BZ40
Pinglestone Cl, Harm. UB7 154 BL80
Pinkcoat Cl, Felt. TW13
off Tanglewood Way 175 BV90
Pinkerton Pl, SW16 181 DK91
Pinkham Way, N11 98 DG52
Pink La, Burn. SL1 130 AH68
Pinkneys Ct, Tap. SL6 130 AG72
Pinks Hill, Swan. BR8 207 FE99
Pinkwell Av, Hayes UB3 155 BR77
Pinkwell La, Hayes UB3 155 BQ77
Sch **Pinkwell Prim Sch**,
Hayes UB3 *off Pinkwell La* 155 BQ77
Pinley Gdns, Dag. RM9
off Stamford Rd 146 EV67
Pinnace Ho, E14
off Manchester Rd 302 F6
Pinnacle, NW9
off Heritage Ave 97 CT54
Pinnacle, The, RM6 126 EY58
Pinnacle Hill, Bexh. DA7 167 FB84
Pinnacle Hill N, Bexh. DA7 167 FB83
PINNACLES, Harl. CM19 51 EN15
Pinnacles, Wal.Abb. EN9 68 EE34
Pinnata Cl, Enf. EN2 82 DQ39
Pinnate Pl, Welw.G.C. AL7 29 CY13
Pinn Cl, Uxb. UB8 134 BK72
Pinnell Rd, SE9 164 EK84
PINNER, HA5 116 BY56
⊖ **Pinner** 116 BY56
Pinner Ct, Pnr. HA5 116 CA56
PINNER GREEN, Pnr. HA5 94 BX54
Pinner Grn, Pnr. HA5 94 BW54
Pinner Gro, Pnr. HA5 116 BY56
Pinner Hill, Pnr. HA5 94 BW53
Pinner Hill Rd, Pnr. HA5 94 BW54
Pinner Pk, Pnr. HA5 94 CA53
Pinner Pk Av, Har. HA2 116 CB55
Pinner Pk Gdns, Har. HA2 94 CC54
Sch **Pinner Pk Inf Sch**,
Pnr. HA5 *off Melbourne Av* 116 CB55
Sch **Pinner Pk Jun Sch**,
Pnr. HA5 *off Melbourne Av* 116 CB55
Pinner Rd, Har. HA1, HA2 116 CB57
Northwood HA6 93 BT53
Pinner HA5 116 BZ56
Watford WD19 76 BX44
Pinner Vw, Har. HA1, HA2 116 CC58
PINNERWOOD PARK,
Pnr. HA5 94 BW52
Sch **Pinner Wd Sch**, Pnr. HA5
off Latimer Gdns 94 BW53
Pinnocks Av, Grav. DA11 191 GH88
Pinn Way, Ruis. HA4 115 BS59
Pinstone Way, Ger.Cr. SL9 113 BB61
Pintail Cl, E6 292 G7
Pintail Rd, Wdf.Grn. IG8 102 EH52
Pintail Way, Hayes UB4 136 BX71
Pinter Ho, SW9 310 B9
Pinto Cl, Borwd. WD6 78 CR44
Pinto Way, SE3 164 EH84
Pioneer Cl, E14 290 C7
Pioneer Pl, Croy. CR0 221 EA109
Pioneer Pt N Twr, Ilf. IG1 125 EP62
Pioneer Pt S Twr, Ilf. IG1 125 EP62
● **Pioneers Ind Pk**, Croy. CR0 201 DL102
Pioneer St, SE15 312 C6
Pioneer Way, W12
off Du Cane Rd 139 CV72
Swanley BR8 207 FE97
Watford WD18 75 BT44
Piper Cl, N7 276 C3
Piper Rd, Kings.T. KT1 198 CN97
Pipers Cl, Burn. SL1 130 AJ69
Cobham KT11 230 BX115
PIPERS END, Hert. SG14 31 DJ13
Pipers End, Hert. SG14 31 DJ13
Virginia Water GU25 192 AX97
Piper's Gdns, Croy. CR0 203 DY101
Pipers Grn, NW9 118 CQ57
Pipers Grn La, Edg. HA8 96 CL48
Piper Way, Ilf. IG1 125 ER60
Pipewell Rd, Cars. SM5 200 DE100
Pippbrook, Dor. RH4 263 CH135
Pippbrook Gdns, Dor. RH4
off London Rd 263 CH135
Pippens, Welw.G.C. AL8 29 CY06
Pippin Cl, NW2 119 CV62
Croydon CR0 203 DZ102
Shenley WD7 62 CL33
Pippins, The, Slou. SL3
off Pickford Dr 133 AZ74
Watford WD25 60 BW34
Pippins Cl, West Dr. UB7 154 BK76
Pippins Ct, Ashf. TW15 175 BP93
Sch **Pippins Sch**, Colnbr. SL3
off Raymond Cl 153 BF81
Pippit Ct, Enf. EN3
off Teal Cl 82 DW37
Piquet Rd, SE20 202 DW96
Pirbright Cres,
New Adgtn CR0 221 EC107
Pirbright Rd, SW18 179 CZ88
Pirie Cl, SE5 311 M10
Pirie St, E16 304 B3
Pirrip Cl, Grav. DA12 191 GM89
Pirton Cl, St.Alb. AL4 43 CJ15
Pishiobury Dr, Saw. CM21 36 EW07
Pishiobury Ms, Saw. CM21 36 EX08
Pitcairn Cl, Rom. RM7 126 FA56
Pitcairn Rd, Mitch. CR4 180 DF94
Pitcairn's Path, Har. HA2
off Eastcote Rd 116 CC62
Pitchfont La, Oxt. RH8 238 EF124
Pitchford St, E15 281 H7
PITCH PLACE, Guil. GU3 242 AT129
Pitch Pond Cl, Knot.Grn HP9 88 AH50
Pit Fm Rd, Guil. GU1 243 BA134
Pitfield Cres, SE28 146 EU74
Pitfield Est, N1 287 M2
Pitfield St, N1 287 N3
Pitfield Way, NW10 138 CQ65
Enfield EN3 82 DW39
Pitfold Cl, SE12 184 EG86
Pitfold Rd, SE12 184 EG86
Pitlake, Croy. CR0 201 DP103
Pitman Ho, SE8
off Tanners Hill 314 A6
Pitman St, SE5 311 J4
Pitmaston Ho, SE13 314 E8
Pitmaston Rd, SE13 314 E8
Pitsea Pl, E1 289 K9
Pitsea St, E1 289 K9
Pitsfield, Welw.G.C. AL8 29 CX06
Pitshanger La, W5 137 CH70
Pitshanger Pk, W13 137 CH69
Pitson Cl, Add. KT15 212 BK105
Pitstone Cl, St.Alb. AL4
off Highview Gdns 43 CJ15
Pitt Cres, SW19 180 DB91
Pitt Dr, St.Alb. AL4 43 CJ23
Pitteway Wk, Hert. SG14
off Port Vale 32 DQ09
Pitt Ho, SW11
off Maysoule Rd 160 DD84
Pittman Cl, Ingrave CM13 109 GC50
Pittman Gdns, Ilf. IG1 125 EQ64
Pittmans Fld, Harl. CM20 35 ET14
Pitt Pl, Epsom KT17 216 CS114
Pitts Rivers Cl, Guil. GU1 243 BB134
Pitt Rd, Croy. CR0 202 DQ99
Epsom KT17 216 CS114
Orpington BR6 223 EQ105
Thornton Heath CR7 202 DQ99
Pitt's Head Ms, W1 297 H3
Pittsmead Av, Brom. BR2 204 EG101
Pitts Rd, Slou. SL1 131 AQ74
Pitt St, W8 295 K4
Pittville Gdns, SE25 202 DU97
Pittwood, Shenf. CM15 109 GA46
Pitwood Grn, Tad. KT20 233 CW120
● **Pitwood Pk Ind Est**,
Tad. KT20 *off Waterfield* 233 CV120
★ **Pitzhanger Manor Ho
& Gall**, W5 137 CJ74
Pix Fm La, Hem.H. HP1 39 BB21
Pixfield Ct, Brom. BR2
off Beckenham La 204 EF96
PIXHAM, Dor. RH4 247 CJ133
● **Pixham End**, Dor. RH4 247 CJ133
Pixham La, Dor. RH4 247 CJ133
Pixholme Gro, Dor. RH4 247 CJ134
Pixies Hill Cres, Hem.H. HP1 39 BF22
Sch **Pixies Hill JMI Sch**,
Hem.H. HP1 *off Hazeldell Rd* 39 BF21
Pixies Hill Rd, Hem.H. HP1 39 BF21
Pixley St, E14 289 P8
Pixton Way, Croy. CR0 221 DY109
Place Fm Av, Orp. BR6 205 ER102
Place Fm Rd, Bletch. RH1 252 DR130
Placehouse La, Couls. CR5 235 DM119
Plackett Way, Slou. SL1 131 AK74
Plain, The, Epp. CM16 70 EV29
Plaines Cl, Slou. SL1 131 AM74
PLAISTOW, E13 291 L2
Brom. BR1 184 EF93
⊖ **Plaistow** 281 M10
Plaistow Gro, E15 281 L9
Bromley BR1 184 EH94
Plaistow La, Brom. BR1 184 EG94
Plaistow Pk Rd, E13 144 EH68
Sch **Plaistow Prim Sch**, E13
off Junction Rd 144 EH68
Plaistow Rd, E13 281 L9
E15 281 L9
Plaitford Cl, Rick. WD3 92 BL47
Plane Av, Nthflt DA11 190 GD87
Planes, The, Cher. KT16 194 BJ101
Plane St, SE26 182 DV90
Plane Tree Cres, Felt. TW13 175 BV90
Planetree Path, E17
off Rosebank Vil 123 EA56
Plane Tree Wk, N2 120 DD55
SE19 *off Lunham Rd* 182 DS93
Plantaganet Pl, Wal.Abb. EN9 67 EB33
Plantagenet Cl, Wor.Pk. KT4 216 CR105
Plantagenet Gdns, Rom. RM6 126 EX59
Plantagenet Pl, Rom. RM6 126 EX59
Plantagenet Rd, Barn. EN5 80 DC42
Plantain Gdns, E11
off Hollydown Way 123 ED62
Plantain Pl, SE1 299 L4
Plantation, The, SE3 315 P9
Plantation Cl, SW4
off King's Av 181 DL85
Greenhithe DA9 189 FT86
Plantation Dr, Orp. BR5 206 EX102
Plantation La, EC3
off Rood La 287 N10
Warlingham CR6 237 DY119
Plantation Rd, Amer. HP6 55 AS37
Erith DA8 167 FG81
Swanley BR8 187 FG94
Plantation Wk, Hem.H. HP1 40 BG17
Plantation Way, Amer. HP6 55 AS37
Plantation Wf, SW11 307 P10
Plashet Gdns, Brwd. CM13 109 GA49
Plashet Gro, E6 144 EJ67
Plashet Rd, E13 281 P8
Plashets, The, Sheering CM22 37 FC07
Sch **Plashet Sch**, E6
off Plashet Gro 144 EL66
Plassy Rd, SE6 183 EB87
Platford Grn, Horn. RM11 128 FL56
Platina St, EC2 287 M4
Platinum Ho, Har. HA1
off Lyon Rd 117 CF58
Platinum Ms, N15
off Crowland Rd 122 DT57
Plato Rd, SW2 161 DL84
Platt, The, SW15 306 D10
Amersham HP7 55 AP40
Platt Meadow, Guil. GU4
off Eustace Rd 243 BD131
Platts Av, Wat. WD17 75 BV41
Platt's Eyot, Hmptn. TW12 196 CA96
Platt's La, NW3 120 DA63
Platts Rd, Enf. EN3 82 DW39
Platt St, NW1 275 N10
Plawsfield Rd, Beck. BR3 203 DX95
Plaxtol Cl, Brom. BR1 204 EJ95
Plaxtol Rd, Erith DA8 166 FA80
Plaxton Ct, E11
off Woodhouse Rd 124 EF62
Playfair St, W6 306 B1
Playfield Av, Rom. RM5 105 FC53
Playfield Cres, SE22 182 DT85
Playfield Rd, Edg. HA8 96 CQ54
Playford Rd, N4 121 DM61
Playgreen Way, SE6 183 EA91
Playground Cl, Beck. BR3
off Churchfields Rd 203 DX96
Playhouse Ct, SE1
off Southwark Br Rd 299 J4
Playhouse Sq, Harl. CM20
off College Gate 51 EQ15
Playhouse Yd, EC4 286 G9
● **Plaza Business Cen**, Enf.
EN3 *off Stockingswater La* 83 DZ40
Plaza Par, NW6
off Kilburn High Rd 273 L10
🔒 **Plaza Shop Cen, The**, W1 285 M8
Pleasance, The, SW15 159 CV84
Pleasance Rd, SW15 179 CV85
Orpington BR5 206 EV96
Pleasant Gro, Croy. CR0 203 DZ104
Pleasant Pl, N1 277 H7
Hersham KT12 214 BW107
West Hyde WD3 91 BE52
Pleasant Ri, Hat. AL9 45 CW15
Pleasant Row, NW1 275 K9
Pleasant Vw, Erith DA8 167 FE78
Pleasant Vw Pl, Orp. BR6
off High St 223 EP106
Pleasant Way, Wem. HA0 137 CJ68
Pleasure Pit Rd, Ashtd. KT21 232 CP118
Plender St, NW1 275 L9
Pleshey Rd, N7 275 N1
Plesman Way, Wall. SM6 219 DL109
Plevna Cres, N15 122 DS58
Plevna Rd, N9 100 DU48
Hampton TW12 196 CB95
Plevna St, E14 302 E6
Pleydell Av, SE19 182 DT94
W6 159 CT77
Pleydell Ct, EC4 286 F9
Pleydell Est, EC1
off Radnor St 287 K3
Pleydell St, EC4 286 F9
Plimley Pl, W12 294 C4
Plimsoll Cl, E14 290 C9
Plimsoll Rd, N4 121 DN62
Plomer Av, Hodd. EN11 33 DZ14
Plough Ct, NW10 139 CV69
Plough Ct, EC3 287 M10
Plough Fm Cl, Ruis. HA4 115 BR58
Plough Hill, Cuffley EN6 65 DL28
● **Plough Ind Est**, Lthd. KT22 231 CG120
Plough La, SE22 182 DT86
SW17 180 DB92
SW19 180 DB92
Downside KT11 229 BU116
Harefield UB9 92 BJ51
Potten End HP4 39 BB16
Purley CR8 219 DL109
Sarratt WD3 57 BF33
Plough La, Stoke Poges SL2 132 AV67
Teddington TW11 177 CG92
Wallington SM6 219 DL105
Plough La Cl, Wall. SM6 219 DL106
Ploughlees La, Slou. SL1 132 AS73
Ploughmans Cl, NW1 275 N8
Ploughmans End, Islw. TW7 177 CD85
Welwyn Garden City AL7 30 DC10
Ploughmans Wk, N2
off Long La 98 DC54
Plough Ms, SW11
off Plough Ter 160 DD84
Plough Pl, EC4 286 F8
Plough Ri, Upmin. RM14 129 FS59
Plough Rd, SW11 308 A10
Epsom KT19 216 CR109
Smallfield RH6 269 DP148
Jct **Plough Rbt**, Hem.H. HP1 40 BK22
Plough St, E1 288 C8
Plough Ter, SW11 160 DD84
Plough Way, SE16 301 K8
Plough Yd, EC2 287 P5
Plover Cl, Berk. HP4 38 AW20
Staines-upon-Thames TW18 173 BF90
Plover Ct, Enf. EN3
off Teal Cl 82 DW36
Plover Gdns, Upmin. RM14 129 FT60
Plover Way, SE16 301 L6
Hayes UB4 136 BX72
Plowden Bldgs, EC4
off Middle Temple La 286 E10
Plowman Cl, N18 100 DR50
Plowman Way, Dag. RM8 126 EW60
Ployters Rd, Harl. CM18 51 EQ18
Plumbers Row, E1 288 C7
Plumbridge St, SE10 314 E6
Plum Cl, Felt. TW13 175 BU88
Sch **Plumcroft Prim Sch**, SE18
off Plum La 165 EQ79
Plum Garth, Brent. TW8 157 CK77
Plum La, SE18 165 EP80
Plummer La, Mitch. CR4 200 DF96
Plummer Rd, SW4 181 DK87
Plummers Cft, Dunt.Grn TN13 256 FE121
Plumpton Av, Horn. RM12 128 FL63
Plumpton Cl, Nthlt. UB5 136 CA65
Plumpton Rd, Hodd. EN11 49 EC15
Plumpton Way, Cars. SM5 200 DE104
PLUMSTEAD, SE18 165 ES78
⇌ **Plumstead** 165 ER77
Plumstead Common Rd, SE18 165 EP79
Plumstead High St, SE18 165 ES77
Sch **Plumstead Manor Sch**,
SE18 *off Old Mill Rd* 165 ER79
Plumstead Rd, SE18 305 P8
Plumtree Cl, Dag. RM10 147 FB65
Wallington SM6 219 DK108
Plumtree Ct, EC4 286 F8
Plumtree Mead, Loug. IG10 85 EN41
Pluto Cl, Slou. SL1 151 AL75
Pluto Ri, Hem.H. HP2 40 BL18
Plymouth Dr, Sev. TN13 257 FJ124
Plymouth Pk, Sev. TN13 257 FJ124
Plymouth Rd, E16 291 N7
Bromley BR1 204 EH95
Chafford Hundred RM16 169 FW77
Slough SL1 131 AL71
Plymouth Wf, E14 302 G8
Plympton Av, NW6 272 G7
Plympton Cl, Belv. DA17
off Halifield Dr 166 EY76
Plympton Pl, NW8 284 C5
Plympton Rd, NW6 272 G7
Plympton St, NW8 284 C5
Plymstock Rd, Well. DA16 166 EW80
Pocket Hill, Sev. TN13 256 FG128
Pocketsdell La, Bov. HP3 56 AX28
Pocklington Cl, NW9 96 CS54
Pocock Av, West Dr. UB7 154 BM76
Pococks La, Eton SL4 152 AS78
Pocock St, SE1 298 G4
Podium, The, E2 289 H2
Podmore Rd, SW18 160 DC84
Poets Chase, Hem.H. HP1
off Laureate Way 40 BH18
Poets Gate, Chsht EN7 66 DR28
Poets Rd, N5 277 L2
Poets Way, Har. HA1
off Blawith Rd 117 CE56
Point, The, Ruislip HA4 115 BU63
Point, The, E17
off Tower Ms 123 EA56
Pointalls Cl, N3 98 DC54
Point Cl, SE10 314 F6
Pointer Cl, SE28 146 EX72
Pointers, The, Ashtd. KT21 232 CL120
Sch **Pointer Sch, The**, SE3 315 N5
Pointers Cl, E14 302 C10
Pointers Hill, Westc. RH4 262 CC138
Pointers Rd, Cob. KT11 229 BQ116
Point Hill, SE10 314 F5
Point of Thomas Path, E1 301 H1
Point Pl, Wem. HA9 138 CP66
Point Pleasant, SW18 160 DA84
Point W, SW7 295 M8
Point Wf La, Brent. TW8
off Town Meadow 158 CL80
Poland Ho, E15 280 G8
Poland St, W1 285 M9
● **Polar Pk**, West Dr. UB7 154 BM80
Polayn Garth, Welw.G.C. AL8 29 CW08
Polebrook Rd, SE3 164 EJ83
Pole Cat All, Brom. BR2 204 EF103
Polecroft La, SE6 183 DZ89
Polehamptons, The,
Hmptn. TW12 196 CC95
Polehanger La, Hem.H. HP1 39 BE18
Pole Hill Rd, E4 101 EC45
Hayes UB4 135 BQ69
Uxbridge UB10 135 BQ69
Pole La, Ong. CM5 53 FE17
Polesden Gdns, SW20 199 CV96
★ **Polesden Lacey, Ho & Gdn**,
Dor. RH5 246 CA130
Polesden La, Ripley GU23 227 BF122
Polesden Rd, Bkhm KT23 246 CB129
Polesden Vw, Bkhm KT23 246 CB127
Poles Hill, Chesh. HP5 54 AN29
Sarratt WD3 57 BE33
Polesteeple Hill, Bigg.H. TN16 238 EK117
Polesworth Ho, W2 283 K6
Polesworth Rd, Dag. RM9 146 EX66
Polhill, Halst. TN13, TN14 241 FC115
Polhill Pk, Halst. TN14 241 FD117
Police Sta La, Bushey WD23
off Sparrows Herne 94 CB45
Police Sta Rd, Hersham KT12 214 BW107
★ **Polish Inst & Sikorski Mus**,
SW7 *off Princes Gate* 296 B5
Jct **Polish War Mem**, Ruis. HA4 135 BV66
Pollard Av, Denh. UB9 113 BF58
Pollard Cl, E16 291 N10
N7 276 D2
Chigwell IG7 104 EU50
Old Windsor SL4 172 AV85
Pollard Hatch, Harl. CM19 51 EP18
Pollard Rd, N20 98 DE47
Morden SM4 200 DD99
Woking GU22 227 BB116
Pollard Row, E2 288 D2
Pollards, Map.Cr. WD3 91 BD50
Pollards Cl, Goffs Oak EN7 66 DQ29
Loughton IG10 84 EJ43
Welwyn Garden City AL7 30 DA09
Pollards Cres, SW16 201 DL97
Pollards Hill E, SW16 201 DM97
Pollards Hill N, SW16 201 DL97
Pollards Hill S, SW16 201 DL97
Pollards Hill W, SW16 201 DL97
Pollards Oak Cres, Oxt. RH8 254 EG132
Pollards Oak Rd, Oxt. RH8 254 EG132
Pollard St, E2 288 D2
Pollards Wd Hill, Oxt. RH8 254 EH130
Pollards Wd Rd, SW16 201 DL96
Oxted RH8 254 EH131
Pollard Wk, Sid. DA14 186 EW93
Pollen St, W1 285 K9
Pollicott Cl, St.Alb. AL4 43 CJ15
Pollitt Dr, NW8 284 A4
★ **Pollock's Toy Mus**, W1 285 M6
Pollyhaugh, Eyns. DA4 208 FL104
Polperro Cl, Orp. BR6
off Cotswold Ri 205 ET100
Polperro Ms, SE11 298 F8
Polsted Rd, SE6 183 DZ87
Polsten Ms, Enf. EN3 83 EA37
Polthorne Est, SE18 165 EQ77
Polthorne Gro, SE18 165 EQ77
Poltimore Rd, Guil. GU2 258 AU136
Polworth Rd, SW16 181 DL92
Polygon, The, SW4
off Old Town 161 DJ84
● **Polygon Business Cen**,
Colnbr. SL3 153 BF82
Polygon Rd, NW1 285 N1
Polytechnic St, SE18 305 M8
Pomell Way, E1 288 B8
Pomeroy Cl, Amer. HP7 55 AR40
Twickenham TW1 157 CH84
Pomeroy Cres, Wat. WD24 75 BV36
Pomeroy St, SE14 313 H5
Pomfret Rd, SE5 311 H10
Pomoja La, N19 121 DK61
Pompadour Cl, Warley CM14
off Queen St 108 FW50
Pompadour Way, Bark. IG11 146 EV68
Pond Cl, N12 98 DE51
SE3 315 M9
Ashtead KT21 232 CL117
Harefield UB9 92 BJ54
Hersham KT12 213 BU107
Pond Cottage La,
W.Wick. BR4 203 EA102
Pond Cotts, SE21 182 DS88
Pond Cft, Hat. AL10 45 CT18
Pondcroft, Welw.G.C. AL7 29 CY10
PONDERS END, Enf. EN3 82 DW43
⇌ **Ponders End** 83 DX43
● **Ponders End Ind Est**,
Enf. EN3 83 DZ42
Ponder St, N7 276 C6
Pond Fm Cl, Walt.Hill KT20 233 CU124
Pond Fm Est, E5
off Millfields Rd 122 DW62
Pond Fld, Welw.G.C. AL7 30 DA06
Pondfield Cres, St.Alb. AL4 43 CH16
Pond Fld End, Loug. IG10 102 EJ45
Pondfield Ho, SE27
off Elder Rd 182 DQ92
Pondfield La, Brwd. CM13 109 GA49
Pondfield Rd, Brom. BR2 204 EE102
Dagenham RM10 127 FB64
Godalming GU7 258 AT144
Kenley CR8 235 DP116
Orpington BR6 205 EP104
Pond Grn, Ruis. HA4 115 BS61
Pond Hill Gdns, Sutt. SM3 217 CY107
Pond La, Chal.St.P. SL9 90 AV53
Peaslake GU5 261 BQ144
Pond Lees Cl, Dag. RM10
off Leys Av 147 FD66
Pond Mead, SE21 182 DR86
Pond Meadow, Guil. GU2 242 AS134
Sch **Pond Meadow Sch**,
Guil. GU1 *off Larch Av* 242 AW131
Pond Pk Rd, Chesh. HP5 54 AP29
Pond Path, Chis. BR7
off Heathfield La 185 EQ93
Pond Piece, Oxshott KT22 214 CB114
Pond Pl, SW3 296 C9
Pond Rd, E15 281 J10
SE3 315 M8
Egham TW20 173 BC93
Hemel Hempstead HP3 58 BN25
Woking GU22 226 AU120
Ponds, The, Wey. KT13
off Ellesmere Rd 213 BS107
Pondside Ave, Wor.Pk. KT4 199 CW102
Pondside Cl, Harling. UB3 155 BR80
Ponds La, Guil. GU5 260 BL142
Pond Sq, N6
off South Gro 120 DG60
Pond St, NW3 274 C2
Pond Wk, Upmin. RM14 129 FS61
Pond Way, Tedd. TW11
off Holmesdale Rd 177 CJ93
Pondwicks, Amer. HP7 55 AP39
Pondwicks Cl, St.Alb. AL1 42 CC21
Pondwood Ri, Orp. BR6 205 ES101
Ponler St, E1 288 E9
Ponsard Rd, NW10 139 CV69
Sch **Ponsbourne St. Mary's
C of E Prim Sch**, Hert. SG13
off Newgate St Village 47 DL24
Ponsford St, E9 279 H4
Ponsonby Pl, SW1 297 P10
Ponsonby Rd, SW15 179 CV87
Ponsonby Ter, SW1 297 P10
Pontefract Rd, Brom. BR1 184 EF92
Pontes Ave, Houns. TW3 156 BZ84
Pontoise Cl, Sev. TN13 256 FF122
Ponton Rd, SW8 309 P3
DLR **Pontoon Dock** 304 C3
Pont St, SW1 296 E7
Pont St Ms, SW1 296 E7
Pontypool Pl, SE1 298 G4
Pontypool Wk, Rom. RM3 106 FJ51
Pony Chase, Cob. KT11 214 BZ113

P

Pool Cl, Beck. BR3 183 EA92
West Molesey KT8 196 BZ99
Pool Ct, SE6 183 EA89
Poole Cl, Ruis. HA4 115 BS61
Poole Ct Rd, Houns. TW4 156 BY82
Poole Ho, SE11
off Lambeth Wk 298 D7
Grays RM16 171 GJ75
Pool End Cl, Shep. TW17 194 BN99
Poole Rd, E9 279 J5
Epsom KT19 216 CR107
Hornchurch RM11 128 FM59
Woking GU21 226 AY117
Pooles Bldgs, EC1 286 E5
Pooles La, SW10 307 N5
Dagenham RM9 146 EY68
Pooles Pk, N4 121 DN61
Sch Pooles Pk Prim Sch, N4
off Lennox Rd 121 DM61
Poole St, N1 277 L9
Poole Way, Hayes UB4 135 BR69
Pooley Av, Egh. TW20 173 BB92
Pooley Dr, SW14
off Sheen La 158 CQ83
POOLEY GREEN, Egh. TW20 173 BC92
Pooley Grn Cl, Egh. TW20 173 BC92
Pooley Grn Rd, Egh. TW20 173 BB92
Pooleys La, N.Mymms AL9 45 CV23
Pool Gro, Croy. CR0 221 DY112
Pool La, Slou. SL1 132 AS73
Poolmans Rd, Wind. SL4 151 AK83
Poolmans St, SE16 301 J4
Pool Rd, Har. HA1 117 CD59
West Molesey KT8 196 BZ100
Poolsford Rd, NW9 118 CS56
Poonah St, E1 289 H9
Pootings Rd, Crock.H. TN8 255 ER134
Pope Cl, SW19 180 DD93
Feltham TW14 175 BT88
Pope Ho, SE16 300 E9
Sch Pope John RC Prim Sch,
W12 off Commonwealth Av 139 CV73
Sch Pope Paul Cath Prim Sch,
Pot.B. EN6 off Baker St 63 CZ33
Pope Rd, Brom. BR2 204 EK99
Popes Av, Twick. TW2 177 CE89
Popes Cl, Amer. HP6 72 AT37
Colnbrook SL3 153 BB80
Popes Dr, N3 98 DA53
Popes Gro, Croy. CR0 203 DZ104
Twickenham TW1, TW2 177 CF89
Pope's Head All, EC3
off Cornhill 287 M9
Popes La, W5 157 CK76
Oxted RH8 254 EE134
Watford WD24 75 BV37
Popes Rd, SW9 161 DN83
Abbots Langley WD5 59 BS31
Pope St, SE1 299 P5
Popham Cl, Han. TW13 176 BZ90
Popham Gdns, Rich. TW9
off Lower Richmond Rd 158 CN83
Popham Rd, N1 277 J9
Popham St, N1 277 H8
● Popin Business Cen,
Wem. HA9 118 CP64
POPLAR, E14 302 C2
DLR Poplar 302 C1
Poplar Av, Amer. HP7 72 AT39
Gravesend DA12 191 GJ91
Leatherhead KT22 231 CH122
Mitcham CR4 200 DF95
Orpington BR6 205 EP103
Southall UB2 156 CB76
West Drayton UB7 134 BM73
Poplar Bath St, E14 290 D10
● Poplar Business Pk, E14 302 E1
Poplar Cl, E9 279 N2
Chesham HP5 54 AQ28
Colnbrook SL3 153 BE81
Epsom KT17 233 CV115
Pinner HA5 94 BX53
South Ockendon RM15 149 FX70
Poplar Ct, SW19 180 DA92
Poplar Cres, Epsom KT19 216 CQ107
Poplar Dr, Bans. SM7 217 CX114
Hutton CM13 109 GC44
Poplar Fm Cl, Epsom KT19 216 CQ107
Poplar Gdns, N.Mal. KT3 198 CR96
Poplar Gro, N11 98 DG51
W6 294 B5
New Malden KT3 198 CR97
Wembley HA9 118 CQ62
Woking GU22 226 AY119
Poplar High St, E14 290 C10
Poplar Ho, Langley SL3 153 AZ78
Poplar Mt, Belv. DA17 167 FB77
Poplar Pl, SE28 146 EW73
W2 283 L10
Hayes UB3 135 BU73
Sch Poplar Prim Sch, SW19
off Poplar Rd S 200 DA97
Poplar Rd, SE24 162 DQ84
SW19 200 DA96
Ashford TW15 175 BQ92
Denham UB9 114 BJ64
Esher KT10 197 CH104
Leatherhead KT22 231 CH122
Shalford GU4 258 AY141
Sutton SM3 199 CZ102
Wooburn Green HP10
Plough La, off Glory Mill La 110 AE56
Poplar Rd S, SW19 200 DA97
Poplar Row, They.B. CM16 85 ES37
Poplars, Welw.G.C. AL7 30 DB08
Poplars, The, N14 81 DH43
Abridge RM4 off Hoe La 86 EV41
Borehamwood WD6
Plough La, off Grove Rd 78 CN39
Cheshunt EN7 66 DS26
Gravesend DA12 191 GL87
Hemel Hempstead HP1 40 BH21
Magdalen Laver CM5 53 FB19
St. Albans AL1 43 CH24
Poplars Av, NW10 272 A5
Hatfield AL10 44 CR18
Poplars Cl, Hat. AL10 44 CQ18
Ruislip HA4 115 BS60
Watford WD25 59 BV32
Poplar Shaw, Wal.Abb. EN9 68 EF33
Poplars Rd, E17 123 EB58
Poplar St, Rom. RM7 127 FC56
Poplar Vw, Wem. HA9
off Magnet Rd 117 CK61
Poplar Wk, SE24 162 DQ84
Caterham CR3 236 DS123
Croydon CR0 202 DQ103
Poplar Way, Felt. TW13 175 BU90
Ilford IG6 125 EQ56
Poppins Ct, EC4 286 G9
Poppleton Rd, E11 124 EE58
Poppy Cl, Barn. EN5 80 DC44
Belvedere DA17 167 FB76
Hemel Hempstead HP1 39 BE19
Northolt UB5 136 BZ65
Pilgrim's Hatch CM15 108 FV43
Wallington SM6 200 DG102
Poppy Dr, Enf. EN1 82 DV42
★ Poppy Factory Mus, The,
Rich. TW10 177 CK86
Poppyfields, Welw.G.C. AL7 30 DC09
Poppy La, Croy. CR0 202 DW101
Poppy Wk, Hat. AL10 45 CT15
Waltham Cross EN7 66 DR28
Porchester Cl, SE5 162 DQ84
Hornchurch RM11 128 FL58
Porchester Gdns, W2 283 L10
Porchester Gdns Ms, W2 283 M9
Porchester Gate, W2
off Bayswater Rd 295 N1
Porchester Mead, Beck. BR3 183 EA93
Porchester Ms, W2 283 M8
Porchester Pl, W2 284 D9
Porchester Rd, W2 283 L8
Kingston upon Thames KT1 198 CP96
Porchester Sq, W2 283 M8
Porchester Sq Ms, W2 283 M8
Porchester Ter, W2 283 N9
Porchester Ter N, W2 283 M8
Porchfield Cl, Grav. DA12 191 GJ89
Sutton SM2 218 DB110
Porch Way, N20 98 DF48
Porcupine Cl, SE9 184 EL89
Porden Rd, SW2 161 DM84
Porlock Av, Har. HA2 116 CC60
Porlock Rd, Enf. EN1 100 DT45
Porlock St, SE1 299 L4
Porridge Pot All, Guil. GU2
off Bury Flds 258 AW136
Porrington Cl, Chis. BR7 205 EM95
Portal Cl, SE27 181 DN90
Ruislip HA4 115 BU63
Uxbridge UB10 134 BL66
Portal Way, W3 138 CR71
Port Av, Green. DA9 189 FV86
Portbury Cl, SE15 312 D7
Port Cres, E13 292 A5
★ Portcullis Ho, SW1
off Bridge St 298 B5
Portcullis Lo Rd, Enf. EN2 82 DR41
Portelet Ct, N1 277 M8
Portelet Rd, E1 289 J3
Porten Rd, W14 294 E7
Porter Cl, Grays RM20 169 FW79
Porter Rd, E6 293 K8
Porters Av, Dag. RM8, RM9 146 EV65
Porters Cl, Brwd. CM14 108 FU46
Portersfield Rd, Enf. EN1 82 DS42
Porters Pk Dr, Shenley WD7 61 CK33
Porter Sq, N19 121 DL60
Porter St, SE1 299 K2
W1 284 F6
Porters Wk, E1 300 F1
Porters Way, N12 98 DE52
West Drayton UB7 154 BM76
Porters Wd, St.Alb. AL3 43 CE16
Porteus Rd, W2 283 P7
Portgate Cl, W9 283 H4
Porthallow Cl, Orp. BR6 223 ET105
Porthcawe Rd, SE26 183 DY91
Port Hill, Hert. SG14 32 DQ09
Orpington BR6 224 EV112
Porthkerry Av, Well. DA16 166 EU84
Portia Way, E3 289 N5
Coll Portico City Learning Cen,
E5 278 G1
Portinscale Rd, SW15 179 CY85
Portland Av, N16 122 DT59
Gravesend DA12 191 GH89
New Malden KT3 199 CT101
Sidcup DA15 186 EU86
● Portland Business Cen,
Datchet SL3 off Manor Ho La 152 AV81
Portland Cl, Rom. RM6 126 EY57
Slough SL2 131 AK70
Worcester Park KT4 199 CV101
● Portland Commercial Est,
Bark. IG11 146 EW68
Portland Ct, SE1
off Falmouth Rd 299 L6
Portland Cres, SE9 184 EL89
Feltham TW13 175 BR91
Greenford UB6 136 CB70
Stanmore HA7 95 CK54
Portland Dr, Chsht EN7 66 DU31
Enfield EN2 82 DS38
Merstham RH1 251 DK129
Portland Gdns, N4 121 DP58
Romford RM6 126 EX57
Portland Gro, SW8 310 C6
Portland Hts, Nthwd. HA6 93 BT49
H Portland Hosp for Women &
Children, The, W1 285 K5
Portland Ho, Merst. RH1 251 DJ129
Portland Ms, W1 285 M9
Portland Pk, Ger.Cr. SL9 112 AX58
Portland Pl, W1 285 J5
Epsom KT17 216 CS112
Greenhithe DA9 169 FW84
Hertford Heath SG13 32 DW11
Sch Portland Pl Sch, W1 285 K6
Portland Ri, N4 121 DP60
Portland Ri Est, N4 121 DP60
Portland Rd, N15 122 DT56
SE9 184 EL89
SE25 202 DU98
W11 294 F2
Ashford TW15 174 BL90
Bromley BR1 184 EJ91
Dorking RH4 263 CG135
Gravesend DA12 191 GH88
Hayes UB4 135 BS69
Kingston upon Thames KT1 198 CL97
Mitcham CR4 200 DE96
Southall UB2 156 BZ76
Portland Sq, E1 300 E2
Portland St, SE17 299 L10
St. Albans AL3 42 CC20
Portland Ter, Rich. TW9 157 CK84
Portland Wk, SE17 311 M2
Portley La, Cat. CR3 236 DS121
Portley Wd Rd, Whyt. CR3 236 DT120
Portman Av, SW14 158 CR83
Portman Cl, W1 284 F8
Bexley DA5 187 FE88
Bexleyheath DA7
off Queen Anne's Gate 166 EX83
St. Albans AL4 43 CJ15
Portman Dr, Wdf.Grn. IG8 102 EK54
Portman Gdns, NW9 96 CR54
Uxbridge UB10 134 BN66
Portman Gate, NW1 284 D5
Portman Hall, Har. HA3 95 CD50
Portman Ho, St.Alb. AL3 43 CD17
Portman Ms S, W1 284 G9
Portman Pl, E2 289 H3
Portman Rd, Kings.T. KT1 198 CM96
Portman Sq, W1 284 F8
Portman St, W1 284 G9
Portmeadow Wk, SE2 166 EX75
Portmeers Cl, E17
off Lennox Rd 123 EA58
Portmore Gdns, Rom. RM5 104 FA50
Portmore Pk Rd, Wey. KT13 212 BN105
Portmore Quays, Wey. KT13
off Weybridge Rd 212 BM105
Portmore Way, Wey. KT13 194 BN104
Portnall Dr, Vir.W. GU25 192 AT99
Portnall Ri, Vir.W. GU25 192 AT99
Portnall Rd, W9 282 G4
Virginia Water GU25 192 AT99
Portnalls Cl, Couls. CR5 235 DH116
Portnalls Ri, Couls. CR5 235 DH116
Portnalls Rd, Couls. CR5 235 DH118
Portnoi Cl, Rom. RM1 105 FD54
Portobello Cl, Chesh. HP5 54 AN29
Portobello Ct, W11 283 H9
Portobello Ms, W11 295 J1
Portobello Rd, W10 282 G8
W11 283 H10
Port of Tilbury, Til. RM18 170 GE84
Porton Ct, Surb. KT6 197 CJ100
Portpool La, EC1 286 E6
Portree Cl, N22 99 DM52
Portree St, E14 291 H8
Portsdown, Edg. HA8
off Rectory La 96 CN50
Portsdown Av, NW11 119 CZ58
Portsdown Ms, NW11 119 CZ58
Portsea Ms, W2 284 D9
Portsea Pl, W2 284 D9
Portsea Rd, Til. RM18 171 GJ81
Portslade Rd, SW8 309 L8
Portsmouth Av, T.Ditt. KT7 197 CG101
Portsmouth Ct, Slou. SL1 132 AS73
Portsmouth Ms, E16 304 B2
Portsmouth Rd, SW15 179 CV87
Cobham KT11 213 BU114
Esher KT10 214 CC105
Guildford GU2, GU3 258 AW138
Kingston upon Thames KT1 197 CJ99
Surbiton KT6 197 CJ99
Thames Ditton KT7 197 CE103
Woking GU23 228 BM119
Portsmouth St, WC2 286 C9
Portsoken St, E1 288 A10
Portswood Pl, SW15
off Danebury Ave 179 CT87
Portugal Gdns, Twick. TW2
off Fulwell Pk Av 176 CC89
Portugal Rd, Wok. GU21 227 AZ116
Portugal St, WC2 286 C9
Port Vale, Hert. SG14 31 DP08
Portway, E15 281 M8
Epsom KT17 217 CU110
Rainham RM13 147 FG67
Portway Cres, Epsom KT17 217 CU109
Portway Gdns, SE18
off Shooters Hill Rd 164 EK81
Sch Portway Prim Sch, E15 281 N9
Postern Grn, Enf. EN2 81 DN40
Postfield, Welw.G.C. AL7 30 DA06
Post Ho La, Bkhm KT23 246 CA125
Post La, Twick. TW2 177 CD88
Post Meadow, Iver SL0 133 BD69
Postmill Cl, Croy. CR0 203 DX104
Post Office App, E7 124 EH64
Post Office Ct, EC3 287 M9
Post Office La, Beac. HP9 89 AK52
George Green SL3 132 AX72
Post Office Rd, Harl. CM20 35 EQ14
Post Office Row, Oxt. RH8 254 EL131
Post Office Wk, Harl. CM20 35 ER14
Post Office Way, SW8 309 N4
Post Rd, Sthl. UB2 156 CB76
Postway Ms, Ilf. IG1
off Clements Rd 125 EP62
Postwood Grn, Hert.Hth SG13 32 DW12
Post Wd Rd, Ware SG12 33 DY08
Potier St, SE1 299 M7
Potiphar Pl, Warley CM14 108 FV49
Potkiln La, Jordans HP9 111 AQ55
POTTEN END, Berk. HP4 39 BC16
Sch Potten End First Sch,
Pott.End HP4 off Church Rd 39 BB17
Potten End Hill, Hem.H. HP1 39 BD16
Potten End HP4 39 BD16
Potter Cl, Mitch. CR4 201 DH96
Potterells, N.Mymms AL9 63 CX25
Potteries, The, Barn. EN5 80 DA43
Ottershaw KT16 211 BE107
Potterne Cl, SW19 179 CX87
POTTERS BAR, EN6 64 DA32
⇌ Potters Bar 64 DA32
H Potters Bar Comm Hosp,
Pot.B. EN6 64 DC34
Potters Cl, SE15 311 P4
Croydon CR0 203 DY102
Loughton IG10 84 EL40
Potters Ct, Pot.B. EN6 64 DA32
Potters Cross, Iver SL0 133 BE69
POTTERS CROUCH,
St.Alb. AL2 60 BX25
Potters Fld, Harl. CM17 52 EX17
St. Albans AL3 43 CE16
Potters Flds, SE1 299 P3
Potters Gro, N.Mal. KT3 198 CQ98
Potters Hts Cl, Pnr. HA5 93 BV52
Potters La, SW16 181 DK93
Barnet EN5 80 DA42
Borehamwood WD6 78 CQ39
Send GU23 227 BB123
Potters Ms, Els. WD6 77 CK44
Potters Rd, SW6 307 N9
Barnet EN5 80 DB42
POTTER STREET, Harl. CM17 52 EW16
Potter St, Harl. CM17 52 EW16
Northwood HA6 93 BU53
Pinner HA5 93 BV53
Potter St Hill, Pnr. HA5 93 BV51
Sch Potter St Prim Sch,
Harl. CM17 off Carters Mead 52 EW17
Potters Way, Reig. RH2 266 DC138
Pottery Cl, SE25 202 DV98
Pottery La, W11 294 E1
Pottery Rd, Bex. DA5 187 FC89
Brentford TW8 158 CL79
Pottery St, SE16 300 E5
Pott St, E2 288 F3
Pouchen End La, Hem.H. HP1 39 BD21
Poulcott, Wrays. TW19 172 AY86
Poulett Gdns, Twick. TW1 177 CG88
Poulett Rd, E6 145 EM68
Poulters Wd, Kes. BR2 222 EK106
Poultney Cl, Shenley WD7 62 CM32
Poulton Av, Sutt. SM1 200 DD104
Poulton Cl, E8 278 E4
Poulton Ct, W3
off Victoria Rd 138 CR71
Poultry, EC2 287 L9
Pound, The, Burn. SL1
off Hogfair La 130 AJ70
Pound Cl, Epsom KT19 216 CR111
Long Ditton KT6 197 CJ102
Lower Nazeing EN9 50 EE23
Orpington BR6 205 ER103
Pound Ct, Ashtd. KT21 232 CM118
Pound Ct Dr, Orp. BR6 205 ER103
Pound Cres, Fetch. KT22 231 CD121
Pound Fm Cl, Esher KT10 197 CD102
Pound Fld, Guil. GU1 242 AX133
Poundfield, Wat. WD25 75 BT35
Poundfield Ct, Wok. GU22
off High St 227 BC121
Poundfield Gdns, Wok. GU22 227 BC120
Poundfield Rd, Loug. IG10 85 EN43
Pound La, NW10 139 CU65
Epsom KT19 216 CR112
Knockholt Pound TN14 240 EX115
Sevenoaks TN13 257 FH124
Shenley WD7 62 CM33
Pound Pk Rd, SE7 304 E9
Pound Pl, SE9 185 EN86
Shalford GU4 259 AZ140
Pound Pl Cl, Shalf. GU4 259 AZ140
Pound Rd, Bans. SM7 233 CZ117
Chertsey KT16 194 BH101
Pound St, Cars. SM5 218 DF106
Poundwell, Welw.G.C. AL7 30 DA10
Pounsley Rd, Dunt.Grn TN13 256 FE121
Pountney Rd, SW11 308 G10
POVEREST, Orp. BR5 205 ET99
Sch Poverest Prim Sch,
St.M.Cray BR5
off Tillingbourne Grn 206 EU99
Poverest Rd, Orp. BR5 205 ET99
Povey Cross Rd, Horl. RH6 268 DD150
Powder Mill La, Dart. DA1 188 FL89
Twickenham TW2 176 BZ88
Powdermill La, Wal.Abb. EN9 67 EB33
Powdermill Ms, Wal.Abb. EN9
off Powdermill La 67 EB33
Powder Mills Pl, Chilw. GU4 259 BC140
Powdermill Way,
Wal.Abb. EN9 67 EB32
Powell Av, Dart. DA2 189 FS89
Powell Cl, Chess. KT9
off Coppard Gdns 215 CK106
Edgware HA8 96 CM51
Guildford GU2 258 AT136
Horley RH6 268 DE147
Sch Powell Corderoy Prim Sch,
Dor. RH4 off Longfield Rd 263 CF137
Powell Gdns, Dag. RM10 126 FA63
Redhill RH1 251 DH132
Powell Pl, E4 83 EB42
Powell Rd, E5 122 DV62
Buckhurst Hill IG9 102 EJ45
Powells Cl, Dor. RH4
off Goodwyns Rd 263 CJ139
Powell's Wk, W4 158 CS79
Power Cl, Guil. GU1 242 AW133
Power Dr, Enf. EN3 83 DZ36
● Powergate Business Pk,
NW10 138 CR69
● Power Ind Est, Erith DA8 167 FG81
Power Rd, W4 158 CN77
Powers Ct, Twick. TW1 177 CK87
Powerscroft Rd, E5 278 G1
Sidcup DA14 186 EW93
Powis Ct, Pot.B. EN6 64 DC34
Powis Gdns, NW11 119 CZ59
W11 283 H8
Powis Ms, W11 283 H8
Powis Pl, WC1 286 B5
Powis Rd, E3 290 D3
Powis Sq, W11 283 H8
Powis St, SE18 305 L7
Powis Ter, W11 283 H8
Powle Ter, Ilf. IG1
off Oaktree Gro 125 ER64
Powlett Pl, NW1 275 H6
Pownall Gdns, Houns. TW3 156 CB84
Pownall Rd, E8 278 B9
Hounslow TW3 156 CB84
Pownsett Ter, Ilf. IG1
off Buttsbury Rd 125 EQ64
Powster Rd, Brom. BR1 184 EH92
Powys Cl, Bexh. DA7 166 EX79
Powys Ct, Borwd. WD6 78 CR41
Powys La, N13 99 DL50
N14 99 DL49
POYLE, Slou. SL3 153 BE81
Poyle La, Burn. SL1 130 AH67
Poyle New Cotts,
Colnbr. SL3 153 BF82
Poyle Pk, Colnbr. SL3 153 BE83
Poyle Rd, Colnbr. SL3 153 BE83
Guildford GU1 258 AY136
● Poyle Tech Cen, Slou. SL3 153 BE82
Poyle Ter, Guil. GU1
off Sydenham Rd 258 AX136
Poynder Rd, Til. RM18 171 GH81
Poynders Ct, SW4
off Poynders Rd 181 DJ86
Poynders Gdns, SW4 181 DJ87
Poynders Hill, Hem.H. HP2 41 BQ21
Poynders Rd, SW4 181 DJ86
Poynes Rd, Horl. RH6 268 DE146
Poynings, The, Iver SL0 153 BF77
Poynings Cl, Orp. BR6 206 EV103
Poynings Rd, N19 121 DJ62
Poynings Way, N12 98 DA50
Romford RM3
off Arlington Gdns 106 FL53
Poyntell Cres, Chis. BR7 205 ER95
Poynter Ho, W11 294 D2
Poynter Rd, Enf. EN1 82 DU43
Poynton Rd, N17 100 DU54
Poyntz Rd, SW11 308 E9
Poyser St, E2 288 F1
Prae, The, Wok. GU22 227 BF118
Prae Cl, St.Alb. AL3 42 CB19
Praed Ms, W2 284 B8
Praed St, W2 284 C7
Praetorian Ct, St.Alb. AL1 42 CC23
Sch Prae Wd Prim Sch,
St.Alb. AL3 off King Harry La 42 CA22
Pragel St, E13 292 B1
Pragnell Rd, SE12 184 EH89
Prague Pl, SW2 181 DL85
Prah Rd, N4 121 DN61
Prairie Cl, Add. KT15 194 BH104
Prairie Rd, Add. KT15 194 BH104
Prairie St, SW8 309 H9
Pratt Ms, NW1 275 L9
Sch Pratts Bottom Prim Sch,
Pr.Bot. BR6
off Hookwood Rd 224 EW111
Pratts La, Hersham KT12
off Molesey Rd 214 BX105
PRATT'S BOTTOM, Orp. BR6 224 EV110
Pratts Pas, Kings.T. KT1
off Clarence St 198 CL96
Pratt St, NW1 275 L9
Pratt Wk, SE11 298 D8
Prayle Gro, NW2 119 CX60
Prebend Gdns, W4 159 CT76
W6 159 CT76
Prebend St, N1 277 J9
Precinct, The, Egh. TW20
off High St 173 BA92
West Molesey KT8
off Victoria Av 196 CB97
Precinct Rd, Hayes UB3 135 BU73
Precincts, The, Burn. SL1 130 AH70
Morden SM4 off Green La 200 DA100
Premier Av, Grays RM16 170 GC75
Premier Cor, W9 282 G1
Premiere Pl, E14 302 A1
● Premier Pk, NW10 138 CP67
Premier Pk Rd, NW10 138 CP68
Premier Pl, Wat. WD18 75 BT43
Sch Prendergast - Hilly Flds Coll,
SE4 off Adelaide Av 163 EA84
Sch Prendergast - Ladywell Flds
Coll, SE4 off Manwood Rd 183 EA86
Prendergast Rd, SE3 315 K10
Prentice Pl, Harl. CM17 52 EW17
Prentis Rd, SW16 181 DK91
Prentiss Ct, SE7 304 E9
Presburg Rd, N.Mal. KT3 198 CS99
Prescelly Pl, Edg. HA8 96 CM53
Prescot St, E1 288 B10
Prescott Av, Petts Wd BR5 205 EP100
Prescott Cl, SW16 181 DL94
Prescott Grn, Loug. IG10 85 EQ41
Prescott Ho, SE17 311 H3
Prescott Pl, SW4 161 DK83
Prescott Rd, Chsht EN8 67 DY27
Colnbrook SL3 153 BE82
Presdales Ct, Ware SG12
off Presdales Dr 33 DY07
Presdales Dr, Ware SG12 33 DX07
Sch Presdales Sch, Ware SG12
off Hoe La 33 DX08
Presentation Ms, SW2 181 DM89
Preshaw Cres, Mitch. CR4
off Lower Grn W 200 DE97
President Dr, E1 300 E2
President St, EC1 287 J2
Prespa Cl, N9
off Hudson Way 100 DW47
Press Ct, SE1 300 C10
Press Rd, NW10 118 CR62
Uxbridge UB8 134 BK65
Prestage Way, E14 290 F10
Prestbury Ct, Wok. GU21
off Muirfield Rd 226 AU118
Prestbury Cres, Bans. SM7 234 DF116
Prestbury Rd, E7 144 EJ66
Prestbury Sq, SE9 185 EM91
Prested Rd, SW11
off St. John's Hill 160 DE84
Prestige Way, NW4
off Heriot Rd 119 CW57
PRESTON, Wem. HA9 117 CK59
Preston Av, E4 101 ED51
Preston Cl, SE1 299 N8
Twickenham TW2 177 CE90
Preston Ct, Walt. KT12 196 BW102
Jct Preston Cross, Lthd. KT23 246 BZ126
Preston Dr, E11 124 EJ57
Bexleyheath DA7 166 EX81
Epsom KT19 216 CS107
Preston Gdns, NW10
off Church Rd 138 CS65
Enfield EN3 83 DY37
Ilford IG1 124 EL58
Preston Gro, Ashtd. KT21 231 CJ117
Preston Hill, Chesh. HP5 54 AR29
Harrow HA3 118 CM58
Preston La, Tad. KT20 233 CV121
Sch Preston Manor High Sch,
Wem. HA9 off Carlton Av E 118 CM61
Sch Preston Pk Prim Sch,
Wem. HA9 off College Rd 117 CK60
Preston Pl, NW2 139 CU65
Richmond TW10 178 CL85
⊖ Preston Road 118 CL60
Preston Rd, E11 124 EE58
SE19 181 DP93
SW20 179 CT94
Harrow HA3 118 CL59
Northfleet DA11 190 GE88
Romford RM3 106 FK49
Shepperton TW17 194 BN99
Slough SL2 132 AW73
Wembley HA9 118 CL61
Prestons Rd, E14 302 F4
Bromley BR2 204 EG104
Preston Waye, Har. HA3 118 CL60
Prestwick Cl, Sthl. UB2
off Ringway 156 BY78
Prestwick Rd, Wat. WD19 94 BX50
Prestwood, Slou. SL2 132 AV72
Prestwood Av, Har. HA3 117 CH56
Prestwood Cl, SE18 166 EU80
Harrow HA3 117 CH56
Prestwood Dr, Rom. RM5 105 FC50
Prestwood Gdns, Croy. CR0 202 DQ101
Prestwood St, N1 287 K1
Pretoria Av, E17 123 DY56
Pretoria Cl, N17 100 DT52
Pretoria Cres, E4 101 EC46
Pretoria Rd, E4 101 EC46
E11 123 ED60
E16 291 L4
N17 100 DT52
SW16 181 DH93

Pretoria Rd, Chertsey KT16 193 BF102
Ilford IG1 125 EP64
Romford RM7 127 FC56
Watford WD18 75 BU42
Pretoria Rd N, N18 100 DT51
Pretty La, Couls. CR5 235 DJ121
Prevost Rd, N11 98 DG47
Prey Heath, Wok. GU22 226 AV123
Prey Heath Cl, Wok. GU22 226 AW124
Prey Heath Rd, Wok. GU22 226 AV124
Price Cl, NW7 97 CY51
SW17 180 DF90
Price Rd, Croy. CR0 219 DP106
Price's Ct, SW11 308 A10
Prices La, Reig. RH2 266 DA137
Prices Ms, N1 276 D8
Price's St, SE1 299 H3
Price Way, Hmptn. TW12
off Victors Dr 176 BY93
Prichard Ct, N7 276 C3
Prichard Ho, SE11
off Hotspur St 298 E9
Pricklers Hill, Barn. EN5 80 DB44
Prickley Wd, Brom. BR2 204 EF102
Priddy Pl, Red. RH1 251 DJ131
Priddy's Yd, Croy. CR0
off Church St 202 DQ103
Prideaux Pl, W3 138 CR73
WC1 286 D2
Prideaux Rd, SW9 310 B10
Pridham Rd, Th.Hth. CR7 202 DR98
Priest Ct, EC2 287 J8
Priestfield Rd, SE23 183 DY90
Priest Hill, Egh. TW20 172 AW90
Old Windsor SL4 172 AW90
Priestland Gdns, Berk. HP4 38 AY17
Priestlands Cl, Horl. RH6 268 DF147
Priestlands Pk Rd, Sid. DA15 185 ET90
Priestley Cl, N16 122 DT59
Priestley Gdns, Rom. RM6 126 EV58
Priestley Rd, Mitch. CR4 200 DG96
Priestley Way, E17 123 DX55
NW2 119 CU60
Priestly Gdns, Wok. GU22 227 BA120
Priestman Pt, E3 290 C3
Sch Priestmead Prim Sch,
Kenton HA3 off Hartford Av 117 CH55
Priest Pk Av, Har. HA2 116 CA61
Priests Av, Rom. RM1 105 FD54
Priests Br, SW14 158 CS84
SW15 158 CS84
Priests Fld, Ingrave CM13 109 GC50
Priests La, Brwd. CM15 108 FY47
Priests Paddock, Knot.Grn HP9 88 AJ50
Prima Rd, SW9 310 E4
Primary Rd, Slou. SL1 151 AR76
Sch Prim Sch, Bark. IG11 146 EU70
Sch Prim Sch, Slou. SL3 132 AV73
Primeplace Ms, Th.Hth. CR7 202 DQ96
Prime Zone Ms, N8 121 DL58
Primley La, Sheering CM22 37 FC06
Primrose Av, Enf. EN2 82 DR39
Horley RH6 269 DH150
Romford RM6 126 EV59
Primrose Cl, E3 290 A1
N3 98 DB54
SE6 183 EC92
Harrow HA2 116 BZ62
Hatfield AL10 45 CV19
Hemel Hempstead HP1 39 BE21
Wallington SM6 201 DH102
Primrose Ct, Brwd. CM14
off White Lyons Rd 108 FW48
Primrose Dr, Hert. SG13 32 DV09
West Drayton UB7 154 BK77
Primrose Fld, Harl. CM18 51 ET18
Primrose Gdns, NW3 274 D4
Bushey WD23 94 CB45
Radlett WD7
Pretoria Rd, off Aldenham Rd 77 CG35
Ruislip HA4 116 BW64
Primrose Glen, Horn. RM11 128 FL56
PRIMROSE HILL, NW8 274 E8
Primrose Hill, EC4 286 F9
Brentwood CM14 108 FW48
Kings Langley WD4 59 BP28
Primrose Hill Ct, NW3 274 E7
Sch Primrose Hill Prim Sch,
NW1 275 H8
Primrose Hill Rd, NW3 274 E6
Primrose Hill Studios, NW1 274 G8
Primrose La, Ald. WD25 77 CD38
Croydon CR0 203 DX102
Primrose Ms, NW1 274 F7
SE3 164 EH80
W5 off St. Mary's Rd 157 CK75
Primrose Path, Chsht EN7 66 DU31
Primrose Pl, Islw. TW7 157 CF82
Primrose Rd, E10 123 EB60
E18 102 EH54
Hersham KT12 214 BW106
Primrose Sq, E9 279 H7
Primrose St, EC2 287 N6
Primrose Wk, SE14 313 M4
Ewell KT17 217 CT108
Primrose Way, Wem. HA0 137 CK68
Primula St, W12 139 CU72
Prince Albert Rd, NW1 284 D1
NW8 284 D1
Prince Albert Sq, Red. RH1 266 DF139
Prince Alberts Wk, Wind. SL4 152 AU81
Prince Arthur Ms, NW3 273 P1
Prince Arthur Rd, NW3 273 P2
Prince Charles Av,
S.Darenth DA4 209 FR96
Prince Charles Dr, NW4 119 CW59
Prince Charles Rd, SE3 315 L6
Prince Charles Way,
Wall. SM6 201 DH104
Prince Consort Cotts,
Wind. SL4 151 AR82
Prince Consort Dr, Chis. BR7 205 ER95
Prince Consort Rd, SW7 295 P6
Princedale Rd, W11 294 F2
Prince Edward Rd, E9 279 P5
Prince Edward St, Berk. HP4 38 AW19
Prince George Av, N14 81 DJ42
Prince George Duke of Kent Ct,
Chis. BR7 off Holbrook La 185 ER94
Prince George Rd, N16 277 P1
Prince George's Av, SW20 199 CW96
Prince George's Rd, SW19 200 DD95
Prince Henry Rd, SE7 164 EK80
★ Prince Henry's Room, EC4 286 E9
Prince Imperial Rd, SE18 165 EM81
Chislehurst BR7 185 EP94
Prince John Rd, SE9 184 EL85
Princelet St, E1 288 B6
Prince of Orange La, SE10 314 E4
Prince of Wales Cl, NW4
off Church Ter 119 CV56
Prince of Wales Dr, SW8 309 K5
SW11 308 E7
Prince of Wales Footpath,
Enf. EN3 83 DY38
Prince of Wales Gate, SW7 296 C4
Prince of Wales Pas, NW1 285 L3
Sch Prince of Wales Prim Sch,
Enf. EN3 off Salisbury Rd 83 DZ37
Prince of Wales Rd, NW5 275 H5
SE3 315 M7
Outwood RH1 267 DN143
Sutton SM1 200 DD103
Prince of Wales Ter, W4 158 CS78
W8 295 M5
Prince Pk, Hem.H. HP1 40 BG21
DLR Prince Regent 292 C10
Prince Regent 292 D10
Prince Regent La, E13 292 C7
E16 292 C7
Prince Regent Ms, NW1 285 L3
Prince Regent Rd,
Houns. TW3 156 CC83
Prince Rd, SE25 202 DS99
Prince Rupert Rd, SE9 165 EM84
Prince's Arc, SW1 297 M2
Princes Av, N3 98 DA53
N10 120 DG55
N13 99 DN50
N22 99 DK53
NW9 118 CP56
W3 158 CN76
Carshalton SM5 218 DF108
Dartford DA2 188 FP88
Enfield EN3 83 DY36
Greenford UB6 136 CB72
Petts Wood BR5 205 ES99
South Croydon CR2 236 DV115
Surbiton KT6 198 CN102
Watford WD18 75 BT43
Woodford Green IG8 102 EH49
Princes Cl, N4 121 DP60
NW9 118 CN56
SW4 off Old Town 161 DJ83
Berkhamsted HP4 38 AU17
Edgware HA8 96 CN50
Eton Wick SL4 151 AM78
North Weald Bassett CM16 71 FC25
Sidcup DA14 186 EX90
South Croydon CR2 236 DV115
Teddington TW11 177 CD91
Princes Ct, SE16 301 N7
SW3 off Brompton Rd 296 E6
Hemel Hempstead HP3 40 BH23
Wembley HA9 118 CL64
● Princes Ct Business Cen, E1 300 F1
Princes Dr, Har. HA1 117 CE55
Prince's Dr, Oxshott KT22 215 CE112
Princesfield Rd, Wal.Abb. EN9 68 EH33
Coll Prince's Foundation, The,
EC2 287 N4
Princes Gdns, SW7 296 B6
W3 138 CN71
W5 137 CJ70
Princes Gate, Harl. CM20 35 ES12
Princes Gate, SW7 296 C5
Princes Gate Ct, SW7 296 B5
Princes Gate Ms, SW7 296 B6
Princes La, N10 121 DH55
Ruislip HA4 115 BS60
Princes Ms, W2 283 L10
Hounslow TW3 156 CA84
Princes Par, Pot.B. EN6
off High St 64 DC32
Princes Pk, Rain. RM13 147 FG66
Princes Pk Av, NW11 119 CY58
Hayes UB3 135 BR73
Princes Pk Circle, Hayes UB3 135 BR73
Princes Pk Cl, Hayes UB3 135 BR73
Princes Pk La, Hayes UB3 135 BR73
Princes Pk Par, Hayes UB3 135 BR73
Princes Pl, SW1 297 M2
W11 294 E2
Princes Plain, Brom. BR2 204 EL101
Sch Princes Plain Prim Sch,
Brom. BR2 off Princes Plain 204 EL101
Princes Ri, SE13 314 F8
Princes Riverside Rd, SE16 301 J2
Princes Rd, N18 100 DW49
SE20 183 DX93
SW14 158 CR83
SW19 180 DA93
W13 off Broomfield Rd 137 CH74
Ashford TW15 174 BM92
Bourne End SL8 110 AC60
Buckhurst Hill IG9 102 EJ47
Dartford DA1, DA2 187 FG86
Egham TW20 173 AZ93
Feltham TW13 175 BT89
Gravesend DA12 191 GJ90
Ilford IG6 125 ER56
Kew TW9 158 CM81
Kingston upon Thames KT2 178 CN94
Redhill RH1 266 DF136
Richmond TW10 178 CM85
Romford RM1 127 FG57
Swanley BR8 187 FG93
Teddington TW11 177 CD91
Weybridge KT13 213 BP106
Int Princes Rd Interchange,
Dart. DA1 188 FP88
H Princess Alexandra Hosp,
Harl. CM20 35 EP14
Princess Alice Way, SE28 165 ER75
Princess Av, Wem. HA9 118 CL61
Windsor SL4 151 AP83
Princess Cl, SE28 146 EX72
Princess Cres, N4 121 DP61
Princess Diana Dr, St.Alb. AL4 43 CK21
Princesses Wk, Kew TW9
off Royal Botanic Gdns 158 CL80
Sch Princess Frederica C of E
Prim Sch, NW10 282 A1
Princess Gdns, Wok. GU22 227 BB116
H Princess Grace Hosp, The, W1 284 G5
Princess Gro, Seer Grn HP9 89 AR49
Princess Louise Cl, W2 284 B6
H Princess Margaret Hosp,
Wind. SL4 151 AR82
Princess May Cl, Guil. GU2 242 AU130
Princess Mary's Rd, Add. KT15 212 BJ105
Sch Princess May Prim Sch,
N16 278 A2
Princess May Rd, N16 277 P1
Princess Ms, NW3 274 B4
Kingston upon Thames KT1 198 CM97
Princess Par, Orp. BR6
off Crofton Rd 205 EN104
Princess Pk Manor, N11 98 DG50
Princess Prec, Horl. RH6
off High St 269 DH148
Princes Sq, W2 283 L10
Princess Rd, NW1 274 G8
NW6 283 J1
Croydon CR0 202 DQ100
Woking GU22 227 BB116
H Princess Royal Uni Hosp,
The, Orp. BR6 205 EN104
Princess St, SE1 299 H7
Princes St, EC2 287 L8
N17 100 DS51
W1 285 K9
Bexleyheath DA7 166 EZ84
Gravesend DA11 191 GH86
Richmond TW9 off Sheen Rd 178 CL85
Slough SL1 152 AV75
Sutton SM1 218 DD105
Ware SG12 33 DX05
Princess Way, Red. RH1 250 DG133
Princes Ter, E13 144 EH67
Prince St, SE8 313 P2
Watford WD17 76 BW41
Princes Vw, Dart. DA1 188 FN88
Princes Way, SW19 179 CX87
Buckhurst Hill IG9 102 EJ47
Croydon CR0 219 DM106
Hutton CM13 109 GA46
Ruislip HA4 116 BY63
West Wickham BR4 222 EF105
Princes Yd, W11 294 F3
Princethorpe Ho, W2 283 K6
Princethorpe Rd, SE26 183 DX91
Princeton Ct, SW15
off Felsham Rd 159 CX83
Princeton St, WC1 286 C6
Principal Cl, N14 99 DJ46
Principal Sq, E9
off Chelmer Rd 279 K2
Pringle Gdns, SW16 181 DJ91
Purley CR8 219 DM110
Sch Prins Willem Alexander Sch,
Wok. GU22
off Old Woking Rd 227 BC117
Printers Av, Wat. WD18 75 BS43
Printers Inn Ct, EC4 286 E8
Printers Ms, E3 279 M9
Printers Rd, SW9 310 D6
Printer St, EC4 286 F8
Printers Way, Harl. CM20 36 EU10
Printing Ho La, Hayes UB3 155 BS75
Printing Ho Sq, Guil. GU1
off Martyr Rd 258 AX135
Printing Ho Yd, E2 287 P2
Print Village, SE15 312 B9
Priolo Rd, SE7 164 EJ78
Prior Av, Sutt. SM2 218 DE108
Prior Bolton St, N1 277 H5
Prior Chase, Bad.Dene RM17 170 FZ77
Prioress Cres, Green. DA9 169 FW84
Prioress Ho, E3
off Bromley High St 290 D2
Prioress Rd, SE27 181 DP90
Prioress St, SE1 299 M7
Prior Gro, Chesh. HP5 54 AQ30
Prior Rd, Ilf. IG1 125 EN62
Priors, The, Ashtd. KT21 231 CK119
Priors Cl, Hert.Hth SG13 32 DV12
Slough SL1 152 AU76
Priors Ct, Wok. GU21 226 AU118
Priors Cft, E17 101 DY54
Woking GU22 227 BA120
Priors Fm La, Nthlt. UB5 136 BZ65
Priors Fld, Nthlt. UB5
off Arnold Rd 136 BY65
Priorsford Av, Orp. BR5 206 EU98
Priors Gdns, Ruis. HA4 116 BW64
Priors Mead, Bkhm KT23 246 CC125
Enfield EN1 82 DS39
Priors Pk, Horn. RM12 128 FJ62
Priors Rd, Wind. SL4 151 AK83
Prior St, SE10 314 E5
Priors Wd Rd, Hert.Hth SG13 32 DW12
Sch Prior Weston Prim Sch, EC1 287 K5
Priory, The, SE3 164 EF84
Croydon CR0 off Epsom Rd 219 DN105
Godstone RH9 252 DV131
Priory Av, E4 101 DZ48
E17 123 EA57
N8 121 DK56
W4 158 CS77
Harefield UB9 114 BJ56
Harlow CM17 36 EW10
Petts Wood BR5 205 ER100
Sutton SM3 217 CX105
Wembley HA0 117 CF63
Priory Cl, E4 101 DZ48
E18 102 EG53
N3 97 CZ53
N14 81 DH43
N20 97 CZ45
SW19 off High Path 200 DB95
Beckenham BR3 203 DY97
Broxbourne EN10 49 DY24
Chislehurst BR7 205 EM95
Dartford DA1 188 FJ85
Denham UB9 114 BG62
Dorking RH4 263 CG138
Hampton TW12 196 BZ95
Harefield UB9 114 BH56
Hayes UB3 135 BV73
Hoddesdon EN11 49 EA18
Horley RH6 268 DF147
Pilgrim's Hatch CM15 108 FU43
Ruislip HA4 115 BT60
Stanmore HA7 95 CF48
Sudbury HA0 117 CF63
Sunbury-on-Thames TW16
Pretoria Rd, off Staines Rd E 175 BU94
Walton-on-Thames KT12 195 BU104
Woking GU21 211 BD113
Sch Priory C of E Prim Sch, The,
SW19 off Queens Rd 180 DB92
Priory Ct, E17 123 DZ55
EC4 off Carter La 287 H9
SW8 309 P7
Berkhamsted HP4 38 AW19
Bushey WD23
off Sparrows Herne 94 CC46
Epsom KT17 off Old Schs La 217 CT109
Guildford GU2
off Portsmouth Rd 258 AW137
Harlow CM18 52 EV17
Priory Ct Est, E17 off Priory Ct 101 DZ54
Priory Ct Ho, SE6 183 EB88
Priory Cres, SE19 182 DQ94
Sutton SM3 217 CX105
Wembley HA0 117
CG62 Priory Dr, SE2 166 EX78
Reigate RH2 266 DA136
Stanmore HA7 95 CF48
Priory Fld Dr, Edg. HA8 96 CP49
Priory Flds, Eyns. DA4 208 FM103
Watford WD17 75 BT39
Priory Gdns, N6 121 DH58
SE25 202 DT98
SW13 159 CT83
W4 158 CS77
W5 off Hanger La 138 CM69
Ashford TW15 175 BR92
Berkhamsted HP4 38 AW19
Dartford DA1 188 FK85
Hampton TW12 176 BZ94
Harefield UB9 114 BJ56
Wembley HA0 117 CG63
Priory Gate, Chsht EN8 67 DZ27
Priory Grn, Stai. TW18 174 BH92
Priory Grn Est, N1 276 C10
Priory Gro, SW8 310 A8
Barnet EN5 80 DA43
Romford RM3 106 FL48
Priory Hts, N1 276 C10
Slough SL1
off Buckingham Av 131 AL72
Priory Hill, Dart. DA1 188 FK86
Wembley HA0 117 CG63
H Priory Hosp, The, SW15 159 CT84
H Priory Hosp Hayes Gro, The,
Hayes BR2 204 EG103
H Priory Hosp N London, N14 99 DL46
Priory Ho, SE7
off Springfield Gro 164 EJ79
Priory La, SW15 178 CS86
Eynsford DA4 208 FM102
Richmond TW9 158 CN80
West Molesey KT8 196 CA98
Priory Ms, SW8 310 A7
Hornchurch RM11 127 FH60
Staines-upon-Thames TW18 174 BH92
Priory Pk, SE3 164 EF83
Priory Pk Rd, NW6 273 H8
Wembley HA0 117 CG63
Priory Path, Rom. RM3 106 FL48
Priory Pl, Dart. DA1 188 FK86
Walton-on-Thames KT12 195 BU104
Priory Post 16 Cen, SE19
off Hermitage Rd 182 DR93
Priory Rd, E6 144 EK67
N8 121 DK56
NW6 273 L8
SW19 180 DD94
W4 158 CR76
Barking IG11 145 ER66
Chalfont St. Peter SL9 112 AX55
Chessington KT9 198 CL104
Croydon CR0 201 DN101
Hampton TW12 176 BZ94
Hounslow TW3 176 CC85
Loughton IG10 84 EL42
Reigate RH2 266 DA136
Richmond TW9 158 CN79
Romford RM3 106 FL48
Slough SL1 130 AJ71
Sutton SM3 217 CX105
Priory Rd N, Dart. DA1 168 FK84
Priory Rd S, Dart. DA1 188 FK85
Sch Priory Sch, SE25
off Tennison Rd 202 DT98
Slough SL1 off Orchard Av 131 AK71
Sch Priory Sch, The, Bans. SM7
off Bolters La 234 DA115
Dorking RH4 off West Bk 263 CF137
Orpington BR5
off Tintagel Rd 206 EW102
Priory Shop Cen, Dart. DA1 188 FL86
Priory St, E3 290 D2
Hertford SG14 32 DR09
Ware SG12 32 DW06
Priory Ter, NW6 273 L8
Sunbury-on-Thames TW16
off Staines Rd E 175 BU94
Priory Vw, Bushey Hth WD23 95 CE45
Priory Wk, SW10 307 P1
Saint Albans AL1 43 CE23
Priory Way, Chal.St.P. SL9 112 AX55
Datchet SL3 152 AV80
Harmondsworth UB7 154 BL79
Harrow HA2 116 CB56
Southall UB2 156 BX76
Priory Wf, Hert. SG14
off Priory St 32 DR09
Priscilla Cl, N15 122 DQ57
Pritchard's Rd, E2 278 D9
Pritchett Cl, Enf. EN3 83 EA37
Priter Rd, SE16 300 D7
Private Rd, Enf. EN1 82 DS43
Privet Dr, Lvsdn WD25 59 BT34
Prize Wk, E20 280 E3
Probyn Rd, SW2 181 DP89
Procter Ho, SE1 300 C10
Procter St, WC1 286 C7
Proctor Cl, Mitch. CR4 200 DG95
Proctor Gdns, Bkhm KT23 246 CB125
Proctors Cl, Felt. TW14 175 BU88
Profumo Rd, Hersham KT12 214 BX106
● Progress Business Cen,
Slou. SL1 131 AK72
● Progress Business Pk,
Croy. CR0 201 DM103
● Progression Cen, The,
Hem.H. HP2 40 BN17
Progress Way, N22 99 DN53
Croydon CR0 201 DM103
Enfield EN1 82 DU43
Prologis Pk, E16 290 F5
● Prologis Pk Heathrow,
West Dr. UB7 155 BP76
Promenade, Edg. HA8 96 CN50
Promenade, The, W4 158 CS81
Promenade App Rd, W4 158 CS80
Promenade de Verdun,
Pur. CR8 219 DK111
Promenade Mans, Edg. HA8
off Hale La 96 CN50
Propeller Cres, Croy. CR0 219 DN106
● Prospect Business Pk,
Loug. IG10 85 ER42
Prospect Cl, SE26 182 DV91
Belvedere DA17 166 FA77
Bushey WD23 95 CD45
Hounslow TW3 156 BZ81
Ruislip HA4 116 BX59
Prospect Cotts, SW18 160 DA84
Prospect Cres, Twick. TW2 176 CC86
Prospect Gro, Grav. DA12 191 GK87
Prospect Hill, E17 123 EB56
Prospect Ho, SW19
off Chapter Way 200 DD95
Prospect La, Eng.Grn TW20 172 AT92
Prospect Pl, Dart. DA1 188 FK86
Prospect Pl, E1 300 G2
N2 120 DD56
N7 276 B1
N17 100 DS52
NW2 off Ridge Rd 119 CZ62
NW3 273 N1
SW20 179 CV94
W4 off Barley Mow Pas 158 CR78
Bromley BR2 204 EH97
Epsom KT17 216 CS113
Gravesend DA12 191 GK87
Grays RM17 170 GB79
Romford RM5 105 FC54
Staines-upon-Thames TW18 173 BF92
Prospect Quay, SW18 160 DA84
Prospect Ring, N2 120 DD55
Prospect Rd, NW2 119 CZ62
Barnet EN5 80 DA43
Cheshunt EN8 66 DW29
Hornchurch RM11 128 FM55
Long Ditton KT6 197 CJ100
St. Albans AL1 43 CD22
Sevenoaks TN13 257 FJ123
Woodford Green IG8 102 EJ50
Prospect St, SE16 300 F6
Prospect Vale, SE18 304 G8
Prospect Way, Hutt. CM13 109 GE42
Prospero Rd, N19 121 DJ60
Prossers, Tad. KT20 233 CX121
Protea Cl, E16 291 L4
Prothero Gdns, NW4 119 CV57
Prothero Rd, SW6 306 F4
Prout Gro, NW10 118 CS63
Prout Rd, E5 122 DV62
Provence St, N1 277 J10
Providence Av, Har. HA2
off Goodwill Dr 116 CA60
Providence Cl, E9 279 K8
Providence Ct, W1 285 H10
Providence La, Harling. UB3 155 BR80
Providence Pl, N1 276 G8
Epsom KT17 216 CS112
Romford RM5 104 EZ54
Woking GU22 212 BG114
Providence Rd, West Dr. UB7 134 BL74
Providence Row, N1
off Pentonville Rd 286 C1
Providence Row Cl, E2
off Ainsley St 288 F3
Providence Sq, SE1
off Jacob St 300 C4
Providence St, Green. DA9 189 FU85
Providence Yd, E2 288 C2
● Provident Ind Est,
Hayes UB3 155 BU75
Province Dr, SE16 301 J5
Provost Est, N1 287 L2
Provost Rd, NW3 274 F6
Provost St, N1 287 L3
Provost Way, Dag. RM8 126 EU63
Prowse Av, Bushey Hth WD23 94 CC47
Prowse Pl, NW1 275 L6
Prudence La, Orp. BR6 223 EN105
Pruden Cl, N14 99 DJ47
Prudent Pas, EC2 287 K8
Prune Hill, Eng.Grn TW20 172 AX94
Prusom St, E1 300 F3
Pryor Cl, Abb.L. WD5 59 BT32
Pryors, The, NW3 120 DD62
★ P.S. Tattershall Castle, SW1 298 B3
H Public Health England
Colindale, NW9 118 CS55
Puck La, Wal.Abb. EN9 67 ED29
Pucknells Cl, Swan. BR8 207 FC95
Puddenhole Cotts, Bet. RH3 248 CN133
Pudding La, EC3 299 M1
Chigwell IG7 103 ET46
Hemel Hempstead HP1 40 BG18
St. Albans AL3 off Market Pl 43 CD20
Seal TN15 off Church St 257 FN121
DLR Pudding Mill Lane 280 C9
Pudding Mill La, E15 280 D9
Puddingstone Dr, St.Alb. AL4 43 CJ22
Puddle Dock, EC4 287 H10
Puddledock La, Dart. DA2 187 FE92
Westerham TN16 255 ET133
PUDDS CROSS, Hem.H. HP3 56 AX29
Puers Fld, Jordans HP9 90 AS51
Puers La, Jordans HP9 90 AS51
Puffin Cl, Bark. IG11 146 EV69
Beckenham BR3 203 DX99
Puffin Ter, Ilf. IG5
off Tiptree Cres 125 EN55
Pulborough Rd, SW18 179 CZ87
Pulborough Way,
Houns. TW4 156 BW84
Pulford Rd, N15 122 DR58
Pulham Av, N2 120 DC56
Broxbourne EN10 49 DX21
Pulham Ho, SW8
off Dorset Rd 310 C5
Puller Rd, Barn. EN5 79 CY40
Hemel Hempstead HP1 40 BG21
Pulleyns Av, E6 293 H2
Pulleys Cl, Hem.H. HP1 39 BF19
Pulleys La, Hem.H. HP1 39 BF19
Pullfields, Chesh. HP5 54 AN30
Pullman Cl, St.Alb. AL1
off Ramsbury Rd 43 CE22
Pullman Ct, SW2 181 DL88
Pullman Gdns, SW15 179 CW86
Pullman Ms, SE12 184 EH90
Pullman Pl, SE9 184 EL85
Pullmans Pl, Stai. TW18 174 BG92
Pulpit Cl, Chesh. HP5 54 AN29
Pulross Rd, SW9 161 DM83
Pulse, The, Colnbr. SL3 153 BE81
Pulse Apts, NW6 273 M3
Pulteney Cl, E3 279 N9
Isleworth TW7
off Gumley Gdns 157 CG83
Pulteney Gdns, E18
off Pulteney Rd 124 EH55
Pulteney Rd, E18 124 EH55
Pulteney Ter, N1 276 D9
Pulton Pl, SW6 307 J5
Puma Ct, E1 288 A6
Pump All, Brent. TW8 157 CK80
Pump Cl, Nthlt. UB5
off Union Rd 136 CA68
Pump Ct, EC4 286 E9

Pumphandle Path, N2 off Tarling Rd 98 DC54
Pump Hill, Loug. IG10 85 EM40
Pump Ho Cl, SE16 301 H5
Bromley BR2 204 EF96
Pumphouse Cres, Wat. WD17 76 BW43
★ Pumphouse Ed Mus, Rotherhithe, SE16 301 M2
Pump Ho Ms, E1 288 C10
Pumping Sta Rd, W4 158 CS80
Pumpkin Hill, Burn. SL1 131 AL65
Pump La, SE14 313 H4
Chesham HP5 54 AS32
Epping Green CM16 51 EP24
Hayes UB3 155 BV75
Orpington BR6 225 FB106
Pump Pail N, Croy. CR0 off Old Town 202 DQ104
Pump Pail S, Croy. CR0 off Southbridge Rd 202 DQ104
Punchard Cres, Enf. EN3 83 EB38
Punch Bowl La, Chesh. HP5 off Red Lion St 54 AQ32
Hemel Hempstead HP2 41 BR17
St. Albans AL3 41 BT16
Punchbowl La, Dor. RH5 263 CK135
Pundersons Gdns, E2 288 F2
Punjab La, Sthl. UB1 off Herbert Rd 136 BZ74
Purbeck Av, N.Mal. KT3 199 CT100
Purbeck Cl, Merst. RH1 251 DK128
Purbeck Ct, Guil. GU2 242 AS134
Purbeck Dr, NW2 119 CY61
Woking GU21 211 AZ114
Purbeck Ho, SW8 off Bolney St 310 C5
Purbeck Rd, Horn. RM11 127 FG60
Purberry Gro, Epsom KT17 217 CT110
Purbrock Av, Wat. WD25 76 BW36
Purbrook Est, SE1 299 P5
Purbrook St, SE1 299 P6
Purcell Cl, Borwd. WD6 77 CK39
Kenley CR8 220 DR114
Purcell Cres, SW6 306 E4
Purcell Ho, Enf. EN1 82 DT38
Purcell Rd, Grnf. UB6 136 CB71
Purcells Av, Edg. HA8 96 CN50
Sch Purcell Sch, The, Bushey WD23 off Aldenham Rd 76 CA41
Purcells Cl, Ashtd. KT21 off Albert Rd 232 CM118
Purcell St, N1 277 N10
Purchese St, NW1 275 P10
Purdom Rd, Welw.G.C. AL7 29 CY12
Purdy St, E3 290 C4
Purelake Ms, SE13 163 ED83
PURFLEET, RM19 168 FP77
⇌ Purfleet 168 FN78
Purfleet Bypass, Purf. RM19 168 FP77
● Purfleet Ind Pk, Aveley RM15 168 FM75
Sch Purfleet Prim Sch, Purf. RM19 off Tank Hill Rd 168 FN77
Purfleet Rd, Aveley RM15 168 FN75
● Purfleet Thames Terminal, Purf. RM19 168 FQ80
Purford Grn, Harl. CM18 52 EU16
Sch Purford Grn Inf Sch, Harl. CM18 off Purford Grn 52 EU17
Sch Purford Grn Jun Sch, Harl. CM18 off Purford Grn 52 EU17
Purkis Cl, Uxb. UB8 off Dawley Rd 135 BQ72
Purkiss Rd, Hert. SG13 32 DQ12
Purland Cl, Dag. RM8 126 EZ60
Purland Rd, SE28 166 EU75
Purleigh Av, Wdf.Grn. IG8 102 EL51
PURLEY, CR8 219 DM111
⇌ Purley 219 DP112
Purley Av, NW2 119 CY62
Purley Bury Av, Pur. CR8 220 DQ110
Purley Bury Cl, Pur. CR8 220 DQ111
Purley Cl, Ilf. IG5 103 EN54
Jct Purley Cross, Pur. CR8 219 DN111
Purley Downs Rd, Pur. CR8 220 DQ110
South Croydon CR2 220 DR111
Purley Hill, Pur. CR8 219 DP112
Purley Knoll, Pur. CR8 219 DM111
⇌ Purley Oaks 220 DQ109
Sch Purley Oaks Prim Sch, S.Croy. CR2 off Bynes Rd 220 DR108
Purley Oaks Rd, S.Croy. CR2 220 DR109
Purley Par, Pur. CR8 off High St 219 DN111
Purley Pk Rd, Pur. CR8 219 DP110
Purley Pl, N1 276 G6
Purley Ri, Pur. CR8 219 DM112
Purley Rd, N9 100 DR48
Purley CR8 219 DN111
South Croydon CR2 220 DR108
Purley Vale, Pur. CR8 219 DP113
H Purley War Mem Hosp, Pur. CR8 219 DN111
Purley Way, Croy. CR0 201 DM101
Purley CR8 219 DN108
🔒 Purley Way Centre, Croy. CR0 201 DN103
Purley Way Cres, Croy. CR0 off Purley Way 201 DM101
Purlieu Way, They.B. CM16 85 ES35
Purlings Rd, Bushey WD23 76 CB43
Purneys Rd, SE9 164 EK84
Purrett Rd, SE18 165 ET78
Pursers Ct, Slou. SL2 132 AS72
Purser's Cross Rd, SW6 307 H6
Pursers La, Peasl. GU5 261 BR142
Pursers Lea, Peasl. GU5 261 BR144
Pursewardens Cl, W13 137 CJ74
Pursley Gdns, Borwd. WD6 78 CN38
Pursley Rd, NW7 97 CV52
Purton Ct, Farn.Royal SL2 131 AQ66
Purton La, Farn.Royal SL2 131 AQ66
Purves Rd, NW10 282 A1
Puteaux Ho, E2 289 J1
PUTNEY, SW15 159 CY84
⇌ Putney 159 CY84
⊖ Putney Bridge 306 G10
Putney Br, SW6 159 CY83
SW15 159 CY83
Putney Br App, SW6 306 F10
Putney Br Rd, SW15 159 CY84
SW18 159 CY84
Putney Common, SW15 306 A10
Putney Gdns, Chad.Hth RM6 off Heathfield Pk Dr 126 EV57
PUTNEY HEATH, SW15 179 CW86
Putney Heath, SW15 179 CW86
Putney Heath La, SW15 179 CX86
Sch Putney High Sch, SW15 off Putney Hill 179 CX85
Putney High St, SW15 159 CX84
Putney Hill, SW15 179 CX86
Putney Pk Av, SW15 159 CU84
Putney Pk La, SW15 159 CV84
Sch Putney Pk Sch, SW15 off Woodborough Rd 159 CV84
Pier Putney Pier 306 E10
Putney Rd, Enf. EN3 83 DX36
Coll Putney Sch of Art & Design, SW15 off Oxford Rd 159 CY84
PUTNEY VALE, SW15 179 CT90
Putney Wf Twr, SW15 159 CY83
Puttenham Cl, Wat. WD19 94 BW48
Putters Cft, Hem.H. HP2 40 BM15
Puttocks Cl, N.Mymms AL9 45 CW23
Puttocks Dr, N.Mymms AL9 45 CW23
Pycroft Way, N9 100 DU49
Pyebush La, Beac. HP9 111 AN56
Pye Cl, Cat. CR3 off St. Lawrence Way 236 DR123
Pyecombe Cor, N12 97 CZ49
PYE CORNER, Harl. CM20 35 ER10
Pyenest Rd, Harl. CM19 51 EP18
Pyghtle, The, Denh. UB9 114 BG60
Pylbrook Rd, Sutt. SM1 200 DA104
Pyle Hill, Wok. GU22 226 AX124
Pylon Way, Croy. CR0 201 DL102
Pym Cl, E.Barn. EN4 80 DD43
Pymers Mead, SE21 182 DQ88
Pymmes Brook Dr, Barn. EN4 80 DE42
Pymmes Cl, N13 99 DM50
N17 100 DV53
Pymmes Gdns N, N9 100 DT48
Pymmes Gdns S, N9 100 DT48
Pymmes Grn Rd, N11 99 DH49
Pymmes Rd, N13 99 DL51
Pym Orchard, Brasted TN16 240 EW124
Pym Pl, Grays RM17 170 GA77
Pynchester Cl, Uxb. UB10 114 BN61
Pyne Rd, Surb. KT6 198 CN102
Pynest Grn La, Wal.Abb. EN9 84 EG38
Pynfolds, SE16 300 F5
Pynham Cl, SE2 166 EU76
Pynnacles Cl, Stan. HA7 95 CH50
Pypers Hatch, Harl. CM20 51 ET15
Sch Pyrcroft Gra Prim Sch, Cher. KT16 off Pyrcroft Rd 193 BE100
Pyrcroft La, Wey. KT13 213 BP106
Pyrcroft Rd, Cher. KT16 193 BF101
PYRFORD, Wok. GU22 227 BE115
Sch Pyrford C of E Prim Sch, Pyrford GU22 off Coldharbour Rd 228 BG116
Pyrford Common Rd, Wok. GU22 227 BD116
Pyrford Ct, Wok. GU22 227 BE117
PYRFORD GREEN, Wok. GU22 228 BH117
Pyrford Heath, Wok. GU22 227 BF116
Pyrford Lock, Wisley GU23 228 BJ116
Pyrford Rd, W.Byf. KT14 212 BG113
Woking GU22 212 BG114
PYRFORD VILLAGE, Wok. GU22 228 BG118
Pyrford Wds, Wok. GU22 227 BE115
Pyrford Wds Cl, Wok. GU22 227 BF115
Pyrford Wds Rd, Wok. GU22 227 BE115
Sch Pyrgo Priory Prim Sch, Harold Hill RM3 off Dagnam Pk Dr 106 FN50
Pyrian Cl, Wok. GU22 227 BD117
Pyrland Rd, N5 277 L2
Richmond TW10 178 CM86
Pyrles Grn, Loug. IG10 85 EP39
Pyrles La, Loug. IG10 85 EP40
Pyrmont Gro, SE27 181 DP90
Pyrmont Rd, W4 158 CN79
Pytchley Cres, SE19 182 DQ93
Pytchley Rd, SE22 162 DS83
Pytt Fld, Harl. CM17 52 EV16

Q

● QED Distribution Pk, Purf. RM19 169 FR77
Quadrangle, The, SE24 182 DQ85
SW10 307 P6
W2 284 C8
Guildford GU2 off The Oval 258 AU135
Horley RH6 269 DH148
Welwyn Garden City AL8 29 CW08
Quadrangle Cl, SE1 299 N8
Quadrangle Ho, E15 281 K5
Quadrangle Ms, Stan. HA7 95 CJ52
Jct Quadrant, The, Epsom KT17 216 CR113
Quadrant, The, SW20 199 CY95
Bexleyheath DA7 166 EX80
Purfleet RM19 168 FQ77
Richmond TW9 178 CL84
Rickmansworth WD3 92 BL45
St. Albans AL4 43 CH17
Sutton SM2 218 DC107
🔒 Quadrant Arc, Rom. RM1 127 FE57
Quadrant Arc, W1 297 M1
Quadrant Cl, NW4 off The Burroughs 119 CV57
● Quadrant Ct, Green. DA9 169 FT84
Quadrant Gro, NW5 274 F3
Quadrant Ho, Sutt. SM2 218 DC107
● Quadrant Pk, Welw.G.C. AL7 29 CZ07
Quadrant Rd, Rich. TW9 157 CK84
Thornton Heath CR7 201 DP98
Quad Rd, Wem. HA9 117 CK62
Quadrant Way, Wey. KT13 212 BM105
Quadrivium Pt, Slou. SL1 131 AQ74
● Quadrum Ind Pk, Peasm. GU3 258 AV141
Quaggy Wk, SE3 164 EG84
Quail Gdns, S.Croy. CR2 221 DY110
Sch Quainton Hall Sch, Har. HA1 off Hindes Rd 117 CE57
Quainton St, NW10 118 CR62
Quaker Cl, Sev. TN13 257 FK123
Quaker Ct, E1 288 A5
EC1 287 L4
Quaker La, Sthl. UB2 156 CA76
Waltham Abbey EN9 67 EC34
Quakers Course, NW9 97 CT53
Quakers Hall La, Sev. TN13 257 FJ122
Quakers La, Islw. TW7 157 CG81
Potters Bar EN6 64 DB30
Quaker's Pl, E7 124 EK64
Quaker St, E1 288 A5
Quakers Wk, N21 82 DR44
Quality Ct, WC2 286 E8
Quality St, Merst. RH1 251 DH128
Quantock Cl, Harling. UB3 155 BR80
St. Albans AL4 43 CJ16
Slough SL3 153 BA78
Quantock Dr, Wor.Pk. KT4 199 CW103
Quantock Gdns, NW2 119 CX61
Quantock Ms, SE15 312 C9
Quantock Rd, Bexh. DA7 off Cumbrian Av 167 FE82
Quantocks, Hem.H. HP2 40 BM17
Quarles Cl, Rom. RM5 104 FA52
Quarles Pk Rd, Chad.Hth RM6 126 EV58
Quarrendon Fm La, Colesh. HP7 55 AQ42
Quarrendon Rd, Amer. HP7 55 AR40
Quarrendon St, SW6 307 K7
Quarr Rd, Cars. SM5 200 DD100
Quarry, The, Bet. RH3 248 CR132
Quarry Cl, Grav. DA11 191 GF87
Lthd. KT22 231 CK121
Oxted RH8 254 EE130
Quarry Cotts, Sev. TN13 256 FG123
Quarry Gdns, Lthd. KT22 231 CK121
Quarry Hill, Grays RM17 170 GA78
Sevenoaks TN15 257 FK123
Sch Quarry Hill Inf Sch, Grays RM17 off Dell Rd 170 GB78
Sch Quarry Hill Jun Sch, Grays RM17 off Bradleigh Av 170 GB78
Quarry Hill Pk, Reig. RH2 250 DC131
Quarry Ms, Purf. RM19 168 FN77
Quarry Pk Rd, Sutt. SM1 217 CZ107
Quarry Ri, Sutt. SM1 217 CZ107
Quarry Rd, SW18 180 DC86
Godstone RH9 252 DW128
Oxted RH8 254 EE130
● Quarryside Business Pk, Red. RH1 251 DH130
Quarry Spring, Harl. CM20 52 EU15
Quarry St, Guil. GU1 258 AX136
Quarterdeck, The, E14 302 A5
Quartermaine Av, Wok. GU22 227 AZ122
Quartermass Cl, Hem.H. HP1 off Quartermass Rd 40 BG19
Quartermass Rd, Hem.H. HP1 40 BG19
Quarts Mews, Dor. RH5 263 CJ138
Quaves Rd, Slou. SL3 152 AV76
Quay La, Green. DA9 169 FV84
Quay Rd, Bark. IG11 145 EP68
Quayside Ho, W10 off Kensal Rd 282 E4
Quayside Wk, Kings.T. KT1 off Bishop's Hall 197 CK96
Quay W, Tedd. TW11 177 CH92
Quebec Av, West. TN16 255 ER126
Quebec Cl, Smallfield RH6 off Alberta Dr 269 DN148
★ Quebec Ho (Wolfe's Ho), West. TN16 255 ER126
★ Quebec Ms, W1 284 F9
Quebec Rd, Hayes UB4 136 BW73
Ilford IG1, IG2 125 EP59
Tilbury RM18 171 GG82
Quebec Sq, West. TN16 255 ER126
Quebec Way, SE16 301 K5
Queen Adelaide Rd, SE20 182 DW93
Queen Alexandra's Ct, SW19 179 CZ92
Queen Alexandra's Way, Epsom KT19 216 CN111
Queen Anne Av, N15 off Suffield Rd 122 DT57
Bromley BR2 204 EF97
Queen Anne Dr, Clay. KT10 215 CE108
Queen Anne Ms, W1 285 K7
Queen Anne Rd, E9 279 J5
Sch Queen Anne Royal Free C of E First Sch, The, Wind. SL4 off Chaucer Cl 151 AR83
Queen Anne's Cl, Twick. TW2 177 CD90
Queen Annes Gdns, W5 158 CL75
Enfield EN1 82 DS44
Leatherhead KT22 off Linden Rd 231 CH121
Queen Anne's Gdns, W4 158 CS76
Mitch. CR4 200 DF97
Queen Anne's Gate, SW1 297 N5
Bexleyheath DA7 166 EX83
Queen Annes Gro, W5 158 CL75
Enfield EN1 100 DR45
Queen Anne's Gro, W4 158 CS76
Queen Anne's Ms, Lthd. KT22 off Fairfield Rd 231 CH121
Queen Annes Pl, Enf. EN1 82 DS44
Queen Annes Rd, Wind. SL4 151 AQ84
Queen Annes Sq, SE1 300 C8
Queen Annes Ter, Lthd. KT22 off Fairfield Rd 231 CH121
Queen Anne St, W1 285 J8
Queen Anne's Wk, WC1 off Queen Sq 286 B5
Queen Anne Ter, E1 off Sovereign Cl 300 F1
Queen Bee Ct, Hat. AL10 44 CR16
Queenborough Gdns, Chis. BR7 185 ER93
Ilford IG2 125 EN56
Queen Caroline Est, W6 306 A1
Queen Caroline St, W6 294 B9
H Queen Charlotte's & Chelsea Hosp, W12 139 CU72
Queen Charlotte St, Wind. SL4 off High St 151 AR81
Queendale Ct, Wok. GU21 off Roundthorn Way 226 AT116
Sch Queen Eleanor's C of E Jun Sch, Guil. GU2 off Queen Eleanor's Rd 258 AU135
Queen Eleanor's Rd, Guil. GU2 258 AT135
Queen Elizabeth Ct, Brox. EN10 off Groom Rd 67 DZ26
Queen Elizabeth Gdns, Mord. SM4 200 DA98
★ Queen Elizabeth Hall & Purcell Room, SE1 298 C2
H Queen Elizabeth Hosp, SE18 164 EL80
★ Queen Elizabeth Olympic Pk, E20 280 C3
Queen Elizabeth Rd, E17 123 DY55
Kingston upon Thames KT2 198 CM95
Queen Elizabeths Cl, N16 122 DR61
Queen Elizabeth's Coll, SE10 314 E4
Queen Elizabeth's Ct, Wal.Abb. EN9 off Greenwich Way 83 EC36
Queen Elizabeths Dr, N14 99 DL46
Queen Elizabeth's Dr, New Adgtn CR0 221 ED110
Queen Elizabeth II Br, Dart. DA1 169 FR82
Purfleet RM19 169 FR82
★ Queen Elizabeth II Conf Cen, SW1 297 P5
H Queen Elizabeth II Hosp, The, Welw.G.C. AL7 30 DA13
Sch Queen Elizabeth II Jubilee Sch, W9 283 H4
Coll Queen Elizabeth's Foundation, Training Coll, Lthd. KT22 off Woodlands Rd 231 CD117
Queen Elizabeth's Gdns, New Adgtn CR0 221 ED110
Sch Queen Elizabeth's Girls' Sch, Barn. EN5 off High St 79 CZ42
★ Queen Elizabeth's Hunting Lo, E4 102 EF45
Sch Queen Elizabeth's Sch, Barn. EN5 off Queens Rd 79 CX41
Queen Elizabeth St, SE1 299 P4
Queen Elizabeths Wk, N16 122 DR61
Queen Elizabeth's Wk, Wall. SM6 219 DK105
Queen Elizabeth Wk, SW13 159 CV81
Windsor SL4 152 AS82
Queen Elizabeth Way, Wok. GU22 227 AZ119
Queenhill Rd, S.Croy. CR2 220 DV110
Queenhithe, EC4 287 K10
Queenhythe Cres, Guil. GU4 242 AX128
Queenhythe Rd, Jacobs Well GU4 242 AX128
Queen Margaret's Gro, N1 277 N3
Uni Queen Mary, Mile End Campus, E1 289 L4
Queen Mary Av, E18 102 EG53
Mord. SM4 199 CX99
Uni Queen Mary - Barts & The London Sch of Med & Dentistry, EC1 287 H5
Royal London Hosp, E1 288 E7
Queen Mary Cl, Rom. RM1 127 FF58
Surbiton KT6 198 CN104
Woking GU22 227 BC116
Queen Mary Ct, Stai. TW19 off Victory Cl 174 BL88
Queen Mary Ho, SW15 179 CU86
Queen Mary Rd, SE19 181 DP93
Shepperton TW17 195 BQ96
Queen Marys Av, Wat. WD18 75 BS42
Queen Mary's Av, Cars. SM5 218 DF108
Queen Marys Bldgs, SW1 off Stillington St 297 M8
Queen Mary's Ct, Wal.Abb. EN9 off Greenwich Way 83 EC35
Queen Marys Dr, New Haw KT15 211 BF110
★ Queen Mary's Gdns, NW1 284 G3
H Queen Mary's Hosp, NW3 120 DC62
Sidcup DA14 186 EU93
H Queen Mary's Hosp for Children, Cars. SM5 200 DC102
H Queen Mary's Hosp (Roehampton), SW15 179 CU86
Queen Mother's Dr, Denh. UB9 113 BF58
Queen of Denmark Ct, SE16 301 N6
Queens Acre, Sutt. SM3 217 CX108
Windsor SL4 151 AR84
Queens All, Epp. CM16 69 ET31
Queens Av, N3 98 DC52
N10 120 DG55
N20 98 DD47
Byfleet KT14 212 BK112
Feltham TW13 176 BW91
Greenford UB6 136 CB72
Stanmore HA7 117 CJ55
Watford WD18 75 BT42
Woodford Green IG8 102 EH50
Queen's Av, N21 99 DP46
Queensberry Ms W, SW7 296 A8
Queensberry Pl, E12 124 EK64
SW7 296 A8
Richmond TW9 off Friars La 177 CK85
Queensberry Way, SW7 296 A8
Queensborough Ms, W2 283 N10
Queensborough Pas, W2 283 N10
Queensborough Studios, W2 283 N10
Queensborough Ter, W2 283 M10
Queensbridge Pk, Islw. TW7 177 CE85
Sch Queensbridge Prim Sch, E8 278 B7
Queensbridge Rd, E2 278 B8
E8 278 B5
QUEENSBURY, Har. HA3 117 CK55
⊖ Queensbury 118 CM55
Queensbury Circle Par, Har. HA3 off Streatfield Rd 118 CL55
Stan. HA7 off Streatfield Rd 118 CL55
Queensbury Rd, NW9 118 CR59
Wembley HA0 138 CM68
Queensbury Sta Par, Edg. HA8 118 CM55
Queensbury St, N1 277 K7
Queen's Circ, SW8 309 J5
SW11 309 J5
Queens Cl, Edg. HA8 96 CN50
Old Windsor SL4 172 AU85
Wallington SM6 off Queens Rd 219 DH106
Walton on the Hill KT20 233 CU124
★ Queen's Club, The (Tennis Cen), W14 306 E1
Queens Club Gdns, W14 306 F2
Sch Queen's C of E Prim Sch, The, Kew TW9 off Cumberland Rd 158 CN80
Sch Queen's Coll, W1 285 J7
Queen's Cotts, Wind. SL4 151 AR84
Queens Ct, SE23 182 DW88
Borwd. WD6 off Bennington Dr 78 CM39
Broxbourne EN10 49 DZ24
Hertford SG13 off Queens Rd 32 DR10
Richmond TW10 178 CM86
St. Albans AL1 43 CH20
Slough SL1 132 AT73
Waltham Cross EN8 off Queens Way 67 DZ34
Weybridge KT13 213 BR106
Woking GU22 off Hill Vw Rd 227 AZ118
Queenscourt, Wem. HA9 118 CL63
Queens Ct Ride, Cob. KT11 213 BU113
Queens Cres, Rich. TW10 178 CM85
St. Albans AL4 43 CH17
Queen's Cres, NW5 274 G5
Queenscroft Rd, SE9 184 EK85
Queensdale Cres, W11 294 D2
Queensdale Pl, W11 294 E2
Queensdale Rd, W11 294 D3
Queensdale Wk, W11 294 E3
Queensdown Rd, E5 122 DV63
Queens Dr, E10 123 EA59
N4 121 DP61
W3 138 CM72
W5 138 CM72
Abbots Langley WD5 59 BT32
Guildford GU2 242 AU131
Oxshott KT22 214 CC111
Surb. KT5 198 CN101
Thames Ditton KT7 197 CG101
Waltham Cross EN8 67 EA34
Queen's Dr, Slou. SL3 133 AZ66
Queens Dr, The, Mill End WD3 91 BF45
Queens Elm Par, SW3 off Old Ch St 296 B10
Queen's Elm Sq, SW3 308 B1
Queensferry Wk, N17 off Jarrow Rd 122 DV56
★ Queen's Gall, The, SW1 297 K5
Queens Gdns, NW4 119 CW57
W2 283 N10
W5 137 CJ71
Dartford DA2 188 FP88
Rain. RM13 147 FD68
Upminster RM14 129 FT58
Queen's Gdns, Houns. TW5 156 BY81
Queensgate, Cob. KT11 214 BX112
Wal.Cr. EN8 67 DZ34
Queens Gate, Wat. WD17 off Lord St 76 BW41
Queen's Gate, SW7 295 P5
Gat. RH6 268 DG152
🔒 Queensgate Cen, Harl. CM20 35 ES11
🔒 Queensgate Centre, Grays RM17 off Orsett Rd 170 GA78
Queens Gate Gdns, SW15 159 CV84
Queensgate Gdns, Chis. BR7 205 ER95
Queen's Gate Gdns, SW7 295 P7
Queensgate Ho, E3 off Hereford Rd 289 P1
Queensgate Ms, Beck. BR3 off Queens Rd 203 DY95
Queen's Gate Ms, SW7 295 P5
Queensgate Pl, NW6 273 J7
Queen's Gate Pl, SW7 295 P7
Queen's Gate Pl Ms, SW7 295 P7
Sch Queen's Gate Sch, SW7 296 A8
Queen's Gate Ter, SW7 295 N6
Queens Gro, NW8 274 A9
Queen's Gro Ms, NW8 274 A9
Queens Gro Rd, E4 101 ED46
Queen's Head Pas, EC4 287 J8
Queen's Head St, N1 277 H9
Queens Head Wk, Brox. EN10 off High Rd Wormley 49 DY23
Queens Head Yd, SE1 299 L3
H Queen's Hosp, Rom. RM7 127 FE59
Queens Ho, Tedd. TW11 177 CF93
★ Queen's Ho, The, SE10 314 G3
★ Queen's Ice & Bowl, W2 295 M1
Queenside Ms, Horn. RM12 128 FL61
Queensland Av, N18 100 DQ51
SW19 200 DB95
Queensland Cl, E17 101 DZ54
Queensland Ho, E16 off Rymill St 305 L3
Queensland Rd, N7 276 E1
Queens La, N10 121 DH55
Ashford TW15 off Clarendon Rd 174 BM91
Sch Queen's Manor Prim Sch, SW6 306 C5
🔒 Queens Mkt, E13 off Green St 144 EJ67
Queensmead, NW8 274 B8
Datchet SL3 152 AV80
Oxshott KT22 214 CC111
Queens Mead, Edg. HA8 96 CM51
Queensmead Av, Epsom KT17 217 CV110
Queensmead Rd, Brom. BR2 204 EF96
Sch Queensmead Sch, S.Ruis. HA4 off Queens Wk 116 BX63
Queensmere Cl, SW19 179 CX89
Queensmere Rd, SW19 179 CX89
Slough SL1 off Wellington St 152 AU75
🔒 Queensmere Shop Cen, Slou. SL1 152 AT75
Queens Ms, W2 283 M10
Queensmill Rd, SW6 306 C5
Sch Queensmill Sch, SW6 307 K9
Queens Par, N11 98 DF50
W5 138 CM72
Queens Par Cl, N11 off Colney Hatch La 98 DF50
⊖ Queen's Park 282 F1
⊖ Queen's Park 282 F1
Sch Queens Pk Comm Sch, NW6 272 C8
Queens Pk Ct, W10 282 D3
Queens Pk Gdns, Felt. TW13 off Vernon Rd 175 BU90
Sch Queen's Pk Prim Sch, W10 282 F4
★ Queens Park Rangers FC, W12 139 CV74
Queens Pk Rd, Cat. CR3 236 DS123
Romford RM3 106 FM53
Queens Pas, Chis. BR7 off High St 185 EP93
Queens Pl, Mord. SM4 200 DA98
Watford WD17 76 BW41
Queen's Prom, Kings.T. KT1 197 CK97
Queen Sq, WC1 286 B5
Queen Sq Pl, WC1 286 B5
Queens Reach, E.Mol. KT8 197 CE98
Queens Ride, SW13 159 CU83
SW15 159 CU83
Queen's Ride, Rich. TW10 178 CP88
Queens Ri, Rich. TW10 178 CM86
Queens Rd, E11 123 ED59
E13 144 EH67
N3 98 DC53
N9 100 DV48
NW4 119 CW57
SE14 312 E6
SE15 312 E6
SW14 158 CR83
SW19 179 CZ93
W5 138 CL72
Barking IG11 145 EQ66
Barnet EN5 79 CX41
Beckenham BR3 203 DY96
Berkhamsted HP4 38 AU18
Brentwood CM14 108 FW48
Bromley BR1 204 EG96

P
Q

Queens Rd, Buckhurst Hill IG9 102 EH47
Chesham HP5 54 AQ30
Chislehurst BR7 185 EP93
Datchet SL3 152 AU81
Egham TW20 173 AZ93
Enfield EN1 82 DS42
Eton Wick SL4 151 AL78
Feltham TW13 175 BV88
Gravesend DA12 191 GJ90
Guildford GU1 242 AX134
Hampton Hill TW12 176 CB91
Hayes UB3 135 BS72
Hersham KT12 213 BV106
Hertford SG13, SG14 32 DR11
Horley RH6 268 DG148
Kings.T. KT2 178 CN94
Loughton IG10 84 EL41
Morden SM4 200 DA98
New Malden KT3 199 CT98
North Weald Bassett CM16 71 FB26
Richmond TW10 178 CM85
Sthl. UB2 156 BX75
Sutton SM2 218 DA110
Twick. TW1 177 CF88
Wall. SM6 219 DH106
Waltham Cross EN8 67 DY34
Ware SG12 33 DZ05
Watford WD17 76 BW42
West Dr. UB7 154 BM75
Weybridge KT13 213 BQ105
Windsor SL4 151 AQ82
Queen's Rd, E17 123 DZ58
N11 99 DL52
Croy. CR0 201 DP100
Erith DA8 167 FE79
Houns. TW3 156 CB83
Slou. SL1 132 AT73
Tedd. TW11 177 CE93
Thames Ditton KT7 197 CF99
Uxb. UB8 134 BJ69
Well. DA16 166 EV82
⇌ Queens Road Peckham 312 F6
⊖ Queens Road Peckham 312 F6
Queens Rd W, E13 281 P10
Queen's Row, SE17 311 L2
Sch Queens' Sch, Bushey WD23 off Aldenham Rd 76 BZ41
Queen's Sq, The, Hem.H. HP2 40 BM20
Queens Ter, E13 144 EH67
Islw. TW7 157 CG84
Queen's Ter, NW8 274 A10
Queens Ter Cotts, W7 off Boston Rd 157 CE75
Queensthorpe Rd, SE26 183 DX91
★ Queen's Twr, SW7 296 A6
Queenstown Gdns, Rain. RM13 147 FF69
Queenstown Ms, SW8 309 J7
Queenstown Rd, SW8 309 J3
⇌ Queenstown Road (Battersea) 309 K6
Queen St, EC4 287 K10
N17 100 DS51
W1 297 J2
Bexleyheath DA7 166 EZ83
Chertsey KT16 194 BG102
Chipperfield WD4 58 BG31
Croydon CR0 220 DQ105
Erith DA8 167 FE79
Gomshall GU5 261 BQ139
Gravesend DA12 191 GH86
Romford RM7 127 FD58
St. Albans AL3 42 CC20
Warley CM14 108 FW50
Queen St Pl, EC4 299 K1
Queensville Rd, SW12 181 DK87
Queens Wk, E4 101 ED46
NW9 118 CQ61
W5 137 CJ70
Ashford TW15 174 BK91
Ruis. HA4 116 BX62
Queen's Wk, SW1 297 L3
Har. HA1 117 CE56
Queen's Wk, The, SE1 298 C3
⊖ Queensway 295 M1
Queensway, NW4 119 CW57
W2 283 M9
Croydon CR0 219 DM107
Enfield EN3 82 DV42
Feltham TW13 176 BW91
Hatfield AL10 45 CU18
Hemel Hempstead HP1, HP2 40 BM18
Petts Wood BR5 205 EQ99
Redhill RH1 250 DF133
Sun.bury-on-Thames TW16 195 BV96
West Wickham BR4 204 EE104
Queens Way, Shenley WD7 62 CL32
Waltham Cross EN8 67 DZ34
Queensway, The, Chal.St.P. SL9 112 AX55
● Queensway Business Cen, Enf. EN3 off Queensway 82 DW42
Queensway N, Hersham KT12 off Robinsway 214 BW105
Queensway S, Hersham KT12 off Trenchard Cl 214 BW106
Queenswell Av, N20 98 DE49
Sch Queenswell Inf & Nurs Sch, N20 off Sweets Way 98 DD47
Sch Queenswell Jun Sch, N20 off Sweets Way 98 DD47
Queenswood Av, E17 101 EC53
Hampton TW12 176 CB93
Hounslow TW3 156 BZ82
Hutton CM13 109 GD43
Thornton Heath CR7 201 DN99
Wallington SM6 219 DK105
Queenswood Cres, Wat. WD25 59 BU33
Queenswood Gdns, E11 124 EG60
Queenswood Pk, N3 97 CY54
Queenswood Rd, SE23 183 DX90
Sidcup DA15 185 ET85
Queen's Wd Rd, N10 121 DH58
Sch Queenswood Sch, Brook.Pk AL9 off Shepherds Way 64 DD28
Queens Yd, WC1 285 M5
Tram Queen Victoria, Sutt. SM3 217 CW105
Queen Victoria Av, Wem. HA0 137 CK66
★ Queen Victoria Mem, SW1 297 L4
Queen Victoria St, EC4 287 H10
Queen Victoria's Wk, Wind. SL4 152 AS81
Queen Victoria Ter, E1 off Sovereign Cl 300 F1
Quemerford Rd, N7 276 C2
Quendell Wk, Hem.H. HP2 40 BL20
Quendon Dr, Wal.Abb. EN9 67 ED33
Quennell Cl, Ashtd. KT21 off Parkers La 232 CM119
Quennell Way, Hutt. CM13 109 GC45
Quentin Pl, SE13 164 EE83
Quentin Rd, SE13 164 EE83
Quentins Dr, Berry's Grn TN16 239 EP116
Quentins Wk, Berry's Grn TN16 off St. Anns Way 239 EP116
Quentin Way, Vir.W. GU25 192 AV98
Quernmore Cl, Brom. BR1 184 EG93
Quernmore Rd, N4 121 DN58
Bromley BR1 184 EG93
Querrin St, SW6 307 N9
Sch Quest Acad, The, S.Croy. CR2 off Farnborough Av 221 DX108
● Questor, Dart. DA1 188 FL89
Quex Ms, NW6 273 K8
Quex Rd, NW6 273 K8
Quickbeams, Welw.G.C. AL7 30 DA06
Quickberry Pl, Amer. HP7 55 AR39
Quickley La, Chorl. WD3 73 BB44
Quickley Ri, Chorl. WD3 73 BC44
Quickmoor La, Kings L. WD4 58 BH33
Quick Rd, W4 158 CS78
Quicks Rd, SW19 180 DB94
Quick St, N1 287 H1
Quick St Ms, N1 286 G1
Quickswood, NW3 274 D6
Quickwood Cl, Rick. WD3 74 BG44
Quiet Cl, Add. KT15 212 BG105
Quiet Nook, Brom. BR2 off Croydon Rd 204 EK104
Quill Hall La, Amer. HP6 72 AT37
Quill La, SW15 159 CX84
Quillot, The, Hersham KT12 213 BT106
Quill St, N4 121 DN62
W5 138 CL69
Quilp St, SE1 299 J4
Quilter Gdns, Orp. BR5 off Tintagel Rd 206 EW102
Quilter Rd, Orp. BR5 206 EW102
Quilters Pl, SE9 185 EQ88
Quilter St, E2 288 C2
SE18 165 ET78
Quilting Ct, SE16 off Poolmans St 301 J4
Quinbrookes, Slou. SL2 132 AW72
Quince Ho, SW16 off Hemlock Cl 201 DK96
Felt. TW13 off High St 175 BV88
Quince Rd, SE13 314 D8
Quinces Cft, Hem.H. HP1 40 BG18
Quince Tree Cl, S.Ock. RM15 149 FW70
Quincy Rd, Egh. TW20 173 BA92
Quinnell Cl, SE18 off Rippolson Rd 165 ET78
Quinta Dr, Barn. EN5 79 CV43
Quintin Av, SW20 199 CZ95
Quintin Cl, Pnr. HA5 off High Rd 115 BV57
Sch Quintin Kynaston Sch, NW8 274 A9
Quinton Cl, Beck. BR3 203 EC97
Hounslow TW5 155 BV80
Wallington SM6 219 DH105
Quinton Rd, T.Ditt. KT7 197 CG102
Quinton St, SW18 180 DC89
Quintrell Cl, Wok. GU21 226 AV117
Quixley St, E14 290 G10
Quorn Rd, SE22 162 DS84

R

Raans Rd, Amer. HP6 72 AT38
Rabbit La, Hersham KT12 213 BU108
Rabbit Row, W8 295 K2
Rabbits Rd, E12 124 EL63
South Darenth DA4 209 FR96
Sch Rabbsfarm Prim Sch, Yiew. UB7 off Gordon Rd 134 BL73
Rabbs Mill Ho, Uxb. UB8 134 BJ68
Rabies Heath Rd, Bletch. RH1 252 DS133
Godstone RH9 252 DU134
Rabournmead Dr, Nthlt. UB5 116 BY64
Raby Rd, N.Mal. KT3 198 CR98
Raby St, E14 289 L8
Raccoon Way, Houns. TW4 156 BW82
Racecourse Way, Gat. RH6 268 DF151
Rachel Cl, Ilf. IG6 125 ER55
Rachels Way, Chesh. HP5 off Cresswell Rd 54 AR34
Rackham Cl, Well. DA16 166 EV82
Rackham Ms, SW16 181 DJ93
Racks Ct, Guil. GU1 258 AX136
Racton Rd, SW6 307 J3
Radbourne Av, W5 157 CJ77
Radbourne Cl, E5 123 DX63
Radbourne Ct, Har. HA3 117 CH58
Radbourne Cres, E17 101 ED54
Radbourne Rd, SW12 181 DK88
Radburn Cl, Harl. CM18 52 EU19
Radcliffe Av, NW10 139 CU68
Enfield EN2 82 DQ39
Radcliffe Gdns, Cars. SM5 218 DE108
Radcliffe Ms, Hmptn H. TW12 off Taylor Cl 176 CC92
Radcliffe Path, SW8 309 K9
Radcliffe Rd, N21 99 DP46
SE1 299 P6
Croydon CR0 202 DT103
Harrow HA3 95 CG54
Radcliffe Sq, SW15 179 CX86
Radcliffe Way, Nthlt. UB5 136 BX69
Radcot Av, Slou. SL3 153 BB76
Radcot Pt, SE23 183 DX90
Radcot St, SE11 310 F1
Raddington Rd, W10 282 F7
Radfield Dr, Dart. DA2 off Teynham Rd 188 FQ87
Radfield Way, Sid. DA15 185 ER87
Radford Rd, SE13 183 EC86
Radford Way, Bark. IG11 145 ET69
Radipole Rd, SW6 306 G6
● Radius Pk, Felt. TW14 155 BT84
Radland Rd, E16 291 M9
Rad La, Abin.Ham. RH5 261 BS141
Peaslake GU5 261 BS140
Radlet Av, SE26 182 DV90
RADLETT, WD7 77 CH35
⇌ Radlett 77 CG35
Radlett Cl, E7 281 M4
Radlett La, Shenley WD7 77 CK35
Sch Radlett Lo Sch, Rad. WD7 off Harper La 61 CH31
Radlett Pk Rd, Rad. WD7 61 CG34
Radlett Pl, NW8 274 C8
Sch Radlett Prep Sch, Rad. WD7 off Watling St 77 CJ38
Radlett Rd, Ald. WD25 76 CB39
St. Albans AL2 61 CE28
Watford WD17, WD24 76 BW41
Radley Av, Ilf. IG3 125 ET63
Radley Cl, Felt. TW14 175 BT88
Radley Ct, SE16 301 K4
Radley Gdns, Har. HA3 118 CL56
Radley Ho, SE2 off Wolvercote Rd 166 EX75
Radley Ms, W8 295 K7
Radley Rd, N17 100 DS54
Radley's La, E18 102 EG54
Radleys Mead, Dag. RM10 147 FB65
Radley Sq, E5 off Dudlington Rd 122 DW61
Radlix Rd, E10 123 EA60
Radnor Av, Har. HA1 117 CE57
Welling DA16 186 EV85
Radnor Cl, Chis. BR7 185 ES93
Mitcham CR4 201 DL98
Radnor Cres, SE18 166 EU79
Ilford IG4 125 EM57
Radnor Gdns, Enf. EN1 82 DS39
Twickenham TW1 177 CF89
Radnor Gro, Uxb. UB10 134 BN68
Radnor Ho, SW16 201 DM96
Radnor La, Holm.St.M. RH5 261 BU144
Radnor Ms, W2 284 B9
Radnor Pl, W2 284 C9
Radnor Rd, NW6 272 E9
SE15 312 C4
Harrow HA1 117 CD57
Twickenham TW1 177 CF89
Weybridge KT13 194 BN104
Radnor St, EC1 287 K3
Radnor Ter, W14 294 G8
Radnor Wk, E14 302 B8
SW3 308 D1
Croydon CR0 203 DZ100
Radnor Way, NW10 138 CP70
Slough SL3 152 AY77
Radolphs, Tad. KT20 233 CX122
Radstock Av, Har. HA3 117 CG55
Radstock Cl, N11 98 DG50
Radstock St, SW11 308 C5
Radstock Way, Merst. RH1 251 DK128
Radstone Ct, Wok. GU22 227 AZ118
Radzan Cl, Dart. DA2 187 FE89
Raebarn Gdns, Barn. EN5 79 CV43
Raeburn Av, Dart. DA1 187 FH85
Surbiton KT5 198 CP100
Raeburn Cl, NW11 120 DC58
Kingston upon Thames KT1 177 CK94
Raeburn Ct, Wok. GU21 off Martin Way 226 AU118
Raeburn Rd, Edg. HA8 96 CN54
Hayes UB4 135 BR68
Sidcup DA15 185 ES86
Raeburn St, SW2 161 DL84
Raeside Cl, Seer Grn HP9 89 AQ51
Rafford Way, Brom. BR1 204 EH96
★ R.A.F. Northolt, Ruis. HA4 115 BT64
Raft Rd, SW18 off North Pas 160 DA84
Ragged Hall La, St.Alb. AL2 42 BZ24
★ Ragged Sch Mus, E3 289 M6
Raggleswood, Chis. BR7 205 EN95
Rag Hill Cl, Tats. TN16 238 EL121
Rag Hill Rd, Tats. TN16 238 EK121
Raglan Av, Wal.Cr. EN8 67 DX34
Raglan Cl, Houns. TW4 176 BZ85
Reigate RH2 250 DC132
Raglan Ct, SE12 184 EG85
South Croydon CR2 219 DP106
Wembley HA9 118 CM63
Raglan Gdns, Wat. WD19 93 BV46
Sch Raglan Inf Sch, Enf. EN1 off Wellington Rd 100 DS45
Sch Raglan Jun Sch, Enf. EN1 off Raglan Rd 100 DS45
Raglan Prec, Cat. CR3 236 DS122
Sch Raglan Prim Sch, Brom. BR2 off Raglan Rd 204 EJ98
Raglan Rd, E17 123 EC57
SE18 305 P10
Belvedere DA17 166 EZ77
Bromley BR2 204 EJ98
Enfield EN1 100 DS45
Knaphill GU21 226 AS118
Reigate RH2 250 DB131
Raglan St, NW5 275 K4
Raglan Ter, Har. HA2 116 CB63
Raglan Way, Nthlt. UB5 136 CC65
Rags La, Chsht EN7 66 DS27
Ragstone Rd, Slou. SL1 151 AR76
Ragwort Ct, SE26 182 DV92
Rahere Ho, EC1 287 J2
Rahn Rd, Epp. CM16 70 EU31
Raider Cl, Rom. RM7 104 FA53
Raikes Hollow, Abin.Ham. RH5 261 BV142
Raikes La, Abin.Ham. RH5 261 BV141
Raikes Ms, NW5 275 L2
Railpit La, Warl. CR6 238 EE115
Railshead Rd, Twick. TW1 157 CH84
Railstore, The, Gidea Pk RM2 128 FJ55
Railton Rd, SE24 161 DN84
Guildford GU2 242 AV130
Railway App, N4 off Wightman Rd 121 DN58
SE1 299 M2
Harrow HA1, HA3 117 CF56
Twickenham TW1 177 CG87
Wallington SM6 219 DH107
Railway Arches, W12 294 A5
Railway Av, SE16 301 H4
Railway Children Wk, SE12 184 EG89
Bromley BR1 184 EG89
Railway Cotts, Rad. WD7 77 CH35
Watford WD24 75 BV39
Railway Ms, E3 290 A3
W10 282 F8
Railway Pas, Tedd. TW11 off Victoria Rd 177 CG93
Railway Pl, Belvedere DA17 166 FA76
Gravesend DA12 off Stone St 191 GH86
Hertford SG13 32 DS09
Railway Ri, SE22 off Grove Vale 162 DS84
Railway Rd, Grnf. UB6 137 CD66
Tedd. TW11 177 CF91
Waltham Cross EN8 67 DY33
Railway Side, SW13 158 CS83
Railway Sq, Brwd. CM14 off Fairfield Rd 108 FW48
Railway St, N1 286 B1
Hertford SG13, SG14 32 DR09
Northfleet DA11 190 GA85
Romford RM6 126 EW60
Railway Ter, E17 101 EC53
SE13 off Ladywell Rd 183 EB85
Kings Langley WD4 58 BN27
Slough SL2 132 AT74
Staines-upon-Thames TW18 173 BD92
Watford WD17 75 BV39
Westerham TN16 255 ER125
Rainborough Cl, NW10 138 CQ65
Rainbow Av, E14 302 C10
Rainbow Cl, Horl. RH6 269 DH146
Rainbow Ct, Wat. WD19 off Oxhey Rd 76 BW44
Woking GU21 off Langmans Way 226 AS116
● Rainbow Ind Est, West Dr. UB7 134 BK73
● Rainbow Ind Pk, SW20 199 CV96
Rainbow Quay, SE16 301 M7
Rainbow Rd, Chaff.Hun. RM16 169 FW77
Matching Tye CM17 37 FE12
Rainbow St, SE5 311 N5
Rainer Cl, Chsht EN8 67 DX29
Raines Ct, N16 off Northwold Rd 122 DT61
Sch Raine's Foundation Sch, Lwr Sch, E2 288 F2
Upr Sch, E2 289 H1
Raine St, E1 300 F2
RAINHAM, RM13 147 FG69
⇌ Rainham 147 FF70
Rainham Cl, SE9 185 ER86
SW11 180 DE86
★ Rainham Hall, Rain. RM13 147 FG70
Rainham Rd, NW10 282 B3
Rainham RM13 147 FE66
Rainham Rd N, Dag. RM10 127 FB61
Rainham Rd S, Dag. RM10 127 FB63
Sch Rainham Village Prim Sch, Rain. RM13 off Upminster Rd S 147 FG70
Rainhill Way, E3 290 B2
Rainsborough Av, SE8 301 L9
Rainsborough Ct, Hert. SG13 off Lilbourne Dr 32 DU08
Rainsford Cl, Stan. HA7 95 CJ49
Rainsford Rd, NW10 138 CP69
Rainsford St, W2 284 C8
Rainsford Way, Horn. RM12 127 FG60
Rainton Rd, SE7 303 P10
Rainville Rd, W6 306 B3
Raisins Hill, Pnr. HA5 116 BW55
Raith Av, N14 99 DK48
Raleana Rd, E14 302 F2
Raleigh Av, Hayes UB4 135 BV71
Wallington SM6 219 DK105
Raleigh Cl, NW4 119 CW57
Erith DA8 167 FF79
Pinner HA5 116 BX59
Ruislip HA4 115 BT61
Slough SL1 131 AN74
Raleigh Ct, SE19 off Lymer Av 182 DT92
Beckenham BR3 203 EB95
Staines-upon-Thames TW18 174 BG91
Wallington SM6 219 DH107
Raleigh Dr, N20 98 DE48
Claygate KT10 215 CD106
Smallfield RH6 269 DN148
Surbiton KT5 198 CQ102
Raleigh Gdns, SW2 off Brixton Hill 181 DM86
Mitcham CR4 200 DF96
Raleigh Ms, N1 off Queen's Head St 277 H9
Orp. BR6 off Osgood Av 223 ET106
Raleigh Rd, N8 121 DN56
SE20 183 DX94
Enfield EN2 82 DR42
Feltham TW13 175 BT90
Richmond TW9 158 CM83
Southall UB2 156 BY78
Sch Raleigh Sch, The, W.Hors. KT24 off Northcote Cres 245 BQ125
Raleigh St, N1 277 H9
Raleigh Way, N14 99 DK46
Feltham TW13 176 BW92
Rale La, E4 off Buxton Rd 101 ED45
Ralliwood Rd, Ashtd. KT21 232 CN119
Ralph Ct, W2 283 M8
Ralph Perring Ct, Beck. BR3 203 EA98
Ralston Ct, Wind. SL4 off Russell St 151 AR81
Ralston St, SW3 308 E1
Ralston Way, Wat. WD19 94 BX47
Rama Cl, SW16 181 DK94
Rama Ct, Har. HA1 117 CE61
Ramac Way, SE7 304 A9
Rama La, SE19 182 DT94
Coll Rambert, SE1 298 E2
Coll Rambert Sch of Ballet & Contemporary Dance, Twick. TW1 off St. Margarets Rd 177 CH85
Rambler Cl, SW16 181 DJ91
Taplow SL6 130 AH72
Rambler La, Slou. SL3 152 AW76
Ramblers La, Harl. CM17 off Crossway 36 EX14
Ramblers Way, Welw.G.C. AL7 30 DB10
Rambling Way, Pott.End HP4 39 BC17
Rame Cl, SW17 180 DG92
Ram Gorse, Harl. CM20 35 EP13
Ramilles Cl, SW2 181 DL86
Ramillies Pl, W1 285 L9
Ramillies Rd, NW7 96 CS47
W4 158 CR77
Sidcup DA15 186 EV86
Ramillies St, W1 285 L9
Ramin Ct, Guil. GU1 242 AW131
Ramney Dr, Enf. EN3 83 DY37
Ramornie Cl, Hersham KT12 214 BZ106
Ramparts, The, St.Alb. AL3 42 CB21
Rampart St, E1 288 E9
Ram Pas, Kings.T. KT1 off High St 197 CK96
Rampayne St, SW1 297 N10
Ram Pl, E9 279 H4
Rampton Cl, E4 101 EA48
Ramsay Cl, Brox. EN10 49 DY21
Ramsay Gdns, Rom. RM3 106 FJ53
Ramsay Pl, Har. HA1 117 CE60
Ramsay Rd, E7 124 EE63
W3 158 CQ76
Ramsbury Rd, St.Alb. AL1 43 CE21
Ramscote La, Bell. HP5 54 AN25
Ramscroft Cl, N9 100 DS45
Ramsdale Rd, SW17 180 DG92
RAMSDEN, Orp. BR5 206 EW102
Ramsden Cl, Orp. BR5 206 EW102
Ramsden Dr, Rom. RM5 104 FA52
Ramsden Rd, N11 98 DF50
SW12 180 DG86
Erith DA8 167 FD80
Orpington BR5 206 EW102
Ramsey Cl, NW9 119 CT58
Brookmans Park AL9 64 DD27
Greenford UB6 117 CD64
Horley RH6 268 DF148
St. Albans AL1 43 CG22
Ramsey Ct, Slou. SL2 off Lower Britwell Rd 131 AK70
Ramsey Ho, SW11 off Maysoule Rd 160 DD84
Ramsey Lo Ct, St.Alb. AL1 43 CE19
Ramsey Pl, Cat. CR3 236 DQ122
Ramsey Rd, Th.Hth. CR7 201 DM100
Ramsey St, E2 288 D4
Ramsey Wk, N1 277 L5
Ramsey Way, N14 99 DJ45
Ramsfort Ho, SE16 off Manor Est 300 E9
Ramsgate Cl, E16 304 A3
Ramsgate St, E8 278 B4
Ramsgill App, Ilf. IG2 125 ET56
Ramsgill Dr, Ilf. IG2 125 ET57
Rams Gro, Rom. RM6 126 EY56
Ramson Ri, Hem.H. HP1 39 BE21
Ram St, SW18 180 DB85
Ramulis Dr, Hayes UB4 136 BX70
Ramus Wd Av, Orp. BR6 223 ES106
Rancliffe Gdns, SE9 164 EL84
Rancliffe Rd, E6 293 H1
Sch Randal Cremer Prim Sch, E2 278 A10
Randal Cres, Reig. RH2 266 DA136
Randall Av, NW2 119 CT62
Randall Cl, SW11 308 C6
Erith DA8 167 FC79
Slough SL3 153 AZ78
Randall Ct, NW7 97 CU52
SW6 off Dairy Cl 307 J7
Randall Dr, Horn. RM12 128 FJ63
Randall Pl, SE10 314 E4
Randall Rd, SE11 298 C10
Randall Row, SE11 298 C9
Randalls Cres, Lthd. KT22 231 CG120
Randalls Dr, Hutt. CM13 109 GE44
Randalls Pk Av, Lthd. KT22 231 CG120
Randalls Pk Dr, Lthd. KT22 off Randalls Rd 231 CG121
Randalls Ride, Hem.H. HP2 40 BK18
Randalls Rd, Lthd. KT22 231 CE119
Randall's Wk, Brick.Wd AL2 60 BZ30
Randalls Way, Lthd. KT22 231 CG121
Randell's Rd, N1 276 B8
Randisbourne Gdns, SE6 183 EB90
Randle Rd, Rich. TW10 177 CJ91
Randlesdown Rd, SE6 183 EA91
Randles La, Knock.P. TN14 240 EX115
Randolph App, E16 292 D9
Randolph Av, W9 283 P4
Randolph Cl, Bexh. DA7 167 FC83
Kingston upon Thames KT2 178 CQ92
Knaphill GU21 off Creston Av 226 AS117
Stoke D'Abernon KT11 230 CA115
Randolph Cres, W9 283 N5
Randolph Gdns, NW6 283 L1
Randolph Gro, Rom. RM6 off Donald Dr 126 EW57
● Randolph Ho, Croy. CR0 202 DQ102
Randolph Ms, W9 283 P5
Randolph Rd, E17 123 EB57
W9 283 N5
Bromley BR2 205 EM102
Epsom KT17 217 CT114
Slough SL3 152 AY76
Southall UB1 156 BZ75
Randolph's La, West. TN16 255 EP126
Randolph St, NW1 275 L7
Randon Cl, Har. HA2 94 CB54
Ranelagh Av, SW6 306 G10
SW13 159 CU82
Ranelagh Br, W2 off Gloucester Ter 283 M7
Ranelagh Cl, Edg. HA8 96 CN49
Ranelagh Dr, Edg. HA8 96 CN49
Twickenham TW1 177 CH85
★ Ranelagh Gdns, SW3 308 G1
Ranelagh Gdns, E11 124 EJ57
SW6 306 G10
W4 158 CQ80
W6 159 CT76
Ilford IG1 125 EN60
Northfleet DA11 191 GF87
Ranelagh Gdns Mans, SW6 off Ranelagh Gdns 306 F10
Ranelagh Gro, SW1 297 H10
Ranelagh Ms, W5 157 CK75
Ranelagh Pl, N.Mal. KT3 198 CS99
Sch Ranelagh Prim Sch, E15 281 K10
Ranelagh Rd, E6 145 EN67
E11 124 EE63
E15 281 K9
N17 122 DS55
N22 99 DM53
NW10 139 CT68
SW1 309 M1
W5 157 CK75
Hemel Hempstead HP2 41 BP20
Redhill RH1 250 DE134
Southall UB1 136 BX74
Wembley HA0 117 CK64
Ranfurly Rd, Sutt. SM1 200 DA103
Sch Rangefield Prim Sch, Downham BR1 off Glenbow Rd 184 EE92
Rangefield Rd, Brom. BR1 184 EE92
Rangemoor Rd, N15 122 DT57
Range Rd, Grav. DA12 191 GL87
Rangers Rd, E4 102 EE45
Loughton IG10 102 EE45
Rangers Sq, SE10 314 G6
Ranger Wk, Add. KT15 off Monks Cres 212 BH106
Range Way, Shep. TW17 194 BN101
Rangeworth Pl, Sid. DA15 off Priestlands Pk Rd 185 ET90
Rangoon St, EC3 288 A9
Rankin Cl, NW9 118 CS55
Rankine Ho, SE1 off Bath Ter 299 J7
Ranleigh Gdns, Bexh. DA7 166 EZ80
Ranmere St, SW12 off Ormeley Rd 181 DH88

Ranmoor Cl, Har. HA1 117 CD56
Ranmoor Gdns, Har. HA1 117 CD56
Ranmore Av, Croy. CR0 202 DT104
Ranmore Cl, Red. RH1 250 DG131
★ Ranmore Common, Dor. RH5 246 CB133
Ranmore Common Rd, Westh. RH5 247 CD133
Ranmore Path, Orp. BR5 206 EU98
Ranmore Rd, Dor. RH4 246 CC134
Sutton SM2 217 CX109
Rannoch Cl, Edg. HA8 96 CP47
Rannoch Rd, W6 306 B2
Rannoch Wk, Hem.H. HP2 40 BK16
Rannock Av, NW9 118 CS59
Ranskill Rd, Borwd. WD6 78 CN39
Ransom Cl, Wat. WD19 94 BW45
● Ransome's Dock Business Cen, SW11 308 D5
Ransom Rd, SE7 304 D10
Ransom Wk, SE7 304 D9
Ranston Cl, Denh. UB9 off Nightingale Way 113 BF58
Ranston St, NW1 284 C6
Rant Meadow, Hem.H. HP3 40 BN22
Ranulf Cl, Harl. CM17 36 EW09
Ranulf Rd, NW2 119 CZ63
Ranwell Cl, E3 279 N9
Ranwell St, E3 279 N9
Ranworth Av, Hodd. EN11 33 EB13
Ranworth Cl, Erith DA8 167 FE82
Hemel Hempstead HP3 off Panxworth Rd 40 BK22
Ranworth Gdns, Pot.B. EN6 63 CX31
Ranworth Rd, N9 100 DW47
Ranyard Cl, Chess. KT9 198 CM104
Raphael Av, Rom. RM1 127 FF55
Tilbury RM18 171 GG80
Raphael Cl, Kings.T. KT1 197 CK98
Shenley WD7 62 CL32
Raphael Dr, Loug. IG10 85 EP40
T.Ditt. KT7 197 CF101
Watford WD24 76 BX40
Sch Raphael Indep Sch, Horn. RM11 off Park La 127 FG59
Raphael Rd, Grav. DA12 191 GK87
Raphael St, SW7 296 E5
Rapier Cl, Purf. RM19 168 FN77
Rasehill Cl, Rick. WD3 74 BJ43
Rashleigh St, SW8 309 K9
Rashleigh Way, Hort.Kir. DA4 208 FQ98
Rasper Rd, N20 98 DC47
Rastell Av, SW2 181 DK89
Ratcliffe Cl, SE12 184 EG87
Uxbridge UB8 134 BK69
Ratcliffe Cross St, E1 289 K9
Ratcliffe La, E14 289 L9
Ratcliffe Orchard, E1 289 K10
Ratcliff Rd, E7 124 EJ64
Rathbone Mkt, E16 291 L7
Rathbone Pl, W1 285 N8
Rathbone St, E16 291 L7
W1 285 M7
Rathcoole Av, N8 121 DM56
Rathcoole Gdns, N8 121 DM57
Sch Rathfern Prim Sch, SE6 off Rathfern Rd 183 DZ88
Rathfern Rd, SE6 183 DZ88
Rathgar Av, W13 137 CH74
Rathgar Cl, N3 97 CZ54
Redhill RH1 266 DG139
Rathgar Rd, SW9 311 H10
Rathlin, Hem.H. HP3 41 BP22
Rathmell Dr, SW4 181 DK86
Rathmore Rd, SE7 304 A10
Gravesend DA11 191 GH87
Rathore Cl, Rom. RM6 126 EX57
Rathwell Path, Borwd. WD6 78 CL39
Rats La, High Beach IG10 84 EH38
Rattray Rd, SW2 161 DN84
Ratty's La, Hodd. EN11 49 ED17
Raul Rd, SE15 312 D8
Raveley St, NW5 275 L1
Ravel Gdns, Aveley RM15 148 FQ72
Ravel Rd, Aveley RM15 148 FQ72
Raven Cl, NW9 96 CS54
Rickmansworth WD3 92 BJ45
Watford WD18 75 BS43
Raven Ct, E5 off Stellman Cl 122 DU62
Hatfield AL10 45 CU19
Ravencroft, Grays RM16 off Alexandra Cl 171 GH75
Ravendale Rd, Sun. TW16 195 BT96
Ravenet St, SW11 309 J7
Ravenfield, Eng.Grn TW20 172 AW93
Ravenfield Rd, SW17 180 DF90
Welwyn Garden City AL7 29 CZ09
Ravenhill Rd, E13 144 EJ68
Ravenna Rd, SW15 179 CX85
Ravenoak Way, Chig. IG7 103 ES50
Ravenor Pk Rd, Grnf. UB6 136 CB69
Sch Ravenor Prim Sch, Grnf. UB6 off Greenway Gdns 136 CA69
Raven Rd, E18 102 EJ54
Raven Row, E1 288 F6
⇌ Ravensbourne 183 ED94
Ravensbourne Av, Beck. BR3 183 ED94
Bromley BR2 183 ED94
Staines-upon-Thames TW19 174 BL88
● Ravensbourne Business Cen, Kes. BR2 222 EK105
Coll Ravensbourne Coll of Design & Communication, SE10 303 K4
Ravensbourne Cres, Rom. RM3 128 FM55
Ravensbourne Gdns, W13 137 CH71
Ilford IG5 103 EN53
Ravensbourne Pk, SE6 183 EA87
Ravensbourne Pk Cres, SE6 183 DZ87
Ravensbourne Pl, SE13 314 D8
Ravensbourne Rd, SE6 183 DZ87
Bromley BR1 204 EG97
Dartford DA1 167 FG83
Twickenham TW1 177 CJ86
Sch Ravensbourne Sch, Rom. RM3 off Neave Cres 106 FK53
Sch Ravensbourne Sch, The, Brom. BR2 off Hayes La 204 EH98
Ravensbourne Ter, Stanw. TW19 off Ravensbourne Av 174 BM88
Ravensbury Av, Mord. SM4 200 DC99
Ravensbury Ct, Mitch. CR4 off Ravensbury Gro 200 DD98
Ravensbury Gro, Mitch. CR4 200 DD98
Ravensbury La, Mitch. CR4 200 DD98
Ravensbury Path, Mitch. CR4 200 DD98
Ravensbury Rd, SW18 180 DA89
Orpington BR5 205 ET98
Ravensbury Ter, SW18 180 DB89
Ravenscar Rd, Brom. BR1 184 EE91
Surbiton KT6 198 CM103
Ravens Cl, Brom. BR2 204 EF96
Enfield EN1 82 DS40
Redhill RH1 250 DF132
Surbiton KT6 197 CK100
Ravens Ct, Berk. HP4 off Benningfield Gdns 38 AY17
Ravenscourt, Brwd. CM15 108 FX46
Sun. TW16 195 BT95
Ravenscourt Av, W6 159 CU77
Ravenscourt Cl, Horn. RM12 off Ravenscourt Dr 128 FL62
Ruislip HA4 115 BQ59
Ravenscourt Dr, Horn. RM12 128 FL62
Ravenscourt Gdns, W6 159 CU77
Ravenscourt Gro, Horn. RM12 128 FL61
⊖ Ravenscourt Park 159 CU77
Ravenscourt Pk, W6 159 CU76
Ravenscourt Pl, W6 159 CV77
Ravenscourt Rd, W6 159 CV77
Orpington BR5 206 EU97
Ravenscourt Sq, W6 159 CU76
Ravenscraig Rd, N11 99 DH49
Ravenscroft, Brox. EN10 49 DZ20
Watford WD25 60 BY34
Ravenscroft Av, NW11 119 CZ59
Wembley HA9 118 CM60
Ravenscroft Cl, E16 291 N6
Ravenscroft Cres, SE9 185 EM90
Ravenscroft Pk, Barn. EN5 79 CX42
Ravenscroft Pt, E9 279 J5
Sch Ravenscroft Prim Sch, E16 291 P5
Ravenscroft Rd, E16 291 P6
W4 158 CQ77
Beckenham BR3 202 DW96
Weybridge KT13 213 BQ111
Sch Ravenscroft Sch, The, N20 off Barnet La 97 CZ45
Ravenscroft St, E2 288 B1
Ravensdale Av, N12 98 DC49
Ravensdale Gdns, SE19 182 DR94
Hounslow TW4 156 BY83
● Ravensdale Ind Est, N16 122 DU58
Ravensdale Ms, Stai. TW18 off Worple Rd 174 BH93
Ravensdale Rd, N16 122 DT59
Hounslow TW4 156 BY83
Ravensdell, Hem.H. HP1 39 BF19
Ravensdon St, SE11 310 F1
Ravensfield, Slou. SL3 152 AX75
Ravensfield Cl, Dag. RM9 126 EX63
Ravensfield Gdns, Epsom KT19 216 CS106
Ravens Gate Ms, Brom. BR2 off Meadow Rd 204 EE96
Ravenshaw St, NW6 273 H3
Ravenshead Cl, S.Croy. CR2 220 DW111
Ravenshill, Chis. BR7 205 EP95
Ravenshurst Av, NW4 119 CW56
Ravenside Cl, N18 101 DX51
Ravenside Retail Pk, N18 101 DX50
Ravens La, Berk. HP4 38 AX19
Ravenslea Rd, SW12 180 DF87
Ravensleigh Gdns, Brom. BR1 off Pike Cl 184 EH92
Ravensmead, Chal.St.P. SL9 91 AZ50
Ravensmead Rd, Brom. BR2 183 ED94
Ravensmede Way, W4 159 CT77
Ravensmere, Epp. CM16 70 EU31
Ravens Ms, SE12 off Ravens Way 184 EG85
Ravenstone, SE17 311 P1
Sch Ravenstone Prim Sch, SW12 off Ravenstone St 181 DH88
Ravenstone Rd, N8 121 DN55
NW9 off West Hendon Bdy 119 CT58
Ravenstone St, SW12 180 DG88
Ravens Wk, E20 280 D4
Ravens Way, SE12 184 EG85
Ravens Wf, Berk. HP4 38 AX19
Ravenswold, Ken. CR8 236 DQ115
Ravenswood, Bex. DA5 186 EY88
Ravenswood Av, Surb. KT6 198 CM103
West Wickham BR4 203 EC102
Ravenswood Cl, Cob. KT11 230 BX115
Romford RM5 105 FB50
Ravenswood Ct, Kings.T. KT2 178 CP93
Woking GU22 227 AZ118
Ravenswood Cres, Har. HA2 116 BZ61
West Wickham BR4 203 EC102
Ravenswood Gdns, Islw. TW7 157 CE81
● Ravenswood Ind Est, E17 off Shernhall St 123 EC56
Ravenswood Pk, Nthwd. HA6 93 BU51
Ravenswood Rd, E17 123 EB56
SW12 181 DH87
Croydon CR0 201 DP104
Sch Ravens Wd Sch, Brom. BR2 off Oakley Rd 204 EK104
Ravensworth Rd, NW10 139 CV69
SE9 185 EM91
Slough SL2 131 AN69
Ravey St, EC2 287 N4
Ravine Gro, SE18 165 ES79
Rav Pinter Cl, N16 122 DS59
Rawdon Dr, Hodd. EN11 49 EA18
Rawlings Cl, Beck. BR3 203 EC99
Orpington BR6 223 ET106
Rawlings Cres, Wem. HA9 118 CP62
Rawlings La, Seer Grn HP9 89 AQ48
Rawlings St, SW3 296 E8
Rawlins Cl, N3 119 CY55
South Croydon CR2 221 DY108
Rawlinson Ho, SE13 off Mercator Rd 163 ED84
Rawlyn Cl, Chaff.Hun. RM16 169 FV78
Rawnsley Av, Mitch. CR4 200 DD99
Rawreth Wk, N1 277 K8
Rawson Ct, SW11 off Strasburg Rd 309 J7
Rawson St, SW11 309 H7
Rawsthorne Cl, E16 305 J3
Rawstone Wk, E13 281 P10
Rawstorne Pl, EC1 286 G2
Rawstorne St, EC1 286 G2
Raybarn Rd, Hem.H. HP1 40 BG18
Rayburn Rd, Horn. RM11 128 FN59
Ray Cl, Chess. KT9 215 CJ107
Raydean Rd, New Barn. EN5 80 DB43
Raydon Rd, Chsht EN8 67 DX32
Raydons Gdns, Dag. RM9 126 EY63
Raydons Rd, Dag. RM9 126 EY64
Raydon St, N19 121 DH61
Rayfield, Epp. CM16 70 EU30
Welwyn Garden City AL8 29 CX06
Rayfield Cl, Brom. BR2 204 EL100
Rayford Av, SE12 184 EF87
Rayford Cl, Dart. DA1 188 FJ85
Ray Gdns, Bark. IG11 146 EU68
Stanmore HA7 95 CH50
Ray Lamb Way, Erith DA8 167 FH79
Raylands Mead, Ger.Cr. SL9 112 AW57
Rayleas Cl, SE18 165 EP81
Rayleigh Av, Tedd. TW11 177 CE93
Rayleigh Cl, N13 100 DR48
Hutton CM13 109 GC44
Rayleigh Ct, Kings.T. KT1 198 CM96
Rayleigh Ri, S.Croy. CR2 220 DS107
Rayleigh Rd, E16 304 B2
N13 100 DQ48
SW19 199 CZ95
Hutton CM13 109 GB44
Woodford Green IG8 102 EJ51
Rayley La, N.Wld Bas. CM16 52 FA24
Sch Ray Lo Prim Sch, Wdf.Grn. IG8 off Snakes La E 102 EK51
Ray Lo Rd, Wdf.Grn. IG8 102 EJ51
Ray Massey Way, E6 off Ron Leighton Way 144 EL67
Raymead, NW4 119 CW56
Raymead Av, Th.Hth. CR7 201 DN99
Raymead Cl, Fetch. KT22 231 CE122
Ray Mead Ct, Maid. SL6 off Boulters La 130 AC70
Raymead Pas, Th.Hth. CR7 off Raymead Av 201 DN99
Ray Mead Rd, Maid. SL6 130 AC72
Raymead Way, Fetch. KT22 231 CE122
Raymer Cl, St.Alb. AL1 43 CE19
Raymere Gdns, SE18 165 ER80
Raymer Wk, Horl. RH6 269 DJ147
Raymond Av, E18 124 EF55
W13 157 CG76
Raymond Bldgs, WC1 286 D6
Raymond Cl, SE26 182 DW92
Abbots Langley WD5 59 BR32
Colnbrook SL3 153 BE81
Raymond Ct, N10 off Pembroke Rd 98 DG52
Potters Bar EN6 off St. Francis Cl 64 DC34
Raymond Cres, Guil. GU2 258 AT135
Raymond Gdns, Chig. IG7 104 EV48
Raymond Rd, E13 144 EJ66
SW19 179 CY93
Beckenham BR3 203 DY98
Ilford IG2 125 ER59
Slough SL3 153 BA76
Raymonds Cl, Welw.G.C. AL7 29 CY11
Raymonds Plain, Welw.G.C. AL7 29 CY11
Raymond Way, Clay. KT10 215 CG107
Raymouth Rd, SE16 300 F8
Rayne Ct, E18 124 EF56
Rayners Av Mobile Home Pk, Loud. HP10 88 AC52
Rayners Cl, Colnbr. SL3 153 BC80
Loudwater HP10 88 AC52
Wembley HA0 117 CK64
Rayners Ct, Grav. DA11 190 GB86
Harrow HA2 116 CA60
Rayners Cres, Nthlt. UB5 135 BV69
Rayners Gdns, Nthlt. UB5 135 BV68
RAYNERS LANE, Har. HA2 116 BZ60
⊖ Rayners Lane 116 BZ59
Rayners La, Har. HA2 116 CB61
Pinner HA5 116 BZ58
Rayners Rd, SW15 179 CY85
Rayner Twrs, E10 123 EA59
Raynes Av, E11 124 EJ59
RAYNES PARK, SW20 199 CV97
⇌ Raynes Park 199 CW96
Sch Raynes Pk High Sch, SW20 off Bushey Rd 199 CV97
Raynham, W2 284 C9
Raynham Av, N18 100 DU51
Raynham Cl, Guil. GU4 243 BB130
Sch Raynham Prim Sch, N18 off Raynham Av 100 DU50
Raynham Rd, N18 100 DU50
W6 159 CV77
Raynham St, Hert. SG13 32 DS08
Raynham Ter, N18 100 DU50
Raynor Cl, Sthl. UB1 136 BZ74
Raynor Pl, N1 277 K7
Raynsford Rd, Ware SG12 33 DY06
Raynton Cl, Har. HA2 116 BY60
Hayes UB4 135 BT70
Raynton Dr, Hayes UB4 135 BT70
Raynton Rd, Enf. EN3 83 DX37
Ray Rd, Rom. RM5 105 FB50
West Molesey KT8 196 CB99
Rays Av, N18 100 DW49
Windsor SL4 151 AM80
Rays Hill, Hort.Kir. DA4 208 FQ98
Rays La, Penn HP10 88 AC47
Rays Rd, N18 100 DW49
West Wickham BR4 203 EC101
Ray St, EC1 286 F5
Ray St Br, EC1 286 F5
Ray Wk, N7 off Andover Rd 121 DM61
Raywood Cl, Harling. UB3 155 BQ80
Reach, The, SE28 165 ES75
Reachview Cl, NW1 275 M7
Read Cl, T.Ditt. KT7 197 CG101
Read Ct, Wal.Abb. EN9 68 EG33
Reade Ct, Farn.Com. SL2 off Victoria Rd 131 AQ65
Readens, The, Bans. SM7 234 DF116
Reading Arch Rd, Red. RH1 250 DF134
Reading Cl, SE22 182 DU86
Reading La, E8 278 E5
Reading Rd, Nthlt. UB5 116 CB64
Sutton SM1 218 DC106
Readings, The, Chorl. WD3 73 BF41
Harlow CM18 51 ET18
Reading Way, NW7 97 CX50
Read Rd, Ashtd. KT21 231 CK117
Reads Cl, Ilf. IG1 off Chapel Rd 125 EP62
Reads Rest La, Tad. KT20 233 CZ119
Read Way, Grav. DA12 191 GK92
Reapers Cl, NW1 275 N8
Reapers Way, Islw. TW7 off Hall Rd 177 CD85
Reardon Ct, N21 100 DQ47
Reardon Path, E1 300 F3
Reardon St, E1 300 E2
Reaston St, SE14 313 H4
Sch Reay Prim Sch, SW9 310 D5
Reckitt Rd, W4 158 CS78
Record St, SE15 312 G2
Recovery St, SW17 180 DE92
Recreation Av, Harold Wd RM3 106 FM54
Romford RM7 127 FC57
Recreation Rd, SE26 183 DX91
Bromley BR2 204 EF96
Guildford GU1 242 AW134
Sidcup DA15 off Woodside Rd 185 ES90
Southall UB2 156 BY77
Recreation Way, Mitch. CR4 201 DK97
Rector St, N1 277 J9
Rectory Chase, Lt.Warley CM13 129 FX56
Rectory Cl, E4 101 EA48
N3 97 CZ53
SW20 199 CW97
Ashtead KT21 232 CM119
Byfleet KT14 212 BL113
Dartford DA1 167 FE84
Essendon AL9 46 DF17
Farnham Royal SL2 131 AQ69
Guildford GU4 243 BD132
Hunsdon SG12 34 EK07
Long Ditton KT6 197 CJ102
Shepperton TW17 194 BN97
Sidcup DA14 186 EV91
Stanmore HA7 95 CH51
Windsor SL4 151 AN81
Rectory Cres, E11 124 EJ58
Rectory Fm Rd, Enf. EN2 81 DM38
Rectory Fld, Harl. CM19 51 EP17
Rectory Fld Cres, SE7 164 EJ80
Rectory Gdns, N8 121 DL56
SW4 309 L10
Chalfont St. Giles HP8 90 AV48
Hatfield AL10 45 CV18
Northolt UB5 136 BZ67
Upminster RM14 129 FR61
Rectory Grn, Beck. BR3 203 DZ95
Rectory Gro, SW4 309 L10
Croydon CR0 201 DP103
Hampton TW12 176 BZ91
Rectory Hill, Amer. HP6, HP7 55 AP39
Rectory La, SW17 180 DG93
Ashtead KT21 232 CM118
Banstead SM7 218 DF114
Berkhamsted HP4 38 AW19
Bookham KT23 246 BZ126
Brasted TN16 240 EW123
Buckland RH3 249 CT131
Byfleet KT14 212 BL113
Edgware HA8 96 CN51
Harlow CM19 51 EP17
Kings Langley WD4 58 BN28
Long Ditton KT6 197 CH102
Loughton IG10 85 EN40
Rickmansworth WD3 92 BK46
Sevenoaks TN13 257 FJ126
Shenley WD7 62 CN33
Shere GU5 260 BM139
Sidcup DA14 186 EV91
Stanmore HA7 95 CH50
Wallington SM6 219 DJ105
Westerham TN16 238 EL123
Rectory Meadow, Sthflt DA13 190 GA93
Rectory Orchard, SW19 179 CY91
Rectory Pk, S.Croy. CR2 220 DS113
Rectory Pk Av, Nthlt. UB5 136 BZ69
Rectory Pl, SE18 305 L7
Rectory Road 122 DT62
Rectory Rd, E12 125 EM64
E17 123 EB55
N16 122 DT62
SW13 159 CU82
W3 138 CP74
Beckenham BR3 203 EA95
Chipstead CR5 250 DD125
Dagenham RM10 146 FA66
Grays RM17 170 GD76
Hayes UB3 135 BU72
Hounslow TW4 155 BV81
Keston BR2 222 EK108
Rickmansworth WD3 92 BK46
Southall UB2 156 BZ76
Sutton SM1 200 DA104
Swanscombe DA10 190 FY87
Taplow SL6 130 AD70
Welwyn Garden City AL8 29 CV06
West Tilbury RM18 171 GK79
Rectory Sq, E1 289 K6
Rectory Way, Amer. HP7 55 AP39
Uxbridge UB10 115 BP62
Rectory Wd, Harl. CM20 35 EQ14
Reculver Ms, N18 100 DU49
Reculver Rd, SE16 301 J10
Red Anchor Cl, SW3 308 C3
Redan Pl, W2 283 L9
Redan St, W14 294 D6
Redan Ter, SE5 311 H8
Redbarn Cl, Pur. CR8 off Whytecliffe Rd N 219 DP111
Red Barracks Rd, SE18 305 K9
Redberry Gro, SE26 182 DW90
Redbourne Av, N3 98 DA53
Redbourne Dr, SE28 146 EX72
Redbourn Rd, Hem.H. HP2 40 BN16
St. Albans AL3 42 CA18
REDBRIDGE, Ilf. IG1 125 EM58
⊖ Redbridge 124 EK58
Coll Redbridge Coll, Rom. RM6 off Little Heath 126 EV57
Coll Redbridge Drama Cen, E18 off Churchfields 102 EG53
● Redbridge Enterprise Cen, Ilf. IG1 125 EQ61
Redbridge Gdns, SE5 311 P5
Redbridge Ho, E16 off University Way 305 N1
Coll Redbridge Inst of Adult Ed, Ilf. IG2 off Gaysham Av 125 EP57
Redbridge La E, Ilf. IG4 124 EK58
Redbridge La W, E11 124 EH58
Coll Redbridge Music Sch, Ilf. IG6 off Fencepiece Rd 103 EQ52
Sch Redbridge Prim Sch, Ilf. IG4 off College Gdns 124 EL57
Jct Redbridge Rbt, Ilf. IG4 124 EJ58
Redburn St, SW3 308 E2
Redbury Cl, Rain. RM13 147 FH70
Redcar Cl, Nthlt. UB5 116 CB64
Redcar Rd, Rom. RM3 106 FM50
Redcar St, SE5 311 J5
Redcastle Cl, E1 288 G10
Red Cedars Rd, Orp. BR6 205 ES101
Redchurch St, E2 288 A4
Redcliffe Cl, SW5 off Old Brompton Rd 307 L1
Redcliffe Ct, E5 off Napoleon Rd 122 DV62
Redcliffe Gdns, SW5 307 M1
SW10 307 M1
W4 158 CP80
Ilford IG1 125 EN60
Redcliffe Ms, SW10 307 M1
Redcliffe Pl, SW10 307 N3
Redcliffe Rd, SW10 307 N1
Sch Redcliffe Sch, SW10 307 N2
Redcliffe Sq, SW10 307 M1
Redcliffe St, SW10 307 M2
Redclose Av, Mord. SM4 200 DA99
Redclyffe Rd, E6 144 EJ67
Redcote Pl, Dor. RH4 247 CK134
Red Cottage Ms, Slou. SL3 152 AW76
Red Ct, Slou. SL1 132 AS74
Redcourt, Wok. GU22 227 BD115
Jct Red Cow, Slou. SL1 152 AT76
Redcroft Rd, Sthl. UB1 136 CC73
Redcross Way, SE1 299 K4
Redden Ct Rd, Rom. RM3 128 FL55
Sch Redden Ct Sch, Harold Wd RM3 off Cotswold Rd 128 FM55
Redding Cl, Dart. DA2 189 FS89
Redding Dr, Amer. HP6 55 AN37
Reddings, Hem.H. HP3 40 BM22
Welwyn Garden City AL8 29 CW08
Reddings, The, NW7 97 CT48
Borehamwood WD6 78 CM41
Reddings Av, Bushey WD23 76 CB43
Reddings Cl, NW7 97 CT49
Sch Reddings Prim & Nurs Sch, The, Hem.H. HP3 off Bennetts End Rd 40 BN22
Reddington Cl, S.Croy. CR2 220 DR109
Reddington Dr, Slou. SL3 152 AY76
Reddington Ho, N1 276 D10
Reddins Rd, SE15 312 C3
Redditch Ct, Hem.H. HP2 40 BM16
Reddons Rd, Beck. BR3 183 DY94
Reddown Rd, Couls. CR5 235 DK118
Reddy Rd, Erith DA8 167 FF79
Rede Ct, Wey. KT13 195 BP104
Redehall Rd, Smallfield RH6 269 DP148
Redenham Ho, SW15 off Tangley Gro 179 CT87
Rede Pl, W2 283 K9
Redesdale Gdns, Islw. TW7 157 CG80
Redesdale St, SW3 308 D2
Redfern Av, Houns. TW4 176 CA87
Redfern Cl, Uxb. UB8 134 BJ67
Redfern Gdns, Rom. RM2 106 FK54
Redfern Rd, NW10 138 CS66
SE6 183 EC87
Redfield La, SW5 295 K8
Redfield Ms, SW5 295 K8
Redford Av, Couls. CR5 219 DH114
Thornton Heath CR7 201 DM98
Wallington SM6 219 DL107
Redford Cl, Felt. TW13 175 BT89
H Redford Lo Psychiatric Hosp, N9 100 DU47
Redford Rd, Wind. SL4 151 AK81
Redford Wk, N1 277 H8
Redford Way, Uxb. UB8 134 BJ66
Redgate Dr, Brom. BR2 204 EH103
Sch Red Gates Sch, Croy. CR0 off Purley Way 219 DN106
Redgate Ter, SW15 179 CY86
Redgrave Cl, Croy. CR0 202 DT100
Redgrave Ct, Denh. UB9 off Patrons Way E 113 BF57
Redgrave Rd, SW15 159 CX83
Redhall Cl, Hat. AL10 45 CT21
Redhall Ct, Cat. CR3 236 DR123
Redhall Dr, Hat. AL10 45 CT22
Redhall End, St.Alb. AL4 off Roestock La 44 CS22
Redhall La, Chan.Cr. WD3 74 BL39
Redheath Cl, Wat. WD25 75 BT35
REDHILL, RH1 250 DG134
⇌ Redhill 250 DG133
Redhill 250 DG133
Red Hill, Chis. BR7 185 EN92
Denham UB9 113 BD61
Redhill Common, Red. RH1 266 DE135
Redhill Dr, Edg. HA8 96 CQ54
Sch Red Hill Prim Sch, Chis. BR7 off Red Hill 185 EP92
Redhill Rd, Cob. KT11 213 BP113
Red Hills, Hodd. EN11 48 DV19
Redhill St, NW1 285 K2
★ Red Ho, The (William Morris Ho), Bexh. DA6 166 EY84
Red Ho Cl, Knot.Grn HP9 88 AH51
Ware SG12 33 DY07
Red Ho La, Bexh. DA6 166 EX84
Walton-on-Thames KT12 195 BU103
Red Ho Rd, Croy. CR0 201 DK100
Redhouse Rd, Tats. TN16 238 EJ120
Red Ho Sq, N1 277 K5
Redington Gdns, NW3 120 DB63
Redington Rd, NW3 120 DB63
Redland Gdns, W.Mol. KT8 off Dunstable Rd 196 BZ98
Redlands, Couls. CR5 235 DL116
Sch Redlands C of E Prim Sch, The, Dor. RH4 off Goodwyns Rd 263 CH139
Redlands Ct, Brom. BR1 184 EF94
Redlands La, Mid Holm. RH5 263 CG142
Sch Redlands Prim Sch, E1 289 H6
Redlands Rd, Enf. EN3 83 DY39
Sevenoaks TN13 256 FF124
Redlands Way, SW2 181 DM87
Red La, Clay. KT10 215 CG107
Dorking RH5 264 CL142
Oxted RH8 254 EH133
Redleaf Cl, Belv. DA17 166 FA79
Fetcham KT22 231 CE124
Red Leaf Cl, Slou. SL3 off Pickford Dr 133 AZ74
Redleaves Av, Ashf. TW15 175 BP93
Redlees Cl, Islw. TW7 157 CG84
Red Leys, Uxb. UB8 134 BL66
● Red Lion Business Pk, Surb. KT6 198 CM103
Red Lion Cl, SE17 311 K2
Aldenham WD25 off Church La 76 CC37
Orpington BR5 206 EW100
Red Lion Ct, EC4 286 F8
Hatfield AL9 45 CW16
Red Lion Cres, Harl. CM17 52 EW17
Red Lion Dr, Hem.H. HP3 58 BM25
Red Lion Hill, N2 98 DD54
Red Lion La, SE18 165 EN80
Chobham GU24 210 AS109
Harlow CM17 52 EW17
Hemel Hempstead HP3 58 BM26
Sarratt WD3 74 BG35

R

Red Lion Par, Pnr. HA5 116 BY55
Red Lion Pl, SE18
 off Shooters Hill Rd 165 EN81
Red Lion Rd, Chobham GU24 210 AS109
 Surbiton KT6 198 CM103
Red Lion Row, SE17 311 K2
Red Lion Sq, SW18
 off Wandsworth High St 180 DA85
 WC1 286 C7
Red Lion St, WC1 286 C6
 Chesham HP5 54 AP32
 Richmond TW9 177 CK85
Red Lion Way,
 Woob.Grn HP10 110 AE57
Red Lion Yd, W1 297 H2
Red Lo Cres, Bex. DA5 187 FD90
Red Lo Gdns, Berk. HP4 38 AU20
Red Lo Rd, Beck. BR3 203 ED100
 Bexley DA5 187 FD90
 West Wickham BR4 203 EC102
Redman Cl, Nthlt. UB5 136 BW68
Redmans La, Shore. TN14 225 FE107
Redmans Rd, E1 288 G6
Redmead La, E1 300 C3
Redmead Rd, Hayes UB3 155 BS77
Redmore Rd, W6 159 CV77
Red Oak Cl, Croy. CR0 203 EA103
 Orpington BR6 205 EP104
Red Oaks Mead,
 They.B. CM16 85 ER37
Red Path, E9 279 M4
Red Pl, W1 284 G10
Redpoll Way, Erith DA18 166 EX76
Red Post Hill, SE21 182 DR85
 SE24 162 DR84
Redricks La, Saw. CM21 35 ES09
Redriffe Rd, E13 281 M9
Redriff Est, SE16 301 M6
Sch Redriff Prim Sch, SE16 301 M4
Redriff Rd, SE16 301 K7
 Romford RM7 105 FB54
Red Rd, Borwd. WD6 78 CM41
 Warley CM14 108 FV49
Redroofs Cl, Beck. BR3 203 EB95
Jct Red Rover, SW15 159 CT83
Redruth Cl, N22 99 DM52
Redruth Gdns, Clay. KT10 215 CF108
 Romford RM3 106 FM50
Redruth Rd, E9 279 H8
 Romford RM3 106 FM50
Redruth Wk, Rom. RM3 106 FN50
Redsan Cl, S.Croy. CR2 220 DR108
Red Sq, N16 122 DR62
Redstart Cl, E6 292 G6
 SE14 313 L4
 New Addington CR0 221 ED110
Redstart Mans, Ilf. IG1
 off Mill Rd 125 EN62
Redstone Hill, Red. RH1 250 DG134
Redstone Hollow, Red. RH1 266 DG135
Redstone Manor, Red. RH1 250 DG134
Redstone Pk, Red. RH1 250 DG134
Redstone Rd, Red. RH1 266 DG135
Redston Rd, N8 121 DK56
REDSTREET, Grav. DA13 190 GB93
Red St, Sthflt DA13 190 GA93
Redtiles Gdns, Ken. CR8 235 DP115
Redvers Rd, N22 99 DN54
 Warlingham CR6 236 DW118
Redvers St, N1 287 P2
Redwald Rd, E5 279 K1
Redway Dr, Twick. TW2 176 CC87
Red Willow, Harl. CM19 51 EM18
Redwing Cl, S.Croy. CR2 221 DX111
Redwing Gdns, W.Byf. KT14 212 BH112
Redwing Gro, Abb.L. WD5 59 BU31
Redwing Ms, SE5 311 J9
Redwing Path, SE28 165 ER75
Redwing Ri, Guil. GU4 243 BD132
Redwing Rd, Wall. SM6 219 DL108
Redwood, Burn. SL1 130 AG68
 Egham TW20 193 BE96
Redwood Chase, S.Ock. RM15 149 FW70
Redwood Cl, E3 280 A10
 N14 99 DK45
 SE16 301 M3
 Kenley CR8 220 DQ114
 St. Albans AL1 43 CJ20
 Sidcup DA15 186 EU87
 Uxbridge UB10 135 BP68
 Watford WD19 94 BW49
Redwood Ct, NW6 272 E7
Redwood Dr, Hem.H. HP3 40 BL22
 Epsom KT19 216 CQ110
Redwood Est, Houns. TW5 155 BV79
Redwood Gdns, E4 83 EB44
 Chigwell IG7 104 EU50
 Slough SL1
 off Godolphin Rd 131 AR73
Redwood Gro, W5 157 CH76
 Chilworth GU4 259 BC140
Redwood Ms, SW4 309 K10
 Ashford TW15 off Napier Wk 175 BR94
Redwood Mt, Reig. RH2 250 DA131
Redwood Pl, Beac. HP9 89 AK54
Redwood Ri, Borwd. WD6 78 CN37
Redwoods, SW15 179 CU88
 Addlestone KT15 212 BG107
 Hertford SG14 32 DQ08
Redwoods, The, Wind. SL4 151 AR83
Redwoods Cl, Buck.H. IG9 102 EH47
Redwood Wk, Surb. KT6 197 CK102
Redwood Way, Barn. EN5 79 CX43
Reece Ms, SW7 296 A8
Reed Av, Orp. BR6 205 ES104
Reed Cl, E16 291 N7
 SE12 184 EG85
 Iver SL0 133 BE72
 London Colney AL2 62 CL27
Reed Ct, Green. DA9 169 FW84
Reed Dr, Red. RH1 266 DG137
Reede Gdns, Dag. RM10 127 FB64
Reede Rd, Dag. RM10 146 FA65
Reede Way, Dag. RM10 127 FB64
⇌ Reedham 219 DM113
Reedham Cl, N17 122 DV56
 Bricket Wood AL2 60 CA29
Reedham Dr, Pur. CR8 219 DM113
Reedham Pk Av, Pur. CR8 235 DN116
Reedham Rd, Burn. SL1 130 AJ69
Reedham St, SE15 312 C9
Reedholm Vil, N16 122 DR63
Reed Ho, SW19
 off Durnsford Rd 180 DB91
Reed Pl, SW4 161 DK84
 Shepperton TW17 194 BM102
 West Byfleet KT14 211 BE113
Reed Pond Wk, Rom. RM2 105 FF54
Reed Rd, N17 100 DT54
Reeds, The, Welw.G.C. AL7 29 CX10
Reeds Cres, Wat. WD24 76 BW40
Reedsfield Cl, Ashf. TW15
 off Reedsfield Rd 175 BP91
Reedsfield Rd, Ashf. TW15 175 BP91
Reeds Meadow, S.Merst. RH1 251 DJ130
Reeds Pl, NW1 275 L6
Sch Reed's Sch, Cob. KT11
 off Sandy La 214 CA112
Reeds Wk, Wat. WD24 76 BW40
Reed Way, Slou. SL1 131 AM73
Reedworth St, SE11 298 F9
Reef Ho, E14
 off Manchester Rd 302 F6
Ree La Cotts, Loug. IG10
 off Englands La 85 EN39
Reenglass Rd, Stan. HA7 95 CK49
Rees Dr, Stan. HA7 96 CL49
Rees Gdns, Croy. CR0 202 DT100
Reesland Cl, E12 145 EN65
Rees St, N1 277 K9
Reets Fm Cl, NW9 118 CS58
Reeve Rd, Reig. RH2 266 DC138
Reeves Av, NW9 118 CR59
Tm Reeves Corner 201 DP103
Reeves Cor, Croy. CR0
 off Roman Way 201 DP103
Reeves Cres, Swan. BR8 207 FD97
Reeves La, Roydon CM19 50 EJ19
Reeves Ms, W1 296 G1
Reeves Rd, E3 290 C4
 SE18 165 EP79
Reflection, The, E16 305 N4
Reform Row, N17 100 DT54
Reform St, SW11 308 E8
Regal Cl, E1 288 D6
 W5 137 CK71
Regal Ct, N18 100 DT50
Regal Cres, Wall. SM6 201 DH104
Regal Dr, N11 99 DH50
Regalfield Cl, Guil. GU2 242 AU130
Regal Ho, SW6
 off Lensbury Av 307 P8
 Ilford IG2 off Royal Cres 125 ER58
Regal La, NW1 275 H9
Regal Pl, E3 289 P3
 SW6 307 M5
Regal Row, SE15 312 G6
Regal Way, Har. HA3 118 CL58
 Watford WD24 76 BW38
Regan Cl, Guil. GU2 242 AV129
Regan Ho, N18 100 DT51
Regan Way, N1 287 N1
Regarder Rd, Chig. IG7 104 EU50
Regarth Av, Rom. RM1 127 FE58
Regatta Ho, Tedd. TW11
 off Twickenham Rd 177 CG91
Regency Cl, W5 138 CL72
 Chigwell IG7 103 EQ50
 Hampton TW12 176 BZ92
Regency Ct, E18 102 EG54
 Brentwood CM14 108 FW47
 Broxbourne EN10
 off Berners Way 49 DZ23
 Harlow CM18 52 EU18
 Hemel Hempstead HP2
 off Alexandra Rd 40 BK20
 Sutton SM1 off Brunswick Rd 218 DB105
Regency Cres, NW4 97 CX54
Regency Dr, Ruis. HA4 115 BS60
 West Byfleet KT14 211 BF113
Regency Gdns, Horn. RM11 128 FJ59
 Walton-on-Thames KT12 196 BW102
 Weybridge KT13 213 BQ106
Regency Ho, SW6
 off The Boulevard 307 P7
Regency Lo, Buck.H. IG9 102 EK47
Regency Ms, NW10 139 CU65
 SW9 311 H5
 Beckenham BR3 203 EC95
 Isleworth TW7 off
 Queensbridge Pk 177 CE85
Regency Pl, SW1 297 P8
Regency St, NW10 138 CS70
 SW1 297 N8
Regency Ter, SW7
 off Fulham Rd 296 A10
Regency Wk, Croy. CR0 203 DY100
 Richmond TW10
 off Grosvenor Rd 178 CL85
Regency Way, Bexh. DA6 166 EX83
 Woking GU22 227 BD115
Regeneration Rd, SE16 301 J9
Regent Av, Uxb. UB10 135 BP66
● Regent Business Cen,
 Hayes UB3 off Pump La 155 BU75
Regent Cl, N12
 off Nether St 98 DC50
 Grays RM16 170 GC75
 Harrow HA3 118 CL58
 Hounslow TW4 155 BV81
 Kings Langley WD4 58 BN29
 New Haw KT15 212 BK109
 Redhill RH1 251 DJ129
 St. Albans AL4 43 CJ16
Coll Regent Coll, Har. HA2
 off Imperial Dr 116 CA59
Regent Ct, Slou. SL1 132 AS72
 Welwyn Garden City AL7 29 CY10
 Windsor SL4 151 AR81
Regent Cres, Red. RH1 250 DF132
Regent Gdns, Ilf. IG3 126 EU58
Regent Gate, Wal.Cr. EN8 67 DX34
● Regent Pk, Lthd. KT22 231 CG118
Regent Pk, Barn. EN4 80 DB39
Regent Pl, SW19
 off Haydons Rd 180 DB92
 W1 285 M10
 Croydon CR0 off Grant Rd 202 DT102
Regent Rd, SE24 181 DP86
 Epping CM16 69 ET30
 Surbiton KT5 198 CM99
Regents Av, N13 99 DM50
Regents Br Gdns, SW8 310 B4
Regents Cl, Hayes UB4 135 BS71
 Radlett WD7 61 CG34
 South Croydon CR2 220 DS107
 Whyteleafe CR3 236 DS118
Regents Dr, Kes. BR2 222 EK106
 Woodford Green IG8 103 EN51
Regents Ms, NW8 273 P10
 Horley RH6 off Victoria Rd 268 DG148
REGENT'S PARK, NW1 285 H1
⊖ Regent's Park 285 J5
★ Regent's Park, The, NW1 284 F1
Regent's Pk Est, NW1 285 K3
Regents Pk Rd, N3 119 CZ55
 NW1 274 F8
Regents Pk Ter, NW1 275 J8
Regents Pl, Loug. IG10 102 EK45
Regent's Pl, SE3 315 N8
Regent Sq, E3 290 C3
 WC1 286 B3
 Belvedere DA17 167 FB77
Regents Row, E8 278 C9
Regent St, NW10 282 D3
 SW1 297 N1
 W1 285 K8
 W4 158 CN78
 Watford WD24 75 BV38
Uni Regent's Uni, NW1 284 G4
Regents Wf, N1 276 C10
Regina Cl, Barn. EN5 79 CX41
Sch Regina Coeli Catholic
 Prim Sch, S.Croy. CR2
 off Pampisford Rd 219 DP108
Reginald Ellingworth St,
 Dag. RM9 146 EV67
Reginald Ms, Harl. CM17
 off Green St 36 EX14
Reginald Rd, E7 281 N6
 SE8 314 A5
 Northwood HA6 93 BT53
 Romford RM3 106 FN53
Reginald Sq, SE8 314 A5
Regina Pt, SE16 301 H6
Regina Rd, N4 121 DM60
 SE25 202 DU97
 W13 137 CG74
 Southall UB2 156 BY77
Regina Ter, W13 137 CG74
Regis Pl, SW2 161 DM84
Regis Rd, NW5 275 J3
Regius Ct, Penn HP10 88 AD47
Regnart Bldgs, NW1 285 M4
Reid Av, Cat. CR3 236 DR121
Reid Cl, Couls. CR5 235 DH116
 Hayes UB3 135 BS72
 Pinner HA5 115 BU56
Reidhaven Rd, SE18 165 ES77
REIGATE, RH2 250 DA134
⇌ Reigate 250 DA133
Reigate Av, Sutt. SM1 200 DA102
● Reigate Business Ms,
 Reig. RH2 off Albert Rd N 249 CZ133
Coll Reigate Coll, Reig. RH2
 off Castlefield Rd 250 DB134
Sch Reigate Gram Sch,
 Reig. RH2 off Reigate Rd 250 DC134
Reigate Heath, Reig. RH2 265 CX135
Reigate Hill, Reig. RH2 250 DB130
Reigate Hill Cl, Reig. RH2 250 DA131
Jct Reigate Hill Interchange,
 Tad. KT20 250 DB129
Sch Reigate Parish Ch Sch,
 Reig. RH2 off Blackborough Rd 250 DC134
Sch Reigate Priory Sch,
 Reig. RH2 off Bell St 250 DA134
Reigate Rd, Bet. RH3 248 CS132
 Bromley BR1 184 EF90
 Dorking RH4 263 CJ135
 Epsom KT17, KT18 217 CT110
 Hookwood RH6 268 DC146
 Ilford IG3 125 ET61
 Leatherhead KT22 231 CJ123
 Redhill RH1 250 DB134
 Reigate RH2 250 DB134
 Sidlow RH2 266 DB141
 Tadworth KT20 233 CX117
Sch Reigate St. Mary's Prep &
 Choir Sch, Reig. RH2
 off Chart La 250 DB134
Sch Reigate Sch, Reig. RH2
 off Pendleton Rd 266 DC137
Reigate Way, Wall. SM6 219 DL106
Reighton Rd, E5 122 DU62
Reindeer Cl, E13 281 P9
Reindorp Cl, Guil. GU2
 off Old Ct Rd 258 AU135
Reinickendorf Av, SE9 185 EQ85
Reizel Cl, N16 122 DT60
Relay Rd, W12 294 B1
Relf Rd, SE15 312 D10
Reliance Sq, EC2 287 P4
Relko Ct, Epsom KT19 216 CR110
Relko Gdns, Sutt. SM1 218 DD106
Relton Ms, SW7 296 D6
Rembrandt Cl, E14 302 G7
 SW1 296 G9
Rembrandt Ct, Epsom KT19 217 CT107
Rembrandt Dr, Nthflt DA11 190 GD90
Rembrandt Rd, SE13 164 EE84
 Edgware HA8 96 CN54
Rembrandt Way, Walt. KT12 195 BV104
Remington Rd, E6 292 G8
 N15 122 DR58
Remington St, N1 287 H1
Remnant St, WC2 286 C8
Remus Cl, St.Alb. AL1 43 CD24
Remus Rd, E3 280 A7
Renaissance Ct, Houns. TW3
 off Prince Regent Rd 156 CC83
Renaissance Wk, SE10 303 M6
Rendel Ho, Bans. SM7 234 DC118
Rendle Cl, Croy. CR0 202 DT99
Rendlesham Av, Rad. WD7 77 CF37
Rendlesham Cl, Ware SG12 32 DV05
Rendlesham Rd, E5 122 DU63
 Enfield EN2 81 DP39
Rendlesham Way, Chorl. WD3 73 BC44
Renforth St, SE16 301 H5
Renfree Way, Shep. TW17 194 BM101
Renfrew Cl, E6 293 L9
Renfrew Ho, E17
 off Sherwood Cl 101 DZ54
Renfrew Rd, SE11 298 G8
 Hounslow TW4 156 BX82
 Kingston upon Thames KT2 178 CP94
Renmans, The, Ashtd. KT21 232 CM116
Renmuir St, SW17 180 DF93
Rennell St, SE13 163 EC83
Rennels Way, Islw. TW7 157 CE82
Renness Rd, E17 123 DY55
Rennets Cl, SE9 185 ES85
Rennets Wd Rd, SE9 185 ER85
Rennie Cl, Ashf. TW15 174 BK90
Rennie Ct, SE1 off Upper Grd 298 G2
 Enfield EN3 off Brunswick Rd 83 EA38
Rennie Dr, Dart. DA1
 off Marsh St N 168 FN82
Rennie Est, SE16 300 F9
Rennie Ho, SE1 off Bath Ter 299 J7
Rennie St, SE1 298 G2
Rennie Ter, Red. RH1 266 DG135
Rennison Cl, Chsht EN7 66 DT27
Renovation, The, E16 305 N4
Renown Cl, Croy. CR0 201 DP102
 Romford RM7 104 FA53
Rensburg Rd, E17 123 DX57
Renshaw Cl, Belv. DA17
 off Grove Rd 166 EZ79
Renters Av, NW4 119 CW58
Renton Dr, Orp. BR5 206 EX101
● Renwick Ind Est, Bark. IG11 146 EV67
Renwick Rd, Bark. IG11 146 EV70
Repens Way, Hayes UB4 136 BX70
Rephidim St, SE1 299 N7
Replingham Rd, SW18 179 CZ88
Reporton Rd, SW6 306 F5
Repository Rd, SE18 165 EM79
Repton Av, Hayes UB3 155 BR77
 Romford RM2 127 FG55
 Wembley HA0 117 CJ63
Repton Cl, Cars. SM5 218 DE106
Repton Ct, Beck. BR3 203 EB95
 Ilford IG5 off Repton Gro 103 EM53
Repton Dr, Rom. RM2 127 FG56
Repton Gdns, Rom. RM2 127 FG55
Repton Grn, St.Alb. AL3 43 CD16
Repton Gro, Ilf. IG5 103 EM53
Repton Pl, Amer. HP7 72 AU39
Repton Rd, Har. HA3 118 CM56
 Orpington BR6 206 EU104
Repton St, E14 289 M8
Repton Way, Crox.Grn WD3 74 BN43
Repulse Cl, Rom. RM5 104 FA53
Reservoir Cl, Green. DA9 189 FW86
 Thornton Heath CR7 202 DR98
Reservoir Rd, N14 81 DJ43
 SE4 313 L9
 Ruislip HA4 115 BQ57
Resham Cl, Sthl. UB2 156 BW76
Residence, Pnr. HA5
 off Marsh Rd 116 BY56
Resolution Wk, SE18 305 J6
Resolution Way, SE8 314 A4
Reson Way, Hem.H. HP1 40 BH21
Restavon Pk,
 Berry's Grn TN16 239 EP116
Restell Cl, SE3 315 K2
Restmor Way, Wall. SM6 200 DG103
Reston Cl, Borwd. WD6 78 CN38
Reston Path, Borwd. WD6 78 CN38
Reston Pl, SW7 295 N5
Restons Cres, SE9 185 ER86
Restoration Sq, SW11 308 B7
Restormel Cl, Houns. TW3 176 CA85
Retcar Cl, N19
 off Dartmouth Pk Hill 121 DH61
Retcar Pl, N19 121 DH61
Retford Cl, Borwd. WD6 78 CN38
 Romford RM3 106 FN51
Retford Path, Rom. RM3 106 FN51
Retford Rd, Rom. RM3 106 FM51
Retford St, N1 287 P1
Retingham Way, E4 101 EB47
Retreat, The, NW9 118 CR57
 SW14 off South Worple Way 158 CS83
 Addlestone KT15 212 BK106
 Amersham HP6 72 AY39
 Brentwood CM14 108 FV46
 Englefield Green TW20 172 AX92
 Fifield SL6 150 AD80
 Grays RM17 170 GB79
 Harrow HA2 116 CA59
 Hutton CM13 109 GB44
 Kings Langley WD4 59 BQ31
 Orpington BR6 224 EV107
 Surbiton KT5 198 CM100
 Thornton Heath CR7 202 DR98
 Worcester Park KT4 199 CV104
Retreat Cl, Har. HA3 117 CJ57
Retreat Pl, E9 279 H5
Retreat Rd, Rich. TW9 177 CK85
Retreat Way, Chig. IG7 104 EV48
Reubens Rd, Hutt. CM13 109 GB44
Reunion Row, E1
 off Tobacco Dock 300 F1
Reuters Plaza, E14 302 B3
Reveley Sq, SE16 301 M5
Revell Cl, Fetch. KT22 230 CB122
Revell Dr, Fetch. KT22 230 CB122
Revell Ri, SE18 165 ET79
Revell Rd, Kings.T. KT1 198 CP95
 Sutton SM1 217 CZ107
Revelon Rd, SE4 163 DY84
Revel Rd, Woob.Grn HP10 110 AD55
Revels Cl, Hert. SG14 32 DR07
Revels Rd, Hert. SG14 32 DR07
Revelstoke Rd, SW18 179 CZ89
Reventlow Rd, SE9 185 EQ88
Reverdy Rd, SE1 300 C9
Reverend Cl, Har. HA2 116 CB62
Revere Way, Epsom KT19 216 CS109
Revesby Rd, Cars. SM5 200 DD100
Review Lodge, Dag. RM10 147 FA68
Review Rd, NW2 119 CT61
 Dagenham RM10 147 FB67
Rewell St, SW6 307 N5
Rewley Rd, Cars. SM5 200 DD100
Rex Av, Ashf. TW15 174 BN93
Rex Cl, Rom. RM5 105 FB52
Rex Pl, W1 297 H1
Reydon Av, E11 124 EJ58
Reynard Cl, SE4 313 M10
 Bromley BR1 205 EM97
Reynard Ct, Pur. CR8 219 DN111
Reynard Dr, SE19 182 DT94
Reynard Pl, SE14
 off Milton Ct Rd 313 M3
Reynardson Rd, N17 100 DQ52
Reynards Way, Brick.Wd AL2 60 BZ29
Reynard Way, Hert. SG13 32 DU09
Reynolah Gdns, SE7 304 B10
Reynolds Av, E12 125 EN64
 Chessington KT9 216 CL108
 Redhill RH1 251 DH132
 Romford RM6 126 EW59
Reynolds Cl, NW11 120 DB59
 SW19 200 DD95
 Carshalton SM5 200 DF102
 Hemel Hempstead HP1 40 BG19
Reynolds Ct, E11
 off Cobbold Rd 124 EF62
 Romford RM6 126 EX55
Reynolds Cres, Sand. AL4 43 CH15
Reynolds Dr, Edg. HA8 118 CM55
Reynolds Ho, Enf. EN1
 off Ayley Cft 82 DU43
Reynolds Pl, SE3 164 EH80
 Richmond TW10
 off Cambrian Rd 178 CM86
Reynolds Rd, SE15 182 DW85
 W4 158 CQ76
 Beaconsfield HP9 88 AJ52
 Hayes UB4 136 BW70
 New Malden KT3 198 CR101
Reynolds Wk, Chesh. HP5
 off Great Hivings 54 AN27
Reynolds Way, Croy. CR0 220 DS105
Rhapsody Cres, Warley CM14 108 FV50
Rheidol Ms, N1 277 J10
Rheidol Ter, N1 277 H10
Rheingold Way, Wall. SM6 219 DL109
Rheola Cl, N17 100 DT53
Rhoda St, E2 288 B4
Rhodes Av, N22 99 DJ53
Sch Rhodes Av Prim Sch, N22
 off Rhodes Av 99 DJ53
Rhodes Cl, Egh. TW20 173 BB92
Rhodesia Rd, E11 123 ED61
 SW9 310 B9
Rhodes Moorhouse Ct,
 Mord. SM4 200 DA100
Rhodes St, N7 276 D3
Rhodes Way, Wat. WD24 76 BX40
Rhodeswell Rd, E14 289 M6
Rhododendron Ride,
 Egh. TW20 172 AT94
 Slough SL3 133 AZ69
Rhodrons Av, Chess. KT9 216 CL106
Rhondda Gro, E3 289 M3
Sch Rhyl Prim Sch, NW5 275 H4
Rhyl Rd, Perivale UB6 137 CF68
Rhyl St, NW5 275 H4
Rhymes, The, Hem.H. HP1 40 BH18
Rhys Av, N11 99 DK52
Rialto Rd, Mitch. CR4 200 DG96
Ribble Cl, Wdf.Grn. IG8
 off Prospect Rd 102 EJ51
Ribbledale, Lon.Col. AL2 62 CM27
Ribblesdale, Dor. RH4
 off Roman Rd 263 CH138
 Hemel Hempstead HP2 40 BL17
Ribblesdale Av, N11 98 DG51
 Northolt UB5 136 CB65
Ribblesdale Rd, N8 121 DM56
 SW16 181 DH93
 Dartford DA2 188 FQ88
Ribbon Dance Ms, SE5 311 M7
Ribbons Wk, E20 280 E3
Ribston Cl, Brom. BR2 205 EM102
 Shenley WD7 61 CK33
Rib Vale, Hert. SG14 32 DR06
Ricardo Path, SE28
 off Byron Cl 146 EW74
Ricardo Rd, Old Wind. SL4 172 AV86
Ricardo St, E14 290 C9
Sch Ricards Lo High Sch,
 SW19 off Lake Rd 179 CZ92
Ricards Rd, SW19 179 CZ92
Ricebridge La, Reig. RH2 265 CV137
Rice Cl, Hem.H. HP2 40 BM19
Rices Cor, Shalf. GU4 259 BA141
Sch Richard Alibon Prim Sch,
 Dag. RM10 off Alibon Rd 126 FA64
Sch Richard Atkins Prim Sch,
 SW2 off New Pk Rd 181 DL87
Sch Richard Challoner Sch,
 N.Mal. KT3 off Manor Dr N 198 CR101
Richard Cl, SE18 305 H9
Sch Richard Cloudesley Sch,
 EC1 287 J5
Sch Richard Cobden Prim Sch,
 NW1 275 M10
Richard Fell Ho, E12
 off Walton Rd 125 EN63
Richard Foster Cl, E17 123 DZ59
Sch Richard Hale Sch,
 Hert. SG13 off Hale Rd 32 DR10
Richard Ho Dr, E16 292 F9
Richard Meyjes Rd, Guil. GU2 258 AS135
Richard Robert Res, The, E15
 off Salway Pl 281 H5
Richard Ryan Pl, Dag. RM9 146 EY67
Richards Av, Rom. RM7 127 FC57
Richards Cl, Bushey WD23 95 CD45
 Harlington UB3 155 BR79
 Harrow HA1 117 CG57
 Uxbridge UB10 134 BN67
Richards Fld, Epsom KT19 216 CR109
Richardson Cl, E8 278 A9
 Greenhithe DA9
 off Steele Av 189 FU85
 London Colney AL2 62 CL27
Richardson Cres, Chsht EN7 65 DP25
Richardson Gdns, Dag. RM10 147 FB65
Richardson Pl, Coln.Hth AL4 44 CP22
Richardson Rd, E15 281 J10
Richardson's Ms, W1 285 L5
Richards Pl, E17 123 EA55
 SW3 296 D8
Richards Rd,
 Stoke D'Ab. KT11 214 CB114
Richards St, Hat. AL10 44 CR16
Richard Stagg Cl, St.Alb. AL1 43 CJ22
Richard St, E1 288 E9
Richards Way, Slou. SL1 131 AN74
Richbell Cl, Ashtd. KT21 231 CK118
Richbell Pl, WC1 286 C6
Richborne Ter, SW8 310 D4
Richborough Cl, Orp. BR5 206 EX98
Richborough Ho, E5
 off Pembury Rd 278 E2
Richborough Rd, NW2 272 D1
Richens Cl, Houns. TW3 157 CD82
Riches Rd, Ilf. IG1 125 EQ61
Richfield Rd, Bushey WD23 94 CC45
Richford Gate, W6 294 A6
Richford Rd, E15 281 L8
Richford St, W6 294 A5
● Rich Ind Est, SE1 299 P7
RICHINGS PARK, Iver SL0 153 BE76
Richings Pl, Iver SL0 153 BE76
Richings Way, Iver SL0 153 BF76
Richland Av, Couls. CR5 218 DG114
Richlands Av, Epsom KT17 217 CU105
Rich La, SW5 307 L1
Richmer Rd, Erith DA8 167 FG80
★ Rich Mix Cen, The, E1
 off Bethnal Grn Rd 288 B4
RICHMOND, TW9 & TW10 178 CL86
⇌ Richmond 158 CL84
⊖ Richmond 158 CL84
⊖ Richmond 158 CL84
⛴ Richmond 177 CK85
Coll Richmond Adult Comm
 Coll, Clifden, Twick. TW1
 off Clifden Rd 177 CF88
 Parkshot, Rich. TW9
 off Parkshot 157 CK84

Richmond Av, E4 101 ED50
N1 276 C8
NW10 272 A5
SW20 199 CY95
Brentwood CM14 108 FW46
Feltham TW14 175 BS86
Uxbridge UB10 135 BP65
Richmond Br, Rich. TW9 177 CK86
Twickenham TW1 177 CK86
Richmond Bldgs, W1 285 N9
Jct Richmond Circ, Rich. TW9 158 CL84
Richmond Cl, E17 123 DZ58
Amersham HP6 72 AT38
Biggin Hill TN16 238 EH119
Borehamwood WD6 78 CR43
Cheshunt EN8 66 DW29
Epsom KT18 216 CS114
Fetcham KT22 230 CC124
Richmond Ct, Brox. EN10 49 DZ20
Hatfield AL10 off Cooks Way 45 CV20
Mitcham CR4 off Phipps Br Rd 200 DD97
Potters Bar EN6 64 DC31
Richmond Cres, E4 101 ED50
N1 276 D8
N9 100 DU46
Epsom KT19 216 CM112
Slough SL1 132 AU74
Staines-upon-Thames TW18 173 BF92
Richmond Dr, Grav. DA12 191 GL89
Shepperton TW17 195 BQ100
Watford WD17 75 BS39
Woodford Green IG8 103 EN52
Richmond Gdns, NW4 119 CU57
Harrow HA3 95 CF51
Richmond Grn, Croy. CR0 201 DL104
Richmond Gro, N1 276 G7
Surbiton KT5 off Ewell Rd 198 CM100
Richmond Hill, Rich. TW10 178 CL86
Richmond Hill Ct, Rich. TW10 178 CL86
Sch Richmond Ho, Hmptn. TW12 off Buckingham Rd 176 BZ92
Richmond Ho, NW1 off Park Village E 285 K1
Richmond Ms, W1 285 N9
Teddington TW11 off Church Rd 177 CF92
★ Richmond Park, Rich. TW10 178 CN88
Richmond Pk, Kings.T. KT2 178 CN88
Loughton IG10 off Fallow Flds 102 EK45
Richmond TW10 178 CN88
Sch Richmond Pk Acad, SW14 off Park Av 158 CS84
Richmond Pk Rd, SW14 178 CQ85
Kingston upon Thames KT2 178 CL94
Richmond Pl, SE18 165 EQ77
Richmond Rd, E4 101 ED46
E7 124 EH64
E8 278 A6
E11 123 ED61
N2 98 DC54
N11 99 DL51
N15 122 DS58
SW20 199 CV95
W5 158 CL75
Coulsdon CR5 235 DH115
Croydon CR0 201 DL104
Grays RM17 170 GC79
Ilford IG1 125 EQ62
Isleworth TW7 157 CG83
Kingston upon Thames KT2 177 CK92
New Barnet EN5 80 DB43
Potters Bar EN6 64 DC31
Romford RM1 127 FF58
Staines-upon-Thames TW18 173 BF92
Thornton Heath CR7 201 DP97
Twickenham TW1 177 CJ86
H Richmond Royal Hosp, Rich. TW9 158 CL83
Richmond St, E13 291 P1
Richmond Ter, SW1 298 A4
Uni Richmond Uni - The American Int Uni In London, Kensington Campus, W8 295 M6
Richmond Hill Campus, Rich. TW10 off Queens Rd 178 CL87
Coll Richmond upon Thames Coll, Twick. TW2 off Egerton Rd 177 CE87
Richmond Wk, St.Alb. AL4 43 CK16
Richmond Way, E11 124 EG61
W12 294 D5
W14 294 D6
Croxley Green WD3 75 BQ42
Fetcham KT22 230 CB123
Richmount Gdns, SE3 164 EG83
Rich St, E14 289 P10
Rickard Cl, NW4 119 CV56
SW2 181 DM88
West Drayton UB7 154 BK76
Rickards Cl, Surb. KT6 198 CL102
Ricketts Hill Rd, Tats. TN16 238 EK118
Rickett St, SW6 307 K2
Rickfield Cl, Hat. AL10 45 CU20
Rickman Ct, Add. KT15 off Rickman Cres 194 BH104
Rickman Cres, Add. KT15 194 BH104
Rickman Hill, Couls. CR5 235 DH118
Rickman Hill Rd, Chipstead CR5 235 DH118
Rickmans La, Stoke P. SL2 112 AS64
Rickman St, E1 289 H4
RICKMANSWORTH, WD3 92 BL45
⇌ Rickmansworth 92 BK45
⊖ Rickmansworth 92 BK45
Rickmansworth La, Chal.St.P. SL9 91 AZ50
Rickmansworth Pk, Rick. WD3 92 BK45
Sch Rickmansworth Pk JMI Sch, Rick. WD3 off Park Rd 92 BL45
Sch Rickmansworth PNEU Sch, Rick. WD3 off The Drive 74 BJ44
Rickmansworth Rd, Amer. HP6 55 AQ37
Chorleywood WD3 73 BE41
Harefield UB9 92 BJ53
Northwood HA6 93 BR52
Pinner HA5 93 BV54
Watford WD17, WD18 75 BS42
Sch Rickmansworth Sch, Crox.Grn WD3 off Scots Hill 74 BM44
Rick Roberts Way, E15 280 F9
Ricksons La, W.Hors. KT24 245 BP127
Rickthorne Rd, N19 121 DL61
Rickwood, Horl. RH6 269 DH147
Rickyard Path, SE9 164 EL84
Ridding La, Grnf. UB6 117 CF64
Riddings, The, Cat. CR3 252 DT125
Riddings La, Harl. CM18 51 ET19
⇌ Riddlesdown 220 DR113
Riddlesdown Av, Pur. CR8 220 DQ112
Sch Riddlesdown High Sch, Pur. CR8 off Dunmail Dr 220 DS114
Riddlesdown Rd, Pur. CR8 220 DQ111
Riddons Rd, SE12 184 EJ90
Ride, The, Brent. TW8 157 CH78
Enfield EN3 82 DW41
Ride La, Far.Grn GU5 260 BK144
Rideout St, SE18 305 J9
Rider Cl, Sid. DA15 185 ES86
Riders Way, Gdse. RH9 252 DW131
Ridgdale St, E3 290 B1
RIDGE, Pot.B. EN6 62 CS34
Ridge, The, Barn. EN5 79 CZ43
Bexley DA5 186 EZ87
Coulsdon CR5 219 DL114
Epsom KT18 232 CP117
Fetcham KT22 231 CD124
Orpington BR6 205 ER103
Purley CR8 219 DJ110
Surbiton KT5 198 CN99
Twickenham TW2 177 CD87
Woking GU22 227 BB117
Woldingham CR3 253 EB126
Ridge Av, N21 100 DQ45
Dartford DA1 187 FF86
Ridgebank, Slou. SL1 131 AM73
Ridgebrook Rd, SE3 164 EJ84
Ridge Cl, NW4 97 CX54
NW9 118 CR56
SE28 165 ER75
Strood Green RH3 264 CP138
Woking GU22 226 AV121
Ridge Crest, Enf. EN2 81 DM39
Ridgecroft Cl, Bex. DA5 187 FC88
Ridgefield, Wat. WD17 75 BS37
Ridgegate Cl, Reig. RH2 250 DD132
RIDGE GREEN, Red. RH1 267 DL137
Ridge Grn, S.Nutfld RH1 267 DL137
Ridge Grn Cl, S.Nutfld RH1 267 DL137
RIDGE HILL, Rad. WD7 62 CQ30
Ridge Hill, NW11 119 CY60
Ridgehurst Av, Wat. WD25 59 BT34
Ridgelands, Fetch. KT22 231 CD124
Ridge La, Wat. WD17 75 BS38
Ridge Langley, S.Croy. CR2 220 DU109
Ridge Lea, Hem.H. HP1 39 BF20
Ridgemead Cl, N14 99 DL47
Ridgemead Rd, Eng.Grn TW20 172 AU90
Ridgemont Gdns, Edg. HA8 96 CQ49
Ridgemont Pl, Horn. RM11 128 FK58
Ridgemount, Guil. GU2 258 AV135
Weybridge KT13 off Oatlands Dr 195 BS103
Ridgemount Av, Couls. CR5 235 DH117
Croydon CR0 203 DX102
Ridgemount Cl, SE20 182 DV94
Ridgemount End, Chal.St.P. SL9 90 AY50
Ridgemount Gdns, Enf. EN2 81 DP40
Ridgemount Way, Red. RH1 266 DD136
Ridge Pk, Pur. CR8 219 DK110
Ridge Rd, N8 121 DM58
N21 100 DQ46
NW2 119 CZ62
Mitcham CR4 181 DH94
Sutton SM3 199 CY102
Ridges, The, Art. GU3 258 AW139
Ridge St, Wat. WD24 75 BV38
Ridge's Yd, Croy. CR0 201 DP104
Ridgeview Cl, Barn. EN5 79 CX44
Ridgeview Lo, Lon.Col. AL2 62 CM28
Ridgeview Rd, N20 98 DB48
Ridge Way, SE19 off Vicars Oak Rd 182 DS93
Crayford DA1 187 FF86
Feltham TW13 176 BY90
Ridgeway, SE28 off Pettman Cres 165 ER77
Berkhamsted HP4 38 AT19
Bromley BR2 204 EG103
Epsom KT19 216 CQ112
Grays RM17 170 GE77
Horsell GU21 226 AX115
Hutton CM13 109 GB46
Iver SL0 133 BF73
Lane End DA2 189 FS92
Rickmansworth WD3 92 BH45
Virginia Water GU25 192 AY99
Welwyn Garden City AL7 30 DA09
Woodford Green IG8 102 EJ49
Ridgeway, The, E4 101 EB47
N3 98 DB52
N11 98 DF49
N14 99 DL47
NW7 97 CU49
NW9 119 CT56
NW11 119 CZ60
W3 158 CN75
Amersham HP7 55 AR40
Chalfont St. Peter SL9 112 AY55
Croydon CR0 201 DM104
Cuffley EN6 64 DE28
Enfield EN2 81 DN39
Fetcham KT22 231 CD123
Gidea Park RM2 127 FG56
Guildford GU1 259 BA135
Harold Wood RM3 106 FL53
Hertford SG14 31 DM08
Horley RH6 268 DG150
Kenton HA3 117 CJ58
North Harrow HA2 116 CA58
Oxshott KT22 214 CC114
Potters Bar EN6 64 DD34
Radlett WD7 77 CF37
Ruislip HA4 115 BU59
St. Albans AL4 43 CH17
Stanmore HA7 95 CJ51
Walton-on-Thames KT12 195 BT102
Watford WD17 75 BS37
Ridge Way, The, S.Croy. CR2 220 DS110
Ridgeway Av, Barn. EN4 80 DF44
Gravesend DA12 191 GH90
Ridgeway Cl, Chesh. HP5 54 AP28
Dorking RH4 263 CG138
Fetcham KT22 231 CE124
Hemel Hempstead HP3 off London Rd 58 BM25
Oxshott KT22 214 CC114
Woking GU21 226 AX116
Ridgeway Ct, Red. RH1 266 DE135
Ridgeway Cres, Orp. BR6 205 ES104
Ridgeway Cres Gdns, Orp. BR6 205 ES103
Ridgeway Dr, Brom. BR1 184 EH91
Dorking RH4 263 CG139
Ridgeway E, Sid. DA15 185 ET85
Ridgeway Gdns, N6 121 DJ59
Ilford IG4 124 EL57
Woking GU21 226 AX115
Sch Ridgeway Prim Sch, S.Croy. CR2 off Southcote Rd 220 DS110
Ridgeway Rd, SW9 161 DP83
Chesham HP5 54 AN28
Dorking RH4 263 CG139
Isleworth TW7 157 CE80
Redhill RH1 250 DE134
Ridgeway Rd N, Islw. TW7 157 CE79
Ridgeways, Harl. CM17 52 EY15
Ridgeway Wk, Nthlt. UB5 off Arnold Rd 136 BY65
Ridgeway W, Sid. DA15 185 ES85
Ridgewell Cl, N1 277 K8
SE26 183 DZ91
Dagenham RM10 147 FB67
Ridgewell Gro, Horn. RM12 off North Weald Cl 147 FH66
Ridgmont Rd, St.Alb. AL1 43 CE21
Ridgmount Gdns, WC1 285 N5
Ridgmount Pl, WC1 285 N6
Ridgmount Rd, SW18 180 DB85
Ridgmount St, WC1 285 N6
Ridgway, SW19 179 CX93
Pyrford GU22 227 BF115
Ridgway, The, Sutt. SM2 218 DD108
Ridgway Gdns, SW19 179 CX93
Ridgway Pl, SW19 179 CY93
Ridgway Rd, Pyrford GU22 227 BF115
Ridgwell Rd, E16 292 D6
Riding, The, NW11 off Golders Grn Rd 119 CZ59
Woking GU21 211 BB114
Riding Ct Rd, Datchet SL3 152 AW80
Riding Hill, S.Croy. CR2 220 DU113
Riding Ho St, W1 285 L7
Riding La, Beac. HP9 88 AF53
Ridings, The, E11 off Malcolm Way 124 EG57
W5 138 CM70
Addlestone KT15 211 BF107
Amersham HP6 55 AR35
Ashtead KT21 231 CK117
Biggin Hill TN16 238 EL117
Chigwell IG7 104 EV49
Cobham KT11 214 CA112
East Horsley KT24 245 BS125
Epsom KT18 232 CS115
Ewell KT17 217 CT109
Hertford SG14 31 DN10
Iver SL0 153 BF77
Kingswood KT20 233 CZ120
Latimer HP5 72 AX36
Reigate RH2 250 DD131
Ripley GU23 228 BG123
Sunbury-on-Thames TW16 195 BU95
Surbiton KT5 198 CN99
Windsor SL4 off River Rd 151 AK80
Ridings Av, N21 81 DP42
Ridings Cl, N6 121 DJ59
Ridings La, Wok. GU23 228 BN123
Ridlands Gro, Oxt. RH8 254 EL130
Ridlands La, Oxt. RH8 254 EK130
Ridlands Ri, Oxt. RH8 254 EL130
Ridler Rd, Enf. EN1 82 DS38
Ridley Av, W13 157 CH76
Ridley Cl, Bark. IG11 145 ET66
Romford RM3 105 FH53
Ridley Rd, E7 124 EJ63
E8 278 A3
NW10 139 CU68
SW19 180 DB94
Bromley BR2 204 EF97
Warlingham CR6 236 DW118
Welling DA16 166 EV81
Ridsdale Rd, SE20 202 DV95
Woking GU21 226 AV117
Riefield Rd, SE9 165 EQ84
Riesco Dr, Croy. CR0 220 DW107
Riffel Rd, NW2 272 A2
Riffhams, Brwd. CM13 109 GB48
Rifle Butts All, Epsom KT18 233 CT115
Rifle Ct, SE11 310 F2
Rifle Pl, W11 off St. Anns Rd 294 D2
Rifle St, E14 290 D7
Riga Ms, E1 off Commercial Rd 288 C8
Rigault Rd, SW6 306 F9
Rigby Cl, Croy. CR0 201 DN104
Rigby Gdns, Grays RM16 171 GH77
Rigby La, Hayes UB3 155 BR75
Rigby Ms, Ilf. IG1 125 EN61
Rigby Pl, Enf. EN3 83 EA37
Rigden St, E14 290 C9
Rigeley Rd, NW10 139 CU69
Rigg App, E10 123 DX60
Rigge Pl, SW4 161 DK84
Riggindale Rd, SW16 181 DK92
Riley Cl, Epsom KT19 216 CP111
Riley Rd, SE1 299 P6
Enfield EN3 82 DW38
Riley St, SW10 308 A4
Rill Ct, Bark. IG11 off Spring Pl 145 EQ68
Sch Rimon Jewish Prim Sch, NW11 119 CZ60
Rinaldo Rd, SW12 181 DH87
Ring, The, W2 284 C10
Ring Cl, Brom. BR1 184 EH94
Ringcroft St, N7 276 E3
Ringers Rd, Brom. BR1 204 EG97
Ringford Rd, SW18 179 CZ85
Ringlet Cl, E16 292 A7
Ringlewell Cl, Enf. EN1 off Central Av 82 DV40
Ringley Av, Horl. RH6 268 DG148
Ringley Pk Av, Reig. RH2 266 DD135
Ringley Pk Rd, Reig. RH2 250 DC134
Ringmer Av, SW6 306 F7
Ringmer Gdns, N19 121 DL61
Ringmer Ho, SE22 off Pytchley Rd 162 DS83
Ringmer Pl, N21 82 DR43
Ringmer Way, Brom. BR1 205 EM99
Ringmore Dr, Guil. GU4 243 BC131
Ringmore Ri, SE23 182 DV87
Ringmore Rd, Walt. KT12 196 BW104
Ringmore Vw, SE23 off Ringmore Ri 182 DV87
Ring Rd, W12 294 A1
Ring Rd N, Gat. RH6 269 DH152
Ring Rd S, Gat. RH6 269 DH152
Ringshall Rd, Orp. BR5 206 EU97
Ringside Ct, SE28 146 EW74
Ringslade Rd, N22 99 DM54
Ringstead Rd, SE6 183 EB87
Sutton SM1 218 DD105
Ringway, N11 99 DJ51
Southall UB2 156 BY78
Ringway Rd, Park St AL2 60 CB27
Ringwold Cl, Beck. BR3 183 DY94
Ringwood Av, N2 98 DF54
Croydon CR0 201 DL101
Hornchurch RM12 128 FK61
Orpington BR6 224 EW110
Redhill RH1 250 DF131
Ringwood Cl, Pnr. HA5 116 BW55
Ringwood Gdns, E14 302 B8
SW15 179 CU89
Ringwood Rd, E17 123 DZ58
Ringwood Way, N21 99 DP46
Hampton Hill TW12 176 CA91
RIPLEY, Wok. GU23 228 BJ122
Ripley Av, Egh. TW20 172 AY93
Ripley Bypass, Wok. GU23 228 BK122
Ripley Cl, Brom. BR1 205 EM99
New Addington CR0 221 EC107
Slough SL3 152 AY77
Sch Ripley C of E Inf Sch, Ripley GU23 off Georgelands 228 BH121
Sch Ripley Ct Sch, Ripley GU23 off Rose La 228 BJ122
Ripley Gdns, SW14 158 CR83
Sutton SM1 218 DC105
Ripley La, W.Hors. KT24 244 BN125
Woking GU23 228 BL123
Ripley Ms, E11 124 EE58
Ripley Rd, E16 292 C8
Belvedere DA17 166 FA77
East Clandon GU4 244 BJ127
Enfield EN2 82 DQ39
Hampton TW12 176 CA94
Ilford IG3 125 ET61
Send GU23 244 BJ127
★ Ripley's Believe It or Not!, W1 297 N1
RIPLEY SPRINGS, Egh. TW20 172 AY93
Ripley Vw, Loug. IG10 85 EP38
Ripley Vil, W5 137 CJ72
Ripley Way, Chsht EN7 66 DV30
Epsom KT19 216 CN111
Hemel Hempstead HP1 39 BE19
Riplington Ct, SW15 179 CU87
Ripon Cl, Guil. GU2 242 AT131
Northolt UB5 116 CA64
Ripon Gdns, Chess. KT9 215 CK106
Ilford IG1 124 EL58
Ripon Rd, N9 100 DV45
N17 122 DR55
SE18 165 EP79
Ripon Way, Borwd. WD6 78 CQ43
St. Albans AL4 43 CK16
Rippersley Rd, Well. DA16 166 EU81
Sch Ripple Inf & Jun Schs, Bark. IG11 off Suffolk Rd 145 ES67
Ripple Rd, Bark. IG11 145 EQ66
Dagenham RM9 146 EV67
● Rippleside Commercial Est, Bark. IG11 146 EW68
Ripplevale Gro, N1 276 D7
Rippolson Rd, SE18 165 ET78
Ripston Rd, Ashf. TW15 175 BR92
Risborough, SE17 off Deacon Way 299 J8
Risborough Dr, Wor.Pk. KT4 199 CU101
Risborough St, SE1 299 H4
Risdens, Harl. CM18 51 EQ19
Risdon St, SE16 301 H5
Rise, The, E11 124 EG57
N13 99 DN49
NW7 97 CT51
NW10 118 CR63
Amersham HP7 55 AQ39
Bexley DA5 186 EW87
Buckhurst Hill IG9 102 EK45
Dartford DA1 167 FF84
East Horsley KT24 245 BS126
Edgware HA8 96 CP50
Elstree WD6 78 CM43
Epsom KT17 217 CT110
Gravesend DA12 191 GL91
Greenford UB6 117 CG64
Greenhithe DA9 189 FU86
Park Street AL2 61 CD25
Sevenoaks TN13 257 FJ129
South Croydon CR2 220 DW109
Tadworth KT20 233 CW121
Uxbridge UB10 134 BM68
Waltham Abbey EN9 off Breach Barn Mobile Home Pk 68 EH30
Risebridge Chase, Rom. RM1 105 FF52
Risebridge Rd, Rom. RM2 105 FF54
Rise Cotts, Ware SG12 off Widford Rd 34 EK05
Risedale Cl, Hem.H. HP3 off Risedale Hill 40 BL23
Risedale Hill, Hem.H. HP3 40 BL23
Risedale Rd, Bexh. DA7 167 FB83
Hemel Hempstead HP3 40 BL23
Riseholme Ho, SE22 off Albrighton Rd 162 DS83
Riseldine Rd, SE23 183 DY86
Rise Pk Boul, Rom. RM1 105 FF53
Sch Rise Pk Inf Sch, Rom. RM1 off Annan Way 105 FD53
Sch Rise Pk Jun Sch, Rom. RM1 off Annan Way 105 FD53
Rise Pk Par, Rom. RM1 105 FE54
Riseway, Brwd. CM15 108 FY48
Rising Hill Cl, Nthwd. HA6 off Ducks Hill Rd 93 BQ51
Risinghill St, N1 276 D10
Risingholme Cl, Bushey WD23 94 CB45
Harrow HA3 95 CE53
Risingholme Rd, Har. HA3 95 CE54
Risings, The, E17 123 ED56
Rising Sun Ct, EC1 287 H7
Risley Av, N17 100 DQ53
Sch Risley Av Prim Sch, N17 off The Roundway 100 DS53
Rita Rd, SW8 310 B3
Ritches Rd, N15 122 DQ57
Ritchie Rd, Croy. CR0 202 DV100
Ritchie St, N1 276 F10
Ritchings Av, E17 123 DY56
Ritcroft Cl, Hem.H. HP3 41 BP21
Ritcroft Dr, Hem.H. HP3 41 BP21
Ritcroft St, Hem.H. HP3 41 BP21
Ritherdon Rd, SW17 180 DG89
Ritson Rd, E8 278 B4
Ritter St, SE18 165 EN79
Ritz Ct, Pot.B. EN6 64 DA31
Ritz Par, W5 off Connell Cres 138 CM70
Rivaz Pl, E9 279 H4
Rivenhall End, Welw.G.C. AL7 30 DC09
Rivenhall Gdns, E18 124 EF56
River App, Edg. HA8 96 CQ53
River Ash Est, Shep. TW17 195 BS101
River Av, N13 99 DP48
Hoddesdon EN11 49 EB16
Thames Ditton KT7 197 CG101
River Bk, N21 100 DQ45
East Molesey KT8 197 CE97
Thames Ditton KT7 197 CF99
West Molesey KT8 196 BZ97
Riverbank, Picc.End HP1 off Piccotts End Rd 40 BJ16
Staines-upon-Thames TW18 173 BF93
Riverbank, The, Wind. SL4 151 AP80
Riverbank Rd, Brom. BR1 184 EG90
Riverbank Way, Brent. TW8 157 CJ79
River Barge Cl, E14 302 F5
● River Brent Business Pk, W7 157 CE76
River Cl, E11 124 EJ58
Guildford GU1 242 AW132
Rainham RM13 147 FH71
Ruislip HA4 115 BT58
Southall UB2 156 CC75
Surbiton KT6 off Catherine Rd 197 CK99
Waltham Cross EN8 67 EA34
● River Ct, Wok. GU21 227 BC115
River Ct, SE1 298 G1
Shepperton TW17 195 BQ101
Taplow SL6 130 AC72
Rivercourt Rd, W6 159 CV77
River Crane Wk, Felt. TW13 176 BX88
Hounslow TW4 176 BX88
River Crane Way, Felt. TW13 off Watermill Way 176 BZ89
Riverdale, SE13 off Lewisham High St 163 EC83
Riverdale Cl, Bark. IG11 146 EV70
Riverdale Dr, SW18 off Knaresborough Dr 180 DB88
Woking GU22 227 AZ121
Riverdale Gdns, Twick. TW1 177 CJ86
Riverdale Rd, SE18 165 ET78
Bexley DA5 186 EZ87
Erith DA8 167 FB78
Feltham TW13 176 BY91
Twickenham TW1 177 CJ86
Riverdene, Edg. HA8 96 CQ48
Riverdene Rd, Ilf. IG1 125 EN62
River Dr, Upmin. RM14 128 FQ58
Riverfield Rd, Stai. TW18 173 BF93
River Front, Enf. EN1 82 DR41
River Gdns, Bray SL6 150 AD75
Carshalton SM5 200 DG103
Feltham TW14 175 BV85
● River Gdns Business Cen, Felt. TW14 off River Gdns 155 BV84
Rivergate Cen, The, Bark. IG11 146 EU70
River Gro Pk, Beck. BR3 203 DZ95
RIVERHEAD, Sev. TN13 256 FD122
Riverhead Cl, E17 101 DX54
Riverhead Dr, Sutt. SM2 218 DA110
Sch Riverhead Infants' Sch, Sev. TN13 off Worships Hill 256 FE123
Riverhill, Cob. KT11 229 BV115
Sevenoaks TN15 257 FL130
Worcester Park KT4 198 CR103
Riverhill Ms, Wor.Pk. KT4 198 CR104
Riverholme Dr, Epsom KT19 216 CR109
River Island Cl, Fetch. KT22 231 CD121
River La, Lthd. KT22 231 CD120
Richmond TW10 177 CK88
Sch Riverley Prim Sch, E10 off Park Rd 123 EA60
Rivermead, Byfleet KT14 212 BM113
East Molesey KT8 196 CC97
Kingston upon Thames KT1 197 CK99
Rivermead Cl, Add. KT15 212 BJ108
Teddington TW11 177 CH92
Rivermead Ct, SW6 306 G10
Rivermead Ho, E9 off Kingsmead Way 279 M2
Rivermead Rd, N18 101 DX51
River Meads, Stans.Abb. SG12 33 EC10
Rivermeads Av, Twick. TW2 176 CA90
Rivermill, SW1 309 P1
Harlow CM20 35 EQ13
River Mt, Walt. KT12 195 BT101
Rivermount Gdns, Guil. GU2 258 AW137
Rivernook Cl, Walt. KT12 196 BW99
River Pk, Berk. HP4 38 AU18
Hemel Hempstead HP1 40 BG22
River Pk Av, Stai. TW18 173 BD91
River Pk Gdns, Brom. BR2 183 ED94
River Pk Rd, N22 99 DM54
River Pk Vw, Orp. BR6 206 EV101
River Pl, N1 277 J7
River Reach, Tedd. TW11 177 CJ92
River Rd, Bark. IG11 145 ES68
Brentwood CM14 108 FS49
Buckhurst Hill IG9 102 EL46
Staines-upon-Thames TW18 193 BF95
Taplow SL6 130 AC73
Windsor SL4 150 AJ80
● River Rd Business Pk, Bark. IG11 145 ET69
Riversdale, Nthflt DA11 190 GE89
Sch Riversdale Prim Sch, SW18 off Merton Rd 180 DA88
Riversdale Rd, N5 121 DP62
Romford RM5 105 FB52
Thames Ditton KT7 197 CG99
Riversdell Cl, Cher. KT16 193 BF101
Riversend Rd, Hem.H. HP3 40 BJ23
Riversfield Rd, Enf. EN1 82 DS41
H Rivers Hosp, The, Saw. CM21 36 EW06
Rivers Ho, Brent. TW8 off Chiswick High Rd 158 CN78
Riverside, Hem.H. HP1 40 BJ22
Riverside, NW4 119 CV59
SE7 304 A7
Chertsey KT16 194 BG97
Dorking RH4 247 CK134
Eynsford DA4 208 FK103
Guildford GU1 242 AX132
Hertford SG14 off The Folly 32 DR09
Horley RH6 268 DG150
London Colney AL2 62 CL27
Richmond TW9, TW10 off Water La 177 CK85
Runnymede TW20 173 BA90
Shepperton TW17 195 BS101
Staines-upon-Thames TW18 193 BF95
Stanstead Abbotts SG12 33 EC11
Twickenham TW1 177 CH88
Wraysbury TW19 172 AW87

R

Riverside,The, E.Mol. KT8 197 CD97
Riverside Av, Brox. EN10 49 EA22
East Molesey KT8 197 CD99
● Riverside Business Cen,
SW18 180 DB88
Guildford GU1 242 AW134
Tilbury RM18 171 GH84
Riverside Cl, E5 122 DW60
W7 137 CE70
Kings Langley WD4 59 BP29
Kingston upon Thames KT1 197 CK98
Orpington BR5 206 EW96
Romford RM1 127 FD56
St. Albans AL1
off Riverside Rd 43 CE22
Staines-upon-Thames TW18 193 BF95
Wallington SM6 201 DH104
Riverside Cotts,
Woob.Moor HP10 110 AE55
Riverside Ct, E4
off Chelwood Cl 83 EB44
SW8 309 P2
Harlow CM17 36 EW09
St. Albans AL1 43 CE22
Riverside Dr, NW11 119 CY58
W4 158 CS80
Bramley GU5 259 BA144
Esher KT10 214 CA105
Mitcham CR4 200 DE99
Richmond TW10 177 CH89
Rickmansworth WD3 92 BK46
Staines-upon-Thames TW18 173 BE92
● Riverside Est, Lon.Col. AL2 62 CL27
Riverside Gdns, N3 119 CY55
W6 159 CV78
Berkhamsted HP4 38 AU18
Enfield EN2 82 DQ40
Old Woking GU22 227 BB121
Wembley HA0 138 CL68
Riverside Hts, Til. RM18 171 GG82
● Riverside Ind Est, Bark. IG11 146 EU69
Dartford DA1 188 FL85
Riverside Mans, E1 300 G1
Riverside Pk, West Dr. UB7 154 BJ76
Weybridge KT13 212 BL106
Riverside Path, Chsht EN8
off Dewhurst Rd 66 DW29
Riverside Pl, Stanw. TW19 174 BK86
Sch Riverside Prim Sch, SE16 300 D5
(shop) Riverside Retail Pk,
Sev. TN14 241 FH119
Riverside Rd, E15 290 F1
N15 122 DU58
SW17 180 DB91
Hersham KT12 214 BX105
St. Albans AL1 43 CE21
Sidcup DA14 186 EY90
Staines-upon-Thames TW18 173 BF94
Stanwell TW19 174 BK85
Watford WD19 75 BV44
Sch Riverside Sch, Bark. IG11 146 EV69
St.P.Cray BR5 off Main Rd 206 EW96
Riverside Twr, SW6 307 P8
Riverside Wk, E14
off Ferry St 314 E1
Bexley DA5 186 EW87
Isleworth TW7 157 CE83
Kingston upon Thames KT1
off High St 197 CK97
Loughton IG10 85 EP44
West Wickham BR4
off The Alders 203 EB102
Windsor SL4 off Farm Yd 151 AR80
Riverside Way, Cowley UB8 134 BH67
Dartford DA1 188 FL85
St. Albans AL2 61 CD32
● Riverside W,
Woob.Grn HP10 110 AE55
Riverside Yd, SW17 180 DC91
Riversmead, Hodd. EN11 49 EA18
Riversmeet, Hert. SG14 31 DP10
Riverstone Cl, Har. HA2 117 CD60
Riverstone Ct, Kings.T. KT2
off Queen Elizabeth Rd 198 CM95
Sch Riverston Sch, SE12
off Eltham Rd 184 EG85
River St, EC1 286 E2
Ware SG12 33 DY06
Windsor SL4 151 AR80
Riverton Cl, W9 283 H3
River Vw, Enf. EN2
off Chase Side 82 DQ41
Grays RM16 171 GG77
Welwyn Garden City AL7 29 CZ05
Sch Riverview C of E Prim
Sch & Nurs, W.Ewell KT19 216 CR105
off Riverview Rd
Riverview Gdns, SW13 159 CV79
Cobham KT11 213 BU113
Twickenham TW1 177 CF89
Riverview Gro, W4 158 CP79
River Vw Hts, SE16 300 C4
Sch Riverview Inf Sch,
Grav. DA12 off Cimba Wd 191 GL91
Sch Riverview Jun Sch,
Grav. DA12 off Cimba Wd 191 GL91
RIVERVIEW PARK, Grav. DA12 191 GK92
Riverview Pk, SE6 183 EA89
Riverview Rd, W4 158 CP80
Epsom KT19 216 CQ105
Greenhithe DA9 189 FU85
River Wk, E4
off Winchester Rd 101 EC52
Denham UB9 114 BJ64
Walton-on-Thames KT12 195 BU100
● Riverwalk Business Pk,
Enf. EN3 83 DZ41
Riverwalk Rd, Enf. EN3 83 DZ42
Riverway, N13 99 DN50
Staines-upon-Thames TW18 194 BH95
River Way, SE10 303 L6
Epsom KT19 216 CR106
Harlow CM20 36 EU10
Loughton IG10 85 EN44
Twickenham TW2 176 CB89
● Riverway Est, Peasm. GU3 258 AW142
River Wey Navigation,
Guil. GU1 242 AX132
Woking GU23 227 BB122
Riverwood La, Chis. BR7 205 ER95
Rivet Ho, SE1 300 B10
Rivett-Drake Cl, Guil. GU2 242 AV130
Rivey Cl, W.Byf. KT14 211 BF114
Rivington Av, Wdf.Grn. IG8 102 EK54
Rivington Ct, NW10 139 CU67
Dagenham RM10
off St. Mark's Pl 147 FB65
Rivington Cres, NW7 97 CT52
Rivington Pl, EC2 287 P3
Rivington St, EC2 287 N3
Rivington Wk, E8 278 D8
Rivulet Rd, N17 100 DQ52
Rixon Cl, Geo.Grn SL3 132 AY72
Rixon Ho, SE18 165 EP79
Rixon St, N7 121 DN62
Rixsen Rd, E12 124 EL64
Sch R.J. Mitchell Prim Sch, The,
Horn. RM12
off Tangmere Cres 147 FH65
Roach Rd, E3 280 A6
Road Ho Est, Old Wok. GU22
off High St 227 BA120
Roads Pl, N19 121 DL61
Roakes Av, Add. KT15 194 BH103
Roan St, SE10 314 E3
Roasthill La, Dorney SL4 151 AK79
Robarts Cl, Pnr. HA5 115 BV57
Robb Rd, Stan. HA7 95 CG51
Robbs Cl, Hem.H. HP1 40 BG17
Robe End, Hem.H. HP1 39 BF18
Robert Adam St, W1 284 G8
Roberta St, E2 288 C2
Robert Av, St.Alb. AL1 42 CB24
Sch Robert Blair Prim Sch, N7 276 B5
Sch Robert Browning
Prim Sch, SE17 299 L10
Robert Burns Ms, SE24
off Mayall Rd 181 DP85
Sch Robert Clack Sch,
Lwr Site, Dag. RM8
off Green La 126 EZ61
Upr Site, Dag. RM8
off Gosfield Rd 126 FA60
Robert Cl, W9 283 P5
Chigwell IG7 103 ET50
Hersham KT12 213 BV106
Potters Bar EN6 63 CY33
Robert Daniels Ct,
They.B. CM16 85 ES37
Robert Dashwood Way, SE17 299 J9
Sch Robert Fitzroy Acad, The,
Croy. CR0 202 DT100
Robert Keen Cl, SE15 312 D7
Robert Lowe Cl, SE14 313 K4
Roberton Dr, Brom. BR1 204 EJ95
Robert Owen Ho, SW6 306 D6
Robert Rd, Hedg. SL2 111 AR61
Robertsbridge Rd, Cars. SM5 200 DC102
Roberts Cl, SE9 185 ER88
SE16 301 K5
Barking IG11 off Tanner St 145 EQ65
Cheshunt EN8
off Norwood Rd 67 DY30
Orpington BR5
off Sholden Gdns 206 EW99
Romford RM3 105 FH53
Stanwell TW19 174 BJ86
Sutton SM3 217 CX108
Thornton Heath CR7
off Kitchener Rd 202 DR97
West Drayton UB7 134 BL74
Roberts La, Chal.St.P. SL9 91 BA50
Roberts Ms, SW1 296 G7
Orpington BR6 206 EU102
Robertson Cl, Brox. EN10 67 DY26
Robertson Ct, Wok. GU21 226 AS118
Robertson Rd, E15 280 F8
E16 291 P7
Berkhamsted HP4 38 AX19
Robertson St, SW8 309 J10
Roberts Pl, Dag. RM10 146 FA65
Robert's Pl, EC1 286 F4
Robert Sq, SE13 163 EC84
Roberts Rd, E17 101 EB53
NW7 97 CY51
Belvedere DA17 166 FA78
Watford WD18 off Tucker St 76 BW43
Robert St, E16 305 N3
NW1 285 K3
SE18 165 ER77
WC2 298 B1
Croydon CR0 off High St 202 DQ104
Robert Sutton Ho, E1
off Tarling St 288 G9
Roberts Way, Eng.Grn TW20 172 AW94
Hatfield AL10 45 CT19
Sch Robertswood Comb Sch,
Chal.St.P. SL9 off Denham La 91 AZ52
Roberts Wd Dr, Chal.St.P. SL9 91 AZ50
Robeson St, E3 289 P6
Robeson Way, Borwd. WD6 78 CQ39
Robina Cl, Bexh. DA6 166 EX84
Northwood HA6 93 BT53
Robina Rd, Brox. EN10 67 DZ25
Robin Cl, NW7 96 CS48
Addlestone KT15 212 BK106
Hampton TW12 176 BY92
Romford RM5 105 FD52
Stanstead Abbotts SG12 33 EC12
Robin Ct, E14 off New Union Cl 302 F6
SE16 300 C8
Wallington SM6 off Carew Rd 219 DJ107
Robin Cres, E6 292 F6
Robin Gdns, Red. RH1 250 DG131
Robin Gro, N6 120 DG61
Brentford TW8 157 CJ79
Harrow HA3 118 CM58
Robin Hill, Berk. HP4 38 AW20
Robin Hill Dr, Chis. BR7 184 EL93
Jct Robin Hood, SW15 178 CS90
Robinhood Cl, Mitch. CR4 201 DJ97
Robin Hood Cl, Slou. SL1 131 AL74
Woking GU21 226 AT118
Robin Hood Cres, Knap. GU21 226 AS117
Robin Hood Dr, Bushey WD23 76 BZ39
Harrow HA3 95 CF52
Robin Hood Gdns, E14 290 F10
Robin Hood Grn, Orp. BR5 206 EU99
Sch Robin Hood Infants' Sch,
Sutt. SM1 off Robin Hood La 218 DA106
Sch Robin Hood Jun Sch, Sutt. SM1
off Thorncroft Rd 218 DB106
Robin Hood La, E14 290 F10
SW15 178 CS91
Bexleyheath DA6 186 EY85
Hatfield AL10 45 CU17
Sutton SM1 218 DA106
Sutton Green GU4 227 AZ124
Robinhood La, Mitch. CR4 201 DJ97
Robin Hood Meadow,
Hem.H. HP2 40 BM15
Sch Robin Hood Prim Sch,
SW15 off Bowness Cres 178 CS92
Robin Hood Rd, SW19 179 CV92
Brentwood CM15 108 FV45
Woking GU21 226 AT118
● Robin Hood Wks, Knap.
GU21 off Robin Hood Rd 226 AS117
Robin Hood Way, SW15 178 CS91
SW20 178 CS91
Greenford UB6 137 CF65
Robin Ho, NW8
off Newcourt St 284 C1
Robinia Av, Nthflt DA11 190 GD87
Robinia Cl, SE20
off Sycamore Gro 202 DU95
Ilford IG6 103 ES51
Robinia Cres, E10 123 EB61
Robin La, NW4 119 CX55
Robin Mead, Welw.G.C. AL7 30 DA06
Robin Pl, Wat. WD25 59 BV32
Robins, The, Harl. CM17 36 EW09
Robins Cl, Lon.Col. AL2 62 CL27
Uxbridge UB8 off Newcourt 134 BJ71
Robins Ct, SE12 184 EJ90
Robinscroft Ms, SE10 314 D7
Robinsfield, Hem.H. HP1 40 BG20
Sch Robinsfield Inf Sch, NW8 274 C10
Robins Gro, W.Wick. BR4 204 EG104
Robins La, They.B. CM16 85 EQ36
Robins Nest Hill, Lt.Berk. SG13 47 DJ19
Robinson Av, Goffs Oak EN7 65 DP28
Robinson Cl, E11 124 EE62
Enfield EN2 82 DQ41
Hornchurch RM12 147 FH66
Woking GU22 227 BC120
Robinson Cres,
Bushey Hth WD23 94 CC46
Robinson Ho, W10 282 D9
Robinson Rd, E2 288 G1
SW17 180 DE93
Dagenham RM10 126 FA63
Robinsons Cl, W13 137 CG71
Robinson St, SW3 308 E2
Robinson Way, Nthflt DA11 190 GA85
Robins Orchard, Chal.St.P. SL9 90 AY51
Robins Rd, Hem.H. HP3 40 BN22
Robins Way, Hat. AL10 45 CT21
Robinsway, Hersham KT12 214 BW105
Waltham Abbey EN9
off Roundhills 68 EE34
Robinswood Cl, Beac. HP9 88 AJ50
Robinswood Ms, N5 276 G3
Robin Way, Cuffley EN6 65 DL28
Guildford GU2 242 AV130
Orpington BR5 206 EV97
Staines-upon-Thames TW18 173 BF90
Robin Willis Way,
Old Wind. SL4 172 AU86
Robinwood Gro, Uxb. UB8 134 BM70
Robinwood Pl, SW15 178 CR91
Roborough Wk, Horn. RM12 148 FJ65
Robsart St, SW9 310 D8
Robson Av, NW10 139 CU67
Robson Cl, E6 292 G8
Chalfont St. Peter SL9 90 AY50
Enfield EN2 81 DP40
Robson Rd, SE27 181 DP90
Robsons Cl, Chsht EN8 66 DW29
Robyns Cft, Nthflt DA11 190 GE90
Robyns Way, Sev. TN13 256 FF122
Rocastle Rd, SE4 183 DY85
Roch Av, Edg. HA8 96 CM54
Rochdale Rd, E17 123 EA59
SE2 166 EV78
Rochdale Way, SE8 314 A4
Rochelle Cl, SW11 160 DD84
Rochelle St, E2 288 A3
Rochemont Wk, E8 278 B9
Roche Rd, SW16 201 DM95
Sch Roche Sch, The, SW18
off Frogmore 180 DA85
Rochester Av, E13 144 EJ67
Bromley BR1 204 EH96
Feltham TW13 175 BT89
Rochester Cl, SW16 181 DL94
Enfield EN1 82 DS39
Sidcup DA15 186 EV86
Rochester Dr, Bex. DA5 186 EZ86
Pinner HA5 116 BX57
Watford WD25 60 BW34
Rochester Gdns, Cat. CR3 236 DS122
Croydon CR0 202 DS104
Ilford IG1 125 EM59
Rochester Ms, NW1 275 L6
Rochester Pl, NW1 275 M6
Rochester Rd, NW1 275 L5
Carshalton SM5 218 DF105
Dartford DA1 188 FN87
Gravesend DA12 191 GL87
Hornchurch RM12 147 FH66
Northwood HA6 115 BT55
Staines-upon-Thames TW18 173 BD92
Rochester Row, SW1 297 M8
Rochester Sq, NW1 275 M6
Rochester St, SW1 297 N7
Rochester Ter, NW1 275 L5
Rochester Wk, SE1 299 L2
Reigate RH2 off Castle Dr 266 DB139
Rochester Way, SE3 164 EH81
SE9 165 EM83
Croxley Green WD3 75 BP42
Dartford DA1 187 FD87
Rochester Way Relief Rd, SE3 164 EH81
SE9 164 EL84
Roche Wk, Cars. SM5 200 DD100
Rochford Av, Loug. IG10 85 EQ41
Romford RM6 126 EW57
Shenfield CM15 109 GA43
Waltham Abbey EN9 67 ED33
Rochford Cl, E6
off Boleyn Rd 144 EK68
Broxbourne EN10 67 DY26
Hornchurch RM12 147 FH65
Rochford Grn, Loug. IG10 85 EQ41
Rochfords Gdns, Slou. SL2 132 AW74
Rochford St, NW5 274 F2
Rochford Wk, E8 278 D6
Rochford Way, Croy. CR0 201 DL100
Taplow SL6 130 AG73
Rockall Ct, Slou. SL3 153 BB76
Rock Av, SW14
off South Worple Way 158 CR83
Rockbourne Rd, SE23 183 DX88
Rockchase Gdns, Horn. RM11 128 FL58
Sch Rockcliffe Manor Prim Sch,
SE18 off Bassant Rd 165 ET79
Rock Cl, Mitch. CR4 200 DD96
Rockdale Gdns, Sev. TN13 257 FH125
Rockdale Rd, Sev. TN13 257 FH125
Rockells Pl, SE22 182 DV86
Rockfield Cl, Oxt. RH8 254 EF131
Rockfield Rd, Oxt. RH8 254 EF129
Rockford Av, Perivale UB6 137 CG68
Rock Gdns, Dag. RM10 127 FB64
Rock Gro Way, SE16 300 D8
Rockhall Rd, NW2 272 C1
Rockhall Way, NW2
off Midland Ter 119 CX62
Rockhampton Cl, SE27 181 DN91
Rockhampton Rd, SE27 181 DN91
South Croydon CR2 220 DS107
Rock Hill, SE26 182 DT91
Orpington BR6 224 FA107
Rockingham Av, Horn. RM11 127 FH58
Rockingham Cl, SW15 159 CT84
Uxbridge UB8 134 BJ67
Rockingham Est, SE1 299 J7
Rockingham Gate,
Bushey WD23 76 CC44
Rockingham Par, Uxb. UB8 134 BJ66
Rockingham Pl, Beac. HP9 89 AM54
Rockingham Rd, Uxb. UB8 134 BH67
Rockingham St, SE1 299 J7
Rockland Rd, SW15 159 CY84
Rocklands Dr, S.Croy. CR2 220 DR108
Stanmore HA7 95 CH54
Rockleigh, Hert. SG14 31 DP09
Rockleigh Ct, Shenf. CM15 109 GA45
Rockley Rd, W14 294 C5
Rockliffe Av, Kings L. WD4 58 BN30
Sch Rockmount Prim Sch, SE19
off Chevening Rd 182 DR93
Rockmount Rd, SE18 165 ET78
SE19 182 DR93
Rockshaw Rd, Merst. RH1 251 DM127
Rocks La, SW13 159 CU81
Rock St, N4 121 DN61
Rockware Av, Grnf. UB6 137 CD67
Rockways, Barn. EN5 79
CT44 Rockwell Gdns, SE19 182 DS92
Rockwell Rd, Dag. RM10 127 FB64
Rockwood Pl, W12 294 B4
Rocky La, Merst. RH1 250 DG129
Reigate RH2 250 DF128
Rocliffe St, N1 287 H1
Rocombe Cres, SE23 182 DW87
Rocque La, SE3 315 M10
Rodborough Rd, NW11 120 DA60
Roden Cl, Harl. CM17 36 EZ11
Roden Ct, N6 121 DK59
Roden Gdns, Croy. CR0 202 DS100
Rodenhurst Rd, SW4 181 DJ86
Roden St, N7 121 DM62
Ilford IG1 125 EN62
Rodeo Cl, Erith DA8 167 FH81
Roderick Rd, NW3 274 F1
Rodgers Cl, Els. WD6 77 CK44
Roding Av, Wdf.Grn. IG8 102 EL51
Roding Ct, Ilf. IG1 125 EN62
Roding Gdns, Loug. IG10 84 EL44
Roding La, Buck.H. IG9 102 EL46
Chigwell IG7 103 EN46
Roding La N, Wdf.Grn. IG8 102 EK54
Roding La S, Ilf. IG4 124 EK56
Woodford Green IG8 124 EK56
Roding Ms, E1 300 D2
Sch Roding Prim Sch,
Dagenham RM8 off Hewett Rd 126 EX63
Dagenham RM9
off Cannington Rd 146 EW65
Woodford Green IG8
off Roding La N 102 EL52
Roding Rd, E5 279 K1
E6 293 N6
Loughton IG10 84 EL43
Rodings, The, Upmin. RM14 129 FR58
Woodford Green IG8 102 EJ51
Rodings Row, Barn. EN5
off Leecroft Rd 79 CY43
⊖ Roding Valley 102 EK49
Sch Roding Valley High Sch,
Loug. IG10 off Alderton Hill 84 EL43
Roding Vw, Buck.H. IG9 102 EK46
Roding Way, Rain. RM13 148 FK68
Rodmarton St, W1 284 F7
Rodmell Cl, Hayes UB4 136 BY70
Rodmell Slope, N12 97 CZ50
Rodmere St, SE10 315 K1
Rodmill La, SW2 181 DL87
Rodney Av, St.Alb. AL1 43 CG22
Rodney Cl, Croy. CR0 201 DP102
New Malden KT3 198 CS99
Pinner HA5 116 BY59
Walton-on-Thames KT12 196 BW102
Rodney Ct, W9 283 P4
Rodney Cres, Hodd. EN11 49 EA15
Rodney Gdns, Pnr. HA5 115 BV57
West Wickham BR4 222 EG105
Rodney Grn, Walt. KT12 196 BW103
Rodney Pl, E17 101 DY54
SE17 299 K8
SW19 200 DC95
Rodney Rd, E11 124 EH56
SE17 299 K8
Mitcham CR4 200 DE96
New Malden KT3 198 CS99
Twickenham TW2 176 CA86
Walton-on-Thames KT12 196 BW103
Rodney St, N1 276 D10
Rodney Way, Colnbr. SL3 153 BE81
Guildford GU1 243 BA133
Romford RM7 104 FA53
Rodona Rd, Wey. KT13 213 BR111
Rodway Rd, SW15 179 CU87
Bromley BR1 204 EH95
Rodwell Cl, Ruis. HA4 116 BW60
Rodwell Ct, Addlestone KT15
off Garfield Rd 212 BJ105
Walton-on-Thames KT12 195 BV104
Rodwell Pl, Edg. HA8 96 CN51
Rodwell Rd, SE22 182 DT86
Roebourne Way, E16 305 L4
Roebuck Cl, Ashtd. KT21 232 CL120
Feltham TW13 175 BV91
Hertford SG13 32 DU09
Reigate RH2 250 DB134
Roebuck Grn, Slou. SL1 131 AL74
Roebuck La, N17 off High Rd 100 DT51
Buckhurst Hill IG9 102 EJ45
Roebuck Rd, Chess. KT9 216 CN106
Ilford IG6 104 EV50
Roedean Av, Enf. EN3 82 DW39
Roedean Cl, Enf. EN3 82 DW39
Orpington BR6 224 EV105
Roedean Cres, SW15 178 CS86
Roedean Dr, Rom. RM1 127 FE56
Roe End, NW9 118 CQ56
Roefields Cl, Felden HP3 40 BG24
ROE GREEN, Hat. AL10 45 CU18
Roe Grn, NW9 118 CQ57
Roe Grn Cl, Hat. AL10 44 CS19
Sch Roe Grn Inf & Jun Schs,
NW9 off Princes Av 118 CP56
Roe Grn La, Hat. AL10 45 CT18
ROEHAMPTON, SW15 179 CU85
Roehampton Cl, SW15 159 CU84
Gravesend DA12 191 GL87
Sch Roehampton C of E Prim Sch,
SW15 off Roehampton La 179 CV87
Roehampton Dr, Chis. BR7 185 EQ93
Roehampton Gate, SW15 178 CS86
Roehampton High St, SW15 179 CV87
Jct Roehampton La, SW15 179 CV88
Roehampton La, SW15 159 CU84
Uni Roehampton Uni - Digby Stuart Coll,
SW15 off Roehampton La 179 CU85
Coll Roehampton Uni - Downshire Ho,
SW15 off Roehampton La 179 CU86
Uni Roehampton Uni - Froebel Coll,
SW15 off Roehampton La 179 CT86
Halls of Res, SW15
off Minstead Gdns 179 CT87
Uni Roehampton Uni - Southlands Coll,
SW15 off Roehampton La 179 CU85
Uni Roehampton Uni - Whitelands Coll,
SW15 off Holybourne Av 179 CU87
Roehampton Vale, SW15 178 CS90
Roe Hill Cl, Hat. AL10 45 CT19
Roehyde Way, Hat. AL10 44 CS20
Roe La, NW9 118 CP56
Roesel Pl, Petts Wd BR5 205 EP99
ROESTOCK, St.Alb. AL4 44 CR23
Roestock Gdns, Coln.Hth AL4 44 CS22
Roestock La, Coln.Hth AL4 44 CR23
Roe Way, Wall. SM6 219 DL107
Rofant Rd, Nthwd. HA6 93 BS51
Roffes La, Chaldon CR3 236 DR124
Roffey Cl, Horl. RH6 268 DF148
Purley CR8 235 DP116
Roffey St, E14 302 E5
Roffords, Wok. GU21 226 AV117
Rogate Ho, E5 off Muir Rd 122 DV62
Sch Roger Ascham Prim Sch,
E17 off Wigton Rd 101 DZ53
Roger Dowley Ct, E2 278 G10
Rogers Cl, Cat. CR3
off Tillingdown Hill 236 DV122
Cheshunt EN7 66 DR26
Coulsdon CR5 235 DP118
Rogers Ct, Swan. BR8 207 FG98
Rogers Est, E2
off Globe Rd 289 H3
Rogers Gdns, Dag. RM10 126 FA64
Rogers Ho, SW1 off Page St 297 P8
Rogers La, Stoke P. SL2 132 AT67
Warlingham CR6 237 DZ118
Rogers Mead, Gdse. RH9
off Ivy Mill La 252 DV132
Rogers Rd, E16 291 M9
SW17 180 DD91
Dagenham RM10 126 FA64
Grays RM17 170 GC77
Rogers Ruff, Nthwd. HA6 93 BQ53
Roger St, WC1 286 D5
Rogers Wk, N12
off Holden Rd 98 DB48
Rojack Rd, SE23 183 DX88
Rokeby Ct, Wok. GU21 226 AT117
Rokeby Gdns, Wdf.Grn. IG8 102 EG53
Rokeby Pl, SW20 179 CV94
Rokeby Rd, SE4 313 N8
Sch Rokeby Sch, E16 291 M6
Kingston upon Thames KT2
off George Rd 178 CQ94
Rokeby St, E15 281 H8
Roke Cl, Ken. CR8 220 DQ114
Rokefield, Dor. RH4 262 CB136
Roke Lo Rd, Ken. CR8 219 DP113
Roke Rd, Ken. CR8 236 DQ115
Roker Pk Av, Uxb. UB10 114 BL63
Rokesby Cl, Well. DA16 165 ER82
Rokesby Pl, Wem. HA0 117 CK64
Rokesby Rd, Slou. SL2 131 AM69
Rokesly Av, N8 121 DL57
Sch Rokesly Inf Sch, N8
off Hermiston Av 121 DL57
Sch Rokesly Jun Sch, N8
off Rokesly Av 121 DL57
Rokewood Ms, Ware SG12 33 DX05
Roland Gdns, SW7 295 P10
Feltham TW13 176 BY90
Roland Ms, E1 289 J6
Roland Rd, E17 123 ED56
Roland St, St.Alb. AL1 43 CG20
Roland Way, SE17 311 M1
SW7 295 P10
Worcester Park KT4 199 CT103
Roles Gro, Rom. RM6 126 EX56
Rolfe Cl, Barn. EN4 80 DE42
Beaconsfield HP9 89 AL54
Rolinsden Way, Kes. BR2 222 EK105
Rollason Way, Brwd. CM14 108 FV48
Rollesby Rd, Chess. KT9 216 CN107
Rollesby Way, SE28 146 EW73
Rolleston Av, Petts Wd BR5 205 EP100
Rolleston Cl, Petts Wd BR5 205 EP101
Rolleston Rd, S.Croy. CR2 220 DR108
Roll Gdns, Ilf. IG2 125 EN57
Rollins St, SE15 313 H2
Rollit Cres, Houns. TW3 176 CA85
Rollit St, N7 276 E2
Rollo Rd, Swan. BR8 187 FF94
Rolls Bldgs, EC4 286 E8
Rolls Cotts, Magd.Lav. CM5
off Hastingwood Rd 53 FB19
Rollscourt Av, SE24 182 DQ85
Rolls Pk Av, E4 101 EA51
Rolls Pk Rd, E4 101 EB50
Jct Rolls Pk Rbt, Chig. IG7 103 ER45
Rolls Pas, EC4 286 E8
Rolls Rd, SE1 300 B10
Rolls Royce Cl, Wall. SM6 219 DL108
Rollswood, Welw.G.C. AL7 29 CY12
Rolt St, SE8 313 L2
Rolvenden Gdns, Brom. BR1 184 EK94
Rolvenden Pl, N17 100 DU52
Romanby Ct, Red. RH1
off Mill St 266 DF135
Roman Cl, W3
off Avenue Gdns 158 CP75
Feltham TW14 176 BW85
Harefield UB9 92 BH53
Rainham RM13 147 FD68
Romanfield Rd, SW2 181 DM87
Roman Gdns, Kings L. WD4 59 BP30
Romanhurst Av, Brom. BR2 204 EE98
Romanhurst Gdns,
Brom. BR2 204 EE98
● Roman Ind Est, Croy. CR0 202 DS101

Roman Ms, Hodd. EN11
off North Rd 49 EA16
Roman Ri, SE19 182 DR93
Sawbridgeworth CM21 36 EX05
Roman Rd, E2 288 G3
E3 289 L1
E6 292 F5
N10 99 DH52
NW2 119 CW62
W4 158 CS77
Brentwood CM15 109 GC41
Dorking RH4 263 CG138
Ilford IG1 145 EP65
Northfleet DA11 190 GC90
Sch Roman Rd Prim Sch, E6 292 F4
Jct Roman Rbt, Harl. CM20 36 EU11
Romans Cl, Guil. GU1 243 BB134
Romans End, St.Alb. AL3 42 CC22
Roman Sq, SE28 146 EU74
Roman St, Hodd. EN11 49 EA16
Romans Way, Wok. GU22 228 BG115
Roman Vale, Harl. CM17 36 EW10
Roman Vil Rd,
Dart. DA2, DA4 188 FQ92
Roman Way, N7 276 D5
SE15 312 G5
Carshalton SM5 218 DF109
Croydon CR0 201 DP103
Dartford DA1 187 FE85
Enfield EN1 82 DT43
Waltham Abbey EN9 83 EB35
● Roman Way Ind Est, N1 276 C6
Romany Ct, Hem.H. HP2
off Wood End Cl 41 BQ19
Romany Gdns, E17
off McEntee Av 101 DY53
Sutton SM3 200 DA101
Romany Ri, Orp. BR5 205 EQ102
Roma Read Cl, SW15 179 CV87
Roma Rd, E17 123 DY55
Romberg Rd, SW17 180 DG90
Romborough Gdns, SE13 183 EC85
Romborough Way, SE13 183 EC85
Rom Cres, Rom. RM7 127 FF59
Romeland, Els. WD6 77 CK44
St. Albans AL3 42 CC20
Waltham Abbey EN9 67 EC33
Romeland Hill, St.Alb. AL3 42 CC20
Romero Cl, SW9 310 D10
Romero Sq, SE3 164 EJ84
Romeyn Rd, SW16 181 DM90
ROMFORD, RM1 - RM7 127 FF57
⇌ Romford 127 FE58
⊖ Romford 127 FE58
Romford Rd, E7 281 M4
E12 124 EL63
E15 281 J6
Aveley RM15 148 FQ73
Chigwell IG7 104 EU48
Romford RM5 104 EY52
● Romford Seedbed Cen,
Rom. RM7 127 FE59
Romford St, E1 288 D7
Romilly Dr, Wat. WD19 94 BY49
Romilly Rd, N4 121 DP61
Romilly St, W1 285 N10
Rommany Rd, SE27 182 DR91
Romney Chase, Horn. RM11 128 FM58
Romney Cl, N17 100 DV53
NW11 120 DC60
SE14 313 H5
Ashford TW15 175 BQ92
Chessington KT9 216 CL105
Harrow HA2 116 CA59
Romney Dr, Brom. BR1 184 EK94
Harrow HA2 116 CA59
Romney Gdns, Bexh. DA7 166 EZ81
Romney Ho, Enf. EN1
off Ayley Cft 82 DU43
Romney Lock, Wind. SL4 152 AS79
Romney Lock Rd, Wind. SL4 151 AR80
Romney Ms, W1 284 G6
Romney Par, Hayes UB4
off Romney Rd 135 BR68
Romney Rd, SE10 314 F3
Hayes UB4 135 BR68
New Malden KT3 198 CR100
Northfleet DA11 190 GE90
Romney Row, NW2
off Brent Ter 119 CX61
Romney St, SW1 297 P7
Romola Rd, SE24 181 DP88
Romsey Cl, Orp. BR6 223 EP105
Slough SL3 153 AZ76
Romsey Dr, Farn.Com. SL2 111 AR62
Romsey Gdns, Dag. RM9 146 EX67
Romsey Rd, W13 137 CG73
Dagenham RM9 146 EX67
Romside Pl, Rom. RM7
off Brooklands La 127 FD56
Romulus Ct, Brent. TW8
off Justin Cl 157 CK80
Romulus Rd, Grav. DA12 191 GJ86
Rom Valley Way, Rom. RM7 127 FE59
Ronald Av, E15 291 K3
Ronald Cl, Beck. BR3 203 DZ98
Ronald Ct, St.Alb. AL2 60 BY29
Ronald Rd, Beac. HP9 89 AM53
Romford RM3 106 FN53
Sch Ronald Ross Prim Sch,
SW19
off Castlecombe Dr 179 CY87
Ronald Ross Rd, Guil. GU2 258 AS135
Ronaldsay Spur, Slou. SL1 132 AS71
Ronalds Rd, N5 276 F3
Bromley BR1 204 EG95
Ronaldstone Rd, Sid. DA15 185 ES86
Ronald St, E1 289 H9
Ronan Way, Denh. UB9 113 BF61
Rona Rd, NW3 274 G1
Ronart St, Wealds. HA3 117 CF55
Rona Wk, N1 277 L5
Rondu Rd, NW2 272 E2
Ronelean Rd, Surb. KT6 198 CM104
Roneo Cor, Horn. RM12 127 FF60
Roneo Link, Horn. RM12 127 FF60
Ronfearn Av, Orp. BR5 206 EX99
Ron Grn Ct, Erith DA8 167 FD79
Ron Leighton Way, E6 144 EL67
Ronneby Cl, Wey. KT13 195 BS104
Ronnie La, E12 125 EN63
Ronsons Way, St.Alb. AL4 43 CF17
Ronson Way, Lthd. KT22 231 CF121
Ron Todd Cl, Dag. RM10 146 FA67
Ronver Rd, SE12 184 EF87
Rood La, EC3 287 N10
Roof of the World Pk
Homes Est, Box H. KT20 248 CP132
Rookby Ct, N21 99 DP47
Rook Cl, Horn. RM12 147 FG66
Wembley HA9 118 CP62
Rookdean, Chipstead TN13 256 FC122
Rookeries Cl, Felt. TW13 175 BV90
Rookery, The, Grays RM20 169 FU79
Rookery Cl, NW9 119 CT57
Fetcham KT22 231 CE124
Rookery Ct, Grays RM20 169 FU79
Rookery Cres, Dag. RM10 147 FB66
Rookery Dr, Chis. BR7 205 EN95
Westcott RH4 262 CA138
Rookery Gdns, Orp. BR5 206 EW99
Rookery Hill, Ashtd. KT21 232 CN118
Outwood RH1 269 DN145
Rookery La, Brom. BR2 204 EK100
Grays RM17 170 GD78
Smallfield RH6 269 DN146
Rookery Mead, Couls. CR5 235 DJ122
Rookery Rd, SW4 161 DJ84
Downe BR6 223 EM110
Staines-upon-Thames TW18 174 BH92
Rookery Vw, Grays RM17 170 GD78
Rookery Way, NW9 119 CT57
Lower Kingswood KT20 249 CZ127
Rookes All, Hert. SG13
off Mangrove Rd 32 DS10
Rookesley Rd, Orp. BR5 206 EX101
Rooke Way, SE10 303 L10
Rookfield Av, N10 121 DJ56
Rookfield Cl, N10 121 DJ56
Rook La, Chaldon CR3 235 DM124
Rookley Cl, Sutt. SM2 218 DB110
Rook Rd, Woob.Grn HP10 110 AD59
Rooks Cl, Welw.G.C. AL8 29 CX10
Sch Rooks Heath Coll,
S.Har. HA2 off Eastcote La 116 CA62
Rooks Hill, Loud. WD3 74 BJ42
Welwyn Garden City AL8 29 CW10
Rooksmead Rd, Sun. TW16 195 BT96
Rooks Nest, Gdse. RH9 253 DY130
Rookstone Rd, SW17 180 DF92
Rook Wk, E6 292 G8
Rookwood Av, Loug. IG10 85 EQ41
New Malden KT3 199 CU98
Wallington SM6 219 DK105
Rookwood Cl, Grays RM17 170 GB77
Merstham RH1 251 DH129
Rookwood Ct, Guil. GU2 258 AW137
Rookwood Gdns, E4 102 EF47
Loughton IG10 85 EQ41
Rookwood Ho, Bark. IG11
off St. Marys 145 ER68
Rookwood Rd, N16 122 DT59
★ Roosevelt Mem, W1 285 H10
Roosevelt Way, Dag. RM10 147 FD65
Rootes Dr, W10 282 C5
Roothill La, Bet. RH3 264 CN140
Ropemaker Pl, EC2 287 L6
Ropemaker Rd, SE16 301 L5
Ropemakers Flds, E14 301 N1
Ropemaker St, EC2 287 L6
Roper La, SE1 299 P4
Ropers Av, E4 101 EC50
Ropers Orchard, SW3 308 B3
Roper St, SE9 185 EM86
Ropers Wk, SW2
off Brockwell Pk Gdns 181 DN87
Roper Way, Mitch. CR4 200 DG96
● Ropery Business Pk, SE7
off Anchor And Hope La 304 C8
Ropery St, E3 289 N5
Rope St, SE16 301 M7
Rope Wk, Sun. TW16 196 BW97
Ropewalk Gdns, E1 288 D9
Ropewalk Ms, E8 278 C7
Rope Yd Rails, SE18 305 N7
Ropley St, E2 288 C1
Rosa Alba Ms, N5
off Kelross Rd 122 DQ63
Rosa Av, Ashf. TW15 174 BN91
Rosalind Franklin Cl
(Surr.Res.Pk), Guil. GU2 258 AS135
Rosaline Rd, SW6 306 F5
Rosamond St, SE26 182 DV90
Rosamund Cl, S.Croy. CR2 220 DR105
Rosamun St, Sthl. UB2 156 BY77
Rosary, The, Egh. TW20 193 BD96
Rosary Cl, Houns. TW3 156 BY82
Rosary Ct, Pot.B. EN6 64 DB30
Rosary Gdns, SW7 295 N9
Ashford TW15 175 BP91
Bushey WD23 95 CE45
Sch Rosary RC Prim Sch, NW3 274 C2
Heston TW5 off The Green 156 CA79
Rosaville Rd, SW6 306 G5
Roscoe St, EC1 287 K5
Roscoff Cl, Edg. HA8 96 CQ53
Roseacre, Oxt. RH8 254 EG134
Roseacre Cl, W13 137 CH71
Hornchurch RM11 128 FM60
Shepperton TW17 194 BN99
Sutton SM1 200 DC103
Roseacre Gdns, Chilw. GU4 259 BF140
Welwyn Garden City AL7 30 DC09
Roseacre Rd, Well. DA16 166 EV83
Rose All, EC2
off New St 287 P7
SE1 299 K2
Rose & Crown Ct, EC2 287 J8
Rose & Crown Yd, SW1 297 M2
Roseary Cl, West Dr. UB7 154 BK77
Rose Av, E18 102 EH54
Gravesend DA12 191 GL88
Mitcham CR4 200 DF95
Morden SM4 200 DC99
Rosebank, SE20 182 DV94
Epsom KT18 216 CQ114
Waltham Abbey EN9 68 EE33
Rose Bk, Brwd. CM14 108 FX48
Rosebank Av, Horn. RM12 128 FJ64
Wembley HA0 117 CF63
Rosebank Cl, N12 98 DE50
Teddington TW11 177 CG93
Rose Bk Cotts, Wok. GU22 226 AY122
Rosebank Gdns, E3 289 M1
Northfleet DA11 190 GE88
Rosebank Rd, E17 123 EB58
W7 157 CE75
Rosebank Vil, E17 123 EA56
Rosebank Wk, NW1 275 P6
SE18 305 H8
Rosebank Way, W3 138 CR72
Rose Bates Dr, NW9 118 CN56
Rosebay Dr, N17 100 DT54
Roseberry Cl, Upmin. RM14 129 FT58
Roseberry Ct, Wat. WD17
off Grandfield Av 75 BU39
Roseberry Gdns, N4 121 DP58
Dartford DA1 188 FJ87
Orpington BR6 205 ES104
Upminster RM14 129 FT59
Roseberry Pl, E8 278 A5
Roseberry St, SE16 300 E9
Rosebery Av, E12 144 EL65
EC1 286 E5
N17 100 DU54
Epsom KT17 216 CS114
Harrow HA2 116 BY63
New Malden KT3 199 CT96
Sidcup DA15 185 ES87
Thornton Heath CR7 202 DQ96
Rosebery Cl, Mord. SM4 199 CX100
Rosebery Ct, EC1
off Rosebery Av 286 E4
Northfleet DA11 191 GF88
Rosebery Cres, Wok. GU22 227 AZ121
Rosebery Gdns, N8 121 DL57
W13 137 CG72
Sutton SM1 218 DB105
● Rosebery Ind Pk, N17 100 DV54
Rosebery Ms, N10 99 DJ54
SW2 off Rosebery Rd 181 DL86
Rosebery Rd, N10 99 DJ54
SW2 181 DL86
Bushey WD23 94 CB45
Epsom KT18 232 CR119
Grays RM17 170 FY79
Hounslow TW3 176 CC85
Kingston upon Thames KT1 198 CP96
Sutton SM1 217 CZ107
Roseberys, Epsom KT18 216 CS114
Sch Rosebery Sch, Epsom
KT18 off White Horse Dr 216 CQ114
Rosebery Sq, EC1 286 E5
Kingston upon Thames KT1 198 CN96
Rosebine Av, Twick. TW2 177 CD87
Rosebriar Cl, Wok. GU22 228 BG116
Rosebriars, Cat. CR3 236 DS120
Esher KT10 214 CC106
Rosebriar Wk, Wat. WD24 75 BT36
Coll Rose Bruford Coll,
Sid. DA15 off Burnt Oak La 186 EV88
Rosebury Rd, SW6 307 M9
Rosebury Sq, Wdf.Grn. IG8 103 EN52
Rosebury Vale, Ruis. HA4 115 BT60
Rose Bushes, Epsom KT17 233 CV116
Rose Ct, E1 288 A7
Amersham HP6
off Chestnut La 55 AS37
Pinner HA5 off Nursery Rd 116 BW55
Waltham Cross EN7 66 DU27
Rosecourt Rd, Croy. CR0 201 DM100
Rosecrest Ct, N15
off High Rd 122 DT55
Rosecroft Av, NW3 120 DA62
Rosecroft Cl, Bigg.H. TN16
off Lotus Rd 239 EM118
Orpington BR5 206 EW100
Rosecroft Dr, Wat. WD17 75 BS36
Rosecroft Gdns, NW2 119 CU62
Twickenham TW2 177 CD88
Rosecroft Rd, Sthl. UB1 136 CA70
Rosecroft Wk, Pnr. HA5 116 BX57
Wembley HA0 117 CK64
Rosedale, Ashtd. KT21 231 CJ118
Caterham CR3 236 DS123
Welwyn Garden City AL7 29 CZ05
Rose Dale, Orp. BR6 205 EP103
Rosedale Av, Chsht EN7 66 DT29
Hayes UB3 135 BR71
Rosedale Cl, SE2 166 EV76
W7 off Boston Rd 157 CF75
Bricket Wood AL2 60 BY30
Dartford DA2 188 FP87
Stanmore HA7 95 CH51
Sch Rosedale Coll, Hayes UB3
off Wood End Grn Rd 135 BS72
Rosedale Ct, N5 276 G1
Rosedale Dr, Dag. RM9 146 EV67
Rosedale Gdns, Dag. RM9 146 EV66
Rosedale Pl, Croy. CR0 203 DX101
Rosedale Rd, E7 124 EJ64
Dagenham RM9 146 EV66
Epsom KT17 217 CU106
Grays RM17 170 GD78
Richmond TW9 158 CL84
Romford RM1 105 FC54
Rosedale Ter, W6
off Dalling Rd 159 CV76
Rosedale Way, Chsht EN7 66 DU29
Rosedene, NW6 272 D8
Rosedene Av, SW16 181 DM90
Croydon CR0 201 DM101
Greenford UB6 136 CA69
Morden SM4 200 DA99
Rosedene Ct, Dart. DA1
off Shepherds La 188 FJ87
Ruislip HA4 115 BS60
Rosedene End, St.Alb. AL2 60 CA26
Rosedene Gdns, Ilf. IG2 125 EN56
Rosedene Ms, Uxb. UB8 134 BJ69
Rosedene Ter, E10 123 EB61
Rosedew Rd, W6 306 C3
Rose Dr, Chesh. HP5 54 AS32
Rose End, Wor.Pk. KT4 199 CX102
Rosefield, Sev. TN13 256 FG124
Rosefield Cl, Cars. SM5 218 DE106
Rosefield Gdns, E14 290 A10
Ottershaw KT16 211 BD107
Rosefield Rd, Stai. TW18 174 BG91
Roseford Ct, W12 294 C5
Rose Gdn Cl, Edg. HA8 96 CL51
Rose Gdns, W5 157 CK76
Feltham TW13 175 BU89
Southall UB1 136 CA70
Stanwell TW19 174 BK87
Watford WD18 75 BU43
Rosegate Ho, E3 289 P1
Rose Glen, NW9 118 CR56
Romford RM7 127 FE60
Rosehart Ms, W11 283 J9
Rose Hatch Av, Rom. RM6 126 EX55
Roseheath, Hem.H. HP1 39 BE19
Roseheath Rd, Houns. TW4 176 BZ85
ROSE HILL, Dor. RH4 263 CG136
ROSEHILL, Sutt. SM1 200 DB102
Jct Rose Hill, Sutt. SM1 200 DB103
Rose Hill, Burnham SL1 130 AG66
Dorking RH4 263 CH136
Sutton SM1 200 DB103
Rosehill, Claygate KT10 215 CG107
Hampton TW12 196 CA95
Rose Hill App, Dor. RH4
off Rose Hill 263 CG136
Rosehill Av, Sutt. SM1 200 DC102
Woking GU21 226 AW116
Rosehill Cl, Hodd. EN11 49 DZ17
Rosehill Ct, Hem.H. HP1
off Green End Rd 40 BG22
Slough SL1 152 AU76
Rosehill Fm Meadow,
Bans. SM7 234 DB115
Rosehill Gdns, Abb.L. WD5 59 BQ32
Greenford UB6 117 CF64
Sutton SM1 200 DB103
Rose Hill Pk W, Sutt. SM1 200 DC102
Rosehill Rd, SW18 180 DC86
Biggin Hill TN16 238 EJ117
Rose Joan Ms, NW6 273 J1
Roseland Cl, N17 100 DR52
Roselands Av, Hodd. EN11 49 DZ15
Sch Roselands Prim Sch,
Hodd. EN11 off High Wd Rd 33 DZ14
Rose La, Ripley GU23 228 BJ121
Romford RM6 126 EX55
Rose Lawn, Bushey Hth WD23 94 CC46
Roseleigh Av, N5 277 H1
Roseleigh Cl, Twick. TW1 177 CK86
Roseley Cotts, Eastwick CM20 35 EP11
Rosemary Av, N3 98 DB54
N9 100 DV46
Enfield EN2 82 DR39
Hounslow TW4 156 BX82
Romford RM1 127 FF55
West Molesey KT8 196 CA97
Rosemary Cl, Croy. CR0 201 DL100
Harlow CM17 36 EW11
Oxted RH8 254 EG133
South Ockendon RM15 149 FW69
Uxbridge UB8 134 BN71
Rosemary Ct, Horl. RH6 268 DE147
Rosemary Cres, Guil. GU2 242 AT130
Rosemary Dr, E14 290 G9
Ilford IG4 124 EK57
London Colney AL2 61 CG26
Rosemary Gdns, SW14
off Rosemary La 158 CQ83
Chessington KT9 216 CL105
Dagenham RM8 126 EZ60
Rosemary La, SW14 158 CQ83
Egham TW20 193 BB97
Horley RH6 269 DH149
Rosemary Rd, SE15 312 B4
SW17 180 DC90
Welling DA16 165 ET81
Rosemary St, N1 277 L8
Rosemead, NW9 119 CT59
Chertsey KT16 194 BH101
Potters Bar EN6 64 DC30
Rosemead Av, Felt. TW13 175 BT89
Mitcham CR4 201 DJ96
Wembley HA9 118 CL64
Rosemead Cl, Red. RH1 266 DD136
Surbiton KT6 198 CN103
Rosemead Gdns, Hutt. CM13 109 GD42
Sch Rosemead Prep Sch, SE21
off Thurlow Pk Rd 182 DQ89
Rosemere Pl, Beck. BR2 204 EE98
Rose Ms, N18 100 DV49
Rosemont Av, N12 98 DC51
Rosemont Rd, NW3 273 N4
W3 138 CP73
New Malden KT3 198 CQ97
Richmond TW10 178 CL86
Wembley HA0 138 CL67
Rosemoor Cl, Welw.G.C. AL7 29 CZ10
Rosemoor St, SW3 296 E9
Rosemount, Harl. CM19 51 EP18
Wallington SM6 219 DJ107
Rosemount Av, W.Byf. KT14 212 BG113
Rosemount Cl, Wdf.Grn. IG8
off Chapelmount Rd 103 EM51
Rosemount Dr, Brom. BR1 205 EM98
Rosemount Pt, SE23
off Dacres Rd 183 DX90
Rosemount Rd, W13 137 CG72
Rosenau Cres, SW11 308 D7
Rosenau Rd, SW11 308 D6
Sch Rosendale Prim Sch, SE21
off Rosendale Rd 182 DQ87
Rosendale Rd, SE21 182 DQ87
SE24 182 DQ87
Roseneath Av, N21 99 DP46
Roseneath Cl, Orp. BR6 224 EW108
Roseneath Pl, SW16
off Curtis Fld Rd 181 DM91
Roseneath Rd, SW11 180 DG86
Roseneath Wk, Enf. EN1 82 DR42
Rosens Wk, Edg. HA8 96 CP48
Rosenthal Rd, SE6 183 EB86
Rosenthorpe Rd, SE15 183 DX85
Rose Pk, Add. KT15 211 BE109
Rose Pk Cl, Hayes UB4 136 BW70
Rosepark Ct, Ilf. IG5 103 EM54
Roserton St, E14 302 E5
Rosery, The, Croy. CR0 203 DX100
Roses, The, Wdf.Grn. IG8 102 EF52
Roses La, Wind. SL4 151 AK82
Rose Sq, SW3 296 B10
Rose St, EC4 287 H8
WC2 286 A10
Northfleet DA11 190 GB86
Rosethorn Cl, SW12 181 DJ87
Rose Tree Ms, Wdf.Grn. IG8
off Chigwell Rd 102 EL51
Rosetree Pl, Hmptn. TW12 196 CA94
Rosetrees, Guil. GU1 259 BA135
Coll Rosetta Arts Centre, E15 291 K3
Rosetta Cl, SW8 310 B5
Sch Rosetta Prim Sch, E16 292 B7
Rosetti Ter, Dag. RM8
off Marlborough Rd 126 EV63
Rose Vale, Hodd. EN11 49 EA17
Rose Valley, Brwd. CM14 108 FW48
Roseveare Rd, SE12 184 EJ91
Rose Vil, Dart. DA1 188 FP87
Roseville Av, Houns. TW3 176 CA85
Roseville Rd, Hayes UB3 155 BU78
Rosevine Rd, SW20 199 CW95
Rose Wk, Pur. CR8 219 DK111
St. Albans AL4 43 CJ18
Slough SL2 131 AP71
Surbiton KT5 198 CP99
West Wickham BR4 203 ED103
Rose Wk, The, Rad. WD7 77 CH37
Rosewarne Cl, Wok. GU21
off Muirfield Rd 226 AU118
Rose Way, SE12 184 EG85
Edgware HA8 96 CQ49
Roseway, SE21 182 DR86
Rosewell Cl, SE20 182 DV94
Rosewood, Dart. DA2 187 FE91
Esher KT10 197 CG103
Sutton SM2 218 DC110
Woking GU22 227 BA119
Rosewood Av, Grnf. UB6 117 CG64
Hornch. RM12 127 FG64
Rosewood Cl, Sid. DA14 186 EW90
Rosewood Ct, Brom. BR1 204 EJ95
Hemel Hempstead HP1 39 BE19
Kings.T. KT2 178 CN94
Romford RM6 126 EW57
Rosewood Dr, Enf. EN2 81 DN35
Shepperton TW17 194 BM99
Rosewood Gdns, SE13
off Morden Hill 314 E8
Rosewood Gro, Sutt. SM1 200 DC103
Rosewood Sq, W12
off Primula St 139 CU72
Rosewood Ter, SE20
off Laurel Gro 182 DW94
Rosewood Way,
Farn.Com. SL2 111 AQ64
Rosher Cl, E15 280 G7
ROSHERVILLE, Grav. DA11 191 GF85
Sch Rosherville C of E Prim Sch,
Nthflt DA11 off London Rd 190 GE86
Rosherville Way, Grav. DA11 190 GE87
Sch Rosh Pinah Jewish Prim Sch,
Edg. HA8 off Glengall Rd 96 CP48
Rosie's Way, S.Ock. RM15 149 FX72
Rosina St, E9 279 J3
Rosing Apts, Brom. BR2
off Homesdale Rd 204 EJ98
Roskell Rd, SW15 159 CX83
Rosken Gro, Farn.Royal SL2 131 AP68
Roslin Rd, W3 158 CP76
● Roslin Sq, W3 158 CP76
Roslin Way, Brom. BR1 184 EG92
Roslyn Cl, Brox. EN10 49 DY21
Mitcham CR4 200 DD96
Roslyn Ct, Wok. GU21
off St. John's Rd 226 AU118
Roslyn Gdns, Rom. RM2 105 FF54
Roslyn Rd, N15 122 DR57
Rosmead Rd, W11 282 F10
Rosoman Pl, EC1 286 F4
Rosoman St, EC1 286 F3
Ross, E16
off Seagull La 291 N10
Rossall Cl, Horn. RM11 127 FG58
Rossall Cres, NW10 138 CM69
Ross Av, Dag. RM8 126 EZ61
Ross Cl, Har. HA3 94 CC52
Hatfield AL10
off Homestead Rd 45 CU15
Hayes UB3 155 BR77
Northolt UB5 117 CD63
Ross Ct, E5 off Napoleon Rd 122 DV63
SW15 179 CX87
Ross Cres, Wat. WD25 75 BU35
Rossdale, Sutt. SM1 218 DE106
Rossdale Dr, N9 82 DW44
NW9 118 CQ60
Rossdale Rd, SW15 159 CW84
Rosse Gdns, SE13
off Desvignes Dr 183 ED86
Rosse Ms, SE3 164 EH81
Rossendale Cl, Enf. EN2 81 DP37
Rossendale St, E5 122 DV61
Rossendale Way, NW1 275 M7
Rossetti Gdns, Couls. CR5 235 DM118
Rossetti Ms, NW8 274 B9
Rossetti Rd, SE16 300 E10
Rossgate, Hem.H. HP1
off Galley Hill 40 BG18
Sch Rossgate Prim Sch,
Hem.H. HP1 off Galley Hill 40 BG18
Ross Haven Pl, Nthwd. HA6 93 BT53
Rossignol Gdns, Cars. SM5 200 DG103
Rossindel Rd, Houns. TW3 176 CA85
Rossington Av, Borwd. WD6 78 CL38
Rossington Cl, Enf. EN1 82 DV38
Rossington St, E5 122 DU61
Rossiter Cl, SE19 182 DQ94
Slou. SL3 152 AY77
Rossiter Flds, Barn. EN5 79 CY44
Rossiter Gro, SW9 161 DN83
Rossiter Rd, SW12 181 DH88
Rossland Cl, Bexh. DA6 187 FB85
Rosslare Cl, West. TN16 255 ER125
Rosslyn Av, E4 102 EF47
SW13 158 CS83
Dagenham RM8 126 EZ59
East Barnet EN4 80 DE44
Feltham TW14 175 BU86
Romford RM3 106 FM54
Rosslyn Cl, Hayes UB3 135 BR71
Sunbury-on-Thames TW16
off Cadbury Rd 175 BS93
West Wickham BR4 204 EF104
Rosslyn Cres, Har. HA1 117 CF57
Wembley HA9 118 CL63
Rosslyn Gdns, Wem. HA9
off Rosslyn Cres 118 CL62
Rosslyn Hill, NW3 274 B1
Rosslyn Ms, NW3 274 B1
Rosslyn Pk, Wey. KT13 213 BR105
Rosslyn Pk Ms, NW3 274 B2
Rosslyn Rd, E17 123 EC56
Barking IG11 145 ER66
Twickenham TW1 177 CJ86
Watford WD18 75 BV41
Rossmore Cl, Enf. EN3 83 DX42
Rossmore Ct, NW1 284 E4
Rossmore Rd, NW1 284 D5
Ross Par, Wall. SM6 219 DH107
Ross Rd, SE25 202 DR97
Cobham KT11 214 BW113
Dartford DA1 187 FG86
Twickenham TW2 176 CB88
Wallington SM6 219 DJ106
Ross Way, SE9 164 EL83
Northwood HA6 93 BT49
Rossway Dr, Bushey WD23 76 CC43
Rosswood Gdns, Wall. SM6 219 DJ107
Rostella Rd, SW17 180 DD91
Rostrevor Av, N15 122 DT58
Rostrevor Gdns, Hayes UB3 135 BS74
Iver SL0 133 BD68
Southall UB2 156 BY78
Rostrevor Ms, SW6 306 G7
Rostrevor Rd, SW6 306 G6
SW19 180 DA92
Roswell Cl, Chsht EN8 67 DY30
Rotary St, SE1 298 G6
Rothbury Av, Rain. RM13 147 FH71
Rothbury Gdns, Islw. TW7 157 CG80
Rothbury Rd, E9 279 P6

R

Rothbury Wk, N17 100 DU52
Roth Dr, Hutt. CM13 109 GB47
Rother Cl, Wat. WD25 60 BW34
Sch Rotherfield Prim Sch, N1 277 K8
Rotherfield Rd, Cars. SM5 218 DG105
Enfield EN3 83 DX37
Rotherfield St, N1 277 K7
Rotherham Wk, SE1 298 G3
Rotherhill Av, SW16 181 DK93
ROTHERHITHE, SE16 301 J6
⊖ Rotherhithe 301 H4
Rotherhithe New Rd, SE16 312 D1
Rotherhithe Old Rd, SE16 301 J7
Sch Rotherhithe Prim Sch, SE16 301 J8
Rotherhithe St, SE16 301 H4
Rotherhithe Tunnel, E1 301 J2
Rotherhithe Tunnel App, E14 289 L10
SE16 300 G5
Rothervale, Horl. RH6 268 DF145
Rotherwick Hill, W5 138 CM70
Rotherwick Rd, NW11 120 DA59
Rotherwood Cl, SW20 199 CY95
Rotherwood Rd, SW15 306 C10
Rothery St, N1 276 G8
Rothery Ter, SW9 310 G5
Rothesay Av, SW20 199 CY96
Greenford UB6 137 CD65
Richmond TW10 158 CP84
Rothesay Rd, SE25 202 DR98
Rothes Rd, Dor. RH4 263 CH135
Rothsay Rd, E7 144 EJ66
Rothsay St, SE1 299 N6
Rothsay Wk, E14 302 B8
Rothschild Rd, W4 158 CQ77
Rothschild St, SE27 181 DP91
Roth Wk, N7 off Durham Rd 121 DN61
Rothwell Gdns, Dag. RM9 146 EW67
Rothwell Ho, Houns. TW5 off Biscoe Cl 156 CA79
Rothwell Rd, Dag. RM9 146 EW67
Rothwell St, NW1 274 F8
Rotten Row, SW1 296 G4
SW7 296 C4
Rotterdam Dr, E14 302 F7
Rouel Rd, SE16 300 C7
Rouge La, Grav. DA12 191 GH88
Rougemont Av, Mord. SM4 200 DA100
Roughdown Av, Hem.H. HP3 40 BG23
Roughdown Rd, Hem.H. HP3 40 BH23
Roughdown Vil Rd, Hem.H. HP3 40 BG23
Roughets La, Bletch. RH1 252 DS129
Godstone RH9 252 DS129
Roughlands, Wok. GU22 227 BE115
Rough Rew, Dor. RH4 263 CH139
Roughs, The, Nthwd. HA6 93 BT48
Roughtallys, N.Wld Bas. CM16 70 EZ27
Roughwood Cl, Wat. WD17 75 BS38
Roughwood La, Ch.St.G. HP8 90 AY45
Roundacre, SW19 179 CX89
Roundaway Rd, Ilf. IG5 103 EM54
Roundburrow Cl, Warl. CR6 236 DU117
ROUND BUSH, Wat. WD25 76 CC38
Roundbush La, Ald. WD25 76 CC38
Roundcroft, Chsht EN7 66 DT26
Roundel Cl, SE4 163 DZ84
Round Gro, Croy. CR0 203 DX101
Roundhay Cl, SE23 183 DX89
Roundheads End, Forty Grn HP9 88 AH51
Roundhedge Way, Enf. EN2 81 DM38
Round Hill, SE26 182 DW89
Roundhill, Wok. GU22 227 BB119
Roundhill Dr, Enf. EN2 81 DM42
Woking GU22 227 BB118
Roundhills, Wal.Abb. EN9 68 EE34
Roundhill Way, Cob. KT11 214 CB111
Guildford GU2 242 AT134
Round House Ct, Chsht EN8 off Hobbs Cl 67 DX29
Roundhouse La, E20 280 E5
Roundings, The, Hert.Hth SG13 32 DV14
Roundlyn Gdns, St.M.Cray BR5 off Lynmouth Ri 206 EV98
Roundmead Av, Loug. IG10 85 EN41
Roundmead Cl, Loug. IG10 85 EN41
Roundmoor Dr, Chsht EN8 67 DX29
Round Oak Rd, Wey. KT13 212 BM105
Roundtable Rd, Brom. BR1 184 EF90
Roundthorn Way, Wok. GU21 226 AT116
Roundtree Rd, Wem. HA0 117 CH64
Roundway, Bigg.H. TN16 off Norheads La 238 EK116
Egham TW20 173 BC92
Roundway, The, N17 100 DQ53
Claygate KT10 215 CF106
Watford WD18 75 BT44
Roundways, Ruis. HA4 115 BT62
Roundwood, Chis. BR7 205 EP96
Kings Langley WD4 58 BL26
Roundwood Av, Hutt. CM13 109 GA46
Uxbridge UB11 135 BQ74
Roundwood Cl, Ruis. HA4 115 BR59
Roundwood Dr, Welw.G.C. AL8 29 CW07
Roundwood Gro, Hutt. CM13 109 GB45
Roundwood Lake, Hutt. CM13 109 GB46
Roundwood Pk, NW10 139 CU66
Roundwood Rd, NW10 139 CT65
Amersham HP6 55 AS38
Roundwood Vw, Bans. SM7 233 CX115
Roundwood Way, Bans. SM7 233 CX115
Rounton Rd, E3 290 B4
Waltham Abbey EN9 68 EE33
Roupell Rd, SW2 181 DM88
Roupell St, SE1 298 F3
Rousden St, NW1 275 L7
Rousebarn La, Rick. WD3 75 BQ41
Rouse Cl, Wey. KT13 213 BT105
Rouse Gdns, SE21 182 DS91
Rous Rd, Buck.H. IG9 102 EL46
Routemaster Cl, E13 292 A2
Routh Ct, Felt. TW14 175 BR88
Routh Rd, SW18 180 DE87
Routh St, E6 293 K7
Rover Av, Ilf. IG6 103 ET51
Rover Ho, N1 off Phillipp St 277 P9
Rowallan Par, Dag. RM8 off Green La 126 EW60
Rowallan Rd, SW6 306 E5
Rowan Av, E4 101 DZ51
Egham TW20 173 BC92
Rowan Cl, SW16 201 DJ95
W5 158 CL75
Ashford TW15 174 BK91
Banstead SM7 233 CX115
Beaconsfield HP9 88 AH54
Bricket Wood AL2 60 CA31
Guildford GU1 242 AV131
Ilford IG1 125 ER64
New Malden KT3 198 CS96
Reigate RH2 266 DC136
St. Albans AL4 44 CL20
Shenley WD7 off Juniper Gdns 62 CL33
Stanmore HA7 95 CF51
Wembley HA0 117 CG62
Rowan Ct, Borwd. WD6 off Theobald St 78 CL39
Rowan Cres, SW16 201 DJ95
Dartford DA1 188 FJ88
Rowan Dr, NW9 119 CU56
Broxbourne EN10 67 DZ25
Rowan Gdns, Croy. CR0 202 DT104
Iver SL0 133 BC68
Rowan Grn, Wey. KT13 213 BR105
Rowan Grn E, Brwd. CM13 109 FZ48
Rowan Grn W, Brwd. CM13 109 FZ49
Rowan Gro, Aveley RM15 148 FQ73
Coulsdon CR5 235 DH121
Rowan Ho, NW3 off Maitland Pk Rd 274 F4
Rowanhurst Dr, Farn.Com. SL2 111 AQ64
Rowan Pl, Amer. HP6 72 AT38
Hayes UB3 135 BT73
Sch Rowan Prep Sch, Rowan Brae, Esher KT10 off Gordon Rd 215 CE108
Rowan Hill, Esher KT10 off Fitzalan Rd 215 CF108
Rowan Rd, SW16 201 DJ96
W6 294 C9
Bexleyheath DA7 166 EY83
Brentford TW8 157 CH80
Swanley BR8 207 FD97
West Drayton UB7 154 BK77
Rowans, Welw.G.C. AL7 30 DA06
Rowans, The, N13 100 DQ48
Aveley RM15 off Purfleet Rd 148 FQ74
Chalfont St. Peter SL9 112 AX55
Hemel Hempstead HP1 40 BG20
Sunbury-on-Thames TW16 175 BT92
Woking GU22 226 AY118
Rowans Cl, Long. DA3 209 FX96
Sch Rowans Prim Sch, Welw.G.C. AL7 off Rowans 30 DA06
Sch Rowans Sch, The, SW20 off Drax Av 179 CU94
Rowans Way, Loug. IG10 85 EM42
Rowan Ter, SE20 off Sycamore Gro 202 DU95
W6 294 C9
Rowantree Cl, N21 100 DR46
Rowantree Rd, N21 100 DR46
Enfield EN2 81 DP40
Rowan Wk, N2 120 DC58
N19 off Bredgar Rd 121 DJ61
W10 282 E4
Barnet EN5 80 DB43
Bromley BR2 205 EM104
Chesham HP5 54 AN30
Hatfield AL10 45 CU21
Hornchurch RM11 128 FK56
Rowan Way, Rom. RM6 126 EW55
Slough SL2 131 AP71
South Ockendon RM15 149 FX70
Rowanwood Av, Sid. DA15 186 EU88
Rowanwood Ms, Enf. EN2 81 DP40
Rowbarns Way, E.Hors. KT24 245 BT130
Rowben Cl, N20 98 DB46
Rowberry Cl, SW6 306 B5
Rowbourne Pl, Cuffley EN6 65 DK28
Rowbury, Gdmg. GU7 258 AU143
Rowcroft, Hem.H. HP1 39 BE21
Rowcross St, SE1 300 A10
Rowdell Rd, Nthlt. UB5 136 CA67
Rowden Pk Gdns, E4 off Rowden Rd 101 EA51
Rowden Rd, E4 101 EA51
Beckenham BR3 203 DY95
Epsom KT19 216 CP105
Rowditch La, SW11 308 G8
Rowdon Av, NW10 139 CV66
Rowdown Cres, New Adgtn CR0 221 ED109
Sch Rowdown Inf Sch, New Adgtn CR0 off Calley Down Cres 221 ED110
Rowdowns Rd, Dag. RM9 146 EZ67
Rowe Gdns, Bark. IG11 145 ET68
Rowe La, E9 278 G2
Rowena Cres, SW11 308 D9
Rowe Wk, Har. HA2 116 CA62
Rowfant Rd, SW17 180 DG88
Rowhedge, Brwd. CM13 109 GA48
Row Hill, Add. KT15 211 BF107
Rowhill Rd, E5 278 F1
Dartford DA2 187 FF93
Swanley BR8 187 FF93
Sch Rowhill Sch, Wilm. DA2 off Stock La 188 FJ91
Rowhurst Av, Add. KT15 212 BH107
Leatherhead KT22 231 CF117
Rowington Cl, W2 283 L6
Rowland Av, Har. HA3 117 CJ55
Rowland Cl, Wind. SL4 151 AK83
Rowland Ct, E16 291 L4
Rowland Cres, Chig. IG7 103 ES49
Rowland Gro, SE26 off Dallas Rd 182 DV90
Rowland Hill Av, N17 100 DQ52
Rowland Hill St, NW3 274 C2
Rowlands Av, Pnr. HA5 94 CA51
Rowlands Cl, N6 120 DG58
NW7 97 CU52
Cheshunt EN8 67 DX30
Rowlands Flds, Chsht EN8 67 DX29
Rowlands Rd, Dag. RM8 126 EZ61
Rowland Wk, Hav.at.Bow. RM4 105 FE48
Rowland Way, SW19 200 DB95
Ashford TW15 off Littleton Rd 175 BQ94
Rowlatt Cl, Dart. DA2 188 FJ91
Rowlatt Ct, St.Alb. AL1 off Hillside Rd 43 CE19
Rowlatt Dr, St.Alb. AL3 42 CA22
Rowlatt Rd, Dart. DA2 off Whitehead Cl 188 FJ90
Rowley Av, Sid. DA15 186 EV87
Rowley Cl, Pyrford GU22 228 BG116
Watford WD19 off Lower Paddock Rd 76 BY44
Wembley HA0 138 CM66
Rowley Ct, Cat. CR3 236 DQ122
Rowley Gdns, N4 122 DQ59
Cheshunt EN8 67 DX28
ROWLEY GREEN, Barn. EN5 79 CT42
Rowley Grn Rd, Barn. EN5 79 CT43
● Rowley Ind Pk, W3 158 CP76
Rowley La, Barn. EN5 79 CT43
Borehamwood WD6 78 CR39
Wexham SL3 132 AW67
Rowley Mead, Thnwd CM16 70 EW25
Rowley Rd, N15 122 DQ57
Rowleys Rd, Hert. SG13 32 DT08
Rowley Wk, Hem.H. HP2 41 BQ15
Rowley Way, NW8 273 M8
Rowlheys Pl, West Dr. UB7 154 BL76
Rowlls Rd, Kings.T. KT1 198 CM97
Rowmarsh Cl, Nthflt DA11 190 GD91
Rowney Gdns, Dag. RM9 146 EW65
Sawbridgeworth CM21 36 EW07
Rowney Rd, Dag. RM9 146 EV65
Rowney Wd, Saw. CM21 36 EW06
Rowntree Clifford Cl, E13 292 A4
Rowntree Cl, NW6 273 K5
Rowntree Path, SE28 off Booth Cl 146 EV73
Rowntree Rd, Twick. TW2 177 CE88
Rows, The, Harl. CM20 off East Gate 35 ER14
Rowse Cl, E15 280 F8
Rowsley Av, NW4 119 CW55
Rowstock Gdns, N7 275 P3
Rowton Rd, SE18 165 EQ80
ROWTOWN, Add. KT15 211 BF108
Rowtown, Add. KT15 211 BF108
Rowzill Rd, Swan. BR8 187 FF93
Roxborough Av, Har. HA1 117 CD59
Isleworth TW7 157 CF80
Roxborough Hts, Har. HA1 off College Rd 117 CE58
Roxborough Pk, Har. HA1 117 CE59
Roxborough Rd, Har. HA1 117 CD57
Roxbourne Cl, Nthlt. UB5 136 BX65
Sch Roxbourne Prim Sch, S.Har. HA2 off Torbay Rd 116 BY61
Roxburgh Av, Upmin. RM14 128 FQ62
Roxburgh Rd, SE27 181 DP92
Roxburn Way, Ruis. HA4 115 BT62
Roxby Pl, SW6 307 K2
ROXETH, Har. HA2 117 CD61
Roxeth Ct, Ashf. TW15 174 BN92
Roxeth Grn Av, Har. HA2 116 CB62
Roxeth Gro, Har. HA2 116 CB63
Roxeth Hill, Har. HA2 117 CD61
Sch Roxeth Prim Sch, Har. HA2 off Brickfields 117 CD61
Roxford Cl, Shep. TW17 195 BS99
Roxley Rd, SE13 183 EB86
Roxton Gdns, Croy. CR0 221 EA106
Roxwell Cl, Slou. SL1 131 AL74
Roxwell Gdns, Hutt. CM13 109 GC43
Roxwell Rd, W12 159 CU75
Barking IG11 146 EU68
● Roxwell Trd Pk, E10 123 DX59
Roxwell Way, Wdf.Grn. IG8 102 EJ52
Roxy Av, Rom. RM6 126 EW59
★ Royal Acad of Arts, W1 297 L1
Coll Royal Acad of Dance, SW11 308 B7
★ Royal Acad of Dramatic Art (R.A.D.A.), WC1 285 P6
Uni Royal Acad of Music, NW1 285 H5
★ Royal Air Force Mus, NW9 97 CU54
DLR Royal Albert 292 G10
Royal Albert Dock, E16 305 J1
★ Royal Albert Hall, SW7 296 A5
Royal Albert Rbt, E16 292 G10
Royal Albert Way, E16 292 F10
Sch Royal Alexandra & Albert Sch, Reig. RH2 off Rocky La 250 DE129
Royal Arc, W1 297 L1
Royal Artillery Barracks, SE18 305 L10
Royal Av, SW3 296 E10
Waltham Cross EN8 67 DY33
Worcester Park KT4 198 CS103
Coll Royal Ballet Sch, The, Upr Sch, WC2 286 B9
Sch Royal Ballet Sch, The, Lwr Sch, Rich. TW10 off Richmond Pk 178 CR88
★ Royal Berkshire Yeomanry Mus (Windsor TA Cen), Wind. SL4 151 AR83
★ Royal Botanic Gdns, Kew, Rich. TW9 158 CL80
H Royal Brompton Hosp, SW3 296 C10
Annexe, SW3 296 B10
Royal Carriage Ms, SE18 off Major Draper Rd 305 P7
Royal Circ, SE27 181 DN90
Royal Cl, N16 122 DS60
SE8 313 N2
SW19 179 CX90
Ilford IG3 126 EU59
Orpington BR6 223 EP105
Uxbridge UB8 134 BM72
Worcester Park KT4 198 CS103
Coll Royal Coll of Anaesthetists, The, WC1 286 C7
Uni Royal Coll of Art, Kensington (Darwin Building), SW7 295 P5
Kensington (Stevens Building), SW7 295 P5
Battersea, SW11 308 C5
Coll Royal Coll of Defence Studies, SW1 297 H6
Coll Royal Coll of Music, SW7 296 A6
Coll Royal Coll of Nursing, W1 285 J8
Coll Royal Coll of Obstetricians & Gynaecologists, NW1 284 E4
Coll Royal Coll of Physicians, NW1 285 K4
★ Royal Coll of Surgeons of England, WC2 286 D8
Royal Coll St, NW1 275 L6
Royal Connaught Dr, Bushey WD23 76 BZ42
Royal Ct, EC3 off Royal Ex Bldgs 287 M9
SE16 301 N6
Hemel Hempstead HP3 40 BL23
Watford WD18 75 BS42
★ Royal Courts of Justice, WC2 286 D9
Royal Cres, W11 294 D3
Ilford IG2 125 ER58
Ruislip HA4 116 BY63
Royal Cres Ms, W11 294 D3
Sch Royal Docks Comm Sch, The, E16 292 D9
Royal Docks Rd, E6 293 P10
★ Royal Dress Collection (Kensington Palace), W8 295 M3
Royal Dr, N11 98 DG50
Epsom KT18 233 CV118
Royal Duchess Ms, SW12 off Dinsmore Rd 181 DH87
Royal Earlswood Pk, Red. RH1 266 DG138
Royale Leisure Pk, W3 138 CN70
Royal Ex, EC3 287 M9
Royal Ex Av, EC3 287 M9
Royal Ex Bldgs, EC3 287 M9
★ Royal Festival Hall, SE1 298 D3
Uni Royal Free & Uni Coll Med Sch, Royal Free Campus, NW3 274 D2
H Royal Free Hosp, The, NW3 274 D2
Royal Gdns, W7 157 CG76
★ Royal Geographical Society, SW7 296 A5
Sch Royal Gram Sch, Guil. GU1 off High St 258 AY135
Royal Herbert Pavilions, SE18 165 EM81
Royal Hill, SE10 314 E4
Uni Royal Holloway Coll, Egh. TW20 off Egham Hill 172 AX93
Inst for Environmental Research, Vir.W. GU25 off Callow Hill 192 AW96
Kingswood Hall of Res, Egh. TW20 off Coopers Hill La 172 AX91
Royal Horticultural Society Cotts, Wisley GU23 off Wisley La 228 BL116
★ Royal Horticultural Society Gdn Wisley, Wok. GU22 228 BL119
★ Royal Horticultural Society (Lawrence Hall), SW1 297 N7
★ Royal Horticultural Society (Lindley Hall), SW1 297 N8
★ Royal Hosp Chelsea & Mus, SW3 308 G1
H Royal Hosp for Neuro-Disability, SW15 179 CY86
Royal Hosp Rd, SW3 308 E2
Royal Jubilee Ct, Rom. RM2 127 FG55
Sch Royal Kent C of E Prim Sch, The, Oxshott KT22 off Oakshade Rd 214 CC114
Royal La, Uxb. UB8 134 BM69
West Drayton UB7 134 BM72
Sch Royal Liberty Sch, The, Gidea Pk RM2 off Upper Brentwood Rd 128 FJ55
H Royal London Homoeopathic Hosp, WC1 286 B6
H Royal London Hosp, The, St. Clements, E3 289 P3
Whitechapel, E1 288 E7
Whitechapel - Dentistry Cen, E1 288 E7
H Royal Marsden Hosp, The, SW3 296 B10
Sutton SM2 218 DC110
Sch Royal Masonic Sch for Girls, The, Rick. WD3 off Chorleywood Rd 74 BK44
Royal Mews, Lon.Col. AL2 61 CK26
★ Royal Mews, The, SW1 297 K6
Coll Royal Military Sch of Music, Twick. TW2 off Kneller Rd 177 CD86
Royal Mint Ct, EC3 300 B1
Royal Mint Pl, E1 288 B10
Royal Mint St, E1 288 B10
Royal Mt Ct, Twick. TW2 177 CE90
★ Royal Nat Inst for the Blind Sunshine Ho Sch, Nthwd. HA6 off Dene Rd 93 BR51
H Royal Nat Orthopaedic Hosp, W1 285 K5
Stanmore HA7 95 CJ47
★ Royal National Rose Society - Gdns of the Rose, The, St.Alb. AL2 60 BY26
H Royal National Throat, Nose & Ear Hosp, WC1 286 C2
Royal Naval Pl, SE14 313 N4
⊖ Royal Oak 283 M7
Royal Oak Ct, N1 287 N2
Royal Oak Ms, Tedd. TW11 off High St 177 CG92
Royal Oak Pl, SE22 182 DV86
Royal Oak Rd, E8 278 E4
Bexleyheath DA6 186 EZ85
Woking GU21 226 AW118
Royal Oak Ter, Grav. DA12 off Constitution Hill 191 GJ88
Royal Oak Yd, SE1 299 N5
★ Royal Observatory Greenwich (Flamsteed Ho), SE10 315 H4
★ Royal Opera Arc, SW1 297 N2
★ Royal Opera Ho, WC2 286 B10
Royal Orchard Cl, SW18 179 CY87
Royal Par, SE3 315 L9
SW6 off Dawes Rd 306 E4
W5 off Western Av 138 CL69
Chislehurst BR7 185 EQ94
Richmond TW9 off Station App 158 CN81
Royal Par Ms, SE3 315 L9
Chislehurst BR7 185 EQ94
Sch Royal Pk Prim Sch, Sid. DA14 off Riverside Rd 186 EY90
Royal Pier Ms, Grav. DA12 off Royal Pier Rd 191 GH86
Royal Pier Rd, Grav. DA12 191 GH86
Royal Pl, SE10 314 F5
Royal Quarter, Kings.T. KT2 198 CL95
Royal Rd, E16 292 E9
SE17 310 G2
Darenth DA2 188 FN92
St. Albans AL1 43 CH20
Sidcup DA14 186 EX90
Teddington TW11 177 CD92
Royal Route, Wem. HA9 118 CN63
Sch Royal Russell Prep Sch, Croy. CR0 off Coombe La 220 DV106
Sch Royal Russell Sen Sch, Croy. CR0 off Coombe La 220 DV107
Sch Royal Sch Hampstead, The, NW3 274 A1
Coll Royal Sch of Needlework, E.Mol. KT8 off Hampton Ct Palace 197 CF98
Royal St, SE1 298 D6
H Royal Surrey Co Hosp, Guil. GU2 242 AS134
Royal Swan Quarter, Lthd. KT22 off Leret Way 231 CH121
Royalty Ms, W1 285 N9
Uni Royal Vet Coll - Boltons Pk Fm, Pot.B. EN6 off Hawkshead Rd 64 DA29
Uni Royal Vet Coll - Camden Campus, Beaumont Animal's Hosp, NW1 275 M9
Royal Coll St, NW1 275 N9
Uni Royal Vet Coll - Hawkshead Campus, N.Mymms AL9 off Hawkshead La 63 CX28
DLR Royal Victoria 291 N10
Royal Victoria Dock, E16 304 A1
● Royal Victoria Patriotic Bldg, SW18 180 DD86
Royal Victoria Pl, E16 304 B2
Royal Victoria Sq, E16 304 A1
Royal Victor Pl, E3 289 K1
Royal Wk, Wall. SM6 off Prince Charles Way 201 DH104
Royce Cl, Brox. EN10 49 DZ21
Royce Gro, Lvsdn WD25 59 BT34
Roycraft Av, Bark. IG11 145 ET68
Roycraft Cl, Bark. IG11 145 ET68
Roycroft Cl, E18 102 EH53
SW2 181 DN88
Roydene Rd, SE18 165 ES79
ROYDON, Harl. CM19 50 EH15
⇌ Roydon 34 EG13
● Roydonbury Ind Est, Harl. CM19 50 EL15
Roydon Cl, SW11 308 F8
Loughton IG10 102 EL45
Roydon Ct, Hersham KT12 213 BU105
ROYDON HAMLET, Harl. CM19 50 EJ19
Roydon Lo Chalet Est, Roydon CM19 34 EJ14
Roydon Marina Village, Roydon CM19 34 EG14
Sch Roydon Prim Sch, Roydon CM19 off Epping Rd 50 EH15
Roydon Rd, Harl. CM19 34 EL14
Stanstead Abbotts SG12 34 EE11
Roydon St, SW11 309 J6
Roy Gdns, Ilf. IG2 125 ES56
Roy Gro, Hmptn. TW12 176 CB93
Royle Bldg, N1 277 J10
Royle Cl, Chal.St.P. SL9 91 AZ52
Romford RM2 127 FH57
Royle Cres, W13 137 CG70
Roy Richmond Way, Epsom KT19 216 CS110
Roy Rd, Nthwd. HA6 93 BT52
Roy Sq, E14 289 M10
Royston Av, E4 101 EA50
Byfleet KT14 212 BL112
Sutton SM1 200 DD104
Wallington SM6 219 DK105
Royston Cl, Hert. SG14 31 DP09
Hounslow TW5 155 BV81
Walton-on-Thames KT12 195 BU102
Royston Ct, SE24 182 DQ86
Richmond TW9 158 CM81
Surbiton KT6 198 CN104
Royston Gdns, Ilf. IG1 124 EK58
Royston Gro, Pnr. HA5 94 BZ51
Royston Par, Ilf. IG1 124 EK58
Royston Pk Rd, Pnr. HA5 94 BZ51
Sch Royston Prim Sch, SE20 off High St 203 DX95
Royston Rd, SE20 203 DX95
Byfleet KT14 212 BL112
Dartford DA1 187 FF86
Richmond TW10 178 CL85
Romford RM3 106 FN52
St. Albans AL1 43 CH21
Roystons, The, Surb. KT5 198 CP99
Royston St, E2 289 H1
Royston Way, Slou. SL1 130 AJ71
Rozel Ct, N1 277 N8
Rozel Rd, SW4 309 L9
Rubastic Rd, Sthl. UB2 156 BW76
Rubeck Cl, Red. RH1 251 DH132
Rubens Pl, SW4 off Dolman St 161 DM84
Rubens Rd, Nthlt. UB5 136 BW68
Rubens St, SE6 183 DZ89
Rubin Pl, Enf. EN3 83 EA37
Ruby Cl, Slou. SL1 151 AN75
Ruby Ms, E17 off Ruby Rd 123 EA55
Ruby Rd, E17 123 EA55
Ruby St, NW10 138 CQ66
SE15 312 E2
Ruby Triangle, SE15 312 E2
Ruby Way, NW9 97 CT53
Ruckholt Cl, E10 123 EB62
Ruckholt Rd, E10 280 B1
Rucklers La, Kings L. WD4 58 BK27
Ruckles Way, Amer. HP7 55 AQ40
Rucklidge Av, NW10 139 CT68
Rudall Cres, NW3 off Willoughby Rd 120 DD63
Ruddington Cl, E5 123 DY63
Ruddlesway, Wind. SL4 151 AK81
Ruddock Cl, Edg. HA8 96 CQ52
Ruddstreet Cl, SE18 305 P9
Ruden Way, Epsom KT17 233 CV116
Rudge Ri, Add. KT15 211 BF106
Rudgwick Keep, Horl. RH6 off Langshott La 269 DJ147
Rudgwick Ter, NW8 274 D9
Rudland Rd, Bexh. DA7 167 FB83
Rudloe Rd, SW12 181 DJ87
Rudolf Pl, SW8 310 B3
Sch Rudolf Steiner Sch - Kings Langley, Kings L. WD4 off Langley Hill 58 BM29
Rudolph Rd, E13 291 M1
NW6 283 K1
Bushey WD23 76 CA44
Rudstone Ho, E3 off Bromley High St 290 C2
Rudsworth Cl, Colnbr. SL3 153 BD80
Rudyard Gro, NW7 96 CQ51
Rue de St. Lawrence, Wal.Abb. EN9 off Quaker La 67 EC34
Ruffets Wd, Grav. DA12 191 GJ93
Ruffetts, The, S.Croy. CR2 220 DV108
Ruffetts Cl, S.Croy. CR2 220 DV108
Ruffetts Way, Tad. KT20 233 CY118
Ruffle Cl, West Dr. UB7 154 BL75
Rufford Cl, Har. HA3 117 CG58
Watford WD17 75 BT37
Rufford St, N1 276 B8
Rufford Twr, W3 138 CP74
● Rufus Business Cen, SW18 180 DB89
Rufus Cl, Ruis. HA4 116 BY62
Rufus St, N1 287 N3
Rugby Av, N9 100 DT46
Greenford UB6 137 CD65
Wembley HA0 117 CH64
Rugby Cl, Har. HA1 117 CE57
★ Rugby Football Union Twickenham, Twick. TW1 177 CE86
Rugby Gdns, Dag. RM9 146 EW65
Rugby La, Sutt. SM2 off Nonsuch Wk 217 CX109

Rugby Rd, NW9 118 CP56
W4 158 CS75
Dagenham RM9 146 EV66
Twickenham TW1 177 CE86
Rugby St, WC1 286 C5
Rugby Way, Crox.Grn WD3 75 BP43
Rugged La, Wal.Abb. EN9 68 EK33
Ruggles-Brise Rd, Ashf. TW15 174 BK92
Rugg St, E14 290 A10
RUISLIP, HA4 115 BS59
⊖ Ruislip 115 BS60
Ruislip Adult Learning Cen, Ruis. HA4 off Sidmouth Dr 115 BU62
Ruislip Cl, Grnf. UB6 136 CB70
RUISLIP COMMON, Ruis. HA4 115 BR57
Ruislip Ct, Ruis. HA4 off Courtfield Gdns 115 BT61
RUISLIP GARDENS, Ruis. HA4 115 BS63
⊖ Ruislip Gardens 115 BU63
Ruislip Gdns Prim Sch, Ruis. HA4 off Stafford Rd 115 BT63
Ruislip High Sch, Ruis. HA4 off Sidmouth Dr 115 BU62
RUISLIP MANOR, Ruis. HA4 115 BU61
⊖ Ruislip Manor 115 BU60
Ruislip Retail Pk, Ruis. HA4 116 BY63
Ruislip Rd, Grnf. UB6 136 CA69
Northolt UB5 136 BX69
Ruislip Rd E, W7 137 CD70
W13 137 CD70
Greenford UB6 137 CD70
Ruislip St, SW17 180 DF91
Rumania Wk, Grav. DA12 191 GM90
Rumballs Cl, Hem.H. HP3 40 BN23
Rumballs Rd, Hem.H. HP3 40 BN23
Rumbold Rd, SW6 307 M5
Hoddesdon EN11 49 EC15
Rum Cl, E1 300 G1
Rumford Ho, SE1 off Bath Ter 299 J6
Rumford Shop Hall, Rom. RM1 off Market Pl 127 FE56
Rumsey Cl, Hmptn. TW12 176 BZ93
Rumsey Ms, N4 121 DP62
Rumsey Rd, SW9 310 D10
Rumsley, Wal.Cr. EN7 66 DU27
Runbury Circle, NW9 118 CR61
Runcie Cl, St.Alb. AL4 43 CG16
Runciman Cl, Orp. BR6 224 EW110
Runcorn Cl, N17 122 DV56
Runcorn Cres, Hem.H. HP2 40 BM16
Runcorn Pl, W11 282 E10
Rundell Cres, NW4 119 CV57
Rundells, Harl. CM18 52 EU19
Rundell Twr, SW8 310 C6
Runes Cl, Mitch. CR4 200 DD98
Runham Rd, Hem.H. HP3 40 BL22
Runnel Ct, Bark. IG11 off Spring Pl 145 EQ68
Runnelfield, Har. HA1 117 CE62
Runnemede Rd, Egh. TW20 173 AZ91
Running Horse Yd, Brent. TW8 off Pottery Rd 158 CL79
Running Waters, Brwd. CM13 109 GA49
Runnymede, SW19 200 DD95
Runnymede Cen, The, Add. KT15 off Chertsey Rd 194 BH103
Runnymede Cl, Twick. TW2 176 CB86
Runnymede Ct, SW15 179 CU88
Croydon CR0 202 DT103
Egham TW20 173 BA91
Runnymede Cres, SW16 201 DK95
Runnymede Gdns, Grnf. UB6 137 CD68
Twickenham TW2 176 CB86
Runnymede Hosp, Cher. KT16 193 BD104
Runnymede Ho, E9 off Kingsmead Way 279 M1
Runnymede Rd, Twick. TW2 176 CB86
Runrig Hill, Amer. HP6 55 AS35
Runsley, Welw.G.C. AL7 29 CZ06
Runtley Wd La, Sutt.Grn GU4 243 AZ125
Runway, The, Hat. AL10 44 CR16
Ruislip HA4 115 BV64
Runway Cl, NW9 off Great Strand 97 CT54
Rupack St, SE16 300 G5
Rupert Av, Wem. HA9 118 CL64
Rupert Ct, W1 285 N10
West Molesey KT8 off St. Peter's Rd 196 CA98
Rupert Gdns, SW9 310 G9
Rupert Rd, N19 off Holloway Rd 121 DK61
NW6 283 H1
W4 158 CS76
Guildford GU2 258 AV135
Rupert St, W1 285 N10
Rural Cl, Horn. RM11 127 FH60
Rural Vale, Nthflt DA11 190 GE87
Rural Way, SW16 181 DH94
Redhill RH1 250 DG134
Rusbridge Cl, E8 278 C2
Ruscoe Dr, Wok. GU22 off Pembroke Rd 227 BA117
Ruscoe Rd, E16 291 L8
Ruscombe Dr, Park St AL2 60 CB26
Ruscombe Gdns, Datchet SL3 152 AU80
Ruscombe Way, Felt. TW14 175 BT87
Rush, The, SW19 off Kingston Rd 199 CZ95
Rusham Ct, Egh. TW20 off Rusham Pk Av 173 BA93
Rusham Pk Av, Egh. TW20 173 AZ93
Rusham Rd, SW12 180 DF86
Egham TW20 173 AZ93
Rushbridge Cl, Croy. CR0 202 DQ100
Rushbrook Cres, E17 101 DZ53
Rushbrook Rd, SE9 185 EQ89
Rushburn, Woob.Grn HP10 110 AF57
Rush Cl, Stans.Abb. SG12 33 EC11
Rush Common Ms, SW2 181 DM87
Rush Cft, Gdmg. GU7 258 AU143
Rushcroft Rd, E4 101 EA52
SW2 161 DN84
Rush Cft Sch, E4 off Rushcroft Rd 101 EB52
Rushden Cl, SE19 182 DR94
Rushdene, SE2 166 EX76
Rushdene Av, Barn. EN4 98 DE45
Rushdene Cl, Nthlt. UB5 136 BW68
Rushdene Cres, Nthlt. UB5 136 BW68
Rushdene Rd, Brwd. CM15 108 FW45
Pinner HA5 116 BX58
Rushdene Wk, Bigg.H. TN16 238 EK117
Rushden Gdns, NW7 97 CW51
Ilford IG5 125 EN55
Rushdon Cl, Grays RM17 170 GA76
Romford RM1 127 FG57
Rush Dr, Wal.Abb. EN9 83 EC36
Rushen Dr, Hert.Hth SG13 32 DW12
Rushen Wk, Cars. SM5 off Paisley Rd 200 DD102
Rushes Mead, Harl. CM18 51 ES17
Uxbridge UB8 off Frays Waye 134 BJ67
Rushet Rd, Orp. BR5 206 EU96
Rushett Cl, T.Ditt. KT7 197 CH102
Rushett Dr, Dor. RH4 263 CH139
Rushett La, Epsom KT18 215 CJ111
Rushett Rd, T.Ditt. KT7 197 CH101
Rushetts Rd, Reig. RH2 266 DC138
Rushey Cl, N.Mal. KT3 198 CR98
Rushey Grn, SE6 183 EB87
Rushey Grn Prim Sch, SE6 off Culverley Rd 183 EB88
Rushey Hill, Enf. EN2 81 DM42
Rushey Mead, SE4 183 EA85
Rushfield, Pot.B. EN6 63 CX33
Sawbridgeworth CM21 36 EY05
Rushford Rd, SE4 183 DZ86
RUSH GREEN, Rom. RM7 127 FC59
Rush Grn Gdns, Rom. RM7 127 FC60
Rush Grn Inf Sch, Rom. RM7 off Dagenham Rd 127 FD60
Rush Grn Jun Sch, Rom. RM7 off Dagenham Rd 127 FE60
Rush Grn Rd, Rom. RM7 127 FC60
Rushgrove Av, NW9 119 CT57
Rushgrove St, SE18 305 K9
Rush Hill Ms, SW11 off Rush Hill Rd 160 DG83
Rush Hill Rd, SW11 160 DG83
Rushleigh Av, Chsht EN8 67 DX31
Rushley Cl, Kes. BR2 222 EK105
Rushmead, E2 288 E3
Richmond TW10 177 CH90
Rushmead Cl, Croy. CR0 220 DT105
Rushmere Av, Upmin. RM14 128 FQ62
Rushmere Ct, Hem.H. HP3 off Ebberns Rd 40 BL24
Wor.Pk. KT4 off The Avenue 199 CU103
Rushmere Ho, SW15 off Fontley Way 179 CU88
Rushmere La, Orch.L. HP5 56 AU28
Rushmere Pl, SW19 179 CX92
Englefield Green TW20 172 AY92
Rushmon Gdns, Walt. KT12 off Collingwood Pl 195 BV104
Rushmoor Cl, Guil. GU2 242 AT131
Pinner HA5 115 BV56
Rickmansworth WD3 92 BK47
Rushmore Cl, Brom. BR1 204 EL97
Rushmore Cres, E5 off Rushmore Rd 123 DX63
Rushmore Hill, Knock.P. TN14 224 EX112
Orpington BR6 224 EW110
Rushmore Prim Sch, E5 off Elderfield Rd 123 DX63
Rushmore Rd, E5 122 DW63
Rusholme Av, Dag. RM10 126 FA62
Rusholme Gro, SE19 182 DS92
Rusholme Rd, SW15 179 CX86
Rushout Av, Har. HA3 117 CH58
Rushton Av, Wat. WD25 75 BU35
Rushton Gro, Harl. CM17 52 EX15
Rushton St, N1 277 M10
Rushworth Rd, Reig. RH2 250 DA133
Rushworth St, SE1 299 H4
Rushy Meadow La, Cars. SM5 200 DE103
Rushy Meadow Prim Sch, Cars. SM5 off Rushy Meadow La 200 DE104
Ruskin Av, E12 144 EL65
Feltham TW14 175 BT86
Richmond TW9 158 CN80
Upminster RM14 128 FQ59
Waltham Abbey EN9 68 EE34
Welling DA16 166 EU83
Ruskin Cl, NW11 120 DB58
Cheshunt EN7 66 DS26
Ruskin Dr, Orp. BR6 205 ES104
Welling DA16 166 EU83
Worcester Park KT4 199 CV103
Ruskin Gdns, W5 137 CK70
Harrow HA3 118 CM56
Romford RM3 105 FH52
Ruskin Gro, Dart. DA1 188 FN85
Welling DA16 166 EU82
Ruskin Pk Ho, SE5 311 M10
Ruskin Rd, N17 100 DT53
Belvedere DA17 166 FA77
Carshalton SM5 218 DF106
Croydon CR0 201 DP103
Grays RM16 171 GG77
Isleworth TW7 157 CF83
Southall UB1 136 BY73
Staines-upon-Thames TW18 173 BF94
Ruskin Wk, N9 100 DU47
SE24 182 DQ85
Bromley BR2 205 EM100
Ruskin Way, SW19 200 DD95
Rusland Av, Orp. BR6 205 ER104
Rusland Hts, Har. HA1 off Rusland Pk Rd 117 CE56
Rusland Pk Rd, Har. HA1 117 CE56
Rusper Cl, NW2 119 CW62
Stanmore HA7 95 CJ49
Rusper Rd, N22 100 DQ54
Dagenham RM9 146 EW65
Russell Av, N22 99 DP54
St. Albans AL3 43 CD20
Russell Cl, NW10 138 CQ66
SE7 164 EJ80
W4 159 CT79
Amersham HP6 72 AX39
Beckenham BR3 203 EB97
Bexleyheath DA7 166 FA84
Brentwood CM15 108 FV45
Dartford DA1 167 FG83
Northwood HA6 93 BQ50
Ruislip HA4 116 BW61
Walton on the Hill KT20 249 CU125
Woking GU21 226 AW115
Russell Ct, SW1 297 M3
Bricket Wood AL2 60 CA30
Chesham HP5 54 AR29
Guildford GU1 242 AW131
Leatherhead KT22 231 CH122
Surbiton KT6 198 CL101
Russell Cres, Wat. WD25 75 BT35
Russellcroft Rd, Welw.G.C. AL8 29 CW08
Russell Dr, Stanw. TW19 174 BK86
Russell Gdns, N20 98 DE47
NW11 119 CY58
W14 294 E6
Richmond TW10 177 CJ89
Sipson UB7 154 BN78
Russell Gdns Ms, W14 294 E5
Russell Grn Cl, Pur. CR8 219 DN110
Russell Gro, NW7 96 CS50
SW9 310 F5
Russell Hill, Pur. CR8 219 DM110
Russell Hill Pl, Pur. CR8 219 DN111
Russell Hill Rd, Pur. CR8 219 DN110
Russell Kerr Cl, W4 158 CQ80
Russell La, N20 98 DE47
Watford WD17 75 BR36
Russell Lo, SE1 off Spurgeon St 299 L6
Russell Mead, Har.Wld HA3 95 CF53
Russell Par, NW11 off Golders Grn Rd 119 CY58
Russell Pl, NW3 274 D2
SE16 301 L7
Hemel Hempstead HP3 40 BH23
Sutton at Hone DA4 208 FN95
Russell Prim Sch, The, Rich. TW10 off Petersham Rd 177 CK88
Russell Rd, E4 101 DZ49
E10 123 EB58
E16 291 P8
E17 123 DZ55
N8 121 DK58
N13 99 DM51
N15 122 DS57
N20 98 DE47
NW9 119 CT58
SW19 180 DA94
W14 294 E6
Buckhurst Hill IG9 102 EH46
Enfield EN1 82 DT38
Gravesend DA12 191 GK86
Grays RM17 170 GA77
Mitcham CR4 200 DE97
Northolt UB5 116 CC64
Northwood HA6 93 BQ49
Shepperton TW17 195 BQ101
Tilbury RM18 170 GE81
Tilbury (cul-de-sac) RM18 171 GF82
Twickenham TW2 177 CF86
Walton-on-Thames KT12 195 BU100
Woking GU21 226 AW115
Russells, Tad. KT20 233 CX122
Russell Sch, The, Chorl. WD3 off Brushwood Dr 73 BB42
Russells Cres, Horl. RH6 268 DG149
Russell's Footpath, SW16 181 DL92
⊖ Russell Square 286 A5
Russell Sq, WC1 286 A5
Longfield DA3 off Cavendish Sq 209 FX97
Russells Ride, Chsht EN8 67 DX31
Russell St, WC2 286 B10
Hertford SG14 32 DQ09
Windsor SL4 151 AR81
Russell's Way, S.Ock. RM15 149 FX72
Russell's Wf Flats, W10 282 G4
Russell Wk, Rich. TW10 off Park Hill 178 CM86
Russell Way, Sutt. SM1 218 DA106
Watford WD19 93 BV45
Russell Wilson Ct, Rom. RM3 off Church Rd 106 FN53
Russet Cl, Chsht EN7 66 DS26
Hersham KT12 196 BX104
Horley RH6 off Carlton Tye 269 DJ148
Staines-upon-Thames TW19 173 BF86
Uxbridge UB10 135 BQ70
Russet Cres, N7 276 C2
Russet Dr, Croy. CR0 203 DY102
St. Albans AL4 43 CJ21
Shenley WD7 62 CL32
Russet Ho Sch, Enf. EN1 off Autumn Cl 82 DV39
Russets, The, Chal.St.P. SL9 off Austenwood Cl 90 AX54
Russets Cl, E4 off Larkshall Rd 101 ED49
Russett Cl, Orp. BR6 224 EV106
Russett Ct, Cat. CR3 252 DU125
Russett Hill, Chal.St.P. SL9 112 AY55
Russetts, Horn. RM11 128 FL56
Russetts Cl, Wok. GU21 227 AZ115
Russett Way, Swan. BR8 207 FD96
Russettwood, Welw.G.C. AL7 30 DD10
Russet Way, N.Holm. RH5 263 CK140
Russia Dock Rd, SE16 301 M3
Russia La, E2 278 G10
Russia Row, EC2 287 K9
Russia Wk, SE16 301 K5
Russington Rd, Shep. TW17 195 BR100
Rusthall Av, W4 158 CR77
Rusthall Cl, Croy. CR0 202 DW100
Rustic Av, SW16 181 DH94
Rustic Cl, Upmin. RM14 129 FS60
Rustic Pl, Wem. HA0 117 CK63
Rustic Wk, E16 292 A8
Rustington Wk, Mord. SM4 199 CZ101
Ruston Av, Surb. KT5 198 CP101
Ruston Gdns, N14 off Byre Rd 80 DG44
Ruston Ms, W11 282 E9
Ruston Rd, SE18 304 G7
Ruston St, E3 279 P8
Rust Sq, SE5 311 L4
Rutford Rd, SW16 181 DL92
Ruth Cl, Stan. HA7 118 CM56
Ruthen Cl, Epsom KT18 216 CP114
Rutherford Cl, Borwd. WD6 78 CQ40
Sutton SM2 218 DD107
Uxbridge UB8 134 BM70
Windsor SL4 151 AM81
Rutherford Sch, S.Croy. CR2 off Melville Av 220 DT106
Rutherford St, SW1 297 N8
Rutherford Twr, Sthl. UB1 136 CB72
Rutherford Way, Bushey Hth WD23 95 CD46
Wembley HA9 118 CN63
Rutherglen Rd, SE2 166 EU79
Rutherwick Cl, Horl. RH6 268 DF148
Rutherwick Ri, Couls. CR5 235 DL117
Rutherwyke Cl, Epsom KT17 217 CU107
Rutherwyk Rd, Cher. KT16 193 BE101
Ruthin Cl, NW9 118 CS58
Ruthin Rd, SE3 315 N2
Ruthven Av, Wal.Cr. EN8 67 DX33
Ruthven St, E9 279 J8
Rutland App, Horn. RM11 128 FN57
Rutland Av, Sid. DA15 186 EU87
Slough SL1 131 AR71
Rutland Cl, SW14 158 CP83
SW19 off Rutland Rd 180 DE94
Ashtead KT21 232 CL117
Bexley DA5 186 EX88
Chessington KT9 216 CM107
Dartford DA1 188 FK87
Rutland Cl, Epsom KT19 216 CR110
Redhill RH1 250 DF133
Rutland Ct, SW7 off Rutland Gdns 296 D5
Chis. BR7 205 EN95
Enfield EN3 82 DW43
Rutland Dr, Horn. RM11 128 FN57
Morden SM4 199 CZ100
Richmond TW10 177 CK88
Rutland Gdns, N4 121 DP58
SW7 296 D5
W13 137 CG71
Croydon CR0 220 DS105
Dagenham RM8 126 EW64
Hemel Hempstead HP2 40 BM19
Rutland Gdns Ms, SW7 296 D5
Rutland Gate, SW7 296 D5
Belvedere DA17 167 FB78
Bromley BR2 204 EF98
Rutland Gate Ms, SW7 296 C5
Rutland Gro, W6 159 CV78
Rutland Ms, NW8 273 M9
Rutland Ms E, SW7 296 C6
Rutland Ms S, SW7 296 C6
Rutland Ms W, SW7 off Ennismore St 296 C6
Rutland Pk, NW2 272 B5
SE6 183 DZ89
Rutland Pk Gdns, NW2 off Rutland Pk 272 B5
Rutland Pk Mans, NW2 off Rutland Pk 272 B5
Rutland Pl, EC1 287 J5
Bushey Heath WD23 off The Rutts 95 CD46
Rutland Rd, E7 144 EK66
E9 279 H8
E11 124 EH57
E17 123 EA58
SW19 180 DE94
Harrow HA1 116 CC58
Hayes UB3 155 BR77
Ilford IG1 125 EP63
Southall UB1 136 CA71
Twickenham TW2 177 CD89
Rutland St, SW7 296 D6
Rutland Wk, SE6 183 DZ89
Rutland Way, Orp. BR5 206 EW100
Rutley Cl, SE17 310 G2
Harold Wood RM3 off Pasteur Dr 106 FK54
Rutlish Rd, SW19 200 DA95
Rutlish Sch, SW20 off Watery La 199 CZ96
Rutson Rd, Byfleet KT14 212 BM114
Rutter Gdns, Mitch. CR4 200 DC98
Rutters Cl, West Dr. UB7 154 BN75
Rutts, The, Bushey Hth WD23 95 CD46
Rutts Ter, SE14 313 J7
Ruvigny Gdns, SW15 306 D10
Ruxbury Rd, Cher. KT16 193 BC100
Ruxley Cl, Epsom KT19 216 CP106
Sidcup DA14 186 EX93
Ruxley Cor, Sid. DA14 186 EY93
Ruxley Cor Ind Est, Sid. DA14 186 EX93
Ruxley Cres, Clay. KT10 215 CH107
Ruxley Gdns, Shep. TW17 195 BQ99
Ruxley La, Epsom KT19 216 CR106
Ruxley Ms, Epsom KT19 216 CP106
Ruxley Ridge, Clay. KT10 215 CG108
Ruxton Cl, Couls. CR5 235 DJ115
Swanley BR8 207 FE97
Ryall Cl, Brick.Wd AL2 60 BY29
Ryalls Ct, N20 98 DF48
Ryan Cl, SE3 164 EJ84
Ruislip HA4 115 BV60
Ryan Dr, Brent. TW8 157 CG79
Ryan Way, Wat. WD24 76 BW39
Ryarsh Cres, Orp. BR6 223 ES105
Rybrook Dr, Walt. KT12 196 BW103
Rycott Path, SE22 off Lordship La 182 DU87
Rycroft, Wind. SL4 151 AM83
Rycroft La, Sev. TN14 256 FE130
Rycroft Way, N17 122 DT55
Ryculff Sq, SE3 315 M8
Rydal Cl, NW4 97 CY53
Purley CR8 220 DR113
Rydal Ct, Wat. WD25 off Grasmere Cl 59 BV32
Rydal Cres, Perivale UB6 137 CH69
Rydal Dr, Bexh. DA7 166 FA81
West Wickham BR4 204 EE103
Rydal Gdns, NW9 118 CS57
SW15 178 CS92
Hounslow TW3 176 CB86
Wembley HA9 117 CJ60
Rydal Rd, SW16 181 DK91
Rydal Way, Egh. TW20 173 BB94
Enfield EN3 82 DW44
Ruislip HA4 116 BW63
RYDE, THE, Hat. AL9 45 CW15
Ryde, The, Hat. AL9 45 CW16
Staines-upon-Thames TW18 194 BH95
Ryde Cl, Ripley GU23 228 BJ121
Ryde Heron, Knap. GU21 226 AS117
RYDENS, Walt. KT12 196 BW103
Rydens Av, Walt. KT12 195 BV103
Rydens Cl, Walt. KT12 196 BW103
Rydens Gro, Hersham KT12 214 BX105
Rydens Pk, Walt. KT12 196 BX103
Rydens Rd, Walt. KT12 196 BX103
Rydens Sch, Hersham KT12 off Hersham Rd 214 BW105
Rydens Way, Wok. GU22 227 BA120
Ryde Pl, Twick. TW1 177 CJ86
Ryder Av, E10 123 EB59
Ryder Cl, Bov. HP3 57 BA28
Bromley BR1 184 EH92
Bushey WD23 76 CB44
Hertford SG13 32 DV08
Ryder Ct, SW1 297 M2
Ryder Dr, SE16 312 E1
Ryder Gdns, Rain. RM13 147 FF65
Ryder Ms, E9 279 H3
Ryders Av, Coln.Hth AL4 44 CS20
Ryder Seed Ms, St.Alb. AL1 off Pageant Rd 43 CD21
Ryders Ter, NW8 273 N10
Ryder St, SW1 297 M2
Ryder Yd, SW1 297 M2
Rydes Av, Guil. GU2 242 AT131
Ryde Sch, The, Hat. AL9 off Pleasant Ri 45 CW15
Rydes Cl, Wok. GU22 227 BC120
RYDESHILL, Guil. GU3 242 AS131
Rydes Hill Cres, Guil. GU2 242 AT130
Rydes Hill Prep Sch, Guil. GU2 off Aldershot Rd 242 AT132
Rydes Hill Rd, Guil. GU2 242 AT132
Ryde Vale Rd, SW12 181 DH89
Rydings, Wind. SL4 151 AM83
Rydon Business Cen, Lthd. KT22 231 CH119
Rydon Ms, SW19 179 CW94
Rydons Cl, SE9 164 EL83
Rydon's La, Couls. CR5 236 DQ120
Rydon St, N1 277 K8
Rydons Way, Red. RH1 266 DG135
Rydon's Wd Cl, Couls. CR5 236 DQ120
Rydston Cl, N7 276 B6
Rye, The, N14 99 DJ45
Ryebridge Cl, Lthd. KT22 231 CG118
Ryebrook Rd, Lthd. KT22 231 CG118
Rye Cl, Bex. DA5 187 FB86
Borwd. WD6 78 CR42
Guildford GU2 242 AS132
Hornchurch RM12 128 FJ64
Ryecotes Mead, SE21 182 DS88
Rye Ct, Slou. SL1 off Alpha St S 152 AU76
Rye Cres, Orp. BR5 206 EW102
Ryecroft, Grav. DA12 191 GL92
Harlow CM19 51 EP15
Hatfield AL10 45 CT20
Ryecroft Av, Ilf. IG5 103 EP54
Twickenham TW2 176 CB87
Ryecroft Cl, Hem.H. HP2 off Poynders Hill 41 BQ21
Ryecroft Ct, St.Alb. AL4 44 CM20
Ryecroft Cres, Barn. EN5 79 CV43
Ryecroft Rd, SE13 183 EC85
SW16 181 DN93
Chesham HP5 54 AN32
Otford TN14 241 FG116
Petts Wood BR5 205 ER100
Ryecroft St, SW6 307 L7
Ryedale, SE22 182 DV86
Ryedale Ct, Sev. TN13 off London Rd 256 FE121
Ryefeld Cl, Hodd. EN11 33 EB13
Rye Fld, Ashtd. KT21 231 CK117
Orpington BR5 206 EX102
Ryefield Av, Uxb. UB10 135 BP66
Ryefield Ct, Nthwd. HA6 off Ryefield Cres 93 BU54
Ryefield Cres, Nthwd. HA6 93 BU54
Ryefield Par, Nthwd. HA6 off Ryefield Cres 93 BU54
Ryefield Path, SW15 179 CU88
Ryefield Prim Sch, Hlgdn UB10 off Ryefield Av 135 BQ67
Ryefield Rd, SE19 182 DQ93
Ryegates, SE15 312 F8
RYE HILL, Harl. CM18 51 ES22
Rye Hill Pk, SE15 162 DW84
Rye Hill Rd, Harl. CM18 51 ES22
Thornwood CM16 52 EU23
Rye Ho, NW7 off Peacock Cl 97 CY50
⇌ Rye House 49 EC15
Ryeland Cl, West Dr. UB7 134 BL72
Ryelands, Horl. RH6 269 DJ147
Welwyn Garden City AL7 29 CZ12
Ryelands Cl, Cat. CR3 236 DS121
Ryelands Ct, Lthd. KT22 231 CG118
Ryelands Cres, SE12 184 EJ86
Ryelands Pl, Wey. KT13 195 BS104
Ryelands Prim Sch, SE25 off Albert Rd 202 DV99
Rye La, SE15 312 C7
Sevenoaks TN14 241 FG117
Rye Oak Prim Sch, SE15 off Whorlton Rd 162 DV83
RYE PARK, Hodd. EN11 49 EB16
Rye Pk Ind Est, Hodd. EN11 off Salisbury Rd 49 EC15
Rye Pas, SE15 312 D10
Ryepeck Meadow Moorings, Shep. TW17 194 BL101
Rye Rd, SE15 163 DX84
Hoddesdon EN11 49 EB15
Stanstead Abbotts SG12 34 EE13
Rye Wk, SW15 179 CX85
Rye Way, Edg. HA8 off Canons Dr 96 CM51
Ryfold Rd, SW19 180 DA90
Ryhope Rd, N11 99 DH49
Rykens La, Bet. RH3 264 CQ139
Rykhill, Grays RM16 171 GH76
Ryland Cl, Felt. TW13 175 BT91
Rylandes Rd, NW2 119 CU62
South Croydon CR2 220 DV109
Ryland Ho, Croy. CR0 202 DQ104
Ryland Rd, NW5 275 J4
Rylett Cres, W12 159 CT76
Rylett Rd, W12 159 CT76
Rylston Rd, N13 100 DR48
SW6 306 G3
Rymer Rd, Croy. CR0 202 DS101
Rymer St, SE24 181 DP86
Rymill Cl, Bov. HP3 57 BA28
Rymill St, E16 305 L3
Rysbrack St, SW3 296 E6
Rysted La, West. TN16 255 EQ126
Rythe Bk Cl, T.Ditt. KT7 197 CH101
Rythe Cl, Chess. KT9 off Nigel Fisher Way 215 CJ108
Claygate KT10 215 CE106
Rythe Ct, T.Ditt. KT7 197 CG101
Rythe Rd, Clay. KT10 215 CD106
Ryvers Comb Sch, Langley SL3 off Trelawney Av 152 AX76
Ryvers Rd, Slou. SL3 153 AZ76

S

★ Saatchi Gall, The, SW3 296 F9
Sabah Ct, Ashf. TW15 174 BN91
Sabbarton St, E16 291 L9
Sabella Ct, E3 289 P1
Sabina Rd, Grays RM16 171 GJ77
Sabine Rd, SW11 308 E10
Sable Cl, Houns. TW4 156 BW83
Sable St, N1 277 H6
Sachfield Dr, Chaff.Hun. RM16 170 FY76
Sach Rd, E5 122 DV61
Sackville Av, Brom. BR2 204 EG102
Sackville Cl, Har. HA2 117 CD62
Sevenoaks TN13 257 FH122

Sackville Ct, Rom. RM3
off Sackville Cres 106 FL53
Sackville Cres, Rom. RM3 106 FL53
Sackville Est, SW16 181 DL90
Sackville Gdns, Ilf. IG1 125 EM60
Sackville Rd, Dart. DA2 188 FK89
Sutton SM2 218 DA108
Sackville St, W1 297 M1
Sacombe Rd, Hem.H. HP1 39 BF18
Sacred Heart Cath Prim Sch, N.Mal. KT3 off Burlington Rd 199 CU98
Sacred Heart Cath Prim Sch & Nurs, Bushey WD23
off Merry Hill Rd 76 BZ44
Sacred Heart High Sch, W6 294 B9
Sacred Heart Language Coll, The, Wealds. HA3 off High St 95 CE54
Sacred Heart of Mary Girls' Sch, Upmin. RM14
off St. Mary's La 128 FP61
Sacred Heart RC Prim Sch, N7 276 D3
N20 off Oakleigh Pk S 98 DE47
SW11 308 D9
SW15 off Roehampton La 179 CU85
Ruislip HA4 off Herlwyn Av 115 BS61
Teddington TW11
off St. Mark's Rd 177 CH94
Ware SG12 off Broadmeads 33 DX06
Sacred Heart RC Sch, SE5 311 J6
Saddington St, Grav. DA12 191 GH87
Saddlebrook Pk, Sun. TW16 175 BS94
Saddle Ms, Croy. CR0 202 DQ101
Saddlers Cl, Arkley EN5 79 CV43
Borehamwood WD6
off Farriers Way 78 CR44
Pinner HA5 94 CA51
Saddlers Ms, SW8
off Portland Gro 310 B6
Hampton Wick KT1 197 CJ95
Wembley HA0 off The Boltons 117 CF63
Saddler's Pk, Eyns. DA4 208 FK104
Saddlers Path, Borwd. WD6 78 CR43
Saddlers Way, Epsom KT18 232 CR119
Saddlescombe Way, N12 98 DA50
Saddleworth Rd, Rom. RM3 106 FJ51
Saddleworth Sq, Rom. RM3 106 FJ51
Saddle Yd, W1 297 J2
Sadleir Rd, St.Alb. AL1 43 CE22
Sadler Cl, Chsht EN7
off Markham Rd 66 DQ25
Mitcham CR4 200 DF96
Sadler Ho, E3
off Bromley High St 290 D2
Sadlers Cl, Guil. GU4 243 BD133
Sadlers Gate Ms, SW15 306 A10
Sadlers Mead, Harl. CM18 52 EU16
Sadlers Ride, W.Mol. KT8 196 CC96
Sadlers Way, Hert. SG14 31 DN09
★ Sadler's Wells Thea, EC1 286 G2
SAE Inst, N7 276 B3
Saffron Av, E14 290 G10
Saffron Cen Sq, Croy. CR0
off Wellesley Rd 202 DQ102
Saffron Cl, NW11 119 CZ57
Croydon CR0 201 DL100
Datchet SL3 152 AV81
Hoddesdon EN11 49 DZ16
Saffron Ct, Felt. TW14
off Staines Rd 175 BQ87
Saffron Grn First Sch, Borwd. WD6 off Nicoll Way 78 CR42
Saffron Hill, EC1 286 F5
Saffron La, Hem.H. HP1 40 BH19
Saffron Platt, Guil. GU2 242 AU130
Saffron Rd, Chaff.Hun. RM16 169 FW77
Romford RM5 105 FC54
Saffron St, EC1 286 F6
Saffron Twr, Croy. CR0 202 DQ224
Saffron Way, Surb. KT6 197 CK102
Sage Cl, E6 293 J7
Sage Ms, SE22
off Lordship La 182 DT85
Sage St, E1 288 G10
Sage Way, WC1 286 C3
Saigasso Cl, E16 292 E9
Sailacre Ho, SE10
off Calvert Rd 164 EF78
Sail Ct, E14
off Newport Av 291 H10
Sailmakers Ct, SW6 307 N10
Sail St, SE11 298 D8
Sainfoin Rd, SW17 180 DG89
Sainsbury Cen, The, Cher. KT16 off Guildford St 194 BG101
Sainsbury Rd, SE19 182 DS92
St. Adrian's RC Prim Sch & Nurs, St.Alb. AL1 off Watling Vw 42 CC23
St. Agatha's Cath Prim Sch, Kings.T. KT2 off St. Agatha's Dr 178 CM93
St. Agatha's Dr, Kings.T. KT2 178 CM93
St. Agathas Gro, Cars. SM5 200 DF102
St. Agnells Ct, Hem.H. HP2 40 BN16
St. Agnells La, Hem.H. HP2 40 BM15
St. Agnes Cl, E9 278 G9
St. Agnes Pl, SE11 310 G3
St. Agnes RC Prim Sch, E3 290 C2
St. Agnes' RC Prim Sch, NW2 off Thorverton Rd 119 CY62
St. Agnes Well, EC1 off Old St 287 M4
St. Aidan's Cath Prim Sch, Couls. CR5 off Portnalls Rd 235 DJ116
Ilford IG1 off Benton Rd 125 ER60
St. Aidans Ct, W13
off St. Aidans Rd 157 CJ75
Barking IG11 off Choats Rd 146 EV69
St. Aidan's Prim Sch, N4
off Albany Rd 121 DN59
St. Aidans Rd, W13 157 CH75
St. Aidan's Rd, SE22 182 DV86
St. Aidan's Way, Grav. DA12 191 GL90
St. Alban & Stephen RC Inf & Nurs Sch, St.Alb. AL1
off Vanda Cres 43 CF21
St. Alban & Stephen RC Jun Sch, St.Alb. AL1
off Cecil Rd 43 CG20
≠ St. Albans Abbey 43 CD22
St. Albans Av, E6 293 K2
Felt. TW13 176 BX92
Upminster RM14 129 FS60
Weybridge KT13 194 BN104
St. Alban's Av, W4 158 CR77
★ St. Albans Cath, St.Alb. AL3 43 CD20
St. Albans Catholic Prim Sch, Harl. CM20 off First Av 35 ET13
St. Alban's Catholic Prim Sch, E.Mol. KT8 off Beauchamp Rd 196 CC99
St. Alban's Cath Prim Sch, Horn. RM12
off Heron Flight Av 147 FH66
≠ St. Albans City 43 CE20
St. Albans City Hosp, St.Alb. AL3 42 CC18
St. Albans Cl, NW11 120 DA60
Gravesend DA12 191 GK90
Windsor SL4 off St. Alban's St 151 AR81
St. Alban's C of E Prim Sch, EC1 286 E6
St. Albans Ct, EC2 287 K8
St. Albans Cres, N22 99 DN53
St. Alban's Cres, Wdf.Grn. IG8 102 EG52
● St. Albans Enterprise Cen, St.Alb. AL3 off Long Spring 43 CF16
St. Albans Gdns, Grav. DA12 191 GK90
St. Alban's Gdns, Tedd. TW11 177 CG92
St. Albans Girls' Sch, St.Alb. AL3 off Sandridgebury La 43 CE16
St. Albans Gro, W8 295 M6
St. Alban's Gro, Cars. SM5 200 DE101
St. Albans High Sch for Girls, St.Alb. AL1 off Townsend Av 43 CE19
St. Albans Hill, Hem.H. HP3 40 BL23
St. Albans La, NW11 120 DA60
Bedmond WD5 59 BT26
St. Albans Music Sch, St.Alb. AL3 off Townsend Dr 43 CD17
★ St. Albans Organ Mus, St.Alb. AL1 off Camp Rd 43 CH21
St. Alban's Pl, N1 276 G9
St. Albans Retail Pk, St.Alb. AL1 43 CD22
St. Albans Rd, NW5 120 DG62
NW10 138 CS67
Barnet EN5 79 CX39
Coopersale CM16 70 EX29
Dancers Hill EN6 79 CV35
Dartford DA1 188 FM87
Hemel Hempstead HP2, HP3 40 BN21
Ilford IG3 125 ET60
Lon.Col. AL2 62 CN28
Reigate RH2 250 DA133
Sandridge AL4 43 CF17
Shenley WD7 62 CN28
South Mimms EN6 63 CV34
Wat. WD17, WD24, WD25 75 BV40
St. Alban's Rd, Kings.T. KT2 178 CL93
Sutt. SM1 217 CZ105
Wdf.Grn. IG8 102 EG52
St. Albans Rd E, Hat. AL10 45 CV17
St. Albans Rd Inf Sch, Dart. DA1 off St. Albans Rd 188 FM86
St. Albans Rd W, Hat. AL10 44 CR18
Roe Green AL10 45 CT17
St. Albans Sch, St.Alb. AL3
off Abbey Gateway 42 CC20
St. Albans St, SW1 297 N1
St. Alban's St, Wind. SL4 151 AR81
St. Albans Ter, W6 306 E2
St. Alban's Vil, NW5
off Highgate Rd 120 DG62
St. Albert the Gt RC Prim Sch, Hem.H. HP3 off Acorn Rd 40 BN21
St. Alfege Pas, SE10 314 E3
St. Alfege Rd, SE7 164 EK79
St. Alfege with St. Peter's C of E Prim Sch, SE10 314 E3
St. Aloysius' Coll, N6
off Hornsey La 121 DJ60
St. Aloysius RC Inf Sch, NW1 285 N2
St. Aloysius RC Jun Sch, NW1 285 M1
St. Alphage Gdns, EC2 287 K7
St. Alphage Highwalk, EC2 287 L7
St. Alphage Wk, Edg. HA8 96 CQ54
St. Alphege Rd, N9 100 DW45
St. Alphonsus Rd, SW4 161 DJ84
St. Amunds Cl, SE6 183 EA91
St. Andrew & St. Francis C of E Prim Sch, NW2 off Belton Rd 139 CU65
St. Andrew Ms, Hert. SG14 32 DQ09
St. Andrew's & St. Mark's C of E Jun Sch, Surb. KT6
off Maple Rd 197 CK99
St. Andrews Av, Horn. RM12 127 FG64
Wembley HA0 117 CG63
Windsor SL4 151 AM82
St. Andrews Cl, NW2 119 CV62
SE16 312 F1
SE28 146 EX72
SW19 180 DB93
N.Wld Bas. CM16 53 FC16
Old Windsor SL4 172 AU86
Reig. RH2 off St. Marys Rd 266 DB135
Ruislip HA4 116 BX61
Stan. HA7 95 CJ54
Thames Ditton KT7 197 CH102
Woking GU21 226 AW117
St. Andrew's Cl, N12 98 DC49
Islw. TW7 157 CD81
Shep. TW17 195 BR98
Wrays. TW19 172 AY87
St. Andrews C of E High Sch, Croy. CR0 off Warrington Rd 219 DP105
St. Andrew's C of E Prim Sch, N1 276 D8
N14 off Chase Rd 99 DK46
N20 off Totteridge Village 97 CZ47
SW9 310 B9
Enfield EN1 off Churchbury La 82 DS40
North Weald Bassett CM16
off School Grn La 71 FC25
Stanstead Abbotts SG12
off Mill Race 33 ED11
Uxbridge UB8
off Nursery Waye 134 BK67
St. Andrews Ct, Colnbr. SL3
off High St 153 BD80
Watford WD17 75 BV39
St. Andrew's Ct, SW18 180 DC89
St. Andrews Cres, Wind. SL4 151 AM82
St. Andrews Dr, Orp. BR5 206 EV100
St. Albans AL1 43 CH23
Stanmore HA7 95 CJ53
St. Andrews Gdns, Cob. KT11 214 BW113
St. Andrew's Gro, N16 122 DR60
St. Andrew's Hill, EC4 287 H10
St. Andrews Meadow, Harl. CM18 51 ET16
St. Andrews Ms, SE3 315 N4
SW12 off Emmanuel Rd 181 DK88
St. Andrew's Ms, N16 122 DS60
St. Andrews Pl, NW1 285 K4
Shenfield CM15 109 FZ47
St. Andrew's Prim Sch, Cob. KT11 off Lockhart Rd 214 BW113
St. Andrews Rd, E11 124 EE58
E13 292 A3
E17 101 DX54
N9 100 DW45
NW9 118 CR60
NW10 139 CV65
NW11 119 CZ58
W3 138 CS73
W7 off Churchfield Rd 157 CE75
W14 306 F2
Carshalton SM5 200 DE104
Coulsdon CR5 234 DG116
Croydon CR0
off Lower Coombe St 220 DQ105
Enfield EN1 82 DR41
Hem.H. HP3 off West Valley Rd 40 BJ24
Ilford IG1 125 EM59
Romford RM7 127 FD58
Sidcup DA14 186 EX90
Til. RM18 170 GE81
Uxbridge UB10 134 BM66
Watford WD19 94 BX48
St. Andrew's Rd, Grav. DA12 191 GJ87
Surb. KT6 197 CK100
St. Andrew's RC Prim Sch, SW16 off Polworth Rd 181 DL92
St. Andrew's Sch, Lthd. KT22 off Grange Rd 231 CK120
Woking GU21
off Wilson Way 226 AX116
St. Andrews Sq, W11 282 E9
St. Andrew's Sq, Surb. KT6 197 CK100
St. Andrews Twr, Sthl. UB1 136 CC73
St. Andrew St, EC4 286 F7
Hertford SG14 32 DQ09
St. Andrews Wk, Cob. KT11 229 BV115
St. Andrews Way, E3 290 C5
Oxted RH8 254 EL130
Slough SL1 131 AK73
St. Angela's Ursuline Sch, E7 off St. Georges Rd 144 EH65
St. Anna Rd, Barn. EN5
off Sampson Av 79 CX43
St. Annes Av, Stanw. TW19 174 BK87
St. Annes Boul, Red. RH1 251 DH132
St. Anne's Cath High Sch for Girls, Upr Sch, N13
off Oakthorpe Rd 99 DN49
Lwr Sch, Enf. EN2
off London Rd 82 DR42
St. Anne's Catholic Prim Sch, Bans. SM7 off Court Rd 234 DA116
Chertsey KT16
off Free Prae Rd 194 BG102
St. Annes Cl, Chsht EN7 66 DU28
St. Anne's Cl, N6 120 DG62
Wat. WD19 94 BW49
St. Anne's C of E Prim Sch, SW18 off St. Ann's Hill 180 DB85
St. Anne's Ct, W1 285 N9
St. Anne's Dr, Red. RH1 250 DG133
St. Annes Dr N, Red. RH1 250 DG132
St. Annes Gdns, NW10 138 CM69
St. Anne's Mt, Red. RH1 250 DG133
St. Annes Pk, Brox. EN10 49 EA20
St. Annes Pas, E14 289 N9
St. Anne's Prim Sch, E1 288 C5
St. Annes Ri, Red. RH1 250 DG133
St. Annes Rd, E11 123 ED61
St. Anne's Rd, Hare. UB9 114 BJ55
London Colney AL2 61 CK27
Wembley HA0 117 CK64
St. Anne's RC Prim Sch, SE11 310 C2
St. Anne's Row, E14 289 P9
St. Anne St, E14 289 P9
St. Anne's Way, Red. RH1
off St. Anne's Dr 250 DG133
St. Ann's, Bark. IG11 145 EQ67
St. Anns Cl, Cher. KT16 193 BF100
St. Ann's C of E Prim Sch, N15 off Avenue Rd 122 DR57
St. Ann's Cres, SW18 180 DC86
St. Ann's Gdns, NW5 274 G4
St. Ann's Heath Jun Sch, Vir.W. GU25 off Sandhills La 192 AY99
St. Ann's Hill, SW18 180 DB85
St. Anns Hill Rd, Cher. KT16 193 BC100
St. Ann's Hosp, N15 122 DQ57
St. Ann's La, SW1 297 P6
St. Ann's Ms, Cher. KT16 193 BE101
St. Ann's Pk Rd, SW18 180 DC86
St. Ann's Pas, SW13 158 CS83
St. Anns Rd, N9 100 DT47
W11 294 D1
Cher. KT16 193 BF100
St. Ann's Rd, N15 121 DP57
SW13 159 CT82
Bark. IG11 off Axe St 145 EQ67
Har. HA1 117 CE58
St. Ann's Shop Cen, Har. HA1 117 CE58
St. Ann's St, SW1 297 P6
St. Ann's Ter, NW8 274 B10
St. Anns Vil, W11 294 D3
St. Anns Way, Berry's Grn TN16 239 EP116
South Croydon CR2 219 DP107
St. Anselm's Cath Prim Sch, Dartford DA1
off Littlebrook Manor Way 188 FN85
Harrow HA1
off Roxborough Pk 117 CE59
St. Anselm's Pl, W1 285 J9
St. Anselms Rd, Hayes UB3 155 BT75
St. Anselms RC Prim Sch, Sthl. UB2 off Church Av 156 BZ76
St. Anselm's RC Prim Sch, SW17 off Tooting Bec Rd 180 DG90
St. Anthonys Av, Hem.H. HP3 41 BP22
Woodford Green IG8 102 EJ51
St. Anthony's Cath Prim Sch, SE20 off Genoa Rd 202 DV95
SE22 off Etherow St 182 DU86
Farnham Royal SL2
off Farnham Rd 131 AQ70
Woodford Green IG8
off Mornington Rd 102 EG49
St. Anthonys Cl, E1 300 C2
SW17 off College Gdns 180 DE89
St. Anthonys Ct, Beac. HP9
off Walkwood Ri 110 AJ55
St. Anthony's Hosp, Sutt. SM3 199 CX102
St. Anthony's Prep Sch, NW3 274 A2
St. Anthony's RC Prim Sch, Wat. WD18 off Croxley Vw 75 BS43
St. Anthony's Way, Felt. TW14 155 BT84
St. Antony's Rd, E7 144 EH66
St. Antony's RC Prim Sch, E7 off Upton Av 144 EH66
St. Arvans Cl, Croy. CR0 202 DS104
St. Asaph Rd, SE4 313 J10
St. Aubins Ct, N1
off De Beauvoir Est 277 M8
St. Aubyns Av, Houns. TW3 176 CA85
St. Aubyn's Av, SW19 179 CZ92
St. Aubyns Cl, Orp. BR6 205 ET104
St. Aubyns Gdns, Orp. BR6 205 ET103
St. Aubyn's Rd, SE19 182 DT93
St. Aubyn's Sch, Wdf.Grn. IG8 off Bunces La 102 EF52
St. Audrey Av, Bexh. DA7 166 FA82
St. Audreys Cl, Hat. AL10 45 CV21
St. Audreys Grn, Welw.G.C. AL7 29 CZ10
St. Augustine of Canterbury C of E Prim Sch, Belv. DA17
off St. Augustine's Rd 166 EZ76
St. Augustine Rd, Grays RM16 171 GH77
St. Augustines Av, Brom. BR2 204 EL99
Wem. HA9 118 CL62
St. Augustine's Av, W5 138 CL68
S.Croy. CR2 220 DQ107
St. Augustine's Cath Prim Sch, Ilf. IG2 off Cranbrook Rd 125 EP57
St. Augustines Cl, Brox. EN10 49 DZ20
St. Augustine's C of E High Sch, NW6 283 K1
St. Augustine's C of E Prim Sch, NW6 273 L10
St. Augustines Ct, SE1 300 E10
St. Augustines Dr, Brox. EN10 49 DZ19
St. Augustine's Path, N5 277 K1
St. Augustine's Priory Sch, W5 off Hillcrest Rd 138 CM71
St. Augustines Rd, NW1 275 N6
St. Augustine's Rd, Belv. DA17 166 EZ77
St. Augustine's RC Prim Sch, SE6 off Dunfield Rd 183 EC92
W6 306 F3
Hoddesdon EN11
off Riversmead 49 EA17
St. Austell Cl, Edg. HA8 96 CM54
St. Austell Rd, SE13 314 F8
St. Awdry's Rd, Bark. IG11 145 ER66
St. Awdry's Wk, Bark. IG11
off Station Par 145 EQ66
St. Barnabas & St. Philip's C of E Prim Sch, W8 295 J7
St. Barnabas Cl, SE22
off East Dulwich Gro 182 DS85
Beckenham BR3 203 EC96
St. Barnabas C of E Prim Sch, SW1 297 H10
St. Barnabas Ct, Har. HA3 94 CC53
St. Barnabas Gdns, W.Mol. KT8 196 CA99
St. Barnabas Ms, SW1
off St. Barnabas St 297 H10
St. Barnabas Rd, E17 123 EA58
Mitcham CR4 180 DG94
Sutton SM1 218 DD106
Woodford Green IG8 102 EH53
St. Barnabas St, SW1 297 H10
St. Barnabas Ter, E9 279 J3
St. Barnabas Vil, SW8 310 B6
St. Bartholomew's Catholic Prim Sch, Swan. BR8 off Sycamore Dr 207 FE97
St. Bartholomews Cl, SE26 182 DW91
St. Bartholomew's C of E Prim Sch, SE26 off The Peak 182 DW91
St. Bartholomews Ct, Guil. GU1 259 AZ135
St. Bartholomew's Hosp, EC1 287 H7
St. Bartholomew's Rd, E6 144 EL67
★ St. Bartholomew-the-Great Ch, EC1 287 H7
St. Bart's Cl, St.Alb. AL4 43 CK21
St. Bede's Cath Prim Sch, Chad.Hth RM6 off Canon Av 126 EW57
St. Bede's C of E Jun Sch, Send GU23 off Bush La 227 BD124
St. Bede's RC Inf Sch, SW12 off Thornton Rd 181 DK88
St. Bede's Sch, Red. RH1
off Carlton Rd 250 DE131
St. Benedict's Av, Grav. DA12 191 GK89
St. Benedict's Cl, SW17
off Church La 180 DG92
St. Benedict's Sch, Nurs & Jun Sch, W5
off Montpelier Av 137 CJ71
Sen Sch & 6th Form, W5
off Eaton Ri 137 CK71
St. Benet's Cl, SW17
off College Gdns 180 DE89
St. Benet's Gro, Cars. SM5 200 DC101
St. Benet's Pl, EC3 287 M10
St. Benjamins Dr, Pr.Bot. BR6 224 EW109
St. Bernadette Cath Prim Sch, Uxb. UB10 off Long La 135 BP67
St. Bernadette RC Nurs & Prim Sch, Lon.Col. AL2
off Walsingham Way 61 CK27
St. Bernadette's Catholic Prim Sch, Kenton HA3 off Clifton Rd 118 CM56
St. Bernadette's RC Jun Sch, SW12 off Atkins Rd 181 DJ87
St. Bernards, Croy. CR0 202 DS104
St. Bernard's Cl, SE27 182 DR91
St. Bernard's Conv Sch, Slou. SL3 off Langley Rd 152 AW75
St. Bernard's Hosp, Sthl. UB1 157 CD75
St. Bernard's Prep Sch, Slou. SL1 off Hawtrey Cl 152 AV75
St. Bernards Rd, St.Alb. AL3 43 CD19
Slough SL3 152 AW76
St. Bernard's Rd, E6 144 EK67
St. Blaise Av, Brom. BR1 204 EH96
St. Bonaventure's Cath Comp Sch, E7 281 P7
St. Boniface RC Prim Sch, SW17 off Undine St 180 DF92
St. Botolph Rd, Nthflt DA11 190 GC90
St. Botolph Row, EC3 288 A9
St. Botolph's Av, Sev. TN13 256 FG124
St. Botolph's C of E Prim Sch, Nthflt DA11 off Dover Rd 190 GD87
St. Botolph's Rd, Sev. TN13 256 FG124
St. Botolph St, EC3 288 A9
St. Brelades Cl, Dor. RH4 263 CG138
St. Brelades Ct, N1
off Balmes Rd 277 M8
St. Brelades Pl, St.Alb. AL4
off Harvesters 43 CK16
St. Brides Av, EC4 286 G9
Edgware HA8 96 CM53
★ St. Bride's Ch, EC4 286 G9
St. Brides Cl, Erith DA18
off St. Katherines Rd 166 EX75
St. Bride's Pas, EC4
off Salisbury Ct 286 G9
St. Bride St, EC4 286 G8
St. Catharines Rd, Brox. EN10 49 EA19
St. Catherine of Siena Cath Prim Sch, Wat. WD25
off Horseshoe La 60 BX33
St. Catherines, Wok. GU22 226 AW119
St. Catherine's Bletchingley Village Sch, Bletch. RH1
off Coneybury 252 DS133
St. Catherine's Cath Sch for Girls, Bexh. DA6
off Watling St 167 FB84
St. Catherines Cl, SW17 180 DE89
Chessington KT9 215 CK107
St. Catherine's C of E Prim Sch, Hodd. EN11 off Haslewood Av 49 EA17
Ware SG12 off Park Rd 32 DV05
St. Catherines Ct, Felt. TW13 175 BU88
St. Catherines Cross, Bletch. RH1 252 DS134
St. Catherines Dr, SE14 313 K9
Guildford GU2 258 AV138
St. Catherines Fm Ct, Ruis. HA4 115 BQ58
St. Catherines Hill, Guil. GU2
off Portsmouth Rd 258 AW138
St. Catherine's Ms, SW3 296 E8
St. Catherines Pk, Guil. GU1 259 AZ136
St. Catherines Rd, E4 101 EA47
Ruislip HA4 115 BR57
St. Catherine's RC Prim Sch, Barn. EN5 off Vale Dr 80 DA42
West Drayton UB7
off Money La 154 BK75
St. Catherine's Sch, Sen Sch, Bramley GU5
off Station Rd 259 AZ144
Twickenham TW1
off Cross Deep 177 CG89
St. Cecelia's Pl, SE3 315 N1
St. Cecilia Rd, Grays RM16 171 GH77
St. Cecilia's Cl, Sutt. SM3 199 CY102
St. Cecilia's RC Prim Sch, Sutt. SM3 off London Rd 199 CX103
St. Cecilia's, Wandsworth Sch, SW18 off Sutherland Gro 179 CZ87
St. Chad's Cath Prim Sch, SE25 off Alverston Gdns 202 DS99
St. Chads Cl, Long Dit. KT6 197 CJ101
St. Chad's Dr, Grav. DA12 191 GL90
St. Chad's Gdns, Rom. RM6 126 EY59
St. Chad's Pl, WC1 286 B2
St. Chad's Rd, Rom. RM6 126 EY58
Tilbury RM18 171 GG80
St. Chad's St, WC1 286 B2
St. Charles Borromeo Catholic Prim Sch, Wey. KT13
off Portmore Way 194 BN104
St. Charles Catholic 6th Form Coll, W10 282 D7
St. Charles Ct, Wey. KT13 212 BN106
St. Charles Hosp, W10 282 D6
St. Charles Pl, W10 282 E7
Weybridge KT13 212 BN106
St. Charles Rd, Brwd. CM14 108 FV46
St. Charles RC Prim Sch, W10 282 D6
St. Charles Sq, W10 282 E6
St. Christina's Sch, NW8 274 D10
St. Christopher Rd, Uxb. UB8 134 BK71
St. Christopher's Cl, Islw. TW7 157 CE81
St. Christopher's Dr, Hayes UB3 135 BV73
St. Christophers Gdns, Th.Hth. CR7 201 DN97
St. Christophers Ms, Wall. SM6 219 DJ106
St. Christopher's Pl, W1 285 H8
St. Christopher's Sch, NW3 274 B3
Epsom KT18 off Downs Rd 216 CS114
Wembley HA9
off Wembley Pk Dr 118 CM62
St. Christopher's The Hall Sch, Beck. BR3 off Bromley Rd 203 EC96
St. Clair Cl, Ilf. IG5 103 EM54
Oxted RH8 253 EC130
Reigate RH2 250 DC134
St. Clair Dr, Wor.Pk. KT4 199 CV104
St. Clair Rd, E13 292 B1
St. Clair's Rd, Croy. CR0 202 DS103
● St. Clare Business Pk, Hmptn. TW12 176 CC93
St. Clare St, EC3 288 A9
St. Clement Cl, Uxb. UB8 134 BK72
★ St. Clement Danes Ch, WC2 286 D9
St. Clement Danes C of E Prim Sch, WC2 286 C9
St. Clement Danes Sch, Chorl. WD3 off Chenies Rd 73 BD40
St. Clements & St. James C of E Prim Sch, W11 294 E2
St. Clements Av, Grays RM20 169 FV79
St. Clement's Catholic Prim Sch, Ewell KT17 off Fennells Mead 217 CT109
St. Clement's Cl, Nthflt DA11
off Coldharbour Rd 191 GF90
St. Clement's C of E Jun Sch, Wal.Cr. EN8 off Cheshunt Wash 67 DY27
St. Clements Ct, EC4
off Clements La 287 M10
N7 276 E5
Purfleet RM19 168 FN77
St. Clements Hts, SE26 182 DU90
St. Clement's La, WC2 286 D9
St. Clements Rd, Grays RM20 169 FW80
Greenhithe DA9 169 FW84
St. Clements St, N7 276 E5
St. Clements Way, Grays RM20 169 FT79
Greenhithe DA9 189 FU85
St. Clements Yd, SE22
off Archdale Rd 182 DT85
St. Cloud Rd, SE27 182 DQ91
St. Columba's Cath Boys' Sch, Bexh. DA6 off Halcot Av 187 FB85
St. Columba's Cl, Grav. DA12 191 GL90
St. Columba's Coll, St.Alb. AL3 off King Harry La 42 CC22

S

St. Crispins Cl, NW3 274 D1
Southall UB1 136 BZ72
St. Crispins Way, Ott. KT16 211 BC109
St. Cross Ct, Hodd. EN11 49 EA19
St. Cross RC Prim Sch, Hodd. EN11 off Upper Marsh La 49 EA19
St. Cross St, EC1 286 F6
St. Cuthbert La, Uxb. UB8 134 BK72
St. Cuthbert Mayne Catholic Jun Sch, Hem.H. HP1 off Clover Way 40 BH19
St. Cuthbert's Catholic Prim Sch, Eng.Grn TW20 off Bagshot Rd 172 AW94
St. Cuthberts Cl, Eng.Grn TW20 172 AX92
St. Cuthberts Gdns, Pnr. HA5 off Westfield Pk 94 BZ52
St. Cuthberts Rd, N13 99 DN51
NW2 272 G4
Hoddesdon EN11 33 EC14
St. Cuthbert with St. Matthias C of E Prim Sch, SW5 295 L10
St. Cyprian's Greek Orthodox Prim Sch, Th.Hth. CR7 off Springfield Rd 202 DQ95
St. Cyprian's St, SW17 180 DF91
St. David Cl, Uxb. UB8 134 BK71
St. Davids, Couls. CR5 235 DM117
St. Davids Cl, SE16 312 F1
Hemel Hempstead HP3 41 BR21
Iver SL0 133 BD67
Wem. HA9 118 CQ62
St. David's Cl, Reig. RH2 250 DC133
W.Wick. BR4 203 EB101
St. David's Coll, W.Wick. BR4 off Beckenham Rd 203 EB101
St. David's Ct, E17 123 EC55
St. David's Cres, Grav. DA12 191 GK91
St. Davids Dr, Edg. HA8 96 CM53
St. David's Dr, Brox. EN10 49 DZ19
Eng.Grn TW20 172 AW94
St. Davids Ms, E3 off Morgan St 289 M3
St. Davids Pl, NW4 119 CV59
St. Davids Rd, Swan. BR8 187 FF93
St. David's Sch, Ashf. TW15 off Church Rd 174 BM90
Purley CR8 off Woodcote Valley Rd 219 DM111
St. Davids Sq, E14 302 D10
St. Denis Rd, SE27 182 DR91
St. Denys Cl, Pur. CR8 219 DP110
St. Dionis Rd, SW6 307 H8
St. Dominic's 6th Form Coll, Har.Hill HA1 off Mount Pk Av 117 CE61
St. Dominic's RC Prim Sch, E9 279 L4
NW5 274 F3
St. Donatts Rd, SE14 313 N7
St. Dunstans, Sutt. SM1 off Cheam Rd 217 CZ107
St. Dunstan's All, EC3 off Great Tower St 287 N10
St. Dunstans Av, W3 138 CR73
St. Dunstan's Catholic Prim Sch, Wok. GU22 off Onslow Cres 227 BA117
St. Dunstans Cl, Hayes UB3 155 BT77
St. Dunstan's C of E Prim Sch, Cheam SM3 off Anne Boleyn's Wk 217 CY108
St. Dunstan's Coll, SE6 off Stanstead Rd 183 EA88
St. Dunstan's Ct, EC4 off Fleet St 286 F9
St. Dunstan's Dr, Grav. DA12 191 GL91
St. Dunstans Gdns, W3 138 CR73
St. Dunstan's Hill, EC3 off Great Tower St 299 N1
Sutton SM1 217 CY106
St. Dunstan's La, EC3 299 N1
Beckenham BR3 203 EC100
St. Dunstans Rd, SE25 202 DT98
W6 306 C1
W7 157 CE75
Houns. TW4 156 BW82
Hunsdon SG12 34 EK07
St. Dunstan's Rd, E7 144 EJ65
Felt. TW13 175 BT90
St. Ebba's Hosp, Epsom KT19 216 CQ109
St. Edith Cl, Epsom KT18 216 CQ114
St. Edmunds, Berk. HP4 38 AW20
St. Edmunds Av, Ruis. HA4 115 BR58
St. Edmunds Cl, NW8 274 E9
SW17 off College Gdns 180 DE89
Erith DA18 off St. Katherines Rd 166 EX75
St. Edmunds Dr, Stan. HA7 95 CG53
St. Edmund's La, Twick. TW2 176 CB87
St. Edmunds Rd, N9 100 DU45
Dartford DA1 168 FM84
Ilford IG1 125 EM58
St. Edmund's RC Prim Sch, E14 302 B8
N9 off Hertford Rd 100 DV46
Whitton TW2 off Nelson Rd 176 CB87
St. Edmunds Sq, SW13 306 A3
St. Edmunds Ter, NW8 274 D10
St. Edmunds Wk, St.Alb. AL4 43 CJ21
St. Edmunds Way, Harl. CM17 36 EW11
St. Edward's Catholic First Sch, Wind. SL4 off Parsonage La 151 AN81
St. Edwards Cl, NW11 120 DA58
New Addington CR0 221 ED111
St. Edward's C of E Comp Sch, Rom. RM7 off London Rd 126 FA58
St. Edward's C of E Prim Sch, Rom. RM1 off Havering Dr 127 FE56
St. Edward's RC Prim Sch, E13 off Green St 144 EJ67
NW1 284 D5
St. Edward's Royal Free Ecumenical Mid Sch, Wind. SL4 off Parsonage La 151 AN81
St. Edwards Way, Rom. RM1 127 FD57
St. Egberts Way, E4 101 EC46
St. Elizabeth Dr, Epsom KT18 216 CQ114
St. Elizabeth's Catholic Prim Sch, Rich. TW10 off Queens Rd 178 CM86
St. Elizabeth's Prim Sch, E2 279 H10
St. Elmo Cl, Slou. SL2 off St. Elmo Cres 131 AR70
St. Elmo Cres, Slou. SL2 131 AR70
St. Elmo Rd, W12 139 CT74
St. Elmos Rd, SE16 301 L4
St. Elphege's RC Infants' & Jun Schs, Wall. SM6 off Mollison Dr 219 DL107
St. Erkenwald Ms, Bark. IG11 off St. Erkenwald Rd 145 ER67
St. Erkenwald Rd, Bark. IG11 145 ER67
St. Ermin's Hill, SW1 297 N6
St. Ervans Rd, W10 282 F6
St. Ethelbert's Catholic Prim Sch, Slou. SL2 off Wexham Rd 132 AV72
St. Etheldredas Dr, Hat. AL10 45 CW18
St. Eugene de Mazenod RC Prim Sch, NW6 273 K7
St. Faiths Cl, Enf. EN2 82 DQ39
St. Faith's C of E Prim Sch, SW18 off Alma Rd 180 DC85
St. Faith's Rd, SE21 181 DP88
St. Fidelis Cath Prim Sch, Erith DA8 off Bexley Rd 167 FC79
St. Fidelis Rd, Erith DA8 167 FD77
St. Fillans Rd, SE6 183 EC88
St. Francesca Cabrini RC Prim Sch, SE23 off Honor Oak Pk 182 DW86
St. Francis Av, Grav. DA12 191 GL91
St. Francis Cath Prim Sch, SE15 312 D4
Caterham CR3 off Whyteleafe Rd 236 DT121
St. Francis Cl, Berk. HP4 38 AU18
Petts Wood BR5 205 ES100
Potters Bar EN6 64 DC33
Watford WD19 93 BV46
St. Francis de Sales RC Inf & Jun Schs, N17 off Church Rd 100 DT52
St. Francis of Assisi RC Prim Sch, W11 294 D1
St. Francis Pl, SW12 off Malwood Rd 181 DH86
St. Francis Rd, SE22 162 DS84
Denham UB9 113 BF58
Erith DA8 off West St 167 FD77
St. Francis' RC Prim Sch, E15 281 J3
St. Francis Way, Grays RM16 171 GJ77
Ilford IG1 125 ES63
St. Francis Xavier 6th Form Coll, SW12 off Malwood Rd 181 DH86
St. Frideswides Ms, E14 290 E9
St. Gabriel's Cl, E11 124 EH61
E14 290 C7
St. Gabriel's C of E Prim Sch, SW1 309 L1
St. Gabriels Manor, SE5 off Cormont Rd 310 G6
St. Gabriels Rd, NW2 272 C3
St. George's, SW17 off Cranmer Ter 180 DD92
St. George's, Har. HA1 117 CE58
St. Georges Av, E7 144 EH66
N7 121 DK63
NW9 118 CQ56
Grays RM17 170 GC77
Hornchurch RM11 128 FM59
Southall UB1 136 BZ73
St. George's Av, W5 157 CK75
Wey. KT13 213 BP107
St. George's Bickley C of E Prim Sch, Brom. BR1 off Tylney Rd 204 EK96
St. George's Cath Prim Sch, Enfield EN2 off Gordon Rd 82 DR40
Harrow HA1 off Sudbury Hill 117 CF62
St. George's Cath RC Prim Sch, SE1 298 G6
St. George's Cath School, Maida Vale, W9 283 M1
St. George's Cen, Grav. DA11 191 GH86
St. Georges Circ, SE1 298 G6
St. Georges Cl, NW11 119 CZ58
SE28 off Redbourne Dr 146 EX72
Horl. RH6 269 DH148
Wembley HA0 117 CG62
St. George's Cl, SW8 309 M6
Wey. KT13 213 BQ106
Windsor SL4 151 AL81
St. George's C of E Inf Sch, Amer. HP7 off White Lion Rd 72 AT39
St. George's C of E Prim Sch, SE5 311 N4
SW8 309 M5
St. George's C of E Sch, Grav. DA11 off Meadow Rd 191 GG89
St. George's Coll, Add. KT15 off Weybridge Rd 194 BK104
Jun Sch, Wey. KT13 off Thames St 195 BP104
St. Georges Ct, E6 293 J4
EC4 286 G8
SW7 295 N6
St. Georges Cres, Grav. DA12 191 GK91
St. George's Cres, Slou. SL1 131 AK73
St. Georges Dr, Uxb. UB10 114 BM62
Watford WD19 94 BY48
St. George's Dr, SW1 297 K9
St. Georges Flds, W2 284 D9
St. Georges Gdns, Epsom KT17 217 CT114
St. George's Gdns, Surb. KT6 198 CP103
St. Georges Gro, SW17 180 DD90
St. George's Hanover Sq Prim Sch, W1 297 H1
ST. GEORGE'S HILL, Wey. KT13 213 BQ110
St. George's Hosp, SW17 180 DD92
Hornchurch RM12 128 FK63
St. Georges Ind Est, Kings.T. KT2 177 CK92
St. George's Ind Est, N22 99 DP52
St. Georges La, EC3 off Pudding La 287 M10
St. George's Lo, Wey. KT13 213 BR106
St. Georges Ms, NW1 274 F7
SE1 298 F6
SE8 301 N8
St. Georges Pl, Esher KT10 214 CC105
Twickenham TW1 off Church St 177 CG88
St. Georges Rd, E7 144 EH65
E10 123 EC62
N9 100 DU48
N13 99 DM48
NW11 119 CZ58
SE1 298 F6
W4 158 CS75
W7 137 CF74
Addlestone KT15 212 BJ105
Brom. BR1 205 EM96
Dagenham RM9 126 EY64
Enfield EN1 82 DT38
Hemel Hempstead HP3 40 BJ24
Ilford IG1 125 EM59
Redhill RH1 267 DK142
St. Georges Rd, Richmond TW9 158 CM83
Swanley BR8 207 FF98
Twickenham TW1 177 CH85
Wallington SM6 219 DH106
Watford WD24 75 BV38
St. George's Rd, SW19 179 CZ93
Beck. BR3 203 EB95
Felt. TW13 176 BX91
Kings.T. KT2 178 CN94
Mitcham CR4 201 DH97
Petts Wood BR5 205 ER100
Sev. TN13 257 FH122
Sidcup DA14 186 EX93
Wey. KT13 213 BR107
St. Georges Rd W, Brom. BR1 204 EL95
St. George's Sch, Wind. SL4 off Windsor Castle 151 AR80
St. Georges Sq, E7 144 EH66
E14 289 L10
SE8 301 N8
St. George's Sq, SW1 297 N10
New Malden KT3 off High St 198 CS97
St. George's Sq Ms, SW1 309 N1
St. Georges Ter, NW1 274 F7
St. George St, W1 285 K9
St. Georges Wk, Croy. CR0 202 DQ104
St. Georges Way, SE15 311 N3
St. George the Martyr C of E Prim Sch, WC1 286 C5
St. George Wf, SW8 310 A1
St. George Wharf Pier, SW8 310 A1
St. Gerards Cl, SW4 181 DJ85
St. German's Pl, SE3 315 N7
St. Germans Rd, SE23 183 DY88
St. Gilda's RC Jun Sch, N8 off Oakington Way 121 DL59
St. Giles Av, Dag. RM10 147 FB66
South Mimms EN6 63 CV32
Uxbridge UB10 115 BQ63
St. Giles Cl, Dag. RM10 off St. Giles Av 147 FB66
Hounslow TW5 156 BY80
Orpington BR6 223 ER106
St. Giles C of E Inf Sch, Ashtd. KT21 off Dene Rd 232 CM118
St. Giles' C of E Prim Sch, S.Mimms EN6 off Blanche La 63 CU32
St. Giles Ct, WC2 off St. Giles High St 286 A8
St. Giles High St, WC2 285 P8
St. Giles Pas, WC2 285 P9
St. Giles Rd, SE5 311 N5
St. Giles' Sch, S.Croy. CR2 off Pampisford Rd 219 DP107
St. Gilles Ho, E2 289 J1
St. Gothard Rd, SE27 182 DR91
St. Gregory Cl, Ruis. HA4 116 BW63
St. Gregory's Catholic Science Coll, Kenton HA3 off Donnington Rd 117 CK57
St. Gregorys Cres, Grav. DA12 191 GL89
St. Gregory's RC Prim Sch, W5 off Woodfield Rd 137 CK71
St. Helena Rd, SE16 301 J9
St. Helena St, WC1 286 E3
St. Helen's Catholic Inf Sch, E17 off Shernhall St 123 EC57
Brentwood CM14 off Queens Rd 108 FX47
St. Helen's Catholic Jun Sch, Brwd. CM15 off Sawyers Hall La 108 FX45
St. Helen's Catholic Prim Sch, E13 291 N4
St. Helens Cl, Uxb. UB8 134 BK72
St. Helen's Coll, Uxb. UB10 off Parkway 135 BP66
St. Helens Ct, Epp. CM16 off Hemnall St 70 EU30
Rainham RM13 147 FG70
St. Helens Cres, SW16 off St. Helens Rd 201 DM95
St. Helens Gdns, W10 282 C7
St. Helen's Ms, Brwd. CM15 108 FX47
St. Helens Pl, E10 123 DY59
EC3 287 N8
St. Helens Rd, SW16 201 DM95
Erith DA18 166 EX75
Ilford IG1 125 EM58
St. Helen's Rd, W13 off Dane Rd 137 CJ74
St. Helen's RC Prim Sch, SW9 310 E10
St. Helen's Sch, Nthwd. HA6 off Eastbury Rd 93 BS51
ST. HELIER, Cars. SM5 200 DD101
St. Helier 200 DA100
St. Helier Av, Mord. SM4 200 DC101
St. Helier Hosp, Cars. SM5 200 DC102
St. Helier Rd, Sand. AL4 43 CH15
St. Heliers Av, Houns. TW3 176 CA85
St. Heliers Rd, E10 123 EC58
St. Hildas Av, Ashf. TW15 174 BL92
St. Hildas Cl, NW6 272 D7
SW17 180 DE89
Horley RH6 269 DH148
St. Hilda's Rd, SW13 159 CV79
St. Hilda's Sch, Bushey WD23 off High St 94 CB45
St. Hilda's Way, Grav. DA12 191 GK91
St. Huberts Cl, Ger.Cr. SL9 112 AY60
St. Huberts La, Ger.Cr. SL9 113 AZ61
St. Hughe's Cl, SW17 180 DE89
St. Hughs Rd, SE20 off Ridsdale Rd 202 DV95
St. Ignatius RC Prim Sch, N15 off St. Ann's Rd 122 DT58
St. Ignatius Coll, Enf. EN1 off Turkey St 82 DV37
St. Ignatius RC Prim Sch, Sun. TW16 off Green St 195 BU95
St. Ives Cl, Rom. RM3 106 FM52
St. Ivian Ct, N10 off Colney Hatch La 98 DG54
St. Ivians Dr, Rom. RM2 127 FG55
St. James' & St. Michael's C of E Prim Sch, W2 283 P10
St. James Av, N20 98 DE48
W13 137 CG74
Epsom KT17 217 CT111
Sutton SM1 218 DA106
St. James' Cath High Sch, NW9 off Great Strand 97 CT53
St. James' Cath Prim Sch, Orp. BR5 off Maybury Cl 205 EP99
St. James Cen, Harl. CM20 36 EU11
St. James Cl, N20 98 DE48
NW8 off St. James's Ter 274 E9
SE18 off Congleton Gro 165 EQ78
Barnet EN4 80 DD42
St. James Cl, Epsom KT18 216 CS114
New Malden KT3 199 CT99
Ruislip HA4 116 BW61
Woking GU21 226 AU118
St. James' C of E Jun Sch, E7 281 N2
St. James C of E Prim Sch, N10 off Woodside Av 120 DG56
St. James C of E Prim Sch, Wey. KT13 off Grotto Rd 195 BQ104
St. James' C of E Prim Sch, SE16 300 C6
Enfield EN3 off Frederick Cres 82 DW40
Harlow CM18 off Paringdon Rd 51 ER19
St. James Ct, Green. DA9 189 FT86
St. James Dr, Rom. RM3 106 FL51
St. James Gdns, Lt.Hth RM6 126 EV56
Wembley HA0 137 CK66
St. James Gate, NW1 275 P7
St. James Gro, SW11 308 F8
St. James Hatcham C of E Prim Sch, SE14 313 M6
St. James Indep Sch for Sen Boys, Twick. TW1 off Cross Deep 177 CG89
St. James Indep Schs for Jun Boys & Girls & Sen Girls, W14 294 F8
St. James La, Green. DA9 189 FS88
St. James Ms, E14 302 F7
E17 123 DY57
Weybridge KT13 213 BP105
St. James Oaks, Grav. DA11 191 GG87
St. James Pl, Dart. DA1 off Spital St 188 FK86
Slough SL1 off Greenfern Av 130 AJ72
St. James Rd, E15 281 L2
N9 100 DV47
Brentwood CM14 108 FW48
Carshalton SM5 200 DE104
Goffs Oak EN7 66 DQ28
Kingston upon Thames KT1 198 CL96
Mitcham CR4 180 DG94
Purley CR8 219 DP113
Sevenoaks TN13 257 FH122
Surbiton KT6 197 CK100
Sutton SM1 218 DA106
Watford WD18 75 BV43
ST. JAMES'S, SW1 297 N3
St. James's, SE14 313 M6
St. James's & Lucie Clayton Coll, SW5 295 N9
St. James's Av, E2 289 H1
Beckenham BR3 203 DY97
Gravesend DA11 191 GG87
Hampton Hill TW12 176 CC92
St. James's Cath Prim Sch, Twick. TW2 off Stanley Rd 177 CD90
St. James's Cl, SW17 180 DF89
St. James's Cotts, Rich. TW9 off Paradise Rd 178 CL85
St. James's Ct, SW1 297 M6
St. James's Cres, SW9 310 F10
St. James's Dr, SW12 180 DF88
SW17 180 DF88
St. James's Gdns, W11 294 E2
St. James's La, N10 121 DH56
St. James's Mkt, SW1 297 N1
★ St. James's Palace, SW1 297 M4
★ St. James's Park, SW1 297 N4
St. James's Park 297 N5
St. James's Pk, Croy. CR0 202 DQ101
St. James's Pas, EC3 287 P9
St. James's Pl, SW1 297 L3
Grav. DA11 191 GF86
St. James's Rd, SE1 300 D10
SE16 300 D6
Croydon CR0 201 DP101
Gravesend DA11 191 GG86
Hampton Hill TW12 176 CB92
St. James's Sq, SW1 297 M2
St. James's St, E17 123 DY57
SW1 297 L2
Gravesend DA11 191 GG86
St. James's Ter, NW8 274 E10
St. James's Ter Ms, NW8 274 E9
St. James Street 123 DY57
St. James St, W6 306 A1
St. James's Wk, EC1 286 G4
St. James Ter, SW12 180 DG88
St. James the Gt Cath Prim & Nurs Sch, Th.Hth. CR7 off Windsor Rd 201 DP96
St. James the Gt Cath Prim Sch, SE15 312 B6
St. James Wk, Iver SL0 153 BE75
St. James Way, Sid. DA14 186 EY92
St. Jeromes Gro, Hayes UB3 135 BQ72
St. Joachim's RC Prim Sch, E16 292 C9
St. Joan of Arc Cath Sch, Rick. WD3 off High St 92 BL45
St. Joan of Arc RC Prim Sch, N5 off Northolme Rd 122 DQ63
St. Joans Rd, N9 100 DT46
St. John & St. James C of E Prim Sch, E9 278 G3
N18 off Grove St 100 DT50
St. John Baptist Prim Sch, Downham BR1 off Beachborough Rd 183 EC91
St. John Bosco Sch, SW11 308 C7
St. John Evangelist RC Prim Sch, N1 276 G10
St. John Fisher Cath Prim Sch, Erith DA18 off Kale Rd 166 EY76
Pinner HA5 off Melrose Rd 116 CA56
Loughton IG10 off Burney Dr 85 EQ40
St. John Fisher Rd, Erith DA18 166 EX76
St. John Fisher RC Prim Sch, SW20 off Grand Dr 199 CX99
Perivale UB6 off Thirlmere Av 137 CJ69
St. Albans AL4 off Hazelmere Rd 43 CJ17
St. John of Jerusalem C of E Prim Sch, E9 279 H7
St. Johns 314 B8
St. Johns, N.Holm. RH5 263 CH140
ST. JOHN'S, SE8 314 A8
ST. JOHN'S, Wok. GU21 226 AV118
St. John's, Red. RH1 266 DE136
St. John's & St. Clement's C of E Prim Sch, SE15 off Adys Rd 162 DU83
St. John's (Angell Town) C of E Prim Sch, SW9 310 F9
St. Johns Av, N11 98 DF50
Lthd. KT22 231 CH121
Warley CM14 108 FX49
St. John's Av, NW10 139 CT67
SW15 179 CX85
Epsom KT17 217 CT112
Harlow CM17 36 EW11
St. John's Beaumont Sch, Old Wind. SL4 off Priest Hill 172 AV89
St. John's Catholic Comp Sch, Grav. DA12 off Rochester Rd 191 GK88
St. John's Catholic Prim Sch, Grav. DA12 off Rochester Rd 191 GK87
Mill End WD3 off Berry La 92 BH46
St. John's Ch Rd, E9 278 G3
Wotton RH5 off Coast Hill 262 BZ139
St. Johns Cl, N14 81 DJ44
Berry's Grn TN16 off St. Johns Ri 239 EP116
Hem.H. HP1 off Anchor La 40 BH22
Leatherhead KT22 231 CJ120
Rain. RM13 147 FG66
St. John's Cl, SW6 307 J4
Guil. GU2 off St. John's Rd 258 AU135
Pot.B. EN6 64 DC33
Uxb. UB8 134 BH67
Wembley HA9 118 CL64
St. John's C of E Prim Sch, N11 off Crescent Rd 98 DF49
N20 off Swan La 98 DC47
SE20 off Maple Rd 182 DW94
Buckhurst Hill IG9 off High Rd 102 EH46
Caterham CR3 off Markfield Rd 252 DV125
Croydon CR0 off Spring Pk Rd 203 DX104
Enfield EN2 off Theobalds Pk Rd 81 DP36
Kingston upon Thames KT1 off Portland Rd 198 CL97
Lemsford AL8 off Lemsford Village 29 CT10
Sevenoaks TN13 off Bayham Rd 257 FK123
Welwyn AL6 off Hertford Rd 29 CZ05
St. John's C of E School, Stanmore, Stan. HA7 off Green La 95 CG49
St. John's C of E Walham Grn Prim Sch, SW6 306 F6
St. Johns Cotts, Rich. TW9 off Kew Foot Rd 158 CL83
St. John's Cotts, SE20 off Maple Rd 182 DW94
St. Johns Ct, Buck.H. IG9 102 EH46
Hert. SG14 off St. John's St 32 DR09
Nthwd. HA6 off Murray Rd 93 BS52
St. Albans AL1 43 CH19
Westcott RH4 off St. John's Rd 262 CC137
St. John's Ct, Egh. TW20 173 BA92
Islw. TW7 157 CF82
Wok. GU21 off St. Johns Hill Rd 226 AU119
St. John's Cres, SW9 310 E10
St. Johns Dr, SW18 180 DB88
Walton-on-Thames KT12 196 BW102
Windsor SL4 151 AM82
St. John's Est, N1 287 M1
SE1 300 A5
St. John's Gdns, W11 294 G1
★ St. John's Gate & Mus of the Order of St. John, EC1 286 G5
St. Johns Gro, N19 121 DJ61
SW13 off Terrace Gdns 159 CT82
Richmond TW9 off Kew Foot Rd 158 CL84
St. John's Highbury Vale C of E Prim Sch, N5 off Conewood St 121 DP62
St. John's Hill, SW11 160 DD84
Coulsdon CR5 235 DN117
Purley CR8 235 DN116
Sevenoaks TN13 257 FJ123
St. John's Hill Gro, SW11 160 DD84
St. Johns Hill Rd, Wok. GU21 226 AU119
★ St. John's Jerusalem, Dart. DA4 188 FP94
St. Johns La, EC1 286 G5
Great Amwell SG12 33 EA09
St. Johns Lo, Wok. GU21 226 AU119
St. John's Lye, Wok. GU21 226 AT119
St. John's Ms, W11 283 J9
Woking GU21 226 AU119
St. Johns Par, Sid. DA14 186 EU91
St. John's Pk, SE3 315 M5
St. Johns Pk Home Est, Enf. EN2 81 DP37
St. John's Pas, SW19 off Ridgway Pl 179 CY93
St. John's Path, EC1 286 G5
St. Johns Pathway, SE23 off Devonshire Rd 182 DW88
St. John's Pl, EC1 286 G5
St. John's Prep Sch, Pot.B. EN6 off The Ridgeway 64 DE34
St. John's Prim Sch, E2 288 G1
W13 off Felix Rd 137 CG73
Knaphill GU21 off Victoria Rd 226 AS118
Redhill RH1 off Pendleton Rd 266 DE136
St. John's R. C. Sch, Wdf.Grn. IG8 off Turpins La 103 EN50
St. Johns Ri, Berry's Grn TN16 239 EP116
Woking GU21 226 AV119
St. Johns Rd, E16 291 N8
NW11 119 CZ58
Croy. CR0 off Waddon Rd 201 DP104
E.Mol. KT8 197 CD98
Erith DA8 167 FD78
Grav. DA12 191 GK87
Grays RM16 171 GH78
Hem.H. HP1 40 BG22
Ilford IG2 125 ER59
Lthd. KT22 231 CJ121
Loughton IG10 85 EM40
New Malden KT3 198 CQ97
Rom. RM5 105 FC50
Sid. DA14 186 EV91
Slough SL2 132 AU74
Southall UB2 156 BY76
Sutton SM1 200 DA103
Uxbridge UB8 134 BH67
Watford WD17 75 BV40
Wind. SL4 151 AN82

St. John's Rd, E4 101 EB48
E6 off Ron Leighton Way 144 EL67
E17 101 EB54
N15 122 DS58
SE20 182 DW94
SW11 160 DE84
SW19 179 CY94
Barking IG11 145 ES67
Carshalton SM5 200 DE104
Dart. DA2 188 FQ87
Epp. CM16 69 ET30
Felt. TW13 176 BY91
Guil. GU2 258 AT135
Hampton Wick KT1 197 CJ96
Harrow HA1 117 CF58
Islw. TW7 157 CE82
Petts Wd BR5 205 ER100
Redhill RH1 266 DF136
Richmond TW9 158 CL84
Sev. TN13 257 FH121
Well. DA16 166 EV83
Wembley HA9 117 CK63
Westcott RH4 262 CC137
Wok. GU21 226 AV118
Sch St. John's RC Prim Sch, SE16 301 L5
Sch St. John's Sch, Lthd. KT22 off Epsom Rd 231 CH121
Northwood HA6 off Wieland Rd 93 BV51
Coll St. John's Seminary, Won. GU5 off Cranleigh Rd 259 BC144
Sch St. John's Sen Sch, Enf. EN2 off The Ridgeway 80 DG35
St. John's Sq, EC1 286 G5
St. John's St, Gdmg. GU7 258 AT144
Hertford SG14 32 DR09
St. Johns Ter, E7 144 EH65
SE18 165 EQ79
SW15 off Kingston Vale 178 CS90
W10 282 D4
St. John's Ter, Enf. EN2 82 DR37
Redhill RH1 off St. John's Ter Rd 266 DF136
St. John's Ter Rd, Red. RH1 266 DF136
St. John St, EC1 287 H5
Sch St. John's Upr Holloway C of E Prim Sch, N19 off Pemberton Gdns 121 DK61
St. John's Vale, SE8 314 B8
St. Johns Vil, N19 121 DK61
St. John's Vil, W8 295 M7
St. Johns Wk, Harl. CM17 36 EW11
Sch St. John's Walworth C of E Prim Sch, SE17 299 K9
St. John's Waterside, Wok. GU21 off Copse Rd 226 AT118
St. Johns Way, N19 121 DK60
St. John's Way, Cher. KT16 194 BG102
St. Johns Well Ct, Berk. HP4 38 AV18
St. Johns Well La, Berk. HP4 38 AV18
ST. JOHN'S WOOD, NW8 284 A2
⊖ St. John's Wood 274 A10
St. John's Wd Ct, NW8 284 B3
St. John's Wd High St, NW8 284 B1
St. John's Wd Pk, NW8 274 B9
St. John's Wd Rd, NW8 284 A4
St. John's Wd Ter, NW8 274 C10
Sch St. John the Baptist C of E Jun Sch, Hmptn W. KT1 off Lower Teddington Rd 177 CK94
Sch St. John the Baptist C of E Prim Sch, N1 287 N1
Great Amwell SG12 off Hillside La 33 EA10
Sch St. John the Baptist Sch, Wok. GU22 off Elmbridge La 227 BA119
Sch St. John the Divine C of E Prim Sch, SE5 310 G4
Sch St. John Vianney RC Prim Sch, N15 off Stanley Rd 121 DP56
Sch St. Joseph's Catholic Comb Sch, Chal.St.P. SL9 off Priory Rd 112 AW55
Sch St. Joseph's Catholic High Sch, Slou. SL2 off Shaggy Calf La 132 AU73
Sch St. Joseph's Cath Infants' & Jun Schs, SE5 311 J4
Sch St. Joseph's Cath Inf Sch, E10 off Marsh La 123 EA61
Sch St. Joseph's Cath Jun Sch, E10 off Vicarage Rd 123 EB60
Sch St. Joseph's Cath Prim Sch, Bark. IG11 off Broadway 145 EQ67
Bromley BR1 off Plaistow La 184 EH94
Crayford DA1 off Old Rd 167 FE84
Dagenham RM9 off Connor Rd 126 EZ63
Dorking RH4 off Norfolk Rd 263 CG136
Epsom KT18 off Rosebank 216 CQ114
Guildford GU2 off Aldershot Rd 242 AT132
Harrow HA3 off Dobbin Cl 95 CG54
Hertford SG14 off North Rd 31 DN08
Kingston upon Thames KT1 off Fairfield S 198 CM96
Northfleet DA11 off Springhead Rd 190 GD87
South Oxhey WD19 off Ainsdale Rd 94 BW48
Upminster RM14 off St. Mary's La 128 FP61
Sch St. Joseph's Catholic Prim Sch Redhill, Red. RH1 off Linkfield La 250 DE133
St. Josephs Cl, W10 282 F7
St. Joseph's Cl, Orp. BR6 223 ET105
Sch St. Joseph's Coll, SE19 off Beulah Hill 181 DP93
Sch St. Joseph's Conv Prep Sch, Grav. DA12 off Old Rd E 191 GJ89
Sch St. Joseph's Conv Sch, E11 off Cambridge Pk 124 EG58
St. Josephs Ct, SE2 166 EX79
St. Joseph's Ct, SE7 164 EH79
St. Josephs Dr, Sthl. UB1 136 BY74
St. Josephs Grn, Welw.G.C. AL7 29 CX12
St. Joseph's Gro, NW4 119 CV56
Sch St. Joseph's In The Pk Sch, Hertingfordbury SG14 off St. Mary's La 31 DN11
St. Joseph's Ms, Beac. HP9 89 AM53
Sch St. Joseph's Prim Sch, SE8 314 A4
SW3 296 E9
St. Josephs Rd, N9 100 DV45
St. Joseph's Rd, Wal.Cr. EN8 67 DY33
Sch St. Joseph's RC Inf & Jun Schs, NW4 off Watford Way 119 CV56
Sch St. Joseph's RC Inf Sch, SE19 off Crown Dale 182 DQ93
Wembley HA9 off Waverley Av 118 CM64
Sch St. Joseph's RC Jun Sch, SE19 off Woodend 182 DQ93
Wembley HA9 off Chatsworth Av 118 CM64
Sch St. Joseph's RC Prim Sch, N19 off Dartmouth Pk Hill 121 DH60
NW10 off Goodson Rd 138 CS66
SE1 299 K4
SE10 303 K10
Bermondsey, SE16 300 C5
Rotherhithe, SE16 301 H7
SW15 off Oakhill Rd 180 DA85
W7 off York Av 137 CE74
W9 283 N3
WC2 286 B8
Waltham Cross EN8 off Royal Av 67 DY32
St. Josephs St, SW8 309 K6
St. Joseph's Vale, SE3 315 H9
Sch St. Joseph the Worker Catholic Prim Sch, Hutt. CM13 off Highview Cres 109 GC44
Sch St. Jude's & St. Paul's C of E Prim Sch, N1 277 N4
St. Judes Cl, Eng.Grn TW20 172 AW92
Sch St. Jude's C of E Prim Sch, SE1 298 G6
SE24 off Regent Rd 181 DP85
Sch St. Jude's C of E Sch, Eng.Grn TW20 off Bagshot Rd 172 AW93
St. Jude's Rd, E2 288 F1
Englefield Green TW20 172 AW90
St. Jude St, N16 277 P3
ST. JULIANS, St.Alb. AL1 43 CD23
St. Julians, Sev. TN15 257 FN128
St. Julian's Cl, SW16 181 DN91
St. Julian's Fm Rd, SE27 181 DN91
St. Julians Rd, St.Alb. AL1 43 CD22
St. Julian's Rd, NW6 273 H7
St. Justin Cl, Orp. BR5 206 EX97
★ St. Katharine Docks, E1 300 B1
Pier St. Katharine's Pier 300 A2
St. Katharines Prec, NW1 275 J10
St. Katharine's Way, E1 300 B2
Sch St. Katherine's Knockholt C of E Prim Sch, Knock. TN14 off Main Rd 240 EV117
St. Katherines Rd, Cat. CR3 252 DU125
Erith DA18 166 EX75
St. Katherine's Row, EC3 off Fenchurch St 287 P9
St. Katherine's Wk, W11 294 D2
St. Katherines Way, Berk. HP4 38 AT16
St. Keverne Rd, SE9 184 EL91
St. Kilda Rd, W13 137 CG74
Orpington BR6 205 ET102
St. Kilda's Rd, N16 122 DR60
Brentwood CM15 108 FV45
Harrow HA1 117 CE58
St. Kitts Ter, SE19 182 DS92
St. Laurence Cl, NW6 272 D9
Orpington BR5 206 EX97
Uxbridge UB8 134 BJ71
St. Laurence Dr, Brox. EN10 49 DZ23
St. Laurence Way, Slou. SL1 152 AU76
St. Lawrence Cl, Abb.L. WD5 59 BS30
Bovingdon HP3 57 BA27
Edgware HA8 96 CM52
Sch St. Lawrence C of E Jun Sch, E.Mol. KT8 off Church Rd 196 CC98
St. Lawrence Ct, Abb.L. WD5 off St. Lawrence Cl 59 BS30
St. Lawrence Dr, Pnr. HA5 115 BV58
★ St. Lawrence Jewry Ch, EC2 287 K8
Sch St. Lawrence Prim Sch, Eff. KT24 off Lower Rd 246 BX127
Feltham TW13 off Victoria Rd 175 BV88
St. Lawrence Rd, Upmin. RM14 128 FQ61
St. Lawrence St, E14 302 F2
St. Lawrence's Way, Reig. RH2 off Church St 250 DA134
St. Lawrence Ter, W10 282 E6
St. Lawrence Way, SW9 310 F7
Bricket Wood AL2 60 BZ30
Caterham CR3 236 DQ123
St. Leonards Av, E4 101 ED51
Harrow HA3 117 CJ56
Windsor SL4 151 AQ82
St. Leonards Cl, Bushey WD23 76 BY42
Grays RM17 170 FZ79
Hertford SG14 32 DS07
St. Leonard's Cl, Well. DA16 166 EU83
Sch St. Leonard's C of E Prim Sch, SW16 off Mitcham La 181 DK92
St. Leonards Ct, N1 287 M2
St. Leonards Gdns, Ilf. IG1 125 EQ64
St. Leonard's Gdns, Houns. TW5 156 BY80
St. Leonards Hill, Wind. SL4 151 AK84
St. Leonards Ri, Orp. BR6 223 ES105
St. Leonards Rd, E14 290 D7
NW10 138 CR70
W13 137 CJ73
Amersham HP6 55 AS35
Claygate KT10 215 CF107
Croydon CR0 201 DP104
Epsom KT18 233 CW119
Hertford SG14 32 DR07
Nazeing EN9 68 EE25
T.Ditt. KT7 197 CG100
Windsor SL4 151 AQ82
St. Leonard's Rd, SW14 158 CP83
Surb. KT6 197 CK99
St. Leonards Sq, NW5 275 H5
St. Leonard's Sq, Surb. KT6 197 CK99
St. Leonards St, E3 290 D2
St. Leonard's Ter, SW3 308 E1
St. Leonards Wk, SW16 181 DM94
Iver SL0 153 BF76
St. Leonards Way, Horn. RM11 127 FH61
St. Loo Av, SW3 308 D2
St. Louis Cl, Pot.B. EN6 64 DC33
St. Louis Rd, SE27 182 DQ91
St. Loy's Rd, N17 100 DS54
St. Lucia Dr, E15 281 L8
St. Luke Cl, Uxb. UB8 134 BK72
ST. LUKE'S, EC1 287 K4
St. Lukes Av, Enf. EN2 82 DR38
St. Luke's Av, SW4 161 DK84
Ilf. IG1 125 EP64
Sch St. Luke's Catholic Prim Sch, Harl. CM19 off Pyenest Rd 51 EQ17
St. Lukes Cl, Lane End DA2 189 FS92
Swanley BR8 207 FD96
St. Luke's Cl, EC1 287 K4
SE25 202 DV100
Sch St. Luke's C of E Prim Sch, EC1 287 K3
SE27 off Linton Gro 182 DQ92
W9 282 G2
Kingston upon Thames KT2 off Acre Rd 198 CM95
Sch St. Luke's C of E (VA) Prim Sch, E16 291 M8
St. Lukes Ct, Hat. AL10 45 CV17
St. Lukes Est, EC1 287 L3
H St. Luke's Hosp for the Clergy, W1 285 L5
St. Lukes Ms, W11 283 H8
Sch St. Luke's Prim Sch, E14 302 G9
St. Lukes Rd, W11 283 H7
Old Windsor SL4 172 AU86
Whyteleafe CR3 off Whyteleafe Hill 236 DT118
St. Lukes Sq, E16 291 M9
Guildford GU1 259 AZ135
St. Luke's St, SW3 296 C10
H St. Luke's Woodside Hosp, N10 120 DG56
St. Luke's Yd, W9 282 G1
St. Magnus Ct, Hem.H. HP3 41 BP22
St. Malo Av, N9 100 DW48
Sch St. Margaret Clitherow RC Prim Sch, NW10 off Quainton St 118 CR63
SE28 off Cole Cl 146 EV74
St. Margaret Dr, Epsom KT18 216 CR114
ST. MARGARETS, Twick. TW1 177 CG85
ST. MARGARETS, Ware SG12 33 EB10
St. Margarets, Bark. IG11 145 ER67
Guildford GU1 243 AZ133
≠ St. Margarets (SG12) 33 EC11
≠ St. Margarets (TW1) 177 CH86
St. Margarets Av, N15 121 DP56
N20 98 DC47
Ashford TW15 175 BP92
Berry's Green TN16 off St. Anns Way 239 EP116
Harrow HA2 116 CC62
Sidcup DA15 185 ER90
Uxb. UB8 134 BN70
St. Margaret's Av, Sutt. SM3 199 CY104
St. Margarets Cl, EC2 off Lothbury 287 L8
Berkhamsted HP4 38 AX20
Dartford DA2 189 FR89
Iver SL0 133 BD68
Orpington BR6 224 EV105
Penn HP10 88 AC47
Sch St. Margaret's C of E Prim Sch, SE18 off St. Margaret's Gro 165 EQ78
Barking IG11 off North St 145 EQ66
St. Margaret's Ct, SE1 299 K3
St. Margaret's Cres, SW15 179 CV85
Gravesend DA12 191 GL90
St. Margaret's Dr, Twick. TW1 177 CH85
St. Margarets Gate, Iver SL0 off St. Margarets Cl 133 BD68
St. Margarets Gro, Twick. TW1 177 CG86
St. Margaret's Gro, E11 124 EF62
SE18 165 EQ79
H St. Margaret's Hosp, Epp. CM16 70 EV29
St. Margarets La, W8 295 L7
Sch St. Margaret's Lee C of E Prim Sch, SE13 off Lee Ch St 164 EE84
St. Margarets Pas, SE13 off Church Ter 164 EE83
St. Margarets Path, SE18 165 EQ78
St. Margarets Rd, E12 124 EJ61
SE4 163 DZ84
W7 157 CE75
Coulsdon CR5 235 DH121
Edgware HA8 96 CP50
Isleworth TW7 157 CH84
S.Darenth DA2, DA4 189 FS93
Twick. TW1 157 CH84
St. Margaret's Rd, N17 122 DS55
NW10 282 A1
Nthflt DA11 190 GE89
Ruislip HA4 115 BR58
Stans.Abb. SG12 33 EA13
Jct St. Margarets Rbt, Twick. TW1 177 CH85
Sch St. Margaret's Sch, NW3 off Kidderpore Gdns 120 DB63
Tadworth KT20 off Tadworth Ct 233 CX121
Sch St. Margaret's Sch Bushey, Bushey WD23 off Merry Hill Rd 94 CA45
Prep Sch, Bushey WD23 off Merry Hill Rd 94 CA46
St. Margarets Sq, SE4 off Adelaide Av 163 DZ84
St. Margaret's St, SW1 298 A5
St. Margaret's Ter, SE18 165 EQ78
St. Margarets Way, Hem.H. HP2 41 BR20
St. Margaret Way, Slou. SL1 151 AM75
St. Marks Av, Nthflt DA11 191 GF87
Sch St. Mark's Catholic Sch, Houns. TW3 off Bath Rd 156 BZ83
St. Marks Cl, SE10 314 E5
SW6 307 J7
W11 282 E9
Coln.Hth AL4 44 CP22
Harrow HA1 117 CH59
St. Mark's Cl, Barn. EN5 80 DB41
Sch St. Mark's C of E Acad, Mitch. CR4 off Acacia Rd 201 DH96
Sch St. Mark's C of E Prim Sch, N19 off Sussex Way 121 DL61
SE11 310 D2
SE25 off Albert Rd 202 DU98
Bromley BR2 off Aylesbury Rd 204 EG97
St. Marks Cres, NW1 275 H8
St. Mark's Gate, E9 279 P7
St. Mark's Gro, SW10 307 M3
St. Mark's Hill, Surb. KT6 198 CL100
H St. Mark's Hosp, Har. HA1 117 CH59
St. Marks Pl, W11 282 F9
Wind. SL4 151 AQ82
St. Mark's Pl, SW19 off Wimbledon Hill Rd 179 CZ93
Dag. RM10 147 FB65
Sch St. Mark's Prim Sch, W7 off Lower Boston Rd 157 CE75
Mitcham CR4 off St. Marks Rd 200 DF96
St. Marks Ri, E8 278 B3
St. Marks Rd, SE25 off Coventry Rd 202 DU98
W7 157 CE75
W10 282 D8
W11 282 E9
Bromley BR2 204 EH97
Enfield EN1 82 DT44
Mitch. CR4 200 DF96
Wind. SL4 151 AQ82
St. Mark's Rd, W5 138 CL74
Epsom KT18 233 CW118
Tedd. TW11 177 CH94
St. Marks Sq, NW1 274 G8
St. Mark St, E1 288 B9
Sch St. Mark's W Essex Catholic Sch, Harl. CM18 off Tripton Rd 51 ES16
St. Martha's Av, Wok. GU22 227 AZ121
Sch St. Martha's Conv Sen Sch, Had.Wd EN4 off Camlet Way 80 DA39
St. Marthas Ct, Chilw. GU4 off Nursery Gdns 259 BB140
St. Martin Cl, Uxb. UB8 134 BK72
★ St. Martin-in-the-Fields Ch, WC2 298 A1
Sch St. Martin-in-the-Fields High Sch for Girls, SW2 off Tulse Hill 181 DP88
Sch St. Martin of Porres RC Prim Sch, N11 off Blake Rd 99 DJ51
St. Martins, Nthwd. HA6 93 BR50
St. Martins App, Ruis. HA4 115 BS59
St. Martins Av, E6 292 E1
Epsom KT18 216 CS114
St. Martins Cl, NW1 275 L8
East Horsley KT24 245 BS129
Enfield EN1 82 DV39
Epsom KT17 217 CT113
Erith DA18 off St. Helens Rd 166 EX75
St. Martin's Cl, Wat. WD19 94 BW49
West Drayton UB7 off St. Martin's Rd 154 BK76
Sch St. Martin's C of E Inf & Jun Schs, Epsom KT18 off Worple Rd 232 CR115
Sch St. Martin's C of E Prim Sch, Pixham La, Dor. RH4 off Pixham La 247 CJ134
Ranmore Rd, Dor. RH4 off Ranmore Rd 263 CG135
St. Martin's Ct, WC2 off St. Martin's La 286 A10
Ashford TW15 174 BJ92
St. Martin's Ctyd, WC2 286 A10
St. Martins Dr, Walt. KT12 196 BW104
St. Martins Est, SW2 181 DN88
St. Martins La, Beck. BR3 203 EB99
St. Martin's La, WC2 286 A10
St. Martin's-le-Grand, EC1 287 J8
St. Martins Meadow, Brasted TN16 240 EW123
St. Martins Ms, Dor. RH4 off Church St 263 CG136
Pyrford GU22 228 BG116
St. Martin's Ms, WC2 298 A1
St. Martin's Pl, WC2 298 A1
St. Martins Rd, N9 100 DV47
Dart. DA1 188 FM86
Hoddesdon EN11 49 EC17
St. Martin's Rd, SW9 310 C8
West Dr. UB7 154 BJ76
Sch St. Martin's Sch, Hutt. CM13 off Hanging Hill La 109 GC46
Northwood HA6 off Moor Pk Rd 93 BR50
St. Martin's St, WC2 297 P1
St. Martins Ter, N10 off Pages La 98 DG54
St. Martins Wk, Dor. RH4 off High St 263 CH136
St. Martins Way, SW17 180 DC90
Sch St. Mary Abbots C of E Prim Sch, W8 295 L5
St. Mary Abbots Pl, W8 295 H7
St. Mary Abbots Ter, W14 295 H7
Sch St. Mary & All Saints C of E Prim Sch, Beac. HP9 off Maxwell Rd 89 AL52
Sch St. Mary & St. Joseph's Cath Sch, Sid. DA14 off Chislehurst Rd 186 EU92
Sch St. Mary & St. Michael Prim Sch, E1 288 G9
Sch St. Mary & St. Pancras C of E Prim Sch, NW1 285 N1
St. Mary at Hill, EC3 299 N1
★ St. Mary at Hill Ch, EC3 299 N1
St. Mary Av, Wall. SM6 200 DG104
St. Mary Axe, EC3 287 N9
St. Marychurch St, SE16 300 G5
ST. MARY CRAY, Orp. BR5 206 EW99
≠ St. Mary Cray 206 EU98
Sch St. Mary Cray Prim Sch, St.M.Cray BR5 off High St 206 EW100
St. Mary Graces Ct, E1 288 B10
St. Marylebone Cl, NW10 off Craven Pk 138 CS67
Sch St. Marylebone C of E Sch, W1 285 H6
★ St. Mary-le-Bow Ch, EC2 287 K9
Sch St. Mary Magdalene Acad, N7 276 E4
Sch St. Mary Magdalene C of E Prim Sch, SE15 312 E9
SE18 305 L8
Sch St. Mary Magdalene's Cath Prim Sch, SW14 off Worple St 158 CR83
Sch St. Mary Magdalene's C of E Prim Sch, W2 283 L6
Sch St. Mary Magdalen's Cath Prim Sch, SE4 off Howson Rd 163 DY84
Sch St. Mary Magdalen's RC Jun Sch, NW2 off Linacre Rd 139 CV65
St. Mary Newington Cl, SE17 off Surrey Sq 299 P10
Sch St. Mary of the Angels RC Prim Sch, W2 283 J8
St. Mary Rd, E17 123 EA56
St. Marys, Bark. IG11 145 ER67
Sch St. Mary's & St. John's C.E. Prim Sch, NW4 off Prothero Gdns 119 CV57
Sch St. Mary's & St. Peter's C of E Prim Sch, Tedd. TW11 off Somerset Rd 177 CF92
St. Marys App, E12 125 EM64
St. Marys Av, E11 124 EH58
Shenf. CM15 109 GA43
St. Mary's Av, N3 97 CY54
Bromley BR2 204 EE97
Northwood HA6 93 BS50
Stanw. TW19 174 BK87
Teddington TW11 177 CF93
St. Mary's Av Cen, Sthl. UB2 156 CB77
St. Mary's Av N, Sthl. UB2 156 CB77
St. Mary's Av S, Sthl. UB2 156 CB77
Sch St. Mary's Bryanston Sq C of E Prim Sch, W1 284 E6
Sch St. Mary's Cath Inf Sch, Croy. CR0 off Bedford Pk 202 DR102
Sch St. Mary's Cath Jun Sch, E17 off Shernhall St 123 EC55
Croydon CR0 off Sydenham Rd 202 DR102
Sch St. Mary's Cath Prim Sch, E4 off Station Rd 101 ED46
SW19 off Russell Rd 180 DA94
Beckenham BR3 off Westgate Rd 183 EC94
Hornchurch RM12 off Hornchurch Rd 127 FG60
Uxbridge UB8 off Rockingham Cl 134 BJ67
St. Mary's Ch Rd, Hat. AL9 63 CU25
St. Marys Cl, Chess. KT9 216 CM108
Epsom KT17 217 CU108
Grays RM17 off Dock Rd 170 GD79
Orp. BR5 206 EV96
Wat. WD18 off Church St 76 BW42
St. Mary's Cl, N17 100 DU53
Fetch. KT22 231 CD123
Gravesend DA12 191 GJ89
Hare. UB9 114 BH55
Loughton IG10 84 EL42
Oxt. RH8 254 EE129
Stanwell TW19 174 BK87
Sunbury-on-Thames TW16 off Green Way 195 BU98
Sch St. Mary's C of E Comb Sch, Amer. HP7 off School La 55 AP39
Sch St. Mary's C of E First Sch, Nthch HP4 off New Rd 38 AS17
Sch St. Mary's C of E High Sch, NW4 off Downage 119 CW55
Sch St. Mary's C of E Inf Sch, N8 off Church La 121 DM56
Sch St. Mary's C of E Jun Sch, N8 off Rectory Gdns 121 DL56
Oxted RH8 off Silkham Rd 254 EE128
Sch St. Mary's C of E Prim Sch, E17 off The Drive 123 EB56
E17 off Brooke Rd 123 EC56
N1 277 H8
N3 off Dollis Pk 97 CZ52
NW10 off Garnet Rd 138 CS65
SE13 off Lewisham High St 183 EC85
SW15 off Felsham Rd 159 CX83
Barnet EN4 off Littlegrove 80 DE44
Byfleet KT14 off Hart Rd 212 BL113
Chessington KT9 off Church La 216 CM107
North Mymms AL9 off Dellsome La 45 CV23
Rickmansworth WD3 off Stockers Fm Rd 92 BK48
Shenfield CM15 off Hall La 109 FZ44
Slough SL1 off Yew Tree Rd 152 AU76
Swanley BR8 off St. Marys Rd 207 FE98
Inf Site, Twick. TW1 off Amyand Pk Rd 177 CG87
Jun Site, Twick. TW1 off Richmond Rd 177 CH88
Sch St. Mary's C of E Prim School, Stoke Newington, N16 off Lordship Rd 122 DS61
Univ St. Mary's Coll, Twick. TW1 off Waldegrave Rd 177 CF90
St. Mary's Copse, Wor.Pk. KT4 198 CS103
St. Marys Ct, E6 293 J3
St. Mary's Ct, SE7 164 EK80
W5 off St. Mary's Rd 157 CK75
Beaconsfield HP9 off Malthouse Sq 111 AM55
St. Marys Cres, Islw. TW7 157 CD80
St. Mary's Cres, NW4 119 CV55
Hayes UB3 135 BT73
Stanw. TW19 174 BK87
St. Marys Dr, Felt. TW14 175 BQ87
St. Mary's Dr, Sev. TN13 256 FE123
St. Marys Est, SE16 off St. Marychurch St 300 G5
Sch St. Mary's Farnham Royal C of E Prim Sch, Farn.Royal SL2 off Church Rd 131 AQ69
St. Mary's Gdns, SE11 298 F8
St. Mary's Gate, W8 295 L7
St. Marys Grn, N2 120 DC55
Biggin Hill TN16 238 EJ118
St. Marys Gro, Bigg.H. TN16 238 EJ118
St. Mary's Gro, N1 277 H5
SW13 159 CV83
W4 158 CP79
Rich. TW9 158 CM84
Sch St. Mary's Hare Pk Sch, Gidea Pk RM2 off South Dr 128 FJ55
Sch St. Mary's High Sch, Croydon CR0 off Woburn Rd 202 DQ102
H St. Mary's Hosp, W2 284 B8
Sch St. Mary's Kilburn C of E Prim Sch, NW6 273 K8
St. Mary's La, Hert. SG14 31 DM11
Upminster RM14 128 FN61
St. Marys Mans, W2 284 A6
St. Mary's Ms, NW6 273 L7
Richmond TW10 off Wiggins La 177 CJ89
St. Mary's Mt, Cat. CR3 236 DT124
St. Marys Path, N1 277 H8
St. Mary's Pl, SE9 off Eltham High St 185 EN86
W5 157 CK75
W8 295 L7
St. Marys Rd, E10 123 EC62
E13 144 EH68
N8 off High St 121 DL56
N9 100 DW46
NW11 119 CY59
E.Mol. KT8 197 CD99
Ilf. IG1 125 EQ61
Leatherhead KT22 231 CH122
Long Ditton KT6 197 CJ101
Reigate RH2 266 DB135
Surb. KT6 197 CK100
Swanley BR8 207 FD98
Wey. KT13 213 BR105
St. Mary's Rd, NW10 138 CS67
SE15 312 G7
SE25 202 DS97
SW19 (Wimbledon) 179 CY92
W5 157 CK75
Barnet EN4 98 DF45

St. Mary's Rd, Bexley DA5 187 FC88
Cheshunt EN8 66 DW29
Denham UB9 113 BF58
Grays RM16 171 GH77
Greenhithe DA9 189 FS85
Harefield UB9 114 BH56
Hayes UB3 135 BT73
Hemel Hempstead HP2 40 BK19
Slou. SL3 132 AY74
South Croydon CR2 220 DR110
Wat. WD18 75 BV42
Wok. GU21 226 AW117
Worcester Park KT4 198 CS103
St. Mary's RC Inf Sch, N15 off Hermitage Rd 122 DR58
St. Mary's RC Infants' Sch, Cars. SM5 off West St 218 DF105
St. Mary's RC Jun Sch, N15 off Hermitage Rd 122 DR57
Carshalton SM5 off Shorts Rd 218 DF106
St. Mary's RC Prim Sch, NW6 273 J10
SE9 off Glenure Rd 185 EN85
SW4 off Crescent La 161 DJ84
SW8 309 K6
W4 off Duke Rd 158 CS78
W10 282 E5
W14 294 D7
Enfield EN3 off Durants Rd 83 DX42
Isleworth TW7 off South St 157 CG83
Tilbury RM18 off Calcutta Rd 171 GF82
St. Mary's Sch, NW3 274 A3
Gerrards Cross SL9 off Packhorse Rd 112 AY56
St. Marys Sq, W2 284 A6
St. Mary's Sq, W5 off St. Mary's Rd 157 CK75
St. Marys Ter, W2 284 A6
St. Mary's Twr, EC1 off Fortune St 287 K5
St. Mary St, SE18 305 K8
St. Marys Vw, Har. HA3 117 CJ57
St. Mary's Vw, Wat. WD18 76 BW42
St. Marys Wk, St.Alb. AL4 43 CH16
St. Mary's Wk, SE11 298 F8
Bletchingley RH1 252 DR133
Hayes UB3 135 BT73
St. Mary's Way, Chal.St.P. SL9 90 AX54
Chesham HP5 54 AP31
Chigwell IG7 103 EN50
Guildford GU2 242 AS132
St. Matthew Acad, SE3 315 J10
St. Matthew Cl, Uxb. UB8 134 BK72
St. Matthew's Av, Surb. KT6 198 CL102
St. Matthews Cl, Rain. RM13 147 FG66
Watford WD19 76 BX44
St. Matthew's C of E Inf Sch, Cob. KT11 off Downside Rd 229 BV118
St. Matthews C of E Prim Sch, Red. RH1 off Linkfield La 250 DF132
St. Matthew's C of E Prim Sch, SW1 297 P6
Enfield EN3 off South St 82 DW43
St. Matthew's C of E Prim Sch, Surb. KT6 off Langley Rd 198 CL101
St. Matthew's Dr, Brom. BR1 205 EM97
St. Matthews Prim Sch, SW20 off Cottenham Pk Rd 199 CU95
St. Matthew's Prim Sch, Yiew. UB7 off High St 134 BL74
St. Matthews Rd, W5 off The Common 138 CL74
St. Matthew's Rd, SW2 161 DM84
Red. RH1 250 DF133
St. Matthew's Row, E2 288 C3
St. Matthew St, SW1 297 N7
St. Matthias Cl, NW9 119 CT57
St. Matthias C of E Prim Sch, E2 288 B4
N16 277 N2
St. Maur Rd, SW6 307 H6
St. Mawes Cl, Crox.Grn WD3 75 BP42
St. Mellion Cl, SE28 146 EX72
St. Merryn Cl, SE18 165 ER80
St. Meryl Sch, Carp.Pk WD19 off The Mead 94 BY48
St. Michael & All Angels C of E Acad, SE5 311 J5
St. Michael & St. Martin RC Prim Sch, Houns. TW4 off Belgrave Rd 156 BZ83
St. Michael at Bowes C of E Jun Sch, N13 off Tottenhall Rd 99 DN51
St. Michael Cath Prim Sch, Ashf. TW15 off Feltham Hill Rd 174 BN92
St. Michael's, Oxt. RH8 254 EG129
St. Michael's All, EC3 287 M9
St. Michaels Av, N9 100 DW45
Hemel Hempstead HP3 41 BP21
St. Michael's Av, Wem. HA9 138 CN65
St. Michael's Camden Town C of E Prim Sch, NW1 275 L8
St. Michael's Catholic Coll, SE16 300 D5
St. Michael's Catholic Gram Sch, N12 off Nether St 98 DC50
St. Michael's Catholic High Sch, Wat. WD25 off High Elms La 60 BX32
St. Michaels Cl, E16 292 E7
N12 98 DE50
Aveley RM15 148 FQ73
Bromley BR1 204 EL97
Erith DA18 off St. Helens Rd 166 EX75
Harlow CM20 35 ES14
Walton-on-Thames KT12 196 BW103
Worcester Park KT4 199 CT103
St. Michael's Cl, N3 97 CZ54
St. Michael's C of E First Sch, Mick. RH5 off School La 247 CJ127
N6 off North Rd 120 DG59
N22 off Bounds Grn Rd 99 DM53
SE26 off Champion Rd 183 DY91
SW18 off Granville Rd 179 CZ87
Enfield EN2 off Brigadier Hill 82 DQ39
St. Albans AL3 off St. Michaels St 42 CB20
St. Michael's C of E Prim Sch, Well. DA16 off Wrotham Rd 166 EW81
St. Michael's Ct, Slou. SL2 131 AK70
St. Michaels Cres, Pnr. HA5 116 BY58
St. Michaels Dr, Wat. WD25 59 BV33
St. Michaels Gdns, W10 282 E7
St. Michael's Grn, Beac. HP9 89 AL52
St. Michael's Ms, SW1 296 G9
St. Michaels Rd, NW2 119 CW63
Brox. EN10 49 DZ20
Caterham CR3 236 DR122
Croydon CR0 202 DQ102
St. Michaels Rd, Grays RM16 171 GH78
Wallington SM6 219 DJ107
Welling DA16 166 EV83
St. Michael's Rd, SW9 310 C8
Ashford TW15 174 BN92
Wok. GU21 211 BD114
St. Michael's RC Prim Sch, E6 off Howard Rd 145 EM68
St. Michaels St, W2 284 B8
St. Albans AL3 42 CB20
St. Michaels Ter, N22 99 DL54
St. Michaels Vw, Hat. AL10 off Homestead Rd 45 CV16
St. Michaels Way, Pot.B. EN6 64 DB30
St. Mildred's Ct, EC2 off Poultry 287 L9
St. Mildreds Rd, SE12 184 EE87
Guildford GU1 243 AZ133
St. Monica's Rd, Kgswd KT20 233 CZ121
St. Monica's RC Prim Sch, N1 287 N2
N14 off Cannon Rd 99 DL48
St. Nazaire Cl, Egh. TW20 off Mullens Rd 173 BC92
St. Neots Cl, Borwd. WD6 78 CN38
St. Neots Rd, Rom. RM3 106 FM52
St. Nicholas Av, Bkhm KT23 246 CB125
Hornchurch RM12 127 FG62
St. Nicholas Cen, Sutt. SM1 off St. Nicholas Way 218 DB106
St. Nicholas Cl, Amer. HP7 72 AV39
Elstree WD6 77 CK44
Uxbridge UB8 134 BK72
St. Nicholas C of E Prim Sch, Els. WD6 off St. Nicholas Cl 77 CK44
Shepperton TW17 off Manor Fm Av 195 BP100
St. Nicholas Cres, Pyrford GU22 228 BG116
St. Nicholas Dr, Sev. TN13 257 FH126
Shepperton TW17 194 BN101
St. Nicholas Glebe, SW17 180 DG93
St. Nicholas Grn, Harl. CM17 36 EW14
St. Nicholas Gro, Ingrave CM13 109 GC50
St. Nicholas Hill, Lthd. KT22 231 CH122
St. Nicholas Ho, Enf. EN2 81 DH35
St. Nicholas Mt, Hem.H. HP1 39 BF20
St. Nicholas Pl, Loug. IG10 85 EN42
St. Nicholas Prep Sch, SW7 296 B5
St. Nicholas Rd, SE18 165 ET78
Sutton SM1 218 DB106
Thames Ditton KT7 197 CF100
St. Nicholas Sch, Harl. CM17 off Hobbs Cross Rd 36 EY12
Merstham RH1 off Taynton Dr 251 DK129
Purley CR8 off Reedham Dr 219 DN113
St. Nicholas St, SE8 313 P7
St. Nicholas Way, Sutt. SM1 218 DB105
St. Nicolas' C of E Comb Sch, Tap. SL6 off Rectory Rd 130 AE70
St. Nicolas C of E Inf Sch, Guil. GU2 off Portsmouth Rd 258 AW136
St. Nicolas La, Chis. BR7 204 EL95
St. Ninian's Ct, N20 98 DF48
St. Norbert Grn, SE4 163 DY84
St. Norbert Rd, SE4 163 DY84
St. Normans Way, Epsom KT17 217 CU110
St. Olaf's Rd, SW6 306 F5
St. Olaves Cl, Stai. TW18 173 BF94
St. Olaves Ct, EC2 287 L9
St. Olave's Est, SE1 299 P4
St. Olaves Gdns, SE11 298 E8
St. Olave's Gram Sch, Orp. BR6 off Goddington La 206 EV104
St. Olave's Prep Sch, SE9 off Southwood Rd 185 EP89
St. Olaves Rd, E6 145 EN67
St. Olave's Wk, SW16 201 DJ96
St. Olav's Sq, SE16 300 G6
St. Omer Ridge, Guil. GU1 259 BA135
St. Omer Rd, Guil. GU1 259 BA135
St. Osmund's Cath Prim Sch, SW13 off Church Rd 159 CT81
St. Oswald's Pl, SE11 310 C1
St. Oswald's Rd, SW16 201 DP95
St. Oswulf St, SW1 297 P9
ST. PANCRAS, WC1 286 A3
St. Pancras Commercial Cen, NW1 off Pratt St 275 M8
St. Pancras Hosp, NW1 275 N9
Saint Pancras International 286 A1
St. Pancras Way, NW1 275 M8
St. Patrick's Cath Prim Sch, E17 off Longfield Av 123 DY56
NW5 275 K4
Collier Row RM5 off Lowshoe La 105 FB53
St. Patrick's Ct, Wdf.Grn. IG8 102 EE52
St. Patrick's Gdns, Grav. DA12 191 GK90
St. Patricks Pl, Grays RM16 171 GJ77
St. Patrick's RC Prim Sch, SE18 off Griffin Rd 165 ER77
St. Paul & All Hallows C.E. Inf & Jun Schs, N17 off Park La 100 DU52
St. Paul Cl, Uxb. UB8 134 BK71
St. Paulinus C of E Prim Sch, Cray. DA1 off Iron Mill La 167 FE84
St. Paul's 287 J8
St. Paul's Acad, SE2 off Wickham La 166 EU79
St. Paul's All, EC4 off St. Paul's Chyd 287 H9
St. Pauls Av, Har. HA3 118 CM57
Slough SL2 132 AT73
St. Paul's Av, NW2 139 CV65
SE16 301 K2
St. Paul's Cath, EC4 287 J9
St. Paul's Catholic Coll, Sun. TW16 off Green St 195 BU95
St. Paul's Cath Prim Sch, T.Ditt. KT7 off Hampton Ct Way 197 CE101
St. Paul's Cath Sch, EC4 287 J9
St. Paul's Chyd, EC4 287 H9
St. Pauls Cl, Add. KT15 212 BG106
Aveley RM15 148 FQ73
Borehamwood WD6 78 CQ43
Chess. KT9 215 CK105
Harlington UB3 155 BR78
Swans. DA10 190 FY87
St. Paul's Cl, SE7 164 EK78
W5 158 CM75
Ashf. TW15 175 BQ92
Cars. SM5 200 DE102
Houns. TW3 156 BY82
St. Paul's C of E Comb Sch, Woob.Grn HP10 off Stratford Dr 110 AD59
St. Paul's C of E Jun Sch, Kings.T. KT2 off Princes Rd 178 CN94
St. Pauls C of E Prim Sch, Chess. KT9 off Orchard Rd 216 CL105
St. Paul's C of E Prim Sch, E1 288 D10
N11 off The Avenue 99 DH50
N21 off Ringwood Way 99 DP45
NW3 274 E7
NW7 off The Ridgeway 97 CV49
SE17 311 J1
W6 294 A10
Addlestone KT15 off School La 212 BG105
Brentford TW8 off St. Paul's Rd 157 CK79
St. Paul's C of E Prim Sch, Chipper. WD4 off The Common 58 BG31
Dorking RH4 off St. Pauls Rd W 263 CH137
Hunton Bridge WD4 off Langleybury La 59 BQ34
Swanley BR8 off School La 207 FH95
St. Pauls Ct, Chipper. WD4 off The Common 58 BG31
St. Paul's Ct, W14 294 D9
St. Pauls Ctyd, SE8 off Mary Ann Gdns 314 A3
ST. PAUL'S CRAY, Orp. BR5 206 EU96
St. Paul's Cray C of E Prim Sch, St.P.Cray BR5 off Buttermere Rd 206 EX97
St. Pauls Cray Rd, Chis. BR7 205 ER95
St. Paul's Cres, NW1 275 P6
St. Pauls Dr, E15 280 G3
St. Paul's Girls' Sch, W6 294 C8
St. Pauls Ms, Dor. RH4 263 CH137
St. Paul's Ms, NW1 275 P6
St. Pauls Pl, Aveley RM15 148 FQ73
St. Albans AL1 43 CG20
St. Paul's Pl, N1 277 L4
St. Paul's Prep Sch, SW13 off Lonsdale Rd 159 CU78
St. Pauls Ri, N13 99 DP51
St. Pauls Rd, Hem.H. HP2 40 BK19
Wok. GU22 227 BA117
St. Paul's Rd, N1 276 G5
N17 100 DU52
Barking IG11 145 EQ67
Brentford TW8 157 CK79
Erith DA8 167 FC80
Rich. TW9 158 CM83
Staines-upon-Thames TW18 173 BD92
Thornton Heath CR7 202 DQ97
St. Pauls Rd E, Dor. RH4 263 CH137
St. Pauls Rd W, Dor. RH4 263 CG137
St. Paul's RC Prim Sch, N22 off Bradley Rd 99 DM54
Cheshunt EN7 off Park La 66 DV27
St. Paul's Sch, SW13 off Lonsdale Rd 159 CU78
St. Paul's Shrubbery, N1 277 L4
St. Pauls Sq, Brom. BR2 204 EG96
St. Paul's Ter, SE17 311 H2
St. Paul St, N1 277 J9
St. Pauls Wk, Kings.T. KT2 off Alexandra Rd 178 CN94
St. Pauls Way, E3 289 N7
E14 289 N7
Wal.Abb. EN9 off Rochford Av 67 ED33
Watford WD24 76 BW40
St. Paul's Way, N3 98 DB52
St. Paul's Way Trust Sch, E3 290 A6
St. Paul's with St. Luke's Prim Sch, E3 289 P6
St. Paul's with St. Michael's C of E Prim Sch, E8 278 D8
St. Pauls Wd Hill, Orp. BR5 205 ES96
St. Peter & Paul's Cath Prim Sch, Ilf. IG1 off Gordon Rd 125 ER62
St. Peter & St. Paul Cath Prim Sch, St.P.Cray BR5 off St. Pauls Wd Hill 205 ES96
St. Peter & St. Paul C of E Inf Sch, Chaldon CR3 off Rook La 251 DN125
St. Peter & St. Paul RC Prim Sch, Mitch. CR4 off Cricket Grn 200 DF98
St. Peter & St. Paul's RC Prim Sch, EC1 287 H4
St. Peter Chanel Cath Prim Sch, Sid. DA14 off Baugh Rd 186 EW92
St. Peter in Chains RC Inf Sch, N8 off Elm Gro 121 DL58
St. Peter's All, EC3 287 M9
St. Peters Av, N18 100 DU49
Berry's Green TN16 239 EP116
St. Peter's Av, E2 288 D1
E17 124 EE56
St. Petersburgh Ms, W2 283 L10
St. Petersburgh Pl, W2 283 L10
St. Peter's Catholic Comp Sch, Guil. GU1 off Horseshoe La E 243 BC133
St. Peter's Cath Prim Sch, Dag. RM9 off Goresbrook Rd 146 EZ67
Leatherhead KT22 off Grange Rd 231 CJ120
Romford RM1 off Dorset Av 127 FE55
St. Peters Cl, SW17 180 DE89
Bushey Hth WD23 95 CD46
Chalfont St. Peter SL9 off Lewis La 90 AY53
Chislehurst BR7 185 ER94
Hatfield AL10 45 CU17
Ilford IG2 125 ES56
Mill End WD3 92 BH46
Old Windsor SL4 off Church Rd 172 AU85
St.Alb. AL1 43 CD19
Staines-upon-Thames TW18 173 BF93
Swanscombe DA10 190 FZ87
Woking GU22 227 BC120
St. Peter's Cl, E2 288 D1
Barn. EN5 79 CV43
Burnham SL1 130 AH70
Ruis. HA4 116 BX61
St. Peter's C of E Comb Sch, Burn. SL1 off Minniecroft Rd 130 AH69
St. Peter's C of E Inf Sch, Tand. RH8 off Tandridge La 253 EA133
St. Peter's C of E Mid Sch, Old Wind. SL4 off Crimp Hill Rd 172 AT86
St. Peter's C of E Prim Sch, SE17 311 L1
W6 off St. Peter's Rd 159 CU77
W9 283 J5
Mill End WD3 off Church La 92 BH46
South Weald CM14 off Wigley Bush La 108 FS47
St. Peters Ct, Chal.St.P. SL9 off High St 90 AY53
SE3 off Eltham Rd 184 EF85
SE4 313 P9
West Molesey KT8 196 CA98
St. Peter's Ct, NW4 119 CW57
St. Peter's Eaton Sq C of E Prim Sch, SW1 297 K7
St. Peter's Gdns, SE27 181 DN90
St. Peter's Gro, W6 159 CU77
St. Peter's Hosp, Cher. KT16 193 BD104
St. Peters La, St.P.Cray BR5 206 EU96
St. Peters Ms, N4 121 DP57
St. Peter's Pl, W9 283 L5
St. Peter's Prim Sch, E1 300 G2
South Croydon CR2 off Normanton Rd 220 DS107
St. Peters Rd, N9 100 DW46
Kings.T. KT1 198 CN96
St. Albans AL1 43 CE20
Southall UB1 136 CA71
Twickenham TW1 177 CH85
Uxbridge UB8 134 BK71
Warley CM14 off Crescent Rd 108 FV49
Wok. GU22 227 BB121
St. Peter's Rd, W6 159 CU78
Croydon CR0 220 DR105
Grays RM16 171 GH77
W.Mol. KT8 196 CA98
St. Peter's RC Prim Sch, SE18 305 N10
St. Peter's Sch, St.Alb. AL1 off Cottonmill La 43 CE21
St. Peter's Sq, E2 288 D1
W6 159 CU78
St. Peters St, N1 277 H9
St. Albans AL1 43 CD20
St. Peter's St, S.Croy. CR2 220 DR106
St. Peter's St Ms, N1 277 H10
St. Peters Ter, SW6 306 F5
St. Peter's Vil, W6 159 CT77
St. Peters Way, W5 137 CK71
Chorl. WD3 73 BB43
Harlington UB3 155 BR78
St. Peter's Way, N1 277 P7
Add. KT15 194 BG104
Chertsey KT16 211 BD105
St. Philip Howard RC Prim Sch, Hat. AL10 off Woods Av 45 CV18
St. Philip's Av, Wor.Pk. KT4 199 CV103
St. Philips Gate, Wor.Pk. KT4 199 CV103
St. Philip Sq, SW8 309 J8
St. Philips Rd, Surb. KT6 197 CK100
St. Philip's Rd, E8 278 C5
St. Philip's Sch, SW7 295 P9
Chessington KT9 off Harrow Cl 215 CK107
St. Philip St, SW8 309 J10
St. Philip's Way, N1 277 K8
St. Philomena's Cath Prim Sch, Orp. BR5 off Chelsfield Rd 206 EW101
St. Philomena's Sch, Cars. SM5 off Pound St 218 DF106
St. Pinnock Av, Stai. TW18 194 BG95
St. Quentin Ho, SW18 off Fitzhugh Gro 180 DD86
St. Quentin Rd, Well. DA16 165 ET83
St. Quintin Av, W10 282 B7
St. Quintin Gdns, W10 282 A7
St. Quintin Rd, E13 292 A1
St. Raphaels Ct, St.Alb. AL1 off Avenue Rd 43 CE19
St. Raphael's RC Prim Sch, Nthlt. UB5 off Hartfield Av 135 BV68
St. Raphael's Way, NW10 118 CQ64
St. Regis Cl, N10 99 DH54
St. Richard's with St. Andrew's C of E Prim Sch, Rich. TW10 off Ashburnham Rd 177 CH90
St. Robert Southwell Cath Prim Sch, NW9 off Slough La 118 CQ58
St. Ronan's Cl, Barn. EN4 80 DD38
St. Ronans Cres, Wdf.Grn. IG8 102 EG52
St. Ronans Vw, Dart. DA1 188 FM87
St. Rose's Catholic Inf Sch, Hem.H. HP1 off Green End Rd 40 BG22
St. Rule St, SW8 309 L8
St. Saviour's & St. Olave's Sch, SE1 299 M7
St. Saviour's C of E Inf Sch, W5 off The Grove 137 CK74
St. Saviour's C of E Prim Sch, E17 off Verulam Av 123 DZ59
SE24 off Herne Hill Rd 162 DQ83
W9 283 M5
St. Saviour's Ct, Pur. CR8 off Old Lo La 219 DM113
St. Saviours Ct, Har. HA1 117 CD57
St. Saviour's Est, SE1 300 A6
St. Saviours Pl, Guil. GU1 off Leas Rd 242 AW134
St. Saviour's Prim Sch, E14 290 C7
St. Saviours Rd, Croy. CR0 202 DQ100
St. Saviour's Rd, SW2 181 DM85
St. Saviour's RC Prim Sch, SE13 off Bonfield Rd 163 EC84
St. Saviours Vw, St.Alb. AL1 off Summerhill Ct 43 CF19
St. Scholastica's RC Prim Sch, E5 off Kenninghall Rd 122 DU62
Saints Cl, SE27 off Wolfington Rd 181 DP91
Saints Dr, E7 124 EK64
St. Silas Pl, NW5 274 G5
St. Silas St Est, NW5 274 G4
St. Simon's Av, SW15 179 CW85
ST. STEPHENS, St.Alb. AL3 42 CC22
St. Stephens Av, E17 123 EC57
W12 159 CV75
W13 137 CH72
St.Alb. AL3 42 CB22
St. Stephen's Av, Ashtd. KT21 232 CL116
St. Stephen's Cath Prim Sch, Well. DA16 off Deepdene Rd 166 EU82
St. Stephens Cl, E17 123 EB57
NW8 274 D9
St. Albans AL3 42 CB23
Southall UB1 136 CA71
St. Stephen's C of E Jun Sch, Twick. TW1 off Winchester Rd 177 CH86
St. Stephen's C of E Prim Sch, SE8 314 B8
SW8 310 C4
W2 283 K7
W12 294 A4
St. Stephens Cres, W2 283 K8
Brentwood CM13 109 GA49
Thornton Heath CR7 201 DN97
St. Stephens Gdn Est, W2 283 J8
St. Stephens Gdns, SW15 off Manfred Rd 179 CZ85
W2 283 K7
Twickenham TW1 177 CJ86
St. Stephens Gro, SE13 314 F10
St. Stephens Hill, St.Alb. AL1 42 CC22
St. Stephens Ms, W2 283 K7
St. Stephen's Par, E7 off Green St 144 EJ66
St. Stephen's Pas, Twick. TW1 off Richmond Rd 177 CJ86
St. Stephen's Prim Sch, E6 off Whitfield Rd 144 EJ66
St. Stephens Rd, E3 279 N10
E6 144 EJ66
W13 137 CH72
Enf. EN3 83 DX37
Hounslow TW3 176 CA86
St. Stephen's Rd, E17 123 EB57
Barn. EN5 79 CX43
West Dr. UB7 134 BK74
St. Stephens Row, EC4 287 L9
St. Stephens Ter, SW8 310 C5
St. Stephen's Wk, SW7 295 N8
Saints Wk, Grays RM16 171 GJ77
St. Swithin's La, EC4 287 L10
St. Swithun's Rd, SE13 183 ED85
St. Swithun Wells RC Prim Sch, Hlgdn HA4 off Hunters Hill 116 BX62
St. Teresa Cath Prim Sch, The, Dag. RM8 off Bowes Rd 126 EW63
St. Teresa's Cath Prim Sch, Harrow Weald HA3 off Long Elmes 94 CC53
Borehamwood WD6 off Brook Rd 78 CP40
St. Teresa's Prep Sch, Dor. RH5 off Effingham Hill 246 BX132
St. Teresa's RC Prim Sch, Mord. SM4 off Montacute Rd 200 DD100
St. Teresa's Sch, Dor. RH5 off Effingham Hill 246 BX132
St. Teresa Wk, Grays RM16 171 GH76
St. Theresa Cl, Epsom KT18 216 CQ114
St. Theresa's Cl, E9 123 EA63
St. Theresa's Rd, Felt. TW14 155 BT84
St. Theresa's RC Prim Sch, N3 off East End Rd 120 DB55
St. Thomas à Becket RC Prim Sch, SE2 off Mottisfont Rd 166 EU76
St. Thomas Becket Cath Prim Sch, SE25 off Becket Cl 202 DU100
St. Thomas' Catholic Prim Sch, Sev. TN13 off South Pk 257 FH125
St. Thomas Cl, Chilw. GU4 259 BC140
Wok. GU21 off St. Mary's Rd 226 AW117
St. Thomas' Cl, Surb. KT6 198 CM102
St. Thomas C of E Prim Sch, W10 282 F5
St. Thomas Ct, Bex. DA5 186 FA87
St. Thomas Dr, E.Clan. GU4 off The Street 244 BL131
Orpington BR5 205 EQ102
St. Thomas' Dr, Pnr. HA5 94 BY53
St. Thomas Gdns, Ilf. IG1 145 EQ65
St. Thomas' Hosp, SE1 298 C6
St. Thomas' Med Sch & the Nightingale Sch, SE1 298 C7
St. Thomas Ms, SE7 304 G9
St. Thomas More Cath Prim Sch, Bexh. DA7 off Sheldon Rd 166 EZ82
St. Thomas More RC Prim Sch, SE9 off Appleton Rd 164 EL83
Berkhamsted HP4 off Greenway 38 AU19
St. Thomas More RC Sch, N22 off Glendale Av 99 DN52
SE9 off Footscray Rd 185 EN86
St. Thomas More Sch, SW3 296 E9
St. Thomas of Canterbury Cath Prim Sch, SW6 306 G4
Grays RM17 off Ward Av 170 GB77
Guildford GU1 off Horseshoe La W 243 BB134
Mitcham CR4 off Commonside E 200 DG97
St. Thomas of Canterbury C of E Inf & Jun Schs, Brwd. CM15 off Sawyers Hall La 108 FX45
St. Thomas Rd, E16 291 N8
N14 99 DK45
Belv. DA17 167 FC75
Brentwood CM14 108 FX47
Northfleet DA11 off St. Margaret's Rd 190 GE89
St. Thomas' Rd, W4 158 CQ79
St. Thomas's Av, Grav. DA11 191 GH88
St. Thomas's Cl, Wal.Abb. EN9 68 EH33
St. Thomas's Gdns, NW5 274 G4
St. Thomas's Ms, SW18 off West Hill 180 DA85
Guil. GU1 off St. Catherines Pk 259 AZ136
St. Thomas's Pl, E9 278 G6
St. Thomas's Rd, N4 121 DN61
NW10 138 CS67
St. Thomas's Sq, E9 278 F6
St. Thomas St, SE1 299 L3
St. Thomas's Way, SW6 306 G4
St. Thomas the Apostle Coll, SE15 312 G8
St. Thomas Wk, Colnbr. SL3 153 BD80
St. Timothy's Ms, Brom. BR1 off Wharton Rd 204 EH95
St. Ursula Gro, Pnr. HA5 116 BX57
St. Ursula Rd, Sthl. UB1 136 CA72
St. Ursula's Cath Inf Sch, Harold Hill RM3 off Straight Rd 106 FJ51
St. Ursula's Conv Sch, SE10 314 G5
St. Ursula's Jun Sch, Harold Hill RM3 off Straight Rd 105 FH51
St. Vincent Cl, SE27 181 DP92
St. Vincent de Paul RC Prim Sch, SW1 297 L7
St. Vincent Dr, St.Alb. AL1 43 CG23
St. Vincent Rd, Twick. TW2 176 CC86
Walton-on-Thames KT12 195 BV104
St. Vincents Av, Dart. DA1 188 FN85
St. Vincent's Cath Prim Sch, SE9 off Harting Rd 184 EL91
Dagenham RM8 off Burnside Rd 126 EW61

ST. VINCENT'S HAMLET, Brwd. CM14 106 FP46
St. Vincents La, NW7 97 CW50
St. Vincents Rd, Dart. DA1 188 FN86
Sch St. Vincent's RC Prim Sch, NW7 off The Ridgeway 97 CW50
W1 285 H7
W3 off Pierrepoint Rd 138 CP73
St. Vincent St, W1 285 H7
St. Vincents Way, Pot.B. EN6 64 DC33
St. Wilfrids Cl, Barn. EN4 80 DE43
St. Wilfrids Rd, Barn. EN4 80 DD43
Sch St. William of York RC Prim Sch, SE23 off Brockley Pk 183 DY88
St. Williams Ct, N1 off Gifford St 276 B7
St. Winefride's Av, E12 125 EM64
Sch St. Winefride's RC Prim Sch, E12 off Church Rd 125 EM64
St. Winifreds, Ken. CR8 236 DQ115
Sch St. Winifred's Catholic Jun Sch, SE12 off Newstead Rd 184 EF86
Sch St. Winifred's Catholic Nurs & Inf Sch, SE12 off Effingham Rd 184 EE85
St. Winifreds Cl, Chig. IG7 103 EQ50
St. Winifred's Rd, Bigg.H. TN16 239 EM118
Teddington TW11 177 CH93
St. Yon Ct, St.Alb. AL4 43 CK20
Sakins Cft, Harl. CM18 51 ET18
Sakura Dr, N22 99 DK53
Saladin Dr, Purf. RM19 168 FN77
Salamanca Pl, SE1 298 C9
Barking IG11 146 EV68
Salamanca St, SE1 298 B9
Salamander Cl, Kings.T. KT2 177 CJ92
Salamander Quay, Hare. UB9 92 BG52
Salamons Way, Rain. RM13 147 FE72
Salbrook Rd, Salf. RH1 266 DG142
Salcombe Dr, Mord. SM4 199 CX102
Romford RM6 126 EZ58
Salcombe Gdns, NW7 97 CW51
Salcombe Pk, Loug. IG10 84 EK43
Sch Salcombe Prep Sch, Inf Dept, N14 off Green Rd 81 DH43
Jun Dept, N14 off Chase Side 99 DH45
Salcombe Rd, E17 123 DZ59
N16 277 P2
Ashford TW15 174 BL91
Salcombe Vil, Rich. TW10 off The Vineyard 178 CL85
Salcombe Way, Hayes UB4 135 BS69
Ruislip HA4 115 BU61
Salcot Cres, New Adgtn CR0 221 EC110
Salcote Rd, Grav. DA12 191 GL92
Salcott Rd, SW11 180 DE85
Croydon CR0 201 DL104
Salehurst Cl, Har. HA3 118 CL57
Salehurst Rd, SE4 183 DZ86
Salem Pl, Croy. CR0 202 DQ104
Northfleet DA11 190 GD87
Salem Rd, W2 283 M10
Salento Cl, N3 98 DA52
Sale Pl, W2 284 C7
Salesian Gdns, Cher. KT16 194 BG102
Sch Salesian Sch, Cher. KT16 off Highfield Rd 194 BG102
Sale St, E2 288 C4
Salford Rd, SW2 181 DK88
SALFORDS, Red. RH1 266 DF142
⇌ Salfords 266 DG142
Sch Salfords Prim Sch, Salf. RH1 off Copsleigh Av 266 DG140
Salfords Way, Red. RH1 266 DG142
Salhouse Cl, SE28 off Rollesby Way 146 EW72
Salisbury Av, N3 119 CZ55
Barking IG11 145 ER66
St. Albans AL1 43 CH19
Slough SL2 131 AQ70
Sutton SM1 217 CZ107
Swanley BR8 207 FG98
Salisbury Cl, SE17 299 L8
Amersham HP7 55 AS39
Potters Bar EN6 64 DC32
Upminster RM14 129 FT61
Worcester Park KT4 199 CT104
Salisbury Ct, EC4 286 G9
Edgware HA8 96 CM49
Salisbury Cres, Chsht EN8 67 DX32
Salisbury Gdns, SW19 179 CY94
Buckhurst Hill IG9 102 EK47
Welwyn Garden City AL7 29 CZ10
Salisbury Hall Dr, Hat. AL10 44 CR16
Salisbury Hall Gdns, E4 101 EA51
Salisbury Ho, E14 290 C8
Salisbury Ms, SW6 306 G5
Bromley BR2 204 EL99
Salisbury Pl, SW9 311 H5
W1 284 E6
West Byfleet KT14 212 BJ111
Sch Salisbury Prim Sch, E12 off Romford Rd 124 EL64
Salisbury Rd, E4 101 EA48
E7 281 N5
E10 123 EC61
E12 124 EK64
E17 123 EC57
N4 121 DP57
N22 99 DP53
SE25 202 DU100
SW19 179 CY94
W13 157 CG75
Banstead SM7 218 DB114
Barnet EN5 79 CY41
Bexley DA5 186 FA88
Bromley BR2 204 EL99
Carshalton SM5 218 DF107
Dagenham RM10 147 FB65
Dartford DA2 188 FQ88
Enfield EN3 83 DZ37
Feltham TW13 176 BW88
Godstone RH9 252 DW131
Gravesend DA11 191 GF88
Grays RM17 170 GC79
Harrow HA1 117 CD57
Hoddesdon EN11 49 EC15
Hounslow TW4 156 BW83
Ilford IG3 125 ES61
London Heathrow Airport TW6 175 BQ85
New Malden KT3 198 CR97
Pinner HA5 115 BU56
Richmond TW9 158 CL84
Romford RM2 127 FH57
Salisbury Rd, Southall UB2 156 BY77
Uxbridge UB8 134 BH68
Watford WD24 75 BV38
Welwyn Garden City AL7 29 CZ10
Woking GU22 226 AY119
Worcester Park KT4 199 CT104
Sch Salisbury Sch, Lwr Sch, N9 off Turin Rd 100 DW45
Upr Sch, N9 off Nightingale Rd 100 DW45
Salisbury Sq, EC4 286 F9
Hatfield AL9 off Park St 45 CW17
Hertford SG14 off Railway St 32 DR09
Salisbury St, NW8 284 B5
W3 158 CQ75
Salisbury Ter, SE15 313 H10
Salisbury Wk, N19 121 DJ61
Salix Cl, Fetch. KT22 230 CB123
Sunbury-on-Thames TW16 off Oak Gro 175 BV94
Salix La, Wdf.Grn. IG8 102 EL53
Salix Rd, Grays RM17 170 GD79
Salliesfield, Twick. TW2 177 CD86
Sally Murray Cl, E12 125 EN63
Salmen Rd, E13 291 M1
Salmon Cl, Welw.G.C. AL7 30 DA06
Salmond Cl, Stan. HA7 95 CG51
Salmonds Gro, Ingrave CM13 109 GC50
Salmon La, E14 289 L8
Salmon Meadow Footpath, Hem.H. HP3 40 BK24
Salmon Rd, Belv. DA17 166 FA78
Dartford DA1 168 FM83
Salmons La, Whyt. CR3 236 DU119
Salmons La W, Cat. CR3 236 DS120
Salmons Rd, N9 100 DU46
Chessington KT9 215 CK107
Effingham KT24 245 BV129
Salmon St, E14 289 N9
NW9 118 CP60
Salomons Rd, E13 292 C6
Salop Rd, E17 123 DX58
Saltash Cl, Sutt. SM1 217 CZ105
Saltash Rd, Ilf. IG6 103 ER52
Welling DA16 166 EW81
Salt Box Hill, Bigg.H. TN16 222 EH113
Salt Box Rd, Guil. GU3, GU4 242 AT129
Saltcoats Rd, W4 158 CS75
Saltcote Cl, Dart. DA1 187 FE86
Saltcroft Cl, Wem. HA9 118 CP60
Salter Cl, Har. HA2 116 BZ62
Salterford Rd, SW17 180 DG93
Saltern Ct, Bark. IG11 off Puffin Cl 146 EV69
Salter Rd, SE16 301 J3
Salters Cl, Berk. HP4 38 AT17
Rickmansworth WD3 92 BL46
Salters Gdns, Wat. WD17 75 BU39
Salters Hall Ct, EC4 287 L10
Salters Hill, SE19 182 DR92
Salters Rd, E17 123 ED56
W10 282 C5
Salter St, E14 290 A10
NW10 139 CU69
Salter St Alleyway, NW10 off Hythe Rd 139 CU70
Salterton Rd, N7 121 DL62
Saltford Cl, Erith DA8 167 FE78
Salt Hill Av, Slou. SL1 131 AQ74
Salthill Cl, Uxb. UB8 114 BL64
Salt Hill Dr, Slou. SL1 131 AQ74
Salt Hill Way, Slou. SL1 131 AQ74
Saltings, The, Green. DA9 169 FW84
Saltley Cl, E6 293 H8
Salton Cl, N3 off East End Rd 98 DA54
Saltoun Rd, SW2 161 DN84
Saltram Cl, N15 122 DT56
Saltram Cres, W9 283 H2
Saltwell St, E14 290 B10
Saltwood Cl, Orp. BR6 224 EW105
Saltwood Gro, SE17 311 L1
Sch Salusbury Prim Sch, NW6 272 G9
Salusbury Rd, NW6 282 G1
Salutation Rd, SE10 303 K8
Sch Salvatorian Coll, Wealds. HA3 off High St 95 CE54
Salvia Gdns, Perivale UB6 137 CG68
Salvin Rd, SW15 159 CX83
Salway Cl, Wdf.Grn. IG8 102 EF52
Salway Pl, E15 281 H5
Salway Rd, E15 281 H5
Salwey Cres, Brox. EN10 49 DZ20
Samantha Cl, E17 123 DZ59
Samantha Ms, Hav.at.Bow. RM4 105 FE48
Sam Bartram Cl, SE7 304 D10
Sambrook Ho, SE11 298 E9
Sambruck Ms, SE6 183 EB88
Samels Ct, W6 off South Black Lion La 159 CU78
Samford Ho, N1 276 E9
Samford St, NW8 284 B5
Samian Gate, St.Alb. AL3 42 BZ22
Samira Cl, E17 off Colchester Rd 123 DZ58
Samos Rd, SE20 202 DV96
Samphire Ct, Grays RM17 off Salix Rd 170 GE79
Sample Oak La, Chilw. GU4 259 BE140
Sampson Av, Barn. EN5 79 CX43
Sampson Cl, Belv. DA17 off Carrill Way 166 EX76
Sampsons Ct, Shep. TW17 off Linden Way 195 BQ99
Sampsons Grn, Slou. SL2 131 AM69
Sampson St, E1 300 D3
Samson St, E13 292 C1
Samuel Cl, E8 278 B8
SE14 313 J3
SE18 305 H8
Stanmore HA7 95 CG47
Samuel Gray Gdns, Kings.T. KT2 197 CK95
Samuel Johnson Cl, SW16 181 DM91
Samuel Lewis Trust Dws, N1 276 F5
SW3 296 C9
SW6 307 K4
W14 294 F8
Samuel Lewis Trust Est, SE5 off Warner Rd 311 K7
Sch Samuel Rhodes Sch Sec Dept, N5 122 DQ64
Sch Samuel Ryder Acad, St.Alb. AL1 off Drakes Dr 43 CH23
Samuels Ct, W6 159 CU78
Samuel Sq, St.Alb. AL1 off Pageant Rd 43 CD21
Samuel St, SE15 312 A4
SE18 305 J8
Sancroft Cl, NW2 119 CV62
Sancroft Rd, Har. HA3 95 CF54
Sancroft St, SE11 298 D10
Sanctuary, The, SW1 297 P5
Bexley DA5 186 EX86
Morden SM4 200 DA100
Sanctuary Cl, Dart. DA1 188 FJ86
Harefield UB9 92 BJ52
Sanctuary Ms, E8 278 B5
Sanctuary Rd, Lon.Hthrw Air. TW6 174 BN86
Sanctuary St, SE1 299 K5
Sandall Cl, W5 138 CL70
Sandall Ho, E3 279 M10
Sandall Rd, NW5 275 M5
W5 138 CL70
Sandalls Spring, Hem.H. HP1 39 BF18
Sandal Rd, N18 100 DU50
New Malden KT3 198 CR99
Sandal St, E15 281 J8
Sandalwood, Guil. GU2 258 AV135
Sandalwood Av, Cher. KT16 193 BD104
Sandalwood Cl, E1 289 L5
Sandalwood Dr, Ruis. HA4 115 BQ59
Sandalwood Rd, Felt. TW13 175 BV90
Sanday Cl, Hem.H. HP3 41 BP22
Sandbach Pl, SE18 165 EQ78
Sandbanks, Felt. TW14 175 BS88
Sandbanks Hill, Bean DA2 189 FV93
Sandbourne Av, SW19 200 DB97
Sandbourne Rd, SE4 313 L8
Sandbrook Cl, NW7 96 CR51
Sandbrook Rd, N16 122 DS62
Sandby Grn, SE9 164 EL83
Sandcliff Rd, Erith DA8 167 FD77
Sandcroft Cl, N13 99 DP51
Sandcross La, Reig. RH2 265 CZ137
Sch Sandcross Prim Sch, Reig. RH2 off Sandcross La 265 CZ137
Reig. RH2 off Alexander Rd 266 DA137
Sandells Av, Ashf. TW15 175 BQ91
Sandell St, SE1 298 E4
Sandels Way, Beac. HP9 89 AK51
Sandelswood End, Beac. HP9 89 AK50
Sandelswood Gdns, Beac. HP9 89 AK51
Sandeman Gdns, Ware SG12 33 DY05
Sanderling Way, Green. DA9 189 FU85
Sanders Cl, Hmptn H. TW12 176 CC92
Hemel Hempstead HP3 40 BM24
London Colney AL2 61 CK27
Sanders Ct, Brwd. CM14 108 FW49
Sch Sanders Draper Sch, The, Horn. RM12 off Suttons La 128 FK63
Sandersfield Gdns, Bans. SM7 234 DA115
Sandersfield Rd, Bans. SM7 234 DB115
Sanders La, NW7 97 CX52
Hounslow TW4 176 BZ85
Sanderson Cl, NW5 275 J1
Sanderson Rd, Uxb. UB8 134 BJ65
Sandersons Av, Bad.Mt TN14 224 FA110
Sandersons La, W4 off Chiswick High Rd 158 CR78
Sanderson Sq, Brom. BR1 205 EN97
Sanders Pl, St.Alb. AL1 43 CG21
Sanders Rd, Hem.H. HP3 40 BM23
SANDERSTEAD, S.Croy. CR2 220 DT111
⇌ Sanderstead 220 DR109
Sanderstead Av, NW2 119 CY61
Sanderstead Cl, SW12 181 DJ87
Sanderstead Ct Av, S.Croy. CR2 220 DU113
Sanderstead Hill, S.Croy. CR2 220 DS111
Sanderstead Rd, E10 123 DY60
Orpington BR5 206 EV100
South Croydon CR2 220 DR108
Sanders Way, N19 off Sussex Way 121 DK60
Sandes Pl, Lthd. KT22 231 CG118
Sandfield Gdns, Th.Hth. CR7 201 DP97
Sandfield Pas, Th.Hth. CR7 202 DQ97
Sch Sandfield Prim Sch, Guil. GU1 off York Rd 258 AX135
Sandfield Rd, St.Alb. AL1 43 CG20
Thornton Heath CR7 201 DP97
Sandfields, Send GU23 227 BD124
Sandfield Ter, Guil. GU1 258 AX135
Sandford Av, N22 100 DQ52
Loughton IG10 85 EQ41
Sandford Cl, E6 293 J4
Sandford Ct, N16 122 DS60
Sandford Rd, E6 293 H2
Bexleyheath DA7 166 EY84
Bromley BR2 204 EG98
Sandford St, SW6 307 M5
Sandgate Cl, Rom. RM7 127 FD59
Sandgate Ho, E5 278 F1
W5 137 CJ71
Sandgate La, SW18 180 DE88
Sandgate Rd, Well. DA16 166 EW80
Sandgates, Cher. KT16 193 BE103
Sandgate St, SE15 312 E2
Sandham Pt, SE18 305 P9
Sandhills, Wall. SM6 219 DK105
Sandhills, The, SW10 off Limerston St 307 P2
Sandhills Ct, Vir.W. GU25 192 AY99
Sandhills La, Vir.W. GU25 192 AY99
Sandhills Meadow, Shep. TW17 195 BQ101
Sandhills Rd, Reig. RH2 266 DA136
Sandhurst Av, Har. HA2 116 CB58
Surbiton KT5 198 CP101
Sandhurst Cl, NW9 118 CN55
South Croydon CR2 220 DS109
Sandhurst Dr, Ilf. IG3 125 ET63
Sch Sandhurst Inf & Jun Schs, SE6 off Minard Rd 184 EE88
Sandhurst Rd, N9 82 DW44
NW9 118 CN55
SE6 183 ED88
Bexley DA5 186 EX85
Orpington BR6 206 EU104
Sidcup DA15 185 ET90
Tilbury RM18 171 GJ82
Sandhurst Way, S.Croy. CR2 220 DS108
Sandifer Dr, NW2 119 CX62
Sandifield, Hat. AL10 45 CU21
Sandiford Rd, Sutt. SM3 199 CZ103
Sandiland Cres, Brom. BR2 204 EF103
Tra Sandilands 202 DT103
Sandilands, Croy. CR0 202 DU103
Sevenoaks TN13 256 FD122
Sandilands Rd, SW6 307 L7
Sandison St, SE15 312 B10
Sandlands Gro, Walt.Hill KT20 233 CU123
Sandlands Rd, Walt.Hill KT20 233 CU123
Sandland St, WC1 286 D7
Sandlers End, Slou. SL2 131 AP70
Sandlewood Cl, Barn. EN5 79 CT43
Sandling Ri, SE9 185 EN90
Sandlings, The, N22 99 DN54
Sandlings Cl, SE15 312 E9
Sandmartin Way, Wall. SM6 200 DG101
Sandmere Cl, Hem.H. HP2 off St. Albans Rd 40 BN21
Sandmere Rd, SW4 161 DL84
Sandon Cl, Esher KT10 197 CD101
Sandon Rd, Chsht EN8 66 DW30
Sandow Cres, Hayes UB3 155 BT76
Sandown Av, Dag. RM10 147 FC65
Esher KT10 214 CC106
Hornchurch RM12 128 FK61
Sandown Cl, Houns. TW5 155 BU81
Sandown Ct, Sutt. SM2 off Grange Rd 218 DB108
Sandown Dr, Cars. SM5 218 DG109
Sandown Gate, Esher KT10 196 CC104
● Sandown Ind Pk, Esher KT10 196 CA103
★ Sandown Park Racecourse, Esher KT10 196 CB104
Sandown Rd, SE25 202 DV99
Coulsdon CR5 234 DG116
Esher KT10 214 CC105
Gravesend DA12 191 GJ93
Slough SL2 131 AM71
Watford WD24 76 BW38
● Sandown Rd Ind Est, Wat. WD24 76 BW37
Sandown Way, Nthlt. UB5 136 BY65
Sandpiper Cl, E17 101 DX53
SE16 301 N4
Greenhithe DA9 189 FU85
Sandpiper Ct, E14 off Stewart St 302 F6
Sandpiper Dr, Erith DA8 167 FH80
Sandpiper Ho, West Dr. UB7 off Wraysbury Dr 134 BK73
Sandpiper Rd, S.Croy. CR2 221 DX111
Sutton SM1 217 CZ106
Sandpipers, The, Grav. DA12 191 GK89
Sandpiper Way, Orp. BR5 206 EX98
Sandpit Hall Rd, Chobham GU24 210 AU112
Sandpit La, Brwd. CM14, CM15 108 FT46
St. Albans AL1, AL4 43 CJ18
Sandpit Pl, SE7 305 H10
Sandpit Rd, Brom. BR1 184 EE92
Dartford DA1 168 FJ84
Redhill RH1 266 DE135
Welwyn Garden City AL7 29 CY11
Sandpits La, Penn HP10 88 AC48
Sandpits Rd, Croy. CR0 221 DX105
Richmond TW10 177 CK89
Sandra Cl, N22 100 DQ53
Hounslow TW3 176 CB85
Sandridgebury La, St.Alb. AL3 43 CE16
Sandridge Cl, Barn. EN4 80 DE37
Harrow HA1 117 CE56
● Sandridge Gate Business Cen, St.Alb. AL4 43 CF16
● Sandridge Pk, Port.Wd AL3 43 CF15
Sandridge Rd, St.Alb. AL1 43 CE18
Sandridge St, N19 121 DJ61
Sandringham Av, SW20 199 CY95
Harlow CM19 50 EL15
Sandringham Cl, SW19 179 CX88
Enfield EN1 82 DS40
Ilford IG6 125 EQ55
Woking GU22 228 BG116
Sandringham Ct, W9 283 P3
Kingston upon Thames KT2 off Skerne Wk 197 CK95
Slough SL1 131 AK72
Sandringham Cres, Har. HA2 116 CA61
St. Albans AL4 43 CJ15
Sandringham Dr, Ashf. TW15 174 BK91
Dartford DA2 187 FE89
Welling DA16 165 ES82
Sandringham Flats, WC2 off Charing Cross Rd 285 P10
Sandringham Gdns, N8 121 DL58
N12 98 DC51
Hounslow TW5 155 BU81
Ilford IG6 125 EQ55
West Molesey KT8 196 CA98
Sandringham Lo, Hodd. EN11 off Taverners Way 49 EA17
Sandringham Ms, W5 off High St 137 CK73
Hampton TW12 196 BZ95
Sandringham Pk, Cob. KT11 214 BZ112
Sch Sandringham Prim Sch, E7 off Sandringham Rd 124 EJ64
Sandringham Rd, E7 124 EJ64
E8 278 A3
E10 123 ED58
N22 122 DQ55
NW2 139 CV65
NW11 119 CY59
Barking IG11 145 ET65
Bromley BR1 184 EG92
London Heathrow Airport TW6 174 BL85
Northolt UB5 136 CA66
Pilgrim's Hatch CM15 108 FV43
Potters Bar EN6 64 DB30
Thornton Heath CR7 202 DQ99
Watford WD24 76 BW37
Worcester Park KT4 199 CU104
Sch Sandringham Sch, St.Alb. AL4 off The Ridgeway 43 CH16
Sandringham Way, Wal.Cr. EN8 67 DX34
Sandrock Pl, Croy. CR0 221 DX105
Sandrock Rd, SE13 314 B10
Westcott RH4 262 CB138
Sandroyd Way, Cob. KT11 214 CA113
SANDS END, SW6 307 N7
Sand's End La, SW6 307 M6
Sands Fm Dr, Burn. SL1 130 AJ70
Sandstone La, E16 292 B10
Sandstone Pl, N19 121 DH61
Sandstone Rd, SE12 184 EH89
Sands Way, Wdf.Grn. IG8 102 EL51
Sandtoft Rd, SE7 164 EH79
Sandway Path, St.M.Cray BR5 off Okemore Gdns 206 EW98
Sandway Rd, Orp. BR5 206 EW98
Sandwell Cres, NW6 273 K4
Sandwich St, WC1 286 A3
Sandwick Cl, NW7 97 CU52
Sandy Bk Rd, Grav. DA12 191 GH88
Sandy Bury, Orp. BR6 205 ER104
Sandy Cl, Hert. SG14 31 DP09
Woking GU22 off Sandy La 227 BC117
Sandycombe Rd, Felt. TW14 175 BU88
Richmond TW9 158 CN83
Sandycoombe Rd, Twick. TW1 177 CJ86
Sandycroft, SE2 166 EU79
Sandy Cft, Epsom KT17 217 CW110
Sandycroft Rd, Amer. HP6 72 AV39
Sandy Dr, Cob. KT11 214 CA111
Feltham TW14 175 BS88
Sandy Gro, Borwd. WD6 78 CM40
Sandy Hill Av, SE18 165 EP78
Sandy Hill Rd, SE18 305 N9
Wallington SM6 219 DJ109
Sandyhill Rd, Ilf. IG1 125 EP63
Sandy La, Alb.Hth GU5 260 BJ141
Aveley RM15 148 FM73
Bean DA2 189 FW89
Betchworth RH3 264 CS135
Bletchingley RH1 251 DP132
Bushey WD23 76 CC41
Chadwell St. Mary RM16 171 GH79
Chobham GU24 210 AS109
Cobham KT11 214 CA112
Guildford GU3 258 AU139
Harrow HA3 118 CM58
Kingston upon Thames KT1 177 CG94
Kingswood KT20 234 DA123
Leatherhead KT22 214 CA112
Limpsfield RH8 254 EH127
Mitcham CR4 200 DG95
Northwood HA6 93 BU50
Orpington BR6 206 EU101
Oxted RH8 253 EC129
Pyrford GU22 227 BF117
Reigate RH2 265 CW135
Richmond TW10 177 CJ89
St. Paul's Cray BR5 206 EX95
Send GU23 227 BC123
Sevenoaks TN13 257 FJ123
Shere GU5 260 BN139
Sidcup DA14 186 EX94
South Nutfield RH1 267 DK135
Sutton SM2 217 CY108
Teddington TW11 177 CG94
Virginia Water GU25 192 AY98
Walton-on-Thames KT12 195 BV100
Watford WD25 76 CC41
West Thurrock RM20 off London Rd W Thurrock 169 FV79
Westerham TN16 255 ER125
Woking GU22 227 BC116
Sandy La Caravan Site, Wat. WD25 off Sandy La 76 CC41
Sandy La Est, Rich. TW10 177 CK89
Sandy La N, Wall. SM6 219 DK107
Sandy La S, Wall. SM6 219 DK107
Sandy Lo, Nthwd. HA6 93 BS47
Sandy Lo La, Nthwd. HA6 93 BR47
Sandy Lo Rd, Rick. WD3 93 BP47
Sandy Lo Way, Nthwd. HA6 93 BS50
Sandy Mead, Epsom KT19 216 CN109
Maidenhead SL6 150 AC78
Sandymount Av, Stan. HA7 95 CJ50
Sandy Ridge, Chis. BR7 185 EN93
Sandy Ri, Chal.St.P. SL9 90 AY53
Sandy Rd, NW3 120 DB62
Addlestone KT15 212 BG107
Sandys Ct, Hounslow TW4 off Bath Rd 156 BY82
Sandy's Row, E1 287 P7
Sandy Way, Cob. KT11 214 CA112
Croydon CR0 203 DZ104
Walton-on-Thames KT12 195 BT102
Woking GU22 227 BC117
Sanfoin End, Hem.H. HP2 40 BN18
Sanford La, N16 off Lawrence Bldgs 122 DT61
Sanford St, SE14 313 L3
Sanford Ter, N16 122 DT62
Sanford Wk, N16 off Sanford Ter 122 DT61
SE14 313 L3
Sangam Cl, Sthl. UB2 156 BY76
Sanger Av, Chess. KT9 216 CL106
Sanger Dr, Send GU23 227 BC123
Sangers Dr, Horl. RH6 268 DF148
Sangers Wk, Horl. RH6 off Sangers Dr 268 DF148
Sangley Rd, SE6 183 EB87
SE25 202 DS98
Sangora Rd, SW11 160 DD84
San Ho, E9 279 K5
San Juan Dr, Chaff.Hun. RM16 169 FW77
San Luis Dr, Chaff.Hun. RM16 169 FW77
San Marcos Dr, Chaff.Hun. RM16 169 FW77
Sansom Rd, E11 124 EE61
Sansom St, SE5 311 M5
Sans Wk, EC1 286 F4
Santers La, Pot.B. EN6 63 CY33
Santiago Way, Chaff.Hun. RM16 169 FX78
Santley St, SW4 161 DM84
Santos Rd, SW18 180 DA85
Santway, The, Stan. HA7 95 CE50
Sanville Gdns, Stans.Abb. SG12 33 EC11
Sanway Cl, Byfleet KT14 212 BL114
Sanway Rd, Byfleet KT14 212 BL114
● Sapcote Trd Cen, NW10 119 CT64
Saperton Wk, SE11 298 D8
Sapho Pk, Grav. DA12 191 GM91
Saphora Cl, Orp. BR6 223 ER106
Sappers Cl, Saw. CM21 36 EZ05
Sapperton Ct, EC1 287 J4
Sapphire Cl, E6 293 K8
Dagenham RM8 126 EW60
Sapphire Ct, NW9 off Ruby Way 97 CT53
Sapphire Rd, NW10 138 CQ66
SE8 301 M9
Sappho Ct, Wok. GU21 off Langmans Way 226 AS116
Saracen Cl, Croy. CR0 202 DR100
● Saracen Ind Area, Hem.H. HP2 41 BP18
Saracens Head, Hem.H. HP2 off Adeyfield Rd 40 BN19
Saracen's Head Yd, EC3 287 P9
★ Saracens RFC, Wat. WD18 75 BV43
Saracen St, E14 290 B9
Sara Ct, Beck. BR3 203 EB95
Sara Cres, Green. DA9 169 FU84
Sch Sarah Bonnell Sch, E15 281 K5
Sarah Ho, SW15 159 CT84
Sara Ho, Erith DA8 off Larner Rd 167 FE80
Sara La Ct, N1 off Stanway St 277 P10
Sara Pk, Grav. DA12 191 GL91
Saratoga Rd, E5 122 DW63
● Sarbir Ind Pk, Harl. CM20 36 EW10

S

Sardinia St, WC2 286 C9
Sarel Way, Horl. RH6 269 DH146
Sargeant Cl, Uxb. UB8 134 BK69
Sarita Cl, Har. HA3 95 CD54
Sarjant Path, SW19
off Queensmere Rd 179 CX89
Sark Cl, Houns. TW5 156 CA80
Sark Ho, N1 off Clifton Rd 277 K5
Enfield EN3 off Eastfield Rd 83 DX38
Sark Twr, SE28 165 EQ75
Sark Wk, E16 292 B8
Sarnesfield Ho, SE15 312 E3
Sarnesfield Rd, Enf. EN2
off Church St 82 DR41
SARRATT, Rick. WD3 74 BG35
Sarratt Bottom, Sarratt WD3 73 BE36
Sch Sarratt C of E Sch,
Sarratt WD3 off The Green 74 BG36
Sarratt La, Rick. WD3 74 BH40
Sarratt Rd, Rick. WD3 74 BM41
Sarre Av, Horn. RM12 148 FJ65
Sarre Rd, NW2 272 G2
Orpington BR5 206 EW99
Sarsby Dr, Stai. TW19 173 BA89
Sarsen Av, Houns. TW3 156 BZ82
Sarsfeld Rd, SW12 180 DF88
Sarsfield Rd, Perivale UB6 137 CH68
Sartor Rd, SE15 163 DX84
● Sarum Complex, Uxb. UB8 134 BH68
Sarum Grn, Wey. KT13 195 BS104
Sch Sarum Hall Sch, NW3 274 C6
Sarum Pl, Hem.H. HP2 40 BL16
Sarum Ter, E3 289 N5
Satanita Cl, E16 292 E8
Satchell Mead, NW9 97 CT53
Satchwell Rd, E2 288 C3
Satinwood Ct, Hem.H. HP3 40 BL22
Satis Ct, Epsom KT17 217 CT111
Sattar Ms, N16
off Clissold Rd 122 DR62
Saturn Ho, E3
off Garrison Rd 280 A9
Saturn Way, Hem.H. HP2 40 BM18
Sauls Grn, E11
off Napier Rd 124 EE62
Saunder Cl, Chsht EN8
off Welsummer Way 67 DX27
Saunders Cl, E14 289 P10
Ilford IG1 125 ER60
Northfleet DA11 190 GE89
Saunders Copse, Wok. GU22 226 AV122
Saunders La, Wok. GU22 226 AS122
Saunders Ness Rd, E14 302 F10
Saunders Rd, SE18 165 ET78
Uxbridge UB10 134 BM66
Saunders St, SE11 298 E9
Saunders Way, SE28
off Oriole Way 146 EV73
Dartford DA1 188 FM89
Saunderton Rd, Wem. HA0 117 CH64
Saunton Av, Hayes UB3 155 BT80
Saunton Rd, Horn. RM12 127 FG61
Savage Gdns, E6 293 K9
EC3 287 P10
Savannah Cl, SE15 312 A5
Savay Cl, Denh. UB9 114 BG59
Savay La, Denh. UB9 114 BG58
Savera Cl, Sthl. UB2 156 BW76
Savernake Rd, N9 82 DU44
NW3 274 F1
Savery Dr, Long Dit. KT6 197 CJ101
Savile Cl, N.Mal. KT3 198 CS99
Thames Ditton KT7 197 CF102
Savile Gdns, Croy. CR0 202 DT103
Savile Row, W1 285 L10
Savill Cl, Chsht EN7
off Markham Rd 66 DQ25
Saville Cl, Epsom KT19 216 CP111
Saville Cres, Ashf. TW15 175 BR93
Saville Ho, E16
off Robert St 305 N3
Saville Rd, E16 305 H3
W4 158 CR76
Romford RM6 126 EZ58
Twickenham TW1 177 CF88
Saville Row, Brom. BR2 204 EF102
Enfield EN3 83 DX40
Savill Gdns, SW20
off Bodnant Gdns 199 CU97
Savill Ms, Eng.Grn TW20 172 AX93
Savill Row, Wdf.Grn. IG8 102 EF51
Savona Cl, SW19 179 CY94
Savona Est, SW8 309 L5
Savona St, SW8 309 L5
Savoy Av, Hayes UB3 155 BS78
Savoy Bldgs, WC2 298 C1
Jct Savoy Circ, W3 139 CT73
Savoy Cl, E15 281 J8
Edgware HA8 96 CN50
Harefield UB9 92 BK54
Savoy Ct, Har. HA2
off Station Rd 116 CB57
WC2 298 B1
Savoy Hill, WC2 298 C1
Savoy Ms, SW9 310 A9
St. Albans AL1 42 CB23
Savoy Pl, W12 off Bourbon La 294 C3
WC2 298 B1
Savoy Rd, Dart. DA1 188 FK85
Savoy Row, WC2 286 C10
Savoy Steps, WC2
off Savoy Row 298 C1
Savoy St, WC2 286 C10
Savoy Way, WC2 298 C1
Savoy Wd, Harl. CM19 51 EN20
Sawbill Cl, Hayes UB4 136 BX71
SAWBRIDGEWORTH, CM21 36 EW05
Sawells, Brox. EN10 49 DZ21
Sawkins Cl, SW19 179 CY89
Sawley Rd, W12 139 CU74
Saw Mill Way, N16 122 DU58
Sawmill Yd, E3 279 M9
Sawpit La, E.Clan. GU4 244 BL131
Sawtry Cl, Cars. SM5 200 DD101
Sawtry Way, Borwd. WD6 78 CN38
Sawyer Cl, N9 100 DU47
Sawyers Chase, Abridge RM4 86 EV41
Sawyers Cl, Dag. RM10 147 FC65
Windsor SL4 151 AL80
Sawyers Ct, Wal.Cr. EN8
off Sturlas Way 67 DY33
Sawyers Gro, Brwd. CM15 108 FX46
Sch Sawyers Hall Coll of Science &
Tech, The, Brwd. CM15
off Sawyers Hall La 108 FW45
Sawyers Hall La, Brwd. CM15 108 FW45
Sawyer's Hill, Rich. TW10 178 CP87
Sawyers La, Els. WD6 77 CH40
Potters Bar EN6 63 CX34
Sawyers Lawn, W13 137 CF72
Sawyer St, SE1 299 J4
Sawyers Way, Hem.H. HP2 40 BM20
Saxby Rd, SW2 181 DL87
Saxham Rd, Bark. IG11 145 ES68
Saxley, Horl. RH6
off Ewelands 269 DJ147
Saxlingham Rd, E4 101 ED48
Saxon Av, Felt. TW13 176 BZ89
Saxonbury Av, Sun. TW16 195 BV97
Saxonbury Cl, Mitch. CR4 200 DD97
Saxonbury Gdns,
Long Dit. KT6 197 CJ102
Saxon Cl, E17 123 EA59
Amersham HP6 55 AR38
Brentwood CM13 109 GA48
Northfleet DA11 190 GC90
Otford TN14 241 FF117
Romford RM3 106 FM54
Slough SL3 153 AZ75
Surbiton KT6 197 CK100
Uxbridge UB8 134 BM71
Saxon Ct, Borwd. WD6 78 CL40
Whyteleafe CR3
off Godstone Rd 236 DU119
Saxon Dr, W3 138 CP72
Saxonfield Cl, SW2 181 DM87
Saxon Gdns, Sthl. UB1 136 BY73
Taplow SL6 130 AD70
Saxon Pl, Hort.Kir. DA4 208 FQ99
Sch Saxon Prim Sch,
Shep. TW17 off Briar Rd 194 BN99
Saxon Rd, E3 289 N1
E6 293 J5
N22 99 DP53
SE25 202 DR99
Ashford TW15 175 BR93
Bromley BR1 184 EF94
Hawley DA2 188 FL91
Ilford IG1 145 EP65
Kingston upon Thames KT2 198 CL95
Southall UB1 136 BY74
Walton-on-Thames KT12 196 BX104
Wembley HA9 118 CQ62
Saxons, Tad. KT20 233 CX121
Saxon Shore Way, Grav. DA12 191 GM86
Saxon Ter, SE6
off Neuchatel Rd 183 DZ89
Saxon Wk, Sid. DA14 186 EW93
Saxon Way, N14 81 DK44
Harmondsworth UB7 154 BJ79
Old Windsor SL4 172 AV86
Reigate RH2 249 CZ133
Waltham Abbey EN9 67 EC33
Saxony Par, Hayes UB3 135 BQ71
Saxton Cl, SE13 163 ED83
Saxton Ms, Wat. WD17 75 BU40
Saxville Rd, Orp. BR5 206 EV97
Sayer Cl, Green. DA9 189 FU85
Sayers Cl, Fetch. KT22 230 CC124
Sayers Gdns, Berk. HP4 38 AU16
Sayers Wk, Rich. TW10
off Stafford Pl 178 CM87
Sayesbury La, N18 100 DU50
Sayesbury Rd, Saw. CM21 36 EX05
Sayes Ct, SE8 313 P2
Addlestone KT15 212 BJ106
Sayes Ct Fm Dr, Add. KT15 212 BH106
Sch Sayes Ct Jun Sch, Add.
KT15 off Sayes Ct Fm Dr 212 BH106
Sayes Ct Rd, Orp. BR5 206 EU98
Sayes Ct St, SE8 313 P2
Sayes Gdns, Saw. CM21 36 EZ05
Sayward Cl, Chesh. HP5 54 AR29
Scadbury Gdns, Orp. BR5 206 EU96
Scadbury Pk, Chis. BR7 185 ET93
Scads Hill Cl, Orp. BR6 205 ET100
Scafell Rd, Slou. SL2 131 AM71
Scala St, W1 285 M6
Scales Rd, N17 122 DT55
Scammell Way, Wat. WD18 75 BT44
Scampston Ms, W10 282 D8
Scandrett St, E1 300 E3
Scarab Cl, E16 303 L1
Scarba Wk, N1 277 L5
Scarborough Cl, Bigg.H. TN16 238 EJ118
Sutton SM2 217 CZ111
Scarborough Dr, Crox.Grn WD3 75 BP42
Scarborough Rd, E11 123 ED60
N4 121 DN59
N9 100 DW45
London Heathrow Airport
TW6 off Southern Perimeter Rd 175 BQ86
Scarborough St, E1 288 B9
Scarborough Way, Slou. SL1 151 AP75
Scarbrook Rd, Croy. CR0 202 DQ104
Sch Scargill Inf & Jun Schs,
Rain. RM13 off Mungo Pk Rd 147 FG65
Scarle Rd, Wem. HA0 137 CK65
Scarlet Cl, E20 280 D3
St. Paul's Cray BR5 206 EV98
Scarlet Rd, SE6 184 EE90
Scarlett Cl, Wok. GU21 226 AT118
Scarlette Manor Way, SW2
off Papworth Way 181 DN87
Scarsbrook Rd, SE3 164 EK83
Scarsdale Pl, W8 295 L6
Scarsdale Rd, Har. HA2 116 CC62
Scarsdale Vil, W8 295 K7
Scarth Rd, SW13 159 CT83
Scatterdells La, Chipper. WD4 57 BF30
Scawen Cl, Cars. SM5 218 DG105
Scawen Rd, SE8 313 L1
Scawfell St, E2 288 B1
Scaynes Link, N12 98 DA50
Sceaux Gdns, SE5 311 P6
Sceptre Rd, E2 289 H3
Uni Schiller Int Uni, SE1 298 E3
Schofield Wk, SE3
off Dornberg Cl 164 EH80
Scholars Cl, Barn. EN5 79 CY42
Scholars Ms, Welw.G.C. AL8 29 CX07
Scholars Pl, N16 122 DS62
Walton-on-Thames KT12 196 BW102
Scholars Rd, E4 101 EC46
SW12 181 DJ88
Scholars Wk, Chal.St.P. SL9 90 AY51
Guildford GU2 258 AV135
Hatfield AL10 45 CU21
Langley SL3 153 BA75
Scholars Way, Amer. HP6 72 AT38
Dagenham RM9 126 EU63
Romford RM2 127 FG57
Scholefield Rd, N19 121 DK60
Schomberg Ho, SW1
off Page St 297 P8
Schonfeld Sq, N16 122 DR61
Schoolbank Rd, SE10 303 L8
Schoolbell Ms, E3 289 M1
School Cl, Chesh. HP5 54 AP28
Essendon AL9 off School La 46 DF17
Guildford GU1 242 AX132
School Cres, Cray. DA1 167 FF84
Schoolfield Rd, Grays RM20 169 FU79
School Gdns, Pott.End HP4 39 BB17
Schoolgate Dr, Mord. SM4 200 DB99
School Grn La,
N.Wld Bas. CM16 71 FC25
School Hill, Merst. RH1 251 DJ128
Schoolhouse Gdns, Loug. IG10 85 EP42
Schoolhouse La, E1 289 J10
School Ho La, Tedd. TW11 177 CH94
Schoolhouse Yd, SE18
off Bloomfield Rd 165 EP78
School La, Add. KT15 212 BG105
Amersham Old Town HP7 55 AM39
Bean DA2 189 FW90
Bricket Wood AL2 60 CA31
Bushey WD23 94 CB45
Caterham CR3 252 DT126
Chalfont St. Giles HP8 90 AV47
Chalfont St. Peter SL9 90 AX54
Chigwell IG7 103 ET49
East Clandon GU4 244 BL131
Egham TW20 173 BA92
Essendon AL9 46 DE17
Fetcham KT22 231 CD122
Harlow CM20 35 ES12
Hatfield AL10 45 CV17
Horton Kirby DA4 208 FQ98
Kingston upon Thames KT1
off School Rd 197 CJ95
Longfield DA3 209 FT100
Magdalen Laver CM5 53 FD17
Mickleham RH5 247 CJ127
Ockham GU23 229 BP122
Pinner HA5 116 BY56
Seal TN15 257 FM121
Seer Green HP9 89 AR51
Shepperton TW17 195 BP100
Slough SL2 132 AT73
Stoke Poges SL2 132 AV67
Surbiton KT6 198 CN102
Swanley BR8 207 FH95
Tewin AL6 30 DE06
Walton on the Hill KT20
off Chequers La 249 CU125
Welling DA16 166 EV83
West Horsley KT24 245 BP129
Westcott RH4 263 CD137
School Mead, Abb.L. WD5 59 BS32
School Meadow, Guil. GU2 242 AS132
Coll School of Economic
Science, W1 285 H8
Coll School of Horticulture,
Rich. TW9 off Kew Grn 158 CM80
Uni School of Oriental & African Studies,
Russell Sq Campus, WC1 285 P5
Vernon Sq Campus, WC1 286 D2
Uni School of Pharmacy, WC1 286 B4
Sch School of the Islamic
Republic of Iran, The, NW6 283 J1
School Pas, Kings.T. KT1 198 CM96
Southall UB1 136 BZ74
School Rd, E12 off Sixth Av 125 EM63
NW10 138 CR70
Ashford TW15 175 BP93
Chislehurst BR7 205 EQ95
Dagenham RM10 146 FA67
East Molesey KT8 197 CD98
Hampton Hill TW12 176 CC93
Harmondsworth UB7 154 BK79
Hounslow TW3 156 CC83
Kingston upon Thames KT1 197 CJ95
Ongar CM5 71 FG32
Penn HP10 88 AC47
Potters Bar EN6 64 DC30
Wooburn Green HP10 110 AE57
School Rd Av, Hmptn H. TW12 176 CC93
School Row, Hem.H. HP1 39 BF21
School Sq, SE10
off Greenroof Way 303 M7
School Wk, Horl. RH6
off Thornton Cl 268 DE148
Slough SL2 off Grasmere Av 132 AV73
Sunbury-on-Thames TW16 195 BT98
School Way, N12 98 DC49
Dagenham RM8 126 EW62
Schoolway,
N12 (Woodhouse Rd) 98 DD51
Schooner Cl, E14 302 G7
SE16 301 J4
Barking IG11 146 EV69
Schooner Ct, Dart. DA2 168 FQ84
Schrier, Bark. IG11
off Ripple Rd 145 EQ66
Schroder Ct, Eng.Grn TW20 172 AV92
Schubert Rd, SW15 179 CZ85
Elstree WD6 77 CK44
Schurlock Pl, Twick. TW2 177 CD89
★ Science Mus, SW7 296 B7
Scilla Ct, Grays RM17 170 GD79
Scillonian Rd, Guil. GU2 258 AU135
Jct Scilly Isles, Esher KT10 197 CE103
● Scimitar Pk, Harl. CM19 34 EL14
Sclater St, E1 288 A4
Scoble Pl, N16 278 B1
Scoles Cres, SW2 181 DN88
★ Scoop at More London, SE1
off Tooley St 299 P3
Scope Way, Kings.T. KT1 198 CL98
Scoresby St, SE1 298 G3
Scorton Av, Perivale UB6 137 CG68
Scotch Common, W13 137 CG71
Scoter Cl, Wdf.Grn. IG8 102 EH52
Scot Gro, Pnr. HA5 94 BX52
Scotia Rd, SW2 181 DN87
Scotland Br Rd,
New Haw KT15 212 BG111
Scotland Grn, N17 100 DT54
Scotland Grn Rd, Enf. EN3 83 DX43
Scotland Grn Rd N, Enf. EN3 83 DX42
Scotland Pl, SW1 298 A2
Scotland Rd, Buck.H. IG9 102 EJ46
Scotlands Dr, Farn.Com. SL2 131 AP65
Scotney Cl, Orp. BR6 223 EN105
Scotney Cl, Crox.Grn WD3 75 BP42
Orpington BR6 223 EN105
Scotney Wk, Horn. RM12
off Bonington Rd 128 FK64
Scotscraig, Rad. WD7 77 CF35
Scotsdale Cl, Petts Wd BR5 205 ES98
Sutton SM3 217 CY108
Scotsdale Rd, SE12 184 EH85
Scotshall La, Warl. CR6 221 EC114
Scots Hill, Crox.Grn WD3 74 BM44
Scots Hill Cl, Crox.Grn WD3 74 BM44
Scotsmill La, Crox.Grn WD3 74 BM44
Scotswood Cl, Beac. HP9 89 AK50
Scotswood St, EC1 286 F4
Scotswood Wk, N17 100 DU52
Scott Av, SW15 179 CY86
Stanstead Abbotts SG12 33 EB11
Scott Cl, SW16 201 DM95
Epsom KT19 216 CQ106
Farnham Common SL2 111 AQ64
Guildford GU2 242 AU132
Saint Albans AL3 42 CA22
West Drayton UB7 154 BM77
Scott Ct, SW8
off Silverthorne Rd 309 K9
W3 off Petersfield Rd 158 CR75
Scott Cres, Erith DA8
off Cloudesley Rd 167 FF81
Harrow HA2 116 CB60
Scott Ellis Gdns, NW8 284 A3
Scottes La, Dag. RM8
off Valence Av 126 EX60
Scott Fm Cl, T.Ditt. KT7 197 CH102
Scott Gdns, Houns. TW5 156 BX80
Scott Ho, E13 281 P10
N18 100 DU50
Scott Lidgett Cres, SE16 300 C5
Scott Rd, Edg. HA8 96 CP54
Gravesend DA12 191 GK92
Grays RM16 171 GG77
Scott Russell Pl, E14 302 C10
Scotts Av, Brom. BR2 203 ED96
Sunbury-on-Thames TW16 175 BS94
Scotts Cl, Horn. RM12 off Rye Cl 128 FJ64
Staines-upon-Thames TW19 174 BK88
Ware SG12 33 DX07
Scotts Dr, Hmptn. TW12 176 CB94
Scotts Fm Rd, Epsom KT19 216 CQ107
Scotts La, Brom. BR2 203 ED97
Walton-on-Thames KT12 214 BX105
Sch Scotts Pk Prim Sch,
Brom. BR1 off Orchard Rd 204 EJ95
Scotts Pas, SE18 off Spray St 305 P8
Sch Scotts Prim Sch, Horn.
RM12 off Bonington Rd 128 FJ64
Scotts Rd, E10 123 EC60
W12 159 CV75
Bromley BR1 184 EG94
Southall UB2 156 BW76
Ware SG12 33 DX07
Scott St, E1 288 E5
Scotts Vw, Welw.G.C. AL8 29 CW10
Scotts Way, Sev. TN13 256 FE122
Sunbury-on-Thames TW16 175 BS93
Scottswood Cl, Bushey WD23
off Scottswood Rd 76 BY40
Scottswood Rd, Bushey WD23 76 BY40
Scott Trimmer Way,
Houns. TW3 156 BY82
Scottwell Dr, NW9 119 CT57
Sch Scott Wilkie Prim Sch, E16 292 E8
Scoulding Rd, E16 291 M8
Scouler St, E14 302 G1
Scout App, NW10 118 CS63
Scout La, SW4
off Old Town 161 DJ83
Scout Way, NW7 96 CR49
Scovell Cres, SE1 299 J5
Scovell Rd, SE1 299 J5
Scratchers La, Fawk.Grn DA3 209 FR103
Scrattons Ter, Bark. IG11 146 EX67
Scriveners Cl, Hem.H. HP2 40 BL20
Scriven St, E8 278 B8
Scrooby St, SE6 183 EB86
Scrubbitts Pk Rd, Rad. WD7 77 CG35
Scrubbitts Sq, Rad. WD7 77 CG35
Scrubs La, NW10 139 CU69
W10 139 CU69
Scrutton Cl, SW12 181 DK87
Scrutton St, EC2 287 N5
Scudamore La, NW9 118 CQ55
Scudders Hill, Fawk.Grn DA3 209 FV100
Scutari Rd, SE22 182 DW85
Scylla Cres,
Lon.Hthrw Air. TW6 175 BP87
Scylla Pl, St.John's GU21
off Church Rd 226 AU119
Scylla Rd, SE15 312 D10
London Heathrow Airport
TW6 175 BP86
Seaborough Rd, Grays RM16 171 GJ76
Seabright St, E2 288 E3
Seabrook Ct, Pot.B. EN6 64 DA32
Seabrook Dr, W.Wick. BR4 204 EE103
Seabrooke Ri, Grays RM17 170 GB79
Seabrook Gdns, Rom. RM7 126 FA59
Seabrook Rd, Dag. RM8 126 EX62
Kings Langley WD4 59 BR27
Seaburn Cl, Rain. RM13 147 FE68
Seacole Cl, W3 138 CR71
Seacon Twr, E14 301 P5
Seacourt Rd, SE2 166 EX75
Slough SL3 153 BB77
Seacroft Gdns, Wat. WD19 94 BX48
Seafield Rd, N11 99 DK49
Seaford Cl, Ruis. HA4 115 BR61
Seaford Rd, E17 123 EB55
N15 122 DR57
W13 137 CH74
Enfield EN1 82 DS42
London Heathrow Airport
TW6 174 BK85
Seaford St, WC1 286 B3
Seaforth Av, N.Mal. KT3 199 CV99
Seaforth Cl, Rom. RM1 105 FE52
Seaforth Cres, N5 277 J2
Seaforth Dr, Wal.Cr. EN8 67 DX34
Seaforth Gdns, N21 99 DM45
Epsom KT19 217 CT105
Woodford Green IG8 102 EJ50
Seaforth Pl, SW1
off Buckingham Gate 297 M6
Seager Pl, SE8 314 B6
Seagrave Cl, E1 289 J7
Seagrave Rd, SW6 307 K2
Beaconsfield HP9 88 AJ51
Seagry Rd, E11 124 EG58
Seagull Cl, Bark. IG11 146 EU69
Seagull La, E16 291 P10
SEAL, Sev. TN15 257 FN121
Sealand Rd,
Lon.Hthrw Air. TW6 174 BN86
Sealand Wk, Nthlt. UB5
off Wayfarer Rd 136 BY69
Seal Dr, Seal TN15 257 FM121
Seale Hill, Reig. RH2 266 DA136
Seal Hollow Rd, Sev. TN13, TN15 257 FJ124
★ Sea Life London
Aquarium, SE1 298 C4
Sealy Rd, Grays RM17 170 GA78
Seal Rd, Sev. TN14, TN15 257 FJ121
Seal St, E8 278 B1
Sealy Way, Hem.H. HP3 40 BK24
Seaman Cl, Park St AL2 61 CD25
Searches La, Bedmond WD5 59 BV28
Searchwood Rd, Warl. CR6 236 DV118
Searle Pl, N4 121 DM60
Searles Cl, SW11 308 D5
Searles Dr, E6 293 N7
Searles Rd, SE1 299 M8
Sears St, SE5 311 L4
Seasalter Ct, Beck. BR3
off Kingsworth Cl 203 DY99
Seasons Cl, W7 137 CE74
Seasprite Cl, Nthlt. UB5 136 BX69
Seaton Av, Ilf. IG3 125 ES64
Seaton Cl, E13 291 P5
SE11 298 F10
SW15 179 CV88
Twickenham TW2 177 CD86
Seaton Dr, Ashf. TW15 174 BL89
Seaton Gdns, Ruis. HA4 115 BU62
Sch Seaton Ho Sch, Sutt. SM2
off Banstead Rd S 218 DD110
Seaton Pt, E5 122 DU63
Seaton Rd, Dart. DA1 187 FG87
Hayes UB3 155 BR77
Hemel Hempstead HP3 40 BK23
London Colney AL2 61 CK26
Mitcham CR4 200 DE96
Twickenham TW2 176 CC86
Welling DA16 166 EW80
Wembley HA0 138 CL68
Seaton Sq, NW7
off Tavistock Av 97 CX52
Seaton St, N18 100 DU50
Seawall Ct, Bark. IG11
off Dock Rd 145 EQ68
Sebastian Av, Shenf. CM15 109 GA44
Sebastian Ct, Bark. IG11
off Meadow Rd 145 ET66
Sebastian St, EC1 287 H3
Sebastopol Rd, N9 100 DU49
Sebbon St, N1 277 H7
Sebergham Gro, NW7 97 CU52
Sebert Rd, E7 124 EH64
Sebright Pas, E2 288 D1
Sch Sebright Prim Sch, E2 278 C10
Sebright Rd, Barn. EN5 79 CX40
Hemel Hempstead HP1 40 BG21
Secker Cres, Har. HA3 94 CC53
Secker St, SE1 298 E3
Second Av, E12 124 EL63
E13 291 N2
E17 123 EA57
N18 100 DW49
NW4 119 CX56
SW14 158 CS83
W3 139 CT74
W10 282 F4
Dagenham RM10 147 FB67
Enfield EN1 82 DT43
Grays RM20 169 FU79
Harlow CM18 51 ES15
Hayes UB3 135 BT74
Romford RM6 126 EW57
Waltham Abbey EN9 off Breach
Barn Mobile Home Pk 68 EH30
Walton-on-Thames KT12 195 BV100
Watford WD25 76 BX35
Wembley HA9 117 CK61
Second Cl, W.Mol. KT8 196 CC98
Second Cres, Slou. SL1 131 AQ71
Second Cross Rd, Twick. TW2 177 CE89
Second Way, Wem. HA9 118 CP63
Sedan Way, SE17 299 N10
Sedcombe Cl, Sid. DA14 186 EV91
Sedcote Rd, Enf. EN3 82 DW43
Sedding St, SW1 296 G8
Seddon Highwalk, EC2
off The Barbican 287 J6
Seddon Ho, EC2
off The Barbican 287 J6
Seddon Rd, Mord. SM4 200 DD99
Seddon St, WC1 286 D3
Sedgebrook Rd, SE3 164 EK82
Sedgecombe Av, Har. HA3 117 CJ57
Sedge Ct, Grays RM17 170 GE80
Sedgefield Cl, Rom. RM3 106 FM49
Sedgefield Cres, Rom. RM3 106 FM49
Sedgeford Rd, W12 139 CT74
Sedge Gdns, Bark. IG11 146 EU69
Sedge Grn, Lwr Naze. EN9 50 EE20
Roydon CM19 50 EE20
Sedgehill Rd, SE6 183 EA91
Sch Sedgehill Sch, SE6
off Sedgehill Rd 183 EB92
Sedgemere Av, N2 120 DC55
Sedgemere Rd, SE2 166 EW76
Sedgemoor Dr, Dag. RM10 126 FA63
Sedge Rd, N17 100 DW52
Sedgeway, SE6 184 EF88
Sedgewood Cl, Brom. BR2 204 EF101
Sedgmoor Pl, SE5 311 P5
Sedgwick Av, Uxb. UB10 135 BP66
Sedgwick Rd, E10 123 EC61
Sedgwick St, E9 279 J3
Sedleigh Rd, SW18 179 CZ86
Sedlescombe Rd, SW6 307 H3
Sedley, Sthflt DA13 190 GA93
Sedley Cl, Enf. EN1 82 DV38
Sedley Gro, Hare. UB9 114 BJ56
Sedley Pl, W1 285 J9
Sedley Ri, Loug. IG10 85 EM40
Sch Sedley's C of E Prim Sch,
Sthflt DA13 off Church St 190 GA92
Sedum Cl, NW9 118 CP57
Seeley Dr, SE21 182 DS91
Seeleys, Harl. CM17 36 EW12
Seeleys Cl, Beac. HP9 88 AJ51
Seeleys La, Beac. HP9
off Seeleys Wk 89 AK52
Seeleys Rd, Beac. HP9 88 AJ50
Seeleys Wk, Beac. HP9 88 AJ52
Seelig Av, NW9 119 CU59
Seely Rd, SW17 180 DG93
SEER GREEN, Beac. HP9 89 AR52
⇌ Seer Green & Jordans 89 AR52
Sch Seer Grn C of E Comb Sch,
Seer Grn HP9 off School La 89 AQ51
Seer Grn La, Jordans HP9 90 AS52
Seer Mead, Seer Grn HP9 89 AR52
Seething La, EC3 299 P1
Seething Wells La, Surb. KT6 197 CJ100
Sefton Av, NW7 96 CR50
Harrow HA3 95 CD53

S

Sefton Cl, Petts Wd BR5 205 ET98
St. Albans AL1
off Blenheim Rd 43 CF19
Stoke Poges SL2 132 AT66
Sefton Ct, Welw.G.C. AL8 29 CV11
Sefton Paddock, Stoke P. SL2 132 AU66
● Sefton Pk, Stoke P. SL2 132 AU66
Sefton Rd, Croy. CR0 202 DU102
Epsom KT19 216 CR110
Petts Wood BR5 205 ET98
Sefton St, SW15 306 B9
Sefton Way, Uxb. UB8 134 BJ72
Segal Cl, SE23 183 DY87
Segrave Cl, Wey. KT13 212 BN108
Sekforde St, EC1 286 G5
Sekhon Ter, Felt. TW13 176 CA90
Selah Dr, Swan. BR8 207 FC95
Selan Gdns, Hayes UB4 135 BV71
Selbie Av, NW10 119 CT64
Selborne Av, E12
off Walton Rd 125 EN63
Bexley DA5 186 EY88
Selborne Gdns, NW4 119 CU56
Perivale UB6 137 CG67
Sch Selborne Prim Sch, Perivale
UB6 off Conway Cres 137 CF68
Selborne Rd, E17 123 DZ57
N14 99 DL48
N22 99 DM53
SE5 311 L8
Croydon CR0 202 DS104
Ilford IG1 125 EN61
New Malden KT3 198 CS96
Sidcup DA14 186 EV91
Selborne Wk, E17
off The Mall Walthamstow 123 DZ56
Selbourne Av, E17 123 DZ56
New Haw KT15 212 BH110
Surbiton KT6 198 CM103
Selbourne Cl, New Haw KT15 212 BH109
Selbourne Rd, Guil. GU4 243 BA131
Selbourne Sq, Gdse. RH9 252 DW130
Selby Av, St.Alb. AL3 43 CD20
Selby Chase, Ruis. HA4 115 BV61
Selby Cl, E6 292 G7
Chessington KT9 216 CL108
Chislehurst BR7 185 EN93
Selby Gdns, Sthl. UB1 136 CA70
Selby Grn, Cars. SM5 200 DE101
Selby Rd, E11 124 EE62
E13 292 B6
N17 100 DS51
SE20 202 DU96
W5 137 CH70
Ashford TW15 175 BQ93
Carshalton SM5 200 DE101
Selby Sq, W10 282 F2
Selby St, E1 288 D5
Selby Wk, Wok. GU21
off Wyndham Rd 226 AV118
Selcroft Rd, Pur. CR8 219 DP112
Selden Hill, Hem.H. HP2 40 BK21
Selden Rd, SE15 313 H9
Selden Wk, N7
off Durham Rd 121 DM61
Seldon Ho, SW8 309 L5
Sele Mill, Hert. SG14 31 DP09
Sele Rd, Hert. SG14 31 DP09
Sch Sele Sch, The, Hert. SG14
off Welwyn Rd 31 DM09
★ Selfridges, W1 284 G9
SELHURST, SE25 202 DS100
⇌ Selhurst 202 DS99
Selhurst Cl, SW19 179 CX88
Woking GU21 227 AZ115
Selhurst New Rd, SE25 202 DS100
Selhurst Pl, SE25 202 DS100
Selhurst Rd, N9 100 DR48
SE25 202 DS99
Selinas La, Dag. RM8 126 EY59
Selkirk Dr, Erith DA8 167 FE81
Selkirk Rd, SW17 180 DE91
Twickenham TW2 176 CC89
Sell Cl, Chsht EN7
off Gladding Rd 66 DQ26
Sellers Cl, Borwd. WD6 78 CQ39
Sellers Hall Cl, N3 98 DA52
Sch Sellincourt Prim Sch, SW17
off Sellincourt Rd 180 DE93
Sellincourt Rd, SW17 180 DE92
Sellindge Cl, Beck. BR3 183 DZ94
Sellons Av, NW10 139 CT67
Sells Cl, Guil. GU1 259 AZ136
Sells Rd, Ware SG12 33 DZ05
Sellwood Dr, Barn. EN5 79 CX43
Sellwood St, SW2
off Brockwell Pk Row 181 DN87
SELSDON, S.Croy. CR2 220 DW110
Selsdon Av, S.Croy. CR2 220 DR107
Selsdon Cl, Rom. RM5 105 FC53
Surbiton KT6 198 CL99
Selsdon Cres, S.Croy. CR2 220 DW109
Selsdon Pk Rd, S.Croy. CR2 221 DX109
Sch Selsdon Prim Sch,
S.Croy. CR2 off Addington Rd 220 DW109
Selsdon Rd, E11 124 EG59
E13 144 EJ67
NW2 119 CT61
SE27 181 DP90
New Haw KT15 212 BG111
South Croydon CR2 220 DR106
● Selsdon Rd Ind Est,
S.Croy. CR2
off Selsdon Rd 220 DR108
Selsdon Way, E14 302 D7
Selsea Pl, N16 277 P2
Selsey Cres, Well. DA16 166 EX81
Selsey St, E14 290 A7
Selvage La, NW7 96 CR50
Selway Cl, Pnr. HA5 115 BV56
Selway Ho, SW8
off South Lambeth Rd 310 B6
Selwood Cl, Stanw. TW19 174 BJ86
Selwood Gdns, Stanw. TW19 174 BJ86
Selwood Pl, SW7 296 A10
Selwood Rd, Brwd. CM14 108 FT48
Chessington KT9 215 CK105
Croydon CR0 202 DV103
Sutton SM3 199 CZ102
Woking GU22 227 BB120
Selwood Ter, SW7 296 A10
Selworthy Cl, E11 124 EG57
Selworthy Ho, SW11 308 B6
Selworthy Rd, SE6 183 DZ90
Selwyn Av, E4 101 EC51
Hatfield AL10 44 CR19
Ilford IG3 125 ES58
Richmond TW9 158 CL83
Selwyn Cl, Houns. TW4 156 BY84
Windsor SL4 151 AL82
Selwyn Ct, SE3 315 L10
Edgware HA8 96 CP52
Selwyn Cres, Hat. AL10 44 CS18
Welling DA16 166 EV84
Selwyn Dr, Hat. AL10 44 CR18
Selwyn Pl, Orp. BR5 206 EV97
Sch Selwyn Prim Sch, E4
off Selwyn Av 101 EC51
E13 281 P8
Selwyn Rd, E3 289 N1
E13 144 EH67
NW10 138 CR66
New Malden KT3 198 CR99
Tilbury RM18 off Dock Rd 171 GF82
Semaphore Rd, Guil. GU1 258 AY136
Semley Gate, E9
off Osborne Rd 279 P4
Semley Pl, SW1 297 H9
SW16 off Semley Rd 201 DM96
Semley Rd, SW16 201 DL96
Semper Cl, Knap. GU21 226 AS117
Semper Rd, Grays RM16 171 GJ75
Sempill Rd, Hem.H. HP3 40 BL23
Senate St, SE15 313 H9
Senator Wk, SE28
off Garrick Dr 165 ER76
SEND, Wok. GU23 227 BC124
Sendall Ct, SW11 160 DD83
Send Barns La, Send GU23 227 BD124
Send Cl, Send GU23 227 BC123
Sch Send C of E First Sch, Send
GU23 off Send Barns La 227 BE124
SENDGROVE, Wok. GU23 243 BC126
Send Hill, Send GU23 243 BC125
SEND MARSH, Wok. GU23 227 BF124
Send Marsh Grn, Send M.
GU23 off Send Marsh Rd 227 BF123
Send Marsh Rd, Wok. GU23 227 BF123
Send Par Cl, Send GU23
off Send Rd 227 BC123
Send Rd, Send GU23 227 BB122
Seneca Rd, Th.Hth. CR7 202 DQ98
Senga Rd, Wall. SM6 200 DG102
Senhouse Rd, Sutt. SM3 199 CX104
Senior St, W2 283 L6
Senlac Rd, SE12 184 EH88
Sennen Rd, Enf. EN1 100 DT45
Sennen Wk, SE9 184 EL90
Senrab St, E1 289 J8
Sentamu Cl, SE24 181 DP88
Sentinel Cl, Nthlt. UB5 136 BY70
Sentinel Pt, SW8
off St. George Wf 310 A2
Sentinel Sq, NW4 119 CW56
Sentis Ct, Nthwd. HA6
off Carew Rd 93 BT51
September Way, Stan. HA7 95 CH51
Sequoia Cl, Bushey Hth WD23
off Giant Tree Hill 95 CD46
Sequoia Gdns, Orp. BR6 205 ET101
Sequoia Pk, Pnr. HA5 94 CB51
Serbin Cl, E10 123 EC59
Serenaders Rd, SW9 310 F9
Serenity Cl, Har. HA2 116 CB61
Seren Park Gdns, SE3 315 K2
Sergeants Grn La, Wal.Abb. EN9 68 EJ33
Sergeants Pl, Cat. CR3 236 DQ122
Sergehill La, Bedmond WD5 59 BT27
Serjeants Inn, EC4 286 F9
Serle St, WC2 286 D8
Sermed Ct, Slou. SL2 132 AW74
Sermon Dr, Swan. BR8 207 FC97
Sermon La, EC4 287 J9
★ Serpentine, The, W2 296 C3
Serpentine Ct, Sev. TN13 257 FK122
★ Serpentine Gall, W2 296 B3
Serpentine Grn, Merst. RH1
off Malmstone Av 251 DK129
Serpentine Rd, W2 296 E3
Sevenoaks TN13 257 FJ123
★ Serpentine Sackler Gallery,
W8 296 C2
Service Rd, The, Pot.B. EN6 64 DA32
Serviden Dr, Brom. BR1 204 EK95
Sch Servite RC Prim Sch, SW10 307 N2
Setchell Rd, SE1 300 A8
Setchell Way, SE1 300 A8
Seth St, SE16 301 H5
Seton Gdns, Dag. RM9 146 EW66
Settle Pt, E13 281 N1
Settle Rd, E13 281 N10
Romford RM3 106 FN49
Settlers Ct, E14
off Newport Av 291 H10
Settles St, E1 288 D7
Settrington Rd, SW6 307 L9
Seven Acres, Cars. SM5 200 DE103
Northwood HA6 93 BU51
Swanley BR8 207 FD100
Seven Arches App, Wey. KT13 212 BM108
Seven Arches Rd, Brwd. CM14 108 FX48
Seven Hills Cl, Walt. KT12 213 BS109
Seven Hills Rd, Cob. KT11 213 BS111
Iver SL0 133 BC65
Walton-on-Thames KT12 213 BS109
Seven Hills Rd S, Cob. KT11 213 BS113
SEVEN KINGS, Ilf. IG3 125 ES59
⇌ Seven Kings 125 ES60
Sch Seven Kings High Sch,
Ilf. IG2 off Ley St 125 ER59
Seven Kings Rd, Ilf. IG3 125 ET61
Seven Kings Way, Kings.T. KT2 198 CL95
Sch Seven Mills Prim Sch, E14 302 B5
SEVENOAKS, TN13 - TN15 257 FJ125
⇌ Sevenoaks 256 FG124
Sevenoaks 257 FJ125
Coll Sevenoaks Adult Ed Cen,
Sev. TN13 off Bradbourne Rd 257 FH122
● Sevenoaks Business Cen,
Sev. TN14 257 FH121
Sevenoaks Bypass, Sev. TN14 256 FC123
Sevenoaks Cl, Bexh. DA7 167 FC84
Romford RM3 106 FJ49
Sutton SM2 218 DA110
SEVENOAKS COMMON,
Sev. TN13 257 FH129
Sevenoaks Ct, Nthwd. HA6 93 BQ52
H Sevenoaks Hosp, Sev. TN13 257 FJ121
Sevenoaks Ho, SE25 202 DU97
★ Sevenoaks Mus, Sev. TN13 257 FJ125
Sch Sevenoaks Prep Sch,
Godden Grn TN15
off Fawke Common Rd 257 FN126
Sch Sevenoaks Prim Sch, Sev.
TN13 off Bradbourne Pk Rd 257 FH122
Sevenoaks Rd, SE4 183 DY86
Orpington BR6 223 ET106
Otford TN14 241 FH116
Pratt's Bottom BR6 223 ET108
Sch Sevenoaks Sch, Sev. TN13
off High St 257 FJ126
Sevenoaks Way, Orp. BR5 186 EW94
Sidcup DA14 186 EW94
Sevens Cl, Berk. HP4 38 AX19
Seven Sea Gdns, E3 290 C6
Sevenseas Rd,
Lon.Hthrw Air. TW6 175 BQ86
Seven Sisters, N15 122 DT57
⇌ Seven Sisters 122 DS57
Seven Sisters 122 DS57
⊖ Seven Sisters 122 DS57
Sch Seven Sisters Prim Sch,
N15 off South Gro 122 DR57
Seven Sisters Rd, N4 121 DM62
N7 121 DM62
N15 122 DQ59
Seven Stars Cor, W12
off Goldhawk Rd 159 CU76
Seven Stars Yd, E1 288 B6
Seventh Av, E12 125 EM63
Hayes UB3 135 BU74
Severalls Av, Chesh. HP5 54 AQ30
Severnake Cl, E14 302 B8
Severn Av, W10 282 F2
Romford RM2 127 FH55
Severn Cres, Slou. SL3 153 BB78
Severn Dr, Enf. EN1 82 DU38
Esher KT10 197 CG103
Upminster RM14 129 FR58
Walton-on-Thames KT12 196 BX103
Severnmead, Hem.H. HP2 40 BL17
Severn Rd, Aveley RM15 148 FQ72
Severns Fld, Epp. CM16 70 EU29
Severnvale, Lon.Col. AL2
off Thamesdale 62 CM27
Severn Way, NW10 119 CT64
Watford WD25 60 BW34
Severus Rd, SW11 160 DE84
Seville Ms, N1 277 N7
Seville St, SW1 296 F5
Sevington Rd, NW4 119 CV58
Sevington St, W9 283 L5
Seward Rd, W7 157 CG75
Beckenham BR3 203 DX96
SEWARDSTONE, E4 83 EC39
SEWARDSTONEBURY, E4 84 EE42
Sewardstone Cl, E4 83 EC39
Sewardstone Gdns, E4 83 EC39
Sewardstone Grn, E4 84 EE42
Sewardstone Rd, E2 279 H10
E4 101 EB45
Waltham Abbey EN9 83 EC38
Jct Sewardstone Rbt,
Wal.Abb. EN9 83 ED35
Sewardstone St, Wal.Abb. EN9 67 EC34
Seward St, EC1 287 H4
Sewdley St, E5 123 DX62
Sewell Cl, Chaff.Hun. RM16 169 FW78
St. Albans AL4 44 CL20
Sewell Harris Cl, Harl. CM20 35 ET14
Sewell Rd, SE2 166 EU76
Sewells, Welw.G.C. AL8 29 CY05
Sewell St, E13 291 P2
Sextant Av, E14 302 G8
Sexton Cl, Chsht EN7
off Shambrook Rd 66 DQ25
Rainham RM13 off Blake Cl 147 FF67
Sexton Ct, E14
off Newport Av 291 H10
Sexton Rd, Til. RM18 171 GF81
Seymer Rd, Rom. RM1 127 FD55
Seymore Ms, SE14
off New Cross Rd 313 N5
Seymour Av, N17 100 DU54
Caterham CR3 236 DQ123
Epsom KT17 217 CV109
Morden SM4 199 CX101
Seymour Chase, Epp. CM16
off Boleyn Row 70 EV29
Seymour Cl, E.Mol. KT8 196 CC99
Loughton IG10 84 EL44
Pinner HA5 94 BZ53
Seymour Ct, E4 102 EF47
N10 98 DG54
N16 off Cazenove Rd 122 DU60
Seymour Cres, Hem.H. HP2 40 BL20
Seymour Dr, Brom. BR2 205 EM102
Seymour Gdns, SE4 313 L10
Feltham TW13 176 BW91
Ilford IG1 125 EM60
Ruislip HA4 116 BX60
Surbiton KT5 198 CM99
Twickenham TW1 177 CH87
Seymour Gro, Watford WD19 94 BW45
Seymour Ms, W1 284 G8
Ewell KT17 217 CU110
Sawbridgeworth CM21 36 EY08
Seymour Pl, SE25 202 DV98
W1 284 E7
Hornchurch RM11 128 FK59
Seymour Rd, E4 101 EB46
E6 144 EK68
E10 123 DZ60
N3 98 DB52
N8 121 DN57
N9 100 DV47
SW18 179 CZ87
SW19 179 CX89
W4 158 CQ77
Carshalton SM5 218 DG106
Chalfont St. Giles HP8 90 AW49
East Molesey KT8 196 CC99
Hampton Hill TW12 176 CC92
Kingston upon Thames KT1 197 CK95
Mitcham CR4 200 DG101
Northchurch HP4 38 AS17
Northfleet DA11 191 GF88
St. Albans AL3 43 CE17
Slough SL1 151 AR75
Tilbury RM18 171 GF81
Seymours, Harl. CM19 51 EM18
Seymours, The, Loug. IG10 85 EN39
Seymour St, SE18 165 EQ76
W1 284 E9
W2 284 E9
Seymour Ter, SE20 202 DV95
Seymour Vil, SE20 202 DV95
Seymour Wk, SW10 307 N2
Swanscombe DA10 190 FY87
Seymour Way, Sun. TW16 175 BS93
Seyssel St, E14 302 F8
Shaa Rd, W3 138 CR73
Shacklands Rd, Sev. TN14 225 FB111
Shackleford Rd, Wok. GU22 227 BA121
Shacklegate La, Tedd. TW11 177 CE91
Shackleton Cl, SE23
off Featherstone Av 182 DV89
Shackleton Ct, E14
off Maritime Quay 302 B10
W12 159 CV75
Shackleton Rd, Slou. SL1 132 AT73
Southall UB1 136 BZ73
Shackleton Wk, Guil. GU2
off Humbolt Cl 242 AT134
Shackleton Way, Abb.L. WD5
off Lysander Way 59 BU32
Welwyn Garden City AL7 30 DD09
SHACKLEWELL, N16 278 A1
Shacklewell Grn, E8 278 B1
Shacklewell La, E8 278 A2
N16 278 A2
Sch Shacklewell Prim Sch, E8 278 A1
Shacklewell Rd, N16 278 B1
Shacklewell Row, E8 278 B1
Shacklewell St, E2 288 B4
Shadbolt Av, E4 101 DY50
Shadbolt Cl, Wor.Pk. KT4 199 CT103
Shad Thames, SE1 300 A3
SHADWELL, E1 300 G1
⊖ Shadwell 288 F10
DLR Shadwell 288 F10
Shadwell Ct, Nthlt. UB5
off Shadwell Dr 136 BZ68
Shadwell Dr, Nthlt. UB5 136 BZ69
Shadwell Gdns Est, E1 288 G10
Shadwell Pierhead, E1 301 H1
Shadwell Pl, E1 288 G10
Shady Bush Cl, Bushey WD23 94 CC45
Shady La, Wat. WD17 75 BV40
Shaef Way, Tedd. TW11 177 CG94
Shafter Rd, Dag. RM10 147 FC65
Shaftesbury, Loug. IG10 84 EK41
Shaftesbury Av, W1 285 N10
WC2 285 N10
Enfield EN3 83 DX40
Feltham TW14 175 BU86
Kenton HA3 117 CK58
New Barnet EN5 80 DC42
South Harrow HA2 116 CB60
Southall UB2 156 CA77
Shaftesbury Circle, S.Har. HA2
off Shaftesbury Av 116 CC60
Shaftesbury Ct, N1 287 L1
SE1 off Alderney Ms 299 L6
Shaftesbury Cres, Stai. TW18 174 BK94
Shaftesbury Gdns, NW10 138 CS70
Sch Shaftesbury High Sch,
Har.Wld HA3 off Headstone La 94 CB53
Shaftesbury La, Dart. DA1 168 FP84
Shaftesbury Ms, SW4 181 DJ85
W8 295 K7
Sch Shaftesbury Pk Prim Sch,
SW11 308 G9
Shaftesbury Pl, W14 295 H9
Shaftesbury Pt, E13 291 P1
Sch Shaftesbury Prim Sch, E7
off Shaftesbury Rd 144 EJ66
Shaftesbury Quay, Hert. SG14
off Railway St 32 DR09
Shaftesbury Rd, E4 101 ED46
E7 144 EJ66
E10 123 EA60
E17 123 EB58
N18 100 DS51
N19 121 DL60
Beckenham BR3 203 DZ96
Carshalton SM5 200 DD101
Epping CM16 69 ET29
Richmond TW9 158 CL83
Romford RM1 127 FF58
Watford WD17 76 BW41
Woking GU22 227 BA117
Shaftesburys, The, Bark. IG11 145 EQ67
Shaftesbury St, N1 287 K1
Shaftesbury Way, Kings L. WD4 59 BQ28
Twickenham TW2 177 CD90
Shaftesbury Waye, Hayes UB4 135 BV71
Shafto Ms, SW1 296 E7
Shafton Rd, E9 279 K8
Shaggy Calf La, Slou. SL2 132 AU73
Shakespeare Av, N11 99 DJ50
NW10 138 CR67
Feltham TW14 175 BU86
Hayes UB4 135 BV70
Tilbury RM18 171 GH82
Shakespeare Cres, E12 145 EM65
Shakespeare Dr, Borwd. WD6 78 CN42
Har. HA3 118 CM58
Shakespeare Gdns, N2 120 DF56
● Shakespeare Ind Est,
Wat. WD24 75 BU38
Shakespeare Rd, E17 101 DX54
N3 off Popes Dr 98 DA53
NW7 97 CT49
NW10 138 CR67
SE24 181 DP85
W3 138 CQ74
W7 137 CF73
Addlestone KT15 212 BK105
Bexleyheath DA7 166 EY81
Dartford DA1 168 FN84
Romford RM1 127 FF58
★ Shakespeare's Globe Thea,
SE1 299 J1
Shakespeare Sq, Ilf. IG6 103 EQ51
Shakespeare St, Wat. WD24 75 BV38
Shakespeare Twr, EC2 287 K6
Shakespeare Way, Felt. TW13 176 BW91
Shakspeare Ms, N16
off Shakspeare Wk 122 DS63
Shakspeare Wk, N16 277 N1
Shalbourne Sq, E9 279 N4
Shalcomb St, SW10 307 P3
Shalcross Dr, Chsht EN8 67 DZ30
Shalden Ho, SW15
off Tunworth Cres 179 CT86
Shaldon Dr, Mord. SM4 199 CY99
Ruislip HA4 116 BW62
Shaldon Rd, Edg. HA8 96 CM53
Shaldon Way, Walt. KT12 196 BW104
Shale Ct, E15
off Romford Rd 281 L5
Shale Grn, Merst. RH1
off Bletchingley Rd 251 DK129
Shalfleet Dr, W10 282 C10
SHALFORD, Guil. GU4 258 AX141
⇌ Shalford 258 AY140
Shalford Cl, Orp. BR6 223 EQ105
Sch Shalford Inf Sch,
Guil. GU4 off Station Row 258 AY140
Shalford Rd, Guil. GU1, GU4 258 AX137
Shalimar Gdns, W3 138 CQ73
Shalimar Rd, W3 138 CQ73
Shallcross Cres, Hat. AL10 45 CU21
Shallons Rd, SE9 185 EP91
Shalstone Rd, SW14 158 CP83
Shalston Vil, Surb. KT6 198 CM100
Shambles, The, Sev. TN13
off London Rd 257 FJ125
Shambrook Rd, Chsht EN7 65 DP25
Shamrock Cl, Fetch. KT22 231 CD121
Shamrock Ho, SE26
off Talisman Sq 182 DU91
Shamrock Rd, Croy. CR0 201 DM100
Gravesend DA12 191 GL87
Shamrock St, SW4 309 N10
Shamrock Way, N14 99 DH46
Shandon Rd, SW4 181 DJ86
Shand St, SE1 299 N4
Shandy St, E1 289 K5
Shanklin Cl, Chsht EN7 66 DT29
Shanklin Gdns, Wat. WD19 94 BW49
Shanklin Ho, E17
off Sherwood Cl 101 DZ54
Shanklin Rd, N8 121 DK57
N15 122 DU56
Shannon Cl, NW2 119 CX62
Southall UB2 156 BX78
● Shannon Commercial Cen,
N.Mal. KT3 off Beverley Way 199 CU98
Jct Shannon Cor, N.Mal. KT3 199 CU98
Shannon Cor Retail Pk,
N.Mal. KT3 199 CU98
Shannon Gro, SW9 161 DM84
Shannon Pl, NW8 274 D10
Shannon Way, Aveley RM15 148 FQ73
Beckenham BR3 183 EB93
Shantock Hall La, Bov. HP3 56 AY29
Shantock La, Bov. HP3 56 AX30
Shap Cres, Cars. SM5 200 DF102
Shapland Way, N13 99 DM50
Sch Shapla Prim Sch, E1 288 C10
Shapwick Cl, N11 98 DF50
★ Shard, The, SE1 299 M3
Shardcroft Av, SE24 181 DP85
Shardeloes Rd, SE4 313 N9
SE14 313 N8
Sharland Cl, Th.Hth. CR7
off Dunheved Rd N 201 DN100
Sharland Rd, Grav. DA12 191 GJ89
Sharman Ct, Sid. DA14 186 EU91
Sharman Row, Slou. SL3 153 AZ78
Sharnbrooke Cl, Well. DA16 166 EW83
Sharnbrook Ho, W14 307 J2
Sharney Av, Slou. SL3 153 BB76
Sharon Cl, Bkhm KT23 230 CA124
Epsom KT19 216 CQ113
Long Ditton KT6 197 CJ102
Sharon Gdns, E9 278 G8
Sharon Rd, W4 158 CR78
Enfield EN3 83 DY40
Sharpcroft, Hem.H. HP2 40 BK18
Sharpe Cl, W7 off Templeman Rd 137 CF71
Sharpecroft, Harl. CM19 51 EQ15
Sharpes La, Hem.H. HP1 39 BB21
Sharpleshall St, NW1 274 F7
Sharpness Cl, Hayes UB4 136 BY71
Sharps La, Ruis. HA4 115 BR60
Sharp Way, Dart. DA1 168 FM83
Sharratt St, SE15 313 H2
Sharsted St, SE17 310 G1
Sharvel La, Nthlt. UB5 135 BU67
Shavers Pl, SW1 297 N1
Shaw Av, Bark. IG11 146 EY68
Shawbridge, Harl. CM19 51 EQ18
Shawbrooke Rd, SE9 184 EJ85
Shawbury Cl, NW9 96 CS54
Shawbury Rd, SE22 182 DT85
Shaw Cl, SE28 146 EV74
Bushey Heath WD23 95 CE47
Cheshunt EN8 66 DW28
Epsom KT17 217 CT111
Hornchurch RM11 127 FH60
Ottershaw KT16 211 BC107
South Croydon CR2 220 DT112
Staines-upon-Thames TW19 174 BL88
Shaw Ct, SW11 160 DD83
Morden SM4 200 DC101
Windsor SL4 172 AU85
Shaw Cres, E14 289 M7
Hutton CM13 109 GD43
South Croydon CR2 220 DT112
Tilbury RM18 171 GH81
Shaw Dr, Walt. KT12 196 BW101
Shawfield Ct, West Dr. UB7 154 BL76
Shawfield Pk, Brom. BR1 204 EK96
Shawfield St, SW3 308 D1
Shawford Ct, SW15 179 CU87
Shawford Rd, Epsom KT19 216 CR107
Shaw Gdns, Bark. IG11 146 EY68
Slough SL3 153 AZ78
Shaw Gro, Couls. CR5 236 DQ120
Shaw Ho, E16 off Claremont St 305 M3
N17 off Queen St 100 DS51
Banstead SM7 234 DC118
Sch Shawley Comm Prim Sch,
Epsom KT18 off Shawley Way 233 CW118
Shawley Cres, Epsom KT18 233 CW118
Shawley Way, Epsom KT18 233 CV118
Shaw Path, Brom. BR1
off Shroffold Rd 184 EF90
Sch Shaw Prim Sch,
S.Ock. RM15 off Avon Grn 149 FV72
Shaw Rd, SE22 162 DS84
Bromley BR1 184 EF90
Enfield EN3 83 DX39
Tatsfield TN16 238 EJ120
Shaws, The, Welw.G.C. AL7 30 DC10
Shaws Cotts, SE23 183 DY90
Shaw Sq, E17 101 DY53
Shaw Way, Wall. SM6 219 DL108
Shaxton Cres, New Adgtn CR0 221 EC109
Sheares Hoppit,
Hunsdon SG12 34 EK05
Shearing Dr, Cars. SM5
off Stavordale Rd 200 DC101
Shearling Way, N7 276 B4
Shearman Rd, SE3 164 EF84
Jct Shears, The, Sun. TW16 175 BS94
Shears Cl, Dart. DA1 188 FJ89
Shears Ct, Sun. TW16
off Staines Rd W 175 BS94
Sch Shears Grn Inf Sch,
Nthflt DA11 off Packham Rd 191 GF90
Sch Shears Grn Jun Sch,
Nthflt DA11 off White Av 191 GF90
Shearsmith Ho, E1 288 D10
Shearwater Cl, Bark. IG11 146 EU69
Shearwater Rd, Sutt. SM1 217 CZ106
Shearwater Way, Hayes UB4 136 BX72

Shearwood Cres, Dart. DA1 167 FF83
Sheath La, Oxshott KT22 214 CB113
Sheaveshill Av, NW9 118 CS56
Sheba Pl, E1 288 B5
Sheehy Way, Slou. SL2 132 AV73
Sheen Common, SW14 178 CP85
Sheen Common Dr, Rich. TW10 158 CN84
Sheen Ct, Rich. TW10 158 CN84
Sheen Ct Rd, Rich. TW10 158 CN84
Sheendale Rd, Rich. TW9 158 CM84
Sheenewood, SE26 182 DV92
Sheen Gate Gdns, SW14 158 CQ84
Sheen Gate Mans Pas, SW14
off East Sheen Av 158 CR84
Sheen Gro, N1 276 E8
Sheen La, SW14 158 CQ83
Sch Sheen Mt Prim Sch, SW14
off West Temple Sheen 178 CP85
Sheen Pk, Rich. TW9 158 CM84
Sheen Rd, Orp. BR5 205 ET98
Richmond TW9, TW10 178 CL85
Sheen Way, Wall. SM6 219 DM106
Sheen Wd, SW14 178 CQ85
Sheepbarn La, Warl. CR6 222 EF112
Sheepcot Dr, Wat. WD25 60 BW34
Sheepcote, Welw.G.C. AL7 30 DA12
Sheepcote Cl, Beac. HP9 88 AJ51
Hounslow TW5 155 BU80
Sheepcote Gdns, Denh. UB9 114 BG58
Sheepcote La, SW11 308 E9
Burnham SL1 110 AF62
Orpington BR5 206 EZ99
Swanley BR8 206 EZ98
Wheathampstead AL4 28 CL07
Wooburn Green HP10 110 AG61
Sheepcote Rd, Eton Wick SL4 151 AN78
Harrow HA1 117 CF58
Hemel Hempstead HP2 40 BM20
Windsor SL4 151 AL82
Sheepcotes Rd, Rom. RM6 126 EX56
Sheepcot La, Wat. WD25 59 BV34
Sheepfold La, Amer. HP7 55 AR39
Sheepfold Rd, Guil. GU2 242 AT131
Sheephouse Grn, Wotton RH5 262 BZ140
Sheephouse La, Dor. RH5 262 BZ139
Sheephouse Rd, Hem.H. HP3 40 BM22
Sheephouse Way, N.Mal. KT3 198 CS101
Sheeplands Av, Guil. GU1 243 BC132
Sheep La, E8 278 E9
Sheep Wk, Epsom KT18 232 CR122
Reigate RH2 249 CY131
Shepperton TW17 194 BM101
Sheep Wk, The, Wok. GU22 227 BE118
Sheepwalk La, E.Hors. KT24 245 BT134
Sheep Wk Ms, SW19 179 CX93
Sheer Cft, Chesh. HP5 54 AM29
SHEERING, B.Stort. CM22 37 FC07
Sch Sheering C of E Prim Sch,
Sheering CM22 off The Street 37 FD06
Sheering Dr, Harl. CM17 36 EX12
Sheering Hall Dr, Harl. CM17 36 FA08
Sheering Lwr Rd, Harl. CM17 36 EZ09
Sawbridgeworth CM21 36 FA06
Sheering Mill La, Saw. CM21 36 EZ05
Sheering Rd, Harl. CM17 36 EY11
Hatfield Heath CM22 37 FF05
Sheerness Ms, E16 305 P4
SHEERWATER, Wok. GU21 211 BC113
Hem.H. HP3 40 BJ24
Sheerwater Av, Wdhm KT15 211 BE112
Sheerwater Rd, E16 292 E6
West Byfleet KT14 211 BE112
Woking GU21 211 BE112
Woodham KT15 211 BE112
Sheethanger La, Felden HP3 40 BG24
Sheet St, Wind. SL4 151 AR82
Sheffield Dr, Rom. RM3 106 FN50
Sheffield Gdns, Rom. RM3 106 FN50
Sheffield Rd, Lon.Hthrw Air.
TW6 off Shrewsbury Rd 175 BQ86
Slough SL1 131 AQ72
Sheffield Sq, E3 289 P2
Sheffield St, WC2 286 C9
Sheffield Ter, W8 295 J3
Shefton Ri, Nthwd. HA6 93 BU52
Sheila Cl, Rom. RM5 105 FB52
Sheila Rd, Rom. RM5 105 FB52
Sheilings, The, Horn. RM11 128 FM57
Shelbourne Cl, Pnr. HA5 116 BZ55
Shelbourne Pl, Beck. BR3 183 DZ94
Shelbourne Rd, N17 100 DV54
Shelburne Dr, Houns. TW4
off Hanworth Rd 176 CA86
Shelburne Rd, N7 121 DM63
Shelbury Cl, Sid. DA14 186 EU90
Shelbury Rd, SE22 182 DV85
Sheldon Av, N6 120 DE59
Ilford IG5 103 EP54
Sheldon Cl, SE12 184 EH85
SE20 202 DV95
Cheshunt EN7 66 DS26
Harlow CM17 52 EY15
Reigate RH2 266 DB135
Sheldon Ct, SW8
off Thorncroft St 310 A5
Guildford GU1
off Lower Edgeborough Rd 259 AZ135
Sheldon Pl, E2 288 D1
Sheldon Rd, N18 100 DS49
NW2 272 D1
Bexleyheath DA7 166 EZ81
Dagenham RM9 146 EY66
Sheldon Sq, W2 283 P7
Sheldon St, Croy. CR0 202 DQ104
Sheldon Way, Berk. HP4 38 AU18
Sheldrake Cl, E16 305 J3
Sheldrake Pl, W8 295 J4
Sheldrick Cl, SW19 200 DD96
Shelduck Cl, E15 281 M2
Sheldwich Ter, Brom. BR2 204 EL100
Shelford, Kings.T. KT1
off Burritt Rd 198 CN96
Shelford Pl, N16 122 DR62
Shelford Ri, SE19 182 DT94
Shelford Rd, Barn. EN5 79 CW44
Shelgate Rd, SW11 180 DE85
Shellbank La, Dart. DA2 189 FU93
★ Shell Cen, SE1 298 D3
Shell Cl, Brom. BR2 204 EL100
Shellduck Cl, NW9 off Swan Dr 96 CS54
Shelley Av, E12 144 EL65
Greenford UB6 137 CD69
Hornchurch RM12 127 FF61
Shelley Cl, SE15 312 F8
Banstead SM7 233 CX115
Borehamwood WD6 78 CN42
Coulsdon CR5 235 DM117
Edgware HA8 96 CN49
Greenford UB6 137 CD69
Shelley Cl, Hayes UB4 135 BU71
Northwood HA6 93 BT50
Orpington BR6 205 ES104
Slough SL3 153 AZ78
Wooburn Moor HP10
off Falcons Cft 110 AE55
Shelley Ct, N4 121 DM60
Waltham Abbey EN9
off Bramley Shaw 68 EF33
Shelley Cres, Houns. TW5 156 BX82
Southall UB1 136 BZ72
Shelley Dr, Well. DA16 165 ES81
Shelley Gdns, Wem. HA0 117 CJ61
Shelley Gro, Loug. IG10 85 EM42
Shelley Ho, SW1 309 M2
Shelley La, Hare. UB9 92 BG53
Shelley Pl, Til. RM18 171 GH81
Shelley Rd, NW10 138 CR67
Chesham HP5 54 AP29
Hutton CM13 109 GD45
Shelleys La, Knock. TN14 239 ET116
Shelley Way, SW19 180 DD93
Shellfield Cl, Stai. TW19 174 BG85
Shellgrove Est, N16 277 P2
Shellness Rd, E5 278 F2
Shell Rd, SE13 163 EB83
Shellwood Dr, N.Holm. RH5 263 CJ140
Shellwood Rd, SW11 308 E9
Leigh RH2 264 CQ141
Shelmerdine Cl, E3 290 A6
Shelson Av, Felt. TW13 175 BT90
Shelton Av, Warl. CR6 236 DW117
Shelton Cl, Guil. GU2 242 AU129
Warlingham CR6 236 DW117
Shelton Rd, SW19 200 DA95
Shelton St, WC2 286 A9
Shelvers Grn, Tad. KT20 233 CW121
Shelvers Hill, Tad. KT20
off Ashurst Rd 233 CV121
Shelvers Spur, Tad. KT20 233 CW121
Shelvers Way, Tad. KT20 233 CW121
Shenden Cl, Sev. TN13 257 FJ128
Shenden Way, Sev. TN13 257 FJ128
Shendish Edge, Hem.H. HP3
off London Rd 58 BM25
SHENFIELD, Brwd. CM15 109 GA45
⇌ Shenfield 109 GA45
Shenfield Cl, Couls. CR5
off Woodfield Cl 235 DJ119
Shenfield Common, Brwd. CM15 108 FY48
Shenfield Cres, Brwd. CM15 108 FY47
Shenfield Gdns, Hutt. CM13 109 GB44
Shenfield Grn, Shenf. CM15 109 GA45
Sch Shenfield High Sch,
Shenf. CM15 off Alexander La 109 GA43
Shenfield Ho, SE18
off Shooters Hill Rd 164 EK80
Shenfield Pl, Shenf. CM15 108 FY45
Shenfield Rd, Brwd. CM15 108 FX46
Woodford Green IG8 102 EH52
Shenfield St, N1 287 P1
SHENLEY, Rad. WD7 62 CN33
Shenley Av, Ruis. HA4 115 BT61
Shenleybury, Shenley WD7 62 CL30
Shenleybury Cotts,
Shenley WD7 62 CL31
Shenley Cl, S.Croy. CR2 220 DT110
Shenley Hill, Rad. WD7 77 CG35
Shenley La, Lon.Col. AL2 61 CJ27
Sch Shenley Prim Sch,
Shenley WD7 off London Rd 62 CM34
Shenley Rd, SE5 311 P7
Borehamwood WD6 78 CN42
Dartford DA1 188 FN86
Hounslow TW5 156 BY81
Radlett WD7 61 CH34
Shenstone Cl, Dart. DA1 167 FD84
Shenstone Dr, Burn. SL1 131 AK70
Shenstone Gdns, Rom. RM3 106 FJ53
Shenstone Hill, Berk. HP4 38 AX18
Sch Shenstone Sch, Cray. DA1
off Old Rd 167 FD84
Shepcot Ho, N14 81 DJ44
Shepherd Cl, Abb.L. WD5 59 BT30
Hanworth TW13 176 BY91
Shepherdess Pl, N1 287 K2
Shepherdess Wk, N1 277 K10
Shepherd Ho, E16 305 N1
Shepherd Mkt, W1 297 J2
Sch Shepherd Prim Sch, Mill End
WD3 off Shepherds La 92 BG46
SHEPHERD'S BUSH, W12 294 B2
⇌ Shepherd's Bush 294 D4
Ⓞ Shepherd's Bush 294 D4
⊖ Shepherd's Bush 294 C4
Shepherds Bush Grn, W12 294 B4
Shepherds Bush Mkt, W12 294 A5
⊖ Shepherd's Bush Market 294 A3
Shepherds Bush Pl, W12 294 C4
Shepherds Bush Rd, W6 294 B9
Shepherds Cl, N6 121 DH58
W1 off Lees Pl 284 G10
Beaconsfield HP9 89 AM54
Cowley UB8 134 BJ70
Leatherhead KT22 232 CL124
Orpington BR6
off Stapleton Rd 205 ET104
Romford RM6 126 EX57
Shepperton TW17 195 BP100
Stanmore HA7 95 CG50
Shepherds Ct, W12 294 C4
Hertford SG14 32 DQ06
Shepherds Farm,
Rickmansworth WD3 92 BG46
Shepherds Grn, Chis. BR7 185 ER94
Hemel Hempstead HP1 39 BE21
Shepherds Hill, N6 121 DH58
Guildford GU2 242 AU132
Merstham RH1 251 DJ126
Romford RM3 106 FN54
Shepherds Ho,
N7 off York Way 276 A5
Shepherds La, E9 279 J3
SE28 145 ES74
Beaconsfield HP9 89 AM54
Dart. DA1 187 FG88
Guildford GU2 242 AT131
Rickmansworth WD3 91 BF45
Shepherd's La, Brwd. CM14 108 FS45
Shepherds Path, Nthlt. UB5
off Cowings Mead 136 BY65
Shepherd's Pl, W1 284 G10
Shepherds Rd, Wat. WD18 75 BT41
Shepherd St, W1 297 J3
Northfleet DA11 190 GD87
Shepherds Wk, NW2 119 CU61
NW3 274 A2
Bushey Heath WD23 95 CD47
Shepherds' Wk, Epsom KT18 232 CP121
Shepherds Way, Brook.Pk AL9 64 DC27
Chesham HP5 54 AR33
Rickmansworth WD3 92 BH45
Shalford GU4 258 AY138
South Croydon CR2 221 DX108
Shepiston La, Hayes UB3 155 BR77
West Drayton UB7 155 BQ77
Shepley Cl, Cars. SM5 200 DG104
Shepley Ms, Enf. EN3 83 EA37
Sheppard Cl, Enf. EN1 82 DV38
Kingston upon Thames KT1
off Beaufort Rd 198 CL98
Sheppard Dr, SE16 300 E10
Sheppards, Harl. CM19
off Heighams 51 EM18
Sheppards Cl, St.Alb. AL3 43 CE17
Sheppard St, E16 291 M4
SHEPPERTON, TW17 194 BN101
⇌ Shepperton 195 BQ99
● Shepperton Business Pk,
Shep. TW17 195 BQ99
Shepperton Cl, Borwd. WD6 78 CR39
Shepperton Ct, Shep. TW17 195 BP100
Shepperton Ct Dr, Shep. TW17 195 BP99
Shepperton Rd, N1 277 K8
Petts Wood BR5 205 EQ100
Staines-upon-Thames TW18 194 BJ97
Shepperton Studios,
Shep. TW17 194 BM97
Sheppey Cl, Erith DA8 167 FH80
Sheppey Gdns, Dag. RM9
off Sheppey Rd 146 EW66
Sheppey Rd, Dag. RM9 146 EV66
Sheppeys La, Bedmond WD5 59 BS28
Sheppy Pl, Grav. DA12 191 GH87
Shepton Hos, E2
off Welwyn St 289 H2
Sherard Ct, N7
off Manor Gdns 121 DL62
Sherard Rd, SE9 184 EL85
Sherards Orchard, Harl. CM19 51 EP17
● Sheraton Business Cen,
Perivale UB6 137 CH68
Sheraton Cl, Els. WD6 78 CM43
Sheraton Dr, Epsom KT19 216 CQ113
Sheraton Ms, Wat. WD18 75 BS42
Sheraton St, W1 285 N9
Sherborne Av, Enf. EN3 82 DW40
Southall UB2 156 CA77
Sherborne Cl, Colnbr. SL3 153 BE81
Epsom KT18 233 CW117
Hayes UB4 136 BW72
Sherborne Ct, Guil. GU2
off The Mount 258 AW136
Sherborne Cres, Cars. SM5 200 DE101
Sherborne Gdns, NW9 118 CN55
W13 137 CH72
Romford RM5 104 FA50
Sherborne Ho, SW8
off Bolney St 310 C5
Sherborne La, EC4 287 L10
Sherborne Pl, Nthwd. HA6 93 BR51
Sherborne Rd, Chess. KT9 216 CL106
Feltham TW14 175 BR87
Orpington BR5 205 ET98
Sutton SM3 200 DA103
Sherborne St, N1 277 L8
Sherborne Wk, Lthd. KT22
off Windfield 231 CJ121
Sherborne Way, Crox.Grn WD3 75 BP42
Sherboro Rd, N15 122 DT58
Sherbourne, Albury GU5 260 BK139
Sherbourne Cl, Hem.H. HP2 40 BL21
Sherbourne Cotts, Albury GU5 260 BL138
Watford WD18 off Lammas Rd 76 BW43
Sherbourne Dr, Wind. SL4 151 AM84
Sherbourne Gdns, Shep. TW17 195 BS101
Sherbourne Pl, Stan. HA7 95 CG51
Sherbourne Wk, Farn.Com. SL2 111 AQ63
Sherbrooke Cl, Bexh. DA6 166 FA84
Sherbrooke Rd, SW6 306 F5
Sherbrooke Way, Wor.Pk. KT4 199 CV101
Sherbrook Gdns, N21 99 DP45
SHERE, Guil. GU5 260 BN139
Shere Av, Sutt. SM2 217 CW110
Shere Cl, Chess. KT9 215 CK106
North Holmwood RH5 263 CJ140
Sch Shere C of E Inf Sch,
Shere GU5 off Gomshall La 260 BN139
Sheredan Rd, E4 101 ED50
Sheredes Dr, Hodd. EN11 49 DZ19
Sch Sheredes Prim Sch,
Hodd. EN11 off Benford Rd 49 DZ19
Sch Sheredes Sch,
Hodd. EN11 off Cock La 49 DZ18
Shere La, Shere GU5 260 BN139
★ Shere Mus, Guil. GU5 260 BN139
Shere Rd, Guil. GU4, GU5 260 BL138
Ilford IG2 125 EN57
West Horsley KT24 245 BP130
Sherfield Av, Rick. WD3 92 BK47
Sherfield Cl, N.Mal. KT3 198 CP98
Sherfield Gdns, SW15 179 CT86
Sherfield Ms, Hayes UB3 135 BS72
Sherfield Rd, Grays RM17 170 GB79
Sheridan Cl, Hem.H. HP1 40 BH21
Romford RM3 105 FH52
Swanley BR8 off Willow Av 207 FF97
Uxbridge UB10 off Alpha Rd 135 BQ70
Sheridan Ct, Houns. TW4
off Vickers Way 176 BY85
Northolt UB5 116 CB64
Sheridan Cres, Chis. BR7 205 EP96
Sheridan Dr, Reig. RH2 250 DB132
Sheridan Gdns, Har. HA3 117 CK58
Sheridan Hts, E1
off Spencer Way 288 F9
Sheridan Ho, Lthd. KT22
off Highbury Dr 231 CG121
Sheridan Ms, E11
off Woodbine Pl 124 EH58
Sheridan Pl, SW13 159 CT82
Bromley BR1 204 EK96
Hampton TW12 196 CB95
Sheridan Rd, E7 124 EF62
E12 124 EL64
SW19 199 CZ95
Belvedere DA17 166 FA77
Bexleyheath DA7 166 EY83
Richmond TW10 177 CJ90
Watford WD19 94 BX45
Sheridans Rd, Bkhm KT23 246 CC126
Sheridan Ter, Nthlt. UB5 116 CB64
Sheridan Wk, NW11 120 DA58
Broxbourne EN10 49 DY20
Carshalton SM5
off Carshalton Pk Rd 218 DF106
Sheridan Way, Beck. BR3
off Turners Meadow Way 203 DZ95
Sheriff Way, Wat. WD25 59 BU33
Sch Sheringdale Prim Sch,
SW18 off Standen Rd 179 CZ88
Sheringham Av, E12 125 EM63
N14 81 DK43
Feltham TW13 175 BU90
Romford RM7 127 FC58
Twickenham TW2 176 BZ88
Sheringham Ct, Hayes UB3 155 BT75
Sheringham Dr, Bark. IG11 125 ET64
Sch Sheringham Jun Sch, E12
off Sheringham Av 125 EM63
Sheringham Rd, N7 276 D4
SE20 202 DV97
Sheringham Twr, Sthl. UB1 136 CB73
Sherington Av, Pnr. HA5 94 CA52
Sch Sherington Prim Sch, SE7
off Sherington Rd 164 EH79
Sherington Rd, SE7 164 EH79
Sherland Rd, Twick. TW1 177 CF88
Sherlies Av, Orp. BR6 205 ES103
Sherlock Cl, SW16 201 DM96
★ Sherlock Holmes Mus, NW1 284 F5
Sherlock Ms, W1 284 G6
Shermanbury Cl, Erith DA8 167 FF80
Sherman Gdns,
Chad.Hth RM6 126 EW58
Sherman Rd, Brom. BR1 204 EG95
Slough SL1 132 AS71
Shernbroke Rd, Wal.Abb. EN9 68 EF34
Shernhall St, E17 123 EC57
Sherpa Rd, Hem.H. HP2 40 BN19
Sherrard Rd, E7 144 EJ65
E12 144 EK65
Sherrards, Welw.G.C. AL8 29 CV06
Sherrards Mansion,
Welw.G.C. AL8 off Sherrards 29 CV06
Sherrards Ms,
Welw.G.C. AL8 off Sherrards 29 CV06
SHERRARDSPARK,
Welw.G.C. AL8 29 CV07
Sherrardspark Rd,
Welw.G.C. AL8 29 CW07
Sherrards Way, Barn. EN5 80 DA43
Sherrick Grn Rd, NW10 119 CV64
Sherriff Cl, Esher KT10 196 CB103
Sherriff Rd, NW6 273 K5
Sherringham Av, N17 100 DU54
Sherrin Rd, E10 123 EA63
Sherrock Gdns, NW4 119 CU56
Sherry Ms, Bark. IG11 145 ER66
Sherwin Rd, SE14 313 J7
Sherwood Av, E18 124 EH55
SW16 181 DK94
Greenford UB6 137 CE65
Hayes UB4 135 BV70
Potters Bar EN6 63 CY32
Ruislip HA4 115 BS58
St. Albans AL4 43 CH17
Sherwood Cl, E17 101 DZ54
SW13 off Lower Common S 159 CV83
W13 137 CH74
Bexley DA5 186 EW86
Fetcham KT22 230 CC122
Slough SL3 152 AY76
Sherwood Ct, Colnbr. SL3
off High St 153 BD80
Watford WD25 off High Rd 59 BU34
Sherwood Cres, Reig. RH2 266 DB138
Sherwood Gdns, E14 302 B8
SE16 312 D1
Barking IG11 145 ER66
Sherwood Ho, Harl. CM18
off Bush Fair 51 ET17
Sherwood Pk Av, Sid. DA15 186 EU87
Sch Sherwood Pk Prim Sch,
Sid. DA15 off Sherwood Pk Av 186 EV86
Sherwood Pk Rd, Mitch. CR4 201 DJ98
Sutton SM1 218 DA106
Sch Sherwood Pk Sch,
Wall. SM6 off Streeters La 201 DK104
Sherwood Pl, Hem.H. HP2
off Turnpike Grn 40 BM16
Sherwood Rd, NW4 119 CW55
SW19 179 CZ94
Coulsdon CR5 235 DJ116
Croydon CR0 202 DV101
Hampton Hill TW12 176 CC92
Harrow HA2 116 CC61
Ilford IG6 125 ER56
Knaphill GU21 226 AS117
Welling DA16 165 ES82
Sch Sherwood Sch, The,
Mitch. CR4 off Abbotts Rd 201 DJ98
Sherwoods Rd, Wat. WD19 94 BY45
Sherwood St, N20 98 DD48
W1 285 M10
Sherwood Ter, N20 98 DD48
Sherwood Way, Epsom KT19 216 CM112
W.Wick. BR4 203 EB103
Shetland Cl, Borwd. WD6 78 CR44
Guildford GU4
off Weybrook Dr 243 BB129
Shetland Rd, E3 289 N1
Shevon Way, Brwd. CM14 108 FT49
Shewens Rd, Wey. KT13 213 BR105
Shey Copse, Wok. GU22 227 BC117
Shield Dr, Brent. TW8 157 CG79
Shieldhall St, SE2 166 EW77
Shield Rd, Ashf. TW15 175 BQ91
Shifford Path, SE23 183 DX90
Shilburn Way, Wok. GU21 226 AU118
Shillibeer Pl, W1 284 D6
Shillibeer Wk, Chig. IG7 103 ET48
Shillingford Cl, NW7 97 CX52
Shillingford St, N1 277 H7
Shillitoe Av, Pot.B. EN6 63 CX32
Shimmings, The, Guil. GU1 243 BA133
Shinecroft, Otford TN14 241 FG116
Shinfield St, W12 282 A9
Shingle Ct, Wal.Abb. EN9 68 EG33
Shinglewell Rd, Erith DA8 166 FA80
Shinners Cl, SE25 202 DU99
Ship All, W4 off Thames Rd 158 CN79
Ship & Half Moon Pas, SE18 305 N6
Ship & Mermaid Row, SE1 299 M4
Shipfield Cl, Tats. TN16 238 EJ121
Ship Hill, H.Wyc. HP10 111 AL60
Tatsfield TN16 238 EJ121
Shipka Rd, SW12 181 DH88
Ship La, SW14 158 CQ82
Aveley RM15 169 FR75
Mountnessing CM13 109 GF41
Purfleet RM19 169 FS76
Sutton at Hone DA4 208 FK95
Swanley BR8 208 FK95
Ship La Caravan Site,
Aveley RM15 169 FR76
SHIPLEY BRIDGE, Horl. RH6 269 DM153
Shipman Rd, E16 292 B9
SE23 183 DX89
Ship St, SE8 314 A6
Ship Tavern Pas, EC3 287 N10
Shipton Cl, Dag. RM8 126 EX62
Shipton St, E2 288 B2
Shipwright Rd, SE16 301 L5
Shipwright Yd, SE1 299 N3
Ship Yd, E14 302 C10
Weybridge KT13 off High St 213 BP105
Shirburn Cl, SE23
off Tyson Rd 182 DW87
Shirbutt St, E14 290 C10
Shirebrook Rd, SE3 164 EK82
Shire Cl, Brox. EN10
off Groom Rd 67 DZ26
Shire Ct, Epsom KT17 217 CT108
Erith DA18
off St. John Fisher Rd 166 EX76
Shirehall Cl, NW4 119 CX58
Shirehall Gdns, NW4 119 CX58
Shirehall La, NW4 119 CX58
Shirehall Pk, NW4 119 CX58
Shirehall Rd, Dart. DA2 188 FK92
Shire Horse Way, Islw. TW7 157 CF83
Shire La, Chal.St.P. SL9 91 BD54
Chorleywood WD3 73 BB43
Denham UB9 113 BE55
Keston BR2 223 EM108
Orpington BR6 223 ER107
Shiremeade, Els. WD6 78 CM43
Shire Ms, Whitton TW2 176 CC86
● Shire Pk, Welw.G.C. AL7 29 CY07
Shire Pl, SW18 180 DB87
Redhill RH1 266 DF136
Shires, The, Ham TW10 178 CL91
Watford WD25 59 BV31
Shires Cl, Ashtd. KT21 231 CK118
Shires Ho, Byfleet KT14 212 BL113
Shirland Ms, W9 283 H3
Shirland Rd, W9 283 J3
SHIRLEY, Croy. CR0 203 DX104
Shirley Av, Bex. DA5 186 EX87
Cheam SM2 217 CZ109
Coulsdon CR5 235 DP119
Croydon CR0 202 DW102
Redhill RH1 266 DF139
Sutton SM1 218 DE105
Windsor SL4 151 AM81
Shirley Ch Rd, Croy. CR0 203 DX104
Shirley Cl, E17
off Addison Rd 123 EB57
Broxbourne EN10 49 DZ24
Cheshunt EN8 66 DW29
Dartford DA1 168 FJ84
Hounslow TW3 176 CC85
Shirley Ct, Croy. CR0 203 DX104
Shirley Cres, Beck. BR3 203 DY98
Shirley Dr, Houns. TW3 176 CC85
Shirley Gdns, W7 137 CF74
Barking IG11 145 ES65
Hornchurch RM12 128 FJ61
Shirley Gro, N9 100 DW45
SW11 160 DG83
Shirley Hts, Wall. SM6 219 DJ109
Sch Shirley High Sch, Croy.
CR0 off Shirley Ch Rd 203 DX104
Shirley Hills Rd, Croy. CR0 221 DX106
Shirley Ho Dr, SE7 164 EJ80
H Shirley Oaks Hosp,
Croy. CR0 202 DW101
Shirley Oaks Rd, Croy. CR0 203 DX102
Shirley Pk Rd, Croy. CR0 202 DV102
Shirley Rd, E15 281 K6
W4 158 CR75
Abbots Langley WD5 59 BT32
Croydon CR0 202 DV101
Enfield EN2 82 DQ41
St. Albans AL1 43 CF21
Sidcup DA15 185 ES90
Wallington SM6 219 DJ109
Watford WD17 75 BU39
Shirley St, E16 291 L8
Shirley Way, Croy. CR0 203 DY104
Shirlock Rd, NW3 274 F1
Shirwell Cl, NW7 97 CX52
Shobden Rd, N17 100 DR53
Shobroke Cl, NW2 119 CW62
Shoebury Rd, E6 145 EM66
Shoe La, EC4 286 F8
Harlow CM17 52 EZ16
Sholden Gdns, Orp. BR5 206 EW99
Sholto Rd, Lon.Hthrw Air. TW6 174 BM85
Shona Ho, E13 292 C6
Shonks Mill Rd, Nave. RM4 87 FG37
Shooters Av, Har. HA3 117 CJ56
Shooters Dr, Lwr Naze. EN9 50 EE22
Shooters Hill, SE18 165 EN81
Welling DA16 165 EN81
Coll Shooters Hill Post 16 Campus,
SE18 off Red Lion La 165 EN81
Shooters Hill Rd, SE3 315 M6
SE10 314 F7
SE18 164 EH80
SHOOTER'S HILL, SE18 165 EQ81
Shooters Rd, Enf. EN2 81 DP39
Shootersway, Berk. HP4 38 AU20
Shootersway La, Berk. HP4 38 AT20
Shootersway Pk, Berk. HP4 38 AT20
Shoot Up Hill, NW2 272 E3
Shophouse La, Albury GU5 260 BK144
Shoplands, Welw.G.C. AL8 29 CX05
Shord Hill, Ken. CR8 236 DR116
Shore, The, Nthflt DA11 190 GD85
Rosherville DA11 191 GF86
Shore Cl, Felt. TW14 175 BU87
Hampton TW12
off Stewart Cl 176 BY92
Shorediche Cl, Uxb. UB10 114 BM62
SHOREDITCH, E1 288 A5
Ⓞ Shoreditch High Street 287 P5
Shoreditch High St, E1 287 P5
Shoreditch Ho, N1 287 M3
Shore Gro, Felt. TW13 176 CA89
SHOREHAM, Sev. TN14 225 FG111
⇌ Shoreham 225 FG111
Shoreham Cl, SW18
off Ram St 180 DB85
Bexley DA5 186 EX88
Croydon CR0 202 DW100
Shoreham La, Halst. TN14 224 EZ112
Orpington BR6 224 FA107
Sevenoaks TN13 256 FF122
Shoreham Pl, Shore. TN14 225 FG112

S

Shoreham Ri, Slou. SL2 off Lower Britwell Rd 131 AK70
Shoreham Rd, Orp. BR5 206 EV95
Sevenoaks TN14 225 FH111
Shoreham Rd E, Lon.Hthrw Air. TW6 174 BL85
Shoreham Rd W, Lon.Hthrw Air. TW6 174 BL85
Shoreham Village Sch, Shore. TN14 off Church St 225 FF111
Shoreham Way, Brom. BR2 204 EG100
Shore Pl, E9 278 G7
Shore Pt, Buck.H. IG9 102 EH47
Shore Rd, E9 278 G7
Shores Rd, Wok. GU21 210 AY114
Shore Way, SW9 310 F8
Shorncliffe Rd, SE1 300 A10
Shorndean St, SE6 183 EC88
Shorne Cl, Orp. BR5 206 EX98
Sidcup DA15 186 EV86
Shornefield Cl, Brom. BR1 205 EN97
Shornells Way, SE2 off Willrose Cres 166 EW78
Shorrolds Rd, SW6 307 H4
Shortacres, Red. RH1 251 DM133
Shortcroft Rd, Epsom KT17 217 CT108
Shortcrofts Rd, Dag. RM9 146 EZ65
Shorter Av, Shenf. CM15 109 FZ44
Shorter St, E1 288 A10
Shortfern, Slou. SL2 132 AW72
Shortgate, N12 97 CZ49
Short Hedges, Houns. TW3, TW5 156 CB81
Short Hill, Har. HA1 off High St 117 CE60
SHORTLANDS, Brom. BR1 204 EE97
⇌ Shortlands 204 EE96
Shortlands, W6 294 C9
Harlington UB3 155 BR79
Shortlands Cl, N18 100 DR48
Belvedere DA17 166 EZ76
Shortlands Gdns, Brom. BR2 204 EE96
Shortlands Grn, Welw.G.C. AL7 29 CZ10
Shortlands Gro, Brom. BR2 203 ED97
Shortlands Rd, E10 123 EB59
Bromley BR2 203 ED97
Kingston upon Thames KT2 178 CM94
Short La, Brick.Wd AL2 60 BZ30
Oxted RH8 254 EH132
Staines-upon-Thames TW19 174 BM88
Shortmead Dr, Chsht EN8 67 DY31
Short Path, SE18 off Long Wk 165 EP79
Short Rd, E11 124 EE61
W4 158 CS79
London Heathrow Airport TW6 174 BL86
Shorts Cft, NW9 118 CP56
Shorts Gdns, WC2 286 A9
Shorts Rd, Cars. SM5 218 DE105
Short St, NW4 off New Brent St 119 CW56
SE1 298 F4
Short Wall, E15 290 F2
Shortway, N12 98 DE51
Amersham HP6 55 AR37
Chesham HP5 54 AP29
Short Way, SE9 164 EL83
Twickenham TW2 176 CC87
Shortwood Av, Stai. TW18 174 BH90
Shortwood Common, Stai. TW18 174 BH91
Shortwood Inf Sch, Stai. TW18 off Stanwell New Rd 174 BH90
Shotfield, Wall. SM6 219 DH107
Shothanger Way, Bov. HP3 57 BC26
Shott Cl, Sutt. SM1 off Turnpike La 218 DC106
Shottendane Rd, SW6 307 J6
Shottery Cl, SE9 184 EL90
Shottfield Av, SW14 158 CS84
Shoulder of Mutton All, E14 289 M10
Shouldham St, W1 284 D7
Showers Way, Hayes UB3 135 BU74
Shrapnel Cl, SE18 164 EL80
Shrapnel Rd, SE9 165 EM83
SHREDING GREEN, Iver SL0 133 BB72
Shrewsbury Av, SW14 158 CQ84
Harrow HA3 118 CL56
Shrewsbury Cl, Surb. KT6 198 CL103
Shrewsbury Ct, EC1 off Whitecross St 287 K5
Shrewsbury Ho Sch, Surb. KT6 off Ditton Rd 198 CL103
Shrewsbury La, SE18 165 EP81
Shrewsbury Ms, W2 283 J7
Shrewsbury Rd, E7 124 EK64
N11 99 DJ51
NW10 off Shakespeare Rd 138 CR67
W2 283 J8
Beckenham BR3 203 DY97
Carshalton SM5 200 DE100
London Heathrow Airport TW6 175 BQ86
Redhill RH1 250 DE134
Shrewsbury St, W10 282 B5
Shrewsbury Wk, Islw. TW7 off South St 157 CG83
Shrewton Rd, SW17 180 DF94
Shrimpton Cl, Beac. HP9 89 AK49
Shrimpton Rd, Beac. HP9 89 AK49
Shroffold Rd, Brom. BR1 184 EE91
Shropshire Cl, Mitch. CR4 201 DL98
Shropshire Ho, N18 100 DV50
Shropshire Pl, WC1 285 M5
Shropshire Rd, N22 99 DM52
Shroton St, NW1 284 C6
Shrubberies, The, E18 102 EG54
Chigwell IG7 103 EQ50
Shrubbery, The, E11 124 EH57
Hemel Hempstead HP1 39 BE19
Upminster RM14 128 FQ62
Shrubbery Cl, N1 277 K9
Shrubbery Gdns, N21 99 DP45
Shrubbery Rd, N9 100 DU48
SW16 181 DL91
Gravesend DA12 191 GH88
South Darenth DA4 209 FR95
Southall UB1 136 BZ74
Shrubhill Rd, Hem.H. HP1 39 BF21
Shrubland Gro, Wor.Pk. KT4 199 CW104
Shrubland Rd, E8 278 B8
E10 123 EA59
E17 123 EA57
Banstead SM7 233 CZ116
Shrublands, Brook.Pk AL9 64 DB26
Shrublands, The, Pot.B. EN6 63 CY33
Shrublands Av, Berk. HP4 38 AU19
Croydon CR0 221 EA105
Shrublands Cl, N20 98 DD46
SE26 182 DW90
Chigwell IG7 103 EQ51
Shrublands Rd, Berk. HP4 38 AU18
Shrubsall Cl, SE9 184 EL88
Shrubs Rd, Rick. WD3 92 BM51
Shuna Wk, N1 off St. Paul's Rd 277 L4
Shurland Av, Barn. EN4 80 DD44
Shurland Gdns, SE15 312 B4
Shurlock Av, Swan. BR8 207 FD96
Shurlock Dr, Orp. BR6 223 EQ105
Shuters Sq, W14 306 G1
Shuttle Cl, Sid. DA15 185 ET87
Shuttlemead, Bex. DA5 186 EZ87
Shuttle Rd, Dart. DA1 167 FG83
Shuttle St, E1 288 C5
Shuttleworth Rd, SW11 308 B8
Siamese Ms, N3 98 DA53
Siani Ms, N8 121 DP56
Sibella Rd, SW4 309 N9
Sibford Ct, Mitch. CR4 off Lower Grn W 200 DF97
Sibley Cl, Bexh. DA6 186 EY85
Bromley BR1 204 EL99
Sibley Ct, Uxb. UB8 135 BQ71
Sibley Gro, E12 144 EL66
Sibneys Grn, Harl. CM18 51 ES19
Sibthorpe Rd, SE12 184 EH86
North Mymms AL9 45 CX24
Sibthorp Rd, Mitch. CR4 off Holborn Way 200 DF96
Sibton Rd, Cars. SM5 200 DE101
Sicilian Av, WC1 286 B7
Sicklefield Cl, Chsht EN7 66 DT26
Sidbury St, SW6 306 E6
SIDCUP, DA14 & DA15 185 ET91
⇌ Sidcup 186 EU89
Sidcup Arts & Adult Ed Cen, Sid. DA14 off Alma Rd 186 EV90
Sidcup Bypass, Chis. BR7 185 ES91
Orpington BR5 186 EX94
Sidcup DA14 185 ES91
Sidcup High St, Sid. DA14 186 EU91
Sidcup Hill, Sid. DA14 186 EV91
Sidcup Hill Gdns, Sid. DA14 off Sidcup Hill 186 EW92
Sidcup Pl, Sid. DA14 186 EU92
Sidcup Rd, SE9 184 EK87
SE12 184 EH85
● Sidcup Tech Cen, Sid. DA14 186 EX92
Siddeley Dr, Houns. TW4 156 BY83
Siddeley Rd, E17 off Fulbourne Rd 101 EC54
Siddons La, NW1 284 F5
Siddons Rd, N17 100 DU53
SE23 183 DY89
Croydon CR0 201 DN104
Side Rd, E17 123 DZ57
Denham UB9 113 BD59
Sideways La, Hkwd RH6 268 DD149
Sidewood Rd, SE9 185 ER88
Sidford Cl, Hem.H. HP1 39 BF20
Sidford Ho, SE1 off Briant Est 298 D7
Sidford Pl, SE1 298 D7
Sidi Ct, N15 121 DP55
Sidings, The, E11 123 EC60
Dunton Green TN13 241 FE120
Hatfield AL10 44 CS19
Loughton IG10 84 EL44
Staines-upon-Thames TW18 174 BH91
Sidings Apts, The, E16 305 M4
Sidings Ct, Hert. SG14 32 DQ09
Sidings Ms, N7 121 DN62
Siding Way, Lon.Col. AL2 61 CH26
SIDLOW, Reig. RH2 266 DB141
Sidmouth Av, Islw. TW7 157 CE82
Sidmouth Cl, Wat. WD19 93 BV47
Sidmouth Dr, Ruis. HA4 115 BU62
Sidmouth Par, NW2 off Sidmouth Rd 272 A7
Sidmouth Rd, E10 123 EC62
NW2 272 B6
Orpington BR5 206 EV99
Welling DA16 166 EW80
Sidmouth St, WC1 286 B3
Sidney Av, N13 99 DM50
Sidney Cl, Uxb. UB8 134 BJ66
Sidney Ct, Wal.Cr. EN8 off Queens Way 67 DZ34
Sidney Elson Way, E6 293 L1
Sidney Gdns, Brent. TW8 157 CJ79
Sidney Gro, EC1 286 G1
Sidney Rd, E7 124 EG62
N22 99 DM52
SE25 202 DU99
SW9 310 C9
Beckenham BR3 203 DY96
Harrow HA2 116 CC55
Staines-upon-Thames TW18 174 BG91
Theydon Bois CM16 85 ER36
Twickenham TW1 177 CG86
Walton-on-Thames KT12 195 BU101
Windsor SL4 150 AJ83
Sidney Sq, E1 288 G7
Sidney St, E1 288 G8
Sidney Webb Ho, SE1 299 M6
Sidworth St, E8 278 F7
Siebert Rd, SE3 315 P3
Siege Ho, E1 off Sidney St 288 F8
Siemens Brothers Way, E16 303 N1
Siemens Rd, SE18 304 F7
Sienna Cl, Chess. KT9 215 CK107
Sigdon Pas, E8 278 D3
Sigdon Rd, E8 278 D3
Sigers, The, Pnr. HA5 115 BV58
Signal Bldg, Hayes UB3 off Station Rd 155 BT76
Signal Ho, Har. HA1 off Lyon Rd 117 CF58
Signmakers Yd, NW1 275 K9
Sigrist Sq, Kings.T. KT2 198 CL95
Silbury Av, Mitch. CR4 200 DE95
Silbury Ho, SE26 off Sydenham Hill Est 182 DU90
Silbury St, N1 287 L2
Silchester Manor Sch, Tap. SL6 off Bath Rd 130 AD72
Silchester Rd, W10 282 D9
Silecroft Rd, Bexh. DA7 166 FA81
Silent Pool Junct, Guil. GU5 260 BK138
Silesia Bldgs, E8 278 F6
Silex St, SE1 299 H5
Silk Br Retail Pk, NW9 119 CT58
Silk Cl, SE12 184 EG85
Silkfield Rd, NW9 118 CS57
Silkham Rd, Oxt. RH8 253 ED127
Silkin Ms, SE15 312 D5
Silk Ms, SE11 off Kennington Rd 310 F1
Silk Mill Ct, Wat. WD19 off Silk Mill Rd 93 BV45
Silk Mill Rd, Wat. WD19 93 BV45
Silk Mills Cl, Sev. TN14 257 FJ121
Silk Mills Pas, SE13 314 D8
Silk Mills Path, SE13 314 D9
Silk Mills Sq, E9 279 P4
Silkmore La, W.Hors. KT24 244 BN125
Silkstream Rd, Edg. HA8 96 CQ53
Silk St, EC2 287 K6
Silk Weaver Way, E2 278 F10
Silo Cl, Gdmg. GU7 258 AT143
Silo Dr, Gdmg. GU7 258 AT143
Silo Rd, Gdmg. GU7 258 AT143
Silsden Cres, Ch.St.G. HP8 off London Rd 90 AX48
Silsoe Ho, NW1 off Park Village E 285 K1
Silsoe Rd, N22 99 DM54
Silverbeck Way, Stanw.M. TW19 174 BG85
Silver Birch Av, E4 101 DZ51
North Weald Bassett CM16 70 EY27
Silver Birch Cl, N11 98 DG51
SE6 183 DZ90
SE28 146 EU74
Dartford DA2 187 FE91
Uxbridge UB10 114 BL63
Woodham KT15 211 BE112
Silver Birch Ct, Chsht EN8 67 DX31
Silver Birches, Hutt. CM13 109 GA46
Silver Birch Gdns, E6 293 J5
Silver Birch Ms, Ilf. IG6 off Fencepiece Rd 103 EQ51
Upminster RM14 129 FS60
Silverbirch Wk, NW3 274 F5
Silvercliffe Gdns, Barn. EN4 80 DE42
Silver Cl, SE14 313 L4
Harrow HA3 95 CD52
Kingswood KT20 233 CY124
● Silver Ct, Welw.G.C. AL7 30 DA08
Silver Cres, W4 158 CP77
Silverdale, NW1 285 L2
SE26 182 DW91
Enfield EN2 81 DL42
Silverdale Av, Ilf. IG3 125 ES57
Oxshott KT22 214 CC114
Walton-on-Thames KT12 195 BT104
Silverdale Cl, W7 137 CE74
Brockham RH3 264 CP138
Northolt UB5 116 BZ64
Sutton SM1 217 CZ105
Silverdale Ct, Stai. TW18 off Leacroft 174 BH92
Silverdale Dr, SE9 184 EL89
Hornchurch RM12 127 FH64
Sunbury-on-Thames TW16 195 BV96
Silverdale Gdns, Hayes UB3 155 BU75
● Silverdale Ind Est, Hayes UB3 off Silverdale Rd 155 BU75
Silverdale Rd, E4 101 ED51
Bexleyheath DA7 167 FB82
Bushey WD23 76 BY43
Hayes UB3 155 BU75
Petts Wood BR5 205 EQ98
St. Paul's Cray BR5 206 EU97
Silver Dell, Wat. WD24 75 BT35
Silverfield, Brox. EN10 49 DZ22
Silvergate, Epsom KT19 216 CQ106
● Silverglade Business Pk, Chess. KT9 215 CJ112
Silverhall St, Islw. TW7 157 CG83
Silver Hill, Ch.St.G. HP8 90 AV47
Well End WD6 78 CQ36
Silverholme Cl, Har. HA3 117 CK59
Silver Jubilee Way, Houns. TW4 155 BV82
Silverlands Cl, Ott. KT16 193 BD104
Silverland St, E16 305 K3
Silver La, Pur. CR8 219 DK112
West Wickham BR4 203 ED103
Silverlea Gdns, Horl. RH6 269 DJ149
Silverleigh Rd, Th.Hth. CR7 201 DM98
Silverlocke Rd, Grays RM17 170 GD79
Silvermead, E18 off Churchfields 102 EG53
Silvermere Av, Rom. RM5 105 FB51
Silvermere Dr, N18 101 DX51
Silvermere Rd, SE6 183 EB86
Silver Pl, W1 285 M10
Watford WD18 off Metropolitan Ms 75 BS42
Silver Rd, SE13 163 EB83
W12 294 C1
Gravesend DA12 191 GL89
Silversmiths Way, Wok. GU21 226 AW118
Silver Spring Cl, Erith DA8 167 FB79
Silverstead La, West. TN16 239 ER121
Silverstone Cl, Red. RH1 off Goodwood Rd 250 DF132
Silverston Way, Stan. HA7 95 CJ51
⇌ Silver Street 100 DT50
Silver St, N18 100 DS49
Abridge RM4 86 EV41
Enfield EN1 82 DR41
Goffs Oak EN7 66 DR30
Waltham Abbey EN9 67 EC33
Silverthorn Dr, Hem.H. HP3 41 BP24
Silverthorne Rd, SW8 309 J8
Silverthorn Gdns, E4 101 EA47
Silverton Rd, W6 306 C3
SILVERTOWN, E16 304 C4
Silvertown Way, E16 291 K8
Silver Tree Cl, Walt. KT12 195 BU104
Silvertree La, Grnf. UB6 137 CD69
Silver Trees, Brick.Wd AL2 60 BZ30
Silver Wk, SE16 301 N3
Silver Way, Hlgdn UB10 135 BP68
Romford RM7 127 FB55
● Silverwing Ind Est, Croy. CR0 219 DM106
Silverwood Cl, Beck. BR3 183 EA94
Croydon CR0 221 DZ109
Northwood HA6 93 BQ53
Silverwood Cotts, Shere GU5 260 BL138
Silvester Rd, SE22 182 DT85
Silvesters, Harl. CM19 51 EM17
Silvester St, SE1 299 K5
Silvocea Way, E14 291 H9
Silwood Est, SE16 off Concorde Way 301 J9
Silwood St, SE16 301 H9
Sime Cl, Guil. GU3 242 AT130
Simla Ho, SE1 299 M5
Simmil Rd, Clay. KT10 215 CE106
Simmonds Ri, Hem.H. HP3 40 BK22
Simmons Cl, N20 98 DE46
Chessington KT9 215 CJ107
Slough SL3 off Common Rd 153 BA77
Simmons Ct, Guil. GU1 242 AW130
Simmons Dr, Dag. RM8 126 EY62
Simmons Gate, Esher KT10 214 CC106
Simmons La, E4 101 ED47
Simmons Pl, Stai. TW18 off Chertsey La 173 BE92
Simmons Rd, SE18 305 N10
Simmons Way, N20 98 DE47
Simms Cl, Cars. SM5 200 DE103
Simms Gdns, N2 98 DC54
Simms Rd, SE1 300 C9
Simnel Rd, SE12 184 EH87
Simon Balle Sch, Hert. SG13 off Mangrove Rd 32 DS10
Simon Cl, W11 283 H10
Simon Ct, N11 off Ringway 99 DJ51
Simon Dean, Bov. HP3 57 BA27
Simonds Rd, E10 123 EA61
Simone Cl, Brom. BR1 204 EK95
Simone Dr, Ken. CR8 236 DQ116
Simon Marks Jewish Prim Sch, N16 off Cazenove Rd 122 DT61
Simons Cl, Ott. KT16 211 BC107
Simons Wk, E15 281 H3
Englefield Green TW20 172 AW94
Simplemarsh Ct, Add. KT15 off Simplemarsh Rd 212 BH105
Simplemarsh Rd, Add. KT15 212 BG105
Simplicity La, Harl. CM17 36 EX14
Simpson Cl, N21 off Macleod Rd 81 DL43
Croy. CR0 202 DQ99
Simpson Dr, W3 138 CR72
Simpson Rd, Houns. TW4 176 BZ86
Rainham RM13 147 FF65
Richmond TW10 177 CJ91
Simpsons Rd, E14 302 D1
Bromley BR2 204 EG97
Simpson St, SW11 308 C8
Simpsons Way, Slou. SL1 132 AS74
Simpson Way, Long Dit. KT6 197 CJ100
Simrose Ct, SW18 off Wandsworth High St 180 DA85
Sims Cl, Rom. RM1 127 FF56
Sims Wk, SE3 164 EF84
Sinclair Ct, Beck. BR3 183 EA94
Sinclair Dr, Sutt. SM2 218 DB109
Sinclair Gdns, W14 294 D5
Sinclair Gro, NW11 119 CX58
Sinclair Pl, SE4 183 EA86
Sinclair Rd, E4 101 DZ50
W14 294 D5
Windsor SL4 151 AQ83
Sinclair Way, Lane End DA2 189 FR91
Sinclare Cl, Enf. EN1 82 DT39
Sincots Rd, Red. RH1 off Lower Br Rd 250 DF134
Sinderby Cl, Borwd. WD6 78 CL39
Singapore Rd, W13 137 CG74
Singer St, EC2 287 M3
Singlegate Prim Sch, SW19 off South Gdns 180 DD94
Singles Cross La, Knock.P. TN14 224 EW114
SINGLE STREET, West. TN16 239 EN115
Single St, Berry's Grn TN16 239 EP115
Singleton Cl, SW17 180 DF94
Croydon CR0 off St. Saviours Rd 202 DQ101
Hornchurch RM12 off Carfax Rd 127 FF63
Singleton Rd, Dag. RM9 126 EZ64
Singleton Scarp, N12 98 DA50
SINGLEWELL, Grav. DA12 191 GK93
Singlewell Prim Sch, Grav. DA12 off Mackenzie Way 191 GK93
Singlewell Rd, Grav. DA11 191 GH89
Singret Pl, Cowley UB8 134 BJ70
Sinnott Rd, E17 101 DX53
Sion-Manning RC Girls' Sch, W10 282 E7
Sion Rd, Twick. TW1 177 CH88
SIPSON, West Dr. UB7 154 BN79
Sipson Cl, Sipson UB7 154 BN79
Sipson La, Harling. UB3 154 BN79
Sipson UB7 154 BN79
Sipson Rd, West Dr. UB7 154 BN78
Sipson Way, Sipson UB7 154 BN80
Sir Alexander Cl, W3 139 CT74
Sir Alexander Rd, W3 139 CT74
Sir Cyril Black Way, SW19 180 DA94
Sirdar Rd, N22 121 DP55
W11 294 D1
Mitcham CR4 off Grenfell Rd 180 DG93
Sirdar Strand, Grav. DA12 191 GM92
Sir Francis Drake Prim Sch, SE8 313 L1
Sir Francis Way, Brwd. CM14 108 FV47
Sir Frederic Osborn Sch, Welw.G.C. AL7 off Herns La 30 DB08
Sir George Monoux Coll, E17 off Chingford Rd 101 EB54
Sir Giles Gilbert Scott Bldg, The, SW15 179 CY86
Sir Henry Peek's Dr, Slou. SL2 131 AN65
Sirinham Pt, SW8 310 C3
Sirius Rd, Nthwd. HA6 93 BU50
Sir James Black Ho, SE5 off Coldharbour La 311 L8
Sir John Cass's Foundation & Redcoat Sch, E1 289 K7
Sir John Cass's Foundation C of E Prim Sch, EC3 288 A9
Sir John Heron Prim Sch, E12 off School Rd 125 EM63
Sir John Kirk Cl, SE5 311 J4
Sir John Lillie Prim Sch, SW6 306 F3
Sir John Lyon Ho, EC4 off Gardners La 287 J10
Sir John Newsom Way, Welw.G.C. AL7 29 CY12
★ Sir John Soane's Mus, WC2 off Lincoln's Inn Flds 286 C8
Sir Martin Bowles Ho, SE18 off Calderwood St 305 M8
Sir Robert Ms, Slou. SL3 off Cheviot Rd 153 BA78
Sir Steve Redgrave Br, E16 305 N1
Sir Thomas Abney Sch, N16 off Fairholt Rd 122 DR60
Sir Thomas More Est, SW3 308 B3
Sir William Burrough Prim Sch, E14 289 M8
Sir William Perkin's Sch, Cher. KT16 off Guildford Rd 193 BF102
Sise La, EC4 287 L9
Siskin Cl, Borwd. WD6 78 CN42
Bushey WD23 76 BY42
Sisley Rd, Bark. IG11 145 ES67
Sispara Gdns, SW18 179 CZ86
Sissinghurst Cl, Brom. BR1 184 EE92
Sissinghurst Rd, Croy. CR0 202 DU101
Sissulu Ct, E6 144 EJ67
Sister Mabel's Way, SE15 312 C4
Sisters Av, SW11 160 DF84
Sistova Rd, SW12 181 DH88
Sisulu Pl, SW9 161 DN83
Sittingbourne Av, Enf. EN1 82 DR44
Sitwell Gro, Stan. HA7 95 CF50
Siverst Cl, Nthlt. UB5 136 CB65
Sivill Ho, E2 288 B2
Siviter Way, Dag. RM10 147 FB66
Siward Rd, N17 100 DR53
SW17 180 DC90
Bromley BR2 204 EH97
Six Acres, Hem.H. HP3 40 BN23
Six Acres Est, N4 121 DN61
Six Bells La, Sev. TN13 257 FJ126
● Six Bridges Trd Est, SE1 312 D1
Sixpenny Ct, Bark. IG11 145 EQ65
Sixth Av, E12 125 EM63
W10 282 E3
Hayes UB3 135 BT74
Watford WD25 76 BX35
Sixth Cross Rd, Twick. TW2 176 CC90
Skardu Rd, NW2 272 E2
Skarnings Ct, Wal.Abb. EN9 68 EG33
Skeena Hill, SW18 179 CY87
Skeet Hill La, Orp. BR5, BR6 206 EY103
Skeffington Rd, E6 144 EL67
Skeffington St, SE18 165 EQ76
Skelbrook St, SW18 180 DB89
Skelgill Rd, SW15 159 CZ84
Skelley Rd, E15 281 L7
Skelton Cl, E8 278 B5
Beaconsfield HP9 110 AG55
Skelton Rd, E7 281 P5
Skeltons La, E10 123 EB59
Skelwith Rd, W6 306 B3
Skenfrith Ho, SE15 312 E3
Skerne Rd, Kings.T. KT2 197 CK95
Skerne Wk, Kings.T. KT2 197 CK95
Sketchley Gdns, SE16 301 J10
Sketty Rd, Enf. EN1 82 DS41
Skibbs La, Orp. BR5, BR6 206 EZ103
Skid Hill La, Warl. CR6 222 EF113
Skidmore Way, Rick. WD3 92 BL46
Skiers St, E15 281 J9
Skiffington Cl, SW2 181 DN88
Skillet Hill, Wal.Abb. EN9 84 EH35
Skimpans Cl, N.Mymms AL9 45 CX24
Skinner Pl, SW1 296 G9
★ Skinners' Hall, EC4 off Dowgate Hill 287 L10
Skinners La, EC4 287 K10
Ashtead KT21 231 CK118
Hounslow TW5 156 CB81
Skinner St, EC1 286 F3
Skinney La, Hort.Kir. DA4 208 FQ97
Skip La, Hare. UB9 114 BL60
Skippers Cl, Green. DA9 189 FV85
Skipsea Ho, SW18 180 DD86
Skipsey Av, E6 293 K3
Skipton Cl, N11 98 DG51
Skipton Dr, Hayes UB3 155 BQ76
Skipton Way, Horl. RH6 269 DH145
Skipworth Rd, E9 279 H8
Skomer Wk, N1 off Ashby Gro 277 K6
Sky Apts, E9 123 DZ64
● Sky Business Pk, Egh. TW20 off Eversley Way 193 BC96
Skydmore Path, Slou. SL2 off Umberville Way 131 AM69
Skylark Av, Green. DA9 189 FU86
Skylark Rd, Denh. UB9 113 BC60
Skylines Village, E14 302 E5
Sky Peals Rd, Wdf.Grn. IG8 101 ED53
Skyport Dr, Harm. UB7 154 BK80
Skyswood Prim Sch, St.Alb. AL4 off Chandlers Rd 43 CJ16
Skys Wd Rd, St.Alb. AL4 43 CH16
Skyvan Cl, Lon.Hthrw Air. TW6 175 BQ85
● Skyway 14, Colnbr. SL3 153 BF83
Slacksbury Hatch, Harl. CM19 off Helions Rd 51 EP15
Slade, The, SE18 165 ES79
Sladebrook Rd, SE3 164 EK83
Slade Ct, Ott. KT16 211 BD107
Radlett WD7 77 CG35
Sladedale Rd, SE18 165 ES78
Slade End, They.B. CM16 85 ES36
Slade Gdns, Erith DA8 167 FF81
⇌ Slade Green 167 FG81
Slade Grn Prim Sch, Erith DA8 off Slade Grn Rd 167 FG80
Slade Grn Rd, Erith DA8 167 FG80
Slade Ho, Houns. TW4 176 BZ86
Slade Oak La, Denh. UB9 113 BD59
Gerrards Cross SL9 113 BB55
Slade Rd, Ott. KT16 211 BD107
Slades Cl, Enf. EN2 81 DN41
Slades Dr, Chis. BR7 185 EQ90
Slades Gdns, Enf. EN2 81 DN40
Slades Hill, Enf. EN2 81 DN41
Slades Ri, Enf. EN2 81 DN41
Slade Twr, E10 123 EA61
Slade Wk, SE17 311 H3
Slade Way, Mitch. CR4 200 DG95
Slagrove Pl, SE13 183 EA85
Slaidburn St, SW10 307 P3
Slaithwaite Rd, SE13 163 EC84
Slaney Pl, N7 276 E2
Slaney Rd, Rom. RM1 127 FE57
Slapleys, Wok. GU22 226 AX120
Slater Cl, SE18 305 M9
Slattery Rd, Felt. TW13 176 BW88
Sleaford Grn, Wat. WD19 94 BX48
Sleaford Ho, E3 290 B5
Sleaford St, SW8 309 L4
Sleapcross Gdns, Smallford AL4 44 CP21
SLEAPSHYDE, St.Alb. AL4 44 CP21
Sleapshyde La, Smallford AL4 44 CP21
Sleddale, Hem.H. HP2 40 BL17
Sledmere Ct, Felt. TW14 off Kilross Rd 175 BS88
Sleepers Fm Rd, Grays RM16 171 GH75
Sleets End, Hem.H. HP1 40 BH18
Slewins Cl, Horn. RM11 128 FJ57
Slewins La, Horn. RM11 128 FJ57

Slievemore Cl, SW4
off Voltaire Rd 161 DK83
Slimmons Dr, St.Alb. AL4 43 CG16
Slines Oak Rd, Warl. CR6 237 EA119
Woldingham CR3 237 EA123
Slingsby Pl, WC2 286 A10
Slip, The, West. TN16 255 EQ126
Slipe La, Brox. EN10 49 DZ24
Slippers Hill, Hem.H. HP2 40 BK19
Slippers Pl, SE16 300 F6
Slippers Pl Est, SE16 300 F7
Slipshatch Rd, Reig. RH2 265 CX138
Slipshoe St, Reig. RH2
off West St 250 DA134
Sloane Av, SW3 296 D9
Sloane Ct E, SW3 296 G10
Sloane Ct W, SW3 296 G10
Sloane Gdns, SW1 296 G9
Orpington BR6 205 EQ104
Sloane Hosp, The,
Beck. BR3 203 ED95
Sloane Ms, N8 121 DL57
Sloane Square 296 G9
Sloane Sq, SW1 296 G9
Sloane St, SW1 296 F6
Sloane Ter, SW1 296 F8
Sloane Wk, Croy. CR0 203 DZ100
Sloansway, Welw.G.C. AL7 29 CZ06
Slocock Hill, Wok. GU21 226 AW117
Slocum Cl, SE28 146 EW73
SLOUGH, SL1 - SL3 132 AS74
Slough 132 AT74
Slough & Eton C of E Sch,
Slou. SL1 off Ragstone Rd 151 AR76
Slough Business Pk,
Slou. SL1 131 AQ73
Slough Gram Sch,
Slou. SL3 off Lascelles Rd 152 AV76
Slough Interchange,
Slou. SL2 132 AU74
Slough Islamic Sch,
Slou. SL2 off Wexham Rd 132 AV73
Slough La, NW9 118 CQ58
Buckland RH3 249 CU133
Epping CM16 53 FD24
Headley KT18 248 CQ125
Slough Mus, Slou. SL1 152 AU75
Slough Retail Pk, Slou. SL1 131 AP74
Slough Rd, Datchet SL3 152 AU78
Eton SL4 151 AR78
Iver SL0 133 BE68
Slough Trd Est, Slou. SL1 131 AN72
Slowmans Cl, Park St AL2 60 CC28
Slyfield Ct, Guil. GU1
off Slyfield Grn 242 AY131
Slyfield Grn, Guil. GU1 242 AX130
Slyfield Ind Est, Guil. GU1 242 AY130
Sly St, E1 288 E9
Smaldon Cl, West Dr. UB7
off Walnut Av 154 BN76
Small Acre, Hem.H. HP1 39 BF20
Smallberry Av, Islw. TW7 157 CF82
Smallberry Grn Prim Sch,
Islw. TW7 off Turnpike Way 157 CG81
Smallbrook Ms, W2 284 A9
Smallcroft, Welw.G.C. AL7 30 DB08
Smalley Cl, N16 122 DT62
Smalley Rd Est, N16
off Smalley Cl 122 DT61
SMALLFIELD, Horl. RH6 269 DP149
Smallfield Rd, Horl. RH6 269 DH148
SMALLFORD, St.Alb. AL4 44 CP19
Smallford La, Smallford AL4 44 CP21
Small Grains, Fawk.Grn DA3 209 FV104
Smallholdings Rd,
Epsom KT17 217 CW114
Smallmead, Horl. RH6 269 DH148
Small's Hill Rd, Leigh RH2 265 CU141
Smallwood Cl, Wheat. AL4 28 CL08
Smallwood Prim Sch, SW17
off Smallwood Rd 180 DD91
Smallwood Rd, SW17 180 DD91
Smardale Rd, SW18
off Alma Rd 180 DC85
Smarden Cl, Belv. DA17
off Essenden Rd 166 FA78
Smarden Gro, SE9 185 EM91
Smart Cl, Rom. RM3 105 FH53
Smarts Grn, Chsht EN7 66 DT27
Smarts Heath La, Wok. GU22 226 AU123
Smarts Heath Rd, Wok. GU22 226 AT123
Smarts La, Loug. IG10 84 EK42
Smarts Pl, N18 100 DU50
Smart's Pl, WC2 286 B8
Smarts Rd, Grav. DA12 191 GH89
Smart St, E2 289 J2
Smead Way, SE13 163 EB83
Smeaton Cl, Chess. KT9 215 CK107
Waltham Abbey EN9 68 EE32
Smeaton Ct, SE1 299 J7
Smeaton Dr, Wok. GU22 227 BB120
Smeaton Rd, SW18 180 DA87
Enfield EN3 83 EA37
Woodford Green IG8 103 EM50
Smeaton St, E1 300 E2
Smedley St, SW4 309 P8
SW8 309 P8
Smeed Rd, E3 280 A7
Smiles Pl, SE13 314 E8
Woking GU22 227 BB116
Smitham Bottom La, Pur. CR8 219 DJ111
Smitham Downs Rd, Pur. CR8 219 DK113
Smitham Prim Sch,
Couls. CR5 off Portnalls Rd 235 DJ116
Smithbarn Cl, Horl. RH6 269 DH147
Smith Cl, SE16 301 J3
Smithers, The, Brock. RH3 264 CP136
Smithfield, Hem.H. HP2 40 BK18
Smithfield St, EC1 286 G7
Smithies Rd, SE2 166 EV77
Smith Rd, Reig. RH2 265 CZ137
Smiths Caravan Site, Thnwd CM16 70 EW25
Smith's Ct, W1 285 M10
Smiths Cres, Smallford AL4 44 CP21
Smiths Fm Est, Nthlt. UB5 136 CA68
Smiths La, Chsht EN7 66 DR26
Crockham Hill TN8 255 EQ133
Windsor SL4 151 AL82
Smithson Rd, N17 100 DR53
Smiths Pt, E13 281 N9
Smith Sq, SW1 298 A7
Smith St, SW3 296 E10
Surbiton KT5 198 CM100
Watford WD18 76 BW42
Smiths Yd, SW18
off Summerley St 180 DC89
Smith's Yd, Croy. CR0
off St. Georges Wk 202 DQ104
Smith Ter, SW3 308 E1

Smithwood Cl, SW19 179 CY88
Smithy Cl, Lwr Kgswd KT20 249 CZ126
Smithy La, Lwr Kgswd KT20 249 CZ127
Smithy St, E1 288 G6
Smithy St Prim Sch, E1 289 H6
Smock Wk, Croy. CR0 202 DQ100
Smokehouse Yd, EC1 287 H6
Smoke La, Reig. RH2 266 DB136
SMOKY HOLE, Guil. GU5 261 BR144
Smoothfield Ct, Houns. TW3
off Hibernia Rd 156 CA84
Smugglers Wk, Green. DA9 189 FV85
Smugglers Way, SW18 160 DB84
Smug Oak Grn Business Cen,
Brick.Wd AL2 60 CA29
Smug Oak La, St.Alb. AL2 60 CB30
Smyrks Rd, SE17 311 P1
Smyrna Rd, NW6 273 J7
Smythe Cl, N9 100 DU48
Smythe Rd, Sutt.H. DA4 208 FN95
Smythe St, E14 290 D10
Snag La, Cudham TN14 223 ES109
Snakeley Cl, Loud. HP10 88 AC54
Snakes La, Barn. EN4 81 DH41
Snakes La E, Wdf.Grn. IG8 102 EJ51
Snakes La W, Wdf.Grn. IG8 102 EG51
Snakey La, Felt. TW13 175 BU91
Snape Spur, Slou. SL1 132 AS72
SNARESBROOK, E11 124 EE57
Snaresbrook 124 EG57
Snaresbrook Coll, E18
off Woodford Rd 124 EG55
Snaresbrook Dr, Stan. HA7 95 CK49
Snaresbrook Prim Sch, E18
off Meadow Wk 124 EG56
Snaresbrook Rd, E11 124 EE56
Snarsgate St, W10 282 A7
Snatts Hill, Oxt. RH8 254 EF129
Sneath Av, NW11 119 CZ59
Snelling Av, Nthflt DA11 190 GE89
Snellings Rd, Hersham KT12 214 BW106
Snells La, Amer. HP7 72 AV39
Snells Pk, N18 100 DT51
Snells Wd Ct, Amer. HP7 72 AW40
Sneyd Rd, NW2 272 A2
Sniggs La, Penn HP10
off Beacon Hill 88 AD50
Snipe Cl, Erith DA8 167 FH80
Snodland Cl, Downe BR6
off Mill La 223 EN110
Snowberry Cl, E15 281 H1
Barnet EN5 79 CZ41
Snowbury Rd, SW6 307 M9
Snowden Av, Hlgdn UB10 135 BP68
Snowden Cl, Wind. SL4 151 AK84
Snowden Hill, Nthflt DA11 190 GA85
Snowden St, EC2
off Finsbury Mkt 287 N5
Snowdon Cres, Hayes UB3 155 BQ76
Snowdon Dr, NW9 118 CS58
Snowdon Rd, Lon.Hthrw Air. TW6
off Southern Perimeter Rd 175 BQ85
Snowdown Cl, SE20 203 DX95
Snowdrop Cl, Hmptn. TW12
off Gresham Rd 176 CA93
Snowdrop Path, Rom. RM3 106 FK52
Snowerhill Rd, Bet. RH3 264 CS136
Snow Hill, EC1 286 G7
Snowhill Cotts, Chesh. HP5 38 AT24
Snow Hill Ct, EC1 287 H8
Snowman Ho, NW6 273 L8
Snowsfields, SE1 299 M4
Snowsfields Prim Sch,
SE1 299 N4
Snowshill Rd, E12 124 EL64
Snowy Fielder Waye, Islw. TW7 157 CH82
Soames Pl, Barn. EN4 80 DB40
Soames St, SE15 162 DT83
Soames Wk, N.Mal. KT3 198 CS95
Soane Cl, W5 157 CK75
Soap Ho La, Brent. TW8
off Ferry La 158 CL79
Socket La, Brom. BR2 204 EH100
SOCKETT'S HEATH,
Grays RM16 170 GD76
Soham Rd, Enf. EN3 83 DZ37
SOHO, W1 285 N10
Soho Cres, Woob.Grn HP10 110 AD59
Soho Mills Ind Est,
Woob.Grn HP10 110 AD59
Soho Parish Sch, W1 285 N10
Soho Sq, W1 285 N8
Soho St, W1 285 N8
Sojourner Truth Cl, E8 278 F5
Solander Gdns, E1 288 G10
Solar Way, Enf. EN3 83 DZ36
Soldene Ct, N7 276 C4
Solebay St, E1 289 L5
Solecote, Bkhm KT23 246 CA125
Sole Fm Av, Bkhm KT23 246 BZ125
Sole Fm Cl, Bkhm KT23 230 BZ124
Sole Fm Rd, Bkhm KT23 246 BZ125
Solefield Sch, Sev. TN13
off Solefields Rd 257 FJ126
Solefields Rd, Sev. TN13 257 FH128
Solent Ri, E13 291 N3
Solent Rd, NW6 273 J3
Soleoak Dr, Sev. TN13 257 FH127
Solesbridge Cl, Chorl. WD3 73 BF41
Solesbridge La, Rick. WD3 74 BG40
Soley Ms, WC1 286 E2
Solna Av, SW15 179 CW85
Solna Rd, N21 100 DR46
Solomon Av, N9 100 DU49
Solomons Ct, N12
off High Rd 98 DC52
Solomons Hill, Rick. WD3
off Northway 92 BK45
Solomon's Pas, SE15 162 DV84
Solom's Ct Rd, Bans. SM7 234 DD117
Solon New Rd, SW4 161 DL84
Solon Rd, SW2 161 DL84
Solway, Hem.H. HP2 40 BM18
Solway Cl, E8 278 B5
Hounslow TW4 156 BY83
Solway Rd, N22 99 DP53
SE22 162 DU84
Somaford Gro, Barn. EN4 80 DD44
Somali Rd, NW2 272 G1
Somborne Ho, SW15
off Fontley Way 179 CU87
Somerby Cl, Brox. EN10 49 EA21
Somerby Rd, Bark. IG11 145 ER66
Somercoates Cl, Barn. EN4 80 DE41
Somerden Rd, Orp. BR5 206 EX101
Somerfield Cl, Tad. KT20 233 CY119
Somerfield Rd, N4 121 DP61
Somerfield St, SE16 301 J10
Somerford Cl, Eastcote HA5 115 BU56

Somerford Gro, N16 278 A1
N17 100 DU52
Somerford Gro Est, N16 278 A1
Somerford Pl, Beac. HP9 89 AK52
Somerford St, E1 288 E5
Somerford Way, SE16 301 L5
Somerhill Av, Sid. DA15 186 EV87
Somerhill Rd, Well. DA16 166 EV82
Someries Rd, Hem.H. HP1 39 BF18
Somerleyton Pas, SW9 161 DP84
Somerleyton Rd, SW9 161 DN84
Somersby Gdns, Ilf. IG4 125 EM57
Somers Cl, NW1 275 N10
Reigate RH2 250 DA133
Somers Cres, W2 284 C9
Somerset Av, SW20 199 CV96
Chessington KT9 215 CK105
Welling DA16 185 ET85
Somerset Cl, N17 100 DR54
Epsom KT19 216 CS109
Hersham KT12
off Queens Rd 213 BV106
New Malden KT3 198 CS100
Sutt. SM3 199 CW104
Woodford Green IG8 102 EG53
Somerset Est, SW11 308 B6
Somerset Gdns, N6 120 DG59
N17 100 DS52
SE13 314 C9
SW16 201 DM97
Hornchurch RM11 128 FN60
Teddington TW11 177 CE92
Wem. HA0 117 CJ64
Somerset Hall, N17 100 DS52
Somerset Ho, WC2 286 C10
Somerset Ho, SW19 179 CX90
Somerset Rd, E17 123 EA57
N17 122 DT55
N18 100 DT50
NW4 119 CW56
SW19 179 CY91
W4 158 CR76
W13 137 CH74
Brentford TW8 157 CJ79
Dartford DA1 187 FH86
Enfield EN3 83 EA38
Harrow HA1 116 CC58
Kingston upon Thames KT1 198 CM96
New Barnet EN5 80 DB43
Orpington BR6 206 EU101
Redhill RH1 266 DD136
Southall UB1 136 BZ71
Teddington TW11 177 CE92
Somerset Sq, W14 294 F5
Somerset Way, Iver SL0 153 BF75
Somerset Waye, Houns. TW5 156 BY79
Somersham, Welw.G.C. AL7 30 DD09
Somersham Rd, Bexh. DA7 166 EY82
Somers Heath Prim Sch,
S.Ock. RM15 off Foyle Dr 149 FU73
Somers Ms, W2 284 C9
Somers Pl, SW2 181 DM87
Reigate RH2 250 DA133
Somers Rd, E17 123 DZ56
SW2 181 DM86
North Mymms AL9 45 CW24
Reigate RH2 249 CZ133
Somers Sq, N.Mymms AL9 45 CW23
SOMERS TOWN, NW1 285 P2
Somers Way, Bushey WD23 94 CC45
Somerswey, Shalf. GU4 258 AY142
Somerton Av, Rich. TW9 158 CP83
Somerton Cl, Pur. CR8 235 DN115
Somerton Rd, NW2 119 CY62
SE15 162 DV84
Somertons Cl, Guil. GU2 242 AU131
Somertrees Av, SE12 184 EH89
Somervell Rd, Har. HA2 116 BZ64
Somerville Av, SW13 159 CV79
Somerville Cl, SW9 310 D8
Somerville Rd, SE20 183 DX94
Cobham KT11 214 CA114
Dartford DA1 188 FM86
Eton SL4 151 AQ78
Romford RM6 126 EW58
Sommer's Ct, Ware SG12
off Crane Mead 33 DY07
Sommerville Ct, Borwd. WD6
off Alconbury Cl 78 CM39
Sonderburg Rd, N7 121 DM61
Sondes Fm, Dor. RH4 263 CF136
Sondes Pl Dr, Dor. RH4 263 CF136
Sondes St, SE17 311 L2
Songhurst Cl, Croy. CR0 201 DM100
Sonia Cl, Wat. WD19 94 BW45
Sonia Ct, Har. HA1 117 CF58
Sonia Gdns, N12 98 DC49
NW10 119 CT63
Hounslow TW5 156 CA80
Sonic Ct, Guil. GU1 242 AW133
Sonnets, The, Hem.H. HP1 40 BH19
Sonning Gdns, Hmptn. TW12 176 BY93
Sonning Rd, SE25 202 DU100
Soothouse Spring, St.Alb. AL3 43 CF16
Soper Cl, E4 101 DZ50
SE23 183 DX88
Soper Dr, Cat. CR3 236 DR123
Soper Ms, Enf. EN3
off Harston Dr 83 EA38
Soper Sq, Harl. CM17
off Square St 36 EW14
Sopers Rd, Cuffley EN6 65 DM29
Sophia Cl, N7 276 C4
Sophia Rd, E10 123 EB60
E16 292 A8
Sophia Sq, SE16 301 L1
Sophie Gdns, Slou. SL3 152 AX75
Soprano Ct, E15
off Plaistow Rd 281 L9
Soprano Way, Esher KT10 197 CH104
Sopwell La, St.Alb. AL1 43 CD21
Sopwith Av, Chess. KT9 216 CL106
Sopwith Cl, Bigg.H. TN16 238 EK116
Kingston upon Thames KT2 178 CM92
Sopwith Dr, W.Byf. KT14 212 BL111
Weybridge KT13 212 BL111
Sopwith Rd, Houns. TW5 156 BW80
Sopwith Way, SW8 309 J4
Kingston upon Thames KT2 198 CL95
Sorbie Cl, Wey. KT13 213 BR107
Sorbus Rd, Brox. EN10 67 DZ25
Sorrel Bk, Croy. CR0 221 DY110
Sorrel Cl, SE28 146 EU74
Sorrel Ct, Grays RM17
off Salix Rd 170 GD79
Sorrel Gdns, E6 292 G6
Sorrel La, E14 291 H9
Sorrell Cl, SE14 313 L4
SW9 310 F8

Sorrel Wk, Rom. RM1 127 FF55
Sorrel Way, Nthflt DA11 190 GE91
Sorrento Rd, Sutt. SM1 200 DB104
Sospel Ct, Farn.Royal SL2 131 AQ68
Sotheby Rd, N5 121 DP62
Sotheran Cl, E8 278 D8
Sotheron Rd, SW6 307 M5
Watford WD17 76 BW40
Soudan Rd, SW11 308 E7
Souldern Rd, W14 294 D7
Souldern St, Wat. WD18 75 BU43
Sounds Lo, Swan. BR8 207 FC100
South Access Rd, E17 123 DY59
Southacre Way, Pnr. HA5 94 BW53
SOUTH ACTON, W3 158 CN76
South Acton 158 CQ76
South Acton Est, W3 158 CP75
South Africa Rd, W12 139 CV74
South Albert Rd, Reig. RH2 249 CZ133
SOUTHALL, UB1 & UB2 136 BX74
Southall 156 BZ75
Southall & W London Coll,
Sthl. UB1 off Beaconsfield Rd 136 BY74
Southall Cl, Ware SG12 33 DX05
Southall Enterprise Centre,
Sthl. UB2 off Bridge Rd 156 CA75
Southall La, Houns. TW5 155 BV79
Southall UB2 155 BV79
Southall Pl, SE1 299 L5
Southall Way, Brwd. CM14 108 FT49
Southam Ms, Crox.Grn. WD3 75 BP44
Southampton Bldgs, WC2 286 E8
Southampton Gdns,
Mitch. CR4 201 DL99
Southampton Ms, E16 304 A2
Southampton Pl, WC1 286 B7
Southampton Rd, NW5 274 F3
Southampton Rd E,
Lon.Hthrw Air. TW6 174 BN86
Southampton Rd W,
Lon.Hthrw Air. TW6 174 BL86
Southampton Row, WC1 286 B6
Southampton St, WC2 286 B10
Southampton Way, SE5 311 M4
Southam St, W10 282 F5
South App, Nthwd. HA6 93 BR48
South Audley St, W1 297 H1
South Av, E4 101 EB45
Carshalton SM5 218 DG108
Egham TW20 173 BC93
Richmond TW9
off Sandycombe Rd 158 CN82
Southall UB1 136 BZ73
Whiteley Village KT12 213 BS110
South Av Gdns, Sthl. UB1 136 BZ73
South Bk, Chis. BR7 185 EQ90
Surbiton KT6 198 CL100
Westerham TN16 255 ER126
Southbank, Hext. BR8 187 FF94
Thames Ditton KT7 197 CH101
Southbank Business Cen,
SW8 309 P3
Southbank Int Sch -
Hampstead Campus, NW3 273 P4
Southbank Int Sch -
Kensington Campus, W11 295 J1
Southbank Int Sch - Westminster
Campus, Conway St, W1 285 L5
Portland Pl, W1 285 J6
South Bk Rd, Berk. HP4 38 AT17
South Bk Ter, Surb. KT6 198 CL100
South Bank Twr, SE1 298 F2
SOUTH BEDDINGTON,
Wall. SM6 219 DK107
South Bermondsey 300 G10
South Birkbeck Rd, E11 123 ED62
South Black Lion La, W6 159 CU78
South Bolton Gdns, SW5 295 M10
South Bookham Sch,
Bkhm KT23 off Oakdene Cl 246 CC127
South Border, The, Pur. CR8 219 DK111
SOUTHBOROUGH, Brom. BR2 205 EM100
Southborough Cl, Surb. KT6 197 CK102
Southborough La, Brom. BR2 204 EL99
Southborough Prim Sch,
Brom. BR2
off Southborough La 205 EN99
Southborough Rd, E9 279 J8
Bromley BR1 204 EL97
Surbiton KT6 198 CL102
Southborough Sch,
Surb. KT6 off Hook Rd 198 CL104
Southbourne, Brom. BR2 204 EG101
Southbourne Av, NW9 96 CQ54
Southbourne Cl, Pnr. HA5 116 BY59
Southbourne Cres, NW4 119 CY56
Southbourne Gdns, SE12 184 EH85
Ilford IG1 125 EQ64
Ruislip HA4 115 BV60
Southbridge Pl, Croy. CR0 220 DQ105
Southbridge Rd, Croy. CR0 220 DQ105
Southbridge Way, Sthl. UB2 156 BY75
Southbrook, Saw. CM21 36 EY06
Southbrook Dr, Chsht EN8 67 DX28
Southbrook Ms, SE12 184 EF86
Southbrook Rd, SE12 184 EF86
SW16 201 DL95
Southbury 82 DV42
Southbury Av, Enf. EN1 82 DU43
Southbury Cl, Horn. RM12 128 FK64
Southbury Prim Sch, Enf. EN3
off Swansea Rd 82 DW42
Southbury Rd, Enf. EN1, EN3 82 DR41
South Camden City Learning Cen,
NW1 275 N10
South Camden
Comm Sch, NW1 275 N10
South Carriage Dr, SW1 296 E4
SW7 296 B5
SOUTH CHINGFORD, E4 101 DZ50
Southchurch Rd, E6 293 J1
South Circular Rd, SE6 (A205) 183 ED87
SE9 (A205) 165 EM83
SE12 (A205) 184 EH86
SE18 (A205) 165 EN79
SE21 (A205) 182 DS88
SE22 (A205) 182 DV88
SE23 (A205) 183 DZ88
SW2 (A205) 181 DN88
SW4 (A205) 180 DG85
SW11 (A3) 180 DE85
SW12 (A205) 181 DN88
SW14 (A205) 158 CS84
SW15 (A205) 159 CW84
SW18 (A3) 180 DE85
W4 (A205) 158 CN78
Brentford (A205) TW8 158 CN78
Richmond (A205) TW9 158 CP82
South City Ct, SE15 311 P4

Southcliffe Dr, Chal.St.P. SL9 90 AY50
South Cl, N6 121 DH58
Barnet EN5 79 CZ41
Bexleyheath DA6 166 EX84
Dagenham RM10 146 FA67
Morden SM4 200 DA100
Pinner HA5 116 BZ59
St. Albans AL2 60 CB25
Slough SL1
off St. George's Cres 131 AK73
Twickenham TW2 176 CA90
West Drayton UB7 154 BM76
Woking GU21 226 AW116
South Cl Grn, Merst. RH1 251 DH129
South Colonnade, The, E14 302 B2
Southcombe St, W14 294 E8
South Common Rd, Uxb. UB8 134 BL65
Southcote, Wok. GU21 226 AX115
Southcote Av, Felt. TW13 175 BT89
Surbiton KT5 198 CP101
Southcote Ri, Ruis. HA4 115 BR59
Southcote Rd, E17 123 DX57
N19 121 DJ63
SE25 202 DV100
South Croydon CR2 220 DS110
South Merstham RH1 251 DJ129
South Cottage Dr, Chorl. WD3 73 BF43
South Cottage Gdns,
Chorl. WD3 73 BF43
Southcott Ms, NW8 284 C1
Southcott Rd, Tedd. TW11 197 CJ95
South Countess Rd, E17 123 DZ55
South Cres, E16 290 G5
WC1 285 N7
South Cft, Eng.Grn TW20 172 AV92
Southcroft, Slou. SL2 131 AP70
Southcroft Av, Well. DA16 165 ES83
West Wickham BR4 203 EC103
Southcroft Rd, SW16 180 DG93
SW17 180 DG93
Orpington BR6 205 ES104
South Cross Rd, Ilf. IG6 125 EQ57
South Croxted Rd, SE21 182 DR90
SOUTH CROYDON, CR2 220 DQ107
South Croydon 220 DR106
Southdale, Chig. IG7 103 ER51
SOUTH DARENTH, Dart. DA4 209 FR95
Southdean Gdns, SW19 179 CZ89
South Dene, NW7 96 CR48
Southdene, Halst. TN14 224 EY113
Southdown Av, W7 157 CG76
Southdown Ct, Hat. AL10 45 CV21
Southdown Cres, Har. HA2 116 CB60
Ilford IG2 125 ES57
Southdown Dr, SW20 179 CX94
Southdown Rd, SW20 199 CX95
Carshalton SM5 218 DG109
Hatfield AL10 45 CU21
Hersham KT12 214 BY105
Hornchurch RM11 127 FH59
Woldingham CR3 237 DZ122
Southdowns, S.Darenth DA4 209 FR96
South Dr, Bans. SM7 218 DE113
Beaconsfield HP9 110 AH55
Coulsdon CR5 235 DK115
Cuffley EN6 65 DL30
Dorking RH5 263 CJ136
Orpington BR6 223 ES106
Romford RM2 128 FJ55
Ruislip HA4 115 BS60
St. Albans AL4 43 CK20
Sutton SM2 217 CY110
Virginia Water GU25 192 AU102
Warley CM14 108 FX49
South Ealing 157 CJ76
South Ealing Rd, W5 157 CK75
South Eastern Av, N9 100 DT48
South Eaton Pl, SW1 297 H8
South Eden Pk Rd, Beck. BR3 203 EB100
South Edwardes Sq, W8 295 H7
SOUTHEND, SE6 183 EB91
South End, W8 295 M6
Bookham KT23 246 CB126
Croydon CR0 220 DQ105
Southend Arterial Rd,
Brwd. CM13 129 FV57
Hornchurch RM11 106 FK54
Romford RM2, RM3 106 FK54
Upminster RM14 129 FR57
South End Cl, NW3 274 D1
Southend Cl, SE9 185 EP86
Southend Cres, SE9 185 EN86
South End Grn, NW3 274 D1
Southend La, SE6 183 DZ91
SE26 183 DZ91
Waltham Abbey EN9 68 EH34
Southend Rd, E4 101 DY50
E6 145 EM66
E17 101 EB53
E18 102 EG53
Beckenham BR3 183 EA94
Grays RM17 170 GC77
Woodford Green IG8 102 EJ54
South End Rd, NW3 274 C1
Hornchurch RM12 147 FH65
Rainham RM13 147 FG67
South End Row, W8 295 M6
Southerland Cl, Wey. KT13 213 BQ105
Southern Av, SE25 202 DT97
Feltham TW14 175 BU88
Redhill RH1 266 DG141
Southern Dr, Loug. IG10 85 EM44
Southerngate Way, SE14 313 L4
Southern Gro, E3 289 N4
Southernhay, Loug. IG10 84 EK43
Southern Lo, Harl. CM19 51 EQ18
Southern Perimeter Rd,
Lon.Hthrw Air. TW6 175 BR85
Southern Pl, Har. HA1 117 CF63
Swanley BR8 207 FD98
Southern Rd, E13 292 B1
N2 120 DF56
Southern Rd Prim Sch,
E13 off Southern Rd 144 EH68
Southern Row, W10 282 E5
Southerns La, Chipstead CR5 250 DC125
Southern St, N1 276 C10
Southern Way, SE10 303 M8
Harlow CM17, CM18 51 ER18
Romford RM7 126 FA58
Southernwood Cl, Hem.H. HP2 40 BN19
Southerton Rd, W6 294 A7
Southerton Way, Shenley WD7 62 CL33
South Esk Rd, E7 144 EJ65

S

Southey Ms, E16 303 P2
Southey Rd, N15 122 DS57
SW9 310 E6
SW19 180 DA94
Southey St, SE20 183 DX94
Southey Wk, Til. RM18 171 GH81
Southfield, Barn. EN5 79 CX44
Welwyn Garden City AL7 29 CX11
Southfield Av, Wat. WD24 76 BW38
Southfield Cl, Dorney SL4 150 AJ76
Uxbridge UB8 134 BN69
Southfield Cotts, W7
off Oaklands Rd 157 CF75
Southfield Gdns, Burn. SL1 130 AH71
Twickenham TW1 177 CF91
Southfield Pk, Har. HA2 116 CB56
Sch **Southfield Pk Prim Sch**,
Epsom KT19 *off Long Gro Rd* 216 CQ111
Southfield Pl, Wey. KT13 213 BP108
Sch **Southfield Prim Sch**, W4
off Southfield Rd 158 CS75
Southfield Rd, N17
off The Avenue 100 DS54
W4 158 CS76
Chislehurst BR7 205 ET97
Enfield EN3 82 DV44
Hoddesdon EN11 49 EA15
Waltham Cross EN8 67 DY32
SOUTHFIELDS, SW18 180 DA88
⊖ **Southfields** 179 CZ88
Southfields, NW4 119 CU55
East Molesey KT8 197 CE100
Swanley BR8 187 FE94
Southfields Av, Ashf. TW15 175 BP93
Sch **Southfields Sch**, Hat. AL10
off Travellers La 45 CV21
Sch **Southfields Comm Coll**, SW18
off Merton Rd 180 DA88
Southfields Ct, SW19 179 CY88
Sutton SM1
off Sutton Common Rd 200 DA103
Southfields Grn, Grav. DA11 191 GH92
Southfields Ms, SW18
off Southfields Rd 180 DA86
Southfields Pas, SW18 180 DA86
Southfields Rd, SW18 180 DA86
Woldingham CR3 237 EB123
Southfield Way, St.Alb. AL4 43 CK18
SOUTHFLEET, Grav. DA13 190 GB93
Southfleet Rd, Bean DA2 189 FW91
Northfleet DA11 191 GF89
Orpington BR6 205 ES104
Swanscombe DA10 190 FZ87
South Gdns, SW19 180 DD94
Wembley HA9 *off The Avenue* 118 CM61
South Gate, Harl. CM20 51 ER15
SOUTHGATE, N14 99 DJ47
⊖ **Southgate** 99 DJ46
Southgate, Purf. RM19 168 FQ77
Southgate Av, Felt. TW13 175 BR91
Southgate Circ, N14
off The Bourne 99 DK46
Southgate Gro, N1 277 M7
Southgate Rd, N1 277 M8
Potters Bar EN6 64 DC33
Sch **Southgate Sch**, Cockfos. EN4
off Sussex Way 81 DH43
South Gipsy Rd, Well. DA16 166 EX83
South Glade, The, Bex. DA5 186 EZ88
South Grn, NW9
off Clayton Fld 96 CS53
Slough SL1 132 AS73
⇌ **South Greenford** 137 CE69
South Gro, E17 123 DZ57
N6 120 DG60
N15 122 DR57
Chertsey KT16 193 BF100
South Gro Ho, N6 120 DG60
Sch **South Gro Prim Sch**, E17
off Ringwood Rd 123 DZ58
SOUTH HACKNEY, E9 278 F7
South Hall Cl, Fnghm DA4 208 FM101
South Hall Dr, Rain. RM13 147 FH71
SOUTH HAMPSTEAD, NW6 273 M6
⊖ **South Hampstead** 273 P7
Sch **South Hampstead High Sch**,
NW3 273 P5
Jun Dept, NW3 273 P4
SOUTH HAREFIELD, Uxb. UB9 114 BJ56
Sch **South Harringay Inf Sch**,
N4 *off Pemberton Rd* 121 DP57
Sch **South Harringay Jun Sch**,
N4 *off Mattison Rd* 121 DP57
SOUTH HARROW, Har. HA2 116 CB62
⊖ **South Harrow** 116 CC62
SOUTH HATFIELD, Hat. AL10 45 CU20
South Hill, Chis. BR7 185 EM93
Guildford GU1 258 AX136
South Hill Av, Har. HA1, HA2 116 CC62
South Hill Gro, Har. HA1 117 CE63
South Hill Pk, NW3 274 C1
South Hill Pk Gdns, NW3 120 DE63
Sch **South Hill Prim Sch**,
Hem.H. HP1 *off Heath La* 40 BJ21
South Hill Rd, Brom. BR2 204 EE97
Gravesend DA12 191 GH88
Hemel Hempstead HP1 40 BJ20
Southholme Cl, SE19 202 DS95
SOUTH HOLMWOOD,
Dor. RH5 263 CJ144
SOUTH HORNCHURCH,
Rain. RM13 147 FE67
South Huxley, N18 100 DR50
Southill La, Pnr. HA5 115 BU56
Southill Rd, Chis. BR7 184 EL94
Southill St, E14 290 D8
South Island Pl, SW9 310 D5
SOUTH KENSINGTON, SW7 295 N9
⊖ **South Kensington** 296 B8
South Kensington Sta Arc, SW7
off Pelham St 296 B8
South Kent Av, Nthflt DA11 190 GC86
⊖ **South Kenton** 117 CJ60
⊖ **South Kenton** 117 CJ60
SOUTH LAMBETH, SW8 310 B6
South Lambeth Est, SW8
off Dorset Rd 310 C5
South Lambeth Pl, SW8 310 B2
South Lambeth Rd, SW8 310 B3
Southland Rd, SE18 165 ET80
Southlands Av, Horl. RH6 268 DF147
Orpington BR6 223 ER105
Southlands Cl, Couls. CR5 235 DM117
Southlands Dr, SW19 179 CX89
Southlands Gro, Brom. BR1 204 EL97
Southlands La, Tand. RH8 253 EB134
Southlands Rd,
Brom. BR1, BR2 204 EJ99
Denham UB9 113 BF63
Iver SL0 113 BF64
Southland Way, Houns. TW3 177 CD85
South La, Kings.T. KT1 197 CK97
New Malden KT3 198 CR98
South La W, N.Mal. KT3 198 CR98
South Lawns Apts, Wat. WD25
off Holbrook Gdns 76 CB36
SOUTHLEA, Slou. SL3 152 AV82
Southlea Rd, Datchet SL3 152 AV81
Windsor SL4 152 AU84
South Ley, Welw.G.C. AL7 29 CY12
South Ley Ct, Welw.G.C. AL7
off South Ley 29 CY12
South Lo, NW8 284 A2
SW7 *off Knightsbridge* 296 D5
South Lo Av, Mitch. CR4 201 DL98
South Lo Cres, Enf. EN2 81 DK42
South Lo Dr, N14 81 DL43
South Lo Rd, Walt. KT12 213 BU109
★ **South London Art Gall**, SE5 311 P6
South Loop Rd, Uxb. UB8 134 BK70
Southly Cl, Sutt. SM1 200 DA104
South Mall, N9
off Edmonton Grn Shop Cen 100 DU48
South Mead, NW9 97 CT53
Epsom KT19 216 CS108
Redhill RH1 250 DF131
Southmead Cres, Chsht EN8 67 DY30
Southmead Gdns, Tedd. TW11 177 CG93
South Meadow La, Eton SL4 151 AQ80
South Meadows, Wem. HA9 118 CL64
Sch **Southmead Prim Sch**, SW19
off Princes Way 179 CY88
Southmead Rd, SW19 179 CY88
Southmere Dr, SE2 166 EX75
SOUTH MERSTHAM, Red. RH1 251 DJ130
⇌ **South Merton** 199 CZ97
SOUTH MIMMS, Pot.B. EN6 63 CT32
South Molton La, W1 285 J9
South Molton Rd, E16 291 P8
South Molton St, W1 285 J9
Southmont Rd, Esher KT10 197 CE103
Southmoor Way, E9 279 P4
South Mundells,
Welw.G.C. AL7 29 CZ08
SOUTH NORWOOD, SE25 202 DT97
Coll **South Norwood CETS Cen**,
SE25 *off Sandown Rd* 202 DV99
South Norwood Hill, SE25 202 DS96
Sch **South Norwood Prim Sch**,
SE25 *off Crowther Rd* 202 DU98
SOUTH NUTFIELD, Red. RH1 267 DL136
South Oak Rd, SW16 181 DM91
SOUTH OCKENDON, RM15 149 FW70
Southold Ri, SE9 185 EM90
Southolm St, SW11 309 J7
South Ordnance Rd, Enf. EN3 83 EA37
Southover, N12 98 DA49
Bromley BR1 184 EG92
SOUTH OXHEY, Wat. WD19 94 BW48
South Par, SW3 296 B10
W4 158 CR77
Edgware HA8
off Mollison Way 96 CN54
SOUTH PARK, Reig. RH2 265 CZ138
South Pk, SW6 307 K9
Gerrards Cross SL9 113 AZ57
Sevenoaks TN13 257 FH125
South Pk Av, Chorl. WD3 73 BF43
South Pk Cres, SE6 184 EF88
Gerrards Cross SL9 112 AY56
Ilford IG1 125 ER62
South Pk Dr, Bark. IG11 125 ES63
Gerrards Cross SL9 112 AY56
Ilford IG3 125 ES63
South Pk Gdns, Berk. HP4 38 AV18
South Pk Gro, N.Mal. KT3 198 CQ98
South Pk Hill Rd, S.Croy. CR2 220 DR106
South Pk Ms, SW6 307 L10
Sch **South Pk Prim Sch**,
Seven Kings IG3 *off Water La* 125 ES62
South Pk Rd, SW19 180 DA93
Ilford IG1 125 ER62
South Pk Ter, Ilf. IG1 125 ER62
South Pk Vw, Ger.Cr. SL9 113 AZ56
South Pk Way, Ruis. HA4 136 BW65
South Path, Wind. SL4 151 AQ81
South Penge Pk Est, SE20 202 DV96
South Perimeter Rd, Uxb. UB8
off Kingston La 134 BL69
South Pier Rd, Gat. RH6 269 DH152
South Pl, EC2 287 M6
Enfield EN3 82 DW43
Harlow CM20 36 EU12
Surbiton KT5 198 CM101
Waltham Abbey EN9
off Sun St 67 EC33
South Pl Ms, EC2 287 M7
South Pt, Sutt. SM1 218 DC107
Southport Rd, SE18 165 ER77
DLR **South Quay** 302 D5
● **South Quay Plaza**, E14 302 C4
South Quay Sq, E14 302 C4
South Ridge, Wey. KT13 213 BP110
Southridge Pl, SW20 179 CX94
South Riding, Brick.Wd AL2 60 CA30
South Ri, Cars. SM5 218 DE109
Sch **South Ri Prim Sch**, SE18
off Brewery Rd 165 ER78
South Ri Way, SE18 165 ER78
South Rd, N9 100 DU46
SE23 183 DX89
SW19 180 DC93
W5 157 CK77
Amersham HP6 55 AQ36
Chadwell Heath RM6 126 EY58
Chorleywood WD3 73 BC43
Edgware HA8 96 CP53
Englefield Green TW20 172 AW93
Erith DA8 167 FF79
Feltham TW13 176 BX92
Guildford GU2 242 AV132
Hampton TW12 176 BY93
Harlow CM20 36 EU12
Little Heath RM6 126 EW57
Reigate RH2 266 DB135
St. George's Hill KT13 213 BP109
South Ockendon RM15 149 FW72
Southall UB1 156 BZ75
Twickenham TW2 177 CD90
West Drayton UB7 154 BM76
Weybridge KT13 213 BQ106
Woking GU21 210 AX114
South Row, SE3 315 M8
SOUTH RUISLIP, Ruis. HA4 116 BW63
⇌ **South Ruislip** 116 BW63
⊖ **South Ruislip** 116 BW63
Southsea Av, Wat. WD18 75 BU42
Southsea Rd, Kings.T. KT1 198 CL98
South Sea St, SE16 301 N6
South Side, W6 159 CT76
Chertsey KT16 194 BG97
Southside, Chal.St.P. SL9 112 AX55
Southside Common, SW19 179 CW93
Southside Shop Cen, SW18 180 DB86
Southspring, Sid. DA15 185 ER87
South Sq, NW11 120 DB58
WC1 286 E7
Southstand Apts, N5
off Avenell Rd 121 DP63
South Sta App, S.Nutfld RH1 267 DL136
SOUTH STIFFORD,
Grays RM20 169 FW78
SOUTH STREET, West. TN16 239 EM119
South St, W1 297 H2
Brentwood CM14 108 FW47
Bromley BR1 204 EG96
Dorking RH4 263 CG137
Enfield EN3 83 DX43
Epsom KT18 216 CR113
Gravesend DA12 191 GH87
Hertford SG14 32 DR09
Isleworth TW7 157 CG83
Rainham RM13 147 FC68
Romford RM1 127 FF58
Staines-upon-Thames TW18 173 BF92
Stanstead Abbotts SG12 33 EC11
South Tenter St, E1 288 B10
South Ter, SW7 296 C8
Dorking RH4 263 CH137
Surbiton KT6 198 CL100
Coll **South Thames Coll**,
Mord. SM4 *off London Rd* 200 DA99
Roehampton Cen, SW15
off Roehampton La 179 CU86
Tooting Cen, SW17
off Tooting High St 180 DE92
Wandsworth Cen, SW18
off Wandsworth High St 180 DB85
SOUTH TOTTENHAM, N15 122 DS57
⇌ **South Tottenham** 122 DT57
South Vale, SE19 182 DS93
Harrow HA1 117 CE63
Southvale Rd, SE3 315 K9
South Vw, Brom. BR1 204 EH96
Epsom KT19 216 CN110
Southview Av, NW10 119 CT64
South Vw Av, Til. RM18 171 GG81
Southview Cl, SW17 180 DG92
Cheshunt EN7 66 DS26
Swanley BR8 207 FF98
South Vw Cl, Bex. DA5 186 EZ86
South Vw Ct, Wok. GU22
off Constitution Hill 226 AY118
Southview Cres, Ilf. IG2 125 EP58
South Vw Dr, E18 124 EH55
Upminster RM14 128 FN62
Southview Gdns, Wall. SM6 219 DJ108
South Vw Rd, N8 121 DK55
Ashtead KT21 231 CK119
Dartford DA2 188 FK90
Gerrards Cross SL9 112 AX56
Grays RM20 169 FW79
Loughton IG10 85 EM44
Pinner HA5 93 BV51
Southview Rd, Brom. BR1 183 ED91
Warlingham CR6 236 DU119
Woldingham CR3 237 EB124
Southviews, S.Croy. CR2 221 DX109
South Vil, NW1 275 P5
Southville, SW8 309 P6
Southville Cl, Epsom KT19 216 CR109
Feltham TW14 175 BS88
Southville Cres, Felt. TW14 175 BS88
Sch **Southville Inf & Nurs & Jun Schs**,
Felt. TW14 *off Bedfont La* 175 BT88
Southville Rd, Felt. TW14 175 BS88
Thames Ditton KT7 197 CG101
South Wk, Hayes UB3
off Middleton Rd 135 BR71
Reigate RH2 *off Chartway* 250 DB134
West Wickham BR4 204 EE104
SOUTHWARK, SE1 299 H3
⊖ **Southwark** 298 G3
Coll **Southwark Adult Ed**,
Nunhead Cen, SE15
off Whorlton Rd 162 DV83
Thomas Calton Cen, SE15 312 C9
Southwark Br, EC4 299 K2
SE1 299 K2
Southwark Br Rd, SE1 299 H6
★ **Southwark Cath**, SE1 299 L2
Southwark Pk, SE16 300 F7
Southwark Pk Est, SE16 300 F8
Sch **Southwark Pk Prim Sch**,
SE16 300 F7
Southwark Pk Rd, SE16 300 B8
Southwark Pl, Brom. BR1 205 EM97
Southwark St, SE1 299 H2
Southwater Cl, E14 289 N8
Beckenham BR3 183 EB94
South Way, N9 100 DW47
N11 *off Ringway* 99 DJ51
Abbots Langley WD5 59 BT33
Beaconsfield HP9 110 AG55
Croydon CR0 203 DY104
Harrow HA2 116 CA56
Hayes BR2 204 EG101
Purfleet RM19 169 FS76
Wembley HA9 118 CN64
Southway, N20 98 DA47
NW11 120 DB58
SW20 199 CW98
Carshalton SM5 218 DD110
Guildford GU2 242 AT134
Hatfield AL10 45 CU22
Wallington SM6 219 DJ105
Southway Cl, W12 159 CV75
Southway Ct, Guil. GU2 242 AS134
SOUTH WEALD, Brwd. CM14 108 FS47
South Weald Dr, Wal.Abb. EN9 67 ED33
South Weald Rd, Brwd. CM14 108 FU48
Southwell Av, Nthlt. UB5 136 CA65
Southwell Cl, Chaff.Hun. RM16 169 FW78
Southwell Gdns, SW7 295 N8
Southwell Gro Rd, E11 124 EE61
Southwell Rd, SE5 311 J10
Croydon CR0 201 DN100
Kenton HA3 117 CK58
South Western Rd, Twick. TW1 177 CG86
Southwest Rd, E11 123 ED60
South Wf Rd, W2 284 A8
Southwick Ms, W2 284 B8
Southwick Pl, W2 284 C9
Southwick St, W2 284 C8
SOUTH WIMBLEDON, SW19 180 DB94
⊖ **South Wimbledon** 180 DB94
Southwold Dr, Bark. IG11 126 EU64
Sch **Southwold Prim Sch**, E5
off Detmold Rd 122 DW61
Southwold Rd, E5 122 DV61
Bexley DA5 187 FB86
Watford WD24 76 BW38
Southwold Spur, Slou. SL3 153 BC75
Southwood Av, N6 121 DH59
Coulsdon CR5 235 DJ115
Kingston upon Thames KT2 198 CQ95
Ottershaw KT16 211 BC108
Southwood Cl, Brom. BR1 205 EM98
Worcester Park KT4 199 CX102
Southwood Dr, Surb. KT5 198 CQ101
SOUTH WOODFORD, E18 102 EF54
⊖ **South Woodford** 102 EG54
Southwood Gdns, Esher KT10 197 CG104
Ilford IG2 125 EP56
Southwood La, N6 120 DG59
Southwood Lawn Rd, N6 120 DG59
Southwood Pk, N6 120 DG59
Sch **Southwood Prim Sch**,
Dag. RM9 *off Keppel Rd* 126 EY63
Southwood Rd, SE9 185 EP89
SE28 146 EV74
Southwood Smith St, N1 276 G9
South Worple Av, SW14 158 CS83
South Worple Way, SW14 158 CR83
Soval Ct, Nthwd. HA6 93 BR52
● **Sovereign Business Cen**,
Enf. EN3 83 DZ40
Sovereign Cl, E1 300 F1
W5 137 CJ71
Purley CR8 219 DM110
Ruislip HA4 115 BS60
Sovereign Ct, Harl. CM19
off Rosemount 51 EP18
West Molesey KT8 196 BZ98
Sovereign Cres, SE16 301 L1
Sovereign Gro, Wem. HA0 117 CK62
Sovereign Hts, Slou. SL3 153 BA79
Sovereign Ms, E2 278 A10
Barnet EN4 80 DF41
Sovereign Pk, NW10 138 CP70
St. Albans AL4 43 CK21
Sovereign Pl, Har. HA1 117 CF57
Sovereign Rd, Bark. IG11 146 EW69
Sowerby Cl, SE9 184 EL85
Sowrey Av, Rain. RM13 147 FF65
Soyer Ct, Wok. GU21
off Raglan Rd 226 AS118
● **Spaces Business Cen**, SW8 309 K6
Space Waye, Felt. TW14 175 BV85
Spackmans Way, Slou. SL1 151 AQ76
Spa Cl, SE25 202 DS95
Spa Dr, Epsom KT18 216 CN114
Spafield St, EC1 286 E4
Spa Grn Est, EC1 286 F2
Spa Hill, SE19 202 DR95
Spalding Cl, Edg. HA8 96 CS52
Spalding Rd, NW4 119 CW58
SW17 181 DH92
Spalt Cl, Hutt. CM13 109 GB47
Spanby Rd, E3 290 B5
Spaniards Cl, NW11 120 DD60
Spaniards End, NW3 120 DC60
Spaniards Rd, NW3 120 DC61
Spanish Pl, W1 285 H8
Spanish Rd, SW18 180 DC85
Spareleaze Hill, Loug. IG10 85 EM43
Sparepenny La, Dart. DA4 208 FL102
Sparkbridge Rd, Har. HA1 117 CE56
Sparkes Cl, Brom. BR2 204 EH98
Sparke Ter, E16 291 L8
Sparkford Gdns, N11 98 DG50
Sparkford Ho, SW11 308 B6
Sparks Cl, W3 138 CR72
Dagenham RM8 126 EX61
Hampton TW12 *off Victors Dr* 176 BY93
Spa Rd, SE16 300 A7
Sparrow Cl, Hmptn. TW12 176 BY93
Sparrow Dr, Orp. BR5 205 EQ102
Sparrow Fm Dr, Felt. TW14 176 BX87
Sch **Sparrow Fm Inf & Nurs Sch**,
Felt. TW14 *off Denham Rd* 176 BW87
Sch **Sparrow Fm Jun Sch**,
Felt. TW14 *off Sparrow Fm Dr* 176 BW87
Sparrow Fm Rd, Epsom KT17 217 CU105
Sparrow Grn, Dag. RM10 127 FB62
Sparrows Herne, Bushey WD23 94 CB45
Sparrows La, SE9 185 EQ87
Sparrows Mead, Red. RH1 250 DG131
Sparrows Way, Bushey WD23 94 CC45
Sparrowswick Ride, St.Alb. AL3 42 CC15
Sparrow Wk, Wat. WD25
off Gullet Wd Rd 75 BU35
Sparsholt Rd, N19 121 DL60
Barking IG11 145 ES67
Spartan Cl, Wall. SM6 219 DL108
Sparta St, SE10 314 D7
Sch **Spa Sch**, SE1 300 C9
★ **Speaker's Cor**, W2 284 F10
Speaker's Ct, Croy. CR0
off St. James's Rd 202 DR102
Spearman St, SE18 165 EN79
Spear Ms, SW5 295 K9
Spearpoint Gdns, Ilf. IG2 125 ET56
Spears Rd, N19 121 DL60
Speart La, Houns. TW5 156 BY80
Spectacle Wks, E13 292 C2
Spectrum Ho, Enf. EN3
off Tysoe Av 83 DY36
Spectrum Pl, SE17 311 L2
Spedan Cl, NW3 120 DB62
Speechly Ms, E8 278 B2
Speedbird Way, Harm. UB7 154 BH80
Speedgate Hill,
Fawk.Grn DA3 209 FU103
Speed Highwalk, EC2 287 K6
off Silk St
Speed Ho, EC2
off The Barbican 287 L6
● **Speedway Ind Est**,
Hayes UB3 155 BR75
Speedwell Cl, Guil. GU4 243 BB131
Hemel Hempstead HP1
off Campion Rd 39 BE21
Speedwell Ct, Grays RM17 170 GE80
Speedwell St, SE8 314 A5
Speedy Pl, WC1 286 A3
Speer Rd, T.Ditt. KT7 197 CF99
Speirs Cl, N.Mal. KT3 199 CT100
Spekehill, SE9 185 EM90
Speke Rd, Th.Hth. CR7 202 DR96
Speldhurst Cl, Brom. BR2 204 EF99
Speldhurst Rd, E9 279 J7
W4 158 CR76
Spellbrook Wk, N1 277 K8
Spelman St, E1 288 C6
Spelthorne Gro, Sun. TW16 175 BT94
Sch **Spelthorne Inf & Nurs Sch**,
Ashf. TW15 *off Chertsey Rd* 175 BS93
Sch **Spelthorne Jun Sch**,
Ashf. TW15 *off Feltham Hill Rd* 175 BR93
Spelthorne La, Ashf. TW15 195 BQ95
Spence Av, Byfleet KT14 212 BL114
Spence Cl, SE16 301 N5
Spencer Av, N13 99 DM51
Cheshunt EN7 66 DS26
Hayes UB4 135 BU71
Spencer Cl, N3 97 CZ54
NW10 138 CM69
Epsom KT18 232 CS119
Orpington BR6 205 ES103
Uxbridge UB8 134 BJ69
Woking GU21 211 BC113
Woodford Green IG8 102 EJ50
Spencer Ctyd, N3
off Regents Pk Rd 97 CZ54
Spencer Dr, N2 120 DC58
Spencer Gdns, SE9 185 EM85
SW14 178 CQ85
Englefield Green TW20 172 AX92
Spencer Gate, St.Alb. AL1 43 CE18
Spencer Hill, SW19 179 CY93
Spencer Hill Rd, SW19 179 CY94
★ **Spencer Ho**, SW1 297 L3
Spencer Ms, SW8 310 C7
W6 306 E2
Spencer Pk, SW18 180 DD85
Spencer Pas, E2 278 E10
Spencer Pl, N1 276 G6
Croydon CR0 202 DR101
Spencer Ri, NW5 121 DH63
Spencer Rd, E6 144 EK67
E17 101 EC54
N8 121 DM57
N11 99 DH49
N17 100 DU53
SW18 160 DD84
SW20 199 CV95
W3 138 CQ74
W4 158 CQ80
Beddington Corner CR4 200 DG101
Bromley BR1 184 EE94
Caterham CR3 236 DR121
Cobham KT11 229 BV115
East Molesey KT8 196 CC99
Harrow HA3 95 CE54
Ilford IG3 125 ET60
Isleworth TW7 157 CD81
Mitcham CR4 200 DG97
Rainham RM13 147 FD69
Slough SL3 153 AZ76
South Croydon CR2 220 DS106
Twickenham TW2 177 CE90
Wembley HA0 117 CJ61
Spencers Cft, Harl. CM18 52 EV17
Spencer St, EC1 286 G3
Gravesend DA11 191 GG87
Hertford SG13 32 DS08
St. Albans AL3 43 CD20
Southall UB2 156 BX75
Spencer Wk, NW3 273 P1
SW15 159 CX84
Rickmansworth WD3 74 BJ43
Tilbury RM18 171 GG82
Spencer Way, E1 288 F9
Hemel Hempstead HP1 40 BG17
Redhill RH1 266 DG139
Spencer Yd, SE3 315 L9
Spenser Av, Wey. KT13 212 BN108
Spenser Cres, Upmin. RM14 128 FQ59
Spenser Gro, N16 277 N1
Spenser Ms, SE21 182 DR88
Spenser Rd, SE24 181 DN85
Spenser St, SW1 297 M6
Spensley Wk, N16 122 DR62
Speranza St, SE18 165 ET78
Sperling Rd, N17 100 DS54
Spert St, E14 289 L10
Speyhawk Pl, Pot.B. EN6 64 DB30
Speyside, N14 81 DJ44
Spey St, E14 290 F7
Spey Way, Rom. RM1 105 FE52
Spezia Rd, NW10 139 CU68
Sphere, The, E16 291 L9
● **Sphere Ind Est**, St.Alb. AL1 43 CG20
Spice Quay Hts, SE1 300 B3
Spicer Cl, SW9 311 H8
Walton-on-Thames KT12 196 BW100
Spicersfield, Chsht EN7 66 DU27
Spicers Fld, Oxshott KT22 215 CD113
Spicers La, Harl. CM17
off Wayre St 36 EW11
Spicer St, St.Alb. AL3 42 CC20
Spice's Yd, Croy. CR0 220 DQ105
Spielman Rd, Dart. DA1 168 FM84
Spiers Way, Horl. RH6 269 DH150
Spigurnell Rd, N17 100 DR53
Spikes Br Moorings,
Hayes UB4 136 BY73
Spikes Br Rd, Sthl. UB1 136 BY72
Spilsby Rd, Rom. RM3 106 FK52
Spindle Cl, SE18 305 H7
Epsom KT19 216 CR109
Spindles, Til. RM18 171 GG80
Spindlewood Gdns, Croy. CR0 220 DS105
Spindlewoods, Tad. KT20 233 CV122
Spindrift Av, E14 302 C8
Spinel Cl, SE18 165 ET78
Spingate Cl, Horn. RM12 128 FK64
Spinnaker Cl, Bark. IG11 146 EV69
Spinnells Rd, Har. HA2 116 BZ60
Spinners Wk, Wind. SL4 151 AQ81
Spinney, Slou. SL1 131 AP74
Spinney, The, N21 99 DN45
SW16 181 DK90
Aldenham WD25 77 CD38
Barnet EN5 80 DB40
Beaconsfield HP9 111 AK55
Berkhamsted HP4 38 AT20
Bookham KT23 230 CB124
Broxbourne EN10 49 DZ19
Chesham HP5 54 AR29
Epsom KT18 233 CV119
Gerrards Cross SL9 112 AX60
Guildford GU2 *off Southway* 242 AU133
Headley KT18 248 CQ126
Hertford SG13 32 DT09
Horley RH6 268 DG146
Hutton CM13 109 GC44
Loughton IG10 85 EP42
Northwood HA6 93 BU51

Spinney,The, Oxshott KT22 214 CC112
Potters Bar EN6 64 DD31
Purley CR8 219 DP111
Send GU23 244 BJ127
Sidcup DA14 186 EY92
Stanmore HA7 96 CL49
Sunbury-on-Thames TW16 195 BU95
Sutton SM3 217 CW105
Swanley BR8 207 FE96
Watford WD17 75 BU39
Welwyn Garden City AL7 29 CY10
Wembley HA0 117 CG62
Spinney Cl, Beck. BR3 203 EB98
Cobham KT11 214 CA111
New Malden KT3 198 CS99
Rainham RM13 147 FE68
West Drayton UB7 134 BL73
Worcester Park KT4 199 CT104
Spinneycroft, Oxshott KT22 231 CD115
Spinney Dr, Felt. TW14 175 BQ87
Spinney Gdns, SE19 182 DT92
Dagenham RM9 126 EY64
Spinney Hill, Add. KT15 211 BE106
Sch Spinney Inf Sch, Harl. CM20
off Cooks Spinney 36 EU14
Sch Spinney Jun Sch, Harl. CM20
off Cooks Spinney 36 EU14
Spinney Oak, Brom. BR1 204 EL96
Ottershaw KT16 211 BD107
Spinneys,The, Brom. BR1 205 EM96
Spinneys Dr, St.Alb. AL3 42 CB22
Spinney St, Hert. SG13 32 DU09
Spinney Way, Cudham TN14 223 ER111
Spinning Wk,The, Shere GU5 260 BN139
Spinning Wheel Mead,
Harl. CM18 52 EU18
H Spire Bushey Hosp,
Bushey WD23 95 CF46
Spire Cl, Grav. DA12 191 GH88
H Spire Gatwick Pk Hosp,
Horl. RH6 268 DE149
● Spire Grn Cen, Harl. CM19 50 EL16
H Spire Hartswood Hosp,
Warley CM13 107 FV51
Spire Ho, W2 283 P10
Spire Pl, Warl. CR6 237 DY118
H Spire Roding Hosp, Ilf. IG4 124 EK55
Spires,The, Dart. DA1 188 FK89
Spires Shop Cen,The,
Barn. EN5 79 CY41
Spirit Quay, E1 300 D2
SPITALBROOK, Hodd. EN11 49 EA19
★ Spitalfields City Fm, E1 288 C5
Spital Heath, Dor. RH4 263 CJ135
Spital La, Brwd. CM14 108 FT48
Spital Sq, E1 287 P6
Spital St, E1 288 C6
Dartford DA1 188 FK86
Spital Yd, E1 287 P6
● Spitfire Business Pk,
Croy. CR0 219 DN107
Spitfire Cl, Slou. SL3 153 BA77
● Spitfire Est, Houns. TW5 156 BW78
Spitfire Rd, Wall. SM6 219 DL108
Spitfire Way, Houns. TW5 156 BW78
Splendour Wk, SE16
off Verney Rd 312 G1
Spode Ho, SE11
off Lambeth Wk 298 E7
Spode Wk, NW6 273 M3
Spondon Rd, N15 122 DU56
Spook Hill, N.Holm. RH5 263 CH141
Spoonbill Way, Hayes UB4
off Cygnet Way 136 BX71
Spooners Dr, Park St AL2 60 CC27
Spooners Ms, W3
off Churchfield Rd 138 CR74
Spooner Wk, Wall. SM6 219 DK106
Sporle Ct, SW11 160 DD83
Sportsbank St, SE6 183 EC87
Sportsman Ms, E2 278 C9
Spotted Dog Path, E7 281 P5
Spottiswood Ct, Croy. CR0
off Pawson's Rd 202 DQ100
Spottons Gro, N17 100 DQ53
Spout Hill, Croy. CR0 221 EA106
Spout La, Crock.H. TN8 255 EQ134
Staines-upon-Thames TW19 174 BG85
Spout La N, Stai. TW19 154 BH84
Spratt Hall Rd, E11 124 EG58
Spratts All, Ott. KT16 211 BE107
Spratts La, Ott. KT16 211 BE107
Spray La, Twick. TW2 177 CE86
Spray St, SE18 305 P8
Spread Eagle Wk Shop Cen,
Epsom KT19 off High St 216 CR113
Spreighton Rd, W.Mol. KT8 196 CB98
Spriggs Oak, Epp. CM16
off Palmers Hill 70 EU29
Sprimont Pl, SW3 296 E10
Springall St, SE15 312 F5
Springate Fld, Slou. SL3 152 AY75
Spring Av, Egh. TW20 172 AY93
Springbank, N21 81 DM44
Springbank Av, Horn. RM12 128 FJ64
Springbank Rd, SE13 183 ED86
Springbank Wk, NW1 275 P6
Springbottom La,
Bletch. RH1 251 DN127
Springbourne Ct, Beck. BR3 203 EC95
Spring Br Ms, W5
off Spring Br Rd 137 CK73
Spring Br Rd, W5 137 CK73
Spring Cl, Barn. EN5 79 CX43
Borehamwood WD6 78 CN39
Dagenham RM8 126 EX60
Godalming GU7 258 AS143
Harefield UB9 92 BK53
Latimer HP5 72 AX36
Springclose La, Sutt. SM3 217 CY107
Springcopse Rd, Reig. RH2 266 DC135
Spring Cotts, Surb. KT6 197 CK99
Spring Ct, Guil. GU2
off Dayspring 242 AV130
Sidcup DA15 off Station Rd 186 EU90
Spring Ct Rd, Enf. EN2 81 DN38
Springcroft Av, N2 120 DF56
Spring Cfts, Bushey WD23 76 CA43
Springdale Ms, N16 277 L1
Springdale Rd, N16 277 L1
Spring Dr, Maid. SL6 130 AE65
Pinner HA5 115 BU58
Springett Ho, SW2
off St. Matthew's Rd 181 DN85
Spring Fm Cl, Rain. RM13 148 FK69
Springfield, E5 122 DV60
Bushey Heath WD23 95 CD46
Epping CM16 69 ET32
Oxted RH8 253 ED130
Springfield Av, N10 121 DJ55
SW20 199 CZ97
Hampton TW12 176 CB93
Hutton CM13 109 GE45
Swanley BR8 207 FF98
Springfield Cl, N12 98 DB50
Chesham HP5 54 AQ33
Croxley Green WD3 75 BP43
Knaphill GU21 226 AS118
Potters Bar EN6 64 DD31
Stanmore HA7 95 CG48
Windsor SL4 151 AP82
Sch Springfield Comm Prim Sch,
N16 off Castlewood Rd 122 DU58
Springfield Ct, Wall. SM6
off Springfield Rd 219 DH106
Springfield Dr, Ilf. IG2 125 EQ58
Leatherhead KT22 231 CE119
Springfield Gdns, E5 122 DV60
NW9 118 CR57
Bromley BR1 205 EM98
Ruislip HA4 115 BV60
Upminster RM14 128 FP62
West Wickham BR4 203 EB103
Woodford Green IG8 102 EJ52
Springfield Gro, SE7 164 EJ79
Sunbury-on-Thames TW16 195 BT95
Springfield Gro Est, SE7 164 EJ79
Springfield La, NW6 273 L9
Weybridge KT13 213 BP105
Springfield Meadows,
Wey. KT13 213 BP105
Springfield Mt, NW9 118 CS57
Springfield Par Ms, N13
off Hazelwood La 99 DN49
Springfield Pl, Ger.Cr. SL9 112 AY57
New Malden KT3 198 CQ98
Sch Springfield Prim Sch,
Sun. TW16 off Nursery Rd 195 BT96
Springfield Ri, SE26 182 DV90
Springfield Rd, E4 102 EE46
E6 145 EM66
E15 291 K2
E17 123 DZ58
N11 99 DH50
N15 122 DU56
NW8 273 N9
SE26 182 DV92
SW19 179 CZ92
W7 137 CE74
Ashford TW15 174 BM92
Berkhamsted HP4 38 AT16
Bexleyheath DA7 167 FB83
Bromley BR1 205 EM98
Chesham HP5 54 AQ33
Cheshunt EN8 67 DY32
Epsom KT17 217 CW110
Grays RM16 170 GD75
Guildford GU1 258 AY135
Harrow HA1 117 CE58
Hayes UB4 136 BW74
Hemel Hempstead HP2 40 BM19
Kingston upon Thames KT1 198 CL97
St. Albans AL1 43 CG21
Slough SL3 153 BB80
Smallford AL4 44 CP20
Teddington TW11 177 CG92
Thornton Heath CR7 202 DQ95
Twickenham TW2 176 CA88
Wallington SM6 219 DH106
Watford WD25 off Haines Way 59 BV33
Welling DA16 166 EV83
Westcott RH4 262 CB137
Windsor SL4 151 AP82
● Springfield Rd Business Cen,
Hayes UB4 136 BW74
Springfields, Amer. HP6 55 AQ37
Broxbourne EN10 49 DZ19
Waltham Abbey EN9 68 EE34
Welwyn Garden City AL8 29 CV11
Springfields Cl, Cher. KT16 194 BH102
H Springfield Uni Hosp, SW17 180 DE89
Springfield Wk, NW6 273 L9
Orpington BR6
off Place Fm Av 205 ER102
Spring Gdns, N5 277 J3
SW1 297 P2
Biggin Hill TN16 238 EJ118
Dorking RH4 263 CG136
Hornchurch RM12 127 FH63
Orpington BR6 224 EV107
Romford RM7 127 FC57
Wallington SM6 219 DJ106
Watford WD25 76 BW35
West Molesey KT8 196 CC99
Wooburn Green HP10 110 AE55
Woodford Green IG8 102 EJ52
● Spring Gdns Business Pk,
Rom. RM7 127 FC57
Spring Glen, Hat. AL10 45 CT19
SPRING GROVE, Islw. TW7 157 CF81
Spring Gro, SE19
off Alma Pl 182 DT94
W4 158 CN78
Fetcham KT22 230 CB123
Godalming GU7 258 AS143
Gravesend DA12 191 GH88
Hampton TW12 off Plevna Rd 196 CB95
Loughton IG10 84 EK44
Mitcham CR4 200 DG95
Spring Gro Cres, Houns. TW3 156 CC81
Sch Spring Gro Prim Sch,
Islw. TW7 off Star Rd 157 CD82
Spring Gro Rd, Houns. TW3 156 CB81
Isleworth TW7 156 CB81
Richmond TW10 178 CM85
Springhall La, Saw. CM21 36 EY06
Sch Springhallow Sch, W13
off Compton Cl 137 CG72
Springhall Rd, Saw. CM21 36 EY05
Springhaven Cl, Guil. GU1 243 BA134
● Springhead Enterprise Pk,
Nthflt DA11 190 GC88
Springhead Parkway,
Nthflt. DA11 190 GC89
Springhead Rd, Erith DA8 167 FF79
Northfleet DA11 190 GC87
Spring Hill, E5 122 DU59
SE26 182 DW91
Springhill Cl, SE5 162 DR83
Spring Hills, Harl. CM20 35 EN14
Springholm Cl, Bigg.H. TN16 238 EJ118
Springhurst Cl, Croy. CR0 221 DZ105
Spring Lake, Stan. HA7 95 CH49
Spring La, E5 122 DV60
N10 120 DG55
SE25 202 DV100
Farnham Royal SL2 131 AP66
Hemel Hempstead HP1 39 BF18
Spring La, Oxted RH8 253 ED131
Slough SL1 131 AM74
Springle La, Hailey SG13 33 DZ12
Sch Springmead JMI Sch,
Welw.G.C. AL7 off Hilly Flds 30 DC08
Spring Ms, W1 284 F6
Epsom KT17 off Old Schs La 217 CT109
Richmond TW9
off Rosedale Rd 158 CL84
Spring Pk Av, Croy. CR0 203 DX103
Spring Pk Dr, N4 122 DQ60
Springpark Dr, Beck. BR3 203 EC97
Sch Spring Pk Prim Sch,
Croy. CR0 off Bridle Rd 203 EA104
Spring Pk Rd, Croy. CR0 203 DX103
Spring Pas, SW15 306 C10
Spring Path, NW3 274 A3
Spring Pl, N3
off Windermere Av 98 DA54
NW5 275 J3
Barking IG11 145 EQ68
Cobham KT11 214 BY113
Springpond Rd, Dag. RM9 126 EY64
Springrice Rd, SE13 183 EC86
Spring Ri, Egh. TW20 172 AY93
Spring Rd, Felt. TW13 175 BT90
Springs,The, Brox. EN10 67 DY25
Hertford SG13 32 DT08
Springshaw Cl, Sev. TN13 256 FD123
Spring Shaw Rd, Orp. BR5 206 EU95
Springside Ct, Guil. GU1 242 AW133
Spring St, W2 284 A9
Epsom KT17 217 CT109
Spring Ter, Rich. TW9 178 CL85
Spring Tide Cl, SE15 312 D6
Spring Vale, Bexh. DA7 167 FB84
Greenhithe DA9 189 FW86
Springvale Av, Brent. TW8 157 CK78
Springvale Cl, Bkhm KT23 246 CB126
Spring Vale Cl, Swan. BR8 207 FF95
Springvale Est, W14 294 D7
Spring Vale N, Dart. DA1 188 FK87
Springvale Retail Pk,
Orp. BR5 206 EW97
Spring Vale S, Dart. DA1 188 FK87
Springvale Ter, W14 294 D7
Springvale Way, Orp. BR5 206 EW97
● Spring Valley Enterprise Cen,
Port.Wd AL3 43 CE16
Spring Vw Rd, Ware SG12 32 DW07
Spring Vil Rd, Edg. HA8 96 CN52
Spring Wk, E1 288 D6
Broxbourne EN10 48 DW22
Horley RH6 off Court Lo Rd 268 DF148
Springwater Cl, SE18 165 EN81
Springway, Har. HA1 117 CD59
Spring Way, SE5 311 J7
Hem.H. HP2 41 BP18
Springwell Av, NW10 139 CT67
Mill End WD3 92 BG47
Springwell Cl, SW16
off Etherstone Rd 181 DN91
Springwell Ct, Houns. TW4 156 BX82
Stanstead Abbotts SG12 33 EC11
Springwell Hill, Hare. UB9 92 BH51
Sch Springwell Inf & Nurs Sch,
Heston TW5 off Speart La 156 BY80
Sch Springwell Jun Sch, Heston TW5
off Vicarage Fm Rd 156 BY80
Springwell La, Hare. UB9 92 BG49
Rickmansworth WD3 92 BG49
Springwell Rd, SW16 181 DN91
Hounslow TW4,TW5 156 BX81
Springwood, Chsht EN7 66 DU26
Springwood Cl, E3 290 A1
Harefield UB9 92 BK53
Springwood Cres, Edg. HA8 96 CP47
Springwood Pl, Wey. KT13 213 BP108
Spring Wds, Vir.W. GU25 192 AV98
Springwood Wk, St.Alb. AL4 43 CK17
Springwood Way, Rom. RM1 127 FG57
Sprowston Ms, E7 281 N4
Sprowston Rd, E7 281 P3
Spruce Cl, Red. RH1 250 DF133
Spruce Ct, W5 158 CL76
Sprucedale Cl, Swan. BR8 207 FE96
Sprucedale Gdns, Croy. CR0 221 DX105
Wallington SM6 219 DK109
Spruce Hill, Harl. CM18 51 ES20
Spruce Hills Rd, E17 101 EC54
Spruce Pk, Brom. BR2
off Cumberland Rd 204 EF98
Spruce Rd, Bigg.H. TN16 238 EK116
Spruce Way, Park St AL2 60 CB27
Sprules Rd, SE4 313 L9
Spur,The, Chsht EN8
off Welsummer Way 67 DX28
Slough SL1 131 AK71
Walton-on-Thames KT12 196 BW103
Spur Cl, Abb.L. WD5 59 BR33
Abridge RM4 86 EV41
Spurfield, W.Mol. KT8 196 CB97
Spurgate, Hutt. CM13 109 GA47
Spurgeon Av, SE19 202 DR95
Spurgeon Cl, Grays RM17 170 GC79
Spurgeon Rd, SE19 202 DR95
Coll Spurgeon's Coll, SE25
off South Norwood Hill 202 DS96
Spurgeon St, SE1 299 L7
Spurling Rd, SE22 162 DT84
Dagenham RM9 146 EZ65
Spurrell Av, Bex. DA5 187 FD91
Spur Rd, N15
off Philip La 122 DR56
SE1 298 E4
SW1 297 L5
Barking IG11 145 EQ68
Edgware HA8 96 CL49
Feltham TW14 175 BV85
Isleworth TW7 157 CH80
Orpington BR6 206 EU103
Spur Rd Est, Edg. HA8
off Green La 96 CM49
Spurstowe Rd, E8 278 E3
Spurstowe Ter, E8 278 E3
Squadrons App, Horn. RM12 148 FJ65
Square,The, E10 123 EC62
W6 306 B1
Broxbourne EN10 49 DY23
Carshalton SM5 218 DG106
Caterham CR3
off Godstone Rd 236 DU124
Guildford GU2 258 AT136
Hemel Hempstead HP1
off Marlowes 40 BK20
Ilford IG1 125 EN59
Loug. IG10 85 EP42
Potten End HP4 39 BB16
Richmond TW9 177 CK85
Square,The,
Sawbridgeworth CM21 36 EY05
Sevenoaks TN13
off Amherst Hill 256 FE122
Shere GU5 260 BN139
Swanley BR8 207 FD97
Tatsfield TN16 238 EJ120
Uxbridge UB11 135 BR74
Watford WD24 75 BV37
West Drayton UB7 154 BH81
Weybridge KT13 213 BQ105
Wisley GU23 228 BL116
Woodford Green IG8 102 EG50
● Square One, Sthl. UB2 156 BW77
Square Rigger Row, SW11
off York Pl 160 DC83
Square St, Harl. CM17 36 EW14
Squarey St, SW17 180 DC90
Squerryes,The, Cat. CR3 236 DS121
★ Squerryes Ct & Gdns,
West. TN16 255 EQ128
Squerryes Mede, West. TN16 255 EQ127
Squire Gdns, NW8 284 A3
Squires,The, Rom. RM7 127 FC58
Squires Br Rd, Shep. TW17 194 BM98
Squires Ct, SW19 180 DA91
Chertsey KT16
off Springfields Cl 194 BH102
Squires Fld, Swan. BR8 207 FF95
Squires La, N3 98 DB54
Squires Mt, NW3
off East Heath Rd 120 DD62
Squires Rd, Shep. TW17 194 BM98
Squire's Wk, Ashf. TW15 175 BR94
Squires Way, Dart. DA2 187 FD91
Squires Wd Dr, Chis. BR7 184 EL94
Squirrel Chase, Hem.H. HP1 39 BE19
Squirrel Cl, Houns. TW4 156 BW82
Squirrel Keep, W.Byf. KT14 212 BH112
Squirrel Ms, W13 137 CG73
Squirrels,The, SE13 163 ED83
Bushey WD23 77 CD44
Hertford SG13 32 DU09
Pinner HA5 116 BZ55
Welwyn Garden City AL7 30 DC10
Squirrels Chase, Orsett RM16
off Hornsby La 171 GG75
Squirrels Cl, N12 98 DC49
Orpington BR6 205 ES102
Swanscombe BR8 207 FF97
Uxbridge UB10 134 BN66
Squirrels Grn, Bkhm KT23 230 CA123
Worcester Park KT4 199 CT102
Squirrels Heath Av, Rom. RM2 127 FH55
Sch Squirrels Heath Inf & Jun Schs,
Rom. RM2 off Salisbury Rd 127 FH57
Squirrels Heath La,
Horn. RM11 128 FJ56
Romford RM2 128 FJ56
Squirrels Heath Rd, Rom. RM3 128 FL55
Squirrels La, Buck.H. IG9 102 EK48
● Squirrels Trd Est,
Hayes UB3 155 BU76
Squirrels Way, Epsom KT18 232 CR115
Squirrel Wd, W.Byf. KT14 212 BH112
Squirries St, E2 288 D2
Stable Cl, Epsom KT18 232 CS119
Kingston upon Thames KT2 178 CM93
Northolt UB5 136 CA68
Stable La, Seer Grn HP9 89 AQ51
Stable Ms, NW5 275 J4
Twickenham TW1 177 CF88
Stables,The, Ald. WD25 76 CB36
Buckhurst Hill IG9 102 EJ45
Cobham KT11 214 BZ114
Guildford GU1
off Old Fm Rd 242 AX131
Stables End, Orp. BR6 205 EQ104
Stables Ms, SE27 182 DQ92
Stable St, NW1 276 A9
Stables Way, SE11 298 E10
Stable Wk, N1
off Wharfdale Rd 141 DL68
N2 off Old Fm Rd 98 DD53
Stable Way, W10 282 B9
Stable Yd, SW1 297 L4
SW9 310 D9
SW15 306 B10
Stable Yd Rd, SW1 297 L3
Staburn Ct, Edg. HA8 96 CQ54
Stacey Av, N18 100 DW49
Stacey Cl, E10 123 ED57
Gravesend DA12 191 GL92
Stacey St, N7 121 DN62
WC2 285 P9
Stackfield, Harl. CM20 36 EU12
Stackhouse St, SW3 296 E6
Stacklands, Welw.G.C. AL8 29 CV11
Stack Rd, Hort.Kir. DA4 209 FR97
Stacy Path, SE5 311 N5
Staddon Cl, Beck. BR3 203 DY98
● Stadium Business Cen,
Wem. HA9 118 CP62
Stadium Retail Pk,
Wem. HA9 118 CN62
Stadium Rd, NW2 119 CV59
SE18 164 EL80
Stadium Rd E, NW2 119 CW59
Stadium St, SW10 307 P5
Stadium Way, Dart. DA1 187 FE85
Harlow CM19 35 EM14
Watford WD18 75 BV43
Wembley HA9 118 CM63
Staffa Rd, E10 123 DY60
Stafford Av, Horn. RM11 128 FK55
Slough SL2 131 AQ70
Stafford Cl, E17 123 DZ58
N14 81 DJ43
NW6 283 J3
Caterham CR3 236 DT123
Chafford Hundred RM16 169 FW77
Cheshunt EN8 66 DV29
Greenhithe DA9 189 FT85
Sutton SM3 217 CY107
Taplow SL6 130 AH72
Stafford Ct, SW8
off Allen Edwards Dr 310 A5
W8 295 J6
Stafford Cripps Ho, E2 289 H3
SW6 off Clem Attlee Ct 307 H3
● Stafford Cross Business Pk,
Croy. CR0 219 DM106
Stafford Dr, Brox. EN10 49 EA20
Stafford Gdns, Croy. CR0 219 DM106
● Stafford Ind Est,
Horn. RM11 128 FK55
Stafford Pl, SW1 297 L6
Richmond TW10 178 CM87
Stafford Ri, Cat. CR3 236 DU122
Stafford Rd, E3 289 N1
E7 144 EJ66
NW6 283 J2
Caterham CR3 236 DT122
Croydon CR0 219 DN105
Harrow HA3 94 CC52
New Malden KT3 198 CQ97
Ruislip HA4 115 BT63
Sidcup DA14 185 ES91
Wallington SM6 219 DJ107
Staffords, Harl. CM17 36 EY11
Staffordshire St, SE15 312 D6
Staffords Pl, Horl. RH6 269 DH150
Stafford St, W1 297 L2
Stafford Ter, W8 295 J6
Stafford Way, Sev. TN13 257 FJ127
Staff St, EC1 287 M3
Stagbury Av, Chipstead CR5 234 DE118
Stagbury Cl, Chipstead CR5 234 DE119
Stag Cl, Edg. HA8 96 CP54
Staggart Grn, Chig. IG7 103 ET51
Stagg Hill, Barn. EN4 80 DD35
Potters Bar EN6 80 DD35
Stag Grn Av, Hat. AL9 45 CW16
STAG HILL, Guil. GU2 258 AU135
Stag Hill, Guil. GU2 258 AU135
Jct Stag La, SW15 179 CT89
Stag La, NW9 118 CQ55
SW15 179 CT89
Berkhamsted HP4 38 AU18
Buckhurst Hill IG9 102 EH47
Chorleywood WD3 73 BC44
Edgware HA8 96 CP54
Sch Stag La Inf & Jun Schs,
Edg. HA8 off Collier Dr 96 CN54
Stag Leys, Ashtd. KT21 232 CL120
Stag Leys Cl, Bans. SM7 234 DD115
Stag Ride, SW19 179 CT90
Stagshaw Ho, SE22
off Pytchley Rd 162 DS83
Stags Way, Islw. TW7 157 CF79
Stainash Cres, Stai. TW18 174 BH92
Stainash Par, Stai. TW18
off Kingston Rd 174 BH92
Stainbank Rd, Mitch. CR4 201 DH97
Stainby Cl, West Dr. UB7 154 BL76
Stainby Rd, N15 122 DT56
Stainer Rd, Borwd. WD6 77 CK39
⇌ Staines 174 BG92
Staines 173 BF92
Staines Av, Sutt. SM3 199 CX103
Staines Br, Stai. TW18 173 BE92
Staines Bypass, Ashf. TW15 174 BH91
Staines-upon-Thames
TW18,TW19 174 BH91
Staines Grn, Hert. SG14 31 DK11
Staines La, Cher. KT16 193 BF99
Staines La Cl, Cher. KT16 193 BF100
Sch Staines Prep Sch,
Stai. TW18 off Gresham Rd 174 BG92
Staines Rd, Cher. KT16 193 BF97
Feltham TW14 175 BR87
Hounslow TW3,TW4 156 CB83
Ilford IG1 125 EQ63
Staines-upon-Thames TW18 194 BH95
Twickenham TW2 176 CA90
Wraysbury TW19 172 AY87
Staines Rd E, Sun. TW16 175 BU94
Staines Rd W, Ashf. TW15 175 BP93
Sunbury-on-Thames TW16 175 BP93
STAINES-UPON-THAMES,
TW18 & TW19 174 BG91
Staines Wk, Sid. DA14
off Evry Rd 186 EW93
Stainford Cl, Ashf. TW15 175 BR92
Stainforth Rd, E17 123 EA56
Ilford IG2 125 ER59
Staining La, EC2 287 K8
Stainmore Cl, Chis. BR7 205 ER95
Stainsbury St, E2 289 H1
Stainsby Rd, E14 290 A8
Stains Cl, Chsht EN8 67 DY28
Stainton Rd, SE6 183 ED86
Enfield EN3 82 DW39
Stainton Wk, Wok. GU21
off Inglewood 226 AW118
Stairfoot La, Chipstead TN13 256 FC122
Staithes Way, Tad. KT20 233 CV120
Stakescorner Rd,
Littleton GU3 258 AU142
ST. ALBANS, AL1 - AL4 43 CE20
Stalbridge St, NW1 284 D6
Stalham St, SE16 300 F7
Stalham Way, Ilf. IG6 103 EP53
Stalisfield Pl, Downe BR6
off Mill La 223 EN110
Stambourne Way, SE19 182 DS94
West Wickham BR4 203 EC104
⊖ Stamford Brook 159 CT77
Stamford Brook Av, W6 159 CT76
Stamford Brook Gdns, W6
off Stamford Brook Rd 159 CT76
Stamford Brook Rd, W6 159 CT76
Stamford Cl, N15 122 DU56
NW3 off Hampstead Sq 120 DC62
Harrow HA3 95 CE52
Potters Bar EN6 64 DD32
Southall UB1 136 CA73
Stamford Cotts, SW10 307 M4
Stamford Ct, W6 159 CU77
Stamford Dr, Brom. BR2 204 EF98
Stamford Gdns, Dag. RM9 146 EW66
Stamford Grn, Epsom KT18 216 CP113
Sch Stamford Grn Prim Sch,
Epsom KT19 off Christ Ch Mt 216 CP112
Stamford Grn Rd,
Epsom KT18 216 CP113
Stamford Gro E, N16 122 DU60
Stamford Gro W, N16 122 DU60
STAMFORD HILL, N16 122 DS60
Stamford Hill 122 DS59
Stamford Hill, N16 122 DT61
Stamford Hill Est, N16 122 DT60
Sch Stamford Hill Prim Sch,
N15 off Berkeley Rd 122 DR58
Stamford Rd, E6 144 EL67
N1 277 P6
N15 122 DU57
Dagenham RM9 146 EV67
Walton-on-Thames KT12
off Kenilworth Dr 196 BX104
Watford WD17 75 BV40
Stamford St, SE1 298 E3
Stamp Pl, E2 288 A2

S

Stanard Cl, N16 122 DS59
STANBOROUGH, Welw.G.C. AL8 29 CT12
Stanborough Av, Borwd. WD6 78 CN37
Stanborough Cl, Borwd. WD6 78 CN38
Hampton TW12 176 BZ93
Welwyn Garden City AL8 29 CW10
Stanborough Grn, Welw.G.C. AL8 29 CW11
Stanborough Ms, Welw.G.C. AL8 29 CX11
Stanborough Pk, Wat. WD25 75 BV35
Stanborough Pas, E8 278 A4
Stanborough Prim Sch, Wat. WD25 off Appletree Wk 76 BW35
Stanborough Rd, Houns. TW3 157 CD83
Welwyn Garden City AL8 29 CV12
Stanborough Sch, Wat. WD25 off Stanborough Pk 75 BV35
Welwyn Garden City AL8 off Lemsford La 29 CV11
Stanbridge Pl, N21 99 DP47
Stanbridge Rd, SW15 159 CW83
Stanbrook Rd, SE2 166 EV75
Gravesend DA11 191 GF88
Stanburn Inf & Jun Schs, Stan. HA7 off Abercorn Rd 95 CJ52
Stanbury Av, Wat. WD17 75 BS37
Stanbury Rd, SE15 312 F7
Stancroft, NW9 118 CS56
Standale Gro, Ruis. HA4 115 BQ57
● Standard Ind Est, E16 305 J4
Standard Pl, EC2 287 P3
Standard Rd, NW10 138 CQ70
Belvedere DA17 166 FA78
Bexleyheath DA6 166 EY84
Downe BR6 223 EN110
Enfield EN3 83 DY38
Hounslow TW4 156 BY83
Standen Av, Horn. RM12 128 FK62
Standen Rd, SW18 179 CZ87
Standfield, Abb.L. WD5 59 BS31
Standfield Gdns, Dag. RM10 off Standfield Rd 146 FA65
Standfield Rd, Dag. RM10 126 FA64
Standingford, Harl. CM19 51 EP20
Standish Ho, SE3 off Elford Cl 164 EJ84
Standish Rd, W6 159 CU77
Standlake Pt, SE23 183 DX90
Standring Ri, Hem.H. HP3 40 BH23
Stane Cl, SW19 180 DB94
Stane Gro, SW9 310 A9
Stane St, Lthd. KT22 248 CL126
Mickleham RH5 247 CK127
Stane Way, SE18 164 EK80
Epsom KT17 217 CU110
Stanfield Ho, NW8 off Frampton St 284 B4
Stanfield Rd, E3 289 M1
Stanfields Ct, Harl. CM20 off Broadfield 35 ES14
Stanford Cl, Hmptn. TW12 176 BZ93
Romford RM7 127 FB58
Ruislip HA4 115 BQ58
Woodford Green IG8 102 EL50
Stanford Ct, SW6 307 M7
Waltham Abbey EN9 68 EG33
Stanford Gdns, Aveley RM15 149 FR74
Stanford Ms, E8 278 C3
Stanford Pl, SE17 299 N9
Stanford Prim Sch, SW16 off Chilmark Rd 201 DK95
Stanford Rd, N11 98 DF50
SW16 201 DK96
W8 295 M6
Grays RM16 170 GD76
Stanford St, SW1 297 N9
Stanford Way, SW16 201 DK96
Stangate, SE1 298 C6
Stangate Cres, Borwd. WD6 78 CS43
Stangate Gdns, Stan. HA7 95 CH49
Stanger Rd, SE25 202 DU98
Stanham Pl, Dart. DA1 off Crayford Way 167 FG84
Stanham Rd, Dart. DA1 188 FJ85
Stanhope Av, N3 119 CZ55
Bromley BR2 204 EF102
Harrow HA3 95 CD53
Stanhope Cl, SE16 301 K4
Stanhope Gdns, N4 121 DP58
N6 121 DH58
NW7 97 CT50
SW7 295 P8
Dagenham RM8 126 EZ62
Ilford IG1 125 EM60
Stanhope Gate, W1 297 H2
Stanhope Gro, Beck. BR3 203 DZ99
Stanhope Heath, Stanw. TW19 174 BJ86
Stanhope Ms E, SW7 295 P8
Stanhope Ms S, SW7 295 P9
Stanhope Ms W, SW7 295 P8
Stanhope Par, NW1 off Stanhope St 285 L2
Stanhope Pk Rd, Grnf. UB6 136 CC70
Stanhope Pl, W2 284 E9
Stanhope Prim Sch, Grnf. UB6 off Mansell Rd 136 CC70
Stanhope Rd, E17 123 EB57
N6 121 DJ58
N12 98 DC50
Barnet EN5 79 CW44
Bexleyheath DA7 166 EY82
Carshalton SM5 218 DG108
Croydon CR0 202 DS104
Dagenham RM8 126 EZ61
Greenford UB6 136 CC71
Rainham RM13 147 FG68
St. Albans AL1 43 CF21
Sidcup DA15 186 EU91
Slough SL1 131 AK72
Swanscombe DA10 190 FZ85
Waltham Cross EN8 67 DY33
Stanhope Row, W1 297 J3
Stanhopes, Oxt. RH8 254 EH128
Stanhope St, NW1 285 L3
Stanhope Ter, W2 284 B10
Stanhope Way, Sev. TN13 256 FD122
Stanwell TW19 174 BJ86
Stanier Cl, W14 307 H1
Stanier Ri, Berk. HP4 38 AT16
Staniland Dr, Wey. KT13 212 BM111
Stanlake Ms, W12 294 A3
Stanlake Rd, W12 139 CV74
Stanlake Vil, W12 294 A3
Stanley Av, Bark. IG11 145 ET68
Beckenham BR3 203 EC96
Chesham HP5 54 AP31
Dagenham RM8 126 EZ60
Greenford UB6 136 CC67
New Malden KT3 199 CU99
Romford RM2 127 FG56
St. Albans AL2 60 CA25
Wembley HA0 138 CL66
Stanley Cl, SE9 185 EQ88
SW8 310 C3
Coulsdon CR5 235 DM117
Greenhithe DA9 189 FS85
Hornchurch RM12 off Stanley Rd 128 FJ61
Romford RM2 127 FG56
Uxbridge UB8 134 BK67
Wembley HA0 138 CL66
Stanley Cotts, Slou. SL2 132 AT74
Stanley Ct, Cars. SM5 off Stanley Pk Rd 218 DG108
Stanley Cres, W11 282 G10
Gravesend DA12 191 GK92
Stanleycroft Cl, Islw. TW7 157 CE81
Stanley Dr, Hat. AL10 45 CV20
Stanley Gdns, NW2 272 B3
W3 138 CS74
W11 282 G10
Borehamwood WD6 78 CL39
Hersham KT12 214 BW107
Mitcham CR4 off Ashbourne Rd 180 DG93
South Croydon CR2 220 DU112
Wallington SM6 219 DJ107
Stanley Gdns Ms, W11 283 H10
Stanley Gdns Rd, Tedd. TW11 177 CE92
Stanley Grn E, Slou. SL3 153 AZ77
Stanley Grn W, Slou. SL3 153 AZ77
Stanley Gro, SW8 309 H9
Croydon CR0 201 DN100
Stanley Hill, Amer. HP7 55 AR40
Stanley Hill Av, Amer. HP7 55 AR39
Stanley Inf & Nurs Sch, Tedd. TW11 off Strathmore Rd 177 CE91
Stanley Jun Sch, Tedd. TW11 off Stanley Rd 177 CE91
Stanley Pk Dr, Wem. HA0 138 CM66
Stanley Pk High Sch, Cars. SM5 off Stanley Pk Rd 218 DG107
Stanley Pk Rd, Cars. SM5 218 DF108
Wallington SM6 219 DH107
Stanley Rd, E4 101 ED46
E10 123 EB58
E12 124 EL64
E18 102 EF53
N2 120 DD55
N9 100 DT46
N10 99 DH52
N11 99 DK51
N15 121 DP56
NW9 off West Hendon Bdy 119 CU59
SW14 158 CP84
SW19 180 DA94
W3 158 CQ76
Ashford TW15 174 BL92
Bromley BR2 204 EH98
Carshalton SM5 218 DG108
Croydon CR0 201 DN101
Enfield EN1 82 DS41
Grays RM17 170 GB78
Harrow HA2 116 CC61
Hertford SG13 32 DS09
Hornchurch RM12 128 FJ61
Hounslow TW3 156 CC84
Ilford IG1 125 ER61
Mitcham CR4 180 DG94
Morden SM4 200 DA98
Northfleet DA11 190 GE88
Northwood HA6 93 BU53
Orpington BR6 206 EU102
Sidcup DA14 186 EU90
Southall UB1 136 BY73
Sutton SM2 218 DB107
Swanscombe DA10 190 FZ86
Teddington TW11 177 CE91
Twickenham TW2 177 CD90
Watford WD17 76 BW41
Wembley HA9 138 CM65
Woking GU21 227 AZ116
Stanley Rd N, Rain. RM13 147 FE67
Stanley Rd S, Rain. RM13 147 FF68
Stanley Sq, Cars. SM5 218 DF109
Stanley St, SE8 313 P5
Caterham CR3 236 DQ121
Stanley Ter, N19 121 DL61
Stanley Way, Orp. BR5 206 EV99
Stanliff Ho, E14 302 B6
Stanmer St, SW11 308 D7
STANMORE, HA7 95 CG50
⊖ Stanmore 95 CK50
Stanmore Chase, St.Alb. AL4 43 CK21
Stanmore Coll, Stan. HA7 off Elm Pk 95 CJ51
Stanmore Gdns, Rich. TW9 158 CM83
Sutton SM1 200 DC104
Stanmore Hall, Stan. HA7 95 CH48
Stanmore Hill, Stan. HA7 95 CG48
Stanmore Rd, E11 124 EF60
N15 121 DP56
Belvedere DA17 167 FC77
Richmond TW9 158 CM83
Watford WD24 75 BV39
Stanmore St, N1 276 C8
Stanmore Ter, Beck. BR3 203 EA96
Stanmore Twrs, Stan. HA7 off Church Rd 95 CJ50
Stanmore Way, Loug. IG10 85 EN39
Stanmount Rd, St.Alb. AL2 60 CA25
Stannard Ho, SW19 off Plough La 180 DC91
Stannard Ms, E8 278 C4
Stannard Rd, E8 278 C4
Stannary St, SE11 310 F2
Stannet Way, Wall. SM6 219 DJ105
Stannington Path, Borwd. WD6 78 CN39
Stansbury Sq, W10 282 F2
Stansfeld Rd, E6 292 F7
E16 292 F7
Stansfield Ho, SE1 300 B9
Stansfield Rd, SW9 161 DM83
Hounslow TW4 155 BV82
Stansgate Rd, Dag. RM10 126 FA61
STANSTEAD ABBOTTS, Ware SG12 33 ED11
Stanstead Bury, Stans.Abb. SG12 34 EF12
Stanstead Cl, Brom. BR2 204 EF99
Caterham CR3 236 DS124
Stanstead Dr, Hodd. EN11 49 EB15
Stanstead Gro, SE6 off Stanstead Rd 183 DZ88
Stanstead Manor, Sutt. SM1 218 DA107
Stanstead Rd, E11 124 EH57
SE6 183 DX88
SE23 183 DX88
Caterham CR3 252 DR125
Hertford SG13 32 DT08
Hoddesdon EN11 49 EB16
Hunsdon SG12 34 EG09
London Heathrow Airport TW6 174 BM86
Stanstead Abbotts SG12 34 EH12
Ware SG12 32 DW09
Stansted Cl, Horn. RM12 147 FH65
Stansted Cres, Bex. DA5 186 EX88
Stanswood Gdns, SE5 311 P5
● Stanta Business Cen, St.Alb. AL3 off Soothouse Spring 43 CF16
Stanthorpe Cl, SW16 181 DL92
Stanthorpe Rd, SW16 181 DL92
Stanton Av, Tedd. TW11 177 CE93
Stanton Cl, Epsom KT19 216 CP106
Orpington BR5 206 EW101
St. Albans AL4 43 CK16
Worcester Park KT4 199 CX102
Stanton Ct, Dag. RM10 off St. Mark's Pl 146 FA65
Stanton Ho, SE16 301 N4
Stanton Rd, SE26 off Stanton Way 183 DZ91
SW13 159 CT82
SW20 199 CX96
Croydon CR0 202 DQ101
Stantons, Harl. CM20 51 EN15
Stanton Sq, SE26 off Stanton Way 183 DZ91
Stantons Wf, Bramley GU5 259 BA144
Stanton Way, SE26 183 DZ91
Slough SL3 152 AY77
Stants Vw, Hert. SG13 off Rowleys Rd 32 DT08
Stanway Cl, Chig. IG7 103 ES50
Stanway Ct, N1 287 P1
Stanway Gdns, W3 138 CN74
Edgware HA8 96 CQ50
Stanway Rd, Wal.Abb. EN9 68 EG33
Stanway St, N1 277 P10
STANWELL, Stai. TW19 174 BL87
Stanwell Cl, Stanw. TW19 174 BK86
Stanwell Flds C of E Prim Sch, Stanw. TW19 off Clare Rd 174 BL87
Stanwell Gdns, Stanw. TW19 174 BK86
STANWELL MOOR, Stai. TW19 174 BG85
Stanwell Moor Rd, Stai. TW19 174 BH85
Stanwell New Rd, Stai. TW18 174 BH90
Stanwell Rd, Ashf. TW15 174 BL89
Feltham TW14 175 BQ87
Horton SL3 153 BA83
Stanwick Rd, W14 294 G9
Stanworth St, SE1 300 A5
Stanwyck Dr, Chig. IG7 103 EQ50
Stanwyck Gdns, Rom. RM3 105 FH50
Stapenhill Rd, Wem. HA0 117 CH62
Staple Cl, Bex. DA5 187 FD90
Staplefield Cl, SW2 181 DL88
Pinner HA5 94 BY52
Stapleford, Welw.G.C. AL7 30 DD09
STAPLEFORD ABBOTTS, Rom. RM4 87 FC43
Stapleford Abbotts Prim Sch, Stap.Abb. RM4 off Stapleford Rd 87 FB43
★ Stapleford Aerodrome, Rom. RM4 86 EZ40
Stapleford Av, Ilf. IG2 125 ES57
Stapleford Cl, E4 101 EC48
SW19 179 CY87
Kingston upon Thames KT1 198 CN97
Stapleford Ct, Sev. TN13 256 FF123
Stapleford Gdns, Rom. RM5 104 FA51
Stapleford Rd, Rom. RM4 87 FB42
Wembley HA0 137 CK66
STAPLEFORD TAWNEY, Rom. RM4 87 FC37
Staple Hill Rd, Chob.Com. GU24 210 AS105
Staplehurst Cl, Reig. RH2 266 DC138
Staplehurst Rd, SE13 184 EE85
Carshalton SM5 218 DE108
Reigate RH2 266 DC138
Staple Inn, WC1 286 E7
Staple Inn Bldgs, WC1 286 E7
Staple La, Shere GU5 244 BK132
Staples, The, Swan. BR8 207 FH95
Staples Cl, SE16 301 L2
Staples Cor, NW2 119 CV60
● Staples Cor Retail Pk, NW2 off Geron Way 119 CV61
Staples Rd, Loug. IG10 84 EL41
Staples Rd Inf Sch, Loug. IG10 off Staples Rd 84 EL41
Staples Rd Jun Sch, Loug. IG10 off Staples Rd 84 EL41
Staple St, SE1 299 M5
Stapleton Cl, Pot.B. EN6 64 DD31
Stapleton Cres, Rain. RM13 147 FG65
Stapleton Gdns, Croy. CR0 219 DN106
Stapleton Hall Rd, N4 121 DM59
Stapleton Rd, SW17 180 DG90
Bexleyheath DA7 166 EZ80
Borehamwood WD6 78 CN38
Orpington BR6 205 ET104
Staple Tye Shop Cen, Harl. CM18 51 EQ18
Staple Tye Shop Ms, Harl. CM18 off Perry Rd 51 EQ18
Stapley Rd, Belv. DA17 166 FA78
St. Albans AL3 43 CD19
Stapylton Rd, Barn. EN5 79 CY41
Star All, EC3 287 P10
Star & Garter Hill, Rich. TW10 178 CL88
Starboard Av, Green. DA9 189 FV86
Starboard Way, E14 302 B6
Starbuck Cl, SE9 185 EN87
● Star Business Cen, Rain. RM13 off Marsh Way 147 FD71
Starch Ho La, Ilf. IG6 103 ER54
Star Cl, Enf. EN3 82 DW44
Starcross St, NW1 285 M3
Star Est, Grays RM16 171 GH78
Starfield Rd, W12 159 CU75
Star Hill, Dart. DA1 187 FE85
Woking GU22 226 AW119
Star Hill Rd, Dunt.Grn TN14 240 EZ116
Star Holme Ct, Ware SG12 33 DY06
Starhurst Sch, Dor. RH5 off Chart La S 263 CJ138
Starkey Cl, Chsht EN7 off Shambrook Rd 66 DQ25
Starks Fld Prim Sch, N9 off Church St 100 DS47
Star La, E16 291 J5
Coulsdon CR5 234 DG122
Epping CM16 70 EU30
Orpington BR5 206 EW98
Star Lane 291 J5
Starlight Way, Lon.Hthrw Air. TW6 175 BQ85
St. Albans AL4 43 CJ22
Starling Cl, Buck.H. IG9 102 EG46
Croydon CR0 203 DY100
Pinner HA5 116 BW55
Starling La, Cuffley EN6 65 DM28
Starling Pl, Wat. WD25 60 BW25
Starlings, The, Oxshott KT22 214 CC113
Starling Wk, Hmptn. TW12 off Oak Av 176 BY92
Starmans Cl, Dag. RM9 146 EY67
Star Path, Nthlt. UB5 off Brabazon Rd 136 CA68
Star Pl, E1 300 B1
Star Prim Sch, E16 291 K5
Star Rd, W14 306 G2
Isleworth TW7 157 CD82
Uxbridge UB10 135 BQ70
Starrock La, Chipstead CR5 234 DF120
Starrock Rd, Couls. CR5 235 DH119
Star St, E16 291 M6
W2 284 B8
Ware SG12 33 DY06
Starts Cl, Orp. BR6 205 EN104
Starts Hill Av, Farnboro. BR6 223 EP106
Starts Hill Rd, Orp. BR6 205 EN104
Starveall Cl, West Dr. UB7 154 BM76
Star Wf, NW1 275 M8
Starwood Cl, W.Byf. KT14 212 BJ111
Star Yd, WC2 286 E8
State Fm Av, Orp. BR6 223 EP105
Staten Bldg, E3 off Fairfield Rd 280 B10
Staten Gdns, Twick. TW1 177 CF88
Statham Ct, N7 121 DL62
Statham Gro, N16 off Green Las 122 DR63
N18 100 DS50
Station App, E4 (Chingford) off Station Rd 102 EE45
E4 (Highams Pk) off The Avenue 101 ED51
E7 off Woodgrange Rd 124 EH63
E11 (Snaresbrook) off High St 124 EG57
N11 off Friern Barnet Rd 99 DH50
N12 (Woodside Pk) 98 DB49
N16 (Stoke Newington) off Stamford Hill 122 DT61
NW10 off Station Rd 139 CT69
SE1 298 D3
SE3 off Kidbrooke Pk Rd 164 EH83
SE9 (Mottingham) 185 EM88
SE26 (Lwr Sydenham) off Worsley Br Rd 183 DZ92
SE26 (Sydenham) off Sydenham Rd 182 DW91
SW6 306 F10
SW16 181 DK92
SW20 199 CW96
W7 137 CE74
Amersham HP6 55 AQ38
Ashford TW15 174 BM91
Barnehurst DA7 167 FC82
Beckenham BR3 off Rectory Rd 203 EA95
Belmont SM2 off Brighton Rd 218 DB110
Berkhamsted HP4 off Brownlow Rd 38 AW18
Bexley DA5 off Bexley High St 186 FA87
Bexleyheath DA7 off Avenue Rd 166 EY82
Bromley BR1 off High St 204 EG97
Buckhurst Hill IG9 off Cherry Tree Ri 102 EK49
Carpenders Park WD19 off Prestwick Rd 94 BX48
Cheam SM2 217 CY108
Chelsfield BR6 224 EV106
Cheshunt EN8 67 DZ30
Chipstead CR5 234 DF118
Chislehurst BR7 205 EN95
Chorleywood WD3 73 BD42
Coulsdon CR5 235 DK116
Croy. CR0 off George St 202 DR103
Crayford DA1 187 FF86
Dartford DA1 188 FL86
Debden IG10 85 EQ42
Denham UB9 off Middle Rd 113 BD59
Dorking RH4 247 CJ134
Dunton Green TN13 241 FE120
East Horsley KT24 245 BS126
Elmstead Woods BR7 184 EL93
Epping CM16 70 EU31
Epsom KT19 216 CR113
Ewell East KT17 217 CV110
Ewell West KT19 off Chessington Rd 217 CT109
Gerrards Cross SL9 112 AY57
Gomshall GU5 261 BR139
Grays RM17 170 GA79
Greenford UB6 137 CD66
Guildford GU1 258 AY135
Hampton TW12 off Milton Rd 196 CA95
Harlow (Harl. Mill) CM20 36 EW10
Harlow (Harl. Town) CM20 35 EQ12
Harrow HA1 117 CE59
Hatch End HA5 off Uxbridge Rd 94 CA52
Hayes BR2 204 EG102
Hayes UB3 off Station Rd 155 BT75
Hemel Hempstead HP3 40 BG23
High Barnet EN5 off Barnet Hill 80 DA42
Hinchley Wood KT10 197 CF104
Horley RH6 269 DH148
Kenley CR8 off Hayes La 220 DQ114
Kingston upon Thames KT1 198 CN95
Leatherhead KT22 231 CG121
Little Chalfont HP7 off Chalfont Sta Rd 72 AX39
Loughton IG10 84 EL43
New Barnet EN5 80 DC42
Northwood HA6 93 BS52
Orpington BR6 205 ET103
Station App, Oxshott KT22 214 CC113
Oxted RH8 254 EE128
Pinner HA5 116 BY55
Purley CR8 219 DN111
Radlett WD7 off Shenley Hill 77 CG35
Richmond TW9 158 CN81
Ruislip HA4 115 BS60
St. Mary Cray BR5 206 EV98
Shalford GU4 off Horsham Rd 258 AY140
Shepperton TW17 195 BQ100
Slough SL3 153 BA75
South Croydon CR2 off Sanderstead Rd 220 DR109
South Ruislip HA4 115 BV64
Staines-upon-Thames TW18 174 BG92
Stoneleigh KT19 217 CU106
Sunbury-on-Thames TW16 195 BU95
Swanley BR8 207 FE98
Tadworth KT20 233 CW122
Theydon Bois CM16 85 ES36
Upminster RM14 128 FQ61
Virginia Water GU25 192 AX98
Waltham Cross EN8 67 DY34
Wembley HA0 137 CH65
West Byfleet KT14 212 BG112
West Drayton UB7 134 BL74
West Wickham BR4 203 EC102
Weybridge KT13 212 BN107
Whyteleafe CR3 236 DU117
Woking GU22 227 AZ117
Woodford Green IG8 off The Broadway 102 EH51
Worcester Park KT4 199 CU102
Station App E, Earls. RH1 off Earlsbrook Rd 266 DF136
Station App N, Sid. DA15 186 EU89
Station App Path, SE9 off Glenlea Rd 185 EM85
Station App Rd, W4 158 CQ80
Coulsdon CR5 235 DK115
Gatwick RH6 off London Rd 269 DH151
Station App W, Earls. RH1 off Earlswood Rd 266 DF136
Station Av, SW9 311 H10
Caterham CR3 236 DU124
Epsom KT19 216 CS109
Kew TW9 off Station App 158 CN81
New Malden KT3 198 CS97
Walton-on-Thames KT12 213 BU105
Station Cl, N3 98 DA53
N12 (Woodside Pk) 98 DB49
Brookmans Park AL9 63 CY26
Hampton TW12 196 CB95
Potters Bar EN6 63 CZ31
Station Ct, SW6 307 N7
Station Cres, N15 122 DR56
SE3 315 N1
Ashford TW15 174 BK90
Wembley HA0 137 CH65
Stationers' Crown Wds Acad, SE9 off Rifield Rd 185 EQ85
Stationers Hall Ct, EC4 off Ludgate Hill 287 H9
Stationers Pl, Hem.H. HP3 58 BL25
● Station Est, E18 off George La 102 EH54
Station Est, Beck. BR3 off Elmers End Rd 203 DX98
Station Est Rd, Felt. TW14 175 BV88
Station Footpath, Kings L. WD4 59 BP31
Station Forecourt, Rick. WD3 off Rectory Rd 92 BK45
Station Gar Ms, SW16 off Estreham Rd 181 DK93
Station Gdns, W4 158 CQ80
Station Gro, Wem. HA0 138 CL65
Station Hill, Brom. BR2 204 EG103
They.B. CM16 off Abridge Rd 85 ET37
Station Ho Ms, N9 100 DU49
Station La, E20 280 E5
Hornchurch RM12 128 FK62
Station Ms Ter, SE3 off Halstow Rd 315 N1
Station Par, E11 124 EG57
N14 off High St 99 DK46
NW2 272 B4
SW12 off Balham High Rd 180 DG88
W3 138 CN72
W5 off Uxbridge Rd 138 CM74
Ashford TW15 off Woodthorpe Rd 174 BM91
Barking IG11 145 EQ66
Barnet EN4 off Cockfosters Rd 80 DG42
Beaconsfield HP9 89 AK52
Denham UB9 114 BG59
East Horsley KT24 off Ockham Rd S 245 BS126
Edgware HA8 96 CL52
Feltham TW14 175 BV87
Har. HA3 95 CG54
Hornchurch RM12 off Rosewood Av 127 FH63
Nthlt. HA2 116 CB63
Nthlt. UB5 off Dorchester Rd 116 CB63
Richmond TW9 158 CN81
Rom. RM1 off South St 127 FE58
Sevenoaks TN13 off London Rd 256 FG124
Virginia Water GU25 192 AX98
Station Pas, E18 off Cowslip Rd 102 EH54
SE15 312 G6
Station Path, E8 278 F4
Staines-upon-Thames TW18 173 BF91
Station Pl, N4 off Seven Sisters Rd 121 DN61
Godalming GU7 off Summers Rd 258 AT144
Station Ri, SE27 off Norwood Rd 181 DP89
Station Rd, E4 (Chingford) 101 ED46
E7 124 EG63
E12 124 EK63
E17 123 DY58
N3 98 DA53
N11 99 DH50
N17 122 DU55
N19 121 DJ62
N21 99 DP46
N22 99 DM54
NW4 119 CU58
NW7 96 CS50
NW10 139 CT68
SE13 314 E10
SE20 182 DW93
SE25 (Norwood Junct.) 202 DT98
SW13 159 CU83

Station Rd, SW19 200 DC95
W5 138 CM72
W7 (Hanwell) 137 CE74
Addlestone KT15 212 BJ105
Amersham HP6, HP7 55 AQ38
Ashford TW15 174 BM91
Barkingside IG6 125 ER55
Beaconsfield HP9 89 AK52
Belmont SM2 218 DA110
Belvedere DA17 166 FA76
Berkhamsted HP4 38 AW18
Betchworth RH3 248 CS131
Bexleyheath DA7 166 EY83
Borehamwood WD6 78 CN42
Bramley GU5 259 AZ144
Brasted TN16 240 EV123
Brentford TW8 157 CJ79
Bricket Wood AL2 60 CA31
Bromley BR1 204 EG95
Broxbourne EN10 49 DZ20
Carshalton SM5 218 DF105
Chadwell Heath RM6 126 EX59
Chertsey KT16 193 BF102
Chesham HP5 54 AP31
Chessington KT9 216 CL106
Chigwell IG7 103 EP48
Chobham GU24 210 AT111
Cippenham SL1 131 AL72
Claygate KT10 215 CD106
Crayford DA1 187 FF86
Croydon CR0 202 DQ102
Cuffley EN6 65 DM29
Dorking RH4 263 CG135
Dunton Green TN13 241 FE120
Edgware HA8 96 CN51
Egham TW20 173 BA92
Epping CM16 69 ET31
Esher KT10 197 CD103
Eynsford DA4 208 FK104
Farncombe GU7 258 AT144
Gerrards Cross SL9 112 AY57
Gidea Park RM2 127 FH56
Gomshall GU5 261 BQ139
Greenhithe DA9 169 FU84
Halstead TN14 224 EZ111
Hampton TW12 196 CA95
Hampton Wick KT1 197 CJ95
Harlow CM17 36 EW11
Harold Wood RM3 106 FM53
Harrow HA1 117 CF59
Hayes UB3 155 BS77
Hemel Hempstead HP1 40 BH22
Horley RH6 269 DH148
Hounslow TW3 156 CB84
Ilford IG1 125 EP62
Kenley CR8 220 DQ114
Kings Langley WD4 59 BP29
Kingston upon Thames KT2 198 CN95
Langley SL3 153 BA76
Leatherhead KT22 231 CG121
Letty Green SG14 30 DG12
Loudwater HP10 88 AC53
Loughton IG10 84 EL42
Merstham RH1 251 DJ128
Motspur Park KT3 199 CV99
New Barnet EN5 80 DB43
North Harrow HA2 116 CB57
North Mymms AL9 63 CX25
North Weald Bassett CM16 71 FB27
Northfleet DA11 190 GB86
Orpington BR6 205 ET103
Otford TN14 241 FH116
Radlett WD7 77 CG35
Redhill RH1 250 DG133
Rickmansworth WD3 92 BK45
St. Paul's Cray BR5 206 EW98
Shalford GU4 258 AY140
Shepperton TW17 195 BQ99
Shoreham TN14 225 FG111
Shortlands BR2 204 EE96
Sidcup DA15 186 EU91
Smallford AL4 44 CP19
South Darenth DA4 208 FP96
Southfleet DA13 190 GA91
Stanstead Abbotts SG12 33 EA11
Stoke D'Abernon KT11 230 BY117
Sunbury-on-Thames TW16 175 BU94
Swanley BR8 207 FE98
Taplow SL6 130 AF72
Teddington TW11 177 CF92
Thames Ditton KT7 197 CF101
Twickenham TW1 177 CF88
Upminster RM14 128 FQ61
Uxbridge UB8 134 BJ70
Waltham Abbey EN9 67 EA34
Waltham Cross EN8 67 EA34
Ware SG12 33 DX06
Watford WD17 75 BV40
West Byfleet KT14 212 BG112
West Drayton UB7 134 BK74
West Wickham BR4 203 EC102
Whyteleafe CR3 236 DT118
Woldingham CR3 237 DZ123
Wraysbury TW19 173 AZ86
Station Rd E, Oxt. RH8 254 EE128
Station Rd N, Belv. DA17 167 FB76
Egham TW20 173 BA92
Merstham RH1 251 DJ128
Station Rd S, Merst. RH1 251 DJ128
Station Rd W, Oxt. RH8 254 EE129
Station Row, Shalf. GU4 258 AY140
Station Sq, Petts Wd BR5 205 EQ99
Station St, E15 280 G6
E16 305 N3
Station Ter, NW10 282 C1
SE5 311 K6
Dorking RH4 off Chalkpit La 263 CG135
Park Street AL2 off Park St 61 CD26
Station Vw, Grnf. UB6 137 CD67
Guildford GU1 258 AW135
Station Way, SE15 312 C8
off Blenheim Gro
Cheam SM3 217 CY107
Claygate KT10 215 CE107
Epsom KT19 216 CR113
Roding Valley IG9 102 EJ49
St. Albans AL1 43 CF20
Station Yd, Denh. UB9 114 BG59
Smallford AL4 44 CP20
Twickenham TW1 177 CG87
Staunton Rd, Kings.T. KT2 178 CL93
Slough SL2 131 AR71
Staunton St, SE8 313 P2
★ Stave Hill Ecological Pk, SE16 301 L4
Staveley Cl, E9 279 H2
N7 276 B1
SE15 312 F6
Staveley Gdns, W4 158 CR81
Staveley Rd, W4 158 CR80
Ashford TW15 175 BR93
Staveley Way, Knap. GU21 226 AS117
Staverton Rd, NW2 272 A6
Hornchurch RM11 128 FK58
Stave Yd Rd, SE16 301 L3
Stavordale Rd, N5 121 DP63
Carshalton SM5 200 DC101
Stayne End, Vir.W. GU25 192 AU98
Stayner's Rd, E1 289 J4
Stayton Rd, Sutt. SM1 200 DA104
Steadfast Rd, Kings.T. KT1 197 CK95
Stead St, SE17 299 L9
Steam Fm La, Felt. TW14 155 BT84
Stean St, E8 278 A8
Stebbing Ho, W11 294 D2
Stebbing Way, Bark. IG11 146 EU68
Stebondale St, E14 302 F10
Sch Stebon Prim Sch, E14 290 A7
Stedham Pl, WC1 286 A8
Stedman Cl, Bex. DA5 187 FE90
Uxbridge UB10 114 BN62
Steed Cl, Horn. RM11 127 FH61
Steedman St, SE17 299 J9
Steeds Rd, N10 98 DF53
Steeds Way, Loug. IG10 84 EL41
Steele Av, Green. DA9 189 FT85
Steele Rd, E11 124 EE63
N17 122 DS55
NW10 138 CQ68
W4 158 CQ76
Isleworth TW7 157 CG84
Steeles Ms N, NW3 274 E5
Steeles Ms S, NW3 274 F5
Steeles Rd, NW3 274 E5
Steele Wk, Erith DA8 167 FB79
Steels La, Oxshott KT22 214 CB114
Steel's La, E1 289 H9
Steelyard Pas, EC4 299 L1
Steen Way, SE22 182 DS85
off East Dulwich Gro
Steep Cl, Orp. BR6 223 ET107
Steep Hill, SW16 181 DK90
Croydon CR0 220 DS105
Steeplands, Bushey WD23 94 CB45
Steeple Cl, SW6 306 F9
SW19 179 CY92
Steeple Ct, E1 288 F4
off Coventry Rd
Egham TW20 173 BA92
off The Chantries
Steeple Gdns, Add. KT15 212 BH106
off Weatherall Cl
Steeple Hts Dr, Bigg.H. TN16 238 EK117
Steeplestone Cl, N18 100 DQ50
Steeple Wk, N1 277 K8
Steerforth St, SW18 180 DB89
Steering Cl, N9 100 DW46
Steers Mead, Mitch. CR4 200 DF95
Steers Way, SE16 301 M5
Stella Cl, Uxb. UB8 135 BP71
Stellar Ho, N17 100 DT51
Stella Rd, SW17 180 DF93
Stelling Rd, Erith DA8 167 FD80
Stellman Cl, E5 122 DU62
Stembridge Rd, SE20 202 DV96
Sten Cl, Enf. EN3 83 EA37
Stents La, Cob. KT11 230 BZ120
Stepbridge Path, Wok. GU21 226 AX117
off Goldsworth Rd
Stepgates, Cher. KT16 194 BH101
Stepgates Cl, Cher. KT16 194 BH101
Sch Stepgates Comm Sch, Cher. KT16 off Stepgates 194 BH101
Stephan Cl, E8 278 D8
Stephen Av, Rain. RM13 147 FG65
Stephen Cl, Egh. TW20 173 BC93
Orpington BR6 205 ET104
Stephendale Rd, SW6 307 M8
Sch Stephen Hawking Sch, E14 289 M9
Stephen Ms, W1 285 N7
Stephen Pl, SW4 309 L10
Stephen Rd, Bexh. DA7 167 FC83
Stephens Cl, Rom. RM3 106 FJ50
Stephenson Av, Til. RM18 171 GG81
Stephenson Cl, E3 290 C3
Hoddesdon EN11 49 ED17
Welling DA16 166 EU82
Stephenson Ct, Ware SG12 33 DY07
Stephenson Dr, Wind. SL4 151 AP80
Stephenson Ho, SE1 299 J6
off Bath Ter
Stephenson Rd, E17 123 DY57
W7 137 CF72
Twickenham TW2 176 CA87
Stephenson St, E16 291 J5
NW10 138 CS69
Stephenson Way, NW1 285 M4
Watford WD24 76 BX41
Stephenson Wf, Hem.H. HP3 58 BL25
Stephen's Rd, E15 281 K9
Stephen St, W1 285 N7
Stephyns Chambers, Hem.H. HP1 40 BJ21
off Waterhouse St
STEPNEY, E1 289 J7
Stepney Causeway, E1 289 K9
Stepney City, E1 288 G7
off Jubilee St
Stepney Cl, Mitch. CR4 200 DG95
⊖ Stepney Green 289 J5
Stepney Grn, E1 289 H6
Sch Stepney Greencoat C of E Prim Sch, E14 289 N8
Sch Stepney Grn Sch, E1 289 K7
Stepney High St, E1 289 K7
Stepney Way, E1 288 E7
Sterling Av, Edg. HA8 96 CM49
Waltham Cross EN8 67 DX34
Sterling Cl, NW10 139 CU66
Sterling Gdns, SE14 313 L3
● Sterling Ind Est, Dag. RM10 127 FB63
Sterling Pl, W5 158 CL77
Weybridge KT13 213 BS105
Sterling Rd, Enf. EN2 82 DR39
Sterling St, SW7 296 D6
Sterling Way, N18 100 DR50
★ Sternberg Cen, N3 98 DB54
Stern Cl, Bark. IG11 146 EW68
Sterndale Rd, W14 294 C7
Dartford DA1 188 FM87
Sterne St, W12 294 C4
Sternhall La, SE15 312 D10
Sternhold Av, SW2 181 DK89
Sterry Cres, Dag. RM10 126 FA64
off Alibon Rd
Sterry Dr, Epsom KT19 216 CS105
Thames Ditton KT7 197 CE100
Sterry Gdns, Dag. RM10 146 FA65
Sterry Rd, Bark. IG11 145 ET67
Dagenham RM10 126 FA63
Sterry St, SE1 299 L5
Steucers La, SE23 183 DY87
Steve Biko La, SE6 183 EA91
Steve Biko Rd, N7 121 DN62
Steve Biko Way, Houns. TW3 156 CA83
Stevedale Rd, Well. DA16 166 EW82
Stevedore St, E1 300 E2
Stevenage Cres, Borwd. WD6 78 CL39
Stevenage Ri, Hem.H. HP2 40 BM16
Stevenage Rd, E6 145 EN65
SW6 306 C5
Stevens Av, E9 279 H4
Stevens Cl, Beck. BR3 183 EA93
Bexley DA5 187 FD91
Epsom KT17 216 CS113
Hampton TW12 176 BY93
Pnr. HA5 116 BW57
Potters Bar EN6 63 CX33
Steven's Cl, Lane End DA2 189 FS92
Stevens Grn, Bushey Hth WD23 94 CC46
Stevens La, Clay. KT10 215 CG108
Stevenson Cl, Barn. EN5 80 DD44
Erith DA8 167 FH80
Stevenson Cres, SE16 300 D10
Stevenson Rd, Hedg. SL2 111 AR61
Stevens Pl, Pur. CR8 219 DP113
Stevens Rd, Dag. RM8 126 EV62
Stevens St, SE1 299 P6
Steven's Wk, Croy. CR0 221 DY111
Stevens Way, Amer. HP7 55 AP40
Chigwell IG7 103 ES49
Steventon Rd, W12 139 CT73
Steward Cl, Chsht EN8 67 DY30
STEWARDS, Harl. CM18 51 ER19
Stewards Cl, Epp. CM16 70 EU33
Stewards Grn La, Epp. CM16 70 EV32
Stewards Grn Rd, Epp. CM16 70 EU33
Stewards Holte Wk, N11 99 DH49
off Coppies Gro
Sch Stewards Sch, Harl. CM18 51 ER19
off Parnall Rd
Steward St, E1 287 P7
🔒 Stewards Wk, Rom. RM1 127 FE57
off Western Rd
Stewart, Tad. KT20 233 CX121
Stewart Av, Shep. TW17 194 BN98
Slough SL1 132 AT71
Upminster RM14 128 FP62
Stewart Cl, NW9 118 CQ58
Abbots Langley WD5 59 BT32
Chislehurst BR7 185 EP92
Fifield SL6 150 AD81
Hampton TW12 176 BY92
Woking GU21 226 AT117
Stewart Cl, Denh. UB9 113 BF58
off Patrons Way West
Sch Stewart Fleming Prim Sch, SE20 off Witham Rd 202 DW97
Sch Stewart Headlam Prim Sch, E1 288 E4
Stewart Pl, Ware SG12 33 DX06
Stewart Rainbird Ho, E12 125 EN64
Stewart Rd, E15 280 F1
Stewartsby Cl, N18 100 DQ50
Stewart's Dr, Farn.Com. SL2 111 AP64
Stewart's Gro, SW3 296 B10
Stewart's Rd, SW8 309 L5
Stewart St, E14 302 F5
Stew La, EC4 287 J10
Steyne Rd, W3 138 CQ74
Steyning Cl, Ken. CR8 235 DP116
Steyning Gro, SE9 185 EM91
Steynings Way, N12 98 DA50
Steyning Way, Houns. TW4 156 BW84
Steynton Av, Bex. DA5 186 EX89
Stickland Rd, Belv. DA17 166 FA77
Stickleton Cl, Grnf. UB6 136 CB69
Stifford Hill, N.Stfd RM16 149 FX74
South Ockendon RM15 149 FW73
Sch Stifford Prim Sch, Grays RM17 off Parker Rd 170 FY78
Stifford Rd, S.Ock. RM15 149 FR74
Stile Cft, Harl. CM18 52 EU17
Stilecroft Gdns, Wem. HA0 117 CH62
Stile Hall Gdns, W4 158 CN78
Stile Hall Mans, W4 158 CN78
off Wellesley Rd
Stile Hall Par, W4 158 CN78
off Chiswick High Rd
Stile Meadow, Beac. HP9 89 AL52
Stile Path, Sun. TW16 195 BU98
Stile Rd, Slou. SL3 152 AX76
Stiles Cl, Brom. BR2 205 EM100
Erith DA8 off Riverdale Rd 167 FB78
Stillingfleet Rd, SW13 159 CU79
Stillington St, SW1 297 M8
Sch Stillness Inf & Jun Schs, SE23 off Brockley Ri 183 DY86
Stillness Rd, SE23 183 DY86
Stilton Path, Borwd. WD6 78 CN38
Jct Stilwell Dr, Uxb. UB8 134 BM70
Jct Stilwell Rbt, Uxb. UB8 135 BP72
Stipularis Dr, Hayes UB4 136 BX70
Stirling Av, Pnr. HA5 116 BY59
Wallington SM6 219 DL108
Stirling Cl, SW16 201 DJ95
Banstead SM7 233 CZ117
Rainham RM13 147 FH69
Sidcup DA14 185 ES91
Uxbridge UB8 134 BJ69
off Ferndale Cres
Windsor SL4 151 AK82
Jct Stirling Cor, Barn. EN5 78 CR44
Stirling Dr, Cat. CR3 236 DQ121
Orpington BR6 224 EV106
Stirling Gro, Houns. TW3 156 CC82
● Stirling Ind Cen, Borwd. WD6 78 CR43
🔒 Stirling Retail Pk, Borwd. WD6 78 CR44
Stirling Rd, E13 292 A1
E17 123 DY55
N17 100 DU53
N22 99 DP53
SW9 310 A9
W3 158 CP76
Harrow HA3 117 CF55
Hayes UB3 135 BV73
London Heathrow Airport TW6 174 BM86
Slough SL1 131 AP72
Twickenham TW2 176 CA87
Stirling Rd Path, E17 123 DY55
Stirling Wk, N.Mal. KT3 198 CQ99
Surbiton KT5 198 CP100
Stirling Way, Abb.L. WD5 59 BU32
Borehamwood WD6 78 CR44
Croydon CR0 201 DL101
Welwyn Garden City AL7 30 DE09
Stites Hill Rd, Couls. CR5 235 DP120
Stiven Cres, Har. HA2 116 BZ62
Stoat Cl, Hert. SG13 32 DU09
Stoats Nest Rd, Couls. CR5 219 DL114
Stoats Nest Village, Couls. CR5 235 DL115
Stockbreach Cl, Hat. AL10 45 CU17
Stockbreach Rd, Hat. AL10 45 CU17
Stockbury Rd, Croy. CR0 202 DW100
Stockdale Rd, Dag. RM8 126 EZ61
Stockdales Rd, Eton Wick SL4 151 AM77
Stockdove Way, Perivale UB6 137 CF69
Stocker Gdns, Dag. RM9 146 EW66
Stockers Fm Rd, Rick. WD3 92 BK48
Stockers La, Wok. GU22 227 AZ120
★ Stock Exchange, EC4 287 H8
Stockfield, Horl. RH6 269 DH147
Stockfield Av, Hodd. EN11 49 EA15
Stockfield Rd, SW16 181 DM90
Claygate KT10 215 CE106
Stockford Av, NW7 97 CX52
Stockham's Cl, S.Croy. CR2 220 DR111
Stock Hill, Bigg.H. TN16 238 EK116
Stockholm Ho, E1 288 E10
Stockholm Rd, SE16 313 H1
Stockholm Way, E1 300 C2
Stockhurst Cl, SW15 306 B9
Stocking La, Bayford SG13 47 DN18
Stockings La, Lt.Berk. SG13 47 DK18
Stockingswater La, Enf. EN3 83 DY41
Stockland Rd, Rom. RM7 127 FD58
Stock La, Dart. DA2 188 FJ91
Stockleigh Hall, NW8 274 E10
off Prince Albert Rd
Sch Stockley Acad, Yiew. UB7 134 BM72
off Apple Tree Av
Stockley Cl, West Dr. UB7 155 BP75
Stockley Fm Rd, West Dr. UB7 155 BP76
off Stockley Rd
● Stockley Pk, Uxb. UB11 135 BP74
Jct Stockley Pk Rbt, Uxb. UB11 134 BN74
Stockley Rd, Uxb. UB8 135 BP73
West Drayton UB7 155 BP77
Stock Orchard Cres, N7 276 C2
Stock Orchard St, N7 276 C3
Stockport Rd, SW16 201 DK95
Heronsgate WD3 91 BC45
Stocksbridge Cl, Chsht EN7 66 DS26
Stocks Cl, Horl. RH6 269 DH149
Stocksfield Rd, E17 123 EC55
Stocks Meadow, Hem.H. HP2 40 BN19
Stocks Pl, E14 289 P10
Hillingdon UB10 134 BN67
Stock St, E13 291 N1
Stockton Cl, New Barn. EN5 80 DC42
Stockton Gdns, N17 100 DQ52
NW7 96 CR48
Stockton Ho, E2 288 E2
off Ellsworth St
Stockton Rd, N17 100 DQ52
N18 100 DU51
Reigate RH2 266 DA137
STOCKWELL, SW9 310 E9
⊖ Stockwell 310 B8
Stockwell Av, SW9 161 DM83
Stockwell Cl, Brom. BR1 204 EH96
Cheshunt EN7 66 DU28
Edgware HA8 96 CQ54
Stockwell Gdns, SW9 310 C7
Stockwell Gdns Est, SW9 310 B8
Stockwell Grn, SW9 310 C9
Stockwell La, SW9 310 D9
Cheshunt EN7 66 DU28
Stockwell Ms, SW9 310 C9
off Stockwell Rd
Stockwell Pk Cres, SW9 310 D8
Stockwell Pk Est, SW9 310 D9
Stockwell Pk Rd, SW9 310 C7
Sch Stockwell Pk Sch, SW9 310 C7
Stockwell Pk Wk, SW9 310 D10
Sch Stockwell Prim Sch, SW9 310 D10
Stockwell Rd, SW9 310 C8
Stockwells, Tap. SL6 130 AD70
Stockwell St, SE10 314 F3
Stockwell Ter, SW9 310 C7
Stocton Cl, Guil. GU1 242 AW133
Stocton Rd, Guil. GU1 242 AW133
Stodart Rd, SE20 202 DW95
Stofield Gdns, SE9 184 EK90
off Aldersgrove Av
Stoford Cl, SW19 179 CY87
Stoke Av, Ilf. IG6 104 EU51
Stoke Cl, Stoke D'Ab. KT11 230 BZ116
Stoke Common Rd, Fulmer SL3 112 AU63
Stoke Ct Dr, Stoke P. SL2 132 AS67
STOKE D'ABERNON, Cob. KT11 230 BZ116
Stoke Flds, Guil. GU1 242 AX134
off Stoke Rd
Stoke Gdns, Slou. SL1 132 AS74
STOKE GREEN, Slou. SL2 132 AU70
Stoke Grn, Stoke P. SL2 132 AU70
Stoke Gro, Guil. GU1 242 AX134
off Stoke Rd
Stoke Hosp, Guil. GU1 242 AX134
off Stoke Rd
Stoke Ms, Guil. GU1 258 AX135
off Stoke Rd
Stoke Mill Cl, Guil. GU1 242 AX132
off Mangles Rd
Stokenchurch St, SW6 307 L7
STOKE NEWINGTON, N16 122 DS61
⇌ Stoke Newington 122 DT61
Stoke Newington Ch St, N16 122 DR62
Stoke Newington Common, N16 122 DT62
Stoke Newington High St, N16 122 DT62
Stoke Newington Rd, N16 278 A2
Sch Stoke Newington Sch, N16 off Clissold Rd 122 DR62
Stoke Pk Av, Farn.Royal SL2 131 AQ69
Stoke Pl, NW10 139 CT69
STOKE POGES, Slou. SL2 132 AT66
Stoke Poges La, Slou. SL1, SL2 132 AS72
Sch Stoke Poges Sch, The, Stoke P. SL2 off Rogers La 132 AT66
Stoke Rd, Cob. KT11 230 BW115
Guildford GU1 242 AX133
Kingston upon Thames KT2 178 CQ94
Rainham RM13 148 FK68
Slough SL2 132 AT71
Walton-on-Thames KT12 196 BW104
Stokers Cl, Gat. RH6 268 DE151
Stokesay, Slou. SL2 132 AT73
Stokesby Rd, Chess. KT9 216 CM107
Stokesheath Rd, Oxshott KT22 214 CC111
Stokesley Ri, Woob.Grn HP10 110 AE55
Stokesley St, W12 139 CT72
Stokes Ridings, Tad. KT20 233 CX123
Stokes Rd, E6 292 G5
Croydon CR0 203 DX100
Stoke Wd, Stoke P. SL2 112 AT63
Stoll Cl, NW2 119 CW62
Stompond La, Walt. KT12 195 BU103
Stomp Rd, Burn. SL1 130 AJ71
Stoms Path, SE6 183 EA92
off Maroons Way
Stonard Rd, N13 99 DN48
Dagenham RM8 126 EV64
Stonards Hill, Epp. CM16 70 EW31
Loughton IG10 85 EM44
Stondon Pk, SE23 183 DY87
Stondon Wk, E6 144 EK68
STONE, Green. DA9 189 FT85
Stonebank, Welw.G.C. AL8 29 CX08
off Stonehills
Stonebanks, Walt. KT12 195 BU101
STONEBRIDGE, NW10 138 CP67
Dor. RH5 264 CL139
Stonebridge Common, E8 278 A7
Stonebridge Fld, Eton SL4 151 AP78
Stonebridge Flds, Shalf. GU4 258 AX141
Stonebridge Ms, SE19 182 DR94
⇌ Stonebridge Park 138 CN66
⊖ Stonebridge Park 138 CN66
Stonebridge Pk, NW10 138 CR66
Sch Stonebridge Prim Sch, The, NW10 off Shakespeare Av 138 CQ67
Stonebridge Rd, N15 122 DS57
Northfleet DA11 190 GA85
🔒 Stonebridge Shop Cen, NW10 off Shakespeare Rd 138 CR67
Stonebridge Way, Wem. HA9 138 CP65
Stonebridge Wf, Shalf. GU4 258 AX141
Stone Bldgs, WC2 286 D7
Stone Castle Dr, Green. DA9 189 FU86
Stonechat Ms, Green. DA9 189 FU86
Stonechat Sq, E6 293 H6
Stone Cl, SW4 309 M9
Dagenham RM8 126 EZ61
West Drayton UB7 134 BM74
Stonecot Cl, Sutt. SM3 199 CY102
Stonecot Hill, Sutt. SM3 199 CY102
Stonecourt Cl, Horl. RH6 269 DJ148
Stone Cres, Felt. TW14 175 BT87
Stonecroft Av, Iver SL0 133 BE72
Stonecroft Cl, Barn. EN5 79 CV42
Stonecroft Rd, Erith DA8 167 FC80
Stonecroft Way, Croy. CR0 201 DL101
Stonecrop Cl, NW9 118 CR55
Stonecrop Rd, Guil. GU4 243 BC132
Stone Cross, Harl. CM20 35 ER14
off Post Office Rd
Stonecross, St.Alb. AL1 43 CE19
Stonecross Cl, St.Alb. AL1 43 CE19
⇌ Stone Crossing 189 FS85
Stonecross Rd, Hat. AL10 45 CV16
Stonecutter St, EC4 286 G8
Stonefield, N4 121 DM61
Stonefield Cl, Bexh. DA7 166 FA83
Ruislip HA4 116 BY64
Stonefield St, N1 276 F8
Stonefield Way, SE7 164 EK80
off Greenbay Rd
Ruislip HA4 116 BY63
Stonegate Cl, Orp. BR5 206 EW97
off Main Rd
Stonegrove, Edg. HA8 96 CL49
Stonegrove Est, Edg. HA8 96 CM49
off Lacey Dr
Stonegrove Gdns, Edg. HA8 96 CM50
Stonehall Av, Ilf. IG1 124 EL58
● Stonehall Business Pk, Match.Grn CM17 37 FH10
Stone Hall Gdns, W8 295 L7
Stone Hall Pl, W8 295 L7
Stone Hall Rd, N21 99 DM45
Stoneham Rd, N11 99 DJ51
STONEHILL, Cher. KT16 210 AY107
● Stonehill Business Pk, N18 101 DX51
off Silvermere Dr
Stonehill Cl, SW14 178 CR85
Bookham KT23 246 CA125
Stonehill Cres, Ott. KT16 210 AY107
Stonehill Grn, Dart. DA2 187 FC94
Stonehill Rd, SW14 178 CQ85
W4 158 CN78
Chobham GU24 210 AW108
Ottershaw KT16 211 BA105
Stonehills, Welw.G.C. AL8 29 CX09
Stonehills Ct, SE21 182 DS90
Stonehill Wds Pk, Sid. DA14 187 FB93
Stonehorse Rd, Enf. EN3 82 DW43
Jct Stonehouse Cor, Purf. RM19 169 FR79
Stone Ho Ct, EC3 287 N8
Stone Ho Gdns, Cat. CR3 252 DS125
Stonehouse La, Halst. TN14 224 EX109
Purfleet RM19 169 FS78
Stonehouse Rd, Halst. TN14 224 EW110
Stoneings La, Knock. TN14 239 ET118
🔒 Stone Lake Retail Pk, SE7 304 D9
Jct Stone Lake Rbt, SE7 304 C9
Stonelea Rd, Hem.H. HP3 40 BM23
STONELEIGH, Epsom KT17 217 CU106
⇌ Stoneleigh 217 CU106
Stoneleigh Av, Enf. EN1 82 DV39
Worcester Park KT4 217 CU105
Stoneleigh Bdy, Epsom KT17 217 CU106
Stoneleigh Cl, Wal.Cr. EN8 67 DX33
Stoneleigh Cres, Epsom KT19 217 CT106
Stoneleigh Dr, Hodd. EN11 33 EB14
Stoneleigh Ms, E3 289 M1
Stoneleigh Pk, Wey. KT13 213 BQ106
Stoneleigh Pk Av, Croy. CR0 203 DX100
Stoneleigh Pk Rd, Epsom KT19 217 CT107
Stoneleigh Pl, W11 294 D1
Stoneleigh Rd, N17 122 DT55
Bromley BR1 205 EP97
Carshalton SM5 200 DE101
Ilford IG5 124 EL55
Oxted RH8 254 EL130
Stoneleigh St, W11 282 D10
Stoneleigh Ter, N19 121 DH61

Stoneley Cres, Green. DA9 169 FW84
Stonells Rd, SW11 *off Chatham Rd* 180 DF85
Stonemasons Cl, N15 122 DR56
Stoneness Rd, Grays RM20 169 FV79
Stonenest St, N4 121 DM60
Stone Pk Av, Beck. BR3 203 EA98
Stone Pl, Wor.Pk. KT4 199 CU103
Stone Pl Rd, Green. DA9 189 FS85
Stone Rd, Brom. BR2 204 EF99
Stone St. Mary's C of E Prim Sch, Stone DA9 *off Hayes Rd* 189 FS87
Stones All, Wat. WD18 75 BV42
Stones Cross Rd, Swan. BR8 207 FC99
Stones End St, SE1 299 J5
Stones La, Westc. RH4 262 CC137
Stones Rd, Epsom KT17 216 CS112
Stone St, Grav. DA11 191 GH86
Stoneswood Rd, Oxt. RH8 254 EH130
Stonewall, E6 293 M7
Stonewood, Bean DA2 189 FW90
Stonewood Rd, Erith DA8 167 FE78
Stoney All, SE18 165 EN82
Stoneyard La, E14 302 C1
Stoney Br Dr, Wal.Abb. EN9 68 EG34
Stoney Brook, Guil. GU2 242 AS133
Stoney Cl, Nthch HP4 38 AT17
Stoney Cl, Couls. CR5 235 DJ122
Stoneycroft, Hem.H. HP1 40 BG20
Welwyn Garden City AL7 30 DA08
Stoneycroft Cl, SE12 184 EF87
Stoneycroft Rd, Wdf.Grn. IG8 102 EL51
Stoneydeep, Tedd. TW11 *off Twickenham Rd* 177 CG91
Stoneydown, E17 123 DY56
Stoneydown Av, E17 123 DY56
Stoneydown Pk Prim Sch, E17 *off Pretoria Av* 123 DY56
Stoneyfield, Ger.Cr. SL9 112 AW60
Stoneyfield Rd, Couls. CR5 235 DM117
Stoneyfields Gdns, Edg. HA8 96 CQ49
Stoneyfields La, Edg. HA8 96 CQ50
Stoney Gro, Chesh. HP5 54 AR30
Stoneylands Ct, Egh. TW20 173 AZ92
Stoneylands Rd, Egh. TW20 173 AZ92
Stoney La, E1 287 P8
SE19 *off Church Rd* 182 DT93
Bovingdon HP3 57 BB27
Chipperfield WD4 57 BE30
East Burnham SL2 131 AN67
Hemel Hempstead HP1 39 BB23
Stoney Meade, Slou. SL1 *off Weekes Dr* 131 AP74
Stoney St, SE1 299 L2
Stonhouse St, SW4 161 DK83
Stonny Cft, Ashtd. KT21 232 CM117
Stonor Rd, W14 294 G9
Stonycroft Cl, Enf. EN3 *off Brimsdown Av* 83 DY40
Stony Dean Sch, Amer. HP7 *off Orchard End Av* 72 AT39
Stony La, Amer. HP6 72 AY38
Stony Path, Loug. IG10 85 EM40
Stonyrock La, Dor. RH5 246 BY131
Stonyshotts, Wal.Abb. EN9 68 EE34
Stony Wd, Harl. CM18 51 ES16
Stoop Ct, W.Byf. KT14 212 BH112
Stopes St, SE15 312 B5
Stopford Rd, E13 281 P8
SE17 311 H1
Store Rd, E16 305 L4
Storers Quay, E14 302 G9
Store St, E15 281 H3
WC1 285 N7
Storey Cl, Uxb. UB10 114 BQ61
Storey Ct, NW8 *off St. John's Wd Rd* 284 A3
Storey Rd, E17 123 DZ56
N6 120 DF58
Storey's Gate, SW1 297 P5
Storey St, E16 305 M3
Hemel Hempstead HP3 40 BK24
Stories Ms, SE5 311 N9
Stories Rd, SE5 311 N10
Stork Rd, E7 281 M5
Storksmead Rd, Edg. HA8 96 CS52
Storks Rd, SE16 300 D7
Stormont Ho Sch, E5 278 E1
Stormont Rd, N6 120 DF59
SW11 160 DG83
Stormont Sch, Pot.B. EN6 *off The Causeway* 64 DD31
Stormont Way, Chess. KT9 215 CJ106
Stormount Dr, Hayes UB3 155 BQ75
Stornaway Rd, Slou. SL3 153 BC77
Stornaway Strand, Grav. DA12 191 GM91
Stornoway, Hem.H. HP3 41 BP22
Storr Gdns, Hutt. CM13 109 GD43
Storrington Rd, Croy. CR0 202 DT102
Stortford Rd, Hodd. EN11 49 EB16
Stort Mill, Harl. CM20 36 EV09
Stort Twr, Harl. CM20 35 ET13
Story St, N1 276 C7
Stothard Pl, E1 *off Spital Yd* 287 P6
Stothard St, E1 288 G4
Stott Cl, SW18 180 DD86
STOUGHTON, Guil. GU2 242 AV131
Stoughton Av, Sutt. SM3 217 CX106
Stoughton Cl, SE11 298 D9
SW15 *off Bessborough Rd* 179 CU88
Stoughton Inf Sch, Guil. GU2 *off Stoughton Rd* 242 AV131
Stoughton Rd, Guil. GU1, GU2 242 AU131
Stour Av, Sthl. UB2 156 CA76
Stourcliffe St, W1 284 E9
Stour Cl, Kes. BR2 222 EJ105
Slough SL1 151 AP76
Stourhead Cl, SW19 179 CX87
Stourhead Gdns, SW20 199 CU97
Stourhead Ho, SW1 *off Tachbrook St* 297 N10
Stour Rd, E3 280 A7
Dagenham RM10 126 FA61
Dartford DA1 167 FG83
Grays RM16 171 GG78
Stourton Av, Felt. TW13 176 BZ91
Stour Way, Upmin. RM14 129 FS58
Stovell Rd, Wind. SL4 151 AP80
Stow, The, Harl. CM20 35 ET13
Stowage, SE8 314 B3
Stow Cres, E17 101 DY52
Stowe Ct, Dart. DA2 188 FQ87
Stowe Cres, Ruis. HA4 115 BP58
Stowe Gdns, N9 100 DT46
Stowell Av, New Adgtn CR0 221 ED110
Stowe Pl, N15 122 DS55
Stowe Rd, W12 159 CV75
Orpington BR6 224 EV105
Slough SL1 131 AL73
Stowford Coll, Sutt. SM2 *off Brighton Rd* 218 DC108
Stowting Rd, Orp. BR6 223 ES105
Stox Mead, Har. HA3 95 CD53
Stracey Rd, E7 281 P1
NW10 138 CR67
Strachan Pl, SW19 179 CW93
Stradbroke Dr, Chig. IG7 103 EN51
Stradbroke Gro, Buck.H. IG9 102 EK46
Ilford IG5 124 EL55
Stradbroke Pk, Chig. IG7 103 EP51
Stradbroke Rd, N5 277 K1
Stradbrook Cl, Har. HA2 *off Stiven Cres* 116 BZ62
Stradella Rd, SE24 182 DQ86
Strafford Av, Ilf. IG5 103 EN54
Strafford Cl, Pot.B. EN6 64 DA32
Strafford Gate, Pot.B. EN6 64 DA32
Strafford Rd, W3 158 CQ75
Barnet EN5 79 CY41
Hounslow TW3 156 BZ83
Twickenham TW1 177 CG87
Strafford St, E14 302 A4
Strahan Rd, E3 289 M2
Straight, The, Sthl. UB1 156 BX75
Straight Bit, Flack.Hth HP10 110 AC55
Straight Rd, Old Wind. SL4 172 AU85
Romford RM3 106 FJ52
Straightsmouth, SE10 314 E4
Strait Rd, E6 293 K10
Straker's Rd, SE15 162 DV84
STRAND, WC2 286 A10
Strand, WC2 298 A1
Strand Cl, Epsom KT18 232 CR119
Strand Ct, SE18 *off Strandfield Cl* 165 ES78
Strand Dr, Rich. TW9 158 CP80
Strandfield Cl, SE18 165 ES78
Strand Ho, SE28 *off Merbury Cl* 145 ER74
Strand La, WC2 286 D10
Strand on the Grn, W4 158 CN79
Strand on the Grn Br, Rich. TW9 158 CP80
Strand-on-the-Grn Inf & Nurs & Jun Schs, W4 *off Thames Rd* 158 CN79
Strand Pl, N18 100 DR49
Strand Sch App, W4 *off Thames Rd* 158 CN79
Strangeways, Wat. WD17 75 BS36
Strangways Ter, W14 294 G6
Stranraer Gdns, Slou. SL1 132 AS74
Stranraer Rd, Lon.Hthrw Air. TW6 174 BL86
Stranraer Way, N1 276 B7
Strasburg Rd, SW11 309 H7
Stratfield Dr, Brox. EN10 49 DY19
Stratfield Pk Cl, N21 99 DP45
Stratfield Rd, Borwd. WD6 78 CN41
Slough SL1 152 AU75
STRATFORD, E15/E20 280 F5
Stratford 280 G6
Stratford 280 G6
Stratford 280 G6
Stratford 280 G6
Stratford 280 G6
Stratford Av, W8 295 K7
Uxbridge UB10 134 BM68
Stratford Cen, The, E15 281 H6
Stratford Cl, Bark. IG11 146 EU66
Dagenham RM10 147 FC66
Slough SL2 131 AK70
Stratford Ct, N.Mal. KT3 198 CR98
Stratford Dr, Woob.Grn HP10 110 AD59
Stratford Gro, SW15 159 CX84
Stratford High Street 280 G7
Stratford Ho Av, Brom. BR1 204 EL97
Stratford International 280 D5
● **Stratford Office Village, The**, E15 281 J6
Stratford Pl, W1 285 J9
Stratford Rd, E13 281 M9
NW4 119 CX56
W8 295 K8
Hayes UB4 135 BV70
London Heathrow Airport TW6 175 BP86
Southall UB2 156 BY77
Thornton Heath CR7 201 DN98
Watford WD17 75 BU40
Stratford Sch, E7 281 P6
Stratford Vil, NW1 275 M6
Stratford Way, Brick.Wd AL2 60 BZ29
Hemel Hempstead HP3 40 BH23
Watford WD17 75 BT40
Stratford Workshops, E15 *off Burford Rd* 281 H8
Strathan Cl, SW18 179 CY86
Strathaven Rd, SE12 184 EH86
Strathblaine Rd, SW11 160 DD84
Strathbrook Rd, SW16 181 DM94
Strathcona Av, Bkhm KT23 246 BY128
Strathcona Cl, Flack.Hth HP10 110 AC56
Strathcona Rd, Wem. HA9 117 CK61
Strathcona Way, Flack.Hth HP10 110 AC56
Strathdale, SW16 181 DM92
Strathdon Dr, SW17 180 DD90
Strathearn Av, Hayes UB3 155 BT80
Twickenham TW2 176 CB88
Strathearn Pl, W2 284 B10
Strathearn Rd, SW19 180 DA92
Sutton SM1 218 DA106
Stratheden Par, SE3 *off Stratheden Rd* 315 P5
Stratheden Rd, SE3 315 N6
Strathfield Gdns, Bark. IG11 145 ER65
Strathleven Rd, SW2 181 DL85
Strathmore Cl, Cat. CR3 236 DS121
Strathmore Gdns, N3 98 DB53
W8 295 K2
Edgware HA8 96 CP54
Hornchurch RM12 127 FF60
Strathmore Rd, SW19 180 DA90
Croydon CR0 202 DQ101
Teddington TW11 177 CE91
Strathmore Sch, Rich. TW10 *off Meadlands Dr* 177 CK89
Strathnairn St, SE1 300 D9
Strathray Gdns, NW3 274 C5
Strath Ter, SW11 160 DE84
Strathville Rd, SW18 180 DB89
Strathyre Av, SW16 201 DN97
Stratton Av, Enf. EN2 82 DR37
Wallington SM6 219 DK109
Stratton Chase Dr, Ch.St.G. HP8 90 AU47
Stratton Cl, SW19 200 DA96
Bexleyheath DA7 166 EY83
Edgware HA8 96 CM52
Hounslow TW3 156 BZ81
Walton-on-Thames KT12 *off St. Johns Dr* 196 BW102
Stratton Ct, Surb. KT6 *off Adelaide Rd* 198 CL99
Strattondale St, E14 302 E6
Stratton Dr, Bark. IG11 125 ET64
Stratton Gdns, Sthl. UB1 136 BZ72
Stratton Rd, SW19 200 DA96
Beaconsfield HP9 88 AH53
Bexleyheath DA7 166 EY83
Romford RM3 106 FN50
Sunbury-on-Thames TW16 195 BT96
Stratton St, W1 297 K2
Stratton Ter, West. TN16 *off High St* 255 EQ127
Stratton Wk, Rom. RM3 106 FN50
Strauss Rd, W4 158 CR75
Strawberry Cres, Lon.Col. AL2 61 CH26
Strawberry Fld, Hat. AL10 45 CU21
Strawberry Flds, Farnboro. BR6 223 EP106
Swanley BR8 207 FE95
Ware SG12 32 DV05
STRAWBERRY HILL, Twick. TW1 177 CE90
Strawberry Hill 177 CE90
Strawberry Hill, Chess. KT9 215 CK07
Twickenham TW1 177 CF90
Strawberry Hill Cl, Twick. TW1 177 CF90
★ **Strawberry Hill Ho**, Twick. TW1 177 CF90
Strawberry Hill Rd, Twick. TW1 177 CF90
Strawberry La, Cars. SM5 200 DF104
Strawberry Vale, N2 98 DD53
Twickenham TW1 177 CG90
Straw Cl, Cat. CR3 236 DQ123
Strawfields, Welw.G.C. AL7 30 DB08
Strawmead, Hat. AL10 45 CV16
Strawson Ct, Horl. RH6 268 DF147
Strayfield Rd, Enf. EN2 81 DP37
Streakes Fld Rd, NW2 119 CU61
Stream Cl, Byfleet KT14 212 BK112
Streamdale, SE2 166 EU79
Stream La, Edg. HA8 96 CP50
Streamline Ms, SE22 182 DU88
Streamside, Slou. SL1 *off Richards Way* 131 AM74
Streamside Cl, N9 100 DT46
Bromley BR2 204 EG98
Streamway, Belv. DA17 166 FA79
Streatfield Av, E6 145 EM67
Streatfield Rd, Har. HA3 117 CK55
STREATHAM, SW16 181 DL91
Streatham 181 DL92
Streatham & Clapham High Sch, Jun Dept, SW2 *off Wavertree Rd* 181 DM88
SW16 *off Abbotswood Rd* 181 DK90
Streatham Cl, SW16 181 DL89
Streatham Common 181 DK94
Streatham Common N, SW16 181 DL92
Streatham Common S, SW16 181 DL93
Streatham Ct, SW16 181 DL90
Streatham High Rd, SW16 181 DL92
STREATHAM HILL, SW2 181 DM87
Streatham Hill 181 DL89
Streatham Hill, SW2 181 DL89
STREATHAM PARK, SW16 181 DJ91
Streatham Pl, SW2 181 DL87
Streatham Rd, SW16 200 DG95
Mitcham CR4 200 DG95
Streatham St, WC1 285 P8
STREATHAM VALE, SW16 181 DK94
Streatham Vale, SW16 181 DJ94
Streatham Wells Prim Sch, SW2 *off Palace Rd* 181 DN89
Streathbourne Rd, SW17 180 DG89
Streatley Pl, NW3 *off New End* 120 DC63
Streatley Rd, NW6 272 G7
Street, The, Albury GU5 260 BH139
Ashtead KT21 232 CL119
Betchworth RH3 264 CS135
Chipperfield WD4 58 BG31
East Clandon GU4 244 BK131
Effingham KT24 246 BX127
Fetcham KT22 231 CD122
Horton Kirby DA4 208 FP98
Shalford GU4 258 AY139
Sheering CM22 37 FC07
West Clandon GU4 244 BH131
West Horsley KT24 245 BP129
Wonersh GU5 259 BA144
Streeters La, Wall. SM6 201 DK104
Streetfield Ms, SE3 315 P10
St John's Inf & Nurs Sch, Rad. WD7 *off Gills Hill La* 77 CF36
Streimer Rd, E15 280 F10
Strelley Way, W3 138 CS73
Stretton Mans, SE8 314 B1
Stretton Pl, Amer. HP6 72 AT38
Stretton Rd, Croy. CR0 202 DS101
Richmond TW10 177 CJ89
Stretton Way, Borwd. WD6 78 CL38
Strickland Av, Dart. DA1 168 FL83
Strickland Row, SW18 180 DD87
Strickland St, SE8 314 B7
Strickland Way, Orp. BR6 223 ET105
Stride Rd, E13 291 M1
Strides Ct, Ott. KT16 *off Brox Rd* 211 BC107
Strimon Cl, N9 100 DW47
Stringers Av, Jacobs Well GU4 242 AX128
Stringer's Common, Guil. GU1, GU4 242 AV129
Stringhams Copse, Ripley GU23 227 BF124
Stripling Way, Wat. WD18 75 BU44
Strode Cl, N10 98 DG52
Strode Rd, E7 124 EG63
N17 100 DS54
NW10 139 CU65
SW6 306 D4
Strodes Coll, Egh. TW20 *off High St* 173 AZ92
Strodes Coll La, Egh. TW20 173 AZ92
Strodes Cres, Stai. TW18 174 BJ92
Strode St, Egh. TW20 173 BA91
Stroma Cl, Hem.H. HP3 41 BQ22
Stroma Ct, Slou. SL1 *off Lincoln Way* 131 AK73
Strone Rd, E7 144 EJ65
E12 144 EK65
Strone Way, Hayes UB4 136 BY70
Strongbow Cres, SE9 185 EM85
Strongbow Rd, SE9 185 EM85
Strongbridge Cl, Har. HA2 116 CA60
Stronsa Rd, W12 159 CT75
Stronsay Cl, Hem.H. HP3 *off Northend* 41 BQ22
Strood Av, Rom. RM7 127 FD60
STROOD GREEN, Bet. RH3 264 CP138
Stroud Cl, Wind. SL4 151 AK83
Stroud Cres, SW15 179 CU90
STROUDE, Vir.W. GU25 193 AZ96
Stroude Rd, Egh. TW20 173 BA93
Virginia Water GU25 192 AY98
Stroudes Cl, Wor.Pk. KT4 198 CS101
Stroud Fld, Nthlt. UB5 136 BY65
Stroud Gate, Har. HA2 116 CB63
STROUD GREEN, N4 121 DM58
Stroud Grn Gdns, Croy. CR0 202 DW101
Stroud Grn Prim Sch, N4 *off Woodstock Rd* 121 DN60
Stroud Grn Rd, N4 121 DM60
Stroud Grn Way, Croy. CR0 202 DV101
Stroudley Wk, E3 290 C2
Stroud Rd, SE25 202 DU100
SW19 180 DA90
Strouds Cl, Chad.Hth RM6 126 EV57
Stroudwater Pk, Wey. KT13 213 BP107
Stroud Way, Ashf. TW15 *off Courtfield Rd* 175 BP93
● **Stroud Wd Business Cen**, Frog. AL2 *off Frogmore* 61 CE27
Strouts Pl, E2 288 A2
Struan Gdns, Wok. GU21 226 AY115
Strutton Grd, SW1 297 N6
Struttons Av, Nthflt DA11 191 GF89
Strype St, E1 288 A7
Stuart Av, NW9 119 CU59
W5 138 CM74
Bromley BR2 204 EG102
Harrow HA2 116 BZ62
Walton-on-Thames KT12 195 BV102
Stuart Cl, Pilg.Hat. CM15 108 FV43
Swanley BR8 187 FF94
Uxbridge UB10 134 BN65
Windsor SL4 151 AM82
Stuart Ct, Els. WD6 *off High St* 77 CK44
Stuart Cres, N22 99 DM53
Croydon CR0 203 DZ104
Hayes UB3 135 BQ72
Reigate RH2 266 DA137
Stuart Evans Cl, Well. DA16 166 EW83
Stuart Gro, Tedd. TW11 177 CE92
Stuart Mantle Way, Erith DA8 167 FD80
Stuart Pl, Mitch. CR4 200 DF95
Stuart Rd, NW6 283 J3
SE15 162 DW84
SW19 180 DA90
W3 138 CQ74
Barking IG11 145 ET66
East Barnet EN4 98 DE45
Gravesend DA11 191 GG86
Grays RM17 170 GB78
Harrow HA3 95 CF54
Reigate RH2 266 DA137
Richmond TW10 177 CH89
Thornton Heath CR7 202 DQ98
Warlingham CR6 236 DV120
Welling DA16 166 EV81
Stuarts Cl, Hem.H. HP3 *off Marriotts Way* 40 BK22
Stuart Twr, W9 283 P3
Stuart Way, Chsht EN7 66 DV31
Staines-upon-Thames TW18 174 BH93
Virginia Water GU25 192 AU97
Windsor SL4 151 AL82
Stubbers La, Upmin. RM14 149 FR65
Stubbins Hall La, Wal.Abb. EN9 67 EB28
Stubbs Cl, NW9 118 CQ57
Stubbs Dr, SE16 300 E10
Stubbs End Cl, Amer. HP6 55 AS36
Stubbs Hill, Knock.P. TN14 224 EW113
Stubbs La, Lwr Kgswd KT20 249 CZ128
Stubbs Ms, Dag. RM8 126 EV63
Stubbs Pt, E13 292 A5
Stubbs Way, SW19 *off Ruskin Way* 200 DD95
Stubbs Wd, Amer. HP6 55 AS36
Stubs Cl, Dor. RH4 263 CJ138
Stubs Hill, Dor. RH4 263 CJ139
Stucley Pl, NW1 275 K7
Stucley Rd, Houns. TW5 156 CC80
Studdridge St, SW6 307 K9
Studd St, N1 276 G8
Stud Grn, Wat. WD25 59 BV32
Studholme Ct, NW3 273 K1
Studholme St, SE15 312 E5
Studio Ms, NW4 *off Glebe Cres* 119 CW56
Studio Pl, SW1 296 F5
Studios, The, Bushey WD23 76 CA44
Studios Rd, Shep. TW17 194 BM97
Studio Way, Borwd. WD6 78 CQ40
Studland, SE17 299 L10
Studland Cl, Sid. DA15 185 ET90
Studland Ho, E14 289 L8
Studland Rd, SE26 183 DX92
W7 137 CD72
Byfleet KT14 212 BM113
Kingston upon Thames KT2 178 CL93
Studland St, W6 159 CV77
Studley Av, E4 101 ED52
Studley Cl, E5 279 L3
Studley Ct, E14 *off Jamestown Way* 303 H1
Sidcup DA14 186 EV92
Studley Dr, Ilf. IG4 124 EK58
Studley Est, SW4 310 A7
Studley Gra Rd, W7 157 CE75
Studley Rd, E7 144 EH65
SW4 310 A7
Dagenham RM9 146 EX66
Study Prep Sch, The, Spencer Ho, SW19 *off Peek Cres* 179 CX92
Wilberforce Ho, SW19 *off Camp Rd* 179 CW92
Study Sch, The, N.Mal. KT3 *off Thetford Rd* 198 CS99
Stukeley Rd, E7 144 EH66
Stukeley St, WC1 286 B8
WC2 286 B8
Stump Rd, Epp. CM16 70 EW27
Stumps Hill La, Beck. BR3 183 EA93
Stumps La, Whyt. CR3 236 DS117
Stumpwell La, Penn HP10 88 AD48
Sturdy Rd, SE15 312 E9
Sturge Av, E17 101 EB54
Sturgeon Rd, SE17 311 J1
Sturges Fld, Chis. BR7 185 ER93
Sturgess Av, NW4 119 CV59
Sturge St, SE1 299 J4
Sturla Cl, Hert. SG14 31 DP08
Sturlas Way, Wal.Cr. EN8 67 DX33
Sturmer Cl, St.Alb. AL4 43 CJ21
Sturmer Way, N7 276 C2
Sturminster Cl, Hayes UB4 136 BW72
Sturrock Cl, N15 122 DR56
Sturry St, E14 290 C9
Sturt Ct, Guil. GU4 243 BB132
Sturts La, Walt.Hill KT20 249 CT127
Sturt St, N1 287 K1
Stutfield St, E1 288 D9
Stychens Cl, Bletch. RH1 252 DQ133
Stychens La, Bletch. RH1 252 DQ132
Stylecroft Rd, Ch.St.G. HP8 90 AX47
Styles End, Bkhm KT23 246 CB127
Styles Gdns, SW9 311 H10
Styles Way, Beck. BR3 203 EC98
Stylus Ho, E1 *off Devonport St* 289 H9
Styventon Pl, Cher. KT16 193 BF101
Subrosa Dr, Merst. RH1 251 DH130
● **Subrosa Pk**, Merst. RH1 251 DH130
Succombs Hill, Warl. CR6 236 DV120
Whyteleafe CR3 236 DV120
Succombs Pl, Warl. CR6 236 DV120
Sudbourne Prim Sch, SW2 *off Hayter Rd* 181 DM85
Sudbourne Rd, SW2 181 DL85
Sudbrooke Rd, SW12 180 DF86
Sudbrook Gdns, Rich. TW10 177 CK90
Sudbrook La, Rich. TW10 178 CL88
SUDBURY, Wem. HA0 117 CG64
Sudbury, E6 293 M8
Sudbury & Harrow Road 117 CH64
Sudbury Av, Wem. HA0 117 CK62
Sudbury Ct, SW8 *off Allen Edwards Dr* 310 A6
Sudbury Ct Dr, Har. HA1 117 CF62
Sudbury Ct Rd, Har. HA1 117 CF62
Sudbury Cres, Brom. BR1 184 EG93
Wembley HA0 117 CH64
Sudbury Cft, Wem. HA0 117 CF63
Sudbury Gdns, Croy. CR0 220 DS105
Sudbury Hts Av, Grnf. UB6 117 CF64
Sudbury Hill 117 CE63
Sudbury Hill, Har. HA1 117 CE61
Sudbury Hill Cl, Wem. HA0 117 CF63
Sudbury Hill Harrow 117 CE63
Sudbury Ho, SW18 *off Wandsworth High St* 180 DB85
Sudbury Prim Sch, Sudbury, Wem. HA0 *off Watford Rd* 117 CH63
Sudbury Rd, Bark. IG11 125 ET64
Sudbury Town 137 CH65
Sudeley St, N1 287 H1
Sudicamps Ct, Wal.Abb. EN9 68 EG33
Sudlow Rd, SW18 160 DA84
Sudrey St, SE1 299 J5
Suez Av, Grnf. UB6 137 CF68
Suez Rd, Enf. EN3 83 DY42
Suffield Cl, S.Croy. CR2 221 DX112
Suffield Rd, E4 101 EB48
N15 122 DT57
SE20 202 DW96
Suffolk Cl, Borwd. WD6 78 CR43
Horley RH6 268 DG149
London Colney AL2 61 CJ25
Slough SL1 131 AL72
Suffolk Ct, E10 123 EA59
Ilford IG3 125 ES58
Suffolk Dr, Guil. GU4 243 BB129
Suffolk La, EC4 287 L10
Suffolk Pk Rd, E17 123 DY56
Suffolk Pl, SW1 297 P2
Suffolk Rd, E13 291 M3
N15 122 DR58
NW10 138 CS66
SE25 202 DT98
SW13 159 CT80
Barking IG11 145 ER66
Dagenham RM10 127 FC64
Dartford DA1 188 FL86
Enfield EN3 82 DV43
Gravesend DA12 191 GK86
Harrow HA2 116 BZ58
Ilford IG3 125 ES58
Potters Bar EN6 63 CY32
Sidcup DA14 186 EW93
Worcester Park KT4 199 CT103
Suffolks Prim Sch, Enf. EN1 *off Brick La* 82 DV40
Suffolk St, E7 281 N2
SW1 297 P2
Suffolk Way, Horn. RM11 128 FN56
Sevenoaks TN13 257 FJ125
Sugar Bakers Ct, EC3 *off Creechurch La* 287 P9
Sugar Ho La, E15 280 F10
Sugar La, Berk. HP4 39 AZ22
Hemel Hempstead HP1 39 BB22
Sugar Loaf Wk, E2 288 G2
Sugar Quay Wk, EC3 299 P1
Sugden Rd, SW11 160 DG83
Thames Ditton KT7 197 CH102
Sugden Way, Bark. IG11 145 ET68
Sulgrave Gdns, W6 294 B5
Sulgrave Rd, W6 294 B5
Sulina Rd, SW2 181 DL87
Sulivan Ct, SW6 307 J9
● **Sulivan Enterprise Cen**, SW6 *off Sulivan Rd* 160 DA83
Sulivan Prim Sch, SW6 307 J9
Sulivan Rd, SW6 160 DA83
Sulkin Ho, E2 *off Knottisford St* 289 J2
Sullivan Av, E16 292 E6
Sullivan Cl, SW11 308 C10
Dartford DA1 187 FH86
Hayes UB4 136 BW71
Sullivan Cres, Hare. UB9 92 BK54
Sullivan Ho, SW1 *off Churchill Gdns* 309 K1
Sullivan Rd, SE11 298 F8
Tilbury RM18 171 GG81
Sullivans Reach, Walt. KT12 195 BT101
Sullivan Way, Els. WD6 77 CJ44
Sultan Rd, E11 124 EH56
Sultan St, SE5 311 J4
Beckenham BR3 203 DX96

S

Sultan Ter, N22
off Vincent Rd 99 DN54
Sumatra Rd, NW6 273 K4
Sumburgh Rd, SW12 180 DG86
Sumburgh Way, Slou. SL1 132 AS71
Summer Av, E.Mol. KT8 197 CE99
Summer Cl, Byfleet KT14 212 BM114
Summer Ct, Hem.H. HP2
off Townsend 40 BK18
Summercourt Rd, E1 289 H8
Summer Crossing, T.Ditt. KT7 197 CE98
Summerdale, Welw.G.C. AL8 29 CX05
Summerene Cl, SW16 181 DJ94
Summerfield, Ashtd. KT21 231 CK119
Hatfield AL10 45 CU21
Summerfield Av, NW6 272 F10
Summerfield Cl, Add. KT15
off Spinney Hill 211 BF106
London Colney AL2 61 CJ26
Summerfield La,
Long Dit. KT6 197 CK103
Summerfield Pl, Ott. KT16
off Crawshaw Rd 211 BD107
Summerfield Rd, W5 137 CH70
Loughton IG10 84 EK44
Watford WD25 75 BU35
Summerfields Av, N12 98 DE51
Summerfield St, SE12 184 EF87
Summer Gdns,
East Molesey KT8 197 CE99
Uxbridge UB10 115 BQ61
Summer Gro, Els. WD6 77 CK44
West Wickham BR4 204 EE103
Summerhayes Cl, Wok. GU21 210 AY114
Summerhays, Cob. KT11 214 BX113
Summer Hill, Chis. BR7 205 EN96
Elstree WD6 78 CN43
Summerhill Cl, Orp. BR6 205 ES104
Summerhill Ct, St.Alb. AL1 43 CF19
Summerhill Gro, Enf. EN1 82 DS44
Summerhill Rd, N15 122 DR56
Dartford DA1 188 FK87
Summer Hill Vil, Chis. BR7 205 EN95
Summerhill Way, Mitch. CR4 200 DG95
Summerhouse Av, Houns. TW5 156 BY81
Summerhouse Dr, Bex. DA5 187 FD91
Dartford DA2 187 FD91
Summerhouse La, Ald. WD25 76 CC40
Harefield UB9 92 BG52
Harmondsworth UB7 154 BK79
Summerhouse Rd, N16 122 DS61
Summerhouse Way,
Abb.L. WD5 59 BT30
Summerland Gdns, N10 121 DH55
Summerlands Av, W3 138 CQ73
Summerlands Rd, St.Alb. AL4 43 CJ16
Summerlay Cl, Kgswd KT20 233 CY120
Summerlea, Slou. SL1 131 AP74
Summerleas Cl, Hem.H. HP2 40 BL20
Summerlee Av, N2 120 DF56
Summerlee Gdns, N2 120 DF56
Summerley St, SW18 180 DB89
Summerly Av, Reig. RH2
off Burnham Dr 250 DA133
Summer Pl, Chal.St.P. SL9 90 AY52
Wat. WD18 *off Tolpits La* 75 BT44
Summer Rd, E.Mol. KT8 197 CE99
Thames Ditton KT7 197 CF99
Summersbury Dr, Shalf. GU4 258 AY142
Summersbury Hall, Shalf. GU4
off Summersbury Dr 258 AY142
Summersby Rd, N6 121 DH58
Summers Cl, Sutt. SM2
off Overton Rd 218 DA108
Wembley HA9 118 CP60
Weybridge KT13 212 BN111
[Sch] **Summerside Prim Sch**, N12
off Crossway 98 DD51
Summerskill Cl, SE15
off Manaton Cl 312 E10
Summerskille Cl, N9 100 DV47
Summers La, N12 98 DD52
Summers Rd, Burn. SL1 130 AJ69
Godalming GU7 258 AT144
Summers Row, N12 98 DE51
Summers St, EC1 286 E5
SUMMERSTOWN, SW17 180 DB90
Summerstown, SW17 180 DC90
Summerswood Cl, Ken. CR8
off Longwood Rd 236 DR116
Summerswood La,
Borwd. WD6 62 CS34
[Sch] **Summerswood Prim Sch**,
Borwd. WD6 *off Furzehill Rd* 78 CP42
Summerton Way, SE28 146 EX72
Summer Trees, Sun. TW16
off The Avenue 195 BV95
Summerville Gdns, Sutt. SM1 217 CZ107
Summerwood Rd, Islw. TW7 177 CF85
Summit, The, Loug. IG10 85 EM39
Summit Av, NW9 118 CR57
Summit Cl, N14 99 DJ47
NW9 118 CR56
Edgware HA8 96 CN52
Summit Ct, NW2 272 F4
Summit Dr, Wdf.Grn. IG8 102 EK54
Summit Est, N16 122 DU59
Summit Pl, Wey. KT13 212 BN108
Summit Rd, E17 123 EB56
Northolt UB5 136 CA66
Potters Bar EN6 63 CY30
Summit Way, N14 99 DH47
SE19 182 DS94
Sumner Av, SE15 312 B6
Sumner Cl, Fetch. KT22 231 CD124
Orpington BR6 223 EQ105
Sumner Ct, SW8
off Darsley Dr 310 A6
Sumner Gdns, Croy. CR0 201 DN102
Sumner Pl, SW7 296 B9
Addlestone KT15 212 BG106
Sumner Pl Ms, SW7 296 B9
Sumner Rd, SE15 312 B3
Croydon CR0 201 DN102
Harrow HA1 116 CC59
Sumner Rd S, Croy. CR0 201 DN102
SUMNERS, Harl. CM19 51 EN19
Sumners Fm Cl, Harl. CM19 51 EN20
Sumner St, SE1 299 H2
Sumpter Cl, NW3 273 P5
Sumpter Yd, St.Alb. AL1 43 CD20
Sun All, Rich. TW9
off Kew Rd 158 CL84
Sunbeam Cres, W10 282 B5
Sunbeam Rd, NW10 138 CQ70
SUNBURY, Sun. TW16 195 BV97
⇌ **Sunbury** 195 BT95
[Coll] **Sunbury Adult Learning Cen**,
Sun. TW16 *off The Avenue* 195 BV95
Sunbury Av, NW7 96 CR50
SW14 158 CR84
Sunbury Cl, Walt. KT12 195 BU100
Sunbury Ct, Sun. TW16 196 BX96
Sunbury Ct Island, Sun. TW16 196 BX97
Sunbury Ct Ms, Sun. TW16
off Lower Hampton Rd 196 BX97
Sunbury Ct Rd, Sun. TW16 196 BW96
Sunbury Cres, Felt. TW13
off Ryland Cl 175 BT91
[Jct] **Sunbury Cross**, Sun. TW16 175 BT94
● **Sunbury Cross Cen**,
Sun. TW16 175 BT94
Sunbury Gdns, NW7 96 CR50
Sunbury La, SW11 308 B6
Walton-on-Thames KT12 195 BU100
Sunbury Lock Ait, Walt. KT12 195 BV98
[Sch] **Sunbury Manor Sch**,
Sun. TW16 *off Nursery Rd* 195 BT95
Sunbury Rd, Eton SL4 151 AR79
Feltham TW13 175 BT90
Sutton SM3 199 CX104
Sunbury St, SE18 305 K7
Sunbury Way, Han. TW13 176 BW92
● **Sunbury Workshops**, E2
off Swanfield St 288 A3
Sun Ct, EC3 287 M9
Erith DA8 167 FF82
Suncroft Pl, SE26 182 DW90
Chessington KT9 216 CL108
Sundale Av, S.Croy. CR2 220 DW110
Sunderland Av, St.Alb. AL1 43 CG18
Sunderland Ct, SE22 182 DU87
Sunderland Gro, Lvsdn WD25 59 BT34
Sunderland Mt, SE23 183 DX89
Sunderland Rd, SE23 183 DX88
W5 157 CK76
Sunderland Ter, W2 283 L8
Sunderland Way, E12 124 EK61
Sundew Av, W12 139 CU73
Sundew Cl, W12 139 CU73
Sundew Ct, Grays RM17
off Salix Rd 170 GD79
Sundew Rd, Hem.H. HP1 39 BE21
Sundial Av, SE25 202 DT97
Sundon Cres, Vir.W. GU25 192 AV99
Sundorne Rd, SE7 164 EH78
Sundown Av, S.Croy. CR2 220 DT111
Sundown Rd, Ashf. TW15 175 BQ92
Sundra Wk, E1 289 J5
SUNDRIDGE, Brom. BR1 184 EJ93
Sev. TN14 240 EZ124
Sundridge Av, Brom. BR1 204 EK95
Chislehurst BR7 184 EK94
Welling DA16 165 ER82
Sundridge Cl, Dart. DA1 188 FN86
Sundridge Hill, Sev. TN14 240 EW118
Sundridge Ho, Brom. BR1
off Burnt Ash La 184 EH92
Sundridge La, Sev. TN14 240 EV117
⇌ **Sundridge Park** 184 EH94
Sundridge Pl, Croy. CR0
off Inglis Rd 202 DU102
Sundridge Rd, Croy. CR0 202 DT101
Dunton Green TN14 240 FA120
Woking GU22 227 BA119
Sunfields Pl, SE3 164 EH80
Sunflower Way, Rom. RM3 106 FK53
Sun Hill, Fawk.Grn DA3 209 FU104
Woking GU22 226 AU121
[Jct] **Sun-In-The-Sands**, SE3 164 EH80
Sunken Rd, Croy. CR0 220 DW106
Sunkist Way, Wall. SM6 219 DL109
Sunland Av, Bexh. DA6 166 EY84
Sun La, SE3 164 EH80
Gravesend DA12 191 GJ89
Sunleigh Rd, Wem. HA0 138 CL67
Sunley Gdns, Perivale UB6 137 CG67
Sunlight Cl, SW19 180 DC93
Sunlight Sq, E2 288 F3
Sunmead Cl, Fetch. KT22 231 CF122
Sunmead Rd, Hem.H. HP2 40 BK18
Sunbury-on-Thames TW16 195 BU97
Sunna Gdns, Sun. TW16 195 BV96
Sunningdale, N14 99 DK50
Sunningdale Av, W3 138 CS73
Barking IG11 145 ER67
Feltham TW13 176 BY89
Rainham RM13 147 FH70
Ruislip HA4 116 BW60
Sunningdale Cl, E6 293 J2
SE16 312 E1
SE28 146 EY72
Stanmore HA7 95 CG52
Surbiton KT6 *off Culsac Rd* 198 CL103
Sunningdale Gdns, NW9 118 CQ57
W8 295 K7
Sunningdale Ms,
Welw.G.C. AL7 29 CY05
Sunningdale Rd, Brom. BR1 204 EL98
Rainham RM13 147 FG66
Sutton SM1 217 CZ105
Sunningfields Cres, NW4 97 CV54
Sunningfields Rd, NW4 97 CV54
Sunning Hill, Nthflt DA11 190 GE89
Sunninghill Ct, W3
off Bollo Br Rd 158 CQ75
Sunninghill Rd, SE13 314 C9
Sunnings La, Upmin. RM14 148 FQ65
Sunningvale Av, Bigg.H. TN16 238 EJ115
Sunningvale Cl, Bigg.H. TN16 238 EK116
Sunny Bk, SE25 202 DU97
Warlingham CR6 237 DY117
Sunnybank, Epsom KT18 232 CQ116
[Sch] **Sunny Bk Prim Sch**,
Pot.B. EN6 *off Field Vw Rd* 64 DA34
Sunnybank Rd, Pot.B. EN6 64 DA33
Sunnybank Vil, Red. RH1 252 DT132
Sunny Cres, NW10 138 CQ66
Sunny Cft, Harl. CM18 51 ET18
Sunnycroft Gdns,
Upmin. RM14 129 FT59
Sunnycroft Rd, SE25 202 DU97
Hounslow TW3 156 CB82
Southall UB1 136 CA71
Sunnydale, Orp. BR6 205 EN103
Sunnydale Gdns, NW7 96 CR51
Sunnydale Rd, SE12 184 EH85
Sunnydell, St.Alb. AL2 60 CB26
Sunnydene Av, E4 101 ED50
Ruislip HA4 115 BU60
Sunnydene Cl, Rom. RM3 106 FM52
Sunnydene Gdns, Wem. HA0 137 CJ65
Sunnydene Rd, Pur. CR8 219 DP113
Sunnydene St, SE26 183 DY91
[Sch] **Sunnydown Sch**, Cat. CR3
off Whyteleafe Rd 236 DT121
Sunnyfield, NW7 97 CT49
Hatfield AL9 45 CX15
Sunnyfield Rd, Chis. BR7 206 EU97
[Sch] **Sunnyfields Prim Sch**, NW4
off Hatchcroft 119 CV55
Sunny Gdns Par, NW4
off Great N Way 97 CW54
Sunny Gdns Rd, NW4 97 CV54
Sunny Hill, NW4 119 CV55
Sunnyhill Cl, E5 123 DY63
[Sch] **Sunnyhill Prim Sch**, SW16
off Sunnyhill Rd 181 DM91
Sunnyhill Rd, SW16 181 DL91
Hemel Hempstead HP1 40 BH20
West Hyde WD3 91 BD51
Sunnyhurst Cl, Sutt. SM1 200 DA104
Sunnymead Av, Mitch. CR4 201 DJ97
Sunnymead Rd, NW9 118 CR59
SW15 179 CV85
SUNNYMEADS, Stai. TW19 152 AY84
⇌ **Sunnymeads** 152 AY83
Sunnymede, Chig. IG7 104 EV48
Sunnymede Av, Cars. SM5 218 DD111
Chesham HP5 54 AS28
Epsom KT19 216 CS109
Sunnymede Dr, Ilf. IG6 125 EP56
Sunny Ms, Rom. RM5 105 FC52
Sunny Nook Gdns,
S.Croy. CR2 220 DR107
Sunny Pl, NW4
off Sunny Gdns Rd 119 CW56
Sunny Ri, Chaldon CR3 236 DR124
Sunny Rd, The, Enf. EN3 83 DX39
Sunnyside, NW2 119 CZ62
SW19 179 CY93
Lower Nazeing EN9 50 EF22
Walton-on-Thames KT12 196 BW99
Sunnyside Cotts, Chesh. HP5 56 AU26
Sunnyside Dr, E4 101 EC45
Sunnyside Gdns,
Upmin. RM14 128 FQ61
Sunnyside Pas, SW19 179 CY93
Sunnyside Pl, SW19
off Sunnyside 179 CY93
Sunnyside Rd, E10 123 EA60
N19 121 DK59
W5 137 CK74
Chesham HP5 54 AP30
Epping CM16 69 ET32
Ilford IG1 125 EQ62
Teddington TW11 177 CD91
Sunnyside Rd E, N9 100 DU48
Sunnyside Rd N, N9 100 DT48
Sunnyside Rd S, N9 100 DT48
Sunnyside Ter, NW9
off Edgware Rd 118 CR55
Sunny Vw, NW9 118 CR56
Sunny Way, N12 98 DE52
Sun Pas, SE16 300 C6
Windsor SL4
off Bachelors Acre 151 AR81
Sunray Av, SE24 162 DR84
Bromley BR2 204 EL100
Hutton CM13 109 GE44
Surbiton KT5 198 CP103
West Drayton UB7 154 BK75
Sunrise Av, Horn. RM12 128 FJ62
Sunrise Cl, E20 280 E3
Feltham TW13 *off Exeter Rd* 176 BZ90
Sunrise Cres, Hem.H. HP3 40 BL23
Sun Rd, W14 306 G1
Swanscombe DA10 190 FZ86
Sunset Av, E4 101 EB46
Woodford Green IG8 102 EF49
Sunset Cl, Erith DA8 167 FH80
Sunset Ct, Wdf.Grn. IG8
off Navestock Cres 102 EJ52
Sunset Dr, Hav.at.Bow. RM4 105 FH50
Sunset Gdns, SE25 202 DT96
Sunset Ms, Rom. RM5 105 FC51
Sunset Rd, SE5 162 DQ84
SE28 166 EU75
Sunset Vw, Barn. EN5 79 CY40
Sunshine Way, Mitch. CR4 200 DF96
Sun Sq, Hem.H. HP1
off High St 40 BK19
Sunstone Gro, Merst. RH1 251 DL129
Sun St, EC2 287 N7
Sawbridgeworth CM21 36 EZ06
Waltham Abbey EN9 67 EC33
Sun Wk, E1 300 C1
Sunwell Cl, SE15 312 E7
Superior Dr, Grn St Grn BR6 223 ET107
SURBITON, KT5 & KT6 198 CM101
⇌ **Surbiton** 197 CK100
Surbiton Ct, Surb. KT6 197 CJ100
Surbiton Cres, Kings.T. KT1 198 CL98
Surbiton Hall Cl, Kings.T. KT1 198 CL98
[Sch] **Surbiton High Sch**,
Kings.T. KT1 *off Surbiton Cres* 198 CL98
Surbiton Hill Pk, Surb. KT5 198 CN99
Surbiton Hill Rd, Surb. KT6 198 CL98
[Sch] **Surbiton Jun Girls' Sch**,
Kings.T. KT1 *off Surbiton Rd* 198 CL98
Surbiton Par, Surb. KT6
off St. Mark's Hill 198 CL100
Surbiton Plaza, Surb. KT6
off St. Marys Rd 197 CK100
[Sch] **Surbiton Prep Sch**, Surb. KT6
off Avenue Elmers 198 CL99
Surbiton Rd, Kings.T. KT1 198 CL98
Surlingham Cl, SE28 146 EX73
Surly Hall Wk, Wind. SL4 151 AM81
Surma Cl, E1 288 E5
Surman Cres, Hutt. CM13 109 GC45
Surmans Cl, Dag. RM9 146 EW67
Surrendale Pl, W9 283 K5
Surrey Av, Slou. SL2 131 AQ71
Surrey Canal Rd, SE14 313 H2
SE15 313 H2
Surrey Cl, N3 119 CY55
Surrey Cres, W4 158 CN78
★ **Surrey Docks Fm**, SE16 301 N5
Surrey Dr, Horn. RM11 128 FN56
Surrey Gdns, N4 122 DQ58
Effingham Junction KT24 229 BT123
Surrey Gro, SE17 311 N1
Sutton SM1 200 DD104
Surrey Hills Av, Box H. KT20 248 CQ130
● **Surrey Hills Business Pk**,
Wotton RH5 262 BZ139
Surrey Hills Pk, Box H. KT20 248 CP130
[Coll] **Surrey Inst of Art & Design, The**,
Epsom KT18 *off Ashley Rd* 216 CS114
Surrey La, SW11 308 C7
Surrey La Est, SW11 308 C6
Surrey Ms, SE27
off Hamilton Rd 182 DS91
Surrey Mt, SE23 182 DV88
⊖ **Surrey Quays** 301 J8
Surrey Quays Rd, SE16 301 H6
🛍 **Surrey Quays Shop Cen**,
SE16 301 J7
Surrey Rd, SE15 183 DX85
Barking IG11 145 ES67
Dagenham RM10 127 FB64
Harrow HA1 116 CC57
West Wickham BR4 203 EB102
Surrey Row, SE1 298 G4
Surrey Sq, SE17 299 N10
[Sch] **Surrey Sq Inf & Jun Schs**,
SE17 299 N10
Surrey St, E13 292 B3
WC2 286 D10
Croydon CR0 202 DQ104
Surrey Ter, SE17 299 P9
Surrey Twrs, Add. KT15
off Garfield Rd 212 BJ106
Surrey Water Rd, SE16 301 K3
Surridge Cl, Rain. RM13 148 FJ69
Surridge Gdns, SE19
off Hancock Rd 182 DR93
Surr St, N7 276 B3
Sury Basin, Kings.T. KT2 198 CL95
Susan Cl, Rom. RM7 127 FC55
Susan Constant Ct, E14
off Newport Av 291 H10
Susan Lawrence Ho, E12
off Walton Rd 125 EN63
Susannah St, E14 290 D9
Susan Rd, SE3 164 EH82
Susan Wd, Chis. BR7 205 EN95
Sussex Av, Islw. TW7 157 CE83
Romford RM3 106 FM52
Sussex Border Path,
Horl. RH6 268 DF150
Sussex Cl, N19 121 DL61
Chalfont St. Giles HP8 90 AV47
Hoddesdon EN11
off Roman St 49 EA16
Ilford IG4 125 EM58
New Malden KT3 198 CS98
Reigate RH2 266 DD135
Slough SL1 152 AV75
Twickenham TW1
off Westmorland Cl 177 CH86
Sussex Ct, Add. KT15
off Garfield Rd 212 BJ106
Sussex Cres, Nthlt. UB5 136 CA65
Sussex Gdns, N4 122 DQ57
N6 120 DF57
W2 284 A10
Chessington KT9 215 CK107
[Sch] **Sussex Ho Sch**, SW1 296 E8
Sussex Keep, Slou. SL1
off Sussex Cl 152 AV75
Sussex Ms, SE6
off Ravensbourne Pk 183 EA87
Sussex Ms E, W2 284 B9
Sussex Ms W, W2 284 B10
Sussex Pl, NW1 284 E3
W2 284 B9
W6 294 A10
Erith DA8 167 FB80
New Malden KT3 198 CS98
Slough SL1 152 AV75
Sussex Ring, N12 98 DA50
Sussex Rd, E6 145 EN67
Carshalton SM5 218 DF107
Dartford DA1 188 FN87
Erith DA8 167 FB80
Harrow HA1 116 CC57
Mitcham CR4 *off Lincoln Rd* 201 DL99
New Malden KT3 198 CS98
Orpington BR5 206 EW100
Sidcup DA14 186 EV92
South Croydon CR2 220 DR107
Southall UB2 156 BX76
Uxbridge UB10 115 BQ63
Warley CM14 108 FV49
Watford WD24 75 BU38
West Wickham BR4 203 EB102
Sussex Sq, W2 284 B10
Sussex St, E13 292 B3
SW1 309 K1
Sussex Way, N7 121 DL61
N19 121 DL60
Cockfosters EN4 80 DG43
Sutcliffe Cl, NW11 120 DB57
Bushey WD23 76 CC42
Sutcliffe Ho, Hayes UB3 135 BU72
Sutcliffe Rd, SE18 165 ES79
Welling DA16 166 EW82
Sutherland Av, W9 283 N3
W13 137 CH72
Biggin Hill TN16 238 EK117
Cuffley EN6 65 DK28
Hayes UB3 155 BU77
Jacobs Well GU4 242 AX128
Petts Wood BR5 205 ET100
Sunbury-on-Thames TW16 195 BT96
Welling DA16 165 ES84
Sutherland Cl, Barn. EN5 79 CY42
Greenhithe DA9 189 FT85
Sutherland Ct, NW9 118 CP57
Welwyn Garden City AL7 29 CZ08
Sutherland Dr, SW19 200 DD95
Burpham GU4 243 AZ131
Sutherland Gdns, SW14 158 CS83
Sunbury-on-Thames TW16
off Sutherland Av 195 BT96
Worcester Park KT4 199 CV102
Sutherland Gro, SW18 179 CY86
Teddington TW11 177 CE92
Sutherland Pl, W2 283 J8
Sutherland Rd, E17 101 DX54
N9 100 DU46
N17 100 DU52
W4 158 CS79
W13 137 CG72
Belvedere DA17 166 FA76
Croydon CR0 201 DN101
Enfield EN3 83 DX43
Southall UB1 136 BZ72
Sutherland Rd Path, E17 123 DX55
Sutherland Row, SW1 297 K10
Sutherland Sq, SE17 311 J1
Sutherland St, SW1 297 J10
Sutherland Wk, SE17 311 K1
Sutherland Way, Cuffley EN6 65 DK28
Sutlej Rd, SE7 164 EJ80
Sutterton St, N7 276 C5
SUTTON, SM1 - SM3 218 DB107
⇌ **Sutton** 218 DC107
SUTTON ABINGER, Dor. RH5 261 BU143
SUTTON AT HONE, Dart. DA4 208 FN95
[Sch] **Sutton at Hone C of E Prim Sch**,
Sutt.H. DA4 *off Church Rd* 188 FN94
Sutton Av, Slou. SL3 152 AW75
Woking GU21 226 AS119
Sutton Cl, Beck. BR3 203 EB95
Broxbourne EN10 49 DY19
Loughton IG10 102 EL45
Pinner HA5 115 BU57
[Coll] **Sutton Coll of Learning for Adults**,
Sutton Cen, Sutt. SM1
off St. Nicholas Way 218 DB106
Sutton W Cen, Sutt. SM1
off Robin Hood La 218 DA106
⇌ **Sutton Common** 200 DB103
Sutton Common Rd,
Sutt. SM1, SM3 199 CZ101
Sutton Ct, W4 158 CQ79
Sutton SM2 218 DC107
Ware SG12 *off Crane Mead* 33 DY07
Sutton Ct Rd, E13 292 C3
W4 158 CQ80
Sutton SM1 218 DC107
Uxbridge UB10 135 BP67
Sutton Cres, Barn. EN5 79 CX43
Sutton Dene, Houns. TW3 156 CB81
Sutton Est, SW3 296 D10
W10 282 A6
Sutton Est, The, N1 276 G6
Sutton Gdns, Bark. IG11
off Sutton Rd 145 ES68
Croydon CR0 202 DT99
Merstham RH1 251 DK129
[Sch] **Sutton Gram Sch for Boys**,
Sutt. SM1 *off Manor La* 218 DC106
SUTTON GREEN, Guil. GU4 243 AZ125
Sutton Grn, Bark. IG11
off Sutton Rd 145 ES67
Sutton Grn Rd, Sutt.Grn GU4 242 AY126
Sutton Gro, Sutt. SM1 218 DD105
Sutton Hall Rd, Houns. TW5 156 CA80
Sutton Hts, Sutt. SM2 218 DD108
[Sch] **Sutton High Sch**, Sutt. SM1
off Cheam Rd 218 DB107
Sutton Hill, Guil. GU4 243 BC129
[H] **Sutton Hosp**, Sutt. SM2 218 DB110
★ **Sutton Ho**, E9 278 G3
Sutton Ho, Hem.H. HP2 40 BL16
Sutton La, EC1 287 H5
Abinger Common RH5 261 BV143
Banstead SM7 234 DB115
Hounslow TW3 156 BZ83
Slough SL3 153 BC78
Sutton SM2 218 DB111
Sutton La N, W4 158 CQ78
Sutton La S, W4 158 CQ79
Sutton Par, NW4
off Church Rd 119 CW56
Sutton Pk, Sutt.Grn GU4 243 AZ127
Sutton Pk Rd, Sutt. SM1 218 DB107
Sutton Path, Borwd. WD6 78 CN40
★ **Sutton Pl**, Guil. GU4 243 BA127
Sutton Pl, E9 278 G3
Abinger Hammer RH5 261 BT143
Dartford DA4 188 FN92
Slough SL3 153 BB79
Sutton Rd, E13 291 M4
E17 101 DX53
N10 98 DG54
Barking IG11 145 ES68
Hounslow TW5 156 CA81
St. Albans AL1 43 CH21
Watford WD17 76 BW41
Sutton Row, W1 285 P8
Suttons Av, Horn. RM12 128 FJ62
● **Suttons Business Pk**,
Rain. RM13 147 FD69
Suttons Gdns, Horn. RM12 128 FK62
Suttons La, Horn. RM12 128 FK64
[Sch] **Suttons Prim Sch**,
Horn. RM12 *off Suttons La* 128 FK63
Sutton Sq, E9 278 G3
Hounslow TW5 156 BZ81
Sutton St, E1 288 G10
Sutton's Way, EC1 287 K5
Sutton Wk, SE1 298 D3
Sutton Way, W10 282 A5
Hounslow TW5 156 BZ81
Swabey Rd, Slou. SL3 153 BA77
Swaby Rd, SW18 180 DC88
Swaffham Way, N22 99 DP52
[Sch] **Swaffield Prim Sch**, SW18
off St. Ann's Hill 180 DC86
Swaffield Rd, SW18 180 DB87
Sevenoaks TN13 257 FJ122
Swain Cl, SW16 181 DH93
Swain Rd, Th.Hth. CR7 202 DQ99
Swains Cl, West Dr. UB7 154 BL75
Swains La, N6 120 DG62
Swainson Rd, W3 159 CT75
Swains Rd, SW17 180 DF94
Swain St, NW8 284 C4
Swaisland Dr, Cray. DA1 187 FF85
Swaisland Rd, Dart. DA1 187 FH85
Swakeleys Dr, Uxb. UB10 114 BM63
Swakeleys Rd, Ickhm UB10 114 BM62
[Jct] **Swakeleys Rbt**, Uxb. UB9 114 BL63
[Sch] **Swakeleys Sch**, Hlgdn UB10
off Clifton Gdns 135 BP68
Swale Cl, Aveley RM15 148 FQ72
Swaledale Cl, N11
off Ribblesdale Av 98 DG51
Swaledale Rd, Dart. DA2 188 FQ88
Swale Rd, Dart. DA1 167 FG83
Swaley's Way, S.Ock. RM15 149 FX72
Swallands Rd, SE6 183 EA90
Swallow Cl, SE14 313 H7
Bushey WD23 94 CC46
Chafford Hundred RM16 169 FW77
Erith DA8 167 FE81
Greenhithe DA9 189 FT85
Rickmansworth WD3 92 BJ45
Staines-upon-Thames TW18 173 BF91
Swallow Ct, W13 *off Gurnell Gro* 137 CF70
Hert. SG14 32 DQ09
Swallowdale, Iver SL0 133 BD69
South Croydon CR2 221 DX109
Swallowdale La, Hem.H. HP2 41 BP17
[Sch] **Swallow Dell Prim Sch**,
Welw.G.C. AL7
off Blackthorn Rd 30 DA10
Swallow Dr, NW10
off Kingfisher Way 138 CR65
Northolt UB5 136 CA68
Swallow End, Welw.G.C. AL7 29 CZ09
Swallowfield, NW1
off Munster Sq 285 K3
Englefield Green TW20
off Heronfield 172 AV93

S

Swallowfield Rd, SE7 164 EH78
Swallow Flds, Iver SL0 133 BD70
Swallowfields, Nthflt DA11 190 GE90
Welwyn Garden City AL7 29 CZ09
Swallowfield Way, Hayes UB3 155 BR75
Swallow Gdns, SW16 181 DK92
Hatfield AL10 45 CU20
Swallow Ho, NW8
off Allitsen Rd 274 C10
Swallow La, Mid Holm. RH5 263 CH142
St. Albans AL1 43 CH23
Swallow Pk Cl, Surb. KT6 198 CM104
Swallow Pas, W1
off Swallow Pl 285 K9
Swallow Pl, W1 285 K9
Swallows, Harl. CM17 36 EW11
Swallows, The, Welw.G.C. AL7 29 CZ05
Swallows Oak, Abb.L. WD5 59 BT31
Swallow St, E6 293 H7
W1 297 M1
Iver SL0 133 BD69
Swallowtail Cl, Orp. BR5 206 EX98
Swallowtail Wk, Berk. HP4
off Springfield Rd 38 AT16
Swallow Wk, Horn. RM12
off Heron Flight Av 147 FH65
Sch Swaminarayan Sch, The, NW10
off Brentfield Rd 138 CR65
Swanage Ho, SW8 310 C5
Swanage Rd, E4 101 EC52
SW18 180 DC86
Swanage Waye, Hayes UB4 136 BW72
Swan All, Wat. WD18
off Lower High St 76 BW43
Swan & Pike Rd, Enf. EN3 83 EA38
Swan App, E6 292 G7
Swan Av, Upmin. RM14 129 FT60
Swanbourne Dr, Horn. RM12 128 FJ64
Swanbridge Rd, Bexh. DA7 166 FA81
● Swan Business Pk,
Dart. DA1 168 FJ84
● Swan Cen, The, SW17
off Rosemary Rd 180 DC90
Swan Cl, E17 101 DY53
Chesham HP5 54 AP27
Croydon CR0 202 DS101
Feltham TW13 176 BY91
Orpington BR5 206 EU97
Rickmansworth WD3
off Parsonage Rd 92 BK45
Swan Ct, SW3 308 D1
Guildford GU1 242 AX132
Hemel Hempstead HP1
off Waterhouse St 40 BJ21
Swandon Way, SW18 180 DB85
Swan Dr, NW9 96 CS54
Swanfield Rd, Wal.Cr. EN8 67 DY33
Swanfield St, E2 288 A3
Swanhill, Welw.G.C. AL7 30 DA06
Jct Swan Junct, The,
W.Wick. BR4 203 EC103
Swanland Rd, N.Mymms AL9 63 CV28
South Mimms EN6 63 CV33
Swan La, EC4 299 L1
N20 98 DC48
Dartford DA1 187 FF87
Guildford GU1 258 AX135
Loughton IG10 102 EJ45
Sch Swanlea Sch, E1 288 E6
SWANLEY, BR8 207 FE98
⇌ Swanley 207 FD98
Swanley Bar La, Pot.B. EN6 64 DB28
Swanley Bypass, Sid. DA14 207 FC97
Swanley BR8 207 FC97
Swanley Cen, Swan. BR8 207 FE97
Swanley Cres, Pot.B. EN6 64 DB29
Swanley La, Swan. BR8 207 FF97
Swanley Rd, Well. DA16 166 EW81
SWANLEY VILLAGE,
Swan. BR8 208 FJ95
Swanley Village Rd,
Swan. BR8 207 FH95
Swan Mead, SE1 299 N7
Hemel Hempstead HP3 58 BM25
Swan Ms, SW6
off Purser's Cross Rd 307 J6
Romford RM7 127 FB56
Swan Mill Gdns, Dor. RH4 247 CJ134
Swanns Meadow, Bkhm KT23 246 CA126
Swan Pas, E1
off Cartwright St 300 B1
Swan Path, E10
off Jesse Rd 123 EC60
Kingston upon Thames KT1
off Villiers Rd 198 CM97
Swan Pl, SW13 159 CT82
West.TN16 255 ER127
Swan Rd, SE16 301 H4
SE18 304 F7
Feltham TW13 176 BY92
Iver SL0 133 BF72
Southall UB1 136 CB72
West Drayton UB7 154 BK75
Swans Cl, St.Alb. AL4 44 CL21
SWANSCOMBE, DA10 190 FZ86
⇌ Swanscombe 190 FZ85
● Swanscombe Business Cen,
Swans. DA10 190 FY85
Swanscombe Ho, W11
off St. Anns Rd 294 D2
Swanscombe Rd, W4 158 CS78
W11 294 D3
Swanscombe St, Swans. DA10 190 FY87
Swansea Cl, Coll.Row RM5 105 FD52
Swansea Ct, E16 305 P3
Swansea Rd, Enf. EN3 82 DW42
London Heathrow Airport TW6
off Shrewsbury Rd 175 BR86
Swanshope, Loug. IG10 85 EP40
Swansland Gdns, E17
off McEntee Av 101 DY53
Swansmere Cl, Walt. KT12 196 BW102
Swans Rd, Wal.Cr. EN8 67 DX34
Swanston Path, Wat. WD19 94 BW48
Swan St, SE1 299 K6
Isleworth TW7 157 CH83
Swan Ter, Wind. SL4
off Mill La 151 AN80
Swanton Gdns, SW19 179 CX88
Swanton Rd, Erith DA8 167 FB80
Sch Swan Valley Comm Sch,
Swans. DA10 off Southfleet Rd 190 FZ87
Swan Wk, Rom. RM1
off Market Pl 127 FE57
Swan Wk, SW3 308 E2
Shepperton TW17 195 BS101
Swan Way, Enf. EN3 83 DX40
● Swan Wf Business Cen,
Uxb. UB8 off Waterloo Rd 134 BJ68
Swanwick Cl, SW15 179 CT87
Swanworth La, Mick. RH5 247 CH128
Swan Yd, N1 276 G5
Sward Rd, Orp. BR5 206 EU100
Swaton Rd, E3 290 B5
Swaylands Rd, Belv. DA17 166 FA79
Swaynesland Rd, Eden. TN8 255 EM134
Swaynes La, Guil. GU1 243 BE134
Swaything Cl, N18 100 DV49
Swaythling Ho, SW15
off Tunworth Cres 179 CT86
Swedenborg Gdns, E1 288 D10
Sweden Gate, SE16 301 L7
Sch Swedish Sch, The, SW13
off Lonsdale Rd 159 CT79
Sweeney Cres, SE1 300 B5
Sweeps Ditch Cl, Stai. TW18 194 BG95
Sweeps La, Egh. TW20 173 AZ92
Orpington BR5 206 EX99
Sweet Briar, Welw.G.C. AL7 30 DA11
Sweetbriar Cl, Hem.H. HP1 40 BG17
Sweet Briar Grn, N9 100 DT48
Sweet Briar Gro, N9 100 DT48
Sweet Briar La, Epsom KT18 216 CR114
Sweet Briar Wk, N18 100 DT49
Sweetcroft La, Uxb. UB10 134 BN66
Sweet La, Peasl. GU5 261 BR143
Sweetmans Av, Pnr. HA5 116 BX55
Sweets Way, N20 98 DD47
Swetenham Wk, SE18
off Raglan Rd 165 EQ78
Swete St, E13 291 P1
Sweyne Rd, Swans. DA10 190 FY86
Sweyn Pl, SE3 315 P9
Sweyns, Harl. CM17 52 EW17
Swievelands Rd,
Bigg.H. TN16 238 EH119
Swift Cl, E17 101 DY52
SE28 146 EV73
Harrow HA2 116 CB61
Hayes UB3 135 BT72
Slough SL1 131 AM73
Stanstead Abbotts SG12 33 EC12
Upminster RM14 129 FS60
Swiftfields, Welw.G.C. AL7 29 CZ08
Swift Rd, Felt. TW13 176 BY90
Southall UB2 156 BZ76
Swiftsden Way, Brom. BR1 184 EE93
Swift St, SW6 306 F6
Swiftsure Rd,
Chaff.Hun. RM16 169 FW77
SWILLET, THE, Rick. WD3 73 BB44
Swinbrook Rd, W10 282 F6
Swinburne Ct, SE5
off Basingdon Way 162 DR84
Swinburne Cres, Croy. CR0 202 DW100
Swinburne Gdns, Til. RM18 171 GH82
Swinburne Rd, SW15 159 CU84
Swinderby Rd, Wem. HA0 138 CL65
Swindon Cl, Ilf. IG3
off Salisbury Rd 125 ES61
Romford RM3 106 FM50
Swindon Gdns, Rom. RM3 106 FM50
Swindon La, Rom. RM3 106 FM50
Swindon Rd,
Lon.Hthrw Air. TW6 175 BQ85
Swindon St, W12 139 CV74
Swinfield Cl, Felt. TW13 176 BY91
Swinford Gdns, SW9 310 G10
Swingate La, SE18 165 ES79
Sch Swing Gate First & Nurs Sch,
Berk. HP4 off Swing Gate La 38 AX20
Swing Gate La, Berk. HP4 38 AX22
Swinnerton St, E9 279 L3
Swinton Cl, Wem. HA9 118 CP60
Swinton Pl, WC1 286 C2
Swinton St, WC1 286 C2
Swires Shaw, Kes. BR2 222 EK105
Swiss Av, Wat. WD18 75 BS42
Swiss Cl, Wat. WD18 75 BS41
⊖ Swiss Cottage 274 A6
Sch Swiss Cottage Sch, NW8 274 B7
Swiss Ct, W1 297 P1
Swiss Ter, NW6 274 A6
Switch Ho, E14 291 H10
Swithland Gdns, SE9 185 EN91
Sword Cl, Brox. EN10 49 DX20
Swyncombe Av, W5 157 CH77
Swynford Gdns, NW4 119 CU56
Sch Sybil Elgar Sch, W5
off Florence Rd 138 CL73
Southall UB2 off Havelock Rd 156 BZ76
Sybil Ms, N4 121 DP58
Sybil Phoenix Cl, SE8 301 K10
Sch Sybourn Infants' Sch, E17
off Sybourn St 123 DZ59
Sch Sybourn Jun Sch, E17
off Sybourn St 123 DZ59
Sybourn St, E17 123 DZ59
Sycamore App, Crox.Grn WD3 75 BQ43
Sycamore Av, E3 279 N8
W5 157 CK76
Hatfield AL10 45 CU19
Hayes UB3 135 BS73
Sidcup DA15 185 ET86
Upminster RM14 128 FN62
Sycamore Cl, E16 291 J5
N9 100 DU49
SE9 184 EL89
W3 off Bromyard Av 138 CS74
Amersham HP6 55 AR37
Barnet EN4 80 DD44
Bushey WD23 76 BY40
Carshalton SM5 218 DF105
Chalfont St. Giles HP8 90 AU48
Cheshunt EN7 66 DT27
Edgware HA8 off Ash Cl 96 CQ49
Feltham TW13 175 BU90
Fetcham KT22 231 CE123
Gravesend DA12 191 GK87
Loughton IG10 85 EP40
Northolt UB5 136 BY67
South Croydon CR2 220 DS106
Tilbury RM18 171 GG81
Watford WD25 75 BV35
West Drayton UB7 134 BM73
Sycamore Ct, Surb. KT6
off Penners Gdns 198 CL101
Sycamore Dene, Chesh. HP5 54 AR28
Sycamore Dr, Brwd. CM14
off Copperfield Gdns 108 FW46
Park Street AL2 61 CD27
Swanley BR8 207 FE97
Sycamore Fld, Harl. CM19 51 EN19
Sycamore Gdns, W6 159 CV75
Mitcham CR4 200 DD96
Sycamore Gro, NW9 118 CQ59
SE6 183 EC86
SE20 182 DU94
New Malden KT3 198 CR97
Romford RM2 105 FG54
Sycamore Hill, N11 98 DG51
Sycamore Ho, NW3
off Maitland Pk Vil 274 F4
Warlingham CR6
off East Parkside 237 EB115
Sycamore Ms, SW4 161 DJ83
Sycamore Path, E17
off Poplars Rd 123 EB58
Sycamore Pl, Brom. BR1 205 EN97
Sycamore Ri, Bans. SM7 217 CX114
Berkhamsted HP4 38 AX20
Chalfont St. Giles HP8 90 AU48
Sycamore Rd, SW19 179 CW93
Amersham HP6 55 AR37
Chalfont St. Giles HP8 90 AU48
Croxley Green WD3 75 BQ43
Dartford DA1 188 FK88
Guildford GU1 242 AX134
Sycamores, The, Aveley RM15
off Dacre Av 149 FR74
Bookham KT23 230 CC124
Hemel Hempstead HP3 39 BF23
Radlett WD7 61 CH34
Sycamore St, EC1 287 J5
Sycamore Wk, W10 282 E4
Englefield Green TW20 172 AV93
George Green SL3 132 AY72
Ilford IG6 off Civic Way 125 EQ56
Reigate RH2 266 DC137
Sycamore Way, S.Ock. RM15 149 FX70
Teddington TW11 177 CJ93
Thornton Heath CR7 201 DN99
SYDENHAM, SE26 182 DW92
⇌ Sydenham 182 DW91
Sydenham 182 DW91
Sydenham Av, N21
off Fleming Dr 81 DM43
SE26 182 DV92
Sydenham Cl, Rom. RM1 127 FF56
Sydenham Gdns, Slou. SL1 151 AQ76
Sch Sydenham High Sch, SE26
off Westwood Hill 182 DV92
Jun Dept, SE26
off Westwood Hill 182 DV91
⇌ Sydenham Hill 182 DT90
Sydenham Hill, SE23 182 DV88
SE26 182 DU90
Sydenham Hill Est, SE26 182 DU90
Sydenham Pk, SE26 182 DW90
Sydenham Pk Rd, SE26 182 DW90
Sydenham Pl, SE27
off Lansdowne Hill 181 DP90
Sydenham Ri, SE23 182 DV89
Sydenham Rd, SE26 182 DW91
Croydon CR0 202 DR101
Guildford GU1 258 AX136
Sch Sydenham Sch, SE26
off Dartmouth Rd 182 DV90
Sydmons Ct, SE23 182 DW87
Sydner Ms, N16 122 DT63
Sydner Rd, N16 122 DT63
Sydney Av, Pur. CR8 219 DM112
Sydney Chapman Way,
Barn. EN5 79 CZ40
Sydney Cl, SW3 296 B9
Sydney Cres, Ashf. TW15 175 BP93
Sydney Gro, NW4 119 CW57
Slough SL1 131 AQ72
Sydney Ms, SW3 296 B9
Sydney Pl, SW7 296 B9
Guildford GU1 259 AZ135
Sydney Rd, E11
off Mansfield Rd 124 EH58
N8 121 DN56
N10 98 DG53
SE2 166 EW76
SW20 199 CX96
W13 137 CG74
Bexleyheath DA6 166 EX84
Enfield EN2 82 DR42
Feltham TW14 175 BU88
Guildford GU1 259 AZ135
Ilford IG6 103 EQ54
Richmond TW9 158 CL84
Sidcup DA14 185 ES91
Sutton SM1 218 DA105
Teddington TW11 177 CF92
Tilbury RM18 171 GG82
Watford WD18 75 BS43
Woodford Green IG8 102 EG49
Sch Sydney Russell Comp Sch,
Dag. RM9 off Parsloes Av 126 EX64
Sydney St, SW3 296 C10
Syke Cluan, Iver SL0 153 BE75
Syke Ings, Iver SL0 153 BE76
Sykes Dr, Stai. TW18 174 BH92
Sykes Rd, Slou. SL1 131 AP72
Sylvana Cl, Uxb. UB10 134 BM67
Sylvan Av, N3 98 DA54
N22 99 DM52
NW7 97 CT51
Hornchurch RM11 128 FL58
Romford RM6 126 EZ58
Sylvan Cl, Chaff.Hun. RM16 170 FY77
Hemel Hempstead HP3 40 BN21
Oxted RH8 254 EH129
South Croydon CR2 220 DV110
Woking GU22 227 BB117
Sylvan Ct, N12 98 DB49
Sylvandale, Welw.G.C. AL7 30 DC10
Sylvan Est, SE19 202 DT95
Sylvan Gdns, Surb. KT6 197 CK101
Sylvan Gro, NW2 272 D1
SE15 312 F4
Sylvan Hill, SE19 202 DS95
Sylvan Ms, Green. DA9
off Watermans Way 169 FV84
Sylvan Rd, E7 281 P4
E11 124 EG57
E17 123 EA57
SE19 202 DT95
Ilford IG1 125 EQ61
Sylvan Wk, Brom. BR1 205 EM97
Sylvan Way, Chig. IG7 104 EV48
Dagenham RM8 126 EV62
Redhill RH1 266 DG135
Welwyn Garden City AL7 30 DC10
West Wickham BR4 222 EE105
Sylverdale Rd, Croy. CR0 201 DP104
Purley CR8 219 DP113
Sylvester Av, Chis. BR7 185 EM93
Sylvester Gdns, Ilf. IG6 104 EV50
Sylvester Path, E8 278 F4
Sylvester Rd, E8 278 F4
E17 123 DZ59
N2 98 DC54
Wembley HA0 117 CJ64
Sylvestres, Rvrhd TN13 256 FD121
Sylvestrus Cl, Kings.T. KT1 198 CN95
Sylvia Av, Hutt. CM13 109 GC47
Pinner HA5 94 BZ51
Sylvia Ct, Wem. HA9
off Harrow Rd 138 CP66
Sylvia Gdns, Wem. HA9 138 CP66
Sch Sylvia Young Thea Sch,
NW1 284 D5
Symes Ms, NW1 275 L10
Symington Ho, SE1 299 L7
Symington Ms, E9 279 K2
Symister Ms, N1 287 N3
Symonds Ct, Chsht EN8 67 DX28
Symonds Hyde, Hat. AL10 28 CP13
Symons Cl, SE15 312 G9
Symons St, SW3 296 F9
Symphony Cl, Edg. HA8 96 CP52
Symphony Ms, W10 282 F2
Syon Gate Way, Brent. TW8 157 CG80
★ Syon Ho & Pk, Brent. TW8 157 CJ81
⇌ Syon Lane 157 CG80
Syon La, Islw. TW7 157 CH80
Syon Pk Gdns, Islw. TW7 157 CF80
Sch Syon Pk Sch, Islw. TW7
off Twickenham Rd 157 CH81
Syon Vista, Rich. TW9 157 CK81
Syracuse Av, Rain. RM13 148 FL69
Uni Syracuse Uni - London Program,
WC1 286 B6
Syringa Ct, Grays RM17 170 GD80
Sythwood, Wok. GU21 226 AV117
Sch Sythwood Prim Sch,
Horsell GU21 off Sythwood 226 AV116

T

Tabard Cen, SE1
off Prioress St 299 M7
Tabard Gdns Est, SE1 299 M5
Tabard St, SE1 299 L5
Tabarin Way, Epsom KT17 233 CW116
Tabernacle Av, E13 291 N5
Tabernacle St, EC2 287 M5
Tableer Av, SW4 181 DJ85
Tabley Rd, N7 121 DL63
Tabor Gdns, Sutt. SM3 217 CZ107
Tabor Gro, SW19 179 CY94
Tabor Rd, W6 159 CV76
Tabors Ct, Shenf. CM15
off Shenfield Rd 109 FZ45
Tabrums Way, Upmin. RM14 129 FS59
Tachbrook Est, SW1 309 P1
Tachbrook Ms, SW1 297 L8
Tachbrook Rd, Felt. TW14 175 BT87
Southall UB2 156 BX77
Uxbridge UB8 134 BJ68
Tachbrook St, SW1 297 M9
Tack Ms, SE4 314 A10
Tadema Ho, NW8 284 B5
Tadema Rd, SW10 307 P4
Tadlows Cl, Upmin. RM14 128 FP64
Tadmor Cl, Sun. TW16 195 BT98
Tadmor St, W12 294 C3
Tadorne Rd, Tad. KT20 233 CW121
TADWORTH, KT20 233 CV121
⇌ Tadworth 233 CW122
Tadworth Av, N.Mal. KT3 199 CT99
Tadworth Cl, Tad. KT20 233 CX122
Tadworth Par, Horn. RM12
off Maylands Av 127 FH63
Sch Tadworth Prim Sch, Tad. KT20
off Tadworth St 233 CX122
Tadworth Rd, NW2 119 CU61
Tadworth St, Tad. KT20 233 CW123
Taeping St, E14 302 C8
Taffy's How, Mitch. CR4 200 DE97
Taft Way, E3 290 D2
Tagalie Pl, Shenley WD7 62 CL32
Tagg's Island, Hmptn. TW12 197 CD96
Tagore Cl, Har. HA3 117 CF55
Tailworth St, E1 288 C7
Tait Ct, SW8
off Darsley Dr 309 P6
Tait Rd, Croy. CR0 202 DS101
● Tait Rd Ind Est, Croy. CR0 202 DS101
Tait St, E1 288 E9
Takeley Cl, Rom. RM5 105 FD54
Waltham Abbey EN9 67 ED33
Takhar Ms, SW11 308 D9
Talacre Rd, NW5 275 H4
Jct Talbot, The,
N.Wld Bas. CM16 53 FD24
Talbot Av, N2 120 DD55
Slough SL3 153 AZ76
Watford WD19 94 BY45
Talbot Cl, N15 122 DT56
Mitcham CR4 201 DJ98
Reigate RH2 266 DB135
Talbot Ct, EC3 287 M10
Hemel Hempstead HP3
off Forest Av 40 BK22
Talbot Cres, NW4 119 CU57
Talbot Gdns, Ilf. IG3 126 EU61
Talbot Ho, E14 290 C8
N7 off Harvist Est 121 DN62
Talbot Pl, SE3 315 J8
Datchet SL3 152 AW81
Talbot Rd, E6 145 EN68
E7 124 EG63
N6 120 DG58
N15 122 DT56
N22 99 DJ54
SE22 162 DS84
W2 283 K8
W11 283 H8
W13 137 CG73
Ashford TW15 174 BK92
Carshalton SM5 218 DG106
Dagenham RM9 146 EZ65
Harrow HA3 95 CF54
Hatfield AL10 45 CU15
Isleworth TW7 157 CG84
Rickmansworth WD3 92 BL46
Southall UB2 156 BY77
Thornton Heath CR7 202 DR98
Twickenham TW2 177 CE88
Wembley HA0 117 CK64
Talbot Sq, W2 284 B9
Talbot St, Hert. SG13 32 DS09
Talbot Wk, NW10
off Garnet Rd 138 CS65
W11 282 E9
Talbot Yd, SE1 299 L3
Talbrook, Brwd. CM14 108 FT48
Talehangers Cl, Bexh. DA6 166 EX84
Taleworth Cl, Ashtd. KT21 231 CK120
Taleworth Pk, Ashtd. KT21 231 CK120
Taleworth Rd, Ashtd. KT21 231 CK119
Talfourd Pl, SE15 312 A7
Talfourd Rd, SE15 312 A7
Talford Way, Red. RH1 266 DF137
Talgarth Rd, W6 294 B10
W14 294 D10
Talgarth Wk, NW9 118 CS57
Talia Ho, E14 off New Union Cl 302 F6
Talisman Cl, Ilf. IG3 126 EV60
Talisman Sq, SE26 182 DU91
Talisman Way, Epsom KT17 233 CW116
Wembley HA9 118 CM62
Tallack Cl, Har. HA3 95 CE52
Tallack Rd, E10 123 DZ60
Tall Elms Cl, Brom. BR2 204 EF99
Tallents Cl, Sutt.H. DA4 188 FP94
Tallis Cl, E16 292 A9
Tallis Ct, Gidea Pk RM2 128 FJ55
Tallis Gro, SE7 164 EH79
Tallis St, EC4 286 F10
Tallis Vw, NW10 138 CR65
Tallis Way, Borwd. WD6 77 CK39
Warley CM14 108 FV50
Tall Oaks, Amer. HP6 55 AR37
Tallon Rd, Hutt. CM13 109 GE43
Tallow Cl, Dag. RM9 146 EX65
Tallow Rd, Brent. TW8 157 CJ79
Tall Trees, SW16 201 DM97
Colnbrook SL3 153 BE81
Tall Trees Cl, Horn. RM11 128 FK58
Jct Tally Ho Cor, N12 98 DC50
Tally Rd, Oxt. RH8 254 EL131
Talma Gdns, Twick. TW2 177 CE86
Talmage Cl, SE23
off Tyson Rd 182 DW87
Talman Gro, Stan. HA7 95 CK51
Talma Rd, SW2 161 DN84
Sch Talmud Torah Machzikei Hadass Sch,
E5 off Clapton Common 122 DU59
Talus Cl, Purf. RM19
off Brimfield Rd 169 FR77
Talwin St, E3 290 D3
Tamar Cl, E3 279 P9
Upminster RM14 129 FS58
Tamar Dr, Aveley RM15 148 FQ72
Tamar Grn, Hem.H. HP2 40 BM15
Tamarind Cl, Guil. GU2 242 AU129
Tamarind Yd, E1 300 D2
Tamarisk Cl, St.Alb. AL3
off New Grns Av 43 CD16
South Ockendon RM15 149 FW70
Tamarisk Rd, S.Ock. RM15 149 FW69
Tamarisk Sq, W12 139 CT73
Tamarisk Way, Slou. SL1 151 AN75
Tamarix Cres, Lon.Col. AL2 61 CG26
Tamar Sq, Wdf.Grn. IG8 102 EH51
Tamar St, SE7 304 G8
Tamar Way, N17
off Park Vw Rd 122 DU55
Slough SL3 153 BB78
Tamblin Way, Hat. AL10 44 CS17
Tamerton Sq, Wok. GU22 226 AY119
Tamesis Gdns, Wor.Pk. KT4 198 CS102
Tamesis Strand, Grav. DA12 191 GL92
Tamian Way, Houns. TW4 156 BW84
Tamworth Av, Wdf.Grn. IG8 102 EE51
Tamworth La, Mitch. CR4 201 DH96
Tamworth Pk, Mitch. CR4 201 DH98
Tamworth Pl, Croy. CR0 202 DQ103
Tamworth Rd, Croy. CR0 201 DP103
Hertford SG13 32 DS08
Tamworth St, SW6 307 J2
Tancred Rd, N4 121 DP58
Tandem Cen, SW19 200 DD95
Tandem Way, SW19 200 DD95
TANDRIDGE, Oxt. RH8 253 EA133
Tandridge Ct, Cat. CR3 236 DU122
Tandridge Dr, Orp. BR6 205 ER102
Tandridge Gdns, S.Croy. CR2 220 DT113
Tandridge Hill La, Gdse. RH9 253 DZ128
Tandridge La, Tand. RH8 253 EA131
Tandridge Pl, Orp. BR6 205 ER102
Tandridge Rd, Warl. CR6 237 DX119
Tanfield Av, NW2 119 CT63
Tanfield Cl, Chsht EN7 66 DU27
Tanfield Rd, Croy. CR0 220 DQ105
Tangent Link, Harold Hill RM3 106 FK53
Tangent Rd, Rom. RM3
off Ashton Rd 106 FK53
Tangier La, Eton SL4 151 AR79
Tangier Rd, Guil. GU1 259 BA135
Richmond TW10 158 CP83
Tangier Way, Tad. KT20 233 CY117
Tangier Wd, Tad. KT20 233 CY118
Tangleberry Cl, Brom. BR1 204 EL98
Tangle Tree Cl, N3 98 DB54
Tanglewood Cl, Croy. CR0 202 DW104
Longcross KT16 192 AV104
Stanmore HA7 95 CE47
Uxbridge UB10 134 BN69
Woking GU22 227 BD116
Tanglewood Way, Felt. TW13 175 BV90
Tangley Gro, SW15 179 CT87
Tangley La, Guil. GU3 242 AT130
Tangley Pk Rd, Hmptn. TW12 176 BZ93
Tanglyn Av, Shep. TW17 195 BP99
Tangmere Cres, Horn. RM12 147 FH65
Tangmere Gdns, Nthlt. UB5 136 BW68
Tangmere Gro, Kings.T. KT2 177 CK92
Tangmere Way, NW9 96 CS54
Tanhouse Rd, Oxt. RH8 253 ED132
Tanhouse Way, Colnbr. SL3 153 BD80
Tanhurst Wk, SE2
off Alsike Rd 166 EX76
Tankerton Rd, Surb. KT6 198 CM103
Tankerton St, WC1 286 B3
Tankerton Ter, Croy. CR0
off Mitcham Rd 201 DM101
Tankerville Rd, SW16 181 DK93
Tank Hill Rd, Purf. RM19 168 FN78
Tank La, Purf. RM19 168 FN77
Tankridge Rd, NW2 119 CV61
Tanner Pt, E13 281 N9
Tanners Cl, St.Alb. AL3 42 CC19
Walton-on-Thames KT12 195 BV100
Tanners Ct, Brock. RH3 264 CQ138
Tanners Cres, Hert. SG13 32 DQ11
Tanners Dean, Lthd. KT22 231 CJ122
Tanners End La, N18 100 DS49
Tannersfield, Shalf. GU4 258 AY142
Tanners Hill, SE8 313 P7
Abbots Langley WD5 59 BT31
Tanners La, Ilf. IG6 125 EQ55
Tanners Meadow, Brock. RH3 264 CP138

S T

Tanners Ms, SE8 313 P7
Tanner St, SE1 299 P5
Barking IG11 145 EQ65
Tanners Way, Hunsdon SG12 34 EJ06
Tanners Wd Cl, Abb.L. WD5
off Tanners Wd La 59 BS32
Sch Tanners Wd JMI Sch, Abb.L. WD5 off Hazelwood La 59 BS32
Tanners Wd La, Abb.L. WD5 59 BS32
Tanners Yd, E2 288 E1
Tannery, The, Red. RH1 250 DE134
Tannery Cl, Beck. BR3 203 DX99
Dagenham RM10 127 FB62
Tannery La, Bramley GU5 258 AY144
Send GU23 227 BF122
Tannington Ter, N5 121 DN62
Tannoy Sq, SE27 182 DR91
Tannsfeld Rd, SE26 183 DX92
Tannsfield Dr, Hem.H. HP2 40 BM18
Tannsmore Cl, Hem.H. HP2 40 BM18
Tansley Cl, N7 275 P2
Tanswell Est, SE1 298 E5
Tanswell St, SE1 298 E5
Tansy Cl, E6 293 M9
Guildford GU4 243 BC132
Romford RM3 106 FL51
Tansycroft, Welw.G.C. AL7 30 DB08
Tantallon Rd, SW12 180 DG88
Tant Av, E16 291 L8
Tantony Gro, Rom. RM6 126 EX55
Tanworth Cl, Nthwd. HA6 93 BQ51
Tanworth Gdns, Pnr. HA5 93 BV54
Tanyard La, Bex. DA5 186 FA88
Tanyard Way, Horl. RH6 269 DH146
Tanys Dell, Harl. CM20 36 EU12
Sch Tany's Dell Comm Prim Sch, Harl. CM20 off Mowbray Rd 36 EU12
Tanza Rd, NW3 120 DF63
Tapestry Cl, Sutt. SM2 218 DB108
TAPLOW, Maid. SL6 130 AE70
⇌ Taplow 130 AF72
Taplow, NW3 274 B7
SE17 299 M10
Taplow Common Rd, Burn. SL1 130 AG67
Taplow Rd, N13 100 DQ49
Taplow SL6 130 AG71
Taplow St, N1 287 K1
Tapners Rd, Bet. RH3 265 CT139
Leigh RH2 265 CT139
Tapper Wk, N1 276 A8
Tappesfield Rd, SE15 312 G10
Tapp St, E1 288 E4
Tapster St, Barn. EN5 79 CZ42
Tara Ms, N8 121 DK58
Taransay, Hem.H. HP3 41 BP22
Taransay Wk, N1 277 L4
Tarbay La, Oakley Grn SL4 150 AH82
Tarbert Ms, N15 122 DS57
Tarbert Rd, SE22 182 DS85
Tarbert Wk, E1 288 G10
Target Cl, Felt. TW14 175 BS86
Jct Target Rbt, Nthlt. UB5 off Western Av 136 BZ67
Tarham Cl, Horl. RH6 268 DE146
Tariff Cres, SE8 301 N8
Tariff Rd, N17 100 DU51
Tarleton Gdns, SE23 182 DV88
Tarling Cl, Sid. DA14 186 EV90
Tarling Rd, E16 291 M9
N2 98 DC54
Tarling St, E1 288 G9
Tarling St Est, E1 288 G9
Tarnbank, Enf. EN2 81 DL43
Tarn St, SE1 299 J7
Tarnwood Pk, SE9 185 EM88
Tarnworth Rd, Rom. RM3 106 FN50
Tarpan Way, Brox. EN10 67 DZ26
Tarquin Ho, SE26 182 DU91
Tarragon Cl, SE14 313 L4
Tarragon Dr, Guil. GU2 242 AU129
Tarragon Gro, SE26 183 DX93
Tarrant Pl, W1 284 E7
Tarrington Cl, SW16 181 DK90
Tartar Rd, Cob. KT11 214 BW113
Tarver Rd, SE17 311 H1
Tarves Way, SE10 314 D4
Taryn Gro, Brom. BR1 205 EM97
Tash Pl, N11 99 DH50
Sch TASIS, The American Sch in England, Thorpe TW20 off Coldharbour La 193 BC97
Tasker Cl, Harling. UB3 155 BQ80
Tasker Ho, Bark. IG11 off Dovehouse Mead 145 ER68
Tasker Rd, NW3 274 E3
Grays RM16 171 GH76
Tasman Ct, E14 off Westferry Rd 302 C9
Sunbury-on-Thames TW16 175 BS94
Tasmania Ho, Til. RM18 off Hobart Rd 171 GG81
Tasmania Ter, N18 100 DQ51
Tasman Rd, SW9 161 DL83
Tasman Wk, E16 292 E9
Tasso Rd, W6 306 E2
Tatam Rd, NW10 138 CQ66
Tatchbury Ho, SW15 off Tunworth Cres 179 CT86
Tate & Lyle Jetty, E16 304 G5
★ Tate Britain, SW1 298 A9
Tate Cl, Lthd. KT22 231 CJ123
Tate Gdns, Bushey WD23 95 CE45
★ Tate Modern, SE1 299 H2
Tate Rd, E16 305 J3
Chalfont St. Peter SL9 91 AZ50
Sutton SM1 218 DA106
Tatham Pl, NW8 274 B10
TATLING END, Ger.Cr. SL9 113 BB61
Tatnell Rd, SE23 183 DY86
TATSFIELD, West. TN16 238 EL120
Tatsfield App Rd, Tats. TN16 238 EH123
Tatsfield Av, Lwr Naze. EN9 49 ED23
Tatsfield La, Tats. TN16 239 EM121
Sch Tatsfield Prim Sch, Tats. TN16 238 EJ121
TATTENHAM CORNER, Epsom KT18 233 CV118
⇌ Tattenham Corner 233 CV118
Tattenham Cor Rd, Epsom KT18 233 CT117
Tattenham Cres, Epsom KT18 233 CU118
Tattenham Gro, Epsom KT18 233 CV118
Tattenham Way, Tad. KT20 233 CX118
Tattersall Cl, SE9 184 EL85
Tattle Hill, Hert. SG14 31 DL05
Tatton Cl, Cars. SM5 200 DG102
Tatton Cres, N16 122 DT59
Tatton St, Harl. CM17 36 EW14
Tatum St, SE17 299 M9
Tauber Cl, Els. WD6 78 CM42
Tauheed Cl, N4 122 DQ61
Taunton Av, SW20 199 CV96
Caterham CR3 236 DT123
Hounslow TW3 156 CC82
Taunton Cl, Bexh. DA7 167 FD82
Ilford IG6 103 ET51
Sutton SM3 200 DA102
Taunton Dr, N2 98 DC54
Enfield EN2 81 DN41
Taunton La, Couls. CR5 235 DN119
Taunton Ms, NW1 284 E5
Taunton Pl, NW1 284 E4
Taunton Rd, SE12 184 EE85
Greenford UB6 136 CB67
Northfleet DA11 190 GA85
Romford RM3 106 FJ49
Taunton Vale, Grav. DA12 191 GK90
Taunton Way, Stan. HA7 118 CL55
Tavern Cl, Cars. SM5 200 DE101
Taverners, Hem.H. HP2 40 BL18
Taverners Cl, W11 294 E3
Taverner Sq, N5 277 J1
Taverners Way, E4 102 EE46
Hoddesdon EN11 49 EA17
Tavern La, SW9 310 F8
Tavern Quay, SE16 off Sweden Gate 301 L8
Tavistock Av, E17 123 DY55
NW7 97 CX52
Perivale UB6 137 CG68
St. Albans AL1 42 CC23
Tavistock Cl, N16 277 P3
Potters Bar EN6 64 DD31
Romford RM3 106 FK53
St. Albans AL1 43 CD24
Staines-upon-Thames TW18 174 BK94
Tavistock Ct, WC2 off Tavistock St 286 B10
Tavistock Cres, W11 283 H7
Mitcham CR4 201 DL98
Tavistock Gdns, Ilf. IG3 125 ES63
Tavistock Gate, Croy. CR0 202 DR102
Tavistock Gro, Croy. CR0 202 DR101
Tavistock Ms, E18 off Tavistock Pl 124 EG56
N19 off Tavistock Terr 121 DL62
Tavistock Pl, E18 124 EG56
N14 81 DH44
WC1 285 P4
Tavistock Rd, E7 124 EF63
E15 281 L5
E18 124 EG55
N4 122 DR58
NW10 139 CT68
W11 282 G8
Bromley BR2 204 EF98
Carshalton SM5 200 DD102
Croydon CR0 202 DR102
Edgware HA8 96 CN53
Uxbridge UB10 115 BQ64
Watford WD24 76 BX39
Welling DA16 166 EW81
West Drayton UB7 134 BK74
Tavistock Sq, WC1 285 P4
Tavistock St, WC2 286 B10
Tavistock Ter, N19 121 DK62
Tavistock Twr, SE16 301 L7
Tavistock Wk, Cars. SM5 off Tavistock Rd 200 DD102
Taviton St, WC1 285 N4
Tavy Cl, SE11 298 F10
Tawney Common, They.Mt CM16 70 FA32
Tawney La, Ong. CM5 71 FC32
Stapleford Tawney RM4 87 FD35
Tawney Rd, SE28 146 EV73
Tawneys Rd, Harl. CM18 51 ES16
Tawny Av, Upmin. RM14 128 FP64
Tawny Cl, W13 137 CH74
Feltham TW13 off Chervil Cl 175 BU90
Tawny Way, SE16 301 K8
Tayben Av, Twick. TW2 177 CE86
Taybridge Rd, SW11 160 DG83
Tayburn Cl, E14 290 E8
Tayfield Cl, Uxb. UB10 115 BQ62
Tayler Cotts, Ridge EN6 off Crossoaks La 63 CT34
Tayles Hill, Epsom KT17 off Tayles Hill Dr 217 CT110
Tayles Hill Dr, Epsom KT17 217 CT110
Taylifers, Harl. CM19 51 EN20
Taylor Av, Rich. TW9 158 CP82
Taylor Cl, N17 100 DU52
SE8 313 N2
Epsom KT19 216 CN111
Hampton Hill TW12 176 CC92
Harefield UB9 off High St 92 BJ53
Hounslow TW3 156 CC81
Orpington BR6 223 ET105
Romford RM5 104 FA52
St. Albans AL4 43 CG16
Taylor Pl, E3 off Payne Rd 290 C1
Taylor Rd, Ashtd. KT21 231 CK117
Mitcham CR4 180 DE94
Wallington SM6 219 DH106
Taylor Row, Dart. DA2 188 FJ90
Noak Hill RM3 off Cummings Hall La 106 FJ47
Taylors Av, Hodd. EN11 49 EA18
Taylors Bldgs, SE18 305 P8
Taylors Cl, Sid. DA14 185 ET91
Taylors Ct, Felt. TW13 175 BU89
Taylors Grn, W3 138 CS72
Taylors La, SE26 182 DV91
Barnet EN5 79 CZ39
Taylors Rd, Chesh. HP5 54 AR29
Taymount Ri, SE23 182 DW89
Taynton Dr, Merst. RH1 251 DK129
Tayport Cl, N1 276 B7
Tayside Dr, Edg. HA8 96 CP48
Tay Way, Rom. RM1 105 FF53
Taywood Rd, Nthlt. UB5 136 BZ69
Teak Cl, SE16 301 M3
Teal Av, Orp. BR5 206 EX98
Tealby Ct, N7 276 C4
Teal Cl, E16 292 E7
Enfield EN3 82 DW37
South Croydon CR2 221 DX111
Teal Ct, Wall. SM6 off Carew Rd 219 DJ107
Teal Dr, Nthwd. HA6 93 BQ52
Teale St, E2 278 D10
Tealing Dr, Epsom KT19 216 CR105
Teal Pl, Sutt. SM1 off Sandpiper Rd 217 CZ106
Teal St, SE10 303 M6
Teal Way, Hem.H. HP3 58 BM25
● Teardrop Cen, Swan. BR8 207 FH99
Teasel Cl, Croy. CR0 203 DX102
Teasel Cres, SE28 145 ES74
Teasel Way, E15 291 K2
Teazle Meade, Thnwd CM16 70 EV25
Teazle Wd Hill, Lthd. KT22 231 CE117
Teazlewood Pk, Lthd. KT22 231 CG117
Tebworth Rd, N17 100 DT52
● Technology Pk, The, NW9 118 CR55
Teck Cl, Islw. TW7 157 CG82
Tedder Cl, Chess. KT9 215 CJ107
Ruislip HA4 off West End Rd 115 BV64
Uxbridge UB10 134 BM66
Tedder Rd, Hem.H. HP2 40 BN19
South Croydon CR2 220 DW108
TEDDINGTON, TW11 177 CG93
⇌ Teddington 177 CG93
Teddington Cl, Epsom KT19 216 CR110
Teddington Lock, Tedd. TW11 177 CG91
H Teddington Mem Hosp, Tedd. TW11 177 CE93
Teddington Pk, Tedd. TW11 177 CF92
Teddington Pk Rd, Tedd. TW11 177 CF91
Sch Teddington Sch, Tedd. TW11 off Broom Rd 177 CK93
Tedworth Gdns, SW3 308 E1
Tedworth Sq, SW3 308 E1
Tee, The, W3 138 CS72
Tees Av, Perivale UB6 137 CE68
Tees Cl, Upmin. RM14 129 FR59
Teesdale, Hem.H. HP2 40 BL17
Teesdale Av, Islw. TW7 157 CG81
Teesdale Cl, E2 288 D1
Teesdale Gdns, SE25 202 DS96
Isleworth TW7 157 CG81
Teesdale Rd, E11 124 EF58
Dartford DA2 188 FQ88
Slough SL2 131 AM71
Teesdale St, E2 288 E1
Teesdale Yd, E2 278 D10
Tees Dr, Rom. RM3 106 FK48
Tee Side, Hert. SG13 32 DV08
Teeswater Ct, Erith DA18 off Middle Way 166 EX76
Teevan Cl, Croy. CR0 202 DU101
Teevan Rd, Croy. CR0 202 DU101
Tegan Cl, Sutt. SM2 218 DA108
Teggs La, Wok. GU22 227 BF116
Teign Ms, SE9 184 EL89
Teignmouth Cl, SW4 161 DK84
Edgware HA8 96 CM54
Teignmouth Gdns, Perivale UB6 137 CF68
Teignmouth Par, Perivale UB6 off Teignmouth Gdns 137 CH68
Teignmouth Rd, NW2 272 C3
Welling DA16 166 EW82
Sch Teikyo Sch UK Teikyo Women's Coll London, Stoke P. SL2 off Framewood Rd 132 AX66
Telcote Way, Ruis. HA4 off Woodlands Av 116 BW59
★ Telecom Twr, W1 285 L6
Telegraph Hill, NW3 120 DB62
Telegraph La, Clay. KT10 215 CF107
Telegraph Ms, Ilf. IG3 126 EU60
Telegraph Path, Chis. BR7 185 EP92
Telegraph Pl, E14 302 C8
Telegraph Rd, SW15 179 CV87
Telegraph St, EC2 287 L8
Telegraph Track, Cars. SM5 218 DG110
Telemann Sq, SE3 164 EH83
Telephone Pl, SW6 307 H2
Telfer Cl, W3 off Church Rd 158 CQ75
Sch Telferscot Prim Sch, SW12 off Telferscot Rd 181 DK88
Telferscot Rd, SW12 181 DK88
Telford Av, SW2 181 DL88
Telford Cl, E17 123 DY59
SE19 off St. Aubyn's Rd 182 DT93
Watford WD25 76 BX35
Telford Ct, Guil. GU1 243 AZ134
St. Albans AL1 43 CE21
Telford Dr, Slou. SL1 151 AN75
Walton-on-Thames KT12 196 BW101
Telford Ho, SE1 299 J7
Telford Rd, N11 99 DJ51
NW9 off West Hendon Bdy 119 CU58
SE9 185 ER89
W10 282 E6
London Colney AL2 61 CJ27
Southall UB1 136 CB73
Twickenham TW2 176 CA87
Telfords Yd, E1 300 D1
Telford Ter, SW1 309 L2
Telford Way, W3 138 CS71
Hayes UB4 136 BY71
Telham Rd, E6 293 L1
Tell Gro, SE22 162 DT84
Tellisford, Esher KT10 214 CB105
Tellson Av, SE18 164 EL81
Telscombe Cl, Orp. BR6 205 ES103
Telston La, Otford TN14 241 FF117
Temair Ho, SE10 off Tarves Way 314 D4
Temeraire Pl, Brent. TW8 158 CM78
Temeraire St, SE16 301 H5
Temperance St, St.Alb. AL3 42 CC20
Temperley Rd, SW12 180 DG87
Tempest Av, Pot.B. EN6 64 DC32
Tempest Mead, N.Wld Bas. CM16 71 FB27
Tempest Rd, Egh. TW20 173 BC93
Tempest Way, Rain. RM13 147 FG65
Templar Ct, NW8 off St. John's Wd Rd 284 A3
Templar Dr, SE28 146 EX72
Gravesend DA11 191 GG92
Templar Ho, NW2 272 G4
Harrow HA2 off Northolt Rd 117 CD61
Templar Pl, Hmptn. TW12 176 CA94
Templars Av, NW11 119 CZ58
Templars Ct, Dart. DA1 188 FN85
Templars Cres, N3 98 DA54
Templars Dr, Har. HA3 95 CD51
Templars Ho, E16 off University Way 305 P1
Templar St, SE5 311 H7
⊖ Temple 286 D10
★ Temple, The, EC4 286 E10
Temple Av, EC4 286 F10
N20 98 DD45
Croydon CR0 203 DZ103
Dagenham RM8 126 FA60
Temple Bk, Harl. CM20 36 EV09
★ Temple Bar, EC4 287 H9
★ Temple Bar Mem, EC4 286 E9
Temple Bar Rd, Wok. GU21 226 AT119
Temple Cl, E11 124 EE59
N3 97 CZ54
SE28 165 EQ76
Cheshunt EN7 66 DU31
Epsom KT19 216 CR112
Watford WD17 75 BT40
Templecombe Ms, Wok. GU22 off Dorchester Ct 227 BA116
Templecombe Rd, E9 278 G8
Templecombe Way, Mord. SM4 199 CY99
Temple Ct, E1 off Rectory Sq 289 J6
SW8 off Thorncroft St 310 A5
Hertford SG14 32 DR06
Potters Bar EN6 63 CY31
Templecroft, Ashf. TW15 175 BR93
Templedene Av, Stai. TW18 174 BH94
Temple Dws, E2 off Temple Yd 288 E1
Templefield Cl, Add. KT15 212 BH107
● Temple Flds, Harl. CM20 36 EU11
Temple Flds, Hert. SG14 32 DR06
Temple Fortune Hill, NW11 120 DA57
Temple Fortune La, NW11 120 DA58
Temple Fortune Mans, NW11 off Finchley Rd 119 CZ57
Temple Fortune Par, NW11 off Finchley Rd 119 CZ57
Temple Gdns, N21 off Barrowell Grn 99 DP47
NW11 119 CZ58
Dagenham RM8 126 EX62
Rickmansworth WD3 93 BP49
Staines-upon-Thames TW18 193 BF95
Temple Gro, NW11 120 DA58
Enfield EN2 81 DP41
Temple Hill, Dart. DA1 188 FM86
Sch Temple Hill Comm Prim & Nurs Sch, Dart. DA1 off St. Edmunds Rd 188 FN85
Temple Hill Sq, Dart. DA1 188 FM85
Templehof Av, NW2 119 CW59
Temple La, EC4 286 F9
Templeman Cl, Pur. CR8 off Croftleigh Av 235 DP116
Templeman Rd, W7 137 CF71
Temple Mead, Hem.H. HP2 40 BK18
Roydon CM19 50 EH15
Templemead Cl, W3 138 CS72
Temple Mead Cl, Stan. HA7 95 CH51
Templemead Ho, E9 off Kingsmead Way 279 M1
Templemere, Wey. KT13 195 BR104
Temple Mills La, E20, E15 280 E2
Temple of Mithras, EC4 off Queen Victoria St 287 L9
Templepan La, Chan.Cr. WD3 74 BL37
Temple Pk, Uxb. UB8 134 BN69
Temple Pl, WC2 286 D10
Templer Av, Grays RM16 171 GG77
Temple Rd, E6 144 EL67
N8 121 DM56
NW2 119 CW63
W4 158 CQ76
W5 157 CK76
Biggin Hill TN16 238 EK117
Croydon CR0 220 DR105
Epsom KT19 216 CR112
Hounslow TW3 156 CB84
Richmond TW9 158 CM83
Windsor SL4 151 AQ82
Temple Sheen, SW14 178 CQ85
Temple Sheen Rd, SW14 158 CP84
Temple St, E2 288 E1
Templeton Av, E4 101 EA49
Templeton Cl, N16 277 P2
SE19 202 DR95
Templeton Ct, NW7 off Kingsbridge Dr 97 CX52
Borwd. WD6 off Eaton Way 78 CM39
Templeton Pl, SW5 295 K9
Templeton Rd, N15 122 DR58
Temple Vw, St.Alb. AL3 42 CC18
Temple Way, Farn.Com. SL2 111 AQ64
Sutton SM1 200 DD104
Temple W Ms, SE11 298 G7
Templewood, W13 137 CH71
Welwyn Garden City AL8 29 CX06
Templewood Av, NW3 120 DB62
Temple Wd Dr, Red. RH1 250 DF131
Templewood Gdns, NW3 120 DB62
Templewood Gate, Farn.Com. SL2 111 AQ64
Templewood La, Slou. SL2 112 AS63
Templewood Pk, Slou. SL2 112 AT63
Templewood Pt, NW2 119 CZ61
Sch Templewood Prim Sch, Welw.G.C. AL8 off Pentley Pk 29 CX07
Temple Yd, E2 288 E1
Tempsford, Welw.G.C. AL7 30 DD09
Tempsford Av, Borwd. WD6 78 CR42
Tempsford Cl, Enf. EN2 off Gladbeck Way 82 DQ41
Tempus, Har. HA2 116 CC61
Tempus Ct, E18 102 EG53
Temsford Cl, Har. HA2 94 CC54
Ten Acre, Wok. GU21 off Chirton Wk 226 AU118
Ten Acre La, Egh. TW20 193 BC96
Ten Acres, Fetch. KT22 231 CD124
Ten Acres Cl, Fetch. KT22 231 CD124
Tenbury Cl, E7 off Romford Rd 124 EK64
Tenbury Ct, SW2 181 DK88
Tenby Av, Har. HA3 95 CH54
Tenby Cl, N15 122 DT56
Romford RM6 126 EY58
Tenby Gdns, Nthlt. UB5 136 CA65
Tenby Rd, E17 123 DY57
Edgware HA8 96 CM53
Enfield EN3 82 DW41
Romford RM6 126 EY58
Welling DA16 166 EX81
Tenchleys La, Oxt. RH8 254 EK131
Tench St, E1 300 E3
Tenda Rd, SE16 300 E9
Tendring Ms, Harl. CM18 51 ES16
Tendring Rd, Harl. CM18 51 EQ17
Tendring Way, Rom. RM6 126 EW57
Tenham Av, SW2 181 DK88
Tenison Ct, W1 285 L10
Tenison Way, SE1 298 E3
Tennand Cl, Chsht EN7 66 DT26
Tenniel Cl, W2 283 N9
Guildford GU2 242 AV132
Tennis Ct La, E.Mol. KT8 off Hampton Ct Way 197 CE97
Tennison Av, Borwd. WD6 78 CP43
Tennison Cl, Couls. CR5 235 DP120
Tennison Rd, SE25 202 DT98
Tennis St, SE1 299 L4
Tenniswood Rd, Enf. EN1 82 DT39
Tennyson Av, E11 124 EG59
E12 144 EL66
NW9 118 CQ55
Grays RM17 170 GB76
New Malden KT3 199 CV99
Twickenham TW1 177 CF88
Waltham Abbey EN9 68 EE34
Tennyson Cl, Enf. EN3 83 DX43
Feltham TW14 175 BT86
Welling DA16 165 ES81
Tennyson Rd, E10 123 EB61
E15 281 J6
E17 123 DZ58
NW6 272 G8
NW7 97 CU50
SE20 183 DX94
SW19 180 DC93
W7 137 CF73
Addlestone KT15 212 BL105
Ashford TW15 174 BL92
Dartford DA1 188 FN85
Hounslow TW3 156 CC82
Hutton CM13 109 GC45
Romford RM3 106 FJ52
St. Albans AL2 60 CA26
Tennyson St, SW8 309 J9
Tennyson Wk, Nthflt DA11 190 GD90
Tilbury RM18 171 GH82
Tennyson Way, Horn. RM12 127 FF61
Slough SL2 131 AL70
Tensing Av, Nthflt DA11 190 GE90
Tensing Rd, Sthl. UB2 156 CA76
Tentelow La, Sthl. UB2 156 CA78
Tenterden Cl, NW4 119 CX55
SE9 185 EM91
Tenterden Dr, NW4 119 CX55
Tenterden Gdns, NW4 119 CX55
Croydon CR0 202 DU101
Tenterden Gro, NW4 119 CW56
Tenterden Rd, N17 100 DT52
Croydon CR0 202 DU101
Dagenham RM8 126 EZ61
Tenterden St, W1 285 K9
Tenter Grd, E1 288 A7
Tenter Pas, E1 288 B9
Tent Peg La, Orp. BR5 205 EQ99
Tent St, E1 288 E4
Tenzing Rd, Hem.H. HP2 40 BN20
Tequila Wf, E14 off Commercial Rd 289 M9
Terborch Way, SE22 off East Dulwich Gro 182 DS85
Tercel Path, Chig. IG7 104 EV49
Teredo St, SE16 301 K7
Terence Cl, Grav. DA12 191 GM88
Terence Ct, Belv. DA17 off Nuxley Rd 166 EZ79
Teresa Gdns, Wal.Cr. EN8 66 DW34
Teresa Ms, E17 123 EA56
Teresa Wk, N10 off Connaught Gdns 121 DH57
Terling Cl, E11 124 EF62
Terling Rd, Dag. RM8 126 FA61
Terlings, The, Brwd. CM14 108 FU48
Terling Wk, N1 277 J8
Jct Terminal Four Rbt, Lon.Hthrw Air. TW6 175 BQ86
Terminus Pl, SW1 297 K7
Terminus St, Harl. CM20 35 ER14
Tern Gdns, Upmin. RM14 129 FS60
Tern Way, Brwd. CM14 108 FS49
Terrace, The, E4 off Chingdale Rd 102 EE48
N3 off Hendon La 97 CZ54
NW6 273 J8
SW13 158 CS82
Addlestone KT15 212 BL106
Bray SL6 150 AC76
Dorking RH5 263 CJ137
Gravesend DA12 191 GH86
Sevenoaks TN13 256 FD122
Woodford Green IG8 off Broadmead Rd 102 EG51
Terrace Apts, N5 off Drayton Pk 276 F2
Terrace Gdns, SW13 159 CT82
Watford WD17 75 BV40
Terrace La, Rich. TW10 178 CL86
Terrace Rd, E9 279 H6
E13 281 P9
Walton-on-Thames KT12 195 BU101
Terraces, The, Dart. DA2 188 FQ87
Terrace St, Grav. DA12 191 GH86
Terrace Wk, Dag. RM9 126 EY64
Terrapin Rd, SW17 181 DH90
Terretts Pl, N1 276 G7
Terrick Rd, N22 99 DL53
Terrick St, W12 139 CV72
Terrilands, Pnr. HA5 116 BZ55
Terront Rd, N15 122 DQ57
Tersha St, Rich. TW9 158 CM84
Tessa Sanderson Pl, SW8 309 K10
Tessa Sanderson Way, Grnf. UB6 off Lilian Board Way 117 CD64
Testard Rd, Guil. GU2 258 AW136
Testers Cl, Oxt. RH8 254 EH132
Testerton Wk, W11 282 D10
Testwood Rd, Wind. SL4 151 AK81
Tetbury Pl, N1 276 G9
Tetcott Rd, SW10 307 N4
Tetherdown, N10 120 DG55
Coll Tetherdown Adult Ed Cen, N10 off Tetherdown 120 DG55
Sch Tetherdown Prim Sch, N10 off Grand Av 120 DG56
Tethys Rd, Hem.H. HP2 40 BM17
Tetty Way, Brom. BR2 204 EG96
Teversham La, SW8 310 B6
Teviot Av, Aveley RM15 148 FQ72
Teviot Cl, Guil. GU2 242 AU131
Welling DA16 166 EV81
Teviot St, E14 290 E6
TEWIN, Welw. AL6 30 DE05
Tewin Cl, St.Alb. AL4 43 CJ16
Tewin Ct, Welw.G.C. AL7 29 CZ08
Sch Tewin Cowper C of E Prim Sch, Tewin AL6 off Cannons Meadow 30 DE05
Tewin Mill Ho, Tewin AL6 30 DE07
Tewin Rd, Hem.H. HP2 41 BQ20
Welwyn Garden City AL7 29 CZ09
Tewin Water, Welw. AL6 30 DB05

T

Tewkesbury Av, SE23 182 DV88
Pinner HA5 116 BY57
Tewkesbury Cl, N15 off Pulford Rd 122 DR58
Barnet EN4 off Approach Rd 80 DD42
Byfleet KT14 212 BK111
Loughton IG10 84 EL44
Tewkesbury Gdns, NW9 118 CP55
Tewkesbury Rd, N15 122 DR58
W13 137 CG73
Carshalton SM5 200 DD102
Tewkesbury Ter, N11 99 DJ51
Tewson Rd, SE18 165 ES78
Teynham Av, Enf. EN1 82 DR44
Teynham Grn, Brom. BR2 204 EG99
Teynham Rd, Dart. DA2 188 FQ87
Teynton Ter, N17 100 DQ53
Thackeray Av, N17 100 DU54
Tilbury RM18 171 GH81
Thackeray Cl, SW19 179 CX94
Isleworth TW7 157 CG82
Uxbridge UB8 135 BP72
Thackeray Dr, Rom. RM6 126 EU59
Thackeray Rd, E6 144 EK68
SW8 309 J9
Thackeray St, W8 295 M5
Thackrah Cl, N2 off Tarling Rd 98 DC54
Thakeham Cl, SE26 182 DV92
Thalia Cl, SE10 315 H2
Thalmassing Cl, Hutt. CM13 109 GB47
Thame Rd, SE16 301 K4
Thames Av, SW10 307 P6
Chertsey KT16 194 BG97
Dagenham RM9 147 FB70
Hemel Hempstead HP2 40 BM15
Perivale UB6 137 CF68
Windsor SL4 151 AR80
Wor.Pk. 199 CW102
Thames Bk, SW14 158 CQ82
Thamesbank Pl, SE28 146 EW72
★ Thames Barrier Information & Learning Cen, SE18 304 E6
Thames Christian Coll, SW11 308 B10
Thames Circle, E14 302 B8
Thames Cl, Cher. KT16 194 BH101
Hampton TW12 196 CB96
Rainham RM13 147 FH72
Thames Ct, W.Mol. KT8 196 CB96
Thames Cres, W4 158 CS80
Thamesdale, Lon.Col. AL2 62 CM27
THAMES DITTON, KT7 197 CF100
⇌ Thames Ditton 197 CF101
Thames Ditton Inf Sch, T.Ditt. KT7 off Speer Rd 197 CF100
Thames Ditton Island, T.Ditt. KT7 197 CG99
Thames Ditton Jun Sch, T.Ditt. KT7 off Mercer Cl 197 CF101
Thames Dr, Grays RM16 171 GG78
Ruislip HA4 115 BQ58
Thames Edge Ct, Stai. TW18 off Clarence St 173 BE91
● Thames Europort, Dart. DA2 169 FS84
Thames Eyot, Twick. TW1 177 CG88
Thamesfield Ct, Shep. TW17 195 BQ101
Thames Gate, Dart. DA1 188 FN85
Thamesgate Cl, Rich. TW10 177 CH91
Thamesgate Shop Cen, Grav. DA11 off New Rd 191 GH86
Thames Gateway, Dag. RM9 146 EZ68
Rainham RM13 147 FG72
South Ockendon RM15 168 FP75
Thames Gateway Coll, CEME Campus, Rain. RM13 off Marsh Way 147 FD70
● Thames Gateway Pk, Dag. RM9 146 EZ69
Thameshill Av, Rom. RM5 105 FC54
Thameside, Cher. KT16 194 BJ101
Staines-upon-Thames TW18 194 BH97
Teddington TW11 177 CK94
● Thameside Cen, Brent. TW8 158 CM79
● Thameside Ind Est, E16 304 F4
Thameside Inf Sch, Grays RM17 off Manor Rd 170 GC79
Thameside Jun Sch, Grays RM17 off Manor Rd 170 GC79
Thameside Wk, SE28 145 ET72
Thames Link, SE16 301 J3
THAMESMEAD, SE28 145 ET73
Thames Mead, Walt. KT12 195 BU101
Windsor SL4 151 AL81
Thamesmead Cen, Erith DA18 off Yarnton Way 166 EY75
THAMESMEAD NORTH, SE28 146 EX72
Thames Meadow, Shep. TW17 195 BR102
West Molesey KT8 196 CA96
Thamesmead Sch, Shep. TW17 off Manygate La 195 BQ100
Thamesmead Spine Rd, Belv. DA17 167 FB75
THAMESMEAD WEST, SE28 165 ER75
Thamesmere Dr, SE28 146 EU73
Thames Pl, SW15 159 CX83
Thames Pt, SW6 307 P7
Thamespoint, Tedd. TW11 177 CK94
Thames Quay, SW10 307 P7
Thames Rd, E16 304 E3
W4 158 CN79
Barking IG11 145 ET69
Dartford DA1 167 FG82
Grays RM17 170 GB80
Slough SL3 153 BA77
Thames Side, Kings.T. KT1 197 CK95
Windsor SL4 151 AR80
Thames St, SE10 314 D2
Greenhithe DA9 169 FT84
Hampton TW12 196 CB95
Kingston upon Thames KT1 197 CK96
Staines-upon-Thames TW18 173 BE91
Sunbury-on-Thames TW16 195 BV98
Walton-on-Thames KT12 195 BT101
Weybridge KT13 195 BP103
Windsor SL4 151 AR81
Thames Tunnel Mills, SE16 off Rotherhithe St 300 G4
Thamesvale Cl, Houns. TW3 156 CA83
Thames Valley Nuffield Hosp, Wexham SL2 132 AW67
Thames Valley Nuffield Hosp, The, Wexham Pk Hall, Wexham SL3 132 AV68
Thames Vw, Grays RM16 171 GG78
Ilford IG1 off Axon Pl 125 EQ61
Thames Vw Inf Sch, Bark. IG11 off Bastable Av 146 EU68
Thames Vw Jun Sch, Bark. IG11 off Bastable Av 145 ET68
Thamesview Sch, Grav. DA12 off Thong La 191 GM90
Thames Village, W4 158 CQ81
Thames Way, Grav. DA11 190 GB86
Thames Wf, E16 303 L2
Thamley, Purf. RM19 168 FN77
Thanescroft Gdns, Croy. CR0 202 DS104
Thanet Dr, Kes. BR2 off Phoenix Dr 204 EK104
Thanet Pl, Croy. CR0 220 DQ105
Thanet Rd, Bex. DA5 186 FA87
Erith DA8 167 FE80
Thanet St, WC1 286 A3
Thane Vil, N7 121 DM62
Thane Wks, N7 121 DM62
Thanington Ct, SE9 185 ES86
Thanstead Copse, Loud. HP10 88 AC53
Thanstead Ct, Loud. HP10 88 AC53
Thant Cl, E10 123 EB62
Tharp Rd, Wall. SM6 219 DK106
Thatcham Gdns, N20 98 DC45
Thatcher Cl, West Dr. UB7 off Classon Cl 154 BL75
Thatcher Ct, Dart. DA1 off Heath St 188 FK87
Thatchers Cl, Horl. RH6 off Wheatfield Way 269 DH146
Loughton IG10 85 EQ40
Thatchers Cft, Hem.H. HP2 40 BL16
Thatchers Way, Islw. TW7 177 CD85
Thatches Gro, Rom. RM6 126 EY56
Thavies Inn, EC1 286 F8
Thaxted Ct, N1 287 L1
SE16 off Abbeyfield Rd 300 G8
Thaxted Grn, Hutt. CM13 109 GC43
Thaxted Ho, Dag. RM10 147 FB66
Thaxted Pl, SW20 179 CX94
Thaxted Rd, SE9 185 EQ89
Buckhurst Hill IG9 102 EL45
Thaxted Wk, Rain. RM13 off Ongar Way 147 FF67
Thaxted Way, Wal.Abb. EN9 67 ED33
Thaxton Rd, W14 307 H2
Thayers Fm Rd, Beck. BR3 203 DY95
Thayer St, W1 285 H7
Thaynesfield, Pot.B. EN6 64 DD31
★ Theatre Royal, WC2 286 B9
Theatre Sq, E15 281 H5
Theatre St, SW11 308 F10
Theberton St, N1 276 F8
Theed St, SE1 298 E3
Thele Av, Stans.Abb. SG12 33 ED11
Theleway Cl, Hodd. EN11 33 EB14
Thellusson Way, Rick. WD3 91 BF45
Thelma Cl, Grav. DA12 191 GM92
Thelma Gdns, SE3 164 EK81
Feltham TW13 176 BY90
Thelma Gro, Tedd. TW11 177 CG93
Theobald Cres, Har. HA3 94 CB53
Theobald Rd, E17 123 DZ59
Croydon CR0 201 DP103
Theobalds Av, N12 98 DC49
Grays RM17 170 GC78
Theobalds Cl, Cuffley EN6 65 DM30
Theobalds Ct, N4 off Queens Dr 122 DQ62
Theobalds Grove 67 DX32
Theobalds La, Chsht EN7, EN8 66 DV32
Theobalds Pk Rd, Enf. EN2 81 DP35
Theobalds Rd, Cuffley EN6 65 DL30
Theobald's Rd, WC1 286 C6
Theobald St, SE1 299 L7
Borehamwood WD6 78 CM40
Radlett WD7 77 CH36
Theodora Way, Pnr. HA5 115 BT55
Theodore Rd, SE13 183 EC86
Thepps Cl, S.Nutfld RH1 267 DM137
Therapia Lane 201 DL101
Therapia La, Croy. CR0 201 DL100
Therapia Rd, SE22 182 DW86
Theresa Rd, W6 159 CU77
Theresas Wk, S.Croy. CR2 off St. Mary's Rd 220 DR110
Therfield Ct, N4 off Brownswood Rd 122 DQ61
Therfield Rd, St.Alb. AL3 43 CD16
Therfield Sch, Lthd. KT22 off Dilston Rd 231 CG119
Thermopylae Gate, E14 302 D9
Theseus Wk, N1 287 H1
Thesiger Rd, SE20 183 DX94
Thessaly Ho, SW8 309 L5
Thessaly Rd, SW8 309 L5
Thetford Cl, N13 99 DP52
Thetford Gdns, Dag. RM9 146 EX66
Thetford Rd, Ashf. TW15 174 BL91
Dagenham RM9 146 EX67
New Malden KT3 198 CR100
Thetis Ter, Rich. TW9 off Kew Grn 158 CN79
Theven St, E1 off Globe Rd 289 H4
THEYDON BOIS, Epp. CM16 85 ET36
⊖ Theydon Bois 85 ET36
Theydon Bois Prim Sch, They.B. CM16 off Orchard Dr 85 ES36
Theydon Bower, Epp. CM16 70 EU31
Theydon Ct, Wal.Abb. EN9 68 EG33
Theydon Gdns, Rain. RM13 147 FE66
THEYDON GARNON, Epp. CM16 86 EW35
Theydon Gate, They.B. CM16 off Coppice Row 85 ES36
Theydon Gro, Epp. CM16 70 EU30
Woodford Green IG8 102 EJ51
THEYDON MOUNT, Epp. CM16 70 FA34
Theydon Pk Rd, They.B. CM16 85 ES39
Theydon Pl, Epp. CM16 69 ET31
Theydon Rd, E5 122 DW61
Epping CM16 69 ER34
Theydon St, E17 123 DZ59
Thicket, The, West Dr. UB7 134 BL72
Thicket Cres, Sutt. SM1 218 DC105
Thicket Gro, SE20 off Anerley Rd 182 DU94
Dagenham RM9 146 EW65
Thicket Rd, SE20 182 DU94
Sutton SM1 218 DC105
Thicketts, Sev. TN13 257 FJ123
Thickthorne La, Stai. TW18 174 BJ94
Thieves La, Hert. SG14 31 DM10
Ware SG12 32 DW08
Third Av, E12 124 EL63
E13 291 P2
E17 123 EA57
W3 139 CT74
W10 282 F4
Dagenham RM10 147 FB67
Enfield EN1 82 DT43
Grays RM20 169 FU79
Harlow CM18, CM19 51 EM16
Hayes UB3 135 BT74
Romford RM6 126 EW57
Waltham Abbey EN9 off Breach Barn Mobile Home Pk 68 EH30
Watford WD25 76 BX35
Wembley HA9 117 CK61
Third Cl, W.Mol. KT8 196 CB98
Third Cres, Slou. SL1 131 AQ71
Third Cross Rd, Twick. TW2 177 CD89
Third Way, Wem. HA9 118 CP63
Thirkleby Cl, Slou. SL1 131 AQ74
Thirleby Rd, NW7 97 CY50
SW1 297 M7
Edgware HA8 96 CR53
Thirlmere Av, Perivale UB6 137 CJ69
Slough SL1 130 AJ71
Thirlmere Cl, Egh. TW20 173 BB94
Thirlmere Dr, St.Alb. AL1 43 CH22
Thirlmere Gdns, Nthwd. HA6 93 BQ51
Wembley HA9 117 CJ60
Thirlmere Ho, Islw. TW7 off Summerwood Rd 177 CF85
Thirlmere Ri, Brom. BR1 184 EF93
Thirlmere Rd, N10 99 DH53
SW16 181 DK91
Bexleyheath DA7 167 FC82
Thirlstane, St.Alb. AL1 43 CE19
Thirsk Cl, Nthlt. UB5 136 CA65
Thirsk Rd, SE25 202 DR98
SW11 160 DG83
Borehamwood WD6 78 CN37
Mitcham CR4 180 DG94
Thirston Path, Borwd. WD6 78 CN40
Thirza Rd, Dart. DA1 188 FM86
Thistlebrook, SE2 166 EW76
● Thistlebrook Ind Est, SE2 166 EW75
Thistle Cl, Hem.H. HP1 39 BE21
Thistlecroft, Hem.H. HP1 40 BH21
Thistlecroft Gdns, Stan. HA7 95 CK53
Thistlecroft Rd, Hersham KT12 214 BW105
Thistledene, T.Ditt. KT7 197 CE100
West Byfleet KT14 211 BF113
Thistledene Av, Har. HA2 116 BY62
Romford RM5 105 FB50
Thistledown, Grav. DA12 191 GK93
Thistle Dr, Hat. AL10 45 CT15
Thistlefield Cl, Bex. DA5 186 EX88
Thistle Gro, SW10 295 P10
Welwyn Garden City AL7 30 DC12
Thistlemead, Chis. BR7 205 EP96
Thistle Mead, Loug. IG10 85 EN41
Thistle Rd, Grav. DA12 191 GL87
Thistles, The, Hem.H. HP1 40 BH19
Leatherhead KT22 231 CJ122
Thistlewaite Rd, E5 122 DV62
Thistlewood Cl, N7 121 DM61
Thistlewood Cres, New Adgtn CR0 221 ED112
Thistleworth Cl, Islw. TW7 157 CD80
Thistley Cl, N12 98 DE51
Coulsdon CR5 235 DK122
Thistley Ct, SE8 off Glaisher St 314 C2
Thomas a'Beckett Cl, Wem. HA0 117 CF63
Thomas Arnold Prim Sch, Dag. RM9 off Rowdowns Rd 146 EZ66
Thomas Av, Cat. CR3 236 DQ121
Thomas Baines Rd, SW11 160 DD83
Thomas Buxton Inf & Jun Schs, E1 288 D5
Thomas Cl, Brwd. CM15 108 FY48
Thomas Coram Mid Sch, The, Berk. HP4 off Swing Gate La 38 AX21
Thomas Cribb Ms, E6 293 K8
Thomas Darby Ct, W11 282 E9
Thomas Dean Rd, SE26 183 DZ91
Thomas Dinwiddy Rd, SE12 184 EH89
Thomas Doyle St, SE1 298 G6
Thomas Dr, Rom. RM2 128 FJ56
Grav. DA12 191 GK89
Thomas Fairchild Comm Sch, N1 277 K10
Thomas Gamuel Prim Sch, E17 off Colchester Rd 123 EA58
Thomas Harding Jun Sch, Chesh. HP5 off Fullers Hill 54 AP32
Thomas Hardy Ho, N22 99 DM52
Thomas Hollywood Ho, E2 288 G1
Thomas Jacomb Pl, E17 123 DZ56
Thomas Jones Prim Sch, W11 282 E9
Thomas Knyvett Coll, Ashf. TW15 off Stanwell Rd 174 BL90
Thomas La, SE6 183 EA87
Thomas More Bldg, The, Ruis. HA4 115 BS60
Thomas More Cath Sch, Pur. CR8 off Russell Hill Rd 219 DN110
Thomas More Ho, EC2 off The Barbican 287 J7
Thomas More Sq, E1 off Thomas More St 300 C1
Thomas More St, E1 300 C1
Thomas More Way, N2 120 DC55
Thomas N Ter, E16 off Barking Rd 291 L7
Thomas Pl, W8 295 L7
Thomas Rd, E14 289 P8
Crayford DA1 167 FG82
Wooburn Green HP10 110 AD59
● Thomas Rd Ind Est, E14 290 A7
Thomas Rochford Way, Chsht EN8 67 DZ27
Thomas's Acad, SW6 307 H8
Thomas Sims Ct, Horn. RM12 127 FH64
Thomas's School, Battersea, SW11 308 B7
Thomas's School, Clapham, SW11 off Broomwood Rd 180 DF86
Thomas's School, Fulham, SW6 307 L10
Thomas's School, Kensington, Lwr Sch, W8 295 N6
Prep Sch, W8 295 M6
Thomas St, SE18 305 M8
Thomas Tallis Sch, SE3 off Kidbrooke Pk Rd 164 EH83
Thomas Wall Cl, Sutt. SM1 off Clarence Rd 218 DB106
Thomas Willingale Sch, Loug. IG10 off The Broadway 85 EQ41
Thompkins La, Farn.Royal SL2 131 AM66
Thompson Av, Rich. TW9 158 CN83
Thompson Cl, Ilf. IG1 off High Rd 125 EQ61
Slough SL3 153 BA77
Sutton SM3 off Barrington Rd 200 DA102
Thompson Ho, W3 off Larden Rd 158 CS75
Thompson Rd, SE22 182 DT86
Dagenham RM9 126 EZ62
Hounslow TW3 156 CB84
Thompsons Av, SE5 311 J4
Thompsons Cl, Chsht EN7 66 DT29
Thompson's La, High Beach IG10 84 EF39
Thompson Way, Rick. WD3 92 BG45
Thomson Cres, Croy. CR0 201 DN102
Thomson Rd, Har. HA3 117 CE55
Thong La, Grav. DA12 191 GM90
Thorburn Sq, SE1 300 C9
Thorburn Way, SW19 200 DC95
Thoresby St, N1 287 K2
Thorkhill Gdns, T.Ditt. KT7 197 CG102
Thorkhill Rd, T.Ditt. KT7 197 CH101
Thorley Cl, W.Byf. KT14 212 BG114
Thorley Gdns, Wok. GU22 212 BG114
Thornaby Gdns, N18 100 DU51
Thornaby Pl, Woob.Grn HP10 110 AE55
Thornash Cl, Wok. GU21 226 AW115
Thornash Rd, Wok. GU21 226 AW115
Thornash Way, Wok. GU21 226 AW115
Thorn Av, Bushey Hth WD23 94 CC46
Thorn Bk, Guil. GU2 258 AU136
Thornbank Cl, Stai. TW19 174 BG85
Thornberry Way, Guil. GU1 243 AZ130
Thornbridge Rd, Iver SL0 133 BC67
Thornbrook, Thnwd CM16 70 EX25
Thornbury Av, Islw. TW7 157 CD80
Thornbury Cl, N16 277 P2
NW7 off Kingsbridge Dr 97 CX52
Hoddesdon EN11 33 EB13
Thornbury Gdns, Borwd. WD6 78 CQ42
Thornbury Rd, SW2 181 DL86
Isleworth TW7 157 CD81
Thornbury Sq, N6 121 DJ60
Thornby Rd, E5 122 DW62
Thorncliffe Rd, SW2 181 DL86
Southall UB2 156 BZ78
Thorn Cl, Brom. BR2 205 EN100
Northolt UB5 136 BZ69
Thorncombe Rd, SE22 182 DS85
Thorncroft, Eng.Grn TW20 172 AW94
Hemel Hempstead HP3 41 BP22
Hornchurch RM11 127 FH58
Thorncroft Cl, Couls. CR5 off Waddington Av 235 DN119
Thorncroft Dr, Lthd. KT22 231 CH123
Thorncroft Rd, Sutt. SM1 218 DB105
Thorncroft St, SW8 310 A5
Thorndales, Warley CM14 108 FX49
Thorndean St, SW18 180 DC89
Thorndene Av, N11 98 DG46
Thorndike, Slou. SL2 131 AN71
Thorndike Av, Nthlt. UB5 136 BX67
Thorndike Cl, SW10 307 N4
Thorndike Ho, SW1 off Vauxhall Br Rd 297 N10
Thorndike Rd, N1 277 K5
Thorndike St, SW1 297 N9
Thorndon Cl, Orp. BR5 205 ET96
Thorndon Ct, Gt Warley CM13 107 FW51
Thorndon Gdns, Epsom KT19 216 CS105
Thorndon Gate, Ingrave CM13 109 GC50
Thorndon Rd, Orp. BR5 205 ET96
Thorn Dr, Geo.Grn SL3 132 AY72
Thorndyke Ct, Pnr. HA5 off Westfield Pk 94 BZ52
Thorne Cl, E11 124 EE63
E16 291 N8
Ashford TW15 175 BQ94
Claygate KT10 215 CG108
Erith DA8 167 FC79
Hemel Hempstead HP1 40 BH22
Thorneloe Gdns, Croy. CR0 219 DN106
Thorne Pas, SW13 158 CS82
Thorne Rd, SW8 310 A5
Thornes Cl, Beck. BR3 203 EC97
Thorne St, E16 291 M8
SW13 158 CS83
Thornet Wd Rd, Brom. BR1 205 EN97
THORNEY, Iver SL0 154 BH76
Thorney Cres, SW11 308 B5
Thorneycroft Cl, Walt. KT12 196 BW100
Thorneycroft Dr, Enf. EN3 83 EA38
Thorney Hedge Rd, W4 158 CP77
Thorney La N, Iver SL0 133 BF74
Thorney La S, Iver SL0 153 BF75
Thorney Mill Rd, Iver SL0 154 BG76
West Drayton UB7 154 BG76
Thorney St, SW1 298 A8
Thornfield Av, NW7 97 CY53
Thornfield Rd, W12 159 CV75
Banstead SM7 234 DA117
Thornford Rd, SE13 183 EC85
Thorngate Rd, W9 283 K4
Thorngrove Rd, E13 144 EH67
Thornham Gro, E15 280 G3
Thornham St, SE10 314 D3
Thornhaugh Ms, WC1 285 P5
Thornhaugh St, WC1 285 P6
Thornhill, N.Wld Bas. CM16 71 FC26
Thornhill Av, SE18 165 ES80
Surbiton KT6 198 CL103
Thornhill Br Wf, N1 276 C9
Thornhill Cl, Amer. HP7 55 AP40
Thornhill Ct, Slou. SL3 off Maplin Pk 153 AZ76
Thornhill Cres, N1 276 C7
Thornhill Gdns, E10 123 EB61
Barking IG11 145 ES66
Thornhill Gro, N1 276 D7
Thornhill Prim Sch, N1 276 E7
Thornhill Rd, E10 123 EB61
N1 276 E6
Croydon CR0 202 DQ101
Northwood HA6 93 BQ49
Surbiton KT6 198 CL103
Uxbridge UB10 114 BM63
Thornhill Sq, N1 276 D7
Thornhill Way, Shep. TW17 194 BN99
Thorn La, Rain. RM13 148 FK68
Thornlaw Rd, SE27 181 DN91
Thornleas Pl, E.Hors. KT24 off Station App 245 BS126
Thornley Cl, N17 100 DU52
Thornley Dr, Har. HA2 116 CB61
Thornley Pl, SE10 315 J1
Thorn Mead, Hem.H. HP2 40 BK20
Thornridge, Brwd. CM14 108 FV45
Thornsbeach Rd, SE6 183 EC88
Thornsett Pl, SE20 202 DV96
Thornsett Rd, SE20 202 DV96
SW18 180 DB89
Thornside, Edg. HA8 96 CN51
Thorns Meadow, Brasted TN16 240 EW123
Thorn Ter, SE15 off Nunhead Gro 162 DW83
Thornton Av, SW2 181 DK88
W4 158 CS77
Croydon CR0 201 DM100
West Drayton UB7 154 BM76
Thornton Cl, Guil. GU2 242 AU130
Horley RH6 268 DE148
West Drayton UB7 154 BM76
Thornton Ct, SW20 199 CX99
Thornton Cres, Couls. CR5 235 DN119
Thornton Dene, Beck. BR3 203 EA96
Thornton Gdns, SW12 181 DK88
Thornton Gro, Pnr. HA5 94 CA51
THORNTON HEATH, CR7 201 DP98
⇌ Thornton Heath 202 DQ98
Thornton Heath 201 DN99
Thornton Heath Pond, Th.Hth. CR7 201 DN99
Thornton Hill, SW19 179 CY94
Thornton Ho, SE17 299 M9
Thornton Pl, W1 284 F6
Horley RH6 268 DE148
Thornton Rd, E11 123 ED61
N18 100 DW48
SW12 181 DK87
SW14 158 CR83
SW19 179 CX93
Barnet EN5 79 CY41
Belvedere DA17 167 FB77
Bromley BR1 184 EG92
Carshalton SM5 200 DD102
Croydon CR0 201 DM101
Ilford IG1 125 EP63
Potters Bar EN6 64 DC30
Thornton Heath CR7 201 DM101
Thornton Rd E, SW19 off Thornton Rd 179 CX93
● Thornton Rd Ind Est, Croy. CR0 201 DL100
Thornton Row, Th.Hth. CR7 off London Rd 201 DN99
Thorntons Fm Av, Rom. RM7 127 FD60
Thornton Side, Red. RH1 251 DH131
Thornton St, SW9 310 E8
Hertford SG14 32 DR09
St. Albans AL3 42 CC19
Thornton Wk, Horl. RH6 off Thornton Pl 268 DE148
Thornton Way, NW11 120 DB57
Thorntree Prim Sch, SE7 304 F10
Thorntree Rd, SE7 164 EK78
Thornville Gro, Mitch. CR4 200 DC96
Thornville St, SE8 314 A7
THORNWOOD, Epp. CM16 70 EW25
Thornwood Cl, E18 102 EH54
Thornwood Gdns, W8 295 J4
Thornwood Rd, SE13 184 EE85
Epping CM16 70 EV29
Thorogood Gdns, E15 281 K3
Thorogood Way, Rain. RM13 147 FE67
Thorold Cl, S.Croy. CR2 221 DX110
Thorold Rd, N22 99 DL52
Ilford IG1 125 EP61
Thoroughfare, The, Walt.Hill KT20 249 CU125
Thorparch Rd, SW8 309 P6
THORPE, Egh. TW20 193 BC97
Thorpebank Rd, W12 139 CU74
Thorpe Bypass, Egh. TW20 193 BB96
Thorpe Cl, W10 282 F8
New Addington CR0 221 EC111
Orpington BR6 205 ES103
Thorpe C of E Inf Sch, Thorpe TW20 off The Bence 193 BB97
Thorpe Coombe Hosp, E17 123 EC55
Thorpe Cres, E17 101 DZ54
Watford WD19 94 BW45
Thorpedale Gdns, Ilf. IG2, IG6 125 EN56
Thorpedale Rd, N4 121 DL60
Thorpefield Cl, St.Alb. AL4 43 CK17
THORPE GREEN, Egh. TW20 193 BA98
Thorpe Hall Prim Sch, E17 off Hale End Rd 101 EC53
Thorpe Hall Rd, E17 101 EC53
Thorpe Ho Sch, Ger.Cr. SL9 off Oval Way 112 AY56
● Thorpe Ind Est, Egh. TW20 193 BC96
THORPE LEA, Egh. TW20 173 BB93
Thorpe Lea Prim Sch, Egh. TW20 off Huntingfield Way 173 BD93
Thorpe Lea Rd, Egh. TW20 173 BB93
Thorpe Lo, Horn. RM11 128 FK59
★ Thorpe Park, Cher. KT16 193 BE98
Thorpe Rd, E6 145 EM67
E7 124 EF63
E17 101 EC54
N15 122 DS58
Barking IG11 145 ER66
Chertsey KT16 193 BD99
Kingston upon Thames KT2 178 CL94
St. Albans AL1 43 CD21
Staines-upon-Thames TW18 173 BD93
Thorpes Cl, Guil. GU2 242 AU131
Thorpeside Cl, Stai. TW18 193 BE96
Thorpe Wk, Grnf. UB6 137 CE68
Thorpewood Av, SE26 182 DV89
Thorpland Av, Uxb. UB10 115 BQ62
Thorsden Cl, Wok. GU22 226 AY118
Thorsden Ct, Wok. GU22 off Guildford Rd 226 AY118
Thorsden Way, SE19 off Oaks Av 182 DS92
Thorverton Rd, NW2 119 CY62
Thoydon Rd, E3 289 L1
Thrale Rd, SW16 181 DJ92
Thrale St, SE1 299 K3
Thrasher Cl, E8 278 A8
Thrawl St, E1 288 B7
Threadneedle St, EC2 287 M9
Three Arches Pk, Red. RH1 266 DF138
Three Arch Rd, Red. RH1 266 DF138
Three Barrels Wk, EC4 299 K1
Three Bridges Path, Kings.T. KT1 off Portland Rd 198 CL97
Three Bridges Prim Sch, Sthl. UB2 off Melbury Av 156 CB76

T

Three Cherry Trees La,
Hem.H. HP2 41 BP16
Three Cl La, Berk. HP4 38 AW20
Three Colts Cor, E2 288 C4
Three Colts La, E2 288 E4
Three Colt St, E14 289 P9
Three Cors, Bexh. DA7 167 FB82
Hemel Hempstead HP3 40 BN22
Three Cranes Wk, EC4
off Bell Wf La 299 K1
Three Cups Yd, WC1 286 D7
Three Forests Way,
Broad.Com. EN9 50 EL21
Chigwell IG7 104 EW48
Epping CM16 51 EM23
Harlow CM19 50 EH18
Loughton IG10 off The Clay Rd 84 EK38
Mark Hall North CM20 36 EU10
Romford RM4 104 EW48
Waltham Abbey EN9 84 EK36
Ware SG12 34 EL12
Three Gates, Guil. GU1 243 BC132
Three Gates Rd,
Fawk.Grn DA3 209 FU102
Three Horseshoes Rd,
Harl. CM19 51 EP17
Three Households,
Ch.St.G. HP8 90 AT49
Three Kings Rd, Mitch. CR4 200 DG97
Three Kings Yd, W1 285 J10
Three Meadows Ms, Har. HA3 95 CF53
Three Mill La, E3 290 E2
Three Oak La, SE1 300 A4
Three Oaks Cl, Uxb. UB10 114 BM62
Three Pears Rd, Guil. GU1 243 BE134
Three Quays Wk, EC3 299 P1
Three Valleys Way,
Bushey WD23 76 BX43
THRESHERS BUSH,
Harl. CM17 53 FB16
Threshers Bush, Harl. CM17 36 FA14
Threshers Pl, W11 282 E10
Thriffwood, SE26 182 DW90
Thrift, The, Bean DA2 189 FW90
Thrift Fm La, Borwd. WD6 78 CP40
Thriftfield, Hem.H. HP2 40 BK18
Thrift Grn, Brwd. CM13
off Knight's Way 109 GA48
Thrift La, Cudham TN14 239 ER117
Ware SG12 33 DZ08
Thrifts Mead, They.B. CM16 85 ES37
Thrift Vale, Guil. GU4 243 BD131
Thrigby Rd, Chess. KT9 216 CM107
Throckmorton Rd, E16 292 B9
Throgmorton Av, EC2 287 M8
Throgmorton St, EC2 287 M8
Throstle Pl, Wat. WD25 60 BW32
Thrower Pl, Dor. RH5 263 CJ138
Throwley Cl, SE2 166 EW76
Throwley Rd, Sutt. SM1 218 DB106
Throwley Way, Sutt. SM1 218 DB105
Thrums, The, Wat. WD24 75 BV37
Thrupp Cl, Mitch. CR4 201 DH96
Thrupps Av, Hersham KT12 214 BX106
Thrupps La, Hersham KT12 214 BX106
Thrush Av, Hat. AL10 45 CU20
Thrush Grn, Har. HA2 116 CA56
Rickmansworth WD3 92 BJ45
Thrush La, Cuffley EN6 65 DL28
Thrush St, SE17 299 J10
Thumbswood, Welw.G.C. AL7 30 DA12
Thumpers, Hem.H. HP2 40 BL18
Thundercourt, Ware SG12 33 DX05
Thunderer Rd, Dag. RM9 146 EY70
Thundridge Cl, Welw.G.C. AL7
off Amwell Common 30 DB10
Thurbarn Rd, SE6 183 EB92
Thurgood Rd, Hodd. EN11 49 EA15
Thurland Ho, SE16 off Manor Est 300 E9
Thurland Rd, SE16 300 C6
Thurlby Cl, Har. HA1
off Gayton Rd 117 CG58
Woodford Green IG8 103 EM50
Thurlby Rd, SE27 181 DN91
Wembley HA0 137 CK65
Thurleigh Av, SW12 180 DG86
Thurleigh Rd, SW12 180 DG86
Thurleston Av, Mord. SM4 199 CY99
Thurlestone Av, N12 98 DF51
Ilford IG3 125 ET63
Thurlestone Cl, Shep. TW17 195 BQ100
Thurlestone Rd, SE27 181 DN90
Thurloe Cl, SW7 296 C8
Thurloe Gdns, Rom. RM1 127 FF58
Thurloe Pl, SW7 296 B8
Thurloe Pl Ms, SW7 296 B8
Thurloe Sq, SW7 296 C8
Thurloe St, SW7 296 B8
Thurloe Wk, Grays RM17 170 GA76
Thurlow Cl, E4
off Higham Sta Av 101 EB51
Thurlow Gdns, Ilf. IG6 103 ER51
Wembley HA0 117 CK64
Thurlow Hill, SE21 182 DQ88
Thurlow Pk Rd, SE21 181 DP88
Thurlow Rd, NW3 274 A2
W7 157 CG75
Thurlow St, SE17 299 M10
Thurlow Ter, NW5 274 G3
Thurlstone Rd, Ruis. HA4 115 BU62
Thurlton Ct, Wok. GU21
off Chobham Rd 226 AY116
Thurnby Ct, Twick. TW2 177 CE90
Thurnham Way, Tad. KT20 233 CW120
Coll Thurrock Adult Comm Coll - Grays
Adult Ed Cen, Grays RM17
off Richmond Rd 170 GB78
Coll Thurrock & Basildon Coll,
Woodview Campus, Grays RM16
off Woodview 171 GF77
● Thurrock Commercial Centre,
S.Ock. RM15 168 FM75
Thurrock Pk Way, Til. RM18 170 GD80
● Thurrock Trade Pk,
Grays RM20 169 FU80
Thursby Rd, Wok. GU21 226 AU118
Thursland Rd, Sid. DA14 186 EY92
Thursley Cres,
New Adgtn CR0 221 ED108
Thursley Gdns, SW19 179 CX89
Thursley Rd, SE9 185 EM90
Thurso Cl, Rom. RM3 106 FP51
Thurso Ho, NW6 283 L1
Thurso St, SW17 180 DD91
Thurstan Rd, SW20 179 CV94
Thurstans, Harl. CM19 51 EP20
Thurston Rd, SE13 314 D9
Slough SL1 132 AS72
Southall UB1 136 BZ72
Thurtle Rd, E2 278 B9
Thwaite Cl, Erith DA8 167 FC79
Thyer Cl, Orp. BR6
off Isabella Dr 223 EQ105
Thyme Cl, SE3 164 EJ83
Thyme Ct, Guil. GU4
off Mallow Cres 243 BB131
Thyra Gro, N12 98 DB51
Tibbatts Rd, E3 290 C4
Tibbenham Pl, SE6 183 EA89
Tibbenham Wk, E13 291 M1
Tibberton Sq, N1 277 J7
Tibbets Cl, SW19 179 CX88
Jct Tibbet's Cor, SW15 179 CX87
Tibbet's Cor Underpass, SW15
off West Hill 179 CX87
Tibbet's Ride, SW15 179 CX87
Tibbles Cl, Wat. WD25 76 BY35
Tibbs Hill Rd, Abb.L. WD5 59 BT30
Tiber Cl, E3 280 A9
Tiber Gdns, N1 276 B9
Tiberius Sq, St.Alb. AL3 42 CA22
Ticehurst Cl, Orp. BR5 186 EU94
Ticehurst Rd, SE23 183 DY89
Tichborne, Map.Cr. WD3 91 BD50
Tichmarsh, Epsom KT19 216 CQ110
Tickenhall Dr, Harl. CM17 52 EX15
Tickford Cl, SE2
off Ampleforth Rd 166 EW75
Tidal Basin Rd, E16 303 M1
Tide Cl, Mitch. CR4 200 DG95
Tideham Ho, SE28
off Merbury Cl 145 ER74
Sch Tidemill Academy, SE8 314 B4
Tidemill Way, SE8 314 B4
Tidenham Gdns, Croy. CR0 202 DS104
Tideslea Path, SE28 145 ER74
Tideslea Twr, SE28 165 ER75
Tideswell Rd, SW15 179 CW85
Croydon CR0 203 EA104
Tideway Cl, Rich. TW10 177 CH91
● Tideway Ind Est, SW8 309 M3
Tideway Wk, SW8 309 L3
Tidey St, E3 290 B6
Tidford Rd, Well. DA16 165 ET82
Tidlock Ho, SE28 165 ER75
Tidworth Ho, SE22
off Albrighton Rd 162 DS83
Tidworth Rd, E3 290 A4
Tidy's La, Epp. CM16 70 EV29
Tiepigs La, Brom. BR2 204 EE103
West Wickham BR4 204 EE103
Tierney Rd, SW2 181 DL88
Sch Tiffin Girl's Sch, The,
Kings.T. KT2 off Richmond Rd 178 CL93
Sch Tiffin Sch for Boys,
Kings.T. KT2
off Queen Elizabeth Rd 198 CM96
Tiger Cl, Bark. IG11 146 EV68
Tiger Moth Way, Hat. AL10 44 CR17
Tiger Way, E5 122 DV63
Tigris Cl, N9 100 DW47
Tilbrook Rd, SE3 164 EJ83
Tilburstow Hill Rd, Gdse. RH9 252 DW132
TILBURY, RM18 171 GG81
Tilbury Cl, SE15 312 B4
Orpington BR5 206 EV96
Pinner HA5 94 BZ52
Coll Tilbury Energy & Environment Cen,
Til. RM18 off Fort Rd 171 GK83
★ Tilbury Fort, Til. RM18 171 GJ84
Sch Tilbury Manor Jun Sch,
Til. RM18 off Dickens Av 171 GH80
Tilbury Mead, Harl. CM18 52 EU17
Tilbury Rd, E6 293 J1
E10 123 EC59
⇌ Tilbury Town 170 GE82
Tilbury Wk, Slou. SL3 153 BB76
Tildesley Rd, SW15 179 CW86
Tilecroft, Welw.G.C. AL8 29 CX06
Tile Fm Rd, Orp. BR6 205 ER104
Tilegate Rd, Harl. CM18 51 ET17
Ongar CM5 53 FC19
Tilehouse Cl, Borwd. WD6 78 CM41
Sch Tilehouse Comb Sch, Denh.
UB9 off Nightingale Way 113 BF58
Tilehouse La, Denh. UB9 113 BE58
Gerrards Cross SL9 113 BE53
West Hyde WD3 113 BE53
Tilehouse Rd, Guil. GU4 258 AY138
Tilehouse Way, Denh. UB9 113 BF59
Tilehurst La, Dor. RH5 264 CL137
Tilehurst Pt, SE2
off Yarnton Way 166 EW75
Tilehurst Rd, SW18 180 DD88
Sutton SM3 217 CY106
Tilekiln Cl, Chsht EN7 66 DS29
Tile Kiln Cl, Hem.H. HP3 41 BP21
Tile Kiln Cres, Hem.H. HP3 41 BP21
Tile Kiln La, N6 121 DJ60
N13 100 DQ50
Bexley DA5 187 FC89
Harefield UB9 115 BP59
Hemel Hempstead HP3 40 BN21
Tilers Cl, S.Merst. RH1 251 DJ131
Tiler's Wk, Reig. RH2 266 DC138
Tiler's Way, Reig. RH2 266 DC138
Tile Yd, E14 289 P9
Tileyard Rd, N7 276 A6
Tilford Av, New Adgtn CR0 221 EC109
Tilford Gdns, SW19 179 CX89
Tilgate Common, Bletch. RH1 252 DQ133
Tilia Cl, Sutt. SM1 217 CZ106
Tilia Rd, E5 278 F1
Tilia Wk, SW9 161 DP84
Tillage Cl, St.Alb. AL4 43 CK22
Till Av, Fnghm DA4 208 FM102
Tiller Rd, E14 302 A6
Tillett Cl, NW10 138 CQ65
Tillett Sq, SE16 301 M5
Tillett Way, E2 288 C2
Tilley La, Headley KT18 232 CQ123
Tilley Rd, Felt. TW13 175 BU88
Tillingbourne Gdns, N3 119 CZ55
Tillingbourne Grn, Orp. BR5 206 EU98
Sch Tillingbourne Jun Sch,
Chilw. GU4 off New Rd 259 BB141
Tillingbourne Rd, Shalf. GU4 258 AY140
Tillingbourne Way, N3
off Tillingbourne Gdns 119 CZ56
Tillingdown Hill, Cat. CR3 236 DU122
Tillingdown La, Cat. CR3 236 DV124
Tillingham Ct, Wal.Abb. EN9 68 EG33
Tillingham Way, N12 98 DA49
Tilling Rd, NW2 119 CW60
Tillings Cl, SE5 311 K7
Tilling Way, Wem. HA9 117 CK61
Tillman St, E1 288 F9
Tilloch St, N1 276 C7
Tillotson Ct, SW8
off Wandsworth Rd 310 A5
Tillotson Rd, N9 100 DT47
Harrow HA3 94 CB52
Ilford IG1 125 EN59
Tillwicks Rd, Harl. CM18 52 EU17
Tilly's La, Stai. TW18 173 BF91
Tilmans Mead, Fnghm DA4 208 FM101
Tilney Cl, Lthd. KT22
off Randalls Cres 231 CG120
Tilney Ct, EC1 287 K4
Tilney Dr, Buck.H. IG9 102 EG47
Tilney Gdns, N1 277 M5
Tilney Rd, Dag. RM9 146 EZ65
Southall UB2 156 BW77
Tilney St, W1 297 H2
Tilson Cl, SE5 311 N4
Tilson Gdns, SW2 181 DL87
Tilson Ho, SW2 181 DL87
Tilson Rd, N17 100 DU53
Tilston Cl, E11
off Matcham Rd 124 EF62
Tilstone Av, Eton Wick SL4 151 AL78
Tilstone Cl, Eton Wick SL4 151 AL78
Tilsworth Rd, Beac. HP9 110 AJ55
Tilsworth Wk, St.Alb. AL4
off Larkswood Ri 43 CJ15
Tilt Cl, Cob. KT11 230 BY116
Tilthams Cor Rd, Gdmg. GU7 258 AV143
Tilthams Grn, Gdmg. GU7 258 AV143
Tiltman Pl, N7 121 DM62
Tilt Meadow, Cob. KT11 230 BY116
Tilton St, SW6 306 F3
Tilt Rd, Cob. KT11 230 BW115
Tiltwood, The, W3 138 CQ73
Tilt Yd App, SE9 185 EM86
Timber Cl, Bkhm KT23 246 CC126
Chislehurst BR7 205 EN96
Stanstead Abbotts SG12 33 EB10
Woking GU22 211 BF114
Timber Ct, Grays RM17
off Columbia Wf Rd 170 GA79
Timbercroft, Epsom KT19 216 CS105
Welwyn Garden City AL7 29 CZ06
Timbercroft La, SE18 165 ES79
Sch Timbercroft Prim Sch, SE18
off Timbercroft La 165 ES80
Timberdene, NW4 97 CX54
Timberdene Av, Ilf. IG6 103 EP53
Timberham Fm Rd, Gat. RH6 268 DD151
Timberham Way, Horl. RH6 268 DE152
Timberhill, Ashtd. KT21 232 CL119
Timber Hill Cl, Ott. KT16 211 BC108
Timber Hill Rd, Cat. CR3 236 DU124
Timberidge, Loud. WD3 74 BJ42
Timberland Cl, SE15 312 C5
Timberland Rd, E1
off Hainton Cl 288 F9
Timber La, Cat. CR3
off Timber Hill Rd 236 DU124
Timberling Gdns, S.Croy. CR2
off St. Mary's Rd 220 DR110
Timber Mill Way, SW4 309 N10
Timber Orchard, Waterf. SG14 31 DN05
Timber Pond Rd, SE16 301 K3
Timberslip Dr, Wall. SM6 219 DK109
Timber St, EC1 287 J4
Timbertop Rd, Bigg.H. TN16 238 EJ118
Timber Wf, E2 278 A9
Timberwharf Rd, N16 122 DU58
Timberwood, Slou. SL2 111 AR62
Timbrell Pl, SE16 301 N3
Time Sq, E8 278 A3
Times Sq, Sutt. SM1 218 DB106
Times Sq, E1 288 C9
Times Sq Shop Cen, Sutt. SM1
off High St 218 DB106
Timms Cl, Brom. BR1 205 EM98
Timothy Cl, SW4
off Elms Rd 181 DJ85
Bexleyheath DA6 186 EY85
Timothy Ho, Erith DA18
off Kale Rd 166 EY75
Timperley Gdns, Red. RH1 250 DE132
Timplings Row, Hem.H. HP1 40 BH18
Timsbury Wk, SW15 179 CU88
Timsway, Stai. TW18 173 BF92
Tindale Cl, S.Croy. CR2 220 DR111
Tindall Cl, Rom. RM3 106 FM54
Tindall Ms, Horn. RM12 128 FJ62
Tindal St, SW9 310 G6
Tinderbox All, SW14 158 CR83
Tine Rd, Chig. IG7 103 ES50
Tingeys Top La, Enf. EN2 81 DN36
Tinkers La, Roydon CM19 50 EJ20
Windsor SL4 151 AK82
Tinniswood Cl, N5
off Drayton Pk 276 E2
Tinsey Cl, Egh. TW20 173 BB92
Tinsley Cl, SE25 202 DV97
Tinsley Est, Wat. WD18 75 BS42
Tinsley Rd, E1 289 H6
Tintagel Cl, Epsom KT17 217 CT114
Hemel Hempstead HP2 40 BK15
Tintagel Cres, SE22 162 DT84
Tintagel Dr, Stan. HA7 95 CK49
Tintagel Gdns, SE22
off Oxonian St 162 DT84
Tintagel Rd, Orp. BR5 206 EW103
Tintagel Way, Wok. GU22 227 BA116
Tintells La, W.Hors. KT24 245 BP128
Tintern Av, NW9 118 CP55
Tintern Cl, SW15 179 CY85
SW19 180 DC94
Slough SL1 151 AQ76
Tintern Ct, W13
off Green Man La 137 CG73
Tintern Gdns, N14 99 DL45
Tintern Path, NW9
off Ruthin Cl 118 CS58
Tintern Rd, N22 100 DQ53
Carshalton SM5 200 DD102
Tintern St, SW4 161 DL84
Tintern Way, Har. HA2 116 CB60
Tinto Rd, E16 291 P5
Tinwell Ms, Borwd. WD6 78 CQ43
Tinworth St, SE11 298 B10
Tippendell La, St.Alb. AL2 60 CB26
Tippetts Cl, Enf. EN2 82 DQ39
Tipthorpe Rd, SW11 308 G10
Tipton Cotts, Add. KT15
off Oliver Cl 212 BH105
Tipton Dr, Croy. CR0 220 DS105
Tiptree Cl, E4
off Mapleton Rd 101 EC48
Hornchurch RM11 128 FN60
Tiptree Cres, Ilf. IG5 125 EN55
Tiptree Dr, Enf. EN2 82 DR42
Tiptree Est, Ilf. IG5 125 EN55
Tiptree Rd, Ruis. HA4 115 BV63
Tiree Cl, Hem.H. HP3 41 BP22
Tirlemont Rd, S.Croy. CR2 220 DQ108
Tirrell Rd, Croy. CR0 202 DQ100
Tisbury Ct, W1
off Rupert St 285 N10
Tisbury Rd, SW16 201 DL96
Tisdall Pl, SE17 299 M9
Tissington Ct, SE16
off Rotherhithe New Rd 301 J9
Titan Rd, Grays RM17 170 GA78
Hemel Hempstead HP2 40 BM17
Titchborne Row, W2 284 D9
Titchfield Rd, NW8 274 D9
Carshalton SM5 200 DD102
Enfield EN3 83 DY37
Titchfield Wk, Cars. SM5
off Titchfield Rd 200 DD101
Titchwell Rd, SW18 180 DD87
Tite Hill, Egh. TW20 172 AX92
Tite St, SW3 308 E1
Tithe Barn Cl, Kings.T. KT2 198 CM95
St. Albans AL1 42 CC23
Tithe Barn Ct, Abb.L. WD5 59 BT29
Tithe Barn Dr, Maid. SL6 150 AE78
Tithebarns La, Send GU23 244 BG126
Tithe Barn Way, Nthlt. UB5 135 BV68
Tithe Cl, NW7 97 CU53
Hayes UB4 135 BT71
Maidenhead SL6 150 AC78
Virginia Water GU25 192 AX100
Walton-on-Thames KT12 195 BV100
Tithe Ct, Slou. SL3 153 BA77
Tithe Fm Av, Har. HA2 116 CA62
Tithe Fm Cl, Har. HA2 116 CA62
Tithelands, Harl. CM19 51 EM18
Tithe La, Wrays. TW19 173 BA86
Tithe Meadows, Vir.W. GU25 192 AW100
Tithepit Shaw La, Warl. CR6 236 DV115
Tithe Wk, NW7 97 CU53
Titian Av, Bushey Hth WD23 95 CE45
Titley Cl, E4 101 EA50
Titmus Cl, Uxb. UB8 135 BQ72
Titmuss Av, SE28 146 EV73
Titmuss St, W12
off Goldhawk Rd 159 CW75
TITSEY, Oxt. RH8 254 EH125
Titsey Hill, Titsey RH8 238 EF123
Titsey Rd, Oxt. RH8 254 EH125
Tiverton Av, Ilf. IG5 125 EN55
Tiverton Cl, Croy. CR0
off Exeter Rd 202 DT101
Tiverton Dr, SE9 185 EQ88
Tiverton Gro, Rom. RM3 106 FN50
Tiverton Ho, Enf. EN3 83 DX41
Sch Tiverton Prim Sch, N15
off Pulford Rd 122 DR58
Tiverton Rd, N15 122 DR58
N18 100 DS50
NW10 272 C9
Edgware HA8 96 CM54
Hounslow TW3 156 CC82
Potters Bar EN6 64 DD31
Ruislip HA4 115 BU62
Thornton Heath CR7
off Willett Rd 201 DN99
Wembley HA0 138 CL68
Tiverton St, SE1 299 J7
Tiverton Way, NW7 97 CX52
Chessington KT9 215 CJ106
Tivoli Ct, SE16 301 N4
Tivoli Gdns, SE18 304 G8
Tivoli Ms, Grav. DA12 191 GH88
Tivoli Rd, N8 121 DK57
SE27 182 DQ92
Hounslow TW4 156 BY84
Toad La, Houns. TW4 156 BZ84
Tobacco Dock, E1 300 E1
Tobacco Quay, E1 300 E1
Tobago St, E14 302 A4
Tobermory Cl, Slou. SL3 152 AY77
Tobin Cl, NW3 274 D6
Epsom KT19 216 CP111
Toby La, E1 289 L5
Toby Way, Surb. KT5 198 CP103
Tockley Rd, Burn. SL1 130 AH68
Todd Brook, Harl. CM19 51 EP16
Todd Cl, Rain. RM13 148 FK70
Todds Cl, Horl. RH6 268 DE146
Todds Wk, N7
off Andover Rd 121 DM61
Todhunter Ter, Barn. EN5
off Prospect Rd 80 DA42
Toft Av, Grays RM17 170 GD77
Tokenhouse Yd, EC2 287 L8
Token Yd, SW15 159 CY84
TOKYNGTON, Wem. HA9 138 CP65
Tokyngton Av, Wem. HA9 138 CN65
Toland Sq, SW15 179 CU85
Tolcarne Dr, Pnr. HA5 115 BV55
Toldene Ct, Couls. CR5 235 DM120
Toley Av, Wem. HA9 118 CL59
Tolhurst Dr, W10 282 F2
Toll Bar Ct, Sutt. SM2 218 DB109
Tollbridge Cl, W10 282 F4
Tolldene Cl, Knap. GU21
off Robin Hood Rd 226 AS117
Tollers La, Couls. CR5 235 DM119
Tollesbury Gdns, Ilf. IG6 125 ER55
Tollet St, E1 289 J4
Tollgate, Guil. GU1 243 BD133
Tollgate Av, Red. RH1 266 DF139
Tollgate Cl, Chorl. WD3 73 BF41
Tollgate Dr, SE21 182 DS89
Hayes UB4 136 BX73
Tollgate Gdns, NW6 273 L10
Tollgate Ho, NW6 273 K10
Sch Tollgate Prim Sch, E13 292 D4
Tollgate Rd, E6 292 E7
E16 292 C6
Colney Heath AL4 44 CS24
Dartford DA2 189 FR87
Dorking RH4 263 CH139
North Mymms AL9 63 CU25
Waltham Cross EN8 83 DX35
Tollhouse La, Wall. SM6 219 DJ109
Tollhouse Way, N19 121 DJ61
Tollington Pk, N4 121 DM61
Tollington Pl, N4 121 DM61
Tollington Rd, N7 121 DM63
Tollington Way, N7 121 DL62
Tollpit End, Hem.H. HP1 40 BG17
Tolmers Av, Cuffley EN6 65 DL28
Tolmers Gdns, Cuffley EN6 65 DL29
Tolmers Ms, Newgate St SG13 65 DL25
Tolmers Pk, Newgate St SG13 65 DL25
Tolmers Rd, Cuffley EN6 65 DL27
Tolmers Sq, NW1 285 M4
Tolpaide Ho, SE11 298 E9
Tolpits Cl, Wat. WD18 75 BT43
Tolpits La, Wat. WD18 75 BT44
Tolpuddle Av, E13
off Rochester Av 144 EJ67
Tolpuddle St, N1 276 E10
Tolsford Rd, E5 278 F2
Tolson Rd, Islw. TW7 157 CG83
Tolvaddon, Wok. GU21
off Cardingham 226 AU117
Tolverne Rd, SW20 199 CW95
TOLWORTH, Surb. KT6 198 CN103
⇌ Tolworth 198 CP103
Tolworth Bdy, Surb. KT6 198 CP102
Tolworth Cl, Surb. KT6 198 CP102
Tolworth Gdns, Rom. RM6 126 EX57
Sch Tolworth Girls' Sch & Cen for
Cont Ed, Surb. KT6
off Fullers Way N 198 CM104
H Tolworth Hosp, Surb. KT6 198 CN103
Sch Tolworth Infants' Sch,
Surb. KT6 off School La 198 CM102
Jct Tolworth Junct, Surb. KT5 198 CP103
Sch Tolworth Jun Sch,
Surb. KT6 off Douglas Rd 198 CM102
Tolworth Pk Rd, Surb. KT6 198 CM103
Tolworth Ri N, Surb. KT5
off Elmbridge Av 198 CQ101
Tolworth Ri S, Surb. KT5
off Warren Dr S 198 CQ102
Tolworth Rd, Surb. KT6 198 CL103
Tolworth Twr, Surb. KT6 198 CP103
Tomahawk Gdns, Nthlt. UB5
off Javelin Way 136 BX69
Tom Coombs Cl, SE9 164 EL84
Tom Cribb Rd, SE28 165 EQ76
Tom Gros St, E15 281 H3
Tom Hood Cl, E15 281 H3
Sch Tom Hood Sch, E11
off Terling Cl 124 EF62
Tom Jenkinson Rd, E16 303 P2
Tomkins Cl, Borwd. WD6
off Tallis Way 78 CL39
Tomkyns La, Upmin. RM14 129 FR56
Tomlin Cl, Epsom KT19 216 CR111
Tomlin Rd, Slou. SL2 131 AL70
Tomlins Gro, E3 290 B2
Tomlinson Cl, E2 288 B3
W4 158 CP78
Tomlins Orchard, Bark. IG11 145 EQ67
Tomlins Ter, E14 289 M8
Tomlins Wk, N7
off Briset Way 121 DM61
Tomlyns Cl, Hutt. CM13 109 GE44
Tom Mann Cl, Bark. IG11 145 ES67
Tom Nolan Cl, E15 291 K1
● Tomo Ind Est, Uxb. UB8 134 BJ72
Tompion Ho, EC1
off Percival St 287 H4
Tompion St, EC1 286 G3
Toms Cft, Hem.H. HP2 40 BL21
Tomsfield, Hat. AL10 44 CS19
Toms Hill, Kings L. WD4 74 BL36
Rickmansworth WD3 74 BL36
Toms La, Bedmond WD5 59 BR28
Kings Langley WD4 59 BP29
Tom Smith Cl, SE10 315 J2
Tomswood Ct, Ilf. IG6 103 EQ53
Tomswood Hill, Ilf. IG6 103 EP52
Tomswood Rd, Chig. IG7 103 EN51
Tom Thumbs Arch, E3
off Malmesbury Rd 290 A1
Tom Williams Ho, SW6
off Clem Attlee Ct 306 G3
Tonbridge Cl, Bans. SM7 218 DF114
Tonbridge Cres, Har. HA3 118 CL56
Tonbridge Ho, SE25 202 DU97
Tonbridge Rd, Harold Hill RM3 106 FK52
Sevenoaks TN13 257 FJ127
West Molesey KT8 196 BY98
Tonbridge St, WC1 286 A2
Tonbridge Wk, WC1
off Bidborough St 286 A2
Tonfield Rd, Sutt. SM3 199 CZ102
Tonge Cl, Beck. BR3 203 EA99
Tonsley Hill, SW18 180 DB85
Tonsley Pl, SW18 180 DB85
Tonsley Rd, SW18 180 DB85
Tonsley St, SW18 180 DB85
Tonstall Rd, Epsom KT19 216 CR110
Mitcham CR4 200 DG96
Tony Cannell Ms, E3 289 N3
Tooke Cl, Pnr. HA5 94 BY53
Tookey Cl, Har. HA3 118 CM59
Took's Ct, EC4 286 E8
Tooley St, SE1 299 M2
Northfleet DA11 190 GD87
Toorack Rd, Har. HA3 95 CD54
TOOT HILL, Ong. CM5 71 FF30
Toot Hill Rd, Ong. CM5 71 FF29
⇌ Tooting 180 DG93
⊖ Tooting Bec 180 DF90
Jct Tooting Bec, SW17 180 DF90
Tooting Bec Gdns, SW16 181 DK91
Tooting Bec Rd, SW16 180 DG90
SW17 180 DG90
⊖ Tooting Broadway 180 DE92
Jct Tooting Bdy, SW17 180 DE91
TOOTING GRAVENEY, SW17 180 DE93
Tooting Gro, SW17 180 DE92
Tooting High St, SW17 180 DE93
Tooting Mkt, SW17
off Tooting High St 180 DF91
Tootswood Rd, Brom. BR2 204 EE99
Tooveys Mill Cl, Kings L. WD4 58 BN28
Topaz Cl, Slou. SL1
off Pearl Gdns 131 AP74
Topaz Ct, E11
off High Rd Leytonstone 124 EE60
Topaz Ho, E15
off Romford Rd 281 L5
Topaz Wk, NW2
off Marble Dr 119 CX59
Topcliffe Dr, Orp. BR6 223 ER105
Top Dartford Rd, Dart. DA2 187 FF94
Swanley BR8 187 FF94
Top Fm Cl, Beac. HP9 88 AG54
Topham Sq, N17 100 DQ53
Topham St, EC1 286 E4
Top Ho Ri, E4
off Parkhill Rd 101 EC45
Topiary, The, Ashtd. KT21 232 CL120
Topiary Sq, Rich. TW9 158 CM83
Topland Rd, Chal.St.P. SL9 90 AX52
Toplands Av, Aveley RM15 148 FP74

T

Topley St, SE9 164 EK84
Topmast Pt, E14 302 A5
Top Pk, Beck. BR3 204 EE99
Gerrards Cross SL9 112 AW58
Topping La, Uxb. UB8 134 BK69
Topp Wk, NW2 119 CW61
Topsfield Cl, N8 121 DK57
Topsfield Par, N8
off Tottenham La 121 DL57
Topsfield Rd, N8 121 DL57
Topsham Rd, SW17 180 DF90
Torbay Rd, NW6 272 G7
Harrow HA2 116 BY61
Torbay St, NW1 275 K7
Torbitt Way, Ilf. IG2 125 ET57
Torbridge Cl, Edg. HA8 96 CL52
Torbrook Cl, Bex. DA5 186 EY86
Torcross Dr, SE23 182 DW89
Torcross Rd, Ruis. HA4 115 BV62
Tor Gdns, W8 295 J4
Tor Gro, SE28 145 ES74
Torin Ct, Eng.Grn TW20 172 AW92
Torkildsen Way, Harl. CM20 35 ER13
Torland Dr, Oxshott KT22 215 CD114
Tor La, Wey. KT13 213 BQ111
Tormead Cl, Sutt. SM1 218 DA107
Tormead Rd, Guil. GU1 243 AZ134
Sch Tormead Sch,
Jun Sch, Guil. GU1
off Cranley Rd 243 AZ134
Sen Sch, Guil. GU1
off Cranley Rd 243 AZ134
Tormount Rd, SE18 165 ES79
Tornay Ho, N1
off Priory Grn Est 276 C10
Toronto Av, E12 125 EM63
Toronto Dr, Smallfield RH6 269 DN148
Toronto Ho, SE16 301 J5
Toronto Rd, Ilf. IG1 125 EP60
Tilbury RM18 171 GG82
Torquay Gdns, Ilf. IG4 124 EK56
Torquay Spur, Slou. SL2 131 AP70
Torquay St, W2 283 L7
Torrance Cl, SE7 164 EK79
Hornchurch RM11 127 FH60
Torrens Cl, Guil. GU2 242 AU131
Torrens Rd, E15 281 L4
SW2 181 DM85
Torrens Sq, E15 281 K4
Torrens St, EC1 286 F1
Torrens Wk, Grav. DA12 191 GL92
Torres Sq, E14
off Maritime Quay 302 B10
Torre Wk, Cars. SM5 200 DE102
Torrey Dr, SW9 310 F8
Torriano Av, NW5 275 N3
Torriano Cotts, NW5 275 M3
Sch Torriano Inf Sch, NW5 275 N4
Sch Torriano Jun Sch, NW5 275 N3
Torriano Ms, NW5 275 M2
Torridge Gdns, SE15 162 DW84
Torridge Rd, Slou. SL3 153 BB79
Thornton Heath CR7 201 DP99
Torridge Wk, Hem.H. HP2
off The Dee 40 BM15
Torridon Cl, Wok. GU21 226 AV117
Torridon Ho, NW6 283 L1
Sch Torridon Inf Sch, SE6
off Torridon Rd 183 ED89
Sch Torridon Jun Sch, SE6
off Hazelbank Rd 183 ED89
Torridon Rd, SE6 183 ED88
SE13 183 ED87
Torrington Av, N12 98 DD50
Torrington Cl, N12 98 DD49
Claygate KT10 215 CE107
Torrington Dr, Har. HA2 116 CB63
Loughton IG10 85 EQ42
Potters Bar EN6 64 DD32
Torrington Gdns, N11 99 DJ51
Loughton IG10 85 EQ42
Perivale UB6 137 CJ67
Torrington Gro, N12 98 DE50
Torrington Pk, N12 98 DC50
Torrington Pl, E1 300 D2
WC1 285 M6
Torrington Rd, E18 124 EG55
Berkhamsted HP4 38 AV19
Claygate KT10 215 CE107
Dagenham RM8 126 EZ60
Perivale UB6 137 CJ67
Ruislip HA4 115 BT62
Torrington Sq, WC1 285 P5
Croydon CR0
off Tavistock Gro 202 DR101
Torrington Way, Mord. SM4 200 DA100
Tor Rd, Well. DA16 166 EW81
Torr Rd, SE20 183 DX94
Tortoiseshell Way, Berk. HP4 38 AT17
Torver Rd, Har. HA1 117 CE56
Torver Way, Orp. BR6 205 ER104
Torwood Cl, Berk. HP4 38 AT19
Torwood La, Whyt. CR3 236 DT120
Torwood Rd, SW15 179 CU85
Torworth Rd, Borwd. WD6 78 CM39
Tothill Ho, SW1
off Page St 297 P8
Tothill St, SW1 297 N5
Totnes Rd, Well. DA16 166 EV80
Totnes Wk, N2 120 DD56
Tottan Ter, E1 289 K8
Sch Tottenhall Inf Sch, N13
off Tottenhall Rd 99 DN51
Tottenhall Rd, N13 99 DN51
TOTTENHAM, N17 100 DS53
⊖ Tottenham Court Road 285 N8
Tottenham Ct Rd, W1 285 M5
Tottenham Grn E, N15 122 DT56
TOTTENHAM HALE, N17 122 DV55
⇌ Tottenham Hale 122 DV55
⊖ Tottenham Hale 122 DV55
Bus Tottenham Hale, N17 122 DT56
Tottenham Hale Retail Pk,
N15 122 DU56
★ Tottenham Hotspur FC, N17 100 DT52
Tottenham Hotspur Training Cen,
Enf. EN2 82 DU35
Tottenham La, N8 121 DL57
Tottenham Ms, W1 285 M6
Tottenham Rd, N1 277 N5
Tottenham St, W1 285 M7
Totterdown St, SW17 180 DF91
TOTTERIDGE, N20 97 CY46
⊖ Totteridge & Whetstone 98 DB47
Totteridge Common, N20 97 CU47
Totteridge Grn, N20 98 DA47
Totteridge Ho, SW11 308 B9
Totteridge La, N20 98 DA47
Totteridge Rd, Enf. EN3 83 DX37
Totteridge Village, N20 97 CY46
Totternhoe Cl, Har. HA3 117 CJ57
Totton Rd, Th.Hth. CR7 201 DN97
Toucan Cl, NW10 138 CN69
Toulmin Dr, St.Alb. AL3 42 CC16
Toulmin St, SE1 299 J5
Toulon St, SE5 311 J4
Tournay Rd, SW6 307 H4
Tours Pas, SW11 160 DD84
Tourtel Yd, Nthflt. DA11 190 GC89
Toussaint Wk, SE16 300 D6
Tovey Av, Hodd. EN11 49 EA15
Tovey Cl, Lon.Col. AL2 61 CK26
Lower Nazeing EN9 50 EE23
Tovil Cl, SE20 202 DU96
Tovy Ho, SE1 312 C1
Towcester Rd, E3 290 D5
Tower, The, Couls. CR5 235 DK122
● Tower 42, EC2 287 N8
Tower Br, E1 300 A3
SE1 300 A3
Tower Br App, E1 300 A2
★ Tower Br Exhib, SE1 300 A3
Tower Br Ms, Har. HA1
off Greenford Rd 117 CF63
Tower Br Piazza, SE1 300 A3
Sch Tower Br Prim Sch, SE1 300 A4
Tower Br Rd, SE1 299 N7
Tower Br Wf, E1 300 C3
Tower Bldgs, E1
off Brewhouse La 300 F3
Tower Cl, NW3 274 B2
SE20 182 DV94
Berkhamsted HP4 38 AU20
Flackwell Heath HP10 110 AC56
Gravesend DA12 191 GL92
Hertford Heath SG13 32 DW13
Horley RH6 268 DF148
Ilford IG6 103 EP51
North Weald Bassett CM16 53 FD24
Orpington BR6 205 ET103
Woking GU21 226 AX117
Tower Ct, WC2 286 A9
Brentwood CM14 108 FV47
Egham TW20
off The Chantries 173 BA92
Tower Cft, Eyns. DA4 208 FL103
Tower Gdns, Clay. KT10 215 CG108
Tower Gdns Rd, N17 100 DQ53
Towergate Cl, Uxb. UB8 114 BL64
DLR Tower Gateway 288 B10
Tower Gro, Wey. KT13 195 BS103
Coll Tower Hamlets Coll,
Arbour Sq Cen, E1 289 J8
Bethnal Grn Cen, E2 288 C3
East India Dock Rd, E14 290 D9
Poplar Cen, E14 302 C1
Tower Hamlets Rd, E7 281 M1
E17 123 EA55
Tower Hts, Hodd. EN11
off Amwell St 49 EA17
TOWER HILL, Dor. RH4 263 CH138
⊖ Tower Hill 287 P10
Tower Hill, EC3 300 A1
Brentwood CM14 108 FW47
Chipperfield WD4 57 BE29
Dorking RH4 263 CH138
Gomshall GU5 261 BQ140
Tower Hill La, Goms. GU5 261 BQ140
Sandridge AL4 28 CM10
Tower Hill Ri, Goms. GU5 261 BQ140
Tower Hill Rd, Dor. RH4 263 CH138
Tower Hill Ter, EC3
off Byward St 299 P1
Tower Ho, Slou. SL1 152 AS75
Uxb. UB8 off High St 134 BJ66
Sch Tower Ho Sch, SW14
off Sheen La 158 CQ84
Tower La, Wem. HA9
off Main Dr 117 CK62
Tower Ms, E17 123 EA56
Tower Mill Rd, SE15 311 N3
★ Tower of London, EC3 300 A1
Tower Pk Rd, Cray. DA1 187 FF85
★ Tower Pier, EC3 299 P2
Tower Pl, Warl. CR6 237 EA115
● Tower Pl E, EC3 299 P1
● Tower Pl W, EC3 299 P1
Tower Pt, Enf. EN2 82 DR42
Tower Retail Pk, Cray. DA1 187 FF85
Tower Ri, Rich. TW9
off Jocelyn Rd 158 CL83
Tower Rd, NW10 139 CU66
Belvedere DA17 167 FC77
Bexleyheath DA7 167 FB84
Coleshill HP7 55 AN43
Dartford DA1 188 FJ86
Epping CM16 69 ES30
Orpington BR6 205 ET103
Tadworth KT20 233 CW123
Twickenham TW1 177 CF90
Ware SG12 33 DY05
Towers, The, Ken. CR8 236 DQ115
Towers Av, Hlgdn UB10 135 BQ69
● Towers Business Pk, Wem. HA9
off Carey Way 118 CQ63
Sch Towers Inf Sch, Horn. RM11
off Osborne Rd 128 FJ59
Sch Towers Jun Sch, Horn. RM11
off Windsor Rd 128 FJ59
Towers Pl, Rich. TW9 178 CL85
Towers Rd, Grays RM17 170 GC78
Hemel Hempstead HP2 40 BL19
Pinner HA5 94 BY53
Southall UB1 136 CA70
Tower St, WC2 285 P9
Hertford SG14 32 DQ07
Towers Wk, Wey. KT13 213 BP107
Towers Wd, S.Darenth DA4 209 FR95
Tower Ter, N22 off Mayes Rd 99 DM54
SE4 off Foxberry Rd 163 DY84
Tower Vw, Bushey Hth WD23 95 CE45
Croydon CR0 203 DX101
Towfield Rd, Felt. TW13 176
BZ89 Towing Path, Guil. GU1 258 AW138
Towing Path Wk, N1 276 A10
Town, The, Enf. EN2 82 DR41
Town Br Ct, Chesh. HP5 54 AP32
off Watermeadow
Town Cen, Hat. AL10 45 CU17
Towncourt Cres, Petts Wd BR5 205 EQ99
Towncourt La, Petts Wd BR5 205 ER100
Town Ct Path, N4 122 DQ60
Town End, Cat. CR3 236 DS122
Town End Cl, Cat. CR3 236 DS122
Towney Mead, Nthlt. UB5 136 BZ68
Towney Mead Ct, Nthlt. UB5
off Towney Mead 136 BZ68
Sch Town Fm Prim Sch,
Stanw. TW19
off St. Mary's Cres 174 BK87
Town Fm Way, Stanw. TW19
off Town La 174 BK87
Townfield, Chesh. HP5 54 AP32
Rickmansworth WD3 92 BJ45
Townfield Cor, Grav. DA12 191 GJ88
Townfield Ct, Dor. RH4
off Horsham Rd 263 CG137
Town Fld La, Ch.St.G. HP8 90 AW48
Townfield Rd, Dor. RH4 263 CG137
Hayes UB3 135 BT74
Townfields, Hat. AL10 45 CU17
Townfield Sq, Hayes UB3 135 BT74
Town Fld Way, Islw. TW7 157 CG82
Towngate, Cob. KT11 230 BY115
Town Hall App, N16 277 M1
Town Hall App Rd, N15 122 DT56
Town Hall Av, W4 158 CR78
Town Hall Rd, SW11 160 DF83
Townholm Cres, W7 157 CF76
Town La, Stanw. TW19 174 BK86
Wooburn Green HP10 110 AD59
Townley Ct, E15 281 L5
Sch Townley Gram Sch for Girls,
Bexh. DA6 off Townley Rd 186 EZ85
Townley Rd, SE22 182 DS85
Bexleyheath DA6 186 EZ85
Townley St, SE17 299 L10
Town Mead, Bletch. RH1 252 DR133
● Townmead Business Cen,
SW6 307 N10
Town Meadow, Brent. TW8 157 CK79
Townmead Rd, SW6 307 N9
Richmond TW9 158 CP82
Waltham Abbey EN9 67 EC34
Town Mill Ms, Hert. SG14
off Millbridge 32 DQ09
Town Path, Egh. TW20 173 BA92
Town Pier, Grav. DA11
off West St 191 GH86
Town Quay, Bark. IG11 145 EP67
Town Rd, N9 100 DV47
TOWNSEND, St.Alb. AL3 43 CD17
Townsend, Hem.H. HP2 40 BK18
Townsend Av, N14 99 DK49
St. Albans AL1 43 CE19
Sch Townsend C of E Sch, St.Alb.
AL3 off Sparrowswick Ride 42 CC15
Townsend Dr, St.Alb. AL3 43 CD18
● Townsend Ind Est, NW10 138 CQ68
Townsend La, NW9 118 CR59
Woking GU22
off St. Peters Rd 227 BB121
Townsend Ms, SW18
off Waynflete St 180 DC89
Sch Townsend Prim Sch, SE17 299 N8
Townsend Rd, N15 122 DT57
Ashford TW15 174 BL92
Chesham HP5 54 AP30
Southall UB1 136 BY74
Townsend St, SE17 299 M9
Townsend Way, Nthwd. HA6 93 BT52
Townsend Yd, N6 121 DH60
Townshend Cl, Sid. DA14 186 EV93
Townshend Est, NW8 274 C10
Townshend Rd, NW8 274 C9
Chislehurst BR7 185 EP92
Richmond TW9 158 CM84
Townshend St, Hert. SG13 32 DS09
Townshend Ter, Rich. TW9 158 CM84
Townshott Cl, Bkhm KT23 246 CA125
Townslow La, Wisley GU23 228 BK116
Townson Av, Nthlt. UB5 135 BU69
Townson Way, Nthlt. UB5
off Townson Av 135 BU68
Town Sq, Bark. IG11
off Clockhouse Av 145 EQ67
Erith DA8 off Pier Rd 167 FE79
Woking GU21 off Church St E 227 AZ117
Town Sq Cres, Bluewater DA9 189 FT87
Town Tree Rd, Ashf. TW15 174 BN92
Towpath, Shep. TW17 194 BM103
Towpath Rd, N18 101 DX51
Towpath Wk, E9 279 N2
Towpath Way, Croy. CR0 202 DT100
Towton Rd, SE27 182 DQ89
Toynbec Cl, Chis. BR7
off Beechwood Ri 185 EP91
Toynbee Rd, SW20 199 CY95
Toynbee St, E1 288 A7
Toyne Way, N6 120 DF58
Tozer Wk, Wind. SL4 151 AK83
Tracery, The, Bans. SM7 234 DB115
Tracey Av, NW2 272 A2
Tracious Cl, Wok. GU21
off Sythwood 226 AV116
Tracious La, Wok. GU21 226 AV116
Tracy Av, Slou. SL3 153 AZ78
Tracy Ct, Stan. HA7 95 CJ52
Tracyes Rd, Harl. CM18 52 EV17
● Trade City, Wey. KT13 212 BL110
● Trade City Bus Pk,
Uxb. UB8 134 BJ68
Trade Cl, N13 99 DN49
Trader Rd, E6 293 N9
Tradescant Rd, SW8 310 B5
Trading Est Rd, NW10 138 CQ70
Trafalgar Av, N17 100 DS51
SE15 312 B1
Broxbourne EN10 49 DZ21
Worcester Park KT4 199 CX102
● Trafalgar Business Cen,
Bark. IG11 145 ET70
Trafalgar Cl, SE16 301 L8
Trafalgar Ct, E1 301 H1
Cobham KT11 213 BU113
Trafalgar Dr, Walt. KT12 195 BV104
Trafalgar Gdns, E1 289 K6
W8 295 L6
Trafalgar Gro, SE10 315 H2
Sch Trafalgar Inf Sch, Twick. TW2
off Elmsleigh Rd 177 CD89
Sch Trafalgar Jun Sch, Twick. TW2
off Elmsleigh Rd 177 CD89
Trafalgar Ms, E9 279 N4
Trafalgar Pl, E11 124 EG56
N18 100 DU50
Trafalgar Rd, SE10 315 H2
SW19 180 DB94
Dartford DA1 188 FL89
Gravesend DA11 191 GG87
Rainham RM13 147 FF68
Twickenham TW2 177 CD89
Trafalgar Sq, SW1 297 P2
WC2 297 P2
Trafalgar St, SE17 299 L10
Trafalgar Ter, Har. HA1
off Nelson Rd 117 CE60
● Trafalgar Trd Est, Enf. EN3 83 DY42
Trafalgar Way, E14 302 E2
Croydon CR0 201 DM103
Trafalgar Way Retail Pk,
Croy. CR0 201 DM103
Trafford Cl, Ilf. IG6 103 ET51
Shenley WD7 62 CL32
Trafford Rd, Th.Hth. CR7 201 DM99
Trafford Way, Beck. BR3 183 EA93
Trahorn Cl, E1 288 E5
Tralee Ct, SE16 300 E10
Tram Cl, SE24
off Hinton Rd 161 DP83
● Tramsheds Ind Est,
Croy. CR0 201 DK101
Tramway Av, E15 281 J6
N9 100 DV45
Tramway Cl, SE20 202 DW95
Tramway Ho, Erith DA8
off Stonewood Rd 167 FE78
Tramway Path, Mitch. CR4 200 DF99
Tranby Pl, E9 279 K3
Tranley Ms, NW3 274 D2
Tranmere Rd, N9 100 DT45
SW18 180 DC89
Twickenham TW2 176 CB87
Tranquil Dale, Buckland RH3 249 CT132
Tranquil La, Har. HA2 116 CB60
Tranquil Pas, SE3 315 L9
Tranquil Ri, Erith DA8
off West St 167 FE78
Tranquil Vale, SE3 315 K9
Transept St, NW1 284 C7
Transmere Cl, Petts Wd BR5 205 EQ100
Transmere Rd, Petts Wd BR5 205 EQ100
Transom Cl, SE16 301 M8
Transom Sq, E14 302 C9
Transport Av, Brent. TW8 157 CG78
Tranton Rd, SE16 300 D6
Trappes Ho, SE16
off Manor Est 300 E9
Trapps La, Chesh. HP5 54 AR32
Traps Hill, Loug. IG10 85 EM41
Traps La, N.Mal. KT3 198 CS95
Trapstyle Rd, Ware SG12 32 DU05
Trasher Mead, Dor. RH4 263 CJ139
Travellers Cl, N.Mymms AL9 45 CW23
Travellers La, Hat. AL10 45 CU19
North Mymms AL9 45 CW22
Travellers Way, Houns. TW4 156 BW82
Travers Cl, E17 101 DX53
Travers Rd, N7 121 DN62
Travic Rd, Slou. SL2 131 AM69
Travis Ct, Farn.Royal SL2 131 AP69
Treachers Cl, Chesh. HP5 54 AP31
Jct Treacle Mine Rbt,
Grays RM16 170 FZ75
Treacy Cl, Bushey Hth WD23 94 CC47
Treadgold St, W11 282 D10
Treadway St, E2 288 E1
Treadwell Rd, Epsom KT18 232 CS115
Treasury Cl, Wall. SM6 219 DK106
Treaty Cen, Houns. TW3 156 CB83
Treaty St, N1 276 C9
Trebble Rd, Swans. DA10 190 FY86
Trebeck St, W1 297 J2
Trebellan Dr, Hem.H. HP2 40 BM19
Trebovir Rd, SW5 295 K10
Treby St, E3 289 N5
Trecastle Way, N7 275 P1
Tredegar Ms, E3 289 N2
Tredegar Rd, E3 289 N1
N11 99 DK52
Dartford DA2 187 FG89
Tredegar Sq, E3 289 N2
Tredegar Ter, E3 289 N2
Trederwen Rd, E8 278 D8
Tredown Rd, SE26 182 DW92
Tredwell Cl, SW2
off Hillside Rd 181 DM89
Bromley BR2 204 EL98
Tredwell Rd, SE27 181 DP91
Treebourne Rd, Bigg.H. TN16 238 EJ117
Treeby Ct, Enf. EN3
off George Lovell Dr 83 EA37
Treebys Av, Jacobs Well GU4 242 AX128
Tree Cl, Rich. TW10 177 CK88
Sch Treehouse Sch, N10
off Woodside Av 120 DG56
Treelands, N.Holm. RH5 263 CJ139
Treemount Ct, Epsom KT17 216 CS113
Treen Av, SW13 159 CT83
Tree Rd, E16 292 C8
Treeside Cl, West Dr. UB7 154 BK77
Tree Tops, Brwd. CM15 108 FW46
Treetops, Grav. DA12 191 GH92
Whyteleafe CR3 236 DU118
Treetops Cl, SE2 166 EY78
Northwood HA6 93 BR50
Treetops Vw, Loug. IG10 102 EK45
Treeview Cl, SE19 202 DS95
Treewall Gdns, Brom. BR1 184 EH91
Tree Way, Reig. RH2 250 DB131
Trefgarne Rd, Dag. RM10 126 FA61
Trefil Wk, N7 121 DL63
Trefoil Ho, Erith DA18
off Kale Rd 166 EY75
Trefoil Rd, SW18 180 DC85
Trefusis Wk, Wat. WD17 75 BS39
Tregaron Av, N8 121 DL58
Tregaron Gdns, N.Mal. KT3 198 CS98
Tregarthen Pl, Lthd. KT22 231 CJ121
Tregarth Pl, Wok. GU21 226 AT117
Tregarvon Rd, SW11 160 DG84
Tregelles Rd, Hodd. EN11 33 EA14
Tregenna Av, Har. HA2 116 BZ63
Tregenna Cl, N14 81 DJ43
Tregenna Ct, Har. HA2 116 CA63
Tregony Rd, Orp. BR6 223 ET105
Trego Rd, E9 279 P6
Tregothnan Rd, SW9 310 A10
Tregunter Rd, SW10 307 N2
Trehaven Par, Reig. RH2
off Hornbeam Rd 266 DB137
Trehearn Rd, Ilf. IG6 103 ER52
Treherne Ct, SW17 180 DG91
Trehern Rd, SW14 158 CR83
Trehurst St, E5 279 L2
Trelawn Cl, Ott. KT16 211 BC108
Trelawney Av, Slou. SL3 152 AX76
Trelawney Cl, E17
off Orford Rd 123 EB56
Trelawney Est, E9 278 G5
Trelawney Gro, Wey. KT13 212 BN107
Trelawney Rd, Ilf. IG6 103 ER52
Trelawn Rd, E10 123 EC62
SW2 181 DN85
Trellick Twr, W10 282 G5
Trellis Sq, E3 289 P2
Treloar Gdns, SE19
off Hancock Rd 182 DR93
Tremadoc Rd, SW4 161 DK84
Tremaine Cl, SE4 314 A9
Tremaine Gro, Hem.H. HP2 40 BL16
Tremaine Rd, SE20 202 DV96
Trematon Pl, Tedd. TW11 177 CJ94
Trematon Wk, N1 276 B10
Tremlett Gro, N19 121 DJ62
Tremlett Ms, N19 121 DJ62
Tremolo Grn, Dag. RM8 126 EY60
Trenance, Wok. GU21
off Cardingham 226 AU117
Trenance Gdns, Ilf. IG3 126 EU62
Trenchard Av, Ruis. HA4 115 BV63
Trenchard Cl, NW9
off Fulbeck Dr 96 CS53
Hersham KT12 214 BW106
Stanmore HA7 95 CG51
Trenchard Ct, Mord. SM4
off Green La 200 DA100
Trenchard St, SE10 315 H1
Trenches La, Slou. SL3 133 BA73
Trenchold St, SW8 310 A3
Trenear Cl, Orp. BR6 224 EU105
Trenham Dr, Warl. CR6 236 DW116
Trenholme Cl, SE20 182 DV94
Trenholme Ct, Cat. CR3 236 DU122
Trenholme Rd, SE20 182 DV94
Trenholme Ter, SE20 182 DV94
Trenmar Gdns, NW10 139 CV69
Trent Av, W5 157 CJ76
Upminster RM14 129 FR58
Trentbridge Cl, Ilf. IG6 103 ET51
Trent Cl, Shenley WD7
off Edgbaston Dr 62 CL32
Sch Trent C of E Prim Sch,
Cockfos. EN4 off Church Way 80 DF42
Trent Gdns, N14 81 DH44
Trentham Ct, W3
off Victoria Rd 138 CR71
Trentham Cres, Wok. GU22 227 BA121
Trentham Dr, Orp. BR5 206 EU98
Trentham Rd, Red. RH1 266 DF136
Trentham St, SW18 180 DA88
★ Trent Park Country Pk,
Barn. EN4 80 DG40
Trent Rd, SW2 181 DM85
Buckhurst Hill IG9 102 EH46
Slough SL3 153 BB79
Trent Way, Hayes UB4 135 BS69
Worcester Park KT4 199 CW104
Trentwood Side, Enf. EN2 81 DM41
Treport St, SW18 180 DB87
Tresco Cl, Brom. BR1 184 EE93
Trescoe Gdns, Har. HA2 116 BY59
Romford RM5 105 FC50
Tresco Gdns, Ilf. IG3 126 EU61
Tresco Rd, SE15 162 DV84
Berkhamsted HP4 38 AT19
Tresham Cres, NW8 284 C4
Tresham Rd, Bark. IG11 145 ET66
Tresham Wk, E9 279 H2
Tresilian Av, N21 81 DM43
Tresilian Sq, Hem.H. HP2 40 BM15
Tresillian Way, Wok. GU21 226 AU116
Tressell Cl, N1 277 H7
Tressillian Cres, SE4 314 A10
Tressillian Rd, SE4 163 DZ84
Tresta Wk, Wok. GU21 226 AU115
Trestis Cl, Hayes UB4
off Jollys La 136 BY71
Treston Ct, Stai. TW18 173 BF92
Treswell Rd, Dag. RM9 146 EY67
Tretawn Gdns, NW7 96 CS49
Tretawn Pk, NW7 96 CS49
Trevalga Way, Hem.H. HP2 40 BL16
Trevanion Rd, W14 294 F10
Treve Av, Har. HA1 116 CC59
Trevellance Way, Wat. WD25 60 BW33
Trevelyan Av, E12 125 EM63
Trevelyan Cl, Dart. DA1 168 FM84
Trevelyan Ct, Wind. SL4 151 AP82
Trevelyan Cres, Har. HA3 117 CK59
Trevelyan Gdns, NW10 272 A9
Trevelyan Ho, E2
off Morpeth St 289 J3
Sch Trevelyan Mid Sch,
Wind. SL4 off Wood Cl 151 AQ84
Trevelyan Rd, E15 281 K1
SW17 180 DE92
Trevelyan Way, Berk. HP4 38 AV17
Trevera Ct, Wal.Cr. EN8
off Eleanor Rd 67 DY33
Trevereux Hill, Oxt. RH8 255 EM131
Treveris St, SE1 298 G3
Treverton St, W10 282 D5
Treves Cl, N21 81 DM43
Treville St, SW15 179 CV87
Treviso Rd, SE23
off Farren Rd 183 DY89
Trevithick Cl, Felt. TW14 175 BT88
Trevithick Dr, Dart. DA1 168 FM84
Trevithick Ho, SE16 300 F9
Trevithick St, SE8 314 A2
Trevithick Way, E3 290 B3
Trevone Gdns, Pnr. HA5 116 BY58
Trevor Cl, Brom. BR2 204 EF101
East Barnet EN4 80 DD43
Harrow HA3 off Kenton La 95 CF52
Isleworth TW7 177 CF85
Northolt UB5 136 BW68
Trevor Cres, Ruis. HA4 115 BT63
Trevor Gdns, Edg. HA8 96 CR53
Northolt UB5 136 BW68
Ruislip HA4
off Clyfford Rd 115 BU63
Trevor Pl, SW7 296 D5
Trevor Rd, SW19 179 CY94
Edgware HA8 96 CR53
Hayes UB3 155 BS75
Woodford Green IG8 102 EG52
Trevor Sq, SW7 296 E5
Trevor St, SW7 296 D5
Trevor Wk, SW7
off Trevor Sq 296 E5
Trevose Av, W.Byf. KT14 211 BF114
Trevose Rd, E17 101 ED53
Trevose Way, Wat. WD19 94 BW48
Trewarden Av, Iver SL0 133 BD68
Trewenna Dr, Chess. KT9 215 CK106
Potters Bar EN6 64 DD32
Trewince Rd, SW20 199 CW95
Trewint St, SW18 180 DC89

Trewsbury Ho, SE2
off Hartslock Dr 166 EX75
Trewsbury Rd, SE26 183 DX92
Triandra Way, Hayes UB4 136 BX71
Triangle, The, EC1 287 H4
N13 off Green Las 99 DM49
Barking IG11 off Tanner St 145 EQ65
Kingston upon Thames KT1
off Kenley Rd 198 CQ96
Woking GU21 226 AW118
● Triangle Business Cen, NW10
off Enterprise Way 139 CU69
Triangle Ct, E16 292 E6
Triangle Est, SE11 310 E1
Triangle Ms, West Dr. UB7 134 BM74
Triangle Pas, Barn. EN4
off Station App 80 DC42
Triangle Pl, SW4 161 DK84
Triangle Rd, E8 278 E8
● Triangle Wks, N9
off Centre Way 100 DW47
Tricorn Ho, SE28
off Miles Dr 145 ER74
● Trident Cen, Wat. WD24 76 BW39
Trident Gdns, Nthlt. UB5
off Jetstar Way 136 BX69
Trident Ho, SE28
off Merbury Rd 145 ER74
● Trident Ind Est, Colnbr. SL3 153 BE83
Hoddesdon EN11 49 EC17
Trident Rd, Wat. WD25 59 BT34
Trident St, SE16 301 K8
Trident Way, Sthl. UB2 155 BV76
Trigg's Cl, Wok. GU22 226 AX119
Trigg's La, Wok. GU21, GU22 226 AW118
Trig La, EC4 287 J10
Trigo Ct, Epsom KT19
off Blakeney Cl 216 CR111
Trigon Rd, SW8 310 D4
Trilby Rd, SE23 183 DX89
Trimmer Wk, Brent. TW8 158 CL79
Trim St, SE14 313 N3
Trinder Gdns, N19 121 DL60
Trinder Ms, Tedd. TW11 177 CG92
Trinder Rd, N19 121 DL60
Barnet EN5 79 CW43
Trindles Rd, S.Nutfld RH1 267 DM136
Tring Av, W5 138 CM74
Southall UB1 136 BZ72
Wembley HA9 138 CN65
Tring Cl, Ilf. IG2 125 EQ57
Romford RM3 106 FM49
Tring Gdns, Rom. RM3 106 FL49
Tring Grn, Rom. RM3 106 FM49
Tringham Cl, Ott. KT16 211 BC107
Tring Wk, Rom. RM3 106 FL49
Trinidad Gdns, Dag. RM10 147 FD66
Trinidad St, E14
off Limehouse Causeway 289 P10
Trinity Av, N2 120 DD55
Enfield EN1 82 DT44
Trinity Buoy Wf, E14 303 L1
● Trinity Business Pk, E4
off Trinity Way 101 DZ51
Sch Trinity Cath High Sch,
Lwr Sch, Wdf.Grn. IG8
off Sydney Rd 102 EG49
Upr Sch, Wdf.Grn. IG8
off Mornington Rd 102 EG49
Trinity Ch Pas, SW13 159 CV79
Trinity Ch Rd, SW13 159 CV79
Trinity Ch Sq, SE1 299 K6
Trinity Chyd, Guil. GU1
off High St 258 AX135
Trinity Cl, E8 278 B4
E11 124 EE61
NW3 274 A1
SE13 163 ED84
SW4 off The Pavement 161 DJ84
Bromley BR2 204 EL102
Hounslow TW4 156 BY84
Northwood HA6 93 BS51
South Croydon CR2 220 DS109
Stanwell TW19 174 BJ86
Coll Trinity Coll of Music, SE10 314 F2
Trinity Cotts, Rich. TW9
off Trinity Rd 158 CM83
Trinity Ct, N1 277 N8
N18 100 DT51
NW2 272 A1
SE7 304 E9
Rick. WD3 92 BL47
Trinity Cres, SW17 180 DF89
Trinity Dr, Uxb. UB8 135 BQ72
Trinity Gdns, E16 291 M6
SW9 161 DM84
Dartford DA1
off Summerhill Rd 188 FK86
Trinity Gate, Guil. GU1
off Epsom Rd 258 AY135
Trinity Gro, SE10 314 E6
Hertford SG14 32 DQ07
Trinity Hall Cl, Wat. WD24 76 BW41
★ Trinity Ho, EC3 287 P10
Trinity Ho, SE1
off Bath Ter 299 K6
Trinity La, Wal.Cr. EN8 67 DY32
Trinity Ms, SE20 202 DV95
W10 282 D8
Hemel Hempstead HP2 41 BR21
Trinity Path, SE26 182 DW90
Trinity Pl, EC3 300 A1
Bexleyheath DA6 166 EZ84
Windsor SL4 151 AQ82
Sch Trinity Prim Sch, SE13 183 ED85
Trinity Ri, SW2 181 DN88
Trinity Rd, N2 120 DD55
N22 99 DL53
SW17 180 DF89
SW18 180 DD85
SW19 180 DA93
Gravesend DA12 191 GJ87
Hertford Heath SG13 32 DW12
Ilford IG6 125 EQ55
Richmond TW9 158 CM83
Southall UB1 136 BY74
Ware SG12 33 DY05
Sch Trinity St. Mary's C of E Prim Sch,
SW12 off Balham Pk Rd 180 DG88
Sch Trinity St. Stephen C of E First Sch,
Wind. SL4
off Vansittart Rd 151 AP81
Sch Trinity Sch, SE13 184 EF85
Belvedere DA17 off Erith Rd 167 FC77
Dagenham RM10
off Heathway 126 FA63
Sch Trinity Sch of John Whitgift,
Croy. CR0 off Shirley Rd 202 DW103
Trinity Sq, EC3 299 P1
Trinity St, E16 291 N7
SE1 299 K5
Enfield EN2 82 DQ40
Trinity Wk, NW3 273 P5
Hemel Hempstead HP2 41 BR21
Hertford Heath SG13 32 DW12
Trinity Way, E4 101 DZ51
W3 138 CS73
Trio Pl, SE1 299 K5
Tripps Hill, Ch.St.G. HP8 90 AU48
Tripps Hill Cl, Ch.St.G. HP8 90 AU48
Tripton Rd, Harl. CM18 51 ES16
Tristan Ct, Wem. HA0
off King George Cres 117 CK64
Tristan Sq, SE3 164 EE83
Tristram Cl, E17 123 ED55
Tristram Dr, N9 100 DU48
Tristram Rd, Brom. BR1 184 EF91
● Triton Sq, NW1 285 L4
Triton Wk, Hem.H. HP2 40 BM18
Tritton Av, Croy. CR0 219 DL105
Tritton Rd, SE21 182 DR90
Trittons, Tad. KT20 233 CW121
Triumph Cl, Chaff.Hun. RM16 169 FW77
Harlington UB3 155 BQ80
Triumph Ho, Bark. IG11 146 EU69
Triumph Rd, E6 293 K8
● Triumph Trd Est, N17 100 DU51
Trivett Cl, Green. DA9 189 FU85
Trocette Mansion, SE1
off Bermondsey St 299 P6
Trodd's La, Guil. GU1 259 BF135
Trojan Way, Croy. CR0 201 DM104
Trolling Down Hill, Dart. DA2 188 FP89
Troon Cl, SE16 300 F10
SE28 off Fairway Dr 146 EX72
Troon St, E1 289 L8
Troopers Dr, Rom. RM3 106 FK49
Trosley Av, Grav. DA11 191 GH89
Trosley Rd, Belv. DA17 166 FA79
Trossachs Rd, SE22 182 DS85
Trothy Rd, SE1 300 D8
Trotsworth Av, Vir.W. GU25 192 AX98
Trotsworth Ct, Vir.W. GU25 192 AX98
Trotters Bottom, Barn. EN5 79 CU37
Trotters Gap, Stans.Abb. SG12 33 ED11
Trotters La, Mimbr. GU24 210 AV112
Trotters Rd, Harl. CM18 52 EU17
Trotter Way, Epsom KT19 216 CN112
Trott Rd, N10 98 DF52
Trotts La, West. TN16 255 EQ127
Trott St, SW11 308 C7
Trotwood, Chig. IG7 103 ER51
Trotwood Cl, Shenf. CM15
off Middleton Rd 108 FY46
Troughton Rd, SE7 304 A10
Troutbeck Cl, Slou. SL2 132 AU73
Troutbeck Rd, SE14 313 L6
Trout La, West Dr. UB7 134 BJ73
Trout Ri, Loud. WD3 74 BH41
Trout Rd, West Dr. UB7 134 BK74
Troutstream Way, Loud. WD3 74 BH42
Trouvere Pk, Hem.H. HP1 40 BH18
Trouville Rd, SW4 181 DJ86
Trowbridge Est, E9 279 N4
Trowbridge Rd, E9 279 P5
Romford RM3 106 FK51
Trowers Way, Red. RH1 251 DH131
Trowley Ri, Abb.L. WD5 59 BS31
Trowlock Av, Tedd. TW11 177 CJ93
Trowlock Island, Tedd. TW11 177 CK92
Trowlock Way, Tedd. TW11 177 CK93
Troy Cl, Tad. KT20 233 CV120
Troy Ct, SE18 305 P9
W8 295 J6
Troy Rd, SE19 182 DR93
Troy Town, SE15 312 D10
TRS Apts, Sthl. UB2 156 BY75
Trubshaw Rd, Sthl. UB2
off Havelock Rd 156 CB76
Trueman Cl, Edg. HA8 96 CQ52
Trueman Rd, Ken. CR8 236 DR120
Truesdale Dr, Hare. UB9 114 BJ56
Truesdale Rd, E6 293 K9
Truesdales, Uxb. UB10 115 BQ61
Trulock Ct, N17 100 DU52
Trulock Rd, N17 100 DU52
Truman's Rd, N16 277 P2
Truman Wk, E3 290 D4
Trumpers Way, W7 157 CE76
Trumper Way, Slou. SL1 131 AM74
Uxbridge UB8 134 BJ67
Trumpets Hill Rd, Reig. RH2 265 CU135
Trumpington Dr, St.Alb. AL1 43 CD23
Trumpington Rd, E7 124 EF63
Trumps Grn Av, Vir.W. GU25 192 AX100
Trumps Grn Cl, Vir.W. GU25
off Trumpsgreen Rd 192 AY99
Sch Trumps Grn Inf Sch,
Vir.W. GU25 off Crown Rd 192 AX100
Trumpsgreen Rd, Vir.W. GU25 192 AX100
Trumps Mill La, Vir.W. GU25 193 AZ100
Trump St, EC2 287 K9
Trundlers Way,
Bushey Hth WD23 95 CE46
Trundle St, SE1 299 J4
Trundleys Rd, SE8 301 K10
Trundleys Ter, SE8 301 K9
Trunks All, Swan. BR8 207 FB96
Trunley Heath Rd,
Bramley GU5 258 AW144
Truro Gdns, Ilf. IG1 124 EL59
Truro Rd, E17 123 DZ56
N22 99 DL52
Gravesend DA12 191 GK90
Truro St, NW5 274 G5
Truro Wk, Rom. RM3 106 FJ51
Truro Way, Hayes UB4 135 BS69
Truslove Rd, SE27 181 DN92
Trussley Rd, W6 294 A7
Trustees Cl, Denh. UB9
off Patrons Way West 113 BF58
Trustees Way, Denh. UB9 113 BF57
Trustons Gdns, Horn. RM11 127 FG59
Trust Rd, Wal.Cr. EN8 67 DY34
Trust Wk, SE21
off Peabody Hill 181 DP88
Tryfan Cl, Ilf. IG4 124 EK57
Tryon Cres, E9 278 G8
Tryon St, SW3 296 E10
Trys Hill, Lyne KT16 193 AZ103
Trystings Cl, Clay. KT10 215 CG107
Tuam Rd, SE18 165 ER79
Tubbenden Cl, Orp. BR6 205 ES103
Tubbenden Dr, Orp. BR6 223 ER105
Sch Tubbenden Inf Sch,
Orp. BR6 off Sandy Bury 205 ER104
Sch Tubbenden Jun Sch,
Orp. BR6 off Sandy Bury 205 ER104
Tubbenden La, Orp. BR6 205 ES104
Tubbenden La S, Orp. BR6 223 ER106
Tubbs Cft, Welw.G.C. AL7 30 DB10
Tubbs Rd, NW10 139 CT68
Tubs Hill Par, Sev. TN13 256 FG124
Tubwell Rd, Stoke P. SL2 132 AV67
Tucker Rd, Ott. KT16 211 BD107
Tucker St, Wat. WD18 76 BW43
Tuckey Gro, Ripley GU23 227 BF124
Tuck Rd, Rain. RM13 147 FG65
Tudor Av, Chsht EN7 66 DU31
Hampton TW12 176 CA93
Romford RM2 127 FG55
Watford WD24 76 BX38
Worcester Park KT4 199 CV104
Tudor Circle, Gdmg. GU7 258 AS144
Tudor Cl, N6 121 DJ59
NW3 274 C3
NW7 97 CU51
NW9 118 CQ61
SW2 181 DM86
Ashford TW15 174 BL91
Banstead SM7 233 CY115
Bookham KT23 230 CA124
Cheshunt EN7 66 DV31
Chessington KT9 216 CL106
Chigwell IG7 103 EN49
Chislehurst BR7 205 EM95
Cobham KT11 214 BZ113
Coulsdon CR5 235 DN118
Dartford DA1 187 FH86
Epsom KT17 217 CT110
Hatfield AL10 44 CS21
Hunsdon SG12 34 EK07
Northfleet DA11 190 GE88
Pinner HA5 115 BU57
Shenfield CM15 109 FZ44
Smallfield RH6 269 DP148
South Croydon CR2 236 DV115
Sutton SM3 217 CX106
Wallington SM6 219 DJ108
Woking GU22 227 BA117
Woodford Green IG8 102 EH50
Tudor Ct, E17 123 DY59
Borehamwood WD6 78 CL40
Crockenhill BR8 207 FC101
Egham TW20
off The Chantries 173 BA92
Feltham TW13 176 BW91
Tudor Ct N, Wem. HA9 118 CN64
Sch Tudor Ct Prim Sch,
Chaff.Hun. RM16
off Bark Burr Rd 170 FZ75
Tudor Ct S, Wem. HA9 118 CN64
Tudor Cres, Enf. EN2 81 DP39
Ilford IG6 103 EP51
Tudor Dr, Kings.T. KT2 178 CL92
Morden SM4 199 CX100
Romford RM2 127 FG56
Walton-on-Thames KT12 196 BX102
Watford WD24 76 BX38
Wooburn Green HP10 110 AD55
● Tudor Enterprise Pk, Har. HA3
off Tudor Rd 117 CD55
● Tudor Est, NW10 138 CP68
Tudor Gdns, NW9 118 CQ61
SW13 off Treen Av 158 CS83
W3 138 CN72
Harrow HA3 off Tudor Rd 95 CD54
Romford RM2 127 FG56
Slough SL1 130 AJ72
Twickenham TW1 177 CF88
Upminster RM14 128 FQ61
West Wickham BR4 203 EC104
Tudor Gro, E9 278 G7
N20 98 DE48
Tudor Ho, Surb. KT6
off Lenelby Rd 198 CN102
Tudor La, Old Wind. SL4 172 AW87
Tudor Manor Gdns, Wat. WD25 60 BX32
Tudor Ms, Rom. RM1
off Eastern Rd 127 FF57
Tudor Par, Rick. WD3
off Berry La 92 BG45
Tudor Pk, Amer. HP6 55 AR37
Tudor Pl, Mitch. CR4 180 DE94
Sch Tudor Prim Sch, N3
off Queens Rd 98 DC53
Hemel Hempstead HP3
off Redwood Dr 40 BL22
Southall UB1 off Tudor Rd 136 BY73
Tudor Ri, Brox. EN10 49 DY21
Tudor Rd, E4 101 EB51
E6 144 EJ67
E9 278 F8
N9 100 DV45
SE19 182 DT94
SE25 202 DV99
Ashford TW15 175 BR93
Barking IG11 145 ET67
Barnet EN5 80 DA41
Beckenham BR3 203 EB97
Godalming GU7 258 AS144
Hampton TW12 176 CA94
Harrow HA3 95 CD54
Hayes UB3 135 BR72
Hazlemere HP15 88 AC45
Hounslow TW3 157 CD84
Kingston upon Thames KT2 178 CN94
Pinner HA5 94 BW54
St. Albans AL3 43 CE16
Southall UB1 136 BY73
Wheathampstead AL4 28 CL07
Tudors, The, Reig. RH2 250 DC131
Tudor Sq, Hayes UB3 135 BR71
Tudor St, EC4 286 F10
Tudor Wk, Bex. DA5 186 EY86
Leatherhead KT22 231 CF120
Watford WD24 76 BX37
Weybridge KT13
off West Palace Gdns 195 BP104
Tudor Wks, Hayes UB4
off Beaconsfield Rd 136 BW74
Tudor Way, N14 99 DK46
W3 158 CN75
Hertford SG14 31 DN09
Petts Wood BR5 205 ER100
Rickmansworth WD3 92 BG46
Uxbridge UB10 134 BN65
Waltham Abbey EN9 67 ED33
Windsor SL4 151 AL81
Tudor Well Cl, Stan. HA7 95 CH50
Tudway Rd, SE3 164 EH83
Tuffnell Ct, Chsht EN8
off Coopers Wk 67 DX28
Tufnail Rd, Dart. DA1 188 FM86
TUFNELL PARK, N7 121 DK63
⊖ Tufnell Park 121 DJ63
Sch Tufnell Pk Prim Sch, N7 275 P1
Tufnell Pk Rd, N7 121 DJ63
N19 121 DJ63
Tufter Rd, Chig. IG7 103 ET50
Tufton Gdns, W.Mol. KT8 196 CB96
Tufton Rd, E4 101 EA49
Tufton St, SW1 297 P6
Tugboat St, SE28 165 ES75
Tugela Rd, Croy. CR0 202 DR100
Tugela St, SE6 183 DZ89
Tugmutton Cl, Orp. BR6 223 EP105
Tugswood Cl, Couls. CR5 235 DK121
Tuilerie St, E2 278 C10
Coll Tuition Cen, The, NW4
off Lodge Rd 119 CW56
Sch Tuke Sch, SE15 312 E7
Tulip Cl, E6 293 J7
Croydon CR0 203 DX102
Hampton TW12
off Partridge Rd 176 BZ93
Pilgrim's Hatch CM15
off Poppy Cl 108 FV43
Romford RM3 106 FJ51
Southall UB2 off Chevy Rd 156 CC75
Tulip Ct, Pnr. HA5 116 BW55
Tulip Gdns, Ilf. IG1 145 EP65
Tulip Tree Ct, Sutt. SM2
off The Crescent 218 DA111
Tulip Way, West Dr. UB7 154 BK77
Tull St, Mitch. CR4 200 DF101
Tulse Cl, Beck. BR3 203 EC97
TULSE HILL, SE21 182 DQ88
⇌ Tulse Hill 181 DP89
Coll Tulse Hill, SW2 181 DP88
Tulse Hill, SW2 181 DN86
Tulse Hill Est, SW2 181 DN86
Tulsemere Rd, SE27 182 DQ89
Tulyar Cl, Tad. KT20 233 CV120
Tumber St, Headley KT18 248 CQ125
Tumbler Rd, Harl. CM18 52 EU17
Tumblewood Rd, Bans. SM7 233 CY116
Tumbling Bay, Walt. KT12 195 BU100
Tummons Gdns, SE25 202 DS96
Tump Ho, SE28 145 ES74
Tuncombe Rd, N18 100 DS49
Tunfield Rd, Hodd. EN11 33 EB14
Tunis Rd, W12 139 CV74
Tunley Grn, E14
off Burdett Rd 289 P7
Tunley Rd, NW10 138 CS67
SW17 180 DG88
Tunmarsh La, E13 292 B2
Tunmers End, Chal.St.P. SL9 90 AW53
Tunnan Leys, E6 293 M8
Tunnel Av, SE10 303 H4
● Tunnel Av Trd Est, SE10 303 H5
Tunnel Gdns, N11 99 DJ52
Tunnel Rd, SE16 300 G4
Reigate RH2 off Church St 250 DA134
Tunnel Wd Cl, Wat. WD17 75 BT37
Tunnel Wd Rd, Wat. WD17 75 BT37
Tunnmeade, Harl. CM20 36 EU14
Tunsgate, Guil. GU1 258 AX136
Tunsgate Sq, Guil. GU1
off High St 258 AX136
Tuns La, Slou. SL1 151 AQ76
Tunstall Av, Ilf. IG6 104 EU51
Tunstall Cl, Orp. BR5 223 ES105
Tunstall Rd, SW9 161 DM84
Croydon CR0 202 DS102
Tunstall Wk, Brent. TW8 158 CL79
Tunstock Way, Belv. DA17 166 EY76
Tunworth Cl, NW9 118 CQ58
Tunworth Cres, SW15 179 CT86
Tun Yd, SW8 309 K10
Tupelo Rd, E10 123 EB61
Tuppy St, SE28 165 EQ76
Tupwood Ct, Cat. CR3 252 DU125
Tupwood La, Cat. CR3 252 DU125
Tupwood Scrubbs Rd,
Cat. CR3 252 DU128
Turenne Cl, SW18 160 DC84
Turfhouse La, Chobham GU24 210 AS109
Turin Rd, N9 100 DW45
Turin St, E2 288 C3
Turkey Oak Cl, SE19 202 DS95
Turkey Street 82 DW37
Turkey St, Enf. EN1, EN3 82 DV37
Turks Cl, Uxb. UB8 134 BN69
Turks Head Ct, Eton SL4
off High St 151 AR80
Turk's Head Yd, EC1 286 G6
Turks Row, SW3 296 F10
Turle Rd, N4 121 DM60
SW16 201 DL96
Turlewray Cl, N4 121 DM60
Turley Cl, E15 281 K9
Turmore Dale, Welw.G.C. AL8 29 CW10
Turnagain La, EC4 286 G8
Dartford DA2 187 FG90
Turnage Rd, Dag. RM8 126 EY60
Turnberry Cl, NW4 97 CX54
SE16 312 F1
Turnberry Ct, Wat. WD19 94 BW48
Turnberry Dr, Brick.Wd AL2 60 BY30
Turnberry Quay, E14 302 D6
Turnberry Way, Orp. BR6 205 ER102
Turnbull Cl, Green. DA9 189 FS87
Turnbury Cl, SE28 146 EX72
Turnchapel Ms, SW4
off Cedars Rd 161 DH83
Turner Av, N15 122 DS56
Bigg.H. TN16 222 EJ112
Mitcham CR4 200 DF95
Twickenham TW2 176 CC90
Turner Cl, NW11 120 DB58
SW9 311 H6
Guildford GU4 243 AZ131
Hayes UB4 135 BQ68
Wembley HA0 117 CK64
Turner Ct, N15
off St. Ann's Rd 122 DR57
Dartford DA1 188 FJ85
Turner Cres, Croy. CR0 202 DQ100
Turner Dr, NW11 120 DB58
Turner Ho, E14
off Cassilis Rd 302 B5
Turner Ms, Sutt. SM2 218 DB108
Turner Pl, SW11 180 DE85
Turner Rd, E17 123 EC55
Bean DA2 189 FV90
Bushey WD23 76 CC42
Edgware HA8 118 CM55
Hornchurch RM12 127 FF61
New Malden KT3 198 CR101
Slough SL3 152 AW75
Turners Cl, N20 98 DF48
Staines-upon-Thames TW18 174 BH92
Turners Ct, Abridge RM4 86 EV41
Turners Gdns, Sev. TN13 257 FJ128
Turners Hill, Chsht EN8 67 DX30
Hemel Hempstead HP2 40 BL21
Turners La, Hersham KT12 213 BV107
Turners Meadow Way,
Beck. BR3 203 DZ95
Turners Rd, E3 289 N7
Turner St, E1 288 E7
E16 291 L9
Turners Wk, Chesh. HP5 54 AQ30
Turners Way, Croy. CR0 201 DN103
Turners Wd, NW11 120 DC60
Turners Wd Dr, Ch.St.G. HP8 90 AX48
Turneville Rd, W14 306 G2
Sch Turney Prim & Sec Spec Sch,
SE21 off Turney Rd 182 DQ87
Turney Rd, SE21 182 DR87
Turneys Orchard, Chorl. WD3 73 BD43
TURNFORD, Brox. EN10 67 DZ26
Coll Turnford, Brox. EN10 67 DY25
Sch Turnford Sch, Chsht EN8
off Mill La 67 DY28
Turnford Vil, Turnf. EN10 67 DZ26
Turnham Cl, Guil. GU2 258 AW138
⊖ Turnham Green 158 CS77
Turnham Grn Ter, W4 158 CS77
Turnham Grn Ter Ms, W4 158 CS77
Sch Turnham Prim Sch, SE4
off Turnham Rd 163 DY84
Turnham Rd, SE4 183 DY85
Turnmill St, EC1 286 F5
Turnoak Av, Wok. GU22 226 AY120
Turnoak La, Wok. GU22 226 AY120
Turnoak Pk, Wind. SL4 151 AL84
Turnors, Harl. CM20 51 EQ15
Turnpike Cl, SE8 313 P4
Turnpike Dr, Orp. BR6 224 EW109
Turnpike Grn, Hem.H. HP2 40 BL16
Turnpike Ho, EC1 287 H3
⊖ Turnpike Lane 121 DN55
Turnpike Lane 121 DP55
Turnpike La, N8 121 DM56
Sutton SM1 218 DC106
Uxbridge UB10 134 BL69
West Tilbury RM18 171 GK78
Turnpike Link, Croy. CR0 202 DS103
Turnpike Ms, N8 121 DN56
Turnpike Way, Islw. TW7 157 CG81
Turnpin La, SE10 314 F3
Turnstone Cl, E13 291 N3
NW9 off Kestrel Cl 96 CS54
Ickenham UB10 115 BP64
South Croydon CR2 221 DY110
Turnstones, The, Grav. DA12 191 GK89
Watford WD25 76 BY36
Turp Av, Grays RM16 170 GC75
Turpentine La, SW1 297 K10
Turpin Av, Rom. RM5 104 FA52
Turpin Cl, Enf. EN3 83 EA37
Turpington Cl, Brom. BR2 204 EL100
Turpington La, Brom. BR2 204 EL101
Turpin Ho, SW11 309 J6
Turpin La, Erith DA8 167 FG80
Turpin Rd, Felt. TW14
off Staines Rd 175 BT86
Turpins Cl, Hert. SG14 31 DM09
Turpins La, Wdf.Grn. IG8 103 EM50
Turpin Way, N19 121 DK61
Wallington SM6 219 DH108
Turquand St, SE17 299 K9
Turret Gro, SW4 309 L10
Turton Rd, Wem. HA0 118 CL64
Turton Way, Slou. SL1 151 AR76
Turville Ct, Bkhm KT23
off Proctor Gdns 246 CB125
Turville St, E2 288 A4
Tuscan Ho, E2 289 H2
Tuscan Rd, SE18 165 ER78
Tuscany Ho, E17
off Sherwood Cl 101 DZ54
Ilf. IG3 126 EU58
Tuskar St, SE10 315 J1
Tussauds Cl, Crox.Grn WD3 74 BN43
Tustin Est, SE15 312 G3
Tuttlebee La, Buck.H. IG9 102 EG47
Tutts Cl, Dor. RH4 263 CH135
Tuxford Cl, Borwd. WD6 78 CL38
Twankhams All, Epp. CM16
off Hemnall St 70 EU30
Tweed Cl, Berk. HP4 38 AV18
Tweeddale Gro, Uxb. UB10 115 BQ62
Sch Tweeddale Prim Sch,
Cars. SM5
off Tweeddale Rd 200 DD101
Tweeddale Rd, Cars. SM5 200 DD102
Tweed Glen, Rom. RM1 105 FD52
Tweed Grn, Rom. RM1 105 FD52
Tweed La, Strood Grn RH3 264 CP139
Tweedmouth Rd, E13 292 A1
Tweed Rd, Slou. SL3 153 BA79
Tweed Way, Rom. RM1 105 FD52
Tweedy Cl, Enf. EN1 82 DT43
Tweedy Rd, Brom. BR1 204 EF95
Tweenways, Chesh. HP5 54 AR30
Tweezer's All, WC2 286 E10
Twelve Acre Cl, Bkhm KT23 230 BZ124
Twelve Acre Ho, E12
off Grantham Rd 125 EN62
Twelve Acres, Welw.G.C. AL7 29 CY11
● Twelvetrees Business Pk,
E3 290 G5
Twelvetrees Cres, E3 290 E4
Twentyman Cl, Wdf.Grn. IG8 102 EG50
TWICKENHAM, TW1 & TW2 177 CG89
⇌ Twickenham 177 CF87
Sch Twickenham Acad,
Whitton TW2 off Percy Rd 176 CB89
Twickenham Br, Rich. TW9 177 CJ85
Twickenham TW1 177 CJ85
Twickenham Cl, Croy. CR0 201 DM104
Twickenham Gdns, Grnf. UB6 117 CG64
Harrow HA3 95 CE52
Sch Twickenham Prep Sch,
Hmptn. TW12 off High St 196 CC95
Twickenham Rd, E11 123 ED61
Feltham TW13 176 BZ90
Isleworth TW7 157 CG83
Richmond TW9 157 CJ84
Teddington TW11 177 CG92
● Twickenham Trd Est,
Twick. TW1 177 CF86
Twig Folly Cl, E2 289 K1
Twigg Cl, Erith DA8 167 FE80
Twilley St, SW18 180 DB87
Twinches La, Slou. SL1 131 AP74

T

Twine Cl, Bark. IG11
off Thames Rd 146 EV69
Twine Ct, E1 288 G10
Twineham Grn, N12 98 DA49
Twine Ter, E3
off Ropery St 289 N5
Twining Av, Twick. TW2 176 CC90
Twinn Rd, NW7 97 CY51
Twinoaks, Cob. KT11 214 CA113
Twin Tumps Way, SE28 146 EU73
Twisden Rd, NW5 121 DH63
Twisleton Ct, Dart. DA1
off Priory Hill 188 FK86
Twitchells La, Jordans HP9 90 AT51
Twitten Gro, Brom. BR1 205 EM97
TWITTON, Sev. TN14 241 FF116
Twitton La, Otford TN14 241 FD115
Twitton Meadows,
Otford TN14 241 FE116
Two Acres, Welw.G.C. AL7 29 CZ11
Two Beeches, Hem.H. HP2 40 BM15
Two Dells La, Chesh. HP5 38 AT24
Two Mile Dr, Slou. SL1 131 AK74
Two River's Ct, Felt. TW14 175 BR86
Two Rivers Retail Pk,
Stai. TW18 173 BE91
Two Waters Prim Sch,
Hem.H. HP3 off High Ridge Cl 58 BK25
Two Waters Rd, Hem.H. HP3 40 BJ22
Two Waters Way, Hem.H. HP3 40 BJ24
Twybridge Way, NW10 138 CQ66
Twycross Ms, SE10 303 K9
Twyford Abbey Rd, NW10 138 CM69
Twyford Av, N2 120 DF55
W3 138 CN73
Twyford C of E High Sch, W3
off Twyford Cres 138 CP74
Twyford Cres, W3 138 CN74
Twyford Ho, N15 122 DS58
Twyford Pl, WC2 286 C8
Twyford Rd, Cars. SM5 200 DD102
Harrow HA2 116 CB60
Ilford IG1 125 EQ64
St. Albans AL4 43 CJ16
Twyford St, N1 276 C8
Twyner Cl, Horl. RH6 269 DK147
Twynersh Av, Cher. KT16 193 BF100
Twysdens Ter, N.Mymms AL9
off Dellsome La 45 CW24
Tyas Rd, E16 291 L5
Tybenham Rd, SW19 200 DA97
Tyberry Rd, Enf. EN3 82 DV41
Tyburn La, Har. HA1 117 CE59
Tyburns, The, Hutt. CM13 109 GC47
Tyburn Way, W1 284 F10
Tycehurst Hill, Loug. IG10 85 EM42
Tychbourne Dr, Guil. GU4 243 BC131
Tydcombe Rd, Warl. CR6 236 DW119
TYE GREEN, Harl. CM18 51 ES17
Tye Grn Village, Harl. CM18 51 ES18
Tye La, Headley KT18 248 CR127
Orpington BR6 223 EQ106
Tadworth KT20 248 CS128
Tyers Est, SE1 299 N4
Tyers Gate, SE1 299 N4
Tyers St, SE11 298 C10
Tyers Ter, SE11 310 C1
Tyeshurst Cl, SE2 166 EY78
Tyfield Cl, Chsht EN8 66 DW30
Tykeswater La, Els. WD6 77 CJ39
Tylecroft Rd, SW16 201 DL96
Tyle Grn, Horn. RM11 128 FL56
Tylehost, Guil. GU2 242 AU130
Tylehurst Dr, Red. RH1 266 DF135
Tylehurst Gdns, Ilf. IG1 125 EQ64
Tyle Pl, Old Wind. SL4 172 AU85
Tyler Cl, E2 278 A10
Erith DA8 167 FB80
Nthflt. DA11 190 GC89
Tyler Gdns, Add. KT15 212 BJ105
Tyler Gro, Dart. DA1
off Spielman Rd 168 FM84
Tyler Rd, Sthl. UB2
off McNair Rd 156 CB76
TYLERS CAUSEWAY,
Hert. SG13 47 DK22
Tylers Causeway,
Newgate St SG13 47 DH23
Tylers Cl, Gdse. RH9 252 DV130
Kings Langley WD4 58 BL28
Loughton IG10 102 EL45
Tyler's Ct, W1 285 N9
Tylers Cres, Horn. RM12 128 FJ64
Tylersfield, Abb.L. WD5 59 BT31
Tylers Gate, Har. HA3 118 CL58
Tylers Grn First Sch,
Penn HP10 off School Rd 88 AD47
Tylers Grn Rd, Swan. BR8 207 FC100
Tylers Hill Rd, Chesh. HP5 56 AT30
Tylers Path, Cars. SM5
off Rochester Rd 218 DF105
Tylers Rd, Roydon CM19 50 EJ19
Tyler St, SE10 315 K1
Tylers Way, Wat. WD25 77 CD42
Tyler Wk, Slou. SL3
off Gilbert Way 153 AZ78
Tyler Way, Brwd. CM14 108 FV46
Tylney Av, SE19 182 DT92
Tylney Cl, Chig. IG7 103 ET49
Tylney Cft, Harl. CM19 51 EP17
Tylney Rd, E7 124 EJ63
Bromley BR1 204 EK96
Tylsworth Cl, Amer. HP6 55 AR38
Tymberwood Acad,
Grav. DA12 off Cerne Rd 191 GM90
Tymperley Ct, SW19
off Windlesham Gro 179 CY88
Tynan Cl, Felt. TW14 175 BU88
Tyndale Ct, E14 302 C10
Tyndale La, N1 276 G6
Tyndale Ms, Slou. SL1 151 AP75
Tyndale Ter, N1 276 G6
Tyndall Rd, E10 123 EC61
Welling DA16 165 ET83
Tyne Cl, Upmin. RM14 129 FR58
Tynedale, Lon.Col. AL2
off Thamesdale 62 CM27
Tynedale Cl, Dart. DA2 189 FR88
Tynedale Rd, Strood Grn RH3 264 CP138
Tyne Gdns, Aveley RM15 148 FQ73
Tyneham Cl, SW11 309 H10
Tyneham Rd, SW11 309 H9
Tynemouth Cl, E6 293 N9
Tynemouth Dr, Enf. EN1 82 DU38
Tynemouth Rd, N15 122 DT56
SE18 165 ET78
Mitcham CR4 180 DG94
Tynemouth St, SW6 307 N8
Tyne St, E1
off Old Castle St 288 B8
Tynley Gro, Jacobs Well GU4 242 AX128
Tynsdale Rd, NW10 138 CS66
Tynwald Ho, SE26
off Sydenham Hill Est 182 DU90
Type St, E2 289 J1
Typhoon Way, Wall. SM6 219 DL108
Typleden Cl, Hem.H. HP2 40 BK18
Tyrawley Rd, SW6 307 L6
Tyre La, NW9 118 CS56
Tyrell Cl, Har. HA1 117 CE63
Tyrell Ct, Cars. SM5 218 DF105
Tyrell Gdns, Wind. SL4 151 AM83
Tyrell Ri, Warley CM14 108 FW50
Tyrells Cl, Upmin. RM14 128 FN61
Tyrells Pl, Guil. GU1 259 AZ135
Tyrols Rd, SE23
off Wastdale Rd 183 DX88
Tyrone Rd, E6 293 K1
Tyron Way, Sid. DA14 185 ES91
Tyrrell Av, Well. DA16 186 EU85
Tyrrell Rd, SE22 162 DU84
Tyrrells Hall Cl, Grays RM17 170 GD79
TYRRELL'S WOOD, Lthd. KT22 232 CM123
Tyrrell Sq, Mitch. CR4 200 DE95
Tyrrel Way, NW9 119 CT59
Tyrwhitt Ct, Guil. GU2
off Henderson Av 242 AV130
Tyrwhitt Rd, SE4 163 EA83
Tysea Cl, Harl. CM18 51 ET18
Tysea Hill, Stap.Abb. RM4 105 FF45
Tysea Rd, Harl. CM18 51 ET18
Tysoe Av, Enf. EN3 83 DZ36
Tysoe St, EC1 286 E3
Tyson Rd, SE23 182 DW87
Tyssen Comm Prim Sch,
N16 off Oldhill St 122 DU60
Tyssen Pas, E8 278 A4
Tyssen Pl, S.Ock. RM15 149 FW69
Tyssen Rd, N16 122 DT62
Tyssen St, E8 278 B4
N1 277 P10
Tythebarn Cl, Guil. GU4
off Dairyman's Wk 243 BB129
Tytherton Rd, N19 121 DK62
TYTTENHANGER, St.Alb. AL4 43 CK23
Tyttenhanger Grn, Tytten. AL4 43 CK23

U

Uamvar St, E14 290 D6
Uckfield Gro, Mitch. CR4 200 DG95
Uckfield Rd, Enf. EN3 83 DX37
UCL Academy, The, NW3
off Adelaide Rd 274 B7
Udall Gdns, Rom. RM5 104 FA51
Udall St, SW1 297 M9
Udney Pk Rd, Tedd. TW11 177 CG92
Uffington Rd, NW10 139 CU67
SE27 181 DN91
Ufford Cl, Har. HA3 94 CB52
Ufford Rd, Har. HA3 94 CB52
Ufford St, SE1 298 F4
Ufton Gro, N1 277 M6
Ufton Rd, N1 277 M7
Uhura Sq, N16 122 DS62
Ujima Ct, SW16 181 DL91
Ullathorne Rd, SW16 181 DJ91
Ulleswater Rd, N14 99 DL49
Ullin St, E14 290 E7
Ullswater Business Pk,
Couls. CR5 235 DL116
Ullswater Cl, SW15 178 CR91
Bromley BR1 184 EE93
Hayes UB4 135 BS68
Slough SL1
off Buttermere Av 130 AJ71
Ullswater Ct, Har. HA2 116 CA59
Ullswater Cres, SW15 178 CR91
Coulsdon CR5 235 DL116
Ullswater Rd, SE27 181 DP89
SW13 159 CU80
Hemel Hempstead HP3 41 BQ22
Ullswater Way, Horn. RM12 127 FG64
Ulstan Cl, Wold. CR3 237 EA123
Ulster Gdns, N13 100 DQ49
Ulster Pl, NW1 285 J5
Ulster Ter, NW1 285 J5
Ulundi Rd, SE3 315 K3
Ulva Rd, SW15 179 CX85
Ulverscroft Rd, SE22 182 DT85
Ulverston, Purf. RM19 168 FQ78
Ulverston Cl, St.Alb. AL1 43 CF20
Ulverstone Rd, SE27 181 DP89
Ulverston Rd, E17 101 ED54
Ulwin Av, Byfleet KT14 212 BL113
Ulysses Pl, E20 280 E3
Ulysses Rd, NW6 273 H2
Umberstones, Vir.W. GU25 192 AX100
Umberston St, E1 288 E8
Umberville Way, Slou. SL2 131 AM70
Umbria St, SW15 179 CU86
Umbriel Pl, E13 291 P1
Umfreville Rd, N4 121 DP58
Underacres Cl, Hem.H. HP2 40 BN19
Undercliff Rd, SE13 314 B10
UNDERHILL, Barn. EN5 80 DA43
Underhill, Barn. EN5 80 DA43
Underhill Inf Sch,
Barn. EN5 off Mays La 79 CY43
Underhill Jun Sch,
Barn. EN5 off Mays La 79 CY43
Underhill Pk Rd, Reig. RH2 250 DA131
Underhill Pas, NW1 275 K8
Underhill Rd, SE22 182 DV86
Underhill St, NW1 275 K9
Underne Av, N14 99 DH47
UNDERRIVER, Sev. TN15 257 FN130
Underriver Ho Rd,
Undrvr TN15 257 FP130
Undershaft, EC3 287 N9
Undershaw Rd, Brom. BR1 184 EE90
Underwood, New Adgtn CR0 221 EC106
Underwood, The, SE9 185 EM89
Underwood Rd, E1 288 C5
E4 101 EB50
Caterham CR3 252 DS126
Woodford Green IG8 102 EK52
Underwood Row, N1 287 K2
Underwood St, N1 287 K2
Undine Rd, E14 302 D8
Undine St, SW17 180 DF92
Uneeda Dr, Grnf. UB6 137 CD67
Unicorn Pas, SE1
off Tooley St 299 P3
Unicorn Prim Sch, Beck. BR3
off Creswell Dr 203 EB99
Unicorn Sch, Rich. TW9
off Kew Rd 158 CM81
Unicorn Wk, Green. DA9 189 FT85
Union Business Pk,
Uxb. UB8 134 BH66
Union Cl, E11 123 ED63
Union Cotts, E15 281 K6
Union Ct, EC2 287 N8
Richmond TW9 off Eton St 178 CL85
Union Dr, E1 289 M4
Union Gro, SW8 309 N9
Union Jack Club, SE1 298 E4
Union La, Islw. TW7 157 CG81
Union Pk, SE10 315 L1
Uxbridge UB8 134 BJ72
Union Rd, N11 99 DK51
SW4 309 N8
SW8 309 N8
Bromley BR2 204 EK99
Croydon CR0 202 DQ101
Northolt UB5 136 CA68
Romford RM7 127 FD58
Wembley HA0 138 CL65
Union Sq, N1 277 J9
Union St, SE1 299 H3
Barnet EN5 79 CY42
Kingston upon Thames KT1 197 CK96
Union Wk, E2 287 P2
Union Wf, N1 287 J1
West Drayton UB7
off Bentinck Rd 134 BL74
Unity Cl, NW10 139 CU65
SE19 off Crown Dale 182 DQ92
New Addington CR0 221 EB109
Unity Ct, SE1
off Mawbey Pl 300 B10
Unity Ms, SE2 166 EU78
Unity Rd, Enf. EN3 82 DW37
Unity Ter, Har. HA2
off Scott Cres 116 CB60
Unity Trd Est, Wdf.Grn. IG8 124 EK55
Unity Way, SE18 304 E6
Unity Wf, SE1 300 B4
University Cl, NW7 97 CT52
Bushey WD23 76 CA42
University Coll Hosp, NW1 285 M4
Elizabeth Garrett Anderson
Wing, NW1 285 M4
Hosp for Tropical Diseases,
WC1 285 M5
Macmillan Cancer Cen, WC1 285 M5
Private Wing, WC1 285 M5
University Coll London, WC1 285 N4
Arthur Stanley Ho, W1 285 M6
Eastman Dental Inst, WC1 286 C3
Inst of Ophthalmology, EC1 287 L3
Ludwig Inst for Cancer
Research, W1 285 M6
Prankerd Ho, NW1 285 M4
Ramsay Hall, W1 285 L5
Slade Research Cen, WC1 285 P5
The Inst of Neurology, WC1 286 B5
The Warburg Inst, WC1 285 P5
Windeyer Bldg, W1 285 M6
Wolfson Ho, NW1 285 M3
Wolfson Inst for
Biomedical Research, WC1 285 M5
University Coll Sch,
Jun Branch, NW3 off Holly Hill 120 DC63
Sen Sch, NW3 273 N2
University Gdns, Bex. DA5 186 EZ87
University Hosp Lewisham,
SE13 183 EB85
University of Cumbria,
Tower Hamlets E3 289 N5
University of E London -
London Docklands Campus,
E16 293 M10
University of E London -
Stratford Campus,
Arthur Edwards Bldg, E15 281 K4
Cen for Clinical Ed, E15 281 K5
Duncan Ho, E15 280 G8
Sch of Ed, E15 281 K4
Student Services Cen, E15 281 K4
Uni Ho, E15 281 K5
University of Greenwich -
Avery Hill Campus,
Mansion Site, SE9
off Bexley Rd 185 EQ86
Southwood Site, SE9
off Avery Hill Rd 185 EQ87
University of Greenwich -
Maritime Greenwich Campus,
Cooper Bldg, SE10 314 G2
Old Royal Naval Coll, SE10 314 G2
University of Hertfordshire,
Bayfordbury Fld Sta &
Observatory, Hert. SG13
off Lower Hatfield Rd 31 DN14
College La Campus, Hat. AL10
off College La 45 CT20
de Havilland Campus,
Hat. AL10 off Mosquito Way 44 CR18
University of London,
Canterbury Hall, WC1 286 A3
Commonwealth Hall, WC1 286 A3
Hughes Parry Hall, WC1 286 A3
International Hall, WC1 286 B5
Senate Ho, WC1 285 P6
Stewart Ho, WC1 285 P6
Union, WC1 285 N5
University of Surrey,
Frances Harrison Ho, Guil. GU2
off Gill Av 258 AS135
HPRU, Guil. GU2 off Gill Av 258 AS135
Manor Pk Campus, Guil. GU2 258 AS135
Post Grad Med Sch, Guil. GU2
off Gill Av 258 AS135
Sch of Acting, Guil. GU2
off Gill Av 242 AU134
Stag Hill Campus, Guil. GU2
off Alresford Rd 242 AV134
Surrey Sports Pk, Guil. GU2 258 AS136
Wealden Ho, Guil. GU2
off Gill Av 258 AS135
University of West London,
Brentford Site TW8
off Boston Manor Rd 157 CJ78
Ealing Site W5
off St. Mary's Rd 137 CK74
Vestry Hall W5
off Ranelagh Rd 157 CK75
University of Westminster -
Cavendish Campus, W1 285 L6
University of Westminster -
Harrow Campus, Har. HA1
off Watford Rd 117 CG59
University of Westminster -
Marylebone Campus, NW1 284 G6
University of Westminster -
Regent Campus, W1 285 K8
Great Portland St, W1 285 K6
Little Titchfield St, W1 285 L7
Riding Ho St, W1 285 L7
University Pl, Erith DA8
off Belmont Rd 167 FC80
University Rd, SW19 180 DD93
University Sq Stratford, E15 281 J5
University St, WC1 285 M5
University Way, E16 305 M1
Dartford DA1 168 FP84
Unstead La, Bramley GU5 258 AW144
Unstead Wd, Peasm. GU3 258 AW142
Unwin Av, Felt. TW14 175 BR85
Unwin Cl, SE15 312 C3
Unwin Rd, SW7 296 B6
Isleworth TW7 157 CE83
Unwin Way, Stan. HA7 96 CL52
Upbrook Ms, W2 283 P9
Upcerne Rd, SW10 307 P5
Upchurch Cl, SE20 182 DV94
Up Cor, Ch.St.G. HP8 90 AW47
Up Cor Cl, Ch.St.G. HP8 90 AV47
Upcroft, Wind. SL4 151 AP83
Upcroft Av, Edg. HA8 96 CQ50
Updale Cl, Pot.B. EN6 63 CY33
Updale Rd, Sid. DA14 185 ET91
Upfield, Croy. CR0 202 DV103
Horley RH6 268 DG149
Upfield Cl, Horl. RH6 268 DG150
Upfield Rd, W7 137 CF71
Upfolds Grn, Guil. GU4 243 BC130
Upgrove Manor Way, SW2
off Trinity Ri 181 DN87
Uphall Prim Sch, Ilf. IG1
off Uphall Rd 125 EP64
Uphall Rd, Ilf. IG1 125 EP64
Upham Pk Rd, W4 158 CS77
Uphavering Ho, Horn. RM12 127 FH61
Uphill Dr, NW7 96 CS50
NW9 118 CQ57
Uphill Gro, NW7 96 CS49
Uphill Rd, NW7 96 CS49
Upland Av, Chesh. HP5 54 AP28
Upland Ct Rd, Rom. RM3 106 FM54
Upland Dr, Brook.Pk AL9 64 DB25
Epsom KT18 233 CW118
Upland Ms, SE22 182 DU85
Upland Prim Sch, Bexh. DA7
off Church Rd 166 EZ83
Upland Rd, E13 291 M4
SE22 182 DU85
Bexleyheath DA7 166 EZ83
Caterham CR3 237 EB120
Epping CM16 69 ET25
South Croydon CR2 220 DR106
Sutton SM2 218 DD108
Uplands, Ashtd. KT21 231 CK120
Beckenham BR3 203 EA96
Croxley Green WD3 74 BM44
Ware SG12 33 DZ05
Welwyn Garden City AL8 29 CW05
Uplands, The, Brick.Wd AL2 60 BY30
Gerrards Cross SL9 112 AY60
Loughton IG10 85 EM41
Ruislip HA4 115 BU60
Uplands Av, E17
off Blackhorse La 101 DX54
Uplands Business Pk, E17 101 DX54
Uplands Cl, SE18 165 EP78
SW14 off Monroe Dr 178 CP85
Gerrards Cross SL9 112 AY60
Sevenoaks TN13 256 FF123
Uplands Dr, Oxshott KT22 215 CD113
Uplands End, Wdf.Grn. IG8 102 EL52
Uplands Pk Rd, Enf. EN2 81 DN41
Uplands Rd, N8 121 DM57
East Barnet EN4 98 DG46
Guildford GU1 243 BB134
Kenley CR8 236 DQ116
Orpington BR6 206 EV102
Romford RM6 126 EX55
Warley CM14 108 FY50
Woodford Green IG8 102 EL52
Uplands Way, N21 81 DN43
Sevenoaks TN13 256 FF123
Upland Way, Epsom KT18 233 CW118
UPMINSTER, RM14 128 FQ62
Upminster 128 FQ61
Upminster 128 FQ61
Upminster 128 FQ61
Upminster Bridge 128 FN61
Upminster Inf Sch,
Upmin. RM14 off St. Mary's La 128 FQ62
Upminster Jun Sch,
Upmin. RM14 off St. Mary's La 128 FQ62
Upminster Rd,
Horn. RM11, RM12 128 FM61
Upminster RM14 128 FM61
Upminster Rd N, Rain. RM13 148 FJ69
Upminster Rd S, Rain. RM13 147 FG70
Upminster Tithe Barn Ms
of Nostalgia, Upmin. RM14 128 FQ59
Upminster Trd Pk,
Upmin. RM14 129 FX59
Upney 145 ET66
Upney Cl, Horn. RM12
off Tylers Cres 128 FK64
Upney La, Bark. IG11 145 ES65
Upnor Way, SE17 299 P10
Uppark Dr, Ilf. IG2 125 EQ58
Upper Abbey Rd, Belv. DA17 166 EZ77
Upper Addison Gdns, W14 294 E4
Upper Ashlyns Rd, Berk. HP4 38 AV20
Upper Bk St, E14 302 C3
Upper Bardsey Wk, N1
off Bardsey Wk 277 K4
Upper Barn, Hem.H. HP3 40 BM23
Upper Belgrave St, SW1 297 H6
Upper Belmont Rd, Chesh. HP5 54 AP28
Upper Berenger Wk, SW10
off Blantyre St 308 A4
Upper Berkeley St, W1 284 E9
Upper Beulah Hill, SE19 202 DS95
Upper Blantyre Wk, SW10
off Blantyre St 308 A4
Upper Bourne End La,
Hem.H. HP1 57 BA25
Upper Bray Rd, Bray SL6 150 AC77
Upper Brentwood Rd,
Rom. RM2 128 FJ56
Upper Br Rd, Red. RH1 250 DE134
Upper Brighton Rd, Surb. KT6 197 CK100
Upper Brockley Rd, SE4 313 P8
Upper Brook St, W1 296 G1
Upper Butts, Brent. TW8 157 CJ79
Upper Caldy Wk, N1
off Clifton Rd 142 DQ65
Upper Camelford Wk, W11
off St. Marks Rd 139 CY72
Upper Cavendish Av, N3 120 DA55
Upper Cheyne Row, SW3 308 C3
Upper Ch Hill, Green. DA9 189 FS85
Upper Clabdens, Ware SG12 33 DZ05
UPPER CLAPTON, E5 122 DV60
Upper Clapton Rd, E5 122 DV60
Upper Clarendon Wk, W11
off Clarendon Wk 139 CY72
Upper Cornsland, Brwd. CM14 108 FX48
Upper Ct Rd, Epsom KT19 216 CQ111
Woldingham CR3 237 EA123
Upper Culver Rd, St.Alb. AL1 43 CE18
Upper Dagnall St, St.Alb. AL3 43 CD20
Upper Dartrey Wk, SW10
off Blantyre St 308 A4
Upper Dengie Wk, N1
off Popham Rd 142 DQ67
Upper Dr, Beac. HP9 89 AK50
Biggin Hill TN16 238 EJ118
Upper Dunnymans, Bans. SM7
off Basing Rd 217 CZ114
Upper Edgeborough Rd,
Guil. GU1 259 AZ135
UPPER EDMONTON, N18 100 DU51
UPPER ELMERS END,
Beck. BR3 203 DZ100
Upper Elmers End Rd,
Beck. BR3 203 DY98
Upper Fairfield Rd,
Lthd. KT22 231 CH121
Upper Fm Rd, W.Mol. KT8 196 BZ98
Upperfield Rd, Welw.G.C. AL7 29 CZ11
Upper Forecourt, Gat. RH6 269 DH152
Upper Fosters, NW4
off New Brent St 119 CW57
UPPER GATTON, Reig. RH2 250 DC127
Upper George St, Chesh. HP5
off Frances St 54 AQ30
Upper Gladstone Rd,
Chesh. HP5 54 AQ30
Upper Grn E, Mitch. CR4 200 DF97
Upper Grn Rd, Tewin AL6 30 DE05
Upper Grn W, Mitch. CR4
off London Rd 200 DF97
Upper Grosvenor St, W1 296 G1
Upper Grotto Rd, Twick. TW1 177 CF89
Upper Grd, SE1 298 E2
Upper Gro, SE25 202 DS98
Upper Gro Rd, Belv. DA17 166 EZ79
Upper Guild Hall, Bluewater
DA9 off Bluewater Shop Cen 189 FT87
Upper Guildown Rd,
Guil. GU2 258 AV137
Upper Gulland Wk, N1
off Nightingale Rd 277 K5
UPPER HALLIFORD,
Shep. TW17 195 BS97
Upper Halliford 195 BS96
Upper Halliford Bypass,
Shep. TW17 195 BS99
Upper Halliford Grn,
Shep. TW17 195 BS98
Upper Halliford Rd,
Shep. TW17 195 BS96
Upper Hall Pk, Berk. HP4 38 AX20
Upper Hampstead Wk, NW3
off New End 120 DC63
Upper Ham Rd, Kings.T. KT2 177 CK91
Richmond TW10 177 CK91
Upper Handa Wk, N1
off Handa Wk 277 K4
Upper Harestone, Cat. CR3 252 DU127
Upper Hawkwell Wk, N1
off Popham Rd 142 DQ67
Upper Heath Rd, St.Alb. AL1 43 CF18
Upper High St, Epsom KT17 216 CS113
Upper Highway, Abb.L. WD5 59 BR33
Kings Langley WD4 59 BQ32
Upper Hill Ri, Rick. WD3 74 BH44
Upper Hitch, Wat. WD19 94 BY46
UPPER HOLLOWAY, N19 121 DJ62
Upper Holloway 121 DK61
Upper Holly Hill Rd,
Belv. DA17 167 FB78
Upper Hook, Harl. CM18 51 ET17
Upper James St, W1 285 M10
Upper John St, W1 285 M10
Upper Lattimore Rd,
St.Alb. AL1 43 CE20
Upper Lees Rd, Slou. SL2 131 AP69
Upper Lismore Wk, N1
off Mull Wk 277 K5
Upper Lo Way, Couls. CR5
off Netherne Dr 235 DK122
Upper Mall, W6 159 CU78
Upper Manor Rd, Gdmg. GU7 258 AS144
Upper Marlborough Rd,
St.Alb. AL1 43 CE20
Upper Marsh, SE1 298 D6
Upper Marsh La, Hodd. EN11 49 EA18
Upper Meadow, Chesh. HP5
off Stanley Av 54 AP30
Gerrards Cross SL9 112 AW60
Upper Mealines, Harl. CM18 52 EU18
Upper Montagu St, W1 284 E6
Upper Mulgrave Rd,
Sutt. SM2 217 CY108
Upper N St, E14 290 B10
UPPER NORWOOD, SE19 182 DR94
Upper Paddock Rd, Wat. WD19 76 BY44
Upper Palace Rd, E.Mol. KT8 196 CC97
Upper Pk, Harl. CM20 35 EP14
Loughton IG10 84 EK42
Upper Pk Rd, N11 99 DH50
NW3 274 E4
Belvedere DA17 167 FB77
Bromley BR1 184 EH95
Kingston upon Thames KT2 178 CN93
Upper Phillimore Gdns, W8 295 J5
Upper Pillory Down,
Cars. SM5 218 DG113
Upper Pines, Bans. SM7 234 DF117
Upper Rainham Rd,
Horn. RM12 127 FF63
Upper Ramsey Wk, N1
off Ramsey Wk 277 L5
Upper Rawreth Wk, N1
off Popham Rd 142 DQ67
Upper Richmond Rd, SW15 159 CY84
Upper Richmond Rd W, SW14 158 CP84
Richmond TW10 158 CN84
Upper Riding, Beac. HP9 88 AG54

Upper Rd, E13 291 N2
Denham UB9 113 BD59
Wallington SM6 219 DK106
Upper Rose Gall, Bluewater DA9 *off Bluewater Shop Cen* 189 FU87
Upper Rose Hill, Dor. RH4 263 CH137
Upper Ryle, Brwd. CM14 108 FV45
Upper St. Martin's La, WC2 286 A10
Upper Sales, Hem.H. HP1 39 BF21
Upper Sawley Wd, Bans. SM7 217 CZ114
Upper Selsdon Rd, S.Croy. CR2 220 DT108
Upper Sheridan Rd, Belv. DA17 *off Coleman Rd* 166 FA77
Upper Shirley Rd, Croy. CR0 202 DW103
Upper Shot, Welw.G.C. AL7 30 DA08
Upper Shott, Chsht EN7 66 DT26
Upper Sq, Islw. TW7 157 CG83
Upper Sta Rd, Rad. WD7 77 CG35
Upper Stoneyfield, Harl. CM19 51 EP15
Upper St, N1 276 F10
Shere GU5 260 BM138
Upper Sunbury Rd, Hmptn. TW12 196 BY95
Upper Sutton La, Houns. TW5 156 CA80
Upper Swaines, Epp. CM16 69 ET30
UPPER SYDENHAM, SE26 182 DU91
Upper Tachbrook St, SW1 297 L8
Upper Tail, Wat. WD19 94 BY48
Upper Talbot Wk, W11 *off Talbot Wk* 139 CY72
Upper Teddington Rd, Kings.T. KT1 197 CJ95
Upper Ter, NW3 120 DC62
Upper Thames St, EC4 287 H10
Upper Thames Wk, Bluewater DA9 *off Bluewater Shop Cen* 189 FT88
Upper Tollington Pk, N4 121 DN60
Upperton Rd, Guil. GU2 258 AW136
Sidcup DA14 185 ET92
Upperton Rd E, E13 292 D2
Upperton Rd W, E13 292 C3
UPPER TOOTING, SW17 180 DE90
Upper Tooting Pk, SW17 180 DF89
Upper Tooting Rd, SW17 180 DF91
Upper Town Rd, Grnf. UB6 136 CB70
Upper Tulse Hill, SW2 181 DM87
Upper Vernon Rd, Sutt. SM1 218 DD106
Upper Wk, Vir.W. GU25 192 AY98
UPPER WALTHAMSTOW, E17 123 EB56
Upper Walthamstow Rd, E17 123 ED56
Upper Warlingham 236 DU118
Upper W St, Reig. RH2 249 CZ134
Upper Whistler Wk, SW10 *off Blantyre St* 307 P4
Upper Wickham La, Well. DA16 166 EV80
Upper Wimpole St, W1 285 J6
Upper Woburn Pl, WC1 285 P3
Upper Woodcote Village, Pur. CR8 219 DK112
Uppingham Av, Stan. HA7 95 CH53
Upsdell Av, N13 99 DN51
UPSHIRE, Wal.Abb. EN9 68 EJ32
Upshirebury Grn, Wal.Abb. EN9 *off Horseshoe Hill* 68 EK33
Upshire Prim Foundation Sch, Wal.Abb. EN9 *off Upshire Rd* 68 EH33
Upshire Rd, Wal.Abb. EN9 68 EF32
Upshot La, Wok. GU22 227 BF117
Upstall St, SE5 311 H7
UPTON, E7 144 EH66
Slou. SL1 152 AU76
Upton, Wok. GU21 226 AV117
Upton Av, E7 281 P6
St. Albans AL3 43 CD19
Upton Cl, NW2 119 CY62
Bexley DA5 186 EZ86
Park Street AL2 61 CD25
Slough SL1 152 AT76
Upton Ct, SE20 *off Blean Gro* 182 DW94
Upton Ct Rd, Slou. SL3 152 AU76
Upton Cross Prim Sch, E13 *off Churston Av* 144 EH67
Upton Dene, Sutt. SM2 218 DB108
Upton Gdns, Har. HA3 117 CH57
Upton Hosp, Slou. SL1 152 AT76
Upton Ho Sch, Wind. SL4 *off St. Leonards Rd* 151 AQ82
Upton La, E7 281 P8
Upton Lo Cl, Bushey WD23 94 CC45
UPTON PARK, E6 144 EJ67
Slou. SL1 152 AT76
Upton Park 144 EH67
Upton Pk, Slou. SL1 152 AT76
Upton Pk Rd, E7 144 EH66
Upton Prim Sch, Bexh. DA6 *off Upton Rd* 186 EZ85
Upton Rd, N18 100 DU50
SE18 165 EQ79
Bexley DA5 186 EZ86
Bexleyheath DA6 166 EY84
Hounslow TW3 156 CA83
Slough SL1 152 AU76
Thornton Heath CR7 202 DR96
Watford WD18 75 BV42
Upton Rd S, Bex. DA5 186 EZ86
Upway, N12 98 DE52
Chalfont St. Peter SL9 91 AZ53
Upwood Rd, SE12 184 EF86
SW16 201 DL95
Uranus Rd, Hem.H. HP2 40 BM18
Urban Av, Horn. RM12 128 FJ62
Urban Ms, N4 121 DP59
Urdang Acad, The, EC1 286 F3
Urlwin St, SE5 311 J3
Urlwin Wk, SW9 310 F7
Urmston Dr, SW19 179 CY88
Urnfield Cl, Guil. GU1 243 BB134
Ursula Gould Way, E14 290 B7
Ursula Ms, N4 121 DP60
Ursula St, SW11 308 C7
Ursuline Conv Prep Sch, SW20 *off The Downs* 179 CX94
Ursuline High Sch, SW20 *off Crescent Rd* 199 CX95
Urswick Gdns, Dag. RM9 146 EY66
Urswick Rd, E9 278 G2
Dagenham RM9 146 EX66
Urswick Sch, The, E9 278 G5
Usborne Ms, SW8 310 C4
Usher Rd, E3 279 P10
Usherwood Cl, Box H. KT20 248 CP131
Usk Rd, SW11 160 DC84
Aveley RM15 148 FQ72
Usk St, E2 289 J2
Utah Bldg, SE13 *off Deals Gateway* 314 C6
Utopia Village, NW1 274 G8
Uvedale Cl, New Adgtn CR0 *off Uvedale Cres* 221 ED111
Uvedale Cres, New Adgtn CR0 221 ED111
Uvedale Rd, Dag. RM10 126 FA62
Enfield EN2 82 DR43
Oxted RH8 254 EF129
Uverdale Rd, SW10 307 P5
UXBRIDGE, UB8 - UB11 134 BK66
Uxbridge 134 BK66
Uxbridge Business Pk, Uxb. UB8 114 BJ64
Uxbridge Coll, Hayes Comm Campus, Hayes UB3 *off Coldharbour La* 135 BU73
Uxbridge Campus, Uxb. UB8 *off Park Rd* 134 BL65
Uxbridge High Sch, Uxb. UB8 *off The Greenway* 134 BK68
UXBRIDGE MOOR, Iver SL0 134 BG67
Uxb. UB8 134 BG67
Uxbridge Rd, W3 138 CL73
W5 137 CJ73
W5 (Ealing Com.) 138 CL73
W7 137 CE74
W12 294 B4
W13 137 CH74
Feltham TW13 176 BW89
Hampton TW12 176 CA91
Harrow HA3 94 CC52
Hayes UB4 136 BW73
Iver SL0 132 AY71
Kingston upon Thames KT1 197 CK98
Pinner HA5 94 CB52
Rickmansworth WD3 91 BF47
Slough SL1, SL2, SL3 152 AU75
Southall UB1 136 CA74
Stanmore HA7 95 CF51
Uxbridge UB10 134 BN69
Uxbridge St, W8 295 J2
Uxendon Cres, Wem. HA9 118 CL60
Uxendon Hill, Wem. HA9 118 CM60
Uxendon Manor Prim Sch, Kenton HA3 *off Vista Way* 118 CL57

V

Vache La, Ch.St.G. HP8 90 AW47
Vache Ms, Ch.St.G. HP8 90 AX46
Vaillant Rd, Wey. KT13 213 BQ105
Valance Av, E4 102 EF46
Valan Leas, Brom. BR2 204 EE97
Vale, The, N10 98 DG53
N14 99 DK45
NW11 119 CX62
SW3 308 A2
W3 138 CR74
Brentwood CM14 108 FW46
Chalfont St. Peter SL9 90 AX53
Coulsdon CR5 219 DK114
Croydon CR0 203 DX103
Feltham TW14 175 BV86
Hounslow TW5 156 BY79
Ruislip HA4 116 BW63
Sunbury-on-Thames TW16 175 BU93
Woodford Green IG8 102 EG52
Vale Av, Borwd. WD6 78 CP43
Vale Border, Croy. CR0 221 DX111
Vale Cl, N2 120 DF55
W9 283 N3
Chalfont St. Peter SL9 90 AX53
Epsom KT18 232 CS119
Orpington BR6 223 EN105
Pilgrim's Hatch CM15 108 FT43
Weybridge KT13 195 BR104
Woking GU21 226 AY116
Vale Cotts, SW15 178 CS90
Vale Ct, W9 *off The Vale* 139 CT74
W9 283 N3
Weybridge KT13 195 BR104
Vale Cres, SW15 178 CS90
Vale Cft, Clay. KT10 215 CE109
Pinner HA5 116 BY57
Vale Dr, Barn. EN5 79 CZ42
Vale End, SE22 *off Grove Vale* 162 DS84
Vale Fm Rd, Wok. GU21 226 AX117
Vale Gro, N4 122 DQ59
W3 *off The Vale* 138 CR74
Slough SL1 152 AS76
Vale Ind Est, Wat. WD18 93 BP46
Vale Ind Pk, SW16 201 DJ95
Vale La, W3 138 CN71
Valence Av, Dag. RM8 126 EX62
Valence Circ, Dag. RM8 126 EX62
Valence Dr, Chsht EN7 66 DU28
Valence Ho Mus, Dag. RM8 126 EX62
Valence Inf & Jun Schs, Dag. RM8 *off Bonham Rd* 126 EX61
Valence Rd, Erith DA8 167 FD80
Valence Sch, West. TN16 *off Westerham Rd* 255 ET126
Valence Wd Rd, Dag. RM8 126 EX62
Valencia Rd, Stan. HA7 95 CJ49
Valency Cl, Nthwd. HA6 93 BT49
Valentia Pl, SW9 *off Brixton Sta Rd* 161 DN84
Valentine Av, Bex. DA5 186 EY89
Valentine Ct, SE23 183 DX89
Valentine Ho, E3 *off Garrison Rd* 279 P9
Valentine Pl, SE1 298 G4
Valentine Rd, E9 279 J5
Harrow HA2 116 CC62
Valentine Row, SE1 298 G5
Valentines High Sch, Ilf. IG2 *off Cranbrook Rd* 125 EN58
Valentines Rd, Ilf. IG1 125 EP60
Valentines Way, Rom. RM7 127 FE61
Valentine Way, Ch.St.G. HP8 90 AX48
Valentyne Cl, New Adgtn CR0 222 EE111
Vale of Health, NW3 120 DD62
Vale Par, SW15 *off Kingston Vale* 178 CS90
Vale Prim Sch, The, Epsom KT18 *off Beaconsfield Rd* 232 CS119
Valerian Wk, N11 *off Nurserymans Rd* 98 DG47
Valerian Way, E15 291 K3
Valerie Cl, St.Alb. AL1 43 CH20
Valerie Ct, Bushey WD23 94 CC45
Sutton SM2 *off Stanley Rd* 218 DB108
Vale Ri, NW11 119 CZ60
Chesham HP5 54 AQ28
Vale Rd, E7 144 EH65
N4 122 DQ59
Bromley BR1 205 EN96
Vale Rd, Bushey WD23 76 BY43
Chesham HP5 54 AQ27
Claygate KT10 215 CE109
Dartford DA1 187 FH88
Epsom KT19 217 CT105
Mitcham CR4 201 DK97
Northfleet DA11 190 GD87
Sutton SM1 218 DB105
Weybridge KT13 195 BR104
Windsor SL4 151 AM80
Worcester Park KT4 217 CT105
Vale Rd N, Surb. KT6 198 CL103
Vale Rd S, Surb. KT6 198 CL103
Vale Row, N5 *off Gillespie Rd* 121 DP62
Vale Royal, N7 276 A7
Valery Pl, Hmptn. TW12 176 CA94
Vale Sch, The, SW7 295 N7
Valeside, Hert. SG14 31 DN10
Vale St, SE27 182 DR90
Valeswood Rd, Brom. BR1 184 EF92
Vale Ter, N4 122 DQ58
Valetta Gro, E13 281 N10
Valetta Rd, W3 158 CS75
Valette St, E9 278 F4
Valiant Cl, Nthlt. UB5 *off Ruislip Rd* 136 BX69
Romford RM7 104 FA54
Valiant Ho, SE7 304 D10
Valiant Path, NW9 96 CS53
Valiant Way, E6 293 J7
Vallance Rd, E1 288 D3
E2 288 D3
N22 99 DJ54
Vallentin Rd, E17 123 EC56
Valley, The, Guil. GU2 *off Portsmouth Rd* 258 AW138
Valley Av, N12 98 DD49
Valley Cl, Dart. DA1 187 FF86
Hertford SG13 32 DR10
Loughton IG10 85 EM44
Pinner HA5 93 BV54
Waltham Abbey EN9 67 EC32
Ware SG12 32 DV05
Valley Ct, Cat. CR3 *off Beechwood Gdns* 236 DU122
Kenley CR8 *off Hayes La* 220 DQ114
Valley Dr, NW9 118 CN58
Gravesend DA12 191 GK91
Sevenoaks TN13 257 FH125
Valleyfield Rd, SW16 181 DM92
Valley Flds Cres, Enf. EN2 81 DN40
Valley Gdns, SW19 180 DD94
Greenhithe DA9 189 FV86
Wembley HA0 138 CM66
Valley Gdns, The, Egh. TW20 192 AS96
Valley Grn, The, Welw.G.C. AL8 29 CW08
Valley Gro, SE7 304 D10
Valley Hill, Loug. IG10 102 EL45
Valley Ind Pk, Kings L. WD4 59 BP28
Valleylink Est, Enf. EN3 *off Meridian Way* 83 DY44
Valley Ms, Twick. TW1 *off Cross Deep* 177 CG89
Valley Pt Ind Est, Croy. CR0 201 DL101
Valley Prim Sch, Brom. BR2 *off Beckenham La* 204 EF96
Valley Ri, Wat. WD25 59 BV33
Valley Rd, SW16 181 DM91
Belvedere DA17 167 FB77
Bromley BR2 204 EE96
Dartford DA1 187 FF86
Erith DA8 167 FD77
Fawkham Green DA3 209 FV102
Kenley CR8 236 DR115
Northchurch HP4 38 AT17
Orpington BR5 206 EV95
Rickmansworth WD3 74 BG43
St. Albans AL3 43 CE15
Uxbridge UB10 134 BL68
Welwyn Garden City AL8 29 CV10
Valley Side, E4 101 EA47
Valleyside, Hem.H. HP1 39 BF20
Valley Side Par, E4 *off Valley Side* 101 EA47
Valley Vw, Barn. EN5 79 CY44
Biggin Hill TN16 238 EJ118
Chesham HP5 54 AN29
Goffs Oak EN7 66 DQ28
Greenhithe DA9 189 FV86
Valley Vw Gdns, Ken. CR8 236 DS115
Valley Wk, Crox.Grn WD3 75 BQ43
Croydon CR0 202 DW103
Valley Way, Ger.Cr. SL9 112 AW58
Valliere Rd, NW10 139 CV69
Valliers Wd Rd, Sid. DA15 185 ER88
Vallings Pl, Surb. KT6 197 CH101
Vallis Way, W13 137 CG71
Chessington KT9 215 CK105
Valmar Rd, SE5 311 K7
Valmar Trd Est, SE5 311 K7
Val McKenzie Av, N7 *off Parkside Cres* 121 DN62
Valnay St, SW17 180 DF92
Valognes Av, E17 101 DY53
Valonia Gdns, SW18 179 CZ86
Vambery Rd, SE18 165 EQ79
Vanbrough Cres, Nthlt. UB5 136 BW67
Vanbrugh Cl, E16 292 E7
Vanbrugh Dr, Walt. KT12 196 BW101
Vanbrugh Flds, SE3 315 L3
Vanbrugh Hill, SE3 315 L2
SE10 315 K1
Vanbrugh Pk, SE3 315 L5
Vanbrugh Pk Rd, SE3 315 M4
Vanbrugh Pk Rd W, SE3 315 L4
Vanbrugh Rd, W4 158 CR76
Vanbrugh Ter, SE3 315 M6
Vanburgh Cl, Orp. BR6 205 ES102
Vancouver Cl, Epsom KT19 216 CQ111
Orpington BR6 224 EU105
Vancouver Ct, Smallfield RH6 269 DN148
Vancouver Rd, SE23 183 DY89
Broxbourne EN10 67 DY25
Edgware HA8 96 CP53
Hayes UB4 135 BV70
Richmond TW10 177 CJ91
Vanda Cres, St.Alb. AL1 43 CF21
Vanderbilt Rd, SW18 180 DB88
Vanderville Gdns, N2 98 DC54
Vandome Cl, E16 292 A9
Vandon Pas, SW1 297 M6
Vandon St, SW1 297 M6
Van Dyck Av, N.Mal. KT3 198 CR101
Vandyke Cl, SW15 179 CX87
Redhill RH1 250 DF131
Vandyke Cross, SE9 184 EL85
Vandy St, EC2 287 N5
Vane Cl, NW3 274 A1
Harrow HA3 118 CM58
Vanessa Cl, Belv. DA17 166 FA78
Vanessa Wk, Grav. DA12 191 GM92
Vanessa Way, Bex. DA5 187 FD90
Vane St, SW1 297 M8
Van Gogh Cl, Islw. TW7 *off Twickenham Rd* 157 CG83
Van Gogh Wk, SW9 310 D6
Vanguard Cl, E16 291 P7
Croydon CR0 201 DP102
Romford RM7 105 FB54
Vanguard Ho, E8 278 F6
Vanguard St, SE8 314 A6
Vanguard Way, Cat. CR3 237 EB121
Wallington SM6 219 DL108
Warlingham CR6 237 EB121
Vanneck Sq, SW15 179 CU85
Vanner Pt, E9 279 J5
Vanners Par, Byfleet KT14 *off Brewery La* 212 BL113
Vanoc Gdns, Brom. BR1 184 EG91
Vanquish Cl, Twick. TW2 176 CA87
Vanquisher Wk, Grav. DA12 191 GM90
Vansittart Est, Wind. SL4 151 AQ81
Vansittart Rd, E7 281 M1
Windsor SL4 151 AP80
Vansittart St, SE14 313 M4
Vanston Pl, SW6 307 J4
Vantage Bldg, Hayes UB3 *off Station Rd* 155 BT75
Vantage Ms, E14 302 F3
Northwood HA6 93 BR51
Vantage Pl, W8 295 K7
Feltham TW14 175 BU86
Vantage Pt, S.Croy. CR2 220 DR109
Vantage Rd, Slou. SL1 131 AP74
Vantorts Cl, Saw. CM21 36 EY05
Vantorts Rd, Saw. CM21 36 EY06
Vant Rd, SW17 180 DF92
Varcoe Gdns, Hayes UB3 135 BR72
Varcoe Rd, SE16 312 F1
Vardens Rd, SW11 160 DD84
Varden St, E1 288 E8
Vardon Cl, W3 138 CR72
Varley Dr, Twick. TW1 157 CH84
Varley Par, NW9 118 CS56
Varley Rd, E16 292 B8
Varley Way, Mitch. CR4 200 DD96
Varna Rd, SW6 306 F4
Hampton TW12 196 CB95
Varndell St, NW1 285 L2
Varnell Cl, Chsht EN7 66 DU27
Hemel Hempstead HP1 39 BF20
Varney Rd, Hem.H. HP1 39 BF20
Varnishers Yd, N1 286 B1
Varsity Dr, Twick. TW1 177 CE85
Varsity Row, SW14 158 CQ82
Vartry Rd, N15 122 DR58
Vassall Rd, SW9 310 E5
Vauban Est, SE16 300 B7
Vauban St, SE16 300 B7
Vaughan Av, NW4 119 CU57
W6 159 CT77
Hornchurch RM12 128 FK63
Vaughan Cl, Dart. DA1 188 FK87
Hampton TW12 *off Oak Av* 176 BY93
Vaughan Ct, Guil. GU2 *off Railton Rd* 242 AV130
Vaughan Gdns, Eton Wick SL4 *off Moores La* 151 AM77
Ilford IG1 125 EM59
Vaughan Prim Sch, Har. HA1 *off Vaughan Rd* 116 CC58
Vaughan Rd, E15 281 L5
SE5 311 J9
Harrow HA1 116 CC59
Thames Ditton KT7 197 CH101
Welling DA16 165 ET82
Vaughan St, SE16 301 N5
Vaughan Way, E1 300 C1
Dorking RH4 263 CG136
Slough SL2 131 AL70
Vaughan Williams Cl, SE8 314 A5
Vaughan Williams Way, Warley CM14 107 FU51
Vaux Cres, Hersham KT12 213 BV107
VAUXHALL, SE11 310 B1
Vauxhall 310 B2
Vauxhall 310 B2
Vauxhall Br, SE1 310 A1
SW1 310 A1
Vauxhall Br Rd, SW1 297 M8
Vauxhall Cl, Nthflt DA11 191 GF87
Vauxhall Gdns, S.Croy. CR2 220 DQ107
Vauxhall Gdns Est, SE11 310 C1
Vauxhall Gro, SW8 310 C2
Vauxhall Pl, Dart. DA1 188 FL87
Vauxhall Prim Sch, SE11 298 D10
Vauxhall Rd, Hem.H. HP2 40 BN20
Vauxhall St, SE11 298 D10
Vauxhall Wk, SE11 298 C10
Vawdrey Cl, E1 288 G5
Veals Mead, Mitch. CR4 200 DE95
Vectis Gdns, SW17 *off Vectis Rd* 181 DH93
Vectis Rd, SW17 181 DH93
Veda Rd, SE13 163 EA84
Vega Cres, Nthwd. HA6 93 BT50
Vegal Cres, Eng.Grn TW20 172 AW92
Vega Rd, Bushey WD23 94 CC45
Veitch Cl, Felt. TW14 175 BT88
Veldene Way, Har. HA2 116 BZ62
Velde Way, SE22 *off East Dulwich Gro* 182 DS85
Velizy Av, Harl. CM20 51 ER15
Vellacott Cl, Purf. RM19 169 FR79
Vellacott Ho, W12 139 CV72
Velletri Ho, E2 289 J1
Vellum Dr, Cars. SM5 200 DG104
Velocity Way, Enf. EN3 83 DZ36
Venables Cl, Dag. RM10 127 FB63
Venables St, NW8 284 B5
Vencourt Pl, W6 159 CU78
Venetian Rd, SE5 311 K9
Venetia Rd, N4 121 DP58
W5 157 CK75
Venette Cl, Rain. RM13 147 FH71
Venice Av, Wat. WD18 75 BS42
Venice Wk, W2 283 P6
Venner Cl, Red. RH1 250 DG133
Venner Rd, SE26 182 DW93
Venners Cl, Bexh. DA7 167 FE82
Venn St, SW4 161 DJ84
Ventnor Av, Stan. HA7 95 CH53
Ventnor Dr, N20 98 DB48
Ventnor Gdns, Bark. IG11 145 ES65
Ventnor Rd, SE14 313 K5
Sutton SM2 218 DB108
Venton Cl, Wok. GU21 226 AV117
Ventura Pk, Coln.St AL2 61 CF29
Venture Cl, Bex. DA5 186 EY87
Venture Ct, Grav. DA12 191 GK86
Venue St, E14 290 E6
Venus Cl, Slou. SL2 131 AM70
Venus Hill, Bov. HP3 57 BA31
Venus Ho, E3 *off Garrison Rd* 280 A9
E14 *off Crews St* 302 A8
Venus Ms, Mitch. CR4 200 DE97
Venus Rd, SE18 305 J7
Veny Cres, Horn. RM12 128 FK64
Vera Av, N21 81 DN43
Vera Ct, Wat. WD19 94 BX45
Vera Lynn Cl, E7 281 P1
Vera Rd, SW6 306 F7
Verbena Cl, E16 291 L4
South Ockendon RM15 149 FW72
West Drayton UB7 *off Magnolia St* 154 BK78
Verbena Gdns, W6 159 CU78
Verdant La, SE6 184 EE88
Verdayne Av, Croy. CR0 203 DX102
Verdayne Gdns, Warl. CR6 236 DW116
Verderers Rd, Chig. IG7 104 EU50
Verdi Cres, W10 282 F1
Verdun Rd, SE18 166 EU79
SW13 159 CU79
Verdure Cl, Wat. WD25 60 BY32
Vereker Dr, Sun. TW16 195 BU97
Vereker Rd, W14 306 F1
Vere Rd, Loug. IG10 85 EQ42
Vere St, W1 285 J9
Veridion Way, Erith DA18 166 EZ75
Verity Cl, W11 282 E9
Veritys, Hat. AL10 45 CU18
Vermeer Gdns, SE15 *off Elland Rd* 162 DW84
Vermont Cl, Enf. EN2 81 DP42
Vermont Rd, SE19 182 DR93
SW18 180 DB86
Slough SL2 131 AM70
Sutton SM1 200 DB104
Verney Cl, Berk. HP4 38 AT18
Verney Gdns, Dag. RM9 126 EY63
Verney Rd, SE16 312 D2
Dagenham RM9 126 EY64
Slough SL3 153 BA77
Verney St, NW10 118 CR62
Verney Way, SE16 312 E1
Vernham Rd, SE18 165 EQ79
Vernon Av, E12 125 EM63
SW20 199 CX96
Enfield EN3 83 DY36
Woodford Green IG8 102 EH52
Vernon Cl, Epsom KT19 216 CQ107
Orpington BR5 206 EV97
Ottershaw KT16 211 BD107
St. Albans AL1 43 CE21
Staines-upon-Thames TW19 174 BL88
Vernon Ct, Stan. HA7 *off Vernon Dr* 95 CH53
Vernon Cres, Barn. EN4 80 DG44
Brentwood CM13 109 GA48
Vernon Dr, Cat. CR3 236 DQ122
Harefield UB9 92 BJ53
Stanmore HA7 95 CG53
Vernon Ms, E17 *off Vernon Rd* 123 DZ56
W14 294 F9
Vernon Pl, WC1 286 B7
Vernon Ri, WC1 286 D2
Greenford UB6 117 CD64
Vernon Rd, E3 279 P10
E11 124 EE60
E15 281 K6
E17 123 DZ57
N8 121 DN55
SW14 158 CR83
Bushey WD23 76 BY43
Feltham TW13 175 BT89
Ilford IG3 125 ET60
Romford RM5 105 FC50
Sutton SM1 218 DC106
Swanscombe DA10 190 FZ86
Vernon Sq, WC1 286 D2
Vernon St, W14 294 E9
Vernon Wk, Tad. KT20 233 CX120
Vernon Way, Guil. GU2 242 AT133
Vernon Yd, W11 282 G10
Vern Pl, Tats. TN16 *off Ship Hill* 238 EJ121
Veroan Rd, Bexh. DA7 166 EY82
Verona Cl, Uxb. UB8 134 BJ72
Verona Ct, W4 *off Chiswick La* 158 CS78
Verona Dr, Surb. KT6 198 CL103
Verona Gdns, Grav. DA12 191 GL91
Verona Rd, E7 281 P6
Veronica Cl, Rom. RM3 106 FJ52
Veronica Gdns, SW16 201 DJ95
Veronica Rd, SW17 181 DH90
Veronique Gdns, Ilf. IG6 125 EP57
Verralls, Wok. GU22 227 BB117
Verran Rd, SW12 181 DH87
Ver Rd, St.Alb. AL3 42 CC20
Versailles Rd, SE20 182 DU94
Verulam Av, E17 123 DZ58
Purley CR8 219 DJ112
Verulam Bldgs, WC1 286 D6
Verulam Cl, Welw.G.C. AL7 29 CZ09
Verulam Ct, NW9 119 CU59
Verulam Ho, W6 *off Hammersmith Gro* 294 A5
Verulam Ind Est, St.Alb. AL1 43 CF22
Verulamium Mus & Pk, St.Alb. AL3 42 CB20
Verulam Pas, Wat. WD17 75 BV40
Verulam Rd, Grnf. UB6 136 CA70
St. Albans AL3 42 CB19
Verulam Sch, St.Alb. AL1 *off Brampton Rd* 43 CG19
Verulam St, WC1 286 E6
Verwood Dr, Barn. EN4 80 DF41
Verwood Lo, E14 *off Manchester Rd* 302 F8
Verwood Rd, Har. HA2 94 CC54
Veryan, Wok. GU21 226 AU117
Veryan Cl, Orp. BR5 206 EW98
Vesage Ct, EC1 286 F7
Vesey Path, E14 290 D9
Vespan Rd, W12 159 CU75
Vesta Av, St.Alb. AL1 42 CC23
Vesta Ct, SE1 *off Morocco St* 299 N5

Vesta Ho, E3 off Garrison Rd 280 A9
Vesta Rd, SE4 313 L9
Hemel Hempstead HP2
off Saturn Way 40 BM18
Vestris Rd, SE23 183 DX89
Vestry Ms, SE5 311 N7
Vestry Rd, E17 123 EB56
SE5 311 N7
Vestry St, N1 287 L2
Vevers Rd, Reig. RH2 266 DB137
Vevey St, SE6 183 DZ89
Vexil Cl, Purf. RM19 169 FR77
Veysey Cl, Hem.H. HP1
off Halwick Cl 40 BH22
Veysey Gdns, Dag. RM10 126 FA62
Viaduct Pl, E2 288 E3
Viaduct Rd, Ware SG12 33 DY06
Viaduct St, E2 288 E3
Viaduct Way, Welw.G.C. AL7 29 CZ06
Vian Av, Enf. EN3 83 DY35
Vian St, SE13 314 D10
Vibart Gdns, SW2 181 DM87
Vibart Wk, N1 276 B8
Vibia Cl, Stanw. TW19 174 BK87
Vicarage Av, SE3 315 P5
Egham TW20 173 BB93
Vicarage Causeway,
Hert.Hth SG13 32 DV11
Vicarage Cl, Bkhm KT23 246 CA125
Brentwood CM14 108 FS49
Erith DA8 167 FC79
Hemel Hempstead HP1 40 BJ22
Kingswood KT20 233 CY124
Northaw EN6 64 DF30
Northolt UB5 136 BZ66
Potters Bar EN6 63 CY32
Ruislip HA4 115 BR59
St. Albans AL1 42 CC23
Seer Green HP9 89 AQ52
Worcester Park KT4 198 CS102
Vicarage Ct, W8
off Vicarage Gate 295 L4
Egham TW20 173 BB93
Feltham TW14 175 BQ87
Vicarage Cres, SW11 308 A7
Egham TW20 173 BB92
Vicarage Dr, SW14 178 CR85
Barking IG11 145 EQ66
Beckenham BR3 203 EA95
Bray SL6 150 AC75
Northfleet DA11 190 GC86
Vicarage Fm Rd,
Houns. TW3, TW5 156 BY82
Vicarage Flds, Walt. KT12 196 BW100
Vicarage Fld Shop Cen,
Bark. IG11 145 EQ66
Vicarage Gdns, SW14
off Vicarage Rd 178 CQ85
W8 295 K3
Mitcham CR4 200 DE97
Potten End HP4 39 BB16
Vicarage Gate, W8 295 L4
Guildford GU2 258 AU136
Vicarage Gate Ms, Tad. KT20 233 CY124
Vicarage Gro, SE5 311 M6
Vicarage Hill, West. TN16 255 ER126
Vicarage La, E6 293 K2
E15 281 K8
Bovingdon HP3 57 BB26
Chigwell IG7 103 EQ47
Dunton Green TN13
off London Rd 241 FD119
Epsom KT17 217 CU109
Horley RH6 268 DF147
Ilford IG1 125 ER60
Kings Langley WD4 58 BM29
Laleham TW18 194 BH97
Leatherhead KT22 231 CH122
North Weald Bassett CM16 52 FA24
Send GU23 243 BC126
Wraysbury TW19 172 AY88
Vicarage Par, N15
off West Grn Rd 122 DQ56
Vicarage Pk, SE18 165 EQ78
Vicarage Path, N8 121 DL59
Vicarage Pl, Slou. SL1 152 AU76
Sch Vicarage Prim Sch, E6 293 K2
Vicarage Rd, E10 123 EB60
E15 281 L6
N17 100 DU52
NW4 119 CU58
SE18 165 EQ78
SW14 178 CQ85
Bexley DA5 187 FB88
Coopersale CM16 70 EW29
Croydon CR0 201 DN104
Dagenham RM10 147 FB65
Egham TW20 173 BB93
Hampton Wick KT1 197 CJ95
Hornchurch RM12 127 FG60
Kingston upon Thames KT1 197 CK96
Potten End HP4 39 BA16
Staines-upon-Thames TW18 173 BE91
Sunbury-on-Thames TW16 175 BT92
Sutton SM1 218 DB105
Teddington TW11 177 CG92
Twickenham TW2 177 CE89
Ware SG12 33 DY06
Watford WD18 75 BU44
Whitton TW2 176 CC86
Woking GU22 227 AZ121
Woodford Green IG8 102 EL52
Vicarage Sq, Grays RM17 170 GA79
Vicarage Wk, SW11 308 A7
Reigate RH2 off Chartway 250 DB134
Vicarage Way, NW10 118 CR62
Colnbrook SL3 153 BC80
Gerrards Cross SL9 113 AZ58
Harrow HA2 116 CA59
Vicarage Wd, Harl. CM20 36 EU14
Vicars Br Cl, Wem. HA0 138 CL68
Vicars Cl, E9 278 G9
E15 281 N8
Enfield EN1 82 DS40
Sch Vicar's Grn Prim Sch,
Wem. HA0 off Lily Gdns 137 CJ68
Vicars Hill, SE13 163 EB84
Vicars Moor La, N21 99 DN45
Vicars Oak Rd, SE19 182 DS93
Vicars Rd, NW5 274 G2
Vicars Wk, Dag. RM8 126 EV62
Viceroy Cl, N2 120 DE55
Viceroy Ct, NW8 274 D10
Croy. CR0 off Dingwall Rd 202 DR102
Viceroy Par, N2
off High Rd 120 DE56
Viceroy Rd, SW8 310 A6
Vickers Cl, Wall. SM6 219 DM108
Vickers Dr N, Wey. KT13 212 BL110
Vickers Dr S, Wey. KT13 212 BL111
Vickers Rd, Erith DA8 167 FD78
Vickers Way, Houns. TW4 176 BY85
Vickery's Wf, E14 290 A8
Victor Cl, Horn. RM12 128 FK60
Victor Ct, Horn. RM12 128 FK60
Rainham RM13
off Askwith Rd 147 FD68
Victor Gdns, Horn. RM12 128 FK60
Victor Gro, Wem. HA0 138 CL66
⇌ Victoria 297 K8
⊖ Victoria 297 K8
★ Victoria & Albert Mus, SW7 296 B7
Victoria Arc, SW1
off Terminus Pl 297 K7
Victoria Av, E6 144 EK67
EC2 287 P7
N3 97 CZ53
Barnet EN4 80 DD42
Gravesend DA12
off Sheppy Pl 191 GH87
Grays RM16 170 GC75
Hounslow TW3 176 BZ85
Romford RM5 105 FB51
South Croydon CR2 220 DQ110
Surbiton KT6 197 CK101
Uxbridge UB10 135 BP66
Wallington SM6 200 DG104
Wembley HA9 138 CP65
West Molesey KT8 196 CA97
Victoria Bus Sta 297 K7
H Victoria Cen, Rom. RM1 127 FF56
Victoria Cl, SE22
off Underhill Rd 182 DU85
Barnet EN4 80 DD42
Cheshunt EN8 67 DX30
Grays RM16 170 GC75
Hayes UB3 135 BR72
Horley RH6 268 DG148
Rickmansworth WD3 92 BK45
West Molesey KT8
off Victoria Av 196 CA97
Weybridge KT13 195 BR104
Victoria Coach Sta 297 J9
Sch Victoria C of E First Sch,
Berk. HP4 off Prince Edward St 38 AW19
Victoria Cotts, Rich. TW9 158 CM81
Victoria Ct, Red. RH1 266 DG137
Wembley HA9 138 CN65
Victoria Cres, N15 122 DS57
SE19 182 DS93
SW19 179 CZ94
Iver SL0 134 BG73
Victoria Dock Rd, E16 292 B10
Victoria Dr, SW19 179 CX87
Slough SL1, SL2 131 AL65
South Darenth DA4 209 FR96
Victoria Embk, EC4 298 C1
SW1 298 B4
WC2 298 C1
★ Victoria Embankment Gdns,
WC2 298 B1
Victoria Gdns, W11 295 J2
Biggin Hill TN16 238 EJ115
Hounslow TW5 156 BY81
Victoria Gate, Harl. CM17 52 EW15
Victoria Gate Gdns, SE10 314 D5
Victoria Gro, N12 98 DC50
W8 295 N6
Victoria Gro Ms, W2 295 K1
Victoria Hill Rd, Swan. BR8 207 FF95
Victoria Ho, SW8
off South Lambeth Rd 310 B4
Romford RM2 128 FJ56
● Victoria Ind Est, NW10 138 CS69
W3 138 CR71
● Victoria Ind Pk, Dart. DA1 188 FL85
Sch Victoria Jun Sch, Felt. TW13
off Victoria Rd 175 BV88
Victoria La, Barn. EN5 79 CZ42
Harlington UB3 155 BQ78
Victoria Mans, SW8
off South Lambeth Rd 310 B4
Victoria Ms, E8 278 C4
NW6 273 J8
SW4 off Victoria Ri 161 DH84
SW18 180 DC88
Bayfordbury SG13 31 DN14
Englefield Green TW20 172 AW93
Victoria Mills Studios, E15 280 G8
Victorian Gro, N16 122 DS62
Victorian Hts, SW8
off Thackeray Rd 309 K9
Victorian Rd, N16 122 DS62
Victoria Par, SE10 314 D2
★ Victoria Park, E9 279 L8
● Victoria Pk Ind Cen, E9 279 P6
Victoria Pk Rd, E9 278 F9
Victoria Pk Sq, E2 288 G2
Victoria Pas, NW8 284 A4
Watford WD18 75 BV42
Victoria Pl, SW1 297 K8
Victoria Pl, Epsom KT17 216 CS112
Richmond TW9 177 CK85
Victoria Pt, E13 281 N10
Victoria Retail Pk, Ruis. HA4 116 BX64
Victoria Ri, SW4 161 DH83
Victoria Rd, E4 102 EE46
E11 124 EE63
E13 291 N1
E17 101 EC54
E18 102 EH54
N4 121 DM59
N9 100 DT49
N15 122 DU56
N18 100 DT49
N22 99 DJ53
NW4 119 CW56
NW6 273 H9
NW7 97 CT50
NW10 138 CR71
SW14 158 CR83
W3 138 CR71
W5 137 CH71
W8 295 N7
Addlestone KT15 212 BK105
Barking IG11 145 EP65
Barnet EN4 80 DD42
Berkhamsted HP4 38 AW20
Bexleyheath DA6 166 FA84
Bromley BR2 204 EK99
Buckhurst Hill IG9 102 EK47
Bushey WD23 94 CB46
Chesham HP5 54 AQ31
Victoria Rd, Chislehurst BR7 185 EN92
Coulsdon CR5 235 DK115
Dagenham RM10 127 FB64
Dartford DA1 188 FK85
Erith DA8 167 FE79
Eton Wick SL4 151 AM78
Farnham Common SL2 131 AQ65
Feltham TW13 175 BV88
Guildford GU1 242 AY134
Horley RH6 268 DG148
Kingston upon Thames KT1 198 CM96
Mitcham CR4 180 DE94
Northfleet DA11 191 GF88
Redhill RH1 266 DG135
Romford RM1 127 FE58
Ruislip HA4 116 BW64
Sevenoaks TN13 257 FH125
Sidcup DA15 185 ET90
Slough SL2 132 AV74
Southall UB2 156 BZ76
Staines-upon-Thames TW18 173 BE90
Surbiton KT6 197 CK100
Sutton SM1 218 DD106
Teddington TW11 177 CG93
Twickenham TW1 177 CH87
Uxbridge UB8 134 BJ66
Waltham Abbey EN9 67 EC34
Warley CM14 108 FW49
Watford WD24 75 BV38
Weybridge KT13 195 BR104
Woking GU22 226 AY117
Victoria Scott Ct, Dart. DA1 167 FE83
● Victoria Sq, St.Alb. AL1 43 CF21
Victoria Sq, SW1 297 K6
Victoria Steps, Brent. TW8
off Kew Br Rd 158 CM79
Victoria St, E15 281 J6
SW1 297 L7
Belvedere DA17 166 EZ78
Englefield Green TW20 172 AW93
St. Albans AL1 43 CD20
Slough SL1 152 AT75
Windsor SL4 151 AQ81
Victoria's Way, S.Ock. RM15 149 FW72
Victoria Ter, N4 121 DN60
NW10 off Old Oak La 138 CS70
Dorking RH4 off South St 263 CG136
Harrow HA1 117 CE60
Victoria Vil, Rich. TW9 158 CM83
Victoria Way, SE7 304 A10
Ruislip HA4 116 BX64
Weybridge KT13 195 BR104
Woking GU21 226 AY117
Victoria Wf, E14 301 M1
Victoria Yd, E1 288 D9
Victor Rd, NW10 139 CV69
SE20 183 DX94
Harrow HA2 116 CC55
Teddington TW11 177 CE91
Windsor SL4 151 AQ83
Victors Cres, Hutt. CM13 109 GB47
Victors Dr, Hmptn. TW12 176 BY93
Sch Victor Seymour Infants' Sch,
Cars. SM5 off Denmark Rd 218 DF105
Victors Way, Barn. EN5 79 CZ41
Victor Vil, N9 100 DR48
Victor Wk, NW9 96 CS54
Hornchurch RM12
off Abbs Cross Gdns 128 FK60
Victor Way, Coln.St AL2 61 CF31
Victory Av, Mord. SM4 200 DC99
● Victory Business Cen,
Islw. TW7 157 CF83
Victory Cl, Chaff.Hun. RM16 169 FW77
Staines-upon-Thames TW19 174 BL88
Victory Ms, Sthl. UB2 156 BY76
Victory Par, E20 280 D3
Victory Pk Rd, Add. KT15 212 BJ105
Victory Pl, E14 289 M10
SE17 299 L8
SE19 off Westow St 182 DS93
Sch Victory Prim Sch, SE17 299 K8
Victory Rd, E11 124 EH56
SW19 180 DC94
Berkhamsted HP4
off Gossoms End 38 AU18
Chertsey KT16 194 BG102
Rainham RM13 147 FG68
Victory Rd Ms, SW19
off Victory Rd 180 DC94
Victory Wk, SE8 314 A6
Victory Way, SE16 301 M5
Dartford DA2 168 FQ84
Hounslow TW5 156 BW78
Romford RM7 105 FB54
Vidler Cl, Chess. KT9
off Merritt Gdns 215 CJ107
Vienna Cl, Ilf. IG5 124 EK55
View, The, SE2 166 EY78
View Cl, N6 120 DF59
Biggin Hill TN16 238 EJ116
Chigwell IG7 103 ER50
Harrow HA1 117 CD56
View Cres, N8 121 DK57
Viewfield Cl, Har. HA3 118 CL59
Viewfield Rd, SW18 179 CZ86
Bexley DA5 186 EW88
Viewland Rd, SE18 165 ET78
Viewlands Av, West. TN16 239 ES120
View Rd, N6 120 DF59
Potters Bar EN6 64 DC32
Viga Rd, N21 81 DN44
Vigerons Way, Grays RM16 171 GH77
Viggory La, Wok. GU21 226 AW115
Vigilant Cl, SE26 182 DU91
Vigilant Way, Grav. DA12 191 GL92
Vignoles Rd, Rom. RM7 126 FA59
Vigors Cft, Hat. AL10 45 CT19
Vigo St, W1 297 L1
Viking Cl, E3 289 M1
Viking Ct, SW6 307 K2
Viking Gdns, E6 292 G5
Viking Pl, E10 123 DZ60
Sch Viking Prim Sch, Nthlt. UB5
off Radcliffe Way 136 BX69
Viking Rd, Nthflt DA11 190 GC90
Southall UB1 136 BY73
Viking Way, Erith DA8 167 FC76
Pilgrim's Hatch CM15 108 FV45
Rainham RM13 147 FG70
Villa Ct, Dart. DA1
off Greenbanks 188 FL89
Villacourt Rd, SE18 166 EU80
Village, The,
Bluewater DA9 189 FT87
Slough SL1 152 AT75
Village, The, SE7 164 EJ79
Village Arc, E4
off Station Rd 101 ED46
Village Cl, E4 101 EC50
NW3 274 B3
Hoddesdon EN11 49 ED15
Weybridge KT13 195 BR104
Village Ct, E17
off Eden Rd 123 EB57
Village Gdns, Epsom KT17 217 CT110
Village Grn Av, Bigg.H. TN16 238 EL117
Village Grn Rd, Dart. DA1 167 FG84
Village Grn Way, Bigg.H. TN16
off Main Rd 238 EL117
Village Hts, Wdf.Grn. IG8 102 EF50
Sch Village Infants' Sch,
Dag. RM10 off Ford Rd 146 FA66
Village La, Hedg. SL2 111 AR60
Village Ms, NW9 118 CR61
Village Pk Cl, Enf. EN1 82 DS44
Village Rd, N3 97 CY53
Coleshill HP7 55 AM44
Denham UB9 113 BF61
Dorney SL4 150 AH76
Egham TW20 193 BC97
Enfield EN1 82 DS44
Village Row, Sutt. SM2 218 DA108
Village Sq, The, Couls. CR5
off Netherne Dr 235 DK122
Village Way, NW10 118 CR63
SE21 182 DR86
Amersham HP7 72 AX40
Ashford TW15 174 BM91
Beckenham BR3 203 EA96
Ilford IG6 125 EQ55
Pinner HA5 116 BY59
South Croydon CR2 220 DU113
Village Way E, Har. HA2 116 BZ59
Villa Rd, SW9 310 E10
Villas Rd, SE18 165 EQ77
Villa St, SE17 311 M1
Villiers, The, Wey. KT13 213 BR107
Villiers Av, Surb. KT5 198 CM99
Twickenham TW2 176 BZ88
Villiers Cl, E10 123 EA61
Surbiton KT5 198 CM98
Villiers Ct, N20
off Buckingham Av 98 DC45
Villiers Cres, St.Alb. AL4 43 CK17
Villiers Gro, Sutt. SM2 217 CX109
Sch Villiers High Sch, Sthl. UB1
off Boyd Av 136 BZ74
Villiers Path, Surb. KT5 198 CL99
Villiers Rd, NW2 139 CU65
Beckenham BR3 203 DX96
Isleworth TW7 157 CE82
Kingston upon Thames KT1 198 CM97
Slough SL2 131 AR71
Southall UB1 136 BZ74
Watford WD19 76 BY44
Villiers St, WC2 298 A1
Hertford SG13 32 DS09
Villier St, Uxb. UB8 134 BK68
Vimy Cl, Houns. TW4 176 BZ85
Vincam Cl, Twick. TW2 176 CA87
Vince Ct, N1
off Charles Sq 287 M3
Vincent Av, Cars. SM5 218 DD111
Croydon CR0 221 DY111
Surbiton KT5 198 CP102
Vincent Cl, SE16 301 L5
Barnet EN5 80 DA41
Bromley BR2 204 EH98
Chertsey KT16 193 BE101
Cheshunt EN8 67 DY28
Esher KT10 196 CB104
Fetcham KT22 230 CB123
Ilford IG6 103 EQ51
Sidcup DA15 185 ES88
Sipson UB7 154 BN79
Vincent Dr, Dor. RH4 263 CG137
Shepperton TW17 195 BS97
Uxbridge UB10 134 BM67
Vincent Gdns, NW2 119 CT62
Vincent Grn, Couls. CR5 234 DF120
★ Vincentia Ct, SW11 307 P9
Vincent La, Dor. RH4 263 CG136
Vincent Ms, E3
off Menai Pl 280 A10
Vincent Rd, E4 101 ED51
N15 122 DQ56
N22 99 DN54
SE18 305 N8
W3 158 CQ76
Chertsey KT16 193 BE101
Coulsdon CR5 235 DJ116
Croydon CR0 202 DS101
Dagenham RM9 146 EY66
Dorking RH4 263 CG136
Hounslow TW4 156 BX82
Isleworth TW7 157 CD81
Kingston upon Thames KT1 198 CN97
Rainham RM13 148 FJ70
Stoke D'Abernon KT11 230 BY116
Wembley HA0 138 CM66
Vincent Row, Hmptn H. TW12 176 CC93
Vincents Cl, Chipstead CR5 234 DF120
Vincents Dr, Dor. RH4
off Nower Rd 263 CG137
Vincents Path, Nthlt. UB5
off Arnold Rd 136 BY65
Vincent Sq, N22 99 DN54
SW1 297 M8
Biggin Hill TN16 222 EJ113
Vincent St, E16 291 M7
SW1 297 N8
Vincents Wk, Dor. RH4
off Arundel Rd 263 CG136
Vincent Ter, N1 276 G10
● Vincent Wks, Dor. RH4 263 CG136
Vincenzo Cl, N.Mymms AL9 45 CW23
Vince St, EC1 287 M3
Vine, The, Sev. TN13 257 FH124
Vine Av, Sev. TN13 257 FH124
Vine Cl, E5
off Rendlesham Rd 122 DU63
Staines-upon-Thames TW19 174 BG85
Surbiton KT5 198 CM100
Sutton SM1 200 DC104
Welwyn Garden City AL8 29 CY07
West Drayton UB7 154 BN77
Vine Ct, E1 288 D7
Harrow HA3 118 CL58
Vine Ct Rd, Sev. TN13 257 FJ124
Vinegar All, E17 123 EB56
Vine Gdns, Ilf. IG1 125 EQ64
Vinegar St, E1 300 E2
Vinegar Yd, SE1 299 N4
Vine Gate, Farn.Com. SL2 131 AQ65
Vine Gro, Harl. CM20 35 ER10
Uxbridge UB10 134 BN66
Vine Hill, EC1 286 E5
Vine La, SE1 299 P3
Uxbridge UB10 134 BM67
Vine Pl, W5
off St. Mark's Rd 138 CL74
Hounslow TW3 156 CB84
Viner Cl, Walt. KT12 196 BW100
Vineries, The, N14 81 DJ44
SE6 183 EA88
Enfield EN1 82 DS41
Vineries Bk, NW7 97 CV50
Vineries Cl, Dag. RM9 146 FA65
Sipson UB7 154 BN79
Vine Rd, E15 281 L6
SW13 159 CT83
East Molesey KT8 196 CC98
Orpington BR6 223 ET107
Stoke Poges SL2 132 AT65
Vinery Way, W6 159 CV76
Vines Av, N3 98 DB53
Vine Sq, W14 307 H1
Vine St, EC3 288 A10
W1 297 M1
Romford RM7 127 FC57
Uxbridge UB8 134 BK67
Vine St Br, EC1 286 F5
Vine Way, Brwd. CM14 108 FW46
Vine Yd, SE1 299 K4
Vineyard, The, Hert. SG14 32 DR07
Richmond TW10 178 CL85
Ware SG12 33 EA05
Welwyn Garden City AL8 29 CX07
Vineyard Av, NW7 97 CY52
Vineyard Cl, SE6 183 EA88
Kingston upon Thames KT1 198 CM97
Vineyard Gro, N3 98 DB53
Vineyard Hill, Northaw EN6 64 DG29
Vineyard Hill Rd, SW19 180 DA91
Vineyard Pas, Rich. TW9
off Paradise Rd 178 CL85
Vineyard Path, SW14 158 CR83
Sch Vineyard Prim Sch, The,
Rich. TW10 off Friars Stile Rd 178 CL86
Vineyard Rd, Felt. TW13 175 BU90
Vineyard Row, Hmptn W. KT1 197 CJ95
Vineyards Rd, Northaw EN6 64 DF30
Vineyard Wk, EC1 286 E4
Viney Bk, Croy. CR0 221 DZ109
Viney Rd, SE13 163 EB83
Vining St, SW9 161 DN84
Vinlake Av, Uxb. UB10 114 BM62
Vinson Cl, Orp. BR6 206 EU102
Vintage Ms, E4
off Cherrydown Ave 101 EA49
Vintners Ct, EC4 287 K10
Vintners Pl, EC4
off Vintners Ct 287 K10
Vintry Ms, E17
off Cleveland Pk Cres 123 EA56
Viola Av, SE2 166 EV77
Feltham TW14 176 BW86
Staines-upon-Thames TW19 174 BK88
Viola Cl, S.Ock. RM15 149 FW69
Viola Sq, W12 139 CT73
Violet Av, Enf. EN2 82 DR38
Uxbridge UB8 134 BM71
Violet Cl, E16 291 K5
SE8 313 N2
Sutton SM3 199 CY102
Wallington SM6 200 DG102
Violet Gdns, Croy. CR0 219 DP106
Violet Hill, NW8 283 N1
Violet La, Croy. CR0 219 DP106
Violet Rd, E3 290 C5
E17 123 EA58
E18 102 EH54
Violet St, E2 288 F4
Violet Way, Loud. WD3 74 BJ42
Virgil Dr, Brox. EN10 49 DZ23
Virgil Pl, W1 284 E7
Virgil St, SE1 298 D6
Virginia Av, Vir.W. GU25 192 AW99
Virginia Beeches, Vir.W. GU25 192 AW97
Virginia Cl, Ashtd. KT21
off Skinners La 231 CK118
Bromley BR2 203 ED97
New Malden KT3
off Willow Rd 198 CQ98
Romford RM5 105 FC52
Staines-upon-Thames TW18
off Blacksmiths La 194 BJ97
Weybridge KT13 213 BQ107
Virginia Dr, Vir.W. GU25 192 AW99
Virginia Gdns, Ilf. IG6 103 EQ54
Virginia Pl, Cob. KT11 213 BU114
Sch Virginia Prim Sch, E2 288 A3
Virginia Rd, E2 288 A3
Thornton Heath CR7 201 DP95
Virginia St, E1 300 D1
Virginia Wk, SW2 181 DM86
Gravesend DA12 191 GK93
VIRGINIA WATER, GU25 192 AX99
⇌ Virginia Water 192 AY99
Sch Virgo Fidelis Conv Sen Sch,
SE19 off Central Hill 182 DR93
Sch Virgo Fidelis Prep Sch,
SE19 off Central Hill 182 DR93
Viridian Apts, SW8 309 L5
Visage Apts, NW3 274 B7
Viscount Cl, N11 99 DH50
Viscount Dr, E6 293 J6
Viscount Gdns, W.Byf. KT14 212 BL112
Viscount Gro, Nthlt. UB5 136 BX69
Viscount Rd, Stanw. TW19 174 BK88
Viscount St, EC1 287 J5
Viscount Way,
Lon.Hthrw Air. TW6 155 BS84
Vista, The, E4 101 ED45
SE9 184 EK86
Sidcup DA14 185 ET92
Vista Av, Enf. EN3 83 DX40
Vista Bldg, The, SE18 305 M8
Vista Dr, Ilf. IG4 124 EK57
Vista Ho, SW19
off Chapter Way 200 DD95
Vista Office Cen, TW4 156 BW83
Vista Way, Har. HA3 118 CL58
Vitae, W6
off Goldhawk Rd 159 CU76
Sch Vita et Pax Sch, N14
off Priory Cl 81 DH43
Sch Vittoria Prim Sch, N1 276 E10
Viveash Cl, Hayes UB3 155 BT76
Vivian Av, NW4 119 CV57
Wembley HA9 118 CN64
Vivian Cl, Wat. WD19 93 BU46
Vivian Comma Cl, N4 121 DP62
Vivian Ct, W9 273 L10
Vivian Gdns, Wat. WD19 93 BU46
Wembley HA9 118 CN64

V

Vivian Rd, E3 279 L10
Vivian Sq, SE15 312 E10
Vivian Way, N2 120 DD57
Vivien Cl, Chess. KT9 216 CL108
Vivien Ct, N9
off Galahad Rd 100 DU47
Vivienne Cl, Twick. TW1 177 CJ86
Vixen Ct, Hat. AL10 45 CV16
Vixen Dr, Hert. SG13 32 DU09
Voce Rd, SE18 165 ER80
Voewood Cl, N.Mal. KT3 199 CT100
Vogan Cl, Reig. RH2 266 DB137
Vogans Mill, SE1 300 B4
Volta Cl, N9
off Hudson Way 100 DW48
Voltaire Bldgs, SW18 180 DB88
Voltaire Rd, SW4 161 DK83
Voltaire Way, Hayes UB3 135 BS73
Volt Av, NW10 138 CR69
Volta Way, Croy. CR0 201 DM102
Voluntary Pl, E11 124 EG58
Vorley Rd, N19 121 DJ61
Voss Ct, SW16 181 DL93
Voss St, E2 288 D3
● Voyager Business Est, SE16
off Spa Rd 300 C6
Voyagers Cl, SE28 146 EW72
Voysey Cl, N3 119 CY55
Voysey Sq, E3 290 C6
Vulcan Cl, E6 293 M9
Vulcan Gate, Enf. EN2 81 DN40
Vulcan Rd, SE4 313 N8
Vulcan Sq, E14 302 B9
Vulcan Ter, SE4 313 N8
Vulcan Way, N7 276 D4
New Addington CR0 222 EE110
Wallington SM6 219 DL109
Vyne, The, Bexh. DA7 167 FB83
Vyner Rd, W3 138 CR73
Vyners Sch, Ickhm UB10
off Warren Rd 114 BM63
Vyner St, E2 278 F10
Vyners Way, Uxb. UB10 114 BN64
Vyse Cl, Barn. EN5 79 CW42

W

Wacketts, Chsht EN7 66 DU27
Wadbrook St, Kings.T. KT1 197 CK96
Wadding St, SE17 299 L9
Waddington Av, Couls. CR5 235 DN120
Waddington Cl, Couls. CR5 235 DP119
Enfield EN1 82 DS42
Waddington Rd, E15 281 H3
St. Albans AL3 43 CD20
Waddington St, E15 281 H4
Waddington Way, SE19 182 DQ94
WADDON, Croy. CR0 201 DN103
⇌ Waddon 219 DN105
Waddon Cl, Croy. CR0 201 DN104
Waddon Ct Rd, Croy. CR0 219 DN105
Waddon Marsh 201 DN103
Waddon Marsh Way,
Croy. CR0 201 DM102
Waddon New Rd, Croy. CR0 201 DP104
Waddon Pk Av, Croy. CR0 219 DN105
Waddon Rd, Croy. CR0 201 DN104
Waddon Way, Croy. CR0 219 DP107
Wade, The, Welw.G.C. AL7 29 CZ12
Wade Av, Orp. BR5 206 EX101
Wade Dr, Slou. SL1 131 AN74
Wades, The, Hat. AL10 45 CU21
Wades Gro, N21 99 DN45
Wades Hill, N21 81 DN44
Wades La, Tedd. TW11
off High St 177 CG92
Wadesmill Rd, Chap.End SG12 32 DQ06
Hertford SG14 32 DQ06
Wadeson St, E2 278 F10
Wades Pl, E14 290 C10
Wadeville Av, Rom. RM6 126 EZ59
Wadeville Cl, Belv. DA17 166 FA79
Wadham Av, E17 101 EB52
Wadham Cl, Shep. TW17 195 BQ101
Wadham Gdns, NW3 274 C8
Greenford UB6 137 CD65
Wadham Ms, SW14 158 CQ82
Wadham Rd, E17 101 EB53
SW15 159 CY84
Abbots Langley WD5 59 BT31
Wadhurst Cl, SE20 202 DV96
Wadhurst Rd, SW8 309 L6
W4 158 CR76
Wadley Cl, Hem.H. HP2
off White Hart Dr 40 BM21
Wadley Rd, E11 124 EE59
● Wadsworth Business Cen,
Grnf. UB6 137 CJ68
Wadsworth Cl, Enf. EN3 83 DX43
Perivale UB6 137 CJ68
Wadsworth Rd, Perivale UB6 137 CH68
Wager St, E3 289 N5
Waggon Cl, Guil. GU2 242 AS133
Waggoners Rbt,
Houns. TW5 155 BV81
Waggon Ms, N14
off Chase Side 99 DJ46
Waggon Rd, Barn. EN4 80 DC37
Waghorn Rd, E13 144 EJ67
Harrow HA3 117 CK55
Waghorn St, SE15 312 C10
Wagner St, SE15 312 G4
Wagon Rd, Barn. EN4 80 DB36
Wagon Way, Loud. WD3 74 BJ41
Wagstaff Gdns, Dag. RM9 146 EW66
Wagtail Cl, NW9 96 CS54
Enfield EN1 82 DV39
Wagtail Gdns, S.Croy. CR2 221 DY110
Wagtail Wk, Beck. BR3 203 EC99
Wagtail Way, Orp. BR5 206 EX98
Waid Cl, Dart. DA1 188 FM86
Waight Cl, Hat. AL10 44 CS16
Waights Ct, Kings.T. KT2 198 CL95
Wain Cl, Pot.B. EN6 64 DB29
Wainfleet Av, Rom. RM5 105 FC54
Wainford Cl, SW19
off Windlesham Gro 179 CX88
Wainwright Av, Hutt. CM13 109 GD44
Wainwright Gro, Islw. TW7 157 CD84
Waite Davies Rd, SE12 184 EF87
Waite St, SE15 312 A2
Waithman St, EC4 286 G9
Wake Arms, Epp. CM16 85 EM36
Wake Cl, Guil. GU2 242 AV129
Wakefield Cl, Byfleet KT14 212 BL112
Wakefield Cres, Stoke P. SL2 132 AT66
Wakefield Gdns, SE19 182 DS94
Ilford IG1 124 EL58
Wakefield Ms, WC1 286 B3
Wakefield Rd, N11 99 DK50
N15 122 DT57
Greenhithe DA9 189 FW85
Richmond TW10 177 CK85
Wakefield St, E6 144 EK67
N18 100 DU50
WC1 286 B4
Wakefields Wk, Chsht EN8 67 DY31
Wakeford Cl, SW4 181 DJ85
Bexley DA5 186 EX87
Wakehams Hill, Pnr. HA5 116 BZ55
Wakeham St, N1 277 L5
Wakehurst Path, Wok. GU21 211 BC114
Wakehurst Rd, SW11 180 DE85
Wakeling La, Wem. HA0 117 CH62
Wakeling Rd, W7 137 CF71
Wakeling St, E14 289 L9
Wakelin Rd, E15 281 J10
Wakely Cl, Bigg.H. TN16 238 EJ118
Wakeman Rd, NW10 282 C2
Wakemans Hill Av, NW9 118 CR57
Wakerfield Cl, Horn. RM11 128 FM57
Wakering Rd, Bark. IG11 145 EQ66
Wakerley Cl, E6 293 J9
Wake Rd, High Beach IG10 84 EJ38
Wakley St, EC1 286 G2
Walberswick St, SW8 310 B5
Walbrook, EC4 287 L10
Walbrook Building, The, EC4 287 L10
Walbrook Ho, N9 100 DW47
Walbrook Wf, EC4
off Bell Wf La 299 K1
Walburgh St, E1 288 E9
Walburton Rd, Pur. CR8 219 DJ113
Walcorde Av, SE17 299 K9
Walcot Ho, SE22
off Albrighton Rd 162 DS83
Walcot Rd, Enf. EN3 83 DZ40
Walcot Sq, SE11 298 F8
Walcott St, SW1 297 M8
Waldair Ct, E16 305 N4
Waldair Wf, E16 305 N4
Waldeck Gro, SE27 181 DP90
Waldeck Rd, N15 121 DP56
SW14
off Lower Richmond Rd 158 CQ83
W4 158 CN79
W13 137 CH72
Dartford DA1 188 FM86
Waldeck Ter, SW14
off Lower Richmond Rd 158 CQ83
Waldegrave Av, Tedd. TW11
off Waldegrave Rd 177 CF92
Waldegrave Ct, Upmin. RM14 128 FP60
Waldegrave Gdns, Twick. TW1 177 CF89
Upminster RM14 128 FP60
Waldegrave Pk, Twick. TW1 177 CF91
Waldegrave Rd, N8 121 DN55
SE19 182 DT94
W5 138 CM72
Bromley BR1 204 EL98
Dagenham RM8 126 EW61
Teddington TW11 177 CF91
Twickenham TW1 177 CF91
Waldegrave Sch for Girls,
Twick. TW2 off Fifth Cross Rd 177 CD90
Waldegrove, Croy. CR0 202 DT104
Waldemar Av, SW6 306 F7
W13 137 CJ74
Waldemar Rd, SW19 180 DA92
Walden Av, N13 100 DQ49
Chislehurst BR7 185 EM91
Rainham RM13 147 FD68
Waldenbury Pl, Beac. HP9 110 AG55
Walden Cl, Belv. DA17 166 EZ78
Walden Ct, SW8
off Wandsworth Rd 309 P6
Walden Gdns, Th.Hth. CR7 201 DM97
Waldenhurst Rd, Orp. BR5 206 EX101
Walden Par, Chis. BR7
off Walden Rd 185 EM93
Walden Pl, Welw.G.C. AL8 29 CX07
Walden Rd, N17 100 DR53
Chislehurst BR7 185 EM93
Hornchurch RM11 128 FK58
Welwyn Garden City AL8 29 CX07
Waldens Cl, Orp. BR5 206 EX101
Waldenshaw Rd, SE23 182 DW88
Waldens Pk Rd, Wok. GU21 226 AW116
Waldens Rd, Orp. BR5 206 EY101
Woking GU21 226 AX117
Walden St, E1 288 E8
Walden Way, NW7 97 CX51
Hornchurch RM11 128 FK58
Ilford IG6 103 ES52
Waldo Cl, SW4 181 DJ85
Waldo Pl, Mitch. CR4 180 DE94
Waldorf Cl, S.Croy. CR2 219 DP109
Waldo Rd, NW10 139 CU69
Bromley BR1 204 EK97
Waldram Cres, SE23 182 DW88
Waldram Pk Rd, SE23 183 DX88
Waldram Pl, SE23
off Waldram Cres 182 DW88
Waldrist Way, Erith DA18 166 EZ75
Waldron Gdns, Brom. BR2 203 ED97
Waldronhyrst, S.Croy. CR2 219 DP105
Waldron Ms, SW3 308 B2
Waldron Rd, SW18 180 DC90
Harrow HA1, HA2 117 CE60
Waldrons, The, Croy. CR0 219 DP105
Oxted RH8 254 EF131
Waldrons Path, S.Croy. CR2 220 DQ105
Waldrons Yd, Har. HA2
off Northolt Rd 117 CD61
Waldstock Rd, SE28 146 EU73
Waleran Cl, Stan. HA7 95 CF51
Walerand Rd, SE13 314 F9
Waleran Flats, SE1 299 N8
Wales Av, Cars. SM5 218 DF106
Wales Cl, SE15 312 E4
Wales Fm Rd, W3 138 CR71
Waleton Acres, Wall. SM6 219 DJ107
Waley St, E1 289 K6
Walfield Av, N20 98 DB45
Walford Rd, N16 122 DS63
North Holmwood RH5 263 CH140
Uxbridge UB8 134 BJ68
Walfords Cl, Harl. CM17 36 EW12
Walfrey Gdns, Dag. RM9 146 EY66
WALHAM GREEN, SW6 307 L5
Walham Grn Ct, SW6 307 L5
Walham Gro, SW6 307 J4
Walham Ri, SW19 179 CY93
Walham Yd, SW6 307 J4
Walk, The, Eton Wick SL4 151 AN78
Hertford SG14 32 DQ08
off Chelmsford Rd 31 DN10
Walk, The, Hornchurch RM11 128 FM61
Potters Bar EN6 64 DA32
Sunbury-on-Thames TW16 175 BT94
Tandridge RH8 253 EA133
Walkden Rd, Chis. BR7 185 EN92
Walker Cl, N11 99 DJ49
SE18 165 EQ77
W7 137 CE74
Dartford DA1 167 FF83
Feltham TW14 175 BT87
Hampton TW12
off Fearnley Cres 176 BZ93
New Addington CR0 221 EC108
Walker Cres, Slou. SL3 153 AZ78
Walker Gro, Hat. AL10 44 CR17
Walker Ms, SW2 off Effra Rd 181 DN85
Walker Prim Sch, N14
off Waterfall Rd 99 DK47
Walkers Ct, E8 278 C4
W1 285 N10
Walkerscroft Mead, SE21 182 DQ88
Walkers Pl, SW15
off Felsham Rd 159 CY84
Walkfield Dr, Epsom KT18 233 CV117
Walkley Rd, Dart. DA1 187 FH85
Walks, The, N2 120 DD55
Walkwood End, Beac. HP9 88 AJ54
Walkwood Ri, Beac. HP9 110 AJ55
Walkynscroft, SE15 312 F8
Wallace Cl, SE28
off Haldane Rd 146 EX73
Shepperton TW17 195 BR98
Uxbridge UB10 134 BL68
★ Wallace Collection, W1 284 G8
Wallace Ct, Enf. EN3
off Eden Cl 83 EA37
Wallace Cres, Cars. SM5 218 DF106
Wallace Flds, Epsom KT17 217 CT112
Wallace Flds Inf Sch,
Ewell KT17 off Wallace Flds 217 CU113
Wallace Flds Jun Sch,
Ewell KT17 off Dorling Dr 217 CU112
Wallace Gdns, Swans. DA10 190 FY86
Wallace Rd, N1 277 K4
Grays RM17 170 GA76
Wallace Sq, Couls. CR5
off Cayton Rd 235 DK122
Wallace Wk, Add. KT15 212 BJ105
Wallace Way, N19
off Giesbach Rd 121 DK61
Romford RM1 105 FD53
Wallasey Cres, Uxb. UB10 114 BN61
● Wallbrook Business Cen,
Houns. TW4 off Green La 155 BV83
Wallbutton Rd, SE4 313 L9
Wallcote Av, NW2 119 CX60
Walled Gdn, The, Bet. RH3 264 CR135
Tadworth KT20 233 CX122
Walled Gdn Cl, Beck. BR3 203 EB98
Wall End Rd, E6 145 EM66
Wallenger Av, Rom. RM2 127 FH55
Waller Dr, Nthwd. HA6 93 BU54
Waller La, Cat. CR3 236 DT123
Waller Rd, SE14 313 J7
Beaconsfield HP9 89 AM53
Wallers Cl, Dag. RM9 146 EY67
Woodford Green IG8 103 EM51
Waller's Hoppet, Loug. IG10 84 EL40
Wallers Way, Hodd. EN11 33 EB14
Waller Way, SE10 314 D4
Wallfield All, Hert. SG13 32 DQ10
Wallflower St, W12 139 CT73
Wallgrave Rd, SW5 295 L8
Wall Hall Dr, Ald. WD25 76 CB36
Wall Hall Fm Cotts, Ald. WD25
off Pelham La 76 CB36
Wall Hall Mansion,
Ald. WD25 76 CB36
Wallhouse Rd, Erith DA8 167 FH80
Wallingford Av, W10 282 C7
Wallingford Rd, Uxb. UB8 134 BH68
Wallingford Wk, St.Alb. AL1 43 CD23
WALLINGTON, SM6 219 DJ106
⇌ Wallington 219 DH107
Wallington Cl, Ruis. HA4 115 BQ58
Wallington Cor, Wall. SM6
off Manor Rd N 219 DH105
Wallington Co Gram Sch,
Wall. SM6 off Croydon Rd 219 DH105
Wallington Grn,
Wall. SM6 off Croydon Rd 219 DH105
Wallington High Sch for Girls,
Wall. SM6 off Woodcote Rd 219 DH109
Wallington Rd, Chesh. HP5 54 AP30
Ilford IG3 125 ET59
Wallington Sq, Wall. SM6
off Woodcote Rd 219 DH107
Wallis All, SE1 299 K4
Wallis Cl, SW11 160 DD83
Dartford DA2 187 FF90
Hornchurch RM11 127 FH60
Wallis Ct, Slou. SL1 152 AU75
● Wallis Ho, Brent. TW8 158 CL78
Wallis Ms, N8
off Courcy Rd 121 DN55
Fetcham KT22 231 CG122
Wallis Pk, Nthflt DA11 190 GB85
Wallis Rd, E9 279 P5
Lon.Hthrw Air. TW6
off Western Perimeter Rd 154 BH82
Southall UB1 136 CB72
Wallis's Cotts, SW2 181 DL87
Wallman Pl, N22
off Bounds Grn Rd 99 DM53
Wallorton Gdns, SW14 158 CR84
Wallside, EC2
off The Barbican 287 K7
Wall St, N1 277 M5
Wallwood Rd, E11 123 ED60
Wallwood St, E14 289 P7
Walmar Cl, Barn. EN4 80 DD39
Walmer Cl, E4 101 EB47
Farnborough BR6
off Tubbenden La S 223 ER105
Romford RM7 105 FB54
Walmer Gdns, W13 157 CG75
Walmer Ho, N9 100 DT45
Walmer Pl, W1 284 E6
Walmer Rd, W10 282 B9
W11 282 E10
Walmer St, W1 284 E6
Walmer Ter, SE18 165 EQ77
Walmgate Rd, Perivale UB6 137 CH67
Walmington Fold, N12 98 DA51
Walm La, NW2 272 B5
Walmsley Ho, SW16
off Colson Way 181 DJ91
Walney Wk, N1 277 K4
Walnut Av, West Dr. UB7 154 BN76
Walnut Cl, SE8 313 P3
Carshalton SM5 218 DF106
Epsom KT18 233 CT115
Eynsford DA4 208 FK104
Hayes UB3 135 BS73
Ilford IG6 125 EQ56
Park Street AL2 60 CB27
Walnut Ct, W5 158 CL75
Welwyn Garden City AL7 29 CY12
Walnut Dr, Kgswd KT20 233 CY123
Walnut Gdns, E15 281 H2
Walnut Grn, Bushey WD23 76 BZ40
Walnut Gro, Bans. SM7 217 CX114
Enfield EN1 82 DR43
Harlow CM20 35 EP14
Hemel Hempstead HP2 40 BK20
Hornchurch RM12 128 FK60
Welwyn Garden City AL7 29 CY12
Wooburn Green HP10 110 AE57
Walnut Ms, Sutt. SM2 218 DC108
Wooburn Green HP10 110 AE57
Walnut Rd, E10 123 EA61
Walnuts, The, Orp. BR6
off High St 206 EU102
Walnut Shop Cen, Orp. BR6 206 EU102
Walnuts Rd, Orp. BR6 206 EU102
Walnut Tree Av, Dart. DA1 188 FL89
Mitcham CR4
off De'Arn Gdns 200 DE97
Walnut Tree Cl, SW13 159 CT81
Banstead SM7 217 CY112
Cheshunt EN8 67 DX31
Chislehurst BR7 205 EQ95
Fetcham KT23 247 CD125
Guildford GU1 242 AW134
Hoddesdon EN11 49 EA17
Uxbridge UB10 114 BL63
Westerham TN16 255 ER126
Walnut Tree Cotts, SW19
off Church Rd 179 CY92
Walnut Tree Gdns, Gdmg. GU7 258 AS144
Walnut Tree La, Byfleet KT14 212 BK112
Walnut Tree Pk, Guil. GU1 242 AW134
Walnut Tree Pl, Send GU23 227 BD123
Walnut Tree Rd, SE10 315 K1
Brentford TW8 158 CL79
Dagenham RM8 126 EX61
Erith DA8 167 FE78
Hounslow TW5 156 BZ79
Shepperton TW17 195 BQ96
Walnut Tree Wk, SE11 298 E8
Ware SG12 33 DX09
Walnut Tree Wk Prim Sch,
SE11 298 E8
Walnut Way, Buck.H. IG9 102 EK48
Ruislip HA4 136 BW65
Swanley BR8 207 FD96
Walpole Av, Chipstead CR5 234 DF118
Richmond TW9 158 CM82
Walpole Cl, W13 157 CJ75
Grays RM17 off Palmers Dr 170 GC77
Pinner HA5 94 CA51
Walpole Cres, Tedd. TW11 177 CF92
Walpole Gdns, W4 158 CQ78
Twickenham TW2 177 CE89
Walpole Ho, SE1
off Westminster Br Rd 298 E5
Walpole Ms, NW8 274 A9
SW19 off Walpole Rd 180 DD93
Walpole Pk, W5 137 CJ74
Weybridge KT13 212 BN108
Walpole Pl, SE18 305 N9
Teddington TW11 177 CF92
Walpole Rd, E6 144 EJ66
E17 123 DY56
E18 102 EF53
N17 (Downhills Way) 122 DQ55
N17 (Lordship La) 100 DQ54
SW19 180 DD93
Bromley BR2 204 EK99
Croydon CR0 202 DR103
Old Windsor SL4 172 AV87
Slough SL1 131 AK72
Surbiton KT6 198 CL101
Teddington TW11 177 CF92
Twickenham TW2 177 CE89
Walpole St, SW3 296 E10
Walrond Av, Wem. HA9 118 CL64
Walrus Rd, Lon.Hthrw Air. TW6
off Western Perimeter Rd 154 BH83
Walsham Cl, N16
off Clarke Path 122 DU60
SE28 146 EX73
Walsham Rd, SE14 313 J8
Feltham TW14 175 BV87
Walsh Cres, New Adgtn CR0 222 EE112
Walshford Way, Borwd. WD6 78 CN38
Walsingham Cl, Hat. AL10 45 CT17
Walsingham Gdns,
Epsom KT19 216 CS105
Walsingham Pk, Chis. BR7 205 ER96
Walsingham Pl, SW4
off Clapham Common W Side 160 DF84
SW11 180 DG86
Walsingham Rd, E5 122 DU62
W13 137 CG74
Enfield EN2 82 DR42
Mitcham CR4 200 DF99
New Addington CR0 221 EC110
Orpington BR5 206 EV95
Walsingham Wk, Belv. DA17 166 FA79
Walsingham Way, Lon.Col. AL2 61 CJ27
Walter Rodney Cl, E6
off Stevenage Rd 145 EM65
Walters Cl, SE17 299 K9
Cheshunt EN7 65 DP25
Hayes UB3 155 BT75
Walters Ho, SE17 310 G3
Walters Mead, Ashtd. KT21 232 CL117
Walters Rd, SE25 202 DS98
Enfield EN3 82 DW43
Walter St, E2 289 J3
Kingston upon Thames KT2
off Sopwith Way 198 CL95
Walters Way, SE23 183 DX86
Walters Yd, Brom. BR1 204 EG96
Walter Ter, E1 289 K8
Walterton Rd, W9 283 H5
Walter Wk, Edg. HA8 96 CQ51
WALTHAM ABBEY, EN9 84 EF35
★ Waltham Abbey (ruins),
Wal.Abb. EN9 67 EC33
Waltham Av, NW9 118 CN58
Guildford GU2 242 AV131
Hayes UB3 155 BQ76
Waltham Cl, Dart. DA1 187 FG86
Hutton CM13
off Bannister Dr 109 GC44
Orpington BR5 206 EX102
WALTHAM CROSS, EN7 & EN8 67 DZ33
⇌ Waltham Cross 67 DY34
Waltham Cross 67 DY34
Waltham Dr, Edg. HA8 96 CN54
Waltham Forest Coll, E17
off Forest Rd 123 EB55
Waltham Forest Construction
Training Cen, E17 123 ED62
Waltham Gdns, Enf. EN3 82 DW36
Waltham Gate, Wal.Cr. EN8 67 DZ26
Waltham Holy Cross Inf Sch,
Wal.Abb. EN9 off Quendon Dr 67 ED33
Waltham Holy Cross Jun Sch,
Wal.Abb. EN9 off Quendon Dr 67 ED33
Waltham Pk Way, E17 101 EA53
Waltham Rd, Cars. SM5 200 DD101
Caterham CR3 236 DV122
Nazeing Gate EN9 68 EF26
Southall UB2 156 BY76
Woodford Green IG8 102 EL51
WALTHAMSTOW, E17 101 EB54
Walthamstow Acad, E17
off Billet Rd 101 DZ53
Walthamstow Av, E4 101 DZ52
● Walthamstow Business Cen,
E17 101 EC54
⇌ Walthamstow Central 123 EA56
Walthamstow Central 123 EA56
Walthamstow Central 123 EA56
Walthamstow Central 123 EA56
Walthamstow Hall Sch,
Jun Sch, Sev. TN13
off Bradbourne Pk Rd 257 FH122
Sen Sch, Sev. TN13
off Holly Bush La 257 FJ123
Walthamstow Queens Road 123 DZ57
Walthamstow Sch for Girls,
E17 off Church Hill 123 EB56
Waltham Way, E4 101 DZ49
Waltheof Av, N17 100 DR53
Waltheof Gdns, N17 100 DR53
Walton Av, Har. HA2 116 BZ64
New Malden KT3 199 CT98
Sutton SM3 199 CZ104
Wembley HA9 118 CP62
Walton Br, Shep. TW17 195 BS101
Walton-on-Thames KT12 195 BS101
Walton Br Rd, Shep. TW17 195 BS101
Walton Cl, E5
off Orient Way 123 DX62
NW2 119 CV61
SW8 310 B4
Harrow HA1 117 CD56
Walton Comm Hosp,
Walt. KT12 195 BV103
Walton Ct, Wok. GU21 227 BA116
Walton Cres, Har. HA2 116 BZ63
Walton Dr, NW10 138 CR65
Harrow HA1 117 CD56
Walton Gdns, W3 138 CP71
Feltham TW13 175 BT91
Hutton CM13 109 GC43
Waltham Abbey EN9 67 EB33
Wembley HA9 118 CL61
Walton Grn, New Adgtn CR0 221 EC108
Walton La, Farn.Royal SL2 131 AL69
Shepperton TW17 195 BR101
Walton-on-Thames KT12 195 BQ102
Weybridge KT13 195 BP103
Walton Leigh Sch, Walt. KT12
off Queens Rd 213 BT105
Walton Oak Sch, Walt. KT12
off Ambleside Av 196 BW102
WALTON-ON-THAMES, KT12 195 BT103
⇌ Walton-on-Thames 213 BU105
WALTON ON THE HILL,
Tad. KT20 249 CT125
Walton-on-the-Hill Prim Sch,
Walt.Hill KT20 off Walton St 233 CV124
Walton Pk, Walt. KT12 196 BX103
Walton Pk La, Walt. KT12 196 BX103
Walton Pl, SW3 296 E6
Walton Rd, E12 125 EN63
E13 144 EJ68
N15 122 DT56
Bushey WD23 76 BX42
East Molesey KT8 196 CA98
Epsom Downs KT18 233 CT118
Harrow HA1 117 CD56
Headley KT18 232 CQ121
Hoddesdon EN11 49 EB15
Romford RM5 104 EZ52
Sidcup DA14 186 EW89
Walton-on-Thames KT12 196 BW99
Ware SG12 33 DX07
West Molesey KT8 196 BY99
Woking GU21 227 AZ116
Walton St, SW3 296 D8
Enfield EN2 82 DR39
St. Albans AL1 43 CF19
Walton on the Hill KT20 233 CU124
Walton Ter, Borwd. WD6
off Watford Rd 77 CK44
Wok. GU21 227 BB115
Walton Way, W3 138 CP71
Mitcham CR4 201 DJ98
Walt Whitman Cl, SE24
off Shakespeare Rd 161 DP84
Walverns Cl, Wat. WD19 76 BW44
WALWORTH, SE17 299 J10
Walworth Acad, SE1 311 P1
★ Walworth Garden Fm - Horticultural
Training Cen, SE17 311 H1
Walworth Pl, SE17 311 K1
Walworth Rd, SE1 299 J8
SE17 299 J8
Walwyn Av, Brom. BR1 204 EK97
Wambrook Cl, Hutt. CM13 109 GC46
Wanborough Dr, SW15 179 CV88
Wanderer Dr, Bark. IG11 146 EV69
Wander Wf, Kings L. WD4 59 BP30
Wandle Bk, SW19 180 DD93
Croydon CR0 201 DL104
Wandle Ct, Epsom KT19 216 CQ105
Wandle Ct Gdns, Croy. CR0 201 DL104
Wandle Park 201 DN103
Wandle Rd, SW17 180 DE89
Beddington CR0 201 DL104
Croydon CR0 202 DQ104
Morden SM4 200 DC98
Wallington SM6 201 DH103
Wandle Side, Croy. CR0 201 DM104
Wallington SM6 201 DH104
● Wandle Tech Pk, Mitch. CR4 200 DF101

● Wandle Trd Est, Mitch. CR4
off Budge La 200 DF101
Sch Wandle Valley Sch, Cars. SM5
off Welbeck Rd 200 DE101
Wandle Way, SW18 180 DB88
Mitcham CR4 200 DF99
Wandon Rd, SW6 307 M5
WANDSWORTH, SW18 179 CZ85
Wandsworth Br, SW6 160 DB83
SW18 160 DB83
Wandsworth Br Rd, SW6 307 L6
⇌ Wandsworth Common 180 DF88
Wandsworth Common, SW12 180 DE86
Wandsworth Common W Side,
SW18 180 DC85
Wandsworth High St, SW18 180 DA85
★ Wandsworth Mus, SW18 180 DA85
Wandsworth Plain, SW18 180 DB85
Riv Wandsworth Riverside
Quarter Pier 160 DA84
Wandsworth Rd, SW8 310 A2
Wandsworth Road 309 M9
⇌ Wandsworth Town 160 DB84
Jct Wandsworth Town, SW18 180 DA85
Wangey Rd, Rom. RM6 126 EX59
Wanless Rd, SE24 162 DQ83
Wanley Rd, SE5 162 DR84
Wanlip Rd, E13 292 A4
Wanmer Ct, Reig. RH2
off Birkheads Rd 250 DA133
Wannions Cl, Chesh. HP5 56 AU30
Wannock Gdns, Ilf. IG6 103 EP52
Wansbeck Rd, E3 279 P6
E9 279 P6
Wansbury Way, Swan. BR8 207 FG99
Wansdown Pl, SW6 307 L4
Wansey St, SE17 299 K9
Wansford Cl, Brwd. CM14 108 FT48
Wansford Grn, Wok. GU21 226 AT117
Wansford Pk, Borwd. WD6 78 CS42
Wansford Rd, Wdf.Grn. IG8 102 EJ53
WANSTEAD, E11 124 EH59
⊖ Wanstead 124 EH58
Sch Wanstead Ch Prim Sch, E11
off Church Path 124 EG57
Wanstead Cl, Brom. BR1 204 EJ96
Sch Wanstead High Sch, E11
off Redbridge La W 124 EJ58
Wanstead La, Ilf. IG1 124 EK58
Wanstead Park 124 EH63
Wanstead Pk, E11 124 EK59
Wanstead Pk Av, E12 124 EK61
Wanstead Pk Rd, Ilf. IG1 125 EM60
Wanstead Pl, E11 124 EG58
Wanstead Rd, Brom. BR1 204 EJ96
Wansunt Rd, Bex. DA5 187 FC88
Wantage Rd, SE12 184 EF85
Wantz La, Rain. RM13 147 FH70
Wantz Rd, Dag. RM10 127 FB63
Waplings, The, Tad. KT20 233 CV124
WAPPING, E1 300 D2
⊖ Wapping 300 G3
Wapping Dock St, E1 300 F3
Wapping High St, E1 300 C3
Wapping La, E1 300 F1
Wapping Wall, E1 300 G2
Wapseys La, Hedg. SL2 112 AS58
Wapshott Rd, Stai. TW18 173 BE93
Warbank Cl, New Adgtn CR0 222 EE111
Warbank Cres,
New Adgtn CR0 222 EE110
Warbank La, Kings.T. KT2 179 CT94
Warbeck Rd, W12 139 CV74
Warberry Rd, N22 99 DM54
Warblers Grn, Cob. KT11 214 BZ114
Warboys App, Kings.T. KT2 178 CP93
Warboys Cres, E4 101 EC50
Warboys Rd, Kings.T. KT2 178 CP93
Warburton Cl, N1 277 N4
Harrow HA3 95 CD51
Warburton Ho, E8
off Warburton Rd 278 E8
Warburton Rd, E8 278 E8
Twickenham TW2 176 CB88
Warburton St, E8 278 E8
Warburton Ter, E17 101 EB54
War Coppice Rd, Cat. CR3 252 DR127
Wardalls Gro, SE14 313 H4
Ward Av, Grays RM17 170 GA77
Ward Cl, Chsht EN7 66 DU27
Erith DA8 167 FD79
Iver SL0 153 BF72
South Croydon CR2 220 DS106
Ware SG12 32 DW05
Wardell Cl, NW7 96 CS52
Wardell Fld, NW9 96 CS53
Warden Av, Har. HA2 116 BZ60
Romford RM5 105 FC50
Warden Rd, NW5 275 H4
Wardens Fld Cl,
Grn St Grn BR6 223 ES107
Wardens Gro, SE1 299 J3
Ward Gdns, Harold Wd RM3
off Whitmore Av 106 FL54
Slough SL1 131 AL73
Ward Hatch, Harl. CM20 36 EU12
Ward La, Warl. CR6 236 DW116
Wardle St, E9 279 J3
Wardley St, SW18 180 DB87
Wardo Av, SW6 306 E7
Wardour Ms, W1 285 M9
Wardour St, W1 285 N10
Ward Pl, Amer. HP7 55 AP40
Ward Pt, SE11 298 E9
Ward Rd, E15 280 G8
N19 121 DJ62
Watford WD24 75 BU36
Wardrobe Pl, EC4
off St. Andrew's Hill 287 H9
Wardrobe Ter, EC4 287 H9
Ward Royal, Wind. SL4 151 AQ81
Wards Dr, Sarratt WD3 73 BF36
Wards La, Els. WD6 77 CG40
Ward's Pl, Egh. TW20 173 BC93
Wards Rd, Ilf. IG2 125 ER59
Ward St, Guil. GU1
off Martyr Rd 258 AX135
Wards Wf App, E16 304 E4
WARE, SG12 33 DX06
⇌ Ware 33 DY07
Wareham Cl, Houns. TW3 156 CB84
Wareham Ho, SW8 310 C4
Warehams La, Hert. SG14 32 DQ10
Warehouse W, E16 292 A10
Waremead Rd, Ilf. IG2 125 EP57
★ Ware Mus, Ware SG12 33 DX06
Warenford Way, Borwd. WD6 78 CN39
Warenne Hts, Red. RH1 266 DD136
Warenne Rd, Fetch. KT22 230 CC122
WARE PARK, Ware SG12 32 DT06
Ware Pk Rd, Hert. SG14 32 DR07
Ware Pt Dr, SE28 165 ER75
Ware Rd, Chad.Spr. SG12 32 DU08
Hailey SG13 32 EA12
Hertford SG13, SG14 32 DS09
Hoddesdon EN11 33 EA14
Widford SG12 33 EC05
Warescot Cl, Brwd. CM15 108 FV45
Warescot Rd, Brwd. CM15 108 FV45
Wareside Cl, Welw.G.C. AL7 30 DB10
Warfield Rd, NW10 282 C3
Feltham TW14 175 BS87
Hampton TW12 196 CB95
Warfield Yd, NW10 282 C3
Wargrave Av, N15 122 DT58
Wargrave Rd, Har. HA2 116 CC62
Warham Rd, N4 121 DN57
Harrow HA3 95 CF54
Otford TN14 241 FH116
South Croydon CR2 219 DP106
Warham St, SE5 311 H4
Waring Cl, Orp. BR6 223 ET107
Waring Dr, Orp. BR6 223 ET107
Waring Rd, Sid. DA14 186 EW93
Waring St, SE27 182 DQ91
Warkworth Gdns, Islw. TW7 157 CG80
Warkworth Rd, N17 100 DR52
Warland Rd, SE18 165 ER80
WARLEY, Brwd. CM14 108 FW50
Warley Av, Dag. RM8 126 EZ59
Hayes UB4 135 BU71
Warley Cl, E10 123 DZ60
Warley Gap, Lt.Warley CM13 107 FV52
Warley Hill,
Brwd. CM13, CM14 107 FV51
● Warley Hill Business Pk,
Gt Warley CM13 off The Dr 107 FW51
Warley Mt, Warley CM14 108 FW49
Sch Warley Prim Sch,
Warley CM14 off Chindits La 108 FW50
Warley Rd, N9 100 DW47
Great Warley CM13 107 FT54
Hayes UB4 135 BU72
Ilford IG5 103 EN53
Upminster RM14 106 FQ54
Woodford Green IG8 102 EH52
Warley St, E2 289 J2
Great Warley CM13 129 FW58
Upminster RM14 129 FW58
Warley St Flyover,
Brwd. CM13 129 FX57
Warley Wds Cres, Brwd. CM14
off Crescent Rd 108 FV49
WARLINGHAM, CR6 237 DX118
Sch Warlingham Pk Sch, Warl.
CR6 off Chelsham Common 237 EA116
Warlingham Rd, Th.Hth. CR7 201 DP98
Sch Warlingham Sch, Warl. CR6
off Tithepit Shaw La 236 DV116
Warlock Rd, W9 283 J4
Warlow Cl, Enf. EN3 83 EA37
Warlters Cl, N7
off Warlters Rd 121 DL63
Warlters Rd, N7 121 DL63
Warltersville Rd, N19 121 DL59
Warltersville Way, Horl. RH6 269 DJ150
Warmark Rd, Hem.H. HP1 39 BE18
Warmington Cl, E5
off Denton Way 123 DX62
Warmington Rd, SE24 182 DQ86
Warmington St, E13 291 P4
Warminster Gdns, SE25 202 DU96
Warminster Rd, SE25 202 DT96
Warminster Sq, SE25 202 DU96
Warminster Way, Mitch. CR4 201 DH95
Warmwell Av, NW9 96 CS53
Warndon St, SE16 301 H9
Warneford Ct, NW9
off Annesley Ave 118 CR55
Warneford Pl, Wat. WD19 76 BY44
Warneford Rd, Har. HA3 117 CK55
Lon.Hthrw Air. TW6 154 BH82
Warneford St, E9 278 F8
Warne Pl, Sid. DA15
off Shorne Cl 186 EV86
Warner Av, Sutt. SM3 199 CY103
Warner Cl, E15 281 K3
NW9 119 CT59
Barnet EN4 80 DE37
Hampton TW12
off Tangley Pk Rd 176 BZ92
Harlington UB3 155 BR80
Slough SL1 131 AL74
Warner Ho, SE13 314 D8
Warner Par, Hayes UB3 155 BR80
Warner Pl, E2 288 D1
Warner Rd, E17 123 DY56
N8 121 DK56
SE5 311 J7
Bromley BR1 184 EF94
Ware SG12 32 DW07
Warners Av, Hodd. EN11 49 DZ19
Warners Cl, Wdf.Grn. IG8 102 EG50
WARNERS END, Hem.H. HP1 39 BE19
Warners End Rd, Hem.H. HP1 40 BG20
Warners La, Albury GU5 260 BL141
Kingston upon Thames KT2 177 CK91
Warners Path, Wdf.Grn. IG8 102 EG50
Warner St, EC1 286 E5
Warner Ter, E14 290 B7
Warner Yd, EC1 286 E5
Warnford Ho, SW15
off Tunworth Cres 178 CS86
● Warnford Ind Est,
Hayes UB3 155 BS75
Warnford Rd, Orp. BR6 223 ET106
Warnham Ct Rd, Cars. SM5 218 DF108
Warnham Rd, N12 98 DE50
Warple Ms, W3
off Warple Way 158 CS75
Warple Way, W3 138 CS74
Warren, The, E12 124 EL63
Ashtead KT21 232 CL119
Carshalton SM5 218 DD109
Chalfont St. Peter SL9 91 AZ52
Chesham HP5 54 AL28
East Horsley KT24 245 BT130
Gravesend DA12 191 GK91
Hayes UB4 135 BU72
Hounslow TW5 156 BZ80
Kings Langley WD4 58 BM29
Kingswood KT20 233 CY123
Oxshott KT22 214 CC112
Warren, The, Park Street AL2
off How Wd 60 CC28
Radlett WD7 61 CG33
Worcester Park KT4 216 CR105
Warren Av, E10 123 EC62
Bromley BR1 184 EE94
Orpington BR6 223 ET106
Richmond TW10 158 CP84
South Croydon CR2 221 DX108
Sutton SM2 217 CZ110
Warren Cl, N9 101 DX45
SE21 182 DQ87
Bexleyheath DA6 186 FA85
Esher KT10 214 CB105
Hatfield AL10 45 CV15
Hayes UB4 136 BW71
Slough SL3 152 AY76
Wembley HA9 117 CK61
Sch Warren Comp Sch, The,
Chad.Hth RM6
off Whalebone La N 126 EZ57
Warren Ct, N17
off High Cross Rd 122 DU55
SE7 164 EJ78
Ashtead KT21 off Ashfield Cl 232 CL119
Chigwell IG7 103 ER49
Sevenoaks TN13 257 FJ125
Weybridge KT13 212 BN106
Warren Cres, N9 100 DT45
Warren Cutting, Kings.T. KT2 178 CR94
Warren Dale, Welw.G.C. AL8 29 CX06
Sch Warren Dell Prim Sch,
S.Oxhey WD19 off Gosforth La 94 BW48
Sch Warrender Prim Sch,
Ruis. HA4 off Old Hatch Manor 115 BT59
Warrender Rd, N19 121 DJ62
Chesham HP5 54 AS29
Warrender Way, Ruis. HA4 115 BU59
Warren Dr, Grnf. UB6 136 CB70
Hornchurch RM12 127 FG62
Kingswood KT20 233 CZ122
Orpington BR6 224 EV106
Ruislip HA4 116 BX59
Warren Dr, The, E11 124 EJ59
Warren Dr N, Surb. KT5 198 CP102
Warren Dr S, Surb. KT5 198 CQ102
Warreners La, Wey. KT13 213 BR109
Warren Fm Home Pk,
Wok. GU22 228 BH119
Warren Fld, Epp. CM16 70 EU32
Iver SL0 133 BC68
Warrenfield Cl, Chsht EN7 66 DU31
Warren Flds, Stan. HA7
off Valencia Rd 95 CJ49
Warren Footpath, Twick. TW1 177 CK87
Warren Gdns, E15 280 G3
Orpington BR6 224 EU106
Warrengate La, S.Mimms EN6 63 CW31
Warrengate Rd, N.Mymms AL9 63 CW28
Warren Grn, Hat. AL10 45 CV15
Warren Gro, Borwd. WD6 78 CR42
Warren Hastings Ct, Grav. DA11
off Pier Rd 191 GF86
Warren Hts, Chaff.Hun. RM16 170 FY77
Loughton IG10 84 EJ43
Warren Hill, Epsom KT18 232 CR116
Loughton IG10 84 EJ44
Warren Ho, E3 290 C2
W14 295 H8
Warren Ho Conf Cen,
Kings.T. KT2 178 CQ93
Warrenhurst Gdns, Wey. KT13 213 BR107
Warrenhyrst, Guil. GU1
off Warren Rd 259 BA135
Sch Warren Jun Sch,
Chad.Hth RM6 off Gordon Rd 126 EZ57
Warren La, SE18 305 N7
Albury GU5 260 BJ139
Grays RM16 169 FX77
Oxshott KT22 214 CC111
Oxted RH8 254 EF134
Stanmore HA7 95 CF48
Woking GU22 228 BH118
Warren La Gate, SE18 305 N7
Warren Lo, Kgswd KT20 233 CY124
Warren Mead, Bans. SM7 233 CW115
Sch Warren Mead Inf Sch,
Bans. SM7 off Partridge Mead 233 CX115
Sch Warren Mead Jun Sch,
Nork SM7 off Roundwood Way 233 CX115
Warren Ms, W1 285 L5
Warrenne Rd, Brock. RH3 264 CP136
Warrenne Way, Reig. RH2 250 DA134
Warren Pk, Box H. KT20 248 CQ131
Kingston upon Thames KT2 178 CQ93
Warlingham CR6 237 DX118
Warren Pk Rd, Hert. SG14 32 DQ08
Sutton SM1 218 DD107
Warren Pond Rd, E4 102 EF46
Sch Warren Prim Sch,
Chaff.Hun. RM16 off Gilbert Rd 169 FW76
Warren Ri, N.Mal. KT3 198 CR95
Warren Rd, E4 101 EC47
E10 123 EC62
E11 124 EJ60
NW2 119 CT61
SW19 180 DE93
Ashford TW15 175 BS94
Banstead SM7 217 CW114
Bexleyheath DA6 186 FA85
Bromley BR2 204 EG103
Bushey Heath WD23 94 CC46
Croydon CR0 202 DS102
Dartford DA1 188 FK90
Godalming GU7 258 AS144
Guildford GU1 259 AZ135
Ilford IG6 125 ER57
Kingston upon Thames KT2 178 CQ93
New Haw KT15 212 BG110
Orpington BR6 223 ET106
Purley CR8 219 DP111
Reigate RH2 250 DB133
St. Albans AL1 42 CC24
Sidcup DA14 186 EW90
Southfleet DA13 190 GB92
Twickenham TW2 176 CC86
Uxbridge UB10 114 BL63
Sch Warren Rd Prim Sch,
Orp. BR6 off Warren Rd 223 ET106
Warrens Shawe La, Edg. HA8 96 CP46
⊖ Warren Street 285 M4
Warren St, W1 285 K5
Warren Ter, Grays RM16
off Arterial Rd W Thurrock 169 FX75
Hertford SG14 32 DR07
Romford RM6 126 EX56
Warren Wk, SE7 164 EJ79
Warren Way, Edg. HA8 96 CP54
Weybridge KT13 213 BQ106
Warren Wd Cl, Brom. BR2 204 EF103
Warren Wd Ms, Hat. AL9 46 DD22
Warriner Av, Horn. RM12 128 FK61
Warriner Dr, N9 100 DU48
Warriner Gdns, SW11 308 F7
Warrington Av, Slou. SL1 131 AQ72
Warrington Cres, W9 283 N5
Warrington Gdns, W9 283 N5
Hornchurch RM11 128 FJ58
Warrington Rd, Croy. CR0 201 DP104
Dagenham RM8 126 EX61
Harrow HA1 117 CE57
Richmond TW10 177 CK85
Warrington Spur,
Old Wind. SL4 172 AV87
Warrington Sq, Dag. RM8 126 EX61
Warrior Av, Grav. DA12 191 GJ91
Warrior Cl, SE28 145 ER74
Warrior Sq, E12 125 EN63
Warsaw Cl, Ruis. HA4
off Glebe Av 135 BV65
Warsdale Dr, NW9
off Mardale Dr 118 CR57
Warspite Rd, SE18 304 G6
Warton Rd, E15 280 E8
Warwall, E6 293 N8
⊖ Warwick Avenue 283 N5
Warwick Av, W2 283 N5
W9 283 N5
Cuffley EN6 65 DK27
Edgware HA8 96 CP48
Egham TW20 193 BC95
Harrow HA2 116 BZ63
Slough SL2 131 AQ70
Staines-upon-Thames TW18 174 BJ93
Warwick Bldg, SW8 309 J4
Warwick Chambers, W8
off Pater St 295 J6
Warwick Cl, Barn. EN4 80 DD43
Bexley DA5 186 EZ87
Bushey Heath WD23
off Magnaville Rd 95 CE45
Cuffley EN6 65 DK27
Hampton TW12 176 CC94
Hertford SG13 32 DQ11
Hornchurch RM11 128 FM56
Orpington BR6 206 EU104
South Holmwood RH5 263 CH144
Warwick Ct, SE15 312 D9
WC1 286 D7
Chorleywood WD3 73 BF41
Surbiton KT6 198 CL103
Warwick Cres, W2 283 N6
Hayes UB4 135 BT70
Warwick Deeping, Ott. KT16 211 BC106
Warwick Dene, W5 138 CL74
Warwick Dr, SW15 159 CV83
Cheshunt EN8 67 DX28
Warwick Est, W2 283 L7
Warwick Gdns, N4 122 DQ57
W14 295 H7
Ashtead KT21 231 CJ117
Barnet EN5 79 CZ38
Ilford IG1 125 EP60
Romford RM2 128 FJ55
Thames Ditton KT7 197 CF99
Thornton Heath CR7
off London Rd 201 DN97
Warwick Gro, E5 122 DV60
Surbiton KT5 198 CM101
Warwick Ho St, SW1 297 P2
Warwick La, EC4 287 H9
Rainham RM13 148 FM68
Upminster RM14 148 FP68
Woking GU21 226 AU119
Warwick Ms, Crox.Grn WD3 74 BN44
Warwick Pas, EC4 287 H8
Warwick Pl, W5
off Warwick Rd 157 CK75
W9 283 N6
Northfleet DA11 190 GB85
Uxbridge UB8 134 BJ66
Warwick Pl N, SW1 297 L9
🔒 Warwick Quad Shop Mall,
Red. RH1 off London Rd 250 DG133
Warwick Rd, E4 101 EA50
E11 124 EH57
E12 124 EL64
E15 281 M5
E17 101 DZ53
N11 99 DK51
N18 100 DS49
SE20 202 DV97
SW5 294 G8
W5 157 CK75
W14 294 G8
Ashford TW15 174 BL92
Barnet EN5 80 DB42
Beaconsfield HP9 89 AK52
Borehamwood WD6 78 CR41
Coulsdon CR5 219 DJ114
Enfield EN3 83 DZ37
Hounslow TW4 155 BV83
Kingston upon Thames KT1 197 CJ95
New Malden KT3 198 CQ97
Rainham RM13 148 FJ70
Redhill RH1 250 DF133
St. Albans AL1 43 CF18
Sidcup DA14 186 EV92
Southall UB2 156 BZ76
Sutton SM1 218 DC105
Thames Ditton KT7 197 CF99
Thornton Heath CR7 201 DN97
Twickenham TW2 177 CE88
Welling DA16 166 EW83
West Drayton UB7 154 BL75
Warwick Row, SW1 297 K6
Warwicks Bench, Guil. GU1 258 AX136
Warwicks Bench La,
Guil. GU1 258 AY137
Warwicks Bench Rd,
Guil. GU1 258 AY137
Sch Warwick Sch, The,
Red. RH1 off Noke Dr 250 DG133
Warwickshire Path, SE8 313 P4
Warwick Sq, EC4 287 H8
SW1 297 L10
Warwick Sq Ms, SW1 297 L9
Warwick St, W1 285 M10
Warwick Ter, SE18 165 ER79
Warwick Way, SW1 297 L9
Croxley Green WD3 75 BQ42
Dartford DA1 188 FL89
WARWICK WOLD, Red. RH1 251 DN129
Warwick Wold Rd, Red. RH1 251 DN128
Warwick Yd, EC1 287 K5
Wash, The, Hert. SG14 32 DR09
Wash Hill, Woob.Grn HP10 110 AE60
Wash Hill Lea, Woob.Grn HP10 110 AD59
Washington Av, E12 124 EL63
Hemel Hempstead HP2 40 BM15
Washington Bldg, SE13
off Deals Gateway 314 C6
Washington Cl, E3 290 D2
Reigate RH2 250 DA131
Washington Dr, Slou. SL1 131 AK73
Windsor SL4 151 AL83
Washington Rd, E6
off St. Stephens Rd 144 EJ66
E18 102 EF54
SW13 159 CU80
Kingston upon Thames KT1 198 CN96
Lon.Hthrw Air. TW6
off Wayfarer Rd 154 BH82
Worcester Park KT4 199 CV103
Washington Row, Amer. HP7
off London Rd W 55 AQ40
Wash La, S.Mimms EN6 63 CV33
Washneys Rd, Orp. BR6 224 EV113
Washpond La, Warl. CR6 237 EC118
Wash Rd, Hutt. CM13 109 GD44
Wasp Grn La, Outwood RH1 267 DP143
Wasp Rd, Lon.Hthrw Air. TW6
off Wayfarer Rd 154 BH82
Wastdale Rd, SE23 183 DX88
Watchfield Ct, W4 158 CQ78
Watchgate, Lane End DA2 189 FR91
Watchlytes, Welw.G.C. AL7 30 DC09
Sch Watchlytes Sch,
Welw.G.C. AL7 off Watchlytes 30 DC09
Watchmead, Welw.G.C. AL7 30 DA09
Watcombe Cotts, Rich. TW9 158 CN79
Watcombe Pl, SE25
off Albert Rd 202 DV98
Watcombe Rd, SE25 202 DV99
Waterbank Rd, SE6 183 EC91
Waterbeach, Welw.G.C. AL7 30 DD08
Waterbeach Cl, Slou. SL1 131 AR72
Waterbeach Rd, Dag. RM9 146 EW65
Slough SL1 131 AR72
Waterbourne Way, Ken. CR8 220 DR114
Water Brook La, NW4 119 CW57
Watercress Pl, N1 277 P7
Watercress Rd, Chsht EN7 66 DR26
Watercress Way, Wok. GU21 226 AV117
Watercroft Rd, Halst. TN14 224 EZ110
Jct Waterdale, Wat. WD25 60 BX30
Waterdale, Hert. SG13 32 DQ11
Waterdale Rd, SE2 166 EU79
Waterdales, Nthflt DA11 190 GD88
Waterdell Pl, Rick. WD3
off Uxbridge Rd 92 BG47
Waterden Cl, Guil. GU1 259 AZ135
Waterden Rd, E20 280 B3
Guildford GU1 258 AY135
WATER END, Hat. AL9 63 CV26
Water End Cl, Borwd. WD6 78 CM40
Waterend La, Ayot St.P. AL6 28 CQ07
Wheathampstead AL4 28 CQ07
Water End Rd, Pott.End HP4 39 BB17
Waterer Gdns, Tad. KT20 233 CX118
Waterer Ri, Wall. SM6 219 DK107
Waterfall Cl, N14 99 DJ48
Hoddesdon EN11 49 DZ16
Virginia Water GU25 192 AU97
Waterfall Cotts, SW19 180 DD93
Waterfall Rd, N11 99 DH49
N14 99 DJ48
SW19 180 DD93
Waterfall Ter, SW17 180 DE93
Waterfield, Herons. WD3 91 BC45
Tadworth KT20 233 CV119
Welwyn Garden City AL7 30 DB08
Waterfield Cl, SE28 146 EV74
Belvedere DA17 166 FA76
Waterfield Dr, Warl. CR6 236 DW119
Waterfield Gdns, SE25 202 DR98
Waterfield Grn, Tad. KT20 233 CW120
Waterfields, Lthd. KT22 231 CH119
Watford WD17 76 BX42
🔒 Waterfields Retail Pk,
Wat. WD17 76 BX42
Waterfields Way, Wat. WD17 76 BX42
WATERFORD, Hert. SG14 31 DM05
Waterford Cl, Cob. KT11 214 BY111
Waterford Common,
Waterf. SG14 31 DP05
Waterford Grn, Welw.G.C. AL7 30 DB09
Waterford Rd, SW6 307 M6
Waterford Way, NW10 119 CV64
Waterfront, The, Els. WD6 77 CH44
Hertford SG14 32 DR09
Waterfront Apts, W9 283 L5
Waterfront Ms, N1
off Arlington Av 277 K10
● Waterfront Studios
Business Cen, E16 303 N2
🔒 Water Gdns, Harl. CM20 51 ER15
Water Gdns, Stan. HA7 95 CH51
Water Gdns, The, W2 284 D8
Watergardens, The,
Kings.T. KT2 178 CQ93
Water Gdns Sq, SE16 301 J5
Watergate, EC4 286 G10
Watergate, The, Wat. WD19 94 BX47
Sch Watergate Sch, SE6
off Lushington Rd 183 EB92
Watergate St, SE8 314 A3
Watergate Wk, WC2 298 B2
● Waterglade Ind Pk,
Grays RM20 169 FT78
Waterglades, Knot.Grn HP9 88 AJ49
Waterhall Av, E4 102 EE49
Waterhall Cl, E17 101 DX53
Waterhead Cl, Erith DA8 167 FE80
Waterhouse Cl, E16 292 E6
NW3 274 B2
W6 294 D10
Waterhouse La, Bletch. RH1 252 DT132
Kenley CR8 236 DQ119
Kingswood KT20 233 CY121
Waterhouse Moor, Harl. CM18 51 ES16
Waterhouse Sq, EC1 286 E7
Waterhouse St, Hem.H. HP1 40 BJ20
Wateridge Cl, E14 302 A7
Wateringbury Cl, Orp. BR5 206 EV97
Water La, E15 281 K4
EC3 299 N1
N9 100 DV46
NW1 275 K7
SE14 313 H4
Abinger Hammer RH5 261 BV143
Albury GU5 260 BH137
Berkhamsted HP4 38 AW19
Bookham KT23 246 BY125
Bovingdon HP3 57 BA29
Chesham HP5 54 AP32
Cobham KT11 230 BY115

W

Water La, Hertford SG14 32 DQ10
Ilford IG3 125 ES62
Kings Langley WD4 59 BP29
Kingston upon Thames KT1 197 CK95
Purfleet RM19 168 FN77
Redhill RH1 251 DP130
Richmond TW9 177 CK85
Roydon CM19 50 EL19
Shoreham TN14 225 FF112
Sidcup DA14 186 EZ89
Titsey RH8 254 EG126
Twickenham TW1
off The Embankment 177 CG88
Watford WD17 76 BW42
Westerham TN16 255 ER127
Sch **Water La Prim Sch**,
Harl. CM19 *off Broadley Rd* 51 EN19
Water Lily Cl, Sthl. UB2
off Navigator Dr 156 CC75
⇌ **Waterloo** 298 E4
⊖ **Waterloo** 298 E4
Waterloo Br, SE1 298 C1
WC2 298 C1
Waterloo Cl, E9 279 H2
Feltham TW14 175 BT88
⇌ **Waterloo East** 298 E3
Waterloo Est, E2 278 G10
Waterloo Gdns, E2 278 G10
N1 276 G7
Romford RM7 127 FD58
Waterloo Pas, NW6 273 H7
Waterloo Pl, SW1 297 N2
Kew TW9 *off Kew Grn* 158 CN79
Richmond TW9
off The Quadrant 158 CL84
Waterloo Rd, E6 144 EJ66
E7 281 M2
E10 123 EA59
NW2 119 CU60
SE1 298 E4
Brentwood CM14 108 FW46
Epsom KT19 216 CR112
Ilford IG6 103 EQ54
Romford RM7 127 FE57
Sutton SM1 218 DD106
Uxbridge UB8 134 BJ67
Waterloo St, Grav. DA12 191 GJ87
Waterloo Ter, N1 276 G7
Waterlow Ct, NW11
off Heath Cl 120 DB59
Waterlow Rd, N19 121 DJ60
Reigate RH2 266 DC135
Waterman Cl, Wat. WD19 75 BV44
Waterman Ct, Slou. SL1 131 AL74
Watermans, Rom. RM1 127 FF57
● **Watermans, The**,
Stai. TW18 173 BE91
★ **Watermans Art Cen**,
Brent. TW8 158 CL79
Waterman's Cl, Kings.T. KT2
off Woodside Rd 178 CL94
Waterman St, SW15 159 CX83
Watermans Wk, SE16 301 L6
Waterman's Wk, EC4
off Allhallows La 299 L1
Watermans Way, Green. DA9 169 FV84
North Weald Bassett CM16 70 FA27
Waterman Way, E1 300 E2
Watermark Way, Hert. SG13 32 DT09
Water Mead, Chipstead CR5 234 DF117
Watermead, Felt. TW14 175 BS88
Tadworth KT20 233 CV121
Woking GU21 226 AT116
Watermead Ho, E9
off Kingsmead Way 279 M2
Watermead La, Cars. SM5
off Middleton Rd 200 DF101
Watermeadow, Chesh. HP5 54 AP32
Watermeadow Cl, Erith DA8 167 FH80
Watermeadow La, SW6 307 N9
Water Meadows, Frog. AL2
off Frogmore 61 CE28
Watermead Rd, SE6 183 EC91
Watermead Way, N17 122 DV55
Watermen's Sq, SE20 182 DW94
Water Ms, SE15 162 DW84
● **Watermill Business Cen**,
Enf. EN3 83 DZ40
Watermill Cl, Brasted TN16 240 EW124
Richmond TW10 177 CJ90
Watermill La, N18 100 DS50
Hertford SG14 32 DR06
Watermill La N, Hert. SG14 32 DQ06
Watermill Way, SW19 200 DC95
Feltham TW13 176 BZ89
Water Mill Way,
S.Darenth DA4 208 FP96
Watermint Cl, Orp. BR5
off Wagtail Way 206 EX98
Watermint Quay, N16 122 DU59
Waterperry La,
Chobham GU24 210 AT110
Water Rd, Wem. HA0 138 CM67
Water Row, Ware SG12 33 DX06
Waters Dr, Rick. WD3 92 BL46
Staines-upon-Thames TW18 173 BF90
Watersedge, Epsom KT19 216 CQ105
Waters Edge Ct, Erith DA8
off Erith High St 167 FF78
Watersfield Way, Edg. HA8 95 CK52
Waters Gdns, Dag. RM10 126 FA64
WATERSIDE, Chesh. HP5 54 AR32
Waterside, Beck. BR3 203 EA95
Berkhamsted HP4
off Holliday St 38 AX19
Chesham HP5 54 AQ32
Dartford DA1 187 FE85
Gravesend DA11 190 GE86
Horley RH6 268 DG146
London Colney AL2 62 CL27
Radlett WD7 61 CH34
Uxbridge UB8 134 BJ71
Welwyn Garden City AL7 30 DA07
Wooburn Green HP10 110 AE56
Water Side, Kings L. WD4 58 BN29
Waterside Av, Beck. BR3
off Brockwell Av 203 EB99
● **Waterside Business Cen**,
Islw. TW7 *off Railshead Rd* 157 CH84
Waterside Cl, E3 279 N8
SE16 300 D5
SE28 145 ET74
Barking IG11 126 EU63
Harold Wood RM3 106 FN52
Northolt UB5 136 BZ69
Shepperton TW17 195 BQ95
Surbiton KT6 *off Culsac Rd* 198 CL103
Sch **Waterside Comb Sch**,
Chesh. HP5 *off Blackhorse Av* 54 AR33
Waterside Ct, SE13
off Weardale Rd 163 ED84
Kings Langley WD4
off Water Side 59 BP29
Waterside Dr, Langley SL3 153 AZ75
Walton-on-Thames KT12 195 BU99
Waterside Ms, Guil. GU1 242 AW132
Harefield UB9 92 BG51
Waterside Path, SW18
off Smugglers Way 160 DB84
Waterside Pl, NW1 275 H8
Sawbridgeworth CM21 36 FA05
Waterside Pt, SW11 308 D4
Waterside Rd, Guil. GU1 242 AX131
Southall UB2 156 CA76
Sch **Waterside Sch**, SE18
off Robert St 165 ER78
Waterside Twr, SW6 307 P8
● **Waterside Trd Cen**, W7 157 CE76
Waterside Way, SW17 180 DC91
Woking GU21
off Winnington Way 226 AV118
Waterslade, Red. RH1 250 DE134
Watersmeet, Harl. CM19 51 EP19
Watersmeet Cl, Guil. GU4
off Cotts Wd Dr 243 BA129
Watersmeet Way, SE28 146 EW72
Waterson Rd, Grays RM16 171 GH77
Waterson St, E2 287 P2
Waters Pl, SW15 306 B9
Watersplash Cl, Kings.T. KT1 198 CL97
Watersplash Ct, Lon.Col. AL2
off Thamesdale 62 CM27
Watersplash La, Hayes UB3 155 BU77
Hounslow TW5 155 BV78
Watersplash Rd, Shep. TW17 194 BN98
Waters Rd, SE6 184 EE90
Kingston upon Thames KT1 198 CP96
Waters Sq, Kings.T. KT1 198 CP97
Waterstone Way, Green. DA9 189 FU86
Water St, WC2 286 D10
Waterton, Swan. BR8 207 FD98
Waterton Av, Grav. DA12 191 GL87
Water Twr Cl, Uxb. UB8 114 BL64
Water Twr Hill, Croy. CR0 220 DR105
Water Twr Pl, N1 276 F9
Water Twr Rd,
Gt Warley CM14 108 FW50
Water Vw, Horl. RH6
off Carlton Tye 269 DJ148
Waterview Cl, Bexh. DA6 186 EX85
Waterview Ho, E14 289 M7
Waterway Av, SE13 163 EB83
● **Waterway Business Pk**,
Hayes UB3 155 BR75
Waterway Rd, Lthd. KT22 231 CG122
● **Waterways Business Cen**,
Enf. EN3 83 EA38
Jct **Waterworks Cor**, E18 102 EE54
Waterworks Cotts, Brox. EN10 49 DY22
Waterworks La, E5 123 DX61
Waterworks Rd, SW2 181 DL86
Waterworks Yd, Croy. CR0
off Surrey St 202 DQ104
Watery La, SW20 199 CZ96
Broxbourne EN10 67 DY25
Flamstead AL3 61 CK28
Hatfield AL10 44 CS19
Lyne KT16 193 BD101
Northolt UB5 136 BW68
Sidcup DA14 186 EV93
Wooburn Green HP10 88 AE54
Wates Way, Brwd. CM15 108 FX46
Mitcham CR4 200 DF100
● **Wates Way Ind Est**,
Mitch. CR4 200 DF100
Wateville Rd, N17 100 DQ53
WATFORD, WD17 - WD19;
WD24 & WD25 75 BT41
⊖ **Watford** 75 BT41
🔒 **Watford Arches Retail Pk**,
Wat. WD17 76 BX43
● **Watford Business Pk**,
Wat. WD18 75 BS44
Watford Bypass, Borwd. WD6 95 CG45
Watford Cl, SW11 308 D6
Guildford GU1 243 AZ134
Watford Fld Rd, Wat. WD17 76 BW43
★ **Watford FC**, Wat. WD18 75 BV43
H **Watford Gen Hosp**,
Wat. WD18 75 BV43
Sch **Watford Gram Sch for Boys**,
Wat. WD18
off Rickmansworth Rd 75 BT42
Sch **Watford Gram Sch for Girls**,
Wat. WD18 *off Lady's Cl* 76 BW43
WATFORD HEATH, Wat. WD19 94 BY46
Watford Heath, Wat. WD19 94 BX45
Watford High Street 76 BW42
Watford Ho La, Wat. WD17
off Clarendon Rd 75 BV41
⇌ **Watford Junction** 76 BW40
Watford Junction 76 BW40
● **Watford Metro Cen**,
Wat. WD18 93 BQ45
★ **Watford Mus**, Wat. WD17 76 BW42
⇌ **Watford North** 76 BW37
Watford Rd, E16 291 P7
Croxley Green WD3 75 BQ43
Elstree WD6 77 CJ44
Harrow HA1 117 CG61
Kings Langley WD4 59 BP32
Northwood HA6 93 BT52
Radlett WD7 77 CE36
St. Albans AL1, AL2 60 CA27
Wembley HA0 117 CG61
Watford Way, NW4 119 CU56
NW7 97 CT51
Wathen Rd, Dor. RH4 263 CH135
Watkin Ms, Enf. EN3 83 EA37
Watkin Rd, Wem. HA9 118 CP62
Watkins Cl, Nthwd. HA6
off Chestnut Av 93 BT53
Watkinson Rd, N7 276 C4
Watkins Ri, Pot.B. EN6
off The Walk 64 DB32
Watkins Way, Dag. RM8 126 EY60
Watling Av, Edg. HA8 96 CR52
Watling Cl, Hem.H. HP2 40 BL17
Watling Ct, EC4 287 K9
Borehamwood WD6 77 CK44
Watling Fm Cl, Stan. HA7 95 CJ46
Watling Gdns, NW2 272 F5
Watling Knoll, Rad. WD7 61 CF33
Watlings Cl, Croy. CR0 203 DY100
Watling St, EC4 287 J9
SE15 311 P3
Bexleyheath DA6 167 FB84
Dartford DA1, DA2 188 FP87
Watling St, Elstree WD6 77 CJ40
Gravesend
DA11, DA12, DA13 191 GL94
Radlett WD7 61 CF32
St. Albans AL1, AL2 60 CC25
Watling St Caravan Site (Travellers),
Park St AL2 60 CC25
Watlington Gro, SE26 183 DY92
Watlington Rd, Harl. CM17 36 EX11
Watling Vw, St.Alb. AL1 42 CC24
Sch **Watling Vw Sch**, St.Alb. AL1
off Watling Vw 43 CD24
Watney Cl, Pur. CR8 219 DM113
Watney Cotts, SW14
off Lower Richmond Rd 158 CQ83
Watney Mkt, E1 288 F9
Watney Rd, SW14 158 CQ83
Watneys Rd, Mitch. CR4 201 DK99
Watney St, E1 288 F9
Watson Av, E6 145 EN66
St. Albans AL3 43 CF17
Sutton SM3 199 CY103
Watson Cl, N16 277 M2
SW19 180 DE93
Grays RM20 169 FU81
Watson Gdns,
Harold Wd. RM3 106 FK54
Watson Ho, Har. HA1 117 CF57
Watson Pl, SE25 202 DT99
Watson Rd, Westc. RH4 262 CC137
Watsons Ms, W1 284 D7
Watsons Rd, N22 99 DM53
Watson's St, SE8 314 A5
Watson St, E13 144 EH68
Watson's Wk, St.Alb. AL1 43 CE21
Sch **Wattenden Prim Sch, The**,
Pur. CR8 *off Old Lo La* 235 DP116
Wattendon Rd, Ken. CR8 235 DP116
Wattisfield Rd, E5 122 DW62
Wattleton Rd, Beac. HP9 89 AK54
Watton Rd, Ware SG12 32 DW05
Watts Cl, N15 122 DS57
Tadworth KT20 233 CX122
Watts Cres, Purf. RM19 168 FQ77
Watts Down Cl, E13 281 N9
Watts Fm Par, Chobham GU24
off Barnmead 210 AT110
Watts Gro, E3 290 C6
Watts La, Chis. BR7 205 EP95
Tadworth KT20 233 CX122
Teddington TW11 177 CG92
Watts La, Horsell GU21 226 AU115
Watts Mead, Tad. KT20 233 CX122
Watts Rd, T.Ditt. KT7 197 CG101
Watts St, E1 300 F2
SE15 312 B6
Watts Way, SW7 296 B6
Wat Tyler Rd, SE3 314 F8
SE10 314 F8
Wauthier Cl, N13 99 DP50
Wavell Cl, Chsht EN8 67 DY27
Wavell Dr, Sid. DA15 185 ES86
Wavell Gdns, Slou. SL2 131 AM69
Wavell Rd, Beac. HP9 89 AP54
Wavel Ms, N8 121 DK56
NW6 273 L7
Wavel Pl, SE26
off Sydenham Hill 182 DT91
Wavendene Av, Egh. TW20 173 BB94
Wavendon Av, W4 158 CR78
Waveney, Hem.H. HP2 40 BM15
Waveney Av, SE15 162 DV84
Waveney Cl, E1 300 D2
Waverley Av, E4 101 DZ49
E17 123 ED55
Kenley CR8 236 DS116
Surbiton KT5 198 CP100
Sutton SM1 200 DB103
Twickenham TW2 176 BZ88
Wembley HA9 118 CM64
Waverley Cl, E18 102 EJ53
Bromley BR2 204 EK99
Hayes UB3 155 BR77
West Molesey KT8 196 CA99
Waverley Ct, Wok. GU22 226 AY118
Waverley Cres, SE18 165 ER78
Romford RM3 106 FJ51
Waverley Dr, Cher. KT16 193 BD104
Virginia Water GU25 192 AU97
Waverley Gdns, E6 293 H7
NW10 138 CM69
Barking IG11 145 ES68
Grays RM16 170 GA75
Ilford IG6 103 EQ54
Northwood HA6 93 BU53
Waverley Gro, N3 119 CX55
● **Waverley Ind Pk**, Har. HA1 117 CD55
Waverley Pl, N4 121 DP60
NW8 274 A10
Leatherhead KT22
off Church Rd 231 CH122
Waverley Rd, E17 123 EC55
E18 102 EJ53
N8 121 DK58
N17 100 DV52
SE18 165 EQ78
SE25 202 DV98
Enfield EN2 81 DP42
Epsom KT17 217 CV106
Harrow HA2 116 BZ60
Oxshott KT22 214 CB114
Rainham RM13 147 FH69
St. Albans AL3 43 CD18
Slough SL1 131 AQ71
Southall UB1 136 CA73
Stoke D'Abernon KT11 214 CB114
Weybridge KT13 212 BN106
Sch **Waverley Sch**, Enf. EN3
off The Ride 82 DW42
Waverley Vil, N17 100 DT54
Waverley Wk, W2 283 K6
Waverley Way, Cars. SM5 218 DE107
Waverton Ho, E3 279 P8
Waverton Rd, SW18 180 DC87
Waverton St, W1 297 H2
Wavertree Ct, SW2
off Streatham Hill 181 DL88
Wavertree Rd, E18 102 EG54
SW2 181 DL88
Waxham, NW3 274 F2
Waxlow Cres, Sthl. UB1 136 CA72
Waxlow Rd, NW10 138 CQ68
Waxlow Way, Nthlt. UB5 136 BZ70
Waxwell Cl, Pnr. HA5 94 BX54
Waxwell La, Pnr. HA5 94 BX54
Way, The, Reig. RH2 250 DD133
Wayborne Gro, Ruis. HA4 115 BQ58
Waycross Rd, Upmin. RM14 129 FS58
Waye Av, Houns. TW5 155 BU81
Wayfarer Rd,
Lon.Hthrw Air. TW6 154 BH82
Nthlt. UB5 136 BX70
Wayfarers Pk, Berk. HP4 38 AT19
Wayfaring Grn, Bad.Dene RM17
off Curling La 170 FZ78
Wayfield Link, SE9 185 ER86
Wayford St, SW11 308 D9
Wayland Av, E8 278 D3
Wayland Ho, SW9 310 E8
Waylands, Hayes UB3 135 BR71
Swanley BR8 207 FF98
Wraysbury TW19 172 AY86
Waylands Cl, Knock.P. TN14 240 EY115
Waylands Mead, Beck. BR3 203 EB95
Wayleave, The, SE28 146 EV73
Waylen Gdns, Dart. DA1 168 FM82
Waylett Ho, SE11 310 E1
Waylett Pl, SE27 181 DP90
Wembley HA0 117 CK63
Wayman Ct, E8 278 E5
Wayne Cl, Orp. BR6 205 ET104
Wayneflete Ms,
Hersham KT12 214 BY105
Wayneflete Pl, Esher KT10
off More La 196 CB104
Wayneflete Twr Av,
Esher KT10 196 CA104
Waynflete Av, Croy. CR0 201 DP104
Waynflete Sq, W10 282 C10
Waynflete St, SW18 180 DC89
Wayre, The, Harl. CM17 36 EW11
Wayre St, Harl. CM17 36 EW11
Wayside, NW11 119 CY60
SW14 178 CQ85
Chipperfield WD4 58 BH30
New Addington CR0 221 EB107
Potters Bar EN6 64 DD33
Shenley WD7 61 CK33
Wayside, The, Hem.H. HP3 41 BQ21
Wayside Av, Bushey WD23 77 CD44
Hornchurch RM12 128 FK61
Wayside Cl, N14 81 DJ44
Romford RM1 127 FF55
● **Wayside Commercial Est**,
Bark. IG11 146 EU67
Wayside Ct, Twick. TW1 177 CJ86
Wembley HA9 118 CN62
Woking GU21
off Langmans Way 226 AS116
Wayside Gdns, SE9
off Wayside Gro 185 EM91
Dagenham RM10 126 FA64
Gerrards Cross SL9 112 AX59
Wayside Gro, SE9 185 EM91
Wayside Ms, Ilf. IG2
off Gaysham Av 125 EN57
Wayville Rd, Dart. DA1 188 FP87
Way Volante, Grav. DA12 191 GL91
Weald, The, Chis. BR7 185 EM93
Weald Br Rd, N.Wld Bas. CM16 53 FD24
Weald Cl, SE16 300 E10
Brentwood CM14 108 FU48
Bromley BR2 204 EL103
Istead Rise DA13 190 GE94
Shalford GU4 *off Station Rd* 258 AY140
★ **Weald Country Pk**,
Brwd. CM14 108 FS45
● **Weald Hall Fm Commercial
Cen**, Hast. CM17 70 EZ25
Weald Hall La, Thnwd CM16 70 EW25
Sch **Weald Inf & Jun Schs**,
Har. HA3 *off Robin Hood Dr* 95 CF52
Weald La, Har. HA3 95 CD54
Wealdon Ct, Guil. GU2
off Chapelhouse Cl 242 AS134
Weald Pk Way, S.Wld CM14 108 FS48
Weald Ri, Har. HA3 95 CF52
Weald Rd, Brwd. CM14 107 FR46
Sevenoaks TN13 257 FH129
Uxbridge UB10 134 BN68
Weald Sq, E5 122 DU61
WEALDSTONE, Har. HA3 117 CF55
Wealdstone Rd, Sutt. SM3 199 CZ103
Weald Way, Cat. CR3 252 DS128
Hayes UB4 135 BS69
Reigate RH2 266 DC138
Romford RM7 127 FB58
Wealdway, Grav. DA13 191 GH93
Wealdwood Gdns, Pnr. HA5
off Highbanks Rd 94 CB51
Weale Rd, E4 101 ED48
Weall Cl, Pur. CR8 219 DM113
Weall Grn, Wat. WD25 59 BV32
Weardale Av, Dart. DA2 188 FQ89
Weardale Gdns, Enf. EN2 82 DR39
Weardale Rd, SE13 163 ED84
Wear Pl, E2 288 E3
Wearside Rd, SE13 163 EB84
Weasdale Ct, Wok. GU21
off Roundthorn Way 226 AT116
Weatherall Cl, Add. KT15 212 BH106
Weatherbury Ho, N19
off Wedmore St 121 DK62
Weatherhill Cl, Horl. RH6 269 DM148
Weatherhill Common,
Smallfield RH6 269 DM147
Weatherhill Rd,
Smallfield RH6 269 DM148
Weatherill Cl, Guil. GU1 243 BB134
Weatherley Cl, E3 289 P6
Weaver Cl, E6 293 N10
Croydon CR0 220 DT105
Weavers Almshouses, E11
off New Wanstead 124 EG58
Weavers Cl, Grav. DA11 191 GG88
Isleworth TW7 157 CE84
Weavers La, SE1 299 P3
Sevenoaks TN14 257 FJ121
Weavers Orchard, Sthflt DA13 190 GA93
Weavers Ter, SW6 307 K3
Weaver St, E1 288 C5
Weavers Way, NW1 275 N8
Weaver Wk, SE27 181 DP91
Webb Cl, W10 282 A5
Chesham HP5 54 AP30
Slough SL3 152 AX77
Webber Cl, Els. WD6
off Rodgers Cl 77 CK44
Erith DA8 167 FH80
Webber Row, SE1 298 F5
Webber St, SE1 298 F4
Webb Est, E5 122 DU59
Webb Gdns, E13 291 P4
Webb Ho, SW8 309 P5
Webb Pl, NW10 139 CT69
Webb Rd, SE3 315 M2
Webb's All, Sev. TN13, TN15 257 FJ125
Webbscroft Rd, Dag. RM10 127 FB63
Webbs Rd, SW11 180 DF85
Hayes UB4 135 BV69
Webb St, SE1 299 N7
Webheath Est, NW6 273 H6
Webley Ct, Enf. EN3 *off Sten Cl* 83 EA37
Webster Cl, Horn. RM12 128 FK62
Oxshott KT22 214 CB114
Waltham Abbey EN9 68 EG33
Webster Gdns, W5 137 CK74
Webster Rd, E11 123 EC62
SE16 300 D7
Websters Cl, Wok. GU22 226 AU120
Wedderburn Rd, NW3 274 A3
Barking IG11 145 ER67
Wedgewood Cl, Epp. CM16 70 EU30
Northwood HA6 93 BQ52
Wedgewood Dr, Harl. CM17 52 EX16
Wedgwood Ho, SE11 298 E7
Wedgwood Ms, W1 285 P9
Wedgwood Pl, Cob. KT11 213 BU114
Wedgwoods, Tats. TN16
off Redhouse Rd 238 EJ121
Wedgwood Wk, NW6
off Dresden Cl 273 M3
Wedgwood Way, SE19 182 DQ94
Wedhey, Harl. CM19 51 EQ15
Wedlake Cl, Horn. RM11 128 FL60
Wedlake St, W10 282 F4
Wedmore Av, Ilf. IG5 103 EN53
Wedmore Gdns, N19 121 DK61
Wedmore Ms, N19 121 DK62
Wedmore Rd, Grnf. UB6 137 CD69
Wedmore St, N19 121 DK62
Wednesbury Gdns, Rom. RM3 106 FM52
Wednesbury Grn, Rom. RM3
off Wednesbury Gdns 106 FM52
Wednesbury Rd, Rom. RM3 106 FM52
Weech Rd, NW6 273 J1
Weedington Rd, NW5 274 G2
Weedon Cl, Chal.St.P. SL9 90 AV53
Weedon La, Amer. HP6 55 AN36
Weekes Dr, Slou. SL1 131 AP74
Weekley Sq, SW11
off Thomas Baines Rd 160 DD83
Weigall Rd, SE12 164 EG84
Weighhouse St, W1 285 H9
Weighton Rd, SE20 202 DV96
Harrow HA3 95 CD53
Weihurst Gdns, Sutt. SM1 218 DD106
Weimar St, SW15 159 CY83
Weind, The, They.B. CM16 85 ES36
Weirdale Av, N20 98 DF47
Weir Est, SW12 181 DJ87
Weir Hall Av, N18 100 DR51
Weir Hall Gdns, N18 100 DR50
Weir Hall Rd, N17 100 DR50
N18 100 DR50
Weir Pl, Stai. TW18 193 BE95
Weir Rd, SW12 181 DJ87
SW19 180 DB90
Bexley DA5 187 FB87
Chertsey KT16 194 BH101
Walton-on-Thames KT12 195 BU100
Weirside Gdns, West Dr. UB7 134 BK74
Weir's Pas, NW1 285 P2
Weiss Rd, SW15 159 CX83
Welbeck Av, Brom. BR1 184 EG91
Hayes UB4 135 BV70
Sidcup DA15 186 EU88
Welbeck Cl, N12 98 DD50
Borehamwood WD6 78 CN41
Epsom KT17 217 CU108
New Malden KT3 199 CT99
Welbeck Rd, E6 292 E2
Barnet EN4 80 DD44
Carshalton SM5 200 DE102
Harrow HA2 116 CB60
Sutton SM1 200 DD103
Welbeck St, W1 285 J8
Welbeck Wk, Cars. SM5
off Welbeck Rd 200 DE102
Welbeck Way, W1 285 J8
Sch **Welbourne Prim Sch**, N17
off High Cross Rd 122 DU55
Welby St, SE5 311 H7
Welch Ho, Enf. EN3
off Beaconsfield Rd 83 DX37
Welch Pl, Pnr. HA5 94 BW53
Welclose St, St.Alb. AL3 42 CC20
Welcomes Rd, Ken. CR8 236 DQ115
Welcote Dr, Nthwd. HA6 93 BR51
Welden, Slou. SL2 132 AW72
Welders La, Chal.St.P. SL9 90 AT52
Jordans HP9 90 AT52
Weldon Cl, Ruis. HA4 135 BV65
Weldon Dr, W.Mol. KT8 196 BZ98
Weldon Way, Merst. RH1 251 DK129
Weld Pl, N11 99 DH50
Welfare Rd, E15 281 K6
Welford Cl, E5 *off Denton Way* 123 DX62
Welford Ho, Nthlt. UB5
off Waxlow Way 136 BZ70
Welford Pl, SW19 179 CY91
Welham Cl, Borwd. WD6 78 CN39
N.Mymms AL9 45 CW24
Welham Ct, N.Mymms AL9
off Dixons Hill Rd 45 CW24
WELHAM GREEN, Hat. AL9 45 CV23
⇌ **Welham Green** 45 CX23
Welham Manor, N.Mymms AL9 45 CW24
Welham Rd, SW16 180 DG92
SW17 180 DG92
Welhouse Rd, Cars. SM5 200 DE102
Welkin Grn, Hem.H. HP2
off Wood End Cl 41 BQ19
Wellacre Rd, Har. HA3 117 CH58
Wellan Cl, Sid. DA15 186 EV85
Welland Cl, Slou. SL3 153 BA79
Welland Gdns, Perivale UB6 137 CF68
Welland Ms, E1 300 D2
Welland Rd, Lon.Hthrw Air. TW6
off Wayfarer Rd 154 BH82
Wellands, Hat. AL10 45 CU16
Wellands Cl, Brom. BR1 205 EM96
Welland St, SE10 314 E2
Well App, Barn. EN5 79 CW43
Wellbank, Tap. SL6
off Rectory Rd 130 AE70
Wellbrook Rd, Orp. BR6 223 EN105
Wellbury Ter, Hem.H. HP2 41 BQ20
Wellby Cl, N9 100 DU46
Well Cl, SW16 181 DM91
Ruislip HA4 *off Parkfield Cres* 116 BY62
Woking GU21 226 AW117

Wellclose Sq, E1 288 D10
Wellclose St, E1 300 D1
Wellcome Av, Dart. DA1 168 FM84
Wellcome Trust, NW1 285 N4
Well Cottage Cl, E11 124 EJ59
Well Ct, EC4 287 K9
SW16 181 DM91
Wellcroft, Hem.H. HP1
off Gadebridge Rd 40 BH19
Wellcroft Cl, Welw.G.C. AL7 30 DA11
Wellcroft Rd, Slou. SL1 131 AP74
Welwyn Garden City AL7 30 DA11
Welldon Cres, Har. HA1 117 CE58
Welldon Pk Inf Sch,
S.Har. HA2 off Kingsley Rd 116 CC63
Welldon Pk Jun Sch,
S.Har. HA2 off Wyvenhoe Rd 116 CC63
WELL END, Borwd. WD6 78 CR38
Well End Rd, Borwd. WD6 78 CQ37
Wellen Ri, Hem.H. HP3 40 BL23
Weller Cl, Amer. HP6 55 AS37
Weller Ms, Brom. BR2 204 EH98
Enfield EN2 81 DN39
Weller Pl, Downe BR6 223 EN111
Weller Rd, Amer. HP6 55 AS37
Wellers Cl, West. TN16 255 EQ127
Wellers Ct, Shere GU5 260 BN139
Wellers Gro, Chsht EN7 66 DU28
Weller St, SE1 299 J4
Wellesford Cl, Bans. SM7 233 CZ117
Wellesley, Harl. CM19 51 EN20
Wellesley Av, W6 159 CV76
Iver SL0 153 BF76
Northwood HA6 93 BT50
Wellesley Cl, SE7
off Wellington Gdns 164 EJ78
Wellesley Cor, Nthflt. DA11 190 GB88
Wellesley Ct, W9 283 N2
Sutton SM3 off Stonecot Hill 199 CY102
Wellesley Ct Rd, Croy. CR0 202 DR103
Wellesley Cres, Pot.B. EN6 63 CY33
Twickenham TW2 177 CE89
Wellesley Gro, Croy. CR0 202 DR103
Wellesley Pk Ms, Enf. EN2 81 DP40
Wellesley Pas, Croy. CR0
off Wellesley Rd 202 DQ103
Wellesley Path, Slou. SL1
off Wellesley Rd 152 AU75
Wellesley Pl, NW1 285 N3
Wellesley Road 202 DQ103
Wellesley Rd, E11 124 EG57
E17 123 EA58
N22 99 DN54
NW5 274 G3
W4 158 CN78
Brentwood CM14 108 FW46
Croydon CR0 202 DQ102
Harrow HA1 117 CE57
Ilford IG1 125 EP61
Slough SL1 152 AU75
Sutton SM2 218 DC107
Twickenham TW2 177 CD90
Wellesley St, E1 289 J7
Wellesley Ter, N1 287 K2
Welley Av, Wrays. TW19 152 AY84
Welley Rd, Horton SL3 152 AY84
Wraysbury TW19 172 AX85
Well Fm Rd, Cat. CR3 236 DU119
Wellfield Av, N10 121 DH55
Wellfield Cl, Hat. AL10 45 CU17
Wellfield Gdns, Cars. SM5 218 DE109
Wellfield Rd, SW16 181 DL91
Hatfield AL10 45 CU16
Wellfields, Loug. IG10 85 EN41
Wellfield Wk, SW16 181 DM92
Wellfit St, SE24
off Hinton Rd 161 DP83
Wellgarth, Grnf. UB6 137 CH65
Welwyn Garden City AL7 29 CY10
Wellgarth Rd, NW11 120 DB60
Well Gro, N20 98 DC45
Well Hall Par, SE9
off Well Hall Rd 165 EM84
Well Hall Rd, SE9 165 EM83
Well Hall Rbt, SE9 164 EL83
WELL HILL, Orp. BR6 225 FB107
Well Hill, Orp. BR6 225 FB107
Well Hill La, Orp. BR6 225 FB108
Well Hill Rd, Sev. TN14 225 FC107
Wellhouse La, Barn. EN5 79 CW42
Betchworth RH3 264 CQ138
Wellhouse Rd, Beck. BR3 203 DZ98
Wellhurst Cl, Orp. BR6 223 ET108
WELLING, DA16 166 EU83
Welling 166 EU82
Welling High St, Well. DA16 166 EV83
Welling Sch, Well. DA16
off Elsa Rd 166 EV81
Wellings Ho, Hayes UB3 135 BV74
★ Wellington Arch, W1 297 H4
Wellington Av, E4 101 EA47
N9 100 DV48
N15 122 DT58
Hounslow TW3 176 CA85
Pinner HA5 94 BZ53
Sidcup DA15 186 EU86
Virginia Water GU25 192 AV99
Worcester Park KT4 199 CW104
Wellington Bldgs, SW1 309 H1
Wellington Cl, SE14 313 J7
W11 283 J9
Dagenham RM10 147 FC66
Walton-on-Thames KT12 195 BT102
Watford WD19 94 BZ48
Wellington Cotts,
E.Hors. KT24 245 BS129
Wellington Ct, NW8 284 A1
Ashford TW15
off Wellington Rd 174 BL92
Staines-upon-Thames TW19
off Clare Rd 174 BL87
Surb. KT6 off Glenbuck Rd 198 CL100
Wellington Cres, N.Mal. KT3 198 CQ97
Wellington Dr, Dag. RM10 147 FC66
Purley CR8 219 DM110
Welwyn Garden City AL7 30 DC09
Wellington Gdns, SE7 164 EJ79
Twickenham TW2 177 CD91
Wellington Gro, SE10 314 G5
Wellington Hill,
High Beach IG10 84 EG37
Wellington Hosp, NW8 284 B1
Wellington Ho, Gidea Pk RM2
off Kidman Cl 128 FJ55
Wellingtonia Av,
Hav.at.Bow. RM4 105 FE48
Wellington Ms, SE7 164 EJ79
SE22 162 DU84
SW16 off Woodbourne Av 181 DK90
★ Wellington Mus, W1 296 G4
Wellington Par, Sid. DA15 186 EU85
● Wellington Pk Est, NW2 119 CU61
Wellington Pas, E11 124 EG57
Wellington Pl, N2 120 DE57
NW8 284 B2
Broxbourne EN10 48 DW23
Cobham KT11 214 BZ112
Warley CM14 108 FW50
Wellington Prim Sch, E3 290 A3
Hounslow TW3 off Sutton La 156 BZ82
Wellington Rd, E6 145 EM68
E7 281 M1
E10 123 DY60
E11 124 EG57
E17 123 DY55
NW8 274 A10
NW10 282 D3
SW19 180 DA89
W5 157 CJ76
Ashford TW15 174 BL92
Belvedere DA17 166 EZ78
Bexley DA5 186 EX86
Bromley BR2 204 EJ98
Caterham CR3 236 DQ122
Croydon CR0 201 DP101
Dartford DA1 188 FJ86
Enfield EN1 82 DS42
Feltham TW14 175 BS85
Hampton TW12 177 CD91
Harrow HA3 117 CE55
London Colney AL2 61 CK26
North Weald Bassett CM16 70 FA27
Orpington BR5 206 EV100
Pinner HA5 94 BZ53
St. Albans AL1 43 CH21
Tilbury RM18 171 GG83
Twickenham TW2 177 CD91
Uxbridge UB8 134 BJ67
Watford WD17 75 BV40
Wellington Rd N, Houns. TW4 156 BZ83
Wellington Rd S, Houns. TW4 156 BZ84
Wellington Row, E2 288 B2
Wellington Sq, N1 276 C8
SW3 296 E10
Wellington St, SE18 305 L9
WC2 286 B10
Gravesend DA12 191 GJ87
Hertford SG14 31 DP08
Slough SL1 152 AT75
Wellington Ter, E1 300 E2
W2 off Notting Hill Gate 295 L1
Harrow HA1 off West St 117 CD60
Knaphill GU21 off Victoria Rd 226 AS118
Wellington Way, E3 290 A3
Horley RH6 268 DF146
Weybridge KT13 212 BN110
Welling Way, SE9 165 ER83
Welling DA16 165 ER83
Well La, SW14 178 CQ85
Harlow CM19 35 EN14
Harlow CM20 51 EN15
Pilgrim's Hatch CM15 108 FT41
Woking GU21 226 AW117
Wellmeade Dr, Sev. TN13 257 FH127
Wellmeadow Rd, SE6 184 EE87
SE13 184 EE86
W7 157 CG77
Wellow Wk, Cars. SM5 200 DD102
Well Pas, NW3 120 DD62
Well Path, Wok. GU21
off Well La 226 AW117
Well Rd, NW3 120 DD62
Barnet EN5 79 CW43
Northaw EN6 64 DE28
Well Row, Bayford SG13 47 DM17
Wells, The, N14 99 DK45
Wells Cl, Chsht EN7
off Bloomfield Rd 66 DQ25
Leatherhead KT23 230 CB124
Northolt UB5 off Yeading La 136 BW69
St. Albans AL3
off Artisan Cres 42 CC19
South Croydon CR2 220 DS106
Windsor SL4 151 AN81
Wells Ct, Northfleet DA11 190 GB88
Romford RM1 off Regarth Av 127 FE58
Wells Dr, NW9 118 CR60
Wellsfield, Bushey WD23 76 BY43
Wells Gdns, Dag. RM10 127 FB64
Ilford IG1 124 EL59
Rainham RM13 147 FF65
Wells Ho Rd, NW10 138 CS71
Wellside Cl, Barn. EN5 79 CW42
Wellside Gdns, SW14
off Well La 178 CQ85
Wells Ms, W1 285 M7
Wellsmoor Gdns, Brom. BR1 205 EN97
Wells Pk Rd, SE26 182 DU90
Wells Pk Sch & Training Cen,
Chig. IG7 off Lambourne Rd 103 ET49
Wells Path, Hayes UB4 135 BS69
Wells Pl, SW18 180 DC87
Merstham RH1 251 DH130
Westerham TN16 255 EQ127
Wells Prim Sch, Wdf.Grn. IG8
off Barclay Oval 102 EG49
Wellspring Cres, Wem. HA9 118 CP62
Wellspring Ms, SE26 182 DV91
Wellspring Way, Wat. WD17 76 BW43
Wells Ri, NW8 274 E9
Wells Rd, W12 294 A5
Bromley BR1 205 EM96
Epsom KT18 216 CN114
Guildford GU4 243 BC131
Wells Sq, WC1 286 C3
Wells St, W1 285 L7
Wellstead Av, N9 100 DW45
Wellstead Rd, E6 293 L1
Wells Ter, N4 121 DN61
Wellstones, Wat. WD17 75 BV41
Wellstones Yd, Wat. WD17
off Wellstones 75 BV41
Well St, E9 278 F7
E15 281 J4
Wells Way, SE5 311 M2
SW7 296 A6
Wellswood Cl, Hem.H. HP2 41 BP19
Wells Yd S, N7 276 E2
Well Wk, NW3 120 DD63
Well Way, Epsom KT18 232 CN115
Wellwood Rd, Ilf. IG3 126 EU60
Welmar Ms, SW4 161 DK84
Welsford St, SE1 300 C10
Welsh Cl, E13 291 N3
Welshpool Ho, E8 278 D8
Welshpool St, E8 278 D8
Welsh Sch, The, NW10
off Shakespeare Av 138 CQ67
Welshside Wk, NW9
off Fryent Gro 118 CS58
Welstead Way, W4 159 CT77
Welsummer Way, Chsht EN8 67 DX27
● Weltech Business Cen,
Welw.G.C. AL7 30 DA09
Weltje Rd, W6 159 CU78
Welton Rd, SE18 165 ES80
Welwyn Av, Felt. TW14 175 BT86
Welwyn Ct, Hem.H. HP2 40 BM16
WELWYN GARDEN CITY,
AL7 & AL8 29 CX09
Welwyn Garden City 29 CY09
Welwyn Garden City 29 CX08
Welwyn Rd, Hert. SG14 30 DG08
Welwyn St, E2 289 H2
Welwyn Way, Hayes UB4 135 BS70
WEMBLEY, HA0 & HA9 118 CL64
★ Wembley Arena, Wem. HA9 118 CN63
Wembley Central 118 CL64
Wembley Central 118 CL64
Wembley Central 118 CL64
● Wembley Commercial Cen,
Wem. HA9 117 CK61
Wembley High Tech Coll,
Wem. HA0 off East La 117 CJ62
Wembley Hill Rd, Wem. HA9 118 CM64
WEMBLEY PARK, Wem. HA9 118 CM61
Wembley Park 118 CN62
Wembley Pk Boul, Wemb. HA9 118 CN63
● Wembley Pk Business Cen,
Wem. HA9 118 CP62
Wembley Pk Dr, Wemb. HA9 118 CM62
Wembley Pt, Wem. HA9 138 CP66
Wembley Prim Sch,
Wem. HA9 off East La 118 CL62
Wembley Retail Pk,
Wemb. HA9 118 CP63
Wembley Rd, Hmptn. TW12 176 CA94
★ Wembley Stadium,
Wem. HA9 118 CN63
Wembley Stadium 118 CM64
Wembley Way, Wem. HA9 138 CP65
Wemborough Rd, Stan. HA7 95 CJ52
Wembury Rd, N6 121 DH59
Wemyss Rd, SE3 315 L9
Wend, The, Couls. CR5 219 DK114
Croydon CR0 221 DZ111
Wendela Cl, Wok. GU22 227 AZ118
Wendela Ct, Har. HA1 117 CE62
Wendell Pk Prim Sch, W12
off Cobbold Rd 159 CT75
Wendell Rd, W12 159 CT75
Wendle Ct, SW8 310 A3
Wendle Sq, SW11 308 D6
Wendley Dr, New Haw KT15 211 BF110
Wendling, NW5 274 F2
Wendling Rd, Sutt. SM1 200 DD102
Wendon St, E3 279 P8
Wendover, SE17 299 N10
Wendover Cl, Hayes UB4 136 BX70
St. Albans AL4
off Highview Gdns 43 CJ15
Wendover Ct, W3 138 CP70
Wendover Dr, N.Mal. KT3 199 CT100
Wendover Gdns, Brwd. CM13 109 GB47
Wendover Pl, Stai. TW18 173 BD92
Wendover Rd, NW10 139 CT68
SE9 164 EK83
Bromley BR2 204 EH97
Burnham SL1 130 AH71
Staines-upon-Thames TW18 173 BC92
Wendover Way, Bushey WD23 76 CC44
Hornchurch RM12 128 FJ64
Orpington BR6
off Glendower Cres 206 EU100
Welling DA16 186 EU85
Wendron Cl, Wok. GU21 226 AU118
Wendy Cl, Enf. EN1 82 DT44
Wendy Cres, Guil. GU2 242 AU132
Wendy Way, Wem. HA0 138 CL67
Wengeo La, Ware SG12 32 DV05
Wenham Gdns, Hutt. CM13
off Bannister Dr 109 GC44
Wenham Ho, SW8
off Ascalon St 309 L5
Wenham Pl, Hat. AL10 45 CU17
Wenlack Cl, Denh. UB9 114 BG62
Wenlock Ct, N1 287 M1
Wenlock Edge, Dor. RH4 263 CJ138
Wenlock Gdns, NW4 119 CU56
Wenlock Rd, N1 277 J10
Edgware HA8 96 CP52
Wenlock St, N1 287 K1
WENNINGTON, Rain. RM13 148 FK73
Wennington Rd, E3 289 K1
Rainham RM13 147 FG70
Wensley Av, Wdf.Grn. IG8 102 EF52
Wensley Cl, N11 98 DG51
SE9 185 EM86
Romford RM5 104 FA50
Wensleydale, Hem.H. HP2 40 BM17
Wensleydale Av, Ilf. IG5 102 EL54
Wensleydale Gdns,
Hmptn. TW12 176 CB94
Wensleydale Pas,
Hmptn. TW12 196 CA95
Wensleydale Rd, Hmptn. TW12 176 CA93
Wensley Rd, N18 100 DV51
Wensum Way, Rick. WD3 92 BK46
● Wenta Business Cen,
Watford WD24 76 BX37
Wentbridge Path, Borwd. WD6 78 CN38
Wentland Cl, SE6 183 ED89
Wentland Rd, SE6 183 ED89
WENTWORTH, Vir.W. GU25 192 AS100
Wentworth Av, N3 98 DA52
Elstree WD6 78 CM43
Slough SL2 131 AN68
Wentworth Av Shop Par,
Slou. SL2 off Wentworth Av 131 AN69
Wentworth Cl, N3 98 DB52
SE28 146 EX72
Ashford TW15
off Reedsfield Rd 175 BP91
Gravesend DA11 191 GG92
Hayes BR2 off Hillside La 204 EG103
Long Ditton KT6 197 CK103
Morden SM4 200 DA101
Orpington BR6 223 ES106
Potters Bar EN6 64 DA31
Ripley GU23 228 BH121
Watford WD17 75 BT38
Wentworth Cotts, Brox. EN10 49 DY22
Wentworth Ct, Surb. KT6
off Culsac Rd 198 CL103
Wentworth Cres, SE15 312 D5
Hayes UB3 155 BR76
Wentworth Dene, Wey. KT13 213 BP106
Wentworth Dr, Dart. DA1 187 FG86
Lon.Hthrw Air. TW6
off Widgeon Rd 154 BH83
Pinner HA5 115 BU57
Virginia Water GU25 192 AT98
Watford WD19 94 BX50
Wentworth Gdns, N13 99 DP49
★ Wentworth Golf Course,
Vir.W. GU25 192 AT100
Wentworth Hill, Wem. HA9 118 CM60
● Wentworth Ind Ct, Slou. SL2
off Goodwin Rd 131 AN69
Wentworth Ms, E3 289 M4
W3 138 CS72
Wentworth Pk, N3 98 DA52
Wentworth Pl, Grays RM16 170 GD76
Stanmore HA7
off Greenacres Dr 95 CH51
Wentworth Prim Sch,
Dart. DA1 off Wentworth Dr 187 FG87
Wentworth Rd, E12 124 EK63
NW11 119 CZ58
Barnet EN5 79 CX41
Croydon CR0 201 DN101
Hertford SG13 32 DQ12
Southall UB2 156 BW77
Wentworth St, E1 288 A8
Wentworth Way, Pnr. HA5 116 BX56
Rainham RM13 147 FH69
South Croydon CR2 220 DU114
Wenvoe Av, Bexh. DA7 167 FB82
Wepham Cl, Hayes UB4 136 BX71
Wernbrook St, SE18 165 EQ79
Werndee Rd, SE25 202 DU98
Werneth Hall Rd, Ilf. IG5 125 EM55
Werrington St, NW1 285 M1
Werter Rd, SW15 159 CY84
Wescott Way, Uxb. UB8 134 BJ68
Wesleyan Pl, NW5 275 J1
Wesley Apts, SW8
off Wandsworth Rd 309 P6
Wesley Av, E16 303 P2
NW10 138 CR69
Hertford SG13 off Hale Rd 32 DR10
Hounslow TW3 156 BY82
Wesley Cl, N7 121 DM61
SE17 299 H9
Epsom KT19 216 CQ106
Goffs Oak EN7 66 DQ28
Harrow HA2 116 CC61
Horley RH6 268 DG146
Orpington BR5 206 EW97
Reigate RH2 265 CZ135
Wesley Ct, SW19 180 DB94
Wesley Dr, Egh. TW20 173 BA93
Wesley Hill, Chesh. HP5 54 AP30
Wesley Rd, E10 123 EC59
NW10 138 CQ67
Hayes UB3 135 BU73
Leatherhead KT22 231 CJ122
★ Wesley's Ho, EC1 287 L5
Wesley Sq, W11 282 E9
Wesley St, W1 285 H7
Wessels, Tad. KT20 233 CX121
Wessex Av, SW19 200 DA96
Wessex Cl, Ilf. IG3 125 ES58
Kingston upon Thames KT1 198 CP95
Thames Ditton KT7 197 CF103
Wessex Ct, Wem. HA9 118 CM61
Wessex Dr, Erith DA8 167 FE81
Pinner HA5 94 BY52
Wessex Gdns, NW11 119 CY60
Wessex Gdns Prim Sch, NW11
off Wessex Gdns 119 CY60
Wessex Ho, SE1 300 B10
Wessex La, Grnf. UB6 137 CD68
Wessex St, E2 289 H3
Wessex Wk, Dart. DA2
off Sandringham Dr 187 FE89
Wessex Way, NW11 119 CY59
Wessonmead, SE5
off Camberwell Rd 311 K5
West 12 Shop Cen, W12 294 C4
Westacott, Hayes UB4 135 BS71
Westacott Cl, N19 121 DK60
West Acres, Amer. HP7 55 AR40
Westacres, Esher KT10 214 BZ108
WEST ACTON, W3 138 CN72
West Acton 138 CN72
West Acton Prim Sch, W3
off Noel Rd 138 CP72
Westall Cl, Hert. SG13 32 DQ10
Westall Ms, Hert. SG13
off West St 32 DQ10
Westall Rd, Loug. IG10 85 EP41
Westanley Av, Amer. HP7 55 AR39
West App, Petts Wd BR5 205 EQ99
West Arbour St, E1 289 H8
West Ashtead Prim Sch,
Ashtd. KT21 off Taleworth Rd 232 CL120
West Av, E17 123 EB56
N3 98 DA51
NW4 119 CX57
Hayes UB3 135 BT73
Penn HP10 88 AC46
Pinner HA5 116 BZ58
Redhill RH1 266 DG140
St. Albans AL2 60 CB25
Southall UB1 136 BZ73
Wallington SM6 219 DL106
Whiteley Village KT12 213 BS109
West Av Rd, E17 123 EA56
West Bk, N16 122 DS59
Barking IG11
off Highbridge Rd 145 EP67
Dorking RH4 263 CF137
Enfield EN2 82 DQ40
Westbank Rd, Hmptn H. TW12 176 CC93
WEST BARNES, N.Mal. KT3 199 CU99
West Barnes La, SW20 199 CV96
New Malden KT3 199 CV97
Westbeech Rd, N22 121 DN55
Westbere Dr, Stan. HA7 95 CK49
Westbere Rd, NW2 272 G2
Westbourne Av, W3 138 CR72
Sutton SM3 199 CY103
Westbourne Br, W2 283 N7
Westbourne Cl, Hayes UB4 135 BV70
Westbourne Cres, W2 284 A10
Westbourne Cres Ms, W2 284 A10
Westbourne Dr, SE23 183 DX89
Brentwood CM14 108 FT49
Westbourne Gdns, W2 283 L8
WESTBOURNE GREEN, W2 283 J7
Westbourne Gro, W2 283 K9
W11 283 H10
Westbourne Gro Ms, W11 283 J9
Westbourne Gro Ter, W2 283 L8
Westbourne Ho, Houns. TW5 156 CA79
Westbourne Ms, St.Alb. AL1
off London Rd 43 CD20
Westbourne Park 283 H6
Westbourne Pk Ms, W2 283 L8
Westbourne Pk Pas, W2 283 K7
Westbourne Pk Rd, W2 283 K7
W11 282 F9
Westbourne Pk Vil, W2 283 K7
Westbourne Pl, N9 100 DV48
Westbourne Prim Sch,
Sutt. SM1 off Anton Cres 200 DA104
Westbourne Rd, N7 276 E5
SE26 183 DX93
Bexleyheath DA7 166 EY80
Croydon CR0 202 DT100
Feltham TW13 175 BT90
Staines-upon-Thames TW18 174 BH94
Uxbridge UB8 135 BP70
Westbourne St, W2 284 A10
Westbourne Ter, SE23
off Westbourne Dr 183 DX89
W2 283 P8
Westbourne Ter Ms, W2 283 N8
Westbourne Ter Rd, W2 283 N7
West Br Cl, W12
off Percy Rd 139 CU74
Westbridge Prim Sch,
SW11 308 C6
Westbridge Rd, SW11 308 B7
WEST BROMPTON, SW10 307 L2
West Brompton 307 K1
West Brompton 307 K1
West Brompton 307 K1
Westbrook, Maid. SL6 150 AE78
Westbrook Av, Hmptn. TW12 176 BZ94
Westbrook Cl, Barn. EN4 80 DD41
Westbrook Cres, Cockfos. EN4 80 DD41
Westbrook Dr, Orp. BR5 206 EW102
Westbrooke Cres, Well. DA16 166 EW83
Westbrooke Rd, Sid. DA15 185 ER89
Welling DA16 166 EV83
Westbrooke Sch, Well. DA16
off South Gipsy Rd 166 EX83
Westbrook Hay Prep Sch,
Hem.H. HP1 off London Rd 39 BD24
Westbrook Prim Sch,
Heston TW5 off Westbrook Rd 156 BZ80
Westbrook Rd, SE3 164 EH81
Hounslow TW5 156 BZ80
Staines-upon-Thames TW18
off South St 173 BF92
Thornton Heath CR7 202 DR95
Westbrook Sq, Barn. EN4
off Westbrook Cres 80 DD41
West Burrowfield,
Welw.G.C. AL7 29 CX11
Westbury, Chsht EN8
off Turners Hill 67 DX30
Westbury Av, N22 121 DP55
Claygate KT10 215 CF107
Southall UB1 136 CA70
Wembley HA0 138 CL66
Westbury Cl, Ruis. HA4 115 BU59
Shepperton TW17
off Burchetts Way 195 BP100
Whyteleafe CR3
off Station App 236 DU118
Westbury Dr, Brwd. CM14 108 FV47
Westbury Gro, N12 98 DA51
Westbury Ho Sch, N.Mal. KT3
off Westbury Rd 198 CR99
Westbury La, Buck.H. IG9 102 EJ47
Westbury Lo Cl, Pnr. HA5 116 BX55
Westbury Par, SW12
off Balham Hill 181 DH86
Westbury Pl, Brent. TW8 157 CK79
Westbury Ri, Harl. CM17 52 EX16
Westbury Rd, E7 124 EH64
E17 123 EA56
N11 99 DL51
N12 98 DA51
SE20 203 DX95
W5 138 CL72
Barking IG11 145 ER67
Beckenham BR3 203 DY97
Brentwood CM14 108 FW47
Bromley BR1 204 EK95
Buckhurst Hill IG9 102 EJ47
Croydon CR0 202 DR100
Feltham TW13 176 BX88
Ilford IG1 125 EM61
New Malden KT3 198 CR98
Northwood HA6 93 BS49
Watford WD18 75 BV43
Wembley HA0 138 CL66
Westbury St, SW8 309 L9
Westbury Ter, E7 144 EH65
Upminster RM14 129 FS61
Westerham TN16 255 EQ127
Westbush Cl, Hodd. EN11 33 DZ14
WEST BYFLEET, KT14 212 BH113
West Byfleet 212 BG112
West Byfleet Comm Inf Sch,
W.Byf. KT14 off Camphill Rd 212 BH112
West Byfleet Jun Sch,
W.Byf. KT14 off Camphill Rd 212 BH112
Westcar La, Hersham KT12 213 BV107
West Carriage Dr, W2 296 B3
West Cen Av, W10
off Harrow Rd 139 CV69
West Cen St, WC1 286 A8
West Chantry, Har. HA3
off Chantry Rd 94 CB53
Westchester Dr, NW4 119 CX55
WEST CLANDON, Guil. GU4 244 BH129
Westcliffe Apts, W2 284 B7
West Cl, N9 100 DT48
Ashford TW15 174 BL91
Barnet EN5 79 CV43
Cockfosters EN4 80 DG42
Greenford UB6 136 CC68
Hampton TW12 off Oak Av 176 BY93
Hoddesdon EN11 49 EA16
Rainham RM13 147 FH70
Wembley HA9 118 CM60
Westcombe Av, Croy. CR0 201 DL100
Westcombe Ct, SE3 315 L4
Westcombe Dr, Barn. EN5 80 DA43
Westcombe Hill, SE3 315 P2
SE10 315 N1
Westcombe Lo Dr, Hayes UB4 135 BR71
Westcombe Park 315 P1
Westcombe Pk Rd, SE3 315 K3
West Common, Ger.Cr. SL9 112 AX57

West Common Cl, Ger.Cr. SL9 112 AY57
West Common Rd, Brom. BR2 204 EG103
Keston BR2 222 EH105
Uxbridge UB8 114 BK64
Westcoombe Av, SW20 199 CT95
Westcote Ri, Ruis. HA4 115 BQ59
Westcote Rd, SW16 181 DJ92
Epsom KT19 216 CP111
WESTCOTT, Dor. RH4 262 CC138
Westcott, Welw.G.C. AL7 30 DD08
West Cotts, NW6 273 K3
Westcott Av, Nthflt DA11 191 GG90
Westcott Cl, N15 122 DT58
Bromley BR1 204 EL99
New Addington CR0
off Castle Hill Av 221 EB109
Westcott C of E First Sch, Westc. RH4 off School La 263 CD137
Westcott Common, Westc. RH4 262 CB138
Westcott Cres, W7 137 CE72
Westcott Ho, E14 290 B10
Westcott Keep, Horl. RH6
off Langshott La 269 DJ147
Westcott Rd, SE17 310 G2
Dorking RH4 263 CE137
Westcott St, Westc. RH4 262 CB137
Westcott Way, Sutt. SM2 217 CW110
WESTCOURT, Grav. DA12 191 GL89
Westcourt, Sun. TW16 195 BV96
West Ct, SE18
off Prince Imperial Rd 165 EM81
Hounslow TW5 156 CC80
Wembley HA0 117 CJ61
Westcourt Cen, The, Grav. DA12 off Jubilee Cres 191 GL89
Westcourt Prim Sch, Grav. DA12 off Silver Rd 191 GL89
West Cres, Wind. SL4 151 AM81
West Cres Rd, Grav. DA12 191 GH86
Westcroft, Slou. SL2 131 AP70
Westcroft Cl, NW2 272 F2
Enfield EN3 82 DW38
Westcroft Ct, Brox. EN10 49 EA19
Westcroft Gdns, Mord. SM4 199 CZ97
Westcroft Rd, Cars. SM5 218 DG105
Wallington SM6 218 DG105
Westcroft Sq, W6 159 CU77
Westcroft Way, NW2 119 CY63
West Cromwell Rd, SW5 295 J9
W14 294 G10
West Cross Cen, Brent. TW8 157 CG79
West Cross Route, W10 282 C10
W11 282 C10
West Cross Way, Brent. TW8 157 CH79
West Croydon 202 DQ102
West Croydon 202 DQ102
West Croydon 202 DQ102
West Croydon 202 DQ102
Westdale Pas, SE18 165 EP79
Westdale Rd, SE18 165 EP79
Westdean Av, SE12 184 EH88
Westdean Cl, SW18 180 DB85
Westdene, Hersham KT12 213 BV105
West Dene, Sutt. SM3
off Park La 217 CY107
West Dene Dr, Rom. RM3 106 FK50
Westdene Way, Wey. KT13 195 BS104
West Down, Bkhm KT23 246 CB127
Westdown Rd, E15 123 EC63
SE6 183 EA87
WEST DRAYTON, UB7 154 BK76
West Drayton 134 BL74
West Drayton Pk Av, West Dr. UB7 154 BL76
West Drayton Prim Sch, West Dr. UB7 off Kingston La 154 BL75
West Drayton Rd, Hayes End UB8 135 BP71
West Dr, SW16 181 DJ91
Carshalton SM5 218 DD110
Cheam SM2 217 CX109
Harrow HA3 95 CD51
Tadworth KT20 233 CX118
Virginia Water GU25 192 AT101
Watford WD25 75 BV36
West Dr Gdns, Har. HA3 95 CD51
WEST DULWICH, SE21 182 DR90
West Dulwich 182 DR88
West Ealing 137 CH73
West Eaton Pl, SW1 296 G8
West Eaton Pl Ms, SW1 296 G8
Wested La, Swan. BR8 207 FG101
West Ella Rd, NW10 138 CS66
WEST END, Esher KT10 214 BZ107
Hat. AL9 46 DC18
West End Av, E10 123 EC57
Pinner HA5 116 BX56
West End Cl, NW10 138 CQ66
West End Ct, Pnr. HA5 116 BX56
Stoke Poges SL2 132 AT67
West End Gdns, Esher KT10 214 BZ106
Northolt UB5 136 BW68
West End La, NW6 273 K9
Barnet EN5 79 CX42
Esher KT10 214 BZ107
Essendon AL9 46 DC18
Harlington UB3 155 BQ80
Pinner HA5 116 BX55
Stoke Poges SL2 132 AS67
West End Rd, Brox. EN10 48 DS23
Northolt UB5 136 BW66
Ruislip HA4 115 BV64
Southall UB1 136 BY74
Westerdale, Hem.H. HP2 40 BL17
Westerdale Rd, SE10 315 N1
Westerfield Rd, N15 122 DT57
Westerfolds Cl, Wok. GU22 227 BC116
Westergate Rd, SE2 166 EY79
WESTERHAM, TN16 255 EQ126
Westerham Av, N9 100 DR48
Westerham Cl, Add. KT15 212 BJ107
Sutton SM2 218 DA110
Westerham Dr, Sid. DA15 186 EV86
Westerham Hill, West. TN16 239 EN121
Westerham Rd, E10 123 EB58
Keston BR2 222 EK107
Oxted RH8 254 EF129
Sevenoaks TN13 256 FC123
Westerham TN16 255 EM128
Westerham Trade Cen, West. TN16 off The Flyer's Way 255 ER126
Westerley Cres, SE26 183 DZ92
Westerley Ware, Rich. TW9
off Kew Grn 158 CN79
Westermain, New Haw KT15 212 BJ110
Western Av, NW11 119 CX58
W3 138 CR71
W5 138 CM69
Western Av, Brentwood CM14 108 FW46
Chertsey KT16 194 BG97
Dagenham RM10 147 FC65
Denham UB9 114 BJ63
Egham TW20 193 BB97
Epping CM16 69 ET32
Greenford UB6 137 CF69
Ickenham UB10 135 BP65
Northolt UB5 136 BZ67
Romford RM2 106 FJ54
Ruislip HA4 135 BP65
Western Av Business Pk, W3
off Mansfield Rd 138 CP70
Western Av Underpass, W5
off Western Av 138 CM69
Western Beach Apts, E16 303 N2
Western Cl, Cher. KT16
off Western Av 194 BG97
Western Ct, N3
off Huntly Dr 98 DA51
Western Cross Cl, Green. DA9
off Johnsons Way 189 FW86
Western Dr, Shep. TW17 195 BR100
Wooburn Green HP10 110 AE58
Western Eye Hosp, NW1 284 E6
Western Gdns, W5 138 CN73
Brentwood CM14 108 FW47
Western Gateway, E16 303 N1
Western Ho Prim Sch, Slou. SL1 off Richards Way 131 AL74
Western Int Mkt, Sthl. UB2 155 BV77
Western La, SW12 180 DG87
Western Ms, W9 283 H5
Western Par, New Barn. EN5
off Great N Rd 80 DA43
Reigate RH2 off Prices La 266 DB137
Western Pathway, Horn. RM12 148 FJ65
Western Perimeter Rd, Lon.Hthrw Air. TW6 154 BH83
Western Pl, SE16 301 H4
Western Rd, E13 144 EJ67
E17 123 EC57
N2 120 DF56
N22 99 DM54
NW10 138 CQ70
SW9 161 DN83
SW19 200 DD95
W5 137 CK73
Brentwood CM14 108 FW47
Epping CM16 69 ET32
Lower Nazeing EN9 50 EE22
Mitcham CR4 200 DD95
Romford RM1 127 FE57
Southall UB2 156 BX76
Sutton SM1 218 DA106
Western Ter, W6
off Chiswick Mall 159 CU78
Western Trd Est, NW10 138 CQ70
Western Vw, Hayes UB3 155 BT75
Westernville Gdns, Ilf. IG2 125 EQ59
Western Way, SE28 165 ER76
Barnet EN5 80 DA44
WEST EWELL, Epsom KT19 216 CS108
West Ewell Inf Sch, W.Ewell KT19 off Ruxley La 216 CR106
West Fm Av, Ashtd. KT21 231 CJ118
West Fm Cl, Ashtd. KT21 231 CJ119
West Fm Dr, Ashtd. KT21 231 CK119
Westferry 290 A10
Westferry Circ, E14 302 A2
Westferry Rd, E14 301 P2
WESTFIELD, Wok. GU22 227 AZ122
Westfield, Abin.Ham. RH5 261 BS143
Ashtead KT21 232 CM118
Harlow CM18 51 ES16
Hatfield AL9 46 DA23
Loughton IG10 84 EJ43
Reigate RH2 250 DB131
Sevenoaks TN13 257 FJ122
Welwyn Garden City AL7 30 DA08
Westfield Ave, E20 280 E5
South Croydon CR2 220 DR113
Watford WD24 76 BW37
Woking GU22 226 AY121
Westfield Cl, NW9 118 CQ55
SW10 307 N5
Enfield EN3 83 DY41
Gravesend DA12 191 GJ93
Sutton SM1 217 CZ105
Waltham Cross EN8 67 DZ31
Westfield Common, Wok. GU22 226 AY122
Westfield Comm Prim Sch, Hodd. EN11 off Westfield Rd 49 DZ16
Westfield Comm Tech Coll, Wat. WD18 off Tolpits La 75 BT44
Westfield Ct, St.Alb. AL4 43 CK17
Westfield Dr, Bkhm KT23 230 CA122
Harrow HA3 117 CK57
Westfield First Sch, Berk. HP4
off Durrants La 38 AT18
Westfield Gdns, Dor. RH4 263 CG136
Harrow HA3 117 CK56
Romford RM6 126 EW58
Westfield Gro, Wok. GU22 226 AY120
Westfield La, Geo.Grn SL3 132 AX73
Harrow HA3 117 CK57
Westfield London, W12 294 C3
Westfield Par, New Haw KT15 212 BK110
Westfield Pk, Pnr. HA5 94 BZ52
Westfield Pk Dr, Wdf.Grn. IG8 102 EL51
Westfield Prim Sch, Wok. GU22 off Bonsey La 226 AY121
Westfield Rd, NW7 96 CR48
W13 137 CG74
Beaconsfield HP9 88 AJ54
Beckenham BR3 203 DZ96
Berkhamsted HP4 38 AS17
Bexleyheath DA7 167 FC82
Croydon CR0 201 DP103
Dagenham RM9 126 EY63
Guildford GU1 242 AY130
Hertford SG14 31 DP07
Hoddesdon EN11 49 DZ16
Mitcham CR4 200 DF96
Slough SL2 131 AP70
Surbiton KT6 197 CK99
Sutton SM1 217 CZ105
Walton-on-Thames KT12 196 BY101
Woking GU22 226 AX122
Westfields, SW13 159 CT83
St. Albans AL3 42 CA22
Westfields Av, SW13 158 CS83
Westfields Rd, W3 138 CP71
Westfield Stratford City, E15 280 E5
Westfield St, SE18 304 E7
Westfield Wk, Wal.Cr. EN8 67 DZ31
Westfield Way, E1 289 L3
W12 294 C2
Ruislip HA4 115 BS62
Woking GU22 226 AY122
West Finchley 98 DB51
West Gdn Pl, W2 284 D9
West Gdns, E1 300 F1
SW17 180 DE93
Epsom KT17 216 CS110
Westgate, E16 291 P10
West Gate, W5 138 CL69
Harlow CM20 51 EQ15
Westgate Cl, Epsom KT18
off Chalk La 232 CR115
Westgate Ct, SW9
off Canterbury Cres 161 DN83
Waltham Cross EN8
Western Av, off Holmesdale 83 DX35
Westgate Cres, Slou. SL1 131 AM73
Westgate Est, Felt. TW14 174 BN88
Westgate Houe, Islw. TW7
off London Rd 157 CD82
Westgate Prim Sch, Dart. DA1
off Summerhill Rd 188 FK87
Westgate Retail Pk, Slou. SL1 131 AN73
Westgate Rd, SE25 202 DV98
Beckenham BR3 203 EB96
Dartford DA1 188 FK86
Westgate Sch, Slou. SL1
off Cippenham La 131 AN74
Westgate St, E8 278 E8
Westgate Ter, SW10 307 M1
Westglade Ct, Har. HA3 117 CK57
West Gorse, Croy. CR0 221 DY112
WEST GREEN, N15 122 DQ55
West Grn Pl, Grnf. UB6
off Uneeda Dr 137 CD67
West Grn Prim Sch, N15
off Woodlands Pk Rd 122 DQ56
West Grn Rd, N15 121 DP56
West Gro, SE10 314 F6
Hersham KT12 213 BV105
Woodford Green IG8 102 EJ51
Westgrove La, SE10 314 F6
West Gro Prim Sch, N14
off Chase Rd 99 DK45
West Halkin St, SW1 296 G6
West Hallowes, SE9 184 EK88
Westhall Pk, Warl. CR6 236 DW119
West Hall Rd, Rich. TW9 158 CP81
Westhall Rd, Warl. CR6 236 DV119
WEST HAM, E15 281 M7
West Ham 291 K2
West Ham 291 K2
West Ham 291 J2
West Ham Ch Prim Sch, E15 281 L8
West Ham La, E15 281 J7
West Ham Pk, E7 281 N6
WEST HAMPSTEAD, NW6 273 L3
West Hampstead 273 K5
West Hampstead 273 L5
West Hampstead Ms, NW6 273 L5
West Hampstead (Thameslink) 273 K4
West Ham United FC, E13 144 EJ68
West Harding St, EC4 286 F8
West Harold, Swan. BR8 207 FD97
WEST HARROW, Har. HA1 116 CC59
West Harrow 116 CC58
West Hatch High Sch, Chig. IG7 off High Rd 103 EM50
West Hatch Manor, Ruis. HA4 115 BT60
Westhay Gdns, SW14 178 CP85
WEST HEATH, SE2 166 EX79
West Heath, Oxt. RH8 254 EG130
West Heath Av, NW11 120 DA60
West Heath Cl, NW3 120 DA62
Dartford DA1
off West Heath Rd 187 FF86
West Heath Dr, NW11 120 DA60
West Heath Gdns, NW3 120 DA61
West Heath La, Sev. TN13 257 FH128
West Heath Rd, NW3 120 DA61
SE2 166 EW79
Dartford DA1 187 FF86
WEST HENDON, NW9 118 CS59
West Hendon Bdy, NW9 119 CT58
West Herts Business Cen, Borwd. WD6 off Brook Rd 78 CP41
West Herts Coll, Dacorum Campus, Hem.H. HP1
off Marlowes 40 BJ19
Watford Campus, Wat. WD17
off Hempstead Rd 75 BU41
West Hill, SW15 179 CX87
SW18 180 DA85
Dartford DA1 188 FK86
Downe BR6 223 EM112
Epsom KT19 216 CQ113
Harrow HA2 117 CE61
Oxted RH8 253 ED130
South Croydon CR2 220 DS110
Wembley HA9 118 CM60
West Hill Av, Epsom KT19 216 CQ112
West Hill Bk, Oxt. RH8 253 ED130
Westhill Cl, Grav. DA12
off Leith Pk Rd 191 GH88
West Hill Ct, N6 120 DG62
West Hill Dr, Dart. DA1 188 FJ86
West Hill Pk, N6 120 DF61
West Hill Prim Sch, SW18
off Merton Rd 180 DA85
Dartford DA1 off Dartford Rd 188 FJ86
Westhill Ri, Dart. DA1 188 FK86
West Hill Rd, SW18 180 DA86
Woking GU22 226 AX119
Westhill Rd, Hodd. EN11 49 DZ16
West Hill Sch, Lthd. KT22
off Kingston Rd 231 CG118
West Hill Way, N20 98 DB46
Westholm, NW11 120 DB56
West Holme, Erith DA8 167 FC81
Westholme, Orp. BR6 205 ES101
Westholme Gdns, Ruis. HA4 115 BU60
Westhorne Av, SE9 184 EJ86
SE12 184 EG87
Westhorpe Gdns, NW4 119 CW55
Westhorpe Rd, SW15 159 CW83
WEST HORSLEY, Lthd. KT24 245 BP127
West Ho Cl, SW19 179 CY88
WESTHUMBLE, Dor. RH5 247 CG131
Westhumble St, Westh. RH5 247 CH131
Westhurst Dr, Chis. BR7 185 EP92
WEST HYDE, Rick. WD3 91 BE52
West Hyde La, Chal.St.P. SL9 91 AZ52
West India Av, E14 302 A2
West India Dock Rd, E14 289 P9
West India Quay 302 C1
West Kensington 294 G10
West Kensington Ct, W14 294 G10
West Kent Av, Nthflt DA11 190 GC86
West Kent Cold Storage, Dunt.Grn TN14 241 FF120
WEST KILBURN, W9 282 G2
Westlake Cl, N13 99 DN48
Hayes UB4 136 BY70
Westlake Rd, Wem. HA9 117 CK61
Westland Av, Horn. RM11 128 FL60
Westland Cl, Lvsdn WD25 59 BT34
Stanwell TW19 174 BL86
Westland Dr, Brom. BR2 204 EF103
Brookmans Park AL9 63 CY27
Westland Ho, E16
off Rymill St 305 L3
Westland Pl, N1 287 L2
Westland Rd, Wat. WD17 75 BV40
Westlands Av, Slou. SL1 130 AJ72
Westlands Cl, Hayes UB3 155 BU77
Slough SL1 off Westlands Av 130 AJ72
Westlands Ct, Epsom KT18 232 CQ115
Westlands Ter, SW12
off Gaskarth Rd 181 DJ86
Westlands Way, Oxt. RH8 253 ED127
West La, SE16 300 E5
Abinger Hammer RH5 262 BX139
West Lawn Apts, Ald. WD25
off Broadfield Way 76 CB36
Westlea Av, Wat. WD25 76 BY37
Westlea Cl, Brox. EN10 49 DZ24
Westlea Rd, W7 157 CG76
Broxbourne EN10 49 DZ23
Westleas, Horl. RH6 268 DE146
West Lea Sch, N9
off Haselbury Rd 100 DS48
Westlees Cl, N.Holm. RH5 263 CJ139
Westleigh Av, SW15 179 CV85
Coulsdon CR5 234 DG116
Westleigh Dr, Brom. BR1 204 EL95
Westleigh Gdns, Edg. HA8 96 CN53
Westlinks, Wem. HA0
off Alperton La 137 CK68
Westlinton Cl, NW7 97 CY51
West Lo Av, W3 138 CN74
West Lo Prim Sch, Pnr. HA5 off West End La 116 BX56
West Lo Sch, Sid. DA15
off Station Rd 186 EU90
West London Acad, Nthlt. UB5 off Compton Cres 136 BY67
West London Coll, W1 285 H9
Westlyn Cl, Rain. RM13 148 FJ69
Westly Wd, Welw.G.C. AL7 30 DA08
Westmacott Dr, Felt. TW14 175 BT88
West Mall, N9 off Plevna Rd 100 DU48
W8 295 K2
West Malling Way, Horn. RM12 128 FJ64
Westmark Pt, SW15
off Norley Vale 179 CV88
Westmead, SW15 179 CV86
Windsor SL4 151 AP83
Woking GU21 226 AV117
West Mead, Epsom KT19 216 CS107
Ruislip HA4 116 BW63
Welwyn Garden City AL7 30 DB12
Westmead Cor, Cars. SM5
off Colston Av 218 DE105
Westmead Dr, Red. RH1 266 DG142
Westmeade Cl, Chsht EN7 66 DV29
Westmead Rd, Sutt. SM1 218 DD105
West Meads, Guil. GU2 258 AT135
Horley RH6 269 DJ148
Westmede, Chig. IG7 103 EQ51
Westmere Dr, NW7 96 CR48
West Mersea Cl, E16 304 A3
West Ms, N17 100 DV51
SW1 297 K9
West Middlesex Uni Hosp, Islw. TW7 157 CG82
West Mill, Grav. DA11 191 GF86
WESTMINSTER, SW1 297 L6
Westminster 298 B5
Westminster Abbey, SW1 298 A6
Westminster Abbey Choir Sch, SW1 297 P6
Westminster Abbey Mus, SW1 298 A6
Westminster Acad, W2 283 K6
Westminster Adult Ed Service, Ebury Br Cen, SW1 297 J10
Frith St Cen, W1 285 P9
Westminster Av, Th.Hth. CR7 201 DP96
Westminster Br, SE1 298 B5
SW1 298 B5
Westminster Br Rd, SE1 298 D5
Westminster Business Sq, SE11 off Durham St 310 C1
Westminster Cath, SW1 297 L7
Westminster Cath Choir Sch, SW1 297 M7
Westminster Cath RC Prim Sch, SW1 297 P10
Westminster City Hall, SW1 297 M6
Westminster City Sch, SW1 297 M6
Westminster Cl, Felt. TW14 175 BU88
Ilford IG6 103 ER54
Teddington TW11 177 CG92
Westminster Ct, St.Alb. AL1 42 CC22
Waltham Cross EN8
off Eleanor Way 67 DZ33
Westminster Dr, N13 99 DL50
Westminster Gdns, E4 102 EE46
SW1 298 A8
Barking IG11 145 ES68
Ilford IG6 103 EQ54
Westminster Kingsway Coll, Castle La Cen, SW1 297 M6
Kings Cross Cen, WC1 286 C3
Peter St Cen, W1 285 N10
Regent's Pk Cen, NW1 285 L4
Vincent Sq Cen, SW1 297 N8
Westminster Palace Gdns, SW1
off Artillery Row 297 N7
Westminster Pier 298 B4
Westminster Rd, N9 100 DV46
W7 137 CE74
Sutton SM1 200 DD103
Westminster Sch, SW1 298 A6
Westminster Under Sch, SW1 297 N9
Westmoat Cl, Beck. BR3 183 EC94
WEST MOLESEY, KT8 196 BZ99
Westmont Rd, Esher KT10 197 CE103
Westmoor Gdns, Enf. EN3 83 DX40
Westmoor Rd, Enf. EN3 83 DX40
Westmoor St, SE7 304 D7
Westmore Grn, Tats. TN16 238 EJ121
Westmoreland Av, Horn. RM11 128 FJ57
Welling DA16 165 ES83
Westmoreland Dr, Sutt. SM2 218 DB109
Westmoreland Pl, Brom. BR1 204 EG97
Westmoreland Pl, SW1 309 K1
W5 137 CK71
Westmoreland Rd, NW9 118 CN56
SE17 311 K2
SW13 159 CT81
Bromley BR1, BR2 204 EE99
Westmoreland St, W1 285 H7
Westmoreland Ter, SE20 182 DV94
SW1 309 K1
Westmoreland Wk, SE17 311 M2
Westmore Rd, Tats. TN16 238 EJ121
Westmorland Cl, E12 124 EK61
Epsom KT19 216 CS110
Twickenham TW1 177 CH86
Westmorland Rd, E17 123 EA58
Harrow HA1 116 CB57
Westmorland Sq, Mitch. CR4
off Westmorland Way 201 DL99
Westmorland Way, Mitch. CR4 201 DK98
West Mt, Guil. GU2
off The Mount 258 AW136
Westmount Apts, Wat. WD18
off Linden Av 75 BT42
Westmount Av, Amer. HP7 55 AQ39
Westmount Rd, SE9 165 EM82
WEST NORWOOD, SE27 182 DQ90
West Norwood 181 DP90
West Oak, Beck. BR3 203 ED95
Westoe Rd, N9 100 DV47
Weston Av, Add. KT15 212 BG105
Grays RM20 169 FT77
Thames Ditton KT7 197 CE101
West Molesey KT8 196 BY97
Weston Cl, Couls. CR5 235 DM120
Godalming GU7 258 AS144
Hutton CM13 109 GC45
Potters Bar EN6 63 CZ32
Weston Ct, N4
off Queens Dr 122 DQ62
N20 off Farnham Cl 98 DC45
Weston Dr, Cat. CR3 236 DQ122
Stanmore HA7 95 CH53
West One Shop Cen, W1 285 H9
Weston Flds, Albury GU5 260 BJ139
Weston Gdns, Islw. TW7 157 CD81
Woking GU22 227 BE116
WESTON GREEN, T.Ditt. KT7 197 CF102
Weston Grn, Dag. RM9 126 EZ63
Thames Ditton KT7 197 CE102
Weston Grn Rd, Esher KT10 197 CD102
Thames Ditton KT7 197 CE102
Weston Gro, Brom. BR1 204 EF95
Weston Lea, W.Hors. KT24 245 BR125
Weston Pk, N8 121 DL58
Kingston upon Thames KT1
off Clarence St 198 CL96
Thames Ditton KT7 197 CE102
Weston Pk Cl, T.Ditt. KT7 197 CE102
Weston Pk Prim Sch, N8
off Denton Rd 121 DM57
Weston Ri, WC1 286 D1
Weston Rd, W4 158 CQ76
Bromley BR1 184 EF94
Dagenham RM9 126 EY63
Enfield EN2 82 DR39
Epsom KT17 216 CS111
Guildford GU2 242 AV133
Slough SL1 131 AM71
Thames Ditton KT7 197 CE102
Weston St, SE1 299 M5
Weston Wk, E8 278 F7
Weston Way, Wok. GU22 227 BE116
Weston Yd, Albury GU5 260 BJ139
Westover Cl, Sutt. SM2 218 DB109
Westover Hill, NW3 120 DA61
Westover Rd, SW18 180 DC86
Westow Hill, SE19 182 DS93
Westow St, SE19 182 DS93
West Palace Gdns, Wey. KT13 195 BP104
West Pk, SE9 184 EL89
West Pk Av, Rich. TW9 158 CN81
West Pk Cl, Houns. TW5 156 BZ79
Romford RM6 126 EX57
West Pk Hill, Brwd. CM14 108 FU48
West Pk Hosp, Epsom KT19 216 CM112
West Pk Rd, Epsom KT19 216 CM112
Richmond TW9 158 CN81
Southall UB2 136 CC74
West Parkside, SE10 303 M7
Warlingham CR6 237 EA115
West Pk Wk, E20 280 E3
West Pier, E1 300 E3
West Pl, Harl. CM20 36 EU12
West Pl, SW19 179 CW92
West Pt, SE1 300 C10
Slough SL1 131 AK74
Westpoint Apts, N8
off Turnpike La 121 DM56
West Pt Cl, Houns. TW4 156 BZ83
Westpoint Trd Est, W3 138 CP71
Westpole Av, Cockfos. EN4 80 DG42
Westport Rd, E13 292 A5
Westport St, E1 289 K8
West Poultry Av, EC1 286 G7
West Quarters, W12 139 CU72
West Quay Dr, Hayes UB4 136 BY71
West Ramp, Lon.Hthrw Air. TW6 154 BN81
Westray, Hem.H. HP3 41 BQ22
Westridge Cl, Chesh. HP5 54 AM30
Hemel Hempstead HP1 39 BF20
West Ridge Gdns, Grnf. UB6 136 CC68
West Riding, Brick.Wd AL2 60 BZ30
West Rd, E15 281 M9
N17 100 DV51
SW3 308 F1
SW4 181 DK85
W5 138 CL71
Barnet EN4 98 DG46
Berkhamsted HP4 38 AU18
Chadwell Heath RM6 126 EX58
Chessington KT9 215 CJ112
Feltham TW14 175 BR86
Guildford GU1 258 AY135
Harlow CM20 36 EU11
Kingston upon Thames KT2 198 CQ95
Reigate RH2 266 DB135
Rush Green RM7 127 FD59

West Rd,
South Ockendon RM15 149 FV69
West Drayton UB7 154 BM76
Weybridge KT13 213 BP109
Westrow, SW15 179 CW85
West Row, W10 282 E4
Westrow Dr, Bark. IG11 145 ET65
Westrow Gdns, Ilf. IG3 125 ET61
⇌ **West Ruislip** 115 BQ61
⊖ **West Ruislip** 115 BQ61
West Shaw, Long. DA3 209 FX96
West Sheen Vale, Rich. TW9 158 CM84
Westside, NW4 97 CV54
West Side, Turnf. EN10 67 DY25
Westside Apts, Ilf. IG1
off Roden St 125 EN62
● **West Side Business Cen**,
Harl. CM19 50 EL16
West Side Common, SW19 179 CW92
DLR **West Silvertown** 303 P3
West Smithfield, EC1 286 G7
West Spur Rd, Uxb. UB8 134 BK69
West Sq, SE11 298 G7
Harlow CM20 35 EQ14
Iver SL0 *off High St* 133 BF72
Weststand Apts, N5
off Avenell Rd 121 DP62
West St, E2 288 F1
E11 124 EE62
E17 123 EB57
WC2 285 P9
Bexleyheath DA7 166 EZ84
Brentford TW8 157 CJ79
Bromley BR1 224 EG95
Carshalton SM5 200 DF104
Croydon CR0 220 DQ105
Dorking RH4 263 CG136
Epsom KT18 216 CR113
Erith DA8 167 FD77
Ewell KT17 216 CS110
Gravesend DA11 191 GG86
Grays RM17 170 GA79
Harrow HA1 117 CD60
Hertford SG13 32 DQ10
Reigate RH2 249 CY133
Sutton SM1 218 DB106
Ware SG12 33 DX06
Watford WD17 75 BV40
Woking GU21 *off Church St E* 227 AZ117
West St La, Cars. SM5 218 DF105
⇌ **West Sutton** 218 DA105
West Temple Sheen, SW14 158 CP84
West Tenter St, E1 288 B9
Coll **West Thames Coll**,
Islw. TW7 *off London Rd* 157 CE81
Feltham Skills Cen, Felt. TW13
off Boundaries Rd 176 BX88
● **West Thamesmead Business Pk**,
SE28 165 ET76
Sch **West Thornton Prim Sch**,
Croy. CR0 *off Rosecourt Rd* 201 DM100
WEST THURROCK,
Grays RM20 169 FU78
Sch **West Thurrock Prim Sch**,
W.Thur. RM20 *off The Rookery* 169 FU79
West Thurrock Way,
Grays RM20 169 FT77
WEST TILBURY, Til. RM18 171 GL79
West Twrs, Pnr. HA5 116 BX58
Sch **West Twyford Prim Sch**,
NW10 *off Twyford Abbey Rd* 138 CN68
Westvale Ms, W3 138 CS74
West Valley Rd, Hem.H. HP3 58 BJ25
West Vw, NW4 119 CW56
Ashtead KT21 231 CJ119
Chesham HP5 54 AR29
Feltham TW14 175 BQ87
Hatfield AL10 45 CU16
Loughton IG10 85 EM41
West Vw Av, Whyt. CR3
off Station Rd 236 DT118
Westview Cl, NW10 119 CT64
W7 137 CE72
W10 282 B8
Rainham RM13 148 FJ69
Redhill RH1 266 DE136
West Vw Ct, Els. WD6
off High St 77 CK44
Westview Cres, N9 100 DS45
Westview Dr, Wdf.Grn. IG8 102 EK54
West Vw Gdns, Els. WD6
off High St 77 CK44
Westview Ri, Hem.H. HP2 40 BK19
West Vw Rd, Crock. BR8 207 FD100
Dartford DA1 188 FM86
St. Albans AL3 43 CD19
Swanley BR8 207 FG98
Westview Rd, Warl. CR6 236 DV119
Westville Rd, W12 159 CU75
Thames Ditton KT7 197 CG102
West Wk, W5 138 CL71
East Barnet EN4 98 DG45
Harlow CM20 35 EQ14
Hayes UB3 135 BU74
West Way, The, Sutt. SM1
off Cheam Rd 218 DB106
Westward Ho, Guil. GU1 243 AZ132
Sch **Westward Prep Sch**,
Walt. KT12 *off Hersham Rd* 195 BV103
Westward Rd, E4 101 DZ50
Westward Way, Har. HA3 118 CL58
West Warwick Pl, SW1 297 L9
WEST WATFORD, Wat. WD18 75 BU42
West Way, N18 100 DR49
NW10 118 CR62
Beaconsfield HP9 88 AF54
Brentwood CM14 108 FU48
Carshalton SM5 218 DD110
Croydon CR0 203 DY103
Edgware HA8 96 CP51
Hounslow TW5 156 BZ81
Petts Wood BR5 205 ER99
Pinner HA5 116 BX56
Rickmansworth WD3 92 BH46
Ruislip HA4 115 BT60
Shepperton TW17 195 BR100
West Wickham BR4 203 ED100
🔒 **Westway**, Rom. RM1
off South St 127 FE57
Westway, SW20 199 CV97
W2 283 J6
W9 283 J6
W10 282 F8
W12 139 CU73
Westway, Caterham CR3 236 DR122
Gatwick RH6 269 DH152
Guildford GU2 242 AT132
Westway Cl, SW20 199 CV97
West Way Gdns, Croy. CR0 203 DX103
Westway Gdns, Red. RH1 250 DG131
Westways, Epsom KT19 217 CT105
Westerham TN16 255 EQ126
🔒 **Westway Shop Pk**,
Grnf. UB6 137 CE67
Westwell Cl, Orp. BR5 206 EX102
Westwell Rd, SW16 181 DL93
Westwell Rd App, SW16
off Westwell Rd 181 DL93
Westwick Cl, Hem.H. HP2 41 BR21
Westwick Gdns, W14 294 C5
Hounslow TW4 155 BV82
WEST WICKHAM, BR4 203 EC103
⇌ **West Wickham** 203 EC101
Westwick Pl, Wat. WD25 60 BW34
Westwick Row, Hem.H. HP2 41 BR20
Sch **West Wimbledon Prim Sch**,
SW20 *off Bodnant Gdns* 199 CV97
Westwood Av, SE19 202 DQ95
Brentwood CM14 108 FU49
Harrow HA2 116 CB63
Woodham KT15 211 BF112
Westwood Cl, Amer. HP6 72 AX39
Bromley BR1 204 EK97
Esher KT10 196 CC104
Potters Bar EN6 64 DA30
Ruislip HA4 115 BP58
Westwood Ct, Guil. GU2
off Hillcrest Rd 242 AT133
Westwood Dr, Amer. HP6 72 AX39
Westwood Gdns, SW13 159 CT83
Westwood Hill, SE26 182 DU92
Westwood La, Sid. DA15 186 EU85
Welling DA16 165 ET83
Coll **Westwood Language Coll for Girls**, SE19 *off Spurgeon Rd* 182 DR94
Westwood Pk, SE23 182 DV87
● **Westwood Pk Trd Est**, W3 138 CN71
Westwood Pl, SE26 182 DU91
Westwood Rd, E16 304 A3
SW13 159 CT83
Coulsdon CR5 235 DK118
Ilford IG3 125 ET60
Southfleet DA13 190 FY93
West Woodside, Bex. DA5 186 EY87
Westwood Way, Sev. TN13 256 FF122
West Yoke, Ash TN15 209 FX103
Wetheral Dr, Stan. HA7 95 CH53
Wetherall Ms, St.Alb. AL1
off Watsons Wk 43 CE21
Wetherby Cl, Nthlt. UB5 136 CB65
Wetherby Gdns, SW5 295 N9
Wetherby Ms, SW5 295 L10
Wetherby Pl, SW7 295 N9
Sch **Wetherby Pre-Prep Sch**,
W2 295 K1
Wetherby Rd, Borwd. WD6 78 CL39
Enfield EN2 82 DQ39
Wetherby Way, Chess. KT9 216 CL108
Wetherden St, E17 123 DZ59
Wetherell Dr, Burn. SL1 130 AH71
Wetherell Rd, E9 279 K8
Wetherill Rd, N10 98 DG53
Wetherly Cl, Harl. CM17 36 EZ11
Wettern Cl, S.Croy. CR2
off Purley Oaks Rd 220 DS110
Wetton Pl, Egh. TW20 173 AZ92
Wexfenne Gdns, Wok. GU22 228 BH116
Wexford Rd, SW12 180 DF87
Sch **Wexham Ct Prim Sch**,
Wexham SL3 *off Church La* 132 AW71
Wexham Lo, Wexham SL2 132 AV71
H **Wexham Pk Hosp**, Slou. SL2 132 AW70
Wexham Pk La, Wexham SL3 132 AW70
Wexham Pl, Wexham SL2 132 AX65
Wexham Rd, Slou. SL1, SL2 132 AV71
Sch **Wexham Sch**, Slou. SL2
off Norway Dr 132 AW71
● **Wexham Springs**,
Wexham SL2 132 AW66
WEXHAM STREET, Slou. SL3 132 AW67
Wexham St, Slou. SL2, SL3 132 AW67
Wexham Wds, Wexham SL3 132 AW71
Wey Av, Cher. KT16 194 BG97
Weybank, Wisley GU23 228 BL116
Wey Barton, Byfleet KT14 212 BM113
Weybourne Pl, S.Croy. CR2 220 DR110
Weybourne St, SW18 180 DC89
WEYBRIDGE, KT13 212 BN105
⇌ **Weybridge** 212 BN107
● **Weybridge Business Pk**,
Add. KT15 212 BL105
Weybridge Ct, SE16 312 D1
H **Weybridge Hosp**, Wey. KT13 212 BN105
Weybridge Pk, Wey. KT13 212 BN106
Weybridge Pt, SW11 308 F8
Weybridge Rd, Add. KT15 194 BK104
Thornton Heath CR7 201 DN98
Weybridge KT13 194 BL104
Weybrook Dr, Guil. GU4 243 BB129
Wey Cl, W.Byf. KT14
off Broadoaks Cres 212 BH113
Wey Ct, Epsom KT19 216 CQ105
New Haw KT15 212 BK109
Weydown Cl, SW19 179 CY88
Guildford GU2 242 AU129
Weydown La, Guil. GU2
off Cumberland Av 242 AU129
Sch **Weyfield Prim Sch**,
Guil. GU1 *off School Cl* 242 AX131
Weyhill Rd, E1 288 D8
Wey Ho, Nthlt. UB5
off Taywood Rd 136 BZ69
Sch **Wey Ho Sch**, Bramley GU5
off Horsham Rd 258 AY143
Weylands Cl, Walt. KT12 196 BZ102
Weylands Pk, Wey. KT13 213 BR107
Wey La, Chesh. HP5 54 AP32
Weylea Av, Guil. GU4 243 BA131
Weylond Rd, Dag. RM8 126 EZ62
Wey Manor Rd,
New Haw KT15 212 BK109
Weyman Rd, SE3 164 EJ81
Weymead Cl, Cher. KT16 194 BJ102
Wey Meadows, Wey. KT13 212 BL106
Weymede, Byfleet KT14 212 BM112
Weymouth Av, NW7 96 CS50
W5 157 CJ76
Weymouth Cl, E6 293 N9
Weymouth Ct, Sutt. SM2 218 DA108
Weymouth Dr,
Chaff.Hun. RM16 169 FX78
Weymouth Ho, SW8 310 C5
Weymouth Ms, W1 285 J6
Weymouth Rd, Hayes UB4 135 BS69
Weymouth St, W1 285 H7
Hemel Hempstead HP3 40 BK24
Weymouth Ter, E2 278 B10
Weymouth Wk, Stan. HA7 95 CG51
🔒 **Wey Retail Pk**, Byfleet KT14 212 BL112
Wey Rd, Wey. KT13 194 BM104
Weyside Cl, Byfleet KT14 212 BM112
Weyside Gdns, Guil. GU1 242 AV132
Weyside Rd, Guil. GU1 242 AV132
Weystone Rd, Wey. KT13
off Weybridge Rd 212 BM105
Weyver Ct, St.Alb. AL1
off Avenue Rd 43 CE19
● **Weyvern Pk**, Peasm. GU3
off Old Portsmouth Rd 258 AV142
Weyview Cl, Guil. GU1 242 AW132
Wey Vw Ct, Guil. GU1
off Walnut Tree Cl 258 AW135
Whadcote St, N4 121 DN61
Whaddon Ho, SE22
off Albrighton Rd 162 DS83
Whalebone Av, Rom. RM6 126 EZ58
Whalebone Ct, EC2 287 L8
Whalebone Gro, Rom. RM6 126 EZ58
Whalebone La, E15 281 J7
Whalebone La N, Rom. RM6 126 EY57
Whalebone La S, Dag. RM8 126 EZ59
Romford RM6 126 EZ59
Whales Yd, E15 281 J7
Whaley Rd, Pot.B. EN6 64 DC33
Wharfdale Cl, N11 98 DG51
Wharfdale Ct, E5
off Pedro St 123 DX63
Wharfdale Rd, N1 276 B10
Wharfedale, Hem.H. HP2 40 BL17
Wharfedale Gdns, Th.Hth. CR7 201 DM98
Wharfedale Rd, Dart. DA2 188 FQ88
Wharfedale St, SW10 307 L1
Wharf Ho, Erith DA8
off West St 167 FE78
Wharf La, E14 289 N9
Rickmansworth WD3 92 BL46
Ripley GU23 228 BJ118
Send GU23 227 BC123
Twickenham TW1 177 CG88
Wharf Pl, E2 278 D9
Wharf Rd, N1 277 J10
N1 (King's Cross) 276 A10
Brentwood CM14 108 FW48
Broxbourne EN10 49 DZ23
Enfield EN3 83 DY44
Gravesend DA12 191 GL86
Grays RM17 170 FZ79
Guildford GU1 242 AW134
Hemel Hempstead HP1 40 BH22
Wraysbury TW19 172 AW87
Wharf Rd S, Grays RM17 170 FZ79
Wharfside Cl, Erith DA8 167 FF78
Wharfside Pt S, E14 290 E10
Wharfside Rd, E16 291 J7
Wharf St, E16 291 J7
SE8 163 EA78
Wharf Way, Hunt.Br WD4 59 BQ33
Wharley Hook, Harl. CM18 51 ET18
Wharncliffe Dr, Sthl. UB1 137 CD74
Wharncliffe Gdns, SE25 202 DS96
Wharncliffe Ms, SW4 181 DK86
Wharncliffe Rd, SE25 202 DS96
Wharton Cl, NW10 138 CS65
Wharton Cotts, WC1
off Wharton St 286 D3
Wharton Rd, Brom. BR1 204 EH95
Wharton St, WC1 286 D3
Whateley Cl, Guil. GU2 242 AV129
Whateley Rd, SE20 183 DX94
SE22 182 DT85
Whatley Av, SW20 199 CY97
Whatman Rd, SE23 183 DX87
Whatmore Cl, Stai. TW19 174 BG86
Wheatash Rd, Add. KT15 194 BH103
Wheatbarn, Welw.G.C. AL7 30 DB08
Wheatbutts, The,
Eton Wick SL4 151 AM77
Wheat Cl, Sand. AL4 43 CG16
Wheatcroft, Chsht EN7 66 DV28
Wheatcroft Ct, Sutt. SM1
off Cleeve Way 200 DB102
Sch **Wheatcroft Sch**,
Hert. SG13 *off Stanstead Rd* 32 DU08
Wheatfield, Hat. AL10
off Stonecross Rd 45 CV17
Hemel Hempstead HP2 40 BK18
Wheatfields, E6 293 N8
Enfield EN3 83 DY40
Harlow CM17 36 EW09
Sch **Wheatfields Inf & Nurs Sch**,
St.Alb. AL4 *off Downes Rd* 43 CH16
Sch **Wheatfields Jun Sch**,
St.Alb. AL4 *off Downes Rd* 43 CH16
Wheatfield Way, Horl. RH6 269 DH147
Kingston upon Thames KT1 198 CL96
WHEATHAMPSTEAD,
St.Alb. AL4 28 CL06
Wheathill Rd, SE20 202 DV97
Wheat Knoll, Ken. CR8 236 DQ116
Wheatland Ho, SE22
off Albrighton Rd 162 DS83
Wheatlands, Houns. TW5 156 CA79
Wheatlands Rd, SW17
off Stapleton Rd 180 DG90
Slough SL3 152 AV76
Wheatley Cl, NW4 97 CU54
Greenhithe DA9
off Steele Av 189 FU85
Hornchurch RM11 128 FK58
Sawbridgeworth CM21 36 EW06
Welwyn Garden City AL7 30 DA11
Wheatley Cres, Hayes UB3 135 BU73
Wheatley Dr, Wat. WD25 60 BW34
Wheatley Gdns, N9 100 DS47
Wheatley Ho, SW15
off Tangley Gro 179 CU87
Wheatley Ms, E.Mol. KT8 197 CD98
Wheatley Rd, Islw. TW7 157 CF83
Welwyn Garden City AL7 29 CZ10
Wheatleys, St.Alb. AL4 43 CJ18
Wheatleys Eyot, Sun. TW16 195 BU99
Wheatley St, W1 285 H7
Wheatley Ter Rd, Erith DA8 167 FF79
Wheatley Way, Chal.St.P. SL9 90 AY51
Wheat Sheaf Cl, E14 302 C8
Wheatsheaf Cl, Nthlt. UB5 116 BY64
Ottershaw KT16 211 BD107
Woking GU21 226 AY116
Wheatsheaf Hill, Halst. TN14 224 EZ109
Wheatsheaf La, SW6 306 B4
SW8 310 B4
Staines-upon-Thames TW18 173 BF94
Wheatsheaf Rd,
Hunsdon SG12 34 EK06
Romford RM1 127 FF58
Wheatsheaf Ter, SW6 307 H5
Wheatstone Cl, Mitch. CR4 200 DE95
Slough SL3 152 AU76
Wheatstone Rd, W10 282 F6
Erith DA8 167 FD78
Wheeler Av, Oxt. RH8 253 ED129
Penn HP10 88 AC47
Wheeler Cl, Wdf.Grn. IG8
off Chigwell Rd 103 EM50
Wheeler Gdns, N1 276 B8
Wheeler Pl, Brom. BR2 204 EH98
Wheelers, Epp. CM16 69 ET29
Wheelers Cl, Lwr Naze. EN9 50 EE22
Wheelers Cross, Bark. IG11 145 ER68
Wheelers Dr, Ruis. HA4
off Wallington Cl 115 BQ58
Wheelers Fm Gdns,
N.Wld Bas. CM16 71 FB26
Wheelers La, Brock. RH3 264 CP136
Epsom KT18 216 CP113
Hemel Hempstead HP3 40 BL22
Smallfield RH6 269 DN149
Wheelers Orchard,
Chal.St.P. SL9 90 AY51
Wheel Fm Dr, Dag. RM10 127 FC62
Wheelock Cl, Erith DA8 167 FB80
Wheelwright Cl, Bushey WD23
off Ashfield Av 76 CB44
Wheelwright St, N7 276 C6
Whelan Way, Wall. SM6 201 DK104
Wheler St, E1 288 A5
Whellock Rd, W4 158 CS76
WHELPLEY HILL, Chesh. HP5 56 AX26
Whelpley Hill Pk, Whel.Hill HP5 56 AX26
Whenman Av, Bex. DA5 187 FC89
Whernside Cl, SE28 146 EW73
Wherwell Rd, Guil. GU2 258 AW136
WHETSTONE, N20 98 DB47
Whetstone Cl, N20 98 DD47
Whetstone Pk, WC2 286 C8
Whetstone Rd, SE3 164 EJ82
Whewell Rd, N19 121 DL61
Whichcote Gdns, Chesh. HP5 54 AR33
Whichcote St, SE1 298 E3
Whichert Cl, Knot.Grn HP9 88 AJ49
Whidborne Cl, SE8 314 B9
Whidborne St, WC1 286 B3
Whielden Cl, Amer. HP7 55 AP40
Whielden Gate, Winch.Hill HP7 55 AL43
Whielden Grn, Amer. HP7 55 AP40
Whielden Hts, Amer. HP7 55 AN41
Whielden La, Amer. HP7 55 AL43
Whielden St, Amer. HP7 55 AN41
Whiffins Gra, Ch.Lang. CM17 52 EY16
Whiffins Orchard,
Cooper. CM16 70 EX29
Whimbrel Cl, SE28 146 EW73
South Croydon CR2 220 DR111
Whimbrel Way, Hayes UB4 136 BX72
Whinchat Rd, SE28 165 ER76
Whinfell Cl, SW16 181 DK92
Whinfell Way, Grav. DA12 191 GM91
Whinneys Rd, Loud. HP10 88 AC52
Whinyates Rd, SE9 164 EL83
Whipley Cl, Guil. GU4
off Weybrook Dr 243 BB129
Whippendell Cl, Orp. BR5 206 EV95
Whippendell Hill,
Kings L. WD4 58 BJ30
Whippendell Rd, Wat. WD18 75 BU43
Whippendell Way, Orp. BR5 206 EV95
Jct **Whipps Cross**, E17 123 ED57
Whipps Cross Rd, E11 123 ED57
H **Whipps Cross University Hospital**, E11 123 ED58
Whiskin St, EC1 286 G3
Whisperwood, Loud. WD3 74 BH41
Whisperwood Cl, Har. HA3 95 CE52
Whistler Gdns, Edg. HA8 96 CM54
Whistler Ms, SE15 312 B5
Dagenham RM8
off Fitzstephen Rd 126 EV64
Whistlers Av, SW11 308 B5
Whistlers Ct, Wold. CR3 253 ED125
Whistler St, N5 276 G2
Whistler Twr, SW10 307 P4
Whistler Wk, SW10
off Blantyre St 307 P4
Whiston Rd, E2 278 A10
Whitacre Ms, SE11 310 F1
Whitakers Way, Loug. IG10 85 EM39
Whitbread Cl, N17 100 DU53
Whitbread Rd, SE4 163 DY84
Whitburn Rd, SE13 163 EB84
Whitby Av, NW10 138 CP69
Whitby Cl, Bigg.H. TN16 238 EH119
Greenhithe DA9 189 FU85
Whitby Ct, N7 276 B1
Whitby Gdns, NW9 118 CN55
Sutton SM1 200 DD103
Whitby Rd, SE18 305 J8
Harrow HA2 116 CC62
Ruislip HA4 115 BV62
Slough SL1 131 AQ73
Sutton SM1 200 DD103
Whitby St, E1 288 A4
Whitcher Cl, SE14 313 L3
Whitcher Pl, NW1 275 L5
Whitchurch Av, Edg. HA8 96 CM52
Whitchurch Cl, Edg. HA8 96 CM51
Sch **Whitchurch First & Jun Schs**,
Stan. HA7 *off Wemborough Rd* 95 CK52
Whitchurch Gdns, Edg. HA8 96 CM51
Whitchurch La, Edg. HA8 95 CK52
Whitchurch Rd, W11 282 D10
Romford RM3 106 FK49
Whitcomb Ct, WC2
off Whitcomb St 297 P1
Whitcomb St, WC2 297 P1
Whitcome Ms, Rich. TW9 158 CP81
Whiteadder Way, E14 302 D8
Whitear Wk, E15 281 H4
White Av, Nthflt DA11 191 GF90
Whitebarn La, Dag. RM10 146 FA67
Whitebeam Av, Brom. BR2 205 EN100
Whitebeam Cl, SW9 310 D5
Shenley WD7
off Mulberry Gdns 62 CM33
Waltham Cross EN7 66 DS26
Whitebeam Dr, Reig. RH2 266 DB137
South Ockendon RM15 149 FW69
Whitebeam Ho, NW3
off Maitland Pk Rd 274 F4
Whitebeams, Hat. AL10 45 CU21
White Beams, Park St AL2 60 CC28
White Beam Way, Tad. KT20 233 CU121
White Bear Pl, NW3
off New End Sq 120 DD63
Whiteberry Rd, Dor. RH5 262 CB143
White Br Av, Mitch. CR4 200 DD98
Whitebridge Cl, Felt. TW14 175 BT86
Sch **White Br Comm Inf Sch, The**,
Loug. IG10 *off Greensted Rd* 103 EM45
Sch **White Br Jun Sch, The**,
Loug. IG10 *off Greensted Rd* 103 EM45
Whitebroom Rd, Hem.H. HP1 39 BE18
WHITE BUSHES, Red. RH1 267 DH139
White Butts Rd, Ruis. HA4 116 BX62
WHITECHAPEL, E1 288 C9
⊖ **Whitechapel** 288 E6
⊖ **Whitechapel** 288 E6
★ **Whitechapel Art Gall**, E1 288 B8
Whitechapel High St, E1 288 B8
Whitechapel Rd, E1 288 C8
White Ch La, E1 288 C8
White Ch Pas, E1 288 C8
⊖ **White City** 294 B1
⊖ **White City** 294 B2
White City Cl, W12 294 A1
White City Est, W12 139 CV73
White City Rd, W12 282 A10
White Cl, Slou. SL1 131 AR74
White Conduit St, N1 276 F10
Whitecote Rd, Sthl. UB1 136 CB72
White Craig Cl, Pnr. HA5 94 CA50
Whitecroft, Horl. RH6
off Woodhayes 269 DH147
St. Albans AL1 43 CH23
Swanley BR8 207 FE96
Whitecroft Cl, Beck. BR3 203 ED98
Whitecroft Way, Beck. BR3 203 EC99
Whitecross Pl, EC2 287 M6
Whitecross St, EC1 287 K4
★ **White Cube**, N1
off Hoxton Sq 287 N3
★ **White Cube**, SW1 297 M2
White Down Rd, Dor. RH5 262 BW135
Whitefield Av, NW2 119 CW59
Purley CR8 235 DN116
Whitefield Cl, SW15 179 CY86
Orpington BR5 206 EW97
Whitefields, Cat. CR3 236 DS121
Sch **Whitefield Sch**, NW2
off Claremont Rd 119 CX59
Sch **Whitefield Schs & Cen**, E17
off Macdonald Rd 101 ED54
Whitefields Rd, Chsht EN8 66 DW28
Whitefoot La, Brom. BR1 183 EC91
Whitefoot Ter, Brom. BR1 184 EE90
Whiteford Rd, Slou. SL2 132 AS71
White Friars, Sev. TN13 256 FG127
Whitefriars Av, Har. HA3 95 CE54
Sch **Whitefriars Comm Sch**,
Wealds. HA3 *off Whitefriars Av* 95 CE54
Whitefriars Dr, Har. HA3 95 CD54
● **Whitefriars Ind Est**,
Harrow HA3 95 CD54
Whitefriars St, EC4 286 F9
White Gdns, Dag. RM10 146 FA65
Whitegate Gdns, Har. HA3 95 CF52
White Gates, Horn. RM12 128 FJ61
Whitegates, Whyt. CR3
off Court Bushes Rd 236 DU119
Woking GU22 *off Loop Rd* 227 AZ120
Whitegates Cl, Crox.Grn WD3 74 BN42
Whitegate Way, Tad. KT20 233 CV120
Whitehall, SW1 298 A2
White Hall, Abridge RM4
off Market Pl 86 EV41
Whitehall Cl, Borwd. WD6 78 CN42
Chigwell IG7 104 EU48
Lower Nazeing EN9 50 EE22
Uxbridge UB8 134 BJ67
Whitehall Ct, SW1 298 A3
Whitehall Cres, Chess. KT9 215 CK106
Whitehall Fm La, Vir.W. GU25 192 AY96
Whitehall Gdns, E4 102 EE46
SW1 298 A3
W3 138 CN74
W4 158 CP79
Sch **Whitehall Inf Sch**,
Uxb. UB8 *off Cowley Rd* 134 BJ67
Sch **Whitehall Jun Sch**,
Uxb. UB8 *off Cowley Rd* 134 BJ68
Whitehall La, Buck.H. IG9 102 EG47
Egham TW20 173 AZ94
Erith DA8 167 FF82
Grays RM17 170 GC78
South Park RH2 265 CZ138
Wraysbury TW19 173 BA86
Whitehall Pk, N19 121 DJ60
Whitehall Pk Rd, W4 158 CP79
Whitehall Pl, E7 281 P2
SW1 298 A3
Wallington SM6
off Bernard Rd 219 DH105
Sch **Whitehall Prim Sch**, E4
off Normanton Pk 102 EE47
Whitehall Rd, E4 102 EE47
W7 157 CG75
Bromley BR2 204 EK99
Grays RM17 170 GC77
Harrow HA1 117 CE59
Thornton Heath CR7 201 DN99
Uxbridge UB8 134 BK67
Woodford Green IG8 102 EE47
Jct **Whitehall Rbt**, Harl. CM19 51 EM16
Whitehall St, N17 100 DT52
Whitehands Cl, Hodd. EN11 49 DZ17
White Hart Av, SE18 165 ET76
SE28 165 ET76
White Hart Cl, Ch.St.G. HP8 90 AU48
Sevenoaks TN13 257 FJ128
White Hart Ct, EC2 287 N7
Ripley GU23 228 BJ121
White Hart Dr, Hem.H. HP2 40 BM21
⇌ **White Hart Lane** 100 DT52
White Hart La, N17 100 DR52
N22 99 DN53
NW10 *off Church Rd* 139 CT65
SW13 158 CS83
Romford RM7 104 FA53
White Hart Meadow,
Beac. HP9 89 AL54
White Hart Meadows,
Ripley GU23 228 BJ121
White Hart Rd, SE18 165 ES77
Hemel Hempstead HP2 40 BN21
Orpington BR6 206 EU101
Slough SL1 151 AR76
Jct **White Hart Rbt**, Nthlt. UB5 136 BX68
White Hart Row, Cher. KT16
off Heriot Rd 194 BG101
White Hart Slip, Brom. BR1
off Market Sq 204 EG96

W

White Hart St, EC4 287 H8
SE11 298 F10
White Hart Wd, Sev. TN13 257 FJ129
White Hart Yd, SE1 299 L3
Gravesend DA11 *off High St* 191 GH86
Whitehaven, Slou. SL1 132 AT73
Whitehaven Cl, Brom. BR2 204 EG98
Goffs Oak EN7 66 DS28
Whitehaven St, NW8 284 C5
Whitehead Cl, N18 100 DR50
SW18 180 DC87
Dartford DA2 188 FJ90
Whitehead's Gro, SW3 296 D10
Whiteheart Av, Uxb. UB8 135 BQ71
Whiteheath Av, Ruis. HA4 115 BQ59
Sch Whiteheath Inf Sch,
Ruis. HA4 *off Ladygate La* 115 BP58
Sch Whiteheath Jun Sch,
Ruis. HA4 *off Whiteheath Av* 115 BP58
White Hedge Dr, St.Alb. AL3 42 CC19
White Heron Ms, Tedd. TW11 177 CF93
White Hill, Beac. HP9 110 AG55
Chesham HP5 54 AQ31
Chipstead CR5 234 DC124
Hemel Hempstead HP1 39 BF21
Northwood HA6 92 BN51
Rickmansworth WD3 92 BN51
South Croydon CR2
off St. Mary's Rd 220 DR109
Whitehill, Berk. HP4 38 AX18
Welwyn AL6 29 CU05
Whitehill Cl, Berk. HP4
off Whitehill 38 AX18
White Hill Cl, Cat. CR3 252 DS125
Chesham HP5 54 AQ30
White Hill Ct, Berk. HP4
off Whitehill 38 AX18
Sch Whitehill Infants' & Nurs Sch,
Grav. DA12 *off Sun La* 191 GJ90
Sch Whitehill Jun Sch,
Grav. DA12 *off Sun La* 191 GJ90
White Hill La, Bletch. RH1 252 DR127
Whitehill La, Grav. DA12 191 GK90
Ockham GU23 229 BQ123
Whitehill Par, Grav. DA12 191 GJ90
Whitehill Pl, Vir.W. GU25 192 AY99
White Hill Rd, Berk. HP4 38 AV21
Chesham HP5 56 AX26
Whitehill Rd, Dart. DA1 187 FG85
Gravesend DA12 191 GJ89
Longfield DA3 209 FX96
Southfleet DA13 209 FX96
Whitehills Rd, Loug. IG10 85 EN41
White Horse All, EC1 286 G6
White Horse Dr, Epsom KT18 216 CQ114
White Horse Hill, Chis. BR7 185 EN91
White Horse La, E1 289 J5
London Colney AL2 62 CL25
Ripley GU23 228 BJ121
Whitehorse La, SE25 202 DR98
Sch Whitehorse Manor - Brigstock Site Sch, TH.Hth. CR7 201 DP99
Sch Whitehorse Manor Inf & Jun Schs, Th.Hth. CR7
off Whitehorse Rd 202 DR98
White Horse Ms, SE1 298 F6
Enf. EN3 83 DX40
White Horse Rd, E1 289 L9
E6 293 K2
Windsor SL4 151 AK83
Whitehorse Rd, Croy. CR0 202 DR100
Thornton Heath CR7 202 DR100
White Horse St, W1 297 J3
White Horse Yd, EC2 287 L8
Whitehouse Apts, SE1
off Belvedere Rd 298 D3
Whitehouse Av, Borwd. WD6 78 CP41
White Ho Cl, Chal.St.P. SL9 90 AY52
Whitehouse Cl,
Woob.Grn HP10 88 AE54
White House Ct, Amer. HP6 55 AQ37
White Ho Dr, Guil. GU1 243 BB134
Stanmore HA7 95 CJ49
Sch Whitings Hill Prim Sch,
Whitehouse La, Bedmond WD5 59 BV26
Wooburn Green HP10 88 AE54
White Ho La, Enf. EN2
off Brigadier Hill 82 DQ39
Jacobs Well GU4 242 AX129
Sevenoaks TN14 256 FF130
White Ho Rd, Sev. TN14 256 FF130
Whitehouse Way, N14 99 DH47
Iver SL0 133 BD69
Slough SL3 152 AW76
Whitehurst Dr, N18 101 DX51
White Kennett St, E1 287 P8
White Knights Rd, Wey. KT13 213 BQ108
White Knobs Way, Cat. CR3 252 DU125
Whitelands Av, Chorl. WD3 73 BC42
Whitelands Cres, SW18 179 CY87
Whitelands Ho, SW3 296 E10
Whitelands Way, Rom. RM3 106 FK54
White La, Guil. GU4, GU5 259 BC136
Oxted RH8 238 EH123
Warlingham CR6 238 EH123
Whiteleaf Rd, Hem.H. HP3 40 BJ23
Whiteledges, W13 137 CJ72
Whitelegg Rd, E13 291 M1
Whiteley, Wind. SL4 151 AL80
Whiteley Rd, SE19 182 DR92
Whiteleys Shop Cen, W2 283 L9
Whiteleys Way, Han. TW13 176 CA90
WHITELEY VILLAGE,
Walt. KT12 213 BS110
White Lion Cl, Amer. HP7 72 AU39
White Lion Ct, EC3 287 N9
White Lion Gate, Cob. KT11 213 BU114
White Lion Hill, EC4 287 H10
White Lion Hos, Hat. AL10
off Robin Hood La 45 CU17
White Lion Rd, Amer. HP7 72 AT38
White Lion Sq, Hat. AL10
off Robin Hood La 45 CV17
White Lion St, N1 286 E1
Hemel Hempstead HP3 40 BK24
White Lion Wk, Guil. GU1
off High St 258 AX136
White Lo, SE19 181 DP94
White Lo Cl, N2 120 DD58
Isleworth TW7 157 CG82
Sevenoaks TN13 257 FH123
Sutton SM2 218 DC108
White Lo Gdns, Red. RH1 266 DG142
White Lyon Ct, EC2 287 J6
White Lyons Rd, Brwd. CM14 108 FW47
Whitemore Rd, Guil. GU1 242 AX130
White Oak Dr, Beck. BR3 203 EC96
White Oak Gdns, Sid. DA15 185 ET87
Sch White Oak Prim Sch,
Swan. BR8 *off Hilda May Av* 207 FE96
White Oaks, Bans. SM7 218 DB113
Whiteoaks La, Grnf. UB6 137 CD68
● White Oak Sq, Swan. BR8 207 FE97
White Orchards, N20 97 CZ45
Stanmore HA7 95 CG50
Whitepit La, H.Wyc. HP10 110 AE57
Jct White Post Cor,
Rain. RM13 148 FL68
White Post Fld, Saw. CM21 36 EX05
White Post Hill, Fnghm DA4 208 FN101
Whitepost Hill, Red. RH1 250 DE134
White Post La, E9 279 P6
SE13 163 EA83
White Post St, SE15 313 H4
White Rd, E15 281 K6
Betchworth RH3 248 CN133
Box Hill KT20 248 CN133
White Rose La, Wok. GU22 227 AZ117
Whites Av, Ilf. IG2 125 ES58
Whites Cl, Green. DA9 189 FW86
Whites Grds, SE1 299 P5
Whites Grds Est, SE1
off Whites Grds 299 P4
White Shack La, Chan.Cr. WD3 74 BM37
Whites La, Datchet SL3 152 AV79
Whites Meadow, Brom. BR1
off Blackbrook La 205 EN98
White's Row, E1 288 A7
White's Sq, SW4
off Nelson's Row 161 DK84
White Star Cl, Gdmg. GU7 258 AT144
Whitestile Rd, Brent. TW8 157 CJ78
Whitestone La, NW3 120 DC62
Whitestone Wk, NW3
off North End Way 120 DC62
Hemel Hempstead HP1
off Fennycroft Rd 40 BG17
Whitestone Way, Croy. CR0 201 DN104
White St, Sthl. UB1 156 BX75
White Stubbs Fm, Brox. EN10 48 DU21
White Stubbs La, Bayford SG13 47 DK21
Broxbourne EN10 47 DP21
White Swan Ms, W4
off Bennett St 158 CS79
Whitethorn, Welw.G.C. AL7 30 DB10
Whitethorn Av, Couls. CR5 234 DG115
West Drayton UB7 134 BL73
Whitethorn Gdns, Croy. CR0 202 DV103
Enfield EN2 82 DR43
Hornchurch RM11 128 FJ58
Whitethorn Pl, West Dr. UB7 134 BM74
Whitethorn St, E3 290 B5
White Twr Way, E1 289 L6
Whitewaits, Harl. CM20 35 ES14
White Way, Bkhm KT23 246 CB126
Whiteways Ct, Stai. TW18
off Pavilion Gdns 174 BH94
Whitewebbs La, Enf. EN2 82 DS35
Whitewebbs Pk, Enf. EN2 82 DQ35
Whitewebbs Rd, Enf. EN2 81 DP35
Whitewebbs Way, Orp. BR5 205 ET95
Whitewood Cotts, Tats. TN16 238 EJ120
Whitewood Rd, Berk. HP4 38 AU19
Whitfield Cl, Guil. GU2 242 AU131
Whitfield Cres, Dart. DA2 188 FQ87
Whitfield Pl, W1 285 L5
Whitfield Rd, E6 144 EJ66
Bexleyheath DA7 166 EZ80
Whitfield St, W1 285 N7
Whitfield Way, Mill End WD3 91 BF46
Whitford Gdns, Mitch. CR4 200 DF97
Whitgift Av, S.Croy. CR2 219 DP106
Whitgift Cen, Croy. CR0 202 DQ103
Whitgift Ho, SW11
off Randall Cl 308 C6
Sch Whitgift Sch, S.Croy. CR2
off Haling Pk Rd 220 DQ106
Whitgift St, SE11 298 C8
Croydon CR0 202 DQ104
Whit Hern Ct, Chsht EN8 66 DW30
Whiting Av, Bark. IG11 145 EP66
Whitings, Ilf. IG2 125 ER57
Barn. EN5 *off Whitings Rd* 79 CW43
Whitings Rd, Barn. EN5 79 CW43
Whitings Way, E6 293 L6
Whitland Rd, Cars. SM5 200 DD102
Whitlars Dr, Kings L. WD4 58 BM28
Whitley Cl, Abb.L. WD5 59 BU32
Stanwell TW19 174 BL86
Whitley Ho, SW1 309 M1
Whitley Rd, N17 100 DS54
Hoddesdon EN11 49 EB15
Whitlock Dr, SW19 179 CY87
Whitman Rd, E3 289 M4
Whitmead Cl, S.Croy. CR2 220 DS107
Whitmoor Common,
Worp. GU3 242 AV127
Whitmoor La, Guil. GU4 242 AX126
Whitmore Av, Harold Wd RM3 106 FL54
Whitmore Cl, N11 99 DH50
Whitmore Est, N1 277 P9
Whitmore Gdns, NW10 272 A10
Sch Whitmore High Sch,
Har. HA2 *off Porlock Av* 116 CC60
Sch Whitmore Prim Sch, N1 277 M9
Whitmore Rd, N1 277 N9
Beckenham BR3 203 DZ97
Harrow HA1 116 CC59
Whitmores Cl, Epsom KT18 232 CQ115
Whitmore's Wd, Hem.H. HP2 41 BP19
Whitmore Way, Horl. RH6 268 DE147
Whitnell Way, SW15 179 CX85
Whitney Av, Ilf. IG4 124 EK56
Whitney Ho, SE22
off Albrighton Rd 162 DS83
Whitney Rd, E10 123 EB59
Whitney Wk, Sid. DA14 186 EY93
Whitstable Cl, Beck. BR3 203 DZ95
Ruislip HA4 115 BS61
Whitstable Ho, W10 282 D9
Whitstable Pl, Croy. CR0 220 DQ105
Whitstone La, Beck. BR3 203 EB99
Whittaker Av, Rich. TW9
off Hill St 177 CK85
Whittaker Rd, E6 144 EJ66
Slough SL2 131 AK70
Sutton SM3 199 CZ104
Whittaker St, SW1 296 G9
Whittaker Way, SE1 300 D9
Whitta Rd, E12 124 EK63
Whittell Gdns, SE26 182 DW90
Whittenham Cl, Slou. SL2 132 AU74
Whittets Ait, Wey. KT13
off Jessamy Rd 194 BN103
Sch Whittingham Comm Prim Sch,
E17 *off Higham Hill Rd* 101 DY53
Whittingstall Rd, SW6 307 H7
Hoddesdon EN11 49 EB15
Whittington Av, EC3 287 N9
Hayes UB4 135 BT71
Whittington Ct, N2 120 DF57
H Whittington Hosp, N19 121 DJ61
Whittington Ms, N12 98 DC49
Whittington Rd, N22 99 DL52
Hutton CM13 109 GC44
Whittington Way, Pnr. HA5 116 BY57
Whittlebury Cl, Cars. SM5 218 DF108
Whittle Cl, E17 123 DY58
Leavesden WD25 59 BT34
Southall UB1 136 CB72
Whittle Parkway, Slou. SL1 131 AK72
Whittle Rd, Houns. TW5 156 BW80
Lon.Hthrw Air. TW6
off Western Perimeter Rd 154 BH83
Southall UB2 *off Post Rd* 156 CB75
Whittlesea Cl, Har. HA3 94 CC52
Whittlesea Path, Har. HA3 94 CC53
Whittlesea Rd, Har. HA3 94 CC53
Whittlesey St, SE1 298 E3
WHITTON, Twick. TW2 176 CB87
⇌ Whitton 176 CC87
Whitton Av E, Grnf. UB6 117 CE64
Whitton Av W, Grnf. UB6 116 CC64
Northolt UB5 116 CC64
Whitton Cl, Grnf. UB6 137 CH65
Whitton Dene, Houns. TW3 176 CB85
Isleworth TW7 177 CD85
Whitton Dr, Grnf. UB6 137 CG65
Whitton Manor Rd, Islw. TW7 176 CC85
Whitton Rd, Houns. TW3 156 CB84
Twickenham TW1, TW2 177 CF86
Jct Whitton Rd Rbt, Twick. TW1 177 CF86
Whitton Wk, E3 290 A2
Whitton Waye, Houns. TW3 176 CA86
Whitwell Rd, E13 291 N3
Watford WD25 76 BX35
Whitworth Cres, Enf. EN3 83 EA37
Whitworth Ho, SE1 299 K7
Whitworth Rd, SE18 165 EN80
SE25 202 DS97
Whitworth St, SE10 303 K10
Whopshott Av, Wok. GU21 226 AW116
Whopshott Cl, Wok. GU21 226 AW116
Whopshott Dr, Wok. GU21 226 AW116
Whorlton Rd, SE15 162 DV83
Whybridge Cl, Rain. RM13 147 FE67
Sch Whybridge Inf Sch,
Rain. RM13 *off Ford La* 147 FG67
Sch Whybridge Jun Sch,
Rain. RM13
off Blacksmiths La 147 FF67
Whybrow Gdns, Berk. HP4 38 AY17
Whychcote Pt, NW2
off Claremont Rd 119 CW59
Whymark Av, N22 121 DN55
Whytebeam Vw, Whyt. CR3 236 DT118
Whytecliffe Rd N, Pur. CR8 219 DP111
Whytecliffe Rd S, Pur. CR8 219 DN111
Whytecroft, Houns. TW5 156 BX80
WHYTELEAFE, Cat. CR3 236 DS118
⇌ Whyteleafe 236 DT117
● Whyteleafe Business Village,
Whyt. CR3 *off Whyteleafe Hill* 236 DT117
Whyteleafe Hill, Whyt. CR3 236 DT118
Whyteleafe Rd, Cat. CR3 236 DS120
Sch Whyteleafe Sch,
Whyt. CR3 *off Whyteleafe Hill* 236 DT118
⇌ Whyteleafe South 236 DU119
Whyte Ms, Sutt. SM3 217 CY108
Whyteville Rd, E7 144 EH65
Wichling Cl, Orp. BR5 206 EX102
Wick, The, Hert. SG14 31 DP06
Wickenden Rd, Sev. TN13 257 FJ122
Wicken's Meadow,
Dunt.Grn TN14 241 FF119
Wickersley Rd, SW11 309 H9
Wickers Oake, SE19 182 DT91
Wicker St, E1 288 E9
Wicket, The, Croy. CR0 221 EA106
Wicket Rd, Perivale UB6 137 CG69
Wickets, The, Ashf. TW15 174 BL91
Wickets End, Shenley WD7 62 CL33
Wickets Way, Ilf. IG6 103 ET51
Wickford Cl, Rom. RM3
off Wickford Dr 106 FM50
Wickford Dr, Rom. RM3 106 FM50
Wickford St, E1 288 G4
Wickford Way, E17 123 DX56
Wickham Av, Croy. CR0 203 DY103
Sutton SM3 217 CW106
Wickham Chase, W.Wick. BR4 203 ED101
Wickham Cl, E1 289 H7
Enfield EN3 82 DV41
Harefield UB9 92 BK53
Horley RH6 268 DF147
New Malden KT3 199 CT99
Sch Wickham Common Prim Sch,
W.Wick. BR4
off Gates Grn Rd 222 EG105
Wickham Ct, St.Alb. AL1 43 CH18
Wickham Ct Rd, W.Wick. BR4 203 EC103
Sch Wickham Ct Sch,
W.Wick. BR4 *off Layhams Rd* 222 EE105
Wickham Cres, W.Wick. BR4 203 EC103
Wickham Fld, Otford TN14 241 FF116
Wickham Gdns, SE4 163 DZ83
Wickham La, SE2 166 EU78
Egham TW20 173 BA94
Welling DA16 166 EU78
Wickham Ms, SE4 313 P9
Wickham Rd, E4 101 EC52
SE4 313 P9
Beckenham BR3 203 EB96
Croydon CR0 203 DX103
Grays RM16 171 GJ75
Harrow HA3 95 CD54
Wickham St, SE11 298 C10
Welling DA16 165 ES82
Wickhams Wf, Ware SG12
off Crane Mead 33 DY06
Wickham Way, Beck. BR3 203 EC98
Wicklands Rd, Hunsdon SG12 34 EK07
Wick La, E3 280 A10
Englefield Green TW20 172 AT92
Wickliffe Av, N3 97 CY54
Wickliffe Gdns, Wem. HA9 118 CP61
Wicklow St, WC1 286 C2
Wick Rd, E9 279 J5
Englefield Green TW20 172 AV94
Teddington TW11 177 CH94
Wicks Cl, SE9 184 EK91
Wicksteed Cl, Bex. DA5 187 FD90
Wicksteed Ho, SE1 299 K7
Brentford TW8
off Green Dragon La 158 CM78
Wick Way, St.Alb. AL1 43 CH17
Wickway Ct, SE15 312 A3
Wickwood St, SE5 311 H9
Widbury Barns, Ware SG12 33 EA07
Widbury Gdns, Ware SG12 33 DZ06
Widbury Hill, Ware SG12 33 DZ06
Wid Cl, Hutt. CM13 109 GD43
Widdecombe Av, Har. HA2 116 BY61
Widdenham Rd, N7 276 C1
Widdin St, E15 281 H7
Widecombe Cl, Rom. RM3 106 FK53
Widecombe Gdns, Ilf. IG4 124 EL56
Widecombe Rd, SE9 184 EL90
Widecombe Way, N2 120 DD57
Widecroft Rd, Iver SL0 133 BE72
Widegate St, E1 287 P7
Widenham Cl, Pnr. HA5 116 BW57
Widewater Pl, Hare. UB9 114 BH57
Wide Way, Mitch. CR4 201 DK97
Widewing Cl, Tedd. TW11 177 CH94
Widford Rd, Hunsdon SG12 34 EK05
Welwyn Garden City AL7 30 DB09
Widgeon Cl, E16 292 A8
Widgeon Rd, Erith DA8 167 FH80
Lon.Hthrw Air. TW6 154 BH82
Widgeon Way, Wat. WD25 76 BY36
Widley Rd, W9 283 K3
Widmoor, Woob.Grn HP10 110 AE60
WIDMORE, Brom. BR1 204 EH97
Widmore Dr, Hem.H. HP2 40 BN18
WIDMORE GREEN, Brom. BR1 204 EJ95
Widmore Lo Rd, Brom. BR1 204 EK96
Widmore Rd, Brom. BR1 204 EG96
Uxbridge UB8 135 BP70
Widvale Rd, Mtnsg CM15 109 GC41
Widworthy Hayes, Hutt. CM13 109 GB46
Wieland Rd, Nthwd. HA6 93 BU52
Wigan Ho, E5 122 DV60
Wigeon Path, SE28 165 ER76
Wigeon Way, Hayes UB4 136 BX72
Wiggenhall Rd, Wat. WD18 75 BV43
Wiggenhall Rd Goods Yd,
Wat. WD18 75 BV44
Wiggie La, Red. RH1 250 DG132
Wiggins La, Rich. TW10 177 CJ89
Wiggins Mead, NW9 97 CT52
Wigginton Av, Wem. HA9 138 CP65
Wightman Rd, N4 121 DN57
N8 121 DN56
Wighton Ms, Islw. TW7 157 CE82
Wigley Bush La, S.Wld CM14 108 FS47
Wigley Rd, Felt. TW13 176 BX88
Wigmore Ct, W13
off Singapore Rd 137 CG74
Wigmore Pl, W1 285 J8
Wigmore Rd, Cars. SM5 200 DD103
Wigmores N, Welw.G.C. AL8 29 CX08
Wigmores S, Welw.G.C. AL8 29 CX09
Wigmore St, W1 284 G9
Wigmore Wk, Cars. SM5 200 DD103
Wigram Rd, E11 124 EJ58
Wigram Sq, E17 101 EC54
Wigston Cl, N18 100 DS50
Wigston Rd, E13 292 A4
Wigton Gdns, Stan. HA7 96 CL53
Wigton Pl, SE11 310 F1
Wigton Rd, E17 101 DZ53
Romford RM3 106 FL49
Wigton Way, Rom. RM3 106 FL49
Wilberforce Ct, Edg. HA8 96 CM49
Keston BR2 222 EK107
Wilberforce Ms, SW4 161 DK84
Sch Wilberforce Prim Sch,
W10 282 F2
Wilberforce Rd, N4 121 DP61
NW9 119 CU58
Wilberforce Wk, E15 281 K3
Wilberforce Way, SW19 179 CX93
SE25 202 DT98
Gravesend DA12 191 GK92
Wilbraham Pl, SW1 296 F8
Wilbur Rd, Lon.Hthrw Air. TW6
off Wayfarer Rd 154 BH82
Wilbury Av, Sutt. SM2 217 CZ110
Sch Wilbury Prim Sch, N18
off Wilbury Way 100 DR50
Wilbury Rd, Wok. GU21 226 AX117
Wilbury Way, N18 100 DR50
Wilby Ms, W11 295 H2
Wilcon Way, Wat. WD25 60 BX34
Wilcot Av, Wat. WD19 94 BY45
Wilcot Cl, Wat. WD19
off Wilcot Av 94 BY45
Wilcox Cl, SW8 310 B4
Borehamwood WD6 78 CQ39
Wilcox Gdns, Shep. TW17 194 BM97
Wilcox Pl, SW1 297 M7
Wilcox Rd, SW8 310 A4
Sutton SM1 218 DB105
Teddington TW11 177 CD91
Wildacres, Nthwd. HA6 93 BT49
West Byfleet KT14 212 BJ111
Wildbank Ct, Wok. GU22
off White Rose La 227 AZ118
Wildberry Cl, W7 157 CG77
Wildcat Rd, Lon. Hthrw Air TW6
off Widgeon Rd 154 BH83
Wild Ct, WC2 286 C8
Wildcroft Dr, N.Holm. RH5 263 CK139
Wildcroft Gdns, Edg. HA8 95 CK51
Wildcroft Rd, SW15 179 CW87
Wilde Cl, E8 278 C8
Tilbury RM18
off Coleridge Rd 171 GJ82
Wilde Pl, N13 99 DP51
SW18 180 DD87
Wilder Cl, Ruis. HA4 115 BV60
Wilderness, The, Berk. HP4 38 AW19
East Molesey KT8 196 CC99
Hampton Hill TW12 176 CB91
off Park Rd
WILDERNESSE, Sev. TN15 257 FL122
Wildernesse Av, Sev. TN15 257 FL122
Wildernesse Mt, Sev. TN13 257 FK122
Wilderness Ms, SW4 161 DH84
Wilderness Rd, Chis. BR7 185 EP94
Guildford GU2 258 AT135
Oxted RH8 254 EE130
Wilde Rd, Erith DA8 167 FB80
Wilders Cl, Wok. GU21 226 AW118
Wilderton Rd, N16 122 DS59
Wildfell Rd, SE6 183 EB87
Wild Goose Dr, SE14 313 H7
Wild Grn N, Slou. SL3
off Verney Rd 153 BA77
Wild Grn S, Slou. SL3 153 BA77
Wild Hatch, NW11 120 DA58
WILDHILL, Hat. AL9 46 DD21
Wild Hill, Hat. AL9 46 DC21
Wildhill Rd, Hat. AL9 45 CY23
Wild Oaks Cl, Nthwd. HA6 93 BT51
Wild's Rents, SE1 299 N6
Wild St, WC2 286 B9
Wildwood, Nthwd. HA6 93 BR51
Wildwood Av, Brick.Wd AL2 60 BZ30
Wildwood Cl, SE12 184 EF87
East Horsley KT24 245 BT125
Woking GU22 227 BF115
Wildwood Ct, Ken. CR8 236 DR115
Wildwood Gro, NW3
off North End Way 120 DC60
Wildwood Ri, NW11 120 DC60
Wildwood Rd, NW11 120 DC59
Wildwood Ter, NW3 120 DC60
Wilford Cl, Enf. EN2 82 DR41
Northwood HA6 93 BR52
Wilford Rd, Slou. SL3 152 AY77
Wilfred Av, Rain. RM13 147 FG71
Wilfred Owen Cl, SW19 180 DC93
Wilfred St, SW1 297 L6
Gravesend DA12 191 GH86
Woking GU21 226 AX117
Wilfred Turney Est, W6
off Hammersmith Gro 159 CW75
Wilfrid Gdns, W3 138 CQ71
Wilhelmina Av, Couls. CR5 235 DJ119
Wilkes Rd, Brent. TW8 158 CL79
Hutton CM13 109 GD43
Wilkes St, E1 288 B6
Wilkins Cl, Hayes UB3 155 BT78
Mitcham CR4 200 DE95
Wilkins Grn La, Hat. AL10 44 CQ19
Smallford AL4 44 CP20
Wilkins Gro, Welw.G.C. AL8 29 CX10
Wilkins Ho, SW1
off Churchill Gdns 309 L2
Wilkinson Cl, Chsht EN7 66 DQ26
Dartford DA1 168 FM84
Uxbridge UB10 135 BP67
Wilkinson Gdns, SE25 202 DS95
Wilkinson Rd, E16 292 D8
Wilkinson St, SW8 310 C5
Wilkinson Way, W4 158 CR75
Hemel Hempstead HP3 40 BM24
WILKIN'S GREEN, Hat. AL10 44 CQ19
Wilkin St, NW5 275 J4
Wilkin St Ms, NW5 275 J4
Wilks Way, Brasted TN16 240 EV124
Wilks Av, Dart. DA1 188 FM89
Wilks Gdns, Croy. CR0 203 DY102
Wilks Pl, N1 287 P1
Willan Rd, N17 100 DR54
Willan Wall, E16 291 L10
Willard St, SW8 309 J10
Willats Cl, Cher. KT16 193 BF100
Willcocks Cl, Chess. KT9 198 CL104
Willcott Rd, W3 138 CP74
Will Crooks Gdns, SE9 164 EJ84
Willen Fld Rd, NW10 138 CQ68
Willenhall Av, New Barn. EN5 80 DC44
Willenhall Dr, Hayes UB3 135 BS73
Willenhall Rd, SE18 165 EP78
Willersley Av, Orp. BR6 205 ER104
Sidcup DA15 185 ET88
Willersley Cl, Sid. DA15 185 ET88
WILLESDEN, NW10 139 CT65
WILLESDEN GREEN, NW10 139 CV66
⊖ Willesden Green 272 B4
⇌ Willesden Junction 139 CT69
⊖ Willesden Junction 139 CT69
Willesden La, NW2 272 B5
NW6 272 F7
Willes Rd, NW5 275 K4
Willett Cl, Nthlt. UB5
off Broomcroft Av 136 BW69
Petts Wood BR5 205 ES100
Willett Ho, E13
off Queens Rd W 144 EG68
Willett Pl, Th.Hth. CR7
off Willett Rd 201 DN99
Willett Rd, Th.Hth. CR7 201 DN99
Willetts La, Denh. UB9 113 BF63
Willetts Ms, Hodd. EN11 49 EA16
Willett Way, Petts Wd BR5 205 ER99
Willey Broom La,
Chaldon CR3 251 DN125
Willey Fm La, Chaldon CR3 252 DQ126
Willey La, Chaldon CR3 252 DR125
William Ash Cl, Dag. RM9 146 EV65
William Atkinson Ho, N17
off Beaufoy Rd 100 DS52
William Barefoot Dr, SE9 185 EN91
Sch William Bellamy Inf Sch,
Dag. RM10 *off Frizlands La* 126 FA61
Sch William Bellamy Jun Sch,
Dag. RM10 *off Frizlands La* 126 FA61
William Bonney Est, SW4 161 DK84
Coll William Booth Coll, SE5 311 M9
William Booth Rd, SE20 202 DU95
Sch William Byrd Prim Sch,
Harling. UB3 *off Victoria La* 155 BR79
William Carey Way, Har. HA1 117 CE59
Sch William C. Harvey Sch,
N17 *off Adams Rd* 100 DR54
William Cl, N2 98 DD54
SE13 314 F9
SW6 306 F4
Romford RM5 105 FC53
Southall UB2 *off Windmill Av* 156 CC75
William Cory Prom, Erith DA8 167 FE78
William Ct, Hem.H. HP3
off King Edward St 40 BK24
William Covell Cl, Enf. EN2 81 DM38
Sch William Davies Prim Sch,
E7 *off Stafford Rd* 144 EK65
Sch William Davis Prim Sch, E2 288 C4
William Dr, Stan. HA7 95 CG51
William Dunbar Ho, NW6 282 G1
William Dyce Ms, SW16
off Babington Rd 181 DK91
William Ellis Cl, Old Wind. SL4 172 AU85
Sch William Ellis Sch, NW5
off Highgate Rd 120 DG62
William Ellis Way, SE16 300 D7
William Evans Rd,
Epsom KT19 216 CN111
William Evelyn Ct,
Wotton RH5 262 BZ139
Sch William Ford C of E Jun Sch,
Dag. RM10 *off Ford Rd* 146 FA66
William Foster La, Well. DA16 166 EU82
William IV St, WC2 298 A1
William Gdns, SW15 179 CV85
Smallfield RH6 269 DN148
William Gro, Slou. SL2 131 AR70

William Guy Gdns, E3 290 D3
William Harvey Ho, SW19 off Whitlock Dr 179 CY88
William Henry Wk, SW8 309 N3
Sch William Hogarth Sch, The, W4 off Duke Rd 158 CS78
William Hunter Way, Brwd. CM14 108 FW47
William Margrie Cl, SE15 312 D8
Sch William Martin C of E Inf & Nurs Sch, Harl. CM18 off Tawneys Rd 51 ES17
Sch William Martin C of E Jun Sch, Harl. CM18 off Tawneys Rd 51 ET17
William Ms, SW1 296 F5
William Morley Cl, E6 144 EK67
Coll William Morris 6th Form, W6 306 C1
William Morris Cl, E17 123 DZ55
★ William Morris Gall, E17 off Lloyd Pk 123 EA55
Sch William Morris Prim Sch, Mitch. CR4 off Recreation Way 201 DK97
Sch William Morris Sch, E17 off Folly La 101 DY53
William Morris Way, SW6 307 N10
William Moulder Ct, Chesh. HP5 54 AP28
William Nash Ct, Orp. BR5 off Brantwood Way 206 EW97
Sch William Patten Prim Sch, N16 off Stoke Newington Ch St 122 DT61
Sch William Penn Sch, The, Slou. SL2 off Penn Rd 131 AR70
William Perkin Ct, Grnf. UB6 off Greenford Rd 137 CE65
William Petty Way, Orp. BR5 206 EW102
William Pl, E3 279 N10
William Rainbird Ho, N17 off Beaufoy Rd 100 DT52
William Rd, NW1 285 L3
SW19 179 CY94
Caterham CR3 236 DR122
Guildford GU1 242 AW134
Sutton SM1 218 DC106
William Rushbrooke Ho, SE16 off Eveline Lowe Est 300 C8
William Russell Ct, Wok. GU21 226 AS118
Williams Av, E17 101 DZ53
William Saville Ho, NW6 283 H1
Williams Bldgs, E2 288 G4
Williams Cl, N8 off Coolhurst Rd 121 DK58
Addlestone KT15 off Monks Cres 212 BH106
Williams Dr, Houns. TW3 156 CA84
William Sellars Cl, Cat. CR3 236 DS121
Williams Gro, N22 99 DN53
Long Ditton KT6 197 CJ101
Williams La, SW14 158 CQ83
Mord. SM4 200 DC99
Williamson Cl, SE10 303 L10
Williamson Rd, N4 121 DP58
Watford WD24 75 BU36
Williamson St, N7 276 B1
Williamson Way, Rick. WD3 92 BG46
Williams Sq, SE16 301 M1
Williams Rd, W13 137 CG73
Oxted RH8 254 EG133
Southall UB2 156 BY77
Williams Ter, Croy. CR0 219 DN107
William St, E10 123 EB58
N17 100 DT52
SW1 296 F5
Barking IG11 145 EQ66
Berkhamsted HP4 38 AX19
Bushey WD23 76 BX41
Carshalton SM5 200 DE104
Gravesend DA12 191 GH87
Grays RM17 170 GB79
Slough SL1 132 AT74
Windsor SL4 151 AR81
Williams Wk, Guil. GU2 off Grange Rd 242 AV130
Williams Way, Dart. DA2 187 FD89
Radlett WD7 77 CJ35
William Swayne Pl, Guil. GU1 off Station App 258 AY135
Sch William Torbitt Prim Sch, Ilf. IG2 off Eastern Av 125 ET57
Sch William Tyndale Prim Sch, N1 277 H6
Willifield Way, NW11 119 CZ56
Willingale Cl, Hutt. CM13 off Fairview Av 109 GE44
Loughton IG10 off Willingale Rd 85 EQ40
Woodford Green IG8 102 EJ51
Willingale Rd, Loug. IG10 85 EQ41
Willingdon Rd, N22 99 DP54
Willinghall Cl, Wal.Abb. EN9 67 ED32
Willingham Cl, NW5 275 M3
Willingham Ter, NW5 275 M3
Willingham Way, Kings.T. KT1 198 CN97
Willington Ct, E5 off Mandeville St 123 DY62
Willington Rd, SW9 161 DL83
Sch Willington Sch, SW19 off Worcester Rd 179 CZ92
Willis Av, Sutt. SM2 218 DE107
Willis Cl, Epsom KT18 216 CP113
Willis Ho, E12 off Grantham Rd 125 EN62
Willis Rd, E15 281 L10
Croydon CR0 202 DQ101
Erith DA8 167 FC77
Willis St, E14 290 D9
Willmore End, SW19 200 DB95
Willoners, Slou. SL2 131 AN70
Willoughby Av, Croy. CR0 219 DM105
Willoughby Cl, Brox. EN10 49 DY21
Willoughby Ct, Lon.Col. AL2 61 CK26
Willoughby Dr, Rain. RM13 147 FE66
Willoughby Gro, N17 100 DV52
Willoughby Ho, EC2 off The Barbican 287 L7
Willoughby La, N17 100 DV52
Willoughby Ms, SW4 off Wixs La 161 DH84
Willoughby Pk Rd, N17 100 DV52
Willoughby Pas, E14 302 A2
Willoughby Rd, N8 121 DN55
NW3 274 A1
Kingston upon Thames KT2 198 CM95
Slough SL3 153 BA76
Twickenham TW1 177 CK86
Willoughbys, The, SW14 off Upper Richmond Rd W 158 CS83
Willoughby St, WC1 286 A7
Willoughby Way, SE7 304 A8
Willow Av, SW13 159 CT82
Denham UB9 114 BJ64
Sidcup DA15 186 EU86
Swanley BR8 207 FF97
West Drayton UB7 134 BM73
Willow Bk, SW6 306 F10
Richmond TW10 177 CH90
Woking GU22 226 AY122
Willowbank Gdns, Tad. KT20 233 CV122
Willowbank Pl, Pur. CR8 off Kingsdown Av 219 DP109
Willowbay Cl, Barn. EN5 79 CX44
Willow Brean, Horl. RH6 268 DE147
Willow Br Rd, N1 277 J5
Willowbrook, Eton SL4 151 AR77
Willowbrook Est, SE15 off Shurland Gdns 312 B4
Sch Willow Brook Prim Sch, E10 off Church Rd 123 EA60
Sch Willowbrook Prim Sch, Hutt. CM13 off Brookfield Cl 109 GD44
Willowbrook Rd, SE15 312 B3
Southall UB2 156 CA76
Staines-upon-Thames TW19 174 BL89
● Willow Cen, Mitch. CR4 200 DF99
Willow Chase, Chesh. HP5 54 AP30
Willow Cl, SE6 off Verdant La 184 EF88
Banstead SM7 217 CY114
Bexley DA5 186 EZ86
Brentford TW8 157 CJ79
Bromley BR2 205 EM99
Buckhurst Hill IG9 102 EK48
Chalfont St. Peter SL9 90 AY54
Chertsey KT16 193 BE103
Cheshunt EN7 66 DS26
Colnbrook SL3 153 BC80
Erith DA8 off Willow Rd 167 FG81
Flackwell Heath HP10 110 AC57
Hornchurch RM12 127 FH62
Hutton CM13 109 GB44
Orpington BR5 206 EV101
Thornton Heath CR7 201 DP100
Woodham KT15 211 BF111
Willow Cor, Bayford SG13 47 DM18
Willow Cotts, Mitch. CR4 201 DJ97
Richmond TW9 off Kew Grn 158 CN79
Willow Ct, EC2 287 N4
Edgware HA8 96 CL49
Hemel Hempstead HP3 40 BL24
Horley RH6 269 DH145
Sawbridgeworth CM21 36 EX06
Willowcourt Av, Har. HA3 117 CH57
Willow Cres, St.Alb. AL1 43 CJ20
Willow Cres E, Denh. UB9 114 BJ64
Willow Cres W, Denh. UB9 114 BJ64
Willowdene, N6 off View Rd 120 DF59
Cheshunt EN8 67 DY27
Willow Dene, Bushey Hth WD23 95 CE45
Pilgrim's Hatch CM15 108 FT43
Pinner HA5 94 BX54
Willowdene Cl, Twick. TW2 176 CC87
Willowdene Ct, Warley CM14 108 FW49
Sch Willow Dene Sch, SE18 off Swingate La 165 ES81
Willow Dr, Barn. EN5 79 CY42
Ripley GU23 228 BG124
Willow Edge, Kings L. WD4 58 BN29
Willow End, N20 98 DA47
Northwood HA6 93 BU51
Surbiton KT6 198 CL102
Willow Fm La, SW15 off Queens Ride 159 CV83
Willowfield, Harl. CM18 51 ER17
Sch Willowfield Sch, E17 off Clifton Av 123 DX55
Willowfields Cl, SE18 165 ES78
Willow Gdns, Houns. TW3 156 CA81
Ruislip HA4 115 BT61
Willow Glade, Reig. RH2 off Hornbeam Rd 266 DB137
Willow Grn, NW9 off Clayton Fld 96 CS53
Borehamwood WD6 78 CR43
North Holmwood RH5 263 CH140
Willow Gro, E13 281 N10
Chislehurst BR7 185 EN93
Ruislip HA4 115 BT61
Willowhayne Dr, Walt. KT12 195 BV101
Willowhayne Gdns, Wor.Pk. KT4 199 CW104
Willowherb Wk, Rom. RM3 off Clematis Cl 106 FJ52
Willow Ho, NW3 off Maitland Pk Vil 274 F4
Warlingham CR6 off East Parkside 237 EB115
Willow La, SE18 305 K8
Amersham HP7 72 AT41
Guildford GU1 off Boxgrove Rd 243 BA133
Mitcham CR4 200 DF99
Watford WD18 75 BU43
● Willow La Ind Est, Mitch. CR4 200 DF99
Willow Lo, Rom. RM7 off Cottons App 127 FD57
Willowmead, Chig. IG7 104 EU48
Hertford SG14 31 DN10
Staines-upon-Thames TW18 194 BH95
Willow Mead, Dor. RH4 263 CG135
Sawbridgeworth CM21 36 EY06
Willowmead Cl, W5 137 CK71
Woking GU21 226 AU116
Willowmere, Esher KT10 214 CC105
Willow Mt, Croy. CR0 off Langton Way 202 DS104
Willow Pk, Otford TN14 241 FF117
Stoke Poges SL2 132 AU66
Willow Path, Wal.Abb. EN9 68 EE34
Willow Pl, SW1 297 M8
Eton SL4 151 AQ78
Hastingwood CM17 52 EZ19
Willow Rd, NW3 120 DD63
W5 158 CL75
Colnbrook SL3 153 BE82
Dartford DA1 188 FJ88
Enfield EN1 82 DS41
Erith DA8 167 FG81
Godalming GU7 258 AT143
New Malden KT3 198 CQ98
Redhill RH1 266 DC137
Romford RM6 126 EY58
Wallington SM6 219 DH108
Willows, The, Amer. HP6 55 AP35
Buckhurst Hill IG9 102 EK48
Byfleet KT14 212 BL113
Claygate KT10 215 CE107
Grays RM17 170 GE79
Guildford GU4 off Collier Way 243 BD132
Mill End WD3 off Uxbridge Rd 92 BG47
St. Albans AL1 43 CH24
Watford WD19 off Brookside Rd 93 BV45
Weybridge KT13 194 BN104
Windsor SL4 151 AK80
Willows Av, Mord. SM4 200 DB99
Willows Cl, Pnr. HA5 94 BW54
Willowside, Lon.Col. AL2 62 CL27
Willows Path, Epsom KT18 216 CP114
Windsor SL4 150 AJ81
Willows Riverside Pk, Wind. SL4 150 AJ80
Sch Willows Sch, The, Hayes UB4 off Stipularis Dr 136 BX70
Willow St, E4 101 ED45
EC2 287 N4
Romford RM7 127 FC56
Willow Tree Cl, E3 279 M9
SW18 off Cargill Rd 180 DB88
Abridge RM4 86 EV41
Hayes UB4 136 BW70
Northolt UB5 136 BY65
Uxbridge UB10 115 BQ62
Willow Tree La, Hayes UB4 136 BW70
Willowtree Marina, Hayes UB4 136 BY72
Willow Tree Pl, Chal.St.P. SL9 90 AV54
Sch Willow Tree Prim Sch, Nthlt. UB5 off Arnold Rd 136 BY65
Jct Willow Tree Rbt, Hayes UB4 136 BX71
Willow Tree Wk, Brom. BR1 204 EH95
Willowtree Way, Th.Hth. CR7 off Kensington Av 201 DN95
Willow Vale, W12 139 CU74
Chislehurst BR7 185 EP93
Fetcham KT22 230 CB123
Willow Vw, SW19 200 DD95
Ware SG12 33 DY07
Willow Wk, E17 123 DZ57
N2 98 DD54
N15 121 DP56
N21 81 DM44
SE1 299 P8
Box Hill KT20 off Oak Dr 248 CQ130
Chertsey KT16 193 BG101
Dartford DA1 188 FJ85
Englefield Green TW20 172 AW92
Fetcham KT22 230 CC124
Orpington BR6 205 EP104
Redhill RH1 off Ash Dr 267 DH136
Shere GU5 260 BN139
Sutton SM3 199 CZ104
Upminster RM14 129 FS60
Willow Way, N3 98 DB52
SE26 182 DV90
W11 294 D1
Box Hill KT20 off Oak Dr 248 CP130
Epsom KT19 216 CR107
Godstone RH9 252 DV132
Guildford GU1 242 AV130
Hatfield AL10 45 CT21
Hemel Hempstead HP1 40 BH18
Potters Bar EN6 64 DB33
Radlett WD7 77 CE36
Romford RM3 106 FP51
St. Albans AL2 60 CA27
Sunbury-on-Thames TW16 195 BU98
Twickenham TW2 176 CB89
Wembley HA0 117 CG62
West Byfleet KT14 212 BJ111
Woking GU22 226 AX121
Willow Wd Cl, Burn. SL1 130 AH68
Willow Wd Cres, SE25 202 DS100
Willrose Cres, SE2 166 EW78
Wills Cres, Houns. TW3 176 CB86
Wills Gro, NW7 97 CU50
Willson Rd, Eng.Grn TW20 172 AV92
Wilman Gro, E8 278 D6
Wilmar Cl, Hayes UB4 135 BR70
Uxbridge UB8 134 BK66
Wilmar Gdns, W.Wick. BR4 203 EB102
Wilmcote Ho, W2 283 K6
Wilmer Cl, Kings.T. KT2 178 CM92
Wilmer Cres, Kings.T. KT2 178 CM92
Wilmer Gdns, N1 277 N9
Wilmerhatch La, Epsom KT18 232 CP118
Wilmer Ho, E3 279 M10
Wilmer Lea Cl, E15 280 G7
Wilmer Pl, N16 122 DT61
Wilmer Way, N14 99 DK50
WILMINGTON, Dart. DA2 188 FK91
Sch Wilmington Acad, Wilm. DA2 off Common La 187 FH90
Wilmington Av, W4 158 CR80
Orpington BR6 206 EW103
Wilmington Cl, Wat. WD17 75 BV41
Wilmington Ct Rd, Dart. DA2 187 FG90
Wilmington Gdns, Bark. IG11 145 ER65
Sch Wilmington Gram Sch for Boys, Wilm. DA2 off Common La 187 FH90
Sch Wilmington Prim Sch, Wilm. DA2 off Common La 187 FH90
Wilmington Sq, WC1 286 E3
Wilmington St, WC1 286 E3
Wilmot Cl, N2 98 DC54
SE15 312 C5
Wilmot Grn, Gt Warley CM13 107 FW51
Wilmot Pl, NW1 275 L6
W7 137 CE74
Wilmot Rd, E10 123 EB61
N17 122 DR55
Burnham SL1 130 AH69
Carshalton SM5 218 DF106
Dartford DA1 187 FG85
Purley CR8 219 DN112
Wilmots Cl, Reig. RH2 250 DC133
Wilmot St, E2 288 E4
Wilmot Way, Bans. SM7 218 DA114
Wilmount St, SE18 305 N9
Wilna Rd, SW18 180 DC87
Wilsham St, W11 294 D2
Wilshaw Cl, NW4 119 CU55
Wilshaw St, SE14 314 A6
Wilshere Av, St.Alb. AL1 42 CC23
Wilsman Rd, S.Ock. RM15 149 FW68
Wilsmere Dr, Har.Wld HA3 95 CE52
Northolt UB5 116 BY64
Wilson Av, Mitch. CR4 180 DE94
Wilson Cl, S.Croy. CR2 off Bartlett St 220 DR106
Wembley HA9 118 CM59
Wilson Dr, Ott. KT16 211 BB106
Wembley HA9 118 CM59
Wilson Gdns, Har. HA1 116 CC59
Wilson Gro, SE16 300 E5
Wilson Ho, SE7 off Springfield Gro 164 EJ79
Wilson La, Dart. DA4 209 FT96
Wilson Rd, E6 292 E2
SE5 311 N7
Chessington KT9 216 CM107
Ilford IG1 125 EM59
Wilsons, Tad. KT20 233 CX121
Wilsons Cor, Brwd. CM15 108 FX47
Wilsons Pl, E14 289 N9
Wilsons Rd, W6 294 D10
Sch Wilson's Sch, Wall. SM6 off Mollison Dr 219 DL107
Wilson St, E17 123 EC57
EC2 287 M6
N21 99 DN45
Wilson Way, Wok. GU21 226 AX116
Wilstone Cl, Hayes UB4 136 BY70
Wilstone Dr, St.Alb. AL4 43 CJ15
Wilthorne Gdns, Dag. RM10 off Acre Rd 147 FB66
Wilton Av, W4 158 CS78
Wilton Cl, Harm. UB7 154 BK79
Wilton Cres, SW1 296 G5
SW19 179 CZ95
Beaconsfield HP9 89 AL52
Hertford SG13 32 DQ12
Windsor SL4 151 AK84
Wilton Dr, Rom. RM5 105 FC52
Wilton Est, E8 278 D5
Wilton Gdns, Walt. KT12 196 BX102
West Molesey KT8 196 CA97
Wilton Gro, SW19 179 CZ94
New Malden KT3 199 CT100
Wilton Ho, SE22 off Albrighton Rd 162 DS83
Wilton La, Jordans HP9 89 AR52
Wilton Ms, SW1 297 H6
Wilton Par, Felt. TW13 off High St 175 BV88
Wilton Pk, Beac. HP9 89 AP53
Wilton Pk Ct, SE18 off Prince Imperial Rd 165 EN81
Wilton Pl, E4 101 EC51
SW1 296 G5
New Haw KT15 212 BK109
Wilton Rd, N10 98 DG54
SE2 166 EW76
SW1 297 K7
SW19 180 DE94
Beaconsfield HP9 89 AL51
Cockfosters EN4 80 DF42
Hounslow TW4 156 BX83
Ilford IG1 125 EP63
Redhill RH1 266 DF135
Wilton Row, SW1 296 G5
Wilton Sq, N1 277 L8
Wilton St, SW1 297 J6
Wilton Ter, SW1 296 G6
Wilton Vil, N1 277 L9
Wilton Way, E8 278 C5
Hertford SG13 32 DQ11
Wiltshire Av, Horn. RM11 128 FM56
Slough SL2 131 AQ70
Wiltshire Cl, NW7 97 CT50
SW3 296 E8
Dartford DA2 189 FR87
Wiltshire Gdns, N4 122 DQ58
Twickenham TW2 176 CC88
Wiltshire La, Pnr. HA5 115 BT55
Wiltshire Rd, SW9 161 DN83
Orpington BR6 206 EU101
Thornton Heath CR7 201 DN97
Wiltshire Row, N1 277 L9
Wilverley Cres, N.Mal. KT3 198 CS100
Wimbart Rd, SW2 181 DM87
WIMBLEDON, SW19 179 CY93
⇌ Wimbledon 179 CZ93
⊖ Wimbledon 179 CZ93
Tra Wimbledon 179 CZ93
★ Wimbledon (All England Tenn & Croquet Club), SW19 179 CY91
Wimbledon Br, SW19 179 CZ93
⇌ Wimbledon Chase 199 CY96
Sch Wimbledon Chase Prim Sch, SW19 off Merton Hall Rd 199 CY95
Sch Wimbledon Coll, SW19 off Edge Hill 179 CX94
★ Wimbledon Common, SW19 179 CT91
Sch Wimbledon Common Prep Sch, SW19 off Ridgway 179 CX94
Sch Wimbledon High Sch, SW19 off Mansel Rd 179 CZ93
Wimbledon Hill Rd, SW19 179 CY93
WIMBLEDON PARK, SW19 179 CZ90
⊖ Wimbledon Park 180 DA90
Wimbledon Pk, SW19 179 CZ89
Wimbledon Pk Est, SW19 179 CY88
Sch Wimbledon Pk Prim Sch, SW19 off Havana Rd 180 DB89
Wimbledon Pk Rd, SW18 179 CZ87
SW19 179 CZ88
Wimbledon Pk Side, SW19 179 CX89
Wimbledon Rd, SW17 180 DC91
Coll Wimbledon Sch of Art, SW19 off Merton Hall Rd 199 CY95
● Wimbledon Stadium Business Cen, SW17 180 DB90
★ Wimbledon Windmill Mus, SW19 179 CV89
Wimbolt St, E2 288 C2
Wimborne Av, Chis. BR7 205 ET98
Hayes UB4 135 BV72
Orpington BR5 205 ET98
Redhill RH1 266 DF139
Southall UB2 156 CA77
Wimborne Cl, SE12 184 EF85
Buckhurst Hill IG9 102 EH47
Epsom KT17 216 CS113
Sawbridgeworth CM21 36 EX05
Worcester Park KT4 199 CW102
Wimborne Dr, NW9 118 CN55
Pinner HA5 116 BX59
Wimborne Gdns, W13 137 CH72
Wimborne Gro, Wat. WD17 75 BS37
Wimborne Ho, SW8 310 D5
Wimborne Rd, N9 100 DU47
N17 100 DS54
Wimborne Way, Beck. BR3 203 DX97
Wimbourne Ct, N1 277 L10
Wimbourne St, N1 277 L10
Wimpole Cl, Brom. BR2 204 EJ98
Kingston upon Thames KT1 198 CM96
Wimpole Ms, W1 285 J6
Wimpole Rd, West Dr. UB7 134 BK74
Wimpole St, W1 285 J8
Wimshurst Cl, Croy. CR0 201 DL102
Winans Wk, SW9 310 E9
Wincanton Cres, Nthlt. UB5 116 CA64
Wincanton Gdns, Ilf. IG6 125 EP55
Wincanton Rd, SW18 179 CZ87
Romford RM3 106 FK48
Winchcombe Rd, Cars. SM5 200 DD101
Winchcomb Gdns, SE9 164 EK83
Winchdells, Hem.H. HP3 40 BN23
Winchelsea Av, Bexh. DA7 166 EZ80
Winchelsea Cl, SW15 179 CX85
Winchelsea Rd, E7 124 EG62
N17 122 DS55
NW10 138 CR67
Winchelsey Ri, S.Croy. CR2 220 DT107
Winchendon Rd, SW6 306 G5
Teddington TW11 177 CD91
Winchester Av, NW6 272 F8
NW9 118 CN55
Hounslow TW5 156 BZ79
Upminster RM14 129 FT60
Winchester Cl, E6 293 J9
SE17 299 H9
Amersham HP7 55 AS39
Bromley BR2 204 EF97
Colnbrook SL3 153 BE81
Enfield EN1 82 DS43
Esher KT10 214 CA105
Kingston upon Thames KT2 178 CP94
Waltham Abbey EN9 off Highbridge St 67 EB33
Winchester Ct, E17 off Billet Rd 101 DY53
Winchester Cres, Grav. DA12 191 GK90
Winchester Dr, Pnr. HA5 116 BX57
Winchester Gro, Sev. TN13 257 FH123
Winchester Ho, SE18 off Shooters Hill Rd 164 EK80
Winchester Ms, NW3 274 B6
Worcester Park KT4 199 CX103
Winchester Pk, Brom. BR2 204 EF97
Winchester Pl, E8 278 A3
N6 121 DH60
Winchester Rd, E4 101 EC52
N6 121 DH60
N9 100 DU46
NW3 274 B6
Bexleyheath DA7 166 EX82
Bromley BR2 204 EF97
Feltham TW13 176 BZ90
Harrow HA3 118 CL56
Hayes UB3 155 BS80
Ilford IG1 125 ER62
Northwood HA6 115 BT55
Orpington BR6 224 EW105
Twickenham TW1 177 CH86
Walton-on-Thames KT12 195 BU102
Winchester Sq, SE1 299 L2
Winchester St, SW1 297 K10
W3 138 CQ74
Winchester Wk, SE1 299 L2
Winchester Way, Crox.Grn WD3 75 BP43
Winchet Wk, Croy. CR0 202 DW100
Winchfield Cl, Har. HA3 117 CJ58
Winchfield Ho, SW15 off Highcliffe Dr 179 CT86
Winchfield Rd, SE26 183 DY92
Winchfield Way, Rick. WD3 92 BJ45
Winchilsea Cres, W.Mol. KT8 196 CC96
WINCHMORE HILL, N21 99 DM45
⇌ Winchmore Hill 99 DN46
Winchmore Hill Rd, N14 99 DK46
N21 99 DK46
Sch Winchmore Sch, N21 off Laburnum Gro 100 DQ47
Winchstone Cl, Shep. TW17 194 BM98
Winckley Cl, Har. HA3 118 CM57
Wincott St, SE11 298 F8
Wincrofts Dr, SE9 165 ER84
Windall Cl, SE19 202 DU95
Windborough Rd, Cars. SM5 218 DG108
Windermere Av, N3 120 DA55
NW6 272 F9
SW19 200 DB97
Harrow HA3 117 CJ59
Hornchurch RM12 127 FG64
Purfleet RM19 168 FQ78
Ruislip HA4 116 BW59
St. Albans AL1 43 CH22
Wembley HA9 117 CJ59
Windermere Cl, Chorl. WD3 73 BC43
Dartford DA1 187 FH88
Egham TW20 173 BB94
Feltham TW14 175 BT88
Hemel Hempstead HP3 41 BQ21
Orpington BR6 205 EP104
Staines-upon-Thames TW19 174 BK89
Windermere Ct, SW13 159 CT79
Kenley CR8 235 DP115
Wembley HA9 off Windermere Av 117 CJ59
Windermere Gdns, Ilf. IG4 124 EL57
Windermere Gro, Wem. HA9 off Windermere Av 117 CJ60
Windermere Ho, Islw. TW7 off Summerwood Rd 177 CF85
Windermere Pt, SE15 312 G4
Sch Windermere Prim Sch, St.Alb. AL1 off Windermere Av 43 CH22
Windermere Rd, N10 99 DH53
N19 121 DJ61
SW15 178 CS91
SW16 201 DJ95
W5 157 CJ76
Bexleyheath DA7 167 FC82
Coulsdon CR5 235 DL115
Croydon CR0 202 DT102
Southall UB1 136 BZ71
West Wickham BR4 204 EE103
Windermere Way, Reig. RH2 250 DD133
Slough SL1 130 AJ71
West Drayton UB7 134 BL74
Winders Rd, SW11 308 C8
Windfield, Lthd. KT22 231 CH121
Windfield Cl, SE26 183 DX91
Windgates, Guil. GU4 off Tychbourne Dr 243 BC131
Windham Av, New Adgtn CR0 221 ED110
Windham Rd, Rich. TW9 158 CM83
Wind Hill, Magd.Lav. CM5 53 FF20
Windhill, Welw.G.C. AL7 30 DA08
Windhover Way, Grav. DA12 191 GL91
Windings, The, S.Croy. CR2 220 DT111
Winding Shot, Hem.H. HP1 40 BG19
Winding Way, Dag. RM8 126 EW62
Harrow HA1 117 CE63

Windlass Pl, SE8 301 M9
Windlebrook Pk, Lyne KT16 193 AZ103
Windlesham Gro, SW19 179 CX88
Windley Cl, SE23 182 DW89
Windmill All, W4
off Windmill Rd 158 CS77
Windmill Av, Epsom KT17 217 CT111
St. Albans AL4 43 CJ16
Southall UB2 156 CC75
Windmill Br Ho, Croy. CR0 202 DR102
● **Windmill Business Village**, Sun.TW16
off Brooklands Cl 195 BS95
Windmill Centre, Sthl. UB2 136 CC74
Windmill Cl, SE1 300 D8
SE13 314 F8
Caterham CR3 236 DQ121
Epsom KT17 217 CT112
Horley RH6 269 DH148
Long Ditton KT6 197 CH102
Sunbury-on-Thames TW16 175 BS94
Upminster RM14 128 FN61
Waltham Abbey EN9 68 EE34
Windsor SL4 151 AP82
Windmill Ct, NW2 272 F4
Ruis. HA4 *off West Way* 115 BT60
Windmill Dr, NW2 119 CY62
SW4 181 DH85
Croxley Green WD3 74 BM44
Keston BR2 222 EJ105
Leatherhead KT22 231 CJ123
Reigate RH2 250 DD132
Windmill End, Epsom KT17 217 CT112
Windmill Fld, Ware SG12 33 DX07
Windmill Flds, Harl. CM17 36 EZ11
Windmill Gdns, Enf. EN2 81 DN41
Windmill Grn, Shep. TW17 195 BS101
Windmill Gro, Croy. CR0 202 DQ101
WINDMILL HILL, Grav. DA11 191 GG88
Windmill Hill, NW3 120 DC62
Chipperfield WD4 57 BF32
Coleshill HP7 89 AM45
Enfield EN2 81 DP41
Ruislip HA4 115 BT59
Windmill Ho, E14 302 A8
Windmill La, E15 281 H4
Barnet EN5 79 CT44
Bushey Heath WD23 95 CE46
Cheshunt EN8 67 DX30
Epsom KT17 217 CT112
Greenford UB6 136 CC71
Isleworth TW7 157 CE77
Long Ditton KT6 197 CH100
Southall UB2 156 CC76
Windmill Ms, W4 158 CS77
Windmill Pas, W4 158 CS77
Windmill Ri, Kings.T. KT2 178 CP94
Windmill Rd, N18 100 DR49
SW18 180 DD86
SW19 179 CV88
W4 158 CS77
W5 157 CJ77
Brentford TW8 157 CK78
Chalfont St. Peter SL9 90 AX52
Croydon CR0 202 DQ101
Fulmer SL3 112 AX64
Hampton Hill TW12 176 CB92
Hemel Hempstead HP2 40 BL21
Mitcham CR4 201 DJ99
Sevenoaks TN13 257 FH130
Slough SL1 131 AR74
Sunbury-on-Thames TW16 195 BS95
Windmill Rd W, Sun. TW16 195 BS96
Windmill Row, SE11 310 E1
Windmill Shott, Egh. TW20
off Rusham Rd 173 AZ93
Windmill St, W1 285 N7
Bushey Heath WD23 95 CE46
Gravesend DA12 191 GH86
Windmill Wk, SE1 298 F3
Windmill Way, Reig. RH2 250 DD132
Ruislip HA4 115 BT60
Windmill Wd, Amer. HP6 55 AN37
Windmore Av, Pot.B. EN6 63 CW31
Windmore Cl, Wem. HA0 117 CG64
Windover Av, NW9 118 CR56
Windridge Cl, St.Alb. AL3 42 CA22
Windrose Cl, SE16 301 J4
Windrush, N.Mal. KT3 198 CP98
Windrush Av, Slou. SL3 153 BB76
Windrush Cl, N17 100 DS53
SW11 *off Maysoule Rd* 160 DD84
W4 158 CQ81
Uxbridge UB10 114 BM63
Windrushes, Cat. CR3 252 DU125
Windrush La, SE23 183 DX90
Sch **Windrush Prim Sch**, SE28
off Bentham Rd 146 EV74
Windrush Rd, NW10 138 CR67
Sch **Windrush Sch - Charlton**, SE7 304 F8
Windrush Sq, SW2
off Rushcroft Rd 161 DN84
Winds End Cl, Hem.H. HP2 40 BN18
Windsock Cl, SE16 301 N8
Windsock Way, Lon.Hthrw Air. TW6 *off Western Perimeter Rd* 154 BH82
WINDSOR, SL4 152 AS82
⇌ **Windsor & Eton Central** 151 AR81
Windsor & Eton Relief Rd, Wind. SL4 151 AP80
⇌ **Windsor & Eton Riverside** 151 AR80
Windsor Av, E17 101 DY54
SW19 200 DC95
Edgware HA8 96 CP49
Grays RM16 170 GB75
New Malden KT3 198 CQ99
Sutton SM3 199 CY104
Uxbridge UB10 135 BP67
West Molesey KT8 196 CA97
Sch **Windsor Boys' Sch, The**, Wind. SL4
off Maidenhead Rd 151 AP81
★ **Windsor Castle**, Wind. SL4 152 AS80
● **Windsor Cen, The**, SE27 182 DQ91
Windsor Cl, N3 97 CY54
SE27 182 DQ91
Borehamwood WD6 78 CN39
Bovingdon HP3 57 BA28
Brentford TW8 157 CH79
Cheshunt EN7 66 DU30
Chislehurst BR7 185 EP92
Guildford GU2 258 AT136
Harrow HA2 116 CA62
Hemel Hempstead HP2 40 BL22
Lon.Hthrw Air. TW6
off Western Perimeter Rd 154 BH83
Northwood HA6 93 BU54
Windsor Ct, N14 99 DJ45
Borehamwood. WD6
off Rutherford Cl 78 CQ40
Pnr. HA5 *off Westbury Lo Cl* 116 BX55
Sunbury-on-Thames TW16 175 BU94
Windsor Ct Rd, Chobham GU24 210 AS109
Windsor Cres, Har. HA2 116 CA63
Loudwater HP10 88 AC53
Wembley HA9 118 CP62
Windsor Dr, Ashf. TW15 174 BK91
Barnet EN4 80 DF44
Dartford DA1 187 FG86
Hertford SG14 31 DM09
Orpington BR6 224 EU107
Windsor End, Beac. HP9 111 AM55
Windsor Gdns, W9 283 J6
Croydon CR0
off Richmond Rd 201 DL104
Hayes UB3 155 BR76
Sch **Windsor Girls' Sch**, Wind. SL4 *off Imperial Rd* 151 AN83
★ **Windsor Great Pk**, Ascot SL5, Egh. TW20 & Wind. SL4 172 AS93
Windsor Gt Pk, Ascot SL5 172 AS93
Egham TW20 172 AS93
Windsor Gro, SE27 182 DQ91
Windsor Hill, Woob.Grn HP10 110 AF58
Windsor Ho, N1 277 J10
Bushey WD23
off Royal Connaught Dr 76 BZ42
Windsor La, Burn. SL1 130 AJ70
Wooburn Green HP10 110 AE58
Windsor Ms, SE6 183 EC88
SE23 183 DY88
Windsor Pk Rd, Hayes UB3 155 BT80
Windsor Pl, SW1 297 M7
Chertsey KT16 *off Windsor St* 194 BG100
Harlow CM20 36 EU11
★ **Windsor Racecourse (Royal)**, Wind. SL4 151 AM79
Windsor Rd, E4
off Chivers Rd 101 EB49
E7 124 EH64
E10 123 EB61
E11 124 EG60
N3 97 CY54
N7 121 DL62
N13 99 DN48
N17 100 DU54
NW2 139 CV65
W5 138 CL73
Barnet EN5 79 CX44
Beaconsfield HP9 111 AN57
Bexleyheath DA6 166 EY84
Chesham HP5 54 AP28
Chobham GU24 210 AS109
Dagenham RM8 126 EY62
Datchet SL3 152 AT80
Enfield EN3 83 DX36
Englefield Green TW20 173 AZ90
Eton SL4 151 AR79
Gerrards Cross SL9 112 AW60
Gravesend DA12 191 GH90
Harrow HA3 95 CD53
Hornchurch RM11 128 FJ59
Hounslow TW4 155 BV82
Ilford IG1 125 EP63
Kingston upon Thames KT2 178 CL94
Old Windsor SL4 172 AX88
Pilgrim's Hatch CM15 108 FV44
Richmond TW9 158 CM82
Slough SL1 152 AS76
Southall UB2 156 BZ76
Stoke Poges SL2 112 AU63
Sunbury-on-Thames TW16 175 BU93
Teddington TW11 177 CD92
Thornton Heath CR7 201 DP96
Water Oakley SL4 150 AF79
Watford WD24 76 BW38
Worcester Park KT4 199 CU103
Wraysbury TW19 172 AY86
Windsors, The, Buck.H. IG9 102 EL47
Windsor St, N1 277 H8
Chertsey KT16 194 BG100
Uxbridge UB8 134 BJ66
Windsor Ter, N1 287 K2
Windsor Wk, SE5 311 M9
Walton-on-Thames KT12
off King George Av 196 BX102
Weybridge KT13 213 BP106
Windsor Way, W14 294 D8
Rickmansworth WD3 92 BG46
Woking GU22 227 BC116
Windsor Wf, E9 279 P3
Windsor Wd, Wal.Abb. EN9
off Monkswood Av 68 EE33
Windspoint Dr, SE15 312 E3
Winds Ridge, Send GU23 243 BC125
Windus Rd, N16 122 DT60
Windus Wk, N16 122 DT60
Windward Cl, Enf. EN3
off Bullsmoor La 83 DX35
Windycroft Cl, Pur. CR8 219 DK113
Windy Hill, Hutt. CM13 109 GC46
Windy Ridge, Brom. BR1 204 EL95
Windy Ridge Cl, SW19 179 CX92
Wine Cl, E1 300 G1
Wine Office Ct, EC4 286 F8
Winern Glebe, Byfleet KT14 212 BK113
Winery La, Kings.T. KT1 198 CM97
Winey Cl, Chess. KT9
off Nigel Fisher Way 215 CJ108
Winfield Mobile Home Pk, Wat. WD25 76 CB39
Winford Dr, Brox. EN10 49 DZ22
Winford Ho, E3 279 P7
Winford Par, Sthl. UB1
off Telford Rd 136 CB72
Winforton St, SE10 314 E6
Winfrith Rd, SW18 180 DC87
Wingate Cres, Croy. CR0 201 DK100
Wingate Rd, W6 159 CV76
Ilford IG1 125 EP64
Sidcup DA14 186 EW92
Wingate Sq, SW4
off Old Town 161 DJ84
Wingate Way, St.Alb. AL1 43 CG21
Wing Cl, N.Wld Bas. CM16 70 FA27
Wingfield, Bad.Dene RM17 170 FZ78
Wingfield Bk, Nthflt DA11 190 GC89
Wingfield Cl, Brwd. CM13
off Pondfield La 109 GA48
New Haw KT15 212 BH110
Wingfield Ct, E14
off Newport Av 302 G1
Banstead SM7 234 DA115
Wingfield Gdns, Upmin. RM14 129 FT58
Wingfield Ho, NW6
off Tollgate Gdns 273 L10
Wingfield Ms, SE15 312 C10
Sch **Wingfield Prim Sch**, SE3
off Moorehead Way 164 EH83
Wingfield Rd, E15 281 J1
E17 123 EB57
Gravesend DA12 191 GH87
Kingston upon Thames KT2 178 CN93
Wingfield St, SE15 312 C10
Wingfield Way, Ruis. HA4 135 BV65
Wingford Rd, SW2 181 DL86
Wingletye La, Horn. RM11 128 FM60
Wingmore Rd, SE24 162 DQ83
Wingrave Cres, Brwd. CM14 108 FS49
Wingrave Rd, W6 306 B3
Wingrove Dr, Purf. RM19 168 FP78
Wingrove Rd, SE6 184 EE89
Wings Cl, Sutt. SM1 218 DA105
Wings Rd, Lon.Hthrw Air. TW6
off Wayfarer Rd 154 BH83
Wing Way, Brwd. CM14
off Geary Dr 108 FW46
Winifred Av, Horn. RM12 128 FK63
Winifred Cl, Barn. EN5 79 CT44
Winifred Gro, SW11 160 DF84
Winifred Pl, N12
off High Rd 98 DC50
Winifred Rd, SW19 200 DA95
Coulsdon CR5 234 DG116
Dagenham RM8 126 EY61
Dartford DA1 187 FH85
Erith DA8 167 FE78
Hampton Hill TW12 176 CA91
Hemel Hempstead HP3 40 BK24
Winifred St, E16 305 K3
Winifred Ter, E13 291 N1
Enfield EN1 100 DT45
Winkers Cl, Chal.St.P. SL9 91 AZ53
Winkers La, Chal.St.P. SL9 91 AZ53
Winkfield Rd, E13 292 A1
N22 99 DN53
Winkley St, E2 288 E1
Winkwell, Hem.H. HP2 39 BD22
Winkworth Pl, Bans. SM7
off Bolters La 217 CZ114
Winkworth Rd, Bans. SM7 217 CZ114
Winlaton Rd, Brom. BR1 183 ED91
Winmill Rd, Dag. RM8 126 EZ62
Winnards, Wok. GU21
off Abercorn Way 226 AV118
Winn Common Rd, SE18 165 ES79
Winnett St, W1 285 N10
Winningales Ct, Ilf. IG5
off Vienna Cl 124 EL55
Winnings Wk, Nthlt. UB5
off Arnold Rd 136 BY65
Winnington Cl, N2 120 DD58
Winnington Rd, N2 120 DD59
Enfield EN3 82 DW38
Winnington Way, Wok. GU21 226 AV118
Winnipeg Dr, Grn St Grn BR6 223 ET107
Winnipeg Way, Brox. EN10 67 DY25
Winnock Rd, West Dr. UB7 134 BK74
Winn Rd, SE12 184 EG88
Winns Av, E17 123 DY55
Winns Ms, N15 122 DS56
Sch **Winns Prim Sch**, E17
off Fleeming Rd 101 DZ54
Winns Ter, E17 101 EA54
Winsbeach, E17 123 ED55
Winscombe Cres, W5 137 CK70
Winscombe St, N19 121 DH61
Winscombe Way, Stan. HA7 95 CG50
Winsford Rd, SE6 183 DZ90
Winsford Ter, N18 100 DR50
Winsham Gro, SW11 180 DG85
Winslade Rd, SW2 181 DL85
Winsland Ms, W2 284 A8
Winsland St, W2 284 A8
Winsley St, W1 285 L8
Winslow, SE17 311 N1
Winslow Cl, NW10
off Neasden La N 118 CS62
Pinner HA5 115 BV58
Winslow Gro, E4 102 EE47
Winslow Rd, W6 306 B2
Winslow Way, Felt. TW13 176 BX90
Walton-on-Thames KT12 196 BW104
Sch **Winsor Prim Sch**, E6 293 L9
Winsor Ter, E6 293 L7
Winstanley Cl, Cob. KT11 213 BV114
Winstanley Est, SW11 308 B10
Winstanley Rd, SW11 160 DD83
Winstanley Wk, Cob. KT11
off Winstanley Cl 213 BV114
Winstead Gdns, Dag. RM10 127 FC64
Winston Av, NW9 118 CS59
Sch **Winston Churchill Sch, The**, St.John's GU21
off Hermitage Rd 226 AT118
Winston Churchill Way, Chsht EN8 66 DW33
Winston Cl, Green. DA9 189 FT86
Harrow HA3 95 CF51
Romford RM7 127 FB56
Winston Ct, Har. HA3 94 CB52
Winston Dr, Bigg.H. TN16
off Polesteeple Hill 238 EK117
Stoke D'Abernon KT11 230 BY116
Winstone Cl, Amer. HP6 54 AP34
Winston Gdns, Berk. HP4 38 AT19
Winston Rd, N16 277 M2
Winston Wk, W4
off Beaconsfield Rd 158 CR76
Winston Way, Ilf. IG1 125 EP62
Old Woking GU22 227 BB120
Potters Bar EN6 64 DA34
Sch **Winston Way Prim Sch**, Ilf. IG1 *off Winston Way* 125 EQ61
Winstre Rd, Borwd. WD6 78 CN39
Winter Av, E6 144 EL67
Winterborne Av, Orp. BR6 205 ER104
Winterbourne Gro, Wey. KT13 213 BQ107
Sch **Winterbourne Inf & Nurs Sch**, Th.Hth. CR7
off Winterbourne Rd 201 DN98
Sch **Winterbourne Jun Boys' Sch**, Th.Hth. CR7
off Winterbourne Rd 201 DN98
Sch **Winterbourne Jun Girls' Sch**, Th.Hth. CR7
off Winterbourne Rd 201 DN98
Winterbourne Ms, Oxt. RH8
off Brook Hill 253 EC130
Winterbourne Rd, SE6 183 DZ88
Dagenham RM8 126 EW61
Thornton Heath CR7 201 DN98
Winter Box Wk, Rich. TW10 158 CM84
Winterbrook Rd, SE24 182 DQ86
Winterburn Cl, N11 98 DG51
Winter Cl, Epsom KT17 216 CS112
Winterdown Gdns, Esher KT10 214 BZ107
Winterdown Rd, Esher KT10 214 BZ107
Winterfold Cl, SW19 179 CY89
Wintergarden, Bluewater DA9
off Bluewater Parkway 189 FU87
Winter Gdn Cres, Bluewater DA9 189 FU87
Winter Gdn Ho, WC2
off Macklin St 286 B8
Wintergreen Cl, E6 292 G7
Winterhill Way, Guil. GU4 243 BB130
Winters Cft, Grav. DA12 191 GK93
Winterscroft Rd, Hodd. EN11 49 DZ16
Wintersells Rd, Byfleet KT14 212 BK110
Winterslow Rd, SW9 310 G6
Winters Rd, T.Ditt. KT7 197 CH101
Winterstoke Gdns, NW7 97 CU50
Winterstoke Rd, SE6 183 DZ88
Winters Way, Wal.Abb. EN9 68 EG33
Winterton Ho, E1 288 F9
Winterton Pl, SW10 307 P2
Winterwell Rd, SW2 181 DL85
Winthorpe Gdns, Borwd. WD6 78 CM39
Winthorpe Rd, SW15 159 CY84
Winthrop St, E1 288 E6
Winthrop Wk, Wem. HA9
off Everard Way 118 CL62
Winton App, Crox.Grn WD3 75 BQ43
Winton Av, N11 99 DJ52
Winton Cl, N9 101 DX45
Winton Cres, Crox.Grn WD3 75 BP43
Winton Dr, Chsht EN8 67 DY29
Croxley Green WD3 75 BP44
Winton Gdns, Edg. HA8 96 CM52
Sch **Winton Prim Sch**, N1 286 C1
Winton Rd, Orp. BR6 223 EP105
Ware SG12 33 DZ06
Winton Way, SW16 181 DN92
Wintoun Path, Slou. SL2 131 AL70
Winvale, Slou. SL1 152 AS76
Winwood, Slou. SL2 132 AW72
Wireless Rd, Bigg.H. TN16 238 EK115
Wirrall Ho, SE26
off Sydenham Hill Est 182 DU90
Wirral Wd Cl, Chis. BR7 185 EN93
Wirra Way, Lon.Hthrw Air. TW6
off Wayfarer Rd 154 BH82
Wisbeach Rd, Croy. CR0 202 DR99
Wisborough Rd, S.Croy. CR2 220 DT109
Wisdom Dr, Hert. SG13 32 DS09
Wisdons Cl, Dag. RM10 127 FB60
Wise La, NW7 97 CV51
West Drayton UB7 154 BK77
Wiseman Ct, SE19 182 DS92
Wiseman Rd, E10 123 EA61
Wisemans Gdns, Saw. CM21 36 EW06
Wise Rd, E15 280 F9
Wise's La, Hat. AL9 63 CW27
Wiseton Rd, SW17 180 DE88
Wishart Rd, SE3 164 EK81
Wishaw Wk, N13
off Elvendon Rd 99 DL51
Wishbone Way, Wok. GU21 226 AT116
Wishford Ct, Ashtd. KT21
off The Marld 232 CM118
Sch **Wishmore Cross Sch**, Chobham GU24 *off Alpha Rd* 210 AT110
WISLEY, Wok. GU23 228 BL116
Wisley Common, Wok. GU23 228 BN117
Wisley Ct, S.Croy. CR2
off Sanderstead Rd 220 DR110
Jct **Wisley Interchange**, Cob. KT11 229 BQ116
Wisley La, Wisley GU23 228 BL116
Wisley Rd, SW11 180 DG85
Orpington BR5 186 EU94
Wissants, Harl. CM19 51 EP19
Wistaria Cl, Orp. BR6 205 EP103
Pilgrim's Hatch CM15 108 FW43
Wistaria Dr, Lon.Col. AL2 61 CH26
Wisteria Apts, E9
off Chatham Pl 278 G4
Wisteria Cl, NW7 97 CT51
Ilford IG1 125 EP64
Wisteria Gdns, Swan. BR8 207 FD96
Wisteria Rd, SE13 163 ED84
Wistlea Cres, Coln.Hth AL4 44 CP22
Witanhurst La, N6 120 DG60
Witan St, E2 288 F3
Witches La, Sev. TN13 256 FD122
Witchford, Welw.G.C. AL7 30 DD09
Witcombe Pt, SE15 312 E7
Witham Cl, Loug. IG10 84 EL44
Witham Rd, SE20 202 DW97
W13 137 CG74
Dagenham RM10 126 FA64
Isleworth TW7 157 CD81
Romford RM7 127 FH57
Withens Cl, Orp. BR5 206 EW98
Witherby Cl, Croy. CR0 220 DS106
Wither Dale, Horl. RH6 268 DE147
Witheridge La, Knot.Grn HP9 88 AF48
Penn HP10 88 AF48
Witherings, The, Horn. RM11 128 FL57
Witherington Rd, N5 276 F3
Withers Cl, Chess. KT9
off Coppard Gdns 215 CJ107
Withers Mead, NW9 97 CT53
Witherston Way, SE9 185 EN89
Withey Brook, Hkwd RH6 268 DD150
Withey Cl, Wind. SL4 151 AL81
Witheygate Av, Stai. TW18 174 BH93
Withey Meadows, Hkwd RH6 268 DD150
Withies, The, Knap. GU21 226 AS117
Leatherhead KT22 231 CH120
Withybed Cor, Walt.Hill KT20 233 CV123
Withycombe Rd, SW19 179 CX87
Withycroft, Geo.Grn SL3 132 AY72
Withy La, Ruis. HA4 115 BQ57
Withy Mead, E4 101 ED48
Withy Pl, Park St AL2 60 CC28
Witley Cres, New Adgtn CR0 221 EC107
Witley Gdns, Sthl. UB2 156 BZ77
● **Witley Ind Est**, Sthl. UB2
off Witley Gdns 156 BZ77
Witley Pt, SW15
off Wanborough Dr 179 CV88
Witley Rd, N19 121 DJ61
Witney Cl, Pnr. HA5 94 BZ51
Uxbridge UB10 114 BM63
Witney Path, SE23 183 DX90
Wittenham Way, E4 101 ED48
Wittering Cl, Kings.T. KT2 177 CK92
Wittering Wk, Horn. RM12 148 FJ65
Wittersham Rd, Brom. BR1 184 EF92
Wivenhoe Cl, SE15 312 E10
Wivenhoe Ct, Houns. TW3 156 BZ84
Wivenhoe Rd, Bark. IG11 146 EU68
Wiverton Rd, SE26 182 DW93
Wix Hill, W.Hors. KT24 245 BP130
Wix Hill Cl, W.Hors. KT24 245 BP131
Sch **Wix Prim Sch**, SW4
off Wixs La 161 DH83
Wix Rd, Dag. RM9 146 EX67
Wixs La, SW4 161 DH84
Woburn Av, Horn. RM12 127 FG63
Purley CR8 *off High St* 219 DN111
Theydon Bois CM16 85 ES37
Woburn Cl, SE28
off Summerton Way 146 EX72
SW19 180 DC93
Bushey WD23 76 CC43
Woburn Ct, SE16
off Masters Dr 312 F1
Woburn Hill, Add. KT15 194 BJ103
Woburn Pk, Add. KT15 194 BK103
Woburn Pl, WC1 285 P4
Woburn Rd, Cars. SM5 200 DE102
Croydon CR0 202 DQ102
Woburn Sq, WC1 285 P5
Woburn Wk, WC1 285 P3
Wodeham Gdns, E1 288 D6
Wodehouse Av, SE5 312 A6
Wodehouse Rd, Dart. DA1 168 FN84
Wodeland Av, Guil. GU2 258 AV136
Woffington Cl, Kings.T. KT1 197 CJ95
Wokindon Rd, Grays RM16 171 GH76
WOKING, GU22 - GU24 227 AZ117
⇌ **Woking** 227 AZ117
Coll **Woking Adult Learning Cen**, Wok. GU22 *off Bonsey La* 226 AX121
● **Woking Business Pk**, Wok. GU21 227 BB115
Woking Cl, SW15 159 CT84
Coll **Woking Coll**, Wok. GU22
off Rydens Way 227 BA120
H **Woking Comm Hosp**, Wok. GU22 227 AZ118
Sch **Woking High Sch**, Horsell GU21 *off Morton Rd* 226 AX115
H **Woking Nuffield Hosp, The**, Wok. GU21 210 AY114
Woking Rd, Guil. GU1, GU4 242 AX130
Wold, The, Wold. CR3 237 EA122
Woldham Pl, Brom. BR2 204 EJ98
Woldham Rd, Brom. BR2 204 EJ98
WOLDINGHAM, Cat. CR3 237 EB122
⇌ **Woldingham** 237 DX122
WOLDINGHAM GARDEN VILLAGE, Cat. CR3 237 DY121
Woldingham Rd, Wold. CR3 236 DV120
Sch **Woldingham Sch**, Wold. CR3 *off Marden Pk* 253 DY125
Wolds Dr, Orp. BR6 223 EN105
Wolfe Cl, Brom. BR2 204 EG100
Hayes UB4 135 BV69
Wolfe Cres, SE7 164 EK78
SE16 301 J5
Wolfendale Cl, S.Merst. RH1 251 DJ130
Wolferton Rd, E12 125 EM63
Wolffe Gdns, E15 281 L5
Sch **Wolf Flds Prim Sch**, Sthl. UB2 *off Norwood Rd* 156 BZ77
Wolffram Cl, SE13 184 EE85
Wolfington Rd, SE27 181 DP91
Wolf La, Wind. SL4 151 AK83
Wolfs Hill, Oxt. RH8 254 EG131
Sch **Wolfson Hillel Prim Sch**, N14 *off Chase Rd* 81 DK44
Wolf's Row, Oxt. RH8 254 EH130
Wolfs Wd, Oxt. RH8 254 EG132
Wolftencroft Cl, SW11 308 B10
Wollaston Cl, SE1 299 J8
Wolmer Cl, Edg. HA8 96 CP49
Wolmer Gdns, Edg. HA8 96 CN48
Wolseley Av, SW19 180 DA89
Wolseley Gdns, W4 158 CP79
Wolseley Rd, E7 144 EH66
N8 121 DK58
N22 99 DM53
W4 158 CQ77
Harrow HA3 117 CE55
Mitcham CR4 200 DG101
Romford RM7 127 FD59
Wolseley St, SE1 300 B5
Wolsey Av, E6 293 L3
E17 123 DZ55
Cheshunt EN7 66 DT29
Thames Ditton KT7 197 CF99
● **Wolsey Business Pk**, Wat. WD18 93 BR45
Wolsey Cl, SE2 166 EW75
SW20 179 CV94
Hounslow TW3 156 CC84
Kingston upon Thames KT2 198 CP95
Southall UB2 156 CC76
Worcester Park KT4 217 CU105
Wolsey Cres, Green. DA9
off The Ri 189 FU86
Morden SM4 199 CY101
New Addington CR0 221 EC109
Wolsey Dr, Kings.T. KT2 178 CL92
Walton-on-Thames KT12 196 BX102
Wolsey Gdns, Ilf. IG6 103 EQ51
Wolsey Gro, Edg. HA8 96 CR52
Esher KT10 214 CB105
Sch **Wolsey Inf Sch**, Croy. CR0
off King Henry's Dr 221 EC108
Sch **Wolsey Jun Sch**, New Adgtn CR0
off King Henry's Dr 221 EC108
Wolsey Ms, NW5 275 L4
Orpington BR6 223 ET106
Wolsey Pl Shop Cen, Wok. GU21
off Commercial Way 227 AZ117
Wolsey Rd, N1 277 M3
Ashford TW15 174 BL91
East Molesey KT8 197 CD98
Enfield EN1 82 DV40
Esher KT10 214 CB105
Hampton Hill TW12 176 CB93
Hemel Hempstead HP2 40 BK21
Northwood HA6 93 BQ47
Sunbury-on-Thames TW16 175 BT94
Wolsey St, E1 288 G7
Wolsey Wk, Wok. GU21 226 AY117
Wolsey Way, Chess. KT9 216 CN106
Wolsley Cl, Dart. DA1 187 FE85
Wolstan Cl, Denh. UB9 114 BG62

W

Wolstonbury, N12 98 DA50
Wolvens La, Dor. RH4, RH5 262 CA140
Wolvercote Rd, SE2 166 EX75
Wolverley St, E2 288 E3
Wolverton, SE17 299 M10
Wolverton Av, Kings.T. KT2 198 CN95
Wolverton Cl, Horl. RH6 268 DF150
Wolverton Gdns, W5 138 CM73
W6 294 C8
Horley RH6 268 DF149
Wolverton Rd, Stan. HA7 95 CH51
Wolverton Way, N14 81 DJ43
Wolves La, N13 99 DN52
N22 99 DN52
Wombwell Gdns, Nthflt DA11 190 GE89
WOMBWELL PARK,
Grav. DA11 190 GD89
Womersley Rd, N8 121 DM58
WONERSH, Guil. GU5 259 BB144
Wonersh Common, Won. GU5 259 BB141
Wonersh Common Rd,
Won. GU5 259 BB142
Wonersh Way, Sutt. SM2 217 CX109
Wonford Cl, Kings.T. KT2 198 CS95
Walton on the Hill KT20 249 CU126
Wonham La, Bet. RH3 264 CS135
Wonham Way, Guil. GU5 261 BR139
Wonnacott Pl, Enf. EN3 83 DX36
Wontford Rd, Pur. CR8 235 DN115
Wontner Cl, N1 277 J7
Wontner Rd, SW17 180 DF89
WOOBURN, H.Wyc. HP10 110 AD58
Wooburn Cl, Uxb. UB8
off Aldenham Dr 135 BP70
Wooburn Common,
Woob.Grn HP10 110 AH59
Wooburn Common Rd,
Slou. SL1 110 AH61
Wooburn Green HP10 110 AH61
Wooburn Gra, Woob.Grn HP10 110 AD60
WOOBURN GREEN,
H.Wyc. HP10 110 AF56
Wooburn Grn La, Beac. HP9 110 AG56
● Wooburn Ind Pk,
Woob.Grn HP10 110 AD59
Wooburn Manor Pk,
Woob.Grn HP10 110 AE58
Wooburn Mead,
Woob.Grn HP10 110 AE57
Wooburn Ms, Woob.Grn HP10 110 AE58
Wooburn Town,
Woob.Grn HP10 110 AD59
Woodall Cl, E14 290 D10
Chessington KT9 215 CK108
Woodall Rd, Enf. EN3 83 DX44
Wood Av, Purf. RM19 168 FQ77
Woodbank, Rick. WD3 74 BJ44
Woodbank Av, Ger.Cr. SL9 112 AX58
Woodbank Dr, Ch.St.G. HP8 90 AX48
Woodbank Rd, Brom. BR1 184 EF90
Woodbastwick Rd, SE26 183 DX92
Woodberry Av, N21 99 DN47
Harrow HA2 116 CB56
Woodberry Cl, NW7 97 CX52
Sunbury-on-Thames TW16 175 BU93
Woodberry Cres, N10 121 DH55
Woodberry Down, N4 122 DQ59
Epping CM16 70 EU29
Sch Woodberry Down Comm Prim
Sch, N4 off Woodberry Gro 122 DQ59
Woodberry Down Est, N4 122 DQ59
Woodberry Gdns, N12 98 DC51
Woodberry Gro, N4 122 DQ59
N12 98 DC51
Bexley DA5 187 FD90
Woodberry Way, E4 101 EC46
N12 98 DC51
Woodbine Cl, Harl. CM19 51 EQ17
Twickenham TW2 177 CD89
Waltham Abbey EN9 84 EJ35
Woodbine Gro, SE20 182 DV94
Enfield EN2 82 DR38
Woodbine La, Wor.Pk. KT4 199 CV104
Woodbine Pl, E11 124 EG58
Woodbine Rd, Sid. DA15 185 ES88
Woodbines Av, Kings.T. KT1 197 CK97
Woodbine Ter, E9 279 H4
Woodborough Rd, SW15 159 CV84
Woodbourne Av, SW16 181 DK90
Woodbourne Cl, SW16
off Woodbourne Av 181 DL90
Woodbourne Dr, Clay. KT10 215 CF107
Woodbourne Gdns, Wall. SM6 219 DH108
Woodbridge Av, Lthd. KT22 231 CG118
● Woodbridge Business Pk,
Guil. GU1 242 AW133
Woodbridge Cl, N7 121 DM61
NW2 119 CU62
Romford RM3 106 FK49
Woodbridge Ct, Wdf.Grn. IG8 102 EL52
Woodbridge Gro, Lthd. KT22 231 CG118
Sch Woodbridge High Sch &
Language Coll, Wdf.Grn. IG8
off St. Barnabas Rd 102 EH52
WOODBRIDGE HILL,
Guil. GU2 242 AU132
Woodbridge Hill, Guil. GU2 242 AV133
Woodbridge Hill Gdns,
Guil. GU2 242 AU133
Woodbridge La, Rom. RM3 106 FK48
Woodbridge Meadows,
Guil. GU1 242 AW133
Woodbridge Rd, Bark. IG11 125 ET64
Guildford GU1 242 AW133
Woodbridge St, EC1 286 G4
Woodbrook Gdns,
Wal.Abb. EN9 68 EE33
Woodbrook Rd, SE2 166 EU79
Woodburn Cl, NW4 119 CX57
Woodbury Cl, E11 124 EH56
Biggin Hill TN16 239 EM118
Bourne End SL8 110 AC59
Croydon CR0 202 DT103
Woodbury Dr, Sutt. SM2 218 DC110
Woodbury Gdns, SE12 184 EH90
Woodbury Hill, Loug. IG10 84 EL41
Woodbury Hollow, Loug. IG10 84 EL40
Woodbury Pk Rd, W13 137 CH70
Woodbury Rd, E17 123 EB56
Biggin Hill TN16 239 EM118
Woodbury St, SW17 180 DE92
Woodchester Pk, Knot.Grn HP9 88 AJ50
Woodchester Sq, W2 283 L6
Woodchurch Cl, Sid. DA14 185 ER90
Woodchurch Dr, Brom. BR1 184 EK94
Woodchurch Rd, NW6 273 K7
Wood Cl, E2 288 C4
NW9 118 CR59
Bexley DA5 187 FE90
Harrow HA1 117 CD59
Hatfield AL10 45 CV18
Redhill RH1 266 DG143
Windsor SL4 151 AQ84
Woodclyffe Dr, Chis. BR7 205 EN96
Woodcock Ct, Har. HA3 118 CL59
Woodcock Dell Av, Har. HA3 117 CK59
Woodcock Hill, Berk. HP4 38 AS18
Harrow HA3 117 CK59
Rickmansworth WD3 92 BL50
Sandridge AL4 44 CN15
● Woodcock Hill Ind Est,
Rick. WD3 92 BL49
Woodcocks, E16 292 D7
Woodcombe Cres, SE23 182 DW88
Wood Common, Hat. AL10 45 CV15
WOODCOTE, Epsom KT18 232 CQ116
Pur. CR8 219 DK111
Woodcote, Guil. GU2 258 AV138
Horley RH6 269 DH147
Woodcote Av, NW7 97 CW51
Hornchurch RM12 127 FG63
Thornton Heath CR7 201 DP98
Wallington SM6 219 DH108
Woodcote Cl, Chsht EN8 66 DW30
Enfield EN3 82 DW44
Epsom KT18 216 CR114
Kingston upon Thames KT2 178 CM92
Woodcote Dr, Orp. BR6 205 ER102
Purley CR8 219 DK110
Woodcote End, Epsom KT18 232 CR115
Woodcote Grn, Wall. SM6 219 DJ109
Woodcote Grn Rd,
Epsom KT18 232 CQ116
Woodcote Gro, Couls. CR5 219 DH112
Woodcote Gro Rd, Couls. CR5 235 DK115
Sch Woodcote High Sch,
Couls. CR5 off Meadow Ri 219 DK113
Woodcote Hurst,
Epsom KT18 232 CQ116
Woodcote La, Pur. CR8 219 DK111
Woodcote Lawns, Chesh. HP5
off Little Hivings 54 AN27
Woodcote Ms, Loug. IG10 102 EK45
Wallington SM6 219 DH107
WOODCOTE PARK,
Couls. CR5 219 DH113
Woodcote Pk, Epsom KT18 232 CQ117
Woodcote Pk Av, Pur. CR8 219 DJ112
Woodcote Pk Rd,
Epsom KT18 232 CQ116
Woodcote Pl, SE27 181 DP92
Sch Woodcote Prim Sch,
Couls. CR5 off Dunsfold Ri 219 DK114
Woodcote Rd, E11 124 EG59
Epsom KT18 216 CR114
Purley CR8 219 DJ109
Wallington SM6 219 DH107
Woodcote Side, Epsom KT18 232 CP115
Woodcote Valley Rd, Pur. CR8 219 DK113
Woodcott Ho, SW15
off Ellisfield Dr 179 CU87
Wood Ct, W12
off Heathstan Rd 139 CU72
Edg. HA8 off South Rd 96 CP53
Wood Cres, Hem.H. HP3 40 BK21
Woodcrest Rd, Pur. CR8 219 DL113
Woodcrest Wk, Reig. RH2 250 DE132
Woodcroft, N21 99 DM46
SE9 185 EM90
Greenford UB6 137 CG65
Harlow CM18 51 EQ17
Woodcroft Av, NW7 96 CS52
Woodcroft Cl, SE9 185 EN86
Woodcroft Cres, Uxb. UB10 135 BP67
Woodcroft Ms, SE8 301 L9
Sch Woodcroft Prim Sch,
Edg. HA8 off Goldbeaters Gro 96 CS52
Woodcroft Rd, Chesh. HP5 54 AR28
Thornton Heath CR7 201 DP99
Sch Woodcroft Sch, Loug. IG10
off Whitakers Way 85 EM39
Woodcutter Pl, St.Alb. AL2 60 CC27
Woodcutters Av, Grays RM16 170 GC75
Woodcutters Cl, Horn. RM11 128 FK56
Wood Dr, Chis. BR7 184 EL93
Sevenoaks TN13 256 FF126
Woodedge Cl, E4 102 EF46
Jct Wooden Br, Guil. GU2 242 AU133
Woodend, SE19 182 DQ93
Esher KT10 196 CC103
Leatherhead KT22 247 CJ125
Sutton SM1 200 DC103
Wood End, Hayes UB3 135 BS72
Park Street AL2 60 CC28
Swanley BR8 207 FC98
Woodend, The, Wall. SM6 219 DH109
Wood End Av, Har. HA2 116 CB63
Wood End Cl, Farn.Com. SL2 111 AR62
Hemel Hempstead HP2 41 BQ19
Northolt UB5 117 CD64
Woodend Cl, Wok. GU21 226 AU119
Woodend Gdns, Enf. EN2 81 DL42
Wood End Gdns, Nthlt. UB5 116 CC64
Wood End Grn Rd, Hayes UB3 135 BR71
Sch Wood End Inf Sch,
Nthlt. UB5 off Whitton Av W 117 CD64
Sch Wood End Jun Sch,
Grnf. UB6 off Vernon Ri 117 CD64
Wood End La, Nthlt. UB5 136 CB65
Woodend Pk, Cob. KT11 230 BX115
Sch Wood End Pk Comm Sch,
Hayes UB3
off Judge Heath La 135 BQ73
Woodend Rd, E17 101 EC54
Wood End Rd, Har. HA1 117 CD63
Wood End Way, Nthlt. UB5 116 CC64
Wooder Gdns, E7 281 N1
Wooderson Cl, SE25 202 DS98
Woodfall Av, Barn. EN5 79 CZ43
Woodfall Dr, Dart. DA1 167 FE84
Woodfall Rd, N4 121 DN60
Woodfall St, SW3 308 E1
Wood Fm Rd, Hem.H. HP2 40 BL20
Woodfarrs, SE5 162 DR84
Wood Fld, NW3 274 E3
Woodfield, Ashtd. KT21 231 CK117
Woodfield Av, NW9 118 CS56
SW16 181 DK90
W5 137 CJ70
Carshalton SM5 218 DG107
Gravesend DA11 191 GH88
Northwood HA6 93 BS49
Wembley HA0 117 CJ62
Woodfield Cl, SE19 182 DQ94
Ashtead KT21 231 CK117
Coulsdon CR5 235 DJ119
Enfield EN1 82 DS42
Redhill RH1 250 DE133
Woodfield Cres, W5 137 CJ70
Woodfield Dr, E.Barn. EN4 98 DG46
Hemel Hempstead HP3 41 BR22
Romford RM2 127 FG56
Woodfield Gdns, Hem. H. HP3 41 BQ22
New Malden KT3 199 CT99
Woodfield Gro, SW16 181 DK90
Woodfield Hill, Couls. CR5 235 DH119
Woodfield La, SW16 181 DK90
Ashtead KT21 232 CL116
Hatfield AL9 46 DD23
Hertford SG13 46 DD23
Woodfield Pk, Amer. HP6 55 AN37
Woodfield Pl, W9 283 H5
Woodfield Ri, Bushey WD23 95 CD45
Woodfield Rd, W5 137 CJ70
W9 283 H6
Ashtead KT21 231 CK117
Hounslow TW4 155 BV82
Radlett WD7 77 CG36
Thames Ditton KT7 197 CF103
Welwyn Garden City AL7 29 CZ09
Woodfields, Sev. TN13 256 FD122
Woodfields, The, S.Croy. CR2 220 DT111
Sch Woodfield Sch, NW9
off Glenwood Av 118 CS60
Hemel Hempstead HP3
off Malmes Cft 41 BQ22
Merstham RH1
off Sunstone Gro 251 DL129
Woodfield Ter, Hare. UB9 92 BH54
Thornwood CM16 70 EW25
Woodfield Way, N11 99 DK52
Hornchurch RM12 128 FK60
Redhill RH1 250 DE132
St. Albans AL4 43 CJ17
Woodfines, The, Horn. RM11 128 FK58
⊖ Woodford 102 EH51
Woodford 102 EH51
Woodford Av, Ilf. IG2, IG4 125 EM57
Woodford Green IG8 124 EK55
WOODFORD BRIDGE,
Wdf.Grn. IG8 103 EM52
Woodford Br Rd, Ilf. IG4 124 EK55
Sch Woodford Co High Sch for Girls,
Wdf.Grn. IG8
off High Rd Woodford Grn 102 EF51
Woodford Ct, W12 294 C4
Waltham Abbey EN9 68 EG33
Woodford Cres, Pnr. HA5 93 BV54
WOODFORD GREEN, IG8 102 EF49
Sch Woodford Grn Prep Sch,
Wdf.Grn. IG8 off Glengall Rd 102 EG51
Sch Woodford Grn Prim Sch,
Wdf.Grn. IG8 off Sunset Av 102 EG50
Woodford New Rd, E17 124 EE56
E18 102 EE53
Woodford Green IG8 102 EE53
Woodford Pl, Wem. HA9 118 CL60
Woodford Rd, E7 124 EH63
E18 124 EG56
Watford WD17 75 BV40
● Woodford Trd Est,
Wdf.Grn. IG8 102 EJ54
Woodford Way, Slou. SL2 131 AN69
WOODFORD WELLS,
Wdf.Grn. IG8 102 EH49
Woodgate, Wat. WD25 59 BV33
Woodgate Av, Chess. KT9 215 CK106
Northaw EN6 65 DH33
Woodgate Cl, Cob. KT11 213 BV113
Woodgate Ct, Horn. RM11 128 FK55
Woodgate Cres, Stanmore HA7 95 CF53
Stanstead Abbotts SG12 33 ED11
Nthwd. HA6 93 BU51
Woodgate Dr, SW16 181 DK94
Woodgate Ms, Wat. WD17 75 BU39
Woodgavil, Bans. SM7 233 CZ116
Woodger Cl, Guil. GU4 243 BC132
Woodger Ct, Croy. CR0
off Lion Rd 202 DQ99
Woodger Rd, W12 294 B5
Woodgers Gro, Swan. BR8 207 FF96
Woodget Cl, E6 292 G8
Woodgrange Av, N12 98 DD51
W5 138 CN74
Enfield EN1 82 DU44
Harrow HA3 117 CJ57
Woodgrange Cl, Har. HA3 117 CK57
Woodgrange Gdns, Enf. EN1 82 DU44
Sch Woodgrange Inf Sch, E7
off Sebert Rd 124 EH63
Woodgrange Park 124 EK64
Woodgrange Rd, E7 281 P2
Woodgrange Ter, Enf. EN1 82 DU44
WOOD GREEN, N22 99 DL53
⊖ Wood Green 99 DM54
Woodgreen Rd, Wal.Abb. EN9 84 EJ35
Wood Grn Way, Chsht EN8 67 DY31
WOODHALL, Welw.G.C. AL7 29 CY11
Woodhall, NW1 285 L3
Woodhall Av, SE21 182 DT90
Pinner HA5 94 BY54
Woodhall Cl, Hert. SG14 32 DQ07
Uxbridge UB8 114 BK64
Woodhall Ct, Welw.G.C. AL7 29 CY10
Woodhall Cres, Horn. RM11 128 FM59
Woodhall Dr, SE21 182 DT90
Pinner HA5 94 BX53
Woodhall Gate, Pnr. HA5 94 BX52
Woodhall Ho, SW18
off Fitzhugh Gro 180 DD86
Woodhall La, Hem.H. HP2 40 BL19
Shenley WD7 78 CL35
Watford WD19 94 BX49
Welwyn Garden City AL7 29 CY10
Woodhall Par, Welw.G.C. AL7 29 CZ11
Sch Woodhall Prim Sch,
S.Oxhey WD19
off Woodhall La 94 BY49
Woodhall Rd, Pnr. HA5 94 BX52
WOODHAM, Add. KT15 211 BF111
Woodham Ct, E18 124 EF56
Woodham Gate, Wok. GU21 211 BC113
Woodham La, Add. KT15 212 BG110
Woking GU21 211 BB114
Woodham Lock, W.Byf. KT14 211 BF112
Woodham Pk Rd,
Wdhm KT15 211 BF109
Woodham Pk Way,
Wdhm KT15 211 BF111
Woodham Ri, Wok. GU21 211 AZ114
Woodham Rd, SE6 183 EC90
Woking GU21 226 AY115
Woodham Way,
Stans.Abb. SG12 33 EC11
Woodham Waye, Wok. GU21 211 BB113
WOODHATCH, Reig. RH2 266 DC137
Woodhatch Cl, E6 292 G7
Woodhatch Rd, Red. RH1 266 DB137
Reigate RH2 266 DB137
Woodhatch Spinney,
Couls. CR5 235 DL116
Woodhaven Gdns, Ilf. IG6
off Brandville Gdns 125 EQ56
Woodhaw, Egh. TW20 173 BB91
Woodhayes, Horl. RH6 269 DH147
Woodhayes Rd, SW19 179 CW94
Woodhead Dr, Orp. BR6
off Sherlies Av 205 ES103
Woodheyes Rd, NW10 118 CR64
Woodhill, SE18 305 H8
Harlow CM18 51 ES18
Send GU23 243 BD125
Woodhill Av, Ger.Cr. SL9 113 BA58
Woodhill Ct, Send GU23 243 BD125
Woodhill Cres, Har. HA3 117 CK58
Sch Woodhill Prim Sch, SE18 305 H9
Wood Ho, SW17 off Laurel Cl 180 DE92
Woodhouse Av, Perivale UB6 137 CF68
Woodhouse Cl, SE22 162 DU84
Hayes UB3 155 BS76
Perivale UB6 137 CF68
Coll Woodhouse Coll, N12
off Woodhouse Rd 98 DD51
Woodhouse Eaves,
Nthwd. HA6 93 BU50
Woodhouse Gro, E12 144 EL65
Wood Ho La, Brox. EN10 48 DT21
Woodhouse La,
Holm.St.M. RH5 261 BU143
Woodhouse Rd, E11 124 EF62
N12 98 DD51
Woodhurst Av, Petts Wd BR5 205 EQ100
Watford WD25 76 BX35
Woodhurst Dr, Denh. UB9 113 BF57
Woodhurst La, Oxt. RH8 254 EE130
Woodhurst Pk, Oxt. RH8 254 EE130
Woodhurst Rd, SE2 166 EU78
W3 138 CQ73
Woodhyrst Gdns, Ken. CR8 235 DP115
Woodies La, N.Mal. KT3 198 CR100
Woodin Cl, Dart. DA1 188 FK86
Wooding Gro, Harl. CM19 51 EP15
Woodington Cl, SE9 185 EN86
Woodknoll Dr, Chis. BR7 205 EM95
Woodland App, Grnf. UB6 137 CG65
Woodland Av, Hem.H. HP1 40 BH21
Hutton CM13 109 GC43
Slough SL1 131 AR73
Windsor SL4 151 AM84
Woodland Chase,
Crox.Grn WD3 93 BP45
Woodland Cl, NW9 118 CQ58
SE19 182 DS93
Epsom KT19 216 CS107
Hemel Hempstead HP1 40 BH21
Hutton CM13 109 GC43
Ickenham UB10 115 BP61
Weybridge KT13 213 BR105
Woodford Green IG8 102 EH48
Woodland Ct, N7 276 B4
Oxt. RH8 253 ED128
Woodland Cres, SE10 315 J2
SE16 301 J5
Woodland Dr, E.Hors. KT24 245 BT127
St. Albans AL4 43 CJ18
Watford WD17 75 BT39
Woodland Gdns, N10 121 DH57
Isleworth TW7 157 CE82
South Croydon CR2 220 DW111
Woodland Glade,
Farn.Com. SL2 111 AR62
Woodland Gra, Iver SL0 153 BE76
Woodland Gro, SE10 315 J1
Epping CM16 70 EU31
Weybridge KT13 213 BR105
Woodland Hts, SE3 315 K2
Woodland Hill, SE19 182 DS93
Woodland La, Chorl. WD3 73 BD41
Woodland Ms, SW16 181 DL90
Woodland Mt, Hert. SG13 32 DT09
Woodland Pl, Chorl. WD3 73 BF42
Hemel Hempstead HP1 40 BH21
Woodland Ri, N10 121 DH56
Greenford UB6 137 CG65
Oxted RH8 254 EE130
Sevenoaks TN15 257 FL123
Welwyn Garden City AL8 29 CW07
Woodland Rd, E4 101 EC46
N11 99 DH50
SE19 182 DS92
Hertford Heath SG13 32 DV12
Loughton IG10 84 EL41
Maple Cross WD3 91 BD50
Thornton Heath CR7 201 DN98
WOODLANDS, Islw. TW7 157 CE82
Woodlands, NW11 119 CY58
SW20 199 CW98
Brookmans Park AL9 64 DB26
Epping CM16 70 EU31
Gerrards Cross SL9 113 AZ57
Harrow HA2 116 CA56
Horley RH6 269 DJ147
Park Street AL2 60 CC27
Radlett WD7 61 CG34
Send Marsh GU23
off Clandon Rd 243 BF125
Woking GU22
off Constitution Hill 226 AY118
Woodlands, The, N14 99 DH46
SE13 183 ED87
SE19 182 DQ94
Amersham HP6 55 AQ35
Beckenham BR3 203 EC95
Esher KT10 196 CC103
Guildford GU1 243 BC133
Isleworth TW7 157 CF82
Orpington BR6 224 EV107
Smallfield RH6 269 DP148
Wallington SM6 219 DH109
Woodlands Av, E11 124 EH60
N3 98 DC52
W3 138 CP74
Berkhamsted HP4 38 AW20
Hornchurch RM11 128 FK57
New Malden KT3 198 CQ95
Redhill RH1 266 DF135
Romford RM6 126 EY58
Ruislip HA4 116 BW60
Sidcup DA15 185 ES88
West Byfleet KT14 211 BF113
Worcester Park KT4 199 CT103
Woodlands Cl, NW11 119 CY57
Borehamwood WD6 78 CP42
Bromley BR1 205 EM96
Claygate KT10 215 CF108
Dorking RH4 263 CF137
East Horsley KT24 245 BT127
Gerrards Cross SL9 113 BA58
Grays RM16 170 GE76
Guildford GU1 242 AY130
Hoddesdon EN11 49 EA18
Ottershaw KT16 211 BB110
Swanley BR8 207 FF97
Woodlands Copse,
Ashtd. KT21 231 CK116
Woodlands Ct, Wok. GU22
off Constitution Hill 226 AY119
Woodlands Dr, Beac. HP9 88 AJ51
Hoddesdon EN11 49 EA19
Kings Langley WD4 59 BQ28
Stanmore HA7 95 CF51
Sunbury-on-Thames TW16 196 BW96
Sch Woodlands First & Mid Sch,
Edg. HA8 off Bransgrove Rd 96 CM53
Woodlands Gdns,
Epsom KT18 233 CW117
Woodlands Glade, Beac. HP9 88 AJ51
Woodlands Gro, Couls. CR5 234 DG117
Isleworth TW7 157 CE82
Woodlands Hill, Beac. HP9 111 AL58
Sch Woodlands Inf Sch, Ilf. IG1
off Loxford La 125 ER64
Sch Woodlands Jun Sch, Ilf. IG1
off Loxford La 125 ER64
Woodlands La,
Stoke D'Ab. KT11 230 CA117
Woodlands Par, Ashf. TW15 175 BQ93
Woodlands Pk, Add. KT15 211 BF106
Bexley DA5 187 FC91
Box Hill KT20 248 CP131
Guildford GU1 243 BB132
Woking GU21
off Blackmore Cres 211 BC114
Woodlands Pk Rd, N15 121 DP57
SE10 315 J2
Woodlands Pl, Cat. CR3 252 DU126
Sch Woodlands Prim Sch,
Borwd. WD6 off Alban Cres 78 CN39
Woodlands Ri, Swan. BR8 207 FF96
Woodlands Rd, E11 124 EE61
E17 123 EC55
N9 100 DW46
SW13 159 CT83
Bexleyheath DA7 166 EY83
Bookham KT23 246 BY128
Bromley BR1 204 EL96
Bushey WD23 76 BY43
Enfield EN2 82 DR39
Epsom KT18 232 CN115
Guildford GU1 242 AX130
Harold Wood RM3 106 FN53
Harrow HA1 117 CF57
Hemel Hempstead HP3 58 BN27
Hertford SG13 32 DT09
Ilford IG1 125 EQ62
Isleworth TW7 157 CE82
Leatherhead KT22 231 CD117
Orpington BR6 224 EU107
Redhill RH1 266 DF135
Romford RM1 127 FF55
Southall UB1 136 BX74
Surbiton KT6 197 CK101
Virginia Water GU25 192 AW98
West Byfleet KT14 211 BF114
Woodlands Rd E, Vir.W. GU25 192 AW98
Woodlands Rd W, Vir.W. GU25 192 AW97
Sch Woodlands Sch,
Gt Warley CM13 off Warley St 129 FX56
Leatherhead KT22
off Fortyfoot Rd 231 CJ122
Woodlands St, SE13 183 ED87
Woodland St, E8 278 B4
Woodlands Vw, Bad.Mt TN14 224 FA110
Dorking RH5 263 CH142
Woodlands Way, SW15 179 CZ85
Ashtead KT21 232 CN116
Box Hill KT20 248 CQ130
Woodland Ter, SE7 304 G9
Woodland Vw, Chesh. HP5 54 AR32
Godalming GU7 258 AS142
Woodland Wk, NW3 274 D2
SE10 315 K1
Bromley BR1 184 EE91
Epsom KT19 216 CN107
Woodland Way, N21 99 DN47
NW7 96 CS51
SE2 166 EX77
Bedmond WD5 59 BT27
Caterham CR3 252 DS128
Croydon CR0 203 DY102
Goffs Oak EN7 65 DP28
Greenhithe DA9 169 FU84
Kingswood KT20 233 CY122
Mitcham CR4 180 DG94
Morden SM4 199 CZ98
Petts Wood BR5 205 EQ98
Purley CR8 219 DN113
Surbiton KT5 198 CP103
Theydon Bois CM16 85 ER35
West Wickham BR4 221 EB105
Weybridge KT13 213 BR106
Woodford Green IG8 102 EH48
⊖ Wood Lane 294 B1
Wood La, N6 121 DH58
NW9 118 CS59
W12 282 B10
Caterham CR3 236 DR124
Dagenham RM8, RM9, RM10 126 EW63
Hedgerley SL2 112 AS61
Hemel Hempstead HP2 40 BK21
Hornchurch RM12 127 FG64
Isleworth TW7 157 CF80
Iver SL0 133 BC71
Lane End DA2 189 FR91
Ruislip HA4 115 BR60
Slough SL1 151 AM76
Stanmore HA7 95 CG48
Tadworth KT20 233 CZ116
Ware SG12 33 EA05
Weybridge KT13 213 BQ109
Woodford Green IG8 102 EF50
Wood La Cl, Iver SL0 133 BB69
Wood La End, Hem.H. HP2 40 BN19
Sch Woodlane High Sch, W12
off Du Cane Rd 139 CV72
Woodlawn Cl, SW15 179 CZ85
Woodlawn Cres, Twick. TW2 176 CB89
Woodlawn Dr, Felt. TW13 176 BX89
Woodlawn Gro, Wok. GU21 227 AZ115
Woodlawn Rd, SW6 306 C4

W

Woodlea, St.Alb. AL2
off Hammers Gate 60 CA25
Woodlea Dr, Brom. BR2 204 EE99
Woodlea Gro, Nthwd. HA6 93 BQ51
Sch **Woodlea Prim Sch**,
Wold. CR3 *off Long Hill* 237 EA122
Woodlea Rd, N16 122 DS62
Woodlee Cl, Vir.W. GU25 192 AW96
Woodleigh, E18
off Churchfields 102 EG53
Woodleigh Av, N12 98 DE51
Woodleigh Gdns, SW16 181 DL90
Woodley Cl, SW17
off Arnold Rd 180 DF94
Woodley Hill, Chesh. HP5 54 AR34
Woodley La, Cars. SM5 200 DD104
Woodley Rd, Orp. BR6 206 EW103
Ware SG12 33 DZ05
Wood Lo Gdns, Brom. BR1 184 EL94
Wood Lo La, W.Wick. BR4 203 EC104
Woodmancote Gdns,
W.Byf. KT14 212 BG113
Woodman La, E4 84 EE43
Woodman Ms, Rich. TW9 158 CP81
Woodman Path, Ilf. IG6 103 ES51
Woodman Rd, Couls. CR5 235 DJ115
Hemel Hempstead HP3 40 BL22
Warley CM14 108 FW50
Woodmans Gro, NW10 119 CT64
Woodmans Ms, W12 139 CV71
WOODMANSTERNE,
Bans. SM7 234 DD115
⇌ **Woodmansterne** 235 DH116
Woodmansterne La,
Bans. SM7 234 DB115
Carshalton SM5 218 DF112
Wallington SM6 219 DH111
Sch **Woodmansterne Prim Sch**,
SW16 *off Stockport Rd* 201 DK95
Banstead SM7
off Carshalton Rd 218 DF114
Woodmansterne Rd, SW16 201 DK95
Carshalton SM5 218 DE109
Coulsdon CR5 235 DJ115
Woodmansterne St,
Bans. SM7 234 DE115
Woodman St, E16 305 M3
Woodman Way, Horl. RH6 269 DJ146
Wood Meads, Epp. CM16 70 EU29
Woodmere, SE9 185 EM88
Woodmere Av, Croy. CR0 203 DX101
Watford WD24 76 BX38
Woodmere Cl, SW11
off Lavender Hill 160 DG83
Croydon CR0 203 DX101
Woodmere Gdns, Croy. CR0 203 DX101
Woodmere Way, Beck. BR3 203 ED99
Woodmill Ms, Hodd. EN11
off Whittingstall Rd 49 EB15
Woodmill Rd, E5 122 DW61
Woodmount, Swan. BR8 207 FC101
Woodnook Rd, SW16 181 DH92
Woodpecker Cl, N9 82 DV44
Bushey WD23 94 CC46
Cobham KT11 214 BY112
Harrow HA3 95 CF53
Hatfield AL10 45 CT21
Woodpecker Dr, Green. DA9 189 FU86
Woodpecker Ms, SE13
off Mercator Rd 163 ED84
Woodpecker Mt, Croy. CR0 221 DY109
Woodpecker Rd, SE14 313 L3
SE28 146 EW73
Woodpecker Way, Wok. GU22 226 AX123
Woodplace Cl, Couls. CR5 235 DJ119
Woodplace La, Couls. CR5 235 DJ118
Wood Pond Cl, Seer Grn HP9 89 AQ51
Woodquest Av, SE24 182 DQ85
Woodredon Cl, Roydon CM19
off Epping Rd 50 EH16
Woodredon Fm La,
Wal.Abb. EN9 84 EK35
Wood Retreat, SE18 165 ER80
Woodridden Hill,
Wal.Abb. EN9 84 EK35
Wood Ride, Barn. EN4 80 DD39
Petts Wood BR5 205 ER98
Woodridge Cl, Enf. EN2 81 DN39
Sch **Woodridge Prim Sch**, N12
off Southover 98 DA48
Woodridge Way, Nthwd. HA6 93 BS51
Wood Riding, Wok. GU22
off Pyrford Wds 227 BF115
Woodridings Av, Pnr. HA5 94 BZ53
Woodridings Cl, Pnr. HA5 94 BY52
Woodriffe Rd, E11 123 ED59
Wood Ri, Guil. GU3 242 AS132
Pinner HA5 115 BU57
Wood Rd, NW10 138 CQ66
Biggin Hill TN16 238 EJ118
Godalming GU7 258 AT144
Shepperton TW17 194 BN98
Woodrow, SE18 305 J9
Woodrow Av, Hayes UB4 135 BT71
Woodrow Cl, Perivale UB6 137 CH66
Woodrow Ct, N17
off Heybourne Rd 100 DV52
Woodroyd Av, Horl. RH6 268 DF149
Woodroyd Gdns, Horl. RH6 268 DF150
Woodruff Av, Guil. GU1 243 BA131
Woodrush Cl, SE14 313 L4
Woodrush Way, Rom. RM6 126 EX56
Woods, The, Nthwd. HA6 93 BU50
Radlett WD7 61 CH34
Uxbridge UB10 115 BP63
Woods Av, Hat. AL10 45 CV18
Wood's Bldgs, E1 288 E6
Woods Dr, Slou. SL2 111 AM64
Woodseer St, E1 288 B6
Woodsford, SE17 311 L1
Woodsford Sq, W14 294 F5
Woodshire Rd, Dag. RM10 127 FB62
Woodshore Cl, Vir.W. GU25 192 AV100
Woodshots Meadow,
Wat. WD18 75 BR43
WOODSIDE, SE25 202 DU100
WOODSIDE, Hat. AL9 45 CZ21
WOODSIDE, Wat. WD25 59 BT33
Tra **Woodside** 202 DV100
Woodside, NW11 120 DA57
SW19 179 CZ93
Buckhurst Hill IG9 102 EJ47
Cheshunt EN7 66 DU31
Elstree WD6 78 CM42
Fetcham KT22 230 CB122
Flackwell Heath HP10 110 AC57
Hertford Heath SG13 32 DW12
Lower Kingswood KT20 249 CZ128
Orpington BR6 224 EU106
Woodside,
Thornwood CM16 70 EX27
Walton-on-Thames KT12
off Ashley Rd 195 BU102
Watford WD24 75 BU36
West Horsley KT24 245 BQ126
Woodside Av, N6 120 DF57
N10 120 DF57
N12 98 DC49
SE25 202 DV100
Amersham HP6 55 AR36
Beaconsfield HP9 88 AJ52
Chislehurst BR7 185 EQ92
Esher KT10 197 CE101
Flackwell Heath HP10 110 AC57
Hersham KT12 213 BV105
Wembley HA0 138 CL67
Woodside Cl, Amer. HP6 55 AR37
Beaconsfield HP9 88 AJ52
Bexleyheath DA7 167 FD84
Caterham CR3 236 DS124
Chalfont St. Peter SL9 90 AY54
Hutton CM13 109 GD43
Rainham RM13 148 FJ70
Ruislip HA4 115 BR58
Stanmore HA7 95 CH50
Surbiton KT5 198 CQ101
Wembley HA0 138 CL67
● **Woodside Commercial Est**,
Thnwd CM16 70 EX26
Woodside Ct, N12 98 DB49
Woodside Ct Rd, Croy. CR0 202 DU101
Woodside Cres, Sid. DA15 185 ES90
Smallfield RH6 269 DN148
Woodside Dr, Dart. DA2 187 FE91
Woodside End, Wem. HA0 138 CL67
Woodside Gdns, E4 101 EB50
N17 100 DS54
Woodside Gra Rd, N12 98 DB49
Woodside Grn, SE25 202 DV100
Hatfield AL9 46 DA21
Woodside Gro, N12 98 DC48
Sch **Woodside High Sch**, N22
off White Hart La 99 DP52
Woodside Hill, Chal.St.P. SL9 90 AY54
Sch **Woodside Junior, Inf & Nurs Schs**,
Croy. CR0 *off Morland Rd* 202 DU101
Sch **Woodside Jun Sch**,
Amer. HP6 *off Mitchell Wk* 55 AS38
Woodside La, N12 98 DB48
Bexley DA5 186 EX86
Hatfield AL9 45 CZ21
Woodside Ms, SE22 182 DT86
⊖ **Woodside Park** 98 DB49
Woodside Pk, SE25 202 DU99
Woodside Pk Av, E17 123 ED56
Woodside Pk Rd, N12 98 DB49
Woodside Pl, Hat. AL9 45 CZ21
Wembley HA0 138 CL67
Sch **Woodside Prim Acad**, E17 123 EC56
Sch **Woodside Prim Sch**,
Chsht EN7 *off Jones Rd* 65 DP29
Grays RM16
off Grangewood Av 171 GF76
Woodside Rd, E13 292 C4
N22 99 DM52
SE25 202 DV100
Abbots Langley WD5 59 BV31
Amersham HP6 55 AR37
Beaconsfield HP9 88 AJ52
Bexleyheath DA7 167 FD84
Bricket Wood AL2 60 BZ30
Bromley BR1 204 EL99
Cobham KT11 214 CA113
Guildford GU2 242 AT133
Kingston upon Thames KT2 178 CL94
New Malden KT3 198 CR96
Northwood HA6 93 BT52
Purley CR8 219 DK113
Sevenoaks TN13 256 FG123
Sidcup DA15 185 ES90
Sundridge TN14 240 EX124
Sutton SM1 200 DC104
Watford WD25 59 BV31
Woodford Green IG8 102 EG49
Sch **Woodside Sch**, Belv. DA17
off Halt Robin Rd 167 FB77
Sch **Woodside Sch, The**, E17
off Wood St 123 EC55
Woodside Way, Croy. CR0 202 DV100
Mitcham CR4 201 DH95
Penn HP10 88 AC46
Redhill RH1 266 DG135
Salfords RH1 266 DG140
Virginia Water GU25 192 AV97
Woods Ms, W1 284 F10
Woodsome Lo, Wey. KT13 213 BQ107
Woodsome Rd, NW5 120 DG62
Woods Pl, SE1 299 P7
Woodspring Rd, SW19 179 CY89
Woods Rd, SE15 312 E7
Woodstead Gro, Edg. HA8 96 CL51
Woodstock, W.Clan. GU4 244 BH128
Jct **Woodstock, The**, Sutt. SM3 199 CY101
Woodstock Av, NW11 119 CY59
W13 157 CG76
Isleworth TW7 177 CG85
Romford RM3 106 FP50
Slough SL3 152 AX77
Southall UB1 136 BZ69
Sutton SM3 199 CZ101
Woodstock Cl, Bex. DA5 186 EZ88
Hertford Heath SG13
off Hogsdell La 32 DV11
Stanmore HA7 96 CL54
Woking GU21 226 AY116
Woodstock Ct, SE12 184 EG86
Woodstock Cres, N9 82 DV44
Woodstock Dr, Uxb. UB10 114 BL63
Woodstock Gdns, Beck. BR3 203 EB95
Hayes UB4 135 BT71
Ilford IG3 126 EU61
Woodstock Gro, W12 294 D4
Coll **Woodstock Ho**, Long Dit. KT6
off Woodstock La N 197 CJ103
Woodstock La N,
Long Dit. KT6 197 CJ103
Woodstock La S, Chess. KT9 215 CJ105
Claygate KT10 215 CH106
Woodstock Ms, W1 285 H7
Woodstock Ri, Sutt. SM3 199 CZ101
Woodstock Rd, E7 144 EJ66
E17 101 ED54
N4 121 DN60
NW11 119 CZ59
W4 158 CS76
Broxbourne EN10 49 DY19
Bushey Heath WD23 95 CF45
Carshalton SM5 218 DG106
Woodstock Rd, Coulsdon CR5
off Chipstead Valley Rd 235 DH116
Croydon CR0 202 DR104
Wembley HA0 138 CM66
Woodstock Rd N, St.Alb. AL1 43 CH18
Woodstock Rd S, St.Alb. AL1 43 CH20
Woodstock St, W1 285 J9
Woodstock Ter, E14 290 D10
Woodstock Way, Mitch. CR4 201 DH96
Woodstone Av, Epsom KT17 217 CU106
⊙ **Wood Street** 123 EC56
Jct **Wood Street**, E17 101 EC54
Wood St, E17 123 EC55
EC2 287 K9
W4 158 CS78
Barnet EN5 79 CW42
Grays RM17 170 GC79
Kingston upon Thames KT1 197 CK95
Merstham RH1 251 DJ129
Mitcham CR4 200 DG101
Swanley BR8 208 FJ96
Woodsway, Oxshott KT22 215 CE114
Woodsyre, SE26 182 DT91
Woodthorpe Rd, SW15 159 CV84
Ashford TW15 174 BL91
Woodtree Cl, NW4 97 CW54
Wood Vale, N10 121 DJ57
SE23 182 DV88
Hatfield AL10 45 CV18
Woodvale Av, SE25 202 DT97
Wood Vale Est, SE23 182 DW86
Woodvale Est, SE27 182 DQ92
Woodvale Pk, St.Alb. AL1 43 CH20
Woodvale Wk, SE27 182 DQ92
Woodvale Way, NW11 119 CX62
Woodview, Chess. KT9 215 CJ111
Grays RM16, RM17 170 GE76
Wood Vw, Cuffley EN6 65 DL27
Hemel Hempstead HP1 40 BH18
Woodview Av, E4 101 EC49
Woodview Cl, N4 121 DP59
SW15 178 CR91
Ashtead KT21 232 CN116
Orpington BR6 205 EQ103
South Croydon CR2 220 DV114
Wood View Ms, Rom. RM1 105 FD53
Woodview Rd, Swan. BR8 207 FC96
Woodville Cl, SE3 164 EH81
SE12 184 EG85
Teddington TW11 177 CG91
Woodville Ct, Wat. WD17 75 BU40
Woodville Gdns, NW11 119 CX59
W5 138 CL72
Ilford IG6 125 EP55
Ruislip HA4 115 BQ59
Woodville Gro, Well. DA16 166 EU83
Woodville Pl, Grav. DA12 191 GH87
Hertford SG14 31 DP07
Woodville Rd, E11 124 EF60
E17 123 DY56
E18 102 EH54
N16 277 N3
NW6 273 H10
NW11 119 CX59
W5 137 CK72
Barnet EN5 80 DB41
Morden SM4 200 DA98
Richmond TW10 177 CH90
Thornton Heath CR7 202 DQ98
Woodville St, SE18 305 H9
Woodvill Rd, Lthd. KT22 231 CH120
Wood Wk, Chorl. WD3 73 BE40
Woodward Av, NW4 119 CU57
Woodward Cl, Clay. KT10 215 CF107
Grays RM17 170 GB77
Woodwarde Rd, SE22 182 DS86
Woodward Gdns, Dag. RM9
off Woodward Rd 146 EW66
Stanmore HA7 95 CF52
Woodward Hts, Grays RM17 170 GB77
Woodward Rd, Dag. RM9 146 EV66
Woodwards, Harl. CM19 51 EQ17
Woodward Ter, Green. DA9 189 FS86
Woodway, Beac. HP9 88 AF54
Brentwood CM13, CM15 109 GA46
Guildford GU1 243 BB133
Wood Way, Orp. BR6 205 EN103
Woodway Cres, Har. HA1 117 CG58
Woodwaye, Wat. WD19 94 BW45
Woodwell St, SW18
off Huguenot Pl 180 DC85
Wood Wf, SE10 314 D2
Wood Wf Apts, SE10
off Horseferry Pl 314 E2
Woodwicks, Map.Cr. WD3 91 BD50
Woodyard, The, Epp. CM16 70 EW28
Woodyard Cl, NW5 275 H3
Woodyard La, SE21 182 DS87
Woodyates Rd, SE12 184 EG86
Woodyers Cl, Won. GU5 259 BB144
Woolacombe Rd, SE3 164 EJ81
Woolacombe Way, Hayes UB3 155 BS77
Woolborough La,
Outwood RH1 267 DM143
Woolbrook Rd, Dart. DA1 187 FE86
Wooldridge Cl, Felt. TW14 175 BQ88
Wooler St, SE17 311 L1
Woolf Cl, SE28 146 EV74
Woolf Ms, WC1 285 P4
Woolf Wk, Til. RM18
off Brennan Rd 171 GJ82
Woolhampton Way, Chig. IG7 104 EV48
Woolhams, Cat. CR3 252 DT126
Woollam Cres, St.Alb. AL3 42 CC16
Woollard St, Wal.Abb. EN9 67 EC34
Woollaston Rd, N4 121 DP58
WOOLLENSBROOK,
Hodd. EN11 49 DX15
Woollens Gro, Hodd. EN11 49 DZ16
Woollett Cl, Cray. DA1 167 FG84
Woolman Rd, Wat. WD17 75 BU38
Woolmans Cl, Brox. EN10 49 DZ22
Woolmead Av, NW9 119 CU59
Woolmer Cl, Borwd. WD6 78 CN38
Woolmerdine Ct, Bushey WD23 76 BX41
Woolmer Dr, Hem.H. HP2 41 BQ20
Woolmer Gdns, N18 100 DU51
Woolmer Rd, N18 100 DU50
Woolmers La, Letty Grn SG14 31 DH13
Woolmers Pk,
Hert. SG13, SG14 31 DH14
Woolmers Pk Ms,
Letty Grn SG14 31 DH14
Sch **Woolmore Prim Sch**, E14 290 F10
Woolmore St, E14 290 E10
Woolneigh St, SW6 307 L10
Woolpack Ho, Enf. EN3 83 DX37
Woolridge Way, E9 279 H6
Wool Rd, SW20 179 CV93
Woolstaplers Way, SE16 300 C8
Woolston Cl, E17
off Riverhead Cl 101 DX54
Woolstone Rd, SE23 183 DY89
WOOLWICH, SE18 305 M6
⇌ **Woolwich Arsenal** 305 P8
DLR **Woolwich Arsenal** 305 P8
Riv **Woolwich Arsenal Pier** 305 P6
Woolwich Ch St, SE18 304 G7
★ **Woolwich Common**, SE18 165 EM80
Woolwich Common, SE18 165 EN79
Woolwich Ct, Enf. EN3
off Hodson Pl 83 EA38
⇌ **Woolwich Dockyard** 305 J8
● **Woolwich Dockyard Ind Est**,
SE18 305 H7
Woolwich Ferry Pier, E16 305 K5
Woolwich Foot Tunnel, E16 305 L5
SE18 305 L5
Woolwich Garrison, SE18 164 EL79
Woolwich High St, SE18 305 L7
Woolwich Manor Way, E6 293 K5
E16 305 N3
Woolwich Mkt, SE18 305 N8
Woolwich New Rd, SE18 165 EN78
Sch **Woolwich Poly Sch**, SE28
off Hutchins Rd 146 EU74
Woolwich Rd, SE2 166 EX79
SE7 304 D9
SE10 303 L10
Belvedere DA17 166 EX79
Bexleyheath DA6, DA7 166 FA84
● **Woolwich Trade Pk**, SE28 165 ER76
Wooster Gdns, E14 290 G8
Wooster Ms, Har. HA2
off Fairfield Dr 116 CC55
Wooster Pl, SE1 299 M8
Wooster Rd, Beac. HP9 88 AJ51
Wootton Cl, Epsom KT18 233 CT115
Hornchurch RM11 128 FK57
Wootton Dr, Hem.H. HP2 40 BM15
Wooburn Green HP10 110 AE55
Wootton Gro, N3 98 DA53
Wootton Pl, Esher KT10 214 CC105
Wootton St, SE1 298 F4
Worbeck Rd, SE20 202 DV96
Worcester Av, N17 100 DU52
Upminster RM14 129 FT61
Worcester Cl, NW2
off Newfield Ri 119 CV62
SE20 202 DU95
Croydon CR0 203 DZ103
Greenhithe DA9 169 FV84
Istead Rise DA13 191 GF94
Mitcham CR4 200 DG96
Worcester Ct, Walt. KT12 196 BW103
Worcester Cres, NW7 96 CS48
Woodford Green IG8 102 EH50
Worcester Dr, W4 158 CS75
Ashford TW15 175 BP93
Worcester Gdns, SW11
off Grandison Rd 180 DF85
Greenford UB6 136 CC65
Ilford IG1 124 EL59
Slough SL1 151 AR75
Worcester Park KT4 198 CS104
Worcester Ho, SE11
off Kennington Rd 298 E7
Worcester Ms, NW6 273 M4
WORCESTER PARK, KT4 199 CT103
⇌ **Worcester Park** 199 CU102
Worcester Pk Rd, Wor.Pk. KT4 198 CQ104
Worcester Rd, E12 125 EM63
E17 101 DX54
SW19 179 CZ92
Cowley UB8 134 BJ71
Guildford GU2 242 AT132
Hatfield AL10 45 CT17
Reigate RH2 249 CZ133
Sutton SM2 218 DB107
Worcesters Av, Enf. EN1 82 DU38
Sch **Worcesters Prim Sch**,
Enf. EN1 *off Goat La* 82 DT38
Wordsworth Av, E12 144 EL66
E18 124 EF55
Greenford UB6 137 CD68
Kenley CR8 *off Valley Rd* 236 DR115
Wordsworth Cl, Rom. RM3 106 FJ53
Saint Albans AL3 42 CB22
Tilbury RM18 171 GJ82
Wordsworth Dr, Sutt. SM3 217 CW105
Wordsworth Gdns,
Borwd. WD6 78 CN43
Wordsworth Mead, Red. RH1 250 DG132
Wordsworth Pl, NW5 274 F3
Wordsworth Rd, N16 277 P2
SE1 300 A9
SE20 183 DX94
Addlestone KT15 212 BK105
Hampton TW12 176 BZ91
Slough SL2 131 AK70
Wallington SM6 219 DJ107
Welling DA16 165 ES81
Wordsworth Wk, NW11 119 CZ56
Wordsworth Way, Dart. DA1 168 FN84
West Drayton UB7 154 BL77
Worfield St, SW11 308 D5
Worgan St, SE11 298 C10
SE16 301 K7
Workers Rd, Harl. CM17 53 FB16
Ongar CM5 53 FD17
Coll **Working Men's Coll, The**,
NW1 275 M10
Worland Rd, E15 281 K6
World Cargo Cen, Gat. RH6 268 DD152
World's End, Cob. KT11 213 BU114
Worlds End La, N21 81 DM43
Enfield EN2 81 DM43
Orpington BR6 223 ET107
World's End Pas, SW10 308 A4
World's End Pl, SW10
off King's Rd 307 P4
WORLD'S END, Enf. EN2 81 DN41
Worley Pl, Seer Grn HP9 89 AR50
Worley Rd, St.Alb. AL3 42 CC19
Worleys Dr, Orp. BR6 223 ER105
Worlidge St, W6 294 A10
Worlingham Rd, SE22 162 DT84
Sch **Wormholt Pk Prim Sch**,
W12 *off Bryony Rd* 139 CU73
Wormholt Rd, W12 139 CU73
WORMLEY, Brox. EN10 49 DY24
Wormleybury, Brox. EN10 48 DW23
Wormley Ct, Wal.Abb. EN9 68 EG33
Wormley Lo Cl, Brox. EN10 49 DZ23
Sch **Wormley Prim Sch**,
Brox. EN10 *off Cozens La E* 49 DZ22
WORMLEY WEST END,
Brox. EN10 48 DS22
Wormwood St, EC2 287 N8
Wormyngford Ct, Wal.Abb. EN9
off Ninefields 68 EG33
Wornington Rd, W10 282 E5
Woronzow Rd, NW8 274 B9
Worple, The, Wrays. TW19 173 AZ86
Worple Av, SW19 179 CX94
Isleworth TW7 177 CG85
Staines-upon-Thames TW18 174 BH93
Worple Cl, Har. HA2 116 BZ60
Sch **Worple Prim Sch**,
Islw. TW7 *off Queens Ter* 157 CG84
Worple Rd, SW19 179 CY94
SW20 199 CW96
Epsom KT18 216 CS114
Isleworth TW7 157 CG84
Leatherhead KT22 231 CH123
Staines-upon-Thames TW18 174 BH94
Worple Rd Ms, SW19 179 CZ93
⇌ **Worplesdon** 226 AV124
Worplesdon Rd,
Guil. GU2, GU3 242 AT129
Worple St, SW14 158 CR83
Worple Way, Har. HA2 116 BZ60
Richmond TW10 178 CL85
Worrall La, Uxb. UB10 134 BL65
Worrin Cl, Shenf. CM15 109 FZ46
Worrin Pl, Shenf. CM15 109 FZ46
Worrin Rd, Shenf. CM15 109 FZ47
Worsfold Cl, Send GU23 227 BB123
Worships Hill, Sev. TN13 256 FE123
Worship St, EC2 287 M5
Worslade Rd, SW17 180 DD91
Sch **Worsley Br Jun Sch**,
Beck. BR3 *off Brackley Rd* 183 EA94
Worsley Br Rd, SE26 183 DZ91
Beckenham BR3 183 DZ92
Worsley Gra, Chis. BR7 185 EQ93
Worsley Gro, E5 122 DU63
Worsley Rd, E11 124 EE63
Worsopp Dr, SW4 181 DJ85
Worsted Grn, Merst. RH1 251 DJ129
Worth Cl, Orp. BR6 223 ES105
Worthfield Cl, Epsom KT19 216 CR108
Worth Gro, SE17 311 L1
Worthies, The, Amer. HP7 55 AP40
Worthing Cl, E15 281 J9
Grays RM17 170 FY79
Worthing Rd, Houns. TW5 156 BZ79
Worthington Cl, Mitch. CR4 201 DH97
Worthington Rd, Surb. KT6 198 CM102
Worthy Down Ct, SE18
off Prince Imperial Rd 165 EN81
Wortley Rd, E6 144 EK66
Croydon CR0 201 DN101
Worton Gdns, Islw. TW7 157 CD82
● **Worton Hall Est**, Islw. TW7 157 CE84
Worton Rd, Islw. TW7 157 CE83
Worton Way, Houns. TW3 157 CD82
Isleworth TW7 156 CC81
WOTTON, Dor. RH5 262 BZ139
Wotton Dr, Dor. RH5 262 BZ139
Wotton Grn, Orp. BR5 206 EX98
Wotton Rd, NW2 119 CW63
SE8 313 P3
Wotton Way, Sutt. SM2 217 CW110
Wouldham Rd, E16 291 L8
Grays RM20 170 FY79
Wrabness Way, Stai. TW18 194 BH95
Wragby Rd, E11 124 EE62
Wrampling Pl, N9 100 DU46
Wrangley Ct, Wal.Abb. EN9 68 EG33
Wrangthorn Wk, Croy. CR0
off Fernleigh Cl 219 DN105
Wray Av, Ilf. IG5 125 EN55
Wray Cl, Horn. RM11 128 FJ59
Wray Common, Reig. RH2 250 DD132
Sch **Wray Common Prim Sch**,
Reig. RH2 *off Kendal Cl* 250 DD133
Wray Common Rd, Reig. RH2 250 DC133
Wray Cres, N4 121 DL61
Wrayfield Av, Reig. RH2 250 DC133
Wrayfield Rd, Sutt. SM3 199 CX104
Wraylands Dr, Reig. RH2 250 DD132
Wray La, Reig. RH2 250 DC130
Wraymead Pl, Reig. RH2
off Wray Pk Rd 250 DB133
Wray Mill Pk, Reig. RH2 250 DD132
Wray Pk Rd, Reig. RH2 250 DB133
Wray Rd, Sutt. SM2 217 CZ109
WRAYSBURY, Stai. TW19 173 AZ86
⇌ **Wraysbury** 173 BA86
Wraysbury Cl, Houns. TW4 176 BY85
Wraysbury Dr, West Dr. UB7 134 BK73
Wraysbury Gdns, Stai. TW18 173 BE91
Sch **Wraysbury Prim Sch**,
Wrays. TW19 *off Welley Rd* 172 AY86
Wraysbury Rd,
Stai. TW18, TW19 173 BC90
Wrays Way, Hayes UB4 135 BS70
Wrekin Rd, SE18 165 EQ80
Sch **Wren Acad**, N12
off Hilton Av 98 DD50
Wren Av, NW2 272 B2
Southall UB2 156 BZ77
Wren Cl, E16 291 M8
N9 *off Chaffinch Cl* 101 DX46
Lon.Hthrw Air. TW6
off Widgeon Rd 154 BH83
Orpington BR5 206 EX97
South Croydon CR2 221 DX109
Wren Ct, Slou. SL3 153 BA76
Warlingham CR6 236 DW117
Wren Cres, Add. KT15 212 BK106
Bushey WD23 94 CC46
Wren Dr, Wal.Abb. EN9 68 EG34
West Drayton UB7 154 BK76
Wren Gdns, Dag. RM9 126 EX64
Hornchurch RM12 127 FF60
Wren Landing, E14 302 B2
Wren La, Ruis HA4 115 BV58
Wren Ms, SE13
off Lee High Rd 164 EE84
Wren Path, SE28 165 ER76
Wren Pl, Brwd. CM14 108 FX48
Wren Rd, SE5 311 L7
Dagenham RM9 126 EX64
Sidcup DA14 186 EW91
Wrens, The, Harl. CM19 51 EP15
Wrens Av, Ashf. TW15 175 BQ92
Wrens Cft, Nthflt DA11 190 GE91
Wrensfield, Hem.H. HP1 40 BG21
Wrensfield Cl, Wat. WD17 75 BT37
Wrens Hill, Oxshott KT22 230 CC115

HERTFORDSHIRE
AYLESBURY VALE
DACORUM
ST. ALBANS
WELWYN
HATFIELD
BUCKINGHAMSHIRE
CHILTERN
WYCOMBE
THREE RIVERS
WATFORD
HERTSMERE
BARNET
SOUTH BUCKS
HARROW
HILLINGDON
BRENT
CAMDEN
EALING
WESTMINSTER
KENSINGTON & CHELSEA
HAMMERSMITH & FULHAM
SLOUGH
WINDSOR & MAIDENHEAD
HOUNSLOW
RICHMOND UPON THAMES
WANDSWORTH
WOKINGHAM
BRACKNELL FOREST
SPELTHORNE
KINGSTON UPON THAMES
MERTON
RUNNYMEDE
ELMBRIDGE
SUTTON
SURREY HEATH
EPSOM & EWELL
HART
WOKING
REIGATE & BANSTEAD
HAMPSHIRE
RUSHMOOR
GUILDFORD
MOLE VALLEY
SURREY
EAST HANTS
WAVERLEY
CRAWLEY
WEST
GREATER LONDON

HERTFORDSHIRE
WARE
SAWBRIDGEWORTH
SHEERING
UTTLESFORD
LEADEN RODING
BRAINTREE
HATFIELD PEVEREL
FORD
OLD HARLOW
HARLOW
HARLOW
M11
HODDESDON
ESSEX
EPPING
FOREST
CHELMSFORD
BROXBOURNE
LOWER NAZEING
MALDON
CHELMSFORD
MALDON
BROXBOURNE
NORTH WEALD BASSETT
CHIPPING ONGAR
EPPING
CHESHUNT
WALTHAM ABBEY
THEYDON BOIS
KELVEDON HATCH
INGATESTONE
SOUTH WOODHAM FERRERS
M25
M11
ENFIELD
ABRIDGE
LOUGHTON
BRENTWOOD
IELD
STAPLEFORD ABBOTTS
CHIGWELL
BRENTWOOD
BILLERICAY
WICKFORD
ROCHFORD
ONTON
WALTHAM FOREST
WOODFORD
COLLIER ROW
HAROLD HILL
BASILDON
RAYLEIGH
GREEN
EY
REDBRIDGE
BASILDON
CASTLE POINT
R
WALTHAMSTOW
WANSTEAD
ROMFORD
HAVERING
LAINDON
STOKE NEWINGTON
LEYTON
ILFORD
HORNCHURCH
UPMINSTER
SOUTH BENFLEET
HACKNEY
BARKING & DAGENHAM
DAGENHAM
THURROCK
HACKNEY
WEST HAM
BARKING
CANVEY ISLAND
TOWER HAMLETS
EAST HAM
NEWHAM
STANFORD-LE-HOPE
SOUTH OCKENDON
STEPNEY
London City
RAINHAM
AVELEY
RIVER THAMES
CHADWELL ST. MARY
WOOLWICH
ERITH
PURFLEET
GRAYS
SOUTHWARK
PECKHAM
GREENWICH
TILBURY
MEDWAY
GREENWICH
BEXLEY
DARTFORD
NORTHFLEET
GRAVESEND
LEWISHAM
BEXLEYHEATH
CATFORD
HOO
SIDCUP
DARTFORD
GRAVESHAM
BECKENHAM
CHISLEHURST
SOUTH DARENTH
SWANLEY
BROMLEY
LONGFIELD
CHATHAM
GILLINGHAM
ON
RAMSDEN
ORPINGTON
FARNINGHAM
MEOPHAM
ROYDON
BROMLEY
M25
ADDINGTON
FARNBOROUGH
CHELSFIELD
M20
CROYDON
WEST KINGSDOWN
CULVERSTONE GREEN
M2
DOWNE
M25
OTFORD
WROTHAM
BIGGIN HILL
KEMSING
WARLINGHAM
KNOCKHOLT
M26
M20
WEST MALLING
IGHTHAM
MAIDSTONE
TATSFIELD
TONBRIDGE & MALLING
CATERHAM
SEVENOAKS
M25
WESTERHAM
OXTED
MEREWORTH
GODSTONE
SHIPBOURNE
MAIDSTONE
SEVENOAKS
TANDRIDGE
KENT
EAST PECKHAM
TONBRIDGE
EDENBRIDGE
LINGFIELD
SOUTHBOROUGH
TUNBRIDGE WELLS
HOLTYE COMMON
EAST SUSSEX
ROYAL TUNBRIDGE WELLS
SSEX
MID SUSSEX